# OFFICIAL

# BASEBALL REGISTER

PUBLISHER

## C. C. JOHNSON SPINK

EDITORS

## JOE MARCIN

## DICK BYERS

PUBLISHED BY

# The Sporting News

**1212 NORTH LINDBERGH BLVD.**
**P. O. BOX 56** • **ST. LOUIS, MISSOURI 63166**

Copyright © 1977
The Sporting News Publishing Company
a Times Mirror company

ISBN 0-89204-022-X

# Table
## *of*
# CONTENTS

*On the cover: Joe Morgan, THE SPORTING NEWS 1976*
*Major League Player of the Year.*
*Photograph by Carl Skalak.*

### EXPLANATION OF ABBREVIATIONS

G—Games played. Pos.—Position. AB—At Bats. R—Runs, H—Hits. 2B—Two-Base Hits. 3B—Three-Base Hits. HR—Home Runs. RBI—Runs Batted In. B.A.—Batting Average. PO—Putouts. A—Assists. E—Errors. F.A.—Fielding Average. IP—Innings Pitched. W—Won. L—Lost. Pct.—Percentage. R—Runs. ER—Earned Runs. SO—Strikeouts. BB—Bases on Balls. ERA—Earned-Run Average.

# Active Players

*—Denotes led league.  ●—Tied for lead. Mark before position (where more than one position is given) denotes where played as leader in department shown.

### DONALD WILLIAM AASE
Name pronounced AH-see.

### (Don)

Born September 8, 1954, at Orange, Calif.
Height, 6.03. Weight, 190.
Throws and bats righthanded.
Hobbies—Hunting and camping.
Attended California State University, Fullerton, Calif.
Led International League pitchers in games started with 29 in 1975.
Led Carolina League pitchers in games started with 30 and in complete games with 18 in 1974.
Tied for California League lead in shutouts with 4 in 1974.
Named Carolina League Pitcher of the Year in 1974.

| Year     Club | League | G. | IP. | W. | L. | Pct. | H. | R. | ER. | SO. | BB. | ERA. |
|---|---|---|---|---|---|---|---|---|---|---|---|---|
| 1972—Williamsport | NYP | 12 | 62 | 0 | ●10 | .000 | 60 | 48 | 40 | 40 | 34 | 5.81 |
| 1973—Winter Haven | Florida St. | 29 | 170 | 12 | ●15 | .444 | 153 | 82 | 68 | 127 | 73 | 3.60 |
| 1974—Winston-Salem | Carolina | 32 | *230 | *17 | 8 | .680 | 185 | 72 | 62 | *176 | 84 | *2.43 |
| 1975—Pawtucket | Int'national | 29 | 186 | 8 | 13 | .381 | 173 | 85 | 75 | 125 | 88 | 3.63 |
| 1976—Pawtucket† | Int'national | 10 | 54 | 5 | 2 | .714 | 42 | 23 | 20 | 40 | 34 | 3.33 |

†On disabled list, June 23 through remainder of season.

### WILLIAM GLENN ABBOTT
(Known by middle name.)

Born February 16, 1951, at Little Rock, Ark.
Height, 6.06. Weight, 210.
Throws and bats righthanded.
Hobbies—Hunting, fishing and golf.
Attended State College of Arkansas, Conway, Ark.

| Year    Club | League | G. | IP. | W. | L. | Pct. | H. | R. | ER. | SO. | BB. | ERA. |
|---|---|---|---|---|---|---|---|---|---|---|---|---|
| 1970—Coos Bay-North Bend | Northwest | 14 | 101 | 8 | 3 | .727 | 106 | 55 | 43 | 92 | 40 | 3.83 |
| 1971—Burlington | Midwest | 24 | 179 | 11 | 10 | .524 | 166 | 67 | 54 | 195 | 52 | 2.72 |
| 1972—Birmingham | Southern | 13 | 97 | 3 | 8 | .273 | 84 | 38 | 27 | 78 | 31 | 2.51 |
| 1972—Iowa | Am. Assoc. | 15 | 107 | 6 | 8 | .429 | 90 | 42 | 40 | 62 | 35 | 3.36 |
| 1973—Tucson | P. Coast | 29 | 206 | *18 | 8 | .692 | 219 | 97 | 80 | 120 | 67 | 3.50 |
| 1973—Oakland | American | 5 | 19 | 1 | 0 | 1.000 | 16 | 8 | 8 | 6 | 7 | 3.79 |
| 1974—Tucson | P. Coast | 11 | 85 | 6 | 2 | .750 | 109 | 44 | 39 | 39 | 25 | 4.13 |
| 1974—Oakland | American | 19 | 96 | 5 | 7 | .417 | 89 | 38 | 38 | 38 | 34 | 3.00 |
| 1975—Tucson | P. Coast | 4 | 30 | 2 | 2 | .500 | 30 | 14 | 12 | 18 | 11 | 3.60 |
| 1975—Oakland | American | 30 | 114 | 5 | 5 | .500 | 109 | 61 | 54 | 51 | 50 | 4.26 |
| 1976—Oakland† | American | 19 | 62 | 2 | 4 | .333 | 87 | 41 | 38 | 27 | 16 | 5.52 |
| Major League Totals | | 73 | 291 | 13 | 16 | .448 | 301 | 148 | 132 | 122 | 107 | 4.08 |

†Selected by Seattle Mariners from Oakland A's in American League expansion draft, November 5, 1976.

#### CHAMPIONSHIP SERIES RECORD

| Year    Club | League | G. | IP. | W. | L. | Pct. | H. | R. | ER. | SO. | BB. | ERA. |
|---|---|---|---|---|---|---|---|---|---|---|---|---|
| 1975—Oakland | American | 1 | 1 | 0 | 0 | .000 | 0 | 0 | 0 | 0 | 0 | 0.00 |

### GLENN CHARLES ADAMS

Born October 4, 1947, at Northbridge, Mass.
Height, 6.01. Weight, 185.
Throws right and bats lefthanded.
Hobbies—Hunting and playing scrabble.
Attended Springfield College, Springfield, Mass.

| Year    Club | League | Pos. | G. | AB. | R. | H. | 2B. | 3B. | HR. | RBI. | B.A. | PO. | A. | E. | F.A. |
|---|---|---|---|---|---|---|---|---|---|---|---|---|---|---|---|
| 1968—Greensboro | Carol. | OF | 129 | 451 | 58 | 132 | 23 | 4 | 3 | 51 | .293 | 139 | 11 | 12 | .926 |
| 1969—Savannah | South. | OF | 36 | 121 | 13 | 27 | 6 | 1 | 1 | 12 | .223 | 56 | 2 | 3 | .951 |
| 1969—Peninsula | Carol. | OF | 71 | 247 | 32 | 69 | 5 | 0 | 4 | 23 | .279 | 92 | 3 | 6 | .941 |
| 1970—Columbus | South. | OF | 83 | 234 | 32 | 69 | 10 | 2 | 2 | 20 | .295 | 74 | 6 | 5 | .941 |
| 1971—Columbus | South. | OF | 24 | 81 | 13 | 31 | 7 | 0 | 2 | 10 | .383 | 24 | 2 | 1 | .963 |
| 1971—Okla. City† | A.A. | OF | 59 | 161 | 14 | 50 | 9 | 0 | 0 | 19 | .311 | 61 | 2 | 2 | .969 |
| 1972— | | | | | | (Did not play) | | | | | | | | | |
| 1973—Amarillo | Tex. | OF | 110 | 415 | 59 | 129 | 32 | 2 | 3 | 52 | .311 | 88 | 1 | 4 | .957 |
| 1974—Phoenix | P.C. | OF | 127 | 432 | 79 | 152 | 26 | 1 | 13 | 105 | *.352 | 26 | 1 | 0 | 1.000 |
| 1975—Phoenix | P.C. | DH | 19 | 67 | 9 | 20 | 4 | 1 | 1 | 8 | .299 | 0 | 0 | 0 | .000 |
| 1975—San Francisco | Nat. | OF | 61 | 90 | 10 | 27 | 2 | 1 | 4 | 15 | .300 | 31 | 1 | 2 | .941 |
| 1976—San Francisco‡ | Nat. | OF | 69 | 74 | 2 | 18 | 4 | 0 | 0 | 3 | .243 | 3 | 0 | 0 | 1.000 |
| Major League Totals | | | 130 | 164 | 12 | 45 | 6 | 1 | 4 | 18 | .274 | 34 | 1 | 2 | .946 |

†Released by Houston Astros' organization, January 20, 1972; signed as a free agent by San Francisco Giants' organization, December 23, 1972.
‡Sold to Minnesota Twins, December 6, 1976.

## ROBERT MELVIN ADAMS, JR.
### (Bob)

Born January 6, 1952, at Pittsburgh, Pa.
Height, 6.02. Weight, 200.
Throws and bats righthanded.
Attended University of California at Los Angeles, Los Angeles, Calif.
Led Southern League in passed balls with 25 in 1974.

| Year Club | League | Pos. | G. | AB. | R. | H. | 2B. | 3B. | HR. | RBI. | B.A. | PO. | A. | E. | F.A. |
|---|---|---|---|---|---|---|---|---|---|---|---|---|---|---|---|
| 1973-Lakeland ..........Fla. St. | | 3B-OF | 68 | 241 | 27 | 74 | 10 | 4 | 1 | 28 | .307 | 61 | 95 | 13 | .923 |
| 1973-Montgomery.....South. | | 3B | 5 | 16 | 0 | 3 | 0 | 0 | 0 | 0 | .188 | 3 | 15 | 1 | .947 |
| 1974-Evansville ........A.A. | | C | 27 | 85 | 9 | 21 | 2 | 1 | 2 | 13 | .247 | 87 | 17 | 2 | .981 |
| 1974-Montgomery.....South. | | C-1B | 83 | 297 | 30 | 78 | 11 | 1 | 2 | 29 | .263 | 295 | 45 | 13 | .963 |
| 1975-Montgomery† ....South. | | C | 89 | 297 | 30 | 84 | 11 | 0 | 3 | 26 | .283 | 370 | 43 | 7 | .983 |
| 1976-Montgomery......South. | | OF-C | 7 | 30 | 6 | 7 | 2 | 0 | 1 | 6 | .233 | 8 | 2 | 0 | 1.000 |
| 1976-Evansville ........A.A. | | C-1B-OF | 105 | 338 | 32 | 89 | 16 | 4 | 5 | 44 | .263 | 549 | 59 | 14 | .977 |

†On disabled list, April 23 to May 3 and June 4 to July 7, 1975.
Listed on Detroit Tigers' 1977 spring roster.

## WILLIE MAYS AIKENS

Born October 14, 1954, at Seneca, S. C.
Height, 6.03. Weight, 220.
Throws left and bats righthanded.
Attended Southern Carolina State College, Orangeburg, S.C.
Led Midwest League in sacrifice flies with 9 in 1975.
Led Texas League in total bases with 285 in 1976.

| Year Club | League | Pos. | G. | AB. | R. | H. | 2B. | 3B. | HR. | RBI. | B.A. | PO. | A. | E. | F.A. |
|---|---|---|---|---|---|---|---|---|---|---|---|---|---|---|---|
| 1975-Davenport ........Midw. | | 1B | 125 | 443 | 69 | 126 | 17 | 1 | 17 | •91 | .284 | 1038 | 53 | •26 | .977 |
| 1976-El Paso ...........Texas | | 1B | 133 | 514 | •99 | 163 | 24 | 4 | •30 | •117 | .317 | 971 | 52 | 20 | .981 |

Invited to California Angels' 1977 spring camp.

## JEFFREY ALLAN ALBERT
### (Jeff)

Born May 6, 1954, at Brooklyn, N.Y.
Height, 6.03. Weight, 195.
Throws and bats righthanded.
Hobbies—Music and fishing.
Attended C. W. Post College, Glendale, N.Y.
Tied for Northwest League lead in shutouts with 3 in 1976.

| Year Club | League | G. | IP. | W. | L. | Pct. | H. | R. | ER. | SO. | BB. | ERA. |
|---|---|---|---|---|---|---|---|---|---|---|---|---|
| 1976-Bellingham† .......................Northwest | | 14 | 102 | 8 | 3 | .727 | 87 | 42 | 32 | 92 | 22 | 2.82 |

†Traded with outfielder Bill Buckner and Infielder Ivan DeJesus to Chicago Cubs for outfielder Rick Monday and pitcher Mike Garman, January 11, 1977.

## VICTOR ALBURY

Name pronounced All-berry.
### (Vic)

Born May 12, 1947, at Key West, Fla.
Height, 6.00 Weight, 185.
Throws and bats lefthanded.
Led Florida State League in shutouts with 6 in 1969.

| Year Club | League | G. | IP. | W. | L. | Pct. | H. | R. | ER. | SO. | BB. | ERA. |
|---|---|---|---|---|---|---|---|---|---|---|---|---|
| 1966— | | | (Out of Organized Baseball) | | | | | | | | | |
| 1967-68— | | | (In Military Service) | | | | | | | | | |
| 1969-Key West...........................Florida St. | | 31 | 186 | 12 | 10 | .545 | 145 | 68 | 48 | 155 | 106 | 2.32 |
| 1970-Salt Lake City.....................P. Coast | | 21 | 47 | 2 | 4 | .333 | 69 | 47 | 44 | 27 | 33 | 8.43 |
| 1970-Lodi† ...................................California | | 17 | 92 | 5 | 6 | .455 | 103 | 54 | 46 | 80 | 36 | 4.50 |
| 1971-Charlotte...............................Southern | | •66 | 135 | 12 | 7 | .632 | 95 | 31 | 26 | 130 | 67 | 1.73 |
| 1972-Tacoma§ ..............................P. Coast | | 12 | 18 | 0 | 2 | .000 | 20 | 11 | 10 | 18 | 12 | 5.00 |
| 1973-Tacoma† ..............................P. Coast | | 29 | 142 | 8 | 11 | .421 | 118 | 65 | 63 | 115 | 75 | 3.99 |
| 1973-Minnesota ..........................American | | 14 | 23 | 1 | 0 | 1.000 | 13 | 7 | 7 | 13 | 19 | 2.74 |
| 1974-Minnesota ..........................American | | 32 | 164 | 8 | 9 | .471 | 159 | 83 | 75 | 85 | 80 | 4.12 |
| 1975-Minnesota ..........................American | | 32 | 135 | 6 | 7 | .462 | 115 | 82 | 68 | 72 | 97 | 4.53 |
| 1976-Minnesota x ......................American | | 23 | 50 | 3 | 1 | .750 | 51 | 22 | 20 | 23 | 24 | 3.60 |
| Major League Totals ............... | | 101 | 372 | 18 | 17 | .514 | 338 | 194 | 170 | 193 | 220 | 4.11 |

†Appeared in one game as a first baseman.
‡Drafted from San Diego Padres' organization by Charlotte (Minnesota Twins' organization), November 30, 1970.
§On disabled list, April 13 through July 1.
xOn disabled list, May 13 through June 6.

### RECORD AS FIRST BASEMAN

| Year Club | League | Pos. | G. | AB. | R. | H. | 2B. | 3B. | HR. | RBI. | B.A. | PO. | A. | E. | F.A. |
|---|---|---|---|---|---|---|---|---|---|---|---|---|---|---|---|
| 1965-Dubuque† .........Midw. | | 1B | 52 | 172 | 18 | 40 | 7 | 0 | 4 | 24 | .233 | 342 | 42 | 11 | .972 |
| 1971-Charlotte .........South. | | P-1B | 78 | 65 | 9 | 23 | 3 | 0 | 3 | 17 | .354 | 20 | 18 | 3 | .927 |

†Released by Cleveland Indians' organization; signed as free agent by San Diego Padres, March 17, 1969.

## SANTO ALCALA

Name pronounced AL-kuh-luh.

Born December 23, 1952, at San Pedro de Macoris, Dominican Republic.
Height, 6.05. Weight, 195.
Throws and bats righthanded.
Tied for Eastern League lead in games started by pitchers with 27 in 1973.

| Year Club | League | G. | IP. | W. | L. | Pct. | H. | R. | ER. | SO. | BB. | ERA. |
|---|---|---|---|---|---|---|---|---|---|---|---|---|
| 1970—Bradenton Reds | Gulf Coast | 11 | 72 | 4 | 6 | .400 | 74 | 34 | 24 | 54 | 40 | 3.00 |
| 1971—Sioux Falls | Northern | 20 | 41 | 0 | 2 | .000 | 43 | 42 | 24 | 48 | 36 | 5.27 |
| 1972—Key West | Florida St. | 29 | 176 | 7 | •14 | .333 | 152 | 75 | 59 | •176 | 59 | 3.02 |
| 1972—Three Rivers | Eastern | 4 | 29 | 2 | 1 | .667 | 14 | 3 | 2 | 18 | 7 | 0.62 |
| 1973—Three Rivers | Eastern | 30 | 190 | 7 | •13 | .350 | 168 | 91 | 83 | 115 | 85 | 3.93 |
| 1974—Indianapolis | Am. Assoc. | 32 | 161 | 12 | 11 | .522 | 152 | 84 | 75 | 113 | 74 | 4.19 |
| 1975—Indianapolis | Am. Assoc. | 27 | 173 | 13 | 12 | .520 | 144 | 61 | 53 | 118 | 64 | 2.76 |
| 1976—Cincinnati | National | 30 | 132 | 11 | 4 | .733 | 131 | 72 | 69 | 67 | 67 | 4.70 |
| Major League Totals | | 30 | 132 | 11 | 4 | .733 | 131 | 72 | 69 | 67 | 67 | 4.70 |

## DOYLE LAFAYETTE ALEXANDER

Born September 4, 1950, at Cordova, Ala.
Height, 6.02. Weight, 200.
Throws and bats righthanded.
Hobbies—Hunting, fishing, golf and working on cars.
Attended Jefferson State Junior College, Pinson, Ala.

| Year Club | League | G. | IP. | W. | L. | Pct. | H. | R. | ER. | SO. | BB. | ERA. |
|---|---|---|---|---|---|---|---|---|---|---|---|---|
| 1968—Tri-City | Northwest | 13 | 70 | 3 | •9 | .250 | 66 | 47 | 32 | 58 | 47 | 4.11 |
| 1969—Daytona Beach | Florida St. | 30 | 185 | 13 | 9 | .591 | 154 | 75 | 56 | 140 | 100 | 2.72 |
| 1969—Albuquerque | Texas | 3 | 15 | 0 | 3 | .000 | 19 | 10 | 10 | 3 | 12 | 6.00 |
| 1970—Albuquerque | Texas | 10 | 80 | 4 | 3 | .571 | 72 | 29 | 28 | 60 | 20 | 3.15 |
| 1970—Spokane | P. Coast | 19 | 137 | 9 | 7 | .563 | 137 | 66 | 55 | 78 | 26 | 3.61 |
| 1971—Spokane | P. Coast | 15 | 110 | 6 | 3 | .667 | 114 | 49 | 42 | 65 | 31 | 3.44 |
| 1971—Los Angeles† | National | 17 | 92 | 6 | 6 | .500 | 105 | 45 | 39 | 30 | 18 | 3.82 |
| 1972—Baltimore | American | 35 | 106 | 6 | 8 | .429 | 78 | 36 | 29 | 49 | 30 | 2.46 |
| 1973—Baltimore‡ | American | 29 | 175 | 12 | 8 | .600 | 169 | 85 | 75 | 63 | 52 | 3.86 |
| 1974—Baltimore | American | 30 | 114 | 6 | 9 | .400 | 127 | 65 | 51 | 40 | 43 | 4.03 |
| 1975—Baltimore | American | 32 | 133 | 8 | 8 | .500 | 127 | 47 | 45 | 46 | 47 | 3.05 |
| 1976—Balt.§-N.Y. x | American | 30 | 201 | 13 | 9 | .591 | 172 | 81 | 75 | 58 | 63 | 3.36 |
| National League Totals | | 17 | 92 | 6 | 6 | .500 | 105 | 45 | 39 | 30 | 18 | 3.82 |
| American League Totals | | 156 | 729 | 45 | 42 | .517 | 673 | 314 | 275 | 256 | 235 | 3.40 |
| Major League Totals | | 173 | 821 | 51 | 48 | .515 | 778 | 359 | 314 | 286 | 253 | 3.44 |

†Traded with Pitcher Bob O'Brien, Catcher Sergio Robles and First Baseman-Outfielder Royle Stillman to Baltimore Orioles for Pitcher Pete Richert and Outfielder Frank Robinson, December 2, 1971.

‡On disabled list, July 10 to August 6, 1973.

§Traded with Pitchers Kenny Holtzman and Grant Jackson, Catcher Elrod Hendricks and Pitcher Jimmy Freeman, latter assigned from Rochester to Syracuse, to New York Yankees for Pitchers Rudy May, Tippy Martinez, Dave Pagan, Scott McGregor and Catcher Rick Dempsey, June 15, 1976.

xPlayed out option year and granted free agency, November 1, 1976; signed as free agent by Texas Rangers, November 23, 1976.

### CHAMPIONSHIP SERIES RECORD

| Year Club | League | G. | IP. | W. | L. | Pct. | H. | R. | ER. | SO. | BB. | ERA. |
|---|---|---|---|---|---|---|---|---|---|---|---|---|
| 1973—Baltimore | American | 1 | 3⅔ | 0 | 1 | .000 | 5 | 3 | 2 | 1 | 0 | 4.91 |

### WORLD SERIES RECORD

| Year Club | League | G. | IP. | W. | L. | Pct. | H. | R. | ER. | SO. | BB. | ERA. |
|---|---|---|---|---|---|---|---|---|---|---|---|---|
| 1976—New York | American | 1 | 6 | 0 | 1 | .000 | 9 | 5 | 5 | 1 | 2 | 7.50 |

## GARY WAYNE ALEXANDER

Born March 27, 1953, at Los Angeles, Calif.
Height, 6.02. Weight, 195.
Throws and bats righthanded.
Hobbies—Music, cars and clothes.
Attended Los Angeles Harbor Junior College, Wilmington, Calif.
Led Midwest League batters in strikeouts with 126 in 1973.
Named California League Player of the Year in 1974.
Named Texas League Player of the Year in 1975.

| Year Club | League | Pos. | G. | AB. | R. | H. | 2B. | 3B. | HR. | RBI. | B.A. | PO. | A. | E. | F.A. |
|---|---|---|---|---|---|---|---|---|---|---|---|---|---|---|---|
| 1972—Great Falls | Pion. | OF-C | 55 | 136 | 14 | 28 | 6 | 1 | 2 | 14 | .206 | 117 | 7 | 8 | .939 |
| 1973—Decatur | Midw. | OF-C | 123 | 406 | 68 | 106 | 16 | 5 | 17 | 66 | .261 | 178 | 7 | 14 | .930 |
| 1974—Fresno† | Calif. | •C-OF | 103 | 356 | 84 | 106 | 15 | 3 | •27 | 95 | .298 | 475 | 54 | •27 | .951 |
| 1975—Phoenix | P.C. | OF | 7 | 14 | 2 | 2 | 1 | 0 | 0 | 1 | .143 | 0 | 0 | 0 | .000 |
| 1975—Lafayette | Tex. | C-OF | 103 | 346 | 80 | 114 | 24 | 1 | •23 | 81 | .329 | 275 | 22 | 11 | .964 |
| 1975—San Francisco | Nat. | C | 3 | 3 | 1 | 0 | 0 | 0 | 0 | 0 | .000 | 2 | 0 | 0 | 1.000 |
| 1976—Phoenix | P.C. | C-1B | 109 | 360 | 59 | 115 | 18 | 12 | 17 | 76 | .319 | 398 | 63 | 13 | .972 |
| 1976—San Francisco | Nat. | C | 23 | 73 | 12 | 13 | 1 | 1 | 2 | 7 | .178 | 92 | 16 | 4 | .964 |
| Major League Totals | | | 26 | 76 | 13 | 13 | 1 | 1 | 2 | 0 | .171 | 94 | 16 | 4 | .965 |

†On disabled list, August 5 through remainder of season.

— 5 —

## MATTHEW ALEXANDER, JR.
### (Matt)

Born January 30, 1947, at Shreveport, La.
Height, 5.11.  Weight, 170.
Throws right and bats right and lefthanded.
Hobbies—Billiards and cars.
Attended Grambling College, Grambling, La.
Major League stolen bases: 1973 (2), 1974 (8), 1975 (17), 1976 (20). Total—47.
Led Texas League in stolen bases with 38 and tied for lead in double plays by outfielders with 4 in 1972.

| Year Club | League | Pos. | G. | AB. | R. | H. | 2B. | 3B. | HR. | RBI. | B.A. | PO. | A. | E. | F.A. |
|---|---|---|---|---|---|---|---|---|---|---|---|---|---|---|---|
| 1968—Caldwell | Pion. | 2-S-3 | 35 | 142 | 27 | 37 | 3 | 2 | 1 | 10 | .261 | 55 | 75 | 8 | .942 |
| 1969—Quincy | Midw. | 3B | 71 | 266 | 65 | 73 | 13 | 5 | 8 | 32 | .274 | •63 | 112 | 19 | .902 |
| 1969—San Antonio | Tex. | 3-1-SS | 30 | 109 | 17 | 33 | 3 | 2 | 1 | 13 | .303 | 81 | 42 | 8 | .939 |
| 1970-71—Chicago | Nat. | | | | | (In Military Service) | | | | | | | | | |
| 1972—Midland | Tex. | OF-2-3 | 124 | 460 | 78 | 124 | 18 | 2 | 5 | 45 | .270 | 262 | 65 | 13 | .962 |
| 1973—Wichita | A.A. | O-3-2 | 106 | 427 | 61 | 132 | 22 | 3 | 2 | 51 | .309 | 114 | 60 | 14 | .926 |
| 1973—Chicago | Nat. | OF | 12 | 5 | 4 | 1 | 0 | 0 | 0 | 1 | .200 | 2 | 0 | 0 | 1.000 |
| 1974—Wichita | A.A. | O-2-S | 30 | 120 | 26 | 33 | 2 | 1 | 2 | 12 | .275 | 68 | 27 | 3 | .969 |
| 1974—Chicago | Nat. | 3-O-2 | 45 | 54 | 15 | 11 | 2 | 1 | 0 | 0 | .204 | 13 | 24 | 3 | .925 |
| 1975—Wichita† | A.A. | OF | 7 | 32 | 4 | 8 | 0 | 0 | 2 | 8 | .250 | 25 | 1 | 0 | 1.000 |
| 1975—Oakland‡ | Amer. | O-2-3 | 63 | 10 | 16 | 1 | 0 | 0 | 0 | 0 | .100 | 7 | 2 | 1 | .900 |
| 1976—Oakland | Amer. | OF-DH | 61 | 30 | 16 | 1 | 0 | 0 | 0 | 0 | .033 | 23 | 0 | 0 | 1.000 |
| National League Totals | | | 57 | 59 | 19 | 12 | 2 | 1 | 0 | 1 | .203 | 15 | 24 | 3 | .929 |
| American League Totals | | | 124 | 40 | 32 | 2 | 0 | 0 | 0 | 0 | .050 | 30 | 2 | 1 | .970 |
| Major League Totals | | | 181 | 99 | 51 | 14 | 2 | 1 | 0 | 1 | .141 | 45 | 26 | 4 | .947 |

†Traded by Chicago Cubs to Oakland Athletics for a player to be named later, April 28, 1975; Athletics sent Pitcher Howell (Buddy) Copeland to Cubs, May 2, 1975, to complete deal.
‡On disabled list, June 4 to July 4, 1975.

## DON THOMAS ALFANO
### (Donnie)

Born October 1, 1955, at Visalia, Calif.
Height, 6.02. Weight, 195.
Throws and bats lefthanded.
Hobbies—Hunting and gun collecting.
Son of Don R. Alfano, infielder with Chicago Cubs' organization, 1946-1950.

| Year Club | League | G. | IP. | W. | L. | Pct. | H. | R. | ER. | SO. | BB. | ERA. |
|---|---|---|---|---|---|---|---|---|---|---|---|---|
| 1974—Walla Walla | Northw. | 1 | 1 | 0 | 0 | .000 | 1 | 0 | 0 | 3 | 1 | 0.00 |
| 1976—Amarillo | Texas | 28 | 48 | 3 | 1 | .750 | 54 | 28 | 22 | 36 | 35 | 4.13 |

#### RECORD AS INFIELDER-OUTFIELDER

| Year Club | League | Pos. | G. | AB. | R. | H. | 2B. | 3B. | HR. | RBI. | B.A. | PO. | A. | E. | F.A. |
|---|---|---|---|---|---|---|---|---|---|---|---|---|---|---|---|
| 1974—Walla Walla | Northw. | 1B | 76 | 265 | 40 | 76 | 13 | 0 | 8 | 47 | .287 | 579 | •44 | 15 | .976 |
| 1975—Alexandria | Texas | OF-1B | 26 | 95 | 7 | 20 | 4 | 0 | 0 | 5 | .211 | 50 | 1 | 0 | 1.000 |
| 1975—Reno | Calif. | 1B | 92 | 347 | 47 | 109 | 23 | 4 | 9 | 74 | .314 | 796 | 44 | 11 | .987 |
| 1976—Amarillo | Texas | OF-1B | 50 | 62 | 6 | 15 | 3 | 1 | 0 | 11 | .242 | 28 | 2 | 0 | 1.000 |

Listed on San Diego Padres' 1977 spring roster.

## MICHAEL WILLIAM ALLEN
### (Mike)

Born August 31, 1954, at Philadelphia, Pa.
Height, 6.03. Weight, 200.
Throws and bats righthanded.
Attended West Chester State, West Chester, Pa.
Led Northwest League in shutouts with 4 in 1973.

| Year Club | League | G. | IP. | W. | L. | Pct. | H. | R. | ER. | SO. | BB. | ERA. |
|---|---|---|---|---|---|---|---|---|---|---|---|---|
| 1972—Tri-City | Northwest | 14 | 75 | 1 | 8 | .111 | 74 | 61 | 44 | 57 | 46 | 5.28 |
| 1973—Alexandria† | Texas | | | | | Did not play. | | | | | | |
| 1973—Walla Walla | Northwest | 14 | 115 | 9 | 3 | .750 | 82 | 24 | 22 | 72 | 44 | •1.72 |
| 1974—Alexandria | Texas | 24 | 154 | 8 | 13 | .381 | 172 | 100 | 82 | 86 | 53 | 4.79 |
| 1976—Amarillo‡ | Texas | 15 | 83 | 7 | 4 | .636 | 85 | 29 | 23 | 33 | 15 | 2.52 |

†On disabled list from beginning of season until May 31, 1973.
‡On disabled list, April 16 to May 15 and July 3 to August 4, 1976. Traded to Houston Astros for Pitcher Paul Siebert, January 25, 1977.
Listed on Houston Astros' spring roster.

## RICHARD ANTHONY ALLEN
### (Dick)

Born March 8, 1942, at Wampum, Pa.
Height, 5.11. Weight, 187.
Throws and bats righthanded.
Brother of Hank Allen, former utilityman with Washington Senators, Milwaukee Brewers
and Chicago White Sox, and Ron Allen, former first baseman with
Philadelphia Phillies and St. Louis Cardinals.

Established major league records for most times, four or more strikeouts, game, league (13), 1964 (2), 1966, 1968 (7), 1969 (2), 1970; and most times, four or more strikeouts, game, season (7), April 13, May 1, 9, June 29, July 16, 21, August 19, 1968.

Tied major league records for most games, rookie season (162), 1964; most strikeouts in nine-inning game (5), June 28, 1964 (first game); by making 200 or more hits in rookie season (201), 1964; for most consecutive seasons, 100 or more strikeouts (9), 1972; and for most strikeouts, two consecutive games (more than 18 innings), 8, May 24 (5), May 26 (3), 1970, 19 innings.

Established National League record for most total bases, rookie season (352), 1964.

Tied National League records for most walks, game (5), August 16, 1968; and most years, 100 or more strikeouts (8), 1971.

Hit three home runs in a game, September 29, 1968.

Led National League in total bases with 352 in 1964; led third basemen in double plays with 29 in 1965; led in strikeouts with 138 in 1964 and 150 in 1965; led in slugging percentage with .632 in 1966.

Led American League in slugging percentage with .603 in 1972 and .563 in 1974.

Tied for American League lead in bases on balls by batters with 99 in 1972.

Led International League in total bases with 299 in 1963.

Named American League Most Valuable Player in 1972.

Named National League Rookie of the Year, 1964 by Baseball Writers' Association and National League Rookie Player of the Year by THE SPORTING NEWS, 1964.

Named first baseman on THE SPORTING NEWS American League All-Star Team, 1972 and 1974.

Named THE SPORTING NEWS American League Player of the Year, 1972.

Received reported $60,000 bonus to sign with Philadelphia Phillies, 1960.

| Year Club | League | Pos. | G. | AB. | R. | H. | 2B. | 3B. | HR. | RBI. | B.A. | PO. | A. | E. | F.A. |
|---|---|---|---|---|---|---|---|---|---|---|---|---|---|---|---|
| 1960—Elmira† | NYP | SS | 88 | 320 | 56 | 90 | 19 | 10 | 8 | 42 | .281 | 141 | 173 | •48 | .867 |
| 1961—Magic Valley | Pion. | 2B | 117 | 460 | 101 | 146 | 17 | 8 | 21 | 94 | .317 | •258 | •298 | •27 | .953 |
| 1962—Williamsport | East. | OF-2B | 132 | 511 | 97 | 168 | •32 | 10 | 20 | 109 | .329 | 255 | 59 | 17 | .949 |
| 1963—Philadelphia | Nat. | OF-3B | 10 | 24 | 6 | 7 | 2 | 1 | 0 | 2 | .292 | 10 | 0 | 2 | .833 |
| 1964—Philadelphia | Nat. | 3B | 162 | 632 | •125 | 201 | 38 | •13 | 29 | 91 | .318 | 154 | 325 | •41 | .921 |
| 1965—Philadelphia | Nat. | 3B-SS | 161 | 619 | 93 | 187 | 31 | 14 | 20 | 85 | .302 | 130 | 305 | 26 | .944 |
| 1966—Philadelphia | Nat. | 3B-OF | 141 | 524 | 112 | 166 | 25 | 10 | 40 | 110 | .317 | 146 | 182 | 14 | .959 |
| 1967—Philadephia‡ | Nat. | •3-2B-SS | 122 | 463 | 89 | 142 | 31 | 10 | 23 | 77 | .307 | 95 | 249 | •35 | .908 |
| 1968—Philadelphia | Nat. | OF-3B | 152 | 521 | 87 | 137 | 17 | 9 | 33 | 90 | .263 | 215 | 20 | 12 | .951 |
| 1969—Philadelphia§ | Nat. | 1B | 118 | 438 | 79 | 126 | 23 | 3 | 32 | 89 | .288 | 1024 | 54 | 16 | .985 |
| 1970—St. Louis x | Nat. | 1-3-OF | 122 | 459 | 88 | 128 | 17 | 5 | 34 | 101 | .279 | 708 | 109 | 18 | .978 |
| 1971—Los Angeles y | Nat. | 3B-O-1 | 155 | 549 | 82 | 162 | 24 | 1 | 23 | 90 | .295 | 382 | 151 | 21 | .962 |
| 1972—Chicago | Amer. | 1B-3B | 148 | 506 | 90 | 156 | 28 | 5 | •37 | •113 | .308 | 1235 | 69 | 7 | .995 |
| 1973—Chicago z | Amer. | 1B-2B | 72 | 250 | 39 | 79 | 20 | 3 | 16 | 41 | .316 | 601 | 46 | 4 | .994 |
| 1974—Chicago a b | Amer. | •1B-2B | 128 | 462 | 84 | 139 | 23 | 1 | •32 | 88 | .301 | 998 | 50 | •16 | .985 |
| 1975—Philadelphia | Nat. | 1B | 119 | 416 | 54 | 97 | 21 | 3 | 12 | 62 | .233 | 900 | 70 | •18 | .982 |
| 1976—Philadelphia c d | Nat. | 1B | 85 | 298 | 52 | 80 | 16 | 1 | 15 | 49 | .268 | 671 | 44 | 8 | .989 |
| American League Totals | | | 348 | 1218 | 213 | 374 | 71 | 9 | 85 | 242 | .307 | 2834 | 165 | 27 | .991 |
| National League Totals | | | 1347 | 4943 | 867 | 1433 | 245 | 70 | 261 | 846 | .290 | 4435 | 1509 | 211 | .966 |
| Major League Totals | | | 1695 | 6161 | 1080 | 1807 | 316 | 79 | 346 | 1088 | .293 | 7269 | 1674 | 238 | .974 |

†On disabled list, July 6 through July 16, 1960.

‡On disabled list from August 28 through end of season after suffering severe cuts on right hand in accident, August 25.

§Traded with Infielder Octavio (Cookie) Rojas and Pitcher Jerry Johnson for Catcher Tim McCarver, Pitcher Joe Hoerner, Outfielder Curt Flood and Outfielder Byron Browne to St. Louis Cardinals, October 7, 1969. Flood refused to report and the Cardinals sent First Baseman Guillermo Montanez and a player to be named later to Philadelphia to complete the deal, April 8, 1970. Pitcher James Robert Browning was sent "as the player to be named later" from the Cardinals to Philadelphia, August 30, 1970. Was placed on suspended list, June 25 through July 20, 1970.

xTraded to Los Angeles Dodgers for Infielder Ted Sizemore and Catcher Bob Stinson, October 5, 1970.

yTraded to Chicago White Sox for Pitcher Tommy John and Infielder Steve Huntz (latter assigned to Spokane), December 2, 1971.

zOn supplemental disabled list, June 29 to July 31; on disabled list, August 26 through remainder of season.

aTraded to Atlanta Braves for $5,000 and a player to be named later, December 3, 1974; Braves sent Catcher Jim Essian to White Sox, May 15, 1975, to complete deal.

bTraded with Catcher Johnny Oates by Atlanta Braves to Philadelphia Phillies for Catcher Jim Essian, Outfielder Barry Bonnell (assigned from Spartanburg to Greenwood), a player to be named later and an estimated $150,000, May 7, 1975; deal was completed with a cash payment.

cOn supplemental disabled list, April 30 through May 15, and July 26 through September 3, 1976.

dPlayed out option year and granted free agency, November 5, 1976; signed with Oakland A's, March 16, 1977.

### CHAMPIONSHIP SERIES

| Year Club | League | Pos. | G. | AB. | R. | H. | 2B. | 3B. | HR. | RBI. | B.A. | PO. | A. | E. | F.A. |
|---|---|---|---|---|---|---|---|---|---|---|---|---|---|---|---|
| 1976—Philadelphia | Nat. | 1B | 3 | 9 | 1 | 2 | 0 | 0 | 0 | 0 | .222 | 28 | 0 | 1 | .966 |

### ALL-STAR GAME RECORD

| Year League | Pos. | AB. | R. | H. | 2B. | 3B. | HR. | RBI. | B.A. | PO. | A. | E. | F.A. |
|---|---|---|---|---|---|---|---|---|---|---|---|---|---|
| 1965—National | 3B | 3 | 0 | 1 | 0 | 0 | 0 | 0 | .333 | 0 | 1 | 0 | 1.000 |
| 1966—National | PH | 1 | 0 | 0 | 0 | 0 | 0 | 0 | .000 | 0 | 0 | 0 | .000 |
| 1967—National | 3B | 4 | 1 | 1 | 0 | 0 | 1 | 1 | .250 | 1 | 2 | 0 | 1.000 |
| 1970—National | 1B | 3 | 0 | 0 | 0 | 0 | 0 | 0 | .000 | 4 | 0 | 0 | 1.000 |
| 1972—American | 1B | 3 | 0 | 0 | 0 | 0 | 0 | 0 | .000 | 4 | 0 | 0 | 1.000 |
| 1974—American | 1B | 2 | 0 | 1 | 0 | 0 | 0 | 1 | .500 | 2 | 0 | 0 | 1.000 |
| All-Star Game Totals | | 16 | 1 | 3 | 0 | 0 | 1 | 2 | .188 | 10 | 3 | 0 | 1.000 |

Named to American League All-Star Team for 1973; replaced due to an injury.

## WILLIAM FRANCIS ALMON
### (Bill)

Born November 21, 1952, at Providence, R. I.
Height, 6.03. Weight, 180.
Throws and bats righthanded.
Attended Brown University, Providence, R. I.

Tied for Pacific Coast League lead in stolen bases with 33 in 1975.
Received reported $100,000 bonus to sign with San Diego Padres, 1974.

| Year Club | League | Pos. | G. | AB. | R. | H. | 2B. | 3B. | HR. | RBI. | B.A. | PO. | A. | E. | F.A. |
|---|---|---|---|---|---|---|---|---|---|---|---|---|---|---|---|
| 1974—Hawaii | P.C. | SS | 14 | 36 | 6 | 8 | 0 | 0 | 0 | 3 | .222 | 16 | 33 | 7 | .875 |
| 1974—Alexandria | Tex. | SS | 25 | 97 | 9 | 18 | 2 | 2 | 0 | 5 | .186 | 48 | 70 | 8 | .937 |
| 1974—San Diego | Nat. | SS | 16 | 38 | 4 | 12 | 1 | 0 | 0 | 3 | .316 | 13 | 30 | 4 | .915 |
| 1975—Hawaii | P.C. | SS | 144 | 496 | 76 | 113 | 22 | 0 | 1 | 47 | .228 | *288 | 456 | *48 | .939 |
| 1975—San Diego | Nat. | SS | 6 | 10 | 0 | 4 | 0 | 0 | 0 | 0 | .400 | 6 | 5 | 0 | 1.000 |
| 1976—Hawaii | P.C. | SS | 129 | 454 | 67 | 132 | 16 | 2 | 3 | 44 | .291 | *248 | 395 | *36 | .947 |
| 1976—San Diego | Nat. | SS | 14 | 57 | 6 | 14 | 3 | 0 | 1 | 6 | .246 | 23 | 52 | 3 | .962 |
| Major League Totals | | | 36 | 105 | 10 | 30 | 4 | 0 | 1 | 9 | .286 | 42 | 87 | 7 | .948 |

## SANTOS ALOMAR (CONDE)
Name pronounced AL-o-mar.

### (Sandy)

Born October 19, 1943, at Salinas, Puerto Rico.
Height, 5.08. Weight, 155.
Throws right and bats left and righthanded.
Hobbies—Dominoes and records.
Brother of Rafael, Demetrio and Antonio Alomar, former minor league players.

Established major league record for most at bats, season, without being hit by pitch, 689, in 1971.
Major League stolen bases: 1964 (1), 1965 (12), 1966 (0), 1967 (2), 1968 (21), 1969 (20), 1970 (35), 1971 (39), 1972 (20), 1973 (25), 1974 (8), 1975 (28), 1976 (12). Total—223.
Led American League second basemen in double plays with 119 in 1970.
Led Texas League shortstops in double plays with 92 in 1963.
Named Player of the Year in Pioneer League, 1962.

| Year Club | League | Pos. | G. | AB. | R. | H. | 2B. | 3B. | HR. | RBI. | B.A. | PO. | A. | E. | F.A. |
|---|---|---|---|---|---|---|---|---|---|---|---|---|---|---|---|
| 1960—Eau Claire† | North. | | | | | (Restricted List) | | | | | | | | | |
| 1961—Davenport‡ | Midw. | SS | 77 | 299 | 48 | 83 | 19 | 3 | 4 | 31 | .278 | 107 | 195 | 34 | .899 |
| 1962—Boise | Pion. | SS | 129 | *535 | 83 | •176 | 31 | 2 | 3 | 72 | .329 | *195 | *304 | *60 | .893 |
| 1963—Austin | Texas | SS | 136 | *583 | 84 | 170 | 18 | *12 | 5 | 65 | .292 | *255 | *417 | *61 | .917 |
| 1964—Denver | P.C. | SS | 154 | *620 | 86 | 163 | 18 | *22 | 3 | 40 | .263 | 235 | 476 | *42 | .944 |
| 1964—Milwaukee | Nat. | SS | 19 | 53 | 3 | 13 | 1 | 0 | 0 | 6 | .245 | 27 | 60 | 3 | .967 |
| 1965—Milwaukee | Nat. | SS-2B | 67 | 108 | 16 | 26 | 1 | 1 | 0 | 8 | .241 | 68 | 114 | 5 | .973 |
| 1965—Atlanta | Int. | SS-2B | 66 | 267 | 40 | 65 | 7 | 9 | 0 | 20 | .243 | 123 | 206 | 20 | .943 |
| 1966—Atlanta | Nat. | 2B-SS | 31 | 44 | 4 | 4 | 1 | 0 | 0 | 2 | .091 | 30 | 34 | 1 | .985 |
| 1966—Richmond§x | Int. | 3-SS-2B | 103 | 395 | 49 | 96 | 16 | 6 | 5 | 26 | .243 | 124 | 233 | 23 | .939 |
| 1967—New York | Nat. | SS-3-2B | 15 | 22 | 1 | 0 | 0 | 0 | 0 | 0 | .000 | 16 | 18 | 0 | 1.000 |
| 1967—Jacksonville y | Int. | S-3-1-2-O | 85 | 316 | 29 | 66 | 8 | 0 | 1 | 24 | .209 | 140 | 250 | 23 | .944 |
| 1967—Chicago | Amer. | SS-2B | 12 | 15 | 4 | 3 | 0 | 0 | 0 | 0 | .200 | 11 | 14 | 1 | .962 |
| 1968—Chicago | Amer. | •2-3-S-O | 133 | 363 | 41 | 92 | 8 | 2 | 0 | 12 | .253 | 210 | 264 | •20 | .960 |
| 1969—Chi. z-Calif. | Amer. | 2B | 156 | 617 | 68 | 153 | 12 | 2 | 1 | 34 | .248 | 344 | 401 | *23 | .970 |
| 1970—California | Amer. | 2-S-3B | •162 | 672 | 82 | 169 | 18 | 2 | 2 | 36 | .251 | 391 | 481 | 20 | .978 |
| 1971—California | Amer. | 2B-SS | *162 | *689 | 77 | 179 | 24 | 3 | 4 | 42 | .260 | 393 | 530 | 17 | .982 |
| 1972—California | Amer. | 2B-SS | 155 | 610 | 65 | 146 | 20 | 3 | 1 | 25 | .239 | 353 | 394 | 17 | .978 |
| 1973—California | Amer. | 2B-SS | 136 | 470 | 45 | 112 | 7 | 1 | 0 | 28 | .238 | 290 | 355 | 17 | .974 |
| 1974—Calif. a-N.Y. | Amer. | 2-S-3-O | 122 | 333 | 47 | 87 | 8 | 1 | 1 | 28 | .261 | 222 | 241 | 11 | .977 |
| 1975—New York | Amer. | *2B-SS | 151 | 489 | 61 | 117 | 18 | 4 | 2 | 39 | .239 | 341 | 370 | 11 | *.985 |
| 1976—New York b | Amer. | IN-O-DH | 67 | 163 | 20 | 39 | 4 | 0 | 1 | 10 | .239 | 95 | 114 | 7 | .968 |
| National League Totals | | | 132 | 227 | 24 | 43 | 3 | 1 | 0 | 16 | .189 | 141 | 226 | 9 | .976 |
| American League Totals | | | 1256 | 4421 | 510 | 1097 | 119 | 18 | 12 | 254 | .248 | 2650 | 3164 | 144 | .976 |
| Major League Totals | | | 1388 | 4648 | 534 | 1140 | 122 | 19 | 12 | 270 | .245 | 2791 | 3390 | 153 | .976 |

†On restricted list, May 1 through October 15, 1960.
‡On restricted list, March 17 through June 4, 1961. On disabled list, July 9 through July 25, 1961.
§Recalled by Atlanta Braves September 1, 1966; sent to Houston Astros, February 25, 1967, to complete deal in which Braves traded Pitcher Arnold Umbach (transferred from Richmond to Oklahoma City) and Third Baseman Ed Mathews to Astros for Outfielder Dave Nicholson (transferred from Oklahoma City to Richmond) and Pitcher Bob Bruce, December 31, 1966.
xTraded by Houston Astros to New York Mets for Infielder-Outfielder Derrell Griffith, March 24, 1967.
yRecalled by New York Mets and sold to Chicago White Sox, August 15, 1967, to complete deal in which White Sox obtained Third Baseman Ken Boyer from Mets for cash and Infielder Billy Southworth, July 22, 1967; the trade also included Catcher J. C. Martin being sent by White Sox to Mets, November 27, 1967.
zTraded with Pitcher Bob Priddy to California Angels for Second Baseman Bobby Knoop, May 14, 1969.
aSold to New York Yankees, July 8, 1974.
bTraded to Texas Rangers for Infielders Greg Pryor and Brian Doyle and cash estimated at $25,000, February 17, 1977.

### CHAMPIONSHIP SERIES RECORD

| Year Club | League | Pos. | G. | AB. | R. | H. | 2B. | 3B. | HR. | RBI. | B.A. | PO. | A. | E. | F.A. |
|---|---|---|---|---|---|---|---|---|---|---|---|---|---|---|---|
| 1976—New York | Amer. | PH-R-DH | 2 | 1 | 0 | 0 | 0 | 0 | 0 | 0 | .000 | 0 | 0 | 0 | .000 |

### ALL-STAR GAME RECORD

| Year League | Pos. | AB. | R. | H. | 2B. | 3B. | HR. | RBI. | B.A. | PO. | A. | E. | F.A. |
|---|---|---|---|---|---|---|---|---|---|---|---|---|---|
| 1970—American | 2B | 1 | 0 | 0 | 0 | 0 | 0 | 0 | .000 | 0 | 2 | 0 | 1.000 |

## WENDELL ALSTON
### (Dell)

Born September 22, 1952, at White Plains, N.Y.
Height, 6.00. Weight, 180.
Throws right and bats lefthanded.
Hobby—Dancing.
Attended Concordia Junior College, Bronxville, N.Y., and Concordia Teachers College, River Forest, Ill.,
received Bachelor of Arts Degree in Elementary Education.

| Year Club | League | Pos. | G. | AB. | R. | H. | 2B. | 3B. | HR. | RBI. | B.A. | PO. | A. | E. | F.A. |
|---|---|---|---|---|---|---|---|---|---|---|---|---|---|---|---|
| 1973—Oneonta ............NYP | | OF-2B | 61 | 246 | 59 | 79 | 13 | 3 | 4 | 34 | .321 | 96 | 43 | 12 | .921 |
| 1974—Ft. Lauderdale ..Fla.St. | | OF-3B | 120 | 431 | 68 | 127 | 15 | 12 | 2 | 52 | .295 | 168 | 11 | 8 | .957 |
| 1974—West Haven ......East. | | OF | 119 | 452 | *77 | 139 | 18 | 7 | 6 | 47 | .308 | 181 | 12 | 8 | .960 |
| 1976—Syracuse ..........Int. | | OF-PH | 130 | 516 | 87 | 145 | 26 | 9 | 12 | 66 | .281 | 183 | 6 | 11 | .945 |

Invited to New York Yankees' 1977 spring camp.

## LUIS CESAR ALVARADO

Born January 15, 1949, at LaJas, Puerto Rico.
Height, 5.09. Weight, 162.
Throws and bats righthanded.
Hobby—Reading comics.
Tied for Midwest League lead in double plays by shortstop with 60 in 1967.
Named Most Valuable Player in International League, 1969.

| Year Club | League | Pos. | G. | AB. | R. | H. | 2B. | 3B. | HR. | RBI. | B.A. | PO. | A. | E. | F.A. |
|---|---|---|---|---|---|---|---|---|---|---|---|---|---|---|---|
| 1967—Waterloo ..........Midw. | | SS | 118 | 437 | 59 | 97 | 15 | 3 | 8 | 43 | .222 | 172 | *340 | 25 | *.953 |
| 1968—Pittsfield ..........East. | | SS | 129 | 486 | 55 | *125 | 16 | 1 | 0 | 29 | .257 | 156 | ●395 | 25 | .957 |
| 1968—Boston ..............Amer. | | SS | 11 | 46 | 3 | 6 | 2 | 0 | 0 | 1 | .130 | 14 | 26 | 1 | .976 |
| 1969—Louisville ..........Int. | | SS | 137 | *568 | *89 | *166 | *30 | 8 | 4 | 62 | .292 | 201 | 406 | 14 | *.977 |
| 1969—Boston ..............Amer. | | SS | 6 | 5 | 0 | 0 | 0 | 0 | 0 | 0 | .000 | 4 | 6 | 0 | 1.000 |
| 1970—Louisville ..........Int. | | SS | 69 | 294 | 43 | 59 | 12 | 1 | 2 | 23 | .201 | 95 | 210 | 11 | .965 |
| 1970—Boston† ...........Amer. | | 3B-SS | 59 | 183 | 19 | 41 | 11 | 0 | 1 | 10 | .224 | 45 | 134 | 8 | .957 |
| 1971—Chicago ...........Amer. | | SS-2B | 99 | 264 | 22 | 57 | 14 | 1 | 0 | 8 | .216 | 120 | 238 | 13 | .965 |
| 1972—Chicago ...........Amer. | | S-2-3 | 103 | 254 | 30 | 54 | 4 | 1 | 4 | 29 | .213 | 107 | 234 | 15 | .958 |
| 1973—Chicago ...........Amer. | | 2-S-3 | 79 | 203 | 21 | 47 | 7 | 2 | 0 | 20 | .232 | 120 | 158 | 9 | .969 |
| 1974—St. Louis‡ ......Nat. | | SS | 17 | 36 | 3 | 5 | 2 | 0 | 0 | 1 | .139 | 16 | 33 | 1 | .980 |
| 1974—Chi.§-Cleve. .....Amer. | | 2-S-3 | 69 | 124 | 13 | 26 | 2 | 0 | 0 | 12 | .210 | 88 | 114 | 10 | .953 |
| 1975—O.C. x-Tulsa ......A.A. | | *2-3-S | 117 | 462 | 58 | 111 | 16 | 0 | 3 | 64 | .240 | 243 | 288 | 4 | *.993 |
| 1976—Tulsa ...............A.A. | | 2-3-OF | 130 | 490 | 65 | 137 | 38 | 2 | 11 | 72 | .280 | 249 | 332 | 18 | .970 |
| 1976—St. Louis y .......Nat. | | 2B | 16 | 42 | 5 | 12 | 1 | 0 | 0 | 3 | .286 | 22 | 22 | 3 | .936 |
| National League Totals ................. | | | 33 | 78 | 8 | 17 | 3 | 0 | 0 | 4 | .218 | 38 | 55 | 4 | .959 |
| American League Totals ............... | | | 426 | 1079 | 108 | 231 | 40 | 4 | 5 | 80 | .214 | 498 | 910 | 56 | .962 |
| Major League Totals ..................... | | | 459 | 1157 | 116 | 248 | 43 | 4 | 5 | 84 | .214 | 536 | 965 | 60 | .962 |

†Traded with Second Baseman Mike Andrews to Chicago White Sox for Shortstop Luis Aparicio, December 1, 1970.
‡Traded to St. Louis Cardinals for Pitcher Ken Tatum, April 26, 1974.
§Traded with Infielder Ed Crosby to Cleveland Indians for Shortstop Jack Heidemann, May 31, 1974.
xTraded by Cleveland Indians to St. Louis Cardinals for a player to be named later, May 27, 1975; Cardinals sent Infielder-Outfielder Doug Howard to Indians, September 30, 1975, to complete deal.
ySold to Detroit Tigers, November 6, 1976; sold to New York Mets, March 25, 1977.

## LARRY EUGENE ANDERSEN

Born May 6, 1953, at Portland, Ore.
Height, 6.03. Weight, 200.
Throws and bats righthanded.
Hobbies—Music and airplanes.
Attended Bellevue Community College, Bellevue, Wash.
Pitched 6-0 no-hit victory against Victoria, June 1, 1974.

| Year Club | League | G. | IP. | W. | L. | Pct. | H. | R. | ER. | SO. | BB. | ERA. |
|---|---|---|---|---|---|---|---|---|---|---|---|---|
| 1971—Reno.....................................California | | 7 | 24 | 1 | 0 | 1.000 | 37 | 20 | 18 | 10 | 9 | 6.75 |
| 1971—Sarasota Indians ..................Gulf Coast | | 4 | 15 | 0 | 3 | .000 | 15 | 7 | 5 | 10 | 7 | 3.00 |
| 1972—Reno.....................................California | | 27 | 124 | 4 | 14 | .222 | 166 | 102 | 90 | 79 | 57 | 6.53 |
| 1973—Reno.....................................California | | 29 | 164 | 10 | 8 | .556 | 173 | 91 | 72 | 115 | 67 | 3.95 |
| 1974—San Antonio .........................Texas | | 25 | 169 | 10 | 6 | .625 | 176 | 84 | 72 | 64 | 51 | 3.83 |
| 1975—Oklahoma City ....................Am. Assoc. | | 25 | 156 | 10 | 11 | .476 | 179 | 87 | 73 | 64 | 52 | 4.21 |
| 1975—Cleveland .............................American | | 3 | 6 | 0 | 0 | .000 | 4 | 3 | 3 | 4 | 2 | 4.50 |
| 1976—Toledo..................................Int'national | | 6 | 23 | 0 | 2 | .000 | 47 | 33 | 33 | 8 | 6 | 12.91 |
| 1976—Williamsport ........................Eastern | | 21 | 133 | 9 | 6 | .600 | 117 | 47 | 40 | 74 | 34 | 2.71 |
| Major League Totals ............................. | | 3 | 6 | 0 | 0 | .000 | 4 | 3 | 3 | 4 | 2 | 4.50 |

## LAWRENCE DENNIS ANDERSON
### (Larry)

Born December 3, 1952, at Maywood, Calif.
Height, 6.03. Weight, 200.
Throws and bats righthanded.
Hobby—Fishing.
Led Pacific Coast League in wild pitches with 27 in 1975 and 25 in 1976.
Led Pacific Coast League in hit batsmen with 9 in 1975.

| Year Club | League | G. | IP. | W. | L. | Pct. | H. | R. | ER. | SO. | BB. | ERA. |
|---|---|---|---|---|---|---|---|---|---|---|---|---|
| 1971—Newark | NYP | 13 | 69 | 4 | 7 | .364 | 64 | 60 | •51 | 74 | 57 | 6.65 |
| 1972—Danville | Midwest | 18 | 92 | 3 | 4 | .429 | 70 | 42 | 35 | 97 | 65 | 3.42 |
| 1973—Danville† | Midwest | 16 | 100 | 6 | 5 | .545 | 58 | 33 | 25 | 101 | 54 | 2.25 |
| 1973—Shreveport | Texas | 3 | 22 | 2 | 1 | .667 | 19 | 11 | 10 | 28 | 8 | 4.09 |
| 1974—Sacramento | P. Coast | 9 | 33 | 0 | 5 | .000 | 43 | 42 | 40 | 17 | 34 | 10.91 |
| 1974—Shreveport‡ | Texas | 19 | 107 | 7 | 8 | .467 | 98 | 60 | 48 | 81 | 46 | 4.04 |
| 1974—Milwaukee | American | 2 | 2 | 0 | 0 | .000 | 2 | 0 | 0 | 3 | 1 | 0.00 |
| 1975—Thetford Mines | Eastern | 8 | 56 | 3 | 4 | .429 | 43 | 23 | 21 | 38 | 23 | 3.38 |
| 1975—Sacramento | P. Coast | 19 | 110 | 7 | 9 | .438 | 107 | 70 | 67 | 87 | 95 | 5.48 |
| 1975—Milwaukee | American | 8 | 30 | 1 | 0 | 1.000 | 36 | 18 | 17 | 13 | 6 | 5.10 |
| 1976—Spokane§ | P. Coast | 34 | 145 | 9 | 11 | .450 | 158 | 110 | 99 | 89 | 100 | 6.14 |
| Major League Totals | | 10 | 32 | 1 | 0 | 1.000 | 38 | 18 | 17 | 16 | 7 | 4.78 |

†On temporary inactive list, June 15 to July 3, 1973.
‡Played in one game as a catcher.
§Selected by Toronto Blue Jays from Milwaukee Brewers in American League expansion draft, November 5, 1976. Assigned to Chicago White Sox' organization, January 5, 1976, to complete deal which sent Catcher Phil Roof to Toronto, October 21, 1976.

## MICHAEL ALLEN ANDERSON
### (Mike)

Born June 22, 1951, at Florence, S. C.
Height, 6.02. Weight, 200.
Throws and bats righthanded.
Hobby—Golf.
Attended University of Tampa, Tampa, Fla.

Led Appalachian League first basemen in double plays with 35 in 1969 and tied for Pacific Coast League lead in double plays by outfielders with 3 in 1971.
Named Pacific Coast League Rookie of the Year in 1971.

| Year Club | League | Pos. | G. | AB. | R. | H. | 2B. | 3B. | HR. | RBI. | B.A. | PO. | A. | E. | F.A. |
|---|---|---|---|---|---|---|---|---|---|---|---|---|---|---|---|
| 1969—Pulaski | Appal. | 1B | 64 | 231 | 51 | 84 | 18 | •6 | 10 | 60 | .364 | 431 | 32 | 5 | •.989 |
| 1970—Peninsula | Carol. | OF-1-3 | 118 | 402 | 77 | 126 | 19 | 4 | 22 | 67 | .313 | 505 | 53 | 11 | .981 |
| 1971—Eugene | P.C. | OF | 134 | 482 | 111 | 161 | 28 | 10 | 36 | 100 | .334 | •319 | 14 | 6 | .982 |
| 1971—Philadelphia | Nat. | OF | 26 | 89 | 11 | 22 | 5 | 1 | 2 | 5 | .247 | 67 | 1 | 1 | .986 |
| 1972—Eugene | P.C. | OF-1B | 88 | 309 | 60 | 92 | 14 | 1 | 17 | 56 | .298 | 224 | 11 | 6 | .975 |
| 1972—Philadelphia | Nat. | OF | 36 | 103 | 8 | 20 | 5 | 1 | 2 | 5 | .194 | 68 | 6 | 1 | .987 |
| 1973—Philadelphia† | Nat. | OF | 87 | 193 | 32 | 49 | 9 | 1 | 9 | 28 | .254 | 99 | 4 | 2 | .981 |
| 1974—Philadelphia | Nat. | OF-1B | 145 | 395 | 35 | 99 | 22 | 2 | 5 | 34 | .251 | 240 | 12 | 5 | .981 |
| 1975—Philadelphia‡ | Nat. | OF-1B | 115 | 247 | 24 | 64 | 10 | 3 | 4 | 28 | .259 | 170 | 6 | 4 | .978 |
| 1976—St. Louis | Nat. | OF-1B | 86 | 199 | 17 | 58 | 8 | 1 | 1 | 12 | .291 | 136 | 7 | 3 | .979 |
| Major League Totals | | | 495 | 1226 | 127 | 312 | 59 | 9 | 23 | 112 | .254 | 780 | 36 | 16 | .981 |

†On disabled list, July 26 to August 19, 1973.
‡Traded to St. Louis Cardinals for Pitcher Ron Reed, December 9, 1975.

## FRED ANDREWS, III

Born May 4, 1952, at Lafayette, La.
Height, 5.08. Weight, 163.
Throws and bats righthanded.
Hobby—Music.

Led Western Carolinas League shortstops in double plays with 58 in 1972.
Tied for Appalachian League lead in sacrifice hits with 6 in 1970.

| Year Club | League | Pos. | G. | AB. | R. | H. | 2B. | 3B. | HR. | RBI. | B.A. | PO. | A. | E. | F.A. |
|---|---|---|---|---|---|---|---|---|---|---|---|---|---|---|---|
| 1970—Pulaski | Appal. | SS-3 | 53 | 194 | 36 | 60 | 10 | 1 | 1 | 24 | .309 | 62 | 112 | 21 | .892 |
| 1971—Spartanburg | W. Car. | •SS-2-O | 105 | 355 | 46 | 94 | 15 | 3 | 4 | 33 | .265 | •166 | •284 | •42 | .915 |
| 1972—Spartanburg | W. Car. | •SS-2B | 92 | 365 | 67 | 103 | 15 | 3 | 3 | 43 | .282 | 134 | 274 | •35 | .921 |
| 1972—Reading | East. | SS | 40 | 137 | 10 | 33 | 6 | 0 | 0 | 10 | .241 | 47 | 146 | 12 | .941 |
| 1973—Reading† | East. | 2B-SS | 110 | 335 | 48 | 76 | 15 | 4 | 1 | 38 | .227 | 194 | 292 | 34 | .935 |
| 1974—Reading | East. | •2B-SS | 128 | •506 | 85 | 138 | 25 | 7 | 14 | 56 | .273 | •298 | •341 | •29 | .957 |
| 1974—Toledo | Int. | 2B | 4 | 12 | 0 | 2 | 1 | 0 | 0 | 2 | .167 | 5 | 7 | 0 | 1.000 |
| 1975—Toledo | Int. | 2B | 119 | 430 | 44 | 111 | 23 | 4 | 5 | 36 | .258 | •287 | 328 | 21 | .967 |
| 1976—Oklahoma City‡ | A.A. | 2B | 97 | 360 | 46 | 107 | 20 | 4 | 2 | 48 | .297 | 210 | 231 | 15 | .967 |
| 1976—Philadelphia | Nat. | 2B | 4 | 6 | 1 | 4 | 0 | 0 | 0 | 0 | .667 | 7 | 3 | 0 | 1.000 |
| Major League Totals | | | 4 | 6 | 1 | 4 | 0 | 0 | 0 | 0 | .667 | 7 | 3 | 0 | 1.000 |

†On disabled list, June 11 to June 23, 1973.
‡On disabled list, April 16 to April 26, and June 24 to July 14, 1976.

## ROBERT PATRICK ANDREWS
### (Rob)

Born December 11, 1952, at Santa Monica, Calif.
Height, 6.00. Weight, 185.
Throws and bats righthanded.
Hobbies—Golf, surfing and water skiing.
Attended El Camino College, Torrance, Calif.

Brother of Mike Andrews, former second baseman with Boston Red Sox, Chicago White Sox and Oakland Athletics.
Led Southern League second basemen in double plays with 107 in 1973.
Led International League second basemen in double plays with 99 in 1974.
Led International League in sacrifice hits with 11 in 1974.

| Year Club | League | Pos. | G. | AB. | R. | H. | 2B. | 3B. | HR. | RBI. | B.A. | PO. | A. | E. | F.A. |
|---|---|---|---|---|---|---|---|---|---|---|---|---|---|---|---|
| 1971—Stockton ............Calif. | | 2-O-S-3 | 110 | 331 | 39 | 84 | 8 | 1 | 1 | 28 | .254 | 186 | 207 | 23 | .945 |
| 1972—Lodi ..................Calif. | | •2B-OF | 128 | 489 | 79 | 145 | 18 | 5 | 2 | 59 | .297 | 266 | 370 | 17 | •.974 |
| 1973—Asheville ..........South. | | 2B | 138 | 541 | •98 | •167 | 25 | 11 | 4 | 80 | •.309 | 293 | •456 | •25 | .968 |
| 1974—Rochester† ........Int. | | 2B | •144 | •540 | 84 | •165 | 10 | 6 | 5 | 55 | .306 | •337 | 370 | 24 | .967 |
| 1975—Houston ............Nat. | | 2B-SS | 103 | 277 | 29 | 66 | 5 | 4 | 0 | 19 | .238 | 193 | 249 | 10 | .978 |
| 1976—Memphis ..........Int. | | 2B | 22 | 80 | 16 | 26 | 3 | 3 | 2 | 14 | .325 | 38 | 75 | 3 | .974 |
| 1976—Houston‡ ..........Nat. | | 2B-SS | 109 | 410 | 42 | 105 | 8 | 5 | 0 | 23 | .256 | 228 | 356 | 14 | .976 |
| Major League Totals ..................... | | | 212 | 687 | 71 | 171 | 13 | 9 | 0 | 42 | .249 | 421 | 605 | 24 | .977 |

†Traded with Infielder Enos Cabell by Baltimore Orioles to Houston Astros for First Baseman Lee May and Outfielder Jay Schlueter, December 3, 1974.
‡Traded with a player to be named later to San Francisco Giants for Outfielder Willie Crawford and Infielder Rob Sperring, March 26, 1977.

## JOAQUIN ANDUJAR
Name pronounced Wah-Keen AHN-doo-hahr.
### (Jack)
Born December 21, 1952, at San Pedro de Macoris, Dominican Republic.
Height, 6.00. Weight, 170.
Throws and bats righthanded.

| Year Club | League | G. | IP. | W. | L. | Pct. | H. | R. | ER. | SO. | BB. | ERA. |
|---|---|---|---|---|---|---|---|---|---|---|---|---|
| 1970—Bradenton Reds....................Gulf Coast | | 12 | 82 | 3 | 5 | .375 | •86 | •58 | •38 | 88 | 56 | 4.17 |
| 1971—Sioux Falls ..........................Northern | | 19 | 75 | 4 | 7 | .364 | 61 | 67 | 53 | 82 | 63 | 6.36 |
| 1972—Three Rivers.......................Eastern | | 22 | 112 | 7 | 6 | .538 | 87 | 59 | 44 | 101 | 73 | 3.54 |
| 1973—Indianapolis .......................Am. Assoc. | | 11 | 40 | 2 | 5 | .286 | 42 | 45 | 40 | 23· | 45 | 8.93 |
| 1973—Three Rivers† .....................Eastern | | 10 | 59 | 5 | 2 | .714 | 38 | 29 | 13 | 39 | 38 | 1.98 |
| 1974—Indianapolis .......................Am. Assoc. | | 33 | 111 | 8 | 8 | .500 | 85 | 62 | 44 | 92 | 93 | 3.57 |
| 1975—Three Rivers‡§ ...................Eastern | | 18 | 62 | 4 | 8 | .333 | 57 | 36 | 28 | 44 | 40 | 4.06 |
| 1976—Houston .............................National | | 28 | 172 | 9 | 10 | .474 | 163 | 74 | 69 | 59 | 75 | 3.61 |
| Major League Totals .............................. | | 28 | 172 | 9 | 10 | .474 | 163 | 74 | 69 | 59 | 75 | 3.61 |

†On disabled list, August 5 to August 15, 1973.
‡On disabled list, May 11 to July 4, 1975.
§Traded by Cincinnati Reds to Houston Astros for two minor league players to be named later, October 25, 1975; Astros sent Pitchers Carlos Alfonso and Luis Sanchez to Reds, December 11, 1975, to complete deal.

## NORMAN STANLEY ANGELINI
### (Norm)
Born September 24, 1947, at San Francisco, Calif.
Height, 5.11. Weight, 180.
Throws and bats lefthanded.
Hobbies—Fishing, hunting and motorcycles.
Attended College of San Mateo, San Francisco, Calif., San Francisco State,
San Francisco, Calif., and Washington State University, Pullman, Wash.
Led American Association in saves with 20 in 1975.

| Year Club | League | G. | IP. | W. | L. | Pct. | H. | R. | ER. | SO. | BB. | ERA. |
|---|---|---|---|---|---|---|---|---|---|---|---|---|
| 1969—Winnipeg.............................Northern | | 13 | 72 | 5 | 3 | .625 | 58 | 33 | 24 | 74 | 18 | 3.00 |
| 1970—San José† ...........................California | | 21 | 129 | 8 | 8 | .500 | 115 | 47 | 38 | 136 | 34 | 2.65 |
| 1971—Elmira ...............................Eastern | | 26 | 70 | 5 | 6 | .455 | 53 | 21 | 13 | 79 | 18 | 1.67 |
| 1972—Omaha ...............................Am. Assoc. | | 19 | 51 | 4 | 2 | .667 | 27 | 9 | 8 | 66 | 22 | 1.41 |
| 1972—Kansas City........................American | | 21 | 16 | 2 | 1 | .667 | 13 | 4 | 4 | 16 | 12 | 2.25 |
| 1973—Omaha ...............................Am. Assoc. | | 22 | 55 | 2 | 3 | .400 | 63 | 35 | 29 | 58 | 37 | 4.75 |
| 1973—Kansas City........................American | | 7 | 4 | 0 | 0 | .000 | 2 | 2 | 2 | 3 | 7 | 4.50 |
| 1974—Jacksonville .......................Southern | | •56 | 105 | 9 | 7 | .563 | 85 | 41 | 29 | 94 | 59 | 2.49 |
| 1975—Omaha‡ .............................Am. Assoc. | | 54 | 69 | 3 | 8 | .273 | 58 | 35 | 34 | 71 | 43 | 4.43 |
| 1976—Richmond ..........................Int'national | | 42 | 74 | 6 | 5 | .545 | 71 | 43 | 30 | 67 | 40 | 3.65 |
| Major League Totals .............................. | | 28 | 20 | 2 | 1 | .667 | 15 | 6 | 6 | 19 | 19 | 2.70 |

†On temporary inactive list, April 13 to May 30, 1970.
‡Traded with Pitcher Al Autry by Kansas city Royals to Atlanta Braves for Pitcher Ray Sadecki, September 4, 1975, to complete deal in which Braves obtained Pitcher Bruce Dal Canton on waivers from Royals, June 20, 1975.
Invited to Atlanta Braves' 1977 spring camp.

## ROBERT JOHN APODACA
Name pronounced ap-poh-DACK-uh.
### (Bob)
Born January 31, 1950, at Los Angeles, Calif.
Height, 5.11. Weight, 175.
Throws and bats righthanded.
Attended Cerritos College, Norwalk, Calif., and California State University,
Los Angeles, Calif.

| Year   Club | League | G. | IP. | W. | L. | Pct. | H. | R. | ER. | SO. | BB. | ERA. |
|---|---|---|---|---|---|---|---|---|---|---|---|---|
| 1971–Visalia ...............................California | | 13 | 70 | 7 | 1 | .875 | 62 | 28 | 28 | 52 | 16 | 3.60 |
| 1972–Memphis ............................Texas | | 20 | 157 | 11 | 7 | .611 | 145 | 61 | 49 | 125 | 40 | 2.81 |
| 1973–Tidewater .........................Int'national | | 34 | 80 | 6 | 3 | .667 | 63 | 20 | 16 | 45 | 28 | 1.80 |
| 1973–New York ...........................National | | 1 | 0 | 0 | 0 | .000 | 0 | 1 | 1 | 0 | 2 | ....... |
| 1974–New York ..........................National | | 35 | 103 | 6 | 6 | .500 | 92 | 47 | 40 | 54 | 42 | 3.50 |
| 1975–New York† ........................National | | 46 | 85 | 3 | 4 | .429 | 66 | 18 | 14 | 45 | 28 | 1.48 |
| 1976–New York ..........................National | | 43 | 90 | 3 | 7 | .300 | 71 | 34 | 28 | 45 | 29 | 2.80 |
| Major League Totals ............................. | | 125 | 278 | 12 | 17 | .414 | 229 | 100 | 83 | 144 | 101 | 2.69 |

†On disabled list, March 27 to April 18 and June 29 to July 27, 1975.

## ANTONIO RAFAEL ARMAS (MACHADO)
### (Tony)

Born July 12, 1953, at Anzoategui, Venezuela.
Height, 5.11. Weight, 182.
Throw and bats righthanded.

| Year   Club | League | Pos. | G. | AB. | R. | H. | 2B. | 3B. | HR. | RBI. | B.A. | PO. | A. | E. | F.A. |
|---|---|---|---|---|---|---|---|---|---|---|---|---|---|---|---|
| 1971–Monroe..............W. Car. | | OF | 31 | 88 | 7 | 20 | 3 | 0 | 1 | 10 | .227 | 37 | 3 | 6 | .870 |
| 1971–Bradenton Pir ..Gulf C. | | OF | 43 | 169 | 12 | 39 | 3 | 3 | 0 | 17 | .231 | •98 | 5 | 3 | .972 |
| 1972–Gastonia............W. Car. | | OF | 117 | 399 | 50 | 106 | 18 | 4 | 9 | 51 | .266 | 165 | 7 | 8 | .956 |
| 1973–Sherbrooke† ......East. | | OF | 84 | 302 | 46 | 91 | 15 | 5 | 11 | 45 | .301 | 150 | 6 | 8 | .951 |
| 1974–Thetford Mines..East. | | OF | •137 | 476 | 64 | 132 | 26 | 3 | 15 | 81 | .277 | •329 | 18 | 10 | .972 |
| 1975–Charleston ........Int. | | OF | 128 | 450 | 65 | 135 | 28 | 4 | 12 | 72 | .300 | 220 | •14 | 3 | .987 |
| 1976–Charleston ........Int. | | OF-1B | 114 | 409 | 62 | 96 | 24 | 1 | 21 | 67 | .235 | 210 | 8 | 7 | .969 |
| 1976–Pittsburgh ........Nat. | | OF | 4 | 6 | 0 | 2 | 0 | 0 | 0 | 1 | .333 | 3 | 0 | 0 | 1.000 |
| Major League Totals ..................... | | | 4 | 6 | 0 | 2 | 0 | 0 | 0 | 1 | .333 | 3 | 0 | 0 | 1.000 |

†On disabled list, May 27 to July 12, 1973.

## EDISON ROSANDA ARMBRISTER
### (Ed)

Born July 4, 1948, at Nassau, Bahamas.
Height, 6.03. Weight, 175.
Throws and bats righthanded.
Hobbies–Swimming, basketball, dancing and track.

Tied for Southern League lead in double plays by outfielders with 4 in 1970 and tied for American Association lead with 4 in 1972.

| Year   Club | League | Pos. | G. | AB. | R. | H. | 2B. | 3B. | HR. | RBI. | B.A. | PO. | A. | E. | F.A. |
|---|---|---|---|---|---|---|---|---|---|---|---|---|---|---|---|
| 1967–Cocoa† ..............Fla. St. | | OF | 100 | 336 | 27 | 71 | 8 | 5 | 1 | 32 | .211 | 150 | 5 | 9 | .945 |
| 1968–Cocoa ................Fla. St. | | OF | 129 | 472 | 75 | 123 | 17 | 3 | 2 | 32 | .261 | 169 | 6 | 12 | .936 |
| 1969–Peninsula ..........Carol. | | OF | 126 | 420 | 59 | 114 | 11 | 8 | 8 | 30 | .271 | 244 | 19 | •17 | .939 |
| 1970–Columbus .........South. | | O-3 | 127 | 428 | 58 | 102 | 13 | 8 | 8 | 46 | .238 | 213 | 40 | 17 | .937 |
| 1971–Columbus .........South. | | O-3 | 121 | 403 | 58 | 120 | 21 | 2 | 9 | 42 | .298 | 124 | 67 | 15 | .927 |
| 1972–Indianapolis ......A.A. | | O-3 | 133 | 460 | 69 | 138 | 26 | •11 | 7 | 43 | .300 | 235 | 22 | 14 | .948 |
| 1973–Indianapolis ......A.A. | | OF | 125 | 448 | 86 | 138 | 22 | 8 | 10 | 72 | .308 | 175 | 13 | 11 | .945 |
| 1973–Cincinnati..........Nat. | | OF | 18 | 37 | 5 | 8 | 0 | 1 | 1 | 5 | .216 | 21 | 1 | 2 | .917 |
| 1974–Indianapolis ......A.A. | | OF | 125 | 427 | 64 | 123 | 22 | 8 | 13 | 73 | .288 | 176 | 7 | 5 | .973 |
| 1974–Cincinnati..........Nat. | | OF | 9 | 7 | 0 | 2 | 0 | 0 | 0 | 0 | .286 | 1 | 0 | 0 | 1.000 |
| 1975–Cincinnati..........Nat. | | OF | 59 | 65 | 9 | 12 | 1 | 0 | 0 | 2 | .185 | 13 | 0 | 2 | .867 |
| 1976–Cincinnati..........Nat. | | OF | 73 | 78 | 20 | 23 | 3 | 2 | 2 | 7 | .295 | 31 | 4 | 1 | .972 |
| Major League Totals ..................... | | | 159 | 187 | 34 | 45 | 7 | 3 | 3 | 14 | .241 | 66 | 5 | 5 | .934 |

†On disabled list, July 13 through July 28, 1967.
‡Traded by Houston Astros with Pitcher Jack Billingham, Outfielder Cesar Geronimo, Infielder Denis Menke and Second Baseman Joe Morgan to Cincinnati Reds for First Baseman Lee May, Second Baseman Tommy Helms and Outfielder Jim Stewart, November 29, 1971.

### CHAMPIONSHIP SERIES RECORD

| Year   Club | League | Pos. | G. | AB. | R. | H. | 2B. | 3B. | HR. | RBI. | B.A. | PO. | A. | E. | F.A. |
|---|---|---|---|---|---|---|---|---|---|---|---|---|---|---|---|
| 1973–Cincinnati..........Nat. | | PH-OF | 3 | 6 | 0 | 1 | 0 | 0 | 0 | 0 | .167 | 3 | 0 | 0 | 1.000 |
| 1975–Cincinnati..........Nat. | | PH | 2 | 0 | 0 | 0 | 0 | 0 | 0 | 1 | .000 | 0 | 0 | 0 | .000 |
| 1976–Cincinnati..........Nat. | | PH | 1 | 0 | 0 | 0 | 0 | 0 | 0 | 0 | .000 | 0 | 0 | 0 | .000 |
| Championship Series Totals ............ | | | 6 | 6 | 0 | 1 | 0 | 0 | 0 | 1 | .167 | 3 | 0 | 0 | 1.000 |

### WORLD SERIES RECORD

| Year   Club | League | Pos. | G. | AB. | R. | H. | 2B. | 3B. | HR. | RBI. | B.A. | PO. | A. | E. | F.A. |
|---|---|---|---|---|---|---|---|---|---|---|---|---|---|---|---|
| 1975–Cincinnati..........Nat. | | PH | 4 | 1 | 1 | 0 | 0 | 0 | 0 | 0 | .000 | 0 | 0 | 0 | .000 |

---

## *DID YOU KNOW —*

That the National League record for hitting 30 or more home runs in consecutive seasons is held by Eddie Mathews? Playing for the Milwaukee Braves, he blasted at least 30 round-trippers every year from 1953 through 1961, nine seasons.

---

## JOHN THOMAS ARNOLD

Born November 10, 1956, at Effingham, Ill.
Height, 6.03. Weight, 200.
Throws and bats lefthanded.
Hobby—Hunting.

| Year Club | League | G. | IP. | W. | L. | Pct. | H. | R. | ER. | SO. | BB. | ERA. |
|---|---|---|---|---|---|---|---|---|---|---|---|---|
| 1974—Sarasota Indians | Gulf Coast | 11 | 64 | 4 | 4 | .500 | 59 | 26 | 24 | 56 | 28 | 3.38 |
| 1975—San Jose | California | 26 | 177 | 12 | 7 | .632 | 151 | 67 | 62 | 109 | 80 | 3.15 |
| 1976—Williamsport | Eastern | 6 | 27 | 1 | 3 | .250 | 34 | 20 | 18 | 12 | 26 | 6.00 |
| 1976—San Jose | California | 17 | 93 | 6 | 8 | .429 | 84 | 76 | 59 | 74 | 74 | 5.71 |

Listed on Cleveland Indians' 1977 spring roster.

## FERNANDO ARROYO
### (Fred)

Born March 21, 1952, at Sacramento, Calif.
Height, 6.02½. Weight, 195.
Throws and bats righthanded.
Hobbies—Music, fishing and sports in general.
Pitched 5-0 perfect game against West Palm Beach, July 8, 1971.

| Year Club | League | G. | IP. | W. | L. | Pct. | H. | R. | ER. | SO. | BB. | ERA. |
|---|---|---|---|---|---|---|---|---|---|---|---|---|
| 1970—Bristol | Appalachian | 9 | 61 | 4 | 1 | .800 | 45 | 28 | 14 | 53 | 21 | 2.07 |
| 1971—Lakeland | Fla. State | 25 | 193 | 11 | 11 | .500 | 153 | 71 | 54 | 117 | 53 | 2.52 |
| 1972—Montgomery | Southern | 28 | 157 | 8 | 9 | .471 | 142 | 81 | 67 | 82 | 55 | 3.84 |
| 1973—Montgomery | Southern | 23 | 159 | 9 | 8 | .529 | 153 | 71 | 54 | 74 | 50 | 3.06 |
| 1974—Evansville | Am. Assoc. | 35 | 87 | 6 | 4 | .600 | 93 | 50 | 41 | 45 | 45 | 4.24 |
| 1975—Evansville | Am. Assoc. | 11 | 86 | 5 | 4 | .556 | 82 | 37 | 25 | 44 | 18 | 2.62 |
| 1975—Detroit | American | 14 | 53 | 2 | 1 | .667 | 56 | 28 | 27 | 25 | 22 | 4.58 |
| 1976—Evansville | Am. Assoc. | 44 | 102 | 5 | 8 | .385 | 120 | 74 | 54 | 56 | 41 | 4.76 |
| Major League Totals | | 14 | 53 | 2 | 1 | .667 | 56 | 28 | 27 | 25 | 22 | 4.58 |

## ALAN DEAN ASHBY

Born July 8, 1951, at Long Beach, Calif.
Height, 6.02. Weight, 190.
Throws right and bats lefthanded.
Hobbies—Golf, basketball and football.
Attended Harbor Junior College, Wilmington, Calif.
Led California League catchers in double plays with 12 in 1971.

| Year Club | League | Pos. | G. | AB. | R. | H. | 2B. | 3B. | HR. | RBI. | B.A. | PO. | A. | E. | F.A. |
|---|---|---|---|---|---|---|---|---|---|---|---|---|---|---|---|
| 1969—Sara. Indians | Gulf C. | C | 48 | 117 | 10 | 28 | 3 | 1 | 0 | 14 | .239 | 219 | 20 | 2 | *.992 |
| 1970—Reno† | Calif. | C | 40 | 121 | 15 | 23 | 5 | 1 | 3 | 18 | .190 | 321 | 27 | 7 | .980 |
| 1971—Jacksonville | South. | C | 13 | 35 | 4 | 7 | 2 | 0 | 0 | 8 | .200 | 76 | 6 | 1 | .988 |
| 1971—Reno‡ | Calif. | C-3B | 77 | 239 | 52 | 70 | 14 | 1 | 18 | 60 | .293 | 492 | 59 | 10 | .982 |
| 1972—Portland | P. C. | C | 95 | 291 | 33 | 65 | 9 | 2 | 9 | 28 | .223 | 601 | 50 | 8 | .988 |
| 1973—Ok.C.§-Evan. | A. A. | C-OF | 41 | 124 | 20 | 28 | 8 | 0 | 3 | 16 | .226 | 253 | 26 | 2 | .993 |
| 1973—Cleveland | Amer. | C | 11 | 29 | 4 | 5 | 1 | 0 | 1 | 3 | .172 | 45 | 0 | 1 | .978 |
| 1974—Oklahoma City | A. A | C | 66 | 211 | 26 | 60 | 19 | 1 | 2 | 24 | .284 | 405 | 33 | 8 | .982 |
| 1974—Cleveland | Amer. | C | 10 | 7 | 1 | 1 | 0 | 0 | 0 | 0 | .143 | 12 | 0 | 0 | 1.000 |
| 1975—Cleveland | Amer. | C-1-3 | 90 | 254 | 32 | 57 | 10 | 1 | 5 | 32 | .224 | 450 | 43 | 6 | .988 |
| 1976—Cleveland xy | Amer. | C-3-1 | 89 | 247 | 26 | 59 | 5 | 1 | 4 | 32 | .239 | 476 | 52 | 7 | .987 |
| Major League Totals | | | 200 | 537 | 63 | 122 | 16 | 2 | 10 | 67 | .227 | 983 | 95 | 14 | .987 |

†On military list, January 1 through May 23, 1970.
‡On temporary inactive list, August 27 through September 13, 1971.
§Option transferred to Evansville, May 22, 1973.
xOn supplemental disabled list, August 9 through November 5, 1976.
yTraded with Outfielder-First Baseman Doug Howard (Toledo) to Toronto Blue Jays for Pitcher Al Fitzmorris, November 5, 1976.

## THOMAS STEVEN ASHFORD
### (Tucker)

Born December 4, 1954, at Memphis, Tenn.
Height, 6.01. Weight, 195.
Throws and bats righthanded.
Hobbies—Golf, basketball and billiards.
Attended University of Mississippi, University, Miss., and
Shelby State Community College, Memphis, Tenn.

| Year Club | League | Pos. | G. | AB. | R. | H. | 2B. | 3B. | HR. | RBI. | B.A. | PO. | A. | E. | F.A. |
|---|---|---|---|---|---|---|---|---|---|---|---|---|---|---|---|
| 1974—Walla Walla | N'west | S-O-3B | 77 | 263 | 56 | 64 | 7 | 2 | 4 | 30 | .243 | 123 | 159 | 26 | .916 |
| 1975—Alexandria | Texas | SS | 120 | 376 | 33 | 89 | 12 | 1 | 3 | 38 | .237 | 58 | 92 | 16 | .904 |
| 1976—Amarillo | Texas | 3B-SS | 132 | 519 | 91 | 141 | 29 | 0 | 12 | 67 | .272 | *112 | 288 | *38 | .913 |
| 1976—San Diego | Nat. | 3B | 4 | 5 | 0 | 3 | 1 | 0 | 0 | 0 | .600 | 1 | 2 | 0 | 1.000 |
| Major League Totals | | | 4 | 5 | 0 | 3 | 1 | 0 | 0 | 0 | .600 | 1 | 2 | 0 | 1.000 |

## BRIAN HANLY ASSELSTINE
Name pronounced ASS-ul-styn.

Born September 23, 1953, at Santa Barbara, Calif.
Height, 6.01. Weight, 175.
Throws right and bats lefthanded.
Hobbies—Fishing, hunting, golf, water skiing and music.
Attended Allan Hancock College, Santa Maria, Calif.

| Year Club | League | Pos. | G. | AB. | R. | H. | 2B. | 3B. | HR. | RBI. | B.A. | PO. | A. | E. | F.A. |
|---|---|---|---|---|---|---|---|---|---|---|---|---|---|---|---|
| 1973—Savannah | South. | OF | 15 | 47 | 5 | 7 | 1 | 0 | 1 | 3 | .149 | 27 | 0 | 0 | 1.000 |
| 1973—Greenwood | W. Car. | OF | 2 | 2 | 0 | 0 | 0 | 0 | 0 | 0 | .000 | 0 | 0 | 0 | .000 |
| 1974—Savannah | South. | OF | 126 | 508 | 82 | 133 | 11 | 4 | 6 | 35 | .262 | 294 | 9 | 10 | .968 |
| 1975—Richmond† | Int. | •OF-SS | 122 | 444 | 66 | 126 | 21 | 2 | 1 | 22 | .284 | 284 | 6 | •12 | .960 |
| 1976—Richmond | Int. | OF-2B | 122 | 458 | 73 | 134 | 23 | 5 | 5 | 58 | .293 | 237 | 9 | 5 | .980 |
| 1976—Atlanta | Nat. | OF | 11 | 33 | 2 | 7 | 0 | 0 | 1 | 3 | .212 | 19 | 0 | 0 | 1.000 |
| Major League Totals | | | 11 | 33 | 2 | 7 | 0 | 0 | 1 | 3 | .212 | 19 | 0 | 0 | 1.000 |

†On disabled list, July 1 to July 19, 1975.


## WILLIAM CECIL GLENN ATKINSON
### (Bill)

Born October 4, 1954, at Chatham, Ontario, Canada.
Height, 5.07½. Weight, 165.
Throws right and bats lefthanded.
Hobby—Watching sports.

| Year Club | League | G. | IP. | W. | L. | Pct. | H. | R. | ER. | SO. | BB. | ERA. |
|---|---|---|---|---|---|---|---|---|---|---|---|---|
| 1972—Jamestown | NYP | 19 | 25 | 3 | 3 | .500 | 21 | 11 | 10 | 27 | 11 | 3.60 |
| 1973—West Palm Beach | Florida St. | 35 | 113 | 8 | 7 | .533 | 99 | 49 | 36 | 69 | 33 | 3.03 |
| 1974—Quebec City | Eastern | 33 | 141 | 7 | 8 | .467 | 133 | 81 | 58 | 66 | 65 | 3.70 |
| 1975—Memphis | Inter'tional | 49 | 106 | 3 | 4 | .429 | 94 | 38 | 33 | 72 | 36 | 2.80 |
| 1976—Denver | Am. Assoc. | 51 | 79 | 6 | 3 | .667 | 79 | 36 | 35 | 61 | 47 | 3.99 |
| 1976—Montreal | National | 4 | 5 | 0 | 0 | .000 | 3 | 0 | 0 | 4 | 1 | 0.00 |
| Major League Totals | | 4 | 5 | 0 | 0 | .000 | 3 | 0 | 0 | 4 | 1 | 0.00 |


## FREDERICK STEVEN AUERBACH
### (Rick)

Born February 15, 1950, at Woodland Hills, Calif.
Height, 6.00. Weight, 175.
Throws and bats righthanded.
Hobbies—Hunting, trapping and taxidermy.
Attended Pierce Junior College, Woodland Hills, Calif., and
Mesa Community College, Mesa, Ariz.

| Year Club | League | Pos. | G. | AB. | R. | H. | 2B. | 3B. | HR. | RBI. | B.A. | PO. | A. | E. | F.A. |
|---|---|---|---|---|---|---|---|---|---|---|---|---|---|---|---|
| 1969—Billings | Pion. | SS | 12 | 49 | 12 | 14 | 4 | 0 | 3 | 9 | .286 | 14 | 29 | 6 | .878 |
| 1969—Clinton | Midw. | SS | 63 | 203 | 37 | 46 | 8 | 3 | 1 | 20 | .227 | 93 | 117 | 21 | .909 |
| 1970—Clinton | Midw. | SS | 28 | 117 | 26 | 38 | 5 | 1 | 1 | 5 | .325 | 53 | 79 | 7 | .950 |
| 1970—Portland | P. C. | SS | 80 | 300 | 52 | 90 | 15 | 2 | 3 | 19 | .300 | 119 | 242 | 26 | .933 |
| 1971—Evansville | A. A. | SS | 63 | 227 | 41 | 56 | 10 | 5 | 3 | 18 | .247 | 81 | 191 | 9 | .968 |
| 1971—Milwaukee | Amer. | SS | 79 | 236 | 22 | 48 | 10 | 0 | 1 | 9 | .203 | 120 | 193 | 12 | .963 |
| 1972—Milwaukee† | Amer. | SS | 153 | 554 | 50 | 121 | 16 | 3 | 2 | 30 | .218 | 256 | 452 | 30 | .959 |
| 1973—Albuquerque‡ | P. C. | SS-3B | 74 | 255 | 45 | 64 | 7 | 3 | 1 | 26 | .251 | 124 | 196 | 21 | .938 |
| 1973—Milwaukee§ | Amer. | SS | 6 | 10 | 2 | 1 | 1 | 0 | 0 | 0 | .100 | 4 | 6 | 2 | .833 |
| 1974—Los Angeles | Nat. | S-2-3 | 45 | 73 | 12 | 25 | 0 | 0 | 1 | 4 | .342 | 38 | 60 | 8 | .925 |
| 1975—Los Angeles x | Nat. | S-2-3 | 85 | 170 | 18 | 38 | 9 | 0 | 0 | 12 | .224 | 82 | 137 | 9 | .961 |
| 1976—Los Angeles | Nat. | S-3-2 | 36 | 47 | 7 | 6 | 0 | 0 | 0 | 1 | .128 | 41 | 50 | 6 | .938 |
| National League Totals | | | 166 | 290 | 37 | 69 | 9 | 0 | 1 | 17 | .238 | 161 | 247 | 23 | .947 |
| American League Totals | | | 238 | 800 | 74 | 170 | 27 | 3 | 3 | 39 | .213 | 380 | 651 | 44 | .959 |
| Major League Totals | | | 404 | 1090 | 111 | 239 | 36 | 3 | 4 | 56 | .219 | 541 | 898 | 67 | .956 |

†Traded to Los Angeles Dodgers for Infielder Tim Johnson, April 24, 1973.
‡On disabled list, June 22 to July 2, 1973; purchased by Milwaukee Brewers, September 4, 1973.
§Sold to Los Angeles Dodgers, October 27, 1973.
xOn supplemental disabled list, June 30 to July 17, 1975.
yTraded to New York Mets for Pitchers Rick Sander and Hank Webb, February 7, 1977.

CHAMPIONSHIP SERIES RECORD

| Year Club | League | Pos. | G. | AB. | R. | H. | 2B. | 3B. | HR. | RBI. | B.A. | PO. | A. | E. | F.A. |
|---|---|---|---|---|---|---|---|---|---|---|---|---|---|---|---|
| 1974—Los Angeles | Nat. | PH | 1 | 1 | 0 | 1 | 1 | 0 | 0 | 0 | 1.000 | 0 | 0 | 0 | .000 |

WORLD SERIES RECORD

| Year Club | League | Pos. | G. | AB. | R. | H. | 2B. | 3B. | HR. | RBI. | B.A. | PO. | A. | E. | F.A. |
|---|---|---|---|---|---|---|---|---|---|---|---|---|---|---|---|
| 1974—Los Angeles | Nat. | PR | 1 | 0 | 0 | 0 | 0 | 0 | 0 | 0 | .000 | 0 | 0 | 0 | .000 |

## GERALD LEE AUGUSTINE
### (Jerry)
Born July 24, 1952, at Green Bay, Wis.
Height, 6.00. Weight, 185.
Throws and bats lefthanded.
Hobbies—Reading, playing the guitar and outdoor activities.
Attended University of Wisconsin at La Crosse, La Crosse, Wis.;
received Bachelor of Science degree in Education.

| Year   Club | League | G. | IP. | W. | L. | Pct. | H. | R. | ER. | SO. | BB. | ERA. |
|---|---|---|---|---|---|---|---|---|---|---|---|---|
| 1974—Danville | Midwest | 13 | 88 | 7 | 4 | .636 | 81 | 34 | 25 | 52 | 34 | 2.56 |
| 1975—Sacramento† | P. Coast | 15 | 79 | 4 | 3 | .571 | 90 | 49 | 42 | 27 | 40 | 4.78 |
| 1975—Milwaukee | American | 5 | 27 | 2 | 0 | 1.000 | 26 | 9 | 9 | 8 | 12 | 3.00 |
| 1976—Milwaukee | American | 39 | 172 | 9 | 12 | .429 | 167 | 69 | 63 | 59 | 56 | 3.30 |
| Major League Totals | | 44 | 199 | 11 | 12 | .478 | 193 | 78 | 72 | 67 | 68 | 3.26 |

†On disabled list from beginning of season until June 28, 1975.

## DOUGLAS REAGAN AULT
### (Doug)
Born March 9, 1950, at Beaumont, Tex.
Height, 6.03. Weight, 200.
Throws left and bats righthanded.
Hobbies—Golf, fishing and hunting.
Attended Panola Junior College, Carthage, Tex. and Texas Tech University, Lubbock, Tex.

Led Pacific Coast League in total bases with 278 in 1976.

| Year   Club | League | Pos. | G. | AB. | R. | H. | 2B. | 3B. | HR. | RBI. | B.A. | PO. | A. | E. | F.A. |
|---|---|---|---|---|---|---|---|---|---|---|---|---|---|---|---|
| 1973—Gastonia | W. Car. | OF | 130 | 464 | 66 | 128 | 22 | 5 | •19 | •88 | .276 | 168 | 9 | 5 | .973 |
| 1974—Pittsfield | East. | OF-1B | 132 | 455 | 60 | 119 | 19 | 3 | 15 | 72 | .262 | 586 | 30 | 10 | .984 |
| 1975—Pittsfield | East. | 1B | 75 | 277 | 42 | 78 | 13 | 3 | 11 | 56 | .282 | 596 | 43 | 10 | .985 |
| 1975—Spokane | P.C. | 1B | 48 | 175 | 23 | 60 | 8 | 2 | 7 | 37 | .343 | 403 | 41 | 13 | .972 |
| 1976—Sacramento | P. C. | 1B | 143 | 536 | •112 | 168 | 25 | 5 | 25 | 83 | .313 | •1259 | •99 | 13 | .991 |
| 1976—Texas† | Amer. | 1B-DH | 9 | 20 | 0 | 6 | 1 | 0 | 0 | 0 | .300 | 23 | 0 | 0 | 1.000 |
| Major League Totals | | | 9 | 20 | 0 | 6 | 1 | 0 | 0 | 0 | .300 | 23 | 0 | 0 | 1.000 |

†Selected by Toronto Blue Jays from Texas Rangers in American League expansion draft, November 5, 1976.

## PAUL DAVID AUSMAN
Name pronounced, AWZ-mun.

Born August 24, 1955, at Eau Claire, Wis.
Height, 6.02. Weight, 180.
Throws and bats lefthanded.
Hobbies—Basketball and football.

Led California League in saves with 12 in 1975.

| Year   Club | League | G. | IP. | W. | L. | Pct. | H. | R. | ER. | SO. | BB. | ERA. |
|---|---|---|---|---|---|---|---|---|---|---|---|---|---|
| 1973—Newark† | NYP | 8 | 14 | 0 | 0 | .000 | 28 | 18 | 15 | 9 | 8 | 9.64 |
| 1974—Wisconsin Rapids‡ | Midwest | 35 | 55 | 8 | 2 | .800 | 45 | 20 | 15 | 53 | 27 | 2.45 |
| 1975—Reno | California | 47 | 90 | 6 | 3 | .667 | 88 | 39 | 25 | 92 | 42 | 2.50 |
| 1976—Orlando§ | Southern | 12 | 33 | 2 | 1 | .667 | 39 | 19 | 15 | 19 | 16 | 4.09 |
| 1976—Tacoma | P. Coast | 10 | 17 | 0 | 0 | .000 | 11 | 3 | 1 | 8 | 7 | 0.53 |

†Released by Milwaukee Brewers' organization, December 12, 1973; signed as free agent by Minnesota Twins' organization, April 3, 1974.
‡Drafted by Alexandria (San Diego Padres' organization) from Minnesota Twins' organization, December 2, 1974; returned to Minnesota Twins' organization, April 8, 1975.
§On disabled list, June 14 through July 1, 1976.
Listed on Minnesota Twins' 1977 spring roster.

## ALBERT AUTRY, JR.
### (Al)
Born February 29, 1952, at Modesto, Calif.
Height, 6.05. Weight, 225.
Throws and bats righthanded.
Hobbies—Hunting and fishing.
Attended Arizona State University, Tempe, Ariz.

Tied for Southern League lead in games started by pitchers with 29 in 1972.

| Year   Club | League | G. | IP. | W. | L. | Pct. | H. | R. | ER. | SO. | BB. | ERA. |
|---|---|---|---|---|---|---|---|---|---|---|---|---|---|
| 1969—Winnipeg | Northern | 8 | 30 | 0 | 5 | .000 | 43 | 34 | 30 | 40 | 28 | 9.00 |
| 1970—Waterloo† | Midwest | 3 | 11 | 1 | 0 | 1.000 | 13 | 8 | 6 | 15 | 10 | 4.91 |
| 1970—Billings | Pioneer | 7 | 43 | 2 | 5 | .286 | 41 | 40 | 30 | 49 | 42 | 6.28 |
| 1971—Waterloo | Midwest | 3 | 20 | 1 | 2 | .333 | 11 | 6 | 2 | 28 | 12 | 0.90 |
| 1971—San Jose | California | 22 | 134 | 8 | 11 | .421 | 116 | 84 | 61 | 149 | 85 | 4.10 |
| 1972—Jacksonville | Southern | 29 | 184 | 11 | 13 | .458 | 152 | 79 | 68 | 173 | 76 | 3.33 |
| 1973—Omaha | Am. Assoc. | 28 | 153 | 9 | 11 | .450 | 161 | 114 | •104 | 136 | 104 | 6.12 |
| 1974—Jacksonville | Southern | 19 | 137 | 10 | 5 | .667 | 104 | 57 | 44 | 124 | 66 | 2.89 |

| Year Club | League | G. | IP. | W. | L. | Pct. | H. | R. | ER. | SO. | BB. | ERA. |
|---|---|---|---|---|---|---|---|---|---|---|---|---|
| 1974—Omaha | Am. Assoc. | 8 | 46 | 2 | 4 | .333 | 52 | 25 | 23 | 22 | 33 | 4.50 |
| 1975—Omaha | Am. Assoc. | 23 | 137 | 9 | 7 | .563 | 140 | 73 | 60 | 81 | 63 | 3.94 |
| 1976—Richmond | Int'national | 32 | 161 | 9 | 6 | .600 | 142 | 58 | 51 | 109 | 77 | 2.85 |
| 1976—Atlanta | National | 1 | 5 | 1 | 0 | 1.000 | 4 | 3 | 3 | 3 | 3 | 5.40 |
| Major League Totals | | 1 | 5 | 1 | 0 | 1.000 | 4 | 3 | 3 | 3 | 3 | 5.40 |

†On disabled list, June 6 to July 22, 1970.

‡Traded with Pitcher Norm Angelini by Kansas City Royals to Atlanta Braves for Pitcher Ray Sadecki, September 4, 1975, to complete deal in which Braves obtained Pitcher Bruce Dal Canton on waivers from Royals, June 20, 1975.

## RAMON ANTONIO AVILES (MIRANDA)

Born January 22, 1952, at Manati, Puerto Rico.
Height, 5.09. Weight, 155.
Throws and bats righthanded.
Hobby—Music.
Attended University of Puerto Rico, Arecibo, Puerto Rico.
Led Western Carolinas League shortstops in double plays with 56 in 1971.

| Year Club | League | Pos. | G. | AB. | R. | H. | 2B. | 3B. | HR. | RBI. | B.A. | PO. | A. | E. | F.A. |
|---|---|---|---|---|---|---|---|---|---|---|---|---|---|---|---|
| 1970—Greenville | W. Car. | SS-2B | 94 | 304 | 47 | 90 | 9 | 2 | 0 | 38 | .296 | 136 | 245 | 32 | .922 |
| 1971—Winston-Salem | Carol. | SS | 33 | 116 | 19 | 29 | 1 | 3 | 0 | 8 | .250 | 48 | 105 | 13 | .922 |
| 1971—Greenville | W. Car. | SS | 91 | 313 | 33 | 92 | 9 | 1 | 0 | 33 | .294 | 154 | 271 | 30 | .934 |
| 1972—Pawtucket | East. | 2B | 106 | 339 | 29 | 62 | 5 | 0 | 0 | 24 | .183 | 253 | 255 | 16 | •.969 |
| 1973—Bristol | East. | SS-2-3B | 109 | 353 | 39 | 79 | 13 | 1 | 0 | 28 | .224 | 178 | 316 | 18 | .946 |
| 1974—Bristol | East. | SS-3B | 118 | 373 | 48 | 92 | 12 | 3 | 0 | 33 | .247 | 174 | 282 | 32 | .934 |
| 1975—Pawtucket | Int. | SS-OF | 123 | 287 | 20 | 63 | 6 | 1 | 1 | 22 | .220 | 177 | 333 | 23 | .957 |
| 1976—Rhode Is. | Int. | SS | 134 | 421 | 50 | 108 | 17 | 3 | 2 | 42 | .257 | 238 | 452 | 35 | .952 |

Listed on Boston Red Sox' 1977 spring roster.

## BENIGNO FELIX AYALA

Name pronounced eye-AL-uh.

### (Benny)

Born February 7, 1951, at Yauco, Puerto Rico.
Height, 6.01. Weight, 175.
Throws and bats righthanded.
Attended Puerto Rico Junior College, Rio Piedras, P. R.
Hit home run in first major league at bat, August 27, 1974.

| Year Club | League | Pos. | G. | AB. | R. | H. | 2B. | 3B. | HR. | RBI. | B.A. | PO. | A. | E. | F.A. |
|---|---|---|---|---|---|---|---|---|---|---|---|---|---|---|---|
| 1971—Visalia | Calif. | 3B | 21 | 46 | 3 | 10 | 0 | 1 | 1 | 8 | .217 | 8 | 16 | 7 | .774 |
| 1971—Pompano Beach | Fla. St. | 3B-OF | 63 | 208 | 38 | 58 | 7 | 4 | 8 | 34 | .279 | 57 | 59 | 17 | .872 |
| 1972—Visalia | Calif. | 1B-OF | 113 | 348 | 68 | 79 | 15 | 2 | 19 | 66 | .227 | 442 | 38 | 22 | .956 |
| 1973—Memphis | Texas | OF | 136 | 462 | 69 | 119 | 17 | 6 | 17 | 68 | .258 | 44 | 5 | 3 | .942 |
| 1974—Tidewater | Int. | OF | 92 | 288 | 41 | 79 | 21 | 1 | 11 | 40 | .274 | 125 | 4 | •16 | .890 |
| 1974—New York | Nat. | OF | 23 | 68 | 9 | 16 | 1 | 0 | 2 | 8 | .235 | 37 | 1 | 3 | .927 |
| 1975—Tidewater† | Int. | OF | 65 | 177 | 24 | 49 | 13 | 0 | 6 | 28 | .277 | 66 | 1 | 4 | .944 |
| 1976—Tidewater | Int. | OF-1B | 87 | 293 | 41 | 66 | 9 | 2 | 12 | 48 | .225 | 47 | 2 | 3 | .942 |
| 1976—New York‡ | Nat. | OF | 22 | 26 | 2 | 3 | 0 | 0 | 1 | 2 | .115 | 7 | 1 | 1 | .889 |
| Major League Totals | | | 45 | 94 | 11 | 19 | 1 | 0 | 3 | 10 | .202 | 44 | 2 | 4 | .920 |

†On disabled list, April 22 to May 29, 1975.

‡Traded to St. Louis Cardinals' organization and assigned to New Orleans for infielder Doug Clarey, latter assigned from New Orleans to Tidewater, March 30, 1977.

## MICHAEL JAMES BACSIK

Named pronounced Bassik.

### (Mike)

Born April 1, 1952, at Dallas, Tex.
Height, 6.02. Weight, 188.
Throws and bats righthanded.
Hobbies—Golf and tennis.
Attended Trinity University, San Antonio, Tex.; received Bachelor of Arts degree
in Business Administration and Marketing

| Year Club | League | G. | IP. | W. | L. | Pct. | H. | R. | ER. | SO. | BB. | ERA. |
|---|---|---|---|---|---|---|---|---|---|---|---|---|
| 1973—Sarasota Rangers | Gulf Coast | 8 | 23 | 2 | 0 | 1.000 | 13 | 13 | 10 | 31 | 14 | 3.91 |
| 1974—Gastonia | W. Carol. | 25 | 170 | •15 | 5 | •.750 | •183 | 93 | •80 | 121 | 59 | 4.24 |
| 1975—Spokane | P. Coast | 19 | 110 | 6 | 10 | .375 | 135 | 82 | 67 | 48 | 38 | 5.48 |
| 1975—Texas | American | 7 | 27 | 1 | 2 | .333 | 28 | 17 | 11 | 13 | 9 | 3.67 |
| 1976—Sacramento | P. Coast | 12 | 77 | 4 | 3 | .571 | 101 | 51 | 39 | 43 | 31 | 4.56 |
| 1976—Texas | American | 23 | 55 | 3 | 2 | .600 | 66 | 31 | 26 | 21 | 26 | 4.25 |
| Major League Totals | | 30 | 82 | 4 | 4 | .500 | 94 | 48 | 37 | 34 | 35 | 4.06 |

## JOSE ANTONIO BAEZ

Born December 31, 1953, at San Cristobal, Dominican Republic.
Height, 5.08. Weight, 150.
Throws and bats righthanded.
Hobbies—Music and reading.
Cousin of Manny Mota, outfielder with Los Angeles Dodgers.
Led Florida State League second basemen in double plays with 67 in 1973.
Led California League second basemen in double plays with 116 in 1974.
Led Eastern League second basemen in total chances with 648 and double plays with 83 in 1975.

| Year Club League | Pos. | G. | AB. | R. | H. | 2B. | 3B. | HR. | RBI. | B.A. | PO. | A. | E. | F.A. |
|---|---|---|---|---|---|---|---|---|---|---|---|---|---|---|
| 1972—Daytona Beach..Fla. St. | | 3 | 4 | 0 | 0 | 0 | 0 | 0 | 0 | .000 | .... | .... | .... | .... |
| 1972—Ogden ..............Pion. | C-3B | 38 | 109 | 19 | 26 | 9 | 2 | 0 | 12 | .239 | 119 | 34 | 5 | .968 |
| 1973—Daytona Beach..Fla. St. | 2B | 124 | 422 | 62 | 129 | 13 | 5 | 4 | 39 | .306 | 260 | 300 | 24 | .959 |
| 1974—Bakersfield........Calif. | 2B | 125 | 506 | 101 | •167 | •34 | 4 | 4 | 55 | •.330 | 328 | 373 | 33 | .955 |
| 1974—Albuquerque......P.C. | 3B-2B | 4 | 12 | 1 | 3 | 0 | 0 | 0 | 0 | .250 | 4 | 7 | 0 | 1.000 |
| 1975—Waterbury ........East. | 2B | 114 | 441 | 64 | 127 | 20 | •9 | 2 | 37 | .288 | 289 | •337 | 22 | .966 |
| 1976—Albuquerque†‡ ..P.C. | 2B-3B | 107 | 392 | 54 | 121 | 30 | 4 | 4 | 49 | .309 | 223 | 330 | 21 | .963 |

†On disabled list, August 8 through September 7, 1976.
‡Sold by Los Angeles Dodgers' organization to Seattle Mariners' October 25, 1976.

## STANLEY RAYMOND BAHNSEN
### (Stan)

Born December 15, 1944, at Council Bluffs, Ia.
Height, 6.02. Weight, 198.
Throws and bats righthanded.
Hobbies—Fishing, hunting and pocket billiards.
Attended University of Nebraska, Lincoln, Neb.

Pitched seven-inning, 1-0 no-hit victory against Richmond, July 17, 1966.
Pitched seven-inning, 8-0 perfect game against Buffalo, July 9, 1967.
Named THE SPORTING NEWS American League Rookie Pitcher of the Year, 1968.
Named American League Rookie of the Year by the Baseball Writers' Association of America, 1968.
Received reported $30,000 bonus to sign with New York Yankees, 1965.

| Year Club | League | G. | IP. | W. | L. | Pct. | H. | R. | ER. | SO. | BB. | ERA. |
|---|---|---|---|---|---|---|---|---|---|---|---|---|
| 1965—Columbus ...........Southern | | 11 | 53 | 2 | 2 | .500 | 47 | 21 | 16 | 39 | 29 | 2.72 |
| 1966—Toledo...............Int'national | | 26 | 170 | 10 | 7 | .588 | 141 | 67 | 55 | 151 | 71 | 2.91 |
| 1966—New York ...........American | | 4 | 23 | 1 | 1 | .500 | 15 | 9 | 9 | 16 | 7 | 3.52 |
| 1967—Syracuse ...........Int'national | | 26 | 138 | 9 | 11 | .450 | 122 | 64 | 54 | 115 | 41 | 3.52 |
| 1968—New York ...........American | | 37 | 267 | 17 | 12 | .586 | 216 | 72 | 61 | 162 | 68 | 2.06 |
| 1969—New York ...........American | | 40 | 221 | 9 | 16 | .360 | 222 | 102 | 94 | 130 | 90 | 3.83 |
| 1970—New York ...........American | | 36 | 233 | 14 | 11 | .560 | 227 | 100 | 86 | 116 | 75 | 3.32 |
| 1971—New York† ...........American | | 36 | 242 | 14 | 12 | .538 | 221 | 99 | 90 | 110 | 72 | 3.35 |
| 1972—Chicago...............American | | 43 | 252 | 21 | 16 | .568 | 263 | 107 | 101 | 157 | 73 | 3.61 |
| 1973—Chicago...............American | | 42 | 282 | 16 | •21 | .462 | 290 | 128 | 112 | 120 | 117 | 3.57 |
| 1974—Chicago...............American | | 38 | 216 | 12 | 15 | .444 | 230 | 128 | 113 | 102 | 110 | 4.71 |
| 1975—Chicago‡-Oakland ..............American | | 33 | 167 | 10 | 13 | .435 | 166 | 91 | 81 | 80 | 77 | 4.37 |
| 1976—Oakland ...............American | | 35 | 143 | 8 | 7 | .533 | 124 | 55 | 53 | 82 | 43 | 3.34 |
| Major League Totals ..................... | | 344 | 2046 | 124 | 124 | .500 | 1974 | 891 | 800 | 1075 | 732 | 3.52 |

†Traded to Chicago White Sox for Infielder-Outfielder Rich McKinney, December 2, 1971.
‡Traded with Pitcher Lee (Skip) Pitlock to Oakland Athletics for Pitcher Dave Hamilton and Infielder-Outfielder Chet Lemon, June 15, 1975.

## ROBERT SHERWOOD BAILEY
### (Bob)

Born October 13, 1942, at Long Beach, Calif.
Height, 6.00. Weight, 190.
Throws and bats righthanded.
Hobby—Golf.
Son of Paul "Buck" Bailey, minor league infielder, 1939-40.

Tied National League record for most home runs, bases full, one month, 2, July, 1973.
Led National League third basemen in double plays with 38 in 1963.
Named Minor League Player of the Year by THE SPORTING NEWS, 1962.
Named Player of the Year and Rookie of the Year in International League, 1962.
Received reported $135,000 bonus to sign with Pittsburgh Pirates, 1961.

| Year Club League | Pos. | G. | AB. | R. | H. | 2B. | 3B. | HR. | RBI. | B.A. | PO. | A. | E. | F.A. |
|---|---|---|---|---|---|---|---|---|---|---|---|---|---|---|
| 1961—Asheville ..........Sally | SS | 75 | 218 | 39 | 48 | 12 | 1 | 9 | 31 | .220 | 140 | 204 | 27 | .927 |
| 1962—Columbus..........Int. | •3B-SS | 153 | 548 | 109 | 164 | 31 | 7 | 28 | •108 | .299 | 178 | 363 | •34 | .941 |
| 1962—Pittsburgh ........Nat. | 3B | 14 | 42 | 6 | 7 | 2 | 1 | 0 | 6 | .167 | 10 | 25 | 3 | .921 |
| 1963—Pittsburgh ........Nat. | 3B-SS | 154 | 570 | 60 | 130 | 15 | 3 | 12 | 45 | .228 | 118 | 337 | 33 | .932 |
| 1964—Pittsburgh ........Nat. | 3B-O-S | 143 | 530 | 73 | 149 | 26 | 3 | 11 | 51 | .281 | 117 | 224 | 23 | .937 |
| 1965—Pittsburgh ........Nat. | 3B-OF | 159 | 626 | 87 | 160 | 28 | 3 | 11 | 49 | .256 | 119 | 247 | 23 | .941 |
| 1966—Pittsburgh†........Nat. | 3B-OF | 126 | 380 | 51 | 106 | 19 | 3 | 13 | 46 | .279 | 81 | 202 | 12 | .959 |
| 1967—Los Angeles ......Nat. | 3-O-1-S | 116 | 322 | 21 | 73 | 8 | 2 | 4 | 28 | .227 | 94 | 154 | 16 | .939 |
| 1968—Los Angeles‡ ....Nat. | 3-S-OF | 105 | 322 | 24 | 73 | 9 | 3 | 8 | 39 | .227 | 81 | 164 | 13 | .950 |
| 1969—Montreal§..........Nat. | 1-OF-3 | 111 | 358 | 46 | 95 | 16 | 6 | 9 | 53 | .265 | 715 | 67 | 8 | .990 |
| 1970—Montreal ..........Nat. | 3-OF-1 | 131 | 352 | 77 | 101 | 19 | 3 | 28 | 84 | .287 | 179 | 86 | 8 | .971 |
| 1971—Montreal ..........Nat. | •3-OF-1 | 157 | 545 | 65 | 137 | 21 | 4 | 14 | 83 | .251 | 177 | 204 | 14 | •.965 |
| 1972—Montreal ..........Nat. | 3-OF-1 | 143 | 489 | 55 | 114 | 10 | 4 | 16 | 57 | .233 | 95 | 251 | 22 | .940 |

| Year | Club | League | Pos. | G. | AB. | R. | H. | 2B. | 3B. | HR. | RBI. | B.A. | PO. | A. | E. | F.A. |
|------|------|--------|------|-----|------|-----|------|-----|-----|-----|------|------|------|------|-----|------|
| 1973-Montreal | .........Nat. | | 3B-OF | 151 | 513 | 77 | 140 | 25 | 4 | 26 | 86 | .273 | 94 | 275 | 17 | .956 |
| 1974-Montreal | .........Nat. | | OF-3B | 152 | 507 | 69 | 142 | 20 | 2 | 20 | 73 | .280 | 139 | 125 | 10 | .964 |
| 1975-Montreal x | ......Nat. | | OF-3B | 106 | 227 | 23 | 62 | 5 | 0 | 5 | 30 | .273 | 89 | 10 | 2 | .980 |
| 1976-Cincinnati | .........Nat. | | OF-3B | 69 | 124 | 17 | 37 | 6 | 1 | 6 | 23 | .298 | 39 | 14 | 3 | .946 |
| Major League Totals | ...................... | | | 1837 | 5907 | 751 | 1526 | 229 | 42 | 183 | 753 | .258 | 2147 | 2385 | 207 | .956 |

†Traded with Shortstop Gene Michael to Los Angeles Dodgers for Shortstop Maury Wills, December 1, 1966.

‡Sold to Montreal Expos, October 21, 1968.

§On disabled list, April 17 to May 16, 1969.

xOn disabled list, March 30, to April 27, 1975. Traded to Cincinnati Reds for Pitcher Clay Kirby, December 12, 1975.

## ROBERT MICHAEL BAILOR
### (Bob)

Born July 10, 1951, at Connellsville, Pa.
Height, 5.11. Weight, 170.
Throws and bats righthanded.
Hobbies—Hunting and fishing.
Attended California State College, California, Pa.

Led California League in stolen bases with 63 in 1972.
Led Southern League shortstops in double plays with 85 in 1973 and tied for International League lead with 64 in 1975.

| Year | Club | League | Pos. | G. | AB. | R. | H. | 2B. | 3B. | HR. | RBI. | B.A. | PO. | A. | E. | F.A. |
|------|------|--------|------|-----|------|-----|------|-----|-----|-----|------|------|------|------|-----|------|
| 1970-Bluefield | .........Appal. | | 2-O-3-S-P | 46 | 121 | 18 | 33 | 3 | 0 | 0 | 8 | .273 | 53 | 43 | 6 | .941 |
| 1971-Aberdeen | .........North. | | S-3-O-2 | 68 | 268 | •71 | •91 | 11 | 2 | 2 | 50 | •.340 | 92 | 140 | 32 | .879 |
| 1972-Lodi | .................Calif. | | •S-O-2 | 129 | 528 | 95 | 153 | 16 | 3 | 2 | 34 | .290 | •241 | 330 | •54 | .914 |
| 1973-Asheville | .........South. | | SS | 115 | 468 | 77 | 137 | 23 | 3 | 0 | 29 | .293 | •222 | 386 | 22 | •.965 |
| 1973-Rochester | .........Int. | | SS | 17 | 47 | 5 | 13 | 1 | 0 | 1 | 4 | .277 | 30 | 34 | 4 | .941 |
| 1974-Rochester | .........Int. | | S-O-3-2 | 96 | 330 | 45 | 76 | 13 | 3 | 1 | 25 | .230 | 174 | 160 | 13 | .963 |
| 1975-Rochester | .........Int. | | SS | 129 | •501 | 68 | 147 | 19 | 6 | 5 | 39 | .293 | 198 | •386 | •32 | .948 |
| 1975-Baltimore | .........Amer. | | SS-2B | 5 | 7 | 0 | 1 | 0 | 0 | 0 | 0 | .143 | 5 | 9 | 0 | 1.000 |
| 1976-Rochester† | .......Int. | | 3-SS-OF | 36 | 103 | 21 | 32 | 10 | 1 | 1 | 12 | .311 | 10 | 24 | 0 | 1.000 |
| 1976-Baltimore‡ | ......Amer. | | SS-DH | 9 | 6 | 2 | 2 | 0 | 1 | 0 | 0 | .333 | 0 | 0 | 0 | .000 |
| Major League Totals | ...................... | | | 14 | 13 | 2 | 3 | 0 | 1 | 0 | 0 | .231 | 5 | 9 | 0 | 1.000 |

†On supplemental disabled list, April 14 through June 7; on disabled list, June 8 through August 1, 1976.

‡Selected by Toronto Blue Jays from Baltimore Orioles in American League expansion draft, November 5, 1976.

PITCHING RECORD

| Year | Club | League | G. | IP. | W. | L. | Pct. | H. | R. | ER. | SO. | BB. | ERA. |
|------|------|--------|-----|-----|-----|-----|------|-----|-----|-----|-----|-----|------|
| 1970-Bluefield | .............................Appal. | | 1 | 1 | 0 | 0 | .000 | 7 | 8 | 8 | 1 | 2 | 72.00 |

## CHARLES DOUGLAS BAIR
### (Doug)

Born August 22, 1949, at Defiance, O.
Height, 6.00. Weight, 170.
Throws and bats righthanded.
Hobbies—Hunting and fishing.
Attended Bowling Green State University, Bowling Green, O.; received
Bachelor of Science degree in Industrial Education.

Led Carolina League pitchers in complete games with 15 in 1972.
Named Carolina League Pitcher of the Year in 1972.

| Year | Club | League | G. | IP. | W. | L. | Pct. | H. | R. | ER. | SO. | BB. | ERA. |
|------|------|--------|-----|-----|-----|-----|------|-----|-----|-----|-----|-----|------|
| 1971-Salem† | ...............................Carolina | | 6 | 29 | 2 | 3 | .400 | 35 | 22 | 19 | 18 | 26 | 5.90 |
| 1971-Waterbury | ...........................Eastern | | 1 | 7 | 1 | 0 | 1.000 | 5 | 0 | 0 | 2 | 0 | 0.00 |
| 1972-Salem | ...............................Carolina | | 24 | 180 | 15 | 7 | .682 | 170 | •86 | 57 | 186 | •95 | 2.85 |
| 1972-Charleston | ........................Int'national | | 1 | 4 | 0 | 1 | .000 | 5 | 3 | 3 | 5 | 0 | 6.75 |
| 1973-Charleston | ........................Int'national | | 26 | 158 | 7 | 11 | .389 | 173 | 103 | 77 | 94 | 87 | 4.39 |
| 1974-Charleston‡ | ........................Int'national | | 26 | 170 | 7 | •16 | .350 | 166 | 87 | 77 | 117 | 91 | 4.08 |
| 1975-Charleston | ........................Int'national | | 26 | 167 | 9 | 12 | .429 | 157 | 72 | 56 | 113 | 58 | 3.02 |
| 1976-Charleston | ........................Int'national | | 45 | 122 | 7 | 10 | .412 | 102 | 48 | 43 | 108 | 57 | 3.17 |
| 1976-Pittsburgh§ | ........................National | | 4 | 6 | 0 | 0 | .000 | 4 | 4 | 4 | 4 | 5 | 6.00 |
| Major League Totals | ................................ | | 4 | 6 | 0 | 0 | .000 | 4 | 4 | 4 | 4 | 5 | 6.00 |

†On temporary inactive list, June 23 to July 22, 1971.

‡Conditionally released by Pittsburgh Pirates' organziation to Detroit Tigers' organization, December 17, 1974; returned by Tigers to Pirates, March 28, 1975.

§Traded with Pitchers Doc Medich, Dave Giusti and Rick Langford, Infielder Mitchell Page and Outfielder Tony Armas to Oakland A's for Infielders Phil Garner and Tommy Helms, and Pitcher Chris Batton, March 15, 1977.

## JACK EDWARD BAKER

Born May 4, 1950, at Birmingham, Ala.
Height, 6.05. Weight, 225.
Throws and bats righthanded.
Hobbies—Reading, hunting and golf.
Attended Auburn University, Auburn, Ala.; received Bachelor
of Science degree in Business Administration.

Led International League first basemen in double plays with 102 in 1975.

| Year Club | League | Pos. | G. | AB. | R. | H. | 2B. | 3B. | HR. | RBI. | B.A. | PO. | A. | E. | F.A. |
|---|---|---|---|---|---|---|---|---|---|---|---|---|---|---|---|
| 1971—Williamsport......NYP | | 1B | 61 | 205 | 35 | 51 | 8 | 4 | 12 | 45 | .249 | 445 | 24 | •15 | .969 |
| 1972—Winter Haven ....Fla. St. | | 1B | 125 | 456 | 70 | 124 | 20 | 4 | •27 | •89 | .272 | 1007 | 46 | 17 | .984 |
| 1973—Winston-Salem† Carol. | | 1B | 84 | 235 | 29 | 58 | 7 | 0 | 10 | 32 | .247 | 622 | 42 | 7 | .990 |
| 1974—Bristol ..............East. | | 1B | 128 | 435 | 69 | 119 | 11 | 0 | •27 | •105 | .274 | •1134 | 42 | 17 | .986 |
| 1975—Pawtucket ........Int. | | 1B | 132 | 456 | 42 | 115 | 20 | 3 | 18 | 63 | .252 | 1080 | 75 | •20 | .983 |
| 1976—Rhode Island ....Int. | | 1B | 133 | 469 | 72 | 119 | 16 | 0 | 36 | 80 | .254 | 1049 | 84 | 9 | .992 |
| 1976—Boston ..............Amer. | | 1B-DH | 12 | 23 | 1 | 3 | 0 | 0 | 1 | 2 | .130 | 48 | 3 | 1 | .981 |
| Major League Totals ..................... | | | 12 | 23 | 1 | 3 | 0 | 0 | 1 | 2 | .130 | 48 | 3 | 1 | .981 |

†On disabled list, August 1 through remainder of season.

## JOHNNIE B. BAKER, JR.
## (Dusty)

Born June 15, 1949, At Riverside, Calif.
Height, 6.02. Weight, 190.
Throws and bats righthanded.
Hobbies—Fishing and hunting.
Attended American River Junior College, Sacramento, Calif.

Tied major league records for most plate appearances and most at bats in an inning, 3, September 20, 1972 (second game of doubleheader).
Led National League outfielders in total chances with 407 in 1973.

| Year Club | League | Pos. | G. | AB. | R. | H. | 2B. | 3B. | HR. | RBI. | B.A. | PO. | A. | E. | F.A. |
|---|---|---|---|---|---|---|---|---|---|---|---|---|---|---|---|
| 1967—Austin ..............Texas | | OF | 9 | 39 | 6 | 9 | 1 | 0 | 0 | 1 | .231 | 17 | 0 | 1 | .944 |
| 1968—W. Palm B'ch† ..Fla. St. | | OF | 6 | 21 | 2 | 4 | 0 | 0 | 0 | 2 | .190 | 6 | 2 | 0 | 1.000 |
| 1968—Greenwood ........W. Car. | | OF | 52 | 199 | 45 | 68 | 11 | 3 | 6 | 39 | .342 | 82 | 1 | 3 | .965 |
| 1968—Atlanta..............Nat. | | OF | 6 | 5 | 0 | 2 | 0 | 0 | 0 | 0 | .400 | 0 | 0 | 0 | .000 |
| 1969—Shreveport ........Texas | | OF | 73 | 265 | 40 | 68 | 5 | 1 | 9 | 31 | .257 | 135 | 10 | 3 | .980 |
| 1969—Richmond..........Int. | | OF-3B | 25 | 89 | 7 | 22 | 4 | 0 | 0 | 8 | .247 | 40 | 9 | 4 | .925 |
| 1969—Atlanta ..............Nat. | | OF | 3 | 7 | 0 | 0 | 0 | 0 | 0 | 0 | .000 | 2 | 0 | 0 | 1.000 |
| 1970—Richmond..........Int. | | OF | 118 | 461 | 97 | 150 | 29 | 3 | 11 | 51 | .325 | 236 | 10 | 7 | .972 |
| 1970—Atlanta..............Nat. | | OF | 13 | 24 | 3 | 7 | 0 | 0 | 0 | 4 | .292 | 11 | 1 | 3 | .800 |
| 1971—Richmond..........Int. | | OF-3B | 80 | 341 | 62 | 106 | 23 | 2 | 11 | 41 | .311 | 136 | 13 | 4 | .974 |
| 1971—Atlanta ..............Nat. | | OF | 29 | 62 | 2 | 14 | 2 | 0 | 0 | 4 | .226 | 29 | 1 | 0 | 1.000 |
| 1972—Atlanta‡ ...........Nat. | | OF | 127 | 446 | 62 | 143 | 27 | 2 | 17 | 76 | .321 | 344 | 8 | 4 | .989 |
| 1973—Atlanta ..............Nat. | | OF | 159 | 604 | 101 | 174 | 29 | 4 | 21 | 99 | .288 | •390 | 10 | 7 | .983 |
| 1974—Atlanta ..............Nat. | | OF | 149 | 574 | 80 | 147 | 35 | 0 | 20 | 69 | .256 | 359 | 10 | 7 | .981 |
| 1975—Atlanta§ ...........Nat. | | OF | 142 | 494 | 63 | 129 | 18 | 2 | 19 | 72 | .261 | 287 | 10 | 3 | .990 |
| 1976—Los Angeles ......Nat. | | OF | 112 | 384 | 36 | 93 | 13 | 0 | 4 | 39 | .242 | 254 | 3 | 1 | .996 |
| Major League Totals ..................... | | | 740 | 2600 | 347 | 709 | 124 | 8 | 81 | 363 | .273 | 1676 | 43 | 25 | .986 |

†On restricted list from beginning of season until June 13, 1968.
‡On Military List, June 17 to July 3, 1972.
§Traded with First Baseman-Third Baseman Ed Goodson to Los Angeles Dodgers for Outfielder Jimmy Wynn, Second Baseman Lee Lacy, First Baseman-Outfielder Tom Paciorek and Infielder Jerry Royster, November 17, 1975.

## RICKEY ALAN BALDWIN
## (Rick)

Born June 1, 1953, at Fresno, Calif.
Height, 6.03. Weight, 180.
Throws right and bats lefthanded.

| Year Club | League | G. | IP. | W. | L. | Pct. | H. | R. | ER. | SO. | BB. | ERA. |
|---|---|---|---|---|---|---|---|---|---|---|---|---|
| 1971—Marion ................Ap'plachian | | 10 | 52 | 4 | 4 | .500 | 50 | 20 | 17 | 29 | 8 | 2.94 |
| 1972—Visalia .................California | | 27 | 164 | 12 | 8 | .600 | 172 | 109 | 90 | 105 | 79 | 4.94 |
| 1973—Memphis ..............Texas | | 29 | 121 | 9 | 8 | .529 | 133 | 65 | 53 | 66 | 43 | 3.94 |
| 1974—Victoria† ..............Texas | | 40 | 96 | 9 | 5 | .643 | 96 | 43 | 34 | 54 | 40 | 3.23 |
| 1975—New York ............National | | 54 | 97 | 3 | 5 | .375 | 97 | 39 | 36 | 54 | 34 | 3.34 |
| 1976—New York ............National | | 11 | 23 | 0 | 0 | .000 | 14 | 6 | 6 | 9 | 10 | 2.35 |
| 1976—Tidewater ............Int'national | | 46 | 74 | 8 | 4 | .667 | 53 | 20 | 19 | 35 | 36 | 2.31 |
| Major League Totals .............................. | | 65 | 120 | 3 | 5 | .375 | 111 | 45 | 42 | 63 | 44 | 3.15 |

†Played in one game as a second baseman.

## ROBERT LAMONT BALDWIN, SR.
## (Billy)

Born June 9, 1951, at Tazwell, Va.
Height, 6.00. Weight, 180.
Throws and bats lefthanded.
Hobbies—Horseback riding, hunting and fishing.
Attended Southern University, Baton Rouge, La.

Tied for Florida State League lead in sacrifice hits with 12 in 1972.

| Year Club | League | Pos. | G. | AB. | R. | H. | 2B. | 3B. | HR. | RBI. | B.A. | PO. | A. | E. | F.A. |
|---|---|---|---|---|---|---|---|---|---|---|---|---|---|---|---|
| 1972—Lakeland ..........Fla. St. | | OF-1B | 118 | 414 | 34 | 115 | 14 | 9 | 5 | 47 | .278 | 223 | 13 | 4 | .983 |
| 1972—Montgomery ......South. | | OF-1B | 5 | 9 | 0 | 1 | 0 | 0 | 0 | 0 | .111 | 9 | 1 | 0 | 1.000 |
| 1973—Clinton ..............Midw. | | OF-1B | 120 | 473 | 66 | 133 | 21 | 2 | 13 | 76 | .281 | 257 | 17 | 8 | .972 |
| 1974—Lakeland ..........Fla. St. | | OF-1B | 130 | 490 | 61 | •150 | 16 | •12 | 7 | 68 | .306 | 255 | 12 | 6 | .978 |
| 1975—Montgomery ......South. | | OF | 78 | 322 | 45 | 97 | 9 | 4 | 15 | 48 | .301 | 154 | 5 | 3 | .981 |

| Year | Club | League | Pos. | G. | AB. | R. | H. | 2B. | 3B. | HR. | RBI. | B.A. | PO. | A. | E. | F.A. |
|---|---|---|---|---|---|---|---|---|---|---|---|---|---|---|---|---|
| 1975—Evansville ........A. A. | | | OF | 14 | 62 | 9 | 19 | 2 | 1 | 1 | 7 | .306 | 29 | 2 | 1 | .969 |
| 1975—Detroit† ............Amer. | | | OF | 30 | 95 | 8 | 21 | 3 | 0 | 4 | 8 | .221 | 53 | 4 | 1 | .983 |
| 1976—Tidewater.........Int. | | | OF | 133 | 495 | 66 | 134 | 20 | 5 | 17 | 72 | .271 | 259 | 11 | 4 | .985 |
| 1976—New York.........Nat. | | | OF | 9 | 22 | 4 | 6 | 1 | 1 | 1 | 5 | .273 | 12 | 1 | 1 | .929 |
| American League Totals ................ | | | | 30 | 95 | 8 | 21 | 3 | 0 | 4 | 8 | .221 | 53 | 4 | 1 | .983 |
| National League Totals ................. | | | | 9 | 22 | 4 | 6 | 1 | 1 | 1 | 5 | .273 | 12 | 1 | 1 | .929 |
| Major League Totals ....................... | | | | 39 | 117 | 12 | 27 | 4 | 1 | 5 | 13 | .231 | 65 | 5 | 2 | .972 |

†Traded with Pitcher Mickey Lolich to New York Mets for Outfielder Rusty Staub and Pitcher Bill Laxton, December 12, 1975.

## SALVATORE LEONARD BANDO
### (Sal)

Born February 13, 1944, at Cleveland, O.
Height, 6.00. Weight, 205.
Throws and bats righthanded.
Hobby—Sports.
Attended Arizona State University, Tempe, Ariz.

Tied major league record for fewest doubles, season, for leader in doubles, 32, in 1973.
Led American League third basemen in double plays with 36 in 1975.
Led American League in sacrifice flies with 13 in 1974.
Named third baseman on THE SPORTING NEWS American League All-Star Team, 1973 and 1974.
Received reported $30,000 bonus to sign with Kansas City Athletics, 1965.

| Year | Club | League | Pos. | G. | AB. | R. | H. | 2B. | 3B. | HR. | RBI. | B.A. | PO. | A. | E. | F.A. |
|---|---|---|---|---|---|---|---|---|---|---|---|---|---|---|---|---|
| 1965—Burlington ........Midw. | | | 3B | 60 | 221 | 28 | 58 | 10 | 2 | 6 | 35 | .262 | 39 | 127 | 11 | .938 |
| 1966—Mobile .............South. | | | 3B | 119 | 393 | 55 | 109 | 11 | 4 | 12 | 50 | .277 | 65 | 179 | 18 | .931 |
| 1966—Kansas City ......Amer. | | | 3B | 11 | 24 | 1 | 7 | 1 | 1 | 0 | 1 | .292 | 5 | 23 | 2 | .933 |
| 1967—Vancouver .........P.C. | | | 3B | 116 | 371 | 39 | 108 | 14 | 2 | 9 | 55 | .291 | 85 | 231 | 19 | .943 |
| 1967—Kansas City ......Amer. | | | 3B | 47 | 130 | 11 | 25 | 3 | 2 | 0 | 6 | .192 | 43 | 96 | 6 | .959 |
| 1968—Oakland ...........Amer. | | | *3B-OF | ●162 | 605 | 67 | 152 | 25 | 5 | 9 | 67 | .251 | *188 | 272 | 17 | .964 |
| 1969—Oakland ...........Amer. | | | 3B | ●162 | 609 | 106 | 171 | 25 | 3 | 31 | 113 | .281 | 178 | 321 | ●24 | .954 |
| 1970—Oakland ...........Amer. | | | 3B | 155 | 502 | 93 | 132 | 20 | 2 | 20 | 75 | .263 | *158 | 258 | 20 | .954 |
| 1971—Oakland ...........Amer. | | | 3B | 153 | 538 | 75 | 146 | 23 | 1 | 24 | 94 | .271 | 141 | 267 | 12 | .971 |
| 1972—Oakland ...........Amer. | | | 3B-2B | 152 | 535 | 64 | 126 | 20 | 3 | 15 | 77 | .236 | 124 | 337 | 20 | .958 |
| 1973—Oakland ...........Amer. | | | 3B | ●162 | 592 | 97 | 170 | ●32 | 3 | 29 | 98 | .287 | 126 | 281 | 22 | .949 |
| 1974—Oakland ...........Amer. | | | 3B | 146 | 498 | 84 | 121 | 21 | 2 | 22 | 103 | .243 | 113 | 287 | 23 | .946 |
| 1975—Oakland ...........Amer. | | | 3B | ●160 | 562 | 64 | 129 | 24 | 1 | 15 | 78 | .230 | 122 | 314 | 15 | .967 |
| 1976—Oakland† .........Amer. | | | 3-SS-DH | 158 | 550 | 75 | 132 | 18 | 2 | 27 | 84 | .240 | 127 | 310 | 17 | .962 |
| Major League Totals ....................... | | | | 1468 | 5145 | 737 | 1311 | 212 | 25 | 192 | 996 | .255 | 1325 | 2766 | 178 | .958 |

†Played out option year and granted free agency, November 1, 1976; signed as free agent by Milwaukee Brewers, November 19, 1976.

### CHAMPIONSHIP SERIES RECORD

| Year | Club | League | Pos. | G. | AB. | R. | H. | 2B. | 3B. | HR. | RBI. | B.A. | PO. | A. | E. | F.A. |
|---|---|---|---|---|---|---|---|---|---|---|---|---|---|---|---|---|
| 1971—Oakland ...........Amer. | | | 3B | 3 | 11 | 3 | 4 | 2 | 0 | 1 | 1 | .364 | 6 | 2 | 0 | 1.000 |
| 1972—Oakland ...........Amer. | | | 3B | 5 | 20 | 0 | 4 | 0 | 0 | 0 | 0 | .200 | 6 | 16 | 0 | 1.000 |
| 1973—Oakland ...........Amer. | | | 3B | 5 | 18 | 2 | 3 | 0 | 0 | 2 | 3 | .167 | 7 | 10 | 0 | 1.000 |
| 1974—Oakland ...........Amer. | | | 3B | 4 | 13 | 4 | 3 | 0 | 0 | 2 | 2 | .231 | 3 | 8 | 0 | 1.000 |
| 1975—Oakland ...........Amer. | | | 3B | 3 | 12 | 1 | 6 | 2 | 0 | 0 | 2 | .500 | 3 | 11 | 1 | .933 |
| Championship Series Totals ............ | | | | 20 | 74 | 10 | 20 | 4 | 0 | 5 | 8 | .270 | 25 | 47 | 1 | .986 |

### WORLD SERIES RECORD

Tied World Series record for most assists, third baseman, inning, 3, October 16, 1974.

| Year | Club | League | Pos. | G. | AB. | R. | H. | 2B. | 3B. | HR. | RBI. | B.A. | PO. | A. | E. | F.A. |
|---|---|---|---|---|---|---|---|---|---|---|---|---|---|---|---|---|
| 1972—Oakland ...........Amer. | | | 3B | 7 | 26 | 2 | 7 | 1 | 0 | 0 | 1 | .269 | 3 | 12 | 1 | .938 |
| 1973—Oakland ...........Amer. | | | 3B | 7 | 26 | 5 | 6 | 1 | 1 | 0 | 1 | .231 | 6 | 14 | 1 | .952 |
| 1974—Oakland ...........Amer. | | | 3B | 5 | 16 | 3 | 1 | 0 | 0 | 0 | 2 | .063 | 2 | 10 | 0 | 1.000 |
| World Series Totals ....................... | | | | 19 | 68 | 10 | 14 | 2 | 1 | 0 | 4 | .206 | 11 | 36 | 2 | .959 |

### ALL-STAR GAME RECORD

| Year | League | Pos. | AB. | R. | H. | 2B. | 3B. | HR. | RBI. | B.A. | PO. | A. | E. | F.A. |
|---|---|---|---|---|---|---|---|---|---|---|---|---|---|---|
| 1969—American ............................ | | 3B | 3 | 0 | 1 | 0 | 0 | 0 | 0 | .333 | 0 | 1 | 0 | 1.000 |
| 1972—American ............................ | | 3B | 2 | 0 | 0 | 0 | 0 | 0 | 0 | .000 | 1 | 1 | 0 | 1.000 |
| 1973—American ............................ | | 3B | 1 | 0 | 0 | 0 | 0 | 0 | 0 | .000 | 0 | 1 | 0 | 1.000 |
| All-Star Game Totals ....................... | | | 6 | 0 | 1 | 0 | 0 | 0 | 0 | .167 | 1 | 3 | 0 | 1.000 |

Named to American League All-Star Team for 1974 game; replaced due to injury.

## EDWARD NORMAN BANE
### (Eddie)

Born March 22, 1952, at Great Lakes, Ill.
Height, 5.10. Weight, 170.
Throws left and bats righthanded.
Hobby—Golf.
Attended Arizona State University, Tempe, Ariz.

Led Pacific Coast League pitchers in games started with 31 in 1975.
Received reported $55,000 bonus to sign with Minnesota Twins, 1973.

| Year Club | League | G. | IP. | W. | L. | Pct. | H. | R. | ER. | SO. | BB. | ERA. |
|---|---|---|---|---|---|---|---|---|---|---|---|---|
| 1973—Minnesota ...............American | American | 23 | 60 | 0 | 5 | .000 | 62 | 40 | 33 | 42 | 30 | 4.95 |
| 1974—Tacoma....................P. Coast | P. Coast | 27 | 142 | 10 | 8 | .556 | 146 | 83 | 66 | 104 | 69 | 4.18 |
| 1975—Tacoma....................P. Coast | P. Coast | 32 | 199 | 15 | 11 | .577 | 200 | 118 | 89 | 106 | 83 | 4.03 |
| 1975—Minnesota ...............American | American | 4 | 28 | 3 | 1 | .750 | 28 | 11 | 9 | 14 | 15 | 2.89 |
| 1976—Tacoma....................P. Coast | P. Coast | 14 | 78 | 4 | 5 | .444 | 79 | 49 | 32 | 40 | 41 | 3.69 |
| 1976—Minnesota ...............American | American | 17 | 79 | 4 | 7 | .364 | 92 | 52 | 45 | 24 | 39 | 5.13 |
| Major League Totals ............... | | 44 | 167 | 7 | 13 | .350 | 182 | 103 | 87 | 80 | 84 | 4.69 |

## ALAN BANNISTER

Born September 3, 1951, at Montebello, Calif.
Height, 5.11. Weight, 170
Throws and bats righthanded.
Hobbies—Movies, cars and all sports.
Attended Arizona State University, Tempe, Ariz., and California State University
at Long Beach, Long Beach, Calif.
Received reported $85,000 bonus to sign with Philadelphia Phillies, 1973.

| Year Club | League | Pos. | G. | AB. | R. | H. | 2B. | 3B. | HR. | RBI. | B.A. | PO. | A. | E. | F.A. |
|---|---|---|---|---|---|---|---|---|---|---|---|---|---|---|---|
| 1973—Eugene..............P.C. | P.C. | 2-3-S-O | 130 | 460 | 72 | 105 | 17 | 2 | 4 | 46 | .228 | 207 | 342 | 27 | .953 |
| 1974—Toledo ..............Int. | Int. | *SS-OF | 94 | 343 | 56 | 99 | 17 | 7 | 4 | 40 | .289 | 164 | 173 | *27 | .926 |
| 1974—Philadelphia ......Nat. | Nat. | OF-SS | 26 | 25 | 4 | 3 | 0 | 0 | 0 | 1 | .120 | 10 | 0 | 0 | 1.000 |
| 1975—Toledo ..............Int. | Int. | OF | 101 | 335 | 50 | 74 | 7 | 3 | 5 | 27 | .221 | 209 | 3 | 6 | .972 |
| 1975—Philadelphia† ....Nat. | Nat. | O-S-2 | 24 | 61 | 10 | 16 | 3 | 1 | 0 | 0 | .262 | 54 | 4 | 2 | .967 |
| 1976—Iowa..................A.A. | A.A. | 3B | 32 | 118 | 24 | 29 | 6 | 0 | 3 | 12 | .246 | 64 | 106 | 9 | .950 |
| 1976—Chicago ...........Amer. | Amer. | O-I-DH | 73 | 145 | 19 | 36 | 6 | 2 | 0 | 8 | .248 | 92 | 36 | 5 | .962 |
| American League Totals ................. | | | 73 | 145 | 19 | 36 | 6 | 2 | 0 | 8 | .248 | 92 | 36 | 5 | .962 |
| National League Totals ................. | | | 50 | 86 | 14 | 19 | 3 | 1 | 0 | 1 | .221 | 64 | 4 | 2 | .971 |
| Major League Totals ...................... | | | 123 | 231 | 33 | 55 | 9 | 3 | 0 | 9 | .238 | 156 | 40 | 7 | .966 |

†Traded with Pitchers Dick Ruthven and Roy Thomas to Chicago White Sox for Pitcher Jim Kaat and Shortstop Mike Buskey, December 10, 1975.

## FLOYD FRANKLIN BANNISTER

Born June 10, 1955, at Pierre, S. Dakota.
Height, 6.01. Weight, 190.
Throws and bats lefthanded.
Attended Arizona State University, Tempe, Ariz.

| Year Club | League | G. | IP. | W. | L. | Pct. | H. | R. | ER. | SO. | BB. | ERA. |
|---|---|---|---|---|---|---|---|---|---|---|---|---|
| 1976—Covington ..............Ap'lachian | Ap'lachian | 3 | 13 | 0 | 0 | .000 | 3 | 0 | 0 | 27 | 2 | 0.00 |
| 1976—Columbus ..............Southern | Southern | 3 | 24 | 1 | 0 | 1.000 | 16 | 4 | 4 | 20 | 14 | 1.50 |
| 1976—Memphis................Int'national | Int'national | 1 | 6 | 1 | 0 | 1.000 | 7 | 1 | 1 | 6 | 3 | 1.50 |

Invited to Houston Astros' 1977 spring camp.

## RAYMOND DOUGLAS BARE
### (Ray)

Born April 15, 1949, at Miami, Fla.
Height, 6.02. Weight, 193.
Throws and bats righthanded.
Hobbies—Golf, skin diving and trap and skeet shooting.
Attended University of South Florida, Tampa, Fla., and Miami-Dade (North)
Community College, Miami, Fla.

| Year Club | League | G. | IP. | W. | L. | Pct. | H. | R. | ER. | SO. | BB. | ERA. |
|---|---|---|---|---|---|---|---|---|---|---|---|---|
| 1969—St. Petersburg.................Florida St. | Florida St. | 21 | 113 | 6 | 5 | .545 | 100 | 41 | 33 | 71 | 35 | 2.63 |
| 1970—Arkansas...........................Texas | Texas | 29 | 179 | 10 | 13 | .435 | 195 | 86 | 78 | 98 | 55 | 3.92 |
| 1971—Tulsa ...................Am. Assoc. | Am. Assoc. | 33 | 156 | 6 | 11 | .353 | 176 | *102 | 80 | 68 | 46 | 4.62 |
| 1972—Tulsa ...................Am. Assoc. | Am. Assoc. | 29 | 82 | 6 | 5 | .545 | 78 | 28 | 23 | 47 | 26 | 2.52 |
| 1972—St. Louis ...........................National | National | 14 | 17 | 0 | 1 | .000 | 18 | 2 | 1 | 5 | 6 | 0.53 |
| 1973—Tulsa ...................Am. Assoc. | Am. Assoc. | 41 | 102 | 7 | 8 | .467 | 108 | 53 | 41 | 74 | 51 | 3.62 |
| 1974—Tulsa ...................Am. Assoc. | Am. Assoc. | 19 | 127 | 12 | 4 | *.750 | 111 | 45 | 33 | 67 | 44 | *2.34 |
| 1974—St. Louis† .........................National | National | 10 | 24 | 1 | 2 | .333 | 25 | 17 | 16 | 6 | 9 | 6.00 |
| 1975—Detroit ......................American | American | 29 | 151 | 8 | 13 | .381 | 174 | 81 | 75 | 71 | 47 | 4.47 |
| 1976—Detroit ......................American | American | 30 | 134 | 7 | 8 | .467 | 157 | 85 | 69 | 59 | 51 | 4.63 |
| National League Totals............................ | | 24 | 41 | 1 | 3 | .250 | 43 | 19 | 17 | 11 | 15 | 3.73 |
| American League Totals........................ | | 59 | 285 | 15 | 21 | .417 | 331 | 166 | 144 | 140 | 98 | 4.55 |
| Major League Totals ............................... | | 83 | 326 | 16 | 24 | .400 | 374 | 185 | 161 | 151 | 113 | 4.44 |

Sold via waivers to Detroit Tigers, April 4, 1975.

---

## *DID YOU KNOW* —

That the first extra-inning game in the National League was played between Hartford and Boston on April 29, 1876? It went 10 innings and Hartford won, 3-2.

## JEFFREY EVERETT BARKER
### (Jeff)

Born March 25, 1955, at Pasadena, Calif.
Height, 6.01. Weight, 195.
Throws and bats righthanded.
Hobby—Motorcycle riding.
Brother of Ken Barker, pitcher in California Angels'
organization, 1971 through 1974.

| Year Club | League | G. | IP. | W. | L. | Pct. | H. | R. | ER. | SO. | BB. | ERA. |
|---|---|---|---|---|---|---|---|---|---|---|---|---|
| 1973—Newark | NYP | 11 | 57 | 2 | 4 | .333 | 69 | 49 | 33 | 30 | 18 | 5.21 |
| 1974—Danville | Midwest | 23 | 161 | 11 | 9 | .550 | 154 | 65 | 52 | 144 | 39 | 2.91 |
| 1975—Sacramento† | P.Coast | 8 | 35 | 2 | 2 | .500 | 43 | 35 | 30 | 21 | 13 | 7.71 |
| 1976—Spokane‡ | P.Coast | 2 | 3 | 0 | 0 | .000 | 6 | 4 | 4 | 0 | 4 | 12.00 |

†On disabled list, June 11 to September 2, 1975.
‡On disabled list, April 17 through August 2, 1976.
Listed on Milwaukee Brewers' 1977 spring roster.


## LEONARD HAROLD BARKER, II
### (Len)

Born July 7, 1955, at Ft. Knox, Ky.
Height, 6.05. Weight, 225.
Throws and bats righthanded.
Hobbies—Hunting and fishing.

Led Western Carolinas League in shutouts with 5 in 1974.

| Year Club | League | G. | IP. | W. | L. | Pct. | H. | R. | ER. | SO. | BB. | ERA. |
|---|---|---|---|---|---|---|---|---|---|---|---|---|
| 1973—Sarasota Rangers | Gulf Coast | 11 | 59 | •7 | 1 | •.875 | 34 | 13 | 9 | 54 | 27 | 1.37 |
| 1974—Gastonia | W. Carol. | 20 | 124 | 11 | 7 | .611 | 101 | 57 | 46 | 140 | 53 | 3.34 |
| 1975—Pittsfield | Eastern | 24 | 159 | 7 | 12 | .368 | 117 | 72 | 51 | 133 | 109 | 2.89 |
| 1976—Sacramento | P. Coast | 27 | 141 | 11 | 10 | .524 | 140 | 103 | 87 | 92 | 96 | 5.55 |
| 1976—Texas | American | 2 | 15 | 1 | 0 | 1.000 | 7 | 4 | 4 | 7 | 6 | 2.40 |
| Major League Totals | | 2 | 15 | 1 | 0 | 1.000 | 7 | 4 | 4 | 7 | 6 | 2.40 |


## JAMES LELAND BARR
### (Jim)

Born February 10, 1948, at Lynwood, Calif.
Height, 6.03. Weight, 215.
Throws and bats righthanded.
Hobbies—Woodworking and Water skiing.
Attended University of Southern California, Los Angeles, Calif.;
received Bachelor of Arts degree in Business Administration.
Brother of Mark Barr, pitcher in Boston Red Sox' organization.

Set major league record for most batters retired, consecutive, season, 41, August 23-29, 1972.

| Year Club | League | G. | IP. | W. | L. | Pct. | H. | R. | ER. | SO. | BB. | ERA. |
|---|---|---|---|---|---|---|---|---|---|---|---|---|
| 1970—Amarillo | Texas | 14 | 98 | 6 | 5 | .545 | 107 | 51 | 36 | 48 | 23 | 3.31 |
| 1971—Phoenix | P. Coast | 47 | 79 | 6 | 3 | .667 | 72 | 36 | 33 | 71 | 26 | 3.76 |
| 1971—San Francisco | National | 17 | 35 | 1 | 1 | .500 | 33 | 15 | 14 | 16 | 5 | 3.60 |
| 1972—San Francisco | National | 44 | 179 | 8 | 10 | .444 | 166 | 66 | 57 | 86 | 41 | 2.87 |
| 1973—San Francisco | National | 41 | 231 | 11 | 17 | .393 | 240 | 105 | 98 | 88 | 49 | 3.82 |
| 1974—San Francisco | National | 44 | 240 | 13 | 9 | .591 | 223 | 81 | 73 | 84 | 47 | 2.74 |
| 1975—San Francisco | National | 35 | 244 | 13 | 14 | .481 | 244 | 94 | 83 | 77 | 58 | 3.06 |
| 1976—San Francisco | National | 37 | 252 | 15 | 12 | .556 | 260 | 104 | 81 | 75 | 60 | 2.89 |
| Major League Totals | | 218 | 1181 | 61 | 63 | .492 | 1166 | 465 | 406 | 426 | 260 | 3.09 |

CHAMPIONSHIP SERIES RECORD

| Year Club | League | G. | IP. | W. | L. | Pct. | H. | R. | ER. | SO. | BB. | ERA. |
|---|---|---|---|---|---|---|---|---|---|---|---|---|
| 1971—San Francisco | National | 1 | 1 | 0 | 0 | .000 | 3 | 1 | 1 | 2 | 0 | 9.00 |


## STEVEN CHARLES BARR
### (Steve)

Born September 8, 1951, at St. Louis, Mo.
Height, 6.04. Weight, 200.
Throws and bats lefthanded.

Led Eastern League in complete games with 15 and tied for lead in wild pitches with 19 in 1974.

| Year Club | League | G. | IP. | W. | L. | Pct. | H. | R. | ER. | SO. | BB. | ERA. |
|---|---|---|---|---|---|---|---|---|---|---|---|---|
| 1969—Jamestown | NYP | 9 | 28 | 0 | 4 | .000 | 34 | 35 | 26 | 21 | 30 | 8.36 |
| 1970—Greenville† | W. Carol. | 15 | 74 | 3 | 4 | .429 | 72 | 52 | 36 | 61 | 55 | 4.38 |
| 1971—Winter Haven‡ | Florida St. | 10 | 36 | 1 | 1 | .500 | 38 | 29 | 24 | 22 | 32 | 6.00 |
| 1972—Winston-Salem | Carolina | 19 | 118 | 8 | 9 | .471 | 102 | 64 | 55 | 79 | 45 | 4.19 |
| 1973—Bristol | Eastern | 20 | 132 | 7 | 10 | .412 | 117 | 62 | 47 | 95 | 73 | 3.20 |
| 1973—Pawtucket | Int'national | 3 | 14 | 1 | 0 | 1.000 | 18 | 10 | 9 | 9 | 6 | 5.79 |
| 1974—Bristol | Eastern | 25 | •191 | •16 | 8 | .667 | 143 | 62 | 52 | 155 | 80 | 2.45 |

| Year Club | League | G. | IP. | W. | L. | Pct. | H. | R. | ER. | SO. | BB. | ERA. |
|---|---|---|---|---|---|---|---|---|---|---|---|---|
| 1974—Boston .................................American | | 1 | 9 | 1 | 0 | 1.000 | 7 | 4 | 4 | 3 | 6 | 4.00 |
| 1975—Pawtucket§ ...........................Int'national | | 23 | 148 | 6 | 12 | .333 | 128 | 65 | 48 | 110 | 80 | 2.92 |
| 1975—Boston x .............................American | | 3 | 7 | 0 | 1 | .000 | 11 | 9 | 2 | 2 | 7 | 2.57 |
| 1976—Texas y................................American | | 20 | 68 | 2 | 6 | .250 | 70 | 51 | 42 | 27 | 44 | 5.56 |
| Major League Totals .............................. | | 24 | 84 | 3 | 7 | .300 | 88 | 64 | 48 | 32 | 57 | 5.14 |

†On disabled list, June 26 through remainder of season.
‡On suspended list from beginning of season until July 9.
§On temporary inactive list, April 24 to May 20, 1975.
xTraded with Outfielder Juan Beniquez, a minor league player to be named later and an estimated $200,000 to Texas Rangers for Pitcher Ferguson Jenkins, November 17, 1975; Red Sox sent Pitcher Craig Skok to Rangers, December 12, 1975, to complete deal.
ySelected by Seattle Mariners from Texas Rangers in American League expansion draft, November 5, 1976.

## FRANCISCO JAVIER BARRIOS (JIMENEZ)

Born June 10, 1953, at Hermosillo, Mexico.
Height, 5.11. Weight, 155.
Throws and bats righthanded.
Led Mexican Center League in hit batsmen with 10 in 1972.

| Year Club | League | G. | IP. | W. | L. | Pct. | H. | R. | ER. | SO. | BB. | ERA. |
|---|---|---|---|---|---|---|---|---|---|---|---|---|
| 1971—San Luis Potosi ....................Mex. Cent. | | 18 | 90 | 6 | 4 | .600 | 76 | 45 | 32 | 43 | 32 | 3.20 |
| 1971—Mexicali ..............................Mex. North. | | 22 | 113 | 7 | 4 | .636 | 103 | 38 | 34 | 71 | 44 | 2.71 |
| 1972—Zacatecas ...........................Mex. Cent. | | 19 | 97 | 5 | •9 | .357 | 102 | •70 | •60 | 55 | 41 | 5.57 |
| 1972—Jalisco ................................Mexican | | 8 | 23 | 1 | 1 | .500 | 23 | 15 | 12 | 11 | 14 | 4.70 |
| 1973—Jalisco† ...............................Mexican | | 33 | 198 | 10 | 12 | .455 | 157 | 70 | 52 | 158 | 98 | 2.36 |
| 1973—Phoenix‡§ ...........................P. Coast | | 6 | 30 | 2 | 1 | .667 | 36 | 18 | 15 | 9 | 10 | 4.50 |
| 1974—Knoxville ............................Southern | | 26 | 124 | 9 | 5 | .643 | 112 | 60 | 54 | 84 | 58 | 3.92 |
| 1974—Chicago...............................American | | 2 | 2 | 0 | 0 | .000 | 7 | 6 | 6 | 2 | 2 | 27.00 |
| 1975—Jalisco ................................Mexican | | 31 | 183 | 10 | 12 | .455 | 169 | 77 | 55 | 138 | 85 | 2.70 |
| 1975—Denver ...............................Am. Assoc. | | 3 | 23 | 2 | 0 | 1.000 | 21 | 10 | 10 | 12 | 9 | 3.91 |
| 1976—Chicago...............................American | | 35 | 142 | 5 | 9 | .357 | 136 | 72 | 68 | 81 | 46 | 4.31 |
| Major League Totals ............................... | | 37 | 144 | 5 | 9 | .357 | 143 | 78 | 74 | 83 | 48 | .462 |

†Conditionally released to Phoenix (San Francisco Giants' organization), August 9, 1973.
‡Returned to Jalisco, September 6, 1973.
§Traded with Pitcher Manuel Lugo by Jalisco to Chicago White Sox for Infielder Rudy Hernandez, December 4, 1973.

## RANDY WILLIAM BASS

Born March 13, 1954, at Lawton, Okla.
Height, 6.01. Weight, 210.
Throws right and bats lefthanded.
Hobbies—Hunting, fishing and golf.
Led Florida East Coast League in total bases with 106 and in walks with 59 in 1972.
Led Carolina League first basemen in double plays with 107 in 1974.

| Year Club | League | Pos. | G. | AB. | R. | H. | 2B. | 3B. | HR. | RBI. | B.A. | PO. | A. | E. | F.A. |
|---|---|---|---|---|---|---|---|---|---|---|---|---|---|---|---|
| 1972—Melb'ne Twins ..Fla.E.C. | | 1B | 59 | 199 | •47 | 61 | •15 | 0 | •10 | •41 | .307 | •527 | 14 | •11 | •.980 |
| 1973—Wis. Rapids ......Midw. | | 1B | 114 | 388 | 83 | 112 | 23 | 1 | •21 | 86 | .289 | •988 | 59 | 19 | .982 |
| 1974—Lynchburg ........Carol. | | 1B | 133 | 461 | 89 | 118 | 17 | 1 | •30 | •112 | .256 | •1237 | •84 | 17 | .987 |
| 1975—Tacoma ............P.C. | | 1B | 120 | 397 | 64 | 102 | 14 | 5 | 18 | 80 | .257 | 795 | 74 | 6 | .993 |
| 1976—Tacoma ............P.C. | | 1B | 141 | 451 | 73 | 126 | 15 | 3 | 21 | 76 | .279 | 569 | 51 | 3 | .995 |

Listed on Minnesota Twins' 1977 spring roster.

## CHRISTOPHER SEAN BATTON

### (Chris)

Born August 24, 1954, at Los Angeles, Calif.
Height, 6.04. Weight, 195.
Throws and bats righthanded.
Hobbies—Music, movies and basketball.
Attended West Los Angeles College, Culver City, Calif.
Twin brother of John Batton, pitcher in Minnesota Twins' organization, 1974.
Tied for Southern League lead in games started with 28 and in shutouts with 4 in 1975.

| Year Club | League | G. | IP. | W. | L. | Pct. | H. | R. | ER. | SO. | BB. | ERA. |
|---|---|---|---|---|---|---|---|---|---|---|---|---|
| 1972—Coos Bay-North Bend ..........Northwest | | 15 | 53 | 0 | 6 | .000 | 64 | 47 | 37 | 47 | 37 | 6.28 |
| 1973—Burlington† .........................Midwest | | 10 | 64 | 4 | 5 | .444 | 51 | 24 | 19 | 61 | 30 | 2.67 |
| 1974—Burlington..........................Midwest | | 24 | 140 | 6 | 12 | .333 | 133 | •87 | 64 | 120 | 66 | 4.11 |
| 1975—Birmingham ......................Southern | | 29 | 190 | 13 | 10 | .565 | 192 | 89 | 77 | 96 | •109 | 3.65 |
| 1976—Tucson‡ ............................P. Coast | | 24 | 157 | 10 | 12 | .455 | 182 | 106 | 94 | 77 | 82 | 5.39 |
| 1976—Oakland§............................American | | 2 | 4 | 0 | 0 | .000 | 5 | 4 | 4 | 4 | 3 | 9.00 |
| Major League Totals ............................. | | 2 | 4 | 0 | 0 | .000 | 5 | 4 | 4 | 4 | 3 | 9.00 |

†On disabled list, July 17 through remainder of season.
‡On disabled list, May 22 through June 1, 1976.
§Traded with Infielders Phil Garner and Tommy Helms to Pittsburgh Pirates for Pitchers Doc Medich, Dave Giusti, Rick Langford and Doug Bair, Infielder Mitchell Page and Outfielder Tony Armas, March 15, 1977.

## DONALD EDWARD BAYLOR
### (Don)

Born June 28, 1949, at Austin, Tex.
Height, 6.01. Weight, 195.
Throws and bats righthanded.
Hobbies—Fishing and reading poetry.
Attended Miami-Dade Junior College, Miami, Fla., and Blinn Junior
College, Brenham, Tex.

Established major league record for most times caught stealing, inning, 2, June 15, 1974 (9th inning).
Tied modern league records for most hits, two consecutive games, 9, August 13-14, 1973, and most long hits, opening game of season, 4, April 6, 1973 (2 doubles, 1 triple, 1 home run).
Major League stolen bases: 1970 (1), 1971 (0), 1972 (24), 1973 (32), 1974 (29), 1975 (32), 1976 (52). Total—170.
Led Appalachian League in stolen bases with 26 and total bases with 135 in 1967.
Led International League in total bases with 296 in 1970.
Named by THE SPORTING NEWS as Minor League Player of the Year, 1970.

| Year Club League | Pos. | G. | AB. | R. | H. | 2B. | 3B. | HR. | RBI. | B.A. | PO. | A. | E. | F.A. |
|---|---|---|---|---|---|---|---|---|---|---|---|---|---|---|
| 1967—Bluefield ..........Appal. | OF | •67 | 246 | 50 | •85 | 10 | •8 | 8 | 47 | *.346 | 106 | 5 | 5 | .957 |
| 1968—Stockton ............Calif. | OF | 68 | 244 | 52 | 90 | 6 | 3 | 7 | 40 | .369 | 135 | 3 | 7 | .952 |
| 1968—Elmira ..............East. | OF | 6 | 24 | 4 | 8 | 1 | 1 | 1 | 3 | .333 | 10 | 1 | 0 | 1.000 |
| 1968—Rochester..........Int. | OF | 15 | 46 | 4 | 10 | 2 | 0 | 0 | 4 | .217 | 29 | 1 | 4 | .882 |
| 1969—Miami ..............Fla.St. | OF | 17 | 56 | 13 | 21 | 5 | 4 | 3 | 24 | .375 | 30 | 2 | 3 | .914 |
| 1969—Dal.-Ft. Worth ..Texas | OF | 109 | 406 | 71 | 122 | 17 | •10 | 11 | 57 | .300 | 241 | 7 | •13 | .950 |
| 1970—Rochester..........Int. | OF | •140 | 508 | •127 | 166 | •34 | •15 | 22 | 107 | .327 | 286 | 5 | 7 | .977 |
| 1970—Baltimore.........Amer. | OF | 8 | 17 | 4 | 4 | 0 | 0 | 0 | 4 | .235 | 15 | 0 | 0 | 1.000 |
| 1971—Rochester..........Int. | OF | 136 | 492 | 104 | 154 | •31 | 10 | 20 | 95 | .313 | 210 | 4 | 9 | .960 |
| 1971—Baltimore.........Amer. | OF | 1 | 2 | 0 | 0 | 0 | 0 | 0 | 1 | .000 | 4 | 0 | 0 | 1.000 |
| 1972—Baltimore.........Amer. | OF-1B | 102 | 320 | 33 | 81 | 13 | 3 | 11 | 38 | .253 | 206 | 4 | 5 | .977 |
| 1973—Baltimore.........Amer. | OF-1B | 118 | 405 | 64 | 116 | 20 | 4 | 11 | 51 | .286 | 228 | 10 | 6 | .975 |
| 1974—Baltimore.........Amer. | OF-1B | 137 | 489 | 66 | 133 | 22 | 1 | 10 | 59 | .272 | 260 | 2 | 5 | .981 |
| 1975—Baltimore†........Amer. | OF-1B | 145 | 524 | 79 | 148 | 21 | 6 | 25 | 76 | .282 | 286 | 8 | 5 | .983 |
| 1976—Oakland‡ .........Amer. | OF-1-DH | 157 | 595 | 85 | 147 | 25 | 1 | 15 | 68 | .247 | 781 | 45 | 12 | .986 |
| Major League Totals ..................... | | 668 | 2352• | 331 | 629 | 101 | 15 | 72 | 697 | .267 | 1780 | 69 | 33 | .982 |

†Traded with Pitchers Mike Torrez and Paul Mitchell to Oakland Athletics for Outfielder Reggie Jackson and Pitchers Ken Holtzman and Bill Van Bommel, April 2, 1976.
‡Played out option year and granted free agency, November 1, 1976; signed as free agent by California Angels, November 16, 1976.


## CHARLES ALFONZO BEAMON
### (Charlie)

Born December 4, 1953, at Oakland, Calif.
Height, 6.01. Weight, 183.
Throws and bats lefthanded.
Hobbies—Music, basketball and billiards.
Attended Laney Junior College, Oakland, Calif.

| Year Club League | Pos. | G. | AB. | R. | H. | 2B. | 3B. | HR. | RBI. | B.A. | PO. | A. | E. | F.A. |
|---|---|---|---|---|---|---|---|---|---|---|---|---|---|---|
| 1974—Sarasota Royals Gulf C. | 1B-OF | 47 | 159 | 31 | 49 | 6 | 4 | 0 | 27 | .308 | 142 | 12 | 3 | .981 |
| 1975—Waterloo .........Midw. | 1B-OF | 109 | 370 | 57 | 113 | 16 | 4 | 1 | 63 | .305 | 808 | 65 | 12 | .986 |
| 1976—Jacksonville† ....South. | OF-1B | •138 | 500 | 58 | 143 | 12 | 0 | 1 | 47 | .286 | 479 | 49 | 9 | .983 |

†Drafted from Kansas City Royals' organization by Seattle Mariners, December 6, 1976.


## MICHAEL RICHARD BEARD
### (Mike)

Born June 21, 1950, at Little Rock, Ark.
Height, 6.01. Weight, 190.
Throws and bats lefthanded.
Attended University of Texas, Austin, Tex., and University of
Arkansas at Little Rock, Little Rock, Ark.

| Year Club League | G. | IP. | W. | L. | Pct. | H. | R. | ER. | SO. | BB. | ERA. |
|---|---|---|---|---|---|---|---|---|---|---|---|
| 1971—Savannah ...........................Southern | 10 | 57 | 4 | 4 | .500 | 46 | 20 | 17 | 38 | 23 | 2.68 |
| 1971—Richmond ..........................Int'national | 1 | 9 | 1 | 0 | 1.000 | 6 | 2 | 2 | 4 | 2 | 2.00 |
| 1972—Richmond ..........................Int'national | 28 | 137 | 6 | •14 | .300 | 172 | 95 | 73 | 83 | 55 | 4.80 |
| 1973—Richmond† .........................Int'national | 9 | 57 | 1 | 6 | .143 | 55 | 34 | 26 | 31 | 27 | 4.11 |
| 1974—Savannah ...........................Southern | 47 | 124 | 9 | 10 | .474 | 99 | 50 | 33 | 82 | 40 | •2.40 |
| 1974—Atlanta ...............................National | 6 | 9 | 0 | 0 | .000 | 5 | 3 | 3 | 7 | 1 | 3.00 |
| 1975—Richmond ..........................Int'national | 13 | 25 | 2 | 1 | .667 | 20 | 9 | 8 | 16 | 9 | 2.88 |
| 1975—Atlanta ...............................National | 34 | 70 | 4 | 0 | 1.000 | 71 | 31 | 25 | 27 | 28 | 3.21 |
| 1976—Richmond ..........................Int'national | 14 | 21 | 2 | 0 | 1.000 | 24 | 8 | 7 | 8 | 6 | 3.00 |
| 1976—Atlanta ...............................National | 30 | 34 | 0 | 2 | .000 | 38 | 18 | 16 | 8 | 14 | 4.24 |
| Major League Totals ............................. | 70 | 113 | 4 | 2 | .667 | 114 | 52 | 44 | 42 | 43 | 3.50 |

†On disabled list, June 1 through remainder of season.

## GARY RAY BEARE

Born August 22, 1952, at San Diego, Calif.
Height, 6.04. Weight, 205.
Throws and bats righthanded.
Hobby—Food.
Attended San Diego Mesa Junior College, San Diego, Calif.; and
Long Beach State University, Long Beach, Calif.

| Year Club | League | G. | IP. | W. | L. | Pct. | H. | R. | ER. | SO. | BB. | ERA. |
|---|---|---|---|---|---|---|---|---|---|---|---|---|
| 1974—Newark | NYP | 14 | 76 | 4 | 4 | .500 | 73 | 44 | 37 | 71 | 58 | 4.38 |
| 1975—Thetford Mines | Eastern | 36 | 92 | 3 | 9 | .250 | 95 | 49 | 35 | 61 | 57 | 3.42 |
| 1976—Pittsfield | Eastern | 22 | 139 | 10 | 10 | .500 | 138 | 55 | 46 | 71 | 47 | 2.98 |
| 1976—Spokane | P. Coast | 6 | 40 | 1 | 4 | .200 | 33 | 15 | 13 | 36 | 15 | 2.93 |
| 1976—Milwaukee | American | 6 | 41 | 2 | 3 | .400 | 43 | 16 | 15 | 32 | 15 | 3.29 |
| Major League Totals | | 6 | 41 | 2 | 3 | .400 | 43 | 16 | 15 | 32 | 15 | 3.29 |

## MARK HENRY BELANGER

Name pronounced Bel-LAN-ger.
Born June 8, 1944, at Pittsfield, Mass.
Height, 6.02. Weight, 179.
Throws and bats righthanded.
Hobbies—Announcing on radio station in home city and
coaching basketball.
Attended University of Tampa, Tampa, Fla.

Established major league record for highest fielding percentage, shortstop, lifetime, .975, 1976.
Tied major league record for most doubles, inning, 2, August 18, 1969, 2nd inning.
Led American League shortstops in total chances with 794 in 1973 and 808 in 1974.
Led American League in sacrifice hits with 15 in 1973 and 23 in 1975.
Tied for American League lead in double plays by shortstops with 105 in 1975.
Led Northern League shortstops in double plays with 76 in 1964.
Led Eastern League in stolen bases with 29 in 1965.
Named Rookie of the Year in Northern League, 1964.
Named shortstop on THE SPORTING NEWS American League All-Star Team, 1976.
Named shortstop on THE SPORTING NEWS American League All-Star fielding teams, 1969, 1971, 1973, 1974, 1975, and 1976.
Received reported $35,000 bonus to sign with Baltimore Orioles, 1962.

| Year Club | League | Pos. | G. | AB. | R. | H. | 2B. | 3B. | HR. | RBI. | B.A. | PO. | A. | E. | F.A. |
|---|---|---|---|---|---|---|---|---|---|---|---|---|---|---|---|
| 1962—Bluefield | Appal. | SS | 47 | 151 | 44 | 45 | 7 | 1 | 3 | 23 | .298 | 58 | 123 | 20 | .900 |
| 1962—Elmira | East. | SS | 8 | 22 | 0 | 1 | 0 | 0 | 0 | 0 | .045 | 10 | 16 | 3 | .897 |
| 1963—Baltimore† | Amer. | | | | | (In Military Service) | | | | | | | | | |
| 1964—Aberdeen | North. | SS | 117 | *465 | 79 | 105 | 21 | 6 | 4 | 28 | .226 | *186 | 335 | 23 | *.958 |
| 1965—Elmira | East. | SS | 125 | 481 | 84 | 110 | 16 | 5 | 2 | 33 | .229 | *217 | 428 | 21 | *.968 |
| 1965—Baltimore | Amer. | SS | 11 | 3 | 1 | 1 | 0 | 0 | 0 | 0 | .333 | 1 | 1 | 0 | 1.000 |
| 1966—Rochester | Int. | SS | 139 | 504 | 80 | 132 | 12 | 6 | 6 | 38 | .262 | 242 | 387 | 17 | *.974 |
| 1966—Baltimore | Amer. | SS | 8 | 19 | 2 | 3 | 1 | 0 | 0 | 0 | .158 | 9 | 20 | 0 | 1.000 |
| 1967—Baltimore‡ | Amer. | S-2-3B | 69 | 184 | 19 | 32 | 5 | 0 | 1 | 10 | .174 | 100 | 138 | 9 | .964 |
| 1968—Baltimore‡‡ | Amer. | SS | 145 | 472 | 40 | 98 | 13 | 0 | 2 | 21 | .208 | 248 | 444 | 22 | .969 |
| 1969—Baltimore | Amer. | SS | 150 | 530 | 76 | 152 | 17 | 4 | 2 | 50 | .287 | 251 | 449 | 23 | .968 |
| 1970—Baltimore | Amer. | SS | 145 | 459 | 53 | 100 | 6 | 5 | 1 | 36 | .218 | 212 | 412 | 19 | .970 |
| 1971—Baltimore | Amer. | SS | 150 | 500 | 67 | 133 | 19 | 4 | 0 | 35 | .266 | 280 | 443 | 16 | .978 |
| 1972—Baltimore | Amer. | SS | 113 | 285 | 36 | 53 | 9 | 1 | 2 | 16 | .186 | 180 | 285 | 12 | .975 |
| 1973—Baltimore | Amer. | SS | 154 | 470 | 60 | 106 | 15 | 1 | 0 | 27 | .226 | 241 | *530 | 23 | .971 |
| 1974—Baltimore | Amer. | SS | 155 | 493 | 54 | 111 | 14 | 4 | 5 | 36 | .225 | 243 | *552 | 13 | *.984 |
| 1975—Baltimore | Amer. | SS | 152 | 442 | 44 | 100 | 11 | 1 | 3 | 27 | .226 | 259 | 508 | 17 | .978 |
| 1976—Baltimore | Amer. | SS | 153 | 522 | 66 | 141 | 22 | 2 | 1 | 40 | .270 | 239 | *545 | 14 | .982 |
| Major League Totals | | | 1405 | 4379 | 518 | 1030 | 132 | 22 | 17 | 298 | .235 | 2263 | 4327 | 168 | .975 |

†On military list, April 11, 1963 through March 6, 1964.
‡On military list, July 1 through July 17, 1967.
‡‡On military list, June 16 through June 25, 1968.

### CHAMPIONSHIP SERIES RECORD

| Year Club | League | Pos. | G. | AB. | R. | H. | 2B. | 3B. | HR. | RBI. | B.A. | PO. | A. | E. | F.A. |
|---|---|---|---|---|---|---|---|---|---|---|---|---|---|---|---|
| 1969—Baltimore | Amer. | SS | 3 | 15 | 4 | 4 | 0 | 1 | 1 | 1 | .267 | 4 | 9 | 0 | 1.000 |
| 1970—Baltimore | Amer. | SS | 3 | 12 | 5 | 4 | 0 | 0 | 0 | 1 | .333 | 6 | 14 | 0 | 1.000 |
| 1971—Baltimore | Amer. | SS | 3 | 8 | 1 | 2 | 0 | 0 | 0 | 1 | .250 | 6 | 11 | 0 | 1.000 |
| 1973—Baltimore | Amer. | SS | 5 | 16 | 0 | 2 | 0 | 0 | 0 | 1 | .125 | 8 | 17 | 0 | 1.000 |
| 1974—Baltimore | Amer. | SS | 4 | 9 | 0 | 0 | 0 | 0 | 0 | 0 | .000 | 7 | 12 | 1 | .950 |
| Championship Series Totals | | | 18 | 60 | 10 | 12 | 0 | 1 | 1 | 4 | .200 | 31 | 63 | 1 | .989 |

### WORLD SERIES RECORD

| Year Club | League | Pos. | G. | AB. | R. | H. | 2B. | 3B. | HR. | RBI. | B.A. | PO. | A. | E. | F.A. |
|---|---|---|---|---|---|---|---|---|---|---|---|---|---|---|---|
| 1969—Baltimore | Amer. | SS | 5 | 15 | 2 | 3 | 0 | 0 | 0 | 1 | .200 | 7 | 14 | 0 | 1.000 |
| 1970—Baltimore | Amer. | SS | 5 | 19 | 0 | 2 | 0 | 0 | 0 | 1 | .105 | 11 | 14 | 1 | .962 |
| 1971—Baltimore | Amer. | SS | 7 | 21 | 4 | 5 | 0 | 1 | 0 | 0 | .238 | 10 | 20 | 3 | .909 |
| World Series Totals | | | 17 | 55 | 6 | 10 | 0 | 1 | 0 | 2 | .182 | 28 | 48 | 4 | .950 |

### ALL-STAR GAME RECORD

| Year League | | Pos. | AB. | R. | H. | 2B. | 3B. | HR. | RBI. | B.A. | PO. | A. | E. | F.A. |
|---|---|---|---|---|---|---|---|---|---|---|---|---|---|---|
| 1976—American | | SS | 1 | 0 | 0 | 0 | 0 | 0 | 0 | .000 | 1 | 1 | 0 | 1.000 |

## DAVID GUS BELL
### (Buddy)

Born August 27, 1951, at Pittsburgh, Pa.
Height, 6.02. Weight, 190.
Throws and bats righthanded.
Hobby—Sports in general.
Attended Xavier University, Cincinnati, O., and Miami University, Oxford, O.
Son of Gus Bell, outfielder with Pittsburgh Pirates, Cincinnati Reds, New York Mets
and Milwaukee Braves, 1950 through 1964.

Tied major league record for first home run in majors, bases filled, April 22, 1972.
Led American League third basemen in double plays with 44 in 1973.
Led Gulf Coast League second basemen in double plays with 26 in 1969.
Named Rookie of the Year in American Association, 1971.

| Year Club | League | Pos. | G. | AB. | R. | H. | 2B. | 3B. | HR. | RBI. | B.A. | PO. | A. | E. | F.A. |
|---|---|---|---|---|---|---|---|---|---|---|---|---|---|---|---|
| 1969—Sarasota Ind. | ....Gulf C. | 2B | 51 | 170 | 18 | 39 | 4 | •3 | 3 | 24 | .229 | 119 | 108 | 7 | •.970 |
| 1970—Sumter | ..............W. Car. | 3-2-S | 121 | 442 | 81 | 117 | 19 | 3 | 12 | 75 | .265 | 116 | 189 | 27 | .919 |
| 1971—Wichita | ............A.A. | •3-2-S-O | 129 | 470 | 65 | 136 | 23 | 1 | 11 | 59 | .289 | •139 | 203 | 16 | .955 |
| 1972—Cleveland | ........Amer. | OF-3B | 132 | 466 | 49 | 119 | 21 | 1 | 9 | 36 | .255 | 284 | 23 | 3 | .990 |
| 1973—Cleveland | ........Amer. | •3B-OF | 156 | 631 | 86 | 169 | 23 | 7 | 14 | 59 | .268 | •146 | 363 | 22 | .959 |
| 1974—Cleveland† | ........Amer. | 3B | 116 | 423 | 51 | 111 | 15 | 1 | 7 | 46 | .262 | 112 | 274 | 15 | .963 |
| 1975—Cleveland | ........Amer. | 3B | 153 | 553 | 66 | 150 | 20 | 4 | 10 | 59 | .271 | •146 | 330 | 25 | .950 |
| 1976—Cleveland | ........Amer. | 3B | 159 | 604 | 75 | 170 | 26 | 2 | 7 | 60 | .281 | 104 | 330 | 20 | .956 |
| Major League Totals | ..................... | | 716 | 2677 | 327 | 719 | 105 | 15 | 47 | 260 | .268 | 792 | 1320 | 85 | .961 |

†On disabled list, May 27 to June 17 and August 8 to September 1, 1974.

### ALL-STAR GAME RECORD

| Year League | Pos. | AB. | R. | H. | 2B. | 3B. | HR. | RBI. | B.A. | PO. | A. | E. | F.A. |
|---|---|---|---|---|---|---|---|---|---|---|---|---|---|
| 1973—American | ........................... | PH | 1 | 0 | 1 | 0 | 1 | 0 | 0 | 1.000 | 0 | 0 | 0 | .000 |

## KEVIN ROBERT BELL

Born July 13, 1955, at Los Angeles, Calif.
Height, 6.00. Weight, 195.
Throws and bats righthanded.
Attended Mount San Antonio Junior College, Walnut, Calif.
Son of Donald Robert Bell, former shortstop in Cleveland Indians' organization.

| Year Club | League | Pos. | G. | AB. | R. | H. | 2B. | 3B. | HR. | RBI. | B.A. | PO. | A. | E. | F.A. |
|---|---|---|---|---|---|---|---|---|---|---|---|---|---|---|---|
| 1974—Appleton | ............Midw. | 3B | 77 | 283 | 46 | 78 | 11 | 1 | 15 | 59 | .276 | 59 | 151 | 18 | .921 |
| 1975—Appleton | ............Midw. | 3B | 67 | 239 | 32 | 68 | 16 | 4 | 8 | 42 | .285 | 57 | 137 | 25 | .886 |
| 1975—Knoxville | ..........South. | 3B | 66 | 224 | 31 | 68 | 15 | 1 | 11 | 41 | .304 | 68 | 117 | 7 | .964 |
| 1976—Iowa | ..................A.A. | 3B | 51 | 165 | 24 | 47 | 12 | 0 | 4 | 24 | .285 | 39 | 100 | 16 | .897 |
| 1976—Chicago | ............Amer. | 3B-DH | 68 | 230 | 24 | 57 | 7 | 6 | 5 | 20 | .248 | 70 | 124 | 6 | .970 |
| Major League Totals | ..................... | | 68 | 230 | 24 | 57 | 7 | 6 | 5 | 20 | .248 | 70 | 124 | 6 | .970 |

## ROBERT EDWARD BELLOIR

Name pronounced BELL-wah.
### (Rob)

Born July 13, 1948, at Heidelberg, West Germany.
Height, 5.10. Weight, 165.
Throws and bats righthanded.
Hobby—Reading.
Attended Mercer University, Macon, Ga.; received Bachelor of Arts
degree in English.

Led Texas League shortstops in double plays with 78 in 1974.

| Year Club | League | Pos. | G. | AB. | R. | H. | 2B. | 3B. | HR. | RBI. | B.A. | PO. | A. | E. | F.A. |
|---|---|---|---|---|---|---|---|---|---|---|---|---|---|---|---|
| 1969—Monroe | ..............W. Car. | SS | 58 | 195 | 19 | 44 | 1 | 0 | 1 | 26 | .226 | 103 | 168 | 11 | .961 |
| 1969—Waterbury | ........East. | SS-3B | 17 | 41 | 2 | 9 | 0 | 0 | 0 | 3 | .220 | 20 | 37 | 2 | .966 |
| 1970—Savannah† | ........South. | SS | 18 | 47 | 3 | 10 | 0 | 1 | 0 | 5 | .213 | 28 | 42 | 2 | .972 |
| 1971—Jacksonville | ......South. | | | | | (On Military List) | | | | | | | | | |
| 1972—Elmira | ..............East. | SS | 101 | 273 | 29 | 54 | 6 | 1 | 0 | 15 | .198 | 102 | 260 | 30 | .923 |
| 1973—San Antonio | ......Tex. | S-3-O-P | 114 | 311 | 48 | 81 | 8 | 2 | 0 | 21 | .260 | 166 | 276 | 27 | .942 |
| 1974—San Antonio | ......Tex. | SS | 128 | 408 | 36 | 103 | 10 | 2 | 2 | 36 | .252 | 204 | 379 | 21 | •.965 |
| 1975—San Antonio‡ | ....Tex. | SS | 58 | 221 | 16 | 48 | 15 | 2 | 1 | 27 | .217 | 87 | 215 | 17 | .947 |
| 1975—Richmond | .........Int. | SS | 36 | 122 | 16 | 31 | 5 | 1 | 1 | 8 | .254 | 40 | 114 | 7 | .957 |
| 1975—Atlanta | ..............Nat. | SS-2B | 43 | 105 | 11 | 23 | 2 | 1 | 0 | 9 | .219 | 39 | 106 | 13 | .918 |
| 1976—Richmond | .........Int. | SS-3B | 35 | 93 | 16 | 24 | 4 | 0 | 2 | 9 | .258 | 41 | 67 | 5 | .956 |
| 1976—Atlanta | ..............Nat. | SS-3B-2B | 30 | 60 | 5 | 12 | 2 | 0 | 0 | 4 | .200 | 25 | 41 | 4 | .943 |
| Major League Totals | ..................... | | 73 | 165 | 16 | 35 | 4 | 1 | 0 | 13 | .212 | 64 | 147 | 17 | .925 |

†On temporary inactive list from beginning of season until June 10 and from July 8 through remainder of season.

‡Traded by Cleveland Indians to Atlanta Braves, June 16, 1975, to complete deal in which Braves obtained Pitcher John Odom and a player to be named later from Indians for Pitcher Roric Harrison, June 7, 1975.

### PITCHING RECORD

| Year Club | League | G. | IP. | W. | L. | Pct. | H. | R. | ER. | SO. | BB. | ERA. |
|---|---|---|---|---|---|---|---|---|---|---|---|---|
| 1973—San Antonio | ......................Texas | 1 | 1 | 0 | 0 | .000 | 0 | 0 | 0 | 2 | 1 | 0.00 |

# JOHNNY LEE BENCH

Born December 7, 1947, at Oklahoma City, Okla.
Height, 6.01. Weight, 197.
Throws and bats righthanded.
Hobbies—Golf, bowling, singing and playing cards.

Established major league record for most games, catcher, rookie season (154), 1968.
Tied major league record for most consecutive seasons leading league in sacrifice flies, 2, 1973.
Established National League record for most stolen bases, no caught stealing, season, 11, in 1975.
Tied National League records for most home runs, 5 consecutive games (7), May 30-June 3, 1972; most seasons leading league, sacrifice flies, 3, 1973; and most home runs, bases full, month, 2, May, 1975.
Hit three home runs in a game, July 26, 1970 and May 9, 1973.
Led National League in total bases with 315 in 1974.
Led National League catchers in double plays with 16 in 1974.
Led National League in passed balls with 18 in 1968 and tied for lead with 10 in 1973.
Led National League in sacrifice flies with 11 in 1970 and 12 in 1972.
Named Minor League Player of the Year by THE SPORTING NEWS, 1967.
Named THE SPORTING NEWS National League Rookie Player of the Year, 1968.
Named catcher on THE SPORTING NEWS National League All-Star fielding teams, 1968, 1969, 1970, 1971, 1972, 1973, 1974, 1975, 1976.
Named catcher on THE SPORTING NEWS National League All-Star Teams, 1968, 1969, 1970, 1972, 1973, 1974 and 1975.
Named National League Rookie of the Year by the Baseball Writers' Association of America, 1968.
Most Valuable Player in National League, 1970 and 1972.
Named by THE SPORTING NEWS as Major League Player of the Year, 1970.
Named by THE SPORTING NEWS as National League Player of the Year, 1970.
Named Player of the Year in Carolina League, 1966.

| Year | Club | League | Pos. | G. | AB. | R. | H. | 2B. | 3B. | HR. | RBI. | B.A. | PO. | A. | E. | F.A. |
|------|------|--------|------|----|-----|----|----|-----|-----|-----|------|------|-----|----|----|------|
| 1965—Tampa | Fla. St. | C-OF | 68 | 214 | 29 | 53 | 13 | 1 | 2 | 35 | .248 | 415 | 40 | 6 | .987 |
| 1966—Peninsula | Carol. | C | 98 | 350 | 59 | 103 | 16 | 0 | 22 | 68 | .294 | 692 | •87 | •17 | .979 |
| 1966—Buffalo† | Int. | C | 1 | 0 | 0 | 0 | 0 | 0 | 0 | 0 | .000 | 2 | 0 | 0 | 1.000 |
| 1967—Buffalo‡ | Int. | •C-3-O-1 | 98 | 344 | 39 | 89 | 17 | 2 | 23 | 68 | .259 | 577 | •82 | 13 | .981 |
| 1967—Cincinnati | Nat. | C | 26 | 86 | 7 | 14 | 3 | 1 | 1 | 6 | .163 | 175 | 16 | 1 | .995 |
| 1968—Cincinnati | Nat. | C | 154 | 564 | 67 | 155 | 40 | 2 | 15 | 82 | .275 | •942 | •102 | 9 | .991 |
| 1969—Cincinnati§ | Nat. | C | 148 | 532 | 83 | 156 | 23 | 1 | 26 | 90 | .293 | 793 | 76 | 7 | .992 |
| 1970—Cincinnati | Nat. | C-O-1-3 | 158 | 605 | 97 | 177 | 35 | 4 | •45 | •148 | .293 | 854 | 78 | 15 | .984 |
| 1971—Cincinnati x | Nat. | C-O-1-3 | 149 | 562 | 80 | 134 | 19 | 2 | 27 | 61 | .238 | 735 | 67 | 10 | .988 |
| 1972—Cincinnati | Nat. | C-O-1-3 | 147 | 538 | 87 | 145 | 22 | 2 | •40 | •125 | .270 | 791 | 63 | 10 | .988 |
| 1973—Cincinnati | Nat. | C-O-1-3 | 152 | 557 | 83 | 141 | 17 | 3 | 25 | 104 | .253 | 757 | 63 | 6 | .993 |
| 1974—Cincinnati | Nat. | C-3-1 | 160 | 621 | 108 | 174 | 38 | 2 | 33 | •129 | .280 | 794 | 123 | 9 | .990 |
| 1975—Cincinnati | Nat. | C-O-1 | 142 | 530 | 83 | 150 | 39 | 1 | 28 | 110 | .283 | 646 | 52 | 8 | .989 |
| 1976—Cincinnati | Nat. | •C-O-1 | 135 | 465 | 62 | 109 | 24 | 1 | 16 | 74 | .234 | •655 | 60 | 4 | •.994 |
| Major League Totals | | | 1371 | 5060 | 757 | 1355 | 260 | 19 | 258 | 929 | .268 | 7142 | 700 | 79 | .990 |

†On disabled list, July 31 through September 6, 1966. On military list, November 7, 1966 through April 9, 1967.
‡On temporary inactive list, July 29 through August 14, 1967.
§On military list, July 11 through July 18, 1969.
xOn military list, June 13 through June 17, 1971.

## CHAMPIONSHIP SERIES RECORD

| Year | Club | League | Pos. | G. | AB. | R. | H. | 2B. | 3B. | HR. | RBI. | B.A. | PO. | A. | E. | F.A. |
|------|------|--------|------|----|-----|----|----|-----|-----|-----|------|------|-----|----|----|------|
| 1970—Cincinnati | Nat. | C | 3 | 9 | 2 | 2 | 0 | 0 | 1 | 1 | .222 | 20 | 3 | 0 | 1.000 |
| 1972—Cincinnati | Nat. | C | 5 | 18 | 3 | 6 | 1 | 1 | 1 | 2 | .333 | 28 | 3 | 1 | .969 |
| 1973—Cincinnati | Nat. | C | 5 | 19 | 1 | 5 | 2 | 0 | 1 | 1 | .263 | 31 | 2 | 0 | 1.000 |
| 1975—Cincinnati | Nat. | C | 3 | 13 | 1 | 1 | 0 | 0 | 0 | 0 | .077 | 18 | 4 | 0 | 1.000 |
| 1976—Cincinnati | Nat. | C | 3 | 12 | 3 | 4 | 1 | 0 | 1 | 1 | .333 | 11 | 4 | 0 | 1.000 |
| Championship Series Totals | | | 19 | 71 | 10 | 18 | 4 | 1 | 4 | 5 | .254 | 108 | 16 | 1 | .992 |

## WORLD SERIES RECORD

| Year | Club | League | Pos. | G. | AB. | R. | H. | 2B. | 3B. | HR. | RBI. | B.A. | PO. | A. | E. | F.A. |
|------|------|--------|------|----|-----|----|----|-----|-----|-----|------|------|-----|----|----|------|
| 1970—Cincinnati | Nat. | C | 5 | 19 | 3 | 4 | 0 | 0 | 1 | 3 | .211 | 36 | 3 | 0 | 1.000 |
| 1972—Cincinnati | Nat. | C | 7 | 23 | 4 | 6 | 1 | 0 | 1 | 1 | .261 | 41 | 7 | 1 | .980 |
| 1975—Cincinnati | Nat. | C | 7 | 29 | 5 | 6 | 2 | 0 | 1 | 4 | .207 | 44 | 6 | 0 | 1.000 |
| 1976—Cincinnati | Nat. | C | 4 | 15 | 4 | 8 | 1 | 1 | 2 | 6 | .533 | 18 | 2 | 0 | 1.000 |
| World Series Totals | | | 23 | 86 | 16 | 24 | 4 | 1 | 5 | 14 | .279 | 139 | 18 | 1 | .994 |

## ALL-STAR GAME RECORD

| Year | League | Pos. | AB. | R. | H. | 2B. | 3B. | HR. | RBI. | B.A. | PO. | A. | E. | F.A. |
|------|--------|------|-----|----|----|-----|-----|-----|------|------|-----|----|----|------|
| 1968—National | | C | 0 | 0 | 0 | 0 | 0 | 0 | 0 | .000 | 2 | 0 | 0 | 1.000 |
| 1969—National | | C | 3 | 2 | 2 | 0 | 0 | 1 | 2 | .667 | 4 | 0 | 0 | 1.000 |
| 1970—National | | C | 3 | 0 | 0 | 0 | 0 | 0 | 0 | .000 | 5 | 1 | 0 | 1.000 |
| 1971—National | | C | 4 | 1 | 2 | 0 | 0 | 1 | 2 | .500 | 5 | 0 | 0 | 1.000 |
| 1972—National | | C | 2 | 0 | 1 | 0 | 0 | 0 | 0 | .500 | 3 | 0 | 0 | 1.000 |
| 1973—National | | C | 3 | 1 | 1 | 0 | 0 | 1 | 1 | .333 | 3 | 0 | 0 | 1.000 |
| 1974—National | | C | 3 | 1 | 2 | 0 | 0 | 0 | 0 | .667 | 7 | 0 | 1 | .875 |
| 1975—National | | C | 4 | 0 | 1 | 0 | 0 | 0 | 1 | .250 | 10 | 1 | 0 | 1.000 |
| 1976—National | | C | 2 | 0 | 1 | 0 | 0 | 0 | 0 | .500 | 1 | 0 | 0 | 1.000 |
| All Star Game Totals | | | 24 | 5 | 10 | 0 | 0 | 3 | 6 | .417 | 40 | 2 | 1 | .977 |

## JUAN JOSE BENIQUEZ (TORRES)
Name pronounced Be-NE-Kez.

Born May 13, 1950, at San Sebastian, Puerto Rico.
Height, 5.11. Weight, 160.
Throws and bats righthanded.
Set major league record for most errors, shortstop, two consecutive games, 6, July 13-14, 1972.
Led Florida State League shortstops in double plays with 51 in 1969.
Led International League in sacrifice hits with 11 in 1971.

| Year Club | League | Pos. | G. | AB. | R. | H. | 2B. | 3B. | HR. | RBI. | B.A. | PO. | A. | E. | F.A. |
|---|---|---|---|---|---|---|---|---|---|---|---|---|---|---|---|
| 1969–Winter Haven | ....Fla. St. | *S-2 | 120 | 426 | 59 | 111 | 15 | *14 | 2 | 59 | .261 | 175 | *373 | *49 | .918 |
| 1969–Winston-Salem | ..Carol. | SS | 2 | 10 | 0 | 2 | 0 | 0 | 0 | 0 | .200 | 2 | 6 | 0 | 1.000 |
| 1970–Winston-Salem | ..Carol. | SS | 92 | 335 | 53 | 91 | 12 | 2 | 9 | 37 | .272 | 144 | 275 | 35 | .923 |
| 1970–Pawtucket | ........East. | SS | 56 | 233 | 29 | 58 | 5 | 3 | 4 | 25 | .249 | 105 | 167 | 29 | .904 |
| 1971–Louisville | ..........Int. | SS | 132 | 534 | 82 | 149 | 12 | *16 | 4 | 51 | .279 | 205 | 364 | *55 | .912 |
| 1971–Boston | ..............Amer. | SS | 16 | 57 | 8 | 17 | 2 | 0 | 0 | 4 | .298 | 24 | 27 | 6 | .895 |
| 1972–Louisville | ..........Int. | SS | 66 | 277 | 40 | 82 | 10 | 7 | 5 | 32 | .296 | 114 | 172 | 21 | .932 |
| 1972–Boston | ..............Amer. | SS | 33 | 99 | 10 | 24 | 4 | 1 | 1 | 8 | .242 | 38 | 88 | 14 | .900 |
| 1973–Pawtucket | ........Int. | O-S-2-3 | 131 | 440 | 80 | 131 | 24 | 4 | 13 | 52 | *.298 | 196 | 176 | 26 | .934 |
| 1974–Boston† | ...........Amer. | OF | 106 | 389 | 60 | 104 | 14 | 3 | 5 | 33 | .267 | 264 | 4 | 6 | .978 |
| 1975–Boston†§ | ...........Amer. | OF-3B | 78 | 254 | 43 | 74 | 14 | 4 | 2 | 17 | .291 | 110 | 17 | 1 | .992 |
| 1976–Texas | ..............Amer. | OF-2B | 145 | 478 | 49 | 122 | 14 | 4 | 0 | 33 | .255 | *411 | *18 | 7 | .984 |
| Major League Totals | ...................... | | 378 | 1277 | 170 | 341 | 48 | 12 | 8 | 95 | .267 | 847 | 154 | 34 | .967 |

†On disabled list, July 3 to July 28, 1974.
‡On supplemental disabled list, July 2 to July 18, 1975.
§Traded with Pitcher Steve Barr, a minor league player to be named later and an estimated $200,000 to Texas Rangers for Pitcher Ferguson Jenkins, November 17, 1975; Red Sox sent Pitcher Craig Skok to Rangers, December 12, 1975, to complete deal.

CHAMPIONSHIP SERIES RECORD

| Year Club | League | Pos. | G. | AB. | R. | H. | 2B. | 3B. | HR. | RBI. | B.A. | PO. | A. | E. | F.A. |
|---|---|---|---|---|---|---|---|---|---|---|---|---|---|---|---|
| 1975–Boston | ..............Amer. | DH | 3 | 12 | 2 | 3 | 0 | 0 | 0 | 1 | .250 | 0 | 0 | 0 | .000 |

WORLD SERIES RECORD

| Year Club | League | Pos. | G. | AB. | R. | H. | 2B. | 3B. | HR. | RBI. | B.A. | PO. | A. | E. | F.A. |
|---|---|---|---|---|---|---|---|---|---|---|---|---|---|---|---|
| 1975–Boston | ..............Amer. | OF-PH | 3 | 8 | 0 | 1 | 0 | 0 | 0 | 1 | .125 | 6 | 1 | 0 | 1.000 |

## DAVID BRUCE BERGMAN
### (Dave)

Born June 6, 1953, at Evanston, Ill.
Height, 6.01. Weight, 188.
Throws and bats lefthanded.
Attended Illinois State University, Normal, Ill.
Named Eastern League Player of the Year in 1975.
Named New York-Pennsylvania League Player of the Year in 1974.

| Year Club | League | Pos. | G. | AB. | R. | H. | 2B. | 3B. | HR. | RBI. | B.A. | PO. | A. | E. | F.A. |
|---|---|---|---|---|---|---|---|---|---|---|---|---|---|---|---|
| 1974–Oneonta | ...........NYP | 1B | 56 | 201 | 60 | 70 | 6 | •7 | 10 | 48 | *.348 | 494 | *29 | 8 | *.985 |
| 1975–West Haven | ......East. | 1B-OF | 124 | 399 | 76 | 124 | 15 | 6 | 11 | 60 | *.311 | 610 | 61 | 5 | .993 |
| 1975–New York | .........Amer. | OF | 7 | 17 | 0 | 0 | 0 | 0 | 0 | 0 | .000 | 10 | 1 | 1 | .917 |
| 1976–Syracuse | .........Int. | *1B-OF | 134 | 455 | 68 | 134 | 23 | 2 | 7 | 65 | .295 | *1201 | 82 | 10 | .992 |
| Major League Totals | ...................... | | 7 | 17 | 0 | 0 | 0 | 0 | 0 | 0 | .000 | 10 | 1 | 1 | .917 |

## VICTOR HUGO BERNAL
Name pronounced Burr-NALL.

Born October 6, 1953, at Los Angeles, Calif.
Height, 6.01. Weight, 175.
Throws and bats righthanded.
Attended California Poly State University, Pomona, Calif.
Led Texas League in saves with 19 in 1976.

| Year Club | League | G. | IP. | W. | L. | Pct. | H. | R. | ER. | SO. | BB. | ERA. |
|---|---|---|---|---|---|---|---|---|---|---|---|---|
| 1975–Walla Walla | ........................Northwest | 10 | 53 | 4 | 3 | .571 | 55 | 21 | 19 | 59 | 13 | 3.23 |
| 1976–Amarillo | .............................Texas | 44 | 68 | 5 | 7 | .417 | 65 | 33 | 31 | 55 | 24 | 4.10 |

Invited to San Diego Padres' 1977 spring camp.

## DWIGHT VERN BERNARD

Born May 31, 1952, at Mt. Vernon, Ill.
Height, 6.02. Weight, 170.
Throws and bats righthanded.
Hobbies–Hunting and fishing.
Attended Belmont College, Nashville, Tenn.

| Year Club | League | G. | IP. | W. | L. | Pct. | H. | R. | ER. | SO. | BB. | ERA. |
|---|---|---|---|---|---|---|---|---|---|---|---|---|
| 1974–Victoria† | .............................Texas | 14 | 103 | 7 | 4 | .636 | 85 | 43 | 35 | 60 | 58 | 3.06 |
| 1975–Tidewater‡ | .........................Int'national | 27 | 126 | 9 | 9 | .500 | 96 | 51 | 46 | 70 | 77 | 3.29 |
| 1976–Tidewater | ..........................Int'national | 15 | 90 | 1 | 9 | .100 | 109 | 74 | 64 | 47 | 61 | 6.40 |
| 1976–Jackson | ..............................Texas | 9 | 54 | 2 | 5 | .286 | 48 | 28 | 25 | 33 | 32 | 4.17 |

†Played one game as outfielder.
‡On disabled list, July 20 through August 4, 1975.
Invited to New York Mets 1977 spring camp.

## JUAN RAMON BERNHARDT (CORADIN)
### (Moncho)
(Nicknamed by mother.)

Born August 31, at San Pedro de Maeoris, Dominican Republic.
Height, 5.11. Weight, 160.
Throws and bats righthanded.
Hobbies—Music and fishing.
Brother of Carlos Juan Bernhardt, former pitcher in New York Yankees' organization.

| Year Club | League | Pos. | G. | AB. | R. | H. | 2B. | 3B. | HR. | RBI. | B.A. | PO. | A. | E. | F.A. |
|---|---|---|---|---|---|---|---|---|---|---|---|---|---|---|---|
| 1971—Key West† .......Fla. St. | | 3-1-O-S | 97 | 329 | 25 | 82 | 15 | 2 | 1 | 31 | .249 | 328 | 129 | 15 | .968 |
| 1972—Ft. Laud. ........Fla. St. | | 1-O-3-S | 121 | 444 | 65 | 128 | 18 | 2 | 2 | 43 | .288 | 461 | 78 | 10 | .982 |
| 1973—Ft. Laud.‡ .......Fla. St. | | 3-1-O | 37 | 101 | 13 | 43 | 4 | 0 | 1 | 13 | .337 | 118 | 37 | 9 | .945 |
| 1974—West Haven§ ....East. | | 2B | 60 | 184 | 20 | 37 | 6 | 1 | 3 | 19 | .201 | 84 | 107 | 10 | .950 |
| 1975—West Haven ......East. | | 1B-2B | 41 | 160 | 16 | 51 | 10 | 1 | 1 | 28 | .319 | 267 | 42 | 11 | .966 |
| 1975—Syracuse .........Int. | | O-3-1 | 79 | 297 | 22 | 90 | 19 | 1 | 4 | 44 | .303 | 190 | 73 | 7 | .974 |
| 1976—Syracuse .........Int. | | 3-1-O-2 | 101 | 380 | 41 | 115 | 24 | 0 | 8 | 57 | .303 | 231 | 187 | 19 | .956 |
| 1976—New York x ......Amer. | | OF-3-DH | 10 | 21 | 1 | 4 | 1 | 0 | 0 | 1 | .190 | 4 | 1 | 1 | .833 |
| Major League Totals ...................... | | | 10 | 21 | 1 | 4 | 1 | 0 | 0 | 1 | .190 | 4 | 1 | 1 | .833 |

†On disabled list, April 15 to May 1, 1971.
‡On disabled list, April 10 to July 13, 1973.
§On disabled list, August 7 to August 30, 1974.
xSelected by Seattle Mariners from New York Yankees in American League expansion draft, November 5, 1976.

## DALE ANTHONY BERRA

Born December 13, 1956, at Ridgewood, N. J.
Height, 6.00. Weight, 180.
Throws and bats righthanded.
Son of Yogi Berra, coach with New York Yankees.
Led New York-Pennsylvania League in sacrifice flies with 8 in 1975.
Tied for New York-Pennsylvania League lead in double plays by third basemen with 13 in 1975.
Led Western Carolinas League third basemen in double plays with 27 in 1976.

| Year Club | League | Pos. | G. | AB. | R. | H. | 2B. | 3B. | HR. | RBI. | B.A. | PO. | A. | E. | F.A. |
|---|---|---|---|---|---|---|---|---|---|---|---|---|---|---|---|
| 1975—Niagara Falls ....NYP | | 3B | 67 | •269 | 36 | 69 | 6 | 4 | 3 | •49 | .257 | 67 | 137 | 24 | .895 |
| 1976—Charleston ........W. Car. | | 3B | •139 | 527 | 78 | 157 | 28 | 5 | 16 | 89 | .298 | 129 | •269 | •41 | .907 |

Listed on Pittsburgh Pirates' 1977 spring roster.

## KURT ANTHONY BEVACQUA
Name pronounced Buh-VAHK-wuh.

Born January 23, 1947, at Miami Beach, Fla.
Height, 6.01. Weight, 185.
Throws and bats righthanded.
Hobbies—Hunting, fishing, golf and billiards.
Attended Miami-Dade (North) Community College, Miami, Fla.
Led American Association third basemen in double plays with 26 in 1970.
Tied for Southern League lead in double plays by third basemen with 24 in 1969.

| Year Club | League | Pos. | G. | AB. | R. | H. | 2B. | 3B. | HR. | RBI. | B.A. | PO. | A. | E. | F.A. |
|---|---|---|---|---|---|---|---|---|---|---|---|---|---|---|---|
| 1967—Tampa ...............Fla. St. | | 2B | 65 | 217 | 13 | 48 | 2 | 1 | 0 | 11 | .221 | 119 | 143 | 10 | .963 |
| 1968—Tampa ...............Fla. St. | | 2-1B | 91 | 219 | 18 | 55 | 11 | 2 | 2 | 26 | .251 | 264 | 74 | 7 | .980 |
| 1969—Asheville ..........South. | | 3B | 133 | 490 | 72 | 155 | 26 | 6 | 16 | 91 | .316 | •129 | 245 | 29 | .928 |
| 1970—Indianapolis ......A.A. | | •O-INF | 135 | 482 | 62 | 126 | 26 | 5 | 15 | 67 | .261 | •157 | •216 | 21 | •.947 |
| 1971—Ind.†-Wichita ....A.A. | | 3-S-2-O | 60 | 235 | 36 | 71 | 16 | 1 | 9 | 38 | .302 | 107 | 130 | 11 | .956 |
| 1971—Cleveland ..........Amer. | | 2-O-3-S | 55 | 137 | 9 | 28 | 3 | 1 | 3 | 13 | .204 | 77 | 72 | 5 | .968 |
| 1972—Portland ............P.C. | | 3-2-O-S | 145 | 537 | 57 | 168 | 27 | 7 | 9 | 72 | .313 | 223 | 252 | 30 | .941 |
| 1972—Cleveland‡ ........Amer. | | OF-3 | 19 | 35 | 2 | 4 | 0 | 0 | 1 | 1 | .114 | 11 | 5 | 1 | .941 |
| 1973—Kansas City§ .....Amer. | | 3-2-O-1 | 99 | 276 | 39 | 71 | 8 | 3 | 2 | 40 | .257 | 120 | 90 | 9 | .959 |
| 1974—Pittsburgh x ......Nat. | | 3B-OF | 18 | 35 | 1 | 4 | 1 | 0 | 0 | 0 | .114 | 8 | 13 | 1 | .955 |
| 1974—Kansas City y .....Amer. | | 1-3-2-S | 39 | 90 | 10 | 19 | 0 | 0 | 0 | 3 | .211 | 90 | 29 | 5 | .960 |
| 1975—Milwaukee ........Amer. | | 3-2-S-1 | 104 | 258 | 30 | 59 | 14 | 0 | 2 | 24 | .229 | 157 | 168 | 13 | .962 |
| 1976—Milwaukee ........Amer. | | 2B-DH | 12 | 7 | 3 | 1 | 0 | 0 | 0 | 0 | .143 | 0 | 6 | 0 | 1.000 |
| 1976—Spokane z.........P.C. | | 3-S-2-1 | 95 | 356 | 70 | 120 | 24 | 0 | 12 | 49 | .337 | 116 | 197 | 22 | .934 |
| National League Totals ................ | | | 18 | 35 | 1 | 4 | 1 | 0 | 0 | 0 | .114 | 8 | 13 | 1 | .955 |
| American League Totals ................ | | | 328 | 803 | 93 | 182 | 25 | 4 | 8 | 81 | .227 | 455 | 370 | 33 | .962 |
| Major League Totals ...................... | | | 346 | 838 | 94 | 186 | 26 | 4 | 8 | 81 | .222 | 463 | 383 | 34 | .961 |

†Traded by Cincinnati Reds to Cleveland Indians for Outfielder Charles Bradford, May 8, 1971.
‡Traded to Kansas City Royals for Pitcher Mike Hedlund, November 2, 1972.
§Traded with Catcher-Outfielder Ed Kirkpatrick and First Baseman Winston Cole to Pittsburgh Pirates for Pitcher Nelson Briles and Infielder Fernando Gonzalez, December 4, 1973.
xTraded to Kansas City Royals for cash and Infielder Cal Meier, July 8, 1974.
ySold to Milwaukee Brewers for an undisclosed amount of cash, March 6, 1975.
zSold by Milwaukee Brewers to Seattle Mariners for an undisclosed amount of cash, October 22, 1976; released, March 28, 1977.

## JAMES BLAIR BIBBY
### (Jim)

Born October 10, 1944, at Franklinton, N. C.
Height, 6.04. Weight, 225.
Throws and bats righthanded.
Attended Fayetteville State College, Fayetteville, N. C., and Lynchburg College, Lynchburg, Va.
Brother of Henry Bibby, guard for New Orleans Jazz.

Pitched 6-0 no-hit victory against Oakland Athletics, July 30, 1973.
Led American Association in hit batsmen with 12 in 1972.
Led International League in wild pitches with 20 in 1971.

| Year Club | League | G. | IP. | W. | L. | Pct. | H. | R. | ER. | SO. | BB. | ERA. |
|---|---|---|---|---|---|---|---|---|---|---|---|---|
| 1965—Marion | Ap'lachian | 13 | 24 | 2 | 3 | .400 | 30 | 35 | 30 | 24 | 27 | 11.25 |
| 1966—Greenville | Carolina | | | | | (In Military Service) | | | | | | |
| 1967—Jacksonville | Int'national | | | | | (In Military Service) | | | | | | |
| 1968—Raleigh-Durham | Carolina | 23 | 131 | 7 | 7 | .500 | 79 | 49 | 41 | 118 | 74 | 2.82 |
| 1969—Memphis | Texas | 17 | 122 | 10 | 6 | .625 | 94 | 58 | 45 | 115 | 57 | 3.32 |
| 1969—Tidewater | Int'national | 11 | 75 | 4 | 4 | .500 | 64 | 33 | 29 | 65 | 34 | 3.48 |
| 1970—Tidewater | Int'national | | | | | (On disabled list) | | | | | | |
| 1971—Tidewater† | Int'national | 27 | 76 | ●15 | 6 | .174 | 145 | 87 | 79 | 150 | 109 | 4.04 |
| 1972—Tulsa | Am. Assoc. | 27 | 195 | 13 | 9 | .591 | 155 | 76 | 67 | 208 | 76 | 3.09 |
| 1972—St. Louis | National | 6 | 40 | 1 | 3 | .250 | 29 | 18 | 15 | 28 | 19 | 3.38 |
| 1973—St. Louis‡ | National | 6 | 16 | 0 | 2 | .000 | 19 | 17 | 17 | 12 | 17 | 9.56 |
| 1973—Texas | American | 26 | 180 | 9 | 10 | .474 | 121 | 73 | 65 | 155 | 106 | 3.25 |
| 1974—Texas | American | 41 | 264 | 19 | 19 | .500 | 255 | 146 | ●139 | 149 | 113 | 4.74 |
| 1975—Texas§-Cleveland | American | 36 | 181 | 7 | 15 | .318 | 172 | 89 | 78 | 93 | 78 | 3.88 |
| 1976—Cleveland | American | 34 | 163 | 13 | 7 | .650 | 162 | 61 | 58 | 84 | 56 | 3.20 |
| National League Totals | | 12 | 56 | 1 | 5 | .167 | 48 | 35 | 32 | 40 | 36 | 5.14 |
| American League Totals | | 137 | 788 | 48 | 51 | .485 | 710 | 369 | 340 | 481 | 353 | 3.88 |
| Major League Totals | | 149 | 844 | 49 | 56 | .467 | 758 | 404 | 372 | 521 | 389 | 3.97 |

†Traded by New York Mets with Pitchers Rich Folkers and Charlie Hudson and Outfielder-First Baseman Art Shamsky to St. Louis Cardinals for Pitchers Chuck Taylor and Harry Parker, Infielder Tom Coulter and Outfielder Jim Beauchamp, October 18, 1971.

‡Traded to Texas Rangers for Pitcher Mike Nagy and Catcher John Wockenfuss (both assigned from Spokane to Tulsa), June 6, 1973.

§Traded with Pitchers Jackie Brown and Rick Waits and an estimated $100,000 to Cleveland Indians for Pitcher Gaylord Perry, June 12, 1975.

## LAWRENCE DAVID BIITTNER
### (Larry)

Born July 27, 1947, at Pocahontas, Ia.
Height, 6.02. Weight, 205.
Throws and bats lefthanded.
Hobbies—Hunting and fishing.
Attended Buena Vista College, Storm Lake, Ia.; received Bachelor of Arts degree
in Physical Education.

Led International League in sacrifice flies with 9 in 1974.

| Year Club | League | Pos. | G. | AB. | R. | H. | 2B. | 3B. | HR. | RBI. | B.A. | PO. | A. | E. | F.A. |
|---|---|---|---|---|---|---|---|---|---|---|---|---|---|---|---|
| 1968—Savannah | South. | OF-1B | 58 | 199 | 24 | 57 | 12 | 2 | 1 | 21 | .286 | 160 | 6 | 3 | .982 |
| 1969—Savannah† | South. | OF | 14 | 44 | 4 | 9 | 2 | 0 | 0 | 2 | .205 | 13 | 2 | 1 | .938 |
| 1970—Pittsfield | East. | 1B-OF | 102 | 388 | 51 | 126 | 27 | 6 | 9 | 62 | .325 | 658 | 46 | 6 | .992 |
| 1970—Washington | Amer. | PH | 2 | 2 | 0 | 0 | 0 | 0 | 0 | 0 | .000 | 0 | 0 | 0 | .000 |
| 1971—Denver | A.A. | 1B | 25 | 101 | 20 | 36 | 10 | 2 | 2 | 18 | .356 | 223 | 28 | 3 | .988 |
| 1971—Washington‡ | Amer. | OF-1B | 66 | 171 | 12 | 44 | 4 | 1 | 0 | 16 | .257 | 83 | 7 | 6 | .938 |
| 1972—Texas | Amer. | 1B-OF | 137 | 382 | 34 | 99 | 18 | 1 | 3 | 31 | .259 | 503 | 41 | 8 | .986 |
| 1973—Texas§ | Amer. | OF-1B | 83 | 258 | 19 | 65 | 8 | 2 | 1 | 12 | .252 | 234 | 20 | 2 | .992 |
| 1974—Memphis | Int. | 1B-OF | 94 | 303 | 53 | 99 | 16 | 1 | 3 | 48 | .327 | 413 | 36 | 6 | .987 |
| 1974—Montreal | Nat. | OF | 18 | 26 | 2 | 7 | 1 | 0 | 0 | 3 | .269 | 7 | 1 | 0 | 1.000 |
| 1975—Montreal | Nat. | OF | 121 | 346 | 34 | 109 | 13 | 5 | 3 | 28 | .315 | 166 | 8 | 5 | .972 |
| 1976—Mont.y-Chi.y | Nat. | 1B-OF | 89 | 224 | 23 | 53 | 14 | 1 | 0 | 18 | .237 | 283 | 35 | 5 | .984 |
| American League Totals | | | 288 | 813 | 65 | 208 | 30 | 4 | 4 | 59 | .256 | 820 | 68 | 16 | .982 |
| National League Totals | | | 228 | 596 | 59 | 169 | 28 | 6 | 3 | 49 | .284 | 456 | 44 | 10 | .980 |
| Major League Totals | | | 516 | 1409 | 124 | 377 | 58 | 10 | 7 | 108 | .268 | 1276 | 112 | 26 | .982 |

†On military list, February 2, 1969, to August 8, 1969.
‡On military list August 3 through August 24.
§Traded to Montreal Expos for Pitcher Pat Jarvis, December 20, 1973.
yTraded with Pitcher Steve Renko to Chicago Cubs for First Baseman Andy Thornton, May 17, 1976.
yOn supplemental disabled list, July 26 through August 10, 1976.

## JOHN EUGENE BILLINGHAM
### (Jack)

Born February 21, 1943, at Orlando, Fla.
Height, 6.04½. Weight, 210.
Throws and bats righthanded.
Hobbies—Fishing, bowling and golf.
Distant cousin of Hall of Fame pitcher Christy Mathewson.

Led National League in hit batsmen with 16 in 1971.
Led National League in shutouts with 7 in 1973.
Tied for National League lead in games started by pitchers with 40 in 1973.

| Year Club | League | G. | IP. | W. | L. | Pct. | H. | R. | ER. | SO. | BB. | ERA. |
|---|---|---|---|---|---|---|---|---|---|---|---|---|
| 1961–Orlando† | Florida St. | 12 | 56 | 1 | 6 | .143 | 53 | 37 | 28 | 30 | 37 | 4.50 |
| 1962–St. Petersburg‡ | Florida St. | 22 | 68 | 1 | 5 | .167 | 74 | 52 | 39 | 58 | 39 | 5.16 |
| 1963–Salisbury§ | W. Carol. | 31 | 142 | 9 | 6 | .600 | 124 | 72 | 55 | 136 | 53 | 3.49 |
| 1964–Santa Barbara | California | 16 | 22 | 1 | 1 | .500 | 17 | 12 | 12 | 31 | 10 | 4.91 |
| 1964–St. Petersburg | Florida St. | 32 | 105 | 7 | 3 | .700 | 63 | 21 | 12 | 126 | 27 | 1.03 |
| 1965–Spokane | P. Coast | 6 | 20 | 0 | 0 | .000 | 17 | 9 | 8 | 20 | 10 | 3.60 |
| 1965–Albuquerque | Texas | 39 | 86 | 7 | 3 | .700 | 68 | 29 | 17 | 67 | 27 | 1.78 |
| 1966–Spokane | P. Coast | 50 | 106 | 6 | 9 | .400 | 107 | 47 | 45 | 84 | 41 | 3.82 |
| 1967–Spokane | P. Coast | 51 | 123 | 7 | 4 | .636 | 98 | 46 | 41 | 108 | 46 | 3.00 |
| 1968–Los Angeles x-y | National | 50 | 71 | 3 | 0 | 1.000 | 54 | 18 | 17 | 46 | 30 | 2.15 |
| 1969–Houston | National | 52 | 83 | 6 | 7 | .462 | 92 | 45 | 39 | 71 | 29 | 4.23 |
| 1970–Houston | National | 46 | 188 | 13 | 9 | .591 | 190 | 102 | 83 | 134 | 63 | 3.97 |
| 1971–Houston z | National | 33 | 228 | 10 | 16 | .385 | 205 | 98 | 86 | 139 | 68 | 3.39 |
| 1972–Cincinnati | National | 36 | 218 | 12 | 12 | .500 | 197 | 83 | 77 | 137 | 64 | 3.18 |
| 1973–Cincinnati | National | 40 | •293 | 19 | 10 | .655 | 257 | 112 | 99 | 155 | 95 | 3.04 |
| 1974–Cincinnati | National | 36 | 212 | 19 | 11 | .633 | 233 | 105 | 93 | 103 | 64 | 3.95 |
| 1975–Cincinnati | National | 33 | 208 | 15 | 10 | .600 | 222 | 100 | 95 | 79 | 76 | 4.11 |
| 1976–Cincinnati | National | 34 | 177 | 12 | 10 | .545 | 190 | 96 | 85 | 76 | 62 | 4.32 |
| Major League Totals | | 360 | 1678 | 109 | 85 | .562 | 1640 | 759 | 674 | 940 | 551 | 3.62 |

†On temporary inactive list, June 12 through June 23, 1961.
‡On disabled list, June 2 through June 4, and from July 24 through August 5, 1962.
§On disabled list, May 26 through June 5, 1963.
xSelected by Montreal Expos from Los Angeles Dodgers in expansion draft, October 5, 1968.
ySent with Pitcher Drannon (Skip) Guinn and cash by Montreal Expos to Houston Astros to complete earlier deal in which Donn Clendenon refused to report to Houston, April 8, 1969.
zTraded with Second Baseman Joe Morgan, Infielder Denis Menke and Outfielders Cesar Geronimo and Ed Armbrister to Cincinnati Reds for First Baseman Lee May, Second Baseman Tommy Helms and Outfielder Jim Stewart, November 29, 1971.

### CHAMPIONSHIP SERIES RECORD

| Year Club | League | G. | IP. | W. | L. | Pct. | H. | R. | ER. | SO. | BB. | ERA. |
|---|---|---|---|---|---|---|---|---|---|---|---|---|
| 1972–Cincinnati | National | 1 | 4⅔ | 0 | 0 | .000 | 5 | 2 | 2 | 4 | 2 | 3.86 |
| 1973–Cincinnati | National | 2 | 12 | 0 | 1 | .000 | 9 | 6 | 6 | 9 | 4 | 4.50 |
| Championship Series Totals | | 3 | 16⅔ | 0 | 1 | .000 | 14 | 8 | 8 | 13 | 6 | 4.32 |

### WORLD SERIES RECORD

| Year Club | League | G. | IP. | W. | L. | Pct. | H. | R. | ER. | SO. | BB. | ERA. |
|---|---|---|---|---|---|---|---|---|---|---|---|---|
| 1972–Cincinnati | National | 3 | 13⅔ | 1 | 0 | 1.000 | 6 | 1 | 0 | 11 | 4 | 0.00 |
| 1975–Cincinnati | National | 3 | 9 | 0 | 0 | .000 | 8 | 2 | 1 | 7 | 5 | 1.00 |
| 1976–Cincinnati | National | 1 | 2⅔ | 1 | 0 | 1.000 | 0 | 0 | 0 | 1 | 0 | 0.00 |
| World Series Totals | | 7 | 25⅓ | 2 | 0 | 1.000 | 14 | 3 | 1 | 19 | 9 | 0.36 |

### ALL-STAR GAME RECORD

Member of National League All-Star Team for the 1973 game; did not play.

## JAMES DOUGLAS BIRD
### (Doug)

Born March 5, 1950, at Pomona, Calif.
Height, 6.04. Weight, 180.
Throws and bats righthanded.
Hobbies—Hunting and fishing.
Attended Mesa Community College, Mesa, Ariz., and Mount San Antonio Junior College, Walnut, Calif.

Tied for California League lead in games started with 27 and in shutouts with 3 in 1971.

| Year Club | League | G. | IP. | W. | L. | Pct. | H. | R. | ER. | SO. | BB. | ERA. |
|---|---|---|---|---|---|---|---|---|---|---|---|---|
| 1969–Winnipeg | Northern | 16 | 99 | 6 | 2 | .750 | 105 | 45 | 38 | 88 | 17 | 3.45 |
| 1970–San Jose | California | 3 | 10 | 0 | 2 | .000 | 10 | 10 | 7 | 14 | 3 | 6.30 |
| 1970–Waterloo | Midwest | 22 | 147 | 11 | 9 | .550 | 122 | 49 | 30 | 149 | 32 | •1.84 |
| 1971–San Jose | California | 29 | •182 | •15 | 9 | .625 | 175 | 84 | 69 | 143 | 48 | 3.41 |
| 1972–Jacksonville | Southern | 24 | 122 | 10 | 7 | .588 | 117 | 43 | 33 | 72 | 32 | 2.43 |
| 1972–Omaha | Am. Assoc. | 7 | 9 | 1 | 1 | .500 | 9 | 4 | 3 | 13 | 5 | 3.00 |
| 1973–Omaha | Am. Assoc. | 4 | 6 | 1 | 0 | 1.000 | 5 | 0 | 0 | 3 | 1 | 0.00 |
| 1973–Kansas City | American | 54 | 102 | 4 | 4 | .500 | 81 | 37 | 34 | 83 | 30 | 3.00 |
| 1974–Kansas City | American | 55 | 92 | 7 | 6 | .538 | 100 | 31 | 28 | 62 | 27 | 2.74 |
| 1975–Kansas City | American | 51 | 105 | 9 | 6 | .600 | 100 | 42 | 38 | 81 | 40 | 3.26 |
| 1976–Kansas City | American | 39 | 198 | 12 | 10 | .545 | 191 | 90 | 74 | 107 | 31 | 3.36 |
| Major League Totals | | 199 | 497 | 32 | 26 | .552 | 472 | 200 | 174 | 333 | 128 | 3.15 |

### CHAMPIONSHIP SERIES RECORD

| Year Club | League | G. | IP. | W. | L. | Pct. | H. | R. | ER. | SO. | BB. | ERA. |
|---|---|---|---|---|---|---|---|---|---|---|---|---|
| 1976–Kansas City | American | 1 | 4⅔ | 1 | 0 | 1.000 | 4 | 1 | 1 | 1 | 0 | 1.93 |

# TIMOTHY P. BLACKWELL
## (Tim)

Born August 19, 1952, at San Diego, Calif.
Height, 5.11. Weight, 180.
Throws right and bats left and righthanded.
Hobbies—Tennis, golf and basketball.
Attended Grossmont College, El Cajon, Calif.

Tied for Eastern League lead in double plays by catchers with 12 in 1973.

| Year Club | League | Pos. | G. | AB. | R. | H. | 2B. | 3B. | HR. | RBI. | B.A. | PO. | A. | E. | F.A. |
|---|---|---|---|---|---|---|---|---|---|---|---|---|---|---|---|
| 1970—Jamestown | NYP | 3B-C | 28 | 81 | 8 | 19 | 3 | 2 | 0 | 10 | .235 | 33 | 30 | 5 | .926 |
| 1971—Greenville | W. Car. | C-0-3 | 55 | 140 | 18 | 25 | 6 | 0 | 0 | 10 | .179 | 230 | 24 | 5 | .981 |
| 1972—Winston-Salem† | Carol. | C | 60 | 177 | 25 | 44 | 14 | 3 | 3 | 26 | .249 | 357 | 15 | 9 | .976 |
| 1973—Bristol | East. | C-OF | 102 | 318 | 39 | 90 | 15 | 0 | 5 | 38 | .283 | 502 | 63 | 5 | .991 |
| 1974—Pawtucket | Int. | C | 50 | 140 | 12 | 29 | 8 | 0 | 0 | 17 | .207 | 302 | 24 | 6 | .982 |
| 1974—Boston | Amer. | C | 44 | 122 | 9 | 30 | 1 | 1 | 0 | 8 | .246 | 182 | 21 | 6 | .971 |
| 1975—Boston‡ | Amer. | C | 59 | 132 | 15 | 26 | 3 | 2 | 0 | 6 | .197 | 230 | 23 | 4 | .984 |
| 1976—Philadelphia | Nat. | C | 4 | 8 | 0 | 2 | 0 | 0 | 0 | 1 | .250 | 17 | 0 | 0 | 1.000 |
| 1976—Reading | East. | •C-OF | 91 | 299 | 29 | 74 | 10 | 2 | 2 | 25 | .247 | 427 | •64 | 10 | .980 |
| American League Totals | | | 103 | 254 | 24 | 56 | 4 | 3 | 0 | 14 | .220 | 412 | 44 | 10 | .979 |
| National League Totals | | | 4 | 8 | 0 | 2 | 0 | 0 | 0 | 1 | .250 | 17 | 0 | 0 | 1.000 |
| Major League Totals | | | 107 | 262 | 24 | 58 | 4 | 3 | 0 | 15 | .221 | 429 | 44 | 10 | .979 |

†On disabled list, May 24 to June 16, 1972.
‡Sold to Philadelphia Phillies, April 19, 1976.

# DENNIS HERMAN BLAIR

Born June 5, 1954, at Middletown, O.
Height, 6.04. Weight, 185.
Throws and bats righthanded.
Hobbies—Hiking, cycling and music.
Attended California State University, San Bernardino, Calif.

| Year Club | League | G. | IP. | W. | L. | Pct. | H. | R. | ER. | SO. | BB. | ERA. |
|---|---|---|---|---|---|---|---|---|---|---|---|---|
| 1972—Jamestown | NYP | 1 | 4 | 0 | 0 | .000 | 6 | 5 | 3 | 0 | 1 | 6.75 |
| 1972—Cocoa Expos | Fla. E. C't | 5 | 33 | 1 | 0 | 1.000 | 29 | 20 | 9 | 21 | 23 | 2.45 |
| 1972—West Palm Beach | Florida St. | 6 | 31 | 1 | 3 | .250 | 34 | 18 | 16 | 13 | 9 | 4.65 |
| 1973—West Palm Beach | Florida St. | 10 | 64 | 4 | 3 | .571 | 45 | 27 | 16 | 55 | 24 | 2.25 |
| 1973—Quebec City | Eastern | 15 | 86 | 3 | 9 | .250 | 78 | 38 | 31 | 45 | 39 | 3.24 |
| 1974—Memphis | Int. | 9 | 54 | 5 | 0 | 1.000 | 37 | 11 | 11 | 47 | 24 | 1.83 |
| 1974—Montreal | National | 22 | 146 | 11 | 7 | .611 | 113 | 61 | 53 | 76 | 72 | 3.27 |
| 1975—Montreal | National | 30 | 163 | 8 | 15 | .348 | 150 | 77 | 69 | 82 | 106 | 3.81 |
| 1976—Denver | Am. Assoc. | 25 | 122 | 9 | 4 | .692 | 131 | 73 | 61 | 91 | 84 | 4.50 |
| 1976—Montreal | National | 5 | 16 | 0 | 2 | .000 | 21 | 11 | 7 | 9 | 11 | 3.94 |
| Major League Totals | | 57 | 325 | 19 | 24 | .442 | 284 | 149 | 129 | 167 | 189 | 3.57 |

# PAUL L. D. BLAIR

Born February 1, 1944, at Cushing, Okla.
Height, 6.00. Weight, 172.
Throws and bats righthanded.
Attended East Los Angeles Junior College, Los Angeles, Calif.

Tied major league record for fewest sacrifices, season, for leader in sacrifices (no sacrifice flies), 13, in 1969.
Hit three home runs in a game, April 29, 1970 against Chicago White Sox.
Tied for American League lead in sacrifice hits with 13 in 1969.
Led California League outfielders in double plays with 7 in 1962.
Led Eastern League in stolen bases with 34 in 1964.
Named outfielder on THE SPORTING NEWS American League All-Star fielding teams, 1967-69-70-71-72-73-74-75.
Named as center fielder on THE SPORTING NEWS American League All-Star Team, 1969 and 1974.

| Year Club | League | Pos. | G. | AB. | R. | H. | 2B. | 3B. | HR. | RBI. | B.A. | PO. | A. | E. | F.A. |
|---|---|---|---|---|---|---|---|---|---|---|---|---|---|---|---|
| 1962—Santa Barbara† | Calif. | O-3-S | 122 | 417 | 69 | 95 | 11 | 3 | 17 | 63 | .228 | 191 | 37 | 14 | .942 |
| 1963—Stockton | Calif. | OF-INF | 139 | 540 | 126 | 175 | 30 | 10 | 16 | 77 | .324 | 250 | 72 | 17 | .950 |
| 1964—Rochester | Int. | OF | 23 | 69 | 6 | 9 | 1 | 1 | 2 | 5 | .130 | 35 | 2 | 1 | .974 |
| 1964—Elmira | East. | •OF-3B | 108 | 415 | 81 | 129 | 18 | 11 | 5 | 52 | •.311 | 249 | 13 | 5 | •.981 |
| 1964—Baltimore | Amer. | OF | 8 | 1 | 0 | 0 | 0 | 0 | 0 | 0 | .000 | 2 | 0 | 0 | 1.000 |
| 1965—Baltimore | Amer. | OF | 119 | 364 | 49 | 85 | 19 | 2 | 5 | 25 | .234 | 241 | 5 | 2 | .992 |
| 1965—Rochester | Int. | OF | 37 | 143 | 17 | 47 | 6 | 5 | 4 | 21 | .329 | 81 | 2 | 3 | .965 |
| 1966—Baltimore | Amer. | OF | 133 | 303 | 35 | 84 | 20 | 2 | 6 | 33 | .277 | 204 | 4 | 2 | .990 |
| 1967—Baltimore | Amer. | OF | 151 | 552 | 72 | 162 | 27 | •12 | 11 | 64 | .293 | •369 | 13 | 6 | .985 |
| 1968—Baltimore | Amer. | OF-3B | 141 | 421 | 48 | 89 | 22 | 1 | 7 | 38 | .211 | 272 | 11 | 3 | .990 |
| 1969—Baltimore | Amer. | OF | 150 | 625 | 102 | 178 | 32 | 5 | 26 | 76 | .285 | •407 | 14 | 5 | .988 |
| 1970—Baltimore‡ | Amer. | OF-3B | 133 | 480 | 79 | 128 | 24 | 2 | 18 | 65 | .267 | 368 | 10 | 5 | .987 |
| 1971—Baltimore | Amer. | OF | 142 | 516 | 75 | 135 | 24 | 8 | 10 | 44 | .262 | 331 | 4 | 3 | .991 |
| 1972—Baltimore | Amer. | OF | 142 | 477 | 47 | 111 | 20 | 8 | 8 | 49 | .233 | 337 | 10 | 3 | .991 |
| 1973—Baltimore | Amer. | OF | 146 | 500 | 73 | 140 | 25 | 3 | 10 | 64 | .280 | 344 | 4 | 4 | .990 |
| 1974—Baltimore | Amer. | OF | 151 | 552 | 77 | 144 | 27 | 4 | 17 | 62 | .261 | 447 | 7 | 7 | .985 |
| 1975—Baltimore | Amer. | OF-1B | 140 | 440 | 51 | 96 | 13 | 4 | 5 | 31 | .218 | 327 | 8 | 3 | .991 |
| 1976—Baltimore§ | Amer. | OF-DH | 145 | 375 | 29 | 74 | 16 | 0 | 3 | 16 | .197 | 327 | 6 | 7 | .979 |
| Major League Totals | | | 1700 | 5606 | 737 | 1426 | 269 | 51 | 126 | 567 | .254 | 4001 | 106 | 50 | .988 |

†Drafted by Baltimore Orioles from Syracuse (New York Mets' organization), November 26, 1962.
‡On disabled list, May 31 through June 21, 1970.
§Traded to New York Yankees for Outfielders Elliott Maddox and Rick Bladt, latter assigned to Rochester, January 20, 1976.

## CHAMPIONSHIP SERIES RECORD

| Year    Club       League | Pos. | G. | AB. | R. | H. | 2B. | 3B. | HR. | RBI. | B.A. | PO. | A. | E. | F.A. |
|---|---|---|---|---|---|---|---|---|---|---|---|---|---|---|
| 1969–Baltimore..........Amer. | OF | 3 | 15 | 1 | 6 | 2 | 0 | 1 | 6 | .400 | 8 | 0 | 0 | 1.000 |
| 1970–Baltimore..........Amer. | OF | 3 | 13 | 0 | 1 | 0 | 0 | 0 | 0 | .077 | 4 | 0 | 0 | 1.000 |
| 1971–Baltimore..........Amer. | OF | 3 | 9 | 1 | 3 | 1 | 0 | 0 | 2 | .333 | 5 | 0 | 0 | 1.000 |
| 1973–Baltimore..........Amer. | OF | 5 | 18 | 2 | 3 | 0 | 0 | 0 | 0 | .167 | 8 | 0 | 0 | 1.000 |
| 1974–Baltimore..........Amer. | OF | 4 | 14 | 3 | 4 | 0 | 0 | 1 | 2 | .286 | 7 | 0 | 0 | 1.000 |
| Championship Series Totals ............ | | 18 | 69 | 7 | 17 | 3 | 0 | 2 | 10 | .246 | 32 | 0 | 0 | 1.000 |

## WORLD SERIES RECORD

Tied World Series record for most hits, 5-game series, 9, in 1970.

| Year    Club       League | Pos. | G. | AB. | R. | H. | 2B. | 3B. | HR. | RBI. | B.A. | PO. | A. | E. | F.A. |
|---|---|---|---|---|---|---|---|---|---|---|---|---|---|---|
| 1966–Baltimore..........Amer. | OF | 4 | 6 | 2 | 1 | 0 | 0 | 1 | 1 | .167 | 9 | 0 | 0 | 1.000 |
| 1969–Baltimore..........Amer. | OF | 5 | 20 | 1 | 2 | 0 | 0 | 0 | 0 | .100 | 7 | 0 | 0 | 1.000 |
| 1970–Baltimore..........Amer. | OF | 5 | 19 | 5 | 9 | 1 | 0 | 0 | 3 | .474 | 18 | 0 | 1 | .947 |
| 1971–Baltimore..........Amer. | PR-OF | 4 | 9 | 2 | 3 | 1 | 0 | 0 | 0 | .333 | 6 | 2 | 1 | .889 |
| World Series Totals ....................... | | 18 | 54 | 10 | 15 | 2 | 0 | 1 | 4 | .278 | 40 | 2 | 2 | .955 |

## ALL-STAR GAME RECORD

| Year    League | Pos. | AB. | R. | H. | 2B. | 3B. | HR. | RBI. | B.A. | PO. | A. | E. | F.A. |
|---|---|---|---|---|---|---|---|---|---|---|---|---|---|
| 1969–American ........................... | OF | 2 | 0 | 0 | 0 | 0 | 0 | 0 | .000 | 2 | 0 | 0 | 1.000 |
| 1973–American ........................... | OF | 0 | 0 | 0 | 0 | 0 | 0 | 0 | .000 | 1 | 0 | 0 | 1.000 |
| All-Star Game Totals ...................... | | 2 | 0 | 0 | 0 | 0 | 0 | 0 | .000 | 3 | 0 | 0 | 1.000 |

## LARVELL BLANKS

Born January 28, 1950, at Del Rio, Tex.
Height, 5.08. Weight, 164.
Throws and bats righthanded.
Attended Sul Ross State University, Alpine, Tex., and Mesa Community College, Mesa, Ariz.
Nephew of Sid Blanks, former halfback with Houston Oilers, Boston Patriots
and Houston Texans.

| Year    Club       League | Pos. | G. | AB. | R. | H. | 2B. | 3B. | HR. | RBI. | B.A. | PO. | A. | E. | F.A. |
|---|---|---|---|---|---|---|---|---|---|---|---|---|---|---|
| 1969–Magic Valley ....Pion. | S-2-3-O | ●72 | 260 | 43 | 75 | ●15 | 4 | 9 | ●60 | .283 | 97 | 179 | 24 | .920 |
| 1970–Greenwood........W. Car. | 3-2-S | 116 | 437 | 79 | 121 | 16 | 3 | 15 | 69 | .277 | 104 | 232 | 16 | .955 |
| 1971–Savannah ..........South. | 2B | 134 | 477 | 58 | 106 | 22 | 3 | 14 | 48 | .222 | 295 | 333 | 17 | .974 |
| 1972–Savannah ..........South. | SS-2B | 83 | 271 | 38 | 77 | 17 | 3 | 6 | 34 | .284 | 108 | 230 | 13 | .963 |
| 1972–Atlanta..............Nat. | 2-SS-3 | 33 | 85 | 10 | 28 | 5 | 0 | 1 | 7 | .329 | 49 | 74 | 0 | 1.000 |
| 1973–Richmond..........Int. | 2-3-S | 100 | 366 | 45 | 91 | 21 | 1 | 6 | 35 | .249 | 185 | 247 | 17 | .962 |
| 1973–Atlanta..............Nat. | 3-2-S | 17 | 18 | 1 | 4 | 0 | 0 | 0 | 0 | .222 | 1 | 3 | 0 | 1.000 |
| 1974–Richmond..........Int. | ●S-3-2 | 136 | 466 | 72 | 126 | ●29 | 4 | 14 | 47 | .270 | 167 | ●414 | 22 | .964 |
| 1974–Atlanta..............Nat. | SS | 3 | 8 | 0 | 2 | 0 | 0 | 0 | 1 | .250 | 1 | 7 | 1 | .889 |
| 1975–Atlanta† ...........Nat. | SS-2B | 141 | 471 | 49 | 110 | 13 | 3 | 3 | 38 | .234 | 212 | 438 | 27 | .960 |
| 1976–Cleveland..........Amer. | 3-S-2-DH | 104 | 328 | 45 | 92 | 8 | 7 | 5 | 41 | .280 | 152 | 214 | 11 | .971 |
| National League Totals ................. | | 194 | 582 | 60 | 144 | 18 | 3 | 4 | 46 | .247 | 263 | 522 | 28 | .966 |
| American League Totals ............... | | 104 | 328 | 45 | 92 | 8 | 7 | 5 | 41 | .280 | 152 | 214 | 11 | .971 |
| Major League Totals ...................... | | 298 | 910 | 105 | 236 | 26 | 10 | 9 | 87 | .259 | 415 | 736 | 39 | .967 |

†Traded with Outfielder Ralph Garr to Chicago White Sox for Outfielder Ken Henderson and Pitchers Dick Ruthven and Danny Osborn, December 12, 1975. Traded by Chicago White Sox to Cleveland Indians for Second Baseman Jack Brohamer, December 12, 1975.

## RONALD MARK BLOMBERG

Name pronounced Bloomberg.

### (Ron)

Born August 23, 1948, at Atlanta, Ga.
Height, 6.01. Weight, 205.
Throws right and bats lefthanded.
Hobbies–Fishing and golf.
Attended DeKalb Junior College, Clarkston, Ga.

Led Appalachian League in sacrifice flies with 6 in 1967.
Received reported $60,000 bonus to sign with New York Yankees, 1967.

| Year    Club       League | Pos. | G. | AB. | R. | H. | 2B. | 3B. | HR. | RBI. | B.A. | PO. | A. | E. | F.A. |
|---|---|---|---|---|---|---|---|---|---|---|---|---|---|---|
| 1967–Johnson City ....Appal. | ●1-O | 66 | 236 | ●51 | 70 | 12 | 3 | 10 | ●55 | .297 | ●521 | 22 | 8 | .985 |
| 1968–Kinston ...........Carol. | OF | 105 | 359 | 41 | 90 | 10 | 4 | 7 | 43 | .251 | 181 | 8 | 7 | .964 |
| 1969–Manchester†......East. | OF | 107 | 384 | 63 | 109 | 17 | 7 | 19 | 52 | .284 | 146 | 4 | 7 | .955 |
| 1969–New York..........Amer. | OF | 4 | 6 | 0 | 3 | 0 | 0 | 0 | 0 | .500 | 2 | 0 | 0 | 1.000 |
| 1970–Syracuse ..........Int. | OF | 92 | 289 | 50 | 79 | 13 | 2 | 10 | 38 | .273 | 124 | 11 | 4 | .971 |
| 1971–Syracuse ..........Int. | OF | 48 | 138 | 24 | 45 | 9 | 3 | 6 | 20 | .326 | 48 | 1 | 2 | .961 |
| 1971–New York..........Amer. | OF | 64 | 199 | 30 | 64 | 6 | 2 | 7 | 31 | .322 | 96 | 1 | 3 | .970 |
| 1972–New York..........Amer. | 1B | 107 | 299 | 36 | 80 | 22 | 1 | 14 | 49 | .268 | 813 | 32 | 13 | .985 |
| 1973–New York..........Amer. | 1B | 100 | 301 | 45 | 99 | 13 | 1 | 12 | 57 | .329 | 359 | 28 | 8 | .980 |

| Year | Club | League | Pos. | G. | AB. | R. | H. | 2B. | 3B. | HR. | RBI. | B.A. | PO. | A. | E. | F.A. |
|------|------|--------|------|----|----|----|----|-----|-----|-----|------|------|-----|----|----|------|
| 1974–New York | | Amer. | OF | 90 | 264 | 39 | 82 | 11 | 2 | 10 | 48 | .311 | 32 | 2 | 0 | 1.000 |
| 1975–New York‡ | | Amer. | O-DH-PH | 34 | 106 | 18 | 27 | 8 | 2 | 4 | 17 | .255 | 2 | 0 | 0 | 1.000 |
| 1976–New York§ | | Amer. | DH | 1 | 2 | 0 | 0 | 0 | 0 | 0 | 0 | .000 | 0 | 0 | 0 | .000 |
| Major League Totals | | | | 400 | 1177 | 168 | 355 | 60 | 8 | 47 | 202 | .302 | 1304 | 63 | 24 | .983 |

†On temporary inactive list, July 11 through July 29, 1969.
‡On supplemental disabled list, May 16 to June 13 and July 31 to October 3, 1975.
§On disabled list April 8 through September 3, 1976.

## VIDA ROCHELLE BLUE, JR.

Born July 28, 1949, at Mansfield, La.
Height, 6.00. Weight, 195.
Throws left and bats left and righthanded.
Hobbies–Hunting and fishing.
Attended Southern University, Baton Rouge, La.

Pitched seven-inning, 4-0 no-hit victory against Appleton, June 19, 1968.
Pitched 6-0 no-hit victory against Minnesota Twins, September 21, 1970.
Led American League in shutouts with 8 in 1971.
Won American League Cy Young Memorial Award, 1971.
Named lefthanded pitcher on THE SPORTING NEWS American League All-Star Team, 1971.
Named American League Pitcher of the Year by THE SPORTING NEWS, 1971.
Named Most Valuable Player in American League, 1971.

| Year | Club | League | G. | IP. | W. | L. | Pct. | H. | R. | ER. | SO. | BB. | ERA. |
|------|------|--------|----|----|----|----|------|----|----|-----|-----|-----|------|
| 1968–Burlington | | Midwest | 24 | 152 | 8 | •11 | .421 | 102 | 67 | 42 | *231 | 80 | 2.49 |
| 1969–Birmingham | | Southern | 15 | 104 | 10 | 3 | .769 | 80 | 40 | 37 | 112 | 52 | 3.20 |
| 1969–Oakland | | American | 12 | 42 | 1 | 1 | .500 | 49 | 34 | 29 | 24 | 18 | 6.21 |
| 1970–Iowa | | Am. Assoc. | 17 | 133 | 12 | 3 | *.800 | 88 | 40 | 32 | *165 | 55 | 2.17 |
| 1970–Oakland | | American | 6 | 39 | 2 | 0 | 1.000 | 20 | 12 | 9 | 35 | 12 | 2.08 |
| 1971–Oakland | | American | 39 | 312 | 24 | 8 | .750 | 209 | 73 | 63 | 301 | 88 | *1.82 |
| 1972–Oakland† | | American | 25 | 151 | 6 | 10 | .375 | 117 | 55 | 47 | 111 | 48 | 2.80 |
| 1973–Oakland | | American | 37 | 264 | 20 | 9 | .690 | 214 | 108 | 96 | 158 | 105 | 3.27 |
| 1974–Oakland | | American | 40 | 282 | 17 | 15 | .531 | 246 | 118 | 102 | 174 | 98 | 3.26 |
| 1975–Oakland | | American | 39 | 278 | 22 | 11 | .667 | 243 | 103 | 93 | 189 | 99 | 3.01 |
| 1976–Oakland | | American | 37 | 298 | 18 | 13 | .581 | 268 | 90 | 78 | 166 | 63 | 2.36 |
| Major League Totals | | | 235 | 1666 | 110 | 67 | .621 | 1366 | 593 | 517 | 1158 | 531 | 2.79 |

†On restricted list, March 30 through April 27, 1972.

### CHAMPIONSHIP SERIES RECORD

| Year | Club | League | G. | IP. | W. | L. | Pct. | H. | R. | ER. | SO. | BB. | ERA. |
|------|------|--------|----|----|----|----|------|----|----|-----|-----|-----|------|
| 1971–Oakland | | American | 1 | 7 | 0 | 1 | .000 | 7 | 5 | 5 | 8 | 2 | 6.43 |
| 1972–Oakland | | American | 4 | 5⅓ | 0 | 0 | .000 | 4 | 0 | 0 | 5 | 1 | 0.00 |
| 1973–Oakland | | American | 2 | 7 | 0 | 1 | .000 | 8 | 8 | 8 | 3 | 5 | 10.29 |
| 1974–Oakland | | American | 1 | 9 | 1 | 0 | 1.000 | 2 | 0 | 0 | 7 | 0 | 0.00 |
| 1975–Oakland | | American | 1 | 3 | 0 | 0 | .000 | 6 | 3 | 3 | 2 | 0 | 9.00 |
| Championship Series Totals | | | 9 | 31⅓ | 1 | 2 | .333 | 27 | 16 | 16 | 25 | 8 | 4.60 |

### WORLD SERIES RECORD

| Year | Club | League | G. | IP. | W. | L. | Pct. | H. | R. | ER. | SO. | BB. | ERA. |
|------|------|--------|----|----|----|----|------|----|----|-----|-----|-----|------|
| 1972–Oakland | | American | 4 | 8⅔ | 0 | 1 | .000 | 8 | 4 | 4 | 5 | 5 | 4.15 |
| 1973–Oakland | | American | 2 | 11 | 0 | 1 | .000 | 10 | 6 | 6 | 8 | 3 | 4.91 |
| 1974–Oakland | | American | 2 | 13⅔ | 0 | 1 | .000 | 10 | 5 | 5 | 9 | 7 | 3.29 |
| World Series Totals | | | 8 | 33⅓ | 0 | 3 | .000 | 28 | 15 | 15 | 22 | 15 | 4.05 |

### ALL-STAR GAME RECORD

| Year | League | IP. | W. | L. | Pct. | H. | R. | ER. | SO. | BB. | ERA. |
|------|--------|-----|----|----|------|----|----|-----|-----|-----|------|
| 1971–American | | 3 | 1 | 0 | 1.000 | 2 | 3 | 3 | 3 | 0 | 9.00 |
| 1975–American | | 2 | 0 | 0 | .000 | 5 | 2 | 2 | 1 | 0 | 9.00 |
| All-Star Game Totals | | 5 | 1 | 0 | 1.000 | 7 | 5 | 5 | 4 | 0 | 9.00 |

## RIK AALBERT BLYLEVEN
### (Bert)

Born April 6, 1951, at Zeist, The Netherlands.
Height, 6.03. Weight, 200.
Throws and bats righthanded.
Hobbies–Bowling, golf, basketball and pool.

Tied American League record for most consecutive strikeouts, start of game, 6, September 16, 1970.
Led American League in shutouts with 9 in 1973.
Named by THE SPORTING NEWS as American League Rookie Pitcher of the Year for 1970.

| Year | Club | League | G. | IP. | W. | L. | Pct. | H. | R. | ER. | SO. | BB. | ERA. |
|------|------|--------|----|----|----|----|------|----|----|-----|-----|-----|------|
| 1969–Sarasota Twins | | Gulf Coast | 7 | 32 | 2 | 2 | .500 | 31 | 13 | 10 | 39 | 11 | 2.81 |
| 1969–Orlando | | Florida St. | 6 | 37 | 5 | 0 | 1.000 | 26 | 6 | 6 | 41 | 14 | 1.46 |
| 1970–Evansville | | Am. Assoc. | 8 | 54 | 4 | 2 | .667 | 48 | 18 | 15 | 63 | 12 | 2.50 |
| 1970–Minnesota | | American | 27 | 164 | 10 | 9 | .526 | 143 | 66 | 58 | 135 | 47 | 3.18 |
| 1971–Minnesota | | American | 38 | 278 | 16 | 15 | .516 | 267 | 95 | 87 | 224 | 59 | 2.82 |
| 1972–Minnesota | | American | 39 | 287 | 17 | 17 | .500 | 247 | 93 | 87 | 228 | 69 | 2.73 |
| 1973–Minnesota | | American | 40 | 325 | 20 | 17 | .541 | 296 | 109 | 91 | 258 | 67 | 2.52 |

| Year Club | League | G. | IP. | W. | L. | Pct. | H. | R. | ER. | SO. | BB. | ERA. |
|---|---|---|---|---|---|---|---|---|---|---|---|---|
| 1974—Minnesota | American | 37 | 281 | 17 | 17 | .500 | 244 | 99 | 83 | 249 | 77 | 2.66 |
| 1975—Minnesota | American | 35 | 276 | 15 | 10 | .600 | 219 | 104 | 92 | 233 | 84 | 3.00 |
| 1976—Minnesota†-Texas | American | 36 | 298 | 13 | 16 | .448 | 283 | 106 | 95 | 219 | 81 | 2.87 |
| Major League Totals | | 252 | 1908 | 108 | 101 | .517 | 1699 | 672 | 593 | 1546 | 484 | 2.80 |

†Traded with Shortstop Danny Thompson to Texas Rangers for Pitcher Bill Singer, Infielders Roy Smalley and Mike Cubbage and Pitcher Jim Gideon, assigned to Tacoma, and a reported $250,000 cash, June 1, 1976.

### CHAMPIONSHIP SERIES RECORD

| Year Club | League | G. | IP. | W. | L. | Pct. | H. | R. | ER. | SO. | BB. | ERA. |
|---|---|---|---|---|---|---|---|---|---|---|---|---|
| 1970—Minnesota | American | 1 | 2 | 0 | 0 | .000 | 2 | 1 | 0 | 2 | 0 | 0.00 |

### ALL-STAR GAME RECORD

| Year League | IP. | W. | L. | Pct. | H. | R. | ER. | SO. | BB. | ERA. |
|---|---|---|---|---|---|---|---|---|---|---|
| 1973—American | 1 | 0 | 1 | .000 | 2 | 2 | 2 | 0 | 2 | 18.00 |

## BRUCE ANTON BOCHTE
Name pronounced Bock-tee.

Born November 12, 1950, at Pasadena, Calif.
Height, 6.03. Weight, 195.
Throws and bats lefthanded.
Hobbies—Reading, tennis and collecting tropical fish.
Attended University of Santa Clara, Santa Clara, Calif.;
received Bachelor of Science Degree in Commerce.

| Year Club | League | Pos. | G. | AB. | R. | H. | 2B. | 3B. | HR. | RBI. | B.A. | PO. | A. | E. | F.A. |
|---|---|---|---|---|---|---|---|---|---|---|---|---|---|---|---|
| 1972—Stockton | Calif. | 1B-OF | 72 | 266 | 36 | 87 | 14 | 2 | 11 | 42 | .327 | 470 | 27 | 9 | .982 |
| 1973—El Paso | Texas | 1B-OF | 122 | 417 | 57 | 133 | 32 | 4 | 10 | 79 | .319 | 775 | 41 | 11 | .987 |
| 1974—Salt Lake City | P.C. | OF-1B | 92 | 332 | 55 | 118 | 15 | 2 | 9 | 56 | .355 | 218 | 12 | 6 | .975 |
| 1974—California | Amer. | OF-1B | 57 | 196 | 24 | 53 | 4 | 1 | 5 | 26 | .270 | 248 | 9 | 5 | .981 |
| 1975—California† | Amer. | 1B | 107 | 375 | 41 | 107 | 19 | 3 | 3 | 48 | .285 | 850 | 51 | 12 | .987 |
| 1976—California | Amer. | OF-1-DH | 146 | 466 | 53 | 120 | 17 | 1 | 2 | 49 | .258 | 651 | 42 | 7 | .990 |
| Major League Totals | | | 310 | 1037 | 118 | 280 | 40 | 5 | 10 | 123 | .270 | 1749 | 102 | 24 | .987 |

†On disabled list, June 24 to August 13, 1975.

## THOMAS WINTON BOGGS

Born October 25, 1955, at Poughkeepsie, N.Y.
Height, 6.02. Weight, 195.
Throws and bats righthanded.
Hobby—Water skiing.

Tied for Gulf Coast League lead in shutouts with 2 in 1974.
Led Pacific Coast League pitchers in double plays with 5 in 1976.

| Year Club | League | G. | IP. | W. | L. | Pct. | H. | R. | ER. | SO. | BB. | ERA. |
|---|---|---|---|---|---|---|---|---|---|---|---|---|
| 1974—Sarasota Rangers | Gulf Coast | 10 | 64 | 5 | 2 | .714 | 50 | 21 | 18 | 55 | 35 | 2.53 |
| 1975—Pittsfield | Eastern | 24 | 162 | 10 | 11 | .476 | 153 | 84 | 63 | 100 | 73 | 3.50 |
| 1976—Sacramento | P. Coast | 18 | 115 | 6 | 11 | .353 | 153 | 101 | 88 | 77 | 60 | 6.89 |

Listed on Texas Rangers' 1977 spring roster.

## BRUCE ARMAND BOISCLAIR
Name pronounced BOH-clair.

Born December 9 1952, at Putnam, Conn.
Height, 6.03. Weight, 200.
Throws and bats lefthanded.
Hobbies—Bicycle riding and all sports.

| Year Club | League | Pos. | G. | AB. | R. | H. | 2B. | 3B. | HR. | RBI. | B.A. | PO. | A. | E. | F.A. |
|---|---|---|---|---|---|---|---|---|---|---|---|---|---|---|---|
| 1970—Marion | Appal. | OF-P | 40 | 117 | 15 | 33 | 5 | 2 | 0 | 10 | .282 | 49 | 3 | 0 | 1.000 |
| 1971—Pompano Bch. | Fla. St. | OF-1B | 129 | 401 | 64 | 108 | 18 | 4 | 0 | 47 | .269 | 163 | 6 | 4 | .977 |
| 1972—Visalia† | Calif. | 1B-OF | 88 | 328 | 64 | 114 | 19 | 4 | 4 | 32 | .348 | 473 | 26 | 9 | .982 |
| 1973—Memphis | Texas | OF-1B | 19 | 63 | 10 | 13 | 2 | 0 | 1 | 7 | .206 | 71 | 5 | 2 | .974 |
| 1973—Tidewater | Int. | OF | 80 | 243 | 31 | 62 | 11 | 0 | 2 | 23 | .255 | 112 | 3 | 2 | .983 |
| 1974—Tidewater‡ | Int. | OF-1B | 107 | 297 | 27 | 71 | 8 | 4 | 5 | 31 | .239 | 181 | 8 | 4 | .979 |
| 1974—New York | Nat. | OF | 7 | 12 | 0 | 3 | 1 | 0 | 0 | 1 | .250 | 10 | 2 | 1 | .923 |
| 1975—Tidewater | Int. | OF | 127 | 453 | 62 | 126 | 16 | 5 | 4 | 37 | .278 | 264 | 9 | 4 | .986 |
| 1976—New York | Nat. | OF | 110 | 286 | 42 | 82 | 13 | 3 | 2 | 13 | .287 | 156 | 3 | 3 | .981 |
| Major League Totals | | | 117 | 298 | 42 | 85 | 14 | 3 | 2 | 14 | .285 | 166 | 5 | 4 | .977 |

†On military list from beginning of season to May 12.
‡On temporary inactive list, June 14 to June 29, 1974.

### PITCHING RECORD

| Year Club | League | G. | IP. | W. | L. | Pct. | H. | R. | ER. | SO. | BB. | ERA. |
|---|---|---|---|---|---|---|---|---|---|---|---|---|
| 1970—Marion | Appal. | 1 | 4 | 0 | 0 | .000 | 7 | 5 | 5 | 1 | 2 | 11.25 |

## DANNY JON BOITANO

Name pronounced boy-TAHN-oh.

Born March 22, 1953, at Sacramento, Calif.
Height, 6.00. Weight, 185.
Throws and bats righthanded.
Hobby—Hunting ducks.
Attended Fresno City College, Fresno, Calif.

Pitched 2-0 no-hit victory against Elmira, August 21, 1973.

| Year Club | League | G. | IP. | W. | L. | Pct. | H. | R. | ER. | SO. | BB. | ERA. |
|---|---|---|---|---|---|---|---|---|---|---|---|---|
| 1973—Auburn | NYP | 14 | 104 | 8 | 3 | .727 | 73 | 41 | 24 | 95 | 47 | 2.08 |
| 1974—Rocky Mount | Carolina | 17 | 94 | 3 | 10 | .231 | 99 | 68 | 59 | 82 | 55 | 5.65 |
| 1974—Spartanburg | W. Carol. | 5 | 21 | 0 | 1 | .000 | 26 | 15 | 12 | 20 | 9 | 5.14 |
| 1975—Reading | Eastern | 40 | 78 | 10 | 3 | .769 | 59 | 31 | 29 | 63 | 32 | 3.35 |
| 1976—Oklahoma City | Am. Assoc. | 50 | 70 | 3 | 5 | .375 | 65 | 39 | 33 | 50 | 54 | 4.24 |

Listed on Philadelphia Phillies' 1977 spring roster.

## BOBBY LEE BONDS

Born March 15, 1946, at Riverside, Calif.
Height, 6.01. Weight, 195.
Throws and bats righthanded.
Hobbies—Singing, dancing and listening to records.
Attended Riverside City College, Riverside, Calif.
Brother of Robert V. Bonds, Jr., 13th round draft choice
of Kansas City Chiefs in 1965.

Established major league records for most strikeouts, batter, season, 189 in 1970; most home runs as lead-off batter of game, season, 11 in 1973; and most home runs, first batter of game, lifetime, 32, 1975.
Tied major league record for most chances accepted, right fielder, game—10, May 28, 1976.
Tied American League record for most putouts, right fielder, game—9, May 28, 1976.
Major league stolen bases: 1968 (16), 1969 (45), 1970 (48), 1971 (26), 1972 (44), 1973 (43), 1974 (41), 1975 (30), 1976 (30). Total—323.
Led National League in total bases with 341 in 1973.
Led National League outfielders in double plays with 7 in 1970.
Led National League batters in strikeouts with 187 in 1969, 189 in 1970 and 148 in 1973.
Led California League batters in strikeouts with 146 in 1966.
Hit grand slam home run in first major league game; first rookie to do so in 20th century (in his third at bat), June 25, 1968.
Only player in major league history to hit 30 or more home runs and steal 30 or more bases in the same season on three occasions (32 home runs and 45 stolen bases in 1969; 39 home runs and 43 stolen bases in 1973; 32 home runs and 30 stolen bases in 1975).
Tied for National League lead in double plays by outfielders with 5 in 1973.
Named by THE SPORTING NEWS as National League Player of the Year, 1973.
Named as outfielder on THE SPORTING NEWS National League All-Star Team, 1973.
Named as outfielder on THE SPORTING NEWS National League All-Star fielding teams, 1971, 1973 and 1974.

| Year Club | League | Pos. | G. | AB. | R. | H. | 2B. | 3B. | HR. | RBI. | B.A. | PO. | A. | E. | F.A. |
|---|---|---|---|---|---|---|---|---|---|---|---|---|---|---|---|
| 1965—Lexington | W. Car. | OF | 112 | 418 | ★103 | 135 | 12 | 11 | 25 | 86 | .323 | 200 | 14 | 12 | .947 |
| 1965—Fresno | Calif. | OF | 7 | 32 | 6 | 7 | 0 | 0 | 1 | 2 | .219 | 16 | 0 | 1 | .941 |
| 1966—Fresno† | Calif. | OF | 117 | 455 | 93 | 119 | 12 | 6 | 26 | 91 | .262 | 181 | 15 | 10 | .951 |
| 1967—Waterbury | East. | *O-1B | 137 | 476 | 65 | 124 | 19 | 8 | 15 | 68 | .261 | 229 | 13 | ★11 | .957 |
| 1968—Phoenix | P.C. | OF | 60 | 219 | 47 | 81 | 16 | 7 | 8 | 47 | .370 | 156 | 7 | 2 | .988 |
| 1968—San Francisco | Nat. | OF | 81 | 307 | 55 | 78 | 10 | 5 | 9 | 35 | .254 | 169 | 6 | 4 | .978 |
| 1969—San Francisco | Nat. | OF | 158 | 622 | ●120 | 161 | 25 | 6 | 32 | 90 | .259 | 339 | 9 | 8 | .978 |
| 1970—San Francisco | Nat. | OF | 157 | 663 | 134 | 200 | 36 | 10 | 26 | 78 | .302 | 326 | 14 | 11 | .969 |
| 1971—San Francisco | Nat. | OF | 155 | 619 | 110 | 178 | 32 | 4 | 33 | 102 | .288 | 329 | 10 | 2 | ★.994 |
| 1972—San Francisco | Nat. | OF | 153 | 626 | 118 | 162 | 29 | 5 | 26 | 80 | .259 | 345 | 8 | 8 | .978 |
| 1973—San Francisco | Nat. | OF | 160 | 643 | ★131 | 182 | 34 | 4 | 39 | 96 | .283 | 346 | 12 | 11 | .970 |
| 1974—San Francisco‡ | Nat. | OF | 150 | 567 | 97 | 145 | 22 | 8 | 21 | 71 | .256 | 305 | 11 | 11 | .966 |
| 1975—New York§ | Amer. | OF | 145 | 529 | 93 | 143 | 26 | 3 | 32 | 85 | .270 | 287 | 12 | 4 | .987 |
| 1976—California x | Am. | OF-DH | 99 | 378 | 48 | 100 | 10 | 3 | 10 | 54 | .265 | 199 | 9 | 5 | .977 |
| National League Totals | | | 1014 | 4047 | 765 | 1106 | 188 | 42 | 186 | 552 | .273 | 2159 | 70 | 55 | .976 |
| American League Totals | | | 244 | 907 | 141 | 243 | 36 | 6 | 42 | 139 | .268 | 486 | 21 | 9 | .982 |
| Major League Totals | | | 1258 | 4954 | 906 | 1349 | 224 | 48 | 228 | 691 | .272 | 2645 | 91 | 64 | .977 |

†On disabled list, April 28 to May 17, 1966.
‡Traded to New York Yankees for Outfielder Bobby Murcer, October 21, 1974.
§Traded to California Angels for Outfielder Mickey Rivers and Pitcher Ed Figueroa, December 11, 1975.
xOn supplemental disabled list, April 2 to April 19, 1976; on emergency disabled list, August 9 to October 14, 1976.

### CHAMPIONSHIP SERIES RECORD

| Year Club | League | Pos. | G. | AB. | R. | H. | 2B. | 3B. | HR. | RBI. | B.A. | PO. | A. | E. | F.A. |
|---|---|---|---|---|---|---|---|---|---|---|---|---|---|---|---|
| 1971—San Francisco | Nat. | OF | 3 | 8 | 0 | 2 | 0 | 0 | 0 | 0 | .250 | 3 | 0 | 1 | .750 |

### ALL-STAR GAME RECORD

| Year League | Pos. | AB. | R. | H. | 2B. | 3B. | HR. | RBI. | B.A. | PO. | A. | E. | F.A. |
|---|---|---|---|---|---|---|---|---|---|---|---|---|---|
| 1971—National | OF | 1 | 0 | 0 | 0 | 0 | 0 | 0 | .000 | 0 | 0 | 0 | .000 |
| 1973—National | OF | 2 | 1 | 2 | 1 | 0 | 1 | 2 | 1.000 | 0 | 0 | 0 | .000 |
| 1975—American | OF | 3 | 0 | 0 | 0 | 0 | 0 | 0 | .000 | 0 | 1 | 0 | 1.000 |
| All-Star Game Totals | | 6 | 1 | 2 | 1 | 0 | 1 | 2 | .333 | 0 | 1 | 0 | 1.000 |

## WILLIAM GORDON BONHAM
### (Bill)
Born October 1, 1948, at Glendale, Calif.
Height, 6.03. Weight, 195.
Throws and bats righthanded.
Hobby—Basketball.
Attended University of California at Los Angeles.

Tied major league records for most balks, season, 8, 1974; and most strikeouts, inning, 4, July 31, 1974 (1st game, 2nd inning).

| Year | Club | League | G. | IP. | W. | L. | Pct. | H. | R. | ER. | SO. | BB. | ERA. |
|---|---|---|---|---|---|---|---|---|---|---|---|---|---|
| 1970—Huron | | Northern | 18 | 39 | 3 | 3 | .500 | 27 | 20 | 13 | 69 | 24 | 3.00 |
| 1971—Tacoma | | P. Coast | 8 | 11 | 2 | 1 | .667 | 9 | 4 | 3 | 12 | 2 | 2.45 |
| 1971—Chicago | | National | 33 | 60 | 2 | 1 | .667 | 63 | 38 | 31 | 41 | 36 | 4.65 |
| 1972—Wichita | | Am. Assoc. | 18 | 125 | 10 | 4 | .714 | 120 | 57 | 49 | 116 | 41 | 3.53 |
| 1972—Chicago | | National | 19 | 58 | 1 | 1 | .500 | 56 | 22 | 20 | 49 | 25 | 3.10 |
| 1973—Chicago | | National | 44 | 152 | 7 | 5 | .583 | 126 | 55 | 51 | 121 | 64 | 3.02 |
| 1974—Chicago | | National | 44 | 243 | 11 | •22 | .333 | 246 | 133 | 104 | 191 | 109 | 3.85 |
| 1975—Chicago | | National | 38 | 229 | 13 | 15 | .464 | 254 | •133 | •120 | 165 | 109 | 4.72 |
| 1976—Chicago | | National | 32 | 196 | 9 | 13 | .409 | 215 | 102 | 93 | 110 | 96 | 4.27 |
| Major League Totals | | | 210 | 938 | 43 | 57 | .430 | 960 | 483 | 419 | 677 | 439 | 4.02 |

## ROBERT BARRY BONNELL
### (Known by middle name.)
Born October 27, 1953, at Cincinnati, O.
Height, 6:03. Weight, 190.
Throws and bats righthanded.
Hobbies—Flying, photography and amateur radio.
Attended Ohio State University, Columbus, O.
Brother of Glenn Bonnell, infielder in Cincinnati Reds' organization.

| Year | Club | League | Pos. | G. | AB. | R. | H. | 2B. | 3B. | HR. | RBI. | B.A. | PO. | A. | E. | F.A. |
|---|---|---|---|---|---|---|---|---|---|---|---|---|---|---|---|---|
| 1975—Spart.†-Green. | ..W.C. | | OF | 124 | 457 | 86 | 148 | 20 | 6 | 12 | 80 | •.324 | 276 | 19 | 12 | .961 |
| 1976—Savannah | | South. | OF | 51 | 188 | 31 | 42 | 6 | 2 | 6 | 23 | .223 | 117 | 6 | 5 | .961 |
| 1976—Richmond | | Int. | OF | 66 | 227 | 36 | 64 | 13 | 2 | 5 | 31 | .282 | 134 | 4 | 3 | .979 |

†Traded with Catcher Jim Essian and cash by Philadelphia Phillies to Atlanta Braves for First Baseman Dick Allen and Catcher Johnny Oates, May 7, 1975.
Invited to Atlanta Braves' 1977 spring camp.

## ROBERT RAYMOND BOONE
### (Bob)
Born November 19, 1947, at San Diego, Calif.
Height, 6.03. Weight, 200.
Throws and bats righthanded.
Hobbies—Fishing, golf and basketball.
Attended Stanford University, Palo Alto, Calif.; received Bachelor of Arts degree in Psychology.
Son of Raymond Otis Boone, former major league infielder and presently Boston Red Sox scout.
Brother of Rodney Alan Boone, catcher-outfielder in Kansas City Royal and Houston Astro organization, 1972 through 1975.

Led National League catchers in total chances with 924 in 1974.
Set Pacific Coast League modern (since 1958) record for errors by catcher with 24 and tied modern record for most times throwing out runners trying to steal with 41 in 1972.
Led Pacific Coast League catchers in passed balls with 18 and in double plays with 13 in 1972.
Tied for Carolina League lead in double plays by third basemen with 18 in 1969.
Named catcher on THE SPORTING NEWS National League All-Star Team, 1976.

| Year | Club | League | Pos. | G. | AB. | R. | H. | 2B. | 3B. | HR. | RBI. | B.A. | PO. | A. | E. | F.A. |
|---|---|---|---|---|---|---|---|---|---|---|---|---|---|---|---|---|
| 1969—Raleigh-Dur. | | Carol. | 3B | 80 | 300 | 45 | 90 | 13 | 1 | 5 | 46 | .300 | 71 | 160 | 20 | .920 |
| 1970—Reading† | | East. | 3B | 20 | 80 | 12 | 23 | 2 | 0 | 2 | 10 | .288 | 28 | 38 | 7 | .904 |
| 1971—Reading‡ | | East. | 3B-C-S | 92 | 328 | 41 | 87 | 14 | 3 | 4 | 37 | .265 | 206 | 138 | 17 | .953 |
| 1972—Eugene | | P. C. | C | 138 | 513 | 77 | 158 | 32 | 4 | 17 | 67 | .308 | •699 | •77 | •24 | .970 |
| 1972—Philadelphia | | Nat. | C | 16 | 51 | 4 | 14 | 1 | 0 | 1 | 4 | .275 | 66 | 7 | 5 | .936 |
| 1973—Philadelphia | | Nat. | C | 145 | 521 | 42 | 136 | 20 | 2 | 10 | 61 | .261 | 868 | •89 | 10 | .990 |
| 1974—Philadelphia | | Nat. | C | 146 | 488 | 41 | 118 | 24 | 3 | 3 | 52 | .242 | •825 | 77 | •22 | .976 |
| 1975—Philadelphia | | Nat. | C-3B | 97 | 289 | 28 | 71 | 14 | 2 | 2 | 20 | .246 | 459 | 48 | 5 | .990 |
| 1976—Philadelphia | | Nat. | C-1B | 121 | 361 | 40 | 98 | 18 | 2 | 4 | 54 | .271 | 587 | 39 | 6 | .990 |
| Major League Totals | | | | 525 | 1710 | 155 | 437 | 77 | 9 | 20 | 191 | .256 | 2805 | 260 | 48 | .984 |

†On military list, May 26 through remainder of season.
‡On disabled list from beginning of season until June 4, 1971.

### CHAMPIONSHIP SERIES RECORD

| Year | Club | League | Pos. | G. | AB. | R. | H. | 2B. | 3B. | HR. | RBI. | B.A. | PO. | A. | E. | F.A. |
|---|---|---|---|---|---|---|---|---|---|---|---|---|---|---|---|---|
| 1976—Philadelphia | | Nat. | C | 3 | 7 | 0 | 2 | 0 | 0 | 0 | 1 | .286 | 8 | 0 | 0 | 1.000 |

### ALL-STAR GAME RECORD

| Year | League | Pos. | AB. | R. | H. | 2B. | 3B. | HR. | RBI. | B.A. | PO. | A. | E. | F.A. |
|---|---|---|---|---|---|---|---|---|---|---|---|---|---|---|
| 1976—National | | C | 2 | 0 | 0 | 0 | 0 | 0 | 0 | .000 | 5 | 0 | 0 | 1.000 |

## PEDRO BORBON (RODRIGUEZ)

Name pronounced bor-BOHN.

Born December 2, 1946, at Valverde Mao, Dominican Republic.
Height, 6.02. Weight, 185.
Throws and bats righthanded.
Hobby—Rooster fights.

| Year    Club | League | G. | IP. | W. | L. | Pct. | H. | R. | ER. | SO. | BB. | ERA. |
|---|---|---|---|---|---|---|---|---|---|---|---|---|
| 1966—Cedar Rapids | Midwest | 38 | 69 | 6 | 1 | .857 | 53 | 22 | 15 | 58 | 16 | 1.96 |
| 1967—St. Petersburg | Florida St. | 36 | 63 | 5 | 4 | .556 | 52 | 22 | 16 | 50 | 17 | 2.29 |
| 1968—Modesto† | California | *65 | 100 | 8 | 5 | .615 | 99 | 34 | 26 | 96 | 22 | 2.34 |
| 1969—California‡§ | American | 22 | 41 | 2 | 3 | .400 | 55 | 31 | 28 | 20 | 11 | 6.15 |
| 1970—Indianapolis | Am. Assoc. | 32 | 71 | 5 | 2 | .714 | 81 | 27 | 26 | 53 | 29 | 3.30 |
| 1970—Cincinnati | National | 12 | 17 | 0 | 2 | .000 | 21 | 15 | 13 | 6 | 6 | 6.88 |
| 1971—Indianapolis | Am. Assoc. | 56 | 97 | 12 | 6 | .667 | 101 | 34 | 33 | 75 | 20 | 3.06 |
| 1971—Cincinnati | National | 3 | 4 | 0 | 0 | .000 | 3 | 3 | 2 | 4 | 1 | 4.50 |
| 1972—Cincinnati | National | 62 | 122 | 8 | 3 | .727 | 115 | 45 | 43 | 48 | 32 | 3.17 |
| 1973—Cincinnati | National | 80 | 121 | 11 | 4 | .733 | 137 | 33 | 29 | 60 | 35 | 2.16 |
| 1974—Cincinnati | National | 73 | 139 | 10 | 7 | .588 | 133 | 54 | 50 | 53 | 32 | 3.24 |
| 1975—Cincinnati | National | 67 | 125 | 9 | 5 | .643 | 145 | 47 | 41 | 29 | 21 | 2.95 |
| 1976—Cincinnati | National | 69 | 121 | 4 | 3 | .571 | 135 | 49 | 45 | 53 | 31 | 3.35 |
| American League Totals | | 22 | 41 | 2 | 3 | .400 | 55 | 31 | 28 | 20 | 11 | 6.15 |
| National League Totals | | 366 | 649 | 42 | 24 | .636 | 689 | 246 | 223 | 253 | 258 | 3.09 |
| Major League Totals | | 388 | 690 | 44 | 27 | .260 | 744 | 277 | 251 | 273 | 269 | 3.27 |

†Drafted by California Angels from Tulsa (St. Louis Cardinals' organziation), December 2, 1968.
‡On disabled list, May 7 through June 5, 1969.
§Traded with Pitchers Jim McGlothlin and Vern Geishert to Cincinnati Reds for Outfielder Alex Johnson and Infielder Chico Ruiz, November 25, 1969. Completed transaction of October 24, 1969, in which California acquired Pitcher Mel Queen from Indianapolis, Reds' affiliate.

### CHAMPIONSHIP SERIES RECORD

| Year    Club | League | G. | IP. | W. | L. | Pct. | H. | R. | ER. | SO. | BB. | ERA. |
|---|---|---|---|---|---|---|---|---|---|---|---|---|
| 1972—Cincinnati | National | 3 | 4⅓ | 0 | 0 | .000 | 2 | 1 | 1 | 1 | 0 | 2.08 |
| 1973—Cincinnati | National | 4 | 4⅔ | 1 | 0 | 1.000 | 3 | 0 | 0 | 3 | 0 | 0.00 |
| 1975—Cincinnati | National | 1 | 1 | 0 | 0 | .000 | 0 | 0 | 0 | 1 | 0 | 0.00 |
| 1976—Cincinnati | National | 2 | 4⅓ | 0 | 0 | .000 | 4 | 0 | 0 | 0 | 1 | 0.00 |
| Championship Series Totals | | 10 | 14⅓ | 1 | 0 | 1.000 | 9 | 1 | 1 | 5 | 1 | 0.63 |

### WORLD SERIES RECORD

| Year    Club | League | G. | IP. | W. | L. | Pct. | H. | R. | ER. | SO. | BB. | ERA. |
|---|---|---|---|---|---|---|---|---|---|---|---|---|
| 1972—Cincinnati | National | 6 | 7 | 0 | 1 | .000 | 7 | 3 | 3 | 4 | 2 | 3.86 |
| 1975—Cincinnati | National | 3 | 3 | 0 | 0 | .000 | 3 | 3 | 2 | 1 | 2 | 6.00 |
| 1976—Cincinnati | National | 1 | 1⅔ | 0 | 0 | .000 | 0 | 0 | 0 | 0 | 0 | 0.00 |
| World Series Totals | | 10 | 11⅔ | 0 | 1 | .000 | 10 | 6 | 5 | 5 | 4 | 3.86 |

## GLENN DENNIS BORGMANN

Born May 25, 1950, at Paterson, N. J.
Height, 6.02. Weight, 210.
Throws and bats righthanded.
Hobbies—Fishing, hunting and playing cards.
Attended Miami-Dade (North) Community College, Miami, Fla., and
University of South Alabama, Mobile, Ala.

| Year    Club | League | Pos. | G. | AB. | R. | H. | 2B. | 3B. | HR. | RBI. | B.A. | PO. | A. | E. | F.A. |
|---|---|---|---|---|---|---|---|---|---|---|---|---|---|---|---|
| 1971—Wis. Rapids | Midw. | C-1B | 55 | 182 | 27 | 64 | 8 | 0 | 7 | 28 | .352 | 348 | 45 | 6 | .985 |
| 1971—Charlotte | South. | C-OF | 22 | 70 | 10 | 18 | 4 | 1 | 3 | 15 | .257 | 113 | 7 | 0 | 1.000 |
| 1972—Tacoma | P. C. | C-1B | 66 | 235 | 37 | 79 | 13 | 0 | 12 | 39 | .336 | 440 | 39 | 3 | .994 |
| 1972—Minnesota | Amer. | C | 56 | 175 | 11 | 41 | 4 | 0 | 3 | 14 | .234 | 304 | 31 | 12 | .965 |
| 1973—Tacoma | P. C. | C | 136 | 485 | 69 | 133 | 18 | 3 | 8 | 71 | .274 | 570 | 63 | 12 | .981 |
| 1973—Minnesota | Amer. | C | 12 | 34 | 7 | 9 | 2 | 0 | 0 | 9 | .265 | 55 | 2 | 0 | 1.000 |
| 1974—Minnesota | Amer. | C | 128 | 345 | 33 | 87 | 8 | 1 | 3 | 45 | .252 | 652 | 52 | 2 | *.997 |
| 1975—Minnesota | Amer. | C | 125 | 352 | 34 | 73 | 15 | 2 | 2 | 33 | .207 | 618 | 81 | 8 | .989 |
| 1976—Minnesota | Amer. | C | 24 | 65 | 10 | 16 | 3 | 0 | 1 | 6 | .246 | 110 | 13 | 3 | .976 |
| Major League Totals | | | 345 | 971 | 95 | 226 | 32 | 3 | 9 | 107 | .233 | 1739 | 179 | 25 | .987 |

## RICHARD ALAN BOSETTI

Name pronounced boh-SET-ee.

### (Rick)

Born August 5, 1953, at Redding, Calif.
Height, 5.11. Weight, 185.
Throws and bats righthanded.
Attended Shasta College, Redding, Calif.

Led New York-Pennsylvania League third basemen in double plays with 16 in 1973.
Led New York-Pennsylvania League in total bases with 125 and in stolen bases with 27 in 1973.
Led American Association in stolen bases with 42 in 1976.

| Year Club League | Pos. | G. | AB. | R. | H. | 2B. | 3B. | HR. | RBI. | B.A. | PO. | A. | E. | F.A. |
|---|---|---|---|---|---|---|---|---|---|---|---|---|---|---|
| 1973—Spartanburg ......W. Car. | 3B | 26 | 79 | 4 | 18 | 4 | 0 | 0 | 5 | .228 | 14 | 25 | 11 | .780 |
| 1973—Auburn..............NYP | *3B-2B | 67 | *282 | *68 | 94 | 13 | 3 | 4 | 34 | .333 | 34 | *158 | *30 | .881 |
| 1974—Rocky Mount ....Carol. | 3B | 37 | 157 | 27 | 39 | 5 | 2 | 1 | 11 | .248 | 26 | 73 | 15 | .868 |
| 1974—Reading ...........East. | OF-3B | 93 | 308 | 37 | 82 | 15 | 4 | 4 | 35 | .266 | 82 | 92 | 12 | .935 |
| 1975—Reading ...........East. | OF-3B | 110 | 432 | 73 | 118 | 21 | 5 | 6 | 34 | .273 | 233 | 18 | 6 | .977 |
| 1976—Oklahoma City† A.A. | OF | 123 | *504 | 82 | *154 | 25 | 6 | 5 | 52 | .306 | *273 | 12 | 9 | .969 |
| 1976—Philadelphia ......Nat. | OF | 13 | 18 | 6 | 5 | 1 | 0 | 0 | 0 | .278 | 9 | 1 | 0 | 1.000 |
| Major League Totals ..................... | | 13 | 18 | 6 | 5 | 1 | 0 | 0 | 0 | .278 | 9 | 1 | 0 | 1.000 |

†On disabled list, June 10 through June 20, 1976.

## THADDIS BOSLEY, JR.

Born September 17, 1956, at Oceanside, Calif.
Height, 6.03. Weight, 175.
Throws and bats lefthanded.
Hobby—Music; composing, playing and singing.
Attended Mira Costa Community College, Oceanside, Calif.

Led Pioneer League in base on balls with 71 in 1974.
Led California League in stolen bases with 90 in 1976.
Named California League Player of the Year, 1976.

| Year Club League | Pos. | G. | AB. | R. | H. | 2B. | 3B. | HR. | RBI. | B.A. | PO. | A. | E. | F.A. |
|---|---|---|---|---|---|---|---|---|---|---|---|---|---|---|
| 1974—Idaho Falls........Pion. | OF | 68 | 223 | 55 | 54 | 3 | 4 | 0 | 14 | .242 | 101 | 4 | *11 | .905 |
| 1975—Quad Cities† ......Midw. | OF | 108 | 379 | 67 | 113 | 12 | 3 | 1 | 50 | .298 | 206 | 2 | 4 | *.981 |
| 1976—Salinas ..............Calif. | OF | 134 | 527 | 105 | 171 | 26 | 4 | 2 | 72 | *.324 | 285 | 13 | 7 | *.977 |

†On disabled list, April 19 through May 6, 1975.
Listed on California Angels' 1977 spring roster.

## RICHARD ALLEN BOSMAN
### (Dick)

Born February 17, 1944, at Kenosha, Wis.
Height, 6.02½. Weight, 205.
Throws and bats righthanded.
Hobbies—Drag racing, water skiing, hunting and fishing.
Attended University of Wisconsin, Madison, Wis.
Second cousin of Duane Kuiper, second baseman with Cleveland Indians.

Pitched 4-0 no-hit victory against Oakland Athletics, July 19, 1974.

| Year Club | League | G. | IP. | W. | L. | Pct. | H. | R. | ER. | SO. | BB. | ERA. |
|---|---|---|---|---|---|---|---|---|---|---|---|---|
| 1963—Kingsport† .........................Ap'lachian | | 21 | 46 | 3 | 3 | .500 | 50 | 26 | 18 | 66 | 23 | 3.52 |
| 1964—Lexington‡ ..........................W. Carol. | | 35 | 129 | 8 | 5 | .615 | 100 | 62 | 46 | 132 | 77 | 3.21 |
| 1965—York ...................................Eastern | | 42 | 144 | 6 | 8 | .429 | 136 | 69 | 59 | 86 | 70 | 3.69 |
| 1966—York ...................................Eastern | | 16 | 121 | 8 | 5 | .615 | 96 | 50 | 45 | 78 | 46 | 3.35 |
| 1966—Washington .........................American | | 13 | 39 | 2 | 6 | .250 | 60 | 36 | 33 | 20 | 12 | 7.62 |
| 1967—Hawaii ...............................P. Coast | | 26 | 196 | 12 | 11 | .522 | 185 | 72 | 60 | 115 | 41 | 2.76 |
| 1967—Washington .........................American | | 7 | 51 | 3 | 1 | .750 | 38 | 12 | 10 | 25 | 10 | 1.76 |
| 1968—Washington .........................American | | 46 | 139 | 2 | 9 | .182 | 139 | 63 | 57 | 63 | 35 | 3.69 |
| 1969—Buffalo ...............................Int'national | | 1 | 2 | 0 | 0 | .000 | 6 | 3 | 3 | 2 | 0 | 13.50 |
| 1969—Washington .........................American | | 31 | 193 | 14 | 5 | .737 | 156 | 59 | 47 | 99 | 39 | *2.19 |
| 1970—Washington .........................American | | 36 | 231 | 16 | 12 | .571 | 212 | 81 | 77 | 134 | 71 | 3.00 |
| 1971—Washington .........................American | | 35 | 237 | 12 | 16 | .429 | 245 | 110 | 98 | 113 | 71 | 3.72 |
| 1972—Texas‡‡..............................American | | 29 | 173 | 8 | 10 | .444 | 183 | 87 | 70 | 105 | 48 | 3.64 |
| 1973—Texas§-Cleveland.................American | | 29 | 137 | 3 | 13 | .188 | 172 | 98 | 86 | 55 | 46 | 5.65 |
| 1974—Cleveland ...........................American | | 25 | 127 | 7 | 5 | .583 | 126 | 69 | 58 | 56 | 29 | 4.11 |
| 1975—Cleveland x-Oakland ...........American | | 28 | 151 | 11 | 6 | .647 | 145 | 67 | 61 | 53 | 32 | 3.64 |
| 1976—Oakland y ...........................American | | 27 | 112 | 4 | 2 | .667 | 118 | 54 | 51 | 34 | 19 | 4.10 |
| Major League Totals ............................. | | 306 | 1590 | 82 | 85 | .491 | 1594 | 736 | 648 | 757 | 412 | 3.67 |

†Drafted by San Francisco Giants from Columbus (Pittsburgh Pirates' organization), December 2, 1963.
‡Drafted from San Francisco Giants' organization by York (Washington Senators' organization), November 30, 1964.
‡‡On disabled list, July 8 through July 29, 1972.
§Traded with Outfielder Ted Ford (assigned to Oklahoma City) to Cleveland Indians for Pitcher Steve Dunning, May 10, 1973.
xTraded with Pitcher Jim Perry to Oakland Athletics for Pitcher Johnny (Blue Moon) Odom and cash, May 20, 1975.
yReleased March 26, 1977.

### CHAMPIONSHIP SERIES RECORD

| Year Club | League | G. | IP. | W. | L. | Pct. | H. | R. | ER. | SO. | BB. | ERA. |
|---|---|---|---|---|---|---|---|---|---|---|---|---|
| 1975—Oakland ..............................American | | 1 | ⅓ | 0 | 0 | .000 | 0 | 0 | 0 | 0 | 0 | 0.00 |

## LYMAN WESLEY BOSTOCK

Born November 22, 1950, at Birmingham, Ala.
Height, 6.01. Weight, 180.
Throws right and bats lefthanded.
Attended California State University, Northridge, Calif.
Son of Lyman Bostock, Sr., who played in Negro professional leagues for Birmingham Black Barons, Chicago American Giants and New York Cubans, 1940 through 1949.

| Year Club League | Pos. | G. | AB. | R. | H. | 2B. | 3B. | HR. | RBI. | B.A. | PO. | A. | E. | F.A. |
|---|---|---|---|---|---|---|---|---|---|---|---|---|---|---|
| 1972—Charlotte ..........W. Car. | OF | 57 | 177 | 27 | 52 | 12 | 2 | 0 | 27 | .294 | 75 | 5 | 3 | .964 |
| 1973—Orlando† ..........South. | OF | 85 | 297 | 49 | 93 | 18 | 2 | 5 | 37 | .313 | 160 | 4 | 5 | .970 |
| 1974—Tacoma ............P.C. | OF | 128 | 475 | 73 | 158 | 17 | 2 | 7 | 56 | .333 | 242 | 9 | 12 | .954 |
| 1975—Tacoma ............P.C. | OF | 22 | 92 | 16 | 36 | 5 | 0 | 0 | 13 | .391 | 55 | 0 | 2 | .965 |
| 1975—Minnesota‡ .......Amer. | OF | 98 | 369 | 52 | 104 | 21 | 5 | 0 | 29 | .282 | 188 | 3 | 3 | .985 |
| 1976—Minnesota ........Amer. | OF | 128 | 474 | 75 | 153 | 21 | 9 | 4 | 60 | .323 | 320 | 10 | 4 | .988 |
| Major League Totals ..................... | | 226 | 843 | 127 | 257 | 42 | 14 | 4 | 89 | .305 | 508 | 13 | 7 | .987 |

†On disabled list, May 16 to June 5, 1973.
‡On disabled list, May 4 to June 4, 1975.

## KENNETH GEORGE BOSWELL
### (Ken)

Born February 23, 1946, at Austin, Tex.
Height, 6.00. Weight, 170.
Throws right and bats lefthanded.
Attended Sam Houston State College, Huntsville, Tex.

Established major league record for highest fielding average, second baseman, 100 or more games, .996, 1970.
Established National League records for most errorless games, consecutive, second baseman, season, 85, April 30 through September 26, 1970, 391 chances accepted; and longest game with no chances by a second baseman, 13 innings, August 7, 1972.
Named Rookie of the Year in New York-Pennsylvania League, 1965.

| Year Club League | Pos. | G. | AB. | R. | H. | 2B. | 3B. | HR. | RBI. | B.A. | PO. | A. | E. | F.A. |
|---|---|---|---|---|---|---|---|---|---|---|---|---|---|---|
| 1965—Auburn..............NYP | 2B | 73 | 298 | 49 | 85 | 20 | 1 | 7 | 33 | .285 | 140 | 186 | 14 | .959 |
| 1966—Williamsport......East. | 2B | 63 | 241 | 43 | 72 | 15 | 3 | 1 | 36 | .299 | 163 | 193 | 19 | .949 |
| 1966—Jacksonville ......Int. | 2-3-SS | 80 | 298 | 28 | 76 | 9 | 3 | 2 | 22 | .255 | 145 | 199 | 13 | .964 |
| 1967—New York.........Nat. | 2B-3B | 11 | 40 | 2 | 9 | 3 | 0 | 1 | 4 | .225 | 12 | 34 | 1 | .979 |
| 1967—Jacksonville ......Int. | 2B | 52 | 197 | 19 | 49 | 9 | 2 | 3 | 15 | .249 | 118 | 120 | 9 | .964 |
| 1968—New York†.......Nat. | 2B | 75 | 284 | 37 | 74 | 7 | 2 | 4 | 11 | .261 | 154 | 203 | 13 | .965 |
| 1969—New York‡........Nat. | 2B | 102 | 362 | 48 | 101 | 14 | 7 | 3 | 32 | .279 | 190 | 229 | 18 | .959 |
| 1970—New York‡........Nat. | 2B | 105 | 351 | 32 | 89 | 13 | 2 | 5 | 44 | .254 | 204 | 244 | 2 | .996 |
| 1971—New York.........Nat. | 2B | 116 | 392 | 46 | 107 | 20 | 1 | 5 | 40 | .273 | 191 | 234 | 12 | .973 |
| 1972—New York.........Nat. | 2B | 100 | 355 | 35 | 75 | 9 | 1 | 9 | 33 | .211 | 208 | 183 | 4 | .990 |
| 1973—New York.........Nat. | 3B-2B | 76 | 110 | 12 | 25 | 2 | 1 | 2 | 14 | .227 | 15 | 33 | 2 | .960 |
| 1974—New York§........Nat. | 2-3-O | 96 | 222 | 19 | 48 | 6 | 1 | 2 | 15 | .216 | 94 | 113 | 6 | .972 |
| 1975—Houston ...........Nat. | 2B-3B | 86 | 178 | 16 | 43 | 8 | 2 | 0 | 21 | .242 | 54 | 103 | 6 | .963 |
| 1976—Houston ...........Nat. | 3-2-OF | 91 | 126 | 12 | 33 | 8 | 1 | 0 | 18 | .262 | 8 | 21 | 2 | .935 |
| Major League Totals ..................... | | 858 | 2420 | 259 | 604 | 90 | 18 | 31 | 222 | .250 | 1130 | 1397 | 66 | .974 |

†On disabled list with broken finger on right hand from June 25 through August 19.
‡On military list, July 14 to August 3, 1970.
§Traded to Houston Astros for Outfielder Bob Gallagher, October 29, 1974.

### CHAMPIONSHIP SERIES RECORD

| Year Club League | Pos. | G. | AB. | R. | H. | 2B. | 3B. | HR. | RBI. | B.A. | PO. | A. | E. | F.A. |
|---|---|---|---|---|---|---|---|---|---|---|---|---|---|---|
| 1969—New York.........Nat. | 2B | 3 | 12 | 4 | 4 | 0 | 0 | 2 | 5 | .333 | 3 | 2 | 1 | .833 |
| 1973—New York.........Nat. | PH | 1 | 1 | 0 | 0 | 0 | 0 | 0 | 0 | .000 | 0 | 0 | 0 | .000 |
| Championship Series Totals ............ | | 4 | 13 | 4 | 4 | 0 | 0 | 2 | 5 | .308 | 3 | 2 | 1 | .833 |

### WORLD SERIES RECORD

Tied World Series record for most pinch-hits, series, 3, 1973.

| Year Club League | Pos. | G. | AB. | R. | H. | 2B. | 3B. | HR. | RBI. | B.A. | PO. | A. | E. | F.A. |
|---|---|---|---|---|---|---|---|---|---|---|---|---|---|---|
| 1969—New York.........Nat. | 2B | 1 | 3 | 1 | 1 | 0 | 0 | 0 | 0 | .333 | 0 | 1 | 0 | 1.000 |
| 1973—New York.........Nat. | PH | 3 | 3 | 1 | 3 | 0 | 0 | 0 | 0 | 1.000 | 0 | 0 | 0 | .000 |
| World Series Totals ..................... | | 4 | 6 | 2 | 4 | 0 | 0 | 0 | 0 | .667 | 0 | 1 | 0 | 1.000 |

## LAWRENCE ROBERT BOWA
### (Larry)

Born December 6, 1945, at Sacramento, Calif.
Height, 5.11. Weight, 155.
Throws right and bats left and righthanded.
Hobbies—Golf and billiards.
Attended Sacramento City College, Sacramento, Calif.
Son of Paul Bowa, former minor league infielder and manager,
and nephew of Frank Bowa, former minor league infielder.

Tied major league record for most at bats, game, since 1900, 7, July 12, 1975.
Established National League records for highest fielding percentage, shortstop, season (.9874), 1972; fewest errors, season, 150 or more games, by shortstop, 9, 1972.
Established major league record for highest fielding percentage, shortstop, lifetime (1,000 + games), .979.
Major League stolen bases: 1970 (24), 1971 (28), 1972 (17), 1973 (10), 1974 (39), 1975 (24), 1976 (30). Total 172.
Led National League in sacrifice hits with 18 in 1972.
Led National League shortstops in total chances with 843 in 1971.
Tied for National League lead in double plays by shortstops with 97 in 1971.
Led Pacific Coast League in stolen bases with 48 in 1969.
Led Eastern League shortstops in double plays with 77 in 1968.
Named shortstop on THE SPORTING NEWS National League All-Star fielding team, 1972.
Named shortstop on THE SPORTING NEWS National League All-Star Team, 1975.

| Year | Club | League | Pos. | G. | AB. | R. | H. | 2B. | 3B. | HR. | RBI. | B.A. | PO. | A. | E. | F.A. |
|---|---|---|---|---|---|---|---|---|---|---|---|---|---|---|---|---|
| 1966–Spartanburg | ......W. Car. | | SS | 97 | 429 | 70 | 134 | 14 | 4 | 2 | 36 | .312 | 138 | 284 | 12 | *.972 |
| 1966–San Diego | ..........P.C. | | SS | 5 | 19 | 0 | 6 | 0 | 1 | 0 | 1 | .316 | 13 | 20 | 2 | .943 |
| 1967–Bakersfield† | ......Calif. | | SS-2B | 7 | 32 | 4 | 6 | 2 | 0 | 0 | 3 | .188 | 15 | 12 | 1 | .964 |
| 1967–Reading | ............East. | | SS | 22 | 89 | 11 | 25 | 4 | 0 | 0 | 9 | .281 | 35 | 79 | 9 | .927 |
| 1968–Reading | ............East. | | SS | 133 | 480 | 47 | 116 | 14 | 2 | 3 | 36 | .242 | 192 | ●395 | 24 | .961 |
| 1969–Eugene | ..............P.C. | | *SS-2 | 135 | 568 | 80 | 163 | 11 | 6 | 1 | 26 | .287 | *215 | *469 | 18 | *.974 |
| 1970–Philadelphia | ......Nat. | | SS-2B | 145 | 547 | 50 | 137 | 17 | 6 | 0 | 34 | .250 | 202 | 418 | 13 | .979 |
| 1971–Philadelphia | ......Nat. | | SS | 159 | *650 | 74 | 162 | 18 | 5 | 0 | 25 | .249 | 272 | *560 | 11 | *.987 |
| 1972–Philadelphia | ......Nat. | | SS | 152 | 579 | 67 | 145 | 11 | *13 | 1 | 31 | .250 | 212 | 494 | 9 | *.987 |
| 1973–Philadelphia‡ | ....Nat. | | SS | 122 | 446 | 42 | 94 | 11 | 3 | 0 | 23 | .211 | 191 | 361 | 12 | .979 |
| 1974–Philadelphia | ......Nat. | | SS | 162 | 669 | 97 | 184 | 19 | 10 | 1 | 36 | .275 | 256 | 462 | 12 | *.984 |
| 1975–Philadelphia§ | ....Nat. | | SS | 136 | 583 | 79 | 178 | 18 | 9 | 2 | 38 | .305 | 227 | 403 | 25 | .962 |
| 1976–Philadelphia | ......Nat. | | SS | 156 | 624 | 71 | 155 | 15 | 9 | 0 | 49 | .248 | 180 | 492 | 17 | .975 |
| Major League Totals | ...................... | | | 1032 | 4098 | 480 | 1055 | 109 | 55 | 4 | 236 | .257 | 1540 | 3190 | 99 | .979 |

†In military service from beginning of season to July 18.
‡On disabled list, July 26 to September 1, 1973.
§On supplemental disabled list, May 27 to June 23, 1975.

### CHAMPIONSHIP SERIES RECORD

| Year | Club | League | Pos. | G. | AB. | R. | H. | 2B. | 3B. | HR. | RBI. | B.A. | PO. | A. | E. | F.A. |
|---|---|---|---|---|---|---|---|---|---|---|---|---|---|---|---|---|
| 1976–Philadelphia | ......Nat. | | SS | 3 | 8 | 1 | 1 | 1 | 0 | 0 | 1 | .125 | 2 | 11 | 0 | 1.000 |

### ALL-STAR GAME RECORD

| Year | League | Pos. | AB. | R. | H. | 2B. | 3B. | HR. | RBI. | B.A. | PO. | A. | E. | F.A. |
|---|---|---|---|---|---|---|---|---|---|---|---|---|---|---|
| 1974–National | ............................. | SS | 2 | 0 | 0 | 0 | 0 | 0 | 0 | .000 | 2 | 0 | 0 | 1.000 |
| 1975–National | ............................. | SS | 0 | 1 | 0 | 0 | 0 | 0 | 0 | .000 | 2 | 0 | 0 | 1.000 |
| 1976–National | ............................. | SS | 1 | 0 | 0 | 0 | 0 | 0 | 0 | .000 | 2 | 1 | 0 | 1.000 |
| All-Star Game Totals | ...................... | | 3 | 1 | 0 | 0 | 0 | 0 | 0 | .000 | 6 | 1 | 0 | 1.000 |

## STEPHEN SHADDON BOWLING
### (Steve)

Born June 26, 1952, at Tulsa, Okla.
Height, 6.00. Weight, 185.
Throws and bats righthanded.
Hobbies–Golf and fishing.
Attended University of Tulsa, Tulsa, Okla.

Led New York-Pennsylvania League outfielders in double plays with 6 in 1974.
Led Pacific Coast League outfielders in double plays with 4 in 1976.

| Year | Club | League | Pos. | G. | AB. | R. | H. | 2B. | 3B. | HR. | RBI. | B.A. | PO. | A. | E. | F.A. |
|---|---|---|---|---|---|---|---|---|---|---|---|---|---|---|---|---|
| 1974–Newark | ............NYP | | OF | 67 | 215 | 49 | 64 | 11 | 2 | *12 | 35 | .298 | *157 | 10 | 6 | .965 |
| 1975–Sacramento | ......P.C. | | OF | 139 | 447 | 70 | 106 | 12 | 1 | 20 | 61 | .237 | 298 | 13 | 5 | .984 |
| 1976–Spokane | ...........P.C. | | OF | 137 | 470 | 59 | 125 | 25 | 7 | 16 | 92 | .266 | 290 | 16 | 4 | .987 |
| 1976–Milwaukee† | ......Amer. | | OF-DH | 14 | 42 | 4 | 7 | 2 | 0 | 0 | 2 | .167 | 38 | 1 | 1 | .975 |
| Major League Totals | ...................... | | | 14 | 42 | 4 | 7 | 2 | 0 | 0 | 2 | .167 | 38 | 1 | 1 | .975 |

†Selected by Toronto Blue Jays in American League expansion draft, November 5, 1976.
Listed on Toronto Blue Jays' 1977 spring roster.

## STEPHEN RUSSELL BRAUN, III
### (Steve)

Born May 8, 1948, at Trenton, N. J.
Height, 5.10. Weight, 180.
Throws right and bats lefthanded.

Led Gulf Coast League second basemen in double plays with 47 in 1967.

| Year | Club | League | Pos. | G. | AB. | R. | H. | 2B. | 3B. | HR. | RBI. | B.A. | PO. | A. | E. | F.A. |
|---|---|---|---|---|---|---|---|---|---|---|---|---|---|---|---|---|
| 1966–Sarasota Twins | ..Gulf C. | | 2B | 45 | 152 | 23 | 35 | 5 | *5 | 0 | 15 | .230 | 70 | 85 | *16 | .906 |
| 1967–Wis. Rapids | ......Midw. | | 2B | 10 | 9 | 1 | 2 | 1 | 0 | 0 | 2 | .222 | 0 | 0 | 0 | .000 |
| 1967–Sar. Twins† | ......Gulf C. | | 2B | 54 | 184 | 37 | 45 | 6 | *8 | 1 | 13 | .245 | *111 | *153 | *14 | .950 |
| 1970–Lynchburg | ........Carol. | | *3-2B | 118 | 387 | 52 | 108 | 24 | 1 | 4 | 43 | .279 | 109 | 253 | 29 | *.926 |
| 1971–Minnesota | ........Amer. | | 3-2-S-O | 128 | 343 | 51 | 87 | 12 | 2 | 5 | 35 | .254 | 107 | 193 | 13 | .958 |
| 1972–Minnesota | ........Amer. | | 3-2-S-O | 121 | 402 | 40 | 116 | 21 | 0 | 2 | 50 | .289 | 110 | 207 | 13 | .961 |
| 1973–Minnesota | ........Amer. | | 3B-OF | 115 | 361 | 46 | 102 | 28 | 5 | 6 | 42 | .283 | 86 | 175 | 16 | .942 |
| 1974–Minnesota | ........Amer. | | OF-3B | 129 | 453 | 53 | 127 | 12 | 1 | 8 | 40 | .280 | 195 | 47 | 12 | .953 |
| 1975–Minnesota | ........Amer. | | O-1-3-2 | 136 | 453 | 70 | 137 | 18 | 3 | 11 | 45 | .302 | 271 | 14 | 10 | .966 |
| 1976–Minnesota‡ | ........Amer. | | OF-3-DH | 122 | 417 | 73 | 120 | 12 | 3 | 3 | 61 | .288 | 71 | 32 | 6 | .945 |
| Major League Totals | ........................... | | | 751 | 2429 | 333 | 689 | 103 | 14 | 35 | 273 | .284 | 840 | 668 | 70 | .956 |

†On military list, September 6, 1967, to September 23, 1969.
‡Selected by Seattle Mariners in American League expansion draft, November 5, 1976.
Listed on Seattle Mariners' 1977 spring roster.

---

## *DID YOU KNOW* —
That Joe Jackson hit .408 for Cleveland in 1911 but failed to lead the American League in batting? Detroit's Ty Cobb led the circuit with .420.

---

## GEORGE HOWARD BRETT

Born May 15, 1953, at Wheeling, W. Va.
Height, 6.00. Weight, 195.
Throws right and bats lefthanded.
Hobbies—Horses and surfing.
Attended El Camino College, Torrance, Calif.
Brother of Ken Brett, pitcher with Chicago White Sox, and John Brett,
former third baseman in Boston Red Sox' organization.

Tied major league record for most consecutive seasons leading major leagues, three-base hits—2.
Led California League in sacrifice hits with 8 in 1972.
Led American League batters in total bases with 298 in 1976.
Named third baseman on THE SPORTING NEWS American League All-Star Team, 1976.

| Year Club | League | Pos. | G. | AB. | R. | H. | 2B. | 3B. | HR. | RBI. | B.A. | PO. | A. | E. | F.A. |
|---|---|---|---|---|---|---|---|---|---|---|---|---|---|---|---|
| 1971—Billings ............ | Pion. | SS-3B | 68 | 258 | 44 | 75 | 8 | 5 | 5 | 44 | .291 | 87 | 140 | 28 | .890 |
| 1972—San José† ......... | Calif. | •3-S-2 | 117 | 431 | 66 | 118 | 13 | 5 | 10 | 68 | .274 | 101 | •213 | •30 | .913 |
| 1973—Omaha ............. | A.A. | 3B-OF | 117 | 405 | 66 | 115 | 16 | 4 | 8 | 64 | .284 | 92 | 219 | 26 | .923 |
| 1973—Kansas City ...... | Amer. | 3B | 13 | 40 | 2 | 5 | 2 | 0 | 0 | 0 | .125 | 9 | 28 | 1 | .974 |
| 1974—Omaha ............. | A.A. | 3B | 16 | 64 | 9 | 17 | 2 | 0 | 2 | 14 | .266 | 8 | 31 | 4 | .907 |
| 1974—Kansas City ...... | Amer. | 3B-SS | 133 | 457 | 49 | 129 | 21 | 5 | 2 | 47 | .282 | 102 | 279 | 21 | .948 |
| 1975—Kansas City ...... | Amer. | •3B-SS | 159 | •634 | 84 | •195 | 35 | •13 | 11 | 89 | .308 | 132 | 356 | •26 | .949 |
| 1976—Kansas City ...... | Amer. | •3B-SS | 159 | •645 | 94 | •215 | 34 | •14 | 7 | 67 | •.333 | •146 | 350 | 26 | .950 |
| Major League Totals ..................... | | | 464 | 1776 | 229 | 544 | 92 | 32 | 20 | 203 | .306 | 389 | 1013 | 74 | .950 |

†On disabled list, April 29 to May 11, 1972.

### CHAMPIONSHIP SERIES RECORD

| Year Club | League | Pos. | G. | AB. | R. | H. | 2B. | 3B. | HR. | RBI. | B.A. | PO. | A. | E. | F.A. |
|---|---|---|---|---|---|---|---|---|---|---|---|---|---|---|---|
| 1976—Kansas City ...... | Amer. | 3B | 5 | 18 | 4 | 8 | 1 | 1 | 1 | 5 | .444 | 3 | 7 | 3 | .769 |

### ALL-STAR GAME RECORD

| Year League | Pos. | AB. | R. | H. | 2B. | 3B. | HR. | RBI. | B.A. | PO. | A. | E. | F.A. |
|---|---|---|---|---|---|---|---|---|---|---|---|---|---|
| 1976—American ........................... | 3B | 2 | 0 | 0 | 0 | 0 | 0 | 0 | .000 | 0 | 1 | 0 | 1.000 |

## KENNETH ALVEN BRETT
### (Ken)

Born September 18, 1948, at Brooklyn, N. Y.
Height, 6.00. Weight, 195.
Throws and bats lefthanded.
Hobbies—Golf and photography.
Attended Boston University, Boston, Mass.
Brother of George Brett, Kansas City Royals' third baseman, and John Brett, former third
baseman in Boston Red Sox' organization.

Established major league record for most consecutive games, home runs by pitcher, 4, June
9-13-18-23, 1973.
Tied for International League lead in wild pitches with 12 in 1969.
Received reported $85,000 bonus to sign with Boston Red Sox, 1969.

| Year Club | League | G. | IP. | W. | L. | Pct. | H. | R. | ER. | SO. | BB. | ERA. |
|---|---|---|---|---|---|---|---|---|---|---|---|---|
| 1966—Oneonta ..................... | NYP | 14 | 62 | 1 | 4 | .200 | 75 | 49 | 40 | 53 | 39 | 5.81 |
| 1967—Winston-Salem ................... | Carolina | 11 | 64 | 4 | 4 | .500 | 42 | 19 | 16 | 77 | 38 | 2.25 |
| 1967—Pittsfield ............................. | Eastern | 18 | 125 | 10 | 7 | .588 | 87 | 30 | 25 | 142 | 59 | 1.80 |
| 1967—Boston ............................. | American | 1 | 2 | 0 | 0 | .000 | 3 | 1 | 1 | 2 | 0 | 4.50 |
| 1968—Louisville† ......................... | Int'national | 9 | 29 | 2 | 1 | .667 | 25 | 12 | 10 | 20 | 13 | 3.10 |
| 1969—Louisville .......................... | Int'national | 25 | 129 | 7 | 5 | .583 | 122 | 58 | 47 | 81 | 56 | 3.28 |
| 1969—Boston ............................. | American | 8 | 39 | 2 | 3 | .400 | 41 | 24 | 23 | 23 | 22 | 5.31 |
| 1970—Boston ............................. | American | 41 | 139 | 8 | 9 | .471 | 118 | 71 | 63 | 155 | 79 | 4.08 |
| 1971—Boston‡ ............................. | American | 29 | 59 | 0 | 3 | .000 | 57 | 38 | 35 | 57 | 35 | 5.34 |
| 1972—Milwaukee§ ......................... | American | 26 | 133 | 7 | 12 | .368 | 121 | 76 | 67 | 74 | 49 | 4.53 |
| 1973—Philadelphia x ..................... | National | 31 | 212 | 13 | 9 | .591 | 206 | 91 | 81 | 111 | 74 | 3.44 |
| 1974—Pittsburgh ......................... | National | 27 | 191 | 13 | 9 | .591 | 192 | 81 | 70 | 96 | 52 | 3.30 |
| 1975—Pittsburgh y z ..................... | National | 23 | 118 | 9 | 5 | .643 | 110 | 47 | 44 | 47 | 43 | 3.36 |
| 1976—N.Y. a-Chicago ................... | American | 29 | 203 | 10 | 12 | .455 | 173 | 82 | 74 | 92 | 76 | 3.28 |
| American League Totals............... | | 134 | 575 | 27 | 39 | .409 | 513 | 292 | 263 | 403 | 261 | 4.12 |
| National League Totals............... | | 81 | 521 | 35 | 23 | .603 | 508 | 219 | 195 | 254 | 169 | 3.37 |
| Major League Totals ................... | | 215 | 1096 | 62 | 62 | .500 | 1021 | 511 | 458 | 657 | 430 | 3.76 |

†On disabled list with arm trouble for six weeks of season.
‡Traded with Catcher Don Pavletich, Pitcher Jim Lonborg, First Baseman George Scott and Outfielders
Billy Conigliaro and Joe Lahoud to Milwaukee Brewers for Pitchers Marty Pattin and Lew Krausse and Outfielders Tommy Harper and Pat Skrable, October 11, 1971.
§Traded with Pitchers Jim Lonborg, Ken Sanders and Earl Stephenson to Philadelphia Phillies for Infielders Don Money and John Vukovich and Pitcher Billy Champion, October 31, 1972.
xTraded to Pittsburgh Pirates for Infielder Dave Cash, September 18, 1973.
yOn disabled list, March 25 to April 16 and June 5 to June 26, 1975.
zTraded with Pitcher Dock Ellis and Second Baseman Willie Randolph to New York Yankees for Pitcher
Doc Medich, December 11, 1975.
aTraded with Outfielder Rich Coggins to Chicago White Sox for Outfielder Carlos May, May 18, 1976.

| Year Club | League | G. | IP. | W. | L. | Pct. | H. | R. | ER. | SO. | BB. | ERA. |
|---|---|---|---|---|---|---|---|---|---|---|---|---|
| 1974—Pittsburgh............National | | 1 | 2⅓ | 0 | 0 | .000 | 3 | 2 | 2 | 1 | 2 | 7.71 |
| 1975—Pittsburgh............National | | 2 | 2⅓ | 0 | 0 | .000 | 1 | 0 | 0 | 1 | 0 | 0.00 |
| Championship Series Totals ............ | | 3 | 4⅔ | 0 | 0 | .000 | 4 | 2 | 2 | 2 | 2 | 3.86 |

WORLD SERIES RECORD

| Year Club | League | G. | IP. | W. | L. | Pct. | H. | R. | ER. | SO. | BB. | ERA. |
|---|---|---|---|---|---|---|---|---|---|---|---|---|
| 1967—Boston ...............American | | 2 | 1⅓ | 0 | 0 | .000 | 0 | 0 | 0 | 1 | 1 | 0.00 |

ALL-STAR GAME RECORD

| Year League | IP. | W. | L. | Pct. | H. | R. | ER. | SO. | BB. | ERA. |
|---|---|---|---|---|---|---|---|---|---|---|
| 1974—National ....................... | 2 | 1 | 0 | 1.000 | 1 | 0 | 0 | 0 | 1 | 0.00 |

## DANIEL LEE BRIGGS
### (Dan)

Born November 18, 1952, at Scotia, Calif.
Height, 6.00. Weight, 180.
Throws and bats lefthanded.
Attended University of California at Berkeley, Berkeley, Calif.

| Year Club | League | Pos. | G. | AB. | R. | H. | 2B. | 3B. | HR. | RBI. | B.A. | PO. | A. | E. | F.A. |
|---|---|---|---|---|---|---|---|---|---|---|---|---|---|---|---|
| 1970—Idaho Falls........Pion. | | *1B-P | 62 | 190 | 44 | 58 | 11 | 1 | 4 | 34 | .305 | 389 | 31 | *24 | .946 |
| 1971—Quad Cities ......Midw | | 1B-P | 29 | 82 | 8 | 14 | 2 | 0 | 0 | 5 | .171 | 177 | 8 | 7 | .964 |
| 1971—Idaho Falls........Pion. | | 1B | 51 | 180 | 25 | 46 | 5 | 7 | 3 | 22 | .256 | 401 | 26 | *21 | .953 |
| 1972—Stockton ............Calif. | | •OF-1B | 131 | 449 | 66 | 104 | 14 | 3 | 18 | 56 | .232 | 383 | 23 | •27 | .938 |
| 1973—Salinas ............Calif. | | 1B | 101 | 360 | 62 | 106 | 18 | 5 | 11 | 59 | .294 | 854 | 55 | 13 | .986 |
| 1973—El Paso ............Tex. | | 1B-OF | 40 | 150 | 22 | 47 | 12 | 2 | 5 | 18 | .313 | 306 | 20 | 9 | .973 |
| 1974—El Paso ...........Tex. | | 1B | 53 | 216 | 49 | 76 | 18 | 5 | 13 | 55 | .352 | 454 | 31 | 12 | .975 |
| 1974—Salt Lake C. ......P.C. | | 1B | 83 | 317 | 40 | 88 | 13 | 10 | 4 | 56 | .278 | 726 | 49 | 15 | .981 |
| 1975—Salt Lake C.† ....P.C. | | 1B-OF | 80 | 260 | 45 | 84 | 12 | 2 | 1 | 37 | .323 | 352 | 36 | 7 | .982 |
| 1975—California..........Amer. | | 1B-OF | 13 | 31 | 3 | 7 | 1 | 0 | 1 | 3 | .226 | 49 | 1 | 2 | .961 |
| 1976—Salt Lake C. ......P.C. | | 1B-OF | 56 | 219 | 41 | 66 | 14 | 3 | 7 | 42 | .301 | 398 | 34 | 6 | .986 |
| 1976—California..........Amer. | | 1-OF-DH | 77 | 248 | 19 | 53 | 13 | 2 | 1 | 14 | .214 | 358 | 26 | 5 | .987 |
| Major League Totals ..................... | | | 90 | 279 | 22 | 60 | 14 | 2 | 2 | 17 | .215 | 407 | 27 | 7 | .986 |

†On disabled list, June 2 to July 27, 1975.

PITCHING RECORD

| Year Club | League | G. | IP. | W. | L. | Pct. | H. | R. | ER. | SO. | BB. | ERA. |
|---|---|---|---|---|---|---|---|---|---|---|---|---|---|
| 1970—Idaho Falls ...........Pioneer | | 7 | 28 | 2 | 0 | 1.000 | 20 | 8 | 4 | 33 | 19 | 1.29 |
| 1971—Quad Cities ..........Midwest | | 1 | 2 | 0 | 0 | .000 | 2 | 0 | 0 | 3 | 1 | 0.00 |

## NELSON KELLEY BRILES

Born August 5, 1943, at Dorris, Calif.
Height, 5.11. Weight, 200.
Throws and bats righthanded.
Hobbies—All sports, music, dramatics and languages.
Attended Santa Clara University, Santa Clara, Calif., and
Chico State College, Chico, Calif.
Received reported $65,000 bonus to sign with St. Louis Cardinals, 1963.

| Year Club | League | G. | IP. | W. | L. | Pct. | H. | R. | ER. | SO. | BB. | ERA. |
|---|---|---|---|---|---|---|---|---|---|---|---|---|---|
| 1964—Tulsa ...................Texas | | 28 | 171 | 11 | 6 | .647 | 148 | 71 | 53 | 132 | 61 | 2.79 |
| 1965—St. Louis ...............National | | 37 | 82 | 3 | 3 | .500 | 79 | 33 | 32 | 52 | 26 | 3.51 |
| 1966—St. Louis ...............National | | 49 | 154 | 4 | 15 | .211 | 162 | 65 | 55 | 100 | 54 | 3.21 |
| 1967—St. Louis ...............National | | 49 | 155 | 14 | 5 | *.737 | 139 | 45 | 42 | 94 | 40 | 2.44 |
| 1968—St. Louis ...............National | | 33 | 244 | 19 | 11 | .633 | 251 | 90 | 76 | 141 | 55 | 2.80 |
| 1969—St. Louis ...............National | | 36 | 228 | 15 | 13 | .536 | 218 | 104 | 89 | 126 | 63 | 3.51 |
| 1970—St. Louis†‡ ...............National | | 30 | 107 | 6 | 7 | .462 | 129 | 84 | 74 | 59 | 36 | 6.22 |
| 1971—Pittsburgh...............National | | 37 | 136 | 8 | 4 | .667 | 131 | 51 | 46 | 76 | 35 | 3.04 |
| 1972—Pittsburgh...............National | | 28 | 196 | 14 | 11 | .560 | 185 | 83 | 67 | 120 | 43 | 3.08 |
| 1973—Pittsburgh§ ...............National | | 33 | 219 | 14 | 13 | .519 | 201 | 87 | 69 | 94 | 51 | 2.84 |
| 1974—Kansas City x ...............American | | 18 | 103 | 5 | 7 | .417 | 118 | 48 | 46 | 41 | 21 | 4.02 |
| 1975—Kansas City y ...............American | | 24 | 112 | 6 | 6 | .500 | 127 | 60 | 53 | 73 | 25 | 4.26 |
| 1976—Texas ...............American | | 32 | 210 | 11 | 9 | .550 | 224 | 87 | 76 | 98 | 47 | 3.26 |
| American League Totals........................... | | 74 | 425 | 22 | 22 | .500 | 469 | 195 | 175 | 212 | 93 | 3.71 |
| National League Totals............................. | | 332 | 1521 | 97 | 82 | .542 | 1495 | 642 | 550 | 862 | 403 | 3.25 |
| Major League Totals ...................... | | 406 | 1946 | 119 | 104 | .534 | 1964 | 837 | 725 | 1074 | 496 | 3.35 |

†On disabled list, June 14 through July 7, 1970.
‡Traded with Outfielder Vic Davalillo to Pittsburgh Pirates for Outfielder Matty Alou and Pitcher George Brunet, January 29, 1971.
§Traded with Infielder Fernando Gonzalez to Kansas City Royals for Utilityman Kurt Bevacqua, Catcher-Outfielder Ed Kirkpatrick and First Baseman Winston Cole, December 4, 1973.
xOn disabled list from beginning of season until April 11 and from April 23 to June 28, 1974.
yTraded to Texas Rangers for Second Baseman Dave Nelson, November 11, 1975.

| Year Club | League | G. | IP. | W. | L. | Pct. | H. | R. | ER. | SO. | BB. | ERA. |
|---|---|---|---|---|---|---|---|---|---|---|---|---|
| 1972—Pittsburgh | National | 1 | 6 | 0 | 0 | .000 | 6 | 2 | 2 | 3 | 1 | 3.00 |

### WORLD SERIES RECORD

| Year Club | League | G. | IP. | W. | L. | Pct. | H. | R. | ER. | SO. | BB. | ERA. |
|---|---|---|---|---|---|---|---|---|---|---|---|---|
| 1967—St. Louis | National | 2 | 11 | 1 | 0 | 1.000 | 7 | 2 | 2 | 4 | 1 | 1.64 |
| 1968—St. Louis | National | 2 | 11⅓ | 0 | 1 | .000 | 13 | 7 | 7 | 7 | 4 | 5.56 |
| 1971—Pittsburgh | National | 1 | 9 | 1 | 0 | 1.000 | 2 | 0 | 0 | 2 | 2 | 0.00 |
| World Series Totals | | 5 | 31⅓ | 2 | 1 | .667 | 22 | 9 | 9 | 13 | 7 | 2.59 |

## PETER SVEN BROBERG
### (Pete)

Born March 2, 1950, at West Palm Beach, Fla.
Height, 6.03. Weight, 205.
Throws and bats righthanded.
Hobby—Squash.
Attended Darmouth College, Hanover, N. H.; received Bachelor of Arts degree.

Led American League in hit batsmen with 13 in 1972 and 16 in 1975.
Received reported $150,000 bonus to sign with Washington Senators, 1971.

| Year Club | League | G. | IP. | W. | L. | Pct. | H. | R. | ER. | SO. | BB. | ERA. |
|---|---|---|---|---|---|---|---|---|---|---|---|---|
| 1971—Washington | American | 18 | 125 | 5 | 9 | .357 | 104 | 57 | 48 | 89 | 53 | 3.46 |
| 1972—Texas | American | 39 | 176 | 5 | 12 | .294 | 153 | 93 | 84 | 133 | 85 | 4.30 |
| 1973—Spokane | P. Coast | 13 | 79 | 6 | 3 | .667 | 71 | 42 | 34 | 50 | 39 | 3.87 |
| 1973—Texas | American | 22 | 119 | 5 | 9 | .357 | 130 | 77 | 74 | 57 | 66 | 5.60 |
| 1974—Spokane | P. Coast | 14 | 88 | 4 | 5 | .444 | 93 | 51 | 44 | 77 | 42 | 4.50 |
| 1974—Texas† | American | 12 | 29 | 0 | 4 | .000 | 29 | 29 | 26 | 15 | 13 | 8.07 |
| 1975—Milwaukee | American | 38 | 220 | 14 | 16 | .467 | 219 | 114 | 101 | 100 | 106 | 4.13 |
| 1976—Milwaukee‡ | American | 20 | 92 | 1 | 7 | .125 | 99 | 59 | 51 | 28 | 72 | 4.99 |
| Major League Totals | | 149 | 762 | 28 | 57 | .326 | 734 | 429 | 384 | 422 | 395 | 4.54 |

†Traded to Milwaukee Brewers for Pitcher Clyde Wright, December 5, 1974.
‡Selected by Seattle Mariners in American League expansion draft, November 5, 1976.

## LOUIS CLARK BROCK
### (Lou)

Born June 18, 1939, at El Dorado, Ark.
Height, 5.11½. Weight, 172.
Throws and bats lefthanded.
Attended Southern University, Baton Rouge, La.
Cousin of Dale Brock, outfielder in St. Louis Cardinals' organization.

Established following major league records: most consecutive years, leading league, errors by outfielder (5), 1968; most consecutive years, 50 or more stolen bases (12), 1976; most seasons leading league, errors by outfielder (7), 1973; most seasons, 50 or more stolen bases, lifetime (12), 1976; most seasons leading majors, stolen bases (6), 1974; most times caught stealing lifetime, 266, 1976; and most stolen bases, season, since 1900 (118), 1974.

Established National League records for most seasons and consecutive seasons, 600 or more at bats (11), 1974; and most stolen bases, lifetime, since 1900 (809), 1975.

Tied National League record for most years, 100 or more strikeouts (9), 1973.

Major League stolen bases: 1961 (0), 1962 (16), 1963 (24), 1964 (43), 1965 (63), 1966 (74), 1967 (52), 1968 (62), 1969 (53), 1970 (51), 1971 (64), 1972 (63), 1973 (70), 1974 (118), 1975 (56), 1976 (56). Total 865.

Led National League outfielders in double plays with 7 in 1963.

Led National League in stolen bases with 74 in 1966, 52 in 1967, 62 in 1968, 53 in 1969, 64 in 1971, 63 in 1972, 70 in 1973 and 118 in 1974.

One of three players in major league history to steal 50 or more bases and hit 20 or more home runs in the same season (52 stolen bases and 21 home runs in 1967).

Led Northern League in total bases with 268 in 1961.

Named National League and Major League Player of the Year by THE SPORTING NEWS, 1974.

Named as outfielder on THE SPORTING NEWS National League All-Star Team, 1974.

Received reported $30,000 bonus to sign with Chicago Cubs, 1961.

| Year Club | League | Pos. | G. | AB. | R. | H. | 2B. | 3B. | HR. | RBI. | B.A. | PO. | A. | E. | F.A. |
|---|---|---|---|---|---|---|---|---|---|---|---|---|---|---|---|
| 1961—St. Cloud | North. | OF | •128 | 501 | •117 | •181 | •33 | 6 | 14 | 82 | •.361 | •277 | 14 | 14 | .954 |
| 1961—Chicago | Nat. | OF | 4 | 11 | 1 | 1 | 0 | 0 | 0 | 0 | .091 | 6 | 0 | 2 | .750 |
| 1962—Chicago | Nat. | OF | 123 | 434 | 73 | 114 | 24 | 7 | 9 | 35 | .263 | 243 | 7 | 9 | .965 |
| 1963—Chicago | Nat. | OF | 148 | 547 | 79 | 141 | 19 | 11 | 9 | 37 | .258 | 269 | 17 | 8 | .973 |
| 1964—Chi.†-St. Louis | Nat. | OF | 155 | 634 | 111 | 200 | 30 | 11 | 14 | 58 | .315 | 266 | 15 | •14 | .953 |
| 1965—St. Louis | Nat. | OF | 155 | 631 | 107 | 182 | 35 | 8 | 16 | 69 | .288 | 272 | 11 | •12 | .959 |
| 1966—St. Louis | Nat. | OF | 156 | 643 | 94 | 183 | 24 | 12 | 15 | 46 | .285 | 269 | 9 | •19 | .936 |
| 1967—St. Louis | Nat. | OF | 159 | •689 | •113 | 206 | 32 | 12 | 21 | 76 | .299 | 272 | 12 | •13 | .956 |
| 1968—St. Louis | Nat. | OF | 159 | 660 | 92 | 184 | •46 | •14 | 6 | 51 | .279 | 269 | 9 | •14 | .952 |
| 1969—St. Louis | Nat. | OF | 157 | 655 | 97 | 195 | 33 | 10 | 12 | 47 | .298 | 255 | 7 | 14 | .949 |
| 1970—St. Louis | Nat. | OF | 155 | 664 | 114 | 202 | 29 | 5 | 13 | 57 | .304 | 247 | 9 | 10 | .962 |
| 1971—St. Louis | Nat. | OF | 157 | 640 | •126 | 200 | 37 | 7 | 7 | 61 | .313 | 262 | 7 | 14 | .951 |
| 1972—St. Louis | Nat. | OF | 153 | 621 | 81 | 193 | 26 | 8 | 3 | 42 | .311 | 253 | 6 | •13 | .952 |

| Year | Club | League | Pos. | G. | AB. | R. | H. | 2B. | 3B. | HR. | RBI. | B.A. | PO. | A. | E. | F.A. |
|---|---|---|---|---|---|---|---|---|---|---|---|---|---|---|---|---|
| 1973—St. Louis | | Nat. | OF | 160 | 650 | 110 | 193 | 29 | 8 | 7 | 63 | .297 | 310 | 3 | •12 | .963 |
| 1974—St. Louis | | Nat. | OF | 153 | 635 | 105 | 194 | 25 | 7 | 3 | 48 | .306 | 283 | 8 | 10 | .967 |
| 1975—St. Louis | | Nat. | OF | 136 | 528 | 78 | 163 | 27 | 6 | 3 | 47 | .309 | 247 | 5 | 9 | .966 |
| 1976—St. Louis | | Nat. | OF | 133 | 498 | 73 | 150 | 24 | 5 | 4 | 67 | .301 | 221 | 6 | 4 | .983 |
| Major League Totals | | | | 2263 | 9140 | 1454 | 2701 | 440 | 131 | 142 | 804 | .296 | 3944 | 131 | 177 | .958 |

†Traded to St. Louis Cardinals with Pitchers Jack Spring and Paul Toth for Pitchers Ernie Broglio and Bobby Shantz and Outfielder Doug Clemens, June 15, 1964; Toth assigned to Jacksonville.

### WORLD SERIES RECORD

Established World Series record for most stolen bases, seven-game Series (7), 1967 and 1968.
Tied following World Series records: Most hits, game (4), and most one-base hits, game (4), October 4, 1967; most stolen bases game (3), October 12, 1967, and October 5, 1968; most stolen bases, inning (2), October 12, 1967, fifth inning; most runs, seven-game Series (8), 1967; most hits, seven-game Series (13), 1968; most total bases, seven-game Series (24), 1968; most long hits, seven-game Series (6), 1968; most stolen bases, total series (14), 1968; most times reached first base seven-game Series (13) 1968.

| Year | Club | League | Pos. | G. | AB. | R. | H. | 2B. | 3B. | HR. | RBI. | B.A. | PO. | A. | E. | F.A. |
|---|---|---|---|---|---|---|---|---|---|---|---|---|---|---|---|---|
| 1964—St. Louis | | Nat. | OF | 7 | 30 | 2 | 9 | 2 | 0 | 1 | 5 | .300 | 8 | 1 | 1 | .900 |
| 1967—St. Louis | | Nat. | OF | 7 | 29 | 8 | 12 | 2 | 1 | 1 | 3 | .414 | 13 | 0 | 1 | 1.000 |
| 1968—St. Louis | | Nat. | OF | 7 | 28 | 6 | 13 | 3 | 1 | 2 | 5 | .464 | 13 | 0 | 1 | .929 |
| World Series Totals | | | | 21 | 87 | 16 | 34 | 7 | 2 | 4 | 13 | .391 | 34 | 1 | 2 | .946 |

### ALL-STAR GAME RECORD

| Year | League | Pos. | AB. | R. | H. | 2B. | 3B. | HR. | RBI. | B.A. | PO. | A. | E. | F.A. |
|---|---|---|---|---|---|---|---|---|---|---|---|---|---|---|
| 1967—National | | OF | 2 | 0 | 0 | 0 | 0 | 0 | 0 | .000 | 1 | 0 | 0 | 1.000 |
| 1971—National | | PH | 1 | 0 | 0 | 0 | 0 | 0 | 0 | .000 | 0 | 0 | 0 | .000 |
| 1974—National | | PH | 1 | 1 | 1 | 0 | 0 | 0 | 0 | 1.000 | 0 | 0 | 0 | .000 |
| 1975—National | | OF | 3 | 1 | 1 | 0 | 0 | 0 | 0 | .333 | 2 | 0 | 0 | 1.000 |
| All-Star Game Totals | | | 7 | 2 | 2 | 0 | 0 | 0 | 0 | .286 | 3 | 0 | 0 | 1.000 |

Member of National League All-Star Team for the 1972 game; did not play.

## JOHN ANTHONY BROHAMER, JR.

Name pronounced Bro-hammer.

### (Jack)

Born February 26, 1950, at Maywood, Calif.
Height, 5.09. Weight, 165.
Throws right and bats lefthanded.
Hobbies—Hunting, fishing and golf.
Attended Golden West College, Huntington Beach, Calif.

Tied for California League lead in sacrifice flies with 8 in 1969.

| Year | Club | League | Pos. | G. | AB. | R. | H. | 2B. | 3B. | HR. | RBI. | B.A. | PO. | A. | E. | F.A. |
|---|---|---|---|---|---|---|---|---|---|---|---|---|---|---|---|---|
| 1968—Rock Hill | | W. Car. | SS | 78 | 296 | 62 | 86 | 21 | 5 | 3 | 33 | .291 | 138 | 206 | 23 | .937 |
| 1968—Reno | | Calif. | 2B-SS | 32 | 101 | 11 | 27 | 6 | 1 | 2 | 9 | .267 | 49 | 50 | 8 | .925 |
| 1969—Reno | | Calif. | •SS-2 | 133 | 501 | 75 | 139 | 19 | 4 | 10 | 64 | .277 | 161 | •396 | 45 | .925 |
| 1970—Savannah | | South. | SS-2 | 75 | 269 | 31 | 63 | 17 | 5 | 4 | 22 | .234 | 105 | 188 | 17 | .945 |
| 1970—Wichita | | A.A. | 3-SS-2 | 40 | 146 | 24 | 34 | 7 | 1 | 2 | 17 | .233 | 58 | 78 | 8 | .944 |
| 1971—Wichita† | | A.A. | 2-3-SS | 103 | 355 | 45 | 93 | 14 | 5 | 4 | 44 | .262 | 172 | 245 | 8 | .981 |
| 1972—Cleveland | | Amer. | 2B-3B | 136 | 527 | 49 | 123 | 13 | 2 | 5 | 35 | .233 | 285 | 395 | 16 | .977 |
| 1973—Cleveland | | Amer. | 2B | 102 | 300 | 29 | 66 | 12 | 1 | 4 | 29 | .220 | 215 | 279 | 15 | .971 |
| 1974—Cleveland‡ | | Amer. | 2B | 101 | 315 | 33 | 85 | 11 | 1 | 2 | 30 | .270 | 203 | 269 | 6 | .987 |
| 1975—Cleveland§ | | Amer. | 2B | 69 | 217 | 15 | 53 | 5 | 0 | 6 | 16 | .244 | 166 | 162 | 8 | .976 |
| 1976—Chicago | | Amer. | 2B-3B | 119 | 354 | 33 | 89 | 12 | 2 | 7 | 40 | .251 | 265 | 338 | 10 | .984 |
| Major League Totals | | | | 527 | 1713 | 159 | 416 | 53 | 6 | 24 | 150 | .243 | 1134 | 1443 | 55 | .979 |

†On disabled list, May 17 through June 1, 1971.
‡On supplemental disabled list, July 31 to August 15 and August 19 to September 4, 1974.
§On supplemental disabled list, June 4 to July 4, 1975.
xTraded to Chicago White Sox for Infielder Larvell Blanks, December 12, 1975.

## JACKIE GENE BROWN

Born May 31, 1943 at Holdenville, Okla.
Height, 6.02. Weight, 190.
Throws and bats righthanded.
Hobbies—Golf, fishing and hunting.
Brother of Paul Brown, pitcher for Philadelphia Phillies, 1961 through 1963 and 1968.

Led California League pitchers in games started with 32 in 1965.

| Year | Club | League | G. | IP. | W. | L. | Pct. | H. | R. | ER. | SO. | BB. | ERA. |
|---|---|---|---|---|---|---|---|---|---|---|---|---|---|
| 1962—Miami† | | Florida St. | 7 | 10 | 0 | 1 | .000 | 13 | 10 | 7 | 12 | 8 | 6.30 |
| 1963—Spartanburg‡ | | W. Carol. | 19 | 101 | 5 | 10 | .333 | 109 | 66 | 52 | 100 | 47 | 4.63 |
| 1964—Bakersfield | | California | 6 | 26 | 1 | 1 | .500 | 33 | 23 | 19 | 17 | 13 | 6.58 |
| 1964—Miami | | Florida St. | 23 | 152 | 8 | 10 | .444 | 118 | 55 | 34 | 124 | 61 | 2.01 |
| 1965—Bakersfield | | California | 33 | 236 | 15 | 11 | .577 | •228 | 117 | 96 | 214 | 110 | 3.66 |
| 1966—Macon | | Southern | 24 | 95 | 3 | 5 | .375 | 87 | 60 | 51 | 91 | 63 | 4.83 |

| Year Club | League | G. | IP. | W. | L. | Pct. | H. | R. | ER. | SO. | BB. | ERA. |
|---|---|---|---|---|---|---|---|---|---|---|---|---|
| 1967—Tidewater§ | Carolina | 17 | 73 | 5 | 5 | .500 | 62 | 33 | 31 | 53 | 26 | 3.82 |
| 1968—Tidewater x-Burlington | Carolina | 24 | 61 | 2 | 4 | .333 | 55 | 34 | 27 | 79 | 34 | 3.98 |
| 1968—Savannah | Southern | 5 | 21 | 3 | 1 | .750 | 19 | 11 | 8 | 19 | 8 | 3.43 |
| 1969—Savannah | Southern | 24 | 142 | 9 | 7 | .563 | 119 | 50 | 41 | 103 | 70 | 2.60 |
| 1970—Denver | Am. Assoc. | 12 | 71 | 6 | 1 | .857 | 68 | 24 | 20 | 56 | 27 | 2.54 |
| 1970—Washington | American | 24 | 57 | 2 | 2 | .500 | 49 | 28 | 25 | 47 | 37 | 3.95 |
| 1971—Denver | Am. Assoc. | 14 | 91 | 6 | 4 | .600 | 90 | 47 | 40 | 85 | 40 | 3.96 |
| 1971—Washington | American | 14 | 47 | 3 | 4 | .429 | 60 | 34 | 31 | 21 | 27 | 5.94 |
| 1972—Denver | Am. Assoc. | 32 | 165 | 6 | •17 | .261 | •212 | •120 | •101 | 128 | 60 | 5.51 |
| 1973—Spokane | P. Coast | 19 | 96 | 10 | 1 | .909 | 76 | 28 | 25 | 84 | 44 | 2.34 |
| 1973—Texas | American | 25 | 67 | 5 | 5 | .500 | 82 | 31 | 29 | 45 | 25 | 3.90 |
| 1974—Texas y | American | 35 | 217 | 13 | 12 | .520 | 219 | 97 | 86 | 134 | 74 | 3.57 |
| 1975—Texas z-Cleveland | American | 42 | 140 | 6 | 7 | .462 | 142 | 77 | 66 | 76 | 64 | 4.24 |
| 1976—Cleveland a | American | 32 | 180 | 9 | 11 | .450 | 193 | 94 | 85 | 104 | 55 | 4.25 |
| Major League Totals | | 172 | 708 | 38 | 41 | .481 | 745 | 361 | 322 | 427 | 282 | 4.09 |

†On temporary inactive list, May 25 to August 7, 1962.
‡On disabled list, June 11 to July 18, 1963.
§On disabled list, May 5 to May 31; on temporary inactive list, July 15 to July 28, 1967.
xReleased by Philadelphia Phillies' organization, May 16, 1968; signed as free agent by Washington Senators' organization, May 17, 1968.
yOn temporary inactive list from beginning of season until April 29, 1974.
zTraded with Pitchers Jim Bibby and Rick Waits and an estimated $100,000 to Cleveland Indians for Pitcher Gaylord Perry, June 12, 1975.
aTraded to Montreal Expos for First Baseman Andre Thornton, December 10, 1976.

## OLLIE LEE BROWN

Born February 11, 1944, at Tuscaloosa, Ala.
Height, 6.02. Weight, 205.
Throws and bats righthanded.
Hobby—Golf.
Attended Long Beach City College, Long Beach, Calif.
Brother of Willie Brown, present assistant coach with Tampa Bay Buccaneers,
and former halfback at University of Southern California and with
Los Angeles Rams and Philadelphia Eagles, and Oscar Lee Brown,
former outfielder with Atlanta Braves.
Led California League in total bases with 324 in 1964.
Named Most Valuable Player in California League, 1964.

| Year Club | League | Pos. | G. | AB. | R. | H. | 2B. | 3B. | HR. | RBI. | B.A. | PO. | A. | E. | F.A. |
|---|---|---|---|---|---|---|---|---|---|---|---|---|---|---|---|
| 1962—Salem | Appal. | OF | 5 | 12 | 1 | 2 | 0 | 0 | 0 | 2 | .167 | 2 | 0 | 1 | .667 |
| 1962—Decatur | Midw. | OF | 64 | 235 | 37 | 54 | 13 | 2 | 10 | 29 | .230 | 98 | 3 | 10 | .910 |
| 1963—Decatur | Midw. | P-OF | 59 | 92 | 25 | 28 | 2 | 0 | 6 | 26 | .304 | 17 | 32 | 4 | .925 |
| 1964—Fresno | Calif. | OF | 133 | 483 | •111 | 159 | 23 | •11 | •40 | •133 | .329 | 189 | 9 | 9 | .957 |
| 1965—Tacoma | P.C. | OF | 139 | 518 | 76 | 152 | 30 | 1 | 27 | 81 | .293 | 242 | •15 | 8 | .970 |
| 1965—San Francisco | Nat. | OF | 6 | 10 | 0 | 2 | 1 | 0 | 0 | 0 | .200 | 4 | 0 | 0 | 1.000 |
| 1966—San Francisco | Nat. | OF | 115 | 348 | 32 | 81 | 7 | 1 | 7 | 33 | .233 | 163 | 12 | 4 | .978 |
| 1966—Phoenix | P.C. | OF | 27 | 105 | 23 | 36 | 9 | 1 | 9 | 29 | .343 | 48 | 2 | 3 | .943 |
| 1967—San Francisco | Nat. | OF | 120 | 412 | 44 | 110 | 12 | 1 | 13 | 53 | .267 | 190 | 5 | 3 | .985 |
| 1968—San Francisco | Nat. | OF | 40 | 95 | 7 | 22 | 4 | 0 | 0 | 11 | .232 | 32 | 1 | 0 | 1.000 |
| 1968—Phoenix†‡ | P.C. | OF | 25 | 84 | 19 | 21 | 6 | 0 | 3 | 10 | .250 | 41 | 0 | 1 | .976 |
| 1969—San Diego | Nat. | OF | 151 | 568 | 76 | 150 | 18 | 3 | 20 | 61 | .264 | 269 | 14 | 7 | .976 |
| 1970—San Diego | Nat. | OF | 139 | 534 | 79 | 156 | 34 | 1 | 23 | 89 | .292 | 258 | 12 | 10 | .964 |
| 1971—San Diego | Nat. | OF | 145 | 484 | 36 | 132 | 16 | 0 | 9 | 55 | .273 | 263 | 9 | 5 | .982 |
| 1972—San Diego§ | Nat. | OF | 23 | 70 | 3 | 12 | 2 | 0 | 0 | 3 | .171 | 34 | 1 | 0 | 1.000 |
| 1972—Oak. x-Milw. | Amer. | OF-3B | 86 | 233 | 26 | 63 | 9 | 0 | 4 | 29 | .270 | 147 | 8 | 1 | .994 |
| 1973—Milwaukee y | Amer. | OF | 97 | 296 | 28 | 83 | 10 | 1 | 7 | 32 | .280 | 1 | 0 | 0 | 1.000 |
| 1974—Hous. z-Phila. | Nat. | OF | 70 | 168 | 19 | 39 | 6 | 2 | 7 | 19 | .232 | 73 | 1 | 3 | .961 |
| 1975—Philadelphia | Nat. | OF | 84 | 145 | 19 | 44 | 12 | 0 | 6 | 26 | .303 | 67 | 0 | 0 | 1.000 |
| 1976—Philadelphia | Nat. | OF | 92 | 209 | 30 | 53 | 10 | 1 | 5 | 30 | .254 | 105 | 7 | 6 | .949 |
| National League Totals | | | 985 | 3043 | 345 | 801 | 122 | 9 | 90 | 380 | .263 | 1458 | 62 | 38 | .976 |
| American League Totals | | | 183 | 529 | 54 | 146 | 19 | 1 | 11 | 61 | .276 | 148 | 8 | 1 | .994 |
| Major League Totals | | | 1168 | 3572 | 399 | 947 | 141 | 10 | 101 | 441 | .265 | 1606 | 70 | 39 | .972 |

†On disqualified list from June 26 through August 1 after refusing to report to Phoenix.
‡Recalled by San Francisco Giants; selected by San Diego Padres from San Francisco in expansion draft, October 14, 1968.
§Traded to Oakland A's for Pitcher Mike Kilkenny, Catcher-First Baseman Curt Blefary and a player to be named later, May 17, 1972; Athletics assigned Outfielder Greg Schubert from Iowa to Hawaii, September 11, 1972, to complete deal.
xReleased on waivers to Milwaukee Brewers, June 29, 1972.
yTraded with Outfielder Joe Lahoud, Pitchers Skip Lockwood and Gary Ryerson, and Catcher Ellie Rodriguez to California Angels for Pitchers Clyde Wright and Steve Barber, Outfielder Ken Berry, Catcher Art Kusnyer and a player to be named later, October 22, 1973. Sold by California to Houston Astros, March 28, 1974.
zSold via waivers to Philadelphia Phillies for $40,000, June 23, 1974.

### CHAMPIONSHIP SERIES RECORD

| Year Club | League | Pos. | G. | AB. | R. | H. | 2B. | 3B. | HR. | RBI. | B.A. | PO. | A. | E. | F.A. |
|---|---|---|---|---|---|---|---|---|---|---|---|---|---|---|---|
| 1976—Philadelphia | Nat. | OF | 1 | 2 | 0 | 0 | 0 | 0 | 0 | 0 | .000 | 2 | 0 | 0 | 1.000 |

Pitched 8-0 no-hit victory against Wisconsin Rapids, August 13, 1963.
Led Midwest League in wild pitches with 24 in 1963.

| Year Club | League | G. | IP. | W. | L. | Pct. | H. | R. | ER. | SO. | BB. | ERA. |
|---|---|---|---|---|---|---|---|---|---|---|---|---|
| 1963—Decatur.................................Midwest | | 21 | 123 | 9 | 8 | .529 | 94 | 79 | 65 | 107 | *132 | 4.76 |

## THOMAS MICHAEL BRUNO
### (Tom)

Born January 26, 1953, at Chicago, Ill.
Height, 6.05. Weight, 210.
Throws and bats righthanded.
Hobbies—Hunting and fishing.
Attended Eastern Illinois University, Charleston, Ill.

Pitched seven-inning, 5-0 no-hit victory against Columbus, July 5, 1974.
Pitches seven-inning, 2-0 no-hit victory against Danville, August 23, 1972.

| Year Club | League | G. | IP. | W. | L. | Pct. | H. | R. | ER. | SO. | BB. | ERA. |
|---|---|---|---|---|---|---|---|---|---|---|---|---|
| 1972—Sarasota Royals ..................Gulf Coast | | 5 | 41 | 5 | 0 | 1.000 | 28 | 11 | 8 | 43 | 13 | 1.76 |
| 1972—Waterloo .............................Midwest | | 6 | 40 | 3 | 1 | .750 | 28 | 18 | 10 | 29 | 13 | 2.25 |
| 1973—San Jose .............................California | | 42 | 137 | 13 | 8 | .619 | 156 | 79 | 62 | 121 | 42 | 4.07 |
| 1974—Jacksonville ........................Southern | | 17 | 118 | 5 | 7 | .417 | 113 | 56 | 45 | 81 | 33 | 3.43 |
| 1974—Omaha ...............................Am. Assoc. | | 13 | 55 | 2 | 6 | .250 | 61 | 35 | 28 | 33 | 12 | 4.58 |
| 1975—Jacksonville ........................Southern | | 4 | 31 | 1 | 3 | .250 | 24 | 10 | 7 | 12 | 15 | 2.03 |
| 1975—Omaha ...............................Am. Assoc. | | 23 | 156 | 9 | 12 | .429 | 157 | 76 | 65 | 112 | 55 | 3.75 |
| 1976—Omaha ...............................Am. Assoc. | | 20 | 114 | 9 | 4 | .692 | 115 | 59 | 48 | 79 | 38 | 3.79 |
| 1976—Kansas City† ........................American | | 12 | 17 | 1 | 0 | 1.000 | 20 | 13 | 13 | 11 | 9 | 6.88 |
| Major League Totals ................................. | | 12 | 17 | 1 | 0 | 1.000 | 20 | 13 | 13 | 11 | 9 | 6.88 |

†Selected by Toronto Blue Jays in American League expansion draft, November 5, 1976.

## WARREN SCOTT BRUSSTAR

Born February 2, 1952, at Oakland, Calif.
Height, 6.03. Weight, 200.
Throws and bats righthanded.
Hobbies—Sports and music.
Attended Napa Junior College, Napa, Calif., and Fresno State
University, Fresno, Calif.

| Year Club | League | G. | IP. | W. | L. | Pct. | H. | R. | ER. | SO. | BB. | ERA. |
|---|---|---|---|---|---|---|---|---|---|---|---|---|
| 1974—Spartanburg ........................W. Carol. | | 22 | 42 | 2 | 4 | .333 | 39 | 23 | 9 | 34 | 24 | 1.93 |
| 1975—Rocky Mount† .....................Carolina | | 25 | 162 | ●14 | 8 | .636 | 117 | 61 | 40 | 123 | 94 | 2.22 |
| 1976—Reading ...............................Eastern | | 27 | *199 | 10 | *17 | .370 | 167 | 83 | 60 | 119 | *90 | 2.71 |

†On disabled list, May 29 through June 9, 1976.
Listed on Philadelphia Phillies' 1977 spring roster.

## DEREK ROSZELL BRYANT

Born October 9, 1951, at Lexington, Ky.
Height, 5.11. Weight, 185.
Throws and bats righthanded.
Attended University of Kentucky, Lexington, Ky.

Led Southern League outfielders in chances accepted with 311 in 1974.
Tied for Southern League lead in stolen bases with 42 in 1976.

| Year Club | League | Pos. | G. | AB. | R. | H. | 2B. | 3B. | HR. | RBI. | B.A. | PO. | A. | E. | F.A. |
|---|---|---|---|---|---|---|---|---|---|---|---|---|---|---|---|
| 1973—Burlington ........Midw. | | OF | 66 | 246 | 50 | 77 | 4 | 3 | 0 | 36 | .313 | 116 | 3 | 6 | .952 |
| 1974—Birmingham ......South. | | OF | 132 | 510 | 68 | 136 | 23 | 4 | 4 | 45 | .267 | *299 | 12 | 14 | .957 |
| 1975—Birmingham ......South. | | OF | 134 | *509 | 64 | *147 | 25 | 4 | 1 | 58 | .289 | 235 | 10 | 4 | .984 |
| 1976—Chattanooga ......South. | | OF-2B | 134 | 467 | 70 | 141 | 14 | ●10 | 2 | 50 | .302 | 215 | 11 | ●10 | .957 |

Listed on Oakland A's 1977 spring roster.

## STEPHEN ROBERT BRYE
### (Steve)

Born February 4, 1949, at Alameda, Calif.
Height, 6.00. Weight, 190.
Throws and bats righthanded.
Hobbies—Sports and music.
Attended Merritt College, Oakland, Calif., and Portland Community College,
Portland, Ore.

Led Northern League in total bases with 147 in 1967.
Tied for Pacific Coast League lead in double plays by outfielders with 3 in 1971.
Named Player of the Year in Northern League, 1967.
Received reported $47,000 bonus to sign with Minnesota Twins, 1967.

| Year Club | League | Pos. | G. | AB. | R. | H. | 2B. | 3B. | HR. | RBI. | B.A. | PO. | A. | E. | F.A. |
|---|---|---|---|---|---|---|---|---|---|---|---|---|---|---|---|
| 1967—St. Cloud ..........North. | | 3B | 67 | 264 | *59 | *82 | *16 | *5 | ●13 | 46 | .311 | *55 | 117 | 19 | .901 |
| 1968—Sarasota Twins..Gulf C. | | 3B | 4 | 12 | 1 | 4 | 1 | 2 | 0 | 3 | .333 | 2 | 2 | 2 | .667 |
| 1968—Orlando† .........Fla. St. | | 3B | 49 | 159 | 27 | 53 | 11 | 2 | 6 | 31 | .333 | 35 | 133 | 7 | .960 |
| 1969—Red Springs ......Carol. | | 1-3-O-2 | 106 | 389 | 48 | 91 | 16 | 1 | 7 | 40 | .234 | 518 | 124 | 17 | .974 |
| 1970—Charlotte ..........South. | | OF | 106 | 374 | 52 | 115 | 17 | ●10 | 6 | 48 | *.307 | 212 | 6 | 8 | .965 |

| Year Club League | Pos. | G. | AB. | R. | H. | 2B. | 3B. | HR. | RBI. | B.A. | PO. | A. | E. | F.A. |
|---|---|---|---|---|---|---|---|---|---|---|---|---|---|---|
| 1970–Minnesota ........Amer. | OF | 9 | 11 | 1 | 2 | 1 | 0 | 0 | 2 | .182 | 4 | 0 | 0 | 1.000 |
| 1971–Portland............P.C. | OF | 128 | 483 | 96 | 164 | 27 | 8 | 13 | 81 | .340 | 219 | *21 | 6 | .976 |
| 1971–Minnesota ........Amer. | OF | 28 | 107 | 10 | 24 | 1 | 0 | 3 | 11 | .224 | 53 | 4 | 2 | .966 |
| 1972–Minnesota‡ .......Amer. | OF | 100 | 253 | 18 | 61 | 9 | 3 | 0 | 12 | .241 | 170 | 9 | 1 | .994 |
| 1973–Minnesota ........Amer. | OF | 92 | 278 | 39 | 73 | 9 | 5 | 6 | 33 | .263 | 209 | 4 | 3 | .986 |
| 1974–Minnesota ........Amer. | OF | 135 | 488 | 52 | 138 | 32 | 1 | 2 | 41 | .283 | 301 | 10 | 1 | *.997 |
| 1975–Minnesota§ .......Amer. | OF | 86 | 246 | 41 | 62 | 13 | 1 | 9 | 34 | .252 | 112 | 7 | 2 | .983 |
| 1976–Minnesota x ......Amer. | OF-DH | 87 | 258 | 33 | 68 | 11 | 0 | 2 | 23 | .264 | 147 | 1 | 2 | .987 |
| Major League Totals ..................... | | 537 | 1641 | 194 | 428 | 76 | 10 | 22 | 156 | .261 | 996 | 35 | 11 | .989 |

†On suspended list, June 23 through July 1. On military list, October 17, 1968, through March 14, 1969.
‡On military list, June 9 through June 27, 1972.
§On disabled list, July 5 to July 26, 1975.
xSold to Milwaukee Brewers, March 21, 1977.

## WILLIAM JOSEPH BUCKNER
### (Bill)

Born December 14, 1949, at Vallejo, Calif.
Height, 6.00. Weight, 185.
Throws and bats lefthanded.
Hobby–Hunting.
Attended University of Southern California, Los Angeles, Calif., and
Arizona State University, Tempe, Ariz.
Brother of Jim Buckner, outfielder in Baltimore Orioles' organization.

Led Pioneer League first basemen in double plays with 37 in 1968.

| Year Club League | Pos. | G. | AB. | R. | H. | 2B. | 3B. | HR. | RBI. | B.A. | PO. | A. | E. | F.A. |
|---|---|---|---|---|---|---|---|---|---|---|---|---|---|---|
| 1968–Ogden ..............Pion. | 1B | *64 | *256 | 54 | *88 | 10 | *8 | 4 | 41 | *.344 | 468 | 28 | 4 | *.992 |
| 1969–Albuquerque .......Texas | OF-1B | 70 | 257 | 44 | 79 | 7 | 3 | 7 | 50 | .307 | 220 | 15 | 3 | .987 |
| 1969–Spokane ...........P.C. | OF-1B | 36 | 143 | 21 | 45 | 1 | 1 | 2 | 27 | .315 | 128 | 12 | 5 | .966 |
| 1969–Los Angeles ......Nat. | PH | 1 | 1 | 0 | 0 | 0 | 0 | 0 | 0 | .000 | 0 | 0 | 0 | .000 |
| 1970–Spokane ...........P.C. | 1B-OF | 111 | 465 | 78 | 156 | 33 | 2 | 3 | 74 | .335 | 582 | 22 | 7 | .989 |
| 1970–Los Angeles ......Nat. | OF-1B | 28 | 68 | 6 | 13 | 3 | 1 | 0 | 4 | .191 | 37 | 1 | 0 | 1.000 |
| 1971–Los Angeles ......Nat. | OF-1B | 108 | 358 | 37 | 99 | 15 | 1 | 5 | 41 | .277 | 235 | 11 | 1 | .996 |
| 1972–Los Angeles ......Nat. | OF-1B | 105 | 383 | 47 | 122 | 14 | 3 | 5 | 37 | .319 | 434 | 22 | 4 | .991 |
| 1973–Los Angeles ......Nat. | 1B-OF | 140 | 575 | 68 | 158 | 20 | 0 | 8 | 46 | .275 | 981 | 50 | 3 | .997 |
| 1974–Los Angeles ......Nat. | OF-1B | 145 | 580 | 83 | 182 | 30 | 3 | 7 | 58 | .314 | 284 | 5 | 7 | .976 |
| 1975–Los Angeles† ....Nat. | OF | 92 | 288 | 30 | 70 | 11 | 2 | 6 | 31 | .243 | 138 | 4 | 2 | .986 |
| 1976–Los Angeles‡ ....Nat. | OF-1B | 154 | 642 | 76 | 193 | 28 | 4 | 7 | 60 | .301 | 315 | 7 | 5 | .985 |
| Major League Totals ..................... | | 773 | 2895 | 347 | 837 | 121 | 14 | 38 | 277 | .289 | 2424 | 100 | 22 | .991 |

†On supplemental disabled list, April 21 to May 12, 1975.
‡Traded with Infielder Ivan DeJesus and Pitcher Jeff Albert to Chicago Cubs for Outfielder Rick Monday and Pitcher Mike Garman, January 11, 1977.

CHAMPIONSHIP SERIES RECORD

| Year Club League | Pos. | G. | AB. | R. | H. | 2B. | 3B. | HR. | RBI. | B.A. | PO. | A. | E. | F.A. |
|---|---|---|---|---|---|---|---|---|---|---|---|---|---|---|
| 1974–Los Angeles ......Nat. | OF | 4 | 18 | 0 | 3 | 1 | 0 | 0 | 0 | .167 | 6 | 0 | 0 | 1.000 |

WORLD SERIES RECORD

| Year Club League | Pos. | G. | AB. | R. | H. | 2B. | 3B. | HR. | RBI. | B.A. | PO. | A. | E. | F.A. |
|---|---|---|---|---|---|---|---|---|---|---|---|---|---|---|
| 1974–Los Angeles ......Nat. | OF | 5 | 20 | 1 | 5 | 1 | 0 | 1 | 1 | .250 | 11 | 0 | 0 | 1.000 |

## TERRY CHARLES BULLING

Born December 15, 1952, at Lynwood, Calif.
Height, 6.01. Weight, 200.
Throws and bats righthanded.
Hobbies–Fishing, bowling and golf.
Attended Golden West Junior College, Huntington Beach, Calif., and
California State University, Los Angeles, Calif.

Led Midwest League batters in walks with 102 in 1976.

| Year Club League | Pos. | G. | AB. | R. | H. | 2B. | 3B. | HR. | RBI. | B.A. | PO. | A. | E. | F.A. |
|---|---|---|---|---|---|---|---|---|---|---|---|---|---|---|
| 1974–Wis. Rapids†......Midw. | C | 4 | 12 | 1 | 3 | 0 | 0 | 0 | 3 | .250 | 31 | 1 | 1 | .970 |
| 1975–Wis. Rapids ......Midw. | C | 104 | 296 | 31 | 71 | 11 | 0 | 9 | 40 | .240 | *596 | 51 | 13 | .980 |
| 1976–Wis. Rapids ......Midw. | C | 112 | 352 | 85 | 109 | 13 | 2 | 8 | 50 | .310 | *623 | *105 | 17 | .977 |

†On temporary inactive list, July 8 through August 30, 1974.
Listed on Minnesota Twins' 1977 spring roster.

## ALONZA BENJAMIN BUMBRY
### (Al)

Born April 21, 1947, at Fredericksburg, Va.
Height, 5.08. Weight, 170.
Throws right and bats lefthanded.
Hobbies–Sports in general and corresponding.
Attended Virginia State College, Petersburg, Va.; received Bachelor of Science degree
in Physical Education.

Tied modern major league record for most triples, game, 3, September 22, 1973.
Named American League Rookie Player of the Year by THE SPORTING NEWS, 1973.
Named American League Rookie of the Year by Baseball Writers' Association of America, 1973.
Named International League Most Valuable Player in 1972.
Named Northern League Player of the Year in 1971.

| Year Club | League | Pos. | G. | AB. | R. | H. | 2B. | 3B. | HR. | RBI. | B.A. | PO. | A. | E. | F.A. |
|---|---|---|---|---|---|---|---|---|---|---|---|---|---|---|---|
| 1969—Stockton† ..........Calif. | | OF-1 | 35 | 73 | 19 | 13 | 4 | 0 | 0 | 3 | .178 | 31 | 3 | 2 | .944 |
| 1970— ........................ | | | | (In Military Service.) | | | | | | | | | | | |
| 1971—Aberdeen ..........North. | | OF | 66 | 247 | 68 | 83 | 14 | 6 | 6 | 53 | .336 | 85 | 5 | 5 | .947 |
| 1972—Asheville ..........South. | | OF | 26 | 121 | 26 | 42 | 4 | 4 | 4 | 10 | .347 | 60 | 4 | 3 | .955 |
| 1972—Rochester..........Int. | | OF | 108 | 435 | 83 | 150 | 29 | •15 | 6 | 47 | •.345 | 198 | 14 | 0 | •1.000 |
| 1972—Baltimore ..........Amer. | | OF | 9 | 11 | 5 | 4 | 0 | 1 | 0 | 0 | .364 | 4 | 0 | 0 | 1.000 |
| 1973—Baltimore ..........Amer. | | OF | 110 | 356 | 73 | 120 | 15 | •11 | 7 | 34 | .337 | 134 | 2 | 3 | .978 |
| 1974—Baltimore ..........Amer. | | OF | 94 | 270 | 35 | 63 | 10 | 3 | 1 | 19 | .233 | 115 | 7 | 6 | .953 |
| 1975—Baltimore ..........Amer. | | OF-3B | 114 | 349 | 47 | 94 | 19 | 4 | 2 | 32 | .269 | 70 | 2 | 0 | 1.000 |
| 1976—Baltimore ..........Amer. | | OF-DH | 133 | 450 | 71 | 113 | 15 | 7 | 9 | 36 | .251 | 251 | 9 | 3 | .989 |
| Major League Totals ...................... | | | 460 | 1436 | 231 | 394 | 59 | 26 | 19 | 121 | .274 | 574 | 20 | 12 | .980 |

†On temporary inactive list, June 16, 1969. Transferred to military list, July 22, 1969 through June 3, 1971.

### CHAMPIONSHIP SERIES RECORD

| Year Club | League | Pos. | G. | AB. | R. | H. | 2B. | 3B. | HR. | RBI. | B.A. | PO. | A. | E. | F.A. |
|---|---|---|---|---|---|---|---|---|---|---|---|---|---|---|---|
| 1973—Baltimore ..........Amer. | | OF | 2 | 7 | 1 | 0 | 0 | 0 | 0 | 0 | .000 | 4 | 1 | 1 | .833 |
| 1974—Baltimore ..........Amer. | | PR-PH | 2 | 1 | 0 | 0 | 0 | 0 | 0 | 0 | .000 | 0 | 0 | 0 | .000 |
| Championship Series Totals ............ | | | 4 | 8 | 1 | 0 | 0 | 0 | 0 | 0 | .000 | 4 | 1 | 1 | .833 |

## THOMAS HENRY BURGMEIER
### (Tom)

Born August 2, 1943, at St. Paul, Minn.
Height, 5.11. Weight, 190.
Throws and bats lefthanded.
Hobbies—Fishing and hunting.

Led Pacific Coast League pitchers in complete games with 15 in 1967.

| Year Club | League | G. | IP. | W. | L. | Pct. | H. | R. | ER. | SO. | BB. | ERA. |
|---|---|---|---|---|---|---|---|---|---|---|---|---|
| 1962—Modesto ...........................California | | 34 | 197 | 12 | 11 | .522 | 204 | 122 | 95 | 210 | 100 | 4.34 |
| 1963—San Antonio .......................Texas | | 6 | 34 | 1 | 4 | .200 | 46 | 27 | 24 | 19 | 14 | 6.35 |
| 1963—Durham ...........................Carolina | | 15 | 76 | 3 | 9 | .250 | 98 | 55 | 40 | 43 | 30 | 4.74 |
| 1964—Modesto†-San Jose................California | | 22 | 122 | 8 | 7 | .533 | 149 | 82 | 67 | 89 | 30 | 4.94 |
| 1965—Seattle ...........................P. Coast | | 22 | 129 | 8 | 7 | .533 | 114 | 57 | 46 | 94 | 32 | 3.21 |
| 1966—Seattle ...........................P. Coast | | 12 | 41 | 2 | 5 | .286 | 50 | 31 | 28 | 23 | 16 | 6.15 |
| 1966—El Paso...........................Texas | | 16 | 73 | 4 | 8 | .333 | 87 | 52 | 40 | 40 | 28 | 4.93 |
| 1967—Seattle ...........................P. Coast | | 32 | 230 | 11 | 14 | .440 | 199 | 81 | 71 | 114 | 44 | 2.78 |
| 1968—California‡§.........................American | | 56 | 73 | 1 | 4 | .200 | 65 | 41 | 35 | 33 | 24 | 4.32 |
| 1969—Kansas City‡ .......................American | | 31 | 54 | 3 | 1 | .750 | 67 | 31 | 25 | 23 | 21 | 4.17 |
| 1970—Omaha ...........................Am. Assoc. | | 10 | 22 | 3 | 1 | .750 | 10 | 3 | 3 | 9 | 7 | 1.23 |
| 1970—Kansas City.........................American | | 41 | 68 | 6 | 6 | .500 | 59 | 31 | 24 | 43 | 23 | 3.18 |
| 1971—Kansas City.........................American | | 67 | 88 | 9 | 7 | .563 | 71 | 23 | 17 | 44 | 30 | 1.74 |
| 1972—Kansas City.........................American | | 51 | 55 | 6 | 2 | .750 | 67 | 32 | 26 | 18 | 33 | 4.25 |
| 1973—Omaha‡ ...........................Am. Assoc. | | 24 | 61 | 2 | 4 | .333 | 75 | 35 | 35 | 31 | 19 | 5.16 |
| 1973—Kansas City x .....................American | | 6 | 0 | 0 | 0 | .000 | 13 | 6 | 6 | 4 | 4 | 5.40 |
| 1974—Minnesota ...........................American | | 50 | 92 | 5 | 3 | .625 | 92 | 46 | 46 | 34 | 26 | 4.50 |
| 1975—Minnesota ...........................American | | 46 | 76 | 5 | 8 | .385 | 76 | 32 | 26 | 41 | 23 | 3.08 |
| 1976—Minnesota ...........................American | | 57 | 115 | 8 | 1 | .889 | 95 | 36 | 32 | 45 | 29 | 2.50 |
| Major League Totals ............................... | | 405 | 631 | 43 | 32 | .573 | 605 | 278 | 237 | 285 | 213 | 3.38 |

†Released by Houston Colt .45s' organization, June 10, 1964; signed as free agent by Los Angeles Angels' organization, July 22, 1964.
‡Appeared as outfielder in one game.
§Selected by Kansas City Royals from California Angels in expansion draft, October 15, 1968.
xTraded to Minnesota Twins for Pitcher Ken Gill, October 24, 1973.

## GLENN LAWRENCE BURKE

Born November 16, 1952, at Oakland, Calif.
Height, 6.00. Weight, 195.
Throws and bats righthanded.
Hobbies—Basketball, football and air hockey.
Attended Merritt College, Oakland, Calif., and University of Nevada, Reno, Nev.

Led Florida State League in stolen bases with 42 in 1973 and Eastern League with 48 in 1975.
Led Pacific Coast League in stolen bases with 63 in 1976.

| Year Club | League | Pos. | G. | AB. | R. | H. | 2B. | 3B. | HR. | RBI. | B.A. | PO. | A. | E. | F.A. |
|---|---|---|---|---|---|---|---|---|---|---|---|---|---|---|---|
| 1972—Ogden ..............Pion. | | OF | 14 | 45 | 5 | 9 | 1 | 0 | 0 | 5 | .200 | 17 | 0 | 3 | .850 |
| 1972—Spokane ...........Northw. | | OF | 41 | 141 | 31 | 48 | 9 | 1 | 2 | 16 | .340 | 48 | 3 | 2 | .962 |
| 1973—Bakersfield........Calif. | | OF | 11 | 34 | 6 | 6 | 1 | 1 | 1 | 3 | .176 | 17 | 3 | 0 | 1.000 |
| 1973—Daytona Beach ..Fla. St. | | OF | 110 | 372 | 68 | 115 | 17 | 2 | 10 | 57 | .309 | 184 | 14 | 6 | .971 |
| 1974—Waterbury ........East. | | OF | 51 | 153 | 19 | 38 | 5 | 2 | 1 | 14 | .248 | 65 | 1 | 2 | .971 |
| 1974—Bakersfield........Calif. | | OF | 66 | 263 | 46 | 89 | 17 | 0 | 7 | 46 | .338 | 97 | 6 | 2 | .981 |
| 1975—Waterbury‡ ......East. | | OF | 119 | 478 | 66 | 129 | 14 | 2 | 12 | 49 | .270 | 211 | 7 | 4 | .982 |
| 1976—Albuquerque .....P.C. | | OF | 116 | 467 | 72 | 140 | 17 | 10 | 7 | 53 | .300 | 258 | 9 | 7 | .974 |
| 1976—Los Angeles ......Nat. | | OF | 25 | 46 | 9 | 11 | 2 | 0 | 0 | 5 | .239 | 33 | 0 | 1 | .971 |
| Major League Totals ...................... | | | 25 | 46 | 9 | 11 | 2 | 0 | 0 | 5 | .239 | 33 | 0 | 1 | .971 |

†On disabled list, April 24 to May 7, 1975.

## RICHARD PAUL BURLESON
### (Rick)

Born April 29, 1951, at Lynwood, Calif.
Height, 5.10. Weight, 160.
Throws and bats righthanded.
Hobby—Sports in general.
Attended Cerritos Junior College, Norwalk, Calif.

Led Eastern League shortstops in double plays with 80 in 1972.

| Year | Club | League | Pos. | G. | AB. | R. | H. | 2B. | 3B. | HR. | RBI. | B.A. | PO. | A. | E. | F.A. |
|------|------|--------|------|-----|------|-----|-----|-----|-----|-----|------|------|-----|------|-----|------|
| 1970—Winter Haven | ....Fla. St. | | SS | 118 | 419 | 42 | 92 | 13 | 4 | 1 | 29 | .220 | 188 | *400 | 38 | .939 |
| 1971—Greenville | ........W. Car. | | SS | 29 | 118 | 24 | 31 | 4 | 2 | 2 | 12 | .263 | 32 | 68 | 11 | .901 |
| 1971—Winston-Salem† | Carol. | | SS | 77 | 299 | 35 | 82 | 14 | 2 | 4 | 30 | .274 | 118 | 262 | 23 | .943 |
| 1972—Pawtucket | ........East. | | SS | 136 | 488 | 59 | 115 | 26 | 0 | 9 | 51 | .236 | *191 | 380 | 23 | *.961 |
| 1973—Pawtucket | ........Int. | | *SS-2B | *146 | 477 | 58 | 120 | 20 | 1 | 6 | 45 | .252 | 241 | 431 | 25 | *.964 |
| 1974—Pawtucket | ...........Int. | | SS | 10 | 41 | 7 | 14 | 4 | 0 | 1 | 4 | .341 | 10 | 36 | 3 | .939 |
| 1974—Boston | .............Amer. | | S-2-3 | 114 | 384 | 36 | 109 | 22 | 0 | 4 | 44 | .284 | 209 | 329 | 21 | .962 |
| 1975—Boston | .............Amer. | | SS | 158 | 580 | 66 | 146 | 25 | 1 | 6 | 62 | .252 | 267 | 498 | 29 | .963 |
| 1976—Boston | .............Amer. | | SS | 152 | 540 | 75 | 157 | 27 | 1 | 7 | 42 | .291 | 274 | 478 | 34 | .957 |
| Major League Totals | ...................... | | | 424 | 1504 | 177 | 412 | 74 | 2 | 17 | 148 | .274 | 750 | 1305 | 84 | .961 |

†On disabled list, June 1 through June 19.

#### CHAMPIONSHIP SERIES RECORD

| Year | Club | League | Pos. | G. | AB. | R. | H. | 2B. | 3B. | HR. | RBI. | B.A. | PO. | A. | E. | F.A. |
|------|------|--------|------|-----|------|-----|-----|-----|-----|-----|------|------|-----|------|-----|------|
| 1975—Boston | .............Amer. | | SS | 3 | 9 | 2 | 4 | 2 | 0 | 0 | 1 | .444 | 4 | 12 | 1 | .941 |

#### WORLD SERIES RECORD

| Year | Club | League | Pos. | G. | AB. | R. | H. | 2B. | 3B. | HR. | RBI. | B.A. | PO. | A. | E. | F.A. |
|------|------|--------|------|-----|------|-----|-----|-----|-----|-----|------|------|-----|------|-----|------|
| 1975—Boston | .............Amer. | | SS | 7 | 24 | 1 | 7 | 1 | 0 | 0 | 2 | .292 | 9 | 19 | 1 | .966 |

## BERTRAM RAY BURRIS
### (Known by middle name.)

Born August 22, 1950, at Idabel, Okla.
Height, 6.05. Weight, 200.
Throws and bats righthanded.
Hobby—Basketball.
Attended Southwestern State, Weatherford, Okla.; received Bachelor of Arts
degree in Recreational Leadership.

| Year | Club | League | G. | IP. | W. | L. | Pct. | H. | R. | ER. | SO. | BB. | ERA. |
|------|------|--------|-----|------|-----|-----|------|-----|-----|-----|------|------|------|
| 1972—Midland | ...............................Texas | | 14 | 95 | 7 | 5 | .583 | 98 | 43 | 37 | 91 | 20 | 3.51 |
| 1973—Wichita | ...............................Am. Assoc. | | 8 | 59 | 4 | 3 | .571 | 72 | 45 | 37 | 34 | 19 | 5.64 |
| 1973—Chicago | ...............................National | | 31 | 65 | 1 | 1 | .500 | 65 | 22 | 21 | 57 | 27 | 2.91 |
| 1974—Wichita | ...............................Am. Assoc. | | 7 | 46 | 2 | 3 | .400 | 52 | 33 | 26 | 34 | 23 | 5.09 |
| 1974—Chicago | ...............................National | | 40 | 75 | 3 | 5 | .375 | 91 | 61 | 55 | 40 | 26 | 6.60 |
| 1975—Chicago | ...............................National | | 36 | 238 | 15 | 10 | .600 | 259 | 121 | 109 | 108 | 73 | 4.12 |
| 1976—Chicago | ...............................National | | 37 | 249 | 15 | 13 | .536 | 251 | 102 | 86 | 112 | 70 | 3.11 |
| Major League Totals | ............................... | | 144 | 627 | 34 | 29 | .540 | 666 | 306 | 271 | 317 | 196 | 3.89 |

## JEFFREY ALAN BURROUGHS
### (Jeff)

Born March 7, 1951, at Long Beach, Calif.
Height, 6.02. Weight, 195.
Throws and bats righthanded.
Hobby—Fishing.
Attended Long Beach City College, Long Beach, Calif.

Led American League batters in strikeouts with 155 in 1975.
Led American League outfielders in double plays with 5 in 1974.
Led American League in sacrifice flies with 11 in 1973.
Named Most Valuable Player in American League, 1974.
Named American League Player of the Year by THE SPORTING NEWS, 1974.
Named as outfielder on THE SPORTING NEWS American League All-Star Team, 1974.
Received reported $88,000 bonus to sign with Washington Senators, 1969.

| Year | Club | League | Pos. | G. | AB. | R. | H. | 2B. | 3B. | HR. | RBI. | B.A. | PO. | A. | E. | F.A. |
|------|------|--------|------|-----|------|-----|-----|-----|-----|-----|------|------|------|-----|-----|------|
| 1969—Wytheville | ........Appal. | | 1B-OF | 52 | 183 | 41 | 65 | 16 | 4 | 6 | 48 | .355 | 192 | 12 | 10 | .953 |
| 1970—Denver | .............A.A. | | O-3-1 | 115 | 390 | 64 | 105 | 17 | 6 | 17 | 71 | .269 | 250 | 52 | 16 | .950 |
| 1970—Washington | ........Amer. | | OF | 6 | 12 | 1 | 2 | 0 | 0 | 0 | 1 | .167 | 5 | 0 | 0 | 1.000 |
| 1971—Denver | ..............A.A. | | OF | 81 | 298 | 51 | 87 | 13 | 3 | 12 | 58 | .292 | 108 | 7 | 10 | .920 |
| 1971—Washington | ........Amer. | | OF | 59 | 181 | 20 | 42 | 9 | 0 | 5 | 25 | .232 | 82 | 3 | 3 | .966 |
| 1972—Denver† | .............A.A. | | OF | 84 | 307 | 60 | 93 | 13 | 2 | 24 | 59 | .303 | 118 | 5 | 5 | .961 |
| 1972—Texas | ...............Amer. | | OF-1B | 22 | 65 | 4 | 12 | 1 | 0 | 1 | 3 | .185 | 33 | 2 | 2 | .946 |
| 1973—Texas | ...............Amer. | | OF-1B | 151 | 526 | 71 | 147 | 17 | 1 | 30 | 85 | .279 | 320 | 14 | 8 | .977 |
| 1974—Texas | ...............Amer. | | OF-1B | 152 | 554 | 84 | 167 | 33 | 2 | 25 | *118 | .301 | 242 | 11 | 8 | .969 |
| 1975—Texas | ...............Amer. | | OF | 152 | 585 | 81 | 132 | 20 | 0 | 29 | 94 | .226 | 249 | 10 | 9 | .966 |
| 1976—Texas‡ | .............Amer. | | OF-DH | 158 | 604 | 71 | 143 | 22 | 2 | 18 | 86 | .237 | 289 | 12 | 4 | .987 |
| Major League Totals | ...................... | | | 700 | 2527 | 332 | 645 | 102 | 5 | 108 | 412 | .255 | 1220 | 52 | 34 | .974 |

†On supplemental disabled list, April 27 through May 16, 1972.
‡Traded to Atlanta Braves for Outfielders Ken Henderson and Dave May, Pitchers Carl Morton, Rogelio

Moret and Adrian Devine, and cash estimated at $250,000, December 9, 1976.

| Year League | Pos. | AB. | R. | H. | 2B. | 3B. | HR. | RBI. | B.A. | PO. | A. | E. | F.A. |
|---|---|---|---|---|---|---|---|---|---|---|---|---|---|
| 1974—American ........................... | OF | 0 | 0 | 0 | 0 | 0 | 0 | 0 | .000 | 1 | 0 | 0 | 1.000 |

## JIM SCOTT BURTON

Born October 27, 1949, at Royal Oak, Mich.
Height, 6.03. Weight, 195.
Throws left and bats righthanded.
Attended University of Michigan, Ann Arbor, Mich.; received
Bachelor of Science degree in Education.

Led International League in wild pitches with 18 in 1976.
Pitched 2-0 no-hit victory against Tidewater, June 8, 1975.

| Year Club | League | G. | IP. | W. | L. | Pct. | H. | R. | ER. | SO. | BB. | ERA. |
|---|---|---|---|---|---|---|---|---|---|---|---|---|
| 1971—Pawtucket............................Eastern | Eastern | 14 | 89 | 7 | 5 | .583 | 64 | 31 | 28 | 71 | 35 | 2.83 |
| 1972—Pawtucket............................Eastern | Eastern | 21 | 150 | 11 | 7 | .611 | 128 | 59 | 51 | 104 | 62 | 3.06 |
| 1972—Louisville ............................Int'national | Int'national | 6 | 32 | 2 | 4 | .333 | 38 | 20 | 17 | 26 | 11 | 4.78 |
| 1973—Bristol† ...............................Eastern | Eastern | 24 | 86 | 4 | 11 | .267 | 91 | 57 | 49 | 56 | 59 | 5.13 |
| 1974—Pawtucket‡ .........................Int'national | Int'national | 24 | 149 | 7 | 13 | .350 | 109 | 61 | 58 | •146 | 68 | 3.50 |
| 1975—Pawtucket............................Int'national | Int'national | 12 | 94 | 8 | 2 | .800 | 51 | 20 | 16 | 73 | 32 | 1.53 |
| 1975—Boston ...............................American | American | 29 | 53 | 1 | 2 | .333 | 58 | 30 | 17 | 39 | 19 | 2.89 |
| 1976—Rhode Island .......................Int'national | Int'national | •28 | 169 | 11 | 7 | .611 | 167 | •110 | •105 | 106 | •112 | 5.59 |
| Major League Totals ............................. | | 29 | 53 | 1 | 2 | .333 | 58 | 30 | 17 | 39 | 19 | 2.89 |

†On disabled list, June 29 to July 17, 1973.
‡On disabled list, April 24 to May 7, 1974.
Listed on Roston Red Sox' 1977 spring roster.

| Year Club | League | G. | IP. | W. | L. | Pct. | H. | R. | ER. | SO. | BB. | ERA. |
|---|---|---|---|---|---|---|---|---|---|---|---|---|
| 1975—Boston ...............................American | American | 2 | 1 | 0 | 1 | .000 | 1 | 1 | 1 | 0 | 3 | 9.00 |

## STEVEN LEE BUSBY
### (Steve)

Born September 29, 1949, at Burbank, Calif.
Height, 6.02. Weight, 205.
Throws and bats righthanded.
Hobbies—Golf and bowling.
Attended University of Southern California, Los Angeles, Calif.
Fourth-cousin of Jim Busby, coach with Chicago White Sox.

Established American League record for most consecutive batsmen retired, season, 33, June 19-24, 1974.
Pitched 2-0 no-hit victory against Milwaukee Brewers, June 19, 1974.
Pitched 3-0 no-hit victory against Detroit Tigers, April 27, 1973.
Led American Association pitchers in complete games with 17 in 1972.
Tied for American Association lead in games started by pitchers with 30 and in wild pitches with 13 in 1972.
**Named American League Rookie Pitcher of the Year by** THE SPORTING NEWS, **1973.**

| Year Club | League | G. | IP. | W. | L. | Pct. | H. | R. | ER. | SO. | BB. | ERA. |
|---|---|---|---|---|---|---|---|---|---|---|---|---|
| 1971—San Jose ...............................California | California | 8 | 40 | 4 | 1 | .800 | 31 | 14 | 3 | 50 | 14 | 0.68 |
| 1972—Omaha ..............................Am. Assoc. | Am. Assoc. | 30 | •217 | 12 | 14 | .462 | 197 | 87 | 77 | •221 | 64 | 3.20 |
| 1972—Kansas City...........................American | American | 5 | 40 | 3 | 1 | .750 | 28 | 9 | 7 | 31 | 8 | 1.58 |
| 1973—Kansas City...........................American | American | 37 | 238 | 16 | 15 | .516 | 246 | 125 | 112 | 174 | 105 | 4.24 |
| 1974—Kansas City...........................American | American | 38 | 292 | 22 | 14 | .611 | 284 | 118 | 110 | 198 | 92 | 3.39 |
| 1975—Kansas City...........................American | American | 34 | 260 | 18 | 12 | .600 | 233 | 96 | 89 | 160 | 81 | 3.08 |
| 1976—Kansas City† .......................American | American | 13 | 72 | 3 | 3 | .500 | 58 | 42 | 35 | 29 | 49 | 4.38 |
| Major League Totals ............................. | | 127 | 902 | 62 | 45 | .579 | 849 | 390 | 353 | 592 | 335 | 3.52 |

†On disabled list, March 25 through April 17, 1976; and emergency disabled list July 10 through October 19, 1976.

| Year League | IP. | W. | L. | Pct. | H. | R. | ER. | SO. | BB. | ERA. |
|---|---|---|---|---|---|---|---|---|---|---|
| 1975—American ..................................................... | 2 | 0 | 0 | .000 | 4 | 1 | 1 | 0 | 0 | 4.50 |

Member of American League All-Star Team in 1974 game; did not play.

## MICHAEL THOMAS BUSKEY
### (Mike)

Born January 13, 1950, at San Francisco, Calif.
Height, 5.11. Weight, 160.
Throws and bats righthanded.
Hobbies—Tennis, skiing, fishing and golf.
Attended University of San Francisco, San Francisco, Calif.; received
Bachelor of Arts degree in English.

Led Midwest League in sacrifice hits with 12 in 1972 and Southern League with 12 in 1973.

Led American Association shortstops in double plays with 91 in 1976.
Tied for Gulf Coast League lead in sacrifice hits with 4 in 1971.

| Year Club | League | Pos. | G. | AB. | R. | H. | 2B. | 3B. | HR. | RBI. | B.A. | PO. | A. | E. | F.A. |
|---|---|---|---|---|---|---|---|---|---|---|---|---|---|---|---|
| 1971—Sarasota W.S. ....Gulf C. | | •2B-SS | 46 | 179 | 27 | 53 | 5 | 0 | 0 | 16 | .296 | •99 | 106 | 15 | .932 |
| 1972—Appleton............Midw. | | •S-2-3 | 122 | 441 | 74 | 117 | 17 | 2 | 2 | 41 | .265 | •204 | 332 | 34 | •.940 |
| 1973—Knoxville .........South. | | SS-2B | 136 | 510 | 82 | 130 | 17 | 2 | 2 | 48 | .255 | 290 | 468 | 34 | .957 |
| 1973—Iowa.................A.A. | | SS | 2 | 4 | 0 | 0 | 0 | 0 | 0 | 0 | .000 | 2 | 3 | 0 | 1.000 |
| 1974—Knoxville .........South. | | SS | 77 | 276 | 44 | 77 | 8 | 4 | 1 | 24 | .279 | 130 | 225 | 18 | .952 |
| 1974—Iowa.................A.A. | | SS | 38 | 119 | 20 | 31 | 4 | 2 | 2 | 12 | .261 | 65 | 110 | 12 | .936 |
| 1975—Denver† ............A.A. | | SS | 133 | 448 | 67 | 109 | 15 | •9 | 2 | 43 | .243 | •245 | 393 | 24 | .964 |
| 1976—Oklahoma City ..A.A. | | SS | 122 | 387 | 54 | 104 | 25 | 4 | 2 | 45 | .269 | 194 | •379 | 29 | .952 |

†Traded with Pitcher Jim Kaat by Chicago White Sox to Philadelphia Phillies for Outfielder-Infielder Alan Bannister and Pitchers Dick Ruthven and Roy Thomas, December 10, 1975.
Listed on Philadelphia Phillies' 1977 spring roster.

### THOMAS WILLIAM BUSKEY
### (Tom)

Born February 20, 1947, at Harrisburg, Pa.
Height, 6.03. Weight, 215.
Throws and bats righthanded.
Hobby—Bowling.
Attended University of North Carolina, Chapel Hill, N. C.; received Bachelor of Arts degree in Education.
Tied for Florida State League lead in shutouts with 5 in 1970.

| Year Club | League | G. | IP. | W. | L. | Pct. | H. | R. | ER. | SO. | BB. | ERA. |
|---|---|---|---|---|---|---|---|---|---|---|---|---|
| 1969—Johnson City .......................Ap'lachian | | 5 | 41 | 5 | 0 | •1.000 | 25 | 8 | 6 | 51 | 4 | 1.32 |
| 1969—Fort Lauderdale .................Florida St. | | 7 | 48 | 3 | 3 | .500 | 49 | 17 | 12 | 29 | 9 | 2.25 |
| 1970—Fort Lauderdale† ...............Florida St. | | 18 | 133 | 10 | 5 | .667 | 98 | 37 | 29 | 81 | 19 | 1.96 |
| 1970—Kinston ...............................Carolina | | 2 | 13 | 1 | 1 | .500 | 7 | 2 | 2 | 5 | 3 | 1.38 |
| 1971—Manchester ..........................Eastern | | 21 | 122 | 7 | 5 | .583 | 104 | 46 | 37 | 76 | 28 | 2.73 |
| 1971—Syracuse ..........................Int'national | | 9 | 21 | 0 | 3 | .000 | 36 | 22 | 21 | 8 | 11 | 9.00 |
| 1972—West Haven..........................Eastern | | 24 | 137 | 9 | 5 | .643 | 123 | 55 | 43 | 83 | 27 | 2.82 |
| 1973—Syracuse ..........................Int'national | | 30 | 87 | 6 | 4 | .600 | 76 | 34 | 28 | 52 | 28 | 2.90 |
| 1973—New York ...........................American | | 8 | 17 | 0 | 1 | .000 | 18 | 12 | 10 | 8 | 4 | 5.29 |
| 1974—New York‡-Cleveland ..........American | | 55 | 99 | 2 | 7 | .222 | 103 | 40 | 37 | 43 | 36 | 3.36 |
| 1975—Cleveland§ ..........................American | | 50 | 77 | 5 | 3 | .625 | 69 | 27 | 22 | 29 | 29 | 2.57 |
| 1976—Cleveland ............................American | | 39 | 94 | 5 | 4 | .556 | 88 | 42 | 38 | 32 | 34 | 3.64 |
| Major League Totals ............................... | | 152 | 287 | 12 | 15 | .444 | 178 | 121 | 107 | 112 | 103 | 3.36 |

†On temporary inactive list, April 17 to June 9, 1970.
‡Traded with Pitchers Fritz Peterson, Steve Kline and Fred Beene to Cleveland Indians for First Baseman Chris Chambliss and Pitchers Dick Tidrow and Cecil Upshaw, April 26, 1974.
§On disabled list, July 25 to September 1, 1975.

### JEFFREY ALLAN BYRD
### (Jeff)

Born November 11, 1956, at La Mesa, Calif.
Height, 6.03. Weight, 195.
Throws and bats righthanded.
Hobbies—Sports and camping.

| Year Club | League | G. | IP. | W. | L. | Pct. | H. | R. | ER. | SO. | BB. | ERA. |
|---|---|---|---|---|---|---|---|---|---|---|---|---|
| 1974—Sarasota Rangers .................Gulf Coast | | 9 | 47 | 4 | 1 | .800 | 23 | 17 | 15 | 34 | 39 | 2.87 |
| 1975—Anderson ...........................W. Carol. | | 22 | 141 | 7 | 11 | .389 | 115 | 78 | 62 | 82 | 104 | 3.96 |
| 1976—San Antonio† ........................Texas | | 26 | 143 | 7 | 11 | .389 | 152 | 106 | 83 | 86 | 107 | 5.22 |

†Selected by Toronto Blue Jays from Texas Rangers in American League expansion draft, November 5, 1976.

### ENOS MILTON CABELL, JR.

Born October 8, 1949, at Fort Riley, Kan.
Height, 6.05. Weight, 190.
Throws and bats righthanded.
Hobby—Sports in general.
Attended Harbor Junior College, San Pedro, Calif.
Led Appalachian League in total bases with 149 in 1969.
Named Rookie of the Year in Appalachian League, 1969.
Named Player of the Year in Texas League, 1971.

| Year Club | League | Pos. | G. | AB. | R. | H. | 2B. | 3B. | HR. | RBI. | B.A. | PO. | A. | E. | F.A. |
|---|---|---|---|---|---|---|---|---|---|---|---|---|---|---|---|
| 1969—Bluefield .........Appal. | | 1B | •69 | •270 | •62 | •101 | 14 | 2 | 10 | 43 | .374 | •471 | 30 | 9 | .982 |
| 1970—Stockton ...........Calif. | | •1B-OF | 138 | 517 | 78 | 147 | 25 | 6 | 10 | 67 | .284 | 844 | •81 | •33 | .966 |
| 1971—Dall-Ft. Worth ..Tex. | | •1-3-O | 140 | 521 | 65 | •162 | 24 | 6 | 6 | 79 | •.311 | 1135 | •122 | •20 | .984 |
| 1972—Rochester..........Int. | | •1-0-3-S | 141 | •540 | 82 | 145 | 26 | 9 | 8 | 66 | .269 | 893 | •110 | 11 | •.989 |
| 1972—Baltimore.........Amer. | | 1B | 3 | 5 | 0 | 0 | 0 | 0 | 0 | 1 | .000 | 7 | 0 | 0 | 1.000 |
| 1973—Rochester..........Int. | | 1-3-2 | 60 | 229 | 43 | 81 | 9 | 1 | 2 | 24 | .354 | 510 | 47 | 10 | .982 |

| Year Club League | Pos. | G. | AB. | R. | H. | 2B. | 3B. | HR. | RBI. | B.A. | PO. | A. | E. | F.A. |
|---|---|---|---|---|---|---|---|---|---|---|---|---|---|---|
| 1973—Baltimore..........Amer. | 1B-3B | 32 | 47 | 12 | 10 | 2 | 0 | 1 | 3 | .213 | 111 | 4 | 1 | .991 |
| 1974—Baltimore..........Amer. | 1-O-3-2 | 80 | 174 | 24 | 42 | 4 | 2 | 3 | 17 | .241 | 223 | 45 | 4 | .985 |
| 1975—Houston ............Nat. | O-1-3 | 117 | 348 | 43 | 92 | 17 | 6 | 2 | 43 | .264 | 197 | 58 | 6 | .977 |
| 1976—Houston ............Nat. | 3B-1B | 144 | 586 | 85 | 160 | 13 | 7 | 2 | 43 | .273 | 131 | 263 | 17 | .959 |
| American League Totals ................ | | 115 | 226 | 36 | 52 | 6 | 2 | 4 | 21 | .230 | 341 | 49 | 5 | .987 |
| National League Totals ................. | | 261 | 934 | 128 | 252 | 30 | 13 | 4 | 86 | .270 | 328 | 321 | 23 | .966 |
| Major League Totals ..................... | | 376 | 1160 | 164 | 304 | 36 | 15 | 8 | 107 | .262 | 669 | 370 | 28 | .974 |

†Traded with Second Baseman Rob Andrews to Houston Astros for First Baseman Lee May and Outfielder Jay Schlueter, December 3, 1974.

CHAMPIONSHIP SERIES RECORD

| Year Club League | Pos. | G. | AB. | R. | H. | 2B. | 3B. | HR. | RBI. | B.A. | PO. | A. | E. | F.A. |
|---|---|---|---|---|---|---|---|---|---|---|---|---|---|---|
| 1974—Baltimore..........Am | O-PH-PR | 3 | 4 | 0 | 1 | 0 | 0 | 0 | 0 | .250 | 2 | 0 | 0 | 1.000 |

## CRAIG CACEK

Born August 10, 1954, at Hollywood, Calif.
Height, 6.01. Weight, 200.
Throws and bats righthanded.
Hobbies—Tennis, hiking, reading and bicycling.
Attended Pierce Junior College, Woodland Hills, Calif.

| Year Club League | Pos. | G. | AB. | R. | H. | 2B. | 3B. | HR. | RBI. | B.A. | PO. | A. | E. | F.A. |
|---|---|---|---|---|---|---|---|---|---|---|---|---|---|---|
| 1972—Marion ..............Appal. | OF | 61 | 202 | 37 | 54 | 7 | 4 | 9 | 27 | .267 | 63 | 3 | 5 | .930 |
| 1973—Pompano Beach Fla. St. | OF | 138 | 465 | 76 | 134 | 24 | 3 | 5 | 64 | .288 | 178 | 9 | 6 | .969 |
| 1974—Visalia ..............Calif. | 1B-OF | 139 | 483 | ∗112 | 152 | 26 | 2 | 22 | 93 | .315 | ∗1106 | ●71 | ∗22 | .981 |
| 1975—Jackson† ..........Texas | 1B | 129 | 432 | 63 | 135 | 20 | 7 | 4 | 57 | .313 | ∗1085 | ∗70 | 16 | .986 |
| 1976—Memphis ..........Int. | 1B-OF | 132 | 475 | 85 | 154 | 24 | 1 | 8 | 63 | .324 | 1200 | ∗106 | 18 | .986 |

†Traded for catcher Manual Lantiqua by New York Mets' organization to Houston Astros' organization, December 23, 1975.

Listed on Houston Astros' 1977 spring roster.

## RALPH MICHAEL CALDWELL
### (Mike)

Born January 22, 1949, at Tarboro, N. C.
Height, 6.00. Weight, 185.
Throws left and bats righthanded.
Hobby—Model airplanes.
Attended North Carolina State University, Raleigh, N. C.
Son of Ralph Franklin Caldwell, former minor league catcher.

| Year Club League | G. | IP. | W. | L. | Pct. | H. | R. | ER. | SO. | BB. | ERA. |
|---|---|---|---|---|---|---|---|---|---|---|---|
| 1971—Tri-City...............................Northwest | 2 | 11 | 2 | 0 | 1.000 | 9 | 2 | 2 | 19 | 5 | 1.64 |
| 1971—Lodi ...................................California | 17 | 32 | 4 | 1 | .800 | 31 | 14 | 13 | 38 | 12 | 3.66 |
| 1971—San Diego .........................National | 6 | 7 | 1 | 0 | 1.000 | 4 | 0 | 0 | 5 | 3 | 0.00 |
| 1972—San Diego ..........................National | 42 | 164 | 7 | 11 | .389 | 183 | 92 | 73 | 102 | 49 | 4.01 |
| 1973—San Diego† ........................National | 55 | 149 | 5 | 14 | .263 | 146 | 77 | 62 | 86 | 53 | 3.74 |
| 1974—San Francisco .....................National | 31 | 189 | 14 | 5 | .737 | 176 | 80 | 62 | 83 | 63 | 2.95 |
| 1975—San Francisco .....................National | 38 | 163 | 7 | 13 | .350 | 194 | 102 | 87 | 57 | 48 | 4.80 |
| 1976—San Francisco‡ ...................National | 50 | 107 | 1 | 7 | .125 | 145 | 74 | 58 | 55 | 20 | 4.88 |
| Major League Totals ............................. | 122 | 779 | 35 | 50 | .412 | 848 | 425 | 342 | 388 | 236 | 3.95 |

†Traded to San Francisco Giants for First Baseman Willie McCovey and Outfielder Bernie Williams (latter on Phoenix roster), October 25, 1973.

‡Traded with Pitcher John D'Acquisto and Catcher Dave Rader to St. Louis Cardinals for Outfielder Willie Crawford, Pitcher John Curtis, and Infielder-Outfielder Vic Harris, October 26, 1976. Traded to Cincinnati Reds' organization for Pitcher Pat Darcy, March 29, 1977.

## RICK LAMAR CAMP

Born June 10, 1953, at Trion, Ga.
Height, 6.01. Weight, 185.
Throws and bats righthanded.
Attended West Georgia College, Carrollton, Ga.

| Year Club League | G. | IP. | W. | L. | Pct. | H. | R. | ER. | SO. | BB. | ERA. |
|---|---|---|---|---|---|---|---|---|---|---|---|
| 1974—Kingsport ...........................Ap'plachian | 7 | 43 | 3 | 2 | .600 | 44 | 23 | 15 | 52 | 16 | 3.14 |
| 1975—Savannah ...........................Southern | 25 | 176 | 12 | 10 | .545 | 161 | 68 | 56 | 100 | 62 | 2.86 |
| 1976—Richmond ...........................Int'national | 49 | 164 | 10 | 11 | .476 | 177 | 90 | 78 | 85 | 68 | 4.28 |
| 1976—Atlanta ...............................National | 5 | 11 | 0 | 1 | .000 | 13 | 9 | 8 | 6 | 2 | 6.55 |
| Major League Totals ............................. | 5 | 11 | 0 | 1 | .000 | 13 | 9 | 8 | 6 | 2 | 6.55 |

Invited to Atlanta Braves' 1977 spring camp.

---

**DID YOU KNOW —**
That the 1927 Philadelphia A's had 11 players who batted .300 or better for the season while appearing in 50 or more games?

# DAGOBERTO BLANCO CAMPANERIS
## (Bert and Campy)

Born March 9, 1942, at Pueblo Nuevo, Matanzas, Cuba.
Height, 5,10. Weight, 160.
Throws and bats righthanded.
Hobby—Fishing.
Cousin of Jose Cardenal, Chicago Cubs' outfielder.

Established major league record for most double plays, shortstop, extra-inning game (6), September 13, 1970, first game (11 innings).

Tied major league record for most home runs first game in majors (2), July 23, 1964, against Minnesota Twins. Campaneris hit Jim Kaat's first pitch of game for homer, and added No. 2 in the seventh inning.

Tied modern major league record for most triples, game (3), August 29, 1967.

Established American League record for: fewest hits, season, for leader in hits, 177, in 1968; most time caught stealing, lifetime, 157, 1976.

Tied following American League records: Most positions played, one season (9), 1965 and most positions played, one game (9), September 8, 1965; most home runs as leadoff batter, season, 6, in 1970.

On August 13, 1962, pitching in relief for Daytona Beach against Ft. Lauderdale, Campaneris pitched right-handed to the righthanded batters and lefthanded to the lefthanded batters. In two innings he gave up one run and one hit while walking two and striking out four.

Major League stolen bases: 1964 (10), 1965 (51), 1966 (52), 1967 (55), 1968 (62), 1969 (62), 1970 (42), 1971 (34), 1972 (52), 1973 (34), 1974 (34), 1975 (24), 1976 (54). Total—566.

Led American League in stolen bases with 51 in 1965, 52 in 1966, 55 in 1967, 62 in 1968, 42 in 1970 and 52 in 1972.

Led American League in sacrifice hits with 20 in 1972.

Led American League shortstops in total chances with 795 in 1972.

Named shortstop on THE SPORTING NEWS American League All-Star Team, 1973 and 1974.

| Year—Club | League | Pos. | G. | AB. | R. | H. | 2B. | 3B. | HR. | RBI. | B.A. | PO. | A. | E. | F.A. |
|---|---|---|---|---|---|---|---|---|---|---|---|---|---|---|---|
| 1962—Daytona Beach ..Fl. St. | | O-1-C-S | 100 | 334 | 59 | 97 | 15 | 2 | 1 | 33 | .290 | 384 | 68 | 24 | .950 |
| 1962—Binghamton ......Ea. | | I-OF-P | 13 | 44 | 11 | 16 | 3 | 0 | 0 | 3 | .364 | 12 | 4 | 2 | .889 |
| 1963—Lewiston ..........Northw. | | PH | 11 | 6 | 2 | 0 | 0 | 0 | 0 | 1 | .000 | 0 | 0 | 0 | .000 |
| 1963—Binghamton ......Ea. | | SS-C-1B | 35 | 117 | 21 | 36 | 5 | 1 | 0 | 12 | .308 | 99 | 49 | 12 | .925 |
| 1964—Birmingham ......South. | | SS | 86 | 354 | 69 | 115 | 18 | •11 | 6 | 40 | .325 | 163 | 229 | 23 | .945 |
| 1964—Kansas City ......Amer. | | SS-O-3 | 67 | 269 | 27 | 69 | 14 | 3 | 4 | 22 | .257 | 102 | 108 | 8 | .963 |
| 1965—Kansas City .....Amer. | | SS-OF† | 144 | 578 | 67 | 156 | 23 | •12 | 6 | 42 | .270 | 258 | 276 | 35 | .938 |
| 1966—Kansas City ......Amer. | | SS | 142 | 573 | 82 | 153 | 29 | 10 | 5 | 42 | .267 | 283 | 350 | 19 | .971 |
| 1967—Kansas City ......Amer. | | SS | 147 | 601 | 85 | 149 | 29 | 6 | 3 | 32 | .248 | •259 | 365 | •30 | .954 |
| 1968—Oakland ..........Amer. | | •SS-OF | 159 | •642 | 87 | •177 | 25 | 9 | 4 | 38 | .276 | •283 | 458 | •34 | .956 |
| 1969—Oakland ..........Amer. | | SS | 135 | 547 | 71 | 142 | 15 | 2 | 2 | 25 | .260 | 220 | 391 | 21 | .967 |
| 1970—Oakland ..........Amer. | | SS | 147 | 603 | 97 | 168 | 28 | 4 | 22 | 64 | .279 | 267 | 414 | 19 | .973 |
| 1971—Oakland‡ .........Amer. | | SS | 134 | 569 | 80 | 143 | 18 | 4 | 5 | 47 | .251 | 231 | 303 | •26 | .954 |
| 1972—Oakland ..........Amer. | | SS | 149 | •625 | 85 | 150 | 25 | 2 | 8 | 32 | .240 | •283 | 494 | 18 | .977 |
| 1973—Oakland ..........Amer. | | SS | 151 | 601 | 89 | 150 | 17 | 6 | 4 | 46 | .250 | 228 | 496 | 23 | .969 |
| 1974—Oakland§ .........Amer. | | SS | 134 | 527 | 77 | 153 | 18 | 8 | 2 | 41 | .290 | 207 | 423 | 22 | .966 |
| 1975—Oakland ..........Amer. | | SS | 137 | 509 | 69 | 135 | 15 | 3 | 4 | 46 | .265 | 199 | 378 | 23 | .962 |
| 1976—Oakland x.........Amer. | | SS | 149 | 536 | 67 | 137 | 14 | 1 | 1 | 52 | .256 | 231 | 490 | 23 | .969 |
| Major League Totals ...................... | | | 1795 | 7180 | 983 | 1882 | 270 | 70 | 70 | 529 | .262 | 3051 | 4946 | 301 | .964 |

†On September 8 against the California Angels, Campaneris played one inning at each of the nine positions.
‡On disabled list, July 3 to July 23, 1971.
§On supplemental disabled list, July 28 to August 12, 1974.
xPlayed out option year, and granted free agency, November 1, 1976; signed as free agent by Texas Rangers, November 17, 1976.

## CHAMPIONSHIP SERIES RECORD

| Year—Club | League | Pos. | G. | AB. | R. | H. | 2B. | 3B. | HR. | RBI. | B.A. | PO. | A. | E. | F.A. |
|---|---|---|---|---|---|---|---|---|---|---|---|---|---|---|---|
| 1971—Oakland ...........Amer. | | SS | 3 | 12 | 0 | 2 | 1 | 0 | 0 | 0 | .167 | 3 | 6 | 0 | 1.000 |
| 1972—Oakland ...........Amer. | | SS | 2 | 7 | 3 | 3 | 0 | 0 | 0 | 0 | .429 | 3 | 7 | 0 | 1.000 |
| 1973—Oakland ...........Amer. | | SS | 5 | 21 | 3 | 7 | 1 | 0 | 2 | 3 | .333 | 6 | 15 | 1 | .955 |
| 1974—Oakland ...........Amer. | | SS | 4 | 17 | 0 | 3 | 0 | 0 | 0 | 3 | .176 | 3 | 17 | 0 | 1.000 |
| 1975—Oakland ...........Amer. | | SS | 3 | 11 | 1 | 0 | 0 | 0 | 0 | 0 | .000 | 2 | 10 | 0 | 1.000 |
| Championship Series Totals ............ | | | 17 | 68 | 7 | 15 | 2 | 0 | 2 | 6 | .221 | 17 | 55 | 1 | .986 |

## WORLD SERIES RECORD

| Year—Club | League | Pos. | G. | AB. | R. | H. | 2B. | 3B. | HR. | RBI. | B.A. | PO. | A. | E. | F.A. |
|---|---|---|---|---|---|---|---|---|---|---|---|---|---|---|---|
| 1972—Oakland ...........Amer. | | SS | 7 | 28 | 1 | 5 | 0 | 0 | 0 | 0 | .179 | 17 | 15 | 1 | .970 |
| 1973—Oakland ...........Amer. | | SS | 7 | 31 | 6 | 9 | 0 | 1 | 1 | 3 | .290 | 10 | 28 | 1 | .974 |
| 1974—Oakland ...........Amer. | | SS | 5 | 17 | 1 | 6 | 2 | 0 | 0 | 2 | .353 | 6 | 16 | 2 | .917 |
| World Series Totals ...................... | | | 19 | 76 | 8 | 20 | 2 | 1 | 1 | 5 | .263 | 33 | 59 | 4 | .958 |

## ALL-STAR GAME RECORD

| Year—League | Pos. | AB. | R. | H. | 2B. | 3B. | HR. | RBI. | B.A. | PO. | A. | E. | F.A. |
|---|---|---|---|---|---|---|---|---|---|---|---|---|---|
| 1968—American ........................... | SS | 1 | 0 | 0 | 0 | 0 | 0 | 0 | .000 | 1 | 0 | 0 | 1.000 |
| 1973—American ........................... | SS | 3 | 0 | 0 | 0 | 0 | 0 | 0 | .000 | 1 | 2 | 0 | 1.000 |
| 1974—American ........................... | SS | 4 | 0 | 0 | 0 | 0 | 0 | 0 | .000 | 2 | 3 | 0 | 1.000 |
| 1975—American ........................... | SS | 2 | 0 | 2 | 0 | 0 | 0 | 0 | 1.000 | 3 | 2 | 0 | 1.000 |
| All-Star Game Totals ...................... | | 10 | 0 | 2 | 0 | 0 | 0 | 0 | .200 | 7 | 7 | 0 | 1.000 |

Member of American League All-Star Team for the 1972 game; did not play.

| Year Club | League | G. | IP. | W. | L. | Pct. | H. | R. | ER. | SO. | BB. | ERA. |
|---|---|---|---|---|---|---|---|---|---|---|---|---|
| 1962—Daytona Beach ................... | Florida St. | 3 | 6 | 0 | 0 | .000 | 5 | 2 | 2 | 6 | 2 | 3.00 |
| 1962—Binghamton........................ | Eastern | 1 | 2 | 0 | 0 | .000 | 2 | 5 | 1 | 0 | 4 | 4.50 |
| 1965—Kansas City........................ | American | 1 | 1 | 0 | 0 | .000 | 1 | 1 | 1 | 1 | 2 | 9.00 |
| Major League Totals .............................. | | 1 | 1 | 0 | 0 | .000 | 1 | 1 | 1 | 1 | 2 | 9.00 |

## WILLIAM RICHARD CAMPBELL
### (Bill)

Born August 9, 1948, at Highland Park, Mich.
Height, 6.03½. Weight, 190.
Throws and bats righthanded.
Hobby—Coaching girls' basketball team.
Attended Mount San Antonio Junior College, Walnut, Calif.

Led Southern League pitchers in complete games with 14 and tied for lead in games started with 29 in 1972.
Established American League record for most innings pitched, relief pitcher, sesason–168, 1976.
Tied American League record for most games won, relief pitcher, season–17, 1976.
Named by THE SPORTING NEWS as American League Fireman of the Year, 1976.

| Year Club | League | G. | IP. | W. | L. | Pct. | H. | R. | ER. | SO. | BB. | ERA. |
|---|---|---|---|---|---|---|---|---|---|---|---|---|
| 1971—Wisconsin Rapids† ............... | Midwest | 9 | 63 | 5 | 3 | .625 | 42 | 13 | 8 | 91 | 19 | 1.14 |
| 1972—Charlotte.......................... | Southern | 29 | 219 | 13 | 10 | .565 | 181 | 74 | 59 | *204 | 69 | 2.42 |
| 1973—Tacoma............................. | P. Coast | 18 | 133 | 10 | 5 | .667 | 123 | 63 | 54 | 110 | 46 | 3.65 |
| 1973—Minnesota ......................... | American | 28 | 52 | 3 | 3 | .500 | 44 | 20 | 18 | 42 | 20 | 3.12 |
| 1974—Minnesota ......................... | American | 63 | 120 | 8 | 7 | .533 | 109 | 37 | 35 | 89 | 55 | 2.63 |
| 1975—Minnesota‡ ........................ | American | 47 | 121 | 4 | 6 | .400 | 119 | 58 | 51 | 76 | 46 | 3.79 |
| 1976—Minnesota ......................... | American | *78 | 168 | 17 | 5 | *.773 | 145 | 63 | 56 | 115 | 62 | 3.00 |
| Major League Totals ............................. | | 216 | 461 | 32 | 21 | .604 | 417 | 178 | 160 | 322 | 183 | 3.12 |

†On disabled list, June 14, 1971 through remainder of season.
‡Played out option year in 1976; signed as free agent by Boston Red Sox, November 6, 1976.

## CARDELL CAMPER

Born July 6, 1952, at Boley, Okla.
Height, 6.03. Weight, 208.
Throws and bats righthanded.
Attended Glendale Community College, Glendale, Ariz.

| Year Club | League | G. | IP. | W. | L. | Pct. | H. | R. | ER. | SO. | BB. | ERA. |
|---|---|---|---|---|---|---|---|---|---|---|---|---|
| 1973—St. Petersburg..................... | Florida St. | 4 | 11 | 0 | 1 | .000 | 9 | 11 | 7 | 11 | 10 | 5.73 |
| 1973—Sarasota Cardinals .............. | Gulf State | 12 | 69 | 4 | 6 | .400 | 53 | 26 | 21 | 59 | 47 | 2.74 |
| 1974—St. Petersburg..................... | Florida St. | 23 | 157 | 11 | 6 | .647 | 122 | 58 | 46 | 84 | 84 | 2.64 |
| 1975—St. Petersburg..................... | Florida St. | 13 | 88 | 8 | 2 | .800 | 77 | 30 | 25 | 46 | 34 | 2.56 |
| 1975—Arkansas............................ | Texas | 13 | 75 | 6 | 6 | .500 | 79 | 34 | 23 | 43 | 41 | 2.76 |
| 1976—Arkansas† ........................ | Texas | 7 | 35 | 1 | 3 | .250 | 33 | 22 | 20 | 25 | 25 | 5.14 |
| 1976—Toledo............................... | Int'national | 18 | 95 | 4 | 8 | .333 | 101 | 65 | 57 | 58 | 40 | 5.40 |

†Traded by St. Louis Cardinals' organization to Cleveland Indians' organization for Outfielder Nelson Garcia, May 23, 1976.
Listed on Cleveland Indians' 1977 winter roster.

## JOHN ROBERT CANDELARIA

Born November 6, 1953, at Brooklyn, N.Y.
Height, 6.07. Weight, 218.
Throws and bats lefthanded.
Hobbies—Records, fishing, hunting and basketball.

Pitched 2-0 no-hit victory against Los Angeles Dodgers, August 9, 1976.
Received reported $40,000 bonus to sign with Pittsburgh Pirates, 1973.

| Year Club | League | G. | IP. | W. | L. | Pct. | H. | R. | ER. | SO. | BB. | ERA. |
|---|---|---|---|---|---|---|---|---|---|---|---|---|
| 1973—Charleston ......................... | W. Carol. | 18 | 95 | 10 | 2 | *.833 | 84 | 45 | 40 | 60 | 38 | 3.79 |
| 1974—Salem ................................ | Carolina | 25 | 154 | 11 | 8 | .579 | 146 | 80 | 63 | 147 | 63 | 3.68 |
| 1974—Charleston ......................... | Int'national | 1 | 11 | 0 | 0 | .000 | 7 | 2 | 2 | 10 | 1 | 1.64 |
| 1975—Charleston ......................... | Int'national | 10 | 61 | 7 | 1 | .875 | 53 | 15 | 12 | 48 | 17 | 1.77 |
| 1975—Pittsburgh.......................... | National | 18 | 121 | 8 | 6 | .571 | 95 | 47 | 37 | 95 | 36 | 2.75 |
| 1976—Pittsburgh.......................... | National | 32 | 220 | 16 | 7 | .696 | 173 | 87 | 77 | 138 | 60 | 3.15 |
| Major League Totals .............................. | | 50 | 341 | 24 | 13 | .649 | 268 | 134 | 114 | 233 | 96 | 3.01 |

CHAMPIONSHIP SERIES RECORD

| Year Club | League | G. | IP. | W. | L. | Pct. | H. | R. | ER. | SO. | BB. | ERA. |
|---|---|---|---|---|---|---|---|---|---|---|---|---|
| 1975—Pittsburgh.......................... | National | 1 | 7⅔ | 0 | 0 | .000 | 3 | 3 | 3 | 14 | 2 | 3.52 |

**DID YOU KNOW —**

The Miller Huggins led National League batsmen in bases on balls with 116 in 1910? Huggins played for the St. Louis club.

## JOSEPH JEROME CANNON

Born July 13, 1953, at Camp Lejeune, N. C.
Height, 6.03. Weight, 193.
Throws right and bats lefthanded.
Hobbies—Golf, hunting and fishing.
Attended Pensacola Junior College, Pensacola, Fla.
Cousin of Willie Broughton, infielder with San Francisco Giants' organization,
and Pittsburgh Pirates' organization, 1957 through 1961.

| Year Club | League | Pos. | G. | AB. | R. | H. | 2B. | 3B. | HR. | RBI. | B.A. | PO. | A. | E. | F.A. |
|---|---|---|---|---|---|---|---|---|---|---|---|---|---|---|---|
| 1974—Covington | Appal. | OF | 66 | 280 | 55 | 84 | 13 | 8 | 6 | 40 | .300 | 66 | 136 | 6 | .928 |
| 1974—Cedar Rapids | Midw. | OF | 11 | 38 | 2 | 7 | 2 | 1 | 0 | 1 | .184 | 20 | 0 | 0 | 1.000 |
| 1975—Dubuque | Midw. | OF | 119 | 346 | 47 | 72 | 8 | 5 | 6 | 37 | .208 | 160 | 17 | 12 | .937 |
| 1976—Columbus | South. | OF | 127 | 478 | 64 | 142 | 13 | 4 | 2 | 40 | .297 | 238 | 12 | 8 | .969 |

Listed on Houston Astros' 1977 spring roster.

## DOUGLAS EDMUND CAPILLA
### (Doug)

Born January 7, 1952, at Honolulu, Hawaii.
Height, 5.10. Weight, 180.
Throws and bats lefthanded.
Hobbies—Fishing, swimming and dancing.
Attended West Valley College, Saratoga, Calif.

Pitched seven-inning, 1-0 no-hit victory against Appleton, May 31, 1972.
Tied for Midwest League lead in hit batsmen with 12 and tied for lead in wild pitches with 25 in 1972.

| Year Club | League | G. | IP. | W. | L. | Pct. | H. | R. | ER. | SO. | BB. | ERA. |
|---|---|---|---|---|---|---|---|---|---|---|---|---|
| 1970—Great Falls† | Pioneer | 17 | 38 | 2 | 5 | .286 | 24 | 37 | 28 | 69 | 57 | 6.63 |
| 1971—Fresno‡ | California | | | | | | Did not play. | | | | | |
| 1972—Decatur | Midwest | 26 | 161 | 6 | 12 | .333 | 134 | ∗100 | ∗84 | 192 | ●125 | 4.70 |
| 1973—Fresno§ | California | 24 | 86 | 4 | 7 | .364 | 86 | 67 | 42 | 112 | 74 | 4.40 |
| 1974—Arkansas | Texas | 20 | 88 | 6 | 6 | .500 | 87 | 72 | 60 | 78 | 84 | 6.14 |
| 1975—St. Petersburg | Florida St. | 8 | 51 | 3 | 4 | .429 | 38 | 20 | 12 | 45 | 39 | 2.12 |
| 1975—Arkansas | Texas | 16 | 80 | 3 | 5 | .375 | 91 | 51 | 41 | 48 | 34 | 4.61 |
| 1976—Tulsa | Am. Assoc. | 49 | 57 | 4 | 4 | .500 | 59 | 38 | 31 | 58 | 45 | 4.89 |
| 1976—St. Louis | National | 7 | 8 | 1 | 0 | 1.000 | 8 | 5 | 5 | 5 | 4 | 5.63 |
| Major League Totals | | 7 | 8 | 1 | 0 | 1.000 | 8 | 5 | 5 | 5 | 4 | 5.63 |

†Played in five games as an outfielder.
‡On suspended list, May 18, 1971 to March 2, 1972.
§Drafted from San Francisco Giants' organization by Arkansas (St. Louis Cardinals' organization), December 3, 1973.

## GEORGE ANGELO CAPPUZZELLO

Born January 1, 1954, at Youngstown, O.
Height, 6.00. Weight, 185.
Throws left and bats righthanded.
Hobby—Golf.
Attended Youngstown State University, Youngstown, O.

| Year Club | League | G. | IP. | W. | L. | Pct. | H. | R. | ER. | SO. | BB. | ERA. |
|---|---|---|---|---|---|---|---|---|---|---|---|---|
| 1973—Anderson | W. Carol. | 25 | 117 | 9 | 5 | .643 | 118 | 54 | 37 | 89 | 54 | 2.85 |
| 1974—Lakeland | Florida St. | 4 | 4 | 0 | 0 | .000 | 5 | 6 | 5 | 4 | 8 | 11.25 |
| 1974—Dubuque | Midwest | 24 | 136 | 7 | 11 | .389 | 120 | 70 | 44 | 137 | 69 | 2.91 |
| 1975—Lakeland | Florida St. | 16 | 110 | 5 | 8 | .385 | 92 | 46 | 31 | 89 | 64 | 2.54 |
| 1975—Montgomery | Southern | 8 | 32 | 0 | 3 | .000 | 27 | 17 | 13 | 23 | 20 | 3.66 |
| 1976—Montgomery | Southern | 17 | 117 | 7 | 7 | .500 | 102 | 57 | 46 | 105 | 65 | 3.54 |
| 1976—Evansville | Am. Assoc. | 11 | 49 | 1 | 4 | .200 | 50 | 22 | 15 | 37 | 20 | 2.76 |

Listed on Detroit Tigers' 1977 spring roster.

## LEE WILLIAM CAPRA
### (Buzz)

(Named by father because he thought his son swung a bat like a buzz saw.)

Born October 1, 1947, at Chicago, Ill.
Height, 5.11. Weight, 168.
Throws and bats righthanded.
Hobbies—Art, water skiing and basketball.
Attended Illinois State University, Normal, Ill.; received Bachelor of Arts
degree in Education.

Led International League in shutouts with 6 in 1971.

| Year Club | League | G. | IP. | W. | L. | Pct. | H. | R. | ER. | SO. | BB. | ERA. |
|---|---|---|---|---|---|---|---|---|---|---|---|---|
| 1969—Pompano Beach† | Florida St. | 18 | 57 | 8 | 2 | .800 | 49 | 24 | 17 | 54 | 31 | 2.68 |
| 1970—Visalia | California | 24 | 129 | 9 | 5 | .643 | 106 | 56 | 46 | 157 | 30 | 3.21 |
| 1971—Memphis | Texas | 5 | 32 | 3 | 0 | 1.000 | 17 | 4 | 2 | 43 | 10 | 0.56 |
| 1971—Tidewater | Int'national | 20 | 140 | 13 | 3 | .813 | 99 | 38 | 34 | 113 | 38 | ∗2.19 |
| 1971—New York | National | 3 | 5 | 0 | 1 | .000 | 3 | 6 | 5 | 6 | 5 | 9.00 |

| Year Club | League | G. | IP. | W. | L. | Pct. | H. | R. | ER. | SO. | BB. | ERA. |
|---|---|---|---|---|---|---|---|---|---|---|---|---|
| 1972—Tidewater ...........................Int'national | | 11 | 80 | 5 | 2 | .714 | 71 | 32 | 30 | 59 | 33 | 3.38 |
| 1972—New York ...........................National | | 14 | 53 | 3 | 2 | .600 | 50 | 27 | 27 | 45 | 27 | 4.58 |
| 1973—Tidewater ...........................Int'national | | 10 | 68 | 4 | 5 | .444 | 65 | 34 | 28 | 69 | 30 | 3.71 |
| 1973—New York‡ ..........................National | | 24 | 42 | 2 | 7 | .222 | 35 | 18 | 18 | 35 | 28 | 3.86 |
| 1974—Atlanta ...............................National | | 39 | 217 | 16 | 8 | .667 | 163 | 67 | 55 | 137 | 84 | *2.28 |
| 1975—Atlanta§ .............................National | | 12 | 78 | 4 | 7 | .364 | 77 | 41 | 37 | 35 | 28 | 4.27 |
| 1976—Richmond x..........................Int'national | | 4 | 14 | 2 | 1 | .667 | 13 | 8 | 8 | 6 | 8 | 5.14 |
| 1976—Atlanta ...............................National | | 5 | 9 | 0 | 1 | .000 | 9 | 9 | 9 | 4 | 6 | 9.00 |
| Major League Totals ............................... | | 97 | 404 | 25 | 26 | .490 | 337 | 168 | 151 | 262 | 178 | 3.36 |

†Appeared as shortstop in 4 games; as second baseman in 1 game.
‡Sold to Atlanta Braves for an estimated $35,000, March 26, 1974.
§On disabled list, June 10 through October 21, 1975.
xOn disabled list, April 7 to June 29, and July 17 to August 31, 1976.

### ALL-STAR GAME RECORD

Member of National League All-Star Team in 1974 game; did not play.

## BERNARDO CARBO
### (Bernie)

Born August 5, 1947, at Detroit, Mich.
Height, 6.00. Weight, 185.
Throws right and bats lefthanded.
Hobby—Sports.

Led Southern League batters in walks with 91 in 1968.
Led Carolina League batters in walks with 108 and third basemen in double plays with 27 in 1966.
Tied for Southern League lead in double plays by outfielders with 3 in 1968.
Named Most Valuable Player in American Association, 1969.
Named to THE SPORTING NEWS Minor League All-Star Team, 1969.
Named THE SPORTING NEWS National League Rookie Player of the Year, 1970.

| Year Club | League | Pos. | G. | AB. | R. | H. | 2B. | 3B. | HR. | RBI. | B.A. | PO. | A. | E. | F.A. |
|---|---|---|---|---|---|---|---|---|---|---|---|---|---|---|---|
| 1965—Tampa ..............Fla. St. | | 3B | 71 | 211 | 25 | 46 | 2 | 4 | 0 | 19 | .218 | 66 | 124 | 16 | .922 |
| 1966—Peninsula .........Carol. | | 3B | 132 | 402 | 66 | 108 | *30 | 1 | 15 | 57 | .269 | 80 | *270 | *41 | .895 |
| 1967—Knoxville ..........So. | | *3B-OF | 93 | 279 | 23 | 56 | 5 | 7 | 2 | 27 | .201 | 59 | 150 | *31 | .871 |
| 1968—Asheville ..........South. | | *OF-3 | 127 | 417 | 87 | 117 | 20 | 7 | 20 | 66 | .281 | 153 | *34 | 9 | .954 |
| 1969—Indianapolis ......A. A. | | OF | 111 | 404 | 83 | 145 | ●37 | 2 | 21 | 76 | *.359 | 191 | 16 | 6 | .972 |
| 1969—Cincinnati..........Nat. | | PH-PR | 4 | 3 | 0 | 0 | 0 | 0 | 0 | 0 | .000 | 0 | 0 | 0 | .000 |
| 1970—Cincinnati..........Nat. | | OF | 125 | 365 | 54 | 113 | 19 | 3 | 21 | 63 | .310 | 177 | 8 | 4 | .979 |
| 1971—Cincinnati..........Nat. | | OF | 106 | 310 | 33 | 68 | 20 | 1 | 5 | 20 | .219 | 154 | 7 | 3 | .982 |
| 1972—Cinn.†-St. L. .......Nat. | | *OF-3B | 118 | 323 | 44 | 81 | 13 | 1 | 7 | 34 | .251 | 171 | ●16 | 6 | .969 |
| 1973—St. Louis‡ .........Nat. | | OF | 111 | 308 | 42 | 88 | 18 | 0 | 8 | 40 | .286 | 171 | 11 | 4 | .978 |
| 1974—Boston ..............Amer. | | OF | 117 | 338 | 40 | 84 | 20 | 0 | 12 | 61 | .249 | 164 | 5 | 1 | .994 |
| 1975—Boston ..............Amer. | | OF | 107 | 319 | 64 | 82 | 21 | 3 | 15 | 50 | .257 | 157 | 7 | 4 | .976 |
| 1976—Bos.§-Mil. x ......Amer. | | DH-OF | 86 | 238 | 25 | 56 | 11 | 0 | 5 | 21 | .235 | 72 | 5 | 0 | 1.000 |
| American League Totals ................ | | | 310 | 895 | 129 | 222 | 52 | 3 | 32 | 132 | .248 | 393 | 17 | 5 | .984 |
| National League Totals ................... | | | 464 | 1309 | 173 | 350 | 70 | 5 | 41 | 157 | .267 | 673 | 42 | 17 | .977 |
| Major League Totals .................... | | | 774 | 2204 | 302 | 572 | 122 | 8 | 73 | 289 | .260 | 1066 | 59 | 22 | .981 |

†Traded to St. Louis Cardinals for First Baseman Joe Hague, May 18, 1972.
‡Traded with Pitcher Rick Wise to Boston Red Sox for Outfielder Reggie Smith and Pitcher Ken Tatum, October 26, 1973.
§Traded with undisclosed amount of cash to Milwaukee Brewers' for Outfielder Bobby Darwin and Pitcher Tom Murphy, June 3, 1976.
xTraded with First Baseman George Scott to Boston Red Sox for First Baseman Cecil Cooper, December 6, 1976.

### CHAMPIONSHIP SERIES RECORD

| Year Club | League | Pos. | G. | AB. | R. | H. | 2B. | 3B. | HR. | RBI. | B.A. | PO. | A. | E. | F.A. |
|---|---|---|---|---|---|---|---|---|---|---|---|---|---|---|---|
| 1970—Cincinnati..........Nat. | | OF | 2 | 6 | 0 | 0 | 0 | 0 | 0 | 0 | .000 | 0 | 0 | 0 | .000 |

### WORLD SERIES RECORD

| Year Club | League | Pos. | G. | AB. | R. | H. | 2B. | 3B. | HR. | RBI. | B.A. | PO. | A. | E. | F.A. |
|---|---|---|---|---|---|---|---|---|---|---|---|---|---|---|---|
| 1970—Cincinnati..........Nat. | | OF-PH | 4 | 8 | 0 | 0 | 0 | 0 | 0 | 0 | .000 | 4 | 0 | 0 | 1.000 |
| 1975—Boston ..............Amer. | | PH-OF | 4 | 7 | 3 | 3 | 1 | 0 | 2 | 4 | .429 | 1 | 1 | 0 | 1.000 |
| World Series Totals ...................... | | | 8 | 15 | 3 | 3 | 1 | 0 | 2 | 4 | .200 | 5 | 1 | 0 | 1.000 |

## JOSE DOMEC CARDENAL

Name pronounced Car-duh-NAHL.

Born October 7, 1943, at Matanzas, Cuba.
Height, 5.10. Weight, 151.
Throws and bats righthanded.
Hobbies—Movies and sports cars.
Cousin of Dagoberto (Bert) Campaneris, Texas Rangers' shortstop.

Tied major league record for most unassisted double plays, outfielder, season (2), 1968.
Major League stolen bases: 1963 (0), 1964 (2), 1965 (37), 1966 (24), 1967 (10), 1968 (40), 1969 (36), 1970 (26), 1971 (21), 1972 (25), 1973 (19), 1974 (23), 1975 (34), 1976 (23). Total—320.

Led Sophomore League in total bases with 336 and stolen bases with 64 in 1961.
Led Pacific Coast League outfielders in double plays with 6 in 1962.
Tied for Pacific Coast League lead in stolen bases with 40 in 1964.

| Year | Club | League | Pos. | G. | AB. | R. | H. | 2B. | 3B. | HR. | RBI. | B.A. | PO. | A. | E. | F.A. |
|---|---|---|---|---|---|---|---|---|---|---|---|---|---|---|---|---|
| 1961–El Paso | ............ | Soph. | O-IN-P | 128 | 502 | *159 | 178 | *39 | 7 | *35 | 108 | .355 | 196 | 132 | 34 | .906 |
| 1961–Eugene | .............. | Northw. | OF | 9 | 25 | 2 | 7 | 1 | 0 | 0 | 1 | .280 | 12 | 1 | 1 | .929 |
| 1962–Tacoma | ............ | P. C. | O-3-1B | 121 | 391 | 55 | 87 | 16 | 6 | 16 | 41 | .223 | 208 | 22 | 9 | .962 |
| 1963–San Francisco | ..Nat. | | OF | 9 | 5 | 1 | 1 | 0 | 0 | 0 | 2 | .200 | 0 | 0 | 0 | .000 |
| 1963–El Paso | ............ | Tex. | OF-3B | 125 | 475 | 112 | 148 | 27 | 5 | 36 | 95 | .312 | 258 | 47 | 21 | .936 |
| 1964–Tacoma | ............ | P. C. | OF-2B | 132 | 464 | 70 | 134 | 18 | 3 | 12 | 54 | .289 | 262 | 13 | 9 | .968 |
| 1964–San Francisco† | ..Nat. | | OF | 20 | 15 | 3 | 0 | 0 | 0 | 0 | 0 | .000 | 8 | 2 | 1 | .909 |
| 1965–California | ......... | Amer. | •OF-3-2 | 134 | 512 | 58 | 128 | 23 | 2 | 11 | 57 | .250 | 287 | 13 | •11 | .965 |
| 1966–California | ......... | Amer. | OF | 154 | 561 | 67 | 155 | 15 | 3 | 16 | 48 | .276 | 351 | 10 | 3 | .992 |
| 1967–California‡ | ........ | Amer. | OF | 108 | 381 | 40 | 90 | 13 | 5 | 6 | 27 | .236 | 195 | 10 | 3 | .986 |
| 1968–Cleveland | ......... | Amer. | OF | 157 | 583 | 78 | 150 | 21 | 7 | 7 | 44 | .257 | 367 | 12 | 10 | .974 |
| 1969–Cleveland§ | ........ | Amer. | OF-3B | 146 | 557 | 75 | 143 | 26 | 3 | 11 | 45 | .257 | 329 | 12 | 6 | .983 |
| 1970–St. Louis | ......... | Nat. | OF | 148 | 552 | 73 | 162 | 32 | 6 | 10 | 74 | .293 | 276 | 6 | 9 | .969 |
| 1971–St. Louis x | ........ | Nat. | OF | 89 | 301 | 37 | 73 | 12 | 4 | 7 | 48 | .243 | 181 | 9 | 6 | .969 |
| 1971–Milwaukee y | ...... | Amer. | OF | 53 | 198 | 20 | 51 | 10 | 0 | 3 | 32 | .258 | 133 | 6 | 3 | .979 |
| 1972–Chicago | ............ | Nat. | OF | 143 | 533 | 96 | 155 | 24 | 6 | 17 | 70 | .291 | 223 | 11 | 7 | .971 |
| 1973–Chicago | ............ | Nat. | OF | 145 | 522 | 80 | 158 | 33 | 2 | 11 | 68 | .303 | 234 | 13 | 5 | .980 |
| 1974–Chicago | ............ | Nat. | OF | 143 | 542 | 75 | 159 | 35 | 3 | 13 | 72 | .293 | 262 | 15 | 10 | .965 |
| 1975–Chicago | ............ | Nat. | OF | 154 | 574 | 85 | 182 | 30 | 2 | 9 | 68 | .317 | 313 | 14 | 8 | .976 |
| 1976–Chicago | ............ | Nat. | OF | 136 | 521 | 64 | 156 | 25 | 2 | 8 | 47 | .299 | 246 | 10 | 5 | .981 |
| National League Totals | ................ | | | 987 | 3565 | 514 | 1046 | 191 | 25 | 75 | 449 | .293 | 1473 | 80 | 51 | .973 |
| American League Totals | .............. | | | 752 | 2792 | 338 | 717 | 108 | 20 | 54 | 253 | .257 | 1662 | 63 | 36 | .980 |
| Major League Totals | ...................... | | | 1739 | 6357 | 852 | 1763 | 299 | 45 | 129 | 702 | .277 | 3405 | 143 | 87 | .976 |

†Traded to Los Angeles Angels for Catcher Jack Hiatt, November 21, 1964.
‡Traded to Cleveland Indians for Outfielder Chuck Hinton, November 29, 1967.
§Traded to St. Louis Cardinals for Outfielder Vada Pinson, November 20, 1969.
xTraded with Infielder Dick Schofield (latter on Tulsa roster) and Pitcher Bob Reynolds (assigned to Evansville) to Milwaukee Brewers for Shortstop Ted Kubiak and Pitcher Charlie Loseth (assigned from Raleigh-Durham to St. Petersburg), July 29, 1971.
yTraded to Chicago Cubs for Pitcher Jim Colborn, Outfielder Brock Davis and Pitcher Earl Stephenson, latter assigned to Evansville, December 3, 1971.

### PITCHING RECORD

| Year | Club | League | G. | IP. | W. | L. | Pct. | H. | R. | ER. | SO. | BB. | ERA. |
|---|---|---|---|---|---|---|---|---|---|---|---|---|---|
| 1961–El Paso | ............... | Soph. | 1 | 1 | 0 | 0 | .000 | 1 | 0 | 0 | 1 | 2 | 0.00 |

# RODNEY CLINE CAREW
## (Rod)

Born October 1, 1945, at Gatun, Panama.
Height, 6.00. Weight, 175.
Throws right and bats lefthanded.

Tied following major league records: most times stealing home, season, 7, 1969, and most stolen bases, inning, 3, May 18, 1969 (3rd inning).
Led American League first basemen in double plays with 149 in 1976.
Major league stolen bases: 1967 (5), 1968 (12), 1969 (19 ), 1970 (4), 1971 (6), 1972 (12), 1973 (41), 1974 (38), 1975 (35), 1976 (49). Total–221.
Named American League Rookie Player of the Year by THE SPORTING NEWS, 1967.
Named American League Rookie of the Year by the Baseball Writers' Association of America, 1967.
Named second baseman on THE SPORTING NEWS American League All-Star Team, 1967-68-69-72-73-74-75.

| Year | Club | League | Pos. | G. | AB. | R. | H. | 2B. | 3B. | HR. | RBI. | B.A. | PO. | A. | E. | F.A. |
|---|---|---|---|---|---|---|---|---|---|---|---|---|---|---|---|---|
| 1964–Melb'rne Twins | Coc. Rk. | | 2B | 37 | 123 | 17 | 40 | 5 | •3 | 0 | 21 | .325 | 86 | 48 | 7 | .950 |
| 1965–Orlando | ............ | Fla. St. | 2B | 125 | 439 | 57 | 133 | 20 | 8 | 1 | 52 | .303 | 290 | 328 | •28 | .957 |
| 1966–Wilson | .............. | Carol. | 2B | 112 | 383 | 64 | 112 | 19 | 3 | 1 | 30 | .292 | 248 | 275 | 21 | .961 |
| 1967–Minnesota† | ........ | Amer. | 2B | 137 | 514 | 66 | 150 | 22 | 7 | 8 | 51 | .292 | 289 | 314 | 15 | .976 |
| 1968–Minnesota‡ | ........ | Amer. | •2B-SS | 127 | 461 | 46 | 126 | 27 | 2 | 1 | 42 | .273 | 266 | 285 | •18 | .968 |
| 1969–Minnesota§ | ........ | Amer. | 2B | 123 | 458 | 79 | 152 | 30 | 4 | 8 | 56 | *.332 | 244 | 302 | 17 | .970 |
| 1970–Minnesota x | ...... | Amer. | 2B-1B | 51 | 191 | 27 | 70 | 12 | 3 | 4 | 28 | .366 | 79 | 122 | 8 | .962 |
| 1971–Minnesota | ....... | Amer. | 2B-3B | 147 | 577 | 88 | 177 | 16 | 10 | 2 | 48 | .307 | 324 | 331 | 16 | .976 |
| 1972–Minnesota | ....... | Amer. | 2B | 142 | 535 | 61 | 170 | 21 | 6 | 0 | 51 | *.318 | 331 | 378 | 16 | .978 |
| 1973–Minnesota | ....... | Amer. | 2B | 149 | 580 | 98 | *203 | 30 | •11 | 6 | 62 | *.350 | 383 | 413 | 13 | .984 |
| 1974–Minnesota | ....... | Amer. | 2B | 153 | 599 | 86 | *218 | 30 | 5 | 3 | 55 | *.364 | 375 | 416 | *33 | .960 |
| 1975–Minnesota | ....... | Amer. | 2B-1B | 143 | 535 | 89 | 192 | 24 | 4 | 14 | 80 | *.359 | 408 | 377 | 21 | .974 |
| 1976–Minnesota | ....... | Amer. | 1B-2B | 156 | 605 | 97 | 200 | 29 | 12 | 9 | 90 | .331 | 1398 | 110 | 16 | .990 |
| Major League Totals | ...................... | | | 1328 | 5055 | 737 | 1658 | 241 | 64 | 55 | 563 | .328 | 4097 | 3048 | 173 | .976 |

†On military list, August 5 through August 21, 1967.
‡On military list, June 8 through June 24, 1968.
§On military list, August 17 through September 1, 1969.
xOn disabled list, June 24 through September 1, 1970.

### CHAMPIONSHIP SERIES RECORD

| Year | Club | League | Pos. | G. | AB. | R. | H. | 2B. | 3B. | HR. | RBI. | B.A. | PO. | A. | E. | F.A. |
|---|---|---|---|---|---|---|---|---|---|---|---|---|---|---|---|---|
| 1969–Minnesota | ....... | Amer. | 2B | 3 | 14 | 0 | 1 | 0 | 0 | 0 | 0 | .071 | 6 | 3 | 1 | .900 |
| 1970–Minnesota | ....... | Amer. | PH | 2 | 2 | 0 | 0 | 0 | 0 | 0 | 0 | .000 | 0 | 0 | 0 | .000 |
| Championship Series Totals | ............ | | | 5 | 16 | 0 | 1 | 0 | 0 | 0 | 0 | .063 | 6 | 3 | 1 | .900 |

## ALL-STAR GAME RECORD

| Year | League | Pos. | AB. | R. | H. | 2B. | 3B. | HR. | RBI. | B.A. | PO. | A. | E. | F.A. |
|---|---|---|---|---|---|---|---|---|---|---|---|---|---|---|
| 1967–American | | 2B | 3 | 0 | 0 | 0 | 0 | 0 | 0 | .000 | 2 | 3 | 0 | 1.000 |
| 1968–American | | 2B | 3 | 0 | 0 | 0 | 0 | 0 | 0 | .000 | 2 | 2 | 0 | 1.000 |
| 1969–American | | 2B | 3 | 0 | 0 | 0 | 0 | 0 | 0 | .000 | 0 | 2 | 0 | 1.000 |
| 1971–American | | 2B | 1 | 1 | 0 | 0 | 0 | 0 | 0 | .000 | 1 | 2 | 0 | 1.000 |
| 1972–American | | 2B | 2 | 0 | 1 | 0 | 0 | 0 | 1 | .500 | 2 | 3 | 0 | 1.000 |
| 1973–American | | 2B | 3 | 0 | 0 | 0 | 0 | 0 | 0 | .000 | 5 | 1 | 0 | 1.000 |
| 1974–American | | 2B | 1 | 1 | 0 | 0 | 0 | 0 | 0 | .000 | 0 | 1 | 0 | 1.000 |
| 1975–American | | 2B | 5 | 0 | 1 | 0 | 0 | 0 | 0 | .200 | 3 | 1 | 0 | 1.000 |
| 1976–American | | 1B | 3 | 0 | 0 | 0 | 0 | 0 | 0 | .000 | 9 | 2 | 0 | 1.000 |
| All-Star Game Totals | | | 24 | 2 | 2 | 0 | 0 | 0 | 1 | .083 | 24 | 17 | 0 | 1.000 |

Named to American League All-Star Team in 1970; replaced due to injury.

## STEVEN NORMAN CARLTON
### (Steve)

Born December 22, 1944, at Miami, Fla.
Height, 6.04. Weight, 210.
Throws and bats lefthanded.
Hobbies–Hunting, pool and winter sports.
Attended Miami-Dade Community College, Miami, Fla.

Tied modern major league record for most strikeouts in one game, nine innings, 19, September 15, 1969.
Tied modern National League record for most games won, season, by lefthander, 27, 1972.
Led National League pitchers in games started with 41 and in complete games with 30 in 1972.
Tied for National League lead in games started with 40 and tied for lead in complete games with 18 in 1973.
Won National League Cy Young Memorial Award, 1972.
Named lefthanded pitcher on THE SPORTING NEWS National League All-Star Team, 1969-71-72.
Named THE SPORTING NEWS National League Pitcher of the Year, 1972.

| Year | Club | League | G. | IP. | W. | L. | Pct. | H. | R. | ER. | SO. | BB. | ERA. |
|---|---|---|---|---|---|---|---|---|---|---|---|---|---|
| 1964–Rock Hill | | W. Carol. | 11 | 79 | 10 | 1 | .909 | 39 | 17 | 9 | 91 | 36 | 1.03 |
| 1964–Winnipeg | | Northern | 12 | 75 | 4 | 4 | .500 | 63 | 40 | 28 | 79 | 48 | 3.36 |
| 1964–Tulsa | | Texas | 4 | 24 | 1 | 1 | .500 | 16 | 13 | 7 | 21 | 18 | 2.63 |
| 1965–St. Louis | | National | 15 | 25 | 0 | 0 | .000 | 27 | 7 | 7 | 21 | 8 | 2.52 |
| 1966–Tulsa | | P. Coast | 19 | 128 | 9 | 5 | .643 | 110 | 65 | 51 | 108 | 54 | 3.59 |
| 1966–St. Louis | | National | 9 | 52 | 3 | 3 | .500 | 56 | 22 | 18 | 25 | 18 | 3.12 |
| 1967–St. Louis | | National | 30 | 193 | 14 | 9 | .609 | 173 | 71 | 64 | 168 | 62 | 2.98 |
| 1968–St. Louis | | National | 34 | 232 | 13 | 11 | .542 | 214 | 87 | 77 | 162 | 61 | 2.99 |
| 1969–St. Louis | | National | 31 | 236 | 17 | 11 | .607 | 185 | 66 | 57 | 210 | 93 | 2.17 |
| 1970–St. Louis | | National | 34 | 254 | 10 | •19 | .345 | 239 | 123 | 105 | 193 | 109 | 3.72 |
| 1971–St. Louis† | | National | 37 | 273 | 20 | 9 | .690 | 275 | 120 | 108 | 172 | 98 | 3.56 |
| 1972–Philadelphia | | National | 41 | •346 | •27 | 10 | .730 | •257 | 84 | 76 | •310 | 87 | •1.98 |
| 1973–Philadelphia | | National | 40 | •293 | 13 | •20 | .394 | •293 | •146 | •127 | 223 | 113 | 3.90 |
| 1974–Philadelphia | | National | 39 | 291 | 16 | 13 | .552 | 249 | 118 | 104 | •240 | •136 | 3.22 |
| 1975–Philadelphia | | National | 37 | 255 | 15 | 14 | .517 | 217 | 116 | 101 | 192 | 104 | 3.56 |
| 1976–Philadelphia | | National | 35 | 253 | 20 | 7 | •.741 | 224 | 94 | 88 | 195 | 72 | 3.13 |
| Major League Totals | | | 382 | 2703 | 168 | 126 | .571 | 2409 | 1054 | 932 | 2111 | 961 | 3.10 |

†Traded to Philadelphia Phillies for Pitcher Rick Wise, February 25, 1972.

## CHAMPIONSHIP SERIES RECORD

| Year | Club | League | G. | IP. | W. | L. | Pct. | H. | R. | ER. | SO. | BB. | ERA. |
|---|---|---|---|---|---|---|---|---|---|---|---|---|---|
| 1976–Philadelphia | | National | 1 | 7 | 0 | 1 | .000 | 8 | 5 | 5 | 6 | 5 | 6.43 |

## WORLD SERIES RECORD

| Year | Club | League | G. | IP. | W. | L. | Pct. | H. | R. | ER. | SO. | BB. | ERA. |
|---|---|---|---|---|---|---|---|---|---|---|---|---|---|
| 1967–St. Louis | | National | 1 | 6 | 0 | 1 | .000 | 3 | 1 | 0 | 5 | 2 | 0.00 |
| 1968–St. Louis | | National | 2 | 4 | 0 | 0 | .000 | 7 | 3 | 3 | 3 | 1 | 6.75 |
| World Series Totals | | | 3 | 10 | 0 | 1 | .000 | 10 | 4 | 3 | 8 | 3 | 2.70 |

## ALL-STAR GAME RECORD

| Year | League | IP. | W. | L. | Pct. | H. | R. | ER. | SO. | BB. | ERA. |
|---|---|---|---|---|---|---|---|---|---|---|---|
| 1968–National | | 1 | 0 | 0 | .000 | 0 | 0 | 0 | 1 | 0 | 0.00 |
| 1969–National | | 3 | 1 | 0 | 1.000 | 2 | 2 | 2 | 2 | 1 | 6.00 |
| 1972–National | | 1 | 0 | 0 | .000 | 0 | 0 | 0 | 0 | 1 | 0.00 |
| All-Star Game Totals | | 5 | 1 | 0 | 1.000 | 2 | 2 | 2 | 3 | 2 | 3.60 |

Member of National League All-Star Team in 1971 and 1974 games; did not play.

## DONALD GEORGE CARRITHERS
### (Don)

Born September 15, 1949, at Lynwood, Calif.
Height, 6.03. Weight, 205.
Throws and bats righthanded.
Hobbies–Hunting, fishing and pool.

Tied National League record for most wild pitches, inning (3), May 23, 1972, 6th inning.

| Year Club | League | G. | IP. | W. | L. | Pct. | H. | R. | ER. | SO. | BB. | ERA. |
|---|---|---|---|---|---|---|---|---|---|---|---|---|
| 1967—Salt Lake City | Pioneer | 18 | 57 | 4 | 5 | .444 | 59 | 42 | 29 | 68 | 39 | 4.58 |
| 1968—Decatur | Midwest | 15 | 98 | 6 | 6 | .500 | 82 | 35 | 30 | 82 | 37 | 2.76 |
| 1968—Fresno | California | 8 | 71 | 7 | 0 | 1.000 | 60 | 19 | 17 | 61 | 24 | 2.15 |
| 1969—Phoenix | P. Coast | 30 | 107 | 3 | 12 | .200 | 150 | 86 | 73 | 66 | 53 | 6.14 |
| 1970—Phoenix | P. Coast | 24 | 67 | 9 | 1 | .900 | 70 | 19 | 16 | 52 | 20 | 2.15 |
| 1970—San Francisco | National | 11 | 22 | 2 | 1 | .667 | 31 | 19 | 18 | 14 | 14 | 7.36 |
| 1971—Phoenix | P. Coast | 16 | 111 | 7 | 3 | .700 | 109 | 59 | 49 | 66 | 48 | 3.97 |
| 1971—San Francisco | National | 22 | 80 | 5 | 3 | .625 | 77 | 48 | 36 | 41 | 37 | 4.05 |
| 1972—San Francisco | National | 25 | 90 | 4 | 8 | .333 | 108 | 66 | 58 | 42 | 42 | 5.80 |
| 1973—San Francisco† | National | 25 | 58 | 1 | 2 | .333 | 64 | 40 | 31 | 36 | 35 | 4.81 |
| 1974—Memphis | Int'national | 16 | 107 | 7 | 6 | .538 | 96 | 39 | 29 | 90 | 44 | 2.44 |
| 1974—Montreal | National | 22 | 60 | 5 | 2 | .714 | 56 | 22 | 20 | 31 | 17 | 3.00 |
| 1975—Memphis | Int'national | 12 | 70 | 3 | 5 | .375 | 62 | 28 | 18 | 34 | 17 | 2.31 |
| 1975—Montreal‡ | National | 19 | 101 | 5 | 3 | .625 | 90 | 39 | 37 | 37 | 38 | 3.30 |
| 1976—Montreal§ | National | 34 | 140 | 6 | 12 | .333 | 153 | 84 | 69 | 71 | 78 | 4.44 |
| Major League Totals | | 158 | 551 | 28 | 31 | .475 | 579 | 318 | 269 | 272 | 261 | 4.39 |

†Traded to Montreal Expos for Catcher John Boccabella, March 27, 1974.
‡On disabled list, June 15 to July 20, 1975.
§Sold to Minnesota Twins, April 6, 1977.

CHAMPIONSHIP SERIES RECORD

| Year Club | League | G. | IP. | W. | L. | Pct. | H. | R. | ER. | SO. | BB. | ERA. |
|---|---|---|---|---|---|---|---|---|---|---|---|---|
| 1971—San Francisco | National | 1 | *0 | 0 | 0 | .000 | 3 | 3 | 3 | 0 | 0 | ....... |

*Pitched to three batters in seventh inning of second game.

## CLAY PALMER CARROLL

Born May 2, 1941, at Clanton, Ala.
Height, 6.01. Weight, 205.
Throws and bats righthanded.
Hobbies—Fishing and hunting.

Led National League in saves with 37 in 1972.
Led Pioneer League pitchers in complete games with 16 in 1962.
Named THE SPORTING NEWS National League Fireman of the Year, 1972.

| Year Club | League | G. | IP. | W. | L. | Pct. | H. | R. | ER. | SO. | BB. | ERA. |
|---|---|---|---|---|---|---|---|---|---|---|---|---|
| 1961—Davenport | Midwest | 21 | 122 | 7 | 10 | .412 | 123 | 73 | 57 | 94 | 43 | 4.20 |
| 1962—Boise | Pioneer | 31 | 181 | *14 | 7 | .667 | 158 | 93 | 77 | 223 | 78 | 3.83 |
| 1963—Denver | P. Coast | 18 | 70 | 3 | 7 | .300 | 82 | 55 | 43 | 41 | 25 | 5.53 |
| 1963—Austin | Texas | 17 | 112 | 8 | 4 | .667 | 104 | 57 | 44 | 64 | 30 | 3.54 |
| 1964—Denver | P. Coast | 21 | 127 | 8 | 8 | .500 | 129 | 56 | 49 | 87 | 35 | 3.47 |
| 1964—Austin | Texas | 3 | 17 | 2 | 0 | 1.000 | 10 | 4 | 3 | 14 | 2 | 1.59 |
| 1964—Milwaukee | National | 11 | 20 | 2 | 0 | 1.000 | 15 | 4 | 4 | 17 | 3 | 1.80 |
| 1965—Milwaukee | National | 19 | 35 | 0 | 1 | .000 | 35 | 18 | 17 | 16 | 13 | 4.37 |
| 1965—Atlanta | Int'national | 13 | 93 | 3 | 6 | .333 | 85 | 28 | 25 | 52 | 32 | 2.42 |
| 1966—Atlanta | National | *73 | 144 | 8 | 7 | .533 | 127 | 45 | 38 | 67 | 29 | 2.38 |
| 1967—Atlanta | National | 42 | 93 | 6 | 12 | .333 | 111 | 62 | 57 | 35 | 29 | 5.52 |
| 1967—Richmond | Int'national | 4 | 22 | 2 | 0 | 1.000 | 16 | 2 | 2 | 13 | 5 | 0.82 |
| 1968—Atlanta†-Cincinnati | National | 68 | 144 | 7 | 8 | .467 | 128 | 50 | 43 | 71 | 38 | 2.69 |
| 1969—Cincinnati | National | 71 | 151 | 12 | 6 | .667 | 149 | 70 | 59 | 90 | 78 | 3.52 |
| 1970—Cincinnati | National | 65 | 104 | 9 | 4 | .692 | 104 | 38 | 30 | 63 | 27 | 2.60 |
| 1971—Cincinnati‡ | National | 61 | 94 | 10 | 4 | .714 | 78 | 26 | 26 | 64 | 42 | 2.49 |
| 1972—Cincinnati | National | ●65 | 96 | 6 | 4 | .600 | 89 | 27 | 24 | 51 | 32 | 2.25 |
| 1973—Cincinnati | National | 53 | 93 | 8 | 8 | .500 | 111 | 47 | 38 | 41 | 34 | 3.68 |
| 1974—Cincinnati | National | 57 | 101 | 12 | 5 | .706 | 96 | 27 | 24 | 46 | 30 | 2.14 |
| 1975—Cincinnati‡ | National | 56 | 96 | 7 | 5 | .583 | 93 | 30 | 28 | 44 | 32 | 2.63 |
| 1976—Chicago§ | American | 29 | 77 | 4 | 4 | .500 | 67 | 26 | 22 | 38 | 24 | 2.57 |
| American League Totals | | 29 | 77 | 4 | 4 | .500 | 67 | 26 | 22 | 38 | 24 | 2.57 |
| National League Totals | | 641 | 1171 | 87 | 64 | .576 | 1136 | 444 | 388 | 605 | 387 | 2.98 |
| Major League Totals | | 670 | 1248 | 91 | 68 | .572 | 1203 | 470 | 410 | 643 | 411 | 2.96 |

†Traded with Pitcher Tony Cloninger and Infielder Woody Woodward to Cincinnati Reds for Infielder Bob Johnson and Pitchers Milt Pappas and Ted Davidson, June 11, 1968.
‡Traded to Chicago White Sox for Pitcher Rich Hinton and Catcher Jeff Sovern, December 12, 1975.
§On disabled list, July 4 through August 3, 1976; Traded to St. Louis Cardinals for Pitcher Lerrin LaGrow, March 23, 1977.

CHAMPIONSHIP SERIES RECORD

| Year Club | League | G. | IP. | W. | L. | Pct. | H. | R. | ER. | SO. | BB. | ERA. |
|---|---|---|---|---|---|---|---|---|---|---|---|---|
| 1970—Cincinnati | National | 2 | 1⅓ | 0 | 0 | .000 | 2 | 0 | 0 | 2 | 0 | 0.00 |
| 1972—Cincinnati | National | 2 | 2⅔ | 1 | 1 | .500 | 2 | 1 | 1 | 0 | 3 | 3.38 |
| 1973—Cincinnati | National | 3 | 7 | 1 | 0 | 1.000 | 5 | 1 | 1 | 2 | 1 | 1.29 |
| 1975—Cincinnati | National | 1 | 1 | 0 | 0 | .000 | 0 | 0 | 0 | 1 | 1 | 0.00 |
| Championship Series Totals | | 8 | 12 | 2 | 1 | .667 | 9 | 2 | 2 | 5 | 5 | 1.50 |

WORLD SERIES RECORD

| Year Club | League | G. | IP. | W. | L. | Pct. | H. | R. | ER. | SO. | BB. | ERA. |
|---|---|---|---|---|---|---|---|---|---|---|---|---|
| 1970—Cincinnati | National | 4 | 9 | 1 | 0 | 1.000 | 5 | 0 | 0 | 11 | 2 | 0.00 |
| 1972—Cincinnati | National | 5 | 5⅔ | 0 | 1 | .000 | 6 | 1 | 1 | 3 | 4 | 1.59 |
| 1975—Cincinnati | National | 5 | 5⅔ | 1 | 0 | 1.000 | 4 | 2 | 2 | 3 | 2 | 3.18 |
| World Series Totals | | 14 | 20⅓ | 2 | 1 | .667 | 15 | 3 | 3 | 17 | 8 | 1.33 |

Member of National League All-Star Team for the 1971 and 1972 games; did not play.

## THOMAS MICHAEL CARROLL
### (Tom)

Born November 5, 1952, at Oriskany, N. Y.
Height, 6.04. Weight, 185.
Throws right and bats lefthanded.
Attended Duquesne University, Pittsburgh, Pa.

Pitched 2-0 no-hit victory against Omaha, May 24, 1974.
Tied for American Association lead in shutouts with 4 in 1973.

| Year | Club | League | G. | IP. | W. | L. | Pct. | H. | R. | ER. | SO. | BB. | ERA. |
|------|------|--------|----|----|----|----|------|----|----|-----|-----|-----|------|
| 1970—Sioux Falls | ......................... | North. | 12 | 86 | 4 | 5 | .444 | 69 | 51 | 27 | 63 | 54 | 2.83 |
| 1971—Tampa | ............................... | Florida St. | 28 | 192 | •18 | 5 | .783 | 147 | 63 | 51 | 148 | 81 | 2.39 |
| 1972—Three Rivers | ....................... | Eastern | 19 | 104 | 6 | 10 | .375 | 106 | 54 | 39 | 62 | 52 | 3.38 |
| 1973—Indianapolis | ...................... | Am. Assoc. | 29 | 174 | 15 | 9 | .625 | 151 | 91 | 75 | 137 | 97 | 3.88 |
| 1974—Indianapolis | ...................... | Am. Assoc. | 16 | 97 | 8 | 4 | .667 | 79 | 55 | 53 | 68 | 71 | 4.92 |
| 1974—Cincinnati | ........................... | National | 16 | 78 | 4 | 3 | .571 | 68 | 44 | 32 | 37 | 44 | 3.69 |
| 1975—Indianapolis† | ...................... | Am. Assoc. | 16 | 102 | 6 | 6 | .500 | 79 | 41 | 35 | 58 | 45 | 3.09 |
| 1975—Cincinnati | ........................... | National | 12 | 47 | 4 | 1 | .800 | 52 | 28 | 26 | 14 | 26 | 4.98 |
| 1976—Indianapolis‡§ | ..................... | Am. Assoc. | 27 | 149 | 9 | 12 | .429 | 159 | 103 | 89 | 83 | 88 | 5.38 |
| Major League Totals | ................................ | | 28 | 125 | 8 | 4 | .667 | 120 | 72 | 58 | 51 | 70 | 4.18 |

†On suspended list, April 7, to April 20, 1975.
‡On suspended list, June 6 through June 9, 1976.
§Traded to Pittsburgh Pirates' organization for Pitcher Jim Sadowski, November 6, 1976; drafted by Montreal Expos, December 6, 1976. Sold to Pittsburgh Pirates, April 5, 1977.

## GARY EDMUND CARTER

Born April 8, 1954, at Culver City, Calif.
Height, 6.02. Weight, 205.
Throws and bats righthanded.
Brother of Gordon Carter, outfielder in San Francisco Giants'
organization, 1972 and 1973.

Led International League catchers in double plays with 15 in 1974.
Named National League Rookie Player of the Year by THE SPORTING NEWS, 1975.

| Year | Club | League | Pos. | G. | AB. | R. | H. | 2B. | 3B. | HR. | RBI. | B.A. | PO. | A. | E. | F.A. |
|------|------|--------|------|----|----|----|----|-----|-----|-----|------|------|-----|----|----|------|
| 1972—Cocoa Expos. | ....Fla.E.C. | | C-1-3 | 18 | 71 | 6 | 17 | 3 | 0 | 2 | 9 | .239 | 111 | 12 | 10 | .925 |
| 1972—W. Palm Beach | Fla. St. | | C | 20 | 50 | 9 | 16 | 2 | 2 | 0 | 5 | .320 | 84 | 12 | 2 | .980 |
| 1973—Quebec City | ......East. | | C-1-O | 130 | 439 | 65 | 111 | 16 | 1 | 15 | 68 | .253 | 823 | 75 | 20 | .978 |
| 1973—Peninsula | ..........Int. | | C | 8 | 25 | 2 | 7 | 2 | 0 | 0 | 1 | .280 | 5 | 1 | 0 | 1.000 |
| 1974—Memphis | ..........Int. | | *C-1-3 | 135 | 441 | 62 | 118 | 14 | 7 | 23 | 83 | .268 | *908 | *76 | 12 | *.988 |
| 1974—Montreal | .........Nat. | | C-OF | 9 | 27 | 5 | 11 | 0 | 1 | 1 | 6 | .407 | 28 | 4 | 0 | 1.000 |
| 1975—Montreal | .........Nat. | | O-C-3 | 144 | 503 | 58 | 136 | 20 | 1 | 17 | 68 | .270 | 430 | 38 | 9 | .981 |
| 1976—Montreal† | .........Nat. | | C-OF | 91 | 311 | 31 | 68 | 8 | 1 | 6 | 38 | .219 | 364 | 42 | 2 | .995 |
| Major League Totals | ..................... | | | 244 | 841 | 94 | 215 | 28 | 3 | 24 | 112 | .256 | 822 | 84 | 11 | .988 |

†On disabled list, June 6 through July 22, 1976.

| Year | League | Pos. | AB. | R. | H. | 2B. | 3B. | HR. | RBI. | B.A. | PO. | A. | E. | F.A. |
|------|--------|------|-----|----|----|-----|-----|-----|------|------|-----|----|----|------|
| 1975—National | ............................. | OF | 0 | 0 | 0 | 0 | 0 | 0 | 0 | .000 | 1 | 0 | 0 | 1.000 |

## RICARDO ADOLFO JACOBO CARTY
Name pronounced CAR-tee.
### (Rico)

Born September 1, 1939, at San Pedro de Macoris, Dominican Republic.
Height, 6.02. Weight, 190.
Throws and bats righthanded.
Attended Collegio San Esteban, Santo Domingo, Dominican Republic.

Hit three home runs in a game, May 31, 1970.
Led Northern League catchers in passed balls with 35 in 1961.

| Year | Club | League | Pos. | G. | AB. | R. | H. | 2B. | 3B. | HR. | RBI. | B.A. | PO. | A. | E. | F.A. |
|------|------|--------|------|----|----|----|----|-----|-----|-----|------|------|-----|----|----|------|
| 1960—Davenport | ........Midw. | | C-2B | 25 | 60 | 9 | 14 | 2 | 2 | 3 | 15 | .233 | 101 | 11 | 10 | .918 |
| 1961—Eau Claire | ........North. | | C | 110 | 342 | 69 | 102 | 19 | 1 | 11 | 39 | .298 | *636 | 65 | *29 | .960 |
| 1962—Yakima | ..........Northw | | C | 108 | 352 | 68 | 129 | 21 | 6 | 17 | 79 | .366 | *789 | 61 | *15 | .983 |
| 1963—Toronto | ...........Int. | | C | 21 | 63 | 12 | 14 | 2 | 0 | 4 | 11 | .222 | 99 | 9 | 2 | .982 |
| 1963—Austin | ............Tex. | | OF-C | 111 | 391 | 85 | 128 | 32 | 3 | 27 | 100 | .327 | 186 | 13 | 8 | .961 |
| 1963—Milwaukee | .......Nat. | | PH | 2 | 2 | 0 | 0 | 0 | 0 | 0 | 0 | .000 | 0 | 0 | 0 | .000 |
| 1964—Milwaukee | .......Nat. | | OF | 133 | 455 | 72 | 150 | 28 | 4 | 22 | 88 | .330 | 176 | 5 | 4 | .978 |
| 1965—Milwaukee | .......Nat. | | OF | 83 | 271 | 37 | 84 | 18 | 1 | 10 | 35 | .310 | 112 | 3 | 5 | .958 |
| 1966—Atlanta | .............Nat. | | O-C-1-3 | 151 | 521 | 73 | 170 | 25 | 2 | 15 | 76 | .326 | 318 | 16 | 10 | .971 |
| 1967—Atlanta | .............Nat. | | OF-1B | 134 | 444 | 41 | 113 | 16 | 2 | 15 | 64 | .255 | 267 | 9 | 11 | .962 |
| 1968—Atlanta† | ...........Nat. | | | | | | (On Disabled List) | | | | | | | | | |

| Year Club League | Pos. | G. | AB. | R. | H. | 2B. | 3B. | HR. | RBI. | B.A. | PO. | A. | E. | F.A. |
|---|---|---|---|---|---|---|---|---|---|---|---|---|---|---|
| 1969-Atlanta.............Nat. | OF | 104 | 304 | 47 | 104 | 15 | 0 | 16 | 58 | .342 | 118 | 0 | 6 | .952 |
| 1970-Atlanta.............Nat. | OF | 136 | 478 | 84 | 175 | 23 | 3 | 25 | 101 | *.366 | 219 | 5 | 6 | .974 |
| 1971-Atlanta ............Nat. | | | | | | (On Disabled List) | | | | | | | | |
| 1972-Atlanta‡§ ........Nat. | OF | 86 | 271 | 31 | 75 | 12 | 2 | 6 | 29 | .277 | 139 | 3 | 3 | .979 |
| 1973-Tex. xy-Oak. a ..Amer. | OF | 93 | 314 | 25 | 73 | 13 | 0 | 4 | 34 | .232 | 87 | 2 | 0 | 1.000 |
| 1973-Chicago z .........Nat. | OF | 22 | 70 | 4 | 15 | 0 | 0 | 1 | 8 | .214 | 36 | 0 | 2 | .947 |
| 1974-Cordoba b.........Mex. | 1B-OF | 122 | 401 | 61 | 142 | 33 | 0 | 11 | 72 | .354 | 518 | 16 | 6 | .989 |
| 1974-Cleveland.........Amer. | 1B | 33 | 91 | 6 | 33 | 5 | 0 | 1 | 16 | .363 | 64 | 1 | 1 | .985 |
| 1975-Cleveland.........Amer. | 1B-OF | 118 | 383 | 57 | 118 | 19 | 1 | 18 | 64 | .308 | 209 | 15 | 3 | .987 |
| 1976-Cleveland c ......Amer. | DH-1-OF | 152 | 552 | 67 | 171 | 34 | 0 | 13 | 83 | .310 | 81 | 3 | 0 | 1.000 |
| National League Totals ................. | | 851 | 2816 | 389 | 886 | 137 | 14 | 110 | 459 | .315 | 1385 | 41 | 47 | .968 |
| American League Totals ............... | | 396 | 1340 | 155 | 395 | 71 | 1 | 36 | 197 | .295 | 441 | 21 | 4 | .991 |
| Major League Totals ...................... | | 1247 | 4156 | 544 | 1281 | 208 | 15 | 146 | 656 | .308 | 1826 | 62 | 51 | .974 |

†Missed season due to tuberculosis.
‡Placed on disabled list, July 18 through August 20, 1972.
§Traded to Texas Rangers for Pitcher Jim Panther, October 27, 1972.
xOn disabled list, July 23 to August 13, 1973.
ySold to Chicago Cubs, August 13, 1973.
zSold to Oakland Athletics, September 11, 1973.
aUnconditionally released, December 12, 1973; signed as free agent by Cordoba (Mexican League), April 5, 1974.
bSold to Cleveland Indians, August 17, 1974.
cSelected by Toronto Blue Jays in American League expansion draft, November 5, 1976; traded to Cleveland Indians for Infielder-Outfielder John Lowenstein and Catcher Rick Cerone, December 6, 1976.

### CHAMPIONSHIP SERIES RECORD

| Year Club League | Pos. | G. | AB. | R. | H. | 2B. | 3B. | HR. | RBI. | B.A. | PO. | A. | E. | F.A. |
|---|---|---|---|---|---|---|---|---|---|---|---|---|---|---|
| 1969-Atlanta.............Nat. | OF | 3 | 10 | 4 | 3 | 2 | 0 | 0 | 0 | .300 | 3 | 0 | 0 | 1.000 |

### ALL-STAR GAME RECORD

| Year League | Pos. | AB. | R. | H. | 2B. | 3B. | HR. | RBI. | B.A. | PO. | A. | E. | F.A. |
|---|---|---|---|---|---|---|---|---|---|---|---|---|---|
| 1970-National ........................... | OF | 1 | 0 | 0 | 0 | 0 | 0 | 0 | .000 | 0 | 0 | 0 | .000 |

## DAVID CASH, JR.
### (Dave)

Born June 11, 1948, at Utica, N. Y.
Height, 6.00. Weight, 175.
Throws and bats righthanded.

Established major league records for most at bats, season, 699 in 1975; and fewest sacrifice hits, season (most at bats), 0, in 1975.
Tied major league record for most seasons, consecutive, leading major leagues, at bats—3, 1974-1976.
Established National League record for most games, consecutive, second basemen, lifetime—443, 1974-1976.
Tied National League records: most seasons leading league, at bats, since 1900—3, 1974-1976; most seasons, consecutive, leading league, at bats—3, 1974-1976.
Led National League second basemen in double plays with 141 in 1974, 126 in 1975 and 110 in 1976.
Led National League second basemen in total chances with 937 in 1974 and 898 in 1975.

| Year Club League | Pos. | G. | AB. | R. | H. | 2B. | 3B. | HR. | RBI. | B.A. | PO. | A. | E. | F.A. |
|---|---|---|---|---|---|---|---|---|---|---|---|---|---|---|
| 1966-Salem...............Appal | 2B-SS | 58 | 192 | 23 | 51 | 7 | 2 | 2 | 25 | .266 | 93 | 127 | 17 | .928 |
| 1967-Gastonia...........W. Car. | *S-2 | 114 | 442 | 80 | *148 | 17 | 3 | 4 | 38 | *.335 | *203 | 274 | 29 | .943 |
| 1968-Salem...............Carol. | 2B-SS | 124 | 473 | 68 | 131 | 20 | 1 | 6 | 59 | .277 | 307 | 343 | 21 | .969 |
| 1969-Columbus ..........Int. | 2B | 115 | 426 | 57 | 124 | 17 | *12 | 4 | 49 | .291 | 262 | 342 | 10 | *.984 |
| 1969-Pittsburgh .......Nat. | 2B | 18 | 61 | 8 | 17 | 3 | 1 | 0 | 4 | .279 | 37 | 60 | 1 | .990 |
| 1970-Columbus ..........Int. | 2B | 35 | 128 | 20 | 40 | 3 | 2 | 1 | 16 | .313 | 89 | 86 | 5 | .972 |
| 1970-Pittsburgh†........Nat. | 2B | 64 | 210 | 30 | 66 | 7 | 6 | 1 | 28 | .314 | 147 | 156 | 8 | .974 |
| 1971-Pittsburgh‡.......Nat. | 2B-3-S | 123 | 478 | 79 | 138 | 17 | 4 | 2 | 34 | .289 | 254 | 333 | 10 | .983 |
| 1972-Pittsburgh§.......Nat. | 2B | 99 | 425 | 58 | 120 | 22 | 4 | 3 | 30 | .282 | 260 | 342 | 5 | .992 |
| 1973-Pittsburgh x ......Nat. | 2B-3B | 116 | 436 | 59 | 118 | 21 | 2 | 2 | 31 | .271 | 244 | 311 | 12 | .979 |
| 1974-Philadelphia .....Nat. | 2B | 162 | *687 | 89 | 206 | 26 | 11 | 2 | 58 | .300 | 396 | *519 | 22 | .977 |
| 1975-Philadelphia .....Nat. | 2B •162 | | *699 | 111 | *213 | 40 | 3 | 4 | 57 | .305 | *400 | 481 | 17 | .981 |
| 1976-Philadelphia y ..Nat. | 2B | 160 | *666 | 92 | 189 | 14 | *12 | 1 | 56 | .284 | 407 | 424 | 10 | *.988 |
| Major League Totals ...................... | | 904 | 3662 | 526 | 1067 | 150 | 43 | 15 | 298 | .291 | 2145 | 2626 | 85 | .982 |

†On military list, June 27 through July 13, 1970.
‡On military list, July 10 through July 26, 1971.
§On military list, July 8 through July 24, 1972.
xTraded to Philadelphia Phillies for Pitcher Ken Brett, October 18, 1973.
yPlayed out option year, signed as free agent with Montreal Expos, November 17, 1976.

### CHAMPIONSHIP SERIES RECORD

| Year Club League | Pos. | G. | AB. | R. | H. | 2B. | 3B. | HR. | RBI. | B.A. | PO. | A. | E. | F.A. |
|---|---|---|---|---|---|---|---|---|---|---|---|---|---|---|
| 1970-Pittsburgh .......Nat. | 2B | 2 | 8 | 1 | 1 | 1 | 0 | 0 | 0 | .125 | 6 | 8 | 0 | 1.000 |
| 1971-Pittsburgh .......Nat. | 2B | 4 | 19 | 5 | 8 | 2 | 0 | 0 | 1 | .421 | 11 | 11 | 1 | .957 |
| 1972-Pittsburgh .......Nat. | 2B | 5 | 19 | 0 | 4 | 0 | 0 | 0 | 3 | .211 | 5 | 10 | 1 | .938 |
| 1976-Philadelphia .....Nat. | 2B | 3 | 13 | 1 | 4 | 1 | 0 | 0 | 1 | .308 | 8 | 8 | 0 | 1.000 |
| Championship Series Totals ........... | | 14 | 59 | 7 | 17 | 4 | 0 | 0 | 5 | .288 | 30 | 37 | 2 | .971 |

| Year   Club        League | Pos. | G. | AB. | R. | H. | 2B. | 3B. | HR. | RBI. | B.A. | PO. | A. | E. | F.A. |
|---|---|---|---|---|---|---|---|---|---|---|---|---|---|---|
| 1971—Pittsburgh ........Nat. | 2B | 7 | 30 | 2 | 4 | 1 | 0 | 0 | 1 | .133 | 20 | 23 | 0 | 1.000 |

ALL-STAR GAME RECORD

| Year   League | Pos. | AB. | R. | H. | 2B. | 3B. | HR. | RBI. | B.A. | PO. | A. | E. | F.A. |
|---|---|---|---|---|---|---|---|---|---|---|---|---|---|
| 1974—National ............................. | PH-2B | 1 | 0 | 0 | 0 | 0 | 0 | 0 | .000 | 0 | 1 | 0 | 1.000 |
| 1975—National ............................. | 2B | 1 | 0 | 0 | 0 | 0 | 0 | 0 | .000 | 0 | 0 | 0 | .000 |
| 1976—National ............................. | 2B | 1 | 1 | 1 | 0 | 0 | 0 | 0 | 1.000 | 1 | 1 | 0 | 1.000 |
| All-Star Game Totals ....................... | | 3 | 1 | 1 | 0 | 0 | 0 | 0 | .333 | 1 | 2 | 0 | 1.000 |

## ESTEBAN MANUEL ANTONIO CASTILLO

Born April 1, 1957, at Santo Domingo, Dominican Republic.
Height, 5.09. Weight, 160.
Throws right and bats right and lefthanded.
Hobby—Horse racing.

| Year   Club        League | Pos. | G. | AB. | R. | H. | 2B. | 3B. | HR. | RBI. | B.A. | PO. | A. | E. | F.A. |
|---|---|---|---|---|---|---|---|---|---|---|---|---|---|---|
| 1973—Marion ..............Appal. | 3B-2B | 10 | 19 | 1 | 2 | 0 | 0 | 0 | 1 | .105 | 8 | 10 | 2 | .900 |
| 1974—Marion ..............Appal. | 3B-2B | 42 | 144 | 19 | 42 | 6 | 1 | 1 | 21 | .292 | 41 | 55 | 9 | .914 |
| 1975—Wausau ............Midw. | 3B | 68 | 212 | 28 | 69 | 9 | 4 | 1 | 34 | .325 | 39 | 109 | 19 | .886 |
| 1976—Arkansas ..........Tex. | 3-2-1B | 116 | 355 | 36 | 99 | 11 | 2 | 0 | 35 | .279 | 130 | 194 | 15 | .956 |

Listed on St. Louis Cardinals' 1977 spring roster.

## WILLIAM RADHAMES CASTRO (CHECO)
### (Bill)

Born December 13, 1953, at Barrero, Santiago, Dominican Republic.
Height, 6.00. Weight, 175.
Throws and bats righthanded.
Hobbies—Hunting, music and volleyball.
Led Midwest League in saves with 17 in 1972.

| Year   Club | League | G. | IP. | W. | L. | Pct. | H. | R. | ER. | SO. | BB. | ERA. |
|---|---|---|---|---|---|---|---|---|---|---|---|---|
| 1971—Newark...............................NYP | | 9 | 13 | 0 | 1 | .000 | 20 | 7 | 6 | 10 | 6 | 4.15 |
| 1972—Danville ............................Midwest | | 45 | 74 | 10 | 9 | .526 | 59 | 31 | 25 | 66 | 26 | 3.04 |
| 1973—Danville ............................Midwest | | 46 | 114 | 11 | 4 | ●.733 | 96 | 33 | 23 | 104 | 24 | 1.82 |
| 1974—Sacramento.........................P. Coast | | 50 | 105 | 9 | 5 | .643 | 133 | 68 | 55 | 52 | 35 | 4.71 |
| 1974—Milwaukee ........................American | | 8 | 18 | 0 | 0 | .000 | 19 | 10 | 9 | 10 | 5 | 4.50 |
| 1975—Milwaukee† ........................American | | 18 | 75 | 3 | 2 | .600 | 78 | 28 | 21 | 25 | 17 | 2.52 |
| 1976—Milwaukee‡ ........................American | | 39 | 70 | 4 | 6 | .400 | 70 | 29 | 27 | 23 | 19 | 3.47 |
| Major League Totals ............................. | | 65 | 163 | 7 | 8 | .467 | 167 | 67 | 57 | 58 | 41 | 3.15 |

†On disabled list, July 23 to September 1, 1975.
‡On disabled lise, May 19 through June 9, 1976.

## WILLIAM HOLLAND CAUDILL
### (Bill)

Born July 13, 1956, at Santa Monica, Calif.
Height, 6.01. Weight, 190.
Throws and bats righthanded.
Hobbies—Hunting and fishing.
Pitched six-inning, 4-0 no-hit victory against Winter Haven, May 14, 1975.
Led Florida State League in complete games with 12 in 1975.

| Year   Club | League | G. | IP. | W. | L. | Pct. | H. | R. | ER. | SO. | BB. | ERA. |
|---|---|---|---|---|---|---|---|---|---|---|---|---|
| 1974—Sarasota Cardinals ..............Gulf Coast | | 8 | 30 | 1 | 0 | 1.000 | 18 | 9 | 4 | .228 | 13 | 1.80 |
| 1975—St. Petersburg.....................Fla. St. | | 25 | 163 | ●14 | 8 | .636 | 123 | 63 | 57 | ●153 | 87 | 3.15 |
| 1976—Arkansas† ...........................Texas | | 27 | 140 | 6 | 15 | .286 | 128 | 79 | 69 | ●140 | 84 | 4.44 |

†Traded from St. Louis Cardinals' organization to Cincinnati Reds' organization for Infielder-Outfielder Joel Youngblood, March 28, 1977.

## WAYNE HOWARD CAUGHEY
Name pronounced CAW-hee

Born February 2, 1954, at Brainerd, Minn.
Height, 6.00, Weight, 175.
Throws right and bats lefthanded.
Hobbies—Hunting and fishing.
Attended St. Cloud State University, St. Cloud, Minn.

| Year   Club        League | Pos. | G. | AB. | R. | H. | 2B. | 3B. | HR. | RBI. | B.A. | PO. | A. | E. | F.A. |
|---|---|---|---|---|---|---|---|---|---|---|---|---|---|---|
| 1974—Wis. Rapids ......Midw. | SS-3B | 27 | 57 | 4 | 13 | 2 | 0 | 0 | 4 | .228 | 16 | 39 | 6 | .902 |
| 1974—Elizabethton ......Appal. | SS-3-2 | 60 | 222 | 45 | 61 | 12 | 4 | 2 | 32 | .275 | 67 | 156 | 15 | .937 |
| 1975—Wis. Rapids ......Midw. | 2-SS-3 | 127 | 461 | 70 | 113 | 13 | 1 | 5 | 38 | .245 | 246 | 385 | 29 | .956 |
| 1976—Orlando ............South. | SS-2-3 | 96 | 323 | 40 | 80 | 8 | 6 | 1 | 29 | .248 | 158 | 233 | 24 | .942 |

†On disabled list, May 25 through June 8, 1974.
Listed on Minnesota Twins' 1977 spring roster.

# CESAR CEDENO
Name pronounced Suh-DAYN-yo.

Born February 25, 1951, at Santo Domingo, Dominican Republic.
Height, 6.02. Weight, 190.
Throw and bats righthanded.

Tied major league record for most doubles, inning, 2, April 9, 1973 (1st game, 6th inning).
Led National League outfielders in total chances with 460 in 1974.
Led National League outfielders in double plays with 5 in 1976.
Only player in major league history to steal 50 or more bases and hit 20 or more home runs in the same season on three occasions (55 stolen bases and 22 home runs in 1972; 56 stolen bases and 25 home runs in 1973; 57 stolen bases and 26 home runs in 1974).
Major league stolen bases: 1970 (17), 1971 (20), 1972 (55), 1973 (56), 1974 (57), 1975 (50), 1976 (58). Total—313.
Named outfielder on THE SPORTING NEWS National League All-Star fielding team, 1972, 1973, 1974, 1975 and 1976.
Named outfielder on THE SPORTING NEWS National League All-Star Team, 1972 and 1976.

| Year | Club | League | Pos. | G. | AB. | R. | H. | 2B. | 3B. | HR. | RBI. | B.A. | PO. | A. | E. | F.A. |
|------|------|--------|------|-----|------|-----|------|-----|-----|-----|------|------|------|-----|-----|------|
| 1968—Covington | .........Appal. | | OF | 36 | 131 | 23 | 49 | 5 | 6 | 0 | 21 | .374 | 49 | •8 | 7 | .891 |
| 1968—Cocoa | ...............Fla. St. | | OF | 69 | 180 | 19 | 46 | 8 | 2 | 0 | 16 | .256 | 70 | 4 | 7 | .914 |
| 1969—Peninsula | .........Carol. | | 1-OF | 142 | 497 | 62 | 136 | •32 | 3 | 5 | 39 | .274 | 761 | 52 | 17 | .980 |
| 1970—Houston | ............Nat. | | OF | 90 | 355 | 46 | 110 | 21 | 4 | 7 | 42 | .310 | 211 | 1 | 7 | .968 |
| 1971—Houston | ............Nat. | | OF-1B | 161 | 611 | 85 | 161 | •40 | 6 | 10 | 81 | .264 | 348 | 6 | 4 | .989 |
| 1972—Houston | ............Nat. | | OF | 139 | 559 | 103 | 179 | •39 | 8 | 22 | 82 | .320 | 345 | 9 | 7 | .981 |
| 1973—Houston | ............Nat. | | OF | 139 | 525 | 86 | 168 | 35 | 2 | 25 | 70 | .320 | 357 | 10 | 7 | .981 |
| 1974—Houston | ............Nat. | | OF | 160 | 610 | 95 | 164 | 29 | 5 | 26 | 102 | .269 | •446 | 11 | 3 | .993 |
| 1975—Houston† | .........Nat. | | OF | 131 | 500 | 93 | 144 | 31 | 3 | 13 | 63 | .288 | 322 | 8 | 6 | .982 |
| 1976—Houston | ............Nat. | | OF | 150 | 575 | 89 | 171 | 26 | 5 | 18 | 83 | .297 | 377 | 11 | 8 | .980 |
| Major League Totals | ...................... | | | 970 | 3735 | 597 | 1097 | 221 | 33 | 121 | 523 | .294 | 2406 | 56 | 42 | .983 |

## ALL-STAR GAME RECORD

| Year | League | Pos. | AB. | R. | H. | 2B. | 3B. | HR. | RBI. | B.A. | PO. | A. | E. | F.A. |
|------|--------|------|-----|-----|-----|-----|-----|-----|------|------|-----|-----|-----|------|
| 1972—National | ............................ | OF | 2 | 1 | 1 | 0 | 0 | 0 | 0 | .500 | 0 | 0 | 0 | .000 |
| 1973—National | ............................ | OF | 3 | 0 | 1 | 0 | 0 | 0 | 1 | .333 | 3 | 0 | 0 | 1.000 |
| 1974—National | ............................ | OF | 2 | 0 | 0 | 0 | 0 | 0 | 0 | .000 | 2 | 0 | 0 | 1.000 |
| 1976—National | ............................ | OF | 2 | 1 | 1 | 0 | 0 | 1 | 2 | .500 | 1 | 0 | 0 | 1.000 |
| All-Star Game Totals | ...................... | | 9 | 2 | 3 | 0 | 0 | 1 | 3 | .333 | 6 | 0 | 0 | 1.000 |

# RICHARD ALDO CERONE
## (Rick)

Born May 19, 1954, at Newark, N. J.
Height, 5.11. Weight, 190.
Throws and bats righthanded.
Hobbies—Golf, swimming and tennis.
Attended Seton Hall University, South Orange, N. J.; received Bachelor of Science degree in Physical Education.

Received reported $60,000 bonus to sign with Cleveland Indians, 1975.

| Year | Club | League | Pos. | G. | AB. | R. | H. | 2B. | 3B. | HR. | RBI. | B.A. | PO. | A. | E. | F.A. |
|------|------|--------|------|-----|-----|-----|-----|-----|-----|-----|------|------|-----|-----|-----|------|
| 1975—Okla. City | .........A.A. | | C-OF | 46 | 140 | 22 | 35 | 6 | 1 | 2 | 13 | .250 | 178 | 30 | 3 | .986 |
| 1975—Cleveland | .........Amer. | | C | 7 | 12 | 1 | 3 | 1 | 0 | 0 | 0 | .250 | 18 | 1 | 0 | 1.000 |
| 1976—Toledo† | ............Int. | | C | 96 | 339 | 38 | 86 | 19 | 0 | 11 | 49 | .254 | 351 | 50 | 18 | .957 |
| 1976—Cleveland‡ | ........Amer. | | C-DH | 7 | 16 | 1 | 2 | 0 | 0 | 0 | 1 | .125 | 25 | 1 | 1 | .963 |
| Major League Totals | ...................... | | | 14 | 28 | 2 | 5 | 1 | 0 | 0 | 1 | .178 | 43 | 2 | 1 | .978 |

†On disabled list May 13 through May 24, 1976.
‡Traded with Infielder-Outfielder John Lowenstein to Toronto Blue Jays for Outfielder Rico Carty, December 6, 1976.

# RONALD CHARLES CEY
Name pronounced Say.
## (Ron)

Born February 15, 1948, at Tacoma, Wash.
Height, 5.09. Weight, 185.
Throws and bats righthanded.
Attended Washington State University, Pullman, Wash., and Western Washington State College, Bellingham, Wash.

Led National League third basemen in double plays with 39 in 1973.
Led Pacific Coast League batters in bases on balls with 117 in 1972.
Led California League third basemen in double plays with 22 in 1969.
Led Northwest League in sacrifice flies with 7 in 1968.
Tied for Pacific Coast League lead in double plays by third basemen with 24 in 1972.

| Year | Club | League | Pos. | G. | AB. | R. | H. | 2B. | 3B. | HR. | RBI. | B.A. | PO. | A. | E. | F.A. |
|------|------|--------|------|-----|-----|-----|-----|-----|-----|-----|------|------|-----|------|-----|-------|
| 1968—Tri-City | ...........Northw. | | 3B | 74 | 254 | 50 | 76 | 11 | 4 | 9 | •62 | .299 | 46 | •175 | 10 | •.957 |
| 1969—Albuquerque | ......Texas | | 3B | 13 | 32 | 8 | 5 | 1 | 0 | 0 | 2 | .156 | 13 | 19 | 1 | .970 |
| 1969—Bakersfield | ........Calif. | | 3B | 98 | 353 | 68 | 117 | 16 | 1 | 22 | 56 | .331 | 82 | 197 | 22 | .927 |

— 64 —

| Year Club League | Pos. | G. | AB. | R. | H. | 2B. | 3B. | HR. | RBI. | B.A. | PO. | A. | E. | F.A. |
|---|---|---|---|---|---|---|---|---|---|---|---|---|---|---|
| 1970—Albuquerque......Texas | 3B | 71 | 239 | 31 | 79 | 22 | 1 | 4 | 56 | .331 | 44 | 132 | 10 | .946 |
| 1971—Spokane ...........P. C. | 3B | 137 | 500 | 85 | 164 | 26 | 4 | 32 | ∗123 | .328 | 95 | 283 | 24 | ∗.940 |
| 1971—Los Angeles ......Nat. | PH | 2 | 2 | 0 | 0 | 0 | 0 | 0 | 0 | .000 | 0 | 0 | 0 | .000 |
| 1972—Albuquerque......P. C. | 3B-2B | 142 | 496 | 99 | 163 | 25 | 7 | 23 | 103 | .329 | ∗108 | ∗279 | 21 | .949 |
| 1972—Los Angeles ......Nat. | 3B | 11 | 37 | 3 | 10 | 1 | 0 | 1 | 3 | .270 | 7 | 20 | 3 | .900 |
| 1973—Los Angeles ......Nat. | 3B | 152 | 507 | 60 | 124 | 18 | 4 | 15 | 80 | .245 | 111 | ∗328 | 18 | .961 |
| 1974—Los Angeles ......Nat. | 3B | 159 | 577 | 88 | 151 | 20 | 2 | 18 | 97 | .262 | 155 | 365 | 22 | .959 |
| 1975—Los Angeles ......Nat. | 3B | 158 | 566 | 72 | 160 | 29 | 2 | 25 | 101 | .283 | 144 | 309 | 19 | .960 |
| 1976—Los Angeles ......Nat. | 3B | 145 | 502 | 69 | 139 | 18 | 3 | 23 | 80 | .277 | 111 | 334 | 16 | .965 |
| Major League Totals ..................... | | 627 | 2191 | 292 | 584 | 86 | 11 | 82 | 361 | .267 | 528 | 1356 | 78 | .960 |

### CHAMPIONSHIP SERIES RECORD

| Year Club League | Pos. | G. | AB. | R. | H. | 2B. | 3B. | HR. | RBI. | B.A. | PO. | A. | E. | F.A. |
|---|---|---|---|---|---|---|---|---|---|---|---|---|---|---|
| 1974—Los Angeles ......Nat. | 3B | 4 | 16 | 2 | 5 | 3 | 0 | 1 | 1 | .313 | 2 | 4 | 2 | .750 |

### WORLD SERIES RECORD

| Year Club League | Pos. | G. | AB. | R. | H. | 2B. | 3B. | HR. | RBI. | B.A. | PO. | A. | E. | F.A. |
|---|---|---|---|---|---|---|---|---|---|---|---|---|---|---|
| 1974—Los Angeles ......Nat. | 3B | 5 | 17 | 1 | 3 | 0 | 0 | 0 | 0 | .176 | 5 | 9 | 1 | .933 |

### ALL-STAR GAME RECORD

| Year League | Pos. | AB. | R. | H. | 2B. | 3B. | HR. | RBI. | B.A. | PO. | A. | E. | F.A. |
|---|---|---|---|---|---|---|---|---|---|---|---|---|---|
| 1974—National ............................ | 3B | 2 | 0 | 1 | 1 | 0 | 0 | 2 | .500 | 0 | 0 | 0 | .000 |
| 1975—National ............................ | 3B | 3 | 0 | 1 | 0 | 0 | 0 | 0 | .333 | 0 | 1 | 0 | 1.000 |
| 1976—National ............................ | 3B | 0 | 0 | 0 | 0 | 0 | 0 | 0 | .000 | 0 | 0 | 0 | .000 |
| All-Star Game Totals ....................... | | 5 | 0 | 2 | 1 | 0 | 0 | 2 | .400 | 0 | 1 | 0 | 1.000 |

## DAVID LEE CHALK
### (Dave)

Born August 30, 1950, at Del Rio, Tex.
Height, 5.10. Weight, 175.
Throws and bats righthanded.
Hobby—Sports in general.
Attended University of Texas, Austin, Tex.

| Year Club League | Pos. | G. | AB. | R. | H. | 2B. | 3B. | HR. | RBI. | B.A. | PO. | A. | E. | F.A. |
|---|---|---|---|---|---|---|---|---|---|---|---|---|---|---|
| 1972—Shreveport ........Tex. | 3B-2B | 76 | 265 | 31 | 67 | 11 | 0 | 3 | 25 | .253 | 63 | 155 | 15 | .936 |
| 1973—El Paso ............Tex. | SS-2B | 48 | 174 | 34 | 51 | 6 | 1 | 4 | 18 | .293 | 85 | 183 | 10 | .964 |
| 1973—Salt Lake C. ......P.C. | SS | 92 | 330 | 46 | 78 | 8 | 2 | 5 | 38 | .236 | 118 | 290 | 21 | .951 |
| 1973—California .........Amer. | SS | 24 | 69 | 14 | 16 | 2 | 0 | 0 | 6 | .232 | 36 | 66 | 4 | .962 |
| 1974—California .........Amer. | ●SS-3B | 133 | 465 | 44 | 117 | 9 | 3 | 5 | 31 | .252 | 200 | 350 | ●34 | .942 |
| 1975—California .........Amer. | 3B | 149 | 513 | 59 | 140 | 24 | 2 | 3 | 56 | .273 | 108 | 333 | 11 | .976 |
| 1976—California .........Amer. | SS-3B | 142 | 438 | 39 | 95 | 14 | 1 | 0 | 33 | .217 | 176 | 387 | 17 | .971 |
| Major League Totals ..................... | | 448 | 1485 | 156 | 368 | 49 | 6 | 8 | 126 | .248 | 520 | 1136 | 66 | .962 |

### ALL-STAR GAME RECORD

| Year League | Pos. | AB. | R. | H. | 2B. | 3B. | HR. | RBI. | B.A. | PO. | A. | E. | F.A. |
|---|---|---|---|---|---|---|---|---|---|---|---|---|---|
| 1974—American ........................... | 3B | 1 | 0 | 0 | 0 | 0 | 0 | 0 | .000 | 0 | 0 | 0 | .000 |

Member of American League All-Star Team for 1975 game; did not play.

## CARROLL CHRISTOPHER CHAMBLISS
### (Chris)

Born December 26, 1948, at Dayton, O.
Height, 6.01. Weight, 200.
Throws right and bats lefthanded.
Hobby—Collecting phonograph records.
Attended Mira Costa Junior College, Oceanside, Calif., and University of California
at Los Angeles, Los Angeles, Calif.

Led American League first basemen in total chances with 1,565 in 1973.
Named by THE SPORTING NEWS as American League Rookie Player of the Year, 1971.
Named by the Baseball Writers' Association as American League Rookie of the Year, 1971.
Named American Association Rookie of the Year in 1970.
Named first baseman on THE SPORTING NEWS American League All-Star Team, 1976.

| Year Club League | Pos. | G. | AB. | R. | H. | 2B. | 3B. | HR. | RBI. | B.A. | PO. | A. | E. | F.A. |
|---|---|---|---|---|---|---|---|---|---|---|---|---|---|---|
| 1970—Wichita† ...........A. A. | OF-1B | 105 | 383 | 60 | 131 | 17 | 8 | 7 | 52 | ∗342 | 413 | 21 | 13 | .971 |
| 1971—Wichita ...........A.A. | OF-1B | 13 | 42 | 8 | 12 | 3 | 0 | 2 | 6 | .286 | 42 | 3 | 0 | 1.000 |
| 1971—Cleveland .........Amer. | 1B | 111 | 415 | 49 | 114 | 20 | 4 | 9 | 48 | .275 | 943 | 55 | 8 | .992 |
| 1972—Cleveland‡ .......Amer. | 1B | 121 | 466 | 51 | 136 | 27 | 2 | 6 | 44 | .292 | 1109 | 56 | 8 | .993 |
| 1973—Cleveland .........Amer. | 1B | 155 | 572 | 70 | 156 | 30 | 2 | 11 | 53 | .273 | 1437 | 114 | ∗14 | .991 |
| 1974—Cleve.§-N. Y. ....Amer. | 1B | 127 | 467 | 46 | 119 | 20 | 3 | 6 | 50 | .255 | 1035 | 84 | 11 | .990 |
| 1975—New York.........Amer. | 1B | 150 | 562 | 66 | 171 | 38 | 4 | 9 | 72 | .304 | 1222 | 106 | 12 | .991 |
| 1976—New York.........Amer. | 1B-DH | 156 | 641 | 79 | 188 | 32 | 6 | 17 | 96 | .293 | 1440 | 109 | 9 | .994 |
| Major League Totals ..................... | | 820 | 3123 | 361 | 884 | 167 | 21 | 58 | 363 | .283 | 7186 | 524 | 62 | .992 |

†On disabled list, May 25 through June 16, 1970.
‡On military list, June 23 through June 30, 1972.
§Traded with Pitchers Dick Tidrow and Cecil Upshaw to New York Yankees for Fritz Peterson, Steve Kline, Fred Beene and Tom Buskey, April 26, 1974.

## CHAMPIONSHIP SERIES RECORD

| Year Club League | Pos. | G. | AB. | R. | H. | 2B. | 3B. | HR. | RBI. | B.A. | PO. | A. | E. | F.A. |
|---|---|---|---|---|---|---|---|---|---|---|---|---|---|---|
| 1976–New York..........Amer. | 1B | 5 | 21 | 5 | 11 | 1 | 1 | 2 | 8 | .524 | 50 | 3 | 1 | .981 |

## WORLD SERIES RECORD

| Year Club League | Pos. | G. | AB. | R. | H. | 2B. | 3B. | HR. | RBI. | B.A. | PO. | A. | E. | F.A. |
|---|---|---|---|---|---|---|---|---|---|---|---|---|---|---|
| 1976–New York..........Amer. | 1B | 4 | 16 | 1 | 5 | 1 | 0 | 0 | 1 | .313 | 26 | 3 | 1 | .967 |

## ALL-STAR GAME RECORD

| Year League | Pos. | AB. | R. | H. | 2B. | 3B. | HR. | RBI. | B.A. | PO. | A. | E. | F.A. |
|---|---|---|---|---|---|---|---|---|---|---|---|---|---|
| 1976–American ........................... | PH | 1 | 0 | 0 | 0 | 0 | 0 | 0 | .000 | 0 | 0 | 0 | .000 |

## ROBERT MICHAEL CHAMPION
### (Mike)

Born February 10, 1955, at Montgomery, Ala.
Height, 6.00. Weight, 185.
Throws and bats righthanded.
Hobby–Music.
Led Pacific Coast League second basemen in double plays with 113 in 1976.

| Year Club League | Pos. | G. | AB. | R. | H. | 2B. | 3B. | HR. | RBI. | B.A. | PO. | A. | E. | F.A. |
|---|---|---|---|---|---|---|---|---|---|---|---|---|---|---|
| 1973–Walla Walla ......Northw. | SS | 66 | 268 | 49 | 74 | 9 | •5 | 2 | 39 | .276 | 95 | ★165 | 27 | .906 |
| 1974–Alexandria ........Texas | •SS-2B | 86 | 250 | 16 | 56 | 6 | 4 | 0 | 17 | .224 | 114 | 161 | •33 | .893 |
| 1975–Alexandria ........Texas | 2B | 125 | 403 | 54 | 117 | 23 | 4 | 4 | 36 | .290 | ★303 | 262 | 25 | .958 |
| 1976–Hawaii ..............P. C. | ★2B-SS | 141 | 501 | 68 | 134 | 21 | 5 | 9 | 65 | .267 | 317 | ★454 | ★23 | ★.971 |
| 1976–San Diego..........Nat. | 2B | 11 | 38 | 4 | 9 | 2 | 0 | 1 | 2 | .237 | 23 | 24 | 3 | .940 |
| Major League Totals ...................... | | 11 | 38 | 4 | 9 | 2 | 0 | 1 | 2 | .237 | 23 | 24 | 3 | .940 |

## DARREL LEE CHANEY

Name pronounced CHAY-nee.

Born March 9, 1948, at Hammond, Ind.
Height, 6.01. Weight, 185.
Throws right and bats right and lefthanded.
Hobby–Bowling.
Led Northern League shortstops in double plays with 35 in 1966.
Led Southern League batters in strikeouts with 159 in 1968.

| Year Club League | Pos. | G. | AB. | R. | H. | 2B. | 3B. | HR. | RBI. | B.A. | PO. | A. | E. | F.A. |
|---|---|---|---|---|---|---|---|---|---|---|---|---|---|---|
| 1966–Sioux Falls ........North. | SS | 57 | 218 | 24 | 45 | 4 | 3 | 3 | 14 | .206 | ★117 | ★147 | 19 | .933 |
| 1967–Knoxville† ........South. | SS | 26 | 90 | 10 | 17 | 0 | 1 | 1 | 7 | .189 | 42 | 58 | 10 | .909 |
| 1968–Asheville ..........South. | 2B-SS | 132 | 468 | 64 | 108 | 21 | 7 | 23 | 78 | .231 | 256 | 359 | 31 | .952 |
| 1969–Cincinnati..........Nat. | SS | 93 | 209 | 21 | 40 | 5 | 2 | 0 | 15 | .191 | 115 | 191 | 17 | .947 |
| 1970–Cincinnati..........Nat. | SS-2-3 | 57 | 95 | 7 | 22 | 3 | 0 | 1 | 4 | .232 | 56 | 90 | 9 | .942 |
| 1971–Indianapolis ......A. A. | SS | 120 | 459 | 73 | 127 | 17 | 9 | 3 | 38 | .277 | ★215 | 346 | 24 | ★.959 |
| 1971–Cincinnati..........Nat. | SS-2-3 | 10 | 24 | 2 | 3 | 0 | 0 | 0 | 1 | .125 | 16 | 21 | 0 | 1.000 |
| 1972–Cincinnati..........Nat. | SS-2-3 | 83 | 196 | 29 | 49 | 7 | 2 | 2 | 19 | .250 | 100 | 178 | 10 | .965 |
| 1973–Cincinnati..........Nat. | SS-2-3 | 105 | 227 | 27 | 41 | 7 | 1 | 0 | 14 | .181 | 123 | 246 | 14 | .963 |
| 1974–Cincinnati..........Nat. | 3-2-S | 117 | 135 | 27 | 27 | 6 | 1 | 2 | 16 | .200 | 90 | 135 | 9 | .962 |
| 1975–Cincinnati‡ ........Nat. | SS-2-3 | 71 | 160 | 18 | 35 | 6 | 0 | 2 | 26 | .219 | 77 | 164 | 7 | .972 |
| 1976–Atlanta..............Nat. | ★SS-3-2 | 153 | 496 | 42 | 125 | 20 | 8 | 1 | 50 | .252 | 243 | 468 | ★37 | .950 |
| Major League Totals ...................... | | 689 | 1542 | 173 | 342 | 54 | 14 | 8 | 145 | .222 | 820 | 1493 | 103 | .957 |

†On military list, May 29, 1967 through February 27, 1968.
‡Traded to Atlanta Braves for Outfielder-First Baseman Mike Lum, December 12, 1975.

## CHAMPIONSHIP SERIES RECORD

| Year Club League | Pos. | G. | AB. | R. | H. | 2B. | 3B. | HR. | RBI. | B.A. | PO. | A. | E. | F.A. |
|---|---|---|---|---|---|---|---|---|---|---|---|---|---|---|
| 1972–Cincinnati..........Nat. | SS | 5 | 16 | 3 | 3 | 0 | 0 | 0 | 1 | .188 | 8 | 16 | 3 | .889 |
| 1973–Cincinnati..........Nat. | SS | 5 | 9 | 0 | 0 | 0 | 0 | 0 | 0 | .000 | 2 | 10 | 0 | 1.000 |
| Championship Series Totals ............ | | 10 | 25 | 3 | 3 | 0 | 0 | 0 | 1 | .120 | 10 | 26 | 3 | .923 |

## WORLD SERIES RECORD

| Year Club League | Pos. | G. | AB. | R. | H. | 2B. | 3B. | HR. | RBI. | B.A. | PO. | A. | E. | F.A. |
|---|---|---|---|---|---|---|---|---|---|---|---|---|---|---|
| 1970–Cincinnati..........Nat. | SS | 3 | 1 | 0 | 0 | 0 | 0 | 0 | 0 | .000 | 1 | 2 | 0 | 1.000 |
| 1972–Cincinnati..........Nat. | SS-PH | 4 | 7 | 0 | 0 | 0 | 0 | 0 | 0 | .000 | 5 | 11 | 0 | 1.000 |
| 1975–Cincinnati..........Nat. | PH | 2 | 2 | 0 | 0 | 0 | 0 | 0 | 0 | .000 | 0 | 0 | 0 | .000 |
| World Series Totals ...................... | | 9 | 10 | 0 | 0 | 0 | 0 | 0 | 0 | .000 | 6 | 13 | 0 | 1.000 |

---

## DID YOU KNOW —

That Joe Medwick of the St. Louis Cardinals set a National League record when he got 64 two-base hits during the 1936 season?

## CHARLES JOSEPH CHANT
### (Charlie)

Born August 7, 1951, at Bell Gardens, Calif.
Height, 6.00. Weight, 190.
Throws and bats righthanded.
Hobby—Sports in general.

| Year Club | League | Pos. | G. | AB. | R. | H. | 2B. | 3B. | HR. | RBI. | B.A. | PO. | A. | E. | F.A. |
|---|---|---|---|---|---|---|---|---|---|---|---|---|---|---|---|
| 1969—Tri-City | Northw. | 3-S-2 | 37 | 111 | 25 | 30 | 4 | 0 | 2 | 11 | .270 | 41 | 66 | 18 | .856 |
| 1970—CoosB-N. Ben | Northw. | *OF-SS | 76 | 284 | 50 | 89 | 12 | 2 | 8 | 38 | .313 | 97 | *13 | ●11 | .909 |
| 1971—Burlington | Midw. | OF | 111 | 442 | 70 | 126 | 13 | 3 | 9 | 53 | .285 | 182 | *17 | 9 | .957 |
| 1972—Birmingham | South. | OF | 123 | 379 | 45 | 80 | 14 | 2 | 10 | 46 | .211 | 196 | 12 | 11 | .950 |
| 1973—Tucson | P. C. | OF | 126 | 453 | 71 | 126 | 13 | 6 | 4 | 51 | .278 | 269 | 13 | *14 | .953 |
| 1974—Tucson | P. C. | OF | 128 | 485 | 83 | 122 | 31 | 3 | 9 | 69 | .252 | 270 | 24 | 13 | .958 |
| 1975—Tucson | P. C. | OF | 135 | 505 | 75 | 145 | 27 | 5 | 5 | 69 | .287 | 279 | *18 | 9 | .971 |
| 1975—Oakland† | Amer. | OF | 5 | 5 | 1 | 0 | 0 | 0 | 0 | 0 | .000 | 1 | 0 | 0 | 1.000 |
| 1976—Tulsa | A. A. | OF | 59 | 185 | 20 | 52 | 12 | 0 | 4 | 31 | .281 | 106 | 6 | 4 | .966 |
| 1976—St. Louis | Nat. | OF | 15 | 14 | 0 | 2 | 0 | 0 | 0 | 0 | .143 | 15 | 1 | 0 | 1.000 |
| American League Totals | | | 5 | 5 | 1 | 0 | 0 | 0 | 0 | 0 | .000 | 1 | 0 | 0 | 1.000 |
| National League Totals | | | 15 | 14 | 0 | 2 | 0 | 0 | 0 | 0 | .143 | 15 | 1 | 0 | 1.000 |
| Major League Totals | | | 20 | 19 | 1 | 2 | 0 | 0 | 0 | 0 | .105 | 16 | 1 | 0 | 1.000 |

†Traded to St. Louis Cardinals for Infielder Larry Lintz, October 28, 1975.


## ANTONIO SILVIO CHEVEZ
### (Tony)

Born June 20, 1954, at Telica, Nicaragua.
Height, 5.11. Weight, 177.
Throws and bats righthanded.

| Year Club | League | G. | IP. | W. | L. | Pct. | H. | R. | ER. | SO. | BB. | ERA. |
|---|---|---|---|---|---|---|---|---|---|---|---|---|
| 1974—Miami | Florida St. | *41 | 109 | 9 | 6 | .600 | 87 | 34 | 19 | 57 | 33 | *1.57 |
| 1975—Miami | Florida St. | 33 | 156 | 14 | 6 | .700 | 136 | 52 | 36 | 70 | 30 | 2.08 |
| 1976—Miami | Florida St. | 13 | 94 | 9 | 2 | .818 | 73 | 27 | 22 | 88 | 18 | 2.11 |
| 1976—Charlotte | Southern | 11 | 77 | 7 | 3 | .700 | 58 | 20 | 16 | 42 | 19 | 1.87 |

Listed on Baltimore Orioles' 1977 spring roster.


## RICHARD FRANCIS CHILES
### (Rich)

Born November 22, 1949, at Sacramento, Calif.
Height, 6.00. Weight, 175.
Throws and bats lefthanded.
Attended Sacramento City College, Sacramento, Calif.
Cousin of George Kelly, star first baseman for New York Giants, Cincinnati Reds
and Brooklyn Dodgers, 1915-1932, and member of Baseball Hall of Fame.

| Year Club | League | Pos. | G. | AB. | R. | H. | 2B. | 3B. | HR. | RBI. | B.A. | PO. | A. | E. | F.A. |
|---|---|---|---|---|---|---|---|---|---|---|---|---|---|---|---|
| 1968—Covington | Appal. | OF | 32 | 121 | 44 | 54 | 11 | 5 | 6 | 42 | .446 | 48 | 4 | 3 | .945 |
| 1968—Oklahoma City | P.C. | OF | 43 | 164 | 17 | 43 | 6 | 2 | 2 | 11 | .262 | 84 | 2 | 2 | .977 |
| 1969—Peninsula | Carol. | OF | 35 | 128 | 8 | 31 | 6 | 0 | 2 | 15 | .242 | 54 | 5 | 2 | .967 |
| 1969—Oklahoma City† | A.A. | OF | 60 | 216 | 35 | 61 | 8 | 4 | 3 | 22 | .282 | 113 | 3 | 7 | .943 |
| 1970—Oklahoma City | A.A. | OF | 108 | 414 | 56 | 126 | 24 | *11 | 1 | 36 | .304 | 150 | 9 | 4 | .975 |
| 1971—Oklahoma City | A.A. | OF | 3 | 12 | 1 | 2 | 1 | 0 | 0 | 0 | .167 | 6 | 0 | 0 | 1.000 |
| 1971—Houston | Nat. | OF | 67 | 119 | 12 | 27 | 5 | 1 | 2 | 15 | .227 | 35 | 0 | 0 | 1.000 |
| 1972—Oklahoma City | A.A. | OF | 115 | 419 | 59 | 110 | 21 | 5 | 7 | 44 | .263 | 180 | 7 | 4 | .979 |
| 1972—Houston‡ | Nat. | OF | 9 | 11 | 0 | 3 | 1 | 0 | 0 | 2 | .273 | 4 | 0 | 0 | 1.000 |
| 1973—Tucson | P.C. | OF | 100 | 370 | 53 | 102 | 16 | 3 | 6 | 41 | .276 | 153 | 8 | 5 | .970 |
| 1973—New York§ | Nat. | OF | 8 | 25 | 2 | 3 | 2 | 0 | 0 | 1 | .120 | 22 | 1 | 0 | 1.000 |
| 1974—Hawaii x | P.C. | OF | 88 | 304 | 50 | 84 | 16 | 0 | 11 | 47 | .276 | 119 | 10 | 3 | .977 |
| 1975— | | | | | | | Did not play. | | | | | | | | |
| 1976—Memphis | Int. | OF | 79 | 288 | 40 | 87 | 14 | 1 | 9 | 47 | .302 | 96 | 9 | 5 | .955 |
| 1976—Houston y | Nat. | OF | 5 | 4 | 1 | 2 | 1 | 0 | 0 | 0 | .500 | 1 | 0 | 0 | 1.000 |
| Major League Totals | | | 89 | 159 | 15 | 35 | 9 | 1 | 2 | 18 | .220 | 62 | 1 | 0 | 1.000 |

†On temporary inactive list, June 9 through June 28, 1969.

‡Traded with Pitcher Walter Harris (assigned from Oklahoma City to Tidewater) to New York Mets for Outfielder Tommie Agee, November 27, 1972.

§Released April 6, 1974; signed as free agent by San Diego Padres' organization, May 15, 1974.

xReleased by San Diego Padres' organization, March 29, 1975; signed as free agent by Houston Astros' organization, 1976.

yOn supplemental disabled list, July 11 through July 30, 1976. Drafted by Minnesota Twins' organization, December 6, 1976.


## LARRY RICHARD CHRISTENSON

Born November 10, 1953, at Everett, Wash.
Height, 6.04. Weight, 220.
Throws and bats righthanded.
Hobbies—Fishing and hunting.

| Year Club | League | G. | IP. | W. | L. | Pct. | H. | R. | ER. | SO. | BB. | ERA. |
|---|---|---|---|---|---|---|---|---|---|---|---|---|
| 1972–Pulaski ............................Ap'lachian | | 8 | 38 | 4 | 2 | .667 | 27 | 26 | 12 | 42 | 14 | 2.84 |
| 1973–Eugene ...........................P. Coast | | 16 | 100 | 7 | 6 | .538 | 109 | 65 | 57 | 64 | 54 | 5.13 |
| 1973–Philadelphia .......................National | | 10 | 34 | 1 | 4 | .200 | 53 | 25 | 25 | 11 | 20 | 6.62 |
| 1974–Toledo...............................Int'national | | 27 | 172 | 11 | 9 | .550 | 131 | 77 | 63 | 137 | 82 | 3.30 |
| 1974–Philadelphia .....................National | | 10 | 23 | 1 | 1 | .500 | 20 | 11 | 11 | 18 | 15 | 4.30 |
| 1975–Toledo† ............................Int'national | | 2 | 12 | 2 | 0 | 1.000 | 5 | 0 | 0 | 10 | 3 | 0.00 |
| 1975–Philadelphia .....................National | | 29 | 172 | 11 | 6 | .647 | 149 | 73 | 70 | 88 | 45 | 3.66 |
| 1976–Philadelphia .....................National | | 32 | 169 | 13 | 8 | .619 | 199 | 77 | 69 | 54 | 42 | 3.67 |
| Major League Totals ............................ | | 81 | 398 | 26 | 19 | .578 | 421 | 186 | 175 | 171 | 122 | 3.96 |

†On disabled list, April 11 to April 30, 1975.

## JAMES CLANCY
## (Jim)

Born December 18, 1955, at Chicago, Ill.
Height, 6.04. Weight, 180.
Throws and bats righthanded.
Hobby–Playing guitar.

| Year Club | League | G. | IP. | W. | L. | Pct. | H. | R. | ER. | SO. | BB. | ERA. |
|---|---|---|---|---|---|---|---|---|---|---|---|---|
| 1974–Sarasota Rangers ...............Gulf Coast | | 9 | 53 | 3 | 3 | .500 | 40 | 21 | 16 | 58 | 28 | 2.72 |
| 1975–Anderson ...........................W. Carol. | | 23 | 148 | 6 | 13 | .316 | 139 | 85 | 63 | 109 | 91 | 3.83 |
| 1976–San Antonio†‡ ......................Texas | | 23 | 125 | 6 | 8 | .429 | 133 | 94 | 89 | 77 | 98 | 6.41 |

†On disabled list, June 15 through June 26, 1976.
‡Selected by Toronto Blue Jays from Texas Rangers in American League expansion draft, November 5, 1976.
Listed on Toronto Blue Jays' 1977 spring roster.

## DOUGLAS WILLIAM CLAREY
## (Doug)

Born April 20, 1954, at Los Angeles, Calif.
Height, 6.00. Weight, 180.
Throws and bats righthanded.

Led Midwest League second basemen in double plays with 80 in 1974 and Texas League with 74 in 1975.

| Year Club League | Pos. | G. | AB. | R. | H. | 2B. | 3B. | HR. | RBI. | B.A. | PO. | A. | E. | F.A. |
|---|---|---|---|---|---|---|---|---|---|---|---|---|---|---|
| 1972–Melb'rne Twins Fl. E.C. | SS | 49 | 185 | 35 | 41 | 6 | 0 | 1 | 18 | .222 | 58 | ∗159 | 24 | .900 |
| 1973–Geneva..............NYP | 2B | 65 | 232 | 34 | 55 | 7 | 0 | 5 | 24 | .237 | 131 | ∗176 | ∗24 | .927 |
| 1974–Wis. Rapids†......Midw. | 2B | 120 | 427 | 47 | 99 | 18 | 2 | 9 | 57 | .232 | 272 | ∗319 | 23 | ∗.963 |
| 1975–Arkansas .........Texas | ∗2B-3B | 130 | 433 | 51 | 89 | 17 | 2 | 3 | 44 | .206 | 284 | ∗334 | ∗32 | .951 |
| 1976–St. Petersburg ..Fla. St. | 3B | 3 | 8 | 0 | 3 | 0 | 0 | 0 | 1 | .375 | 1 | 2 | 2 | .600 |
| 1976–St. Louis .........Nat. | 2B | 9 | 4 | 2 | 1 | 0 | 0 | 1 | 2 | .250 | 3 | 1 | 0 | 1.000 |
| 1976–Tulsa‡ .............A.A. | 3-2-S | 63 | 167 | 29 | 38 | 8 | 2 | 7 | 31 | .228 | 46 | 98 | 12 | .923 |
| Major League Totals ...................... | | 9 | 4 | 2 | 1 | 0 | 0 | 1 | 2 | .250 | 3 | 1 | 0 | 1.000 |

†Drafted from Minnesota Twins' organization by Arkansas (St. Louis Cardinals' organization), December 2, 1974.
‡Traded by St. Louis Cardinals' organization to Tidewater (New York Mets' organization) for Outfielder Benny Ayala, March 30, 1977.

## JACK ANTHONY CLARK

Born November 10, 1955, at New Brighton, Pa.
Height, 6.02. Weight, 185.
Throws and bats righthanded.
Hobby–Music.

Led Texas League third basemen in double plays with 29 in 1975.
Led California League in total bases with 254 in 1974 and Texas League with 239 in 1975.

| Year Club League | Pos. | G. | AB. | R. | H. | 2B. | 3B. | HR. | RBI. | B.A. | PO. | A. | E. | F.A. |
|---|---|---|---|---|---|---|---|---|---|---|---|---|---|---|
| 1973–Great Falls........Pion. | O-P-3 | 65 | 234 | 46 | 75 | 20 | 1 | 9 | 54 | .321 | 73 | 9 | 1 | .988 |
| 1974–Fresno .............Calif. | 3B | 131 | 495 | 88 | 156 | 23 | 9 | ∗117 | 77 | .315 | 100 | 204 | ∗53 | .852 |
| 1975–Lafayette .........Texas | ∗3B-OF | 126 | 466 | 94 | 141 | 25 | 2 | ●23 | 77 | .303 | ∗107 | ∗279 | ∗56 | ∗.873 |
| 1975–San Francisco ..Nat. | Of-3B | 8 | 17 | 3 | 4 | 0 | 0 | 0 | 2 | .235 | 8 | 1 | 0 | 1.000 |
| 1976–Phoenix ...........P.C. | OF-3B | 131 | 470 | 111 | 152 | 29 | ∗16 | 17 | 86 | .323 | 188 | 23 | 9 | .959 |
| 1976–San Francisco ..Nat. | OF | 26 | 102 | 14 | 23 | 6 | 2 | 2 | 10 | .225 | 71 | 3 | 1 | .987 |
| Major League Totals ..................... | | 34 | 119 | 17 | 27 | 6 | 2 | 2 | 12 | .227 | 79 | 4 | 1 | .988 |

### PITCHING RECORD

| Year Club | League | G. | IP. | W. | L. | Pct. | H. | R. | ER. | SO. | BB. | ERA. |
|---|---|---|---|---|---|---|---|---|---|---|---|---|
| 1973–Great Falls ........................Pioneer | | 5 | 15 | 0 | 2 | .000 | 24 | 24 | 10 | 17 | 19 | 6.00 |

## KENNETH EARL CLAY
## (Kenny)

Born April 6, 1954, at Lynchburg, Va.
Height, 6.03. Weight, 185.
Throws and bats righthanded.

Led Florida State League in hit batsmen with 13 and tied for lead in complete games with 11 in 1973.
Tied for Appalachian League lead in games started with 13 and in shutouts with 2 in 1972.

| Year | Club | League | G. | IP. | W. | L. | Pct. | H. | R. | ER. | SO. | BB. | ERA. |
|------|------|--------|-----|-----|-----|-----|------|-----|-----|-----|-----|-----|------|
| 1972–Johnson City | ...................... | Ap'lachian | 13 | 91 | 7 | 2 | .778 | 69 | 32 | 30 | 66 | 53 | 2.97 |
| 1973–Fort Lauderdale | ................ | Florida St. | 24 | 158 | 10 | 10 | .500 | 129 | 61 | 40 | 97 | 80 | 2.28 |
| 1974–West Haven† | ...................... | Eastern | 31 | 155 | 5 | •13 | .278 | 160 | •103 | •84 | 99 | 77 | 4.88 |
| 1975–West Haven | ......................... | Eastern | 15 | 106 | 10 | 2 | .833 | 83 | 39 | 31 | 77 | 44 | 2.63 |
| 1975–Syracuse | ............................ | Int'national | 9 | 48 | 3 | 5 | .375 | 60 | 34 | 32 | 32 | 27 | 6.00 |
| 1976–Syracuse | ............................ | Int'national | 30 | 168 | 11 | 8 | .579 | 202 | 94 | 77 | 87 | 67 | 4.13 |

†Played in one game as an outfielder.
Listed on New York Yankees' 1977 spring roster.

## REGINALD LESLIE CLEVELAND
### (Reggie)

Born May 23, 1948, at Swift Current, Saskatchewan, Canada.
Height, 6.01. Weight, 195.
Throws and bats righthanded.
Hobbies–Reading and skin diving.

Led Northwest League pitchers in games started with 19 in 1967.
Tied for Northwest League lead in complete games with 11 in 1967 and tied for Texas League lead with 13 in 1969.
Named THE SPORTING NEWS National League Rookie Pitcher of the Year, 1971.

| Year | Club | League | G. | IP. | W. | L. | Pct. | H. | R. | ER. | SO. | BB. | ERA. |
|------|------|--------|-----|-----|-----|-----|------|-----|-----|-----|-----|-----|------|
| 1966–St. Petersburg | ...................... | Florida St. | 3 | 5 | 0 | 0 | .000 | 3 | 0 | 0 | 2 | 2 | 0.00 |
| 1966–Eugene | ................. | Northwest | 11 | 18 | 0 | 1 | .000 | 16 | 11 | 11 | 16 | 16 | 5.50 |
| 1967–St. Petersburg | .................... | Florida St. | 2 | 11 | 0 | 2 | .000 | 9 | 6 | 6 | 4 | 3 | 4.91 |
| 1967–Lewiston | ............................. | Northwest | 20 | •146 | 8 | 10 | .444 | •125 | 75 | 47 | 82 | 64 | 2.90 |
| 1968–St. Petersburg | ................... | Florida St. | 27 | 185 | •15 | 10 | .600 | 152 | 71 | 57 | 135 | 68 | 2.77 |
| 1969–Arkansas | ............................ | Texas | 23 | 170 | 15 | 6 | .714 | 156 | 75 | 64 | 103 | 62 | 3.39 |
| 1969–Tulsa | ................. | Am. Assoc. | 6 | 48 | 3 | 3 | .500 | 39 | 19 | 15 | 30 | 23 | 2.81 |
| 1969–St. Louis | ............................. | National | 1 | 4 | 0 | 0 | .000 | 7 | 4 | 4 | 3 | 1 | 9.00 |
| 1970–Tulsa | ............................. | Am. Assoc. | 24 | 155 | 12 | 8 | .600 | 165 | 78 | 69 | 106 | 49 | 4.01 |
| 1970–St. Louis | ............................. | National | 16 | 26 | 0 | 4 | .000 | 31 | 27 | 22 | 22 | 18 | 7.62 |
| 1971–St. Louis | ............................. | National | 34 | 222 | 12 | 12 | .500 | 238 | 107 | 99 | 148 | 53 | 4.01 |
| 1972–St. Louis | ............................. | National | 33 | 231 | 14 | 15 | .483 | 229 | •120 | 101 | 153 | 60 | 3.94 |
| 1973–St. Louis† | ............................. | National | 32 | 224 | 14 | 10 | .583 | 211 | 88 | 75 | 122 | 61 | 3.01 |
| 1974–Boston | ............................. | American | 41 | 221 | 12 | 14 | .462 | 234 | 121 | 106 | 103 | 69 | 4.32 |
| 1975–Boston | ............................. | American | 31 | 171 | 13 | 9 | .591 | 173 | 90 | 84 | 78 | 52 | 4.42 |
| 1976–Boston | ............................. | American | 41 | 170 | 10 | 9 | .526 | 159 | 73 | 58 | 76 | 61 | 3.07 |
| American League Totals | ......................... | | 113 | 562 | 35 | 32 | .522 | 566 | 284 | 248 | 257 | 182 | 3.97 |
| National League Totals | ........................... | | 116 | 707 | 40 | 41 | .494 | 716 | 346 | 301 | 448 | 193 | 3.83 |
| Major League Totals | ............................. | | 229 | 1269 | 75 | 73 | .507 | 1282 | 630 | 549 | 705 | 375 | 3.89 |

†Traded with Pitcher Diego Segui and Infielder Terry Hughes to Boston Red Sox for Pitchers Lynn McGlothen, John Curtis and Mike Garman, December 7, 1973.

CHAMPIONSHIP SERIES RECORD

| Year | Club | League | G. | IP. | W. | L. | Pct. | H. | R. | ER. | SO. | BB. | ERA. |
|------|------|--------|-----|-----|-----|-----|------|-----|-----|-----|-----|-----|------|
| 1975–Boston | ............................. | American | 1 | 5 | 0 | 0 | .000 | 7 | 3 | 3 | 2 | 1 | 5.40 |

WORLD SERIES RECORD

| Year | Club | League | G. | IP. | W. | L. | Pct. | H. | R. | ER. | SO. | BB. | ERA. |
|------|------|--------|-----|-----|-----|-----|------|-----|-----|-----|-----|-----|------|
| 1975–Boston | ............................. | American | 3 | 6⅔ | 0 | 1 | .000 | 7 | 5 | 5 | 5 | 3 | 6.75 |

## EUGENE ANTHONY CLINES
### (Gene)

Born October 6, 1946, at San Pablo, Calif.
Height, 5.09. Weight, 170.
Throws and bats righthanded.
Hobby–Collecting records.

Led Eastern League in stolen bases with 63 in 1969 and 32 in 1970.

| Year | Club | League | Pos. | G. | AB. | R. | H. | 2B. | 3B. | HR. | RBI. | B.A. | PO. | A. | E. | F.A. |
|------|------|--------|------|-----|-----|-----|-----|-----|-----|-----|------|------|-----|-----|-----|------|
| 1966–Salem | ................ | Appal. | OF-3 | 52 | 176 | 37 | •63 | 6 | •4 | 1 | 28 | .358 | 47 | 30 | 10 | .885 |
| 1967–Raleigh† | ............ | Carol. | O-3-2B | 83 | 290 | 34 | 75 | 7 | 4 | 4 | 29 | .259 | 111 | 102 | 20 | .914 |
| 1968–York | ................ | East. | •OF-3B | 137 | •494 | 46 | 119 | 12 | 2 | 4 | 33 | .241 | 209 | •31 | 10 | .960 |
| 1969–York | ................ | East. | •3B-2-O | 135 | 470 | 86 | 126 | 10 | 8 | 5 | 47 | .268 | •153 | •224 | 39 | .906 |
| 1970–Waterbury | ........ | East. | OF | 95 | 371 | 62 | 115 | 19 | 3 | 6 | 42 | .310 | 233 | •15 | 5 | .980 |
| 1970–Pittsburgh | | Nat. | OF | 31 | 37 | 4 | 15 | 2 | 0 | 0 | 3 | .405 | 4 | 0 | 0 | 1.000 |
| 1971–Pittsburgh | ........ | Nat. | OF | 97 | 273 | 52 | 84 | 12 | 4 | 1 | 24 | .308 | 146 | 8 | 3 | .981 |
| 1972–Pittsburgh | ........ | Nat. | OF | 107 | 311 | 52 | 104 | 15 | 6 | 0 | 17 | .334 | 131 | 7 | 6 | .958 |
| 1973–Pittsburgh‡ | ........ | Nat. | OF | 110 | 304 | 42 | 80 | 11 | 3 | 1 | 23 | .263 | 145 | 6 | 5 | .968 |
| 1974–Pittsburgh§ | ........ | Nat. | OF | 107 | 276 | 29 | 62 | 5 | 1 | 0 | 14 | .225 | 177 | 6 | 2 | .989 |
| 1975–New York x | ...... | Nat. | OF | 82 | 203 | 25 | 46 | 6 | 3 | 0 | 10 | .227 | 98 | 9 | 2 | .982 |
| 1976–Texas y | ........ | Amer. | OF-DH | 116 | 446 | 52 | 123 | 12 | 3 | 0 | 38 | .276 | 215 | 9 | 3 | .987 |
| American League Totals | ................ | | | 116 | 446 | 52 | 123 | 12 | 3 | 0 | 38 | .276 | 215 | 9 | 3 | .987 |
| National League Totals | ................ | | | 534 | 1404 | 204 | 391 | 51 | 17 | 2 | 91 | .278 | 701 | 36 | 18 | .976 |
| Major League Totals | ..................... | | | 650 | 1850 | 256 | 514 | 63 | 20 | 2 | 129 | .278 | 916 | 45 | 21 | .979 |

†On temporary inactive list, May 2 through June 10, 1967.
‡On disabled list, July 11 to August 1, 1973.

§Traded to New York Mets for Catcher Duffy Dyer, October 21, 1974.
xTraded to Texas Rangers for Outfielder Joe Lovitto, December 12, 1975.
yTraded with cash to Chicago Cubs for Pitcher Darold Knowles, February 5, 1977.

### CHAMPIONSHIP SERIES RECORD

| Year | Club | League | Pos. | G. | AB. | R. | H. | 2B. | 3B. | HR. | RBI. | B.A. | PO. | A. | E. | F.A. |
|------|------|--------|------|----|-----|----|----|----|----|----|----|------|-----|----|----|------|
| 1971–Pittsburgh | ........Nat. | | OF | 1 | 3 | 1 | 1 | 0 | 0 | 1 | 1 | .333 | 1 | 0 | 0 | 1.000 |
| 1972–Pittsburgh | ........Nat. | | PH-PR | 3 | 2 | 1 | 0 | 0 | 0 | 0 | 0 | .000 | 0 | 0 | 0 | .000 |
| 1974–Pittsburgh | ........Nat. | | OF-PR | 2 | 1 | 1 | 0 | 0 | 0 | 0 | 0 | .000 | 0 | 0 | 0 | .000 |
| Championship Series Totals | ............ | | | 6 | 6 | 3 | 1 | 0 | 0 | 1 | 1 | .167 | 1 | 0 | 0 | 1.000 |

### WORLD SERIES RECORD

| Year | Club | League | Pos. | G. | AB. | R. | H. | 2B. | 3B. | HR. | RBI. | B.A. | PO. | A. | E. | F.A. |
|------|------|--------|------|----|-----|----|----|----|----|----|----|------|-----|----|----|------|
| 1971–Pittsburgh | ........Nat. | | OF | 3 | 11 | 2 | 1 | 0 | 1 | 0 | 0 | .091 | 6 | 0 | 0 | 1.000 |

### PITCHING RECORD

| Year | Club | League | G. | IP. | W. | L. | Pct. | H. | R. | ER. | SO. | BB. | ERA. |
|------|------|--------|----|-----|----|----|------|----|----|-----|-----|-----|------|
| 1969–York | ................................... | Eastern | 1 | 2 | 0 | 0 | .000 | 2 | 1 | 0 | 0 | 0 | 0.00 |

## DAVID EUGENE CLYDE
### (Dave)

Born April 22, 1955, at Kansas City, Kan.
Height, 6.01. Weight, 195.
Throws and bats lefthanded.
Hobbies—Model building, golf and hunting.
Attended Texas A & M University, College Station, Tex.
Received reported $125,000 bonus to sign with Texas Rangers, 1973.

| Year | Club | League | G. | IP. | W. | L. | Pct. | H. | R. | ER. | SO. | BB. | ERA. |
|------|------|--------|----|-----|----|----|------|----|----|-----|-----|-----|------|
| 1973–Texas | ................................... | American | 18 | 93 | 4 | 8 | .333 | 106 | 63 | 52 | 74 | 54 | 5.03 |
| 1974–Texas | ................................... | American | 28 | 117 | 3 | 9 | .250 | 129 | 64 | 57 | 52 | 47 | 4.38 |
| 1975–Pittsfield | ............................. | Eastern | 22 | 161 | 12 | 8 | .600 | 145 | 68 | 55 | 131 | 94 | 3.07 |
| 1975–Texas | ................................... | American | 1 | 7 | 0 | 1 | .000 | 6 | 3 | 2 | 2 | 6 | 2.57 |
| 1976–Sacramento | ......................... | P. Coast | 5 | 27 | 0 | 4 | .000 | 38 | 29 | 26 | 21 | 18 | 8.67 |
| Major League Totals | ............................... | | 47 | 217 | 7 | 18 | .280 | 241 | 130 | 111 | 128 | 107 | 4.60 |

Listed on Texas Rangers' 1977 spring roster.

## ROGER KARL COE

Born September 11, 1952, at Cincinnati, O.
Height, 6.03. Weight, 190.
Throws left and bats righthanded.
Hobbies—Automobiles and cooking.
Attended University of Toledo, Toledo O.

| Year | Club | League | G. | IP. | W. | L. | Pct. | H. | R. | ER. | SO. | BB. | ERA. |
|------|------|--------|----|-----|----|----|------|----|----|-----|-----|-----|------|
| 1974–Walla Walla | ......................... | Northwest | 18 | 105 | 8 | 5 | .615 | 119 | 63 | 49 | 84 | 48 | 4.20 |
| 1975–Alexandria | ......................... | Texas | 7 | 10 | 2 | 0 | 1.000 | 10 | 5 | 3 | 6 | 10 | 2.70 |
| 1975–Reno† | ................................. | California | 10 | 40 | 3 | 3 | .500 | 50 | 29 | 24 | 15 | 16 | 5.40 |
| 1976–Amarillo†‡ | ............................. | Texas | 20 | 123 | 7 | 3 | .700 | 135 | 62 | 51 | 31 | 46 | 3.73 |

†On disabled list, May 28 through June 26, 1975.
‡On disabled list, April 14 through May 11, 1976.
Listed on San Diego Padres' 1977 spring roster.

## NATHAN COLBERT, JR.
### (Nate)

Born April 9, 1946, at St. Louis, Mo.
Height, 6.01½. Weight, 210.
Throws and bats righthanded.
Hobbies—Music, playing cards and checkers.
Attended St. Louis Baptist College, St. Louis, Mo.

Set major league record for most total bases, doubleheader (22), August 1, 1972; most runs batted in, doubleheader (13), August 1, 1972.
Tied major league record for most home runs, doubleheader (5), August 1, 1972; most home runs, two consecutive games (5), August 1, 1972 (dh).
Set National League record for most runs batted in, two consecutive games (13), August 1, 1972 (dh).
Tied National League record for most home runs, one week (Sunday through Saturday), 8, July 30, first game, through August 5, 1972, 9 games.
Hit three home runs in game, August 1, 1972 (second game).
Led National League first basemen in double plays with 125 in 1971.
Led Texas League in strikeouts with 143 and in stolen bases with 26 in 1967.

| Year | Club | League | Pos. | G. | AB. | R. | H. | 2B. | 3B. | HR. | RBI. | B.A. | PO. | A. | E. | F.A. |
|------|------|--------|------|----|-----|----|----|----|----|----|----|------|-----|----|----|------|
| 1964–Sarasota Cards | ..Sar. Rk. | | 1-OF | 45 | 83 | 20 | 18 | 3 | 1 | 2 | 13 | .217 | 182 | 19 | 2 | .990 |
| 1965–Cedar Rapids†‡ | ..Midwest | | 1B | 81 | 285 | 46 | 78 | 7 | 2 | 9 | 45 | .274 | 601 | 39 | 10 | .985 |
| 1966–Houston | ...........Nat. | | PH | 19 | 7 | 3 | 0 | 0 | 0 | 0 | 0 | .000 | 0 | 0 | 0 | .000 |
| 1967–Amarillo | ...........Texas | | O-1-3 | 120 | 434 | 82 | 127 | 18 | 4 | *28 | 67 | .293 | 390 | 25 | 10 | .976 |
| 1967–Oklahoma City | ..P. C. | | OF | 2 | 5 | 0 | 0 | 0 | 0 | 0 | 0 | .000 | 2 | 0 | 0 | 1.000 |

| Year Club League | Pos. | G. | AB. | R. | H. | 2B. | 3B. | HR. | RBI. | B.A. | PO. | A. | E. | F.A. |
|---|---|---|---|---|---|---|---|---|---|---|---|---|---|---|
| 1968−Oklahoma City ..P. C. | OF-1-3B | 92 | 322 | 52 | 85 | 15 | 4 | 14 | 44 | .264 | 232 | 16 | 2 | .992 |
| 1968−Houston§ ..........Nat. | OF-1B | 20 | 53 | 5 | 8 | 1 | 0 | 0 | 4 | .151 | 62 | 1 | 2 | .969 |
| 1969−San Diego x ......Nat. | 1B | 139 | 483 | 64 | 123 | 20 | 9 | 24 | 66 | .255 | 1217 | 87 | 13 | .990 |
| 1970−San Diego..........Nat. | 1B-3B | 156 | 572 | 84 | 148 | 17 | 6 | 38 | 86 | .259 | 1406 | 90 | 14 | .991 |
| 1971−San Diego..........Nat. | 1B | 156 | 565 | 81 | 149 | 25 | 3 | 27 | 84 | .264•1372 | | 106 | 10 | .993 |
| 1972−San Diego..........Nat. | 1B | 151 | 563 | 87 | 141 | 27 | 2 | 38 | 111 | .250 | 1290 | •103 | 6 | .996 |
| 1973−San Diego..........Nat. | 1B | 145 | 529 | 73 | 143 | 25 | 2 | 22 | 80 | .270 | 1300 | •98 | 11 | .992 |
| 1974−San Diego y ......Nat. | 1B-OF | 119 | 368 | 53 | 76 | 16 | 0 | 14 | 54 | .207 | 605 | 52 | 9 | .986 |
| 1975−Detroit z...........Amer. | 1B | 45 | 156 | 16 | 23 | 4 | 2 | 4 | 18 | .147 | 407 | 22 | 8 | .982 |
| 1975−Montreal ..........Nat. | 1B | 38 | 81 | 10 | 14 | 4 | 1 | 4 | 11 | .173 | 151 | 9 | 2 | .988 |
| 1976−Montreal a ........Nat. | OF-1B | 14 | 40 | 5 | 8 | 2 | 0 | 2 | 6 | .200 | 66 | 6 | 2 | .973 |
| 1976−Tucson ..............P. C. | 1B | 64 | 210 | 35 | 52 | 12 | 1 | 12 | 44 | .248 | 493 | 21 | 6 | .988 |
| 1976−Oakland b..........Amer. | DH | 2 | 5 | 0 | 0 | 0 | 0 | 0 | 0 | .000 | 0 | 0 | 0 | .000 |
| American League Totals ................ | | 47 | 161 | 16 | 23 | 4 | 2 | 4 | 18 | .143 | 407 | 22 | 8 | .982 |
| National League Totals ................. | | 957 | 3261 | 465 | 810 | 137 | 23 | 169 | 502 | .248 | 7469 | 552 | 69 | .991 |
| Major League Totals ...................... | | 1004 | 3422 | 481 | 833 | 141 | 25 | 173 | 520 | .243 | 7876 | 574 | 77 | .991 |

†On disabled list with broken hand, July 22 through end of season.
‡Drafted by Houston Astros from Jacksonville (St. Louis Cardinals' organization), November 29, 1965.
§Selected by San Diego Padres from Houston Astros in expansion draft, October 14, 1968.
xOn military list, June 12 to June 30, 1969.
yTraded to Detroit Tigers for Shortstop Eddie Brinkman, Outfielder Dick Sharon and Pitcher Bob Strampe, November 18, 1974.
zSold to Montreal Expos, June 15, 1975.
aUnconditionally released, June 2, 1976; signed as free agent by Oakland A's, and assigned to Tucson, June 9, 1976.
bPlayed out option year and granted free agency, November 1, 1976.
Invited to Toronto Blue Jays 1977 spring training camp.

### ALL-STAR GAME RECORD

| Year League | Pos. | AB. | R. | H. | 2B. | 3B. | HR. | RBI. | B.A. | PO. | A. | E. | F.A. |
|---|---|---|---|---|---|---|---|---|---|---|---|---|---|
| 1971−National ............................. | PH | 1 | 0 | 0 | 0 | 0 | 0 | 0 | .000 | 0 | 0 | 0 | .000 |
| 1972−National ............................. | PH | 0 | 1 | 0 | 0 | 0 | 0 | 0 | .000 | 0 | 0 | 0 | .000 |
| 1973−National ............................. | PH | 1 | 0 | 0 | 0 | 0 | 0 | 0 | .000 | 0 | 0 | 0 | .000 |
| All-Star Game Totals ....................... | | 2 | 1 | 0 | 0 | 0 | 0 | 0 | .000 | 0 | 0 | 0 | .000 |

## JAMES WILLIAM COLBORN
### (Jim)

Born May 22, 1946, at Santa Paula, Calif.
Height, 6.00. Weight, 195.
Throws and bats righthanded.
Hobbies−Outdoor sports (fishing, camping) and cooking.
Attended Whittier College, Whittier, Calif.; received Bachelor of Arts
degree in Sociology. Also attended University of Washington,
Seattle, Wash. (graduate work), and did one year of graduate studies
at the University of Edinburgh, Edinburgh, Scotland (Rotary
Foundation Fellowship).

| Year Club | League | G. | IP. | W. | L. | Pct. | H. | R. | ER. | SO. | BB. | ERA. |
|---|---|---|---|---|---|---|---|---|---|---|---|---|
| 1967−Lodi ......................................California | | 16 | 99 | 7 | 3 | .700 | 91 | 41 | 37 | 106 | 37 | 3.36 |
| 1968−San Antonio ........................Texas | | 2 | 4 | 0 | 1 | .000 | 11 | 9 | 8 | 3 | 5 | 18.00 |
| 1968−Lodi .....................................California | | 31 | 152 | 12 | 6 | .667 | 143 | 64 | 54 | 171 | 53 | 3.20 |
| 1969−Tacoma...............................P. Coast | | 21 | 146 | 8 | 7 | .533 | 132 | 57 | 37 | 80 | 54 | •2.28 |
| 1969−Chicago...............................National | | 6 | 15 | 1 | 0 | 1.000 | 15 | 6 | 5 | 4 | 9 | 3.00 |
| 1970−Chicago...............................National | | 34 | 73 | 3 | 1 | .750 | 88 | 37 | 29 | 50 | 23 | 3.58 |
| 1971−Tacoma...............................P. Coast | | 32 | 124 | 8 | 9 | .471 | 128 | 59 | 54 | 109 | 31 | 3.92 |
| 1971−Chicago† ............................National | | 14 | 10 | 0 | 1 | .000 | 18 | 8 | 8 | 2 | 3 | 7.20 |
| 1972−Milwaukee ..........................American | | 39 | 148 | 7 | 7 | .500 | 135 | 53 | 51 | 97 | 43 | 3.10 |
| 1973−Milwaukee ..........................American | | 43 | 314 | 20 | 12 | .625 | 297 | 133 | 111 | 135 | 87 | 3.18 |
| 1974−Milwaukee ..........................American | | 33 | 224 | 10 | 13 | .435 | 230 | 104 | 101 | 83 | 60 | 4.06 |
| 1975−Milwaukee ..........................American | | 36 | 206 | 11 | 13 | .458 | 215 | 111 | 98 | 79 | 65 | 4.28 |
| 1976−Milwaukee ..........................American | | 32 | 226 | 9 | 15 | .375 | 232 | 97 | 93 | 101 | 54 | 3.70 |
| National League Totals............................. | | 54 | 98 | 4 | 2 | .667 | 121 | 51 | 42 | 56 | 35 | 3.86 |
| American League Totals........................... | | 183 | 1118 | 57 | 60 | .487 | 1109 | 498 | 454 | 495 | 309 | 3.65 |
| Major League Totals ...................... | | 237 | 1216 | 61 | 62 | .496 | 1230 | 549 | 496 | 551 | 344 | 3.67 |

†Traded with Outfielder Brock Davis and Pitcher Earl Stephenson (latter assigned to Evansville) to Milwaukee Brewers for Outfielder Jose Cardenal, December 3, 1971.
‡Traded with Catcher Darrell Porter, and a player to be named later to Kansas City Royals for Outfielder Jim Wohlford and Infielder Jamie Quirk, December 6, 1976; Pitcher Bob McClure was sent to Milwaukee to complete deal, March 15, 1977.

### ALL-STAR GAME RECORD

Member of American League All-Star Team for 1973 game; did not play.

---

**DID YOU KNOW—**
That Walter Johnson struck out 3,508 batters during his major league career? It's an all-time pitching record.

---

# DAVID LEE COLEMAN

Born October 26, 1950, at Dayton, O.
Height, 6.01. Weight, 195.
Throws and bats righthanded.
Hobby—Fishing.

| Year Club | League | Pos. | G. | AB. | R. | H. | 2B. | 3B. | HR. | RBI. | B.A. | PO. | A. | E. | F.A. |
|---|---|---|---|---|---|---|---|---|---|---|---|---|---|---|---|
| 1970—Winter Haven† | ..Fla. St. | 3B-OF | 94 | 354 | 48 | 93 | 13 | 5 | 6 | 51 | .263 | 79 | 186 | 28 | .904 |
| 1971—Winston-Salem‡ | Carol. | 3B-OF | 25 | 85 | 7 | 17 | 1 | 0 | 2 | 7 | .200 | 12 | 35 | 4 | .922 |
| 1972—Winston-Salem | ..Carol. | OF-1-3 | 119 | 395 | 60 | 100 | 18 | 1 | 14 | 52 | .253 | 434 | 45 | 10 | .980 |
| 1973—Bristol | ..............East. | 1-OF-3 | 133 | 454 | 69 | 129 | ●28 | 4 | 8 | 65 | .284 | 1032 | 57 | 12 | .989 |
| 1974—Pawtucket | ........Int. | 1B-3B-2B | 131 | 429 | 60 | 108 | 17 | 2 | 13 | 49 | .252 | 547 | 75 | 18 | .972 |
| 1975—Pawtucket | ........Int. | OF-1-3 | 70 | 164 | 21 | 29 | 8 | 0 | 3 | 11 | .177 | 95 | 6 | 2 | .980 |
| 1975—Bristol | ..............East. | 1B | 64 | 210 | 32 | 53 | 11 | 3 | 6 | 28 | .252 | 567 | 25 | 5 | .992 |
| 1976—Rhode Island | ....Int. | OF-1B | ●138 | 515 | 73 | 143 | 29 | 6 | 12 | 66 | .278 | 359 | 17 | 6 | .984 |

†On temporary inactive list, June 11 through June 30, 1970.
‡On temporary inactive list, June 4 through September 10, 1971.
Listed on Boston Red Sox' 1977 spring roster.

# JOSEPH HOWARD COLEMAN
## (Joe)

Born February 3, 1947, at Boston, Mass.
Height, 6.03. Weight, 195.
Throws and bats righthanded.
Hobby—Golf.
Son of Joseph Patrick Coleman, former pitcher with Philadelphia
Athletics, Baltimore Orioles and Detroit Tigers in 1940s and 1950s.
Led American League in wild pitches with 15 in 1975.
Led American League in hit basemen with 10 in 1973 and 12 in 1974.
Received reported $75,000 bonus to sign with Washington Senators, 1965.

| Year Club | League | G. | IP. | W. | L. | Pct. | H. | R. | ER. | SO. | BB. | ERA. |
|---|---|---|---|---|---|---|---|---|---|---|---|---|
| 1965—Burlington | ............Carolina | 12 | 75 | 2 | 10 | .167 | 82 | 49 | 38 | 49 | 38 | 4.56 |
| 1965—Washington | ............American | 2 | 18 | 2 | 0 | 1.000 | 9 | 3 | 3 | 7 | 8 | 1.50 |
| 1966—York | ............Eastern | 32 | 199 | 7 | ∗19 | .269 | 191 | ∗111 | ∗83 | 109 | 79 | 3.75 |
| 1966—Washington | ............American | 1 | 9 | 1 | 0 | 1.000 | 6 | 2 | 2 | 4 | 2 | 2.00 |
| 1967—Washington | ............American | 28 | 134 | 8 | 9 | .471 | 154 | 78 | 69 | 77 | 47 | 4.63 |
| 1967—York | ............Eastern | 4 | 32 | 0 | 3 | .000 | 31 | 10 | 8 | 23 | 12 | 2.25 |
| 1968—Washington | ............American | 33 | 223 | 12 | 16 | .429 | 212 | 98 | 81 | 139 | 51 | 3.27 |
| 1969—Washington | ............American | 40 | 248 | 12 | 13 | .480 | 222 | 102 | 90 | 182 | 100 | 3.27 |
| 1970—Washington† | ............American | 39 | 219 | 8 | 12 | .400 | 190 | 98 | 87 | 152 | 89 | 3.58 |
| 1971—Detroit | ............American | 39 | 286 | 20 | 9 | .690 | 241 | 106 | 100 | 236 | 96 | 3.15 |
| 1972—Detroit | ............American | 40 | 280 | 19 | 14 | .576 | 216 | 99 | 87 | 222 | 110 | 2.80 |
| 1973—Detroit | ............American | 40 | 288 | 23 | 15 | .605 | 283 | 125 | 113 | 202 | 93 | 3.53 |
| 1974—Detroit | ............American | 41 | 286 | 14 | 12 | .538 | 272 | ∗160 | 137 | 177 | 158 | 4.31 |
| 1975—Detroit | ............American | 31 | 201 | 10 | 18 | .357 | 234 | 137 | 124 | 125 | 85 | 5.55 |
| 1976—Detroit‡ | ............American | 12 | 67 | 2 | 5 | .286 | 80 | 44 | 36 | 38 | 34 | 4.84 |
| 1976—Chicago§ | ............National | 39 | 79 | 2 | 8 | .200 | 72 | 43 | 36 | 66 | 35 | 4.10 |
| American League Totals | | 346 | 2259 | 131 | 123 | .516 | 2119 | 1052 | 929 | 1561 | 873 | 3.70 |
| National League Totals | | 39 | 79 | 2 | 8 | .200 | 72 | 43 | 36 | 66 | 35 | 4.10 |
| Major League Totals | | 385 | 2338 | 133 | 131 | .504 | 2191 | 1095 | 965 | 1627 | 908 | 3.71 |

†Traded with Pitcher Jim Hannan, Shortstop Ed Brinkman and Third Baseman Aurelio Rodriguez to Detroit Tigers for Pitchers Denny McLain and Norm McRae, Third Baseman Don Wert and Infielder-Outfielder Elliott Maddox, October 9, 1970.
‡Traded to Chicago White Sox for cash and player to be named later, June 8, 1976.
§Traded to Oakland A's for Pitcher Jim Todd, March 15, 1977.

### CHAMPIONSHIP SERIES RECORD

| Year Club | League | G. | IP. | W. | L. | Pct. | H. | R. | ER. | SO. | BB. | ERA. |
|---|---|---|---|---|---|---|---|---|---|---|---|---|
| 1972—Detroit | ............American | 1 | 9 | 1 | 0 | 1.000 | 7 | 0 | 0 | 14 | 3 | 0.00 |

### ALL-STAR GAME RECORD

Named to American League All-Star Team for 1972 game; replaced due to injury.

# DAVID S. COLLINS
## (Dave)

Born October 20, 1952, at Rapid City, S. D.
Height, 5.11. Weight, 175.
Throws left and bats left and righthanded.
Hobbies—Weight lifting, basketball and hunting.
Attended Mesa Community College, Mesa, Ariz.

Major league stolen bases: 1975 (24), 1976 (32). Total—56.
Led Pioneer League outfielders in double plays with 3 in 1972.
Named Most Valuable Player in Pioneer League, 1972.

| Year Club | League | Pos. | G. | AB. | R. | H. | 2B. | 3B. | HR. | RBI. | B.A. | PO. | A. | E. | F.A. |
|---|---|---|---|---|---|---|---|---|---|---|---|---|---|---|---|
| 1972—Idaho Falls | ........Pion. | ∗OF-1B | 68 | 252 | 40 | 69 | 8 | ∗8 | 1 | 27 | .274 | 101 | ∗11 | 3 | .974 |
| 1973—Quad Cities† | ......Midw. | OF | 110 | 387 | 61 | 100 | 15 | 7 | 4 | 49 | .258 | 229 | 10 | 11 | .956 |

| Year Club | League | Pos. | G. | AB. | R. | H. | 2B. | 3B. | HR. | RBI. | B.A. | PO. | A. | E. | F.A. |
|---|---|---|---|---|---|---|---|---|---|---|---|---|---|---|---|
| 1974–Salinas ...........Calif. | | OF-1B | 39 | 143 | 30 | 49 | 3 | 5 | 1 | 21 | .343 | 109 | 0 | 5 | .956 |
| 1974–El Paso ...........Texas | | 1B-OF | 82 | 324 | 64 | 114 | 15 | 4 | 4 | 49 | *.352 | 381 | 14 | 12 | .971 |
| 1975–Salt Lake City ..P.C. | | OF | 51 | 193 | 41 | 60 | 7 | 6 | 0 | 24 | .311 | 58 | 2 | 1 | .984 |
| 1975–California ..........Amer. | | OF | 93 | 319 | 41 | 85 | 13 | 4 | 3 | 29 | .266 | 159 | 3 | 2 | .988 |
| 1976–Salt Lake City ..P.C. | | OF | 35 | 136 | 28 | 49 | 13 | 4 | 0 | 12 | .360 | 50 | 3 | 2 | .964 |
| 1976–California‡ ........Amer. | | OF-DH | 99 | 365 | 45 | 96 | 12 | 1 | 4 | 28 | .263 | 160 | 3 | 1 | .994 |
| Major League Totals ..................... | | | 192 | 684 | 86 | 181 | 25 | 5 | 7 | 57 | .265 | 319 | 6 | 3 | .991 |

†On disabled list, May 21 to May 31, 1973.

‡Selected by Seattle Mariners in special American League expansion draft, November 5, 1976.

## DONALD EDWARD COLLINS
### (Don)

Born September 15, 1952, at Lyons, Ga.
Height 6.02. Weight, 195.
Throws left and bats righthanded.
Hobbies–Reading, music and watching television.
Attended South Georgia College, Douglas, Ga.

| Year Club | League | G. | IP. | W. | L. | Pct. | H. | R. | ER. | SO. | BB. | ERA. |
|---|---|---|---|---|---|---|---|---|---|---|---|---|
| 1972–Wytheville...............Ap'lachian | | 8 | 50 | 5 | 1 | .833 | 34 | 19 | 16 | 57 | 19 | 2.88 |
| 1973–Greenwood ..........................W. Carol. | | 22 | 114 | 4 | 10 | .286 | 117 | 54 | 41 | 107 | 83 | 3.24 |
| 1974–Savannah ...........................Southern | | 22 | 110 | 6 | 8 | .429 | 116 | 77 | 59 | 65 | 83 | 4.83 |
| 1975–Savannah ...........................Southern | | 24 | 157 | 8 | 7 | .533 | 153 | 66 | 55 | 79 | 69 | 3.15 |
| 1976–Richmond† ..........................Int'national | | 23 | 88 | 4 | 6 | .400 | 109 | 58 | 49 | 40 | 50 | 5.01 |

†On disabled list August 20 through September 2, 1976.

Listed on Atlanta Braves' 1977 spring roster.

## ROBERT PASQUALI COLUCCIO, JR.

Name pronounced Co-LU-che-o.

### (Bob)

Born October 2, 1951, at Centralia, Wash.
Height, 5.11. Weight, 185.
Throws and bats righthanded.
Hobbies–Music, dogs, golf and tennis.
Attended Mesa Community College, Mesa, Ariz.

| Year Club | League | Pos. | G. | AB. | R. | H. | 2B. | 3B. | HR. | RBI. | B.A. | PO. | A. | E. | F.A. |
|---|---|---|---|---|---|---|---|---|---|---|---|---|---|---|---|---|
| 1969–Billings ............Pion. | | OF-3B | 63 | 213 | 36 | 52 | 11 | 2 | 3 | 23 | .244 | 93 | 34 | 14 | .901 |
| 1970–Clinton† ............Midw. | | 2B | 63 | 238 | 37 | 66 | 11 | 2 | 7 | 37 | .277 | 132 | 160 | 12 | .961 |
| 1971–Evansville ........A.A. | | 2B-O | 35 | 125 | 20 | 28 | 6 | 0 | 2 | 9 | .224 | 74 | 93 | 9 | .949 |
| 1971–Reading ............East. | | 2-3-S-O | 72 | 221 | 23 | 46 | 10 | 3 | 4 | 18 | .208 | 114 | 195 | 14 | .957 |
| 1972–Evansville ........A.A. | | *OF-2 | 135 | 496 | *79 | 149 | 19 | 7 | 9 | 58 | .300 | *281 | 20 | 7 | *.977 |
| 1973–Milwaukee ........Amer. | | OF | 124 | 438 | 65 | 98 | 21 | 8 | 15 | 58 | .224 | 236 | 12 | 2 | .992 |
| 1974–Milwaukee ........Amer. | | OF | 138 | 394 | 42 | 88 | 13 | 4 | 6 | 31 | .223 | 346 | 10 | 4 | .989 |
| 1975–Milw.‡-Chi.§ ......Amer. | | OF | 83 | 223 | 30 | 45 | 4 | 3 | 5 | 18 | .202 | 149 | 5 | 2 | .987 |
| 1976–Iowa....................A.A. | | Of-3B | 125 | 356 | 55 | 87 | 20 | 9 | 8 | 48 | .244 | 229 | 13 | 3 | .988 |
| Major League Totals ..................... | | | 345 | 1055 | 137 | 231 | 38 | 15 | 26 | 107 | .219 | 731 | 27 | 8 | .990 |

†On restricted list from beginning of season until June 19, 1970.

‡Traded to Chicago White Sox for Outfielder Bill Sharp, May 8, 1975.

§On supplemental disabled list, July 1 to August 6, 1975.

Listed on Chicago White Sox' 1977 spring roster.

## DAVID ISMAEL CONCEPCION (BONITEZ)

Name pronounced con-sep-see-OHN.

### (Dave)

Born June 17, 1948, at Oeurrare de la Costa, Aragua, Venezuela.
Height, 6.02. Weight, 173.
Throws and bats righthanded.
Hobby–Hunting.
Attended College Augustin Codazzi

Tied major league records for most stolen bases, pinch-runner, inning, 2, July 7, 1974 (1st game, 7th inning); and most double plays, shortstop, game, 5, June 25, 1975.

Led National League shortstops in total chances with 805 in 1974, and with 836 in 1976.

Major League stolen bases: 1970 (10), 1971 (9), 1972 (13), 1973 (22), 1974 (41), 1975 (33), 1976 (21). Total–149.

Led Southern League shortstops in double plays with 64 in 1969.

Named shortstop on THE SPORTING NEWS National League All-Star fielding team, 1974, 1975 and 1976.

Named shortstop on THE SPORTING NEWS National League All-Star Team, 1974 and 1976.

| Year Club | League | Pos. | G. | AB. | R. | H. | 2B. | 3B. | HR. | RBI. | B.A. | PO. | A. | E. | F.A. |
|---|---|---|---|---|---|---|---|---|---|---|---|---|---|---|---|---|
| 1968–Tampa ..............Fla. St. | | *S-2B | 120 | 329 | 47 | 77 | 11 | 1 | 0 | 22 | .234 | 151 | 239 | 20 | *.951 |
| 1969–Asheville ..........South. | | SS | 96 | 340 | 47 | 100 | 11 | 5 | 1 | 37 | .294 | *157 | *292 | *29 | *.939 |
| 1969–Indianapolis ......A.A. | | S-2-3-O | 42 | 167 | 29 | 57 | 7 | 1 | 0 | 17 | .341 | 76 | 128 | 9 | .958 |
| 1970–Cincinnati..........Nat. | | SS-2B | 101 | 265 | 38 | 69 | 6 | 3 | 1 | 19 | .260 | 144 | 247 | 22 | .947 |
| 1971–Cincinnati† ........Nat. | | S-2-3-O | 130 | 327 | 24 | 67 | 4 | 4 | 1 | 20 | .205 | 182 | 310 | 13 | .974 |

| Year | Club | League | Pos. | G. | AB. | R. | H. | 2B. | 3B. | HR. | RBI. | B.A. | PO. | A. | E. | F.A. |
|---|---|---|---|---|---|---|---|---|---|---|---|---|---|---|---|---|
| 1972—Cincinnati | Nat. | | SS-3-2 | 119 | 378 | 40 | 79 | 13 | 2 | 2 | 29 | .209 | 197 | 372 | 19 | .968 |
| 1973—Cincinnati | Nat. | | SS-OF | 89 | 328 | 39 | 94 | 18 | 3 | 8 | 46 | .287 | 167 | 292 | 12 | .975 |
| 1974—Cincinnati | Nat. | | *SS-OF | 160 | 594 | 70 | 167 | 25 | 1 | 14 | 82 | .281 | 239 | *536 | 30 | .963 |
| 1975—Cincinnati | Nat. | | SS-3B | 140 | 507 | 62 | 139 | 23 | 1 | 5 | 49 | .274 | 241 | 446 | 16 | .977 |
| 1976—Cincinnati | Nat. | | SS | 152 | 576 | 74 | 162 | 28 | 7 | 9 | 69 | .281 | 304 | 506 | 27 | .968 |
| Major League Totals | | | | 891 | 2975 | 347 | 777 | 117 | 21 | 40 | 314 | .261 | 1474 | 2709 | 139 | .968 |

†On disabled list March 21 through April 20, 1971.
‡On disabled list July 22 through remainder of season.

## CHAMPIONSHIP SERIES RECORD

| Year | Club | League | Pos. | G. | AB. | R. | H. | 2B. | 3B. | HR. | RBI. | B.A. | PO. | A. | E. | F.A. |
|---|---|---|---|---|---|---|---|---|---|---|---|---|---|---|---|---|
| 1970—Cincinnati | Nat. | | PR-SS | 3 | 0 | 0 | 0 | 0 | 0 | 0 | 0 | .000 | 1 | 1 | 0 | 1.000 |
| 1972—Cincinnati | Nat. | | PH-S-PR | 3 | 2 | 0 | 0 | 0 | 0 | 0 | 0 | .000 | 0 | 0 | 0 | .000 |
| 1975—Cincinnati | Nat. | | SS | 3 | 11 | 2 | 5 | 0 | 0 | 1 | 1 | .455 | 6 | 8 | 1 | .933 |
| 1976—Cincinnati | Nat. | | SS | 3 | 10 | 4 | 2 | 1 | 0 | 0 | 0 | .200 | 2 | 12 | 0 | 1.000 |
| Championship Series Totals | | | | 12 | 23 | 6 | 7 | 1 | 0 | 1 | 1 | .304 | 9 | 21 | 1 | .968 |

## WORLD SERIES RECORD

| Year | Club | League | Pos. | G. | AB. | R. | H. | 2B. | 3B. | HR. | RBI. | B.A. | PO. | A. | E. | F.A. |
|---|---|---|---|---|---|---|---|---|---|---|---|---|---|---|---|---|
| 1970—Cincinnati | Nat. | | SS | 3 | 9 | 0 | 3 | 0 | 1 | 0 | 3 | .333 | 2 | 2 | 0 | 1.000 |
| 1972—Cincinnati | Nat. | | S-PR-PH | 6 | 13 | 2 | 4 | 0 | 1 | 0 | 2 | .308 | 4 | 11 | 1 | .938 |
| 1975—Cincinnati | Nat. | | SS | 7 | 28 | 3 | 5 | 1 | 0 | 1 | 4 | .179 | 12 | 22 | 1 | .971 |
| 1976—Cincinnati | Nat. | | SS | 4 | 14 | 1 | 5 | 1 | 1 | 0 | 3 | .357 | 6 | 11 | 1 | .944 |
| World Series Totals | | | | 20 | 64 | 6 | 17 | 2 | 3 | 1 | 12 | .266 | 24 | 46 | 3 | .959 |

## ALL STAR GAME RECORD

| Year | League | Pos. | AB. | R. | H. | 2B. | 3B. | HR. | RBI. | B.A. | PO. | A. | E. | F.A. |
|---|---|---|---|---|---|---|---|---|---|---|---|---|---|---|
| 1975—National | | SS | 2 | 0 | 1 | 0 | 0 | 0 | 0 | .500 | 1 | 1 | 1 | .667 |
| 1976—National | | SS | 2 | 0 | 1 | 0 | 0 | 0 | 0 | .500 | 2 | 3 | 0 | 1.000 |
| All-Star Totals | | | 4 | 0 | 2 | 0 | 0 | 0 | 0 | .500 | 3 | 4 | 1 | .750 |

Named to National League All-Star Team for the 1973 game; replaced due to an ankle injury.

## CECIL CELESTER COOPER

Born December 20, 1949, at Brenham, Tex.
Height, 6.01. Weight, 185.
Throws and bats lefthanded.
Attended Prairie View A&M College, Prairie View, Tex.

Tied major league record for most strikeouts, extra-inning game, 6, June 14, 1974 (15 innings).
Named Midwest League Player of the Year in 1970.

| Year | Club | League | Pos. | G. | AB. | R. | H. | 2B. | 3B. | HR. | RBI. | B.A. | PO. | A. | E. | F.A. |
|---|---|---|---|---|---|---|---|---|---|---|---|---|---|---|---|---|
| 1968—Jamestown | NYP | | 1B | 26 | 84 | 16 | 38 | 6 | 0 | 0 | 6 | .452 | 130 | 0 | 1 | .992 |
| 1969—Greenville† | W. Car. | | 1-O | 62 | 212 | 27 | 63 | 12 | 2 | 1 | 18 | .297 | 434 | 32 | 8 | .983 |
| 1970—Danville‡ | Midw. | | 1-OF | 114 | 420 | 86 | 141 | 16 | 8 | 3 | 39 | *336 | 535 | 33 | 12 | .979 |
| 1971—Winston-Salem | Carol. | | 1B | 42 | 153 | 31 | 58 | 6 | 3 | 6 | 26 | .379 | 359 | 21 | 5 | .987 |
| 1971—Pawtucket | East. | | 1B-OF | 98 | 367 | 55 | 126 | 21 | 2 | 10 | 60 | .343 | 740 | 35 | 12 | .985 |
| 1971—Boston | Amer. | | 1B | 14 | 42 | 9 | 13 | 4 | 1 | 0 | 3 | .310 | 82 | 3 | 1 | .988 |
| 1972—Louisville | Int. | | 1B | 134 | 515 | 86 | *162 | *31 | 9 | 10 | 78 | .315 | 1102 | 78 | *17 | .986 |
| 1972—Boston | Amer. | | 1B | 12 | 17 | 0 | 4 | 1 | 0 | 0 | 2 | .235 | 19 | 0 | 0 | 1.000 |
| 1973—Pawtucket | Int. | | 1B | 128 | 450 | 68 | 132 | 27 | 1 | 15 | 77 | .293 | 1082 | 84 | 12 | .990 |
| 1973—Boston | Amer. | | 1B | 30 | 101 | 12 | 24 | 2 | 0 | 3 | 11 | .238 | 227 | 17 | 4 | .984 |
| 1974—Boston | Amer. | | 1B | 121 | 414 | 55 | 114 | 24 | 1 | 8 | 43 | .275 | 637 | 40 | 12 | .983 |
| 1975—Boston | Amer. | | 1B | 106 | 305 | 49 | 95 | 17 | 6 | 14 | 44 | .311 | 197 | 20 | 1 | .995 |
| 1976—Boston§ | Amer. | | 1B-DH | 123 | 451 | 66 | 127 | 22 | 6 | 15 | 78 | .282 | 600 | 42 | 4 | .994 |
| Major League Totals | | | | 406 | 1330 | 191 | 377 | 70 | 14 | 40 | 181 | .283 | 1762 | 122 | 22 | .988 |

†On temporary inactive list, April 13 through June 4.
‡Drafted by St. Louis Cardinals from Louisville (Boston Red Sox' organization), November 30, 1970. Returned to Boston organization, April 5, 1971.
§Traded to Milwaukee Brewers' for First Baseman George Scott and Outfielder Bernie Carbo, December 6, 1976.

## CHAMPIONSHIP SERIES RECORD

| Year | Club | League | Pos. | G. | AB. | R. | H. | 2B. | 3B. | HR. | RBI. | B.A. | PO. | A. | E. | F.A. |
|---|---|---|---|---|---|---|---|---|---|---|---|---|---|---|---|---|
| 1975—Boston | Amer. | | 1B | 3 | 10 | 0 | 4 | 2 | 0 | 0 | 1 | .400 | 24 | 1 | 1 | .962 |

## WORLD SERIES RECORD

| Year | Club | League | Pos. | G. | AB. | R. | H. | 2B. | 3B. | HR. | RBI. | B.A. | PO. | A. | E. | F.A. |
|---|---|---|---|---|---|---|---|---|---|---|---|---|---|---|---|---|
| 1975—Boston | Amer. | | 1B-PH | 5 | 19 | 0 | 1 | 1 | 0 | 0 | 1 | .053 | 40 | 1 | 0 | 1.000 |

## TIMOTHY MICHAEL CORCORAN
### (Tim)

Born March 19, 1953, at Glendale, Calif.
Height, 5.11. Weight, 175.
Throws and bats lefthanded.
Attended Mount San Antonio Junior College, Walnut, Calif.

| Year Club | League | Pos. | G. | AB. | R. | H. | 2B. | 3B. | HR. | RBI. | B.A. | PO. | A. | E. | F.A. |
|---|---|---|---|---|---|---|---|---|---|---|---|---|---|---|---|
| 1974–Bristol ..............Appal. | | OF | 27 | 92 | 20 | 34 | 6 | 0 | 3 | 25 | .370 | 32 | 0 | 0 | 1.000 |
| 1974–Lakeland .........Fla. St. | | OF | 36 | 126 | 15 | 34 | 1 | 3 | 1 | 16 | .270 | 71 | 3 | 1 | .987 |
| 1975–Montgomery .....South. | | OF-1B | 122 | 388 | 42 | 95 | 20 | 3 | 3 | 36 | .245 | 283 | 21 | 4 | .987 |
| 1976–Montgomery ......South. | | OF-1B | 129 | 437 | 66 | 135 | 25 | 5 | 5 | 60 | .309 | 607 | 49 | 5 | .992 |

Listed on Detroit Tigers' 1977 spring roster.

## TERRY STANTON CORNUTT

Born October 2, 1952, at Roseburg, Ore.
Height, 6.02. Weight, 195.
Throws right and bats righthanded.
Hobbies–Hunting, fishing and golf.
Attended Linn-Benton Community College, Albany, Ore.

| Year Club | League | G. | IP. | W. | L. | Pct. | H. | R. | ER. | SO. | BB. | ERA. |
|---|---|---|---|---|---|---|---|---|---|---|---|---|
| 1972–Great Falls .........................Pioneer | | 14 | 67 | 3 | 4 | .429 | 60 | 38 | 23 | 63 | 39 | 3.09 |
| 1973–Fresno†...............................California | | 12 | 65 | 3 | 4 | .429 | 66 | 29 | 22 | 41 | 28 | 3.05 |
| 1974–Fresno .............................California | | 20 | 47 | 3 | 2 | .600 | 47 | 17 | 12 | 42 | 20 | 2.30 |
| 1974–Amarillo ............................Texas | | 8 | 38 | 2 | 1 | .667 | 40 | 18 | 13 | 16 | 15 | 3.08 |
| 1975–Lafayette ...........................Texas | | 42 | 111 | 6 | 4 | .600 | 92 | 44 | 35 | 77 | 44 | 2.84 |
| 1976–Phoenix.............................P. Coast | | 41 | 97 | 7 | 0 | 1.000 | 90 | 45 | 37 | 56 | 48 | 3.43 |

†On Millitary list, February 23 through July 5, 1973.
Listed on San Francisco Giants' 1977 spring roster.

## VICTOR CROSBY CORRELL, JR.
### (Vic)

Born February 5, 1946, at Florence, S. C.
Height, 5.10. Weight, 185.
Throws and bats righthanded.
Hobbies–Golf, hunting, fishing and other outdoor sports.
Attended Georgia Southern, Statesboro, Ga.; received Bachelor of Science degree in Recreation.

Led International League catchers in passed balls with 17 and in total chances with 972 in 1972.
Led Western Carolinas League catchers in double plays with 8 in 1968.
Tied for Western Carolinas League lead in sacrifice flies with 8 in 1968.

| Year Club | League | Pos. | G. | AB. | R. | H. | 2B. | 3B. | HR. | RBI. | B.A. | PO. | A. | E. | F.A. |
|---|---|---|---|---|---|---|---|---|---|---|---|---|---|---|---|
| 1967–Rock Hill .........W. Car. | | C | 60 | 180 | 23 | 43 | 3 | 3 | 4 | 15 | .239 | 360 | 31 | 11 | .973 |
| 1968–Rock Hill .........W. Car. | | ★C-1 | 105 | 301 | 47 | 86 | 17 | 2 | 16 | 66 | .286 | 643 | ★73 | 14 | .981 |
| 1969–Waterbury .......East. | | C-OF | 94 | 271 | 20 | 57 | 4 | 0 | 6 | 33 | .210 | 405 | 45 | 17 | .964 |
| 1970–Savannah† .......South. | | C | 116 | 371 | 31 | 85 | 15 | 3 | 8 | 41 | .229 | 647 | 71 | ★17 | .977 |
| 1971–Asheville‡.........South. | | C-OF | 113 | 337 | 52 | 92 | 20 | 0 | 22 | 58 | .273 | 440 | 38 | 6 | .988 |
| 1972–Louisville .........Int. | | ★C-OF | 137 | 491 | 64 | 133 | 25 | 0 | 10 | 65 | .271 | ★894 | ★68 | 10 | .990 |
| 1972–Boston ..............Amer. | | C | 1 | 4 | 1 | 2 | 0 | 0 | 0 | 1 | .500 | 9 | 1 | 0 | 1.000 |
| 1973–Pawtucket§ ......Int. | | C | 95 | 284 | 30 | 52 | 11 | 0 | 10 | 41 | .183 | 415 | 33 | 5 | .989 |
| 1974–Atlanta.............Nat. | | C | 73 | 202 | 20 | 48 | 15 | 1 | 4 | 29 | .238 | 282 | 40 | 4 | .988 |
| 1975–Atlanta.............Nat. | | C | 103 | 325 | 37 | 70 | 12 | 1 | 11 | 39 | .215 | 413 | 63 | 13 | .973 |
| 1976–Atlanta.............Nat. | | C | 69 | 200 | 26 | 45 | 6 | 2 | 5 | 16 | .225 | 319 | 36 | 7 | .981 |
| American League Totals ................ | | | 1 | 4 | 1 | 2 | 0 | 0 | 0 | 1 | .500 | 9 | 1 | 0 | 1.000 |
| National League Totals .................. | | | 245 | 727 | 83 | 163 | 33 | 4 | 20 | 84 | .224 | 1014 | 139 | 24 | .980 |
| Major League Totals ...................... | | | 246 | 731 | 84 | 165 | 33 | 4 | 20 | 85 | .226 | 1023 | 140 | 24 | .980 |

†Released by Cleveland Indians' organization, April 5, 1971; signed as free agent by Chicago White Sox' organization, April 11, 1971.
‡Drafted from Asheville (Chicago White Sox' organization) by Louisville (Boston Red Sox' organization), November 29, 1971.
§On disabled list, April 13 to April 25, 1973. Traded by Boston Red Sox to Atlanta Braves for Infielder Chuck Goggin, March 26, 1974.

## BARRY LEE CORT

Born April 15, 1956, at Ontario, Canada.
Height, 6.05. Weight, 210.
Throws and bats righthanded.
Hobbies–Golf, tennis and swimming.

| Year Club | League | G. | IP. | W. | L. | Pct. | H. | R. | ER. | SO. | BB. | ERA. |
|---|---|---|---|---|---|---|---|---|---|---|---|---|
| 1974–Newark.............................NYP | | 14 | 103 | 8 | 3 | .727 | 76 | 31 | 26 | ★123 | 56 | 2.27 |
| 1975–Burlington..........................Midwest | | 24 | 188 | 14 | 9 | .609 | 161 | 85 | 67 | 152 | 75 | 3.21 |
| 1976–Pittsfield† ..........................Eastern | | 25 | 148 | 14 | 5 | .737 | 144 | 55 | 46 | 68 | 45 | 2.80 |

†On disabled list, May 30 through June 13, 1976.
Listed on Milwaukee Brewers' 1977 spring roster.

---

## DID YOU KNOW —

That Babe Ruth had a slugging average of .847 in 1920? It's the all-time major league record for one season.

---

## DONALD RAY COSEY
### (Don)

Born February 15, 1956, at San Rafael, Calif.
Height, 5.10. Weight, 185.
Throws and bats lefthanded.
Hobbies—Bicycling and cards.

Led Northwest League in strikeouts with 64 in 1974.

| Year | Club | League | Pos. | G. | AB. | R. | H. | 2B. | 3B. | HR. | RBI. | B.A. | PO. | A. | E. | F.A. |
|---|---|---|---|---|---|---|---|---|---|---|---|---|---|---|---|---|
| 1973—Lewiston† | | Northw. | OF | 47 | 114 | 9 | 15 | 2 | 0 | 0 | 10 | .132 | 28 | 0 | 3 | .903 |
| 1974—Lewiston | | Northw. | OF | 80 | 292 | 39 | 76 | 9 | 3 | 7 | 33 | .260 | •192 | 8 | 7 | .966 |
| 1975—Modesto | | Calif. | OF | 106 | 397 | 69 | 108 | 17 | 2 | 13 | 49 | .272 | 177 | 9 | 3 | .984 |
| 1976—Modesto‡ | | Calif. | OF | 91 | 373 | 73 | 114 | 19 | 3 | 25 | 69 | .306 | 195 | 6 | 12 | .944 |

†On disabled list, July 12 through July 22, 1973.
‡On disabled list, August 3 through September 2, 1976.
Listed on Oakland A's 1977 spring roster.

## MICHAEL JOHN COSGROVE
### (Mike)

Born February 17, 1951, at Phoenix, Ariz.
Height, 6.01. Weight, 180.
Throws and bats lefthanded.
Hobby—Working with hands.
Attending Phoenix College, Phoenix, Ariz.

Led Florida State League in wild pitches with 22 in 1970.

| Year | Club | League | G. | IP. | W. | L. | Pct. | H. | R. | ER. | SO. | BB. | ERA. |
|---|---|---|---|---|---|---|---|---|---|---|---|---|---|
| 1970—Cocoa | | Florida St. | 30 | 113 | 7 | 11 | .389 | 112 | 62 | 50 | 81 | 81 | 3.98 |
| 1971—Cocoa | | Florida St. | 25 | 172 | 13 | 9 | .591 | 119 | 62 | 52 | •231 | 101 | 2.72 |
| 1972—Columbus | | Southern | 18 | 129 | 7 | 8 | .467 | 124 | 68 | 56 | 125 | 71 | 3.91 |
| 1972—Oklahoma City | | Am. Assoc. | 7 | 48 | 4 | 2 | .667 | 38 | 17 | 14 | 44 | 22 | 2.63 |
| 1972—Houston | | National | 7 | 14 | 0 | 1 | .000 | 16 | 8 | 7 | 7 | 3 | 4.50 |
| 1973—Denver | | Am. Assoc. | 22 | 105 | 7 | 11 | .389 | 128 | 88 | 71 | 70 | 62 | 6.09 |
| 1973—Houston | | National | 13 | 10 | 1 | 1 | .500 | 11 | 2 | 2 | 2 | 8 | 1.80 |
| 1974—Denver | | Am. Assoc. | 6 | 37 | 1 | 2 | .333 | 27 | 21 | 14 | 27 | 15 | 3.41 |
| 1974—Houston | | National | 45 | 90 | 7 | 3 | .700 | 76 | 35 | 35 | 47 | 39 | 3.50 |
| 1975—Iowa | | Am. Assoc. | 17 | 43 | 2 | 6 | .250 | 49 | 40 | 35 | 27 | 30 | 7.33 |
| 1975—Houston | | National | 32 | 71 | 1 | 2 | .333 | 62 | 24 | 24 | 32 | 37 | 3.04 |
| 1976—Houston | | National | 22 | 90 | 3 | 4 | .429 | 106 | 63 | 55 | 34 | 58 | 5.50 |
| Major League Totals | | | 119 | 275 | 12 | 11 | .522 | 271 | 132 | 123 | 122 | 145 | 4.03 |

## ALFRED EDWARD COWENS, JR.
### (Al)

Born October 25, 1951, at Los Angeles, Calif.
Height, 6.02. Weight, 200.
Throws and bats righthanded.
Hobbies—Hunting and fishing.

Named Southern League Player of the Year, 1973.

| Year | Club | League | Pos. | G. | AB. | R. | H. | 2B. | 3B. | HR. | RBI. | B.A. | PO. | A. | E. | F.A. |
|---|---|---|---|---|---|---|---|---|---|---|---|---|---|---|---|---|
| 1969—Kingsport | | Appal. | 3-S-O | 51 | 180 | 30 | 53 | 6 | 1 | 2 | 30 | .294 | 48 | 85 | 16 | .893 |
| 1970—Billings | | Pion. | OF-SS | 62 | 237 | 45 | 67 | 9 | 5 | 7 | 47 | .283 | 82 | 20 | 5 | .953 |
| 1971—Waterloo | | Midw. | 3-1-O | 16 | 48 | 5 | 14 | 5 | 0 | 0 | 5 | .292 | 37 | 12 | 3 | .942 |
| 1971—San Jose | | Calif. | OF | 99 | 380 | 60 | 108 | 14 | 5 | 8 | 66 | .284 | 138 | 14 | 3 | •.981 |
| 1972—Waterloo | | Midw. | 3B | 8 | 31 | 5 | 7 | 1 | 0 | 0 | 3 | .226 | 5 | 17 | 2 | .917 |
| 1972—San Jose | | Calif. | O-3-1 | 83 | 307 | 36 | 86 | 17 | 2 | 5 | 53 | .280 | 134 | 53 | 10 | .949 |
| 1972—Jacksonville | | South. | OF | 35 | 120 | 17 | 24 | 2 | 1 | 4 | 9 | .200 | 48 | 5 | 2 | .964 |
| 1973—Jacksonville | | South. | O-1-3 | 135 | 491 | 91 | 142 | 25 | 7 | 16 | 81 | .289 | 444 | 52 | 18 | .965 |
| 1974—Kansas City | | Amer. | OF-3B | 110 | 269 | 28 | 65 | 7 | 1 | 1 | 25 | .242 | 151 | 14 | 3 | .982 |
| 1975—Kansas City | | Amer. | OF | 120 | 328 | 44 | 91 | 13 | 8 | 4 | 42 | .277 | 214 | 4 | 5 | .978 |
| 1976—Kansas City | | Amer. | OF-DH | 152 | 581 | 71 | 154 | 23 | 6 | 3 | 59 | .265 | 329 | 13 | 5 | .986 |
| Major League Totals | | | 382 | 1178 | 143 | 310 | 43 | 15 | 8 | 126 | .263 | 694 | 31 | 13 | .982 |

CHAMPIONSHIP SERIES RECORD

| Year | Club | League | Pos. | G. | AB. | R. | H. | 2B. | 3B. | HR. | RBI. | B.A. | PO. | A. | E. | F.A. |
|---|---|---|---|---|---|---|---|---|---|---|---|---|---|---|---|---|
| 1976—Kansas City | | Amer. | OF | 5 | 21 | 3 | 4 | 0 | 1 | 0 | 0 | .190 | 15 | 0 | 0 | 1.000 |

## LARRY EUGENE COX

Born September 11, 1947, At Bluffton, O.
Height, 5.11 Weight, 190.
Throws and bats righthanded.
Hobbies—Basketball, football, billiards, hunting and fishing.

Led Northern League catchers in double plays with 5 in 1966.

| Year | Club | League | Pos. | G. | AB. | R. | H. | 2B. | 3B. | HR. | RBI. | B.A. | PO. | A. | E. | F.A. |
|---|---|---|---|---|---|---|---|---|---|---|---|---|---|---|---|---|
| 1966—Huron | | North. | C | 54 | 155 | 21 | 34 | 9 | 0 | 0 | 15 | .219 | 497 | 45 | •12 | .978 |
| 1967—Spartanburg† | | W.Car. | C-P | 57 | 155 | 20 | 28 | 5 | 0 | 2 | 19 | .181 | 382 | 30 | 10 | .976 |

| Year | Club | League | Pos. | G. | AB. | R. | H. | 2B. | 3B. | HR. | RBI. | B.A. | PO. | A. | E. | F.A. |
|---|---|---|---|---|---|---|---|---|---|---|---|---|---|---|---|---|
| 1967–Tidewater | .........Carol. | | PH | 2 | 0 | 0 | 0 | 0 | 0 | 0 | 0 | .000 | 0 | 0 | 0 | .000 |
| 1968–Spartanburg | ......W.Car. | | P-C | 11 | 15 | 1 | 3 | 1 | 0 | 1 | 2 | .200 | 26 | 4 | 2 | .938 |
| 1969–Raleigh-Dur | .......Carol. | | C-P | 73 | 240 | 19 | 46 | 9 | 0 | 0 | 16 | .192 | 458 | 43 | 7 | .986 |
| 1970–Reading‡ | .........East. | | C | 59 | 189 | 22 | 41 | 3 | 1 | 5 | 27 | .217 | 289 | 25 | 7 | .978 |
| 1970–Eugene | ..............P.C. | | C | 16 | 40 | 4 | 5 | 0 | 0 | 0 | 2 | .125 | 62 | 6 | 1 | .986 |
| 1971–Eugene | ..............P.C. | | C | 6 | 18 | 2 | 4 | 0 | 0 | 0 | 1 | .222 | 33 | 5 | 0 | 1.000 |
| 1971–Reading | ...........East. | | C-OF | 75 | 238 | 17 | 54 | 7 | 1 | 2 | 29 | .227 | 390 | 42 | 7 | .984 |
| 1972–Hawaii | ..............P.C. | | C | 110 | 363 | 34 | 83 | 12 | 6 | 7 | 38 | .229 | 604 | 64 | 15 | .978 |
| 1973–Reading | ..............East. | | C | 28 | 59 | 7 | 17 | 3 | 1 | 1 | 8 | .288 | 143 | 16 | 1 | .994 |
| 1973–Eugene | ..............P.C. | | C | 60 | 185 | 30 | 43 | 9 | 1 | 2 | 20 | .232 | 336 | 41 | 6 | .984 |
| 1973–Philadelphia | ......Nat. | | C | 1 | 0 | 0 | 0 | 0 | 0 | 0 | 0 | .000 | 1 | 0 | 0 | 1.000 |
| 1974–Toledo | ..............Int. | | C | 32 | 90 | 14 | 23 | 2 | 1 | 3 | 16 | .256 | 192 | 25 | 4 | .982 |
| 1974–Philadelphia§ | ....Nat. | | C | 30 | 53 | 5 | 9 | 2 | 0 | 0 | 4 | .170 | 90 | 9 | 1 | .990 |
| 1975–Toledo | ..............Int. | | C | 32 | 80 | 5 | 10 | 2 | 0 | 0 | 1 | .125 | 168 | 19 | 4 | .979 |
| 1975–Philadelphia x | ..Nat. | | C | 11 | 5 | 0 | 1 | 0 | 0 | 0 | 1 | .200 | 10 | 0 | 0 | 1.000 |
| 1976–Tacoma y | .........P.C. | | C | 135 | 457 | 61 | 121 | 22 | 5 | 12 | 66 | .265 | 641 | 104 | 23 | .970 |
| Major League Totals | ...................... | | | 42 | 58 | 5 | 10 | 2 | 0 | 0 | 5 | .172 | 101 | 9 | 1 | .991 |

†On disabled list, July 19 to July 29, 1967; on temporary inactive list, August 1 to August 4, 1967.
‡On disabled list, July 24 to August 10, 1970.
§On supplemental disabled list, August 14 to September 11, 1974.
xTraded to Minnesota Twins for Shortstop Sergio Ferrer, October 24, 1975.
ySold to Seattle Mariners, October 22, 1976.

PITCHING RECORD

| Year | Club | League | G. | IP. | W. | L. | Pct. | H. | R. | ER. | SO. | BB. | ERA. |
|---|---|---|---|---|---|---|---|---|---|---|---|---|---|
| 1967–Spartanburg | ......................W. Carol. | | 1 | 1 | 0 | 0 | .000 | 1 | 0 | 0 | 0 | 1 | 0.00 |
| 1968–Spartanburg | ......................W. Carol. | | 7 | 21 | 2 | 0 | 1.000 | 15 | 6 | 5 | 20 | 18 | 2.14 |
| 1968–Huron† | ...............................Northern | | 4 | 27 | 1 | 2 | .333 | 25 | 16 | 10 | 22 | 12 | 3.33 |
| 1969–Raleigh-Durham | .................Carolina | | 1 | 4 | 0 | 0 | .000 | 1 | 0 | 0 | 3 | 8 | 0.00 |

†On temporary inactive list, July 12 to September 3, 1968.


## WILLIAM TED COX
(Known by middle name.)

Born January 24, 1955, at Midwest City, Okla.
Height, 6.03. Weight, 195.
Throws and bats righthanded.
Hobbies–Golf and racquet ball.
Tied for New York-Pennsylvania League lead in double plays by shortstops with 34 in 1973.

| Year | Club | League | Pos. | G. | AB. | R. | H. | 2B. | 3B. | HR. | RBI. | B.A. | PO. | A. | E. | F.A. |
|---|---|---|---|---|---|---|---|---|---|---|---|---|---|---|---|---|
| 1973–Elmira | ..............NYP | | SS | 58 | 205 | 28 | 60 | 8 | 5 | 0 | 24 | .293 | 105 | 166 | 18 | •.938 |
| 1974–Winter Haven | ....Fla. St. | | SS-3B | 103 | 340 | 39 | 83 | 11 | 2 | 6 | 39 | .244 | 103 | 233 | 22 | .939 |
| 1975–Winston-Salem | ..Carol. | | 3B | 137 | 505 | 63 | •154 | 23 | 5 | 10 | 80 | •.305 | •125 | 287 | 25 | .943 |
| 1976–Bristol | ..............East. | | 3B | 110 | 399 | 39 | 111 | 13 | 3 | 3 | 53 | .278 | 73 | 208 | 14 | .952 |

Listed on Boston Red Sox' 1977 spring roster.


## GERALD ALLEN CRAM
(Jerry)

Born December 9, 1947, at Los Angeles, Calif.
Height, 6.00. Weight, 180.
Throws and bats righthanded.
Hobbies–Golf, water skiing and bowling.
Attended Riverside City College, Riverside, Calif.
Nephew of Jim Rice, former infielder in Pittsburgh Pirate, San Francisco Giant and Detroit Tiger organizations.
Struck out nine consecutive batters in relief against Duluth-Superior, July 19, 1967.
Tied for Carolina League lead in complete games by pitchers with 14 in 1968.

| Year | Club | League | G. | IP. | W. | L. | Pct. | H. | R. | ER. | SO. | BB. | ERA. |
|---|---|---|---|---|---|---|---|---|---|---|---|---|---|
| 1967–St. Cloud | ....................Northern | | 24 | 70 | 6 | 2 | .750 | 55 | 27 | 21 | 94 | 23 | 2.70 |
| 1968–Wilson† | ................................Carolina | | 30 | 208 | •16 | 10 | .615 | 164 | 74 | 58 | 204 | 48 | 2.51 |
| 1969–High Point-Thomasville | ........Carolina | | 8 | 57 | 6 | 1 | .857 | 45 | 13 | 8 | 69 | 13 | 1.26 |
| 1969–Omaha | ............................Am. Assoc. | | 20 | 126 | 10 | 4 | .714 | 144 | 62 | 59 | 96 | 37 | 4.21 |
| 1969–Kansas City | ..........................Amer. | | 5 | 17 | 0 | 1 | .000 | 15 | 8 | 6 | 10 | 6 | 3.18 |
| 1970–Omaha | .............................Am. Assoc. | | 30 | 171 | 7 | 9 | .438 | 190 | 80 | 61 | 115 | 57 | 3.21 |
| 1971–Omaha | .............................Am. Assoc. | | 27 | 120 | 5 | 11 | .313 | 137 | 71 | 58 | 89 | 35 | 4.35 |
| 1972–Omaha‡ | .............................Am. Assoc. | | 26 | 62 | 3 | 4 | .429 | 45 | 23 | 21 | 29 | 28 | 3.05 |
| 1973–Tidewater§ | .........................Int'national | | 30 | 66 | 6 | 0 | 1.000 | 67 | 29 | 27 | 34 | 30 | 3.68 |
| 1974–Tidewater | .........................Int'national | | 36 | 71 | 4 | 6 | .400 | 76 | 27 | 23 | 54 | 13 | 2.92 |
| 1974–New York | ..........................National | | 10 | 22 | 0 | 1 | .000 | 22 | 4 | 4 | 8 | 4 | 1.64 |
| 1975–Tidewater | .........................Int'national | | 31 | 50 | 8 | 1 | .889 | 43 | 20 | 16 | 24 | 16 | 2.88 |
| 1975–New York x | ........................National | | 4 | 5 | 0 | 1 | .000 | 7 | 3 | 3 | 2 | 2 | 5.40 |

| Year Club | League | G. | IP. | W. | L. | Pct. | H. | R. | ER. | SO. | BB. | ERA. |
|---|---|---|---|---|---|---|---|---|---|---|---|---|
| 1976—Omaha | Am. Assoc. | 51 | 102 | 11 | 3 | .786 | 100 | 45 | 39 | 58 | 28 | 3.44 |
| 1976—Kansas City | American | 4 | 4 | 0 | 0 | .000 | 8 | 3 | 3 | 2 | 0 | 6.75 |
| American League Totals | | 9 | 21 | 0 | 1 | .000 | 23 | 11 | 9 | 12 | 6 | 3.86 |
| National League Totals | | 14 | 27 | 0 | 2 | .000 | 29 | 7 | 7 | 10 | 6 | 2.33 |
| Major League Totals | | 23 | 48 | 0 | 3 | .000 | 52 | 18 | 16 | 22 | 12 | 3.00 |

†Recalled by Minnesota Twins: selected by Kansas City Royals from Minnesota in expansion draft. October 15, 1968.

‡Traded by Kansas City Athletics to New York Mets for Pitcher Barry Raziano, February 1, 1973.

§On disabled list, August 16 to August 27, 1973.

xTraded to Kansas City Royals for Pitcher Randy Hammon, January 9, 1976.

## JAMES FREDERICK CRAWFORD
### (Jim)

Born September 29, 1950, at Mt. Prospect, Ill.
Height, 6.03. Weight, 200.
Throws and bats lefthanded.
Hobbies—Golf and water skiing.
Attended Arizona State University, Tempe, Ariz.; received Bachelor
of Arts degree in Education.

Led Appalachian League pitchers in complete games with 9 in 1972.
Tied for American Association lead in games started by pitchers with 29 in 1974.

| Year Club | League | G. | IP. | W. | L. | Pct. | H. | R. | ER. | SO. | BB. | ERA. |
|---|---|---|---|---|---|---|---|---|---|---|---|---|
| 1972—Covington | Ap'lachian | 11 | 85 | 7 | 3 | .700 | 48 | 26 | 15 | *123 | 18 | *1.59 |
| 1972—Columbus | Southern | 2 | 12 | 1 | 1 | .500 | 8 | 4 | 2 | 13 | 6 | 1.50 |
| 1973—Houston | National | 48 | 70 | 2 | 4 | .333 | 69 | 41 | 35 | 56 | 33 | 4.50 |
| 1974—Denver | Am. Assoc. | 32 | 187 | 11 | 10 | .524 | *208 | *118 | *103 | 121 | 68 | .4.96 |
| 1975—Iowa | Am. Assoc. | 1 | 6 | 0 | 0 | .000 | 5 | 3 | 1 | 4 | 3 | 1.50 |
| 1975—Houston† | National | 44 | 87 | 3 | 5 | .375 | 92 | 40 | 35 | 37 | 37 | 3.62 |
| 1976—Detroit | American | 32 | 109 | 1 | 8 | .111 | 115 | 65 | 55 | 68 | 43 | 4.54 |
| American League Totals | | 32 | 109 | 1 | 8 | .111 | 115 | 65 | 55 | 68 | 43 | 4.54 |
| National League Totals | | 92 | 157 | 5 | 9 | .357 | 161 | 81 | 70 | 93 | 70 | 4.01 |
| Major League Totals | | 124 | 266 | 6 | 17 | .261 | 276 | 146 | 125 | 161 | 113 | 4.23 |

†Traded with Catcher Milt May and Pitcher Dave Roberts to Detroit Tigers for Outfielder Leon Roberts, Catcher Terry Humphrey and Pitchers Gene Pentz and Mark Lemongello, December 6, 1975.

## WILLIE MURPHY CRAWFORD

Born September 7, 1946, at Los Angeles, Calif.
Height, 6.01. Weight, 200.
Throws and bats lefthanded.
Cousin of Curtis Rowe, forward with Boston Celtics.

Led Texas League batters in strikeouts with 186 in 1966.
Received reported $100,000 bonus to sign with Los Angeles Dodgers, 1964.

| Year Club | League | Pos. | G. | AB. | R. | H. | 2B. | 3B. | HR. | RBI. | B.A. | PO. | A. | E. | F.A. |
|---|---|---|---|---|---|---|---|---|---|---|---|---|---|---|---|
| 1964—Santa Barbara | Calif. | OF | 65 | 258 | 58 | 84 | 16 | 5 | 6 | 26 | .326 | 125 | 4 | 6 | .956 |
| 1964—Los Angeles | Nat. | OF | 10 | 16 | 3 | 5 | 1 | 0 | 0 | 0 | .313 | 7 | 0 | 0 | 1.000 |
| 1965—Los Angeles | Nat. | OF | 52 | 27 | 10 | 4 | 0 | 0 | 0 | 0 | .148 | 7 | 0 | 0 | 1.000 |
| 1966—Albuquerque | Texas | OF | •140 | 509 | *94 | 135 | 20 | *14 | 15 | 65 | .265 | 218 | 11 | *13 | .946 |
| 1966—Los Angeles | Nat. | PR | 6 | 0 | 1 | 0 | 0 | 0 | 0 | 0 | .000 | 0 | 0 | 0 | .000 |
| 1967—Albuquerque | Texas | OF | 123 | 469 | *93 | 143 | 20 | 9 | 21 | 67 | .305 | 198 | 7 | 5 | .976 |
| 1967—Los Angeles | Nat. | OF | 4 | 4 | 0 | 1 | 0 | 0 | 0 | 0 | .250 | 0 | 0 | 1 | 1.000 |
| 1968—Spokane | P.C. | OF | 87 | 322 | 57 | 95 | 18 | 9 | 2 | 25 | .295 | 221 | 5 | 5 | .978 |
| 1968—Los Angeles | Nat. | OF | 61 | 175 | 25 | 44 | 12 | 1 | 4 | 14 | .251 | 78 | 6 | 3 | .966 |
| 1969—Los Angeles | Nat. | OF | 129 | 389 | 64 | 96 | 17 | 5 | 11 | 41 | .247 | 177 | 5 | 5 | .973 |
| 1970—Los Angeles | Nat. | OF | 109 | 299 | 48 | 70 | 8 | 6 | 8 | 40 | .234 | 160 | 9 | 7 | .960 |
| 1971—Los Angeles | Nat. | OF | 114 | 342 | 64 | 96 | 16 | 6 | 9 | 40 | .281 | 146 | 5 | 3 | .981 |
| 1972—Los Angeles | Nat. | OF | 96 | 243 | 28 | 61 | 1 | 3 | 8 | 27 | .251 | 111 | 2 | 2 | .983 |
| 1973—Los Angeles | Nat. | OF | 145 | 457 | 75 | 135 | 26 | 2 | 14 | 66 | .295 | 250 | 13 | 6 | .978 |
| 1974—Los Angeles | Nat. | OF | 139 | 468 | 73 | 138 | 23 | 4 | 11 | 61 | .295 | 225 | 3 | 8 | .966 |
| 1975—Los Angeles | Nat. | OF | 124 | 373 | 46 | 98 | 15 | 2 | 9 | 46 | .263 | 201 | 2 | 2 | .990 |
| 1976—St. Louis‡ | Nat. | OF | 120 | 392 | 49 | 119 | 17 | 5 | 9 | 50 | .304 | 209 | 6 | 4 | .982 |
| Major League Totals | | | 1109 | 3185 | 486 | 867 | 142 | 34 | 83 | 385 | .272 | 1571 | 51 | 41 | .975 |

†Traded to St. Louis Cardinals for Second Baseman Ted Sizemore, March 2, 1976.

‡Traded with Pitcher John Curtis and Infielder-Outfielder Vic Harris to San Francisco Giants for Pitchers John D'Acquisto and Mike Caldwell and Catcher Dave Rader, October 20, 1976; traded with Infielder Rob Sperring to Houston Astros for Second Baseman Rob Andrews and a player to be named later, March 26, 1977.

### CHAMPIONSHIP SERIES RECORD

| Year Club | League | Pos. | G. | AB. | R. | H. | 2B. | 3B. | HR. | RBI. | B.A. | PO. | A. | E. | F.A. |
|---|---|---|---|---|---|---|---|---|---|---|---|---|---|---|---|
| 1974—Los Angeles | Nat. | OF-PH | 2 | 4 | 1 | 1 | 0 | 0 | 0 | 1 | .250 | 0 | 0 | 0 | .000 |

### WORLD SERIES RECORD

| Year Club | League | Pos. | G. | AB. | R. | H. | 2B. | 3B. | HR. | RBI. | B.A. | PO. | A. | E. | F.A. |
|---|---|---|---|---|---|---|---|---|---|---|---|---|---|---|---|
| 1965—Los Angeles | Nat. | PH | 2 | 2 | 0 | 1 | 0 | 0 | 0 | 0 | .500 | 0 | 0 | 0 | .000 |
| 1974—Los Angeles | Nat. | OF-PH | 3 | 6 | 1 | 2 | 0 | 0 | 1 | 1 | .333 | 1 | 0 | 1 | 1.000 |
| World Series Totals | | | 5 | 8 | 1 | 3 | 0 | 0 | 1 | 1 | .375 | 1 | 0 | 0 | 1.000 |

## PATRICK ALAN CRISTELLI
### (Pat)

Born September 27, 1952, at Canon City, Colo.
Height, 6.03. Weight, 195.
Throws right and bats lefthanded.
Hobbies—Hunting and fishing.
Attended Green River Community College, Auburn, Wash., and
University of Puget Sound, Tacoma, Wash.
Led Texas League in hit batsmen with 9 in 1975.

| Year Club | League | G. | IP. | W. | L. | Pct. | H. | R. | ER. | SO. | BB. | ERA. |
|---|---|---|---|---|---|---|---|---|---|---|---|---|
| 1974—Quad Cities .........................Midwest | | 24 | 176 | 14 | 10 | .583 | 143 | 48 | 39 | 139 | 45 | 1.99 |
| 1975—El Paso...............................Texas | | 24 | 148 | 11 | 10 | .524 | 148 | 87 | 65 | 123 | 76 | 3.95 |
| 1976—Salt Lake City.....................P. Coast | | 27 | 137 | 11 | 10 | .524 | 161 | 101 | 87 | 80 | 72 | 5.72 |

Listed on California Angels' 1977 spring roster.


## WARREN LIVINGSTON CROMARTIE
Name pronounced Kroh-MART-ee.

Born September 29, 1953, at Miami Beach, Fla.
Height, 6.00. Weight, 190.
Throws and bats lefthanded.
Hobbies—Listening to rock music and playing drums.
Attended Miami-Dade (North) Community College, Miami, Fla.
Led Eastern League in total bases with 235 in 1974.

| Year Club League | Pos. | G. | AB. | R. | H. | 2B. | 3B. | HR. | RBI. | B.A. | PO. | A. | E. | F.A. |
|---|---|---|---|---|---|---|---|---|---|---|---|---|---|---|
| 1974—Quebec City ......East. | OF-1B | 129 | 482 | 94 | •164 | 20 | 7 | 13 | 61 | .336 | 389 | 22 | 9 | .979 |
| 1974—Montreal .........Nat. | OF | 8 | 17 | 2 | 3 | 0 | 0 | 0 | 0 | .176 | 8 | 0 | 0 | 1.000 |
| 1975—Memphis ..........Int. | OF-1B | 119 | 400 | 42 | 107 | 16 | 6 | 3 | 38 | .268 | 478 | 35 | 15 | .972 |
| 1976—Denver† ...........A.A. | OF-1B | 107 | 415 | 69 | 140 | 12 | 5 | 8 | 60 | .337 | 274 | 13 | 6 | .980 |
| 1976—Montreal .........Nat. | OF-PH | 33 | 81 | 8 | 17 | 1 | 0 | 0 | 2 | .210 | 61 | 1 | 2 | .969 |
| Major League Totals ...................... | | 41 | 98 | 10 | 20 | 1 | 0 | 0 | 2 | .204 | 69 | 1 | 2 | .972 |

†On suspended list, May 19 through May 21, 1976.


## EDWARD CARLTON CROSBY
### (Ed)

Born May 26, 1949, at Long Beach, Calif.
Height, 6.02. Weight, 175.
Throws right and bats lefthanded.
Hobbies—Golf and coin collecting.
Attended Long Beach City College, Long Beach, Calif.
Led Northwest League shortstops in double plays with 48 in 1969 and American Association shortstops with 99 in 1971.
Led American Association in sacrifice flies with 9 in 1971.

| Year Club | League | Pos. | G. | AB. | R. | H. | 2B. | 3B. | HR. | RBI. | B.A. | PO. | A. | E. | F.A. |
|---|---|---|---|---|---|---|---|---|---|---|---|---|---|---|---|
| 1969—Lewiston ..........N'west | | •SS-2 | 70 | 275 | 57 | 81 | 12 | 3 | 0 | 20 | .295 | 72 | •214 | 25 | .920 |
| 1970—Arkansas .........Texas | | SS | 78 | 300 | 40 | 90 | 17 | 5 | 5 | 31 | .300 | 150 | 225 | 20 | .949 |
| 1970—St. Louis .........Nat. | | SS-3-2 | 38 | 95 | 9 | 24 | 4 | 1 | 0 | 6 | .253 | 44 | 91 | 7 | .951 |
| 1971—Tulsa ................A.A. | | •S-3-1-2 | 135 | 495 | 49 | 142 | 30 | 5 | 4 | 46 | .287 | 228 | •375 | 33 | .948 |
| 1972—St. Louis .........Nat. | | SS-2-3 | 101 | 276 | 27 | 60 | 9 | 1 | 0 | 19 | .217 | 130 | 197 | 10 | .910 |
| 1973—St.L.†-Cin.‡.......Nat. | | SS-2-3 | 58 | 90 | 8 | 16 | 3 | 2 | 0 | 6 | .178 | 36 | 90 | 9 | .933 |
| 1974—Tul.§-Okla. C. ....A.A. | | S-3-2 | 41 | 144 | 21 | 45 | 5 | 4 | 0 | 15 | .313 | 36 | 68 | 5 | .954 |
| 1974—Cleveland .........Amer. | | 3-S-2 | 37 | 86 | 11 | 18 | 3 | 0 | 0 | 6 | .209 | 14 | 53 | 5 | .931 |
| 1975—Cleveland .........Amer. | | S-2-3 | 61 | 128 | 12 | 30 | 3 | 0 | 0 | 7 | .234 | 69 | 126 | 7 | .965 |
| 1976—Tulsa ................AA | | 3-SS-2 | 95 | 259 | 21 | 60 | 4 | 2 | 0 | 26 | .232 | 87 | 208 | 14 | .955 |
| 1976—Cleveland x ......Amer. | | 3B-DH | 2 | 2 | 0 | 1 | 0 | 0 | 0 | 0 | .500 | 0 | 2 | 0 | 1.000 |
| American League Totals ................ | | | 100 | 216 | 23 | 49 | 6 | 0 | 0 | 13 | .227 | 83 | 181 | 12 | .956 |
| National League Totals .................. | | | 197 | 461 | 44 | 100 | 16 | 4 | 0 | 31 | .217 | 210 | 378 | 26 | .958 |
| Major League Totals ...................... | | | 297 | 677 | 67 | 149 | 22 | 4 | 0 | 44 | .220 | 293 | 559 | 38 | .957 |

†Traded with Catcher Gene Dusan (assigned to Indianapolis) to Cincinnati Reds for Pitcher Ed Sprague and a player to be named later, July 27, 1973; Reds assigned First Baseman Roe Skidmore to Tulsa (St. Louis Cardinals' organization), September 30, 1973, to complete deal.

‡Drafted from Indianapolis (Cincinnati Reds' organization) by Philadelphia Phillies, December 3, 1973.. Sold by Philadelphia Phillies to St. Louis Cardinals (assigned to Tulsa), March 29, 1974.

§Traded with Shortstop Luis Alvarado by St. Louis Cardinals to Cleveland Indians for Shortstop Jack Heidemann, May 31, 1974.

xTraded to California Angels for Outfielder Marty Friedman, December 10, 1976; refused to report to Salt Lake City (California Angels' affiliate) and granted free agency; signed with Oakland A's, January 31, 1977. Released March 28, 1977.

### CHAMPIONSHIP SERIES RECORD

| Year Club | League | Pos. | G. | AB. | R. | H. | 2B. | 3B. | HR. | RBI. | B.A. | PO. | A. | E. | F.A. |
|---|---|---|---|---|---|---|---|---|---|---|---|---|---|---|---|
| 1973—Cincinnati..........Nat. | | SS-PH | 3 | 2 | 0 | 1 | 0 | 0 | 0 | 0 | .500 | 1 | 2 | 0 | 1.000 |

# TERRENCE MICHAEL CROWLEY
## (Terry)

Born February 16, 1947, at Staten Island, N. Y.
Height, 6.00. Weight, 170.
Throws and bats lefthanded.
Hobby—Basketball.
Attended Long Island University, Brooklyn, N. Y.
Led International League in total bases with 246 in 1969.

| Year | Club | League | Pos. | G. | AB. | R. | H. | 2B. | 3B. | HR. | RBI. | B.A. | PO. | A. | E. | F.A. |
|------|------|--------|------|-----|-----|-----|-----|-----|-----|-----|------|------|------|-----|-----|------|
| 1966—Miami | | Fla. St. | OF | 19 | 51 | 5 | 13 | 1 | 0 | 0 | 3 | .255 | 15 | 0 | 1 | .938 |
| 1967—Miami | | Fla. St. | 1-O | 135 | 497 | 50 | 130 | •24 | 10 | 3 | 49 | .262 | 1057 | 56 | 23 | .980 |
| 1968—Elmira | | East. | OF-1B | 55 | 181 | 19 | 49 | 8 | 1 | 0 | 22 | .271 | 132 | 5 | 3 | .979 |
| 1968—Rochester | | Int. | OF-1B | 75 | 271 | 37 | 71 | 13 | 3 | 8 | 34 | .262 | 274 | 18 | 6 | .980 |
| 1969—Rochester | | Int. | OF-1B | 132 | 475 | 78 | 134 | 24 | 2 | 28 | 83 | .282 | 247 | 4 | 6 | .977 |
| 1969—Baltimore | | Amer. | 1B-OF | 7 | 18 | 2 | 6 | 0 | 0 | 0 | 3 | .333 | 23 | 2 | 0 | 1.000 |
| 1970—Baltimore | | Amer. | OF-1B | 83 | 152 | 25 | 39 | 5 | 0 | 5 | 20 | .257 | 138 | 6 | 2 | .986 |
| 1971—Rochester | | Int. | 1B-OF | 78 | 259 | 56 | 73 | 9 | 4 | 19 | 63 | .282 | 591 | 47 | 5 | .992 |
| 1971—Baltimore | | Amer. | OF-1B | 18 | 23 | 2 | 4 | 0 | 0 | 0 | 1 | .174 | 7 | 0 | 0 | 1.000 |
| 1972—Baltimore | | Amer. | OF-1B | 97 | 247 | 30 | 57 | 10 | 0 | 11 | 29 | .231 | 170 | 8 | 1 | .994 |
| 1973—Baltimore† | | Amer. | OF-1B | 54 | 131 | 16 | 27 | 4 | 0 | 3 | 15 | .206 | 33 | 5 | 3 | .927 |
| 1974—Cincinnati | | Nat. | OF-1B | 84 | 125 | 11 | 30 | 12 | 0 | 1 | 20 | .240 | 58 | 5 | 2 | .969 |
| 1975—Cincinnati‡ | | Nat. | 1B-OF | 66 | 71 | 8 | 19 | 6 | 0 | 1 | 11 | .268 | 43 | 4 | 0 | 1.000 |
| 1976—Atlanta§ | | Nat. | PH | 7 | 6 | 0 | 0 | 0 | 0 | 0 | 0 | .000 | 0 | 0 | 0 | .000 |
| 1976—Rochester | | Int. | 1B | 20 | 69 | 4 | 18 | 7 | 0 | 2 | 7 | .261 | 14 | 1 | 0 | 1.000 |
| 1976—Baltimore x | | Amer. | 1B-DH | 33 | 61 | 5 | 15 | 1 | 0 | 0 | 5 | .246 | 13 | 2 | 0 | 1.000 |
| American League Totals | | | | 292 | 632 | 80 | 148 | 20 | 0 | 19 | 73 | .234 | 384 | 23 | 6 | .985 |
| National League Totals | | | | 157 | 202 | 19 | 49 | 18 | 0 | 2 | 31 | .242 | 101 | 9 | 2 | .982 |
| Major League Totals | | | | 449 | 834 | 99 | 197 | 38 | 0 | 21 | 104 | .236 | 485 | 32 | 8 | .985 |

†Sold to Texas Rangers for an estimated $100,000, December 6, 1973. Sold by Texas Rangers to Cincinnati Reds, March 19, 1974.
‡Traded to Atlanta Braves for Pitcher Mike Thompson, April 6, 1976.
§Unconditionally released, May 6, 1976; signed as free agent with Baltimore Orioles' organization, May 26, 1976.
xReleased, March 26, 1977.

### CHAMPIONSHIP SERIES RECORD

| Year | Club | League | Pos. | G. | AB. | R. | H. | 2B. | 3B. | HR. | RBI. | B.A. | PO. | A. | E. | F.A. |
|------|------|--------|------|-----|-----|-----|-----|-----|-----|-----|------|------|------|-----|-----|------|
| 1973—Baltimore | | Amer. | PH-OF | 2 | 2 | 0 | 0 | 0 | 0 | 0 | 0 | .000 | 1 | 0 | 0 | 1.000 |
| 1975—Cincinnati | | Nat. | PH | 1 | 0 | 0 | 0 | 0 | 0 | 0 | 0 | .000 | 0 | 0 | 0 | .000 |
| Championship Series Totals | | | | 3 | 2 | 0 | 0 | 0 | 0 | 0 | 0 | .000 | 1 | 0 | 0 | 1.000 |

### WORLD SERIES RECORD

| Year | Club | League | Pos. | G. | AB. | R. | H. | 2B. | 3B. | HR. | RBI. | B.A. | PO. | A. | E. | F.A. |
|------|------|--------|------|-----|-----|-----|-----|-----|-----|-----|------|------|------|-----|-----|------|
| 1970—Baltimore | | Amer. | PH | 1 | 1 | 0 | 0 | 0 | 0 | 0 | 0 | .000 | 0 | 0 | 0 | .000 |
| 1975—Cincinnati | | Nat. | PH | 2 | 2 | 0 | 1 | 0 | 0 | 0 | 0 | .500 | 0 | 0 | 0 | .000 |
| World Series Totals | | | | 3 | 3 | 0 | 1 | 0 | 0 | 0 | 0 | .333 | 0 | 0 | 0 | .000 |

# CIRILO DILAN CRUZ
## (Tommy)

Born February 15, 1951, at Arroyo, Puerto Rico.
Height, 5.09. Weight, 165.
Throws and bats lefthanded.
Brother of Jose Cruz, outfielder with Houston Astros, and Hector Cruz,
third baseman-outfielder with St. Louis Cardinals.

| Year | Club | League | Pos. | G. | AB. | R. | H. | 2B. | 3B. | HR. | RBI. | B.A. | PO. | A. | E. | F.A. |
|------|------|--------|------|-----|-----|-----|-----|-----|-----|-----|------|------|------|-----|-----|------|
| 1969—Sarasota Cards | | Gulf C. | OF | 12 | 34 | 2 | 5 | 0 | 0 | 0 | 0 | .147 | 11 | 2 | 2 | .867 |
| 1970—Sarasota Cards | | Gulf C. | OF | 5 | 14 | 1 | 2 | 0 | 0 | 0 | 2 | .143 | 3 | 0 | 1 | .750 |
| 1970—Lewiston | | Northw. | OF-1B | 43 | 144 | 27 | 44 | 8 | 1 | 5 | 22 | .306 | 46 | 3 | 4 | .925 |
| 1971—St. Petersburg | | Fla. St. | OF | 110 | 416 | 52 | 126 | 14 | 7 | 6 | 49 | .303 | 188 | 10 | 11 | .947 |
| 1971—Tulsa | | A. A. | OF | 15 | 55 | 9 | 9 | 1 | 2 | 0 | 5 | .164 | 20 | 2 | 0 | 1.000 |
| 1972—Arkansas† | | Texas | OF | 77 | 274 | 37 | 73 | 13 | 2 | 6 | 39 | .266 | 117 | 11 | 7 | .948 |
| 1973—Tulsa | | A. A. | OF | 31 | 108 | 12 | 27 | 4 | 0 | 0 | 11 | .250 | 50 | 0 | 5 | .909 |
| 1973—Arkansas | | Texas | OF | 63 | 191 | 14 | 44 | 10 | 0 | 2 | 15 | .230 | 77 | 3 | 2 | .976 |
| 1973—St. Louis‡ | | Nat. | PR-OF | 3 | 0 | 1 | 0 | 0 | 0 | 0 | 0 | .000 | 0 | 0 | 0 | .000 |
| 1974—Pittsfield | | East. | OF | 133 | 469 | 67 | 137 | 31 | 1 | 7 | 53 | .292 | 221 | 14 | 12 | .951 |
| 1975—Spokane | | P. C. | OF | 138 | 524 | 72 | 151 | •35 | 4 | 8 | 87 | .288 | 250 | 14 | 8 | .971 |
| 1976—Sacramento | | P. C. | OF-1B | 127 | 476 | 69 | 154 | 20 | 6 | 13 | 83 | .324 | 219 | 16 | 8 | .967 |
| Major League Totals | | | | 3 | 0 | 1 | 0 | 0 | 0 | 0 | 0 | .000 | 0 | 0 | 0 | .000 |

†On disabled list, August 8 through remainder of season.
‡Traded to Texas Rangers for Pitcher Wilfred (Sonny) Siebert, October 26, 1973.
Listed on Texas Rangers' 1977 spring roster.

---

## DID YOU KNOW —

That Rabbit Maranville of the Boston Braves hit two inside-the-park home runs on July 1, 1919?

## HECTOR DILAN CRUZ

Born April 2, 1953, at Arroyo, Puerto Rico.
Height, 5.11. Weight, 180.
Throws and bats righthanded.
Hobbies—Music, swimming, fishing, and reading.
Brother of Jose Cruz, outfielder for Houston Astros, and Cirilo (Tommy) Cruz,
outfielder for Texas Rangers.
Led Texas League in total bases with 249 in 1973.
Named Texas League Most Valuable Player, 1973.
Named Player of the Year in American Association, 1975.
Named Minor League Player of the Year by THE SPORTING NEWS, 1975.

| Year Club League | Pos. | G. | AB. | R. | H. | 2B. | 3B. | HR. | RBI. | B.A. | PO. | A. | E. | F.A. |
|---|---|---|---|---|---|---|---|---|---|---|---|---|---|---|
| 1970—Sarasota Cards ..Gulf C. | OF | 3 | 9 | 3 | 4 | 0 | 1 | 0 | 2 | .444 | 4 | 0 | 0 | 1.000 |
| 1970—Cedar Rapids ....Midw. | OF | 24 | 41 | 8 | 6 | 0 | 1 | 0 | 1 | .146 | 35 | 2 | 0 | 1.000 |
| 1971—Cedar Rapids ....Midw. | OF | 111 | 406 | 71 | 112 | 21 | 4 | 23 | 68 | .276 | *236 | 10 | 11 | .957 |
| 1972—Modesto ...........Calif. | OF | 83 | 314 | 58 | 88 | 11 | 2 | 22 | 77 | .280 | 164 | 4 | 5 | .971 |
| 1972—Cedar Rapids ....Midw. | OF | 40 | 141 | 22 | 47 | 10 | 2 | 5 | 24 | .333 | 93 | 5 | 2 | .980 |
| 1973—Arkansas ..........Texas | OF | 114 | 403 | *94 | 132 | 21 | 3 | *30 | *105 | .328 | 228 | 12 | 6 | .976 |
| 1973—St. Louis ..........Nat. | OF | 11 | 11 | 1 | 0 | 0 | 0 | 0 | 0 | .000 | 7 | 0 | 0 | 1.000 |
| 1974—Tulsa ...............A. A. | OF | 134 | 459 | 70 | 117 | 17 | 8 | 11 | 72 | .255 | 236 | *15 | 9 | .965 |
| 1975—Tulsa ...............A. A. | 3B-OF | 115 | 435 | 84 | 133 | 30 | 1 | *29 | *116 | .306 | 93 | 197 | 17 | .945 |
| 1975—St. Louis ..........Nat. | 3B-OF | 23 | 48 | 7 | 7 | 2 | 2 | 0 | 6 | .146 | 20 | 4 | 3 | .889 |
| 1976—St. Louis ..........Nat. | 3B | 151 | 526 | 54 | 120 | 17 | 1 | 13 | 71 | .228 | 100 | 270 | *26 | .934 |
| Major League Totals ...................... | | 185 | 585 | 62 | 127 | 19 | 3 | 13 | 77 | .217 | 127 | 274 | 29 | .932 |

## HENRY CRUZ (ACOSTA)

Born February 27, 1952, at Christiansted, St. Croix, Virgin Islands.
Height, 6.00. Weight, 175.
Throws and bats lefthanded.
Hobbies—Swimming, reading and listening to music.
Attended Inter-American University, Fajardo, Virgin Islands.
Led California League outfielders in double plays with 4 in 1972.

| Year Club League | Pos. | G. | AB. | R. | H. | 2B. | 3B. | HR. | RBI. | B.A. | PO. | A. | E. | F.A. |
|---|---|---|---|---|---|---|---|---|---|---|---|---|---|---|
| 1971—Bakersfield† ......Calif. | | | | (Did not play) | | | | | | | | | | |
| 1972—El Paso ...........Texas | OF | 9 | 34 | 2 | 9 | 0 | 0 | 0 | 2 | .265 | 18 | 0 | 1 | .947 |
| 1972—Bakersfield........Calif. | OF | 114 | 405 | 60 | 114 | 19 | 5 | 8 | 56 | .281 | 193 | 10 | 2 | *.990 |
| 1973—Waterbury ........East. | OF | 65 | 210 | 36 | 55 | 12 | 3 | 2 | 20 | .262 | 121 | 7 | 6 | .955 |
| 1973—Albuquerque‡ ....P. C. | OF | 31 | 103 | 16 | 27 | 5 | 1 | 2 | 16 | .262 | 63 | 3 | 1 | .985 |
| 1974—Albuquerque§ ....P. C. | OF | 104 | 392 | 72 | 119 | 15 | 7 | 6 | 50 | .304 | 222 | 7 | 1 | *.996 |
| 1975—Albuquerque......P. C. | OF | 71 | 255 | 44 | 79 | 13 | 3 | 7 | 41 | .310 | 160 | 3 | 8 | .953 |
| 1975—Los Angeles ......Nat. | OF | 53 | 94 | 8 | 25 | 3 | 1 | 0 | 5 | .266 | 48 | 0 | 2 | .960 |
| 1976—Los Angeles ......Nat. | OF | 49 | 88 | 8 | 16 | 2 | 1 | 4 | 14 | .182 | 39 | 1 | 1 | .976 |
| 1976—Albuquerque......P. C. | OF | 24 | 82 | 15 | 25 | 4 | 1 | 1 | 12 | .305 | 38 | 4 | 4 | .913 |
| Major League Totals ...................... | | 102 | 182 | 16 | 41 | 5 | 2 | 4 | 19 | .225 | 87 | 1 | 3 | .967 |

†On disabled list the entire season.
‡On disabled list, August 4 to August 14, 1973.
§On disabled list, July 28 through remainder of season.

## JOSE DILAN CRUZ

Born August 8, 1947, at Arroyo, Puerto Rico.
Height, 6.00. Weight, 175.
Throws and bats lefthanded.
Hobbies—Swimming and fishing.
Brother of Hector Cruz, third baseman-outfielder with St. Louis Cardinals,
and Cirilo (Tommy) Cruz, outfielder with Texas Rangers.
Led National League outfielders in double plays with 5 in 1972.
Led Texas League in total bases with 254 in 1970.

| Year Club League | Pos. | G. | AB. | R. | H. | 2B. | 3B. | HR. | RBI. | B.A. | PO. | A. | E. | F.A. |
|---|---|---|---|---|---|---|---|---|---|---|---|---|---|---|
| 1967—St. Petersburg ..Fla. St. | OF-1B | 78 | 205 | 33 | 57 | 8 | 9 | 1 | 20 | .278 | 113 | 5 | 7 | .944 |
| 1968—Modesto ...........Calif. | OF-SS | 133 | 504 | 101 | 144 | 24 | 10 | 13 | 53 | .286 | 219 | 10 | 11 | .954 |
| 1969—Arkansas† ........Texas | OF | 102 | 400 | 56 | 109 | 18 | 9 | 6 | 49 | .273 | 235 | 16 | 9 | .965 |
| 1970—Arkansas ..........Texas | OF | 133 | 493 | 89 | 148 | *29 | 7 | 21 | 90 | .300 | *276 | 10 | 12 | .960 |
| 1970—St. Louis ..........Nat. | OF | 6 | 17 | 2 | 6 | 1 | 0 | 0 | 1 | .353 | 16 | 0 | 0 | 1.000 |
| 1971—Tulsa ...............A. A. | OF | 67 | 254 | 56 | 83 | 15 | 7 | 15 | 49 | .327 | 146 | 1 | 7 | .955 |
| 1971—St. Louis ..........Nat. | OF | 83 | 292 | 46 | 80 | 13 | 2 | 9 | 27 | .274 | 197 | 2 | 5 | .975 |
| 1972—St. Louis ..........Nat. | OF | 117 | 332 | 33 | 78 | 14 | 4 | 2 | 23 | .235 | 220 | 9 | 5 | .979 |
| 1973—St. Louis ..........Nat. | OF | 132 | 406 | 51 | 92 | 22 | 5 | 10 | 57 | .227 | 276 | 2 | 6 | .979 |
| 1974—St. Louis‡ ........Nat. | OF-1B | 107 | 161 | 24 | 42 | 4 | 3 | 5 | 20 | .261 | 81 | 2 | 2 | .976 |
| 1975—Houston ...........Nat. | OF | 120 | 315 | 44 | 81 | 15 | 2 | 9 | 49 | .257 | 187 | 6 | 4 | .980 |
| 1976—Houston ...........Nat. | OF | 133 | 439 | 49 | 133 | 21 | 5 | 4 | 61 | .303 | 265 | 10 | 8 | .972 |
| Major League Totals ...................... | | 698 | 1962 | 249 | 512 | 90 | 21 | 39 | 238 | .261 | 1242 | 31 | 30 | .977 |

†On disabled list, April 8 through May 12, 1969.
‡Sold to Houston Astros, October 24, 1974.

## JULIO LUIS CRUZ

Born December 2, 1954, at Brooklyn, N. Y.
Height, 5.09. Weight, 165.
Throws right and bats right and lefthanded.
Hobby—Working on cars.
Attended San Bernardino Valley College, San Bernardino, Calif.; received Associate of Arts degree.

| Year Club | League | Pos. | G. | AB. | R. | H. | 2B. | 3B. | HR. | RBI. | B.A. | PO. | A. | E. | F.A. |
|---|---|---|---|---|---|---|---|---|---|---|---|---|---|---|---|
| 1974—Idaho Falls........Pioneer | 2B-S-3 | 72 | 237 | 44 | 57 | 4 | 1 | 0 | 27 | .241 | 137 | 185 | 22 | .936 |
| 1975—Quad Cities ......Midw. | 2B | 108 | 368 | 79 | 96 | 6 | 6 | 0 | 35 | .261 | 228 | 259 | 14 | .972 |
| 1976—Salinas..............Calif. | 2B | 96 | 348 | 92 | 107 | 12 | 3 | 1 | 45 | .307 | 234 | 314 | 10 | *.982 |
| 1976—El Paso ............Texas | 2B | 13 | 49 | 9 | 16 | 4 | 1 | 0 | 9 | .327 | 23 | 21 | 0 | 1.000 |
| 1976—Salt Lake C.† ....P. C. | 2-3-OF | 20 | 69 | 11 | 17 | 2 | 2 | 0 | 6 | .246 | 30 | 47 | 1 | .987 |

†Selected by Seattle Mariners from California Angels in American League expansion draft, November 5, 1976.

## TODD RUBEN CRUZ

Born November 23, 1955, at Highland Park, Mich.
Height, 6.00. Weight, 175.
Throws and bats righthanded.
Hobby—Karate.
Led Carolina League shortstops in double plays with 68 in 1974 and 74 in 1975.
Led Carolina League in strikeouts by batters with 127 and in sacrifice flies with 10 in 1974.
Tied for Appalachian League in strikeouts by batters with 76 in 1973.

| Year Club | League | Pos. | G. | AB. | R. | H. | 2B. | 3B. | HR. | RBI. | B.A. | PO. | A. | E. | F.A. |
|---|---|---|---|---|---|---|---|---|---|---|---|---|---|---|---|
| 1973—Pulaski..............Appal. | SS | 69 | 208 | 29 | 38 | 10 | 1 | 4 | 18 | .183 | 95 | 174 | *49 | .846 |
| 1974—Rocky Mount ....Carol. | SS | 126 | 445 | 34 | 86 | 13 | 6 | 1 | 43 | .193 | *222 | 321 | *49 | .917 |
| 1974—Toledo ..............Int. | SS | 4 | 10 | 1 | 1 | 1 | 0 | 0 | 1 | .100 | 3 | 8 | 2 | .846 |
| 1975—Rocky Mount ....Carol. | SS | 134 | 453 | 57 | 92 | 23 | 1 | 11 | 67 | .203 | *218 | *457 | 41 | *.943 |
| 1976—Reading ............East. | SS | 123 | 424 | 34 | 98 | 126 | 11 | 1 | 5 | .231 | 203 | 388 | 53 | .918 |

Listed on Philadelphia Phillies' 1977 spring roster.

## MICHAEL LEE CUBBAGE
### (Mike)

Born July 21, 1950, at Charlottesville, Va.
Height, 6.00. Weight, 180.
Throws right and bats lefthanded.
Hobbies—Golf and tennis.
Attended University of Virginia, Charlottesville, Va.

| Year Club | League | Pos. | G. | AB. | R. | H. | 2B. | 3B. | HR. | RBI. | B.A. | PO. | A. | E. | F.A. |
|---|---|---|---|---|---|---|---|---|---|---|---|---|---|---|---|
| 1971—Geneva..............NYP | 2-3-S | 56 | 174 | 42 | 60 | 15 | 0 | 8 | 46 | .345 | 116 | 138 | 17 | .937 |
| 1972—Burlington ........Carol. | 2-3-O | 105 | 334 | 50 | 94 | 17 | 2 | 6 | 36 | .281 | 152 | 240 | 19 | .954 |
| 1973—Pittsfield ..........East. | 2-3-O | 109 | 346 | 81 | 108 | 16 | 3 | 13 | 65 | .312 | 188 | 251 | 16 | .965 |
| 1974—Spokane ............P. C. | 2B-3B | 90 | 339 | 62 | 107 | 25 | 2 | 16 | 61 | .316 | 180 | 224 | 13 | .969 |
| 1974—Texas ................Amer. | 3B-2B | 9 | 15 | 0 | 0 | 0 | 0 | 0 | 0 | .000 | 7 | 9 | 1 | .941 |
| 1975—Spokane ............P. C. | 2-3-1 | 56 | 217 | 50 | 68 | 18 | 2 | 10 | 34 | .313 | 120 | 152 | 8 | .971 |
| 1975—Texas ................Amer. | 2B-3B | 58 | 143 | 12 | 32 | 6 | 0 | 4 | 21 | .224 | 68 | 115 | 8 | .958 |
| 1976—Texas†-Minn. ....Amer. | 3-2-DH | 118 | 374 | 42 | 96 | 19 | 5 | 3 | 49 | .257 | 180 | 218 | 19 | .954 |
| Major League Totals ...................... | | 185 | 532 | 54 | 128 | 25 | 5 | 7 | 70 | .241 | 255 | 342 | 28 | .955 |

†Traded with Pitcher Bill Singer, Infielder Roy Smalley and Pitcher Jim Gideon, latter assigned to Tacoma, and a reported $250,000 cash, to Minnesota Twins for Pitcher Bert Blyleven and Shortstop Danny Thompson, June 1, 1976.

## MIGUEL ANGEL CUELLAR

Named pronounced QUAY-yahr.

### (Mike)

Born May 8, 1937, at Santa Clara, Cuba.
Height, 5.11. Weight, 175.
Throws and bats lefthanded.
Hobbies—Painting, comics, movies and music.
Tied major league record for most strikeouts, inning (4), 4th inning, May 29, 1970.
Led American League pitchers in complete games with 21 and tied for lead in games started with 40 in 1970.
Tied for International League lead in shutouts with 5 in 1958.
Named lefthanded pitcher on THE SPORTING NEWS American League All-Star Team, 1969 and 1974.
Co-winner with Denny McLain for the American League Cy Young Memorial Award, 1969.

| Year Club | League | G. | IP. | W. | L. | Pct. | H. | R. | ER. | SO. | BB. | ERA. |
|---|---|---|---|---|---|---|---|---|---|---|---|---|
| 1957—Havana ..............Int'national | 44 | 155 | 8 | 7 | .533 | 122 | 53 | 42 | 74 | 54 | 2.44 |
| 1958—Havana ..............Int'national | 40 | 221 | 13 | 12 | .520 | 204 | 75 | 68 | 98 | 70 | 2.77 |
| 1959—Cincinnati ..........National | 2 | 4 | 0 | 0 | .000 | 7 | 8 | 7 | 5 | 4 | 15.75 |
| 1959—Havana ..............Int'national | 29 | 212 | 10 | 11 | .476 | 184 | 82 | 66 | 111 | 57 | 2.80 |
| 1960—Havana-Jersey City ..............Int'national | 33 | 148 | 6 | 9 | .400 | 146 | 75 | 58 | 77 | 48 | 3.53 |
| 1961—Jersey City-Syracuse ...........Int'national | 28 | 102 | 4 | 10 | .286 | 116 | 64 | 53 | 65 | 32 | 4.68 |
| 1961—Indianapolis† ......................Am. Assoc. | 5 | 16 | 0 | 1 | .000 | 18 | 7 | 7 | 8 | 4 | 3.94 |

| Year Club | League | G. | IP. | W. | L. | Pct. | H. | R. | ER. | SO. | BB. | ERA. |
|---|---|---|---|---|---|---|---|---|---|---|---|---|
| 1962–Monterrey | Mexican | 37 | 155 | 11 | 6 | .647 | 173 | 74 | 62 | *134 | 60 | 3.60 |
| 1963–Knoxville | Sally | 8 | 39 | 1 | 1 | .500 | 33 | 15 | 11 | 39 | 20 | 2.54 |
| 1963–Jacksonville | Int'national | 24 | 126 | 6 | 7 | .462 | 116 | 56 | 53 | 85 | 47 | 3.79 |
| 1964–Jacksonville | Int'national | 10 | 76 | 6 | 1 | .857 | 57 | 17 | 15 | 64 | 16 | 1.78 |
| 1964–St. Louis | National | 32 | 72 | 5 | 5 | .500 | 80 | 43 | 36 | 56 | 33 | 4.50 |
| 1965–Jacksonville‡ | Int'national | 15 | 97 | 9 | 1 | .900 | 74 | 32 | 27 | 91 | 35 | 2.51 |
| 1965–Houston | National | 25 | 56 | 1 | 4 | .200 | 55 | 24 | 22 | 46 | 21 | 3.54 |
| 1966–Houston | National | 38 | 227 | 12 | 10 | .545 | 193 | 79 | 56 | 175 | 52 | 2.22 |
| 1967–Houston | National | 36 | 246 | 16 | 11 | .593 | 233 | 99 | 83 | 203 | 63 | 3.04 |
| 1968–Houston§ | National | 28 | 171 | 8 | 11 | .421 | 152 | 60 | 52 | 133 | 45 | 2.74 |
| 1969–Baltimore | American | 39 | 291 | 23 | 11 | .676 | 213 | 94 | 77 | 182 | 79 | 2.38 |
| 1970–Baltimore | American | 40 | 298 | •24 | 8 | *.750 | 273 | 126 | •115 | 190 | 69 | 3.47 |
| 1971–Baltimore | American | 38 | 292 | 20 | 9 | .690 | 250 | 111 | 100 | 124 | 78 | 3.08 |
| 1972–Baltimore | American | 35 | 248 | 18 | 12 | .600 | 197 | 78 | 71 | 132 | 71 | 2.58 |
| 1973–Baltimore | American | 38 | 267 | 18 | 13 | .581 | 265 | 120 | 97 | 140 | 84 | 3.27 |
| 1974–Baltimore | American | 38 | 269 | 22 | 10 | *.688 | 253 | 106 | 93 | 106 | 86 | 3.11 |
| 1975–Baltimore | American | 36 | 256 | 14 | 12 | .538 | 229 | 112 | 104 | 105 | 84 | 3.66 |
| 1976–Baltimore x | American | 26 | 107 | 4 | 13 | .235 | 129 | 63 | 59 | 32 | 50 | 4.96 |
| American League Totals | | 290 | 2028 | 143 | 88 | .619 | 1809 | 810 | 716 | 1011 | 601 | 3.18 |
| National League Totals | | 161 | 776 | 42 | 41 | .506 | 720 | 313 | 256 | 618 | 218 | 2.97 |
| Major League Totals | | 451 | 2804 | 185 | 129 | .589 | 2529 | 1123 | 972 | 1629 | 819 | 3.12 |

†Released by Cincinnati Reds' organization to Monterrey (Mexican League), April 26, 1962.

‡Recalled by St. Louis Cardinals and traded with Pitcher Ron Taylor to Houston Astros for Pitchers Hal Woodeshick and Chuck Taylor (latter transferred from Oklahoma City to Jacksonville), June 15, 1965.

§Traded with Infielder Elijah (Tom) Johnson to Baltimore Orioles for Outfielder-Catcher Curt Blefary; as part of deal Orioles assigned Outfielder John Mason from Elmira to Oklahoma City and Astros sent Infielder Enzo Hernandez from Oklahoma City to Stockton, December 4, 1968.

xUnconditionally released, December 21, 1976; signed as free agent by California Angels, January 18, 1977. Released, April 5, 1977.

## CHAMPIONSHIP SERIES RECORD

| Year Club | League | G. | IP. | W. | L. | Pct. | H. | R. | ER. | SO. | BB. | ERA. |
|---|---|---|---|---|---|---|---|---|---|---|---|---|
| 1969–Baltimore | American | 1 | 8 | 0 | 0 | .000 | 3 | 3 | 2 | 7 | 1 | 2.25 |
| 1970–Baltimore | American | 1 | 4⅓ | 0 | 0 | .000 | 10 | 6 | 6 | 2 | 1 | 12.46 |
| 1971–Baltimore | American | 1 | 9 | 1 | 0 | 1.000 | 6 | 1 | 1 | 2 | 1 | 1.00 |
| 1973–Baltimore | American | 1 | 10 | 0 | 1 | .000 | 4 | 2 | 2 | 11 | 3 | 1.80 |
| 1974–Baltimore | American | 2 | 12⅔ | 1 | 1 | .500 | 9 | 4 | 4 | 6 | 13 | 2.84 |
| Championship Series Totals | | 6 | 44 | 2 | 2 | .500 | 32 | 16 | 15 | 28 | 19 | 3.07 |

## WORLD SERIES RECORD

| Year Club | League | G. | IP. | W. | L. | Pct. | H. | R. | ER. | SO. | BB. | ERA. |
|---|---|---|---|---|---|---|---|---|---|---|---|---|
| 1969–Baltimore | American | 2 | 16 | 1 | 0 | 1.000 | 13 | 2 | 2 | 13 | 4 | 1.13 |
| 1970–Baltimore | American | 2 | 11⅓ | 1 | 0 | 1.000 | 11 | 7 | 4 | 5 | 2 | 3.18 |
| 1971–Baltimore | American | 2 | 14 | 0 | 2 | .000 | 11 | 7 | 6 | 10 | 6 | 3.86 |
| World Series Totals | | 6 | 41⅓ | 2 | 2 | .500 | 34 | 16 | 12 | 28 | 12 | 2.61 |

## ALL-STAR GAME RECORD

| Year League | | IP. | W. | L. | Pct. | H. | R. | ER. | SO. | BB. | ERA. |
|---|---|---|---|---|---|---|---|---|---|---|---|
| 1967–National | | 2 | 0 | 0 | .000 | 1 | 0 | 0 | 2 | 0 | 0.00 |
| 1971–American | | 2 | 0 | 0 | .000 | 1 | 0 | 0 | 2 | 1 | 0.00 |
| All-Star Game Totals | | 4 | 0 | 0 | .000 | 2 | 0 | 0 | 4 | 1 | 0.00 |

Member of American League All-Star Team in 1970 and 1974 games; did not play.

## ROBERT CUELLAR
### (Bobby)

Born August 20, 1952, at Allice, Texas.
Height, 5.11. Weight, 188.
Throws and bats righthanded.
Hobbies–Golf and pool.
Attended University of Texas at Austin, Austin, Tex.

Led Carolina League in saves with 17 in 1975.

| Year Club | League | G. | IP. | W. | L. | Pct. | H. | R. | ER. | SO. | BB. | ERA. |
|---|---|---|---|---|---|---|---|---|---|---|---|---|
| 1974–Sarasota Rangers | Gulf Coast | 5 | 8 | 0 | 0 | .000 | 11 | 4 | 3 | 10 | 1 | 3.38 |
| 1974–Gastonia | W. Carol. | 17 | 20 | 4 | 1 | .800 | 15 | 11 | 8 | 22 | 10 | 3.60 |
| 1975–Lynchburg | Carolina | 49 | 91 | 9 | 4 | .692 | 70 | 32 | 26 | 73 | 55 | 2.57 |
| 1976–San Antonio | Texas | 48 | 85 | 9 | 5 | .643 | 67 | 30 | 25 | 63 | 31 | 2.65 |

Listed on Texas Rangers' 1977 spring roster.

## JOHN DUFFIELD CURTIS

Born March 9, 1948, at Newton, Mass.
Height, 6.02. Weight, 185.
Throws and bats lefthanded.
Hobbies–Reading and amateur photography.
Attended Clemson University, Clemson, S. C.; received Bachelor of Arts degree in English.

| Year Club | League | G. | IP. | W. | L. | Pct. | H. | R. | ER. | SO. | BB. | ERA. |
|---|---|---|---|---|---|---|---|---|---|---|---|---|
| 1968–Winston-Salem ...............Carolina | | 16 | 103 | 6 | 8 | .429 | 82 | 49 | 39 | 101 | 41 | 3.41 |
| 1969–Greenville ..........................W. Carol. | | 25 | 149 | 6 | *12 | .333 | 141 | *91 | *74 | *158 | *97 | 4.47 |
| 1970–Pawtucket...........................Eastern | | 21 | 138 | 9 | 8 | .529 | 113 | 65 | 57 | 114 | 75 | 3.72 |
| 1970–Boston ................................American | | 1 | 2 | 0 | 0 | .000 | 4 | 4 | 3 | 1 | 1 | 13.50 |
| 1971–Louisville ..........................Int'national | | 27 | 187 | 10 | 12 | .455 | 167 | 99 | 71 | 165 | *111 | 3.42 |
| 1971–Boston ................................American | | 5 | 26 | 2 | 2 | .500 | 30 | 9 | 9 | 19 | 6 | 3.12 |
| 1972–Louisville ..........................Int'national | | 8 | 67 | 4 | 3 | .571 | 55 | 19 | 15 | 64 | 27 | 2.01 |
| 1972–Boston ................................American | | 26 | 154 | 11 | 8 | .579 | 161 | 69 | 64 | 106 | 50 | 3.74 |
| 1973–Boston† ...............................American | | 35 | 221 | 13 | 13 | .500 | 225 | 103 | 88 | 101 | 83 | 3.58 |
| 1974–St. Louis .............................National | | 33 | 195 | 10 | 14 | .417 | 199 | 91 | 82 | 89 | 83 | 3.78 |
| 1975–St. Louis .............................National | | 39 | 147 | 8 | 9 | .471 | 151 | 70 | 56 | 67 | 65 | 3.43 |
| 1976–St. Louis‡ ...........................National | | 37 | 134 | 6 | 11 | .353 | 139 | 68 | 67 | 52 | 65 | 4.50 |
| American League Totals.......................... | | 67 | 403 | 26 | 23 | .531 | 420 | 185 | 164 | 227 | 140 | 3.66 |
| National League Totals........................... | | 109 | 476 | 24 | 34 | .414 | 489 | 229 | 205 | 208 | 213 | 3.88 |
| Major League Totals ............................. | | 176 | 879 | 50 | 57 | .467 | 909 | 414 | 369 | 435 | 353 | 3.78 |

†Traded with Pitchers Mike Garman and Lynn McGlothen to St. Louis Cardinals for Infielder Terry Hughes and Pitchers Reggie Cleveland and Diego Segui, December 7, 1973.

‡Traded with Outfielder Willie Crawford and Infielder-Outfielder Vic Harris to San Francisco Giants for Pitchers John D'Acquisto and Mike Caldwell and Catcher Dave Rader, October 20, 1976.


## JOHN FRANCIS D'ACQUISTO

Name pronounced dee-uh-KWISS-toh.

Born December 24, 1951, at San Diego, Calif.
Height, 6.03. Weight, 205.
Throws and bats righthanded.
Hobbies–Hunting and fishing.
Cousin of Lou Marone, former pitcher with Pittsburgh Pirates.

Pitched seven-inning, 7-0 no-hit victory against Tacoma, May 16, 1973.
Led Pacific Coast League pitchers in games started with 31 and hit batsmen with 11 in 1973.
Led California League in complete games with 17 and tied for lead in hit batsmen with 15 in 1972.
Led Midwest League pitchers in games started with 29 in 1971.
Tied for Pacific Coast League lead in shutouts with 4 and tied for lead in complete games with 14 in 1973.
Named National League Rookie Pitcher of the Year by THE SPORTING NEWS, 1974.

| Year Club | League | G. | IP. | W. | L. | Pct. | H. | R. | ER. | SO. | BB. | ERA. |
|---|---|---|---|---|---|---|---|---|---|---|---|---|
| 1970–Great Falls ..........................Pioneer | | 12 | 55 | 2 | 5 | .286 | 33 | 46 | 32 | 84 | *74 | 5.24 |
| 1971–Decatur...............................Midwest | | 31 | *233 | 10 | ●13 | .435 | *178 | *98 | *81 | *244 | *124 | 3.13 |
| 1972–Fresno ................................California | | 27 | 209 | 17 | 6 | .739 | 184 | 94 | 77 | *245 | 102 | 3.32 |
| 1973–Phoenix...............................P. Coast | | 31 | *212 | 16 | 12 | .571 | 186 | 97 | 84 | 185 | *113 | 3.57 |
| 1973–San Francisco ....................National | | 7 | 28 | 1 | 1 | .500 | 23 | 14 | 11 | 29 | 19 | 3.54 |
| 1974–San Francisco ....................National | | 38 | 215 | 12 | 14 | .462 | 182 | 101 | 90 | 167 | 124 | 3.77 |
| 1975–San Francisco† ..................National | | 10 | 28 | 2 | 4 | .333 | 29 | 35 | 32 | 22 | 34 | 10.29 |
| 1976–San Francisco‡ ..................National | | 28 | 106 | 3 | 8 | .273 | 93 | 69 | 63 | 53 | 102 | 5.35 |
| Major League Totals ............................. | | 83 | 377 | 18 | 27 | .400 | 327 | 219 | 196 | 271 | 279 | 4.68 |

†On disabled list, May 25 to September 2, 1975.

‡Traded with Pitcher Mike Caldwell and Catcher Dave Rader to St. Louis Cardinals for Outfielder Willie Crawford, Infielder-Outfielder Vic Harris and Pitcher John Curtis, October 20, 1976.


## LONNIE PAUL DADE

(Known by middle name.)

Born December 7, 1951, at Seattle, Wash.
Height, 6.01. Weight, 185.
Throws and bats righthanded.
Hobbies–Sports, music and traveling.

Led Pacific Coast League in double plays by third basemen with 41 in 1974.

| Year Club | League | Pos. | G. | AB. | R. | H. | 2B. | 3B. | HR. | RBI. | B.A. | PO. | A. | E. | F.A. |
|---|---|---|---|---|---|---|---|---|---|---|---|---|---|---|---|
| 1970–Idaho Falls† ......Pion. | | 3B | 46 | 158 | 28 | 48 | 7 | 5 | 1 | 35 | .304 | 44 | 84 | 16 | .889 |
| 1971–Shreveport ........Texas | | 3B | 14 | 45 | 10 | 11 | 0 | 2 | 1 | 5 | .244 | 10 | 21 | 3 | .912 |
| 1971–Quad Cities ......Midw. | | 3B | 101 | 355 | 57 | 114 | 21 | 2 | 2 | 51 | .321 | 81 | 166 | 17 | *.936 |
| 1972–Shreveport ........Texas | | 3-O-S-2 | 131 | 491 | 70 | 133 | 15 | 2 | 8 | 55 | .271 | 145 | 209 | 29 | .924 |
| 1973–El Paso ...........Texas | | 2B-SS | 83 | 298 | 51 | 84 | 13 | 4 | 6 | 57 | .282 | 175 | 185 | 21 | .945 |
| 1973–Salt Lake City ..P. C. | | 3B-SS | 41 | 119 | 18 | 34 | 7 | 1 | 1 | 17 | .286 | 24 | 69 | 12 | .886 |
| 1974–Salt Lake City ..P. C. | | *3B-SS | 134 | 504 | 71 | 149 | 21 | 7 | 3 | 53 | .296 | 102 | *275 | 27 | .933 |
| 1975–El Paso‡...........Tex. | | 2B-3B | 100 | 343 | 66 | 114 | 23 | 5 | 16 | 84 | .332 | 155 | 268 | 26 | .942 |
| 1975–Salt Lake City ..P. C. | | 3B-SS | 9 | 33 | 12 | 18 | 5 | 1 | 3 | 14 | .545 | 3 | 8 | 2 | .846 |
| 1975–California .........Amer. | | OF-3B | 11 | 30 | 5 | 6 | 4 | 0 | 0 | 1 | .200 | 8 | 1 | 0 | 1.000 |
| 1976–El Paso‡ ..........P. C. | | 3-2B-OF | 91 | 320 | 66 | 116 | 18 | 4 | 6 | 65 | *.363 | 59 | 133 | 12 | .941 |
| 1976–California§ ........Amer. | | O-2-3-DH | 13 | 9 | 2 | 1 | 0 | 0 | 0 | 1 | .111 | 5 | 4 | 1 | .900 |
| Major League Totals ..................... | | | 24 | 39 | 7 | 7 | 4 | 0 | 0 | 2 | .179 | 13 | 5 | 1 | .947 |

†On temporary inactive list, June 25 through July 5, 1970.

‡On disabled list, May 7 to May 26, 1975.

§Played out option year and granted free agency, November 1, 1976; signed as free agent by Cleveland Indians, February 7, 1977.

## JOHN BRUCE DAL CANTON

(Known by middle name.)

Born June 15, 1942, at California, Pa.
Height, 6.02. Weight, 208.
Throws and bats righthanded.
Hobby—Golf.
Attended California State College, California, Pa., and University of West Virginia,
Morgantown, W. Va.; received Bachelor of Science degree in Education
and Master's Degree in Biology.
Led American League in wild pitches with 16 in 1974.

| Year Club | League | G. | IP. | W. | L. | Pct. | H. | R. | ER. | SO. | BB. | ERA. |
|---|---|---|---|---|---|---|---|---|---|---|---|---|
| 1966—Columbus | Int'national | 14 | 33 | 1 | 1 | .500 | 46 | 15 | 14 | 17 | 16 | 3.82 |
| 1966—Asheville | Southern | 5 | 34 | 2 | 1 | .667 | 31 | 16 | 13 | 21 | 10 | 3.44 |
| 1967—Macon | Southern | 14 | 93 | 5 | 5 | .500 | 73 | 37 | 32 | 68 | 23 | 3.10 |
| 1967—Pittsburgh | National | 8 | 24 | 2 | 1 | .667 | 19 | 5 | 5 | 13 | 10 | 1.88 |
| 1968—Columbus | Int'national | 11 | 24 | 0 | 4 | .000 | 33 | 25 | 22 | 15 | 12 | 8.25 |
| 1968—York | Eastern | 11 | 71 | 5 | 2 | .714 | 59 | 21 | 18 | 52 | 23 | 2.28 |
| 1968—Pittsburgh | National | 7 | 17 | 1 | 1 | .500 | 7 | 4 | 4 | 8 | 6 | 2.12 |
| 1969—Pittsburgh | National | 57 | 86 | 8 | 2 | .800 | 79 | 34 | 32 | 56 | 49 | 3.35 |
| 1970—Pittsburgh† | National | 41 | 85 | 9 | 4 | .692 | 94 | 48 | 43 | 53 | 39 | 4.55 |
| 1971—Kansas City‡ | American | 25 | 141 | 8 | 6 | .571 | 144 | 63 | 54 | 58 | 44 | 3.45 |
| 1972—Kansas City | American | 35 | 132 | 6 | 6 | .500 | 135 | 54 | 50 | 75 | 29 | 3.41 |
| 1973—Kansas City | American | 32 | 97 | 4 | 3 | .571 | 108 | 60 | 52 | 38 | 46 | 4.82 |
| 1974—Kansas City | American | 31 | 175 | 8 | 10 | .444 | 135 | 71 | 61 | 96 | 82 | 3.14 |
| 1975—Kansas City§ | American | 4 | 9 | 0 | 2 | .000 | 23 | 18 | 15 | 5 | 7 | 15.00 |
| 1975—Atlanta | National | 26 | 67 | 2 | 7 | .222 | 63 | 33 | 25 | 38 | 24 | 3.36 |
| 1976—Atlanta x | National | 42 | 73 | 3 | 5 | .375 | 67 | 41 | 29 | 36 | 42 | 3.58 |
| National League Totals | | 181 | 352 | 25 | 20 | .556 | 329 | 165 | 138 | 204 | 170 | 3.53 |
| American League Totals | | 127 | 554 | 26 | 27 | .491 | 545 | 266 | 232 | 272 | 208 | 3.77 |
| Major League Totals | | 308 | 906 | 51 | 47 | .521 | 874 | 431 | 370 | 476 | 378 | 3.68 |

†Traded with Shortstop Freddie Patek and Catcher Jerry May to Kansas City Royals for Pitcher Bob Johnson, Shortstop Jackie Hernandez and Catcher Jim Campanis, December 2, 1970.
‡On disabled list, August 4 through September 1, 1971.
§Released on waivers to Atlanta Braves, June 20, 1975; Royals traded Pitchers Al Autry and Norm Angelini to Braves for Pitcher Ray Sadecki, September 4, 1975, to complete deal.
xReleased, March 30, 1977; signed as free agent by Chicago White Sox, April 4, 1977.

## PATRICK LEONARD DARCY
### (Pat)

Born May 12, 1950, at Troy, O.
Height, 6.04. Weight, 200.
Throws right and bats lefthanded.
Hobbies—Swimming, golf and tennis.
Attended Mesa Community College, Mesa, Ariz., Arizona State University,
Tempe, Ariz., and University of Arizona, Tucson, Ariz.
Pitched 2-0 no hit victory against Charlotte, August 29, 1971.

| Year Club | League | G. | IP. | W. | L. | Pct. | H. | R. | ER. | SO. | BB. | ERA. |
|---|---|---|---|---|---|---|---|---|---|---|---|---|
| 1969—Covington | Ap'lachian | 7 | 28 | 2 | 2 | .500 | 29 | 18 | 17 | 21 | 9 | 5.46 |
| 1970—Williamsport† | NYP | 9 | 56 | 4 | 3 | .571 | 42 | 28 | 23 | 56 | 36 | 3.70 |
| 1970—Raleigh-Durham | Carolina | 4 | 27 | 1 | 2 | .333 | 25 | 7 | 4 | 11 | 14 | 1.33 |
| 1971—Columbus | Southern | 27 | 123 | 5 | 10 | .333 | 110 | 49 | 35 | 100 | 70 | 2.56 |
| 1972—Columbus | Southern | 20 | 129 | 8 | 8 | .500 | 127 | 66 | 49 | 99 | 50 | 3.42 |
| 1972—Oklahoma City | Am. Assoc. | 3 | 16 | 1 | 0 | 1.000 | 8 | 1 | 0 | 18 | 1 | 0.00 |
| 1973—Denver‡§ | Am. Assoc. | 20 | 111 | 5 | 9 | .357 | 101 | 51 | 44 | 76 | 55 | 3.57 |
| 1974—Indianapolis | Am. Assoc. | 26 | 161 | 12 | 7 | .632 | 156 | 71 | 61 | 97 | 71 | 3.41 |
| 1974—Cincinnati | National | 6 | 17 | 1 | 0 | 1.000 | 17 | 7 | 7 | 14 | 8 | 3.71 |
| 1975—Cincinnati | National | 27 | 131 | 11 | 5 | .688 | 134 | 54 | 52 | 46 | 59 | 3.57 |
| 1976—Cincinnati | National | 11 | 39 | 2 | 3 | .400 | 41 | 27 | 27 | 15 | 22 | 6.23 |
| 1976—Indianapolis x | Am. Assoc. | 16 | 103 | 5 | 7 | .417 | 95 | 53 | 49 | 58 | 59 | 4.28 |
| Major League Totals | | 44 | 187 | 14 | 8 | .636 | 192 | 88 | 86 | 75 | 89 | 4.14 |

†On restricted list from beginning of season until June 17.
‡On disabled list, June 4 to June 23, 1973.
§Traded with a player to be named later by Houston Astros to Cincinnati Reds for Infielder Denis Menke, February 18, 1974.
xTraded to St. Louis Cardinals for Pitcher Mike Caldwell, March 29, 1977.

### WORLD SERIES RECORD

| Year Club | League | G. | IP. | W. | L. | Pct. | H. | R. | ER. | SO. | BB. | ERA. |
|---|---|---|---|---|---|---|---|---|---|---|---|---|
| 1975—Cincinnati | National | 2 | 4 | 0 | 1 | .000 | 3 | 2 | 2 | 1 | 2 | 4.50 |

## MICHAEL EDWARD DARR

Born March 23, 1956, at Pomona, Calif.
Height, 6.04. Weight, 190.
Throws and bats righthanded.

| Year Club | League | G. | IP. | W. | L. | Pct. | H. | R. | ER. | SO. | BB. | ERA. |
|---|---|---|---|---|---|---|---|---|---|---|---|---|
| 1974–Bluefield | Ap'lachian | 13 | 82 | 5 | 5 | .500 | 46 | 45 | 34 | 104 | 83 | 3.73 |
| 1975–Miami | Florida St. | 14 | 78 | 2 | 6 | .250 | 69 | 43 | 39 | 62 | 48 | 4.50 |
| 1975–Lodi | California | 7 | 35 | 2 | 2 | .500 | 30 | 21 | 20 | 35 | 27 | 5.14 |
| 1976–Charlotte† | Southern | 27 | 177 | 12 | 12 | .500 | 153 | 86 | 76 | 98 | *120 | 3.86 |

†Selected by Toronto Blue Jays from Baltimore Orioles in expansion draft, November 5, 1976.

## ARTHUR BOBBY LEE DARWIN
### (Bob)

Born February 16, 1943, at Los Angeles, Calif.
Height, 6.02. Weight, 200.
Throws and bats righthanded.

Tied American League record for most times four or more strikeouts, game, season, 5, May 12-June 23-July 14-August 6-August 10, 1972.
Led American League batters in strikeouts with 145 in 1972, 137 in 1973 and 127 in 1974.
Tied for Pacific Coast League lead in double plays by outfielders with 3 in 1971.
Received reported $40,000 bonus to sign with Los Angeles Angels, 1962.

| Year Club | League | Pos. | G. | AB. | R. | H. | 2B. | 3B. | HR. | RBI. | B.A. | PO. | A. | E. | F.A. |
|---|---|---|---|---|---|---|---|---|---|---|---|---|---|---|---|
| 1966–Stockton | Calif. | OF-P | 53 | 122 | 14 | 35 | 3 | 4 | 6 | 23 | .287 | 20 | 0 | 3 | .870 |
| 1969–Spokane | P. C. | P-OF | 21 | 25 | 2 | 4 | 1 | 0 | 0 | 1 | .160 | 5 | 12 | 2 | .895 |
| 1970–Bakersfield† | Calif. | OF-1B | 86 | 303 | 52 | 90 | 9 | 1 | 23 | 70 | .297 | 140 | 9 | 5 | .968 |
| 1971–Spokane | P. C. | OF-P | 91 | 321 | 53 | 94 | 13 | 4 | 17 | 55 | .293 | 145 | 10 | •10 | .939 |
| 1971–Los Angeles‡ | Nat. | OF | 11 | 20 | 2 | 5 | 1 | 0 | 1 | 4 | .250 | 9 | 0 | 0 | 1.000 |
| 1972–Minnesota | Amer. | OF | 145 | 513 | 48 | 137 | 20 | 2 | 22 | 80 | .267 | 289 | 8 | 6 | .980 |
| 1973–Minnesota | Amer. | OF | 145 | 560 | 69 | 141 | 20 | 2 | 18 | 90 | .252 | 233 | 13 | 5 | .980 |
| 1974–Minnesota | Amer. | OF | 152 | 575 | 67 | 152 | 13 | 7 | 25 | 94 | .264 | 254 | 8 | 8 | .970 |
| 1975–Minn.§-Milw.x | Amer. | OF | 103 | 355 | 45 | 83 | 12 | 2 | 13 | 41 | .234 | 110 | 8 | 3 | .975 |
| 1976–Milw.y-Bos. | Amer. | OF-DH | 68 | 179 | 15 | 37 | 8 | 3 | 4 | 18 | .207 | 68 | 2 | 2 | .972 |
| American League Totals | | | 613 | 2182 | 244 | 550 | 73 | 16 | 82 | 323 | .252 | 954 | 39 | 24 | .976 |
| National League Totals | | | 11 | 20 | 2 | 5 | 1 | 0 | 1 | 4 | .250 | 9 | 0 | 0 | 1.000 |
| Major League Totals | | | 624 | 2202 | 246 | 555 | 74 | 16 | 83 | 327 | .252 | 963 | 39 | 24 | .977 |

†On disabled list, May 25 through June 22, 1970.
‡Traded to Minnesota Twins for Outfielder Paul Powell, October 22, 1971.
§Traded to Milwaukee Brewers for Outfielder-First Baseman John Briggs, June 14, 1975.
xOn supplemental disabled list, August 3 to September 5, 1975.
yTraded with Pitcher Tom Murphy to Boston Red Sox for Outfielder Bernie Carbo and cash, June 3, 1976.

### PITCHING RECORD

Led California League in wild pitches with 25 in 1964.

| Year Club | League | G. | IP. | W. | L. | Pct. | H. | R. | ER. | SO. | BB. | ERA. |
|---|---|---|---|---|---|---|---|---|---|---|---|---|
| 1962–San Jose | California | 26 | 153 | 11 | 6 | .647 | 123 | 98 | 70 | 202 | 149 | 4.12 |
| 1962–Los Angeles | American | 1 | 3 | 0 | 1 | .000 | 8 | 6 | 4 | 6 | 4 | 12.00 |
| 1963–Honolulu† | P. Coast | 3 | 13 | 0 | 1 | .000 | 12 | 7 | 7 | 8 | 15 | 4.85 |
| 1963–Stockton‡ | California | 5 | 28 | 4 | 0 | 1.000 | 12 | 7 | 5 | 24 | 21 | 1.61 |
| 1964–Stockton | California | 22 | 100 | 2 | 11 | .154 | 97 | 70 | 52 | 118 | 77 | 4.68 |
| 1965–Elmira | Eastern | 22 | 111 | 9 | 10 | .474 | 86 | 54 | 48 | 89 | 74 | 3.89 |
| 1966–Elmira§ | Eastern | 5 | 16 | 1 | 2 | .333 | 14 | 13 | 13 | 9 | 21 | 7.31 |
| 1966–Stockton | California | 8 | 38 | 1 | 4 | .200 | 36 | 24 | 17 | 25 | 31 | 4.03 |
| 1967–Elmira x | Eastern | 19 | 73 | 4 | 4 | .500 | 54 | 31 | 28 | 36 | 56 | 3.45 |
| 1968–Elmira y | Eastern | 23 | 163 | 10 | 6 | .625 | 118 | 46 | 40 | 112 | 65 | 2.21 |
| 1969–Los Angeles | National | 3 | 4 | 0 | 0 | .000 | 4 | 4 | 4 | 0 | 5 | 9.00 |
| 1969–Spokane | P. Coast | 17 | 61 | 0 | 6 | .000 | 81 | 54 | 44 | 56 | 27 | 6.49 |
| 1971–Spokane | P. Coast | 3 | 5 | 0 | 0 | .000 | 3 | 0 | 0 | 7 | 1 | 0.00 |
| American League Totals | | 1 | 3 | 0 | 1 | .000 | 8 | 6 | 4 | 6 | 4 | 12.00 |
| National League Totals | | 3 | 4 | 0 | 0 | .000 | 4 | 4 | 4 | 0 | 5 | 9.00 |
| Major League Totals | | 4 | 7 | 0 | 1 | .000 | 12 | 10 | 8 | 6 | 9 | 10.29 |

†Claimed on first-year player waivers from Los Angeles Angels by Baltimore Orioles, May 15, 1963.
‡On disabled list, June 30 through August 20, 1963.
§On disabled list, May 22 through June 2, 1966.
xOn disabled list, July 14 through August 2, 1967.
yDrafted by Los Angeles Dodgers from Rochester (Baltimore Orioles' organization), December 2, 1968.

## RICHARD FREMONT DAUER
### (Rich)

Born July 27, 1952, at San Bernardino, Calif.
Height, 6.00. Weight, 180.
Throws and bats righthanded.
Attended San Bernardino Valley College, San Bernardino, Calif., and
University of Southern California, Los Angeles, Calif.

Named International League Most Valuable Player in 1976.

| Year Club | League | Pos. | G. | AB. | R. | H. | 2B. | 3B. | HR. | RBI. | B.A. | PO. | A. | E. | F.A. |
|---|---|---|---|---|---|---|---|---|---|---|---|---|---|---|---|
| 1974–Asheville | South. | 2B-3B | 53 | 180 | 30 | 59 | 7 | 0 | 11 | 35 | .328 | 72 | 104 | 3 | .983 |
| 1975–Rochester | Int. | 2B-3B | 18 | 47 | 2 | 8 | 1 | 0 | 0 | 0 | .170 | 17 | 30 | 2 | .959 |
| 1975–Asheville | South. | 3B-2B | 106 | 374 | 51 | 94 | 13 | 0 | 6 | 44 | .251 | 98 | 195 | 6 | *.980 |

| Year Club League | Pos. | G. | AB. | R. | H. | 2B. | 3B. | HR. | RBI. | B.A. | PO. | A. | E. | F.A. |
|---|---|---|---|---|---|---|---|---|---|---|---|---|---|---|
| 1976—Rochester..........Int. | *2B-O-1 | 132 | *524 | 84 | *176 | 26 | 3 | 11 | 78 | *.336 | 276 | 402 | 18 | *.974 |
| 1976—Baltimore..........Amer. | 2B | 11 | 39 | 0 | 4 | 0 | 0 | 0 | 3 | .103 | 22 | 22 | 0 | 1.000 |
| Major League Totals ..................... | | 11 | 39 | 0 | 4 | 0 | 0 | 0 | 3 | .103 | 22 | 22 | 0 | 1.000 |

## FRANK GERALD DaVANON
### (Jerry)

Born August 21, 1945, at Oceanside, Calif.
Height, 5.11. Weight, 175.
Throws and bats righthanded.
Hobbies—Hunting, fishing and spectator sports.
Attended San Diego City College, San Diego, Calif., San Diego Mesa College, San Diego, Calif., and Westmont College, Santa Barbara, Calif.; received Bachelor of Science degree in Sociology.
Led Florida State League shortstops in double plays with 66 in 1967.

| Year Club League | Pos. | G. | AB. | R. | H. | 2B. | 3B. | HR. | RBI. | B.A. | PO. | A. | E. | F.A. |
|---|---|---|---|---|---|---|---|---|---|---|---|---|---|---|
| 1966—Arkansas ..........Texas | 2B | 8 | 26 | 5 | 9 | 0 | 0 | 0 | 1 | .346 | 22 | 15 | 2 | .949 |
| 1966—Sarasota Cards ..Gulf C. | 2B | 19 | 70 | 10 | 22 | 1 | 2 | 0 | 5 | .314 | 34 | 57 | 4 | .958 |
| 1966—St. Petersburg ..Fla. St. | 2-3-S-O | 15 | 41 | 7 | 17 | 1 | 1 | 0 | 4 | .415 | 20 | 33 | 2 | .964 |
| 1967—St. Petersburg ..Fla. St. | *SS-2 | 133 | 465 | 73 | 117 | 10 | 4 | 3 | 51 | .252 | 255 | 395 | *50 | .929 |
| 1968—Arkansas† ........Texas | *SS-2 | 130 | 425 | 73 | 108 | 16 | 1 | 2 | 32 | .254 | *200 | 337 | ●36 | .937 |
| 1969—S. Diego‡-St. L. Nat. | SS-2B | 40 | 99 | 11 | 20 | 4 | 0 | 1 | 10 | .202 | 63 | 86 | 8 | .949 |
| 1969—Tulsa .................A. A. | 2-S-3 | 70 | 263 | 33 | 74 | 15 | 5 | 1 | 35 | .281 | 87 | 268 | 15 | .959 |
| 1970—Tulsa§ .............A. A. | 2-SS-1 | 76 | 254 | 33 | 59 | 9 | 3 | 3 | 27 | .232 | 169 | 238 | 19 | .955 |
| 1970—St. Louis x ........Nat. | 3B-2B | 11 | 18 | 2 | 2 | 1 | 0 | 0 | 0 | .111 | 8 | 14 | 0 | 1.000 |
| 1971—Baltimore..........Amer. | 2-S-3-1 | 38 | 81 | 14 | 19 | 5 | 0 | 0 | 4 | .235 | 45 | 59 | 4 | .963 |
| 1972—Rochester y ......Int. | 2B-SS | 50 | 180 | 16 | 37 | 7 | 1 | 1 | 18 | .206 | 99 | 145 | 14 | .946 |
| 1972—Salt Lake City ..P. C. | 2-3-S-O | 57 | 178 | 28 | 49 | 10 | 2 | 1 | 17 | .275 | 81 | 123 | 17 | .923 |
| 1973—California..........Amer. | S-2-3 | 41 | 49 | 6 | 12 | 3 | 0 | 0 | 2 | .245 | 29 | 45 | 6 | .925 |
| 1973—Salt Lake City z P. C. | 2B-SS | 29 | 116 | 19 | 35 | 6 | 0 | 1 | 7 | .302 | 77 | 86 | 7 | .959 |
| 1974—Tulsa .................A. A. | 3-2-S | 79 | 304 | 48 | 84 | 14 | 4 | 8 | 34 | .276 | 51 | 167 | 21 | .912 |
| 1974—St. Louis a-b......Nat. | S-3-2-O | 30 | 40 | 4 | 6 | 1 | 0 | 0 | 4 | .150 | 19 | 35 | 5 | .915 |
| 1975—Iowa c .............A. A. | 3-2-S-1 | 90 | 309 | 53 | 96 | 17 | 3 | 0 | 34 | .311 | 92 | 192 | 19 | .937 |
| 1975—Houston ............Nat. | S-2-3 | 32 | 97 | 15 | 27 | 4 | 2 | 1 | 10 | .278 | 54 | 94 | 7 | .955 |
| 1976—Houston d............Nat. | S-2-3 | 61 | 107 | 19 | 31 | 3 | 3 | 1 | 20 | .290 | 53 | 94 | 7 | .955 |
| National League Totals .................. | | 174 | 361 | 51 | 86 | 13 | 5 | 3 | 44 | .238 | 197 | 323 | 27 | .951 |
| American League Totals ............... | | 79 | 130 | 20 | 31 | 8 | 0 | 0 | 6 | .238 | 74 | 104 | 10 | .947 |
| Major League Totals ..................... | | 253 | 491 | 71 | 117 | 21 | 5 | 3 | 50 | .238 | 271 | 427 | 37 | .950 |

†Recalled by St. Louis Cardinals; selected by San Diego Padres from St. Louis in expansion draft, October 14, 1968.
‡Traded with First Baseman Bill Davis (assigned to Tulsa) to St. Louis Cardinals for Shortstop John Sipin and Catcher Sonny Ruberto, May 22, 1969.
§On disabled list, July 7 through August 7, 1970.
xTraded to Baltimore Orioles for Pitcher Moe Drabowsky, November 30, 1970.
yRecalled by Baltimore Orioles; released to Salt Lake City in trade which sent Outfielder Roger Repoz from California to Rochester, June 6.
zTraded by Salt Lake City (California Angels' organization) to Tulsa (St. Louis Cardinals' organization) for Infielder-Outfielder Bill Stein, September 25, 1973.
aSold to Detroit Tigers, January 3, 1975.
bReleased by Detroit Tigers, January 23, 1975; signed as a free agent by Cleveland Indians, February 19, 1975. Sold by Cleveland Indians to Houston Astros, April 9, 1975.
cOn disabled list, June 20 to July 2, 1975.
dTraded with Pitcher Larry Dierker to St. Louis Cardinals for Catcher-Outfielder Joe Ferguson and Outfielder Bobby Detherage, latter assigned to Memphis, November 23, 1976.

## RICHARD EARL DAVIS
### (Dick)

Born September 25, 1953, at Long Beach, Calif.
Height, 6.03. Weight, 190.
Throws and bats righthanded.
Hobby—Music.
Attended Snow College, Ephraim, Utah.
Cousin of Enos Cabell, infielder with Houston Astros' 1975-76.

| Year Club League | Pos. | G. | AB. | R. | H. | 2B. | 3B. | HR. | RBI. | B.A. | PO. | A. | E. | F.A. |
|---|---|---|---|---|---|---|---|---|---|---|---|---|---|---|
| 1972—Newark ............NYP | OF | 37 | 139 | 16 | 40 | 7 | 1 | 1 | 18 | .288 | 41 | 1 | 2 | .955 |
| 1973—Danville ...........Midw. | OF | 101 | 365 | 57 | 100 | 13 | 6 | 8 | 43 | .274 | 138 | 3 | 5 | .966 |
| 1974—Danville ...........Midw. | OF | 114 | 451 | 76 | 118 | 17 | 7 | 11 | 38 | .262 | 161 | 10 | 9 | .950 |
| 1975—Thetford Mines..East | OF | 132 | 455 | 66 | 115 | 23 | 1 | *16 | 67 | .253 | 124 | 4 | 10 | .928 |
| 1976—Pittsfield ..........East. | OF | 126 | 470 | 70 | 136 | 24 | 1 | 16 | 69 | .289 | 157 | 4 | 4 | .976 |

Listed on Milwaukee Brewers' 1977 spring roster.

---

**DID YOU KNOW —**
That the first major league night game was played at Cincinnati on May 24, 1935?

## ROBERT JOHN EUGENE DAVIS
### (Bob)

Born March 1, 1952, at Pryor, Okla.
Height, 6.00. Weight, 190.
Throws and bats righthanded.
Hobbies—Snake hunting and deer hunting.
Attended Northeastern State College, Tahlequah, Okla., and
Claremore Junior College, Claremore, Okla.

Tied for Northwest League lead in total bases with 159 and in sacrifice flies with 6 in 1971.

| Year Club | League | Pos. | G. | AB. | R. | H. | 2B. | 3B. | HR. | RBI. | B.A. | PO. | A. | E. | F.A. |
|---|---|---|---|---|---|---|---|---|---|---|---|---|---|---|---|
| 1970—Tri-City ............ | N'west | *3-2 | 77 | 279 | 58 | 82 | 14 | 3 | 11 | 48 | .294 | *102 | 132 | 28 | .893 |
| 1971—Lodi ................. | Calif. | 1-O-C | 21 | 54 | 6 | 9 | 1 | 0 | 2 | 5 | .167 | 96 | 3 | 1 | .990 |
| 1971—Tri-City ............ | N'west | C-O-2-3 | 75 | 296 | 54 | 97 | 12 | 4 | •14 | *83 | .328 | 318 | 53 | 7 | .981 |
| 1972—Alexandria† ......| Texas | 2-C-1-3 | 54 | 165 | 16 | 35 | 5 | 0 | 4 | 21 | .212 | 140 | 94 | 6 | .975 |
| 1973—San Diego.......... | Nat. | C | 5 | 11 | 1 | 1 | 0 | 0 | 0 | 0 | .091 | 32 | 0 | 2 | .941 |
| 1973—Alexandria ........ | Texas | C-1-O | 118 | 421 | 58 | 119 | 16 | 2 | 12 | 58 | .283 | 839 | 102 | 12 | .987 |
| 1974—Hawaii‡ ............ | P.C. | C-O-1 | 77 | 244 | 32 | 56 | 6 | 2 | 5 | 30 | .230 | 415 | 45 | 9 | .981 |
| 1975—Hawaii .............. | P.C. | C | 94 | 331 | 45 | 109 | 19 | 4 | 6 | 69 | .329 | 499 | 54 | 9 | .984 |
| 1975—San Diego.......... | Nat. | C | 43 | 128 | 6 | 30 | 3 | 2 | 0 | 7 | .234 | 195 | 18 | 3 | .986 |
| 1976—San Diego.......... | Nat. | C | 51 | 83 | 7 | 17 | 0 | 1 | 0 | 5 | .205 | 120 | 19 | 5 | .965 |
| Major League Totals ...................... | | | 99 | 222 | 14 | 48 | 3 | 3 | 0 | 12 | .216 | 347 | 37 | 10 | .975 |

†On disabled list, May 1 through June 10, 1972.
‡On disabled list, July 30 through remainder of season.

## WILLIAM HENRY DAVIS
### (Willie)

Born April 15, 1940, at Mineral Springs, Ark.
Height, 6.02½. Weight, 185.
Throws and bats lefthanded.
Hobbies—Golf, hunting and music.

Tied National League record for fewest triples, season, for leader in triples, 10, in 1962.
Made six hits in one game, May 24, 1973, 19 innings.
Major League stolen bases: 1960 (3), 1961 (12), 1962 (32), 1963 (25), 1964 (41), 1965 (25), 1966 (21), 1967 (20), 1968 (36), 1969 (24), 1970 (38), 1971 (20), 1972 (20), 1973 (17), 1974 (25), 1975 (23), 1976 (14). Total—396.
Led California League in total bases with 304 in 1959.
Led Pacific Coast League in total bases with 347 and stolen bases with 30 in 1960.
Named outfielder on THE SPORTING NEWS National League All-Star Team, 1971.
Named outfielder on THE SPORTING NEWS National League All-Star fielding team, 1971, 1972 and 1973.
Named Minor League Player of the Year by THE SPORTING NEWS, 1960.

| Year Club | League | Pos. | G. | AB. | R. | H. | 2B. | 3B. | HR. | RBI. | B.A. | PO. | A. | E. | F.A. |
|---|---|---|---|---|---|---|---|---|---|---|---|---|---|---|---|
| 1959—Green Bay ........ | I.I.I. | OF | 7 | 30 | 5 | 4 | 0 | 0 | 0 | 1 | .133 | 12 | 2 | 0 | 1.000 |
| 1959—Reno ............... | Calif. | OF | 117 | 513 | *135 | *187 | *40 | *16 | 15 | 90 | *.365 | *302 | 10 | 11 | .966 |
| 1960—Spokane ........... | P.C. | OF | 147 | 624 | *126 | *216 | 43 | *26 | 12 | 75 | *.346 | 384 | 6 | •13 | .968 |
| 1960—Los Angeles ...... | Nat. | OF | 22 | 88 | 12 | 28 | 6 | 1 | 2 | 10 | .318 | 52 | 1 | 1 | .981 |
| 1961—Los Angeles ...... | Nat. | OF | 128 | 339 | 56 | 86 | 19 | 6 | 12 | 45 | .254 | 224 | 4 | 4 | .983 |
| 1962—Los Angeles ...... | Nat. | OF | 157 | 600 | 103 | 171 | 18 | •10 | 21 | 85 | .285 | 379 | 13 | *15 | .963 |
| 1963—Los Angeles ...... | Nat. | OF | 156 | 515 | 60 | 126 | 19 | 8 | 9 | 60 | .245 | 337 | 16 | 8 | .978 |
| 1964—Los Angeles ...... | Nat. | OF | 157 | 613 | 91 | 180 | 23 | 7 | 12 | 77 | .294 | *400 | 16 | 7 | .983 |
| 1965—Los Angeles ...... | Nat. | OF | 142 | 558 | 52 | 133 | 24 | 3 | 10 | 57 | .238 | 318 | 6 | 11 | .967 |
| 1966—Los Angeles ...... | Nat. | OF | 153 | 624 | 74 | 177 | 31 | 6 | 11 | 61 | .284 | 347 | 9 | 11 | .970 |
| 1967—Los Angeles ...... | Nat. | OF | 143 | 569 | 65 | 146 | 27 | 9 | 6 | 41 | .257 | 300 | 6 | 9 | .971 |
| 1968—Los Angeles ...... | Nat. | OF | 160 | 643 | 86 | 161 | 24 | 10 | 7 | 31 | .250 | 345 | 9 | 10 | .973 |
| 1969—Los Angeles ...... | Nat. | OF | 129 | 498 | 66 | 155 | 23 | 8 | 11 | 59 | .311 | 271 | 8 | 6 | .979 |
| 1970—Los Angeles ...... | Nat. | OF | 146 | 593 | 92 | 181 | 23 | •16 | 8 | 93 | .305 | 342 | 12 | 3 | .992 |
| 1971—Los Angeles ...... | Nat. | OF | 158 | 641 | 84 | 198 | 33 | 10 | 10 | 74 | .309 | *404 | 7 | 8 | .981 |
| 1972—Los Angeles ...... | Nat. | OF | 149 | 615 | 81 | 178 | 22 | 7 | 19 | 79 | .289 | 373 | 10 | 5 | .987 |
| 1973—Los Angeles† ...| Nat. | OF | 152 | 599 | 82 | 171 | 29 | 9 | 16 | 77 | .285 | 344 | 6 | 7 | .980 |
| 1974—Montreal‡........ | Nat. | OF | 153 | 611 | 86 | 180 | 27 | 9 | 12 | 89 | .295 | 369 | 8 | •12 | .969 |
| 1975—Texas§ .............. | Amer. | OF | 42 | 169 | 16 | 42 | 8 | 2 | 5 | 17 | .249 | 100 | 1 | 1 | .990 |
| 1975—St. Louis x ....... | Nat. | OF | 98 | 350 | 41 | 102 | 19 | 6 | 6 | 50 | .291 | 187 | 5 | 6 | .970 |
| 1976—San Diego.......... | Nat. | OF | 141 | 493 | 61 | 132 | 18 | 10 | 5 | 46 | .268 | 349 | 6 | 3 | .992 |
| National League Totals ................... | | 2344 | 8949 | 1192 | 2505 | 385 | 135 | 177 | 1034 | .280 | 5341 | 142 | 126 | .978 | |
| American League Totals ................ | | 42 | 169 | 16 | 42 | 8 | 2 | 5 | 17 | .249 | 100 | 1 | 1 | .990 | |
| Major League Totals ...................... | | 2386 | 9118 | 1208 | 2547 | 393 | 137 | 182 | 1051 | .279 | 5441 | 143 | 127 | .978 | |

†Traded to Montreal Expos for Pitcher Mike Marshall, December 5, 1973.
‡Traded to Texas Rangers for Pitcher Don Stanhouse and Infielder Pete Mackanin, December 5, 1974.
§Traded to St. Louis Cardinals for Shortstop Ed Brinkman and Pitcher Tommy Moore, June 4, 1975.
xTraded to San Diego Padres for Outfielder Dick Sharon, October 20, 1975.

### WORLD SERIES RECORD

Established World Series marks for most errors, game, outfielder (3) and most errors, inning, outfielder (3), October 6, 1966, (fifth inning).
Tied World Series mark for most stolen bases in one game (3), October 11, 1965.

| Year Club League | Pos. | G. | AB. | R. | H. | 2B. | 3B. | HR. | RBI. | B.A. | PO. | A. | E. | F.A. |
|---|---|---|---|---|---|---|---|---|---|---|---|---|---|---|
| 1963—Los Angeles ......Nat. | OF | 4 | 12 | 2 | 2 | 2 | 0 | 0 | 3 | .167 | 6 | 0 | 0 | 1.000 |
| 1965—Los Angeles ......Nat. | OF | 7 | 26 | 3 | 6 | 0 | 0 | 0 | 0 | .231 | 11 | 0 | 0 | 1.000 |
| 1966—Los Angeles ......Nat. | OF | 4 | 16 | 0 | 1 | 0 | 0 | 0 | 0 | .063 | 6 | 0 | 3 | .667 |
| World Series Totals ........................ | | 15 | 54 | 5 | 9 | 2 | 0 | 0 | 3 | .167 | 23 | 0 | 3 | .885 |

ALL-STAR GAME RECORD

| Year League | Pos. | AB. | R. | H. | 2B. | 3B. | HR. | RBI. | B.A. | PO. | A. | E. | F.A. |
|---|---|---|---|---|---|---|---|---|---|---|---|---|---|
| 1971—National ............................. | OF | 1 | 0 | 1 | 0 | 0 | 0 | 0 | 1.000 | 2 | 0 | 0 | 1.000 |
| 1973—National ............................. | PH-OF | 2 | 1 | 2 | 0 | 0 | 1 | 2 | 1.000 | 1 | 0 | 0 | 1.000 |
| All-Star Game Totals ........................ | | 3 | 1 | 3 | 0 | 0 | 1 | 2 | 1.000 | 3 | 0 | 0 | 1.000 |

## ANDRE FERNANDO DAWSON

Born July 10, 1954, at Miami, Fla.
Height, 6.03. Weight, 180.
Throws and bats righthanded.
Hobby—Fishing.
Attended Florida A&M University, Tallahassee, Fla.
Nephew of Theodore Taylor, who played in Pittsburgh Pirates' organization, 1967 through 1969.
Led Pioneer League in total bases with 168 and sacrifice flies with 5 in 1975.

| Year Club League | Pos. | G. | AB. | R. | H. | 2B. | 3B. | HR. | RBI. | B.A. | PO. | A. | E. | F.A. |
|---|---|---|---|---|---|---|---|---|---|---|---|---|---|---|
| 1975—Lethbridge ........Pion. | OF | 72 | *300 | 52 | *99 | 14 | 7 | *13 | 50 | .330 | *142 | 7 | *10 | .937 |
| 1976—Quebec City ......East. | OF | 40 | 143 | 27 | 51 | 6 | 0 | 8 | 27 | .357 | 89 | 3 | 6 | .939 |
| 1976—Denver..............A.A. | OF | 74 | 240 | 51 | 84 | 19 | 4 | 20 | 46 | .350 | 97 | 2 | 2 | .980 |
| 1976—Montreal ..........Nat. | OF | 24 | 85 | 9 | 20 | 4 | 1 | 0 | 7 | .235 | 61 | 1 | 2 | .969 |
| Major League Totals ..................... | | 24 | 85 | 9 | 20 | 4 | 1 | 0 | 7 | .235 | 61 | 1 | 2 | .969 |

## DENNIS L. DeBARR

Born January 16, 1953, at Cheyenne, Wyo.
Height, 6.02. Weight, 190.
Throws and bats lefthanded.
Hobbies—Tennis, snow skiing and table tennis.
Attended California State University, Hayward, Calif.

| Year Club League | G. | IP. | W. | L. | Pct. | H. | R. | ER. | SO. | BB. | ERA. |
|---|---|---|---|---|---|---|---|---|---|---|---|
| 1971—Bristol ...............................Ap'lachian | 10 | 36 | 2 | 3 | .400 | 24 | 9 | 8 | 29 | 13 | 2.00 |
| 1972—Lakeland...........................Florida St. | 24 | 129 | 6 | 9 | .400 | 100 | 53 | 45 | 97 | 69 | 3.14 |
| 1972—Montgomery .....................Southern | 1 | 6 | 0 | 0 | .000 | 2 | 1 | 1 | 4 | 5 | 1.50 |
| 1972—Toledo...............................Int'national | 1 | 1 | 0 | 0 | .000 | 1 | 0 | 0 | 1 | 0 | 0.00 |
| 1973—Lakeland...........................Florida St. | 23 | 108 | 5 | 6 | .455 | 100 | 36 | 30 | 55 | 30 | 2.50 |
| 1974—Montgomery .....................Southern | 27 | 81 | 3 | 9 | .250 | 77 | 57 | 35 | 36 | 45 | 3.89 |
| 1975—Montgomery .....................Southern | 18 | 55 | 4 | 3 | .571 | 45 | 17 | 13 | 28 | 22 | 2.13 |
| 1975—Evansville..........................Am. Assoc. | 11 | 64 | 2 | 4 | .333 | 69 | 30 | 29 | 36 | 30 | 4.08 |
| 1976—Montgomery† .....................Southern | 43 | 99 | 11 | 2 | *.846 | 92 | 36 | 26 | 78 | 35 | 2.36 |

†Selected by Toronto Blue Jays from Detroit Tigers in expansion draft, November 5, 1976.

## DOUGLAS VERNON DeCINCES

Name pronounced De-Sinsay.

### (Doug)

Born August 29, 1950, at Burbank, Calif.
Height, 6.03. Weight, 190.
Throws and bats righthanded.
Hobbies—Golf, photography, breeding German shepherd dogs and refinishing antiques.
Attended Pierce Junior College, Woodland Hills, Calif., and University of
California at Los Angeles, Los Angeles, Calif.

| Year Club League | Pos. | G. | AB. | R. | H. | 2B. | 3B. | HR. | RBI. | B.A. | PO. | A. | E. | F.A. |
|---|---|---|---|---|---|---|---|---|---|---|---|---|---|---|
| 1970—Bluefield .........Appal. | INF-P | 54 | 164 | 28 | 48 | 10 | 0 | 4 | 27 | .293 | 105 | 98 | 18 | .919 |
| 1970—Dallas-Ft. W. ....Texas | SS | 11 | 35 | 3 | 6 | 1 | 0 | 0 | 2 | .171 | 25 | 19 | 3 | .936 |
| 1971—Dallas-Ft. W.† ..Texas | 2B-SS | 78 | 235 | 29 | 61 | 10 | 1 | 5 | 29 | .260 | 154 | 164 | 12 | .964 |
| 1972—Asheville ..........So. | *2B-SS | 123 | 396 | 71 | 104 | 23 | 7 | 10 | 60 | .263 | 254 | 314 | *28 | .953 |
| 1973—Rochester..........Int. | *3B-S-2 | 131 | 438 | 79 | 117 | 25 | 3 | 19 | 79 | .267 | 150 | 264 | 17 | *.961 |
| 1973—Baltimore..........Amer. | 3-2-S | 10 | 18 | 2 | 2 | 0 | 0 | 0 | 3 | .111 | 4 | 19 | 2 | .920 |
| 1974—Rochester..........Int. | 3B | 132 | 444 | 70 | 125 | 17 | 4 | 11 | 66 | .282 | 98 | 255 | *32 | .917 |
| 1974—Baltimore..........Amer. | 3B | 1 | 0 | 0 | 0 | 0 | 0 | 0 | 0 | .000 | 0 | 2 | 0 | 1.000 |
| 1975—Baltimore..........Amer. | 3-S-2-1 | 61 | 167 | 20 | 42 | 6 | 3 | 4 | 23 | .251 | 92 | 115 | 7 | .967 |
| 1976—Baltimore..........Amer. | 3-2-1-S | 129 | 440 | 36 | 103 | 17 | 2 | 11 | 42 | .234 | 191 | 257 | 20 | .957 |
| Major League Totals ..................... | | 201 | 626 | 58 | 147 | 23 | 5 | 15 | 68 | .235 | 287 | 393 | 29 | .959 |

†On disabled list, June 25 through July 27, 1971.

PITCHING RECORD

| Year Club League | G. | IP. | W. | L. | Pct. | H. | R. | ER. | SO. | BB. | ERA. |
|---|---|---|---|---|---|---|---|---|---|---|---|
| 1970—Bluefield ...........................Ap'lachian | 1 | 2 | 0 | 1 | .000 | 3 | 2 | 1 | 1 | 1 | 4.50 |

## ARTHUR DENNIS DeFILIPPIS
### (Art)

Born March 7, 1952, at Stamford, Conn.
Height, 6.00. Weight, 178.
Throws and bats lefthanded.
Attended St. Leo College, St. Leo, Fla., and Iona College, New Rochelle, N. Y.
Led Pacific Coast League in home runs allowed with 36 in 1976.

| Year | Club | League | G. | IP. | W. | L. | Pct. | H. | R. | ER. | SO. | BB. | ERA. |
|------|------|--------|----|----|----|----|------|----|----|-----|-----|-----|------|
| 1970—Geneva | | NYP | 13 | 95 | 9 | 2 | •.818 | 46 | 27 | 17 | 139 | 54 | 1.61 |
| 1971—Burlington | | Carolina | 18 | 124 | 7 | 5 | .583 | 93 | 50 | 42 | 120 | 65 | 3.05 |
| 1971—Denver | | Am. Assoc. | 8 | 21 | 1 | 2 | .333 | 30 | 27 | 24 | 18 | 24 | 10.28 |
| 1972—Pittsfield | | Eastern | 29 | 123 | 8 | 9 | .471 | 107 | 72 | 60 | 93 | 85 | 4.39 |
| 1973—Pittsfield | | Eastern | 24 | 146 | 11 | 6 | .647 | 134 | 81 | 73 | 115 | 72 | 4.50 |
| 1974—Pittsfield | | Eastern | 43 | 88 | 4 | 9 | .308 | 79 | 45 | 34 | 79 | 54 | 3.48 |
| 1975—Spokane† | | P. Coast | 31 | 135 | 6 | 7 | .462 | 112 | 62 | 55 | 88 | 84 | 3.67 |
| 1976—Sacramento‡ | | P. Coast | 24 | 109 | 8 | 6 | .571 | 134 | 100 | 89 | 94 | 72 | 7.35 |

†Played in one game as an outfielder.
‡Traded from Texas Rangers' organization to Cincinnati Reds' organization (Indianapolis) for pitcher Mike Thompson, November 8, 1976. Traded to Tacoma (Minnesota Twins' organization) for Outfielder-First Baseman Jack Maloof, March 28, 1977.

## IVAN DeJESUS (ALVAREZ)
Name pronounced day-HAY-soos.

Born January 9, 1953, at Santurce, Puerto Rico.
Height, 5.10. Weight, 170.
Throws and bats righthanded.
Hobbies—Music, swimming and basketball.
Led Florida State League shortstops in double plays with 56 in 1970; led California League shortstops in double plays with 53 in 1971 and with 87 in 1973.
Led Pacific Coast League shortstops in double plays with 114 in 1974.

| Year | Club | League | Pos. | G. | AB. | R. | H. | 2B. | 3B. | HR. | RBI. | B.A. | PO. | A. | E. | F.A. |
|------|------|--------|------|----|-----|----|----|-----|-----|-----|------|------|-----|----|----|------|
| 1970—Daytona Beach | ..Fla. St. | | SS | 123 | 396 | 51 | 92 | 12 | 7 | 2 | 38 | .232 | 164 | 361 | 38 | .933 |
| 1971—Bakersfield | ....Calif. | | *SS-2B | 126 | 462 | 77 | 108 | 16 | 2 | 6 | 30 | .234 | 159 | *323 | *49 | .908 |
| 1972—Daytona Beach | ..Fla. St. | | SS | 131 | 442 | 56 | 108 | 15 | 4 | 7 | 39 | .244 | 187 | *452 | 37 | .945 |
| 1973—Bakersfield | ....Calif. | | SS | 132 | 519 | 77 | 125 | 17 | 1 | 7 | 57 | .241 | 221 | *403 | *47 | .930 |
| 1974—Albuquerque | ......P.C. | | SS | 140 | 510 | 81 | 152 | 17 | 5 | 7 | 55 | .298 | *268 | *479 | 38 | .952 |
| 1974—Los Angeles | ......Nat. | | SS | 3 | 3 | 1 | 1 | 0 | 0 | 0 | 0 | .333 | 1 | 0 | 0 | 1.000 |
| 1975—Albuquerque | ......P.C. | | SS | 62 | 221 | 24 | 60 | 10 | 2 | 1 | 21 | .271 | 97 | 265 | 24 | .938 |
| 1975—Los Angeles | ......Nat. | | SS | 63 | 87 | 10 | 16 | 2 | 1 | 0 | 2 | .184 | 45 | 107 | 4 | .974 |
| 1976—Albuquerque | ......P.C. | | SS-3B | 108 | 405 | 69 | 123 | 27 | 7 | 7 | 64 | .304 | 161 | 341 | 35 | .935 |
| 1976—Los Angeles† | ....Nat. | | SS-3B | 22 | 41 | 4 | 7 | 2 | 1 | 0 | 2 | .171 | 20 | 47 | 3 | .957 |
| Major League Totals | | | | 88 | 131 | 15 | 24 | 4 | 2 | 0 | 4 | .183 | 66 | 154 | 7 | .969 |

†Traded with First Baseman Bill Buckner and Pitcher Jeff Albert to Chicago Cubs for Outfielder Rick Monday and Pitcher Mike Garman, January 11, 1977.

## LUIS FELIPE DELGADO

Born February 2, 1954, in Hatillo, Puerto Rico
Height, 5.11, Weight, 170.
Throws left and bats left and righthanded.
Hobbies—Music, dancing and swimming.
Attended University of Puerto Rico, Rio Piedras, P. R.; received
Bachelor of Science Degree in Physical Education.
Led Carolina League in sacrifice hits with 10 and stolen bases with 52 in 1976.
Tied for Carolina League lead in double plays by outfielder with 5 in 1976.

| Year | Club | League | Pos. | G. | AB. | R. | H. | 2B. | 3B. | HR. | RBI. | B.A. | PO. | A. | E. | F.A. |
|------|------|--------|------|----|-----|----|----|-----|-----|-----|------|------|-----|----|----|------|
| 1973—Winter Haven | ....Fla. St. | | OF | 99 | 277 | 32 | 73 | 6 | 4 | 0 | 25 | .264 | 132 | 5 | 2 | .986 |
| 1974—Winter Haven | ....Fla. St. | | OF | 111 | 364 | 44 | 96 | 1 | 5 | 0 | 27 | .264 | 226 | 9 | 3 | .987 |
| 1975—Winston-Salem | ..Carol. | | OF | 104 | 389 | 63 | 100 | 11 | 4 | 1 | 31 | .257 | 234 | 9 | 8 | .968 |
| 1976—Winston-Salem† | Carol. | | OF | 122 | 486 | 79 | *143 | 21 | 6 | 7 | 48 | .294 | 241 | 11 | 3 | *.988 |

†Selected by Seattle Mariners from Boston Red Sox in expansion draft, November 5, 1976.

## LAWRENCE CALVIN DEMERY
### (Larry)

Born June 4, 1953, at Bakersfield, Calif.
Height, 6.00. Weight, 170.
Throws and bats righthanded.
Hobbies—Basketball, pool, swimming and fixing cars.
Attended Los Angeles City Community College, Los Angeles, Calif.
Son of Artist Demery, minor league pitcher with Bakersfield and Visalia, 1953 through 1955;
he played in Negro professional leagues as an outfielder and pitcher for many years.
Brother of Art Demery, former pitcher in Kansas City Royals' organization.

Led Carolina League pitchers in complete games with 14 and tied for lead in wild pitches with 17 in 1973.

| Year | Club | League | G. | IP. | W. | L. | Pct. | H. | R. | ER. | SO. | BB. | ERA. |
|------|------|--------|----|-----|----|----|------|----|----|-----|-----|-----|------|
| 1972–Gastonia | | W. Carolinas | 24 | 145 | 10 | 6 | .625 | 113 | 80 | 63 | 137 | 119 | 3.91 |
| 1973–Salem | | Carolina | 27 | 182 | 12 | 11 | .522 | 154 | 76 | 57 | 169 | 99 | 2.82 |
| 1973–Charleston | | Int'national | 1 | 8 | 0 | 1 | .000 | 6 | 4 | 3 | 12 | 3 | 3.38 |
| 1974–Charleston | | Int'national | 6 | 48 | 4 | 2 | .667 | 46 | 17 | 15 | 34 | 18 | 2.79 |
| 1974–Pittsburgh | | National | 19 | 95 | 6 | 6 | .500 | 95 | 47 | 45 | 51 | 51 | 4.26 |
| 1975–Pittsburgh | | National | 45 | 115 | 7 | 5 | .583 | 95 | 40 | 37 | 59 | 43 | 2.90 |
| 1976–Pittsburgh | | National | 15 | 145 | 10 | 7 | .588 | 123 | 56 | 51 | 72 | 58 | 3.17 |
| Major League Totals | | | 79 | 355 | 23 | 18 | .561 | 313 | 143 | 133 | 182 | 152 | 3.37 |

CHAMPIONSHIP SERIES RECORD

| Year | Club | League | G. | IP. | W. | L. | Pct. | H. | R. | ER. | SO. | BB. | ERA. |
|------|------|--------|----|-----|----|----|------|----|----|-----|-----|-----|------|
| 1974–Pittsburgh | | National | 2 | 1 | 0 | 0 | .000 | 3 | 4 | 4 | 0 | 2 | 36.00 |
| 1975–Pittsburgh | | National | 1 | 2 | 0 | 0 | .000 | 4 | 4 | 4 | 1 | 1 | 18.00 |
| Championship Series Totals | | | 3 | 3 | 0 | 0 | .000 | 7 | 8 | 8 | 1 | 3 | 24.00 |

## DONALD JOHN DeMOLA
### (Don)

Born July 5, 1952, at Glen Cove, N. Y.
Height, 6.01½. Weight, 188.
Throws and bats righthanded.
Hobbies–Billiards and sports in general.

| Year | Club | League | G. | IP. | W. | L. | Pct. | H. | R. | ER. | SO. | BB. | ERA. |
|------|------|--------|----|-----|----|----|------|----|----|-----|-----|-----|------|
| 1970–Johnson City | | Ap'lachian | 10 | 62 | 3 | 4 | .479 | 54 | 39 | 28 | 67 | 26 | 4.06 |
| 1971–Ft. Lauderdale | | Florida St. | 12 | 50 | 1 | 4 | .200 | 44 | 29 | 25 | 43 | 30 | 4.50 |
| 1971–Oneonta | | NYP | 12 | 68 | 4 | 4 | .500 | 44 | 59 | 31 | 22 | 60 | 36 | 2.91 |
| 1972–Ft. Lauderdale† | | Florida | | | | | (Did not play) | | | | | | |
| 1973–West Palm Beach | | Florida St. | 14 | 54 | 4 | 2 | .667 | 41 | 15 | 13 | 30 | 12 | 2.17 |
| 1973–Quebec City | | Eastern | 29 | 54 | 4 | 4 | .500 | 44 | 17 | 16 | 53 | 31 | 2.67 |
| 1974–Memphis | | Int'national | 9 | 47 | 5 | 1 | .833 | 46 | 11 | 11 | 48 | 17 | 2.11 |
| 1974–Montreal | | National | 25 | 58 | 1 | 0 | 1.000 | 46 | 21 | 20 | 47 | 21 | 3.10 |
| 1975–Montreal | | National | 60 | 98 | 4 | 7 | .364 | 92 | 47 | 45 | 63 | 42 | 4.13 |
| 1976–Denver‡ | | Am. Assoc. | 1 | 2 | 0 | 1 | .000 | 3 | 4 | 4 | 0 | 1 | 18.00 |
| Major League Totals | | | 85 | 156 | 5 | 7 | .417 | 138 | 68 | 65 | 110 | 63 | 3.75 |

†Released by New York Yankees' organization, April 11, 1972; signed as free agent by West Palm Beach (Montreal Expos' organization), January 11, 1973.
‡On emergency disabled list, April 30 through October 25, 1976.
Listed on Montreal Expos' 1977 spring roster.

## JOHN RIKARD DEMPSEY
### (Rick)

Born September 13, 1949, at Fayetteville, Tenn.
Height, 6.00. Weight, 175.
Throws and bats righthanded.
Hobbies–Hunting and fishing.
Attended Pierce Junior College, Woodland Hills, Calif.
Led International League in passed balls with 14 in 1973.
Tied for New York-Pennsylvania League lead in double plays by catchers with 4 in 1968.
Named New York-Pennsylvania League Player of the Year in 1968.

| Year | Club | League | Pos. | G. | AB. | R. | H. | 2B. | 3B. | HR. | RBI. | B.A. | PO. | A. | E. | F.A. |
|------|------|--------|------|----|-----|----|----|-----|-----|-----|------|------|----|----|----|------|
| 1967–Sarasota Twins | | Gulf C. | C-O-1 | 40 | 102 | 9 | 21 | 4 | 3 | 0 | 9 | .206 | 133 | 16 | 2 | .987 |
| 1968–Wis. Rapids | | Midw. | C | 11 | 35 | 12 | 8 | 2 | 0 | 1 | 6 | .229 | 68 | 2 | 1 | .986 |
| 1968–Auburn | | NYP | *C-1-O | 73 | 270 | 48 | 79 | 10 | 7 | 7 | 61 | .293 | *505 | *38 | 7 | *.987 |
| 1969–Wis. Rapids | | Midw. | C | 50 | 151 | 35 | 55 | 11 | 2 | 6 | 31 | .364 | 341 | 30 | •13 | .966 |
| 1969–Minnesota | | Amer. | C | 5 | 6 | 1 | 3 | 1 | 0 | 0 | 0 | .500 | 5 | 0 | 1 | .833 |
| 1970–Charlotte | | South | C-OF-2 | 105 | 351 | 28 | 86 | 20 | 6 | 4 | 42 | .245 | 506 | 76 | 18 | .970 |
| 1970–Minnesota | | Amer. | C | 5 | 7 | 1 | 0 | 0 | 0 | 0 | 0 | .000 | 12 | 0 | 1 | .923 |
| 1971–Charlotte | | South | C-OF | 105 | 338 | 39 | 82 | 16 | 2 | 8 | 47 | .243 | 599 | 65 | 8 | .988 |
| 1971–Minnesota | | Amer. | C | 6 | 13 | 2 | 4 | 1 | 0 | 0 | 0 | .308 | 30 | 4 | 2 | .944 |
| 1972–Tacoma | | P. C. | C-OF | 48 | 161 | 13 | 38 | 6 | 2 | 3 | 18 | .236 | 284 | 33 | 5 | .984 |
| 1972–Minnesota† | | Amer. | C | 25 | 40 | 0 | 8 | 1 | 0 | 0 | 0 | .200 | 67 | 5 | 1 | .986 |
| 1973–Syracuse | | Int. | C-OF-3 | 122 | 387 | 53 | 96 | 14 | 4 | 6 | 47 | .248 | 585 | 69 | 9 | .986 |
| 1973–New York | | Amer. | C | 6 | 11 | 0 | 2 | 0 | 0 | 0 | 0 | .182 | 9 | 0 | 2 | .818 |
| 1974–New York | | Amer. | C-OF | 43 | 109 | 12 | 26 | 3 | 0 | 2 | 12 | .239 | 152 | 22 | 4 | .978 |
| 1975–New York | | Amer. | C-O-3 | 71 | 145 | 18 | 38 | 8 | 0 | 1 | 11 | .262 | 92 | 9 | 3 | .971 |
| 1976–N.Y.‡-Balt. | | Amer. | C-OF | 80 | 216 | 12 | 42 | 2 | 0 | 0 | 12 | .194 | 302 | 39 | 4 | .988 |
| Major League Totals | | | | 241 | 547 | 46 | 123 | 16 | 0 | 3 | 35 | .225 | 669 | 79 | 18 | .976 |

†Released to Syracuse (in trade which sent Outfielder Danny Walton from Syracuse to Minnesota), October 27, 1972.
‡Traded with Pitchers Rudy May, Tippy Martinez, Dave Pagan and Scott McGregor to New York Yankees for Pitchers Ken Holtzman, Doyle Alexander and Grant Jackson, Catcher Ellie Hendricks and Pitcher Jimmy Freehan, latter assigned from Rochester to Syracuse, June 15, 1976.

## JOHN ALLEN DENNY

Born November 8, 1952, at Prescott, Ariz.
Height, 6.03. Weight, 185.
Throws and bats righthanded.
Hobbies—Building model ships and astronomy.
Attended Yavapai College, Prescott, Ariz., and Southern Illinois University, Edwardsville, Ill.

Pitched 8-1 no-hit victory against Midland, May 17, 1973.

| Year Club | League | G. | IP. | W. | L. | Pct. | H. | R. | ER. | SO. | BB. | ERA. |
|---|---|---|---|---|---|---|---|---|---|---|---|---|
| 1970—Sarasota Cardinals ............. | Gulf Coast | 11 | 42 | 2 | 2 | .500 | 32 | 14 | 6 | 43 | 9 | 1.29 |
| 1971—St. Petersburg...................... | Florida St. | 26 | 139 | 8 | 13 | .381 | 123 | 58 | 47 | 77 | 62 | 3.04 |
| 1972—Modesto† .............................. | California | 14 | 92 | 7 | 5 | .583 | 95 | 54 | 45 | 65 | 39 | 4.40 |
| 1973—Arkansas‡ ........................... | Texas | 20 | 147 | 10 | 6 | .625 | 128 | 57 | 51 | 81 | 52 | 3.11 |
| 1974—Tulsa ................................. | Am. Assoc. | 21 | 132 | 9 | 8 | .529 | 127 | 66 | 55 | 79 | 57 | 3.74 |
| 1974—St. Louis ............................ | National | 2 | 2 | 0 | 0 | .000 | 3 | 2 | 0 | 1 | 0 | 0.00 |
| 1975—Tulsa ................................. | Am. Assoc. | 7 | 60 | 3 | 1 | .750 | 47 | 12 | 12 | 44 | 32 | 1.80 |
| 1975—St. Louis ............................ | National | 25 | 136 | 10 | 7 | .588 | 149 | 73 | 60 | 72 | 51 | 3.97 |
| 1976—St. Louis ............................ | National | 30 | 207 | 11 | 9 | .550 | 189 | 71 | 58 | 74 | 74 | *2.52 |
| Major League Totals ............................. | | 57 | 345 | 21 | 16 | .568 | 341 | 146 | 118 | 147 | 125 | 3.08 |

†On disabled list July 17 through remainder of season.
‡On disabled list August 11 through remainder of season.


## RUSSELL EARL DENT
### (Bucky)
(Nicknamed by grandmother; word means "small Indian boy.")

Born November 25, 1951, at Savannah, Ga.
Height, 5.11. Weight, 175.
Throws and bats righthanded.
Attended Miami-Dade (North) Community College, Miami, Fla.

Led American League shortstops in total chances with 838 and tied for lead in double plays with 105 in 1975.
Led Amercian League in sacrifice hits with 23 in 1974.
Tied for American League lead in double plays by shortstops with 108 in 1974.
Led Midwest League in sacrifice hits with 12 and led shortstops in double plays with 51 in 1971; led American Association in sacrifice hits with 12 in 1973.
Tied for Gulf Coast League lead in sacrifice flies with 5 in 1970.

| Year Club | League | Pos. | G. | AB. | R. | H. | 2B. | 3B. | HR. | RBI. | B.A. | PO. | A. | E. | F.A. |
|---|---|---|---|---|---|---|---|---|---|---|---|---|---|---|---|
| 1970—Sarasota W. S. ..G. C. | 3-S-2 | 22 | 77 | 18 | 27 | 2 | 1 | 0 | 13 | .351 | 30 | 55 | 11 | .885 |
| 1970—Appleton............ | Midw. | SS-2 | 39 | 163 | 23 | 42 | 4 | 2 | 3 | 12 | .258 | 53 | 116 | 17 | .909 |
| 1971—Appleton† ......... | Midw. | SS-3 | 83 | 294 | 34 | 68 | 16 | 0 | 1 | 29 | .231 | 109 | 230 | 24 | .934 |
| 1972—Knoxville ......... | South. | SS | 125 | 453 | 58 | 134 | 10 | 6 | 6 | 56 | .296 | 167 | 437 | 31 | .951 |
| 1973—Iowa................. | A. A. | *SS-3B | 95 | 356 | 58 | 105 | 10 | 3 | 3 | 38 | .295 | 137 | 308 | *33 | .931 |
| 1973—Chicago ........... | Amer. | S-2-3 | 40 | 117 | 17 | 29 | 2 | 0 | 0 | 10 | .248 | 55 | 134 | 7 | .964 |
| 1974—Chicago ........... | Amer. | SS | 154 | 496 | 55 | 136 | 15 | 3 | 5 | 45 | .274 | 251 | 499 | 22 | .972 |
| 1975—Chicago ........... | Amer. | SS | 157 | 602 | 52 | 159 | 29 | 4 | 3 | 58 | .264 | *279 | *543 | 16 | *.981 |
| 1976—Chicago‡ ......... | Amer. | SS | 158 | 562 | 44 | 138 | 18 | 4 | 2 | 52 | .246 | 279 | 468 | 18 | .976 |
| Major League Totals ...................... | | 509 | 1777 | 168 | 462 | 64 | 11 | 10 | 165 | .260 | 864 | 1644 | 63 | .975 |

†On military list from beginning of season to May 14, 1971.
‡Traded to New York Yankees for Outfielder Oscar Gamble, Pitchers Bob Polinsky and Dewey Hoyt, and cash estimated at $200,000, April 5, 1977.

### ALL-STAR GAME RECORD

| Year League | Pos. | AB. | R. | H. | 2B. | 3B. | HR. | RBI. | B.A. | PO. | A. | E. | F.A. |
|---|---|---|---|---|---|---|---|---|---|---|---|---|---|
| 1975—American .......................... | SS | 1 | 0 | 0 | 0 | 0 | 0 | 0 | .000 | 0 | 1 | 0 | 1.000 |


## ROBERT WAYNE DETHERAGE
### (Bob)

Born September 20, 1954, at Springfield, Mo.
Height, 6.00. Weight, 180.
Throws and bats righthanded.
Hobby—Car racing.

Tied for Pioneer League lead in double plays by outfielders with 1 in 1973.
Named Most Valuable Player in Pioneer League, 1973.

| Year Club | League | Pos. | G. | AB. | R. | H. | 2B. | 3B. | HR. | RBI. | B.A. | PO. | A. | E. | F.A. |
|---|---|---|---|---|---|---|---|---|---|---|---|---|---|---|---|
| 1973—Daytona Beach ..Fla. St. | OF | 9 | 19 | 1 | 2 | 1 | 0 | 0 | 2 | .105 | 4 | 1 | 0 | 1.000 |
| 1973—Ogden ............. | Pion. | OF-P | 67 | 244 | 43 | *85 | 14 | *7 | 5 | *55 | .348 | 100 | 5 | 6 | .946 |
| 1974—Bakersfield....... | Calif. | OF | 137 | 483 | 95 | 150 | 17 | 7 | 14 | 77 | .311 | 226 | 13 | 12 | .952 |
| 1975—Waterbury ....... | East. | OF | 127 | 433 | 53 | 109 | 21 | 1 | 4 | 35 | .252 | 313 | 11 | 11 | .967 |
| 1976—Waterbury† ...... | East. | OF | 14 | 45 | 9 | 13 | 1 | 0 | 4 | 11 | .289 | 38 | 2 | 1 | .976 |
| 1976—Arkansas ......... | Texas | OF | 41 | 148 | 18 | 44 | 3 | 1 | 3 | 18 | .297 | 74 | 3 | 4 | .951 |
| 1976—Tulsa‡ ............. | A. A. | OF | 21 | 71 | 13 | 15 | 4 | 0 | 1 | 1 | .211 | 27 | 2 | 2 | .935 |

†Traded with Catcher-Outfielder Joe Ferguson and Infielder Freddie Tisdale, latter assigned from Lodi to St. Petersburg, to St. Louis Cardinals for Outfielder Reggie Smith, June 15, 1976.
‡Traded with Catcher-Outfielder Joe Ferguson to Houston Astros for Pitcher Larry Dierker and Infielder Jerry DaVanon, November 23, 1976.

PITCHING RECORD

| Year Club | League | G. | IP. | W. | L. | Pct. | H. | R. | ER. | SO. | BB. | ERA. |
|---|---|---|---|---|---|---|---|---|---|---|---|---|
| 1973—Ogden ...............................Pioneer | | 1 | 1 | 0 | 0 | .000 | 5 | 4 | 2 | 1 | 1 | 18.00 |

## THOMAS ANTHONY DETTORE, JR.

Name pronounced duh-TORR-ee.

### (Tom)

Born November 17, 1947, at Canonsburg, Pa.
Height, 6.04. Weight, 210.
Throws right and bats lefthanded.
Hobby—Sports in general.
Attended Juniata College, Huntingdon, Pa., and California State College, California, Pa.
Tied for Pacific Coast League lead in complete games with 16 in 1976.
Led Western Carolinas League pitchers in complete games with 14 and tied for lead in shutouts with 3 in 1969.
Tied for International League lead in hit batsmen with 13 in 1972.
Named Most Outstanding Pitcher in Western Carolinas League, 1969.

| Year Club | League | G. | IP. | W. | L. | Pct. | H. | R. | ER. | SO. | BB. | ERA. |
|---|---|---|---|---|---|---|---|---|---|---|---|---|
| 1968—Gastonia ............................W. Carol. | | 2 | 6 | 1 | 0 | 1.000 | 5 | 2 | 2 | 7 | 5 | 3.00 |
| 1969—Gastonia ............................W. Carol. | | 19 | 141 | 12 | 3 | .800 | 112 | 51 | 30 | 115 | 56 | •1.91 |
| 1969—Columbus ..........................Int'national | | 3 | 7 | 0 | 0 | .000 | 12 | 3 | 3 | 3 | 5 | 3.86 |
| 1970—Waterbury..........................Eastern | | 23 | 125 | 6 | 11 | .353 | 142 | 82 | 70 | 58 | 61 | 5.04 |
| 1971—Waterbury..........................Eastern | | 21 | 154 | 9 | 8 | .529 | 121 | 60 | 41 | 98 | 57 | 2.40 |
| 1972—Charleston .......................Int'national | | 22 | 159 | 11 | 7 | .611 | 129 | 58 | 54 | 108 | 51 | 3.06 |
| 1973—Charleston .......................Int'national | | 18 | 129 | 9 | 5 | .643 | 91 | 44 | 31 | 72 | 55 | 2.16 |
| 1973—Pittsburgh† ......................National | | 12 | 23 | 0 | 1 | .000 | 33 | 19 | 15 | 13 | 14 | 5.87 |
| 1974—Wichita .............................Am. Assoc. | | 29 | 132 | 5 | 6 | .455 | 111 | 63 | 58 | 104 | 52 | 3.95 |
| 1974—Chicago.............................National | | 16 | 65 | 3 | 5 | .375 | 64 | 39 | 30 | 43 | 31 | 4.15 |
| 1975—Wichita .............................Am. Assoc. | | 13 | 70 | 7 | 1 | .875 | 67 | 24 | 22 | 50 | 28 | 2.83 |
| 1975—Chicago.............................National | | 36 | 85 | 5 | 4 | .556 | 88 | 57 | 51 | 46 | 31 | 5.40 |
| 1976—Chicago‡ ..........................National | | 4 | 7 | 0 | 1 | .000 | 11 | 8 | 8 | 4 | 2 | 10.29 |
| 1976—Hawaii ..............................P. Coast | | 28 | 210 | 11 | •15 | .423 | 222 | 117 | 101 | 105 | 76 | 4.33 |
| Major League Totals ............................. | | 68 | 180 | 8 | 11 | .421 | 196 | 123 | 104 | 106 | 78 | 5.20 |

†Traded to Chicago Cubs for Infielder Paul Popovich and an undisclosed amount of cash, April 1, 1974.
‡Released, April 22, 1976; signed as free agent with Hawaii (San Diego Padres' organization), April 29, 1976.

RECORD AS CATCHER-FIRST BASEMAN

| Year Club | League | Pos. | G. | AB. | R. | H. | 2B. | 3B. | HR. | RBI. | B.A. | PO. | A. | E. | F.A. |
|---|---|---|---|---|---|---|---|---|---|---|---|---|---|---|---|
| 1968—Gastonia............W. Car. | | C-P | 74 | 221 | 23 | 54 | 9 | 2 | 2 | 27 | .244 | 454 | 25 | 11 | .978 |
| 1969—Gastonia............W. Car. | | P-1B | 42 | 69 | 12 | 22 | 3 | 0 | 0 | 9 | .319 | 5 | 13 | 2 | .950 |

## PAUL ADRIAN DEVINE

(Known by middle name.)

Born December 2, 1951, at Galveston, Tex.
Height, 6.04. Weight, 200.
Throws and bats righthanded.
Hobby—Photography.
Attended Sam Houston State University, Huntsville, Tex.

| Year Club | League | G. | IP. | W. | L. | Pct. | H. | R. | ER. | SO. | BB. | ERA. |
|---|---|---|---|---|---|---|---|---|---|---|---|---|
| 1970—Magic Valley.......................Pioneer | | 14 | 66 | 5 | 6 | .455 | 80 | 45 | 38 | 54 | 25 | 5.18 |
| 1971—Greenwood .........................W. Carol. | | 8 | 30 | 2 | 1 | .667 | 23 | 8 | 8 | 24 | 8 | 2.40 |
| 1972—Savannah ...........................Southern | | 25 | 130 | 12 | 8 | .600 | 128 | 54 | 45 | 94 | 29 | 3.12 |
| 1973—Richmond ..........................Int'national | | 13 | 80 | 2 | 7 | .222 | 87 | 43 | 39 | 62 | 41 | 4.39 |
| 1973—Atlanta ..............................National | | 24 | 32 | 2 | 3 | .400 | 45 | 24 | 23 | 15 | 12 | 6.47 |
| 1974—Richmond† .........................Int'national | | 4 | 14 | 0 | 1 | .000 | 19 | 14 | 14 | 4 | 7 | 9.00 |
| 1975—Richmond ..........................Int'national | | 27 | 148 | 10 | 6 | .625 | 148 | 55 | 49 | 82 | 51 | 2.98 |
| 1975—Atlanta ..............................National | | 5 | 16 | 1 | 0 | 1.000 | 19 | 8 | 8 | 8 | 7 | 4.50 |
| 1976—Atlanta‡ ............................National | | 48 | 73 | 5 | 6 | .455 | 72 | 30 | 26 | 48 | 26 | 3.21 |
| Major League Totals ............................. | | 77 | 121 | 8 | 9 | .471 | 136 | 62 | 57 | 71 | 45 | 4.24 |

†On disabled list, April 19 to May 24 and June 9 to June 17, 1974.
‡On disabled list, June 16 to July 21, 1976. Traded with Outfielders Ken Henderson and Dave May, Pitchers Carl Morton and Roger Moret, and cash estimated at $250,000 to Texas Rangers for Outfielder Jeff Burroughs, December 9, 1976.

## BAUDILIO JOSE DIAZ (SEIJAS)

### (Bo)

Born March 23, 1953, at Cua, Miranda, Venezuela.
Height, 5.11. Weight, 185.
Throws and bats righthanded.
Hobby—Music.

| Year | Club | League | Pos. | G. | AB. | R. | H. | 2B. | 3B. | HR. | RBI. | B.A. | PO. | A. | E. | F.A. |
|---|---|---|---|---|---|---|---|---|---|---|---|---|---|---|---|---|
| 1971—Williamsport | NYP | PH | 1 | 1 | 0 | 0 | 0 | 0 | 0 | 0 | .000 | .... | .... | .... | ...... |
| 1971—Pawtucket | East. | PH | 1 | 2 | 0 | 0 | 0 | 0 | 0 | 0 | .000 | .... | .... | .... | ...... |
| 1971—Greenville | W. Car. | C | 10 | 25 | 2 | 5 | 1 | 0 | 0 | 0 | .200 | 35 | 2 | 2 | .949 |
| 1972—Winter Haven | Fla. St. | C | 14 | 44 | 3 | 7 | 1 | 0 | 0 | 0 | .159 | 72 | 7 | 0 | 1.000 |
| 1973—Elmira | NYP | C | 25 | 69 | 3 | 17 | 3 | 0 | 0 | 9 | .246 | 107 | 16 | 1 | .992 |
| 1974—Winter Haven | Fla. St. | C-3B | 97 | 327 | 31 | 79 | 20 | 1 | 1 | 38 | .242 | 476 | 75 | 14 | .975 |
| 1975—Winston-Salem | Carol. | C | 59 | 179 | 22 | 47 | 8 | 1 | 6 | 29 | .263 | 271 | 45 | 9 | .972 |
| 1976—Rhode Island | Int. | C | 62 | 117 | 10 | 29 | 42 | 1 | 0 | 18 | .248 | 222 | 28 | 3 | .988 |

Listed on Boston Red Sox' 1977 spring roster.

## LAWRENCE EDWARD DIERKER

Name pronounced DUR-ker.

### (Larry)

Born September 22, 1946, at Hollywood, Calif.
HEIGHT, 6.04. Weight, 205.
Throws and bats righthanded.
Hobby—Golf.
Attended University of California, Santa Barbara, Calif.
Brother of Richard Dierker, pitcher in Baltimore Orioles' organization,
1972 through 1975.

Pitched 6-0 no-hit victory against Montreal Expos, July 9, 1976.
Led National League in wild pitches with 20 in 1968.

| Year | Club | League | G. | IP. | W. | L. | Pct. | H. | R. | ER. | SO. | BB. | ERA. |
|---|---|---|---|---|---|---|---|---|---|---|---|---|---|
| 1964—Cocoa Colts | Cocoa Rook. | 9 | 39 | 2 | 3 | .400 | 21 | 19 | 14 | 61 | 18 | 3.23 |
| 1964—Houston | National | 3 | 9 | 0 | 1 | .000 | 7 | 4 | 2 | 5 | 3 | 2.00 |
| 1965—Houston | National | 26 | 147 | 7 | 8 | .467 | 135 | 69 | 57 | 109 | 37 | 3.49 |
| 1966—Houston | National | 29 | 187 | 10 | 8 | .556 | 173 | 73 | 66 | 108 | 45 | 3.18 |
| 1967—Houston† | National | 15 | 99 | 6 | 5 | .545 | 95 | 44 | 37 | 68 | 25 | 3.36 |
| 1968—Houston | National | 32 | 234 | 12 | 15 | .444 | 206 | 95 | 86 | 161 | 89 | 3.31 |
| 1969—Houston | National | 39 | 305 | 20 | 13 | .606 | 240 | 97 | 79 | 232 | 72 | 2.33 |
| 1970—Houston | National | 37 | 270 | 16 | 12 | .571 | 263 | 124 | 116 | 191 | 82 | 3.87 |
| 1971—Houston | National | 24 | 159 | 12 | 6 | .667 | 150 | 50 | 48 | 91 | 33 | 2.72 |
| 1972—Houston | National | 31 | 215 | 15 | 8 | .652 | 209 | 87 | 81 | 115 | 51 | 3.39 |
| 1973—Houston‡ | National | 14 | 27 | 1 | 1 | .500 | 27 | 14 | 13 | 18 | 13 | 4.33 |
| 1974—Houston | National | 33 | 224 | 11 | 10 | .524 | 189 | 76 | 72 | 150 | 82 | 2.89 |
| 1975—Houston | National | 34 | 232 | 14 | 16 | .467 | 225 | 109 | 103 | 127 | 91 | 4.00 |
| 1976—Houston§ | National | 28 | 188 | 13 | 14 | .481 | 171 | 85 | 77 | 112 | 72 | 3.69 |
| Major League Totals | | 345 | 2296 | 137 | 117 | .539 | 2090 | 927 | 837 | 1487 | 695 | 3.28 |

†In military service from June 25 through end of season.
‡On disabled list, March 21 to May 22 and June 16 to July 12, 1973.
§Traded with Infielder Jerry DaVanon to St. Louis Cardinals for Catcher-Outfielder Joe Ferguson and Out-fielder Bobby Detherage, latter assigned to Memphis, November 23, 1976.

### ALL-STAR GAME RECORD

| Year | League | IP. | W. | L. | Pct. | H. | R. | ER. | SO. | BB. | ERA. |
|---|---|---|---|---|---|---|---|---|---|---|---|
| 1969—National | | ⅓ | 0 | 0 | .000 | 1 | 0 | 0 | 0 | 0 | 0.00 |

Named to National League All-Star Team for 1971 game; replaced due to injury.

## STEPHEN BRADLEY DILLARD

### (Steve)

Born December8, 1951, at Memphis, Tenn.
Height, 6.01. Weight, 180.
Throws and bats righthanded.
Hobby—Basketball.
AttendedUniversityof Mississippi, Oxford,Miss.

| Year | Club | League | Pos. | G. | AB. | R. | H. | 2B. | 3B. | HR. | RBI. | B.A. | PO. | A. | E. | F.A. |
|---|---|---|---|---|---|---|---|---|---|---|---|---|---|---|---|---|
| 1972—Winston-Salem | Carol. | 3-S-2 | 44 | 114 | 14 | 26 | 0 | 3 | 0 | 9 | .228 | 30 | 56 | 4 | .956 |
| 1973—Winston-Salem | Carol. | *SS-O | 132 | 516 | 84 | 144 | 20 | 8 | 7 | 64 | .279 | *214 | *428 | 43 | *.937 |
| 1974—Bristol | East. | SS-2B | 24 | 28 | 7 | 5 | 2 | 0 | 0 | 4 | .179 | 10 | 23 | 2 | .943 |
| 1974—Pawtucket | Int. | SS | 90 | 338 | 50 | 89 | 11 | 1 | 1 | 14 | .263 | 132 | 233 | 22 | .943 |
| 1975—Pawtucket† | Int. | SS | 57 | 155 | 20 | 30 | 4 | 0 | 0 | 4 | .194 | 53 | 100 | 19 | .890 |
| 1975—Bristol | East. | 2B | 68 | 261 | 34 | 73 | 5 | 2 | 1 | 20 | .280 | 30 | 33 | 3 | .955 |
| 1975—Boston | Amer. | 2B | 1 | 5 | 2 | 2 | 0 | 0 | 0 | 0 | .400 | 5 | 4 | 0 | 1.000 |
| 1976—Boston | Amer. | 3-2-S-DH | 57 | 167 | 22 | 46 | 14 | 0 | 1 | 15 | .275 | 58 | 102 | 11 | .936 |
| 1976—Rhode Island | Int. | 2B | 34 | 135 | 17 | 31 | 5 | 0 | 1 | 9 | .230 | 87 | 107 | 13 | .937 |
| Major League Totals | | 58 | 172 | 24 | 48 | 14 | 0 | 1 | 15 | .279 | 63 | 106 | 11 | .939 |

†On disabled list, May 1 to May 11, 1975.

## *DID YOU KNOW —*

That THE SPORTING NEWS was first published on March 17, 1886?

## MIGUEL ANGEL DILONE (REYES)

Name pronounced De-lo-NAY.

Born November 1, 1954, at Santiago, Dominican Republic.
Height, 5.11. Weight, 160.
Throws right and bats left and righthanded.

Led Western Carolinas League in stolen bases with 95 in 1973, Carolina League with 84 in 1974 and International League with 48 in 1975.
Named Player of the Year in Carolina League, 1974.
Originally signed as a free agent by Pittsburgh Pirates but on a later date the St. Louis Cardinals also signed him not realizing that the Pittsburgh club had a valid contract. The National Association ruled in favor of the Pirates.

| Year Club | League | Pos. | G. | AB. | R. | H. | 2B. | 3B. | HR. | RBI. | B.A. | PO. | A. | E. | F.A. |
|---|---|---|---|---|---|---|---|---|---|---|---|---|---|---|---|
| 1972—Niagara Falls | NYP | OF | 61 | 223 | 50 | 50 | 6 | 0 | 0 | 16 | .224 | 83 | 4 | 5 | .946 |
| 1973—Charleston | W. Car. | OF | 115 | 438 | *94 | 119 | 8 | 5 | 1 | 24 | .272 | 228 | 11 | 7 | .972 |
| 1974—Salem | Carol. | OF | 132 | 532 | 106 | *176 | 28 | 9 | 1 | 47 | .331 | 271 | 8 | 13 | .955 |
| 1974—Pittsburgh | Nat. | PR-OF | 12 | 2 | 3 | 0 | 0 | 0 | 0 | 0 | .000 | 1 | 0 | 0 | 1.000 |
| 1975—Charleston | Int. | OF | 125 | 471 | 61 | 102 | 12 | 5 | 1 | 26 | .217 | 275 | 11 | 6 | .978 |
| 1975—Pittsburgh | Nat. | OF | 18 | 6 | 8 | 0 | 0 | 0 | 0 | 0 | .000 | 3 | 0 | 0 | 1.000 |
| 1976—Charleston | Int. | OF-3B | 100 | 408 | 63 | 137 | 7 | 6 | 1 | 17 | .336 | 202 | 26 | 9 | .962 |
| 1976—Pittsburgh | Nat. | OF | 16 | 17 | 7 | 4 | 0 | 0 | 0 | 0 | .235 | 11 | 0 | 0 | 1.000 |
| Major League Totals | | | 46 | 25 | 18 | 4 | 0 | 0 | 0 | 0 | .160 | 15 | 0 | 0 | 1.000 |

## MICHAEL WAYNE DIMMEL

Name pronounced DIM-ul.

### (Mike)

Born October 16, 1954, at Albert Lea, Minn.
Height, 6.00. Weight, 180.
Throws and bats righthanded.
Hobby—Billiards.
Attended Ball State University, Muncie, Ind.

| Year Club | League | Pos. | G. | AB. | R. | H. | 2B. | 3B. | HR. | RBI. | B.A. | PO. | A. | E. | F.A. |
|---|---|---|---|---|---|---|---|---|---|---|---|---|---|---|---|
| 1973—Ogden | Pion. | OF | 48 | 153 | 20 | 36 | 4 | 3 | 1 | 17 | .235 | 83 | 5 | *9 | .907 |
| 1974—Bakersfield | Calif. | OF | 119 | 473 | 95 | 148 | 17 | 8 | 9 | 53 | .313 | 231 | 14 | 8 | .968 |
| 1974—Waterbury | East. | OF | 18 | 75 | 13 | 20 | 2 | 3 | 1 | 8 | .267 | 41 | 4 | 1 | .978 |
| 1975—Waterbury | East. | OF | 135 | 476 | 69 | 131 | 17 | 6 | 11 | 59 | .275 | 212 | 12 | 11 | .953 |
| 1976—Albuquerque | P.C. | OF | 64 | 236 | 34 | 60 | 6 | 5 | 4 | 27 | .254 | 106 | 6 | 4 | .966 |
| 1976—Waterbury† | East. | OF | 55 | 207 | 20 | 55 | 5 | 3 | 1 | 23 | .266 | 135 | 2 | 7 | .951 |

†Drafted by Baltimore Orioles' organization from Los Angeles Dodgers, December 6, 1976.

## KERRY MICHAEL DINEEN

Born July 1, 1952, at Englewood, N. J.
Height, 5.11. Weight, 165.
Throws and bats lefthanded.
Hobby—Golf.
Attended University of San Diego, Alcala Park, San Diego, Calif.
Distant cousin of Ken Henderson, outfielder with Texas Rangers.

Named New York-Pennsylvania League Player of the Year in 1973.

| Year Club | League | Pos. | G. | AB. | R. | H. | 2B. | 3B. | HR. | RBI. | B.A. | PO. | A. | E. | F.A. |
|---|---|---|---|---|---|---|---|---|---|---|---|---|---|---|---|
| 1973—Oneonta | NYP | OF | 66 | 250 | 46 | 88 | 11 | *10 | 1 | 46 | *.352 | 114 | 3 | 4 | .967 |
| 1974—West Haven | East. | OF | 120 | 456 | 76 | 129 | 22 | 5 | 10 | 55 | .283 | 243 | 9 | 8 | .969 |
| 1974—Syracuse | Int. | OF | 7 | 27 | 1 | 5 | 1 | 1 | 0 | 1 | .185 | 11 | 0 | 0 | 1.000 |
| 1975—Syracuse | Int. | OF | 104 | 348 | 56 | 84 | 9 | 2 | 0 | 30 | .241 | 230 | 8 | 2 | *.992 |
| 1975—New York | Amer. | OF | 7 | 22 | 3 | 8 | 1 | 0 | 0 | 1 | .364 | 19 | 0 | 0 | 1.000 |
| 1976—Syracuse | Int. | OF | 59 | 166 | 21 | 42 | 12 | 3 | 0 | 22 | .253 | 104 | 3 | 2 | .982 |
| 1976—New York† | Amer. | OF | 4 | 7 | 0 | 2 | 0 | 0 | 0 | 1 | .286 | 9 | 0 | 1 | .900 |
| Major League Totals | | | 11 | 29 | 3 | 10 | 1 | 0 | 0 | 2 | .345 | 28 | 0 | 1 | .966 |

†Traded to Philadelphia Phillies for Infielder Sergio Ferrer, March 26, 1977.

## PATRICK EDWARD DOBSON, JR.

### (Pat)

Born February 12, 1942, at Buffalo, N. Y.
Height, 6.03. Weight, 200.
Throws and bats righthanded.

Led National League in sacrifice hits with 19 in 1970.
Led Carolina League in wild pitches with 16 in 1961.
Tied for Alabama-Florida League lead in shutouts with 2 in 1962.
Received reported $35,000 bonus to sign with Detroit Tigers, 1959.

| Year Club | League | G. | IP. | W. | L. | Pct. | H. | R. | ER. | SO. | BB. | ERA. |
|---|---|---|---|---|---|---|---|---|---|---|---|---|
| 1960—Durham | Carolina | 28 | 157 | 7 | 9 | .438 | 145 | 96 | 71 | 137 | 98 | 4.06 |
| 1961—Knoxville | Sally | 6 | 16 | 0 | 1 | .000 | 23 | 17 | 15 | 11 | 16 | 8.44 |
| 1961—Durham | Carolina | 25 | 103 | 4 | 9 | .308 | 104 | 76 | 67 | 71 | 96 | 5.84 |

| Year Club | League | G. | IP. | W. | L. | Pct. | H. | R. | ER. | SO. | BB. | ERA. |
|---|---|---|---|---|---|---|---|---|---|---|---|---|
| 1962—Duluth-Superior...................Northern | | 4 | 5 | 0 | 2 | .000 | 10 | 13 | 11 | 3 | 14 | 19.80 |
| 1962—Montgomery ........................Ala.-Fla. | | 18 | 116 | 8 | 7 | .533 | 90 | 52 | 33 | 124 | 71 | 2.56 |
| 1963—Jamestown ...........................NYP | | 27 | 125 | 7 | 8 | .467 | 135 | 77 | 57 | 158 | 71 | 4.10 |
| 1963—Knoxville ............................Sally | | 10 | 61 | 5 | 1 | .833 | 44 | 14 | 9 | 43 | 27 | 1.33 |
| 1964—Syracuse............................Int'national | | 9 | 35 | 1 | 2 | .333 | 32 | 24 | 21 | 29 | 17 | 5.40 |
| 1964—Knoxville ..........................Southern | | 15 | 91 | 6 | 5 | .545 | 93 | 51 | 40 | 70 | 45 | 3.96 |
| 1965—Syracuse............................Int'national | | 4 | 8 | 0 | 0 | .000 | 4 | 1 | 1 | 6 | 3 | 1.13 |
| 1965—Montgomery ......................Southern | | 17 | 31 | 4 | 1 | .800 | 21 | 9 | 5 | 33 | 14 | 1.45 |
| 1966—Portland ...........................P. Coast | | 31 | 180 | 12 | 9 | .571 | 187 | 82 | 69 | 142 | 61 | 3.45 |
| 1967—Toledo...............................Int'national | | 6 | 49 | 4 | 1 | .800 | 39 | 12 | 8 | 52 | 12 | 1.47 |
| 1967—Detroit ..............................American | | 28 | 49 | 1 | 2 | .333 | 38 | 20 | 16 | 34 | 27 | 2.94 |
| 1968—Detroit ..............................American | | 47 | 125 | 5 | 5 | .385 | 89 | 39 | 37 | 93 | 48 | 2.66 |
| 1969—Detroit† ............................American | | 49 | 105 | 5 | 10 | .333 | 100 | 48 | 42 | 64 | 39 | 3.60 |
| 1970—San Diego‡ .........................National | | 40 | 251 | 14 | 15 | .483 | 257 | 126 | 105 | 185 | 78 | 3.76 |
| 1971—Baltimore ..........................American | | 38 | 282 | 20 | 8 | .714 | 248 | 104 | 91 | 187 | 63 | 2.90 |
| 1972—Baltimore§ ........................American | | 38 | 268 | 16 | •18 | .471 | 220 | 89 | 79 | 161 | 69 | 2.65 |
| 1973—Atlanta x...........................National | | 12 | 58 | 3 | 7 | .300 | 73 | 33 | 32 | 23 | 19 | 4.97 |
| 1973—New York ..........................American | | 22 | 142 | 9 | 8 | .529 | 150 | 72 | 66 | 70 | 34 | 4.18 |
| 1974—New York ..........................American | | 39 | 281 | 19 | 15 | .559 | 282 | 111 | 96 | 157 | 75 | 3.07 |
| 1975—New York y ........................American | | 33 | 208 | 11 | 14 | .440 | 205 | 105 | 94 | 129 | 83 | 4.07 |
| 1976—Cleveland ..........................American | | 35 | 217 | 16 | 12 | .571 | 226 | 98 | 84 | 117 | 65 | 3.48 |
| American League Totals........................... | | 329 | 1677 | 102 | 95 | .518 | 1558 | 686 | 605 | 1012 | 503 | 3.25 |
| National League Totals........................... | | 52 | 309 | 17 | 22 | .436 | 330 | 159 | 137 | 208 | 97 | 3.99 |
| Major League Totals ............................... | | 381 | 1986 | 119 | 117 | .504 | 1888 | 845 | 742 | 1220 | 600 | 3.36 |

†Traded with Shortstop-Outfielder Dave Campbell to San Diego Padres for Pitcher Joe Niekro, December 4, 1969.

‡Traded with Pitcher Tom Dukes to Baltimore Orioles for Pitchers Tom Phoebus, Al Severinsen, Fred Beene and Shortstop Enzo Hernandez, December 1, 1970.

§Traded with Pitcher Roric Harrison, Catcher Johnny Oates and Infielder Dave Johnson to Atlanta Braves for Catcher Earl Williams and Infielder Taylor Duncan, November 30, 1972.

xTraded to New York Yankees for First Baseman Frank Tepedino, Outfielder Wayne Nordhagen (assigned to Richmond) and two players to be named later, June 7, 1973; Braves received Pitcher Alan Closter, September 5, 1973, and Pitcher Dave Cheadle, September 10, 1973, to complete deal.

yTraded to Cleveland Indians for Outfielder Oscar Gamble, November 22, 1975.

### WORLD SERIES RECORD

| Year Club | League | G. | IP. | W. | L. | Pct. | H. | R. | ER. | SO. | BB. | ERA. |
|---|---|---|---|---|---|---|---|---|---|---|---|---|
| 1968—Detroit ..............................American | | 3 | 4⅔ | 0 | 0 | .000 | 5 | 2 | 2 | 0 | 1 | 3.86 |
| 1971—Baltimore ..........................American | | 3 | 6⅔ | 0 | 0 | .000 | 13 | 3 | 3 | 6 | 4 | 4.05 |
| World Series Totals ................................. | | 6 | 11⅓ | 0 | 0 | .000 | 18 | 5 | 5 | 6 | 5 | 3.97 |

### ALL-STAR GAME RECORD

Member of American League All-Star Team for the 1972 game; did not play.

## THOMAS JAMES DONOHUE
### (Tom)

Born November 15, 1952, at Westbury, N. Y.
Height, 6.00. Weight, 185.
Throws and bats righthanded.
Hobbies—Golf and fishing.
Attended Idaho State University, Pocatello, Ida., and Nassau
Community College, Garden City, N. Y.

| Year Club | League | Pos. | G. | AB. | R. | H. | 2B. | 3B. | HR. | RBI. | B.A. | PO. | A. | E. | F.A. |
|---|---|---|---|---|---|---|---|---|---|---|---|---|---|---|---|
| 1972—Quad Cities ......Midw. | | OF | 37 | 86 | 13 | 9 | 1 | 1 | 1 | 7 | .105 | 46 | 2 | 3 | .941 |
| 1972—Idaho Falls........Pion. | | OF | 55 | 204 | 18 | 47 | 7 | 4 | 1 | 10 | .230 | 115 | 2 | 6 | .951 |
| 1973—Quad Cities ......Midw. | | OF-C-3B | 83 | 239 | 26 | 49 | 11 | 0 | 7 | 27 | .205 | 180 | 15 | 7 | .965 |
| 1974—Salinas..............Calif. | | C-OF | 45 | 152 | 19 | 32 | 4 | 3 | 4 | 21 | .211 | 182 | 27 | 4 | .981 |
| 1974—Quad Cities ......Midw. | | OF-C | 38 | 143 | 13 | 26 | 3 | 2 | 3 | 11 | .182 | 144 | 12 | 4 | .975 |
| 1974—El Paso ...........Texas | | C | 4 | 13 | 1 | 2 | 1 | 0 | 0 | 2 | .154 | 14 | 4 | 0 | 1.000 |
| 1975—Salinas..............Calif. | | OF | 8 | 20 | 3 | 6 | 2 | 0 | 1 | 6 | .300 | 8 | 1 | 1 | .900 |
| 1975—El Paso ...........Texas | | C-OF | 100 | 338 | 46 | 91 | 15 | 2 | 12 | 59 | .269 | 340 | 36 | 7 | .982 |
| 1976—El Paso†...........Texas | | C | 37 | 135 | 22 | 44 | 9 | 2 | 3 | 23 | .326 | 146 | 22 | 4 | .977 |

†On disabled list, May 22 through August 19, 1976.
Listed on California Angels' 1977 spring roster.

## ALPHONSO ERWIN DOWNING
### (Al)

Born June 28, 1941, at Trenton, N. J.
Height, 5.11. Weight, 179.
Throws left and bats righthanded.
Hobby—Golf.
Attended Muhlenberg College, Allentown, Pa., and Rider College, Trenton, N. J.

Tied major league record by striking out three batters on nine pitched balls, August 11, 1967 (second inning).

Tied for National League lead in shutouts with 5 in 1971.
Pitched 4-0 no-hit victory against Syracuse, May 12, 1962.
Led International League in games started with 31 and wild pitches with 16 in 1962.
Named by THE SPORTING NEWS as National League Comeback Player of the Year, 1971.

| Year Club | League | G. | IP. | W. | L. | Pct. | H. | R. | ER. | SO. | BB. | ERA. |
|---|---|---|---|---|---|---|---|---|---|---|---|---|
| 1961–Binghamton.........................Eastern | | 12 | 98 | 9 | 1 | .900 | 70 | 28 | 20 | 96 | 50 | 1.84 |
| 1961–New York ............................American | | 5 | 9 | 0 | 1 | .000 | 7 | 8 | 8 | 12 | 12 | 8.00 |
| 1962–Richmond ..........................Int'national | | 32 | 169 | 9 | 13 | .409 | 135 | 87 | 77 | 180 | 113 | 4.10 |
| 1962–New York ...........................American | | 1 | 1 | 0 | 0 | .000 | 0 | 0 | 0 | 1 | 0 | 0.00 |
| 1963–Richmond ..........................Int'national | | 10 | 57 | 3 | 2 | .600 | 40 | 23 | 17 | 64 | 45 | 2.68 |
| 1963–New York ...........................American | | 24 | 176 | 13 | 5 | .722 | 114 | 52 | 50 | 171 | 80 | 2.56 |
| 1964–New York ...........................American | | 37 | 244 | 13 | 8 | .619 | 201 | 104 | 94 | ∗217 | ∗120 | 3.47 |
| 1965–New York ...........................American | | 35 | 212 | 12 | 14 | .462 | 185 | 92 | 80 | 179 | 105 | 3.40 |
| 1966–New York ...........................American | | 30 | 200 | 10 | 11 | .476 | 178 | 90 | 79 | 152 | 79 | 3.56 |
| 1967–New York ...........................American | | 31 | 202 | 14 | 10 | .583 | 158 | 65 | 59 | 171 | 61 | 2.63 |
| 1968–New York† ..........................American | | 15 | 61 | 3 | 3 | .500 | 54 | 24 | 24 | 40 | 20 | 3.54 |
| 1968–Binghamton.........................Eastern | | 5 | 31 | 1 | 4 | .200 | 24 | 17 | 12 | 17 | 16 | 3.48 |
| 1969–New York‡ ..........................American | | 30 | 131 | 7 | 5 | .583 | 117 | 57 | 49 | 85 | 49 | 3.37 |
| 1970–Oak.§-Mil.x .........................American | | 27 | 135 | 5 | 13 | .278 | 118 | 66 | 53 | 79 | 81 | 3.53 |
| 1971–Los Angeles .......................National | | 37 | 262 | 20 | 9 | .690 | 245 | 93 | 78 | 136 | 84 | 2.68 |
| 1972–Los Angeles .......................National | | 31 | 203 | 9 | 9 | .500 | 196 | 81 | 67 | 117 | 67 | 2.97 |
| 1973–Los Angeles .......................National | | 30 | 193 | 9 | 9 | .500 | 155 | 87 | 71 | 124 | 68 | 3.31 |
| 1974–Los Angeles .......................National | | 21 | 98 | 5 | 6 | .455 | 94 | 52 | 40 | 63 | 45 | 3.67 |
| 1975–Los Angeles .......................National | | 22 | 75 | 2 | 1 | .667 | 59 | 31 | 24 | 39 | 28 | 2.88 |
| 1976–Los Angeles .......................National | | 17 | 47 | 1 | 2 | .333 | 43 | 21 | 20 | 30 | 18 | 3.83 |
| National League Totals................... | | 158 | 878 | 46 | 36 | .561 | 792 | 365 | 300 | 509 | 310 | 3.08 |
| American League Totals.......................... | | 235 | 1371 | 77 | 70 | .524 | 1132 | 558 | 496 | 1107 | 607 | 3.26 |
| Major League Totals ............................... | | 393 | 2249 | 123 | 106 | .537 | 1924 | 923 | 796 | 1616 | 917 | 3.19 |

†On disabled list from May 18 through June 17 with stiff shoulder.
‡Traded to Oakland Athletics with Catcher Frank Fernandez for Infielders Danny Cater and Osvaldo Chavarria (transferred from Des Moines to Syracuse), December 5, 1969.
§Traded to Milwaukee Brewers with First Baseman-Outfielder John (Tito) Francona for Outfielder Steve Hovley, June 11, 1970.
xTraded to Los Angeles Dodgers for Outfielder-First Baseman Andy Kosco, February 10, 1971.

### CHAMPIONSHIP SERIES RECORD

| Year Club | League | G. | IP. | W. | L. | Pct. | H. | R. | ER. | SO. | BB. | ERA. |
|---|---|---|---|---|---|---|---|---|---|---|---|---|
| 1974–Los Angeles .......................National | | 1 | 4 | 0 | 0 | .000 | 1 | 0 | 0 | 0 | 1 | 0.00 |

### WORLD SERIES RECORD

| Year Club | League | G. | IP. | W. | L. | Pct. | H. | R. | ER. | SO. | BB. | ERA. |
|---|---|---|---|---|---|---|---|---|---|---|---|---|
| 1963–New York ..........................American | | 1 | 5 | 0 | 1 | .000 | 7 | 3 | 3 | 6 | 1 | 5.40 |
| 1964–New York ..........................American | | 3 | 7⅔ | 0 | 1 | .000 | 9 | 8 | 7 | 5 | 2 | 8.22 |
| 1974–Los Angeles .......................National | | 1 | 3⅔ | 0 | 1 | .000 | 4 | 3 | 1 | 3 | 4 | 2.45 |
| World Series Totals .................................. | | 5 | 16⅓ | 0 | 3 | .000 | 20 | 14 | 11 | 14 | 7 | 6.06 |

### ALL-STAR GAME RECORD

| Year League | IP. | W. | L. | Pct. | H. | R. | ER. | SO. | BB. | ERA. |
|---|---|---|---|---|---|---|---|---|---|---|
| 1967–American ...................................................... | 2 | 0 | 0 | .000 | 2 | 0 | 0 | 2 | 0 | 0.00 |

## BRIAN JAY DOWNING

Born October 9, 1950, at Los Angeles, Calif.
Height, 5.10. Weight, 185.
Throws and bats righthanded.
Hobby–Music.
Attended Cypress Junior College, Cypress, Calif.

| Year Club | League | Pos. | G. | AB. | R. | H. | 2B. | 3B. | HR. | RBI. | B.A. | PO. | A. | E. | F.A. |
|---|---|---|---|---|---|---|---|---|---|---|---|---|---|---|---|
| 1970–Sarasota W. S. ..Gulf C. | | C-OF | 34 | 96 | 16 | 21 | 1 | 1 | 0 | 14 | .219 | 167 | 11 | 1 | .994 |
| 1971–Appleton............Midw. | | 3-C-O | 99 | 333 | 51 | 82 | 6 | 3 | 3 | 22 | .246 | 353 | 98 | 13 | .972 |
| 1972–Knoxville .........South. | | O-3-C | 135 | 442 | 75 | 123 | 24 | 7 | 15 | 67 | .278 | 250 | 123 | 21 | .947 |
| 1973–Iowa..................A. A. | | 3-O-C | 68 | 228 | 34 | 56 | 6 | 1 | 7 | 27 | .246 | 84 | 90 | 8 | .956 |
| 1973–Chicago† .........Amer. | | O-C-3 | 34 | 73 | 5 | 13 | 1 | 0 | 2 | 4 | .178 | 72 | 17 | 5 | .947 |
| 1974–Chicago ...........Amer. | | C-OF | 108 | 293 | 41 | 66 | 12 | 1 | 10 | 39 | .225 | 337 | 30 | 2 | .995 |
| 1975–Chicago ...........Amer. | | C | 138 | 420 | 58 | 101 | 12 | 1 | 7 | 41 | .240 | 730 | 84 | 8 | .990 |
| 1976–Chicago‡ .........Amer. | | C-DH | 104 | 317 | 38 | 81 | 14 | 0 | 3 | 30 | .256 | 450 | 38 | 6 | .988 |
| Major League Totals ..................... | | | 384 | 1103 | 142 | 261 | 39 | 2 | 22 | 114 | .237 | 1589 | 169 | 21 | .988 |

†On disabled list, June 1 to July 9, 1973.
‡On disabled list, July 30 through August 15, 1976.

## BLAKE REGAN DOYLE

Born January 26, 1954, at Glasgow, Ky.
Height, 5.10. Weight, 160.
Throws right and bats lefthanded.
Hobby–Golf.
Attended Western Kentucky University, Bowling Green, Ky.

Brother of Denny and Brian, infielders in Boston Red Sox' and
New York Yankees' organizations, respectively.
Led Appalachian League in stolen bases with 20 in 1972.

| Year Club | League | Pos. | G. | AB. | R. | H. | 2B. | 3B. | HR. | RBI. | B.A. | PO. | A. | E. | F.A. |
|---|---|---|---|---|---|---|---|---|---|---|---|---|---|---|---|
| 1972-Bluefield ..........Appal. | | 2B | 67 | 247 | 46 | 74 | 12 | 2 | 0 | 24 | .300 | *152 | 149 | 16 | .950 |
| 1973-Miami ..............Fla. St. | | 3B-2B | 39 | 98 | 14 | 23 | 2 | 0 | 0 | 7 | .235 | 28 | 53 | 12 | .871 |
| 1973-Lodi .................Calif. | | 2B | 69 | 225 | 23 | 58 | 4 | 1 | 0 | 21 | .258 | 140 | 164 | 10 | .968 |
| 1974-Lodi .................Calif. | | 2B | 125 | 519 | 67 | 143 | 14 | 1 | 0 | 32 | .276 | 325 | 337 | 27 | *.961 |
| 1975-Asheville ..........South. | | 2B | 108 | 354 | 41 | 92 | 9 | 4 | 1 | 31 | .260 | 238 | 344 | •22 | .964 |
| 1976-Charlotte ..........W. Car. | | 2B | 134 | *529 | 72 | *158 | 16 | 5 | 1 | 53 | .299 | 297 | 375 | 24 | .966 |

Listed on Baltimore Orioles' 1977 spring roster.

## ROBERT DENNIS DOYLE
### (Denny)

Born January 17, 1944, at Glasgow, Ky.
Height, 5.10. Weight, 165.
Throws right and bats lefthanded.
Hobby—Golf.
Attended Morehead State University, Morehead, Ky.; received Bachelor of Arts degree
in Physical Education and Geography.
Twin brothers, Blake and Brian, infielders in the Baltimore Oriole and
New York Yankee organizations, respectively.
Tied major league record for fewest putouts, second baseman, extra-inning game, 0, June 14, 1974 (15 innings).
Led Eastern League second basemen in double plays with 76 in 1968.
Led Pacific Coast League in total bases with 257 and led second basemen in double plays with 74 in 1969.
Named Most Valuable Player and Rookie of the Year in Pacific Coast League, 1969.

| Year Club | League | Pos. | G. | AB. | R. | H. | 2B. | 3B. | HR. | RBI. | B.A. | PO. | A. | E. | F.A. |
|---|---|---|---|---|---|---|---|---|---|---|---|---|---|---|---|
| 1966-Spartanburg ......W. Car. | | 2B | 124 | *497 | 94 | *153 | 21 | 5 | 3 | 63 | .308 | *296 | *360 | *37 | .947 |
| 1967-Tidewater..........Carol. | | 2B | 127 | 493 | 79 | 137 | 18 | 4 | 9 | 38 | .278 | 269 | 326 | *22 | .964 |
| 1968-Reading ...........East. | | 2B | 125 | 464 | 45 | 114 | 12 | 5 | 1 | 26 | .246 | *275 | *297 | 15 | *.974 |
| 1969-Eugene..............P. C. | | *2B-SS | 143 | *587 | 91 | *182 | 29 | 14 | 6 | 47 | .310 | *272 | *408 | *21 | .970 |
| 1970-Philadelphia ......Nat. | | 2B | 112 | 413 | 43 | 86 | 10 | 7 | 2 | 16 | .208 | 251 | 228 | 11 | .978 |
| 1971-Philadelphia† ...Nat. | | 2B | 95 | 342 | 34 | 79 | 12 | 1 | 3 | 24 | .231 | 241 | 264 | 17 | .967 |
| 1972-Philadelphia ......Nat. | | 2B | 123 | 442 | 33 | 110 | 14 | 2 | 1 | 26 | .249 | 265 | 288 | 10 | .982 |
| 1973-Philadelphia‡ ....Nat. | | 2B | 116 | 370 | 45 | 101 | 9 | 3 | 3 | 26 | .273 | 231 | 296 | 14 | .974 |
| 1974-California .........Amer. | | 2B-SS | 147 | 511 | 47 | 133 | 19 | 2 | 1 | 34 | .260 | 311 | 405 | 12 | .984 |
| 1975-Calif.§-Boston ....Amer. | | 2-3-S | 97 | 325 | 50 | 97 | 21 | 2 | 4 | 36 | .298 | 155 | 220 | 12 | .969 |
| 1976-Boston ..............Amer. | | 2B | 117 | 432 | 51 | 108 | 15 | 5 | 0 | 26 | .250 | 209 | 311 | 12 | .977 |
| National League Totals ................. | | | 446 | 1567 | 155 | 376 | 45 | 13 | 9 | 92 | .240 | 988 | 1076 | 52 | .975 |
| American League Totals ............... | | | 361 | 1268 | 148 | 338 | 55 | 9 | 5 | 96 | .267 | 675 | 936 | 36 | .978 |
| Major League Totals ...................... | | | 807 | 2835 | 303 | 714 | 100 | 22 | 14 | 188 | •252 | 1663 | 2012 | 88 | .977 |

†On disabled list, August 17 through September 1, 1971.
‡Traded to California Angels for Pitcher Aurelio Monteagudo and Outfielder Chris Coletta (latter assigned from El Paso to Toledo), December 6, 1973, to complete deal in which Phillies obtained Infielder Billy Grabarkewitz, August 14, 1973.
§Traded to Boston Red Sox for a player to be named later, June 14, 1975; Red Sox sent Pitcher Chuck Ross to California Angels, March 5, 1976, to complete deal.

CHAMPIONSHIP SERIES RECORD

| Year Club | League | Pos. | G. | AB. | R. | H. | 2B. | 3B. | HR. | RBI. | B.A. | PO. | A. | E. | F.A. |
|---|---|---|---|---|---|---|---|---|---|---|---|---|---|---|---|
| 1975-Boston ..............Amer. | | 2B | 3 | 11 | 3 | 3 | 0 | 0 | 0 | 2 | .273 | 5 | 8 | 1 | .929 |

WORLD SERIES RECORD

| Year Club | League | Pos. | G. | AB. | R. | H. | 2B. | 3B. | HR. | RBI. | B.A. | PO. | A. | E. | F.A. |
|---|---|---|---|---|---|---|---|---|---|---|---|---|---|---|---|
| 1975-Boston ..............Amer. | | 2B | 7 | 30 | 3 | 8 | 1 | 1 | 0 | 0 | .267 | 13 | 23 | 3 | .923 |

## RICHARD ANTHONY DRAGO
### (Dick)

Born June 25, 1945, at Toledo, O.
Height, 6.01. Weight, 190.
Throws and bats righthanded.
Hobbies—Golf, bowling, fishing.
Attended University of Detroit, Detroit, Mich., and University of Tampa, Tampa, Fla.
Pitched seven-inning, 5-0 no-hit victory against Greensboro, May 15, 1966.
Led Carolina League in shutouts with 7 in 1966 and tied for Southern League lead in shutouts with 4 in 1967.
Tied for Southern League lead in complete games by pitchers with 12 in 1967.

| Year Club | League | G. | IP. | W. | L. | Pct. | H. | R. | ER. | SO. | BB. | ERA. |
|---|---|---|---|---|---|---|---|---|---|---|---|---|
| 1965-Daytona Beach ....................Florida St. | | 14 | 80 | 4 | 7 | .364 | 84 | 42 | 29 | 64 | 28 | 3.26 |
| 1965-Rocky Mount......................Carolina | | 13 | 62 | 1 | 7 | .125 | 66 | 36 | 24 | 41 | 30 | 3.48 |
| 1966-Rocky Mount......................Carolina | | 29 | 186 | 15 | 9 | .625 | 144 | 45 | 37 | 151 | 49 | 1.79 |
| 1967-Montgomery .......................Southern | | 28 | 179 | *15 | 10 | .600 | 171 | 65 | 48 | *134 | 54 | 2.41 |
| 1967-Toledo................................Int'national | | 1 | 3 | 0 | 0 | .000 | 2 | 1 | 1 | 1 | 0 | 3.00 |
| 1968-Toledo† ..............................Int'national | | 27 | 182 | 15 | 8 | .652 | 163 | 77 | 68 | 146 | 43 | 3.36 |

— 98 —

| Year Club | League | G. | IP. | W. | L. | Pct. | H. | R. | ER. | SO. | BB. | ERA. |
|---|---|---|---|---|---|---|---|---|---|---|---|---|
| 1969—Kansas City | American | 41 | 201 | 11 | 13 | .458 | 190 | 95 | 84 | 108 | 65 | 3.76 |
| 1970—Kansas City | American | 35 | 240 | 9 | 15 | .375 | 239 | 110 | 100 | 127 | 72 | 3.75 |
| 1971—Kansas City | American | 35 | 241 | 17 | 11 | .607 | 251 | 84 | 80 | 109 | 46 | 2.99 |
| 1972—Kansas City | American | 34 | 239 | 12 | 17 | .414 | 230 | 88 | 80 | 135 | 51 | 3.01 |
| 1973—Kansas City‡ | American | 37 | 213 | 12 | 14 | .462 | 252 | 116 | 100 | 98 | 76 | 4.23 |
| 1974—Boston | American | 33 | 176 | 7 | 10 | .412 | 165 | 71 | 68 | 90 | 56 | 3.48 |
| 1975—Boston§ | American | 40 | 73 | 2 | 2 | .500 | 69 | 31 | 31 | 43 | 31 | 3.82 |
| 1976—California | American | 43 | 79 | 7 | 8 | .467 | 80 | 42 | 39 | 43 | 31 | 4.44 |
| Major League Totals | | 298 | 1462 | 77 | 90 | .461 | 1476 | 637 | 582 | 753 | 428 | 3.58 |

†Recalled by Detroit Tigers; selected by Kansas City Royals from Detroit in expansion draft, October 15, 1968.

‡Traded to Boston Red Sox for Pitcher Marty Pattin, October 24, 1973.

§Traded to California Angels for Outfielders John Balaz and Dick Sharon and Shortstop Dave Machemer, March 3, 1976.

CHAMPIONSHIP SERIES RECORD

| Year Club | League | G. | IP. | W. | L. | Pct. | H. | R. | ER. | SO. | BB. | ERA. |
|---|---|---|---|---|---|---|---|---|---|---|---|---|
| 1975—Boston | American | 2 | 4⅔ | 0 | 0 | .000 | 2 | 0 | 0 | 2 | 1 | 0.00 |

WORLD SERIES RECORD

| Year Club | League | G. | IP. | W. | L. | Pct. | H. | R. | ER. | SO. | BB. | ERA. |
|---|---|---|---|---|---|---|---|---|---|---|---|---|
| 1975—Boston | American | 2 | 4 | 0 | 1 | .000 | 3 | 1 | 1 | 1 | 1 | 2.25 |

## KEVIN MAURICE DRAKE

Born April 12, 1956, at Nogaya, Japan.
Height, 6.04. Weight, 200.
Throws and bats righthanded.
Hobbies—All sports and youth activities.

| Year Club | League | Pos. | G. | AB. | R. | H. | 2B. | 3B. | HR. | RBI. | B.A. | PO. | A. | E. | F.A. |
|---|---|---|---|---|---|---|---|---|---|---|---|---|---|---|---|
| 1974—Cedar Rapids | Midw. | OF | 25 | 108 | 9 | 24 | 0 | 2 | 0 | 8 | .222 | 48 | 4 | 4 | .929 |
| 1974—Denver | A. A. | OF | 15 | 61 | 12 | 17 | 2 | 1 | 0 | 4 | .279 | 31 | 1 | 2 | .941 |
| 1975—Columbus | South. | OF | 39 | 121 | 12 | 20 | 4 | 0 | 1 | 10 | .165 | 83 | 1 | 5 | .944 |
| 1975—Dubuque | Midw. | OF | 51 | 150 | 22 | 33 | 4 | 0 | 3 | 11 | .220 | 58 | 3 | 5 | .924 |
| 1976—Columbus | South. | OF | 128 | 437 | 50 | 117 | 6 | 4 | 2 | 33 | .268 | 310 | 12 | 5 | .985 |

Listed on Houston Astros' 1977 spring roster.

## ROBERT ALAN DRESSLER
### (Rob)

Born February 2, 1954, at Portland, Ore.
Height, 6.03. Weight, 190.
Throws and bats righthanded.
Hobbies—Camping and listening to classical music.
Attended Portland State University, Portland, Ore.

Led Texas League pitchers in games started with 30 in 1974.
Tied for Pacific Coast League lead in shutouts with 3 in 1975.

| Year Club | League | G. | IP. | W. | L. | Pct. | H. | R. | ER. | SO. | BB. | ERA. |
|---|---|---|---|---|---|---|---|---|---|---|---|---|
| 1972—Great Falls | Pioneer | 14 | 92 | 5 | 7 | .417 | 88 | 44 | 31 | 74 | 38 | 3.03 |
| 1973—Decatur | Midwest | 25 | 182 | 11 | 10 | .524 | 179 | 72 | 57 | 133 | 54 | 2.82 |
| 1974—Amarillo | Texas | 30 | *191 | 11 | 12 | .478 | *214 | 97 | 81 | 125 | 62 | 3.82 |
| 1975—Lafayette | Texas | 6 | 46 | 5 | 1 | .833 | 32 | 11 | 10 | 5 | 9 | 1.96 |
| 1975—Phoenix | P. Coast | 25 | 169 | 8 | 14 | .364 | 174 | 81 | 65 | 91 | 58 | 3.46 |
| 1975—San Francisco | National | 3 | 16 | 1 | 0 | 1.000 | 17 | 3 | 2 | 6 | 4 | 1.13 |
| 1976—Phoenix | P. Coast | 6 | 48 | 5 | 1 | .833 | 46 | 7 | 6 | 18 | 11 | 1.13 |
| 1976—San Francisco | National | 25 | 108 | 3 | 10 | .231 | 125 | 68 | 53 | 33 | 35 | 4.42 |
| Major League Totals | | 28 | 124 | 4 | 10 | .286 | 142 | 71 | 55 | 39 | 39 | 3.99 |

## DANIEL DRIESSEN
### (Dan)

Born July 29, 1951, at Hilton Head, S. C.
Height, 5.11. Weight, 187.
Throws right and bats lefthanded.

| Year Club | League | Pos. | G. | AB. | R. | H. | 2B. | 3B. | HR. | RBI. | B.A. | PO. | A. | E. | F.A. |
|---|---|---|---|---|---|---|---|---|---|---|---|---|---|---|---|
| 1970—Tampa | Fla. St. | 1B | 93 | 242 | 28 | 54 | 2 | 1 | 0 | 20 | .223 | 473 | 37 | 5 | .990 |
| 1971—Tampa | Fla. St. | 1B | 136 | 468 | 72 | 153 | 27 | 9 | 4 | 62 | .327 | 1064 | 86 | 15 | .987 |
| 1972—Three Rivers | East. | *1B-3B | 136 | 481 | 62 | 155 | 37 | 4 | 4 | 65 | .322 | 805 | 138 | 9 | *.991 |
| 1973—Indianapolis | A. A. | 3B-1B | 47 | 181 | 42 | 74 | 14 | 4 | 6 | 46 | .409 | 50 | 97 | 6 | .961 |
| 1973—Cincinnati | Nat. | 3-1-O | 102 | 366 | 49 | 110 | 15 | 2 | 4 | 47 | .301 | 160 | 157 | 12 | .964 |
| 1974—Cincinnati | Nat. | 3-1-O | 150 | 470 | 63 | 132 | 23 | 6 | 7 | 56 | .281 | 186 | 206 | 26 | .938 |
| 1975—Cincinnati† | Nat. | 1B-OF | 88 | 210 | 38 | 59 | 8 | 1 | 7 | 38 | .281 | 309 | 20 | 5 | .985 |
| 1976—Cincinnati | Nat. | 1B-OF | 98 | 219 | 32 | 54 | 11 | 1 | 7 | 44 | .247 | 314 | 23 | 2 | .994 |
| Major League Totals | | 338 | 1265 | 182 | 355 | 57 | 10 | 25 | 185 | .277 | 969 | 406 | 45 | .968 |

†On disabled list, March 23 to April 15, 1975.

| Year Club League | Pos. | G. | AB. | R. | H. | 2B. | 3B. | HR. | RBI. | B.A. | PO. | A. | E. | F.A. |
|---|---|---|---|---|---|---|---|---|---|---|---|---|---|---|
| 1973–Cincinnati..........Nat. | 3B-PR | 4 | 12 | 0 | 2 | 1 | 0 | 0 | 1 | .167 | 3 | 2 | 1 | .833 |
| 1976–Cincinnati..........Nat. | PH | 1 | 1 | 0 | 0 | 0 | 0 | 0 | 0 | .000 | 0 | 0 | 0 | .000 |
| Championship Series Totals ............ | | 5 | 13 | 0 | 2 | 1 | 0 | 0 | 1 | .154 | 3 | 2 | 1 | .833 |

WORLD SERIES RECORD

| Year Club League | Pos. | G. | AB. | R. | H. | 2B. | 3B. | HR. | RBI. | B.A. | PO. | A. | E. | F.A. |
|---|---|---|---|---|---|---|---|---|---|---|---|---|---|---|
| 1975–Cincinnati..........Nat. | PH | 2 | 2 | 0 | 0 | 0 | 0 | 0 | 0 | .000 | 0 | 0 | 0 | .000 |
| 1976–Cincinnati..........Nat. | DH | 4 | 14 | 4 | 5 | 2 | 0 | 1 | 1 | .357 | 0 | 0 | 0 | .000 |
| World Series Totals ....................... | | 6 | 16 | 4 | 5 | 2 | 0 | 1 | 1 | .312 | 0 | 0 | 0 | .000 |

## FRANK THOMAS DUFFY

Born October 14, 1946, at Oakland, Calif.
Height, 6.01. Weight, 180.
Throws and bats righthanded.
Hobby–Playing the guitar.
Attended Stanford University, Palo Alto, Calif.; received Bachelor of Arts degree
in Psychology.

Led American Association in sacrifice hits with 11 in 1970.

| Year Club League | Pos. | G. | AB. | R. | H. | 2B. | 3B. | HR. | RBI. | B.A. | PO. | A. | E. | F.A. |
|---|---|---|---|---|---|---|---|---|---|---|---|---|---|---|
| 1968–Asheville†.........South. | SS | 93 | 346 | 34 | 85 | 12 | 4 | 4 | 25 | .246 | 162 | 259 | 13 | ∗.970 |
| 1969–Indianapolis‡ ....A. A. | SS-3B | 107 | 379 | 61 | 99 | 15 | 3 | 4 | 46 | .261 | 198 | 335 | 28 | .950 |
| 1970–Indianapolis ......A. A. | SS | 117 | 415 | 57 | 109 | 11 | 2 | 7 | 33 | .263 | 208 | 335 | 16 | ∗.971 |
| 1970–Cincinnati..........Nat. | SS | 6 | 11 | 1 | 2 | 2 | 0 | 0 | 0 | .182 | 4 | 12 | 0 | 1.000 |
| 1971–Cin.§-S.F.x ........Nat. | SS-2-3 | 34 | 44 | 4 | 8 | 1 | 0 | 0 | 3 | .182 | 24 | 43 | 3 | .957 |
| 1972–Cleveland ..........Amer. | SS | 130 | 385 | 23 | 92 | 16 | 4 | 3 | 27 | .239 | 197 | 360 | 13 | .977 |
| 1973–Cleveland y ......Amer. | SS | 116 | 361 | 34 | 95 | 16 | 4 | 8 | 50 | .263 | 198 | 377 | 8 | ∗.986 |
| 1974–Cleveland .........Amer. | SS | 158 | 549 | 62 | 128 | 18 | 0 | 8 | 48 | .233 | 242 | 491 | 15 | .980 |
| 1975–Cleveland .........Amer. | SS | 146 | 482 | 44 | 117 | 22 | 2 | 1 | 47 | .243 | 225 | 464 | 16 | .977 |
| 1976–Cleveland .........Amer. | SS | 133 | 392 | 38 | 83 | 11 | 2 | 2 | 30 | .212 | 222 | 344 | 10 | .983 |
| National League Totals .................. | | 40 | 55 | 5 | 10 | 3 | 0 | 0 | 3 | .182 | 28 | 55 | 3 | .965 |
| American League Totals ............... | | 683 | 2169 | 201 | 515 | 83 | 12 | 22 | 202 | .237 | 1084 | 2036 | 62 | .981 |
| Major League Totals ..................... | | 723 | 2224 | 206 | 525 | 86 | 12 | 22 | 205 | .236 | 1112 | 2091 | 65 | .980 |

†On military list, October 12, 1967 through May 6, 1968. On temporary inactive list, July 6 through July 22.
‡On temporary inactive list, July 25 through August 11.
§Traded with Pitcher Vern Geishert (later assigned from Indianapolis to Phoenix) to San Francisco Giants for Outfielder George Foster, May 29, 1971.
xTraded with Pitcher Gaylord Perry to Cleveland Indians for Pitcher Sam McDowell, November 29, 1971.
yOn disabled list, April 9 to May 4, 1973.

CHAMPIONSHIP SERIES RECORD

| Year Club League | Pos. | G. | AB. | R. | H. | 2B. | 3B. | HR. | RBI. | B.A. | PO. | A. | E. | F.A. |
|---|---|---|---|---|---|---|---|---|---|---|---|---|---|---|
| 1971–San Francisco ..Nat. | PH | 1 | 1 | 0 | 0 | 0 | 0 | 0 | 0 | .000 | 0 | 0 | 0 | .000 |

## DANIEL LYNN DUMOULIN
### (Dan)

Born August 20, 1953, at Kokomo, Ind.
Height, 6.00. Weight, 175.
Throws and bats righthanded.
Hobbies–Carpentry and basketball.

| Year Club | League | G. | IP. | W. | L. | Pct. | H. | R. | ER. | SO. | BB. | ERA. |
|---|---|---|---|---|---|---|---|---|---|---|---|---|
| 1974–Billings .............................Pioneer | | 12 | 46 | 4 | 2 | .667 | 43 | 34 | 17 | 29 | 31 | 3.33 |
| 1975–Tampa ...............................Florida St. | | 45 | 84 | 7 | 3 | .700 | 55 | 22 | 19 | 64 | 46 | 2.04 |
| 1976–Three Rivers.......................Eastern | | 38 | 58 | 2 | 1 | .667 | 50 | 27 | 13 | 35 | 26 | 2.02 |

Listed on Cincinnati Reds' 1977 spring roster.

## DAVID EDWIN DUNCAN
### (Dave)

Born September 26, 1945, at Dallas, Tex.
Height, 6.02. Weight, 195.
Throws and bats righthanded.
Hobbies–Hunting, fishing, water skiing and golf.

Tied following major league records: unassisted double play, catcher, game, June 21, 1972; most doubles and most consecutive doubles, game, 4, June 30, 1975 (2nd game of doubleheader).
Tied for Southern League lead in double plays by catchers with 8 in 1967.
Named Most Valuable Player in California League, 1966.
Received reported $65,000 bonus to sign with Kansas City Athletics, 1963.

| Year Club League | Pos. | G. | AB. | R. | H. | 2B. | 3B. | HR. | RBI. | B.A. | PO. | A. | E. | F.A. |
|---|---|---|---|---|---|---|---|---|---|---|---|---|---|---|
| 1963–Daytona Beach ..Fla. St. | C | 47 | 152 | 16 | 22 | 2 | 1 | 4 | 10 | .145 | 250 | 23 | 12 | .958 |
| 1964–Kansas City ......Amer. | C | 25 | 53 | 2 | 9 | 0 | 1 | 1 | 5 | .170 | 99 | 7 | 2 | .981 |
| 1965–Birmingham ......South. | C | 61 | 192 | 20 | 40 | 11 | 2 | 6 | 20 | .208 | 405 | 31 | 9 | .980 |

| Year | Club | League | Pos. | G. | AB. | R. | H. | 2B. | 3B. | HR. | RBI. | B.A. | PO. | A. | E. | F.A. |
|---|---|---|---|---|---|---|---|---|---|---|---|---|---|---|---|---|
| 1965–Lewiston | ......... | N'west | C | 55 | 188 | 30 | 52 | 9 | 1 | 9 | 35 | .277 | 426 | 28 | 7 | .985 |
| 1966–Modesto | ............ | Calif. | C-OF | 121 | 439 | 103 | 119 | 8 | 2 | ∗46 | 112 | .271 | 807 | 61 | 14 | .984 |
| 1967–Birmingham | ...... | South. | C | 95 | 323 | 40 | 78 | 14 | 1 | 13 | 48 | .241 | 552 | 50 | 13 | .979 |
| 1967–Kansas City | ...... | Amer. | C | 34 | 101 | 9 | 19 | 4 | 0 | 5 | 11 | .188 | 176 | 13 | 4 | .979 |
| 1968–Vancouver | ........ | P. C. | C | 35 | 114 | 21 | 36 | 4 | 2 | 6 | 21 | .316 | 177 | 20 | 1 | .995 |
| 1968–Oakland | ........... | Amer. | C | 82 | 246 | 15 | 47 | 4 | 0 | 7 | 28 | .191 | 474 | 41 | 7 | .987 |
| 1969–Oakland | ......... | Amer. | C | 58 | 127 | 11 | 16 | 3 | 0 | 3 | 22 | .126 | 209 | 15 | 4 | .982 |
| 1970–Oakland† | ......... | Amer. | C | 86 | 232 | 21 | 60 | 7 | 0 | 10 | 29 | .259 | 373 | 28 | 9 | .978 |
| 1971–Oakland‡ | ......... | Amer. | C | 103 | 363 | 39 | 92 | 13 | 1 | 15 | 40 | .253 | 678 | 41 | ∗12 | .984 |
| 1972–Oakland§ | ......... | Amer. | C | 121 | 403 | 39 | 88 | 13 | 0 | 19 | 59 | .218 | 661 | 43 | 5 | .993 |
| 1973–Cleveland x | ...... | Amer. | C | 95 | 344 | 43 | 80 | 11 | 1 | 17 | 43 | .233 | 533 | 41 | 7 | .988 |
| 1974–Cleveland y | ...... | Amer. | C-1B | 136 | 425 | 45 | 85 | 10 | 1 | 16 | 46 | .200 | 564 | 48 | 15 | .976 |
| 1975–Baltimore | ......... | Amer. | C | 96 | 307 | 30 | 63 | 7 | 0 | 12 | 41 | .205 | 397 | 41 | 8 | .982 |
| 1976–Baltimore z | ...... | Amer. | C | 93 | 284 | 20 | 58 | 7 | 0 | 4 | 17 | .204 | 371 | 35 | 6 | .985 |
| Major League Totals | ..................... | | | 929 | 2885 | 274 | 617 | 79 | 4 | 109 | 441 | .214 | 4535 | 353 | 79 | .984 |

†On military list August 7 through August 24.

‡On military list July 23 through August 9.

§Traded with Outfielder George Hendrick to Cleveland Indians for Catcher Ray Fosse and Infielder Jack Heidemann, March 24, 1973.

xOn disabled list, July 2 to August 18, 1973.

yTraded with Outfielder Alvin McGrew to Baltimore Orioles for First Baseman Boog Powell and Pitcher Don Hood, February 25, 1975.

zTraded to Chicago White Sox for Outfielder Pat Kelly, November 18, 1976.

CHAMPIONSHIP SERIES RECORD

| Year | Club | League | Pos. | G. | AB. | R. | H. | 2B. | 3B. | HR. | RBI. | B.A. | PO. | A. | E. | F.A. |
|---|---|---|---|---|---|---|---|---|---|---|---|---|---|---|---|---|
| 1971–Oakland | ............. | Amer. | C | 2 | 6 | 0 | 3 | 1 | 0 | 0 | 2 | .500 | 15 | 0 | 0 | 1.000 |
| 1972–Oakland | ............. | Amer. | PH-C | 2 | 2 | 0 | 0 | 0 | 0 | 0 | 0 | .000 | 5 | 1 | 0 | 1.000 |
| Championship Series Totals | ............ | | | 4 | 8 | 0 | 3 | 1 | 0 | 0 | 2 | .375 | 20 | 1 | 0 | 1.000 |

WORLD SERIES RECORD

| Year | Club | League | Pos. | G. | AB. | R. | H. | 2B. | 3B. | HR. | RBI. | B.A. | PO. | A. | E. | F.A. |
|---|---|---|---|---|---|---|---|---|---|---|---|---|---|---|---|---|
| 1972–Oakland | ............. | Amer. | PH-C | 3 | 5 | 0 | 1 | 0 | 0 | 0 | 0 | .200 | 5 | 1 | 0 | 1.000 |

ALL-STAR GAME RECORD

Member of American League All-Star Team for 1971 game; did not play.

## TAYLOR McDOWELL DUNCAN, JR.

Born May 12, 1953, at Memphis, Tenn.
Height, 6.00. Weight, 170.
Throws and bats righthanded.
Hobby–Billiards.
Attended American River College, Sacramento, Calif.

Led Southern League third basemen in double plays with 22 in 1973.
Led International League third baseman in double plays with 28 in 1975.

| Year | Club | League | Pos. | G. | AB. | R. | H. | 2B. | 3B. | HR. | RBI. | B.A. | PO. | A. | E. | F.A. |
|---|---|---|---|---|---|---|---|---|---|---|---|---|---|---|---|---|
| 1971–Wytheville† | ....... | Appal. | SS | 13 | 42 | 10 | 16 | 1 | 1 | 1 | 7 | .381 | 17 | 36 | 0 | 1.000 |
| 1972–Greenwood‡ | ...... | W. Car. | SS | 120 | 423 | 54 | 118 | 15 | 5 | 4 | 47 | .279 | ∗155 | ∗315 | 31 | ∗.938 |
| 1973–Asheville | ......... | South. | 3B | 138 | 485 | 61 | 142 | ●30 | 3 | 9 | 81 | .293 | ∗108 | ∗264 | ∗23 | ∗.942 |
| 1974–Asheville | ......... | South. | 3B | 125 | 445 | 60 | 130 | 25 | 0 | 5 | 58 | .292 | 84 | 187 | 25 | .916 |
| 1975–Rochester | ......... | Int. | 3B | 119 | 384 | 43 | 109 | 16 | 3 | 6 | 54 | .284 | 94 | 222 | ∗19 | .943 |
| 1976–Rochester | ......... | Int. | 3B-SS | 127 | 447 | 50 | 121 | 24 | 2 | 11 | 69 | .271 | 82 | 208 | 13 | .957 |

†On disabled list, July 5 to August 30, 1971.

‡Traded with Catcher-First Baseman Earl Williams by Atlanta Braves to Baltimore Orioles for Pitchers Pat Dobson and Roric Harrison, Second Baseman Dave Johnson and Catcher John Oates, November 30, 1972.
Listed on Baltimore Orioles' 1977 spring roster.

## STEVEN JOHN DUNNING
### (Steve)

Born May 15, 1949, at Denver, Colo.
Height, 6.02. Weight, 205.
Throws and bats righthanded.
Hobbies–Golf, tennis and bridge.
Attended Stanford University, Palo Alto, Calif.

Pitched 10-0 no-hit victory against Sacramento, August 16, 1974.
Led American Association pitchers in complete games with 16 in 1975.

| Year | Club | League | G. | IP. | W. | L. | Pct. | H. | R. | ER. | SO. | BB. | ERA. |
|---|---|---|---|---|---|---|---|---|---|---|---|---|---|
| 1970–Cleveland | .......................... | American | 19 | 94 | 4 | 9 | .308 | 93 | 55 | 52 | 77 | 54 | 4.98 |
| 1971–Cleveland | .......................... | American | 31 | 184 | 8 | 14 | .364 | 173 | 98 | 92 | 132 | 109 | 4.50 |
| 1972–Portland | ........................... | P. Coast | 23 | 132 | 4 | 7 | .364 | 124 | 75 | 70 | 105 | 67 | 4.77 |
| 1972–Cleveland | .......................... | American | 16 | 105 | 6 | 4 | .600 | 98 | 39 | 38 | 52 | 43 | 3.26 |
| 1973–Cleveland†-Texas | ................ | American | 27 | 112 | 2 | 8 | .200 | 118 | 78 | 69 | 48 | 65 | 5.54 |
| 1974–Spokane | ........................... | P. Coast | 22 | 150 | 9 | 7 | .563 | 164 | 96 | 78 | 118 | 70 | 4.68 |
| 1974–Texas‡ | ............................... | American | 1 | 2 | 0 | 0 | .000 | 3 | 5 | 5 | 1 | 3 | 22.50 |
| 1975–Denver§ x | ........................... | Am. Assoc. | 28 | ∗196 | ∗15 | 9 | .625 | 187 | 79 | 76 | ∗139 | 85 | 3.49 |

| Year    Club | League | G. | IP. | W. | L. | Pct. | H. | R. | ER. | SO. | BB. | ERA. |
|---|---|---|---|---|---|---|---|---|---|---|---|---|
| 1976−California y | American | 4 | 6 | 0 | 0 | .000 | 9 | 9 | 5 | 4 | 6 | 7.50 |
| 1976−Denver | Am. Assoc. | 4 | 23 | 3 | 0 | 1.000 | 20 | 7 | 7 | 11 | 5 | 2.74 |
| 1976−Montreal z | National | 32 | 91 | 2 | 6 | .250 | 93 | 50 | 42 | 72 | 33 | 4.15 |
| American League Totals | | 98 | 503 | 20 | 35 | .364 | 494 | 284 | 261 | 314 | 280 | 4.67 |
| National League Totals | | 32 | 91 | 2 | 6 | .250 | 93 | 50 | 42 | 72 | 33 | 4.15 |
| Major League Totals | | 130 | 594 | 22 | 41 | .349 | 587 | 334 | 303 | 386 | 313 | 4.59 |

†Traded to Texas Rangers for Pitcher Dick Bosman and Outfielder Ted Ford (latter assigned from Spokane to Oklahoma City), May 10, 1973.
‡Traded to Chicago White Sox for Pitcher Stan Perzanowski, February 25, 1975.
§Played in six games as a third baseman and one as an outfielder.
xTraded with Third Baseman Bill Melton by Chicago White Sox to California Angels for First Baseman Jim Spencer and Outfielder Morris Nettles, December 11, 1975.
ySold to Montreal Expos' organization, May 5, 1976.
zTraded with Infielder Pat Scanlon and Outfielder Tony Scott to St. Louis Cardinals for Pitchers Bill Grief and Angel Torres, and Outfielder Sam Mejias, November 6, 1976.

## MICHAEL DENNIS DUPREE
### (Mike)

Born May 29, 1953, at Kansas City, Kan.
Height, 6.01. Weight, 185.
Throws and bats righthanded.
Hobbies−Golf and sports in general.
Attended Fresno City College, Fresno, Calif.

| Year    Club | League | G. | IP. | W. | L. | Pct. | H. | R. | ER. | SO. | BB. | ERA. |
|---|---|---|---|---|---|---|---|---|---|---|---|---|
| 1975−Alexandria | Texas | 14 | 33 | 5 | 0 | 1.000 | 30 | 8 | 8 | 31 | 3 | 2.18 |
| 1976−San Diego | National | 12 | 16 | 0 | 0 | .000 | 18 | 17 | 16 | 5 | 7 | 9.00 |
| 1976−Hawaii | P. Coast | 20 | 95 | 4 | 4 | .500 | 90 | 37 | 36 | 60 | 43 | 3.41 |
| Major League Totals | | 12 | 16 | 0 | 0 | .000 | 18 | 17 | 16 | 5 | 7 | 9.00 |

### RECORD AS INFIELDER-OUTFIELDER
Led Northwest League third basemen in double plays with 13 in 1973.
Tied for Texas League lead in double plays by outfielders with 4 in 1975.

| Year    Club | League | Pos. | G. | AB. | R. | H. | 2B. | 3B. | HR. | RBI. | B.A. | PO. | A. | E. | F.A. |
|---|---|---|---|---|---|---|---|---|---|---|---|---|---|---|---|
| 1973−Walla Walla | Northw. | ★3-O-2 | 77 | 291 | 48 | ★102 | 14 | 0 | 4 | 35 | ★.351 | 103 | 144 | 15 | ★.943 |
| 1973−Alexandria | Texas | 3B | 3 | 10 | 0 | 1 | 1 | 0 | 0 | 0 | .100 | 2 | 6 | 1 | .889 |
| 1974−Alexandria† | Texas | 3B-OF | 78 | 282 | 26 | 84 | 19 | 2 | 3 | 30 | .298 | 81 | 87 | 18 | .903 |
| 1975−Alexandria | Tex. | ★OF-P | 124 | 417 | 47 | 111 | 12 | 3 | 0 | 34 | .266 | 211 | ★24 | 3 | ★.987 |

†On disabled list, July 7 to September 3, 1974.
Listed on San Diego Padres' 1977 spring roster.

## JAMES EDWARD DWYER
### (Jimmy)

Born January 3, 1950, at Evergreen Park, Ill.
Height, 5.10. Weight, 175.
Throws and bats lefthanded.
Hobbies−Golf and listening to music.
Attended Southern Illinois University, Carbondale, Ill.; received
Bachelor of Arts degree in Accounting.
Nephew of Don Dwyer, former minor leaguer in New York Giants' organization.

| Year    Club | League | Pos. | G. | AB. | R. | H. | 2B. | 3B. | HR. | RBI. | B.A. | PO. | A. | E. | F.A. |
|---|---|---|---|---|---|---|---|---|---|---|---|---|---|---|---|
| 1971−Cedar Rapids | Midw. | OF | 58 | 201 | 30 | 63 | 6 | 6 | 2 | 15 | .313 | 73 | 3 | 3 | .962 |
| 1972−Modesto | Calif. | OF | 92 | 354 | 87 | 115 | 15 | ★13 | 9 | 45 | .325 | 149 | 8 | 4 | .975 |
| 1972−Arkansas | Texas | OF | 44 | 162 | 16 | 41 | 1 | 0 | 2 | 14 | .253 | 101 | 6 | 2 | .982 |
| 1973−Tulsa | A.A. | OF | 87 | 349 | 63 | 135 | 22 | 8 | 1 | 40 | ★.387 | 127 | 8 | 5 | .964 |
| 1973−St. Louis | Nat. | OF | 28 | 57 | 7 | 11 | 1 | 1 | 0 | 0 | .193 | 32 | 0 | 0 | 1.000 |
| 1974−Tulsa | A.A. | OF-1B | 36 | 119 | 20 | 40 | 7 | 2 | 1 | 15 | .336 | 120 | 13 | 3 | .978 |
| 1974−St. Louis | Nat. | OF-1B | 74 | 86 | 13 | 24 | 1 | 0 | 2 | 11 | .279 | 31 | 3 | 0 | 1.000 |
| 1975−Tulsa | A.A. | OF | 33 | 109 | 17 | 44 | 8 | 2 | 1 | 17 | .404 | 49 | 2 | 2 | .962 |
| 1975−St. L.†−Mont. | Nat. | OF | 81 | 206 | 26 | 56 | 8 | 1 | 3 | 21 | .272 | 104 | 8 | 4 | .966 |
| 1976−Mont.‡−N.Y. § | Nat. | OF-PH | 61 | 105 | 9 | 19 | 3 | 1 | 0 | 5 | .181 | 35 | 0 | 1 | .972 |
| 1976−Tidewater | Int. | OF | 8 | 26 | 0 | 5 | 1 | 0 | 0 | 1 | .192 | 14 | 0 | 1 | .933 |
| Major League Totals | | 244 | 454 | 55 | 110 | 13 | 3 | 5 | 37 | .242 | 202 | 11 | 5 | .977 |

†Traded to Montreal Expos for Infielder Larry Lintz, July 25, 1975.
‡Traded with Outfielder Jose (Pepe) Mangual to New York Mets for Outfielder Del Unser and Infielder Wayne Garrett, July 21, 1976.
§In three-club deal, Cubs traded Outfielder-First Baseman Pete LaCock to Royals, the Mets sent Outfielder Jim Dwyer from Tidewater to Wichita (Cubs' affiliate), and Mets received a player to be named later, December 8, 1976; Royals sent Outfielder Sheldon Mallory to Tidewater to complete deal, December 13, 1976. Released, March 30, 1977.

---

### DID YOU KNOW −
That Christy Mathewson of the New York Giants pitched 10 complete games in World Series competition? It's an all-time record.

## DON ROBERT DYER
### (Duffy)

Born August 15, 1945, at Dayton, O.
Height, 6.00. Weight, 200.
Throws and bats righthanded.
Hobbies—Golf and billiards.
Attended Arizona State University, Tempe, Ariz.
Led National League catchers in double plays with 12 in 1972.
Led Eastern League catchers in double plays with 11 in 1967.

| Year | Club | League | Pos. | G. | AB. | R. | H. | 2B. | 3B. | HR. | RBI. | B.A. | PO. | A. | E. | F.A. |
|------|------|--------|------|----|-----|----|----|-----|-----|-----|------|------|-----|----|----|------|
| 1966 | Williamsport | East. | C | 22 | 52 | 3 | 9 | 2 | 0 | 0 | 1 | .173 | 86 | 12 | 0 | 1.000 |
| 1966 | Greenville | W. Car. | C | 19 | 57 | 7 | 14 | 0 | 1 | 0 | 2 | .246 | 169 | 5 | 0 | 1.000 |
| 1967 | Williamsport | East. | C-OF | 106 | 346 | 26 | 67 | 12 | 3 | 1 | 28 | .194 | 689 | 73 | 10 | .987 |
| 1968 | Jacksonville | Int. | ●C-3B | 111 | 339 | 39 | 78 | 10 | 4 | 16 | 43 | .230 | 654 | 65 | ●11 | .985 |
| 1968 | New York | Nat. | C | 1 | 3 | 0 | 1 | 0 | 0 | 0 | 0 | .333 | 8 | 0 | 0 | 1.000 |
| 1969 | Tidewater | Int. | C | 35 | 112 | 22 | 35 | 6 | 1 | 5 | 26 | .313 | 155 | 15 | 0 | 1.000 |
| 1969 | New York | Nat. | C | 29 | 74 | 5 | 19 | 3 | 1 | 3 | 12 | .257 | 105 | 10 | 1 | .991 |
| 1970 | New York | Nat. | C | 59 | 148 | 8 | 31 | 1 | 0 | 2 | 12 | .209 | 294 | 20 | 3 | .991 |
| 1971 | New York | Nat. | C | 59 | 169 | 13 | 39 | 7 | 1 | 2 | 18 | .231 | 336 | 21 | 3 | .992 |
| 1972 | New York | Nat. | C-OF | 94 | 325 | 33 | 75 | 17 | 3 | 8 | 36 | .231 | 690 | 61 | 6 | .992 |
| 1973 | New York | Nat. | C | 70 | 189 | 9 | 35 | 6 | 1 | 1 | 9 | .185 | 308 | 26 | 2 | .994 |
| 1974 | New York† | Nat. | C | 63 | 142 | 14 | 30 | 1 | 1 | 0 | 10 | .211 | 196 | 19 | 4 | .982 |
| 1975 | Pittsburgh | Nat. | C | 48 | 132 | 8 | 30 | 5 | 2 | 3 | 16 | .227 | 187 | 14 | 2 | .990 |
| 1976 | Pittsburgh | Nat. | C-PH | 69 | 184 | 12 | 41 | 8 | 0 | 3 | 9 | .223 | 279 | 37 | 2 | .994 |
| | Major League Totals | | | 492 | 1366 | 102 | 301 | 48 | 9 | 22 | 122 | .220 | 2403 | 208 | 23 | .991 |

†Traded to Pittsburgh Pirates for Outfielder Gene Clines, October 21, 1974.

### CHAMPIONSHIP SERIES RECORD

| Year | Club | League | Pos. | G. | AB. | R. | H. | 2B. | 3B. | HR. | RBI. | B.A. | PO. | A. | E. | F.A. |
|------|------|--------|------|----|-----|----|----|-----|-----|-----|------|------|-----|----|----|------|
| 1975 | Pittsburgh | Nat. | PH | 1 | 0 | 0 | 0 | 0 | 0 | 0 | 1 | .000 | 0 | 0 | 0 | .000 |

### WORLD SERIES RECORD

| Year | Club | League | Pos. | G. | AB. | R. | H. | 2B. | 3B. | HR. | RBI. | B.A. | PO. | A. | E. | F.A. |
|------|------|--------|------|----|-----|----|----|-----|-----|-----|------|------|-----|----|----|------|
| 1969 | New York | Nat. | PH | 1 | 1 | 0 | 0 | 0 | 0 | 0 | 0 | .000 | 0 | 0 | 0 | .000 |

## MICHAEL ANTHONY EASLER
### (Mike)

Born November 29, 1950, at Cleveland, O.
Height, 6.01. Weight, 198.
Throws right and bats lefthanded.
Hobbies—Table tennis and bowling.
Attended Cleveland State University, Cleveland, O.
Brother-in-law of Cliff Johnson, catcher-first baseman with Houston Astros.

| Year | Club | League | Pos. | G. | AB. | R. | H. | 2B. | 3B. | HR. | RBI. | B.A. | PO. | A. | E. | F.A. |
|------|------|--------|------|----|-----|----|----|-----|-----|-----|------|------|-----|----|----|------|
| 1969 | Covington | Appla. | OF-3B | 33 | 113 | 21 | 36 | 7 | 2 | 0 | 11 | .319 | 25 | 10 | 4 | .897 |
| 1970 | Cocoa† | Fla. St. | OF | 96 | 314 | 30 | 79 | 11 | 4 | 1 | 24 | .252 | 142 | 5 | 7 | .955 |
| 1971 | Cocoa‡ | Fla. St. | OF | 109 | 392 | 61 | 115 | 15 | 5 | 11 | 68 | .293 | 153 | 14 | 8 | .954 |
| 1972 | Columbus | South. | OF | 106 | 372 | 52 | 100 | 11 | 4 | 13 | 46 | .269 | 149 | 7 | 8 | .951 |
| 1973 | Columbus | South. | OF | 48 | 168 | 27 | 52 | 11 | 1 | 6 | 32 | .310 | 81 | 2 | 1 | .988 |
| 1973 | Denver | A. A. | OF | 48 | 176 | 24 | 50 | 11 | 2 | 7 | 26 | .284 | 74 | 2 | 6 | .927 |
| 1973 | Houston | Nat. | OF | 6 | 7 | 1 | 0 | 0 | 0 | 0 | 0 | .000 | 1 | 0 | 1 | .500 |
| 1974 | Denver | A. A. | OF | 100 | 367 | 75 | 104 | 18 | 8 | 19 | 63 | .283 | 172 | 7 | 5 | .973 |
| 1974 | Houston | Nat. | PH | 15 | 15 | 0 | 1 | 0 | 0 | 0 | 0 | .067 | 0 | 0 | 0 | .000 |
| 1975 | Iowa§-Tulsa | A. A. | OF | 113 | 415 | 69 | 130 | 31 | 6 | 15 | 69 | .313 | 161 | 6 | 8 | .954 |
| 1975 | Houston x | Nat. | PH | 5 | 5 | 0 | 0 | 0 | 0 | 0 | 0 | .000 | 0 | 0 | 0 | .000 |
| 1976 | Tulsa y | A. A. | OF | 118 | 378 | 75 | 133 | 31 | 2 | 26 | 77 | ★.352 | 172 | ★16 | 8 | .959 |
| 1976 | California z | Amer. | DH | 21 | 54 | 6 | 13 | 1 | 1 | 0 | 4 | .241 | 0 | 0 | 0 | .000 |
| | National League Totals | | | 26 | 27 | 1 | 1 | 0 | 0 | 0 | 0 | .037 | 1 | 0 | 1 | .500 |
| | American League Totals | | | 21 | 54 | 6 | 13 | 1 | 1 | 0 | 4 | .241 | 0 | 0 | 0 | .000 |
| | Major League Totals | | | 47 | 81 | 7 | 14 | 1 | 1 | 0 | 5 | .173 | 1 | 0 | 1 | .500 |

†On temporary inactive list, May 13 through May 25.
‡On temporary inactive list, May 25 through June 14.
§Loaned by Houston Astros' organization to St. Louis Cardinals' organization, June 25, 1975.
xTraded to St. Louis Cardinals for Pitcher Mike Barlow, September 30, 1975.
ySold to California Angels, September 3, 1976.
zSold to Pittsburgh Pirates, April 4, 1977.

## JAMES MORRIS EASTERLY
### (Jamie)

Born February 17, 1953, at Houston, Tex.
Height, 5.09. Weight, 180.
Throws left and bats left and righthanded.
Hobbies—Golf and watching television.
Attended Sam Houston State University, Huntsville, Tex.

| Year Club | League | G. | IP. | W. | L. | Pct. | H. | R. | ER. | SO. | BB. | ERA. |
|---|---|---|---|---|---|---|---|---|---|---|---|---|
| 1971—Greenwood | W. Carol. | 8 | 29 | 3 | 0 | 1.000 | 14 | 3 | 2 | 33 | 9 | 0.62 |
| 1972—Greenwood | W. Carol. | 7 | 24 | 1 | 0 | 1.000 | 11 | 0 | 0 | 29 | 13 | 0.00 |
| 1972—Savannah† | Southern | 2 | 4 | 0 | 1 | .000 | 7 | 2 | 2 | 4 | 4 | 4.50 |
| 1973—Savannah‡ | Southern | 15 | 67 | 5 | 3 | .625 | 62 | 40 | 28 | 53 | 41 | 3.76 |
| 1974—Richmond | Int'national | 26 | 138 | 9 | 6 | .600 | 115 | 48 | 39 | 84 | 75 | 2.54 |
| 1974—Atlanta | National | 3 | 3 | 0 | 0 | .000 | 6 | 7 | 5 | 0 | 4 | 15.00 |
| 1975—Richmond | Int'national | 2 | 10 | 1 | 1 | .500 | 11 | 3 | 2 | 4 | 6 | 1.80 |
| 1975—Atlanta | National | 21 | 69 | 2 | 9 | .182 | 73 | 47 | 38 | 34 | 42 | 4.96 |
| 1976—Richmond | Int'national | 33 | 137 | 7 | 6 | .583 | 133 | 56 | 45 | 91 | 88 | 2.96 |
| 1976—Atlanta | National | 4 | 22 | 1 | 1 | .500 | 23 | 12 | 12 | 11 | 13 | 4.91 |
| Major League Totals | | 28 | 94 | 3 | 10 | .231 | 102 | 66 | 55 | 45 | 59 | 5.27 |

†On disabled list, April 11 to April 27, July 7 to July 28 and August 5 through remainder of season.
‡On disabled list, April 24 to May 12 and May 24 to July 9, 1973.

### RAWLINS JACKSON EASTWICK, III
### (Rawly)

Born October 24, 1950, at'Camden, N. J.
Height, 6.03. Weight, 175.
Throws and bats righthanded.
Hobbies—Painting and drawing.

Tied following major league records: most seasons leading league, saves—2, 1975-1976; most seasons, consecutive, leading league, saves—2, 1975-1976.
Tied for National League lead in saves with 22 in 1975.
Led Eastern League in saves with 20 in 1972.
Led National League in saves with 26 in 1976.
Named by THE SPORTING NEWS as National League Fireman of the Year, 1976.

| Year Club | League | G. | IP. | W. | L. | Pct. | H. | R. | ER. | SO. | BB. | ERA. |
|---|---|---|---|---|---|---|---|---|---|---|---|---|
| 1969—Bradenton Reds | Gulf Coast | 10 | 29 | 1 | 4 | .200 | 41 | 23 | 16 | 15 | 10 | 4.97 |
| 1970—Tampa | Florida St. | 37 | 101 | 2 | 9 | .182 | 93 | 53 | 39 | 70 | 45 | 3.48 |
| 1971—Raleigh-Durham | Carolina | 23 | 41 | 3 | 2 | .600 | 35 | 19 | 19 | 41 | 24 | 4.17 |
| 1971—Three Rivers | Eastern | 19 | 37 | 1 | 1 | .500 | 32 | 22 | 22 | 30 | 14 | 5.35 |
| 1972—Three Rivers | Eastern | •66 | 119 | 9 | 9 | .500 | 86 | 37 | 31 | 90 | 37 | 2.34 |
| 1973—Indianapolis | Am. Assoc. | 43 | 121 | 9 | 7 | .563 | 116 | 58 | 52 | 83 | 34 | 3.87 |
| 1974—Indianapolis | Am. Assoc. | 47 | 117 | 8 | 7 | .533 | 115 | 62 | 52 | 79 | 39 | 4.00 |
| 1974—Cincinnati | National | 8 | 18 | 0 | 0 | .000 | 12 | 5 | 4 | 14 | 5 | 2.00 |
| 1975—Indianapolis | Am. Assoc. | 13 | 20 | 1 | 0 | 1.000 | 11 | 8 | 3 | 14 | 4 | 1.35 |
| 1975—Cincinnati | National | 58 | 90 | 5 | 3 | .625 | 77 | 26 | 26 | 61 | 25 | 2.60 |
| 1976—Cincinnati | National | 71 | 108 | 11 | 5 | .688 | 93 | 30 | 25 | 70 | 27 | 2.08 |
| Major League Totals | | 137 | 216 | 16 | 8 | .667 | 182 | 61 | 55 | 145 | 57 | 2.29 |

CHAMPIONSHIP SERIES RECORD

| Year Club | League | G. | IP. | W. | L. | Pct. | H. | R. | ER. | SO. | BB. | ERA. |
|---|---|---|---|---|---|---|---|---|---|---|---|---|
| 1975—Cincinnati | National | 2 | 3⅔ | 1 | 0 | 1.000 | 2 | 0 | 0 | 1 | 2 | 0.00 |
| 1976—Cincinnati | National | 2 | 3 | 1 | 0 | 1.000 | 7 | 5 | 4 | 1 | 2 | 12.00 |
| Championship Series Totals | | 4 | 6⅔ | 2 | 0 | 1.000 | 9 | 5 | 4 | 2 | 4 | 5.40 |

WORLD SERIES RECORD

| Year Club | League | G. | IP. | W. | L. | Pct. | H. | R. | ER. | SO. | BB. | ERA. |
|---|---|---|---|---|---|---|---|---|---|---|---|---|
| 1975—Cincinnati | National | 5 | 8 | 2 | 0 | 1.000 | 6 | 2 | 2 | 4 | 3 | 2.25 |

### DENNIS LEE ECKERSLEY

Born October 3, 1954, at Oakland, Calif.
Height, 6.02. Weight, 190.
Throws and bats righthanded.
Hobby—Music.
Son-in-law of Al Jacinto, former infielder in Chicago White Sox' organization.

Led California League pitchers in games started with 31 and tied for lead in shutouts with 5 in 1973.
Led Texas League in hit batsmen with 10 in 1974.
Named American League Rookie Pitcher of the Year by THE SPORTING NEWS, 1975.
Received reported $32,000 bonus to sign with Cleveland Indians, 1972.

| Year Club | League | G. | IP. | W. | L. | Pct. | H. | R. | ER. | SO. | BB. | ERA. |
|---|---|---|---|---|---|---|---|---|---|---|---|---|
| 1972—Reno | California | 12 | 75 | 5 | 5 | .500 | 87 | 46 | 40 | 56 | 33 | 4.80 |
| 1973—Reno | California | 31 | 202 | 12 | 8 | .600 | 182 | 97 | 82 | 218 | 91 | 3.65 |
| 1974—San Antonio | Texas | 23 | 167 | •14 | 3 | •.842 | 141 | 66 | 63 | •163 | 60 | 3.40 |
| 1975—Cleveland | American | 34 | 187 | 13 | 7 | .650 | 147 | 61 | 54 | 152 | 90 | 2.60 |
| 1976—Cleveland | American | 36 | 199 | 13 | 12 | .520 | 155 | 82 | 76 | 200 | 78 | 3.44 |
| Major League Totals | | 70 | 386 | 26 | 19 | .578 | 302 | 143 | 130 | 352 | 168 | 3.03 |

## DID YOU KNOW —
That 14 players have hit home runs in their first time at bat during a World Series? Only one player has hit homers his first TWO at-bats in the World Series. Can you name him? The record is listed in this book.

## EDWARD MICHAEL EDEN
### (Mike)

Born May 22, 1949, at Fort Clayton, Canal Zone.
Height, 5.10. Weight, 170.
Throws right and bats left and righthanded.
Hobbies—Golf, tennis and fishing.
Attended Brevard Junior College, Cocoa, Fla., and
Southern Illinois University, Carbondale, Ill.

| Year    Club | League | Pos. | G. | AB. | R. | H. | 2B. | 3B. | HR. | RBI. | B.A. | PO. | A. | E. | F.A. |
|---|---|---|---|---|---|---|---|---|---|---|---|---|---|---|---|
| 1972–Decatur ............ | Midw. | 2-3-OF | 65 | 249 | 46 | 66 | 9 | 2 | 5 | 22 | .265 | 87 | 150 | 11 | .956 |
| 1973–Fresno ............. | Calif. | 3-2-OF | 138 | 529 | 89 | •159 | 17 | 7 | 0 | 54 | .301 | 140 | 223 | 19 | .950 |
| 1974–Amarillo........... | Texas | SS-3B | 99 | 372 | 64 | 110 | 11 | 2 | 4 | 34 | .296 | 132 | 285 | 29 | .935 |
| 1974–Phoenix ............ | P.C. | 3B-2B | 32 | 131 | 24 | 41 | 8 | 3 | 0 | 15 | .313 | 26 | 54 | 2 | .976 |
| 1975–Phoenix ............ | P.C. | 3B-SS | 121 | 450 | 64 | 144 | 24 | 9 | 1 | 49 | .320 | 43 | 140 | 12 | .938 |
| 1976–Phoenix† .......... | P.C. | OF-3B | 56 | 212 | 34 | 69 | 13 | 3 | 0 | 20 | .325 | 46 | 24 | 6 | .921 |
| 1976–Richmond.......... | Int. | SS-3-OF | 54 | 191 | 37 | 58 | 7 | 4 | 3 | 17 | .304 | 71 | 122 | 13 | .937 |
| 1976–Atlanta‡ ........... | Nat. | 2B | 5 | 8 | 0 | 0 | 0 | 0 | 0 | 1 | .000 | 2 | 5 | 0 | 1.000 |
| Major League Totals ..................... | | | 5 | 8 | 0 | 0 | 0 | 0 | 0 | 1 | .000 | 2 | 5 | 0 | 1.000 |

†Traded by San Francisco Giants' organization with Shortstop Craig Robinson, First Baseman Willie Montanez, and Outfielder Jerald Brown to Atlanta Braves' organization for Infielders Darrell Evans and Marty Perez, June 13, 1976.
‡Sold to Oakland A's, March 10, 1977.


## CLAUDE L. EDGE
### (Butch)

Born July 18, 1956, at Houston, Tex.
Height, 6.03. Weight, 203.
Throws and bats righthanded.
Hobbies—Hunting, fishing and music.
Attended American River College, Sacramento, Calif.
Cousin of Alvin Edge, minor league pitcher with the Milwaukee Brewers' organization.

| Year    Club | League | G. | IP. | W. | L. | Pct. | H. | R. | ER. | SO. | BB. | ERA. |
|---|---|---|---|---|---|---|---|---|---|---|---|---|
| 1974–Newark† .............................. | N.Y.-Pa. | 10 | 53 | 3 | 7 | .300 | 44 | 41 | 26 | 50 | 49 | 4.42 |
| 1975–Burlington.......................... | Midwest | 17 | 105 | 4 | 7 | .364 | 87 | 50 | 39 | 82 | 54 | 3.34 |
| 1976–Spokane‡............................ | P. Coast | 1 | 1 | 0 | 0 | .000 | 4 | 2 | 2 | 0 | 1 | 54.00 |
| 1976–Burlington§ ......................... | Midwest | 5 | 10 | 0 | 1 | .000 | 11 | 5 | 2 | 12 | 7 | 1.80 |

†On disabled list, August 16 through September 3, 1974.
‡On temporary inactive list, April 21 through July 14, 1976.
§Selected by Toronto Blue Jays from Milwaukee Brewers in American League expansion draft, November 5, 1976.


## DAVID LEONARD EDWARDS
### (Dave)

Born February 24, 1954, at Los Angeles, Calif.
Height, 6.00. Weight, 170
Throws and bats righthanded.
Hobbies—Golf, bowling, music and cars.
Attended Los Angeles City Community College, Los Angeles, Calif.
Led Florida State League outfielders in double plays with 6 in 1973.

| Year    Club | League | Pos. | G. | AB. | R. | H. | 2B. | 3B. | HR. | RBI. | B.A. | PO. | A. | E. | F.A. |
|---|---|---|---|---|---|---|---|---|---|---|---|---|---|---|---|
| 1971–Sarasota Twins.. | Gulf C. | OF | 29 | 96 | 11 | 19 | 1 | 2 | 0 | 10 | .198 | 34 | 0 | 3 | .919 |
| 1972–Orlando ............ | Fla. St. | OF-SS | 43 | 143 | 19 | 31 | 2 | 1 | 0 | 3 | .217 | 81 | 5 | 4 | .956 |
| 1972–Melb'rne Twins | Fla.E.C. | OF | 53 | 192 | 40 | 60 | 6 | 2 | 4 | 33 | •.313 | 86 | 5 | 5 | .948 |
| 1973–Ft. Lauderdale .. | Fla. St. | OF | 137 | 457 | 84 | 132 | 17 | 4 | 10 | 44 | .289 | 215 | 12 | 8 | .966 |
| 1974–Lynchburg ........ | Carol. | OF | 124 | 417 | 77 | 102 | 19 | 6 | 3 | 34 | .245 | 274 | 9 | 9 | .969 |
| 1975–Reno ................ | Calif. | OF | 137 | 481 | 103 | 147 | 21 | 9 | 7 | 75 | .306 | •320 | 13 | 7 | .979 |
| 1976–Orlando† .......... | South. | OF | 55 | 209 | 32 | 61 | 10 | 5 | 3 | 26 | .292 | 134 | 6 | 3 | .979 |

†On disabled list, July 1 through July 11, 1976.
Listed on Minnesota Twins' 1977 spring roster.


## MICHAEL LEWIS EDWARDS
### (Mike)

Born August 27, 1952, at Fort Lewis, Wash.
Height, 5.10. Weight, 154.
Throws and bats righthanded.
Hobbies—Golf, bowling, and playing various musical instruments.
Attended University of California at Los Angeles, Los Angeles, Calif.
Led New York-Pennsylvania League second basemen in double plays with 60 in 1974.

| Year    Club | League | Pos. | G. | AB. | R. | H. | 2B. | 3B. | HR. | RBI. | B.A. | PO. | A. | E. | F.A. |
|---|---|---|---|---|---|---|---|---|---|---|---|---|---|---|---|
| 1974–Niagara Falls .... | NYP | 2B | 69 | •275 | 43 | 86 | 11 | •7 | 3 | 28 | .313 | •196 | 166 | 12 | •.968 |
| 1975–Shreveport ........ | Texas | 2B-SS | 93 | 368 | 57 | 112 | 26 | 3 | 3 | 41 | .304 | 194 | 221 | 13 | •.970 |
| 1975–Charleston ........ | Int. | 2B | 31 | 132 | 11 | 37 | 6 | 1 | 1 | 15 | .280 | 48 | 84 | 4 | .971 |
| 1976–Charleston ........ | Int. | 2B-SS | 62 | 223 | 24 | 46 | 3 | 2 | 3 | 21 | .206 | 133 | 146 | 7 | .975 |
| 1976–Shreveport ........ | Texas | 2B-SS | 53 | 209 | 28 | 67 | 12 | 2 | 4 | 23 | .321 | 103 | 157 | 18 | .935 |

# RANDY LEE ELLIOTT

Born June 5, 1951, at Camarillo, Calif.
Height, 6.02. Weight, 195.
Throws and bats righthanded.

Led Texas League in slugging percentage with .544 and in total bases with 258 in 1972.
Led Pioneer League first basemen in double plays with 42 in 1969.
Tied for California League lead in double plays by outfielders with 3 in 1970.
Tied for Pioneer League lead in sacrifice flies with 5 in 1969.
Named Texas League Most Valuable Player, 1972.

| Year Club | League | Pos. | G. | AB. | R. | H. | 2B. | 3B. | HR. | RBI. | B.A. | PO. | A. | E. | F.A. |
|---|---|---|---|---|---|---|---|---|---|---|---|---|---|---|---|
| 1969–Salt Lake City ..Pion. | | 1B | 63 | 225 | 42 | 68 | 8 | •9 | 4 | 50 | .302 | •459 | •29 | 9 | •.982 |
| 1970–Lodi | Calif. | •OF-1 | 132 | 481 | 68 | 135 | 20 | 6 | 14 | 51 | .281 | 241 | •21 | 10 | .963 |
| 1971–Lodi | Calif. | OF | 126 | 481 | 89 | 126 | 25 | 4 | 14 | 75 | .262 | 194 | •16 | 12 | .946 |
| 1972–Alexandria | Texas | OF-1B | 138 | 474 | 84 | 159 | •32 | 5 | 19 | •85 | *.335 | 208 | 16 | 7 | .970 |
| 1972–San Diego | Nat. | OF | 14 | 49 | 5 | 10 | 3 | 1 | 0 | 6 | .204 | 29 | 0 | 0 | 1.000 |
| 1973–Hawaii† | P.C. | OF | 29 | 99 | 14 | 28 | 6 | 0 | 2 | 15 | .283 | 53 | 3 | 0 | 1.000 |
| 1974–Hawaii | P.C. | OF-1B | 112 | 392 | 70 | 126 | 22 | 7 | 11 | 69 | .321 | 265 | 30 | 4 | .987 |
| 1974–San Diego | Nat. | OF-1B | 13 | 33 | 5 | 7 | 1 | 0 | 1 | 2 | .212 | 10 | 0 | 0 | 1.000 |
| 1975–Hawaii‡ | P.C. | OF | 95 | 338 | 63 | 93 | 22 | 3 | 12 | 60 | .275 | 140 | 9 | 7 | .955 |
| 1976–S.L.C. y-Pho. ....P.C. | | | | | | | (Did not play) | | | | | | | | |
| Major League Totals | | | 27 | 82 | 10 | 17 | 4 | 1 | 1 | 8 | .207 | 39 | 0 | 0 | 1.000 |

†On disabled list, May 28 through September 7, 1973.
‡On disabled list, August 1 through September 24, 1975; released, February 26, 1976; signed as free agent with Salt Lake City (California Angels' organization) March 4, 1976.
yOn inactive list, April 17 through May 6, 1976; released, May 6, 1976; signed as free agent with Phoenix (San Francisco Giants' organization), September 3, 1976.
Invited to San Francisco Giants' 1977 spring camp.

# DOCK PHILLIP ELLIS, JR.

Born March 11, 1945, at Los Angeles, Calif.
Height, 6.03. Weight, 205.
Throws right and bats left and righthanded.
Hobbies—Fishing, dancing and listening to music.
Attended Los Angeles Harbor Junior College, Wilmington, Calif.

Tied major league record for most hit batsmen, inning, 3, May 1, 1974 (1st inning).
Pitched 2-0 no-hit victory against San Diego Padres, June 12, 1970.
Tied for Carolina League lead in complete games by pitchers with 15 in 1965.
Named American League Comeback Player of the Year by THE SPORTING NEWS, 1976.

| Year Club | League | G. | IP. | W. | L. | Pct. | H. | R. | ER. | SO. | BB. | ERA. |
|---|---|---|---|---|---|---|---|---|---|---|---|---|
| 1964–Batavia† | NYP | 16 | 121 | 6 | 7 | .462 | 128 | 73 | 43 | 130 | 39 | 3.20 |
| 1965–Kinston | Carolina | 25 | 186 | 14 | 8 | .636 | 147 | 56 | 41 | 149 | 69 | •1.98 |
| 1965–Columbus | Int'national | 1 | 3 | 0 | 0 | .000 | 4 | 0 | 0 | 4 | 2 | 0.00 |
| 1966–Asheville | Southern | 24 | 160 | 10 | 9 | .526 | 138 | 62 | 49 | 145 | 44 | 2.76 |
| 1967–Columbus | Int'national | 20 | 100 | 5 | 7 | .417 | 91 | 57 | 51 | 77 | 51 | 4.59 |
| 1967–Macon | Southern | 3 | 16 | 2 | 0 | 1.000 | 11 | 5 | 5 | 16 | 8 | 2.81 |
| 1968–Columbus | Int'national | 19 | 23 | 2 | 1 | .667 | 14 | 7 | 6 | 24 | 11 | 2.35 |
| 1968–Pittsburgh | National | 26 | 104 | 6 | 5 | .545 | 82 | 35 | 29 | 52 | 38 | 2.51 |
| 1969–Pittsburgh | National | 35 | 219 | 11 | 17 | .393 | 206 | 101 | 87 | 173 | 76 | 3.58 |
| 1970–Pittsburgh‡ | National | 30 | 202 | 13 | 10 | .565 | 194 | 81 | 72 | 128 | 87 | 3.21 |
| 1971–Pittsburgh | National | 31 | 227 | 19 | 9 | .679 | 207 | 93 | 77 | 137 | 63 | 3.05 |
| 1972–Pittsburgh | National | 25 | 163 | 15 | 7 | .682 | 156 | 60 | 49 | 96 | 33 | 2.71 |
| 1973–Pittsburgh | National | 28 | 192 | 12 | 14 | .462 | 176 | 86 | 65 | 122 | 55 | 3.05 |
| 1974–Pittsburgh | National | 26 | 177 | 12 | 9 | .571 | 163 | 71 | 62 | 91 | 41 | 3.15 |
| 1975–Pittsburgh§ | National | 27 | 140 | 8 | 9 | .471 | 163 | 69 | 59 | 69 | 43 | 3.79 |
| 1976–New York x | American | 32 | 212 | 17 | 8 | .680 | 195 | 83 | 75 | 65 | 76 | 3.16 |
| National League Totals | | 228 | 1424 | 96 | 80 | .545 | 1347 | 596 | 500 | 868 | 436 | 3.16 |
| American League Totals | | 32 | 212 | 17 | 8 | .680 | 195 | 83 | 75 | 65 | 76 | 3.18 |
| Major League Totals | | 260 | 1636 | 113 | 88 | .562 | 1542 | 679 | 575 | 933 | 512 | 3.16 |

†On disabled list, July 31 through September 22.
‡On disabled list. August 23 through September 13.
§Traded with Pitcher Ken Brett and Second Baseman Willie Randolph to New York Yankees for Pitcher Doc Medich, December 11, 1975.
xTraded with Infielder Marty Perez and Outfielder Larry Murray, on Syracuse roster, to Oakland A's for Pitcher Mike Torrez, April 27, 1977.

## CHAMPIONSHIP SERIES RECORD

| Year Club | League | G. | IP. | W. | L. | Pct. | H. | R. | ER. | SO. | BB. | ERA. |
|---|---|---|---|---|---|---|---|---|---|---|---|---|
| 1970–Pittsburgh | National | 1 | 9⅔ | 0 | 1 | .000 | 9 | 3 | 3 | 1 | 4 | 2.79 |
| 1971–Pittsburgh | National | 1 | 5 | 1 | 0 | 1.000 | 6 | 2 | 2 | 1 | 4 | 3.60 |
| 1972–Pittsburgh | National | 1 | 5 | 0 | 1 | .000 | 5 | 3 | 0 | 3 | 1 | 0.00 |
| 1975–Pittsburgh | National | 1 | 2 | 0 | 0 | .000 | 2 | 0 | 0 | 2 | 0 | 0.00 |
| 1976–New York | American | 1 | 8 | 1 | 0 | 1.000 | 6 | 3 | 3 | 5 | 2 | 3.37 |
| Championship Series Totals | | 5 | 29⅔ | 2 | 2 | .500 | 28 | 11 | 8 | 12 | 11 | 2.43 |

| Year Club | League | G. | IP. | W. | L. | Pct. | H. | R. | ER. | SO. | BB. | ERA. |
|---|---|---|---|---|---|---|---|---|---|---|---|---|
| 1971-Pittsburgh | National | 1 | $2\frac{1}{3}$ | 0 | 1 | .000 | 4 | 4 | 4 | 1 | 1 | 15.43 |
| 1976-New York | American | 1 | $3\frac{1}{3}$ | 0 | 1 | .000 | 7 | 4 | 4 | 1 | 0 | 10.80 |
| World Series Totals | | 2 | $5\frac{2}{3}$ | 0 | 2 | .000 | 11 | 8 | 8 | 2 | 1 | 12.70 |

## ALL-STAR GAME RECORD

| Year League | IP. | W. | L. | Pct. | H. | R. | ER. | SO. | BB. | ERA. |
|---|---|---|---|---|---|---|---|---|---|---|---|
| 1971-National | 3 | 0 | 1 | .000 | 4 | 4 | 4 | 2 | 1 | 12.00 |

## JOHN CHARLES ELLIS

Born August 21, 1948, at New London, Conn.
Height, 6.02. Weight, 215.
Throws and bats righthanded.
Hobbies—Fishing and hunting.
Attended Mitchell College, New London, Conn.

| Year Club | League | Pos. | G. | AB. | R. | H. | 2B. | 3B. | HR. | RBI. | B.A. | PO. | A. | E. | F.A. |
|---|---|---|---|---|---|---|---|---|---|---|---|---|---|---|---|
| 1967-Ft. Laud† | Fla. St. | C | 34 | 107 | 17 | 30 | 6 | 0 | 3 | 20 | .280 | 167 | 11 | 5 | .973 |
| 1968-Ft. Laud† | Fla. St. | C | 70 | 207 | 28 | 51 | 10 | 3 | 6 | 22 | .246 | 327 | 32 | 6 | .984 |
| 1968-Syracuse | Int. | C | 13 | 46 | 7 | 16 | 2 | 0 | 1 | 7 | .348 | 83 | 12 | 0 | 1.000 |
| 1969-Kinston | Carol. | C | 24 | 97 | 17 | 35 | 5 | 1 | 6 | 28 | .361 | 160 | 12 | 1 | .994 |
| 1969-Syracuse§ | Int. | C-OF | 38 | 123 | 24 | 41 | 8 | 3 | 8 | 31 | .333 | 56 | 5 | 2 | .968 |
| 1969-New York | Amer. | C | 22 | 62 | 2 | 18 | 4 | 0 | 1 | 8 | .290 | 83 | 7 | 2 | .978 |
| 1970-New York | Amer. | 1B-3-C | 78 | 226 | 24 | 56 | 12 | 1 | 7 | 29 | .248 | 461 | 41 | 5 | .990 |
| 1971-New York | Amer. | 1B-C | 83 | 238 | 16 | 58 | 12 | 1 | 3 | 34 | .244 | 625 | 35 | 7 | .990 |
| 1972-New York x | Amer. | C-1B | 52 | 136 | 13 | 40 | 5 | 1 | 5 | 25 | .294 | 190 | 12 | 6 | .971 |
| 1973-Cleveland | Amer. | C-1B | 127 | 437 | 59 | 118 | 12 | 2 | 14 | 68 | .270 | 487 | 31 | 10 | .981 |
| 1974-Cleveland y | Amer. | 1B-C | 128 | 477 | 58 | 136 | 23 | 6 | 10 | 64 | .285 | 823 | 55 | 9 | .990 |
| 1975-Cleveland z a | Amer. | C-1B | 92 | 296 | 22 | 68 | 11 | 1 | 7 | 32 | .230 | 413 | 45 | 13 | .972 |
| 1976-Texas b | Amer. | C-DH | 11 | 31 | 4 | 13 | 2 | 0 | 1 | 8 | .419 | 21 | 2 | 0 | 1.000 |
| Major League Totals | | | 593 | 1903 | 198 | 507 | 81 | 12 | 48 | 268 | .266 | 3103 | 228 | 52 | .985 |

†On temporary inactive list, May 26 through May 29. On temporary inactive list, June 2, 1967. Transferred to the military list, June 5 through October 3.

‡On temporary inactive list, April 26 through April 29, May 24 through May 27, June 21 through June 24, July 11 through 28, and August 2 through August 6.

§On temporary inactive list, April 25 through April 28. On military list, June 17 through July 7.

xTraded with Infielder Jerry Kenney, Outfielders Charlie Spikes and Rosendo Torres to Cleveland Indians for Third Baseman Graig Nettles and Catcher Jerry Moses, November 27, 1972.

yOn disabled list, June 1 to June 30, 1974.

zOn supplemental disabled list, August 15 to September 1, 1975.

aTraded to Texas Rangers for Pitcher Stan Thomas and Utilityman Ron Pruitt, December 9, 1975.

bOn disabled list, May 9 through October 6, 1976.

## GEORGE ALBERT ENRIGHT

Born May 9, 1954, at New Britain, Conn.
Height, 5.11. Weight, 175.
Throws and bats righthanded.
Hobbies—Fishing and boating.

| Year Club | League | Pos. | G. | AB. | R. | H. | 2B. | 3B. | HR. | RBI. | B.A. | PO. | A. | E. | F.A. |
|---|---|---|---|---|---|---|---|---|---|---|---|---|---|---|---|
| 1972-Sar. White Sox | Gulf C. | C | 6 | 18 | 2 | 6 | 0 | 0 | 0 | 1 | .333 | 48 | 3 | 0 | 1.000 |
| 1972-Appleton | Midw. | C | 25 | 61 | 5 | 14 | 2 | 0 | 0 | 5 | .230 | 119 | 4 | 3 | .976 |
| 1973-Appleton | Midw. | C-OF-1B | 54 | 127 | 8 | 21 | 2 | 0 | 0 | 8 | .165 | 252 | 20 | 3 | .989 |
| 1974-Appleton | Midw. | C-1B | 63 | 216 | 15 | 55 | 9 | 1 | 1 | 21 | .255 | 373 | 59 | 2 | .995 |
| 1974-Iowa | A. A. | C | 26 | 59 | 7 | 11 | 0 | 2 | 1 | 6 | .186 | 135 | 16 | 1 | .993 |
| 1975-Knoxville | South. | *C-O-1B | *118 | 370 | 36 | 94 | 5 | 1 | 1 | 32 | .254 | 459 | 75 | 5 | .991 |
| 1976-Iowa | A. A. | C | 108 | 271 | 29 | 68 | 9 | 1 | 3 | 29 | .251 | 529 | *56 | 13 | .978 |
| 1976-Chicago | Amer. | C | 2 | 1 | 0 | 0 | 0 | 0 | 0 | 0 | .000 | 4 | 0 | 0 | 1.000 |
| Major League Totals | | | 2 | 1 | 0 | 0 | 0 | 0 | 0 | 0 | .000 | 4 | 0 | 0 | 1.000 |

## TERRENCE ROBERT ERVIN
### (Terry)

Born August 3, 1955, at Los Angeles, Calif.
Height, 6.04. Weight, 190.
Throws and bats righthanded.
Hobby—Teaching baseball to Little Leaguers.

| Year Club | League | Pos. | G. | AB. | R. | H. | 2B. | 3B. | HR. | RBI. | B.A. | PO. | A. | E. | F.A. |
|---|---|---|---|---|---|---|---|---|---|---|---|---|---|---|---|
| 1973-Newark | NYP | OF | 37 | 102 | 9 | 19 | 4 | 1 | 0 | 6 | .186 | 42 | 1 | 6 | .878 |
| 1974-Danville | Midw. | OF | 23 | 50 | 4 | 12 | 3 | 1 | 1 | 8 | .240 | 21 | 0 | 0 | 1.000 |
| 1974-Newark | NYP | OF | 57 | 200 | 29 | 42 | 2 | 1 | 3 | 15 | .210 | 105 | 8 | •9 | .926 |
| 1975-Burlington† | Midw. | OF | 98 | 359 | 61 | 93 | 14 | 4 | 8 | 28 | .259 | 142 | 9 | •9 | .926 |
| 1976-Pittsfield‡ | East. | OF | 40 | 114 | 12 | 25 | 4 | 3 | 1 | 17 | .219 | 72 | 6 | 4 | .951 |
| 1976-Jackson | Texas | OF | 44 | 147 | 14 | 37 | 5 | 1 | 2 | 19 | .252 | 61 | 6 | 4 | .944 |

†On disabled list, May 15 to June 6, 1975.

‡Traded by Milwaukee Brewers with Pitcher Jim Deidel to New York Mets for Infielder Jack Heidemann, June 23, 1976.

## ARNUFLO ACEVEDO ESPINOSA
Name pronounced es-puh-NOH-suh.
### (Nino)
Born August 15, 1953, at Villa Altagracia, Dominican Republic.
Height, 6.00. Weight, 160.
Throws and bats righthanded.
Brother of Juan Acevedo, pitcher in St. Louis Cardinals' organization, 1963.

| Year Club | League | G. | IP. | W. | L. | Pct. | H. | R. | ER. | SO. | BB. | ERA. |
|---|---|---|---|---|---|---|---|---|---|---|---|---|
| 1971–Key West .......................Florida St. | | 41 | 115 | 6 | 12 | .333 | 116 | 53 | 44 | 70 | 32 | 3.44 |
| 1972–Pompano Beach† ...............Florida St. | | 40 | 89 | 8 | 6 | .571 | 115 | 51 | 41 | 64 | 12 | 4.15 |
| 1973–Visalia ...........................California | | 24 | 174 | 10 | 10 | .500 | 184 | 99 | 81 | 109 | 54 | 4.19 |
| 1974–Victoria‡ ...........................Texas | | 25 | 137 | 9 | 8 | .529 | 137 | 66 | 52 | 63 | 26 | 3.42 |
| 1974–New York .........................National | | 2 | 9 | 0 | 0 | .000 | 12 | 5 | 5 | 2 | 0 | 5.00 |
| 1975–Tidewater§ .....................Int'national | | 24 | 141 | 8 | 5 | .615 | 127 | 48 | 41 | 83 | 38 | 2.62 |
| 1975–New York .........................National | | 2 | 3 | 0 | 1 | .000 | 8 | 6 | 6 | 2 | 1 | 18.00 |
| 1976–Tidewater ......................Int'national | | 14 | 108 | 7 | 3 | .700 | 106 | 40 | 35 | 66 | 34 | 2.92 |
| 1976–New York .........................National | | 12 | 42 | 4 | 4 | .500 | 41 | 21 | 17 | 30 | 13 | 3.64 |
| Major League Totals ............... | | 16 | 54 | 4 | 5 | .444 | 61 | 32 | 28 | 34 | 14 | 4.67 |

†On temporary inactive list from beginning of season until April 25, 1972.
‡Played one game at third base.
§On disabled list, April 22 to May 2, 1975.

## JAMES SARKIS ESSIAN, JR.
Name pronounced Ess-ee-en.
### (Jim)
Born January 2, 1951, at Detroit, Mich.
Height, 6.01. Weight, 190.
Throws and bats righthanded.
Hobbies–Music and chess.
Attended Arizona State University, Tempe, Ariz.
Led Carolina League catchers in double plays with 13 in 1971.

| Year Club | League | Pos. | G. | AB. | R. | H. | 2B. | 3B. | HR. | RBI. | B.A. | PO. | A. | E. | F.A. |
|---|---|---|---|---|---|---|---|---|---|---|---|---|---|---|---|
| 1970–Pulaski...............Appal. | | ★C-3B | 36 | 119 | 17 | 36 | 9 | 0 | 5 | 30 | .303 | 243 | 21 | 2 | ★.992 |
| 1970–Spartanburg ......W. Car. | | C | 35 | 119 | 19 | 35 | 8 | 2 | 6 | 20 | .294 | 204 | 21 | 5 | .978 |
| 1971–Peninsula .........Carol. | | C | 131 | 429 | 54 | 107 | 20 | 0 | 12 | 46 | .249 | ★856 | 68 | ★22 | .977 |
| 1972–Reading ............East. | | C | 96 | 312 | 45 | 79 | 14 | 1 | 4 | 33 | .253 | 512 | 60 | 20 | .966 |
| 1973–Reading ...........East. | | ★C-1-3-O | 105 | 315 | 58 | 92 | 15 | 5 | 10 | 55 | .292 | 609 | 57 | ★22 | .968 |
| 1973–Philadelphia ......Nat. | | C | 2 | 3 | 0 | 0 | 0 | 0 | 0 | 0 | .000 | 0 | 0 | 0 | .000 |
| 1974–Toledo .............Int. | | 1-C-3 | 58 | 181 | 24 | 51 | 4 | 0 | 5 | 24 | .282 | 372 | 50 | 11 | .975 |
| 1974–Philadelphia ......Nat. | | C-1-3 | 17 | 20 | 1 | 2 | 0 | 0 | 0 | 0 | .100 | 38 | 4 | 1 | .977 |
| 1975–Reading ...........East. | | C-3B | 12 | 36 | 5 | 7 | 2 | 0 | 1 | 2 | .194 | 61 | 12 | 1 | .986 |
| 1975–Philadelphia† ....Nat. | | C | 2 | 1 | 1 | 0 | 0 | 0 | 1 | 1.000 | 1 | 1 | 0 | 1.000 |
| 1975–Hawaii ..............P. C. | | C | 40 | 129 | 14 | 27 | 2 | 0 | 2 | 9 | .209 | 228 | 22 | 2 | .992 |
| 1976–Chicago ...........Amer. | | C-1B-3B | 79 | 199 | 20 | 49 | 7 | 0 | 0 | 21 | .246 | 320 | 53 | 10 | .974 |
| Major League Totals ..................... | | | 99 | 223 | 22 | 52 | 7 | 0 | 0 | 22 | .233 | 359 | 58 | 11 | .974 |

†Traded with Outfielder Barry Bonnell and cash to Atlanta Braves for First Baseman Dick Allen and Catcher Johnny Oates, May 7, 1975. Sent by Atlanta Braves to Chicago White Sox, May 15, 1975, to complete deal in which Braves acquired First Baseman Dick Allen from White Sox for $5,000 and a player to be named later, December 3, 1974.

## ANDREW AUGUSTE ETCHEBARREN
Name pronounced ETCH-a-barren.
### (Andy)
Born June 20, 1943, at Whittier, Calif.
Height, 6.02. Weight, 195.
Throws and bats righthanded.
Hobby–Golf.
Tied American League record for most double plays started by catcher, game (2), August 11, 1966.
Led American League catchers in passed balls with 15 in 1966.
Led Eastern League catchers in double plays with 10 and passed balls with 16 in 1962.
Led International League catchers in double plays with 13 in 1965.
Received reported $85,000 bonus to sign with Baltimore Orioles, 1961.

| Year Club | League | Pos. | G. | AB. | R. | H. | 2B. | 3B. | HR. | RBI. | B.A. | PO. | A. | E. | F.A. |
|---|---|---|---|---|---|---|---|---|---|---|---|---|---|---|---|
| 1961–Aberdeen ..........North. | | C | 29 | 76 | 7 | 17 | 1 | 0 | 3 | 5 | .224 | 113 | 13 | 3 | .977 |
| 1962–Elmira ..............East. | | C | 86 | 265 | 36 | 66 | 15 | 2 | 6 | 32 | .249 | 578 | 44 | ●9 | .986 |
| 1962–Baltimore..........Amer. | | C | 2 | 6 | 0 | 2 | 0 | 0 | 0 | 1 | .333 | 7 | 0 | 1 | .875 |
| 1963–Lynchburg ........Sally | | C | 30 | 80 | 9 | 15 | 3 | 0 | 1 | 9 | .188 | 163 | 11 | 5 | .972 |
| 1963–Aberdeen ..........North. | | C | 79 | 278 | 38 | 71 | 9 | 2 | 11 | 48 | .255 | 573 | 58 | 9 | .986 |
| 1964–Elmira ..............East. | | C | 117 | 367 | 40 | 87 | 19 | 5 | 7 | 52 | .237 | 752 | 49 | 12 | .985 |
| 1965–Rochester..........Int. | | C | 140 | 453 | 59 | 112 | 16 | 6 | 6 | 42 | .247★1031 | ★82 | ★22 | .981 |
| 1965–Baltimore..........Amer. | | C | 5 | 6 | 1 | 1 | 0 | 0 | 1 | 4 | .167 | 21 | 2 | 0 | 1.000 |
| 1966–Baltimore..........Amer. | | C | 121 | 412 | 49 | 91 | 14 | 6 | 11 | 50 | .221 | 799 | 65 | 10 | .989 |
| 1967–Baltimore..........Amer. | | C | 112 | 330 | 29 | 71 | 13 | 0 | 7 | 35 | .215 | 673 | 57 | 8 | .989 |

| Year Club League | Pos. | G. | AB. | R. | H. | 2B. | 3B. | HR. | RBI. | B.A. | PO. | A. | E. | F.A. |
|---|---|---|---|---|---|---|---|---|---|---|---|---|---|---|
| 1968–Baltimore† ........Amer. | C | 74 | 189 | 20 | 44 | 11 | 2 | 5 | 20 | .233 | 414 | 29 | 1 | .998 |
| 1969–Baltimore ..........Amer. | C | 73 | 217 | 29 | 54 | 9 | 2 | 3 | 26 | .249 | 380 | 27 | 4 | .990 |
| 1970–Baltimore ..........Amer. | C | 78 | 230 | 19 | 56 | 10 | 1 | 4 | 28 | .243 | 392 | 29 | 7 | .984 |
| 1971–Baltimore ..........Amer. | C | 70 | 222 | 21 | 60 | 8 | 0 | 9 | 29 | .270 | 337 | 24 | 5 | .986 |
| 1972–Baltimore ..........Amer. | C | 71 | 188 | 11 | 38 | 6 | 1 | 2 | 21 | .202 | 334 | 22 | 3 | .992 |
| 1973–Baltimore ..........Amer. | C | 54 | 152 | 16 | 39 | 9 | 1 | 2 | 23 | .257 | 201 | 14 | 2 | .991 |
| 1974–Baltimore ..........Amer. | C | 62 | 180 | 13 | 40 | 8 | 0 | 2 | 15 | .222 | 269 | 19 | 7 | .976 |
| 1975–Balt.‡-Calif.§......Amer. | C | 39 | 120 | 10 | 32 | 1 | 1 | 3 | 20 | .267 | 216 | 17 | 4 | .983 |
| 1976–California ..........Amer. | C | 103 | 247 | 15 | 56 | 9 | 1 | 0 | 21 | .227 | 539 | 46 | 12 | .980 |
| Major League Totals ...... | | 864 | 2499 | 233 | 584 | 98 | 15 | 49 | 293 | .234 | 4582 | 351 | 64 | .987 |

†On disabled list from August 14 through September 19 after suffering broken bone in hand.
‡On supplemental disabled list, April 15 to May 20, 1975. Sold to California Angels, June 15, 1975.
§On supplemental disabled list, June 29 to August 24, 1975.

### CHAMPIONSHIP SERIES RECORD

| Year Club League | Pos. | G. | AB. | R. | H. | 2B. | 3B. | HR. | RBI. | B.A. | PO. | A. | E. | F.A. |
|---|---|---|---|---|---|---|---|---|---|---|---|---|---|---|
| 1969–Baltimore ..........Amer. | C | 2 | 4 | 0 | 0 | 0 | 0 | 0 | 0 | .000 | 11 | 0 | 0 | 1.000 |
| 1970–Baltimore ..........Amer. | C | 2 | 9 | 1 | 1 | 0 | 0 | 0 | 0 | .111 | 19 | 0 | 0 | 1.000 |
| 1971–Baltimore ..........Amer. | PH-C | 2 | 5 | 0 | 0 | 0 | 0 | 0 | 0 | .000 | 11 | 0 | 0 | 1.000 |
| 1973–Baltimore ..........Amer. | C | 4 | 14 | 1 | 5 | 1 | 0 | 1 | 4 | .357 | 30 | 2 | 0 | 1.000 |
| 1974–Baltimore ..........Amer. | C | 2 | 6 | 0 | 2 | 0 | 0 | 0 | 0 | .333 | 7 | 1 | 0 | 1.000 |
| Championship Series Totals ............ | | 12 | 38 | 2 | 8 | 1 | 0 | 1 | 4 | .211 | 78 | 3 | 0 | 1.000 |

### WORLD SERIES RECORD

| Year Club League | Pos. | G. | AB. | R. | H. | 2B. | 3B. | HR. | RBI. | B.A. | PO. | A. | E. | F.A. |
|---|---|---|---|---|---|---|---|---|---|---|---|---|---|---|
| 1966–Baltimore ..........Amer. | C | 4 | 12 | 2 | 1 | 0 | 0 | 0 | 0 | .083 | 32 | 1 | 0 | 1.000 |
| 1969–Baltimore ..........Amer. | C | 2 | 6 | 0 | 0 | 0 | 0 | 0 | 0 | .000 | 16 | 0 | 0 | 1.000 |
| 1970–Baltimore ..........Amer. | C | 2 | 7 | 1 | 1 | 0 | 0 | 0 | 0 | .143 | 10 | 0 | 1 | .909 |
| 1971–Baltimore ..........Amer. | ·C | 1 | 2 | 0 | 0 | 0 | 0 | 0 | 0 | .000 | 6 | 0 | 0 | 1.000 |
| World Series Totals ....................... | | 9 | 27 | 3 | 2 | 0 | 0 | 0 | 0 | .074 | 64 | 1 | 1 | .985 |

### ALL-STAR GAME RECORD
Member of American League All-Star Team in 1966 and 1967 games; did not play.

## DARRELL WAYNE EVANS

Born May 26, 1947, at Pasadena, Calif.
Height, 6.02. Weight, 200.
Throws right and bats lefthanded.
Hobbies–Sports and stamp collecting.
Attended Pasadena City College, Pasadena, Calif.

Established following National League records: most double plays, third baseman, 45, in 1974; most games, consecutive, one or more bases on balls–15, April 9-27, 1976.
Led National League batters in walks with 124 in 1973 and 126 in 1974.
Led National League third basemen in double plays with 45 in 1974 and 41 in 1975.
Led National League third basemen in total chances with 471 in 1973, 578 in 1974 and 578 in 1975.
Named third baseman on THE SPORTING NEWS National League All-Star Team, 1973.
Named Player of the Year in Gulf Coast League, 1967.

| Year Club League | Pos. | G. | AB. | R. | H. | 2B. | 3B. | HR. | RBI. | B.A. | PO. | A. | E. | F.A. |
|---|---|---|---|---|---|---|---|---|---|---|---|---|---|---|
| 1967–Peninsula .........Carol. | 3B | 8 | 28 | 4 | 11 | 1 | 1 | 0 | 6 | .393 | 6 | 13 | 2 | .905 |
| 1967–Bradenton A's ..Gulf C. | 3B-SS | 14 | 45 | 13 | 22 | 3 | 3 | 2 | 11 | .489 | 25 | 30 | 2 | .965 |
| 1967–Leesburg ..........Fla. St. | 3-SS | 39 | 142 | 18 | 37 | 4 | 2 | 0 | 12 | .261 | 49 | 81 | 11 | .922 |
| 1968–Birmingham† ....South. | 3-1-2B | 56 | 187 | 18 | 45 | 6 | 3 | 3 | 25 | .241 | 103 | 101 | 10 | .953 |
| 1969–Richmond ..........Int. | 3B | 59 | 211 | 43 | 76 | 12 | 4 | 7 | 45 | .360 | 51 | 103 | 19 | .890 |
| 1969–Shreveport ........Texas | 3-S-O | 24 | 79 | 14 | 22 | 5 | 4 | 2 | 14 | .278 | 25 | 40 | 3 | .956 |
| 1969–Atlanta .............Nat. | 3B | 12 | 26 | 3 | 6 | 0 | 0 | 0 | 1 | .231 | 4 | 7 | 1 | .917 |
| 1970–Richmond ..........Int. | ∗3-1-O | 120 | 447 | 92 | 134 | 20 | 7 | 20 | 83 | .300 | 99 | 220 | 16 | ∗.952 |
| 1970–Atlanta .............Nat. | 3B | 12 | 44 | 4 | 14 | 1 | 1 | 0 | 9 | .318 | 6 | 26 | 2 | .941 |
| 1971–Richmond ..........Int. | OF-3B | 31 | 101 | 20 | 31 | 2 | 2 | 6 | 30 | .307 | 59 | 11 | 1 | .986 |
| 1971–Atlanta .............Nat. | 3B-OF | 89 | 260 | 42 | 63 | 11 | 1 | 12 | 38 | .242 | 77 | 138 | 14 | .939 |
| 1972–Atlanta‡ ..........Nat. | 3B | 125 | 418 | 67 | 106 | 12 | 0 | 19 | 71 | .254 | 126 | 273 | 25 | .941 |
| 1973–Atlanta .............Nat. | 3B-1B | 161 | 595 | 114 | 167 | 25 | 8 | 41 | 104 | .281 | 266 | 335 | 24 | .962 |
| 1974–Atlanta .............Nat. | 3B | 160 | 571 | 99 | 137 | 21 | 3 | 25 | 79 | .240 | ∗185 | 367 | 26 | .955 |
| 1975–Atlanta .............Nat. | ∗3B-1B | 156 | 567 | 82 | 138 | 22 | 2 | 22 | 73 | .243 | ∗164 | ∗382 | ∗36 | .938 |
| 1976–Atl.§-S.F. ..........Nat. | 1B-3B | 136 | 396 | 53 | 81 | 9 | 1 | 11 | 46 | .205 | 978 | 110 | 10 | .991 |
| Major League Totals ...................... | | 851 | 2877 | 464 | 712 | 101 | 16 | 130 | 421 | .247 | 1806 | 1638 | 138 | .961 |

†Drafted by Atlanta Braves from Vancouver (Oakland Athletics' organization), December 2, 1968.
‡On military list, June 17 through July 3, 1972.
§Traded with Shortstop Marty Perez to San Francisco Giants for First Baseman-Outfielder Willie Montanez, Shortstop Craig Robinson, Infielder Mike Eden (assigned to Richmond) and Outfielder Jake Brown (assigned to Savannah), June 13, 1976.

### ALL-STAR GAME RECORD

| Year League | Pos. | AB. | R. | H. | 2B. | 3B. | HR. | RBI. | B.A. | PO. | A. | E. | F.A. |
|---|---|---|---|---|---|---|---|---|---|---|---|---|---|
| 1973–National ............................ | PH | 0 | 0 | 0 | 0 | 0 | 0 | 0 | .000 | 0 | 0 | 0 | .000 |

# DWIGHT MICHAEL EVANS

Born November 3, 1951, at Santa Monica, Calif.
Height, 6.03. Weight, 210.
Throws and bats righthanded.

Tied American League record for most putouts, rightfielder, game, 9, August 17, 1974.
Led American League outfielders in double plays with 8 in 1975.
Led Western Carolinas League in sacrifice flies with 8 in 1970.
Tied for Carolina League lead in double plays by outfielders with 3 in 1971.
Named Most Valuable Player in International League, 1972.
Named as outfielder on THE SPORTING NEWS American League All-Star fielding team, 1976.

| Year | Club | League | Pos. | G. | AB. | R. | H. | 2B. | 3B. | HR. | RBI. | B.A. | PO. | A. | E. | F.A. |
|---|---|---|---|---|---|---|---|---|---|---|---|---|---|---|---|---|
| 1969–Jamestown | | NYP | OF-3B | 34 | 100 | 13 | 28 | 3 | 2 | 1 | 12 | .280 | 44 | 10 | 3 | .947 |
| 1970–Greenville | | W. Car. | O-3 | 108 | 355 | 69 | 98 | 14 | *11 | 7 | 68 | .276 | 130 | 11 | 7 | .953 |
| 1971–Winston-Salem | | .Carol. | O-1 | 118 | 402 | 63 | 115 | 20 | 4 | 12 | 63 | .286 | 219 | 17 | 10 | .959 |
| 1972–Louisville | | Int. | OF | •144 | 496 | 90 | 149 | 23 | 8 | 17 | *95 | .300 | 270 | 12 | 6 | .979 |
| 1972–Boston | | Amer. | OF | 18 | 57 | 2 | 15 | 3 | 1 | 1 | 6 | .263 | 25 | 3 | 0 | 1.000 |
| 1973–Boston | | Amer. | OF | 119 | 282 | 46 | 63 | 13 | 1 | 10 | 32 | .223 | 178 | 4 | 1 | .995 |
| 1974–Boston | | Amer. | OF | 133 | 463 | 60 | 130 | 19 | 8 | 10 | 70 | .281 | 294 | 8 | 3 | .990 |
| 1975–Boston | | Amer. | OF | 128 | 412 | 61 | 113 | 24 | 6 | 13 | 56 | .274 | 281 | 15 | 4 | .987 |
| 1976–Boston | | Amer. | OF-DH | 146 | 501 | 61 | 121 | 34 | 5 | 17 | 62 | .242 | 324 | 15 | 2 | *994 |
| Major League Totals | | | | 544 | 1715 | 230 | 442 | 93 | 21 | 51 | 226 | .258 | 1102 | 45 | 10 | .990 |

### CHAMPIONSHIP SERIES RECORD

| Year | Club | League | Pos. | G. | AB. | R. | H. | 2B. | 3B. | HR. | RBI. | B.A. | PO. | A. | E. | F.A. |
|---|---|---|---|---|---|---|---|---|---|---|---|---|---|---|---|---|
| 1975–Boston | | Amer. | OF | 3 | 10 | 1 | 1 | 1 | 0 | 0 | 0 | .100 | 7 | 0 | 0 | 1.000 |

### WORLD SERIES RECORD

| Year | Club | League | Pos. | G. | AB. | R. | H. | 2B. | 3B. | HR. | RBI. | B.A. | PO. | A. | E. | F.A. |
|---|---|---|---|---|---|---|---|---|---|---|---|---|---|---|---|---|
| 1975–Boston | | Amer. | OF | 7 | 24 | 3 | 7 | 1 | 1 | 1 | 5 | .292 | 23 | 1 | 0 | 1.000 |

# SAMUEL JAMES EWING

Name pronounced U-ing.

## (Sam)

Born April 9, 1949, at Lewisburg, Tenn.
Height, 6.03. Weight, 195.
Throws and bats lefthanded.
Attended University of Tennessee, Knoxville, Tenn.

| Year | Club | League | Pos. | G. | AB. | R. | H. | 2B. | 3B. | HR. | RBI. | B.A. | PO. | A. | E. | F.A. |
|---|---|---|---|---|---|---|---|---|---|---|---|---|---|---|---|---|
| 1971–Appleton† | | Midw. | OF-1B | 82 | 292 | 49 | 106 | 23 | 4 | 8 | 56 | .363 | 137 | 5 | 5 | .966 |
| 1972–Knoxville | | South. | 1B | 86 | 314 | 46 | 94 | 20 | 1 | 9 | 54 | .299 | 755 | 49 | 14 | .983 |
| 1972–Tucson | | P. C. | 1B | 55 | 192 | 18 | 49 | 10 | 2 | 2 | 28 | .255 | 482 | 32 | 6 | .988 |
| 1973–Iowa | | A. A. | *1B-OF | 123 | 442 | 64 | 129 | 30 | 2 | 12 | 75 | .292 | 934 | 62 | 6 | *.994 |
| 1973–Chicago | | Amer. | 1B | 11 | 20 | 1 | 3 | 1 | 0 | 0 | 2 | .150 | 34 | 4 | 0 | 1.000 |
| 1974–Iowa | | A. A. | OF-1B | 130 | 463 | 64 | 133 | *35 | 2 | 9 | 79 | .287 | 214 | 16 | 8 | .966 |
| 1975–Denver | | A. A. | O-1-3 | 119 | 377 | 62 | 120 | 27 | 4 | 9 | 71 | .318 | 153 | 18 | 4 | .977 |
| 1976–Chicago | | Amer. | DH-1-PH | 19 | 41 | 3 | 9 | 2 | 1 | 0 | 2 | .220 | 4 | 0 | 0 | 1.000 |
| 1976–Iowa‡ | | A. A. | 1-O-C-3 | 101 | 350 | 51 | 123 | 26 | 1 | 15 | 81 | .351 | 380 | 43 | 14 | .968 |
| Major League Totals | | | | 30 | 61 | 4 | 12 | 3 | 1 | 0 | 4 | .197 | 38 | 4 | 0 | 1.000 |

†On disabled list, May 3 to June 10, 1971.
‡Selected by Toronto Blue Jays in American League expansion draft, November 5, 1976.

# WILLIAM ROGER FAHEY

## (Bill)

Born June 14, 1950, at Detroit, Mich.
Height, 6.00. Weight, 200.
Throws right and bats lefthanded.
Hobbies—Hunting and music.
Attended University of Detroit, Detroit, Mich., St. Clair County Community College,
Port Huron, Mich., and University of Tampa, Tampa, Fla.

Led Pacific Coast League in passed balls with 15 in 1973.

| Year | Club | League | Pos. | G. | AB. | R. | H. | 2B. | 3B. | HR. | RBI. | B.A. | PO. | A. | E. | F.A. |
|---|---|---|---|---|---|---|---|---|---|---|---|---|---|---|---|---|
| 1970–Burlington | | Carol. | C | 118 | 377 | 49 | 92 | 10 | 2 | 3 | 36 | .244 | *724 | 76 | 10 | .988 |
| 1971–Pittsfield | | East. | C | 99 | 325 | 44 | 93 | 13 | 4 | 6 | 38 | .286 | 536 | 54 | 6 | *.990 |
| 1971–Denver | | A. A. | C | 4 | 15 | 1 | 4 | 0 | 0 | 1 | 2 | .267 | 19 | 2 | 0 | 1.000 |
| 1971–Washington | | Amer. | C | 2 | 8 | 0 | 0 | 0 | 0 | 0 | 0 | .000 | 8 | 2 | 1 | .909 |
| 1972–Denver | | A. A. | C | 75 | 226 | 28 | 61 | 5 | 4 | 1 | 25 | .270 | 421 | 43 | 6 | .987 |
| 1972–Texas | | Amer. | C | 39 | 119 | 8 | 20 | 2 | 0 | 1 | 10 | .168 | 236 | 26 | 2 | .992 |
| 1973–Spokane | | P. C. | C | 104 | 370 | 45 | 103 | 15 | 2 | 1 | 44 | .278 | 535 | 52 | 8 | *.987 |
| 1974–Spokane | | P. C. | C | 92 | 317 | 39 | 82 | 9 | 2 | 3 | 39 | .259 | 553 | 43 | 3 | *.995 |
| 1974–Texas | | Amer. | C | 6 | 16 | 1 | 4 | 0 | 0 | 0 | 0 | .250 | 21 | 2 | 0 | 1.000 |
| 1975–Texas† | | Amer. | C | 21 | 37 | 3 | 11 | 1 | 1 | 0 | 3 | .297 | 54 | 5 | 1 | .983 |
| 1976–Texas | | Amer. | C | 38 | 80 | 12 | 20 | 2 | 0 | 1 | 9 | .250 | 126 | 19 | 1 | .993 |
| Major League Totals | | | | 106 | 260 | 24 | 55 | 5 | 1 | 2 | 22 | .212 | 445 | 54 | 5 | .990 |

†On disabled list, June 22 to August 14, 1975.

# RONALD RAY FAIRLY
## (Ron)

Born July 12, 1938, at Macon, Ga.
Height, 5.10. Weight, 178.
Throws and bats lefthanded.
Hobby—Golf.
Attended University of Southern California, Los Angeles, Calif.
Son of Carl Fairly, minor league infielder, 1932, 1934 through 1943 and 1947.
Tied major league record for fewest three-base hits, season, 150 or more (0), 1963 and 1967.
Led Pacific Coast League batters in walks with 100 in 1960.
Received reported $60,000 bonus to sign with Los Angeles Dodgers, 1958.

| Year | Club | League | Pos. | G. | AB. | R. | H. | 2B. | 3B. | HR. | RBI. | B.A. | PO. | A. | E. | F.A. |
|---|---|---|---|---|---|---|---|---|---|---|---|---|---|---|---|---|
| 1958—Des Moines | | ......West. | OF | 51 | 172 | 32 | 51 | 7 | 0 | 13 | 41 | .297 | 128 | 7 | 3 | .978 |
| 1958—St. Paul | | ............A. A. | OF | 18 | 57 | 8 | 17 | 2 | 1 | 1 | 8 | .298 | 57 | 1 | 1 | .983 |
| 1958—Los Angeles | | ......Nat. | OF | 15 | 53 | 6 | 15 | 1 | 0 | 2 | 8 | .283 | 33 | 0 | 1 | .971 |
| 1959—Los Angeles | | ......Nat. | OF | 118 | 244 | 27 | 58 | 12 | 1 | 4 | 23 | .238 | 97 | 8 | 4 | .963 |
| 1960—Los Angeles | | ......Nat. | OF | 14 | 37 | 6 | 4 | 0 | 3 | 1 | 3 | .108 | 15 | 1 | 0 | 1.000 |
| 1960—Spokane | | ............P. C. | OF | 147 | 505 | 98 | 153 | 34 | 4 | 27 | 100 | .303 | 299 | •20 | 8 | .976 |
| 1961—Los Angeles | | ......Nat. | OF-1B | 111 | 245 | 42 | 79 | 15 | 2 | 10 | 48 | .322 | 242 | 18 | 3 | .989 |
| 1962—Los Angeles | | ......Nat. | 1B-OF | 147 | 460 | 80 | 128 | 15 | 7 | 14 | 71 | .278 | 1007 | 45 | 11 | .990 |
| 1963—Los Angeles | | ......Nat. | *1B-OF | 152 | 490 | 62 | 133 | 21 | 0 | 12 | 77 | .271 | 946 | 48 | 7 | *.993 |
| 1964—Los Angeles | | ......Nat. | 1B | 150 | 454 | 62 | 116 | 19 | 5 | 10 | 74 | .256 | 1081 | 82 | 15 | .987 |
| 1965—Los Angeles | | ......Nat. | OF-1B | 158 | 555 | 73 | 152 | 28 | 1 | 9 | 70 | .274 | 361 | 13 | 6 | .984 |
| 1966—Los Angeles | | ......Nat. | OF-1B | 117 | 351 | 53 | 101 | 20 | 0 | 14 | 61 | .288 | 264 | 14 | 4 | .986 |
| 1967—Los Angeles | | ......Nat. | OF-1B | 153 | 486 | 45 | 107 | 19 | 0 | 10 | 55 | .220 | 727 | 55 | 11 | .986 |
| 1968—Los Angeles | | ......Nat. | OF-1B | 141 | 441 | 32 | 103 | 15 | 1 | 4 | 43 | .234 | 406 | 26 | 3 | .993 |
| 1969—L.A.†—Mont. | | ......Nat. | 1B-OF | 100 | 317 | 38 | 87 | 16 | 6 | 12 | 47 | .274 | 543 | 46 | 7 | .988 |
| 1970—Montreal‡ | | .........Nat. | 1B-OF | 119 | 385 | 54 | 111 | 19 | 0 | 15 | 61 | .288 | 945 | 90 | 5 | .995 |
| 1971—Montreal | | .........Nat. | 1B-OF | 146 | 447 | 58 | 115 | 23 | 0 | 13 | 71 | .257 | 1116 | 104 | 10 | .992 |
| 1972—Montreal | | .........Nat. | OF-1B | 140 | 446 | 51 | 124 | 15 | 1 | 17 | 68 | .278 | 646 | 46 | 6 | .991 |
| 1973—Montreal | | .........Nat. | OF-1B | 142 | 413 | 70 | 123 | 13 | 1 | 17 | 49 | .298 | 202 | 5 | 5 | .976 |
| 1974—Montreal§ | | .........Nat. | 1B-OF | 101 | 282 | 35 | 69 | 9 | 1 | 12 | 43 | .245 | 603 | 43 | 7 | .989 |
| 1975—St. Louis | | .........Nat. | 1B-OF | 107 | 229 | 32 | 69 | 13 | 2 | 7 | 37 | .301 | 383 | 33 | 8 | .981 |
| 1976—St. Louis x | | .......Nat. | 1B-PH | 73 | 110 | 13 | 29 | 4 | 0 | 0 | 21 | .264 | 174 | 21 | 1 | .995 |
| 1976—Oakland y | | .........Amer. | 1B-PH | 15 | 46 | 9 | 11 | 1 | 0 | 3 | 10 | .239 | 121 | 10 | 0 | 1.000 |
| National League Totals | | ................. | | 2204 | 6445 | 839 | 1723 | 277 | 31 | 183 | 930 | .267 | 9791 | 698 | 114 | .989 |
| American League Totals | | ................ | | 15 | 46 | 9 | 11 | 1 | 0 | 3 | 10 | .239 | 121 | 10 | 0 | 1.000 |
| Major League Totals | | ..................... | | 2219 | 6491 | 848 | 1734 | 278 | 31 | 186 | 940 | .267 | 9912 | 708 | 114 | .989 |

†Traded with Infielder Paul Popovich to Montreal Expos for Infielder Maury Wills and Outfielder Manny Mota, June 11, 1969.
‡On disabled list August 3 through September 4.
§Traded to St. Cardinals for Second Baseman Rudy Kinard and Outfielder-First Baseman Ed Kurpiel, December 6, 1974.
xSold to Oakland A's, September 14, 1976.
y Traded to Toronto Blue Jays for Infielder Mike Weathers and cash estimated at $30,000, February 24, 1977.

## WORLD SERIES RECORD

Tied World Series record of one of more hits each game, seven-game series, 1965.

| Year | Club | League | Pos. | G. | AB. | R. | H. | 2B. | 3B. | HR. | RBI. | B.A. | PO. | A. | E. | F.A. |
|---|---|---|---|---|---|---|---|---|---|---|---|---|---|---|---|---|
| 1959—Los Angeles | | ......Nat. | OF | 6 | 3 | 0 | 0 | 0 | 0 | 0 | 0 | .000 | 0 | 0 | 0 | .000 |
| 1963—Los Angeles | | ......Nat. | OF | 4 | 1 | 0 | 0 | 0 | 0 | 0 | 0 | .000 | 3 | 0 | 0 | 1.000 |
| 1965—Los Angeles | | ......Nat. | OF | 7 | 29 | 7 | 11 | 3 | 0 | 2 | 6 | .379 | 8 | 0 | 0 | 1.000 |
| 1966—Los Angeles | | ......Nat. | OF-1B | 3 | 7 | 0 | 1 | 0 | 0 | 0 | 0 | .143 | 5 | 0 | 1 | .833 |
| World Series Totals | | ....................... | | 20 | 40 | 7 | 12 | 3 | 0 | 2 | 6 | .300 | 16 | 0 | 1 | .941 |

## ALL-STAR GAME RECORD

| Year | League | Pos. | AB. | R. | H. | 2B. | 3B. | HR. | RBI. | B.A. | PO. | A. | E. | F.A. |
|---|---|---|---|---|---|---|---|---|---|---|---|---|---|---|
| 1973—National | .............................. | 1B | 0 | 0 | 0 | 0 | 0 | 0 | 0 | .000 | 4 | 0 | 0 | 1.000 |

# PETER FALCONE
## (Pete)

Born October 1, 1953, at Brooklyn, N. Y.
Height, 6.02. Weight, 190.
Throws and bats lefthanded.
Attended Kingsborough Community College, Brooklyn, N. Y.
Second cousin of Joe Pignatano, coach with New York Mets.

| Year | Club | League | G. | IP. | W. | L. | Pct. | H. | R. | ER. | SO. | BB. | ERA. |
|---|---|---|---|---|---|---|---|---|---|---|---|---|---|
| 1973—Great Falls | ........................Pioneer | | 12 | 72 | 8 | 1 | *.889 | 49 | 19 | 12 | 102 | 53 | *1.50 |
| 1974—Fresno | ..............................California | | 17 | 137 | 10 | 4 | .714 | 116 | 61 | 46 | 172 | 61 | 3.02 |
| 1974—Amarillo | ..............................Texas | | 7 | 37 | 2 | 4 | .333 | 41 | 14 | 11 | 35 | 18 | 2.68 |
| 1975—San Francisco† | ...................National | | 34 | 190 | 12 | 11 | .522 | 171 | 97 | 88 | 131 | 111 | 4.17 |
| 1976—St. Louis | .............................National | | 32 | 212 | 12 | 16 | .429 | 173 | 87 | 76 | 138 | 93 | 3.23 |
| Major League Totals | .............................. | | 66 | 402 | 24 | 27 | .470 | 344 | 184 | 164 | 169 | 204 | 3.67 |

†Traded to St. Louis Cardinals for Third Baseman Ken Reitz, December 8, 1975.

## RONALD SAMUEL FARKAS
### (Ron)

Born July 30, 1953, at Cleveland, O.
Height, 6.00. Weight, 180.
Throws and bats righthanded.
Hobbies—Hunting and fishing.

| Year Club | League | Pos. | G. | AB. | R. | H. | 2B. | 3B. | HR. | RBI. | B.A. | PO. | A. | E. | F.A. |
|---|---|---|---|---|---|---|---|---|---|---|---|---|---|---|---|
| 1972–Melb'rne Twins | Fla. E. | 3B | 52 | 171 | 30 | 51 | 11 | 2 | 2 | 36 | .298 | 36 | *140 | *21 | .893 |
| 1973–Wis. Rapids | Midw. | 3B | 6 | 9 | 0 | 1 | 1 | 0 | 0 | 1 | .111 | 2 | 7 | 0 | 1.000 |
| 1973–Geneva | NYP | 3-SS-2 | 59 | 207 | 38 | 59 | 9 | 3 | 2 | 25 | .285 | 56 | 93 | 17 | .898 |
| 1974–Wis. Rapids | Midw. | SS-2B | 120 | 459 | 88 | 131 | 17 | 4 | 6 | 32 | .285 | *211 | *425 | 41 | *.939 |
| 1975–Reno | Calif. | 3-SS-2 | 135 | 422 | 57 | 99 | 10 | 10 | 6 | 63 | .235 | 269 | 334 | 39 | .939 |
| 1976–Salt Lake City | P. C. | 3B | 7 | 24 | 0 | 4 | 1 | 0 | 0 | 3 | .167 | 4 | 16 | 1 | .952 |
| 1976–El Paso | Texas | 3-SS-2 | 115 | 371 | 77 | 117 | 18 | 6 | 4 | 49 | .315 | 134 | 255 | 34 | .920 |

Listed on St. Louis Cardinals' 1977 spring roster.

## JOSEPH VANCE FERGUSON
### (Joe)

Born September 19, 1946, at San Francisco, Calif.
Height, 6.02. Weight, 200.
Throws and bats righthanded.
Hobbies—Golf and art (sketching).
Attended University of the Pacific, Stockton, Calif.

Established major league record for fewest errors, season, catcher (700 or more chances), 3, 1973.
Led National League catchers in double plays with 17 in 1973.
Tied for National League lead in sacrifice flies with 10 in 1973.
Led Northwest League batters in walks with 54 and strikeouts with 77 in 1968.
Led Florida State League catchers in passed balls with 44 in 1969.

| Year Club | League | Pos. | G. | AB. | R. | H. | 2B. | 3B. | HR. | RBI. | B.A. | PO. | A. | E. | F.A. |
|---|---|---|---|---|---|---|---|---|---|---|---|---|---|---|---|
| 1968–Tri-City | Northw. | OF | 70 | 226 | 44 | 65 | 9 | 4 | *12 | 52 | .288 | 101 | 6 | 2 | .982 |
| 1969–Daytona Beach | F.S. | *C-O-1 | 123 | 391 | 66 | 112 | 21 | 4 | 9 | 58 | .286 | *728 | *90 | *26 | .969 |
| 1970–Albuquerque | Tex. | *C-O-3 | 109 | 364 | 72 | 111 | 20 | 4 | 16 | 65 | .305 | 606 | 83 | 8 | *.989 |
| 1970–Los Angeles | Nat. | C | 5 | 4 | 0 | 1 | 0 | 0 | 0 | 1 | .250 | 9 | 0 | 0 | 1.000 |
| 1971–Spokane | P.C. | C-OF | 60 | 213 | 27 | 54 | 10 | 1 | 10 | 43 | .254 | 345 | 31 | 7 | .982 |
| 1971–Los Angeles | Nat. | C | 36 | 102 | 13 | 22 | 3 | 0 | 2 | 7 | .216 | 167 | 9 | 3 | .983 |
| 1972–Albuquerque | P.C. | C-OF | 123 | 380 | 68 | 99 | 21 | 4 | 10 | 67 | .261 | 516 | 40 | 10 | .982 |
| 1972–Los Angeles | Nat. | C-OF | 8 | 24 | 2 | 7 | 3 | 0 | 1 | 5 | .292 | 42 | 1 | 0 | 1.000 |
| 1973–Los Angeles† | Nat. | *C-OF | 136 | 487 | 84 | 128 | 26 | 0 | 25 | 88 | .263 | 786 | 57 | 5 | *.994 |
| 1974–Los Angeles | Nat. | C-OF | 111 | 349 | 54 | 88 | 14 | 1 | 16 | 57 | .252 | 486 | 40 | 7 | .987 |
| 1975–Los Angeles‡ | Nat. | C-OF | 66 | 202 | 15 | 42 | 2 | 1 | 5 | 23 | .208 | 215 | 20 | 2 | .992 |
| 1976–L.A.§St.L.x | Nat. | C-OF | 125 | 374 | 46 | 79 | 15 | 4 | 10 | 39 | .211 | 409 | 46 | 14 | .970 |
| Major League Totals | | | 487 | 1542 | 214 | 367 | 63 | 6 | 59 | 220 | .238 | 2114 | 173 | 31 | .987 |

†On supplemental disabled list, June 21 to July 10, 1973.
‡On disabled list, July 2 to September 29, 1975.
§Traded with Outfielder Bobby Detherage and Infielder Freddie Tisdale, latter assigned from Lodi to St. Petersburg, to St. Louis Cardinals for Outfielder Reggie Smith, June 15, 1976.
xTraded with Outfielder Bobby Detherage, assigned to Memphis, to Houston Astros for Pitcher Larry Dierker and Infielder Jerry DaVanon, November 23, 1976.

### CHAMPIONSHIP SERIES RECORD

| Year Club | League | Pos. | G. | AB. | R. | H. | 2B. | 3B. | HR. | RBI. | B.A. | PO. | A. | E. | F.A. |
|---|---|---|---|---|---|---|---|---|---|---|---|---|---|---|---|
| 1974–Los Angeles | Nat. | OF-C | 4 | 13 | 3 | 3 | 0 | 0 | 0 | 2 | .231 | 9 | 0 | 1 | .900 |

### WORLD SERIES RECORD

Tied World Series records for most errors, catcher, 5-game series, 2, in 1974, and most errors, catcher, game, 2, October 15, 1974.

| Year Club | League | Pos. | G. | AB. | R. | H. | 2B. | 3B. | HR. | RBI. | B.A. | PO. | A. | E. | F.A. |
|---|---|---|---|---|---|---|---|---|---|---|---|---|---|---|---|
| 1974–Los Angeles | Nat. | OF-C | 5 | 16 | 2 | 2 | 0 | 0 | 1 | 2 | .125 | 14 | 1 | 2 | .882 |

## SERGIO FERRER (MARRERO)

Born January 29, 1951, at Santurce, Puerto Rico.
Height, 5.07. Weight, 145.
Throws right and bats left and righthanded.
Hobby—Listening to music.
Attended University of Puerto Rico, Rio Piedras, Puerto Rico.

Led California League shortstops in double plays with 77 in 1972.

| Year Club | League | Pos. | G. | AB. | R. | H. | 2B. | 3B. | HR. | RBI. | B.A. | PO. | A. | E. | F.A. |
|---|---|---|---|---|---|---|---|---|---|---|---|---|---|---|---|
| 1971–Daytona Beach | Fla.St. | SS | 130 | 467 | 82 | 136 | 11 | 9 | 2 | 43 | .291 | 207 | 429 | 42 | .938 |
| 1972–Bakersfield | Calif. | SS | 119 | 447 | 99 | 135 | 22 | 6 | 4 | 50 | .302 | 190 | *333 | 28 | *.949 |
| 1972–El Paso | Texas | SS | 10 | 31 | 3 | 5 | 1 | 0 | 0 | 1 | .161 | 12 | 21 | 8 | .805 |
| 1973–Waterbury† | East. | SS | 118 | 416 | 69 | 105 | 9 | 2 | 3 | 27 | .252 | 206 | 360 | 31 | .948 |

| ...ar Club | League | Pos. | G. | AB. | R. | H. | 2B. | 3B. | HR. | RBI. | B.A. | PO. | A. | E. | F.A. |
|---|---|---|---|---|---|---|---|---|---|---|---|---|---|---|---|
| .,74–Tacoma ...........P.C. | | SS | 82 | 279 | 46 | 81 | 11 | 1 | 1 | 29 | .290 | 139 | 215 | 29 | .924 |
| 1974–Minnesota ........Amer. | | SS-2B | 24 | 57 | 12 | 16 | 0 | 2 | 0 | 0 | .281 | 18 | 37 | 9 | .859 |
| 1975–Tacoma ...........P.C. | | SS-2B | 47 | 154 | 28 | 33 | 3 | 2 | 1 | 6 | .214 | 87 | 131 | 14 | .940 |
| 1975–Minnesota‡ .......Amer. | | SS-2B | 32 | 81 | 14 | 20 | 3 | 1 | 0 | 2 | .247 | 32 | 62 | 6 | .940 |
| 1976–Okla. City§ ........A.A. | | 2B-SS | 89 | 226 | 33 | 60 | 9 | 0 | 1 | 10 | .265 | 124 | 182 | 18 | .994 |
| Major League Totals ..................... | | | 56 | 138 | 26 | 36 | 3 | 3 | 0 | 2 | .261 | 50 | 99 | 15 | .909 |

†Drafted from Albuquerque (Los Angeles Dodgers' organization) by Minnesota Twins, December 3, 1973.
‡Traded to Philadelphia Phillies for Catcher Larry Cox, October 24, 1975.
§Traded from Philadelphia Phillies' organization to New York Yankees for Outfielder Kerry Dineen, March 26, 1977.

## RAUL FERREYRA (CACERES)

Name pronounced fuh-RAY-ruh.

Born October 10, 1954, at Jima Abajo, Lavega, Dominican Republic.
Height, 6.02. Weight, 185.
Throws and bats righthanded.
Hobby—Movies.

| Year Club | League | G. | IP. | W. | L. | Pct. | H. | R. | ER. | SO. | BB. | ERA. |
|---|---|---|---|---|---|---|---|---|---|---|---|---|
| 1973–Bradenton Reds....................Gulf Coast | | 11 | 50 | 3 | 3 | .500 | 33 | 14 | 12 | 30 | 22 | 2.16 |
| 1974–Billings† .............................Pioneer | | 14 | 58 | 1 | *8 | .111 | 73 | 49 | 38 | 45 | 18 | 5.90 |
| 1975–Tampa .................................Florida St. | | 45 | 89 | 7 | 4 | .636 | 69 | 15 | 11 | 55 | 34 | 1.11 |
| 1976–Three Rivers........................Eastern | | 25 | 44 | 5 | 2 | .714 | 44 | 17 | 14 | 16 | 13 | 2.86 |

†Played in one game as a second baseman.
Listed on Cincinnati Reds' 1977 spring roster.

## MARK STEVEN FIDRYCH

Born August 14, 1954, at Worcester, Mass.
Height, 6.03. Weight, 175.
Throws and bats righthanded.

Led American League in complete games with 24 in 1976.
Named American League Rookie of the Year by Baseball Writers' Association of America, 1976.
Named American League Rookie Pitcher of the Year by THE SPORTING NEWS, 1976.

| Year Club | League | G. | IP. | W. | L. | Pct. | H. | R. | ER. | SO. | BB. | ERA. |
|---|---|---|---|---|---|---|---|---|---|---|---|---|
| 1974–Bristol ..............................Ap'lachian | | 23 | 34 | 3 | 0 | 1.000 | 24 | 13 | 9 | 40 | 16 | 2.38 |
| 1975–Lakeland............................Florida St. | | 17 | 117 | 5 | 9 | .357 | 111 | 58 | 49 | 73 | 50 | 3.77 |
| 1975–Montgomery .......................Southern | | 7 | 14 | 2 | 0 | 1.000 | 15 | 6 | 5 | 11 | 3 | 3.21 |
| 1975–Evansville..........................Am. Assoc. | | 6 | 40 | 4 | 1 | .800 | 27 | 8 | 7 | 29 | 9 | 1.58 |
| 1976–Detroit ..............................American | | 31 | 250 | 19 | 9 | .679 | 217 | 76 | 65 | 97 | 53 | *2.34 |
| Major League Totals .............................. | | 31 | 250 | 19 | 9 | .679 | 217 | 76 | 65 | 97 | 53 | 2.34 |

### ALL-STAR GAME RECORD

| Year League | IP. | W. | L. | Pct. | H. | R. | ER. | SO. | BB. | ERA. |
|---|---|---|---|---|---|---|---|---|---|---|
| 1976–American ...................................... | 2 | 0 | 1 | .000 | 4 | 2 | 2 | 1 | 0 | 9.00 |

## EDUARDO FIGUEROA (PADILLA)

Name pronounced fee-gur-OH-uh.

### (Ed)

Born October 14, 1948, at Ciales, Puerto Rico.
Height, 6.00. Weight, 187.
Throws and bats righthanded.
Hobbies—Music, fishing and basketball.

Tied for Midwest League lead in shutouts with 3 in 1970.

| Year Club | League | G. | IP. | W. | L. | Pct. | H. | R. | ER. | SO. | BB. | ERA. |
|---|---|---|---|---|---|---|---|---|---|---|---|---|
| 1966–Marion ...............................Appal'chian | | 2 | 10 | 1 | 1 | .500 | 16 | 8 | 6 | 6 | 4 | 5.40 |
| 1966–Greenville ..........................W. Carolinas | | 2 | 12 | 1 | 1 | .500 | 13 | 3 | 3 | 10 | 1 | 2.25 |
| 1967–Winter Haven .....................Florida St. | | 26 | 176 | 12 | 5 | .706 | 140 | 50 | 40 | 123 | 44 | 2.05 |
| 1968–Raleigh-Dur.† .....................Carolina | | 7 | 13 | 0 | 2 | .000 | 14 | 10 | 9 | 11 | 7 | 6.23 |
| 1969–................................. | (In Military Service) | | | | | | | | | | | |
| 1970–Decatur...............................Midwest | | 13 | 102 | 8 | 3 | .727 | 86 | 33 | 22 | 85 | 23 | 1.94 |
| 1970–Fresno ...............................California | | 14 | 51 | 1 | 5 | .167 | 55 | 27 | 25 | 47 | 18 | 4.41 |
| 1971–Fresno‡...............................California | | 14 | 101 | 10 | 4 | .714 | 94 | 52 | 41 | 111 | 37 | 3.65 |
| 1971–Amarillo .............................Texas | | 14 | 104 | 8 | 5 | .615 | 85 | 28 | 24 | 91 | 25 | 2.08 |
| 1972–Phoenix...............................P. Coast | | 29 | 139 | 10 | 2 | .833 | 163 | 77 | 66 | 105 | 45 | 4.27 |
| 1973–Phoenix§-S.L.C. ..................P. Coast | | 29 | 150 | 6 | 8 | .429 | 189 | 94 | 69 | 87 | 46 | 4.14 |
| 1974–Salt Lake C. ........................P. Coast | | 4 | 30 | 3 | 0 | 1.000 | 27 | 14 | 8 | 20 | 9 | 2.40 |
| 1974–California ............................American | | 25 | 105 | 2 | 8 | .200 | 119 | 46 | 43 | 49 | 36 | 3.69 |
| 1975–Salt Lake C. ........................P. Coast | | 2 | 15 | 2 | 0 | 1.000 | 5 | 3 | 6 | 3 | 1.80 |
| 1975–California x..........................American | | 33 | 245 | 16 | 13 | .552 | 213 | 96 | 79 | 139 | 84 | 2.90 |
| 1976–New York ............................American | | 34 | 257 | 19 | 10 | .655 | 237 | 101 | 86 | 119 | 94 | 3.01 |
| Major League Totals .............................. | | 92 | 607 | 37 | 31 | .544 | 569 | 243 | 208 | 307 | 214 | 3.08 |

†Released by New York Mets' organization, June 30, 1968; signed as free agent by San Francisco Giants' organization, February 21, 1970.
‡Appeared as outfielder in one game.
§Traded by San Francisco Giants to California Angels for Pitcher Don Rose and Infielder Bruce Christensen, July 6, 1973.
xTraded with Outfielder Mickey Rivers to New York Yankees for Outfielder Bobby Bonds, December 11, 1975.

## CHAMPIONSHIP SERIES RECORD

| Year Club | League | G. | IP. | W. | L. | Pct. | H. | R. | ER. | SO. | BB. | ERA. |
|---|---|---|---|---|---|---|---|---|---|---|---|---|
| 1976—New York ...................American | 2 | 12⅓ | 0 | 1 | .000 | 14 | 8 | 8 | 5 | 2 | 5.84 |

## WORLD SERIES RECORD

| Year Club | League | G. | IP. | W. | L. | Pct. | H. | R. | ER. | SO. | BB. | ERA. |
|---|---|---|---|---|---|---|---|---|---|---|---|---|
| 1976—New York ...................American | 1 | 8 | 0 | 1 | .000 | 6 | 5 | 5 | 2 | 5 | 5.63 |

## ROLAND GLEN FINGERS
### (Rollie)

(Named after a player his father played with.)
Born August 25, 1946, at Steubenville, O.
Height, 6.04. Weight, 190.
Throws and bats righthanded.
Hobby—Golf.
Attended Chaffey Junior College, Alta Loma, Calif.
Son of George M. Fingers, who spent four years in the St. Louis Cardinals' organization, and brother of Gordon Fingers, former pitcher in Oakland Athletics' organization.
Tied for Southern League lead in shutouts with 3 in 1968.

| Year Club | League | G. | IP. | W. | L. | Pct. | H. | R. | ER. | SO. | BB. | ERA. |
|---|---|---|---|---|---|---|---|---|---|---|---|---|
| 1965—Leesburg........................Florida St. | 25 | 175 | 8 | 15 | .348 | 148 | 83 | 58 | 108 | 69 | 2.98 |
| 1966—Modesto ........................California | 22 | 159 | 11 | 6 | .647 | 120 | 61 | 49 | 152 | 43 | 2.77 |
| 1967—Birmingham† ...................Southern | 18 | 102 | 6 | 5 | .545 | 75 | 34 | 25 | 61 | 36 | 2.21 |
| 1968—Birmingham ...................Southern | 18 | 108 | 10 | 4 | .714 | 94 | 38 | 36 | 93 | 28 | 3.00 |
| 1968—Oakland ..........................American | 1 | 1 | 0 | 0 | .000 | 4 | 4 | 4 | 0 | 1 | 36.00 |
| 1969—Oakland ..........................American | 60 | 119 | 6 | 7 | .462 | 116 | 60 | 49 | 61 | 41 | 3.71 |
| 1970—Oakland ..........................American | 45 | 148 | 7 | 9 | .438 | 137 | 65 | 60 | 79 | 48 | 3.65 |
| 1971—Oakland ..........................American | 48 | 129 | 4 | 6 | .400 | 94 | 46 | 43 | 98 | 30 | 3.00 |
| 1972—Oakland ..........................American | 65 | 111 | 11 | 9 | .550 | 85 | 35 | 31 | 113 | 32 | 2.51 |
| 1973—Oakland ..........................American | 62 | 127 | 7 | 8 | .467 | 107 | 41 | 27 | 110 | 39 | 1.91 |
| 1974—Oakland ..........................American | •76 | 119 | 9 | 5 | .643 | 104 | 41 | 35 | 95 | 29 | 2.65 |
| 1975—Oakland ..........................American | •75 | 127 | 10 | 6 | .625 | 95 | 43 | 42 | 115 | 33 | 2.98 |
| 1976—Oakland‡.........................American | 70 | 135 | 13 | 11 | .542 | 118 | 40 | 37 | 113 | 40 | 2.47 |
| Major League Totals .................. | 502 | 1016 | 67 | 61 | .523 | 860 | 375 | 328 | 784 | 293 | 2.91 |

†On disabled list from April 18 through May 31 after suffering fractured jaw and cheekbone when hit by line drive.
‡Played out option year and granted free agency, November 1, 1976; signed as free agent with San Diego Padres, December 14, 1976.

## CHAMPIONSHIP SERIES RECORD

| Year Club | League | G. | IP. | W. | L. | Pct. | H. | R. | ER. | SO. | BB. | ERA. |
|---|---|---|---|---|---|---|---|---|---|---|---|---|
| 1971—Oakland ..........................American | 2 | 2⅓ | 0 | 0 | .000 | 2 | 2 | 2 | 2 | 1 | 7.71 |
| 1972—Oakland ..........................American | 3 | 5⅓ | 1 | 0 | 1.000 | 4 | 1 | 1 | 3 | 1 | 1.69 |
| 1973—Oakland ..........................American | 3 | 4⅔ | 0 | 1 | .000 | 4 | 1 | 1 | 4 | 2 | 1.93 |
| 1974—Oakland ..........................American | 2 | 3 | 0 | 0 | .000 | 3 | 1 | 1 | 3 | 1 | 3.00 |
| 1975—Oakland ..........................American | 1 | 4 | 0 | 1 | .000 | 5 | 3 | 3 | 3 | 1 | 6.75 |
| Championship Series Totals ..................... | 11 | 19⅓ | 1 | 2 | .333 | 18 | 8 | 8 | 15 | 6 | 3.72 |

## WORLD SERIES RECORD

Established World Series records for most total saves, 6, 1972 (2), 1973 (2), 1974 (2); and most total games, relief pitcher, 16, in 1974.

| Year Club | League | G. | IP. | W. | L. | Pct. | H. | R. | ER. | SO. | BB. | ERA. |
|---|---|---|---|---|---|---|---|---|---|---|---|---|
| 1972—Oakland ..........................American | 6 | 10⅓ | 1 | 1 | .500 | 4 | 2 | 2 | 11 | 4 | 1.74 |
| 1973—Oakland ..........................American | 6 | 13⅔ | 0 | 1 | .000 | 13 | 5 | 1 | 8 | 4 | 0.66 |
| 1974—Oakland ..........................American | 4 | 9⅓ | 1 | 0 | 1.000 | 8 | 2 | 2 | 6 | 2 | 1.93 |
| World Series Totals .................................. | 16 | 33⅓ | 2 | 2 | .500 | 25 | 9 | 5 | 25 | 10 | 1.35 |

## ALL-STAR GAME RECORD

| Year League | IP. | W. | L. | Pct. | H. | R. | ER. | SO. | BB. | ERA. |
|---|---|---|---|---|---|---|---|---|---|---|
| 1973—American ...................................................... | 1 | 0 | 0 | .000 | 0 | 0 | 0 | 0 | 0 | 0.00 |
| 1974—American ...................................................... | 1 | 0 | 0 | .000 | 1 | 2 | 2 | 0 | 1 | 18.00 |
| All-Star Game Totals.......................................... | 2 | 0 | 0 | .000 | 1 | 2 | 2 | 0 | 1 | 9.00 |

Member of American League All-Star Team for 1975 game; did not play.

## DID YOU KNOW—

That the New York Giants had a home attendance of 1,600,793 in 1947?

# CARLTON ERNEST FISK

Born December 26, 1947, at Bellows Falls, Vt.
Height, 6.02. Weight, 200.
Throws and bats righthanded.
Hobbies—Sports, reading and woodworking.
Attended University of New Hampshire, Durham, N. H.
Brother of Calvin Fisk, former catcher in Baltimore Orioles' organization.
Brother-in-law of Dick Miller, outfielder with Boston Red Sox. Cousin of
Dave Jennings, punter with New York Giants.
Led American League catchers in total chances with 933 in 1972 and 803 in 1973.
Led International League catchers in double plays with 12 in 1971.
Named American League Rookie of the Year by the Baseball Writers' Association of America, 1972.
Named THE SPORTING NEWS American League Rookie Player of the Year, 1972.
Named catcher on THE SPORTING NEWS American League All-Star Team, 1972.
Named catcher on THE SPORTING NEWS American League All-Star fielding team, 1972.

| Year Club | League | Pos. | G. | AB. | R. | H. | 2B. | 3B. | HR. | RBI. | B.A. | PO. | A. | E. | F.A. |
|---|---|---|---|---|---|---|---|---|---|---|---|---|---|---|---|
| 1967—Greenville† | W. Car. | | | | | (In Military Service) | | | | | | | | | |
| 1968—Waterloo‡ | Midw. | C | 62 | 195 | 31 | 66 | 11 | 2 | 12 | 34 | .338 | 385 | 42 | 8 | .982 |
| 1969—Boston | Amer. | C | 2 | 5 | 0 | 0 | 0 | 0 | 0 | 0 | .000 | 2 | 0 | 0 | 1.000 |
| 1970—Pawtucket | East. | C-O-1 | 93 | 284 | 43 | 65 | 18 | 1 | 12 | 44 | .229 | 482 | 50 | 7 | .987 |
| 1971—Louisville | Int. | C-O-3 | 94 | 308 | 45 | 81 | 10 | 4 | 10 | 43 | .263 | 588 | 51 | 13 | .980 |
| 1971—Boston | Amer. | C | 14 | 48 | 7 | 15 | 2 | 1 | 2 | 6 | .313 | 72 | 6 | 2 | .975 |
| 1972—Boston | Amer. | C | 131 | 457 | 74 | 134 | 28 | •9 | 22 | 61 | .293 | *846 | *72 | ●15 | .984 |
| 1973—Boston | Amer. | C | 135 | 508 | 65 | 125 | 21 | 0 | 26 | 71 | .246 | *739 | 50 | *14 | .983 |
| 1974—Boston§ | Amer. | C | 52 | 187 | 36 | 56 | 12 | 1 | 11 | 26 | .299 | 267 | 26 | 6 | .980 |
| 1975—Boston x | Amer. | C | 79 | 263 | 47 | 87 | 14 | 4 | 10 | 52 | .331 | 347 | 30 | 8 | .979 |
| 1976—Boston | Amer. | C-DH | 134 | 487 | 76 | 124 | 17 | 5 | 17 | 58 | .255 | 649 | 73 | 12 | .984 |
| Major League Totals | | | 547 | 1955 | 305 | 541 | 94 | 20 | 88 | 274 | .277 | 2922 | 257 | 57 | .982 |

†On temporary inactive list, April 17, 1967. Transferred to the military list, May 18, 1967 through April 9, 1968.

‡On temporary inactive list, August 5 through August 20.

§On disabled list from beginning of season until April 26 and from June 28 through remainder of season.

xOn disabled list from beginning of season until June 23, 1975.

## CHAMPIONSHIP SERIES RECORD

| Year Club | League | Pos. | G. | AB. | R. | H. | 2B. | 3B. | HR. | RBI. | B.A. | PO. | A. | E. | F.A. |
|---|---|---|---|---|---|---|---|---|---|---|---|---|---|---|---|
| 1975—Boston | Amer. | C | 3 | 12 | 4 | 5 | 1 | 0 | 0 | 2 | .417 | 15 | 0 | 0 | 1.000 |

## WORLD SERIES RECORD

| Year Club | League | Pos. | G. | AB. | R. | H. | 2B. | 3B. | HR. | RBI. | B.A. | PO. | A. | E. | F.A. |
|---|---|---|---|---|---|---|---|---|---|---|---|---|---|---|---|
| 1975—Boston | Amer. | C | 7 | 25 | 5 | 6 | 0 | 0 | 2 | 4 | .240 | 37 | 3 | 2 | .952 |

## ALL-STAR GAME RECORD

| Year League | Pos. | AB. | R. | H. | 2B. | 3B. | HR. | RBI. | B.A. | PO. | A. | E. | F.A. |
|---|---|---|---|---|---|---|---|---|---|---|---|---|---|
| 1972—American | C | 2 | 1 | 1 | 0 | 0 | 0 | 0 | .500 | 2 | 0 | 0 | 1.000 |
| 1973—American | C | 2 | 0 | 0 | 0 | 0 | 0 | 0 | .000 | 3 | 0 | 0 | 1.000 |
| 1976—American | C | 1 | 0 | 0 | 0 | 0 | 0 | 0 | .000 | 1 | 0 | 0 | 1.000 |
| All-Star Game Totals | | 5 | 1 | 1 | 0 | 0 | 0 | 0 | .200 | 6 | 0 | 0 | 1.000 |

Named to American League All-Star Team for 1974 game; replaced due to injury.

# ALAN JAMES FITZMORRIS
## (Al)

Born March 21, 1946, at Buffalo, N. Y.
Height, 6.02. Weight, 195.
Throws right and bats left and righthanded.
Hobbies—Playing guitar, writing music and singing.
Attended Johnson County Community College, Overland Park, Kan.

| Year Club | League | G. | IP. | W. | L. | Pct. | H. | R. | ER. | SO. | BB. | ERA. |
|---|---|---|---|---|---|---|---|---|---|---|---|---|
| 1966—Fox Cities | Midwest | 4 | 14 | 0 | 0 | .000 | 7 | 2 | 2 | 15 | 7 | 1.29 |
| 1967—Appleton | Midwest | 24 | 190 | 14 | 8 | .636 | 131 | 66 | 48 | 167 | 61 | 2.27 |
| 1968—Lynchburg† | Carolina | 27 | 198 | 11 | 11 | .500 | 152 | 81 | 60 | *214 | 78 | 2.73 |
| 1969—Omaha | Am. Assoc. | 29 | 144 | 10 | 6 | .625 | 147 | 73 | 60 | 95 | 54 | 3.75 |
| 1969—Kansas City | American | 7 | 11 | 1 | 1 | .500 | 9 | 5 | 5 | 3 | 4 | 4.09 |
| 1970—Kansas City | American | 43 | 118 | 8 | 5 | .615 | 112 | 60 | 58 | 47 | 52 | 4.42 |
| 1971—Kansas City | American | 36 | 127 | 7 | 5 | .583 | 112 | 61 | 59 | 53 | 55 | 4.18 |
| 1972—Kansas City | American | 38 | 101 | 2 | 5 | .286 | 99 | 46 | 42 | 51 | 28 | 3.74 |
| 1973—Omaha | Am. Assoc. | 21 | 151 | 9 | 8 | .529 | 132 | 70 | 57 | 100 | 58 | 3.40 |
| 1973—Kansas City | American | 15 | 89 | 8 | 3 | .727 | 88 | 29 | 28 | 26 | 25 | 2.83 |
| 1974—Kansas City | American | 34 | 190 | 13 | 6 | .684 | 189 | 73 | 59 | 53 | 63 | 2.79 |
| 1975—Kansas City | American | 35 | 242 | 16 | 12 | .571 | 239 | 104 | 96 | 78 | 76 | 3.57 |
| 1976—Kansas City‡ | American | 35 | 220 | 15 | 11 | .577 | 227 | 89 | 75 | 80 | 56 | 3.07 |
| Major League Totals | | 243 | 1098 | 70 | 48 | .593 | 1075 | 467 | 422 | 391 | 359 | 3.46 |

†Recalled by Chicago White Sox; selected by Kansas City Royals from Chicago in expansion draft, October 15, 1968.

‡Selected by Toronto Blue Jays in American League expansion draft, November 5, 1976; Traded to Cleveland Indians for Catcher Alan Ashby and Outfielder-First Baseman Doug Howard, latter on Toledo roster, November 5, 1976.

| Year   Club         | League  | Pos. | G. | AB. | R. | H. | 2B. | 3B. | HR. | RBI. | B.A. | PO. | A. | E. | F.A. |
|---------------------|---------|------|-----|-----|----|----|----|----|----|----|------|-----|----|----|------|
| 1965—Sar. W.Sox     | Fla.Rk  | .... | 10 | 24  | 3  | 7  | 1  | 0  | 0  | 3  | .292 | .... | .... | .... | ....  |
| 1965—Clinton        | Midwest | OF   | 37 | 121 | 11 | 27 | 7  | 0  | 1  | 16 | .223 | 56  | 7  | 2  | .969 |
| 1966—Lynchburg      | Carol.  | OF   | 16 | 55  | 4  | 8  | 1  | 0  | 1  | 5  | .145 | 16  | 1  | 1  | .944 |
| 1966—Fox Cities     | Midwest | O-S-P | 104 | 337 | 37 | 80 | 16 | 6  | 5  | 45 | .237 | 130 | 40 | 10 | .944 |
| 1967—Appleton       | Midwest | *P-1-O | 45 | 98 | 14 | 18 | 3  | 0  | 3  | 10 | .184 | *35 | 46 | 2  | .976 |

## MICHAEL KENDALL FLANAGAN
### (Mike)

Born December 16, 1951, at Manchester, N. H.
Height, 6.00. Weight, 188.
Throws and bats lefthanded.
Hobbies—Hunting and fishing.
Attended University of Massachusetts, Amherst, Mass.
Son of Ed Flanagan, Jr., former pitcher in Boston Red Sox' organization.

Tied for Southern League lead in shutouts with 3 in 1974.

| Year   Club        | League      | G. | IP. | W. | L. | Pct. | H. | R. | ER. | SO. | BB. | ERA. |
|--------------------|-------------|----|-----|----|----|------|----|----|----|----|----|------|
| 1973—Miami         | Florida St. | 11 | 61  | 4  | 1  | .800 | 39 | 21 | 15 | 61 | 25 | 2.21 |
| 1974—Miami         | Florida St. | 14 | 103 | 6  | 6  | .500 | 67 | 32 | 24 | 119 | 48 | 2.10 |
| 1974—Asheville     | Southern    | 11 | 84  | 6  | 4  | .600 | 61 | 19 | 17 | 62 | 18 | 1.82 |
| 1975—Rochester     | Int'national | 27 | 173 | 13 | 4  | .765 | 155 | 58 | 48 | 135 | 56 | 2.50 |
| 1975—Baltimore     | American    | 2  | 10  | 0  | 1  | .000 | 9  | 4  | 3  | 7  | 6  | 2.70 |
| 1976—Rochester     | Int'national | 7  | 51  | 6  | 1  | .857 | 40 | 16 | 12 | 24 | 14 | 2.12 |
| 1976—Baltimore     | American    | 20 | 85  | 3  | 5  | .375 | 83 | 41 | 39 | 56 | 33 | 4.13 |
| Major League Totals |            | 22 | 95  | 3  | 6  | .333 | 92 | 45 | 42 | 63 | 39 | 3.98 |

## GILBERTO FLORES (GARCIA)
### (Gil)

Born October 27, 1952, at Ponce, Puerto Rico.
Height, 6.00. Weight, 185.
Throws and bats righthanded.
Hobbies—Music, movies and fishing.
Led California League outfielders in double plays with 5 in 1974.
Tied for Appalachian League lead in double plays by outfielders with 3 in 1971.

| Year   Club        | League    | Pos.   | G. | AB. | R. | H. | 2B. | 3B. | HR. | RBI. | B.A. | PO. | A. | E. | F.A. |
|--------------------|-----------|--------|----|-----|----|----|----|----|----|----|------|-----|----|----|------|
| 1971—Miami†        | Fla. St.  |        |    |     |    | (Did not play) |    |    |    |    |      |     |    |    |      |
| 1971—Bluefield     | Appal.    | *OF-3B | 62 | 205 | 37 | 62 | 11 | 2  | 2  | 17 | .302 | 84  | *46 | 12 | .915 |
| 1972—Miami‡        | Fla. St.  | OF     | 14 | 31  | 3  | 6  | 0  | 0  | 0  | 0  | .194 | 15  | 2  | 1  | .944 |
| 1973—El Paso       | Tex.      | OF-3B  | 90 | 283 | 41 | 80 | 10 | 2  | 0  | 23 | .283 | 106 | 10 | 11 | .913 |
| 1974—Salinas       | Calif.    | OF     | 117 | 414 | 92 | 118 | 16 | 2  | 2  | 45 | .285 | 173 | *18 | *14 | .932 |
| 1975—El Paso       | Tex.      | OF     | 62 | 238 | 51 | 73 | 11 | 6  | 2  | 31 | .307 | 115 | 6  | 6  | .953 |
| 1975—Salt Lake C.  | P.C.      | OF     | 44 | 170 | 34 | 56 | 5  | 3  | 2  | 23 | .329 | 79  | 0  | 4  | .952 |
| 1976—Salt Lake C.§ | P.C.      | OF     | 112 | 468 | 88 | 151 | 16 | 9  | 1  | 48 | .323 | 219 | 8  | 6  | .974 |

†Released by Baltimore Orioles' organization, April 14, 1971; re-signed by Baltimore Orioles' organization, June 22, 1971.
‡Drafted from Baltimore Orioles' organization by Shreveport (California Angels' organization) November 27, 1972.
§On disabled list, April 17 through May 5, 1976.
Listed on California Angels' 1977 spring roster.

## ROBERT DOUGLAS FLYNN, JR.
### (Doug)

Born April 18, 1951, at Lexington, Ky.
Height, 5.11. Weight, 165.
Throws and bats righthanded.
Hobbies—Golf and fishing.
Attended University of Kentucky, Lexington, Ky., and Somerset
Community College, Somerset, Ky.
Son of Robert Douglas Flynn, Sr., former player in Brooklyn Dodgers' organization.

Led Eastern League shortstops in double plays with 97 and tied for league lead in sacrifice flies with 9 in 1973.
Led American Association shortstops in double plays with 91 in 1974.

| Year   Club         | League    | Pos.    | G. | AB. | R. | H. | 2B. | 3B. | HR. | RBI. | B.A. | PO. | A. | E. | F.A. |
|---------------------|-----------|---------|----|-----|----|----|----|----|----|----|------|-----|----|----|------|
| 1972—Tampa          | Fla. St.  | 3-S-2-P | 98 | 313 | 32 | 66 | 12 | 2  | 1  | 37 | .211 | 109 | 240 | 18 | .951 |
| 1973—Three Rivers   | East.     | SS      | *139 | *500 | 52 | 129 | 11 | 0  | 3  | 42 | .258 | *231 | *453 | 34 | .953 |
| 1974—Indianapolis   | A.A.      | SS      | 134 | 458 | 57 | 116 | 13 | 6  | 2  | 34 | .253 | 213 | *392 | 33 | .948 |
| 1975—Cincinnati     | Nat.      | 3-2-S   | 89 | 127 | 17 | 34 | 7  | 0  | 1  | 20 | .268 | 57  | 118 | 2  | .989 |
| 1976—Cincinnati     | Nat.      | 2-3-S   | 93 | 219 | 20 | 62 | 15 | 2  | 1  | 20 | .283 | 107 | 152 | 4  | .985 |
| Major League Totals |           |         | 182 | 346 | 37 | 96 | 22 | 2  | 2  | 40 | .277 | 164 | 270 | 6  | .986 |

PITCHING RECORD

| Year   Club  | League      | G. | IP. | W. | L. | Pct. | H. | R. | ER. | SO. | BB. | ERA. |
|--------------|-------------|----|-----|----|----|------|----|----|----|----|----|------|
| 1972—Tampa   | Florida St. | 1  | 3   | 0  | 0  | .000 | 3  | 1  | 1  | 3  | 1  | 3.00 |

CHAMPIONSHIP SERIES RECORD

| Year   Club     | League   | Pos. | G. | AB. | R. | H. | 2B. | 3B. | HR. | RBI. | B.A. | PO. | A. | E. | F.A. |
|-----------------|----------|------|----|-----|----|----|----|----|----|----|------|-----|----|----|------|
| 1976—Cincinnati | National | 2B   | 1  | 0   | 0  | 0  | 0  | 0  | 0  | 0  | .000 | 0   | 0  | 0  | .000 |

## TIMOTHY JOHN FOLI
### (Tim)

Born December 8, 1950, at Culver City, Calif.
Height, 6.00. Weight, 180
Throws and bats righthanded.
Hobbies—Singing, golfing and fishing.
Brother of Ernie Foli, former infielder-outfielder in California Angel, St. Louis Cardinal,
Houston Astro and Kansas City Athletic organizations.
Led National League shortstops in total chances with 795 in 1972 and 778 in 1975.
Led National League shortstops in double plays with 104 in 1975 and with 102 in 1976.
Led Appalachian League shortstops in double plays with 29 in 1968.
Led California League shortstops in double plays with 72 in 1969.
Received reported $75,000 bonus to sign with New York Mets, 1968.

| Year | Club | League | Pos. | G. | AB. | R. | H. | 2B. | 3B. | HR. | RBI. | B.A. | PO. | A. | E. | F.A. |
|------|------|--------|------|----|-----|----|----|-----|-----|-----|------|------|-----|----|----|------|
| 1968—Marion | | Appal. | *S-1 | 63 | 235 | 38 | 66 | 10 | 3 | 4 | 36 | .281 | *105 | *167 | 23 | *.922 |
| 1968—Memphis | | Texas | SS | 5 | 20 | 4 | 5 | 0 | 0 | 0 | 1 | .250 | 8 | 10 | 2 | .900 |
| 1969—Visalia | | Calif. | SS | 95 | 383 | 60 | 116 | 10 | 0 | 15 | 62 | .303 | 154 | 280 | 36 | .923 |
| 1970—Tidewater | | Int. | SS-2B | 103 | 375 | 63 | 98 | 10 | 4 | 6 | 30 | .261 | 181 | 289 | 20 | .959 |
| 1970—New York | | Nat. | SS-3B | 5 | 11 | 0 | 4 | 0 | 0 | 0 | 1 | .364 | 4 | 10 | 0 | 1.000 |
| 1971—New York† | | Nat. | 2-3-S-O | 97 | 288 | 32 | 65 | 12 | 2 | 0 | 24 | .226 | 150 | 199 | 12 | .967 |
| 1972—Montreal | | Nat. | *SS-2B | 149 | 540 | 45 | 130 | 12 | 2 | 2 | 35 | .241 | *281 | 487 | 27 | .966 |
| 1973—Montreal‡ | | Nat. | S-2-O | 126 | 458 | 37 | 110 | 11 | 0 | 2 | 36 | .240 | 248 | 399 | 27 | .960 |
| 1974—Montreal§ | | Nat. | SS-3B | 121 | 441 | 41 | 112 | 10 | 3 | 0 | 39 | .254 | 220 | 412 | 19 | .971 |
| 1975—Montreal | | Nat. | *SS-2B | 152 | 572 | 64 | 136 | 25 | 2 | 1 | 29 | .238 | *261 | *497 | 21 | .973 |
| 1976—Montreal | | Nat. | SS-3B | 149 | 546 | 41 | 144 | 36 | 1 | 6 | 54 | .264 | 249 | 470 | 18 | .976 |
| Major League Totals | | | | 799 | 2856 | 260 | 701 | 106 | 10 | 11 | 218 | .210 | 1413 | 2474 | 124 | .969 |

†On military list, August 16 through September 1, 1971. Traded with Outfielder Ken Singleton and First
Baseman Mike Jorgensen to the Montreal Expos for Outfielder Rusty Staub, April 5, 1972.
‡On supplemental disabled list, July 9 to August 7, 1973.
§On supplemental disabled list, May 13 to May 29, 1974

## RICHARD NEVIN FOLKERS
### (Rich)

Born October 17, 1946, at Waterloo, Ia.
Height, 6.02. Weight, 180.
Throws and bats lefthanded.
Hobby—All sports.
Attended Ellsworth Junior College, Iowa Falls, Ia., and
Parsons College, Fairfield, Ia.

| Year | Club | League | G. | IP. | W. | L. | Pct. | H. | R. | ER. | SO. | BB. | ERA. |
|------|------|--------|----|-----|----|----|----|----|----|-----|-----|-----|------|
| 1967—Durham | | Carolina | 15 | 81 | 4 | 4 | .500 | 65 | 28 | 28 | 97 | 24 | 3.11 |
| 1968—Memphis | | Texas | 27 | 168 | •13 | 9 | .591 | 153 | 63 | 45 | 142 | 48 | 2.41 |
| 1969—New York | | National | | | | (In Military Service) | | | | | | |
| 1970—Tidewater | | Int'national | 5 | 31 | 4 | 0 | 1.000 | 27 | 15 | 11 | 28 | 5 | 3.19 |
| 1970—New York | | National | 16 | 29 | 0 | 2 | .000 | 36 | 21 | 21 | 15 | 25 | 6.52 |
| 1971—Tidewater† | | Int'national | 24 | 140 | 7 | 11 | .389 | 156 | 87 | 70 | 93 | 50 | 4.50 |
| 1972—Arkansas | | Texas | 22 | 94 | 5 | 4 | .556 | 82 | 36 | 33 | 88 | 29 | 3.16 |
| 1972—Tulsa | | Am. Assoc. | 6 | 22 | 0 | 2 | .000 | 16 | 7 | 7 | 22 | 7 | 2.86 |
| 1972—St. Louis | | National | 9 | 13 | 1 | 0 | 1.000 | 12 | 5 | 5 | 7 | 5 | 3.46 |
| 1973—Tulsa | | Am. Assoc. | 3 | 8 | 1 | 0 | 1.000 | 1 | 0 | 0 | 9 | 3 | 0.00 |
| 1973—St. Louis | | National | 34 | 82 | 4 | 4 | .500 | 74 | 34 | 33 | 44 | 34 | 3.62 |
| 1974—St. Louis‡ | | National | 55 | 90 | 6 | 2 | .750 | 65 | 31 | 30 | 57 | 38 | 3.00 |
| 1975—San Diego | | National | 45 | 142 | 6 | 11 | .353 | 155 | 70 | 66 | 87 | 39 | 4.18 |
| 1976—San Diego§ | | National | 33 | 60 | 2 | 3 | .400 | 67 | 39 | 35 | 26 | 25 | 5.25 |
| Major League Totals | | | 192 | 416 | 19 | 22 | .463 | 409 | 200 | 190 | 236 | 166 | 4.11 |

†Traded with Outfielder Art Shamsky, Pitchers Jim Bibby and Charlie Hudson by New York Mets to St.
Louis Cardinals for Pitchers Chuck Taylor and Harry Parker, Outfielder-First Baseman Jim Beauchamp and
Infielder Tom Coulter, October 18, 1971.
‡Traded with Pitchers Alan Foster and Sonny Siebert to San Diego Padres for Shortstop Ed Brinkman and
a player to be named later, November 18, 1974; Padres assigned Catcher Danny Breeden to Cardinals, Decem-
ber 10, 1974, to complete deal.
§Sold (via waivers) to Milwaukee Brewers, March 23, 1977.

## BARRY CLIFTON FOOTE

Born February 16, 1952, at Smithfield, N. C.
Height, 6.03. Weight, 205.
Throws and bats righthanded.
Attended North Carolina State University, Raleigh, N. C.
Son of Amby Foote, former third baseman-pitcher in Brooklyn Dodger and
Pittsburgh Pirate organizations.
Led National League in sacrifice flies with 12 in 1974.
Tied for National League lead in double plays by catchers with 10 in 1975.
Led Florida State League catchers in double plays with 11 and in passed balls with 31 in 1971.
Led Eastern League catchers in double plays with 21 in 1972.

| Year | Club | League | Pos. | G. | AB. | R. | H. | 2B. | 3B. | HR. | RBI. | B.A. | PO. | A. | E. | F.A. |
|---|---|---|---|---|---|---|---|---|---|---|---|---|---|---|---|---|
| 1970—B'denton Expos | Gulf C. | | C | 46 | 143 | 26 | 38 | 7 | 0 | 3 | 29 | .266 | 268 | 21 | 7 | .976 |
| 1971—W. Palm Beach | Fla. St. | | *C-1B | 115 | 366 | 45 | 84 | 14 | 5 | 8 | 42 | .230 | •677 | *89 | *28 | .965 |
| 1972—Quebec City | ......East. | | *C-OF | 124 | 427 | 62 | 108 | 23 | 0 | 16 | 75 | .253 | 658 | 58 | *25 | .966 |
| 1973—Peninsula | ..........Int. | | C-3-O | 137 | 465 | 63 | 122 | 22 | 2 | 19 | 65 | .262 | 452 | 94 | 12 | .978 |
| 1973—Montreal | .........Nat. | | PH | 6 | 6 | 0 | 4 | 0 | 1 | 0 | 1 | .667 | 0 | 0 | 0 | .000 |
| 1974—Montreal | .........Nat. | | C | 125 | 420 | 44 | 110 | 23 | 4 | 11 | 60 | .262 | 640 | *83 | 12 | .984 |
| 1975—Montreal | .........Nat. | | C | 118 | 387 | 25 | 75 | 16 | 1 | 7 | 30 | .194 | 590 | 50 | 10 | .985 |
| 1976—Montreal† | .........Nat. | | C-3-1 | 105 | 350 | 32 | 82 | 12 | 2 | 7 | 27 | .234 | 487 | 61 | 6 | .989 |
| Major League Totals | | | | 354 | 1163 | 101 | 271 | 51 | 8 | 25 | 118 | .233 | 1717 | 194 | 28 | .986 |

†On disabled list, August 7 through August 23, 1976.

### DARNELL GLENN FORD, SR.
### (Dan)
(Nicknamed by brother because it's easier to say than Darnell.)

Born May 19, 1952, at Los Angeles, Calif.
Height, 6.01. Weight, 185.
Throws and bats righthanded.
Hobbies—Hunting, fishing, horse riding and motor cycles.
Attended Southwestern College, Chula Vista, Calif., and Mesa Community College, Mesa, Ariz.
Led Pacific Coast League outfielders in double plays with 7 in 1973.

| Year | Club | League | Pos. | G. | AB. | R. | H. | 2B. | 3B. | HR. | RBI. | B.A. | PO. | A. | E. | F.A. |
|---|---|---|---|---|---|---|---|---|---|---|---|---|---|---|---|---|
| 1971—Burlington | ........Midw. | | OF | 107 | 397 | 75 | 106 | 21 | 4 | 14 | 80 | .267 | 186 | 11 | 10 | .952 |
| 1972—Burlington† | ......Midw. | | OF | 72 | 246 | 55 | 87 | 15 | 4 | 18 | 61 | .354 | 137 | 4 | 8 | .946 |
| 1973—Tucson | .............P. C. | | OF | 128 | 465 | 80 | 136 | 21 | 12 | 14 | 70 | .292 | 310 | •16 | 11 | .967 |
| 1974—Tucson‡§ | ..........P. C. | | OF | 115 | 428 | 62 | 117 | 11 | 9 | 12 | 65 | .273 | 263 | 11 | 14 | .951 |
| 1975—Minnesota | ........Amer. | | OF | 130 | 440 | 72 | 123 | 21 | 1 | 15 | 59 | .280 | 246 | 3 | 3 | .988 |
| 1976—Minnesota | ........Amer. | | OF-DH | 145 | 514 | 87 | 137 | 24 | 7 | 20 | 86 | .267 | 267 | 6 | 9 | .968 |
| Major League Totals | | | | 275 | 954 | 159 | 260 | 45 | 8 | 35 | 145 | .273 | 513 | 9 | 12 | .978 |

†On temporary inactive list, April 15 to May 20, 1972.
‡On temporary inactive list, July 12 to August 2, 1974.
§Traded with Pitcher Dennis Myers by Oakland Athletics to Minnesota Twins for First Baseman Pat Bourque, October 23, 1974.

### EDWARD JOSEPH FORD
### (Eddie)

Born July 18, 1953, at New York City, N. Y.
Height, 6.01. Weight, 170.
Throws right and bats left and righthanded.
Hobby—Television.
Attended University of South Carolina, Columbia, S. C.; and St. John's University, Queens, N. Y.
Son of Whitey Ford, former pitcher in New York Yankees' organization, 1947-1967;
pitching instructor for Yankees, 1967-1976.

| Year | Club | League | Pos. | G. | AB. | R. | H. | 2B. | 3B. | HR. | RBI. | B.A. | PO. | A. | E. | F.A. |
|---|---|---|---|---|---|---|---|---|---|---|---|---|---|---|---|---|
| 1974—Bristol | .............East. | | SS | 27 | 75 | 7 | 12 | 1 | 0 | 0 | 2 | .160 | 31 | 75 | 5 | .955 |
| 1974—Elmira | .............NYP | | SS | 40 | 154 | 24 | 35 | 3 | 0 | 3 | 19 | .227 | 58 | 141 | 12 | .943 |
| 1975—Bristol | .............East. | | SS | 110 | 354 | 47 | 89 | 14 | 0 | 5 | 31 | .251 | 154 | 267 | 40 | .913 |
| 1976—Bristol | .............East. | | SS | 111 | 356 | 47 | 88 | 8 | 4 | 3 | 38 | .247 | 193 | 356 | 27 | *.953 |

Listed on Boston Red Sox 1977 spring roster.

### JOHN DEWEY FORRY, JR.

Born May 26, 1952, at Sacramento, Calif.
Height, 6.02. Weight, 205.
Throws and bats righthanded.
Hobby—Photography.

| Year | Club | League | G. | IP. | W. | L. | Pct. | H. | R. | ER. | SO. | BB. | ERA. |
|---|---|---|---|---|---|---|---|---|---|---|---|---|---|
| 1972—Daytona Beach† | ..................Florida St. | | 10 | 38 | 3 | 2 | .600 | 32 | 13 | 12 | 23 | 15 | 2.84 |
| 1973—Bakersfield | ...........................California | | 36 | 64 | 9 | 3 | .750 | 52 | 28 | 23 | 50 | 44 | 3.23 |
| 1974—Waterbury | .............................Eastern | | 37 | 69 | 3 | 5 | .375 | 74 | 45 | 30 | 43 | 42 | 3.91 |
| 1975—Waterbury | .............................Eastern | | 33 | 80 | 5 | 5 | .500 | 70 | 19 | 14 | 53 | 28 | 1.58 |
| 1976—Albuquerque‡ | ......................P. Coast | | 32 | 69 | 4 | 4 | .500 | 63 | 33 | 32 | 42 | 35 | 4.17 |

#### RECORD AS OUTFIELDER

| Year | Club | League | Pos. | G. | AB. | R. | H. | 2B. | 3B. | HR. | RBI. | B.A. | PO. | A. | E. | F.A. |
|---|---|---|---|---|---|---|---|---|---|---|---|---|---|---|---|---|
| 1970—Ogden | ..............Pioneer | | OF | 53 | 151 | 30 | 39 | 4 | 1 | 3 | 24 | .258 | 40 | 1 | 3 | .932 |
| 1971—Daytona Beach | ..Fla. St. | | OF | 119 | 281 | 35 | 61 | 10 | 2 | 2 | 36 | .217 | 139 | 11 | 7 | .955 |
| 1972—Daytona Beach | ..Fla. St. | | OF | 18 | 19 | 4 | 3 | 1 | 0 | 0 | 3 | .158 | 8 | 1 | 0 | 1.000 |

†On military list, June 6 through October 26, 1972.
‡On disabled list, August 24 through September 7, 1976.
Listed on Los Angeles Dodgers' 1977 spring roster.

# KENNETH ROTH FORSCH
## (Ken)

Born September 8, 1946, at Sacramento, Calif.
Height, 6.04. Weight, 205.
Throws and bats righthanded.
Hobbies—Hunting and fishing.
Attended Sacramento City College, Sacramento, Calif., and Oregon
State University, Corvallis, Ore.
Brother of Bob Forsch, pitcher with St. Louis Cardinals.
Led Southern League in shutouts with 5 in 1970.

| Year Club | League | G. | IP. | W. | L. | Pct. | H. | R. | ER. | SO. | BB. | ERA. |
|---|---|---|---|---|---|---|---|---|---|---|---|---|
| 1968—Greensboro | Carolina | 3 | 6 | 0 | 0 | .000 | 6 | 2 | 2 | 6 | 3 | 3.00 |
| 1968—Williamsport | NYP | 4 | 26 | 1 | 2 | .333 | 14 | 6 | 4 | 40 | 9 | 1.38 |
| 1969—Peninsula† | Carolina | 17 | 94 | 6 | 5 | .545 | 67 | 40 | 33 | 100 | 53 | 3.16 |
| 1970—Columbus | Southern | 22 | 167 | ●13 | 8 | .619 | 135 | 48 | 38 | 152 | 39 | 2.05 |
| 1970—Oklahoma City | Am. Assoc. | 5 | 40 | 4 | 0 | 1.000 | 25 | 7 | 7 | 37 | 10 | 1.58 |
| 1970—Houston | National | 4 | 24 | 1 | 2 | .333 | 28 | 15 | 15 | 13 | 5 | 5.63 |
| 1971—Houston | National | 33 | 188 | 8 | 8 | .500 | 162 | 60 | 53 | 131 | 53 | 2.54 |
| 1972—Houston | National | 30 | 156 | 6 | 8 | .429 | 163 | 75 | 68 | 113 | 62 | 3.92 |
| 1973—Houston | National | 46 | 201 | 9 | 12 | .429 | 197 | 101 | 94 | 149 | 74 | 4.21 |
| 1974—Houston | National | 70 | 103 | 8 | 7 | .533 | 98 | 38 | 32 | 48 | 37 | 2.80 |
| 1975—Houston‡ | National | 34 | 109 | 4 | 8 | .333 | 114 | 42 | 39 | 54 | 30 | 3.22 |
| 1976—Houston | National | 52 | 92 | 4 | 3 | .571 | 76 | 23 | 22 | 49 | 26 | 2.15 |
| Major League Totals | | 269 | 871 | 40 | 48 | .454 | 838 | 354 | 323 | 557 | 287 | 3.34 |

†On disabled list, June 11 to July 11, 1969.
‡On disabled list, July 31 to September 22, 1975.

# ROBERT HERBERT FORSCH
## (Bob)

Born January 13, 1950, at Sacramento, Calif.
Height, 6.03. Weight, 200.
Throws and bats righthanded.
Hobbies—Hunting and fishing.
Attended Sacramento City College, Sacramento, Calif.
Brother of Ken Forsch, pitcher with Houston Astros.
Pitched 5-0 no-hit victory against Denver, May 25, 1973.
Pitched seven-inning, 4-0 no-hit victory against Memphis, May 13, 1972.
Led Midwest League in hit batsmen with 11 in 1971 and tied for Texas League with 10 in 1972.
Received reported $25,000 bonus to sign with St. Louis Cardinals, 1968.

| Year Club | League | G. | IP. | W. | L. | Pct. | H. | R. | ER. | SO. | BB. | ERA. |
|---|---|---|---|---|---|---|---|---|---|---|---|---|
| 1970—Cedar Rapids | Midwest | 1 | 3 | 0 | 0 | .000 | 6 | 4 | 4 | 1 | 2 | 12.00 |
| 1970—Lewiston | Northwest | 7 | 28 | 2 | 3 | .400 | 32 | 22 | 13 | 15 | 17 | 4.18 |
| 1971—Cedar Rapids | Midwest | 23 | 158 | 11 | 7 | .611 | 140 | 74 | 55 | 134 | 41 | 3.13 |
| 1972—Arkansas | Texas | 24 | 153 | 8 | 10 | .444 | 158 | 85 | *74 | 109 | 47 | 4.35 |
| 1973—Tulsa | Am. Assoc. | 27 | 166 | 12 | 12 | .500 | 169 | 91 | 81 | 124 | 66 | 4.36 |
| 1974—Tulsa | Am. Assoc. | 15 | 103 | 8 | 5 | .615 | 95 | 49 | 42 | 71 | 33 | 3.67 |
| 1974—St. Louis | National | 19 | 100 | 7 | 4 | .636 | 84 | 38 | 33 | 39 | 34 | 2.97 |
| 1975—St. Louis | Mational | 34 | 230 | 15 | 10 | .600 | 213 | 89 | 73 | 108 | 70 | 2.86 |
| 1976—St. Louis | National | 33 | 194 | 8 | 10 | .444 | 209 | 112 | 85 | 76 | 71 | 3.94 |
| Major League Totals | | 86 | 524 | 30 | 24 | .556 | 506 | 239 | 191 | 223 | 175 | 3.28 |

### RECORD AS INFIELDER

| Year Club | League | Pos. | G. | AB. | R. | H. | 2B. | 3B. | HR. | RBI. | B.A. | PO. | A. | E. | F.A. |
|---|---|---|---|---|---|---|---|---|---|---|---|---|---|---|---|
| 1968—Sarasota Cards | Gulf C. | 3B | 44 | 143 | 17 | 32 | 5 | 0 | 0 | 16 | .224 | 29 | 80 | 12 | *.901 |
| 1969—Lewiston | Northw. | 3-O-2 | 26 | 74 | 11 | 15 | 3 | 0 | 3 | 10 | .203 | 12 | 45 | 13 | .814 |
| 1969—Modesto | Calif. | 3B-OF | 33 | 119 | 8 | 28 | 2 | 0 | 1 | 7 | .235 | 33 | 58 | 6 | .938 |
| 1970—Modesto | Calif. | 3B-OF | 20 | 47 | 4 | 7 | 3 | 0 | 1 | 1 | .149 | 19 | 20 | 3 | .929 |
| 1970—Cedar Rapids | Midw. | 3-1-P | 19 | 34 | 2 | 3 | 2 | 0 | 0 | 1 | .088 | 9 | 19 | 3 | .903 |
| 1970—Lewiston | Northw. | P-S-2-3 | 18 | 30 | 5 | 4 | 0 | 1 | 0 | 3 | .133 | 9 | 13 | 6 | .786 |

### ALL-STAR GAME RECORD

| Year League | | IP. | W. | L. | Pct. | H. | R. | ER. | SO. | BB. | ERA. |
|---|---|---|---|---|---|---|---|---|---|---|---|
| 1976—National | | 1 | 0 | 0 | .000 | 0 | 0 | 0 | 1 | 0 | .000 |

# TERRY JAY FORSTER

Born January 14, 1952, at Sioux Falls, S. D.
Height, 6.03. Weight, 210.
Throws and bats lefthanded.
Hobbies—Skiing, music, painting and golf.
Attended Grossmont College, El Cajon, Calif.
Led American League in saves with 24 in 1974.
Named American League Fireman of the Year by THE SPORTING NEWS, 1974.

| Year | Club | League | G. | IP. | W. | L. | Pct. | H. | R. | ER. | SO. | BB. | ERA. |
|------|------|--------|----|-----|----|----|------|----|----|-----|-----|-----|------|
| 1970–Appleton | | Midwest | 10 | 54 | 6 | 1 | .857 | 30 | 11 | 8 | 42 | 29 | 1.33 |
| 1971–Chicago | | American | 45 | 50 | 2 | 3 | .400 | 46 | 23 | 22 | 48 | 23 | 3.96 |
| 1972–Chicago | | American | 62 | 100 | 6 | 5 | .545 | 75 | 31 | 25 | 104 | 44 | 2.25 |
| 1973–Chicago | | American | 51 | 173 | 6 | 11 | .353 | 174 | 69 | 62 | 120 | 78 | 3.23 |
| 1974–Chicago | | American | 59 | 134 | 7 | 8 | .467 | 120 | 57 | 54 | 105 | 48 | 3.63 |
| 1975–Chicago† | | American | 17 | 37 | 3 | 3 | .500 | 30 | 12 | 9 | 32 | 24 | 2.19 |
| 1976–Chicago‡ | | American | 29 | 111 | 2 | 12 | .143 | 126 | 61 | 54 | 70 | 41 | 4.38 |
| Major League Totals | | | 263 | 605 | 26 | 42 | .382 | 571 | 253 | 226 | 479 | 258 | 3.36 |

†On disabled list, May 25 to July 1, July 26 to August 17 and August 18 to September 29, 1975.

‡Traded with Pitcher Rich Gossage to Pittsburgh Pirates for Outfielder Richie Zisk and Pitcher Silvio Martinez, December 10, 1976.

## RAYMOND EARL FOSSE

Name pronounced FOSS-ee.

### (Ray)

Born April 4, 1947, at Marion, Ill.
Height, 6.02. Weight, 215.
Throws and bats righthanded.
Hobby–Golf.
Attended Southern Illinois University, Carbondale, Ill.

Led American League catchers in double plays with 16 in 1971.
Tied for American League lead in passed balls with 17 in 1970.
Led California League catchers in double plays with 10 in 1966.
Tied for Pacific Coast League lead in double plays by catchers with 14 in 1968.
Named catcher on THE SPORTING NEWS American League All-Star Team, 1970.
Named catcher on THE SPORTING NEWS American League All-Star fielding team, 1970 and 1971.

| Year | Club | League | Pos. | G. | AB. | R. | H. | 2B. | 3B. | HR. | RBI. | B.A. | PO. | A. | E. | F.A. |
|------|------|--------|------|----|-----|----|----|-----|-----|-----|------|------|-----|----|----|------|
| 1965–Reading | | East. | C | 55 | 178 | 19 | 39 | 3 | 1 | 3 | 11 | .219 | 342 | 22 | 5 | .986 |
| 1966–Reno | | Calif. | C | 116 | 418 | 61 | 127 | 15 | 5 | 1 | 54 | .304 | ★838 | 79 | 15 | .984 |
| 1967–Portland† | | P.C. | C | 75 | 211 | 18 | 55 | 8 | 4 | 2 | 28 | .261 | 382 | 28 | 4 | .990 |
| 1967–Cleveland | | Amer. | C | 7 | 16 | 0 | 1 | 0 | 0 | 0 | 0 | .063 | 46 | 7 | 0 | 1.000 |
| 1968–Portland‡ | | P.C. | ★C-OF | 103 | 339 | 44 | 102 | 16 | 0 | 9 | 42 | .301 | 566 | ★71 | 8 | .988 |
| 1968–Cleveland | | Amer. | C | 1 | 0 | 0 | 0 | 0 | 0 | 0 | 0 | .000 | 1 | 0 | 0 | 1.000 |
| 1969–Cleveland§ | | Amer. | C | 37 | 116 | 11 | 20 | 3 | 0 | 2 | 9 | .172 | 237 | 18 | 6 | .977 |
| 1970–Cleveland | | Amer. | C | 120 | 450 | 62 | 138 | 17 | 1 | 18 | 61 | .307 | ★854 | 70 | 10 | .989 |
| 1971–Cleveland | | Amer. | ★C-1B | 133 | 486 | 53 | 134 | 21 | 1 | 12 | 62 | .276 | 767 | ★73 | 10 | .988 |
| 1972–Cleveland x | | Amer. | C-1B | 134 | 457 | 42 | 110 | 20 | 1 | 10 | 41 | .241 | 740 | 71 | 12 | .985 |
| 1973–Oakland | | Amer. | C | 143 | 492 | 37 | 126 | 23 | 2 | 7 | 52 | .256 | 712 | 63 | 10 | .987 |
| 1974–Oakland y | | Amer. | C | 69 | 204 | 20 | 40 | 8 | 3 | 4 | 23 | .196 | 299 | 28 | 9 | .973 |
| 1975–Oakland z | | Amer. | C-1-2 | 82 | 136 | 14 | 19 | 3 | 2 | 0 | 12 | .140 | 253 | 15 | 5 | .982 |
| 1976–Cleveland a | | Amer. | C-1-DH | 90 | 276 | 26 | 83 | 9 | 1 | 2 | 30 | .301 | 493 | 43 | 7 | .987 |
| Major League Totals | | | | 816 | 2633 | 265 | 671 | 104 | 11 | 55 | 290 | .255 | 4402 | 388 | 69 | .986 |

†On restricted list, February 6 through June 13.

‡On disabled list, April 19 through May 22.

§On disabled list, June 13 through September 1.

xTraded with Infielder Jack Heidemann to Oakland A's for Catcher Dave Duncan and Outfielder George Hendrick, March 24, 1973.

yOn disabled list, June 6 through August 22, 1974.

zSold to Cleveland Indians, December 8, 1975.

aOn disabled list, April 14 to May 1 and June 30 to July 16, 1976.

### CHAMPIONSHIP SERIES RECORD

| Year | Club | League | Pos. | G. | AB. | R. | H. | 2B. | 3B. | HR. | RBI. | B.A. | PO. | A. | E. | F.A. |
|------|------|--------|------|----|-----|----|----|-----|-----|-----|------|------|-----|----|----|------|
| 1973–Oakland | | Amer. | C | 5 | 11 | 2 | 1 | 1 | 0 | 0 | 3 | .091 | 25 | 4 | 0 | 1.000 |
| 1974–Oakland | | Amer. | C | 4 | 12 | 1 | 4 | 1 | 0 | 1 | 3 | .333 | 21 | 3 | 0 | 1.000 |
| 1975–Oakland | | Amer. | C | 1 | 2 | 0 | 0 | 0 | 0 | 0 | 0 | .000 | 3 | 0 | 0 | 1.000 |
| Championship Series Totals | | | | 10 | 25 | 3 | 5 | 2 | 0 | 1 | 6 | .200 | 49 | 7 | 0 | 1.000 |

### WORLD SERIES RECORD

| Year | Club | League | Pos. | G. | AB. | R. | H. | 2B. | 3B. | HR. | RBI. | B.A. | PO. | A. | E. | F.A. |
|------|------|--------|------|----|-----|----|----|-----|-----|-----|------|------|-----|----|----|------|
| 1973–Oakland | | Amer. | C | 7 | 19 | 0 | 3 | 1 | 0 | 0 | 0 | .158 | 32 | 3 | 0 | 1.000 |
| 1974–Oakland | | Amer. | C | 5 | 14 | 1 | 2 | 0 | 0 | 1 | 1 | .143 | 27 | 1 | 0 | 1.000 |
| World Series Totals | | | | 12 | 33 | 1 | 5 | 1 | 0 | 1 | 1 | .152 | 59 | 4 | 0 | 1.000 |

### ALL-STAR GAME RECORD

| Year | League | Pos. | AB. | R. | H. | 2B. | 3B. | HR. | RBI. | B.A. | PO. | A. | E. | F.A. |
|------|--------|------|-----|----|----|-----|-----|-----|------|------|-----|----|----|------|
| 1970–American | | C | 2 | 1 | 1 | 0 | 0 | 0 | 1 | .500 | 7 | 0 | 0 | 1.000 |

Named to American League All-Star Team for 1971 game; replaced due to injury.

---

## DID YOU KNOW —

That there have been 502 home runs hit in World Series play? The American League teams have hit 300, the National League teams have hit 202.

# ALAN BENTON FOSTER

Bron December 8, 1946, at Pasadena, Calif.
Height, 6.00. Weight, 185.
Throws and bats righthanded.
Hobbies—Car racing, singing and playing guitar.
Attended University of California, Los Angeles, Calif., and University of
California, Santa Barbara, Calif.

Pitched seven-inning, 1-0 no-hit victory against Seattle, August 16, 1967, and 1-0 no-hit victory against Seattle, September 1, 1967.
Received reported $100,000 bonus to sign with Los Angeles Dodgers, 1965.

| Year Club | League | G. | IP. | W. | L. | Pct. | H. | R. | ER. | SO. | BB. | ERA. |
|---|---|---|---|---|---|---|---|---|---|---|---|---|
| 1965–Santa Barbara | California | 8 | 47 | 5 | 2 | .714 | 33 | 23 | 22 | 54 | 18 | 4.21 |
| 1966–Albuquerque | Texas | 23 | 132 | 11 | 5 | .688 | 108 | 50 | 42 | 125 | 65 | 2.86 |
| 1967–Los Angeles | National | 4 | 17 | 0 | 1 | .000 | 10 | 4 | 4 | 15 | 3 | 2.12 |
| 1967–Spokane | P. Coast | 23 | 142 | 10 | 9 | .526 | 102 | 62 | 55 | 127 | 61 | 3.49 |
| 1968–Spokane | P. Coast | 16 | 104 | 8 | 5 | .615 | 76 | 41 | 30 | 87 | 38 | 2.60 |
| 1968–Los Angeles† | National | 3 | 16 | 1 | 1 | .500 | 11 | 4 | 3 | 10 | 2 | 1.69 |
| 1969–Los Angeles | National | 24 | 103 | 3 | 9 | .250 | 119 | 55 | 50 | 59 | 29 | 4.37 |
| 1970–Los Angeles‡ | National | 33 | 199 | 10 | 13 | .435 | 200 | 104 | 94 | 83 | 81 | 4.25 |
| 1971–Cleveland§ | American | 36 | 182 | 8 | 12 | .400 | 158 | 93 | 84 | 97 | 82 | 4.15 |
| 1972–Salt Lake City | P. Coast | 25 | 110 | 8 | 8 | .500 | 105 | 55 | 52 | 108 | 42 | 4.25 |
| 1972–California x | American | 8 | 13 | 0 | 1 | .000 | 12 | 8 | 7 | 11 | 6 | 4.85 |
| 1973–St. Louis | National | 35 | 204 | 13 | 9 | .591 | 195 | 82 | 71 | 106 | 63 | 3.13 |
| 1974–St. Louis y | National | 31 | 162 | 7 | 10 | .412 | 167 | 81 | 70 | 78 | 61 | 3.89 |
| 1975–San Diego z | National | 17 | 45 | 3 | 1 | .750 | 41 | 14 | 12 | 20 | 21 | 2.40 |
| 1976–San Diego a | National | 26 | 87 | 3 | 6 | .333 | 75 | 36 | 31 | 22 | 35 | 3.21 |
| National League Totals | | 173 | 833 | 40 | 50 | .444 | 818 | 380 | 335 | 393 | 295 | 3.62 |
| American League Totals | | 44 | 195 | 8 | 13 | .381 | 170 | 101 | 91 | 108 | 88 | 4.20 |
| Major League Totals | | 217 | 1028 | 48 | 63 | .432 | 988 | 481 | 426 | 501 | 393 | 3.73 |

†On disabled list from July 24 through August 31.
‡Traded with Pitcher Ray Lamb to Cleveland Indians for Catcher Duane (Duke) Sims, December 11, 1970.
§Traded with Outfielders Vada Pinson and Frank Baker to California Angels for Catcher Jerry Moses and Outfielder Alex Johnson, October 5, 1971.
xSold to St. Louis Cardinals, February 6, 1973.
yTraded with Pitchers Rich Folkers and Sonny Siebert to San Diego Padres for Shortstop Ed Brinkman and a player to be named later, November 18, 1974; Padres assigned Catcher Danny Breeden to Cardinals, December 10, 1974, to complete deal.
zOn disabled list, July 20 through October 1, 1975.
aReleased, March 29, 1977.


# GEORGE ARTHUR FOSTER

Born December 1, 1948, at Tuscaloosa, Ala.
Height, 6:02. Weight, 195.
Throws and bats righthanded.
Hobbies—Records and sports in general.
Attended El Camino College, Torrance, Calif.

Tied National League record for most times grounding into double play rookie season, 20, 1971.
Led Northwest League outfielders in double plays with 4 in 1968.
Led California League outfielders in chances accepted with 281 in 1969.
Named National League Player of the Year by THE SPORTING NEWS, 1976.
Named as outfielder on THE SPORTING NEWS National League All-Star Team, 1976.

| Year Club | League | Pos. | G. | AB. | R. | H. | 2B. | 3B. | HR. | RBI. | B.A. | PO. | A. | E. | F.A. |
|---|---|---|---|---|---|---|---|---|---|---|---|---|---|---|---|
| 1968–Medford | Northw. | OF | 72 | 253 | 47 | 70 | 9 | 5 | 3 | 30 | .277 | *142 | 6 | 5 | .967 |
| 1969–Fresno | Calif. | OF | 121 | 449 | 68 | 144 | 5 | 8 | 14 | 85 | .321 | *267 | 14 | 4 | *.986 |
| 1969–San Francisco | Nat. | OF | 9 | 5 | 1 | 2 | 0 | 0 | 0 | 1 | .400 | 3 | 0 | 0 | 1.000 |
| 1970–Phoenix† | P.C. | OF | 114 | 403 | 54 | 124 | 18 | 6 | 8 | 66 | .308 | 202 | 5 | 9 | .958 |
| 1970–San Francisco | Nat. | OF | 9 | 19 | 2 | 6 | 1 | 1 | 1 | 4 | .316 | 10 | 0 | 0 | 1.000 |
| 1971–S.F.‡-Cin. | Nat. | OF | 140 | 473 | 50 | 114 | 23 | 4 | 13 | 58 | .241 | 315 | 9 | 5 | .985 |
| 1972–Cincinnati | Nat. | OF | 59 | 145 | 15 | 29 | 4 | 1 | 2 | 12 | .200 | 71 | 1 | 2 | .973 |
| 1973–Indianapolis | A.A. | OF | 134 | 496 | 77 | 130 | 26 | 1 | 15 | 60 | .262 | *332 | 7 | 10 | .971 |
| 1973–Cincinnati | Nat. | OF | 17 | 39 | 6 | 11 | 3 | 0 | 4 | 9 | .282 | 19 | 1 | 0 | 1.000 |
| 1974–Cincinnati | Nat. | OF | 106 | 276 | 31 | 73 | 18 | 0 | 7 | 41 | .264 | 172 | 2 | 2 | .989 |
| 1975–Cincinnati | Nat. | OF-1B | 134 | 463 | 71 | 139 | 24 | 4 | 23 | 78 | .300 | 299 | 11 | 3 | .990 |
| 1976–Cincinnati | Nat. | OF-1B | 144 | 562 | 86 | 172 | 21 | 9 | 29 | 121 | .306 | 322 | 9 | 2 | *.994 |
| Major League Totals | | | 618 | 1982 | 262 | 546 | 94 | 19 | 79 | 324 | .275 | 1211 | 33 | 14 | .989 |

†On disabled list June 10 to June 30, 1970.
‡Traded to Cincinnati Reds for Shortstop Frank Duffy and Pitcher Vern Geishert (latter assigned from Indianapolis to Phoenix), May 29, 1971.

## CHAMPIONSHIP SERIES RECORD

| Year Club | League | Pos. | G. | AB. | R. | H. | 2B. | 3B. | HR. | RBI. | B.A. | PO. | A. | E. | F.A. |
|---|---|---|---|---|---|---|---|---|---|---|---|---|---|---|---|
| 1972–Cincinnati | Nat. | PR | 1 | 0 | 1 | 0 | 0 | 0 | 0 | 0 | .000 | 0 | 0 | 0 | .000 |
| 1975–Cincinnati | Nat. | OF | 3 | 11 | 3 | 4 | 0 | 0 | 0 | 0 | .364 | 7 | 0 | 0 | 1.000 |
| 1976–Cincinnati | Nat. | OF | 3 | 12 | 2 | 2 | 0 | 0 | 2 | 4 | .167 | 7 | 0 | 0 | 1.000 |
| Championship Series Totals | | | 7 | 23 | 6 | 6 | 0 | 0 | 2 | 4 | .261 | 14 | 0 | 0 | 1.000 |

## WORLD SERIES RECORD

| Year Club | League | Pos. | G. | AB. | R. | H. | 2B. | 3B. | HR. | RBI. | B.A. | PO. | A. | E. | F.A. |
|---|---|---|---|---|---|---|---|---|---|---|---|---|---|---|---|
| 1972—Cincinnati.........Nat. | | PR-OF | 2 | 0 | 0 | 0 | 0 | 0 | 0 | 0 | .000 | 0 | 0 | 0 | .000 |
| 1975—Cincinnati.........Nat. | | OF | 7 | 29 | 1 | 8 | 1 | 0 | 0 | 2 | .276 | 13 | 1 | 0 | 1.000 |
| 1976—Cincinnati.........Nat. | | OF | 4 | 14 | 3 | 6 | 1 | 0 | 0 | 4 | .429 | 14 | 0 | 0 | 1.000 |
| World Series Totals ...................... | | | 13 | 43 | 4 | 14 | 2 | 0 | 0 | 6 | .326 | 27 | 1 | 0 | 1.000 |

## ALL-STAR GAME RECORD

| Year League | Pos. | AB. | R. | H. | 2B. | 3B. | HR. | RBI. | B.A. | PO. | A. | E. | F.A. |
|---|---|---|---|---|---|---|---|---|---|---|---|---|---|
| 1976—National ............................. | OF | 3 | 1 | 1 | 0 | 0 | 1 | 3 | .333 | 0 | 0 | 0 | .000 |

## LARRY JOEL FOSTER

Born February 23, 1951, at Gadsden, Ala.
Height, 5.11. Weight, 190.
Throws and bats righthanded.
Hobbies—Golf, hunting and fishing.
Attended Jacksonville State University, Jacksonville, Ala.; received
Bachelor of Science Degree in Education.
Brother of Max Foster, minor league infielder with Sioux Falls,
Cincinnati Reds' organization, 1966.
Named Most Valuable Player in Gulf Coast League, 1973.
Named Most Valuable Player in Southern League, 1976.

| Year Club | League | Pos. | G. | AB. | R. | H. | 2B. | 3B. | HR. | RBI. | B.A. | PO. | A. | E. | F.A. |
|---|---|---|---|---|---|---|---|---|---|---|---|---|---|---|---|
| 1973—Appleton............Midw. | | OF | 14 | 40 | 2 | 6 | 0 | 0 | 1 | 1 | .150 | 15 | 2 | 1 | .944 |
| 1973—Sarasota W.Sox..Gulf C. | | OF | 41 | 128 | 31 | 49 | 5 | 4 | 3 | 30 | *.383 | 67 | 3 | 4 | .946 |
| 1974—Appleton...........Midw. | | OF | 72 | 216 | 44 | 71 | 11 | 2 | 6 | 31 | .329 | 86 | 7 | 6 | .939 |
| 1974—Knoxville .........South. | | OF | 37 | 106 | 14 | 27 | 3 | 3 | 3 | 14 | .255 | 50 | 3 | 3 | .946 |
| 1975—Knoxville .........South. | | OF | 67 | 213 | 35 | 60 | 9 | 3 | 6 | 40 | .282 | 102 | 4 | 1 | .991 |
| 1975—Denver .............A.A. | | OF-1B | 37 | 98 | 17 | 22 | 3 | 1 | 4 | 11 | .224 | 54 | 1 | 2 | .965 |
| 1976—Knoxville .........South. | | OF-1B | 106 | 338 | 53 | 105 | 14 | 1 | 13 | 57 | *.311 | 190 | 13 | 6 | .971 |

Listed on Chicago White Sox' spring roster.

## LEONARD NORRIS FOSTER
### (Leo)

Born February 2, 1951, at Covington, Ky.
Height, 5.11. Weight, 162.
Throws and bats righthanded.
Attended University of Cincinnati, Cincinnati, O.

| Year Club | League | Pos. | G. | AB. | R. | H. | 2B. | 3B. | HR. | RBI. | B.A. | PO. | A. | E. | F.A. |
|---|---|---|---|---|---|---|---|---|---|---|---|---|---|---|---|
| 1969—Greenwood ........W. Car. | | SS | 55 | 192 | 17 | 44 | 5 | 1 | 2 | 33 | .229 | 81 | 150 | 17 | .931 |
| 1970—Shreveport† ......Tex. | | S-O-2 | 69 | 251 | 35 | 66 | 9 | 5 | 4 | 15 | .263 | 85 | 181 | 26 | .911 |
| 1971—Richmond‡ ........Int. | | SS | 33 | 89 | 11 | 16 | 3 | 0 | 1 | 6 | .180 | 38 | 77 | 9 | .927 |
| 1971—Savannah .........South. | | SS | 32 | 125 | 14 | 37 | 6 | 1 | 1 | 6 | .296 | 41 | 103 | 11 | .929 |
| 1971—Atlanta .............Nat. | | SS | 9 | 10 | 1 | 0 | 0 | 0 | 0 | 0 | .000 | 1 | 8 | 1 | .900 |
| 1972—Richmond§ ........Int. | | SS | 99 | 365 | 44 | 85 | 7 | 3 | 2 | 18 | .233 | 122 | 292 | 26 | .941 |
| 1973—Richmond x ......Int. | | SS | 101 | 300 | 28 | 63 | 6 | 1 | 2 | 23 | .210 | 150 | 274 | 19 | .957 |
| 1973—Atlanta .............Nat. | | SS | 3 | 6 | 1 | 1 | 1 | 0 | 0 | 0 | .167 | 5 | 1 | 0 | 1.000 |
| 1974—Atlanta y .........Nat. | | S-2-3-O | 72 | 112 | 16 | 22 | 2 | 0 | 1 | 5 | .196 | 49 | 92 | 6 | .959 |
| 1975—Tidewater z ......Int. | | 2B-SS | 95 | 307 | 42 | 77 | 8 | 4 | 2 | 25 | .251 | 170 | 247 | 18 | .959 |
| 1976—Tidewater.........Int. | | S-3-2 | 71 | 230 | 26 | 66 | 11 | 1 | 5 | 39 | .287 | 95 | 160 | 17 | .938 |
| 1976—New York.........Nat. | | 3-S-2 | 24 | 59 | 11 | 12 | 2 | 0 | 1 | 15 | .203 | 18 | 42 | 2 | .968 |
| Major League Totals ...................... | | | 108 | 187 | 29 | 35 | 5 | 0 | 2 | 20 | .187 | 73 | 143 | 9 | .960 |

†On disabled list, May 30 through July 28.
‡On disabled list, May 6 through June 5.
§On disabled list, May 7 through May 22 and July 3 through July 15.
xOn disabled list, May 12 to May 22 and May 25 to June 9, 1973.
yTraded to New York Mets for Catcher Joe Nolan, April 4, 1975.
zOn disabled list, April 19 to May 2, 1975.

## STEVEN RAYMOND FOUCAULT
Name pronounced Foo-calt.
### (Steve)

Born October 3, 1949, at Duluth, Minn.
Height, 6.00. Weight, 205.
Throws and bats lefthanded.
Hobby—Sports in general.
Attended South Georgia Junior College, Douglas, Ga..

| Year Club | League | G. | IP. | W. | L. | Pct. | H. | R. | ER. | SO. | BB. | ERA. |
|---|---|---|---|---|---|---|---|---|---|---|---|---|
| 1970—Anderson ..........................W. Carol. | | 33 | 65 | 3 | 3 | .500 | 49 | 25 | 10 | 58 | 25 | 1.38 |
| 1970—Pittsfield............................Eastern | | 2 | 2 | 0 | 0 | .000 | 3 | 1 | 1 | 3 | 0 | 4.50 |
| 1971—Burlington..........................Carolina | | 15 | 27 | 1 | 2 | .333 | 33 | 23 | 19 | 22 | 10 | 6.33 |

| Year Club | League | G. | IP. | W. | L. | Pct. | H. | R. | ER. | SO. | BB. | ERA. |
|---|---|---|---|---|---|---|---|---|---|---|---|---|
| 1971-Anderson ............W. Carol. | 27 | 51 | 4 | 2 | .667 | 50 | 23 | 20 | 56 | 16 | 3.53 |
| 1972-Burlington............Carolina | 23 | 40 | 7 | 0 | 1.000 | 20 | 4 | 2 | 55 | 17 | 0.45 |
| 1972-Denver ...............Am. Assoc. | 25 | 42 | 3 | 2 | .600 | 33 | 17 | 13 | 39 | 24 | 2.79 |
| 1973-Texas† ................American | 32 | 56 | 2 | 4 | .333 | 54 | 26 | 24 | 28 | 31 | 3.86 |
| 1974-Texas .................American | 69 | 144 | 8 | 9 | .471 | 123 | 51 | 36 | 106 | 40 | 2.25 |
| 1975-Texas .................American | 59 | 107 | 8 | 4 | .667 | 96 | 57 | 49 | 56 | 55 | 4.12 |
| 1976-Texas .................American | 46 | 76 | 8 | 8 | .500 | 68 | 31 | 28 | 41 | 25 | 3.32 |
| Major League Totals ............. | 206 | 383 | 26 | 25 | .510 | 341 | 165 | 137 | 231 | 151 | 3.22 |

On disabled list, July 3 to August 31, 1973.

### RECORD AS THIRD BASEMAN-OUTFIELDER

| Year Club | League | Pos. | G. | AB. | R. | H. | 2B. | 3B. | HR. | RBI. | B.A. | PO. | A. | E. | F.A. |
|---|---|---|---|---|---|---|---|---|---|---|---|---|---|---|---|
| 1969-Wytheville ........Appal. | 3B | 4 | 7 | 0 | 2 | 0 | 0 | 0 | 0 | .286 | 0 | 0 | 0 | .000 |
| 1970-Anderson ..........W. C. | P-3-O | 45 | 41 | 4 | 14 | 1 | 0 | 0 | 1 | .341 | 9 | 13 | 2 | .917 |

## KENNETH DOUGLAS FRAILING
## (Ken)

Born January 19, 1948, at Marion, Wis.
Height, 6.00. Weight, 182.
Throws and bats lefthanded.
Hobbies—Reading and listening to music.
Attended Wisconsin State University, Stevens Point, Wis., and Wisconsin
State University, River Falls, Wis.

| Year Club | League | G. | IP. | W. | L. | Pct. | H. | R. | ER. | SO. | BB. | ERA. |
|---|---|---|---|---|---|---|---|---|---|---|---|---|
| 1966-Sarasota White Sox ..............Gulf Coast | 10 | 48 | 1 | •5 | .167 | 45 | 34 | 26 | 52 | •39 | 4.88 |
| 1966-Fox Cities ...........................Midwest | 1 | 7 | 0 | 1 | .000 | 11 | 5 | 5 | 9 | 3 | 6.43 |
| 1967-Appleton .........................Midwest | 15 | 99 | 4 | 7 | .364 | 99 | 51 | 28 | 78 | 41 | 2.55 |
| 1968-Appleton† ...........................Midwest | 15 | 90 | 5 | 3 | .625 | 85 | 40 | 33 | 79 | 29 | 3.30 |
| 1969-Lynchburg‡ .........................Carolina | 14 | 78 | 5 | 4 | .556 | 82 | 29 | 27 | 48 | 29 | 3.12 |
| 1970-Mobile...............................Southern | 22 | 146 | 4 | 9 | .308 | 141 | 55 | 44 | 77 | 40 | 2.71 |
| 1971-Tucson ...............................P. Coast | 28 | 124 | 6 | 9 | .400 | 175 | 89 | 83 | 67 | 49 | 6.02 |
| 1972-Tucson§ ...............................P. Coast | 30 | 158 | 8 | 10 | .444 | 199 | 89 | 82 | 90 | 45 | 4.67 |
| 1972-Chicago...............................American | 4 | 3 | 1 | 0 | 1.000 | 3 | 1 | 1 | 1 | 1 | 3.00 |
| 1973-Iowa ...............................Am. Assoc. | 23 | 145 | 11 | 3 | •.786 | 144 | 51 | 46 | 107 | 49 | 2.86 |
| 1973-Chicago x ...........................American | 10 | 18 | 0 | 0 | .000 | 18 | 6 | 4 | 15 | 7 | 2.00 |
| 1974-Chicago..............................National | 55 | 125 | 6 | 9 | .400 | 150 | 65 | 54 | 71 | 43 | 3.89 |
| 1975-Chicago..............................National | 41 | 53 | 2 | 5 | .286 | 61 | 37 | 32 | 39 | 26 | 5.43 |
| 1976-Wichita ..............................Am. Assoc. | 10 | 52 | 2 | 3 | .400 | 57 | 30 | 26 | 25 | 12 | 4.50 |
| 1976-Chicago..............................National | 6 | 19 | 1 | 2 | .333 | 20 | 7 | 5 | 10 | 5 | 2.37 |
| American League Totals........................... | 14 | 21 | 1 | 0 | 1.000 | 21 | 7 | 5 | 16 | 8 | 2.14 |
| National League Totals.......................... | 102 | 197 | 9 | 16 | .360 | 231 | 109 | 91 | 120 | 74 | 4.16 |
| Major League Totals ............................. | 116 | 218 | 10 | 16 | .385 | 252 | 116 | 96 | 136 | 82 | 3.96 |

†On restricted list, March 15 to June 10, 1968.
‡On military list June 26, 1969, through January 23, 1970.
§On temporary inactive list, July 20 to August 10, 1972.

xTraded with Pitcher Steve Stone, Catcher Steve Swisher and a player to be named later to Chicago Cubs
for Third Baseman Ron Santo, December 11, 1973; White Sox sent Pitcher Jim Kremmel to Cubs, December 18,
1973, to complete deal.

## ROGER VERNON FREED

Born June 2, 1946, at Los Angeles, Calif.
Height, 6.00. Weight, 200.
Throws and bats righthanded.
Attended Mount San Antonio Junior College, Walnut, Calif.

Led Northern League batters in walks with 61 in 1967 and American Association with 89 in 1973.
Led California League batters in strikeouts with 152 in 1968.
Led Texas League in total bases with 230 and in walks with 87 in 1969.
Led American Association in total bases with 274 in 1976.
Tied for Northern League lead in sacrifice flies with 4 in 1967.
Named Most Valuable Player in International League, 1970.

| Year Club | League | Pos. | G. | AB. | R. | H. | 2B. | 3B. | HR. | RBI. | B.A. | PO. | A. | E. | F.A. |
|---|---|---|---|---|---|---|---|---|---|---|---|---|---|---|---|
| 1966-Aberdeen ..........North. | OF | 68 | 233 | 44 | 62 | 8 | 2 | •13 | •58 | .266 | 89 | 10 | 1 | .990 |
| 1967-Stockton ...........Calif. | OF | 49 | 122 | 17 | 22 | 5 | 1 | 3 | 11 | .180 | 58 | 5 | 5 | .955 |
| 1967-Aberdeen ..........North. | OF | •70 | 238 | 47 | 72 | 12 | 3 | •13 | 46 | .303 | 78 | 6 | 7 | .923 |
| 1968-Stockton ...........Cal. | O-1-3-C | 139 | 487 | 88 | 131 | 14 | 3 | 31 | 103 | .269 | 452 | 75 | 14 | .974 |
| 1969-Dallas-Ft. W. ....Texas | •O-3-1-C | 132 | 449 | 76 | 134 | 24 | 3 | 22 | 90 | .298 | 265 | •24 | 5 | •.983 |
| 1970-Rochester ..........Int. | OF-1B | 138 | 503 | 96 | •168 | 30 | 6 | 24 | •130 | .334 | 243 | 13 | 3 | .988 |
| 1970-Baltimore† .........Am. | 1B-OF | 4 | 13 | 0 | 2 | 0 | 0 | 0 | 1 | .154 | 25 | 1 | 0 | 1.000 |
| 1971-Philadelphia ......Nat. | OF-C | 118 | 348 | 23 | 77 | 12 | 1 | 6 | 37 | .221 | 185 | 4 | 2 | .990 |
| 1972-Philadelphia‡ .....Nat. | OF | 73 | 129 | 10 | 29 | 4 | 0 | 6 | 18 | .225 | 64 | 4 | 2 | .971 |
| 1973-Oklahoma City§ A.A. | O-3-2 | 128 | 418 | 81 | 116 | 13 | 1 | 30 | 96 | .278 | 84 | 14 | 7 | .933 |
| 1974-Indianapolis ......A.A. | OF-1B | 120 | 359 | 53 | 92 | 17 | 1 | 19 | 71 | .256 | 189 | 12 | 2 | .990 |
| 1974-Cincinnati x ......Nat. | 1B | 6 | 6 | 1 | 2 | 0 | 0 | 1 | 3 | .333 | 2 | 0 | 0 | 1.000 |
| 1975-Monterrey ........Mex. | O-1-C | 103 | 330 | 56 | 94 | 12 | 1 | 19 | 58 | .285 | 176 | 9 | 4 | .979 |

| Year Club League | Pos. | G. | AB. | R. | H. | 2B. | 3B. | HR. | RBI. | B.A. | PO. | A. | E. | F.A. |
|---|---|---|---|---|---|---|---|---|---|---|---|---|---|---|
| 1976–Denver ..............A.A. | 1B-OF | 122 | 398 | 88 | 123 | 21 | 2 | *42 | *102 | .309 | 920 | 68 | 15 | .985 |
| 1976–Montreal y .......Nat. | 1-OF-PH | 8 | 15 | 0 | 3 | 1 | 0 | 0 | 1 | .200 | 25 | 1 | 0 | 1.000 |
| American League Totals ................ | | 4 | 13 | 0 | 2 | 0 | 0 | 0 | 1 | .154 | 25 | 1 | 0 | 1.000 |
| National League Totals ................. | | 205 | 498 | 34 | 111 | 17 | 1 | 13 | 59 | .223 | 276 | 9 | 4 | .986 |
| Major League Totals ..................... | | 209 | 511 | 34 | 113 | 17 | 1 | 13 | 60 | .221 | 301 | 10 | 4 | .987 |

†Traded to Philadelphia Phillies for Pitcher Grant Jackson, Outfielder Sam Parrilla and Catcher-Outfielder Jim Hutto, December 16, 1970.

‡Traded with Outfielder Oscar Gamble to Cleveland Indians for Outfielder Del Unser and Infielder Terry Wedgewood, November 30, 1972.

§Traded by Cleveland Indians to Cincinnati Reds for Pitcher Steve Blateric, December 12, 1973.

xSold to Monterrey (Mexican League), April 8, 1975.

yDrafted by St. Louis Cardinals from Denver (Montreal Expos' organization), December 6, 1976.

## JAMES LOUIS FREGOSI
Name Pronounced Free-GO-see.
### (Jim)
Born April 4, 1942, at San Francisco, Calif.
Height, 6.02. Weight, 197.
Throws and bats righthanded.
Hobbies–Golf, bowling and basketball.
Attended Menlo College, Menlo Park, Calif.

Tied major league record for most double plays started by shortstop, nine-inning game (5), May 1, 1966, first game.
Tied major league record for fewest stolen bases, 150 or more games, season (0), 1970.
Tied American League record for most games, season, shortstop (162), 1966.
Led American League in sacrifice hits with 15 in 1965.
Led American League shortstops in double plays with 125 in 1966 and tied for lead with 92 in 1968.
Tied American Association shortstops for lead in double plays with 100 in 1961.
Named shortstop on THE SPORTING NEWS American League All-Star Teams, 1964 and 1967.
Named shortstop on THE SPORTING NEWS American League All-Star fielding team, 1967.

| Year Club League | Pos. | G. | AB. | R. | H. | 2B. | 3B. | HR. | RBI. | B.A. | PO. | A. | E. | F.A. |
|---|---|---|---|---|---|---|---|---|---|---|---|---|---|---|
| 1960–Alpine† ..............Soph. | IN-OF | 112 | 404 | 96 | 108 | 17 | 7 | 6 | 58 | .267 | 198 | 261 | 39 | .922 |
| 1961–Dal-Ft. Worth ....A. A. | SS | 150 | 516 | 54 | 131 | 18 | 4 | 6 | 50 | .254 | 247 | *495 | *53 | .933 |
| 1961–Los Angeles ......Amer. | SS | 11 | 27 | 7 | 6 | 0 | 0 | 0 | 3 | .222 | 12 | 22 | 2 | .944 |
| 1962–Dal-Ft. Worth ....A. A. | SS-OF | 64 | 219 | 25 | 62 | 9 | 3 | 1 | 14 | .283 | 94 | 164 | 22 | .921 |
| 1962–Los Angeles ......Amer. | SS | 58 | 175 | 15 | 51 | 3 | 4 | 3 | 23 | .291 | 96 | 150 | 15 | .943 |
| 1963–Los Angeles ......Amer. | SS | 154 | 592 | 83 | 170 | 29 | 12 | 9 | 50 | .287 | 271 | 446 | 27 | .964 |
| 1964–Los Angeles ......Amer. | SS | 147 | 505 | 86 | 140 | 22 | 9 | 18 | 72 | .277 | 225 | 421 | 23 | .966 |
| 1965–California.........Amer. | SS | 161 | 602 | 66 | 167 | 19 | 7 | 15 | 64 | .277 | *312 | 481 | 26 | .968 |
| 1966–California.........Amer. | *S-1B | 162 | 611 | 78 | 154 | 32 | 7 | 13 | 67 | .252 | 299 | *531 | ●35 | .960 |
| 1967–California.........Amer. | SS | 151 | 590 | 75 | 171 | 23 | 6 | 9 | 56 | .290 | 258 | 435 | 25 | .965 |
| 1968–California.........Amer. | SS | 159 | 614 | 77 | 150 | 21 | *13 | 9 | 49 | .244 | 273 | 454 | 29 | .962 |
| 1969–California.........Amer. | SS | 161 | 580 | 78 | 151 | 22 | 6 | 12 | 47 | .260 | 255 | 465 | 21 | .972 |
| 1970–California.........Amer. | SS-1B | 158 | 601 | 95 | 167 | 33 | 5 | 22 | 82 | .278 | 313 | 475 | 20 | .975 |
| 1971–California‡§ ......Amer. | S-1-O | 107 | 347 | 31 | 81 | 15 | 1 | 5 | 33 | .233 | 241 | 251 | 22 | .957 |
| 1972–New York.........Nat. | 3-S-1 | 101 | 340 | 31 | 79 | 15 | 4 | 5 | 32 | .232 | 91 | 162 | 15 | .944 |
| 1973–New York x ......Nat. | S-3-1-O | 45 | 124 | 7 | 29 | 4 | 1 | 0 | 11 | .234 | 47 | 70 | 9 | .929 |
| 1973–Texas.................Amer. | 3-1-S | 45 | 157 | 25 | 42 | 6 | 2 | 6 | 16 | .268 | 98 | 53 | 5 | .968 |
| 1974–Texas.................Amer. | 1B-3B | 78 | 230 | 31 | 60 | 5 | 0 | 12 | 34 | .261 | 331 | 73 | 5 | .988 |
| 1975–Texas.................Amer. | 1B-3B | 77 | 191 | 25 | 50 | 5 | 0 | 7 | 33 | .262 | 356 | 35 | 6 | .985 |
| 1976–Texas.................Amer. | 1-2-DH | 58 | 133 | 17 | 31 | 7 | 0 | 2 | 12 | .233 | 183 | 18 | 2 | .990 |
| American League Totals ................ | | 1687 | 5955 | 789 | 1591 | 242 | 72 | 142 | 641 | .267 | 3523 | 4310 | 263 | .968 |
| National League Totals ................. | | 146 | 464 | 38 | 108 | 19 | 5 | 5 | 43 | .233 | 138 | 232 | 24 | .939 |
| Major League Totals ..................... | | 1833 | 6419 | 827 | 1699 | 261 | 77 | 147 | 684 | .265 | 3661 | 4542 | 287 | .966 |

†Selected by Los Angeles Angels off Boston Red Sox roster in American League expansion draft, December 14, 1960.

‡On disabled list July 12 through August 5.

§Traded to New York Mets for Pitchers Nolan Ryan and Don Rose, Outfielder Leroy Stanton and Catcher Francisco Estrada, December 10, 1971.

xTraded to Texas Rangers for a player to be named later, July 11, 1973.

### ALL-STAR GAME RECORD

| Year League | Pos. | AB. | R. | H. | 2B. | 3B. | HR. | RBI. | B.A. | PO. | A. | E. | F.A. |
|---|---|---|---|---|---|---|---|---|---|---|---|---|---|
| 1964–American ........................... | SS | 4 | 1 | 1 | 0 | 0 | 0 | 1 | .250 | 4 | 1 | 0 | 1.000 |
| 1966–American ........................... | SS | 2 | 0 | 0 | 0 | 0 | 0 | 0 | .000 | 0 | 1 | 0 | 1.000 |
| 1967–American ........................... | SS | 4 | 0 | 1 | 0 | 0 | 0 | 0 | .250 | 2 | 3 | 0 | 1.000 |
| 1968–American ........................... | SS | 3 | 0 | 1 | 1 | 0 | 0 | 0 | .333 | 1 | 6 | 0 | 1.000 |
| 1969–American ........................... | SS | 1 | 0 | 0 | 0 | 0 | 0 | 0 | .000 | 0 | 0 | 0 | .000 |
| 1970–American ........................... | PH | 1 | 0 | 0 | 0 | 0 | 0 | 0 | .000 | 0 | 0 | 0 | .000 |
| All Star Game Totals ..................... | | 15 | 1 | 3 | 1 | 0 | 0 | 1 | .200 | 7 | 11 | 0 | 1.000 |

## DID YOU KNOW —
That Casey Stengel was the manager for 10 All-Star Games? It's an all-time All-Star Game record.

## DAVID JAMES FREISLEBEN
Name pronounced FRYS-leb-un.
### (Dave)
Born October 31, 1951, at Coraopolis, Pa.
Height, 6.00. Weight, 200.
Throws and bats righthanded.
Hobbies—Golf, hunting and playing pool.
Pitched 7-inning, 1-0 no-hit game; lost to Albuquerque, June 22, 1973.
Led Northwest League in shutouts with 4 in 1971.
Led Texas League in complete games with 18 in 1972 and tied for Pacific Coast League lead with 14 in 1973.

| Year | Club | League | G. | IP. | W. | L. | Pct. | H. | R. | ER. | SO. | BB. | ERA. |
|------|------|--------|----|-----|----|----|------|----|----|-----|-----|-----|------|
| 1971—Tri-City | | Northwest | 13 | 97 | 7 | 3 | .700 | 90 | 37 | 32 | 111 | 54 | 2.97 |
| 1972—Alexandria | | Texas | 27 | *190 | *17 | 9 | .654 | 146 | 60 | 49 | 163 | 55 | *2.32 |
| 1973—Hawaii | | P. Coast | 27 | 195 | 16 | 8 | .667 | 148 | 73 | 61 | *206 | 89 | *2.82 |
| 1974—Hawaii | | P. Coast | 3 | 14 | 2 | 1 | .667 | 8 | 7 | 6 | 14 | 9 | 3.86 |
| 1974—San Diego | | National | 33 | 212 | 9 | 14 | .391 | 194 | 100 | 86 | 130 | 112 | 3.65 |
| 1975—San Diego | | National | 36 | 181 | 5 | 14 | .263 | 206 | 102 | 86 | 77 | 82 | 4.28 |
| 1976—Hawaii | | P. Coast | 7 | 41 | 2 | 3 | .400 | 46 | 25 | 21 | 23 | 18 | 4.61 |
| 1976—San Diego | | National | 34 | 172 | 10 | 13 | .435 | 163 | 73 | 67 | 81 | 66 | 3.51 |
| Major League Totals | | | 103 | 565 | 24 | 41 | .369 | 563 | 275 | 239 | 288 | 260 | 3.81 |

## JESUS MARIA FRIAS (ANDUJAR)
Name pronounced FREE-uhs.
### (Pepe)
Born July 14, 1948, at San Pedro de Macoris, Dominican Republic.
Height, 5.11. Weight, 160.
Throws and bats righthanded.
Hobby—Music.
Led Southern League shortstops in double plays with 68 in 1970.
Led Eastern League in sacrifice hits with 15 in 1971.
Tied for American Association lead in double plays by shortstops with 88 in 1972.

| Year | Club | League | Pos. | G. | AB. | R. | H. | 2B. | 3B. | HR. | RBI. | B.A. | PO. | A. | E. | F.A. |
|------|------|--------|------|----|-----|----|----|-----|-----|-----|------|------|-----|----|----|------|
| 1967—Decatur† | | Midw. | 2B | 15 | 44 | 5 | 8 | 0 | 0 | 0 | 1 | .182 | 19 | 39 | 6 | .906 |
| 1967—Salt Lake City‡ | | Pion. | 2B | 4 | 8 | 0 | 1 | 0 | 0 | 0 | 0 | .125 | 4 | 4 | 1 | .889 |
| 1968—Daytona Beach§ | | Fla. St. | | | | | (Did not play) | | | | | | | | | |
| 1969—Decatur x | | Midw. | SS-3B | 44 | 128 | 10 | 24 | 5 | 1 | 0 | 12 | .188 | 42 | 95 | 21 | .867 |
| 1970—Jacksonville | | South. | SS | 136 | 492 | 42 | 125 | 13 | 2 | 0 | 44 | .254 | *204 | *432 | *32 | *.952 |
| 1971—Winnipeg | | Int. | SS | 12 | 40 | 5 | 7 | 0 | 0 | 0 | 2 | .175 | 19 | 25 | 2 | .957 |
| 1971—Quebec City | | East. | SS | 126 | 463 | 50 | 111 | 20 | 5 | 1 | 29 | .240 | 179 | *425 | 25 | .960 |
| 1972—Evansville | | A. A. | SS | 132 | 424 | 53 | 93 | 14 | 3 | 2 | 41 | .219 | •215 | 401 | 34 | .948 |
| 1973—Montreal | | Nat. | S-2-3-O | 100 | 225 | 19 | 52 | 10 | 1 | 0 | 22 | .231 | 122 | 215 | 15 | .957 |
| 1974—Montreal | | Nat. | S-3-2-O | 75 | 112 | 12 | 24 | 4 | 1 | 0 | 7 | .214 | 64 | 115 | 5 | .973 |
| 1975—Montreal | | Nat. | S-3-2 | 51 | 64 | 4 | 8 | 2 | 0 | 0 | 4 | .125 | 55 | 67 | 7 | .946 |
| 1976—Montreal | | Nat. | S-2-3-O | 76 | 113 | 7 | 28 | 5 | 0 | 0 | 8 | .248 | 81 | 116 | 11 | .947 |
| Major League Totals | | | | 302 | 514 | 42 | 112 | 21 | 2 | 0 | 41 | .218 | 322 | 513 | 38 | .956 |

†On disabled list, May 18 through June 10, 1967.
‡Released by San Francisco Giants' organization, July 1, 1967; signed as free agent by Los Angeles Dodgers' organization, November 13, 1967.
§Released by Los Angeles Dodgers' organization, April 1, 1968; signed as free agent by San Francisco Giants' organization, October 22, 1968.
xReleased by San Francisco Giants' organization, July 1, 1969; signed as free agent by Montreal Expos' organization, August 27, 1969.

## CARL DAVID FROST
### (Dave)
Born November 17, 1952, at Long Beach Calif.
Height, 6.06. Weight, 235.
Throws and bats righthanded.
Hobbies—Fishing and skin diving.
Attended Stanford University, Stanford, Calif., received
Bachelor of Arts degree in Political Science.

| Year | Club | League | G. | IP. | W. | L. | Pct. | H. | R. | ER. | SO. | BB. | ERA. |
|------|------|--------|----|-----|----|----|------|----|----|-----|-----|-----|------|
| 1974—Sarasota W. Sox | | Gulf Coast | 10 | 45 | 2 | 3 | .400 | 35 | 14 | 9 | 33 | 18 | 1.80 |
| 1974—Knoxville | | Southern | 1 | 3 | 0 | 0 | .000 | 2 | 1 | 1 | 1 | 3 | 3.00 |
| 1975—Knoxville | | Southern | 28 | 171 | 5 | 14 | .263 | 157 | 73 | 61 | 100 | 68 | 3.21 |
| 1976—Knoxville | | Southern | 20 | 136 | 8 | 7 | .533 | 121 | 43 | 36 | 88 | 32 | 2.38 |

†On disabled list, April 13 through May 24, 1976.
Listed on Chicago White Sox' 1977 spring roster.

## WOODROW THOMPSON FRYMAN
### (Woodie)

Born April 12, 1940, at Ewing, Ky.
Height, 6.02½. Weight, 200.
Throws left and bats righthanded.
Hobbies—Hunting and fishing.

| Year Club | League | G. | IP. | W. | L. | Pct. | H. | R. | ER. | SO. | BB. | ERA. |
|---|---|---|---|---|---|---|---|---|---|---|---|---|
| 1965—Batavia | NYP | 6 | 30 | 3 | 1 | .750 | 13 | 5 | 5 | 45 | 14 | 1.50 |
| 1965—Columbus | Int'national | 6 | 34 | 0 | 3 | .000 | 32 | 15 | 14 | 29 | 15 | 3.71 |
| 1966—Pittsburgh | National | 36 | 182 | 12 | 9 | .571 | 182 | 86 | 77 | 105 | 47 | 3.81 |
| 1967—Pittsburgh† | National | 28 | 113 | 3 | 8 | .273 | 121 | 67 | 51 | 74 | 44 | 4.06 |
| 1968—Philadelphia | National | 34 | 214 | 12 | 14 | .462 | 198 | 78 | 66 | 151 | 64 | 2.78 |
| 1969—Philadelphia | National | 36 | 228 | 12 | 15 | .444 | 243 | 123 | 112 | 150 | 89 | 4.42 |
| 1970—Philadelphia‡ | National | 27 | 128 | 8 | 6 | .571 | 122 | 61 | 58 | 97 | 43 | 4.08 |
| 1971—Philadelphia | National | 37 | 149 | 10 | 7 | .588 | 133 | 61 | 56 | 104 | 46 | 3.38 |
| 1972—Philadelphia§ | National | 23 | 120 | 4 | 10 | .286 | 131 | 64 | 58 | 69 | 39 | 4.35 |
| 1972—Detroit | American | 16 | 114 | 10 | 3 | .769 | 93 | 31 | 26 | 72 | 31 | 2.05 |
| 1973—Detroit | American | 34 | 170 | 6 | 13 | .316 | 200 | 106 | 101 | 119 | 64 | 5.35 |
| 1974—Detroit x | American | 27 | 142 | 6 | 9 | .400 | 120 | 73 | 68 | 92 | 67 | 4.31 |
| 1975—Montreal | National | 38 | 157 | 9 | 12 | .429 | 141 | 69 | 58 | 118 | 68 | 3.32 |
| 1976—Montreal y | National | 34 | 216 | 13 | 13 | .500 | 218 | 89 | 81 | 123 | 76 | 3.38 |
| National League Totals | | 293 | 1507 | 83 | 94 | .469 | 1489 | 698 | 617 | 991 | 516 | 3.68 |
| American League Totals | | 77 | 426 | 22 | 25 | .468 | 413 | 210 | 195 | 283 | 162 | 4.12 |
| Major League Totals | | 370 | 1933 | 105 | 119 | .469 | 1902 | 908 | 812 | 1274 | 678 | 3.78 |

†Traded with Pitchers Harold Clem and Bill Laxton and Infielder Don Money to Philadelphia Phillies for Pitcher Jim Bunning, December 15, 1967.
‡On disabled list July 29 through August 31.
§Released on waivers to Detroit Tigers, August 2, 1972.
xTraded to Montreal Expos for Pitcher Tom Walker and Catcher Terry Humphrey, December 4, 1974.
yTraded with Pitcher Dale Murray to Cincinnati Reds for First Baseman Tony Perez and Pitcher Will McEnaney, December 16, 1976.

### CHAMPIONSHIP SERIES RECORD

| Year Club | League | G. | IP. | W. | L. | Pct. | H. | R. | ER. | SO. | BB. | ERA. |
|---|---|---|---|---|---|---|---|---|---|---|---|---|
| 1972—Detroit | American | 2 | 12⅓ | 0 | 2 | .000 | 11 | 6 | 5 | 8 | 2 | 3.65 |

### ALL-STAR GAME RECORD

Member of National League All-Star Team in 1968 game; did not play.

## RIGOBERTO FUENTES (PEAT)
### (Tito)

Born January 4, 1944, at Havana, Cuba.
Height, 5.11½. Weight, 183.
Throws right and bats left and righthanded.
Hobbies—Records, playing with children and managing Little League team.
Tied major league record for most times hit by pitch, game, 3, September 13, 1973.
Established National League records for highest fielding percentage by second baseman, season, .993, and fewest errors by second baseman (800 or more chances), season, 6, 1973.

| Year Club | League | Pos. | G. | AB. | R. | H. | 2B. | 3B. | HR. | RBI. | B.A. | PO. | A. | E. | F.A. |
|---|---|---|---|---|---|---|---|---|---|---|---|---|---|---|---|
| 1962—Lakeland | Fla. St. | 2B | 68 | 255 | 25 | 56 | 6 | 0 | 2 | 24 | .220 | 203 | 172 | 24 | .940 |
| 1962—Salem | Appal. | 2B | 7 | 29 | 7 | 9 | 1 | 0 | 2 | 6 | .310 | 15 | 16 | 4 | .886 |
| 1963—Decatur | Midw. | 2B | 73 | 299 | 68 | 101 | 15 | 5 | 7 | 37 | .338 | 183 | 181 | 15 | .960 |
| 1963—El Paso | Texas | 2B | 7 | 25 | 3 | 6 | 0 | 1 | 1 | 5 | .240 | 21 | 17 | 2 | .950 |
| 1964—El Paso | Texas | 2B | 67 | 277 | 62 | 96 | 18 | 5 | 8 | 40 | .347 | 147 | 200 | 16 | .956 |
| 1964—Tacoma | P. C. | 2B | 79 | 273 | 28 | 65 | 11 | 4 | 7 | 21 | .238 | 188 | 174 | 12 | .968 |
| 1965—Tacoma | P. C. | SS-2B | 96 | 394 | 61 | 119 | 25 | 5 | 20 | 41 | .302 | 168 | 252 | 26 | .942 |
| 1965—San Francisco | Nat. | SS-2-3 | 26 | 72 | 12 | 15 | 1 | 0 | 0 | 1 | .208 | 27 | 49 | 5 | .938 |
| 1966—San Francisco | Nat. | SS-2B | 133 | 541 | 63 | 141 | 21 | 3 | 9 | 40 | .261 | 283 | 403 | 30 | .958 |
| 1967—San Francisco | Nat. | 2B-SS | 133 | 344 | 27 | 72 | 12 | 1 | 5 | 29 | .209 | 276 | 315 | 12 | .980 |
| 1968—Phoenix† | P. C. | 2-S-3B | 21 | 85 | 17 | 28 | 5 | 3 | 1 | 10 | .329 | 41 | 71 | 4 | .966 |
| 1969—Phoenix | P. C. | SS-3B | 42 | 162 | 30 | 55 | 9 | 2 | 0 | 25 | .340 | 87 | 133 | 16 | .932 |
| 1969—San Francisco | Nat. | 3B-SS | 67 | 183 | 28 | 54 | 4 | 3 | 1 | 14 | .295 | 50 | 117 | 13 | .928 |
| 1970—San Francisco | Nat. | 2-SS-3 | 123 | 435 | 49 | 116 | 13 | 7 | 2 | 32 | .267 | 202 | 324 | 19 | .965 |
| 1971—San Francisco | Nat. | 2B | 152 | 630 | 63 | 172 | 28 | 6 | 4 | 52 | .273 | 373 | 465 | •23 | .973 |
| 1972—San Francisco | Nat. | 2B | 152 | 572 | 64 | 151 | 33 | 6 | 7 | 53 | .264 | 361 | 417 | •29 | .964 |
| 1973—San Francisco | Nat. | •2B-3B | 160 | 656 | 78 | 182 | 25 | 5 | 6 | 63 | .277 | 386 | •479 | 6 | •.993 |
| 1974—San Francisco‡ | Nat. | 2B | 108 | 390 | 33 | 97 | 15 | 2 | 0 | 22 | .249 | 238 | 287 | 11 | .979 |
| 1975—San Diego | Nat. | 2B | 146 | 565 | 57 | 158 | 21 | 3 | 4 | 43 | .280 | 389 | 448 | 26 | .970 |
| 1976—San Diego§ | Nat. | 2B | 135 | 520 | 48 | 137 | 18 | 0 | 2 | 36 | .263 | 339 | 387 | •22 | .971 |
| Major League Totals | | | 1335 | 4908 | 522 | 1295 | 191 | 36 | 40 | 385 | .264 | 2924 | 3691 | 196 | .971 |

†On disabled list with broken leg from May 10 through September 7.
‡Traded with Pitcher Butch Metzger to San Diego Padres for Second Baseman Derrel Thomas, December 6, 1974.
§Played out option year and granted free agency, November 1, 1976; signed as free agent with Detroit Tigers, February 23, 1977.

### CHAMPIONSHIP SERIES RECORD

| Year Club | League | Pos. | G. | AB. | R. | H. | 2B. | 3B. | HR. | RBI. | B.A. | PO. | A. | E. | F.A. |
|---|---|---|---|---|---|---|---|---|---|---|---|---|---|---|---|
| 1971—San Francisco | Nat. | 2B | 4 | 16 | 4 | 5 | 1 | 0 | 1 | 2 | .313 | 9 | 5 | 1 | .933 |

## JAMES H. FULLER
### (Jim)

Born November 28, 1950, at Bethesda, Md.
Height, 6.03. Weight, 220.
Throws and bats righthanded.
Attended San Diego Community College, San Diego, Calif.
Brother of Tom Fuller, former catcher in Chicago White Sox' organization.

Established American League record for most strikeouts, consecutive plate appearances, season (non-pitcher), 8, September 25-28, 1973.
Led Florida State League in total bases with 298 in 1971 and led International League with 279 in 1973.
Led International League batters in strikeouts with 197 in 1973 and 133 in 1975.
Tied for Florida State League lead in double plays by outfielders with 6 in 1971.
Named Most Valuable Player in Florida State League, 1971.
Named International League Most Valuable Player, 1973.

| Year | Club | League | Pos. | G. | AB. | R. | H. | 2B. | 3B. | HR. | RBI. | B.A. | PO. | A. | E. | F.A. |
|------|------|--------|------|----|-----|----|----|-----|-----|-----|------|------|-----|----|----|------|
| 1970—Miami | .............. | Fla. St. | 1B-OF | 114 | 373 | 42 | 92 | 20 | 6 | 9 | 64 | .247 | 867 | 54 | 17 | .982 |
| 1971—Miami | .............. | Fla. St. | OF | •141 | 488 | •105 | •159 | ●28 | 6 | •33 | •110 | .326 | 206 | 17 | 9 | .961 |
| 1972—Rochester | ......... | Int. | OF | 49 | 171 | 22 | 39 | 5 | 1 | 11 | 37 | .228 | 88 | 5 | 4 | .959 |
| 1972—Asheville | .......... | South. | OF | 80 | 292 | 54 | 79 | 19 | 4 | 23 | 70 | .271 | 125 | 9 | 9 | .937 |
| 1973—Rochester | ......... | Int. | OF | 144 | 515 | 96 | 127 | 25 | 5 | •39 | •108 | .247 | 258 | 11 | •12 | .957 |
| 1973—Baltimore | ......... | Amer. | OF-1B | 9 | 26 | 2 | 3 | 0 | 0 | 2 | 4 | .115 | 20 | 2 | 0 | 1.000 |
| 1974—Rochester | ......... | Int. | OF-1B | 25 | 90 | 11 | 25 | 9 | 0 | 5 | 16 | .278 | 54 | 2 | 2 | .966 |
| 1974—Baltimore | ......... | Amer. | OF-1B | 64 | 189 | 17 | 42 | 11 | 0 | 7 | 28 | .222 | 131 | 4 | 6 | .957 |
| 1975—Rochester | ......... | Int. | OF-1B | 113 | 362 | 51 | 77 | 7 | 5 | 17 | 50 | .213 | 203 | 14 | 6 | .973 |
| 1976—Rochester‡ | ........ | Int. | OF | 78 | 269 | 46 | 61 | 9 | 2 | 19 | 55 | .227 | 93 | 5 | 8 | .925 |
| Major League Totals | ..................... | | | 73 | 215 | 19 | 45 | 11 | 0 | 9 | 32 | .209 | 151 | 6 | 6 | .963 |

†On disabled list, July 15 through August 23, 1976. Unconditionally released October 15, signed as free agent with Houston Astros, November 29, 1976.

## ROBERT JOSEPH GALLASSO
Name pronounced Ga-LASS-o
### (Bob)

Born January 13, 1952, at Connellsville, Pa.
Height, 6.01. Weight, 205.
Throws right and bats lefthanded.
Hobbies—Golf and fishing.
Attended Robert Morris College, Pittsburgh, Pa.
Father, Robert Galasso, Sr., pitcher in Pittsburgh Pirates' organization, 1949.

Led California League in wild pitches with 31 in 1972, Northern League with 20 in 1971 and Southern League with 29 in 1973.

| Year | Club | League | G. | IP. | W. | L. | Pct. | H. | R. | ER. | SO. | BB. | ERA. |
|------|------|--------|----|-----|----|----|------|----|----|----|-----|-----|------|
| 1970—Bluefield† | ........................... | Ap'lachian | 10 | 43 | 3 | 3 | .500 | 33 | 25 | 17 | 32 | 39 | 3.56 |
| 1971—Key West | ........................... | Florida St. | 18 | 50 | 1 | 6 | .143 | 62 | 61 | 46 | 44 | 44 | 8.28 |
| 1971—Aberdeen | ........................... | Northern | 23 | 72 | 5 | 4 | .556 | 60 | 69 | 50 | 93 | •94 | 6.25 |
| 1972—Lodi | .................................... | California | 26 | 154 | 8 | 14 | .364 | 147 | 91 | 71 | 132 | 90 | 4.15 |
| 1973—Asheville | ............................ | Southern | 27 | 160 | 9 | •15 | .375 | 156 | •108 | 82 | 101 | •104 | 4.61 |
| 1974—Asheville | ............................ | Southern | 24 | 150 | 8 | 13 | .381 | 144 | 93 | 74 | 88 | 89 | 4.44 |
| 1975—Rochester | ........................... | Int'national | 30 | 155 | 9 | 7 | .563 | 135 | 55 | 49 | 68 | 88 | 2.85 |
| 1976—Rochester‡ | ......................... | Int'national | 25 | 141 | 13 | 5 | •.722 | 132 | 70 | 54 | 75 | 66 | 3.45 |

†Played in two games as an outfielder.
‡Selected by Seattle Mariners from Baltimore Orioles in American League expansion draft, November 5, 1976.

## OSCAR CHARLES GAMBLE

Born December 20, 1949, at Ramer, Ala.
Height, 5:11. Weight, 165.
Throws right and bats lefthanded.
Hobbies—Hunting, fishing and dancing.

| Year | Club | League | Pos. | G. | AB. | R. | H. | 2B. | 3B. | HR. | RBI. | B.A. | PO. | A. | E. | F.A. |
|------|------|--------|------|----|-----|----|----|-----|-----|-----|------|------|-----|----|----|------|
| 1968—Caldwell | ........... | Pion. | OF | 34 | 94 | 18 | 25 | 2 | 0 | 2 | 12 | .266 | 42 | 4 | 4 | .920 |
| 1969—San Antonio | ...... | Texas | OF | 119 | 477 | 62 | 142 | •32 | 3 | 7 | 32 | .298 | 247 | 10 | 8 | .970 |
| 1969—Chicago† | ......... | Nat. | OF | 24 | 71 | 6 | 16 | 1 | 1 | 1 | 5 | .225 | 41 | 1 | 4 | .913 |
| 1970—Eugene | ............. | P.C. | OF | 28 | 108 | 26 | 32 | 7 | 2 | 1 | 8 | .296 | 54 | 3 | 0 | 1.000 |
| 1970—Philadelphia | ...... | Nat. | OF | 88 | 275 | 31 | 72 | 12 | 4 | 1 | 19 | .262 | 148 | 4 | 7 | .956 |
| 1971—Eugene | ............. | P.C. | OF | 39 | 138 | 30 | 40 | 5 | 2 | 4 | 20 | .290 | 65 | 4 | 3 | .958 |
| 1971—Philadelphia | ...... | Nat. | OF | 92 | 280 | 24 | 62 | 11 | 1 | 6 | 23 | .221 | 125 | 4 | 4 | .970 |
| 1972—Eugene | ............. | P.C. | OF | 42 | 144 | 30 | 42 | 8 | 1 | 8 | 20 | .292 | 67 | 8 | 1 | .987 |
| 1972—Philadelphia‡ | ....Nat. | | OF-1B | 74 | 135 | 17 | 32 | 5 | 2 | 1 | 13 | .237 | 54 | 2 | 0 | 1.000 |
| 1973—Cleveland | ......... | Amer. | OF | 113 | 390 | 56 | 104 | 11 | 3 | 20 | 44 | .267 | 67 | 1 | 2 | .971 |
| 1974—Cleveland | ......... | Amer. | OF | 135 | 454 | 74 | 132 | 16 | 4 | 19 | 59 | .291 | 19 | 1 | 0 | 1.000 |
| 1975—Cleveland§ | ......... | Amer. | OF | 121 | 348 | 60 | 91 | 16 | 3 | 15 | 45 | .261 | 146 | 8 | 2 | .987 |
| 1976—New York x | ...... | Amer. | OF-DH | 110 | 340 | 43 | 79 | 13 | 1 | 17 | 57 | .232 | 199 | 10 | 4 | .981 |
| National League Totals | ................. | | | 278 | 761 | 78 | 182 | 29 | 8 | 9 | 60 | .239 | 368 | 11 | 15 | .962 |
| American League Totals | ................ | | | 479 | 1532 | 233 | 406 | 56 | 11 | 71 | 205 | .265 | 431 | 20 | 8 | .982 |
| Major League Totals | ..................... | | | 757 | 2293 | 311 | 588 | 85 | 19 | 80 | 265 | .256 | 799 | 31 | 23 | .973 |

‡Traded with Outfielder Roger Freed to Cleveland Indians for Outfielder Del Unser and Infielder Terry Wedgewood, November 30, 1972.
§Traded to New York Yankees for Pitcher Pat Dobson, November 22, 1975.
xTraded with Pitchers Bob Polinsky and Dewey Hoyt, and cash estimated at $250,000 to Chicago White Sox for Shortstop Bucky Dent, April 5, 1977.

### CHAMPIONSHIP SERIES RECORD

| Year Club | League | Pos. | G. | AB. | R. | H. | 2B. | 3B. | HR. | RBI. | B.A. | PO. | A. | E. | F.A. |
|---|---|---|---|---|---|---|---|---|---|---|---|---|---|---|---|
| 1976–New York..........Am. | | OF-PH | 3 | 8 | 1 | 2 | 1 | 0 | 0 | 1 | .250 | 4 | 0 | 2 | .667 |

### WORLD SERIES RECORD

| Year Club | League | Pos. | G. | AB. | R. | H. | 2B. | 3B. | HR. | RBI. | B.A. | PO. | A. | E. | F.A. |
|---|---|---|---|---|---|---|---|---|---|---|---|---|---|---|---|
| 1976–New York..........Am. | | PH-OF | 3 | 8 | 0 | 1 | 0 | 0 | 0 | 1 | .125 | 3 | 0 | 0 | 1.000 |

## JAMES ELMER GANTNER
### (Jim)

Born January 5, 1954, at Fond du Lac, Wis.
Height, 6.00. Weight, 180.
Throws right and bats lefthanded.
Hobbies–Hunting and fishing.
Attended University of Wisconsin (Oshkosh), Oshkosh, Wis.

| Year Club | League | Pos. | G. | AB. | R. | H. | 2B. | 3B. | HR. | RBI. | B.A. | PO. | A. | E. | F.A. |
|---|---|---|---|---|---|---|---|---|---|---|---|---|---|---|---|
| 1974–Newark ............NYP | | SS-3B | 62 | 177 | 35 | 54 | 6 | 2 | 5 | 21 | .305 | 64 | 134 | 14 | .934 |
| 1975–Theford Mines ..East. | | 3B-SS | 138 | 456 | 61 | 117 | 17 | 0 | 12 | 48 | .257 | 129 | 317 | 33 | .931 |
| 1976–Pittsfield ..........East. | | 3B-SS | 126 | 403 | 56 | 118 | 21 | 1 | 6 | 53 | .293 | 120 | 294 | 20 | *.954 |
| 1976–Milwaukee ........Amer. | | 3B | 26 | 69 | 6 | 17 | 1 | 0 | 0 | 7 | .246 | 17 | 37 | 1 | .982 |
| Major League Totals ...................... | | | 26 | 69 | 6 | 17 | 1 | 0 | 0 | 7 | .246 | 17 | 37 | 1 | .982 |

## HENRY EUGENE GARBER
### (Gene)

Born November 13, 1947, at Lancaster, Pa.
Height, 5.10. Weight, 175.
Throws and bats righthanded.
Hobbies–Basketball and football.
Attended Elizabethtown College, Elizabethtown, Pa.; received Bachelor's degree in History and Political Science.

Tied for International League lead in complete games by pitchers with 13 in 1972.

| Year Club | League | G. | IP. | W. | L. | Pct. | H. | R. | ER. | SO. | BB. | ERA. |
|---|---|---|---|---|---|---|---|---|---|---|---|---|
| 1965–Salem ...................................Ap'lachian | | 1 | ⅔ | 0 | 0 | .000 | 0 | 0 | 0 | 2 | 2 | 0.00 |
| 1965–Batavia ...............................NYP | | 11 | 72 | 4 | 3 | .571 | 71 | 42 | 28 | 40 | 31 | 3.50 |
| 1966–Raleigh ...............................Carolina | | 16 | 94 | 4 | 4 | .500 | 106 | 53 | 48 | 76 | 28 | 4.60 |
| 1967–Raleigh ...............................Carolina | | 18 | 138 | 8 | 6 | .571 | 103 | 41 | 29 | 68 | 47 | 1.89 |
| 1968–York .....................................Eastern | | 16 | 118 | 7 | 2 | .778 | 79 | 33 | 21 | 86 | 30 | 1.60 |
| 1968–Columbus ...........................Int'national | | 23 | 59 | 5 | 1 | .833 | 62 | 21 | 16 | 32 | 17 | 2.44 |
| 1969–York .....................................Eastern | | 11 | 73 | 5 | 3 | .625 | 61 | 40 | 25 | 57 | 40 | 3.08 |
| 1969–Pittsburgh...........................National | | 2 | 5 | 0 | 0 | .000 | 6 | 3 | 3 | 3 | 1 | 5.40 |
| 1969–Columbus† ...........................Int'national | | 17 | 123 | 7 | 6 | .538 | 116 | 51 | 42 | 74 | 37 | 3.07 |
| 1970–Columbus ...........................Int'national | | 30 | 95 | 5 | 2 | .714 | 96 | 57 | 50 | 75 | 38 | 4.74 |
| 1970–Pittsburgh...........................National | | 14 | 22 | 0 | 3 | .000 | 22 | 13 | 13 | 7 | 10 | 5.32 |
| 1971–Charleston‡.........................Int'national | | 24 | 170 | 14 | 6 | .700 | *184 | 85 | 79 | 105 | 54 | 4.18 |
| 1972–Charleston .........................Int'national | | 20 | 163 | 14 | 3 | *.824 | 131 | 49 | 41 | 103 | 45 | *2.26 |
| 1972–Pittsburgh§ .........................National | | 4 | 6 | 0 | 0 | .000 | 7 | 5 | 5 | 3 | 3 | 7.50 |
| 1973–Kansas City.........................American | | 48 | 153 | 9 | 9 | .500 | 164 | 78 | 72 | 60 | 49 | 4.24 |
| 1974–Kansas City x .....................American | | 17 | 28 | 1 | 2 | .333 | 35 | 21 | 15 | 14 | 13 | 4.82 |
| 1974–Toledo .................................Int'national | | 3 | 22 | 2 | 1 | .667 | 19 | 7 | 1 | 17 | 3 | 0.41 |
| 1974–Philadelphia .......................National | | 34 | 48 | 4 | 0 | 1.000 | 39 | 15 | 11 | 27 | 31 | 2.06 |
| 1975–Philadelphia .......................National | | *71 | 110 | 10 | 12 | .455 | 104 | 48 | 44 | 69 | 27 | 3.60 |
| 1976–Philadelphia .......................National | | 59 | 93 | 9 | 3 | .750 | 78 | 33 | 29 | 92 | 30 | 2.81 |
| American League Totals.......................... | | 65 | 181 | 10 | 11 | .476 | 199 | 99 | 87 | 74 | 62 | 4.33 |
| National League Totals............................ | | 184 | 284 | 23 | 18 | .561 | 256 | 117 | 105 | 201 | 102 | 3.33 |
| Major League Totals ............................. | | 249 | 465 | 33 | 29 | .532 | 455 | 216 | 192 | 275 | 164 | 3.72 |

†On military list, September 2, 1969, through February 18, 1970.
‡On temporary inactive list, June 24, 1971 through July 12, 1971.
§Released to Kansas City Royals (in trade which sent Pitcher Jim Rooker from Omaha to Pittsburgh Pirates), October 25, 1972.
xSold to Philadelphia Phillies, July 12, 1974.

### CHAMPIONSHIP SERIES RECORD

| Year Club | League | G. | IP. | W. | L. | Pct. | H. | R. | ER. | SO. | BB. | ERA. |
|---|---|---|---|---|---|---|---|---|---|---|---|---|
| 1976–Philadelphia .......................National | | 2 | ⅔ | 0 | 1 | .000 | 2 | 2 | 1 | 0 | 1 | 13.50 |

## ALFONSO RAFAEL GARCIA
### (Kiko)
(Nicknamed by grandparents.)

Born October 14, 1953, at Martinez, Calif.
Height, 5.11. Weight, 180.
Throws and bats righthanded.
Led Southern League shortstops in double plays with 105 in 1974.
Led International League second basemen in double plays with 71 in 1975.

| Year | Club | League | Pos. | G. | AB. | R. | H. | 2B. | 3B. | HR. | RBI. | B.A. | PO. | A. | E. | F.A. |
|------|------|--------|------|-----|-----|-----|-----|-----|-----|-----|------|------|-----|-----|-----|------|
| 1971–Bluefield | | Appal. | SS | 56 | 203 | 35 | 51 | 3 | *5 | 2 | 23 | .251 | 95 | 128 | 24 | .503 |
| 1971–Stockton | | Calif. | SS | 4 | 14 | 1 | 4 | 0 | 1 | 0 | 2 | .286 | 8 | 13 | 2 | .913 |
| 1972–Miami | | Fla.St. | SS-3B | 126 | 445 | 51 | 112 | 15 | 6 | 2 | 39 | .252 | 176 | 416 | 40 | .937 |
| 1973–Lodi | | Calif. | SS | 129 | 494 | 89 | 128 | 15 | 10 | 3 | 36 | .259 | *237 | 361 | 43 | .933 |
| 1974–Asheville | | South. | SS | 135 | 511 | 68 | 140 | 18 | 5 | 7 | 53 | .274 | *250 | *510 | 48 | .941 |
| 1975–Rochester | | Int. | 2B-SS | 122 | 405 | 34 | 99 | 11 | 1 | 3 | 32 | .244 | 260 | 255 | 25 | .953 |
| 1976–Rochester | | Int. | SS | 130 | 450 | 75 | 124 | 11 | 10 | 3 | 44 | .276 | 241 | 473 | 38 | .949 |
| 1976–Baltimore | | Amer. | SS | 11 | 32 | 2 | 7 | 1 | 1 | 1 | 4 | .219 | 15 | 27 | 0 | 1.000 |
| Major League Totals | | | | 11 | 32 | 2 | 7 | 1 | 1 | 1 | 4 | .219 | 15 | 27 | 0 | 1.000 |

## PEDRO GARCIA (DELFI)

Born April 17, 1950, at Guayama, Puerto Rico.
Height, 5.10. Weight, 175.
Throws and bats righthanded.
Hobby–Listening to music.
Tied major league record for fewest doubles, season, for leader in doubles, 32, in 1973.

| Year | Club | League | Pos. | G. | AB. | R. | H. | 2B. | 3B. | HR. | RBI. | B.A. | PO. | A. | E. | F.A. |
|------|------|--------|------|-----|-----|-----|-----|-----|-----|-----|------|------|-----|-----|-----|------|
| 1969–Clinton† | | Midw. | SS | 10 | 23 | 2 | 3 | 0 | 0 | 0 | 4 | .130 | 8 | 10 | 4 | .818 |
| 1969–Billings | | Pion. | *2-S-3 | 69 | 234 | 46 | 58 | ●15 | 2 | *10 | 32 | .248 | *138 | 145 | 23 | .925 |
| 1970–Clinton | | Midw. | 2-S-O | 54 | 181 | 26 | 44 | 5 | 0 | 4 | 16 | .243 | 99 | 120 | 6 | .973 |
| 1970–Newark | | NYP | SS-3-2 | 51 | 164 | 46 | 50 | 9 | 5 | *14 | 36 | .305 | 66 | 92 | 11 | .935 |
| 1971–Danville | | Midw. | 2-S | 57 | 210 | 44 | 56 | 10 | 7 | 12 | 41 | .267 | 140 | 144 | 13 | .956 |
| 1971–Evansville | | A.A. | 2B | 72 | 236 | 25 | 50 | 14 | 5 | 9 | 35 | .212 | 148 | 199 | 12 | .967 |
| 1972–Evansville | | A.A. | *2B-SS | 128 | 458 | 60 | 122 | 25 | 3 | 14 | 51 | .266 | 281 | *348 | 16 | .975 |
| 1973–Milwaukee | | Amer. | 2B | 160 | 580 | 67 | 142 | ●32 | 5 | 15 | 54 | .245 | 405 | 470 | *27 | .970 |
| 1974–Milwaukee | | Amer. | 2B | 141 | 452 | 46 | 90 | 15 | 4 | 12 | 54 | .199 | 382 | 365 | 23 | .970 |
| 1975–Milwaukee‡ | | Amer. | 2B | 98 | 302 | 40 | 68 | 15 | 2 | 6 | 38 | .225 | 230 | 293 | 8 | .985 |
| 1976–Milw.§-Det | | Amer. | 2B | 118 | 333 | 33 | 68 | 17 | 3 | 4 | 29 | .204 | 242 | 314 | 22 | .962 |
| Major League Totals | | | | 517 | 1667 | 186 | 368 | 79 | 14 | 37 | 175 | .221 | 1259 | 1442 | 80 | .971 |

†On temporary inactive list, May 22 through May 28.
‡On supplemental disabled list, July 11 to August 3, 1975.
§Traded to Detroit Tigers for Second Baseman Gary Sutherland, June 10, 1976. Released, December 16, 1976; signed as free agent by Toronto Blue Jays, January 3, 1977.

## ARTHUR JUNIOR GARDNER
### (Art)

Born September 21, 1952, at Madden, Miss.
Height, 5.11. Weight, 175.
Throws and bats lefthanded.
Hobbies–Dancing, music and playing all sports.
Attended Jackson State College, Jackson, Miss.
Led American Association outfielders in double plays with 6 in 1975.
Tied for Appalachian League lead in stolen bases with 18 in 1971.

| Year | Club | League | Pos. | G. | AB. | R. | H. | 2B. | 3B. | HR. | RBI. | B.A. | PO. | A. | E. | F.A. |
|------|------|--------|------|-----|-----|-----|-----|-----|-----|-----|------|------|-----|-----|-----|------|
| 1971–Covington | | Appal. | OF | 68 | *264 | 45 | 80 | 14 | 4 | 2 | 31 | .303 | *120 | 5 | ●9 | .933 |
| 1972–Cocoa | | Fla.St. | OF | 103 | 378 | 63 | 100 | 10 | 7 | 4 | 34 | .265 | 146 | 15 | *14 | .920 |
| 1973–Cedar Rapids† | | Midw. | OF | 26 | 94 | 16 | 28 | 9 | 0 | 1 | 15 | .298 | 42 | 3 | 2 | .957 |
| 1973–Columbus | | South. | OF | 66 | 214 | 27 | 54 | 4 | 2 | 3 | 24 | .252 | 101 | 10 | 9 | .925 |
| 1974–Columbus | | South. | OF | 78 | 257 | 36 | 61 | 4 | 5 | 6 | 31 | .237 | 154 | 7 | 7 | .958 |
| 1975–Iowa | | A.A. | OF | 135 | 518 | 66 | 136 | 21 | 7 | 7 | 54 | .263 | 286 | *21 | 10 | .968 |
| 1975–Houston | | Nat. | OF | 13 | 31 | 3 | 6 | 0 | 0 | 0 | 2 | .194 | 14 | 0 | 0 | 1.000 |
| 1976–Memphis‡ | | Int. | OF | 118 | 496 | 73 | 141 | 23 | 4 | 8 | 54 | .284 | 265 | 12 | 21 | .930 |
| Major League Totals | | | | 13 | 31 | 3 | 6 | 0 | 0 | 0 | 2 | .194 | 14 | 0 | 0 | 1.000 |

†On temporary inactive list, May 25 to June 12, 1973.
‡On temporary inactive list, June 24 to July 14, 1976.

## VASSIE GARDNER, JR.

Born September 17, 1955, at Los Angeles, Calif.
Height, 6.02. Weight, 180.
Throws and bats righthanded.
Hobbies–Reading and bicycling.
Tied for Gulf Coast League lead in double plays by outfielders with 3 in 1973.

| Year | Club | League | Pos. | G. | AB. | R. | H. | 2B. | 3B. | HR. | RBI. | B.A. | PO. | A. | E. | F.A. |
|------|------|--------|------|-----|-----|-----|-----|-----|-----|-----|------|------|-----|-----|-----|------|
| 1973–Sar. Indians | | Gulf C. | OF | 47 | 155 | 27 | 43 | 7 | 1 | 1 | 13 | .277 | 70 | 6 | 6 | .927 |
| 1974–Reno | | Calif. | OF | 116 | 415 | 56 | 107 | 13 | 5 | 2 | 48 | .258 | 204 | 9 | 13 | .942 |

| Year | Club | League | Pos. | G. | AB. | R. | H. | 2B. | 3B. | HR. | RBI. | B.A. | PO. | A. | E. | F.A. |
|------|------|--------|------|----|----|----|----|----|----|----|----|----|----|----|----|----|
| 1975—San Jose | | Calif. | OF | 134 | 506 | 74 | 140 | 15 | ∗13 | 3 | 75 | .277 | 209 | 10 | 4 | .982 |
| 1976—Toledo | | Int. | OF | 62 | 235 | 29 | 55 | 13 | 1 | 1 | 23 | .234 | 107 | 2 | 4 | .965 |
| 1976—Williamsport | | East. | OF | 74 | 270 | 36 | 72 | 14 | 2 | 3 | 42 | .267 | 152 | 3 | 7 | .957 |

Listed on Cleveland Indians' 1977 spring roster.

## MARCUS WAYNE GARLAND
(Known by middle name.)

Born October 26, 1950, at Nashville, Tenn.
Height, 6.00. Weight, 200.
Throws and bats righthanded.
Attended Gulf Coast Junior College, Panama City, Fla.

Pitched 5-0 no-hit victory against Charleston, April 20, 1974.
Led Texas League pitchers in complete games with 20 and tied for lead in shutouts with 6 in 1971.

| Year | Club | League | G. | IP. | W. | L. | Pct. | H. | R. | ER. | SO. | BB. | ERA. |
|------|------|--------|----|----|----|----|----|----|----|----|----|----|----|
| 1969—Miami | | Florida St. | 9 | 63 | 4 | 3 | .571 | 60 | 31 | 23 | 46 | 39 | 3.29 |
| 1970—Dallas-Ft. Worth | | Texas | 21 | 140 | 7 | 10 | .412 | 122 | 63 | 55 | 107 | 63 | 3.54 |
| 1971—Dallas-Ft. Worth | | Texas | 26 | 211 | ∗19 | 5 | ∗.792 | 140 | 43 | 40 | 154 | 50 | ∗1.71 |
| 1972—Rochester | | Int'national | 26 | 152 | 7 | 9 | .438 | 159 | 69 | 64 | 136 | 49 | 3.79 |
| 1973—Rochester† | | Int'national | 25 | 164 | 10 | 11 | .476 | 164 | 79 | 65 | 141 | 69 | 3.57 |
| 1973—Baltimore | | American | 4 | 16 | 0 | 1 | .000 | 14 | 8 | 7 | 10 | 7 | 3.94 |
| 1974—Rochester | | Int'national | 6 | 35 | 2 | 2 | .500 | 36 | 24 | 21 | 16 | 17 | 5.40 |
| 1974—Baltimore | | American | 20 | 91 | 5 | 5 | .500 | 68 | 37 | 30 | 40 | 26 | 2.97 |
| 1975—Baltimore | | American | 29 | 87 | 2 | 5 | .286 | 80 | 37 | 36 | 46 | 31 | 3.72 |
| 1976—Baltimore‡ | | American | 38 | 232 | 20 | 7 | .741 | 224 | 81 | 69 | 113 | 64 | 2.68 |
| Major League Totals | | | 91 | 426 | 27 | 18 | .600 | 386 | 163 | 142 | 209 | 128 | 3.00 |

†On disabled list, May 6 to May 18 and June 18 to June 28, 1973.
‡Played out option year and granted free agency, November 1, 1976; signed as free agent with Cleveland Indians, November 19, 1976.

### CHAMPIONSHIP SERIES RECORD

| Year | Club | League | G. | IP. | W. | L. | Pct. | H. | R. | ER. | SO. | BB. | ERA. |
|------|------|--------|----|----|----|----|----|----|----|----|----|----|----|
| 1974—Baltimore | | American | 1 | ⅔ | 0 | 0 | .000 | 1 | 0 | 0 | 0 | 1 | 0.00 |

## MICHAEL DOUGLAS GARMAN
(Mike)

Born September 16, 1949, at Caldwell, Idaho.
Height, 6.03. Weight, 210.
Throws and bats righthanded.
Hobbies—Hunting and fishing.
Attended College of Idaho, Caldwell, Idaho.
Son of Houston Stephen Garman, former pitcher in Pittsburgh Pirates' organization.
Brother of Steve Garman, former third baseman in San Francisco Giants' organization.

Tied for Carolina League lead in wild pitches with 20 in 1969 and tied for International League lead with 19 in 1970.
Received reported $50,000 bonus to sign with Boston Red Sox, 1967.

| Year | Club | League | G. | IP. | W. | L. | Pct. | H. | R. | ER. | SO. | BB. | ERA. |
|------|------|--------|----|----|----|----|----|----|----|----|----|----|----|
| 1967—Winston-Salem | | Carolina | 6 | 24 | 1 | 3 | .250 | 19 | 20 | 18 | 19 | 41 | 6.75 |
| 1967—Greenville | | W. Carol. | 1 | 1 | 0 | 1 | .000 | 3 | 3 | 2 | 1 | 2 | 18.00 |
| 1968—Greenville | | W. Carol. | 20 | 99 | 5 | 7 | .417 | 92 | 52 | 41 | 61 | 62 | 3.73 |
| 1969—Winston-Salem | | Carolina | 29 | 162 | 10 | 12 | .455 | 127 | 71 | 56 | ∗183 | 89 | 3.11 |
| 1969—Boston | | American | 2 | 12 | 1 | 0 | 1.000 | 13 | 6 | 6 | 10 | 10 | 4.50 |
| 1970—Louisville | | Int'national | 28 | 156 | 7 | 13 | .350 | 154 | 103 | 83 | 127 | 132 | 4.79 |
| 1971—Louisville | | Int'national | 29 | 129 | 8 | 7 | .533 | 124 | 72 | 60 | 128 | 88 | 4.19 |
| 1971—Boston | | American | 3 | 19 | 1 | 1 | .500 | 15 | 8 | 8 | 6 | 9 | 3.79 |
| 1972—Louisville | | Int'national | 39 | 149 | 11 | 9 | .550 | 139 | 74 | 70 | 118 | 69 | 4.23 |
| 1972—Boston | | American | 3 | 3 | 0 | 1 | .000 | 4 | 4 | 4 | 1 | 2 | 12.00 |
| 1973—Boston† | | American | 12 | 22 | 0 | 0 | .000 | 32 | 15 | 13 | 9 | 15 | 5.32 |
| 1974—St. Louis | | National | 64 | 82 | 7 | 2 | .778 | 66 | 26 | 24 | 45 | 27 | 2.63 |
| 1975—St. Louis‡ | | National | 66 | 79 | 3 | 8 | .273 | 73 | 31 | 21 | 48 | 48 | 2.39 |
| 1976—Chicago§ | | National | 47 | 76 | 2 | 4 | .333 | 79 | 48 | 42 | 37 | 35 | 4.97 |
| American League Totals | | | 20 | 56 | 2 | 3 | .500 | 64 | 33 | 31 | 26 | 36 | 4.98 |
| National League Totals | | | 177 | 237 | 12 | 14 | .462 | 218 | 105 | 87 | 130 | 110 | 3.30 |
| Major League Totals | | | 197 | 293 | 14 | 16 | .467 | 282 | 138 | 118 | 156 | 146 | 3.62 |

†Traded with Pitchers John Curtis and Lynn McGlothen to St. Louis Cardinals for Pitchers Diego Segui and Reggie Cleveland and Infielder Terry Hughes, December 7, 1973.
‡Traded with a player to be named later to Chicago Cubs for Shortstop Don Kessinger, October 27, 1975; Cubs obtained Infielder Bobby Hrapmann from Cardinals, April 5, 1976, to complete deal.
§Traded with Outfielder-First Baseman Rick Monday to Los Angeles Dodgers for First Baseman-Outfielder Bill Buckner, Shortstop Ivan DeJesus and Pitcher Jeff Albert, January 11, 1977.

---

## DID YOU KNOW —

That in the 1967 All-Star Game, Roberto Clemente struck out four consecutive times?

## PHILIP MASON GARNER
### (Phil)

Born April 30, 1949, at Jefferson City, Tenn.
Height, 5.10. Weight, 180.
Throws and bats righthanded.
Hobbies—Golf, leathercrafts and playing the guitar.
Attended University of Tennessee, Knoxville, Tenn.; received Bachelor
of Science degree in General Business.
Led Pacific Coast League third basemen in double plays with 23 in 1973.
Led American League shortstops in total chances with 865 in 1976.

| Year Club | League | Pos. | G. | AB. | R. | H. | 2B. | 3B. | HR. | RBI. | B.A. | PO. | A. | E. | F.A. |
|---|---|---|---|---|---|---|---|---|---|---|---|---|---|---|---|
| 1971—Burlington..........Midw. | 3B | 116 | 439 | 73 | 122 | 22 | 4 | 11 | 70 | .278 | *122 | 203 | 29 | .918 |
| 1972—Birmingham......South. | 3B | 71 | 264 | 45 | 74 | 10 | 6 | 12 | 40 | .280 | 74 | 116 | 13 | .936 |
| 1972—Iowa..................A.A. | 3B | 70 | 247 | 33 | 60 | 18 | 4 | 9 | 22 | .243 | 50 | 140 | 10 | .950 |
| 1973—Tucson ..............P.C. | *3B-2B | 138 | 516 | 87 | 149 | 23 | 12 | 14 | 73 | .289 | *107 | *270 | *35 | .915 |
| 1973—Oakland ...........Amer. | 3B | 9 | 5 | 0 | 0 | 0 | 0 | 0 | 0 | .000 | 2 | 3 | 0 | 1.000 |
| 1974—Tucson ..............P.C. | 3B-SS | 96 | 388 | 78 | 128 | 29 | 10 | 11 | 51 | .330 | 92 | 182 | 15 | .948 |
| 1974—Oakland ...........Amer. | 3-S-2 | 30 | 28 | 4 | 5 | 1 | 0 | 0 | 1 | .179 | 11 | 24 | 1 | .972 |
| 1975—Oakland ...........Amer. | *2B-SS | ●160 | 488 | 46 | 120 | 21 | 5 | 6 | 54 | .246 | 355 | 427 | *26 | .968 |
| 1976—Oakland† .........Amer. | 2B | 159 | 555 | 54 | 145 | 29 | 12 | 8 | 74 | .261 | 378 | *465 | 22 | .975 |
| Major League Totals ..................... | | 358 | 1076 | 104 | 270 | 51 | 17 | 14 | 129 | .251 | 746 | 919 | 49 | .971 |

†Traded with Infielder Tommy Helms and Pitcher Chris Batton to Pittsburgh Pirates for Pitchers Doc Medich, Dave Giusti, Rick Langford and Doug Bair, Infielder Mitchell Page and Outfielder Tony Armas, March 15, 1977.

### CHAMPIONSHIP SERIES RECORD

| Year Club | League | Pos. | G. | AB. | R. | H. | 2B. | 3B. | HR. | RBI. | B.A. | PO. | A. | E. | F.A. |
|---|---|---|---|---|---|---|---|---|---|---|---|---|---|---|---|
| 1975—Oakland ...........Amer. | 2B | 3 | 5 | 0 | 0 | 0 | 0 | 0 | 0 | .000 | 7 | 4 | 1 | .917 |

### ALL-STAR GAME RECORD

| Year League | Pos. | AB. | R. | H. | 2B. | 3B. | HR. | RBI. | B.A. | PO. | A. | E. | F.A. |
|---|---|---|---|---|---|---|---|---|---|---|---|---|---|
| 1976—American ........................... | 2B | 1 | 0 | 0 | 0 | 0 | 0 | 0 | .000 | 1 | 1 | 0 | 1.000 |

## RALPH ALLEN GARR

Born December 12, 1945, at Monroe, La.
Height, 5.11. Weight, 185.
Throws right and bats lefthanded.
Attended Grambling College, Grambling, La.; received Bachelor of
Science degree in Physical Education.
Tied major league record for most at-bats, extra-inning game, 11, May 4, 1973 (20 innings).
Tied National League record for most consecutive seasons, leading league, triples, 2, 1975.
Major League stolen bases: 1968 (1), 1969 (1), 1970 (5), 1971 (30), 1972 (25), 1973 (35), 1974 (26), 1975 (14), 1976 (14). Total—151.
Led National League in sacrifice hits with 18 in 1971.
Led International League in stolen bases with 63 in 1969 and 39 in 1970.
Tied for Texas League lead in stolen bases with 32 and led outfielders in double plays with 6 in 1968.

| Year Club | League | Pos. | G. | AB. | R. | H. | 2B. | 3B. | HR. | RBI. | B.A. | PO. | A. | E. | F.A. |
|---|---|---|---|---|---|---|---|---|---|---|---|---|---|---|---|
| 1967—Austin ..............Texas | 2B-OF | 58 | 234 | 37 | 64 | 9 | 3 | 3 | 18 | .274 | 103 | 11 | 16 | .930 |
| 1968—Shreveport ........Texas | OF | 127 | 485 | 76 | 142 | 20 | 6 | 2 | 35 | .293 | 222 | 11 | 12 | .951 |
| 1968—Atlanta..............National | PH | 11 | 7 | 3 | 2 | 0 | 0 | 0 | 0 | .286 | 0 | 0 | 0 | .000 |
| 1969—Richmond..........Int. | OF | 106 | 438 | 64 | 144 | 12 | 5 | 2 | 25 | *.329 | 197 | 10 | 9 | .958 |
| 1969—Atlanta..............National | OF | 22 | 27 | 6 | 6 | 1 | 0 | 0 | 2 | .222 | 6 | 0 | 1 | .857 |
| 1970—Richmond..........Int. | OF | 98 | 391 | 83 | 151 | 26 | 3 | 7 | 51 | *.386 | 182 | 7 | 6 | .969 |
| 1970—Atlanta..............National | OF | 37 | 96 | 18 | 27 | 3 | 0 | 0 | 8 | .281 | 43 | 0 | 0 | 1.000 |
| 1971—Atlanta..............National | OF | 154 | 639 | 101 | 219 | 24 | 6 | 9 | 44 | .343 | 315 | 15 | 11 | .968 |
| 1972—Atlanta..............National | OF | 134 | 554 | 87 | 180 | 22 | 0 | 12 | 53 | .325 | 246 | 8 | 10 | .962 |
| 1973—Atlanta..............National | OF | 148 | 668 | 94 | 200 | 32 | 6 | 11 | 55 | .299 | 293 | 9 | 10 | .968 |
| 1974—Atlanta..............National | OF | 143 | 606 | 87 | *214 | 24 | *17 | 11 | 54 | *.353 | 255 | 8 | 9 | .967 |
| 1975—Atlanta†..............National | OF | 151 | 625 | 74 | 174 | 26 | *11 | 6 | 31 | .278 | 298 | 12 | *11 | .966 |
| 1976—Chicago ...........Amer. | OF-DH | 136 | 527 | 63 | 158 | 22 | 6 | 4 | 36 | .300 | 254 | 7 | 6 | .978 |
| American League Totals .............. | | 136 | 527 | 63 | 158 | 22 | 6 | 4 | 36 | .300 | 254 | 7 | 6 | .978 |
| National League Totals .................. | | 800 | 3222 | 470 | 1022 | 132 | 40 | 49 | 247 | .317 | 1456 | 52 | 52 | .967 |
| Major League Totals ..................... | | 936 | 3749 | 533 | 1180 | 154 | 46 | 53 | 283 | .315 | 1710 | 59 | 58 | .968 |

†Traded with Infielder Larvell Blanks to Chicago White Sox for Outfielder Ken Henderson and Pitchers Dick Ruthven and Danny Osborn, December 12, 1975.

### ALL-STAR GAME RECORD

| Year League | Pos. | AB. | R. | H. | 2B. | 3B. | HR. | RBI. | B.A. | PO. | A. | E. | F.A. |
|---|---|---|---|---|---|---|---|---|---|---|---|---|---|
| 1974—National ........................... | PH-OF | 3 | 0 | 0 | 0 | 0 | 0 | 0 | .000 | 0 | 0 | 0 | .000 |

## RONALD WAYNE GARRETT
### (Known by middle name.)

Born December 3, 1947, at Brooksville, Fla.
Height, 6.00. Weight, 175.
Throws right and bats lefthanded.
Hobbies—Fishing and hunting.
Brother of Adrian Garrett, outfielder-catcher with Hiroshima Carp of the Japanese Baseball League, and Jim Garrett, former infielder in Atlanta Braves' organization.

Led Florida State League shortstops in double plays with 66 in 1966.

| Year | Club | League | Pos. | G. | AB. | R. | H. | 2B. | 3B. | HR. | RBI. | B.A. | PO. | A. | E. | F.A. |
|---|---|---|---|---|---|---|---|---|---|---|---|---|---|---|---|---|
| 1965–Sar. Braves | | Fla.Rk. | SS | 43 | 134 | 22 | 36 | 5 | 1 | 0 | 15 | .269 | 65 | 137 | 15 | .931 |
| 1966–W. Palm Beach | Fla.St. | | SS | 129 | 446 | 38 | 89 | 12 | 0 | 3 | 30 | .200 | 208 | 355 | *44 | .928 |
| 1967–Kinston | | Carol. | SS | 56 | 199 | 13 | 49 | 6 | 1 | 2 | 20 | .246 | 98 | 151 | 16 | .940 |
| 1967–W. Palm Beach | Fla.St. | | 2-S-O | 46 | 154 | 23 | 36 | 5 | 1 | 0 | 15 | .234 | 112 | 132 | 11 | .957 |
| 1968–Shreveport† | | Texas | 2B-3B | 131 | 456 | 49 | 109 | 17 | 4 | 4 | 44 | .239 | 218 | 310 | 24 | .957 |
| 1969–New York | | Nat. | 3-2B-SS | 124 | 400 | 38 | 87 | 11 | 3 | 1 | 39 | .218 | 147 | 218 | 11 | .971 |
| 1970–New York | | Nat. | 3-2-SS | 114 | 366 | 74 | 93 | 17 | 4 | 12 | 45 | .254 | 152 | 205 | 12 | .967 |
| 1971–Tidewater‡ | | Int. | SS-3B | 11 | 44 | 9 | 10 | 1 | 0 | 3 | 5 | .227 | 20 | 28 | 1 | .980 |
| 1971–New York | | Nat. | 3B-2B | 56 | 202 | 20 | 43 | 2 | 0 | 1 | 11 | .213 | 48 | 100 | 4 | .974 |
| 1972–New York | | Nat. | 3B-2B | 111 | 298 | 41 | 69 | 13 | 3 | 2 | 29 | .232 | 114 | 188 | 14 | .956 |
| 1973–New York | | Nat. | 3-S-2 | 140 | 504 | 76 | 129 | 20 | 3 | 16 | 58 | .256 | 102 | 313 | 26 | .941 |
| 1974–New York | | Nat. | 3B-SS | 151 | 522 | 55 | 117 | 14 | 3 | 13 | 53 | .224 | 123 | 349 | 20 | .959 |
| 1975–New York§ | | Nat. | 3-S-2 | 107 | 274 | 49 | 73 | 8 | 3 | 6 | 34 | .266 | 65 | 162 | 8 | .966 |
| 1976–N.Y. x-Mont. | | Nat. | 3-2-S | 139 | 428 | 51 | 99 | 12 | 2 | 6 | 37 | .231 | 195 | 314 | 15 | .971 |
| Major League Totals | | | | 942 | 2994 | 404 | 710 | 97 | 21 | 57 | 306 | .237 | 946 | 1849 | 110 | .962 |

†Drafted by New York Mets from Richmond (Atlanta Braves' organization), December 2, 1968.
‡On military list, March 1 through July 6, 1971.
§On supplemental disabled list, May 27 to June 11, 1975.
xTraded with Outfielder Del Unser to Montreal Expos for Outfielders Jim Dwyer and Jose Mangual, July 21, 1976.

### CHAMPIONSHIP SERIES RECORD

| Year | Club | League | Pos. | G. | AB. | R. | H. | 2B. | 3B. | HR. | RBI. | B.A. | PO. | A. | E. | F.A. |
|---|---|---|---|---|---|---|---|---|---|---|---|---|---|---|---|---|
| 1969–New York | | Nat. | 3B | 3 | 13 | 3 | 5 | 2 | 0 | 1 | 3 | .385 | 1 | 6 | 0 | 1.000 |
| 1973–New York | | Nat. | 3B | 5 | 23 | 1 | 2 | 1 | 0 | 0 | 1 | .087 | 4 | 6 | 1 | .909 |
| Championship Series Totals | | | | 8 | 36 | 4 | 7 | 3 | 0 | 1 | 4 | .194 | 5 | 12 | 1 | .944 |

### WORLD SERIES RECORD

Tied World Series record for most times struck out, 7-game series, 11, 1973.

| Year | Club | League | Pos. | G. | AB. | R. | H. | 2B. | 3B. | HR. | RBI. | B.A. | PO. | A. | E. | F.A. |
|---|---|---|---|---|---|---|---|---|---|---|---|---|---|---|---|---|
| 1969–New York | | Nat. | 3B | 2 | 1 | 0 | 0 | 0 | 0 | 0 | 0 | .000 | 1 | 0 | 1 | .500 |
| 1973–New York | | Nat. | 3B | 7 | 30 | 4 | 5 | 0 | 0 | 2 | 2 | .167 | 4 | 19 | 3 | .885 |
| World Series Totals | | | | 9 | 31 | 4 | 5 | 0 | 0 | 2 | 2 | .161 | 5 | 19 | 4 | .857 |

## STEVEN PATRICK GARVEY
## (Steve)

Born December 22, 1948, at Tampa, Fla.
Height, 5.10. Weight, 195.
Throws and bats righthanded.
Hobby–Golf.
Attended Michigan State University, East Lansing, Mich.

Tied following major league records: most games, first baseman, season–162, 1976; most unassisted double plays, first baseman, game–2, August 31, 1976.
Established National League record for fewest errors, first baseman, season (1,500 + total chances)–3, 1976.
Led National League first basemen in total chances with 1606 in 1974 and 1585 in 1975.
Led Pioneer League in total bases with 151, led third basemen in double plays with 10 and tied for league lead in sacrifice flies with 4 in 1968.
Named Most Valuable Player in National League, 1974.
Named first baseman on THE SPORTING NEWS National League All-Star Team, 1974 and 1975.
Named first baseman on THE SPORTING NEWS National League All-Star fielding team, 1974, 1975 and 1976.

| Year | Club | League | Pos. | G. | AB. | R. | H. | 2B. | 3B. | HR. | RBI. | B.A. | PO. | A. | E. | F.A. |
|---|---|---|---|---|---|---|---|---|---|---|---|---|---|---|---|---|
| 1968–Ogden | | Pion. | 3B | 62 | 216 | 49 | 73 | 12 | 3 | *20 | *59 | .338 | *51 | *109 | *23 | .874 |
| 1969–Albuquerque | | Texas | 3B-1B | 83 | 316 | 51 | 118 | 18 | 2 | 14 | 85 | .373 | 348 | 86 | 20 | .956 |
| 1969–Los Angeles | | Nat. | PH | 3 | 3 | 0 | 1 | 0 | 0 | 0 | 0 | .333 | 0 | 0 | 0 | .000 |
| 1970–Spokane | | P.C. | *3-2-O | 95 | 376 | 71 | 120 | 26 | 5 | 15 | 87 | .319 | 103 | 178 | *26 | .915 |
| 1970–Los Angeles | | Nat. | 3B-2B | 34 | 93 | 8 | 25 | 5 | 0 | 1 | 6 | .269 | 23 | 59 | 5 | .943 |
| 1971–Los Angeles† | | Nat. | 3B | 81 | 225 | 27 | 51 | 12 | 1 | 7 | 26 | .227 | 53 | 161 | 14 | .939 |
| 1972–Los Angeles | | Nat. | *3B-1B | 96 | 294 | 36 | 79 | 14 | 2 | 9 | 30 | .269 | 104 | 189 | *28 | .913 |
| 1973–Los Angeles | | Nat. | 1B-OF | 114 | 349 | 37 | 106 | 17 | 3 | 8 | 50 | .304 | 731 | 27 | 7 | .991 |
| 1974–Los Angeles | | Nat. | 1B | 156 | 642 | 95 | 200 | 32 | 3 | 21 | 111 | .312 | *1536 | 62 | 8 | .995 |
| 1975–Los Angeles | | Nat. | 1B | 160 | 659 | 85 | 210 | 38 | 6 | 18 | 95 | .319 | *1500 | 77 | 8 | *.995 |
| 1976–Los Angeles | | Nat. | 1B | 162 | 631 | 85 | 200 | 37 | 4 | 13 | 80 | .317 | *1583 | 67 | 3 | *.998 |
| Major League Totals | | | | 806 | 2896 | 373 | 872 | 155 | 19 | 77 | 398 | .301 | 5530 | 642 | 73 | .988 |

†On disabled list, June 23 to July 26, 1971.

### CHAMPIONSHIP SERIES RECORD

| Year | Club | League | Pos. | G. | AB. | R. | H. | 2B. | 3B. | HR. | RBI. | B.A. | PO. | A. | E. | F.A. |
|---|---|---|---|---|---|---|---|---|---|---|---|---|---|---|---|---|
| 1974–Los Angeles | | Nat. | 1B | 4 | 18 | 4 | 7 | 1 | 0 | 2 | 5 | .389 | 40 | 2 | 1 | .977 |

### WORLD SERIES RECORD

Established World Series record for most singles, 5-game series, 8, in 1974.

| Year | Club | League | Pos. | G. | AB. | R. | H. | 2B. | 3B. | HR. | RBI. | B.A. | PO. | A. | E. | F.A. |
|---|---|---|---|---|---|---|---|---|---|---|---|---|---|---|---|---|
| 1974–Los Angeles | | Nat. | 1B | 5 | 21 | 2 | 8 | 0 | 0 | 0 | 1 | .381 | 34 | 3 | 0 | 1.000 |

| Year | League | Pos. | AB. | R. | H. | 2B. | 3B. | HR. | RBI. | B.A. | PO. | A. | E. | F.A. |
|------|--------|------|-----|----|----|-----|-----|-----|------|------|-----|----|----|------|
| 1974–National | | 1B | 4 | 1 | 2 | 1 | 0 | 0 | 1 | .500 | 6 | 2 | 0 | 1.000 |
| 1975–National | | 1B | 3 | 1 | 2 | 0 | 0 | 1 | 1 | .667 | 4 | 1 | 0 | 1.000 |
| 1976–National | | 1B | 3 | 1 | 1 | 0 | 1 | 0 | 1 | .333 | 6 | 0 | 0 | 1.000 |
| All-Star Game Totals | | | 10 | 3 | 5 | 1 | 1 | 1 | 3 | .500 | 16 | 3 | 0 | 1.000 |

## THEODORE JARED GARVIN
### (Jerry)

Born October 21, 1955, at Oakland, Calif.
Height, 6.03. Weight, 195.
Throws and bats lefthanded.
Hobbies–Swimming and Music.

Led California League in complete games with 17, and tied for lead in shutouts with 3 in 1975.

| Year | Club | League | G. | IP. | W. | L. | Pct. | H. | R. | ER. | SO. | BB. | ERA. |
|------|------|--------|----|-----|----|----|------|----|----|-----|-----|-----|------|
| 1974–Wisconsin Rapids | | Midwest | 27 | 163 | 14 | 7 | .667 | 168 | 82 | 68 | 138 | 44 | 3.75 |
| 1975–Reno | | California | 25 | *201 | *17 | 5 | *.773 | 188 | 77 | 57 | 129 | 56 | 2.55 |
| 1976–Orlando | | Southern | 25 | 178 | 11 | 9 | .550 | 163 | 73 | 67 | 91 | 50 | 3.39 |
| 1976–Tacoma† | | P. Coast | 7 | 55 | 0 | 4 | .000 | 52 | 27 | 25 | 36 | 22 | 4.09 |

†Selected by Toronto Blue Jays from Minnesota Twins in expansion draft, November 5, 1976.

## CLARENCE EDWIN GASTON
### (Cito)

Born March 17, 1944, at San Antonio, Tex.
Height, 6.03. Weight, 210.
Throws and bats righthanded.
Hobby–All sports.

Led New York-Pennsylvania League in total bases with 255 in 1966.

| Year | Club | League | Pos. | G. | AB. | R. | H. | 2B. | 3B. | HR. | RBI. | B.A. | PO. | A. | E. | F.A. |
|------|------|--------|------|----|-----|----|----|-----|-----|-----|------|------|-----|----|----|------|
| 1964–Binghamton | | NYP | OF | 11 | 21 | 1 | 5 | 2 | 0 | 1 | 4 | .238 | 8 | 0 | 1 | .889 |
| 1964–Greenville | | W. Car. | OF | 49 | 165 | 15 | 38 | 6 | 3 | 0 | 16 | .230 | 62 | 5 | 5 | .931 |
| 1965–W. Palm Beach | | Fla. St. | OF | 70 | 202 | 14 | 38 | 5 | 3 | 0 | 9 | .188 | 111 | 4 | 5 | .958 |
| 1966–Batavia | | NYP | OF | 114 | 433 | 84 | 143 | 18 | 5 | *28 | *104 | .330 | 214 | 12 | 13 | .946 |
| 1966–Austin | | Texas | OF | 4 | 10 | 2 | 3 | 1 | 1 | 0 | 4 | .300 | 10 | 0 | 0 | 1.000 |
| 1967–Austin | | Texas | OF | 136 | 505 | 72 | 154 | 24 | 6 | 10 | 70 | .305 | 274 | 8 | 12 | .959 |
| 1967–Atlanta | | Nat. | OF | 9 | 25 | 1 | 3 | 0 | 1 | 0 | 1 | .120 | 7 | 1 | 2 | .800 |
| 1968–Richmond | | Int. | OF | 21 | 71 | 9 | 17 | 4 | 0 | 2 | 8 | .239 | 43 | 0 | 0 | 1.000 |
| 1968–Shreveport† | | Texas | OF | 96 | 340 | 49 | 95 | 15 | 4 | 6 | 57 | .279 | 203 | 3 | 9 | .958 |
| 1969–San Diego | | Nat. | OF | 129 | 391 | 20 | 90 | 11 | 7 | 2 | 28 | .230 | 243 | 12 | 11 | .959 |
| 1970–San Diego | | Nat. | OF | 146 | 584 | 92 | 186 | 26 | 9 | 29 | 93 | .318 | 310 | 7 | 8 | .975 |
| 1971–San Diego | | Nat. | OF | 141 | 518 | 57 | 118 | 13 | 9 | 17 | 61 | .228 | 271 | 8 | 5 | .982 |
| 1972–San Diego‡ | | Nat. | OF | 111 | 379 | 30 | 102 | 14 | 0 | 7 | 44 | .269 | 158 | 10 | 4 | .977 |
| 1973–San Diego | | Nat. | OF | 133 | 476 | 51 | 119 | 18 | 4 | 16 | 57 | .250 | 198 | 16 | ●12 | .947 |
| 1974–San Diego§ | | Nat. | OF | 106 | 267 | 19 | 57 | 11 | 0 | 6 | 33 | .213 | 119 | 7 | 1 | .992 |
| 1975–Atlanta | | Nat. | OF-1B | 64 | 141 | 17 | 34 | 4 | 0 | 6 | 15 | .241 | 80 | 2 | 3 | .965 |
| 1976–Atlanta | | Nat. | OF-1B | 69 | 134 | 15 | 39 | 4 | 0 | 4 | 25 | .291 | 58 | 2 | 1 | .984 |
| Major League Totals | | | | 908 | 2915 | 302 | 748 | 101 | 30 | 87 | 357 | .257 | 1444 | 65 | 47 | .970 |

†Recalled by Atlanta Braves; selected by San Diego Padres from Atlanta in expansion draft, October 14, 1968.
‡On supplemental disabled list, May 17 to June 2, 1972.
§Traded to Atlanta Braves for Pitcher Danny Frisella, November 7, 1974.

### ALL-STAR GAME RECORD

| Year | League | Pos. | AB. | R. | H. | 2B. | 3B. | HR. | RBI. | B.A. | PO. | A. | E. | F.A. |
|------|--------|------|-----|----|----|-----|-----|-----|------|------|-----|----|----|------|
| 1970–National | | OF | 2 | 0 | 0 | 0 | 0 | 0 | 0 | .000 | 2 | 0 | 0 | 1.000 |

## JOHN DAVID GEISEL
### (Dave)

Born January 18, 1955, at Windber, Pa.
Height, 6.03. Weight, 210.
Throws and bats lefthanded.
Hobbies–Cooking and listening to music.

| Year | Club | League | G. | IP. | W. | L. | Pct. | H. | R. | ER. | SO. | BB. | ERA. |
|------|------|--------|----|-----|----|----|------|----|----|-----|-----|-----|------|
| 1974–Midland | | Texas | 24 | 150 | 12 | 7 | .632 | 170 | 72 | 63 | 92 | 37 | 3.78 |
| 1975–Midland | | Texas | 35 | 132 | 8 | 5 | .615 | 149 | 67 | 59 | 75 | 44 | 4.02 |
| 1976–Midland | | Texas | 20 | 107 | 5 | 8 | .385 | 114 | 59 | 44 | 59 | 45 | 3.70 |
| 1976–Wichita | | Am. Assoc. | 9 | 50 | 2 | 4 | .333 | 50 | 33 | 28 | 27 | 25 | 5.04 |

Listed on Chicago Cubs' 1977 spring roster.

---

**DID YOU KNOW —**
That Carl Hubbell of the New York Giants pitched 20 innings in the 1933 World Series and had an earned-run average of 0.00?

# FRANKIE LEONARD GEORGE

Born June 16, 1953, at San Diego, Calif.
Height, 6.00. Weight, 190.
Throws and bats righthanded.
Hobbies—Embroidery and playing the guitar.

| Year Club League | Pos. | G. | AB. | R. | H. | 2B. | 3B. | HR. | RBI. | B.A. | PO. | A. | E. | F.A. |
|---|---|---|---|---|---|---|---|---|---|---|---|---|---|---|
| 1971—Idaho Falls........Pion. | OF | 41 | 149 | 25 | 44 | 10 | 2 | 4 | 19 | .295 | 38 | 4 | 4 | .913 |
| 1972—Quad Cities ......Midw. | OF | 101 | 392 | 71 | 119 | 14 | 7 | 15 | 53 | .304 | 203 | 8 | *20 | .913 |
| 1973—El Paso ...........Texas | OF | 121 | 455 | 78 | 120 | 22 | 4 | 10 | 62 | .264 | 158 | 9 | 11 | .938 |
| 1974—El Paso ...........Texas | OF | 40 | 157 | 27 | 61 | 16 | 1 | 2 | 29 | .389 | 50 | 5 | 4 | .932 |
| 1974—Salt Lake City ..P.C. | OF | 76 | 265 | 38 | 79 | 16 | 1 | 5 | 35 | .298 | 82 | 5 | 11 | .888 |
| 1975—Salt Lake City ..P.C. | OF-1B | 105 | 331 | 61 | 84 | 13 | 1 | 8 | 47 | .254 | 140 | 7 | 10 | .936 |
| 1976—Salt Lake City ..P.C. | OF-2B | 113 | 421 | 79 | 124 | 22 | 3 | 12 | 74 | .295 | 192 | 8 | 5 | .976 |

Listed on California Angels' 1977 spring roster.

# CESAR FRANCISCO GERONIMO

Name pronounced juh-RON-uh-moh.

Born March 11, 1948, at El Seibo, Dominican Republic.
Height, 6.02. Weight, 164.
Throws and bats lefthanded.

Led National League outfielders in total chances with 423 and double plays with 5 in 1975.
Named as outfielder on THE SPORTING NEWS National League All-Star fielding team, 1974, 1975 and 1976.

| Year Club League | Pos. | G. | AB. | R. | H. | 2B. | 3B. | HR. | RBI. | B.A. | PO. | A. | E. | F.A. |
|---|---|---|---|---|---|---|---|---|---|---|---|---|---|---|
| 1967—Oneonta† .........NYP | OF | 10 | 1 | 1 | 0 | 0 | 0 | 1 | .100 | 2 | 0 | 1 | .667 | |
| 1967—Johnson City ....Appal. | OF-P | 18 | 14 | 1 | 1 | 0 | 0 | 0 | 0 | .071 | 5 | 1 | 0 | 1.000 |
| 1968—Ft. Lauderdale‡ Fla. St. | OF | 109 | 324 | 35 | 63 | 11 | 5 | 1 | 27 | .194 | 186 | 17 | 4 | .981 |
| 1969—Houston ............Nat. | OF | 28 | 8 | 8 | 2 | 1 | 0 | 0 | 0 | .250 | 1 | 0 | 0 | 1.000 |
| 1970—Columbus .........South. | OF | 74 | 264 | 26 | 71 | 9 | 4 | 0 | 21 | .269 | 113 | 8 | 2 | .984 |
| 1970—Houston ............Nat. | OF | 47 | 37 | 5 | 9 | 0 | 0 | 0 | 2 | .243 | 23 | 0 | 2 | .920 |
| 1971—Houston§ .........Nat. | OF | 94 | 82 | 13 | 18 | 2 | 2 | 1 | 6 | .220 | 42 | 1 | 1 | .977 |
| 1972—Cincinnati.........Nat. | OF | 120 | 255 | 32 | 70 | 9 | 7 | 4 | 29 | .275 | 150 | 10 | 3 | .982 |
| 1973—Cincinnati.........Nat. | OF | 139 | 324 | 35 | 68 | 14 | 3 | 4 | 33 | .210 | 243 | 9 | 2 | .992 |
| 1974—Cincinnati.........Nat. | OF | 150 | 474 | 73 | 133 | 17 | 8 | 7 | 54 | .281 | 355 | 13 | 5 | .987 |
| 1975—Cincinnati.........Nat. | OF | 148 | 501 | 69 | 129 | 25 | 5 | 6 | 53 | .257 | *408 | 12 | 3 | .993 |
| 1976—Cincinnati.........Nat. | OF | 149 | 486 | 59 | 149 | 24 | 11 | 2 | 49 | .307 | 386 | 4 | 6 | .985 |
| Major League Totals .................... | | 875 | 2167 | 294 | 578 | 92 | 36 | 24 | 226 | .267 | 1608 | 49 | 22 | .987 |

†On disabled list, April 17 through June 20.
‡Drafted by Houston Astros from Syracuse (New York Yankees' organization), December 2, 1968.
§Traded with Second Baseman Joe Morgan, Infielder Denis Menke, Pitcher Jack Billingham and Outfielder Ed Armbrister (latter assigned from Oklahoma City to Indianapolis) to Cincinnati Reds for First Baseman Lee May, Second Baseman Tommy Helms and Infielder Jim Stewart, November 29, 1971.

PITCHING RECORD

| Year Club League | G. | IP. | W. | L. | Pct. | H. | R. | ER. | SO. | BB. | ERA. |
|---|---|---|---|---|---|---|---|---|---|---|---|
| 1967—Johnson City .....................Ap'lachian | 1 | 2 | 0 | 0 | .000 | 3 | 4 | 2 | 1 | 2 | 9.00 |

CHAMPIONSHIP SERIES RECORD

| Year Club League | Pos. | G. | AB. | R. | H. | 2B. | 3B. | HR. | RBI. | B.A. | PO. | A. | E. | F.A. |
|---|---|---|---|---|---|---|---|---|---|---|---|---|---|---|
| 1972—Cincinnati.........Nat. | OF | 5 | 20 | 2 | 2 | 0 | 0 | 1 | 1 | .100 | 11 | 1 | 0 | 1.000 |
| 1973—Cincinnati.........Nat. | OF | 4 | 15 | 0 | 1 | 0 | 0 | 0 | 0 | .067 | 11 | 1 | 0 | 1.000 |
| 1975—Cincinnati.........Nat. | OF | 3 | 10 | 0 | 0 | 0 | 0 | 0 | 1 | .000 | 13 | 0 | 0 | 1.000 |
| 1976—Cincinnati.........Nat. | OF | 3 | 11 | 0 | 2 | 0 | 1 | 0 | 2 | .182 | 10 | 0 | 0 | 1.000 |
| Championship Series Totals ............ | | 15 | 56 | 2 | 5 | 0 | 1 | 1 | 4 | .089 | 45 | 2 | 0 | 1.000 |

WORLD SERIES RECORD

| Year Club League | Pos. | G. | AB. | R. | H. | 2B. | 3B. | HR. | RBI. | B.A. | PO. | A. | E. | F.A. |
|---|---|---|---|---|---|---|---|---|---|---|---|---|---|---|
| 1972—Cincinnati.........Nat. | OF | 7 | 19 | 1 | 3 | 0 | 0 | 0 | 3 | .158 | 9 | 0 | 0 | 1.000 |
| 1975—Cincinnati.........Nat. | OF | 7 | 25 | 3 | 7 | 0 | 1 | 2 | 3 | .280 | 23 | 1 | 0 | 1.000 |
| 1976—Cincinnati.........Nat. | OF | 4 | 13 | 3 | 4 | 2 | 0 | 0 | 1 | .308 | 12 | 0 | 1 | .923 |
| World Series Totals ....................... | | 18 | 57 | 7 | 14 | 2 | 1 | 2 | 7 | .246 | 44 | 1 | 1 | .978 |

# JAMES LESLIE GIDEON
## (Jim)

Born September 26, 1953, at Taylor, Tex.
Height, 6.03. Weight, 195.
Throws and bats righthanded.
Attended University of Texas at Austin, Austin, Tex.

| Year Club League | G. | IP. | W. | L. | Pct. | H. | R. | ER. | SO. | BB. | ERA. |
|---|---|---|---|---|---|---|---|---|---|---|---|
| 1975—Sarasota Rangers ...............Gulf Coast | 2 | 16 | 2 | 0 | 1.000 | 3 | 0 | 0 | 14 | 1 | 0.00 |
| 1975—Spokane ............................P. Coast | 11 | 58 | 4 | 5 | .444 | 58 | 47 | 43 | 28 | 42 | 6.67 |
| 1975—Texas ................................American | 1 | 6 | 0 | 0 | .000 | 7 | 6 | 5 | 2 | 5 | 7.50 |
| 1976—Sac.†-Tac. ........................P. Coast | 27 | 146 | 5 | 9 | .357 | 161 | 115 | 89 | 69 | *120 | 5.49 |
| Major League Totals ............................. | 1 | 6 | 0 | 0 | .000 | 7 | 6 | 5 | 2 | 5 | 7.50 |

†Traded with Pitcher Bill Singer, Infielders Roy Smalley and Mike Cubbage, and a reported $250,000 to Minnesota Twins for Pitcher Bert Blyleven and Shortstop Danny Thompson, June 1, 1976.
Listed on Minnesota Twins' 1977 spring roster.

## RODNEY JOE GILBREATH
### (Rod)

Born September 24, 1952, at Laurel, Miss.
Height, 6.02. Weight, 180.
Throws and bats righthanded.
Hobbies—Hunting, fishing, swimming and collecting antiques.
Attended Jones County Junior College, Ellisville, Miss.
Led National League in sacrifice hits with 20 in 1976.
Led Southern League in stolen bases with 45 in 1972.
Named Western Carolinas League Most Valuable Player, 1971.

| Year Club | League | Pos. | G. | AB. | R. | H. | 2B. | 3B. | HR. | RBI. | B.A. | PO. | A. | E. | F.A. |
|---|---|---|---|---|---|---|---|---|---|---|---|---|---|---|---|
| 1970—Magic Valley | ....Pion. | SS | 56 | 198 | 37 | 55 | 7 | 1 | 9 | 35 | .278 | 62 | 133 | 30 | .867 |
| 1971—Greenwood | ........W. Car. | *3-S | 117 | 433 | 89 | 134 | 19 | 8 | 13 | 59 | .309 | 87 | 229 | *27 | .921 |
| 1972—Savannah | .........South. | *3B-S | 117 | 451 | 79 | 125 | 24 | 5 | 10 | 61 | .277 | *106 | *225 | ●27 | .925 |
| 1972—Atlanta | .............Nat. | 2B-3B | 18 | 38 | 2 | 9 | 1 | 0 | 0 | 1 | .237 | 16 | 26 | 1 | .977 |
| 1973—Richmond† | ........Int. | 3-S-O-2 | 65 | 221 | 29 | 54 | 2 | 3 | 0 | 17 | .244 | 83 | 108 | 2 | .990 |
| 1973—Atlanta | .............Nat. | 3B | 29 | 74 | 10 | 21 | 2 | 1 | 0 | 2 | .284 | 16 | 32 | 2 | .960 |
| 1974—Richmond | ..........Int. | 2B | 138 | 441 | 71 | 112 | 13 | 4 | 5 | 42 | .254 | 335 | 361 | 12 | *.983 |
| 1974—Atlanta | .............Nat. | 2B | 3 | 6 | 2 | 2 | 0 | 0 | 0 | 0 | .333 | 5 | 6 | 0 | 1.000 |
| 1975—Atlanta | .............Nat. | 2-3-S | 90 | 202 | 24 | 49 | 3 | 1 | 2 | 16 | .243 | 127 | 141 | 6 | .978 |
| 1976—Atlanta | .............Nat. | 2-3-S | 116 | 383 | 57 | 96 | 11 | 8 | 1 | 32 | .251 | 245 | 314 | 17 | .970 |
| Major League Totals | ..................... | | 256 | 703 | 95 | 177 | 17 | 10 | 3 | 51 | .252 | 409 | 519 | 26 | .973 |

†On disabled list, August 14 to September 4, 1973.

## DAVID JOHN GIUSTI, JR.

Name pronounced JUST-ee.

### (Dave)

Born November 27, 1939, at Seneca Falls, N. Y.
Height, 5.11½. Weight, 200.
Throws and bats righthanded.
Hobbies—Cooking and golf.
Attended Syracuse University, Syracuse, N. Y.; received Bachelor of Arts degree
and Master's degree in Education.
Established National League record for most saves, lifetime, 133, 1976.
Tied National League record for most wild pitches, inning (3), September 2, 1967 (first inning.)
Led National League in saves with 30 in 1971.
Led Pacific Coast League in shutouts with 7 in 1963.
Named by THE SPORTING NEWS as National League Fireman of the Year, 1971.
Received reported $35,000 bonus to sign with Houston Colts, 1961.

| Year Club | League | G. | IP. | W. | L. | Pct. | H. | R. | ER. | SO. | BB. | ERA. |
|---|---|---|---|---|---|---|---|---|---|---|---|---|
| 1961—Jacksonville | .........................Sally | 14 | 118 | 7 | 7 | .500 | 87 | 40 | 30 | 82 | 42 | 2.29 |
| 1961—Houston | .............................Am. Assoc. | 3 | 18 | 2 | 0 | 1.000 | 23 | 6 | 6 | 14 | 3 | 3.00 |
| 1962—Houston | .............................National | 22 | 74 | 2 | 3 | .400 | 82 | 49 | 46 | 43 | 30 | 5.59 |
| 1962—Oklahoma City | ...................Am. Assoc. | 6 | 48 | 2 | 3 | .400 | 40 | 24 | 23 | 32 | 26 | 4.31 |
| 1963—Oklahoma City | ...................P. Coast | 32 | 202 | 13 | 11 | .542 | 181 | 77 | 61 | 165 | 67 | 2.72 |
| 1964—Oklahoma City | ...................P. Coast | 25 | 149 | 10 | 6 | .625 | 151 | 72 | 64 | 127 | 65 | 3.87 |
| 1964—Houston | .............................National | 8 | 26 | 0 | 0 | .000 | 24 | 10 | 9 | 16 | 8 | 3.12 |
| 1965—Houston | .............................National | 38 | 131 | 8 | 7 | .533 | 132 | 67 | 63 | 92 | 46 | 4.33 |
| 1966—Houston | .............................National | 34 | 210 | 15 | 14 | .517 | 215 | 112 | 98 | 131 | 54 | 4.20 |
| 1967—Houston | .............................National | 37 | 222 | 11 | 15 | .423 | 231 | 114 | 103 | 157 | 58 | 4.18 |
| 1968—Houston†‡§ | .............................National | 37 | 251 | 11 | 14 | .440 | 226 | 95 | 89 | 186 | 67 | 3.19 |
| 1969—St. Louis‡‡ | .............................National | 22 | 100 | 3 | 7 | .300 | 96 | 46 | 40 | 62 | 37 | 3.60 |
| 1970—Pittsburgh | ..............................National | 66 | 103 | 9 | 3 | .750 | 98 | 38 | 35 | 85 | 39 | 3.06 |
| 1971—Pittsburgh | ..............................National | 58 | 86 | 5 | 6 | .455 | 79 | 31 | 28 | 55 | 31 | 2.93 |
| 1972—Pittsburgh | ..............................National | 54 | 75 | 7 | 4 | .636 | 59 | 18 | 16 | 54 | 20 | 1.92 |
| 1973—Pittsburgh | ..............................National | 67 | 99 | 9 | 2 | .818 | 89 | 31 | 26 | 64 | 37 | 2.36 |
| 1974—Pittsburgh | ..............................National | 64 | 106 | 7 | 5 | .583 | 101 | 43 | 39 | 53 | 40 | 3.31 |
| 1975—Pittsburgh | ..............................National | 61 | 92 | 5 | 5 | .556 | 79 | 38 | 30 | 38 | 42 | 2.93 |
| 1976—Pittsburgh x | .......................National | 40 | 58 | 5 | 5 | .556 | 59 | 31 | 28 | 24 | 27 | 4.34 |
| Major League Totals | .............................. | 608 | 1633 | 97 | 88 | .524 | 1570 | 723 | 650 | 1060 | 536 | 3.58 |

†Traded with Catcher Dave Adlesh to St. Louis Cardinals for Catchers Tommie Smith (transferred from Tulsa to Oklahoma City) and John Edwards, October 11, 1968.

‡Selected by San Diego Padres from St. Louis Cardinals in expansion draft, October 14, 1968.

§Traded by San Diego Padres to St. Louis Cardinals for Third Baseman Ed Spezio, Outfielder Ron Davis, Catcher Dan Breeden and Pitcher Phil Knuckles, December 3, 1968.

‡‡Traded with Catcher Dave Ricketts to Pittsburgh Pirates for First Baseman-Outfielder Carl Taylor and Outfielder Frank Vanzin (transferred from York to Tulsa), October 21, 1969. On disabled list, May 25 through June 15.

xOn disabled list, June 9 through July 15, 1976; traded with Pitchers Doc Medich, Rick Langford and Doug Bair, and Outfielders Mitchell Page and Tony Armas to Oakland A's for Infielders Phil Garner and Tommy Helms, and Pitcher Chris Batton, March 15, 1977.

### CHAMPIONSHIP SERIES RECORD

| Year Club | League | G. | IP. | W. | L. | Pct. | H. | R. | ER. | SO. | BB. | ERA. |
|---|---|---|---|---|---|---|---|---|---|---|---|---|
| 1970—Pittsburgh | ...........................National | 2 | 2⅓ | 0 | 0 | .000 | 3 | 1 | 1 | 1 | 1 | 3.85 |
| 1971—Pittsburgh | ...........................National | 4 | 5⅓ | 0 | 0 | .000 | 1 | 0 | 0 | 3 | 2 | 0.00 |
| 1972—Pittsburgh | ...........................National | 3 | 2⅔ | 0 | 1 | .000 | 5 | 2 | 2 | 3 | 0 | 6.75 |

| Year Club | League | G. | IP. | W. | L. | Pct. | H. | R. | ER. | SO. | BB. | ERA. |
|---|---|---|---|---|---|---|---|---|---|---|---|---|
| 1974—Pittsburgh | National | 3 | 3⅓ | 0 | 1 | .000 | 13 | 8 | 8 | 1 | 5 | 21.60 |
| 1975—Pittsburgh | National | 1 | 1⅓ | 0 | 0 | .000 | 0 | 0 | 0 | 1 | 0 | 0.00 |
| Championship Series Totals | | 13 | 15 | 0 | 2 | .000 | 22 | 11 | 11 | 9 | 8 | 6.60 |

### WORLD SERIES RECORD

| Year Club | League | G. | IP. | W. | L. | Pct. | H. | R. | ER. | SO. | BB. | ERA. |
|---|---|---|---|---|---|---|---|---|---|---|---|---|
| 1971—Pittsburgh | National | 3 | 5⅓ | 0 | 0 | .000 | 3 | 0 | 0 | 4 | 2 | 0.00 |

### ALL-STAR GAME RECORD

| Year League | IP. | W. | L. | Pct. | H. | R. | ER. | SO. | BB. | ERA. |
|---|---|---|---|---|---|---|---|---|---|---|
| 1973—National | 1 | 0 | 0 | .000 | 0 | 0 | 0 | 0 | 0 | 0.00 |

## EDWARD PAUL GLYNN
## (Ed)

Born June 3, 1953, at Flushing, N. Y.
Height, 6.02. Weight, 180.
Throws left and bats righthanded.
Hobby—All sports.
Attended York College, Jamaica, N. Y.
Pitched seven-inning 3-0 no-hit victory against Iowa, July 15, 1976.

| Year Club | League | G. | IP. | W. | L. | Pct. | H. | R. | ER. | SO. | BB. | ERA. |
|---|---|---|---|---|---|---|---|---|---|---|---|---|
| 1972—Lakeland | Florida St. | 15 | 57 | 1 | 4 | .200 | 52 | 30 | 28 | 54 | 50 | 4.42 |
| 1972—Bristol | Ap'alachian | 11 | 57 | 4 | 2 | .667 | 38 | 35 | 30 | 67 | 46 | 4.74 |
| 1973—Clinton | Midwest | 24 | 135 | 9 | 6 | .600 | 109 | 71 | 68 | 130 | 84 | 4.53 |
| 1974—Clinton | Midwest | 15 | 114 | 8 | 4 | .667 | 104 | 46 | 38 | 104 | 46 | 3.00 |
| 1974—Montgomery | Southern | 9 | 49 | 1 | 4 | .200 | 60 | 44 | 30 | 31 | 29 | 5.51 |
| 1975—Montgomery | Southern | 19 | 127 | 10 | 5 | .667 | 116 | 50 | 44 | 66 | 72 | 3.12 |
| 1975—Evansville | Am. Assoc. | 7 | 40 | 1 | 2 | .333 | 40 | 18 | 11 | 23 | 19 | 2.48 |
| 1975—Detroit | American | 3 | 15 | 0 | 2 | .000 | 11 | 8 | 7 | 8 | 8 | 4.20 |
| 1976—Evansville | Am. Assoc. | 24 | 148 | 9 | 7 | .563 | 146 | 76 | 59 | 92 | 82 | 3.59 |
| 1976—Detroit | American | 5 | 24 | 1 | 3 | .250 | 22 | 18 | 16 | 17 | 20 | 6.00 |
| Major League Totals | | 8 | 39 | 1 | 5 | .167 | 33 | 26 | 23 | 25 | 28 | 5.31 |

## DAVID ALLAN GOLTZ
## (Dave)

Born June 23, 1949, at Pelican Rapids, Minn.
Height, 6.04. Weight, 200.
Throws and bats righthanded.
Hobby—Hunting.
Attended Moorhead State College, Moorhead, Minn.
Pitched seven-inning, 5-0 no-hit victory against Burlington, August 26, 1971.
Led Northern League pitchers in complete games with 12 and tied for lead in games started with 16 in 1968.

| Year Club | League | G. | IP. | W. | L. | Pct. | H. | R. | ER. | SO. | BB. | ERA. |
|---|---|---|---|---|---|---|---|---|---|---|---|---|
| 1967—Sarasota Twins | Gulf Coast | 12 | 72 | •6 | 2 | •.750 | 63 | 23 | 16 | 51 | 14 | •2.00 |
| 1968—St. Cloud | Northern | 16 | •123 | 10 | 3 | .769 | 103 | 39 | 22 | •122 | 29 | 1.61 |
| 1969—Minnesota | American | | | | (In Military Service) | | | | | | | |
| 1970—Charlotte† | Southern | 1 | 2 | 0 | 1 | .000 | 1 | 1 | 0 | 2 | 1 | 0.00 |
| 1970—Orlando | Florida St. | 1 | 6 | 0 | 1 | .000 | 3 | 4 | 4 | 2 | 6 | 6.00 |
| 1971—Orlando | Florida St. | 7 | 53 | 7 | 0 | 1.000 | 49 | 16 | 13 | 34 | 16 | 2.21 |
| 1971—Lynchburg | Carolina | 13 | 87 | 7 | 3 | .700 | 76 | 37 | 32 | 64 | 32 | 3.31 |
| 1972—Tacoma | P. Coast | 19 | 118 | 8 | 8 | .500 | 131 | 65 | 51 | 99 | 42 | 3.89 |
| 1972—Minnesota | American | 15 | 91 | 3 | 3 | .500 | 75 | 30 | 27 | 38 | 26 | 2.67 |
| 1973—Minnesota | American | 32 | 106 | 6 | 4 | .600 | 138 | 68 | 62 | 65 | 32 | 5.26 |
| 1974—Tacoma | P. Coast | 4 | 30 | 3 | 1 | .750 | 25 | 13 | 11 | 26 | 15 | 3.30 |
| 1974—Minnesota | American | 28 | 174 | 10 | 10 | .500 | 192 | 81 | 63 | 89 | 45 | 3.26 |
| 1975—Minnesota | American | 32 | 243 | 14 | 14 | .500 | 235 | 112 | 99 | 128 | 72 | 3.67 |
| 1976—Minnesota | American | 36 | 249 | 14 | 14 | .500 | 239 | 113 | 93 | 133 | 91 | 3.36 |
| Major League Totals | | 143 | 863 | 47 | 45 | .511 | 879 | 404 | 344 | 453 | 266 | 3.59 |

†On disabled list May 26 to June 6 and June 15 to July 13.

## LUIS GOMEZ

Born August 19, 1951, at Guadalajara, Mexico.
Height, 5.09. Weight, 150.
Throws and bats righthanded.
Attended University of California at Los Angeles, Los Angeles, Calif.

| Year Club | League | Pos. | G. | AB. | R. | H. | 2B. | 3B. | HR. | RBI. | B.A. | PO. | A. | E. | F.A. |
|---|---|---|---|---|---|---|---|---|---|---|---|---|---|---|---|
| 1973—Orlando | South. | SS | 76 | 250 | 20 | 56 | 4 | 0 | 0 | 14 | .224 | 105 | 222 | 11 | .967 |
| 1974—Tacoma | P.C. | SS | 12 | 35 | 7 | 8 | 0 | 0 | 0 | 3 | .229 | 17 | 43 | 1 | .984 |
| 1974—Minnesota | Amer. | SS-2B | 82 | 168 | 18 | 35 | 1 | 0 | 0 | 3 | .208 | 97 | 194 | 12 | .960 |
| 1975—Minnesota | Amer. | SS-2B | 89 | 72 | 7 | 10 | 0 | 0 | 0 | 5 | .139 | 55 | 80 | 3 | .978 |
| 1967—Minnesota | Am. | Inf-O-DH | 38 | 57 | 5 | 11 | 1 | 0 | 0 | 3 | .193 | 36 | 58 | 1 | .989 |
| 1976—Tacoma | P.C. | SS-2B | 12 | 32 | 3 | 6 | 1 | 0 | 0 | 0 | .188 | 25 | 34 | 2 | .967 |
| Major League Totals | | | 209 | 297 | 30 | 56 | 2 | 0 | 0 | 11 | .189 | 188 | 332 | 16 | .970 |

## DANIEL DAVID GONZALES
### (Dan)
Born September 30, 1953, at Whittier, Calif.
Height, 6.01. Weight, 195.
Throws right and bats lefthanded.
Attended Fullerton College, Fullerton, Calif.

| Year Club | League | Pos. | G. | AB. | R. | H. | 2B. | 3B. | HR. | RBI. | B.A. | PO. | A. | E. | F.A. |
|---|---|---|---|---|---|---|---|---|---|---|---|---|---|---|---|
| 1972–Rocky Mount | ....Carol. | OF | 65 | 215 | 15 | 51 | 4 | 0 | 0 | 26 | .237 | 100 | 4 | 9 | .920 |
| 1973–Anderson | ....W.C. | OF | 102 | 376 | 39 | 109 | 11 | 2 | 2 | 51 | .290 | 138 | 13 | 3 | .981 |
| 1973–Lakeland | .........Fla. St. | OF | 10 | 20 | 1 | 3 | 0 | 0 | 0 | 0 | .150 | 8 | 0 | 0 | 1.000 |
| 1974–Lakeland† | .........Fla. St. | OF | 101 | 358 | 35 | 93 | 9 | 2 | 4 | 46 | .260 | 161 | 8 | 4 | .977 |
| 1975–Montgomery | ......South. | OF | 123 | 467 | 45 | 123 | 19 | •11 | 10 | 54 | .263 | 181 | 11 | 2 | •.990 |
| 1975–Evansville | ........A.A. | OF | 7 | 27 | 4 | 10 | 0 | 0 | 0 | 2 | .370 | 12 | 0 | 0 | 1.000 |
| 1976–Montgomery | ......South. | OF | 77 | 271 | 26 | 79 | 10 | 3 | 4 | 31 | .292 | 98 | 8 | 2 | .981 |
| 1976–Evansville | ........A.A. | OF | 37 | 108 | 15 | 33 | 6 | 0 | 3 | 14 | .306 | 40 | 1 | 4 | .911 |

†On disabled list, July 1 to July 11, 1974.
Listed on Detroit Tigers' 1977 spring roster.

## JOSE FERNANDO GONZALEZ
(Known by middle name.)
Born June 19, 1950, at Utuado, Puerto Rico.
Height, 5.10. Weight, 170.
Throws and bats righthanded.
Hobbies–Basketball, skin diving and table tennis.
Attended University of Puerto Rico, Rio Piedras, Puerto Rico.
Named Most Valuable Player in Eastern League, 1972.

| Year Club | League | Pos. | G. | AB. | R. | H. | 2B. | 3B. | HR. | RBI. | B.A. | PO. | A. | E. | F.A. |
|---|---|---|---|---|---|---|---|---|---|---|---|---|---|---|---|
| 1969–Clinton† | ...........Midw. | S-O-2-3 | 88 | 262 | 43 | 65 | 7 | 5 | 1 | 31 | .248 | 91 | 137 | 26 | .898 |
| 1970– | | | | | (Out of Baseball) | | | | | | | | | | |
| 1971–Salem | ...............Carol. | S-2-3 | 122 | 422 | 65 | 136 | 18 | •13 | 8 | 66 | .308 | 164 | 306 | 40 | .922 |
| 1972–Sherbrooke | ........Ea. | •3-2-O-S | •140 | 517 | 89 | •172 | •42 | 4 | 11 | 86 | •.333 | •146 | 241 | 29 | .930 |
| 1972–Pittsburgh | ........Nat. | 3B | 3 | 2 | 0 | 0 | 0 | 0 | 0 | 0 | .000 | 0 | 1 | 1 | .500 |
| 1973–Charleston | ........Int. | 2B-3B | 48 | 174 | 20 | 52 | 6 | 2 | 0 | 16 | .299 | 82 | 99 | 12 | .938 |
| 1973–Pittsburgh‡ | .......Nat. | 3B | 37 | 49 | 5 | 11 | 0 | 1 | 1 | 5 | .224 | 5 | 7 | 1 | .923 |
| 1974–K.C.§-N.Y. | ........Amer. | 2-3-S | 60 | 142 | 12 | 29 | 6 | 1 | 1 | 9 | .204 | 104 | 105 | 5 | .977 |
| 1974–Syracuse x | ........Int. | 3B-2B | 37 | 133 | 14 | 30 | 8 | 0 | 2 | 15 | .226 | 32 | 72 | 7 | .937 |
| 1975–Poza Rica y | ......Mex. | 2B-SS | 95 | 370 | 38 | 101 | 20 | 6 | 3 | 40 | .273 | 256 | 227 | 23 | .955 |
| 1975–Charleston | ........Int. | 3B-2B | 45 | 154 | 21 | 43 | 9 | 3 | 1 | 21 | .279 | 31 | 72 | 5 | .954 |
| 1976–Charleston | ........Int. | 3-2-O | 119 | 443 | 53 | 142 | •31 | 4 | 13 | 70 | .321 | 120 | 178 | 11 | .964 |
| National League Totals | .................. | | 40 | 51 | 5 | 11 | 0 | 1 | 1 | 5 | .216 | 5 | 8 | 2 | .867 |
| American League Totals | ............... | | 60 | 142 | 12 | 29 | 6 | 1 | 1 | 9 | .204 | 104 | 105 | 5 | .977 |
| Major League Totals | ...................... | | 100 | 193 | 17 | 40 | 6 | 2 | 2 | 14 | .207 | 109 | 113 | 7 | .969 |

†Released by Milwaukee Brewers' organization, April 15, 1970; signed as free agent by Pittsburgh Pirates' organization, January 7, 1971.
‡Traded with Pitcher Nelson Briles to Kansas City Royals for Infielder Kurt Bevacqua, Catcher-First Baseman Ed Kirkpatrick and First Baseman Winston Cole (latter assigned from Kingsport to Salem), December 4, 1973.
§Sold to New York Yankees, May 5, 1974.
xReleased by New York Yankees' organization to Poza Rica (Mexican League), March 5, 1975.
yReleased to Charleston (Pittsburgh Pirates' organization), July 17, 1975.
Listed on Pittsburgh Pirates' 1977 spring roster.

## JULIO CESAR GONZALEZ (HERNANDEZ)
### (Cesar)
Born December 25, 1953, at Caguas, Puerto Rico.
Height, 5.11. Weight, 162.
Throws and bats righthanded.
Hobby–Reading.

Led Midwest League shortstops in double plays with 63 in 1973.

| Year Club | League | Pos. | G. | AB. | R. | H. | 2B. | 3B. | HR. | RBI. | B.A. | PO. | A. | E. | F.A. |
|---|---|---|---|---|---|---|---|---|---|---|---|---|---|---|---|
| 1972–Quincy | .............Midw. | SS | 96 | 346 | 39 | 82 | 14 | 7 | 7 | 37 | .237 | 111 | 248 | 45 | .889 |
| 1973–Quincy | .............Midw. | SS | •125 | •492 | 81 | 146 | 16 | 8 | 5 | 39 | .297 | •190 | •342 | •61 | .897 |
| 1974–Key West | .........Fla. St. | SS-2B | 87 | 333 | 26 | 74 | 12 | 2 | 1 | 20 | .222 | 145 | 222 | 29 | .926 |
| 1975–Midland | ...........Texas | 3-SS-2 | 81 | 324 | 37 | 88 | 13 | 2 | 2 | 27 | .272 | 95 | 174 | 24 | .918 |
| 1975–Wichita | ...........A.A. | 2B-3B | 56 | 171 | 13 | 35 | 5 | 0 | 0 | 11 | .205 | 90 | 128 | 10 | .956 |
| 1976–Wichita† | ...........A.A. | 2-SS-3 | 128 | 484 | 49 | 136 | 12 | 5 | 3 | 41 | .281 | 264 | 372 | 38 | .943 |

†Traded to Houston Astros for Outfielder Greg Gross, December 8, 1976.

## ORLANDO EUGENE GONZALEZ
Born November 11, 1951, at Havana, Cuba.
Height, 6.02. Weight, 175.
Throws and bats righthanded.
Hobby–Music.
Attended Miami-Dade Junior College–South, Miami, Fla., and University of Miami, Coral Gables, Fla.

| Year  Club       League | Pos. | G. | AB. | R. | H. | 2B. | 3B. | HR. | RBI. | B.A. | PO. | A. | E. | F.A. |
|---|---|---|---|---|---|---|---|---|---|---|---|---|---|---|
| 1974—San Antonio ......Texas | 1B | 64 | 233 | 28 | 65 | 8 | 1 | 1 | 17 | .279 | 538 | 40 | 4 | .993 |
| 1975—San Antonio ......Texas | 1B | 54 | 210 | 38 | 66 | 11 | 3 | 1 | 22 | .314 | 517 | 37 | 8 | .986 |
| 1975—Oklahoma City ..A.A. | OF-1B | 85 | 297 | 40 | 91 | 15 | 3 | 0 | 29 | .306 | 231 | 16 | 3 | .988 |
| 1976—Toledo .............Int. | OF-1B | 98 | 357 | 49 | 111 | 17 | 4 | 1 | 45 | .311 | 494 | 47 | 9 | .984 |
| 1976—Cleveland .........Amer. | 1-O-DH | 28 | 68 | 5 | 17 | 2 | 0 | 0 | 4 | .250 | 123 | 8 | 1 | .992 |
| Major League Totals ..................... | | 28 | 68 | 5 | 17 | 2 | 0 | 0 | 4 | .250 | 123 | 8 | 1 | .992 |

## JAMES EDWARD GOODSON
### (Ed)

Born January 25, 1948, at Pulaski, Va.
Height, 6.03. Weight, 185.
Throws right and bats lefthanded.
Hobbies—Hunting and fishing.
Attended East Tennessee State University, Johnson City, Tenn.;
received Bachelor of Science degree in Biology.

Led California League first basemen in double plays with 84 in 1970.
Tied for California League lead in sacrifice flies with 8 in 1970.
Received reported bonus of $50,000 to sign with San Francisco Giants, 1968.

| Year  Club       League | Pos. | G. | AB. | R. | H. | 2B. | 3B. | HR. | RBI. | B.A. | PO. | A. | E. | F.A. |
|---|---|---|---|---|---|---|---|---|---|---|---|---|---|---|
| 1968—Salt Lake City ..Pion. | SS | 32 | 116 | 12 | 31 | 5 | 2 | 3 | 15 | .267 | 38 | 85 | 12 | .911 |
| 1969—Great Falls........Pion. | SS | 4 | 9 | 2 | 4 | 0 | 0 | 0 | 4 | .444 | 2 | 5 | 0 | 1.000 |
| 1969—Decatur ...........M'west | 1-SS | 60 | 214 | 32 | 61 | 11 | 6 | 1 | 26 | .285 | 426 | 46 | 10 | .979 |
| 1970—Fresno .............Calif. | *1B-3B | 127 | 506 | 66 | 159 | •28 | 5 | 19 | 94 | .314 | *1121 | 57 | 14 | *.988 |
| 1970—San Francisco ..Nat. | 1B | 7 | 11 | 1 | 3 | 0 | 0 | 0 | 0 | .273 | 14 | 2 | 1 | .941 |
| 1971—Phoenix ...........P.C. | 3B-1B | 86 | 323 | 40 | 95 | 16 | 10 | 7 | 56 | .294 | 202 | 119 | 19 | .944 |
| 1971—San Francisco ..Nat. | 1B | 20 | 42 | 4 | 8 | 1 | 0 | 0 | 1 | .190 | 81 | 7 | 0 | 1.000 |
| 1972—Phoenix ...........P.C. | 1B | 32 | 108 | 18 | 42 | 14 | 1 | 0 | 24 | .389 | 206 | 18 | 2 | .991 |
| 1972—San Francisco†..Nat. | 1B | 58 | 150 | 15 | 42 | 1 | 1 | 6 | 30 | .280 | 299 | 27 | 3 | .991 |
| 1973—San Francisco ..Nat. | 3B | 102 | 384 | 37 | 116 | 20 | 1 | 12 | 53 | .302 | 64 | 171 | 23 | .911 |
| 1974—San Francisco‡..Nat. | 1B-3B | 98 | 298 | 25 | 81 | 15 | 0 | 6 | 48 | .272 | 600 | 46 | 2 | .997 |
| 1975—S.F.§-Atl. x........Nat. | 1B-3B | 86 | 197 | 15 | 41 | 9 | 0 | 2 | 16 | .208 | 240 | 52 | 6 | .980 |
| 1976—Los Angeles ......Nat. | 3-1-O-2 | 83 | 118 | 8 | 27 | 4 | 0 | 3 | 17 | .229 | 17 | 27 | 7 | .863 |
| Major League Totals ..................... | | 454 | 1200 | 105 | 318 | 50 | 2 | 29 | 165 | .265 | 1315 | 332 | 42 | .975 |

†Placed on supplemental disabled list, August 23, 1972 (out for remainder of season).
‡On supplemental disabled list, April 22 to May 11, 1974.
§Traded to Atlanta Braves for Shortstop Craig Robinson, June 11, 1975.
xTraded with Outfielder Dusty Baker to Los Angeles Dodgers for Outfielder Jimmy Wynn, Second Baseman Lee Lacy, First Baseman-Outfielder Tom Paciorek and Infielder Jerry Royster, November 17, 1975.

## DANNY KAY GOODWIN

Born September 2, 1953, at St. Louis, Mo.
Height, 6.01. Weight, 195.
Throws right and bats lefthanded.
Attended Southern University, Baton Rouge, La.; received
Bachelor of Science degree in Zoology.

Received bonus reported in excess of $100,000 to sign with California Angels, 1975.

| Year  Club       League | Pos. | G. | AB. | R. | H. | 2B. | 3B. | HR. | RBI. | B.A. | PO. | A. | E. | F.A. |
|---|---|---|---|---|---|---|---|---|---|---|---|---|---|---|
| 1975—El Paso ...........Texas | C-1-O | 46 | 138 | 10 | 38 | 6 | 0 | 2 | 18 | .275 | 224 | 10 | 3 | .987 |
| 1975—California.........Amer. | DH-PH | 4 | 10 | 0 | 1 | 0 | 0 | 0 | 0 | .100 | 0 | 0 | 0 | .000 |
| 1976—Salinas .............Calif. | C | 38 | 139 | 24 | 43 | 7 | 2 | 2 | 30 | .309 | 168 | 13 | 10 | .948 |
| 1976—El Paso ...........Texas | C-PH | 63 | 220 | 43 | 67 | 17 | 0 | 6 | 39 | .305 | 195 | 12 | 4 | .981 |
| Major League Totals ..................... | | 4 | 10 | 0 | 1 | 0 | 0 | 0 | 0 | .100 | 0 | 0 | 0 | .000 |

Listed on California Angels' 1977 spring roster.

## MICHAEL WILLIAM GORDON
### (Mike)

Born September 11, 1953, at Leominister, Mass.
Height, 6.03. Weight, 215.
Throws right and bats left and righthanded.
Hobbies—Fishing, bowling and reading.

| Year  Club       League | Pos. | G. | AB. | R. | H. | 2B. | 3B. | HR. | RBI. | B.A. | PO. | A. | E. | F.A. |
|---|---|---|---|---|---|---|---|---|---|---|---|---|---|---|
| 1972—Brad'ton Cubs ..Gulf C. | C | 42 | 108 | 14 | 21 | 5 | 2 | 2 | 19 | .194 | 247 | 21 | 6 | .978 |
| 1973—Quincy .............Midw. | C-1B | 108 | 316 | 33 | 57 | 14 | 1 | 11 | 39 | .180 | 693 | 64 | 13 | .983 |
| 1974—Key West .........Fla. St. | C | 84 | 250 | 23 | 45 | 5 | 1 | 6 | 25 | .180 | 413 | 42 | 14 | .970 |
| 1975—Key West .........Fla. St. | C-1B | 109 | 340 | 37 | 82 | 10 | 3 | 5 | 40 | .241 | 393 | 35 | 12 | .973 |
| 1976—Midland ...........Texas | C-1B | 120 | 430 | 47 | 106 | 23 | 3 | 10 | 61 | .247 | 608 | 70 | 13 | .981 |

Listed on Chicago Cubs' 1977 spring roster.

---

## *DID YOU KNOW—*

That Henry Aaron's first major league home run was hit off the St. Louis Cardinals' Vic Raschi on April 25, 1954?

## ROBERT JOHN GORINSKI
### (Bob)

Born January 7, 1952, at Latrobe, Pa.
Height, 6.03. Weight, 215.
Throws and bats righthanded.
Hobbies—Hunting and fishing.

Led Midwest League in total bases with 243 in 1971 and Southern League with 238 in 1974.
Led Carolina League batters in strikeouts with 147 in 1972, Southern League with 128 in 1974 and Pacific Coast League with 130 in 1976.
Tied for Southern League lead in sacrifice flies with 8 in 1974.
Received reported $68,000 bonus to sign with Minnesota Twins, 1970.

| Year | Club | League | Pos. | G. | AB. | R. | H. | 2B. | 3B. | HR. | RBI. | B.A. | PO. | A. | E. | F.A. |
|------|------|--------|------|-----|-----|-----|-----|-----|-----|-----|------|------|-----|-----|-----|------|
| 1970—Sarasota Twins | ..Gulf C. | | OF | 60 | 210 | 33 | 50 | 7 | 2 | •6 | 30 | .238 | 75 | 4 | 1 | *.988 |
| 1971—Wis. Rapids | ......Midw. | | OF | 120 | 486 | 65 | 126 | 25 | 1 | 30 | 76 | .259 | 173 | 14 | 14 | .930 |
| 1972—Lynchburg | ........Carol. | | OF | 125 | 457 | 69 | 105 | 17 | 4 | *23 | 91 | .230 | 155 | 15 | 7 | .960 |
| 1973—Orlando | ............South. | | OF | 102 | 344 | 38 | 73 | 16 | 0 | 8 | 43 | .212 | 187 | 8 | 5 | .975 |
| 1974—Orlando | ............South. | | OF | 132 | 521 | 68 | 145 | 18 | 3 | •23 | *100 | .278 | 202 | 11 | 3 | *.986 |
| 1975—Tacoma† | .........P.C. | | OF | 89 | 304 | 44 | 71 | 7 | 2 | 13 | 38 | .234 | 131 | 7 | 7 | .952 |
| 1975—Denver | ..............A.A. | | OF | 35 | 114 | 14 | 37 | 8 | 0 | 7 | 24 | .325 | 54 | 2 | 2 | .966 |
| 1976—Tacoma | ............P.C. | | OF | 138 | 544 | 93 | 155 | 21 | 2 | *28 | *110 | .285 | 199 | 8 | 13 | .941 |

†Option transferred to Denver, July 28, 1975.
Listed on Minnesota Twins' 1977 spring roster.

## RICHARD MICHAEL GOSSAGE

Last name pronounced to rhyme with sausage.

### (Rich)

Born July 5, 1951, at Colorado Springs, Colo.
Height, 6.03. Weight, 215.
Throws and bats righthanded.
Hobby—Hunting.
Attended Southern Colorado State College, Pueblo, Colo.

Led American League in saves with 26 in 1975.
Led Midwest League in complete games with 15 and shutouts with 7 in 1971.
Named American League Fireman of the Year by THE SPORTING NEWS, 1975.
Named Midwest League Player of the Year, 1971.

| Year | Club | League | G. | IP. | W. | L. | Pct. | H. | R. | ER. | SO. | BB. | ERA. |
|------|------|--------|-----|-----|-----|-----|------|-----|-----|-----|-----|-----|------|
| 1970—Sarasota White Sox | ..............Gulf Coast | | 3 | 16 | 0 | 0 | .000 | 11 | 6 | 5 | 21 | 4 | 2.81 |
| 1970—Appleton | ...............................Midwest | | 10 | 35 | 0 | 3 | .000 | 41 | 27 | 23 | 21 | 19 | 5.91 |
| 1971—Appleton | ...............................Midwest | | 25 | 187 | *18 | 2 | *.900 | 141 | 48 | 38 | 149 | 50 | *1.83 |
| 1972—Chicago | ...................................American | | 36 | 80 | 7 | 1 | .875 | 72 | 44 | 38 | 57 | 44 | 4.28 |
| 1973—Iowa | ....................................Am. Assoc. | | 12 | 71 | 5 | 4 | .556 | 59 | 32 | 29 | 66 | 28 | 3.68 |
| 1973—Chicago | ...................................American | | 20 | 50 | 0 | 4 | .000 | 57 | 44 | 41 | 33 | 37 | 7.38 |
| 1974—Appleton | ...............................Midwest | | 2 | 8 | 0 | 2 | .000 | 8 | 6 | 3 | 5 | 4 | 3.38 |
| 1974—Chicago | ...................................American | | 39 | 89 | 4 | 6 | .400 | 92 | 45 | 41 | 64 | 47 | 4.15 |
| 1975—Chicago | ...................................American | | 62 | 142 | 9 | 8 | .529 | 99 | 32 | 29 | 130 | 70 | 1.84 |
| 1976—Chicago† | ...............................American | | 31 | 224 | 9 | 17 | .346 | 214 | 104 | 98 | 135 | 90 | 3.94 |
| Major League Totals | ............................. | | 188 | 585 | 29 | 36 | .446 | 534 | 269 | 247 | 419 | 188 | 3.80 |

†Traded with Pitcher Terry Forster to Pittsburgh Pirates for Outfielder Richie Zisk and Pitcher Silvio Martinez, December 10, 1976.

### ALL-STAR GAME RECORD

| Year | League | IP. | W. | L. | Pct. | H. | R. | ER. | SO. | BB. | ERA. |
|------|--------|-----|-----|-----|------|-----|-----|-----|-----|-----|------|
| 1975—American | ..................................... | 1 | 0 | 0 | .000 | 1 | 1 | 1 | 0 | 0 | 9.00 |

## MICHAEL LEE GRACE
### (Mike)

Born June 14, 1956, at Pontiac, Mich.
Height, 6.00. Weight, 175.
Throws and bats righthanded.
Hobbies—Golf and hunting.

| Year | Club | League | Pos. | G. | AB. | R. | H. | 2B. | 3B. | HR. | RBI. | B.A. | PO. | A. | E. | F.A. |
|------|------|--------|------|-----|-----|-----|-----|-----|-----|-----|------|------|-----|-----|-----|------|
| 1974—Billings | ............Pion. | | 3B | 73 | 261 | 46 | 68 | 8 | 6 | 3 | 27 | .261 | *90 | *139 | *15 | *.939 |
| 1975—Tampa | ..............Fla.St. | | 3B-SS | 118 | 380 | 29 | 87 | 5 | 6 | 2 | 41 | .229 | 111 | 286 | 21 | .950 |
| 1976—Three Rivers | ....East. | | 3B | 132 | 430 | 38 | 102 | 14 | 3 | 3 | 45 | .237 | *123 | *294 | 23 | .948 |

Listed on Cincinnati Reds' 1977 spring roster.

## WAYNE ALLAN GRANGER

Born March 15, 1944, at Springfield, Mass.
Height, 6.02. Weight, 165.
Throws and bats righthanded.
Hobby—Golf.
Attended Springfield College, Springfield, Mass.

Led National League in saves with 35 in 1970.
Named THE SPORTING NEWS National League Fireman of the Year, 1969 and 1970.
Received reported $20,000 bonus to sign with St. Louis Cardinals, 1965.

| Year Club | League | G. | IP. | W. | L. | Pct. | H. | R. | ER. | SO. | BB. | ERA. |
|---|---|---|---|---|---|---|---|---|---|---|---|---|
| 1965—Tulsa | Texas | 7 | 38 | 2 | 2 | .500 | 34 | 23 | 20 | 22 | 8 | 4.74 |
| 1965—Raleigh | Carolina | 24 | 162 | 9 | 10 | .474 | 131 | 69 | 49 | 117 | 41 | 2.72 |
| 1966—Arkansas | Texas | 47 | 95 | 11 | 2 | .846 | 66 | 21 | 19 | 57 | 30 | 1.80 |
| 1967—Tulsa | P. Coast | 57 | 113 | 8 | 7 | .533 | 111 | 45 | 38 | 70 | 38 | 3.03 |
| 1968—Tulsa | P. Coast | 14 | 25 | 4 | 3 | .571 | 16 | 6 | 6 | 19 | 3 | 2.16 |
| 1968—St. Louis† | National | 34 | 44 | 4 | 2 | .667 | 40 | 14 | 11 | 27 | 12 | 2.25 |
| 1969—Cincinnati | National | *90 | 145 | 9 | 6 | .600 | 143 | 64 | 45 | 68 | 40 | 2.79 |
| 1970—Cincinnati‡ | National | 67 | 85 | 6 | 5 | .545 | 79 | 33 | 25 | 38 | 27 | 2.65 |
| 1971—Cincinnati§ | National | *70 | 100 | 7 | 6 | .538 | 94 | 39 | 37 | 51 | 28 | 3.33 |
| 1972—Minnesota x | American | 63 | 90 | 4 | 6 | .400 | 83 | 42 | 30 | 45 | 28 | 3.00 |
| 1973—St. Louis y | National | 33 | 47 | 2 | 4 | .333 | 50 | 29 | 22 | 14 | 21 | 4.21 |
| 1973—New York z | American | 7 | 15 | 0 | 1 | .000 | 19 | 7 | 3 | 10 | 3 | 1.80 |
| 1974—Iowa | Am. Assoc. | 33 | 111 | 10 | 3 | .769 | 114 | 42 | 40 | 76 | 19 | 3.24 |
| 1974—Chicago a | American | 5 | 8 | 0 | 0 | .000 | 16 | 8 | 7 | 4 | 3 | 7.88 |
| 1975—Houston b | National | 55 | 74 | 2 | 5 | .286 | 76 | 39 | 30 | 30 | 23 | 3.65 |
| 1976—Montreal | National | 27 | 32 | 1 | 0 | 1.000 | 32 | 15 | 13 | 16 | 16 | 3.66 |
| 1976—Denver c | Am. Assoc. | 26 | 44 | 3 | 1 | .750 | 42 | 16 | 12 | 18 | 15 | 2.45 |
| American League Totals | | 75 | 113 | 4 | 7 | .364 | 118 | 57 | 40 | 59 | 34 | 3.19 |
| National League Totals | | 376 | 527 | 31 | 28 | .525 | 514 | 233 | 183 | 244 | 167 | 3.13 |
| Major League Totals | | 451 | 640 | 35 | 35 | .500 | 632 | 290 | 223 | 303 | 201 | 3.14 |

†Traded with Outfielder Bob Tolan to Cincinnati Reds for Outfielder Vada Pinson, October 11, 1968.
‡Played in one game as an outfielder.
§Traded to Minnesota Twins for Pitcher Tom Hall, December 3, 1971.
xTraded to St. Louis Cardinals for Outfielder Larry Hisle and Pitcher John Cumberland (latter assigned from Arkansas to Tacoma), November 29, 1972.
yTraded to New York Yankees for two players to be named later, August 7, 1973; Cardinals received cash and Yankees assigned Pitcher Ken Crosby to Tulsa, September 12, 1973, to complete deal.
zUnconditionally released, March 26, 1974; signed as free agent by Chicago White Sox, April 3, 1974.
aReleased, October 23, 1974; signed as a free agent by Houston Astros' organization, February 10, 1975.
bReleased, December 9, 1975; signed as free agent by Montreal Expos, February 14, 1976.
cReleased, February 9, 1977; signed as free agent with Atlanta Braves, February 17, 1977.

### CHAMPIONSHIP SERIES RECORD

| Year Club | League | G. | IP. | W. | L. | Pct. | H. | R. | ER. | SO. | BB. | ERA. |
|---|---|---|---|---|---|---|---|---|---|---|---|---|
| 1970—Cincinnati | National | 1 | ⅔ | 0 | 0 | .000 | 1 | 0 | 0 | 0 | 0 | 0.00 |

### WORLD SERIES RECORD

Tied World Series records for most hit batsmen, inning (2), eighth inning, October 9, 1968, and most hit batsmen, game (2), October 9, 1968.

| Year Club | League | G. | IP. | W. | L. | Pct. | H. | R. | ER. | SO. | BB. | ERA. |
|---|---|---|---|---|---|---|---|---|---|---|---|---|
| 1968—St. Louis | National | 1 | 2 | 0 | 0 | .000 | 0 | 0 | 0 | 1 | 1 | 0.00 |
| 1970—Cincinnati | National | 2 | 1⅓ | 0 | 0 | .000 | 7 | 5 | 5 | 1 | 1 | 33.75 |
| World Series Totals | | 3 | 3⅓ | 0 | 0 | .000 | 7 | 5 | 5 | 2 | 2 | 13.50 |

## GARY GEORGE GRAY

Born September 21, 1952, at New Orleans, La.
Height, 6.00. Weight, 187.
Throws and bats righthanded.
Hobbies—Hunting and playing checkers.
Attended Oklahoma City Southwestern Junior College, Oklahoma City, Okla., and
Southeastern Oklahoma State University, Durant, Okla.

| Year Club | League | Pos. | G. | AB. | R. | H. | 2B. | 3B. | HR. | RBI. | B.A. | PO. | A. | E. | F.A. |
|---|---|---|---|---|---|---|---|---|---|---|---|---|---|---|---|
| 1974—Sar. Rangers | Gulf C. | 1B-3B | 52 | 184 | 32 | 57 | 10 | 3 | 0 | 34 | .310 | 257 | 29 | 13 | .956 |
| 1975—Anderson | W. Car. | 1B | 135 | 487 | 79 | 147 | •27 | 1 | 18 | 95 | .302 | 1138 | 71 | *27 | .978 |
| 1976—San Antonio | Texas | 1-OF-3 | 124 | 443 | 74 | 135 | 27 | 8 | 19 | 109 | .305 | 222 | 13 | 6 | .975 |

Listed on Texas Rangers' 1977 spring roster.

## MONROE DUKE GREENFIELD

Born December 21, 1952, at Coeur d' Alene, Idaho.
Height, 6.04. Weight, 195.
Throws and bats righthanded.
Hobbies—Hunting and sports.
Attended North Idaho College, Coeur d' Alene, Idaho, and Gonzaga
University, Spokane, Wash.

| Year Club | League | G. | IP. | W. | L. | Pct. | H. | R. | ER. | SO. | BB. | ERA. |
|---|---|---|---|---|---|---|---|---|---|---|---|---|
| 1974—Great Falls | Pioneer | 14 | 99 | 7 | 7 | .500 | 84 | 49 | 31 | 84 | 50 | 2.82 |
| 1975—Fresno | California | 19 | 106 | 6 | 8 | .429 | 97 | 57 | 44 | 64 | 58 | 3.74 |
| 1976—Fresno | California | 47 | 114 | 12 | 9 | .571 | 111 | 48 | 31 | 92 | 47 | *2.45 |

Listed on San Francisco Giants' 1977 spring roster.

---

### DID YOU KNOW —

That the office of the Commissioner of Baseball is located at 75 Rockefeller Plaza, New York, New York 10019. The telephone number is 586-7400 (Area Code 212).

# WILLIAM BRILEY GREIF
Name pronounced GRIFE.
## (Bill)

Born April 25, 1950, at Ft. Stockton, Tex.
Height, 6.05. Weight, 205.
Throws right and bats right and lefthanded.
Hobbies—Reading about hypnosis and psychic phenomena.
Attended University of Texas, Austin, Tex., Texas Tech University,
Lubbock, Tex., and Arizona State University, Tempe, Ariz.; received degree in Psychology.
Led National League in hit batsmen with 14 in 1974.

| Year Club | League | G. | IP. | W. | L. | Pct. | H. | R. | ER. | SO. | BB. | ERA. |
|---|---|---|---|---|---|---|---|---|---|---|---|---|
| 1968—Covington | Ap'lachian | 15 | 76 | 5 | 4 | .556 | 64 | 31 | 24 | 92 | 29 | 2.84 |
| 1969—Peninsula† | Carolina | 11 | 30 | 1 | 4 | .200 | 23 | 20 | 11 | 27 | 17 | 3.30 |
| 1970—Columbus | Southern | 27 | 190 | 10 | 12 | .455 | *177 | *82 | 61 | 131 | 54 | 2.89 |
| 1971—Oklahoma City | Am. Assoc. | 21 | 137 | 8 | 9 | .471 | 134 | 70 | 55 | 152 | 47 | 3.61 |
| 1971—Houston‡ | National | 7 | 16 | 1 | 1 | .500 | 18 | 10 | 9 | 14 | 8 | 5.06 |
| 1972—San Diego | National | 34 | 125 | 5 | 16 | .238 | 143 | 86 | 78 | 91 | 47 | 5.62 |
| 1973—San Diego | National | 36 | 199 | 10 | 17 | .370 | 181 | 88 | 71 | 120 | 62 | 3.21 |
| 1974—San Diego | National | 43 | 226 | 9 | 19 | .321 | 244 | 126 | 117 | 137 | 95 | 4.66 |
| 1975—San Diego | National | 59 | 72 | 4 | 6 | .400 | 74 | 44 | 31 | 43 | 38 | 3.88 |
| 1976—San Diego§-St. Louis x | National | 52 | 77 | 2 | 8 | .200 | 87 | 48 | 45 | 37 | 37 | 5.26 |
| Major League Totals | | 231 | 715 | 31 | 67 | .316 | 747 | 402 | 351 | 442 | 287 | 4.42 |

†On restricted list February 21 through May 29.
‡Traded with Infielder Derrel Thomas and Pitcher Mark Schaeffer to San Diego Padres for Pitcher Dave Roberts, December 3, 1971.
§Traded to St. Louis Cardinals for Outfielder Luis Melendez, May 19, 1976.
xTraded with Outfielder Sam Mejias and Pitcher Angel Torres to Montreal Expos for Pitcher Steve Dunning, Infielder Pat Scanlon and Outfielder Tony Scott, November 6, 1976. Released, March 30, 1977.


# ROBERT ANTHONY GRICH
## (Bobby)

Born January 15, 1949, at Muskegon, Mich.
Height, 6.02. Weight, 180.
Throws and bats righthanded.
Hobby—Hunting.
Attended University of California at Los Angeles, Los Angeles, Calif., and
Fresno State University, Fresno, Calif.

Established major league records for highest fielding average by second baseman, season, .995, in 1973; and most putouts, second baseman, season, 484, in 1974.
Tied major league record for fewest errors by second baseman (800 or more chances), season, 5, 1973.
Tied American League record for most games, second baseman, season, 162, 1973.
Hit three home runs in a game, June 18, 1974, against Minnesota Twins.
Led American League second basemen in double plays with 130 in 1973, 132 in 1974 and 122 in 1975.
Led American League second basemen in total chances with 945 in 1973, 957 in 1974 and 928 in 1975.
Led International League in total bases with 299 and led shortstops in double plays with 81 in 1971.
Named International League Most Valuable Player in 1971.
Named by THE SPORTING NEWS as Minor League Player of the Year, 1971.
Named second baseman on THE SPORTING NEWS American League All-Star fielding team, 1973, 1974, 1975 and 1976.
Named second baseman on THE SPORTING NEWS American League All-Star Team, 1976.

| Year Club | League | Pos. | G. | AB. | R. | H. | 2B. | 3B. | HR. | RBI. | B.A. | PO. | A. | E. | F.A. |
|---|---|---|---|---|---|---|---|---|---|---|---|---|---|---|---|
| 1967—Bluefield | Appal. | SS | 58 | 213 | 43 | 54 | 10 | 4 | 3 | 26 | .254 | 74 | 126 | 24 | .893 |
| 1968—Stockton | Calif. | SS | 113 | 426 | 63 | 97 | 18 | 2 | 8 | 44 | .228 | 205 | *379 | 35 | .943 |
| 1969—Dal.-Ft. Worth† | Texas | SS | 121 | 413 | 60 | 128 | 16 | 8 | 2 | 50 | .310 | *199 | 368 | 29 | .951 |
| 1970—Rochester | Int. | 2B-SS | 63 | 235 | 67 | 90 | 11 | 3 | 9 | 42 | .383 | 144 | 199 | 9 | .974 |
| 1970—Baltimore | Amer. | SS-2-3 | 30 | 95 | 11 | 20 | 1 | 3 | 0 | 8 | .211 | 56 | 79 | 7 | .951 |
| 1971—Rochester | Int. | SS | 130 | 473 | *124 | 159 | 26 | 9 | *32 | 83 | *.336 | *238 | *394 | 17 | *.974 |
| 1971—Baltimore | Amer. | SS-2 | 7 | 30 | 7 | 9 | 0 | 0 | 1 | 6 | .300 | 11 | 31 | 0 | 1.000 |
| 1972—Baltimore | Amer. | S-2-1-3 | 133 | 460 | 66 | 128 | 21 | 3 | 12 | 50 | .278 | 299 | 338 | 20 | .970 |
| 1973—Baltimore | Amer. | 2B ●162 | 581 | 82 | 146 | 29 | 7 | 12 | 50 | .251 | *431 | *509 | 5 | *.995 |
| 1974—Baltimore | Amer. | 2B | 160 | 582 | 92 | 153 | 29 | 6 | 19 | 82 | .263 | *484 | *453 | 20 | .979 |
| 1975—Baltimore | Amer. | 2B | 150 | 524 | 81 | 136 | 26 | 4 | 13 | 57 | .260 | *423 | *484 | 21 | .977 |
| 1976—Baltimore‡ | Amer. | *2-3-DH | 144 | 518 | 93 | 138 | 31 | 4 | 13 | 54 | .266 | *389 | 400 | 12 | .985 |
| Major League Totals | | | 786 | 2790 | 432 | 730 | 137 | 27 | 70 | 307 | .262 | 2093 | 2294 | 85 | .981 |

†On military list, September 2, 1969 through April 1, 1970.
‡Played out option year and granted free agency, November 1, 1976; signed as free agent with California Angels, November 24, 1976.

## CHAMPIONSHIP SERIES RECORD

| Year Club | League | Pos. | G. | AB. | R. | H. | 2B. | 3B. | HR. | RBI. | B.A. | PO. | A. | E. | F.A. |
|---|---|---|---|---|---|---|---|---|---|---|---|---|---|---|---|
| 1973—Baltimore | Amer. | 2B | 5 | 20 | 1 | 2 | 0 | 0 | 1 | 1 | .100 | 16 | 9 | 0 | 1.000 |
| 1974—Baltimore | Amer. | 2B | 4 | 16 | 2 | 4 | 1 | 0 | 1 | 2 | .250 | 13 | 12 | 1 | .962 |
| Championship Series Totals | | | 9 | 36 | 3 | 6 | 1 | 0 | 2 | 3 | .167 | 29 | 21 | 1 | .980 |

| Year League | Pos. | AB. | R. | H. | 2B. | 3B. | HR. | RBI. | B.A. | PO. | A. | E. | F.A. |
|---|---|---|---|---|---|---|---|---|---|---|---|---|---|
| 1972–American | SS | 4 | 0 | 0 | 0 | 0 | 0 | 0 | .000 | 0 | 3 | 0 | 1.000 |
| 1974–American | 2B | 3 | 0 | 1 | 0 | 0 | 0 | 0 | .333 | 0 | 2 | 0 | 1.000 |
| 1976–American | 2B | 2 | 0 | 0 | 0 | 0 | 0 | 0 | .000 | 1 | 1 | 0 | 1.000 |
| All-Star Game Totals | | 9 | 0 | 1 | 0 | 0 | 0 | 0 | .111 | 1 | 6 | 0 | 1.000 |

# THOMAS ALAN GRIEVE
## (Tom)

Born March 4, 1948, at Pittsfield, Mass.
Height, 6.02. Weight, 190.
Throws and bats righthanded.
Hobby–Fishing.
Attended University of Michigan, Ann Arbor, Mich.
Received reported $60,000 bonus to sign with Washington Senators, 1966.

| Year Club | League | Pos. | G. | AB. | R. | H. | 2B. | 3B. | HR. | RBI. | B.A. | PO. | A. | E. | F.A. |
|---|---|---|---|---|---|---|---|---|---|---|---|---|---|---|---|
| 1967–Burlington | Carol. | OF | 13 | 29 | 1 | 4 | 1 | 0 | 0 | 0 | .138 | 22 | 1 | 2 | .920 |
| 1967–Geneva | NYP | OF | 58 | 208 | 40 | 49 | 6 | 4 | 6 | 44 | .236 | 91 | 5 | 6 | .941 |
| 1968–Salisbury† | W. Car. | OF | 67 | 245 | 41 | 71 | 12 | 1 | 8 | 26 | .290 | 116 | 8 | 7 | .947 |
| 1968–Burlington | Carol. | OF | 9 | 27 | 6 | 8 | 1 | 0 | 3 | 5 | .296 | 8 | 0 | 2 | .800 |
| 1969–Buffalo‡ | Int. | OF | 99 | 331 | 53 | 81 | 16 | 0 | 11 | 43 | .245 | 213 | 5 | 4 | .982 |
| 1970–Denver | A. A. | OF | 51 | 182 | 39 | 51 | 4 | 2 | 13 | 29 | .280 | 123 | 5 | 6 | .955 |
| 1970–Washington | Amer. | OF | 47 | 116 | 12 | 23 | 5 | 1 | 3 | 10 | .198 | 46 | 0 | 3 | .939 |
| 1971–Denver | A. A. | OF | 93 | 316 | 64 | 86 | 14 | 5 | 19 | 61 | .272 | 174 | 15 | 3 | .984 |
| 1972–Texas§ | Amer. | OF | 64 | 142 | 12 | 29 | 2 | 1 | 3 | 11 | .204 | 60 | 6 | 1 | .985 |
| 1973–Texas | Amer. | OF | 66 | 123 | 22 | 38 | 6 | 0 | 7 | 21 | .309 | 68 | 0 | 0 | 1.000 |
| 1974–Texas | Amer. | OF-1B | 84 | 259 | 30 | 66 | 10 | 4 | 9 | 32 | .255 | 64 | 5 | 0 | 1.000 |
| 1975–Texas | Amer. | OF | 118 | 369 | 46 | 102 | 17 | 1 | 14 | 61 | .276 | 93 | 3 | 1 | .990 |
| 1976–Texas | Amer. | DH-OF | 149 | 546 | 57 | 139 | 23 | 3 | 20 | 81 | .255 | 112 | 4 | 2 | .983 |
| Major League Totals | | | 528 | 1555 | 179 | 397 | 63 | 10 | 56 | 216 | .255 | 443 | 18 | 7 | .985 |

†On temporary inactive list, April 15 through April 28.
‡On temporary inactive list, April 18 through April 28.
§On military list, May 16 through June 6.

# GEORGE KENNETH GRIFFEY
## (Ken)

Born April 10, 1950, at Donora, Pa.
Height, 6.00. Weight, 185.
Throws and bats lefthanded.
Hobby–Drawing cartoons.

Tied major league record for most at bats, game, since 1900, 7, June 13, 1975.
Major League stolen bases: 1973 (4), 1974 (9), 1975 (16), 1976 (34). Total–63.
Led American Association in stolen bases with 43 in 1973.
Tied for Eastern League lead in double plays by outfielders with 6 in 1972.
Named as outfielder on THE SPORTING NEWS National League All-Star Team, 1976.

| Year Club | League | Pos. | G. | AB. | R. | H. | 2B. | 3B. | HR. | RBI. | B.A. | PO. | A. | E. | F.A. |
|---|---|---|---|---|---|---|---|---|---|---|---|---|---|---|---|---|
| 1969–Bradenton Reds | Gulf C. | *OF-1 | 49 | 153 | 22 | 43 | *11 | 1 | 1 | 12 | .281 | 57 | 4 | *10 | .859 |
| 1970–Sioux Falls | North. | OF | 51 | 164 | 20 | 40 | 2 | 1 | 2 | 24 | .244 | 76 | 2 | 7 | .918 |
| 1971–Tampa | Fla. St. | OF | 88 | 281 | 60 | 96 | 7 | 11 | 3 | 33 | .342 | 137 | 13 | 8 | .949 |
| 1971–Three Rivers | East. | OF | 9 | 32 | 1 | 13 | 1 | 2 | 0 | 4 | .406 | 17 | 0 | 1 | .944 |
| 1972–Three Rivers | East. | ●OF-SS | 128 | 472 | *96 | 150 | 21 | 3 | 14 | 52 | .318 | 212 | 10 | ●15 | .937 |
| 1973–Indianapolis | A. A. | OF | 107 | 397 | 88 | 130 | 18 | 5 | 10 | 58 | .327 | 171 | 11 | 6 | .968 |
| 1973–Cincinnati | Nat. | OF | 25 | 86 | 19 | 33 | 5 | 1 | 3 | 14 | .384 | 25 | 1 | 0 | 1.000 |
| 1974–Indianapolis | A. A. | OF | 43 | 162 | 34 | 54 | 6 | 4 | 5 | 18 | .333 | 70 | 4 | 1 | .987 |
| 1974–Cincinnati | Nat. | OF | 88 | 227 | 24 | 57 | 9 | 5 | 2 | 19 | .251 | 115 | 5 | 0 | 1.000 |
| 1975–Cincinnati | Nat. | OF | 132 | 463 | 95 | 141 | 15 | 9 | 4 | 46 | .305 | 202 | 6 | 7 | .967 |
| 1976–Cincinnati | Nat. | OF | 148 | 562 | 111 | 189 | 28 | 9 | 6 | 74 | .336 | 270 | 10 | 6 | .976 |
| Major League Totals | | | 393 | 1338 | 249 | 420 | 57 | 24 | 15 | 153 | .314 | 612 | 22 | 13 | .980 |

### CHAMPIONSHIP SERIES RECORD

| Year Club | League | Pos. | G. | AB. | R. | H. | 2B. | 3B. | HR. | RBI. | B.A. | PO. | A. | E. | F.A. |
|---|---|---|---|---|---|---|---|---|---|---|---|---|---|---|---|---|
| 1973–Cincinnati | Nat. | OF-PH | 3 | 7 | 0 | 1 | 1 | 0 | 0 | 0 | .143 | 2 | 0 | 0 | 1.000 |
| 1975–Cincinnati | Nat. | OF | 3 | 12 | 3 | 4 | 1 | 0 | 0 | 4 | .333 | 4 | 1 | 0 | 1.000 |
| 1976–Cincinnati | Nat. | OF | 3 | 13 | 2 | 5 | 0 | 1 | 0 | 2 | .385 | 11 | 0 | 0 | 1.000 |
| Championship Series Totals | | | 9 | 32 | 5 | 10 | 2 | 1 | 0 | 6 | .312 | 17 | 1 | 0 | 1.000 |

### WORLD SERIES RECORD

| Year Club | League | Pos. | G. | AB. | R. | H. | 2B. | 3B. | HR. | RBI. | B.A. | PO. | A. | E. | F.A. |
|---|---|---|---|---|---|---|---|---|---|---|---|---|---|---|---|---|
| 1975–Cincinnati | Nat. | OF | 7 | 26 | 4 | 7 | 3 | 1 | 0 | 4 | .269 | 10 | 1 | 0 | 1.000 |
| 1976–Cincinnati | Nat. | OF | 4 | 17 | 2 | 1 | 0 | 0 | 0 | 1 | .059 | 5 | 0 | 0 | 1.000 |
| World Series Totals | | | 11 | 43 | 6 | 8 | 3 | 1 | 0 | 5 | .186 | 15 | 1 | 0 | 1.000 |

### ALL-STAR GAME RECORD

| Year League | Pos. | AB. | R. | H. | 2B. | 3B. | HR. | RBI. | B.A. | PO. | A. | E. | F.A. |
|---|---|---|---|---|---|---|---|---|---|---|---|---|---|
| 1976–National | OF | 1 | 1 | 1 | 0 | 0 | 1 | 1 | 1.000 | 1 | 0 | 0 | 1.000 |

# ALFREDO CLAUDINO GRIFFIN

Born June 10, 1957, at Dominican Republic City, Dominican Republic.
Height, 5.11.   Weight, 160.
Throws right and bats left and righthanded.
Hobby—Music.

| Year   Club   League | Pos. | G. | AB. | R. | H. | 2B. | 3B. | HR. | RBI. | B.A. | PO. | A. | E. | F.A. |
|---|---|---|---|---|---|---|---|---|---|---|---|---|---|---|
| 1974—Sarasota Ind. ....Gulf C. | SS | 49 | 158 | 17 | 41 | 1 | 0 | 0 | 11 | .259 | 67 | 133 | 25 | .889 |
| 1975—San Jose...........Calif. | SS | 124 | 358 | 42 | 82 | 4 | 3 | 0 | 25 | .229 | 189 | 281 | 47 | .909 |
| 1976—San Jose...........Calif. | SS | 64 | 224 | 40 | 58 | 3 | 1 | 0 | 17 | .259 | 91 | 145 | 24 | .908 |
| 1976—Williamsport......East. | SS | 58 | 200 | 22 | 55 | 3 | 0 | 0 | 17 | .275 | 86 | 172 | 17 | .938 |
| 1976—Toledo .............Int. | SS | 22 | 88 | 5 | 19 | 7 | 1 | 0 | 6 | .216 | 44 | 71 | 7 | .943 |
| 1976—Cleveland .........Amer. | SS-DH | 12 | 4 | 0 | 1 | 0 | 0 | 0 | 0 | .250 | 1 | 2 | 1 | .750 |
| Major League Totals ..................... | | 12 | 4 | 0 | 1 | 0 | 0 | 0 | 0 | .250 | 1 | 2 | 1 | .750 |

# DOUGLAS LEE GRIFFIN, JR.
## (Doug)

Born June 4, 1947, at South Gate, Calif.
Height, 6.00.   Weight, 160.
Throws and bats righthanded.
Hobbies—Fishing and hunting.

Led Pacific Coast League in stolen bases with 35 in 1970.
Named second baseman on THE SPORTING NEWS American League All-Star fielding team, 1972.

| Year   Club   League | Pos. | G. | AB. | R. | H. | 2B. | 3B. | HR. | RBI. | B.A. | PO. | A. | E. | F.A. |
|---|---|---|---|---|---|---|---|---|---|---|---|---|---|---|
| 1965—Idaho Falls........Pion. | 2B | 31 | 70 | 9 | 14 | 2 | 1 | 0 | 8 | .200 | 46 | 53 | 6 | .943 |
| 1966—Quad Cities†......Midw. | 2B | 98 | 373 | 66 | 103 | 17 | 5 | 0 | 33 | .276 | 190 | 216 | 17 | .960 |
| 1966-68— | | | | | (Served in U. S. Navy) | | | | | | | | | |
| 1969—Quad Cities ......Midw. | 2B | 60 | 224 | 36 | 56 | 10 | 0 | 4 | 23 | .250 | 137 | 137 | 10 | .965 |
| 1969—El Paso ............Texas | 2B | 50 | 182 | 33 | 56 | 3 | 3 | 1 | 11 | .308 | 110 | 120 | 7 | .970 |
| 1970—Hawaii .............P.C. | •2B-SS | 139 | 552 | 119 | 180 | 20 | 7 | 9 | 60 | .326 | 299 | 337 | •23 | .965 |
| 1970—California‡ ........Amer. | 2B-3B | 18 | 55 | 2 | 7 | 1 | 0 | 0 | 4 | .127 | 24 | 42 | 2 | .971 |
| 1971—Boston‡‡...........Amer. | 2B | 125 | 483 | 51 | 118 | 23 | 2 | 3 | 27 | .244 | 311 | 344 | 9 | .986 |
| 1972—Boston§ ...........Amer. | 2B | 129 | 470 | 43 | 122 | 12 | 1 | 2 | 35 | .260 | 321 | 331 | 15 | .978 |
| 1973—Boston x...........Amer. | 2B | 113 | 396 | 43 | 101 | 14 | 5 | 1 | 33 | .255 | 294 | 284 | 6 | .990 |
| 1974—Boston y...........Amer. | 2B-SS | 93 | 312 | 35 | 83 | 12 | 4 | 0 | 33 | .266 | 180 | 243 | 9 | .979 |
| 1975—Boston ............Amer. | 2B-SS | 100 | 287 | 21 | 69 | 6 | 0 | 1 | 29 | .240 | 195 | 215 | 14 | .967 |
| 1976—Boston ............Amer. | 2B-DH | 49 | 127 | 14 | 24 | 2 | 0 | 0 | 4 | .189 | 77 | 98 | 2 | .989 |
| Major League Totals ..................... | | 627 | 2130 | 209 | 524 | 70 | 12 | 7 | 165 | .246 | 1402 | 1557 | 57 | .981 |

†On military list, October 2, 1966 through October 18, 1968.

‡Traded with Pitcher Ken Tatum and Outfielder Jarvis Tatum to Boston Red Sox for Outfielder Tony Conigliaro, Catcher Jerry Moses and Pitcher Ray Jarvis, October 11, 1970.

‡‡On supplemental disabled list, June 30 through July 27.

§On supplemental disabled list, August 9 through September 1.

xOn disabled list, May 24 to July 13, 1973.

yOn disabled list, April 30 to July 1, 1974.

### WORLD SERIES RECORD

| Year   Club   League | Pos. | G. | AB. | R. | H. | 2B. | 3B. | HR. | RBI. | B.A. | PO. | A. | E. | F.A. |
|---|---|---|---|---|---|---|---|---|---|---|---|---|---|---|
| 1975—Boston .............Amer. | PH | 1 | 1 | 0 | 0 | 0 | 0 | 0 | 0 | .000 | 0 | 0 | 0 | .000 |

# THOMAS JAMES GRIFFIN
## (Tom)

Born February 22, 1948, at Los Angeles, Calif.
Height, 6.03.   Weight, 200.
Throws and bats righthanded.
Attended Los Angeles Valley Junior College, Van Nuys, Calif., and
Pierce Junior College, Woodland Hills, Calif.

Named by THE SPORTING NEWS as National League Rookie Pitcher of the Year, 1969.

| Year   Club | League | G. | IP. | W. | L. | Pct. | H. | R. | ER. | SO. | BB. | ERA. |
|---|---|---|---|---|---|---|---|---|---|---|---|---|
| 1966—Bismarck-Mandan ................Northern | | 11 | 46 | 3 | 5 | .375 | 44 | 33 | 29 | 66 | 29 | 5.67 |
| 1966—Amarillo ............................Texas | | 2 | 7 | 0 | 1 | .000 | 9 | 4 | 4 | 6 | 7 | 5.14 |
| 1967—Oklahoma City ..................P. Coast | | 8 | 34 | 0 | 5 | .000 | 38 | 25 | 22 | 30 | 27 | 5.82 |
| 1967—Asheville† ...........................Carolina | | 12 | 58 | 3 | 4 | .429 | 66 | 43 | 36 | 50 | 23 | 5.59 |
| 1968—Oklahoma City ..................P. C. | | 29 | 168 | 7 | 14 | .333 | 157 | 91 | 81 | 144 | 94 | 4.34 |
| 1969—Houston ............................National | | 31 | 188 | 11 | 10 | .524 | 156 | 80 | 74 | 200 | 93 | 3.54 |
| 1970—Oklahoma City ..................Am. Assoc. | | 5 | 28 | 3 | 2 | .600 | 23 | 14 | 4 | 27 | 16 | 1.29 |
| 1970—Houston ............................National | | 23 | 111 | 3 | 13 | .188 | 118 | 72 | 71 | 72 | 72 | 5.76 |
| 1971—Oklahoma City ..................Am. Assoc. | | 16 | 107 | 6 | 8 | .429 | 101 | 43 | 37 | 90 | 48 | 3.11 |
| 1971—Houston ............................National | | 10 | 38 | 0 | 6 | .000 | 44 | 22 | 20 | 29 | 20 | 4.74 |
| 1972—Houston ............................National | | 39 | 94 | 5 | 4 | .556 | 92 | 39 | 34 | 83 | 38 | 3.26 |
| 1973—Houston‡ ...........................National | | 25 | 100 | 4 | 6 | .400 | 83 | 51 | 46 | 69 | 46 | 4.14 |
| 1974—Houston ............................National | | 34 | 211 | 14 | 10 | .583 | 202 | 97 | 83 | 110 | 89 | 3.54 |
| 1975—Houston§ ...........................National | | 17 | 79 | 3 | 8 | .273 | 89 | 52 | 47 | 56 | 46 | 5.35 |
| 1976—Houston x-San Diego ..........National | | 31 | 112 | 9 | 6 | .600 | 100 | 56 | 51 | 69 | 79 | 4.10 |
| Major League Totals ................................ | | 210 | 933 | 49 | 63 | .438 | 884 | 469 | 426 | 688 | 483 | 4.11 |

†On disabled list, June 13 to July 27, 1967.

‡On disabled list, May 27 to June 21, 1973.

§On disabled list, July 2 to October 3, 1975.

xSold via waivers to San Diego Padres, August 3, 1976.

## STEPHEN JOSEPH GRILLI
### (Steve)

Born May 2, 1949, at Brooklyn, N. Y.
Height, 6.02. Weight, 175.
Throws and bats righthanded.
Attended Gannon College, Erie, Pa.

| Year | Club | League | G. | IP. | W. | L. | Pct. | H. | R. | ER. | SO. | BB. | ERA. |
|------|------|--------|----|----|----|----|------|----|----|-----|-----|-----|------|
| 1971 | Lakeland | Florida St. | 8 | 59 | 5 | 0 | 1.000 | 38 | 16 | 13 | 47 | 32 | 1.98 |
| 1971 | Rocky Mount | Carolina | 24 | 67 | 3 | 5 | .375 | 66 | 28 | 23 | 48 | 34 | 3.09 |
| 1972 | Montgomery | Southern | 20 | 115 | 11 | 3 | .786 | 85 | 27 | 22 | 94 | 48 | 1.72 |
| 1972 | Toledo | Int'national | 15 | 45 | 4 | 3 | .571 | 51 | 29 | 23 | 30 | 36 | 4.60 |
| 1973 | Toledo | Int'national | 6 | 21 | 1 | 2 | .333 | 26 | 19 | 15 | 12 | 9 | 6.43 |
| 1973 | Montgomery | Southern | 21 | 147 | 12 | 7 | .632 | 127 | 55 | 42 | 106 | 60 | 2.57 |
| 1974 | Evansville | Am. Assoc. | 31 | 109 | 6 | 7 | .462 | 108 | 62 | 50 | 80 | 86 | 4.13 |
| 1975 | Evansville | Am. Assoc. | 44 | 102 | 11 | 4 | .733 | 84 | 40 | 34 | 66 | 63 | 3.00 |
| 1975 | Detroit | American | 3 | 7 | 0 | 0 | .000 | 3 | 2 | 1 | 5 | 6 | 1.29 |
| 1976 | Detroit | American | 36 | 66 | 3 | 1 | .750 | 63 | 43 | 34 | 36 | 41 | 4.64 |
| | Major League Totals | | 39 | 73 | 3 | 1 | .750 | 66 | 45 | 35 | 41 | 47 | 4.32 |

## ROSS ALBERT GRIMSLEY, II

Born January 7, 1950, at Topeka, Kan.
Height, 6.03. Weight, 200.
Throws and bats lefthanded.
Hobby—Hunting.
Attended Jackson State Community College, Jackson, Tenn.
Son of Ross Grimsley, pitcher for Chicago White Sox, 1951.

| Year | Club | League | G. | IP. | W. | L. | Pct. | H. | R. | ER. | SO. | BB. | ERA. |
|------|------|--------|----|----|----|----|------|----|----|-----|-----|-----|------|
| 1969 | Sioux Falls | Northern | 18 | 103 | 9 | 4 | .692 | 84 | 38 | 32 | 97 | 34 | 2.80 |
| 1970 | Indianapolis | Am. Assoc. | 29 | 188 | 11 | 8 | .579 | 140 | 65 | 57 | 162 | 59 | •2.73 |
| 1971 | Indianapolis | Am. Assoc. | 6 | 43 | 6 | 0 | 1.000 | 31 | 15 | 14 | 40 | 8 | 2.95 |
| 1971 | Cincinnati | National | 26 | 161 | 10 | 7 | .538 | 151 | 67 | 64 | 67 | 43 | 3.58 |
| 1972 | Indianapolis | Am. Assoc. | 4 | 20 | 1 | 1 | .500 | 26 | 9 | 9 | 9 | 15 | 4.05 |
| 1972 | Cincinnati | National | 30 | 198 | 14 | 8 | .636 | 194 | 73 | 67 | 79 | 50 | 3.05 |
| 1973 | Cincinnati† | National | 38 | 242 | 13 | 10 | .565 | 245 | 96 | 87 | 90 | 68 | 3.24 |
| 1974 | Baltimore | American | 40 | 296 | 18 | 13 | .581 | 267 | 111 | 101 | 158 | 76 | 3.07 |
| 1975 | Baltimore | American | 35 | 197 | 10 | 13 | .435 | 210 | 95 | 89 | 89 | 47 | 4.07 |
| 1976 | Baltimore | American | 28 | 137 | 8 | 7 | .533 | 143 | 66 | 60 | 41 | 35 | 3.94 |
| | National League Totals | | 94 | 601 | 37 | 25 | .597 | 590 | 236 | 218 | 236 | 161 | 3.26 |
| | American League Totals | | 103 | 632 | 36 | 33 | .522 | 620 | 272 | 250 | 288 | 158 | 3.56 |
| | Major League Totals | | 197 | 1233 | 73 | 58 | .557 | 1210 | 508 | 468 | 524 | 319 | 3.42 |

†Traded with Catcher Wally Williams to Baltimore Orioles for Outfielder Merv Rettenmund, Infielder Junior Kennedy and Catcher Bill Wood, December 4, 1973.

### CHAMPIONSHIP SERIES RECORD

| Year | Club | League | G. | IP. | W. | L. | Pct. | H. | R. | ER. | SO. | BB. | ERA. |
|------|------|--------|----|----|----|----|------|----|----|-----|-----|-----|------|
| 1972 | Cincinnati | National | 1 | 9 | 1 | 0 | 1.000 | 2 | 1 | 1 | 5 | 0 | 1.00 |
| 1973 | Cincinnati | National | 2 | 3⅔ | 0 | 1 | .000 | 7 | 5 | 5 | 3 | 2 | 12.27 |
| 1974 | Baltimore | American | 2 | 5⅓ | 0 | 0 | .000 | 1 | 1 | 1 | 2 | 2 | 1.69 |
| | Championship Series Totals | | 5 | 18 | 1 | 1 | .500 | 10 | 7 | 7 | 10 | 4 | 3.50 |

### WORLD SERIES RECORD

| Year | Club | League | G. | IP. | W. | L. | Pct. | H. | R. | ER. | SO. | BB. | ERA. |
|------|------|--------|----|----|----|----|------|----|----|-----|-----|-----|------|
| 1972 | Cincinnati | National | 4 | 7 | 2 | 1 | .667 | 7 | 2 | 2 | 2 | 3 | 2.57 |

## DAVID LYNN GRONLUND

Born August 3, 1954, at Jackson, Minn.
Height, 6.02. Weight, 190.
Throws and bats righthanded.
Attended Riverside City Junior College, Riverside, Calif.

| Year | Club | League | G. | IP. | W. | L. | Pct. | H. | R. | ER. | SO. | BB. | ERA. |
|------|------|--------|----|----|----|----|------|----|----|-----|-----|-----|------|
| 1973 | Jamestown | NYP | 11 | 48 | 2 | 1 | .667 | 60 | 33 | 28 | 47 | 18 | 5.25 |
| 1974 | West Palm Beach | Fla.St. | 24 | 177 | 13 | 7 | .650 | 128 | 58 | 52 | 127 | 73 | 2.64 |
| 1974 | Memphis | Int'national | 2 | 8 | 1 | 0 | 1.000 | 5 | 1 | 0 | 5 | 2 | 0.00 |
| 1975 | Quebec City | Eastern | 21 | 129 | 5 | 10 | .333 | 136 | 73 | 60 | 71 | 57 | 4.19 |
| 1976 | Quebec City | Eastern | 6 | 36 | 3 | 1 | .750 | 24 | 15 | 11 | 27 | 0 | 2.75 |
| 1976 | Denver | Am. Assoc. | 19 | 106 | 10 | 3 | .769 | 107 | 60 | 51 | 54 | 52 | 4.33 |

Listed on Montreal Expos' 1977 spring roster.

## JEFFREY JOHN GROSE
### (Jeff)

Born December 15, 1954, at Kingston, Pa.
Height, 6.00. Weight, 180.
Throws and bats lefthanded.
Nephew of Bob Grose, former player in Philadelphia Phillies' organization.

| Year | Club | League | G. | IP. | W. | L. | Pct. | H. | R. | ER. | SO. | BB. | ERA. |
|------|------|--------|----|----|----|----|------|----|----|-----|-----|-----|------|
| 1972 | Marion | Ap'lachian | 11 | 62 | 4 | 3 | .571 | 52 | 39 | 33 | 68 | 46 | 4.79 |

| Year   Club | League | G. | IP. | W. | L. | Pct. | H. | R. | ER. | SO. | BB. | ERA. |
|-------------|--------|----|-----|----|----|------|----|----|-----|-----|-----|------|
| 1973—Batavia | NYP | 10 | 43 | 3 | 2 | .600 | 31 | 14 | 11 | 58 | 35 | 2.30 |
| 1974—Anderson | W. Carol. | 21 | 129 | 8 | 8 | .500 | 93 | 50 | 39 | 111 | 81 | 2.72 |
| 1975—Jackson | Texas | 24 | 145 | 13 | 8 | .619 | 149 | 74 | 57 | 87 | 85 | 3.54 |
| 1976—Tidewater | Int'national | 26 | 120 | 3 | 12 | .200 | 115 | 78 | 61 | 85 | 88 | 4.58 |

Listed on New York Mets' 1977 spring roster.

## GREGORY EUGENE GROSS
### (Greg)

Born August 1, 1952, at York, Pa.
Height, 5.10. Weight, 165.
Throws and bats lefthanded.
Hobby—Golf.

Established major league record for most times caught stealing, rookie season, 20, in 1974.
Tied for Appalachian League lead in double plays by outfielders with 3 in 1970.
Named National League Rookie Player of the Year by THE SPORTING NEWS, 1974.
Named Appalachian League Rookie of the Year in 1970.

| Year   Club | League | Pos. | G. | AB. | R. | H. | 2B. | 3B. | HR. | RBI. | B.A. | PO. | A. | E. | F.A. |
|-------------|--------|------|----|-----|----|----|-----|-----|-----|------|------|-----|----|----|------|
| 1970—Covington | Appal. | OF | 54 | 211 | 40 | •74 | 8 | 3 | 2 | 27 | .351 | 93 | •10 | 3 | .972 |
| 1971—Columbus | South. | OF-1B | 132 | 494 | 57 | 144 | 14 | 4 | 2 | 33 | .291 | 244 | 13 | 9 | .966 |
| 1972—Columbus | South. | OF | 101 | 367 | 55 | 111 | 14 | 2 | 0 | 25 | .302 | 172 | 9 | 3 | .984 |
| 1972—Okla. City | A.A. | OF | 28 | 109 | 15 | 27 | 4 | 0 | 0 | 8 | .248 | 64 | 4 | 1 | .986 |
| 1973—Denver | A.A. | OF | 131 | 528 | 98 | •174 | 25 | 6 | 0 | 55 | .330 | 226 | 11 | 10 | .960 |
| 1973—Houston | Nat. | OF | 14 | 39 | 5 | 9 | 2 | 1 | 0 | 1 | .231 | 13 | 2 | 0 | 1.000 |
| 1974—Houston | Nat. | OF | 156 | 589 | 78 | 185 | 21 | 8 | 0 | 36 | .314 | 296 | 15 | 2 | .994 |
| 1975—Houston† | Nat. | OF | 132 | 483 | 67 | 142 | 14 | 10 | 0 | 41 | .294 | 216 | 14 | 10 | .958 |
| 1976—Houston‡ | Nat. | OF | 128 | 426 | 52 | 122 | 12 | 3 | 0 | 27 | .286 | 208 | 13 | 5 | .978 |
| Major League Totals | | | 430 | 1537 | 202 | 458 | 49 | 22 | 0 | 105 | .298 | 733 | 44 | 17 | .978 |

†On supplemental disabled list, April 2 to April 24, 1975.
‡Traded to Chicago Cubs for Infielder Julio Gonzalez, December 8, 1976.

## WAYNE DALE GROSS

Born January 14, 1952, at Riverside, Calif.
Height, 6.02. Weight, 210.
Throws right and bats lefthanded.
Hobbies—Fishing and skiing.
Attended California State University, Pomona, Calif.

| Year   Club | League | Pos. | G. | AB. | R. | H. | 2B. | 3B. | HR. | RBI. | B.A. | PO. | A. | E. | F.A. |
|-------------|--------|------|----|-----|----|----|-----|-----|-----|------|------|-----|----|----|------|
| 1973—Lewiston | Northw. | 1B | 8 | 29 | 4 | 7 | 2 | 0 | 1 | 1 | .241 | 58 | 4 | 0 | 1.000 |
| 1973—Burlington | Midw. | 1B-OF | 56 | 187 | 27 | 44 | 8 | 3 | 4 | 36 | .235 | 426 | 19 | 4 | .991 |
| 1974—Birmingham | South. | 1-OF-3 | 105 | 316 | 36 | 77 | 12 | 2 | 14 | 54 | .244 | 503 | 42 | 15 | .973 |
| 1975—Birmingham | South. | OF-1B | 130 | 435 | 69 | 121 | 23 | 2 | 19 | 71 | .278 | 193 | 16 | 13 | .941 |
| 1976—Tucson | P.C. | 3-1-OF | 115 | 395 | 77 | 128 | 30 | 7 | 19 | 75 | .324 | 273 | 164 | 16 | .965 |
| 1976—Oakland | Amer. | 1-DH-OF | 10 | 18 | 0 | 4 | 0 | 0 | 0 | 1 | .222 | 30 | 1 | 1 | .969 |
| Major League Totals | | | 10 | 18 | 0 | 4 | 0 | 0 | 0 | 1 | .222 | 30 | 1 | 1 | .969 |

Listed on Oakland Athletics' 1977 spring roster.

## ROBERT CHARLES GROSSMAN
### (Bob)

Born June 19, 1951, at San Diego, Calif.
Height, 6.04. Weight, 210.
Throws and bats righthanded.
Attended University of Maryland, College Park, Md.

Led Texas League in wild pitches with 22 in 1974.

| Year   Club | League | G. | IP. | W. | L. | Pct. | H. | R. | ER. | SO. | BB. | ERA. |
|-------------|--------|----|-----|----|----|------|----|----|-----|-----|-----|------|
| 1972—Portland | P. Coast | 6 | 15 | 0 | 1 | .000 | 17 | 16 | 13 | 19 | 16 | 7.80 |
| 1972—Elmira | Eastern | 10 | 57 | 1 | 3 | .250 | 55 | 36 | 33 | 58 | 41 | 5.21 |
| 1973—San Antonio† | Texas | 26 | 128 | 5 | 12 | .294 | 128 | 96 | 72 | 157 | 95 | 5.06 |
| 1974—San Antonio | Texas | 22 | 133 | 9 | 11 | .450 | 131 | 82 | 76 | 118 | 75 | 5.14 |
| 1975—San Antonio | Texas | 17 | 105 | 6 | 6 | .500 | 118 | 75 | 65 | 57 | 79 | 5.57 |
| 1975—Oklahoma City | Am. Assoc. | 7 | 23 | 0 | 5 | .000 | 33 | 32 | 28 | 14 | 24 | 10.96 |
| 1976—Williamsport‡ | Eastern | 21 | 75 | 3 | 6 | .333 | 81 | 53 | 44 | 43 | 62 | 5.28 |

†On temporary inactive list, from beginning of season until April 27.
‡On disabled list, April 16 through May 1, 1976.
Listed on Cleveland Indians' 1977 spring roster.

## GERALD WAYNE GROTE
### (Jerry)

Born October 6, 1942, at San Antonio, Tex.
Height, 5.10. Weight, 185.
Throws and bats righthanded.
Hobbies—Bowling, hunting and fishing.
Attended Trinity University, San Antonio, Tex.

Established following major league records: most chances accepted, catcher, 2 consecutive games (31),

April 21-22, 1970; most putouts, catcher, game (20), April 22, 1970 (9-inns.); most putouts, catcher, consecutive, game (10), April 22, 1970.

Established following National League records: most innings, game, catcher (24); most innings, game, catcher, no errors (24); most innings, game, no passed balls (24), April 15, 1968.

Led Texas League catchers in passed balls with 21 in 1963.

| Year | Club | League | Pos. | G. | AB. | R. | H. | 2B. | 3B. | HR. | RBI. | B.A. | PO. | A. | E. | F.A. |
|------|------|--------|------|----|-----|----|----|-----|-----|-----|------|------|-----|----|----|------|
| 1963—San Antonio | | Texas | C | 121 | 384 | 50 | 103 | 22 | 5 | 14 | 62 | .268 | ∗792 | 57 | 18 | .979 |
| 1963—Houston | | Nat. | C | 3 | 5 | 0 | 1 | 0 | 0 | 0 | 1 | .200 | 10 | 0 | 0 | 1.000 |
| 1964—Houston | | Nat. | C | 100 | 298 | 26 | 54 | 9 | 3 | 3 | 24 | .181 | 522 | 52 | 9 | .985 |
| 1965—Oklahoma City† | P.C. | | 3B-C | 118 | 374 | 43 | 99 | 23 | 1 | 11 | 47 | .265 | 402 | 126 | 16 | .971 |
| 1966—New York | | Nat. | C-3B | 120 | 317 | 26 | 75 | 12 | 2 | 3 | 31 | .237 | 519 | 55 | 11 | .981 |
| 1967—New York | | Nat. | C | 120 | 344 | 25 | 67 | 8 | 0 | 4 | 23 | .195 | 609 | 62 | 7 | .990 |
| 1968—New York | | Nat. | C | 124 | 404 | 29 | 114 | 18 | 0 | 3 | 31 | .282 | 754 | 60 | 5 | .994 |
| 1969—New York | | Nat. | C | 113 | 365 | 38 | 92 | 12 | 3 | 6 | 40 | .252 | 718 | 63 | 7 | .991 |
| 1970—New York | | Nat. | C | 126 | 415 | 38 | 106 | 14 | 1 | 2 | 34 | .255 | ∗855 | 46 | 8 | .991 |
| 1971—New York | | Nat. | C | 125 | 403 | 35 | 109 | 25 | 0 | 2 | 35 | .270 | ∗892 | 41 | 9 | .990 |
| 1972—New York | | Nat. | C-3-O | 64 | 205 | 15 | 43 | 5 | 1 | 3 | 21 | .210 | 407 | 43 | 1 | .998 |
| 1973—New York‡ | | Nat. | C-3B | 84 | 285 | 17 | 73 | 10 | 2 | 1 | 32 | .256 | 546 | 37 | 4 | .993 |
| 1974—New York | | Nat. | C | 97 | 319 | 25 | 82 | 8 | 1 | 5 | 36 | .257 | 549 | 36 | 7 | .988 |
| 1975—New York | | Nat. | C | 119 | 386 | 28 | 114 | 14 | 5 | 2 | 39 | .295 | 706 | 55 | 4 | ∗.995 |
| 1976—New York | | Nat. | C-OF | 101 | 323 | 30 | 88 | 14 | 2 | 4 | 28 | .272 | 622 | 49 | 5 | .993 |
| Major League Totals | | | | 1296 | 4069 | 332 | 1018 | 149 | 20 | 38 | 375 | .250 | 7709 | 599 | 77 | .991 |

†Sold to New York Mets, October 19, 1965; deal completed with sale of Pitcher Tom Parsons by Mets to Houston Astros, November 24, 1965.

‡On disabled list, May 12 to July 11, 1973.

### CHAMPIONSHIP SERIES RECORD

| Year | Club | League | Pos. | G. | AB. | R. | H. | 2B. | 3B. | HR. | RBI. | B.A. | PO. | A. | E. | F.A. |
|------|------|--------|------|----|-----|----|----|-----|-----|-----|------|------|-----|----|----|------|
| 1969—New York | | Nat. | C | 3 | 12 | 3 | 2 | 1 | 0 | 0 | 1 | .167 | 22 | 1 | 0 | 1.000 |
| 1973—New York | | Nat. | C | 5 | 19 | 2 | 4 | 0 | 0 | 0 | 2 | .211 | 42 | 1 | 1 | .977 |
| Championship Series Totals | | | | 8 | 31 | 5 | 6 | 1 | 0 | 0 | 3 | .194 | 64 | 2 | 1 | .985 |

### WORLD SERIES RECORD

| Year | Club | League | Pos. | G. | AB. | R. | H. | 2B. | 3B. | HR. | RBI. | B.A. | PO. | A. | E. | F.A. |
|------|------|--------|------|----|-----|----|----|-----|-----|-----|------|------|-----|----|----|------|
| 1969—New York | | Nat. | C | 5 | 19 | 1 | 4 | 2 | 0 | 0 | 1 | .211 | 29 | 2 | 0 | 1.000 |
| 1973—New York | | Nat. | C | 7 | 30 | 2 | 8 | 0 | 0 | 0 | 0 | .267 | 67 | 5 | 0 | 1.000 |
| World Series Totals | | | | 12 | 49 | 3 | 12 | 2 | 0 | 0 | 1 | .245 | 96 | 7 | 0 | 1.000 |

### ALL-STAR GAME RECORD

| Year | League | Pos. | AB. | R. | H. | 2B. | 3B. | HR. | RBI. | B.A. | PO. | A. | E. | F.A. |
|------|--------|------|-----|----|----|-----|-----|-----|------|------|-----|----|----|------|
| 1968—National | | C | 2 | 0 | 0 | 0 | 0 | 0 | 0 | .000 | 3 | 0 | 0 | 1.000 |
| 1974—National | | C | 0 | 0 | 0 | 0 | 0 | 0 | 0 | .000 | 1 | 0 | 0 | 1.000 |
| All-Star Game Totals | | | 2 | 0 | 0 | 0 | 0 | 0 | 0 | .000 | 4 | 0 | 0 | 1.000 |

## JOHN MAYWOOD GRUBB, JR.

Born August 4, 1948, at Richmond, Va.
Height, 6.03. Weight, 180.
Throws right and bats lefthanded.
Hobbies—Golf and playing guitar.
Attended Manatee Junior College, West Bradenton, Fla., and graduated from
Florida State University, Tallahassee, Fla.

Tied for Texas League lead in double plays by outfielders with 4 in 1972.

| Year | Club | League | Pos. | G. | AB. | R. | H. | 2B. | 3B. | HR. | RBI. | B.A. | PO. | A. | E. | F.A. |
|------|------|--------|------|----|-----|----|----|-----|-----|-----|------|------|-----|----|----|------|
| 1971—Lodi | | Calif. | O-3-2 | 116 | 409 | 69 | 126 | 23 | 5 | 12 | 56 | .308 | 158 | 84 | 14 | .945 |
| 1972—Alexandria | | Texas | ∗OF-1B | 126 | 446 | 66 | 132 | 25 | 2 | 10 | 61 | .296 | 205 | 12 | 2 | ∗.991 |
| 1972—San Diego | | Nat. | OF | 7 | 21 | 4 | 7 | 1 | 1 | 0 | 1 | .333 | 16 | 0 | 0 | 1.000 |
| 1973—San Diego | | Nat. | OF-3B | 113 | 389 | 52 | 121 | 22 | 3 | 8 | 37 | .311 | 229 | 11 | 3 | .988 |
| 1974—San Diego | | Nat. | OF-3B | 140 | 444 | 53 | 127 | 20 | 4 | 8 | 42 | .286 | 321 | 8 | 8 | .976 |
| 1975—San Diego | | Nat. | OF | 144 | 553 | 72 | 149 | 36 | 2 | 4 | 38 | .269 | 334 | 3 | 3 | .991 |
| 1976—San Diego† | | Nat. | O-1-2 | 109 | 384 | 54 | 109 | 22 | 1 | 5 | 27 | .284 | 248 | 7 | 6 | .977 |
| Major League Totals | | | | 513 | 1791 | 235 | 513 | 101 | 11 | 25 | 145 | .286 | 1148 | 29 | 20 | .983 |

†On disabled list, April 26 through May 28, 1976; traded with Catcher Fred Kendall and Shortstop Hector Torres to Cleveland Indians for Outfielder George Hendrick, December 8, 1976.

### ALL-STAR GAME RECORD

| Year | League | Pos. | AB. | R. | H. | 2B. | 3B. | HR. | RBI. | B.A. | PO. | A. | E. | F.A. |
|------|--------|------|-----|----|----|-----|-----|-----|------|------|-----|----|----|------|
| 1974—National | | OF | 1 | 0 | 0 | 0 | 0 | 0 | 0 | .000 | 0 | 0 | 0 | .000 |

## MARIO MIGUEL GUERRERO
### Name pronounced Gur-RARE-O.

Born September 28, 1950, at Santo Domingo, Dominican Republic.
Height, 5.11. Weight, 155.
Throws and bats righthanded.
Hobbies—Music and golf.
Attended LaSalle College, Santo Domingo, Dominican Republic.
Brother of Eppy Guerrero, scout for New York Yankees.

Tied major league record for most double plays, game, shortstop, 5, June 2, 1973.
Tied for Carolina League lead in double plays by shortstops with 58 in 1969.

| Year Club | League | Pos. | G. | AB. | R. | H. | 2B. | 3B. | HR. | RBI. | B.A. | PO. | A. | E. | F.A. |
|---|---|---|---|---|---|---|---|---|---|---|---|---|---|---|---|
| 1968—Ft. Lauderdale ..Fla. St. | | SS | 91 | 317 | 28 | 72 | 5 | 1 | 1 | 14 | .237 | 110 | 195 | 25 | .924 |
| 1969—Kinston ...........Carol. | | SS | 132 | 496 | 61 | 140 | 22 | 1 | 3 | 46 | .282 | 180 | 329 | 45 | .919 |
| 1970—Manchester ......East. | | SS | 139 | •555 | 57 | 134 | 19 | 1 | 2 | 38 | .241 | •225 | •355 | •44 | .929 |
| 1971—Syracuse ..........Int. | | SS-3B | 116 | 434 | 53 | 126 | 18 | 1 | 1 | 34 | .290 | 144 | 237 | 27 | .934 |
| 1972—Syra.†-Lou........Int. | | S-3-2 | 131 | 452 | 50 | 132 | 10 | 4 | 2 | 49 | .292 | 169 | 305 | 17 | .965 |
| 1973—Boston ..............Amer. | | SS-2B | 66 | 219 | 19 | 51 | 5 | 2 | 0 | 11 | .233 | 106 | 183 | 8 | .973 |
| 1974—Boston‡ ............Amer. | | SS | 93 | 284 | 18 | 70 | 6 | 2 | 0 | 23 | .246 | 136 | 266 | 13 | .969 |
| 1975—Tulsa ................A.A. | | SS | 31 | 115 | 11 | 32 | 6 | 1 | 0 | 15 | .278 | 44 | 83 | 5 | .962 |
| 1975—St. Louis ..........Nat. | | SS | 64 | 184 | 17 | 44 | 9 | 0 | 0 | 11 | .239 | 76 | 198 | 13 | .955 |
| 1976—Tulsa§ ..............A.A. | | 2B-SS | 29 | 81 | 7 | 19 | 2 | 0 | 2 | 4 | .235 | 45 | 60 | 4 | .963 |
| 1976—California ..........Amer. | | 2-SS-DH | 83 | 268 | 24 | 76 | 12 | 0 | 1 | 18 | .284 | 129 | 172 | 14 | .956 |
| American League Totals ................ | | | 242 | 771 | 61 | 197 | 23 | 4 | 1 | 52 | .256 | 371 | 621 | 35 | .966 |
| National League Totals ................. | | | 64 | 184 | 17 | 44 | 9 | 0 | 0 | 11 | .239 | 76 | 198 | 13 | .955 |
| Major League Totals ..................... | | | 306 | 955 | 78 | 241 | 32 | 4 | 1 | 63 | .252 | 447 | 819 | 48 | .963 |

Major League Totals

†Traded by New York Yankees to Boston Red Sox, June 30, 1972, to complete deal in which Yankees obtained Pitcher Sparky Lyle for Infielder Danny Cater, March 22, 1972.

‡Sold to St. Louis Cardinals and assigned to Tulsa, April 4, 1975; Pitcher Jim Willoughby was sent by Cardinals to Boston Red Sox, July 4, 1975, to complete deal.

§Traded to California Angels for Catcher Ed Jordan, assigned from El Paso to Arkansas, and a player to be named later, May 29, 1976; California assigned First Baseman-Outfielder Ed Kurpiel from Salt Lake City to Tulsa to complete deal, July 30, 1976.

## PEDRO GUERRERO

Born June 29, 1956, at San Pedro de Macoris, Dominican Republic.
Height, 5.11. Weight, 180.
Throws right and bats left and righthanded.

| Year Club | League | Pos. | G. | AB. | R. | H. | 2B. | 3B. | HR. | RBI. | B.A. | PO. | A. | E. | F.A. |
|---|---|---|---|---|---|---|---|---|---|---|---|---|---|---|---|
| 1973—Sarasota Ind.† ..Gulf C. | | 3B-SS | 44 | 153 | 13 | 39 | 2 | 3 | 2 | 22 | .255 | 32 | 82 | 11 | .912 |
| 1974—Orangeburg ......W. Car. | | 3B | 19 | 55 | 3 | 8 | 1 | 0 | 0 | 1 | .145 | 11 | 22 | 5 | .868 |
| 1974—Bellingham........Northw. | | 3B | 82 | 297 | 49 | 94 | •23 | 2 | 3 | 55 | .316 | 69 | 124 | 23 | .894 |
| 1975—Danville ............Midw. | | 3B-OF | 104 | 351 | 81 | 121 | 25 | 5 | 10 | 76 | •.345 | 111 | 168 | 31 | .900 |
| 1976—Waterbury ........East. | | 1B | 132 | 495 | 73 | 151 | •30 | •10 | 5 | 66 | .305 | 1129 | •96 | •19 | .985 |

†Traded by Cleveland Indians to Los Angeles Dodgers for Pitcher Bruce Ellingsen, April 4, 1974.
Listed on Los Angeles Dodgers' 1977 spring roster.

## RONALD AMES GUIDRY
### (Ron)

Born August 28, 1950, at Lafayette, La.
Height, 5.11. Weight, 160.
Throws and bats lefthanded.
Hobbies—Hunting and raising German Shepherd dogs.
Attended University of Southwestern Louisiana, Lafayette, La.

| Year Club | League | G. | IP. | W. | L. | Pct. | H. | R. | ER. | SO. | BB. | ERA. |
|---|---|---|---|---|---|---|---|---|---|---|---|---|
| 1971—Johnson City ......................Ap'lachian | | 7 | 47 | 2 | 2 | .500 | 34 | 13 | 11 | 61 | 27 | 2.11 |
| 1972—Ft. Lauderdale† ...................Florida St. | | 15 | 66 | 2 | 4 | .333 | 53 | 35 | 28 | 61 | 50 | 3.82 |
| 1973—Kinston‡ .............................Carolina | | 20 | 101 | 7 | 6 | .538 | 85 | 53 | 36 | 97 | 70 | 3.21 |
| 1974—West Haven§ ........................Eastern | | 37 | 77 | 2 | 4 | .333 | 80 | 48 | 45 | 79 | 53 | 5.26 |
| 1975—Syracuse .............................Int'national | | 42 | 62 | 6 | 5 | .545 | 46 | 24 | 20 | 76 | 37 | 2.90 |
| 1975—New York ............................American | | 10 | 16 | 0 | 1 | .000 | 15 | 6 | 6 | 15 | 9 | 3.38 |
| 1976—New York ............................American | | 20 | 16 | 0 | 0 | .000 | 20 | 12 | 10 | 12 | 4 | 5.63 |
| 1976—Syracuse .............................Int'national | | 22 | 40 | 5 | 1 | .833 | 16 | 5 | 3 | 50 | 13 | 0.68 |
| Major League Totals ............................... | | 30 | 32 | 0 | 1 | .000 | 35 | 18 | 16 | 27 | 13 | 4.50 |

†Played in one game, as an outfielder.
‡On temporary inactive list, July 13 to August 3, 1973.
§Appeared as an outfielder.

### CHAMPIONSHIP SERIES RECORD

| Year Club | League | Pos. | G. | AB. | R. | H. | 2B. | 3B. | HR. | RBI. | B.A. | PO. | A. | E. | F.A. |
|---|---|---|---|---|---|---|---|---|---|---|---|---|---|---|---|
| 1976—New York.........Amer. | | PR | 0 | 0 | 0 | 0 | 0 | 0 | 0 | 0 | .000 | .... | .... | .... | .... |

## DONALD EDWARD GULLETT
### (Don)

Born January 5, 1951, at Lynn, Ky.
Height, 6.00. Weight, 190.
Throws left and bats righthanded.
Tied National League record for most strikeouts, consecutive, relief pitcher, game (6), August 23, 1970, 2nd game.
Named lefthanded pitcher on THE SPORTING NEWS National League All-Star Team, 1974.

| Year Club | League | G. | IP. | W. | L. | Pct. | H. | R. | ER. | SO. | BB. | ERA. |
|---|---|---|---|---|---|---|---|---|---|---|---|---|
| 1969–Sioux Falls ........................Northern | | 11 | 78 | 7 | 2 | .778 | 49 | 24 | 17 | 87 | 37 | *1.96 |
| 1970–Cincinnati ..........................National | | 44 | 78 | 5 | 2 | .714 | 54 | 23 | 21 | 76 | 44 | 2.42 |
| 1971–Cincinnati ..........................National | | 35 | 218 | 16 | 6 | *.727 | 196 | 73 | 64 | 107 | 64 | 2.64 |
| 1972–Cincinnati ..........................National | | 31 | 135 | 9 | 10 | .474 | .127 | 61 | 59 | 96 | 43 | 3.93 |
| 1973–Cincinnati ..........................National | | 45 | 228 | 18 | 8 | .692 | 198 | 95 | 89 | 153 | 69 | 3.51 |
| 1974–Cincinnati ..........................National | | 36 | 243 | 17 | 11 | .607 | 201 | 93 | 82 | 183 | 88 | 3.04 |
| 1975–Cincinnati† ........................National | | 22 | 160 | 15 | 4 | *.789 | 127 | 49 | 43 | 98 | 56 | 2.42 |
| 1976–Cincinnati‡ ........................National | | 23 | 126 | 11 | 3 | .786 | 119 | 48 | 42 | 64 | 48 | 3.00 |
| Major League Totals ............................... | | 236 | 1188 | 91 | 44 | .674 | 1022 | 442 | 400 | 777 | 412 | 3.03 |

†On disabled list, June 17 to August 18, 1975.
‡Played out option year and granted free agency, November 1, 1976; signed as free agent by New York Yankees, November 18, 1976.

### CHAMPIONSHIP SERIES RECORD

| Year Club | League | G. | IP. | W. | L. | Pct. | H. | R. | ER. | SO. | BB. | ERA. |
|---|---|---|---|---|---|---|---|---|---|---|---|---|
| 1970–Cincinnati ..........................National | | 2 | 3⅔ | 0 | 0 | .000 | 1 | 0 | 0 | 3 | 2 | 0.00 |
| 1972–Cincinnati ..........................National | | 2 | 9 | 0 | 1 | .000 | 12 | 8 | 8 | 5 | 0 | 8.00 |
| 1973–Cincinnati ..........................National | | 3 | 9 | 0 | 1 | .000 | 4 | 2 | 2 | 6 | 3 | 2.00 |
| 1975–Cincinnati ..........................National | | 1 | 9 | 1 | 0 | 1.000 | 8 | 3 | 3 | 5 | 2 | 3.00 |
| 1976–Cincinnati ..........................National | | 1 | 8 | 1 | 0 | 1.000 | 2 | 1 | 1 | 4 | 3 | 1.13 |
| Championship Series Totals ...................... | | 9 | 38⅔ | 2 | 2 | .500 | 27 | 14 | 14 | 23 | 10 | 3.26 |

### WORLD SERIES RECORD

| Year Club | League | G. | IP. | W. | L. | Pct. | H. | R. | ER. | SO. | BB. | ERA. |
|---|---|---|---|---|---|---|---|---|---|---|---|---|
| 1970–Cincinnati ..........................National | | 3 | 6⅔ | 0 | 0 | .000 | 5 | 2 | 1 | 4 | 4 | 1.35 |
| 1972–Cincinnati ..........................National | | 1 | 7 | 0 | 0 | .000 | 5 | 1 | 1 | 4 | 2 | 1.29 |
| 1975–Cincinnati ..........................National | | 3 | 18⅔ | 1 | 1 | .500 | 19 | 9 | 9 | 15 | 10 | 4.34 |
| 1976–Cincinnati ..........................National | | 1 | 7⅓ | 1 | 0 | 1.000 | 5 | 1 | 1 | 4 | 3 | 1.23 |
| World Series Totals ............................... | | 8 | 39⅔ | 2 | 1 | .667 | 34 | 13 | 12 | 27 | 19 | 2.72 |

## LAWRENCE CYRIL GURA
### (Larry)

Born November 26, 1947, at Joliet, Ill.
Height, 6.00. Weight, 185.
Throws left and bats left and righthanded.
Hobbies–Hunting, trapping and fishing.
Attended Arizona State University, Tempe, Ariz.
Tied for International League lead in shutouts with 4 in 1974.
Received reported $50,000 bonus to sign with Chicago Cubs, 1969.

| Year Club | League | G. | IP. | W. | L. | Pct. | H. | R. | ER. | SO. | BB. | ERA. |
|---|---|---|---|---|---|---|---|---|---|---|---|---|
| 1969–Tacoma...............................P. Coast | | 16 | 88 | 4 | 8 | .333 | 79 | 39 | 31 | 47 | 24 | 3.17 |
| 1970–Tacoma...............................P. Coast | | 10 | 61 | 3 | 4 | .429 | 55 | 32 | 27 | 32 | 17 | 3.98 |
| 1970–Chicago...............................National | | 20 | 38 | 1 | 3 | .250 | 35 | 18 | 16 | 21 | 23 | 3.79 |
| 1971–Tacoma...............................P. Coast | | 30 | 190 | 11 | 8 | .579 | 199 | 93 | 75 | 140 | 50 | 3.55 |
| 1971–Chicago...............................National | | 6 | 3 | 0 | 0 | .000 | 6 | 3 | 2 | 2 | 1 | 6.00 |
| 1972–Wichita ............................Am. Assoc. | | 26 | 130 | 11 | 4 | *.733 | 127 | 60 | 53 | 109 | 38 | 3.65 |
| 1972–Chicago...............................National | | 7 | 12 | 0 | 0 | .000 | 11 | 5 | 5 | 13 | 3 | 3.75 |
| 1973–Wichita ............................Am. Assoc. | | 5 | 31 | 1 | 2 | .333 | 38 | 18 | 16 | 29 | 11 | 4.65 |
| 1973–Chicago† ...........................National | | 21 | 65 | 2 | 4 | .333 | 79 | 39 | 35 | 43 | 11 | 4.85 |
| 1974–Spokane‡...........................P. Coast | | 7 | 29 | 1 | 1 | .500 | 34 | 14 | 10 | 25 | 9 | 3.10 |
| 1974–Syracuse .........................Int'national | | 17 | 118 | 7 | 7 | .500 | 89 | 32 | 28 | 97 | 19 | *2.14 |
| 1974–New York ..........................American | | 8 | 56 | 5 | 1 | .833 | 54 | 17 | 15 | 17 | 12 | 2.41 |
| 1975–New York ..........................American | | 26 | 151 | 7 | 8 | .467 | 173 | 65 | 59 | 65 | 41 | 3.52 |
| 1976–Kansas City§ ......................American | | 20 | 63 | 4 | 0 | 1.000 | 47 | 20 | 16 | 22 | 20 | 2.29 |
| National League Totals........................... | | 54 | 118 | 3 | 7 | .300 | 131 | 65 | 58 | 79 | 38 | 4.42 |
| American League Totals........................... | | 54 | 270 | 16 | 9 | .640 | 274 | 102 | 90 | 104 | 73 | 3.00 |
| Major League Totals ............................... | | 108 | 388 | 19 | 16 | .543 | 405 | 167 | 148 | 183 | 111 | 3.43 |

†Traded to Texas Rangers, November 14, 1973 (completion of deal in which Cubs obtained Pitcher Mike Paul, August 31, 1973).
‡Traded by Texas Rangers to New York Yankees for Catcher Duke Sims, May 8, 1974.
§Traded by New York Yankees to Kansas City Royals for Catcher Fran Healy, May 15, 1976.
On disabled list, June 1 to June 23, 1976.

### CHAMPIONSHIP SERIES RECORD

| Year Club | League | G. | IP. | W. | L. | Pct. | H. | R. | ER. | SO. | BB. | ERA. |
|---|---|---|---|---|---|---|---|---|---|---|---|---|
| 1976–Kansas City.......................American | | 2 | 10⅔ | 0 | 1 | .000 | 18 | 6 | 5 | 4 | 1 | 4.22 |

## BRYAN EDMUND HAAS
### (Moose)

Born April 22, 1956, at Baltimore, Md.
Height, 6.00. Weight, 180.
Throws and bats righthanded.
Hobby–Sports.
Attended Catonsville Junior College, Catonsville, Md.

| Year   Club | League | G. | IP. | W. | L. | Pct. | H. | R. | ER. | SO. | BB. | ERA. |
|---|---|---|---|---|---|---|---|---|---|---|---|---|
| 1974—Newark | NYP | 13 | 96 | 5 | 5 | .500 | 91 | 43 | 34 | 89 | 41 | 3.19 |
| 1975—Burlington | Midwest | 25 | 171 | 11 | 8 | .579 | 149 | 66 | 39 | 146 | 49 | 2.05 |
| 1976—Spokane | P. Coast | 30 | 172 | 13 | 9 | .591 | 208 | 116 | *106 | 130 | 86 | 5.55 |
| 1976—Milwaukee | American | 5 | 16 | 0 | 1 | .000 | 12 | 8 | 7 | 9 | 12 | 3.94 |
| Major League Totals | | 5 | 16 | 0 | 1 | .000 | 12 | 8 | 7 | 9 | 12 | 3.94 |

## DENNIS LEROY HAINES
### (Denny)

Born January 24, 1952, at McCloud, Calif.
Height, 6.02. Weight, 214.
Throws right and bats lefthanded.
Hobbies—Hunting, fishing and golfing.
Attended University of Arizona, Tucson, Ariz.; received Bachelor of
Science degree in Recreation.

| Year   Club | League | Pos. | G. | AB. | R. | H. | 2B. | 3B. | HR. | RBI. | B.A. | PO. | A. | E. | F.A. |
|---|---|---|---|---|---|---|---|---|---|---|---|---|---|---|---|
| 1974—Burlington | Midw. | C-1B | 17 | 53 | 9 | 17 | 3 | 0 | 1 | 6 | .321 | 114 | 9 | 1 | .992 |
| 1974—Tucson | P.C. | C | 36 | 104 | 13 | 22 | 6 | 2 | 2 | 11 | .212 | 168 | 12 | 3 | .984 |
| 1975—Birmingham | South. | C | 115 | 366 | 47 | 97 | 15 | 2 | 3 | 48 | .265 | 488 | 72 | 7 | .988 |
| 1975—Tucson | P.C. | | 1 | 1 | 1 | 1 | 0 | 0 | 0 | 0 | 1.000 | | | | |
| 1976—Chattanooga | South. | C-1B | 100 | 311 | 38 | 88 | 11 | 5 | 5 | 44 | .283 | 445 | 36 | 6 | .988 |

Listed on Oakland A's 1977 spring roster.

## JERRY WAYNE HAIRSTON

Born February 16, 1952, at Birmingham, Ala.
Height, 5.10. Weight, 180.
Throws right and bats left and righthanded.
Hobbies—Music, cars and golf.
Attended Lawson State Junior College, Birmingham, Ala.
Son of Sam Hairston, Sr., Chicago White Sox' scout. Brother of John Hairston,
former Chicago Cub catcher, and Sam Hairston, Jr., former second
baseman in Chicago White Sox' organization.

Led Midwest League second basemen in double plays with 77 in 1971.

| Year   Club | League | Pos. | G. | AB. | R. | H. | 2B. | 3B. | HR. | RBI. | B.A. | PO. | A. | E. | F.A. |
|---|---|---|---|---|---|---|---|---|---|---|---|---|---|---|---|
| 1970—Sara. W. Sox | Gulf C. | 2B | 56 | 183 | 37 | 61 | 8 | 2 | 1 | 36 | .333 | 129 | 130 | *19 | .932 |
| 1971—Appleton | Midw. | 2B | 121 | 448 | 86 | 120 | 15 | 4 | 0 | 39 | .268 | *260 | *333 | *31 | .950 |
| 1972—Knoxville | South. | 2-1-O-3 | 132 | 459 | 82 | 134 | 19 | *9 | 10 | 64 | .292 | 591 | 225 | 27 | .968 |
| 1973—Iowa | A.A. | O-2-3-1 | 84 | 274 | 51 | 95 | 18 | 6 | 9 | 65 | .347 | 70 | 36 | 7 | .938 |
| 1973—Chicago | Amer. | OF-1B | 60 | 210 | 25 | 57 | 11 | 1 | 0 | 23 | .271 | 194 | 13 | 5 | .976 |
| 1974—Iowa | A.A. | OF | 42 | 140 | 31 | 53 | 10 | 2 | 5 | 42 | .379 | 48 | 1 | 2 | .961 |
| 1974—Chicago† | Amer. | OF | 45 | 109 | 8 | 25 | 7 | 0 | 0 | 8 | .229 | 24 | 1 | 2 | .926 |
| 1975—Denver | A.A. | DH | 40 | 139 | 28 | 51 | 9 | 0 | 3 | 31 | .367 | 0 | 0 | 0 | .000 |
| 1975—Chicago | Amer. | OF | 69 | 219 | 26 | 62 | 8 | 0 | 0 | 23 | .283 | 111 | 6 | 6 | .951 |
| 1976—Iowa | A.A. | OF-INF | 94 | 325 | 53 | 94 | 24 | 3 | 5 | 64 | .289 | 199 | 13 | 5 | .977 |
| 1976—Chicago | Amer. | OF | 44 | 119 | 20 | 27 | 2 | 2 | 0 | 10 | .227 | 71 | 1 | 2 | .973 |
| Major League Totals | | | 218 | 657 | 79 | 171 | 28 | 3 | 0 | 64 | .260 | 400 | 21 | 15 | .966 |

†On supplemental disabled list, June 27 to July 12, 1974.

## JOHN STEVEN HALE

Born August 5, 1953, at Fresno, Calif.
Height, 6.02. Weight, 195.
Throws right and bats lefthanded.

| Year   Club | League | Pos. | G. | AB. | R. | H. | 2B. | 3B. | HR. | RBI. | B.A. | PO. | A. | E. | F.A. |
|---|---|---|---|---|---|---|---|---|---|---|---|---|---|---|---|
| 1971—Ogden | Pion. | 1B | 41 | 145 | 15 | 33 | 4 | 3 | 2 | 16 | .228 | 304 | 16 | 15 | .955 |
| 1972—Daytona Beach | Fla.St. | OF | 100 | 283 | 42 | 66 | 12 | 6 | 4 | 42 | .233 | 103 | 4 | 5 | .955 |
| 1973—Bakersfield | Calif. | OF | 127 | 421 | 80 | 111 | 27 | 8 | 10 | 67 | .264 | 189 | 11 | 4 | .980 |
| 1974—Waterbury | East. | OF-1B | 117 | 377 | 49 | 102 | 14 | *9 | 8 | 51 | .271 | 293 | 19 | 11 | .966 |
| 1974—Los Angeles | Nat. | OF | 4 | 4 | 2 | 4 | 1 | 0 | 0 | 2 | 1.000 | 0 | 0 | 0 | .000 |
| 1975—Albuquerque | P.C. | OF | 67 | 244 | 38 | 69 | 14 | 5 | 11 | 45 | .283 | 130 | 4 | 6 | .957 |
| 1975—Los Angeles | Nat. | OF | 71 | 204 | 20 | 43 | 7 | 0 | 6 | 22 | .211 | 128 | 2 | 3 | .977 |
| 1976—Albuquerque | P.C. | OF | 103 | 352 | 66 | 113 | 31 | 7 | 12 | 62 | .321 | 167 | 8 | 3 | .983 |
| 1976—Los Angeles | Nat. | OF | 44 | 91 | 4 | 14 | 2 | 1 | 0 | 8 | .154 | 55 | 3 | 1 | .983 |
| Major League Totals | | | 119 | 299 | 26 | 61 | 10 | 1 | 6 | 32 | .204 | 183 | 5 | 4 | .979 |

## EDWARD LOUIS HALICKI
### (Ed)

Born October 4, 1950, at Kearny, N. J.
Height, 6.07. Weight, 225.
Throws and bats righthanded.
Attended Monmouth College, West Long Branch, N. J.

Pitched 6-0 no-hit victory against New York Mets, August 24, 1975 (second game of doubleheader).

| Year   Club | League | G. | IP. | W. | L. | Pct. | H. | R. | ER. | SO. | BB. | ERA. |
|---|---|---|---|---|---|---|---|---|---|---|---|---|
| 1972—Great Falls | Pioneer | 12 | 21 | 0 | 2 | .000 | 15 | 9 | 3 | 29 | 14 | 1.29 |
| 1972—Decatur | Midwest | 7 | 48 | 4 | 2 | .667 | 31 | 20 | 13 | 65 | 24 | 2.44 |

| Year Club | League | G. | IP. | W. | L. | Pct. | H. | R. | ER. | SO. | BB. | ERA. |
|---|---|---|---|---|---|---|---|---|---|---|---|---|
| 1973—Fresno ...........................California | 26 | 182 | 14 | 6 | .700 | 142 | 66 | 54 | 162 | 63 | 2.67 |
| 1974—Phoenix.............................P. Coast | 19 | 123 | 8 | 6 | .571 | 124 | 65 | 59 | 72 | 34 | 4.32 |
| 1974—San Francisco .....................National | 16 | 74 | 1 | 8 | .111 | 84 | 49 | 35 | 40 | 31 | 4.26 |
| 1975—Phoenix.............................P. Coast | 8 | 56 | 5 | 3 | .625 | 46 | 26 | 24 | 55 | 21 | 3.86 |
| 1975—San Francisco ....................National | 24 | 160 | 9 | 13 | .409 | 143 | 76 | 62 | 153 | 59 | 3.49 |
| 1976—San Francisco ....................National | 32 | 186 | 12 | 14 | .462 | 171 | 86 | 75 | 130 | 61 | 3.63 |
| Major League Totals ............................ | 72 | 420 | 22 | 35 | .386 | 398 | 211 | 172 | 323 | 151 | 3.69 |

## TOM EDWARD HALL

Born November 23, 1947, at Thomasville, N. C.
Height, 6.00. Weight, 158.
Throws and bats lefthanded.
Hobby—All sports.
Attended Riverside City College, Riverside, Calif.
Led Gulf Coast League in complete games with 6 and shutouts with 4 in 1966.
Tied for Southern League lead in shutouts with 3 in 1968.

| Year Club | League | G. | IP. | W. | L. | Pct. | H. | R. | ER. | SO. | BB. | ERA. |
|---|---|---|---|---|---|---|---|---|---|---|---|---|
| 1966—Sarasota Twins ..................Gulf Coast | 11 | •79 | •6 | 4 | .600 | 51 | 23 | 17 | •100 | 30 | 1.94 |
| 1966—Orlando..............................Florida St. | 3 | 17 | 1 | 0 | 1.000 | 6 | 4 | 4 | 22 | 10 | 2.12 |
| 1967—Wisconsin Rapids ...............Midwest | 23 | 167 | 14 | 5 | .737 | 117 | 45 | 40 | 177 | 48 | 2.16 |
| 1968—Charlotte...........................Southern | 11 | 73 | 6 | 3 | .667 | 41 | 15 | 11 | 57 | 25 | 1.36 |
| 1968—Minnesota ..........................American | 8 | 30 | 2 | 1 | .667 | 27 | 15 | 8 | 18 | 12 | 2.40 |
| 1969—Denver .............................P. Coast | 7 | 48 | 4 | 1 | .800 | 47 | 18 | 15 | 35 | 12 | 2.81 |
| 1969—Minnesota† .......................American | 31 | 141 | 8 | 7 | .533 | 129 | 63 | 52 | 92 | 50 | 3.32 |
| 1970—Minnesota‡ .......................American | 52 | 155 | 11 | 6 | .647 | 94 | 46 | 44 | 184 | 66 | 2.55 |
| 1971—Minnesota§ .......................American | 48 | 130 | 4 | 7 | .364 | 104 | 54 | 48 | 137 | 58 | 3.32 |
| 1972—Cincinnati ..........................National | 47 | 124 | 10 | 1 | .909 | 77 | 43 | 36 | 134 | 56 | 2.61 |
| 1973—Cincinnati ..........................National | 54 | 104 | 8 | 5 | .615 | 74 | 43 | 40 | 96 | 48 | 3.46 |
| 1974—Cincinnati ..........................National | 40 | 64 | 3 | 1 | .750 | 54 | 32 | 29 | 48 | 30 | 4.08 |
| 1975—Cincinnati x-New York .......National | 36 | 63 | 4 | 3 | .571 | 60 | 39 | 32 | 51 | 33 | 4.57 |
| 1976—New York y ......................National | 5 | 5 | 1 | 1 | .500 | 5 | 3 | 3 | 2 | 5 | 5.40 |
| 1976—Kansas City........................American | 31 | 30 | 1 | 1 | .500 | 28 | 19 | 15 | 25 | 18 | 4.50 |
| American League Totals.......................... | 170 | 486 | 26 | 22 | .542 | 382 | 197 | 167 | 456 | 204 | 3.09 |
| National League Totals........................... | 182 | 360 | 26 | 11 | .703 | 270 | 160 | 140 | 331 | 172 | 3.50 |
| Major League Totals ............................ | 352 | 846 | 52 | 33 | .612 | 652 | 357 | 307 | 787 | 376 | 3.27 |

†On military list, June 13 through July 4.
‡On military list, May 29 through June 15.
§Traded to Cincinnati Reds for Pitcher Wayne Granger, December 3, 1971.
xTraded to New York Mets for Pitcher Mac Scarce, April 15, 1975.
yTraded to Kansas City Royals for Infielder Bryan Jones, assigned from Waterloo to Lynchburg, and cash, May 7, 1976.

### CHAMPIONSHIP SERIES RECORD

| Year Club | League | G. | IP. | W. | L. | Pct. | H. | R. | ER. | SO. | BB. | ERA. |
|---|---|---|---|---|---|---|---|---|---|---|---|---|
| 1969—Minnesota ..........................American | 1 | ⅔ | 0 | 0 | .000 | 0 | 0 | 0 | 0 | 0 | 0.00 |
| 1970—Minnesota ..........................American | 2 | 5⅓ | 0 | 1 | .000 | 6 | 4 | 4 | 6 | 4 | 6.75 |
| 1972—Cincinnati ..........................National | 2 | 7⅓ | 1 | 0 | 1.000 | 3 | 1 | 1 | 8 | 3 | 1.23 |
| 1973—Cincinnati ..........................National | 3 | ⅔ | 0 | 0 | .000 | 3 | 5 | 5 | 1 | 4 | 67.50 |
| 1976—Kansas City........................American | 1 | ⅓ | 0 | 0 | .000 | 1 | 0 | 0 | 0 | 0 | .000 |
| Championship Series Totals ..................... | 9 | 14⅓ | 1 | 1 | .500 | 13 | 10 | 10 | 15 | 11 | 6.28 |

### WORLD SERIES RECORD

| Year Club | League | G. | IP. | W. | L. | Pct. | H. | R. | ER. | SO. | BB. | ERA. |
|---|---|---|---|---|---|---|---|---|---|---|---|---|
| 1972—Cincinnati ..........................National | 4 | 8⅓ | 0 | 0 | .000 | 6 | 0 | 0 | 7 | 2 | 0.00 |

## DAVID EDWARD HAMILTON
### (Dave)

Born December 13, 1947, at Seattle, Wash.
Height, 6.00. Weight, 190.
Throws and bats lefthanded.
Attended Everett Community College, Everett, Wash.

| Year Club | League | G. | IP. | W. | L. | Pct. | H. | R. | ER. | SO. | BB. | ERA. |
|---|---|---|---|---|---|---|---|---|---|---|---|---|
| 1966—Lewiston .......................Northwest | 16 | 90 | 6 | 6 | .500 | 84 | 46 | 41 | 103 | 36 | 4.10 |
| 1967—Burlington..........................Midwest | 15 | 60 | 3 | 5 | .375 | 67 | 37 | 22 | 62 | 29 | 3.30 |
| 1968—Peninsula .........................Carolina | 11 | 67 | 3 | 5 | .375 | 64 | 44 | 33 | 44 | 33 | 4.43 |
| 1968—Leesburg† ........................Florida St. | 10 | 63 | 0 | 7 | .000 | 50 | 28 | 18 | 52 | 32 | 2.57 |
| 1969—Lodi ..............................California | 22 | 135 | 8 | 8 | .500 | 127 | 67 | 62 | 131 | 58 | 4.13 |
| 1969—Birmingham .....................Southern | 5 | 25 | 2 | 2 | .500 | 13 | 3 | 3 | 24 | 6 | 1.08 |
| 1970—Birmingham ......................Southern | 21 | 104 | 6 | 4 | .600 | 88 | 39 | 28 | 86 | 32 | 2.42 |
| 1971—Iowa .............................Am. Assoc. | 30 | 121 | 12 | 4 | •.750 | 98 | 58 | 51 | 88 | 54 | 3.79 |
| 1972—Iowa .............................Am. Assoc. | 8 | 59 | 5 | 1 | .833 | 52 | 19 | 15 | 60 | 23 | 2.29 |
| 1972—Oakland ...........................American | 25 | 101 | 6 | 6 | .500 | 94 | 34 | 33 | 55 | 31 | 2.94 |
| 1973—Tucson ...........................P. Coast | 15 | 105 | 8 | 5 | .615 | 98 | 49 | 44 | 83 | 38 | 3.77 |
| 1973—Oakland ..........................American | 16 | 70 | 6 | 4 | .600 | 74 | 37 | 34 | 34 | 24 | 4.37 |
| 1974—Oakland ..........................American | 29 | 117 | 7 | 4 | .636 | 104 | 45 | 41 | 69 | 48 | 3.15 |

| Year Club | League | G. | IP. | W. | L. | Pct. | H. | R. | ER. | SO. | BB. | ERA. |
|---|---|---|---|---|---|---|---|---|---|---|---|---|
| 1975–Oakland‡-Chicago ...............American | | 41 | 105 | 7 | 7 | .500 | 105 | 42 | 38 | 71 | 47 | 3.26 |
| 1976–Chicago.................................American | | 45 | 90 | 6 | 6 | .500 | 81 | 38 | 36 | 62 | 45 | 3.60 |
| Major League Totals .............................. | | 156 | 483 | 32 | 27 | .542 | 458 | 196 | 182 | 291 | 195 | 3.39 |

†Appeared as first baseman in 5 games and as outfielder in one game.
‡Traded with Infielder-Outfielder Chet Lemon to Chicago White Sox for Pitchers Stan Bahnsen and Lee (Skip) Pitlock, June 15, 1975.

### CHAMPIONSHIP SERIES RECORD

| Year Club | League | G. | IP. | W. | L. | Pct. | H. | R. | ER. | SO. | BB. | ERA. |
|---|---|---|---|---|---|---|---|---|---|---|---|---|
| 1972–Oakland ...........................American | | 1 | 0* | 0 | 0 | .000 | 1 | 0 | 0 | 0 | 1 | 0.00 |

*Pitched to two batters in tenth inning of fourth game.

### WORLD SERIES RECORD

| Year Club | League | G. | IP. | W. | L. | Pct. | H. | R. | ER. | SO. | BB. | ERA. |
|---|---|---|---|---|---|---|---|---|---|---|---|---|
| 1972–Oakland ...........................American | | 2 | 1⅓ | 0 | 0 | .000 | 3 | 4 | 4 | 1 | 1 | 27.00 |

## ISAAC BERNARD HAMPTON
### (Ike)

Born August 22, 1951, at Camden, S. C.
Height, 6.01. Weight, 180.
Throws right and bats left and righthanded.
Hobbies–Fishing and basketball.
Led Pacific Coast League catchers in passed balls with 16 in 1976.

| Year Club League | Pos. | G. | AB. | R. | H. | 2B. | 3B. | HR. | RBI. | B.A. | PO. | A. | E. | F.A. |
|---|---|---|---|---|---|---|---|---|---|---|---|---|---|---|
| 1971–Pompano Beach Fla.St. | C | 110 | 362 | 64 | 95 | 16 | 2 | 11 | 71 | .262 | •675 | 77 | 13 | .983 |
| 1972–Visalia ...............Calif. | *C-3-OF | 101 | 349 | 64 | 88 | 24 | 1 | 21 | 77 | .252 | 656 | •111 | 21 | .973 |
| 1973–Tidewater† ........Int. | C | 18 | 52 | 7 | 11 | 6 | 0 | 1 | 3 | .212 | 100 | 15 | 2 | .983 |
| 1973–Memphis ..........Texas | *C-1B | 88 | 288 | 44 | 62 | 12 | 0 | 9 | 34 | .215 | 451 | 47 | *16 | .969 |
| 1974–Tidewater..........Int. | C | 95 | 303 | 33 | 73 | 8 | 4 | 6 | 26 | .241 | 532 | 59 | 15 | .975 |
| 1974–New York‡ ........Nat. | C | 4 | 4 | 0 | 0 | 0 | 0 | 0 | 1 | .000 | 2 | 0 | 0 | 1.000 |
| 1975–Salt Lake City ..P.C. | C-OF-2 | 76 | 251 | 43 | 65 | 15 | 1 | 10 | 51 | .259 | 240 | 40 | 7 | .976 |
| 1975–California..........Amer. | C-SS-3 | 31 | 66 | 8 | 10 | 3 | 0 | 0 | 4 | .152 | 113 | 15 | 8 | .941 |
| 1976–Salt Lake City ..P.C. | C-3-1-2 | 118 | 364 | 77 | 97 | 23 | 1 | 15 | 60 | .266 | 512 | 84 | 30 | .952 |
| 1976–California..........Amer. | C-SS | 3 | 2 | 0 | 0 | 0 | 0 | 0 | 0 | .000 | 2 | 2 | 0 | 1.000 |
| National League Totals .................. | | 4 | 4 | 0 | 0 | 0 | 0 | 0 | 1 | .000 | 2 | 0 | 0 | 1.000 |
| American League Totals ................ | | 34 | 68 | 8 | 10 | 3 | 0 | 0 | 4 | .147 | 115 | 17 | 8 | .943 |
| Major League Totals ..................... | | 38 | 72 | 8 | 10 | 3 | 0 | 0 | 5 | .139 | 117 | 17 | 8 | .944 |

†On disabled list, May 26 to June 5, 1973.
‡Traded to California Angels for Pitcher Ken Sanders, March 22, 1975.

## STEPHEN ANDREW HAMRICK
### (Steve)

Born April 17, 1952, at Cleveland, O.
Height, 6.01. Weight, 195.
Throws left and bats righthanded.
Hobby–Stamp collecting.
Attended Miami-Dade Junior College, Miami, Fla.; Ohio State University, Columbus, Ohio;
Cornell University, Ithaca, N.Y.; received Bachelor of Arts degree
in Business Administration.

| Year Club | League | G. | IP. | W. | L. | Pct. | H. | R. | ER. | SO. | BB. | ERA. |
|---|---|---|---|---|---|---|---|---|---|---|---|---|
| 1974–Bradenton Cubs...................Gulf Coast | | 11 | 68 | 6 | 2 | .750 | 32 | 14 | 7 | *87 | 24 | *0.93 |
| 1975–Key West ...........................Florida St. | | 15 | 111 | 5 | 6 | .455 | 81 | 29 | 24 | 97 | 53 | 1.95 |
| 1975–Midland.............................Texas | | 13 | 84 | 7 | 2 | .778 | 75 | 39 | 30 | 52 | 48 | 3.21 |
| 1976–Midland.............................Texas | | *29 | 185 | 11 | 11 | .500 | 172 | 104 | 87 | 132 | 112 | 4.23 |

Listed on Chicago Cubs' 1977 spring roster.

## WALLACE LARRY HANEY
### (Known by middle name.)

Born November 19, 1942, at Charlottesville, Va.
Height, 6.02. Weight, 195.
Throws and bats righthanded.
Hobby–Golf.
Brother of George Haney, pitcher in New York Yankees' organization, 1959 through 1963.
Led California League catchers in double plays with 18 and in passed balls with 38 in 1962.
Led Eastern League catchers in double plays with 17 in 1963.
Received reported $60,000 bonus to sign with Baltimore Orioles, 1961.

| Year Club League | Pos. | G. | AB. | R. | H. | 2B. | 3B. | HR. | RBI. | B.A. | PO. | A. | E. | F.A. |
|---|---|---|---|---|---|---|---|---|---|---|---|---|---|---|
| 1961–Bluefield ..........Appal. | C | 47 | 145 | 24 | 37 | 6 | 0 | 6 | 26 | .255 | 356 | 20 | 6 | .984 |
| 1962–Stockton ............Calif. | *C-1B | 123 | 425 | 77 | 109 | 17 | 9 | 18 | 77 | .256 | 966 | *99 | 17 | *.984 |
| 1963–Elmira ...............East. | C | 120 | 404 | 41 | 98 | 19 | 1 | 8 | 40 | .243 | 894 | 85 | 8 | .992 |
| 1964–Elmira† ...........East. | C | 3 | 7 | 0 | 2 | 1 | 0 | 0 | 1 | .286 | 14 | 0 | 0 | 1.000 |
| 1965–Elmira‡ ...........East. | C | 76 | 252 | 23 | 64 | 12 | 3 | 3 | 21 | .254 | 574 | 39 | 9 | .986 |
| 1966–Rochester..........Int. | C | 63 | 197 | 18 | 42 | 6 | 1 | 7 | 25 | .213 | 407 | 27 | 3 | .993 |

| Year Club League | Pos. | G. | AB. | R. | H. | 2B. | 3B. | HR. | RBI. | B.A. | PO. | A. | E. | F.A. |
|---|---|---|---|---|---|---|---|---|---|---|---|---|---|---|
| 1966—Baltimore..........Amer. | C | 20 | 56 | 3 | 9 | 1 | 0 | 1 | 3 | .161 | 123 | 6 | 2 | .985 |
| 1967—Baltimore..........Amer. | C | 58 | 164 | 13 | 44 | 11 | 0 | 3 | 20 | .268 | 311 | 31 | 3 | .991 |
| 1968—Baltimore‡‡ ......Amer. | C | 38 | 89 | 5 | 21 | 3 | 1 | 1 | 5 | .236 | 149 | 18 | 1 | .994 |
| 1969—Seattle§-Oak. ....Amer. | C | 75 | 145 | 11 | 28 | 7 | 0 | 4 | 19 | .193 | 255 | 24 | 6 | .979 |
| 1970—Winnipeg ..........Int. | C-1-3 | 81 | 251 | 21 | 55 | 8 | 2 | 3 | 26 | .219 | 459 | 44 | 8 | .984 |
| 1970—Oakland ............Amer. | C | 2 | 2 | 2 | 0 | 0 | 0 | 0 | 0 | .000 | 6 | 0 | 0 | 1.000 |
| 1971—Iowa..................A.A. | C-3-OF | 102 | 354 | 36 | 95 | 15 | 0 | 10 | 53 | .268 | 528 | 43 | 6 | .990 |
| 1972—Hawaii y ..........P.C. | C-3-1 | 55 | 155 | 22 | 38 | 7 | 1 | 3 | 15 | .245 | 289 | 18 | 0 | 1.000 |
| 1972—Oakland x..........Amer. | C-2B | 5 | 4 | 0 | 0 | 0 | 0 | 0 | 0 | .000 | 4 | 0 | 1 | .800 |
| 1973—Tucson ..............P.C. | C-3B | 75 | 265 | 39 | 76 | 12 | 1 | 2 | 44 | .287 | 370 | 46 | 6 | .966 |
| 1973—Oakland z..........Amer. | C | 2 | 2 | 0 | 1 | 0 | 0 | 0 | 0 | .500 | 3 | 0 | 0 | 1.000 |
| 1973—St. Louis a .......Nat. | C | 2 | 1 | 0 | 0 | 0 | 0 | 0 | 0 | .000 | 2 | 0 | 0 | 1.000 |
| 1974—Oakland ............Amer. | C-3-1 | 76 | 121 | 12 | 20 | 4 | 0 | 2 | 3 | .165 | 219 | 21 | 3 | .968 |
| 1975—Oakland ............Amer. | C-3B | 47 | 26 | 3 | 5 | 0 | 0 | 1 | 2 | .192 | 70 | 4 | 0 | 1.000 |
| 1976—Oakland b..........Amer. | C | 88 | 177 | 12 | 40 | 2 | 0 | 0 | 10 | .226 | 290 | 45 | 9 | .974 |
| American League Totals ............... | | 411 | 786 | 61 | 168 | 28 | 1 | 12 | 62 | .214 | 1430 | 149 | 25 | .984 |
| National League Totals ................. | | 2 | 1 | 0 | 0 | 0 | 0 | 0 | 0 | .000 | 2 | 0 | 0 | 1.000 |
| Major League Totals ..................... | | 413 | 787 | 61 | 168 | 28 | 1 | 12 | 62 | .213 | 1432 | 149 | 25 | .984 |

†On temporary inactive list, May 25 through June 6. In military service most of the season, was taken off military list, February 24, 1965.
‡On disabled list, July 20 through August 10.
‡‡Selected by Seattle Pilots from Baltimore Orioles in expansion draft, October 15, 1968.
§Traded to Oakland Athletics for Infielder John Donaldson, June 13, 1969.
xSold to San Diego Padres' organization, May 30, 1972.
yRecalled by San Diego Padres, September 1, 1972. Sold by San Diego Padres to Oakland A's, September 6, 1972.
zPurchased by St. Louis Cardinals, September 1, 1973.
aSold to Oakland Athletics, March 26, 1974.
bSold to Milwaukee Brewers, December 6, 1976.

### WORLD SERIES RECORD

| Year Club League | Pos. | G. | AB. | R. | H. | 2B. | 3B. | HR. | RBI. | B.A. | PO. | A. | E. | F.A. |
|---|---|---|---|---|---|---|---|---|---|---|---|---|---|---|
| 1974—Oakland ............Amer. | C | 2 | 0 | 0 | 0 | 0 | 0 | 0 | 0 | .000 | 6 | 0 | 0 | 1.000 |

## PRESTON LEE HANNA

Born September 10, 1954, at Pensacola, Fla.
Height, 6.01. Weight, 195.
Throws and bats righthanded.
Hobbies—Hunting, fishing, tennis, yoga and sailing.
Attended Pensacola Junior College, Pensacola, Fla.

| Year Club | League | G. | IP. | W. | L. | Pct. | H. | R. | ER. | SO. | BB. | ERA. |
|---|---|---|---|---|---|---|---|---|---|---|---|---|
| 1972—Wytheville..........................Ap'lachian | | 8 | 36 | 3 | 2 | .600 | 40 | 28 | 26 | 42 | 25 | 6.50 |
| 1973—Greenwood .........................W. Carol. | | 23 | 147 | 8 | 11 | .421 | 138 | 69 | 58 | 130 | 80 | 3.55 |
| 1974—Savannah ...........................Southern | | 27 | 167 | 11 | 6 | .647 | 146 | 80 | 64 | 117 | 117 | 3.45 |
| 1975—Richmond† .........................Int'national | | 26 | 141 | 10 | 10 | .500 | 125 | 73 | 52 | 101 | 92 | 3.32 |
| 1975—Atlanta .............................National | | 4 | 6 | 0 | 0 | .000 | 7 | 1 | 1 | 2 | 5 | 1.50 |
| 1976—Richmond‡ .........................Int'national | | 27 | 126 | 4 | 9 | .308 | 126 | 81 | 74 | 47 | 84 | 5.29 |
| 1976—Atlanta .............................National | | 5 | 8 | 0 | 0 | .000 | 11 | 5 | 4 | 3 | 4 | 4.50 |
| Major League Totals ................................. | | 9 | 14 | 0 | 0 | .000 | 18 | 6 | 5 | 5 | 9 | 3.21 |

†Played in one game as an outfielder.
‡On temporary inactive list, April 16 through April 30, 1976.

## GERALD ELLIS HANNAHS

Born March 6, 1953, at Binghamton, N.Y.
Height, 6.03. Weight, 210.
Throws and bats lefthanded.
Attended University of Arkansas, Fayetteville, Ark.; received Bachelor of Science degree in Finance.

| Year Club | League | G. | IP. | W. | L. | Pct. | H. | R. | ER. | SO. | BB. | ERA. |
|---|---|---|---|---|---|---|---|---|---|---|---|---|
| 1974—Sarasota Expos ...................Gulf Coast | | 9 | 24 | 1 | 1 | .500 | 16 | 9 | 7 | 24 | 12 | 2.63 |
| 1974—West Palm Beach ...............Florida St. | | 4 | 19 | 2 | 1 | .667 | 15 | 7 | 6 | 19 | 12 | 2.84 |
| 1975—Quebec City ......................Eastern | | 19 | 121 | 8 | 3 | .727 | 94 | 43 | 38 | 86 | 66 | 2.83 |
| 1976—Quebec City ......................Eastern | | 26 | 173 | •20 | 6 | .769 | 144 | 56 | 46 | 126 | 88 | 2.39 |
| 1976—Montreal ...........................National | | 3 | 16 | 2 | 0 | 1.000 | 20 | 14 | 12 | 10 | 12 | 6.75 |
| Major League Totals ............................. | | 3 | 16 | 2 | 0 | 1.000 | 20 | 14 | 12 | 10 | 12 | 6.75 |

## STEVEN LOWELL HARGAN
### (Steve)

Born September 8, 1942, at Fort Wayne, Ind.
Height, 6.03. Weight, 193.
Throws and bats righthanded.
Hobbies—Golf, tennis and motorcycles.
Attended Ball State Teachers College, Muncie, Ind., and College of the Desert,
Palm Desert, Calif.

Tied for American League lead in shutouts with 6 in 1967.

| Year Club | League | G. | IP. | W. | L. | Pct. | H. | R. | ER. | SO. | BB. | ERA. |
|---|---|---|---|---|---|---|---|---|---|---|---|---|
| 1961—Selma | Ala.-Fla. | 9 | 43 | 4 | 2 | .667 | 33 | 16 | 11 | 31 | 21 | 2.30 |
| 1962—Burlington | Carolina | 7 | 35 | 1 | 4 | .200 | 37 | 30 | 26 | 25 | 21 | 6.69 |
| 1962—Dubuque | Midwest | 26 | 152 | 8 | 7 | .533 | 135 | 91 | 58 | 140 | 96 | 3.43 |
| 1963—Charleston† | Eastern | 14 | 97 | 8 | 4 | .667 | 81 | 21 | 13 | 72 | 15 | 1.21 |
| 1964—Charleston | Eastern | 3 | 23 | 1 | 2 | .333 | 23 | 10 | 7 | 10 | 10 | 2.74 |
| 1964—Portland | P. Coast | 25 | 156 | 11 | 9 | .550 | 141 | 70 | 60 | 116 | 58 | 3.46 |
| 1965—Portland | P. Coast | 24 | 170 | 13 | 5 | .722 | 157 | 64 | 55 | 135 | 66 | 2.91 |
| 1965—Cleveland | American | 17 | 60 | 4 | 3 | .571 | 55 | 26 | 23 | 37 | 28 | 3.45 |
| 1966—Cleveland | American | 38 | 192 | 13 | 10 | .565 | 173 | 60 | 53 | 132 | 45 | 2.48 |
| 1967—Cleveland | American | 30 | 223 | 14 | 13 | .519 | 180 | 79 | 65 | 141 | 72 | 2.62 |
| 1968—Cleveland | American | 32 | 158 | 8 | 15 | .348 | 139 | 81 | 73 | 78 | 81 | 4.16 |
| 1969—Cleveland | American | 32 | 144 | 5 | 14 | .263 | 145 | 95 | 91 | 76 | 81 | 5.69 |
| 1970—Wichita | Am. Assoc. | 9 | 53 | 4 | 2 | .667 | 58 | 25 | 22 | 27 | 13 | 3.74 |
| 1970—Cleveland‡ | American | 23 | 143 | 11 | 3 | .786 | 101 | 47 | 46 | 72 | 53 | 2.90 |
| 1971—Cleveland§ | American | 37 | 113 | 1 | 13 | .071 | 138 | 83 | 78 | 52 | 56 | 6.21 |
| 1972—Portland | P. Coast | 16 | 76 | 4 | 7 | .364 | 70 | 37 | 32 | 48 | 32 | 3.79 |
| 1972—Cleveland | American | 12 | 20 | 0 | 3 | .000 | 23 | 16 | 13 | 10 | 15 | 5.85 |
| 1973—Oklahoma City x | Am. Assoc. | 41 | 114 | 7 | 8 | .467 | 123 | 76 | 65 | 100 | 42 | 5.12 |
| 1974—Texas | American | 37 | 187 | 12 | 9 | .571 | 202 | 103 | 82 | 98 | 48 | 3.95 |
| 1975—Texas | American | 33 | 189 | 9 | 10 | .474 | 203 | 96 | 80 | 93 | 62 | 3.81 |
| 1976—Texas y | American | 35 | 124 | 8 | 8 | .500 | 127 | 63 | 50 | 63 | 38 | 3.63 |
| Major League Totals | | 326 | 1553 | 85 | 101 | .457 | 1486 | 749 | 654 | 852 | 579 | 3.79 |

†On disabled list April 28 through July 3.
‡On disabled list May 12 through June 3.
§On disabled list May 5 through June 21.
xSold conditionally by Cleveland Indians to Texas Rangers, December 5, 1973; Rangers sent Pitcher Bill Gogolewski to Indians, March 23, 1974, to complete deal.
ySelected by Toronto Blue Jays in American League expansion draft, November 5, 1976.

### ALL-STAR GAME RECORD

Member of American League All-Star Team in 1967 game; did not play.

## GARY LYNN HARGIS

Born November 2, 1956, at Minneapolis, Minn.
Height, 5.11. Weight, 165.
Throws and bats righthanded.
Hobby—Tennis.
Attended Hancock Junior College, Santa Maria, Calif.

| Year Club | League | Pos. | G. | AB. | R. | H. | 2B. | 3B. | HR. | RBI. | B.A. | PO. | A. | E. | F.A. |
|---|---|---|---|---|---|---|---|---|---|---|---|---|---|---|---|
| 1974—Brad. Pirates | Gulf C. | ..... | 1 | 1 | 0 | 0 | 0 | 0 | 0 | 0 | .000 | .... | .... | .... | .... |
| 1974—Niagara Falls | NYP | SS | 62 | 234 | 26 | 69 | 5 | 5 | 2 | 28 | .295 | 63 | 111 | 11 | .941 |
| 1975—Salem | Carol. | SS-3B | 134 | 485 | 66 | 130 | 27 | 1 | 2 | 53 | .268 | 178 | 396 | •46 | .926 |
| 1976—Shreveport | Texas | 2B-SS | 130 | 493 | 51 | 134 | 21 | 1 | 3 | 39 | .272 | 252 | 389 | 17 | .974 |

Listed on Pittsburgh Pirates' 1977 spring roster.

## DUDLEY MICHAEL HARGROVE
### (Mike)

Born October 26, 1949, at Perryton, Tex.
Height, 6.00. Weight, 200.
Throws and bats lefthanded.
Hobbies—Hunting and golf.
Attended Northwestern State University, Alva, Okla.; received Bachelor of Science degree in Education.

Led American League batters in walks with 97 in 1976.
Led Western Carolinas League in total bases with 247 in 1973.
Led Western Carolinas League first basemen in double plays with 118 in 1973 and led New York-Pennsylvania League first basemen with 58 in 1972.
Named American League Rookie Player of the Year by THE SPORTING NEWS, 1974.
Named American League Rookie of the Year by Baseball Writers' Association of America, 1974.
Named Western Carolinas League Player of the Year in 1973.

| Year Club | League | Pos. | G. | AB. | R. | H. | 2B. | 3B. | HR. | RBI. | B.A. | PO. | A. | E. | F.A. |
|---|---|---|---|---|---|---|---|---|---|---|---|---|---|---|---|
| 1972—Geneva | NYP | 1B | •70 | 243 | 38 | 65 | 8 | 0 | 4 | 37 | .267 | •537 | •40 | 10 | •.983 |
| 1973—Gastonia | W. Car. | 1B | •130 | 456 | 88 | •160 | •35 | 8 | 12 | 82 | •.351 | •1121 | •77 | 14 | •.988 |
| 1974—Texas | Amer. | 1B-OF | 131 | 415 | 57 | 134 | 18 | 6 | 4 | 66 | .323 | 638 | 72 | 9 | .987 |
| 1975—Texas | Amer. | OF-1B | 145 | 519 | 82 | 157 | 22 | 2 | 11 | 62 | .303 | 513 | 45 | 13 | .977 |
| 1976—Texas | Amer. | 1B-DH | 151 | 541 | 80 | 155 | 30 | 1 | 7 | 58 | .287 | 1222 | 110 | •21 | .984 |
| Major League Totals | | | 427 | 1475 | 219 | 446 | 70 | 9 | 22 | 186 | .302 | 2373 | 227 | 43 | .984 |

### ALL-STAR GAME RECORD

| Year League | Pos. | AB. | R. | H. | 2B. | 3B. | HR. | RBI. | B.A. | PO. | A. | E. | F.A. |
|---|---|---|---|---|---|---|---|---|---|---|---|---|---|
| 1975—American | PH | 1 | 0 | 0 | 0 | 0 | 0 | 0 | .000 | 0 | 0 | 0 | .000 |

---

# *D I D   Y O U   K N O W —*

That the St. Louis Browns won the American League pennant in 1944?

## LARRY DUANE HARLOW

Born November 13, 1951, at Colorado Springs, Colo.
Height, 6.02. Weight, 185.
Throws and bats lefthanded.
Attended Mesa Community College, Mesa, Ariz.

Led Southern League outfielders in double plays with 5 in 1974 and International League outfielders with 5 in 1975.
Tied for California League lead in double plays by outfielders with 3 in 1973.

| Year Club | League | Pos. | G. | AB. | R. | H. | 2B. | 3B. | HR. | RBI. | B.A. | PO. | A. | E. | F.A. |
|---|---|---|---|---|---|---|---|---|---|---|---|---|---|---|---|
| 1971—Key West .........Fla. St. | | OF-P | 70 | 205 | 22 | 42 | 6 | 2 | 2 | 21 | .205 | 95 | 9 | 7 | .937 |
| 1971—Aberdeen .........North. | | OF | 57 | 217 | 50 | 66 | 8 | 6 | 3 | 34 | .304 | 93 | 5 | 5 | .951 |
| 1972—Lodi .................Calif. | | OF | 131 | 480 | 66 | 112 | 9 | 2 | 2 | 47 | .233 | *274 | 13 | 6 | .980 |
| 1973—Lodi .................Calif. | | OF | 134 | 493 | 88 | 140 | 20 | 11 | 5 | 67 | .284 | *367 | 18 | *18 | .955 |
| 1974—Asheville .........South. | | OF | 134 | 529 | 86 | 147 | 21 | 2 | 4 | 42 | .278 | 284 | *18 | 14 | .956 |
| 1974—Rochester .........Int. | | OF | 4 | 5 | 0 | 1 | 0 | 0 | 0 | 0 | .200 | 5 | 1 | 0 | 1.000 |
| 1975—Rochester.........Int. | | OF | 132 | 424 | 65 | 108 | 11 | 4 | 2 | 31 | .255 | 280 | 10 | 8 | .972 |
| 1975—Baltimore.........Amer. | | OF | 4 | 3 | 1 | 1 | 0 | 0 | 0 | 0 | .333 | 2 | 0 | 0 | 1.000 |
| 1976—Rochester.........Int. | | OF | 130 | 442 | 81 | 109 | 22 | 0 | 7 | 47 | .247 | *.308 | 12 | 9 | .973 |
| Major League Totals | | | 4 | 3 | 1 | 1 | 0 | 0 | 0 | 0 | .333 | 2 | 0 | 0 | 1.000 |

Listed on Baltimore Orioles' 1977 spring roster.

### PITCHING RECORD

| Year Club | League | G. | IP. | W. | L. | Pct. | H. | R. | ER. | SO. | BB. | ERA. |
|---|---|---|---|---|---|---|---|---|---|---|---|---|
| 1971—Key West ..........................Florida St. | | 2 | 1 | 0 | 0 | .000 | 3 | 4 | 0 | 2 | 1 | 0.00 |

## TERRY WALTER HARMON

Born April 12, 1944, at Toledo, O.
Height, 6.02. Weight, 180.
Throws and bats righthanded.
Hobbies—Hunting, fishing and all sports.
Attended Ohio University, Athens, O.; received Bachelor of Science degree in
Physical Education.

Set major league record for most chances accepted by second baseman, game (18), June 12, 1971.

| Year Club | League | Pos. | G. | AB. | R. | H. | 2B. | 3B. | HR. | RBI. | B.A. | PO. | A. | E. | F.A. |
|---|---|---|---|---|---|---|---|---|---|---|---|---|---|---|---|
| 1966—Bakersfield........Calif. | | SS | 77 | 270 | 31 | 78 | 11 | 5 | 0 | 23 | .289 | 102 | 211 | 29 | .915 |
| 1967—Tidewater.........Carol. | | SS | 122 | 427 | 52 | 103 | 16 | 6 | 2 | 28 | .241 | 198 | 350 | 23 | *.960 |
| 1967—Philadelphia .....Nat. | | PR | 2 | 0 | 0 | 0 | 0 | 0 | 0 | 0 | .000 | 0 | 0 | 0 | .000 |
| 1968—Buffalo†...........Int. | | SS-2B | 74 | 245 | 21 | 63 | 11 | 2 | 3 | 30 | .257 | 127 | 220 | 16 | .956 |
| 1969—Philadelphia .....Nat. | | SS-2-3 | 87 | 201 | 25 | 48 | 8 | 1 | 0 | 16 | .239 | 94 | 169 | 7 | .974 |
| 1970—Philadelphia .....Nat. | | SS-2-3 | 71 | 129 | 16 | 32 | 2 | 4 | 0 | 7 | .248 | 64 | 81 | 2 | .986 |
| 1971—Philadelphia .....Nat. | | 2-S-S-3-1 | 79 | 221 | 27 | 45 | 4 | 2 | 0 | 12 | .204 | 144 | 191 | 7 | .980 |
| 1972—Philadelphia .....Nat. | | 2-SS-3 | 73 | 218 | 35 | 62 | 8 | 2 | 2 | 13 | .284 | 116 | 164 | 5 | .982 |
| 1973—Philadelphia .....Nat. | | 2-SS-3 | 72 | 148 | 17 | 31 | 3 | 0 | 0 | 8 | .209 | 100 | 103 | 3 | .985 |
| 1974—Philadelphia .....Nat. | | SS-2B | 27 | 15 | 5 | 2 | 0 | 0 | 0 | 0 | .133 | 9 | 6 | 0 | 1.000 |
| 1975—Philadelphia‡ ....Nat. | | S-2-3 | 48 | 72 | 14 | 13 | 1 | 2 | 0 | 5 | .181 | 32 | 65 | 1 | .990 |
| 1976—Philadelphia .....Nat. | | S-2-3 | 42 | 61 | 12 | 18 | 4 | 1 | 0 | 6 | .295 | 28 | 49 | 3 | .962 |
| Major League Totals | | | 501 | 1065 | 151 | 251 | 30 | 12 | 2 | 67 | .236 | 587 | 828 | 28 | .980 |

†Suffered shoulder separation July 20—out for remainder of season.
‡On disabled list, June 19 to July 11, 1975.

### CHAMPIONSHIP SERIES RECORD

| Year Club | League | Pos. | G. | AB. | R. | H. | 2B. | 3B. | HR. | RBI. | B.A. | PO. | A. | E. | F.A. |
|---|---|---|---|---|---|---|---|---|---|---|---|---|---|---|---|
| 1976—Philadelphia ......Nat. | | PR | 1 | 0 | 1 | 0 | 0 | 0 | 0 | 0 | .000 | 0 | 0 | 0 | .000 |

## COLBERT DALE HARRAH
### (Toby)

Born October 26, 1948, at Sissonville, W. Va.
Height, 6.00. Weight, 180.
Throws and bats righthanded.
Hobbies—Hunting, riding horses and motorcycles.

Named shortstop on THE SPORTING NEWS American League All-Star Team, 1975.

| Year Club | League | Pos. | G. | AB. | R. | H. | 2B. | 3B. | HR. | RBI. | B.A. | PO. | A. | E. | F.A. |
|---|---|---|---|---|---|---|---|---|---|---|---|---|---|---|---|
| 1967—Huron†..............North. | | 2-SS | 63 | 207 | 34 | 53 | 6 | 0 | 3 | 22 | .256 | 136 | 163 | 23 | .929 |
| 1968—Burlington .......Carol. | | SS | 135 | 468 | 73 | 112 | 16 | 3 | 6 | 39 | .239 | 217 | 356 | *50 | .920 |
| 1969—Burlington‡ ......Car. | | SS-2B | 46 | 147 | 27 | 45 | 4 | 2 | 4 | 12 | .306 | 76 | 152 | 10 | .958 |
| 1969—Savannah .........South. | | SS | 28 | 80 | 8 | 19 | 2 | 0 | 2 | 7 | .238 | 36 | 78 | 11 | .912 |
| 1969—Washington........Amer. | | SS | 8 | 1 | 4 | 0 | 0 | 0 | 0 | 0 | .000 | 0 | 0 | 0 | .000 |
| 1970—Pittsfield§.........East. | | SS-3B | 95 | 359 | 57 | 99 | 18 | 1 | 3 | 37 | .276 | 159 | 293 | 27 | .944 |
| 1971—Washington........Amer. | | SS-3B | 127 | 383 | 45 | 88 | 11 | 3 | 2 | 22 | .230 | 187 | 321 | 24 | .955 |
| 1972—Texas x...........Amer. | | SS | 116 | 374 | 47 | 97 | 14 | 3 | 1 | 31 | .259 | 166 | 308 | 20 | .960 |
| 1973—Texas y ...........Amer. | | SS-3B | 118 | 461 | 64 | 120 | 16 | 1 | 10 | 50 | .260 | 155 | 332 | 27 | .947 |
| 1974—Texas...............Amer. | | *SS-3B | 161 | 573 | 79 | 149 | 23 | 2 | 21 | 74 | .260 | *283 | 474 | ●29 | .963 |
| 1975—Texas...............Amer. | | S-3-2 | 151 | 522 | 81 | 153 | 24 | 1 | 20 | 93 | .293 | 253 | 481 | 29 | .962 |
| 1976—Texas...............Amer. | | S-3-DH | 155 | 584 | 64 | 152 | 21 | 1 | 15 | 67 | .260 | ●294 | 481 | *37 | .954 |
| Major League Totals | | | 836 | 2898 | 384 | 759 | 109 | 11 | 69 | 337 | .262 | 1338 | 2397 | 166 | .957 |

†Drafted by Honolulu (Washington Senators' organization) from Reading (Philadelphia Phillies' organization), November 28, 1967.
‡On military list from beginning of season to June 2, 1969.
§On temporary inactive list, July 24 to August 11, 1970.
xOn disabled list, August 14 to September 6, 1972.
yOn supplemental disabled list, July 2 to August 7, 1973.

## ALL-STAR GAME RECORD

| Year League | Pos. | AB. | R. | H. | 2B. | 3B. | HR. | RBI. | B.A. | PO. | A. | E. | F.A. |
|---|---|---|---|---|---|---|---|---|---|---|---|---|---|
| 1976–American .......................... | SS | 2 | 0 | 0 | 0 | 0 | 0 | 0 | .000 | 0 | 0 | 0 | .000 |

Named to American League All-Star Team for the 1972 game; replaced due to an injury.
Member of American League All-Star Team for 1975 game; did not play.

## DERREL McKINLEY HARRELSON
### (Bud)

(Named by brother, who couldn't say Derrel so called him "Bubba"
and it ended up "Bud".)

Born June 6, 1944, at Niles, Calif.
Height, 5.10½. Weight, 155.
Throws right and bats left and righthanded.
Hobby–Golf.
Attended San Francisco State College, San Francisco, Calif.

Tied major league record for most assists, shortstop, extra-inning game, 14, May 24, 1973 (19 innings).
Established National League record for fewest hits, season, 400 or more at bats, 90, in 1972.
Tied National League record for most consecutive errorless games by shortstop, season, 54, June 24 through August 19, 1970 (235 chances accepted).
Named shortstop on THE SPORTING NEWS National League All-Star Team, 1971.
Named shortstop on THE SPORTING NEWS National League All-Star fielding team, 1971.

| Year Club | League | Pos. | G. | AB. | R. | H. | 2B. | 3B. | HR. | RBI. | B.A. | PO. | A. | E. | F.A. |
|---|---|---|---|---|---|---|---|---|---|---|---|---|---|---|---|---|
| 1963–Salinas ...............Calif. | | SS | 36 | 136 | 21 | 30 | 2 | 2 | 1 | 9 | .221 | 41 | 99 | 18 | .886 |
| 1964–Salinas ..............Calif. | | SS | 135 | 441 | 65 | 102 | 12 | 5 | 3 | 48 | .231 | 215 | 347 | 34 | ★.943 |
| 1965–Buffalo ..............Int. | | SS | 131 | 446 | 37 | 112 | 15 | 1 | 2 | 36 | .251 | 243 | 350 | ★31 | .950 |
| 1965–New York...........Nat. | | SS | 19 | 37 | 3 | 4 | 1 | 1 | 0 | 0 | .108 | 28 | 36 | 3 | .955 |
| 1966–Jacksonville ......Int. | | SS | 117 | 389 | 56 | 86 | 8 | 5 | 1 | 26 | .221 | 194 | 379 | 28 | .953 |
| 1966–New York...........Nat. | | SS | 33 | 99 | 20 | 22 | 2 | 4 | 0 | 4 | .222 | 52 | 91 | 1 | .993 |
| 1967–New York...........Nat. | | SS | 151 | 540 | 59 | 137 | 16 | 4 | 1 | 28 | .254 | 254 | 467 | 32 | .958 |
| 1968–New York† ........Nat. | | SS | 111 | 402 | 38 | 88 | 7 | 3 | 0 | 14 | .219 | 199 | 317 | 15 | .972 |
| 1969–New York‡ ........Nat. | | SS | 123 | 395 | 42 | 98 | 11 | 6 | 0 | 24 | .248 | 243 | 347 | 19 | .969 |
| 1970–New York...........Nat. | | SS | 157 | 564 | 72 | 137 | 18 | 8 | 1 | 42 | .243 | ★305 | 401 | 21 | .971 |
| 1971–New York...........Nat. | | SS | 142 | 547 | 55 | 138 | 16 | 6 | 0 | 32 | .252 | 257 | 441 | 16 | .978 |
| 1972–New York§ ........Nat. | | SS | 115 | 418 | 54 | 90 | 10 | 4 | 1 | 24 | .215 | 191 | 334 | 16 | .970 |
| 1973–New York x ......Nat. | | SS | 106 | 356 | 35 | 92 | 12 | 3 | 0 | 20 | .258 | 153 | 315 | 10 | .979 |
| 1974–New York...........Nat. | | SS | 106 | 331 | 48 | 75 | 10 | 0 | 1 | 13 | .227 | 196 | 325 | 17 | .968 |
| 1975–New York y ......Nat. | | SS | 34 | 73 | 5 | 16 | 2 | 0 | 0 | 3 | .219 | 44 | 67 | 7 | .941 |
| 1976–New York...........Nat. | | SS | 118 | 359 | 34 | 84 | 12 | 4 | 1 | 26 | .234 | 183 | 330 | 20 | .962 |
| Major League Totals ...................... | | | 1215 | 4121 | 465 | 981 | 117 | 43 | 5 | 230 | .238 | 2105 | 3471 | 177 | .969 |

†On military list, May 23 to June 12, 1968.
‡On military list, June 25 to July 11, 1969.
§On supplemental disabled list, August 3 to August 25, 1972.
xOn disabled list, June 5 to July 8, 1973; on supplemental disabled list, August 3 to August 18, 1973.
yOn emergency disabled list, May 27 to September 1, 1975.

## CHAMPIONSHIP SERIES RECORD

| Year Club | League | Pos. | G. | AB. | R. | H. | 2B. | 3B. | HR. | RBI. | B.A. | PO. | A. | E. | F.A. |
|---|---|---|---|---|---|---|---|---|---|---|---|---|---|---|---|---|
| 1969–New York...........Nat. | | SS | 3 | 11 | 2 | 2 | 1 | 1 | 0 | 3 | .182 | 6 | 6 | 1 | .923 |
| 1973–New York...........Nat. | | SS | 5 | 18 | 1 | 3 | 0 | 0 | 0 | 2 | .167 | 12 | 14 | 0 | 1.000 |
| Championship Series Totals ............ | | | 8 | 29 | 3 | 5 | 1 | 1 | 0 | 5 | .172 | 18 | 20 | 1 | .974 |

## WORLD SERIES RECORD

| Year Club | League | Pos. | G. | AB. | R. | H. | 2B. | 3B. | HR. | RBI. | B.A. | PO. | A. | E. | F.A. |
|---|---|---|---|---|---|---|---|---|---|---|---|---|---|---|---|---|
| 1969–New York...........Nat. | | SS | 5 | 17 | 1 | 3 | 0 | 0 | 0 | 0 | .176 | 12 | 17 | 0 | 1.000 |
| 1973–New York...........Nat. | | SS | 7 | 24 | 2 | 6 | 1 | 0 | 0 | 1 | .250 | 11 | 24 | 0 | 1.000 |
| World Series Totals ...................... | | | 12 | 41 | 3 | 9 | 1 | 0 | 0 | 1 | .220 | 23 | 41 | 0 | 1.000 |

## ALL-STAR GAME RECORD

| Year League | Pos. | AB. | R. | H. | 2B. | 3B. | HR. | RBI. | B.A. | PO. | A. | E. | F.A. |
|---|---|---|---|---|---|---|---|---|---|---|---|---|---|
| 1970–National .......................... | SS | 3 | 2 | 2 | 0 | 0 | 0 | 0 | .667 | 0 | 4 | 0 | 1.000 |
| 1971–National .......................... | SS | 2 | 0 | 0 | 0 | 0 | 0 | 0 | .000 | 1 | 2 | 0 | 1.000 |
| All-Star Game Totals ...................... | | 5 | 2 | 2 | 0 | 0 | 0 | 0 | .400 | 1 | 6 | 0 | 1.000 |

## DID YOU KNOW —

That the headquarters of the National League, formerly in San Francisco, are now in New York City? The mailing address is 1 Rockefeller Plaza, New York, New York 10019. The telephone is 582-4213 (Area Code 212).

## VICTOR LANIER HARRIS
### (Vic)

Born March 27, 1950, at Los Angeles, Calif.
Height, 6.00. Weight, 170.
Throws right and bats left and righthanded.
Hobbies—All sports, music and records.
Attended Los Angeles Valley Junior College, Van Nuys, Calif.
Led Midwest League in stolen bases with 39 and in sacrifice flies with 8 in 1971.

| Year Club | League | Pos. | G. | AB. | R. | H. | 2B. | 3B. | HR. | RBI. | B.A. | PO. | A. | E. | F.A. |
|---|---|---|---|---|---|---|---|---|---|---|---|---|---|---|---|
| 1970—Coos Bay-N.B'd | N'west | •2-S | 75 | 288 | 63 | 94 | 12 | 0 | 7 | 53 | .326 | 157 | 203 | 20 | •.947 |
| 1971—Burlington ........ | Midw. | 2B | 120 | 444 | 84 | 129 | 27 | 6 | 6 | 55 | .291 | 256 | 298 | 27 | .954 |
| 1972—Birmingham ...... | South. | 2B | 32 | 126 | 17 | 37 | 6 | 1 | 0 | 12 | .294 | 84 | 71 | 6 | .963 |
| 1972—Iowa† ................ | A.A. | 2B | 64 | 249 | 42 | 73 | 9 | 6 | 6 | 25 | .293 | 148 | 161 | 6 | .981 |
| 1972—Texas ................ | Amer. | 2-SS | 61 | 186 | 8 | 26 | 5 | 1 | 0 | 10 | .140 | 113 | 135 | 10 | .961 |
| 1973—Texas‡ ............. | Amer. | O-3-2 | 152 | 555 | 71 | 138 | 14 | 7 | 8 | 44 | .249 | 354 | 79 | 21 | .954 |
| 1974—Chicago§ ......... | Nat. | 2B | 62 | 200 | 18 | 39 | 6 | 3 | 0 | 11 | .195 | 122 | 144 | 16 | .943 |
| 1975—Wichita ............ | A.A. | OF | 32 | 132 | 23 | 32 | 2 | 2 | 1 | 11 | .242 | 63 | 7 | 1 | .986 |
| 1975—Chicago x ......... | Nat. | O-3-2 | 51 | 56 | 6 | 10 | 0 | 0 | 0 | 5 | .179 | 15 | 14 | 2 | .935 |
| 1976—St. Louis y ....... | Nat. | 2-O-3-S | 97 | 259 | 21 | 59 | 12 | 3 | 1 | 19 | .228 | 173 | 103 | 14 | .952 |
| American League Totals | | | 213 | 741 | 79 | 164 | 19 | 8 | 8 | 54 | .221 | 467 | 214 | 31 | .956 |
| National League Totals | | | 210 | 515 | 45 | 108 | 18 | 6 | 1 | 35 | .210 | 310 | 261 | 32 | .947 |
| Major League Totals | | | 423 | 1256 | 124 | 272 | 37 | 14 | 9 | 89 | .216 | 777 | 475 | 63 | .952 |

†Traded with Infielder Orlando Martinez and Pitcher Steve Lawson by Oakland A's to Texas Rangers for First Baseman Don Mincher and Infielder Ted Kubiak, July 20, 1972.
‡Traded with Third Baseman Bill Madlock to Chicago Cubs for Pitcher Ferguson Jenkins, October 25, 1973.
§On disabled list, July 7 through remainder of season.
xTraded to St. Louis Cardinals for Shortstop Mick Kelleher, December 22, 1975.
yTraded with Outfielder Willie Crawford and Pitcher John Curtis to San Francisco Giants for Pitchers John D'Acquisto and Mike Caldwell, and Catcher Dave Rader, October 20, 1976.


## RORIC EDWARD HARRISON

Born September 20, 1946, at Los Angeles, Calif.
Height, 6.03. Weight, 200.
Throws and bats righthanded.
Hobbies—Hunting and fishing.
Attended Pierce Junior College, Woodland Hills, Calif., Santa Monica City
College, Santa Monica, Calif., University of Houston, Houston, Tex.
and Mesa Community College, Mesa, Ariz.
Led Florida Rookie League in hit batsmen with 8 in 1965.

| Year Club | League | G. | IP. | W. | L. | Pct. | H. | R. | ER. | SO. | BB. | ERA. |
|---|---|---|---|---|---|---|---|---|---|---|---|---|
| 1965—Salisbury.............................. | W. Carol. | 5 | 12 | 0 | 1 | .000 | 7 | 12 | 10 | 13 | 16 | 7.50 |
| 1965—Bradenton Astros. ............... | Fla. Rookie | 13 | 62 | 4 | 9 | .667 | 49 | 38 | 32 | 38 | •62 | 4.65 |
| 1966—Cocoa ................................ | Florida St. | 6 | 32 | 1 | 3 | .250 | 31 | 25 | 23 | 28 | 18 | 6.47 |
| 1966—Bismarck-Mandan ............... | Northern | 12 | 56 | 3 | 7 | .300 | 59 | 46 | 31 | 67 | 20 | 4.98 |
| 1967—Asheville† ........................... | Carolina | 4 | 10 | 0 | 0 | .000 | 7 | 3 | 3 | 12 | 3 | 2.70 |
| 1968—Dallas-Ft. Worth ................ | Texas | 9 | 47 | 1 | 5 | .167 | 39 | 30 | 24 | 28 | 28 | 4.60 |
| 1968—Oklahoma City‡.................. | P. Coast | 26 | 107 | 4 | 10 | .286 | 89 | 55 | 48 | 75 | 62 | 4.04 |
| 1969—Oklahoma City§.................. | Am. Assoc. | 3 | 2 | 0 | 0 | .000 | 1 | 0 | 0 | 1 | 2 | 0.00 |
| 1970—Portland x........................... | P. Coast | 31 | 152 | 6 | 11 | .353 | 183 | 112 | 94 | 102 | 98 | 5.57 |
| 1971—Rochester ........................... | Int'national | 25 | 170 | •15 | 5 | .750 | 119 | 65 | 53 | •182 | 74 | 2.81 |
| 1972—Baltimore y........................ | American | 39 | 94 | 3 | 4 | .429 | 68 | 24 | 24 | 62 | 34 | 2.30 |
| 1973—Atlanta .............................. | National | 38 | 177 | 11 | 8 | .579 | 161 | 90 | 82 | 130 | 98 | 4.17 |
| 1974—Atlanta z............................ | National | 20 | 126 | 6 | 11 | .353 | 148 | 70 | 66 | 46 | 49 | 4.71 |
| 1975—Atlanta a............................ | National | 15 | 55 | 3 | 4 | .429 | 58 | 33 | 29 | 22 | 19 | 4.75 |
| 1975—Cleveland b........................ | American | 19 | 126 | 7 | 7 | .500 | 137 | 71 | 67 | 52 | 46 | 4.79 |
| 1976—Tulsa c .............................. | Am. Assoc. | 15 | 55 | 2 | 4 | .333 | 67 | 30 | 29 | 35 | 31 | 4.75 |
| American League Totals........................... | | 58 | 220 | 10 | 11 | .476 | 205 | 95 | 91 | 114 | 80 | 3.72 |
| National League Totals............................ | | 73 | 358 | 20 | 23 | .465 | 367 | 193 | 177 | 198 | 166 | 4.45 |
| Major League Totals .............................. | | 131 | 578 | 30 | 34 | .469 | 572 | 288 | 268 | 312 | 246 | 4.17 |

†In military service most of season.
‡Appeared as outfielder in 2 games.
§Injured most of season. Traded by Houston Astros with Pitcher Horace (Dooley) Womack to Seattle Pilots for Pitcher Jim Bouton, August 24, 1969. Optioned to Portland, April 6, 1970, by Milwaukee Brewers (transferred Seattle franchise) and recalled August 20, 1970.
xTraded by Milwaukee Brewers' organization with Outfielder Marion Jackson to Baltimore Orioles' organization for Pitcher Marcelino Lopez, April 5, 1971.
yTraded with Pitcher Pat Dobson, Catcher Johnny Oates and Infielder Dave Johnson to Atlanta Braves for Catcher Earl Williams and Infielder Taylor Duncan, November 30, 1972.
zOn disabled list, July 25 through October 4, 1974.
aTraded to Cleveland Indians for Pitcher Johnny Odom and a player to be named later, June 7, 1975; Indians assigned Shortstop Rob Belloir to Braves, June 16, 1975, to complete deal.
bTraded to St. Louis Cardinals for Pitcher Harry Parker, April 7, 1976.
cOn disabled list, June 10 through August 14, 1976. Released, March 29, 1977.

## CHARLES OSCAR HARTENSTEIN, JR.
### (Chuck)

Born May 26, 1942, at Seguin, Tex.
Height, 5.11. Weight, 160.
Throws and bats righthanded.
Hobbies—Golf and swimming.
Attended University of Texas, Austin, Tex.; received Bachelor of Arts degree in marketing.

| Year Club | League | G. | IP. | W. | L. | Pct. | H. | R. | ER. | SO. | BB. | ERA. |
|---|---|---|---|---|---|---|---|---|---|---|---|---|
| 1964—St. Cloud | Northern | 18 | 113 | 8 | 5 | .615 | 106 | 50 | 41 | 82 | 46 | 3.27 |
| 1965—Dallas-Ft. Worth | Texas | 28 | 223 | 12 | 7 | .632 | 200 | 66 | 54 | 119 | 46 | *2.18 |
| 1966—Tacoma | P. Coast | 38 | 156 | 3 | 10 | .231 | 134 | 67 | 51 | 81 | 49 | 2.94 |
| 1966—Chicago | National | 5 | 9 | 0 | 0 | .000 | 8 | 2 | 2 | 4 | 3 | 2.00 |
| 1967—Tacoma | P. Coast | 20 | 32 | 3 | 2 | .600 | 34 | 17 | 14 | 23 | 13 | 3.94 |
| 1967—Chicago | National | 45 | 73 | 9 | 5 | .643 | 74 | 27 | 25 | 20 | 17 | 3.08 |
| 1968—Chicago | National | 28 | 36 | 2 | 4 | .333 | 41 | 19 | 18 | 17 | 11 | 4.50 |
| 1968—Tacoma† | P. Coast | 20 | 5 | 2 | 4 | .333 | 50 | 15 | 12 | 29 | 10 | 1.86 |
| 1969—Pittsburgh | National | 56 | 96 | 5 | 4 | .556 | 84 | 42 | 42 | 44 | 27 | 3.94 |
| 1970—Pittsburgh‡ | National | 17 | 24 | 1 | 1 | .500 | 25 | 15 | 12 | 14 | 8 | 4.50 |
| 1970—St. Louis§ | National | 6 | 13 | 0 | 0 | .000 | 24 | 13 | 13 | 9 | 5 | 9.00 |
| 1970—Louisville | Int'national | 3 | 4 | 0 | 0 | .000 | 5 | 1 | 1 | 3 | 1 | 2.25 |
| 1970—Boston x | American | 17 | 19 | 0 | 3 | .000 | 21 | 17 | 17 | 12 | 12 | 8.05 |
| 1971—Tucson y | P. Coast | 49 | 65 | 5 | 6 | .454 | 74 | 31 | 26 | 33 | 18 | 3.60 |
| 1972—Tucson | P. Coast | *74 | 114 | 7 | 5 | .583 | 119 | 43 | 38 | 82 | 32 | 3.00 |
| 1973—Phoenix | P. Coast | 43 | 67 | 4 | 3 | .571 | 76 | 30 | 25 | 45 | 13 | 3.36 |
| 1974—Phoenix z | P. Coast | 41 | 72 | 3 | 5 | .375 | 87 | 39 | 29 | 35 | 25 | 3.63 |
| 1975—Hawaii | P. Coast | 27 | 76 | 6 | 2 | .750 | 76 | 26 | 25 | 32 | 12 | 2.96 |
| 1976—Hawaii a | P. Coast | 39 | 96 | 11 | 5 | .688 | 89 | 38 | 34 | 59 | 20 | 3.19 |
| National League Totals | | 157 | 251 | 17 | 14 | .548 | 256 | 118 | 108 | 108 | 71 | 3.87 |
| American League Totals | | 17 | 19 | 0 | 3 | .000 | 21 | 17 | 17 | 12 | 12 | 8.05 |
| Major League Totals | | 174 | 270 | 17 | 17 | .500 | 277 | 135 | 125 | 120 | 83 | 4.17 |

†Traded with Infielder Ron Campbell to Pittsburgh Pirates' organization for Outfielder Manny Jiminez, January 15, 1969.

‡Sold via waivers to St. Louis Cardinals' organization, June 22, 1970.

§Traded to Boston Red Sox' organization, July 14, 1970.

xSold to Chicago White Sox' organization, December 31, 1970.

yTraded by Chicago White Sox' organization to San Francisco Giants' organization for Pitcher Lee Pitlock, February 7, 1973.

zUnconditionally released, April 3, 1975; signed as free agent with San Diego Padres' organization, May 23, 1975.

aSold to Toronto Blue Jays' organization, November 5, 1976.

## PAUL FRANKLIN HARTZELL, JR.

Born November 2, 1953, at Bloomsburg, Pa.
Height, 6.05. Weight, 200.
Throws and bats righthanded.
Attended Lehigh University, Bethlehem, Pa.; received Bachelor of
Science degree in Mechanical Engineering.

| Year Club | League | G. | IP. | W. | L. | Pct. | H. | R. | ER. | SO. | BB. | ERA. |
|---|---|---|---|---|---|---|---|---|---|---|---|---|
| 1975—Quad Cities | Midwest | 24 | 46 | 2 | 1 | .667 | 28 | 14 | 7 | 37 | 12 | 1.37 |
| 1976—California | American | 37 | 166 | 7 | 4 | .636 | 166 | 64 | 51 | 51 | 43 | 2.77 |
| Major League Totals | | 37 | 166 | 7 | 4 | .636 | 166 | 64 | 51 | 51 | 43 | 2.77 |

## DAVID GEORGE HASBACH
### (Dave)

Born February 4, 1952, at Chicago, Ill.
Height, 6.03. Weight, 210.
Throws and bats righthanded.
Hobbies—Piano and guitar playing.
Attended Miami University, Oxford, Ohio; received Bachelor of Science
degree in Business Education.

Pitched seven-inning, 4-0 no-hit victory against Tulsa, June 2, 1976.
Tied Southern League lead in shutouts with 4 in 1975.

| Year Club | League | G. | IP. | W. | L. | Pct. | H. | R. | ER. | SO. | BB. | ERA. |
|---|---|---|---|---|---|---|---|---|---|---|---|---|
| 1974—Sarasota Royals | G. Coast | | | | | Injured—did not play | | | | | | |
| 1975—Jacksonville | Southern | 24 | 164 | 9 | 10 | .474 | 139 | 66 | 57 | 92 | 58 | 3.13 |
| 1975—Omaha | Am. Assoc. | 3 | 23 | 1 | 2 | .333 | 15 | 5 | 5 | 22 | 6 | 1.96 |
| 1976—Omaha† | Am. Assoc. | 13 | 83 | 7 | 4 | .636 | 65 | 36 | 32 | 62 | 31 | 3.47 |

†On disabled list, July 6 through September 15, 1976.
Listed on Kansas City Royals' 1977 spring roster.

## ANDREW EARL HASSLER
### (Andy)

Born October 18, 1951, at Texas City, Tex.
Height, 6.05 Weight, 215.
Throws and bats lefthanded.
Hobbies—Golf, billiards and tennis.

— 157 —

Tied for Pacific Coast League lead in games started with 31 and in wild pitches with 14 in 1972.

| Year Club | League | G. | IP. | W. | L. | Pct. | H. | R. | ER. | SO. | BB. | ERA. |
|---|---|---|---|---|---|---|---|---|---|---|---|---|
| 1970–El Paso | Texas | 22 | 144 | 10 | 7 | .588 | 138 | 80 | 62 | 122 | 87 | 3.88 |
| 1971–Salt Lake City | P. Coast | 9 | 51 | 5 | 1 | .833 | 50 | 34 | 26 | 42 | 39 | 4.59 |
| 1971–California† | American | 6 | 19 | 0 | 3 | .000 | 25 | 10 | 8 | 13 | 15 | 3.79 |
| 1972–Salt Lake City | P. Coast | 32 | 174 | 9 | 10 | .474 | 163 | 106 | 85 | 150 | ∗114 | 4.40 |
| 1973–Salt Lake City | P. Coast | 24 | 163 | 13 | 8 | .619 | 166 | 93 | 76 | 127 | 81 | 4.20 |
| 1973–California | American | 7 | 32 | 0 | 4 | .000 | 33 | 23 | 13 | 19 | 19 | 3.66 |
| 1974–Salt Lake City | P. Coast | 12 | 79 | 5 | 7 | .417 | 98 | 61 | 52 | 52 | 48 | 5.92 |
| 1974–California | American | 23 | 162 | 7 | 11 | .389 | 132 | 64 | 47 | 76 | 79 | 2.61 |
| 1975–California | American | 30 | 133 | 3 | 12 | .200 | 158 | 94 | 88 | 82 | 53 | 5.95 |
| 1976–Calif.‡-K. C. | American | 33 | 147 | 5 | 12 | .294 | 139 | 68 | 59 | 61 | 56 | 3.61 |
| Major League Totals | | 99 | 493 | 15 | 42 | .263 | 487 | 259 | 215 | 251 | 222 | 3.92 |

†On disabled list April 27 through May 12 and June 28 through August 31.
‡Sold to Kansas City Royals, July 5, 1976.

### CHAMPIONSHIP SERIES RECORD

| Year Club | League | G. | IP. | W. | L. | Pct. | H. | R. | ER. | SO. | BB. | ERA. |
|---|---|---|---|---|---|---|---|---|---|---|---|---|
| 1976–Kansas City | American | 2 | 7⅓ | 0 | 1 | .000 | 8 | 6 | 5 | 4 | 6 | 6.14 |

## FRANCIS XAVIER HEALY
### (Fran)

Born September 6, 1946, at Holyoke, Mass.
Height, 6.04. Weight, 210.
Throws and bats righthanded.
Attended Holyoke Community College, Holyoke, Mass., and received Bachelor of Science
degree in History from American International College, Springfield, Mass.
Son of Bernard Healy, outfielder in St. Louis Cardinal system, 1937-38,
and nephew of Francis Healy, catcher with New York Giants and
St. Louis Cardinals, 1930 through 1932 and 1934.

Led American League in passed balls with 21 in 1974.
Tied for Eastern League lead in double plays by catchers with 9 in 1968.

| Year Club | League | Pos. | G. | AB. | R. | H. | 2B. | 3B. | HR. | RBI. | B.A. | PO. | A. | E. | F.A. |
|---|---|---|---|---|---|---|---|---|---|---|---|---|---|---|---|
| 1965–Dubuque† | Midw. | C | 49 | 125 | 8 | 21 | 4 | 0 | 0 | 13 | .168 | 320 | 29 | 10 | .972 |
| 1966–Dubuque | Midw. | C | 48 | 151 | 24 | 39 | 6 | 2 | 5 | 22 | .258 | 301 | 28 | 12 | .965 |
| 1966–Pawtucket | East. | C-OF | 52 | 161 | 22 | 43 | 10 | 2 | 5 | 19 | .267 | 321 | 41 | 5 | .986 |
| 1967–Pawtucket | East. | C-OF | 78 | 245 | 29 | 66 | 11 | 4 | 5 | 37 | .269 | 360 | 36 | 11 | .973 |
| 1968–Waterbury‡ | East. | C-1B-O | 74 | 235 | 18 | 56 · | 7 | 2 | 4 | 16 | .238 | 388 | 42 | 16 | .964 |
| 1969–Omaha | A.A. | C | 64 | 206 | 26 | 58 | 9 | 2 | 3 | 28 | .282 | 376 | 43 | 7 | .984 |
| 1969–Kansas City | Amer. | C | 6 | 10 | 0 | 4 | 1 | 0 | 0 | 0 | .400 | 16 | 1 | 0 | 1.000 |
| 1970–Omaha§ | A. A. | C | 82 | 252 | 35 | 74 | 12 | 1 | 5 | 36 | .294 | 480 | 44 | 15 | .972 |
| 1971–San Francisco | Nat. | C | 47 | 93 | 10 | 26 | 3 | 0 | 2 | 11 | .280 | 104 | 8 | 4 | .966 |
| 1972–San Francisco x | Nat. | C | 45 | 99 | 12 | 15 | 4 | 0 | 1 | 8 | .152 | 174 | 21 | 1 | .995 |
| 1973–Kansas City | Amer. | C | 95 | 279 | 25 | 77 | 15 | 2 | 6 | 34 | .276 | 429 | 43 | 10 | .979 |
| 1974–Kansas City | Amer. | C | 139 | 445 | 59 | 112 | 24 | 2 | 9 | 53 | .252 | 620 | 64 | 16 | .977 |
| 1975–Kansas City | Amer. | C | 56 | 188 | 16 | 48 | 5 | 2 | 2 | 18 | .255 | 258 | 17 | 5 | .982 |
| 1976–K.C. y-N.Y. | Amer. | C-DH | 54 | 144 | 12 | 35 | 3 | 0 | 0 | 10 | .243 | 134 | 20 | 2 | .987 |
| American League Totals | | | 350 | 1066 | 112 | 276 | 48 | 6 | 17 | 115 | .259 | 1457 | 145 | 33 | .980 |
| National League Totals | | | 92 | 192 | 22 | 41 | 7 | 0 | 3 | 19 | .214 | 278 | 29 | 5 | .984 |
| Major League Totals | | | 442 | 1258 | 134 | 317 | 55 | 6 | 20 | 134 | .252 | 1735 | 174 | 38 | .980 |

†On disabled list with leg injury from May 3 through June 14.
‡Recalled by Cleveland Indians; selected by Kansas City Royals from Cleveland in expansion draft, October 15, 1968.
§Traded by Kansas City Royals to San Francisco Giants for Pitcher Bob Garibaldi, October 19, 1970.
xTraded to Kansas City Royals for Pitcher Greg Minton (assigned from Omaha to Phoenix), April 2, 1973.
yTraded to New York Yankees for Pitcher Larry Gura, May 15, 1976.

### PITCHING RECORD

| Year Club | League | G. | IP. | W. | L. | Pct. | H. | R. | ER. | SO. | BB. | ERA. |
|---|---|---|---|---|---|---|---|---|---|---|---|---|
| 1968–Waterbury | Eastern | 1 | 2 | 0 | 0 | .000 | 2 | 1 | 1 | 1 | 3 | 4.50 |

## MICHAEL THOMAS HEATH
### (Mike)

Born February 5, 1955, at Tampa, Fla.
Height, 5.11. Weight, 180.
Throws and bats righthanded.
Hobbies–All sports.

| Year Club | League | Pos. | G. | AB. | R. | H. | 2B. | 3B. | HR. | RBI. | B.A. | PO. | A. | E. | F.A. |
|---|---|---|---|---|---|---|---|---|---|---|---|---|---|---|---|
| 1973–Johnson City | Appal. | S-2-3B | 48 | 166 | 17 | 29 | 5 | 2 | 0 | 10 | .175 | 83 | 137 | 24 | .902 |
| 1974–Oneonta | NYP | SS | 65 | 234 | 51 | 66 | 6 | 3 | 3 | 34 | .282 | 114 | 170 | 27 | .913 |
| 1975–Ft. Lauderdale | Fla. St. | SS | 98 | 376 | 43 | 87 | 7 | 3 | 1 | 23 | .231 | 184 | 256 | 31 | .934 |
| 1976–Ft. Lauderdale† | Fla. St. | SS-3B-C | 80 | 267 | 28 | 71 | 16 | 3 | 2 | 30 | .266 | 144 | 121 | 16 | .943 |

†On disabled list, June 29 through July 13, 1976.
Listed on New York Yankees' 1977 spring roster.

## DAVID WALLACE HEAVERLO
Name pronounced HAV-ur-low.
### (Dave)
Born August 25, 1950, at Ellensburg, Wash.
Height, 6.02. Weight, 200.
Throws and bats righthanded.
Hobbies—Hunting, golf and fishing.
Attended Central Washington, Ellenburg, Wash.; received Bachelor of Arts
degree in Special Education.
Led California League in saves with 17 in 1973.

| Year Club | League | G. | IP. | W. | L. | Pct. | H. | R. | ER. | SO. | BB. | ERA. |
|---|---|---|---|---|---|---|---|---|---|---|---|---|
| 1973—Fresno | California | *63 | 98 | 7 | 5 | .583 | 100 | 39 | 31 | 100 | 31 | 2.85 |
| 1974—Amarillo | Texas | *48 | 85 | 9 | 5 | .643 | 94 | 32 | 25 | 77 | 28 | 2.65 |
| 1975—San Francisco | National | 42 | 64 | 3 | 1 | .750 | 62 | 18 | 17 | 35 | 31 | 2.39 |
| 1976—San Francisco | National | 61 | 75 | 4 | 4 | .500 | 85 | 45 | 37 | 40 | 15 | 4.44 |
| Major League Totals | | 103 | 139 | 7 | 5 | .583 | 147 | 63 | 54 | 75 | 46 | 3.50 |

## RICHARD JOSEPH HEBNER
### (Richie)
Born November 26, 1947, at Norwood, Mass.
Height, 6.01. Weight, 195.
Throws right and bats lefthanded.
Hobbies—Hockey and hunting.
Brother of William Hebner, International League umpire.
Received reported $40,000 bonus to sign with Pittsburgh Pirates, 1966.

| Year Club | League | Pos. | G. | AB. | R. | H. | 2B. | 3B. | HR. | RBI. | B.A. | PO. | A. | E. | F.A. |
|---|---|---|---|---|---|---|---|---|---|---|---|---|---|---|---|
| 1966—Salem† | Appal. | 1B | 26 | 92 | 17 | 33 | 9 | 3 | 4 | 20 | .359 | 167 | 10 | 2 | .989 |
| 1967—Raleigh‡ | Carol. | 3B | 78 | 274 | 45 | 92 | 15 | 6 | 2 | 33 | .336 | 69 | 135 | 17 | .923 |
| 1968—Columbus‡‡ | Int. | *3B-SS | 104 | 381 | 50 | 105 | 20 | 5 | 6 | 51 | .276 | 77 | 224 | *23 | .929 |
| 1968—Pittsburgh | Nat. | PH | 2 | 1 | 0 | 0 | 0 | 0 | 0 | 0 | .000 | 0 | 0 | 0 | .000 |
| 1969—Pittsburgh | Nat. | 3B-1B | 129 | 459 | 72 | 138 | 23 | 4 | 8 | 47 | .301 | 81 | 240 | 19 | .944 |
| 1970—Pittsburgh§ | Nat. | 3B | 120 | 420 | 60 | 122 | 24 | 8 | 11 | 46 | .290 | 64 | 235 | 19 | .940 |
| 1971—Pittsburgh x | Nat. | 3B | 112 | 388 | 50 | 105 | 17 | 8 | 17 | 67 | .271 | 89 | 172 | 14 | .949 |
| 1972—Pittsburgh | Nat. | 3B | 124 | 427 | 63 | 128 | 24 | 4 | 19 | 72 | .300 | 76 | 210 | 9 | .969 |
| 1973—Pittsburgh | Nat. | 3B | 144 | 509 | 73 | 138 | 28 | 1 | 25 | 74 | .271 | 92 | 260 | 23 | .939 |
| 1974—Pittsburgh | Nat. | 3B | 146 | 550 | 97 | 160 | 21 | 6 | 18 | 68 | .291 | 115 | 304 | *28 | .937 |
| 1975—Pittsburgh | Nat. | 3B | 128 | 472 | 65 | 116 | 16 | 4 | 15 | 57 | .246 | 86 | 244 | 19 | .946 |
| 1976—Pittsburgh y | Nat. | 3B | 132 | 434 | 60 | 108 | 21 | 3 | 8 | 51 | .249 | 87 | 236 | 16 | .953 |
| Major League Totals | | | 1037 | 3660 | 540 | 1015 | 174 | 38 | 121 | 482 | .277 | 690 | 1901 | 147 | .946 |

†On temporary inactive list, August 9. On military list, August 18, 1966 through April 6, 1967.
‡On temporary inactive list, May 13 through May 15, June 10 through June 24 and July 20 through August 16.
‡‡On temporary inactive list, July 13 through July 29.
§On military list, August 8 through August 24.
xOn military list, July 25 through August 9.
yPlayed out option year and granted free agency, November 1, 1976; signed as free agent by Philadelphia Phillies, December 15, 1976.

### CHAMPIONSHIP SERIES RECORD

| Year Club | League | Pos. | G. | AB. | R. | H. | 2B. | 3B. | HR. | RBI. | B.A. | PO. | A. | E. | F.A. |
|---|---|---|---|---|---|---|---|---|---|---|---|---|---|---|---|
| 1970—Pittsburgh | Nat. | 3B | 2 | 6 | 0 | 4 | 2 | 0 | 0 | 0 | .667 | 0 | 4 | 0 | 1.000 |
| 1971—Pittsburgh | Nat. | PH-3B | 4 | 17 | 3 | 5 | 1 | 0 | 2 | 4 | .294 | 4 | 3 | 1 | .875 |
| 1972—Pittsburgh | Nat. | 3B | 5 | 16 | 2 | 3 | 1 | 0 | 0 | 1 | .188 | 5 | 11 | 0 | 1.000 |
| 1974—Pittsburgh | Nat. | 3B | 4 | 13 | 1 | 3 | 0 | 0 | 1 | 4 | .231 | 5 | 7 | 0 | 1.000 |
| 1975—Pittsburgh | Nat. | 3B | 3 | 12 | 2 | 4 | 1 | 0 | 0 | 2 | .333 | 0 | 2 | 0 | 1.000 |
| Championship Series Totals | | | 18 | 64 | 8 | 19 | 5 | 0 | 3 | 11 | .297 | 14 | 27 | 1 | .976 |

### WORLD SERIES RECORD

| Year Club | League | Pos. | G. | AB. | R. | H. | 2B. | 3B. | HR. | RBI. | B.A. | PO. | A. | E. | F.A. |
|---|---|---|---|---|---|---|---|---|---|---|---|---|---|---|---|
| 1971—Pittsburgh | Nat. | 3B | 3 | 12 | 2 | 2 | 0 | 0 | 1 | 3 | .167 | 1 | 3 | 1 | .800 |

## JAMES MICHAEL HEGAN
### (Mike)
Born July 21, 1942, at Cleveland, O.
Height, 6.01. Weight, 190.
Throws and bats lefthanded.
Attended Holy Cross College, Worcester, Mass., John Carroll University.
Cleveland, O., and Calvin Coolidge College, Boston, Mass.
Son of Jim Hegan, coach with Detroit Tigers.

Established major league record for most consecutive errorless games by first baseman, 178, September 24, 1970 to June 3, 1973.
Led Pioneer League batters in walks with 112 and first basemen in double plays with 107 in 1963.
Led Southern League batters in strikeouts with 150 in 1964.
Led International League in walks with 98 and first basemen in double plays with 131 in 1966.

Hit for cycle, game (single, double, triple, home run), September 3, 1976.
Received reported $50,000 bonus to sign with New York Yankees, 1961.

| Year | Club | League | Pos. | G. | AB. | R. | H. | 2B. | 3B. | HR. | RBI. | B.A. | PO. | A. | E. | F.A. |
|---|---|---|---|---|---|---|---|---|---|---|---|---|---|---|---|---|
| 1962—Ft. Lauderdale | | Fla. St. | 1B | 121 | 418 | 75 | 128 | 11 | 1 | 3 | 43 | .306 | 1039 | 57 | 7 | •.994 |
| 1963—Idaho Falls | | Pion. | 1B | 126 | 462 | •123 | 149 | 24 | 9 | 28 | 98 | .323 | •929 | 68 | 12 | •.988 |
| 1964—Columbus | | South. | 1B | 139 | 506 | 53 | 118 | 17 | 4 | 10 | 62 | .233 | •1216 | •97 | 9 | .993 |
| 1964—New York | | Amer. | 1B | 5 | 5 | 0 | 0 | 0 | 0 | 0 | 0 | .000 | 17 | 4 | 0 | 1.000 |
| 1965—Toledo | | Int. | 1B | 35 | 106 | 17 | 19 | 2 | 1 | 1 | 3 | .179 | 286 | 13 | 2 | .993 |
| 1965—Columbus | | South. | 1B | 93 | 295 | 35 | 65 | 13 | 3 | 6 | 39 | .220 | 728 | 52 | 3 | .996 |
| 1966—Toledo | | Int. | 1B | 132 | 461 | 71 | 122 | 27 | •11 | 11 | 44 | .265 | •1207 | 87 | 8 | .994 |
| 1966—New York | | Amer. | 1B | 13 | 39 | 7 | 8 | 0 | 1 | 0 | 2 | .205 | 103 | 8 | 1 | .991 |
| 1967—New York† | | Amer. | 1B-OF | 68 | 118 | 12 | 16 | 4 | 1 | 1 | 3 | .136 | 326 | 20 | 0 | 1.000 |
| 1968—Syracuse‡ | | Int. | 1B-OF | 119 | 424 | 83 | 129 | 15 | 10 | 11 | 39 | .304 | 750 | 28 | 5 | .994 |
| 1969—Seattle | | Amer. | OF-1B | 95 | 267 | 54 | 78 | 9 | 6 | 8 | 37 | .292 | 236 | 20 | 6 | .977 |
| 1970—Milwaukee | | Amer. | •1B-O | 148 | 476 | 70 | 116 | 21 | 2 | 11 | 52 | .244 | 1104 | •113 | 7 | .994 |
| 1971—Mil.§-Oak. | | Amer. | 1B-O | 111 | 177 | 24 | 40 | 7 | 1 | 4 | 14 | .226 | 435 | 45 | 1 | .998 |
| 1972—Oakland | | Amer. | 1-OF | 98 | 79 | 13 | 26 | 3 | 1 | 1 | 5 | .329 | 170 | 11 | 0 | 1.000 |
| 1973—Oak. x-N.Y. | | Amer. | 1B-OF | 112 | 202 | 20 | 49 | 5 | 2 | 7 | 19 | .243 | 512 | 31 | 5 | .991 |
| 1974—N.Y. y-Milw. | | Amer. | 1B-OF | 107 | 243 | 24 | 57 | 9 | 1 | 9 | 41 | .235 | 273 | 13 | 1 | .997 |
| 1975—Milwaukee | | Amer. | OF-1B | 93 | 203 | 19 | 51 | 11 | 0 | 5 | 22 | .251 | 241 | 21 | 2 | .992 |
| 1976—Milwaukee | | Amer. | O-1-DH | 80 | 218 | 30 | 54 | 4 | 3 | 5 | 31 | .248 | 88 | 6 | 2 | .979 |
| Major League Totals | | | | 930 | 2027 | 273 | 495 | 73 | 18 | 51 | 226 | .244 | 3505 | 292 | 25 | .993 |

†In military service from beginning of season through May 11.
‡Sold by New York Yankees to Seattle Pilots' organization, June 14, 1968, to report in 1969.
§Sold to Oakland A's, June 14, 1971.
xTraded to New York Yankees for a player to be named later, August 18, 1973; deal was completed when Athletics received a cash payment.
ySold to Milwaukee Brewers, May 13, 1974.

### CHAMPIONSHIP SERIES RECORD

| Year | Club | League | Pos. | G. | AB. | R. | H. | 2B. | 3B. | HR. | RBI. | B.A. | PO. | A. | E. | F.A. |
|---|---|---|---|---|---|---|---|---|---|---|---|---|---|---|---|---|
| 1971—Oakland | | Amer. | PH | 1 | 1 | 0 | 0 | 0 | 0 | 0 | 0 | .000 | 0 | 0 | 0 | .000 |
| 1972—Oakland | | Amer. | PR-1-PH | 3 | 1 | 1 | 0 | 0 | 0 | 0 | 0 | .000 | 1 | 0 | 0 | 1.000 |
| Championship Series Totals | | | | 4 | 2 | 2 | 0 | 0 | 0 | 0 | 0 | .000 | 1 | 0 | 0 | 1.000 |

### WORLD SERIES RECORD

| Year | Club | League | Pos. | G. | AB. | R. | H. | 2B. | 3B. | HR. | RBI. | B.A. | PO. | A. | E. | F.A. |
|---|---|---|---|---|---|---|---|---|---|---|---|---|---|---|---|---|
| 1964—New York | | Amer. | PR-PH | 3 | 1 | 1 | 0 | 0 | 0 | 0 | 0 | .000 | 0 | 0 | 0 | .000 |
| 1972—Oakland | | Amer. | 1-PH | 6 | 5 | 0 | 1 | 0 | 0 | 0 | 0 | .200 | 11 | 1 | 0 | 1.000 |
| World Series Totals | | | | 9 | 6 | 1 | 1 | 0 | 0 | 0 | 0 | .167 | 11 | 1 | 0 | 1.000 |

### ALL-STAR GAME RECORD

Named to American League All-Star Team for 1969 game; replaced due to injury.

## JACK SEALE HEIDEMANN

Name pronounced HYDE-a-min.

Born July 11, 1949, at Brenham, Tex.
Height, 6.00. Weight, 188.
Throws and bats righthanded.
Hobbies—Pool, hunting, fishing and golf.
Attended Blinn Junior College, Brenham, Tex.

Tied for American League lead in sacrifice flies with 10 in 1970.

| Year | Club | League | Pos. | G. | AB. | R. | H. | 2B. | 3B. | HR. | RBI. | B.A. | PO. | A. | E. | F.A. |
|---|---|---|---|---|---|---|---|---|---|---|---|---|---|---|---|---|
| 1967—Rock Hill | | W. Car. | SS | 58 | 210 | 20 | 39 | 8 | 3 | 3 | 20 | .186 | 95 | 149 | 14 | .946 |
| 1968—Reno | | Calif. | SS | 135 | 548 | 105 | 167 | •33 | •13 | 7 | 53 | .305 | 330 | 330 | 39 | .935 |
| 1969—Portland† | | P.C. | SS | 9 | 39 | 6 | 11 | 1 | 0 | 1 | 4 | .282 | 15 | 27 | 3 | .933 |
| 1969—Cleveland | | Amer. | SS | 3 | 3 | 0 | 0 | 0 | 0 | 0 | 0 | .000 | 1 | 5 | 0 | 1.000 |
| 1970—Cleveland | | Amer. | SS | 133 | 445 | 44 | 94 | 14 | 2 | 6 | 37 | .211 | 216 | 354 | 23 | .961 |
| 1971—Wichita | | A.A. | SS | 6 | 24 | 7 | 6 | 0 | 0 | 0 | 2 | .250 | 10 | 14 | 2 | .923 |
| 1971—Cleveland‡ | | Amer. | SS | 81 | 240 | 16 | 50 | 7 | 0 | 0 | 9 | .208 | 113 | 188 | 7 | .977 |
| 1972—Portland | | P.C. | SS-OF | 143 | 515 | 74 | 132 | 23 | 4 | 12 | 50 | .256 | 207 | 400 | 34 | .947 |
| 1972—Cleveland‡‡ | | Amer. | SS | 10 | 20 | 0 | 3 | 0 | 0 | 0 | 0 | .150 | 10 | 17 | 1 | .964 |
| 1973—Tucson x | | P.C. | •SS-OF | 109 | 424 | 55 | 120 | 19 | 1 | 0 | 41 | .283 | 161 | 320 | 17 | •.966 |
| 1974—Cleveland y | | Amer. | 3-S-2-1 | 12 | 11 | 2 | 1 | 0 | 0 | 0 | 0 | .091 | 5 | 6 | 0 | 1.000 |
| 1974—Tulsa | | A.A. | SS-3B | 14 | 54 | 10 | 16 | 6 | 0 | 0 | 3 | .296 | 17 | 35 | 5 | .912 |
| 1974—St. Louis z | | Nat. | SS-3B | 47 | 70 | 8 | 19 | 1 | 0 | 0 | 3 | .271 | 42 | 46 | 3 | .967 |
| 1975—New York | | Nat. | S-3-2 | 61 | 145 | 12 | 31 | 4 | 2 | 1 | 16 | .214 | 72 | 89 | 10 | .942 |
| 1976—Tidewater | | Int. | O-3-2 | 37 | 149 | 26 | 53 | 9 | 1 | 4 | 27 | .356 | 52 | 95 | 9 | .942 |
| 1976—New York a | | Nat. | SS-2B | 5 | 12 | 0 | 1 | 0 | 0 | 0 | 0 | .083 | 5 | 7 | 0 | 1.000 |
| 1976—Milwaukee | | Amer. | 3-2-DH | 69 | 146 | 11 | 32 | 1 | 0 | 2 | 10 | .219 | 74 | 89 | 3 | .982 |
| American League Totals | | | | 308 | 865 | 73 | 180 | 22 | 2 | 8 | 56 | .208 | 419 | 659 | 34 | .969 |
| National League Totals | | | | 113 | 227 | 20 | 51 | 5 | 2 | 1 | 19 | .225 | 119 | 142 | 13 | .952 |
| Major League Totals | | | | 421 | 1092 | 93 | 231 | 27 | 4 | 9 | 75 | .212 | 538 | 801 | 47 | .966 |

†On military list, May 11, 1969 through March 9, 1970.
‡On emergency disabled list, August 4 through October 18.
‡‡Traded with Catcher Ray Fosse to Oakland Athletics for Catcher Dave Duncan and Outfielder George Hendrick, March 24, 1973.

xSold by Oakland A's to Cleveland Indians, March 25, 1974.
yTraded to St. Louis Cardinals for Infielders Ed Crosby and Luis Alvarado, May 31, 1974.
zTraded with Outfielder Mike Vail to New York Mets for Infielder Teddy Martinez, December 11, 1974.
aTraded to Milwaukee Brewers for Pitcher Jim Deidel and Outfielder Terry Ervin, June 23, 1976.

## DOUGLAS WADE HEINOLD
### (Doug)

Born January 12, 1955, at Victoria, Tex.
Height, 6.04. Weight, 175.
Throws and bats righthanded.
Hobbies—Hunting and fishing.
Tied for Eastern League lead in hit batsmen with 9 in 1975.

| Year Club | League | G. | IP. | W. | L. | Pct. | H. | R. | ER. | SO. | BB. | ERA. |
|---|---|---|---|---|---|---|---|---|---|---|---|---|
| 1973—Johnson City | Ap'lachian | 11 | 75 | 5 | 4 | .556 | 83 | 37 | 27 | 73 | 11 | 3.24 |
| 1974—Ft. Lauderdale | Florida St. | 26 | 195 | 11 | 8 | .579 | 150 | 62 | 49 | 108 | 46 | 2.26 |
| 1975—West Haven | Eastern | 23 | 169 | 10 | 7 | .588 | 139 | 60 | 43 | 74 | 36 | 2.29 |
| 1975—Syracuse | Int'national | 1 | 6 | 0 | 1 | .000 | 8 | 3 | 3 | 0 | 1 | 4.50 |
| 1976—Syracuse | Int'national | 17 | 97 | 4 | 9 | .308 | 128 | 59 | 51 | 30 | 33 | 4.93 |
| 1976—West Haven | Eastern | 11 | 74 | 7 | 3 | .700 | 67 | 14 | 11 | 35 | 10 | 1.34 |

Listed on New York Yankees' 1977 spring roster.

## THOMAS KENNETH HEINTZELMAN
### (Tom)

Born November 3, 1946, at St. Charles, Mo.
Height, 6.00. Weight, 185.
Throws and bats righthanded.
Hobbies—Hunting, fishing and golf.
Attended Parsons College, Fairfield, Ia.; received Bachelor of Science
. degree in Physical Education.
Son of Ken Heintzelman, pitcher with Pittsburgh Pirates and Philadelphia Phillies,
1937 through 1942 and 1946 through 1952.
Led Texas League second basemen in double plays with 90 in 1971 and 82 in 1972.

| Year Club | League | Pos. | G. | AB. | R. | H. | 2B. | 3B. | HR. | RBI. | B.A. | PO. | A. | E. | F.A. |
|---|---|---|---|---|---|---|---|---|---|---|---|---|---|---|---|
| 1968—Sarasota Cards | Gulf C. | 2B | 7 | 24 | 3 | 6 | 0 | 0 | 0 | 2 | .250 | 22 | 11 | 4 | .892 |
| 1968—Ced. Rap. | Midw. | 2B-SS | 45 | 165 | 27 | 45 | 4 | 1 | 1 | 11 | .273 | 101 | 125 | 11 | .945 |
| 1969-70— | | | | | (In Military Service) | | | | | | | | | | |
| 1971—Arkansas | Tex. | *2B-SS | 135 | 515 | 56 | 113 | 24 | 2 | 7 | 35 | .219 | *284 | *351 | 21 | .968 |
| 1972—Arkansas | Tex. | *2B-SS | ●139 | 524 | 68 | 138 | 25 | 5 | 4 | 47 | .263 | *329 | 371 | 21 | *.971 |
| 1973—Tulsa | A.A. | 2B-SS | 106 | 408 | 57 | 116 | 17 | 7 | 4 | 58 | .284 | 259 | 334 | 33 | .947 |
| 1973—St. Louis | Nat. | 2B | 23 | 29 | 5 | 9 | 0 | 0 | 0 | 0 | .310 | 8 | 13 | 0 | 1.000 |
| 1974—Tulsa | A.A. | 2-3-S | 55 | 198 | 29 | 51 | 9 | 2 | 3 | 19 | .258 | 97 | 141 | 15 | .941 |
| 1974—St. Louis† | Nat. | 2-3-S | 38 | 74 | 10 | 17 | 4 | 0 | 1 | 6 | .230 | 41 | 56 | 2 | .980 |
| 1975—Phoenix | P.C. | 3B-2B | 123 | 453 | 71 | 111 | 19 | 8 | 5 | 50 | .245 | 155 | 287 | 20 | .957 |
| 1976—Phoenix | P.C. | 2-3-1-S | 136 | 502 | 92 | 139 | 26 | 10 | 15 | 103 | .277 | 369 | 370 | 17 | .978 |
| Major League Totals | | | 61 | 103 | 15 | 26 | 4 | 0 | 1 | 6 | .252 | 49 | 69 | 2 | .983 |

†Traded to San Francisco Giants' organization for Pitcher Jim Willoughby, October 14, 1974.
Listed on San Francisco Giants' 1977 spring roster.

## ROBERT LOWELL HEISE
Name pronounced HIGH-See.
### (Bob)

Born May 12, 1947, at San Antonio, Tex.
Height, 6.00. Weight, 175.
Throws and bats righthanded.
Hobby—Sports.
Attended Vallejo Junior College, Vallejo, Calif.
Led Western Carolinas League in sacrifice hits with 18 in 1966.

| Year Club | League | Pos. | G. | AB. | R. | H. | 2B. | 3B. | HR. | RBI. | B.A. | PO. | A. | E. | F.A. |
|---|---|---|---|---|---|---|---|---|---|---|---|---|---|---|---|
| 1966—Greenville | W. Car. | *2-3B | 122 | 466 | 90 | 132 | 18 | 1 | 6 | 50 | .283 | 191 | 262 | 14 | *.970 |
| 1967—Durham† | Carol. | *2B-SS | 115 | 443 | 53 | 132 | 15 | 1 | 1 | 37 | .298 | 234 | 328 | 11 | *.981 |
| 1967—New York | Nat. | 2-S-3B | 16 | 62 | 7 | 20 | 4 | 0 | 0 | 3 | .323 | 46 | 43 | 3 | .967 |
| 1968—Jacksonville‡ | Int. | 2-S-3B | 114 | 415 | 42 | 104 | 12 | 4 | 2 | 29 | .251 | 210 | 294 | 17 | .967 |
| 1968—New York | Nat. | SS-2B | 6 | 23 | 3 | 5 | 0 | 0 | 0 | 1 | .217 | 6 | 8 | 1 | .933 |
| 1969—Tidewater§ | Int. | SS | 110 | 407 | 52 | 113 | 10 | 3 | 2 | 36 | .278 | 184 | 334 | 25 | .954 |
| 1969—New York x | Nat. | SS | 4 | 10 | 1 | 3 | 1 | 0 | 0 | 0 | .300 | 4 | 5 | 0 | 1.000 |
| 1970—San Francisco y | Nat. | SS-2-3 | 67 | 154 | 15 | 36 | 5 | 1 | 1 | 22 | .234 | 78 | 124 | 13 | .940 |
| 1971—San Francisco z | Nat. | SS-3-2 | 13 | 11 | 2 | 0 | 0 | 0 | 0 | 0 | .000 | 2 | 4 | 1 | .857 |
| 1971—Milwaukee a | Amer. | S-2-3-O | 68 | 189 | 10 | 48 | 7 | 0 | 0 | 7 | .274 | 98 | 159 | 10 | .963 |
| 1972—Milwaukee | Amer. | 2-3-SS | 95 | 271 | 23 | 72 | 10 | 1 | 0 | 12 | .266 | 125 | 170 | 6 | .980 |
| 1973—Milwaukee b | Amer. | S-3-2-1 | 49 | 98 | 8 | 20 | 2 | 0 | 0 | 4 | .204 | 50 | 78 | 5 | .962 |
| 1974—Tulsa | A.A. | 2-SS-3 | 58 | 190 | 28 | 62 | 6 | 1 | 0 | 17 | .326 | 113 | 169 | 9 | .969 |
| 1974—St. Louis c | Nat. | 2B | 3 | 7 | 0 | 1 | 0 | 0 | 0 | 0 | .143 | 7 | 8 | 0 | 1.000 |

| Year | Club | League | Pos. | G. | AB. | R. | H. | 2B. | 3B. | HR. | RBI. | B.A. | PO. | A. | E. | F.A. |
|------|------|--------|------|-----|-----|-----|-----|-----|-----|-----|------|------|-----|-----|-----|------|
| 1974—California d | | ......Amer. | 2-3-SS | 29 | 75 | 7 | 20 | 7 | 0 | 0 | 6 | .267 | 37 | 55 | 0 | 1.000 |
| 1975—Boston | | ...........Amer. | 3-2-S-1 | 63 | 126 | 12 | 27 | 3 | 0 | 0 | 21 | .214 | 52 | 106 | 10 | .940 |
| 1976—Boston e | | ...........Amer. | 3-SS-2 | 32 | 56 | 5 | 15 | 2 | 0 | 0 | 5 | .268 | 27 | 43 | 5 | .933 |
| American League Totals | | ............... | | 336 | 815 | 65 | 202 | 31 | 1 | 0 | 55 | .248 | 389 | 611 | 36 | .965 |
| National League Totals | | .................. | | 109 | 267 | 28 | 65 | 10 | 1 | 1 | 26 | .243 | 143 | 192 | 18 | .949 |
| Major League Totals | | ...................... | | 445 | 1082 | 93 | 267 | 41 | 2 | 1 | 81 | .247 | 532 | 803 | 54 | .961 |

†On temporary inactive list, June 11 through June 24.

‡On temporary inactive list, July 10 through July 20.

xTraded with Outfielder Jim Gosger to San Francisco Giants for Outfielder David Marshall and Pitcher Ray Sadecki, December 12, 1969.

yOn military list, August 8 through August 25.

zTraded to Milwaukee Brewers for Outfielder Floyd Wicker (latter assigned to Phoenix), June 1, 1971.

aOn military list, June 11 through June 30.

bTraded to St. Louis Cardinals for Pitcher Tom Murphy, December 8, 1973.

cTraded to California Angels for a player to be named later, July 31, 1974; Angels sold Infielder-Outfielder Doug Howard to Cardinals, October 7, 1974, to complete deal.

dTraded to Boston Red Sox for Outfielder Tommy Harper, December 2, 1974.

eOn disabled list, April 3 through May 4, 1976. Sold to Kansas City Royals, December 6, 1976.

## TOMMY VANN HELMS

Born May 5, 1941, at Charlotte, N. C.
Height, 5.10. Weight, 173.
Throws and bats righthanded.
Hobbies—Music and golf.

Established National League record for highest fielding percentage, second baseman, lifetime (1,000 or more games), .9831, 1976.

Led National League second basemen in double plays with 107 in 1970, 130 in 1971 and 115 in 1972.

Led Florida State League shortstops in double plays with 93 in 1960 and led Sally League shortstops with 102 in 1962.

Led Three I League in sacrifice hits with 19 in 1961 and Sally League with 18 in 1962.

Named National League Rookie of the Year by the Baseball Writers' Association, 1966.

Named National League Rookie Player of the Year by THE SPORTING NEWS, 1966.

Named second baseman on THE SPORTING NEWS National League All-Star Team, 1968.

Named second baseman on THE SPORTING NEWS National League All-Star Fielding Team, 1970 and 1971.

| Year | Club | League | Pos. | G. | AB. | R. | H. | 2B. | 3B. | HR. | RBI. | B.A. | PO. | A. | E. | F.A. |
|------|------|--------|------|-----|-----|-----|-----|-----|-----|-----|------|------|-----|-----|-----|------|
| 1959—Palatka | | ............Fla.St. | SS | 56 | 210 | 37 | 53 | 3 | 1 | 0 | 16 | .252 | 75 | 151 | 26 | .897 |
| 1960—Palatka | | ............Fla.St. | SS | •137 | •586 | •119 | •171 | •33 | 5 | 3 | 69 | .292 | 217 | •423 | •57 | .918 |
| 1961—Topeka | | ...............I.I.I. | SS | 121 | 484 | 86 | 134 | 13 | 10 | 2 | 57 | .277 | 178 | 378 | •38 | .936 |
| 1962—Macon | | ..............Sally | SS | 139 | •573 | 102 | •195 | •38 | 7 | 1 | 50 | .340 | 245 | •452 | •34 | .953 |
| 1963—San Diego | | .........P.C. | SS-2B | 138 | 471 | 40 | 106 | 21 | 3 | 2 | 39 | .225 | 231 | 395 | 28 | .957 |
| 1964—San Diego | | .........P.C. | SS-2B | 142 | 543 | 57 | 168 | 25 | 9 | 7 | 69 | .309 | 212 | 466 | 32 | .955 |
| 1964—Cincinnati | | .........Nat. | PH | 2 | 1 | 0 | 0 | 0 | 0 | 0 | 0 | .000 | 0 | 0 | 0 | .000 |
| 1965—Cincinnati | | .........Nat. | SS-3-2B | 21 | 42 | 4 | 16 | 2 | 2 | 0 | 6 | .381 | 17 | 22 | 1 | .975 |
| 1965—San Diego | | .........P.C. | SS | 96 | 382 | 48 | 122 | 23 | 3 | 6 | 51 | .319 | 167 | 297 | 13 | .973 |
| 1966—Cincinnati | | .........Nat. | 3B-2B | 138 | 542 | 72 | 154 | 23 | 1 | 9 | 49 | .284 | 155 | 258 | 13 | .969 |
| 1967—Cincinnati | | .........Nat. | 2B-SS | 137 | 497 | 40 | 136 | 27 | 4 | 2 | 35 | .274 | 264 | 347 | 21 | .967 |
| 1968—Cincinnati | | .........Nat. | 2-SS-3B | 127 | 507 | 35 | 146 | 28 | 2 | 2 | 47 | .288 | 322 | 372 | 15 | .979 |
| 1969—Cincinnati | | .........Nat. | 2B-SS | 126 | 480 | 38 | 129 | 18 | 1 | 1 | 40 | .269 | 325 | 347 | 17 | .975 |
| 1970—Cincinnati | | .........Nat. | •2B-SS | 150 | 575 | 42 | 136 | 21 | 1 | 1 | 45 | .237 | 353 | 412 | 13 | •.983 |
| 1971—Cincinnati† | | .........Nat. | 2B | 150 | 547 | 40 | 141 | 26 | 1 | 3 | 52 | .258 | •395 | 468 | 9 | •.990 |
| 1972—Houston | | ............Nat. | 2B | 139 | 518 | 45 | 134 | 20 | 5 | 5 | 60 | .259 | 353 | •441 | 17 | .979 |
| 1973—Houston | | ............Nat. | 2B | 146 | 543 | 44 | 156 | 28 | 2 | 4 | 61 | .287 | 325 | 438 | 9 | .988 |
| 1974—Houston | | ............Nat. | 2B | 137 | 452 | 32 | 126 | 21 | 1 | 5 | 50 | .279 | 308 | 360 | 10 | •.985 |
| 1975—Houston‡§ | | .........Nat. | 2-3-SS | 64 | 135 | 7 | 28 | 2 | 0 | 0 | 14 | .207 | 58 | 109 | 2 | .988 |
| 1976—Pittsburgh x | | ......Nat. | 3-2-SS | 62 | 87 | 10 | 24 | 5 | 1 | 1 | 13 | .276 | 30 | 46 | 3 | .962 |
| Major League Totals | | ...................... | | 1399 | 4926 | 409 | 1326 | 221 | 21 | 33 | 472 | .269 | 2905 | 3620 | 130 | .980 |

†Traded with First Baseman Lee May and Outfielder Jim Stewart to Houston Astros for Infielder Denis Menke, Second Baseman Joe Morgan, Pitcher Jack Billingham and Outfielders Cesar Geronimo and Ed Armbrister (latter assigned from Oklahoma City to Indianapolis), November 29, 1971.

‡On disabled list, March 24 to April 30, 1975.

§Traded to Pittsburgh Pirates for a player to be named later, December 12, 1975; Pirates sent Infielder Art Howe to Astros, January 6, 1976, to complete deal.

xSold to Oakland A's, November 5, 1976; traded with Second Baseman Phil Garner and Pitcher Chris Batton to Pittsburgh Pirates for Pitchers Doc Medich, Dave Giusti, Rick Langford and Doug Bair, Outfielders Mitchell Page and Tony Armas, March 15, 1977.

### CHAMPIONSHIP SERIES RECORD

| Year | Club | League | Pos. | G. | AB. | R. | H. | 2B. | 3B. | HR. | RBI. | B.A. | PO. | A. | E. | F.A. |
|------|------|--------|------|-----|-----|-----|-----|-----|-----|-----|------|------|-----|-----|-----|------|
| 1970—Cincinnati | | .........Nat. | 2B | 3 | 11 | 0 | 3 | 0 | 0 | 0 | 0 | .273 | 11 | 12 | 0 | 1.000 |

### WORLD SERIES RECORD

| Year | Club | League | Pos. | G. | AB. | R. | H. | 2B. | 3B. | HR. | RBI. | B.A. | PO. | A. | E. | F.A. |
|------|------|--------|------|-----|-----|-----|-----|-----|-----|-----|------|------|-----|-----|-----|------|
| 1970—Cincinnati | | .........Nat. | 2B | 5 | 18 | 1 | 4 | 0 | 0 | 0 | 0 | .222 | 10 | 13 | 0 | 1.000 |

### ALL-STAR GAME RECORD

| Year | League | Pos. | AB. | R. | H. | 2B. | 3B. | HR. | RBI. | B.A. | PO. | A. | E. | F.A. |
|------|--------|------|-----|-----|-----|-----|-----|-----|------|------|-----|-----|-----|------|
| 1967—National | ..................... | PH | 1 | 0 | 0 | 0 | 0 | 0 | 0 | .000 | 0 | 0 | 0 | .000 |
| 1968—National | ..................... | 2B | 3 | 0 | 1 | 1 | 0 | 0 | 0 | .333 | 1 | 2 | 0 | 1.000 |
| All-Star Game Totals | ....................... | | 4 | 0 | 1 | 1 | 0 | 0 | 0 | .250 | 1 | 2 | 0 | 1.000 |

## JOSEPH LEE HENDERSON
### (Joe)

Born July 4, 1946, at Lake Cormorant, Miss.
Height, 6.02. Weight, 195.
Throws right and bats lefthanded.

Pitched 10-0 no-hit victory against Wichita, July 31, 1974.

| Year | Club | League | G. | IP. | W. | L. | Pct. | H. | R. | ER. | SO. | BB. | ERA. |
|---|---|---|---|---|---|---|---|---|---|---|---|---|---|
| 1965–Quad Cities | | Midwest | 1 | 1 | 0 | 0 | .000 | 0 | 0 | 0 | 2 | 0 | 0.00 |
| 1966–Quad Cities | | Midwest | 5 | 21 | 1 | 2 | .333 | 17 | 15 | 7 | 19 | 18 | 3.00 |
| 1968–San Jose | | California | 29 | 213 | 17 | 8 | .680 | 188 | 72 | 59 | 186 | •100 | 2.49 |
| 1969–California† | | American | | | | | (Did Not Play) | | | | | | |
| 1970–El Paso‡ | | Texas | 27 | 163 | 12 | 7 | .632 | 165 | 89 | 76 | 124 | 89 | 4.20 |
| 1971–Gomez Palacio§ | | Mexican | 23 | 168 | 10 | 9 | .526 | 182 | 64 | 55 | 56 | 58 | 2.95 |
| 1971–Tucson | | P. Coast | 7 | 30 | 2 | 2 | .500 | 37 | 17 | 16 | 22 | 19 | 4.80 |
| 1972–Tucson | | P. Coast | 18 | 67 | 1 | 6 | .143 | 90 | 57 | 53 | 41 | 26 | 7.12 |
| 1972–Gomez Palacio | | Mexican | 11 | 49 | 6 | 3 | .667 | 58 | 26 | 23 | 39 | 22 | 4.22 |
| 1973–Knoxville | | Southern | 34 | 147 | •17 | 4 | •.810 | 113 | 41 | 34 | 91 | 54 | 2.08 |
| 1974–Iowa | | Am. Assoc. | 27 | 190 | 13 | 8 | .619 | 158 | 81 | 66 | 150 | 69 | 3.13 |
| 1974–Chicago x | | American | 5 | 15 | 1 | 0 | 1.000 | 21 | 15 | 14 | 12 | 11 | 8.40 |
| 1975–Indianapolis | | Am. Assoc. | 45 | 101 | 5 | 4 | .556 | 74 | 32 | 27 | 85 | 50 | 2.41 |
| 1976–Indianapolis | | Am. Assoc. | 54 | 109 | 7 | 3 | .700 | 73 | 29 | 28 | 80 | 66 | 2.31 |
| 1976–Cincinnati | | National | 4 | 11 | 2 | 0 | 1.000 | 9 | 1 | 0 | 7 | 8 | 0.00 |
| American League Totals | | | 5 | 15 | 1 | 0 | 1.000 | 21 | 15 | 14 | 12 | 11 | 8.40 |
| National League Totals | | | 4 | 11 | 2 | 0 | 1.000 | 9 | 1 | 0 | 7 | 8 | 0.00 |
| Major League Totals | | | 9 | 26 | 3 | 0 | 1.000 | 30 | 16 | 14 | 19 | 19 | 4.85 |

†On disabled list, March 10 to April 11, 1969; on voluntary retired list, April 11, 1969 to January 15, 1970.
‡Released by California Angels' organization, April 4, 1971; signed as free agent by Gomez Palacio (Mexican League), April 15, 1971.
§Traded to Chicago White Sox, August 6, 1971, to complete deal in which Gomez Palacio obtained Pitcher Alfredo Mariscal, July 13, 1971.
xSold to Cincinnati Reds' organization, January 2, 1975.

### RECORD AS OUTFIELDER-INFIELDER

Led Midwest League batters in strikeouts with 141 in 1966.

| Year | Club | League | Pos. | G. | AB. | R. | H. | 2B. | 3B. | HR. | RBI. | B.A. | PO. | A. | E. | F.A. |
|---|---|---|---|---|---|---|---|---|---|---|---|---|---|---|---|---|
| 1965–Quad Cities | | Midw. | OF-3-P | 65 | 240 | 37 | 61 | 13 | 5 | 12 | 38 | .254 | 79 | 28 | 13 | .892 |
| 1966–Quad Cities | | Midw. | OF-1-P | 116 | 362 | 47 | 66 | 9 | 4 | 13 | 44 | .182 | 365 | 31 | 14 | .966 |
| 1967–San Jose | | Calif. | OF | 127 | 415 | 44 | 84 | 18 | 2 | 8 | 57 | .202 | 113 | 8 | 6 | .953 |
| 1968–San Jose | | Calif. | P-1B | 37 | 78 | 10 | 18 | 5 | 0 | 1 | 8 | .231 | 14 | 31 | 3 | .938 |
| 1971–Tucson | | P.C. | P-OF | 10 | 14 | 5 | 5 | 0 | 0 | 0 | 1 | .357 | 5 | 5 | 1 | .909 |
| 1972–Tucson | | P.C. | P-OF | 22 | 26 | 1 | 1 | 0 | 0 | 0 | 0 | .038 | 6 | 9 | 0 | 1.000 |
| 1972–Gomez Palacio | | Mex. | P-OF | 18 | 24 | 1 | 3 | 0 | 0 | 0 | 1 | .125 | 6 | 9 | 0 | 1.000 |

## KENNETH JOSEPH HENDERSON
### (Ken)

Born June 15, 1946, at Carroll, Ia.
Height, 6.02. Weight, 185.
Throws right and bats left and righthanded.
Hobbies–Golf and billiards.
Attended West Valley College, Campbell, Calif.
Distant cousin of Kerry Dineen, outfielder with Philadelphia Phillies organization.

Led American League outfielders in total chances with 475 in 1974.

| Year | Club | League | Pos. | G. | AB. | R. | H. | 2B. | 3B. | HR. | RBI. | B.A. | PO. | A. | E. | F.A. |
|---|---|---|---|---|---|---|---|---|---|---|---|---|---|---|---|---|
| 1964–Fresno | | Calif. | OF | 14 | 40 | 5 | 9 | 1 | 0 | 1 | 6 | .225 | 18 | 3 | 1 | .955 |
| 1964–Magic Valley | | Pion. | OF | 31 | 104 | 22 | 19 | 4 | 3 | 0 | 20 | .183 | 65 | 8 | 1 | .986 |
| 1964–Tacoma | | P. C. | OF | 18 | 39 | 3 | 7 | 0 | 0 | 0 | 0 | .179 | 27 | 0 | 3 | .900 |
| 1965–San Francisco | | Nat. | OF | 63 | 73 | 10 | 14 | 1 | 1 | 0 | 7 | .192 | 47 | 2 | 1 | .980 |
| 1966–Phoenix | | P. C. | OF | 133 | 464 | 66 | 126 | 15 | 10 | 13 | 66 | .272 | 286 | 10 | 8 | .974 |
| 1966–San Francisco | | Nat. | OF | 11 | 29 | 4 | 9 | 1 | 1 | 1 | 1 | .310 | 11 | 0 | 1 | .917 |
| 1967–San Francisco | | Nat. | OF | 65 | 179 | 15 | 34 | 3 | 0 | 4 | 14 | .190 | 86 | 3 | 5 | .947 |
| 1967–Phoenix | | P. C. | OF | 41 | 143 | 18 | 38 | 12 | 1 | 3 | 13 | .266 | 99 | 1 | 1 | .990 |
| 1968–Phoenix | | P. C. | OF | 106 | 350 | 53 | 89 | 21 | 5 | 11 | 60 | .254 | 178 | 6 | 4 | .979 |
| 1968–San Francisco | | Nat. | OF | 3 | 3 | 1 | 1 | 0 | 0 | 0 | 0 | .333 | 2 | 0 | 0 | 1.000 |
| 1969–San Francisco | | Nat. | OF-3B | 113 | 374 | 42 | 84 | 14 | 4 | 6 | 44 | .225 | 175 | 12 | 6 | .969 |
| 1970–San Francisco | | Nat. | OF | 148 | 554 | 104 | 163 | 35 | 3 | 17 | 88 | .294 | 272 | 15 | 10 | .966 |
| 1971–San Francisco | | Nat. | OF-1B | 141 | 504 | 80 | 133 | 26 | 6 | 15 | 65 | .264 | 277 | 3 | 10 | .966 |
| 1972–San Francisco† | | Nat. | OF | 130 | 439 | 60 | 113 | 21 | 2 | 18 | 51 | .257 | 247 | 14 | 7 | .974 |
| 1973–Chicago‡ | | Amer. | OF | 73 | 262 | 32 | 68 | 13 | 0 | 6 | 32 | .260 | 102 | 1 | 3 | .972 |
| 1974–Chicago | | Amer. | OF | •162 | 602 | 76 | 176 | 35 | 5 | 20 | 95 | .292 | •462 | 7 | 6 | .987 |
| 1975–Chicago§ | | Amer. | OF | 140 | 513 | 65 | 129 | 20 | 3 | 9 | 53 | .251 | 394 | 7 | 4 | .990 |
| 1976–Atlanta x | | Nat. | OF | 133 | 435 | 52 | 114 | 19 | 0 | 13 | 61 | .262 | 219 | 3 | 3 | .987 |
| National League Totals | | | | 807 | 2590 | 368 | 665 | 120 | 17 | 74 | 331 | .258 | 1336 | 52 | 43 | .970 |
| American League Totals | | | | 375 | 1377 | 173 | 373 | 68 | 8 | 35 | 180 | .271 | 958 | 15 | 13 | .987 |
| Major League Totals | | | | 1182 | 3967 | 541 | 1038 | 188 | 25 | 109 | 511 | .262 | 2294 | 67 | 56 | .977 |

†Traded with Pitcher Steve Stone to Chicago White Sox for Pitcher Tom Bradley, November 29, 1972.
‡On supplemental disabled list, May 26 to June 28, 1973; on disabled list, August 14 through remainder of season.

§Traded with Pitchers Dick Ruthven and Danny Osborn to Atlanta Braves for Outfielder Ralph Garr and Infielder Larvell Blanks, December 12, 1975.

xTraded with Outfielder Dave May, Pitchers Carl Morton, Roger Moret and Adrian Devine, and cash estimated at $250,000 to Texas Rangers for Outfielder Jeff Burroughs, December 9, 1976.

### CHAMPIONSHIP SERIES RECORD

| Year | Club | League | Pos. | G. | AB. | R. | H. | 2B. | 3B. | HR. | RBI. | B.A. | PO. | A. | E. | F.A. |
|------|------|--------|------|-----|-----|-----|-----|-----|-----|-----|------|------|-----|-----|-----|------|
| 1971—San Francisco | ..Nat. | | OF | 4 | 16 | 3 | 5 | 1 | 0 | 0 | 2 | .313 | 4 | 0 | 0 | 1.000 |

## STEPHEN CURTIS HENDERSON
### (Steve)

Born November 18, 1952, at Houston, Tex.
Height, 6.02. Weight, 190.
Throws and bats righthanded.
Hobbies—Music, movies, and sports.
Attended Prairie View A & M University, Prairie View, Tex.

Led Eastern League in total bases with 255 in 1976.

| Year | Club | League | Pos. | G. | AB. | R. | H. | 2B. | 3B. | HR. | RBI. | B.A. | PO. | A. | E. | F.A. |
|------|------|--------|------|-----|-----|-----|-----|-----|-----|-----|------|------|-----|-----|-----|------|
| 1974—Billings | ............Pion. | | OF | 72 | 249 | •60 | 72 | 19 | 5 | •8 | •44 | .289 | 114 | 6 | 6 | •.952 |
| 1975—Tampa | ..............Fla. St. | | OF-SS | 123 | 413 | 59 | 115 | 9 | •16 | 0 | 54 | .278 | 263 | 7 | 8 | .971 |
| 1976—Three Rivers | ....East. | | OF | 134 | 506 | 90 | •158 | 24 | •11 | 17 | 61 | .312 | 260 | 12 | 8 | .971 |

Listed on Cincinnati Reds' 1977 spring roster.

## GEORGE ANDREW HENDRICK, JR.

Born October 18, 1949, at Los Angeles, Calif.
Height, 6.02. Weight, 195.
Throws and bats righthanded.
Attended East Los Angeles Junior College, Los Angeles, Calif.

Hit three home runs in a game, June 19, 1973 against Detroit Tigers.

| Year | Club | League | Pos. | G. | AB. | R. | H. | 2B. | 3B. | HR. | RBI. | B.A. | PO. | A. | E. | F.A. |
|------|------|--------|------|-----|-----|-----|-----|-----|-----|-----|------|------|-----|-----|-----|------|
| 1968—Burlington | ........Midw. | | OF | 103 | 364 | 58 | 119 | •25 | 4 | 5 | 60 | •.327 | 134 | 8 | 8 | .947 |
| 1969—Lodi | ..................Calif. | | OF | 86 | 316 | 47 | 97 | 13 | 2 | 4 | 28 | .307 | 121 | 5 | 4 | .969 |
| 1970—Burlington | ........Midw. | | OF | 54 | 198 | 37 | 61 | 9 | 3 | 12 | 43 | .308 | 80 | 1 | 5 | .942 |
| 1970—Birmingham | ......South. | | OF | 54 | 199 | 30 | 57 | 12 | 0 | 6 | 20 | .286 | 115 | 4 | 5 | .960 |
| 1971—Iowa | ..................A. A. | | OF | 63 | 249 | 57 | 83 | 9 | 2 | 21 | 63 | .333 | 113 | 5 | 3 | .975 |
| 1971—Oakland | ............Amer. | | OF | 42 | 114 | 8 | 27 | 4 | 1 | 0 | 8 | .237 | 52 | 1 | 1 | .981 |
| 1972—Iowa | ..................A. A. | | OF | 8 | 33 | 0 | 9 | 0 | 0 | 0 | 4 | .273 | 14 | 2 | 0 | 1.000 |
| 1972—Oakland† | .........Amer. | | OF | 58 | 121 | 10 | 22 | 1 | 1 | 4 | 15 | .182 | 68 | 0 | 0 | 1.000 |
| 1973—Cleveland‡ | ........Amer. | | OF | 113 | 440 | 64 | 118 | 18 | 0 | 21 | 61 | .268 | 242 | 7 | 3 | .988 |
| 1974—Cleveland | ........Amer. | | OF | 139 | 495 | 65 | 138 | 23 | 1 | 19 | 67 | .279 | 355 | 9 | 4 | .989 |
| 1975—Cleveland | ........Amer. | | OF | 145 | 561 | 82 | 145 | 21 | 2 | 24 | 86 | .258 | 338 | 4 | 6 | .983 |
| 1976—Cleveland§ | ........Amer. | | OF-DH | 149 | 551 | 72 | 146 | 20 | 3 | 25 | 81 | .265 | 288 | 13 | 4 | .987 |
| Major League Totals | | | | 646 | 2282 | 301 | 596 | 87 | 8 | 93 | 318 | .261 | 1343 | 34 | 18 | .987 |

†Traded with Catcher Dave Duncan to Cleveland Indians for Catcher Ray Fosse and Infielder Jack Heidemann, March 24, 1973.

‡On supplemental disabled list, August 14 to September 29, 1973.

§Traded to San Diego Padres for Outfielder Johnny Grubb, Catcher Fred Kendall and Shortstop Hector Torres, December 8, 1976.

### CHAMPIONSHIP SERIES RECORD

| Year | Club | League | Pos. | G. | AB. | R. | H. | 2B. | 3B. | HR. | RBI. | B.A. | PO. | A. | E. | F.A. |
|------|------|--------|------|-----|-----|-----|-----|-----|-----|-----|------|------|-----|-----|-----|------|
| 1972—Oakland | ............Amer. | | PH-OF | 5 | 7 | 2 | 1 | 0 | 0 | 0 | 0 | .143 | 1 | 0 | 0 | 1.000 |

### WORLD SERIES RECORD

| Year | Club | League | Pos. | G. | AB. | R. | H. | 2B. | 3B. | HR. | RBI. | B.A. | PO. | A. | E. | F.A. |
|------|------|--------|------|-----|-----|-----|-----|-----|-----|-----|------|------|-----|-----|-----|------|
| 1972—Oakland | ............Amer. | | OF | 5 | 15 | 3 | 2 | 0 | 0 | 0 | 0 | .133 | 12 | 0 | 0 | 1.000 |

### ALL-STAR GAME RECORD

| Year | League | Pos. | AB. | R. | H. | 2B. | 3B. | HR. | RBI. | B.A. | PO. | A. | E. | F.A. |
|------|--------|------|-----|-----|-----|-----|-----|-----|------|------|-----|-----|-----|------|
| 1974—American | ............................ | OF | 2 | 0 | 1 | 0 | 0 | 0 | 0 | .500 | 3 | 0 | 0 | 1.000 |
| 1975—American | ............................ | PR-OF | 1 | 1 | 1 | 0 | 0 | 0 | 0 | 1.000 | 0 | 0 | 0 | .000 |
| All-Star Game Totals | ....................... | | 3 | 1 | 2 | 0 | 0 | 0 | 0 | .667 | 3 | 0 | 0 | 1.000 |

## ELROD JEROME HENDRICKS
### (Ellie)

Born December 22, 1940, at St. Thomas, Virgin Islands.
Height, 6.01½. Weight, 175.
Throws right and bats lefthanded.
Hobby—Water color painting.

Tied National League record for most bases on balls, game, since 1900 (5), September 16, 1972.
Led Mexican League catchers in double plays with 19 in 1967.
Tied Mexican League catchers for lead in double plays with 9 in 1965.

| Year | Club | League | Pos. | G. | AB. | R. | H. | 2B. | 3B. | HR. | RBI. | B.A. | PO. | A. | E. | F.A. |
|---|---|---|---|---|---|---|---|---|---|---|---|---|---|---|---|---|
| 1959–McCook | | Neb. St. | C | 25 | 34 | 6 | 8 | 1 | 0 | 0 | 3 | .235 | 91 | 7 | 2 | .980 |
| 1960–Wellsville† | | NYP | C | 73 | 217 | 36 | 51 | 8 | 1 | 11 | 36 | .235 | 372 | 36 | 15 | .965 |
| 1961– | | | | | | (Out of Organized Ball) | | | | | | | | | | |
| 1962–Winnipeg | | North. | C | 69 | 213 | 25 | 45 | 7 | 2 | 3 | 22 | .211 | 415 | 43 | 11 | .977 |
| 1963–Winnipeg‡ | | North. | C | 22 | 50 | 10 | 14 | 0 | 0 | 3 | 12 | .280 | 95 | 11 | 2 | .981 |
| 1964–Jalisco | | Mex. | C-OF | 67 | 202 | 43 | 59 | 8 | 4 | 10 | 45 | .292 | 214 | 23 | 9 | .963 |
| 1965–Jalisco | | Mex. | C | 128 | 411 | 100 | 117 | 14 | 8 | 35 | 98 | .285 | 556 | •65 | 6 | .990 |
| 1966–Jalisco | | Mex. | C | 122 | 386 | 78 | 116 | 19 | 2 | 23 | 87 | .301 | 555 | 64 | 6 | .990 |
| 1966–El Paso | | Tex. | C | 18 | 56 | 6 | 15 | 2 | 0 | 3 | 12 | .268 | 119 | 12 | 0 | 1.000 |
| 1967–Jalisco | | Mex. | C | 131 | 434 | •124 | 137 | 18 | 4 | •41 | 112 | .316 | 613 | 63 | 7 | .990 |
| 1967–Seattle§ | | P. C. | C | 13 | 36 | 3 | 8 | 1 | 0 | 2 | 4 | .222 | 59 | 3 | 0 | 1.000 |
| 1968–Baltimore | | Amer. | C | 79 | 183 | 19 | 37 | 8 | 1 | 7 | 23 | .202 | 303 | 21 | 3 | .991 |
| 1969–Baltimore | | Amer. | •C-1B | 105 | 295 | 36 | 72 | 5 | 0 | 12 | 38 | .244 | 488 | 41 | 1 | •.998 |
| 1970–Baltimore | | Amer. | C | 106 | 322 | 32 | 78 | 9 | 0 | 12 | 41 | .242 | 509 | 35 | 8 | .986 |
| 1971–Baltimore | | Amer. | C-1B | 101 | 316 | 33 | 79 | 14 | 1 | 9 | 42 | .250 | 453 | 34 | 7 | .986 |
| 1972–Baltimore x | | Amer. | C | 33 | 84 | 6 | 13 | 4 | 0 | 0 | 4 | .155 | 130 | 15 | 2 | .986 |
| 1972–Chicago y | | Nat. | C | 17 | 43 | 7 | 5 | 1 | 0 | 2 | 6 | .116 | 83 | 7 | 2 | .978 |
| 1973–Baltimore | | Amer. | C | 41 | 101 | 9 | 18 | 5 | 1 | 3 | 15 | .178 | 148 | 9 | 1 | .994 |
| 1974–Baltimore | | Amer. | C-1B | 66 | 159 | 18 | 33 | 8 | 2 | 3 | 8 | .208 | 194 | 13 | 0 | 1.000 |
| 1975–Baltimore | | Amer. | C | 85 | 223 | 32 | 48 | 8 | 2 | 8 | 38 | .215 | 332 | 36 | 2 | .995 |
| 1976–Balt.z-N.Y. | | Amer. | C | 54 | 132 | 8 | 23 | 2 | 0 | 4 | 9 | .174 | 147 | 17 | 3 | .982 |
| American League Totals | | | | 670 | 1815 | 193 | 401 | 63 | 7 | 58 | 218 | .221 | 2704 | 221 | 27 | .991 |
| National League Totals | | | | 17 | 43 | 7 | 5 | 1 | 0 | 2 | 6 | .116 | 83 | 7 | 2 | .978 |
| Major League Totals | | | | 687 | 1858 | 200 | 406 | 64 | 7 | 60 | 224 | .218 | 2787 | 228 | 29 | .990 |

†Released by Milwaukee Braves' organization, September 21, 1960; signed as free agent by Tulsa (St. Louis Cardinals' organization), November 21, 1961.
‡Released by St. Louis Cardinals' organization, June 13, 1963.
§Drafted by Baltimore Orioles from Seattle (California Angels' organization), November 28, 1967.
xTraded to Chicago Cubs for Outfielder H. Thomas Davis, August 18, 1972.
yTraded to Baltimore Orioles for Catcher Francisco Estrada, October 27, 1972.
zTraded with Pitchers Ken Holtzman, Doyle Alexander, Grant Jackson and Jimmy Freeman, latter assigned from Rochester to Syracuse, to New York Yankees for Pitchers Rudy May, Tippy Martinez, Dave Pagan and Scott McGregor, and Catcher Rick Dempsey, June 15, 1976.

## CHAMPIONSHIP SERIES RECORD

| Year | Club | League | Pos. | G. | AB. | R. | H. | 2B. | 3B. | HR. | RBI. | B.A. | PO. | A. | E. | F.A. |
|---|---|---|---|---|---|---|---|---|---|---|---|---|---|---|---|---|
| 1969–Baltimore | | Amer. | C | 3 | 8 | 2 | 2 | 2 | 0 | 0 | 3 | .250 | 18 | 0 | 0 | 1.000 |
| 1970–Baltimore | | Amer. | C | 1 | 5 | 2 | 2 | 0 | 0 | 0 | 0 | .400 | 5 | 0 | 0 | 1.000 |
| 1971–Baltimore | | Amer. | C | 2 | 4 | 1 | 2 | 0 | 0 | 1 | 2 | .500 | 6 | 0 | 0 | 1.000 |
| 1974–Baltimore | | Amer. | C | 3 | 6 | 1 | 1 | 0 | 0 | 0 | 0 | .167 | 11 | 1 | 0 | 1.000 |
| 1976–New York | | Amer. | PH | 1 | 1 | 0 | 1 | 0 | 0 | 0 | 0 | 1.000 | 0 | 0 | 0 | .000 |
| Championship Series Totals | | | | 10 | 24 | 6 | 8 | 2 | 0 | 1 | 5 | .333 | 40 | 1 | 0 | 1.000 |

## WORLD SERIES RECORD

| Year | Club | League | Pos. | G. | AB. | R. | H. | 2B. | 3B. | HR. | RBI. | B.A. | PO. | A. | E. | F.A. |
|---|---|---|---|---|---|---|---|---|---|---|---|---|---|---|---|---|
| 1969–Baltimore | | Amer. | C | 3 | 10 | 1 | 1 | 0 | 0 | 0 | 0 | .100 | 21 | 1 | 0 | 1.000 |
| 1970–Baltimore | | Amer. | C | 3 | 11 | 1 | 4 | 1 | 0 | 1 | 4 | .364 | 17 | 2 | 1 | .950 |
| 1971–Baltimore | | Amer. | C | 6 | 19 | 3 | 5 | 1 | 0 | 0 | 1 | .263 | 40 | 4 | 1 | .978 |
| 1976–Baltimore | | Amer. | PH | 2 | 2 | 0 | 0 | 0 | 0 | 0 | 0 | .000 | 0 | 0 | 0 | .000 |
| World Series Totals | | | | 14 | 42 | 5 | 10 | 2 | 0 | 1 | 5 | .238 | 78 | 7 | 2 | .977 |

## ENZO OCTAVIO HERNANDEZ

Born February 12, 1949, at Valle de Guanape, Venezuela.
Height, 5.08. Weight, 155.
Throws and bats righthanded.
Hobbies–Hunting and attending movies.

Major League stolen bases: 1971 (21), 1972 (24), 1973 (15), 1974 (37), 1975 (20), 1976 (12). Total–129.
Led National League in sacrifice hits with 24 in 1975.
Led Florida State League in sacrifice hits with 19 in 1967.

| Year | Club | League | Pos. | G. | AB. | R. | H. | 2B. | 3B. | HR. | RBI. | B.A. | PO. | A. | E. | F.A. |
|---|---|---|---|---|---|---|---|---|---|---|---|---|---|---|---|---|
| 1967–Cocoa | | Fla. St. | •S-2 | 129 | 449 | 56 | 84 | 7 | 2 | 2 | 23 | .187 | •214 | 329 | 39 | .933 |
| 1968–Greensboro | | Carol. | 2-S-3 | 89 | 323 | 41 | 73 | 11 | 0 | 1 | 12 | .226 | 163 | 201 | 29 | .926 |
| 1968–Okla. City† | | P.C. | PH | 2 | 2 | 0 | 0 | 0 | 0 | 0 | 0 | .000 | 0 | 0 | 0 | .000 |
| 1969–Dal.-Ft. Worth | | Texas | SS | 2 | 6 | 1 | 2 | 0 | 1 | 0 | 1 | .333 | 6 | 9 | 1 | .938 |
| 1969–Miami | | Fla. St. | SS | 107 | 384 | 42 | 95 | 10 | 3 | 0 | 35 | .247 | •187 | 289 | 31 | •.939 |
| 1970–Dal.-Ft. Worth | | Texas | SS | 42 | 156 | 27 | 44 | 8 | 1 | 0 | 9 | .282 | 95 | 98 | 10 | .951 |
| 1970–Rochester‡ | | Int. | SS-2B | 100 | 372 | 61 | 99 | 10 | 4 | 1 | 39 | .266 | 180 | 276 | 26 | .946 |
| 1971–San Diego | | Nat. | SS | 143 | 549 | 58 | 122 | 9 | 3 | 0 | 12 | .222 | 260 | 445 | •33 | .955 |
| 1972–San Diego | | Nat. | SS-OF | 114 | 329 | 33 | 64 | 11 | 2 | 1 | 15 | .195 | 169 | 319 | 19 | .963 |
| 1973–San Diego§ | | Nat. | SS | 70 | 247 | 26 | 55 | 2 | 1 | 0 | 9 | .223 | 106 | 190 | 7 | .977 |
| 1974–San Diego | | Nat. | SS | 147 | 512 | 55 | 119 | 19 | 2 | 0 | 34 | .232 | 229 | 449 | 24 | .966 |
| 1975–San Diego | | Nat. | SS | 116 | 344 | 37 | 75 | 12 | 2 | 0 | 19 | .218 | 168 | 327 | 18 | .965 |
| 1976–San Diego | | Nat. | SS | 113 | 340 | 31 | 87 | 13 | 3 | 1 | 24 | .256 | 132 | 344 | 18 | .964 |
| Major League Totals | | | | 703 | 2321 | 240 | 522 | 66 | 13 | 2 | 113 | .225 | 1064 | 2074 | 119 | .963 |

†Traded with Pitcher Mike Cuellar and Infielder Elijah Johnson by Houston Astros to Baltimore Orioles for Outfielder-Catcher Curt Blefary and Outfielder John Mason, December 4, 1968.

‡Recalled by Baltimore Orioles and traded with Pitchers Tom Phoebus, Fred Beene and Al Severinsen to San Diego Padres for Pitchers Pat Dobson and Tom Dukes, December 1, 1970.
§On supplementary disabled list, June 16 to July 26, 1973.

## KEITH HERNANDEZ

Born October 20, 1953, at San Francisco, Calif.
Height, 6.01. Weight, 185.
Throws and bats lefthanded.
Attended College of San Mateo, San Mateo, Calif.
Son of John Hernandez, former minor league first baseman, and brother of Gary Hernandez, first baseman-outfielder in St. Louis Cardinals' organization.
Led Texas League first basemen in double plays with 101 in 1973.

| Year | Club | League | Pos. | G. | AB. | R. | H. | 2B. | 3B. | HR. | RBI. | B.A. | PO. | A. | E. | F.A. |
|---|---|---|---|---|---|---|---|---|---|---|---|---|---|---|---|---|
| 1972–St. Petersburg† | ..Fla. St. | | 1B | 84 | 309 | 38 | 79 | 16 | 5 | 5 | 41 | .256 | 682 | 52 | 7 | .991 |
| 1972–Tulsa | A.A. | | 1B | 11 | 29 | 5 | 7 | 1 | 0 | 0 | 1 | .241 | 54 | 2 | 0 | 1.000 |
| 1973–Arkansas | Tex. | | 1B | 105 | 388 | 62 | 101 | 20 | 2 | 3 | 52 | .260 | 960 | 61 | 9 | *.991 |
| 1973–Tulsa | A.A. | | 1B | 31 | 120 | 20 | 40 | 6 | 1 | 5 | 25 | .333 | 289 | 15 | 1 | .997 |
| 1974–Tulsa‡ | A.A. | | 1B-OF | 102 | 353 | 67 | 124 | 18 | 6 | 14 | 63 | *.351 | 690 | 50 | 12 | .984 |
| 1974–St. Louis | Nat. | | 1B | 14 | 34 | 3 | 10 | 1 | 2 | 0 | 2 | .294 | 70 | 1 | 2 | .973 |
| 1975–Tulsa | A.A. | | •1B-OF | 85 | 324 | 70 | 107 | 29 | 3 | 10 | 48 | .330 | 597 | 53 | •13 | .980 |
| 1975–St. Louis | Nat. | | 1B | 64 | 188 | 20 | 47 | 8 | 2 | 3 | 20 | .250 | 469 | 36 | 2 | .996 |
| 1976–St. Louis | Nat. | | 1B | 129 | 374 | 54 | 108 | 21 | 5 | 7 | 46 | .289 | 862 | •107 | 10 | .990 |
| Major League Totals | | | | 207 | 596 | 77 | 165 | 30 | 9 | 10 | 68 | .277 | 1401 | 144 | 14 | .991 |

†On disabled list from beginning of season until May 30, 1972.
‡On disabled list, April 16 to May 20, 1974.

## RAMON GONZALEZ HERNANDEZ

Born August 31, 1940, at Carolina, Puerto Rico.
Height, 5.11. Weight, 165.
Throws left and bats left and righthanded.
Attended Julio Vizcarrondo Coronado, Carolina, Puerto Rico.
Pitched seven-inning, 2-0 no-hit victory against El Paso, August 17, 1969.
Led Texas League in hit batsmen with 12 in 1969.

| Year | Club | League | G. | IP. | W. | L. | Pct. | H. | R. | ER. | SO. | BB. | ERA. |
|---|---|---|---|---|---|---|---|---|---|---|---|---|---|
| 1959–Grand Forks | Northern | 31 | 71 | 3 | 6 | .333 | 81 | 74 | 61 | 69 | 63 | 7.73 |
| 1960–Grand Forks† | Northern | 9 | 53 | 4 | 3 | .571 | 44 | 30 | 19 | 42 | 31 | 3.23 |
| 1960–Dubuque‡§ | Midwest | 2 | 5 | 0 | 0 | .000 | 5 | 4 | 4 | 3 | 7 | 7.20 |
| 1961– | (Out of Organized Ball) | | | | | | | | | | | |
| 1962–San Jose | California | 28 | 138 | 7 | 6 | .538 | 117 | 67 | 45 | 161 | 83 | 2.93 |
| 1963–Hawaii | P. Coast | 5 | 13 | 0 | 2 | .000 | 13 | 10 | 6 | 9 | 6 | 4.15 |
| 1963–Reynosa x | Mexican | 7 | 47 | 1 | 4 | .200 | 38 | 22 | 18 | 40 | 28 | 3.45 |
| 1964–San Jose | California | 41 | 94 | 6 | 6 | .500 | 80 | 52 | 46 | 85 | 70 | 4.40 |
| 1965–El Paso | Texas | 43 | 135 | 6 | 7 | .462 | 137 | 71 | 59 | 105 | 42 | 3.93 |
| 1966–Seattle | P. Coast | 6 | 12 | 0 | 2 | .000 | 8 | 7 | 7 | 8 | 3 | 5.25 |
| 1966–El Paso y | Texas | 52 | 121 | 9 | 7 | .563 | 97 | 36 | 29 | 94 | 35 | 2.16 |
| 1967–Atlanta z | National | 46 | 52 | 0 | 2 | .000 | 60 | 27 | 24 | 28 | 14 | 4.15 |
| 1968–Chicago a | National | 8 | 9 | 0 | 0 | .000 | 14 | 11 | 9 | 3 | 0 | 9.00 |
| 1968–Tulsa | P. Coast | 18 | 32 | 2 | 5 | .286 | 32 | 26 | 22 | 31 | 8 | 6.19 |
| 1969–Arkansas b | Texas | 33 | 184 | 10 | 10 | .500 | 155 | 66 | 49 | 133 | 38 | *2.40 |
| 1970–Mexico City Reds c | Mexican | 32 | 79 | 5 | 3 | .625 | 87 | 18 | 16 | 56 | 9 | 1.82 |
| 1971–Charleston | Int'national | 49 | 47 | 2 | 3 | .400 | 49 | 25 | 21 | 43 | 19 | 4.02 |
| 1971–Pittsburgh | National | 10 | 12 | 0 | 1 | .000 | 5 | 1 | 1 | 7 | 2 | 0.75 |
| 1972–Pittsburgh | National | 53 | 70 | 5 | 0 | 1.000 | 50 | 14 | 13 | 47 | 22 | 1.67 |
| 1973–Pittsburgh | National | 59 | 90 | 4 | 5 | .444 | 71 | 27 | 24 | 64 | 25 | 2.40 |
| 1974–Pittsburgh | National | 58 | 69 | 5 | 2 | .714 | 68 | 21 | 21 | 33 | 18 | 2.74 |
| 1975–Pittsburgh | National | 46 | 64 | 7 | 2 | .778 | 62 | 21 | 21 | 43 | 28 | 2.95 |
| 1976–Pitt. d-Chi. | National | 39 | 45 | 2 | 2 | .500 | 44 | 17 | 17 | 18 | 16 | 3.40 |
| Major League Totals | | 319 | 411 | 23 | 14 | .622 | 374 | 139 | 130 | 243 | 125 | 2.85 |

†On disabled list, June 18 through July 2.
‡On suspended list, July 27 to September 1, 1960.
§Purchased from Pittsburgh Pirates' organization by California Angels' organization, December 4, 1961.
xOn temporary inactive list, July 13, 1963. Placed on disqualified list, August 12, 1963 through Jan. 20, 1964.
yDrafted by Atlanta Braves from Seattle (California Angels' organization), November 28, 1966.
zDrafted by Chicago Cubs from Richmond (Atlanta Braves' organization), November 28, 1967.
aSold to St. Louis Cardinals, June 14, 1968.
bOn disqualified list, July 26 through August 5; released by St. Louis Cardinals, March 31, 1970.
cTraded to Pittsburgh Pirates' organization for Pitcher Danny Rivas, February 10, 1971.
dSold to Chicago Cubs, September 8, 1976.

### CHAMPIONSHIP SERIES RECORD

| Year | Club | League | G. | IP. | W. | L. | Pct. | H. | R. | ER. | SO. | BB. | ERA. |
|---|---|---|---|---|---|---|---|---|---|---|---|---|---|
| 1972–Pittsburgh | National | 3 | 3⅓ | 0 | 0 | .000 | 1 | 1 | 1 | 3 | 0 | 2.70 |
| 1974–Pittsburgh | National | 2 | 4⅓ | 0 | 0 | .000 | 3 | 0 | 0 | 2 | 1 | 0.00 |
| 1975–Pittsburgh | National | 1 | ⅔ | 0 | 1 | .000 | 3 | 2 | 2 | 0 | 0 | 27.00 |
| Championship Series Totals | | 6 | 8⅓ | 0 | 1 | .000 | 7 | 3 | 3 | 5 | 1 | 3.24 |

## LARRY DARNELL HERNDON

Born November 3, 1953, at Sunflower, Miss.
Height, 6.03. Weight, 190.
Throws and bats righthanded.
Hobby—Playing pool.
Attended Tennessee State University, Nashville, Tenn.
Led Texas League in stolen bases with 50 in 1974.
Tied for Texas League lead in double plays by outfielders with 4 in 1974.
Named National League Rookie Player of the Year by THE SPORTING NEWS, 1976.

| Year Club | League | Pos. | G. | AB. | R. | H. | 2B. | 3B. | HR. | RBI. | B.A. | PO. | A. | E. | F.A. |
|---|---|---|---|---|---|---|---|---|---|---|---|---|---|---|---|
| 1971—Sarasota Cards | ..Gulf C. | OF | 40 | 138 | 13 | 33 | 2 | 0 | 0 | 8 | .239 | 68 | 4 | 3 | .960 |
| 1972—St. Petersburg | ..Fla. St. | OF | 7 | 28 | 2 | 4 | 0 | 0 | 0 | 0 | .143 | 12 | 1 | 2 | .867 |
| 1972—Sarasota R. B. | ..Gulf C. | OF | 31 | 113 | 16 | 29 | 5 | 3 | 0 | 9 | .257 | 50 | 5 | 3 | .948 |
| 1972—Cedar Rapids† | ..Midw. | OF | 7 | 21 | 1 | 6 | 0 | 0 | 0 | 1 | .286 | 10 | 0 | 0 | 1.000 |
| 1973—St. Petersburg | ..Fla. St. | OF | 141 | 485 | 83 | 139 | 9 | 5 | 3 | 41 | .287 | 233 | 10 | 8 | .968 |
| 1974—Arkansas | .........Tex. | OF | 132 | 498 | 74 | 142 | 16 | •10 | 2 | 41 | .285 | 325 | ∗24 | 16 | .956 |
| 1974—St. Louis | .........Nat. | PR-OF | 12 | 1 | 3 | 1 | 0 | 0 | 0 | 0 | 1.000 | 1 | 0 | 0 | 1.000 |
| 1975—Tulsa‡ | .............A.A. | OF | 22 | 96 | 13 | 23 | 5 | 0 | 1 | 5 | .240 | 35 | 2 | 3 | .867 |
| 1975—Phoenix | ............P.C. | OF | 115 | 427 | 49 | 115 | 6 | 4 | 2 | 44 | .269 | 287 | 10 | 10 | .967 |
| 1976—Phoenix | ............P.C. | OF | 14 | 57 | 8 | 14 | 2 | 1 | 1 | 5 | .246 | 38 | 3 | 0 | 1.000 |
| 1976—San Francisco | ....Nat. | OF | 115 | 337 | 42 | 97 | 11 | 3 | 2 | 23 | .288 | 226 | 8 | 8 | .967 |
| Major League Totals | ...................... | | 127 | 338 | 45 | 98 | 11 | 3 | 2 | 23 | .290 | 227 | 8 | 8 | .967 |

†On disabled list August 11 through remainder of season.
‡Traded with Pitcher Tony Gonzalez by St. Louis Cardinals to San Francisco Giants for Pitcher Ron Bryant, May 9, 1975.

## EDWARD MARTIN HERRMANN
### (Ed)

Born August 27, 1946, at San Diego, Calif.
Height, 6.01. Weight, 205.
Throws right and bats lefthanded.
Hobbies—Cars and guns.
Attended Mesa Junior College, Mesa, Calif.
Tied major league record for most double plays, catcher, 9-inning game, 3, July 4, 1972.
Led American League in passed balls with 19 in 1969, 18 in 1972 and 24 in 1973; tied for lead with 16 in 1971.
Tied for American League lead in double plays by catchers with 11 in 1973.
Tied Sarasota Rookie League catchers for lead in double plays with 2 in 1964.

| Year Club | League | Pos. | G. | AB. | R. | H. | 2B. | 3B. | HR. | RBI. | B.A. | PO. | A. | E. | F.A. |
|---|---|---|---|---|---|---|---|---|---|---|---|---|---|---|---|
| 1964—Sar. Braves† | ......S. Rook | C | 30 | 63 | 9 | 18 | 1 | 1 | 0 | 11 | .286 | 94 | 8 | 3 | .971 |
| 1965—Clinton‡ | ...........Midw. | C | 54 | 156 | 17 | 39 | 4 | 2 | 5 | 22 | .250 | 297 | 31 | 6 | .982 |
| 1966—Lynchburg‡‡ | ......Carol. | C | 51 | 159 | 20 | 42 | 10 | 1 | 7 | 26 | .264 | 274 | 31 | 4 | .987 |
| 1966—Evansville | ........South. | C | 42 | 136 | 13 | 33 | 7 | 2 | 2 | 19 | .243 | 262 | 20 | 3 | .989 |
| 1967—Evansville | ........South. | ∗C-1B | 117 | 386 | 35 | 92 | 18 | 2 | 9 | 53 | .238 | ∗693 | 65 | 8 | ∗.990 |
| 1967—Chicago | ...........Amer. | C | 2 | 3 | 1 | 2 | 1 | 0 | 0 | 1 | .667 | 12 | 1 | 0 | 1.000 |
| 1968—Evansville | ........South. | C | 9 | 29 | 6 | 8 | 1 | 0 | 3 | 5 | .276 | 50 | 7 | 1 | .983 |
| 1968—Hawaii | ..........P.C. | C | 50 | 139 | 16 | 34 | 5 | 0 | 5 | 18 | .245 | 239 | 34 | 7 | .975 |
| 1968—Richmond | ..........Int. | C | 37 | 112 | 10 | 26 | 4 | 2 | 4 | 16 | .232 | 208 | 17 | 1 | .996 |
| 1969—Chicago | ...........Amer. | C | 102 | 290 | 31 | 67 | 8 | 0 | 8 | 31 | .231 | 420 | 41 | 8 | .983 |
| 1970—Chicago | ...........Amer. | C | 96 | 297 | 42 | 84 | 9 | 0 | 19 | 52 | .283 | 433 | 51 | 6 | .988 |
| 1971—Chicago§ | ...........Amer. | C | 101 | 294 | 32 | 63 | 6 | 0 | 11 | 35 | .214 | 556 | 56 | 3 | .995 |
| 1972—Chicago | ...........Amer. | C | 116 | 354 | 23 | 88 | 9 | 0 | 10 | 40 | .249 | 641 | 69 | 8 | .989 |
| 1973—Chicago | ...........Amer. | C | 119 | 379 | 42 | 85 | 17 | 1 | 10 | 39 | .224 | 617 | 70 | 11 | .984 |
| 1974—Chicago x y | ......Amer. | C | 107 | 367 | 32 | 95 | 13 | 1 | 10 | 39 | .259 | 561 | 55 | 8 | .987 |
| 1975—New York z | ......Amer. | C | 80 | 200 | 16 | 51 | 9 | 2 | 6 | 30 | .255 | 121 | 18 | 3 | .979 |
| 1976—California a | ......Amer. | C | 29 | 46 | 5 | 8 | 3 | 0 | 2 | 8 | .174 | 74 | 9 | 4 | .954 |
| 1976—Houston | ..........Nat. | C | 79 | 265 | 14 | 54 | 8 | 0 | 3 | 25 | .204 | 412 | 37 | 6 | .987 |
| American League Totals | ................ | | 752 | 2230 | 224 | 543 | 75 | 4 | 76 | 275 | .243 | 3453 | 370 | 51 | .987 |
| National League Totals | .................. | | 79 | 265 | 14 | 54 | 8 | 0 | 3 | 25 | .204 | 412 | 37 | 6 | .987 |
| Major League Totals | ...................... | | 831 | 2495 | 238 | 597 | 83 | 4 | 79 | 300 | .239 | 384 | 407 | 57 | .987 |

†Drafted by Chicago White Sox from Denver (Milwaukee Braves' organization), November 30, 1964.
‡On disabled list, July 24 through August 28.
‡‡On disabled list, June 21 through July 9.
§On supplemental disabled list, June 6 through June 30.
xOn supplemental disabled list, August 4 to August 20, 1974.
yTraded to New York Yankees for Pitcher Fred Anyzeski, Outfielder-First Baseman John Narron, Outfielder Ken Bennett, Catcher Terry Quinn and cash, April 1, 1975.
zSold to California Angels, February 20, 1976.
aTraded to Houston Astros for Catcher Terry Humphrey and Pitcher Mike Barlow, both assigned to Salt Lake City, June 6, 1976.

### ALL-STAR GAME RECORD

Named to American League All-Star Team for 1974 game; elected not to play.

---

### DID YOU KNOW—
That in the entire history of the American League, no player has ever stolen 50 or more bases and hit 20 or more home runs in the same season?

---

## MARC KEVIN HILL

Born February 18, 1952, at Louisiana, Mo.
Height, 6.03. Weight, 210.
Throws and bats righthanded.
Hobbies—Hunting and fishing.

Led American Association catchers in double plays with 18 in 1974.
Led Gulf Coast League catchers in double plays with 5 in 1970.
Led Florida State League catchers in total chances with 983, total chances accepted with 968 and in double plays with 14 in 1972.

| Year Club | League | Pos. | G. | AB. | R. | H. | 2B. | 3B. | HR. | RBI. | B.A. | PO. | A. | E. | F.A. |
|-----------|--------|------|-----|-----|-----|-----|-----|-----|-----|------|------|------|-----|-----|------|
| 1970—Sarasota Cards | Gulf C | C | 28 | 78 | 6 | 15 | 3 | 0 | 0 | 6 | .192 | 176 | 24 | 2 | .990 |
| 1971—Cedar Rapids | Midw. | C | 87 | 272 | 21 | 63 | 9 | 1 | 1 | 27 | .232 | 572 | 57 | 8 | .987 |
| 1972—St. Petersburg | Fla. St. | C | 124 | 421 | 34 | 104 | 12 | 1 | 8 | 65 | .247 | *876 | *92 | 15 | .985 |
| 1972—Modesto | Calif. | C-1B | 7 | 24 | 2 | 8 | 2 | 0 | 0 | 4 | .333 | 39 | 3 | 0 | 1.000 |
| 1973—Arkansas | Texas | C | 122 | 403 | 41 | 97 | 19 | 2 | 9 | 49 | .241 | *670 | 64 | 8 | .989 |
| 1973—Tulsa | A.A. | C | 9 | 29 | 4 | 12 | 1 | 0 | 3 | 8 | .414 | 61 | 5 | 0 | 1.000 |
| 1973—St. Louis | Nat. | C | 1 | 3 | 0 | 0 | 0 | 0 | 0 | 0 | .000 | 5 | 0 | 0 | 1.000 |
| 1974—Tulsa | A.A. | C-1B | 96 | 327 | 46 | 91 | 16 | 1 | 14 | 58 | .278 | 553 | 61 | 9 | .986 |
| 1974—St. Louis† | Nat. | C | 10 | 21 | 2 | 5 | 1 | 0 | 0 | 2 | .238 | 41 | 5 | 0 | 1.000 |
| 1975—San Francisco | Nat. | C-3B | 72 | 182 | 14 | 39 | 4 | 0 | 5 | 23 | .214 | 282 | 27 | 2 | .994 |
| 1976—San Francisco‡ | Nat. | C-1B | 54 | 131 | 11 | 24 | 5 | 0 | 3 | 15 | .183 | 186 | 24 | 1 | .995 |
| Major League Totals | | | 137 | 337 | 27 | 68 | 10 | 0 | 8 | 40 | .202 | 514 | 56 | 3 | .995 |

†Traded to San Francisco Giants for Pitcher Elias Sosa and Catcher Ken Rudolph, October 14, 1974.
‡On disabled list, August 4 through October 5, 1976.

## RANDALL QUENCY HILL

(Known by middle name.)

Born September 17, 1953, at Dallas, Tex.
Height, 6.00. Weight, 175.
Throws and bats lefthanded.
Hobbies—Bowling and tennis.
Attended Eastfield College, Mesquite, Tex.

Led Eastern League in hit batsmen with 9 in 1974.

| Year Club | League | G. | IP. | W. | L. | Pct. | H. | R. | ER. | SO. | BB. | ERA. |
|-----------|--------|-----|-----|-----|-----|------|-----|-----|-----|-----|-----|------|
| 1972—Auburn | NYP | 15 | 89 | 7 | 3 | .700 | 80 | 38 | 29 | 102 | 42 | 2.93 |
| 1973—Rocky Mount | Carolina | 28 | *203 | 14 | 4 | *.778 | 175 | 81 | 66 | 135 | 100 | 2.93 |
| 1974—Reading | Eastern | 26 | 176 | 13 | 10 | .565 | 157 | 84 | 67 | 99 | 76 | 3.43 |
| 1975—Toledo† | Int'national | 29 | 149 | 10 | 11 | .476 | 147 | 71 | 68 | 89 | 64 | 4.11 |
| 1976—Oklahoma City‡ | Am. Assoc. | 47 | 67 | 5 | 6 | .455 | 63 | 34 | 29 | 42 | 36 | 3.90 |

†On disabled list, April 29 to May 16, 1975.
‡Assigned to Albuquerque, Dodgers' affiliate, January 4, 1977, to complete trade which sent Catcher Johnny Oates from Philadelphia Phillies to Los Angeles Dodgers for Infielder Ted Sizemore, December 20, 1976.

## JOHN FREDERICK HILLER

Born April 8, 1943, at Toronto, Ontario, Canada.
Height, 6.01. Weight, 190.
Throws left and bats righthanded.
Hobby—Most sports.

Established major league record for most saves, season, 38, 1973.
Tied major league record for most games lost, relief pitcher, season, 14, in 1974.
Established American League record for most games won, relief pitcher, season, 17, in 1974.
Tied American League record for most consecutive strikeouts, start of game (6), August 6, 1968.
Named American League Comeback Player of the Year by THE SPORTING NEWS, 1973.
Named American League Fireman of the Year by THE SPORTING NEWS, 1973.

| Year Club | League | G. | IP. | W. | L. | Pct. | H. | R. | ER. | SO. | BB. | ERA. |
|-----------|--------|-----|-----|-----|-----|------|-----|-----|-----|-----|-----|------|
| 1963—Jamestown | NYP | 29 | 181 | 14 | 9 | .609 | 178 | 89 | 81 | 172 | 78 | 4.03 |
| 1964—Duluth-Superior | Northern | 30 | 167 | 10 | *13 | .435 | 167 | 74 | 64 | 137 | 66 | 3.45 |
| 1964—Knoxville | Southern | 3 | 15 | 0 | 3 | .000 | 19 | 13 | 6 | 15 | 4 | 3.60 |
| 1965—Montgomery | Southern | 47 | 103 | 5 | 7 | .417 | 91 | 33 | 29 | 84 | 32 | 2.53 |
| 1965—Detroit | American | 5 | 6 | 0 | 0 | .000 | 5 | 0 | 0 | 4 | 1 | 0.00 |
| 1966—Detroit | American | 1 | 2 | 0 | 0 | .000 | 2 | 2 | 2 | 1 | 2 | 9.00 |
| 1966—Syracuse | Int'national | 54 | 87 | 3 | 7 | .300 | 71 | 46 | 43 | 69 | 33 | 4.45 |
| 1967—Toledo | Int'national | 13 | 45 | 5 | 1 | .833 | 34 | 16 | 15 | 39 | 21 | 3.00 |
| 1967—Detroit | American | 23 | 65 | 4 | 3 | .571 | 57 | 20 | 19 | 49 | 9 | 2.63 |
| 1968—Detroit | American | 39 | 128 | 9 | 6 | .600 | 92 | 37 | 34 | 78 | 51 | 2.39 |
| 1969—Detroit | American | 40 | 99 | 4 | 4 | .500 | 97 | 50 | 44 | 74 | 44 | 4.00 |
| 1970—Detroit | American | 47 | 104 | 6 | 6 | .500 | 82 | 39 | 35 | 89 | 46 | 3.03 |
| 1971† | | | | | | (Did not play) | | | | | | |
| 1972—Detroit‡ | American | 24 | 44 | 1 | 2 | .333 | 39 | 13 | 10 | 26 | 13 | 2.05 |
| 1973—Detroit | American | *65 | 125 | 10 | 5 | .667 | 89 | 21 | 20 | 124 | 39 | 1.44 |
| 1974—Detroit | American | 59 | 150 | 17 | 14 | .548 | 127 | 51 | 44 | 134 | 62 | 2.64 |
| 1975—Detroit§ | American | 36 | 71 | 2 | 3 | .400 | 52 | 20 | 17 | 87 | 36 | 2.15 |
| 1976—Detroit | American | 56 | 121 | 12 | 8 | .600 | 93 | 37 | 32 | 117 | 67 | 2.38 |
| Major League Totals | | 395 | 915 | 65 | 51 | .560 | 735 | 290 | 257 | 783 | 370 | 2.53 |

†Placed on voluntary retired list, March 19. Released by Detroit Tigers, August 31, 1971. Signed by Detroit Tigers, September 9, and placed on voluntary retired list, September 30, 1971.
‡Signed by Detroit Tigers as batting practice pitcher, June 3, 1972. Reinstated as active player, July 8, 1972.
§On disabled list, July 26 to September 1, 1975.

### CHAMPIONSHIP SERIES RECORD

| Year | Club | League | G. | IP. | W. | L. | Pct. | H. | R. | ER. | SO. | BB. | ERA. |
|------|------|--------|----|----|----|----|------|----|----|-----|-----|-----|------|
| 1972 | Detroit | American | 3 | 3⅓ | 1 | 0 | 1.000 | 1 | 0 | 0 | 1 | 1 | 0.00 |

### WORLD SERIES RECORD

| Year | Club | League | G. | IP. | W. | L. | Pct. | H. | R. | ER. | SO. | BB. | ERA. |
|------|------|--------|----|----|----|----|------|----|----|-----|-----|-----|------|
| 1968 | Detroit | American | 2 | 2 | 0 | 0 | .000 | 6 | 4 | 3 | 1 | 3 | 13.50 |

### ALL-STAR GAME RECORD

Member of American League All-Star Team in 1974 game; did not play.

## JOHN DAVID HILTON
### (Dave)

Born September 15, 1950, at Uvalde, Tex.
Height, 6.01. Weight, 190.
Throws and bats righthanded.
Attended Rice University, Houston, Tex.

| Year | Club | League | Pos. | G. | AB. | R. | H. | 2B. | 3B. | HR. | RBI. | B.A. | PO. | A. | E. | F.A. |
|------|------|--------|------|----|-----|----|----|-----|-----|-----|------|------|-----|----|----|------|
| 1971 | Lodi | Calif. | 3-S-2-O | 128 | 493 | 86 | 122 | 30 | 5 | 12 | 56 | .247 | 159 | 249 | 32 | .927 |
| 1972 | Alexandria | Texas | *3-S-2 | 135 | 520 | 75 | 164 | 30 | 6 | 16 | 73 | .315 | 115 | *262 | 21 | *.947 |
| 1972 | San Diego | Nat. | 3B | 13 | 47 | 2 | 10 | 2 | 1 | 0 | 5 | .213 | 12 | 19 | 2 | .939 |
| 1973 | Hawaii | P.C. | 3B-SS | 43 | 146 | 20 | 35 | 7 | 1 | 3 | 11 | .240 | 35 | 67 | 10 | .911 |
| 1973 | Alexandria | Texas | 2B | 45 | 143 | 22 | 39 | 9 | 1 | 7 | 20 | .273 | 90 | 87 | 7 | .962 |
| 1973 | San Diego | Nat. | 3B-2B | 70 | 234 | 21 | 46 | 9 | 0 | 5 | 16 | .197 | 79 | 141 | 6 | .973 |
| 1974 | Hawaii | P.C. | 2B-3B | 74 | 262 | 41 | 86 | 22 | 4 | 4 | 43 | .328 | 124 | 181 | 11 | .965 |
| 1974 | San Diego | Nat. | 3B-2B | 74 | 217 | 17 | 52 | 8 | 2 | 1 | 12 | .240 | 70 | 113 | 12 | .938 |
| 1975 | San Diego† | Nat. | 3B | 4 | 8 | 0 | 0 | 0 | 0 | 0 | 0 | .000 | 2 | 7 | 1 | .900 |
| 1975 | Alexandria | Tex. | 3B-2B | 44 | 151 | 30 | 45 | 14 | 0 | 6 | 27 | .298 | 45 | 99 | 5 | .966 |
| 1975 | Hawaii | P.C. | 2B | 9 | 35 | 7 | 10 | 4 | 0 | 1 | 5 | .286 | 22 | 31 | 0 | 1.000 |
| 1976 | Hawaii‡ | P.C. | 3B-2B | 126 | 475 | 61 | 137 | 27 | 8 | 16 | 77 | .288 | 85 | 257 | 20 | .945 |
| Major League Totals | | | | 161 | 506 | 40 | 108 | 19 | 3 | 6 | 33 | .213 | 163 | 280 | 21 | .955 |

†On disabled list, April 30 to June 27, 1975.
‡Sold to Toronto Blue Jays, October 22, 1976.

## SAMUEL RUSSELL HINDS

Born July 11, 1953, at Fredrick, Md.
Hieght, 6.06. Weight, 215.
Throws and bats righthanded.
Hobbies—Music and fishing.
Attended Broward Junior College, Ft. Lauderdale, Fla.

| Year | Club | League | G. | IP. | W. | L. | Pct. | H. | R. | ER. | SO. | BB. | ERA. |
|------|------|--------|----|----|----|----|------|----|----|-----|-----|-----|------|
| 1974 | Danville | Midwest | 25 | 159 | 9 | 8 | .529 | 151 | 78 | 60 | 113 | 74 | 3.40 |
| 1975 | Thetford Mines | Eastern | 25 | 167 | 6 | 13 | .316 | 153 | 86 | 65 | 98 | 73 | 3.50 |
| 1976 | Pittsfield† | Eastern | 30 | 180 | 12 | 10 | .545 | 177 | 87 | 79 | 85 | 68 | 3.95 |

†On disabled list, July 6 through July 17, 1976.
Listed on Milwaukee Brewers' 1977 spring roster.

## LARRY EUGENE HISLE
### Name pronounced HY-sul.

Born May 5, 1947, at Portsmouth, O.
Height, 6.01. Weight, 193.
Throws and bats righthanded.
Attended Ohio State University, Columbus, O.

Tied major league record for most times struck out rookie season, 152, 1969.
Led Carolina League in total bases with 251 in 1967.

| Year | Club | League | Pos. | G. | AB. | R. | H. | 2B. | 3B. | HR. | RBI. | B.A. | PO. | A. | E. | F.A. |
|------|------|--------|------|----|-----|----|----|-----|-----|-----|------|------|-----|----|----|------|
| 1966 | Huron† | North. | OF | 21 | 60 | 12 | 26 | 5 | 0 | 3 | 13 | .433 | 19 | 1 | 2 | .909 |
| 1967 | Tidewater | Carol. | OF | 136 | 503 | 82 | 152 | 24 | 3 | 23 | 78 | .302 | 274 | 13 | 11 | .963 |
| 1968 | Philadelphia | Nat. | OF | 7 | 11 | 1 | 4 | 1 | 0 | 0 | 1 | .364 | 8 | 0 | 0 | 1.000 |
| 1969 | Philadelphia | Nat. | OF | 145 | 482 | 75 | 128 | 23 | 5 | 20 | 56 | .266 | 324 | 11 | 8 | .977 |
| 1970 | Philadelphia | Nat. | OF | 126 | 405 | 52 | 83 | 22 | 4 | 10 | 44 | .205 | 262 | 5 | 6 | .978 |
| 1971 | Eugene | P. C. | OF | 62 | 186 | 33 | 61 | 17 | 3 | 9 | 30 | .328 | 97 | 4 | 1 | .990 |
| 1971 | Philadelphia§ | Nat. | OF | 36 | 76 | 7 | 15 | 3 | 0 | 0 | 3 | .197 | 48 | 2 | 2 | .962 |
| 1972 | Albuquerque xy | P. C. | OF | 131 | 456 | 87 | 148 | 21 | 9 | 23 | 91 | .325 | 197 | 9 | 8 | .963 |
| 1973 | Minnesota | Amer. | OF | 143 | 545 | 88 | 148 | 25 | 6 | 15 | 64 | .272 | 337 | 11 | 9 | .975 |
| 1974 | Minnesota | Amer. | OF | 143 | 510 | 68 | 146 | 20 | 7 | 19 | 79 | .286 | 279 | 4 | 6 | .979 |
| 1975 | Minnesota z | Amer. | OF | 80 | 255 | 37 | 80 | 9 | 2 | 11 | 51 | .314 | 118 | 2 | 3 | .976 |
| 1976 | Minnesota | Amer. | OF | 155 | 581 | 81 | 158 | 19 | 5 | 14 | 96 | .272 | 361 | 16 | 6 | .984 |
| National League Totals | | | | 314 | 974 | 135 | 230 | 49 | 9 | 30 | 104 | .236 | 642 | 18 | 16 | .974 |
| American League Totals | | | | 521 | 1891 | 274 | 532 | 73 | 20 | 59 | 290 | .281 | 1095 | 33 | 24 | .979 |
| Major League Totals | | | | 835 | 2865 | 409 | 762 | 122 | 29 | 89 | 394 | .266 | 1737 | 51 | 40 | .978 |

†On restricted list, February 25 through June 11. On disabled list, August 12 through September 5.
‡On disabled list from July 2 through August 26 with hepatitis.
§Traded to Los Angeles Dodgers for First Baseman Tommy Hutton, October 22, 1971.
xReleased by Los Angeles Dodgers to St. Louis Cardinals (in trade which sent Pitcher Rudy Arroyo from St. Louis to Los Angeles and Pitcher Greg Millikan from Arkansas to Albuquerque), October 26, 1972.
yTraded by St. Louis Cardinals with Pitcher John Cumberland (latter assigned from Arkansas to Tacoma) to Minnesota Twins for Pitcher Wayne Granger, November 29, 1972.
zOn disabled list, June 27 to July 12 and July 25 to September 2, 1975.

## CLELL LAVERN HOBSON, JR.
### (Butch)

Born August 17, 1951, at Tuscaloosa, Ala.
Height, 6.01. Weight, 190.
Throws and bats righthanded.
Attended University of Alabama, University, Ala.

Led Eastern League in total bases with 201 in 1975.

| Year | Club | League | Pos. | G. | AB. | R. | H. | 2B. | 3B. | HR. | RBI. | B.A. | PO. | A. | E. | F.A. |
|------|------|--------|------|----|-----|----|----|-----|-----|-----|------|------|-----|----|----|------|
| 1973—Winston-Salem | ..Carol. | | 3B-OF | 17 | 39 | 8 | 7 | 2 | 1 | 0 | 5 | .179 | 10 | 10 | 1 | .952 |
| 1974—Winston-Salem | ..Carol. | | O-3-1 | 119 | 423 | 66 | 120 | 18 | 8 | 14 | 74 | .284 | 211 | 79 | 12 | .960 |
| 1975—Bristol | ..............East. | | 3B | •138 | 471 | 68 | 125 | 25 | 3 | 15 | 73 | .265 | 102 | 309 | 28 | .936 |
| 1975—Boston | ..............Amer. | | 3B | 2 | 4 | 0 | 1 | 0 | 0 | 0 | 0 | .250 | 1 | 3 | 0 | 1.000 |
| 1976—Pawtucket | ........Int. | | 3B-SS | 90 | 360 | 56 | 103 | 21 | 1 | 25 | 72 | .286 | 91 | 204 | 15 | .952 |
| 1976—Boston | ..............Amer. | | 3B | 76 | 269 | 34 | 63 | 7 | 5 | 8 | 34 | .234 | 60 | 146 | 14 | .936 |
| Major League Totals | ..................... | | | 78 | 273 | 34 | 64 | 7 | 5 | 8 | 34 | .234 | 61 | 149 | 14 | .938 |

## RONALD WRAY HODGES
### (Ron)

Born June 22, 1949, at Rocky Mount, Va.
Height, 6.01. Weight, 190.
Throws right and bats lefthanded.
Hobby—Hunting.
Attended Appalachian State University, Boone, N. C.

| Year | Club | League | Pos. | G. | AB. | R. | H. | 2B. | 3B. | HR. | RBI. | B.A. | PO. | A. | E. | F.A. |
|------|------|--------|------|----|-----|----|----|-----|-----|-----|------|------|-----|----|----|------|
| 1972—Pompano Beach | Fla. St. | | •C-3-O | 112 | 359 | 59 | 92 | 15 | 4 | 15 | 48 | .256 | 684 | 71 | •18 | .977 |
| 1973—Memphis | ..........Texas | | C | 47 | 139 | 12 | 24 | 4 | 0 | 1 | 11 | .173 | 275 | 3 | 6 | .980 |
| 1973—New York | .........Nat. | | C | 45 | 127 | 5 | 33 | 2 | 0 | 1 | 18 | .260 | 241 | 13 | 2 | .992 |
| 1974—New York | .........Nat. | | C | 59 | 136 | 16 | 30 | 4 | 0 | 4 | 14 | .221 | 227 | 14 | 12 | .953 |
| 1975—Tidewater | .........Int. | | C-O-1 | 95 | 278 | 27 | 74 | 8 | 0 | 2 | 33 | .266 | 431 | 45 | 7 | .986 |
| 1975—New York | .........Nat. | | C | 9 | 34 | 3 | 7 | 1 | 0 | 2 | 4 | .206 | 69 | 1 | 0 | 1.000 |
| 1976—New York† | ........Nat. | | C | 56 | 155 | 21 | 35 | 6 | 0 | 4 | 24 | .226 | 262 | 18 | 7 | .976 |
| Major League Totals | ..................... | | | 169 | 452 | 45 | 105 | 13 | 0 | 11 | 60 | .232 | 799 | 46 | 21 | .976 |

†On disabled list, June 13 through June 28, 1976.

### WORLD SERIES RECORD

| Year | Club | League | Pos. | G. | AB. | R. | H. | 2B. | 3B. | HR. | RBI. | B.A. | PO. | A. | E. | F.A. |
|------|------|--------|------|----|-----|----|----|-----|-----|-----|------|------|-----|----|----|------|
| 1973—New York | .........Nat. | | PH | 1 | 0 | 0 | 0 | 0 | 0 | 0 | 0 | .000 | 0 | 0 | 0 | .000 |

## JOSEPH WALTER HOERNER
### (Joe)

Born November 12, 1936, at Dubuque, Ia.
Height, 6.01. Weight, 200.
Throws left and bats righthanded.
Hobbies—Hunting and fishing.

Tied National League record for most consecutive strikeouts, game, relief pitcher (6), June 1, 1968.
Pitched last eight innings of 14-0 no-hit victory against Winnipeg, June 7, 1957.

| Year | Club | League | G. | IP. | W. | L. | Pct. | H. | R. | ER. | SO. | BB. | ERA. |
|------|------|--------|----|----|----|----|------|----|----|-----|-----|-----|------|
| 1957—Duluth-Superior | ...................Northern | 28 | 185 | 16 | 5 | *.762 | 166 | 63 | 53 | 86 | 71 | 2.58 |
| 1958—Davenport | ......................I.I.I. | 29 | 157 | 8 | 8 | .500 | 176 | 90 | 77 | 85 | 52 | 4.41 |
| 1959—Charleston | .........................Sally | 15 | 28 | 1 | 1 | .500 | 33 | 14 | 10 | 19 | 20 | 3.21 |
| 1959—Duluth-Superior | ...................Northern | 4 | 17 | 1 | 3 | .250 | 23 | 12 | 10 | 14 | 17 | 5.29 |
| 1959—Lincoln | ..............................I.I.I. | 9 | 32 | 2 | 1 | .667 | 29 | 15 | 11 | 21 | 10 | 3.09 |
| 1960—Charleston | .........................Sally | 46 | 157 | 11 | 9 | .550 | 135 | 65 | 52 | 132 | 51 | 2.97 |
| 1961—San Diego | .........................P. Coast | 4 | 9 | 0 | 0 | .000 | 11 | 3 | 3 | 6 | 3 | 3.00 |
| 1961—Charleston† | .........................Sally | 25 | 130 | 6 | 13 | .316 | 141 | 62 | 45 | 86 | 31 | 3.11 |
| 1962—Oklahoma City | ...................Am. Assoc. | 7 | 10 | 0 | 0 | .000 | 22 | 13 | 6 | 9 | 2 | 5.40 |
| 1962—Savannah | .........................Sally | 27 | 94 | 9 | 1 | .900 | 81 | 26 | 26 | 60 | 26 | 2.49 |
| 1963—San Antonio | .........................Texas | 33 | 156 | 11 | 7 | .611 | 153 | 69 | 57 | 126 | 31 | 3.29 |
| 1963—Houston | .............................National | 1 | 3 | 0 | 0 | .000 | 2 | 0 | 0 | 2 | 0 | 0.00 |
| 1964—Houston | .............................National | 7 | 11 | 0 | 0 | .000 | 13 | 11 | 6 | 4 | 6 | 4.91 |
| 1964—Oklahoma City | ...................P. Coast | 51 | 62 | 3 | 3 | .500 | 34 | 11 | 9 | 71 | 20 | 1.31 |
| 1965—Oklahoma City‡ | ...................P. Coast | 53 | 65 | 8 | 3 | .727 | 59 | 22 | 14 | 55 | 14 | 1.94 |
| 1966—St. Louis | .............................National | 57 | 76 | 5 | 1 | .833 | 57 | 16 | 13 | 63 | 21 | 1.54 |
| 1967—St. Louis | .............................National | 57 | 66 | 4 | 4 | .500 | 52 | 25 | 19 | 50 | 20 | 2.59 |

| Year | Club | League | G. | IP. | W. | L. | Pct. | H. | R. | ER. | SO. | BB. | ERA. |
|------|------|--------|----|----|----|----|------|----|----|-----|-----|-----|------|
| 1968–St. Louis | | National | 47 | 49 | 8 | 2 | .800 | 34 | 9 | 8 | 42 | 12 | 1.47 |
| 1969–St. Louis§ | | National | 45 | 53 | 2 | 3 | .400 | 44 | 18 | 17 | 35 | 9 | 2.89 |
| 1970–Philadelphia | | National | 44 | 58 | 9 | 5 | .643 | 53 | 20 | 17 | 39 | 20 | 2.64 |
| 1971–Philadelphia | | National | 49 | 73 | 4 | 5 | .444 | 57 | 19 | 16 | 57 | 21 | 1.97 |
| 1972–Phil.x-Atlanta | | National | 40 | 45 | 1 | 5 | .167 | 55 | 24 | 22 | 31 | 13 | 4.40 |
| 1973–Atlanta y | | National | 20 | 13 | 2 | 2 | .500 | 17 | 9 | 9 | 10 | 4 | 6.23 |
| 1973–Kansas City | | American | 22 | 19 | 2 | 0 | 1.000 | 28 | 11 | 11 | 15 | 13 | 5.21 |
| 1974–Kansas City z | | American | 30 | 35 | 2 | 3 | .400 | 32 | 15 | 15 | 24 | 12 | 3.86 |
| 1975–Philadelphia a | | National | 25 | 21 | 0 | 0 | .000 | 25 | 6 | 6 | 20 | 8 | 2.57 |
| 1976–Texas | | American | 41 | 35 | 0 | 4 | .000 | 41 | 22 | 20 | 15 | 19 | 5.14 |
| National League Totals | | | 392 | 468 | 35 | 27 | .565 | 409 | 157 | 133 | 353 | 134 | 2.56 |
| American League Totals | | | 93 | 89 | 4 | 7 | .364 | 101 | 48 | 46 | 54 | 44 | 4.65 |
| Major League Totals | | | 485 | 557 | 39 | 34 | .534 | 510 | 205 | 179 | 407 | 178 | 2.89 |

†Drafted from Mobile (Chicago White Sox' organization) by Houston Colt .45s, November 27, 1961.
‡Drafted by St. Louis Cardinals from Oklahoma City (Houston Astros' organization), November 29, 1965.
§Traded with Catcher Tim McCarver and Outfielder Curt Flood and Byron Browne to Philadelphia Phillies for First Baseman Richie Allen, Infielder Octavio (Cookie) Rojas and Pitcher Jerry Johnson, October 7, 1969. Flood refused to report and the Cardinals sent First Baseman Guillermo Montanez and a player to be named later to Philadelphia to complete the deal, April 8, 1970. Pitcher James Robert Browning was sent from St. Louis to Philadelphia as the "player to be named later," August 30, 1970.
xTraded with First Baseman Andre Thornton (latter assigned from Eugene to Richmond) to Atlanta Braves for Pitchers Gary Neibauer and Jim Nash, June 15, 1972.
yOn disabled list, April 24 to June 9; purchased by Kansas City Royals, July 18, 1973.
zReleased, December 9, 1974; signed as free agent by Philadelphia Phillies, January 14, 1975.
aReleased, November 5, 1975; signed as a free agent by Texas Rangers, January 6, 1976.

## WORLD SERIES RECORD

| Year | Club | League | G. | IP. | W. | L. | Pct. | H. | R. | ER. | SO. | BB. | ERA. |
|------|------|--------|----|----|----|----|------|----|----|-----|-----|-----|------|
| 1967–St. Louis | | National | 2 | 2⅔ | 0 | 0 | .000 | 4 | 3 | 3 | 0 | 1 | 40.50 |
| 1968–St. Louis | | National | 3 | 4⅔ | 0 | 1 | .000 | 5 | 4 | 2 | 3 | 5 | 3.86 |
| World Series Totals | | | 5 | 5⅓ | 0 | 1 | .000 | 9 | 7 | 5 | 3 | 6 | 8.44 |

## ALL-STAR GAME RECORD

Member of National League All-Star Team in 1970 game; did not play.

## FREDRICK WILLIAM HOLDSWORTH
### (Fred)

Born May 29, 1952, at Detroit, Mich.
Height, 6.01. Weight, 190.
Throws and bats righthanded.
Attended University of Michigan, Ann Arbor, Mich.

Led International League pitchers in games started with 30 in 1973.

| Year | Club | League | G. | IP. | W. | L. | Pct. | H. | R. | ER. | SO. | BB. | ERA. |
|------|------|--------|----|----|----|----|------|----|----|-----|-----|-----|------|
| 1970–Bristol | | Ap'lachian | 8 | 62 | 5 | 1 | .833 | 56 | 14 | 9 | 64 | 15 | ∗1.31 |
| 1970–Lakeland | | Florida St. | 3 | 7 | 0 | 1 | .000 | 7 | 5 | 2 | 5 | 3 | 2.57 |
| 1971–Lakeland | | Florida St. | 9 | 62 | 3 | 5 | .375 | 56 | 22 | 13 | 50 | 14 | 1.89 |
| 1971–Rocky Mount | | Carolina | 18 | 119 | 8 | 4 | .667 | 101 | 47 | 37 | 79 | 32 | 2.80 |
| 1971–Montgomery | | Southern | 3 | 23 | 2 | 1 | .667 | 16 | 10 | 7 | 16 | 3 | 2.74 |
| 1972–Toledo† | | Int'national | 21 | 107 | 7 | 5 | .583 | 119 | 55 | 46 | 83 | 38 | 3.87 |
| 1972–Detroit | | American | 2 | 7 | 0 | 1 | .000 | 10 | 10 | 10 | 5 | 2 | 12.86 |
| 1973–Toledo | | Int'national | 30 | ∗214 | 14 | 10 | .583 | ∗194 | 92 | 81 | 121 | 79 | 3.41 |
| 1973–Detroit | | American | 5 | 15 | 0 | 1 | .000 | 13 | 11 | 11 | 9 | 6 | 6.60 |
| 1974–Evansville | | Am. Assoc. | 21 | 153 | 9 | 6 | .600 | 150 | 72 | 55 | 114 | 38 | 3.24 |
| 1974–Detroit | | American | 8 | 36 | 0 | 3 | .000 | 40 | 20 | 17 | 16 | 14 | 4.25 |
| 1975–Evansville‡ | | Am. Assoc. | 7 | 46 | 2 | 4 | .333 | 47 | 25 | 22 | 39 | 10 | 4.30 |
| 1975–Rochester | | Int'national | 19 | 111 | 4 | 9 | .308 | 99 | 49 | 40 | 99 | 43 | 3.24 |
| 1976–Baltimore | | American | 16 | 40 | 4 | 1 | .800 | 24 | 9 | 9 | 24 | 13 | 2.03 |
| Major League Totals | | | 31 | 98 | 4 | 6 | .400 | 80 | 50 | 47 | 54 | 35 | 4.32 |

†On disabled list, April 14 through May 1, 1972.
‡Traded by Detroit Tigers to Baltimore Orioles for Pitcher Bob Reynolds, May 29, 1975.

## JAMES WILLIAM HOLT
### (Jim)

Born May 27, 1944, at Graham, N. C.
Height, 5.11. Weight, 195.
Throws right and bats lefthanded.

Led American Association outfielders in double plays with 7 in 1969.

| Year | Club | League | Pos. | G. | AB. | R. | H. | 2B. | 3B. | HR. | RBI. | B.A. | PO. | A. | E. | F.A. |
|------|------|--------|------|----|-----|----|----|-----|-----|-----|------|------|-----|----|----|------|
| 1965–Leesburg† | | Fla. St. | | | | | (In Military Service) | | | | | | | | | |
| 1966–Leesburg | | Fla. St. | OF | 126 | 461 | 62 | 132 | 21 | 6 | 4 | 51 | .286 | 172 | ∗20 | 10 | .950 |
| 1967–Peninsula‡ | | Carol. | OF | 129 | 494 | 87 | 154 | 18 | 5 | 8 | 60 | .312 | 287 | 8 | 3 | ●.990 |
| 1968–Minnesota | | Amer. | OF-1B | 70 | 106 | 9 | 22 | 2 | 1 | 0 | 8 | .208 | 35 | 2 | 1 | .974 |
| 1969–Denver | | A.A. | ∗O-3-1 | ●139 | 535 | 98 | 180 | ●37 | 12 | 11 | 87 | .336 | 295 | ∗37 | 10 | ∗.971 |
| 1969–Minnesota | | Amer. | OF-1B | 12 | 14 | 3 | 5 | 0 | 0 | 1 | 2 | .357 | 4 | 0 | 0 | 1.000 |
| 1970–Minnesota | | Amer. | OF-1B | 142 | 319 | 37 | 85 | 9 | 3 | 3 | 40 | .266 | 208 | 2 | 1 | .995 |

– 171 –

| Year Club | League | Pos. | G. | AB. | R. | H. | 2B. | 3B. | HR. | RBI. | B.A. | PO. | A. | E. | F.A. |
|---|---|---|---|---|---|---|---|---|---|---|---|---|---|---|---|
| 1971–Minnesota ........Amer. | | OF-1B | 126 | 340 | 35 | 88 | 11 | 3 | 1 | 29 | .259 | 219 | 4 | 3 | .987 |
| 1972–Tacoma ...........P.C. | | ●OF-1B | 134 | 484 | 53 | 161 | 27 | 6 | 8 | 96 | .333 | 284 | ●23 | 7 | .978 |
| 1972–Minnesota ........Amer. | | OF-1B | 10 | 27 | 6 | 12 | 1 | 0 | 1 | 6 | .444 | 16 | 2 | 1 | .947 |
| 1973–Minnesota ........Amer. | | OF-1B | 132 | 441 | 52 | 131 | 25 | 3 | 11 | 58 | .297 | 415 | 26 | 2 | .995 |
| 1974–Minn.§-Oak. ......Amer. | | 1B-OF | 109 | 239 | 25 | 56 | 11 | 0 | 0 | 16 | .234 | 504 | 49 | 2 | .996 |
| 1975–Tucson .............P.C. | | OF-1B | 8 | 31 | 5 | 7 | 0 | 0 | 0 | 2 | .226 | 27 | 5 | 0 | 1.000 |
| 1975–Oakland ...........Amer. | | 1-O-C | 102 | 123 | 7 | 27 | 3 | 0 | 2 | 16 | .220 | 192 | 18 | 2 | .991 |
| 1976–Tucson .............P.C. | | 1-O-3B | 94 | 312 | 31 | 105 | 22 | 3 | 5 | 34 | .337 | 434 | 22 | 7 | .985 |
| 1976–Oakland ...........Amer. | | DH | 4 | 7 | 0 | 2 | 2 | 0 | 0 | 2 | .286 | .... | .... | .... | ........ |
| Major League Totals .................... | | | 707 | 1616 | 174 | 428 | 64 | 10 | 19 | 177 | .265 | 1593 | 103 | 12 | .993 |

†On temporary inactice list, April 19 through September 28.
‡Drafted by Minnesota Twins from Vancouver (Oakland Athletics' organization), November 28, 1967.
§Traded to Oakland Athletics for First Baseman Pat Bourque, August 19, 1974.

## CHAMPIONSHIP SERIES RECORD

| Year Club | League | Pos. | G. | AB. | R. | H. | 2B. | 3B. | HR. | RBI. | B.A. | PO. | A. | E. | F.A. |
|---|---|---|---|---|---|---|---|---|---|---|---|---|---|---|---|
| 1970–Minnesota ........Am. | | PH-O-PR | 3 | 5 | 0 | 0 | 0 | 0 | 0 | 0 | .000 | 3 | 0 | 1 | .750 |
| 1974–Oakland ...........Am. | | PH-1B | 2 | 0 | 0 | 0 | 0 | 0 | 0 | 0 | .000 | 1 | 0 | 0 | 1.000 |
| 1975–Oakland ...........Am. | | PH-1B | 3 | 3 | 0 | 1 | 1 | 0 | 0 | 0 | .333 | 1 | 2 | 0 | 1.000 |
| Championship Series Totals ............ | | | 8 | 8 | 0 | 1 | 1 | 0 | 0 | 0 | .125 | 5 | 2 | 1 | .875 |

## WORLD SERIES RECORD

| Year Club | League | Pos. | G. | AB. | R. | H. | 2B. | 3B. | HR. | RBI. | B.A. | PO. | A. | E. | F.A. |
|---|---|---|---|---|---|---|---|---|---|---|---|---|---|---|---|
| 1974–Oakland ...........Amer. | | PH-1B | 4 | 3 | 0 | 2 | 0 | 0 | 0 | 2 | .667 | 1 | 0 | 0 | 1.000 |

# KENNETH DALE HOLTZMAN
## (Ken)

Born November 3, 1945, at St. Louis, Mo.
Height, 6.02. Weight, 190.
Throws left and bats righthanded.
Hobbies–Reading and golf.
Attended University of Illinois, Champaign, Ill., and Chicago, Ill.;
received Bachelor of Arts degree in Business Administration

Tied National League record for most consecutive batters stuck out, start of game (5), September 5, 1970.
Pitched 3-0 no-hit victory against Atlanta Braves, August 19, 1969.
Pitched 1-0 no-hit victory against Cincinnati Reds, June 3, 1971.
Named lefthanded pitcher on THE SPORTING NEWS American League All-Star Team, 1973.
Received reported $65,000 bonus to sign with Chicago Cubs, 1965.

| Year Club | League | G. | IP. | W. | L. | Pct. | H. | R. | ER. | SO. | BB. | ERA. |
|---|---|---|---|---|---|---|---|---|---|---|---|---|
| 1965–Treasure Valley ................. | Pioneer | 4 | 27 | 4 | 0 | 1.000 | 14 | 7 | 3 | 44 | 7 | 1.00 |
| 1965–Wenatchee .......................... | Northwest | 8 | 59 | 4 | 3 | .571 | 58 | 25 | 16 | 70 | 24 | 2.44 |
| 1965–Chicago............................... | National | 3 | 4 | 0 | 0 | .000 | 2 | 4 | 1 | 3 | 3 | 2.25 |
| 1966–Chicago............................... | National | 34 | 221 | 11 | 16 | .407 | 194 | 104 | 93 | 171 | 68 | 3.79 |
| 1967–Chicago† ............................. | National | 12 | 93 | 9 | 0 | 1.000 | 76 | 31 | 26 | 62 | 44 | 2.52 |
| 1968–Chicago............................... | National | 34 | 215 | 11 | 14 | .440 | 201 | 89 | 80 | 151 | 76 | 3.35 |
| 1969–Chicago............................... | National | 39 | 261 | 17 | 13 | .567 | 248 | 117 | 104 | 176 | 93 | 3.59 |
| 1970–Chicago............................... | National | 39 | 288 | 17 | 11 | .607 | 271 | 125 | 108 | 202 | 94 | 3.38 |
| 1971–Chicago‡ ............................. | National | 30 | 195 | 9 | 15 | .375 | 213 | 108 | 97 | 143 | 64 | 4.48 |
| 1972–Oakland ............................. | American | 39 | 265 | 19 | 11 | .633 | 232 | 83 | 74 | 134 | 52 | 2.51 |
| 1973–Oakland ............................. | American | 40 | 297 | 21 | 13 | .618 | 275 | 109 | 98 | 157 | 66 | 2.97 |
| 1974–Oakland ............................. | American | 39 | 255 | 19 | 17 | .528 | 273 | 111 | 87 | 117 | 51 | 3.07 |
| 1975–Oakland§............................. | American | 39 | 266 | 18 | 14 | .563 | 217 | 111 | 93 | 122 | 108 | 3.15 |
| 1976–Balt. x-N. Y. ......................American | American | 34 | 247 | 14 | 11 | .560 | 265 | 108 | 100 | 66 | 70 | 3.64 |
| National League Totals............................. | | 191 | 1277 | 74 | 69 | .517 | 1205 | 578 | 509 | 908 | 442 | 3.59 |
| American League Totals........................... | | 191 | 1330 | 91 | 66 | .580 | 1262 | 522 | 452 | 596 | 347 | 3.06 |
| Major League Totals .............................. | | 382 | 2607 | 165 | 135 | .550 | 2467 | 1100 | 961 | 1504 | 789 | 3.32 |

†On military list from May 22 through August 11.
‡Traded to Oakland A's for Outfielder Rick Monday, November 29, 1971.
§Traded with Outfielder Reggie Jackson and Pitcher Bill Van Bommel to Baltimore Orioles for Outfielder Don Baylor and Pitchers Mike Torrez and Paul Mitchell, April 2, 1976.

xTraded with Pitchers Doyle Alexander and Grant Jackson, Catcher Elrod Hendricks and Pitcher Jimmy Freeman (assigned from Rochester to Syracuse) to New York Yankees for Pitchers Rudy May, Tippy Martinez, Dave Pagan and Scott McGregor and Catcher Rick Dempsey, June 15, 1976.

## CHAMPIONSHIP SERIES RECORD

| Year Club | League | G. | IP. | W. | L. | Pct. | H. | R. | ER. | SO. | BB. | ERA. |
|---|---|---|---|---|---|---|---|---|---|---|---|---|
| 1972–Oakland ............................American | American | 1 | 4 | 0 | 1 | .000 | 4 | 2 | 2 | 2 | 2 | 4.50 |
| 1973–Oakland ............................American | American | 1 | 11 | 1 | 0 | 1.000 | 3 | 1 | 1 | 7 | 1 | 0.82 |
| 1974–Oakland ............................American | American | 1 | 9 | 1 | 0 | 1.000 | 5 | 0 | 0 | 3 | 0 | 0.00 |
| 1975–Oakland ............................American | American | 2 | 11 | 0 | 2 | .000 | 12 | 8 | 5 | 7 | 1 | 4.09 |
| Championship Series Totals ..................... | | 5 | 35 | 2 | 3 | .400 | 24 | 11 | 8 | 19 | 6 | 2.06 |

## WORLD SERIES RECORD

| Year Club | League | G. | IP. | W. | L. | Pct. | H. | R. | ER. | SO. | BB. | ERA. |
|---|---|---|---|---|---|---|---|---|---|---|---|---|
| 1972–Oakland ............................American. | American. | 3 | 12⅔ | 1 | 0 | 1.000 | 11 | 3 | 3 | 4 | 2 | 2.13 |
| 1973–Oakland ............................American | American | 3 | 10⅔ | 2 | 1 | .667 | 13 | 5 | 5 | 6 | 5 | 4.22 |
| 1974–Oakland ............................American | American | 2 | 12 | 1 | 0 | 1.00 | 13 | 3 | 2 | 10 | 4 | 1.50 |
| World Series Totals ................................ | | 8 | 35⅓ | 4 | 1 | .800 | 37 | 11 | 10 | 20 | 12 | 2.55 |

| Year League | IP. | W. | L. | Pct. | H. | R. | ER. | SO. | BB. | ERA. |
|---|---|---|---|---|---|---|---|---|---|---|
| 1973—American ...................................................... | ⅔ | 0 | 0 | .000 | 1 | 0 | 0 | 0 | 0 | 0.000 |

Member of American League All-Star Team for the 1972 game; did not play.


## DONALD HARRIS HOOD
### (Don)

Born October 16, 1949, at Florence, S. C.
Height, 6.03. Weight, 188.
Throws and bats lefthanded.
Hobbies—Hunting and fishing.
Attended St. Petersburg Junior College, St. Petersburg, Fla.
Tied for California League lead in shutouts with 5 in 1970.

| Year Club | League | G. | IP. | W. | L. | Pct. | H. | R. | ER. | SO. | BB. | ERA. |
|---|---|---|---|---|---|---|---|---|---|---|---|---|
| 1969—Bluefield .............................Ap'lachian | | 9 | 48 | 5 | 1 | .833 | 53 | 29 | 24 | 54 | 24 | 4.50 |
| 1970—Stockton ..............................California | | 28 | 178 | 10 | 10 | .500 | 165 | 78 | 57 | 196 | 66 | 2.88 |
| 1971—Dallas-Ft. Worth ..................Texas | | 26 | 167 | 11 | 9 | .550 | 146 | 68 | 50 | 96 | 60 | 2.69 |
| 1972—Rochester ...........................Int'national | | 27 | 150 | 9 | 10 | .474 | 160 | 66 | 58 | 84 | 58 | 3.48 |
| 1973—Rochester ...........................Int'national | | 15 | 91 | 4 | 7 | .364 | 75 | 40 | 32 | 62 | 33 | 3.16 |
| 1973—Baltimore ...........................American | | 8 | 32 | 3 | 2 | .600 | 31 | 17 | 14 | 18 | 6 | 3.94 |
| 1974—Baltimore†‡.........................American | | 20 | 57 | 1 | 1 | .500 | 47 | 26 | 22 | 26 | 20 | 3.47 |
| 1975—Cleveland ...........................American | | 29 | 135 | 6 | 10 | .375 | 136 | 76 | 66 | 51 | 57 | 4.40 |
| 1976—Cleveland ...........................American | | 33 | 78 | 3 | 5 | .375 | 89 | 46 | 42 | 32 | 41 | 4.85 |
| Major League Totals | | 90 | 302 | 13 | 18 | .419 | 303 | 165 | 144 | 127 | 124 | 4.29 |

†On restricted list, May 26 to June 4, 1974.
‡Traded with First Baseman Boog Powell to Cleveland Indians for Catcher Dave Duncan and Outfielder Alvin McGrew (assigned to Rochester), February 25, 1974.


## BURT CARLTON HOOTON

Born February 7, 1950, at Greenville, Tex.
Height, 6.01. Weight, 210.
Throws and bats righthanded.
Attended University of Texas, Austin, Tex.
Pitched 4-0 no-hit victory against Philadelphia Phillies, April 16, 1972.

| Year Club | League | G. | IP. | W. | L. | Pct. | H. | R. | ER. | SO. | BB. | ERA. |
|---|---|---|---|---|---|---|---|---|---|---|---|---|
| 1971—Tacoma...............................P. Coast | | 12 | 102 | 7 | 4 | .636 | 73 | 26 | 19 | 135 | 19 | 1.68 |
| 1971—Chicago...............................National | | 3 | 21 | 2 | 0 | 1.000 | 8 | 5 | 5 | 22 | 10 | 2.14 |
| 1972—Chicago...............................National | | 33 | 218 | 11 | 14 | .440 | 201 | 78 | 68 | 132 | 81 | 2.81 |
| 1973—Chicago...............................National | | 42 | 240 | 14 | 17 | .452 | 248 | 107 | 98 | 134 | 73 | 3.68 |
| 1974—Chicago...............................National | | 48 | 176 | 7 | 11 | .389 | 214 | 112 | 94 | 94 | 51 | 4.81 |
| 1975—Chicago†-Los Ang.................National | | 34 | 235 | 18 | 9 | .667 | 190 | 88 | 80 | 153 | 68 | 3.06 |
| 1976—Los Angeles ......................National | | 33 | 227 | 11 | 15 | .423 | 203 | 93 | 82 | 116 | 60 | 3.25 |
| Major League Totals .............................. | | 193 | 1117 | 63 | 66 | .488 | 1064 | 483 | 427 | 651 | 343 | 3.44 |

†Traded to Los Angeles Dodgers for Pitchers Geoffrey Zahn and Eddie Solomon, May 2, 1975.


## DONALD HOPKINS
### (Don)

Born January 9, 1952, at West Point, Miss.
Height, 6.01. Weight, 175.
Throws and bats lefthanded.
Attended Lake Michigan Community College, Benton Harbor, Mich.
Major League stolen bases: 1975 (21), 1976 (1). Total—22.
Led Northern League in stolen bases with 39 in 1971 and New York-Pennsylvania League with 63 in 1972.
Tied for Northern League lead in double plays by outfielders with 2 in 1971.

| Year Club | League | Pos. | G. | AB. | R. | H. | 2B. | 3B. | HR. | RBI. | B.A. | PO. | A. | E. | F.A. |
|---|---|---|---|---|---|---|---|---|---|---|---|---|---|---|---|
| 1970—Brad'ton Expos..Gulf C. | | OF | 22 | 41 | 5 | 11 | 1 | 0 | 0 | 4 | .268 | 5 | 1 | 0 | 1.000 |
| 1971—Watertown .......North. | | OF | 55 | 191 | 35 | 39 | 4 | 0 | 0 | 7 | .204 | 63 | 7 | •13 | .843 |
| 1972—W. P. Beach† ....Fla. St. | | OF | 6 | 14 | 5 | 4 | 0 | 0 | 0 | 0 | .286 | 7 | 0 | 1 | .875 |
| 1972—Jamestown .......NYP | | OF | •70 | •291 | 56 | 75 | 6 | 4 | 0 | 15 | .258 | 117 | 2 | •8 | .937 |
| 1973—Quebec City ......East. | | OF | 53 | 155 | 28 | 32 | 2 | 1 | 0 | 7 | .206 | 75 | 0 | 3 | .962 |
| 1973—W. Palm Beach Fla. St. | | OF | 32 | 102 | 24 | 23 | 2 | 1 | 0 | 3 | .225 | 44 | 0 | 0 | 1.000 |
| 1974—Quebec City ......East. | | OF | 12 | 23 | 4 | 6 | 0 | 0 | 0 | 1 | .261 | 10 | 1 | 0 | 1.000 |
| 1974—Kinston ...........Carol. | | OF | 82 | 319 | 52 | 96 | 11 | 2 | 0 | 15 | .301 | 147 | 8 | 8 | .951 |
| 1974—Memphis‡.........Int. | | OF | 8 | 22 | 5 | 2 | 0 | 0 | 0 | 0 | .091 | 8 | 0 | 0 | 1.000 |
| 1975—Tucson .............P. C. | | OF | 24 | 81 | 15 | 21 | 1 | 1 | 1 | 4 | .259 | 37 | 3 | 2 | .952 |
| 1975—Oakland ...........Amer. | | OF | 82 | 6 | 25 | 1 | 0 | 0 | 0 | 0 | .167 | 3 | 0 | 0 | 1.000 |
| 1976—Tucson .............P. C. | | OF-PH | 98 | 330 | 50 | 87 | 9 | 3 | 0 | 18 | .264 | 179 | 7 | 6 | .969 |
| 1976—Oakland ...........Amer. | | PR | 3 | 0 | 0 | 0 | 0 | 0 | 0 | 0 | .000 | 0 | 0 | 0 | .000 |
| Major League Totals .................... | | | 85 | 6 | 25 | 1 | 0 | 0 | 0 | 0 | .167 | 3 | 0 | 0 | 1.000 |

†On disabled list, May 8 to June 22, 1972.
‡Sold by Montreal Expos to Oakland Athletics, March 28, 1975.

## CHAMPIONSHIP SERIES RECORD

| Year | Club | League | Pos. | G. | AB. | R. | H. | 2B. | 3B. | HR. | RBI. | B.A. | PO. | A. | E. | F.A. |
|------|------|--------|------|----|----|----|----|-----|-----|-----|------|------|-----|----|----|------|
| 1975–Oakland | ...........Amer. | | PR-DH | 1 | 0 | 0 | 0 | 0 | 0 | 0 | 0 | .000 | 0 | 0 | 0 | .000 |

## WILLIE WATTISON HORTON

Born October 18, 1942, at Arno, Va.
Height, 5.10½. Weight, 209.
Throws and bats righthanded.
Hobby—Collecting recordings.

Tied major league record for most putouts by leftfielder, nine-inning game, 11, July 18, 1969.
Hit three home runs in a game, June 9, 1970.
Led Northern League in total bases with 203 in 1962.
Named designated hitter on THE SPORTING NEWS American League All-Star Team, 1975.
Named outfielder on THE SPORTING NEWS American League All-Star Team, 1968.
Received reported $50,000 bonus to sign with Detroit Tigers, 1961.

| Year | Club | League | Pos. | G. | AB. | R. | H. | 2B. | 3B. | HR. | RBI. | B.A. | PO. | A. | E. | F.A. |
|------|------|--------|------|----|----|----|----|-----|-----|-----|------|------|-----|----|----|------|
| 1962–Duluth-Superior | North. | | OF | 123 | 441 | 68 | 130 | 20 | 4 | 15 | 72 | .295 | 184 | 3 | 10 | .949 |
| 1963–Syracuse | ..........Int. | | OF | 21 | 78 | 12 | 17 | 2 | 1 | 2 | 8 | .218 | 40 | 2 | 1 | .977 |
| 1963–Knoxville | ..........Sally | | OF | 118 | 442 | 77 | 147 | 20 | 9 | 14 | 70 | .333 | 183 | 7 | 7 | .964 |
| 1963–Detroit | ..............Amer. | | OF | 15 | 43 | 6 | 14 | 2 | 1 | 1 | 4 | .326 | 13 | 0 | 0 | 1.000 |
| 1964–Syracuse | ..........Int. | | OF-3B | 135 | 490 | 73 | 141 | 16 | 9 | 28 | 99 | .288 | 265 | 6 | 10 | .964 |
| 1964–Detroit | ..............Amer. | | OF | 25 | 80 | 6 | 13 | 1 | 3 | 1 | 10 | .163 | 33 | 0 | 2 | .943 |
| 1965–Detroit | ..............Amer. | | OF-3B | 143 | 512 | 69 | 140 | 20 | 2 | 29 | 104 | .273 | 249 | 9 | 3 | .989 |
| 1966–Detroit | ..............Amer. | | OF | 146 | 526 | 72 | 138 | 22 | 6 | 27 | 100 | .262 | 233 | 4 | 5 | .979 |
| 1967–Detroit | ..............Amer. | | OF | 122 | 401 | 47 | 110 | 20 | 3 | 19 | 67 | .274 | 165 | 5 | 5 | .971 |
| 1968–Detroit | ..............Amer. | | OF | 143 | 512 | 68 | 146 | 20 | 2 | 36 | 85 | .285 | 212 | 6 | 6 | .973 |
| 1969–Detroit | ..............Amer. | | OF | 141 | 508 | 66 | 133 | 17 | 1 | 28 | 91 | .262 | 272 | 8 | 8 | .972 |
| 1970–Detroit† | ...........Amer. | | OF | 96 | 371 | 53 | 113 | 18 | 2 | 17 | 69 | .305 | 154 | 10 | 3 | .982 |
| 1971–Detroit | ..............Amer. | | OF | 119 | 450 | 64 | 130 | 25 | 1 | 22 | 72 | .289 | 176 | 8 | 7 | .963 |
| 1972–Detroit‡ | ...........Amer. | | OF | 108 | 333 | 44 | 77 | 9 | 5 | 11 | 36 | .231 | 131 | 6 | 0 | 1.000 |
| 1973–Detroit§ | | | OF | 111 | 411 | 42 | 130 | 19 | 3 | 17 | 53 | .316 | 160 | 2 | •10 | .942 |
| 1974–Detroit x | .........Amer. | | OF | 72 | 238 | 32 | 71 | 8 | 1 | 15 | 47 | .298 | 106 | 2 | 6 | .947 |
| 1975–Detroit | ..............Amer. | | DH | 159 | 615 | 62 | 169 | 13 | 1 | 25 | 92 | .275 | 0 | 0 | 0 | .000 |
| 1976–Detroit y | .........Amer. | | DH | 114 | 401 | 40 | 105 | 17 | 0 | 14 | 56 | .262 | 0 | 0 | 0 | .000 |
| Major League Totals | ...................... | | | 1514 | 5401 | 671 | 1489 | 211 | 31 | 262 | 886 | .976 | 1904 | 60 | 55 | .973 |

†On disabled list, July 25 through November 8.
‡On supplemental disabled list, May 22 through June 6.
§On supplemental disabled list, May 11 to May 29, 1973.
xOn disabled list, July 12 through remainder of season.
yOn disabled list, June 6 through July 15, 1976.

## CHAMPIONSHIP SERIES RECORD

| Year | Club | League | Pos. | G. | AB. | R. | H. | 2B. | 3B. | HR. | RBI. | B.A. | PO. | A. | E. | F.A. |
|------|------|--------|------|----|----|----|----|-----|-----|-----|------|------|-----|----|----|------|
| 1972–Detroit | ..............Amer. | | O-PH | 5 | 10 | 0 | 1 | 0 | 0 | 0 | 0 | .100 | 6 | 0 | 0 | 1.000 |

## WORLD SERIES RECORD

| Year | Club | League | Pos. | G. | AB. | R. | H. | 2B. | 3B. | HR. | RBI. | B.A. | PO. | A. | E. | F.A. |
|------|------|--------|------|----|----|----|----|-----|-----|-----|------|------|-----|----|----|------|
| 1968–Detroit | ..............Amer. | | OF | 7 | 23 | 6 | 7 | 1 | 1 | 1 | 3 | .304 | 5 | 1 | 1 | .857 |

## ALL-STAR GAME RECORD

| Year | League | Pos. | AB. | R. | H. | 2B. | 3B. | HR. | RBI. | B.A. | PO. | A. | E. | F.A. |
|------|--------|------|----|----|----|-----|-----|-----|------|------|-----|----|----|------|
| 1965–American | ........................... | OF | 3 | 0 | 0 | 0 | 0 | 0 | 0 | .000 | 2 | 0 | 0 | 1.000 |
| 1968–American | ........................... | OF | 2 | 0 | 0 | 0 | 0 | 0 | 0 | .000 | 1 | 0 | 0 | 1.000 |
| 1970–American | ........................... | OF | 2 | 1 | 2 | 0 | 0 | 0 | 0 | 1.000 | 1 | 0 | 0 | 1.000 |
| 1973–American | ........................... | PH | 1 | 0 | 0 | 0 | 0 | 0 | 0 | .000 | 0 | 0 | 0 | .... |
| All-Star Game Totals | ...................... | | 8 | 1 | 2 | 0 | 0 | 0 | 0 | .250 | 4 | 0 | 0 | 1.000 |

## TIMOTHY KENNETH HOSLEY
### (Tim)

Born May 10, 1947, at Spartanburg, S. C.
Height, 5.11. Weight, 190.
Throws and bats righthanded.
Hobbies—Basketball, music and football.

Led International League batters in strikeouts with 123 in 1972.
Led New York-Pennsylvania League in passed balls with 16 in 1967 and tied for Southern League lead with 14 in 1970.
Led New York-Pennsylvania League catchers in double plays with 5 in 1967 and led Carolina League with 11 in 1969.

| Year | Club | League | Pos. | G. | AB. | R. | H. | 2B. | 3B. | HR. | RBI. | B.A. | PO. | A. | E. | F.A. |
|------|------|--------|------|----|----|----|----|-----|-----|-----|------|------|-----|----|----|------|
| 1967–Statesville | ........W. Car. | | C | 8 | 17 | 0 | 4 | 0 | 0 | 0 | 3 | .235 | 25 | 1 | 3 | .897 |
| 1967–Erie† | ................NYP | | •C-3B | 59 | 165 | 26 | 42 | 12 | 2 | 4 | 30 | .255 | 281 | •42 | •17 | .950 |
| 1968–Lakeland | ..........Fla. St. | | C | 98 | 276 | 30 | 66 | 9 | 1 | 7 | 39 | .239 | 540 | 54 | 22 | .964 |

| Year Club League | Pos. | G. | AB. | R. | H. | 2B. | 3B. | HR. | RBI. | B.A. | PO. | A. | E. | F.A. |
|---|---|---|---|---|---|---|---|---|---|---|---|---|---|---|
| 1969—Rocky Mount ....Carol. | C-1B | 130 | 392 | 77 | 105 | 12 | 1 | 27 | 79 | .268 | 820 | 76 | 24 | .974 |
| 1970—Montgomery ......South. | C-O-1 | 110 | 326 | 41 | 70 | 15 | 1 | 20 | 50 | .215 | 650 | 56 | 15 | .979 |
| 1970—Detroit .............Amer. | C | 7 | 12 | 1 | 2 | 0 | 0 | 1 | 2 | .167 | 22 | 3 | 0 | 1.000 |
| 1971—Toledo .............Int. | C-O-1 | 97 | 309 | 47 | 74 | 16 | 3 | 23 | 59 | .239 | 582 | 49 | 11 | .983 |
| 1971—Detroit .............Amer. | C-1B | 7 | 16 | 2 | 3 | 0 | 0 | 2 | 6 | .188 | 26 | 0 | 0 | 1.000 |
| 1972—Toledo‡ ...........Int. | ●C-1B | 132 | 444 | 64 | 108 | 10 | 1 | 24 | 67 | .243 | 960 | 85 | ●17 | .984 |
| 1973—Tucson .............P. C. | C-1B | 60 | 180 | 36 | 54 | 11 | 0 | 12 | 47 | .300 | 271 | 28 | 8 | .974 |
| 1973—Oakland ...........Amer. | C | 13 | 14 | 3 | 3 | 0 | 0 | 0 | 2 | .214 | 19 | 1 | 1 | .952 |
| 1974—Oakland ...........Amer. | C-1B | 11 | 7 | 3 | 2 | 0 | 0 | 0 | 1 | .286 | 13 | 1 | 0 | 1.000 |
| 1974—Tucson§ ...........P. C. | C | 92 | 291 | 53 | 83 | 14 | 2 | 17 | 50 | .285 | 409 | 54 | 11 | .977 |
| 1975—Chicago x .........Nat. | C | 62 | 141 | 22 | 36 | 7 | 0 | 6 | 20 | .255 | 254 | 16 | 9 | .968 |
| 1976—Tucson .............P. C. | C | 62 | 210 | 46 | 67 | 9 | 1 | 15 | 54 | .319 | 208 | 36 | 11 | .957 |
| 1976—Oakland ...........Amer. | C | 37 | 55 | 4 | 9 | 2 | 0 | 1 | 4 | .164 | 79 | 13 | 3 | .968 |
| American League Totals ................ | | 75 | 104 | 13 | 19 | 2 | 0 | 4 | 15 | .183 | 159 | 18 | 4 | .978 |
| National League Totals .................. | | 62 | 141 | 22 | 36 | 7 | 0 | 6 | 20 | .255 | 254 | 16 | 9 | .968 |
| Major League Totals ....................... | | 137 | 245 | 35 | 55 | 9 | 0 | 10 | 35 | .224 | 413 | 34 | 13 | .972 |

†On disabled list, May 17 through June 8, 1967.
‡Purchased from Detroit Tigers by Oakland Athletics, April 2, 1973.
§Drafted from Oakland Athletics' organization by Chicago Cubs, December 2, 1974.
xReleased on waviers to Oakland Athletics, April 20, 1976.

## CHARLES OLIVER HOUGH

Name pronounced Huff.

### (Charlie)

Born January 5, 1948, at Honolulu, Hawaii.
Height, 6.02. Weight, 185.
Throws and bats righthanded.
Hobby—Fishing.

Led Pacific Coast League in saves with 18 in 1970.

| Year Club | League | G. | IP. | W. | L. | Pct. | H. | R. | ER. | SO. | BB. | ERA. |
|---|---|---|---|---|---|---|---|---|---|---|---|---|
| 1966—Ogden ................................ | Pioneer | 21 | 68 | 5 | ●7 | .417 | 82 | 56 | 36 | 68 | 29 | 4.76 |
| 1967—Santa Barbara.................... | California | 20 | 165 | 14 | 4 | ★.778 | 129 | 50 | 41 | 138 | 43 | 2.24 |
| 1967—Albuquerque ....................... | Texas | 7 | 36 | 2 | 1 | .667 | 57 | 31 | 28 | 25 | 10 | 7.00 |
| 1968—Albuquerque ....................... | Texas | 27 | 121 | 6 | 10 | .375 | 145 | 72 | 53 | 74 | 26 | 3.94 |
| 1969—Albuquerque ....................... | Texas | 27 | 163 | 10 | 9 | .526 | 190 | 87 | 74 | 113 | 42 | 4.09 |
| 1970—Spokane .............................. | P. Coast | 49 | 134 | 12 | 8 | .600 | 98 | 43 | 29 | 90 | 44 | 1.95 |
| 1970—Los Angeles ....................... | National | 8 | 17 | 0 | 0 | .000 | 18 | 11 | 10 | 8 | 11 | 5.29 |
| 1971—Spokane‡............................. | P. Coast | 47 | 117 | 10 | 8 | .556 | 95 | 56 | 51 | 104 | 52 | 3.92 |
| 1971—Los Angeles ....................... | National | 4 | 4 | 0 | 0 | .000 | 3 | 3 | 2 | 4 | 3 | 4.50 |
| 1972—Albuquerque§ ..................... | P. Coast | 58 | 125 | 14 | 5 | .737 | 109 | 47 | 33 | 95 | 60 | 2.38 |
| 1972—Los Angeles ....................... | National | 2 | 3 | 0 | 0 | .000 | 2 | 1 | 1 | 4 | 2 | 3.00 |
| 1973—Los Angeles ....................... | National | 37 | 72 | 4 | 2 | .667 | 52 | 24 | 22 | 70 | 45 | 2.75 |
| 1974—Los Angeles ....................... | National | 49 | 96 | 9 | 4 | .692 | 65 | 45 | 40 | 63 | 40 | 3.75 |
| 1975—Los Angeles ....................... | National | 38 | 61 | 3 | 7 | .300 | 43 | 25 | 20 | 34 | 34 | 2.95 |
| 1976—Los Angeles ....................... | National | 77 | 143 | 12 | 8 | .600 | 102 | 43 | 35 | 81 | 77 | 2.20 |
| Major League Totals ............................... | | 215 | 396 | 28 | 21 | .571 | 285 | 152 | 130 | 264 | 212 | 2.95 |

†On temporary inactive list, June 19 to July 1, 1968.
‡On temporary inactive list, July 10 to July 24, 1971.
§Placed on temporary inactive list three times: June 12 through June 15, July 22 through July 24 and August 7 through August 12, 1972.

### CHAMPIONSHIP SERIES RECORD

| Year Club | League | G. | IP. | W. | L. | Pct. | H. | R. | ER. | SO. | BB. | ERA. |
|---|---|---|---|---|---|---|---|---|---|---|---|---|
| 1974—Los Angeles ...................... | National | 1 | 2⅓ | 0 | 0 | .000 | 4 | 2 | 2 | 2 | 0 | 7.71 |

### WORLD SERIES RECORD

| Year Club | League | G. | IP. | W. | L. | Pct. | H. | R. | ER. | SO. | BB. | ERA. |
|---|---|---|---|---|---|---|---|---|---|---|---|---|
| 1974—Los Angeles ...................... | National | 1 | 2 | 0 | 0 | .000 | 0 | 0 | 0 | 0 | 4 | 0.00 |

### RECORD AS FIELDER

| Year Club League | Pos. | G. | AB. | R. | H. | 2B. | 3B. | HR. | RBI. | B.A. | PO. | A. | E. | F.A. |
|---|---|---|---|---|---|---|---|---|---|---|---|---|---|---|
| 1967—Santa Barbara ..Calif. | P-1B | 28 | 72 | 8 | 14 | 2 | 0 | 0 | 4 | .194 | 15 | 25 | 2 | .953 |
| 1968—Albuquerque .....Tex. | P-1-3 | 56 | 83 | 10 | 21 | 4 | 0 | 0 | 6 | .253 | 43 | 25 | 4 | .944 |
| 1969—Albuquerque .....Tex. | P-3B | 31 | 57 | 10 | 12 | 0 | 0 | 1 | 9 | .211 | 10 | 19 | 2 | .935 |
| 1970—Spokane ...........P. C. | P-O-1 | 49 | 33 | 1 | 6 | 0 | 0 | 1 | 3 | .182 | 7 | 28 | 3 | .921 |
| 1971—Spokane ...........P. C. | P-OF | 48 | 36 | 2 | 10 | 0 | 0 | 0 | 3 | .278 | 6 | 20 | 1 | .963 |
| 1972—Albuquerque......P. C. | P-OF | 58 | 34 | 4 | 9 | 1 | 0 | 0 | 5 | .265 | 3 | 27 | 0 | 1.000 |

---

**DID YOU KNOW —**

That Pete Rose of the Cincinnati Reds had 680 at-bats during the 1973 season without hitting one sacrifice fly?

---

## THOMAS ROSS HOUSE
### (Tom)

Born April 29, 1947, at Seattle, Wash.
Height, 5.11. Weight, 185.
Throws and bats lefthanded.
Hobby—Water sports.
Attended University of Southern California, Los Angeles, Calif.; received Bachelor of Science
degree in Marketing and Master's degree in Business Administration.

| Year Club | League | G. | IP. | W. | L. | Pct. | H. | R. | ER. | SO. | BB. | ERA. |
|---|---|---|---|---|---|---|---|---|---|---|---|---|
| 1967—Austin | Texas | 2 | 9 | 0 | 0 | .000 | 5 | 2 | 2 | 9 | 3 | 2.00 |
| 1967—Kinston | Carolina | 5 | 26 | 2 | 2 | .500 | 25 | 11 | 10 | 24 | 15 | 3.46 |
| 1967—Richmond | Int'national | 4 | 5 | 1 | 1 | .500 | 5 | 3 | 3 | 7 | 4 | 5.40 |
| 1968—Shreveport | Texas | 3 | 18 | 2 | 1 | .667 | 14 | 6 | 2 | 18 | 11 | 1.00 |
| 1968—Richmond | Int'national | 21 | 124 | 5 | 7 | .417 | 109 | 55 | 48 | 77 | 38 | 3.48 |
| 1969—Richmond† | Int'national | 21 | 100 | 4 | 7 | .364 | 101 | 49 | 45 | 56 | 54 | 4.05 |
| 1970—Richmond‡ | Int'national | 44 | 83 | 6 | 5 | .545 | 89 | 40 | 38 | 45 | 29 | 4.12 |
| 1971—Richmond | Int'national | 45 | 58 | 7 | 3 | .700 | 64 | 19 | 15 | 49 | 15 | 2.23 |
| 1971—Atlanta | National | 11 | 21 | 1 | 0 | 1.000 | 20 | 8 | 7 | 11 | 3 | 3.00 |
| 1972—Richmond | Int'national | 48 | 62 | 5 | 8 | .385 | 40 | 14 | 10 | 55 | 20 | 1.45 |
| 1972—Atlanta | National | 8 | 9 | 0 | 0 | .000 | 7 | 3 | 3 | 7 | 6 | 3.00 |
| 1973—Atlanta | National | 52 | 67 | 4 | 2 | .667 | 58 | 37 | 35 | 42 | 31 | 4.70 |
| 1974—Atlanta | National | 56 | 103 | 6 | 2 | .750 | 74 | 26 | 22 | 64 | 27 | 1.92 |
| 1975—Atlanta§ | National | 58 | 79 | 7 | 7 | .500 | 79 | 39 | 28 | 36 | 36 | 3.19 |
| 1976—Boston x | American | 36 | 44 | 1 | 3 | .250 | 39 | 22 | 21 | 27 | 19 | 4.30 |
| National League Totals | | 185 | 279 | 18 | 11 | .621 | 238 | 113 | 95 | 160 | 103 | 3.06 |
| American League Totals | | 36 | 44 | 1 | 3 | .250 | 39 | 22 | 21 | 27 | 19 | 4.30 |
| Major League Totals | | 221 | 323 | 19 | 14 | .576 | 277 | 135 | 116 | 187 | 122 | 3.23 |

†On disabled list, June 8 to June 23, 1969.
‡Appeared as an outfielder in one game.
§Traded to Boston Red Sox for Pitcher Roger Moret, December 12, 1975.
xOn disabled list, August 8 through August 29, 1976.

## DOUGLAS LYNN HOWARD
### (Doug)

Born February 6, 1948, at Salt Lake City, Utah.
Height, 6.03. Weight, 185.
Throws and bats righthanded.
Hobby—All sports.
Attended Brigham Young University, Provo, Utah; received Bachelor of Science
degree in Physical Education.
His father, Bob Howard, played for Hollywood in the Pacific Coast League in the 1920s.
Led Texas League first basemen in double plays with 112 in 1971.
Tied for Pacific Coast League lead in sacrifice flies with 12 in 1972.
Named Pacific Coast League Rookie of the Year, 1972.

| Year Club | League | Pos. | G. | AB. | R. | H. | 2B. | 3B. | HR. | RBI. | B.A. | PO. | A. | E. | F.A. |
|---|---|---|---|---|---|---|---|---|---|---|---|---|---|---|---|
| 1970—El Paso | Texas | 1B-O | 16 | 55 | 6 | 11 | 1 | 0 | 1 | 4 | .200 | 136 | 5 | 0 | 1.000 |
| 1970—Quad Cities | Midw. | 1B | 52 | 187 | 33 | 55 | 9 | 1 | 2 | 17 | .294 | 426 | 19 | 8 | .982 |
| 1971—Shreveport | Texas | 1B | 133 | 487 | 53 | 132 | 21 | 2 | 17 | 76 | .271 | 1074 | 71 | 8 | *.993 |
| 1972—Salt Lake City | P.C. | O-3-1-S | 138 | 509 | 86 | 153 | 27 | 5 | 24 | *109 | .301 | 222 | 112 | 9 | .974 |
| 1972—California | Amer. | O-1-3 | 11 | 38 | 4 | 10 | 1 | 0 | 0 | 2 | .263 | 18 | 3 | 1 | .955 |
| 1973—Salt Lake City | P.C. | O-1-3 | 118 | 434 | 67 | 129 | 18 | 7 | 18 | 69 | .297 | 320 | 27 | 5 | .986 |
| 1973—California | Amer. | O-1-3 | 8 | 21 | 2 | 2 | 0 | 0 | 0 | 1 | .095 | 9 | 1 | 0 | 1.000 |
| 1974—S.L.C.† | Tacoma P.C. | 1B-O | 84 | 292 | 36 | 79 | 5 | 2 | 5 | 38 | .271 | 416 | 35 | 5 | .989 |
| 1974—California‡ | Amer. | OF-1B | 22 | 39 | 5 | 9 | 0 | 1 | 0 | 5 | .231 | 29 | 3 | 0 | 1.000 |
| 1975—Tulsa | A.A. | 1-3-O | 90 | 336 | 56 | 110 | 25 | 0 | 14 | 71 | .327 | 597 | 92 | 2 | .997 |
| 1975—St. Louis§ | Nat. | 1B | 17 | 29 | 1 | 6 | 0 | 0 | 1 | 1 | .207 | 60 | 6 | 0 | 1.000 |
| 1976—Toledo | Int. | O-1-3 | 70 | 273 | 33 | 84 | 14 | 0 | 8 | 45 | .308 | 181 | 13 | 1 | .995 |
| 1976—Cleveland x | Amer. | 1-DH-O | 39 | 90 | 7 | 19 | 4 | 0 | 0 | 13 | .211 | 211 | 20 | 2 | .991 |
| American League Totals | | | 80 | 188 | 18 | 40 | 5 | 1 | 0 | 21 | .213 | 267 | 27 | 3 | .990 |
| National League Totals | | | 17 | 29 | 1 | 6 | 0 | 0 | 1 | 1 | .207 | 60 | 6 | 0 | 1.000 |
| Major League Totals | | | 97 | 217 | 19 | 46 | 5 | 1 | 1 | 22 | .212 | 327 | 33 | 3 | .992 |

†Option transferred to Tacoma, June 20, 1974.
‡Sold to St. Louis Cardinals, October 7, 1974, to complete deal in which Angels obtained Infielder Bob Heise
from Cardinals for a player to be named later, July 31, 1974.
§Traded to Cleveland Indians, September 30, 1975, to complete deal in which Cardinals obtained Shortstop
Luis Alvarado from Indians for a player to be named later, May 27, 1975.
xTraded with Catcher Alan Ashby to Toronto Blue Jays for Pitcher Al Fitzmorris, November 5, 1976.

## WILBUR LEON HOWARD

Born January 8, 1949, at Lowell, N. C.
Height, 6.02. Weight, 175.
Throws right and bats right and lefthanded.
Hobbies—Fishing and hunting.
Led New York-Pennsylvania League in stolen bases with 20 in 1969 and led American Association with 42 in
1971.

| Year Club League | Pos. | G. | AB. | R. | H. | 2B. | 3B. | HR. | RBI. | B.A. | PO. | A. | E. | F.A. |
|---|---|---|---|---|---|---|---|---|---|---|---|---|---|---|
| 1969—Newark ............NYP | OF-P | 57 | 181 | 35 | 52 | 5 | 1 | 1 | 15 | .287 | 74 | 4 | 7 | .918 |
| 1970—Clinton .............Midw. | OF | 117 | 469 | 70 | *142 | 17 | 7 | 3 | 34 | .303 | 252 | 6 | 7 | .974 |
| 1970—Portland............P.C. | OF | 7 | 27 | 3 | 9 | 2 | 0 | 0 | 2 | .333 | 18 | 1 | 1 | .950 |
| 1971—Evansville ........A.A. | OF | 128 | *508 | 57 | 122 | 14 | 8 | 6 | 40 | .240 | 220 | 15 | *12 | .951 |
| 1972—Evansville ........A.A. | OF | 129 | *542 | 70 | *155 | 25 | 5 | 8 | 46 | .286 | 241 | 10 | 10 | .962 |
| 1973—Evansville ........A.A. | OF | 130 | 552 | 90 | 149 | 25 | 9 | 6 | 63 | .270 | 290 | 9 | 9 | .971 |
| 1973—Milwaukee† ......Amer. | OF | 16 | 39 | 3 | 8 | 0 | 0 | 0 | 1 | .205 | 29 | 2 | 1 | .969 |
| 1974—Denver..............A.A. | OF | 65 | 279 | 43 | 83 | 19 | 5 | 6 | 32 | .297 | 135 | 5 | 5 | .966 |
| 1974—Houston ............Nat. | OF | 64 | 111 | 19 | 24 | 4 | 0 | 2 | 5 | .216 | 65 | 3 | 0 | 1.000 |
| 1975—Houston ............Nat. | OF | 121 | 392 | 62 | 111 | 16 | 8 | 0 | 21 | .283 | 194 | 7 | 1 | .995 |
| 1976—Houston ............Nat. | O-2-PH | 94 | 191 | 26 | 42 | 7 | 2 | 1 | 18 | .220 | 98 | 8 | 5 | .955 |
| American League Totals ................ | | 16 | 39 | 3 | 8 | 0 | 0 | 0 | 1 | .205 | 29 | 2 | 1 | .969 |
| National League Totals ................ | | 279 | 694 | 107 | 177 | 27 | 10 | 3 | 44 | .255 | 357 | 18 | 6 | .984 |
| Major League Totals ..................... | | 295 | 733 | 110 | 185 | 27 | 10 | 3 | 45 | .252 | 386 | 20 | 7 | .983 |

†Traded to Houston Astros for Pitchers Larry Yount and Don Stratton, March 30, 1974.

### PITCHING RECORD

| Year Club League | G. | IP. | W. | L. | Pct. | H. | R. | ER. | SO. | BB. | ERA. |
|---|---|---|---|---|---|---|---|---|---|---|---|
| 1968—Newark...............NYP | 18 | 86 | 8 | 5 | .615 | 80 | 41 | 37 | 74 | 37 | 3.87 |
| 1969—Clinton ...............Midwest | 4 | 8 | 0 | 0 | .000 | 13 | 13 | 4 | 4 | 6 | 4.50 |
| 1969—Newark...............NYP | 1 | 2 | 0 | 0 | .000 | 4 | 2 | 2 | 0 | 1 | 9.00 |

## ARTHUR HENRY HOWE, JR.
### (Art)

Born December 15, 1946, at Pittsburgh, Pa.
Height, 6.01. Weight, 190.
Throws and bats righthanded.
Hobbies—Golf, handball and tennis.
Attended University of Wyoming, Laramie, Wyo.; received Bachelor
of Science degree in Business Administration.
Led International League third basemen in double plays with 24 in 1972.

| Year Club League | Pos. | G. | AB. | R. | H. | 2B. | 3B. | HR. | RBI. | B.A. | PO. | A. | E. | F.A. |
|---|---|---|---|---|---|---|---|---|---|---|---|---|---|---|
| 1971—Salem................Carol. | ●3B-SS | 114 | 382 | 77 | 133 | 27 | 7 | 12 | 79 | *.348 | ●110 | 221 | 21 | .940 |
| 1972—Charleston† ......Int. | *3-2-S | 109 | 365 | 68 | 99 | 21 | 3 | 14 | 53 | .271 | 105 | 248 | *24 | .936 |
| 1973—Charleston‡ ......Int. | 3-2-S | 119 | 372 | 50 | 85 | 20 | 1 | 8 | 44 | .228 | 141 | 229 | 21 | .946 |
| 1974—Charleston ........Int. | 3B | 60 | 207 | 26 | 70 | 17 | 4 | 8 | 36 | .338 | 35 | 90 | 9 | .933 |
| 1974—Pittsburgh .........Nat. | 3B-SS | 29 | 74 | 10 | 18 | 4 | 1 | 1 | 5 | .243 | 11 | 49 | 4 | .938 |
| 1975—Charleston ........Int. | 3B-2B | 11 | 42 | 4 | 15 | 1 | 3 | 0 | 3 | .357 | 15 | 23 | 1 | .974 |
| 1975—Pittsburgh§........Nat. | 3B-SS | 63 | 146 | 13 | 25 | 9 | 0 | 1 | 10 | .171 | 19 | 89 | 7 | .939 |
| 1976—Memphis ..........Int. | 3B-1B | 74 | 259 | 50 | 92 | 21 | 3 | 12 | 59 | .355 | 93 | 120 | 14 | .934 |
| 1976—Houston ............Nat. | 3B-2B | 21 | 29 | 0 | 4 | 1 | 0 | 0 | 0 | .138 | 17 | 16 | 1 | .970 |
| Major League Totals ..................... | | 113 | 249 | 23 | 47 | 14 | 1 | 2 | 15 | .189 | 47 | 154 | 12 | .944 |

†On disabled list, August 17 to September 2, 1972.
‡On disabled list from beginning of season until May 6, 1973.
§Traded to Houston Astros, January 6, 1976, to complete deal in which Pirates obtained Second Baseman Tommy Helms from Astros for a player to be named later, December 12, 1975.

### CHAMPIONSHIP SERIES RECORD

| Year Club League | Pos. | G. | AB. | R. | H. | 2B. | 3B. | HR. | RBI. | B.A. | PO. | A. | E. | F.A. |
|---|---|---|---|---|---|---|---|---|---|---|---|---|---|---|
| 1974—Pittsburgh ........Nat. | PH | 1 | 1 | 0 | 0 | 0 | 0 | 0 | 0 | .000 | 0 | 0 | 0 | .000 |

## ROY LEE HOWELL

Born December 18, 1953, at Lompoc, Calif.
Height, 6.01. Weight, 190.
Throws right and bats lefthanded.

| Year Club League | Pos. | G. | AB. | R. | H. | 2B. | 3B. | HR. | RBI. | B.A. | PO. | A. | E. | F.A. |
|---|---|---|---|---|---|---|---|---|---|---|---|---|---|---|
| 1972—Pittsfield ..........East. | 3B | 48 | 116 | 12 | 29 | 3 | 0 | 2 | 9 | .250 | 21 | 64 | 9 | .904 |
| 1973—Pittsfield ..........East. | 3-S-O | 96 | 277 | 44 | 67 | 12 | 2 | 15 | 47 | .242 | 51 | 156 | 23 | .900 |
| 1974—Spokane ...........P. C. | 3B | 136 | 513 | 101 | 144 | 23 | 5 | 22 | 80 | .281 | 98 | 247 | 25 | .932 |
| 1974—Texas...............Amer. | 3B | 13 | 44 | 2 | 11 | 1 | 0 | 1 | 3 | .250 | 5 | 24 | 3 | .906 |
| 1975—Texas...............Amer. | 3B | 125 | 383 | 43 | 96 | 15 | 2 | 10 | 51 | .251 | 80 | 214 | 21 | .933 |
| 1976—Texas...............Amer. | 3B-DH | 140 | 491 | 55 | 124 | 28 | 2 | 8 | 53 | .253 | 103 | 245 | *28 | .926 |
| Major League Totals ..................... | | 278 | 918 | 100 | 231 | 44 | 4 | 19 | 107 | .252 | 188 | 483 | 52 | .928 |

†On disabled list, July 29 to August 14, 1973.

## DID YOU KNOW —

That Chuck Klein, playing for the Philadelphia Phillies in 1930, appeared in 156 games and had one or more hits in 135 games? It's a major league record for most games, one or more hits, for a single season.

# DEWEY LAMARR HOYT

Born January 1, 1955, at Columbia, S. C.
Height, 6.03. Weight, 195.
Throws and bats righthanded.

| Year Club | League | G. | IP. | W. | L. | Pct. | H. | R. | ER. | SO. | BB. | ERA. |
|---|---|---|---|---|---|---|---|---|---|---|---|---|
| 1973–Johnson City | Ap'lachian | 12 | 76 | 6 | 6 | .500 | 73 | 44 | 33 | 58 | 40 | 3.91 |
| 1974–Ft. Lauderdale | Florida St. | 23 | 161 | 13 | 4 | .765 | 143 | 66 | 43 | 77 | 60 | 2.40 |
| 1975–Ft. Lauderdale† | Florida St. | 7 | 26 | 2 | 1 | .667 | 24 | 14 | 13 | 12 | 8 | 4.50 |
| 1975–West Haven | Eastern | 8 | 44 | 2 | 4 | .333 | 45 | 25 | 15 | 22 | 13 | 3.07 |
| 1976–West Haven‡ | Eastern | 25 | 180 | 15 | 8 | .652 | 169 | 66 | 50 | 103 | 46 | 2.50 |

†On disabled list, April 16 through June 6, 1975.

‡Traded by New York Yankees with Outfielder Oscar Gamble, Pitcher Bob Polinsky and cash estimated at $250,000 to Chicago White Sox for Shortstop Bucky Dent, April 5, 1977.

# ALAN THOMAS HRABOSKY

Name pronounced Ra-BAH-ski.

## (The Mad Hungarian)

Born July 21, 1949, at Oakland, Calif.
Height, 5.11. Weight, 185.
Throws left and bats righthanded.
Hobbies–Surfing, camping and fishing.
Attended Fullerton Junior College, Fullerton, Calif.

Tied for National League lead in saves with 22 in 1975.
Tied for Texas League lead in hit batsmen with 10 in 1972.
Named National League Fireman of the Year by THE SPORTING NEWS, 1975.

| Year Club | League | G. | IP. | W. | L. | Pct. | H. | R. | ER. | SO. | BB. | ERA. |
|---|---|---|---|---|---|---|---|---|---|---|---|---|
| 1969–Modesto | California | 15 | 98 | 8 | 2 | .800 | 86 | 34 | 27 | 112 | 43 | 2.48 |
| 1969–Arkansas | Texas | 2 | 10 | 1 | 0 | 1.000 | 11 | 8 | 7 | 8 | 4 | 6.30 |
| 1970–Arkansas | Texas | 15 | 91 | 8 | 1 | .889 | 80 | 36 | 33 | 68 | 33 | 3.26 |
| 1970–St. Louis | National | 16 | 19 | 2 | 1 | .667 | 22 | 10 | 10 | 12 | 7 | 4.74 |
| 1971–Tulsa† | Am. Assoc. | 9 | 14 | 1 | 1 | .500 | 23 | 21 | 20 | 7 | 10 | 12.86 |
| 1971–Arkansas | Texas | 8 | 27 | 1 | 0 | 1.000 | 31 | 9 | 9 | 31 | 10 | 3.00 |
| 1971–St. Louis | National | 1 | 2 | 0 | 0 | .000 | 2 | 0 | 0 | 2 | 0 | 0.00 |
| 1972–Arkansas | Texas | 24 | 145 | 7 | 12 | .368 | 134 | 71 | 55 | 142 | 64 | 3.41 |
| 1972–St. Louis | National | 5 | 7 | 1 | 0 | 1.000 | 2 | 0 | 0 | 9 | 3 | 0.00 |
| 1973–Tulsa | Am. Assoc. | 9 | 57 | 3 | 6 | .333 | 60 | 40 | 28 | 56 | 24 | 4.42 |
| 1973–St. Louis | National | 44 | 56 | 2 | 4 | .333 | 45 | 15 | 13 | 57 | 21 | 2.09 |
| 1974–St. Louis | National | 65 | 88 | 8 | 1 | .889 | 71 | 34 | 29 | 82 | 38 | 2.97 |
| 1975–St. Louis | National | 65 | 97 | 13 | 3 | .813 | 72 | 27 | 18 | 82 | 33 | 1.67 |
| 1976–St. Louis | National | 68 | 95 | 8 | 6 | .571 | 89 | 42 | 35 | 73 | 39 | 3.32 |
| Major League Totals | | 264 | 364 | 34 | 15 | .694 | 303 | 128 | 105 | 317 | 141 | 2.60 |

†On military list, January 11 through May 4, 1971.

# CHARLES HUDSON

## (Charlie)

Born August 18, 1949, at Ada, Okla.
Height, 6.03. Weight, 190.
Throws and bats lefthanded.
Hobbies–Hunting and fishing.
Attended East Central State College, Ada, Calif.

Led Carolina League in shutouts with 6 in 1968.
Tied for Pacific Coast League lead in shutouts with 3 in 1975.

| Year Club | League | G. | IP. | W. | L. | Pct. | H. | R. | ER. | SO. | BB. | ERA. |
|---|---|---|---|---|---|---|---|---|---|---|---|---|
| 1967–Marion | Ap'lachian | 6 | 36 | 2 | 0 | 1.000 | 36 | 9 | 7 | 33 | 6 | 1.75 |
| 1967–Winter Haven | Florida St. | 4 | 26 | 2 | 2 | .500 | 19 | 6 | 5 | 26 | 5 | 1.73 |
| 1968–Raleigh-Durham | Carolina | 27 | 174 | ●16 | 7 | .696 | 137 | 56 | 43 | 154 | 42 | 2.22 |
| 1969–Memphis | Texas | 15 | 67 | 2 | 4 | .333 | 57 | 38 | 32 | 46 | 22 | 4.30 |
| 1970–Memphis | Texas | 32 | 79 | 3 | 5 | .375 | 68 | 33 | 26 | 79 | 39 | 2.96 |
| 1971–Tidewater | Int'national | 8 | 11 | 0 | 2 | .000 | 19 | 13 | 13 | 11 | 5 | 10.64 |
| 1971–Memphis† | Texas | 30 | 70 | 1 | 2 | .333 | 63 | 30 | 26 | 78 | 28 | 3.34 |
| 1972–Tulsa | Am. Assoc. | 35 | 59 | 7 | 2 | .778 | 55 | 22 | 18 | 53 | 25 | 2.75 |
| 1972–St. Louis‡ | National | 12 | 12 | 1 | 0 | 1.000 | 10 | 8 | 7 | 4 | 7 | 5.25 |
| 1973–Texas§x | American | 25 | 62 | 4 | 2 | .667 | 59 | 35 | 32 | 34 | 31 | 4.65 |
| 1974–Oklahoma City y | Am. Assoc. | 32 | 87 | 3 | 5 | .375 | 125 | 70 | 66 | 37 | 39 | 6.83 |
| 1975–Salt Lake City | P. Coast | 24 | 160 | 13 | 7 | .650 | 152 | 89 | 76 | 60 | 92 | 4.28 |
| 1975–California | American | 3 | 6 | 0 | 1 | .000 | 7 | 6 | 6 | 0 | 4 | 9.00 |
| 1976–Salt Lake C.z-Tucson | P. Coast | 33 | 137 | 6 | 5 | .545 | 154 | 88 | 75 | 55 | 61 | 4.93 |
| National League Totals | | 12 | 12 | 1 | 0 | 1.000 | 10 | 8 | 7 | 4 | 7 | 5.25 |
| American League Totals | | 28 | 68 | 4 | 3 | .571 | 66 | 41 | 38 | 34 | 35 | 5.03 |
| Major League Totals | | 40 | 80 | 5 | 3 | .625 | 76 | 49 | 45 | 38 | 42 | 5.06 |

†Traded by New York Mets with Pitchers Jim Bibby and Rich Folkers and Outfielder Art Shamsky to St. Louis Cardinals for Pitchers Harry Parker and Chuck Taylor, First Baseman-Outfielder Jim Beauchamp and Infielder Tom Coulter, October 18, 1971.

‡Traded to Texas Rangers for a player to be named later, February 6, 1973; deal was completed when

Rangers traded Pitcher Mike Thompson to Cardinals for Pitcher Mike Nagy, March 31, 1973.
§On disabled list, June 10 to July 27, 1973.
xTraded to Cleveland Indians for Outfielder Ted Ford, April 24, 1974.
yTraded by Cleveland Indians to California Angels for Pitcher Bill Gilbreth, December 4, 1974.
zTraded by California Angels' organization to Oakland A's organization for Pitcher Skip Pitlock, May 19, 1976.

## JAMES MICHAEL HUGHES
### (Jim)

Born July 2, 1951, at Los Angeles, Calif.
Height, 6.03. Weight, 190.
Throws and bats righthanded.
Hobby—Fishing.
Attended West Los Angeles Junior College, Los Angeles, Calif.

Pitched seven-inning, 3-0 perfect game against Rocky Mount (first game of doubleheader), July 30, 1972.
Led Carolina League in shutouts with 5 and tied for lead in games started with 28 in 1972.
Led Northern League in hit batsmen with 6 in 1970.

| Year    Club | League | G. | IP. | W. | L. | Pct. | H. | R. | ER. | SO. | BB. | ERA. |
|---|---|---|---|---|---|---|---|---|---|---|---|---|
| 1969—Sarasota Twins | Gulf Coast | 13 | 63 | 3 | 5 | .375 | 64 | •34 | 26 | 67 | 33 | 3.71 |
| 1970—Orlando | Florida St. | 12 | 53 | 1 | 4 | .200 | 50 | 35 | 24 | 49 | 30 | 4.08 |
| 1970—St. Cloud | Northern | 14 | 71 | 2 | 4 | .333 | 65 | 47 | 33 | 75 | •66 | 4.18 |
| 1971—Wisconsin Rapids | Midwest | 38 | 125 | 6 | 8 | .429 | 111 | 59 | 42 | 119 | 65 | 3.02 |
| 1972—Lynchburg | Carolina | 32 | •192 | 13 | 9 | .591 | 163 | 72 | 55 | 141 | 62 | 2.58 |
| 1973—Tacoma | P. Coast | 32 | 172 | 9 | 11 | .450 | 187 | 102 | 76 | 87 | 72 | 3.98 |
| 1974—Tacoma | P. Coast | 30 | 179 | 10 | 12 | .455 | 189 | 108 | 96 | 116 | 67 | 4.83 |
| 1974—Minnesota | American | 2 | 10 | 0 | 2 | .000 | 8 | 8 | 6 | 8 | 4 | 5.40 |
| 1975—Minnesota | American | 37 | 250 | 16 | 14 | .533 | 241 | 119 | 106 | 130 | 127 | 3.82 |
| 1976—Minnesota | American | 37 | 177 | 9 | 14 | .391 | 190 | 113 | 98 | 87 | 73 | 4.98 |
| Major League Totals | | 76 | 437 | 25 | 30 | .454 | 439 | 240 | 210 | 225 | 204 | 4.32 |

## THOMAS HUBERT HUME, JR.
### (Tom)

Born March 29, 1953, at Cincinnati, O.
Height, 6.01. Weight, 185.
Throws and bats righthanded.
Hobbies—Hunting and fishing.
Attended Manatee Junior College, West Bradenton, Fla.

Tied for Eastern League lead in games started with 27 in 1973.

| Year    Club | League | G. | IP. | W. | L. | Pct. | H. | R. | ER. | SO. | BB. | ERA. |
|---|---|---|---|---|---|---|---|---|---|---|---|---|
| 1972—Tampa† | Florida St. | 23 | 141 | 7 | 11 | .389 | 135 | 69 | 54 | 112 | 68 | 3.45 |
| 1973—Three Rivers | Eastern | 27 | 170 | 7 | 8 | .467 | 186 | 97 | 81 | 103 | 99 | 4.29 |
| 1974—Three Rivers | Eastern | 26 | 157 | 7 | 12 | .368 | •167 | 91 | 77 | 109 | 90 | 4.41 |
| 1975—Three Rivers | Eastern | 7 | 45 | 3 | 2 | .600 | 43 | 20 | 15 | 19 | 15 | 3.00 |
| 1975—Indianapolis | Am. Assoc. | 17 | 100 | 6 | 6 | .500 | 106 | 49 | 45 | 56 | 36 | 4.05 |
| 1976—Indianapolis | Am. Assoc. | 27 | 182 | 9 | 12 | .429 | 178 | 91 | 83 | 111 | 62 | 4.10 |

†Played in one game as a third baseman and in one game as a second baseman.
Listed on Cincinnati Reds' 1977 spring roster.

## TERRYAL GENE HUMPHREY
### (Terry)

Born August 4, 1949, at Chickasha, Okla.
Height, 6.03. Weight, 190.
Throws and bats righthanded.
Hobbies—Golf and fishing.
Attended Los Angeles Junior College, Los Angeles, Calif.

Led Gulf Coast League catchers in double plays with 4 in 1969; led International League in passed balls with 14 in 1971.
Named Gulf Coast League Player of the Year in 1969.

| Year    Club | League | Pos. | G. | AB. | R. | H. | 2B. | 3B. | HR. | RBI. | B.A. | PO. | A. | E. | F.A. |
|---|---|---|---|---|---|---|---|---|---|---|---|---|---|---|---|
| 1969—Braden. Expos | Gulf C. | •C-1B | 45 | 136 | 25 | 40 | 10 | 1 | 1 | 25 | .294 | •280 | •33 | 7 | .978 |
| 1970—Jacksonville | South. | C-1B | 101 | 345 | 36 | 98 | 21 | 2 | 8 | 44 | .284 | 582 | 47 | 10 | .984 |
| 1971—Winnipeg | Int. | •C-1B | 112 | 393 | 41 | 110 | 17 | 3 | 6 | 56 | .280 | 632 | •62 | 6 | .991 |
| 1971—Montreal | Nat. | C | 9 | 26 | 1 | 5 | 1 | 0 | 0 | 1 | .192 | 50 | 3 | 1 | .981 |
| 1972—Montreal | Nat. | C | 69 | 215 | 13 | 40 | 8 | 0 | 1 | 9 | .186 | 322 | 37 | 5 | .986 |
| 1973—Peninsula | Int. | C | 27 | 93 | 9 | 22 | 2 | 1 | 1 | 7 | .237 | 162 | 10 | 1 | .994 |
| 1973—Montreal | Nat. | C | 43 | 90 | 5 | 15 | 2 | 0 | 1 | 9 | .167 | 159 | 9 | 0 | 1.000 |
| 1974—Quebec City | East. | C | 10 | 31 | 3 | 11 | 1 | 0 | 1 | 9 | .355 | 49 | 6 | 1 | .982 |
| 1974—Memphis | Int. | C-3B | 31 | 94 | 4 | 11 | 0 | 0 | 0 | 6 | .117 | 128 | 12 | 3 | .979 |
| 1974—Montreal† | Nat. | C | 20 | 52 | 3 | 10 | 3 | 0 | 0 | 3 | .192 | 85 | 15 | 1 | .990 |
| 1975—Detroit‡§ | Amer. | C | 18 | 41 | 0 | 10 | 0 | 0 | 0 | 1 | .244 | 61 | 9 | 0 | 1.000 |
| 1976—Memphis x | Int. | C | 40 | 135 | 13 | 29 | 3 | 0 | 4 | 21 | .215 | 251 | 17 | 7 | .975 |
| 1976—California | Amer. | C | 71 | 196 | 17 | 48 | 10 | 0 | 1 | 19 | .245 | 397 | 42 | 9 | .980 |
| American League Totals | | | 89 | 237 | 17 | 58 | 10 | 0 | 1 | 20 | .245 | 458 | 51 | 9 | .983 |
| National League Totals | | | 141 | 383 | 22 | 70 | 14 | 0 | 2 | 22 | .183 | 616 | 64 | 7 | .990 |
| Major League Totals | | | 230 | 620 | 39 | 128 | 24 | 0 | 3 | 42 | .206 | 1074 | 115 | 16 | .987 |

†Traded with Pitcher Tom Walker to Detroit Tigers for Pitcher Woodie Fryman, December 4, 1974.

‡On disabled list, June 11 to August 29, 1975.
§Traded with Outfielder Leon Roberts and Pitchers Gene Pentz and Mark Lemongello to Houston Astros for Catcher Milt May and Pitchers Dave Roberts and Jim Crawford, December 6, 1975.
xTraded with Pitcher Mike Barlow to California Angels' organization for Catcher Ed Herrmann, June 6, 1976.

## JAMES AUGUSTUS HUNTER
### (Catfish)
(Nicknamed by Charlie Finley)

Born April 8, 1946, at Hertford, N. C.
Height, 6.00. Weight, 195.
Throws and bats righthanded.
Hobbies—Hunting, fishing and building things.

Pitched 4-0 perfect game victory against Minnesota Twins, May 8, 1968.
Led American League pitchers in complete games with 30 in 1975.
Tied for American League lead in games started by pitchers with 40 in 1970.
Named American League Pitcher of the Year by THE SPORTING NEWS, 1974.
Won American League Cy Young Memorial Award, 1974.
Named righthanded pitcher on THE SPORTING NEWS American League All-Star Team, 1974.
Received reported $75,000 bonus to sign with Kansas City Athletics, 1964.

| Year    Club | League | G. | IP. | W. | L. | Pct. | H. | R. | ER. | SO. | BB. | ERA. |
|---|---|---|---|---|---|---|---|---|---|---|---|---|
| 1964—Daytona Beach | Florida St. | | | | | | (On Disabled List) | | | | | |
| 1965—Kansas City | American | 32 | 133 | 8 | 8 | .500 | 124 | 68 | 63 | 82 | 46 | 4.26 |
| 1966—Kansas City† | American | 30 | 177 | 9 | 11 | .450 | 158 | 87 | 79 | 103 | 64 | 4.02 |
| 1967—Kansas City‡ | American | 35 | 260 | 13 | 17 | .433 | 209 | 91 | 81 | 196 | 84 | 2.80 |
| 1968—Oakland | American | 36 | 234 | 13 | 13 | .500 | 210 | 99 | *87 | 172 | 69 | 3.35 |
| 1969—Oakland | American | 38 | 247 | 12 | 15 | .444 | 210 | 99 | 92 | 150 | 85 | 3.35 |
| 1970—Oakland | American | 40 | 262 | 18 | 14 | .563 | 253 | 124 | 111 | 178 | 74 | 3.81 |
| 1971—Oakland | American | 37 | 274 | 21 | 11 | .656 | 225 | 103 | 90 | 181 | 80 | 2.96 |
| 1972—Oakland | American | 38 | 295 | 21 | 7 | *.750 | 200 | 74 | 67 | 191 | 70 | 2.04 |
| 1973—Oakland§ | American | 36 | 256 | 21 | 5 | *.808 | 222 | 105 | 95 | 124 | 69 | 3.34 |
| 1974—Oakland§ | American | 41 | 318 | ●25 | 12 | .676 | 268 | 97 | 88 | 143 | 45 | *2.49 |
| 1975—New York | American | 39 | *328 | ●23 | 14 | .622 | 248 | 107 | 94 | 177 | 83 | 2.58 |
| 1976—New York | American | 36 | 299 | 17 | 15 | .531 | 268 | 126 | 117 | 173 | 68 | 3.52 |
| Major League Totals | | 438 | 3083 | 201 | 142 | .586 | 2595 | 1180 | 1064 | 1870 | 838 | 3.11 |

†On disabled list from July 26 through August 30 after undergoing appendicitis operation.
‡Appeared as first baseman in one game.
§Declared a free agent by an arbitration panel, December 16, 1974; signed by New York Yankees for an estimated $2.85 million, December 31, 1974.

### CHAMPIONSHIP SERIES RECORD

| Year    Club | League | G. | IP. | W. | L. | Pct. | H. | R. | ER. | SO. | BB. | ERA. |
|---|---|---|---|---|---|---|---|---|---|---|---|---|
| 1971—Oakland | American | 1 | 8 | 0 | 1 | .000 | 7 | 5 | 5 | 6 | 2 | 5.63 |
| 1972—Oakland | American | 2 | 15⅓ | 0 | 0 | .000 | 10 | 2 | 2 | 9 | 5 | 1.17 |
| 1973—Oakland | American | 2 | 16⅓ | 2 | 0 | 1.000 | 12 | 3 | 3 | 6 | 5 | 1.65 |
| 1974—Oakland | American | 2 | 11⅔ | 1 | 1 | .500 | 11 | 6 | 6 | 6 | 2 | 4.63 |
| 1976—New York | American | 2 | 12 | 1 | 1 | .500 | 10 | 6 | 6 | 5 | 1 | 4.50 |
| Championship Series Totals | | 9 | 63⅓ | 4 | 3 | .571 | 50 | 22 | 22 | 32 | 15 | 3.13 |

### WORLD SERIES RECORD

| Year    Club | League | G. | IP. | W. | L. | Pct. | H. | R. | ER. | SO. | BB. | ERA. |
|---|---|---|---|---|---|---|---|---|---|---|---|---|
| 1972—Oakland | American | 3 | 16 | 2 | 0 | 1.000 | 12 | 5 | 5 | 11 | 6 | 2.81 |
| 1973—Oakland | American | 2 | 13⅓ | 1 | 0 | 1.000 | 11 | 3 | 3 | 6 | 4 | 2.03 |
| 1974—Oakland | American | 2 | 7⅔ | 1 | 0 | 1.000 | 5 | 1 | 1 | 5 | 2 | 1.17 |
| 1976—New York | American | 1 | 8⅔ | 0 | 1 | .000 | 10 | 4 | 3 | 5 | 4 | 3.12 |
| World Series Totals | | 8 | 45⅔ | 4 | 1 | .800 | 38 | 13 | 12 | 27 | 16 | 2.36 |

### ALL-STAR GAME RECORD

| Year    League | | IP. | W. | L. | Pct. | H. | R. | ER. | SO. | BB. | ERA. |
|---|---|---|---|---|---|---|---|---|---|---|---|
| 1967—American | | 5 | 0 | 1 | .000 | 4 | 1 | 1 | 4 | 0 | 1.80 |
| 1970—American | | ⅓ | 0 | 0 | .000 | 3 | 3 | 3 | 0 | 0 | 81.00 |
| 1973—American | | 1⅓ | 0 | 0 | .000 | 1 | 0 | 0 | 1 | 0 | 0.00 |
| 1974—American | | 2 | 0 | 0 | .000 | 2 | 1 | 1 | 3 | 1 | 4.50 |
| 1975—American | | 2 | 0 | 1 | .000 | 3 | 2 | 2 | 2 | 0 | 9.00 |
| 1976—American | | 2 | 0 | 0 | .000 | 2 | 2 | 2 | 3 | 0 | 9.00 |
| All-Star Game Totals | | 12⅔ | 0 | 2 | .000 | 15 | 9 | 9 | 13 | 1 | 6.39 |

Member of American League All-Star Team for 1966 and 1972 games; did not play.

## THOMAS GEORGE HUTTON
### (Tommy)

Born April 20, 1946, at Los Angeles, Calif.
Height, 5.11. Weight, 180.
Throws and bats lefthanded.
Hobbies—Basketball and golf.
Attended Pasadena City College, Pasadena, Calif.
Brother-in-law of Dick Ruthven, pitcher with Atlanta Braves.

Led California League first basemen in double plays with 102 in 1965.

— 180 —

Led Texas League in sacrifice flies with 9 in 1966.
Named Most Valuable Player in Pacific Coast League, 1971.
Named Player of the Year in Texas League, 1966.

| Year Club League | Pos. | G. | AB. | R. | H. | 2B. | 3B. | HR. | RBI. | B.A. | PO. | A. | E. | F.A. |
|---|---|---|---|---|---|---|---|---|---|---|---|---|---|---|
| 1965–Santa Barbara ..Calif. | 1B | 132 | 494 | 86 | 145 | 24 | 5 | 20 | 63 | .294 | *991 | *98 | 14 | *.987 |
| 1966–Albuquerque......Texas | 1B | 103 | 385 | 58 | 131 | 24 | 4 | 9 | ●81 | *.340 | 890 | *81 | 7 | *.993 |
| 1966–Spokane ...........P.C. | 1B | 38 | 144 | 18 | 40 | 5 | 2 | 3 | 19 | .278 | 326 | 33 | 2 | .994 |
| 1966–Los Angeles ......Nat. | 1B | 3 | 2 | 0 | 0 | 0 | 0 | 0 | 0 | .000 | 2 | 0 | 0 | 1.000 |
| 1967–Spokane ...........P.C. | *1B-OF | 135 | 442 | 41 | 111 | 18 | 4 | 5 | 45 | .251 | 999 | 82 | 1 | *.999 |
| 1968–Spokane ...........P.C. | 1B | 132 | 439 | 57 | 121 | 26 | 4 | 6 | 64 | .276 | 1081 | 75 | 4 | *.997 |
| 1969–Spokane ...........P.C. | 1-OF-3 | 91 | 225 | 33 | 66 | 10 | 2 | 3 | 28 | .293 | 625 | 53 | 3 | .996 |
| 1969–Los Angeles ......Nat. | 1B | 16 | 48 | 2 | 13 | 0 | 0 | 0 | 4 | .271 | 130 | 19 | 1 | .993 |
| 1970–Spokane† .........P.C. | 1B | 90 | 310 | 51 | 100 | 21 | 5 | 7 | 56 | .323 | 768 | 57 | 8 | .990 |
| 1971–Spokane‡ .........P.C. | 1B | ●145 | 540 | *117 | *190 | *46 | 5 | 19 | 103 | *.352 | *1280 | *114 | 3 | *.998 |
| 1972–Philadelphia ......Nat. | 1B-OF | 134 | 381 | 40 | 99 | 16 | 2 | 4 | 38 | .260 | 648 | 38 | 6 | .991 |
| 1973–Philadelphia ......Nat. | 1B | 106 | 247 | 31 | 65 | 11 | 0 | 5 | 29 | .263 | 527 | 43 | 1 | .998 |
| 1974–Philadelphia ......Nat. | 1B-OF | 96 | 208 | 32 | 50 | 6 | 3 | 4 | 33 | .240 | 285 | 15 | 2 | .993 |
| 1975–Philadelphia ......Nat. | 1B-OF | 113 | 165 | 24 | 41 | 6 | 0 | 3 | 24 | .248 | 316 | 33 | 3 | .991 |
| 1976–Philadelphia ......Nat. | 1B-OF | 95 | 124 | 15 | 25 | 5 | 1 | 1 | 13 | .202 | 294 | 28 | 0 | 1.000 |
| Major League Totals ...... | | 563 | 1175 | 144 | 293 | 44 | 6 | 17 | 141 | .249 | 2202 | 176 | 13 | .994 |

†On disabled list, June 12 through August 1, 1970.
‡Traded by Los Angeles Dodgers to Philadelphia Phillies for Outfielder Larry Hisle and cash, October 22, 1971.

## CHAMPIONSHIP SERIES RECORD

| Year Club League | Pos. | G. | AB. | R. | H. | 2B. | 3B. | HR. | RBI. | B.A. | PO. | A. | E. | F.A. |
|---|---|---|---|---|---|---|---|---|---|---|---|---|---|---|
| 1976–Philadelphia ......Nat. | PH | 1 | 1 | 0 | 0 | 0 | 0 | 0 | 0 | .000 | 0 | 0 | 0 | .000 |

## RECORD AS PITCHER

| Year Club | League | G. | IP. | W. | L. | Pct. | H. | R. | ER. | SO. | BB. | ERA. |
|---|---|---|---|---|---|---|---|---|---|---|---|---|
| 1968–Spokane ...........P. Coast | | 1 | 2 | 0 | 0 | .000 | 2 | 1 | 0 | 0 | 0 | 0.00 |

## DANE CHARLES IORG

Name pronounced Org.

Born May 11, 1950, at Eureka, Calif.
Height, 6.00. Weight, 180.
Throws right and bats lefthanded.
Attended Brigham Young University, Provo, Ut.
Brother of Garth Iorg, second baseman with Toronto Blue Jays' organization, and Lee Iorg, outfielder with New York Mets' organization.

| Year Club League | Pos. | G. | AB. | R. | H. | 2B. | 3B. | HR. | RBI. | B.A. | PO. | A. | E. | F.A. |
|---|---|---|---|---|---|---|---|---|---|---|---|---|---|---|
| 1971–Walla Walla ......Northw. | OF | 77 | 275 | 64 | 101 | ●15 | 6 | 7 | 65 | *.367 | 135 | 10 | 6 | .960 |
| 1972–Reading ...........East. | OF | 15 | 43 | 2 | 6 | 2 | 0 | 0 | 1 | .140 | 18 | 0 | 1 | .947 |
| 1972–Burlington ........Carol. | OF | 92 | 324 | 61 | 104 | 20 | 3 | 8 | 37 | .321 | 119 | 5 | 5 | .961 |
| 1973–Reading ...........East. | OF | 116 | 386 | 64 | 119 | 21 | 6 | 7 | 49 | .308 | 149 | 8 | 5 | .969 |
| 1974–Toledo .............Int. | *1B-OF | 133 | 444 | 53 | 110 | 19 | 3 | 10 | 59 | .248 | 947 | *91 | 9 | .991 |
| 1975–Toledo .............Int. | 1B | 13 | 36 | 7 | 7 | 2 | 0 | 0 | 2 | .194 | 76 | 2 | 0 | 1.000 |
| 1975–Reading ...........East. | 1B | 97 | 319 | 47 | 88 | 19 | 5 | 6 | 59 | .276 | 827 | 44 | 9 | .990 |
| 1976–Oklahoma City ..A. A. | 1B-OF | 120 | 396 | 65 | 129 | 25 | 11 | 11 | 68 | .326 | 731 | 66 | 10 | .988 |

Invited to Philadelphia Phillies' 1977 spring camp.

## GARTH RAY IORG

Name pronounced Org.

Born October 12, 1954, at Arcata, Calif.
Height, 5.11. Weight, 170.
Throws and bats righthanded.
Hobbies–Hunting and fishing.
Attended College of the Redwoods, Eureka, Calif.
Brother of Dane Iorg, first baseman with Philadelphia Phillies, and Lee Iorg, outfielder with New York Mets'organization.

| Year Club League | Pos. | G. | AB. | R. | H. | 2B. | 3B. | HR. | RBI. | B.A. | PO. | A. | E. | F.A. |
|---|---|---|---|---|---|---|---|---|---|---|---|---|---|---|
| 1973–Johnson City ....Appal. | SS-2B | 51 | 169 | 20 | 40 | 3 | 0 | 3 | 13 | .237 | 88 | 120 | 20 | .912 |
| 1974–Ft. Lauderdale ..Fla. St. | SS-2-3 | 102 | 325 | 30 | 70 | 11 | 4 | 0 | 38 | .215 | 134 | 245 | 28 | .931 |
| 1975–Ft. Lauderdale ..Fla. St. | 3-2-SS | 50 | 186 | 10 | 47 | 4 | 2 | 0 | 16 | .253 | 54 | 78 | 11 | .923 |
| 1975–West Haven ......East. | Inf. | 76 | 236 | 19 | 59 | 6 | 2 | 0 | 21 | .250 | 906 | 246 | 35 | .970 |
| 1976–West Haven† ......East. | 2B | 78 | 273 | 31 | 75 | 17 | 1 | 1 | 24 | .275 | 172 | 236 | 18 | .958 |

†Selected by Toronto Blue Jays from New York Yankees in American League expansion draft, November 5, 1976.

## MICHAEL WILSON IVIE
### (Mike)

Born August 8, 1952, at Atlanta, Ga.
Height, 6.04. Weight, 210.
Throws and bats righthanded.
Hobbies–Hunting and fishing.
Led Northwest League in passed balls with 18 in 1970.

Received reported $80,000 bonus to sign with San Diego Padres, 1970.

| Year | Club | League | Pos. | G. | AB. | R. | H. | 2B. | 3B. | HR. | RBI. | B.A. | PO. | A. | E. | F.A. |
|------|------|--------|------|----|-----|----|----|-----|-----|-----|------|------|-----|----|-----|------|
| 1970–Tri-City | ...........Northw. | | ★C-O | 56 | 198 | 29 | 51 | 10 | 0 | 3 | 25 | .258 | ★419 | 4 | ★15 | .968 |
| 1971–Lodi | ..................Calif. | | ★C-3-1 | 102 | 367 | 69 | 112 | 22 | 2 | 15 | 62 | .305 | 685 | ★83 | 22 | .972 |
| 1971–San Diego | .........Nat. | | C | 6 | 17 | 0 | 8 | 0 | 0 | 0 | 3 | .471 | 22 | 2 | 0 | 1.000 |
| 1972–Alexandria | .......Tex. | | ★1B-3B | 133 | 461 | 81 | 134 | 23 | 1 | 24 | 77 | .291 | 1013 | ★86 | ★18 | .984 |
| 1973–Hawaii† | ...........P. Coast | | 1B | 59 | 226 | 33 | 61 | 8 | 3 | 5 | 21 | .270 | 446 | 19 | 7 | .985 |
| 1974–Alexandria | .......Tex. | | 1-O-3 | 108 | 397 | 57 | 116 | 16 | 1 | 18 | 68 | .292 | 586 | 45 | 18 | .972 |
| 1974–San Diego | .........Nat. | | 1B | 12 | 34 | 1 | 3 | 0 | 0 | 1 | 3 | .088 | 67 | 5 | 1 | .986 |
| 1975–San Diego‡ | .......Nat. | | 1-3-C | 111 | 377 | 36 | 94 | 16 | 2 | 8 | 46 | .249 | 540 | 138 | 23 | .967 |
| 1976–San Diego | .........Nat. | | 1-C-3 | 140 | 405 | 51 | 118 | 19 | 5 | 7 | 70 | .291 | 1032 | 71 | 7 | .994 |
| Major League Totals | ...................... | | | 269 | 833 | 88 | 223 | 35 | 7 | 16 | 122 | .268 | 1661 | 216 | 31 | .984 |

†On suspended list, June 14 through remainder of season.
‡On supplemental disabled list. August 17 to September 1, 1975.

## GRANT DWIGHT JACKSON

Born September 28, 1942, at Fostoria, O.
Height, 6.00. Weight, 190.
Throws and bats lefthanded.
Hobbies–Listening to records and working on cars.
Attended Bowling Green State University, Bowling Green, O.
Tied for Northwest League lead in wild pitches with 21 in 1964.

| Year | Club | League | G. | IP. | W. | L. | Pct. | H. | R. | ER. | SO. | BB. | ERA. |
|------|------|--------|----|-----|----|----|------|----|----|-----|-----|-----|------|
| 1962–Bakersfield | .................California | | 29 | 98 | 4 | 5 | .444 | 92 | 75 | 63 | 86 | 71 | 5.79 |
| 1963–Bakersfield | .................California | | 28 | 176 | 12 | 8 | .600 | 164 | 100 | 76 | 159 | 87 | 3.89 |
| 1964–Chattanooga | ......................Southern | | 4 | 14 | 0 | 3 | .000 | 19 | 19 | 15 | 17 | 8 | 9.64 |
| 1964–Eugene | .....................Northwest | | 20 | 134 | 8 | 9 | .471 | 126 | 65 | 55 | 162 | 85 | 3.69 |
| 1965–Arkansas | ..............................P. Coast | | 32 | 155 | 9 | 11 | .450 | 151 | 80 | 68 | 158 | 60 | 3.95 |
| 1965–Philadelphia | .....................National | | 6 | 14 | 1 | 1 | .500 | 17 | 11 | 11 | 15 | 5 | 7.07 |
| 1966–Philadelphia | .....................National | | 2 | 2 | 0 | 0 | .000 | 2 | 1 | 1 | 0 | 3 | 4.50 |
| 1966–San Diego | .....................P. Coast | | 23 | 134 | 10 | 8 | .556 | 126 | 64 | 59 | 132 | 58 | 3.96 |
| 1967–Philadelphia | .....................National | | 43 | 84 | 2 | 3 | .400 | 86 | 40 | 36 | 83 | 43 | 3.86 |
| 1968–Philadelphia | .....................National | | 33 | 61 | 1 | 6 | .143 | 59 | 28 | 20 | 49 | 20 | 2.95 |
| 1969–Philadelphia | .....................National | | 38 | 253 | 14 | 18 | .438 | 237 | 114 | 94 | 180 | 92 | 3.34 |
| 1970–Philadelphia† | .....................National | | 32 | 150 | 5 | 15 | .250 | 170 | 94 | 88 | 104 | 61 | 5.28 |
| 1971–Baltimore | .........................American | | 29 | 78 | 4 | 3 | .571 | 72 | 31 | 27 | 51 | 20 | 3.12 |
| 1972–Baltimore | .........................American | | 32 | 41 | 1 | 1 | .500 | 33 | 14 | 12 | 34 | 9 | 2.63 |
| 1973–Baltimore | .........................American | | 45 | 80 | 8 | 0 | 1.000 | 54 | 18 | 17 | 47 | 24 | 1.91 |
| 1974–Baltimore | .........................American | | 49 | 67 | 6 | 4 | .600 | 48 | 19 | 19 | 56 | 22 | 2.55 |
| 1975–Baltimore | .........................American | | 41 | 48 | 4 | 3 | .571 | 42 | 18 | 18 | 39 | 21 | 3.38 |
| 1976–Baltimore‡ | .........................American | | 13 | 19 | 1 | 1 | .500 | 19 | 11 | 11 | 14 | 9 | 5.21 |
| 1976–New York§ | .........................American | | 21 | 59 | 6 | 0 | 1.000 | 38 | 11 | 11 | 25 | 16 | 1.68 |
| National League Totals | ...................... | | 154 | 564 | 23 | 43 | .348 | 571 | 288 | 250 | 431 | 224 | 3.99 |
| American League Totals | ...................... | | 230 | 392 | 30 | 12 | .714 | 306 | 122 | 115 | 266 | 121 | 2.64 |
| Major League Totals | ...................... | | 384 | 956 | 53 | 55 | .491 | 877 | 410 | 365 | 697 | 345 | 3.44 |

†Traded with Outfielder Jim Hutto and Outfielder Sam Parrilla (latter two assigned to Rochester) to Baltimore Orioles for Outfielder Roger Freed, December 16, 1970.
‡Traded with Pitchers Ken Holtzman and Doyle Alexander, Catcher Ellie Hendricks, and Pitcher Jimmy Freeman (latter assigned to Syracuse), to New New York Yankees for Pitchers Rudy May, Tippy Martinez, Dave Pagan and Scott McGregor and Catcher Rick Dempsey, June 15, 1976.
§Selected by Seattle Mariners in American League expansion draft, November 5, 1976; traded to Pittsburgh Pirates for Infielders Craig Reynolds and Jim Sexton, December 7, 1976.

### CHAMPIONSHIP SERIES RECORD

| Year | Club | League | G. | IP. | W. | L. | Pct. | H. | R. | ER. | SO. | BB. | ERA. |
|------|------|--------|----|-----|----|----|------|----|----|-----|-----|-----|------|
| 1973–Baltimore | .........................American | | 2 | 3 | 1 | 0 | 1.000 | 0 | 0 | 0 | 0 | 1 | 0.00 |
| 1974–Baltimore | .........................American | | 1 | ⅓ | 0 | 0 | .000 | 1 | 2 | 0 | 1 | 0 | 0.00 |
| 1976–New York | .........................American | | 2 | 3⅓ | 0 | 0 | .000 | 4 | 3 | 3 | 3 | 1 | 8.10 |
| Championship Series Totals | ...................... | | 5 | 6⅔ | 1 | 0 | 1.000 | 5 | 5 | 3 | 4 | 2 | 4.05 |

### WORLD SERIES RECORD

| Year | Club | League | G. | IP. | W. | L. | Pct. | H. | R. | ER. | SO. | BB. | ERA. |
|------|------|--------|----|-----|----|----|------|----|----|-----|-----|-----|------|
| 1971–Baltimore | .........................American | | 1 | ⅔ | 0 | 0 | .000 | 0 | 0 | 0 | 0 | 1 | 0.00 |
| 1976–New York | .........................American | | 1 | 3⅔ | 0 | 0 | .000 | 4 | 2 | 2 | 3 | 0 | 4.91 |
| World Series Totals | ............................... | | 2 | 4⅓ | 0 | 0 | .000 | 4 | 2 | 2 | 3 | 1 | 4.15 |

### ALL-STAR GAME RECORD
Member of 1969 National League All-Star Team; did not play.

## REGINALD MARTINEZ JACKSON
### (Reggie)

Born May 18, 1946, at Wyncote, Pa.
Height, 6.00. Weight, 200.
Throws and bats lefthanded.
Hobby–Cars.
Attended Arizona State University, Tempe, Ariz.

Tied major league records for most consecutive years leading league in strikeouts (4), 1968 through 1971, and most strikeouts, nine-inning game (5), September 27, 1968.

Established American League record for most consecutive seasons, 100 or more strikeouts (9), 1968 through 1976.

Tied American League records for most times, four or more strikeouts, game, season (5), April 7 (second game)—April 21—May 18—June 4—September 21 (first game), 1971; and most seasons, 100 or more strikeouts (9), 1976; most consecutive games, one or more home runs (6), July 18-23, 1976; most seasons leading league, errors, outfielder (5), 1968-70-72-75-76.

Hit three home runs in a game, July 2, 1969.

Led American League batters in strikeouts with 171 in 1968, 142 in 1969, 135 in 1970 and 161 in 1971.

Led American League in slugging percentage with .608 in 1969, .531 in 1973 and .502 in 1976.

Tied for American League lead in double plays by outfielders with 5 in 1972.

Led Southern League in total bases with 232 in 1967.

Named Major League Player of the Year by THE SPORTING NEWS, 1973.

Named American League Player of the Year by THE SPORTING NEWS, 1973.

Named American League Most Valuable Player, 1973.

Named outfielder on THE SPORTING NEWS American League All-Star Team, 1969, 1973, 1975 and 1976.

Named Southern League Player of the Year in 1967.

Received reported $90,000 bonus to sign with Kansas City Athletics, 1966.

| Year | Club | League | Pos. | G. | AB. | R. | H. | 2B. | 3B. | HR. | RBI. | B.A. | PO. | A. | E. | F.A. |
|---|---|---|---|---|---|---|---|---|---|---|---|---|---|---|---|---|
| 1966—Lewiston | | Northw. | OF | 12 | 48 | 14 | 14 | 3 | 2 | 2 | 11 | .292 | 23 | 0 | 1 | .958 |
| 1966—Modesto | | Calif. | OF | 56 | 221 | 50 | 66 | 6 | 0 | 21 | 60 | .299 | 108 | 3 | 9 | .925 |
| 1967—Birmingham | | South. | OF | 114 | 413 | *84 | 121 | 26 | *17 | 17 | 58 | .293 | 228 | 3 | *18 | .928 |
| 1967—Kansas City | | Amer. | OF | 35 | 118 | 13 | 21 | 4 | 4 | 1 | 6 | .178 | 55 | 1 | 4 | .933 |
| 1968—Oakland | | Amer. | OF | 154 | 553 | 82 | 138 | 13 | 6 | 29 | 74 | .250 | 269 | 14 | *12 | .959 |
| 1969—Oakland | | Amer. | OF | 152 | 549 | *123 | 151 | 36 | 3 | 47 | 118 | .275 | 278 | 14 | 11 | .964 |
| 1970—Oakland | | Amer. | OF | 149 | 426 | 57 | 101 | 21 | 2 | 23 | 66 | .237 | 251 | 8 | •12 | .956 |
| 1971—Oakland | | Amer. | OF | 150 | 567 | 87 | 157 | 29 | 3 | 32 | 80 | .277 | 285 | 15 | 7 | .977 |
| 1972—Oakland† | | Amer. | OF | 135 | 499 | 72 | 132 | 25 | 2 | 25 | 75 | .265 | 301 | 5 | *9 | .971 |
| 1973—Oakland | | Amer. | OF | 151 | 539 | *99 | 158 | 28 | 2 | *32 | *117 | .293 | 302 | 4 | 9 | .971 |
| 1974—Oakland‡ | | Amer. | OF | 148 | 506 | 90 | 146 | 25 | 1 | 29 | 93 | .289 | 296 | 8 | 10 | .968 |
| 1975—Oakland‡ | | Amer. | OF | 157 | 593 | 91 | 150 | 39 | 3 | •36 | 104 | .253 | 315 | 13 | *12 | .965 |
| 1976—Baltimore§ | | Amer. | OF-DH | 134 | 498 | 84 | 138 | 27 | 2 | 27 | 91 | .277 | 284 | 8 | •11 | .964 |
| Major League Totals | | | | 1365 | 4848 | 798 | 1292 | 247 | 28 | 281 | 824 | .267 | 2636 | 90 | 97 | .966 |

†On supplemental disabled list, August 10 through August 25, 1972.

‡Traded with Pitchers Ken Holtzman and Bill Van Bommel to Baltimore Orioles for Outfielder Don Baylor and Pitchers Mike Torrez and Paul Mitchell, April 2, 1976.

§On disqualified list, April 9 to May 2, 1976. Played out option year and granted free agency, November 1, 1976; signed as free agent with New York Yankees, November 29, 1976.

### CHAMPIONSHIP SERIES RECORD

| Year | Club | League | Pos. | G. | AB. | R. | H. | 2B. | 3B. | HR. | RBI. | B.A. | PO. | A. | E. | F.A. |
|---|---|---|---|---|---|---|---|---|---|---|---|---|---|---|---|---|
| 1971—Oakland | | Amer. | OF | 3 | 12 | 2 | 4 | 1 | 0 | 2 | 2 | .333 | 9 | 1 | 0 | 1.000 |
| 1972—Oakland | | Amer. | OF | 5 | 18 | 1 | 5 | 1 | 0 | 0 | 2 | .278 | 14 | 0 | 1 | .933 |
| 1973—Oakland | | Amer. | OF | 5 | 21 | 0 | 3 | 0 | 0 | 0 | 0 | .143 | 19 | 0 | 0 | 1.000 |
| 1974—Oakland | | Amer. | DH-OF | 4 | 12 | 0 | 2 | 1 | 0 | 0 | 1 | .167 | 0 | 0 | 0 | .000 |
| 1975—Oakland | | Amer. | OF | 3 | 12 | 1 | 5 | 0 | 0 | 1 | 3 | .417 | 5 | 1 | 0 | 1.000 |
| Championship Series Totals | | | | 20 | 75 | 4 | 19 | 3 | 0 | 3 | 8 | .253 | 47 | 2 | 1 | .980 |

### WORLD SERIES RECORD

| Year | Club | League | Pos. | G. | AB. | R. | H. | 2B. | 3B. | HR. | RBI. | B.A. | PO. | A. | E. | F.A. |
|---|---|---|---|---|---|---|---|---|---|---|---|---|---|---|---|---|
| 1973—Oakland | | Amer. | OF | 7 | 29 | 3 | 9 | 3 | 1 | 1 | 6 | .310 | 17 | 0 | 0 | 1.000 |
| 1974—Oakland | | Amer. | OF | 5 | 14 | 3 | 4 | 1 | 0 | 1 | 1 | .286 | 6 | 1 | 1 | .875 |
| World Series Totals | | | | 12 | 43 | 6 | 13 | 4 | 1 | 2 | 7 | .302 | 23 | 1 | 1 | .960 |

### ALL-STAR GAME RECORD

| Year | League | Pos. | AB. | R. | H. | 2B. | 3B. | HR. | RBI. | B.A. | PO. | A. | E. | F.A. |
|---|---|---|---|---|---|---|---|---|---|---|---|---|---|---|
| 1969—American | | OF | 2 | 0 | 0 | 0 | 0 | 0 | 0 | .000 | 2 | 0 | 0 | 1.000 |
| 1971—American | | PH | 1 | 1 | 1 | 0 | 0 | 1 | 2 | 1.000 | 0 | 0 | 0 | .000 |
| 1972—American | | OF | 4 | 0 | 2 | 1 | 0 | 0 | 0 | .500 | 5 | 0 | 0 | 1.000 |
| 1973—American | | OF | 4 | 1 | 1 | 0 | 0 | 0 | 0 | .250 | 0 | 0 | 0 | .000 |
| 1974—American | | OF | 3 | 0 | 0 | 0 | 0 | 0 | 0 | .000 | 3 | 0 | 0 | 1.000 |
| 1975—American | | OF | 3 | 0 | 1 | 0 | 0 | 0 | 0 | .333 | 2 | 0 | 1 | 1.000 |
| All-Star Game Totals | | | 17 | 2 | 5 | 2 | 0 | 1 | 2 | .294 | 12 | 0 | 1 | 1.000 |

## RONNIE D. JACKSON
### (Ron)

Born May 9, 1953, at Birmingham, Ala.

Height, 6.00. Weight, 200.

Throws and bats righthanded.

Attended Lawson State Junior College, Birmingham, Ala.

Brother of Lawrence Jackson, outfielder in Chicago White Sox' organization, 1968 and 1969.

Led Pacific Coast League third basemen in double plays with 31 in 1975.

Led Pioneer League third basemen in double plays with 8 in 1971.

Tied for Texas League lead in double plays by third basemen with 26 in 1973.

| Year | Club | League | Pos. | G. | AB. | R. | H. | 2B. | 3B. | HR. | RBI. | B.A. | PO. | A. | E. | F.A. |
|---|---|---|---|---|---|---|---|---|---|---|---|---|---|---|---|---|
| 1971—Idaho Falls | | Pion. | 3B | •70 | 260 | 36 | 54 | 8 | 0 | 1 | 22 | .208 | *60 | *111 | *32 | .842 |

| Year | Club | League | Pos. | G. | AB. | R. | H. | 2B. | 3B. | HR. | RBI. | B.A. | PO. | A. | E. | F.A. |
|---|---|---|---|---|---|---|---|---|---|---|---|---|---|---|---|---|
| 1972–Quad Cities | ......Midw. | | *3B-SS | *126 | *489 | 62 | 134 | *29 | 7 | 12 | 73 | .274 | *116 | 243 | 30 | .923 |
| 1973–El Paso | ...........Texas | | *3B-SS | 136 | 481 | 75 | 128 | 31 | 4 | 7 | 68 | .266 | *120 | 252 | *36 | .912 |
| 1974–El Paso | ...........Texas | | 3B | 133 | 519 | 84 | 170 | 36 | 8 | 11 | 74 | .328 | 82 | 257 | *33 | .911 |
| 1975–Salt Lake City | ..P.C. | | *3-OF-1 | ●144 | 513 | 82 | 144 | 24 | 5 | 9 | 85 | .281 | *189 | *269 | *26 | *.946 |
| 1975–California | .........Amer. | | OF-3B | 13 | 39 | 2 | 9 | 2 | 0 | 0 | 2 | .231 | 19 | 4 | 2 | .920 |
| 1976–Salt Lake City | ..P.C. | | 3B | 10 | 33 | 9 | 12 | 2 | 0 | 2 | 10 | .364 | 14 | 18 | 2 | .941 |
| 1976–California | .........Amer. | | 3-DH-2-O | 127 | 410 | 44 | 93 | 18 | 3 | 8 | 40 | .227 | 91 | 225 | 16 | .952 |
| Major League Totals | ..................... | | | 140 | 449 | 46 | 102 | 20 | 3 | 8 | 42 | .227 | 110 | 229 | 18 | .950 |

## PHILIP ROBERT JAMES
### (Skip)
(Nicknamed by father.)

Born October 21, 1949, at Elmhurst, Ill.
Height, 6.00. Weight, 185.
Throws and bats lefthanded.
Hobbies—Fishing, reading and golf.
Attended University of Kansas, Lawrence, Kan.
Led California League in total bases with 267 in 1972.
Named California League Player of the Year in 1972.

| Year | Club | League | Pos. | G. | AB. | R. | H. | 2B. | 3B. | HR. | RBI. | B.A. | PO. | A. | E. | F.A. |
|---|---|---|---|---|---|---|---|---|---|---|---|---|---|---|---|---|
| 1971–Decatur | ...........Midw. | | 1B | 77 | 293 | 48 | 72 | 8 | 4 | 9 | 40 | .246 | 650 | 35 | 6 | .991 |
| 1972–Fresno | .............Calif. | | 1B | 132 | 473 | *111 | 138 | 21 | 6 | *32 | *123 | .292 | 945 | 66 | 7 | *.993 |
| 1973–Phoenix | .............P.C. | | 1B | 129 | 379 | 50 | 99 | 19 | 13 | 4 | 56 | .261 | 909 | 63 | 9 | *.991 |
| 1974–Phoenix† | ..........P.C. | | 1B | 122 | 434 | 75 | 124 | 20 | *11 | 9 | 73 | .286 | 1066 | 75 | 5 | *.996 |
| 1975–Phoenix | .............P.C. | | OF-1B | 105 | 817 | 48 | 76 | 9 | 8 | 7 | 51 | .240 | 226 | 24 | 3 | .988 |
| 1976–Phoenix | .............P.C. | | *1B-OF | 130 | 456 | 78 | 136 | 30 | 11 | 6 | 71 | .298 | 1174 | 63 | 9 | *.993 |

†On disabled list, April 21 to May 1, 1974.
Listed on San Francisco Giants' 1977 spring roster.

## IGNACIO ALFREDO JAVIER
Name pronounced Ig-NAH-see-oh HAH-vee-air.

Born February 1, 1954, at San Pedro de Macoris, Dominican Republic.
Height, 5.11. Weight, 170.
Throws and bats righthanded.
Tied for Appalachian League lead in double plays by outfielders with 3 in 1971.

| Year | Club | League | Pos. | G. | AB. | R. | H. | 2B. | 3B. | HR. | RBI. | B.A. | PO. | A. | E. | F.A. |
|---|---|---|---|---|---|---|---|---|---|---|---|---|---|---|---|---|
| 1971–Sumter | ..............W. Car. | | OF | 7 | 20 | 2 | 2 | 0 | 0 | 0 | 1 | .100 | 5 | 0 | 2 | .714 |
| 1971–Covington | .........Appal. | | OF | 52 | 182 | 29 | 43 | 8 | 1 | 3 | 11 | .236 | 60 | 7 | 6 | .918 |
| 1972–Cocoa | ...............Fla. St. | | OF | 23 | 52 | 3 | 14 | 1 | 1 | 0 | 4 | .269 | 23 | 1 | 3 | .889 |
| 1972–Cocoa Astros | ....Fla. E.C. | | OF | 56 | 210 | 34 | 57 | 10 | 3 | 4 | 31 | .271 | 66 | ●8 | 4 | .949 |
| 1973–Cedar Rapids† | ..Midw. | | O-C | 104 | 395 | 65 | 104 | 16 | 3 | 6 | 47 | .263 | 156 | 7 | 11 | .937 |
| 1974–Columbus | .........South. | | OF | 136 | *568 | 71 | 143 | 23 | 5 | 9 | 52 | .252 | 273 | 9 | 14 | .953 |
| 1975–Iowa | ................A. A. | | OF | 13 | 45 | 5 | 12 | 4 | 0 | 1 | 10 | .267 | 20 | 0 | 2 | .909 |
| 1975–Columbus | .........South. | | OF | 117 | 448 | 51 | 135 | 14 | 6 | 9 | 72 | .301 | 202 | 7 | 11 | .950 |
| 1976–Memphis‡ | .........Int. | | OF | 107 | 417 | 54 | 120 | 34 | 3 | 12 | 63 | .288 | 164 | 6 | 5 | .971 |
| 1976–Houston | ...........Nat. | | OF | 8 | 24 | 1 | 5 | 0 | 0 | 0 | 0 | .208 | 7 | 0 | 0 | 1.000 |
| Major League Totals | ..................... | | | 8 | 24 | 1 | 5 | 0 | 0 | 0 | 0 | .208 | 7 | 0 | 0 | 1.000 |

†On disabled list, June 9 to June 19, 1973.
‡On disabled list, May 18 to June 11, 1976.

## JESSE HARRISON JEFFERSON, JR.
Born March 3, 1950, at Midlothian, Va.
Height, 6.03. Weight, 188.
Throws and bats righthanded.
Attended John Tyler Community College, Chester, Va.

| Year | Club | League | G. | IP. | W. | L. | Pct. | H. | R. | ER. | SO. | BB. | ERA. |
|---|---|---|---|---|---|---|---|---|---|---|---|---|---|
| 1968–Bluefield | ...........................Ap'alachian | 16 | 69 | 3 | 7 | .300 | 64 | 65 | 39 | 99 | *66 | 5.09 |
| 1969–Miami | ...............................Florida St. | 2 | 7 | 0 | 0 | .000 | 1 | 2 | 1 | 9 | 8 | 1.29 |
| 1969–Bluefield | ...........................Ap'alachian | 10 | 34 | 0 | *7 | .000 | 29 | 37 | 31 | 54 | 51 | 8.21 |
| 1970–Stockton | ...............................California | 26 | 157 | 8 | *16 | .333 | 129 | 89 | 64 | 177 | *123 | 3.67 |
| 1971–Dallas-Fort Worth | ...............Texas | 27 | 172 | 12 | 11 | .522 | 144 | 84 | 66 | 150 | *109 | 3.45 |
| 1972–Asheville | ..............................Southern | 11 | 71 | 5 | 4 | .556 | 70 | 37 | 26 | 55 | 33 | 3.30 |
| 1972–Rochester | ...........................Int'national | 17 | 103 | 6 | 3 | .667 | 79 | 35 | 28 | 66 | 68 | 2.45 |
| 1973–Rochester | ...........................Int'national | 10 | 66 | 6 | 2 | .750 | 52 | 29 | 25 | 39 | 53 | 3.41 |
| 1973–Baltimore | ...........................American | 18 | 101 | 6 | 5 | .545 | 104 | 53 | 46 | 52 | 46 | 4.10 |
| 1974–Baltimore | ...........................American | 20 | 57 | 1 | 0 | 1.000 | 55 | 30 | 23 | 31 | 38 | 4.42 |
| 1975–Baltimore†-Chicago | .............American | 26 | 115 | 5 | 11 | .313 | 105 | 72 | 63 | 71 | 102 | 4.93 |
| 1976–Chicago‡ | .........................American | 19 | 62 | 2 | 5 | .286 | 86 | 62 | 59 | 30 | 42 | 8.56 |
| Major League Totals | .............................. | 83 | 335 | 14 | 21 | .400 | 350 | 217 | 196 | 184 | 228 | 5.27 |

†Traded to Chicago White Sox for First Baseman Tony Muser, June 15, 1975.
‡Selected by Toronto Blue Jays in American League expansion draft, November 5, 1976.

# FERGUSON ARTHUR JENKINS
## (Fergie)

Born December 13, 1943, at Chatham, Ontario, Canada.
Height, 6.05. Weight, 210.
Throws and bats righthanded.
Tied major league record for most 1-0 games lost, season (5), 1968.
Led American League pitchers in complete games with 29 in 1974.
Led National League pitchers in complete games with 20 in 1967, 24 in 1970 and 30 in 1971.
Led National League pitchers in games started with 40 in 1968 and 42 in 1969; tied for lead in games started with 39 in 1971.
Won National League Cy Young Memorial Award, 1971.
Named American League Comeback Player of the Year by THE SPORTING NEWS, 1974.
Named as pitcher on THE SPORTING NEWS National League All-Star Team, 1967.
Named righthanded pitcher on THE SPORTING NEWS National League All-Star Team, 1971-72.
Named National League Pitcher of the Year by THE SPORTING NEWS, 1971.

| Year Club | League | G. | IP. | W. | L. | Pct. | H. | R. | ER. | SO. | BB. | ERA. |
|---|---|---|---|---|---|---|---|---|---|---|---|---|
| 1962–Miami | Florida St. | 11 | 65 | 7 | 2 | .778 | 34 | 10 | 7 | 69 | 19 | 0.97 |
| 1962–Buffalo | Int'national | 3 | 13 | 1 | 1 | .500 | 18 | 9 | 8 | 6 | 5 | 5.54 |
| 1963–Arkansas | Int'national | 4 | 10 | 0 | 1 | .000 | 13 | 7 | 7 | 13 | 3 | 6.30 |
| 1963–Miami | Florida St. | 20 | 140 | 12 | 5 | .706 | 110 | 66 | 53 | 135 | 59 | 3.41 |
| 1964–Chattanooga | South. | 21 | 139 | 10 | 6 | .625 | 124 | 61 | 48 | 149 | 42 | 3.11 |
| 1964–Arkansas | P. Coast | 11 | 57 | 5 | 5 | .500 | 40 | 27 | 20 | 49 | 34 | 3.16 |
| 1965–Arkansas | P. Coast | 32 | 122 | 8 | 6 | .571 | 104 | 48 | 40 | 112 | 42 | 2.95 |
| 1965–Philadelphia | National | 7 | 12 | 2 | 1 | .667 | 7 | 3 | 3 | 10 | 2 | 2.25 |
| 1966–Philadelphia†-Chicago | National | 61 | 184 | 6 | 8 | .429 | 150 | 77 | 68 | 150 | 52 | 3.33 |
| 1967–Chicago | National | 38 | 289 | 20 | 13 | .606 | 230 | 101 | 90 | 236 | 83 | 2.80 |
| 1968–Chicago | National | 40 | 308 | 20 | 15 | .571 | 255 | 96 | 90 | 260 | 65 | 2.63 |
| 1969–Chicago | National | 43 | 311 | 21 | 15 | .583 | 284 | 122 | 111 | •273 | 71 | 3.21 |
| 1970–Chicago | National | 40 | 313 | 22 | 16 | .579 | 265 | 128 | •118 | 274 | 60 | 3.39 |
| 1971–Chicago | National | 39 | •325 | •24 | 13 | .649 | •304 | 114 | 100 | 263 | 37 | 2.77 |
| 1972–Chicago | National | 36 | 289 | 20 | 12 | .625 | 253 | 111 | •103 | 184 | 62 | 3.21 |
| 1973–Chicago‡ | National | 38 | 271 | 14 | 16 | .467 | 267 | 133 | 117 | 170 | 57 | 3.89 |
| 1974–Texas | American | 41 | 328 | •25 | 12 | .676 | 286 | 117 | 103 | 225 | 45 | 2.83 |
| 1975–Texas§ | American | 37 | 270 | 17 | 18 | .486 | 261 | 130 | 118 | 157 | 56 | 3.93 |
| 1976–Boston | American | 30 | 209 | 12 | 11 | .522 | 201 | 85 | 76 | 142 | 43 | 3.27 |
| National League Totals | | 342 | 2302 | 149 | 109 | .578 | 2015 | 885 | 800 | 1820 | 489 | 3.13 |
| American League Totals | | 108 | 807 | 54 | 41 | .568 | 748 | 332 | 297 | 524 | 144 | 3.31 |
| Major League Totals | | 450 | 3109 | 203 | 150 | .575 | 2763 | 1217 | 1097 | 2344 | 633 | 3.18 |

†Traded with Outfielder Adolfo Phillips and Outfielder-First Baseman John Herrnstein to Chicago Cubs for Pitchers Bob Buhl and Larry Jackson, April 21, 1966.

†Traded with Outfielder Adolfo Phillips and Outfielder-First Baseman John Herrstein to Chicago Cubs for Pitchers Bob Buhl and Larry Jackson, April 21, 1966.

‡Traded to Texas Rangers for Infielders Bill Madlock and Vic Harris, October 25, 1973.

§Traded to Boston Red Sox for Outfielder Juan Beniquez, Pitcher Steve Barr, a minor league player to be named later and an estimated $200,000, November 17, 1975; Red Sox sent Pitcher Craig Skok to Rangers, December 12, 1975, to complete deal.

### ALL-STAR GAME RECORD

| Year League | IP. | W. | L. | Pct. | H. | R. | ER. | SO. | BB. | ERA. |
|---|---|---|---|---|---|---|---|---|---|---|
| 1967–National | 3 | 0 | 0 | .000 | 3 | 1 | 1 | 6 | 0 | 3.00 |
| 1971–National | 1 | 0 | 0 | .000 | 3 | 2 | 2 | 0 | 0 | 18.00 |
| All-Star Game Totals | 4 | 0 | 0 | .000 | 6 | 3 | 3 | 6 | 0 | 6.75 |

Named to National League All-Star Team for 1972 game; did not play.


# THOMAS EDWARD JOHN
## (Tommy)

Born May 22, 1943, at Terre Haute, Ind.
Height, 6.03. Weight, 185.
Throws left and bats righthanded.
Hobbies–Golf, fishing and reading.
Attended Indiana State College, Terre Haute, Ind.
Tied American League record for most hit batsmen, game, nine-innings (4), June 15, 1968.
Tied for American League lead in shutouts with 5 in 1966 and 6 in 1967.
Tied for American League lead in wild pitches with 17 in 1970.
Named National League Comeback Player of the Year by THE SPORTING NEWS, 1976.

| Year Club | League | G. | IP. | W. | L. | Pct. | H. | R. | ER. | SO. | BB. | ERA. |
|---|---|---|---|---|---|---|---|---|---|---|---|---|
| 1961–Dubuque | Midwest | 14 | 88 | 10 | 4 | .714 | 74 | 47 | 31 | 99 | 59 | 3.17 |
| 1962–Charleston | Eastern | 21 | 128 | 6 | 8 | .429 | 129 | 67 | 55 | 114 | 71 | 3.87 |
| 1962–Jacksonville | Int'national | 8 | 34 | 2 | 2 | .500 | 29 | 20 | 18 | 27 | 16 | 4.76 |
| 1963–Charleston | Eastern | 12 | 95 | 9 | 2 | .818 | 85 | 25 | 17 | 45 | 12 | 1.61 |
| 1963–Jacksonville | Int'national | 18 | 102 | 6 | 8 | .429 | 115 | 53 | 40 | 63 | 39 | 3.53 |
| 1963–Cleveland | American | 6 | 20 | 0 | 2 | .000 | 23 | 10 | 5 | 9 | 6 | 2.25 |
| 1964–Cleveland | American | 25 | 94 | 2 | 9 | .182 | 97 | 53 | 41 | 65 | 35 | 3.93 |
| 1964–Portland† | P. Coast | 13 | 74 | 6 | 6 | .500 | 75 | 38 | 35 | 72 | 24 | 4.26 |
| 1965–Chicago | American | 39 | 184 | 14 | 7 | .667 | 162 | 67 | 63 | 126 | 58 | 3.08 |
| 1966–Chicago | American | 34 | 223 | 14 | 11 | .560 | 195 | 76 | 65 | 138 | 57 | 2.62 |

| Year Club | League | G. | IP. | W. | L. | Pct. | H. | R. | ER. | SO. | BB. | ERA. |
|---|---|---|---|---|---|---|---|---|---|---|---|---|
| 1967–Chicago | American | 31 | 178 | 10 | 13 | .435 | 143 | 62 | 49 | 110 | 47 | 2.48 |
| 1968–Chicago‡ | American | 25 | 177 | 10 | 5 | .667 | 135 | 45 | 39 | 117 | 49 | 1.98 |
| 1969–Chicago | American | 33 | 232 | 9 | 11 | .450 | 230 | 91 | 84 | 128 | 90 | 3.26 |
| 1970–Chicago | American | 37 | 269 | 12 | 17 | .414 | 253 | 117 | 98 | 138 | 101 | 3.28 |
| 1971–Chicago§ | American | 38 | 229 | 13 | 16 | .448 | 244 | 115 | 92 | 131 | 58 | 3.62 |
| 1972–Los Angeles | National | 29 | 187 | 11 | 5 | .688 | 172 | 68 | 60 | 117 | 40 | 2.89 |
| 1973–Los Angeles | National | 36 | 218 | 16 | 7 | *.696 | 202 | 88 | 75 | 116 | 50 | 3.10 |
| 1974–Los Angeles x | National | 22 | 153 | 13 | 3 | .813 | 133 | 51 | 44 | 78 | 42 | 2.59 |
| 1975–Los Angeles y | National | | | | | (Did not play) | | | | | | |
| 1976–Los Angeles | National | 31 | 207 | 10 | 10 | .500 | 207 | 76 | 71 | 91 | 61 | 3.09 |
| American League Totals | | 268 | 1606 | 84 | 91 | .480 | 1482 | 636 | 536 | 962 | 501 | 3.00 |
| National League Totals | | 118 | 765 | 50 | 25 | .667 | 714 | 283 | 250 | 402 | 193 | 2.94 |
| Major League Totals | | 386 | 2371 | 134 | 116 | .536 | 2196 | 919 | 786 | 1364 | 694 | 2.98 |

†Traded to Chicago White Sox with Catcher John Romano and Outfielder Tommie Agee for Catcher Camilo Carreon and Outfielder Rocky Colavito, January 20, 1965, as part of three-way deal which saw White Sox obtain Colavito from Kansas City Athletics earlier same day for Outfielders Jim Landis and Mike Hershberger and a pitcher to be named later; White Sox assigned Pitcher Fred Talbot to Athletics, February 10, 1965, to complete deal.

‡On disabled list with torn ligament in left shoulder from August 22 through end of season.

§Traded with Infielder Steve Huntz (latter assigned to Spokane) to Los Angeles Dodgers for Infielder-Outfielder Richie Allen, December 2, 1971.

xOn disabled list, July 17 through remainder of season.

yOn emergency disabled list the entire season.

### ALL-STAR GAME RECORD

| Year League | IP. | W. | L. | Pct. | H. | R. | ER. | SO. | BB. | ERA. |
|---|---|---|---|---|---|---|---|---|---|---|
| 1968–American | ⅔ | 0 | 0 | .000 | 1 | 0 | 0 | 0 | 0 | 0.00 |

## ALEXANDER JOHNSON
### (Alex)

Born December 7, 1942, at Helena, Ark.
Height, 6.00. Weight, 205.
Throws and bats righthanded.
Attended Detroit Institute of Technology, Detroit, Mich.
Brother of Ron Johnson, former New York Giants' and Dallas Cowboys' running back.

Led Florida State League in total bases with 188 in 1962 and Pioneer League with 294 in 1963.
Named THE SPORTING NEWS National League Comeback Player of the Year, 1968.
Named Player of the Year in Pioneer League, 1963.
Named Player of the Year in Florida State League, 1962.

| Year Club | League | Pos. | G. | AB. | R. | H. | 2B. | 3B. | HR. | RBI. | B.A. | PO. | A. | E. | F.A. |
|---|---|---|---|---|---|---|---|---|---|---|---|---|---|---|---|
| 1962–Miami | Fla. St. | OF | 113 | 431 | 60 | 135 | 16 | 11 | 5 | 60 | *.313 | 214 | *19 | 7 | .971 |
| 1963–Magic Valley | Pion. | OF | 120 | 471 | 108 | 155 | 24 | 5 | *35 | *128 | .329 | 189 | 16 | 12 | .945 |
| 1964–Arkansas | P. C. | OF | 90 | 351 | 64 | 111 | 19 | 7 | 21 | 71 | .316 | 154 | 9 | 11 | .937 |
| 1964–Philadelphia | Nat. | OF | 43 | 109 | 18 | 33 | 7 | 1 | 4 | 18 | .303 | 47 | 1 | 1 | .980 |
| 1965–Philadelphia† | Nat. | OF | 97 | 262 | 27 | 77 | 9 | 3 | 8 | 28 | .294 | 109 | 3 | 4 | .966 |
| 1966–St. Louis | Nat. | OF | 25 | 86 | 7 | 16 | 0 | 1 | 2 | 6 | .186 | 23 | 2 | 1 | .962 |
| 1966–Tulsa | P. C. | OF | 80 | 293 | 56 | 104 | 17 | 11 | 14 | 56 | .355 | 124 | 6 | 10 | .929 |
| 1967–St. Louis‡ | Nat. | OF | 81 | 175 | 20 | 39 | 9 | 2 | 1 | 12 | .223 | 91 | 7 | 3 | .970 |
| 1968–Cincinnati | Nat. | OF | 149 | 603 | 79 | 188 | 32 | 6 | 2 | 58 | .312 | 243 | 8 | •14 | .947 |
| 1969–Cincinnati§ | Nat. | OF | 139 | 523 | 86 | 165 | 18 | 4 | 17 | 88 | .315 | 222 | 5 | •18 | .927 |
| 1970–California | Amer. | OF | 156 | 614 | 85 | 202 | 26 | 6 | 14 | 86 | *.329 | 269 | 11 | •12 | .959 |
| 1971–California x | Amer. | OF | 65 | 242 | 19 | 63 | 8 | 0 | 2 | 21 | .260 | 84 | 3 | 7 | .926 |
| 1972–Cleveland y | Amer. | OF | 108 | 356 | 31 | 85 | 10 | 1 | 8 | 37 | .239 | 145 | 4 | 7 | .955 |
| 1973–Texas | Amer. | OF | 158 | 624 | 62 | 179 | 26 | 3 | 8 | 68 | .287 | 72 | 4 | 1 | .987 |
| 1974–Tex. z–N.Y. | Amer. | OF | 124 | 481 | 60 | 138 | 15 | 3 | 5 | 43 | .287 | 168 | 6 | 8 | .956 |
| 1975–New York a | Amer. | OF | 52 | 119 | 15 | 31 | 5 | 1 | 1 | 15 | .261 | 9 | 0 | 0 | 1.000 |
| 1976–Detroit b | Amer. | OF-DH | 125 | 429 | 41 | 115 | 15 | 2 | 6 | 45 | .268 | 159 | 7 | 8 | .954 |
| American League Totals | | | 788 | 2865 | 313 | 813 | 105 | 16 | 44 | 315 | .284 | 906 | 35 | 43 | .956 |
| National League Totals | | | 534 | 1758 | 237 | 518 | 75 | 17 | 34 | 210 | .295 | 735 | 26 | 41 | .949 |
| Major League Totals | | | 1322 | 4623 | 550 | 1331 | 180 | 33 | 78 | 525 | .288 | 1641 | 61 | 84 | .953 |

†Traded with Pitcher Art Mahaffey and Catcher Pat Corrales to St. Louis Cardinals for First Baseman Bill White, Shortstop Dick Groat and Catcher Bob Uecker, October 27, 1965.

‡Traded to Cincinnati Reds for Outfielder Dick Simpson, January 11, 1968.

§Traded with Infielder Chico Ruiz to California Angels for Pitchers Jim McGlothlin, Vern Geishert and Pedro Borbon (deal completes earlier transaction in which Cincinnati sold Pitcher Mel Queen to California), November 25, 1969.

xOn disabled list June 26 through October 1. Traded with Catcher Jerry Moses to Cleveland Indians for Pitcher Alan Foster and Outfielders Vada Pinson and Frank Baker, October 5, 1971.

yTraded to Texas Rangers for Pitchers Vince Colbert and Rich Hinton, March 8, 1973.

zReleased on waivers to New York Yankees, September 9, 1974.

aReleased, September 4, 1975; signed as a free agent by Detroit Tigers, January 7, 1976.

bReleased December 16, 1976.

### ALL-STAR GAME RECORD

| Year League | Pos. | AB. | R. | H. | 2B. | 3B. | HR. | RBI. | B.A. | PO. | A. | E. | F.A. |
|---|---|---|---|---|---|---|---|---|---|---|---|---|---|
| 1970–American | PH | 1 | 0 | 0 | 0 | 0 | 0 | 0 | .000 | 0 | 0 | 0 | .000 |

# CLAIR BARTH JOHNSON
## (Bart)

Born January 3, 1950, at Torrance, Calif.
Height, 6.05. Weight, 215.
Throws and bats righthanded.
Hobbies—Golf and basketball.
Attended Brigham Young University, Provo, Utah.

| Year Club | League | G. | IP. | W. | L. | Pct. | H. | R. | ER. | SO. | BB. | ERA. |
|---|---|---|---|---|---|---|---|---|---|---|---|---|
| 1968—Appleton | Midwest | 12 | 67 | 3 | 5 | .375 | 46 | 27 | 20 | 69 | 28 | 2.69 |
| 1969—Appleton | Midwest | 22 | 170 | 16 | 4 | .800 | 123 | 53 | 41 | ★200 | 59 | 2.17 |
| 1969—Chicago | American | 4 | 22 | 1 | 3 | .250 | 22 | 11 | 8 | 18 | 6 | 3.27 |
| 1970—Tucson | P. Coast | 10 | 61 | 6 | 3 | .667 | 61 | 25 | 19 | 50 | 22 | 2.80 |
| 1970—Mobile | Southern | 4 | 29 | 1 | 1 | .500 | 24 | 5 | 5 | 21 | 7 | 1.55 |
| 1970—Chicago | American | 18 | 90 | 4 | 7 | .364 | 92 | 53 | 48 | 71 | 46 | 4.80 |
| 1971—Chicago | American | 53 | 178 | 12 | 10 | .545 | 148 | 67 | 58 | 153 | 111 | 2.93 |
| 1972—Appleton | Midwest | 5 | 17 | 1 | 0 | 1.000 | 10 | 1 | 1 | 14 | 2 | 0.53 |
| 1972—Chicago | American | 9 | 14 | 0 | 3 | .000 | 18 | 20 | 14 | 9 | 13 | 9.00 |
| 1973—Chicago | American | 22 | 81 | 3 | 3 | .500 | 76 | 39 | 37 | 56 | 40 | 4.11 |
| 1974—Iowa† | Am. Assoc. | 18 | 54 | 3 | 2 | .600 | 64 | 36 | 32 | 38 | 12 | 5.33 |
| 1974—Chicago | American | 18 | 122 | 10 | 4 | .714 | 105 | 42 | 37 | 76 | 32 | 2.73 |
| 1975—Chicago‡ | American | | | | | (Did not play) | | | | | | |
| 1976—Chicago | American | 32 | 211 | 9 | 16 | .360 | 231 | 115 | 111 | 91 | 62 | 4.73 |
| Major League Totals | | 156 | 718 | 39 | 46 | .459 | 692 | 347 | 313 | 474 | 310 | 3.92 |

†On suspended list from beginning of season until April 29, 1974.
‡On disabled list the entire season.

### RECORD AS OUTFIELDER

| Year Club | League | Pos. | G. | AB. | R. | H. | 2B. | 3B. | HR. | RBI. | B.A. | PO. | A. | E. | F.A. |
|---|---|---|---|---|---|---|---|---|---|---|---|---|---|---|---|
| 1972—Appleton | Midw. | O-P | 50 | 143 | 20 | 47 | 10 | 1 | 6 | 25 | .329 | 48 | 8 | 3 | .949 |
| 1972—Knoxville | South. | O-1 | 13 | 47 | 5 | 13 | 6 | 0 | 0 | 4 | .277 | 31 | 2 | 3 | .917 |

# CLIFFORD JOHNSON, JR.
## (Cliff)

Born July 22, 1947, at San Antonio, Tex.
Height, 6.04. Weight, 227.
Throws and bats righthanded.
Hobbies—Horseback riding, basketball and tennis.
Brother-in-law of Mike Easler, outfielder with Pittsburgh organization.
Cousin of Elijah Johnson, former infielder-outfielder in Houston Astro
and Baltimore Oriole organizations.

Led American Association in total bases with 285 in 1973.
Led American Association in passed balls with 17 in 1972 and tied for Southern League lead with 15 in 1971.
Tied for Appalachian League lead in double plays by catchers with 3 in 1967.
Named American Association Player of the Year, 1973.
Named Carolina League Most Valuable Player, 1970.

| Year Club | League | Pos. | G. | AB. | R. | H. | 2B. | 3B. | HR. | RBI. | B.A. | PO. | A. | E. | F.A. |
|---|---|---|---|---|---|---|---|---|---|---|---|---|---|---|---|
| 1967—Cocoa | Fla. St. | C-O | 53 | 156 | 13 | 41 | 5 | 1 | 4 | 20 | .263 | 168 | 13 | 10 | .948 |
| 1967—Covington | Appal. | O-C-1 | 36 | 110 | 21 | 34 | 7 | 2 | 5 | 24 | .309 | 103 | 10 | 6 | .950 |
| 1968—Cocoa | Fla. St. | ★C-O-1 | 117 | 353 | 60 | 102 | 17 | 3 | 10 | 61 | .289 | 641 | 55 | ★26 | .964 |
| 1969—Peninsula | Carol. | C | 103 | 327 | 37 | 75 | 16 | 1 | 11 | 54 | .229 | 615 | 68 | 21 | .970 |
| 1970—Raleigh-Durham | Carol. | C-O | 102 | 343 | 74 | 114 | 24 | 0 | ★27 | ★91 | .332 | 474 | 40 | 9 | .983 |
| 1970—Oklahoma City | A. A. | C-O-1 | 22 | 55 | 12 | 21 | 4 | 1 | 1 | 5 | .382 | 63 | 9 | 2 | .973 |
| 1971—Oklahoma City | A. A. | C-1B | 31 | 105 | 16 | 26 | 5 | 2 | 5 | 15 | .248 | 219 | 20 | 2 | .992 |
| 1971—Columbus | South. | C-1B | 58 | 164 | 16 | 30 | 10 | 0 | 4 | 21 | .183 | 350 | 35 | 5 | .987 |
| 1972—Columbus | South. | C-3-1 | 42 | 160 | 28 | 46 | 11 | 2 | 10 | 38 | .288 | 235 | 36 | 8 | .971 |
| 1972—Oklahoma City | A. A. | ●C-1B | 89 | 313 | 55 | 88 | 12 | 5 | 17 | 59 | .281 | 600 | 59 | ●15 | .978 |
| 1972—Houston | Nat. | C | 5 | 4 | 0 | 1 | 0 | 0 | 0 | 0 | .250 | 6 | 0 | 0 | 1.000 |
| 1973—Denver | A. A. | 1B | 133 | 490 | ★105 | 148 | 30 | 4 | ★33 | ★117 | .302 | 132 | 15 | 4 | .974 |
| 1973—Houston | Nat. | 1B | 7 | 20 | 6 | 6 | 2 | 0 | 2 | 6 | .300 | 47 | 2 | 0 | 1.000 |
| 1974—Houston | Nat. | C-1B | 83 | 171 | 26 | 39 | 4 | 1 | 10 | 29 | .228 | 270 | 18 | 4 | .986 |
| 1975—Houston | Nat. | 1-C-O | 122 | 340 | 52 | 94 | 16 | 1 | 20 | 65 | .276 | 604 | 38 | 12 | .982 |
| 1976—Houston | Nat. | C-O-1 | 108 | 318 | 36 | 72 | 21 | 2 | 10 | 49 | .226 | 468 | 35 | 9 | .982 |
| Major League Totals | | | 325 | 853 | 120 | 212 | 43 | 4 | 42 | 149 | .249 | 1395 | 93 | 25 | .983 |

# DAVID ALLEN JOHNSON
## (Dave)

Born January 30, 1943, at Orlando, Fla.
Height, 6.01. Weight, 182.
Throws and bats righthanded.
Hobbies—Golf, skin diving and flying.
Attended Texas A &M, College Station, Tex., Trinity University, San Antonio, Tex., and Johns
Hopkins University, Baltimore, Md.; received Bachelor of Science degree in Mathematics.

Established major league record for most home runs by second baseman, season, 43, 1973.
Tied major league record for fewest triples, season (150 or more games), 0, 1973.

Led National League second basemen in total chances with 877 and tied for lead in double plays with 106 in 1973.
Led American League second basemen in double plays with 103 in 1971.
Tied for American League lead in sacrifice flies with 8 in 1967.
Led California League shortstops in double plays with 63 in 1962.
Named second baseman on THE SPORTING NEWS American League All-Star fielding team, 1969-70-71.
Named second baseman on THE SPORTING NEWS American League All-Star Team, 1970.
Named second baseman on THE SPORTING NEWS National League All-Star Team, 1973.
Named National League Comeback Player of the Year by THE SPORTING NEWS, 1973.

| Year | Club | League | Pos. | G. | AB. | R. | H. | 2B. | 3B. | HR. | RBI. | B.A. | PO. | A. | E. | F.A. |
|---|---|---|---|---|---|---|---|---|---|---|---|---|---|---|---|---|
| 1962–Stockton | ............ | Calif. | SS | 97 | 343 | 58 | 106 | 18 | ●12 | 10 | 63 | .309 | 135 | 307 | 40 | ★.917 |
| 1963–Elmira | .............. | East. | SS-2B | 63 | 233 | 47 | 76 | 11 | 6 | 13 | 42 | .326 | 115 | 155 | 12 | .957 |
| 1963–Rochester | .......... | Int. | 2B-OF | 63 | 211 | 31 | 52 | 9 | 3 | 6 | 22 | .246 | 141 | 138 | 11 | .962 |
| 1964–Rochester | .......... | Int. | 2B-SS | ●155 | 590 | 87 | 156 | 29 | 14 | 19 | 73 | .264 | 326 | 445 | 39 | .952 |
| 1965–Baltimore | ......... | Amer. | 3-2-SS | 20 | 47 | 5 | 8 | 3 | 0 | 0 | 1 | .170 | 11 | 37 | 3 | .941 |
| 1965–Rochester | .......... | Int. | SS | 52 | 193 | 29 | 58 | 9 | 3 | 4 | 22 | .301 | 96 | 161 | 10 | .963 |
| 1966–Baltimore | ......... | Amer. | ★2B-SS | 131 | 501 | 47 | 129 | 20 | 3 | 7 | 56 | .257 | 294 | 357 | ★20 | .970 |
| 1967–Baltimore | ......... | Amer. | 2B-3B | 148 | 510 | 62 | 126 | 30 | 3 | 10 | 64 | .247 | 344 | 351 | 14 | .980 |
| 1968–Baltimore | ......... | Amer. | 2B-SS | 145 | 504 | 50 | 122 | 24 | 4 | 9 | 56 | .242 | 294 | 370 | 15 | .978 |
| 1969–Baltimore | ......... | Amer. | 2B-SS | 142 | 511 | 52 | 143 | 34 | 1 | 7 | 57 | .280 | 358 | 370 | 12 | .984 |
| 1970–Baltimore | ......... | Amer. | ●2B-SS | 149 | 530 | 68 | 149 | 27 | 1 | 10 | 53 | .281 | ●382 | 391 | 8 | .990 |
| 1971–Baltimore | ......... | Amer. | 2B | 142 | 510 | 67 | 144 | 26 | 1 | 18 | 72 | .282 | 361 | 367 | 12 | .984 |
| 1972–Baltimore† | ....... | Amer. | 2B | 118 | 376 | 31 | 83 | 22 | 3 | 5 | 32 | .221 | 286 | 307 | 6 | ★.990 |
| 1973–Atlanta | .............. | Nat. | 2B | 157 | 559 | 84 | 151 | 25 | 0 | 43 | 99 | .270 | 383 | 464 | ★30 | .966 |
| 1974–Atlanta‡ | ........ | Nat. | 1B-2B | 136 | 454 | 56 | 114 | 18 | 0 | 15 | 62 | .251 | 789 | 231 | 11 | .989 |
| 1975–Yomiuri | ............ | Japan. | 2B | 91 | 289 | 29 | 57 | 7 | 0 | 13 | 38 | .197 | .... | .... | .... | ....... |
| 1976–Yomiuri§ | ......... | Japan. | 2B | 108 | 371 | 48 | 102 | 16 | 2 | 26 | 74 | .275 | .... | .... | .... | ....... |
| American League Totals | ................ | | | 995 | 3489 | 382 | 904 | 186 | 16 | 66 | 391 | .259 | 2330 | 2550 | 90 | .982 |
| National League Totals | ................. | | | 293 | 1013 | 140 | 265 | 43 | 0 | 58 | 161 | .262 | 1172 | 695 | 41 | .979 |
| Major League Totals | ..................... | | | 1288 | 4502 | 522 | 1169 | 229 | 16 | 124 | 552 | .260 | 3502 | 3245 | 131 | .981 |

†Traded with Pitchers Pat Dobson and Roric Harrison and Catcher Johnny Oates to Atlanta Braves for Catcher Earl Williams and Infielder Taylor Duncan, November 30, 1972.
‡Released, April 11, 1975.
§Released, January 21, 1977; signed as free agent with Philadelphia Phillies, February 3, 1977.

## CHAMPIONSHIP SERIES RECORD

| Year | Club | League | Pos. | G. | AB. | R. | H. | 2B. | 3B. | HR. | RBI. | B.A. | PO. | A. | E. | F.A. |
|---|---|---|---|---|---|---|---|---|---|---|---|---|---|---|---|---|
| 1969–Baltimore | .......... | Amer. | 2B | 3 | 13 | 2 | 3 | 0 | 0 | 0 | 0 | .231 | 5 | 11 | 0 | 1.000 |
| 1970–Baltimore | .......... | Amer. | 2B | 3 | 11 | 4 | 4 | 0 | 0 | 2 | 4 | .364 | 11 | 4 | 0 | 1.000 |
| 1971–Baltimore | .......... | Amer. | 2B | 3 | 10 | 2 | 3 | 2 | 0 | 0 | 0 | .300 | 5 | 6 | 1 | .917 |
| Championship Series Totals | ........... | | | 9 | 34 | 8 | 10 | 2 | 0 | 2 | 4 | .294 | 21 | 21 | 1 | .977 |

## WORLD SERIES RECORD

| Year | Club | League | Pos. | G. | AB. | R. | H. | 2B. | 3B. | HR. | RBI. | B.A. | PO. | A. | E. | F.A. |
|---|---|---|---|---|---|---|---|---|---|---|---|---|---|---|---|---|
| 1966–Baltimore | .......... | Amer. | 2B | 4 | 14 | 1 | 4 | 1 | 0 | 0 | 1 | .286 | 12 | 12 | 0 | 1.000 |
| 1969–Baltimore | .......... | Amer. | 2B | 5 | 16 | 1 | 1 | 0 | 0 | 0 | 0 | .063 | 8 | 15 | 0 | 1.000 |
| 1970–Baltimore | .......... | Amer. | 2B | 5 | 16 | 2 | 5 | 2 | 0 | 0 | 2 | .313 | 15 | 9 | 0 | 1.000 |
| 1971–Baltimore | .......... | Amer. | 2B | 7 | 27 | 1 | 4 | 0 | 0 | 0 | 3 | .148 | 18 | 12 | 0 | 1.000 |
| World Series Totals | ...................... | | | 21 | 73 | 5 | 14 | 3 | 0 | 0 | 6 | .192 | 53 | 48 | 0 | 1.000 |

## ALL-STAR GAME RECORD

| Year | League | Pos. | AB. | R. | H. | 2B. | 3B. | HR. | RBI. | B.A. | PO. | A. | E. | F.A. |
|---|---|---|---|---|---|---|---|---|---|---|---|---|---|---|
| 1968–American | ............................ | 2B | 1 | 0 | 0 | 0 | 0 | 0 | 0 | .000 | 1 | 1 | 0 | 1.000 |
| 1970–American | ............................ | 2B | 5 | 0 | 1 | 0 | 0 | 0 | 0 | .200 | 5 | 1 | 0 | 1.000 |
| 1973–National | ............................ | 2B | 1 | 0 | 0 | 0 | 0 | 0 | 0 | .000 | 1 | 1 | 0 | 1.000 |
| All-Star Game Totals | ...................... | | 7 | 0 | 1 | 0 | 0 | 0 | 0 | .143 | 7 | 3 | 0 | 1.000 |

Named to American League All-Star Team for 1969 game; replaced due to injury.

## DAVID CHARLES JOHNSON
### (Dave)

Born October 4, 1949, at Abilene, Tex.
Height, 6.01. Weight, 185.
Throws and bats righthanded.
Hobbies—Leathercraft and hunting.
Attended McMurry College, Abilene, Tex.; received degree in Physical Education.

Led Northern League in wild pitches with 17 in 1968.
Named Northern League Pitcher of the Year, 1969.

| Year | Club | League | G. | IP. | W. | L. | Pct. | H. | R. | ER. | SO. | BB. | ERA. |
|---|---|---|---|---|---|---|---|---|---|---|---|---|---|
| 1967–Bluefield | ............................ | Ap'alachian | 13 | 47 | 3 | 1 | .750 | 45 | 26 | 19 | 40 | 33 | 3.64 |
| 1968–Aberdeen | ............................ | Northern | 17 | 78 | 4 | 8 | .333 | 79 | 45 | 34 | 80 | 38 | 3.92 |
| 1969–Aberdeen† | ............................ | Northern | ★27 | 61 | 6 | 2 | .750 | 53 | 18 | 16 | 69 | 30 | 2.36 |
| 1970–Stockton‡ | ............................ | California | 31 | 76 | 4 | 4 | .500 | 56 | 35 | 23 | 81 | 33 | 2.72 |
| 1971–Stockton | ............................ | California | 34 | 158 | 13 | 12 | .520 | 137 | 92 | 71 | 165 | 75 | 4.04 |
| 1972–Asheville | ............................ | Southern | ★50 | 98 | 7 | 4 | .636 | 91 | 52 | 41 | 89 | 32 | 3.77 |
| 1973–Rochester | ............................ | Int'national | ★49 | 102 | 8 | 5 | .615 | 87 | 42 | 36 | 83 | 51 | 3.18 |
| 1974–Rochester | ............................ | Int'national | 35 | 80 | 7 | 4 | .636 | 51 | 25 | 21 | 76 | 32 | 2.36 |
| 1974–Baltimore | ............................ | American | 11 | 15 | 2 | 2 | .500 | 17 | 5 | 5 | 6 | 5 | 3.00 |

| Year    Club | League | G. | IP. | W. | L. | Pct. | H. | R. | ER. | SO. | BB. | ERA. |
|---|---|---|---|---|---|---|---|---|---|---|---|---|
| 1975–Rochester§ ...................... | Int'national | 28 | 46 | 3 | 1 | .750 | 54 | 35 | 29 | 39 | 25 | 5.67 |
| 1975–Baltimore ......................... | American | 6 | 9 | 0 | 1 | .000 | 8 | 4 | 4 | 4 | 7 | 4.00 |
| 1976–Rochester x........................ | Int'national | 36 | 74 | 11 | 5 | .688 | 65 | 28 | 23 | 44 | 28 | 2.80 |
| Major League Totals ............... | | 17 | 24 | 2 | 3 | .400 | 25 | 9 | 9 | 10 | 12 | 3.38 |

†On restricted list, February 17 through June 17, 1969.
‡On temporary inactive list, April 13 through May 14, 1970.
§On disabled list, July 29 to September 7, 1975.
xOn disabled list, April 16 to May 3, 1976. Sold to Seattle Mariners, September 29, 1976.

### JERRY MICHAEL JOHNSON

Born December 3, 1943, at Miami, Fla.
Height, 6.03. Weight, 200.
Throws and bats righthanded.
Hobbies–Skin diving, hunting, fishing and golf.

| Year    Club | League | G. | IP. | W. | L. | Pct. | H. | R. | ER. | SO. | BB. | ERA |
|---|---|---|---|---|---|---|---|---|---|---|---|---|
| 1963–Salinas† ........................ | California | 11 | 32 | 0 | 0 | .000 | 36 | 28 | 24 | 16 | 19 | 6.75 |
| 1964–Auburn‡ ........................ | NYP | 3 | 10 | 1 | 2 | .333 | 10 | 6 | 6 | 3 | 4 | 5.40 |
| 1964–Williamport..................... | Eastern | 2 | 3 | 0 | 0 | .000 | 3 | 3 | 1 | 1 | 5 | 3.00 |
| 1965–Greenville§ .................... | W. Carolinas | 5 | 35 | 3 | 2 | .600 | 33 | 9 | 6 | 30 | 8 | 1.54 |
| 1966–Jacksonville x .................. | Int'national | 13 | 34 | 2 | 4 | .333 | 26 | 12 | 12 | 21 | 17 | 3.18 |
| 1966–Williamsport ................... | Eastern | 1 | 3 | 0 | 0 | .000 | 3 | 0 | 0 | 2 | 3 | 0.00 |
| 1967–Williamsport .................. | Eastern | 26 | 181 | 10 | 13 | .435 | 153 | •81 | 56 | 151 | 91 | 2.78 |
| 1968–San Diego z..................... | P. Coast | 10 | 74 | 7 | 1 | .875 | 55 | 17 | 16 | 51 | 11 | 1.95 |
| 1968–Philadelphia ................... | National | 16 | 81 | 4 | 4 | .500 | 82 | 33 | 29 | 40 | 29 | 3.22 |
| 1969–Philadelphia a .................. | National | 33 | 147 | 6 | 13 | .316 | 151 | 76 | 70 | 82 | 57 | 4.29 |
| 1970–Tulsa ............................. | Am. Assoc. | 2 | 7 | 1 | 0 | 1.000 | 12 | 4 | 4 | 4 | 1 | 5.14 |
| 1970–St. Louis b-San Francisco ....| National | 40 | 77 | 5 | 4 | .556 | 73 | 43 | 35 | 49 | 41 | 4.09 |
| 1971–San Francisco .................. | National | 67 | 109 | 12 | 9 | .571 | 93 | 42 | 36 | 85 | 48 | 2.97 |
| 1972–San Francisco c ................ | National | 48 | 73 | 8 | 6 | .571 | 73 | 40 | 36 | 57 | 40 | 4.44 |
| 1973–Cleveland d..................... | American | 39 | 60 | 5 | 6 | .455 | 70 | 48 | 41 | 45 | 39 | 6.15 |
| 1974–Denver ........................... | Am. Assoc. | 9 | 48 | 3 | 2 | .600 | 56 | 33 | 26 | 40 | 37 | 4.88 |
| 1974–Houston e ....................... | National | 34 | 45 | 2 | 1 | .667 | 47 | 26 | 24 | 32 | 24 | 4.80 |
| 1975–Hawaii ........................... | P. Coast | 16 | 104 | 10 | 3 | .769 | 83 | 41 | 34 | 61 | 50 | 2.94 |
| 1975–San Diego ....................... | National | 21 | 54 | 3 | 1 | .750 | 60 | 37 | 31 | 18 | 31 | 5.17 |
| 1976–Hawaii ........................... | P. Coast | 17 | 115 | 7 | 8 | .467 | 127 | 69 | 59 | 73 | 36 | 4.62 |
| 1976–San Diego f ..................... | National | 24 | 39 | 1 | 3 | .250 | 39 | 27 | 23 | 27 | 26 | 5.31 |
| National League Totals............. | | 283 | 625 | 41 | 41 | .500 | 618 | 324 | 284 | 390 | 296 | 4.09 |
| American League Totals............ | | 39 | 60 | 5 | 6 | .455 | 70 | 48 | 41 | 45 | 39 | 6.15 |
| Major League Totals ............... | | 322 | 685 | 46 | 47 | .495 | 688 | 372 | 325 | 435 | 335 | 4.27 |

†On disabled list, May 22 to June 4 and June 15 to June 30, 1963.
‡On disabled list, April 27 to May 27, June 9 to June 28 and July 1 to August 3, 1964.
§On military list from beginning of season until June 5; on disabled list, July 23 to August 10, 1965.
xOn disabled list from June 9 through August 17.
yDrafted from New York Mets' organization by San Diego (Philadelphia Phillies' organization), November 28, 1967.
zOn disabled list, May 2 to May 31; On temporary inactive list, April 29 to May 1 and June 28 to July 13, 1968.
aTraded with First Baseman Richie Allen and Infielder Octavio (Cookie) Rojas to St. Louis Cardinals for Catcher Tim McCarver, Outfielders Curt Flood and Byron Browne and Pitcher Joe Hoerner, October 7, 1969. Flood refused to report and the Cardinals sent First Baseman Guillermo Montanez and a player to be named later to Philadelphia to complete the deal, April 8, 1970. Pitcher James Robert Browning was sent from St. Louis to Philadelphia as the "player to be named later" on August 30, 1970.
bTraded to San Francisco Giants for Pitcher Frank Linzy, May 19, 1970.
cSold via waivers to Cleveland Indians, March 6, 1973.
dTraded to Houston Astros for Pitcher Cecil Upshaw, December 3, 1973.
eReleased, October 22, 1974; signed as a free agent by Hawaii (San Diego Padres' organization), February 20, 1975.
fTraded to Toronto Blue Jays for Third Baseman Dave Roberts, February 17, 1977.

### RECORD AS THIRD BASEMAN

| Year    Club | League | Pos. | G. | AB. | R. | H. | 2B. | 3B. | HR. | RBI. | B.A. | PO. | A. | E. | F.A. |
|---|---|---|---|---|---|---|---|---|---|---|---|---|---|---|---|
| 1962–Salisbury .........| W. Car. | 3B | 32 | 109 | 16 | 27 | 5 | 0 | 1 | 9 | .248 | 17 | 29 | 7 | .868 |
| 1963–Salinas ............| Calif. | 3B-P | 34 | 80 | 9 | 19 | 4 | 1 | 0 | 8 | .238 | 11 | 30 | 6 | .872 |
| 1964–Auburn.............| NYP | 3B-P | 20 | 71 | 7 | 20 | 6 | 0 | 0 | 10 | .282 | 15 | 25 | 6 | .870 |
| 1965–Greenville ........| W. Car. | P-3 | 15 | 39 | 5 | 13 | 3 | 2 | 2 | 5 | .333 | 34 | 2 | 0 | 1.000 |

### CHAMPIONSHIP SERIES RECORD

| Year    Club | League | G. | IP. | W. | L. | Pct. | H. | R. | ER. | SO. | BB. | ERA. |
|---|---|---|---|---|---|---|---|---|---|---|---|---|
| 1971–San Francisco ..................... | National | 1 | 1⅓ | 0 | 0 | .000 | 1 | 2 | 2 | 2 | 1 | 13.50 |

### LAMAR JOHNSON, SR.

Born September 2, 1950, at Bessemer, Ala.
Height, 6.02. Weight, 215.
Throws and bats righthanded.
Attended Lawson State Junior College, Birmingham, Ala.
Led Midwest League in total bases with 227 in 1972 and led American Association with 262 in 1975.

Led Gulf Coast League in sacrifice flies with 5 in 1969.
Led Midwest League first basemen in double plays with 98 in 1971 and with 78 in 1972.
Led Northern League first basemen in double plays with 44 in 1970, led Southern League with 128 in 1973 and led American Association with 107 in 1975.

| Year—Club | League | Pos. | G. | AB. | R. | H. | 2B. | 3B. | HR. | RBI. | B.A. | PO. | A. | E. | F.A. |
|---|---|---|---|---|---|---|---|---|---|---|---|---|---|---|---|
| 1968—Sarasota W. Sox | Gulf C. | C-1B | 20 | 47 | 9 | 18 | 2 | 1 | 2 | 7 | .383 | 94 | 9 | 6 | .945 |
| 1969—Sarasota W. Sox | Gulf C. | O-1-C | 45 | 109 | 8 | 25 | 5 | 2 | 1 | 16 | .229 | 61 | 1 | 4 | .939 |
| 1970—Appleton | Midw. | 1B | 7 | 13 | 0 | 3 | 0 | 0 | 0 | 0 | .231 | 11 | 4 | 1 | .938 |
| 1970—Duluth-Superior | North. | 1B | 55 | 221 | 35 | 71 | 10 | 2 | 6 | 44 | .321 | 411 | 27 | 12 | .973 |
| 1971—Appleton | Midw. | 1B | 119 | 442 | 80 | 119 | 22 | 4 | 18 | *97 | .269 | 966 | 41 | •19 | .981 |
| 1972—Knoxville | South. | PH | 2 | 2 | 0 | 0 | 0 | 0 | 0 | 0 | .000 | 0 | 0 | 0 | .000 |
| 1972—Appleton | Midw. | 1B | 114 | 402 | 63 | 126 | 17 | 3 | *26 | *89 | .313 | 900 | 46 | *18 | .981 |
| 1973—Knoxville | South. | 1B | 138 | 491 | 74 | 144 | 24 | 1 | 16 | 93 | .293 | *1187 | *69 | 16 | .987 |
| 1974—Iowa | A. A. | 1B | 122 | 455 | 81 | 137 | 23 | 0 | 20 | *96 | .301 | *1036 | 68 | *20 | .982 |
| 1974—Chicago | Amer. | 1B | 10 | 29 | 1 | 10 | 0 | 0 | 2 | 2 | .345 | 40 | 2 | 0 | 1.000 |
| 1975—Denver | A. A. | 1B | 129 | 485 | 73 | *163 | *35 | 2 | 20 | 101 | *.336 | 939 | 71 | •13 | .987 |
| 1975—Chicago | Amer. | 1B | 8 | 30 | 2 | 6 | 3 | 0 | 1 | 1 | .200 | 46 | 2 | 2 | .960 |
| 1976—Chicago | Amer. | DH-1-OF | 82 | 222 | 29 | 71 | 11 | 1 | 4 | 33 | .320 | 210 | 18 | 4 | .983 |
| Major League Totals | | | 100 | 281 | 32 | 87 | 14 | 1 | 5 | 36 | .310 | 296 | 22 | 6 | .981 |

## ROBERT DALE JOHNSON
### (Bob)

Born April 25, 1943, at Aurora, Ill.
Height, 6.04. Weight, 220.
Throws right and bats lefthanded.

Tied for American League lead in hit batsmen with 11 in 1970.
Tied for Texas League lead in complete games with 13 and shutouts with 5 in 1969.

| Year—Club | League | G. | IP. | W. | L. | Pct. | H. | R. | ER. | SO. | BB. | ERA. |
|---|---|---|---|---|---|---|---|---|---|---|---|---|
| 1964—Auburn† | NYP | 37 | 172 | 10 | 9 | .526 | 182 | 100 | 79 | 146 | 67 | 4.13 |
| 1965—Williamsport | Eastern | 11 | 53 | 3 | 1 | .750 | 45 | 25 | 23 | 28 | 34 | 3.91 |
| 1965—Auburn | NYP | 12 | 86 | 7 | 1 | .875 | 74 | 40 | 33 | 80 | 35 | 3.45 |
| 1966—Jacksonville | Int'national | 16 | 23 | 1 | 3 | .250 | 21 | 15 | 13 | 27 | 18 | 5.09 |
| 1966—Williamsport | Eastern | 19 | 123 | 8 | 3 | .727 | 101 | 50 | 44 | 113 | 48 | 3.22 |
| 1967—Williamsport‡ | Eastern | 13 | 53 | 3 | 1 | .750 | 25 | 7 | 6 | 53 | 23 | 1.02 |
| 1968—§ | | | | | | (In Military Service) | | | | | | |
| 1969—Tidewater | Int'national | 14 | 33 | 0 | 0 | 1.000 | 31 | 24 | 22 | 32 | 13 | 6.00 |
| 1969—Memphis | Texas | 19 | 134 | 13 | 4 | *.765 | 103 | 33 | 22 | 129 | 20 | 1.48 |
| 1969—New York x | National | 2 | 2 | 0 | 0 | .000 | 1 | 0 | 0 | 1 | 1 | 0.00 |
| 1970—Kansas City y | American | 40 | 214 | 8 | 13 | .381 | 178 | 82 | 73 | 206 | 82 | 3.07 |
| 1971—Pittsburgh | National | 31 | 175 | 9 | 10 | .474 | 170 | 73 | 67 | 101 | 55 | 3.45 |
| 1972—Pittsburgh | National | 31 | 116 | 4 | 4 | .500 | 98 | 40 | 38 | 79 | 46 | 2.95 |
| 1973—Pittsburgh z | National | 50 | 92 | 4 | 2 | .667 | 98 | 41 | 37 | 68 | 34 | 3.62 |
| 1974—Cleveland a | American | 14 | 72 | 3 | 4 | .429 | 75 | 42 | 35 | 36 | 37 | 4.38 |
| 1974—Spokane b | P. Coast | 11 | 86 | 5 | 3 | .625 | 86 | 34 | 31 | 40 | 29 | 3.24 |
| 1975—Syracuse c | Int'national | 25 | 57 | 3 | 3 | .500 | 68 | 34 | 33 | 41 | 17 | 5.21 |
| 1976—Omaha d | Am. Assoc. | 22 | 66 | 1 | 5 | .167 | 77 | 42 | 38 | 49 | 22 | 5.18 |
| American League Totals | | 54 | 286 | 11 | 17 | .393 | 253 | 124 | 108 | 242 | 119 | 3.40 |
| National League Totals | | 114 | 385 | 17 | 16 | .515 | 367 | 154 | 142 | 249 | 136 | 3.32 |
| Major League Totals | | 168 | 671 | 28 | 33 | .459 | 620 | 278 | 250 | 491 | 255 | 3.35 |

†On military list, October 12, 1964 through April 19, 1965.
‡On disabled list, May 18 through June 2. On temporary inactive list, June 2 through July 20. On disabled list, July 20 through August 16.
§On temporary inactive list, April 16, 1968. Placed on military list, May 1, 1968 through January 6, 1969.
xTraded with Outfielder Amos Otis to Kansas City Royals for Third Baseman Joe Foy, December 3, 1969.
yTraded with Shortstop Jackie Hernandez and Catcher Jim Campanis (latter assigned from Omaha to Columbus, Ohio) to Pittsburgh Pirates for Pitcher Bruce Dal Canton, Shortstop Freddie Patek and Catcher Jerry May, December 2, 1970.
zTraded to Cleveland Indians for Outfielder Bill Flowers, December 7, 1973.
aReleased on waivers to Texas Rangers, July 1, 1974.
bReleased by Texas Rangers, March 26, 1975; signed as free agent with Syracuse, April 7, 1975.
cReleased by New York Yankees, August 6, 1975.
dSigned as free agent by Kansas City Royals' organization, June 22, 1976; released, September 14, 1976; signed with Atlanta Braves, March 28, 1977.

### CHAMPIONSHIP SERIES RECORD

| Year—Club | League | G. | IP. | W. | L. | Pct. | H. | R. | ER. | SO. | BB. | ERA. |
|---|---|---|---|---|---|---|---|---|---|---|---|---|
| 1971—Pittsburgh | National | 1 | 8 | 1 | 0 | 1.000 | 5 | 1 | 0 | 7 | 3 | 0.00 |
| 1972—Pittsburgh | National | 2 | 6 | 0 | 0 | .000 | 4 | 2 | 2 | 7 | 2 | 3.00 |
| Championship Series Totals | | 3 | 14 | 1 | 0 | 1.000 | 9 | 3 | 2 | 14 | 5 | 1.29 |

### WORLD SERIES RECORD

| Year—Club | League | G. | IP. | W. | L. | Pct. | H. | R. | ER. | SO. | BB. | ERA. |
|---|---|---|---|---|---|---|---|---|---|---|---|---|
| 1971—Pittsburgh | National | 2 | 5 | 0 | 1 | .000 | 5 | 5 | 5 | 3 | 3 | 9.00 |

## *DID YOU KNOW*

That the Pittsburgh Pirates won the National League pennant in 1927?

# THOMAS RAYMOND JOHNSON
## (Tom)

Born April 2, 1951, at St. Paul, Minn.
Height, 6.01. Weight, 185.
Throws and bats righthanded.
Hobbies—Reading and music.
Attended University of Minnesota, Minneapolis, Minn.
Led Carolina League in hit batsmen with 11 in 1973.
Tied for Pacific Coast League lead in saves with 13 in 1975.

| Year Club | League | G. | IP. | W. | L. | Pct. | H. | R. | ER. | SO. | BB. | ERA. |
|---|---|---|---|---|---|---|---|---|---|---|---|---|
| 1970—Auburn† | NYP | 15 | 34 | 1 | 3 | .250 | 49 | 25 | 17 | 38 | 14 | 4.50 |
| 1971—Orlando | Florida St. | 17 | 96 | 3 | 8 | .273 | 110 | 53 | 43 | 71 | 27 | 4.03 |
| 1971—Sarasota Twins | Gulf Coast | 16 | 33 | 5 | 4 | .556 | 32 | 9 | 3 | 32 | 12 | 0.82 |
| 1972—Wisconsin Rapids | Midwest | 24 | 172 | 10 | 12 | .455 | 175 | 88 | 69 | 188 | 53 | 3.61 |
| 1973—Wilson‡ | Carolina | 46 | 116 | 8 | 9 | .471 | 104 | 50 | 34 | 114 | 37 | 2.64 |
| 1974—Orlando | Southern | 42 | 87 | 9 | 7 | .563 | 73 | 21 | 18 | 45 | 30 | 1.86 |
| 1974—Minnesota | American | 4 | 7 | 2 | 0 | 1.000 | 4 | 1 | 0 | 4 | 0 | 0.00 |
| 1975—Tacoma | P. Coast | 33 | 68 | 4 | 2 | .667 | 66 | 23 | 22 | 50 | 20 | 2.91 |
| 1975—Minnesota | American | 18 | 39 | 1 | 2 | .333 | 40 | 23 | 18 | 17 | 21 | 4.15 |
| 1976—Tacoma | P. Coast | 45 | 89 | 7 | 6 | .538 | 75 | 21 | 18 | 65 | 20 | 1.82 |
| 1976—Minnesota | American | 18 | 48 | 3 | 1 | .750 | 44 | 14 | 14 | 37 | 8 | 2.63 |
| Major League Totals | | 40 | 94 | 6 | 3 | .667 | 88 | 38 | 32 | 58 | 29 | 3.06 |

†On temporary inactive list, April 17 to June 24, 1970.
‡On disabled list, May 9 to May 19, 1973.


# TIMOTHY EVALD JOHNSON
## (Tim)

Born July 22, 1949, at Grand Forks, N. D.
Height, 6.03. Weight, 180.
Throws right and bats lefthanded.
Hobby—Motorcycles.
Led California League shortstops in double plays with 69 in 1968.

| Year Club | League | Pos. | G. | AB. | R. | H. | 2B. | 3B. | HR. | RBI. | B.A. | PO. | A. | E. | F.A. |
|---|---|---|---|---|---|---|---|---|---|---|---|---|---|---|---|
| 1968—Bakersfield | Calif. | *SS-OF-2 | 134 | 494 | 57 | 111 | 22 | 2 | 2 | 40 | .225 | •232 | 344 | •41 | .934 |
| 1969—Albuquerque | Texas | SS | 92 | 328 | 33 | 81 | 8 | 2 | 1 | 24 | .247 | 148 | 287 | 32 | .931 |
| 1970—Albuquerque | Texas | SS | 102 | 361 | 45 | 95 | 17 | 8 | 6 | 40 | .263 | 177 | 315 | 11 | •.978 |
| 1971—Spokane | P.C. | SS-2-3 | 98 | 305 | 38 | 75 | 10 | 1 | 2 | 20 | .246 | 141 | 247 | 27 | .935 |
| 1972—El Paso | Texas | SS | 112 | 409 | 46 | 99 | 11 | 3 | 6 | 35 | .242 | 144 | 294 | 35 | .926 |
| 1973—Albuquerque† | P.C. | SS | 8 | 27 | 2 | 7 | 0 | 0 | 0 | 4 | .259 | 9 | 33 | 0 | 1.000 |
| 1973—Milwaukee | Amer. | SS | 136 | 465 | 39 | 99 | 10 | 2 | 0 | 32 | .213 | •253 | 381 | 25 | .962 |
| 1974—Milwaukee | Amer. | S-2-O-3 | 93 | 245 | 25 | 60 | 7 | 7 | 0 | 25 | .245 | 139 | 230 | 9 | .976 |
| 1975—Milwaukee‡ | Amer. | 2-3-S-1 | 38 | 85 | 6 | 12 | 1 | 0 | 0 | 2 | .141 | 38 | 63 | 5 | .953 |
| 1976—Milwaukee | Amer. | 2-3-1 | 105 | 273 | 25 | 75 | 4 | 3 | 0 | 14 | .275 | 165 | 237 | 8 | .980 |
| Major League Totals | | | 372 | 1068 | 95 | 246 | 22 | 12 | 0 | 73 | .230 | 595 | 911 | 47 | .970 |

†Traded by Los Angeles Dodgers to Milwaukee Brewers for Shortstop Rick Auerbach, April 24, 1973.
‡On disabled list, June 24 to July 11 and July 28 to September 26, 1975.


# JOHN WILLIAM JOHNSTONE, JR.
## (Jay)

Born November 20, 1945, at Manchester, Conn.
Height, 6.00. Weight, 185.
Throws right and bats lefthanded.
Hobbies—Hunting and fishing.
Attended Mount San Antonio Junior College, Walnut, Calif.

| Year Club | League | Pos. | G. | AB. | R. | H. | 2B. | 3B. | HR. | RBI. | B.A. | PO. | A. | E. | F.A. |
|---|---|---|---|---|---|---|---|---|---|---|---|---|---|---|---|
| 1963—San Jose | Calif. | OF-S-3 | 48 | 155 | 21 | 39 | 5 | 3 | 1 | 18 | .252 | 51 | 31 | 9 | .901 |
| 1964—San Jose | Calif. | OF | 126 | 454 | 66 | 132 | 27 | •11 | 4 | 48 | .291 | 250 | 14 | 12 | .957 |
| 1965—El Paso | Texas | OF | 35 | 137 | 21 | 39 | 9 | 2 | 1 | 21 | .285 | 82 | 4 | 4 | .956 |
| 1965—San Jose | Calif. | OF | 97 | 356 | 53 | 107 | 17 | 6 | 6 | 60 | .301 | 198 | 11 | 10 | .954 |
| 1966—El Paso | Texas | OF | 7 | 25 | 5 | 9 | 2 | 0 | 1 | 1 | .360 | 19 | 0 | 0 | 1.000 |
| 1966—Seattle | P.C. | OF | 81 | 318 | 60 | 108 | 14 | 7 | 7 | 42 | .340 | 170 | 7 | 4 | .978 |
| 1966—California | Amer. | OF | 61 | 254 | 35 | 67 | 12 | 4 | 3 | 17 | .264 | 114 | 2 | 3 | .975 |
| 1967—California | Amer. | OF | 79 | 230 | 18 | 48 | 7 | 1 | 2 | 10 | .209 | 141 | 3 | 4 | .973 |
| 1967—Seattle | P.C. | OF | 49 | 184 | 21 | 58 | 11 | 1 | 4 | 21 | .315 | 117 | 3 | 4 | .968 |
| 1968—California | Amer. | OF | 41 | 115 | 11 | 30 | 4 | 1 | 0 | 3 | .261 | 58 | 4 | 1 | .984 |
| 1968—Seattle | P.C. | OF | 84 | 314 | 45 | 87 | 15 | 4 | 13 | 56 | .277 | 203 | 11 | 9 | .960 |
| 1969—California | Amer. | OF | 148 | 540 | 64 | 146 | 20 | 5 | 10 | 59 | .270 | 331 | 12 | 6 | .983 |
| 1970—California† | Amer. | OF | 119 | 320 | 34 | 76 | 10 | 5 | 11 | 39 | .238 | 200 | 7 | 4 | .981 |
| 1971—Chicago | Amer. | OF | 124 | 388 | 53 | 101 | 14 | 1 | 16 | 40 | .260 | 232 | 9 | 8 | .968 |
| 1972—Chicago‡ | Amer. | OF | 113 | 261 | 27 | 49 | 9 | 0 | 4 | 17 | .188 | 154 | 5 | 2 | .988 |
| 1973—Tucson | P.C. | OF | 69 | 242 | 58 | 84 | 15 | 5 | 9 | 44 | .347 | 125 | 2 | 6 | .955 |
| 1973—Oakland§ | Amer. | OF-2B | 23 | 28 | 1 | 3 | 1 | 0 | 0 | 3 | .107 | 7 | 0 | 0 | 1.000 |
| 1974—Toledo | Int. | OF-1B | 57 | 155 | 31 | 49 | 15 | 1 | 8 | 35 | .316 | 77 | 6 | 3 | .965 |
| 1974—Philadelphia | Nat. | OF | 64 | 200 | 30 | 59 | 10 | 4 | 6 | 30 | .295 | 88 | 4 | 3 | .968 |

| Year Club League | Pos. | G. | AB. | R. | H. | 2B. | 3B. | HR. | RBI. | B.A. | PO. | A. | E. | F.A. |
|---|---|---|---|---|---|---|---|---|---|---|---|---|---|---|
| 1975–Philadelphia ......Nat. | OF | 122 | 350 | 50 | 115 | 19 | 2 | 7 | 54 | .329 | 152 | 10 | 4 | .976 |
| 1976–Philadelphia ......Nat. | OF-1B | 129 | 440 | 62 | 140 | 38 | 4 | 5 | 53 | .318 | 293 | 10 | 8 | .974 |
| National League Totals ................. | | 315 | 990 | 142 | 314 | 67 | 10 | 18 | 137 | .317 | 533 | 24 | 15 | .974 |
| American League Totals ............... | | 708 | 2136 | 243 | 520 | 77 | 17 | 46 | 188 | .243 | 1237 | 42 | 28 | .979 |
| Major League Totals ...................... | | 1023 | 3126 | 385 | 834 | 144 | 27 | 64 | 325 | .267 | 1770 | 66 | 43 | .977 |

†Traded with Pitcher Tom Bradley and Catcher Tom Egan to Chicago White Sox for Outfielder Ken Berry, Second Baseman Syd O'Brien and Pitcher Billy Wynne, November 30, 1970.

‡Released unconditionally, March 7, 1973; signed as free agent by Oakland Athletics, March 31, 1973.

§Conditionally released to St. Louis Cardinals, January 9, 1974; released by Cardinals, March 26, 1974. Signed as free agent by Philadelphia Phillies (assigned to Toledo), April 3, 1974.

### CHAMPIONSHIP SERIES RECORD

| Year Club League | Pos. | G. | AB. | R. | H. | 2B. | 3B. | HR. | RBI. | B.A. | PO. | A. | E. | F.A. |
|---|---|---|---|---|---|---|---|---|---|---|---|---|---|---|
| 1976–Philadelphia ......Nat. | PH-OF | 3 | 9 | 1 | 7 | 1 | 1 | 0 | 2 | .778 | 3 | 0 | 0 | 1.000 |

## ODELL JONES, JR.

Born January 13, 1953, at Tulare, Calif.
Height, 6.03. Weight, 175.
Throws and bats righthanded.
Hobbies–Swimming, billiards and fishing.

Pitched 7-0 no-hit victory against Pittsfield, April 29, 1974.

| Year Club League | G. | IP. | W. | L. | Pct. | H. | R. | ER. | SO. | BB. | ERA. |
|---|---|---|---|---|---|---|---|---|---|---|---|
| 1972–Niagara Falls ......................NYP | 11 | 79 | 7 | 3 | .700 | 78 | 34 | 27 | 53 | 20 | 3.08 |
| 1973–Charleston .........................W. Carolinas | 10 | 62 | 2 | 3 | .400 | 42 | 22 | 10 | 62 | 29 | 1.45 |
| 1973–Salem ................................Carolina | 11 | 67 | 5 | 4 | .556 | 64 | 40 | 36 | 55 | 38 | 4.84 |
| 1974–Thetford Mines ...................Eastern | 24 | 161 | 11 | 8 | .579 | 103 | 63 | 58 | 153 | •120 | 3.24 |
| 1975–Charleston .........................Int'national | 26 | 188 | •14 | 9 | .609 | 133 | 67 | 56 | •157 | 88 | 2.68 |
| 1975–Pittsburgh ...........................National | 2 | 3 | 0 | 0 | .000 | 1 | 0 | 0 | 2 | 0 | 0.00 |
| 1976–Charleston† .........................National | 16 | 84 | 2 | 7 | .222 | 81 | 49 | 46 | 47 | 43 | 4.93 |
| Major League Totals ............................... | 2 | 3 | 0 | 0 | .000 | 1 | 0 | 0 | 2 | 0 | 0.00 |

†On disabled list, July 13 to August 24, 1976.

## RANDALL LEO JONES
### (Randy)

Born January 12, 1950, at Fullerton, Calif.
Height, 5.11. Weight, 180.
Throws left and bats righthanded.
Attended Chapman College, Orange, Calif.; received Bachelor of Arts degree in Business.

Established major league record for most chances accepted, no errors, pitcher, season, 112, 1976.
Tied major league record for highest fielding percentage, pitcher, season, 1.000, 1976.
Led National League pitchers in complete games with 25 in 1976.
Tied following National League records: most double plays, pitcher, season, 12, 1976; most innings pitched, consecutive, no bases on balls allowed, 68, May 17-June 22, 1976.
Won National League Cy Young Memorial Award, 1976.
Named National League Comeback Player of the Year by THE SPORTING NEWS, 1975.
Named lefthanded pitcher on THE SPORTING NEWS National League All-Star Team, 1975 and 1976.
Named National League Pitcher of the Year by THE SPORTING NEWS, 1976.

| Year Club League | G. | IP. | W. | L. | Pct. | H. | R. | ER. | SO. | BB. | ERA. |
|---|---|---|---|---|---|---|---|---|---|---|---|
| 1972–Tri-City...............................Northwest | 1 | 5 | 1 | 0 | 1.000 | 1 | 0 | 0 | 1 | 2 | 0.00 |
| 1972–Alexandria .........................Texas | 12 | 68 | 3 | 5 | .375 | 53 | 28 | 22 | 63 | 13 | 2.91 |
| 1973–Alexandria .........................Texas | 10 | 67 | 8 | 1 | .889 | 55 | 24 | 15 | 67 | 22 | 2.01 |
| 1973–San Diego ...........................National | 20 | 140 | 7 | 6 | .538 | 129 | 58 | 49 | 77 | 37 | 3.15 |
| 1974–San Diego ...........................National | 40 | 208 | 8 | •22 | .267 | 217 | 118 | 103 | 124 | 78 | 4.46 |
| 1975–San Diego ...........................National | 37 | 285 | 20 | 12 | .625 | 242 | 94 | 71 | 103 | 56 | •2.24 |
| 1976–San Diego ...........................National | •40 | •315 | •22 | 14 | .611 | •274 | 109 | 96 | 93 | 50 | 2.74 |
| Major League Totals ............................... | 137 | 948 | 57 | 54 | .514 | 862 | 379 | 319 | 397 | 221 | 3.03 |

### ALL-STAR GAME RECORD

| Year League | IP. | W. | L. | Pct. | H. | R. | ER. | SO. | BB. | ERA. |
|---|---|---|---|---|---|---|---|---|---|---|
| 1975–National ................................ | 1 | 0 | 0 | .000 | 0 | 0 | 0 | 1 | 0 | 0.00 |
| 1976–National ................................ | 3 | 1 | 0 | 1.000 | 2 | 2 | 0 | 1 | 1 | 0.00 |
| All-Star Game Totals.................... | 4 | 1 | 0 | 1.000 | 2 | 2 | 0 | 2 | 1 | 0.00 |

## ROBERT OLIVER JONES, JR.
### (Bob)

Born October 11, 1949, at Elkton, Md.
Height, 6.03. Weight, 195.
Throws and bats lefthanded.
Hobbies–Football and basketball.

| Year Club League | Pos. | G. | AB. | R. | H. | 2B. | 3B. | HR. | RBI. | B.A. | PO. | A. | E. | F.A. |
|---|---|---|---|---|---|---|---|---|---|---|---|---|---|---|
| 1967–Geneva..............NYP | 1B | 19 | 60 | 5 | 13 | 2 | 1 | 0 | 2 | .217 | 115 | 5 | 0 | 1.000 |
| 1968–Salisbury ..........W. Car. | OF-1B | 102 | 354 | 33 | 87 | 11 | 5 | 5 | 39 | .246 | 327 | 24 | 17 | .954 |
| 1969–Burlington ........Carol. | OF-1B | 39 | 111 | 7 | 22 | 1 | 0 | 1 | 6 | .198 | 73 | 3 | 3 | .962 |

| Year Club | League | Pos. | G. | AB. | R. | H. | 2B. | 3B. | HR. | RBI. | B.A. | PO. | A. | E. | F.A. |
|---|---|---|---|---|---|---|---|---|---|---|---|---|---|---|---|
| 1969–Shelby† | ...........W. Car. | OF-1B | 20 | 74 | 9 | 20 | 3 | 0 | 1 | 7 | .270 | 50 | 2 | 1 | .981 |
| 1970– | ......................... | | | | | (In Military Service) | | | | | | | | | |
| 1971–Anderson | .........W. Car. | 1B-OF | 116 | 424 | 82 | 136 | 19 | 5 | 23 | 77 | .321 | 721 | 27 | 10 | .987 |
| 1972–Denver | ..............A.A. | OF | 118 | 345 | 46 | 99 | 15 | 6 | 5 | 46 | .287 | 159 | 6 | 4 | .976 |
| 1973–Spokane | ...........P.C. | OF | 121 | 437 | 57 | 121 | 25 | 7 | 9 | 71 | .277 | 186 | 6 | 1 | *.995 |
| 1974–Spokane | ...........P.C. | OF | 131 | 466 | 87 | 140 | 18 | 5 | 16 | 91 | .300 | 221 | 9 | 5 | .979 |
| 1974–Texas | ................Amer. | OF | 2 | 5 | 0 | 0 | 0 | 0 | 0 | 0 | .000 | 5 | 0 | 0 | 1.000 |
| 1975–Spokane | ...........P.C. | OF-1B | 109 | 404 | 69 | 112 | 12 | 6 | 17 | 67 | .277 | 210 | 4 | 3 | .986 |
| 1975–Texas | ................Amer. | OF | 9 | 11 | 2 | 1 | 0 | 0 | 0 | 0 | .091 | 6 | 0 | 0 | 1.000 |
| 1976–Sacramento‡ | .....P.C. | OF | 26 | 93 | 16 | 33 | 5 | 2 | 10 | 29 | .355 | 51 | 4 | 1 | .982 |
| 1976–California | ........Amer. | OF-DH | 78 | 166 | 22 | 35 | 6 | 0 | 6 | 17 | .211 | 98 | 6 | 1 | .990 |
| Major League Totals | ..................... | | 89 | 182 | 24 | 36 | 6 | 0 | 6 | 17 | .198 | 109 | 6 | 1 | .991 |

†On military list, August 18, 1969 through February 15, 1971.
‡Sold via waivers to California Angels, May 17, 1976.

## THOMAS FREDERICK JONES
### (Rick)

Born April 16, 1955, at Jacksonville, Fla.
Height, 6.05. Weight, 190.
Throws and bats lefthanded.
Hobbies–Golf, music and fishing.
Son of Marion Jones, minor league performer, 1939 through 1941.
Tied for Carolina League lead in complete games with 14 in 1975.

| Year Club | League | G. | IP. | W. | L. | Pct. | H. | R. | ER. | SO. | BB. | ERA. |
|---|---|---|---|---|---|---|---|---|---|---|---|---|
| 1973–Elmira | ...............................NYP | 17 | 98 | 5 | 3 | .625 | 82 | 32 | 26 | 76 | 38 | 2.39 |
| 1974–Winter Haven | .....................Florida St. | 24 | 133 | 6 | 12 | .333 | 144 | 67 | 54 | 96 | 80 | 3.65 |
| 1975–Winston-Salem | ....................Carolina | 17 | 145 | 13 | 3 | .813 | 107 | 36 | 34 | 118 | 35 | *2.11 |
| 1975–Bristol | ...............................Eastern | 13 | 81 | 7 | 4 | .636 | 67 | 35 | 33 | 59 | 33 | 3.67 |
| 1976–Rhode Island | .......................Int'national | 5 | 20 | 0 | 3 | .000 | 30 | 22 | 22 | 12 | 9 | 9.90 |
| 1976–Boston† | ...............................:American | 24 | 104 | 5 | 3 | .625 | 133 | 48 | 39 | 45 | 26 | 3.38 |
| Major League Totals | ............................. | 24 | 104 | 5 | 3 | .625 | 133 | 48 | 39 | 45 | 26 | 3.38 |

†Selected by Seattle Mariners in American League expansion draft, November 5, 1976.

## RUPPERT SANDERSON JONES

Born March 12, 1955, at Dallas, Tex.
Height, 5.10. Weight, 170.
Throws and bats lefthanded.
Tied for Pioneer League lead in double plays by outfielders with 1 in 1973.

| Year Club | League | Pos. | G. | AB. | R. | H. | 2B. | 3B. | HR. | RBI. | B.A. | PO. | A. | E. | F.A. |
|---|---|---|---|---|---|---|---|---|---|---|---|---|---|---|---|
| 1973–Billings | ............Pion. | OF | 61 | 193 | 45 | 58 | 10 | 4 | 4 | 31 | .301 | 55 | 5 | 5 | .923 |
| 1974–Waterloo | .........Midw. | OF | 68 | 249 | 44 | 88 | 15 | 0 | 13 | 43 | .353 | 94 | 7 | 3 | .971 |
| 1974–San Jose | ...........Calif. | OF | 53 | 191 | 29 | 53 | 7 | 3 | 8 | 45 | .277 | 101 | 2 | 4 | .963 |
| 1975–Omaha | ..............A.A. | OF | 119 | 403 | 62 | 98 | 25 | 5 | 13 | 54 | .243 | 171 | 15 | *13 | .935 |
| 1976–Omaha | ..............A.A. | OF | 102 | 359 | 65 | 94 | 15 | 9 | 19 | 73 | .262 | 243 | 2 | 8 | .968 |
| 1976–Kansas City† | ....Amer. | OF-DH | 28 | 51 | 9 | 11 | 1 | 1 | 1 | 7 | .216 | 21 | 0 | 0 | 1.000 |
| Major League Totals | ..................... | | 28 | 51 | 9 | 11 | 1 | 1 | 1 | 7 | .216 | 21 | 0 | 0 | 1.000 |

†Selected by Seattle Mariners in American League expansion draft, November 5, 1976.

## TIMOTHY BYRON JONES
### (Tim)

Born January 24, 1954, at Sacramento, Calif.
Height, 6.05. Weight, 220.
Throws and bats righthanded.
Hobbies–Fishing, bowling and golfing.
Led Texas League in complete games with 14 in 1975.

| Year Club | League | G. | IP. | W. | L. | Pct. | H. | R. | ER. | SO. | BB. | ERA. |
|---|---|---|---|---|---|---|---|---|---|---|---|---|
| 1972–Bradenton Pirates | ...............Gulf Coast | 11 | 68 | 3 | 4 | .429 | 51 | 30 | 18 | 51 | 36 | 2.38 |
| 1972–Niagara Falls | .....................NYP | 1 | 6 | 0 | 0 | .000 | 5 | 4 | 0 | 6 | 3 | 0.00 |
| 1973–Charleston | .........................W. Carol. | 23 | 172 | 13 | 7 | .650 | 126 | 51 | 42 | 168 | 58 | 2.20 |
| 1974–Thetford Mines† | .................Eastern | 22 | 144 | 11 | 10 | .524 | 146 | 87 | 60 | 106 | 95 | 3.75 |
| 1975–Shreveport | .......................Texas | 24 | 172 | *16 | 6 | .727 | 158 | 73 | 58 | 108 | 62 | 3.03 |
| 1976–Charleston | ........................Int'national | 24 | 161 | 7 | 10 | .412 | 173 | 86 | 65 | 73 | 73 | 3.63 |

†On disqualified list, August 22 through remainder of season.
Listed on Pittsburgh Pirates' 1977 spring roster.

---

## DID YOU KNOW—
That Willie Mays hit 22 home runs in extra-inning games? It's a major
league record for homers in extra-inning games.

## MICHAEL JORGENSEN
### (Mike)

Born August 16, 1948, at Passaic, N. J.
Height, 6.00. Weight, 195.
Throws and bats lefthanded.
Hobbies–Golf and bridge.
Attended St. John's University, Jamaica, N. Y.
Tied for International League lead in sacrifice flies with 8 in 1969.
Named first baseman on THE SPORTING NEWS National League All-Star fielding team, 1973.

| Year | Club | League | Pos. | G. | AB. | R. | H. | 2B. | 3B. | HR. | RBI. | B.A. | PO. | A. | E. | F.A. |
|------|------|--------|------|-----|------|-----|------|-----|-----|-----|------|------|------|-----|-----|------|
| 1966–Marion | | Appal. | 1B | 46 | 150 | 30 | 47 | 0 | 0 | 8 | 37 | .313 | 298 | 16 | 4 | .987 |
| 1967–Winter Haven | | Fla. St. | 1-O | 84 | 302 | 56 | 89 | 11 | 4 | 5 | 41 | .295 | 639 | 29 | 7 | .990 |
| 1968–New York | | Nat. | 1B | 8 | 14 | 0 | 2 | 1 | 0 | 0 | 0 | .143 | 32 | 1 | 0 | 1.000 |
| 1968–Memphis | | Texas | 1B | 28 | 100 | 7 | 16 | 1 | 2 | 0 | 10 | .160 | 211 | 11 | 0 | 1.000 |
| 1968–Raleigh-Dur | | Carol. | 1B-OF | 57 | 213 | 34 | 67 | 13 | 4 | 3 | 27 | .315 | 311 | 25 | 3 | .991 |
| 1969–Tidewater | | Int. | 1B | 105 | 359 | 75 | 104 | 15 | 5 | 21 | 69 | .290 | 882 | 50 | 5 | *.995 |
| 1970–New York | | Nat. | 1B-OF | 76 | 87 | 15 | 17 | 3 | 1 | 3 | 4 | .195 | 145 | 12 | 3 | .981 |
| 1971–Tidewater | | Int. | 1B-OF | 65 | 228 | 50 | 78 | 12 | 1 | 15 | 41 | .342 | 157 | 7 | 3 | .982 |
| 1971–New York† | | Nat. | OF-1B | 45 | 118 | 16 | 26 | 1 | 1 | 5 | 11 | .220 | 64 | 2 | 3 | .957 |
| 1972–Montreal‡ | | Nat. | 1B-OF | 113 | 372 | 48 | 86 | 12 | 3 | 13 | 47 | .231 | 801 | 57 | 6 | .993 |
| 1973–Montreal | | Nat. | *1B-OF | 138 | 413 | 49 | 95 | 16 | 2 | 9 | 47 | .230 | 1002 | 80 | 5 | *.995 |
| 1974–Montreal | | Nat. | 1B-OF | 131 | 287 | 45 | 89 | 16 | 1 | 11 | 59 | .310 | 653 | 54 | 1 | .999 |
| 1975–Montreal | | Nat. | 1B-OF | 144 | 445 | 58 | 116 | 18 | 0 | 18 | 67 | .261 | 1153 | 91 | 7 | .994 |
| 1976–Montreal | | Nat. | 1B-OF | 125 | 343 | 36 | 87 | 13 | 0 | 6 | 23 | .254 | 651 | 58 | 8 | .989 |
| Major League Totals | | | | 780 | 2079 | 267 | 518 | 80 | 8 | 65 | 258 | .249 | 4501 | 355 | 33 | .993 |

†Traded with Infielder Tim Foli and Outfielder Ken Singleton to Montreal Expos for Outfielder Rusty Staub, April 6, 1972.
‡On military list, July 7 to July 10 and July 20 to August 6, 1972.

## VON EVERETT JOSHUA

Born May 1, 1948, at Oakland, Calif.
Height, 5.10. Weight, 170.
Throws and bats lefthanded.
Hobbies–Basketball and fishing.
Attended Laney College, Oakland, Calif., and California State College, Hayward, Calif.

| Year | Club | League | Pos. | G. | AB. | R. | H. | 2B. | 3B. | HR. | RBI. | B.A. | PO. | A. | E. | F.A. |
|------|------|--------|------|-----|------|-----|------|-----|-----|-----|------|------|------|-----|-----|------|
| 1967–Tri-City | | Northw. | OF | 66 | 267 | 57 | ●97 | *17 | *8 | 3 | 40 | *.363 | 139 | 7 | 12 | .924 |
| 1967–Santa Barbara | | Calif. | OF | 8 | 34 | 9 | 13 | 0 | 1 | 0 | 1 | .382 | 18 | 2 | 0 | 1.000 |
| 1968–Albuquerque | | Texas | OF-1B | 74 | 295 | 47 | 88 | 12 | 6 | 5 | 32 | .298 | 150 | 8 | 6 | .963 |
| 1969–Spokane | | P.C. | OF | 107 | 386 | 55 | 107 | 21 | 10 | 2 | 30 | .277 | 201 | 9 | 10 | .955 |
| 1969–Los Angeles | | Nat. | OF | 14 | 8 | 2 | 2 | 0 | 0 | 0 | 0 | .250 | 4 | 0 | 1 | .800 |
| 1970–Spokane | | P.C. | OF | 16 | 53 | 7 | 19 | 4 | 1 | 1 | 9 | .358 | 27 | 2 | 0 | 1.000 |
| 1970–Los Angeles | | Nat. | OF | 72 | 109 | 23 | 29 | 1 | 3 | 1 | 8 | .266 | 47 | 1 | 3 | .941 |
| 1971–Spokane | | P.C. | OF | 56 | 165 | 19 | 44 | 7 | 4 | 2 | 21 | .267 | 82 | 1 | 2 | .976 |
| 1971–Los Angeles† | | Nat. | OF | 11 | 7 | 2 | 0 | 0 | 0 | 0 | 0 | .000 | 7 | 0 | 0 | .000 |
| 1972–Albuquerque | | P.C. | OF | 125 | 484 | 93 | 163 | 29 | 9 | 9 | 76 | *.337 | 193 | 9 | 10 | .953 |
| 1973–Los Angeles‡ | | Nat. | OF | 75 | 159 | 19 | 40 | 4 | 1 | 2 | 17 | .252 | 61 | 2 | 1 | .984 |
| 1974–Los Angeles§ | | Nat. | OF | 81 | 124 | 11 | 29 | 5 | 1 | 1 | 16 | .234 | 33 | 0 | 2 | .943 |
| 1975–San Francisco | | Nat. | OF | 129 | 507 | 75 | 161 | 25 | 10 | 7 | 43 | .318 | 279 | 10 | 2 | *.993 |
| 1976–San Francisco x | | Nat. | OF-PH | 42 | 156 | 13 | 41 | 5 | 2 | 0 | 2 | .263 | 70 | 3 | 4 | .948 |
| 1976–Milwaukee | | Amer. | OF-DH | 107 | 423 | 44 | 113 | 13 | 5 | 5 | 28 | .267 | 268 | 10 | 5 | .982 |
| National League Totals | | | | 424 | 1070 | 145 | 302 | 40 | 17 | 11 | 86 | .282 | 501 | 16 | 13 | .975 |
| American League Totals | | | | 107 | 423 | 44 | 113 | 13 | 5 | 5 | 28 | .267 | 268 | 10 | 5 | .982 |
| Major League Totals | | | | 531 | 1493 | 189 | 415 | 53 | 22 | 16 | 114 | .278 | 769 | 26 | 18 | .978 |

†On military list, June 19 through July 3, 1971.
‡On supplemental disabled list, April 17 to May 14, 1973.
§Released on waivers to San Francisco Giants, January 29, 1975.
xSold to Milwaukee Brewers, June 2, 1976.

### CHAMPIONSHIP SERIES RECORD

| Year | Club | League | Pos. | G. | AB. | R. | H. | 2B. | 3B. | HR. | RBI. | B.A. | PO. | A. | E. | F.A. |
|------|------|--------|------|-----|------|-----|------|-----|-----|-----|------|------|------|-----|-----|------|
| 1974–Los Angeles | | Nat. | PH | 1 | 0 | 0 | 0 | 0 | 0 | 0 | 0 | .000 | 0 | 0 | 0 | .000 |

### WORLD SERIES RECORD

| Year | Club | League | Pos. | G. | AB. | R. | H. | 2B. | 3B. | HR. | RBI. | B.A. | PO. | A. | E. | F.A. |
|------|------|--------|------|-----|------|-----|------|-----|-----|-----|------|------|------|-----|-----|------|
| 1974–Los Angeles | | Nat. | PH | 4 | 4 | 0 | 0 | 0 | 0 | 0 | 0 | .000 | 0 | 0 | 0 | .000 |

## ALFRED HENRY JUTZE
### (Skip)
(Nicknamed by father.)

Born May 28, 1947, at Bayside, N.Y.
Height, 5.11. Weight, 195.
Throws and bats righthanded.
Hobbies–Most sports and coaching kids.
Attended Central Connecticut State College, New Britain, Conn.;
received Bachelor of Science degree in Industrial Education.

Led Florida State League catchers in double plays with 9 in 1969; tied for Texas League lead with 9 in 1970; led Texas League with 10 in 1971.

Led Texas League in passed balls with 28 in 1970.

| Year | Club | League | Pos. | G. | AB. | R. | H. | 2B. | 3B. | HR. | RBI. | B.A. | PO. | A. | E. | F.A. |
|---|---|---|---|---|---|---|---|---|---|---|---|---|---|---|---|---|
| 1968–Sarasota Cards | ..Gulf C. | | C | 6 | 17 | 2 | 2 | 0 | 0 | 0 | 1 | .118 | 31 | 8 | 0 | 1.000 |
| 1968–St. Petersburg | ..Fla. St. | | C | 35 | 90 | 11 | 25 | 4 | 2 | 1 | 11 | .278 | 141 | 13 | 2 | .987 |
| 1969–St. Petersburg | ..Fla. St. | | C-O | 66 | 197 | 14 | 62 | 5 | 1 | 1 | 25 | .315 | 311 | 32 | 4 | .988 |
| 1970–Arkansas | .........Texas | | C | 117 | 412 | 49 | 100 | 17 | 4 | 5 | 41 | .243 | *715 | *87 | 11 | .986 |
| 1971–Arkansas | .........Texas | | *C-1B | 131 | 477 | 44 | 127 | 18 | 3 | 8 | 56 | .266 | *856 | *102 | 5 | *.995 |
| 1972–Tulsa | ...............A.A. | | C | 119 | 426 | 63 | 138 | 25 | 5 | 7 | 55 | .324 | *887 | 49 | 9 | *.990 |
| 1972–St. Louis† | .........Nat. | | C | 21 | 71 | 1 | 17 | 2 | 0 | 0 | 5 | .239 | 93 | 15 | 4 | .964 |
| 1973–Denver | .............A.A. | | C | 14 | 54 | 11 | 11 | 1 | 1 | 2 | 7 | .204 | 105 | 11 | 2 | .983 |
| 1973–Houston | ...........Nat. | | C | 90 | 278 | 18 | 62 | 6 | 0 | 0 | 18 | .223 | 450 | 31 | 8 | .984 |
| 1974–Denver | .............A.A. | | C | 102 | 361 | 47 | 116 | 20 | 6 | 2 | 35 | .321 | 510 | 48 | 5 | .991 |
| 1974–Houston | ...........Nat. | | C | 8 | 13 | 0 | 3 | 0 | 0 | 0 | 1 | .231 | 16 | 2 | 0 | 1.000 |
| 1975–Houston | ...........Nat. | | C | 51 | 93 | 9 | 21 | 2 | 0 | 0 | 6 | .226 | 147 | 15 | 2 | .988 |
| 1976–Houston‡ | .........Nat. | | C | 42 | 92 | 7 | 14 | 2 | 3 | 0 | 6 | .152 | 125 | 21 | 2 | .986 |
| Major League Totals | | | | 212 | 547 | 35 | 117 | 12 | 3 | 0 | 36 | .214 | 831 | 84 | 16 | .983 |

†Traded with Shortstop Milt Ramirez to Houston Astros for Shortstop Ray Busse and Infielder Bob Fenwick, November 28, 1972.

‡Traded to Seattle Mariners for Pitcher Alan Griffin and cash, January 12, 1977.

## JAMES LEE KAAT

Name pronounced Cott.

### (Jim)

Born November 7, 1938, at Zeeland, Mich.
Height, 6.04½. Weight, 215.
Throws and bats lefthanded.
Hobbies—Golf and music.
Attended Hope College, Holland, Mich.

Established major league record for most sacrifice flies allowed, lifetime—109, 1976.

Led American League in hit batsmen with 11 in 1961 and 18 in 1962; tied for league lead in wild pitches with 10 in 1961 and led league with 13 in 1962; led league in games started with 42 in 1965 and 41 in 1966; tied for league lead in shutouts with 5 in 1962; led league in complete games with 19 in 1966.

Led Pioneer League in games started with 30, shutouts with 5, and tied for lead in complete games with 15 in 1958.

Named pitcher on THE SPORTING NEWS American League All-Star fielding teams, 1962-63-64-65-66-67-68-69-70-71-72-73-74-75-76.

Named lefthanded pitcher on THE SPORTING NEWS American League All-Star Team, 1975.

Named pitcher on THE SPORTING NEWS American League All-Star Team, 1966.

Named American League Pitcher of the Year by THE SPORTING NEWS, 1966.

| Year | Club | League | G. | IP. | W. | L. | Pct. | H. | R. | ER. | SO. | BB. | ERA. |
|---|---|---|---|---|---|---|---|---|---|---|---|---|---|
| 1957–Superior | ...........................Neb. St. | 14 | 73 | 5 | 6 | .455 | 65 | 45 | 30 | 95 | 35 | 3.70 |
| 1958–Missoula | ...........................Pioneer | 39 | *223 | 16 | 9 | .640 | 189 | 108 | 74 | *245 | 118 | *2.99 |
| 1959–Chattanooga | ......................Southern | 24 | 134 | 8 | 8 | .500 | 126 | 71 | 61 | 132 | 73 | 4.10 |
| 1959–Washington | ........................American | 3 | 5 | 0 | 2 | .000 | 7 | 9 | 7 | 2 | 4 | 12.60 |
| 1960–Washington | ........................American | 13 | 50 | 1 | 5 | .167 | 48 | 39 | 31 | 25 | 31 | 5.58 |
| 1960–Charleston | ........................Am. Assoc. | 30 | 146 | 7 | 10 | .412 | 154 | 80 | 62 | 106 | 51 | 3.82 |
| 1961–Minnesota | ...........................American | 36 | 201 | 9 | 17 | .346 | 188 | 105 | 87 | 122 | 82 | 3.90 |
| 1962–Minnesota | ...........................American | 39 | 269 | 18 | 14 | .563 | 243 | 106 | 94 | 173 | 75 | 3.14 |
| 1963–Minnesota | ...........................American | 31 | 178 | 10 | 10 | .500 | 195 | 96 | 83 | 105 | 38 | 4.20 |
| 1964–Minnesota | ...........................American | 36 | 243 | 17 | 11 | .607 | 231 | 100 | 87 | 171 | 60 | 3.22 |
| 1965–Minnesota | ...........................American | 45 | 264 | 18 | 11 | .621 | *267 | *121 | 83 | 154 | 63 | 2.83 |
| 1966–Minnesota | ...........................American | 41 | *305 | *25 | 13 | .658 | *271 | 114 | 93 | 205 | 55 | 2.74 |
| 1967–Minnesota | ...........................American | 42 | 263 | 16 | 13 | .552 | *269 | 110 | 89 | 211 | 42 | 3.05 |
| 1968–Minnesota | ...........................American | 30 | 208 | 14 | 12 | .538 | 192 | 78 | 68 | 130 | 40 | 2.94 |
| 1969–Minnesota | ...........................American | 40 | 242 | 14 | 13 | .519 | 252 | 114 | 94 | 139 | 75 | 3.50 |
| 1970–Minnesota | ...........................American | 45 | 230 | 14 | 10 | .583 | 244 | 110 | 91 | 120 | 58 | 3.56 |
| 1971–Minnesota | ...........................American | 39 | 260 | 13 | 14 | .481 | 275 | 104 | 96 | 137 | 47 | 3.32 |
| 1972–Minnesota† | ...........................American | 15 | 113 | 10 | 2 | .833 | 94 | 36 | 26 | 64 | 20 | 2.07 |
| 1973–Minnesota‡-Chicago | ...........American | 36 | 224 | 15 | 13 | .536 | 250 | 124 | 109 | 109 | 43 | 4.38 |
| 1974–Chicago | ...........................American | 42 | 277 | 21 | 13 | .618 | 263 | 106 | 90 | 142 | 63 | 2.92 |
| 1975–Chicago§ | ...........................American | 43 | 304 | 20 | 14 | .588 | *321 | 121 | 105 | 142 | 77 | 3.11 |
| 1976–Philadelphia | .......................National | 38 | 228 | 12 | 14 | .462 | 241 | 95 | 88 | 83 | 32 | 3.47 |
| American League Totals | | | 576 | 3636 | 235 | 187 | .557 | 3610 | 1593 | 1333 | 2151 | 873 | 3.30 |
| National League Totals | | | 38 | 228 | 12 | 14 | .462 | 241 | 95 | 88 | 83 | 32 | 3.47 |
| Major League Totals | | | 614 | 3864 | 247 | 201 | .551 | 3851 | 1688 | 1421 | 2234 | 905 | 3.31 |

†On disabled list, July 6 through September 27.

‡Sold via waivers to Chicago White Sox, August 15, 1973.

§Traded with Shortstop Mike Buskey to Philadelphia Phillies for Outfielder-Infielder Alan Bannister and Pitchers Dick Ruthven and Roy Thomas, December 10, 1975.

### CHAMPIONSHIP SERIES RECORD

| Year | Club | League | G. | IP. | W. | L. | Pct. | H. | R. | ER. | SO. | BB. | ERA. |
|---|---|---|---|---|---|---|---|---|---|---|---|---|---|
| 1970–Minnesota | ...........................American | 1 | 2 | 0 | 1 | .000 | 6 | 4 | 2 | 1 | 2 | 9.00 |
| 1976–Philadelphia | .......................National | 1 | 6 | 0 | 0 | .000 | 2 | 2 | 2 | 1 | 2 | 3.00 |
| Championship Series Totals | | | 2 | 8 | 0 | 1 | .000 | 8 | 6 | 4 | 2 | 4 | 4.50 |

Holds World Series records for most putouts, pitcher, seven game Series (5), 1965 and most putouts, game, nine innings, pitcher (5), October 7, 1965.

| Year Club | League | G. | IP. | W. | L. | Pct. | H. | R. | ER. | SO. | BB. | ERA. |
|---|---|---|---|---|---|---|---|---|---|---|---|---|
| 1965—Minnesota | American | 3 | 14⅓ | 1 | 2 | .333 | 18 | 7 | 6 | 6 | 2 | 3.77 |

## ALL-STAR GAME RECORD

| Year League | | IP. | W. | L. | Pct. | H. | R. | ER. | SO. | BB. | ERA. |
|---|---|---|---|---|---|---|---|---|---|---|---|
| 1966—American | | 2 | 0 | 0 | .000 | 3 | 1 | 1 | 1 | 0 | 4.50 |
| 1975—American | | 2 | 0 | 0 | .000 | 0 | 0 | 0 | 0 | 0 | 0.00 |
| All-Star Game Totals | | 4 | 0 | 0 | .000 | 3 | 1 | 1 | 1 | 0 | 2.25 |

Member of American League All-Star Team in 1962 (second game); did not play.

## MICHAEL HANLEY KAVANAGH
### (Mike)

Born April 13, 1952, at Baltimore, Md.
Height, 6.01. Weight, 185.
Throws and bats righthanded.
Attended Villanova University, Villanova, Pa.

| Year Club | League | G. | IP. | W. | L. | Pct. | H. | R. | ER. | SO. | BB. | ERA. |
|---|---|---|---|---|---|---|---|---|---|---|---|---|
| 1973—Niagara Falls | NYP | 16 | 60 | 1 | 5 | .167 | 56 | 36 | 28 | 57 | 35 | 4.20 |
| 1974—Charleston | W. Carol. | *59 | 104 | 8 | 4 | .667 | 68 | 26 | 15 | 118 | 62 | 1.30 |
| 1974—Thetford Mines | Eastern | 1 | 2 | 0 | 0 | .000 | 6 | 3 | 3 | 2 | 2 | 13.50 |
| 1975—Shreveport | Texas | 17 | 115 | 9 | 6 | .600 | 94 | 59 | 47 | 79 | 72 | 3.68 |
| 1975—Charleston | Int'national | 9 | 36 | 1 | 1 | .500 | 42 | 27 | 24 | 25 | 22 | 6.00 |
| 1976—Salem† | Carolina | 6 | 28 | 2 | 3 | .400 | 33 | 18 | 14 | 18 | 16 | 4.50 |

†On disabled list, April 16 to July 30, 1976.
Listed on Pittsburgh Pirates' 1977 spring roster.

## JOSEPH DONALD KEENER
### (Joe)

Born April 21, 1953, at San Pedro, Calif.
Height, 6.04. Weight, 200.
Throws and bats righthanded.
Hobbies—Volleyball and water and snow skiing.
Attended Antelope Valley College, Lancaster, Calif.

| Year Club | League | G. | IP. | W. | L. | Pct. | H. | R. | ER. | SO. | BB. | ERA. |
|---|---|---|---|---|---|---|---|---|---|---|---|---|
| 1973—Jamestown | NYP | 14 | 99 | 7 | 5 | .583 | 92 | 40 | 34 | 67 | 25 | 3.09 |
| 1974—West Palm Beach | Florida St. | 26 | 206 | *16 | 6 | .727 | 142 | 53 | 41 | 134 | 55 | 1.79 |
| 1974—Memphis | Int'national | 1 | 2 | 0 | 0 | .000 | 1 | 0 | 0 | 2 | 1 | 0.00 |
| 1975—Quebec City | Eastern | 7 | 47 | 4 | 1 | .800 | 40 | 14 | 13 | 24 | 13 | 2.49 |
| 1975—Memphis | Int'national | 19 | 101 | 7 | 5 | .583 | 106 | 51 | 41 | 49 | 25 | 3.65 |
| 1976—Denver | Am. Assoc. | 27 | 176 | *14 | 4 | *.778 | 173 | 74 | 66 | 82 | 59 | 3.38 |
| 1976—Montreal | National | 2 | 4 | 0 | 1 | .000 | 7 | 7 | 5 | 1 | 8 | 11.25 |
| Major League Totals | | 2 | 4 | 0 | 1 | .000 | 7 | 7 | 5 | 1 | 8 | 11.25 |

## MICHAEL DENNIS KEKICH

Name pronounced KEK-ich.

### (Mike)

Born April 2, 1945, at San Diego, Calif.
Height, 6.02. Weight, 205.
Throws left and bats righthanded.
Hobbies—Golf and skiing.

Struck out 11 consecutive batters against Miami, May 28, 1964.

| Year Club | League | G. | IP. | W. | L. | Pct. | H. | R. | ER. | SO. | BB. | ERA. |
|---|---|---|---|---|---|---|---|---|---|---|---|---|
| 1964—Santa Barbara | California | 10 | 62 | 4 | 5 | .444 | 42 | 36 | 29 | 77 | 61 | 4.21 |
| 1964—St. Petersburg | Florida St. | 14 | 85 | 5 | 4 | .556 | 65 | 44 | 28 | 81 | 67 | 2.96 |
| 1964—Spokane | P. Coast | 1 | 3 | 0 | 0 | .000 | 8 | 2 | 2 | 2 | 2 | 6.00 |
| 1965—Los Angeles | National | 5 | 10 | 0 | 1 | .000 | 10 | 12 | 11 | 9 | 13 | 9.90 |
| 1966—Albuquerque | Texas | 6 | 9 | 0 | 0 | .000 | 10 | 4 | 4 | 2 | 6 | 4.00 |
| 1966—Santa Barbara | California | 5 | 18 | 0 | 1 | .000 | 18 | 19 | 14 | 17 | 12 | 7.00 |
| 1967—Santa Barbara | California | 4 | 29 | 3 | 1 | .750 | 12 | 7 | 5 | 40 | 15 | 1.55 |
| 1967—Albuquerque | Texas | 25 | 186 | 14 | 4 | .778 | 190 | 79 | 67 | 138 | 75 | 3.24 |
| 1968—Los Angeles† | National | 25 | 115 | 2 | 10 | .167 | 116 | 54 | 50 | 84 | 46 | 3.91 |
| 1969—New York | American | 28 | 105 | 4 | 6 | .400 | 91 | 58 | 53 | 66 | 49 | 4.54 |
| 1970—New York‡ | American | 26 | 99 | 6 | 3 | .667 | 103 | 59 | 53 | 63 | 55 | 4.82 |
| 1971—New York | American | 37 | 170 | 10 | 9 | .526 | 167 | 89 | 77 | 93 | 82 | 4.08 |
| 1972—New York | American | 29 | 175 | 10 | 13 | .435 | 172 | 77 | 72 | 78 | 76 | 3.70 |
| 1973—New York§-Cleveland x | American | 21 | 65 | 2 | 5 | .286 | 93 | 62 | 54 | 30 | 49 | 7.48 |
| 1974—Spokane | P. Coast | 10 | 58 | 2 | 3 | .400 | 74 | 33 | 32 | 41 | 42 | 4.97 |
| 1974—Nippon | Pacific | 18 | 122 | 5 | 11 | .313 | 104 | .... | 56 | 90 | 88 | 4.13 |
| 1975—Spokane | P. Coast | 14 | 45 | 7 | 4 | .636 | 40 | 20 | 17 | 30 | 25 | 3.40 |

| Year Club | League | G. | IP. | W. | L. | Pct. | H. | R. | ER. | SO. | BB. | ERA. |
|---|---|---|---|---|---|---|---|---|---|---|---|---|
| 1975−Texas y | American | 23 | 31 | 0 | 0 | .000 | 33 | 16 | 13 | 19 | 21 | 3.77 |
| 1976−Nuevo Laredo | Mex. Cent. | 8 | 72 | 3 | 2 | .600 | 45 | 20 | 16 | 67 | 32 | 2.00 |
| National League Totals | | 30 | 125 | 2 | 11 | .154 | 126 | 66 | 61 | 93 | 59 | 4.39 |
| American League Totals | | 164 | 645 | 32 | 36 | .471 | 659 | 361 | 322 | 349 | 332 | 4.49 |
| Major League Totals | | 194 | 770 | 34 | 47 | .420 | 785 | 427 | 383 | 442 | 391 | 4.48 |

†Traded to New York Yankees for Outfielder Andy Kosco, December 4, 1968.
‡On disabled list, April 12 through May 4, 1970.
§Traded to Cleveland Indians for Pitcher Lowell Palmer and a player to be named later, June 12, 1973; Indians' obligation was settled by a cash payment.
xUnconditionally released, March 28, 1974; signed as free agent by Texas Rangers' organization, April 25, 1974. Played in Japan with Nippon Ham Fighters.
yReleased, March 12, 1976; signed as free agent with Nuevo Laredo, June 7, 1976.
Invited to Seattle Mariners' 1977 spring camp.

## MICHAEL DENNIS KELLEHER
### (Mick)

Born July 25, 1947, at Seattle, Wash.
Height, 5.09. Weight, 170.
Throws and bats righthanded.
Hobbies−Basketball, golf and studying the stock market.
Attended Wenatchee Valley College, Wentachee, Wash., and University of
Puget Sound, Tacoma, Wash.

| Year Club | League | Pos. | G. | AB. | R. | H. | 2B. | 3B. | HR. | RBI. | B.A. | PO. | A. | E. | F.A. |
|---|---|---|---|---|---|---|---|---|---|---|---|---|---|---|---|
| 1969−Modesto | Calif. | SS | 76 | 274 | 31 | 58 | 13 | 3 | 1 | 23 | .212 | 119 | 210 | 33 | .909 |
| 1970−Cedar Rapids† | Midw. | SS | 59 | 188 | 23 | 50 | 10 | 3 | 0 | 27 | .266 | 85 | 157 | 10 | .960 |
| 1970−Little Rock | Texas | SS | 21 | 83 | 12 | 18 | 3 | 1 | 0 | 3 | .217 | 44 | 68 | 6 | .949 |
| 1971−Modesto | Calif. | SS | 114 | 429 | 66 | 109 | 20 | 1 | 1 | 45 | .254 | 172 | 301 | 31 | *.938 |
| 1972−Tulsa | A.A. | *S-2B | 113 | 375 | 30 | 91 | 13 | 0 | 0 | 26 | .243 | 166 | 338 | 11 | *.979 |
| 1972−St. Louis | Nat. | SS | 23 | 63 | 5 | 10 | 2 | 1 | 0 | 1 | .159 | 60 | 61 | 2 | .984 |
| 1973−Tulsa | A.A. | SS | 25 | 89 | 9 | 20 | 2 | 0 | 0 | 13 | .225 | 36 | 85 | 7 | .945 |
| 1973−St. Louis‡ | Nat. | SS | 43 | 38 | 4 | 7 | 2 | 0 | 0 | 2 | .184 | 30 | 55 | 4 | .955 |
| 1974−Denver | A.A. | *SS-3B | 105 | 347 | 36 | 82 | 10 | 4 | 0 | 28 | .236 | 150 | 377 | 18 | *.967 |
| 1974−Houston§ | Nat. | SS | 19 | 57 | 4 | 9 | 0 | 0 | 0 | 2 | .158 | 23 | 62 | 5 | .944 |
| 1975−Tulsa | A.A. | *SS-2B | 127 | 420 | 48 | 100 | 17 | 0 | 0 | 27 | .238 | 246 | 376 | 14 | *.978 |
| 1975−St. Louis x | Nat. | SS | 7 | 4 | 0 | 0 | 0 | 0 | 0 | 0 | .000 | 3 | 7 | 1 | .909 |
| 1976−Chicago | Nat. | S-3-2 | 124 | 337 | 28 | 77 | 12 | 1 | 0 | 22 | .228 | 167 | 324 | 12 | .976 |
| Major League Totals | | | 216 | 499 | 41 | 103 | 16 | 2 | 0 | 27 | .206 | 283 | 509 | 24 | .970 |

†On temporary inactive list, April 17 through May 13.
‡Purchased by Houston Astros, October 23, 1973.
§Sold to St. Louis Cardinals, December 13, 1974.
xTraded to Chicago Cubs for Infielder-Outfielder Vic Harris, December 22, 1975.

## HAROLD PATRICK KELLY
### (Pat)

Born July 30, 1944, at Philadelphia, Pa.
Height, 6.01. Weight, 185.
Throws and bats lefthanded.
Hobby−Dancing.
Attended Morgan State College, Baltimore, Md.
Brother of Leroy Kelly, former halfback with Cleveland Browns,
Oakland Raiders and Chicago Fire.

Major League stolen bases: 1967 (0), 1968 (0), 1969 (40), 1970 (34), 1971 (14), 1972 (32), 1973 (22), 1974 (18), 1975 (18), 1976 (15). Total−193.
Led Carolina League batters in walks with 119 and tied for lead in double plays by outfielders with 3 in 1965.
Led Pacific Coast League in stolen bases with 38 in 1968.

| Year Club | League | Pos. | G. | AB. | R. | H. | 2B. | 3B. | HR. | RBI. | B.A. | PO. | A. | E. | F.A. |
|---|---|---|---|---|---|---|---|---|---|---|---|---|---|---|---|
| 1963−Erie | NYP | OF | 69 | 247 | 50 | 70 | 10 | 4 | 4 | 30 | .283 | 137 | 4 | 9 | .940 |
| 1963−Orlando | Fla. St. | OF | 49 | 157 | 27 | 38 | 6 | 3 | 0 | 26 | .242 | 77 | 3 | 0 | 1.000 |
| 1964−Wilson | Carol. | OF | 18 | 49 | 8 | 12 | 3 | 2 | 0 | 8 | .245 | 26 | 1 | 2 | .931 |
| 1964−Wis. Rapids | Midw. | OF | 104 | 387 | 79 | 138 | •26 | 5 | 16 | 70 | .357 | 144 | 10 | 13 | .922 |
| 1965−Wilson | Carol. | OF | 144 | 488 | 101 | 138 | 16 | 9 | 4 | 52 | .283 | 138 | 14 | *22 | .934 |
| 1966−Charlotte | South. | OF | 113 | 392 | 74 | 126 | 23 | 6 | 3 | 55 | .321 | 242 | 9 | 12 | .954 |
| 1967−Minnesota† | Amer. | PH-PR | 8 | 1 | 1 | 0 | 0 | 0 | 0 | 0 | .000 | 0 | 0 | 0 | .000 |
| 1967−Denver | P.C. | OF | 65 | 245 | 42 | 70 | 3 | 2 | 0 | 15 | .286 | 151 | 4 | 6 | .963 |
| 1968−Denver | P.C. | OF | 108 | 396 | 70 | 121 | 21 | 4 | 3 | 31 | .306 | 276 | 14 | 9 | .970 |
| 1968−Minnesota‡ | Amer. | OF | 12 | 35 | 2 | 4 | 2 | 0 | 1 | 2 | .114 | 20 | 1 | 1 | .955 |
| 1969−Kansas City | Amer. | OF | 112 | 417 | 61 | 110 | 20 | 4 | 8 | 32 | .264 | 237 | 12 | 5 | .980 |
| 1970−Kansas City§ | Amer. | OF | 136 | 452 | 56 | 106 | 16 | 1 | 6 | 38 | .235 | 254 | 8 | 10 | .963 |
| 1971−Tucson | P.C. | OF | 75 | 301 | 71 | 107 | 18 | 7 | 6 | 43 | .355 | 159 | 4 | 3 | .982 |
| 1971−Chicago | Amer. | OF | 67 | 213 | 32 | 62 | 6 | 3 | 3 | 22 | .291 | 100 | 7 | 1 | .991 |
| 1972−Chicago | Amer. | OF | 119 | 402 | 57 | 105 | 14 | 7 | 5 | 24 | .261 | 173 | 8 | 6 | .968 |
| 1973−Chicago | Amer. | OF | 144 | 550 | 77 | 154 | 24 | 5 | 1 | 44 | .280 | 254 | 9 | 6 | .978 |
| 1974−Chicago | Amer. | OF | 122 | 424 | 60 | 119 | 16 | 3 | 4 | 21 | .281 | 79 | 2 | 2 | .976 |

| Year | Club | League | Pos. | G. | AB. | R. | H. | 2B. | 3B. | HR. | RBI. | B.A. | PO. | A. | E. | F.A. |
|---|---|---|---|---|---|---|---|---|---|---|---|---|---|---|---|---|
| 1975—Chicago ...........Amer. | | | OF | 133 | 471 | 73 | 129 | 21 | 7 | 9 | 45 | .274 | 222 | 4 | 2 | *.991 |
| 1976—Chicago x .........Amer. | | | DH-OF | 107 | 311 | 42 | 79 | 20 | 3 | 5 | 34 | .254 | 37 | 1 | 2 | .950 |
| Major League Totals ...................... | | | | 960 | 3276 | 461 | 868 | 139 | 33 | 42 | 262 | .265 | 1376 | 52 | 35 | .976 |

†In military service from beginning of season through May 14.
‡Selected by Kansas City Royals from Minnesota Twins in expansion draft, October 15, 1968.
§Traded with Pitcher Don O'Riley to Chicago White Sox for First Baseman-Catcher Gail Hopkins and Out-fielder-First Baseman John Matias, October 13, 1970.
xTraded to Baltimore Orioles for Catcher Dave Duncan, November 18, 1976.

ALL-STAR GAME RECORD

| Year | League | Pos. | AB. | R. | H. | 2B. | 3B. | HR. | RBI. | B.A. | PO. | A. | E. | F.A. |
|---|---|---|---|---|---|---|---|---|---|---|---|---|---|---|
| 1973—American .......................... | | PH | 1 | 0 | 0 | 0 | 0 | 0 | 0 | .000 | 0 | 0 | 0 | .000 |

## STEVEN F. KEMP
### (Steve)

Born August 7, 1954, at San Angelo, Tex.
Height, 6.00. Weight, 195.
Throws and bats lefthanded.
Hobbies—Fishing, golf and most sports.
Attended University of Southern California, Los Angeles, Calif.
Received reported $50,000 bonus to sign with Detroit Tigers, 1976.

| Year | Club | League | Pos. | G. | AB. | R. | H. | 2B. | 3B. | HR. | RBI. | B.A. | PO. | A. | E. | F.A. |
|---|---|---|---|---|---|---|---|---|---|---|---|---|---|---|---|---|
| 1976—Montgomery ......South. | | | OF-1B | 73 | 256 | 41 | 74 | 17 | 2 | 8 | 43 | .289 | 91 | 4 | 2 | .979 |
| 1976—Evansville ........A.A. | | | OF | 52 | 171 | 37 | 66 | 14 | 3 | 11 | 38 | .386 | 91 | 2 | 5 | .945 |

Listed on Detroit Tigers' 1977 spring roster.

## FRED LYN KENDALL

Born January 31, 1949, at Torrance, Calif.
Height, 6.01. Weight, 185.
Throws and bats righthanded.
Hobby—Fishing.
Led Northern League in passed balls with 22 in 1967 and led Southern League with 21 in 1968.
Tied for Northern League lead in double plays by catchers with 6 in 1967 and tied for Eastern League lead with 8 in 1969.

| Year | Club | League | Pos. | G. | AB. | R. | H. | 2B. | 3B. | HR. | RBI. | B.A. | PO. | A. | E. | F.A. |
|---|---|---|---|---|---|---|---|---|---|---|---|---|---|---|---|---|
| 1967—Sioux Falls .......North. | | | C | 63 | 216 | 20 | 65 | 11 | 2 | 2 | 32 | .301 | *491 | *46 | 8 | *.985 |
| 1968—Asheville† .........South. | | | *C-O-1 | 117 | 395 | 38 | 115 | 13 | 2 | 7 | 50 | .291 | *726 | 57 | 6 | .992 |
| 1969—Elmira .............East. | | | *C-O-1 | 136 | 456 | 52 | 128 | 16 | 4 | 10 | 61 | .281 | *743 | *82 | 10 | *.988 |
| 1969—San Diego .........Nat. | | | C | 10 | 26 | 2 | 4 | 0 | 0 | 0 | 0 | .154 | 37 | 5 | 0 | 1.000 |
| 1970—Salt Lake City ..P.C. | | | C-1-3 | 115 | 391 | 49 | 120 | 14 | 2 | 9 | 48 | .307 | 729 | 52 | 4 | .995 |
| 1970—San Diego .........Nat. | | | C-1-O | 4 | 9 | 0 | 0 | 0 | 0 | 0 | 1 | .000 | 7 | 1 | 0 | 1.000 |
| 1971—Hawaii .............P.C. | | | C-1-O | 11 | 34 | 6 | 11 | 3 | 1 | 1 | 6 | .324 | 56 | 3 | 1 | .983 |
| 1971—San Diego .........Nat. | | | C-1-3 | 49 | 111 | 2 | 19 | 1 | 0 | 1 | 7 | .171 | 184 | 14 | 0 | 1.000 |
| 1972—San Diego .........Nat. | | | C-1B | 91 | 273 | 18 | 59 | 3 | 4 | 6 | 18 | .216 | 506 | 41 | 3 | .995 |
| 1973—San Diego .........Nat. | | | C | 145 | 507 | 39 | 143 | 22 | 3 | 10 | 59 | .282 | 749 | 64 | 13 | .984 |
| 1974—San Diego .........Nat. | | | C | 141 | 424 | 32 | 98 | 15 | 2 | 8 | 45 | .231 | 631 | 64 | 12 | .983 |
| 1975—San Diego .........Nat. | | | C | 103 | 286 | 16 | 57 | 12 | 1 | 0 | 24 | .199 | 337 | 38 | 9 | .977 |
| 1976—San Diego‡ .......Nat. | | | C | 146 | 456 | 30 | 112 | 17 | 0 | 2 | 39 | .246 | 582 | 54 | 4 | .994 |
| Major League Totals ...................... | | | | 689 | 2092 | 139 | 492 | 70 | 10 | 27 | 193 | .235 | 3033 | 281 | 41 | .988 |

†Recalled by Cincinnati Reds; selected by San Diego Padres from Cincinnati in expansion draft, October 14, 1968.
‡Traded with Outfielder Johnny Grubb and Shortstop Hector Torres to Cleveland Indians for Outfielder George Hendrick, December 8, 1976.

## MATTHEW LON KEOUGH
### (Matt)

Born July 3, 1955, at Pomona, Calif.
Height, 6.03. Weight, 190.
Throws and bats righthanded.
Hobbies—Hunting and golfing.
Attended University of California Los Angeles, Los Angeles, Calif.
Son of Marty Keough, outfielder with Boston Red Sox' and Cincinnati Reds' organizations, 1952-66, and scout for San Diego Padres' organization, 1967-1976; nephew of Joe Keough, outfielder with Oakland A's and Kansas City Royals' organizations, 1966-72.
Tied for California League lead in sacrifice flies with 9 in 1975.

| Year | Club | League | Pos. | G. | AB. | R. | H. | 2B. | 3B. | HR. | RBI. | B.A. | PO. | A. | E. | F.A. |
|---|---|---|---|---|---|---|---|---|---|---|---|---|---|---|---|---|
| 1974—Burlington ........Midw. | | | SS-1B | 98 | 323 | 31 | 64 | 14 | 2 | 4 | 24 | .198 | 143 | 207 | 34 | .911 |
| 1975—Modesto ...........Calif. | | | SS-3B | 123 | 445 | 73 | 135 | 34 | 2 | 13 | 81 | .303 | 191 | 312 | *57 | .898 |
| 1976—Chattanooga ......South. | | | 3B-SS-1B | 124 | 420 | 43 | 88 | 13 | 3 | 6 | 52 | .210 | *123 | *274 | 25 | .941 |

Listed on Oakland A's 1977 spring roster.

## JAMES LESTER KERN
### (Jim)
Born March 15, 1949, at Gladwin, Mich.
Height, 6.05. Weight, 195.
Throws and bats righthanded.
Hobbies—Hunting, fishing and fly-tying.
Attended Delta Junior College, University Center, Mich., and
Michigan State University, East Lansing, Mich.

Pitched seven-inning, 2-0 no-hit victory against San Jose, May 29, 1971.
Led Western Carolinas League in wild pitches with 25 in 1970 and tied for American Association lead with 17 in 1974.

| Year Club | League | G. | IP. | W. | L. | Pct. | H. | R. | ER. | SO. | BB. | ERA. |
|---|---|---|---|---|---|---|---|---|---|---|---|---|
| 1968—Rock Hill | W. Carol. | 12 | 28 | 0 | 3 | .000 | 29 | 30 | 21 | 25 | 26 | 6.75 |
| 1968—Sarasota Indians | Gulf C | 12 | 45 | 4 | 4 | .500 | 44 | 32 | 19 | 48 | 32 | 3.80 |
| 1969—† | | | | | | (In Military Service) | | | | | | |
| 1970—Reno | California | 4 | 15 | 0 | 0 | .000 | 9 | 12 | 10 | 20 | 20 | 6.00 |
| 1970—Sumter | W. Carol. | 14 | 72 | 5 | 6 | .455 | 57 | 47 | 39 | 71 | 70 | 4.88 |
| 1971—Reno | California | 24 | 100 | 7 | 9 | .438 | 99 | 91 | 73 | 109 | 100 | 6.57 |
| 1972—Elmira | Eastern | 22 | 104 | 3 | 11 | .214 | 87 | 55 | 50 | 90 | 73 | 4.33 |
| 1973—San Antonio | Texas | 25 | 166 | 11 | 7 | .611 | 130 | 76 | 55 | 182 | *129 | 2.98 |
| 1974—Oklahoma City | Am. Assoc. | 25 | 189 | *17 | 7 | .708 | 139 | 63 | 53 | *220 | 104 | 2.52 |
| 1974—Cleveland | American | 4 | 15 | 0 | 1 | .000 | 16 | 9 | 8 | 11 | 14 | 4.80 |
| 1975—Oklahoma City | Am. Assoc. | 3 | 14 | 1 | 1 | .500 | 12 | 10 | 10 | 11 | 11 | 6.43 |
| 1975—Cleveland | American | 13 | 72 | 1 | 2 | .333 | 60 | 31 | 30 | 55 | 45 | 3.75 |
| 1976—Cleveland | American | 50 | 118 | 10 | 7 | .588 | 91 | 38 | 31 | 111 | 50 | 2.36 |
| Major League Totals | | 67 | 205 | 11 | 10 | .524 | 167 | 78 | 69 | 177 | 109 | 3.03 |

†On military list, May 11, 1969 through January 7, 1970.


## JOSEPH THOMAS KERRIGAN
Born November 30, 1954, at Philadelphia, Pa.
Height, 6.05. Weight, 205.
Throws and bats righthanded.
Hobby—Baseball memorabilia.
Attended Temple University, Philadelphia, Pa.
Brother of Tom Kerrigan, catcher in Philadelphia Phillies' organization, 1963

| Year Club | League | G. | IP. | W. | L. | Pct. | H. | R. | ER. | SO. | BB. | ERA. |
|---|---|---|---|---|---|---|---|---|---|---|---|---|
| 1974—Kinston | Carolina | 36 | 128 | 4 | 10 | .286 | 166 | 97 | 66 | 83 | 52 | 4.64 |
| 1975—W. Palm Beach | Fla. St. | 22 | 23 | 0 | 2 | .000 | 24 | 7 | 7 | 24 | 11 | 2.74 |
| 1975—Quebec City | Eastern | 27 | 53 | 6 | 2 | .750 | 38 | 11 | 4 | 28 | 15 | 0.68 |
| 1976—Denver | Am. Assoc. | 22 | 32 | 2 | 0 | 1.000 | 26 | 13 | 12 | 13 | 12 | 3.38 |
| 1976—Montreal | National | 38 | 57 | 2 | 6 | .250 | 63 | 27 | 24 | 22 | 23 | 3.79 |
| Major League Totals | | 38 | 57 | 2 | 6 | .250 | 63 | 27 | 24 | 22 | 23 | 3.79 |


## DONALD EULON KESSINGER
### (Don)
Born July 17, 1942, at Forrest City, Ark.
Height, 6.01. Weight, 170.
Throws right and bats left and righthanded.
Attended University of Mississippi, University, Miss.; received Bachelor of Science
degree in Business Administration.

Tied National League record for most consecutive errorless games by a shortstop, season, 54, April 14 through June 15, first game, 1969 (274 chances accepted).
Led National League shortstops in double plays with 97 in 1968, 101 in 1969 and 109 in 1973; tied for lead with 97 in 1971.
Made six hits in one game, June 17, 1971, 10 innings.
Named shortstop on THE SPORTING NEWS National League All-Star Team, 1968-69-70.
Named shortstop on THE SPORTING NEWS National League All-Star fielding team, 1969-70.
Received reported $25,000 bonus to sign with Chicago Cubs, 1964.

| Year Club | League | Pos. | G. | AB. | R. | H. | 2B. | 3B. | HR. | RBI. | B.A. | PO. | A. | E. | F.A. |
|---|---|---|---|---|---|---|---|---|---|---|---|---|---|---|---|
| 1964—Fort Worth | Texas | SS | 77 | 280 | 28 | 66 | 6 | 2 | 0 | 12 | .236 | 130 | 232 | 28 | .928 |
| 1964—Chicago | Nat. | SS | 4 | 12 | 1 | 2 | 0 | 0 | 0 | 0 | .167 | 3 | 7 | 0 | 1.000 |
| 1965—Dal.-Ft. Worth | Texas | SS | 46 | 193 | 34 | 55 | 6 | 3 | 0 | 14 | .285 | 96 | 152 | 13 | .950 |
| 1965—Chicago | Nat. | SS | 106 | 309 | 19 | 62 | 4 | 3 | 0 | 14 | .201 | 176 | 338 | *28 | .948 |
| 1966—Chicago | Nat. | SS | 150 | 533 | 50 | 146 | 8 | 2 | 1 | 43 | .274 | 202 | *474 | 35 | .951 |
| 1967—Chicago | Nat. | SS | 145 | 580 | 61 | 134 | 10 | 7 | 0 | 42 | .231 | 215 | 457 | 19 | .973 |
| 1968—Chicago | Nat. | SS | 160 | 655 | 63 | 157 | 14 | 7 | 1 | 32 | .240 | 263 | *573 | *33 | .962 |
| 1969—Chicago | Nat. | SS | 158 | 664 | 109 | 181 | 38 | 6 | 4 | 53 | .273 | *266 | *542 | 20 | *.976 |
| 1970—Chicago | Nat. | SS | 154 | 631 | 100 | 168 | 21 | 14 | 1 | 39 | .266 | 257 | *501 | 22 | .972 |
| 1971—Chicago | Nat. | SS | 155 | 617 | 77 | 159 | 18 | 6 | 2 | 38 | .258 | 263 | 512 | 27 | .966 |
| 1972—Chicago | Nat. | SS | 149 | 577 | 77 | 158 | 20 | 6 | 1 | 39 | .274 | 259 | 504 | 28 | .965 |
| 1973—Chicago | Nat. | SS | 160 | 577 | 52 | 151 | 22 | 3 | 0 | 43 | .262 | *274 | 526 | 30 | .964 |
| 1974—Chicago | Nat. | SS | 153 | 599 | 83 | 155 | 20 | 7 | 1 | 42 | .259 | *259 | 476 | 32 | .958 |
| 1975—Chicago† | Nat. | SS-3B | 154 | 601 | 77 | 146 | 26 | 10 | 0 | 46 | .243 | 210 | 464 | 24 | .966 |
| 1976—St. Louis | Nat. | S-2-3 | 145 | 502 | 55 | 120 | 22 | 6 | 1 | 40 | .239 | 266 | 435 | 24 | .967 |
| Major League Totals | | | 1793 | 6857 | 824 | 1739 | 223 | 77 | 12 | 471 | .254 | 2913 | 5809 | 322 | .964 |

†Traded to St. Louis Cardinals for Pitcher Mike Garman and a player to be named later, October 27, 1975; Cubs obtained Infielder Bobby Hrapmann from Cardinals, April 5, 1976, to complete deal.

## ALL-STAR GAME RECORD

| Year League | Pos. | AB. | R. | H. | 2B. | 3B. | HR. | RBI. | B.A. | PO. | A. | E. | F.A. |
|---|---|---|---|---|---|---|---|---|---|---|---|---|---|
| 1968–National | SS | 2 | 0 | 0 | 0 | 0 | 0 | 0 | .000 | 1 | 2 | 0 | 1.000 |
| 1969–National | SS | 3 | 0 | 0 | 0 | 0 | 0 | 0 | .000 | 0 | 0 | 0 | .000 |
| 1970–National | SS | 2 | 0 | 2 | 0 | 0 | 0 | 0 | 1.000 | 0 | 0 | 0 | .000 |
| 1971–National | SS | 2 | 0 | 0 | 0 | 0 | 0 | 0 | .000 | 1 | 1 | 0 | 1.000 |
| 1972–National | SS | 2 | 0 | 0 | 0 | 0 | 0 | 0 | .000 | 0 | 0 | 0 | .000 |
| 1974–National | SS | 1 | 1 | 1 | 0 | 1 | 0 | 1 | 1.000 | 1 | 0 | 0 | 1.000 |
| All-Star Game Totals | | 12 | 1 | 3 | 0 | 1 | 0 | 1 | .250 | 3 | 3 | 0 | 1.000 |

## BRUCE EDWARD KIMM

Born June 29, 1951, at Norway, Ia.
Height, 5.11. Weight, 175.
Throws and bats righthanded.
Attended University of Iowa, Iowa City, Ia.
Led Northern League catchers in double plays with 8 in 1970.

| Year Club League | Pos. | G. | AB. | R. | H. | 2B. | 3B. | HR. | RBI. | B.A. | PO. | A. | E. | F.A. |
|---|---|---|---|---|---|---|---|---|---|---|---|---|---|---|
| 1969–Sarasota W.S.....G.C. | C-OF | 36 | 84 | 9 | 26 | 2 | 0 | 1 | 12 | .310 | 145 | 17 | 5 | .970 |
| 1970–Appleton............Midw. | C | 3 | 8 | 0 | 1 | 0 | 0 | 0 | 0 | .125 | 32 | 1 | 0 | 1.000 |
| 1970–Duluth-Superior North | C | 64 | 238 | 50 | 64 | 12 | 1 | 3 | 43 | .269 | ★571 | ★54 | 6 | ★.990 |
| 1971–Appleton† .........Midw. | C | 54 | 168 | 18 | 28 | 3 | 3 | 2 | 15 | .167 | 440 | 23 | 10 | .979 |
| 1972–Knoxville ..........South. | C | 119 | 353 | 51 | 91 | 5 | 3 | 9 | 55 | .258 | 683 | 56 | 15 | .980 |
| 1972–Tucson‡§ .........P.C. | C | 10 | 19 | 1 | 3 | 1 | 0 | 0 | 0 | .158 | 27 | 2 | 1 | .967 |
| 1973–Montgomery......South. | C-O-2 | 74 | 220 | 33 | 56 | 13 | 4 | 1 | 36 | .255 | 327 | 33 | 9 | .976 |
| 1973–Toledo ..............Int. | C-1-3 | 24 | 62 | 6 | 14 | 2 | 0 | 1 | 7 | .226 | 139 | 13 | 3 | .981 |
| 1974–Montgomery......South. | C | 33 | 111 | 22 | 24 | 2 | 0 | 2 | 14 | .216 | 198 | 16 | 2 | .991 |
| 1974–Evansville ........A.A. | C-OF | 64 | 200 | 27 | 56 | 7 | 5 | 2 | 25 | .280 | 291 | 37 | 4 | .988 |
| 1975–Evansville ........A.A. | ●C-O-1 | 92 | 268 | 35 | 63 | 11 | 2 | 1 | 21 | .235 | 369 | 43 | ●14 | .967 |
| 1975–Tucson ..............P.C. | C | 5 | 15 | 3 | 2 | 0 | 0 | 0 | 0 | .133 | 21 | 5 | 1 | .963 |
| 1976–Evansville ........A.A. | C | 2 | 6 | 1 | 2 | 1 | 0 | 1 | 1 | .333 | 21 | 0 | 0 | 1.000 |
| 1976–Detroit ..............Amer. | C-DH | 63 | 152 | 13 | 40 | 8 | 0 | 1 | 6 | .263 | 256 | 33 | 9 | .970 |
| Major League Totals | | 63 | 152 | 13 | 40 | 8 | 0 | 1 | 6 | .263 | 256 | 33 | 9 | .970 |

†On disabled list, April 25 to June 11, 1971.
‡Traded by Chicago White Sox to California Angels, September 1, 1972, to complete deal in which White Sox obtained Pitcher Eddie Fisher from Angels for Infielder Bruce Miller, August 17, 1972.
§Traded by California Angels' organization to Detroit Tigers' organization for Outfielder Robert Brooks, March 25, 1973.
xOption transferred to Tucson, June 2, 1975.

## DAVID ARTHUR KINGMAN
### (Dave)

Born December 21, 1948, at Pendleton, Ore.
Height, 6.06. Weight, 210.
Throws and bats righthanded.
Hobbies–Hunting and fishing.
Attended Harper College, Palatine, Ill., and University of Southern California, Los Angeles, Calif.

| Year Club League | Pos. | G. | AB. | R. | H. | 2B. | 3B. | HR. | RBI. | B.A. | PO. | A. | E. | F.A. |
|---|---|---|---|---|---|---|---|---|---|---|---|---|---|---|
| 1970–Amarillo............Texas | 1B-OF | 60 | 210 | 41 | 62 | 9 | 1 | 15 | 41 | .295 | 226 | 9 | 9 | .963 |
| 1971–Phoenix ............P. C. | OF-1B | 105 | 392 | 89 | 109 | 29 | 5 | 26 | 99 | .278 | 785 | 40 | 8 | .990 |
| 1971–San Francisco ..Nat. | 1B-OF | 41 | 115 | 17 | 32 | 10 | 2 | 6 | 24 | .278 | 168 | 0 | 4 | .978 |
| 1972–San Francisco ..Nat. | 3-1-OF | 135 | 472 | 65 | 106 | 17 | 4 | 29 | 83 | .225 | 496 | 159 | 22 | .968 |
| 1973–San Francisco ..Nat. | 3-1-P | 112 | 305 | 54 | 62 | 10 | 1 | 24 | 55 | .203 | 313 | 146 | 22 | .954 |
| 1974–San Francisco† ..Nat. | ★1-3-O | 121 | 350 | 41 | 78 | 18 | 2 | 18 | 55 | .223 | 696 | 98 | ★25 | .969 |
| 1975–New York..........Nat. | O-1-3 | 134 | 502 | 65 | 116 | 22 | 1 | 36 | 88 | .231 | 526 | 69 | 14 | .977 |
| 1976–New York‡ ........Nat. | OF-1B | 123 | 474 | 70 | 113 | 14 | 1 | 37 | 86 | .238 | 293 | 18 | 9 | .972 |
| Major League Totals | | 666 | 2218 | 312 | 507 | 91 | 11 | 150 | 391 | .228 | 2492 | 499 | 96 | .969 |

†Sold to New York Mets for an estimated $125,000, February 28, 1975.
‡On disabled list, July 20 to August 27, 1976.

## CHAMPIONSHIP SERIES RECORD

| Year Club League | Pos. | G. | AB. | R. | H. | 2B. | 3B. | HR. | RBI. | B.A. | PO. | A. | E. | F.A. |
|---|---|---|---|---|---|---|---|---|---|---|---|---|---|---|
| 1971–San Francisco ..Nat. | PH-OF | 4 | 9 | 0 | 1 | 0 | 0 | 0 | 0 | .111 | 5 | 0 | 0 | 1.000 |

## ALL-STAR GAME RECORD

| Year League | Pos. | AB. | R. | H. | 2B. | 3B. | HR. | RBI. | B.A. | PO. | A. | E. | F.A. |
|---|---|---|---|---|---|---|---|---|---|---|---|---|---|
| 1976–National | OF | 2 | 0 | 0 | 0 | 0 | 0 | 0 | .000 | 1 | 0 | 0 | 1.000 |

## PITCHING RECORD

| Year Club League | G. | IP. | W. | L. | Pct. | H. | R. | ER. | SO. | BB. | ERA. |
|---|---|---|---|---|---|---|---|---|---|---|---|
| 1973–San Francisco ....................National | 2 | 4 | 0 | 0 | .000 | 3 | 4 | 4 | 4 | 6 | 9.00 |

## CLAYTON LAWS KIRBY, JR.
### (Clay)

Born June 25, 1948, at Washington, D. C.
Height, 6.03. Weight, 175.
Throws and bats righthanded.
Hobby—Building miniature racing cars.
Attended Old Dominion College, Norfolk, Va., and Benjamin
Franklin University, Washington, D. C.
Tied for Gulf Coast League lead in wild pitches with 7 in 1966.

| Year   Club | League | G. | IP. | W. | L. | Pct. | H. | R. | ER. | SO. | BB. | ERA. |
|---|---|---|---|---|---|---|---|---|---|---|---|---|
| 1966—Sarasota Cardinals ............. | Gulf Coast | 9 | 25 | 2 | 3 | .400 | 20 | 20 | 16 | 28 | 14 | 5.76 |
| 1966—St. Petersburg.................... | Florida St. | 3 | 20 | 3 | 0 | 1.000 | 9 | 2 | 2 | 23 | 4 | 0.90 |
| 1967—Modesto ........................... | California | 16 | 74 | 3 | 4 | .429 | 63 | 39 | 36 | 75 | 31 | 4.38 |
| 1968—Arkansas........................... | Texas | 10 | 67 | 5 | 3 | .625 | 51 | 20 | 16 | 59 | 26 | 2.15 |
| 1968—Tulsa†............................... | P. Coast | 19 | 108 | 7 | 6 | .538 | 88 | 49 | 41 | 93 | 60 | 3.42 |
| 1969—San Diego ........................ | National | 35 | 216 | 7 | *20 | .259 | 204 | 108 | 91 | 113 | 100 | 3.79 |
| 1970—San Diego ........................ | National | 36 | 215 | 10 | 16 | .385 | 198 | 118 | 108 | 154 | 120 | 4.52 |
| 1971—San Diego ........................ | National | 38 | 267 | 15 | 13 | .536 | 213 | 99 | 84 | 231 | 103 | 2.83 |
| 1972—San Diego ........................ | National | 34 | 239 | 12 | 14 | .462 | 197 | 87 | 83 | 175 | 116 | 3.13 |
| 1973—San Diego‡ ........................ | National | 34 | 192 | 8 | 18 | .308 | 214 | 122 | 102 | 129 | 66 | 4.78 |
| 1974—Cincinnati ........................ | National | 36 | 231 | 12 | 9 | .571 | 210 | 97 | 84 | 160 | 91 | 3.27 |
| 1975—Cincinnati§ ........................ | National | 26 | 111 | 10 | 6 | .625 | 113 | 63 | 58 | 48 | 54 | 4.70 |
| 1976—Montreal x ........................ | National | 22 | 79 | 1 | 8 | .111 | 81 | 61 | 50 | 51 | 63 | 5.70 |
| Major League Totals ..................... | | 261 | 1550 | 75 | 104 | .419 | 1430 | 755 | 660 | 1061 | 713 | 3.83 |

†Recalled by St. Louis Cardinals; selected by San Diego Padres from St. Louis in expansion draft, October 14, 1968.

‡Traded to Cincinnati Reds for Outfielder Bobby Tolan and Pitcher Dave Tomlin, November 9, 1973.
§Traded to Montreal Expos for Outfielder-Third Baseman Bob Bailey, December 12, 1975.
xUnconditionally released, December 2, 1976; signed as free agent by San Diego Padres.
Invited to San Diego Padres' 1977 spring camp.


## EDGAR LEON KIRKPATRICK
### (Ed)

Born October 8, 1944, at Spokane, Wash.
Height, 6.00. Weight, 199.
Throws right and bats lefthanded.
Hobby—Music.
Tied for American League lead in double plays by catchers with 12 in 1970.
Received reported $20,000 bonus to sign with Los Angeles Angels, 1962.

| Year   Club | League | Pos. | G. | AB. | R. | H. | 2B. | 3B. | HR. | RBI. | B.A. | PO. | A. | E. | F.A. |
|---|---|---|---|---|---|---|---|---|---|---|---|---|---|---|---|
| 1962—San Diego......... | Calif. | C-2B | 19 | 48 | 8 | 17 | 3 | 0 | 3 | 7 | .354 | 120 | 5 | 3 | .977 |
| 1962—Quad Cities ...... | Midw. | C | 45 | 168 | 35 | 64 | 10 | 7 | 9 | 62 | .381 | 333 | 30 | 8 | .978 |
| 1962—Los Angeles ...... | Amer. | C | 3 | 6 | 0 | 0 | 0 | 0 | 0 | 0 | .000 | 10 | 0 | 0 | 1.000 |
| 1963—Los Angeles......Amer. | | C-OF | 34 | 77 | 4 | 15 | 5 | 0 | 2 | 7 | .195 | 82 | 5 | 1 | .989 |
| 1963—Nashville ......... | Sally | OF-C | 47 | 165 | 16 | 50 | 6 | 4 | 6 | 30 | .303 | 125 | 8 | 5 | .964 |
| 1963—Hawaii ............. | P. C. | C-O-3-1 | 49 | 142 | 28 | 50 | 5 | 2 | 8 | 31 | .352 | 219 | 25 | 4 | .984 |
| 1964—Los Angeles ......Amer. | | OF | 75 | 219 | 20 | 53 | 13 | 3 | 2 | 22 | .242 | 90 | 3 | 3 | .969 |
| 1964—Hawaii ............. | P. C. | O-1B-C | 45 | 138 | 19 | 30 | 5 | 0 | 6 | 16 | .217 | 110 | 4 | 3 | .974 |
| 1965—Seattle ............. | P. C. | O-3-1-C | 141 | 508 | 73 | 148 | 29 | 5 | 20 | 82 | .291 | 300 | 75 | 17 | .957 |
| 1965—California.......... | Amer. | OF | 19 | 73 | 8 | 19 | 5 | 0 | 3 | 8 | .260 | 28 | 3 | 1 | .969 |
| 1966—California.......... | Amer. | OF-1B | 117 | 312 | 31 | 60 | 7 | 4 | 9 | 44 | .192 | 169 | 5 | 1 | .994 |
| 1967—Seattle ............. | P. C. | C-OF | 120 | 419 | 48 | 95 | 14 | 0 | 15 | 54 | .227 | 529 | 42 | 10 | .983 |
| 1967—California.......... | Amer. | C-O | 3 | 8 | 0 | 0 | 0 | 0 | 0 | 0 | .000 | 4 | 0 | 0 | 1.000 |
| 1967—Jacksonville ......Int. | | 1B-OF | 17 | 50 | 5 | 7 | 3 | 0 | 1 | 3 | .140 | 103 | 3 | 0 | 1.000 |
| 1968—California†........Am. | | O-C-1B | 89 | 161 | 23 | 37 | 4 | 0 | 1 | 15 | .230 | 62 | 5 | 3 | .957 |
| 1969—Kansas City ......Am. | | O-C-IF | 120 | 315 | 40 | 81 | 11 | 4 | 14 | 49 | .257 | 204 | 13 | 1 | .995 |
| 1970—Kansas City ......Amer. | | *C-O-1 | 134 | 424 | 59 | 97 | 17 | 2 | 18 | 62 | .229 | 626 | 70 | *12 | .983 |
| 1971—Kansas City .....Amer. | | OF-C | 120 | 365 | 46 | 80 | 12 | 1 | 9 | 46 | .219 | 412 | 30 | 8 | .982 |
| 1972—Kansas City ......Amer. | | C-1 | 113 | 364 | 43 | 100 | 15 | 1 | 9 | 43 | .275 | 590 | 49 | 6 | .991 |
| 1973—Kansas City‡ ....Amer. | | OF-C | 126 | 429 | 61 | 113 | 24 | 3 | 6 | 45 | .263 | 264 | 11 | 4 | .986 |
| 1974—Pittsburgh ........Nat. | | 1-O-C | 116 | 271 | 32 | 67 | 9 | 0 | 6 | 38 | .247 | 561 | 32 | 6 | .990 |
| 1975—Pittsburgh ........Nat. | | 1B-OF | 89 | 144 | 15 | 34 | 5 | 0 | 5 | 16 | .236 | 167 | 9 | 0 | 1.000 |
| 1976—Pittsburgh ........Nat. | | 1-O-3-PH | 83 | 146 | 14 | 34 | 9 | 0 | 0 | 16 | .233 | 205 | 17 | 4 | .982 |
| American League Totals ................ | | 953 | 2753 | 335 | 655 | 113 | 18 | 73 | 341 | .238 | 2541 | 194 | 40 | .986 |
| National League Totals ................. | | 288 | 561 | 61 | 135 | 23 | 0 | 11 | 70 | .241 | 933 | 58 | 10 | .990 |
| Major League Totals ..................... | | 1241 | 3324 | 396 | 790 | 136 | 18 | 84 | 411 | .238 | 3474 | 252 | 50 | .987 |

†Traded with Catcher Dennis Paepke to Kansas City Royals for Pitcher Hoyt Wilhelm, December 12, 1968.
‡Traded with Infielder Kurt Bevacqua and First Baseman Winston Cole to Pittsburgh Pirates for Pitcher Nelson Briles and Infielder Fernando Gonzalez, December 4, 1973.

### CHAMPIONSHIP SERIES RECORD

| Year   Club | League | Pos. | G. | AB. | R. | H. | 2B. | 3B. | HR. | RBI. | B.A. | PO. | A. | E. | F.A. |
|---|---|---|---|---|---|---|---|---|---|---|---|---|---|---|---|
| 1974—Pittsburgh .......Nat. | | 1B | 3 | 9 | 0 | 0 | 0 | 0 | 0 | 0 | .000 | 22 | 0 | 0 | 1.000 |
| 1975—Pittsburgh .......Nat. | | PH | 2 | 2 | 0 | 0 | 0 | 0 | 0 | 0 | .000 | 0 | 0 | 0 | .000 |
| Championship Series Totals ........... | | 5 | 11 | 0 | 0 | 0 | 0 | 0 | 0 | .000 | 22 | 0 | 0 | 1.000 |

## DONALD PAUL KIRKWOOD
### (Don)

Born September 24, 1949, at Pontiac, Mich.
Height, 6.03. Weight, 185.
Throws and bats righthanded.
Hobbies—Hunting and fishing.
Attended Oakland Community College, Auburn Heights, Mich., and
Oakland University, Rochester, Mich.
Twin brother of Ron Kirkwood, former minor league pitcher in California Angels' organization.

| Year Club | League | G. | IP. | W. | L. | Pct. | H. | R. | ER. | SO. | BB. | ERA. |
|---|---|---|---|---|---|---|---|---|---|---|---|---|
| 1972–Quad Cities | Midwest | 33 | 77 | 6 | 2 | .750 | 74 | 29 | 24 | 56 | 27 | 2.81 |
| 1973–Salinas | California | 17 | 43 | 3 | 3 | .500 | 31 | 12 | 6 | 35 | 16 | 1.26 |
| 1973–El Paso | Texas | 18 | 48 | 2 | 5 | .286 | 46 | 35 | 22 | 31 | 21 | 4.13 |
| 1974–El Paso | Texas | 35 | 102 | 9 | 4 | .692 | 118 | 50 | 33 | 71 | 39 | 2.91 |
| 1974–California | American | 3 | 7 | 0 | 0 | .000 | 12 | 8 | 7 | 4 | 6 | 9.00 |
| 1975–California | American | 44 | 84 | 6 | 5 | .545 | 85 | 38 | 29 | 49 | 28 | 3.11 |
| 1976–California | American | 28 | 158 | 6 | 12 | .333 | 167 | 91 | 81 | 78 | 57 | 4.61 |
| Major League Totals | | 75 | 249 | 12 | 17 | .414 | 264 | 137 | 117 | 131 | 91 | 4.23 |


## LARRY GRANT KISER

Born July 27, 1949, at Kingsport, Tenn.
Height, 6.04. Weight, 220.
Throws left and bats righthanded.
Hobbies—Hunting, fishing and golf.
Attended University of North Carolina, Chapel Hill, N. C.; received
Bachelor of Science degree in Business Administration.
Led Eastern League in wild pitches with 22 in 1973.

| Year Club | League | G. | IP. | W. | L. | Pct. | H. | R. | ER. | SO. | BB. | ERA. |
|---|---|---|---|---|---|---|---|---|---|---|---|---|
| 1971–Walla Walla† | Northw. | 14 | 88 | 7 | 4 | .636 | 82 | 37 | 28 | 70 | 44 | 2.86 |
| 1972–Spartanburg | W. Carol. | 18 | 131 | 12 | 3 | .800 | 125 | 66 | 48 | 113 | 64 | 3.30 |
| 1972–Burlington | Carolina | 7 | 40 | 2 | 4 | .333 | 35 | 24 | 17 | 44 | 20 | 3.83 |
| 1973–Reading‡ | Eastern | 27 | 139 | 9 | 9 | .500 | 111 | 71 | 51 | 102 | 112 | 3.30 |
| 1974–Toledo | Int'national | 7 | 27 | 1 | 3 | .250 | 24 | 16 | 14 | 17 | 18 | 4.67 |
| 1974–Reading | Eastern | 20 | 129 | 8 | 6 | .571 | 133 | 60 | 49 | 72 | 53 | 3.42 |
| 1975–Reading | Eastern | 12 | 83 | 6 | 5 | .545 | 82 | 45 | 35 | 61 | 37 | 3.80 |
| 1975–Toledo | Int'national | 16 | 99 | 3 | 7 | .300 | 99 | 41 | 31 | 73 | 41 | 2.82 |
| 1976–Oklahoma City§ | Am. Assoc. | 21 | 107 | 4 | 5 | .444 | 107 | 64 | 53 | 64 | 61 | 4.46 |

†Appeared in one game as first baseman.
‡Conditionally released by Philadelphia Phillies to Atlanta Braves, October 26, 1973; returned to Phillies' organization, March 25, 1974.
§On disabled list, August 11 to August 21, 1976.
Listed on Philadelphia Phillies' 1977 spring roster.


## BRUCE EUGENE KISON
Name pronounced Key-son.

Born February 18, 1950, at Pasco, Wash.
Height, 6.05. Weight, 180.
Throws and bats righthanded.
Hobbies—Hunting, fishing, basketball and philately.
Attended Columbia Basin Junior College, Pasco, Wash., Manatee Junior College,
West Bradenton, Fla., and Central Washington State
College, Ellensburgh, Wash.
Led New York-Pennsylvania League in hit batsmen with 13 in 1969, Eastern League with 21 in 1970 and International League with 14 in 1973.

| Year Club | League | G. | IP. | W. | L. | Pct. | H. | R. | ER. | SO. | BB. | ERA. |
|---|---|---|---|---|---|---|---|---|---|---|---|---|
| 1968–Bradenton Pirates | Gulf Coast | 10 | 24 | 2 | 1 | .667 | 24 | 9 | 6 | 9 | 6 | 2.25 |
| 1969–Geneva† | NYP | 13 | 94 | 5 | 2 | .714 | 84 | 48 | 33 | 77 | 39 | 3.16 |
| 1970–Salem | Carolina | 5 | 33 | 3 | 1 | .750 | 17 | 5 | 3 | 26 | 7 | 0.82 |
| 1970–Waterbury | Eastern | 19 | 130 | 10 | 4 | .714 | 93 | 42 | 33 | 82 | 54 | 2.28 |
| 1971–Charleston | Int'national | 12 | 85 | 10 | 1 | .909 | 53 | 29 | 27 | 57 | 38 | 2.86 |
| 1971–Pittsburgh | National | 18 | 95 | 6 | 5 | .545 | 93 | 40 | 36 | 60 | 36 | 3.41 |
| 1972–Pittsburgh‡ | National | 32 | 152 | 9 | 7 | .563 | 123 | 61 | 55 | 102 | 69 | 3.26 |
| 1973–Charleston§ | Int'national | 20 | 114 | 8 | 6 | .571 | 94 | 50 | 50 | 70 | 82 | 3.95 |
| 1973–Pittsburgh | National | 7 | 44 | 3 | 0 | 1.000 | 36 | 17 | 15 | 26 | 24 | 3.07 |
| 1974–Pittsburgh | National | 40 | 129 | 9 | 8 | .529 | 123 | 64 | 50 | 71 | 57 | 3.49 |
| 1975–Pittsburgh | National | 33 | 192 | 12 | 11 | .522 | 160 | 89 | 69 | 89 | 92 | 3.23 |
| 1976–Pittsburgh | National | 31 | 193 | 14 | 9 | .609 | 180 | 83 | 66 | 98 | 52 | 3.08 |
| Major League Totals | | 161 | 805 | 53 | 40 | .570 | 715 | 354 | 291 | 446 | 330 | 3.25 |

†On restricted list, March 13 through June 18.
‡On disabled list, March 29 through April 20.
§On disabled list, June 14 to July 5, 1973.

| Year | Club | League | G. | IP. | W. | L. | Pct. | H. | R. | ER. | SO. | BB. | ERA. |
|------|------|--------|-----|------|-----|-----|-------|-----|-----|-----|-----|-----|------|
| 1971 | Pittsburgh | National | 1 | 4⅔ | 1 | 0 | 1.000 | 2 | 0 | 0 | 3 | 2 | 0.00 |
| 1972 | Pittsburgh | National | 2 | 2⅓ | 1 | 0 | 1.000 | 1 | 0 | 0 | 3 | 0 | 0.00 |
| 1974 | Pittsburgh | National | 1 | 6⅔ | 1 | 0 | 1.000 | 2 | 0 | 0 | 5 | 6 | 0.00 |
| 1975 | Pittsburgh | National | 1 | 2 | 0 | 0 | .000 | 2 | 1 | 1 | 1 | 1 | 4.50 |
| Championship Series Totals | | | 5 | 15⅔ | 3 | 0 | 1.000 | 7 | 1 | 1 | 12 | 9 | 0.57 |

## WORLD SERIES RECORD

| Year | Club | League | G. | IP. | W. | L. | Pct. | H. | R. | ER. | SO. | BB. | ERA. |
|------|------|--------|-----|------|-----|-----|-------|-----|-----|-----|-----|-----|------|
| 1971 | Pittsburgh | National | 2 | 6⅓ | 1 | 0 | 1.000 | 1 | 0 | 0 | 3 | 3 | 0.00 |

## STEVEN JACK KLINE
### (Steve)

Born October 6, 1947, at Wenatchee, Wash.
Height, 6.03. Weight, 200.
Throws and bats righthanded.
Hobby—Fishing.
Attended Washington State University, Pullman, Wash., California State Poly
University, Pomona, Calif., and University of Miami, Coral Gables, Fla.

| Year | Club | League | G. | IP. | W. | L. | Pct. | H. | R. | ER. | SO. | BB. | ERA. |
|------|------|--------|-----|------|-----|-----|-------|-----|-----|-----|-----|-----|------|
| 1966 | Johnson City | Ap'lachian | 2 | 6 | 0 | 0 | .000 | 6 | 2 | 2 | 4 | 1 | 3.00 |
| 1966 | Fort Lauderdale | Florida St. | 12 | 79 | 6 | 6 | .500 | 80 | 36 | 27 | 60 | 10 | 3.08 |
| 1967 | Greensboro† | Carolina | 11 | 71 | 3 | 5 | .375 | 62 | 21 | 17 | 62 | 20 | 2.15 |
| 1968 | Fort Lauderdale | Florida St. | 5 | 30 | 1 | 4 | .200 | 40 | 20 | 13 | 28 | 3 | 3.90 |
| 1968 | Binghamton‡ | Eastern | 14 | 102 | 5 | 6 | .455 | 83 | 31 | 23 | 41 | 23 | 2.03 |
| 1969 | Fort Lauderdale | Florida St. | 2 | 15 | 2 | 0 | 1.000 | 11 | 3 | 2 | 5 | 3 | 1.20 |
| 1969 | Syracuse§ | Int'national | 15 | 54 | 3 | 6 | .333 | 76 | 44 | 42 | 13 | 17 | 7.00 |
| 1970 | Syracuse | Int'national | 11 | 78 | 8 | 2 | .800 | 78 | 27 | 22 | 54 | 13 | 2.54 |
| 1970 | New York | American | 16 | 100 | 6 | 6 | .500 | 99 | 42 | 38 | 49 | 24 | 3.42 |
| 1971 | New York | American | 31 | 222 | 12 | 13 | .480 | 206 | 87 | 73 | 81 | 37 | 2.96 |
| 1972 | New York | American | 32 | 236 | 16 | 9 | .640 | 210 | 79 | 63 | 58 | 44 | 2.40 |
| 1973 | New York x | American | 14 | 74 | 4 | 7 | .364 | 76 | 39 | 33 | 19 | 31 | 4.01 |
| 1974 | New York y-Cleveland z | American | 20 | 97 | 5 | 10 | .333 | 96 | 56 | 50 | 23 | 36 | 4.64 |
| 1975 | Cleveland a | American | | | | | (Did Not Play) | | | | | | |
| 1976 | Toledo b | Int'national | 26 | 157 | 9 | 10 | .474 | 195 | 102 | 88 | 60 | 41 | 5.04 |
| Major League Totals | | | 113 | 729 | 43 | 45 | .489 | 687 | 303 | 257 | 230 | 172 | 3.17 |

†On temporary inactive list, April 17 to June 20, 1967; on disabled list, July 21 to August 12, 1967.
‡On temporary inactive list, May 20 to May 30 and August 10 to August 26, 1968.
§On temporary inactive list, August 1 to August 28, 1969.
xOn disabled list, June 25 to July 28 and August 3 through remainder of season.
yTraded with pitchers Fred Beene, Fritz Peterson and Tom Buskey to Cleveland Indians for First Baseman Chris Chambliss and Pitchers Dick Tidrow and Cecil Upshaw, April 26, 1974.
zOn disabled list, June 28 to July 20 and August 17 to September 10, 1974.
aOn disabled list the entire season.
bSold to Atlanta Braves, December 13, 1976.

## GENE ELLIS KLUTTS
### (Mickey)

Born September 30, 1954, at Montebello, Calif.
Height, 5.11. Weight, 170.
Throws and bats righthanded.

| Year | Club | League | Pos. | G. | AB. | R. | H. | 2B. | 3B. | HR. | RBI. | B.A. | PO. | A. | E. | F.A. |
|------|------|--------|------|-----|------|-----|-----|-----|-----|-----|------|------|-----|-----|-----|------|
| 1972 | Johnson City | Appal. | SS-3B | 54 | 182 | 25 | 46 | 7 | 3 | 3 | 22 | .253 | 54 | 114 | 19 | .898 |
| 1973 | Ft. Lauderdale | Fla.St. | SS-3B | 34 | 94 | 4 | 12 | 1 | 0 | 1 | 9 | .128 | 31 | 57 | 7 | .926 |
| 1973 | Oneonta | NYP | SS-2B | 37 | 135 | 28 | 43 | 7 | 5 | 2 | 22 | .319 | 57 | 107 | 8 | .953 |
| 1974 | Ft. Lauderdale† | Fla.St. | 2B-SS | 85 | 268 | 24 | 61 | 9 | 2 | 5 | 30 | .228 | 101 | 237 | 20 | .944 |
| 1975 | West Haven‡ | East. | 3B-SS | 69 | 221 | 26 | 48 | 10 | 1 | 2 | 23 | .217 | 53 | 180 | 19 | .875 |
| 1976 | Syracuse | Int. | SS-3B | 119 | 430 | 75 | 137 | 22 | 3 | 24 | 80 | .319 | 191 | 293 | 28 | .945 |
| 1976 | New York | Amer. | SS | 2 | 3 | 0 | 0 | 0 | 0 | 0 | 0 | .000 | 4 | 3 | 1 | .875 |
| Major League Totals | | | | 2 | 3 | 0 | 0 | 0 | 0 | 0 | 0 | .000 | 4 | 3 | 1 | .875 |

†On disabled list, May 23 through June 6, 1974.
‡On disabled list, August 2 through September 16, 1975.

## ROBERT CHRISTIAN KNAPP
### (Chris)

Born September 16, 1953, at Cherry Point, N. C.
Height, 6.05. Weight, 200.
Throws and bats righthanded.
Hobby—Carpentry.
Attended Kalamazoo Valley Community College, Kalamazoo, Mich.
and Central Michigan University, Mt. Pleasant, Mich.
Pitched seven inning 3-0, no-hit victory against Evansville, June 13, 1976.

| Year Club | League | G. | IP. | W. | L. | Pct. | H. | R. | ER. | SO. | BB. | ERA. |
|---|---|---|---|---|---|---|---|---|---|---|---|---|
| 1975–Appleton | Midwest | 14 | 87 | 6 | 6 | .500 | 49 | 23 | 19 | 99 | 45 | 1.97 |
| 1975–Chicago | American | 2 | 2 | 0 | 0 | .000 | 2 | 1 | 1 | 3 | 4 | 4.50 |
| 1976–Knoxville | Southern | 11 | 83 | 7 | 3 | .700 | 58 | 26 | 22 | 68 | 42 | 2.39 |
| 1976–Iowa | Am. Assoc. | 11 | 81 | 7 | 2 | .778 | 63 | 24 | 23 | 74 | 28 | 2.56 |
| 1976–Chicago | American | 11 | 52 | 3 | 1 | .750 | 54 | 31 | 28 | 41 | 32 | 4.85 |
| Major League Totals | | 13 | 54 | 3 | 1 | .750 | 56 | 32 | 29 | 44 | 36 | 4.83 |

## ROBERT WESLEY KNEPPER
### (Bob)

Born May 25, 1954, at Akron, O.
Height, 6.03. Weight, 195.
Throws and bats lefthanded.
Hobbies–Hunting, fishing, coin collecting, music and reading.
Led California League pitchers in games started with 30 and tied for lead in complete games with 16 in 1974.
Tied for Pacific Coast League lead in shutouts with 3 in 1976.

| Year Club | League | G. | IP. | W. | L. | Pct. | H. | R. | ER. | SO. | BB. | ERA. |
|---|---|---|---|---|---|---|---|---|---|---|---|---|
| 1972–Great Falls | Pioneer | 12 | 68 | 7 | 1 | .875 | 53 | 20 | 11 | 75 | 19 | 1.46 |
| 1973–Decatur | Midwest | 11 | 79 | 7 | 2 | .778 | 65 | 28 | 17 | 68 | 23 | 1.94 |
| 1973–Fresno | California | 13 | 71 | 2 | 8 | .200 | 78 | 54 | 32 | 66 | 35 | 4.06 |
| 1974–Fresno | California | 30 | *238 | *20 | 5 | •.800 | *239 | 103 | 84 | *247 | 80 | 3.18 |
| 1975–Phoenix | P. Coast | 26 | 155 | 11 | 11 | .500 | 169 | 101 | 79 | 94 | 78 | 4.59 |
| 1976–Phoenix | P. Coast | 29 | 205 | 14 | 10 | .583 | 209 | 105 | 98 | 130 | 64 | 4.30 |
| 1976–San Francisco | National | 4 | 25 | 1 | 2 | .333 | 26 | 9 | 9 | 11 | 7 | 3.24 |
| Major League Totals | | 4 | 25 | 1 | 2 | .333 | 26 | 9 | 9 | 11 | 7 | 3.24 |

## CHARLES RAY KNIGHT
(Known by middle name.)

Born December 28, 1952, at Albany, Ga.
Height, 6.02. Weight, 185.
Throws and bats righthanded.
Hobbies–Hunting, fishing, golfing and chess.
Attended Albany Junior College, Albany, Ga.
Tied for American Association lead in double plays by third basemen with 24 in 1974.

| Year Club | League | Pos. | G. | AB. | R. | H. | 2B. | 3B. | HR. | RBI. | B.A. | PO. | A. | E. | F.A. |
|---|---|---|---|---|---|---|---|---|---|---|---|---|---|---|---|
| 1971–Sioux Falls | North. | O-INF-P | 64 | 239 | 34 | 68 | 5 | 2 | 6 | 31 | .285 | 69 | 79 | 17 | .897 |
| 1972–Three Rivers | East. | O-INF-P | 97 | 302 | 25 | 64 | 8 | 1 | 2 | 35 | .212 | 102 | 142 | 20 | .924 |
| 1973–Three Rivers | East. | O-3-1-2 | 57 | 193 | 41 | 54 | 14 | 2 | 2 | 22 | .280 | 76 | 57 | 7 | .950 |
| 1973–Indianapolis | A.A. | 3-O-1-P | 78 | 253 | 20 | 55 | 10 | 4 | 1 | 16 | .217 | 72 | 126 | 11 | .947 |
| 1974–Indianapolis | A.A. | *3B-OF | 107 | 352 | 36 | 80 | 13 | 4 | 5 | 37 | .227 | 94 | 177 | 11 | *.961 |
| 1974–Cincinnati | Nat. | 3B | 14 | 11 | 1 | 2 | 1 | 0 | 0 | 2 | .182 | 2 | 8 | 0 | 1.000 |
| 1975–Indianapolis | A.A. | *3B-1B | 123 | 434 | 58 | 118 | 16 | 5 | 4 | 48 | .272 | *116 | 227 | 17 | .953 |
| 1976–Indianapolis† | A.A. | 3B-1B | 110 | 396 | 47 | 106 | 24 | 3 | 10 | 41 | .268 | 136 | 181 | 13 | .961 |
| Major League Totals | | | 14 | 11 | 1 | 2 | 1 | 0 | 0 | 2 | .182 | 2 | 8 | 0 | 1.000 |

†On disabled list, June 21 through July 2, 1976.
Listed on Cincinnati Reds' 1977 spring roster.

### PITCHING RECORD

| Year Club | League | G. | IP. | W. | L. | Pct. | H. | R. | ER. | SO. | BB. | ERA. |
|---|---|---|---|---|---|---|---|---|---|---|---|---|
| 1971–Sioux Falls | Northern | 3 | 4 | 1 | 1 | .500 | 5 | 6 | 5 | 4 | 5 | 11.25 |
| 1972–Three Rivers | Eastern | 2 | 4 | 0 | 0 | .000 | 3 | 1 | 1 | 2 | 4 | 2.25 |
| 1973–Indianapolis | Am. Assoc. | 1 | 2 | 0 | 0 | .000 | 2 | 1 | 1 | 0 | 4 | 4.50 |

## DAROLD DUANE KNOWLES

Born December 9, 1941, at Brunswick, Mo.
Height, 6.00. Weight, 185.
Throws and bats lefthanded.
Hobbies–Golf and hunting.
Attended University of Missouri, Columbia, Mo.
Pitched six-inning, 3-0 no-hit loss against San Jose, June 15, 1962.
Led Northern League in hit batsmen with 12 in 1961.

| Year Club | League | G. | IP. | W. | L. | Pct. | H. | R. | ER. | SO. | BB. | ERA. |
|---|---|---|---|---|---|---|---|---|---|---|---|---|
| 1961–Aberdeen | Northern | 23 | 164 | 11 | 5 | .688 | 118 | 79 | 60 | *183 | 106 | 3.29 |
| 1962–Elmira | Eastern | 2 | 9 | 0 | 1 | .000 | 6 | 5 | 4 | 5 | 6 | 4.00 |
| 1962–Charlotte | Sally | 6 | 7 | 0 | 1 | .000 | 9 | 7 | 1 | 4 | 9 | 1.29 |
| 1962–Stockton | California | 23 | 161 | 12 | 7 | .632 | 117 | 60 | 41 | 202 | 80 | *2.29 |
| 1963–Elmira | Eastern | 30 | *201 | •16 | 7 | .696 | 180 | 67 | 61 | 146 | 60 | 2.73 |
| 1964–Rochester | Int'national | 37 | 136 | 6 | 7 | .462 | 130 | 58 | 46 | 104 | 61 | 3.04 |
| 1965–Baltimore | American | 5 | 15 | 0 | 1 | .000 | 14 | 15 | 15 | 12 | 10 | 9.00 |
| 1965–Rochester† | Int'national | 32 | 174 | 11 | 5 | .688 | 160 | 59 | 49 | 155 | 64 | 2.53 |
| 1966–Philadelphia‡ | National | 69 | 100 | 6 | 5 | .545 | 98 | 38 | 34 | 88 | 46 | 3.06 |
| 1967–Washington | American | 61 | 113 | 6 | 8 | .429 | 91 | 37 | 34 | 85 | 52 | 2.71 |
| 1968–Washington§ | American | 32 | 41 | 1 | 1 | .500 | 38 | 11 | 10 | 37 | 12 | 2.20 |
| 1969–Washington | American | 53 | 84 | 9 | 2 | .818 | 73 | 25 | 21 | 59 | 31 | 2.25 |
| 1970–Washington | American | 71 | 119 | 2 | 14 | .125 | 100 | 36 | 27 | 71 | 58 | 2.04 |

| Year Club | League | G. | IP. | W. | L. | Pct. | H. | R. | ER. | SO. | BB. | ERA. |
|---|---|---|---|---|---|---|---|---|---|---|---|---|
| 1971–Wash. x-Oak. | American | 55 | 68 | 7 | 4 | .636 | 57 | 28 | 27 | 56 | 22 | 3.57 |
| 1972–Oakland y | American | 54 | 66 | 5 | 1 | .833 | 49 | 12 | 10 | 36 | 37 | 1.36 |
| 1973–Oakland | American | 52 | 99 | 6 | 8 | .429 | 87 | 44 | 34 | 46 | 49 | 3.09 |
| 1974–Oakland z | American | 45 | 53 | 3 | 3 | .500 | 61 | 29 | 25 | 18 | 35 | 4.25 |
| 1975–Chicago | National | 58 | 88 | 6 | 9 | .400 | 107 | 61 | 57 | 63 | 36 | 5.83 |
| 1976–Chicago a | National | 58 | 72 | 5 | 7 | .417 | 61 | 30 | 23 | 39 | 22 | 2.88 |
| National League Totals | | 185 | 260 | 17 | 21 | .447 | 266 | 129 | 114 | 190 | 104 | 3.95 |
| American League Totals | | 428 | 658 | 39 | 42 | .481 | 570 | 237 | 203 | 420 | 306 | 2.78 |
| Major League Totals | | 613 | 918 | 56 | 63 | .470 | 836 | 366 | 317 | 610 | 410 | 3.11 |

†Recalled by Baltimore Orioles and traded with Outfielder Jackie Brandt to Philadelphia Phillies for Pitcher Jack Baldschun, December 6, 1965.

‡Traded with cash to Washington Senators for Outfielder Don Lock, November 30, 1966.

§In Military service from July 14 through end of season.

xTraded with First Baseman Mike Epstein to Oakland A's for First Baseman Don Mincher, Catcher Frank Fernandez and Pitcher Paul Lindblad, May 8, 1971.

yOn disabled list from September 29 through the end of the season.

zTraded with Pitcher Bob Locker and Second Baseman Manny Trillo to Chicago Cubs for Outfielder-First Baseman Billy Williams, October 23, 1974.

aTraded to Texas Rangers for Outfielder Gene Clines and cash, February 5, 1977.

### CHAMPIONSHIP SERIES RECORD

| Year Club | League | G. | IP. | W. | L. | Pct. | H. | R. | ER. | SO. | BB. | ERA. |
|---|---|---|---|---|---|---|---|---|---|---|---|---|
| 1971–Oakland | American | 1 | ⅓ | 0 | 0 | .000 | 1 | 0 | 0 | 0 | 0 | 0.00 |

### WORLD SERIES RECORD

Established World Series records for consecutive games pitched and most games pitched, 7-game series, 7, 1973.

| Year Club | League | G. | IP. | W. | L. | Pct. | H. | R. | ER. | SO. | BB. | ERA. |
|---|---|---|---|---|---|---|---|---|---|---|---|---|
| 1973–Oakland | American | 7 | 6⅓ | 0 | 0 | .000 | 4 | 1 | 0 | 5 | 5 | 0.00 |

### ALL-STAR GAME RECORD

| Year League | IP. | W. | L. | Pct. | H. | R. | ER. | SO. | BB. | ERA. |
|---|---|---|---|---|---|---|---|---|---|---|
| 1969–American | ⅔ | 0 | 0 | .000 | 0 | 0 | 0 | 0 | 0 | 0.00 |

## KEVIN RICHARD KOBEL

Born October 2, 1953, at Buffalo, N. Y.
Height, 6.01. Weight, 195.
Throws left and bats righthanded.
Attended Mesa Community College, Mesa, Ariz.

| Year Club | League | G. | IP. | W. | L. | Pct. | H. | R. | ER. | SO. | BB. | ERA. |
|---|---|---|---|---|---|---|---|---|---|---|---|---|
| 1971–Newark | NYP | 11 | 60 | 5 | 1 | .833 | 44 | 21 | 17 | 63 | 36 | 2.55 |
| 1972–San Antonio | Texas | 29 | 140 | 3 | ∗15 | .167 | 151 | 84 | 67 | 107 | 56 | 4.31 |
| 1973–Shreveport | Texas | 26 | 167 | 12 | 8 | .600 | 160 | 83 | 63 | 103 | 62 | 3.39 |
| 1973–Milwaukee | American | 2 | 8 | 0 | 1 | .000 | 9 | 8 | 8 | 4 | 8 | 9.00 |
| 1974–Milwaukee | American | 34 | 169 | 6 | 14 | .300 | 166 | 84 | 75 | 74 | 54 | 3.99 |
| 1975–Sacramento† | P. Coast | 7 | 30 | 3 | 2 | .600 | 29 | 11 | 8 | 9 | 7 | 2.40 |
| 1976–Spokane | P. Coast | 32 | 131 | 7 | 12 | .368 | 153 | 86 | 80 | 56 | 43 | 5.50 |
| 1976–Milwaukee | National | 3 | 4 | 0 | 1 | .000 | 6 | 5 | 5 | 1 | 3 | 11.25 |
| Major League Totals | | 39 | 181 | 6 | 16 | .273 | 181 | 97 | 88 | 79 | 65 | 4.38 |

†On disabled list, April 10 to April 21 and May 28 through remainder of season.

## DOUGLAS JAMES KONIECZNY

Name pronounced Kuh-NEZZ-nee.

### (Doug)

Born September 27, 1951, at Detroit, Mich.
Height, 6.03. Weight, 218.
Throws and bats righthanded.
Hobbies–Fishing and leathercrafts.
Attended St. Clair County Community College, Port Huron, Mich., and
Wayne State University, Detroit, Mich.

Led Southern League pitchers in complete games with 17 and tied for lead in games started with 28 in 1973. Named Southern League Pitcher of the Year in 1973.

| Year Club | League | G. | IP. | W. | L. | Pct. | H. | R. | ER. | SO. | BB. | ERA. |
|---|---|---|---|---|---|---|---|---|---|---|---|---|
| 1971–Covington | Ap'lachian | 8 | 48 | 3 | 0 | 1.000 | 27 | 19 | 14 | 78 | 17 | 2.63 |
| 1972–Columbus† | Southern | 22 | 112 | 8 | 9 | .471 | 103 | 61 | 46 | 117 | 65 | 3.70 |
| 1973–Columbus | Southern | 28 | ∗213 | 12 | 12 | .500 | ∗194 | 83 | 63 | ∗222 | 83 | 2.66 |
| 1973–Houston | National | 2 | 13 | 0 | 1 | .000 | 12 | 8 | 8 | 6 | 4 | 5.54 |
| 1974–Denver | Am. Assoc. | 19 | 103 | 3 | 10 | .231 | 128 | 70 | 63 | 97 | 48 | 5.50 |
| 1974–Houston | National | 6 | 16 | 0 | 3 | .000 | 18 | 15 | 14 | 8 | 12 | 7.88 |
| 1975–Houston | National | 32 | 171 | 6 | 13 | .316 | 184 | 93 | 85 | 89 | 87 | 4.47 |
| 1976–Memphis‡ | Int'national | 20 | 105 | 6 | 10 | .375 | 135 | 81 | 71 | 48 | 53 | 6.09 |
| Major League Totals | | 40 | 200 | 6 | 17 | .261 | 214 | 116 | 107 | 103 | 103 | 4.82 |

†On disabled list, July 2 to July 31, 1972.

‡On disabled list, June 28 through July 14, 1976.

# JERRY MARTIN KOOSMAN

Born December 23, 1943, at Appleton, Minn.
Height, 6.03. Weight, 205.
Throws left and bats righthanded.
Hobbies—Flying, golf and water skiing.
Attended Univeristy of Minnesota, Morris, Minn., and
State School of Science, Wahpeton, N. D.

Established National League record for most strikeouts, season, by pitcher as batter (62), 1968.
Tied modern National League record for most shutout games won or tied, rookie season (7), 1968.
Named THE SPORTING NEWS National League Rookie Pitcher of the Year, 1968.

| Year Club | League | G. | IP. | W. | L. | Pct. | H. | R. | ER. | SO. | BB. | ERA. |
|---|---|---|---|---|---|---|---|---|---|---|---|---|
| 1965—Greenville | W. Carol. | 27 | 107 | 5 | 11 | .313 | 101 | 70 | 56 | 128 | 56 | 4.71 |
| 1965—Williamsport | Eastern | 2 | 12 | 0 | 2 | .000 | 11 | 7 | 5 | 11 | 11 | 3.75 |
| 1966—Auburn | NYP | 24 | 170 | 12 | 7 | .632 | 109 | 43 | 26 | 174 | 43 | *1.38 |
| 1967—New York | National | 9 | 22 | 0 | 2 | .000 | 22 | 17 | 15 | 11 | 19 | 6.14 |
| 1967—Jacksonville | Int'national | 25 | 178 | 11 | 10 | .524 | 137 | 60 | 48 | *183 | 46 | 2.43 |
| 1968—New York | National | 35 | 264 | 19 | 12 | .613 | 221 | 72 | 61 | 178 | 69 | 2.08 |
| 1969—New York | National | 32 | 241 | 17 | 9 | .684 | 187 | 66 | 61 | 180 | 68 | 2.28 |
| 1970—New York | National | 30 | 212 | 12 | 7 | .632 | 189 | 87 | 74 | 118 | 71 | 3.14 |
| 1971—New York† | National | 26 | 166 | 6 | 11 | .353 | 160 | 66 | 56 | 96 | 51 | 3.04 |
| 1972—New York | National | 34 | 163 | 11 | 12 | .478 | 155 | 81 | 75 | 147 | 52 | 4.14 |
| 1973—New York | National | 35 | 263 | 14 | 15 | .483 | 234 | 93 | 83 | 156 | 76 | 2.84 |
| 1974—New York | National | 35 | 265 | 15 | 11 | .577 | 258 | 113 | 99 | 188 | 85 | 3.36 |
| 1975—New York | National | 36 | 240 | 14 | 13 | .519 | 234 | 106 | 91 | 173 | 98 | 3.41 |
| 1976—New York | National | 34 | 247 | 21 | 10 | .677 | 205 | 81 | 74 | 200 | 66 | 2.70 |
| Major League Totals | | 306 | 2083 | 129 | 102 | .558 | 1865 | 782 | 689 | 1447 | 655 | 2.98 |

†On disabled list July 7 through August 9.

## CHAMPIONSHIP SERIES RECORD

| Year Club | League | G. | IP. | W. | L. | Pct. | H. | R. | ER. | SO. | BB. | ERA. |
|---|---|---|---|---|---|---|---|---|---|---|---|---|
| 1969—New York | National | 1 | 4⅔ | 0 | 0 | .000 | 7 | 6 | 6 | 5 | 4 | 11.57 |
| 1973—New York | National | 1 | 9 | 1 | 0 | 1.000 | 8 | 2 | 2 | 9 | 0 | 2.00 |
| Championship Series Totals | | 2 | 13⅔ | 1 | 0 | 1.000 | 15 | 8 | 8 | 14 | 4 | 5.27 |

## WORLD SERIES RECORD

| Year Club | League | G. | IP. | W. | L. | Pct. | H. | R. | ER. | SO. | BB. | ERA. |
|---|---|---|---|---|---|---|---|---|---|---|---|---|
| 1969—New York | National | 2 | 17⅔ | 2 | 0 | 1.000 | 7 | 4 | 4 | 9 | 4 | 2.04 |
| 1973—New York | National | 2 | 8⅔ | 1 | 0 | 1.000 | 9 | 3 | 3 | 8 | 7 | 3.12 |
| World Series Totals | | 4 | 26⅓ | 3 | 0 | 1.000 | 16 | 7 | 7 | 17 | 11 | 2.39 |

## ALL-STAR GAME RECORD

| Year League | IP. | W. | L. | Pct. | H. | R. | ER. | SO. | BB. | ERA. |
|---|---|---|---|---|---|---|---|---|---|---|
| 1968—National | ⅓ | 0 | 0 | .000 | 0 | 0 | 0 | 1 | 0 | 0.00 |
| 1969—National | 1⅔ | 0 | 0 | .000 | 1 | 0 | 0 | 1 | 0 | 0.00 |
| All-Star Game Totals | 2 | 0 | 0 | .000 | 1 | 0 | 0 | 2 | 0 | 0.00 |

# EDWARD EMIL KRANEPOOL

Name pronounced KRAIN-pool.

## (Ed)

Born November 8, 1944, at New York, N.Y.
Height, 6.03. Weight, 207.
Throws and bats lefthanded.
Hobby—Athletics.

Tied major league record for most at-bats in doubleheader (more than 18 innings), 14, May 31, 1964, 32 innings.
Received reported $85,000 bonus to sign with New York Mets, 1962.

| Year Club | League | Pos. | G. | AB. | R. | H. | 2B. | 3B. | HR. | RBI. | B.A. | PO. | A. | E. | F.A. |
|---|---|---|---|---|---|---|---|---|---|---|---|---|---|---|---|
| 1962—Syracuse | Int. | 1B | 14 | 48 | 2 | 11 | 1 | 1 | 0 | 4 | .229 | 138 | 10 | 2 | .987 |
| 1962—Knoxville | Sally | OF | 7 | 18 | 4 | 5 | 3 | 0 | 0 | 0 | .278 | 6 | 0 | 0 | 1.000 |
| 1962—Auburn | NYP | 1B | 20 | 77 | 23 | 27 | 2 | 1 | 1 | 18 | .351 | 135 | 8 | 4 | .973 |
| 1962—New York | Nat. | 1B | 3 | 6 | 0 | 1 | 1 | 0 | 0 | 0 | .167 | 9 | 3 | 0 | 1.000 |
| 1963—New York | Nat. | OF-1B | 86 | 273 | 22 | 57 | 12 | 2 | 2 | 14 | .209 | 228 | 18 | 4 | .984 |
| 1963—Buffalo | Int. | OF | 53 | 203 | 28 | 63 | 9 | 8 | 5 | 33 | .310 | 90 | 5 | 1 | .990 |
| 1964—Buffalo | Int. | 1B-OF | 15 | 54 | 7 | 19 | 4 | 1 | 3 | 7 | .352 | 138 | 12 | 1 | .993 |
| 1964—New York | Nat. | 1B-OF | 119 | 420 | 47 | 108 | 19 | 4 | 10 | 45 | .257 | 983 | 80 | 10 | .991 |
| 1965—New York | Nat. | 1B | 153 | 525 | 44 | 133 | 24 | 4 | 10 | 53 | .253 | 1375 | 93 | 12 | .992 |
| 1966—New York | Nat. | 1B-OF | 146 | 464 | 51 | 118 | 15 | 2 | 16 | 57 | .254 | 1180 | 86 | 12 | .991 |
| 1967—New York | Nat. | 1B | 141 | 469 | 37 | 126 | 17 | 1 | 10 | 54 | .269 | 1137 | 87 | 10 | .992 |
| 1968—New York | Nat. | 1B-OF | 127 | 373 | 29 | 86 | 13 | 1 | 3 | 20 | .231 | 924 | 75 | 6 | .994 |
| 1969—New York | Nat. | 1B-OF | 112 | 353 | 36 | 84 | 9 | 2 | 11 | 49 | .238 | 812 | 64 | 6 | .993 |
| 1970—Tidewater | Int. | OF-1B | 47 | 174 | 29 | 54 | 8 | 3 | 7 | 45 | .310 | 91 | 1 | 2 | .979 |
| 1970—New York | Nat. | 1B | 43 | 47 | 2 | 8 | 0 | 0 | 0 | 3 | .170 | 47 | 3 | 0 | 1.000 |
| 1971—New York | Nat. | *1B-OF | 122 | 421 | 61 | 118 | 20 | 4 | 14 | 58 | .280 | 795 | 61 | 2 | *.998 |
| 1972—New York | Nat. | 1B-OF | 122 | 327 | 28 | 88 | 15 | 1 | 8 | 34 | .269 | 705 | 48 | 3 | .996 |
| 1973—New York | Nat. | 1B-OF | 100 | 284 | 28 | 68 | 12 | 2 | 1 | 35 | .239 | 448 | 28 | 2 | .996 |
| 1974—New York | Nat. | OF-1B | 94 | 217 | 20 | 65 | 11 | 1 | 4 | 24 | .300 | 207 | 9 | 5 | .977 |

| Year Club | League | Pos. | G. | AB. | R. | H. | 2B. | 3B. | HR. | RBI. | B.A. | PO. | A. | E. | F.A. |
|---|---|---|---|---|---|---|---|---|---|---|---|---|---|---|---|
| 1975–New York..........Nat. | | 1B-OF | 106 | 325 | 42 | 105 | 16 | 0 | 4 | 43 | .323 | 671 | 46 | 2 | .997 |
| 1976–New York..........Nat. | | 1B-OF | 123 | 415 | 47 | 121 | 17 | 1 | 10 | 49 | .292 | 721 | 35 | 3 | .996 |
| Major League Totals ..................... | | | 1597 | 4919 | 494 | 1286 | 201 | 25 | 103 | 538 | .261 | 10242 | 736 | 77 | .993 |

## CHAMPIONSHIP SERIES RECORD

| Year Club | League | Pos. | G. | AB. | R. | H. | 2B. | 3B. | HR. | RBI. | B.A. | PO. | A. | E. | F.A. |
|---|---|---|---|---|---|---|---|---|---|---|---|---|---|---|---|
| 1969–New York..........Nat. | | 1B | 3 | 12 | 2 | 3 | 1 | 0 | 0 | 1 | .250 | 20 | 3 | 0 | 1.000 |
| 1973–New York..........Nat. | | OF | 1 | 2 | 0 | 1 | 0 | 0 | 0 | 2 | .500 | 2 | 0 | 0 | 1.000 |
| Championship Series Totals ............ | | | 4 | 14 | 2 | 4 | 1 | 0 | 0 | 3 | .286 | 22 | 3 | 0 | 1.000 |

## WORLD SERIES RECORD

| Year Club | League | Pos. | G. | AB. | R. | H. | 2B. | 3B. | HR. | RBI. | B.A. | PO. | A. | E. | F.A. |
|---|---|---|---|---|---|---|---|---|---|---|---|---|---|---|---|
| 1969–New York..........Nat. | | 1B | 1 | 4 | 1 | 1 | 0 | 0 | 1 | 1 | .250 | 7 | 0 | 0 | 1.000 |
| 1973–New York..........Nat. | | PH | 4 | 3 | 0 | 0 | 0 | 0 | 0 | 0 | .000 | 0 | 0 | 0 | .000 |
| World Series Totals ..................... | | | 5 | 7 | 1 | 1 | 0 | 0 | 1 | 1 | .143 | 7 | 0 | 0 | 1.000 |

## ALL-STAR GAME RECORD
Member of National League All-Star Team in 1965 game; did not play.

## KENNETH PETER KRAVEC
### (Ken)

Born July 29, 1951, at Cleveland, O.
Height, 6.02. Weight, 185.
Throws and bats lefthanded.
Hobbies–Golf and listening to music.
Attended Ashland College, Ashland, O.; received Bachelor of Science
degree in Management and Marketing.
Named Pitcher of the Year in Southern League, 1975.

| Year Club | League | G. | IP. | W. | L. | Pct. | H. | R. | ER. | SO. | BB. | ERA. |
|---|---|---|---|---|---|---|---|---|---|---|---|---|
| 1973–Knoxville ...........................Southern | | 13 | 64 | 2 | 8 | .200 | 53 | 44 | 36 | 52 | 65 | 5.06 |
| 1974–Knoxville ...........................Southern | | 27 | 132 | 6 | 6 | .500 | 100 | 58 | 50 | 105 | 79 | 3.41 |
| 1975–Knoxville ...........................Southern | | 28 | 168 | •14 | 7 | .667 | 138 | 52 | 45 | 119 | 78 | 2.41 |
| 1975–Chicago..............................American | | 2 | 4 | 0 | 1 | .000 | 1 | 3 | 3 | 1 | 8 | 6.75 |
| 1976–Iowa ...............................Am. Assoc. | | 24 | 131 | 8 | 5 | .615 | 103 | 68 | 63 | 142 | 89 | 4.33 |
| 1976–Chicago..............................American | | 9 | 50 | 1 | 5 | .167 | 49 | 28 | 27 | 38 | 32 | 4.86 |
| Major League Totals ............................. | | 11 | 54 | 1 | 6 | .143 | 50 | 31 | 30 | 39 | 40 | 5.00 |

## RICHARD ALLEN KREUGER
### (Rick)

Born November 3, 1948, at Wyoming, Mich.
Height, 6.02. Weight, 185.
Throws left and bats righthanded.
Hobbies–Chess and the guitar.
Attended Grand Rapids Junior College, Grand Rapids, Mich., and Michigan State
University, East Lansing, Mich.; received Bachelor of Science degree in Math Education.

| Year Club | League | G. | IP. | W. | L. | Pct. | H. | R. | ER. | SO. | BB. | ERA. |
|---|---|---|---|---|---|---|---|---|---|---|---|---|
| 1971–Greenville...........................W. Carol. | | 35 | ★162 | 10 | 8 | .556 | 160 | 73 | 56 | 115 | 35 | 3.11 |
| 1972–Winston-Salem†....................Carolina | | | | | | (Did not play) | | | | | | |
| 1973–Winston-Salem‡....................Carolina | | 16 | 74 | 8 | 6 | .571 | 61 | 21 | 13 | 44 | 25 | 1.58 |
| 1974–Pawtucket...........................Int'national | | 37 | 155 | 6 | 8 | .429 | 144 | 68 | 53 | 104 | 57 | 3.08 |
| 1975–Pawtucket...........................Int'national | | 33 | 165 | 6 | 15 | .286 | 177 | 71 | 62 | 107 | 50 | 3.38 |
| 1975–Boston ..............................American | | 2 | 4 | 0 | 0 | .000 | 3 | 2 | 2 | 1 | 1 | 4.50 |
| 1976–Rhode Island.......................Int'national | | 35 | 80 | 9 | 4 | .692 | 65 | 28 | 27 | 51 | 35 | 3.04 |
| 1976–Boston ..............................American | | 8 | 31 | 2 | 1 | .667 | 31 | 14 | 14 | 12 | 16 | 4.06 |
| Major League Totals ............................. | | 10 | 35 | 2 | 1 | .667 | 34 | 16 | 16 | 13 | 17 | 4.11 |

†On disabled list, May 3 through remainder of season.
‡On restricted list from beginning of season until June 11, 1973.

## MICHAEL EDWARD KRUKOW
### (Mike)

Born January 21, 1952, at Long Beach, Calif.
Height, 6.05. Weight, 205.
Throws and bats righthanded.
Hobbies–Music, backpacking, golf and raising dogs.
Attended California Poly State University, San Luis Obispo, Calif.
Nephew of Tim Ryan, who played in Pittsburgh Pirates' organization, 1949.

Tied for Gulf Coast League lead in complete games by pitchers with 4 in 1973.

| Year Club | League | G. | IP. | W. | L. | Pct. | H. | R. | ER. | SO. | BB. | ERA. |
|---|---|---|---|---|---|---|---|---|---|---|---|---|
| 1973–Bradenton Cubs...................Gulf Coast | | 13 | 77 | 4 | 3 | .571 | 76 | 32 | 27 | ★80 | 28 | 3.16 |
| 1974–Midland...............................Texas | | 6 | 30 | 1 | 1 | .500 | 42 | 24 | 17 | 21 | 19 | 5.10 |
| 1974–Key West ...........................Florida St. | | 20 | 130 | 5 | 10 | .333 | 121 | 66 | 46 | 94 | 47 | 3.18 |

| Year    Club | League | G. | IP. | W. | L. | Pct. | H. | R. | ER. | SO. | BB. | ERA. |
|---|---|---|---|---|---|---|---|---|---|---|---|---|
| 1975–Midland† ........................... | Texas | 24 | 153 | 13 | 6 | .684 | 143 | 65 | 58 | 100 | 66 | 3.41 |
| 1976–Wichita ............................... | Am. Assoc. | 26 | 144 | 7 | 9 | .438 | 142 | 61 | 53 | 108 | 47 | 3.31 |
| 1976–Chicago ............................. | National | 2 | 4 | 0 | 0 | .000 | 6 | 4 | 4 | 1 | 2 | 9.00 |
| Major League Totals ............................. | | 2 | 4 | 0 | 0 | .000 | 6 | 4 | 4 | 1 | 2 | 9.00 |

†On disabled list, May 19 to June 7, 1975.

## THEODORE RODGER KUBIAK

Name pronounced Q-B-ack.

### (Ted)

Born May 12, 1942, at New Brunswick, N. J.
Height, 6.00. Weight, 175.
Throws right and bats left and righthanded.
Hobby–Art.

Led Florida State League shortstops in double plays with 68 in 1961, Northwest League with 54 in 1963, Southern League with 99 in 1965 and Pacific Coast League with 125 in 1966.

| Year    Club     League | Pos. | G. | AB. | R. | H. | 2B. | 3B. | HR. | RBI. | B.A. | PO. | A. | E. | F.A. |
|---|---|---|---|---|---|---|---|---|---|---|---|---|---|---|
| 1961–Sarasota ............Fla.St. | SS | 138 | 463 | 76 | 117 | 9 | 6 | 0 | 53 | .253 | *242 | *366 | 42 | .935 |
| 1962–Binghamton ......East. | SS | 128 | 428 | 45 | 87 | 10 | 1 | 4 | 30 | .203 | *201 | *350 | 41 | .931 |
| 1963–Binghamton ......East. | SS | 18 | 69 | 6 | 12 | 2 | 0 | 0 | 3 | .174 | 15 | 41 | 7 | .889 |
| 1963–Lewiston ..........Northw. | SS | 111 | 396 | 60 | 117 | 23 | 3 | 5 | 48 | .295 | *156 | *341 | *42 | .922 |
| 1964–Dallas ..............P.C. | SS | 16 | 41 | 6 | 7 | 1 | 0 | 0 | 2 | .171 | 16 | 40 | 2 | .966 |
| 1964–Ft. W.-Austin ....Texas | SS | 105 | 384 | 41 | 82 | 10 | 4 | 2 | 22 | .214 | 164 | 301 | 27 | .945 |
| 1965–Birmingham ......South. | SS | 138 | 526 | 75 | 148 | 17 | 3 | 7 | 38 | .281 | 226 | *414 | 28 | .958 |
| 1966–Vancouver ........P.C. | SS | *149 | 585 | 80 | 152 | 15 | 9 | 2 | 38 | .260 | *281 | *486 | 29 | .964 |
| 1967–Kansas City ......Amer. | SS-2-3 | 53 | 102 | 6 | 16 | 2 | 1 | 0 | 5 | .157 | 37 | 58 | 3 | .969 |
| 1968–Oakland† .........Amer. | 2B-SS | 48 | 120 | 10 | 30 | 5 | 2 | 0 | 8 | .250 | 60 | 78 | 11 | .926 |
| 1969–Oakland‡ .........Amer. | SS-2B | 92 | 305 | 38 | 76 | 9 | 1 | 2 | 27 | .249 | 151 | 215 | 10 | .974 |
| 1970–Milwaukee ........Amer. | 2B-SS | 158 | 540 | 63 | 136 | 9 | 6 | 4 | 41 | .252 | 361 | 412 | 19 | .976 |
| 1971–Milwaukee§ ......Amer. | 2B-SS | 89 | 260 | 26 | 59 | 6 | 5 | 3 | 17 | .227 | 171 | 222 | 14 | .966 |
| 1971–St. Louis x ........Nat. | 2B-SS | 32 | 72 | 8 | 18 | 3 | 2 | 1 | 10 | .250 | 49 | 56 | 4 | .963 |
| 1972–Texas y-Oak. ....Amer. | 2-SS-3 | 97 | 210 | 19 | 43 | 7 | 1 | 0 | 15 | .205 | 156 | 165 | 4 | .988 |
| 1973–Oakland z .........Amer. | 2-SS-3 | 106 | 182 | 15 | 40 | 6 | 1 | 3 | 17 | .220 | 117 | 186 | 8 | .974 |
| 1974–Oakland ...........Amer. | 2-SS-3 | 99 | 220 | 22 | 46 | 3 | 0 | 0 | 18 | .209 | 129 | 175 | 6 | .981 |
| 1975–Oakland a .........Amer. | SS-3-2 | 20 | 28 | 2 | 7 | 1 | 0 | 0 | 4 | .250 | 12 | 31 | 0 | 1.000 |
| 1975–San Diego .........Nat. | 3-2-1 | 87 | 196 | 13 | 44 | 5 | 0 | 0 | 14 | .224 | 51 | 126 | 7 | .962 |
| 1976–San Diego .........Nat. | 3-2-S-1 | 96 | 212 | 16 | 50 | 5 | 2 | 0 | 26 | .236 | 77 | 110 | 4 | .979 |
| American League Totals ................ | | 762 | 1967 | 201 | 453 | 48 | 17 | 12 | 152 | .230 | 1196 | 1542 | 75 | .973 |
| National League Totals ................... | | 215 | 480 | 37 | 112 | 13 | 4 | 1 | 50 | .233 | 177 | 292 | 15 | .969 |
| Major League Totals ..................... | | 977 | 2447 | 238 | 565 | 61 | 21 | 13 | 202 | .231 | 1373 | 1834 | 90 | .973 |

†In military service from June 7 through end of season.

‡Traded with Pitcher George Lauzerique to Seattle Pilots for Pitcher Diego Segui and Shortstop Ray Oyler, December 7, 1969.

§Traded with Pitcher Charlie Loseth (latter assigned from Raleigh-Durham to St. Petersburg) to St. Louis Cardinals for Outfielder Jose Cardenal, Infielder Dick Schofield (on Tulsa roster) and Pitcher Bob Reynolds (latter assigned to Evansville), July 3, 1971.

xTraded to Texas Rangers for Pitcher Joe Grzenda, November 3, 1971.

yTraded with First Baseman Don Mincher to Oakland A's for Infielder Orlando Martinez, Pitcher Steve Lawson and Infielder Vic Harris (latter on Iowa roster), July 20, 1972.

zOn supplemental disabled list, June 25 to July 10, 1973.

aTraded to San Diego Padres for Pitcher Sonny Siebert, May 16, 1975.

CHAMPIONSHIP SERIES RECORD

| Year    Club     League | Pos. | G. | AB. | R. | H. | 2B. | 3B. | HR. | RBI. | B.A. | PO. | A. | E. | F.A. |
|---|---|---|---|---|---|---|---|---|---|---|---|---|---|---|
| 1972–Oakland ............Amer. | 2B-SS | 4 | 4 | 0 | 2 | 0 | 0 | 0 | 1 | .500 | 3 | 8 | 1 | .917 |
| 1973–Oakland ............Amer. | 2B | 3 | 2 | 0 | 0 | 0 | 0 | 0 | 0 | .000 | 0 | 1 | 0 | 1.000 |
| Championship Series Totals ............ | | 7 | 6 | 0 | 2 | 0 | 0 | 0 | 1 | .333 | 3 | 9 | 1 | .923 |

WORLD SERIES RECORD

| Year    Club     League | Pos. | G. | AB. | R. | H. | 2B. | 3B. | HR. | RBI. | B.A. | PO. | A. | E. | F.A. |
|---|---|---|---|---|---|---|---|---|---|---|---|---|---|---|
| 1972–Oakland ............Amer. | 2B | 4 | 3 | 0 | 1 | 0 | 0 | 0 | 0 | .333 | 4 | 3 | 0 | 1.000 |
| 1973–Oakland ............Amer. | 2B | 4 | 3 | 1 | 0 | 0 | 0 | 0 | 0 | .000 | 5 | 7 | 0 | 1.000 |
| World Series Totals ...................... | | 8 | 6 | 1 | 1 | 0 | 0 | 0 | 0 | .167 | 9 | 10 | 0 | 1.000 |

## JOHN ANDREW KUCEK

### (Jack)

Born June 8, 1953, at Warren, O.
Height, 6.02. Weight, 200.
Throws and bats righthanded.
Hobbies–Poetry and music.
Attended Miami University, Oxford, O.

| Year    Club | League | G. | IP. | W. | L. | Pct. | H. | R. | ER. | SO. | BB. | ERA. |
|---|---|---|---|---|---|---|---|---|---|---|---|---|
| 1974–Appleton ...........................Midwest | | 9 | 51 | 5 | 2 | .714 | 33 | 11 | 10 | 49 | 22 | 1.76 |
| 1974–Chicago...............................American | | 9 | 38 | 1 | 4 | .200 | 48 | 25 | 22 | 25 | 21 | 5.21 |
| 1975–Denver ...............................Am. Assoc. | | 6 | 17 | 1 | 2 | .333 | 24 | 13 | 13 | 17 | 3 | 6.88 |

| Year | Club | League | G. | IP. | W. | L. | Pct. | H. | R. | ER. | SO. | BB. | ERA. |
|------|------|--------|----|----|----|----|------|----|----|-----|-----|-----|------|
| 1975–Knoxville | | Southern | 21 | 114 | 10 | 4 | .714 | 93 | 38 | 35 | 77 | 48 | 2.76 |
| 1975–Chicago | | American | 2 | 4 | 0 | 0 | .000 | 9 | 2 | 2 | 2 | 4 | 4.50 |
| 1976–Iowa | | Am. Assoc. | 22 | 124 | 5 | 9 | .357 | 130 | 68 | 58 | 78 | 55 | 4.21 |
| 1976–Chicago | | American | 2 | 5 | 0 | 0 | .000 | 9 | 5 | 5 | 2 | 4 | 9.00 |
| Major League Totals | | | 13 | 47 | 1 | 4 | .200 | 66 | 32 | 29 | 29 | 29 | 5.55 |

## FRED KUHAULUA

Name pronounced KOO-hah-LOO-ah.

Born February 23, 1953, at Honolulu, Hawaii.
Height, 5.11. Weight, 175.
Throws and bats lefthanded.
Hobby–Surfing.
Nephew of Levi Stanley, former defensive tackle with the Hawaiians of World Football League.
Attended Santa Ana College, Santa Ana, Calif.

| Year | Club | League | G. | IP. | W. | L. | Pct. | H. | R. | ER. | SO. | BB. | ERA. |
|------|------|--------|----|----|----|----|------|----|----|-----|-----|-----|------|
| 1972–Great Falls | | Pioneer | 6 | 23 | 1 | 0 | 1.000 | 24 | 15 | 10 | 24 | 8 | 3.91 |
| 1973–Decatur | | Midwest | 22 | 66 | 3 | 3 | .500 | 62 | 36 | 31 | 63 | 39 | 4.23 |
| 1974–Fresno | | California | 23 | 102 | 6 | 6 | .500 | 121 | 80 | 48 | 76 | 59 | 4.24 |
| 1975–Salinas† | | California | 33 | 85 | 3 | 4 | .429 | 88 | 40 | 33 | 59 | 39 | 3.49 |
| 1976–Salinas | | California | 30 | 86 | 3 | 1 | .750 | 70 | 30 | 23 | 103 | 53 | 2.41 |
| 1976–El Paso | | Texas | 13 | 26 | 1 | 2 | .333 | 30 | 15 | 13 | 27 | 24 | 4.50 |

†On disabled list, April 15 through May 1, 1975.
Listed on California Angels' 1977 spring roster.

## DUANE EUGENE KUIPER

Name pronounced KIPE-er.

Born June 19, 1950, at Racine, Wis.
Height, 6.00. Weight, 175.
Throws right and bats lefthanded.
Hobbies–Music and reading.
Attended Indian Hills Community College, Centerville, Ia., and Southern
Illinois University, Carbondale, Ill.; received Bachelor of Arts degree.
Second cousin of Dick Bosman, former pitcher with Oakland Athletics.
Led American Association in stolen bases with 28 in 1974.

| Year | Club | League | Pos. | G. | AB. | R. | H. | 2B. | 3B. | HR. | RBI. | B.A. | PO. | A. | E. | F.A. |
|------|------|--------|------|----|-----|----|----|-----|-----|-----|------|------|-----|----|----|------|
| 1972–Reno | | Calif. | 2-S-3 | 124 | 496 | 89 | 149 | 20 | 3 | 2 | 53 | .300 | 264 | 283 | 18 | .968 |
| 1973–Okla. City | | A. A. | 2B | 18 | 56 | 6 | 9 | 1 | 1 | 0 | 6 | .161 | 42 | 34 | 3 | .962 |
| 1973–San Antonio | | Tex. | 2B | 107 | 395 | 46 | 113 | 11 | 2 | 1 | 42 | .286 | 220 | 317 | 19 | .966 |
| 1974–Okla. City | | A. A. | 2B •135 | | *554 | 83 | 172 | 27 | 5 | 3 | 53 | .310 | 291 | *365 | 11 | .984 |
| 1974–Cleveland | | Amer. | 2B | 10 | 22 | 7 | 11 | 2 | 0 | 0 | 4 | .500 | 16 | 19 | 0 | 1.000 |
| 1975–Okla. City | | A. A. | 2B | 40 | 164 | 18 | 40 | 5 | 0 | 1 | 12 | .244 | 110 | 94 | 3 | .986 |
| 1975–Cleveland† | | Amer. | 2B | 90 | 346 | 42 | 101 | 11 | 1 | 0 | 25 | .292 | 192 | 230 | 12 | .972 |
| 1976–Cleveland | | Amer. | *2-1-DH | 135 | 506 | 47 | 133 | 13 | 6 | 0 | 37 | .263 | 321 | 367 | 11 | *.984 |
| Major League Totals | | | | 235 | 874 | 96 | 245 | 26 | 7 | 0 | 66 | .280 | 529 | 616 | 23 | .980 |

†On supplemental disabled list, July 22 to August 11, 1975.

## EDWARD ANTHONY KURPIEL, JR.

## (Ed)

Born January 19, 1954, at Jamaica, N. Y.
Height, 6.03. Weight, 205.
Throws and bats lefthanded.
Hobbies–Shooting pool and playing golf.
Attended Queensborough Community College, Bayside, N. Y.

Led American Association outfielders in double plays with 4 in 1974.
Led California League in sacrifice flies with 10 in 1972.
Led California League first basemen in double plays with 86 in 1972.
Received reported $75,000 bonus to sign with St. Louis Cardinals, 1971.

| Year | Club | League | Pos. | G. | AB. | R. | H. | 2B. | 3B. | HR. | RBI. | B.A. | PO. | A. | E. | F.A. |
|------|------|--------|------|----|-----|----|----|-----|-----|-----|------|------|-----|----|----|------|
| 1971–Cedar Rapids | | Midw. | 1B | 56 | 191 | 28 | 49 | 8 | 2 | 8 | 34 | .257 | 472 | 30 | 12 | .977 |
| 1972–Modesto | | Cal. | *1B-OF | 130 | 438 | 87 | 112 | 15 | 3 | 22 | 91 | .256 | *1058 | *70 | *20 | .983 |
| 1973–Arkansas | | Texas | OF-1B | 128 | 439 | 55 | 109 | 14 | 3 | 17 | 58 | .248 | 374 | 15 | 15 | .963 |
| 1974–Tulas† | | A. A. | OF | 120 | 393 | 47 | 98 | 23 | 2 | 14 | 53 | .249 | 187 | 8 | *12 | .942 |
| 1975–Memphis‡ | | Int. | 1B | 29 | 80 | 12 | 14 | 1 | 1 | 0 | 9 | .175 | 169 | 18 | 2 | .989 |
| 1975–Evansville§ | | A. A. | 1B-OF | 94 | 296 | 42 | 85 | 15 | 2 | 11 | 57 | .287 | 787 | 41 | 12 | .986 |
| 1976–Salt Lake C. x | | P. C. | 1B | 83 | 263 | 42 | 69 | 16 | 6 | 5 | 37 | .262 | 345 | 33 | 7 | .982 |
| 1976–Tulsa y | | A. A. | OF-1B | 29 | 82 | 14 | 23 | 3 | 0 | 3 | 16 | .280 | 95 | 5 | 3 | .971 |

†Traded with Second Baseman Rudy Kinard by St. Louis Cardinals to Montreal Expos for First Baseman-Outfielder Ron Fairly, December 6, 1974.

‡Traded by Montreal Expos to Detroit Tigers, May 30, 1975, as part of deal in which Expos obtained Outfielder Jim Northrup from Tigers, August 7, 1974.

§Drafted from Detroit Tigers' organization by California Angels, December 8, 1975.

xAssigned to Tulsa (St. Louis Cardinals' organization), July 30, 1976; to complete deal which sent Infielder Mario Guerrero from Tulsa to California Angels for Catcher Ed Jordan, assigned from El Paso to Arkansas, May 29, 1976.
yTraded to New York Mets (assigned to Tidewater) for Outfielder Leon Brown and First Baseman Brock Pemberton (both assigned to New Orleans), December 9, 1976.

PITCHING RECORD

| Year Club | League | G. | IP. | W. | L. | Pct. | H. | R. | ER. | SO. | BB. | ERA. |
|---|---|---|---|---|---|---|---|---|---|---|---|---|
| 1972—Modesto ...........................California | | 1 | 1 | 0 | 0 | .000 | 2 | 3 | 3 | 1 | 3 | 27.00 |

## CRAIG ROBERT KUSICK

Born September 30, 1948, at Milwaukee, Wis.
Height, 6.03. Weight, 220.
Throws and bats righthanded.
Hobbies—Golfing, swimming and handball.
Attended University of Wisconsin, La Crosse, Wis.

Tied major league record for most times hit by pitch, game, 3, August 27, 1975 (11 innings).
Led Pacific Coast League batters in bases on balls with 103 in 1973.

| Year Club | League | Pos. | G. | AB. | R. | H. | 2B. | 3B. | HR. | RBI. | B.A. | PO. | A. | E. | F.A. |
|---|---|---|---|---|---|---|---|---|---|---|---|---|---|---|---|
| 1970—St. Cloud .........North. | | *OF-S | 61 | 201 | 35 | 59 | 13 | 0 | 7 | 41 | .294 | 76 | 7 | *12 | .874 |
| 1971—Lynchburg ........Carol. | | OF-1B | 126 | 378 | 71 | 101 | 23 | 3 | 20 | *91 | .267 | 152 | 10 | 8 | .953 |
| 1972—Charlotte ..........South. | | OF-1B | 134 | 437 | 71 | 123 | 15 | 7 | 17 | 62 | .281 | 267 | 17 | 13 | .956 |
| 1973—Tacoma ............P. C. | | 1B | *144 | 514 | 102 | 157 | 24 | 2 | 27 | 104 | .305 | 1063 | *97 | *23 | .980 |
| 1973—Minnesota ........Amer. | | 1B-OF | 15 | 48 | 4 | 12 | 2 | 0 | 0 | 4 | .250 | 89 | 5 | 1 | .989 |
| 1974—Tacoma ............P. C. | | 1B | 49 | 177 | 44 | 58 | 13 | 2 | 13 | 47 | .328 | 469 | 32 | 3 | .994 |
| 1974—Minnesota ........Amer. | | 1B | 76 | 201 | 36 | 48 | 7 | 1 | 8 | 26 | .239 | 479 | 42 | 2 | .996 |
| 1975—Tacoma ............P. C. | | 1B-OF | 56 | 177 | 20 | 46 | 4 | 0 | 2 | 16 | .260 | 223 | 22 | 2 | .991 |
| 1975—Minnesota ........Amer. | | 1B | 57 | 156 | 14 | 37 | 8 | 0 | 6 | 27 | .237 | 372 | 31 | 4 | .990 |
| 1976—Minnesota ........Amer. | | DH-1B | 109 | 266 | 33 | 69 | 13 | 0 | 11 | 36 | .259 | 109 | 17 | 13 | .977 |
| Major League Totals ..................... | | 257 | 671 | 87 | 166 | 30 | 1 | 25 | 93 | .247 | 1049 | 95 | 20 | .983 |

## ARTHUR WILLIAM KUSNYER
Pronounced Kushner.
### (Art)

Born December 19, 1945, at Akron, O.
Height, 6.02. Weight, 198.
Throws and bats righthanded.
Attended Kent State University, Kent, O.

Led Pacific Coast League catchers in double plays with 14 in 1971.
Led Midwest League in passed balls with 29 in 1968, led Carolina League with 24 in 1969 and tied for Southern League lead with 14 in 1970.

| Year Club | League | Pos. | G. | AB. | R. | H. | 2B. | 3B. | HR. | RBI. | B.A. | PO. | A. | E. | F.A. |
|---|---|---|---|---|---|---|---|---|---|---|---|---|---|---|---|
| 1966—Sar. W. Sox ......Gulf C. | | C | 11 | 20 | 3 | 6 | 2 | 0 | 0 | 0 | .300 | .... | .... | .... | .... |
| 1967—Appleton...........Midw. | | O-C-1 | 81 | 292 | 41 | 73 | 8 | 3 | 7 | 37 | .250 | 206 | 16 | 12 | .949 |
| 1968—Appleton...........Midw. | | C | 99 | 330 | 40 | 82 | 15 | 1 | 5 | 38 | .248 | *705 | *62 | •18 | .977 |
| 1969—Lynchburg ........Carol. | | *C-O | 129 | 435 | 58 | 108 | 19 | 7 | 13 | 66 | .248 | *793 | *87 | *25 | .972 |
| 1970—Mobile .............South. | | C | 122 | 396 | 43 | 99 | 14 | 2 | 12 | 49 | .250 | 650 | *88 | 13 | .983 |
| 1970—Chicago† .........Amer. | | C | 4 | 10 | 0 | 1 | 0 | 0 | 0 | 0 | .100 | 12 | 4 | 1 | .941 |
| 1971—Salt Lake City ..P. C. | | C | 129 | 456 | 73 | 144 | 27 | 3 | 10 | 75 | .316 | *764 | *76 | 12 | .986 |
| 1971—California .........Amer. | | C | 6 | 13 | 0 | 2 | 0 | 0 | 0 | 0 | .154 | 19 | 4 | 1 | .958 |
| 1972—California .........Amer. | | C | 64 | 179 | 13 | 37 | 2 | 1 | 2 | 13 | .207 | 362 | 33 | 10 | .975 |
| 1973—Salt Lake City ..P. C. | | C | 5 | 15 | 1 | 3 | 0 | 0 | 0 | 0 | .200 | 12 | 0 | 1 | .923 |
| 1973—California‡ .......Amer. | | C | 41 | 64 | 5 | 8 | 2 | 0 | 0 | 3 | .125 | 130 | 13 | 3 | .979 |
| 1974—Sacramento ......P. C. | | C | 128 | 440 | 64 | 107 | 10 | 0 | 17 | 63 | .243 | *624 | 60 | *28 | .961 |
| 1975—Spokane ...........P. C. | | C | 128 | 448 | 62 | 118 | 10 | 2 | 25 | 76 | .263 | *720 | 55 | 6 | *.992 |
| 1976—Spokane ...........P. C. | | C | 55 | 203 | 40 | 66 | 9 | 2 | 11 | 45 | .325 | 182 | 14 | 6 | .970 |
| 1976—Milwaukee ........Amer. | | C | 15 | 34 | 2 | 4 | 1 | 0 | 0 | 3 | .118 | 41 | 4 | 3 | .938 |
| Major League Totals ..................... | | 130 | 300 | 20 | 52 | 5 | 1 | 2 | 19 | .173 | 564 | 58 | 18 | .972 |

†Traded to California Angels for Pitcher Steve Kealey and Catcher Dave Adlesh, March 15, 1971.
‡Traded with Pitchers Clyde Wright and Steve Barber, Outfielder Ken Berry and a player to be named later to Milwaukee Brewers for Outfielders Ollie Brown and Joe Lahoud, Pitchers Skip Lockwood and Gary Ryerson and Catcher Ellie Rodriguez, October 22, 1973.

## ROBERT JOSEPH LACEY, JR.
### (Bob)

Born August 25, 1953, at Fredericksburg, Va.
Height, 6.05. Weight, 210.
Throws left and bats righthanded.
Hobbies—Watching cartoons, collecting comic books and albums.
Attended Central Arizona College, Coolidge, Ariz.

| Year Club | League | G. | IP. | W. | L. | Pct. | H. | R. | ER. | SO. | BB. | ERA. |
|---|---|---|---|---|---|---|---|---|---|---|---|---|
| 1972—Coos Bay—North Bend† ........Northwest | | 8 | 39 | 0 | 3 | .000 | 43 | 30 | 25 | 22 | 30 | 5.77 |
| 1973—Key West ...........................Florida St. | | 13 | 90 | 6 | 1 | .857 | 85 | 23 | 13 | 57 | 17 | 1.30 |

| Year Club | League | G. | IP. | W. | L. | Pct. | H. | R. | ER. | SO. | BB. | ERA. |
|---|---|---|---|---|---|---|---|---|---|---|---|---|
| 1973–Burlington | Midwest | 15 | 83 | 7 | 1 | .875 | 86 | 35 | 30 | 63 | 25 | 3.25 |
| 1974–Birmingham | Southern | 32 | 155 | 6 | 13 | .316 | 203 | *111 | 79 | 72 | 35 | 4.59 |
| 1975–Birmingham | Southern | 33 | 68 | 3 | 6 | .333 | 81 | 34 | 28 | 47 | 39 | 3.71 |
| 1975–Tucson | P. Coast | 10 | 35 | 3 | 1 | .750 | 35 | 14 | 12 | 17 | 9 | 3.09 |
| 1976–Tucson‡ | P. Coast | 29 | 105 | 3 | 9 | .250 | 139 | 73 | 69 | 35 | 26 | 5.91 |

†On suspended list, July 31 through remainder of season.
‡On disabled list, June 5 to June 16 and August 4 to September 8, 1976.
Listed on Oakland Athletics' 1977 spring roster.

## RALPH PIERRE LaCOCK, JR.
### (Pete)

Born January 17, 1952, at Burbank, Calif.
Height, 6.03. Weight, 210.
Throws and bats lefthanded.
Hobbies–Automobiles and oceanography.
Son of television personality Peter Marshall, and nephew of actress Joanne Dru.

Led Texas League hitters in bases on balls with 93 in 1972 and 84 in 1971.

| Year Club | League | Pos. | G. | AB. | R. | H. | 2B. | 3B. | HR. | RBI. | B.A. | PO. | A. | E. | F.A. |
|---|---|---|---|---|---|---|---|---|---|---|---|---|---|---|---|
| 1970–Caldwell | Pion. | OF | 69 | 231 | 43 | 65 | 13 | 3 | 4 | 49 | .281 | 76 | 6 | *10 | .981 |
| 1970–Quincy | Midw. | OF | 18 | 13 | 3 | 1 | 0 | 0 | 0 | 2 | .077 | 5 | 0 | 0 | 1.000 |
| 1971–San Antonio | Texas | OF | 131 | 446 | 64 | 119 | 19 | 5 | 7 | 58 | .267 | 187 | 11 | 10 | .952 |
| 1972–Midland | Texas | OF | 129 | 444 | 88 | 136 | 16 | *13 | 8 | 70 | .306 | 216 | 10 | 5 | .978 |
| 1972–Chicago | Nat. | OF | 5 | 6 | 3 | 3 | 0 | 0 | 0 | 4 | .500 | 2 | 0 | 0 | 1.000 |
| 1973–Wichita | A.A. | OF-1B | 130 | 518 | 89 | 154 | 24 | 6 | 9 | 69 | .297 | 238 | 17 | 8 | .970 |
| 1973–Chciago | Nat. | OF | 11 | 16 | 1 | 4 | 1 | 0 | 0 | 3 | .250 | 5 | 1 | 0 | 1.000 |
| 1974–Wichita | A.A. | 1B-OF | 121 | 455 | 95 | 149 | 25 | 4 | 23 | 91 | .327 | 841 | 66 | 11 | .988 |
| 1974–Chicago | Nat. | OF-1B | 35 | 110 | 9 | 20 | 4 | 1 | 1 | 8 | .182 | 134 | 12 | 2 | .986 |
| 1975–Chicago | Nat. | 1B-OF | 106 | 249 | 30 | 57 | 8 | 1 | 6 | 30 | .229 | 479 | 45 | 6 | .989 |
| 1976–Chicago† | Amer. | 1B-OF | 106 | 244 | 34 | 54 | 9 | 2 | 8 | 28 | .221 | 454 | 33 | 13 | .974 |
| Major League Totals | | | 263 | 625 | 77 | 138 | 22 | 4 | 15 | 73 | .221 | 1074 | 91 | 21 | .982 |

†Traded, in three-club deal, to Kansas City Royals, the New York Mets sent Outfielder Jim Dwyer from Tidewater to Wichita, Cub's affiliate, and the Mets were to receive a player to be named later from the Royals, December 8, 1976; Royals assigned Outfielder Sheldon Mallory to Tidewater, Mets' affiliate, to complete deal, December 13, 1976.

## FRANK JOSEPH LaCORTE, JR.

Name pronounced luh-KORT-ee.

Born October 13, 1952, at San Jose, Calif.
Height, 6.01. Weight, 180.
Throws and bats righthanded.
Hobby–Hunting.
Attended Gavilan College, Gilroy, Calif.

| Year Club | League | G. | IP. | W. | L. | Pct. | H. | R. | ER. | SO. | BB. | ERA. |
|---|---|---|---|---|---|---|---|---|---|---|---|---|
| 1973–Greenwood | W. Carol. | 18 | 105 | 7 | 8 | .467 | 70 | 44 | 30 | 109 | 51 | 2.57 |
| 1973–Savannah | Southern | 7 | 30 | 2 | 1 | .667 | 19 | 14 | 12 | 34 | 22 | 3.60 |
| 1974–Savannah | Southern | 23 | 120 | 7 | 8 | .467 | 106 | 76 | 63 | 106 | 89 | 4.73 |
| 1975–Richmond | Int'national | 24 | 128 | 9 | 7 | .563 | 121 | 65 | 61 | 108 | 71 | 4.29 |
| 1975–Atlanta | National | 3 | 14 | 0 | 3 | .000 | 13 | 10 | 8 | 10 | 6 | 5.14 |
| 1976–Richmond | Int'national | 14 | 78 | 3 | 3 | .500 | 91 | 55 | 46 | 77 | 47 | 5.31 |
| 1976–Atlanta | National | 19 | 105 | 3 | 12 | .200 | 97 | 58 | 55 | 79 | 53 | 4.71 |
| Major League Totals | | 22 | 119 | 3 | 15 | .167 | 110 | 68 | 63 | 89 | 59 | 4.76 |

## MICHAEL JAMES LACOSS
### (Mike)

Born May 30, 1956, at Glendale, Calif.
Height, 6.05. Weight, 185.
Throws and bats righthanded.
Hobbies–Hunting and fishing.

| Year Club | League | G. | IP. | W. | L. | Pct. | H. | R. | ER. | SO. | BB. | ERA. |
|---|---|---|---|---|---|---|---|---|---|---|---|---|
| 1974–Billings | Pioneer | 13 | 87 | 6 | 5 | .545 | 81 | 40 | 27 | 58 | 38 | 2.79 |
| 1975–Tampa | Florida St. | 23 | 151 | 4 | 7 | .412 | 131 | 61 | 48 | 72 | 41 | 2.86 |
| 1976–Three Rivers | Eastern | 25 | 162 | 12 | 10 | .545 | 148 | 66 | 53 | 80 | 53 | 2.94 |

Listed on Cincinnati Reds' 1977 spring roster.

---

### DID YOU KNOW –

That Johnny Mize hit three home runs in a game five times during his major league career? Lou Gehrig accomplished the feat four times.

---

## LEONDAUS LACY
### (Lee)

Born April 10, 1949, at Longview, Tex.
Height, 6.01. Weight, 180.
Throws and bats righthanded.
Hobbies—Fishing and hunting.
Attended Laney Junior College, Oakland, Calif.

Led Pioneer League third basemen in double plays with 9 in 1969.

| Year Club | League | Pos. | G. | AB. | R. | H. | 2B. | 3B. | HR. | RBI. | B.A. | PO. | A. | E. | F.A. |
|---|---|---|---|---|---|---|---|---|---|---|---|---|---|---|---|
| 1969—Ogden ..............Pion | | *3-S-2 | 71 | 239 | 43 | 70 | 6 | 7 | 1 | 38 | .293 | *54 | *121 | *27 | .866 |
| 1970—Bakersfield........Calif. | | *SS-3B | 124 | 502 | 96 | 151 | 19 | 5 | 4 | 49 | .301 | 189 | 291 | *66 | .879 |
| 1971—Albuquerque......Texas | | 2-3-S-O | 132 | 488 | 54 | 150 | 17 | 7 | 0 | 57 | .307 | 263 | 358 | 31 | .952 |
| 1972—El Paso ...........Texas | | 2-SS | 68 | 258 | 39 | 96 | 22 | 4 | 1 | 35 | .372 | 123 | 191 | 7 | .978 |
| 1972—Los Angeles ......Nat. | | 2B | 60 | 243 | 34 | 63 | 7 | 3 | 0 | 12 | .259 | 125 | 161 | 8 | .973 |
| 1973—Los Angeles ......Nat. | | 2B | 57 | 135 | 14 | 28 | 2 | 0 | 0 | 8 | .207 | 80 | 85 | 6 | .965 |
| 1974—Los Angeles ......Nat. | | 2B-3B | 48 | 78 | 13 | 22 | 6 | 0 | 0 | 8 | .282 | 38 | 53 | 3 | .968 |
| 1975—Los Angeles† ....Nat. | | 2-O-S | 101 | 306 | 44 | 96 | 11 | 5 | 7 | 40 | .314 | 152 | 75 | 13 | .946 |
| 1976—Atl.‡-L.A. ..........Nat. | | 2-O-3 | 103 | 338 | 42 | 91 | 11 | 3 | 3 | 34 | .269 | 193 | 111 | 9 | .971 |
| Major League Totals ..................... | | | 369 | 1100 | 147 | 300 | 37 | 11 | 10 | 102 | .273 | 588 | 485 | 39 | .965 |

†Traded with Outfielder Jimmy Wynn, First Baseman-Outfielder Tom Paciorek and Infielder Jerry Royster to Atlanta Braves for Outfielder Dusty Baker and First Baseman-Third Baseman Ed Goodson, November 17, 1975.

‡Traded with Pitcher Elias Sosa to Los Angeles Dodgers for Pitcher Mike Marshall, June 23, 1976.

### CHAMPIONSHIP SERIES RECORD

| Year Club | League | Pos. | G. | AB. | R. | H. | 2B. | 3B. | HR. | RBI. | B.A. | PO. | A. | E. | F.A. |
|---|---|---|---|---|---|---|---|---|---|---|---|---|---|---|---|
| 1974—Los Angeles ......Nat. | | PR | 1 | 0 | 0 | 0 | 0 | 0 | 0 | 0 | .000 | 0 | 0 | 0 | .000 |

### WORLD SERIES RECORD

| Year Club | League | Pos. | G. | AB. | R. | H. | 2B. | 3B. | HR. | RBI. | B.A. | PO. | A. | E. | F.A. |
|---|---|---|---|---|---|---|---|---|---|---|---|---|---|---|---|
| 1974—Los Angeles ......Nat. | | PH | 1 | 1 | 0 | 0 | 0 | 0 | 0 | 0 | .000 | 0 | 0 | 0 | .000 |

## LERRIN HARRIS LaGROW

Born July 8, 1948, at Phoenix, Ariz.
Height, 6.05. Weight, 230.
Throws and bats righthanded.
Hobbies—Basketball and golf.
Attended Arizona State University, Tempe Ariz.

Named Southern League Player of the Year in 1970.

| Year Club | League | G. | IP. | W. | L. | Pct. | H. | R. | ER. | SO. | BB. | ERA. |
|---|---|---|---|---|---|---|---|---|---|---|---|---|
| 1969—Montgomery .......................Southern | | 14 | 84 | 2 | 10 | .167 | 79 | 41 | 34 | 59 | 40 | 3.64 |
| 1970—Montgomery .......................Southern | | 19 | 146 | 11 | 4 | *.733 | 111 | 49 | 34 | 126 | 49 | 2.10 |
| 1970—Detroit ...............................American | | 10 | 12 | 0 | 1 | .000 | 16 | 11 | 10 | 7 | 6 | 7.50 |
| 1971—Toledo................................Int'national | | 36 | 69 | 2 | 6 | .250 | 73 | 63 | 46 | 65 | 60 | 6.00 |
| 1972—Toledo................................Int'national | | 22 | 115 | 8 | 6 | .571 | 94 | 43 | 31 | 92 | 59 | 2.43 |
| 1972—Detroit ...............................American | | 16 | 27 | 0 | 1 | .000 | 22 | 4 | 4 | 9 | 6 | 1.33 |
| 1973—Toledo................................Int'national | | 10 | 56 | 5 | 1 | .833 | 57 | 29 | 27 | 40 | 16 | 4.34 |
| 1973—Detroit† ............................American | | 21 | 54 | 1 | 5 | .167 | 54 | 26 | 26 | 33 | 23 | 4.33 |
| 1974—Detroit ..............................American | | 37 | 216 | 8 | 19 | .296 | 245 | 132 | 112 | 85 | 80 | 4.67 |
| 1975—Detroit‡ ............................American | | 32 | 164 | 7 | 14 | .333 | 183 | 105 | 80 | 75 | 66 | 4.39 |
| 1976—Tulsa ................................Am. Assoc. | | 25 | 161 | 6 | 10 | .375 | 171 | 81 | 74 | 108 | 45 | 4.14 |
| 1976—St. Louis§ ........................National | | 8 | 24 | 0 | 1 | .000 | 21 | 4 | 4 | 10 | 7 | 1.50 |
| American League Totals........................... | | 116 | 473 | 16 | 40 | .286 | 520 | 278 | 232 | 209 | 181 | 4.41 |
| National League Totals.......................... | | 8 | 24 | 0 | 1 | .000 | 21 | 4 | 4 | 10 | 7 | 1.50 |
| Major League Totals .............................. | | 124 | 497 | 16 | 41 | .281 | 541 | 282 | 236 | 219 | 188 | 4.27 |

†On disabled list, June 15 to July 10, 1973.
‡Sold to St. Louis Cardinals, April 2, 1976.
§Traded to Chicago White Sox for Pitcher Clay Carroll, March 23, 1977.

### CHAMPIONSHIP SERIES RECORD

| Year Club | League | G. | IP. | W. | L. | Pct. | H. | R. | ER. | SO. | BB. | ERA. |
|---|---|---|---|---|---|---|---|---|---|---|---|---|
| 1972—Detroit ...............................American | | 1 | 1 | 0 | 0 | .000 | 0 | 0 | 0 | 1 | 0 | 0.00 |

## JOSEPH MICHAEL LAHOUD, JR.
### Name pronounced la-WHO.
### (Joe)

Born April 14, 1947, at Danbury, Conn.
Height, 6.01. Weight, 202.
Throws and bats lefthanded.
Hobbies—Bowling, fishing and basketball.
Attended New Haven College, New Haven, Conn.

Led International League batters in walks with 116 in 1970.

| Year Club League | Pos. | G. | AB. | R. | H. | 2B. | 3B. | HR. | RBI. | B.A. | PO. | A. | E. | F.A. |
|---|---|---|---|---|---|---|---|---|---|---|---|---|---|---|
| 1966—Winston-Salem ..Carol. | OF | 62 | 176 | 25 | 46 | 5 | 4 | 3 | 25 | .261 | 51 | 3 | 1 | .982 |
| 1967—Winston-Salem ..Carol. | OF | 99 | 310 | 49 | 89 | 19 | 4 | 16 | 62 | .287 | 119 | 7 | 6 | .955 |
| 1968—Boston .............Amer. | OF | 29 | 78 | 5 | 15 | 1 | 0 | 1 | 6 | .192 | 23 | 2 | 2 | .926 |
| 1968—Louisville .........Int. | OF | 101 | 326 | 47 | 89 | 10 | 4 | 8 | 40 | .273 | 174 | 11 | 8 | .959 |
| 1969—Boston .............Amer. | OF-1B | 101 | 218 | 32 | 41 | 5 | 0 | 9 | 21 | .188 | 91 | 3 | 2 | .979 |
| 1970—Louisville .........Int. | OF | 136 | 454 | 92 | 136 | 19 | 7 | 17 | 93 | .300 | 220 | 4 | 10 | .957 |
| 1970—Boston .............Amer. | OF | 17 | 49 | 6 | 12 | 1 | 0 | 2 | 5 | .245 | 23 | 3 | 1 | .963 |
| 1971—Boston† ...........Amer. | OF | 107 | 256 | 39 | 55 | 9 | 3 | 14 | 32 | .215 | 139 | 4 | 1 | .993 |
| 1972—Milwaukee .......Amer. | OF | 111 | 316 | 35 | 75 | 9 | 3 | 12 | 34 | .237 | 189 | 2 | 5 | .974 |
| 1973—Milwaukee‡ ......Amer. | OF | 96 | 225 | 29 | 46 | 9 | 0 | 5 | 26 | .204 | 85 | 2 | 0 | 1.000 |
| 1974—California.........Amer. | OF | 127 | 325 | 46 | 88 | 16 | 3 | 13 | 44 | .271 | 156 | 6 | 4 | .976 |
| 1975—California§ .......Amer. | OF | 76 | 192 | 21 | 41 | 6 | 2 | 6 | 33 | .214 | 41 | 1 | 0 | 1.000 |
| 1976—Calif. x-Tex. ......Amer. | OF-DH | 80 | 185 | 18 | 37 | 7 | 1 | 1 | 9 | .200 | 54 | 0 | 2 | .964 |
| Major League Totals ..................... | | 724 | 1844 | 231 | 410 | 63 | 12 | 63 | 210 | .222 | 801 | 23 | 17 | .980 |

†Traded with Catcher Don Pavletich, Pitchers Ken Brett and Jim Lonborg, First Baseman George Scott and Outfielder Billy Conigliaro to Milwaukee Brewers for Pitchers Marty Pattin and Lew Krausse and Outfielders Tommy Harper and Pat Skrable, Ocotber 11, 1971.
‡Traded with Pitchers Skip Lockwood and Gary Ryerson, Outfielder Ollie Brown and Catcher Ellie Rodriguez to California Angels for Pitchers Clyde Wright and Steve Barber, Outfielder Ken Berry, Catcher Art Kusnyer and a player to be named later, October 22, 1973.
§On disabled list, August 18 through remainder of season.
xSold to Texas Rangers, June 15, 1976.

## DENNIS PATRICK LAMP

Born September 23, 1952, at Los Angeles, Calif.
Height, 6.04. Weight, 200.
Throws and bats righthanded.
Hobbies—Music and coaching basketball.

| Year Club League | G. | IP. | W. | L. | Pct. | H. | R. | ER. | SO. | BB. | ERA. |
|---|---|---|---|---|---|---|---|---|---|---|---|
| 1971—Caldwell ..............................Pioneer | 14 | 46 | 1 | 2 | .333 | 51 | 39 | 33 | 43 | 32 | 6.46 |
| 1972—Bradenton Cubs....................Gulf Coast | 14 | 70 | 7 | 2 | .778 | 56 | 20 | 15 | 56 | 21 | 1.93 |
| 1973—Quincy ...............................Midwest | 13 | 89 | 6 | 4 | .600 | 67 | 32 | 26 | 71 | 29 | 2.63 |
| 1973—Midland...............................Texas | 9 | 48 | 2 | 4 | .333 | 54 | 29 | 25 | 23 | 11 | 4.69 |
| 1974—Key West ...........................Florida St. | 8 | 49 | 1 | 5 | .167 | 39 | 15 | 8 | 20 | 14 | 1.47 |
| 1974—Midland...............................Texas | 24 | 60 | 1 | 1 | .500 | 70 | 38 | 31 | 42 | 22 | 4.65 |
| 1975—Midland...............................Texas | 37 | 127 | 7 | 5 | .583 | 112 | 52 | 47 | 71 | 54 | 3.33 |
| 1976—Wichita† ..............................Am. Assoc. | 30 | 153 | 8 | *14 | .364 | 182 | 94 | 69 | 98 | 52 | 4.06 |

†Released, March 30, 1977.
Listed on Chicago Cubs' 1977 spring roster.

## RAFAEL SILVIALDO LANDESTOY (SANTANA)

Born May 28, 1953, at Bani, Dominican Republic.
Height, 5.10. Weight, 165.
Throws and bats righthanded.
Hobby—Listening to music.
Led Eastern League shortstops in double plays with 73 in 1975.

| Year Club League | Pos. | G. | AB. | R. | H. | 2B. | 3B. | HR. | RBI. | B.A. | PO. | A. | E. | F.A. |
|---|---|---|---|---|---|---|---|---|---|---|---|---|---|---|
| 1972—Ogden ..............Pion. | OF | 49 | 119 | 13 | 29 | 4 | 2 | 0 | 14 | .244 | 50 | 2 | 4 | .929 |
| 1973—Daytona Beach ..Fla.St. | OF | 96 | 288 | 31 | 84 | 11 | 0 | 0 | 24 | .292 | 145 | 11 | 3 | .981 |
| 1974—Orangeburg ......W. Car. | SS-O-2B | ●134 | 492 | 71 | 135 | 13 | 5 | 2 | 49 | .274 | 264 | 218 | 47 | .911 |
| 1975—Waterbury ........East. | *SS-OF | 130 | 439 | 61 | 123 | 10 | 7 | 0 | 31 | .280 | *203 | *388 | *60 | .908 |
| 1976—Albuquerque......P.C. | S-2-3-O | 140 | 463 | 68 | 128 | 14 | 7 | 2 | 54 | .276 | 226 | 399 | 38 | .943 |

Listed on Los Angeles Dodgers' 1977 spring roster.

## LARRY ROBERT LANDRETH

Born March 11, 1955, at Stratford, Ontario, Canada.
Height, 6.01. Weight, 175.
Throws and bats righthanded.
Hobby—Music.

| Year Club League | G. | IP. | W. | L. | Pct. | H. | R. | ER. | SO. | BB. | ERA. |
|---|---|---|---|---|---|---|---|---|---|---|---|
| 1973—Jamestown ..........................NYP | 14 | 92 | 6 | 4 | .600 | 84 | 44 | 41 | 80 | 37 | 4.01 |
| 1974—West Palm Beach ...............Florida St. | 26 | 188 | 15 | 7 | .682 | 156 | 69 | 53 | 146 | 48 | 2.54 |
| 1974—Quebec City ......................Eastern | 1 | 2 | 0 | 0 | .000 | 4 | 1 | 1 | 3 | 0 | 4.50 |
| 1975—Quebec City ......................Eastern | 25 | 181 | 10 | 12 | .455 | 143 | 78 | 54 | 133 | 85 | 2.69 |
| 1976—Denver ...............................Am. Assoc. | 26 | 155 | 13 | 9 | .591 | 128 | 77 | 64 | 118 | 83 | 3.72 |
| 1976—Montreal ............................National | 3 | 11 | 1 | 2 | .333 | 13 | 8 | 5 | 7 | 10 | 4.09 |
| Major League Totals ............................. | 3 | 11 | 1 | 2 | .333 | 13 | 8 | 5 | 7 | 10 | 4.09 |

## TERRY LEE LANDRUM
### (Tito)

Born October 25, 1954, at Joplin, Mo.
Height, 5.11. Weight, 174.
Throws and bats righthanded.
Hobbies—Coin collecting and playing guitar.
Attended Eastern Oklahoma State College, Wilburton, Okla.

| Year Club League | Pos. | G. | AB. | R. | H. | 2B. | 3B. | HR. | RBI. | B.A. | PO. | A. | E. | F.A. |
|---|---|---|---|---|---|---|---|---|---|---|---|---|---|---|
| 1973–Orangeburg ......W. Car. | OF | 70 | 262 | 30 | 73 | 7 | 3 | 1 | 27 | .279 | 168 | 7 | 1 | .994 |
| 1974–St. Petersburg†..Fla.St. | OF | 87 | 309 | 38 | 73 | 5 | 9 | 3 | 39 | .236 | 214 | 7 | 8 | .965 |
| 1975–St. Petersburg ..Fla.St. | OF | 132 | 435 | 76 | 96 | 21 | 4 | 11 | 45 | .221 | 313 | 5 | 7 | .978 |
| 1976–Arkansas‡ .......Texas | OF | 99 | 359 | 49 | 99 | 13 | 3 | 7 | 45 | .276 | 201 | 12 | 7 | .968 |
| 1976–Tulsa ................A.A. | OF | 9 | 24 | 1 | 6 | 1 | 0 | 0 | 1 | .250 | 17 | 0 | 0 | 1.000 |

†On disabled list, July 19 through September 20, 1974.
‡On disabled list, April 24 through May 10, 1976.
Listed on St. Louis Cardinals' 1977 spring roster.

# MARVIN LANE

Born January 18, 1950, at Sandersville, Ga.
Height, 5.11. Weight, 180.
Throws and bats righthanded.
Hobbies–Basketball and golf.
Attended Arizona State University, Tempe, Ariz.

| Year Club League | Pos. | G. | AB. | R. | H. | 2B. | 3B. | HR. | RBI. | B.A. | PO. | A. | E. | F.A. |
|---|---|---|---|---|---|---|---|---|---|---|---|---|---|---|
| 1969–Lakeland† .........Fla.St. | OF | 11 | 51 | 5 | 12 | 3 | 1 | 0 | 1 | .235 | 25 | 2 | 1 | .964 |
| 1970–Lakeland ..........Fla.St. | OF | 94 | 361 | 52 | 83 | 4 | 6 | 2 | 30 | .230 | 189 | 6 | 2 | .990 |
| 1971–Rocky Mount ....Carol. | OF | 99 | 361 | 59 | 111 | 20 | 5 | 8 | 51 | .307 | 195 | 10 | 4 | .981 |
| 1971–Detroit .............Amer. | OF | 8 | 14 | 0 | 2 | 0 | 0 | 0 | 1 | .143 | 6 | 0 | 0 | 1.000 |
| 1972–Montgomery ......South. | OF | 104 | 369 | 67 | 115 | 21 | 5 | 13 | 63 | .312 | 206 | 4 | 4 | .981 |
| 1972–Detroit .............Amer. | OF | 8 | 6 | 2 | 0 | 0 | 0 | 0 | 0 | .000 | 3 | 0 | 0 | 1.000 |
| 1973–Toledo‡ .............Int. | OF | 80 | 242 | 37 | 56 | 11 | 5 | 5 | 33 | .231 | 189 | 5 | 2 | .990 |
| 1973–Detroit .............Amer. | OF | 6 | 8 | 2 | 2 | 0 | 0 | 1 | 2 | .250 | 7 | 0 | 0 | 1.000 |
| 1974–Evansville ........A.A. | OF | 43 | 158 | 19 | 42 | 1 | 4 | 4 | 17 | .266 | 66 | 1 | 1 | .985 |
| 1974–Detroit .............Amer. | OF | 50 | 103 | 16 | 24 | 4 | 1 | 2 | 9 | .233 | 70 | 3 | 1 | .986 |
| 1975–Evansville ........A.A. | OF-1B | 108 | 324 | 49 | 83 | 22 | 4 | 9 | 42 | .256 | 148 | 6 | 3 | .981 |
| 1976–Evansville ........A.A. | OF-1B | 85 | 276 | 46 | 80 | 13 | 7 | 13 | 61 | .290 | 177 | 6 | 4 | .979 |
| 1976–Detroit§ ...........Amer. | OF | 18 | 48 | 3 | 9 | 1 | 0 | 0 | 5 | .188 | 23 | 1 | 1 | .960 |
| Major League Totals ...................... | | 90 | 179 | 23 | 37 | 5 | 1 | 3 | 17 | .207 | 109 | 4 | 2 | .983 |

†On military list, May 19, 1969 to March 31, 1970.
‡On temporary inactive list, August 3 to August 21, 1973.
§On disabled list, July 28 to August 9 and August 11 to August 21, 1976.
Released, March 28, 1977.

# ROBERT DAVID LANG
## (Chip)
(Nicknamed by father because of chipmunk noises made when baby.)

Born August 21, 1952, at Pittsburgh, Pa.
Height, 6.04. Weight, 205.
Throws and bats righthanded.
Hobbies–Golf, swimming and listening to music.

Pitched 3-0 no-hit victory against West Haven, August 4, 1973.
Led Gulf Coast League pitchers in games started with 13 in 1970.

| Year Club League | G. | IP. | W. | L. | Pct. | H. | R. | ER. | SO. | BB. | ERA. |
|---|---|---|---|---|---|---|---|---|---|---|---|
| 1970–Bradenton Expos .................Gulf Coast | 13 | 74 | 2 | ●7 | .222 | 70 | 42 | 33 | 71 | 29 | 4.01 |
| 1971–West Palm Beach ...............Florida St. | 25 | 157 | 9 | 10 | .474 | 142 | 83 | 49 | 127 | 74 | 2.81 |
| 1971–Quebec City .......................Eastern | 2 | 11 | 0 | 2 | .000 | 7 | 4 | 3 | 12 | 7 | 2.45 |
| 1972–West Palm Beach† .............Florida St. | 9 | 24 | 0 | 3 | .000 | 29 | 27 | 22 | 11 | 17 | 8.25 |
| 1973–Quebec City‡ ......................Eastern | 22 | 102 | 8 | 5 | .615 | 103 | 54 | 41 | 73 | 64 | 3.62 |
| 1974–Quebec City .......................Eastern | 9 | 69 | 5 | 1 | .833 | 53 | 17 | 13 | 57 | 36 | 1.70 |
| 1974–Memphis ...........................Int'national | 16 | 90 | 5 | 7 | .417 | 78 | 39 | 32 | 65 | 42 | 3.20 |
| 1975–Memphis ...........................Int'national | 31 | 184 | 8 | 13 | .381 | 151 | 75 | 60 | 98 | 81 | 2.93 |
| 1975–Montreal ...........................National | 1 | 2 | 0 | 0 | .000 | 2 | 2 | 2 | 2 | 3 | 9.00 |
| 1976–Denver ...........................Am. Assoc. | 8 | 42 | 0 | 3 | .000 | 53 | 37 | 35 | 27 | 23 | 7.50 |
| 1976–Montreal ...........................National | 29 | 62 | 1 | 3 | .250 | 56 | 32 | 29 | 30 | 34 | 4.21 |
| Major League Totals ............................... | 30 | 64 | 1 | 3 | .250 | 58 | 34 | 31 | 32 | 37 | 4.36 |

†On military list, June 2 through remainder of season.
‡On temporary inactive list, July 3 to July 18, 1973.

# RICHARD OTTO LANGE
## (Dick)

Born September 1, 1948, at Harbor Beach, Mich.
Height, 5.10. Weight, 185.
Throws and bats righthanded.
Hobbies–Hunting and fishing.
Attended Central Michigan University, Mount Pleasant, Mich.

Led Pioneer League in winning percentage with 1.000, complete games with 10, shutouts with 3 and wild pitches with 14 in 1970.
Named Pioneer League Player of the Year in 1970.

| Year Club League | G. | IP. | W. | L. | Pct. | H. | R. | ER. | SO. | BB. | ERA. |
|---|---|---|---|---|---|---|---|---|---|---|---|
| 1970–Idaho Falls .........................Pioneer | 14 | 111 | ★13 | 0 | 1.000 | 70 | 28 | 24 | ★151 | 54 | ★1.95 |
| 1971–Shreveport .........................Texas | 8 | 60 | 2 | 3 | .400 | 51 | 17 | 15 | 57 | 12 | 2.25 |
| 1971–Salt Lake City .....................P. Coast | 22 | 125 | 8 | 6 | .571 | 119 | 63 | 53 | 93 | 53 | 3.82 |

| Year Club | League | G. | IP. | W. | L. | Pct. | H. | R. | ER. | SO. | BB. | ERA. |
|---|---|---|---|---|---|---|---|---|---|---|---|---|
| 1972–Salt Lake City† .....................P. | Coast | 33 | 182 | 11 | 11 | .500 | 159 | 71 | 60 | 140 | 71 | •2.97 |
| 1972–California ...........................American | | 2 | 8 | 0 | 0 | .000 | 7 | 4 | 4 | 8 | 2 | 4.50 |
| 1973–Salt Lake City.....................P. | Coast | 13 | 89 | 7 | 6 | .538 | 77 | 38 | 28 | 60 | 35 | 2.83 |
| 1973–California ............................American | | 17 | 53 | 2 | 1 | .667 | 61 | 30 | 26 | 27 | 21 | 4.42 |
| 1974–California ............................American | | 21 | 114 | 3 | 8 | .273 | 111 | 63 | 48 | 57 | 47 | 3.79 |
| 1975–Salt Lake City.....................P. | Coast | 3 | 18 | 0 | 1 | .000 | 18 | 14 | 9 | 7 | 12 | 4.50 |
| 1975–California ............................American | | 30 | 102 | 4 | 6 | .400 | 119 | 70 | 59 | 45 | 53 | 5.21 |
| 1976–Salt Lake City.....................P. | Coast | 30 | 193 | 12 | 7 | .632 | 216 | 102 | 86 | 107 | 65 | 4.01 |
| Major League Totals ............................. | | 70 | 277 | 9 | 15 | .375 | 298 | 167 | 137 | 137 | 123 | 4.45 |

†On disabled list, April 17 through May 4, 1972.
Invited to California Angels' 1977 spring camp.

## JAMES RICK LANGFORD
(Known by middle name.)

Born March 20, 1952, at Farmville, Va.
Height, 6.00. Weight, 180.
Throws and bats righthanded.
Hobbies–Sailing and all water sports.
Attended Manatee Junior College, Bradenton, Fla., and
Florida State University, Tallahassee, Fla.

Pitched seven inning 11-0 no-hit victory against Memphis, May 30, 1976.

| Year Club | League | G. | IP. | W. | L. | Pct. | H. | R. | ER. | SO. | BB. | ERA. |
|---|---|---|---|---|---|---|---|---|---|---|---|---|
| 1973–Bradenton Pirates† .............Gulf | C. | 3 | 10 | 1 | 0 | 1.000 | 5 | 3 | 0 | 10 | 7 | 0.00 |
| 1974–Salem ........................Carolina | | 26 | 174 | 11 | 7 | .611 | 143 | 63 | 52 | 125 | 74 | 2.69 |
| 1975–Shreveport .........................Texas | | 16 | 42 | 5 | 2 | .714 | 40 | 25 | 17 | 39 | 22 | 3.64 |
| 1975–Charleston ....................Int'national | | 13 | 65 | 7 | 2 | .778 | 55 | 26 | 24 | 41 | 20 | 3.32 |
| 1976–Charleston ....................Int'national | | 16 | 121 | 9 | 5 | .643 | 106 | 51 | 43 | 95 | 48 | 3.20 |
| 1976–Pittsburgh‡ ......................National | | 12 | 23 | 0 | 1 | .000 | 27 | 17 | 16 | 17 | 14 | 6.26 |
| Major League Totals ............................. | | 12 | 23 | 0 | 1 | .000 | 27 | 17 | 16 | 17 | 14 | 6.26 |

†On suspended list, July 17 through remainder of season.
‡Traded with Pitchers Doc Medich, Dave Giusti and Doug Bair, Infielder Mitchell Page and Outfielder Tony Armas to Oakland A's for Infielders Phil Garner and Tommy Helms, and Pitcher Chris Batton, March 15, 1977.

## DAVID EUGENE LaROCHE
(Dave)

Born May 14, 1948, at Colorado Springs, Colo.
Height, 6.02. Weight, 200.
Throws and bats lefthanded.
Hobbies–Golf and Basketball.
Attended University of Nevada at Las Vegas, Las Vegas, Nev.

| Year Club | League | G. | IP. | W. | L. | Pct. | H. | R. | ER. | SO. | BB. | ERA. |
|---|---|---|---|---|---|---|---|---|---|---|---|---|
| 1968–Quad Cities .........................Midwest | | 33 | 84 | 5 | 7 | .417 | 76 | 33 | 22 | 80 | 29 | 2.36 |
| 1969–San Jose .............................California | | 11 | 21 | 2 | 1 | .667 | 21 | 11 | 9 | 19 | 8 | 3.68 |
| 1969–El Paso...............................Texas | | 33 | 49 | 6 | 3 | .667 | 43 | 16 | 16 | 46 | 25 | 2.94 |
| 1970–Hawaii ...............................P. | Coast | 22 | 58 | 6 | 0 | 1.000 | 31 | 11 | 8 | 67 | 19 | 1.24 |
| 1970–California ...........................American | | 38 | 50 | 4 | 1 | .800 | 41 | 20 | 19 | 44 | 21 | 3.42 |
| 1971–California† ..........................American | | 56 | 72 | 5 | 1 | .833 | 55 | 21 | 20 | 63 | 27 | 2.50 |
| 1972–Minnesota‡ ..........................American | | 62 | 95 | 5 | 7 | .417 | 72 | 33 | 30 | 79 | 39 | 2.84 |
| 1973–Chicago§ .............................National | | 45 | 54 | 4 | 1 | .800 | 55 | 37 | 35 | 34 | 29 | 5.83 |
| 1974–Wichita ...........................Am. | Assoc. | 6 | 32 | 1 | 3 | .250 | 37 | 19 | 18 | 17 | 7 | 5.06 |
| 1974–Chicago x ...........................National | | 49 | 92 | 5 | 6 | .455 | 103 | 54 | 49 | 49 | 47 | 4.79 |
| 1975–Cleveland .............................American | | 61 | 82 | 5 | 3 | .625 | 61 | 26 | 20 | 94 | 57 | 2.20 |
| 1976–Cleveland ............................American | | 61 | 96 | 1 | 4 | .200 | 57 | 25 | 24 | 104 | 49 | 2.25 |
| American League Totals........................... | | 278 | 395 | 20 | 16 | .556 | 286 | 125 | 113 | 384 | 193 | 2.57 |
| National League Totals............................ | | 94 | 146 | 9 | 7 | .563 | 158 | 91 | 84 | 83 | 76 | 5.18 |
| Major League Totals ............................. | | 372 | 541 | 29 | 23 | .558 | 444 | 216 | 197 | 467 | 269 | 3.28 |

†Traded to Minnesota Twins for Shortstop Leo Cardenas, November 30, 1971.
‡Traded to Chicago Cubs for Pitchers Bill Hands, George (Joe) Decker and Bob Maneely, November 30, 1972.
§On disabled list, March 25 to April 17, 1973.
xTraded with Outfielder Brock Davis to Cleveland Indians for Pitcher Milt Wilcox, February 28, 1975.

### RECORD AS OUTFIELDER

| Year Club | League | Pos. | G. | AB. | R. | H. | 2B. | 3B. | HR. | RBI. | B.A. | PO. | A. | E. | F.A. |
|---|---|---|---|---|---|---|---|---|---|---|---|---|---|---|---|
| 1967–San Jose...........Calif. | | OF | 16 | 55 | 4 | 10 | 2 | 0 | 0 | 6 | .182 | 18 | 1 | 0 | 1.000 |
| 1967–Quad Cities ......Midw. | | OF | 95 | 342 | 39 | 80 | 17 | 0 | 6 | 40 | .234 | 189 | 8 | 8 | .961 |
| 1968–Quad Cities ......Midw. | | P-O-1 | 58 | 98 | 15 | 21 | 3 | 0 | 2 | 9 | .214 | 51 | 18 | 3 | .958 |

```
D I D   Y O U   K N O W —
```
That Vern Kennedy of the Chicago White Sox pitched a 5-0 no-hit victory over the Cleveland Indians on August 31, 1935?

## DANIEL JAMES LARSON
### (Dan)
Born July 4, 1954, at Los Angeles, Calif.
Height, 6.00. Weight, 175.
Throws and bats righthanded.
Hobbies—Backpacking, camping and music.
Attended Whittier College, Whittier, Calif.

| Year | Club | League | G. | IP. | W. | L. | Pct. | H. | R. | ER. | SO. | BB. | ERA. |
|------|------|--------|----|-----|----|----|------|----|----|-----|-----|-----|------|
| 1972—Sarasota Cards. | | Gulf C. | 10 | 57 | 3 | 2 | .600 | 34 | 17 | 9 | 44 | 37 | 1.42 |
| 1973—Modesto | | California | 19 | 100 | 4 | 10 | .286 | 114 | 83 | 63 | 105 | 58 | 5.67 |
| 1973—St. Petersburg | | Florida St. | 6 | 26 | 3 | 1 | .750 | 22 | 14 | 10 | 17 | 12 | 3.46 |
| 1974—Modesto | | California | 22 | 142 | 12 | 6 | .667 | 164 | 96 | 78 | 125 | 61 | 4.94 |
| 1974—Arkansas† | | Texas | 2 | 14 | 2 | 0 | 1.000 | 7 | 5 | 4 | 10 | 6 | 2.57 |
| 1975—Columbus | | Southern | 17 | 132 | 7 | 8 | .467 | 118 | 42 | 32 | 76 | 46 | •2.18 |
| 1975—Iowa | | Am. Assoc. | 12 | 83 | 4 | 6 | .400 | 82 | 42 | 34 | 67 | 45 | 3.69 |
| 1976—Memphis | | Int'national | 17 | 118 | 7 | 4 | .636 | 132 | 68 | 57 | 79 | 60 | 4.35 |
| 1976—Houston | | National | 13 | 92 | 5 | 8 | .385 | 81 | 40 | 31 | 42 | 28 | 3.03 |
| Major League Totals | | | 13 | 92 | 5 | 8 | .385 | 81 | 40 | 31 | 42 | 28 | 3.03 |

†Assigned by St. Louis Cardinals to Houston Astros, October 14, 1974, to complete deal in which Cardinals obtained Pitcher Claude Osteen from Astros for Pitcher Ron Selak and a player to be named later, August 15, 1974.

## GARY ROBERT LAVELLE
Born January 3, 1949, at Sacranton, Pa.
Height, 6.01. Weight, 190.
Throws left and bats right and lefthanded.
Hobby—All sports.
Pitched seven-inning, 4-0 no-hit game against Clinton, August 15, 1969.
Tied for Pacific Coast League lead in shutouts with 3 in 1974.

| Year | Club | League | G. | IP. | W. | L. | Pct. | H. | R. | ER. | SO. | BB. | ERA. |
|------|------|--------|----|-----|----|----|------|----|----|-----|-----|-----|------|
| 1967—Salt Lake City | | Pioneer | 17 | 37 | 3 | 2 | .600 | 37 | 18 | 12 | 32 | 23 | 2.92 |
| 1968—Medford | | Northwest | 13 | 60 | 3 | 3 | .500 | 53 | 33 | 23 | 67 | 42 | 3.45 |
| 1969—Decatur† | | Midwest | 7 | 48 | 4 | 2 | .667 | 41 | 17 | 9 | 30 | 24 | 1.69 |
| 1970—Amarillo | | Texas | 21 | 100 | 6 | 12 | .333 | 99 | 75 | 60 | 64 | 72 | 5.40 |
| 1971—Amarillo | | Texas | 23 | 136 | 11 | 8 | .579 | 132 | 65 | 53 | 77 | 56 | 3.50 |
| 1972—Phoenix | | P. Coast | 37 | 147 | 11 | 14 | .440 | 161 | 91 | 69 | 107 | 55 | 4.22 |
| 1973—Phoenix‡ | | P. Coast | 36 | 101 | 5 | 7 | .417 | 112 | 56 | 51 | 61 | 43 | 4.54 |
| Year | Club | League | G. | IP. | W. | L. | Pct. | H. | R. | ER. | SO. | BB. | ERA. |
| 1974—Phoenix | | P. Coast | 35 | 182 | 8 | •16 | .333 | 228 | 119 | 106 | 105 | 76 | 5.24 |
| 1974—San Francisco | | National | 10 | 17 | 0 | 3 | .000 | 14 | 7 | 4 | 12 | 10 | 2.12 |
| 1975—San Francisco | | National | 65 | 82 | 6 | 3 | .667 | 80 | 30 | 27 | 51 | 48 | 2.96 |
| 1976—San Francisco | | National | 65 | 110 | 10 | 6 | .625 | 102 | 37 | 33 | 71 | 52 | 2.70 |
| Major League Totals | | | 140 | 209 | 16 | 12 | .571 | 196 | 74 | 64 | 134 | 110 | 2.76 |

†On suspended list, April 11, 1969. Transferred to military list through July 5, 1969.
‡On temporary inactive list, June 2 to June 20, 1973.

## WILLIAM HARRY LAXTON
### (Bill)
Born January 5, 1948, at Camden, N. J.
Height, 6.02. Weight, 188.
Throws and bats lefthanded.
Pitched seven-inning, 2-1 no-hit victory against Waterloo, August 25, 1967.
Led Carolina League in wild pitches with 28 in 1968 and tied for Eastern League lead with 15 in 1969.
Led Appalachian Leaaue in hit batsmen with 6 in 1966 and tied for Midwest League lead with 10 in 1967.

| Year | Club | League | G. | IP. | W. | L. | Pct. | H. | R. | ER. | SO. | BB. | ERA. |
|------|------|--------|----|-----|----|----|------|----|----|-----|-----|-----|------|
| 1966—Salem† | | Ap'lachin | 10 | 59 | 1 | 6 | .143 | 41 | 33 | 24 | 79 | •57 | 3.66 |
| 1967—Clinton‡§ | | Midwest | 20 | 89 | 4 | 9 | .308 | 61 | 49 | 37 | 104 | 83 | 3.74 |
| 1968—Tidewater x | | Carolina | 27 | 80 | 3 | 6 | .333 | 52 | 51 | 41 | 90 | 92 | 4.61 |
| 1969—Reading | | Eastern | 20 | 107 | 7 | 9 | .438 | 69 | 46 | 43 | 94 | 105 | 3.62 |
| 1970—Eugene | | Northwest | 15 | 78 | 6 | 5 | .545 | 58 | 41 | 31 | 63 | 93 | 3.58 |
| Year | Club | League | G. | IP. | W. | L. | Pct. | H. | R. | ER. | SO. | BB. | ERA. |
| 1970—Reading | | Eastern | 9 | 37 | 1 | 3 | .250 | 36 | 24 | 23 | 39 | 32 | 5.59 |
| 1970—Philadelphia y | | National | 2 | 2 | 0 | 0 | .000 | 2 | 3 | 3 | 2 | 2 | 13.50 |
| 1971—San Diego | | National | 18 | 28 | 0 | 2 | .000 | 32 | 25 | 21 | 23 | 26 | 6.75 |
| 1972—Alexandria | | Texas | 20 | 88 | 4 | 6 | .400 | 69 | 33 | 31 | 88 | 63 | 3.16 |
| 1973—Alexandria z | | Texas | 25 | 133 | 9 | 8 | .529 | 105 | 67 | 61 | 142 | 94 | 4.11 |
| 1974—Alexandria | | Texas | 13 | 30 | 3 | 0 | 1.000 | 20 | 10 | 8 | 29 | 19 | 2.40 |
| 1974—San Diego a | | National | 30 | 45 | 0 | 1 | .000 | 37 | 22 | 20 | 40 | 38 | 4.00 |
| 1975—Tidewater b | | Int'national | 24 | 130 | 11 | 4 | .733 | 91 | 37 | 36 | 113 | 56 | 2.49 |
| 1976—Detroit c | | American | 26 | 95 | 0 | 5 | .000 | 77 | 49 | 43 | 74 | 51 | 4.07 |
| National League Totals | | | 50 | 75 | 0 | 3 | .000 | 71 | 50 | 44 | 65 | 66 | 5.28 |
| American League Totals | | | 26 | 95 | 0 | 5 | .000 | 77 | 49 | 43 | 74 | 51 | 4.07 |
| Major League Totals | | | 76 | 170 | 0 | 8 | .000 | 148 | 99 | 87 | 139 | 117 | 4.61 |

†On military list, October 31, 1966 through May 1, 1967.
‡On temporary inactive list, June 18 through July 2, 1967.
§Traded with Pitchers Woodie Fryman and Harold Clem and Infielder Don Money by Pittsburgh Pirates to Philadelphia Phillies for Pitcher Jim Bunning, December 15, 1967.
xOn temporary inactive list, June 7 through June 29, 1968.
yDrafted by San Diego Padres from Eugene (Philadelphia Phillies' organization), November 30, 1970.
zPlayed in two games as a first baseman.
aReleased, April 7, 1975; signed as a free agent by New York Mets, April 25, 1975.
bTraded with Outfielder Rusty Staub by New York Mets to Detroit Tigers for Pitcher Mickey Lolich and Outfielder Billy Baldwin, December 12, 1975.
cSelected by Seattle Mariners in American League expansion draft, November 5, 1976.

## WILLIAM FRANCIS LEE, III
### (Bill)

Born December 28, 1946, at Burbank, Calif.
Height, 6.02. Weight, 210.
Throws and bats lefthanded.
Hobbies—Fishing, hunting and golf.
Attended University of Southern California, Los Angeles, Calif., and University of Southern Mississippi, Hattiesburg, Miss.; received Bachelor of Arts degree in Physical Education and Geography from U.S.C.

| Year Club | League | G. | IP. | W. | L. | Pct. | H. | R. | ER. | SO. | BB. | ERA. |
|---|---|---|---|---|---|---|---|---|---|---|---|---|
| 1968—Waterloo | Midwest | 8 | 27 | 1 | 1 | .500 | 14 | 10 | 4 | 31 | 17 | 1.33 |
| 1968—Winston-Salem | Carolina | 8 | 47 | 3 | 3 | .500 | 36 | 23 | 9 | 38 | 19 | 1.72 |
| 1969—Pittsfield | Eastern | 10 | 70 | 6 | 2 | .750 | 48 | 25 | 16 | 48 | 32 | 2.06 |
| 1969—Boston | American | 20 | 52 | 1 | 3 | .250 | 56 | 27 | 26 | 45 | 28 | 4.50 |
| 1970—Boston† | American | 11 | 37 | 2 | 2 | .500 | 48 | 20 | 19 | 19 | 14 | 4.62 |
| 1971—Boston | American | 47 | 102 | 9 | 2 | .818 | 102 | 35 | 31 | 74 | 46 | 2.74 |
| 1972—Boston | American | 47 | 84 | 7 | 4 | .636 | 75 | 31 | 30 | 43 | 32 | 3.21 |
| 1973—Boston | American | 38 | 285 | 17 | 11 | .607 | 275 | 100 | 87 | 120 | 76 | 2.75 |
| 1974—Boston | American | 38 | 282 | 17 | 15 | .531 | *320 | 123 | 110 | 95 | 67 | 3.51 |
| 1975—Boston | American | 41 | 260 | 17 | 9 | .654 | 274 | 123 | 114 | 78 | 69 | 3.95 |
| 1976—Boston‡ | American | 24 | 96 | 5 | 7 | .417 | 124 | 68 | 60 | 29 | 28 | 5.63 |
| Major League Totals | | 266 | 1198 | 75 | 53 | .586 | 1274 | 527 | 477 | 503 | 360 | 3.58 |

†On military list June 5 through October 2.
‡On disabled list, May 21 through July 12, 1976.

### WORLD SERIES RECORD

| Year Club | League | G. | IP. | W. | L. | Pct. | H. | R. | ER. | SO. | BB. | ERA. |
|---|---|---|---|---|---|---|---|---|---|---|---|---|
| 1975—Boston | American | 2 | 14⅓ | 0 | 0 | .000 | 12 | 5 | 5 | 7 | 3 | 3.14 |

### ALL-STAR GAME RECORD
Member of American League All-Star Team in 1973 game; did not play.

## RONALD LeFLORE
### (Ron)

Born June 16, 1948, at Detroit, Mich.
Height, 6.00. Weight, 195.
Throws and bats righthanded.
Hobbies—Reading, chess and woodworking.
Major league stolen bases; 1974 (23), 1975 (28), 1976 (58). Total—109.
Named Most Valuable Player in Florida State League, 1974.

| Year Club | League | Pos. | G. | AB. | R. | H. | 2B. | 3B. | HR. | RBI. | B.A. | PO. | A. | E. | F.A. |
|---|---|---|---|---|---|---|---|---|---|---|---|---|---|---|---|
| 1973—Clinton | Midw. | OF | 32 | 65 | 10 | 18 | 1 | 0 | 1 | 8 | .277 | 17 | 0 | 1 | .944 |
| 1974—Lakeland | Fla. St. | OF | 93 | 386 | *79 | 131 | 11 | 7 | 6 | 38 | *.339 | 202 | 9 | *12 | .946 |
| 1974—Evansville | A. A. | OF | 9 | 34 | 5 | 8 | 1 | 0 | 1 | 3 | .235 | 11 | 0 | 1 | .917 |
| 1974—Detroit | Amer. | OF | 59 | 254 | 37 | 66 | 8 | 1 | 2 | 13 | .260 | 151 | 8 | *11 | .935 |
| 1975—Detroit | Amer. | OF | 136 | 550 | 66 | 142 | 13 | 6 | 8 | 37 | .258 | 317 | 13 | 9 | .973 |
| 1976—Detroit† | Amer. | OF-DH | 135 | 544 | 93 | 172 | 23 | 8 | 4 | 39 | .316 | 381 | 14 | ●11 | .973 |
| Major League Totals | | | 330 | 1348 | 196 | 380 | 44 | 15 | 14 | 89 | .282 | 849 | 35 | 31 | .966 |

†On disabled list, September 15 through October 4, 1976.

### ALL-STAR GAME RECORD

| Year League | Pos. | AB. | R. | H. | 2B. | 3B. | HR. | RBI. | B.A. | PO. | A. | E. | F.A. |
|---|---|---|---|---|---|---|---|---|---|---|---|---|---|
| 1976—American | OF | 2 | 0 | 1 | 0 | 0 | 0 | 0 | .500 | 2 | 0 | 0 | 1.000 |

## DAVID LAWRENCE LEMANCZYK
Name pronounced Luh-MAN-chick.
### (Dave)

Born August 17, 1950, at Syracuse, N. Y.
Height, 6.04. Weight, 230.
Throws and bats righthanded.
Hobby—Furniture building and refinishing.
Attended Hartwick College, Oneonta, N. Y.; received Bachelor of Arts degree in History.
Pitched 3-0 no-hit victory against Asheville, August 8, 1973.

| Year | Club | League | G. | IP. | W. | L. | Pct. | H. | R. | ER. | SO. | BB. | ERA. |
|------|------|--------|----|-----|----|----|------|----|----|-----|-----|-----|------|
| 1972–Lakeland | | Florida St. | 8 | 66 | 7 | 1 | .875 | 44 | 14 | 13 | 55 | 17 | 1.77 |
| 1972–Toledo | | Int'national | 12 | 60 | 5 | 2 | .714 | 55 | 22 | 20 | 32 | 28 | 3.00 |
| 1973–Toledo | | Int'national | 20 | 113 | 6 | 8 | .429 | 115 | 61 | 59 | 84 | 55 | 4.70 |
| 1973–Montgomery | | South. | 4 | 31 | 3 | 1 | .750 | 18 | 8 | 8 | 28 | 14 | 2.32 |
| 1973–Detroit | | American | 1 | 2 | 0 | 0 | .000 | 4 | 3 | 3 | 0 | 0 | 13.50 |
| 1974–Evansville | | Am. Assoc. | 7 | 44 | 2 | 4 | .333 | 45 | 24 | 18 | 38 | 20 | 3.68 |
| 1974–Detroit | | American | 22 | 79 | 2 | 1 | .667 | 79 | 43 | 35 | 52 | 44 | 3.99 |
| 1975–Detroit† | | American | 26 | 109 | 2 | 7 | .222 | 120 | 62 | 54 | 67 | 46 | 4.46 |
| 1976–Evansville | | Am. Assoc. | 7 | 48 | 5 | 2 | .714 | 36 | 16 | 14 | 27 | 18 | 2.63 |
| 1976–Detroit‡ | | American | 20 | 81 | 4 | 6 | .400 | 86 | 47 | 46 | 51 | 34 | 5.11 |
| Major League Totals | | | 69 | 271 | 8 | 14 | .363 | 289 | 155 | 138 | 170 | 124 | 4.58 |

†On disabled list, June 23 to July 17, 1975.
‡Selected by Toronto Blue Jays in American League expansion draft, November 5, 1976.


## JOHNNIE LEE LeMASTER

Born June 19, 1954, at Portsmouth, O.
Height, 6.02. Weight, 165.
Throws and bats righthanded.
Hobbies–Hunting, billiards and all sports.
First-cousin of Ron Salyer, former pitcher in Cleveland Indians' organization.
Led Pacific Coast League shortstops in double plays with 107 in 1975.
Led Pioneer League batters in strikeouts with 71 in 1973.
Led Pioneer League shortstops in double plays with 32 in 1973.

| Year | Club | League | Pos. | G. | AB. | R. | H. | 2B. | 3B. | HR. | RBI. | B.A. | PO. | A. | E. | F.A. |
|------|------|--------|------|----|-----|----|----|-----|-----|-----|------|------|-----|----|----|------|
| 1973–Great Falls | | Pion. | SS | 70 | 250 | 34 | 61 | 8 | 2 | 2 | 33 | .244 | •106 | •178 | •38 | .882 |
| 1974–Decatur | | Midw. | SS | 104 | 399 | 51 | 103 | 14 | 4 | 3 | 28 | .258 | 145 | 280 | •48 | .899 |
| 1974–Fresno | | Calif. | SS | 21 | 84 | 15 | 24 | 3 | 0 | 1 | 4 | .286 | 30 | 68 | 8 | .925 |
| 1975–Phoenix | | P. C. | SS | 143 | 520 | 75 | 152 | 26 | 8 | 4 | 58 | .292 | 207 | •489 | 33 | .955 |
| 1975–San Francisco | | Nat. | SS | 22 | 74 | 4 | 14 | 4 | 0 | 2 | 9 | .189 | 26 | 62 | 3 | .967 |
| 1976–Phoenix | | P. C. | SS | 105 | 380 | 60 | 94 | 14 | 5 | 4 | 35 | .247 | 151 | 349 | 26 | .951 |
| 1976–San Francisco | | Nat. | SS | 33 | 100 | 9 | 21 | 3 | 2 | 0 | 9 | .210 | 54 | 109 | 11 | .937 |
| Major League Totals | | | | 55 | 174 | 13 | 35 | 7 | 2 | 2 | 18 | .201 | 80 | 171 | 14 | .947 |


## CHESTER EARL LEMON
## (Chet)

Born February 12, 1955, at Jackson, Miss.
Height, 6.00. Weight, 190.
Throws and bats righthanded.
Hobbies–Rock and shell collecting and Greek mythology.
Attended Pepperdine University, Malibu, Calif., and Cerritos College, Norwalk, Calif.
Received reported $50,000 bonus to sign with Oakland Athletics, 1972.

| Year | Club | League | Pos. | G. | AB. | R. | H. | 2B. | 3B. | HR. | RBI. | B.A. | PO. | A. | E. | F.A. |
|------|------|--------|------|----|-----|----|----|-----|-----|-----|------|------|-----|----|----|------|
| 1972–Coos Bay-N. B. | | Northw. | SS-3 | 38 | 140 | 33 | 40 | 8 | 1 | 2 | 16 | .286 | 56 | 94 | 16 | .904 |
| 1972–Burlington | | Midw. | 3-SS | 33 | 129 | 18 | 33 | 5 | 0 | 1 | 8 | .256 | 24 | 62 | 13 | .869 |
| 1973–Burlington | | Midw. | 3-SS | 113 | 392 | 73 | 121 | 21 | 1 | 19 | •88 | .309 | 102 | 215 | 36 | .898 |
| 1974–Birmingham† | | South. | 3-SS | 79 | 272 | 52 | 79 | 22 | 2 | 10 | 61 | .290 | 84 | 135 | 23 | .905 |
| 1975–Tucson‡ | | P. C. | 3B-OF | 65 | 243 | 43 | 68 | 7 | 2 | 5 | 33 | .280 | 60 | 70 | 19 | .872 |
| 1975–Denver | | A. A. | 3B-OF | 70 | 254 | 40 | 78 | 15 | 6 | 8 | 49 | .307 | 39 | 76 | 19 | .858 |
| 1975–Chicago | | Amer. | 3B-OF | 9 | 35 | 2 | 9 | 2 | 0 | 0 | 1 | .257 | 5 | 7 | 1 | .923 |
| 1976–Chicago | | Amer. | OF | 132 | 451 | 46 | 111 | 15 | 5 | 4 | 38 | .246 | 353 | 12 | 3 | .992 |
| Major League Totals | | | | 141 | 486 | 48 | 120 | 17 | 5 | 4 | 39 | .247 | 358 | 19 | 4 | .990 |

†On disabled list, July 16 through September 16, 1974.
‡Traded with Pitcher Dave Hamilton by Oakland Athletics to Chicago White Sox for Pitchers Stan Bahnsen and Lee (Skip) Pitlock, June 15, 1975.


## MARK LEMONGELLO

Born July 21, 1955, at Jersey City, N. J.
Height, 6.01. Weight, 180.
Throws and bats righthanded.
Cousin of Mike Lemongello, a professional bowler.

| Year | Club | League | G. | IP. | W. | L. | Pct. | H. | R. | ER. | SO. | BB. | ERA. |
|------|------|--------|----|-----|----|----|------|----|----|-----|-----|-----|------|
| 1974–Lakeland | | Florida St. | 23 | 105 | 6 | 6 | .500 | 94 | 37 | 32 | 59 | 23 | 2.74 |
| 1975–Montgomery | | Southern | 14 | 93 | 6 | 3 | .667 | 90 | 43 | 26 | 44 | 26 | 2.52 |
| 1975–Evansville† | | Am. Assoc. | 15 | 100 | 7 | 4 | .636 | 111 | 49 | 43 | 63 | 25 | 3.87 |
| 1976–Memphis‡ | | Int'national | 30 | 165 | 10 | 6 | .625 | •208 | 102 | 83 | 62 | 51 | 4.53 |
| 1976–Houston | | National | 4 | 29 | 3 | 1 | .750 | 26 | 12 | 9 | 9 | 7 | 2.79 |
| Major League Totals | | | 4 | 29 | 3 | 1 | .750 | 26 | 12 | 9 | 9 | 7 | 2.79 |

†Traded with Outfielder Leon Roberts, Catcher Terry Humphrey and Pitcher Gene Pentz by Detroit Tigers to Houston Astros for Catcher Milt May and Pitchers Jim Crawford and Dave Roberts, December 6, 1975.
‡On temporary inactive list, April 16 to April 26 and July 4 to July 15, 1976.

## MAXIMINO LEON (MOLINA)

Name pronounced LAY-ohn.

### (Max)

Born February 4, 1950, at Villa Acula, Veracruz, Mexico.
Height, 5.11. Weight, 165.
Throws and bats righthanded.
Led Mexican League in hit batsmen with 11 in 1971.

| Year Club | League | G. | IP. | W. | L. | Pct. | H. | R. | ER. | SO. | BB. | ERA. |
|---|---|---|---|---|---|---|---|---|---|---|---|---|
| 1967—Fresnillo | Mex. Cent. | 27 | 165 | 11 | 3 | *.786 | 163 | 74 | 59 | 101 | 55 | 3.32 |
| 1968—Jalisco | Mexican | 8 | 12 | 0 | 0 | .000 | 10 | 8 | 8 | 5 | 7 | 6.00 |
| 1968—Puerto Mexico† | Mex. SE | 25 | 122 | 5 | 6 | .455 | 105 | 45 | 34 | 78 | 48 | 2.51 |
| 1969—Puerto Mexico‡ | Mex. SE | 27 | 151 | 9 | 10 | .474 | 119 | 61 | 46 | 96 | 60 | 2.74 |
| 1969—Jalisco | Mexican | 13 | 30 | 2 | 3 | .400 | 32 | 10 | 7 | 26 | 8 | 2.10 |
| 1970—Jalisco | Mexican | 37 | 182 | 14 | 9 | .609 | 185 | 75 | 58 | 138 | 42 | 2.87 |
| 1971—Jalisco | Mexican | 33 | 179 | 14 | 7 | .667 | 191 | 80 | 66 | 132 | 72 | 3.32 |
| 1972—Jalisco | Mexican | 43 | 218 | 17 | 7 | .708 | 203 | 111 | 78 | 133 | 55 | 3.22 |
| 1972—Savannah‡ | Southern | 6 | 40 | 4 | 1 | .800 | 33 | 12 | 12 | 33 | 11 | 2.70 |
| 1973—Richmond‡ | Int'national | 24 | 105 | 8 | 6 | .571 | 98 | 45 | 41 | 52 | 25 | 3.51 |
| 1973—Atlanta | National | 12 | 27 | 2 | 2 | .500 | 30 | 18 | 16 | 18 | 9 | 5.33 |
| 1974—Richmond | Int'national | 5 | 34 | 3 | 1 | .750 | 30 | 12 | 10 | 20 | 10 | 2.65 |
| 1974—Atlanta | National | 34 | 75 | 4 | 7 | .364 | 68 | 22 | 22 | 38 | 14 | 2.64 |
| 1975—Atlanta | National | 50 | 85 | 2 | 1 | .667 | 90 | 52 | 39 | 53 | 33 | 4.13 |
| 1976—Atlanta§ | National | 30 | 36 | 2 | 4 | .333 | 32 | 15 | 11 | 16 | 15 | 2.75 |
| Major League Totals | | 126 | 223 | 10 | 14 | .417 | 220 | 107 | 88 | 125 | 71 | 3.55 |

†Played in one game as a second baseman.
‡Appeared as an outfielder.
§On disabled list, June 19 through July 24, 1976.

## DENNIS PATRICK LEONARD

Born May 8, 1951, at Brooklyn, N. Y.
Height, 6.01. Weight, 195.
Throws and bats righthanded.
Hobbies—Fishing and bowling.
Attended Iona College, New Rochelle, N. Y.
Pitched seven-inning, 3-0 no-hit victory against Quincy, July 15, 1972.
Pitched 2-0 no-hit victory against Visalia, April 26, 1973.
Led American Association in complete games with 18 and shutouts with 4; also tied for lead in games started with 29 in 1974.
Tied for California League lead in complete games by pitchers with 16 in 1973.

| Year Club | League | G. | IP. | W. | L. | Pct. | H. | R. | ER. | SO. | BB. | ERA. |
|---|---|---|---|---|---|---|---|---|---|---|---|---|
| 1972—Kingsport | Ap'lachian | 4 | 22 | 2 | 1 | .667 | 19 | 9 | 8 | 31 | 6 | 3.27 |
| 1972—Waterloo | Midwest | 10 | 67 | 4 | 3 | .571 | 58 | 28 | 23 | 63 | 26 | 3.09 |
| 1973—San Jose | California | 29 | 206 | *15 | 9 | .625 | 152 | 70 | 59 | 212 | 81 | 2.58 |
| 1974—Omaha | Am. Assoc. | 29 | *223 | 12 | 13 | .480 | 178 | 96 | 86 | 193 | 91 | 3.47 |
| 1974—Kansas City | American | 5 | 22 | 0 | 4 | .000 | 28 | 15 | 13 | 8 | 12 | 5.32 |
| 1975—Omaha | Am. Assoc. | 3 | 19 | 0 | 2 | .000 | 19 | 11 | 9 | 14 | 10 | 4.26 |
| 1975—Kansas City | American | 32 | 212 | 15 | 7 | .682 | 212 | 98 | 89 | 146 | 90 | 3.78 |
| 1976—Kansas City | American | 35 | 259 | 17 | 10 | .630 | 247 | 113 | 101 | 150 | 70 | 3.51 |
| Major League Totals | | 72 | 493 | 32 | 21 | .604 | 487 | 226 | 203 | 304 | 172 | 3.71 |

### CHAMPIONSHIP SERIES RECORD

| Year Club | League | G. | IP. | W. | L. | Pct. | H. | R. | ER. | SO. | BB. | ERA. |
|---|---|---|---|---|---|---|---|---|---|---|---|---|
| 1976—Kansas City | American | 2 | 2⅓ | 0 | 0 | .000 | 9 | 5 | 5 | 0 | 2 | 19.29 |

## JEFFREY N. LEONARD

### (Jeff)

Born September 22, 1955, at Philadelphia, Pa.
Height, 6.02. Weight, 200.
Throws and bats righthanded.
Hobby—Playing drums.

| Year Club | League | Pos. | G. | AB. | R. | H. | 2B. | 3B. | HR. | RBI. | B.A. | PO. | A. | E. | F.A. |
|---|---|---|---|---|---|---|---|---|---|---|---|---|---|---|---|
| 1973—Bellingham | N'west | OF | 55 | 187 | 30 | 52 | 4 | 3 | 2 | 20 | .278 | 46 | 2 | 5 | .906 |
| 1974—Orangeburg | W. Car. | OF | 8 | 15 | 0 | 1 | 0 | 0 | 0 | 1 | .067 | 5 | 1 | 1 | .857 |
| 1974—Bellingham | N'west | OF | 78 | 278 | 47 | 90 | 14 | 4 | 3 | 43 | .324 | 115 | 7 | 6 | .953 |
| 1975—Bakersfield | Calif. | OF | 106 | 320 | 44 | 89 | 11 | 3 | 4 | 37 | .278 | 137 | 5 | 7 | .953 |
| 1976—Lodi | Calif. | OF | 133 | 509 | 93 | 168 | 29 | 9 | 8 | 85 | .330 | 214 | ●13 | *15 | .938 |
| 1976—Albuquerque | P.C. | OF | 7 | 27 | 2 | 8 | 2 | 1 | 1 | 6 | .296 | 14 | 0 | 0 | 1.000 |

Listed on Los Angeles Dodgers' 1977 spring roster.

---

### *DID YOU KNOW—*

That Lou Gehrig hit 23 home runs with the bases filled during his big league career?

---

## RANDY LOUIS LERCH

Born October 9, 1954, at Sacramento, Calif.
Height, 6.05. Weight, 190.
Throws and bats lefthanded.
Hobbies—Hunting and fishing.
Tied for American Association lead in complete games with 11 in 1976.

| Year Club | League | G. | IP. | W. | L. | Pct. | H. | R. | ER. | SO. | BB. | ERA. |
|---|---|---|---|---|---|---|---|---|---|---|---|---|
| 1973—Auburn | NYP | 16 | 96 | 9 | 2 | .818 | 88 | 41 | 31 | 75 | 29 | 2.91 |
| 1974—Rocky Mount | Carolina | 22 | 143 | 7 | 7 | .500 | 150 | 73 | 58 | 114 | 54 | 3.65 |
| 1975—Reading | Eastern | 25 | 177 | *16 | 6 | .727 | 173 | 66 | 53 | 108 | 45 | 2.69 |
| 1975—Philadelphia | National | 3 | 7 | 0 | 0 | .000 | 6 | 5 | 5 | 8 | 1 | 6.43 |
| 1976—Oklahoma City | Am. Assoc. | *29 | *207 | 13 | 11 | .542 | *203 | 91 | 77 | *152 | 47 | 3.35 |
| 1976—Philadelphia | National | 1 | 3 | 0 | 0 | .000 | 3 | 1 | 1 | 0 | 0 | 3.00 |
| Major League Totals | | 4 | 10 | 0 | 0 | .000 | 9 | 6 | 6 | 8 | 1 | 5.40 |

## DENNIS DALE LEWALLYN

Name pronounced loo-ELL-un.

Born August 11, 1953, at Pensacola, Fla.
Height, 6.04. Weight, 200.
Throws and bats righthanded.
Hobbies—Golf and reading.
Attended Chipola Junior College, Marianna, Fla.
Tied for Pacific Coast League lead in shutouts with 3 in 1975.

| Year Club | League | G. | IP. | W. | L. | Pct. | H. | R. | ER. | SO. | BB. | ERA. |
|---|---|---|---|---|---|---|---|---|---|---|---|---|
| 1972—Daytona Beach | Florida St. | 22 | 146 | 11 | 6 | .647 | 120 | 65 | 60 | 122 | 75 | 3.70 |
| 1973—Bakersfield | California | 29 | 175 | 11 | 12 | .478 | 167 | 95 | 75 | 102 | 76 | 3.86 |
| 1974—Waterbury | Eastern | 27 | 138 | 7 | 10 | .412 | 140 | 76 | 66 | 75 | 43 | 4.30 |
| 1975—Albuquerque | P. Coast | 29 | 180 | 13 | 10 | .565 | 207 | 102 | 78 | 81 | 49 | 3.90 |
| 1975—Los Angeles | National | 2 | 3 | 0 | 0 | .000 | 1 | 0 | 0 | 0 | 0 | 0.00 |
| 1976—Albuquerque | P. Coast | 25 | 180 | *15 | 10 | .600 | 207 | 98 | 71 | 62 | 61 | 3.55 |
| 1976—Los Angeles | National | 4 | 17 | 1 | 1 | .500 | 12 | 5 | 4 | 4 | 6 | 2.12 |
| Major League Totals | | 6 | 20 | 1 | 1 | .500 | 13 | 5 | 4 | 4 | 6 | 1.80 |

## SIXTO LEZCANO

Born November 28, 1953, at Arecibo, Puerto Rico.
Height, 5.11. Weight, 175.
Throws and bats righthanded.
Hobbies—Listening to music and reading books.

| Year Club | League | Pos. | G. | AB. | R. | H. | 2B. | 3B. | HR. | RBI. | B.A. | PO. | A. | E. | F.A. |
|---|---|---|---|---|---|---|---|---|---|---|---|---|---|---|---|
| 1971—Newark | NYP | OF-3B | 53 | 152 | 24 | 44 | 5 | 1 | 7 | 23 | .289 | 55 | 11 | 5 | .930 |
| 1972—Danville | Midw. | OF | 114 | 423 | 67 | 114 | 20 | 5 | 10 | 56 | .270 | 147 | 13 | 10 | .941 |
| 1973—Shreveport | Texas | OF | 134 | 458 | 69 | 134 | *35 | *7 | 18 | 90 | .293 | 264 | *17 | 13 | .956 |
| 1974—Sacramento | P.C. | OF | 131 | 508 | 100 | 165 | 23 | 8 | 34 | 99 | .325 | 245 | 24 | 3 | .989 |
| 1974—Milwaukee | Amer. | OF | 15 | 54 | 5 | 13 | 2 | 0 | 2 | 9 | .241 | 32 | 3 | 1 | .972 |
| 1975—Milwaukee | Amer. | OF | 134 | 429 | 55 | 106 | 19 | 3 | 11 | 43 | .247 | 240 | 10 | 6 | .977 |
| 1976—Milwaukee | Amer. | OF-DH | 145 | 513 | 53 | 146 | 19 | 5 | 7 | 56 | .285 | 345 | 10 | 10 | .973 |
| Major League Totals | | | 294 | 996 | 113 | 265 | 40 | 8 | 20 | 108 | .266 | 617 | 23 | 17 | .974 |

## PAUL AARON LINDBLAD

Born August 9, 1941, at Chanute, Kan.
Height, 6.02. Weight, 195.
Throws and bats lefthanded.
Hobby—Mechanical drawing.
Attended Chanute Junior College, Chanute, Kan., and University of Kansas,
Lawrence, Kan.
Brother of Eddie Lindblad, former pitcher in New York Mets' organization.
Established major league record for consecutive errorless games, pitcher, 385, August 17, 1966 to April 30, 1974.

| Year Club | League | G. | IP. | W. | L. | Pct. | H. | R. | ER. | SO. | BB. | ERA. |
|---|---|---|---|---|---|---|---|---|---|---|---|---|
| 1963—Burlington† | Midwest | 14 | 97 | 10 | 2 | .833 | 69 | 32 | 17 | 99 | 23 | 1.58 |
| 1964—Birmingham | Southern | 28 | 187 | 11 | 8 | .579 | 194 | 89 | 69 | 139 | 57 | 3.32 |
| 1965—Vancouver | P. Coast | 28 | 184 | 12 | 11 | .522 | 165 | 87 | 75 | 137 | 65 | 3.67 |
| 1965—Kansas City | American | 4 | 7 | 0 | 1 | .000 | 12 | 9 | 9 | 12 | 0 | 11.57 |
| 1966—Kansas City | American | 38 | 121 | 5 | 10 | .333 | 138 | 63 | 56 | 69 | 37 | 4.17 |
| 1967—Kansas City | American | 46 | 116 | 5 | 8 | .385 | 106 | 59 | 46 | 83 | 35 | 3.57 |
| 1968—Oakland | American | 47 | 56 | 4 | 3 | .571 | 51 | 19 | 15 | 42 | 14 | 2.41 |
| 1969—Oakland | American | 60 | 78 | 9 | 6 | .600 | 72 | 37 | 36 | 64 | 33 | 4.15 |
| 1970—Oakland | American | 62 | 63 | 8 | 2 | .800 | 52 | 23 | 19 | 42 | 28 | 2.71 |
| 1971—Oak.‡-Wash. | American | 51 | 100 | 7 | 4 | .636 | 76 | 32 | 31 | 54 | 31 | 2.79 |
| 1972—Texas‡‡ | American | *66 | 100 | 5 | 8 | .385 | 95 | 31 | 29 | 51 | 29 | 2.61 |
| 1973—Oakland | American | 36 | 78 | 1 | 5 | .167 | 89 | 38 | 32 | 33 | 28 | 3.69 |
| 1974—Oakland | American | 45 | 101 | 4 | 4 | .500 | 85 | 30 | 23 | 46 | 30 | 2.05 |

| Year Club | League | G. | IP. | W. | L. | Pct. | H. | R. | ER. | SO. | BB. | ERA. |
|---|---|---|---|---|---|---|---|---|---|---|---|---|
| 1975—Oakland .............................American | | 68 | 122 | 9 | 1 | .900 | 105 | 44 | 37 | 58 | 43 | 2.73 |
| 1976—Oakland§.............................American | | 65 | 115 | 6 | 5 | .545 | 111 | 50 | 39 | 37 | 24 | 3.05 |
| Major League Totals ............................... | | 588 | 1057 | 63 | 57 | .525 | 992 | 435 | 372 | 591 | 332 | 3.17 |

†On disabled list from July 19 through end of season.

‡Traded with First Baseman Don Mincher and Catcher Frank Fernandez to Washington Senators for First Baseman Mike Epstein and Pitcher Darold Knowles, May 8, 1971.

‡‡Traded to Oakland A's for Outfielder Bill McNulty and a player to be named later, October 30, 1972. The deal was completed with the assignment of Outfielder Brant Alyea from Iowa to Portland November 30, 1972.

§Sold to Texas Rangers for cash estimated at $400,000, February 19, 1977.

### CHAMPIONSHIP SERIES RECORD

| Year Club | League | G. | IP. | W. | L. | Pct. | H. | R. | ER. | SO. | BB. | ERA. |
|---|---|---|---|---|---|---|---|---|---|---|---|---|
| 1975—Oakland ...........................American | | 2 | 4⅔ | 0 | 0 | .000 | 5 | 3 | 0 | 0 | 1 | 0.00 |

### WORLD SERIES RECORD

| Year Club | League | G. | IP. | W. | L. | Pct. | H. | R. | ER. | SO. | BB. | ERA. |
|---|---|---|---|---|---|---|---|---|---|---|---|---|
| 1973—Oakland ...........................American | | 3 | 3⅓ | 1 | 0 | 1.000 | 4 | 0 | 0 | 1 | 1 | 0.00 |

## LARRY LINTZ

Born October 10, 1949, at Martinez, Calif.
Height, 5.10. Weight, 150.
Throws right and bats left and righthanded.
Hobbies—Fishing and listening to soul music.
Attended San Jose State University, San Jose, Calif.

Major League stolen bases: 1973 (12), 1974 (50), 1975 (21), 1976 (31). Total—114.
Led Northern League shortstops in double plays with 43 in 1971.
Led Eastern League in stolen bases with 96 and in strikeouts with 132 in 1972.
Led International League in stolen bases with 48 in 1973.
Tied for Northern League lead in bases on balls with 87 in 1971.

| Year Club | League | Pos. | G. | AB. | R. | H. | 2B. | 3B. | HR. | RBI. | B.A. | PO. | A. | E. | F.A. |
|---|---|---|---|---|---|---|---|---|---|---|---|---|---|---|---|
| 1971—Watertown ........North. | | SS | 65 | 207 | 64 | 58 | 8 | 3 | 1 | 25 | .280 | *126 | *196 | *25 | *.928 |
| 1972—Quebec City ......East. | | SS | 131 | 434 | 88 | 98 | 8 | 2 | 0 | 23 | .226 | 186 | 370 | *39 | .934 |
| 1973—Peninsula .........Int. | | SS | 76 | 248 | 41 | 47 | 2 | 0 | 0 | 7 | .190 | 142 | 336 | 19 | .952 |
| 1973—Montreal ..........Nat. | | 2B-SS | 52 | 116 | 20 | 29 | 1 | 0 | 0 | 3 | .250 | 63 | 114 | 9 | .952 |
| 1974—Montreal ..........Nat. | | 2-S-3 | 113 | 319 | 60 | 76 | 10 | 1 | 0 | 20 | .238 | 169 | 252 | 18 | .959 |
| 1975—Mont.†-St.L.‡ ....Nat. | | 2B-SS | 73 | 150 | 24 | 31 | 1 | 0 | 0 | 4 | .207 | 101 | 132 | 9 | .963 |
| 1976—Oakland ...........Amer. | | DH-2-OF | 68 | 1 | 21 | 0 | 0 | 0 | 0 | 0 | .000 | 2 | 2 | 0 | 1.000 |
| National League Totals ................. | | | 238 | 585 | 104 | 136 | 12 | 1 | 0 | 27 | .232 | 333 | 498 | 36 | .958 |
| American League Totals ............... | | | 68 | 1 | 21 | 0 | 0 | 0 | 0 | 0 | .000 | 2 | 2 | 0 | 1.000 |
| Major League Totals ...................... | | | 306 | 586 | 125 | 136 | 12 | 1 | 0 | 27 | .232 | 335 | 500 | 36 | .959 |

†Traded to St. Louis Cardinals for Outfielder Jimmy Dwyer, July 25, 1975.

‡Traded to Oakland Athletics for Outfielder Charlie Chant, October 28, 1975.

## PEDRO RAFAEL LIRANZO (GIL)
### (Raf)

Born December 28, 1953 at Santiago, Dominican Republic.
Height, 5.11. Weight, 162.
Throws and bats righthanded.

| Year Club | League | Pos. | G. | AB. | R. | H. | 2B. | 3B. | HR. | RBI. | B.A. | PO. | A. | E. | F.A. |
|---|---|---|---|---|---|---|---|---|---|---|---|---|---|---|---|
| 1971—Bluefield .........Appal. | | OF | 27 | 77 | 14 | 24 | 3 | 1 | 1 | 14 | .312 | 17 | 3 | 2 | .909 |
| 1972—Miami .............Fla. St. | | OF | 52 | 169 | 11 | 29 | 4 | 1 | 0 | 24 | .172 | 76 | 3 | 2 | .975 |
| 1972—Bluefield .........Appal. | | OF | 56 | 209 | 36 | 70 | 11 | 1 | 2 | 30 | .335 | 98 | 5 | 6 | .945 |
| 1973—Miami .............Fla. St. | | OF | 136 | 493 | 51 | 125 | 15 | 4 | 3 | 54 | .254 | *306 | *15 | 5 | *.985 |
| 1974—Asheville .........South. | | OF | 123 | 411 | 39 | 102 | 17 | 1 | 4 | 41 | .248 | 278 | 12 | 11 | .963 |
| 1975—Asheville .........South. | | OF | 81 | 279 | 30 | 71 | 18 | 1 | 4 | 29 | .254 | 187 | 15 | 7 | .967 |
| 1976—Charlotte .........South. | | OF | 135 | 486 | 55 | 127 | 25 | ●10 | 9 | 61 | .261 | *318 | 8 | 9 | .973 |

Listed on Baltimore Orioles' 1977 spring roster.

## JOSEPH ANTHONY LIS
### (Joe)

Born August 15, 1946, at Somerville, N. J.
Height, 6.00. Weight, 195.
Throws and bats righthanded.
Hobbies—Sports and working with children.

Led American Association batters in walks with 100 in 1975.
Led California League in total bases with 244 and led third basemen in double plays with 21 in 1967.
Tied for Pacific Coast League lead in double plays by outfielders with 4 in 1970.
Named California League Player of the Year in 1967.

| Year Club | League | Pos. | G. | AB. | R. | H. | 2B. | 3B. | HR. | RBI. | B.A. | PO. | A. | E. | F.A. |
|---|---|---|---|---|---|---|---|---|---|---|---|---|---|---|---|
| 1964—Bakersfield........Calif. | | SS | 7 | 16 | 1 | 3 | 1 | 0 | 0 | 0 | .188 | 2 | 7 | 3 | .750 |
| 1964—Miami .............Fla. St. | | SS | 51 | 161 | 10 | 31 | 4 | 1 | 1 | 10 | .193 | 53 | 62 | 11 | .913 |

| Year | Club | League | Pos. | G. | AB. | R. | H. | 2B. | 3B. | HR. | RBI. | B.A. | PO. | A. | E. | F.A. |
|------|------|--------|------|----|-----|----|----|-----|-----|-----|------|------|-----|----|----|------|
| 1965 | Miami | Fla. St. | 3B | 134 | 492 | 47 | 119 | 20 | 3 | 5 | 57 | .242 | 116 | 235 | 18 | *.951 |
| 1966 | Bakersfield | Calif. | 3-OF | 108 | 334 | 39 | 78 | 21 | 1 | 16 | 62 | .234 | 88 | 127 | 20 | .915 |
| 1967 | Bakersfield | Calif. | *3-S-1-2 | 134 | 467 | 81 | 118 | 23 | 2 | *33 | *90 | .253 | *154 | 227 | *37 | .911 |
| 1968 | Tidewater | Carol. | O-3-1-2 | 140 | 475 | 99 | 139 | 20 | 1 | 32 | 94 | .293 | 215 | 30 | 17 | .935 |
| 1969 | Eugene | P. C. | OF-1B | 106 | 341 | 48 | 94 | 20 | 2 | 12 | 59 | .276 | 195 | 9 | 9 | .976 |
| 1970 | Eugene | P. C. | ●OF-1-3 | 139 | 487 | 102 | 158 | 24 | 5 | *36 | 107 | .324 | 284 | ●18 | ●11 | .965 |
| 1970 | Philadelphia | Nat. | OF | 13 | 37 | 1 | 7 | 2 | 0 | 1 | 4 | .189 | 18 | 0 | 1 | .947 |
| 1971 | Philadelphia | Nat. | OF | 59 | 123 | 16 | 26 | 6 | 0 | 6 | 10 | .211 | 42 | 2 | 1 | .978 |
| 1972 | Eugene | P. C. | OF-1B | 65 | 213 | 65 | 72 | 11 | 2 | 26 | 58 | .338 | 111 | 2 | 2 | .980 |
| 1972 | Philadelphia† | Nat. | 1B-OF | 62 | 140 | 13 | 34 | 6 | 0 | 6 | 18 | .243 | 242 | 16 | 2 | .992 |
| 1973 | Minnesota | Amer. | 1B | 103 | 253 | 37 | 62 | 11 | 1 | 9 | 25 | .245 | 626 | 48 | 9 | .987 |
| 1974 | Minn.‡-Cleve. | Amer. | 1-3-O | 81 | 150 | 20 | 30 | 3 | 0 | 6 | 19 | .200 | 297 | 27 | 4 | .988 |
| 1975 | Okla. City | A. A. | 1-3-O | 130 | 423 | 69 | 116 | 25 | 0 | 18 | 69 | .274 | 832 | 62 | 12 | .987 |
| 1975 | Cleveland | Amer. | 1B | 9 | 13 | 4 | 4 | 2 | 0 | 2 | 8 | .308 | 39 | 2 | 0 | 1.000 |
| 1976 | Toledo | Int. | 1B-3B | 126 | 425 | *93 | 130 | 23 | 1 | 30 | *103 | .306 | 805 | 86 | 8 | .991 |
| 1976 | Cleveland§ | Amer. | 1B-DH | 20 | 51 | 4 | 16 | 1 | 0 | 2 | 7 | .314 | 107 | 8 | 0 | 1.000 |
| | National League Totals | | | 134 | 300 | 30 | 67 | 14 | 0 | 13 | 32 | .223 | 302 | 18 | 4 | .988 |
| | American League Totals | | | 213 | 467 | 65 | 112 | 17 | 1 | 19 | 59 | .240 | 1069 | 85 | 13 | .989 |
| | Major League Totals | | | 347 | 767 | 95 | 179 | 31 | 1 | 32 | 91 | .233 | 1371 | 103 | 17 | .988 |

†Traded with Pitchers Ken Sanders and Ken Reynolds to Minnesota Twins for Infielder-Outfielder Cesar Tovar, November 30, 1972.
‡Sold to Cleveland Indians, June 5, 1974.
§Selected by Seattle Mariners in American League expansion draft, November 5, 1976.

## MARK ALAN LITTELL

Born January 17, 1953, at Gideon, Mo.
Height, 6.03. Weight, 210.
Throws right and bats lefthanded.
Hobbies—Hunting and fishing.
Attended Union University, Jackson, Tenn., and University of Tampa, Tampa, Fla.

Led American Association pitchers in complete games with 15 in 1973.
Named American Association Outstanding Pitcher of the Year in 1973.

| Year | Club | League | G. | IP. | W. | L. | Pct. | H. | R. | ER. | SO. | BB. | ERA. |
|------|------|--------|----|-----|----|----|------|----|----|-----|-----|-----|------|
| 1971 | Billings | Pioneer | 13 | 87 | 5 | 1 | .833 | 76 | 41 | 28 | 69 | 54 | 2.90 |
| 1972 | Waterloo | Midwest | 25 | 153 | 10 | 9 | .526 | 134 | 78 | 59 | *199 | 79 | 3.47 |
| 1973 | Omaha | Am. Assoc. | 22 | 179 | *16 | 6 | .727 | 144 | 58 | 50 | 133 | 81 | *2.51 |
| 1973 | Kansas City | American | 8 | 38 | 1 | 3 | .250 | 44 | 25 | 24 | 16 | 23 | 5.68 |
| 1974 | Omaha† | Am. Assoc. | 16 | 89 | 3 | 9 | .250 | 92 | 58 | 47 | 44 | 43 | 4.75 |
| 1975 | Omaha | Am. Assoc. | 24 | 168 | 13 | 6 | .684 | 160 | 81 | 65 | 128 | 74 | 3.48 |
| 1975 | Kansas City | American | 7 | 24 | 1 | 2 | .333 | 19 | 11 | 10 | 19 | 15 | 3.75 |
| 1976 | Kansas City | American | 60 | 104 | 8 | 4 | .667 | 68 | 26 | 24 | 92 | 60 | 2.08 |
| | Major League Totals | | 75 | 166 | 10 | 9 | .526 | 131 | 62 | 58 | 127 | 98 | 3.14 |

†On disabled list, June 12 to July 1, 1974.

### CHAMPIONSHIP SERIES RECORD

| Year | Club | League | G. | IP. | W. | L. | Pct. | H. | R. | ER. | SO. | BB. | ERA. |
|------|------|--------|----|-----|----|----|------|----|----|-----|-----|-----|------|
| 1976 | Kansas City | American | 1 | 4⅔ | 0 | 1 | .000 | 4 | 1 | 1 | 0 | 1 | 1.93 |

## GENE LOCKLEAR

Born July 19, 1949, at Lumberton, N. C.
Height, 5.11. Weight, 170.
Throws right and bats lefthanded.
Hobby—Art.

Led American Association in slugging percentage with .522 and in total bases with 244 in 1972.
Named Player of the Year in American Association, 1972.
Named Eastern League Most Valuable Player in 1971.

| Year | Club | League | Pos. | G. | AB. | R. | H. | 2B. | 3B. | HR. | RBI. | B.A. | PO. | A. | E. | F.A. |
|------|------|--------|------|----|-----|----|----|-----|-----|-----|------|------|-----|----|----|------|
| 1969 | Tampa | Fla. St. | PH | 5 | 3 | 0 | 0 | 0 | 0 | 0 | 0 | .000 | 0 | 0 | 0 | .000 |
| 1969 | Sioux Falls | North. | OF | 44 | 132 | 24 | 40 | 12 | 0 | 7 | 29 | .303 | 37 | 2 | ●8 | .830 |
| 1970 | Asheville | South. | OF | 46 | 122 | 6 | 20 | 4 | 0 | 2 | 7 | .164 | 52 | 3 | 3 | .948 |
| 1970 | Sioux Falls | North. | OF | 23 | 83 | 12 | 24 | 5 | 2 | 0 | 14 | .289 | 39 | 1 | 2 | .952 |
| 1971 | Three Rivers | East. | OF | 124 | 403 | 72 | 130 | 28 | 5 | 9 | 45 | *.323 | 236 | *17 | ●14 | .948 |
| 1972 | Indianapolis | A.A. | OF | 134 | 467 | 78 | 152 | 31 | 8 | 15 | 65 | *.325 | 189 | 7 | *20 | .907 |
| 1973 | Cin.†-S.D. | Nat. | OF | 96 | 180 | 26 | 42 | 6 | 1 | 3 | 25 | .233 | 81 | 2 | 4 | .954 |
| 1974 | Hawaii‡ | P.C. | OF | 77 | 290 | 63 | 99 | 9 | 1 | 14 | 52 | .341 | 113 | 4 | 9 | .929 |
| 1974 | San Diego | Nat. | OF | 39 | 74 | 7 | 20 | 3 | 2 | 1 | 3 | .270 | 22 | 1 | 0 | 1.000 |
| 1975 | Hawaii | P.C. | OF | 18 | 64 | 17 | 24 | 0 | 1 | 4 | 11 | .375 | 3 | 0 | 1 | .750 |
| 1975 | San Diego | Nat. | OF | 100 | 237 | 31 | 76 | 11 | 1 | 5 | 27 | .321 | 92 | 4 | 3 | .970 |
| 1976 | San Diego§ | Nat. | OF | 43 | 67 | 9 | 15 | 3 | 0 | 0 | 8 | .224 | 20 | 0 | 1 | .952 |
| 1976 | Syracuse | Int. | OF | 16 | 60 | 7 | 18 | 3 | 1 | 2 | 8 | .300 | 14 | 0 | 2 | .875 |
| 1976 | New York | Amer. | OF-DH | 13 | 32 | 2 | 7 | 1 | 0 | 0 | 1 | .219 | 4 | 0 | 0 | 1.000 |
| | National League Totals | | | 278 | 558 | 73 | 153 | 23 | 4 | 9 | 63 | .274 | 215 | 7 | 8 | .965 |
| | American League Totals | | | 13 | 32 | 2 | 7 | 1 | 0 | 0 | 1 | .219 | 4 | 0 | 0 | 1.000 |
| | Major League Totals | | | 291 | 590 | 75 | 160 | 24 | 4 | 9 | 64 | .271 | 219 | 7 | 8 | .966 |

†Traded with Pitcher Mike Johnson (assigned from Indianapolis to Alexandria) to San Diego Padres for Pitcher Fredie Norman, June 12, 1973.
‡On disabled list, May 17 to July 19, 1974.
§Traded to New York Yankees for a player to be named later, July 10, 1976; Yankees assigned Pitcher Rick Sawyer to San Diego Padres to complete deal, July 31, 1976.

## CLAUDE EDWARD LOCKWOOD, JR.
### (Skip)

Born August 17, 1946, at Boston, Mass.
Height, 6.00. Weight, 195.
Throws and bats righthanded.
Hobby—All types of sports.
Attended Merrimack College, Andover, Mass., Boston College, Chestnut Hill, Mass.,
Bryant & Stratton Junior College, Boston, Mass., Marquette University,
Milwaukee, Wis., Emerson College, Boston, Mass., and
Carroll College, Waukesha, Wis.

Received reported $100,000 bonus to sign with Kansas City Athletics, 1964.

| Year | Club | League | G. | IP. | W. | L. | Pct. | H. | R. | ER. | SO. | BB. | ERA. |
|---|---|---|---|---|---|---|---|---|---|---|---|---|---|
| 1966—Modesto | | California | 1 | 1 | 1 | 0 | 1.000 | 0 | 0 | 0 | 1 | 0 | 0.00 |
| 1968—Birmingham | | Southern | 4 | 10 | 0 | 0 | .000 | 13 | 6 | 6 | 8 | 6 | 5.40 |
| 1968—Peninsula§ | | Carolina | 17 | 65 | 6 | 3 | .667 | 58 | 27 | 24 | 40 | 16 | 3.32 |
| 1969—Elmira | | Eastern | 15 | 66 | 6 | 2 | .750 | 66 | 33 | 30 | 53 | 45 | 4.09 |
| 1969—Seattle | | American | 6 | 23 | 0 | 1 | .000 | 24 | 9 | 9 | 10 | 6 | 3.52 |
| 1970—Portland | | P. Coast | 5 | 34 | 4 | 1 | .800 | 29 | 13 | 10 | 24 | 9 | 2.65 |
| 1970—Milwaukee | | American | 27 | 174 | 5 | 12 | .294 | 173 | 91 | 83 | 93 | 79 | 4.29 |
| 1971—Milwaukee | | American | 33 | 208 | 10 | 15 | .400 | 191 | 93 | 77 | 115 | 91 | 3.33 |
| 1972—Milwaukee | | American | 29 | 170 | 8 | 15 | .348 | 148 | 75 | 68 | 106 | 71 | 3.60 |
| 1973—Milwaukee x | | American | 37 | 155 | 5 | 12 | .294 | 164 | 75 | 67 | 87 | 59 | 3.89 |
| 1974—California y z | | American | 37 | 81 | 2 | 5 | .286 | 81 | 42 | 39 | 39 | 32 | 4.33 |
| 1975—Tucson a | | P. Coast | 30 | 84 | 6 | 2 | .750 | 99 | 49 | 41 | 84 | 32 | 4.39 |
| 1975—Tidewater | | Int'national | 3 | 5 | 1 | 0 | 1.000 | 0 | 0 | 0 | 5 | 1 | 0.00 |
| 1975—New York | | National | 24 | 48 | 1 | 3 | .250 | 28 | 9 | 8 | 61 | 25 | 1.50 |
| 1976—New York | | National | 56 | 94 | 10 | 7 | .588 | 62 | 31 | 28 | 108 | 34 | 2.68 |
| American League Totals | | | 169 | 811 | 30 | 60 | .333 | 781 | 385 | 343 | 450 | 338 | 3.81 |
| National League Totals | | | 80 | 142 | 11 | 10 | .524 | 90 | 40 | 36 | 169 | 59 | 2.28 |
| Major League Totals | | | 249 | 953 | 41 | 70 | .369 | 871 | 425 | 379 | 619 | 397 | 3.58 |

### RECORD AS INFIELDER

| Year | Club | League | Pos. | G. | AB. | R. | H. | 2B. | 3B. | HR. | RBI. | B.A. | PO. | A. | E. | F.A. |
|---|---|---|---|---|---|---|---|---|---|---|---|---|---|---|---|---|
| 1964—Burlington | | Midw. | 3B | 64 | 236 | 30 | 49 | 4 | 1 | 5 | 29 | .208 | 47 | 82 | 23 | .849 |
| 1965—Kansas City | | Amer. | 3B | 42 | 33 | 4 | 4 | 0 | 0 | 0 | 0 | .121 | 9 | 4 | 0 | 1.000 |
| 1966—Modesto | | Calif. | OF-3B | 106 | 382 | 53 | 101 | 16 | 3 | 6 | 43 | .264 | 140 | 56 | 20 | .907 |
| 1967—Burlington†‡ | | Midw. | 3-1-S | 58 | 204 | 30 | 50 | 9 | 1 | 5 | 26 | .245 | 117 | 109 | 19 | .922 |
| Major League Totals | | | 42 | 33 | 4 | 4 | 0 | 0 | 0 | 0 | .121 | 9 | 4 | 0 | 1.000 |

†On military list, January 26 through June 23.
‡Drafted by Houston Astros from Vancouver (Oakland Athletics' organization), November 28, 1967; returned to Vancouver, April 3, 1968.
§Recalled by Oakland Athletics; drafted by Seattle Pilots from Oakland in expansion draft, October 15, 1968.
xTraded with Outfielders Ollie Brown and Joe Lahoud, Pitcher Gary Ryerson and Catcher Ellie Rodriguez to California Angels for Pitchers Clyde Wright and Steve Barber, Outfielder Ken Berry, Catcher Art Kusnyer and a player to be named later, October 22, 1973.
yTraded to New York Yankees for Utilityman Bill Sudakis, December 3, 1974; Yankees sent Outfielder Mike Krizmanich to Angels, December 5, 1975, to complete deal.
zReleased by New York Yankees, April 7, 1975; signed as a free agent by Tucson (Oakland Athletics' organization), April 14, 1975.
aSold by Oakland Athletics' organization to New York Mets' organization, July 28, 1975.

## JAMES REYNOLD LONBORG
### (Jim)

Born April 16, 1942, at Santa Maria, Calif.
Height, 6.06. Weight, 210.
Throws and bats righthanded.
Hobbies—Hunting, music and reading.
Attended Stanford University, Palo Alto, Calif.; received Bachelor of Arts degree in Biology.
Led American League in hit batsmen with 19 in 1967 and 14 in 1971.
Tied for American League lead in games started by pitchers with 39 in 1967.
Named American League Pitcher of the Year by THE SPORTING NEWS, 1967.
Named as pitcher on THE SPORTING NEWS American League All-Star Team, 1967.
Won American League Cy Young Memorial Award, 1967.

| Year | Club | League | G. | IP. | W. | L. | Pct. | H. | R. | ER. | SO. | BB. | ERA. |
|---|---|---|---|---|---|---|---|---|---|---|---|---|---|
| 1964—Winston-Salem | | Carolina | 8 | 59 | 6 | 2 | .750 | 47 | 24 | 21 | 61 | 24 | 3.20 |
| 1964—Seattle | | P. Coast | 23 | 132 | 5 | 7 | .417 | 129 | 81 | 71 | 95 | 46 | 4.84 |
| 1965—Boston | | American | 32 | 185 | 9 | 17 | .346 | 193 | 112 | 92 | 113 | 65 | 4.48 |
| 1966—Boston | | American | 45 | 182 | 10 | 10 | .500 | 173 | 86 | 78 | 131 | 55 | 3.86 |

| Year   Club | League | G. | IP. | W. | L. | Pct. | H. | R. | ER. | SO. | BB. | ERA. |
|---|---|---|---|---|---|---|---|---|---|---|---|---|
| 1967—Boston | American | 39 | 273 | •22 | 9 | .710 | 228 | 102 | 96 | *246 | 83 | 3.16 |
| 1968—Boston† | American | 23 | 113 | 6 | 10 | .375 | 89 | 57 | 54 | 73 | 59 | 4.30 |
| 1969—Boston | American | 29 | 144 | 7 | 11 | .389 | 148 | 78 | 72 | 100 | 65 | 4.50 |
| 1970—Louisville | Int'national | 2 | 10 | 1 | 1 | .500 | 12 | 5 | 5 | 8 | 6 | 4.50 |
| 1970—Boston‡ | American | 9 | 34 | 4 | 1 | .800 | 33 | 12 | 12 | 21 | 9 | 3.18 |
| 1971—Louisville | Int'national | 6 | 50 | 4 | 2 | .667 | 28 | 10 | 5 | 43 | 11 | 0.90 |
| 1971—Boston§ | American | 27 | 168 | 10 | 7 | .588 | 167 | 86 | 77 | 100 | 67 | 4.13 |
| 1972—Milwaukee‡‡ | American | 33 | 223 | 14 | 12 | .538 | 197 | 75 | 70 | 143 | 76 | 2.83 |
| 1973—Philadelphia | National | 38 | 199 | 13 | 16 | .448 | 218 | 124 | 108 | 106 | 80 | 4.88 |
| 1974—Philadelphia | National | 39 | 283 | 17 | 13 | .567 | 280 | 113 | 101 | 121 | 70 | 3.21 |
| 1975—Philadelphia | National | 27 | 159 | 8 | 6 | .571 | 161 | 84 | 73 | 72 | 45 | 4.13 |
| 1976—Philadelphia | National | 33 | 222 | 18 | 10 | .643 | 210 | 85 | 76 | 118 | 50 | 3.08 |
| American League Totals | | 237 | 1322 | 82 | 77 | .516 | 1228 | 608 | 551 | 927 | 479 | 3.75 |
| National League Totals | | 137 | 863 | 56 | 45 | .554 | 869 | 406 | 358 | 417 | 245 | 3.73 |
| Major League Totals | | 374 | 2185 | 138 | 122 | .531 | 2097 | 1014 | 909 | 1344 | 724 | 3.74 |

†On restricted and disabled lists with knee injury through May 24.
‡On disabled list, June 8 through July 13 and August 19 through September 9.
§Traded with Catcher Don Pavletich, Pitcher Ken Brett, First Baseman George Scott and Outfielders Billy Conigliaro and Joe Lahoud to Milwaukee Brewers for Pitchers Marty Pattin and Lew Krausse and Outfielders Tommy Harper and Pat Skrable, October 11, 1971.
‡‡Traded with Pitchers Ken Brett, Ken Sanders and Earl Stephenson to Philadelphia Phillies for Infielders Don Money and John Vukovich and Pitcher Billy Champion, October 31, 1972.

CHAMPIONSHIP SERIES TOTALS

| Year   Club | League | G. | IP. | W. | L. | Pct. | H. | R. | ER. | SO. | BB. | ERA. |
|---|---|---|---|---|---|---|---|---|---|---|---|---|
| 1976—Philadelphia | National | 1 | 5⅓ | 0 | 1 | .000 | 2 | 3 | 1 | 2 | 2 | 1.80 |

WORLD SERIES RECORD

| Year   Club | League | G. | IP. | W. | L. | Pct. | H. | R. | ER. | SO. | BB. | ERA. |
|---|---|---|---|---|---|---|---|---|---|---|---|---|
| 1967—Boston | American | 3 | 24 | 2 | 1 | .667 | 14 | 8 | 7 | 11 | 2 | 2.63 |

ALL-STAR GAME RECORD
Member of American League All-Star Team in 1967 game; did not play.


## JOHN ANTHONY LONCHAR

Born September 10, 1952, at Cleveland, O.
Height, 6.04. Weight, 210.
Throws and bats righthanded.
Attended University of Michigan, Ann Arbor, Mich.; received
Bachelor of Arts degree in Business Administration.

| Year   Club | League | Pos. | G. | AB. | R. | H. | 2B. | 3B. | HR. | RBI. | B.A. | PO. | A. | E. | F.A. |
|---|---|---|---|---|---|---|---|---|---|---|---|---|---|---|---|
| 1974—Orlando | South. | C | 40 | 107 | 8 | 18 | 2 | 0 | 0 | 8 | .168 | 171 | 11 | 5 | .973 |
| 1975—Orlando | South. | C | 106 | 332 | 35 | 78 | 10 | 1 | 3 | 19 | .235 | 454 | 73 | 8 | .985 |
| 1976—Orlando† | South. | C | 75 | 224 | 23 | 57 | 10 | 1 | 1 | 28 | .254 | 263 | 39 | 5 | .984 |

†On disabled list, April 13 through May 17, 1976.
Listed on Minnesota Twins' 1977 spring roster.


## DAVID EARL LOPES
### (Dave)

Born May 3, 1946, at East Providence, R. I.
Height, 5.09. Weight, 175.
Throws and bats righthanded.
Hobbies—Basketball and tennis.
Attended Washburn University, Topeka, Kan.;
received Bachelor of Science degree in Education.

Established major league record for most consecutive stolen bases, season, 38, June 10 through August 24, 1975.
Tied major league record for most errors, inning, second baseman, 3, June 2, 1973 (1st inning).
Tied National League records for most stolen bases, game, since 1900, 5, August 24, 1974; and most double plays, second baseman, game, 5, May 18, 1975.
Led National League in stolen bases with 77 in 1975 and 63 in 1976.
Hit three home runs in a game, August 20, 1974, against Chicago Cubs.
Major league stolen bases: 1972 (4), 1973 (36), 1974 (59), 1975 (77), 1976 (63). Total—239.
Led Pacific Coast League in stolen bases with 48 in 1972.

| Year   Club | League | Pos. | G. | AB. | R. | H. | 2B. | 3B. | HR. | RBI. | B.A. | PO. | A. | E. | F.A. |
|---|---|---|---|---|---|---|---|---|---|---|---|---|---|---|---|
| 1968—Daytona Beach | Fla. St. | OF | 82 | 271 | 39 | 67 | 6 | 6 | 5 | 33 | .247 | 109 | 7 | 4 | .967 |
| 1969—Daytona Beach | Fla. St. | OF | 72 | 264 | 53 | 74 | 7 | 4 | 9 | 33 | .280 | 138 | 16 | 7 | .957 |
| 1970—Spokane | P. C. | •OF-2B | 100 | 343 | 48 | 90 | 15 | 4 | 6 | 35 | .262 | 202 | 19 | •12 | .948 |
| 1971—Spokane | P. C. | OF-2B | 94 | 353 | 78 | 108 | 9 | 9 | 6 | 36 | .306 | 157 | 103 | 11 | .959 |
| 1972—Albuquerque† | P. C. | •2-O-S | 104 | 397 | 94 | 126 | 18 | 6 | 11 | 53 | .317 | 213 | 270 | •21 | .958 |
| 1972—Los Angeles | Nat. | 2B | 11 | 42 | 6 | 9 | 4 | 0 | 0 | 1 | .214 | 27 | 27 | 2 | .964 |
| 1973—Los Angeles | Nat. | 2-O-S-3 | 142 | 535 | 77 | 147 | 13 | 5 | 6 | 37 | .275 | 323 | 380 | 11 | .985 |
| 1974—Los Angeles | Nat. | 2B | 145 | 530 | 95 | 141 | 26 | 3 | 10 | 35 | .266 | 309 | 360 | •24 | .965 |

| Year Club | League | Pos. | G. | AB. | R. | H. | 2B. | 3B. | HR. | RBI. | B.A. | PO. | A. | E. | F.A. |
|---|---|---|---|---|---|---|---|---|---|---|---|---|---|---|---|
| 1975–Los Angeles ......Nat. | | 2-O-S | 155 | 618 | 108 | 162 | 24 | 6 | 8 | 41 | .262 | 360 | 386 | 16 | .979 |
| 1976–Los Angeles ......Nat. | | 2B-OF | 117 | 427 | 72 | 103 | 17 | 7 | 4 | 20 | .241 | 254 | 268 | 19 | .965 |
| Major League Totals ..................... | | | 570 | 2152 | 358 | 562 | 84 | 21 | 28 | 134 | .261 | 1273 | 1421 | 72 | .974 |

†On temporary inactive list, June 16 through June 30, 1972.

## CHAMPIONSHIP SERIES RECORD

| Year Club | League | Pos. | G. | AB. | R. | H. | 2B. | 3B. | HR. | RBI. | B.A. | PO. | A. | E. | F.A. |
|---|---|---|---|---|---|---|---|---|---|---|---|---|---|---|---|
| 1974–Los Angeles ......Nat. | | 2B | 4 | 15 | 4 | 4 | 0 | 1 | 0 | 3 | .267 | 9 | 18 | 1 | .964 |

## WORLD SERIES RECORD

Tied World Series records for most stolen bases, inning, 2, October 15, 1974, 1st inning; most putouts, second baseman, game, 8, October 16, 1974; most chances accepted, second baseman, game, 13, October 16, 1974; and most putouts, second baseman, 5-game series, 20, in 1974.

| Year Club | League | Pos. | G. | AB. | R. | H. | 2B. | 3B. | HR. | RBI. | B.A. | PO. | A. | E. | F.A. |
|---|---|---|---|---|---|---|---|---|---|---|---|---|---|---|---|
| 1974–Los Angeles ......Nat. | | 2B | 5 | 18 | 2 | 2 | 0 | 0 | 0 | 0 | .111 | 19 | 9 | 0 | 1.000 |

# CARLOS ANTONIO LOPEZ (MORALES)

Born September 27, 1950, at Mazatlan, Sinaloa, Mexico.
Height, 6.00. Weight, 190.
Throws and bats righthanded.
Hobbies–Fishing and billiards.

| Year Club | League | Pos. | G. | AB. | R. | H. | 2B. | 3B. | HR. | RBI. | B.A. | PO. | A. | E. | F.A. |
|---|---|---|---|---|---|---|---|---|---|---|---|---|---|---|---|
| 1974–El Paso ............Texas | | OF | 128 | 461 | 73 | 136 | 21 | 7 | 14 | 75 | .295 | 149 | 14 | 10 | .942 |
| 1975–El Paso ............Texas | | OF | 112 | 428 | 77 | 140 | 22 | ∗10 | 9 | 78 | .327 | 198 | 9 | 9 | .958 |
| 1975–Salt Lake City ..P. C. | | OF | 15 | 48 | 3 | 12 | 2 | 0 | 1 | 5 | .250 | 27 | 3 | 4 | .882 |
| 1976–Salt Lake City ..P. C. | | OF-1B | 123 | 448 | 95 | 157 | 19 | 12 | 9 | 88 | .350 | 131 | 17 | 5 | .967 |
| 1976–California† ........Amer. | | OF-DH | 9 | 10 | 1 | 0 | 0 | 0 | 0 | 0 | .000 | 4 | 0 | 0 | 1.000 |
| Major League Totals ..................... | | | 9 | 10 | 1 | 0 | 0 | 0 | 0 | 0 | .000 | 4 | 0 | 0 | 1.000 |

†Selected by Seattle Mariners from California Angels in expansion draft, November 5, 1976.

# JUAN LOPEZ (ISAAC)

Born November 6, 1952, at Rio Piedras, Puerto Rico.
Height, 5.11. Weight, 160.
Throws and bats righthanded.
Hobbies–Basketball and movies.

| Year Club | League | Pos. | G. | AB. | R. | H. | 2B. | 3B. | HR. | RBI. | B.A. | PO. | A. | E. | F.A. |
|---|---|---|---|---|---|---|---|---|---|---|---|---|---|---|---|
| 1971–Newark ...........NYP | | PH | 1 | 1 | 0 | 0 | 0 | 0 | 0 | 0 | .000 | 0 | 0 | 0 | .000 |
| 1971–Danville ...........Midw. | | SS | 6 | 11 | 2 | 0 | 0 | 0 | 0 | 0 | .000 | 5 | 7 | 1 | .923 |
| 1972–Danville ...........Midw. | | SS | 99 | 303 | 26 | 56 | 4 | 1 | 0 | 12 | .185 | 128 | 219 | 45 | .885 |
| 1973–Danville ...........Midw. | | SS | 65 | 229 | 36 | 62 | 2 | 3 | 1 | 13 | .271 | 86 | 180 | 17 | .940 |
| 1973–Shreveport ........Texas | | SS | 58 | 218 | 32 | 63 | 8 | 3 | 1 | 16 | .289 | 106 | 195 | 21 | .935 |
| 1974–Sacramento ......P. C. | | SS-3B | 117 | 388 | 48 | 99 | 17 | 1 | 7 | 52 | .255 | 203 | 329 | 34 | .940 |
| 1975–Sacramento ......P. C. | | SS | 131 | ∗542 | 73 | 154 | 19 | 2 | 9 | 59 | .284 | 209 | 392 | 35 | .945 |
| 1976–Spokane ...........P. C. | | SS | 98 | 327 | 28 | 63 | 7 | 4 | 3 | 31 | .193 | 146 | 281 | 23 | .949 |

Listed on Milwaukee Brewers' 1977 spring roster.

# ALBERTO LOUIS

Born May 6, 1956, at Hato Mayor, Dominican Republic.
Height, 5.09. Weight, 175.
Throws and bats righthanded.

| Year Club | League | Pos. | G. | AB. | R. | H. | 2B. | 3B. | HR. | RBI. | B.A. | PO. | A. | E. | F.A. |
|---|---|---|---|---|---|---|---|---|---|---|---|---|---|---|---|
| 1974–Charleston ........W. Car. | | OF | 119 | 366 | 49 | 95 | 9 | 5 | 4 | 35 | .260 | 191 | ●15 | 12 | .945 |
| 1975–Salem...............Carol. | | OF | 83 | 295 | 51 | 89 | 7 | 10 | 7 | 33 | .302 | 183 | 10 | 8 | .960 |
| 1976–Shreveport .......Texas | | OF | 65 | 263 | 47 | 85 | 9 | ∗12 | 4 | 32 | .323 | 133 | 7 | 6 | .959 |
| 1976–Charleston ........Int. | | OF | 31 | 110 | 13 | 33 | 4 | 0 | 1 | 9 | .300 | 63 | 2 | 2 | .970 |

Listed on Pittsburgh Pirates' 1977 spring roster.

# JOHN LEE LOWENSTEIN

Name pronounced Low-in-stine.

Born January 27, 1947, at Wolf Point, Mont.
Height, 6.01. Weight, 175.
Throws right and bats lefthanded.
Hobbies–Golf, traveling and hunting.
Attended University of California, Riverside, Calif.; received Bachelor of Arts
degree in Anthropology.

Major League stolen bases; 1970 (1), 1971 (1), 1972 (2), 1973 (5), 1974 (36), 1975 (15), 1976 (11). Total–71.

| Year Club | League | Pos. | G. | AB. | R. | H. | 2B. | 3B. | HR. | RBI. | B.A. | PO. | A. | E. | F.A. |
|---|---|---|---|---|---|---|---|---|---|---|---|---|---|---|---|
| 1968–Waterbury ........East. | | PH | 3 | 2 | 0 | 0 | 0 | 0 | 0 | 0 | .000 | 0 | 0 | 0 | .000 |
| 1968–Reno ...............Calif. | | 2B-3B | 48 | 164 | 22 | 53 | 8 | 2 | 7 | 38 | .323 | 71 | 106 | 8 | .957 |

| Year Club | League | Pos. | G. | AB. | R. | H. | 2B. | 3B. | HR. | RBI. | B.A. | PO. | A. | E. | F.A. |
|---|---|---|---|---|---|---|---|---|---|---|---|---|---|---|---|
| 1969–Reno† ...............Calif. | | 1B-OF | 26 | 67 | 7 | 19 | 4 | 2 | 1 | 11 | .284 | 93 | 5 | 2 | .980 |
| 1970–Wichita ............A. A. | | 3-S-O-2 | 108 | 369 | 69 | 109 | 15 | 6 | 18 | 52 | .295 | 130 | 218 | 13 | .964 |
| 1970–Cleveland .........Amer. | | 2-3-O-S | 17 | 43 | 5 | 11 | 3 | 1 | 1 | 6 | .256 | 15 | 37 | 2 | .963 |
| 1971–Wichita ............A. A. | | OF-3 | 37 | 125 | 27 | 40 | 8 | 0 | 8 | 24 | .320 | 55 | 4 | 2 | .967 |
| 1971–Cleveland .........Amer. | | 2-O-S | 58 | 140 | 15 | 26 | 5 | 0 | 4 | 9 | .186 | 103 | 66 | 4 | .977 |
| 1972–Cleveland .........Amer. | | OF-1B | 68 | 151 | 16 | 32 | 8 | 1 | 6 | 21 | .212 | 82 | 7 | 0 | 1.000 |
| 1973–Cleveland .........Amer. | | O-2-3-1 | 98 | 305 | 42 | 89 | 16 | 1 | 6 | 40 | .292 | 124 | 85 | 7 | .968 |
| 1974–Cleveland .........Amer. | | O-3-1-2 | 140 | 508 | 65 | 123 | 14 | 2 | 8 | 48 | .242 | 314 | 84 | 6 | .985 |
| 1975–Cleveland .........Amer. | | O-3-2 | 91 | 265 | 37 | 64 | 5 | 1 | 12 | 33 | .242 | 61 | 16 | 2 | .975 |
| 1976–Cleveland‡ .......Amer. | | O-1-DH | 93 | 229 | 33 | 47 | 8 | 2 | 2 | 14 | .205 | 178 | 10 | 7 | .964 |
| Major League Totals ...................... | | | 565 | 1641 | 213 | 392 | 59 | 8 | 39 | 171 | .239 | 877 | 305 | 28 | .977 |

†On military list, January 31 through August 2, 1969.

‡Traded with Catcher Rick Cerone to Toronto Blue Jays for Outfielder Rico Carty, December 6, 1976. Traded to Cleveland Indians for Infielder Hector Torres, March 29, 1977.

## STEPHEN LEE LUEBBER
### (Steve)

Born July 9, 1949, at Clinton, Mo.
Height, 6.03. Weight, 195.
Throws and bats righthanded.
Hobbies–Basketball, golf, tennis, billiards and bowling.
Attended Missouri Southern College, Joplin, Mo.

Led Pacific Coast League in complete games with 15 and tied for lead in shutouts with 3 in 1975.
Led New York-Pennsylvania League in shutouts with 3 in 1968.
Led Pacific Coast League in shutouts with 5 and tied for lead in games started with 31 in 1972.
Led Florida State League pitchers in games started with 30 in 1970.

| Year Club | League | G. | IP. | W. | L. | Pct. | H. | R. | ER. | SO. | BB. | ERA. |
|---|---|---|---|---|---|---|---|---|---|---|---|---|
| 1967–Sarasota Twins ....................Gulf Coast | | 11 | 58 | 4 | 5 | .444 | 31 | 24 | 19 | 58 | ●41 | 2.95 |
| 1968–Auburn ...............................NYP | | 18 | 106 | 8 | 2 | ●.800 | 86 | 30 | 21 | 109 | 48 | 1.78 |
| 1969–Orlando† .............................Florida St. | | 9 | 49 | 1 | 2 | .333 | 60 | 19 | 19 | 22 | 20 | 3.49 |
| 1970–Orlando................................Florida St. | | 34 | ★237 | 17 | 11 | .607 | 184 | 70 | 47 | ★172 | 79 | 1.78 |
| 1971–Charlotte..............................Southern | | 12 | 96 | 9 | 1 | .900 | 61 | 25 | 21 | 86 | 33 | 1.97 |
| 1971–Minnesota ...........................American | | 18 | 68 | 2 | 5 | .286 | 73 | 42 | 38 | 35 | 37 | 5.03 |
| 1972–Tacoma................................P. Coast | | ●31 | ★215 | 13 | 13 | .500 | 200 | 97 | 86 | ★199 | 90 | 3.60 |
| 1972–Minnesota ...........................American | | 2 | 2 | 0 | 0 | .000 | 3 | 0 | 0 | 1 | 2 | 0.00 |
| 1973–Tacoma................................P. Coast | | 11 | 36 | 2 | 4 | .333 | 54 | 34 | 25 | 29 | 21 | 6.25 |
| 1973–Orlando................................Southern | | 8 | 41 | 4 | 3 | .571 | 27 | 24 | 21 | 9 | 34 | 4.61 |
| 1974–Orlando................................Southern | | 26 | 176 | 10 | 6 | .625 | 170 | 87 | 71 | 130 | 90 | 3.63 |
| 1975–Orlando................................Southern | | 6 | 47 | 2 | 2 | .500 | 43 | 16 | 16 | 26 | 15 | 3.06 |
| 1975–Tacoma................................P. Coast | | 24 | 177 | 14 | 7 | .667 | 145 | 62 | 47 | 123 | 79 | ★2.39 |
| 1976–Minnesota ...........................Amer. | | 38 | 119 | 6 | 4 | .444 | 109 | 57 | 53 | 45 | 62 | 4.01 |
| Major League Totals ............................. | | 58 | 189 | 6 | 10 | .375 | 185 | 99 | 91 | 81 | 101 | 4.33 |

†On restricted list, April 28 through June 20, 1969.

## MICHAEL KEN-WAI LUM
### (Mike)

Born October 27, 1945, at Honolulu, Hawaii.
Height, 6.00. Weight, 180.
Throws and bats lefthanded.
Hobby–Horses.
Attended Brigham Young University, Provo, Utah.

Hit three homers in one game, July 3, 1970, first game of a doubleheader vs. San Diego.

| Year Club | League | Pos. | G. | AB. | R. | H. | 2B. | 3B. | HR. | RBI. | B.A. | PO. | A. | E. | F.A. |
|---|---|---|---|---|---|---|---|---|---|---|---|---|---|---|---|
| 1963–Waycross ..........Ga.-Fla. | | OF | 51 | 114 | 17 | 30 | 3 | 2 | 0 | 12 | .263 | 47 | 2 | 4 | .925 |
| 1964–Binghamton ......NYP | | OF | ●127 | 531 | 102 | 163 | 19 | 7 | 18 | 68 | .307 | 254 | 14 | 16 | .944 |
| 1965–Yakima ...........Northw. | | OF | ●139 | 535 | 99 | 153 | ★28 | 7 | 7 | 54 | .286 | ★340 | 13 | 6 | ★.983 |
| 1966–Austin ..............Texas | | OF | 139 | ★541 | 76 | 144 | 19 | 8 | 6 | 48 | .266 | ★374 | 12 | 7 | .982 |
| 1967–Richmond..........Int. | | OF | 109 | 411 | 47 | 104 | 19 | 4 | 11 | 37 | .253 | 219 | 5 | 3 | .987 |
| 1967–Atlanta...............Nat. | | OF | 9 | 26 | 1 | 6 | 0 | 0 | 0 | 1 | .231 | 16 | 1 | 1 | .944 |
| 1968–Atlanta...............Nat. | | OF | 122 | 232 | 22 | 52 | 7 | 3 | 3 | 21 | .224 | 115 | 7 | 3 | .976 |
| 1969–Atlanta...............Nat. | | OF | 121 | 168 | 20 | 45 | 8 | 0 | 1 | 22 | .268 | 119 | 2 | 1 | .992 |
| 1970–Atlanta...............Nat. | | OF | 123 | 291 | 25 | 74 | 17 | 2 | 7 | 38 | .254 | 168 | 3 | 2 | .988 |
| 1971–Atlanta...............Nat. | | OF-1B | 145 | 454 | 56 | 122 | 14 | 1 | 13 | 55 | .269 | 287 | 11 | 3 | .990 |
| 1972–Atlanta...............Nat. | | OF-1B | 123 | 369 | 40 | 84 | 14 | 2 | 9 | 38 | .228 | 247 | 6 | 6 | .977 |
| 1973–Atlanta...............Nat. | | 1B-OF | 138 | 513 | 74 | 151 | 26 | 6 | 16 | 82 | .294 | 833 | 45 | 9 | .990 |
| 1974–Atlanta†..............Nat. | | 1B-OF | 106 | 361 | 50 | 84 | 11 | 2 | 11 | 50 | .233 | 554 | 26 | 4 | .993 |
| 1975–Atlanta‡ ............Nat. | | 1B-OF | 124 | 364 | 32 | 83 | 8 | 2 | 8 | 36 | .228 | 657 | 34 | 5 | .993 |
| 1976–Cincinnati..........Nat. | | OF | 84 | 136 | 15 | 31 | 5 | 1 | 3 | 20 | .228 | 48 | 0 | 0 | 1.000 |
| Major League Totals ..................... | | | 1095 | 2914 | 335 | 732 | 110 | 19 | 71 | 353 | .251 | 3044 | 135 | 34 | .989 |

†On disabled list, April 29 to May 14 and July 2 to July 25, 1974.

‡Traded to Cincinnati Reds for Infielder Darrel Chaney, December 12, 1975.

CHAMPIONSHIP SERIES RECORD

| Year Club League | Pos. | G. | AB. | R. | H. | 2B. | 3B. | HR. | RBI. | B.A. | PO. | A. | E. | F.A. |
|---|---|---|---|---|---|---|---|---|---|---|---|---|---|---|
| 1969—Atlanta..............Nat. | OF | 2 | 2 | 0 | 2 | 1 | 0 | 0 | 0 | 1.000 | 0 | 0 | 0 | .000 |
| 1976—Cincinnati.........Nat. | PH | 1 | 1 | 0 | 0 | 0 | 0 | 0 | 0 | .000 | 0 | 0 | 0 | .000 |
| Championship Series Totals ............ | 3 | 3 | 0 | 2 | 1 | 0 | 0 | 0 | .667 | 0 | 0 | 0 | .000 |

## GREGORY MICHAEL LUZINSKI
### (Greg)

Born November 22, 1950, at Chicago, Ill.
Height, 6.01. Weight, 215.
Throws and bats righthanded.
Hobbies—Bowling and golf.
Brother of Richard Luzinski, outfielder in Philadelphia Phillies' organization.
Led National League in total bases with 322 in 1975.
Led Carolina League hitters in strikeouts with 148 in 1969, Eastern League with 148 in 1970 and Pacific Coast League with 167 in 1971.
Led Carolina League in total bases with 255 in 1969, Eastern League with 287 in 1970 and Pacific Coast League with 319 in 1971.
Led Eastern League first basemen in double plays with 119 in 1970 and Pacific Coast League first basemen with 129 in 1971.
Named left fielder on THE SPORTING NEWS National League All-Star Team, 1975.
Named Eastern League Player of the Year in 1970.

| Year Club League | Pos. | G. | AB. | R. | H. | 2B. | 3B. | HR. | RBI. | B.A. | PO. | A. | E. | F.A. |
|---|---|---|---|---|---|---|---|---|---|---|---|---|---|---|
| 1968—Huron................North. | *1B-3B | 57 | 212 | 22 | 55 | 5 | 0 | *13 | ●43 | .250 | 417 | 26 | 13 | *.971 |
| 1969—Raleigh-Durham Carol. | 1B | 129 | 464 | 75 | 134 | 22 | 3 | *31 | *92 | .289 | 1067 | 67 | ●17 | .985 |
| 1970—Reading ...........East. | 1B | *141 | 471 | *94 | 153 | 25 | 5 | 33 | *120 | *.325 | 1122 | 65 | *21 | .983 |
| 1970—Philadelphia ......Nat. | 1B | 8 | 12 | 0 | 2 | 0 | 0 | 0 | 0 | .167 | 20 | 3 | 0 | 1.000 |
| 1971—Eugene..............P.C. | 1B | 142 | 548 | 104 | 171 | 30 | 5 | 36 | 114 | .312 | 1071 | 76 | ●19 | .984 |
| 1971—Philadelphia ......Nat. | OF | 28 | 100 | 13 | 30 | 8 | 0 | 3 | 15 | .300 | 247 | 34 | 1 | .996 |
| 1972—Philadelphia ......Nat. | OF-1B | 150 | 563 | 66 | 158 | 33 | 5 | 18 | 68 | .281 | 257 | 9 | 12 | .957 |
| 1973—Philadelphia ......Nat. | OF | 161 | 610 | 76 | 174 | 26 | 4 | 29 | 97 | .285 | 262 | 7 | 2 | *.993 |
| 1974—Philadelphia† ....Nat. | OF | 85 | 302 | 29 | 82 | 14 | 1 | 7 | 48 | .272 | 146 | 10 | 3 | .981 |
| 1975—Philadelphia ......Nat. | OF | 161 | 596 | 85 | 179 | 35 | 3 | 34 | *120 | .300 | 248 | 10 | 9 | .966 |
| 1976—Philadelphia ......Nat. | OF | 149 | 533 | 74 | 162 | 28 | 1 | 21 | 95 | .304 | 204 | 8 | 8 | .964 |
| Major League Totals .................... | 742 | 2716 | 343 | 787 | 144 | 14 | 112 | 443 | .290 | 1384 | 81 | 35 | .977 |

†On disabled list, June 6 to August 26, 1974.

CHAMPIONSHIP SERIES RECORD

| Year Club League | Pos. | G. | AB. | R. | H. | 2B. | 3B. | HR. | RBI. | B.A. | PO. | A. | E. | F.A. |
|---|---|---|---|---|---|---|---|---|---|---|---|---|---|---|
| 1976—Philadelphia ......Nat. | OF | 3 | 11 | 2 | 3 | 2 | 0 | 1 | 3 | .273 | 6 | 0 | 0 | 1.000 |

ALL-STAR GAME RECORD

| Year League | Pos. | AB. | R. | H. | 2B. | 3B. | HR. | RBI. | B.A. | PO. | A. | E. | F.A. |
|---|---|---|---|---|---|---|---|---|---|---|---|---|---|
| 1975—National ............................ | PH | 1 | 0 | 0 | 0 | 0 | 0 | 0 | .000 | 0 | 0 | 0 | .000 |
| 1976—National ............................ | OF | 3 | 0 | 0 | 0 | 0 | 0 | 0 | .000 | 0 | 0 | 0 | .000 |
| All-Star Game Totals ...................... | 4 | 0 | 0 | 0 | 0 | 0 | 0 | .000 | 0 | 0 | 0 | .000 |

## ALBERT WALTER LYLE
### (Sparky)
(Nicknamed by father.)

Born July 22, 1944, at Reynoldsville, Pa.
Height, 6.01. Weight, 180.
Throws and bats lefthanded.

Established major league record for most saves, lifetime, 159, 1976.
Tied major league record for most seasons leading league, saves, 2.
Established American League record for most consecutive appearances as relief pitcher, lifetime, 549, 1976.
Led American League in saves with 35 in 1972 and 23 in 1976.
Named THE SPORTING NEWS American League Fireman of the Year, 1972.

| Year Club League | G. | IP. | W. | L. | Pct. | H. | R. | ER. | SO. | BB. | ERA. |
|---|---|---|---|---|---|---|---|---|---|---|---|
| 1964—Bluefield ...............................Ap'lachian | 7 | 33 | 3 | 2 | .600 | 23 | 19 | 16 | 44 | 25 | 4.36 |
| 1964—Fox Cities† ..........................Midwest | 6 | 35 | 3 | 1 | .750 | 30 | 14 | 9 | 51 | 18 | 2.31 |
| 1965—Winston-Salem ...................Carolina | 37 | 87 | 5 | 5 | .500 | 84 | 45 | 41 | 79 | 55 | 4.24 |
| 1966—Pittsfield...............................Eastern | 40 | 74 | 4 | 2 | .667 | 62 | 35 | 30 | 72 | 43 | 3.65 |
| 1967—Toronto ................................Int'national | 16 | 21 | 2 | 2 | .500 | 13 | 5 | 4 | 17 | 14 | 1.71 |
| 1967—Boston .................................American | 27 | 43 | 1 | 2 | .333 | 33 | 13 | 11 | 42 | 14 | 2.30 |
| 1968—Boston .................................American | 49 | 66 | 6 | 1 | .857 | 67 | 25 | 20 | 52 | 14 | 2.73 |
| 1969—Boston .................................American | 71 | 103 | 8 | 3 | .727 | 91 | 33 | 29 | 93 | 48 | 2.53 |
| 1970—Boston .................................American | 63 | 67 | 1 | 7 | .125 | 62 | 37 | 29 | 51 | 34 | 3.90 |
| 1971—Boston‡ ...............................American | 50 | 52 | 6 | 4 | .600 | 41 | 16 | 16 | 37 | 23 | 2.77 |
| 1972—New York .............................American | 59 | 108 | 9 | 5 | .643 | 84 | 25 | 23 | 75 | 29 | 1.92 |
| 1973—New York .............................American | 51 | 82 | 5 | 9 | .357 | 66 | 30 | 23 | 63 | 18 | 2.52 |
| 1974—New York .............................American | 66 | 114 | 9 | 3 | .750 | 93 | 30 | 21 | 89 | 43 | 1.66 |
| 1975—New York .............................American | 49 | 89 | 5 | 7 | .417 | 94 | 34 | 31 | 65 | 36 | 3.13 |
| 1976—New York .............................American | 64 | 104 | 7 | 8 | .467 | 82 | 33 | 26 | 61 | 42 | 2.25 |
| Major League Totals .............................. | 549 | 828 | 57 | 49 | .538 | 713 | 276 | 229 | 628 | 301 | 2.49 |

†Drafted by Boston Red Sox from Rochester (Baltimore Orioles' organization), November 30, 1964.
‡Traded to New York Yankees for First Baseman-Outfielder Danny Cater, March 22, 1972; Yankees sent Infielder Mario Guerrero to Red Sox, June 30, 1972, to complete deal.

### CHAMPIONSHIP SERIES RECORD

| Year Club | League | G. | IP. | W. | L. | Pct. | H. | R. | ER. | SO. | BB. | ERA. |
|---|---|---|---|---|---|---|---|---|---|---|---|---|
| 1976–New York | American | 1 | 1 | 0 | 0 | .000 | 0 | 0 | 0 | 0 | 1 | 0.00 |

### WORLD SERIES RECORD

| Year Club | League | G. | IP. | W. | L. | Pct. | H. | R. | ER. | SO. | BB. | ERA. |
|---|---|---|---|---|---|---|---|---|---|---|---|---|
| 1976–New York | American | 2 | 2⅔ | 0 | 0 | .000 | 1 | 0 | 0 | 3 | 0 | 0.00 |

### ALL-STAR GAME RECORD

| Year League | IP. | W. | L. | Pct. | H. | R. | ER. | SO. | BB. | ERA. |
|---|---|---|---|---|---|---|---|---|---|---|
| 1973–American | 1 | 0 | 0 | .000 | 1 | 0 | 0 | 1 | 0 | 0.00 |

## FREDRIC MICHAEL LYNN
### (Fred)

Born February 3, 1952, at Chicago, Ill.
Height, 6.01. Weight, 185.
Throws and bats lefthanded.
Hobbies—Fishing and golfing.
Attended University of Southern California, Los Angeles, Calif.

Established American League record for most doubles, rookie season, 47, in 1975.
Tied American League record for most total bases, game, 16, June 18, 1975.
Led American League in slugging percentage with .566 in 1975.
Named Most Valuable Player in American League, 1975.
Named American League Rookie of the Year by Baseball Writers' Association of America, 1975.
Named American League Player of the Year and Rookie Player of the Year by THE SPORTING NEWS, 1975.
Named as outfielder on THE SPORTING NEWS American League All-Star fielding team, 1975.
Named center fielder on THE SPORTING NEWS American League All-Star Team, 1975.

| Year Club | League | Pos. | G. | AB. | R. | H. | 2B. | 3B. | HR. | RBI. | B.A. | PO. | A. | E. | F.A. |
|---|---|---|---|---|---|---|---|---|---|---|---|---|---|---|---|
| 1973–Bristol | East. | OF | 53 | 162 | 26 | 42 | 9 | 4 | 6 | 36 | .259 | 79 | 3 | 5 | .943 |
| 1974–Pawtucket | Int. | OF | 124 | 415 | 65 | 117 | 19 | 2 | 21 | 68 | .282 | 247 | 12 | 7 | .974 |
| 1974–Boston | Amer. | OF | 15 | 43 | 5 | 18 | 2 | 2 | 2 | 10 | .419 | 18 | 2 | 0 | 1.000 |
| 1975–Boston | Amer. | OF | 145 | 528 | ★103 | 175 | ★47 | 7 | 21 | 105 | .331 | 404 | 11 | 7 | .983 |
| 1976–Boston | Amer. | OF-DH | 132 | 507 | 76 | 159 | 32 | 8 | 10 | 65 | .314 | 367 | 13 | 6 | .984 |
| Major League Totals | | | 292 | 1078 | 184 | 352 | 81 | 17 | 33 | 180 | .326 | 789 | 26 | 13 | .984 |

### CHAMPIONSHIP SERIES RECORD

| Year Club | League | Pos. | G. | AB. | R. | H. | 2B. | 3B. | HR. | RBI. | B.A. | PO. | A. | E. | F.A. |
|---|---|---|---|---|---|---|---|---|---|---|---|---|---|---|---|
| 1975–Boston | Amer. | OF | 3 | 11 | 1 | 4 | 1 | 0 | 0 | 3 | .364 | 12 | 1 | 1 | .929 |

### WORLD SERIES RECORD

| Year Club | League | Pos. | G. | AB. | R. | H. | 2B. | 3B. | HR. | RBI. | B.A. | PO. | A. | E. | F.A. |
|---|---|---|---|---|---|---|---|---|---|---|---|---|---|---|---|
| 1975–Boston | Amer. | OF | 7 | 25 | 3 | 7 | 1 | 0 | 1 | 5 | .280 | 23 | 1 | 0 | 1.000 |

### ALL-STAR GAME RECORD

| Year League | Pos. | AB. | R. | H. | 2B. | 3B. | HR. | RBI. | B.A. | PO. | A. | E. | F.A. |
|---|---|---|---|---|---|---|---|---|---|---|---|---|---|
| 1975–American | PH-OF | 2 | 0 | 0 | 0 | 0 | 0 | 0 | .000 | 1 | 0 | 0 | 1.000 |
| 1976–American | OF | 3 | 1 | 1 | 0 | 0 | 1 | 1 | .333 | 0 | 0 | 0 | 1.000 |
| All-Star Game Totals | | 5 | 1 | 1 | 0 | 0 | 1 | 1 | .200 | 1 | 0 | 0 | 1.000 |

## FRANK LOUIS MacCORMACK

Born September 21, 1954, at Jersey, City, N. J.
Height, 6.04. Weight, 210.
Throws and bats righthanded.
Attended Rutgers University, New Brunswick, N. J.

| Year Club | League | G. | IP. | W. | L. | Pct. | H. | R. | ER. | SO. | BB. | ERA. |
|---|---|---|---|---|---|---|---|---|---|---|---|---|
| 1974–Lakeland | Florida St. | 26 | 179 | 11 | 11 | .500 | 143 | 67 | 51 | 99 | 92 | 2.56 |
| 1975–Montgomery | Southern | 22 | 67 | 3 | 4 | .429 | 44 | 27 | 17 | 52 | 33 | 2.28 |
| 1975–Evansville | Am. Assoc. | 3 | 19 | 3 | 0 | 1.000 | 12 | 3 | 3 | 31 | 9 | 1.42 |
| 1976–Evansville | Am. Assoc. | 15 | 74 | 4 | 4 | .500 | 63 | 33 | 28 | 60 | 51 | 3.41 |
| 1976–Detroit† | American | 9 | 33 | 0 | 5 | .000 | 35 | 24 | 21 | 14 | 34 | 5.73 |
| Major League Totals | | 9 | 33 | 0 | 5 | .000 | 35 | 24 | 21 | 14 | 34 | 5.73 |

†Selected by Seattle Mariners in American League expansion draft, November 5, 1976.

## KENNETH EDWARD MACHA
### (Ken)

Born September 29, 1950, at Monroeville, Pa.
Height, 6.02. Weight, 210.
Throws and bats righthanded.
Hobbies—Golf, bowling, fishing and music.

Attended University of Pittsburgh, Pittsburgh, Pa.; received
Bachelor of Science degree in Civil Engineering.
Cousin of Hal Newhouser, pitcher with Detroit Tigers and
Cleveland Indians, 1939 through 1955.
Led Eastern League in passed balls with 32 in 1973.
Named Eastern League Player of the Year in 1974.

| Year Club | League | Pos. | G. | AB. | R. | H. | 2B. | 3B. | HR. | RBI. | B.A. | PO. | A. | E. | F.A. |
|---|---|---|---|---|---|---|---|---|---|---|---|---|---|---|---|
| 1972–Salem..............Carol. | | C-3B | 62 | 197 | 20 | 50 | 7 | 2 | 8 | 33 | .254 | 386 | 36 | 13 | .970 |
| 1973–Sherbrooke.......East. | | C-1-O-3 | 106 | 322 | 40 | 86 | 15 | 0 | 12 | 52 | .267 | 551 | 53 | 17 | .973 |
| 1974–Charleston .......Int. | | C-3B | 21 | 65 | 6 | 12 | 3 | 0 | 2 | 10 | .185 | 100 | 13 | 4 | .966 |
| 1974–Thetford Mines..East. | | C-3-1-O | 117 | 386 | 87 | 133 | 22 | 2 | 21 | 100 | •.345 | 531 | 70 | 16 | .974 |
| 1974–Pittsburgh ........Nat. | | C | 5 | 5 | 1 | 3 | 1 | 0 | 0 | 1 | .600 | 1 | 0 | 0 | 1.000 |
| 1975–Charleston ........Int. | | •1-3-O | 138 | 478 | 63 | 128 | 21 | 1 | 14 | 63 | .268 | 1051 | •88 | •22 | .981 |
| 1976–Charleston ........Int. | | 3-C-O-1 | 126 | 458 | 68 | 138 | 29 | 1 | 14 | 77 | .301 | 232 | 116 | 26 | .930 |
| Major League Totals ..................... | | | 5 | 5 | 1 | 3 | 1 | 0 | 0 | 1 | .600 | 1 | 0 | 0 | 1.000 |

## PETER MACKANIN, JR.
Name pronounced Mac-can-un.
### (Pete)
Born August 1, 1951, at Chicago, Ill.
Height, 6.02. Weight, 190.
Throws and bats righthanded.
Hobby–Sports in general.
Attended University of Illinois, Chicago Circle Campus, Ill.

| Year Club | League | Pos. | G. | AB. | R. | H. | 2B. | 3B. | HR. | RBI. | B.A. | PO. | A. | E. | F.A. |
|---|---|---|---|---|---|---|---|---|---|---|---|---|---|---|---|
| 1969–Wytheville ........Appal. | | 3B | 45 | 102 | 22 | 39 | 7 | 1 | 6 | 31 | .241 | •52 | 84 | 11 | .925 |
| 1970–Burlington ........Carol. | | SS-3B | 105 | 361 | 39 | 73 | 9 | 1 | 4 | 42 | .202 | 122 | 258 | 35 | .916 |
| 1971–Burlington ........Carol. | | 2B-SS | 125 | 451 | 49 | 117 | 17 | 7 | 5 | 46 | .259 | 304 | 328 | 26 | .960 |
| 1972–Pittsfield .........East. | | 2-S-3 | 87 | 336 | 47 | 83 | 18 | 1 | 1 | 22 | .247 | 146 | 214 | 21 | .945 |
| 1972–Denver .............A. A. | | 2-S-3 | 29 | 90 | 7 | 19 | 3 | 0 | 0 | 5 | .211 | 47 | 64 | 10 | .917 |
| 1973–Spokane ............P. C. | | SS | 100 | 384 | 57 | 116 | 25 | 5 | 7 | 55 | .302 | 174 | 293 | 31 | .938 |
| 1973–Texas ...............Amer. | | SS-3B | 44 | 90 | 3 | 9 | 2 | 0 | 0 | 2 | .100 | 39 | 88 | 7 | .948 |
| 1974–Spokane ............P. C. | | SS | 140 | 573 | 103 | 167 | 28 | 5 | 28 | 103 | .291 | 234 | 401 | •45 | .934 |
| 1974–Texas† .............Amer. | | SS | 2 | 6 | 0 | 1 | 0 | 1 | 0 | 0 | .167 | 3 | 8 | 0 | 1.000 |
| 1975–Montreal .........Nat. | | 2-3-S | 130 | 448 | 59 | 101 | 19 | 6 | 12 | 44 | .225 | 300 | 411 | 26 | .965 |
| 1976–Montreal .........Nat. | | 2-3-S-O | 114 | 380 | 36 | 85 | 15 | 2 | 8 | 33 | .224 | 203 | 307 | 19 | .964 |
| American League Totals ................ | | | 46 | 96 | 3 | 10 | 2 | 1 | 0 | 2 | .104 | 42 | 96 | 7 | .952 |
| National League Totals .................. | | | 244 | 828 | 95 | 186 | 34 | 8 | 20 | 77 | .225 | 503 | 718 | 45 | .964 |
| Major League Totals ..................... | | | 290 | 924 | 98 | 196 | 36 | 9 | 20 | 79 | .212 | 545 | 814 | 52 | .963 |

†Traded with Pitcher Don Stanhouse to Montreal Expos for Outfielder Willie Davis, December 5, 1974.

## ELLIOTT MADDOX
Born December 21, 1948, at East Orange, N. J.
Height, 5.10. Weight, 180.
Throws and bats righthanded.
Hobbies–Basketball, photography and collecting stereo tapes.
Attended University of Michigan, Ann Arbor, Mich.
Tied for Carolina League lead in double plays by third basemen with 18 in 1969.
Received reported $40,000 bonus to sign with Detroit Tigers, 1968.

| Year Club | League | Pos. | G. | AB. | R. | H. | 2B. | 3B. | HR. | RBI. | B.A. | PO. | A. | E. | F.A. |
|---|---|---|---|---|---|---|---|---|---|---|---|---|---|---|---|
| 1968–Lakeland ..........Fla. St. | | OF | 40 | 118 | 13 | 37 | 3 | 3 | 1 | 19 | .314 | 60 | 6 | 1 | .985 |
| 1968–Rocky Mount ....Carol. | | OF-3 | 34 | 111 | 21 | 33 | 4 | 4 | 0 | 20 | .297 | 60 | 14 | 3 | .961 |
| 1969–Rocky Mount ....Carol. | | •3-O-2 | 118 | 412 | 60 | 124 | 19 | 8 | 4 | 56 | .301 | 138 | •185 | 12 | .964 |
| 1970–Detroit† ...........Amer. | | 3-O-S-2 | 109 | 258 | 30 | 64 | 13 | 4 | 3 | 24 | .248 | 104 | 100 | 14 | .936 |
| 1971–Washington.......Amer. | | OF-3B | 128 | 258 | 38 | 56 | 8 | 2 | 1 | 18 | .217 | 201 | 21 | 3 | .987 |
| 1972–Texas ...............Amer. | | OF | 98 | 294 | 40 | 74 | 7 | 2 | 0 | 10 | .252 | 199 | 7 | 2 | .990 |
| 1973–Texas‡ .............Amer. | | OF-3B | 100 | 172 | 24 | 41 | 1 | 0 | 1 | 17 | .238 | 148 | 14 | 3 | .982 |
| 1974–New York.........Amer. | | O-2-3 | 137 | 466 | 75 | 141 | 26 | 2 | 3 | 45 | .303 | 336 | 19 | 5 | .986 |
| 1975–New York§ .......Amer. | | OF-2B | 55 | 218 | 36 | 67 | 10 | 3 | 1 | 23 | .307 | 158 | 5 | 0 | 1.000 |
| 1976–New York x ......Amer. | | OF-DH | 18 | 46 | 4 | 10 | 2 | 0 | 0 | 3 | .217 | 21 | 2 | 0 | 1.000 |
| Major League Totals ..................... | | | 645 | 1712 | 247 | 453 | 67 | 13 | 9 | 140 | .265 | 1167 | 168 | 27 | .980 |

†Traded with Pitcher Denny McLain, Third Baseman Don Wert and Pitcher Norm McRae to Washington Senators for Shortstop Ed Brinkman, Third Baseman Aurelio Rodriguez and Pitchers Joe Coleman and Jim Hannan, October 9, 1970.

‡On supplemental disabled list, May 16 to May 31, 1973. Sold to New York Yankees for an estimated $35,000, March 23, 1974.

§On disabled list, June 17 to October 3, 1975.

xOn disabled list, April 1 to June 22 and July 1 to September 2, 1976; traded with Outfielder Rick Bladt (assigned from Syracuse to Rochester) to Baltimore Orioles for Outfielder Paul Blair, January 20, 1977.

### CHAMPIONSHIP SERIES RECORD

| Year Club | League | Pos. | G. | AB. | R. | H. | 2B. | 3B. | HR. | RBI. | B.A. | PO. | A. | E. | F.A. |
|---|---|---|---|---|---|---|---|---|---|---|---|---|---|---|---|
| 1976–New York.........Amer. | | OF | 3 | 9 | 0 | 2 | 1 | 0 | 0 | 1 | .222 | 9 | 0 | 0 | 1.000 |

### WORLD SERIES RECORD

| Year Club | League | Pos. | G. | AB. | R. | H. | 2B. | 3B. | HR. | RBI. | B.A. | PO. | A. | E. | F.A. |
|---|---|---|---|---|---|---|---|---|---|---|---|---|---|---|---|
| 1976–New York.........Amer. | | OF-DH | 2 | 5 | 0 | 1 | 0 | 1 | 0 | 0 | .200 | 0 | 0 | 0 | .000 |

## GARRY LEE MADDOX

Born September 1, 1949, at Cincinnati, O.
Height, 6.03. Weight, 190.
Throws and bats righthanded.
Hobbies–Writing and all sports.
Attended Harbor College, Wilmington, Calif.

Major League stolen bases: 1972 (13), 1973 (24), 1974 (21), 1975 (25), 1976 (29). Total–112.
Led National League outfielders in total chances with 456 in 1976.
Led Pioneer League batters in strikeouts with 68 and outfielders in double plays with 2 in 1968.
Named as outfielder on THE SPORTING NEWS National League All-Star fielding team, 1975 and 1976.

| Year Club League | Pos. | G. | AB. | R. | H. | 2B. | 3B. | HR. | RBI. | B.A. | PO. | A. | E. | F.A. |
|---|---|---|---|---|---|---|---|---|---|---|---|---|---|---|
| 1968–Salt Lake City ..Pion. | OF | 58 | 206 | 34 | 52 | 11 | 2 | 5 | 29 | .252 | 98 | 6 | *10 | .912 |
| 1968–Fresno .............Calif. | OF | 5 | 19 | 2 | 6 | 0 | 0 | 0 | 5 | .316 | 7 | 0 | 0 | 1.000 |
| 1969-70– ......... | | | | | (In Military Service) | | | | | | | | | |
| 1971–Fresno .............Calif. | OF | 120 | 475 | 105 | 142 | 25 | 5 | 30 | 106 | .299 | 215 | 13 | 0 | .962 |
| 1972–Phoenix ...........P. C. | OF | 11 | 48 | 16 | 21 | 3 | 2 | 9 | 22 | .438 | 22 | 1 | 2 | .920 |
| 1972–San Francisco ..Nat. | OF | 125 | 458 | 62 | 122 | 26 | 7 | 12 | 58 | .266 | 279 | 7 | 6 | .979 |
| 1973–San Francisco ..Nat. | OF | 144 | 587 | 81 | 187 | 30 | 10 | 11 | 76 | .319 | 370 | 4 | ●12 | .969 |
| 1974–San Francisco ..Nat. | OF | 135 | 538 | 74 | 153 | 31 | 3 | 8 | 50 | .284 | 345 | 3 | 5 | .986 |
| 1975–S.F.†-Phil.‡........Nat. | OF | 116 | 426 | 54 | 116 | 26 | 8 | 5 | 50 | .272 | 325 | 13 | 5 | .985 |
| 1976–Philadelphia .....Nat. | OF | 146 | 531 | 75 | 175 | 37 | 6 | 6 | 68 | .330 | *441 | 10 | 5 | .989 |
| Major League Totals ...................... | | 666 | 2540 | 346 | 753 | 150 | 34 | 42 | 302 | .296 | 1760 | 37 | 33 | .982 |

†Traded to Philadelphia Phillies for First Baseman Willie Montanez, May 4, 1975.
‡On disabled list, May 25 to June 30, 1975.

### CHAMPIONSHIP SERIES RECORD

| Year Club League | Pos. | G. | AB. | R. | H. | 2B. | 3B. | HR. | RBI. | B.A. | PO. | A. | E. | F.A. |
|---|---|---|---|---|---|---|---|---|---|---|---|---|---|---|
| 1976–Philadelphia ......Nat. | OF | 3 | 13 | 2 | 3 | 1 | 0 | 0 | 1 | .231 | 9 | 0 | 0 | 1.000 |

## BILL MADLOCK, JR.

Born January 12, 1951, at Memphis, Tenn.
Height, 5.11. Weight, 180.
Throws and bats righthanded.
Attended Southeastern Community College, Keokuk, Ia.

Led Pacific Coast League in total bases with 268 in 1973.
Named third baseman on THE SPORTING NEWS National League All-Star Team, 1975.

| Year Club League | Pos. | G. | AB. | R. | H. | 2B. | 3B. | HR. | RBI. | B.A. | PO. | A. | E. | F.A. |
|---|---|---|---|---|---|---|---|---|---|---|---|---|---|---|
| 1970–Geneva.............NYP | *SS-3B | 66 | 234 | 44 | 63 | 5 | 1 | 6 | 29 | .269 | *123 | 132 | 25 | .911 |
| 1971–Pittsfield .........East. | *3-2-S-O | 112 | 376 | 62 | 88 | 14 | 2 | 10 | 37 | .234 | 100 | 214 | *34 | .902 |
| 1972–Pittsfield .........East. | 2B-3B | 42 | 131 | 29 | 43 | 13 | 3 | 4 | 26 | .328 | 81 | 88 | 7 | .960 |
| 1972–Denver .............A.A. | 3B-2B | 26 | 61 | 7 | 13 | 3 | 0 | 1 | 9 | .213 | 10 | 30 | 2 | .952 |
| 1973–Spokane ...........P.C. | 2-3-O | 123 | 491 | *119 | 166 | 22 | 7 | 22 | 90 | .338 | 172 | 245 | 25 | .943 |
| 1973–Texas† ...............Amer. | 3B | 21 | 77 | 16 | 27 | 5 | 3 | 1 | 5 | .351 | 13 | 32 | 4 | .918 |
| 1974–Chicago‡ .........Nat. | 3B | 128 | 453 | 65 | 142 | 21 | 5 | 9 | 54 | .313 | 84 | 229 | 18 | .946 |
| 1975–Chicago ...........Nat. | 3B | 130 | 514 | 77 | 182 | 29 | 7 | 7 | 64 | *.354 | 79 | 250 | 20 | .943 |
| 1976–Chicago§ ..........Nat. | 3B | 142 | 514 | 68 | 174 | 36 | 1 | 15 | 84 | *.339 | 107 | 234 | 14 | .961 |
| American League Totals ................ | | 21 | 77 | 16 | 27 | 5 | 3 | 1 | 5 | .351 | 13 | 32 | 4 | .918 |
| National League Totals .................. | | 400 | 1481 | 210 | 498 | 86 | 13 | 31 | 202 | .336 | 270 | 713 | 52 | .950 |
| Major League Totals ...................... | | 421 | 1558 | 226 | 525 | 91 | 16 | 32 | 207 | .337 | 283 | 745 | 56 | .948 |

†Traded with Infielder-Outfielder Vic Harris to Chicago Cubs for Pitcher Ferguson Jenkins, October 25, 1973.
‡On supplemental disabled list, May 4 to June 4, 1974.
§Traded with Infielder Rob Sperring to San Francisco Giants for Outfielder Bobby Murcer, Infielder Steve Ontiveros and Pitcher Andrew Muhlstock, February 11, 1977.

### ALL-STAR GAME RECORD

| Year League | Pos. | AB. | R. | H. | 2B. | 3B. | HR. | RBI. | B.A. | PO. | A. | E. | F.A. |
|---|---|---|---|---|---|---|---|---|---|---|---|---|---|
| 1975–National ............................. | 3B | 2 | 0 | 1 | 0 | 0 | 0 | 2 | .500 | 0 | 0 | 0 | .000 |

## GREGORY JOHN MAHLBURG

Name pronounced MALL-berg

### (Greg)

Born August 8, 1952, at Milwaukee, Wis.
Height, 5.10. Weight, 181.
Throws and bats righthanded.
Hobbies–Antique car restoration, fishing and ice skating.
Attended University of Wisconsin, Madison, Wis.; received
Bachelor of Science degree in Recreational Therapy.

| Year Club League | Pos. | G. | AB. | R. | H. | 2B. | 3B. | HR. | RBI. | B.A. | PO. | A. | E. | F.A. |
|---|---|---|---|---|---|---|---|---|---|---|---|---|---|---|
| 1973–Sar. Rangers ....Gulf C. | C | 34 | 109 | 17 | 27 | 3 | 0 | 1 | 14 | .248 | 215 | 17 | 1 | *.996 |
| 1974–Rocky Mount ....Carol. | C-1B | 100 | 298 | 48 | 87 | 11 | 3 | 2 | 41 | .292 | 658 | 96 | 10 | .987 |
| 1975–Pittsfield .........East. | C-OF-3B | 111 | 324 | 41 | 61 | 9 | 0 | 3 | 27 | .188 | 427 | 62 | 18 | .964 |
| 1976–Sacramento ......P.C. | C | 85 | 247 | 46 | 62 | 8 | 3 | 8 | 23 | .251 | 401 | 34 | 4 | *.991 |

Listed on Texas Rangers' 1977 spring roster.

## SHELDON MALLORY

Born July 16, 1953, at Argo, Ill.
Height, 6.02. Weight, 175.
Throws and bats lefthanded.
Hobbies—Bowling and basketball.
Attended Manatee Junior College, West Bradenton, Fla., and
Illinois State University, Normal, Ill.

Led California League in stolen bases with 72 in 1974 and Southern League with 42 in 1975.
Tied for Pioneer League lead in stolen bases with 31 and in sacrifice flies with 6 in 1972.

| Year Club | League | Pos. | G. | AB. | R. | H. | 2B. | 3B. | HR. | RBI. | B.A. | PO. | A. | E. | F.A. |
|---|---|---|---|---|---|---|---|---|---|---|---|---|---|---|---|
| 1972—Billings ............Pion. | | 1B-OF | 61 | 215 | 53 | 53 | 9 | 5 | 0 | 35 | .247 | 423 | 18 | 11 | .976 |
| 1973—Waterloo ..........Midw. | | OF-1 | 107 | 351 | 82 | 102 | 16 | 6 | 9 | 40 | .291 | 485 | 34 | 12 | .977 |
| 1974—San Jose............Calif. | | OF-1B | 83 | 236 | 50 | 70 | 11 | 5 | 3 | 23 | .297 | 124 | 2 | 5 | .962 |
| 1974—Jacksonville .....South. | | OF-1 | 40 | 124 | 26 | 26 | 4 | 1 | 3 | 20 | .210 | 78 | 3 | 0 | 1.000 |
| 1975—Jacksonville .....South. | | OF-1B | 123 | 432 | 68 | 103 | 18 | 2 | 12 | 56 | .238 | 242 | 10 | 6 | .977 |
| 1976—Omaha†‡ ..........A.A. | | OF | 110 | 346 | 66 | 91 | 22 | 7 | 5 | 29 | .263 | 155 | 8 | 3 | .982 |

†In three-club deal, Chicago Cubs traded Outfielder-First Baseman Pete LaCock to the Kansas City Royals, the New York Mets sent Outfielder Jim Dwyer from Tidewater to Wichita, Cubs' affiliate, and the Mets were to receive a player to be named later from the Royals, December 8, 1976; Royals assigned Outfielder Sheldon'Mallory to Tidewater to complete deal, December 13, 1976.
‡Sold to Oakland A's, April 4, 1977.


## JACK GARTH MALOOF

Born October 12, 1949, at Redlands, Calif.
Height, 6.00. Weight, 175.
Throws and bats lefthanded.
Hobby—Crafts.
Attended La Verne College, La Verne, Calif.; received
Bachelor of Arts degree.

Led Southern League batters in walks with 105 in 1974 and 105 in 1975.
Led Carolina League batters in walks with 86 in 1972.
Led Pacific Coast League batters in walks with 116 in 1976.
Tied for Southern League lead in sacrifice flies with 8 in 1974.
Named Most Valuable Player in New York-Pennsylvania League, 1971.

| Year Club | League | Pos. | G. | AB. | R. | H. | 2B. | 3B. | HR. | RBI. | B.A. | PO. | A. | E. | F.A. |
|---|---|---|---|---|---|---|---|---|---|---|---|---|---|---|---|
| 1971—Auburn..............NYP | | OF | 68 | 256 | •57 | •103 | 9 | 2 | 0 | 25 | •.402 | 141 | 5 | 2 | .986 |
| 1972—Lynchburg ........Carol. | | 1B-OF | 131 | 468 | 82 | 144 | 16 | 8 | 1 | 39 | .308 | 871 | 64 | 8 | .992 |
| 1973—Orlando ...........South. | | OF-1B | 118 | 432 | 69 | 120 | 12 | 3 | 1 | 34 | .278 | 382 | 24 | 5 | .988 |
| 1974—Orlando ...........South. | | 1B-OF | 125 | 427 | 79 | 128 | 20 | 3 | 0 | 48 | .300 | 698 | 42 | 6 | .992 |
| 1975—Orlando ...........South. | | 1B | 119 | 385 | 62 | 122 | 11 | 2 | 1 | 40 | .317 | 896 | 75 | 7 | .993 |
| 1976—Tacoma† ..........P.C. | | 1B-OF | 130 | 445 | 94 | 125 | 18 | 3 | 3 | 39 | .281 | 663 | 54 | 9 | .988 |

†Traded to Indianapolis (Cincinnati Reds' organization) for Pitcher Art DeFilippis, March 28, 1977.


## JOSE MANUEL MANGUAL

Name pronounced mahn-GWHAL.

### (Pepe)

Born May 23, 1952, at Ponce, Puerto Rico.
Height, 5.10. Weight, 157.
Throws and bats righthanded.
Older brother, Angel, former outfielder with Pittsburgh Pirates and Oakland
Athletics. Cousin of Coco Laboy, third baseman with Montreal Expos, 1969 through 1973.

Led International League outfielders in double plays with 7 in 1972.
Led International League in stolen bases with 39 in 1972 and 46 in 1974.
Led Eastern League batters in bases on balls with 90 and in strikeouts with 124 in 1971.

| Year Club | League | Pos. | G. | AB. | R. | H. | 2B. | 3B. | HR. | RBI. | B.A. | PO. | A. | E. | F.A. |
|---|---|---|---|---|---|---|---|---|---|---|---|---|---|---|---|
| 1970—W. Palm Beach | Fla. St. | O-S | 124 | 415 | 73 | 137 | 19 | •18 | 4 | 69 | .330 | 214 | 13 | 2 | .991 |
| 1971—Quebec City .......East. | | OF | •140 | 463 | •80 | 129 | 14 | •8 | 20 | 67 | .279 | 233 | 14 | 10 | .961 |
| 1972—Peninsula ..........Int. | | OF | •144 | 532 | •91 | 139 | 25 | 8 | 16 | 57 | .261 | 276 | 16 | 12 | .961 |
| 1972—Montreal ..........Nat. | | OF | 8 | 11 | 2 | 3 | 0 | 0 | 0 | 0 | .273 | 2 | 0 | 0 | 1.000 |
| 1973—Peninsula ..........Int. | | OF | 91 | 309 | 50 | 80 | 18 | 4 | 9 | 39 | .259 | 164 | 10 | 5 | .972 |
| 1973—Montreal ..........Nat. | | OF | 33 | 62 | 9 | 11 | 2 | 1 | 3 | 7 | .177 | 28 | 0 | 1 | .966 |
| 1974—Memphis ..........Int. | | OF | 120 | 445 | 85 | 130 | 22 | 3 | 17 | 56 | .292 | 174 | 6 | 7 | .963 |
| 1974—Montreal ..........Nat. | | OF | 23 | 61 | 10 | 19 | 3 | 0 | 0 | 4 | .311 | 22 | 0 | 0 | 1.000 |
| 1975—Montreal ..........Nat. | | OF | 140 | 514 | 84 | 126 | 16 | 2 | 9 | 45 | .245 | 308 | 8 | 9 | .972 |
| 1976—Mont.†-N.Y. ......Nat. | | OF | 107 | 317 | 49 | 75 | 14 | 3 | 4 | 25 | .237 | 210 | 5 | 6 | .973 |
| Major League Totals ..................... | | | 311 | 965 | 154 | 234 | 35 | 6 | 16 | 81 | .242 | 570 | 13 | 16 | .973 |

†Traded in waiver deal with Outfielder Jim Dwyer to New York Mets for Outfielder Del Unser ar-Infielder Wayne Garrett, July 21, 1976.

---

**D I D   Y O U   K N O W —**

That there are 163 members in the Baseball Hall of Fame?

---

## PHILIP ANTHONY MANKOWSKI
### (Phil)

Born January 9, 1953, at Buffalo, N.Y.
Height, 6.00. Weight, 180.
Throws right and bats lefthanded.
Hobbies—Music and tennis.
Brother of Paul Mankowski, infielder in Minnesota Twins'
organization, 1966 through 1969.
Son of Ben Mankowski, first baseman in Brooklyn Dodgers' organization, 1940.

| Year    Club          | League   | Pos.  | G.  | AB. | R. | H.  | 2B. | 3B. | HR. | RBI. | B.A. | PO. | A.  | E. | F.A. |
|-----------------------|----------|-------|-----|-----|----|-----|-----|-----|-----|------|------|-----|-----|----|------|
| 1971—Bristol          | Appal.   | 3B    | 14  | 53  | 5  | 20  | 3   | 2   | 0   | 8    | .377 | 17  | 26  | 4  | .915 |
| 1971—Batavia          | NYP      | 3B-1B | 52  | 195 | 20 | 51  | 9   | 0   | 3   | 27   | .262 | 38  | 103 | 14 | .910 |
| 1972—Lakeland         | Fla. St. | 3B    | 110 | 403 | 38 | 110 | 8   | 2   | 2   | 34   | .273 | 71  | 210 | 16 | .946 |
| 1973—Clinton          | Midw.    | 3B    | 121 | 454 | 43 | 105 | 23  | 4   | 2   | 36   | .231 | 77  | 233 | 32 | .906 |
| 1974—Lakeland†        | Fla. St. | 3B    | 64  | 234 | 30 | 60  | 10  | 3   | 5   | 38   | .256 | 45  | 125 | 9  | .950 |
| 1975—Montgomery       | South.   | 3B    | 124 | 407 | 44 | 115 | 18  | 2   | 9   | 49   | .283 | 81  | 257 | 13 | .963 |
| 1976—Evansville       | A.A.     | 3B    | 122 | 413 | 50 | 119 | 21  | 2   | 5   | 49   | .288 | 75  | 217 | 25 | .921 |
| 1976—Detroit          | Amer.    | 3B    | 24  | 85  | 9  | 23  | 2   | 1   | 1   | 4    | .271 | 20  | 47  | 2  | .971 |
| Major League Totals   |          |       | 24  | 85  | 9  | 23  | 2   | 1   | 1   | 4    | .271 | 20  | 47  | 2  | .971 |

†On disabled list, July 11 through September 15, 1974.


## RICHARD EUGENE MANNING
### (Rick)

Born September 2, 1954, at Niagara Falls, N. Y.
Height, 6.01. Weight, 180.
Throws right and bats lefthanded.
Hobbies—Camping and music.
Named outfielder on THE SPORTING NEWS American League All-Star fielding team, 1976.
Received reported $65,000 bonus to sign with Cleveland Indians, 1972.

| Year    Club          | League | Pos.  | G.  | AB. | R.   | H.  | 2B. | 3B. | HR. | RBI. | B.A. | PO. | A.  | E. | F.A.  |
|-----------------------|--------|-------|-----|-----|------|-----|-----|-----|-----|------|------|-----|-----|----|-------|
| 1972—Reno             | Calif. | OF-SS | 57  | 216 | 45   | 52  | 4   | 4   | 3   | 23   | .241 | 71  | 45  | 19 | .859  |
| 1973—Reno             | Calif. | OF-SS | 137 | 486 | •101 | 136 | 40  | •14 | 6   | 67   | .280 | 184 | 8   | 7  | .965  |
| 1974—Oklahoma City    | A. A.  | OF    | 122 | 402 | 58   | 108 | 16  | 5   | 5   | 39   | .269 | 207 | 12  | 8  | .965  |
| 1975—Oklahoma City    | A. A.  | OF    | 30  | 117 | 18   | 37  | 5   | 2   | 0   | 15   | .316 | 62  | 4   | 0  | 1.000 |
| 1975—Cleveland        | Amer.  | OF    | 120 | 480 | 69   | 137 | 16  | 5   | 3   | 35   | .285 | 331 | 12  | 9  | .974  |
| 1976—Cleveland        | Amer.  | OF    | 138 | 552 | 73   | 161 | 24  | 7   | 6   | 43   | .292 | 359 | 8   | 5  | .987  |
| Major League Totals   |        |       | 258 | 1032| 142  | 298 | 40  | 12  | 9   | 78   | .289 | 690 | 20  | 14 | .981  |


## JERRY MANUEL

Born December 23, 1953, at Hahira, Ga.
Height, 6.00. Weight, 165.
Throws right and bats left and righthanded.
Led American Association second basemen in double plays with 81 in 1974 and with 108 in 1975.

| Year    Club          | League   | Pos.    | G.  | AB. | R. | H.  | 2B. | 3B. | HR. | RBI. | B.A. | PO.  | A.   | E. | F.A.  |
|-----------------------|----------|---------|-----|-----|----|-----|-----|-----|-----|------|------|------|------|----|-------|
| 1972—Bristol          | Appal.   | SS      | 67  | 233 | 31 | 56  | 8   | 8   | 4   | 29   | .240 | •112 | •176 | 15 | •.950 |
| 1973—Lakeland         | Fla. St. | SS      | 117 | 433 | 66 | 109 | 17  | 4   | 2   | 28   | .252 | 167  | 349  | 29 | .947  |
| 1973—Toledo           | Int.     | SS      | 27  | 72  | 8  | 20  | 0   | 0   | 0   | 2    | .278 | 44   | 90   | 4  | .971  |
| 1974—Evansville       | A. A.    | 2B      | 127 | 384 | 44 | 81  | 5   | 5   | 1   | 24   | .211 | •315 | 356  | 17 | .975  |
| 1975—Evansville       | A. A.    | 2B      | •137| 501 | 63 | 115 | 10  | 4   | 4   | 43   | .230 | •348 | •394 | 16 | .979  |
| 1975—Detroit          | Amer.    | 2B      | 6   | 18  | 0  | 1   | 0   | 0   | 0   | 0    | .056 | 11   | 23   | 2  | .944  |
| 1976—Detroit          | Amer.    | 2-SS-DH | 54  | 43  | 4  | 6   | 1   | 0   | 0   | 2    | .140 | 40   | 64   | 8  | .928  |
| 1976—Evansville       | A. A.    | 2B      | 11  | 44  | 6  | 8   | 1   | 0   | 1   | 3    | .182 | 25   | 29   | 1  | .982  |
| Major League Totals   |          |         | 60  | 61  | 4  | 7   | 1   | 0   | 0   | 2    | .115 | 51   | 87   | 10 | .932  |


## MICHAEL GRANT MARSHALL
### (Mike)

Born January 15, 1943, at Adrian, Mich.
Height, 5.10. Weight, 180.
Throws and bats righthanded.
Hobby—Chess.
Attended Michigan State University, East Lansing, Mich.;
received Bachelor of Arts and Master's degrees in Education.

Established major league records for most games, season, pitcher, 106; most games, season, relief pitcher, 106; most games, season, no games started, 106; most innings pitched, season, relief pitcher, 208; most seasons, consecutive, leading major leagues in games finished, 3, 1974; most games finished, season, 83, in 1974; and most consecutive games, pitcher, season, 13, June 18 to July 3 (first game), 1974.

Tied following major league records: most seasons leading majors in game finished, 3, 1974; most consecutive seasons leading league in games finished, 4, 1974; most consecutive seasons, leading league, saves, 2, 1974; most seasons, leading saves, 2, 1974; and most games lost, relief pitcher, season, 14, in 1975.

Tied National League record for most seasons leading league in games finished, 4, 1974.
Led National League in saves with 31 in 1973 and 21 in 1974.
Led International League pitchers in complete games with 16 in 1968.

Named National League Fireman of the Year by THE SPORTING NEWS, 1973 and 1974.
Named National League Pitcher of the Year by THE SPORTING NEWS, 1974.
Won National League Cy Young Memorial Award, 1974.

| Year | Club | League | G. | IP. | W. | L. | Pct. | H. | R. | ER. | SO. | BB. | ERA. |
|------|------|--------|----|-----|----|----|------|----|----|-----|-----|-----|------|
| 1965—Chattanooga | | Southern | 8 | 26 | 2 | 4 | .333 | 25 | 15 | 9 | 21 | 13 | 3.12 |
| 1965—Eugene† | | Northw. | 36 | 59 | 6 | 5 | .545 | 53 | 33 | 23 | 63 | 30 | 3.51 |
| 1966—Montgomery | | Southern | 51 | 108 | 11 | 7 | .611 | 84 | 37 | 28 | 81 | 44 | 2.33 |
| 1967—Toledo | | Int'national | 10 | 15 | 2 | 0 | 1.000 | 10 | 1 | 1 | 16 | 5 | 0.60 |
| 1967—Detroit | | American | 37 | 59 | 1 | 3 | .250 | 51 | 15 | 13 | 41 | 20 | 1.98 |
| 1968—Toledo‡ | | Int'national | 31 | *211 | 15 | 9 | .625 | 191 | 85 | 69 | 190 | 52 | 2.94 |
| 1969—Toledo§ | | Int'national | 11 | 87 | 6 | 4 | .600 | 79 | 37 | 30 | 60 | 27 | 3.10 |
| 1969—Seattle x | | American | 20 | 88 | 3 | 10 | .231 | 99 | 54 | 50 | 47 | 35 | 5.11 |
| 1970—Oklahoma City | | Am. Assoc. | 16 | 45 | 4 | 3 | .571 | 32 | 11 | 8 | 42 | 16 | 1.60 |
| 1970—Winnipeg | | Int'national | 9 | 41 | 2 | 1 | .667 | 30 | 13 | 10 | 23 | 19 | 2.20 |
| 1970—Houston y-Montreal | | National | 28 | 70 | 3 | 8 | .273 | 64 | 39 | 30 | 43 | 33 | 3.86 |
| 1971—Montreal | | National | 66 | 111 | 5 | 8 | .385 | 100 | 56 | 53 | 85 | 50 | 4.30 |
| 1972—Montreal | | National | *65 | 116 | 14 | 8 | .636 | 82 | 26 | 23 | 95 | 47 | 1.78 |
| 1973—Montreal z | | National | *92 | 179 | 14 | 11 | .560 | 163 | 52 | 53 | 124 | 75 | 2.66 |
| 1974—Los Angeles | | National | *106 | 208 | 15 | 12 | .556 | 191 | 66 | 56 | 143 | 56 | 2.42 |
| 1975—Los Angeles a | | National | 57 | 109 | 9 | 14 | .391 | 98 | 46 | 40 | 64 | 39 | 3.30 |
| 1976—L. A.b-Atlanta | | National | 54 | 99 | 6 | 4 | .600 | 99 | 48 | 44 | 56 | 39 | 4.00 |
| American League Totals | | | 57 | 147 | 4 | 13 | .235 | 150 | 69 | 63 | 88 | 55 | 3.85 |
| National League Totals | | | 468 | 892 | 66 | 65 | .504 | 797 | 343 | 299 | 610 | 339 | 3.01 |
| Major League Totals | | | 525 | 1039 | 70 | 78 | .473 | 947 | 412 | 362 | 698 | 394 | 3.14 |

†Sold by Philadelphia Phillies' organization to Detroit Tigers' organization, April 11, 1966.
‡Recalled by Detroit; selected by Seattle Pilots from Detroit in expansion draft, October 15, 1968.
§Appeared in one game as an outfielder.
xSold to Houston Astros' organization, November 21, 1969.
yTraded to Montreal Expos for Outfielder Don Bosch, June 23, 1970.
zTraded to Los Angeles Dodgers for Outfielder Willie Davis, December 5, 1973.
aOn disabled list, May 10 to June 6, 1975.
bTraded in waiver deal to Atlanta Braves for Pitcher Elias Sosa and Infielder Lee Lacy, June 23, 1976; on disabled list, August 31 to October 4, 1976.

### RECORD AS SHORTSTOP

| Year | Club | League | Pos. | G. | AB. | R. | H. | 2B. | 3B. | HR. | RBI. | B.A. | PO. | A. | E. | F.A. |
|------|------|--------|------|----|-----|----|----|-----|-----|-----|------|------|-----|----|----|------|
| 1961—Dotham | | Ala.-Fl. | SS | 118 | 425 | 82 | 112 | 15 | 2 | 7 | 51 | .264 | *196 | 281 | *53 | .900 |
| 1962—Bakersfield | | Calif. | SS | 134 | 521 | 85 | 147 | 15 | 3 | 5 | 63 | .282 | 169 | *420 | *68 | .896 |
| 1963—Magic Valley | | Pion. | SS | 107 | 385 | 84 | 117 | 17 | 5 | 14 | 76 | .304 | 152 | 259 | 45 | .901 |
| 1964—Chattanooga | | South. | SS | 133 | 495 | 64 | 136 | 19 | 8 | 5 | 62 | .275 | 213 | 356 | *41 | .933 |

### CHAMPIONSHIP SERIES RECORD

| Year | Club | League | G. | IP. | W. | L. | Pct. | H. | R. | ER. | SO. | BB. | ERA. |
|------|------|--------|----|-----|----|----|------|----|----|-----|-----|-----|------|
| 1974—Los Angeles | | National | 2 | 3 | 0 | 0 | .000 | 0 | 0 | 0 | 1 | 0 | 0.00 |

### WORLD SERIES RECORD

Established World Series records for most games appeared in and most games finished, relief pitcher, 5-game series, 5 in 1974.

| Year | Club | League | G. | IP. | W. | L. | Pct. | H. | R. | ER. | SO. | BB. | ERA. |
|------|------|--------|----|-----|----|----|------|----|----|-----|-----|-----|------|
| 1974—Los Angeles | | National | 5 | 9 | 0 | 1 | .000 | 6 | 1 | 1 | 10 | 1 | 1.00 |

### ALL-STAR GAME RECORD

| Year | League | IP. | W. | L. | Pct. | H. | R. | ER. | SO. | BB. | ERA. |
|------|--------|-----|----|----|------|----|----|-----|-----|-----|------|
| 1974—National | | 2 | 0 | 0 | .000 | 0 | 0 | 0 | 2 | 1 | 0.00 |

Member of National League All-Star Team for 1975 game; did not play.

## JERRY LINDSEY MARTIN

Born May 11, 1949, at Columbia, S. C.
Height, 6.01. Weight, 195.
Throws and bats righthanded.
Attended Spartanburg Junior College, Spartanburg, S. C., and
Furman University, Greenville, S. C.
Son of Barney Martin, Sr., former pitcher in Cincinnati Reds' and New York Giants' organizations, and brother of Mike Martin, pitcher in Philadelphia Phillies' organization.

Led Western Carolinas League in total bases with 240 and tied for lead in sacrifice flies with 7 in 1972.
Tied for Eastern League lead in sacrifice flies with 9 in 1973.
Named Western Carolinas League Most Valuable Player in 1972.

| Year | Club | League | Pos. | G. | AB. | R. | H. | 2B. | 3B. | HR. | RBI. | B.A. | PO. | A. | E. | F.A. |
|------|------|--------|------|----|-----|----|----|-----|-----|-----|------|------|-----|----|----|------|
| 1971—Pulaski | | Appal. | OF | 40 | 156 | 35 | 49 | 8 | 1 | 6 | 28 | .314 | 54 | 1 | 6 | .902 |
| 1972—Spartanburg | | W. Car. | OF | *132 | *513 | 86 | *162 | *30 | 6 | 12 | *112 | .316 | 186 | *15 | 8 | .962 |
| 1973—Reading | | East. | OF-3B | 135 | 460 | 73 | 138 | 23 | 5 | 17 | 86 | .300 | 214 | 11 | 7 | .970 |
| 1974—Toledo | | Int. | OF | 139 | 497 | 67 | 144 | 23 | 4 | 8 | 64 | .290 | 285 | 6 | 3 | .990 |
| 1974—Philadelphia | | Nat. | OF | 13 | 14 | 2 | 3 | 1 | 0 | 0 | 1 | .214 | 5 | 0 | 0 | 1.000 |
| 1975—Toledo | | Int. | OF | 94 | 342 | 64 | 89 | 12 | 4 | 14 | 40 | .260 | 205 | 7 | 3 | .986 |
| 1975—Philadelphia | | Nat. | OF | 57 | 113 | 15 | 24 | 7 | 1 | 2 | 11 | .212 | 90 | 3 | 2 | .979 |
| 1976—Philadelphia | | Nat. | OF-1B | 130 | 121 | 30 | 30 | 7 | 0 | 2 | 15 | .248 | 85 | 0 | 2 | .977 |
| Major League Totals | | | | 200 | 248 | 47 | 57 | 15 | 1 | 4 | 27 | .230 | 180 | 3 | 4 | .979 |

| Year Club League | Pos. | G. | AB. | R. | H. | 2B. | 3B. | HR. | RBI. | B.A. | PO. | A. | E. | F.A. |
|---|---|---|---|---|---|---|---|---|---|---|---|---|---|---|
| 1976–Philadelphia ......Nat. | OF | 1 | 1 | 1 | 0 | 0 | 0 | 0 | 0 | .000 | 1 | 0 | 0 | 1.000 |

## FELIX ANTHONY MARTINEZ
### (Tippy)

Born May 31, 1950, at La Junta, Colo.
Height, 5.10. Weight, 175.
Throws and bats lefthanded.
Hobbies–Tennis, golf and water skiing.
Attended Colorado State University, Fort Collins, Colo.

Tied for Carolina League lead in saves with 15 and in wild pitches with 17 in 1973.

| Year Club | League | G. | IP. | W. | L. | Pct. | H. | R. | ER. | SO. | BB. | ERA. |
|---|---|---|---|---|---|---|---|---|---|---|---|---|
| 1972–Oneonta ...........................NYP | | 2 | 9 | 1 | 0 | 1.000 | 3 | 2 | 2 | 9 | 10 | 2.00 |
| 1972–Kinston ..............................Carolina | | 5 | 20 | 0 | 0 | .000 | 22 | 10 | 10 | 18 | 13 | 4.50 |
| 1973–Kinston ..............................Carolina | | 54 | 105 | 13 | 8 | .619 | 74 | 38 | 31 | 160 | 61 | 2.66 |
| 1974–Syracuse ............................Int'national | | 36 | 64 | 7 | 5 | .583 | 49 | 29 | 27 | 70 | 32 | 3.80 |
| 1974–New York ...........................American | | 10 | 13 | 0 | 0 | .000 | 14 | 7 | 6 | 10 | 9 | 4.15 |
| 1975–Syracuse ............................Int'national | | 14 | 110 | 8 | 2 | .800 | 91 | 39 | 25 | 105 | 35 | 2.05 |
| 1975–New York ...........................American | | 23 | 37 | 1 | 2 | .333 | 27 | 15 | 11 | 20 | 32 | 2.68 |
| 1976–New York† ..........................American | | 11 | 28 | 2 | 0 | 1.000 | 18 | 6 | 6 | 14 | 14 | 1.93 |
| 1976–Baltimore ...........................American | | 28 | 42 | 3 | 1 | .750 | 32 | 13 | 12 | 31 | 28 | 2.57 |
| Major League Totals ............................ | | 72 | 120 | 6 | 3 | .667 | 91 | 41 | 35 | 75 | 83 | 2.62 |

†Traded with Pitchers Rudy May, Dave Pagan and Scott McGregor and Catcher Rick Dempsey to Baltimore Orioles for Pitchers Ken Hotzman, Doyle Alexander and Grant Jackson, Catcher Ellie Hendricks and Pitcher Jimmy Freeman, latter assigned from Rochester to Syracuse, June 15, 1976.

## JOHN ALBERT MARTINEZ
### (Buck)

Born November 7, 1948, at Redding, Calif.
Height, 5.10. Weight, 185.
Throws and bats righthanded.
Hobbies–Golf, hunting and fishing.
Attended Sacramento City College, Sacramento, Calif., and
Sacramento State College, Sacramento, Calif.

| Year Club | League | Pos. | G. | AB. | R. | H. | 2B. | 3B. | HR. | RBI. | B.A. | PO. | A. | E. | F.A. |
|---|---|---|---|---|---|---|---|---|---|---|---|---|---|---|---|
| 1967–Eugene..............Northw. | ●C-O-3 | 77 | 269 | 53 | 96 | 16 | 4 | 2 | 46 | .357 | 294 | ●48 | 8 | .977 |
| 1968–Spartanburg ......W. Car. | C | 8 | 28 | 6 | 11 | 4 | 0 | 0 | 11 | .393 | 51 | 2 | 0 | 1.000 |
| 1968–Tidewater†‡ ......Carol. | C | 36 | 110 | 10 | 31 | 12 | 1 | 1 | 14 | .282 | 272 | 16 | 1 | .997 |
| 1969–Kansas City§ ....Amer. | C-OF | 72 | 205 | 14 | 47 | 6 | 1 | 4 | 23 | .229 | 292 | 26 | 9 | .972 |
| 1970–Kansas City x ....Amer. | C | 6 | 9 | 1 | 1 | 0 | 0 | 0 | 0 | .111 | 20 | 3 | 1 | .958 |
| 1971–Omaha ...............A. A. | C | 75 | 269 | 34 | 77 | 23 | 1 | 5 | 39 | .286 | 502 | 37 | 8 | .985 |
| 1971–Kansas City .......Amer. | C | 22 | 46 | 3 | 7 | 2 | 0 | 0 | 1 | .152 | 84 | 6 | 3 | .968 |
| 1972–Omaha y ..........A. A. | C | 67 | 195 | 23 | 34 | 9 | 0 | 4 | 12 | .174 | 493 | 47 | 6 | .989 |
| 1973–Omaha ...............A. A. | ★C-1B | 82 | 254 | 24 | 69 | 13 | 0 | 5 | 38 | .272 | 522 | 47 | 3 | ★.995 |
| 1973–Kansas City .......Amer. | C | 14 | 32 | 2 | 8 | 1 | 0 | 1 | 6 | .250 | 52 | 4 | 2 | .966 |
| 1974–Kansas City ......Amer. | C | 43 | 107 | 10 | 23 | 3 | 1 | 1 | 8 | .215 | 151 | 16 | 4 | .977 |
| 1975–Kansas City ......Amer. | C | 80 | 226 | 15 | 51 | 9 | 2 | 3 | 23 | .226 | 361 | 39 | 8 | .980 |
| 1976–Kansas City z ....Amer. | C | 95 | 267 | 24 | 61 | 13 | 3 | 5 | 34 | .228 | 420 | 40 | 4 | .991 |
| Major League Totals ...................... | | 332 | 892 | 69 | 198 | 34 | 7 | 14 | 95 | .222 | 1380 | 134 | 31 | .980 |

†Drafted by Houston Astros from San Diego (Philadelphia Phillies' organization), December 2, 1968.
‡Traded with Infielder Mickey Sinnerud and Catcher Tommie Smith (latter two transferred from Oklahoma City to Omaha) by Houston Astros to Kansas City Royals for Catcher John Jones, December 16, 1968.
§On restricted list April 7 through June 17.
xOn military list April 2 through August 10.
yOn disabled list, July 9 through August 25.
zOn disabled list, May 20 through June 5.

| Year Club League | Pos. | G. | AB. | R. | H. | 2B. | 3B. | HR. | RBI. | B.A. | PO. | A. | E. | F.A. |
|---|---|---|---|---|---|---|---|---|---|---|---|---|---|---|
| 1976–Kansas City ......Amer. | C | 5 | 15 | 0 | 5 | 0 | 0 | 0 | 4 | .333 | 15 | 4 | 0 | 1.000 |

## JOSE DENNIS MARTINEZ

Born May 14, 1955, at Granada, Nicaragua.
Height, 6.01. Weight, 160.
Throws and bats righthanded.
Hobby–Music.

Led International League in complete games with 16 in 1976.

| Year Club | League | G. | IP. | W. | L. | Pct. | H. | R. | ER. | SO. | BB. | ERA. |
|---|---|---|---|---|---|---|---|---|---|---|---|---|
| 1974–Miami.................Florida St. | | 25 | 179 | 15 | 6 | .714 | 124 | 48 | 41 | 162 | 53 | 2.06 |
| 1975–Miami.................Florida St. | | 20 | 145 | 12 | 4 | .750 | 125 | 54 | 42 | 114 | 35 | 2.61 |
| 1975–Asheville ............Southern | | 6 | 45 | 4 | 1 | .800 | 45 | 16 | 13 | 18 | 12 | 2.60 |
| 1976–Rochester ...........Int'national | | 25 | 180 | ★14 | 8 | .636 | 148 | 64 | 50 | ★140 | 50 | ★2.50 |
| 1976–Baltimore ...........American | | 4 | 28 | 1 | 2 | .333 | 23 | 8 | 8 | 18 | 8 | 2.57 |
| Major League Totals ............................ | | 4 | 28 | 1 | 2 | .333 | 23 | 8 | 8 | 18 | 8 | 2.57 |

## SILVIO RAMON MARTINEZ

Born August 31, 1955, at Santiago, Dominican Republic.
Height, 5.10. Weight, 170.
Throws and bats righthanded.
Hobby—Fishing.

Led Texas League in shutouts with 7 in 1976.

| Year Club | League | G. | IP. | W. | L. | Pct. | H. | R. | ER. | SO. | BB. | ERA. |
|---|---|---|---|---|---|---|---|---|---|---|---|---|
| 1974—Niagara Falls | NYP | 12 | 67 | 4 | 5 | .444 | 48 | 36 | 24 | 54 | 42 | 3.22 |
| 1975—Charleston | W. Carol. | 19 | 133 | 6 | 9 | .400 | 115 | 63 | 53 | 113 | 55 | 3.59 |
| 1975—Salem | Carolina | 4 | 29 | 2 | 1 | .667 | 25 | 10 | 10 | 28 | 10 | 3.10 |
| 1976—Shreveport | Texas | 16 | 104 | 8 | 4 | .667 | 74 | 29 | 28 | 71 | 33 | 2.42 |
| 1976—Charleston† | Int'national | 8 | 44 | 2 | 4 | .333 | 59 | 30 | 29 | 31 | 18 | 5.93 |

†Traded by Pittsburgh Pirates' organization with Outfielder Richie Zisk to Chicago White Sox for Pitchers Terry Forster and Rich Gossage, December 10, 1976.
Listed on Chicago White Sox' 1977 spring roster.

## TEODORO NOEL MARTINEZ
### (Teddy)

Born December 10, 1947, at Central Barahona, Dominican Republic.
Height, 6.00. Weight, 160.
Throws and bats righthanded.
Hobby—Listening to music.

| Year Club | League | Pos. | G. | AB. | R. | H. | 2B. | 3B. | HR. | RBI. | B.A. | PO. | A. | E. | F.A. |
|---|---|---|---|---|---|---|---|---|---|---|---|---|---|---|---|
| 1967—Winter Haven | Fla. St. | 2-S-3 | 38 | 113 | 12 | 28 | 1 | 0 | 0 | 11 | .248 | 55 | 65 | 9 | .930 |
| 1967—Marion† | Appal. | S-3B | 41 | 139 | 19 | 30 | 0 | 6 | 2 | 18 | .216 | 79 | 170 | 11 | .956 |
| 1968—Visalia | Calif. | SS | 62 | 208 | 19 | 56 | 1 | 1 | 3 | 19 | .269 | 110 | 179 | 24 | .923 |
| 1968—Raleigh-Durham | Carol. | S-2-3 | 59 | 227 | 32 | 75 | 14 | 1 | 1 | 23 | .330 | 103 | 138 | 10 | .960 |
| 1969—Memphis | Tex. | S-3-O | 118 | 418 | 42 | 110 | 12 | 6 | 3 | 34 | .263 | 173 | 277 | 25 | .947 |
| 1970—Tidewater | Int. | 2-S-3 | 116 | 438 | 62 | 134 | 20 | 9 | 3 | 36 | .306 | 201 | 307 | 14 | .973 |
| 1970—New York | Nat. | 2B-SS | 4 | 16 | 0 | 1 | 0 | 0 | 0 | 0 | .063 | 9 | 11 | 0 | 1.000 |
| 1971—Tidewater | Int. | SS | 83 | 337 | 49 | 100 | 12 | 5 | 5 | 27 | .297 | 118 | 218 | 19 | .946 |
| 1971—New York | Nat. | S-2-3-O | 38 | 125 | 16 | 36 | 5 | 2 | 1 | 10 | .288 | 45 | 80 | 3 | .977 |
| 1972—New York | Nat. | 2-S-O-3 | 103 | 330 | 22 | 74 | 5 | 5 | 1 | 19 | .224 | 175 | 194 | 5 | .987 |
| 1973—New York | Nat. | S-O-3-2 | 92 | 263 | 34 | 67 | 11 | 0 | 1 | 14 | .255 | 119 | 139 | 12 | .956 |
| 1974—New York‡ | Nat. | S-3-2-O | 116 | 334 | 32 | 73 | 15 | 7 | 2 | 43 | .219 | 164 | 257 | 20 | .955 |
| 1975—St. Louis§ | Nat. | O-2-3-S | 16 | 21 | 1 | 4 | 2 | 0 | 0 | 2 | .190 | 11 | 3 | 1 | .933 |
| 1975—Oakland | Amer. | S-2-3 | 86 | 87 | 7 | 15 | 0 | 0 | 0 | 3 | .172 | 61 | 81 | 4 | .973 |
| 1976—Indianapolis x | A. A. | O-Inf | 85 | 310 | 45 | 79 | 15 | 2 | 1 | 19 | .255 | 115 | 72 | 6 | .969 |
| National League Totals | | | 369 | 1089 | 105 | 255 | 38 | 14 | 5 | 88 | .234 | 523 | 684 | 41 | .967 |
| American League Totals | | | 86 | 87 | 7 | 15 | 0 | 0 | 0 | 3 | .172 | 61 | 81 | 4 | .973 |
| Major League Totals | | | 455 | 1176 | 112 | 270 | 38 | 14 | 5 | 91 | .230 | 584 | 765 | 45 | .968 |

†Drafted by Houston Astros from Jacksonville (New York Mets' organization), November 28, 1967; returned to Jacksonville, April 3, 1968.
‡Traded to St. Louis Cardinals for Infielder Jack Heidemann and Outfielder Mike Vail, December 11, 1974.
§Traded to Oakland Athletics for Pitcher Steve Staniland and a player to be named later, May 18, 1975; Athletics assigned Pitcher Mike Barlow to Cardinals, May 23, 1975, to complete deal.
xOn disabled list March 29 to May 7, 1976; unconditionally released, May 7, 1976; signed as free agent with Indianapolis (Cincinnati Reds' organization), May 30, 1976; drafted by Los Angeles Dodgers' organization, December 6, 1976.

### CHAMPIONSHIP SERIES RECORD

| Year Club | League | Pos. | G. | AB. | R. | H. | 2B. | 3B. | HR. | RBI. | B.A. | PO. | A. | E. | F.A. |
|---|---|---|---|---|---|---|---|---|---|---|---|---|---|---|---|
| 1975—Oakland | Amer. | PR-2B | 3 | 0 | 0 | 0 | 0 | 0 | 0 | 0 | .000 | 1 | 1 | 0 | 1.000 |

### WORLD SERIES RECORD

| Year Club | League | Pos. | G. | AB. | R. | H. | 2B. | 3B. | HR. | RBI. | B.A. | PO. | A. | E. | F.A. |
|---|---|---|---|---|---|---|---|---|---|---|---|---|---|---|---|
| 1973—New York | Nat. | PR | 2 | 0 | 0 | 0 | 0 | 0 | 0 | 0 | .000 | 0 | 0 | 0 | .000 |

## MICHAEL ANTHONY MARTINSON
### (Marty)

Born April 20, 1956, at Long Beach, Calif.
Height, 6.02. Weight, 195.
Throws and bats righthanded.
Hobby—Guitar.

Attended California State College, Dominguez Hills, Calif.
Tied for Pioneer League lead in sacrifice flies with 5 in 1974.

| Year Club | League | Pos. | G. | AB. | R. | H. | 2B. | 3B. | HR. | RBI. | B.A. | PO. | A. | E. | F.A. |
|---|---|---|---|---|---|---|---|---|---|---|---|---|---|---|---|
| 1974—Idaho Falls | Pion. | C-OF | 62 | 212 | 33 | 53 | 5 | 2 | 2 | 32 | .250 | 366 | 39 | 7 | *.983 |
| 1974—Salinas | Calif. | C | 6 | 19 | 0 | 1 | 0 | 0 | 0 | 0 | .053 | 33 | 6 | 0 | 1.000 |
| 1975—Salinas | Calif. | C | 61 | 193 | 11 | 33 | 2 | 0 | 0 | 18 | .171 | 233 | 50 | 7 | .976 |
| 1975—Quad Cities | Midw. | C | 40 | 126 | 21 | 34 | 3 | 0 | 0 | .18 | .270 | 247 | 28 | 2 | .993 |
| 1976—Quad Cities | Midw. | C | 43 | 152 | 24 | 41 | 6 | 1 | 1 | 20 | .270 | 244 | 27 | 7 | .975 |
| 1976—Salt Lake City | P. C. | C | 53 | 152 | 18 | 32 | 4 | 0 | 0 | 16 | .211 | 274 | 19 | 2 | .993 |

Listed on California Angels' 1977 spring roster.

## JAMES PERCY MASON
### (Jim)

Born August 14, 1950, at Mobile, Ala.
Height, 6.02. Weight, 190.
Throws right and bats lefthanded.
Hobbies—Hunting and fishing.
Attended University of South Alabama, Mobile, Ala.
Tied major league record for most doubles, game, 4, July 8, 1974.

| Year | Club | League | Pos. | G. | AB. | R. | H. | 2B. | 3B. | HR. | RBI. | B.A. | PO. | A. | E. | F.A. |
|---|---|---|---|---|---|---|---|---|---|---|---|---|---|---|---|---|
| 1968—Geneva | | NYP | SS | 60 | 198 | 22 | 43 | 8 | 5 | 2 | 14 | .217 | 79 | 139 | 21 | .912 |
| 1969—Buffalo | | Int. | SS | 35 | 113 | 13 | 26 | 3 | 1 | 1 | 7 | .230 | 63 | 96 | 18 | .898 |
| 1970—Denver | | A.A. | SS | 110 | 382 | 50 | 92 | 16 | 6 | 8 | 43 | .241 | 220 | ★408 | 48 | .929 |
| 1971—Denver | | A.A. | SS-2B | 105 | 403 | 75 | 108 | 17 | 4 | 4 | 36 | .268 | 138 | 314 | 23 | .951 |
| 1971—Washington | | Amer. | SS | 3 | 9 | 0 | 3 | 0 | 0 | 0 | 0 | .333 | 8 | 13 | 1 | .955 |
| 1972—Denver | | A.A. | SS | 86 | 327 | 59 | 89 | 21 | 3 | 5 | 27 | .272 | 148 | 302 | 27 | .943 |
| 1972—Texas | | Amer. | SS-3B | 46 | 147 | 10 | 29 | 3 | 0 | 0 | 10 | .197 | 58 | 106 | 10 | .943 |
| 1973—Texas† | | Amer. | S-2-3 | 92 | 238 | 23 | 49 | 7 | 2 | 3 | 19 | .206 | 143 | 230 | 20 | .949 |
| 1974—New York | | Amer. | SS | 152 | 440 | 41 | 110 | 18 | 6 | 5 | 37 | .250 | 241 | 430 | 25 | .964 |
| 1975—New York | | Amer. | SS-2B | 94 | 223 | 17 | 34 | 3 | 2 | 2 | 16 | .152 | 134 | 209 | 16 | .955 |
| 1976—New York‡ | | Amer. | SS | 93 | 217 | 17 | 39 | 7 | 1 | 1 | 14 | .180 | 128 | 245 | 13 | .966 |
| Major League Totals | | | | 480 | 1274 | 108 | 264 | 38 | 11 | 11 | 96 | .207 | 712 | 1233 | 85 | .958 |

†Sold to New York Yankees for an estimated $100,000, December 6, 1973.
‡Selected by Toronto Blue Jays in American League expansion draft, November 5, 1976.

### CHAMPIONSHIP SERIES RECORD

| Year | Club | League | Pos. | G. | AB. | R. | H. | 2B. | 3B. | HR. | RBI. | B.A. | PO. | A. | E. | F.A. |
|---|---|---|---|---|---|---|---|---|---|---|---|---|---|---|---|---|
| 1976—New York | | Amer. | SS | 2 | 0 | 0 | 0 | 0 | 0 | 0 | 0 | .000 | 1 | 2 | 0 | 1.000 |

### WORLD SERIES RECORD

| Year | Club | League | Pos. | G. | AB. | R. | H. | 2B. | 3B. | HR. | RBI. | B.A. | PO. | A. | E. | F.A. |
|---|---|---|---|---|---|---|---|---|---|---|---|---|---|---|---|---|
| 1976—New York | | Amer. | SS | 3 | 1 | 1 | 1 | 0 | 0 | 1 | 1 | 1.000 | 1 | 2 | 0 | 1.000 |

## JONATHAN TRUMPBOUR MATLACK
### (Jon)

Born January 19, 1950, at West Chester, Pa.
Height, 6.03. Weight, 200.
Throws and bats lefthanded.
Hobby—All sports.
Attended University of Pittsburgh, Pittsburgh, Pa., and West
Chester State College, West Chester, Pa.
Led National League in shutouts with 7 in 1974.
Tied for National League lead in shutouts with 6 in 1976.
Named THE SPORTING NEWS National League Rookie Pitcher of the Year, 1972.
Named 1972 National League Rookie of the Year by Baseball Writers' Association of America.

| Year | Club | League | G. | IP. | W. | L. | Pct. | H. | R. | ER. | SO. | BB. | ERA. |
|---|---|---|---|---|---|---|---|---|---|---|---|---|---|
| 1967—Williamsport | | Eastern | 2 | 5 | 0 | 1 | .000 | 10 | 8 | 8 | 4 | 4 | 14.40 |
| 1968—Raleigh-Dur. | | Carolina | 24 | 173 | 13 | 6 | .684 | 133 | 59 | 53 | 188 | 66 | 2.76 |
| 1969—Tidewater | | Int'national | 26 | 176 | 14 | 7 | .667 | 176 | 83 | 81 | 99 | 66 | 4.14 |
| 1970—Tidewater | | Int'national | 26 | 183 | 12 | 11 | .522 | 168 | 94 | 84 | 146 | 90 | 4.13 |
| 1971—Tidewater | | Int'national | 22 | 152 | 11 | 7 | .611 | 141 | 82 | 67 | 145 | 55 | 3.97 |
| 1971—New York | | National | 7 | 37 | 0 | 3 | .000 | 31 | 18 | 17 | 24 | 15 | 4.14 |
| 1972—New York | | National | 34 | 244 | 15 | 10 | .600 | 215 | 79 | 63 | 169 | 71 | 2.32 |
| 1973—New York | | National | 34 | 242 | 14 | 16 | .467 | 210 | 93 | 86 | 205 | 99 | 3.20 |
| 1974—New York | | National | 34 | 265 | 13 | 15 | .464 | 221 | 82 | 71 | 195 | 76 | 2.41 |
| 1975—New York | | National | 33 | 229 | 16 | 12 | .571 | 224 | 105 | 86 | 154 | 58 | 3.38 |
| 1976—New York | | National | 35 | 262 | 17 | 10 | .630 | 236 | 94 | 86 | 153 | 57 | 2.95 |
| Major League Totals | | | 177 | 1279 | 75 | 66 | .532 | 1137 | 471 | 409 | 900 | 376 | 2.88 |

### CHAMPIONSHIP SERIES RECORD

| Year | Club | League | G. | IP. | W. | L. | Pct. | H. | R. | ER. | SO. | BB. | ERA. |
|---|---|---|---|---|---|---|---|---|---|---|---|---|---|
| 1973—New York | | National | 1 | 9 | 1 | 0 | 1.000 | 2 | 0 | 0 | 9 | 3 | 0.00 |

### WORLD SERIES RECORD

| Year | Club | League | G. | IP. | W. | L. | Pct. | H. | R. | ER. | SO. | BB. | ERA. |
|---|---|---|---|---|---|---|---|---|---|---|---|---|---|
| 1973—New York | | National | 3 | 16⅔ | 1 | 2 | .333 | 10 | 7 | 4 | 11 | 5 | 2.16 |

### ALL-STAR GAME RECORD

| Year | League | IP. | W. | L. | Pct. | H. | R. | ER. | SO. | BB. | ERA. |
|---|---|---|---|---|---|---|---|---|---|---|---|
| 1974—National | | 1 | 0 | 0 | .000 | 1 | 0 | 0 | 0 | 1 | 0.00 |
| 1975—National | | 2 | 1 | 0 | 1.000 | 2 | 0 | 0 | 4 | 0 | 0.00 |
| All-Star Game Totals | | 3 | 1 | 0 | 1.000 | 3 | 0 | 0 | 4 | 1 | 0.00 |

# GARY NATHANIEL MATHEWS

Born July 5, 1950, at San Fernando, Calif.
Height, 6.02. Weight, 200.
Throws and bats righthanded.
Hobbies—Hunting, fishing and dancing.

Led Texas League in total bases with 232 in 1971.
Tied for California League lead in double plays by outfielders with 3 in 1970.
Named National League Rookie Player of the Year by THE SPORTING NEWS, 1973.
Named National League Rookie of the Year by Baseball Writers' Association of America, 1973.

| Year Club | League | Pos. | G. | AB. | R. | H. | 2B. | 3B. | HR. | RBI. | B.A. | PO. | A. | E. | F.A. |
|---|---|---|---|---|---|---|---|---|---|---|---|---|---|---|---|
| 1969—Decatur ...........Midw. | | OF | 53 | 174 | 31 | 56 | 11 | 2 | 8 | 30 | .322 | 63 | 7 | 8 | .897 |
| 1970—Fresno .............Calif. | | OF | 117 | 380 | 77 | 106 | 11 | 5 | 23 | 74 | .279 | 133 | 15 | ★15 | .908 |
| 1971—Amarillo...........Texas | | OF ●142 | 493 | 82 | 138 | ★37 | 6 | 15 | ★86 | .280 | 290 | 10 | 5 | ★.984 |
| 1972—Phoenix ...........P.C. | | OF | 136 | 480 | 101 | 150 | 27 | 8 | 21 | 108 | .313 | 218 | ●16 | ★13 | .947 |
| 1972—San Francisco ..Nat. | | OF | 20 | 62 | 11 | 18 | 1 | 1 | 4 | 14 | .290 | 34 | 0 | 1 | .971 |
| 1973—San Francisco ..Nat. | | OF | 148 | 540 | 74 | 162 | 22 | 10 | 12 | 58 | .300 | 277 | 11 | 5 | .983 |
| 1974—San Francisco ..Nat. | | OF | 154 | 561 | 87 | 161 | 27 | 6 | 16 | 82 | .287 | 281 | 9 | 9 | .970 |
| 1975—San Francisco†..Nat. | | OF | 116 | 425 | 67 | 119 | 22 | 3 | 12 | 58 | .280 | 225 | 11 | 8 | .967 |
| 1976—San Francisco‡..Nat. | | OF | 156 | 587 | 79 | 164 | 28 | 4 | 20 | 84 | .279 | 265 | 8 | 7 | .975 |
| Major League Totals ..................... | | | 594 | 2175 | 318 | 624 | 100 | 24 | 64 | 296 | .287 | 1082 | 39 | 30 | .974 |

†On disabled list, June 5 to July 18, 1975.
‡Played out option year and granted free agency, November 1, 1976; signed as free agent with Atlanta Braves, November 17, 1976.


# CARLOS MAY

Born May 17, 1948, at Birmingham, Ala.
Height, 5.11. Weight, 210.
Throws right and bats lefthanded.
Attended Southern University, Baton Rouge, La.
Brother of Lee May, first baseman with Baltimore Orioles.

Named THE SPORTING NEWS American League Rookie Player of the Year, 1969.

| Year Club | League | Pos. | G. | AB. | R. | H. | 2B. | 3B. | HR. | RBI. | B.A. | PO. | A. | E. | F.A. |
|---|---|---|---|---|---|---|---|---|---|---|---|---|---|---|---|
| 1966—Sara. White Sox | Gulf C. | OF | 16 | 47 | 11 | 20 | 2 | 1 | 0 | 10 | .426 | 41 | 1 | 6 | .875 |
| 1966—Winter Haven ....Fla. St. | | OF | 37 | 118 | 8 | 18 | 1 | 2 | 0 | 4 | .153 | 30 | 0 | 0 | 1.000 |
| 1967—Appleton† ..........Midw. | | OF | 63 | 207 | 45 | 70 | 10 | 6 | 10 | 48 | .338 | 74 | 10 | 5 | .944 |
| 1968—Lynchburg ........Carol. | | OF | 113 | 397 | 62 | 131 | 21 | 7 | 13 | 74 | ★.330 | 223 | 13 | ★22 | .915 |
| 1968—Chicago ...........Amer. | | OF | 17 | 67 | 4 | 12 | 1 | 0 | 0 | 1 | .179 | 24 | 0 | 1 | .960 |
| 1969—Chicago ...........Amer. | | OF | 100 | 367 | 62 | 103 | 18 | 2 | 18 | 62 | .281 | 154 | 10 | 3 | .982 |
| 1970—Chicago ...........Amer. | | OF-1B | 150 | 555 | 83 | 158 | 28 | 4 | 12 | 68 | .285 | 276 | 23 | 4 | .987 |
| 1971—Chicago‡ .........Amer. | | ★1B-OF | 141 | 500 | 64 | 147 | 21 | 7 | 7 | 70 | .294 | 1206 | 72 | ★19 | .985 |
| 1972—Chicago ...........Amer. | | ●OF-1B | 148 | 523 | 83 | 161 | 26 | 3 | 12 | 68 | .308 | 247 | ●15 | 5 | .981 |
| 1973—Chicago ...........Amer. | | OF-1B | 149 | 553 | 62 | 148 | 20 | 0 | 20 | 96 | .268 | 129 | 8 | 1 | .993 |
| 1974—Chicago ...........Amer. | | OF | 149 | 551 | 66 | 137 | 19 | 2 | 8 | 58 | .249 | 245 | 11 | 3 | .988 |
| 1975—Chicago ...........Amer. | | 1B-OF | 128 | 454 | 55 | 123 | 19 | 2 | 8 | 53 | .271 | 580 | 52 | 8 | .988 |
| 1976—Chi.§-N.Y. ........Amer. | | DH-OF-1B | 107 | 351 | 45 | 91 | 13 | 2 | 3 | 43 | .259 | 41 | 0 | 1 | .976 |
| Major League Totals ..................... | | | 1089 | 3921 | 524 | 1080 | 165 | 22 | 88 | 519 | .275 | 2902 | 191 | 45 | .986 |

†On Military List from July 28 through end of season.
‡On supplemental disabled list, July 31 to August 17, 1971.
§Traded to New York Yankees for Outfielder Rich Coggins and Pitcher Ken Brett, May 18, 1976.

## ALL-STAR GAME RECORD

| Year | League | Pos. | AB. | R. | H. | 2B. | 3B. | HR. | RBI. | B.A. | PO. | A. | E. | F.A. |
|---|---|---|---|---|---|---|---|---|---|---|---|---|---|---|
| 1969—American ......................... | | PH | 1 | 0 | 0 | 0 | 0 | 0 | 0 | .000 | 0 | 0 | 0 | .000 |

Member of American League All-Star Team in 1972 game; did not play.

## CHAMPIONSHIP SERIES RECORD

| Year Club | League | Pos. | G. | AB. | R. | H. | 2B. | 3B. | HR. | RBI. | B.A. | PO. | A. | E. | F.A. |
|---|---|---|---|---|---|---|---|---|---|---|---|---|---|---|---|
| 1976—New York..........Amer. | | DH-PH | 3 | 10 | 1 | 2 | 1 | 0 | 0 | 0 | .200 | 0 | 0 | 0 | .000 |

## WORLD SERIES RECORD

| Year Club | League | Pos. | G. | AB. | R. | H. | 2B. | 3B. | HR. | RBI. | B.A. | PO. | A. | E. | F.A. |
|---|---|---|---|---|---|---|---|---|---|---|---|---|---|---|---|
| 1976—New York..........Amer. | | PH-DH | 4 | 9 | 0 | 0 | 0 | 0 | 0 | 0 | .000 | 0 | 0 | 0 | .000 |


# DAVID LaFRANCE MAY
## (Dave)

Born December 23, 1943, at New Castle, Del.
Height, 5.11. Weight, 196.
Throws right and bats lefthanded.
Hobby—All sports.

Tied for American League lead in total bases with 295 in 1973.
Led Midwest League in total bases with 250 in 1964 and Northwest League with 284 in 1965.
Led Northwest League in stolen bases with 32 in 1965.
Named Player of the Year in Midwest League, 1964.

| Year Club | League | Pos. | G. | AB. | R. | H. | 2B. | 3B. | HR. | RBI. | B.A. | PO. | A. | E. | F.A. |
|---|---|---|---|---|---|---|---|---|---|---|---|---|---|---|---|
| 1962–Salem† ..............Appal. | | OF | 59 | 214 | 53 | 81 | 12 | 6 | 5 | 41 | *.379 | 66 | 6 | 1 | *.986 |
| 1963–Stockton ............Calif. | | OF-1B | 40 | 108 | 20 | 27 | 5 | 2 | 2 | 10 | .250 | 46 | 3 | 4 | .925 |
| 1963–Fox Cities ........Midw. | | OF | 71 | 271 | 42 | 84 | 18 | 6 | 4 | 27 | .310 | 105 | 6 | 7 | .941 |
| 1964–Fox Cities ........Midw. | | OF | 122 | 451 | •111 | *166 | •26 | 8 | 14 | 74 | *.368 | 182 | 10 | 11 | .946 |
| 1965–Tri-City ............Northw. | | OF | •139 | 517 | *129 | *173 | •424 | 9 | 23 | 105 | .335 | 248 | 13 | 7 | .974 |
| 1966–Rochester..........Int. | | OF | 119 | 413 | 55 | 113 | 11 | 3 | 11 | 34 | .274 | 148 | 11 | '3 | .981 |
| 1967–Rochester..........Int. | | OF | 93 | 328 | 56 | 104 | 17 | 1 | 11 | 57 | .317 | 156 | 9 | 3 | .982 |
| 1967–Baltimore ..........Amer. | | OF | 36 | 85 | 12 | 20 | 1 | 1 | 1 | 7 | .235 | 30 | 1 | 1 | .969 |
| 1968–Baltimore ..........Amer. | | OF | 84 | 152 | 15 | 29 | 6 | 3 | 0 | 7 | .191 | 62 | 1 | 1 | .984 |
| 1968–Rochester..........Int. | | OF | 31 | 113 | 21 | 35 | 5 | 1 | 4 | 17 | .310 | 52 | 3 | 3 | .948 |
| 1969–Baltimore ..........Amer. | | OF | 78 | 120 | 8 | 29 | 6 | 0 | 3 | 10 | .242 | 43 | 4 | 3 | .940 |
| 1970–Balt.‡-Mil. ........Amer. | | OF | 126 | 373 | 42 | 88 | 8 | 2 | 8 | 37 | .236 | 260 | 6 | 3 | .989 |
| 1971–Milwaukee .......Amer. | | OF | 144 | 501 | 74 | 139 | 20 | 3 | 16 | 65 | .277 | 342 | 10 | 9 | .975 |
| 1972–Milwaukee .......Amer. | | OF | 143 | 500 | 49 | 119 | 20 | 2 | 9 | 45 | .238 | 376 | 9 | 6 | .985 |
| 1973–Milwaukee .......Amer. | | OF | 156 | 624 | 96 | 189 | 23 | 4 | 25 | 93 | .303 | 401 | 9 | 9 | .979 |
| 1974–Milwaukee§ ......Amer. | | OF | 135 | 477 | 56 | 108 | 15 | 1 | 10 | 42 | .226 | 249 | 10 | 3 | .989 |
| 1975–Atlanta ............Nat. | | OF | 82 | 203 | 28 | 56 | 8 | 0 | 12 | 40 | .276 | 103 | 3 | 4 | .964 |
| 1976–Atlanta x ..........Nat. | | OF-PH | 105 | 214 | 27 | 46 | 5 | 3 | 3 | 23 | .215 | 98 | 5 | 3 | .972 |
| American League Totals ................ | | | 902 | 2832 | 352 | 721 | 99 | 16 | 72 | 306 | .255 | 1763 | 50 | 35 | .981 |
| National League Totals .................. | | | 187 | 417 | 55 | 102 | 13 | 3 | 15 | 63 | .245 | 201 | 8 | 7 | .968 |
| Major League Totals ...................... | | | 1089 | 3249 | 407 | 823 | 112 | 19 | 87 | 369 | .253 | 1964 | 58 | 42 | .980 |

†Drafted by Baltimore Orioles from Tacoma (San Francisco Giants' organization), November 26, 1962.
‡Traded to Milwaukee Brewers for Pitchers Dick Baney and Louis Stephen (both assigned from Portland to Rochester), June 15, 1970.
§Traded to Atlanta Braves with a minor league player to be named later for Outfielder Hank Aaron, November 2, 1974; Brewers assigned Pitcher Roger Alexander to Braves, December 2, 1974, to complete deal.
xTraded with Outfielder Ken Henderson, Pitchers Carl Morton, Roger Moret and Adrian Devine and $250,000 cash to Texas Rangers for Outfielder Jeff Burroughs, December 9, 1976.

CHAMPIONSHIP SERIES RECORD

| Year Club | League | Pos. | G. | AB. | R. | H. | 2B. | 3B. | HR. | RBI. | B.A. | PO. | A. | E. | F.A. |
|---|---|---|---|---|---|---|---|---|---|---|---|---|---|---|---|
| 1969–Baltimore ..........Amer. | | PH | 1 | 1 | 0 | 0 | 0 | 0 | 0 | 0 | .000 | 0 | 0 | 0 | .000 |

WORLD SERIES RECORD

| Year Club | League | Pos. | G. | AB. | R. | H. | 2B. | 3B. | HR. | RBI. | B.A. | PO. | A. | E. | F.A. |
|---|---|---|---|---|---|---|---|---|---|---|---|---|---|---|---|
| 1969–Baltimore ..........Amer. | | PH | 2 | 1 | 0 | 0 | 0 | 0 | 0 | 0 | .000 | 0 | 0 | 0 | .000 |

ALL-STAR GAME RECORD

| Year League | Pos. | AB. | R. | H. | 2B. | 3B. | HR. | RBI. | B.A. | PO. | A. | E. | F.A. |
|---|---|---|---|---|---|---|---|---|---|---|---|---|---|
| 1973–American ........................... | OF | 2 | 0 | 0 | 0 | 0 | 0 | 0 | .000 | 0 | 0 | 0 | .000 |

## DAVIS EDWARDS MAY
### (Dave)
Born October 16, 1951, at Covington, Ky.
Height, 6.00 Weight, 175.
Throws and bats righthanded.
Attended Gulf Coast Community College, Panama City, Fla. and
Auburn University, Auburn, Ala.
Tied for Southern League lead in shutouts with 4 in 1976.

| Year Club | League | G. | IP. | W. | L. | Pct. | H. | R. | ER. | SO. | BB. | ERA. |
|---|---|---|---|---|---|---|---|---|---|---|---|---|
| 1975–Wis. Rapids.........................Midwest | | 17 | 93 | 9 | 2 | .818 | 68 | 33 | 28 | 82 | 43 | 2.71 |
| 1976–Orlando...............................Southern | | 18 | 129 | 10 | 5 | .667 | 121 | 52 | 43 | 61 | 53 | 3.00 |
| 1976–Tacoma...............................P. Coast | | 16 | 46 | 7 | 3 | .700 | 50 | 24 | 21 | 22 | 24 | 4.11 |

Invited to Minnesota Twins' 1977 spring camp.


## LEE ANDREW MAY
Born March 23, 1943, at Birmingham, Ala.
Height, 6.03. Weight, 205.
Throws and bats righthanded.
Attended Miles College, Birmingham, Ala.
Brother of Carlos May, outfielder-first baseman with New York Yankees.

Tied following major league records: most home runs, three consecutive games, hitting homer in each game, May 24 (2), May 25 (2), and May 28 (2), 1969; most total bases, inning, 8, and most home runs, inning, 2, April 29, 1974 (6th inning).
Hit three home runs in a game, June 21, 1973 against San Diego Padres.
Led National League batters in strikeouts with 145 in 1972.
Led National League first basemen in double plays with 128 in 1969 and 143 in 1970.
Led National League first basemen in total chances with 1,400 and in double plays with 133 in 1972.
Led American League first basemen in total chances with 1428 and in double plays with 138 in 1975.
Led Carolina League first basemen in double plays with 125 in 1963.
Led Pacific Coast League in total bases with 327 in 1965.
Named National League Rookie Player of the Year by THE SPORTING NEWS, 1967.
Named first baseman on THE SPORTING NEWS National League All-Star Team, 1971.

| Year Club League | Pos. | G. | AB. | R. | H. | 2B. | 3B. | HR. | RBI. | B.A. | PO. | A. | E. | F.A. |
|---|---|---|---|---|---|---|---|---|---|---|---|---|---|---|
| 1961–Tampa ..............Fla. St. | 1-OF | 26 | 77 | 10 | 20 | 2 | 2 | 0 | 9 | .260 | 114 | 7 | 5 | .960 |
| 1962–Tampa ..............Fla. St. | 1B | 89 | 339 | 45 | 88 | 10 | 3 | 10 | 65 | .260 | 674 | 48 | 16 | .978 |
| 1963–Rocky Mount ....Carol. | 1B | 144 | 520 | 79 | 137 | 23 | 4 | 18 | 80 | .263 | *1288 | 74 | *27 | .981 |
| 1964–Macon ..............South. | 1-OF | •140 | 515 | 91 | 156 | 22 | 5 | 25 | *110 | .303 | 1019 | 72 | 20 | .982 |
| 1965–San Diego .........P. C. | 1B-OF | 143 | 558 | 83 | 179 | 32 | 7 | 34 | 103 | .321 | 1165 | 67 | 15 | .988 |
| 1965–Cincinnati.........Nat. | PH | 5 | 4 | 1 | 0 | 0 | 0 | 0 | 0 | .000 | 0 | 0 | 0 | .000 |
| 1966–Cincinnati.........Nat. | 1B | 25 | 75 | 14 | 25 | 5 | 1 | 2 | 10 | .333 | 132 | 9 | 4 | .972 |
| 1966–Buffalo .............Int. | 1B | 128 | 471 | 74 | 146 | 25 | 5 | 16 | 78 | .310 | 1006 | 86 | *16 | .986 |
| 1967–Cincinnati.........Nat. | 1B-OF | 127 | 438 | 54 | 116 | 29 | 2 | 12 | 57 | .265 | 703 | 46 | 6 | .992 |
| 1968–Cincinnati.........Nat. | 1B-OF | 146 | 559 | 78 | 162 | 32 | 1 | 22 | 80 | .290 | 1094 | 73 | 5 | .996 |
| 1969–Cincinnati.........Nat. | 1B-OF | 158 | 607 | 85 | 169 | 32 | 3 | 38 | 110 | .278 | 1395 | 102 | 11 | .993 |
| 1970–Cincinnati.........Nat. | 1B | 153 | 605 | 78 | 153 | 34 | 2 | 34 | 94 | .253 | 1362 | 109 | 10 | .993 |
| 1971–Cincinnati† .......Nat. | 1B | 147 | 553 | 85 | 154 | 17 | 3 | 39 | 98 | .278 | 1261 | 78 | 8 | .994 |
| 1972–Houston ...........Nat. | 1B | 148 | 592 | 87 | 168 | 31 | 2 | 29 | 98 | .284 | *1318 | 76 | 6 | .996 |
| 1973–Houston ...........Nat. | 1B | 148 | 545 | 65 | 147 | 24 | 3 | 28 | 105 | .270 | 1220 | 78 | 9 | .993 |
| 1974–Houston‡ .........Nat. | 1B | 152 | 556 | 59 | 149 | 26 | 0 | 24 | 85 | .268 | 1253 | 88 | 8 | .994 |
| 1975–Baltimore .........Amer. | 1B | 146 | 580 | 67 | 152 | 28 | 3 | 20 | 99 | .262 | *1312 | 106 | 10 | .993 |
| 1976–Baltimore .........Amer. | 1B-DH | 148 | 530 | 61 | 137 | 17 | 4 | 25 | 109 | .258 | 722 | 62 | 3 | .996 |
| National League Totals ................. | | 1209 | 4534 | 606 | 1243 | 230 | 17 | 228 | 737 | .274 | 9738 | 659 | 67 | .994 |
| American League Totals ............... | | 294 | 1110 | 128 | 289 | 45 | 7 | 45 | 208 | .260 | 2034 | 168 | 13 | .994 |
| Major League Totals ...................... | | 1503 | 5644 | 734 | 1532 | 275 | 24 | 273 | 945 | .271 | 11772 | 827 | 80 | .994 |

†Traded with Second Baseman Tommy Helms and Outfielder Jim Stewart to Houston Astros for Infielder Denis Menke, Second Baseman Joe Morgan, Pitcher Jack Billingham and Outfielders Cesar Geronimo and Ed Armbrister, latter assigned from Oklahoma City to Indianapolis, November 29, 1971.

‡Traded with Outfielder Jay Schlueter to Baltimore Orioles for Second Baseman Rob Andrews and Infielder-Outfielder Enos Cabell, December 3, 1974.

CHAMPIONSHIP SERIES RECORD

| Year Club League | Pos. | G. | AB. | R. | H. | 2B. | 3B. | HR. | RBI. | B.A. | PO. | A. | E. | F.A. |
|---|---|---|---|---|---|---|---|---|---|---|---|---|---|---|
| 1970–Cincinnati.........Nat. | 1B | 3 | 12 | 0 | 2 | 1 | 0 | 0 | 2 | .167 | 31 | 1 | 0 | 1.000 |

WORLD SERIES RECORD

Tied World Series record for most runs scored, 5-game series, 6, in 1970.

| Year Club League | Pos. | G. | AB. | R. | H. | 2B. | 3B. | HR. | RBI. | B.A. | PO. | A. | E. | F.A. |
|---|---|---|---|---|---|---|---|---|---|---|---|---|---|---|
| 1970–Cincinnati.........Nat. | 1B | 5 | 18 | 6 | 7 | 2 | 0 | 2 | 8 | .389 | 48 | 3 | 0 | 1.000 |

ALL-STAR GAME RECORD

| Year League | Pos. | AB. | R. | H. | 2B. | 3B. | HR. | RBI. | B.A. | PO. | A. | E. | F.A. |
|---|---|---|---|---|---|---|---|---|---|---|---|---|---|
| 1969–National ............................ | 1B | 1 | 0 | 0 | 0 | 0 | 0 | 0 | .000 | 3 | 0 | 0 | 1.000 |
| 1971–National ............................ | 1B | 1 | 0 | 0 | 0 | 0 | 0 | 0 | .000 | 6 | 0 | 0 | 1.000 |
| 1972–National ............................ | 1B | 4 | 0 | 1 | 0 | 0 | 0 | 1 | .250 | 13 | 2 | 0 | 1.000 |
| All-Star Game Totals ...................... | | 6 | 0 | 1 | 0 | 0 | 0 | 1 | .167 | 22 | 2 | 0 | 1.000 |

## MILTON SCOTT MAY
### (Milt)

Born August 1, 1950, at Gary, Ind.
Height, 6.00. Weight, 185.
Throws right and bats lefthanded.
Hobby–Hunting.
Attended Manatee Junior College, West Bradenton, Fla.
Son of Merrill (Pinky) May, third baseman for Philadelphia Phillies, 1939 through 1943.

Led Western Carolinas League catchers in double plays with 10 in 1969.
Tied for International League lead in passed balls with 10 in 1969.

| Year Club League | Pos. | G. | AB. | R. | H. | 2B. | 3B. | HR. | RBI. | B.A. | PO. | A. | E. | F.A. |
|---|---|---|---|---|---|---|---|---|---|---|---|---|---|---|
| 1968–Brade'n Pirates Gulf C. | C | 52 | 166 | 21 | 40 | 4 | 0 | 0 | 23 | .241 | *337 | 31 | *13 | .966 |
| 1969–Gastonia† .........W. Car. | *C-1 | 86 | 301 | 58 | 87 | 17 | 2 | 11 | 57 | .289 | 485 | *63 | 11 | .980 |
| 1970–Columbus ...........Int. | C | 111 | 397 | 49 | 111 | 14 | 3 | 21 | 86 | .280 | 688 | *69 | 15 | .981 |
| 1970–Pittsburgh ........Nat. | PH | 5 | 4 | 1 | 2 | 1 | 0 | 0 | 2 | .500 | 0 | 0 | 0 | .000 |
| 1971–Pittsburgh‡.......Nat. | C | 49 | 126 | 15 | 35 | 1 | 0 | 6 | 25 | .278 | 168 | 12 | 0 | 1.000 |
| 1972–Pittsburgh§.......Nat. | C | 57 | 139 | 12 | 39 | 10 | 0 | 0 | 14 | .281 | 179 | 21 | 3 | .985 |
| 1973–Pittsburgh x .....Nat. | C | 101 | 283 | 29 | 76 | 8 | 1 | 7 | 31 | .269 | 402 | 36 | 12 | .973 |
| 1974–Houston ...........Nat. | C | 127 | 405 | 47 | 117 | 17 | 4 | 7 | 54 | .289 | 525 | 63 | 4 | *.993 |
| 1975–Houston y .........Nat. | C | 111 | 386 | 29 | 93 | 15 | 1 | 4 | 52 | .241 | 568 | *70 | 9 | .986 |
| 1976–Detroit z...........Amer. | C | 6 | 25 | 2 | 7 | 1 | 0 | 0 | 1 | .280 | 33 | 5 | 0 | 1.000 |
| National League Totals ................. | | 450 | 1343 | 133 | 362 | 52 | 6 | 24 | 178 | .270 | 1842 | 202 | 28 | .986 |
| American League Totals ............... | | 6 | 25 | 2 | 7 | 1 | 0 | 0 | 1 | .280 | 33 | 5 | 0 | 1.000 |
| Major League Totals ...................... | | 456 | 1368 | 135 | 369 | 53 | 6 | 24 | 179 | .270 | 1875 | 207 | 28 | .987 |

†On temporary inactive list, April 13 through April 25 and from August 16 through September 30, 1969.

‡On military list, July 25 through August 8, 1971.

§On military list, July 15 through July 29, 1972.

xTraded to Houston Astros for Pitcher Jerry Reuss, October 31, 1973.

yTraded with Pitchers Dave Roberts and Jim Crawford to Detroit Tigers for Outfielder Leon Roberts, Catcher Terry Humphrey and Pitchers Gene Pentz and Mark Lemongello, December 6, 1975.

zOn disabled list, April 21 through September 3, 1976.

| Year Club League | Pos. | G. | AB. | R. | H. | 2B. | 3B. | HR. | RBI. | B.A. | PO. | A. | E. | F.A. |
|---|---|---|---|---|---|---|---|---|---|---|---|---|---|---|
| 1971–Pittsburgh ........Nat. | PH | 1 | 1 | 0 | 0 | 0 | 0 | 0 | 0 | .000 | 0 | 0 | 0 | .000 |
| 1972–Pittsburgh ........Nat. | C | 1 | 2 | 0 | 1 | 0 | 0 | 0 | 1 | .500 | 8 | 1 | 0 | 1.000 |
| Championship Series Totals ............ | | 2 | 3 | 0 | 1 | 0 | 0 | 0 | 1 | .333 | 8 | 1 | 0 | 1.000 |

WORLD SERIES RECORD

| Year Club League | Pos. | G. | AB. | R. | H. | 2B. | 3B. | HR. | RBI. | B.A. | PO. | A. | E. | F.A. |
|---|---|---|---|---|---|---|---|---|---|---|---|---|---|---|
| 1971–Pittsburgh ........Nat. | PH | 2 | 2 | 0 | 1 | 0 | 0 | 0 | 1 | .500 | 0 | 0 | 0 | .000 |

## RUDOLPH MAY, JR.
### (Rudy)

Born July 18, 1944, at Coffeyville, Kan.
Height, 6.02. Weight, 202.
Throws and bats lefthanded.
Hobby–Playing dominos.
Attended San Francisco State College, San Francisco, Calif.

Led Northern League in wild pitches with 25 in 1963.
Tied for Carolina League lead in shutouts with 4 in 1964.

| Year Club League | G. | IP. | W. | L. | Pct. | H. | R. | ER. | SO. | BB. | ERA. |
|---|---|---|---|---|---|---|---|---|---|---|---|
| 1963–Bismarck-Mandant .............Northern | 24 | 168 | 11 | 11 | .500 | 142 | 100 | •80 | 173 | *120 | 4.29 |
| 1964–Tidewater ...........................Carolina | 20 | 155 | 13 | 6 | .684 | 107 | 52 | 44 | 187 | 98 | 2.55 |
| 1964–Indianapolis‡§ .....................P. Coast | 10 | 52 | 4 | 2 | .667 | 39 | 20 | 16 | 48 | 38 | 2.77 |
| 1965–California ..........................American | 30 | 124 | 4 | 9 | .308 | 111 | 59 | 54 | 76 | 78 | 3.92 |
| 1966–Seattle ...............................P. Coast | 7 | 30 | 3 | 1 | .750 | 36 | 18 | 17 | 12 | 15 | 5.10 |
| 1966–El Paso x .............................Texas | 2 | 5 | 0 | 0 | .000 | 4 | 2 | 2 | 4 | 7 | 3.60 |
| 1967–San Jose ...........................California | 14 | 84 | 7 | 2 | .778 | 62 | 33 | 29 | 51 | 40 | 3.11 |
| 1968–El Paso...............................Texas | 22 | 129 | 8 | 7 | .533 | 133 | 71 | 64 | 112 | 39 | 4.47 |
| 1969–California ..........................American | 43 | 180 | 10 | 13 | .435 | 142 | 81 | 69 | 133 | 66 | 3.45 |
| 1970–California y ........................American | 38 | 209 | 7 | 13 | .350 | 190 | 102 | 93 | 164 | 81 | 4.00 |
| 1971–California z ........................American | 32 | 208 | 11 | 12 | .478 | 160 | 74 | 70 | 156 | 87 | 3.03 |
| 1972–California ..........................American | 35 | 205 | 12 | 11 | .522 | 162 | 79 | 67 | 169 | 82 | 2.94 |
| 1973–California ..........................American | 34 | 185 | 7 | 17 | .292 | 177 | 101 | 90 | 134 | 80 | 4.38 |
| 1974–Calif. a-N.Y. b .....................American | 35 | 141 | 8 | 5 | .615 | 104 | 60 | 50 | 102 | 58 | 3.19 |
| 1975–New York ..........................American | 32 | 212 | 14 | 12 | .538 | 179 | 87 | 72 | 145 | 99 | 3.06 |
| 1976–New York c-Baltimore.........American | 35 | 220 | 15 | 10 | .600 | 205 | 105 | 91 | 109 | 70 | 3.72 |
| Major League Totals ............... | 314 | 1684 | 88 | 102 | .463 | 1430 | 748 | 656 | 1188 | 701 | 3.51 |

†Drafted by Chicago White Sox from Dallas-Fort Worth (Minnesota Twins' organization), December 2, 1963.

‡Traded by Chicago White Sox to Philadelphia Phillies for Catcher Bill Heath and player to be named later, October 15, 1964; Pitcher Joel Gibson was assigned to White Sox, November 23, 1964, to complete deal.

§Traded by Philadelphia Phillies to Los Angeles Angels with First Baseman Costen Shockley for Pitcher Robert (Bo) Belinsky, December 3, 1964.

xOn disabled list June 4 through end of season.

yOn military list July 10 through July 27.

zOn disabled list May 25 through June 17.

aSold to New York Yankees, June 15, 1974.

bOn disabled list, July 11 to August 1, 1974.

cTraded with Pitchers Felix Martinez, Dave Pagan and Scott McGregor and Catcher Rick Dempsey to Baltimore Orioles for Pitchers Ken Holtzman, Doyle Alexander and Grant Jackson, Catcher Ellie Hendricks, and Pitcher Jimmy Freeman, latter assigned from Rochester to Syracuse, June 15, 1976.

## JOHN CLAIBORN MAYBERRY

Born February 18, 1950, at Detroit, Mich.
Height, 6.03. Weight, 215.
Throws and bats lefthanded.
Attended University of Michigan, Ann Arbor, Mich.

Tied American League record for most double plays, first baseman, nine-inning game, 6, May 6, 1972.
Led American League first basemen in total chances with 1,427 in 1972 and with 1,596 in 1976; led in double plays with 141 in 1972 and with 156 in 1973.
Led American League in total bases on balls with 122 in 1973 and with 119 in 1975.
Led American Association first basemen in double plays with 89 in 1969.
Led American League in sacrifice flies with 12 in 1976.
Named first baseman on THE SPORTING NEWS American League All-Star Team, 1973 and 1975.
Received reported $30,000 bonus to sign with Houston Astros, 1967.

| Year Club League | Pos. | G. | AB. | R. | H. | 2B. | 3B. | HR. | RBI. | B.A. | PO. | A. | E. | F.A. |
|---|---|---|---|---|---|---|---|---|---|---|---|---|---|---|
| 1967–Covington ..........Appal. | 1B | 50 | 155 | 23 | 39 | 7 | 0 | 4 | 21 | .252 | 380 | *29 | *11 | .974 |
| 1968–Cocoa ...............Fla. St. | 1B | 64 | 195 | 34 | 66 | 9 | 3 | 14 | 48 | .338 | 479 | 22 | 7 | .986 |
| 1968–Greensboro........Carol. | 1B | 43 | 158 | 31 | 52 | 14 | 1 | 8 | 29 | .329 | 297 | 22 | 3 | .991 |
| 1968–Oklahoma City ..P.C. | 1B | 24 | 78 | 3 | 20 | 0 | 0 | 1 | 5 | .256 | 196 | 12 | 4 | .981 |
| 1968–Houston ...........Nat. | 1B | 4 | 9 | 0 | 0 | 0 | 0 | 0 | 0 | .000 | 25 | 0 | 0 | 1.000 |
| 1969–Oklahoma City ..A.A. | *1B-2B | 123 | 458 | 95 | 139 | 29 | 4 | 21 | 78 | .303 | *1005 | 61 | 11 | *.990 |
| 1969–Houston ...........Nat. | 1B | 5 | 4 | 0 | 0 | 0 | 0 | 0 | 0 | .000 | 0 | 0 | 0 | .000 |
| 1970–Oklahoma City ..A.A. | 1B | 70 | 231 | 55 | 63 | 7 | 3 | 13 | 38 | .273 | 536 | 30 | 8 | .986 |
| 1970–Houston ...........Nat. | 1B | 50 | 148 | 23 | 32 | 3 | 2 | 5 | 14 | .216 | 371 | 35 | 2 | .995 |

| Year Club League | Pos. | G. | AB. | R. | H. | 2B. | 3B. | HR. | RBI. | B.A. | PO. | A. | E. | F.A. |
|---|---|---|---|---|---|---|---|---|---|---|---|---|---|---|
| 1971–Oklahoma City ..A.A. | 1B | 64 | 222 | 50 | 72 | 10 | 3 | 12 | 40 | .324 | 445 | 39 | 4 | .992 |
| 1971–Houston† ..........Nat. | 1B | 46 | 137 | 16 | 25 | 0 | 1 | 7 | 14 | .182 | 317 | 15 | 1 | .997 |
| 1972–Kansas City ......Amer. | 1B | 149 | 503 | 65 | 150 | 24 | 3 | 25 | 100 | .298 | *1338 | 82 | 7 | *.995 |
| 1973–Kansas City ......Amer. | 1B | 152 | 510 | 87 | 142 | 20 | 2 | 26 | 100 | .278 | *1457 | 81 | 9 | .994 |
| 1974–Kansas City ......Amer. | 1B | 126 | 427 | 63 | 100 | 13 | 1 | 22 | 69 | .234 | 963 | 61 | 10 | .990 |
| 1975–Kansas City ......Amer. | 1B | 156 | 554 | 95 | 161 | 38 | 1 | 34 | 106 | .291 | 1199 | 100 | *16 | .988 |
| 1976–Kansas City ......Amer. | 1B-DH | 161 | 594 | 76 | 138 | 22 | 2 | 13 | 95 | .232 | *1484 | 105 | 7 | .996 |
| National League Totals .................. | | 105 | 298 | 39 | 57 | 3 | 3 | 12 | 28 | .191 | 713 | 50 | 3 | .996 |
| American League Totals ............... | | 744 | 2588 | 386 | 691 | 117 | 9 | 120 | 470 | .267 | 6441 | 429 | 49 | .993 |
| Major League Totals ..................... | | 849 | 2886 | 425 | 748 | 120 | 12 | 132 | 498 | .259 | 7154 | 479 | 52 | .993 |

†Traded with Third Baseman Dave Grangaard (latter assigned to Evansville) to Kansas City Royals for Pitchers Jim York and Lance Clemons, December 2, 1971.

### ALL-STAR GAME RECORD

| Year League | Pos. | AB. | R. | H. | 2B. | 3B. | HR. | RBI. | B.A. | PO. | A. | E. | F.A. |
|---|---|---|---|---|---|---|---|---|---|---|---|---|---|
| 1973–American ........................... | 1B | 3 | 0 | 1 | 1 | 0 | 0 | 0 | .333 | 8 | 0 | 0 | 1.000 |
| 1974–American ........................... | PH | 1 | 0 | 0 | 0 | 0 | 0 | 0 | .000 | 0 | 0 | 0 | .000 |
| All-Star Game Totals ..................... | | 4 | 0 | 1 | 1 | 0 | 0 | 0 | .250 | 8 | 0 | 0 | 1.000 |

### CHAMPIONSHIP SERIES RECORD

| Year Club League | Pos. | G. | AB. | R. | H. | 2B. | 3B. | HR. | RBI. | B.A. | PO. | A. | E. | F.A. |
|---|---|---|---|---|---|---|---|---|---|---|---|---|---|---|
| 1976–Kansas City ......Amer. | 1B | 5 | 18 | 4 | 4 | 0 | 0 | 1 | 3 | .222 | 48 | 1 | 0 | 1.000 |

## LEE LOUIS MAZZILLI

Born March 25, 1955, at Brooklyn, N.Y.
Height, 6.01. Weight, 180.
Throws right and bats left and righthanded.
Hobby–Speed skating.
Received reported $50,000 bonus to sign with New York Mets, 1973.
Major League stolen bases: 1976 (5).
Led Texas League in walks with 111 in 1976.

| Year Club League | Pos. | G. | AB. | R. | H. | 2B. | 3B. | HR. | RBI. | B.A. | PO. | A. | E. | F.A. |
|---|---|---|---|---|---|---|---|---|---|---|---|---|---|---|
| 1974–Anderson ..........W. Car. | OF | 132 | 472 | 82 | 127 | 24 | 3 | 11 | 48 | .269 | 227 | 9 | 9 | .963 |
| 1975–Visalia .............Calif. | OF | 125 | 430 | 103 | 121 | 10 | 4 | 13 | 52 | .281 | 185 | 9 | 9 | .956 |
| 1976–Jackson ...........Texas | OF | 131 | 439 | 91 | 128 | 21 | 6 | 13 | 43 | .292 | 262 | 8 | 8 | .971 |
| 1976–New York.........Nat. | OF | 24 | 77 | 9 | 15 | 2 | 0 | 2 | 7 | .195 | 55 | 2 | 1 | .983 |
| Major League Totals ..................... | | 24 | 77 | 9 | 15 | 2 | 0 | 2 | 7 | .195 | 55 | 2 | 1 | .983 |

## JOHN STEPHEN McALLEN

Born April 2, 1952, at Maywood, Calif.
Height, 5.11. Weight, 170.
Throws and bats lefthanded.
Hobbies–Golf and bowling.
Attended Los Angeles City College, Los Angeles, Calif., and
California State University at Los Angeles, Los Angeles, Calif.
Led Northwest League in complete games with 11 in 1973.

| Year Club League | G. | IP. | W. | L. | Pct. | H. | R. | ER. | SO. | BB. | ERA. |
|---|---|---|---|---|---|---|---|---|---|---|---|
| 1973–Walla Walla.........................Northwest | 16 | 106 | 9 | 2 | *.818 | 100 | 42 | 35 | 86 | 44 | 2.97 |
| 1974–Alexandria ........................Texas | 24 | 166 | 5 | *18 | .217 | 182 | 98 | 83 | 90 | 71 | 4.50 |
| 1975–Alexandria ........................Texas | 42 | 57 | 5 | 3 | .625 | 69 | 37 | 28 | 31 | 31 | 4.42 |
| 1976–Hawaii ...............................P. Coast | 25 | 68 | 4 | 0 | 1.000 | 70 | 34 | 31 | 23 | 31 | 4.10 |

Listed on San Diego Padres' 1977 spring roster.

## ARNOLD RAY McBRIDE
### (Bake)

Born February 3, 1949, at Fulton, Mo.
Height, 6.02. Weight, 190.
Throws right and bats lefthanded.
Hobbies–Hunting, fishing and being around kids.
Attended Westminster College, Fulton, Mo.; received Bachelor of Arts degree in Physical Education.
Major League stolen bases: 1973 (0), 1974 (30), 1975 (26), 1976 (5). Total–61.
Named National League Rookie of the Year by Baseball Writers' Association of America, 1974.

| Year Club League | Pos. | G. | AB. | R. | H. | 2B. | 3B. | HR. | RBI. | B.A. | PO. | A. | E. | F.A. |
|---|---|---|---|---|---|---|---|---|---|---|---|---|---|---|
| 1970–Sarasota Cards ..Gulf C. | OF | 17 | 71 | 15 | 30 | 2 | 4 | 2 | 13 | .423 | 27 | 1 | 0 | 1.000 |
| 1970–Modesto ............Calif. | OF | 26 | 85 | 17 | 25 | 4 | 2 | 0 | 7 | .294 | 26 | 1 | 4 | .871 |
| 1971–Modesto ...........Calif. | OF | 118 | 468 | 85 | 142 | 19 | 5 | 8 | 54 | .303 | 181 | 9 | 6 | .969 |
| 1972–Arkansas ..........Texas | OF | 67 | 286 | 51 | 94 | 10 | 4 | 12 | 34 | .329 | 130 | 3 | 3 | .978 |
| 1972–Tulsa ................A.A. | OF | 60 | 232 | 41 | 73 | 14 | 5 | 5 | 24 | .315 | 108 | 5 | 1 | .991 |
| 1973–Tulsa ................A.A. | OF | 58 | 225 | 45 | 65 | 15 | 2 | 6 | 34 | .289 | 111 | 7 | 3 | .975 |
| 1973–St. Louis ..........Nat. | OF | 40 | 63 | 8 | 19 | 3 | 0 | 0 | 5 | .302 | 39 | 1 | 1 | .976 |
| 1974–St. Louis ..........Nat. | OF | 150 | 559 | 81 | 173 | 19 | 5 | 6 | 56 | .309 | 395 | 9 | 4 | .990 |

| Year | Club | League | Pos. | G. | AB. | R. | H. | 2B. | 3B. | HR. | RBI. | B.A. | PO. | A. | E. | F.A. |
|------|------|--------|------|-----|-----|-----|-----|-----|-----|-----|------|------|-----|-----|-----|------|
| 1975–St. Louis | ..........Nat. | | OF | 116 | 413 | 70 | 124 | 10 | 9 | 5 | 36 | .300 | 289 | 4 | 3 | .990 |
| 1976–St. Louis‡ | ..........Nat. | | OF | 72 | 272 | 40 | 91 | 13 | 4 | 3 | 24 | .335 | 201 | 5 | 4 | .981 |
| Major League Totals | ..................... | | | 378 | 1307 | 199 | 407 | 45 | 18 | 14 | 121 | .311 | 924 | 19 | 12 | .987 |

†On supplemental disabled list, May 13 to June 4, 1975.
‡On disabled list, May 9 to May 24 and August 7 through remainder of season.

## JAMES TIMOTHY McCARVER
### (Tim)

Born October 16, 1941, at Memphis, Tenn.
Height, 6.01. Weight, 198.
Throws right and bats lefthanded.
Hobbies–Dancing and collecting matchbooks.
Attended Christian Brothers College, Memphis, Tenn., and Memphis
State University, Memphis, Tenn.

Tied for National League lead in passed balls with 16 in 1963 and led with 18 in 1965.
Named as catcher on THE SPORTING NEWS National League All-Star Team, 1967.
Received reported $75,000 bonus to sign with St. Louis Cardinals, 1959.

| Year | Club | League | Pos. | G. | AB. | R. | H. | 2B. | 3B. | HR. | RBI. | B.A. | PO. | A. | E. | F.A. |
|------|------|--------|------|-----|-----|-----|-----|-----|-----|-----|------|------|-----|-----|-----|------|
| 1959–Keokuk | ..............Midw. | | C | 65 | 275 | 58 | 99 | 6 | 4 | 3 | 24 | .360 | 422 | 37 | 14 | .970 |
| 1959–Rochester | .........Int. | | C | 17 | 70 | 10 | 25 | 1 | 1 | 0 | 8 | .357 | 94 | 9 | 0 | 1.000 |
| 1959–St. Louis | ..........Nat. | | C | 8 | 24 | 3 | 4 | 1 | 0 | 0 | 0 | .167 | 32 | 2 | 1 | .971 |
| 1960–Memphis | ..........South. | | C | 85 | 303 | 45 | 105 | 11 | 2 | 3 | 34 | .347 | 500 | 26 | 4 | .992 |
| 1960–St. Louis | ..........Nat. | | C | 10 | 10 | 3 | 2 | 0 | 0 | 0 | 0 | .200 | 9 | 0 | 0 | 1.000 |
| 1961–S. Juan-Char. | ....Int. | | C | 81 | 275 | 26 | 63 | 10 | 0 | 1 | 27 | .229 | 429 | ★51 | 5 | .990 |
| 1961–St. Louis | ..........Nat. | | C | 22 | 67 | 5 | 16 | 2 | 1 | 1 | 6 | .239 | 86 | 9 | 3 | .969 |
| 1962–Atlanta | ..............Int. | | C | 122 | 382 | 65 | 105 | 17 | 1 | 11 | 57 | .275 | ★685 | 48 | ★11 | .985 |
| 1963–St. Louis | ..........Nat. | | C | 127 | 405 | 39 | 117 | 12 | 7 | 4 | 51 | .289 | 722 | 55 | 5 | .994 |
| 1964–St. Louis | ..........Nat. | | C | 143 | 465 | 53 | 134 | 19 | 3 | 9 | 52 | .288 | 762 | 43 | ●11 | .987 |
| 1965–St. Louis | ..........Nat. | | C | 113 | 409 | 48 | 113 | 17 | 2 | 11 | 48 | .276 | 687 | 43 | 4 | ★.995 |
| 1966–St. Louis | ..........Nat. | | C | 150 | 543 | 50 | 149 | 19 | ●13 | 12 | 68 | .274 | 841 | 62 | 7 | .992 |
| 1967–St. Louis | ..........Nat. | | C | 138 | 471 | 68 | 139 | 26 | 3 | 14 | 69 | .295 | 819 | ★67 | 3 | ★.997 |
| 1968–St. Louis | ..........Nat. | | C | 128 | 434 | 35 | 110 | 15 | 6 | 5 | 48 | .253 | 708 | 54 | 11 | .986 |
| 1969–St. Louis† | ..........Nat. | | C | 138 | 515 | 46 | 134 | 27 | 3 | 7 | 51 | .260 | 925 | 66 | 14 | .986 |
| 1970–Philadelphia‡ | ....Nat. | | C | 44 | 164 | 16 | 47 | 11 | 1 | 4 | 14 | .287 | 314 | 18 | 3 | .991 |
| 1971–Philadelphia | ......Nat. | | C | 134 | 474 | 51 | 132 | 20 | 5 | 8 | 46 | .278 | 673 | 51 | 11 | .985 |
| 1972–Phil.‡‡-Mont.§ | ....Nat. | | C-O-3 | 122 | 391 | 33 | 96 | 13 | 1 | 7 | 34 | .246 | 561 | 47 | 8 | .987 |
| 1973–St. Louis | ..........Nat. | | 1B-C | 130 | 331 | 30 | 88 | 16 | 4 | 3 | 49 | .266 | 608 | 34 | 9 | .986 |
| 1974–St. Louis x | .......Nat. | | C-1B | 74 | 106 | 13 | 23 | 0 | 1 | 0 | 11 | .217 | 126 | 11 | 4 | .972 |
| 1974–Boston | ..............Amer. | | C | 11 | 28 | 3 | 7 | 1 | 0 | 0 | 1 | .250 | 37 | 5 | 0 | 1.000 |
| 1975–Boston y | ...........Amer. | | C-1B | 12 | 21 | 1 | 8 | 2 | 1 | 0 | 3 | .381 | 21 | 4 | 1 | .962 |
| 1975–Philadelphia | .....Nat. | | C-1B | 47 | 59 | 6 | 15 | 2 | 0 | 1 | 7 | .254 | 62 | 5 | 1 | .985 |
| 1976–Philadelphia | .....Nat. | | C-1B | 90 | 155 | 26 | 43 | 11 | 2 | 3 | 29 | .277 | 265 | 9 | 0 | .967 |
| National League Totals | .................. | | | 1618 | 5023 | 525 | 1362 | 211 | 52 | 89 | 583 | .271 | 8200 | 576 | 95 | .989 |
| American League Totals | ............... | | | 23 | 49 | 4 | 15 | 3 | 1 | 0 | 4 | .306 | 58 | 9 | 1 | .985 |
| Major League Totals | ...................... | | | 1641 | 5072 | 529 | 1377 | 214 | 53 | 89 | 587 | .271 | 8258 | 585 | 96 | .989 |

†Traded with Outfielders Curt Flood and Byron Browne and Pitcher Joe Hoerner to Philadelphia Phillies for First Baseman Richie Allen, Infielder Cookie Rojas and Pitcher Jerry Johnson, October 7, 1969. Flood refused to report and the Cardinals sent First Baseman Guillermo Montanez and a player to be named later to Philadelphia to complete the deal, April 8, 1970. Pitcher James Robert Browning was sent from St. Louis to Philadelphia as "the player to be named later," August 30, 1970.
‡On disabled list May 2 through September 1.
‡‡Traded to Montreal Expos for Catcher John Bateman, June 14, 1972.
§Traded to St. Louis Cardinals for Outfielder Jorge Roque, November 6, 1972.
xSold to Boston Red Sox, September 1, 1974.
yReleased, June 23, 1975; signed as a free agent by Philadelphia Phillies, July 1, 1975.

## WORLD SERIES RECORD

Established World Series record for most putouts, catcher, seven-game Series (61), 1964.
Tied following World Series records: Most games, one or more hits, seven-game Series (7), 1964; most chances, catcher, game (18), October 2, 1968; most putouts, catcher, inning (3), second inning and ninth inning October 2, 1968.

| Year | Club | League | Pos. | G. | AB. | R. | H. | 2B. | 3B. | HR. | RBI. | B.A. | PO. | A. | E. | F.A. |
|------|------|--------|------|-----|-----|-----|-----|-----|-----|-----|------|------|-----|-----|-----|------|
| 1964–St. Louis | ..........Nat. | | C | 7 | 23 | 4 | 11 | 1 | 1 | 1 | 5 | .478 | 57 | 1 | 0 | 1.000 |
| 1967–St. Louis | ..........Nat. | | C | 7 | 24 | 3 | 3 | 1 | 0 | 0 | 2 | .125 | 55 | 4 | 0 | 1.000 |
| 1968–St. Louis | ..........Nat. | | C | 7 | 27 | 3 | 9 | 0 | 2 | 1 | 4 | .333 | 61 | 1 | 0 | 1.000 |
| World Series Totals | ...................... | | | 21 | 74 | 10 | 23 | 2 | 3 | 2 | 11 | .311 | 173 | 6 | 0 | 1.000 |

## ALL-STAR GAME RECORD

| Year | League | Pos. | AB. | R. | H. | 2B. | 3B. | HR. | RBI. | B.A. | PO. | A. | E. | F.A. |
|------|--------|------|-----|-----|-----|-----|-----|-----|------|------|-----|-----|-----|------|
| 1966–National | .............................. | C | 1 | 1 | 1 | 0 | 0 | 0 | 0 | 1.000 | 1 | 0 | 0 | 1.000 |
| 1967–National | .............................. | C | 2 | 0 | 2 | 1 | 0 | 0 | 0 | 1.000 | 7 | 1 | 0 | 1.000 |
| All-Star Game Totals | ...................... | | 3 | 1 | 3 | 1 | 0 | 0 | 0 | 1.000 | 8 | 1 | 0 | 1.000 |

## CHAMPIONSHIP SERIES RECORD

| Year | Club | League | Pos. | G. | AB. | R. | H. | 2B. | 3B. | HR. | RBI. | B.A. | PO. | A. | E. | F.A. |
|------|------|--------|------|-----|-----|-----|-----|-----|-----|-----|------|------|-----|-----|-----|------|
| 1976–Philadelphia | ......Nat. | | C-PH | 2 | 4 | 0 | 0 | 0 | 0 | 0 | 0 | .000 | 6 | 0 | 0 | 1.000 |

## STEVEN EARL McCATTY

Born March 20, 1954, at Detroit, Mich.
Height, 6.03. Weight, 195.
Throws and bats righthanded.
Hobbies—Hockey and basketball.
Attended Macomb Community College, Warren, Mich.

| Year | Club | League | G. | IP. | W. | L. | Pct. | H. | R. | ER. | SO. | BB. | ERA. |
|------|------|--------|-----|-----|----|----|------|-----|----|-----|-----|-----|------|
| 1973—Lewiston | | Northwest | 19 | 70 | 2 | 2 | .500 | 83 | 48 | 37 | 49 | 31 | 4.76 |
| 1974—Lewiston | | Northwest | 15 | 96 | 8 | 3 | .727 | 99 | 58 | 35 | 62 | 42 | 3.28 |
| 1975—Modesto | | California | 37 | 126 | 4 | 8 | .333 | 138 | 80 | 64 | 75 | 54 | 4.57 |
| 1976—Chattanooga | | Southern | 36 | 77 | 5 | 4 | .556 | 73 | 44 | 27 | 40 | 31 | 3.16 |
| 1976—Tucson | | P. Coast | 5 | 10 | 1 | 1 | .500 | 13 | 8 | 7 | 5 | 7 | 6.30 |

Listed on Oakland A's 1977 spring roster.

## ROBERT CRAIG McCLURE
## (Bob)

Born April 29, 1952, at Oakland, Calif.
Height, 5.11. Weight, 170.
Throws left and bats righthanded. -
Hobbies—Hunting, fishing and cards.
Attended College of San Mateo, San Mateo, Calif.

Tied for Pioneer League lead in shutouts with 3 in 1973.

| Year | Club | League | G. | IP. | W. | L. | Pct. | H. | R. | ER. | SO. | BB. | ERA. |
|------|------|--------|-----|-----|----|----|------|-----|----|-----|-----|-----|------|
| 1973—Billings | | Pioneer | 14 | 94 | *10 | 2 | .833 | 64 | 41 | 22 | 110 | 67 | 2.11 |
| 1974—Omaha | | Am. Assoc. | 21 | 136 | 5 | 8 | .385 | 140 | 71 | 58 | 88 | 65 | 3.84 |
| 1975—Jacksonville† | | Southern | 9 | 42 | 3 | 2 | .600 | 31 | 18 | 11 | 39 | 23 | 2.36 |
| 1975—Kansas City | | American | 12 | 15 | 1 | 0 | 1.000 | 4 | 0 | 0 | 15 | 14 | 0.00 |
| 1976—Omaha | | Am. Assoc. | 21 | 133 | 9 | 8 | .529 | 133 | 61 | 44 | 91 | 41 | 2.98 |
| 1976—Kansas City‡ | | American | 8 | 4 | 0 | 0 | .000 | 3 | 4 | 4 | 3 | 8 | 9.00 |
| Major League Totals | | | 20 | 19 | 1 | 0 | 1.000 | 7 | 4 | 4 | 18 | 22 | 1.89 |

†On disabled list, April 15 to May 13 and June 5 to July 25, 1975.

‡Assigned to Milwaukee Brewers, March 15, 1977, to complete deal which sent Infielder Jamie Quirk and Outfielder Jim Wohlford to Milwaukee for Pitcher Jim Colborn and Catcher Darrell Porter, December 6, 1976.

## WILLIE LEE McCOVEY

Born January 10, 1938, at Mobile, Ala.
Height, 6.04. Weight, 225.
Throws and bats lefthanded.
Hobbies—Reading comic books and attending motion pictures.

Established major league records for most intentional bases on balls in a season, 45 in 1969 and most seasons 20 or more intentional bases on balls, 5, 1973.

Tied major league records for most home runs, inning, 2, and most total bases, inning, 8, April 12, 1973 (4th inning); most triples, 1st major league game, 2, July 30, 1959; and most home runs, bases full, pinch hitter, lifetime, 3, 1975.

Established National League record for most home runs, first baseman, lifetime, 386, 1976.

Tied National League records for most intentional bases on balls, game, 3, September 3, 1967; and most home runs, bases full, lifetime, 16, 1975.

Tied modern National League record for most hits, first game in majors, 4, July 30, 1959; 2 singles, 2 triples.

Hit three consecutive home runs in a game, on two occasions—September 22, 1963, and April 22, 1964. Hit three home runs in game, September 17, 1966.

Led National League in slugging percentage with .545 in 1968, .656 in 1969 and .612 in 1970.

Led National League batters in bases on balls with 137 in 1970.

Led Georgia State League first basemen in double plays with 73 in 1955.

Led Pacific Coast League first basemen in double plays with 119 in 1958.

Named National League Rookie of the Year by THE SPORTING NEWS and National League Rookie of the Year by Baseball Writers' Association, 1959.

Named first baseman on THE SPORTING NEWS National League All-Star Teams, 1965-68-69-70.

Named by THE SPORTING NEWS as Major League Player of the Year, 1969.

Named Most Valuable Player in National League, 1969.

| Year | Club | League | Pos. | G. | AB. | R. | H. | 2B. | 3B. | HR. | RBI. | B.A. | PO. | A. | E. | F.A. |
|------|------|--------|------|-----|-----|-----|-----|-----|-----|-----|------|------|------|-----|-----|------|
| 1955—Sandersville | | Ga.-St. | 1B | 107 | 410 | 82 | 125 | 24 | 1 | 19 | *113 | .305 | *897 | 51 | 23 | .976 |
| 1956—Danville | | Carol. | 1B | 152 | 519 | 119 | 161 | *38 | 8 | 29 | 89 | .310 | 1273 | 87 | *34 | .976 |
| 1957—Dallas | | Texas | 1B | 115 | 395 | 63 | 111 | 21 | 9 | 11 | 65 | .281 | 960 | 80 | 10 | .990 |
| 1958—Phoenix | | P.C. | 1B | 146 | 527 | 91 | 168 | 37 | 10 | 14 | 89 | .319 | *1171 | 69 | *18 | .986 |
| 1959—Phoenix | | P.C. | 1B | 95 | 349 | 84 | 130 | 26 | 11 | *29 | ●92 | .372 | 896 | 43 | 16 | .983 |
| 1959—San Francisco | | Nat. | 1B | 52 | 192 | 32 | 68 | 9 | 5 | 13 | 38 | .354 | 424 | 29 | 5 | .989 |
| 1960—San Francisco | | Nat. | 1B | 101 | 260 | 37 | 62 | 15 | 3 | 13 | 51 | .238 | 557 | 39 | 9 | .985 |
| 1960—Tacoma | | P.C. | 1B | 17 | 63 | 14 | 18 | 1 | 2 | 3 | 16 | .286 | 149 | 4 | 3 | .980 |
| 1961—San Francisco | | Nat. | 1B | 106 | 328 | 59 | 89 | 12 | 3 | 18 | 50 | .271 | 669 | 55 | 11 | .985 |
| 1962—San Francisco | | Nat. | OF-1B | 91 | 229 | 41 | 67 | 6 | 1 | 20 | 54 | .293 | 186 | 9 | 3 | .985 |
| 1963—San Francisco | | Nat. | *OF-1B | 152 | 564 | 103 | 158 | 19 | 5 | ●44 | 102 | .280 | 363 | 21 | *15 | .962 |
| 1964—San Francisco | | Nat. | OF-1B | 130 | 364 | 55 | 80 | 14 | 1 | 18 | 54 | .220 | 273 | 19 | 14 | .954 |
| 1965—San Francisco | | Nat. | 1B | 160 | 540 | 93 | 149 | 17 | 4 | 39 | 92 | .276 | 1310 | 87 | 13 | .991 |
| 1966—San Francisco | | Nat. | 1B | 150 | 502 | 85 | 148 | 26 | 6 | 36 | 96 | .295 | 1287 | 81 | 22 | .984 |
| 1967—San Francisco | | Nat. | 1B | 135 | 456 | 73 | 126 | 17 | 4 | 31 | 91 | .276 | 1221 | 81 | ●15 | .989 |
| 1968—San Francisco | | Nat. | 1B | 148 | 523 | 81 | 153 | 16 | 4 | *36 | *105 | .293 | 1305 | 103 | *21 | .985 |
| 1969—San Francisco | | Nat. | 1B | 149 | 491 | 101 | 157 | 26 | 2 | *45 | *126 | .320 | 1392 | 79 | 12 | .992 |
| 1970—San Francisco | | Nat. | 1B | 152 | 495 | 98 | 143 | 39 | 2 | 39 | 126 | .289 | 1217 | *134 | *15 | .989 |

| Year Club League | Pos. | G. | AB. | R. | H. | 2B. | 3B. | HR. | RBI. | B.A. | PO. | A. | E. | F.A. |
|---|---|---|---|---|---|---|---|---|---|---|---|---|---|---|
| 1971—San Francisco ..Nat. | 1B | 105 | 329 | 45 | 91 | 13 | 0 | 18 | 70 | .277 | 828 | 63 | *15 | .983 |
| 1972—San Francisco†..Nat. | 1B | 81 | 263 | 30 | 56 | 8 | 0 | 14 | 35 | .213 | 617 | 32 | 9 | .986 |
| 1973—San Francisco‡..Nat. | 1B | 130 | 383 | 52 | 102 | 14 | 3 | 29 | 75 | .266 | 930 | 76 | 12 | .988 |
| 1974—San Diego.........Nat. | 1B | 128 | 344 | 53 | 87 | 19 | 1 | 22 | 63 | .253 | 815 | 47 | 11 | .987 |
| 1975—San Diego.........Nat. | 1B | 122 | 413 | 43 | 104 | 17 | 0 | 23 | 68 | .252 | 979 | 73 | 15 | .986 |
| 1976—San Diego§.......Nat. | 1B | 71 | 202 | 20 | 41 | 9 | 0 | 7 | 36 | .203 | 420 | 44 | 4 | .991 |
| 1976—Oakland x.........Amer. | DH | 11 | 24 | 0 | 5 | 0 | 0 | 0 | 0 | .208 | 10 | 0 | 0 | .000 |
| National League Totals ............... | | 2163 | 6878 | 1101 | 1881 | 296 | 44 | 465 | 1332 | .273 | 14793 | 1072 | 221 | .986 |
| American League Totals ............... | | 11 | 24 | 0 | 5 | 0 | 0 | 0 | 0 | .208 | 0 | 0 | 0 | .000 |
| Major League Totals ..................... | | 2174 | 6902 | 1101 | 1886 | .296 | 44 | 465 | 1332 | .273 | 14793 | 1072 | 22 | .986 |

†Placed on regular disabled list, April 19 through June 2, 1972.
‡Traded with Outfielder Bernie Williams (on Phoenix roster) to San Diego Padres for Pitcher Mike Caldwell, October 25, 1973.
§Sold to Oakland A's, August 30, 1976.
xPlayed out option year and granted free agency; signed as free agent with San Francisco Giants, January 6, 1977.

CHAMPIONSHIP SERIES RECORD

| Year Club League | Pos. | G. | AB. | R. | H. | 2B. | 3B. | HR. | RBI. | B.A. | PO. | A. | E. | F.A. |
|---|---|---|---|---|---|---|---|---|---|---|---|---|---|---|
| 1971—San Francisco ..Nat. | 1B | 4 | 14 | 2 | 6 | 0 | 0 | 2 | 6 | .429 | 34 | 3 | 1 | .974 |

WORLD SERIES RECORD

| Year Club League | Pos. | G. | AB. | R. | H. | 2B. | 3B. | HR. | RBI. | B.A. | PO. | A. | E. | F.A. |
|---|---|---|---|---|---|---|---|---|---|---|---|---|---|---|
| 1962—San Francisco ..Nat. | 1B-OF | 4 | 15 | 2 | 3 | 0 | 1 | 1 | 1 | .200 | 23 | 4 | 2 | .931 |

ALL-STAR GAME RECORD

| Year League | Pos. | AB. | R. | H. | 2B. | 3B. | HR. | RBI. | B.A. | PO. | A. | E. | F.A. |
|---|---|---|---|---|---|---|---|---|---|---|---|---|---|
| 1963—National ............................ | PH | 1 | 0 | 0 | 0 | 0 | 0 | 0 | .000 | 0 | 0 | 0 | .000 |
| 1966—National ............................ | 1B | 3 | 0 | 0 | 0 | 0 | 0 | 0 | .000 | 10 | 1 | 0 | 1.000 |
| 1968—National ............................ | 1B | 4 | 0 | 0 | 0 | 0 | 0 | 0 | .000 | 10 | 0 | 0 | 1.000 |
| 1969—National ............................ | 1B | 4 | 2 | 2 | 0 | 0 | 2 | 3 | .500 | 2 | 0 | 0 | 1.000 |
| 1970—National ............................ | 1B | 2 | 0 | 1 | 0 | 0 | 0 | 1 | .500 | 1 | 0 | 0 | 1.000 |
| 1971—National ............................ | 1B | 2 | 0 | 0 | 0 | 0 | 0 | 0 | .000 | 4 | 0 | 0 | 1.000 |
| All-Star Game Totals ...................... | | 16 | 2 | 3 | 0 | 0 | 2 | 4 | .188 | 27 | 1 | 0 | 1.000 |

## JAMES LARRY McCUTCHIN
### (Jim)

Born February 14, 1953, at Levelland, Tex.
Height, 6.01. Weight, 200.
Throws and bats righthanded.
Hobby—Hunting.
Attended University of Texas, Austin, Tex.
Tied for Gulf Coast League lead in games started with 12 and in complete games with 4 in 1973.

| Year Club | League | G. | IP. | W. | L. | Pct. | H. | R. | ER. | SO. | BB. | ERA. |
|---|---|---|---|---|---|---|---|---|---|---|---|---|
| 1973—Reno.....................................California | | 4 | 8 | 0 | 0 | .000 | 6 | 4 | 2 | 8 | 4 | 2.25 |
| 1973—Sarasota Indians .................Gulf Coast | | 12 | 74 | •7 | 2 | .778 | 72 | 36 | 24 | 58 | 24 | 2.92 |
| 1974—San Antonio ........................Texas | | 2 | 9 | 0 | 1 | .000 | 13 | 9 | 5 | 3 | 4 | 5.00 |
| 1974—Reno† .................................California | | 18 | 88 | 3 | 7 | .300 | 110 | 64 | 53 | 66 | 40 | 5.42 |
| 1975—San Antonio ......................Texas | | 13 | 65 | 4 | 4 | .500 | 76 | 37 | 28 | 25 | 27 | 3.88 |
| 1975—Oklahoma City ...................Am. Assoc. | | 18 | 73 | 4 | 2 | .667 | 65 | 31 | 27 | 33 | 36 | 3.33 |
| 1976—Toledo...............................Int'national | | 31 | 122 | 6 | 10 | .375 | 162 | 89 | 73 | 37 | 63 | 5.39 |

†On disabled list, July 8 to July 30, 1974. On suspended list, August 13 to September 3, 1974.
Listed on Cleveland Indians' 1977 spring roster.

## WILLIAM HENRY McENANEY
Name pronounced MACK-uh-nan-ee.
### (Will)

Born February 14, 1952, at Springfield, O.
Height, 6.00. Weight, 180.
Throws and bats lefthanded.
Tied for Northern League lead in games started by pitchers with 14 in 1970.

| Year Club | League | G. | IP. | W. | L. | Pct. | H. | R. | ER. | SO. | BB. | ERA. |
|---|---|---|---|---|---|---|---|---|---|---|---|---|
| 1970—Sioux Falls ..........................Northern | | 15 | 87 | 3 | *10 | .231 | 104 | *65 | *50 | 71 | 33 | 5.17 |
| 1971—Tampa ...............................Gulf Coast | | 27 | 181 | 14 | 5 | .737 | 159 | 58 | 49 | 105 | 57 | 2.44 |
| 1972—Three Rivers.......................Eastern | | 30 | 138 | 11 | 6 | .647 | 128 | 53 | 43 | 82 | 46 | 2.80 |
| 1973—Indianapolis .......................Am. Assoc. | | 29 | 170 | 9 | 9 | .500 | 196 | 95 | 74 | 105 | 40 | 3.92 |
| 1974—Indianapolis .......................Am. Assoc. | | 29 | 43 | 2 | 1 | .667 | 38 | 12 | 11 | 35 | 21 | 2.30 |
| 1974—Cincinnati ..........................National | | 24 | 27 | 2 | 1 | .667 | 24 | 16 | 13 | 13 | 9 | 4.33 |
| 1975—Cincinnati ..........................National | | 70 | 91 | 5 | 2 | .714 | 92 | 29 | 25 | 48 | 23 | 2.47 |
| 1976—Cincinnati† ........................National | | 55 | 72 | 2 | 6 | .250 | 97 | 44 | 39 | 28 | 23 | 4.88 |
| Major League Totals ............................... | | 149 | 190 | 9 | 9 | .500 | 213 | 89 | 77 | 89 | 55 | 3.65 |

†Traded with First Baseman Tony Perez to Montreal Expos for Pitchers Woodie Fryman and Dale Murray, December 16, 1976.

| Year    Club | League | G. | IP. | W. | L. | Pct. | H. | R. | ER. | SO. | BB. | ERA. |
|---|---|---|---|---|---|---|---|---|---|---|---|---|
| 1975–Cincinnati ..........................National | National | 1 | 1⅓ | 0 | 0 | .000 | 1 | 1 | 1 | 1 | 0 | 6.75 |

### WORLD SERIES RECORD

| Year    Club | League | G. | IP. | W. | L. | Pct. | H. | R. | ER. | SO. | BB. | ERA. |
|---|---|---|---|---|---|---|---|---|---|---|---|---|
| 1975–Cincinnati ..........................National | National | 5 | 6⅔ | 0 | 0 | .000 | 3 | 2 | 2 | 5 | 2 | 2.70 |
| 1976–Cincinnati ..........................National | National | 2 | 4⅔ | 0 | 0 | .000 | 2 | 0 | 0 | 2 | 1 | 0.00 |
| World Series Totals ................................. | | 7 | 11⅓ | 0 | 0 | .000 | 5 | 2 | 2 | 7 | 3 | 1.59 |

## LYNN EVERRATT McGLOTHEN
Name pronounced Mc-LAW-then.

Born March 27, 1950, at Monroe, La.
Height, 6.02.  Weight, 185.
Throws right and bats lefthanded.
Hobbies–Hunting, fishing and listening to music.
Attended Grambling College, Grambling, La.

Led International League pitchers in complete games with 13 in 1971.
Led Carolina League pitchers in complete games with 16 and tied for lead in games started with 29 and in shutouts with 5 in 1970.
Named Carolina League Player of the Year in 1970.

| Year    Club | League | G. | IP. | W. | L. | Pct. | H. | R. | ER. | SO. | BB. | ERA. |
|---|---|---|---|---|---|---|---|---|---|---|---|---|
| 1968–Waterloo ..............................Midwest | Midwest | 17 | 46 | 3 | 2 | .600 | 45 | 20 | 17 | 34 | 36 | 3.33 |
| 1969–Winter Haven .....................Florida St. | Florida St. | 32 | 179 | 15 | 8 | .652 | 161 | 93 | *78 | 153 | 106 | 3.92 |
| 1970–Winston-Salem .................Carol. | Carol. | 31 | *229 | *15 | 7 | .682 | 166 | 63 | 57 | *202 | 91 | 2.24 |
| 1971–Louisville ...........................Int'national | Int'national | 27 | 179 | 10 | 10 | .500 | 162 | 89 | 74 | 151 | 98 | 3.72 |
| 1972–Louisville ...........................Int'national | Int'national | 14 | 108 | 9 | 2 | .818 | 69 | 24 | 23 | 88 | 39 | 1.92 |
| 1972–Boston ...............................American | American | 22 | 145 | 8 | 7 | .533 | 135 | 66 | 55 | 112 | 59 | 3.41 |
| 1973–Pawtucket† ..........................Int'national | Int'national | 9 | 53 | 2 | 4 | .333 | 56 | 26 | 23 | 39 | 18 | 3.91 |
| 1973–Boston‡ ...............................American | American | 6 | 23 | 1 | 2 | .333 | 39 | 23 | 21 | 16 | 8 | 8.22 |
| 1974–St. Louis .............................National | National | 31 | 237 | 16 | 12 | .571 | 212 | 80 | 71 | 142 | 89 | 2.70 |
| 1975–St. Louis .............................National | National | 35 | 239 | 15 | 13 | .536 | 231 | 110 | 104 | 146 | 97 | 3.92 |
| 1976–St. Louis§ ...........................National | National | 33 | 205 | 13 | 15 | .464 | 209 | 96 | 89 | 106 | 68 | 3.91 |
| American League Totals............................ | | 28 | 168 | 9 | 9 | .500 | 174 | 89 | 76 | 128 | 67 | 4.07 |
| National League Totals............................ | | 99 | 681 | 44 | 40 | .524 | 652 | 286 | 264 | 394 | 254 | 3.49 |
| Major League Totals ............................. | | 127 | 849 | 53 | 49 | .520 | 826 | 375 | 340 | 522 | 321 | 3.60 |

†On disabled list, July 3 to August 7, 1973.
‡Traded with Pitchers John Curtis and Mike Garman to St. Louis Cardinals for Pitchers Reggie Cleveland and Diego Segui and Infielder Terry Hughes, December 7, 1973.
§Traded to San Francisco Giants for Third Baseman Ken Reitz, December 10, 1976.

### ALL-STAR GAME RECORD

| Year    League | IP. | W. | L. | Pct. | H. | R. | ER. | SO. | BB. | ERA. |
|---|---|---|---|---|---|---|---|---|---|---|
| 1974–National ........................................................ | 1 | 0 | 0 | .000 | 0 | 0 | 0 | 1 | 0 | 0.000 |

## THOMAS RAY McGOUGH
### (Tom)

Born August 15, 1955, at Johnstown, Pa.
Height, 6.03.  Weight, 190.
Throws and bats righthanded.
Hobbies–Hunting and fishing.
Attended University of Pittsburgh at Johnstown, Johnstown, Pa.

Pitched 1-0 no-hit victory against Shreveport, May 11, 1975.

| Year    Club | League | G. | IP. | W. | L. | Pct. | H. | R. | ER. | SO. | BB. | ERA. |
|---|---|---|---|---|---|---|---|---|---|---|---|---|
| 1973–Sarasota Indians .................Gulf Coast | Gulf Coast | 11 | 68 | 6 | 1 | .857 | 52 | 25 | 18 | 64 | 20 | 2.38 |
| 1974–Reno ..................................California | California | 25 | 183 | 13 | 9 | .591 | 167 | 108 | 83 | 153 | 72 | 4.08 |
| 1975–San Antonio ......................Texas | Texas | 7 | 42 | 2 | 2 | .500 | 43 | 22 | 20 | 23 | 11 | 4.29 |
| 1975–Oklahoma City ...................Am. Assoc. | Am. Assoc. | 18 | 97 | 4 | 11 | .267 | 113 | 67 | 54 | 51 | 48 | 5.01 |
| 1976–Williamsport ......................Eastern | Eastern | 24 | 145 | 7 | 12 | .368 | 172 | 92 | *83 | 57 | 52 | 5.15 |

Listed on Cleveland Indians' 1977 spring roster.

## FRANK EDWIN McGRAW, JR.
### (Tug)
(Named by parents because he tugged on so many things as a baby.)

Born August 30, 1944, at Martinez, Calif.
Height, 6.00.  Weight, 180.
Throws left and bats righthanded.
Attended Vallejo Junior College, Vallejo, Calif.
Brother of Hank McGraw, former outfielder-catcher in New York Met, Chicago Cub,
Philadelphia Phillie and Atlanta Brave organizations.

Pitched seven-inning, 4-0 no-hit victory against Cocoa, July 3, 1964.
Tied for Cocoa Rookie League lead in hit batsmen with 6 in 1964.

| Year    Club | League | G. | IP. | W. | L. | Pct. | H. | R. | ER. | SO. | BB. | ERA. |
|---|---|---|---|---|---|---|---|---|---|---|---|---|
| 1964–Florida Mets | Cocoa Rook. | 8 | 47 | 5 | 2 | .714 | 12 | 11 | 8 | 37 | 52 | 1.53 |
| 1964–Auburn | NYP | 3 | 19 | 1 | 2 | .333 | 17 | 12 | 4 | 14 | 15 | 1.89 |
| 1965–New York | National | 37 | 98 | 2 | 7 | .222 | 88 | 47 | 36 | 57 | 48 | 3.31 |
| 1966–New York | National | 15 | 62 | 2 | 9 | .182 | 72 | 38 | 37 | 34 | 25 | 5.37 |
| 1966–Jacksonville† | Int'national | 11 | 32 | 2 | 2 | .500 | 34 | 16 | 15 | 38 | 9 | 4.22 |
| 1967–Jacksonville | Int'national | 22 | 167 | 10 | 9 | .526 | 111 | 39 | 37 | 161 | 55 | *1.99 |
| 1967–New York | National | 4 | 17 | 0 | 3 | .000 | 13 | 16 | 15 | 18 | 13 | 7.94 |
| 1968–Jacksonville‡ | Int'national | 24 | 166 | 9 | 9 | .500 | 149 | 70 | 63 | 132 | 61 | 3.42 |
| 1969–New York | National | 42 | 100 | 9 | 3 | .750 | 89 | 31 | 25 | 92 | 47 | 2.25 |
| 1970–New York | National | 57 | 91 | 4 | 6 | .400 | 77 | 40 | 33 | 81 | 49 | 3.26 |
| 1971–New York | National | 51 | 111 | 11 | 4 | .733 | 73 | 22 | 21 | 109 | 41 | 1.70 |
| 1972–New York | National | 54 | 106 | 8 | 6 | .571 | 71 | 26 | 20 | 92 | 40 | 1.70 |
| 1973–New York | National | 60 | 119 | 5 | 6 | .455 | 106 | 53 | 51 | 81 | 55 | 3.86 |
| 1974–New York§ | National | 41 | 89 | 6 | 11 | .353 | 96 | 43 | 41 | 54 | 32 | 4.15 |
| 1975–Philadelphia x | National | 56 | 103 | 9 | 6 | .600 | 84 | 38 | 34 | 55 | 36 | 2.97 |
| 1976–Philadelphia | National | 58 | 97 | 7 | 6 | .538 | 81 | 34 | 27 | 76 | 42 | 2.51 |
| Major League Totals | | 475 | 993 | 63 | 67 | .485 | 850 | 388 | 340 | 749 | 428 | 3.08 |

†On disabled list, May 18 to June 11 and June 28 to July 8, 1966.
‡On disabled list, April 20 to April 30, 1968. On temporary inactive list, May 17 to May 20 and July 10 to July 20, 1968.
§On disabled list, May 16 to June 10, 1974. Traded with Outfielders Don Hahn and Dave Schneck to Philadelphia Phillies for Outfielder Del Unser, Pitcher Mac Scarce and Catcher John Stearns, December 3, 1974.
xOn disabled list, March 23 to April 25, 1975.

## CHAMPIONSHIP SERIES RECORD

| Year    Club | League | G. | IP. | W. | L. | Pct. | H. | R. | ER. | SO. | BB. | ERA. |
|---|---|---|---|---|---|---|---|---|---|---|---|---|
| 1969–New York | National | 1 | 3 | 0 | 0 | .000 | 1 | 0 | 0 | 1 | 1 | 0.00 |
| 1973–New York | National | 2 | 5 | 0 | 0 | .000 | 4 | 0 | 0 | 3 | 3 | 0.00 |
| 1976–Philadelphia | National | 2 | 2⅓ | 0 | 0 | .000 | 4 | 3 | 3 | 5 | 1 | 13.50 |
| Championship Series Totals | | 5 | 10⅓ | 0 | 0 | .000 | 9 | 3 | 3 | 9 | 5 | 2.61 |

## WORLD SERIES RECORD

| Year    Club | League | G. | IP. | W. | L. | Pct. | H. | R. | ER. | SO. | BB. | ERA. |
|---|---|---|---|---|---|---|---|---|---|---|---|---|
| 1973–New York | National | 5 | 13⅔ | 1 | 0 | 1.000 | 8 | 5 | 4 | 14 | 9 | 2.63 |

## ALL-STAR GAME RECORD

| Year    League | | IP. | W. | L. | Pct. | H. | R. | ER. | SO. | BB. | ERA. |
|---|---|---|---|---|---|---|---|---|---|---|---|
| 1972–National | | 2 | 1 | 0 | 1.000 | 1 | 0 | 0 | 4 | 0 | 0.00 |

Member of National League All-Star Team for 1975 game; did not play.


## SCOTT HOUSTON McGREGOR

Born January 18, 1954, at Inglewood, Calif.
Height, 6.01. Weight, 190.
Throws left and bats right and lefthanded.
Hobby–Photography.
Attended Loyola Marymount University, Los Angeles, Calif.
Led International League pitchers in complete games with 12 in 1974.
Led Eastern League pitchers in complete games with 14 and tied for lead in games started with 27 in 1973.
Led International League in shutouts with 6 in 1976.
Received reported $80,000 bonus to sign with New York Yankees, 1972.

| Year    Club | League | G. | IP. | W. | L. | Pct. | H. | R. | ER. | SO. | BB. | ERA. |
|---|---|---|---|---|---|---|---|---|---|---|---|---|
| 1972–Ft. Lauderdale | Florida St. | 11 | 79 | 7 | 3 | .700 | 66 | 30 | 24 | 54 | 25 | 2.73 |
| 1973–West Haven | Eastern | 27 | *197 | ●12 | ●13 | .480 | *197 | 95 | 72 | 126 | 63 | 3.29 |
| 1974–Syracuse | Int'national | 27 | *199 | 13 | 10 | .565 | 204 | 88 | 76 | 124 | 75 | 3.44 |
| 1975–Syracuse† | Int'national | 21 | 124 | 6 | 9 | .400 | 134 | 73 | 55 | 72 | 60 | 3.99 |
| 1976–Syracuse‡-Rochester | Int'national | 24 | 162 | 12 | 6 | .667 | 159 | 59 | 55 | 83 | 40 | 3.06 |
| 1976–Baltimore | American | 3 | 15 | 0 | 1 | .000 | 17 | 7 | 6 | 6 | 5 | 3.60 |
| Major League Totals | | 3 | 15 | 0 | 1 | .000 | 17 | 7 | 6 | 6 | 5 | 3.60 |

†On disabled list, August 1 through August 29.
‡Traded with Pitchers Rudy May, Felix Martinez and Dave Pagan, and Catcher Rich Dempsey by New York Yankees to Baltimore Orioles for Pitchers Ken Holtzman, Doyle Alexander and Grant Jackson, Catcher Ellie Hendricks and Pitcher Jimmy Freeman, latter assigned from Rochester to Syracuse, June 15, 1976.


## JOSEPH ANTHONY McINTOSH
### (Joe)

Born August 4, 1951, at Billings, Mont.
Height, 6.02. Weight, 195.
Throws right and bats left and righthanded.
Hobbies–Golf, coins and trains.
Attended Washington State University, Pullman, Wash.; received
Bachelor of Science degree in Zoology.

| Year    Club | League | G. | IP. | W. | L. | Pct. | H. | R. | ER. | SO. | BB. | ERA. |
|---|---|---|---|---|---|---|---|---|---|---|---|---|
| 1973–Walla Walla† | Northwest | 14 | 107 | 8 | 6 | .571 | 93 | 37 | 29 | *117 | 30 | 2.44 |
| 1974–Hawaii | P. Coast | 30 | 152 | 9 | 11 | .450 | 167 | 101 | 89 | 111 | 80 | 5.27 |

| Year    Club | League | G. | IP. | W. | L. | Pct. | H. | R. | ER. | SO. | BB. | ERA. |
|---|---|---|---|---|---|---|---|---|---|---|---|---|
| 1974–San Diego | National | 10 | 37 | 0 | 4 | .000 | 36 | 19 | 15 | 22 | 17 | 3.65 |
| 1975–San Diego‡ | National | 37 | 183 | 8 | 15 | .348 | 195 | 88 | 75 | 71 | 60 | 3.69 |
| 1976–Houston§ | National | | | | | (Did not play) | | | | | | |
| Major League Totals | | 47 | 220 | 8 | 19 | .296 | 231 | 107 | 90 | 93 | 77 | 3.68 |

†On temporary inactive list, July 23 to August 2, 1973.
‡Traded with Pitcher Larry Hardy to Houston Astros for Third Baseman Doug Rader, December 11, 1975.
§On disabled list entire season due to arm injury.

## DAVID LAWRENCE McKAY
### (Dave)

Born March 14, 1950, at Vancouver, British Columbia, Canada.
Height, 6.01 Weight, 195.
Throws and bats righthanded.
Attended Columbia Basin Junior College, Pasco, Wash., and
Creighton University, Omaha, Neb.

Tied major league record by hitting home run, first major league appearance, August 22, 1975.

| Year    Club | League | Pos. | G. | AB. | R. | H. | 2B. | 3B. | HR. | RBI. | B.A. | PO. | A. | E. | F.A. |
|---|---|---|---|---|---|---|---|---|---|---|---|---|---|---|---|
| 1971–Wis. Rapids | Midw. | SS | 65 | 257 | 27 | 58 | 9 | 0 | 3 | 22 | .226 | 126 | 221 | 26 | .930 |
| 1972–Lynchburg† | Carol. | 2-3-S | 90 | 299 | 39 | 64 | 11 | 1 | 5 | 33 | .214 | 145 | 238 | 23 | .943 |
| 1973–Lynchburg | Carol. | 3-S-2 | 107 | 355 | 47 | 79 | 14 | 2 | 10 | 47 | .223 | 107 | 204 | 22 | .934 |
| 1974–Orlando | South. | 3B | 100 | 360 | 59 | 100 | 12 | 2 | 8 | 41 | .278 | 96 | 184 | 15 | .949 |
| 1975–Tacoma | P. C. | SS-3B | 109 | 370 | 56 | 95 | 12 | 2 | 7 | 39 | .257 | 174 | 264 | 31 | .934 |
| 1975–Minnesota | Amer. | 3B | 33 | 125 | 8 | 32 | 4 | 1 | 2 | 16 | .256 | 38 | 70 | 9 | .923 |
| 1976–Minnesota | Amer. | 3-S-DH | 45 | 138 | 8 | 28 | 2 | 0 | 0 | 8 | .203 | 27 | 77 | 10 | .912 |
| 1976–Tacoma‡ | P. C. | 3B-2B | 63 | 211 | 31 | 52 | 6 | 1 | 3 | 22 | .246 | 40 | 123 | 11 | .937 |
| Major League Totals | | | 78 | 263 | 16 | 60 | 6 | 1 | 2 | 24 | .228 | 65 | 147 | 19 | .918 |

†On disabled list, May 15 to June 1, 1972.
‡Selected by Toronto Blue Jays in American League expansion draft, November 5, 1976.

## CHARLES RICHARD McKINNEY
### (Rich)

Born November 22, 1946, at Piqua, O.
Height, 5.11. Weight, 185.
Throws and bats righthanded.
Hobbies–Fishing and trapping.
Attended Ohio University, Athens, O.

Tied American League record for most errors, third baseman, nine-inning game, 4, April 22, 1972.

| Year    Club | League | Pos. | G. | AB. | R. | H. | 2B. | 3B. | HR. | RBI. | B.A. | PO. | A. | E. | F.A. |
|---|---|---|---|---|---|---|---|---|---|---|---|---|---|---|---|
| 1968–Evansville | South. | SS | 86 | 307 | 46 | 80 | 12 | 9 | 7 | 37 | .261 | 118 | 224 | 20 | .945 |
| 1969–Columbus | South. | OF-SS | 11 | 43 | 5 | 14 | 1 | 1 | 3 | 6 | .326 | 11 | 12 | 0 | 1.000 |
| 1969–Tucson | P. C. | SS | 11 | 40 | 2 | 8 | 4 | 0 | 0 | 4 | .200 | 21 | 40 | 5 | .924 |
| 1970–Tucson | P. C. | SS | 62 | 251 | 35 | 76 | 14 | 7 | 6 | 41 | .303 | 101 | 261 | 21 | .945 |
| 1970–Chicago | Amer. | 3B-SS | 43 | 119 | 12 | 20 | 5 | 0 | 4 | 17 | .168 | 34 | 81 | 6 | .950 |
| 1971–Chicago† | Amer. | 2-O-3 | 114 | 369 | 35 | 100 | 11 | 2 | 8 | 46 | .271 | 195 | 171 | 11 | .971 |
| 1972–Syracuse | Int. | 3-O-2 | 86 | 281 | 42 | 84 | 15 | 0 | 16 | 53 | .299 | 60 | 123 | 11 | .943 |
| 1972–New York‡ | Amer. | 3B | 37 | 121 | 10 | 26 | 2 | 0 | 1 | 7 | .215 | 17 | 71 | 8 | .917 |
| 1973–Tucson | P. C. | O-3-2 | 24 | 77 | 8 | 18 | 3 | 0 | 0 | 9 | .234 | 14 | 9 | 1 | .958 |
| 1973–Oakland | Amer. | 3-2-O | 48 | 65 | 9 | 16 | 3 | 0 | 1 | 7 | .246 | 13 | 19 | 2 | .941 |
| 1974–Tucson | P. C. | IF-OF | 116 | 403 | 55 | 115 | 26 | 4 | 7 | 65 | .285 | 277 | 184 | 8 | .983 |
| 1974–Oakland | Amer. | 2B | 5 | 7 | 0 | 1 | 0 | 0 | 0 | 0 | .143 | 1 | 0 | 0 | 1.000 |
| 1975–Tucson | P. C. | OF-2B | 110 | 394 | 57 | 117 | 26 | 3 | 13 | 74 | .297 | 154 | 25 | 6 | .968 |
| 1975–Oakland | Amer. | 1B | 8 | 7 | 0 | 1 | 0 | 0 | 0 | 2 | .143 | 1 | 0 | 0 | 1.000 |
| 1976–Tucson | P. C. | OF-PH | 129 | 458 | 84 | 145 | *34 | 6 | 22 | 95 | .317 | 149 | 13 | 3 | .982 |
| Major League Totals | | | 255 | 688 | 66 | 164 | 21 | 2 | 14 | 79 | .238 | 261 | 342 | 27 | .957 |

†Traded to New York Yankees for Pitcher Stan Bahnsen, December 2, 1971.
‡Released to Oakland A's (completed deal in which New York Yankees acquired Outfielder Matty Alou, November 24, 1972), December 1, 1972.
Invited to Oakland A's 1977 spring camp.

## JOEY RICHARD McLAUGHLIN

Born July 11, 1956, at Tulsa, Okla.
Height, 6.02. Weight, 205.
Throws and bats righthanded.

| Year    Club | League | G. | IP. | W. | L. | Pct. | H. | R. | ER. | SO. | BB. | ERA. |
|---|---|---|---|---|---|---|---|---|---|---|---|---|
| 1974–Kingsport | Ap'lachian | 8 | 34 | 2 | 5 | .286 | 41 | 27 | 20 | 32 | 15 | 5.29 |
| 1975–Greenwood | W. Carol. | 20 | 122 | 12 | 5 | .706 | 112 | 47 | 35 | 59 | 49 | *2.58 |
| 1975–Savannah | Southern | 8 | 53 | 4 | 3 | .571 | 41 | 21 | 20 | 29 | 16 | 3.40 |
| 1976–Savannah | Southern | 24 | 169 | 12 | 8 | .600 | 165 | 69 | 52 | 70 | 44 | 2.77 |
| 1976–Richmond | Int'national | 1 | 1 | 0 | 0 | .000 | 1 | 1 | 1 | 1 | 1 | 9.00 |

Listed on Atlanta Braves' 1977 spring roster.

## MICHAEL DUANE McLAUGHLIN
### (Bo)

Born October 23, 1953, at Oakland, Calif.
Height, 6.05. Weight, 210.
Throws and bats righthanded.
Attended David Lipscomb College, Nashville, Tenn.
Received large bonus to sign with Houston Astros, 1975.

| Year Club | League | G. | IP. | W. | L. | Pct. | H. | R. | ER. | SO. | BB. | ERA. |
|---|---|---|---|---|---|---|---|---|---|---|---|---|
| 1975–Columbus† | Southern | 15 | 95 | 5 | 4 | .556 | 73 | 40 | 35 | 77 | 27 | 3.32 |
| 1976–Memphis | Int'national | 20 | 147 | 8 | 9 | .471 | 137 | 71 | 60 | 117 | 53 | 3.67 |
| 1976–Houston | National | 17 | 79 | 4 | 5 | .444 | 71 | 31 | 25 | 32 | 17 | 2.85 |
| Major League Totals | | 17 | 79 | 4 | 5 | .444 | 71 | 31 | 25 | 32 | 17 | 2.85 |

†On disabled list, July 25 to August 5, 1975.


## THOMAS ERWIN McMILLAN
### (Tommy)

Born September 13, 1951, at Richmond, Va.
Height, 5.09. Weight, 165.
Hobbies–Hunting, fishing, camping and water skiing
Attended Jacksonville University, Jacksonville, Fla.; received
Bachelor of Science degree in Physical Education.

| Year Club | League | Pos. | G. | AB. | R. | H. | 2B. | 3B. | HR. | RBI. | B.A. | PO. | A. | E. | F.A. |
|---|---|---|---|---|---|---|---|---|---|---|---|---|---|---|---|
| 1973–San Antonio | Texas | SS | 44 | 104 | 13 | 24 | 2 | 0 | 0 | 4 | .231 | 53 | 90 | 17 | .894 |
| 1973–Oklahoma City | A. A. | SS | 10 | 38 | 3 | 12 | 3 | 0 | 0 | 5 | .316 | 12 | 18 | 1 | .968 |
| 1974–Oklahoma City | A. A. | SS | 128 | 445 | 59 | 115 | 11 | 5 | 1 | 37 | .258 | ★215 | 362 | ★35 | .943 |
| 1975–Oklahoma City | A. A. | SS | 136 | 503 | 66 | 125 | 14 | 5 | 2 | 58 | .249 | 236 | 363 | 30 | .952 |
| 1976–Toledo | Int. | SS | 107 | 374 | 57 | 91 | 11 | 5 | 3 | 40 | .243 | 174 | 362 | 32 | .944 |
| 1976–Iowa† | A. A. | SS | 23 | 82 | 13 | 17 | 0 | 1 | 0 | 1 | .207 | 33 | 72 | 3 | .972 |

†Selected by Seattle Mariners from Cleveland Indians' organization in American League expansion draft, November 5, 1976.


## KENNETH LEE McMULLEN
### (Ken)

Born June 1, 1942, at Oxnard, Calif.
Height, 6.03. Weight, 193.
Throws and bats righthanded.
Hobby–Golf.

Tied major league records for most assists, nine-inning game, third baseman (11), September 26, 1966, and most double plays started by third baseman, nine-inning game, 4, August 13, 1965.
Led American League third basemen in double plays with 38 in 1967.
Led California League in walks with 107 and led third basemen in double plays with 22 in 1961.
Received reported $60,000 bonus to sign with the Los Angeles Dodgers, 1960.

| Year Club | League | Pos. | G. | AB. | R. | H. | 2B. | 3B. | HR. | RBI. | B.A. | PO. | A. | E. | F.A. |
|---|---|---|---|---|---|---|---|---|---|---|---|---|---|---|---|
| 1961–Reno | Calif. | 3B | 138 | 493 | 109 | 142 | 26 | 4 | 21 | 96 | .288 | ★128 | ★200 | ★35 | .904 |
| 1962–Omaha | A. A. | O-3-1B | 143 | 529 | 77 | 149 | 28 | 4 | 21 | 81 | .282 | 309 | 39 | 13 | .964 |
| 1962–Los Angeles | Nat. | OF | 6 | 11 | 0 | 3 | 0 | 0 | 0 | 0 | .273 | 1 | 0 | 0 | 1.000 |
| 1963–Spokane | P. C. | 3B-OF | 38 | 133 | 14 | 36 | 10 | 1 | 2 | 17 | .271 | 38 | 47 | 8 | .914 |
| 1963–Los Angeles | Nat. | 3-2B-O | 79 | 233 | 16 | 55 | 9 | 0 | 5 | 28 | .236 | 48 | 134 | 13 | .933 |
| 1964–Los Angeles | Nat. | 1-3-OF | 24 | 67 | 3 | 14 | 0 | 0 | 1 | 2 | .209 | 106 | 9 | 3 | .975 |
| 1964–Spokane† | P. C. | OF-1-3B | 93 | 325 | 38 | 76 | 18 | 1 | 14 | 49 | .234 | 272 | 18 | 10 | .967 |
| 1965–Washington | Amer. | 3-OF-1 | 150 | 555 | 75 | 146 | 18 | 6 | 18 | 54 | .263 | 169 | 300 | ★22 | .955 |
| 1966–Washington | Amer. | 3-1-OF | 147 | 524 | 48 | 122 | 19 | 4 | 13 | 54 | .233 | 190 | 284 | 21 | .958 |
| 1967–Washington | Amer. | 3B | 146 | 563 | 73 | 138 | 22 | 2 | 16 | 67 | .245 | 153 | 348 | 18 | .965 |
| 1968–Washington | Amer. | 3B-SS | 151 | 557 | 66 | 138 | 11 | 2 | 20 | 62 | .248 | 194 | 302 | 19 | .963 |
| 1969–Washington | Amer. | 3B | 158 | 562 | 83 | 153 | 25 | 2 | 19 | 87 | .272 | ★185 | 347 | 13 | ●.976 |
| 1970–Wash.‡Cal. | Amer. | 3B | 139 | 481 | 55 | 110 | 11 | 3 | 14 | 64 | .229 | 154 | 306 | 19 | .960 |
| 1971–California | Amer. | 3B | 160 | 593 | 63 | 148 | 19 | 2 | 21 | 68 | .250 | 137 | 344 | 17 | .966 |
| 1972–California‡‡ | Amer. | 3B | 137 | 472 | 36 | 127 | 18 | 1 | 9 | 34 | .269 | 89 | 267 | 11 | .970 |
| 1973–Los Angeles | Nat. | 3B | 42 | 85 | 6 | 21 | 5 | 0 | 5 | 18 | .247 | 5 | 54 | 5 | .922 |
| 1974–Los Angeles | Nat. | 3B-2B | 44 | 60 | 5 | 15 | 1 | 0 | 3 | 12 | .250 | 10 | 14 | 0 | 1.000 |
| 1975–Los Angeles§ | Nat. | 3B-1B | 39 | 46 | 4 | 11 | 1 | 1 | 2 | 14 | .239 | 26 | 12 | 0 | 1.000 |
| 1976–Oakland x | Amer. | 3-1-O-2 | 98 | 186 | 20 | 41 | 6 | 2 | 5 | 23 | .220 | 222 | 39 | 2 | .992 |
| American League Totals | | 1286 | 4493 | 519 | 1123 | 149 | 24 | 135 | 513 | .250 | 1493 | 2537 | 142 | .966 |
| National League Totals | | 234 | 502 | 34 | 119 | 16 | 1 | 16 | 74 | .237 | 196 | 223 | 21 | .952 |
| Major League Totals | | 1520 | 4995 | 553 | 1242 | 165 | 25 | 151 | 587 | .249 | 1689 | 2760 | 163 | 9565 |

†Traded by Los Angeles Dodgers to Washington Senators with Outfielder Frank Howard and Pitchers Phil Ortega and Pete Richert for Pitcher Claude Osteen and Infielder John Kennedy and cash estimated at $100,000, December 4, 1964; deal was completed with transfer of First Baseman Dick Nen to Senators, December 15, 1964.
‡Traded to California Angels for Outfielder Rick Reichardt and Infielder Aurelio Rodriguez, April 26, 1970.
‡‡Traded with Pitcher Andy Messersmith to Los Angeles Dodgers for Outfielder Frank Robinson, Infielders Billy Grabarkewitz and Bob Valentine and Pitchers Bill Singer and Mike Strahler, November 28, 1972.

§Released, March 2, 1976; signed as a free agent by Oakland Athletics, April 5, 1976.
xReleased, February 25, 1977; signed as a free agent by Milwaukee Brewers, February 25, 1977.

CHAMPIONSHIP SERIES RECORD

| Year Club League | Pos. | G. | AB. | R. | H. | 2B. | 3B. | HR. | RBI. | B.A. | PO. | A. | E. | F.A. |
|---|---|---|---|---|---|---|---|---|---|---|---|---|---|---|
| 1974–Los Angeles ......Nat. | PH | 1 | 1 | 0 | 0 | 0 | 0 | 0 | 0 | .000 | 0 | 0 | 0 | .000 |

## HAROLD ABRAHAM McRAE
## (Hal)

Born July 10, 1946, at Avon Park, Fla.
Height, 5.11. Weight, 180.
Throws and bats righthanded.
Attended Florida A&M University, Tallahassee, Fla.

Tied major league record for most long hits, doubleheader, 6, August 27, 1974, 5 doubles, 1 home run.
Named designated hitter on THE SPORTING NEWS American League All-Star Team, 1976.

| Year Club League | Pos. | G. | AB. | R. | H. | 2B. | 3B. | HR. | RBI. | B.A. | PO. | A. | E. | F.A. |
|---|---|---|---|---|---|---|---|---|---|---|---|---|---|---|
| 1965–Tampa ..............Fla. St. | OF | 22 | 65 | 3 | 10 | 3 | 0 | 0 | 4 | .154 | 19 | 0 | 0 | 1.000 |
| 1966–Peninsula† ........Carol. | 2B | 109 | 394 | 65 | 113 | 19 | 4 | 11 | 56 | .287 | 252 | 226 | *28 | .945 |
| 1967–Buffalo† ...........Int. | 2B | 73 | 259 | 30 | 65 | 14 | 3 | 10 | 34 | .251 | 133 | 208 | 23 | .937 |
| 1967–Knoxville ..........South. | 2B | 51 | 186 | 26 | 54 | 10 | 3 | 6 | 25 | .290 | 140 | 136 | 12 | .958 |
| 1968–Indianapolis ......P.C. | 2B-OF | 119 | 444 | 64 | 131 | 31 | 11 | 16 | 65 | .295 | 222 | 307 | 14 | .974 |
| 1968–Cincinnati.........Nat. | 2B | 17 | 51 | 1 | 10 | 1 | 0 | 0 | 2 | .196 | 33 | 30 | 5 | .926 |
| 1969–Indianapolis‡‡....A.A. | OF | 17 | 41 | 2 | 9 | 1 | 0 | 0 | 4 | .220 | 0 | 0 | 0 | .000 |
| 1970–Cincinnati.........Nat. | OF-3-2 | 70 | 165 | 18 | 41 | 6 | 1 | 8 | 23 | .248 | 53 | 7 | 1 | .984 |
| 1971–Cincinnati.........Nat. | OF | 99 | 337 | 39 | 89 | 24 | 2 | 9 | 34 | .264 | 167 | 6 | 6 | .966 |
| 1972–Cincinnati§ | OF-3B | 61 | 97 | 9 | 27 | 4 | 0 | 5 | 26 | .278 | 16 | 14 | 6 | .833 |
| 1973–Kansas City .....Amer. | OF-3B | 106 | 338 | 36 | 79 | 18 | 3 | 9 | 50 | .234 | 101 | 6 | 5 | .955 |
| 1974–Kansas City .....Amer. | OF-3B | 148 | 539 | 71 | 167 | 36 | 4 | 15 | 88 | .310 | 132 | 3 | 7 | .951 |
| 1975–Kansas City .....Amer. | OF-3B | 126 | 480 | 57 | 147 | 38 | 6 | 5 | 71 | .306 | 207 | 7 | 3 | .986 |
| 1976–Kansas City .....Amer. | DH | 149 | 527 | 75 | 175 | 34 | 5 | 8 | 73 | .332 | 63 | 2 | 2 | .970 |
| National League Totals .................. | | 247 | 650 | 67 | 167 | 35 | 3 | 22 | 85 | .257 | 269 | 57 | 18 | .948 |
| American League Totals ................ | | 529 | 1884 | 240 | 568 | 126 | 18 | 37 | 282 | .301 | 503 | 18 | 17 | .968 |
| Major League Totals ................. | | 776 | 2534 | 307 | 735 | 161 | 21 | 59 | 367 | .290 | 772 | 75 | 35 | .960 |

†On disabled list, June 23 through July 6.
‡On disabled list, April 26 through May 7.
‡‡On disabled list, April 18 through May 28 and from July 4 through August 5.
§Traded with Pitcher Wayne Simpson to Kansas City Royals for Pitcher Roger Nelson and Outfielder Richie Scheinblum, November 30, 1972.

CHAMPIONSHIP SERIES RECORD

| Year Club League | Pos. | G. | AB. | R. | H. | 2B. | 3B. | HR. | RBI. | B.A. | PO. | A. | E. | F.A. |
|---|---|---|---|---|---|---|---|---|---|---|---|---|---|---|
| 1970–Cincinnati.........Nat. | PH-OF | 2 | 4 | 0 | 0 | 0 | 0 | 0 | 0 | .000 | 2 | 0 | 0 | 1.000 |
| 1972–Cincinnati.........Nat. | PH | 1 | 0 | 0 | 0 | 0 | 0 | 0 | 0 | .000 | 0 | 0 | 0 | .000 |
| 1976–Kansas City ......Amer. | DH | 5 | 17 | 2 | 2 | 1 | 1 | 0 | 1 | .118 | 5 | 1 | 0 | 1.000 |
| Championship Series Totals ........... | | 8 | 21 | 2 | 2 | 1 | 1 | 0 | 1 | .095 | 7 | 1 | 0 | 1.000 |

WORLD SERIES RECORD

| Year Club League | Pos. | G. | AB. | R. | H. | 2B. | 3B. | HR. | RBI. | B.A. | PO. | A. | E. | F.A. |
|---|---|---|---|---|---|---|---|---|---|---|---|---|---|---|
| 1970–Cincinnati.........Nat. | OF | 3 | 11 | 1 | 5 | 2 | 0 | 0 | 3 | .455 | 2 | 1 | 0 | 1.000 |
| 1972–Cincinnati.........Nat. | PH-OF | 5 | 9 | 1 | 4 | 1 | 0 | 0 | 2 | .444 | 4 | 0 | 0 | 1.000 |
| World Series Totals ..................... | | 8 | 20 | 2 | 9 | 3 | 0 | 0 | 5 | .450 | 6 | 1 | 0 | 1.000 |

ALL-STAR GAME RECORD

| Year League | Pos. | AB. | R. | H. | 2B. | 3B. | HR. | RBI. | B.A. | PO. | A. | E. | F.A. |
|---|---|---|---|---|---|---|---|---|---|---|---|---|---|
| 1975–American .....∶....................... | PH | 1 | 0 | 0 | 0 | 0 | 0 | 0 | .000 | 0 | 0 | 0 | .000 |
| 1976–American ......................... | PH | 1 | 0 | 0 | 0 | 0 | 0 | 0 | .000 | 0 | 0 | 0 | .000 |
| All-Star Game Totals ..................... | | 2 | 0 | 0 | 0 | 0 | 0 | 0 | .000 | 0 | 0 | 0 | .000 |

## GALEN WILLIS McSPADDEN

Born September 4, 1952, at Van Buren, Mo.
Height, 6.01. Weight, 180.
Throws and bats lefthanded.
Hobby–Hunting.
Attended Southeast Missouri State University, Cape Girardeau, Mo., received
Bachelor of Science degree in Secondary Education.

| Year Club League | G. | IP. | W. | L. | Pct. | H. | R. | ER. | SO. | BB. | ERA. |
|---|---|---|---|---|---|---|---|---|---|---|---|
| 1974–Walla Walla.........................Northwest | 10 | 37 | 2 | 2 | .500 | 32 | 16 | 14 | 33 | 17 | 3.41 |
| 1975–Reno...................................California | 22 | 94 | 10 | 2 | .833 | 121 | 53 | 41 | 57 | 33 | 3.93 |
| 1976–Hawaii ............................P. Coast | 4 | 19 | 0 | 1 | .000 | 24 | 12 | 11 | 7 | 6 | 5.21 |
| 1976–Amarillo† ...........................Texas | 19 | 133 | 10 | 7 | .588 | 132 | 55 | 48 | 67 | 44 | 3.25 |

†On disabled list, August 30 through September 23, 1976.
Listed on San Diego Padres' 1977 spring roster.

# LARRY DEAN McWILLIAMS

Born February 10, 1954, at Wichita, Kan.
Height, 6.05. Weight, 180.
Throws and bats lefthanded.
Hobbies—Motorcycles and guitar.
Attended Paris Junior College, Paris, Tex.

| Year Club | League | G. | IP. | W. | L. | Pct. | H. | R. | ER. | SO. | BB. | ERA. |
|---|---|---|---|---|---|---|---|---|---|---|---|---|
| 1974–Greenwood† | W. Carol. | 11 | 64 | 4 | 3 | .571 | 64 | 26 | 20 | 61 | 23 | 2.81 |
| 1975–Greenwood‡ | W. Carol. | 17 | 93 | 8 | 4 | .667 | 83 | 36 | 29 | 71 | 18 | 2.81 |
| 1976–Greenwood | W. Carol. | 8 | 48 | 2 | 2 | .500 | 40 | 19 | 14 | 44 | 13 | 2.63 |
| 1976–Savannah | Southern | 16 | 74 | 3 | 8 | .273 | 82 | 41 | 38 | 37 | 33 | 4.62 |

†On disabled list, July 22 through September 25, 1974.
‡On disabled list, April 11 through June 3, 1975.
Listed on Atlanta Braves' 1977 spring roster.


# GEORGE FRANCIS MEDICH

Name pronounced Med-itch.

## (Doc)

(Nicknamed derived from the fact that he is a medical student in the off-season.)

Born December 9, 1948, at Aliquippa, Pa.
Height, 6.05. Weight, 230.
Throws and bats righthanded.
Hobby—Sports in general.
Attended University of Pittsburgh, Pittsburgh, Pa.; received Bachelor of Science
degree in Chemistry. Studied at University of Pittsburgh School of Medicine.

| Year Club | League | G. | IP. | W. | L. | Pct. | H. | R. | ER. | SO. | BB. | ERA. |
|---|---|---|---|---|---|---|---|---|---|---|---|---|
| 1970–Oneonta | NYP | 4 | 31 | 3 | 1 | .750 | 16 | 10 | 5 | 32 | 14 | 1.45 |
| 1970–Manchester | Eastern | 8 | 42 | 0 | 5 | .000 | 47 | 28 | 23 | 18 | 21 | 4.93 |
| 1971–Kinston† | Carolina | 12 | 74 | 7 | 4 | .636 | 47 | 21 | 20 | 72 | 23 | 2.43 |
| 1972–West Haven‡ | Eastern | 17 | 119 | 11 | 3 | *.786 | 89 | 28 | 19 | 70 | 40 | 1.44 |
| 1972–New York | American | 1 | 0 | 0 | 0 | .000 | 2 | 2 | 2 | 0 | 2 | ..... |
| 1973–New York | American | 34 | 235 | 14 | 9 | .609 | 217 | 84 | 77 | 145 | 74 | 2.95 |
| 1974–New York | American | 38 | 280 | 19 | 15 | .559 | 275 | 122 | 112 | 154 | 91 | 3.60 |
| 1975–New York§ | American | 38 | 272 | 16 | 16 | .500 | 271 | 115 | 106 | 132 | 72 | 3.51 |
| 1976–Pittsburgh x | National | 29 | 179 | 8 | 11 | .421 | 193 | 80 | 70 | 86 | 48 | 3.52 |
| American League Totals | | 111 | 787 | 49 | 40 | .551 | 765 | 323 | 297 | 431 | 239 | 3.40 |
| National League Totals | | 29 | 179 | 8 | 11 | .421 | 193 | 80 | 70 | 86 | 48 | 3.52 |
| Major League Totals | | 140 | 966 | 57 | 51 | .528 | 958 | 403 | 367 | 517 | 287 | 3.43 |

†On temporary inactive list from beginning of season until June 22, 1971.
‡On temporary inactive list from beginning of season until May 22, 1972.
§Traded to Pittsburgh Pirates for Pitchers Ken Brett and Dock Ellis and Second Baseman Willie Randolph, December 11, 1975.
xTraded with Pitchers Dave Giusti, Rick Langford and Doug Bair, Infielder Mitchell Page and Outfielder Tony Armas to Oakland A's for Infielders Phil Garner and Tommy Helms, and Pitcher Chris Batton, March 15, 1977.


# SAMUEL ELIAS MEJIAS

## (Sam)

Born May 9, 1953, at Santiago, Dominican Republic.
Height, 6.00. Weight, 170.
Throws and bats righthanded.
Hobbies—Ping pong and playing the guitar.
Tied for New York-Pennsylvania League lead in double plays by outfielders with 3 in 1972.

| Year Club | League | Pos. | G. | AB. | R. | H. | 2B. | 3B. | HR. | RBI. | B.A. | PO. | A. | E. | F.A. |
|---|---|---|---|---|---|---|---|---|---|---|---|---|---|---|---|
| 1971–Newark | NYP | OF | 66 | 227 | 34 | 59 | 14 | 0 | 4 | 26 | .260 | 98 | 9 | 6 | .947 |
| 1972–Danville | Midw. | OF | 39 | 107 | 13 | 18 | 2 | 0 | 0 | 4 | .168 | 52 | 4 | 0 | 1.000 |
| 1972–Newark | NYP | OF | 59 | 232 | 38 | 72 | 14 | 3 | 5 | 32 | .310 | 118 | 5 | 1 | *.992 |
| 1973–Danville | Midw. | OF | 114 | 432 | 70 | 107 | 16 | 9 | 6 | 39 | .248 | 214 | 14 | 4 | *.983 |
| 1974–Shreveport | Tex. | *OF-P | 134 | 486 | 75 | 128 | 25 | 7 | 12 | 60 | .263 | *326 | 21 | 8 | .977 |
| 1975–Thetford Mines..East. | | OF | 134 | 455 | 56 | 103 | 18 | 3 | 9 | 50 | .226 | 280 | 11 | 8 | .973 |
| 1976–Spokane† | P.C. | OF | 51 | 123 | 13 | 29 | 8 | 0 | 0 | 6 | .236 | 80 | 3 | 5 | .943 |
| 1976–Tulsa | A.A. | OF | 70 | 263 | 49 | 85 | 13 | 3 | 6 | 30 | .323 | 191 | 10 | 6 | .971 |
| 1976–St. Louis‡ | Nat. | OF | 18 | 21 | 1 | 3 | 1 | 0 | 0 | 0 | .143 | 19 | 1 | 0 | 1.000 |
| Major League Totals | | | 18 | 21 | 1 | 3 | 1 | 0 | 0 | 0 | .143 | 19 | 1 | 0 | 1.000 |

†Assigned to Tulsa on June 23 to complete deal which sent Pitcher Danny Frisella to Milwaukee Brewers, June 7, 1976.
‡Traded with Pitchers Bill Greif and Angel Torres to Montreal Expos for Pitcher Steve Dunning, Infielder Pat Scanlon, and Outfielder Tony Scott, November 6, 1976.

## PITCHING RECORD

| Year Club | League | G. | IP. | W. | L. | Pct. | H. | R. | ER. | SO. | BB. | ERA. |
|---|---|---|---|---|---|---|---|---|---|---|---|---|
| 1974–Shreveport | Texas | 1 | 1 | 0 | 0 | .000 | 3 | 3 | 3 | 0 | 0 | 27.00 |

# LUIS ANTONIO MELENDEZ

Born August 11, 1949, at Aibontio, Puerto Rico.
Height, 6.00. Weight, 165.
Throws and bats righthanded.
Tied for Midwest League lead in sacrifice flies with 9 in 1968.

| Year Club | League | Pos. | G. | AB. | R. | H. | 2B. | 3B. | HR. | RBI. | B.A. | PO. | A. | E. | F.A. |
|---|---|---|---|---|---|---|---|---|---|---|---|---|---|---|---|
| 1968–Cedar Rapids ....Midwest | | OF | 113 | 438 | 63 | 120 | 19 | 6 | 6 | 57 | .274 | ∗258 | 8 | 7 | .974 |
| 1969–Arkansas† ........Texas | | OF | 64 | 228 | 40 | 69 | 12 | 6 | 4 | 30 | .303 | 113 | 4 | 6 | .951 |
| 1970–Tulsa ................A.A. | | OF | ∗140 | ∗507 | 77 | ●155 | ∗34 | 8 | 13 | 71 | .306 | ●268 | 8 | 11 | .962 |
| 1970–St. Louis .........Nat. | | OF | 21 | 70 | 11 | 21 | 1 | 0 | 0 | 8 | .300 | 31 | 2 | 0 | 1.000 |
| 1971–St. Louis‡.........Nat. | | OF | 88 | 173 | 25 | 39 | 3 | 1 | 0 | 11 | .225 | 90 | 3 | 4 | .959 |
| 1972–St. Louis .........Nat. | | OF | 118 | 332 | 32 | 79 | 11 | 3 | 5 | 28 | .238 | 206 | 5 | 9 | .959 |
| 1973–St. Louis .........Nat. | | OF | 121 | 341 | 35 | 91 | 18 | 1 | 2 | 35 | .267 | 196 | 8 | 2 | .990 |
| 1974–St. Louis .........Nat. | | OF-SS | 83 | 124 | 15 | 27 | 4 | 3 | 0 | 8 | .218 | 84 | 1 | 2 | .977 |
| 1975–St. Louis .........Nat. | | OF | 110 | 291 | 33 | 77 | 8 | 5 | 2 | 27 | .265 | 169 | 3 | 3 | .983 |
| 1976–St.L.§-S.D. ........Nat. | | OF | 92 | 143 | 15 | 32 | 5 | 0 | 0 | 5 | .224 | 99 | 0 | 1 | .990 |
| Major League Totals ..................... | | | 633 | 1474 | 166 | 366 | 50 | 13 | 9 | 122 | .248 | 875 | 22 | 21 | .977 |

†On disabled list, June 2 through August 2, 1969.
‡On disabled list, August 3 through August 25, 1971.
§Traded to San Diego Padres for Pitcher Bill Greif, May 19, 1976.


# WILLIAM EDWIN MELTON
## (Bill)

Born July 7, 1945, at Gulfport, Miss.
Height, 6.01. Weight, 190.
Throws and bats righthanded.
Hobbies–Golf and hunting.
Attended Citrus College, Azusa, Calif.

Established major league record for consecutive strikeouts, three consecutive games (10), July 24, 24, 28, 1970.
Tied following major league records: Most strikeouts, doubleheader (7), July 24, 1970; most strikeouts, two consecutive 9-inning games (7), July 24, 1970.
Tied American League record for most strikeouts in consecutive official times at bat (11), July 23, 24, 24, 28, 1970.
Hit three home runs in a game, June 24, 1969.
Led Southern League in sacrifice flies with 9 in 1967.

| Year Club | League | Pos. | G. | AB. | R. | H. | 2B. | 3B. | HR. | RBI. | B.A. | PO. | A. | E. | F.A. |
|---|---|---|---|---|---|---|---|---|---|---|---|---|---|---|---|
| 1964–Sar. W. Sox ......Sar. Rk. | | 2-OF | 39 | 112 | 7 | 32 | 5 | 3 | 0 | 10 | .286 | 46 | 46 | 5 | .948 |
| 1965–Sarasota............Fla. St. | | OF | 129 | 393 | 40 | 77 | 13 | 5 | 6 | 49 | .196 | 168 | 8 | 5 | .972 |
| 1966–Fox Cities ........Midw. | | O-1 | 97 | 328 | 56 | 93 | 26 | 3 | 12 | 67 | .284 | 226 | 15 | 8 | .968 |
| 1967–Evansville .......South. | | ∗3-1-O | 134 | 494 | 51 | 124 | 23 | 6 | 9 | 72 | .251 | ∗125 | 290 | 29 | .935 |
| 1968–Hawaii ..............P.C. | | 3B-OF | 63 | 210 | 31 | 54 | 10 | 1 | 10 | 30 | .257 | 52 | 108 | 16 | .909 |
| 1968–Chicago ...........Amer. | | 3B | 34 | 109 | 5 | 29 | 8 | 0 | 2 | 16 | .266 | 17 | 75 | 3 | .968 |
| 1968–Syracuse ..........Int. | | 3-O-1-S | 45 | 147 | 10 | 41 | 7 | 1 | 5 | 32 | .279 | 92 | 57 | 3 | .980 |
| 1969–Chicago ...........Amer. | | 3B-OF | 157 | 556 | 67 | 142 | 26 | 2 | 23 | 87 | .255 | 125 | 325 | 22 | .953 |
| 1970–Chicago ...........Amer. | | OF-3B | 141 | 514 | 74 | 135 | 15 | 1 | 33 | 96 | .263 | 158 | 187 | 18 | .950 |
| 1971–Chicago ...........Amer. | | 3B | 150 | 543 | 72 | 146 | 18 | 2 | ∗33 | 86 | .269 | 116 | 371 | 16 | .968 |
| 1972–Chicago† .........Amer. | | 3B | 57 | 208 | 22 | 51 | 5 | 0 | 7 | 30 | .245 | 47 | 125 | 12 | .935 |
| 1973–Chicago ...........Amer. | | 3B | 152 | 560 | 83 | 155 | 29 | 1 | 20 | 87 | .277 | 115 | 347 | 23 | .953 |
| 1974–Chicago ...........Amer. | | 3B | 136 | 495 | 63 | 120 | 17 | 0 | 21 | 63 | .242 | 100 | 272 | ∗24 | .939 |
| 1975–Chicago‡ .........Amer. | | 3B | 149 | 512 | 62 | 123 | 16 | 0 | 15 | 70 | .240 | 131 | 313 | ●26 | .945 |
| 1976–California§ ........Amer. | | DH-1-3 | 118 | 341 | 41 | 71 | 17 | 3 | 6 | 42 | .208 | 227 | 36 | 3 | .989 |
| Major League Totals ..................... | | | 1094 | 3838 | 479 | 972 | 151 | 9 | 160 | 577 | .253 | 1036 | 2051 | 147 | .954 |

†On supplemental disabled list, June 30 through remainder of season.
‡Traded with Pitcher Steve Dunning to California Angels for First Baseman Jim Spencer and Outfielder Morris Nettles, December 11, 1975.
§On suspended list, July 23 to July 26; traded to Cleveland Indians, December 3, 1976, Pitcher Stan Perzanowski was assigned to California Angels from Cleveland Indians to complete deal, March 27, 1977.

## ALL-STAR GAME RECORD
Member of 1971 American League All-Star Team; did not play.


# MARIO MENDOZA (AIZPURU)

Born December 26, 1950, at Chihuahua, Mexico.
Height, 5.11. Weight, 170.
Throws and bats righthanded.
Hobby–Billiards.

Led Carolina League shortstops in double plays with 79 in 1972.

| Year Club | League | Pos. | G. | AB. | R. | H. | 2B. | 3B. | HR. | RBI. | B.A. | PO. | A. | E. | F.A. |
|---|---|---|---|---|---|---|---|---|---|---|---|---|---|---|---|
| 1970–Brad'n Pirates† Gulf C. | | SS-2B | 47 | 167 | 21 | 44 | 5 | 2 | 0 | 21 | .263 | 60 | 126 | 10 | .949 |
| 1971–Monroe.............W. Car. | | S-3 | 106 | 364 | 45 | 85 | 11 | 1 | 7 | 36 | .234 | 139 | 262 | 30 | .980 |
| 1972–Salem................Carol. | | SS | 136 | 461 | 48 | 102 | 10 | 4 | 3 | 46 | .221 | 211 | 365 | 40 | .935 |
| 1973–Sherbrooke........East. | | SS | 132 | 488 | 54 | 131 | 22 | 2 | 8 | 43 | .268 | 227 | 407 | ∗35 | .948 |
| 1974–Charleston ........Int. | | SS | 2 | 7 | 0 | 0 | 0 | 0 | 0 | 1 | .000 | 4 | 4 | 0 | 1.000 |

| Year Club League | Pos. | G. | AB. | R. | H. | 2B. | 3B. | HR. | RBI. | B.A. | PO. | A. | E. | F.A. |
|---|---|---|---|---|---|---|---|---|---|---|---|---|---|---|
| 1974–Pittsburgh ........Nat. | SS | 91 | 163 | 10 | 36 | 1 | 2 | 0 | 15 | .221 | 77 | 187 | 10 | .964 |
| 1975–Charleston ........Int. | SS | 31 | 106 | 14 | 29 | 7 | 0 | 0 | 8 | .274 | 54 | 68 | 7 | .947 |
| 1975–Pittsburgh ........Nat. | SS-3B | 56 | 50 | 8 | 9 | 1 | 0 | 0 | 2 | .180 | 29 | 70 | 5 | .952 |
| 1976–Pittsburgh ........Nat. | S-3-2 | 50 | 92 | 6 | 17 | 5 | 0 | 0 | 12 | .185 | 42 | 105 | 5 | .967 |
| 1976–Charleston ........Int. | SS-3B | 7 | 29 | 3 | 6 | 0 | 0 | 2 | 4 | .207 | 13 | 11 | 2 | .923 |
| Major League Totals ..................... | | 197 | 305 | 24 | 62 | 7 | 2 | 0 | 29 | .203 | 148 | 362 | 20 | .962 |

†On temporary inactive list, April 6 through July 14, 1970.

## CHAMPIONSHIP SERIES RECORD

| Year Club League | Pos. | G. | AB. | R. | H. | 2B. | 3B. | HR. | RBI. | B.A. | PO. | A. | E. | F.A. |
|---|---|---|---|---|---|---|---|---|---|---|---|---|---|---|
| 1974–Pittsburgh ........Nat. | SS | 3 | 5 | 0 | 1 | 0 | 0 | 0 | 1 | .200 | 4 | 7 | 0 | 1.000 |

# JAMES ANDERSON MERCHANT
## (Andy)

Born August 30, 1950, at Mobile, Ala.
Height, 5.11. Weight, 185.
Throws right and bats lefthanded.
Hobbies–Hunting and fishing.
Attended Auburn University, Auburn, Ala.
Led International League catchers in double plays with 16 in 1975.

| Year Club League | Pos. | G. | AB. | R. | H. | 2B. | 3B. | HR. | RBI. | B.A. | PO. | A. | E. | F.A. |
|---|---|---|---|---|---|---|---|---|---|---|---|---|---|---|
| 1972–Winston-Salem ..Carol. | C | 42 | 121 | 18 | 41 | 9 | 1 | 4 | 21 | .339 | 195 | 18 | 5 | .977 |
| 1973–Bristol ..............East. | C-OF | 70 | 171 | 25 | 46 | 8 | 2 | 2 | 24 | .269 | 225 | 19 | 10 | .961 |
| 1974–Winston-Salem ..Carol. | C-O-1 | 113 | 366 | 49 | 107 | 25 | 2 | 4 | 62 | .292 | 646 | 95 | 10 | .987 |
| 1975–Pawtucket ........Int. | C | 119 | 375 | 31 | 105 | 15 | 0 | 4 | 31 | .280 | 655 | ∗76 | 6 | .992 |
| 1975–Boston ..............Amer. | C | 1 | 4 | 1 | 2 | 0 | 0 | 0 | 0 | .500 | 2 | 1 | 0 | 1.000 |
| 1976–Rhode Island ....Int. | C | 68 | 203 | 34 | 60 | 12 | 0 | 3 | 22 | .296 | 214 | 24 | 0 | 1.000 |
| 1976–Boston ..............Amer. | C | 2 | 2 | 0 | 0 | 0 | 0 | 0 | 0 | .000 | 1 | 0 | 0 | 1.000 |
| Major League Totals ..................... | | 3 | 6 | 1 | 2 | 0 | 0 | 0 | 0 | .333 | 3 | 1 | 0 | 1.000 |

# JOHN ALEXANDER MESSERSMITH
## (Andy)

Born August 6, 1945, at Toms River, N. J.
Height, 6.01. Weight, 200.
Throws and bats righthanded.
Hobby–Golf.
Attended University of California, Berkeley, Calif.
Tied modern major league record for most strikeouts, consecutive, start of game, 6, May 28, 1973.
Led National League in shutouts with 7, games started with 40 and complete games with 19 in 1975.
Tied for American League lead in wild pitches with 16 in 1969.
Named righthanded pitcher on THE SPORTING NEWS National League All-Star Team, 1974.
Named pitcher on THE SPORTING NEWS National League All-Star fielding team, 1974 and 1975.

| Year Club League | G. | IP. | W. | L. | Pct. | H. | R. | ER. | SO. | BB. | ERA. |
|---|---|---|---|---|---|---|---|---|---|---|---|
| 1966–Seattle ..............P. Coast | 18 | 83 | 4 | 6 | .400 | 68 | 36 | 31 | 59 | 36 | 3.36 |
| 1967–El Paso..............Texas | 25 | 139 | 9 | 7 | .563 | 144 | 73 | 67 | 118 | 56 | 4.34 |
| 1968–Seattle ..............P. Coast | 20 | 85 | 6 | 7 | .462 | 70 | 34 | 28 | 86 | 32 | 2.96 |
| 1968–California ..........American | 28 | 81 | 4 | 2 | .667 | 44 | 21 | 20 | 74 | 35 | 2.22 |
| 1969–California ..........American | 40 | 250 | 16 | 11 | .593 | 169 | 81 | 70 | 211 | 100 | 2.52 |
| 1970–California ..........American | 37 | 195 | 11 | 10 | .524 | 144 | 75 | 65 | 162 | 78 | 3.00 |
| 1971–California ..........American | 38 | 277 | 20 | 13 | .606 | 224 | 112 | 92 | 179 | 121 | 2.99 |
| 1972–California† ........American | 25 | 170 | 8 | 11 | .421 | 125 | 56 | 53 | 142 | 68 | 2.81 |
| 1973–Los Angeles ......National | 33 | 250 | 14 | 10 | .583 | 196 | 90 | 75 | 177 | 77 | 2.70 |
| 1974–Los Angeles ......National | 39 | 292 | ●20 | 6 | ∗.769 | 227 | 93 | 84 | 221 | 94 | 2.59 |
| 1975–Los Angeles‡......National | 42 | ∗322 | 19 | 14 | .576 | 244 | 92 | 82 | 213 | 96 | 2.29 |
| 1976–Atlanta ..............National | 29 | 207 | 11 | 11 | .500 | 166 | 83 | 70 | 135 | 74 | 3.04 |
| American League Totals........................... | 168 | 973 | 59 | 47 | .557 | 706 | 345 | 300 | 768 | 402 | 2.77 |
| National League Totals........................... | 143 | 1071 | 64 | 41 | .610 | 833 | 358 | 311 | 746 | 341 | 2.61 |
| Major League Totals ..................... | 311 | 2044 | 123 | 88 | .583 | 1539 | 703 | 611 | 1514 | 743 | 2.69 |

†On disabled list, May 31 through July 19. Traded with Third Baseman Ken McMullen to Los Angeles Dodgers for Outfielder Frank Robinson, Infielders Billy Grabarkewitz and Bob Valentine and Pitchers Bill Singer and Mike Strahler, November 28, 1972.

‡Played out option year and granted free agency, March 16, 1976; signed as free agent by Atlanta Braves for an estimated $1.75 million, April 10, 1976.

## CHAMPIONSHIP SERIES RECORD

| Year Club League | G. | IP. | W. | L. | Pct. | H. | R. | ER. | SO. | BB. | ERA. |
|---|---|---|---|---|---|---|---|---|---|---|---|
| 1974–Los Angeles ......................National | 1 | 7 | 1 | 0 | 1.000 | 8 | 2 | 2 | 0 | 3 | 2.57 |

## WORLD SERIES RECORD

Tied World Series record for most games lost, pitcher, 5-game series, 2 in 1974.

| Year Club League | G. | IP. | W. | L. | Pct. | H. | R. | ER. | SO. | BB. | ERA. |
|---|---|---|---|---|---|---|---|---|---|---|---|
| 1974–Los Angeles ......................National | 2 | 14 | 0 | 2 | .000 | 11 | 8 | 7 | 12 | 7 | 4.50 |

## ALL-STAR GAME RECORD

| Year League | IP. | W. | L. | Pct. | H. | R. | ER. | SO. | BB. | ERA. |
|---|---|---|---|---|---|---|---|---|---|---|
| 1974–National | 3 | 0 | 0 | .000 | 2 | 2 | 2 | 4 | 3 | 6.00 |

Member of American League All-Star Team for 1971 game; did not play.
Member of National League All-Star Team for 1975 game; did not play.

## CLARENCE EDWARD METZGER
### (Butch)
(Nicknamed by older sister.)

Born May 23, 1952, at Lafayette, Ind.
Height, 6.01. Weight, 195.
Throws and bats righthanded.
Hobbies–Hunting and fishing.

Established following major league records: most consecutive games won at start of career for relief pitcher, 12, 1976; most games by pitcher in rookie season, 77, 1976.
Tied for Pacific Coast League lead in games started by pitchers with 28 in 1974.
Named National League Rookie of the Year by Baseball Writers Association of America, 1976.
Named National League Rookie Pitcher of the Year by THE SPORTING NEWS, 1976.
Received reported $27,000 bonus to sign with San Francisco Giants, 1970.

| Year Club | League | G. | IP. | W. | L. | Pct. | H. | R. | ER. | SO. | BB. | ERA. |
|---|---|---|---|---|---|---|---|---|---|---|---|---|
| 1970–Great Falls | Pioneer | 14 | 82 | 2 | •9 | .182 | 80 | 49 | 38 | 92 | 38 | 4.17 |
| 1971–Decatur | Midwest | 13 | 68 | 3 | 7 | .300 | 83 | 64 | 49 | 65 | 48 | 6.49 |
| 1971–Magic Valley | Pioneer | 13 | *106 | 6 | 5 | .545 | 88 | 52 | *46 | 108 | 46 | 3.91 |
| 1972–Decatur | Midwest | 18 | 116 | 4 | 6 | .400 | 107 | 57 | 46 | 117 | 40 | 3.57 |
| 1972–Amarillo | Texas | 5 | 24 | 2 | 1 | .667 | 16 | 6 | 3 | 35 | 3 | 1.13 |
| 1973–Amarillo | Texas | 17 | 131 | 10 | 3 | .769 | 105 | 49 | 40 | 108 | 49 | 2.75 |
| 1973–Phoenix | P. Coast | 13 | 72 | 2 | 5 | .286 | 87 | 41 | 37 | 39 | 22 | 4.63 |
| 1974–Phoenix | P. Coast | 33 | *204 | 12 | 10 | .545 | 209 | 120 | 107 | *148 | 90 | 4.72 |
| 1974–San Francisco† | National | 10 | 13 | 1 | 0 | 1.000 | 11 | 5 | 5 | 5 | 12 | 3.46 |
| 1975–Hawaii | P. Coast | 36 | 169 | 15 | 7 | *.682 | 163 | 86 | 68 | 114 | 78 | 3.62 |
| 1975–San Diego | National | 4 | 5 | 1 | 0 | 1.000 | 6 | 4 | 4 | 6 | 4 | 7.20 |
| 1976–San Diego | National | 77 | 123 | 11 | 4 | .733 | 119 | 44 | 40 | 89 | 52 | 2.93 |
| Major League Totals | | 91 | 141 | 13 | 4 | .765 | 136 | 53 | 49 | 100 | 68 | 3.13 |

†Traded with Second Baseman Tito Fuentes to San Diego Padres for Second Baseman Derrel Thomas, December 6, 1974.

## ROGER HENRY METZGER

Born October 10, 1947, at Fredericksburg, Tex.
Height, 6.00. Weight, 165.
Throws right and bats righthanded.
Hobbies–Water skiing, golf, fishing and hunting.
Attended Arizona State University, Tempe, Ariz., and St. Edward's University, Austin, Tex.;
received degree in Mathematics.

Established major league record for most consecutive errorless games by shortstop, season, 59, June 8–August 15 (1st game), 1976.
Led National League shortstops in double plays with 101 in 1972.
Named shortstop on THE SPORTING NEWS National League All-Star fielding team, 1973.

| Year Club | League | Pos. | G. | AB. | R. | H. | 2B. | 3B. | HR. | RBI. | B.A. | PO. | A. | E. | F.A. |
|---|---|---|---|---|---|---|---|---|---|---|---|---|---|---|---|
| 1969–Tacoma | P. C. | SS | 80 | 250 | 34 | 58 | 3 | 2 | 0 | 15 | .232 | 148 | 276 | 22 | .951 |
| 1970–Tacoma | P. C. | SS | 134 | 492 | 59 | 133 | 20 | 7 | 1 | 32 | .270 | 212 | *483 | 37 | .949 |
| 1970–Chicago† | Nat. | SS | 1 | 2 | 0 | 0 | 0 | 0 | 0 | 0 | .000 | 1 | 4 | 1 | .833 |
| 1971–Houston | Nat. | SS | 150 | 562 | 64 | 132 | 14 | •11 | 0 | 26 | .235 | *275 | 459 | 17 | .977 |
| 1972–Houston | Nat. | SS | 153 | 641 | 84 | 142 | 12 | 3 | 2 | 38 | .222 | 238 | 504 | 22 | .971 |
| 1973–Houston | Nat. | SS | 154 | 580 | 67 | 145 | 11 | *14 | 1 | 35 | .250 | 231 | 429 | 12 | *.982 |
| 1974–Houston‡ | Nat. | SS | 143 | 572 | 66 | 145 | 18 | 10 | 0 | 30 | .253 | 238 | 451 | 17 | .976 |
| 1975–Houston | Nat. | SS | 127 | 450 | 54 | 102 | 7 | 9 | 2 | 26 | .227 | 186 | 441 | 15 | .977 |
| 1976–Houston | Nat. | *SS-2B | 152 | 481 | 37 | 101 | 13 | 8 | 0 | 29 | .210 | 258 | 468 | 10 | *.986 |
| Major League Totals | | | 880 | 3288 | 372 | 767 | 75 | 55 | 5 | 184 | .233 | 1427 | 2756 | 94 | .978 |

†Traded to Houston Astros for Shortstop Hector Torres, October 12, 1970.
‡On supplemental disabled list, April 29 to May 17, 1974.

## DANIEL THOMAS MEYER
### (Dan)

Born August 3, 1952, at Hamilton, O.
Height, 5.11. Weight, 180.
Throws right and bats lefthanded.
Attended Santa Ana College, Santa Ana, Calif., and University
of Arizona, Tucson, Ariz.

Led Appalachian League in total bases with 158 in 1972.
Led American Association in sacrifice flies with 9 in 1974.
Named Appalachian League Player of the Year in 1972.

| Year    Club    League | Pos. | G. | AB. | R. | H. | 2B. | 3B. | HR. | RBI. | B.A. | PO. | A. | E. | F.A. |
|---|---|---|---|---|---|---|---|---|---|---|---|---|---|---|
| 1972–Bristol ..............Appal. | ∗3-2-O | 65 | 235 | 54 | ∗93 | 11 | 6 | 14 | 46 | ∗.396 | 69 | ∗124 | 13 | .937 |
| 1973–Lakeland ..........Fla. St. | 2B | 133 | 473 | 63 | 114 | 17 | 6 | 10 | 59 | .241 | 295 | 297 | 21 | .966 |
| 1974–Evansville ........A. A. | 3-O-1 | 129 | 484 | 75 | 146 | 26 | 7 | 9 | 57 | .302 | 238 | 153 | 22 | .947 |
| 1974–Detroit ..............Amer. | OF | 13 | 50 | 5 | 10 | 1 | 1 | 3 | 7 | .200 | 29 | 0 | 1 | .967 |
| 1975–Detroit† ............Amer. | OF-1B | 122 | 470 | 56 | 111 | 17 | 3 | 8 | 47 | .236 | 571 | 41 | 12 | .981 |
| 1976–Detroit‡ ............Amer. | O-1-DH | 105 | 294 | 37 | 74 | 8 | 4 | 2 | 16 | .252 | 244 | 14 | 2 | .992 |
| Major League Totals ...................... | | 240 | 814 | 98 | 195 | 26 | 8 | 13 | 70 | .240 | 844 | 55 | 15 | .984 |

†On supplemental disabled list, July 20 to August 6, 1975.
‡Selected by Seattle Mariners in Americ⸀ League expansion draft, November 5, 1976.

## LAWRENCE WILLIAM MILBOURNE
Name pronounced MILL-born.
### (Larry)

Born February 14, 1951, at Port Norris, N. J.
Height, 6.00. Weight, 165.
Throws right and bats left and righthanded.
Hobbies–Music and reading.
Attended Glassboro State College, Glassboro, N. J., and Cumberland
County Junior College, Vineland, N. J.
Brother of Monty Milbourne, former minor leaguer in Chicago White Sox' organization.

| Year    Club    League | Pos. | G. | AB. | R. | H. | 2B. | 3B. | HR. | RBI. | B.A. | PO. | A. | E. | F.A. |
|---|---|---|---|---|---|---|---|---|---|---|---|---|---|---|
| 1969–Bluefield† ..........Appal. | SS | •69 | 246 | 49 | 75 | 10 | •6 | 4 | 35 | .305 | 94 | 171 | ∗28 | .904 |
| 1970– ......................... | | | | | (Did not play) | | | | | | | | | |
| 1972–Shreveport‡‡ ....Midw. | ∗2-S-3 | ∗123 | ∗518 | 69 | ∗156 | 23 | 5 | 5 | 38 | .301 | 267 | 256 | 27 | ∗.951 |
| 1971–Decatur‡ .........Texas | 2B | 122 | 416 | 50 | 110 | 14 | 5 | 2 | 36 | .264 | 273 | 314 | 25 | .959 |
| 1973–Tulsa§ ..............A. A. | 2-3-O-S | 111 | 367 | 55 | 104 | 13 | 6 | 5 | 43 | .283 | 158 | 197 | 16 | .957 |
| 1974–Houston ............Nat. | 2-S-O | 112 | 136 | 31 | 38 | 2 | 1 | 0 | 9 | .279 | 102 | 148 | 7 | .973 |
| 1975–Iowa...................A. A. | 2B | 24 | 77 | 9 | 17 | 3 | 1 | 1 | 6 | .221 | 33 | 47 | 8 | .909 |
| 1975–Houston ............Nat. | 2B-SS | 73 | 151 | 17 | 32 | 1 | 2 | 1 | 9 | .212 | 95 | 136 | 10 | .959 |
| 1976–Houston ............Nat. | 2B-PH | 59 | 145 | 22 | 36 | 4 | 0 | 0 | 7 | .248 | 67 | 100 | 6 | .965 |
| 1976–Memphis x .........Int. | 2B-SS | 71 | 292 | 45 | 95 | 12 | 2 | 5 | 31 | .325 | 132 | 245 | 13 | .967 |
| Major League Totals ...................... | | 244 | 432 | 70 | 106 | 7 | 3 | 1 | 25 | .245 | 264 | 384 | 23 | .966 |

†Released by Bluefield (Baltimore Orioles' organization), April 7, 1970; signed as free agent by Decatur (San Francisco Giants' organization), April 2, 1971.
‡Drafted from Amarillo (San Francisco Giants' organization) by Salt Lake City (California Angels' organization), November 29, 1971.
‡‡Drafted from Shreveport (California Angels' organization) by Tulsa (St. Louis Cardinals' organization), November 27, 1972.
§Drafted from Tulsa (St. Louis Cardinals' organization) by Houston Astros, December 3, 1973.
xTraded to Seattle Mariners for Pitcher Roy Thomas, March 30, 1977.

## FELIX BERNARDO MARTINEZ MILLAN
Name Pronounced mee-YAWN.

Born August 21, 1943, at Yabucoa, Puerto Rico.
Height, 5.11. Weight, 172.
Throws and bats righthanded.

Tied major league records for most double plays by second baseman, extra-inning game, 6, August 5, 1971 (17 innings), and most plate appearances, extra-inning game, 12, September 11, 1974 (25 innings).
Made six hits in one game, July 6, 1970, against San Francisco Giants.
Led National League in sacrifice hits with 24 in 1974.
Led Florida State League in sacrifice hits with 16 in 1964.
Named second baseman on THE SPORTING NEWS National League All-Star fielding team, 1969 and 1972.
Named Minor League Player of the Year by THE SPORTING NEWS, 1967.

| Year    Club    League | Pos. | G. | AB. | R. | H. | 2B. | 3B. | HR. | RBI. | B.A. | PO. | A. | E. | F.A. |
|---|---|---|---|---|---|---|---|---|---|---|---|---|---|---|
| 1964–Daytona Beach† Fla. St. | 2B | 95 | 351 | 48 | 102 | 9 | 7 | 1 | 35 | .291 | 198 | 274 | 29 | .942 |
| 1965–Yakima ...........Northw. | 2-SS | 91 | 366 | 65 | 118 | 15 | 6 | 5 | 35 | .322 | 187 | 223 | 25 | .949 |
| 1965–Austin ..............Texas | 2B-3B | 36 | 160 | 22 | 41 | 5 | 1 | 4 | 12 | .256 | 74 | 107 | 12 | .943 |
| 1966–Austin ..............Texas | 2B | 35 | 135 | 17 | 42 | 5 | 1 | 1 | 6 | .311 | 89 | 77 | 3 | .982 |
| 1966–Atlanta..............Nat. | 2-3B-SS | 37 | 91 | 20 | 25 | 6 | 0 | 0 | 5 | .275 | 57 | 56 | 3 | .974 |
| 1966–Richmond..........Int. | 2B-3B | 41 | 170 | 23 | 52 | 10 | 1 | 6 | 29 | .306 | 100 | 137 | 9 | .963 |
| 1967–Richmond..........Int. | 2B-SS | 106 | 435 | 53 | 135 | 10 | 9 | 4 | 41 | .310 | 227 | 316 | 13 | .977 |
| 1967–Atlanta..............Nat. | 2B | 41 | 136 | 13 | 32 | 3 | 3 | 2 | 6 | .235 | 84 | 125 | 6 | .972 |
| 1968–Atlanta..............Nat. | 2B | 149 | 570 | 49 | 165 | 22 | 2 | 1 | 33 | .289 | 330 | 438 | 16 | .980 |
| 1969–Atlanta..............Nat. | 2B | 162 | 652 | 98 | 174 | 23 | 5 | 6 | 57 | .267 | ∗373 | ∗444 | 17 | ∗.980 |
| 1970–Atlanta..............Nat. | 2B | 142 | 590 | 100 | 183 | 25 | 5 | 2 | 37 | .310 | 337 | 359 | 15 | .979 |
| 1971–Atlanta..............Nat. | 2B | 143 | 577 | 65 | 167 | 20 | 8 | 2 | 45 | .289 | 373 | 437 | 15 | .982 |
| 1972–Atlanta‡ ............Nat. | 2B | 125 | 498 | 46 | 128 | 19 | 3 | 1 | 38 | .257 | 273 | 339 | 8 | .987 |
| 1973–New York..........Nat. | 2B | 153 | 638 | 82 | 185 | 23 | 4 | 3 | 37 | .290 | 410 | 411 | 9 | .989 |
| 1974–New York..........Nat. | 2B | 136 | 518 | 50 | 139 | 15 | 2 | 1 | 33 | .268 | 374 | 315 | 15 | .979 |
| 1975–New York..........Nat. | 2B | •162 | 676 | 81 | 191 | 37 | 2 | 1 | 56 | .283 | 379 | 419 | 23 | .972 |
| 1976–New York..........Nat. | 2B | 139 | 531 | 55 | 150 | 25 | 2 | 1 | 35 | .282 | 311 | 315 | 15 | .977 |
| Major League Totals ...................... | | 1389 | 5477 | 659 | 1539 | 218 | 36 | 20 | 382 | .281 | 3301 | 3658 | 142 | .980 |

†Drafted by Milwaukee Braves from Dallas (Kansas City Athletics' organization), November 30, 1964.
‡Traded with Pitcher George Stone to New York Mets for Pitchers Danny Frisella and Gary Gentry, November 2, 1972.

## CHAMPIONSHIP SERIES RECORD

| Year Club | League | Pos. | G. | AB. | R. | H. | 2B. | 3B. | HR. | RBI. | B.A. | PO. | A. | E. | F.A. |
|---|---|---|---|---|---|---|---|---|---|---|---|---|---|---|---|
| 1969-Atlanta | Nat. | 2B | 3 | 12 | 2 | 4 | 1 | 0 | 0 | 0 | .333 | 3 | 9 | 1 | .923 |
| 1973-New York | Nat. | 2B | 5 | 19 | 5 | 6 | 0 | 0 | 0 | 2 | .316 | 9 | 11 | 0 | 1.000 |
| Championship Series Totals | | 8 | 31 | 7 | 10 | 1 | 0 | 0 | 2 | .323 | 12 | 20 | 1 | .970 |

## WORLD SERIES RECORD

Tied World Series record for most at-bats, extra-inning game, no hits, 6, October 14, 1973, 12 innings.

| Year Club | League | Pos. | G. | AB. | R. | H. | 2B. | 3B. | HR. | RBI. | B.A. | PO. | A. | E. | F.A. |
|---|---|---|---|---|---|---|---|---|---|---|---|---|---|---|---|
| 1973-New York | Nat. | 2B | 7 | 32 | 3 | 6 | 1 | 1 | 0 | 1 | .188 | 16 | 13 | 3 | .906 |

## ALL-STAR GAME RECORD

| Year | League | Pos. | AB. | R. | H. | 2B. | 3B. | HR. | RBI. | B.A. | PO. | A. | E. | F.A. |
|---|---|---|---|---|---|---|---|---|---|---|---|---|---|---|
| 1969-National | | 2B | 1 | 1 | 1 | 0 | 0 | 2 | .250 | 1 | 1 | 0 | 1.000 |
| 1971-National | | 2B | 0 | 0 | 0 | 0 | 0 | 0 | 0 | .000 | 1 | 1 | 0 | 1.000 |
| All-Star Game Totals | | 4 | 1 | 1 | 1 | 0 | 0 | 2 | .250 | 2 | 2 | 0 | 1.000 |

Named to National League All-Star Team in 1970; replaced due to injury.

## CHARLES BRUCE MILLER

(Known by middle name.)

Born March 3, 1947, at Fort Wayne, Ind.
Height, 6.01. Weight, 182.
Throws and bats righthanded.
Hobbies–Bridge, dogs, golf, hunting and fishing.
Attended University of Indiana, Bloomington, Ind.; received Bachelor
of Science degree in Education.

Led Pacific Coast League shortstops in double plays with 84 in 1973.
Led Southern League shortstops in double plays with 96 and total chances with 646 in 1971.
Led Northern League shortstops in double plays with 32 and total chances with 296 in 1970.
Tied for Northern League lead in sacrifice flies with 5 in 1970.

| Year Club | League | Pos. | G. | AB. | R. | H. | 2B. | 3B. | HR. | RBI. | B.A. | PO. | A. | E. | F.A. |
|---|---|---|---|---|---|---|---|---|---|---|---|---|---|---|---|
| 1970-Duluth | North. | SS | 69 | 257 | 43 | 71 | 15 | 2 | 3 | 37 | .276 | *107 | *159 | 30 | *.899 |
| 1971-Asheville | South. | SS | 138 | 449 | 59 | 129 | 16 | 1 | 14 | 54 | .287 | *201 | *425 | 20 | .969 |
| 1972-Tucson† | P. C. | SS-3B | 138 | 495 | 60 | 143 | 19 | 3 | 1 | 58 | .289 | 180 | 378 | 33 | .944 |
| 1973-S.L.C.‡-Phx. | P. C. | *SS-3 | 108 | 393 | 50 | 123 | 17 | 6 | 1 | 42 | .313 | *184 | *328 | *32 | .941 |
| 1973-San Francisco | Nat. | 3-2-S | 12 | 21 | 1 | 3 | 0 | 0 | 0 | 2 | .143 | 7 | 14 | 2 | .913 |
| 1974-Phoenix | P. C. | SS | 33 | 140 | 18 | 50 | 5 | 1 | 1 | 19 | .357 | 56 | 103 | 7 | .958 |
| 1974-San Francisco | Nat. | 3-S-2 | 73 | 198 | 19 | 55 | 7 | 1 | 0 | 16 | .278 | 55 | 161 | 12 | .947 |
| 1975-San Francisco | Nat. | 3-2-S | 99 | 309 | 22 | 74 | 6 | 3 | 1 | 31 | .239 | 114 | 186 | 15 | .952 |
| 1976-Phoenix | P. C. | 3-2-S | 87 | 351 | 44 | 92 | 17 | 2 | 2 | 37 | .262 | 118 | 244 | 14 | .963 |
| 1976-San Francisco | Nat. | 2B-3B | 12 | 25 | 1 | 4 | 1 | 0 | 0 | 2 | .160 | 9 | 16 | 2 | .926 |
| Major League Totals | | 196 | 553 | 43 | 136 | 14 | 4 | 1 | 51 | .246 | 185 | 377 | 31 | .948 |

†Traded by Chicago White Sox to California Angels for Pitcher Eddie Fisher, August 17, 1972; White Sox assigned Catcher Bruce Kimm from Knoxville to Salt Lake City, September 1, 1972, to complete deal.

‡Traded by California Angels to San Francisco Giants for Third Baseman Alan Gallagher, April 20, 1973.

## DYAR K. MILLER

Born May 29, 1946, at Batesville, Ind.
Height, 6.01. Weight, 195.
Throws and bats righthanded.
Attended Utah State University, Logan, Utah.

Pitched seven-inning, 10-0 no-hit victory against Amarillo, May 9, 1970.

| Year Club | League | G. | IP. | W. | L. | Pct. | H. | R. | ER. | SO. | BB. | ERA. |
|---|---|---|---|---|---|---|---|---|---|---|---|---|
| 1968-Huron† | Northern | 1 | 1 | 0 | 0 | .000 | 2 | 4 | 3 | 0 | 3 | 27.00 |
| 1969-Stockton | California | 25 | 116 | 4 | 4 | .500 | 80 | 36 | 30 | 111 | 58 | 2.33 |
| 1970-Dallas-Fort Worth | Texas | 26 | 170 | 12 | 10 | .545 | 149 | 69 | 61 | 102 | 83 | 3.23 |
| 1971-Dallas-Fort Worth | Texas | 25 | 88 | 3 | 8 | .273 | 65 | 47 | 34 | 74 | 58 | 3.48 |
| 1972-Asheville‡ | Southern | 15 | 49 | 4 | 1 | .800 | 50 | 25 | 24 | 46 | 27 | 4.41 |
| 1973-Rochester§ | Int'national | 15 | 72 | 6 | 3 | .667 | 53 | 27 | 22 | 41 | 29 | 2.75 |
| 1974-Rochester | Int'national | 28 | 190 | 12 | 8 | .600 | 143 | 65 | 57 | 138 | 95 | 2.70 |
| 1975-Rochester | Int'national | 19 | 41 | 5 | 0 | 1.000 | 24 | 10 | 10 | 38 | 25 | 2.20 |
| 1975-Baltimore | American | 30 | 46 | 6 | 3 | .667 | 32 | 14 | 14 | 33 | 16 | 2.74 |
| 1976-Baltimore | American | 49 | 89 | 2 | 4 | .333 | 79 | 31 | 29 | 37 | 36 | 2.93 |
| Major League Totals | | 79 | 135 | 8 | 7 | .533 | 111 | 45 | 43 | 70 | 52 | 2.87 |

†Released by Philadelphia Phillies' organization, July 28, 1968; signed as free agent by Baltimore Orioles' organization, January 16, 1969.

‡On disabled list from beginning of season until April 24, 1972.

§On disabled list, June 11 to June 25, 1973. On temporary inactive list, August 18 to September 2, 1973.

## RECORD AS CATCHER

| Year Club | League | Pos. | G. | AB. | R. | H. | 2B. | 3B. | HR. | RBI. | B.A. | PO. | A. | E. | F.A. |
|---|---|---|---|---|---|---|---|---|---|---|---|---|---|---|---|
| 1968-Huron† | North. | C | 4 | 7 | 1 | 1 | 0 | 0 | 0 | 0 | .143 | 18 | 3 | 2 | .913 |

## RANDALL SCOTT MILLER
### (Randy)

Born March 18, 1953, at Oxnard, Calif.
Height, 6.01. Weight, 180.
Throws and bats righthanded.
Hobbies—Fishing, golf and surfing.
Attended University of California at San Diego, San Diego, Calif.
Tied for Southern League lead in saves with 19 in 1976.

| Year Club | League | G. | IP. | W. | L. | Pct. | H. | R. | ER. | SO. | BB. | ERA. |
|---|---|---|---|---|---|---|---|---|---|---|---|---|
| 1974—Lodi | California | 15 | 94 | 3 | 6 | .333 | 96 | 45 | 37 | 62 | 29 | 3.54 |
| 1975—Miami | Florida St. | *55 | 98 | 8 | 5 | .615 | 68 | 26 | 20 | 64 | 35 | 1.84 |
| 1976—Charlotte | Southern | 39 | 62 | 3 | 1 | .750 | 47 | 11 | 10 | 43 | 15 | 1.45 |

Listed on Baltimore Orioles' 1977 spring roster.

## RICHARD ALLAN MILLER
### (Rick)

Born April 19, 1948, at Grand Rapids, Mich.
Height, 6.01. Weight, 185.
Throws and bats lefthanded.
Hobbies—paddle ball and most sports activities.
Attended Michigan State University, East Lansing, Mich.
Brother-in-law of Carlton Fisk, catcher for Boston Red Sox.
Led International League batters in bases on balls with 106 in 1971.

| Year Club | League | Pos. | G. | AB. | R. | H. | 2B. | 3B. | HR. | RBI. | B.A. | PO. | A. | E. | F.A. |
|---|---|---|---|---|---|---|---|---|---|---|---|---|---|---|---|
| 1969—Pittsfield | East. | OF | 77 | 221 | 25 | 58 | 7 | 1 | 6 | 32 | .262 | 150 | 8 | 3 | .981 |
| 1970—Pawtucket | East. | OF | 113 | 381 | 69 | 94 | 16 | 4 | 12 | 56 | .247 | 227 | 5 | 5 | .979 |
| 1971—Louisville | Int. | OF | 133 | 461 | 79 | 114 | 24 | 2 | 15 | 58 | .247 | 267 | 21 | 6 | .980 |
| 1971—Boston | Amer. | OF | 15 | 33 | 9 | 11 | 5 | 0 | 1 | 7 | .333 | 30 | 1 | 1 | .969 |
| 1972—Boston | Amer. | OF | 89 | 98 | 13 | 21 | 4 | 1 | 3 | 15 | .214 | 80 | 7 | 3 | .967 |
| 1973—Boston | Amer. | OF | 143 | 441 | 65 | 115 | 17 | 7 | 6 | 43 | .261 | 301 | 4 | 7 | .978 |
| 1974—Boston | Amer. | OF | 114 | 280 | 41 | 73 | 8 | 1 | 5 | 22 | .261 | 253 | 7 | 3 | .989 |
| 1975—Boston | Amer. | OF | 77 | 108 | 21 | 21 | 2 | 1 | 0 | 15 | .194 | 101 | 2 | 2 | .981 |
| 1976—Boston | Amer. | OF-PH | 105 | 269 | 40 | 76 | 15 | 3 | 0 | 27 | .283 | 220 | 4 | 2 | .991 |
| Major League Totals | | | 543 | 1229 | 189 | 317 | 51 | 13 | 15 | 129 | .258 | 985 | 25 | 18 | .982 |

#### WORLD SERIES RECORD

| Year Club | League | Pos. | G. | AB. | R. | H. | 2B. | 3B. | HR. | RBI. | B.A. | PO. | A. | E. | F.A. |
|---|---|---|---|---|---|---|---|---|---|---|---|---|---|---|---|
| 1975—Boston | Amer. | OF-PH | 3 | 2 | 0 | 0 | 0 | 0 | 0 | 0 | .000 | 1 | 0 | 0 | 1.000 |

## ROGER WESLEY MILLER

Born August 1, 1954, at Connellsville, Pa.
Height, 6.02. Weight, 210.
Throws and bats righthanded.
Hobbies—Hunting and fishing.
Tied for Pacific Coast League lead in complete games by pitchers with 11 in 1974.

| Year Club | League | G. | IP. | W. | L. | Pct. | H. | R. | ER. | SO. | BB. | ERA. |
|---|---|---|---|---|---|---|---|---|---|---|---|---|
| 1972—Newark | NYP | 13 | 41 | 1 | 3 | .250 | 37 | 26 | 25 | 43 | 31 | 5.49 |
| 1973—Danville | Midwest | 25 | 103 | 8 | 4 | .667 | 86 | 49 | 38 | 85 | 47 | 3.32 |
| 1974—Sacramento | P. Coast | 32 | 185 | 11 | 5 | .688 | 206 | 118 | 92 | 101 | 86 | 4.48 |
| 1974—Milwaukee | American | 2 | 2 | 0 | 0 | .000 | 3 | 3 | 3 | 2 | 0 | 13.50 |
| 1975—Sacramento† | P. Coast | 23 | 149 | 7 | 12 | .368 | 186 | 111 | 102 | 73 | 57 | 6.16 |
| 1976—Spokane‡ | P. Coast | | | | | | (Did not play) | | | | | |
| Major League Totals | | 2 | 2 | 0 | 0 | .000 | 3 | 3 | 3 | 2 | 0 | 13.50 |

†On disabled list, August 1 through September 2.
‡On disabled list entire season due to elbow injury.
Listed on Milwaukee Brewers' 1977 spring roster.

## JOHN DAVID MILNER

Born December 28, 1949, at Atlanta, Ga.
Height, 6.00. Weight, 185.
Throws and bats lefthanded.
Tied major league record for most plate appearances, extra-inning game, 12, September 11, 1974 (25 innings).
Led Texas League batters in bases on balls with 100 in 1970.

| Year Club | League | Pos. | G. | AB. | R. | H. | 2B. | 3B. | HR. | RBI. | B.A. | PO. | A. | E. | F.A. |
|---|---|---|---|---|---|---|---|---|---|---|---|---|---|---|---|
| 1968—Marion | Appal. | OF | 67 | 234 | 51 | 75 | *18 | 1 | 1 | 28 | .321 | 88 | 7 | 6 | .941 |
| 1969—Pompano Beach | Fla. St. | 1-O | 103 | 8 | 4 | 65 | 12 | 23 | 3 | 2 | 3 | 18 | .354 | 118 | 6 | 0 | 1.000 |
| 1969—Visalia | Calif. | OF-1B | 111 | 393 | 90 | 128 | 20 | 4 | 15 | 63 | .326 | 388 | 26 | 13 | .970 |
| 1970—Memphis | Texas | 1B-O | *136 | 461 | 98 | 137 | 19 | 8 | 20 | 71 | .297 | 792 | 36 | 10 | .988 |
| 1971—Tidewater | Int. | OF-1B | 133 | 497 | 82 | 144 | 27 | 5 | 19 | 87 | .290 | 309 | 12 | 8 | .976 |
| 1971—New York | Nat. | OF | 9 | 18 | 1 | 3 | 1 | 0 | 0 | 1 | .167 | 8 | 1 | 0 | 1.000 |

| Year Club League | Pos. | G. | AB. | R. | H. | 2B. | 3B. | HR. | RBI. | B.A. | PO. | A. | E. | F.A. |
|---|---|---|---|---|---|---|---|---|---|---|---|---|---|---|
| 1972–New York..........Nat. | OF-1B | 117 | 362 | 52 | 86 | 12 | 2 | 17 | 38 | .238 | 233 | 13 | 6 | .976 |
| 1973–New York†........Nat. | 1B-OF | 129 | 451 | 69 | 108 | 12 | 3 | 23 | 72 | .239 | 804 | 51 | 11 | .987 |
| 1974–New York..........Nat. | 1B | 137 | 507 | 70 | 128 | 19 | 0 | 20 | 63 | .252 | 1147 | 77 | 7 | .994 |
| 1975–New York..........Nat. | OF-1B | 91 | 220 | 24 | 42 | 11 | 0 | 7 | 29 | .191 | 267 | 27 | 3 | .990 |
| 1976–New York..........Nat. | OF-1B | 127 | 443 | 56 | 120 | 25 | 4 | 15 | 78 | .271 | 239 | 9 | 3 | .988 |
| Major League Totals ..................... | | 565 | 2001 | 272 | 487 | 80 | 9 | 82 | 281 | .243 | 2698 | 178 | 30 | .990 |

†On supplemental disabled list, April 28 to May 13, 1973.

CHAMPIONSHIP SERIES RECORD

| Year Club League | Pos. | G. | AB. | R. | H. | 2B. | 3B. | HR. | RBI. | B.A. | PO. | A. | E. | F.A. |
|---|---|---|---|---|---|---|---|---|---|---|---|---|---|---|
| 1973–New York..........Nat. | 1B | 5 | 17 | 2 | 3 | 0 | 0 | 0 | 1 | .176 | 37 | 6 | 0 | 1.000 |

WORLD SERIES RECORD

| Year Club League | Pos. | G. | AB. | R. | H. | 2B. | 3B. | HR. | RBI. | B.A. | PO. | A. | E. | F.A. |
|---|---|---|---|---|---|---|---|---|---|---|---|---|---|---|
| 1973–New York..........Nat. | 1B | 7 | 27 | 2 | 8 | 0 | 0 | 0 | 2 | .296 | 66 | 1 | 0 | 1.000 |

## STEPHEN BERNARD MINGORI

Name pronounced Men-GORE-e.

### (Steve)

Born February 29, 1944, at Kansas City, Mo.
Height, 5.10. Weight, 170.
Throws and bats lefthanded.
Hobbies–Reading, hunting and golf.
Attended Kansas State College, Pittsburg, Kan., and University of Missouri
at Kansas City, Kansas City, Mo.

| Year Club | League | G. | IP. | W. | L. | Pct. | H. | R. | ER. | SO. | BB. | ERA. |
|---|---|---|---|---|---|---|---|---|---|---|---|---|
| 1965–Peninsula ..........................Carolina | | 19 | 79 | 4 | 3 | .571 | 79 | 39 | 30 | 62 | 33 | 3.42 |
| 1965–Tampa†...............................Florida St. | | 6 | 16 | 0 | 1 | .000 | 25 | 19 | 11 | 17 | 10 | 6.19 |
| 1966–Peninsula ..........................Carolina | | 26 | 151 | 8 | 12 | .400 | 126 | 62 | 42 | 157 | 52 | 2.50 |
| 1967–Knoxville‡ .........................Southern | | 50 | 81 | 6 | 5 | .545 | 65 | 29 | 24 | 59 | 37 | 2.67 |
| 1968–Indianapolis ......................P. Coast | | 41 | 56 | 3 | 1 | .750 | 40 | 20 | 16 | 71 | 28 | 2.57 |
| 1969–Indianapolis§.....................Am. Assoc. | | 39 | 46 | 2 | 3 | .400 | 43 | 29 | 21 | 51 | 33 | 4.11 |
| 1970–Wichita ..............................Am. Assoc. | | 16 | 21 | 0 | 1 | .000 | 23 | 14 | 10 | 21 | 11 | 4.29 |
| 1970–Savannah ...........................Southern | | 10 | 65 | 6 | 0 | 1.000 | 38 | 6 | 6 | 50 | 8 | 0.83 |
| 1970–Cleveland ...........................American | | 21 | 20 | 1 | 0 | 1.000 | 17 | 8 | 6 | 16 | 12 | 2.70 |
| 1971–Cleveland x ........................American | | 54 | 57 | 1 | 2 | .333 | 31 | 10 | 9 | 45 | 24 | 1.42 |
| 1972–Portland .............................P. Coast | | 6 | 9 | 2 | 0 | 1.000 | 3 | 1 | 1 | 15 | 4 | 1.00 |
| 1972–Cleveland ...........................American | | 41 | 57 | 0 | 6 | .000 | 67 | 28 | 25 | 47 | 36 | 3.95 |
| 1973–Oklahoma City y–Omaha ......Am. Assoc. | | 14 | 23 | 0 | 2 | .000 | 17 | 12 | 11 | 24 | 8 | 4.30 |
| 1973–Cleveland y-Kansas City ......American | | 24 | 68 | 3 | 3 | .500 | 69 | 29 | 27 | 50 | 33 | 3.57 |
| 1974–Omaha ...............................Am. Assoc. | | 5 | 13 | 1 | 0 | 1.000 | 13 | 6 | 6 | 17 | 3 | 4.15 |
| 1974–Kansas City.........................American | | 36 | 67 | 2 | 3 | .400 | 53 | 31 | 21 | 43 | 23 | 2.82 |
| 1975–Kansas City z .....................American | | 36 | 50 | 0 | 3 | .000 | 42 | 21 | 14 | 25 | 20 | 2.52 |
| 1976–Kansas City.........................American | | 55 | 85 | 5 | 5 | .500 | 73 | 23 | 22 | 38 | 25 | 2.33 |
| Major League Totals .............................. | | 267 | 404 | 12 | 22 | .353 | 352 | 150 | 124 | 264 | 173 | 2.76 |

†On disabled list, July 12 to July 24 and August 5 to August 16, 1965.
‡Played two games at first base.
§Traded by Cincinnati Reds to Cleveland Indians for Infielder Jay Ward, February 18, 1970.
xOn disabled list, August 15 to September 7, 1971.
yTraded to Kansas City Royals for Pitcher Mike Jackson, June 8, 1973.
zOn disabled list, August 12 to September 2, 1975.

CHAMPIONSHIP SERIES RECORD

| Year Club | League | G. | IP. | W. | L. | Pct. | H. | R. | ER. | SO. | BB. | ERA. |
|---|---|---|---|---|---|---|---|---|---|---|---|---|
| 1976–Kansas City.........................American | | 3 | 3⅓ | 0 | 0 | .000 | 4 | 1 | 1 | 1 | 0 | 2.70 |

## JAMES EDWARD MINSHALL, JR.

### (Jim)

Born July 4, 1947, at Covington, Ky.
Height, 6.06. Weight, 210.
Throws and bats righthanded.
Hobbies–Hunting and golf.
Attended Eastern Kentucky University, Richmond, Ky.

Pitched 4-0 no-hit victory against High Point-Thomasville, June 16, 1969.
Led Eastern League in hit batsmen with 9 in 1973.

| Year Club | League | G. | IP. | W. | L. | Pct. | H. | R. | ER. | SO. | BB. | ERA. |
|---|---|---|---|---|---|---|---|---|---|---|---|---|
| 1966–Salem ..................................Ap'lachian | | 9 | 36 | 1 | 5 | .167 | 33 | 29 | 24 | 33 | 37 | 6.00 |
| 1967–Salem† ................................Ap'lachian | | 14 | 45 | 2 | 3 | .400 | 33 | 28 | 23 | 47 | 37 | 4.60 |
| 1968–Clinton‡ ..............................Midwest | | 12 | 70 | 4 | 4 | .500 | 56 | 29 | 20 | 67 | 41 | 2.57 |
| 1969–Salem ..................................Carolina | | 18 | 119 | 6 | 3 | .667 | 101 | 51 | 40 | 73 | 63 | 3.03 |
| 1970–Salem ..................................Carolina | | 26 | 124 | 5 | 8 | .385 | 124 | 66 | 57 | 62 | 74 | 4.14 |
| 1971–Salem ..................................Carolina | | 34 | 93 | 2 | 8 | .200 | 82 | 50 | 40 | 100 | 44 | 3.87 |
| 1972–Salem ..................................Carolina | | 26 | 181 | *16 | 1 | *.941 | 166 | 83 | 68 | 136 | 75 | 3.38 |

| Year Club | League | G. | IP. | W. | L. | Pct. | H. | R. | ER. | SO. | BB. | ERA. |
|---|---|---|---|---|---|---|---|---|---|---|---|---|
| 1973–Sherbrooke | Eastern | 24 | 135 | 6 | 11 | .353 | 136 | 77 | 62 | 99 | 91 | 4.13 |
| 1974–Thetford Mines | Eastern | 33 | 42 | 6 | 2 | .750 | 26 | 20 | 19 | 61 | 36 | 4.07 |
| 1974–Charleston | Int'national | 12 | 20 | 2 | 1 | .667 | 8 | 5 | 5 | 21 | 4 | 2.25 |
| 1974–Pittsburgh | National | 5 | 4 | 0 | 1 | .000 | 1 | 1 | 0 | 3 | 2 | 0.00 |
| 1975–Charleston | Int'national | 45 | 65 | 3 | 4 | .429 | 35 | 12 | 10 | 64 | 39 | 1.38 |
| 1975–Pittsburgh | National | 1 | 1 | 0 | 0 | .000 | 0 | 0 | 0 | 2 | 2 | 0.00 |
| 1976–Charleston§ | Int'national | 37 | 77 | 6 | 3 | .667 | 106 | 56 | 46 | 59 | 48 | 5.38 |
| Major League Totals | | 6 | 5 | 0 | 1 | .000 | 1 | 1 | 0 | 5 | 4 | 0.00 |

†On restricted list from beginning of season until June 16, 1967.
‡On restricted list from beginning of season until June 20, 1968.
§Sold to Seattle Mariners, October 15, 1976; released, March 28, 1977.

## GREGORY BRIAN MINTON
### (Greg)

Born July 29, 1951, at Lubbock, Tex.
Height, 6.02. Weight, 190.
Throws right and bats left and righthanded.
Hobbies—Fishing, hunting, golf, racquetball and handball.
Attended San Diego Mesa College, San Diego, Calif.

| Year Club | League | G. | IP. | W. | L. | Pct. | H. | R. | ER. | SO. | BB. | ERA. |
|---|---|---|---|---|---|---|---|---|---|---|---|---|
| 1970–Billings† | Pioneer | 16 | 40 | 1 | 4 | .200 | 37 | 23 | 14 | 36 | 16 | 3.15 |
| 1971–Waterloo | Midwest | 27 | 124 | 11 | 6 | .647 | 118 | 52 | 42 | 117 | 55 | 3.05 |
| 1972–San José‡ | California | 28 | 178 | 12 | 12 | .500 | 182 | 117 | 78 | 153 | 77 | 3.94 |
| 1973–Phoenix | P. Coast | 5 | 13 | 0 | 0 | .000 | 11 | 6 | 6 | 4 | 8 | 4.15 |
| 1973–Amarillo | Texas | 38 | 122 | 5 | 11 | .313 | 138 | 87 | 61 | 77 | 48 | 4.50 |
| 1974–Fresno | California | 13 | 96 | 10 | 1 | .909 | 85 | 32 | 24 | 81 | 18 | 2.25 |
| 1974–Amarillo | Texas | 6 | 29 | 1 | 4 | .200 | 42 | 26 | 19 | 21 | 10 | 5.90 |
| 1975–Phoenix | P. Coast | 42 | 177 | 10 | 6 | .625 | 178 | 73 | 51 | 76 | 76 | 2.59 |
| 1975–San Francisco | National | 4 | 17 | 1 | 1 | .500 | 19 | 14 | 13 | 6 | 11 | 6.88 |
| 1976–San Francisco | National | 10 | 26 | 0 | 3 | .000 | 32 | 18 | 14 | 7 | 12 | 4.85 |
| 1976–Phoenix§ | P. Coast | 13 | 74 | 4 | 5 | .444 | 91 | 57 | 46 | 31 | 32 | 5.59 |
| Major League Totals | | 14 | 43 | 1 | 4 | .200 | 51 | 32 | 27 | 13 | 23 | 5.65 |

†Played in two games as an outfielder.
‡Traded by Kansas City Royals to San Francisco Giants for Catcher Fran Healy, April 2, 1973.
§On disabled list, July 24 through August 5, 1976.

## CRAIG SETON MITCHELL

Born April 14, 1954, at Santa Rosa, Calif.
Height, 6.03. Weight, 195.
Throws and bats righthanded.
Hobbies—Hunting and fishing.
Attended Spokane Falls Community College, Spokane, Wash.

| Year Club | League | G. | IP. | W. | L. | Pct. | H. | R. | ER. | SO. | BB. | ERA. |
|---|---|---|---|---|---|---|---|---|---|---|---|---|
| 1973–Lewiston† | Northwest | 12 | 59 | 1 | •8 | .111 | 56 | 45 | 33 | 42 | 39 | 5.03 |
| 1974–Burlington | Midwest | 22 | 134 | 10 | 6 | .625 | 109 | 55 | 51 | 113 | 51 | 3.43 |
| 1975–Birmingham | Southern | 12 | 76 | 6 | 3 | .667 | 61 | 31 | 24 | 39 | 42 | 2.84 |
| 1975–Tucson | P. Coast | 18 | 90 | 7 | 4 | .636 | 90 | 59 | 48 | 49 | 43 | 4.80 |
| 1975–Oakland | American | 1 | 4 | 0 | 1 | .000 | 6 | 5 | 5 | 2 | 2 | 11.25 |
| 1976–Tucson | P. Coast | 26 | 170 | 8 | 13 | .381 | 178 | 104 | 93 | 105 | 70 | 4.92 |
| 1976–Oakland | American | 1 | 3 | 0 | 0 | .000 | 3 | 1 | 1 | 0 | 0 | 3.00 |
| Major League Totals | | 2 | 7 | 0 | 1 | .000 | 9 | 6 | 6 | 2 | 2 | 7.71 |

†On disabled list, June 18 to July 9, 1973.

## PAUL MICHAEL MITCHELL

Born August 19, 1950, at Worcester, Mass.
Height, 6.01. Weight, 195.
Throws and bats righthanded.
Attended Old Dominion University, Norfolk, Va.; received
Bachelor of Science degree in Education.

Tied for International League lead in wild pitches with 18 in 1973.

| Year Club | League | G. | IP. | W. | L. | Pct. | H. | R. | ER. | SO. | BB. | ERA. |
|---|---|---|---|---|---|---|---|---|---|---|---|---|
| 1972–Asheville | Southern | 26 | 178 | •16 | 8 | .667 | 168 | 73 | 64 | 149 | 53 | 3.24 |
| 1973–Rochester | Int'national | 27 | 152 | 8 | 7 | .533 | 151 | 83 | 70 | 93 | 83 | 4.14 |
| 1974–Rochester | Int'national | 26 | 168 | 14 | 6 | •.700 | 145 | 67 | 54 | 131 | 62 | 2.89 |
| 1975–Rochester | Int'national | 14 | 96 | 10 | 1 | .909 | 73 | 31 | 22 | 78 | 19 | 2.06 |
| 1975–Baltimore† | American | 11 | 57 | 3 | 0 | 1.000 | 41 | 23 | 23 | 31 | 19 | 3.63 |
| 1976–Tucson | P. Coast | 4 | 23 | 3 | 1 | .750 | 22 | 7 | 6 | 17 | 8 | 2.35 |
| 1976–Oakland | American | 26 | 142 | 9 | 7 | .563 | 169 | 74 | 67 | 67 | 30 | 4.25 |
| Major League Totals | | 37 | 199 | 12 | 7 | .632 | 210 | 97 | 90 | 98 | 49 | 4.07 |

†Traded with Outfielder Don Baylor and Pitcher Mike Torrez to Oakland Athletics for Outfielder Reggie Jackson and Pitchers Ken Holtzman and Bill Van Bommel, April 2, 1976.

## GEORGE EUGENE MITTERWALD

Born June 7, 1945, at Berkeley, Calif.
Height, 6.02. Weight, 205.
Throws and bats righthanded.
Hobbies—All sports.
Attended Chabot College, Hayward, Calif.
Hit three home runs in a game, April 17, 1974, against Pittsburgh Pirates.
Led Southern League catchers in passed balls with 20 in 1967.
Tied for Northern League lead in passed balls with 10 in 1965.

| Year—Club | League | Pos. | G. | AB. | R. | H. | 2B. | 3B. | HR. | RBI. | B.A. | PO. | A. | E. | F.A. |
|---|---|---|---|---|---|---|---|---|---|---|---|---|---|---|---|
| 1965—Wis. Rapids | Midw. | C | 1 | 3 | 0 | 1 | 1 | 0 | 0 | 0 | .333 | 5 | 0 | 0 | 1.000 |
| 1965—St. Cloud | North. | C | 37 | 126 | 17 | 41 | 6 | 2 | 3 | 20 | .325 | 273 | 24 | 7 | .977 |
| 1966—Wilson | Carol. | C | 86 | 313 | 35 | 83 | 18 | 2 | 6 | 48 | .265 | 522 | 59 | 13 | .978 |
| 1966—St. Cloud | North. | C | 4 | 15 | 2 | 2 | 0 | 0 | 0 | 0 | .133 | 42 | 1 | 0 | 1.000 |
| 1966—Minnesota | Amer. | C | 3 | 5 | 1 | 1 | 0 | 0 | 0 | 0 | .200 | 13 | 0 | 0 | 1.000 |
| 1967—Charlotte† | South. | C | 104 | 347 | 43 | 84 | 19 | 1 | 8 | 44 | .242 | 550 | •65 | 9 | .986 |
| 1968—Denver | P.C. | •C-OF | 99 | 341 | 50 | 91 | 25 | 4 | 9 | 56 | .267 | 412 | 51 | •12 | .975 |
| 1968—Wis. Rapids | Midw. | C | 5 | 16 | 2 | 2 | 0 | 0 | 1 | 3 | .125 | 38 | 10 | 0 | 1.000 |
| 1968—Minnesota | Amer. | C | 11 | 34 | 1 | 7 | 1 | 0 | 0 | 1 | .206 | 69 | 4 | 3 | .961 |
| 1969—Minnesota‡ | Amer. | C-OF | 69 | 187 | 18 | 48 | 8 | 0 | 5 | 13 | .257 | 340 | 33 | 5 | .987 |
| 1970—Minnesota | Amer. | C | 117 | 369 | 36 | 82 | 12 | 2 | 15 | 46 | .222 | 740 | 62 | 3 | .996 |
| 1971—Minnesota | Amer. | C | 125 | 388 | 38 | 97 | 13 | 1 | 13 | 44 | .250 | 656 | 53 | 10 | .986 |
| 1972—Minnesota | Amer. | C | 64 | 163 | 12 | 30 | 4 | 1 | 1 | 8 | .184 | 272 | 33 | 5 | .984 |
| 1973—Minnesota§ | Amer. | C | 125 | 432 | 50 | 112 | 15 | 0 | 16 | 64 | .259 | 676 | 59 | 6 | .992 |
| 1974—Chicago | Nat. | C | 78 | 215 | 17 | 54 | 7 | 0 | 7 | 28 | .251 | 335 | 40 | 10 | .974 |
| 1975—Chicago | Nat. | C-1B | 84 | 200 | 19 | 44 | 4 | 3 | 5 | 26 | .220 | 315 | 38 | 8 | .978 |
| 1976—Chicago | Nat. | C-1B | 101 | 303 | 19 | 65 | 7 | 0 | 5 | 28 | .215 | 512 | 23 | 4 | .992 |
| American League Totals | | | 514 | 1578 | 156 | 377 | 53 | 4 | 50 | 176 | .239 | 2766 | 244 | 32 | .989 |
| National League Totals | | | 263 | 718 | 55 | 163 | 18 | 3 | 17 | 82 | .227 | 1162 | 101 | 22 | .983 |
| Major League Totals | | | 777 | 2296 | 211 | 540 | 71 | 7 | 67 | 258 | .235 | 3928 | 345 | 54 | .988 |

†On temporary inactive list, June 23 to July 10, 1967
‡On military list, August 1 to August 17, 1969.
§Traded to Chicago Cubs for Catcher Randy Hundley, December 6, 1973.

### CHAMPIONSHIP SERIES RECORD

| Year—Club | League | Pos. | G. | AB. | R. | H. | 2B. | 3B. | HR. | RBI. | B.A. | PO. | A. | E. | F.A. |
|---|---|---|---|---|---|---|---|---|---|---|---|---|---|---|---|
| 1969—Minnesota | Amer. | C | 2 | 7 | 0 | 1 | 0 | 0 | 0 | 0 | .143 | 10 | 4 | 0 | 1.000 |
| 1970—Minnesota | Amer. | C | 2 | 8 | 2 | 4 | 1 | 0 | 0 | 2 | .500 | 16 | 1 | 0 | 1.000 |
| Championship Series Totals | | | 4 | 15 | 2 | 5 | 1 | 0 | 0 | 2 | .333 | 26 | 5 | 0 | 1.000 |

## DAVID ALLAN MOATES
## (DAVE)

Born January 30, 1948, at Great Lakes, Ill.
Height, 5.09. Weight, 170.
Throws and bats lefthanded.
Hobby—Sports in general.
Attended Manatee Junior College, West Bradenton, Fla., and Florida State University,
Tallahassee, Fla.; received Bachelor of Science degree in Physical Education.
Led Pacific Coast League in stolen bases with 42 in 1974.
Tied for Carolina League lead in double plays by outfielders with 3 in 1970.
Tied for Pacific Coast League lead in sacrifice hits with 8 in 1973.

| Year—Club | League | Pos. | G. | AB. | R. | H. | 2B. | 3B. | HR. | RBI. | B.A. | PO. | A. | E. | F.A. |
|---|---|---|---|---|---|---|---|---|---|---|---|---|---|---|---|
| 1969—Wytheville | Appal. | OF | 27 | 101 | 29 | 34 | 11 | 2 | 1 | 12 | .337 | 45 | 1 | 2 | .958 |
| 1970—Burlington | Carol. | •OF-1B | 121 | 440 | 76 | 137 | 14 | 7 | 5 | 70 | .311 | 259 | 16 | 6 | •.979 |
| 1970—Pittsfield | East. | OF | 2 | 10 | 2 | 4 | 0 | 1 | 0 | 1 | .400 | 6 | 0 | 0 | 1.000 |
| 1971—Pittsfield† | East. | OF | 97 | 321 | 41 | 85 | 11 | 3 | 0 | 20 | .265 | 155 | 6 | 8 | .953 |
| 1972—Denver | A.A. | OF | 20 | 47 | 5 | 9 | 2 | 0 | 0 | 3 | .191 | 20 | 0 | 0 | 1.000 |
| 1972—Pittsfield | East. | OF | 90 | 351 | 56 | 98 | 22 | 5 | 4 | 38 | .279 | 169 | 4 | 5 | .972 |
| 1973—Spokane | P.C. | OF | 107 | 414 | 63 | 125 | 18 | 2 | 4 | 63 | .302 | 221 | 14 | 4 | .983 |
| 1974—Spokane | P.C. | OF | 123 | 504 | 95 | 151 | 17 | 8 | 12 | 60 | .300 | 311 | 14 | 11 | .967 |
| 1974—Texas | Amer. | PR | 1 | 0 | 0 | 0 | 0 | 0 | 0 | 0 | .000 | 0 | 0 | 0 | .000 |
| 1975—Spokane | P.C. | OF | 90 | 363 | 58 | 100 | 13 | 2 | 3 | 32 | .275 | 227 | 4 | 5 | .979 |
| 1975—Texas | Amer. | OF | 54 | 175 | 21 | 48 | 9 | 0 | 3 | 14 | .274 | 114 | 6 | 2 | .984 |
| 1976—Texas | Amer. | OF-DH | 85 | 137 | 21 | 33 | 7 | 1 | 0 | 13 | .241 | 106 | 4 | 1 | .991 |
| Major League Totals | | | 140 | 312 | 42 | 81 | 16 | 1 | 3 | 27 | .259 | 220 | 10 | 3 | .987 |

†On disabled list from beginning of season until June 2, 1971.

## RANDALL JAMES MOFFITT
## (Randy)

Born October 13, 1948, at Long Beach, Calif.
Height, 6.03. Weight, 190.
Throws and bats righthanded.
Hobby—Freshwater fishing.
Attended California State College, Long Beach, Calif.
Brother of tennis star Billie Jean King.

| Year Club | League | G. | IP. | W. | L. | Pct. | H. | R. | ER. | SO. | BB. | ERA. |
|---|---|---|---|---|---|---|---|---|---|---|---|---|
| 1970–Fresno† | California | 18 | 135 | 9 | 6 | .600 | 91 | 35 | 24 | 149 | 23 | 1.60 |
| 1971–Phoenix‡ | P. Coast | 42 | 121 | 6 | 7 | .462 | 147 | 78 | 69 | 94 | 48 | 5.13 |
| 1972–Phoenix | P. Coast | 19 | 24 | 1 | 3 | .250 | 22 | 9 | 6 | 24 | 15 | 2.25 |
| 1972–San Francisco | National | 40 | 71 | 1 | 5 | .167 | 72 | 31 | 29 | 37 | 30 | 3.68 |
| 1973–San Francisco | National | 60 | 100 | 4 | 4 | .500 | 86 | 30 | 27 | 65 | 31 | 2.43 |
| 1974–San Francisco | National | 61 | 102 | 5 | 7 | .417 | 99 | 52 | 51 | 49 | 29 | 4.50 |
| 1975–San Francisco | National | 55 | 74 | 4 | 5 | .444 | 73 | 35 | 32 | 39 | 32 | 3.89 |
| 1976–San Francisco | National | 58 | 103 | 6 | 6 | .500 | 92 | 36 | 26 | 50 | 35 | 2.27 |
| Major League Totals | | 274 | 450 | 20 | 27 | .426 | 422 | 184 | 165 | 240 | 157 | 3.30 |

†On military list, February 16 through June 5, 1970.
‡On disabled list, August 22 through September 2, 1971.

## ROBERT JAMES MONDAY, JR.
### (Rick)

Born November 20, 1945, at Batesville, Ark.
Height, 6.03. Weight, 195.
Throws and bats lefthanded.
Hobbies–Golf and hunting.
Attended Arizona State University, Tempe, Ariz.

Established major league record for most strikeouts, two consecutive games, 18 innings (8), April 28, 29, 1970.
Tied major league records for most consecutive strikeouts, 9-inning game (5), April 29, 1970, and most at-bats in doubleheader (more than 18 innings), 14, June 17, 1967, 28 innings.
Tied American League lead for most strikeouts in consecutive times at bat (7), April 28 and 29, 1970.
Hit three home runs in one game, May 16, 1972.
Tied for National League lead in double plays by outfielders with 5 in 1974.
Tied for American League lead in double plays by outfielders with 6 in 1967.
Led Southern League batters in strikeouts with 143 in 1966.
Received reported $104,000 bonus to sign with Kansas City Athletics, 1965.

| Year Club | League | Pos. | G. | AB. | R. | H. | 2B. | 3B. | HR. | RBI. | B.A. | PO. | A. | E. | F.A. |
|---|---|---|---|---|---|---|---|---|---|---|---|---|---|---|---|
| 1965–Lewiston | Northw. | OF-1B | 72 | 247 | 45 | 67 | 12 | 2 | 13 | 44 | .271 | 205 | 6 | 8 | .963 |
| 1966–Mobile | South. | OF | 127 | 469 | 86 | 125 | 16 | 10 | 23 | 72 | .267 | •287 | 10 | 13 | .958 |
| 1966–Kansas City | Amer. | OF | 17 | 41 | 4 | 4 | 1 | 1 | 0 | 2 | .098 | 26 | 1 | 1 | .964 |
| 1967–Kansas City | Amer. | OF | 124 | 406 | 52 | 102 | 14 | 6 | 14 | 58 | .251 | 260 | 14 | 8 | .972 |
| 1968–Oakland | Amer. | OF | 148 | 482 | 56 | 132 | 24 | 7 | 8 | 49 | .274 | 299 | 11 | 7 | .978 |
| 1969–Oakland | Amer. | OF | 122 | 399 | 57 | 108 | 17 | 4 | 12 | 54 | .271 | 262 | 3 | 10 | .964 |
| 1970–Oakland† | Amer. | OF | 112 | 376 | 63 | 109 | 19 | 7 | 10 | 37 | .290 | 257 | 3 | 5 | .981 |
| 1971–Oakland‡ | Amer. | OF | 116 | 355 | 53 | 87 | 9 | 3 | 18 | 56 | .245 | 238 | 6 | 4 | .984 |
| 1972–Chicago | Nat. | OF | 138 | 434 | 68 | 108 | 22 | 5 | 11 | 42 | .249 | 268 | 6 | 1 | •.996 |
| 1973–Chicago | Nat. | OF | 149 | 554 | 93 | 148 | 24 | 5 | 26 | 56 | .267 | 317 | 9 | 9 | .973 |
| 1974–Chicago | Nat. | OF | 142 | 538 | 84 | 158 | 19 | 7 | 20 | 58 | .294 | 302 | 10 | 5 | .984 |
| 1975–Chicago | Nat. | OF | 136 | 491 | 89 | 131 | 29 | 4 | 17 | 60 | .267 | 315 | 6 | 9 | .973 |
| 1976–Chicago§ | Nat. | OF-1B | 137 | 534 | 107 | 145 | 20 | 5 | 32 | 77 | .272 | 587 | 26 | 5 | .992 |
| American League Totals | | | 639 | 2059 | 285 | 542 | 84 | 28 | 62 | 256 | .263 | 1342 | 38 | 35 | .975 |
| National League Totals | | | 702 | 2551 | 441 | 690 | 114 | 26 | 106 | 293 | .270 | 1789 | 57 | 29 | .984 |
| Major League Totals | | | 1341 | 4610 | 726 | 1232 | 198 | 54 | 168 | 549 | .267 | 3131 | 95 | 64 | .980 |

†On military list June 18 through July 8.
‡Traded to Chicago Cubs for Pitcher Ken Holtzman, November 29, 1971.
§Traded with Pitcher Mike Garman to Los Angeles Dodgers for First Baseman-Outfielder Bill Buckner, Shortstop Ivan DeJesus and Pitcher Jeff Albert, January 11, 1977.

### CHAMPIONSHIP SERIES RECORD

| Year Club | League | Pos. | G. | AB. | R. | H. | 2B. | 3B. | HR. | RBI. | B.A. | PO. | A. | E. | F.A. |
|---|---|---|---|---|---|---|---|---|---|---|---|---|---|---|---|
| 1971–Oakland | Amer. | OF | 1 | 3 | 0 | 0 | 0 | 0 | 0 | 0 | .000 | 4 | 0 | 0 | 1.000 |

### ALL-STAR GAME RECORD

| Year League | Pos. | AB. | R. | H. | 2B. | 3B. | HR. | RBI. | B.A. | PO. | A. | E. | F.A. |
|---|---|---|---|---|---|---|---|---|---|---|---|---|---|
| 1968–American | OF | 2 | 0 | 0 | 0 | 0 | 0 | 0 | .000 | 0 | 0 | 0 | .000 |

### PITCHING RECORD

| Year Club | League | G. | IP. | W. | L. | Pct. | H. | R. | ER. | SO. | BB. | ERA. |
|---|---|---|---|---|---|---|---|---|---|---|---|---|
| 1965–Lewiston | Northwest | 1 | 1 | 0 | 0 | .000 | 0 | 0 | 0 | 2 | 2 | 0.00 |

## DONALD WAYNE MONEY
### (Don)

Born June 7, 1947, at Washington, D. C.
Height, 6.01. Weight, 190.
Throws and bats righthanded.
Hobbies–Golf, bowling, hunting and fishing.

Established following major league records: highest fielding percentage, third baseman, season, .9894, 1974; fewest errors, third baseman, season (450 or more chances), 5, 1974; most consecutive errorless games, third baseman, season, 86, April 5 to July 16, 1974; most consecutive errorless chances accepted, third baseman, lifetime, 261, September 28, 1973 (1st game) to July 16, 1974; and most consecutive errorless chances accepted, third baseman, season, 257, April 5 to July 16, 1974.

Established American League record for most consecutive errorless games, third baseman, lifetime, 88, September 28 (2nd game), 1973 to July 16, 1974.

Set National League records for fewest errors by third baseman in 150 or more games, season (10), 1972; most consecutive errorless chances accepted in season by third baseman (163), July 23-September 11, 1972; and highest fielding average by third baseman, season, 150 or more games, .978, in 1972.

Tied for National League lead in double plays by third basemen with 31 in 1972.

Led Appalachian League shortstops in double plays with 34 in 1965 and Carolina League shortstops with 87 in 1967.

Named Most Valuable Player in Carolina League, 1967.

| Year | Club | League | Pos. | G. | AB. | R. | H. | 2B. | 3B. | HR. | RBI. | B.A. | PO. | A. | E. | F.A. |
|---|---|---|---|---|---|---|---|---|---|---|---|---|---|---|---|---|
| 1965–Salem | | Appal. | SS | 66 | 216 | 46 | 52 | 7 | 0 | 6 | 24 | .241 | •88 | •171 | 24 | .915 |
| 1966–Clinton | | Midw. | SS-2 | •125 | 458 | 40 | 108 | 17 | 5 | 7 | 61 | .236 | 186 | 345 | 33 | .941 |
| 1967–Raleigh† | | Carol. | SS | 136 | 480 | 66 | 149 | •37 | 5 | 16 | 86 | .310 | •250 | •418 | 33 | .953 |
| 1968–Philadelphia | | Nat. | SS | 4 | 13 | 1 | 3 | 2 | 0 | 0 | 2 | .231 | 6 | 8 | 0 | 1.000 |
| 1968–San Diego | | P.C. | SS | 127 | 482 | 63 | 146 | 26 | 4 | 9 | 59 | .303 | 226 | 441 | 26 | .962 |
| 1969–Philadelphia | | Nat. | SS | 127 | 450 | 41 | 103 | 22 | 2 | 6 | 42 | .229 | 212 | 443 | 21 | .969 |
| 1970–Philadelphia | | Nat. | 3B-SS | 120 | 447 | 66 | 132 | 25 | 4 | 14 | 66 | .295 | 133 | 236 | 15 | .961 |
| 1971–Philadelphia‡ | | Nat. | 3-O-2 | 121 | 439 | 40 | 98 | 22 | 8 | 7 | 38 | .223 | 167 | 197 | 11 | .970 |
| 1972–Philadelphia‡‡ | | Nat. | •3B-SS | 152 | 536 | 54 | 119 | 16 | 2 | 15 | 52 | .222 | •140 | 316 | 10 | •.978 |
| 1973–Milwaukee | | Amer. | •3B-SS | 145 | 556 | 75 | 158 | 28 | 2 | 11 | 61 | .284 | 146 | 276 | 13 | •.970 |
| 1974–Milwaukee | | Amer. | •3B-2B | 159 | •629 | 85 | 178 | 32 | 3 | 15 | 65 | .283 | 131 | 336 | 5 | •.989 |
| 1975–Milwaukee§ | | Amer. | 3B-SS | 109 | 405 | 58 | 112 | 16 | 1 | 15 | 43 | .277 | 109 | 194 | 15 | .953 |
| 1976–Milwaukee | | Amer. | 3-DH-S | 117 | 439 | 51 | 117 | 18 | 4 | 12 | 62 | .267 | 96 | 202 | 13 | .958 |
| National League Totals | | | | 524 | 1885 | 202 | 455 | 87 | 16 | 42 | 200 | .241 | 658 | 1200 | 57 | .970 |
| American League Totals | | | | 530 | 2029 | 269 | 565 | 94 | 10 | 53 | 231 | .278 | 482 | 1008 | 46 | .970 |
| Major League Totals | | | | 1054 | 3914 | 471 | 1020 | 181 | 26 | 95 | 431 | .261 | 1140 | 2208 | 103 | .970 |

†Recalled by Pittsburgh Pirates; traded with Pitchers Woodie Fryman, Bill Laxton and Harold Clem to Philadelphia Phillies for Pitcher Jim Bunning, December 15, 1967.

‡On military list June 12 through June 30.

‡‡Traded with Infielder John Vukovich and Pitcher Billy Champion to Milwaukee Brewers for Pitchers Ken Brett, Ken Sanders, Jim Lonborg and Earl Stephenson, October 31, 1972.

§On disabled list, May 28 to June 24, 1975.

ALL-STAR GAME RECORD

| Year | League | Pos. | AB. | R. | H. | 2B. | 3B. | HR. | RBI. | B.A. | PO. | A. | E. | F.A. |
|---|---|---|---|---|---|---|---|---|---|---|---|---|---|---|
| 1976–American | | 3B | 1 | 0 | 0 | 0 | 0 | 0 | 0 | .000 | 0 | 1 | 0 | 1.000 |

Member of American League All-Star Team in 1974 game; did not play.

## ISIDRO PEDROZA MONGE
### (Sid)

Born April 11, 1951, at Agua Prieta, Sonora, Mexico.
Height, 6.02. Weight, 185.
Throws left and bats left and righthanded.
Hobbies–Basketball, fishing and hunting.
Pitched 6-0, no-hit victory against Cedar Rapids, May 4, 1971.

| Year | Club | League | G. | IP. | W. | L. | Pct. | H. | R. | ER. | SO. | BB. | ERA. |
|---|---|---|---|---|---|---|---|---|---|---|---|---|---|
| 1970–Idaho Falls | | Pioneer | 17 | 62 | 5 | 1 | .833 | 60 | 35 | 29 | 54 | 42 | 4.21 |
| 1971–Quad Cities | | Midwest | 25 | 169 | 12 | 11 | .522 | 120 | 62 | 45 | 158 | 83 | 2.40 |
| 1972–Shreveport† | | Texas | 24 | 135 | 5 | 10 | .333 | 116 | 62 | 52 | 106 | 73 | 3.47 |
| 1973–El Paso | | Texas | 25 | 147 | 7 | 11 | .389 | 173 | 100 | 75 | 90 | 72 | 4.59 |
| 1974–El Paso | | Texas | 25 | 163 | •14 | 5 | .737 | 182 | 99 | 84 | 111 | 67 | 4.64 |
| 1975–Salt Lake City | | P. Coast | 27 | 167 | 14 | 9 | .609 | 175 | 98 | 86 | 106 | 93 | 4.63 |
| 1975–California | | American | 4 | 24 | 0 | 2 | .000 | 22 | 12 | 11 | 17 | 10 | 4.13 |
| 1976–California | | American | 32 | 118 | 6 | 7 | .462 | 108 | 50 | 44 | 53 | 49 | 3.36 |
| Major League Totals | | | 36 | 142 | 6 | 9 | .400 | 130 | 62 | 55 | 70 | 59 | 3.49 |

†On temporary inactive list, August 10, 1972 through the end of season.

## LAWRENCE JAMES MONROE

Born June 20, 1956, at Detroit, Mich.
Height, 6.04. Weight, 200.
Throws and bats righthanded.
Led Southern League pitchers in wild pitches with 13, and tied for lead in games started with 28 in 1976.

| Year | Club | League | G. | IP. | W. | L. | Pct. | H. | R. | ER. | SO. | BB. | ERA. |
|---|---|---|---|---|---|---|---|---|---|---|---|---|---|
| 1974–Sarasota White Sox | | Gulf Coast | 7 | 28 | 1 | 3 | .250 | 30 | 19 | 14 | 16 | 12 | 4.40 |
| 1974–Appleton | | Midwest | 3 | 24 | 2 | 1 | .667 | 14 | 3 | 3 | 17 | 6 | 1.13 |
| 1975–Appleton† | | Midwest | 23 | 121 | 5 | 11 | .313 | 118 | 66 | 48 | 89 | 48 | 3.57 |
| 1976–Knoxville | | Southern | 29 | 195 | 11 | 14 | .440 | 183 | 73 | 63 | 113 | 75 | 2.91 |
| 1976–Chicago | | American | 8 | 22 | 0 | 1 | .000 | 23 | 11 | 10 | 9 | 13 | 4.09 |
| Major League Totals | | | 8 | 22 | 0 | 1 | .000 | 23 | 11 | 10 | 9 | 13 | 4.09 |

†On disabled list, May 26 through June 14, 1975.

---

**DID YOU KNOW —**

That Babe Ruth of the New York Yankees had 10 hits in 16 times at bat during the 1926 World Series? That comes to a neat batting average of .625.

---

## JOHN EVANS MONTAGUE, JR.
### (Johnny)

Born September 12, 1947, at Newport News, Va.
Height, 6.02. Weight, 205.
Throws and bats righthanded.
Hobby—Hunting.
Attended Old Dominion College, Norfolk, Va.

Pitched seven-inning 1-0 no-hit victory against Oklahoma City, May 25, 1976.
Led American Association pitchers in shutouts with 6, and tied for lead in complete games with 11 in 1976.
Tied for International League lead in complete games by pitchers with 16 in 1973.

| Year Club | League | G. | IP. | W. | L. | Pct. | H. | R. | ER. | SO. | BB. | ERA. |
|---|---|---|---|---|---|---|---|---|---|---|---|---|
| 1968–Aberdeen ...........................Northern | | (On temporary inactive list) | | | | | | | | | | |
| 1969–Miami.................................Florida St. | | 31 | 176 | 12 | 8 | .600 | 130 | 39 | 30 | 166 | 54 | *1.53 |
| 1970–Rochester .........................Int'national | | 26 | 139 | 6 | 9 | .400 | 137 | 82 | 75 | 102 | 60 | 4.86 |
| 1971–Rochester† .........................Int'national | | 28 | 117 | 8 | 6 | .571 | 121 | 62 | 58 | 92 | 36 | 4.46 |
| 1972–Peninsula ..........................Int'national | | 29 | *214 | 9 | 11 | .450 | *216 | 93 | 78 | 149 | 69 | 3.28 |
| 1973–Peninsula ..........................Int'national | | 27 | 194 | *15 | 9 | .625 | 188 | 73 | 67 | 108 | 54 | 3.11 |
| 1973–Montreal............................National | | 4 | 8 | 0 | 0 | .000 | 8 | 3 | 3 | 7 | 2 | 3.38 |
| 1974–Montreal ...........................National | | 46 | 83 | 3 | 4 | .429 | 73 | 37 | 29 | 43 | 38 | 3.14 |
| 1975–Memphis............................Int'national | | 18 | 135 | 7 | 8 | .467 | 114 | 36 | 26 | 68 | 27 | 1.73 |
| 1975–Montreal‡-Philadelphia ........National | | 15 | 23 | 0 | 1 | .000 | 31 | 16 | 16 | 10 | 10 | 6.26 |
| 1976–Oklahoma City§..................Am. Assoc. | | 28 | 194 | ●14 | 6 | .700 | 183 | 72 | 57 | 120 | 51 | 2.64 |
| Major League Totals ................ | | 65 | 114 | 3 | 5 | .375 | 112 | 56 | 48 | 60 | 50 | 3.79 |

†Option transferred by Baltimore Orioles' organization to Peninsula (Montreal Expos' organization), April 4, 1972. Sold by Baltimore Orioles to Montreal Expos, April 13, 1973; Expos assigned Pitcher Mickey Scott to Rochester (Baltimore Orioles' organization), April 4, 1974, to complete deal.
‡Sold via waivers to Philadelphia Phillies, September 2, 1975.
§Sold by Philadelphia Phillies to Seattle Mariners, November 6, 1976.

## GILLERMO NARANJO MONTANEZ

Name pronounced Mon-TAN-yez.

### (Willie)

Born April 1, 1948, at Catano, Puerto Rico.
Height, 6.01. Weight, 185.
Throws and bats lefthanded.

Led National League first basemen in total chances with 1698 in 1976.
Led National League first basemen in double plays with 143 in 1975.
Led National League in sacrifice flies with 13 in 1971.
Led Florida State League first basemen in double plays with 101 in 1967.
Named first baseman on THE SPORTING NEWS National League All-Star Team, 1976.

| Year Club | League | Pos. | G. | AB. | R. | H. | 2B. | 3B. | HR. | RBI. | B.A. | PO. | A. | E. | F.A. |
|---|---|---|---|---|---|---|---|---|---|---|---|---|---|---|---|
| 1965–Sarasota Cards† Sar. Rk. | | 1B | 32 | 81 | 5 | 19 | 0 | 0 | 0 | 8 | .234 | 166 | 9 | 7 | .962 |
| 1966–California.........Amer. | | 1B | 8 | 2 | 2 | 0 | 0 | 0 | 0 | 0 | .000 | 1 | 0 | 0 | 1.000 |
| 1966–Rock Hill .........W. Car. | | O-1 | 93 | 306 | 48 | 86 | 18 | 7 | 11 | 49 | .281 | 177 | 6 | 11 | .943 |
| 1967–St. Petersburg ..Fla. St. | | *1B-O | 134 | 479 | 58 | 129 | 15 | *17 | 5 | 61 | .269 | *1171 | *102 | 13 | *.990 |
| 1968–Modesto ...........Calif. | | 1B | 46 | 174 | 26 | 52 | 8 | 2 | 4 | 18 | .299 | 334 | 33 | 8 | .979 |
| 1969–Tulsa‡§.............A.A. | | 1B | 14 | 56 | 12 | 21 | 4 | 2 | 1 | 7 | .375 | 115 | 12 | 1 | .992 |
| 1970–Eugene x .........P.C. | | *1-OF | 119 | 434 | 65 | 120 | 24 | 9 | 16 | 80 | .276 | 842 | *66 | 5 | .995 |
| 1970–Philadelphia ......Nat. | | OF-1B | 18 | 25 | 3 | 6 | 0 | 0 | 0 | 3 | .240 | 15 | 3 | 0 | 1.000 |
| 1971–Philadelphia ......Nat. | | OF-1B | 158 | 599 | 78 | 153 | 27 | 6 | 30 | 99 | .255 | 377 | 12 | 11 | .972 |
| 1972–Philadelphia ......Nat. | | ●OF-1B | 147 | 531 | 60 | 131 | ●39 | 3 | 13 | 64 | .247 | 429 | ●22 | 6 | .987 |
| 1973–Philadelphia ......Nat. | | 1B-OF | 146 | 552 | 69 | 145 | 16 | 5 | 11 | 65 | .263 | 852 | 58 | 6 | .993 |
| 1974–Philadelphia ......Nat. | | 1B-OF | 143 | 527 | 55 | 160 | 33 | 1 | 7 | 79 | .304 | 1217 | 79 | 10 | .992 |
| 1975–Phil.y-S.F. ........Nat. | | 1B | 156 | 602 | 61 | 182 | 34 | 2 | 10 | 101 | .302 | 1333 | *98 | 10 | .993 |
| 1976–S.F.z-Atl. ..........Nat. | | 1B | *163 | 650 | 74 | 206 | 29 | 2 | 11 | 84 | .317 | 1569 | ●107 | *22 | .987 |
| American League Totals ................ | | | 8 | 2 | 2 | 0 | 0 | 0 | 0 | 0 | .000 | 1 | 0 | 0 | 1.000 |
| National League Totals .................. | | | 931 | 3486 | 400 | 983 | 178 | 19 | 82 | 495 | .282 | 5792 | 379 | 65 | .990 |
| Major League Totals ...................... | | | 939 | 3488 | 402 | 983 | 178 | 19 | 82 | 495 | .282 | 5793 | 379 | 65 | .990 |

†Drafted by California Angels from Jacksonville (St. Louis Cardinals' organization), November 29, 1965; returned to St. Louis organization, May 5, 1966.
‡On disabled list, May 1 through August 25.
§Released to Philadelphia Phillies by St. Louis Cardinals (as partial compensation for Outfielder Curt Flood who refused to report after being traded), April 8, 1970; Cardinals assigned Pitcher Bob Browning to Philadelphia organization, August 31, 1970, to complete deal.
xOn temporary inactive list, May 12 through July 6.
yTraded to San Francisco Giants for Outfielder Garry Maddox, May 4, 1975.
zTraded with Shortstop Craig Robinson, Outfielder Jake Brown, and Infielder Mike Eden to Atlanta Braves for Third baseman-First Baseman Darrell Evans and Shortstop Marty Perez, June 13, 1976.

## JOHN JOSEPH MONTEFUSCO, JR.
### (The Count)

Born May 25, 1950, at Long Branch, N. J.
Height, 6.01. Weight, 180.
Throws and bats righthanded.
Attended Brookdale Community College, Lincroft, N. J.

Pitched 9-0 no-hit victory against Atlanta Braves, September 29, 1976.

Hit home run on first official major league time at bat, September 3, 1974.
Struck out eight consecutive batters against Salt Lake City, August 11, 1974.
Tied for National League lead in shutouts by pitchers with 6 in 1976.
Led Texas League in shutouts with 4 in 1974.
Tied for Pacific Coast League lead in shutouts with 3 in 1974.
Named National League Rookie of the Year by Baseball Writers' Association of America, 1975.
Named National League Rookie Pitcher of the Year by THE SPORTING NEWS, 1975.

| Year Club | League | G. | IP. | W. | L. | Pct. | H. | R. | ER. | SO. | BB. | ERA. |
|---|---|---|---|---|---|---|---|---|---|---|---|---|
| 1973—Decatur | Midwest | 24 | 120 | 9 | 2 | .818 | 94 | 40 | 29 | 126 | 44 | 2.18 |
| 1974—Amarillo | Texas | 19 | 144 | 8 | 9 | .471 | 143 | 61 | 50 | 107 | 37 | 3.13 |
| 1974—Phoenix | P. Coast | 11 | 77 | 7 | 3 | .700 | 60 | 35 | 28 | 90 | 26 | 3.27 |
| 1974—San Francisco | National | 7 | 39 | 3 | 2 | .600 | 41 | 22 | 21 | 34 | 19 | 4.85 |
| 1975—San Francisco | National | 35 | 244 | 15 | 9 | .625 | 210 | 85 | 78 | 215 | 86 | 2.88 |
| 1976—San Francisco | National | 37 | 253 | 16 | 14 | .533 | 224 | 90 | 80 | 172 | 74 | 2.85 |
| Major League Totals | | 79 | 536 | 34 | 25 | .576 | 475 | 197 | 179 | 421 | 179 | 3.01 |

ALL-STAR GAME RECORD

| Year League | IP. | W. | L. | Pct. | H. | R. | ER. | SO. | BB. | ERA. |
|---|---|---|---|---|---|---|---|---|---|---|
| 1976—National | 2 | 0 | 0 | .000 | 0 | 0 | 0 | 2 | 2 | .000 |

## ROBERT EDWARD MONTGOMERY
### (Bob)

Born April 16, 1944, at Davidson, Tenn.
Height, 6.02. Weight, 200.
Throws and bats righthanded.
Hobbies—Flying and playing golf.

Led International League catchers in double plays with 11 in 1970 and tied for league lead with 7 in 1969.
Tied for International League lead in passed balls with 10 in 1970.

| Year Club | League | Pos. | G. | AB. | R. | H. | 2B. | 3B. | HR. | RBI. | B.A. | PO. | A. | E. | F.A. |
|---|---|---|---|---|---|---|---|---|---|---|---|---|---|---|---|
| 1962—Olean | NYP | OF-3B | 46 | 150 | 35 | 41 | 10 | 0 | 2 | 24 | .273 | 60 | 21 | 15 | .844 |
| 1963—Waterloo | Midw. | 3B | 119 | 412 | 71 | 108 | 19 | 4 | 16 | 78 | .262 | 81 | 170 | 37 | .872 |
| 1964—Waterloo | Midw. | C-O | 111 | 418 | 57 | 112 | 24 | 3 | 13 | 85 | .268 | 684 | •91 | •20 | .975 |
| 1964—Seattle | P. C. | .... | 7 | 16 | 0 | 2 | 0 | 0 | 0 | 2 | .125 | .... | .... | .... | ........ |
| 1965—Winston-Salem | Carol. | C-OF | 111 | 360 | 28 | 86 | 12 | 2 | 2 | 40 | .239 | 638 | 78 | 18 | .975 |
| 1966—Toronto | Int. | C | 12 | 34 | 6 | 11 | 0 | 0 | 2 | 5 | .324 | 51 | 4 | 1 | .982 |
| 1966—Pittsfield | East. | C | 65 | 216 | 19 | 63 | 8 | 1 | 5 | 28 | .292 | 389 | 50 | 6 | .987 |
| 1967—Toronto | Int. | C-OF | 90 | 276 | 28 | 65 | 8 | 0 | 8 | 32 | .236 | 357 | 32 | 8 | .980 |
| 1968—Louisville | Int. | C | 48 | 109 | 9 | 31 | 5 | 0 | 0 | 6 | .284 | 173 | 17 | 3 | .984 |
| 1969—Louisville | Int. | C | 103 | 363 | 46 | 106 | 29 | 1 | 4 | 43 | .292 | 414 | 47 | 8 | .983 |
| 1970—Louisville | Int. | •C-OF | 131 | 487 | 71 | 158 | 30 | 3 | 14 | 89 | .324 | •750 | 63 | •16 | .981 |
| 1970—Boston | Amer. | C | 22 | 78 | 8 | 14 | 2 | 0 | 1 | 4 | .179 | 143 | 13 | 3 | .981 |
| 1971—Boston | Amer. | C | 67 | 205 | 19 | 49 | 11 | 2 | 2 | 24 | .239 | 361 | 15 | 4 | .989 |
| 1972—Boston | Amer. | C | 24 | 77 | 7 | 22 | 1 | 0 | 2 | 7 | .286 | 120 | 10 | 2 | .985 |
| 1973—Boston | Amer. | C | 34 | 128 | 18 | 41 | 6 | 2 | 7 | 25 | .320 | 168 | 19 | 5 | .974 |
| 1974—Boston | Amer. | C | 88 | 254 | 26 | 64 | 10 | 0 | 4 | 38 | .252 | 318 | 28 | 8 | .977 |
| 1975—Boston | Amer. | C-1B | 62 | 195 | 16 | 44 | 10 | 1 | 2 | 26 | .226 | 239 | 25 | 5 | .981 |
| 1976—Boston | Amer. | C-PH | 31 | 93 | 10 | 23 | 3 | 1 | 3 | 13 | .247 | 106 | 12 | 2 | .983 |
| Major League Totals | | | 328 | 1030 | 104 | 257 | 43 | 6 | 21 | 137 | .250 | 1455 | 122 | 29 | .982 |

WORLD SERIES RECORD

| Year Club | League | Pos. | G. | AB. | R. | H. | 2B. | 3B. | HR. | RBI. | B.A. | PO. | A. | E. | F.A. |
|---|---|---|---|---|---|---|---|---|---|---|---|---|---|---|---|
| 1975—Boston | Amer. | PH | 1 | 1 | 0 | 0 | 0 | 0 | 0 | 0 | .000 | 0 | 0 | 0 | .000 |

PITCHING RECORD

| Year Club | League | G. | IP. | W. | L. | Pct. | H. | R. | ER. | SO. | BB. | ERA. |
|---|---|---|---|---|---|---|---|---|---|---|---|---|
| 1963—Waterloo | Midwest | 2 | 2 | 0 | 0 | .000 | 4 | 3 | 0 | 2 | 2 | 0.00 |

## ALVIN EARL MOORE
### (Junior)

Born January 25, 1953, at Waskom, Tex.
Height, 5.11. Weight, 185.
Throws and bats righthanded.
Attended College of Alameda, Alameda, Calif.

| Year Club | League | Pos. | G. | AB. | R. | H. | 2B. | 3B. | HR. | RBI. | B.A. | PO. | A. | E. | F.A. |
|---|---|---|---|---|---|---|---|---|---|---|---|---|---|---|---|
| 1971—Wytheville | Appal. | SS-3B | 60 | 210 | 39 | 65 | 7 | 1 | 6 | 37 | .310 | 74 | 135 | 35 | .857 |
| 1972—Greenwood | W. C. | 3B | 117 | 420 | 52 | 126 | 10 | 4 | 5 | 56 | .300 | 91 | 229 | 31 | .912 |
| 1973—Savannah | South. | •2B-3B | 137 | 471 | 65 | 108 | 14 | 1 | 11 | 43 | .229 | •329 | 319 | 16 | •.976 |
| 1974—Savannah | South. | 3B-2B | 135 | 460 | 61 | 119 | 20 | 3 | 9 | 59 | .259 | 118 | 281 | 25 | .941 |
| 1974—Richmond | Int. | 3B-SS | 4 | 11 | 0 | 3 | 0 | 0 | 0 | 0 | .273 | 2 | 7 | 0 | 1.000 |
| 1975—Rochmond | Int. | •2B-3B | 128 | 460 | 60 | 138 | 18 | 5 | 14 | 65 | .300 | 247 | 283 | 18 | •.967 |
| 1976—Richmond | Int. | O-2-3 | 103 | 398 | 58 | 131 | 23 | 3 | 3 | 72 | .329 | 161 | 41 | 7 | .966 |
| 1976—Atlanta | Nat. | 3-O-2 | 20 | 26 | 1 | 7 | 1 | 0 | 0 | 2 | .269 | 7 | 10 | 1 | .944 |
| Major League Totals | | | 20 | 26 | 1 | 7 | 1 | 0 | 0 | 2 | .269 | 7 | 10 | 1 | .944 |

## CHARLES WILLIAM MOORE, JR.
### (Charlie)

Born June 21, 1953, at Birmingham, Ala.
Height, 5.11. Weight, 190.
Throws and bats righthanded.
Hobbies—Hunting, fishing and golf.
Attended University of Alabama, Birmingham, Ala.
Son of Charles William Moore, Sr., former minor league pitcher.
Led Midwest League catchers in double plays with 12 in 1972.
Led New York-Pennsylvania League in passed balls with 16 in 1971 and tied for Midwest League lead with 30 in 1972.

| Year Club | League | Pos. | G. | AB. | R. | H. | 2B. | 3B. | HR. | RBI. | B.A. | PO. | A. | E. | F.A. |
|---|---|---|---|---|---|---|---|---|---|---|---|---|---|---|---|
| 1971—Newark ............ | NYP | C | 60 | 209 | 36 | 62 | 12 | 3 | 6 | 27 | .297 | *439 | *34 | 5 | .990 |
| 1972—Danville ............ | Midw. | *C-1B | 106 | 348 | 56 | 90 | 14 | 4 | 12 | 44 | .259 | *723 | *92 | *25 | .970 |
| 1973—Shreveport ........ | Texas | C | 76 | 271 | 47 | 69 | 14 | 2 | 8 | 45 | .255 | 402 | 46 | 14 | .970 |
| 1973—Evansville ........ | A. A. | C | 50 | 178 | 27 | 52 | 9 | 1 | 7 | 25 | .292 | 274 | 30 | 2 | .993 |
| 1973—Milwaukee ........ | Amer. | C | 8 | 27 | 0 | 5 | 0 | 1 | 0 | 3 | .185 | 48 | 5 | 1 | .981 |
| 1974—Milwaukee ........ | Amer. | C | 72 | 204 | 17 | 50 | 10 | 4 | 0 | 19 | .245 | 229 | 28 | 4 | .985 |
| 1975—Milwaukee ........ | Amer. | C-OF | 73 | 241 | 26 | 70 | 20 | 1 | 1 | 29 | .290 | 234 | 23 | 10 | .963 |
| 1976—Milwaukee ........ | Amer. | C-O-3-DH | 87 | 241 | 33 | 46 | 7 | 4 | 3 | 16 | .191 | 249 | 45 | 9 | .970 |
| Major League Totals .................... | | | 240 | 713 | 76 | 171 | 37 | 10 | 4 | 67 | .240 | 760 | 101 | 24 | .973 |

## DONNIE RAY MOORE

Born February 13, 1954, at Lubbock, Tex.
Height, 6.00. Weight, 175.
Throws right and bats lefthanded.
Hobbies—Hunting, fishing, golf and billiards.
Attended Ranger Junior College, Ranger, Tex.
Led Texas League in games started with 27 and tied for lead in shutouts with 3 in 1975.

| Year Club | League | G. | IP. | W. | L. | Pct. | H. | R. | ER. | SO. | BB. | ERA. |
|---|---|---|---|---|---|---|---|---|---|---|---|---|
| 1973—Bradenton Cubs.................... | Gulf Coast | 4 | 10 | 0 | 1 | .000 | 9 | 5 | 4 | 6 | 6 | 3.60 |
| 1974—Key West† ............................ | Florida St. | 26 | 174 | 11 | 12 | .478 | 167 | 73 | 54 | 97 | 69 | 2.79 |
| 1974—Midland................................ | Texas | 5 | 22 | 0 | 4 | .000 | 32 | 18 | 17 | 9 | 5 | 6.95 |
| 1975—Midland................................ | Texas | 28 | 185 | 14 | 8 | .636 | 191 | 79 | 61 | 123 | 67 | 2.97 |
| 1975—Chicago .............................. | National | 4 | 9 | 0 | 0 | .000 | 12 | 4 | 4 | 8 | 4 | 4.00 |
| 1976—Wichita ............................... | Am. Assoc. | 24 | 152 | 7 | 11 | .389 | 170 | 96 | 80 | 92 | 61 | 4.74 |
| Major League Totals .............................. | | 4 | 9 | 0 | 0 | .000 | 12 | 4 | 4 | 8 | 4 | 4.00 |

†Appeared as an outfielder in two games.

## TOMMY JOE MOORE

Born July 7, 1948, at Lynwood, Calif.
Height, 5.11. Weight, 180.
Throws and bats righthanded.
Hobbies—Hunting, fishing and water skiing.
Attended Cerritos College, Norwalk, Calif.
Pitched seven-inning, 2-0 no-hit victory against Rochester, August 6, 1972.
Pitched seven-inning, 4-0 no-hit victory against Arkansas, June 25, 1971

| Year Club | League | G. | IP. | W. | L. | Pct. | H. | R. | ER. | SO. | BB. | ERA. |
|---|---|---|---|---|---|---|---|---|---|---|---|---|
| 1969—Visalia ............................... | California | 1 | 1 | 0 | 0 | .000 | 0 | 0 | 0 | 0 | 0 | 0.00 |
| 1970—Tidewater ........................... | Int'national | 4 | 12 | 0 | 0 | .000 | 17 | 13 | 13 | 11 | 10 | 9.75 |
| 1970—Pompano Beach.................... | Florida St. | 16 | 82 | 3 | 8 | .273 | 75 | 43 | 33 | 63 | 51 | 3.62 |
| 1971—Memphis.............................. | Texas | 27 | 191 | 11 | 10 | .524 | 142 | 77 | 68 | *160 | 64 | 3.20 |
| 1972—Tidewater ........................... | Int'national | 23 | 148 | 11 | 5 | .688 | 119 | 59 | 46 | 100 | 73 | 2.80 |
| 1972—New York ........................... | National | 3 | 12 | 0 | 0 | .000 | 12 | 4 | 4 | 5 | 1 | 3.00 |
| 1973—Tidewater ........................... | Int'national | 22 | 157 | 9 | 11 | .450 | 148 | 63 | 55 | 101 | 73 | 3.15 |
| 1973—New York ........................... | National | 3 | 3 | 0 | 1 | .000 | 6 | 5 | 4 | 1 | 3 | 12.00 |
| 1974—Tidewater† ......................... | Int'national | 26 | 162 | 7 | 12 | .368 | 147 | 72 | 58 | 131 | ●103 | 3.22 |
| 1975—St. Louis‡ .......................... | National | 10 | 19 | 0 | 0 | .000 | 15 | 10 | 8 | 6 | 12 | 3.79 |
| 1975—Spokane ............................. | P. Coast | 6 | 32 | 1 | 3 | .250 | 23 | 17 | 15 | 14 | 24 | 4.22 |
| 1975—Texas ................................. | American | 12 | 21 | 0 | 2 | .000 | 31 | 21 | 19 | 15 | 12 | 8.14 |
| 1976—Sacramento§ ...................... | P. Coast | 33 | 124 | 10 | 7 | .588 | 123 | 82 | 64 | 80 | 81 | 4.65 |
| National League Totals............................. | | 16 | 34 | 0 | 1 | .000 | 33 | 19 | 16 | 12 | 16 | 4.24 |
| American League Totals............................ | | 12 | 21 | 0 | 2 | .000 | 31 | 21 | 19 | 15 | 12 | 8.14 |
| Major League Totals .............................. | | 28 | 55 | 0 | 3 | .000 | 64 | 40 | 35 | 27 | 28 | 5.73 |

†Traded with Pitcher Ray Sadecki by New York Mets to St. Louis Cardinals for First Baseman-Third Baseman Joe Torre, October 13, 1974.
‡Traded with Shortstop Ed Brinkman to Texas Rangers for Outfielder Willie Davis, June 4, 1975.
§Sold to Seattle Mariners, October 24, 1976.

### RECORD AS OUTFIELDER

Tied for California League lead in sacrifice flies with 8 in 1969.

| Year Club | League | Pos. | G. | AB. | R. | H. | 2B. | 3B. | HR. | RBI. | B.A. | PO. | A. | E. | F.A. |
|---|---|---|---|---|---|---|---|---|---|---|---|---|---|---|---|
| 1967—Marion .............. | Appal. | OF | 59 | 238 | 39 | 69 | 12 | 4 | 3 | 29 | .290 | 70 | *14 | 4 | .955 |
| 1968—Visalia .............. | Calif. | OF | 124 | 471 | 58 | 113 | 13 | 2 | 6 | 41 | .240 | 216 | 12 | *17 | .931 |

| Year | Club | League | Pos. | G. | AB. | R. | H. | 2B. | 3B. | HR. | RBI. | B.A. | PO. | A. | E. | F.A. |
|------|------|--------|------|----|-----|----|----|-----|-----|-----|------|------|-----|----|----|------|
| 1969 | Visalia .............. | Calif. | •OF-P | 117 | 438 | 69 | 125 | 15 | 4 | 16 | 85 | .285 | 182 | •28 | •19 | .917 |
| 1970 | Pompano Beach | Fla. St. | P-OF | 23 | 55 | 3 | 17 | 0 | 2 | 1 | 8 | .309 | 21 | 10 | 3 | .912 |
| 1970 | Memphis ......... | Texas | OF | 9 | 15 | 0 | 1 | 0 | 1 | 0 | 2 | .067 | 11 | 3 | 0 | 1.000 |

## ANDRES MORA (IBARRA)

Born May 25, 1955, at Saltillo, Coahuila, Mexico.
Height, 6.00. Weight, 180.
Throws and bats righthanded.
Led Mexican League in total bases with 288 in 1975.

| Year | Club | League | Pos. | G. | AB. | R. | H. | 2B. | 3B. | HR. | RBI. | B.A. | PO. | A. | E. | F.A. |
|------|------|--------|------|----|-----|----|----|-----|-----|-----|------|------|-----|----|----|------|
| 1971 | Zacatecas ......... | Mex.C. | OF | 56 | 137 | 22 | 42 | 8 | 4 | 1 | 29 | .307 | 62 | 3 | 6 | .951 |
| 1972 | Saltillo† | Mex. | OF | 2 | 1 | 0 | 0 | 0 | 0 | 0 | 0 | .000 | 0 | 0 | 0 | .000 |
| 1973 | W. Palm Beach‡ | Fla.St. | OF | 8 | 21 | 1 | 0 | 0 | 0 | 0 | 0 | .000 | 4 | 0 | 0 | 1.000 |
| 1974 | Saltillo .............. | Mex. | •OF-2B | 132 | 444 | 56 | 138 | 17 | 6 | 14 | 77 | .311 | 195 | 31 | 7 | •.970 |
| 1975 | Saltillo§ ........... | Mex. | •OF-3-2 | 133 | 492 | 82 | 151 | 18 | 7 | •35 | •109 | .307 | 183 | 84 | 9 | •.967 |
| 1976 | Baltimore ......... | Amer. | OF-DH | 73 | 220 | 18 | 48 | 11 | 0 | 6 | 25 | .218 | 55 | 3 | 3 | .951 |
| 1976 | Rochester ......... | Int. | OF-2-3 | 18 | 67 | 17 | 22 | 6 | 0 | 6 | 15 | .328 | 24 | 15 | 1 | .975 |
| | Major League Totals ..................... | | | 73 | 220 | 18 | 48 | 11 | 0 | 6 | 25 | .218 | 55 | 3 | 3 | .951 |

†Conditionally released to Montreal Expos' organization, Februray 28, 1973.
‡On disabled list, May 8 through remainder of season. Returned by Montreal Expos' organization to Mexican League, March 14, 1974.
§Sold to Baltimore Orioles' organization, August 11, 1975.

## JOSE MANUEL MORALES

Born December 30, 1944, at Frederiksted, St. Croix, Virgin Islands.
Height, 6.00. Weight, 205.
Throws and bats righthanded.
Hobbies—Swimming and fishing.

Established following major league records: most games as pinch-hitter, season, 82, 1976; most at bats as pinch-hitter, season, 78, 1976; most hits as pinch-hitter, season, 25, 1976.
Led California League in passed balls with 29 in 1965 and American Association with 21 in 1969.

| Year | Club | League | Pos. | G. | AB. | R. | H. | 2B. | 3B. | HR. | RBI. | B.A. | PO. | A. | E. | F.A. |
|------|------|--------|------|----|-----|----|----|-----|-----|-----|------|------|-----|----|----|------|
| 1964 | Lexington† | W. Car. | C | 73 | 233 | 29 | 56 | 11 | 1 | 3 | 34 | .240 | 640 | 40 | 13 | .981 |
| 1965 | Fresno .............. | Calif. | C | 95 | 321 | 39 | 91 | 13 | 1 | 4 | 48 | .283 | 602 | 61 | •26 | .962 |
| 1966 | Waterbury‡ | East. | C | 64 | 215 | 18 | 54 | 9 | 1 | 7 | 26 | .251 | 319 | 33 | 10 | .972 |
| 1967 | Waterbury ........ | East. | C-OF | 94 | 246 | 19 | 61 | 7 | 4 | 4 | 31 | .248 | 421 | 36 | 14 | .970 |
| 1968 | Amarillo‡‡ | Texas | C | 105 | 307 | 35 | 88 | 22 | 4 | 8 | 41 | .287 | 566 | 70 | •19 | .971 |
| 1969 | Iowa.................. | A.A. | •C-OF | 98 | 363 | 54 | 102 | 11 | 3 | 16 | 61 | .281 | 350 | 60 | •18 | .958 |
| 1970 | Iowa.................. | A.A. | C | 93 | 229 | 36 | 70 | 14 | 0 | 12 | 31 | .306 | 327 | 31 | 9 | .975 |
| 1971 | Iowa§ ............... | A.A. | C-OF | 71 | 153 | 15 | 38 | 7 | 0 | 9 | 22 | .248 | 212 | 18 | 7 | .970 |
| 1972 | Tidewater x y....Int. | | •C-OF-1 | 86 | 256 | 28 | 75 | 18 | 2 | 7 | 48 | .293 | 380 | 15 | •14 | .966 |
| 1973 | Tucson .............. | P.C. | C-1B-3B | 76 | 248 | 37 | 88 | 17 | 2 | 4 | 50 | .355 | 20 | 4 | 5 | .828 |
| 1973 | Oakland z.........Amer. | | DH-PH | 6 | 14 | 0 | 4 | 1 | 0 | 0 | 1 | .286 | 0 | 0 | 0 | .000 |
| 1973 | Montreal ......... | Nat. | PH | 5 | 5 | 0 | 2 | 0 | 0 | 0 | 0 | .400 | 0 | 0 | 0 | .000 |
| 1974 | Memphis .......... | Int. | 1B-C | 66 | 216 | 20 | 60 | 13 | 0 | 6 | 32 | .278 | 442 | 29 | 6 | .987 |
| 1974 | Montreal ......... | Nat. | C | 25 | 26 | 3 | 7 | 4 | 0 | 1 | 5 | .269 | 3 | 1 | 1 | .800 |
| 1975 | Montreal ......... | Nat. | 1-OF-C | 93 | 163 | 18 | 49 | 6 | 1 | 2 | 24 | .301 | 234 | 28 | 4 | .985 |
| 1976 | Montreal ......... | Nat. | 1B-C | 104 | 158 | 12 | 50 | 11 | 0 | 4 | 37 | .316 | 137 | 21 | 3 | .981 |
| | American League Totals ................ | | | 6 | 14 | 0 | 4 | 1 | 0 | 0 | 1 | .286 | 0 | 0 | 0 | .000 |
| | National League Totals .................. | | | 227 | 352 | 33 | 108 | 21 | 1 | 7 | 66 | .307 | 374 | 50 | 8 | .981 |
| | Major League Totals ..................... | | | 233 | 366 | 33 | 112 | 22 | 1 | 7 | 67 | .306 | 374 | 50 | 8 | .981 |

†On disabled list, July 25 through remainder of season.
‡On disabled list, May 28 to June 18 and July 21 through remainder of season.
‡‡Drafted from San Francisco Giants' organization by Vancouver (Oakland Athletics' organization), December 2, 1968.
§Loaned by Oakland Athletics' organization to Tidewater (New York Mets' organization), April 14, 1972.
xOn disabled list, July 12 to July 28, 1972.
yReturned by New York Mets' organization to Oakland Athletics' organization, September 29, 1972.
zPurchased by Montreal Expos, September 18, 1973.

## JULIO RUBEN MORALES
## (Jerry)

Born February 18, 1949, at Yabucoa, Puerto Rico.
Height, 5.10. Weight, 165.
Throws and bats righthanded.
Hobbies—Riding horses and listening to music.

Led Appalachian League outfielders in double plays with 2 in 1966 and tied for lead by Pacific Coast League outfielders with 3 in 1971.
Named Player of the Year in Appalachian League, 1966.

| Year | Club | League | Pos. | G. | AB. | R. | H. | 2B. | 3B. | HR. | RBI. | B.A. | PO. | A. | E. | F.A. |
|------|------|--------|------|----|-----|----|----|-----|-----|-----|------|------|-----|----|----|------|
| 1966 | Marion .............. | Appal. | OF | 38 | 119 | 33 | 41 | 8 | 2 | 1 | 25 | .345 | 78 | 6 | 3 | .966 |
| 1967 | Winter Haven ....Fla.St. | | OF-2-3 | 139 | 501 | 82 | 124 | 11 | 14 | 8 | 48 | .248 | 308 | 56 | 16 | .958 |
| 1968 | Raleigh-Durham Carol. | | OF | 43 | 129 | 18 | 29 | 9 | 1 | 1 | 15 | .225 | 83 | 2 | 3 | .966 |
| 1968 | Visalia† ........... | Calif. | OF | 70 | 250 | 44 | 66 | 7 | 2 | 6 | 33 | .264 | 143 | 9 | 4 | .974 |
| 1969 | Elmira .............. | East. | •OF-SS | 127 | 459 | 62 | 125 | 11 | •12 | 15 | 63 | .272 | •349 | 8 | 7 | .981 |

| Year | Club | League | Pos. | G. | AB. | R. | H. | 2B. | 3B. | HR. | RBI. | B.A. | PO. | A. | E. | F.A. |
|---|---|---|---|---|---|---|---|---|---|---|---|---|---|---|---|---|
| 1969–San Diego | Nat. | | OF | 19 | 41 | 5 | 8 | 2 | 0 | 1 | 6 | .195 | 27 | 2 | 0 | 1.000 |
| 1970–Salt Lake City | P.C. | | OF | 109 | 433 | 50 | 107 | 20 | 7 | 6 | 35 | .247 | 237 | 7 | 4 | •.984 |
| 1970–San Diego | Nat. | | OF | 28 | 58 | 6 | 9 | 0 | 1 | 1 | 4 | .155 | 25 | 0 | 2 | .926 |
| 1971–Hawaii | P.C. | | OF | 137 | 470 | 81 | 128 | 12 | 11 | 11 | 52 | .272 | 285 | 14 | 2 | •.993 |
| 1971–San Diego | Nat. | | OF | 12 | 17 | 1 | 2 | 0 | 0 | 0 | 1 | .118 | 8 | 0 | 0 | 1.000 |
| 1972–San Diego | Nat. | | OF-3B | 115 | 347 | 38 | 83 | 15 | 7 | 4 | 18 | .239 | 214 | 8 | 4 | .982 |
| 1973–San Diego‡ | Nat. | | OF | 122 | 388 | 47 | 109 | 23 | 2 | 9 | 34 | .281 | 214 | 5 | 2 | .991 |
| 1974–Chicago | Nat. | | OF | 151 | 534 | 70 | 146 | 21 | 7 | 15 | 82 | .273 | 266 | 5 | 7 | .975 |
| 1975–Chicago | Nat. | | OF | 153 | 578 | 62 | 156 | 21 | 0 | 12 | 91 | .270 | 273 | 11 | 6 | .979 |
| 1976–Chicago | Nat. | | OF | 140 | 537 | 66 | 147 | 17 | 0 | 16 | 67 | .274 | 273 | 12 | 5 | .983 |
| Major League Totals | | | | 740 | 2500 | 295 | 660 | 99 | 17 | 58 | 303 | .264 | 1300 | 43 | 26 | .981 |

†Recalled by New York Mets; selected by San Diego Padres from New York in expansion draft, October 14, 1968.

‡Traded to Chicago Cubs for Second Baseman Glenn Beckert and Infielder Bob Fenwick (latter assigned from Wichita to Hawaii), November 12, 1973.

## OMAR RENAN MORENO (QUINTERO)
### (YenYe')
(Nicknamed by father.)

Born October 24, 1953, at Puerto Armuelles, Panama.
Height, 6.02. Weight, 180.
Throws and bats lefthanded.
Hobbies–Fishing and playing the guitar.
Led Carolina League in stolen bases with 77 in 1973 and Eastern League with 67 in 1974.

| Year | Club | League | Pos. | G. | AB. | R. | H. | 2B. | 3B. | HR. | RBI. | B.A. | PO. | A. | E. | F.A. |
|---|---|---|---|---|---|---|---|---|---|---|---|---|---|---|---|---|
| 1969–Brad. Pirates | Gulf C. | | OF | 25 | 62 | 7 | 18 | 1 | 0 | 0 | 4 | .290 | 22 | 0 | 3 | .880 |
| 1970–Brad. Pirates | Gulf C. | | OF-1B | 51 | 219 | 32 | 51 | 7 | 4 | 1 | 19 | .233 | 129 | 9 | 8 | .945 |
| 1970–Niagara Falls | NYP | | OF | 10 | 23 | 1 | 4 | 0 | 0 | 0 | 3 | .174 | 10 | 0 | 0 | 1.000 |
| 1971–Brad. Pirates | Gulf C. | | OF | 38 | 101 | 11 | 33 | 5 | 2 | 0 | 9 | .327 | 35 | 4 | 2 | .951 |
| 1972–Gastonia | W. Car. | | OF | 51 | 144 | 18 | 31 | 5 | 2 | 1 | 17 | .215 | 95 | 3 | 3 | .970 |
| 1972–Niagara Falls | NYP | | OF | 68 | 259 | 52 | 75 | 11 | 6 | 2 | 34 | .290 | 87 | 4 | 5 | .948 |
| 1973–Salem | Carol. | | OF | 136 | 529 | •112 | 150 | 22 | 8 | 9 | 56 | .284 | 242 | 14 | 13 | .952 |
| 1973–Charleston | Int. | | OF | 3 | 12 | 1 | 4 | 0 | 1 | 1 | 3 | .333 | 4 | 0 | 0 | 1.000 |
| 1974–Thetford Mines | East. | | OF | 112 | 407 | 88 | 122 | 15 | 6 | 7 | 39 | .300 | 193 | 13 | 9 | .958 |
| 1974–Charleston | Int. | | OF | 23 | 82 | 16 | 18 | 3 | 0 | 0 | 4 | .220 | 40 | 2 | 1 | .977 |
| 1975–Charleston | Int. | | OF | 130 | 447 | 73 | 127 | 20 | 2 | 9 | 51 | .284 | •328 | 10 | 6 | .983 |
| 1975–Pittsburgh | Nat. | | OF | 6 | 6 | 1 | 1 | 0 | 0 | 0 | 0 | .167 | 0 | 0 | 1 | .000 |
| 1976–Charleston | Int. | | OF | 94 | 330 | 70 | 104 | 11 | 7 | 3 | 36 | .315 | 200 | •17 | 1 | •.955 |
| 1976–Pittsburgh | Nat. | | OF | 48 | 122 | 24 | 33 | 4 | 1 | 2 | 12 | .270 | 93 | 3 | 4 | .960 |
| Major League Totals | | | | 54 | 128 | 25 | 34 | 4 | 1 | 2 | 12 | .266 | 93 | 3 | 5 | .950 |

## ROGELIO MORET (TORRES)
### (Roger)

Born September 16, 1949, at Guayama, Puerto Rico.
Height, 6.04. Weight, 170.
Throws left and bats left and righthanded.
Led Florida State League in wild pitches with 21 in 1969.

| Year | Club | League | G. | IP. | W. | L. | Pct. | H. | R. | ER. | SO. | BB. | ERA. |
|---|---|---|---|---|---|---|---|---|---|---|---|---|---|
| 1968–Waterloo | Midwest | 24 | 81 | 6 | 6 | .500 | 73 | 40 | 22 | 75 | 55 | 2.44 |
| 1969–Winter Haven | Florida St. | 25 | 159 | 12 | 6 | .667 | 137 | 73 | 54 | 125 | 106 | 3.06 |
| 1970–Pawtucket | Eastern | 25 | 158 | 11 | 7 | .611 | 130 | 66 | 55 | 124 | •97 | 3.13 |
| 1970–Boston | American | 3 | 8 | 1 | 0 | 1.000 | 7 | 3 | 3 | 2 | 4 | 3.38 |
| 1971–Louisville | Int'national | 23 | 137 | 11 | 8 | .579 | 114 | 65 | 48 | 108 | 93 | 3.15 |
| 1971–Boston | American | 13 | 71 | 4 | 3 | .571 | 50 | 24 | 23 | 47 | 40 | 2.92 |
| 1972–Louisville | Int'national | 24 | 127 | 9 | 6 | .600 | 130 | 74 | 64 | 83 | 53 | 4.54 |
| 1972–Boston | American | 3 | 5 | 0 | 0 | .000 | 5 | 3 | 2 | 4 | 6 | 3.60 |
| 1973–Boston† | American | 30 | 156 | 13 | 2 | .867 | 138 | 60 | 55 | 90 | 67 | 3.17 |
| 1974–Boston | American | 31 | 173 | 9 | 10 | .474 | 158 | 79 | 72 | 111 | 79 | 3.75 |
| 1975–Boston‡ | American | 36 | 145 | 14 | 3 | .824 | 132 | 60 | 58 | 80 | 76 | 3.60 |
| 1976–Atlanta§ | National | 27 | 77 | 3 | 5 | .375 | 84 | 44 | 43 | 30 | 27 | 5.03 |
| American League Totals | | 116 | 558 | 41 | 18 | .695 | 490 | 229 | 213 | 334 | 272 | 3.44 |
| National League Totals | | 27 | 77 | 3 | 5 | .375 | 84 | 44 | 43 | 30 | 27 | 5.03 |
| Major League Totals | | 143 | 635 | 44 | 23 | .657 | 574 | 273 | 256 | 364 | 299 | 3.63 |

†On disabled list, April 22 to May 13, 1973.

‡Traded to Atlanta Braves for Pitcher Tom House, December 12, 1975.

§On disabled list, July 17 to September 12; traded with Outfielders Ken Henderson and Dave May, Pitchers Carl Morton and Adrian Devine, and cash estimated at $250,000 to Texas Rangers for Outfielder Jeff Burroughs, December 9, 1976.

### CHAMPIONSHIP SERIES RECORD

| Year | Club | League | G. | IP. | W. | L. | Pct. | H. | R. | ER. | SO. | BB. | ERA. |
|---|---|---|---|---|---|---|---|---|---|---|---|---|---|
| 1975–Boston | American | 1 | 1 | 1 | 0 | 1.000 | 1 | 0 | 0 | 0 | 1 | 0.00 |

### WORLD SERIES RECORD

| Year | Club | League | G. | IP. | W. | L. | Pct. | H. | R. | ER. | SO. | BB. | ERA. |
|---|---|---|---|---|---|---|---|---|---|---|---|---|---|
| 1975–Boston | American | 3 | 1⅔ | 0 | 0 | .000 | 2 | 0 | 0 | 1 | 3 | 0.00 |

# JOE LEONARD MORGAN

Born September 19, 1943, at Bonham, Tex.
Height, 5.07. Weight, 155.
Throws right and bats lefthanded.
Hobbies—Golf and billiards.
Attended Oakland City College, Oakland City, Ind., and California State University
at Hayward, Hayward, Calif.
First cousin of Marsh White, running back with New York Giants.

Set major league record for most games, consecutive, one or more bases on balls (12), June 11-23, 1972.
Tied National League record for most bases on balls, game (since 1900), 5, June 2, 1966.
Led National League batters in walks with 97 in 1965, 115 in 1972 and 132 in 1975.
Led National League second basemen in total chances with 814 in 1972.
Led National League in slugging percentage with .576 in 1976.
Led National League batters in sacrifice flies with 12 in 1976.
Tied for National League lead in double plays by second basemen with 106 in 1973.
First player to steal 60 or more bases and hit 25 or more home runs in the same season, 1973 and 1976; and one of three players in major league history to steal 50 or more bases and hit 20 or more home runs in same season (67 stolen bases and 26 home runs in 1973 and 60 stolen bases and 27 home runs in 1976).
Made six hits in one game, July 8, 1965, 12 innings.
Major league stolen bases: 1963 (1), 1964 (0), 1965 (20), 1966 (11), 1967 (29), 1968 (3), 1969 (49), 1970 (42), 1971 (40), 1972 (58), 1973 (67), 1974 (58), 1975 (67), 1976 (60). Total—505.
Led Texas League second basemen in double plays with 106 in 1964.
Voted Most Valuable Player in Texas League, 1964.
Named National League Rookie Player of the Year by THE SPORTING NEWS, 1965.
Named Most Valuable Player in National League, 1975 and 1976.
Named National League Player of the Year by THE SPORTING NEWS, 1975.
Named Major League Player of the Year by THE SPORTING NEWS, 1975 and 1976.
Named second baseman on THE SPORTING NEWS National League All-Star Team, 1972, 1974, 1975 and 1976.
Named second baseman on THE SPORTING NEWS National League All-Star fielding team, 1973, 1974, 1975 and 1976.

| Year | Club | League | Pos. | G. | AB. | R. | H. | 2B. | 3B. | HR. | RBI. | B.A. | PO. | A. | E. | F.A. |
|------|------|--------|------|----|-----|----|----|-----|-----|-----|------|------|-----|----|----|------|
| 1963—Modesto | | Calif. | 2B | 45 | 152 | 42 | 40 | 5 | 3 | 5 | 27 | .263 | 81 | 104 | 15 | .925 |
| 1963—Durham | | Carol. | 2B | 95 | 322 | 74 | 107 | 20 | 2 | 13 | 43 | .332 | 217 | 273 | 24 | .953 |
| 1963—Houston | | Nat. | 2B | 8 | 25 | 5 | 6 | 0 | 1 | 0 | 3 | .240 | 15 | 15 | 3 | .909 |
| 1964—San Antonio | | Texas | 2B •140 | 496 | 113 | 160 | •42 | 8 | 12 | 90 | .323 | 319 | 405 | 25 | •.967 |
| 1964—Houston | | Nat. | 2B | 10 | 37 | 4 | 7 | 0 | 0 | 0 | 0 | .189 | 31 | 25 | 3 | .949 |
| 1965—Houston | | Nat. | 2B | 157 | 601 | 100 | 163 | 22 | 12 | 14 | 40 | .271 | 348 | 492 | •27 | .969 |
| 1966—Houston† | | Nat. | 2B | 122 | 425 | 60 | 121 | 14 | 8 | 5 | 42 | .285 | 256 | 316 | 21 | .965 |
| 1967—Houston | | Nat. | 2B-OF | 133 | 494 | 73 | 136 | 27 | 11 | 6 | 42 | .275 | 299 | 344 | 14 | .979 |
| 1968—Houston‡ | | Nat. | 2B-OF | 10 | 20 | 6 | 5 | 0 | 1 | 0 | 0 | .250 | 10 | 6 | 2 | .889 |
| 1969—Houston | | Nat. | 2B-OF | 147 | 535 | 94 | 126 | 18 | 5 | 15 | 43 | .236 | 315 | 328 | 18 | .973 |
| 1970—Houston§ | | Nat. | 2B | 144 | 548 | 102 | 147 | 28 | 9 | 8 | 52 | .268 | 349 | 430 | 17 | .979 |
| 1971—Houston x | | Nat. | 2B | 160 | 583 | 87 | 149 | 27 | •11 | 13 | 56 | .256 | 336 | •482 | 12 | .986 |
| 1972—Cincinnati | | Nat. | 2B | 149 | 552 | •122 | 161 | 23 | 4 | 16 | 73 | .292 | •370 | 436 | 8 | •.990 |
| 1973—Cincinnati | | Nat. | 2B | 157 | 576 | 116 | 167 | 35 | 2 | 26 | 82 | .290 | •417 | 440 | 9 | .990 |
| 1974—Cincinnati | | Nat. | 2B | 149 | 512 | 107 | 150 | 31 | 3 | 22 | 67 | .293 | 344 | 385 | 13 | .982 |
| 1975—Cincinnati | | Nat. | 2B | 146 | 498 | 107 | 163 | 27 | 6 | 17 | 94 | .327 | 356 | 425 | 11 | •.986 |
| 1976—Cincinnati | | Nat. | 2B | 141 | 472 | 113 | 151 | 30 | 5 | 27 | 111 | .320 | 342 | 335 | 13 | .981 |
| Major League Totals | | | | 1633 | 5878 | 1096 | 1652 | 282 | 78 | 169 | 705 | .281 | 3788 | 4459 | 171 | .980 |

†Fractured knee cap, June 25; on disabled list from June 26 through August 5.
‡On disabled list from May 18 through September 14 with strained ligament in left knee. On military list, April 27 through April 29.
§On military list, June 6 through June 20.
xTraded with Pitcher Jack Billingham, Infielder Denis Menke and Outfielders Cesar Geronimo and Ed Armbrister (latter on Columbus roster) to Cincinnati Reds for First Baseman Lee May, Second Baseman Tommy Helms and Outfielder Jim Stewart, November 29, 1971.

## CHAMPIONSHIP SERIES RECORD

| Year | Club | League | Pos. | G. | AB. | R. | H. | 2B. | 3B. | HR. | RBI. | B.A. | PO. | A. | E. | F.A. |
|------|------|--------|------|----|-----|----|----|-----|-----|-----|------|------|-----|----|----|------|
| 1972—Cincinnati | | Nat. | 2B | 5 | 19 | 5 | 5 | 0 | 0 | 2 | 3 | .263 | 11 | 18 | 0 | 1.000 |
| 1973—Cincinnati | | Nat. | 2B | 5 | 20 | 1 | 2 | 1 | 0 | 0 | 1 | .100 | 12 | 27 | 0 | 1.000 |
| 1975—Cincinnati | | Nat. | 2B | 3 | 11 | 2 | 3 | 3 | 0 | 0 | 1 | .273 | 2 | 9 | 0 | 1.000 |
| 1976—Cincinnati | | Nat. | 2B | 3 | 7 | 2 | 0 | 0 | 0 | 0 | 0 | .000 | 9 | 5 | 0 | 1.000 |
| Championship Series Totals | | | | 16 | 57 | 10 | 10 | 4 | 0 | 2 | 5 | .175 | 34 | 59 | 0 | 1.000 |

## WORLD SERIES RECORD

| Year | Club | League | Pos. | G. | AB. | R. | H. | 2B. | 3B. | HR. | RBI. | B.A. | PO. | A. | E. | F.A. |
|------|------|--------|------|----|-----|----|----|-----|-----|-----|------|------|-----|----|----|------|
| 1972—Cincinnati | | Nat. | 2B | 7 | 24 | 4 | 3 | 2 | 0 | 0 | 1 | .125 | 18 | 18 | 1 | .973 |
| 1975—Cincinnati | | Nat. | 2B | 7 | 27 | 4 | 7 | 1 | 0 | 0 | 3 | .259 | 17 | 28 | 0 | 1.000 |
| 1976—Cincinnati | | Nat. | 2B | 4 | 15 | 3 | 5 | 1 | 1 | 1 | 2 | .333 | 13 | 10 | 2 | .920 |
| World Series Totals | | | | 18 | 66 | 11 | 15 | 4 | 1 | 1 | 6 | .227 | 48 | 56 | 3 | .972 |

## ALL-STAR GAME RECORD

| Year | League | Pos. | AB. | R. | H. | 2B. | 3B. | HR. | RBI. | B.A. | PO. | A. | E. | F.A. |
|------|--------|------|-----|----|----|-----|-----|-----|------|------|-----|----|----|------|
| 1970—National | | 2B | 2 | 1 | 1 | 0 | 0 | 0 | 0 | .500 | 1 | 2 | 0 | 1.000 |
| 1972—National | | 2B | 4 | 0 | 1 | 0 | 0 | 0 | 1 | .250 | 3 | 5 | 0 | 1.000 |
| 1973—National | | 2B | 3 | 2 | 1 | 1 | 0 | 0 | 0 | .333 | 2 | 2 | 0 | 1.000 |
| 1974—National | | 2B | 2 | 0 | 1 | 1 | 0 | 0 | 1 | .500 | 3 | 4 | 0 | 1.000 |
| 1975—National | | 2B | 4 | 0 | 1 | 0 | 0 | 0 | 0 | .250 | 0 | 1 | 0 | 1.000 |
| 1976—National | | 2B | 3 | 1 | 1 | 0 | 0 | 0 | 0 | .333 | 2 | 3 | 0 | 1.000 |
| All-Star Game Totals | | | 18 | 4 | 6 | 2 | 0 | 0 | 2 | .333 | 11 | 17 | 0 | 1.000 |

Named to National League All-Star Team for the 1966 game; replaced due to injury.

## JAMES FORREST MORRISON
### (Jim)

Born September 23, 1952, at Pensacola, Fla.
Height, 5.11. Weight, 175.
Throws and bats righthanded.
Attended Georgia Southern, Statesboro, Ga.
Led American Association third basemen in double plays with 22 in 1976.
Led Carolina League in total bases with 239 in 1975.
Led Carolina League third basemen in double plays with 35 in 1975.

| Year Club | League | Pos. | G. | AB. | R. | H. | 2B. | 3B. | HR. | RBI. | B.A. | PO. | A. | E. | F.A. |
|---|---|---|---|---|---|---|---|---|---|---|---|---|---|---|---|
| 1974–Spartanburg ......W. Car. | | 2B | 3 | 8 | 1 | 3 | 1 | 0 | 1 | 3 | .375 | 4 | 5 | 1 | .900 |
| 1974–Rocky Mount ....Carol. | | 3B | 72 | 266 | 30 | 68 | 10 | 1 | 4 | 24 | .256 | 54 | 156 | 19 | .917 |
| 1975–Rocky Mount ....Carol. | | •3b-SS | 140 | 497 | •98 | 143 | 24 | 6 | •20 | 88 | .288 | 135 | •331 | •35 | .930 |
| 1976–Oklahoma City ..A.A. | | 3B-SS | 126 | 422 | 79 | 122 | 17 | 6 | 18 | 71 | .289 | 100 | 239 | 24 | .934 |

Invited to Philadelphia Phillies' 1977 spring camp.

## CARL WENDLE MORTON

Born January 18, 1944, at Kansas City, Mo.
Height, 6.00. Weight, 200.
Throws and bats righthanded.
Hobbies–Golf, bowling and fishing.
Attended University of Oklahoma, Norman, Okla.; and University of Tulsa, Tulsa, Okla.;
received Bachelor of Science degree in Business Administration.

Selected by the Baseball Writers' Association as National League Rookie of the Year, 1970.
Named by THE SPORTING NEWS as National League Rookie Pitcher of the Year, 1970.
Received reported $60,000 bonus to sign with Milwaukee Braves, 1964.

| Year Club | League | G. | IP. | W. | L. | Pct. | H. | R. | ER. | SO. | BB. | ERA. |
|---|---|---|---|---|---|---|---|---|---|---|---|---|
| 1967–Yakima.............................Northwest | | 2 | 1 | 1 | 0 | 1.000 | 3 | 2 | 0 | 1 | 0 | 0.00 |
| 1967–Kinston...........................Carolina | | 24 | 161 | 10 | 9 | .526 | 144 | 69 | 57 | 125 | 63 | 3.19 |
| 1968–Shreveport†.........................Texas | | 26 | 179 | •13 | 5 | •.722 | 160 | 81 | 54 | 130 | 60 | 2.72 |
| 1969–Vancouver..........................P. Coast | | 18 | 133 | 8 | 6 | .571 | 118 | 56 | 52 | 86 | 45 | 3.52 |
| 1969–Montreal ............................National | | 8 | 29 | 0 | 3 | .000 | 29 | 15 | 15 | 16 | 18 | 4.66 |
| 1970–Montreal ............................National | | 43 | 285 | 18 | 11 | .621 | 281 | 123 | 114 | 154 | •125 | 3.60 |
| 1971–Montreal ............................National | | 36 | 214 | 10 | 18 | .357 | 252 | •129 | 114 | 84 | 83 | 4.79 |
| 1972–Montreal‡ ..........................National | | 27 | 172 | 7 | 13 | .350 | 170 | 84 | 75 | 51 | 53 | 3.92 |
| 1973–Atlanta .............................National | | 38 | 256 | 15 | 10 | .600 | 254 | 114 | 97 | 112 | 70 | 3.41 |
| 1974–Atlanta .............................National | | 38 | 275 | 16 | 12 | .571 | •293 | 110 | 96 | 113 | 89 | 3.14 |
| 1975–Atlanta .............................National | | 39 | 278 | 17 | 16 | .515 | •302 | 122 | 108 | 78 | 82 | 3.50 |
| 1976–Atlanta§ ...........................National | | 26 | 140 | 4 | 9 | .308 | 172 | 79 | 65 | 42 | 45 | 4.18 |
| Major League Totals .............................. | | 255 | 1649 | 87 | 92 | .486 | 1753 | 776 | 684 | 650 | 565 | 3.73 |

†Recalled by Atlanta Braves; selected by Montreal Expos from Atlanta in expansion draft, October 14, 1968.
‡Traded to Atlanta Braves for Pitcher Pat Jarvis, February 27, 1973.
§Traded with Pitchers Roger Moret and Adrian Devine, Outfielders Ken Henderson and Dave May, and cash estimated at $250,000 to Texas Rangers for Outfielder Jeff Burroughs, December 9, 1976. Released April 1, 1977.

### RECORD AS OUTFIELDER

| Year Club | League | Pos. | G. | AB. | R. | H. | 2B. | 3B. | HR. | RBI. | B.A. | PO. | A. | E. | F.A. |
|---|---|---|---|---|---|---|---|---|---|---|---|---|---|---|---|---|
| 1965–W. Palm Beach Fla. St. | | OF | 65 | 243 | 23 | 58 | 3 | •10 | 3 | 31 | .239 | 107 | 7 | 4 | .965 |
| 1965–Yakima ............N'west | | OF | 57 | 201 | 30 | 53 | 8 | 2 | 10 | 32 | .264 | 86 | 7 | 8 | .921 |
| 1966–Kinston ............Carol. | | OF | 91 | 317 | 43 | 74 | 14 | 2 | 13 | 40 | .227 | 173 | 14 | 3 | .984 |

## PAUL RICHARD MOSKAU

Name pronounced Mosko.

Born December 20, 1953, at St. Joseph, Mo.
Height, 6.02. Weight, 200.
Throws and bats righthanded.
Hobbies–Fishing, hunting, golf and tennis.
Attended Arizona State University, Tempe, Ariz., and Azusa Pacific College, Azusa, Calif.
Led Eastern League pitchers in shutouts with 6 in 1976.

| Year Club | League | G. | IP. | W. | L. | Pct. | H. | R. | ER. | SO. | BB. | ERA. |
|---|---|---|---|---|---|---|---|---|---|---|---|---|
| 1975–Billings ..............................Pioneer | | 1 | 4 | 0 | 1 | .000 | 3 | 5 | 1 | 6 | 3 | 2.25 |
| 1975–Eugene ..............................Northwest | | 13 | 84 | •10 | 1 | •.909 | 52 | 22 | 14 | •92 | 41 | 1.50 |
| 1976–Three Rivers.......................Eastern | | 26 | 180 | 13 | 6 | .684 | 134 | 42 | 31 | 124 | 58 | •1.55 |

Listed on Cincinnati Reds' 1977 spring roster.

---

## D I D   Y O U   K N O W —

That Pittsburgh Pirate shortstop Glenn Wright made an unassisted triple play against St. Louis on May 7, 1925? Wright caught Bottomley's liner, ran to second to retire Cooney and then tagged Hornsby, who was en route to second.

## MANUEL MOTA (GERONIMO)
### (Manny)

Born February 18, 1938, at Santo Domingo, Dominican Republic.
Height, 5.11. Weight, 168.
Throws and bats righthanded.
Hobby—Golf.
Attended Escuela Salesiana, Don Bosco, Dominican Republic.
Tied major league record for most hits by pinch-hitter, inning (2), September 19, 1967, 9th inning.

| Year Club | League | Pos. | G. | AB. | R. | H. | 2B. | 3B. | HR. | RBI. | B.A. | PO. | A. | E. | F.A. |
|---|---|---|---|---|---|---|---|---|---|---|---|---|---|---|---|
| 1957—Michigan City | ....Midw. | OF | 126 | 471 | 82 | 148 | 23 | 2 | 7 | 91 | .314 | 217 | 20 | 13 | .948 |
| 1958—Danville | ...........Carol. | OF | 103 | 385 | 63 | 116 | 20 | 5 | 8 | 55 | .301 | 167 | ●18 | 7 | .964 |
| 1959—Phoenix | ...........P. C. | OF | 21 | 44 | 9 | 11 | 2 | 1 | 1 | 7 | .250 | 22 | 0 | 2 | .917 |
| 1959—Springfield | ........East. | OF-2B | 65 | 245 | 39 | 77 | 10 | 7 | 3 | 28 | .314 | 118 | 34 | 5 | .968 |
| 1960—Rio Grande Val. | Tex. | ●OF-3 | 141 | 541 | 76 | 166 | 18 | 10 | 4 | 79 | .307 | 316 | ●21 | 9 | .974 |
| 1961—Tacoma | ...........P. C. | OF-1B | 142 | 484 | 64 | 140 | 13 | 4 | 3 | 43 | .289 | 248 | 17 | 4 | .985 |
| 1962—San Francisco | ..Nat. | O-3-2B | 47 | 74 | 9 | 13 | 1 | 0 | 0 | 9 | .176 | 38 | 18 | 2 | .966 |
| 1962—El Paso†‡ | .........Tex. | OF | 30 | 109 | 26 | 38 | 9 | 3 | 7 | 7 | .349 | 51 | 1 | 1 | .981 |
| 1963—Columbus | ..........Int. | OF-2B | 75 | 294 | 46 | 86 | 9 | 3 | 5 | 20 | .293 | 150 | 61 | 4 | .981 |
| 1963—Pittsburgh | ........Nat. | OF-2B | 59 | 126 | 20 | 34 | 2 | 3 | 0 | 7 | .270 | 40 | 1 | 2 | .953 |
| 1964—Pittsburgh | .......Nat. | OF-2B-C | 115 | 271 | 43 | 75 | 8 | 3 | 5 | 32 | .277 | 122 | 5 | 5 | .962 |
| 1965—Pittsburgh | .......Nat. | OF | 121 | 294 | 47 | 82 | 7 | 6 | 4 | 29 | .279 | 127 | 5 | 2 | .985 |
| 1966—Pittsburgh | .......Nat. | OF-3B | 116 | 322 | 54 | 107 | 16 | 7 | 5 | 46 | .332 | 152 | 4 | 1 | .994 |
| 1967—Pittsburgh | .......Nat. | OF-3B | 120 | 349 | 53 | 112 | 14 | 8 | 4 | 56 | .321 | 156 | 14 | 2 | .988 |
| 1968—Pittsburgh§ | .......Nat. | OF-2-3 | 111 | 331 | 35 | 93 | 10 | 2 | 1 | 33 | .281 | 150 | 8 | 3 | .981 |
| 1969—Mont.x-L. A | .....Nat. | OF | 116 | 383 | 41 | 123 | 7 | 5 | 3 | 30 | .321 | 157 | 8 | 8 | .954 |
| 1970—Los Angeles | .....Nat. | OF-3B | 124 | 417 | 63 | 127 | 12 | 6 | 3 | 37 | .305 | 172 | 9 | 5 | .973 |
| 1971—Los Angeles | .....Nat. | OF | 91 | 269 | 24 | 84 | 13 | 5 | 0 | 34 | .312 | 108 | 3 | 4 | .965 |
| 1972—Los Angeles | .....Nat. | OF | 118 | 371 | 57 | 120 | 16 | 5 | 5 | 48 | .323 | 141 | 3 | 1 | .993 |
| 1973—Los Angeles | .....Nat. | OF | 89 | 293 | 33 | 92 | 11 | 2 | 0 | 23 | .314 | 96 | 4 | 0 | 1.000 |
| 1974—Los Angeles | .....Nat. | OF | 66 | 57 | 5 | 16 | 2 | 0 | 0 | 16 | .281 | 1 | 0 | 0 | 1.000 |
| 1975—Los Angeles | .....Nat. | OF | 52 | 49 | 3 | 13 | 1 | 0 | 0 | 10 | .265 | 9 | 0 | 0 | 1.000 |
| 1976—Los Angeles | .....Nat. | OF | 50 | 52 | 1 | 15 | 3 | 0 | 0 | 13 | .288 | 11 | 1 | 0 | 1.000 |
| Major League Totals | ................... | | 1395 | 3658 | 488 | 1106 | 123 | 52 | 30 | 423 | .302 | 1480 | 83 | 35 | .978 |

†Recalled by San Francisco Giants; Traded to Houston Colts with Pitcher Dick LeMay for Second Baseman Joe Amalfitano, November 30, 1962.
‡Traded to Pittsburgh Pirates with cash for Outfielder Howie Goss, April 2, 1963.
§Selected by Montreal Expos from Pittsburgh Pirates in expansion draft, October 14, 1968.
xTraded with Shortstop Maury Wills to Los Angeles Dodgers for Outfielder-First Baseman Ron Fairly and Infielder Paul Popovich, June 11, 1969.

### CHAMPIONSHIP SERIES RECORD

| Year Club | League | Pos. | G. | AB. | R. | H. | 2B. | 3B. | HR. | RBI. | B.A. | PO. | A. | E. | F.A. |
|---|---|---|---|---|---|---|---|---|---|---|---|---|---|---|---|
| 1974—Los Angeles | ......Nat. | PH-OF | 3 | 3 | 0 | 1 | 0 | 0 | 0 | 1 | .333 | 1 | 0 | 0 | 1.000 |

### ALL-STAR GAME RECORD

| Year | League | Pos. | AB. | R. | H. | 2B. | 3B. | HR. | RBI. | B.A. | PO. | A. | E. | F.A. |
|---|---|---|---|---|---|---|---|---|---|---|---|---|---|---|
| 1973—National | ........................... | PH | 1 | 0 | 0 | 0 | 0 | 0 | 0 | .000 | 0 | 0 | 0 | .000 |

## STEVEN RANCE MULLINIKS

Born January 15, 1956, at Tulare, Calif.
Height, 5.11. Weight, 162.
Throws right and bats lefthanded.
Hobbies—Sports.
Son of Harvey Mulliniks, minor leaguer in New York Yankees' organization, 1956-57.

| Year Club | League | Pos. | G. | AB. | R. | H. | 2B. | 3B. | HR. | RBI. | B.A. | PO. | A. | E. | F.A. |
|---|---|---|---|---|---|---|---|---|---|---|---|---|---|---|---|
| 1974—Idaho Falls | ........Pion. | SS | 66 | 202 | 28 | 44 | 8 | 3 | 0 | 24 | .218 | 110 | 170 | 33 | .895 |
| 1975—Quad Cities | ......Midw. | SS | 52 | 186 | 34 | 50 | 6 | 2 | 1 | 21 | .269 | 82 | 136 | 17 | .928 |
| 1975—Salinas | .............Calif. | SS-2B | 59 | 209 | 38 | 54 | 8 | 0 | 0 | 10 | .258 | 88 | 146 | 14 | .944 |
| 1976—El Paso† | ...........Texas | SS-2B | 90 | 333 | 81 | 105 | 22 | 4 | 7 | 51 | .315 | 140 | 247 | 20 | .951 |

†On disabled list, May 4 through June 9 and September 2 through September 24, 1976.
Listed on California Angels' 1977 spring roster.

## JERRY WAYNE MUMPHREY

Born September 9, 1952, at Tyler, Tex.
Height, 6.02. Weight, 185.
Throws right and bats left and righthanded.
Hobbies—Hunting and fishing.
Major League stolen bases: 1976 (22). Total—22.
Led American Association in stolen bases with 44 in 1975.
Led Gulf Coast League batters in strikeouts with 45 in 1971.

| Year Club | League | Pos. | G. | AB. | R. | H. | 2B. | 3B. | HR. | RBI. | B.A. | PO. | A. | E. | F.A. |
|---|---|---|---|---|---|---|---|---|---|---|---|---|---|---|---|
| 1971—Sarasota Cards | ..Gulf C. | OF | 38 | 141 | 20 | 36 | 3 | 2 | 0 | 6 | .255 | 52 | 1 | 3 | .946 |
| 1972—Sarasota Cards | ..Gulf C. | OF | 26 | 111 | 21 | 38 | 5 | 2 | 0 | 12 | .342 | 63 | 2 | 0 | 1.000 |
| 1972—Cedar Rapids | ....Midw. | OF | 11 | 33 | 6 | 6 | 2 | 0 | 0 | 1 | .182 | 15 | 0 | 0 | 1.000 |
| 1972—St. Petersburg | ..Fla. St. | OF | 17 | 44 | 7 | 15 | 2 | 1 | 0 | 1 | .341 | 11 | 1 | ·1 | .923 |

| Year | Club | League | Pos. | G. | AB. | R. | H. | 2B. | 3B. | HR. | RBI. | B.A. | PO. | A. | E. | F.A. |
|------|------|--------|------|-----|-----|-----|-----|-----|-----|-----|------|------|-----|-----|-----|------|
| 1973–St. Petersburg | ..Fla. St. | | OF | 142 | •556 | •93 | •159 | 20 | •9 | 5 | 52 | .286 | 210 | 6 | 4 | 982 |
| 1974–Arkansas | ..........Tex. | | OF | 130 | 507 | 87 | 147 | 21 | 6 | 10 | 54 | .290 | 209 | 11 | 9 | .961 |
| 1974–St. Louis | ..........Nat. | | PR-OF | 5 | 2 | 2 | 0 | 0 | 0 | 0 | 0 | .000 | 0 | 0 | 0 | .000 |
| 1975–Tulsa | ................A. A. | | OF | 127 | 495 | 87 | 141 | 19 | 6 | 8 | 59 | .285 | 248 | 7 | 6 | .977 |
| 1975–St. Louis | ..........Nat. | | OF | 11 | 16 | 2 | 6 | 2 | 0 | 0 | 1 | .375 | 9 | 0 | 0 | 1.000 |
| 1976–Tulsa | ..........A. A. | | OF | 19 | 68 | 14 | 23 | 9 | 1 | 1 | 8 | .338 | 42 | 4 | 0 | 1.000 |
| 1976–St. Louis | ..........Nat. | | OF-PH | 112 | 384 | 51 | 99 | 15 | 5 | 1 | 26 | .258 | 261 | 6 | 2 | .993 |
| Major League Totals | ...................... | | | 128 | 402 | 55 | 105 | 17 | 5 | 1 | 27 | .261 | 270 | 6 | 2 | .993 |

## THURMAN LEE MUNSON

Born June 7, 1947, at Akron, O.
Height, 5.11. Weight, 190.
Throws and bats righthanded.
Attended Kent State University, Kent. O.

Led American League catchers in double plays with 14 in 1975 and tied for lead with 11 in 1973.
Named Most Valuable Player in American league, 1976.
Selected by the Baseball Writers' Association as American League Rookie of the Year, 1970.
Named catcher on THE SPORTING NEWS American League All-Star Team, 1973, 1974, 1975 and 1976.
Named catcher on THE SPORTING NEWS American League All-Star fielding team, 1973, 1974 and 1975.
Named American League Player of the Year by THE SPORTING NEWS, 1976.

| Year | Club | League | Pos. | G. | AB. | R. | H. | 2B. | 3B. | HR. | RBI. | B.A. | PO. | A. | E. | F.A. |
|------|------|--------|------|-----|-----|-----|-----|-----|-----|-----|------|------|-----|-----|-----|------|
| 1968–Binghamton | ......East. | | C | 71 | 226 | 28 | 68 | 12 | 3 | 6 | 37 | .301 | 327 | 53 | 9 | .977 |
| 1969–Syracuse | ..........Int. | | C-2-3 | 28 | 102 | 13 | 37 | 9 | 1 | 2 | 17 | .363 | 81 | 13 | 6 | .940 |
| 1969–New York | ..........Amer. | | C | 26 | 86 | 6 | 22 | 1 | 2 | 1 | 9 | .256 | 119 | 18 | 2 | .986 |
| 1970–New York | ..........Amer. | | C | 132 | 453 | 59 | 137 | 25 | 4 | 6 | 53 | .302 | 631 | •80 | 8 | .989 |
| 1971–New York | ..........Amer. | | •C-OF | 125 | 451 | 71 | 113 | 15 | 4 | 10 | 42 | .251 | 547 | 67 | 1 | •.998 |
| 1972–New York | ..........Amer. | | C | 140 | 511 | 54 | 143 | 16 | 3 | 7 | 46 | .280 | 575 | 71 | •15 | .977 |
| 1973–New York | ..........Amer. | | C | 147 | 519 | 80 | 156 | 29 | 4 | 20 | 74 | .301 | 673 | •80 | 12 | .984 |
| 1974–New York | ..........Amer. | | C | 144 | 517 | 64 | 135 | 19 | 2 | 13 | 60 | .261 | 743 | •75 | •22 | .974 |
| 1975–New York | ..........Amer. | | •C-1-O-3 | 157 | 597 | 83 | 190 | 24 | 3 | 12 | 102 | .318 | 725 | 95 | •23 | .973 |
| 1976–New York | ..........Amer. | | C-DH-O | 152 | 616 | 79 | 186 | 27 | 1 | 17 | 105 | .302 | 546 | 78 | 14 | .978 |
| Major League Totals | ...................... | | | 1023 | 3750 | 496 | 1082 | 156 | 23 | 86 | 491 | .288 | 4559 | 564 | 97 | .981 |

### ALL-STAR GAME RECORD

| Year | League | Pos. | AB. | R. | H. | 2B. | 3B. | HR. | RBI. | B.A. | PO. | A. | E. | F.A. |
|------|--------|------|-----|-----|-----|-----|-----|-----|------|------|-----|-----|-----|------|
| 1971–American | .......................... | C | 0 | 0 | 0 | 0 | 0 | 0 | 0 | .000 | 1 | 0 | 0 | 1.000 |
| 1973–American | .......................... | C | 2 | 0 | 0 | 0 | 0 | 0 | 0 | .000 | 5 | 1 | 0 | 1.000 |
| 1974–American | .......................... | C | 3 | 1 | 1 | 1 | 0 | 0 | 0 | .333 | 7 | 0 | 1 | .875 |
| 1975–American | .......................... | C | 2 | 0 | 1 | 0 | 0 | 0 | 0 | .500 | 1 | 0 | 0 | 1.000 |
| 1976–American | .......................... | C | 2 | 0 | 0 | 0 | 0 | 0 | 0 | .000 | 4 | 0 | 0 | 1.000 |
| All-Star Game Totals | ...................... | | 9 | 1 | 2 | 1 | 0 | 0 | 0 | .222 | 18 | 2 | 1 | .952 |

### CHAMPIONSHIP SERIES RECORD

| Year | Club | League | Pos. | G. | AB. | R. | H. | 2B. | 3B. | HR. | RBI. | B.A. | PO. | A. | E. | F.A. |
|------|------|--------|------|-----|-----|-----|-----|-----|-----|-----|------|------|-----|-----|-----|------|
| 1976–New York | ..........Amer. | | C | 5 | 23 | 3 | 10 | 2 | 0 | 0 | 3 | .435 | 18 | 6 | 2 | .923 |

### WORLD SERIES RECORD

| Year | Club | League | Pos. | G. | AB. | R. | H. | 2B. | 3B. | HR. | RBI. | B.A. | PO. | A. | E. | F.A. |
|------|------|--------|------|-----|-----|-----|-----|-----|-----|-----|------|------|-----|-----|-----|------|
| 1976–New York | ..........Amer. | | C | 4 | 17 | 2 | 9 | 0 | 0 | 0 | 2 | .529 | 21 | 7 | 0 | 1.000 |

## BOBBY RAY MURCER

Born May 20, 1946, at Oklahoma City, Okla.
Height, 5.11. Weight, 180.
Throws right and bats lefthanded.
Hobby–Sports.
Attended University of Oklahoma, Norman, Okla.

Tied the following major league records: Most consecutive home runs, two games (4), June 24, 1970; most home runs, consecutive appearances (4), June 24, 1970, doubleheader; hitting for the cycle, August 29 (1st game), 1972.
Tied American League record for most home runs, doubleheader (4), June 24, 1970.
Hit three home runs in a game, July 13, 1973.
Led American League in total bases with 314 in 1972.
Led American League outfielders in total chances with 396 in 1972.
Led National League in sacrifice flies with 12 in 1975.
Led International League shortstops in double plays with 91 in 1966.
Named outfielder on THE SPORTING NEWS American League All-Star Team, 1971-72-73.
Named outfielder on THE SPORTING NEWS American League All-Star fielding ream, 1972.
Named Player of the Year in Carolina League, 1965.
Received reported $20,000 bonus to sign with New York Yankees, 1964.

| Year | Club | League | Pos. | G. | AB. | R. | H. | 2B. | 3B. | HR. | RBI. | B.A. | PO. | A. | E. | F.A. |
|------|------|--------|------|-----|-----|-----|-----|-----|-----|-----|------|------|-----|-----|-----|------|
| 1964–Johnson City | ....Appal. | | S-2B | 32 | 126 | 34 | 46 | 7 | 4 | 2 | 29 | .365 | 39 | 78 | 34 | .775 |
| 1965–Greensboro† | ......Carol. | | SS | 12 | 478 | 95 | 154 | 30 | 5 | 16 | 90 | .322 | 166 | 320 | •55 | .898 |
| 1965–New York | ..........Amer. | | SS | 11 | 37 | 2 | 9 | 0 | 1 | 1 | 4 | .243 | 28 | 41 | 5 | .932 |
| 1966–New York | ..........Amer. | | SS | 21 | 69 | 3 | 12 | 1 | 1 | 0 | 5 | .174 | 31 | 50 | 6 | .931 |
| 1966–Toledo | ..............Int. | | SS | 133 | 492 | 69 | 131 | 19 | 9 | 15 | 62 | .266 | 207 | 349 | •36 | .939 |
| 1967-68–New York‡ | ....Amer. | | | | | | | | (In Military Service) | | | | | | | |

| Year Club League | Pos. | G. | AB. | R. | H. | 2B. | 3B. | HR. | RBI. | B.A. | PO. | A. | E. | F.A. |
|---|---|---|---|---|---|---|---|---|---|---|---|---|---|---|
| 1969–New York.........Amer. | OF-3B | 152 | 564 | 82 | 146 | 24 | 4 | 26 | 82 | .259 | 235 | 81 | 22 | .935 |
| 1970–New York.........Amer. | OF | 159 | 581 | 95 | 146 | 23 | 3 | 23 | 78 | .251 | 375 | •15 | 3 | .992 |
| 1971–New York.........Amer. | OF | 146 | 529 | 94 | 175 | 25 | 6 | 25 | 94 | .331 | 317 | 10 | 5 | .985 |
| 1972–New York.........Amer. | OF | 153 | 585 | •102 | 171 | 30 | 7 | 33 | 96 | .292 | •382 | 11 | 3 | .992 |
| 1973–New York.........Amer. | OF | 160 | 616 | 83 | 187 | 29 | 2 | 22 | 95 | .304 | 380 | •14 | 6 | .985 |
| 1974–New York§ .......Amer. | OF | 156 | 606 | 69 | 166 | 25 | 4 | 10 | 88 | .274 | 297 | •21 | 7 | .978 |
| 1975–San Francisco ..Nat. | OF | 147 | 526 | 80 | 157 | 29 | 4 | 11 | 91 | .298 | 201 | 10 | 4 | .981 |
| 1976–San Francisco x Nat. | OF | 147 | 533 | 73 | 138 | 20 | 2 | 23 | 90 | .259 | 282 | 11 | 12 | .961 |
| American League Totals ............... | | 958 | 3587 | 530 | 1012 | 157 | 28 | 140 | 542 | .282 | 2045 | 243 | 57 | .976 |
| National League Totals ................. | | 294 | 1059 | 153 | 295 | 49 | 6 | 34 | 181 | .278 | 483 | 21 | 16 | .969 |
| Major League Totals ..................... | | 1252 | 4646 | 683 | 1307 | 206 | 34 | 174 | 723 | .281 | 2528 | 264 | 73 | .974 |

†On disabled list, May 3 through May 15, 1965.
‡On military list, March 6, 1967 through December 6, 1968.
§Traded to San Francisco Giants for Outfielder Bobby Bonds, October 21, 1974.
xTraded with Infielder Steve Ontiveros and Pitcher Andrew Muhlstock to Chicago Cubs for Third Baseman Bill Madlock and Infielder Rob Sperring, February 11, 1977.

### ALL-STAR GAME RECORD

| Year League | Pos. | AB. | R. | H. | 2B. | 3B. | HR. | RBI. | B.A. | PO. | A. | E. | F.A. |
|---|---|---|---|---|---|---|---|---|---|---|---|---|---|
| 1971–American ........................... | OF | 3 | 0 | 1 | 0 | 0 | 0 | 0 | .333 | 1 | 0 | 0 | 1.000 |
| 1972–American ........................... | OF | 3 | 0 | 0 | 0 | 0 | 0 | 0 | .000 | 1 | 0 | 0 | 1.000 |
| 1973–American ........................... | OF | 3 | 0 | 0 | 0 | 0 | 0 | 0 | .000 | 0 | 1 | 0 | 1.000 |
| 1974–American ........................... | OF | 2 | 0 | 0 | 0 | 0 | 0 | 0 | .000 | 0 | 0 | 0 | .000 |
| 1975–National ........................... | OF | 2 | 0 | 0 | 0 | 0 | 0 | 0 | .000 | 1 | 0 | 0 | 1.000 |
| All-Star Game Totals ...................... | | 13 | 0 | 1 | 0 | 0 | 0 | 0 | .077 | 3 | 1 | 0 | 1.000 |

## DALE BRYAN MURPHY

Born March 12, 1956, at Portland, Ore.
Height, 6.04. Weight, 210.
Throws and bats righthanded.
Hobbies–Music, art and reading.
Attended Portland Community College, Portland, Ore.

| Year Club League | Pos. | G. | AB. | R. | H. | 2B. | 3B. | HR. | RBI. | B.A. | PO. | A. | E. | F.A. |
|---|---|---|---|---|---|---|---|---|---|---|---|---|---|---|
| 1974–Kingsport .........Appal. | C | 54 | 181 | 28 | 46 | 7 | 0 | 5 | 31 | .254 | 389 | 28 | 7 | .983 |
| 1975–Greenwood .......W. Car. | C-1B | 131 | 443 | 48 | 101 | 20 | 1 | 5 | 48 | .228 | 723 | 81 | 18 | .978 |
| 1976–Savannah .........South. | C | 104 | 352 | 37 | 94 | 13 | 5 | 12 | 55 | .267 | 444 | 40 | 10 | .980 |
| 1976–Richmond.........Int. | C | 18 | 50 | 10 | 13 | 1 | 1 | 4 | 8 | .260 | 60 | 8 | 4 | .944 |
| 1976–Atlanta.............Nat. | C | 19 | 65 | 3 | 17 | 6 | 0 | 0 | 9 | .262 | 100 | 13 | 3 | .974 |
| Major League Totals ..................... | | 19 | 65 | 3 | 17 | 6 | 0 | 0 | 9 | .262 | 100 | 13 | 3 | .974 |

## DWAYNE KEITH MURPHY

Born March 18, 1955, at Merced, Calif.
Height, 6.01. Weight, 180.
Throws right and bats lefthanded.
Hobby–Automobiles.

| Year Club League | Pos. | G. | AB. | R. | H. | 2B. | 3B. | HR. | RBI. | B.A. | PO. | A. | E. | F.A. |
|---|---|---|---|---|---|---|---|---|---|---|---|---|---|---|
| 1973–Lewiston ..........N'west | OF | 68 | 215 | 25 | 50 | 7 | 2 | 3 | 19 | .233 | 102 | •13 | 6 | .950 |
| 1974–Burlington† ......Mid. | OF | 53 | 150 | 16 | 33 | 6 | 2 | 2 | 10 | .220 | 55 | 2 | 3 | .959 |
| 1975–Modesto ...........Calif. | OF | 126 | 429 | 81 | 125 | 20 | 7 | 8 | 71 | .291 | 250 | 7 | 9 | .966 |
| 1976–Chattanooga ......South. | OF | 68 | 200 | 32 | 52 | 6 | 0 | 1 | 23 | .260 | 138 | 6 | 1 | .993 |
| 1976–Tucson .............P. C. | OF | 52 | 179 | 32 | 42 | 7 | 3 | 2 | 11 | .235 | 125 | 6 | 4 | .970 |

†On disabled list, July 16 through September 16, 1974.
Listed on Oakland A's 1977 spring roster.

## THOMAS ANDREW MURPHY
### (Tom)

Born December 30, 1945, at Cleveland, O.
Height, 6.03. Weight, 205.
Throws and bats righthanded.
Hobbies–Music and reading.
Attended Ohio University, Athens, O.; received Bachelor of Arts degree in English and History.

Pitched 7-0 no-hit victory against Indianapolis, August 25, 1972.
Led American League in hit batsmen with 21 and tied for lead in wild pitches with 16 in 1969; led in wild pitches with 17 in 1971.
Received reported $20,000 bonus to sign with California Angels, 1967.

| Year Club League | G. | IP. | W. | L. | Pct. | H. | R. | ER. | SO. | BB. | ERA. |
|---|---|---|---|---|---|---|---|---|---|---|---|
| 1967–Quad Cities ..........................Midwest | 6 | 50 | 5 | 1 | .833 | 32 | 13 | 13 | 52 | 12 | 2.34 |
| 1967–Seattle ................................P. Coast | 9 | 43 | 0 | 4 | .000 | 33 | 24 | 19 | 42 | 18 | 3.98 |
| 1967–El Paso...............................Texas | 8 | 62 | 2 | 5 | .286 | 50 | 21 | 19 | 51 | 13 | 2.76 |
| 1968–Seattle ..............................P. Coast | 6 | 41 | 1 | 1 | .500 | 35 | 10 | 9 | 33 | 16 | 1.98 |
| 1968–El Paso...............................Texas | 2 | 16 | 2 | 0 | 1.000 | 14 | 9 | 8 | 8 | 11 | 4.50 |

| Year Club | League | G. | IP. | W. | L. | Pct. | H. | R. | ER. | SO. | BB. | ERA. |
|---|---|---|---|---|---|---|---|---|---|---|---|---|
| 1968–California† | American | 15 | 99 | 5 | 6 | .455 | 67 | 30 | 24 | 56 | 28 | 2.18 |
| 1969–California | American | 36 | 216 | 10 | 16 | .385 | 213 | 110 | 101 | 100 | 69 | 4.21 |
| 1970–California | American | 39 | 227 | 16 | 13 | .552 | 223 | 114 | 107 | 99 | 81 | 4.24 |
| 1971–California | American | 37 | 243 | 6 | 17 | .261 | 228 | 108 | 102 | 89 | 82 | 3.78 |
| 1972–Omaha | Am. Assoc. | 12 | 93 | 4 | 6 | .400 | 80 | 36 | 27 | 80 | 22 | 2.61 |
| 1972–Cal.‡-K.C. | American | 24 | 80 | 4 | 4 | .500 | 90 | 32 | 30 | 36 | 24 | 3.38 |
| 1973–Omaha§ | Am. Assoc. | 3 | 10 | 0 | 0 | .000 | 15 | 10 | 7 | 4 | 7 | 6.52 |
| 1973–St. Louis x | National | 19 | 89 | 3 | 7 | .300 | 89 | 38 | 37 | 42 | 22 | 3.74 |
| 1974–Milwaukee | American. | 70 | 123 | 10 | 10 | .500 | 97 | 27 | 26 | 47 | 51 | 1.90 |
| 1975–Milwaukee y | American | 52 | 72 | 1 | 9 | .100 | 85 | 43 | 37 | 32 | 27 | 4.63 |
| 1976–Milw. z-Boston | American | 52 | 99 | 4 | 6 | .400 | 116 | 61 | 46 | 39 | 34 | 4.18 |
| American League Totals | | 325 | 1159 | 56 | 81 | .409 | 1119 | 525 | 473 | 498 | 396 | 3.67 |
| National League Totals | | 19 | 89 | 3 | 7 | .300 | 89 | 38 | 37 | 42 | 22 | 3.74 |
| Major League Totals | | 344 | 1248 | 59 | 88 | .401 | 1208 | 563 | 510 | 540 | 418 | 3.68 |

†On military list from August 19 through end of season.
‡Traded to Kansas City Royals for First Baseman-Outfielder Bob Oliver, May 5, 1972.
§Traded by Kansas City Royals to St. Louis Cardinals for Pitcher Al Santorini (assigned to Omaha), May 8, 1973.
xTraded to Milwaukee Brewers for Infielder Bob Heise, December 7, 1973.
yOn disabled list, June 30 to July 23, 1975.
zTraded with Outfielder Bobby Darwin to Boston Red Sox for Outfielder Bernie Carbo and cash, June 3, 1976.

## DALE ALBERT MURRAY

Born February 2, 1950, at Cuero, Tex.
Height, 6.03. Weight, 205.
Throws and bats righthanded.
Hobbies–Hunting and working on cars.
Attended Blinn Junior College, Brenham, Tex., and Victoria College, Victoria, Tex.

| Year Club | League | G. | IP. | W. | L. | Pct. | H. | R. | ER. | SO. | BB. | ERA. |
|---|---|---|---|---|---|---|---|---|---|---|---|---|
| 1970–Watertown | Northern | 22 | 51 | 4 | 6 | .400 | 50 | 41 | 32 | 48 | 39 | 5.65 |
| 1971–West Palm Beach† | Florida St. | 1 | 1 | 0 | 1 | .000 | 4 | 4 | 4 | 2 | 2 | 36.00 |
| 1972–West Palm Beach | Florida St. | 7 | 10 | 3 | 1 | .750 | 10 | 6 | 6 | 8 | 7 | 5.40 |
| 1972–Quebec City | Eastern | 39 | 108 | 11 | 5 | .688 | 85 | 41 | 29 | 64 | 53 | 2.42 |
| 1973–Peninsula | Int'national | 28 | 150 | 8 | •13 | .381 | 145 | 77 | 71 | 89 | 75 | 4.26 |
| 1974–Memphis | Int'national | 30 | 43 | 4 | 2 | .667 | 34 | 11 | 7 | 36 | 19 | 1.47 |
| 1974–Montreal | National | 32 | 70 | 1 | 1 | .500 | 46 | 12 | 8 | 31 | 23 | 1.03 |
| 1975–Montreal‡ | National | 63 | 111 | 15 | 8 | .652 | 134 | 59 | 49 | 43 | 39 | 3.97 |
| 1976–Montreal§ | National | 81 | 113 | 4 | 9 | .308 | 117 | 47 | 41 | 35 | 37 | 3.27 |
| Major League Totals | | 176 | 294 | 20 | 18 | .526 | 297 | 118 | 98 | 109 | 99 | 3.00 |

†On disabled list, April 16 through September 30, 1971.
‡On disabled list, May 12 to June 17, 1975.
§Traded with Pitcher Woodie Fryman to Cincinnati Reds for First Baseman Tony Perez and Pitcher Will McEnaney, December 16, 1976.

### RECORD AS OUTFIELDER

| Year Club | League | Pos. | G. | AB. | R. | H. | 2B. | 3B. | HR. | RBI. | B.A. | PO. | A. | E. | F.A. |
|---|---|---|---|---|---|---|---|---|---|---|---|---|---|---|---|
| 1970–W. Palm Beach | Fla. St. | OF | 4 | 3 | 0 | 1 | 0 | 0 | 0 | 0 | .333 | 0 | 0 | 0 | .000 |

## EDDIE CLARENCE MURRAY

Born February 24, 1956, at Los Angeles, Calif.
Height, 6.02. Weight, 190.
Throws right and bats left and righthanded.
Hobby–Basketball.
Attended California State University at Los Angeles, Los Angeles, Calif.
Brother of Richard Murray, first baseman in San Francisco Giants' organization;
Leon Murray, first baseman in San Francisco Giants' organization, 1970; and
Charles Murray, outfielder in Houston Colt .45s–Astros' organization, 1962 through 1966 and 1969.
Led Florida State League first basemen in double plays with 113 in 1974.

| Year Club | League | Pos. | G. | AB. | R. | H. | 2B. | 3B. | HR. | RBI. | B.A. | PO. | A. | E. | F.A. |
|---|---|---|---|---|---|---|---|---|---|---|---|---|---|---|---|
| 1973–Bluefield | Appal. | 1B | 50 | 188 | 34 | 54 | 6 | 0 | 11 | 32 | .287 | 421 | 14 | 13 | .971 |
| 1974–Miami | Fla. St. | 1B | 131 | 460 | 64 | 133 | 29 | 7 | 12 | 63 | .289 | •1114 | •51 | •25 | .979 |
| 1974–Asheville | South. | 1B | 2 | 7 | 1 | 2 | 2 | 0 | 0 | 2 | .286 | 17 | 0 | 0 | 1.000 |
| 1975–Asheville | South. | 1B-3B | 124 | 436 | 66 | 115 | 13 | 5 | 17 | 68 | .264 | 637 | 58 | 15 | .979 |
| 1976–Charlotte | South. | 1B | 88 | 299 | 46 | 89 | 15 | 2 | 12 | 46 | .298 | 746 | 45 | 9 | .989 |
| 1976–Rochester | Int. | 1B-O-3 | 54 | 168 | 35 | 46 | 6 | 2 | 11 | 40 | .274 | 291 | 13 | 5 | .984 |

Listed on Baltimore Orioles' 1977 spring roster.

## LARRY A. MURRAY

Born April 1, 1954, at Chicago, Ill.
Height, 6.00. Weight, 180.
Throws right and bats right and lefthanded.
Hobby–Sports in general.
Led New York-Pennsylvania League batters in walks with 66 in 1972.
Led Florida State League in stolen bases with 62 in 1974.

| Year Club League | Pos. | G. | AB. | R. | H. | 2B. | 3B. | HR. | RBI. | B.A. | PO. | A. | E. | F.A. |
|---|---|---|---|---|---|---|---|---|---|---|---|---|---|---|
| 1971—Johnson City ....Appal. | OF-3 | 41 | 128 | 16 | 22 | 4 | 3 | 2 | 8 | .172 | 51 | 14 | 9 | .878 |
| 1972—Ft. Lauderdale ..Fla. St. | OF | 21 | 45 | 6 | 6 | 0 | 0 | 0 | 1 | .133 | 31 | 0 | 0 | 1.000 |
| 1972—Oneonta ...........NYP | OF | •70 | 234 | 60 | 57 | 10 | 3 | 5 | 42 | .244 | •147 | •10 | 6 | .963 |
| 1973—Ft. Lauderdale ..Fla. St. | OF | 122 | 360 | 51 | 91 | 6 | 4 | 2 | 27 | .253 | 178 | 14 | 10 | .950 |
| 1974—Ft. Lauderdale ..Fla. St. | OF | 124 | 401 | 66 | 83 | 14 | 3 | 3 | 35 | .207 | 291 | 9 | 5 | .984 |
| 1974—New York.........Amer. | OF | 6 | 1 | 1 | 0 | 0 | 0 | 0 | 0 | .000 | 0 | 0 | 0 | .000 |
| 1975—West Haven ......East. | OF | 105 | 396 | 60 | 99 | 14 | 4 | 6 | 32 | .250 | 245 | 6 | 7 | .973 |
| 1975—New York.........Amer. | OF | 6 | 1 | 1 | 0 | 0 | 0 | 0 | 0 | .000 | 1 | 0 | 0 | 1.000 |
| 1976—West Haven ......East. | OF | 126 | 472 | •92 | 135 | 26 | 4 | 12 | 55 | .286 | 268 | 12 | 8 | .972 |
| 1976—New York.........Amer. | OF | 8 | 10 | 2 | 1 | 0 | 0 | 0 | 2 | .100 | 9 | 1 | 0 | 1.000 |
| Major League Totals ..................... | | 20 | 12 | 4 | 1 | 0 | 0 | 0 | 2 | .083 | 10 | 1 | 0 | 1.000 |

## ANTHONY JOSEPH MUSER
### (Tony)

Born August 1, 1947, at Van Nuys, Calif.
Height, 6.02. Weight, 185.
Throws and bats lefthanded.
Hobbies—Hunting and fishing.
Attended San Diego Mesa College, San Diego, Calif.

| Year Club League | Pos. | G. | AB. | R. | H. | 2B. | 3B. | HR. | RBI. | B.A. | PO. | A. | E. | F.A. |
|---|---|---|---|---|---|---|---|---|---|---|---|---|---|---|
| 1967—Waterloo ..........Midw | 1B | 68 | 251 | 40 | 71 | 15 | 1 | 6 | 42 | .283 | 674 | 28 | 11 | .985 |
| 1968—Greenville†........W. Car. | 1-O | 33 | 114 | 13 | 31 | 7 | 0 | 2 | 12 | .272 | 223 | 23 | 2 | .992 |
| 1968—Winston-Salem ..Carol. | OF-1B | 7 | 21 | 1 | 8 | 0 | 0 | 0 | 2 | .381 | 13 | 1 | 0 | 1.000 |
| 1969—Louisville ..........Int. | 1B | 120 | 457 | 57 | 129 | 14 | 4 | 7 | 62 | .282 | 1029 | 63 | 15 | .986 |
| 1969—Boston ...........Amer. | 1B | 2 | 9 | 0 | 1 | 0 | 0 | 0 | 1 | .111 | 17 | 3 | 0 | 1.000 |
| 1970—Louisville‡ ........Int. | 1B | 114 | 462 | 66 | 130 | 25 | 7 | 5 | 45 | .281 | 1013 | 45 | 9 | •.992 |
| 1971—Indianapolis ......A. A. | 1B | 85 | 310 | 36 | 91 | 10 | 3 | 3 | 31 | .294 | 720 | 42 | 6 | .992 |
| 1971—Chicago ...........Amer. | 1B | 11 | 16 | 2 | 5 | 0 | 1 | 0 | 0 | .313 | 23 | 3 | 1 | .963 |
| 1972—Tucson .............P. C. | 1B | 83 | 318 | 41 | 86 | 17 | 0 | 3 | 40 | .270 | 680 | 49 | 12 | .984 |
| 1972—Chicago ...........Amer. | 1B-OF | 44 | 61 | 6 | 17 | 2 | 2 | 1 | 9 | .279 | 135 | 7 | 2 | .986 |
| 1973—Chicago ...........Amer. | 1B-OF | 109 | 309 | 38 | 88 | 14 | 3 | 4 | 30 | .285 | 681 | 38 | 6 | .992 |
| 1974—Chicago ...........Amer. | 1B | 103 | 206 | 16 | 60 | 5 | 1 | 1 | 18 | .291 | 419 | 13 | 1 | .998 |
| 1975—Chi.§-Balt. ........Amer. | 1B | 123 | 193 | 22 | 53 | 6 | 0 | 0 | 17 | .275 | 476 | 37 | 3 | .994 |
| 1976—Baltimore.........Amer. | 1-O-DH | 136 | 326 | 25 | 74 | 7 | 1 | 1 | 30 | .227 | 693 | 63 | 7 | .991 |
| Major League Totals ..................... | | 528 | 1120 | 109 | 298 | 34 | 8 | 7 | 105 | .266 | 2444 | 164 | 20 | .992 |

†On military list through July 15.

‡Traded by Boston Red Sox with Pitcher Vicente Romo to Chicago White Sox for Pitcher Danny Murphy and Catcher Duane Josephson, March 30, 1971.

§Traded to Baltimore Orioles for Pitcher Jesse Jefferson, June 15, 1975.

## ROBERT HOWARD MYRICK, JR.
### (Bob)

Born October 1, 1952, at Hattiesburg, Miss.
Height, 6.01. Weight, 195.
Throws left and bats righthanded.
Hobbies—Hunting, fishing and all outdoor activities.
Attended Mississippi State University, Starkville, Miss.
Grand newphew of Charles (Buddy) Myer, infielder with Boston Red Sox and
Washington Senators, 1925 through 1941.

| Year Club League | G. | IP. | W. | L. | Pct. | H. | R. | ER. | SO. | BB. | ERA. |
|---|---|---|---|---|---|---|---|---|---|---|---|
| 1974—Batavia ...............................NYP | 12 | 82 | 3 | 5 | .375 | 88 | 53 | 41 | 62 | 39 | 4.50 |
| 1974—Tidewater .......................Int'national | 2 | 2 | 0 | 0 | .000 | 1 | 0 | 0 | 1 | 2 | 0.00 |
| 1975—Jackson.............................Texas | 22 | 116 | 7 | 4 | .636 | 98 | 54 | 42 | 70 | 49 | 3.26 |
| 1975—Tidewater .......................Int'national | 7 | 11 | 3 | 0 | 1.000 | 7 | 0 | 0 | 9 | 2 | 0.00 |
| 1976—Tidewater .......................Int'national | 13 | 24 | 2 | 0 | 1.000 | 22 | 10 | 7 | 22 | 10 | 2.63 |
| 1976—New York ...........................National | 21 | 28 | 1 | 1 | .500 | 34 | 13 | 10 | 11 | 13 | 3.21 |
| Major League Totals ............................. | 21 | 28 | 1 | 1 | .500 | 34 | 13 | 10 | 11 | 13 | 3.21 |

## WILLIAM GERARD NAHORODNY
Name pronounced Na-ha-rod-knee.
### (Bill)

Born August 31, 1953, at Hamtramck, Mich.
Height, 6.02. Weight, 200.
Throws and bats righthanded.
Hobby—Music.
Attended St. Clair County Community College, Port Huron, Mich.

Led New York-Pennsylvania League catchers in passed balls with 13 and tied for lead in double plays with 6 in 1972.

Tied for New York-Pennsylvania League lead in sacrifice flies with 6 in 1972.

Tied for American Association lead in double plays by catchers with 8 in 1976.

| Year Club League | Pos. | G. | AB. | R. | H. | 2B. | 3B. | HR. | RBI. | B.A. | PO. | A. | E. | F.A. |
|---|---|---|---|---|---|---|---|---|---|---|---|---|---|---|
| 1972—Auburn.............NYP | *C-3B | 69 | 217 | 36 | 57 | 14 | 2 | 6 | 33 | .263 | *532 | ●40 | 13 | *.978 |
| 1973—Rocky Mount ....Carol. | *C-1-3 | 118 | 389 | 40 | 102 | 23 | 1 | 14 | 76 | .262 | 798 | 64 | 10 | *.989 |
| 1974—Reading ............East. | C-1-3 | 110 | 388 | 58 | 93 | 17 | 2 | 19 | 77 | .240 | 642 | 70 | 13 | .982 |
| 1975—Toledo ..............Int. | *C-1B | 125 | 411 | 51 | 105 | 17 | 4 | *19 | 64 | .255 | 691 | 71 | 7 | *.991 |
| 1976—Oklahoma City ..A.A. | *C-1B | 114 | 391 | 74 | 114 | 22 | 3 | 23 | 78 | .292 | *606 | 50 | 7 | .989 |
| 1976—Philadelphia ......Nat. | C | 3 | 5 | 0 | 1 | 1 | 0 | 0 | 0 | .200 | 7 | 0 | 0 | 1.000 |
| Major League Totals ..................... | | 3 | 5 | 0 | 1 | 1 | 0 | 0 | 0 | .200 | 7 | 0 | 0 | 1.000 |

## DAVID EARL NELSON
### (Dave)

Born June 20, 1944, at Fort Sill, Okla.
Height, 5.10. Weight, 160.
Throws and bats righthanded.
Attended Compton Junior College, Compton, Calif., and California
State College, Los Angeles, Calif.

Tied major league record for most stolen bases, inning, 3, August 30, 1974 (1st inning).
Major league stolen bases: 1968 (23), 1969 (4), 1970 (2), 1971 (17), 1972 (51), 1973 (43), 1974 (25), 1975 (6), 1976 (15). Total—186.
Led Eastern League second basemen in double plays with 65 in 1966.
Led California League in stolen bases with 41 in 1965, Eastern League with 57 in 1966 and Pacific Coast League with 29 in 1967.

| Year Club League | Pos. | G. | AB. | R. | H. | 2B. | 3B. | HR. | RBI. | B.A. | PO. | A. | E. | F.A. |
|---|---|---|---|---|---|---|---|---|---|---|---|---|---|---|
| 1964—Dubuque............Midw. | 2B | 120 | 438 | 98 | 111 | 14 | 4 | 8 | 39 | .253 | 274 | 279 | *38 | .936 |
| 1965—Salinas ..............Calif. | 2B | 117 | 429 | 93 | 118 | 9 | 10 | 4 | 29 | .275 | 273 | 279 | 27 | .953 |
| 1966—Pawtucket .........East. | 2B | 129 | 468 | 85 | 114 | 14 | 7 | 3 | 40 | .244 | *335 | *361 | *28 | .961 |
| 1967—Portland...........P.C. | 2B-SS | 103 | 369 | 56 | 103 | 12 | 4 | 1 | 15 | .279 | 205 | 264 | 10 | .979 |
| 1968—Cleveland .........Amer. | 2B-SS | 88 | 189 | 26 | 44 | 4 | 5 | 0 | 19 | .233 | 124 | 127 | 4 | .984 |
| 1969—Cleveland† .......Amer. | 2B-OF | 52 | 123 | 11 | 25 | 0 | 0 | 6 | .203 | 79 | 94 | 6 | .966 |
| 1970—Denver .............A.A. | 3B-2B | 53 | 206 | 36 | 76 | 17 | 6 | 2 | 20 | .369 | 60 | 112 | 11 | .940 |
| 1970—Washington........Amer. | 2B | 47 | 107 | 5 | 17 | 1 | 0 | 0 | 4 | .159 | 64 | 79 | 2 | .986 |
| 1971—Denver .............A.A. | 3B-2B | 50 | 202 | 37 | 62 | 10 | 4 | 2 | 23 | .307 | 58 | 85 | 10 | .935 |
| 1971—Washington........Amer. | 3B-2B | 85 | 329 | 47 | 92 | 11 | 3 | 5 | 33 | .280 | 63 | 150 | 14 | .938 |
| 1972—Texas...............Amer. | 3B-OF | 145 | 499 | 68 | 113 | 16 | 3 | 2 | 28 | .226 | 131 | 222 | 22 | .941 |
| 1973—Texas ...............Amer. | 2B | 142 | 576 | 71 | 165 | 24 | 4 | 7 | 48 | .286 | 327 | 364 | 11 | .984 |
| 1974—Texas‡ .............Amer. | 2B | 121 | 474 | 71 | 112 | 13 | 1 | 3 | 42 | .236 | 295 | 337 | 20 | .969 |
| 1975—Texas§x ...........Amer. | 2B | 28 | 80 | 9 | 17 | 1 | 0 | 2 | 10 | .213 | 56 | 60 | 5 | .959 |
| 1976—Kansas City ......Amer. | 2B-DH | 78 | 153 | 24 | 36 | 4 | 2 | 1 | 17 | .235 | 79 | 90 | 4 | .977 |
| Major League Totals ..................... | | 786 | 2530 | 332 | 621 | 74 | 18 | 20 | 207 | .245 | 1218 | 1523 | 88 | .969 |

†Traded with Pitchers Ron Law and Horacio Pina to Washington Senators for Pitchers Dennis Higgins and Barry Moore, December 5, 1969.
‡On supplemental disabled list, May 12 to June 10, 1974.
§On emergency disabled list, April 27 to August 15, 1975.
xTraded to Kansas City Royals for Pitcher Nelson Briles.

CHAMPIONSHIP SERIES RECORD

| Year Club League | Pos. | G. | AB. | R. | H. | 2B. | 3B. | HR. | RBI. | B.A. | PO. | A. | E. | F.A. |
|---|---|---|---|---|---|---|---|---|---|---|---|---|---|---|
| 1976—Kansas City ......Amer. | PH-DH | 2 | 2 | 0 | 0 | 0 | 0 | 0 | 0 | .000 | 0 | 0 | 0 | .000 |

ALL-STAR GAME RECORD

| Year League | Pos. | AB. | R. | H. | 2B. | 3B. | HR. | RBI. | B.A. | PO. | A. | E. | F.A. |
|---|---|---|---|---|---|---|---|---|---|---|---|---|---|
| 1973—American ........................... | 3B | 0 | 0 | 0 | 0 | 0 | 0 | 0 | .000 | 1 | 0 | 0 | 1.000 |

## ROGER EUGENE NELSON

Born June 7, 1944, at Altadena, Calif.
Height, 6.03. Weight, 200.
Throws and bats righthanded.
Hobby—Bowling.
Attended Mount San Antonio Junior College, Walnut, Calif.

| Year Club League | G. | IP. | W. | L. | Pct. | H. | R. | ER. | SO. | BB. | ERA. |
|---|---|---|---|---|---|---|---|---|---|---|---|
| 1963—Middlesboro ......................Ap'lachian | 16 | 64 | 5 | 4 | .556 | 59 | 41 | 34 | 83 | 50 | 4.78 |
| 1964—Tidewater† ...........................Carolina | 4 | 7 | 0 | 0 | .000 | 9 | 7 | 4 | 3 | 7 | 5.14 |
| 1964—Sarasota ...........................Florida St. | 15 | 65 | 2 | 4 | .333 | 54 | 23 | 17 | 72 | 25 | 2.35 |
| 1965—Tidewater .............................Carolina | 25 | 150 | 9 | 7 | .563 | 125 | 62 | 52 | 120 | 59 | 3.12 |
| 1966—Evansville‡ ..........................Southern | 22 | 131 | 6 | 10 | .375 | 123 | 63 | 55 | 104 | 41 | 3.78 |
| 1967—Indianapolis ........................P. Coast | 37 | 57 | 3 | 3 | .500 | 57 | 33 | 28 | 52 | 18 | 4.42 |
| 1967—Chicago‡‡§ .........................American | 5 | 7 | 0 | 1 | .000 | 4 | 1 | 1 | 4 | 0 | 1.29 |
| 1968—Baltimore ...........................American | 19 | 71 | 4 | 3 | .571 | 49 | 21 | 19 | 70 | 26 | 2.41 |
| 1968—Rochester x..........................Int'national | 4 | 28 | 3 | 0 | 1.000 | 13 | 4 | 4 | 30 | 5 | 1.29 |
| 1969—Kansas City y ......................American | 29 | 193 | 7 | 13 | .350 | 170 | 78 | 71 | 82 | 65 | 3.31 |
| 1970—Kansas City z .......................American | 4 | 9 | 0 | 2 | .000 | 18 | 10 | 10 | 3 | 0 | 10.00 |
| 1971—Omaha ..............................Am. Assoc. | 11 | 64 | 2 | 3 | .400 | 70 | 32 | 27 | 60 | 22 | 3.80 |
| 1971—Kansas City .........................American | 13 | 34 | 0 | 1 | .000 | 35 | 20 | 20 | 29 | 5 | 5.29 |
| 1972—Kansas City a .......................American | 34 | 173 | 11 | 6 | .647 | 120 | 41 | 40 | 120 | 31 | 2.08 |
| 1973—Cincinnati b ........................National | 14 | 55 | 3 | 2 | .600 | 49 | 25 | 21 | 17 | 24 | 3.44 |
| 1974—Cincinnati c d ....................National | 14 | 85 | 4 | 4 | .500 | 67 | 36 | 32 | 42 | 35 | 3.39 |
| 1975—Tucson e .............................P. Coast | 20 | 123 | 7 | 8 | .467 | 125 | 64 | 51 | 78 | 41 | 3.73 |

| Year Club | League | G. | IP. | W. | L. | Pct. | H. | R. | ER. | SO. | BB. | ERA. |
|---|---|---|---|---|---|---|---|---|---|---|---|---|
| 1976—Omaha | Am. Assoc. | 52 | 60 | 6 | 6 | .500 | 49 | 27 | 20 | 56 | 31 | 3.00 |
| 1976—Kansas City | American | 3 | 9 | 0 | 0 | .000 | 4 | 2 | 2 | 4 | 4 | 2.00 |
| American League Totals | | 107 | 496 | 22 | 26 | .458 | 400 | 173 | 163 | 312 | 131 | 2.96 |
| National League Totals | | 28 | 140 | 7 | 6 | .538 | 116 | 61 | 53 | 59 | 59 | 3.41 |
| Major League Totals | | 135 | 636 | 29 | 32 | .475 | 516 | 234 | 216 | 371 | 190 | 3.06 |

†On disabled list, June 23 through July 13.

‡On temporary inactive list, July 28 through September 5. On military list, October 3, 1966 through February 24, 1967.

‡‡On temporary inactive list, August 4 through August 29.

§Traded with Infielder Don Buford and Pitcher Bruce Howard to Baltimore Orioles for Shortstop Luis Aparicio, Outfielder Russ Snyder and First Baseman-Outfielder John Matias (transferred from Rochester to Evansville), November 29, 1967.

xRecalled by Baltimore Orioles; selected by Kansas City Royals from Baltimore in expansion draft, October 15, 1968.

yOn military list, August 7 through August 23.

zOn disabled list, April 20 through May 11 and from June 20 through September 10.

aTraded with Outfielder Richie Scheinblum to Cincinnati Reds for Outfielder Hal McRae and Pitcher Wayne Simpson, November 30, 1972.

bOn disabled list, June 13 to July 21 and August 24 to September 15, 1973.

cOn disabled list, July 1 to September 12, 1974.

dSold to Chicago White Sox, October 25, 1974. Released by Chicago White Sox, March 25, 1975; signed as free agent by Oakland Athletics, April 5, 1975.

eReleased by Oakland Athletics' organization, August 5, 1975; signed as free agent by Kansas City Royals' organization, March 3, 1976.

### CHAMPIONSHIP SERIES RECORD

| Year Club | League | G. | IP. | W. | L. | Pct. | H. | R. | ER. | SO. | BB. | ERA. |
|---|---|---|---|---|---|---|---|---|---|---|---|---|
| 1973—Cincinnati | National | 1 | 2⅓ | 0 | 0 | .000 | 0 | 0 | 0 | 0 | 1 | 0.00 |

## GRAIG NETTLES

Born August 20, 1944, at San Diego, Calif.
Height, 6.00. Weight, 180.
Throws right and bats lefthanded.
Attended San Diego State College, San Diego, Calif.
Brother of Jim Nettles, former outfielder with Minnesota Twins, Detroit Tigers and Cleveland Indians.

Established major league records for most assists by third baseman, season, 412, and most double plays by third baseman, season, 54, 1971.

Tied major league records for most home runs month of April, 11, in 1974; and fewest three-base hits, season, 150 or more games, 0, 1972 and 1973.

Tied American League record for most home runs, double-header, 4, April 14, 1974.

Led American League third basemen in total chances with 545 in 1974.

Led American League in sacrifice flies with 11 in 1975.

Led Southern League third basemen in double plays with 34 in 1967 and led Pacific Coast League third basemen with 20 in 1968.

Led American League third basemen in total chances with 539 and double plays with 30 in 1976.

Named third baseman on THE SPORTING NEWS American League All-Star Team, 1975.

| Year Club | League | Pos. | G. | AB. | R. | H. | 2B. | 3B. | HR. | RBI. | B.A. | PO. | A. | E. | F.A. |
|---|---|---|---|---|---|---|---|---|---|---|---|---|---|---|---|
| 1966—Wis. Rapids | Midw. | 2B-3B | 117 | 413 | 84 | 111 | 19 | 6 | •28 | 75 | .269 | 240 | 245 | 28 | .945 |
| 1967—Charlotte | South. | 3B | 140 | 499 | 69 | 116 | 18 | 4 | •19 | 86 | .232 | 107 | •318 | 24 | .947 |
| 1967—Minnesota | Amer. | PH | 3 | 3 | 0 | 1 | 1 | 0 | 0 | 0 | .333 | 0 | 0 | 0 | .000 |
| 1968—Denver | P.C. | 3-OF-1B | 130 | 451 | 84 | 134 | 17 | •12 | 22 | 83 | .297 | 125 | 266 | 17 | .958 |
| 1968—Minnesota | Amer. | OF-3-1 | 22 | 76 | 13 | 17 | 2 | 1 | 5 | 8 | .224 | 50 | 9 | 2 | .967 |
| 1969—Minnesota† | Amer. | OF-3B | 96 | 225 | 27 | 50 | 9 | 2 | 7 | 26 | .222 | 88 | 44 | 2 | .985 |
| 1970—Cleveland | Amer. | •3B-OF | 157 | 549 | 81 | 129 | 13 | 1 | 26 | 62 | .235 | 135 | 358 | 17 | •.967 |
| 1971—Cleveland | Amer. | 3B | 158 | 598 | 78 | 156 | 18 | 1 | 28 | 86 | .261 | •159 | •412 | 16 | .973 |
| 1972—Cleveland‡ | Amer. | 3B | 150 | 557 | 65 | 141 | 28 | 0 | 17 | 70 | .253 | 114 | •358 | •21 | .957 |
| 1973—New York | Amer. | 3B | 160 | 552 | 65 | 129 | 18 | 0 | 22 | 81 | .234 | 117 | •410 | 26 | .953 |
| 1974—New York | Amer. | •3B-SS | 155 | 566 | 74 | 139 | 21 | 1 | 22 | 75 | .246 | •147 | 377 | 21 | .961 |
| 1975—New York | Amer. | 3B | 157 | 581 | 71 | 155 | 24 | 4 | 21 | 91 | .267 | 135 | •379 | 19 | .964 |
| 1976—New York | Amer. | 3B | 158 | 583 | 88 | 148 | 29 | 2 | •32 | 93 | .254 | 137 | •383 | 19 | .965 |
| Major League Totals | | | 1216 | 4290 | 562 | 1065 | 163 | 12 | 180 | 592 | .248 | 1082 | 2730 | 143 | .964 |

†Traded with Pitchers Dean Chance and Robert L. Miller and Outfielder Ted Uhlaender to Cleveland Indians for Pitchers Luis Tiant and Stan Williams, December 12, 1969.

‡Traded with Catcher Jerry Moses to New York Yankees for Catcher-First Baseman John Ellis, Infielder Jerry Kenney and Outfielders Charlie Spikes and Rosendo Torres, November 27, 1972.

### CHAMPIONSHIP SERIES RECORD

| Year Club | League | Pos. | G. | AB. | R. | H. | 2B. | 3B. | HR. | RBI. | B.A. | PO. | A. | E. | F.A. |
|---|---|---|---|---|---|---|---|---|---|---|---|---|---|---|---|
| 1969—Minnesota | Amer. | PH | 1 | 1 | 0 | 1 | 0 | 0 | 0 | 0 | 1.000 | 0 | 0 | 0 | .000 |
| 1976—New York | Amer. | 3B | 5 | 17 | 2 | 4 | 1 | 0 | 2 | 4 | .235 | 5 | 14 | 0 | 1.000 |
| Championship Series Totals | | | 6 | 18 | 2 | 5 | 1 | 0 | 2 | 4 | .277 | 5 | 14 | 0 | 1.000 |

### WORLD SERIES RECORD

| Year Club | League | Pos. | G. | AB. | R. | H. | 2B. | 3B. | HR. | RBI. | B.A. | PO. | A. | E. | F.A. |
|---|---|---|---|---|---|---|---|---|---|---|---|---|---|---|---|
| 1976—New York | Amer. | 3B | 4 | 12 | 0 | 3 | 0 | 0 | 0 | 2 | .250 | 8 | 8 | 0 | 1.000 |

### ALL-STAR GAME RECORD

| Year League | | Pos. | AB. | R. | H. | 2B. | 3B. | HR. | RBI. | B.A. | PO. | A. | E. | F.A. |
|---|---|---|---|---|---|---|---|---|---|---|---|---|---|---|
| 1975—American | | 3B | 4 | 0 | 1 | 0 | 0 | 0 | 0 | .250 | 2 | 2 | 0 | 1.000 |

## MORRIS NETTLES, JR.

Born January 26, 1952, at Los Angeles, Calif.
Height, 6.01. Weight, 175.
Throws and bats lefthanded.
Attended Santa Monica City College, Santa Monica, Calif.
Major league stolen bases; 1974 (20), 1975 (22). Total–42.
Led Texas League in stolen bases with 41 in 1973.
Tied for Texas League lead in double plays by outfielders with 5 in 1973.

| Year Club | League | Pos. | G. | AB. | R. | H. | 2B. | 3B. | HR. | RBI. | B.A. | PO. | A. | E. | F.A. |
|---|---|---|---|---|---|---|---|---|---|---|---|---|---|---|---|
| 1970–Idaho Falls........ | Pion. | OF | 52 | 203 | 43 | 75 | 10 | 6 | 3 | 29 | *.369 | 110 | 6 | 9 | .928 |
| 1971–Davenport ........ | Midw. | OF | 67 | 243 | 40 | 64 | 8 | 6 | 3 | 19 | .263 | 104 | 2 | 6 | .946 |
| 1971–Shreveport ........ | Texas | OF | 42 | 151 | 22 | 51 | 7 | 2 | 0 | 12 | .338 | 76 | 1 | 5 | .939 |
| 1972–Salt Lake City ..P.C. | | OF | 16 | 25 | 4 | 7 | 1 | 0 | 0 | 1 | .280 | 12 | 1 | 1 | .929 |
| 1972–Shreveport ........ | Texas | OF | 66 | 178 | 19 | 41 | 4 | 1 | 2 | 16 | .230 | 84 | 3 | 5 | .946 |
| 1973–El Paso ............ | Texas | OF | 126 | 470 | 82 | *156 | 19 | 3 | 4 | 59 | *.332 | 301 | 16 | *15 | .955 |
| 1974–Salt Lake City ..P.C. | | OF | 93 | 341 | 69 | 112 | 14 | 6 | 1 | 34 | .328 | 208 | 7 | *15 | .934 |
| 1974–California.......... | Amer. | OF | 56 | 175 | 27 | 48 | 4 | 0 | 0 | 8 | .274 | 99 | 0 | 1 | .990 |
| 1975–Salt Lake City ..P.C. | | OF | 13 | 47 | 9 | 9 | 0 | 1 | 0 | 1 | .191 | 25 | 1 | 1 | .963 |
| 1975–California† ........ | Amer. | OF | 112 | 294 | 50 | 68 | 11 | 0 | 0 | 23 | .231 | 186 | 4 | 5 | .974 |
| 1976–Iowa................ | A.A. | OF | 48 | 100 | 16 | 19 | 5 | 0 | 2 | 8 | .190 | 28 | 2 | 3 | .909 |
| 1976–Toledo ............ | Int. | OF | 65 | 197 | 27 | 50 | 4 | 1 | 0 | 10 | .254 | 131 | 2 | 2 | .985 |
| Major League Totals ..................... | | | 168 | 469 | 77 | 116 | 15 | 0 | 0 | 31 | .247 | 285 | 4 | 6 | .980 |

†Traded with First Baseman Jim Spencer to Chicago White Sox for Third Baseman Bill Melton and Pitcher Steve Dunning, December 11, 1975.
Invited to Chicago White Sox' 1977 spring camp.


## JEFFREY LYNN NEWMAN
### (Jeff)

Born September 11, 1948, at Ft. Worth, Tex.
Height, 6.02. Weight, 215.
Throws and bats righthanded.
Hobbies–Golf and fishing.
Attended Texas Christian University, Ft. Worth, Tex.
Led Texas League catchers in double plays with 10 and in passed balls with 29 in 1973.
Led California League in passed balls with 51 in 1972.

| Year Club | League | Pos. | G. | AB. | R. | H. | 2B. | 3B. | HR. | RBI. | B.A. | PO. | A. | E. | F.A. |
|---|---|---|---|---|---|---|---|---|---|---|---|---|---|---|---|
| 1970–Sara. Indians ....Gulf C. | | 1-3-O | 55 | 195 | 27 | 61 | 9 | 0 | •6 | *53 | .313 | 302 | 33 | 15 | .957 |
| 1971–Reno† .............. | Calif. | O-1-3-C | 67 | 234 | 35 | 63 | 11 | 3 | 16 | 53 | .269 | 173 | 19 | 9 | .955 |
| 1972–Reno ................ | Calif. | *C-1-3 | 107 | 410 | 59 | 106 | 20 | 6 | 20 | 84 | .259 | 718 | 81 | 29 | .965 |
| 1973–San Antonio‡ ....Texas | | C | 112 | 394 | 50 | 97 | 29 | 0 | 13 | 63 | .246 | 668 | *72 | 10 | .987 |
| 1974–Oklahoma City ..A.A. | | C-1B | 57 | 188 | 19 | 46 | 3 | 1 | 7 | 28 | .245 | 292 | 17 | 6 | .981 |
| 1974–Salt Lake City ..P.C. | | C | 28 | 109 | 15 | 33 | 8 | 0 | 4 | 21 | .303 | 30 | 1 | 0 | 1.000 |
| 1975–Toledo§ ............ | Int. | C | 32 | 64 | 7 | 12 | 4 | 0 | 2 | 5 | .188 | 87 | 6 | 2 | .976 |
| 1975–Salt Lake City ..P.C. | | C-1B | 58 | 176 | 24 | 40 | 10 | 0 | 5 | 25 | .227 | 267 | 22 | 12 | .960 |
| 1976–Tucson .............. | P.C. | C | 68 | 231 | 23 | 62 | 11 | 1 | 5 | 38 | .268 | 311 | 26 | 13 | .963 |
| 1976–Oakland ............ | Amer. | C | 43 | 77 | 5 | 15 | 4 | 0 | 0 | 4 | .195 | 140 | 18 | 3 | .981 |
| Major League Totals ..................... | | | 43 | 77 | 5 | 15 | 4 | 0 | 0 | 4 | .195 | 140 | 18 | 3 | .981 |

†On military list, December 24, 1970 through June 13, 1971.
‡On temporary inactive list, May 31 to June 17, 1973.
§Sold to Oakland A's, October 24, 1975.


## STEVEN RICHARD NICOSIA

Name pronounced nuh-KOH-see-uh.
### (Steve)

Born August 6, 1955, at Paterson, N. J.
Height, 5.10. Weight, 185.
Throws and bats righthanded.
Hobbies–Fishing and golf.

| Year Club | League | Pos. | G. | AB. | R. | H. | 2B. | 3B. | HR. | RBI. | B.A. | PO. | A. | E. | F.A. |
|---|---|---|---|---|---|---|---|---|---|---|---|---|---|---|---|
| 1973–Charleston ........W. Car. | | C-OF | 54 | 165 | 22 | 38 | 8 | 2 | 2 | 21 | .230 | 389 | 25 | 7 | .983 |
| 1973–Sherbrooke........ | East. | C | 3 | 9 | 1 | 1 | 0 | 0 | 0 | 0 | .111 | 29 | 1 | 0 | 1.000 |
| 1974–Salem................ | Carol. | *C-1-O | 118 | 413 | 63 | 126 | 16 | 9 | 15 | 92 | .305 | *860 | 89 | *13 | .986 |
| 1975–Shreveport ........ | Tex. | *C-OF | 110 | 370 | 52 | 99 | 15 | 6 | 6 | 39 | .268 | *527 | 45 | 8 | .986 |
| 1976–Charleston ........ | Int. | OF-1B | 117 | 378 | 29 | 99 | 20 | 0 | 8 | 49 | .262 | 616 | 57 | 8 | .988 |

Listed on Pittsburgh Pirates' 1977 spring roster.

---

## *DID YOU KNOW* —

That the head office of the American League is located at 280 Park Avenue, New York, New York 10017? The phone number is 682-7000 (Area Code 212).

## JOSEPH FRANKLIN NIEKRO
### (Joe)

Born November 7, 1944, at Martins Ferry, O.
Height, 6.01. Weight, 190.
Throws and bats righthanded.
Hobbies—Fishing and hunting.
Attended West Liberty State College, West Liberty, W. Va.
Brother of Phil Niekro, pitcher with Atlanta Braves.

Pitched seven-inning, 2-0 perfect game against Tidewater, July 16, 1972 (second game).

| Year Club | League | G. | IP. | W. | L. | Pct. | H. | R. | ER. | SO. | BB. | ERA. |
|---|---|---|---|---|---|---|---|---|---|---|---|---|
| 1966—Treasure Valley | Pioneer | 1 | 4 | 0 | 0 | .000 | 4 | 0 | 0 | 7 | 1 | 0.00 |
| 1966—Quincy | Midwest | 4 | 25 | 1 | 2 | .333 | 17 | 7 | 3 | 14 | 6 | 1.08 |
| 1966—Dallas-Fort Worth | Texas | 12 | 79 | 5 | 4 | .556 | 71 | 28 | 22 | 50 | 15 | 2.51 |
| 1967—Chicago | National | 36 | 170 | 10 | 7 | .588 | 171 | 68 | 63 | 77 | 32 | 3.34 |
| 1968—Chicago | National | 34 | 177 | 14 | 10 | .583 | 204 | 93 | 85 | 65 | 59 | 4.32 |
| 1969—Chicago†-San Diego‡ | National | 41 | 221 | 8 | 18 | .308 | 237 | 100 | 91 | 62 | 51 | 3.71 |
| 1970—Detroit | American | 38 | 213 | 12 | 13 | .480 | 221 | 107 | 96 | 101 | 72 | 4.06 |
| 1971—Detroit | American | 31 | 122 | 6 | 7 | .462 | 136 | 62 | 61 | 43 | 49 | 4.28 |
| 1972—Toledo§ | Int'national | 2 | 14 | 2 | 0 | 1.000 | 6 | 1 | 1 | 11 | 3 | 0.64 |
| 1972—Detroit | American | 18 | 47 | 3 | 2 | .600 | 62 | 20 | 20 | 24 | 8 | 3.83 |
| 1973—Toledo x | Int'national | 26 | 143 | 7 | 10 | .412 | 148 | 74 | 59 | 77 | 47 | 3.71 |
| 1973—Atlanta | National | 20 | 24 | 2 | 4 | .333 | 23 | 11 | 11 | 12 | 11 | 4.13 |
| 1974—Richmond | Int'national | 30 | 52 | 8 | 1 | .889 | 44 | 14 | 12 | 50 | 18 | 2.08 |
| 1974—Atlanta y | National | 27 | 43 | 3 | 2 | .600 | 36 | 19 | 17 | 31 | 18 | 3.56 |
| 1975—Iowa | Am. Assoc. | 7 | 9 | 1 | 0 | 1.000 | 7 | 6 | 5 | 9 | 7 | 5.00 |
| 1975—Houston | National | 40 | 88 | 6 | 4 | .600 | 79 | 32 | 30 | 54 | 39 | 3.07 |
| 1976—Houston | National | 36 | 118 | 4 | 8 | .333 | 107 | 60 | 44 | 77 | 56 | 3.36 |
| National League Totals | | 234 | 841 | 47 | 53 | .470 | 857 | 383 | 341 | 378 | 266 | 3.65 |
| American League Totals | | 87 | 382 | 21 | 22 | .488 | 419 | 189 | 177 | 168 | 129 | 4.17 |
| Major League Totals | | 321 | 1223 | 68 | 75 | .476 | 1276 | 572 | 518 | 546 | 395 | 3.81 |

†Traded with Pitcher Gary Ross and Infielder Francisco Libran to San Diego Padres for Pitcher Dick Selma, April 24, 1969. Libran remained on Cubs' San Antonio farm team but became San Diego property.
‡Traded to Detroit Tigers for Pitcher Pat Dobson and Shortstop-Outfielder Dave Campbell, December 4, 1969.
§On disabled list, August 7 through September 1, 1972.
xPurchased via waivers from Detroit Tigers by Atlanta Braves, August 7, 1973.
ySold to Houston Astros, April 5, 1975.


## PHILIP HENRY NIEKRO
Name pronounced NEE-krow.
### (Phil)

Born April 1, 1939, at Blaine, O.
Height, 6.01. Weight, 180.
Throws and bats righthanded.
Hobbies—Fishing, hunting and basketball.
Brother of Joe Niekro, pitcher with Houston Astros.

Pitched 9-0 no-hit victory against San Diego Padres, August 5, 1973.
Led National League pitchers in complete games with 18 in 1974.
Led National League in wild pitches with 19 in 1967.
Led National League in sacrifice hits with 18 in 1968.
Led National League in hit batsmen with 11 in 1975.

| Year Club | League | G. | IP. | W. | L. | Pct. | H. | R. | ER. | SO. | BB. | ERA. |
|---|---|---|---|---|---|---|---|---|---|---|---|---|
| 1959—Wellsville | NYP | 10 | 35 | 2 | 1 | .667 | 47 | 38 | 29 | 16 | 24 | 7.46 |
| 1959—McCook | Neb. State | *23 | 52 | 7 | 1 | .875 | 35 | 20 | 18 | 48 | 29 | 3.12 |
| 1960—Jacksonville | Sally | 38 | 84 | 6 | 4 | .600 | 66 | 36 | 26 | 52 | 52 | 2.79 |
| 1960—Louisville | Am. Assoc. | 6 | 10 | 1 | 0 | 1.000 | 11 | 5 | 4 | 2 | 9 | 3.60 |
| 1961—Austin | Texas | *51 | 110 | 4 | 4 | .500 | 100 | 45 | 36 | 84 | 53 | 2.95 |
| 1962—Louisville | Am. Assoc. | 49 | 98 | 9 | 6 | .600 | 111 | 50 | 42 | 48 | 41 | 3.86 |
| 1963—Denver | P. Coast | | | (In Military Service) | | | | | | | | |
| 1964—Milwaukee | National | 10 | 15 | 0 | 0 | .000 | 15 | 10 | 8 | 8 | 7 | 4.80 |
| 1964—Denver | P. Coast | 29 | 172 | 11 | 5 | .688 | 172 | 79 | 66 | 119 | 45 | 3.45 |
| 1965—Milwaukee | National | 41 | 75 | 2 | 3 | .400 | 73 | 32 | 24 | 49 | 26 | 2.88 |
| 1966—Atlanta | National | 28 | 50 | 4 | 3 | .571 | 48 | 32 | 23 | 17 | 23 | 4.14 |
| 1966—Richmond | Int'national | 17 | 54 | 3 | 4 | .429 | 43 | 27 | 22 | 36 | 16 | 3.67 |
| 1967—Atlanta | National | 46 | 207 | 11 | 9 | .550 | 164 | 64 | 43 | 129 | 55 | *1.87 |
| 1968—Atlanta | National | 37 | 257 | 14 | 12 | .538 | 228 | 83 | 74 | 140 | 45 | 2.59 |
| 1969—Atlanta | National | 40 | 284 | 23 | 13 | .639 | 235 | 93 | 81 | 193 | 57 | 2.57 |
| 1970—Atlanta | National | 34 | 230 | 12 | 18 | .400 | 222 | 124 | 109 | 168 | 68 | 4.27 |
| 1971—Atlanta | National | 42 | 269 | 15 | 14 | .517 | 248 | 112 | 89 | 173 | 70 | 2.98 |
| 1972—Atlanta | National | 38 | 282 | 16 | 12 | .571 | 254 | 112 | 96 | 164 | 53 | 3.06 |
| 1973—Atlanta | National | 42 | 245 | 13 | 10 | .565 | 214 | 103 | 90 | 131 | 89 | 3.31 |
| 1974—Atlanta | National | 41 | *302 | ●20 | 13 | .606 | 249 | 91 | 80 | 195 | 88 | 2.38 |
| 1975—Atlanta | National | 39 | 276 | 15 | 15 | .500 | 285 | 115 | 98 | 144 | 72 | 3.20 |
| 1976—Atlanta | National | 38 | 271 | 17 | 11 | .607 | 249 | 116 | 99 | 173 | 101 | 3.29 |
| Major League Totals | | 476 | 2763 | 162 | 133 | .549 | 2484 | 1087 | 914 | 1684 | 754 | 2.97 |

— 277 —

## CHAMPIONSHIP SERIES RECORD

| Year Club | League | G. | IP. | W. | L. | Pct. | H. | R. | ER. | SO. | BB. | ERA. |
|---|---|---|---|---|---|---|---|---|---|---|---|---|
| 1969—Atlanta | National | 1 | 8 | 0 | 1 | .000 | 9 | 9 | 4 | 4 | 4 | 4.50 |

## ALL-STAR GAME RECORD

| Year League | IP. | W. | L. | Pct. | H. | R. | ER. | SO. | BB. | ERA. |
|---|---|---|---|---|---|---|---|---|---|---|---|
| 1969—National | 1 | 0 | 0 | .000 | 0 | 0 | 0 | 2 | 0 | 0.00 |

Member of National League All-Star Team for 1975 game; did not play.

## GARY LYNN NOLAN

Born May 27, 1948, at Herlong, Calif.
Height, 6.03. Weight, 200.
Throws and bats righthanded.
Received reported $65,000 bonus to sign with Cincinnati Reds, 1966.

| Year Club | League | G. | IP. | W. | L. | Pct. | H. | R. | ER. | SO. | BB. | ERA. |
|---|---|---|---|---|---|---|---|---|---|---|---|---|
| 1966—Sioux Falls | Northern | 12 | 104 | 7 | 3 | .700 | 76 | 26 | 21 | 163 | 30 | 1.82 |
| 1967—Cincinnati | National | 33 | 227 | 14 | 8 | .636 | 193 | 73 | 65 | 206 | 62 | 2.58 |
| 1968—Tampa | Florida St. | 2 | 5 | 0 | 1 | .000 | 5 | 5 | 2 | 8 | 5 | 3.60 |
| 1968—Cincinnati | National | 23 | 150 | 9 | 4 | .692 | 105 | 48 | 40 | 111 | 49 | 2.40 |
| 1969—Indianapolis | Am. Assoc. | 7 | 31 | 2 | 0 | 1.000 | 18 | 10 | 10 | 34 | 5 | 2.90 |
| 1969—Cincinnati† | National | 16 | 109 | 8 | 8 | .500 | 102 | 45 | 43 | 83 | 40 | 3.55 |
| 1970—Cincinnati | National | 37 | 251 | 18 | 7 | .720 | 226 | 102 | 91 | 181 | 96 | 3.26 |
| 1971—Cincinnati | National | 35 | 245 | 12 | 15 | .444 | 208 | 91 | 86 | 146 | 59 | 3.16 |
| 1972—Cincinnati | National | 25 | 176 | 15 | 5 | *.750 | 147 | 48 | 39 | 90 | 30 | 1.99 |
| 1973—Cincinnati‡ | National | 2 | 10 | 0 | 1 | .000 | 6 | 4 | 4 | 3 | 7 | 3.60 |
| 1974—Indianapolis§ | Am. Assoc. | 2 | 6 | 0 | 0 | .000 | 6 | 4 | 4 | 2 | 3 | 6.00 |
| 1975—Cincinnati | National | 32 | 211 | 15 | 9 | .625 | 202 | 75 | 74 | 74 | 29 | 3.16 |
| 1976—Cincinnati | National | 34 | 239 | 15 | 9 | .625 | 232 | 96 | 92 | 113 | 27 | 3.46 |
| Major League Totals | | 237 | 1618 | 106 | 66 | .616 | 1421 | 582 | 534 | 1007 | 399 | 2.97 |

†On disabled list, June 9 through July 12.
‡On disabled list, March 24 to July 26 and August 9 through remainder of season.
§On disabled list, April 16 to August 14, 1974.

## CHAMPIONSHIP SERIES RECORD

| Year Club | League | G. | IP. | W. | L. | Pct. | H. | R. | ER. | SO. | BB. | ERA. |
|---|---|---|---|---|---|---|---|---|---|---|---|---|
| 1970—Cincinnati | National | 1 | 9 | 1 | 0 | 1.000 | 8 | 0 | 0 | 6 | 4 | 0.00 |
| 1972—Cincinnati | National | 1 | 6 | 0 | 0 | .000 | 4 | 1 | 1 | 4 | 1 | 1.50 |
| 1975—Cincinnati | National | 1 | 6 | 0 | 0 | .000 | 5 | 2 | 2 | 5 | 0 | 3.00 |
| 1976—Cincinnati | National | 1 | 5⅔ | 0 | 0 | .000 | 6 | 1 | 1 | 1 | 2 | 1.59 |
| Championship Series Totals | | 4 | 26⅔ | 1 | 0 | 1.000 | 23 | 4 | 4 | 16 | 7 | 1.35 |

## WORLD SERIES RECORD

| Year Club | League | G. | IP. | W. | L. | Pct. | H. | R. | ER. | SO. | BB. | ERA. |
|---|---|---|---|---|---|---|---|---|---|---|---|---|
| 1970—Cincinnati | National | 2 | 9⅓ | 0 | 1 | .000 | 9 | 8 | 8 | 9 | 3 | 7.71 |
| 1972—Cincinnati | National | 2 | 10⅔ | 0 | 1 | .000 | 7 | 4 | 4 | 3 | 2 | 3.38 |
| 1975—Cincinnati | National | 2 | 6 | 0 | 0 | .000 | 6 | 4 | 4 | 2 | 1 | 6.00 |
| 1976—Cincinnati | National | 1 | 6⅔ | 1 | 0 | 1.000 | 8 | 2 | 2 | 1 | 2 | 2.70 |
| World Series Totals | | 7 | 32⅔ | 1 | 2 | .333 | 30 | 18 | 18 | 15 | 7 | 4.96 |

## ALL-STAR GAME RECORD

Named to National League All-Star Team for the 1972 game; replaced due to injury.

## JOSEPH WILLIAM NOLAN, JR.
### (Joe)

Born May 12, 1951, at St. Louis, Mo.
Height, 6.00. Weight, 180.
Throws right and bats lefthanded.
Hobbies— Golf, hunting and fishing.
Led Texas League catchers in double plays with 10 in 1972.
Tied for Appalachian League lead in double plays by catchers with 3 in 1969.

| Year Club | League | Pos. | G. | AB. | R. | H. | 2B. | 3B. | HR. | RBI. | B.A. | PO. | A. | E. | F.A. |
|---|---|---|---|---|---|---|---|---|---|---|---|---|---|---|---|
| 1969—Marion | Appal. | C | 52 | 160 | 33 | 40 | 5 | 0 | 2 | 19 | .250 | 312 | 30 | 6 | .983 |
| 1970—Pompano Beach Fla. St. | *C-O-3 | 94 | 281 | 38 | 65 | 6 | 4 | 0 | 30 | .231 | 438 | 59 | *18 | .965 |
| 1971—Visalia | Calif. | *C-3-O | 120 | 393 | 76 | 109 | 17 | 3 | 13 | 75 | .277 | *746 | 95 | 17 | .980 |
| 1972—Memphis | Texas | C | 130 | 418 | 51 | 90 | 13 | 3 | 4 | 41 | .215 | *868 | 67 | 12 | .987 |
| 1972—New York | Nat. | C | 4 | 10 | 0 | 0 | 0 | 0 | 0 | 0 | .000 | 12 | 3 | 1 | .938 |
| 1973—Tidewater | Int. | C | 97 | 287 | 34 | 69 | 9 | 1 | 4 | 29 | .240 | 526 | 43 | 10 | .983 |
| 1974—Tidewater† | Int. | C | 57 | 145 | 18 | 39 | 8 | 0 | 5 | 20 | .269 | 274 | 24 | 8 | .974 |
| 1975—Richmond | Int. | C-3-O-2 | 111 | 342 | 41 | 92 | 13 | 0 | 6 | 53 | .269 | 572 | 51 | 7 | .989 |
| 1975—Atlanta | Nat. | C | 4 | 4 | 0 | 1 | 0 | 0 | 0 | 0 | .250 | 2 | 0 | 0 | 1.000 |
| 1976—Richmond‡ | Int. | C | 32 | 87 | 9 | 25 | 6 | 1 | 0 | 9 | .287 | 134 | 14 | 0 | 1.000 |
| Major League Totals | | | 8 | 14 | 0 | 1 | 0 | 0 | 0 | 0 | .071 | 14 | 3 | 1 | .944 |

†Traded by New York Mets to Atlanta Braves for Infielder Leo Foster, April 4, 1975.
‡On disabled list, April 21 through July 14, 1976.

## TIMOTHY CHARLES NORDBROOK
### (Tim)

Born July 7, 1949, at Baltimore, Md.
Height, 6.01. Weight, 170.
Throws and bats righthanded.
Hobbies—Golf, tennis, basketball and billiards.
Attended Loyola University, New Orleans, La.

Led International League shortstops in double plays with 65 in 1974.
Led Southern League shortstops in double plays with 95 in 1972.
Led California League in sacrifice hits with 11 in 1971.

| Year Club | League | Pos. | G. | AB. | R. | H. | 2B. | 3B. | HR. | RBI. | B.A. | PO. | A. | E. | F.A. |
|---|---|---|---|---|---|---|---|---|---|---|---|---|---|---|---|
| 1970—Miami .............Fla.St. | | SS | 9 | 24 | 5 | 3 | 0 | 0 | 0 | 1 | .125 | 13 | 37 | 5 | .909 |
| 1970—Dal.-Ft. Worth ..Texas | | SS | 25 | 69 | 7 | 7 | 1 | 0 | | 7 | .101 | 39 | 55 | 7 | .931 |
| 1970—Stockton ...........Calif. | | SS | 23 | 63 | 4 | 11 | 1 | 0 | 0 | 1 | .175 | 37 | 53 | 3 | .968 |
| 1971—Stockton ...........Calif. | | SS | 100 | 349 | 51 | 100 | 14 | 3 | 1 | 54 | .287 | •180 | 296 | 36 | .930 |
| 1971—Dal.-Ft. Worth ..Texas | | SS | 12 | 35 | 3 | 6 | 0 | 0 | 0 | 1 | .171 | 21 | 29 | 6 | .893 |
| 1972—Asheville ..........South. | | SS | 127 | 474 | 71 | 115 | 20 | 2 | 4 | 45 | .243 | •211 | •442 | •33 | .952 |
| 1973—Miami .............Fla.St. | | 3-SS-2 | 11 | 40 | 6 | 16 | 0 | 0 | 0 | 3 | .400 | 8 | 34 | 3 | .933 |
| 1973—Rochester† ........Int. | | SS-3B | 69 | 167 | 23 | 35 | 0 | 1 | 0 | 10 | .210 | 134 | 181 | 18 | .946 |
| 1973—Indianapolis‡ ....A.A. | | SS-2-3 | 9 | 21 | 1 | 4 | 1 | 0 | 0 | 1 | .190 | 16 | 20 | 1 | .973 |
| 1974—Rochester..........Int. | | •SS-2-3 | 109 | 321 | 35 | 92 | 9 | 1 | 0 | 33 | .287 | 143 | 344 | 12 | •.976 |
| 1974—Baltimore..........Amer. | | SS-2B | 6 | 15 | 4 | 4 | 0 | 0 | 0 | 1 | .267 | 6 | 17 | 0 | 1.000 |
| 1975—Baltimore..........Amer. | | SS-2B | 40 | 34 | 6 | 4 | 1 | 0 | 0 | 0 | .118 | 19 | 51 | 2 | .972 |
| 1976—Balt.§-Calif. x ....Amer. | | SS-2-DH | 32 | 30 | 5 | 5 | 0 | 0 | 0 | 0 | .167 | 23 | 33 | 1 | .982 |
| Major League Totals ..................... | | | 78 | 79 | 15 | 13 | 1 | 0 | 0 | 1 | .164 | 48 | 101 | 3 | .980 |

†Released by Baltimore Orioles' organization to Indianapolis (Cincinnati Reds' organization), May 22, 1973. On temporary inactive list, July 7 to July 25, 1973.

‡Option returned by Cincinnati Reds' organization to Rochester (Baltimore Orioles' organization) in exchange for Infielder Junior Kennedy, June 14, 1973.

§Sold to California Angels, September 9, 1976.

xPlayed out option year and granted free agency, November 1, 1976; signed as free agent by Chicago White Sox, December 2, 1976.

## WAYNE OREN NORDHAGEN

Born July 4, 1948, at Thief River Falls, Minn.
Height, 6.02. Weight, 205.
Throws and bats righthanded.
Hobbies—Fishing, hunting and skin diving.
Attended Treasure Valley Community College, Ontario, Ore., and
Portland State University, Portland, Ore.

| Year Club | League | Pos. | G. | AB. | R. | H. | 2B. | 3B. | HR. | RBI. | B.A. | PO. | A. | E. | F.A. |
|---|---|---|---|---|---|---|---|---|---|---|---|---|---|---|---|
| 1968—Johnson City ....Appal. | | OF | 63 | 213 | 35 | 62 | 9 | 1 | 7 | 34 | .291 | •107 | •8 | 4 | .966 |
| 1969—Kinston† ...........Carol. | | OF | 25 | 90 | 17 | 21 | 1 | 0 | 4 | 9 | .233 | 62 | 3 | 5 | .929 |
| 1970—Kinston ...........Carol. | | OF-1B | 88 | 283 | 31 | 65 | 10 | 3 | 2 | 30 | .230 | 175 | 9 | 10 | .948 |
| 1971—Kinston ...........Carol. | | OF | 114 | 412 | 65 | 121 | 25 | 3 | 14 | 76 | .294 | 224 | 10 | 7 | .971 |
| 1972—West Haven .......East. | | OF | 117 | 414 | 50 | 109 | 21 | 4 | 14 | 73 | .263 | 204 | 14 | •15 | .936 |
| 1973—Syra.‡-Rich. ......Int. | | OF | 130 | 438 | 46 | 115 | 15 | 0 | 13 | 70 | .263 | 222 | 9 | 8 | .967 |
| 1974—Richmond..........Int. | | OF | 112 | 374 | 53 | 108 | 18 | 6 | 16 | 77 | .289 | 192 | 6 | 7 | .966 |
| 1975—Richmond§ ........Int. | | OF-1-3 | 34 | 90 | 8 | 23 | 3 | 0 | 2 | 8 | .256 | 50 | 2 | 0 | 1.000 |
| 1975—Tulsa x y ..........A.A. | | OF | 74 | 268 | 40 | 94 | 19 | 2 | 13 | 60 | .351 | 102 | 7 | 3 | .956 |
| 1976—Ok. City z-Iowa..A.A. | | OF | 99 | 350 | 56 | 106 | 30 | 6 | 11 | 78 | .303 | 182 | 12 | 7 | .965 |
| 1976—Chicago ...........Amer. | | OF-C-DH | 22 | 53 | 6 | 10 | 2 | 0 | 0 | 5 | .189 | 35 | 3 | 1 | .974 |
| Major League Totals ..................... | | | 22 | 53 | 6 | 10 | 2 | 0 | 0 | 5 | .189 | 35 | 3 | 1 | .974 |

†On temporary inactive list, May 10, 1969. Transferred to Military List, May 23, 1969 through remainder of season.

‡Traded with First Baseman Frank Tepedino and two players to be named later by New York Yankees to Atlanta Braves for Pitcher Pat Dobson, June 7, 1973; Braves received Pitcher Alan Closter, September 5, 1973, and Pitcher Dave Cheadle, September 10, 1973, to complete deal.

§Traded by Atlanta Braves to St. Louis Cardinals, June 2, 1975, to complete deal in which Braves obtained Pitchers Elias Sosa and Ray Sadecki from Cardinals for Pitcher Ron Reed and a player to be named later, May 28, 1975.

xOn disabled list, June 22 to July 2, 1975.

ySold by St. Louis Cardinals to Philadelphia Phillies, April 9, 1976.

zTraded by Philadelphia Phillies to Chicago White Sox for Outfielder Rich Coggins, July 14, 1976.

## DANIEL EDMUND NORMAN

Born January 11, 1955, at Los Angeles, Calif.
Height, 6.02. Weight, 195.
Throws and bats righthanded.
Attended Barstow Junior College, Barstow, Calif.

| Year Club | League | Pos. | G. | AB. | R. | H. | 2B. | 3B. | HR. | RBI. | B.A. | PO. | A. | E. | F.A. |
|---|---|---|---|---|---|---|---|---|---|---|---|---|---|---|---|
| 1974—Billings ............Pion. | | OF-1B | 68 | 236 | 34 | 70 | 12 | 5 | 4 | 41 | .297 | 87 | 6 | 8 | .921 |
| 1975—Tampa .............Fla.St. | | OF | 129 | 461 | 71 | 126 | 14 | 10 | 7 | 52 | .273 | 192 | 9 | 5 | .976 |
| 1976—Three Rivers ....East. | | OF | 134 | 491 | 64 | 134 | 20 | 9 | 17 | 63 | .273 | 230 | 13 | 5 | .980 |

Listed on Cincinnati Reds' 1977 spring roster.

## FREDIE HUBERT NORMAN
### (Fred)

Born August 20, 1942, at San Antonio, Tex.
Height, 5.08. Weight, 170.
Throws and bats lefthanded.
Hobbies—Golf, fishing, swimming and automobiles.
Attended Muskegon Junior College, Muskegon, Mich.
Pitched 4-0 no-hit victory against Indianapolis, June 5, 1971.
Received reported $40,000 bonus to sign with Kansas City Athletics, 1961.

| Year Club | League | G. | IP. | W. | L. | Pct. | H. | R. | ER. | SO. | BB. | ERA. |
|---|---|---|---|---|---|---|---|---|---|---|---|---|
| 1961—Shreveport ........................Southern | | 14 | 54 | 1 | 7 | .125 | 45 | 43 | 34 | 46 | 64 | 5.70 |
| 1962—Binghamton......................Eastern | | 11 | 70 | 3 | 5 | .375 | 61 | 41 | 38 | 81 | 53 | 4.89 |
| 1962—Lewiston ..........................Northwest | | 16 | 95 | 7 | 5 | .583 | 66 | 46 | 43 | 147 | 79 | 4.07 |
| 1962—Kansas City......................American | | 2 | 4 | 0 | 0 | .000 | 4 | 1 | 1 | 2 | 1 | 2.25 |
| 1963—Binghamton......................Eastern | | 30 | 198 | 13 | 14 | .481 | 143 | 76 | 68 | •258 | 104 | 3.09 |
| 1963—Kansas City† ......................American | | 2 | 6 | 0 | 1 | .000 | 9 | 9 | 8 | 6 | 7 | 12.00 |
| 1964—Ft. Worth ...........................Texas | | 13 | 57 | 1 | 8 | .111 | 55 | 46 | 44 | 40 | 33 | 6.95 |
| 1964—Chicago.............................National | | 8 | 32 | 0 | 4 | .000 | 34 | 25 | 23 | 20 | 21 | 6.47 |
| 1964—Salt Lake City....................P. Coast | | 15 | 50 | 2 | 6 | .250 | 62 | 50 | 41 | 50 | 30 | 7.38 |
| 1965—Dallas-Ft. Worth ................Texas | | 4 | 7 | 0 | 1 | .000 | 10 | 7 | 7 | 9 | 7 | 9.00 |
| 1965—Wenatchee .........................Northwest | | 25 | 106 | 4 | 4 | .500 | 110 | 74 | 65 | 116 | 63 | 5.52 |
| 1966—Dallas-Ft. Worth ................Texas | | 42 | 191 | 12 | 11 | .522 | 147 | 71 | 58 | •198 | 65 | 2.73 |
| 1966—Chicago.............................National | | 2 | 4 | 0 | 0 | .000 | 5 | 2 | 2 | 6 | 2 | 4.50 |
| 1967—Chicago‡ ...........................National | | 1 | 1 | 0 | 0 | .000 | 0 | 0 | 0 | 3 | 0 | 0.00 |
| 1967—Spokane ............................P. Coast | | 16 | 102 | 8 | 5 | .615 | 91 | 46 | 42 | 77 | 43 | 3.71 |
| 1968—Albuquerque ......................Texas | | 23 | 121 | 6 | 8 | .429 | 124 | 70 | 59 | 86 | 49 | 4.39 |
| 1969—Spokane ............................P. Coast | | 34 | 151 | •13 | 6 | .684 | 128 | 68 | 44 | 134 | 61 | 2.62 |
| 1970—Los Ang.§-St. Louis .............National | | 31 | 63 | 2 | 0 | 1.000 | 66 | 40 | 36 | 47 | 33 | 5.14 |
| 1971—Tulsa ................................Am. Assoc. | | 9 | 62 | 6 | 1 | .857 | 44 | 16 | 15 | 72 | 22 | 2.17 |
| 1971—St. Louis x-San Diego .........National | | 24 | 131 | 3 | 12 | .200 | 121 | 53 | 52 | 81 | 63 | 3.57 |
| 1972—San Diego ........................National | | 42 | 212 | 9 | 11 | .450 | 195 | 88 | 81 | 167 | 88 | 3.44 |
| 1973—San Diego y-Cincinnati .......National | | 36 | 240 | 13 | 13 | .500 | 208 | 102 | 96 | 161 | 101 | 3.60 |
| 1974—Cincinnati .........................National | | 35 | 186 | 13 | 12 | .520 | 170 | 69 | 65 | 141 | 68 | 3.15 |
| 1975—Cincinnati .........................National | | 34 | 188 | 12 | 4 | .750 | 163 | 85 | 78 | 119 | 84 | 3.73 |
| 1976—Cincinnati .........................National | | 33 | 180 | 12 | 7 | .632 | 152 | 71 | 62 | 126 | 70 | 3.10 |
| American League Totals........................... | | 4 | 10 | 0 | 1 | .000 | 13 | 10 | 9 | 8 | 8 | 8.10 |
| National League Totals........................... | | 246 | 1237 | 64 | 63 | .504 | 1114 | 535 | 495 | 771 | 530 | 3.60 |
| Major League Totals ............................... | | 250 | 1247 | 64 | 64 | .500 | 1127 | 545 | 504 | 779 | 538 | 3.64 |

†Traded to Chicago Cubs for Outfielder Nelson Mathews, December 15, 1963.
‡Traded to Los Angeles Dodgers for Pitcher Dick Calmus, April 26, 1967.
§Released on waiver claim to St. Louis Cardinals, September 28, 1970.
xTraded with Outfielder Leron Lee to San Diego Padres for Pitcher Al Santorini, June 1, 1971.
yTraded to Cincinnati Reds for Outfielder Gene Locklear and Pitcher Mike Johnson (latter assigned from Indianapolis to Alexandria), June 12, 1973.

### CHAMPIONSHIP SERIES RECORD

| Year Club | League | G. | IP. | W. | L. | Pct. | H. | R. | ER. | SO. | BB. | ERA. |
|---|---|---|---|---|---|---|---|---|---|---|---|---|
| 1973—Cincinnati ...........................National | | 1 | 5 | 0 | 0 | .000 | 1 | 1 | 1 | 3 | 3 | 1.80 |
| 1975—Cincinnati ...........................National | | 1 | 6 | 1 | 0 | 1.000 | 4 | 1 | 1 | 4 | 5 | 1.50 |
| Championship Series Totals ..................... | | 2 | 11 | 1 | 0 | 1.000 | 5 | 2 | 2 | 7 | 8 | 1.64 |

### WORLD SERIES RECORD

| Year Club | League | G. | IP. | W. | L. | Pct. | H. | R. | ER. | SO. | BB. | ERA. |
|---|---|---|---|---|---|---|---|---|---|---|---|---|
| 1975—Cincinnati ...........................National | | 2 | 4 | 0 | 1 | .000 | 8 | 4 | 4 | 2 | 3 | 9.00 |
| 1976—Cincinnati ...........................National | | 1 | 6⅓ | 0 | 0 | .000 | 9 | 3 | 3 | 2 | 2 | 4.26 |
| World Series Totals ............................... | | 3 | 10⅓ | 0 | 1 | .000 | 17 | 7 | 7 | 4 | 5 | 6.10 |

## JAMES FRANCIS NORRIS
### (Jim)

Born December 20, 1948, at Brooklyn, N.Y.
Height, 5.10. Weight, 175.
Throws and bats lefthanded.
Hobbies—Golf and tennis.
Attended University of Maryland, College Park, Md.;
received Bachelor of Science degree in Business Administration.
Led Gulf Coast League in total bases with 85 in 1971.
Named Gulf Coast Player of Year in 1971.

| Year Club League | Pos. | G. | AB. | R. | H. | 2B. | 3B. | HR. | RBI. | B.A. | PO. | A. | E. | F.A. |
|---|---|---|---|---|---|---|---|---|---|---|---|---|---|---|
| 1971—Sara. Indians ....Gulf C. | OF-1B | 47 | 165 | •34 | •63 | 7 | •6 | 1 | 21 | •.382 | 223 | 13 | 5 | .979 |
| 1971—Jacksonville ......South. | OF-1B | 13 | 37 | 2 | 8 | 1 | 0 | 0 | 4 | .216 | 25 | 2 | 0 | 1.000 |
| 1972—Elmira .............East. | 1B-OF | 106 | 329 | 37 | 76 | 9 | 4 | 2 | 34 | .231 | 794 | 44 | 11 | .987 |
| 1973—San Antonio ......Texas | OF-1B | 116 | 346 | 57 | 94 | 21 | 3 | 6 | 47 | .272 | 178 | 14 | 0 | 1.000 |
| 1974—San Antonio† ....Texas | OF-1B | 82 | 291 | 46 | 85 | 15 | 5 | 5 | 40 | .292 | 214 | 10 | 6 | .974 |
| 1975—Oklahoma City‡ A.A. | OF-1B | 79 | 253 | 32 | 71 | 14 | 4 | 1 | 33 | .281 | 185 | 13 | 4 | .980 |
| 1976—Toledo .............Int. | OF-1B | 133 | 435 | 92 | 139 | 23 | 7 | 7 | 68 | .320 | 233 | 7 | 5 | .980 |

†On disabled list, April 19 through April 30, 1974.
‡On disabled list, July 3 through August 15, 1975.
Listed on Cleveland Indians' 1977 spring roster.

# MICHAEL KELVIN NORRIS
## (Mike)
Born March 19, 1955, at San Francisco, Calif.
Height, 6.02. Weight, 175.
Throws and bats righthanded.
Attended City College of San Francisco, San Francisco, Calif.
Received reported $25,000 bonus to sign with Oakland Athletics, 1973.

| Year | Club | League | G. | IP. | W. | L. | Pct. | H. | R. | ER. | SO. | BB. | ERA. |
|------|------|--------|----|-----|----|----|------|----|----|----|-----|-----|------|
| 1973—Burlington | | Midwest | 20 | 110 | 8 | 4 | .667 | 81 | 38 | 27 | 130 | 40 | 2.21 |
| 1974—Birmingham† | | Southern | 21 | 109 | 7 | 8 | .467 | 107 | 64 | 49 | 103 | 65 | 4.05 |
| 1975—Oakland‡ | | American | 4 | 17 | 1 | 0 | 1.000 | 6 | 2 | 0 | 5 | 8 | 0.00 |
| 1976—Tucson | | P. Coast | 5 | 33 | 2 | 1 | .667 | 28 | 15 | 14 | 19 | 23 | 3.82 |
| 1976—Oakland | | American | 24 | 96 | 4 | 5 | .444 | 91 | 53 | 51 | 18 | 20 | 4.78 |
| Major League Totals | | | 28 | 113 | 5 | 5 | .500 | 97 | 55 | 51 | 23 | 28 | 4.06 |

†On disabled list, June 14 to June 24, 1974.
‡On emergency disabled list, April 28 to September 19, 1975.


# WILLIAM ALEXANDER NORTH
## (Bill)
Born May 15, 1948, at Seattle, Wash.
Height, 5.11. Weight, 185.
Throws right and bats left and righthanded.
Hobbies—Reading and playing pool.
Attended Central Washington State College, Ellensburg, Wash.

Major League stolen bases: 1971 (1), 1972 (6), 1973 (54), 1975 (30), 1976 (75). Total—219.
Led American League in stolen bases with 54 in 1974 and 75 in 1976.
Led American League outfielders in total chances with 452 in 1973 and with 441 in 1975.
Led Texas League in stolen bases with 47 in 1971 and led Pioneer League with 42 in 1969.

| Year | Club | League | Pos. | G. | AB. | R. | H. | 2B. | 3B. | HR. | RBI. | B.A. | PO. | A. | E. | F.A. |
|------|------|--------|------|----|-----|----|----|-----|-----|-----|------|------|-----|----|----|------|
| 1969—Caldwell | | Pion. | OF | 59 | 188 | 67 | 50 | 8 | 1 | 2 | 16 | .266 | 110 | 7 | 9 | .929 |
| 1970—Quincy | | Midw. | OF | 42 | 144 | 31 | 42 | 6 | 3 | 4 | 10 | .292 | 86 | 5 | 2 | .978 |
| 1970—San Antonio | | Texas | OF | 25 | 77 | 14 | 16 | 2 | 1 | 0 | 3 | .208 | 50 | 2 | 3 | .945 |
| 1971—San Antonio | | Texas | OF | 125 | 457 | •91 | 133 | 21 | 7 | 10 | 45 | .291 | 295 | 10 | 9 | .971 |
| 1971—Chicago | | Nat. | OF | 8 | 16 | 3 | 6 | 0 | 0 | 0 | 0 | .375 | 4 | 0 | 0 | 1.000 |
| 1972—Wichita | | A. A. | OF-2B | 28 | 114 | 21 | 40 | 7 | 0 | 0 | 12 | .351 | 81 | 8 | 5 | .947 |
| 1972—Chicago† | | Nat. | OF | 66 | 127 | 22 | 23 | 2 | 3 | 0 | 4 | .181 | 61 | 3 | 3 | .955 |
| 1973—Oakland | | Amer. | OF | 146 | 554 | 98 | 158 | 10 | 5 | 5 | 34 | .285 | •429 | •14 | 9 | .980 |
| 1974—Oakland | | Amer. | OF | 149 | 543 | 79 | 141 | 20 | 5 | 4 | 33 | .260 | 437 | 9 | 4 | .991 |
| 1975—Oakland | | Amer. | OF | 140 | 524 | 74 | 143 | 17 | 5 | 1 | 43 | .273 | •420 | 10 | 11 | .975 |
| 1976—Oakland | | Amer. | OF-DH | 154 | 590 | 91 | 163 | 20 | 5 | 2 | 31 | .276 | 397 | 8 | 9 | .978 |
| National League Totals | | | | 74 | 143 | 25 | 29 | 2 | 3 | 0 | 4 | .203 | 65 | 3 | 3 | .958 |
| American League Totals | | | | 589 | 2211 | 342 | 605 | 67 | 20 | 12 | 141 | .274 | 1683 | 41 | 33 | .981 |
| Major League Totals | | | | 663 | 2354 | 367 | 634 | 69 | 23 | 12 | 145 | .269 | 1748 | 44 | 36 | .980 |

†Traded to Oakland Athletics for Pitcher Bob Locker, November 21, 1972.

### CHAMPIONSHIP SERIES RECORD

| Year | Club | League | Pos. | G. | AB. | R. | H. | 2B. | 3B. | HR. | RBI. | B.A. | PO. | A. | E. | F.A. |
|------|------|--------|------|----|-----|----|----|-----|-----|-----|------|------|-----|----|----|------|
| 1974—Oakland | | Amer. | OF | 4 | 16 | 3 | 1 | 1 | 0 | 0 | 0 | .063 | 14 | 0 | 0 | 1.000 |
| 1975—Oakland | | Amer. | OF | 3 | 10 | 0 | 0 | 0 | 0 | 0 | 1 | .000 | 6 | 1 | 1 | .875 |
| Championship Series Totals | | | | 7 | 26 | 3 | 1 | 1 | 0 | 0 | 1 | .038 | 20 | 1 | 1 | .955 |

### WORLD SERIES RECORD

| Year | Club | League | Pos. | G. | AB. | R. | H. | 2B. | 3B. | HR. | RBI. | B.A. | PO. | A. | E. | F.A. |
|------|------|--------|------|----|-----|----|----|-----|-----|-----|------|------|-----|----|----|------|
| 1974—Oakland | | Amer. | OF | 5 | 17 | 3 | 1 | 0 | 0 | 0 | 0 | .059 | 17 | 0 | 1 | .944 |


# WILLIE NORWOOD
Born November 7, 1950, at Green County, Ala.
Height, 6.00. Weight, 185.
Throws and bats righthanded.
Hobbies—Reading, hiking and music.
Attended Long Beach State University, Long Beach, Calif., and
La Verne College, La Verne, Calif.

Led Carolina League in strikeouts with 140 in 1973.
Tied for Carolina League lead in double plays by outfielder with 3 in 1973.

| Year | Club | League | Pos. | G. | AB. | R. | H. | 2B. | 3B. | HR. | RBI. | B.A. | PO. | A. | E. | F.A. |
|------|------|--------|------|----|-----|----|----|-----|-----|-----|------|------|-----|----|----|------|
| 1972—Orlando | | Fla. St. | OF | 49 | 204 | 26 | 59 | 6 | 2 | 5 | 22 | .289 | 126 | 3 | 12 | .915 |
| 1973—Lynchburg | | Carol. | OF | 126 | 473 | 63 | 130 | 17 | 5 | 16 | 54 | .275 | 240 | •17 | 15 | .945 |
| 1974—Lynchburg | | Carol. | OF | •138 | 502 | 93 | 155 | 25 | 8 | 10 | 91 | .309 | 228 | 9 | •15 | .940 |
| 1975—Orlando | | South. | OF | 128 | 443 | 55 | 115 | 13 | 5 | 11 | 55 | .260 | 262 | 8 | 10 | .964 |
| 1976—Tacoma | | P. C. | OF | 128 | 439 | 84 | 133 | 21 | 2 | 15 | 68 | .303 | 274 | 6 | 8 | .972 |

Listed on Minnesota Twins' 1977 spring roster.

# NYLS WALLACE REX NYMAN

Born March 3, 1954, at Detroit, Mich.
Height, 6.00. Weight, 170.
Throws and bats lefthanded.
Attended American River College, Sacramento, Calif.

Led Gulf Coast League outfielders in double plays with 3 in 1972.
Named Most Valuable Player in Southern League, 1974.

| Year Club | League | Pos. | G. | AB. | R. | H. | 2B. | 3B. | HR. | RBI. | B.A. | PO. | A. | E. | F.A. |
|---|---|---|---|---|---|---|---|---|---|---|---|---|---|---|---|
| 1972–Sarasota W. Sox | Gulf | C | OF | 47 | 177 | 30 | 51 | 3 | 2 | 0 | 20 | .288 | 80 | •10 | 7 | .928 |
| 1973–Appleton† ........Midw. | OF-1B | 92 | 355 | 62 | 112 | 12 | 2 | 2 | 24 | .315 | 274 | 17 | 15 | .951 |
| 1974–Knoxville ........South. | OF | 125 | 510 | •87 | •166 | 25 | •9 | 4 | 69 | •.325 | 288 | 11 | 9 | .971 |
| 1974–Iowa................A. A. | OF | 12 | 43 | 4 | 6 | 0 | 1 | 0 | 3 | .140 | 29 | 1 | 0 | 1.000 |
| 1974–Chicago ...........Amer. | OF | 5 | 14 | 5 | 9 | 2 | 1 | 0 | 4 | .643 | 6 | 1 | 0 | 1.000 |
| 1975–Chicago ...........Amer. | OF | 106 | 327 | 36 | 74 | 6 | 3 | 2 | 28 | .226 | 177 | 6 | 8 | .958 |
| 1976–Iowa................A. A. | OF | 104 | 380 | 60 | 107 | 27 | 4 | 5 | 36 | .282 | 194 | 3 | 0•1.000 | | |
| 1976–Chicago ...........Amer. | OF | 8 | 15 | 2 | 2 | 1 | 0 | 0 | 1 | .133 | 13 | 0 | 0 | 1.000 |
| Major League Totals ...................... | | 119 | 356 | 43 | 85 | 9 | 4 | 2 | 33 | .239 | 196 | 7 | 8 | .962 |

†On disabled list, May 22 to June 8 and June 21 to July 1, 1973.


# JOHNNY LANE OATES

Born January 21, 1946, at Sylva, N. C.
Height, 5.11. Weight, 185.
Throws right and bats lefthanded.
Hobbies–Golf and bowling.
Attended Virginia Tech, Blacksburg, Va.; received Bachelor of Science
degree in Health and Physical Education.

Led National League in passed balls with 15 in 1974.
Tied for National League lead in double plays by catchers with 10 in 1975.

| Year Club | League | Pos. | G. | AB. | R. | H. | 2B. | 3B. | HR. | RBI. | B.A. | PO. | A. | E. | F.A. |
|---|---|---|---|---|---|---|---|---|---|---|---|---|---|---|---|
| 1967–Bluefield .........Appal. | C | 5 | 12 | 5 | 5 | 1 | 0 | 1 | 4 | .417 | 23 | 5 | 0 | 1.000 |
| 1967–Miami .............Fla. St. | C-OF | 48 | 156 | 22 | 45 | 5 | 2 | 3 | 19 | .283 | 271 | 37 | 8 | .975 |
| 1968–Miami .............Fla. St. | C-OF | 70 | 194 | 24 | 51 | 9 | 3 | 0 | 23 | .263 | 384 | 42 | 3 | .993 |
| 1969–Dal.-Ft. W. ........Texas | C | 66 | 191 | 24 | 55 | 12 | 2 | 1 | 18 | .288 | 253 | 42 | 4 | .987 |
| 1970–Rochester.........Int. | C | 9 | 16 | 1 | 6 | 1 | 0 | 0 | 4 | .375 | 24 | 2 | 0 | 1.000 |
| 1970–Baltimore†........Amer. | C | 5 | 18 | 2 | 5 | 0 | 1 | 9 | 2 | .278 | 30 | 1 | 2 | .939 |
| 1971–Rochester.........Int. | C | 114 | 346 | 49 | 96 | 16 | 3 | 7 | 44 | .277 | •648 | •73 | 6 | .992 |
| 1972–Baltimore‡.......Amer. | C | 85 | 253 | 20 | 66 | 12 | 1 | 4 | 21 | .261 | 391 | 31 | 2 | •.995 |
| 1973–Atlanta§ ...........Nat. | C | 93 | 322 | 27 | 80 | 6 | 0 | 4 | 27 | .248 | 409 | 57 | 9 | .981 |
| 1974–Atlanta...........Nat. | C | 100 | 291 | 22 | 65 | 10 | 0 | 1 | 21 | .223 | 434 | 55 | 4 | .992 |
| 1975–Atl.x-Phil. .......Nat. | C | 98 | 287 | 28 | 81 | 15 | 0 | 1 | 25 | .282 | 450 | 45 | 5 | .990 |
| 1976–Philadelphia y ..Nat. | C | 37 | 99 | 10 | 25 | 2 | 0 | 0 | 8 | .253 | 155 | 15 | 1 | .994 |
| American League Totals ................ | | 90 | 271 | 22 | 71 | 12 | 2 | 4 | 23 | .262 | 421 | 32 | 4 | .991 |
| National League Totals ................. | | 328 | 999 | 87 | 251 | 33 | 0 | 6 | 81 | .251 | 1448 | 172 | 19 | .988 |
| Major League Totals ...................... | | 418 | 1270 | 109 | 322 | 45 | 2 | 10 | 104 | .254 | 1869 | 204 | 23 | .989 |

†On military list, April 21 through August 22, 1970.

‡Traded with Pitchers Pat Dobson and Roric Harrison and Second Baseman Dave Johnston to Atlanta
Braves for Catcher Earl Williams and Infielder Taylor Duncan, November 30, 1972.

§On disabled list, July 17 to September 2, 1973.

xTraded with First Baseman Dick Allen to Philadelphia Phillies for Catcher Jim Essian, Outfielder Barry
Bonnell and cash, May 7, 1975.

yOn disabled list April 14 to June 1, 1976; traded with Pitcher R. Quency Hill (assigned to Albuquerque) to
Los Angeles Dodgers for Infielder Ted Sizemore, December 20, 1976.

CHAMPIONSHIP SERIES RECORD

| Year Club | League | Pos. | G. | AB. | R. | H. | 2B. | 3B. | HR. | RBI. | B.A. | PO. | A. | E. | F.A. |
|---|---|---|---|---|---|---|---|---|---|---|---|---|---|---|---|
| 1976–Philadelphia ......Nat. | C | 1 | 1 | 0 | 0 | 0 | 0 | 0 | 0 | .000 | 1 | 0 | 0 | 1.000 |


# JOHNNY LEE ODOM
## (Blue Moon)

Born May 29, 1945, at Macon, Ga.
Height, 5.11. Weight, 180.
Throws and bats righthanded.

Tied for American League lead in wild pitches with 17 in 1968.
Led Northwest League pitchers in games started with 29 in 1965.
Received reported $75,000 bonus to sign with Kansas City Athletics, 1964.

| Year Club | League | G. | IP. | W. | L. | Pct. | H. | R. | ER. | SO. | BB. | ERA. |
|---|---|---|---|---|---|---|---|---|---|---|---|---|
| 1964–Birmingham ......................Southern | 16 | 100 | 6 | 5 | .545 | 102 | 54 | 46 | 69 | 52 | 4.14 |
| 1964–Kansas City......................American | 5 | 17 | 1 | 2 | .333 | 29 | 21 | 19 | 10 | 11 | 10.06 |
| 1965–Lewiston.........................Northwest | 29 | •198 | 11 | 14 | .440 | •207 | •125 | •94 | 184 | 118 | 4.27 |
| 1965–Kansas City......................American | 1 | 1 | 0 | 0 | .000 | 2 | 1 | 1 | 0 | 2 | 9.00 |
| 1966–Mobile...........................Southern | 19 | 140 | 12 | 5 | .706 | 119 | 56 | 48 | 96 | 61 | 3.09 |
| 1966–Kansas City......................American | 14 | 90 | 5 | 5 | .500 | 70 | 31 | 25 | 47 | 53 | 2.50 |
| 1967–Kansas City......................American | 29 | 104 | 3 | 8 | .273 | 94 | 67 | 58 | 67 | 68 | 5.02 |
| 1967–Vancouver.........................P. Coast | 6 | 40 | 3 | 2 | .600 | 39 | 17 | 10 | 35 | 22 | 2.25 |

| Year Club | League | G. | IP. | W. | L. | Pct. | H. | R. | ER. | SO. | BB. | ERA. |
|---|---|---|---|---|---|---|---|---|---|---|---|---|
| 1968–Oakland | American | 32 | 231 | 16 | 10 | .615 | 179 | 74 | 63 | 143 | 98 | 2.45 |
| 1969–Oakland | American | 32 | 231 | 15 | 6 | .714 | 179 | 87 | 75 | 150 | 112 | 2.92 |
| 1970–Oakland† | American | 29 | 156 | 9 | 8 | .529 | 128 | 77 | 66 | 88 | 100 | 3.81 |
| 1971–Oakland‡ | American | 25 | 141 | 10 | 12 | .455 | 147 | 78 | 67 | 69 | 71 | 4.28 |
| 1972–Oakland | American | 31 | 194 | 15 | 6 | .714 | 164 | 62 | 54 | 86 | 87 | 2.51 |
| 1973–Oakland | American | 30 | 150 | 5 | 12 | .294 | 153 | 86 | 75 | 83 | 67 | 4.50 |
| 1974–Oakland | American | 34 | 87 | 1 | 5 | .167 | 85 | 39 | 37 | 52 | 52 | 3.83 |
| 1975–Oakland§-Cleveland x | American | 10 | 21 | 1 | 2 | .333 | 23 | 18 | 18 | 14 | 19 | 7.71 |
| 1975–Atlanta | National | 15 | 56 | 1 | 7 | .125 | 78 | 46 | 44 | 30 | 28 | 7.07 |
| 1976–Richmond y | Int'national | 12 | 74 | 4 | 3 | .571 | 72 | 42 | 29 | 57 | 42 | 3.53 |
| 1976–Iowa | Am. Assoc. | 3 | 21 | 3 | 0 | 1.000 | 21 | 6 | 6 | 18 | 11 | 2.57 |
| 1976–Chicago z | American | 8 | 28 | 2 | 2 | .500 | 31 | 21 | 18 | 18 | 20 | 5.79 |
| American League Totals | | 280 | 1451 | 83 | 78 | .516 | 1284 | 662 | 576 | 827 | 760 | 3.57 |
| National League Totals | | 15 | 56 | 1 | 7 | .125 | 78 | 46 | 44 | 30 | 28 | 7.07 |
| Major League Totals | | 295 | 1507 | 84 | 85 | .497 | 1362 | 708 | 620 | 857 | 788 | 3.70 |

†On disabled list, June 20 to August 4, 1970.
‡On disabled list, March 22 to May 8, 1971.
§Traded with cash to Cleveland Indians for Pitchers Jim Perry and Dick Bosman, May 20, 1975.
xTraded with a player to be named later to Atlanta Braves for Pitcher Roric Harrison, June 7, 1975; Indians sent Shortstop Rob Belloir to Braves, June 16, 1975, to complete deal.
yTraded to Iowa (Chicago White Sox' affiliate) for Catcher Richard Varney, June 15, 1976.
zOn disabled list, August 18 to September 8, 1976; released January 26, 1977.

## CHAMPIONSHIP SERIES RECORD

| Year Club | League | G. | IP. | W. | L. | Pct. | H. | R. | ER. | SO. | BB. | ERA. |
|---|---|---|---|---|---|---|---|---|---|---|---|---|
| 1972–Oakland | American | 2 | 14 | 2 | 0 | 1.000 | 5 | 1 | 0 | 5 | 2 | 0.00 |
| 1973–Oakland | American | 1 | 5 | 0 | 0 | .000 | 6 | 2 | 1 | 4 | 2 | 1.80 |
| 1974–Oakland | American | 1 | 3⅓ | 0 | 0 | .000 | 1 | 0 | 0 | 1 | 0 | 0.00 |
| Championship Series Totals | | 4 | 22⅓ | 2 | 0 | 1.000 | 12 | 3 | 1 | 10 | 4 | 0.40 |

## WORLD SERIES RECORD

| Year Club | League | G. | IP. | W. | L. | Pct. | H. | R. | ER. | SO. | BB. | ERA. |
|---|---|---|---|---|---|---|---|---|---|---|---|---|
| 1972–Oakland | American | 2 | 11⅓ | 0 | 1 | .000 | 5 | 2 | 2 | 13 | 6 | 1.59 |
| 1973–Oakland | American | 2 | 4⅔ | 0 | 0 | .000 | 5 | 2 | 2 | 2 | 2 | 3.86 |
| 1974–Oakland | American | 2 | 1⅓ | 1 | 0 | 1.000 | 0 | 0 | 0 | 2 | 1 | 0.00 |
| World Series Totals | | 6 | 17⅓ | 1 | 1 | .500 | 10 | 4 | 4 | 17 | 9 | 2.08 |

## ALL-STAR GAME RECORD

| Year League | IP. | W. | L. | Pct. | H. | R. | ER. | SO. | BB. | ERA. |
|---|---|---|---|---|---|---|---|---|---|---|
| 1968–American | 2 | 0 | 0 | .000 | 0 | 0 | 0 | 2 | 2 | 0.00 |
| 1969–American | ⅓ | 0 | 0 | .000 | 5 | 5 | 4 | 0 | 0 | 108.00 |
| All-Star Game Totals | 2⅓ | 0 | 0 | .000 | 5 | 5 | 4 | 2 | 2 | 15.43 |

# RONALD JOHN OESTER

Born May 5, 1956, at Cincinnati, O.
Height, 6.02. Weight, 185.
Throws right and bats left and righthanded.
Hobbies—Football, basketball and golf.

| Year Club | League | Pos. | G. | AB. | R. | H. | 2B. | 3B. | HR. | RBI. | B.A. | PO. | A. | E. | F.A. |
|---|---|---|---|---|---|---|---|---|---|---|---|---|---|---|---|
| 1974–Billings | Pion. | SS | 53 | 167 | 23 | 52 | 11 | 1 | 0 | 21 | .311 | 87 | 141 | 27 | .894 |
| 1975–Tampa | Fla. St. | SS | 117 | 375 | 40 | 82 | 3 | 4 | 0 | 25 | .219 | 174 | 358 | 34 | .940 |
| 1976–Three Rivers | East. | SS | 138 | 447 | 57 | 110 | 14 | 4 | 0 | 44 | .246 | *233 | *408 | 38 | .944 |

Listed on Cincinnati Reds' 1977 spring roster.

# ROWLAND JOHNIE OFFICE

Born October 25, 1952, at Sacramento, Calif.
Height, 6.01. Weight, 175.
Throws and bats lefthanded.
Hobbies—Fishing, music and dancing.
Attended Sacramento City College, Sacramento, Calif.

| Year Club | League | Pos. | G. | AB. | R. | H. | 2B. | 3B. | HR. | RBI. | B.A. | PO. | A. | E. | F.A. |
|---|---|---|---|---|---|---|---|---|---|---|---|---|---|---|---|
| 1971–Greenwood | W. Car. | OF | 117 | 394 | 68 | 119 | 23 | 3 | 12 | 68 | .302 | 194 | 3 | 9 | .956 |
| 1972–Savannah | South. | OF | 128 | 416 | 71 | 112 | 19 | 6 | 8 | 52 | .269 | 245 | 9 | 5 | .981 |
| 1972–Atlanta | Nat. | OF | 2 | 5 | 1 | 2 | 0 | 0 | 0 | 0 | .400 | 3 | 0 | 0 | 1.000 |
| 1973–Richmond | Int. | OF-1B | 139 | 461 | 53 | 109 | 17 | 4 | 10 | 43 | .286 | 275 | 7 | 6 | .979 |
| 1974–Atlanta | Nat. | OF | 131 | 248 | 20 | 61 | 16 | 1 | 3 | 31 | .246 | 171 | 0 | 1 | .994 |
| 1975–Atlanta | Nat. | OF | 126 | 355 | 30 | 103 | 14 | 1 | 3 | 30 | .290 | 229 | 6 | 8 | .967 |
| 1976–Atlanta | Nat. | OF | 99 | 359 | 51 | 101 | 17 | 1 | 4 | 34 | .281 | 204 | 3 | 3 | .986 |
| Major League Totals | | | 358 | 967 | 102 | 267 | 47 | 3 | 10 | 95 | .276 | 607 | 9 | 12 | .981 |

## BENJAMIN A. OGLIVIE
### (Ben)

Born February 11, 1949, at Colon, Panama.
Height, 6.01. Weight, 175.
Throws and bats lefthanded.
Hobbies—Swimming, table tennis and electronics.
Attended Bronx Community College, Bronx, N. Y., and Northwestern University, Boston, Mass.
Led Eastern League outfielders in double plays with 5 in 1970.

| Year Club | League | Pos. | G. | AB. | R. | H. | 2B. | 3B. | HR. | RBI. | B.A. | PO. | A. | E. | F.A. |
|---|---|---|---|---|---|---|---|---|---|---|---|---|---|---|---|
| 1968—Jamestown ........NYP | | 1B-OF | 16 | 45 | 7 | 13 | 1 | 0 | 1 | 5 | .289 | 66 | 2 | 2 | .971 |
| 1969—Greenville ........W. Car. | | OF | 106 | 363 | 48 | 115 | 15 | •7 | 8 | 62 | .317 | 128 | 6 | 12 | .918 |
| 1969—Winter Haven ....Fla. St. | | OF | 11 | 32 | 4 | 8 | 1 | 0 | 0 | 5 | .250 | 13 | 1 | 1 | .933 |
| 1970—Pawtucket ........East. | | OF | 115 | 391 | 62 | 91 | 15 | 0 | 10 | 51 | .233 | 172 | 14 | 5 | .974 |
| 1971—Louisville ..........Int. | | OF | 134 | 474 | 82 | 144 | 27 | 7 | 17 | 86 | .304 | 215 | •26 | 12 | .953 |
| 1971—Boston ............Amer. | | OF | 14 | 38 | 2 | 10 | 3 | 0 | 0 | 4 | .263 | 22 | 1 | 1 | .958 |
| 1972—Boston ............Amer. | | OF | 94 | 253 | 27 | 61 | 10 | 2 | 8 | 30 | .241 | 98 | 5 | 2 | .981 |
| 1973—Boston† ...........Amer. | | OF | 58 | 147 | 16 | 32 | 9 | 1 | 2 | 9 | .218 | 56 | 2 | 1 | .983 |
| 1974—Detroit ............Amer. | | OF-1B | 92 | 252 | 28 | 68 | 11 | 3 | 4 | 29 | .270 | 162 | 11 | 5 | .972 |
| 1975—Detroit ............Amer. | | OF-1B | 100 | 332 | 45 | 95 | 14 | 1 | 9 | 36 | .286 | 232 | 8 | 5 | .980 |
| 1976—Detroit ............Amer. | | O-1-DH | 115 | 305 | 36 | 87 | 12 | 3 | 15 | 47 | .285 | 234 | 8 | 3 | .988 |
| Major League Totals ..................... | | | 473 | 1327 | 154 | 353 | 59 | 10 | 38 | 155 | .266 | 804 | 35 | 17 | .980 |

†Traded to Detroit Tigers for Second Baseman Dick McAuliffe, October 23, 1973.


## ALBERT OLIVER, JR.
### (Al)

Born October 14, 1946, at Portsmouth, O.
Height, 6.00. Weight, 195.
Throws and bats lefthanded.
Attended Kent State University, Kent, O.

Tied major league records for most errors by first baseman, inning, 3, May 23, 1969, fourth inning; and most at bats, game, since 1900, 7, September 16, 1975.
Led Western Carolinas League first basemen in double plays with 93 in 1965.
Named center fielder on THE SPORTING NEWS National League All-Star Team, 1975.

| Year Club | League | Pos. | G. | AB. | R. | H. | 2B. | 3B. | HR. | RBI. | B.A. | PO. | A. | E. | F.A. |
|---|---|---|---|---|---|---|---|---|---|---|---|---|---|---|---|
| 1964—Salem† ..............Appal. | | (On disabled list all season due to knee injury) | | | | | | | | | | | | | |
| 1965—Gastonia............W. Car. | | 1B | 123 | •515 | 77 | •159 | 19 | 5 | 10 | 71 | .309 | •1031 | •64 | 21 | .981 |
| 1966—Raleigh‡ ............Carol. | | 1B | 117 | 458 | 66 | 137 | 25 | 4 | 10 | 57 | .299 | 1035 | •75 | 16 | .986 |
| 1967—Macon‡‡ ..........South. | | 1B-O | 38 | 126 | 18 | 28 | 1 | 2 | 1 | 4 | .222 | 267 | 21 | 6 | .980 |
| 1967—Raleigh§ ...........Carol. | | 1B | 40 | 145 | 20 | 43 | 4 | 4 | 2 | 15 | .297 | 365 | 17 | 0 | 1.000 |
| 1968—Columbus ..........Int. | | 1B-OF | 132 | 473 | 61 | 149 | 22 | 13 | 14 | 74 | .315 | 968 | 28 | 16 | .984 |
| 1968—Pittsburgh ..........Nat. | | OF | 4 | 8 | 1 | 1 | 0 | 0 | 0 | 0 | .125 | 3 | 0 | 0 | 1.000 |
| 1969—Pittsburgh ........Nat. | | 1B-OF | 129 | 463 | 55 | 132 | 19 | 2 | 17 | 70 | .285 | 911 | 50 | 9 | .991 |
| 1970—Pittsburgh ........Nat. | | OF-1B | 151 | 551 | 63 | 149 | 33 | 5 | 12 | 83 | .270 | 718 | 52 | 9 | .988 |
| 1971—Pittsburgh ........Nat. | | OF-1B | 143 | 529 | 69 | 149 | 31 | 7 | 14 | 64 | .282 | 497 | 15 | 6 | .988 |
| 1972—Pittsburgh ........Nat. | | OF-1B | 140 | 565 | 88 | 176 | 27 | 4 | 12 | 89 | .312 | 353 | 4 | 5 | .986 |
| 1973—Pittsburgh ........Nat. | | OF-1B | 158 | 654 | 90 | 191 | 38 | 7 | 20 | 99 | .292 | 692 | 36 | 13 | .982 |
| 1974—Pittsburgh ........Nat. | | OF-1B | 147 | 617 | 96 | 198 | 38 | 12 | 11 | 85 | .321 | 702 | 26 | 7 | .990 |
| 1975—Pittsburgh ........Nat. | | OF-1B | 155 | 628 | 90 | 176 | 39 | 8 | 18 | 84 | .280 | 409 | 6 | 5 | .988 |
| 1976—Pittsburgh ........Nat. | | OF-1B | 121 | 443 | 62 | 143 | 22 | 5 | 12 | 61 | .323 | 327 | 4 | 5 | .985 |
| Major League Totals ..................... | | | 1148 | 4458 | 614 | 1315 | 247 | 50 | 116 | 635 | .295 | 4612 | 193 | 59 | .988 |

†On disabled list, June 23 through July 1, 1964. On disabled list, July 16 through September 22, 1964.
‡On temporary inactive list, May 26 through June 15, 1966.
‡‡On military list, January 7 through May 7, 1967.
§On temporary inactive list, June 21 through July 15, 1967.

### CHAMPIONSHIP SERIES RECORD

| Year Club | League | Pos. | G. | AB. | R. | H. | 2B. | 3B. | HR. | RBI. | B.A. | PO. | A. | E. | F.A. |
|---|---|---|---|---|---|---|---|---|---|---|---|---|---|---|---|
| 1970—Pittsburgh ........Nat. | | 1B | 2 | 8 | 0 | 2 | 0 | 0 | 0 | 1 | .250 | 22 | 1 | 0 | 1.000 |
| 1971—Pittsburgh ........Nat. | | PH-OF | 4 | 12 | 2 | 3 | 0 | 0 | 1 | 5 | .250 | 5 | 0 | 0 | 1.000 |
| 1972—Pittsburgh ........Nat. | | OF | 5 | 20 | 3 | 5 | 2 | 1 | 1 | 3 | .250 | 17 | 1 | 0 | 1.000 |
| 1974—Pittsburgh ........Nat. | | OF | 4 | 14 | 1 | 2 | 0 | 0 | 0 | 1 | .143 | 9 | 0 | 0 | 1.000 |
| 1975—Pittsburgh ........Nat. | | OF | 3 | 11 | 1 | 2 | 0 | 0 | 1 | 2 | .182 | 5 | 0 | 0 | 1.000 |
| Championship Series Totals ............ | | | 18 | 65 | 7 | 14 | 2 | 1 | 3 | 12 | .215 | 58 | 2 | 0 | 1.000 |

### WORLD SERIES RECORD

| Year Club | League | Pos. | G. | AB. | R. | H. | 2B. | 3B. | HR. | RBI. | B.A. | PO. | A. | E. | F.A. |
|---|---|---|---|---|---|---|---|---|---|---|---|---|---|---|---|
| 1971—Pittsburgh ........Nat. | | PH-OF | 5 | 19 | 1 | 4 | 2 | 0 | 0 | 2 | .211 | 11 | 0 | 1 | .917 |

### ALL-STAR GAME RECORD

| Year League | Pos. | AB. | R. | H. | 2B. | 3B. | HR. | RBI. | B.A. | PO. | A. | E. | F.A. |
|---|---|---|---|---|---|---|---|---|---|---|---|---|---|
| 1972—National ............................. | OF | 1 | 0 | 0 | 0 | 0 | 0 | 0 | .000 | 0 | 0 | 0 | .000 |
| 1975—National ............................. | PH-OF | 1 | 1 | 1 | 1 | 0 | 0 | 0 | 1.000 | 0 | 0 | 0 | .000 |
| 1976—National ............................. | OF | 1 | 0 | 0 | 0 | 0 | 0 | 0 | .000 | 1 | 0 | 0 | 1.000 |
| All-Star Game Totals ...................... | | 3 | 1 | 1 | 1 | 0 | 0 | 0 | .333 | 1 | 0 | 0 | 1.000 |

## DAVID JACOB OLIVER
### (Dave)

Born April 7, 1951, at Stockton, Calif.
Height,5.11. Weight,175.
Throwsright and bats lefthanded.
Hobbies—Bowling and racquetball.
Attended California Poly State University, San Luis Obispo, Calif.
Led Texas League second basemen in double plays with 92 in 1974.

| Year Club | League | Pos. | G. | AB. | R. | H. | 2B. | 3B. | HR. | RBI. | B.A. | PO. | A. | E. | F.A. |
|---|---|---|---|---|---|---|---|---|---|---|---|---|---|---|---|
| 1973—Reno .................Calif. | | 2B | 74 | 257 | 33 | 71 | 8 | 3 | 0 | 35 | .276 | 131 | 202 | 15 | .957 |
| 1974—San Antonio ......Texas | | 2B | 128 | 481 | 74 | 135 | 10 | 1 | 0 | 34 | .281 | •259 | 357 | 20 | .969 |
| 1975—San Antonio ......Texas | | 2B-3B | 75 | 289 | 34 | 82 | 10 | 0 | 0 | 17 | .284 | 179 | 193 | 15 | .961 |
| 1975—Okla. City.........A. A. | | •3B-2B | 65 | 249 | 36 | 64 | 9 | 1 | 0 | 18 | .257 | 57 | 127 | •23 | .889 |
| 1976—Toledo .............Int. | | 2B-SS | 128 | 486 | 78 | 136 | 12 | 4 | 2 | 42 | .280 | 256 | 443 | 21 | .971 |

Listed on Cleveland Indians' 1977 spring roster.

## LEWIS JAMES OLSEN
### (Lew)

Born February 15, 1955, at Walnut Creek, Calif.
Height, 6.04. Weight, 215.
Throws and bats righthanded.
Hobbies—Photography, fishing and hunting.
Attended Stanford University, Palo Alto, Calif.

| Year Club | League | G. | IP. | W. | L. | Pct. | H. | R. | ER. | SO. | BB. | ERA. |
|---|---|---|---|---|---|---|---|---|---|---|---|---|
| 1973—Billings ............................Pioneer | | 3 | 10 | 0 | 1 | .000 | 3 | 3 | 1 | 13 | 5 | 0.90 |
| 1974—San Jose ...........................California | | 23 | 150 | 11 | 8 | .579 | 138 | 54 | 38 | 84 | 36 | 2.28 |
| 1975—Jacksonville .......................Southern | | 16 | 100 | 2 | 10 | .167 | 95 | 51 | 41 | 34 | 27 | 3.69 |
| 1975—Waterloo ...........................Midwest | | 9 | 65 | 5 | 1 | .833 | 66 | 28 | 24 | 43 | 14 | 3.32 |
| 1976—Omaha ..............................Am Assoc. | | 25 | 155 | 9 | 7 | .563 | 159 | 68 | 58 | 59 | 36 | 3.37 |

Listed on Kansas City Royals' 1977 spring roster.

## STEVEN ROBERT ONTIVEROS
Name pronounced on-tuh-VAIR-us.
### (Steve)

Born October 26, 1951, at Bakersfield, Calif.
Height, 6.00. Weight, 185.
Throws right and bats right and lefthanded.
Hobby—Working with young boys.
Attended Bakersfield College, Bakersfield, Calif.
Brother of Ed Ontiveros, former pitcher in Houston Astros' organization.
Led Midwest League third basemen in double plays with 18 in 1970.
Named Minor League Player of the Year by THE SPORTING NEWS, 1973.

| Year Club | League | Pos. | G. | AB. | R. | H. | 2B. | 3B. | HR. | RBI. | B.A. | PO. | A. | E. | F.A. |
|---|---|---|---|---|---|---|---|---|---|---|---|---|---|---|---|
| 1969—Great Falls........Pion. | | •3B-SS | 61 | 162 | 36 | 45 | 7 | 2 | 2 | 27 | .278 | 34 | 82 | 13 | •.899 |
| 1970—Decatur ...........Midw. | | •3-S-2 | 117 | 417 | 64 | 114 | 23 | 3 | 11 | 52 | .273 | •99 | •226 | 29 | .918 |
| 1971—Fresno .............Calif. | | 3B-SS | 133 | 461 | 103 | 148 | •33 | •10 | 18 | 92 | .321 | 127 | 241 | 36 | .911 |
| 1972—Amarillo...........Texas | | O-1-3 | 138 | 498 | 67 | 143 | 25 | 3 | 12 | 75 | .287 | 477 | 27 | 10 | .981 |
| 1973—Phoenix ...........P. C. | | OF-1B | 113 | 401 | 83 | 143 | •32 | •16 | 10 | 84 | •.357 | 248 | 15 | 9 | .967 |
| 1973—San Francisco ..Nat. | | 1B-OF | 24 | 33 | 3 | 8 | 0 | 0 | 1 | 5 | .242 | 36 | 6 | 0 | 1.000 |
| 1974—San Francisco ..Nat. | | 3-1-O | 120 | 343 | 45 | 91 | 15 | 1 | 4 | 33 | .265 | 225 | 158 | 19 | .953 |
| 1975—San Francisco ..Nat. | | 3-O-1 | 108 | 325 | 21 | 94 | 16 | 0 | 3 | 31 | .289 | 80 | 189 | 21 | .928 |
| 1976—San Francisco†..Nat. | | 3-O-1 | 59 | 74 | 8 | 13 | 3 | 0 | 0 | 5 | .176 | 18 | 8 | 2 | .928 |
| Major League Totals ..................... | | | 311 | 775 | 77 | 206 | 34 | 1 | 8 | 74 | .266 | 359 | 361 | 42 | .945 |

†Traded with Outfielder Bobby Murcer and Pitcher Andrew Muhlstock to Chicago Cubs for Third Baseman Bill Madlock and Infielder Rob Sperring, February 11, 1977.

## JORGE ORTA (NUNEZ)
Named pronounced OR-ta.

Born November 26, 1950, at Mazatlan, Mexico.
Height, 5.10. Weight, 170.
Throws right and bats lefthanded.

| Year Club | League | Pos. | G. | AB. | R. | H. | 2B. | 3B. | HR. | RBI. | B.A. | PO. | A. | E. | F.A. |
|---|---|---|---|---|---|---|---|---|---|---|---|---|---|---|---|
| 1968—Fresnillo .........Mx. Cen. | | 2-S | 20 | 68 | 8 | 18 | 6 | 0 | 0 | 1 | .265 | 29 | 39 | 4 | .944 |
| 1969—S. Luis Potosi...Mx. C. | | (Did not play.) | | | | | | | | | | | | | |
| 1970—Puerto Mex. ......Mx. S.E. | | 2-S | 18 | 43 | 6 | 13 | 1 | 0 | 0 | 3 | .302 | 29 | 28 | 1 | .983 |
| 1971—San Luis Potosi Mx. Cen. | | 2B | 59 | 182 | 55 | 77 | 17 | •7 | 7 | 53 | •.423 | 115 | 108 | 15 | .937 |
| 1971—Mexicali† ..........Mx. No. | | | 58 | 207 | 45 | 75 | 14 | 2 | 16 | 48 | .362 | figures unavailable | | | |
| 1972—Knoxville .........South. | | 2B | 53 | 196 | 41 | 62 | 6 | 7 | 7 | 34 | .316 | 113 | 142 | 9 | .966 |
| 1972—Chicago ...........Amer. | | S-2-3 | 51 | 124 | 20 | 25 | 3 | 1 | 3 | 11 | .202 | 50 | 85 | 8 | .944 |
| 1973—Chicago ...........Amer. | | 2B-SS | 128 | 425 | 46 | 113 | 9 | 10 | 6 | 40 | .266 | 255 | 301 | 18 | .969 |

— 285 —

| Year Club | League | Pos. | G. | AB. | R. | H. | 2B. | 3B. | HR. | RBI. | B.A. | PO. | A. | E. | F.A. |
|---|---|---|---|---|---|---|---|---|---|---|---|---|---|---|---|
| 1974—Chicago ..........Amer. | | 2B-SS | 139 | 525 | 73 | 166 | 31 | 2 | 10 | 67 | .316 | 297 | 313 | 18 | .971 |
| 1975—Chicago ..........Amer. | | 2B | 140 | 542 | 64 | 165 | 26 | 10 | 11 | 83 | .304 | 354 | 354 | 16 | .978 |
| 1976—Chicago ..........Amer. | | O-3-DH | 158 | 636 | 74 | 174 | 29 | 8 | 14 | 72 | .274 | 187 | 111 | 15 | .952 |
| Major League Totals ..................... | | | 616 | 2252 | 277 | 643 | 98 | 31 | 44 | 273 | .286 | 1143 | 1164 | 75 | .968 |

†Sold to Appleton (Chicago White Sox' organization), November 30, 1971.

## ALL-STAR GAME RECORD

Named to American League All-Star Team for 1975 game; replaced due to injury.

## FRANK JOSEPH ORTENZIO, JR.

Born February 24, 1951, at Fresno, Calif.
Height, 6.01. Weight, 215.
Throws and bats righthanded.
Hobbies—Bowling and pool.

Led California League in total bases with 271 in 1971.

| Year Club | League | Pos. | G. | AB. | R. | H. | 2B. | 3B. | HR. | RBI. | B.A. | PO. | A. | E. | F.A. |
|---|---|---|---|---|---|---|---|---|---|---|---|---|---|---|---|
| 1969—Corning ...........NYP | | OF-1B | 38 | 117 | 11 | 30 | 1 | 0 | 4 | 25 | .256 | 130 | 4 | 4 | .971 |
| 1970—Billings ............Pion. | | 1B-OF | 58 | 190 | 45 | 60 | 11 | 2 | 10 | 26 | .316 | 310 | 25 | 16 | .954 |
| 1971—San Jose............Calif. | | 1B | 132 | 472 | 99 | 143 | 22 | 5 | •32 | 103 | .303 | 838 | 63 | 18 | .980 |
| 1972—Jacksonville ......South. | | 1B | 70 | 251 | 47 | 80 | 21 | 1 | 15 | 51 | .319 | 636 | 41 | 8 | .988 |
| 1972—Omaha ..............A. A. | | 1B-OF | 69 | 246 | 30 | 63 | 17 | 2 | 11 | 41 | .256 | 572 | 36 | 5 | .992 |
| 1973—Omaha† ............A. A. | | DH | 8 | 22 | 3 | 5 | 2 | 0 | 0 | 4 | .227 | 0 | 0 | 0 | .000 |
| 1973—Jacksonville ......South. | | OF-1B | 95 | 329 | 59 | 101 | 16 | 2 | 19 | 63 | .307 | 185 | 13 | 7 | .966 |
| 1973—Kansas City ......Amer. | | 1B | 9 | 25 | 1 | 7 | 2 | 0 | 1 | 6 | .280 | 51 | 6 | 1 | .983 |
| 1974—Omaha‡ ...........A. A. | | 1B | 94 | 325 | 43 | 78 | 10 | 3 | 10 | 46 | .240 | 687 | 41 | 10 | .986 |
| 1975—Omaha ..............A. A. | | 1B | 115 | 414 | 48 | 100 | 17 | 2 | 15 | 72 | .242 | 842 | 47 | 7 | .992 |
| 1976—Omaha§ ...........A. A. | | 1B | 129 | 447 | 61 | 113 | 29 | 4 | 14 | 81 | .253 | 1044 | •81 | 10 | .991 |
| Major League Totals ..................... | | | 9 | 25 | 1 | 7 | 2 | 0 | 1 | 6 | .280 | 51 | 6 | 1 | .983 |

†On disabled list, April 13 to April 28 and May 11 to May 22, 1973.
‡On disabled list, July 29 to August 19, 1974.
§Traded from Kansas City Royals' organization to Denver (Montreal Expos' organization) for Second Baseman Rudy Kinard, December 7, 1976.

## AMOS JOSEPH OTIS

Born April 26, 1947, at Mobile, Ala.
Height, 5.11½. Weight, 169.
Throws and bats righthanded.
Hobbies—Bowling, billiards, dancing and fishing.

Major league stolen bases: 1967 (0), 1969 (1), 1970 (33), 1971 (52), 1972 (28), 1973 (13), 1974 (18), 1975 (39), 1976 (26). Total—210.
Led American League in stolen bases with 52 in 1971.
Led American League outfielders in double plays with 6 in 1970 and tied for lead with 4 in 1971.
Led Appalachian League third basemen in double plays with 13 in 1965.
Named outfielder on THE SPORTING NEWS American League All-Star fielding teams, 1971, 1972 and 1974.
Named outfielder on THE SPORTING NEWS American League All-Star Team, 1973.

| Year Club | League | Pos. | G. | AB. | R. | H. | 2B. | 3B. | HR. | RBI. | B.A. | PO. | A. | E. | F.A. |
|---|---|---|---|---|---|---|---|---|---|---|---|---|---|---|---|
| 1965—Harlan ..............Appal. | | 3B | 67 | 252 | 55 | 83 | 11 | 5 | 9 | 39 | .329 | 46 | 76 | 12 | •.910 |
| 1966—Oneonta† .........NYP | | •1-OF-3 | 116 | 419 | 54 | 113 | 17 | 7 | 3 | 46 | .270 | 484 | •74 | 22 | .962 |
| 1967—Jacksonville ......Int. | | O-3-1-2 | 126 | 407 | 62 | 109 | 11 | 7 | 3 | 39 | .268 | 251 | 65 | 8 | .975 |
| 1967—New York..........Nat. | | OF-3B | 19 | 59 | 6 | 13 | 2 | 0 | 0 | 1 | .220 | 23 | 2 | 0 | 1.000 |
| 1968—Jacksonville‡ ....Int. | | OF-1B | 139 | 500 | 76 | 143 | 29 | 4 | 15 | 70 | .286 | 428 | 23 | 9 | .980 |
| 1969—Tidewater.........Int. | | OF | 71 | 248 | 55 | 81 | 14 | 2 | 10 | 43 | .327 | 157 | 9 | 1 | .994 |
| 1969—New York§ ........Nat. | | OF-3B | 48 | 93 | 6 | 14 | 3 | 1 | 0 | 4 | .151 | 49 | 1 | 1 | .982 |
| 1970—Kansas City ......Amer. | | OF | 159 | 620 | 91 | 176 | •36 | 9 | 11 | 58 | .284 | •388 | •15 | 4 | .990 |
| 1971—Kansas City ......Amer. | | OF | 147 | 555 | 80 | 167 | 26 | 4 | 15 | 79 | .301 | •404 | 10 | 4 | .990 |
| 1972—Kansas City ......Amer. | | OF | 143 | 540 | 75 | 158 | 28 | 2 | 11 | 54 | .293 | 351 | 6 | 3 | .992 |
| 1973—Kansas City ......Amer. | | OF | 148 | 583 | 89 | 175 | 21 | 4 | 26 | 93 | .300 | 330 | 10 | 5 | .986 |
| 1974—Kansas City ......Amer. | | OF | 146 | 552 | 87 | 157 | 31 | 9 | 12 | 73 | .284 | 425 | 8 | 6 | .986 |
| 1975—Kansas City x....Amer. | | OF | 132 | 470 | 87 | 116 | 26 | 6 | 9 | 46 | .247 | 310 | 9 | 4 | .988 |
| 1976—Kansas City ......Amer. | | OF | 153 | 592 | 93 | 165 | 40 | 2 | 18 | 86 | .279 | 373 | 5 | 2 | .992 |
| American League Totals ................ | | | 1028 | 3912 | 602 | 1114 | 208 | 36 | 102 | 489 | .285 | 2581 | 63 | 29 | .989 |
| National League Totals .................. | | | 67 | 152 | 12 | 27 | 5 | 1 | 0 | 5 | .178 | 72 | 8 | 1 | .988 |
| Major League Totals ..................... | | | 1095 | 4064 | 614 | 1141 | 213 | 37 | 102 | 494 | .281 | 2653 | 71 | 30 | .989 |

†Drafted by Jacksonville (New York Mets' organization) from Pittsfield (Boston Red Sox' organization), November 28, 1966.
‡On suspended list, May 31 through June 3, 1968.
§Traded with Pitcher Robert D. Johnson to Kansas City Royals for Third baseman Joe Foy, December 3, 1969.
xOn supplemental disabled list, June 25 to July 14, 1975.

## CHAMPIONSHIP SERIES RECORD

| Year Club | League | Pos. | G. | AB. | R. | H. | 2B. | 3B. | HR. | RBI. | B.A. | PO. | A. | E. | F.A. |
|---|---|---|---|---|---|---|---|---|---|---|---|---|---|---|---|
| 1976—Kansas City ......Amer. | | OF | 1 | 1 | 0 | 0 | 0 | 0 | 0 | 0 | .000 | 0 | 0 | 0 | .000 |

| Year League | Pos. | AB. | R. | H. | 2B. | 3B. | HR. | RBI. | B.A. | PO. | A. | E. | F.A. |
|---|---|---|---|---|---|---|---|---|---|---|---|---|---|
| 1970–American | OF | 3 | 0 | 0 | 0 | 0 | 0 | 0 | .000 | 2 | 0 | 0 | 1.000 |
| 1971–American | OF | 1 | 0 | 0 | 0 | 0 | 0 | 0 | .000 | 0 | 0 | 0 | .000 |
| 1973–American | OF | 2 | 0 | 2 | 0 | 0 | 0 | 1 | 1.000 | 0 | 0 | 0 | .000 |
| 1976–American | OF | 1 | 0 | 0 | 0 | 0 | 0 | 0 | .000 | 0 | 0 | 0 | .000 |
| All-Star Game Totals | | 7 | 0 | 2 | 0 | 0 | 0 | 1 | .286 | 2 | 0 | 0 | 1.000 |

Named to American League All-Star Team for the 1972 game; replaced due to injury.

## NATHAN EDWARD OTT
### (Ed)

Born July 11, 1951, at Muncy, Pa.
Height, 5.11. Weight, 185.
Throws right and bats lefthanded.
Hobbies—Hunting and coin collecting.

Led International League in passed balls with 20 in 1975.
Led Carolina League outfielders in double plays with 9 in 1972.
Tied for International League lead in double plays by outfielders with 4 in 1974.

| Year Club | League | Pos. | G. | AB. | R. | H. | 2B. | 3B. | HR. | RBI. | B.A. | PO. | A. | E. | F.A. |
|---|---|---|---|---|---|---|---|---|---|---|---|---|---|---|---|
| 1970–Niagara Falls | NYP | OF | 61 | 206 | 38 | 60 | 9 | 5 | 0 | 24 | .291 | 84 | 8 | 2 | .979 |
| 1971–Monroe | W. Car. | OF | 105 | 356 | 58 | 104 | 12 | 6 | 10 | 48 | .292 | 146 | •16 | 5 | .970 |
| 1972–Salem | Carol. | OF | 133 | 450 | 84 | 137 | 18 | •10 | 7 | 63 | .304 | 211 | 19 | 8 | .966 |
| 1973–Charleston | Int. | OF-C | 126 | 440 | 56 | 115 | 18 | 3 | 6 | 52 | .261 | 203 | 7 | 7 | .968 |
| 1974–Charleston | Int. | •OF-3B | 121 | 423 | 57 | 112 | 13 | 7 | 14 | 49 | .265 | 207 | •31 | 10 | .960 |
| 1974–Pittsburgh | Nat. | OF | 7 | 5 | 1 | 0 | 0 | 0 | 0 | 0 | .000 | 1 | 0 | 0 | 1.000 |
| 1975–Charleston | Int. | •C-OF | 121 | 425 | 66 | 121 | 21 | 5 | 10 | 5 | .285 | •697 | 59 | •21 | .973 |
| 1975–Pittsburgh | Nat. | C | 5 | 5 | 0 | 1 | 0 | 0 | 0 | 0 | .200 | 2 | 0 | 0 | 1.000 |
| 1976–Pittsburgh† | Nat. | C-PH | 27 | 39 | 2 | 12 | 2 | 0 | 0 | 5 | .308 | 20 | 6 | 0 | 1.000 |
| Major League Totals | | | 39 | 49 | 3 | 13 | 2 | 0 | 0 | 5 | .265 | 23 | 6 | 0 | 1.000 |

†On supplemental disabled list, August 10 through September 1, 1976.

## JAMES EDWARD OTTEN, SR.
### (Jim)

Born July 1, 1951, at Lewistown, Mont.
Height, 6.02. Weight, 195.
Throws and bats righthanded.
Hobbies—Hunting, fishing and golf.
Attended Mesa Community College, Mesa, Ariz., and Arizona
State University, Tempe, Ariz.

| Year Club | League | G. | IP. | W. | L. | Pct. | H. | R. | ER. | SO. | BB. | ERA. |
|---|---|---|---|---|---|---|---|---|---|---|---|---|
| 1973–Knoxville | Southern | 14 | 75 | 4 | 8 | .333 | 90 | 50 | 40 | 50 | 43 | 4.80 |
| 1974–Knoxville | Southern | 15 | 75 | 6 | 3 | .667 | 80 | 41 | 35 | 54 | 29 | 4.20 |
| 1974–Iowa | Am. Assoc. | 11 | 76 | 7 | 2 | .778 | 52 | 23 | 19 | 66 | 33 | 2.25 |
| 1974–Chicago | American | 5 | 16 | 0 | 1 | .000 | 22 | 11 | 10 | 11 | 12 | 5.63 |
| 1975–Denver | Am. Assoc. | 28 | 151 | 9 | 9 | .500 | 131 | 79 | 69 | 114 | 71 | 4.11 |
| 1975–Chicago | American | 2 | 5 | 0 | 0 | .000 | 4 | 5 | 4 | 3 | 7 | 7.20 |
| 1976–Iowa | Am. Assoc. | 38 | 133 | 6 | 6 | .500 | 140 | 54 | 43 | 79 | 45 | 2.91 |
| 1976–Chicago | American | 2 | 6 | 0 | 0 | .000 | 9 | 6 | 3 | 3 | 2 | 4.50 |
| Major League Totals | | 9 | 27 | 0 | 1 | .000 | 35 | 22 | 17 | 17 | 21 | 5.67 |

## HAROLD MICHAEL OVERY
### (Mike)

Born January 27, 1951, at Clinton, Ill.
Height, 6.02. Weight, 190.
Throws and bats righthanded.
Hobbies—Hunting, reading and music.
Attended Olivet Nazarene College, Kankakee, Ill.; received
Bachelor of Science degree.

Tied for California League lead in saves with 8 in 1974.

| Year Club | League | G. | IP. | W. | L. | Pct. | H. | R. | ER. | SO. | BB. | ERA. |
|---|---|---|---|---|---|---|---|---|---|---|---|---|
| 1973–Quad Cities | Midwest | 36 | 56 | 5 | 2 | .714 | 47 | 24 | 21 | 73 | 35 | 3.38 |
| 1974–Salinas | California | 40 | 64 | 4 | 7 | .364 | 51 | 38 | 32 | 107 | 56 | 4.50 |
| 1975–El Paso† | Texas | 36 | 78 | 4 | 4 | .500 | 68 | 35 | 23 | 78 | 32 | 2.65 |
| 1976–Salt Lake City | P. Coast | 39 | 79 | 9 | 5 | .643 | 54 | 20 | 18 | 99 | 46 | 2.05 |
| 1976–California | American | 5 | 7 | 0 | 2 | .000 | 6 | 5 | 5 | 8 | 3 | 6.43 |
| Major League Totals | | 5 | 7 | 0 | 2 | .000 | 6 | 5 | 5 | 8 | 3 | 6.43 |

†On disabled list, July 25 to August 16, 1975.

## ROBERT DENNIS OWCHINKO
Name pronounced Oh-CHINK-oh.
### (Bob)
Born January 1, 1955, at Detroit, Mich.
Height, 6.02. Weight, 190.
Throws and bats lefthanded.
Attended Eastern Michigan University, Ypsilanti, Mich.

| Year | Club | League | G. | IP. | W. | L. | Pct. | H. | R. | ER. | SO. | BB. | ERA. |
|------|------|--------|----|-----|----|----|------|----|----|-----|-----|-----|------|
| 1976—Amarillo | | Texas | 13 | 91 | 6 | 2 | .750 | 86 | 36 | 33 | 69 | 38 | 3.26 |
| 1976—San Diego | | National | 2 | 4 | 0 | 2 | .000 | 11 | 8 | 8 | 4 | 3 | 18.00 |
| Major League Totals | | | 2 | 4 | 0 | 2 | .000 | 11 | 8 | 8 | 4 | 3 | 18.00 |

## JOHN LEWIS PACELLA
Born September 15, 1956, at Brooklyn, N.Y.
Height, 6.03. Weight, 195.
Throws and bats righthanded.
Hobbies—Fishing, boating and music.

| Year | Club | League | G. | IP. | W. | L. | Pct. | H. | R. | ER. | SO. | BB. | ERA. |
|------|------|--------|----|-----|----|----|------|----|-----|-----|-----|-----|------|
| 1974—Marion | | Ap'lachian | 12 | 43 | 1 | 7 | .125 | 48 | 31 | 24 | 19 | 32 | 5.02 |
| 1975—Wausau | | Midwest | 19 | 132 | 9 | 8 | .529 | 124 | 71 | 56 | 73 | 58 | 3.82 |
| 1976—Lynchburg | | Carolina | 26 | 185 | 12 | 11 | .522 | 151 | •97 | 67 | 119 | 83 | 3.26 |

Listed on New York Mets' 1977 spring roster.

## THOMAS MARIAN PACIOREK
Name pronounced puh-CHOR-eck.
### (Tom)
Born November 2, 1946, at Detroit, Mich.
Height, 6.04. Weight, 210.
Throws and bats righthanded.
Hobbies—Basketball, golf and football.
Attended University of Houston, Houston, Tex.; received Bachelor of Science degree in Education.
Brother of Mike Paciorek, first baseman in Los Angeles Dodgers' organization.

Led Pacific Coast League in total bases with 310 and tied for lead in sacrifice flies with 12 in 1972.
Named THE SPORTING NEWS Minor League Player of the Year, 1972.

| Year | Club | League | Pos. | G. | AB. | R. | H. | 2B. | 3B. | HR. | RBI. | B.A. | PO. | A. | E. | F.A. |
|------|------|--------|------|----|-----|----|----|-----|-----|-----|------|------|-----|----|----|------|
| 1968—Ogden | | Pion. | OF-1B | 29 | 101 | 25 | 39 | 6 | 3 | 5 | 23 | .386 | 45 | 3 | 2 | .960 |
| 1968—Bakersfield | | Calif. | OF-1B | 38 | 116 | 16 | 32 | 1 | 1 | 0 | 10 | .276 | 44 | 1 | 0 | 1.000 |
| 1969—Bakersfield† | | Calif. | OF-3B | 91 | 359 | 59 | 114 | 20 | 3 | 15 | 53 | .318 | 111 | 44 | 16 | .906 |
| 1970—Spokane | | P.C. | OF | •146 | 549 | 88 | 179 | 36 | 12 | 17 | 101 | .326 | 262 | 5 | 6 | .978 |
| 1970—Los Angeles | | Nat. | OF | 8 | 9 | 2 | 2 | 1 | 0 | 0 | 0 | .222 | 1 | 0 | 0 | 1.000 |
| 1971—Spokane | | P.C. | OF-3B | 144 | 564 | 89 | 172 | 31 | •14 | 15 | 105 | .305 | 240 | 9 | 8 | .969 |
| 1971—Los Angeles | | Nat. | OF | 2 | 2 | 0 | 1 | 0 | 0 | 0 | 1 | .500 | 1 | 0 | 0 | 1.000 |
| 1972—Albuquerque | | P.C. | 1B | 147 | •605 | •125 | •186 | •33 | 5 | •27 | 107 | .307 | •1239 | 80 | •13 | .990 |
| 1972—Los Angeles | | Nat. | 1B-OF | 11 | 47 | 4 | 12 | 4 | 0 | 1 | 6 | .255 | 53 | 3 | 1 | .982 |
| 1973—Los Angeles | | Nat. | OF-1B | 96 | 195 | 26 | 51 | 8 | 0 | 5 | 18 | .262 | 117 | 3 | 2 | .984 |
| 1974—Los Angeles | | Nat. | OF-1B | 85 | 175 | 23 | 42 | 8 | 6 | 1 | 24 | .240 | 85 | 1 | 5 | .945 |
| 1975—Los Angeles‡ | | Nat. | OF | 62 | 145 | 14 | 28 | 8 | 0 | 1 | 5 | .193 | 69 | 0 | 2 | .972 |
| 1976—Atlanta | | Nat. | OF-1-3 | 111 | 324 | 39 | 94 | 10 | 4 | 4 | 36 | .290 | 216 | 10 | 3 | .987 |
| Major League Totals | | | | 375 | 897 | 108 | 230 | 39 | 10 | 12 | 90 | .256 | 542 | 17 | 13 | .977 |

†On restricted list, April 3 through June 3, 1969.
‡Traded with Outfielder Jimmy Wynn, Second Baseman Lee Lacy and Infielder Jerry Royster to Atlanta Braves for Outfielder Dusty Baker and First Baseman-Third Baseman Ed Goodson, November 17, 1975.

CHAMPIONSHIP SERIES RECORD

| Year | Club | League | Pos. | G. | AB. | R. | H. | 2B. | 3B. | HR. | RBI. | B.A. | PO. | A. | E. | F.A. |
|------|------|--------|------|----|-----|----|----|-----|-----|-----|------|------|-----|----|----|------|
| 1974—Los Angeles | | Nat. | PH-OF | 1 | 1 | 0 | 1 | 0 | 0 | 0 | 0 | 1.000 | 0 | 0 | 0 | .000 |

WORLD SERIES RECORD

| Year | Club | League | Pos. | G. | AB. | R. | H. | 2B. | 3B. | HR. | RBI. | B.A. | PO. | A. | E. | F.A. |
|------|------|--------|------|----|-----|----|----|-----|-----|-----|------|------|-----|----|----|------|
| 1974—Los Angeles | | Nat. | PH-PR | 3 | 2 | 1 | 1 | 1 | 0 | 0 | 0 | .500 | 0 | 0 | 0 | .000 |

## DAVID PERCY PAGAN
### (Dave)
Born September 15, 1949, at Nipawin, Saskatchewan, Canada.
Height, 6.02. Weight, 180.
Throws and bats righthanded.
Attended Bellevue Community College, Bellevue, Wash.

| Year | Club | League | G. | IP. | W. | L. | Pct. | H. | R. | ER. | SO. | BB. | ERA. |
|------|------|--------|----|-----|----|----|------|----|-----|-----|-----|-----|------|
| 1970—Johnson City | | Ap'lachian | 4 | 25 | 1 | 1 | .500 | 26 | 16 | 14 | 26 | 12 | 5.04 |
| 1970—Oneonta | | NYP | 9 | 58 | 4 | 3 | .571 | 54 | 26 | 19 | 56 | 11 | 2.95 |
| 1971—Fort Lauderdale | | Florida St. | 26 | 155 | 9 | 10 | .474 | 163 | •93 | •71 | 123 | 76 | 4.12 |
| 1972—Kinston | | Carolina | 26 | 185 | 14 | 9 | .609 | 160 | 65 | 52 | •192 | 56 | •2.53 |
| 1973—West Haven | | Eastern | 12 | 92 | 6 | 2 | .750 | 72 | 23 | 19 | 71 | 39 | 1.86 |

| Year Club | League | G. | IP. | W. | L. | Pct. | H. | R. | ER. | SO. | BB. | ERA. |
|---|---|---|---|---|---|---|---|---|---|---|---|---|
| 1970–Bradenton Pirates ............... | Gulf Coast | 1 | 4 | 0 | 0 | .000 | 7 | 2 | 2 | 2 | 1 | 4.50 |

## HARRY WILLIAM PARKER

Born September 14, 1947, at Highland, Ill.
Height, 6.02. Weight, 190.
Throws and bats righthanded.
Hobbies–Handball and basketball.
Attended University of Illinois, Champaign, Ill., and Tulsa University, Tulsa, Okla.
Brother of Jack Parker, former infielder in Cleveland Indians' organization.

Led International League in shutouts with 5 and tied for lead in complete games with 13 in 1972.

| Year Club | League | G. | IP. | W. | L. | Pct. | H. | R. | ER. | SO. | BB. | ERA. |
|---|---|---|---|---|---|---|---|---|---|---|---|---|
| 1965–Sarasota Cardinals .............. | Florida Rk. | 4 | 21 | 3 | 0 | 1.000 | 12 | 1 | 1 | 17 | 4 | 0.43 |
| 1966–St. Petersburgh† ................. | Florida Rk. | 13 | 86 | 6 | 5 | .545 | 65 | 20 | 15 | 66 | 32 | 1.57 |
| 1967–Modesto‡ ........................... | California | 19 | 132 | 12 | 5 | .706 | 113 | 44 | 41 | 127 | 53 | 2.80 |
| 1968–Arkansas§ .......................... | Texas | 17 | 89 | 6 | 6 | .500 | 83 | 42 | 35 | 50 | 31 | 3.54 |
| 1969–St. Louis x ......................... | National | (In military service) | | | | | | | | | | |
| 1970–Tulsa ................................ | Am. Assoc. | 25 | 148 | 8 | 6 | .571 | 153 | 72 | 59 | 117 | 48 | 3.59 |
| 1970–St. Louis ........................... | National | 7 | 22 | 1 | 1 | .500 | 24 | 13 | 8 | 9 | 15 | 3.27 |
| 1971–Tulsa ................................ | Am. Assoc. | 26 | 180 | 11 | 12 | .478 | 184 | 87 | 74 | 104 | 62 | 3.70 |
| 1971–St. Louis y ......................... | National | 4 | 5 | 0 | 0 | .000 | 6 | 4 | 4 | 2 | 2 | 7.20 |
| 1972–Tidewater z........................ | Int'national | 28 | 200 | 14 | 9 | .609 | 168 | 66 | 58 | 118 | 63 | 2.61 |
| 1973–New York ........................... | National | 38 | 97 | 8 | 4 | .667 | 79 | 40 | 36 | 63 | 36 | 3.34 |
| 1974–New York ........................... | National | 40 | 131 | 4 | 12 | .250 | 145 | 64 | 57 | 58 | 46 | 3.92 |
| 1975–New York a-St. Louis b ....... | National | 32 | 53 | 2 | 4 | .333 | 58 | 30 | 30 | 35 | 29 | 5.09 |
| 1976–Toledo................................ | Int'national | 25 | 159 | 9 | 11 | .450 | 188 | 103 | 90 | 70 | 39 | 5.09 |
| 1976–Cleveland ........................... | American | 3 | 7 | 0 | 0 | .000 | 3 | 0 | 0 | 5 | 0 | .000 |
| Major League Totals ............................... | | 124 | 315 | 15 | 21 | .417 | 315 | 151 | 135 | 172 | 128 | 3.86 |

†On restricted list, January 26 through June 22, 1966.
‡On restricted list, January 13 through June 12, 1967.
§On restricted list, February 2 through June 10, 1968.
xOn military list, April 7, 1969 through January 15, 1970.
yReleased to Tidewater (part of deal which sent Pitcher Charles Taylor, Outfielder-First Baseman Jim Beauchamp, and Infielder Tom Coulter from St. Louis Cardinals to New York Mets for Pitchers Jim Bibby, Rich Folkers, and Charlie Hudson, and Outfielder Art Shamsky), October 18, 1971.
zOn temporary inactive list, August 26 through August 31, 1972.
aOn disabled list, June 24 to July 19, 1975. Released on waivers to St. Louis Cardinals, August 14, 1975.
bTraded to Cleveland Indians for Pitcher Roric Harrison, April 7, 1976.

### CHAMPIONSHIP SERIES RECORD

| Year Club | League | G. | IP. | W. | L. | Pct. | H. | R. | ER. | SO. | BB. | ERA. |
|---|---|---|---|---|---|---|---|---|---|---|---|---|
| 1973–New York ........................... | National | 1 | 1 | 0 | 1 | .000 | 1 | 1 | 1 | 0 | 0 | 9.00 |

### WORLD SERIES RECORD

| Year Club | League | G. | IP. | W. | L. | Pct. | H. | R. | ER. | SO. | BB. | ERA. |
|---|---|---|---|---|---|---|---|---|---|---|---|---|
| 1973–New York ........................... | National | 3 | 3⅓ | 0 | 1 | .000 | 2 | 1 | 0 | 2 | 2 | 0.00 |

## MARTIN ALLEN PARRILL
### (Marty)

Born October 16, 1951, at Springfield, O.
Height, 6.01. Weight, 200.
Throws right and bats lefthanded.
Hobbies–Hunting and camping.
Attended Findlay College, Findlay, O., received Bachelor of
Science degree in pre-dentistry.

Led Florida State League in total bases with 182 in 1975.

| Year Club | League | Pos. | G. | AB. | R. | H. | 2B. | 3B. | HR. | RBI. | B.A. | PO. | A. | E. | F.A. |
|---|---|---|---|---|---|---|---|---|---|---|---|---|---|---|---|
| 1973–Bluefield ..........Appal. | | 3B-1B | 62 | 218 | 38 | 62 | ★17 | 1 | 7 | 37 | .284 | 116 | 87 | 18 | .918 |
| 1974–Miami†..............Fla. St. | | 3B-1B | 107 | 366 | 43 | 95 | 19 | 1 | 5 | 37 | .260 | 36 | 92 | 16 | .889 |
| 1975–Miami ..............Fla. St. | | 3B | 116 | 431 | 62 | 125 | ★24 | 6 | 7 | ★75 | .290 | 69 | 222 | 20 | .936 |
| 1976–Charlotte‡ ........South. | | 3B | 115 | 413 | 50 | 113 | 17 | 2 | 16 | 66 | .274 | 72 | 197 | 14 | ★.951 |

†On disabled list, June 6 through June 23, 1974.
‡On disabled list, April 13 through April 27, 1976.
Listed on Baltimore Orioles' 1977 spring roster.

## LANCE MICHAEL PARRISH

Born June 15, 1956, at McKeesport, Pa.
Height, 6.03. Weight, 210.
Throws and bats righthanded.
Hobbies–Golf and snow skiing.

| Year Club | League | Pos. | G. | AB. | R. | H. | 2B. | 3B. | HR. | RBI. | B.A. | PO. | A. | E. | F.A. |
|---|---|---|---|---|---|---|---|---|---|---|---|---|---|---|---|
| 1974–Bristol ..............Appal. | | 3B | 68 | 253 | 45 | 54 | 11 | 1 | 11 | 46 | .213 | 25 | 83 | 20 | .844 |
| 1975–Lakeland ..........Fla. St. | | C | 100 | 341 | 30 | 75 | 15 | 2 | 5 | 37 | .220 | 460 | 50 | 7 | .986 |
| 1976–Montgomery ......South. | | C | 107 | 340 | 46 | 75 | 9 | 2 | 14 | 55 | .221 | ★600 | ★79 | 11 | ★.984 |

Listed on Detroit Tigers' 1977 spring roster.

## LARRY ALTON PARRISH

Born November 10, 1953, at Winter Haven, Fla.
Height, 6.03. Weight, 200.
Throws and bats righthanded.
Attended Seminole Junior College, Sanford, Fla.
Led Eastern League third basemen in double plays with 32 in 1974.
Led Florida State League in sacrifice flies with 9 in 1973.
Tied for National League lead in double plays by third basemen with 35 in 1976.

| Year | Club | League | Pos. | G. | AB. | R. | H. | 2B. | 3B. | HR. | RBI. | B.A. | PO. | A. | E. | F.A. |
|---|---|---|---|---|---|---|---|---|---|---|---|---|---|---|---|---|
| 1972–W. Palm B'ch | ....Fla. St. | | OF | 2 | 4 | 0 | 1 | 0 | 0 | 0 | 0 | .250 | 2 | 0 | 0 | 1.000 |
| 1972–Jamestown | ........NYP | | OF | 62 | 223 | 32 | 58 | 4 | 3 | 4 | 28 | .260 | 69 | 3 | 3 | .960 |
| 1973–W. Palm B'ch | ....Fla. St. | | *3B-SS | 138 | 481 | 82 | 141 | 14 | 6 | 16 | 33 | .293 | *100 | *292 | 32 | *.925 |
| 1974–Quebec City | ......East. | | 3B | 119 | 437 | 61 | 124 | 14 | 2 | 13 | 77 | .284 | *108 | *277 | •31 | .925 |
| 1974–Montreal | .........Nat. | | 3B | 25 | 69 | 9 | 14 | 5 | 0 | 0 | 4 | .203 | 20 | 51 | 1 | .986 |
| 1975–Montreal | .........Nat. | | 3-S-2 | 145 | 532 | 50 | 146 | 32 | 5 | 10 | 65 | .274 | 105 | 291 | 35 | .919 |
| 1976–Montreal | .........Nat. | | 3B | 154 | 543 | 65 | 126 | 28 | 5 | 11 | 61 | .232 | 122 | 310 | 25 | .945 |
| Major League Totals | ..................... | | | 324 | 1144 | 124 | 286 | 65 | 10 | 21 | 130 | .250 | 247 | 652 | 61 | .936 |

## KEVIN PATRICK PASLEY

Name pronounced PAY-slee.

Born July 22, 1953, at Brooklyn, N. Y.
Height, 6.00. Weight, 190.
Throws and bats righthanded.
Led Pacific Coast League in passed balls with 19 in 1974.
Tied for Eastern League lead in double plays by catchers with 12 in 1973.

| Year | Club | League | Pos. | G. | AB. | R. | H. | 2B. | 3B. | HR. | RBI. | B.A. | PO. | A. | E. | F.A. |
|---|---|---|---|---|---|---|---|---|---|---|---|---|---|---|---|---|
| 1971–Medford† | .........Northw. | | C-O | 24 | 82 | 10 | 23 | 5 | 0 | 0 | 14 | .280 | 163 | 28 | 3 | .985 |
| 1972–Daytona Beach | ..Fla. St. | | *C-O | 126 | 469 | 42 | 129 | 11 | 1 | 0 | 65 | .275 | 873 | 78 | 11 | *.989 |
| 1973–Waterbury | ........East. | | C | 115 | 381 | 24 | 99 | 17 | 2 | 1 | 39 | .260 | *746 | *65 | 12 | .985 |
| 1975–Albuquerque | .....P.C. | | C-OF | 105 | 366 | 50 | 115 | 12 | 4 | 2 | 48 | .314 | 551 | 56 | 9 | .985 |
| 1974–Los Angeles | .....Nat. | | C | 1 | 0 | 0 | 0 | 0 | 0 | 0 | 0 | .000 | 1 | 0 | 0 | 1.000 |
| 1975–Albuquerque‡ | ....P.C. | | C | 98 | 337 | 37 | 84 | 7 | 0 | 2 | 34 | .249 | 492 | 66 | 16 | .972 |
| 1976–Albuquerque | .....P.C. | | C-OF | 122 | 461 | 68 | 148 | 24 | 9 | 2 | 60 | .321 | 566 | 83 | 11 | .983 |
| 1976–Los Angeles | .....Nat. | | C | 23 | 52 | 4 | 12 | 2 | 0 | 0 | 2 | .231 | 86 | 15 | 3 | .971 |
| Major League Totals | ..................... | | | 24 | 52 | 4 | 12 | 2 | 0 | 0 | 2 | .231 | 87 | 15 | 3 | .971 |

†On disabled list, July 23 through remainder of season.
‡On disabled list, April 27 to June 3, 1975.

## STEVEN EARL PATCHIN
### (Patch)

Born March 26, 1950, at Joplin, Mo.
Height, 6.01. Weight, 195.
Throws and bats righthanded.
Hobbies—Bowling, tennis and water skiing.
Attended University of Missouri, Columbia, Mo., and Missouri
Southern College, Joplin, Mo.
Nephew of Ed Patchin, minor leaguer in New York Yankees' organization, 1943-46.
Led Eastern League catchers in passed balls with 22 in 1974.

| Year | Club | League | Pos. | G. | AB. | R. | H. | 2B. | 3B. | HR. | RBI. | B.A. | PO. | A. | E. | F.A. |
|---|---|---|---|---|---|---|---|---|---|---|---|---|---|---|---|---|
| 1971–Medford | ...........Northw. | | C | 13 | 46 | 9 | 13 | 2 | 0 | 0 | 10 | .283 | 105 | 9 | 2 | .983 |
| 1971–Bakersfield | ........Calif. | | C | 48 | 151 | 15 | 42 | 5 | 0 | 4 | 22 | .278 | 348 | 29 | 8 | .979 |
| 1971–Albuquerque | .......Texas | | C | 12 | 32 | 0 | 6 | 2 | 0 | 0 | 4 | .188 | 63 | 6 | 0 | 1.000 |
| 1972–Bakersfield | .......Calif.· | | C | 75 | 242 | 37 | 83 | 9 | 2 | 5 | 44 | .343 | 576 | 44 | 12 | .981 |
| 1972–El Paso | ...........Texas | | C | 48 | 141 | 13 | 38 | 9 | 1 | 1 | 24 | .270 | 348 | 17 | 4 | .989 |
| 1973–Albuquerque | .......P.C. | | C | 90 | 283 | 35 | 76 | 12 | 1 | 4 | 24 | .269 | 467 | 54 | *13 | .976 |
| 1974–Waterbury | ........East. | | C-OF | 112 | 360 | 48 | 101 | 15 | 4 | 7 | 47 | .281 | 536 | 73 | 13 | .979 |
| 1975–Waterbury† | ......East. | | 1B-C | 127 | 435 | 48 | 128 | 24 | 2 | 10 | 67 | .294 | 626 | 51 | *16 | .977 |
| 1976–Omaha | ..............A.A. | | C-1B-OF | 109 | 353 | 47 | 106 | 15 | 4 | 11 | 50 | .300 | 519 | 34 | *15 | .974 |

†Traded by Los Angeles Dodgers to Kansas City Royals for Infielder Ron Washington, December 15, 1975.
Listed on Kansas City Royals' 1977 spring roster.

## FREDDIE JOE PATEK

Born October 9, 1944, at Oklahoma City, Okla.
Height, 5.04. Weight, 165.
Throws and bats righthanded.
Hobbies—Hunting and fishing.
Tied major league record for most double plays, shortstop, 9 innings, 5, May 6, 1972.
Major League stolen bases: 1968 (18), 1969 (15), 1970 (8), 1971 (49), 1972 (33), 1973 (36), 1974 (33), 1975 (32), 1976 (51). Total—275.
Led American League shortstops in double plays with 107 in 1971, 113 in 1972 and 115 in 1973; tied for lead with 108 in 1974.
Led International League in sacrifice hits with 10 and in stolen bases with 42 in 1967.

| Year Club League | Pos. | G. | AB. | R. | H. | 2B. | 3B. | HR. | RBI. | B.A. | PO. | A. | E. | F.A. |
|---|---|---|---|---|---|---|---|---|---|---|---|---|---|---|
| 1966–Gastonia............W. Car. | 2-S | 75 | 294 | 68 | 91 | 8 | 5 | 3 | 20 | .310 | 156 | 201 | 20 | .947 |
| 1966–Columbus..........Int. | SS-3B | 17 | 36 | 3 | 5 | 1 | 0 | 0 | 1 | .139 | 14 | 19 | 5 | .868 |
| 1966–Asheville ..........Sout. | SS | 26 | 64 | 11 | 13 | 0 | 0 | 1 | 5 | .203 | 28 | 49 | 11 | .875 |
| 1967–Columbus ..........Int. | SS-O-2 | 128 | 471 | 77 | 120 | 14 | 5 | 6 | 27 | .255 | 221 | 335 | 27 | .954 |
| 1968–Columbus ..........Int. | SS | 33 | 138 | 21 | 42 | 7 | 1 | 0 | 10 | .304 | 77 | 108 | 5 | .974 |
| 1968–Pittsburgh†.......Nat. | SS-O-3 | 61 | 208 | 31 | 53 | 4 | 2 | 2 | 18 | .255 | 90 | 166 | 6 | .977 |
| 1969–Pittsburgh ........Nat. | SS | 147 | 460 | 48 | 110 | 9 | 1 | 5 | 32 | .239 | 227 | 399 | 30 | .954 |
| 1970–Pittsburgh‡.......Nat. | SS | 84 | 237 | 42 | 58 | 10 | 5 | 1 | 19 | .245 | 122 | 212 | 10 | .971 |
| 1971–Kansas City ......Amer. | SS | 147 | 591 | 86 | 158 | 21 | *11 | 6 | 36 | .267 | *301 | 459 | 25 | .968 |
| 1972–Kansas City§ ....Amer. | SS | 136 | 518 | 59 | 110 | 25 | 4 | 0 | 32 | .212 | 230 | *510 | 22 | .971 |
| 1973–Kansas City x....Amer. | SS | 135 | 501 | 82 | 117 | 19 | 5 | 5 | 45 | .234 | 242 | 503 | 26 | .966 |
| 1974–Kansas City ......Amer. | SS | 149 | 537 | 72 | 121 | 18 | 6 | 3 | 38 | .225 | 250 | 493 | 25 | .967 |
| 1975–Kansas City ......Amer. | SS | 136 | 483 | 58 | 110 | 14 | 5 | 5 | 45 | .228 | 231 | 405 | 27 | .959 |
| 1976–Kansas City ......Amer. | SS | 144 | 432 | 58 | 104 | 19 | 3 | 1 | 43 | .241 | 233 | 426 | 26 | .962 |
| American League Totals ............... | | 847 | 3062 | 415 | 720 | 116 | 34 | 20 | 239 | .235 | 1487 | 2796 | 151 | .966 |
| National League Totals .................. | | 292 | 905 | 121 | 221 | 23 | 8 | 8 | 69 | .244 | 439 | 777 | 46 | .964 |
| Major League Totals ..................... | | 1139 | 3967 | 536 | 941 | 139 | 42 | 28 | 308 | .237 | 1926 | 3573 | 197 | .965 |

†On disabled list, July 11 through August 7, 1968.

‡Traded with Pitcher Bruce Dal Canton and Catcher Jerry May to Kansas City Royals for Pitcher Robert D. Johnson, Shortstop Jackie Hernandez and Catcher Jim Campanis (Latter transferred from Omaha to Columbus), December 2, 1970.

§On disabled list, March 23 through April 25, 1972.

xOn supplemental disabled list, June 11 to June 26, 1973.

## CHAMPIONSHIP SERIES RECORD

| Year Club League | Pos. | G. | AB. | R. | H. | 2B. | 3B. | HR. | RBI. | B.A. | PO. | A. | E. | F.A. |
|---|---|---|---|---|---|---|---|---|---|---|---|---|---|---|
| 1970–Pittsburgh ........Nat. | SS | 1 | 3 | 0 | 0 | 0 | 0 | 0 | 0 | .000 | 1 | 2 | 0 | 1.000 |
| 1976–Kansas City ......Amer. | SS | 5 | 18 | 2 | 7 | 2 | 0 | 0 | 4 | .389 | 13 | 18 | 0 | 1.000 |
| Championship Series Totals ........... | | 6 | 21 | 2 | 7 | 2 | 0 | 0 | 4 | .333 | 14 | 20 | 0 | 1.000 |

## ALL-STAR GAME RECORD

Named to American League All-Star Team for 1972 game; replaced due to injury.

| Year League | Pos. | AB. | R. | H. | 2B. | 3B. | HR. | RBI. | B.A. | PO. | A. | E. | F.A. |
|---|---|---|---|---|---|---|---|---|---|---|---|---|---|
| 1976–American ........................... | SS | 0 | 0 | 0 | 0 | 0 | 0 | 0 | .000 | 0 | 1 | 0 | 1.000 |

## GILBERT THOMAS PATTERSON
### (Gil)

Born September 5, 1955, at Philadelphia, Pa.
Height, 6.01. Weight, 185.
Throws and bats righthanded.
Attended Miami-Dade (South) Junior College, Miami, Fla.

| Year Club | League | G. | IP. | W. | L. | Pct. | H. | R. | ER. | SO. | BB. | ERA. |
|---|---|---|---|---|---|---|---|---|---|---|---|---|
| 1975–Oneonta .............................NYP | | 14 | 106 | 8 | 4 | .667 | 79 | 32 | 23 | 97 | 11 | 1.95 |
| 1976–West Haven.........................Eastern | | 13 | 100 | 9 | 2 | .818 | 67 | 35 | 23 | 64 | 27 | 2.07 |
| 1976–Syracuse ...........................Int'national | | 10 | 77 | 7 | 2 | .778 | 71 | 30 | 25 | 40 | 34 | 2.92 |

Invited to New York Yankees' 1977 spring camp.

## MARTIN WILLIAM PATTIN
### (Marty)

Born April 6, 1943, at Charleston, Ill.
Height, 5.11. Weight, 180
Throws and bats righthanded.
Hobbies–Hunting and fishing.
Attended Eastern Illinois University, Charleston, Ill.; received Bachelor of
Science and Master's degrees in Education.
Did graduate work at Arizona State University, Tempe, Ariz.

| Year Club | League | G. | IP. | W. | L. | Pct. | H. | R. | ER. | SO. | BB. | ERA. |
|---|---|---|---|---|---|---|---|---|---|---|---|---|
| 1965–El Paso..............................Texas | | 13 | 67 | 0 | 6 | .000 | 79 | 42 | 35 | 47 | 25 | 4.70 |
| 1966–Quad Cities ........................Midwest | | 5 | 43 | 4 | 1 | .800 | 23 | 7 | 6 | 52 | 11 | 1.26 |
| 1966–Seattle .............................P. Coast | | 13 | 83 | 9 | 2 | .818 | 75 | 39 | 34 | 62 | 29 | 3.69 |
| 1967–Seattle .............................P. Coast | | 30 | 184 | 12 | 11 | .522 | 169 | 70 | 55 | 140 | 52 | 2.69 |
| 1968–Seattle .............................P. Coast | | 4 | 26 | 1 | 0 | 1.000 | 20 | 10 | 7 | 23 | 8 | 2.42 |
| 1968–California† .........................American | | 52 | 84 | 4 | 4 | .500 | 67 | 27 | 26 | 66 | 37 | 2.79 |
| 1969–Seattle .............................American | | 34 | 159 | 7 | 12 | .368 | 166 | 104 | 99 | 126 | 71 | 5.60 |
| 1970–Milwaukee ..........................American | | 37 | 233 | 14 | 12 | .538 | 204 | 91 | 88 | 161 | 71 | 3.40 |
| 1971–Milwaukee‡..........................American | | 36 | 265 | 14 | 14 | .500 | 225 | 100 | 92 | 169 | 73 | 3.12 |
| 1972–Boston ..............................American | | 38 | 253 | 17 | 13 | .567 | 232 | 102 | 91 | 168 | 65 | 3.24 |
| 1973–Boston§ .............................American | | 34 | 219 | 15 | 15 | .500 | 238 | 112 | 105 | 119 | 69 | 4.32 |
| 1974–Kansas City..........................American | | 25 | 117 | 3 | 7 | .300 | 121 | 55 | 52 | 50 | 28 | 4.00 |
| 1975–Kansas City..........................American | | 44 | 177 | 10 | 10 | .500 | 173 | 77 | 64 | 89 | 45 | 3.25 |
| 1976–Kansas City..........................American | | 44 | 141 | 8 | 14 | .364 | 114 | 51 | 39 | 65 | 38 | 2.49 |
| Major League Totals ..................... | | 344 | 1648 | 92 | 101 | .477 | 1540 | 729 | 656 | 1013 | 497 | 3.58 |

‡Traded with Pitcher Lew Krausse and Outfielders Tommy Harper and Pat Skrable to Boston Red Sox for Catcher Don Pavletich, Pitchers Ken Brett and Jim Lonborg, First Baseman George Scott and Outfielders Billy Conigliaro and Joe Lahoud, October 11, 1971.
§Traded to Kansas City Royals for Pitcher Dick Drago, October 23, 1973.

## CHAMPIONSHIP SERIES RECORD

| Year   Club | League | G. | IP. | W. | L. | Pct. | H. | R. | ER. | SO. | BB. | ERA. |
|---|---|---|---|---|---|---|---|---|---|---|---|---|
| 1976–Kansas City.........................American | | 2 | ⅓ | 0 | 0 | .000 | 0 | 1 | 1 | 0 | 0 | 27.00 |

## ALL-STAR GAME RECORD

Member of American League All-Star Team for 1971 game; did not play.

## LARRY GENE PAYNE

Born February 15, 1954, at Huntsville, Tex.
Height, 6.01. Weight, 190.
Throws and bats righthanded.
Hobbies–Hunting and skiing.
Attended University of Texas, Austin, Tex.
Tied for Florida State League lead in complete games with 11 in 1973.

| Year   Club | League | G. | IP. | W. | L. | Pct. | H. | R. | ER. | SO. | BB. | ERA. |
|---|---|---|---|---|---|---|---|---|---|---|---|---|
| 1972–Bradenton Reds....................Gulf C. | | 5 | 25 | 0 | 2 | .000 | 31 | 22 | 10 | 18 | 8 | 3.60 |
| 1973–Tampa ...............................Florida St. | | 17 | 117 | 10 | 5 | .667 | 90 | 34 | 25 | 96 | 17 | 1.92 |
| 1973–Three Rivers.......................Eastern | | 11 | 72 | 3 | 4 | .429 | 61 | 37 | 22 | 66 | 36 | 2.75 |
| 1974–Three Rivers.......................Eastern | | 26 | 162 | 10 | 6 | .625 | 131 | 72 | 47 | 111 | 71 | 2.61 |
| 1975–Indianapolis ......................Am. Assoc. | | 26 | 154 | 9 | 12 | .429 | 136 | 67 | 54 | 105 | 64 | 3.16 |
| 1976–Indianapolis ......................Am. Assoc. | | 27 | 161 | 9 | 9 | .500 | 147 | 96 | 87 | 128 | 101 | 4.86 |

Listed on Cincinnati Reds' 1977 spring roster.

## MICHAEL JOSEPH PAZIK
## (Mike)

Born January 26, 1950, at Lynn, Mass.
Height, 6.02. Weight, 195.
Throws and bats lefthanded.
Attended Holy Cross College, Worcester, Mass.; received Bachelor of Arts degree in Sociology.
Pitched 5-0 no-hit victory against Rochester, August 31, 1971.
Tied for Pacific Coast League lead in shutouts with 3 in 1975 and with 3 in 1976.

| Year   Club | League | G. | IP. | W. | L. | Pct. | H. | R. | ER. | SO. | BB. | ERA. |
|---|---|---|---|---|---|---|---|---|---|---|---|---|
| 1971–Fort Lauderdale .................Florida St. | | 9 | 58 | 4 | 2 | .667 | 46 | 18 | 15 | 52 | 20 | 2.33 |
| 1971–Syracuse ...........................Int'national | | 4 | 25 | 1 | 3 | .250 | 19 | 9 | 8 | 23 | 14 | 2.88 |
| 1972–Syracuse ...........................Int'national | | 27 | 165 | 10 | 10 | .500 | 172 | 84 | 71 | 93 | 67 | 3.87 |
| 1973–Syracuse ...........................Int'national | | 25 | 167 | 13 | 8 | .619 | 166 | 93 | 84 | 76 | 85 | 4.53 |
| 1974–Syracuse† ..........................Int'national | | 3 | 23 | 2 | 1 | .667 | 23 | 12 | 8 | 17 | 7 | 3.13 |
| 1974–Tacoma..............................P. Coast | | 22 | 152 | 11 | 7 | .611 | 147 | 83 | 70 | 101 | 71 | 4.14 |
| 1975–Tacoma..............................P. Coast | | 20 | 140 | 9 | 9 | .500 | 117 | 61 | 49 | 99 | 46 | 3.15 |
| 1975–Minnesota .........................American | | 5 | 20 | 0 | 4 | .000 | 28 | 20 | 18 | 8 | 10 | 8.10 |
| 1976–Minnesota .........................American | | 5 | 9 | 0 | 0 | .000 | 13 | 9 | 7 | 6 | 4 | 7.00 |
| 1976–Tacoma..............................P. Coast | | 22 | 152 | 14 | 5 | •.737 | 134 | 73 | 70 | 75 | 76 | 4.14 |
| Major League Totals ..................... | | 10 | 29 | 0 | 4 | .000 | 41 | 29 | 25 | 14 | 14 | 7.76 |

†Traded with cash by New York Yankees to Minnesota Twins for Pitcher Dick Woodson, May 3, 1974.

## BROCK PEMBERTON

Born November 5, 1953, at Tulsa, Okla.
Height, 6.03. Weight, 190.
Throws left and bats left and righthanded.
Hobbies–Hunting, fishing and cars.
Son of Cliff "Red" Pemberton, former outfielder in
Brooklyn Dodgers' organization.
Led Texas League first basemen in double plays with 113 in 1974.
Led International League first basemen in double plays with 114 in 1976.

| Year   Club   League | Pos. | G. | AB. | R. | H. | 2B. | 3B. | HR. | RBI. | B.A. | PO. | A. | E. | F.A. |
|---|---|---|---|---|---|---|---|---|---|---|---|---|---|---|
| 1972–Marion ..............Appal. | 1B-P | 30 | 98 | 9 | 23 | 5 | 0 | 0 | 12 | .235 | 182 | 18 | 5 | .976 |
| 1972–Batavia ............NYP | 1B | 28 | 98 | 14 | 26 | 4 | 0 | 1 | 13 | .265 | 202 | 9 | 4 | .981 |
| 1973–Pompano Beach Fla. St. | •1B-P | 141 | 482 | 57 | 128 | •31 | 3 | 7 | 53 | .266•1170 | | 63 | 9 | •.993 |
| 1974–Victoria ...........Texas | •1B-P | 134 | 482 | 67 | 155 | 37 | 9 | 8 | 89 | .322•1176 | | 83 | 19 | .986 |
| 1974–New York.........Nat. | 1B | 11 | 22 | 0 | 4 | 0 | 0 | 0 | 1 | .182 | 31 | 4 | 0 | 1.000 |
| 1975–Tidewater.........Int. | •1B-P | 137 | 474 | 68 | 141 | 24 | 2 | 1 | 55 | .297•1184 | | 66 | 8 | •.994 |
| 1975–New York.........Nat. | PH | 2 | 2 | 0 | 0 | 0 | 0 | 0 | 0 | .000 | 0 | 0 | 0 | .000 |
| 1976–Tidewater† .......Int. | 1B | 138 | 520 | 64 | 151 | 26 | 7 | 3 | 58 | .290 | 1179 | 83 | 13 | .990 |
| Major League Totals ..................... | | 13 | 24 | 0 | 4 | 0 | 0 | 0 | 1 | .167 | 31 | 4 | 0 | 1.000 |

†Traded with Outfielder Leon Brown to St. Louis Cardinals' organization for First Baseman-Outfielder Ed Kurpiel, December 9, 1976.

PITCHING RECORD

| Year | Club | League | G. | IP. | W. | L. | Pct. | H. | R. | ER. | SO. | BB. | ERA. |
|------|------|--------|----|----|----|----|------|----|----|-----|-----|-----|------|
| 1972—Marion | | Ap'lachian | 1 | 2 | 0 | 0 | .000 | 1 | 0 | 0 | 1 | 2 | 0.00 |
| 1973—Pompano Beach | | Florida St. | 2 | 3 | 0 | 0 | .000 | 3 | 1 | 1 | 3 | 0 | 3.00 |
| 1974—Victoria | | Texas | 1 | 2 | 1 | 0 | 1.000 | 4 | 1 | 1 | 1 | 0 | 4.50 |
| 1975—Tidewater | | Int'national | 1 | 1 | 0 | 0 | .000 | 3 | 1 | 1 | 1 | 0 | 9.00 |

## EUGENE DAVID PENTZ
### (Gene)

Born June 21, 1953, at Johnstown, Pa.
Height, 6.00. Weight, 205.
Throws and bats righthanded.
Hobbies—Hunting and fishing.
Attended University of Pittsburgh at Johnstown, Johnstown, Pa.

| Year | Club | League | G. | IP. | W. | L. | Pct. | H. | R. | ER. | SO. | BB. | ERA. |
|------|------|--------|----|----|----|----|------|----|----|-----|-----|-----|------|
| 1971—Bristol | | Ap'lachian | 13 | 71 | 3 | •9 | .250 | 74 | •56 | •47 | 70 | 43 | 5.96 |
| 1972—Lakeland | | Florida St. | 16 | 91 | 4 | 3 | .571 | 78 | 47 | 39 | 73 | 60 | 3.86 |
| 1973—Lakeland | | Florida St. | 23 | 142 | 12 | 5 | .706 | 111 | 54 | 42 | 103 | 75 | 2.66 |
| 1974—Evansville | | Am. Assoc. | | | | | | (On suspended list) | | | | | |
| 1975—Evansville | | Am. Assoc. | 16 | 21 | 2 | 3 | .400 | 22 | 8 | 7 | 17 | 15 | 3.00 |
| 1975—Montgomery | | Southern | 22 | 44 | 4 | 2 | .667 | 23 | 10 | 8 | 43 | 23 | 1.64 |
| 1975—Detroit† | | American | 13 | 25 | 0 | 4 | .000 | 27 | 14 | 9 | 21 | 20 | 3.24 |
| 1976—Houston‡ | | National | 40 | 64 | 3 | 3 | .500 | 62 | 26 | 21 | 36 | 31 | 2.95 |
| American League Totals | | | 13 | 25 | 0 | 4 | .000 | 27 | 14 | 9 | 21 | 20 | 3.24 |
| National League Totals | | | 40 | 64 | 3 | 3 | .500 | 62 | 26 | 21 | 36 | 31 | 2.95 |
| Major League Totals | | | 53 | 89 | 3 | 7 | .300 | 89 | 40 | 30 | 57 | 51 | 3.03 |

†Traded with Outfielder Leon Roberts, Catcher Terry Humphrey and Pitcher Mark Lemongello to Houston Astros for Catcher Milt May and Pitchers Jim Crawford and Dave Roberts, December 6, 1975.
‡On disabled list, April 5 through May 21, 1976.

## CHARLES ANTHONY PEPPER
### (Tony)

Born December 24, 1952, at Washington, D. C.
Height, 6.03. Weight, 210.
Throws and bats lefthanded.
Hobbies—Old automobiles and tailoring.
Led Pacific Coast League first basemen in double plays with 140 in 1975.

| Year | Club | League | Pos. | G. | AB. | R. | H. | 2B. | 3B. | HR. | RBI. | B.A. | PO. | A. | E. | F.A. |
|------|------|--------|------|----|-----|----|----|-----|-----|-----|------|------|-----|----|----|------|
| 1971—Great Falls | | Pion. | 1B | 49 | 138 | 22 | 25 | 6 | 1 | 4 | 27 | .181 | 260 | 18 | 7 | .975 |
| 1972—Decatur | | Midw. | 1B | 62 | 192 | 18 | 42 | 6 | 0 | 2 | 22 | .219 | 404 | 26 | 12 | .973 |
| 1972—Seattle | | Midw. | 1B | 36 | 115 | 12 | 40 | 6 | 0 | 1 | 13 | .348 | 248 | 21 | 5 | .982 |
| 1973—Fresno | | Calif. | 1B | 137 | 477 | 70 | 121 | 21 | 3 | 14 | 77 | .254 | 988 | •64 | •31 | .971 |
| 1974—Amarillo | | Texas | 1B | 126 | 461 | 71 | 134 | 22 | 5 | 19 | 94 | .291 | 1067 | •86 | •24 | .980 |
| 1975—Phoenix | | P. C. | 1B | 134 | 478 | 60 | 121 | 14 | 5 | 8 | 65 | .253•1236 | •83 | •33 | .976 |
| 1976—Lafayette | | Texas | 1B-OF | 121 | 396 | 56 | 102 | 15 | 4 | 13 | 64 | .258 | 734 | 44 | 15 | .981 |

Listed on San Francisco Giants' 1977 spring roster.

## ATANASIO RIGAL PEREZ

Name pronounced PER-ez.

### (Tony)

Born May 14, 1942, at Ciego de Avila, Camaguey, Cuba.
Height, 6.02. Weight, 195.
Throws and bats righthanded.
Tied major league record for most at bats, game, since 1900, 7, June 13, 1975.
Led National League first basemen in total chances with 1416 and double plays with 131 in 1973.
Led National League third basemen in double plays with 35 in 1969 and tied for lead with 33 in 1968.
Led Carolina League third basemen in double plays with 23 in 1962.
Named Most Valuable Player in Pacific Coast League, 1964.
Named third baseman on THE SPORTING NEWS National League All-Star Team, 1970.
Named first baseman on THE SPORTING NEWS National League All-Star Team, 1973.

| Year | Club | League | Pos. | G. | AB. | R. | H. | 2B. | 3B. | HR. | RBI. | B.A. | PO. | A. | E. | F.A. |
|------|------|--------|------|----|-----|----|----|-----|-----|-----|------|------|-----|----|----|------|
| 1960—Geneva† | | NYP | IN-O | 104 | 384 | 82 | 107 | 21 | 4 | 6 | 43 | .279 | 199 | 197 | 31 | .927 |
| 1961—Geneva | | NYP | 3B | 121 | 460 | 110 | •160 | 32 | 7 | 27 | •132 | •.348 | 107 | •232 | •42 | .890 |
| 1962—Rocky Mount‡ | | Carol. | 3B | 100 | 384 | 72 | 112 | 20 | 8 | 18 | 74 | .292 | 88 | 178 | 30 | .899 |
| 1963—San Diego | | P. C. | 3B | 8 | 29 | 4 | 11 | 3 | 1 | 1 | 5 | .379 | 6 | 8 | 1 | .933 |
| 1963—Macon§ | | Sally | 3B | 69 | 256 | 44 | 79 | 19 | 3 | 11 | 48 | .309 | 57 | 100 | 18 | .897 |
| 1964—San Diego | | P. C. | 1-3-OF | 124 | 479 | 96 | 148 | 20 | 8 | 34 | 107 | .309 | 816 | 104 | 19 | .980 |
| 1964—Cincinnati | | Nat. | 1B | 12 | 25 | 1 | 2 | 1 | 0 | 0 | 1 | .080 | 51 | 0 | 1 | .981 |
| 1965—Cincinnati | | Nat. | 1B | 104 | 281 | 40 | 73 | 14 | 4 | 12 | 47 | .260 | 525 | 40 | 6 | .989 |
| 1966—Cincinnati | | Nat. | 1B | 99 | 257 | 25 | 68 | 10 | 4 | 4 | 39 | .265 | 530 | 23 | 6 | .989 |
| 1967—Cincinnati | | Nat. | 3-1-2B | 156 | 600 | 78 | 174 | 28 | 7 | 26 | 102 | .290 | 249 | 234 | 13 | .974 |
| 1968—Cincinnati | | Nat. | 3B | 160 | 625 | 93 | 176 | 25 | 7 | 18 | 92 | .282 | •151 | 343 | •25 | .952 |
| 1969—Cincinnati | | Nat. | 3B | 160 | 629 | 103 | 185 | 31 | 2 | 37 | 122 | .294 | 136 | •342 | •32 | .937 |

— 295 —

| Year | Club | League | Pos. | G. | AB. | R. | H. | 2B. | 3B. | HR. | RBI. | B.A. | PO. | A. | E. | F.A. |
|------|------|--------|------|-----|------|-----|------|-----|-----|-----|------|------|------|------|-----|------|
| 1970–Cincinnati | | Nat. | ★3B-1B | 158 | 587 | 107 | 186 | 28 | 6 | 40 | 129 | .317 | 167 | 292 | ★35 | .929 |
| 1971–Cincinnati | | Nat. | ★3B-1B | 158 | 609 | 72 | 164 | 22 | 3 | 25 | 91 | .269 | 281 | ★308 | 20 | .967 |
| 1972–Cincinnati | | Nat. | 1B | 136 | 515 | 64 | 146 | 33 | 7 | 21 | 90 | .283 | 1207 | 68 | 9 | .993 |
| 1973–Cincinnati | | Nat. | 1B | 151 | 564 | 73 | 177 | 33 | 3 | 27 | 101 | .314 | ★1318 | 85 | ★13 | .991 |
| 1974–Cincinnati | | Nat. | 1B | 158 | 596 | 81 | 158 | 28 | 2 | 28 | 101 | .265 | 1292 | 75 | 6 | ★.996 |
| 1975–Cincinnati | | Nat. | 1B | 137 | 511 | 74 | 144 | 28 | 3 | 20 | 109 | .282 | 1192 | 72 | 9 | .993 |
| 1976–Cincinnati x | | Nat. | 1B | 139 | 527 | 77 | 137 | 32 | 6 | 19 | 91 | .260 | 1158 | 73 | 5 | .996 |
| Major League Totals | | | | 1728 | 6326 | 888 | 1790 | 313 | 54 | 277 | 1115 | .283 | 8257 | 1955 | 180 | .983 |

†On disabled list, June 25 through July 5, 1960.
‡On suspended list, April 13 through April 16, 1962. On disabled list, July 30 through September 4, 1962.
§On suspended list, April 11, 1963. Placed on restricted list, April 23 through June 25, 1963.
xTraded with Pitcher Will McEnaney to Montreal Expos for Pitchers Woodie Fryman and Dale Murray, December 16, 1976.

## CHAMPIONSHIP SERIES RECORD

| Year | Club | League | Pos. | G. | AB. | R. | H. | 2B. | 3B. | HR. | RBI. | B.A. | PO. | A. | E. | F.A. |
|------|------|--------|------|-----|------|-----|------|-----|-----|-----|------|------|------|------|-----|------|
| 1970–Cincinnati | | Nat. | 3B-1B | 3 | 12 | 1 | 4 | 2 | 0 | 1 | 2 | .333 | 6 | 6 | 1 | .923 |
| 1972–Cincinnati | | Nat. | 1B | 5 | 20 | 0 | 4 | 1 | 0 | 0 | 2 | .200 | 45 | 3 | 0 | 1.000 |
| 1973–Cincinnati | | Nat. | 1B | 5 | 22 | 1 | 2 | 0 | 0 | 1 | 2 | .091 | 47 | 4 | 0 | 1.000 |
| 1975–Cincinnati | | Nat. | 1B | 3 | 12 | 3 | 5 | 0 | 0 | 1 | 4 | .417 | 27 | 5 | 0 | 1.000 |
| 1976–Cincinnati | | Nat. | 1B | 3 | 10 | 1 | 2 | 0 | 0 | 0 | 3 | .200 | 27 | 2 | 1 | .967 |
| Championship Series Totals | | | | 19 | 76 | 6 | 17 | 3 | 0 | 3 | 13 | .224 | 152 | 20 | 2 | .988 |

## WORLD SERIES RECORD

| Year | Club | League | Pos. | G. | AB. | R. | H. | 2B. | 3B. | HR. | RBI. | B.A. | PO. | A. | E. | F.A. |
|------|------|--------|------|-----|------|-----|------|-----|-----|-----|------|------|------|------|-----|------|
| 1970–Cincinnati | | Nat. | 3B | 5 | 18 | 2 | 1 | 0 | 0 | 0 | 0 | .056 | 3 | 13 | 1 | .941 |
| 1972–Cincinnati | | Nat. | 1B | 7 | 23 | 3 | 10 | 2 | 0 | 0 | 2 | .435 | 73 | 3 | 1 | .987 |
| 1975–Cincinnati | | Nat. | 1B | 7 | 28 | 4 | 5 | 0 | 0 | 3 | 7 | .179 | 66 | 5 | 1 | .986 |
| 1976–Cincinnati | | Nat. | 1B | 4 | 16 | 1 | 5 | 1 | 0 | 0 | 2 | .313 | 32 | 4 | 0 | 1.000 |
| World Series Totals | | | | 23 | 85 | 10 | 21 | 3 | 0 | 3 | 11 | .247 | 174 | 25 | 3 | .980 |

## ALL-STAR GAME RECORD

| Year | League | Pos. | AB. | R. | H. | 2B. | 3B. | HR. | RBI. | B.A. | PO. | A. | E. | F.A. |
|------|--------|------|-----|-----|-----|-----|-----|-----|------|------|------|-----|-----|------|
| 1967–National | | 3B | 2 | 1 | 1 | 0 | 0 | 1 | 1 | .500 | 0 | 3 | 0 | 1.000 |
| 1968–National | | 3B | 0 | 0 | 0 | 0 | 0 | 0 | 0 | .000 | 0 | 1 | 0 | 1.000 |
| 1969–National | | 3B | 1 | 0 | 0 | 0 | 0 | 0 | 0 | .000 | 1 | 1 | 0 | 1.000 |
| 1970–National | | 3B | 3 | 0 | 0 | 0 | 0 | 0 | 0 | .000 | 1 | 1 | 0 | 1.000 |
| 1974–National | | PH | 1 | 0 | 0 | 0 | 0 | 0 | 0 | .000 | 0 | 0 | 0 | .000 |
| 1975–National | | PH-1B | 1 | 0 | 0 | 0 | 0 | 0 | 0 | .000 | 1 | 1 | 0 | 1.000 |
| 1976–National | | 1B | 0 | 0 | 0 | 0 | 0 | 0 | 0 | .000 | 2 | 0 | 0 | 1.000 |
| All-Star Game Totals | | | 8 | 1 | 1 | 0 | 0 | 1 | 1 | .125 | 5 | 7 | 0 | 1.000 |

## MARTIN ROMAN PEREZ, JR.
### (Marty)

Born February 28, 1947, at Visalia, Calif.
Height, 5.10½. Weight, 160.
Throws and bats righthanded.
Hobbies–Playing billiards and basketball.
Attended College of the Sequoias, Visalia, Calif.

Led Texas League shortstops in double plays with 72 in 1968 and led Pacific Coast League shortstops with 79 in 1969.

| Year | Club | League | Pos. | G. | AB. | R. | H. | 2B. | 3B. | HR. | RBI. | B.A. | PO. | A. | E. | F.A. |
|------|------|--------|------|-----|------|-----|------|-----|-----|-----|------|------|------|------|-----|------|
| 1964–Idaho Falls | | Pion. | SS | 42 | 132 | 18 | 36 | 7 | 3 | 1 | 18 | .273 | 50 | 93 | ★31 | .822 |
| 1965–Quad Cities | | Midw. | SS | 53 | 174 | 19 | 36 | 6 | 1 | 2 | 21 | .207 | 74 | 110 | 34 | .844 |
| 1965–Idaho Falls | | Pion. | SS | 14 | 53 | 15 | 17 | 5 | 2 | 1 | 6 | .321 | 13 | 30 | 9 | .827 |
| 1965–San Jose | | Calif. | SS | 47 | 163 | 18 | 40 | 5 | 2 | 1 | 23 | .245 | 62 | 123 | 19 | .907 |
| 1966–San Jose | | Calif. | SS | 32 | 106 | 10 | 24 | 4 | 1 | 0 | 9 | .226 | 28 | 79 | 8 | .930 |
| 1966–Quad Cities | | Midw. | 2B | 30 | 95 | 8 | 22 | 3 | 1 | 1 | 8 | .232 | 50 | 91 | 5 | .957 |
| 1967–Quad Cities | | Midw. | SS | 100 | 384 | 68 | 111 | 17 | 8 | 3 | 40 | .289 | 166 | 304 | 37 | .927 |
| 1968–El Paso | | Texas | ★SS-2-OF | 116 | 404 | 50 | 102 | 12 | 3 | 5 | 36 | .252 | 171 | ★363 | 29 | .948 |
| 1969–Hawaii | | P.C. | SS | 115 | 411 | 39 | 115 | 18 | 6 | 1 | 40 | .280 | 210 | 410 | 29 | .955 |
| 1969–California | | Amer. | SS-2-3 | 13 | 13 | 3 | 3 | 0 | 0 | 0 | 0 | .231 | 12 | 19 | 0 | 1.000 |
| 1970–Hawaii | | P.C. | SS-OF | 105 | 406 | 54 | 114 | 12 | 3 | 1 | 33 | .281 | 151 | 313 | 22 | .955 |
| 1970–California† | | Amer. | SS | 3 | 3 | 0 | 0 | 0 | 0 | 0 | 1 | .000 | 3 | 2 | 1 | .833 |
| 1971–Atlanta | | Nat. | SS-2B | 130 | 410 | 28 | 93 | 15 | 3 | 4 | 32 | .227 | 195 | 382 | 28 | .954 |
| 1972–Atlanta | | Nat. | SS | 141 | 479 | 33 | 109 | 13 | 1 | 1 | 28 | .228 | 220 | 378 | 27 | .957 |
| 1973–Atlanta | | Nat. | SS | 141 | 501 | 66 | 125 | 15 | 5 | 8 | 57 | .250 | 215 | 416 | 25 | .962 |
| 1974–Atlanta | | Nat. | 2-SS-3 | 127 | 447 | 51 | 116 | 20 | 5 | 2 | 34 | .260 | 236 | 333 | 10 | .983 |
| 1975–Atlanta‡ | | Nat. | 2B-SS | 120 | 461 | 50 | 127 | 14 | 2 | 2 | 34 | .275 | 262 | 349 | 10 | .984 |
| 1976–Atl.§-San F.x | | Nat. | 2-SS-3 | 124 | 428 | 49 | 110 | 17 | 1 | 3 | 32 | .257 | 256 | 357 | 14 | .978 |
| American League Totals | | | | 16 | 16 | 3 | 3 | 0 | 0 | 0 | 1 | .188 | 15 | 21 | 1 | .973 |
| National League Totals | | | | 783 | 2726 | 277 | 680 | 94 | 17 | 20 | 217 | .249 | 1384 | 2215 | 114 | .969 |
| Major League Totals | | | | 799 | 2742 | 280 | 683 | 94 | 17 | 20 | 218 | .249 | 1399 | 2236 | 115 | .969 |

†Released to Atlanta Braves, October 21, 1970. (California received Catcher John Burns, assigned to El Paso, and cash to complete the deal.)

‡On disabled list, August 1 to September 2, 1975.
§Traded with Third Baseman Darrell Evans to San Francisco Giants for First Baseman Willie Montanez, Shortstop Craig Robinson, Outfielder Jake Brown and Infielder Mike Eden, June 13, 1976.
xTraded to New York Yankees for Outfielder Terry Whitfield, March 14, 1977.

## SAMUEL BENEDICT PERLOZZO
Name pronounced Per-LAHZ-oh.
### (Sam)
Born March 4, 1951, at Cumberland, Md.
Height, 5.09. Weight, 170.
Throws and bats righthanded.
Attended George Washington University, Washington, D. C.; received
Bachelor of Science degree in Physical Education and Health.
Brother of Nick Perlozzo, Jr., minor league first baseman with
San Diego Padres' organization, 1970-72.

| Year   Club          League      | Pos. | G.  | AB. | R. | H.  | 2B. | 3B. | HR. | RBI. | B.A. | PO.  | A.  | E. | F.A. |
|----------------------------------|------|-----|-----|----|-----|-----|-----|-----|------|------|------|-----|----|------|
| 1973—Ft. Lauderdale ..Fla.St.    | SS   | 121 | 379 | 50 | 78  | 5   | 3   | 1   | 21   | .206 | 157  | 373 | 27 | ★.952 |
| 1974—Dubuque...........Midw.      | 2-3-SS | 121 | 420 | 55 | 113 | 8   | 1   | 0   | 27   | .269 | 292  | 276 | 30 | .950 |
| 1975—Reno ...............Calif.   | 2B   | 134 | 531 | 99 | 139 | 17  | 5   | 2   | 63   | .262 | ★262 | ★444 | 19 | ★.974 |
| 1976—Orlando ...........South.    | 2B-SS | 126 | 456 | 48 | 123 | 18  | 1   | 0   | 51   | .270 | ★325 | 378 | 6  | ★.992 |

Listed on Minnesota Twins' 1977 spring roster.

## GAYLORD JACKSON PERRY
Born September 15, 1938, at Williamston, N. C.
Height, 6.04½. Weight, 215.
Throws and bats righthanded.
Hobbies—Golf, hunting and fishing.
Attended Campbell College, Buies Creek, N. C.
Brother of Jim Perry, pitcher with Cleveland Indians, Minnesota Twins,
Detroit Tigers and Oakland Athletics, 1959 through 1975.
Tied National League record for most putouts, pitcher, game, 5, July 18, 1970.
Pitched 1-0 no-hit victory against St. Louis Cardinals, September 17, 1968.
Led National League in shutouts with 5 in 1970.
Led National League pitchers in games started with 41 in 1970.
Led American League pitchers in complete games with 29 in 1972 and 29 in 1973.
Led American League in wild pitches with 17 in 1973.
Won American League Cy Young Memorial Award, 1972.
Named righthanded pitcher on THE SPORTING NEWS American League All-Star Team, 1972.
Named Pacific Coast League Pitcher of the Year in 1961.
Received reported $90,000 bonus to sign with San Francisco Giants, 1958.

| Year   Club                League      | G.  | IP.  | W.  | L.  | Pct. | H.   | R.  | ER.  | SO.  | BB. | ERA. |
|----------------------------------------|-----|------|-----|-----|------|------|-----|------|------|-----|------|
| 1958—St. Cloud..............Northern    | 17  | 128  | 9   | 5   | .643 | 97   | 40  | 34   | 111  | 48  | 2.39 |
| 1959—Corpus Christi.........Texas       | 41  | 191  | 10  | 11  | .476 | ★218 | ★120 | 86   | 119  | 69  | 4.05 |
| 1960—Tacoma.................P. Coast     | 1   | 1    | 0   | 0   | .000 | 1    | 1   | 1    | 0    | 0   | 9.00 |
| 1960—Rio Grande Valley......Texas       | 31  | 188  | 9   | 13  | .409 | 164  | 68  | 59   | 120  | 77  | ★2.82 |
| 1961—Tacoma.................P. Coast     | 33  | ★219 | ●16 | 10  | .615 | 208  | 79  | 62   | 95   | 61  | 2.55 |
| 1962—San Francisco .........National    | 13  | 43   | 3   | 1   | .750 | 54   | 29  | 25   | 20   | 14  | 5.23 |
| 1962—Tacoma.................P. Coast     | 22  | 156  | 10  | 7   | .588 | 128  | 56  | 43   | 136  | 56  | ★2.48 |
| 1963—San Francisco .........National    | 31  | 76   | 1   | 6   | .143 | 84   | 41  | 34   | 52   | 29  | 4.03 |
| 1963—Tacoma.................P. Coast     | 1   | 9    | 1   | 0   | 1.000 | 3   | 1   | 1    | 7    | 1   | 1.00 |
| 1964—San Francisco .........National    | 44  | 206  | 12  | 11  | .522 | 179  | 65  | 63   | 155  | 43  | 2.75 |
| 1965—San Francisco .........National    | 47  | 196  | 8   | 12  | .400 | 194  | 105 | 91   | 170  | 70  | 4.18 |
| 1966—San Francisco .........National    | 36  | 256  | 21  | 8   | .724 | 242  | 92  | 85   | 201  | 40  | 2.99 |
| 1967—San Francisco .........National    | 39  | 293  | 15  | 17  | .469 | 231  | 98  | 85   | 230  | 84  | 2.61 |
| 1968—San Francisco .........National    | 39  | 291  | 16  | 15  | .516 | 240  | 93  | 79   | 173  | 59  | 2.44 |
| 1969—San Francisco .........National    | 40  | ★325 | 19  | 14  | .576 | 290  | 115 | 90   | 233  | 91  | 2.49 |
| 1970—San Francisco .........National    | 41  | ★329 | ●23 | 13  | .639 | ★292 | ★138 | 117  | 214  | 84  | 3.20 |
| 1971—San Francisco†.........National    | 37  | 280  | 16  | 12  | .571 | 255  | 116 | 86   | 158  | 67  | 2.76 |
| 1972—Cleveland .............American     | 41  | 343  | ●24 | 16  | .600 | 253  | 79  | 73   | 234  | 82  | 1.92 |
| 1973—Cleveland .............American     | 41  | 344  | 19  | 19  | .500 | 315  | 143 | 129  | 238  | 115 | 3.38 |
| 1974—Cleveland .............American     | 37  | 322  | 21  | 13  | .618 | 230  | 98  | 90   | 216  | 99  | 2.52 |
| 1975—Cleveland‡-Texas.......American     | 37  | 306  | 18  | 17  | .514 | 277  | 127 | 110  | 233  | 70  | 3.24 |
| 1976—Texas .................American     | 32  | 250  | 15  | 14  | .517 | 232  | 93  | 90   | 143  | 52  | 3.24 |
| National League Totals...............    | 367 | 2295 | 134 | 109 | .551 | 2061 | 892 | 755  | 1606 | 581 | 2.96 |
| American League Totals.............      | 188 | 1565 | 97  | 79  | .551 | 1307 | 540 | 492  | 1064 | 418 | 2.83 |
| Major League Totals .................    | 555 | 3860 | 231 | 188 | .551 | 3368 | 1432 | 1247 | 2670 | 999 | 2.91 |

†Traded with Shortstop Frank Duffy to Cleveland Indians for Pitcher Sam McDowell, November 29, 1971.
‡Traded to Texas Rangers for Pitchers Jim Bibby, Jackie Brown and Rick Waits and an estimated $100,000, June 12, 1975.

### CHAMPIONSHIP SERIES RECORD

| Year   Club              League      | G. | IP.   | W. | L. | Pct. | H. | R. | ER. | SO. | BB. | ERA. |
|--------------------------------------|----|-------|----|----|------|----|----|-----|-----|-----|------|
| 1971—San Francisco ...........National | 2 | 14⅔  | 1  | 1  | .500 | 19 | 11 | 10  | 11  | 3   | 6.14 |

| Year League | IP. | W. | L. | Pct. | H. | R. | ER. | SO. | BB. | ERA. |
|---|---|---|---|---|---|---|---|---|---|---|
| 1966–National | 2 | 1 | 0 | 1.000 | 1 | 0 | 0 | 1 | 1 | 0.00 |
| 1970–National | 2 | 0 | 0 | .000 | 4 | 2 | 2 | 0 | 1 | 9.00 |
| 1972–American | 2 | 0 | 0 | .000 | 3 | 2 | 2 | 1 | 0 | 9.00 |
| 1974–American | 3 | 0 | 0 | .000 | 3 | 1 | 1 | 4 | 0 | 3.00 |
| All-Star Game Totals | 9 | 1 | 0 | 1.000 | 11 | 5 | 5 | 6 | 2 | 5.00 |

## KENNETH MICHAEL PERRY
### (Ken)

Born August 26, 1954, at Abbeville, La.
Height, 5.11. Weight, 170.
Throws and bats righthanded.
Led California League batters in strikeouts with 145 in 1974.

| Year Club | League | Pos. | G. | AB. | R. | H. | 2B. | 3B. | HR. | RBI. | B.A. | PO. | A. | E. | F.A. |
|---|---|---|---|---|---|---|---|---|---|---|---|---|---|---|---|
| 1972–Marion | Appal. | 2B-SS | 45 | 148 | 18 | 34 | 4 | 1 | 1 | 11 | .230 | 74 | 107 | 15 | .923 |
| 1972–Visalia | Calif. | 2B | 3 | 8 | 0 | 1 | 0 | 0 | 0 | 0 | .125 | 4 | 5 | 0 | 1.000 |
| 1973–Pompano Beach | Fla.St. | 2-3-SS | 83 | 252 | 34 | 74 | 3 | 3 | 5 | 27 | .294 | 94 | 141 | 24 | .907 |
| 1974–Visalia | Calif. | 2B | 139 | 492 | 80 | 124 | 17 | 5 | 9 | 52 | .252 | 319 | *415 | *51 | .935 |
| 1975–Visalia | Calif. | 2B | 104 | 384 | 81 | 119 | 16 | 6 | 15 | 64 | .310 | 205 | 288 | 27 | .948 |
| 1975–Jackson | Texas | 2B | 33 | 114 | 18 | 26 | 3 | 1 | 1 | 8 | .228 | 71 | 68 | 8 | .946 |
| 1976–Jackson | Texas | 2B | 66 | 245 | 32 | 75 | 13 | 5 | 13 | 43 | .306 | 129 | 200 | 13 | .962 |
| 1976–Tidewater | Int. | 2B | 28 | 99 | 15 | 26 | 5 | 2 | 2 | 10 | .263 | 62 | 73 | 5 | .964 |

Listed on New York Mets' 1977 spring roster.

## STANLEY PERZANOWSKI
### (Stan)

Born August 25, 1950, at East Chicago, Ind.
Height, 6.03. Weight, 190.
Throws and bats righthanded.
Hobbies–Photography and making posters.
Attended Anderson College, Anderson, Ind.
Cousin of Ron Perranoski, pitcher with Los Angeles Dodgers, Minnesota Twins,
Detroit Tigers and California Angels, 1961 through 1973, and presently
minor league pitching instructor for Los Angeles Dodgers.
Led American Association in hit batsmen with 12 in 1974.
Tied for Pacific Coast League lead in hit batsmen with 7 in 1972.
Tied for American Association lead in shutouts with 4 in 1973.

| Year Club | League | G. | IP. | W. | L. | Pct. | H. | R. | ER. | SO. | BB. | ERA. |
|---|---|---|---|---|---|---|---|---|---|---|---|---|
| 1968–Sarasota White Sox | Gulf Coast | 11 | 59 | 2 | 6 | .250 | 50 | 40 | 22 | 32 | 28 | 3.36 |
| 1969–Duluth-Superior | Northern | 14 | 62 | 4 | 4 | .500 | 55 | 32 | 23 | 56 | 36 | 3.34 |
| 1970–Appleton | Midwest | 22 | 139 | 9 | 8 | .529 | 109 | 42 | 33 | 118 | 53 | 2.14 |
| 1970–Tucson | P. Coast | 4 | 13 | 0 | 1 | .000 | 13 | 11 | 9 | 13 | 11 | 6.23 |
| 1971–Asheville | Southern | 13 | 107 | 11 | 0 | 1.000 | 98 | 33 | 30 | 55 | 25 | 2.52 |
| 1971–Tucson | P. Coast | 12 | 76 | 7 | 4 | .636 | 75 | 38 | 36 | 46 | 32 | 4.26 |
| 1971–Chicago | American | 5 | 6 | 0 | 1 | .000 | 14 | 10 | 8 | 5 | 3 | 12.00 |
| 1972–Tucson | P. Coast | 36 | 182 | 5 | *17 | .227 | 192 | *113 | ●96 | 136 | 65 | 4.75 |
| 1973–Iowa | Am. Assoc. | 31 | 208 | 14 | 8 | .636 | 201 | 99 | 85 | 124 | 78 | 3.68 |
| 1974–Iowa | Am. Assoc. | 27 | 152 | 13 | 8 | .619 | 161 | 91 | 80 | 95 | 62 | 4.74 |
| 1974–Chicago† | American | 2 | 2 | 0 | 0 | .000 | 8 | 7 | 5 | 2 | 2 | 22.50 |
| 1975–Spokane | P. Coast | 20 | 113 | 8 | 6 | .571 | 104 | 57 | 48 | 48 | 40 | 3.82 |
| 1975–Texas | American | 12 | 66 | 3 | 3 | .500 | 59 | 25 | 22 | 26 | 25 | 3.00 |
| 1976–Texas‡ | American | 5 | 12 | 0 | 0 | .000 | 20 | 15 | 13 | 6 | 4 | 9.75 |
| 1976–Toledo§ | Int'national | 16 | 66 | 4 | 3 | .571 | 82 | 48 | 42 | 36 | 34 | 5.73 |
| Major League Totals | | 24 | 86 | 3 | 4 | .429 | 101 | 57 | 48 | 39 | 34 | 5.02 |

†Traded to Texas Rangers for Pitcher Steve Dunning, February 25, 1975.
‡Traded with cash to Cleveland Indians' organization for Pitcher Fritz Peterson, June 7, 1976.
§Assigned to Salt Lake City (California Angels' organization), March 27, 1977 to complete deal which sent
Infielder Bill Melton to Cleveland Indians, December 3, 1976.

## FRED INGELS PETERSON
### (Fritz)

(Named to avoid confusion since father and grandfather also were Fred.)

Born February 8, 1942, at Chicago, Ill.
Height, 6.00. Weight, 200.
Throws left and bats left and righthanded.
Hobby–Coaching.
Attended Northern Illinois University, DeKalb, Ill., and Morehead State University, Morehead, Ky.;
received Bachelor of Science degree, Master of Science degree and
Certificate of Advanced Study in Physical Education.

| Year Club | League | G. | IP. | W. | L. | Pct. | H. | R. | ER. | SO. | BB. | ERA. |
|---|---|---|---|---|---|---|---|---|---|---|---|---|
| 1963–Harlan | Ap'achian | 12 | 61 | 4 | 3 | .571 | 62 | 41 | 30 | 80 | 32 | 4.43 |
| 1964–Shelby | W. Carol. | 23 | 155 | 10 | 7 | .588 | 131 | 63 | 47 | 194 | 53 | 2.73 |
| 1965–Greensboro | Carolina | 14 | 108 | 11 | 1 | *.917 | 75 | 19 | 18 | 83 | 26 | 1.50 |
| 1965–Columbus | Southern | 12 | 91 | 5 | 5 | .500 | 64 | 27 | 22 | 62 | 20 | 2.18 |

| Year Club | League | G. | IP. | W. | L. | Pct. | H. | R. | ER. | SO. | BB. | ERA. |
|---|---|---|---|---|---|---|---|---|---|---|---|---|
| 1966–New York | American | 34 | 215 | 12 | 11 | .522 | 196 | 89 | 79 | 96 | 40 | 3.31 |
| 1967–New York | American | 36 | 181 | 8 | 14 | .364 | 179 | 88 | 70 | 102 | 43 | 3.48 |
| 1968–New York | American | 36 | 212 | 12 | 11 | .522 | 187 | 72 | 62 | 115 | 29 | 2.63 |
| 1969–New York | American | 37 | 272 | 17 | 16 | .515 | 228 | 95 | 77 | 150 | 43 | 2.55 |
| 1970–New York | American | 39 | 260 | 20 | 11 | .645 | 247 | 102 | 84 | 127 | 40 | 2.91 |
| 1971–New York | American | 37 | 274 | 15 | 13 | .536 | 269 | 106 | 93 | 139 | 42 | 3.05 |
| 1972–New York | American | 35 | 250 | 17 | 15 | .531 | 270 | 98 | 90 | 100 | 44 | 3.24 |
| 1973–New York | American | 31 | 184 | 8 | 15 | .348 | 207 | 93 | 81 | 59 | 49 | 3.96 |
| 1974–New York†-Cleveland | American | 32 | 160 | 9 | 14 | .391 | 200 | 93 | 78 | 57 | 39 | 4.39 |
| 1975–Cleveland‡ | American | 25 | 146 | 14 | 8 | .636 | 154 | 73 | 64 | 47 | 40 | 3.95 |
| 1976–Cleveland§-Texas x | American | 13 | 62 | 1 | 3 | .250 | 80 | 38 | 35 | 23 | 17 | 5.08 |
| Major League Totals | | 355 | 2216 | 133 | 131 | .504 | 2217 | 947 | 813 | 1015 | 426 | 3.30 |

†Traded with Pitchers Fred Beene, Steve Kline and Tom Buskey to Cleveland Indians for First Baseman Chris Chambliss and Pitchers Dick Tidrow and Cecil Upshaw, April 26, 1974.
‡On disabled list, June 20 to July 18, 1975.
§Traded to Texas Rangers for Pitcher Stan Perzanowski and cash, May 28, 1976; on disabled list June 25 to September 1, 1976.
xUnconditional release, February 2, 1977; signed as free agent by Chicago White Sox, February 15, 1977.

### ALL-STAR GAME RECORD

| Year League | IP. | W. | L. | Pct. | H. | R. | ER. | SO. | BB. | ERA. |
|---|---|---|---|---|---|---|---|---|---|---|
| 1970–American | 0 | 0 | 0 | .000 | 1 | 0 | 0 | 0 | 0 | 0.00 |

## MICHAEL DWAINE PHILLIPS
### (Mike)

Born August 19, 1950, at Beaumont, Tex.
Height, 6.01. Weight, 180.
Throws right and bats right and lefthanded.
Hobby–Hunting.
Attended Phoenix College, Phoenix, Ariz.

| Year Club | League | Pos. | G. | AB. | R. | H. | 2B. | 3B. | HR. | RBI. | B.A. | PO. | A. | E. | F.A. |
|---|---|---|---|---|---|---|---|---|---|---|---|---|---|---|---|
| 1969–Great Falls | Pion. | •SS-2 | 55 | 167 | 23 | 36 | 9 | 1 | 0 | 18 | .216 | 58 | 125 | 13 | •.934 |
| 1970–Fresno | Calif. | SS-2B | 94 | 318 | 26 | 79 | 7 | 3 | 3 | 21 | .248 | 133 | 264 | 34 | .921 |
| 1971–Amarillo | Texas | SS | 89 | 347 | 45 | 81 | 15 | 6 | 2 | 22 | .233 | 116 | 290 | 30 | .931 |
| 1972–Phoenix | P. C. | S-2-3 | 114 | 375 | 57 | 93 | 17 | 7 | 0 | 32 | .248 | 148 | 342 | 41 | .932 |
| 1973–Phoenix | P. C. | SS | 1 | 4 | 1 | 1 | 0 | 0 | 0 | 1 | .250 | 1 | 2 | 0 | 1.000 |
| 1973–San Francisco | Nat. | 3-S-2 | 63 | 104 | 18 | 25 | 3 | 4 | 1 | 9 | .240 | 42 | 69 | 6 | .949 |
| 1974–San Francisco | Nat. | 3-2-S | 100 | 283 | 19 | 62 | 6 | 1 | 2 | 20 | .219 | 125 | 195 | 19 | .944 |
| 1975–S. F.†-N. Y. | Nat. | •S-2-3 | 126 | 414 | 34 | 104 | 10 | 7 | 1 | 29 | .251 | 203 | 364 | •32 | .947 |
| 1976–New York | Nat. | S-3-2 | 87 | 262 | 30 | 67 | 4 | 6 | 4 | 29 | .256 | 115 | 191 | 11 | .965 |
| Major League Totals | | 376 | 1063 | 101 | 258 | 23 | 18 | 8 | 87 | .243 | 485 | 819 | 68 | .950 |

†Released on waivers to New York Mets, May 3, 1975.

## ROBERT MICHAEL PICCIOLO
Name pronounced PEACH-alo.
### (Rob)

Born February 4, 1953, at Santa Monica, Calif.
Height, 6.02. Weight, 185.
Throws and bats righthanded.
Hobby–Music.
Attended Pepperdine University, Malibu, Calif.; received degree in Journalism.
Led Southern League shortstops in double plays with 91 in 1975.

| Year Club | League | Pos. | G. | AB. | R. | H. | 2B. | 3B. | HR. | RBI. | B.A. | PO. | A. | E. | F.A. |
|---|---|---|---|---|---|---|---|---|---|---|---|---|---|---|---|
| 1975–Birmingham | South. | SS | 133 | 488 | 55 | 135 | 23 | 6 | 3 | 62 | .277 | •278 | •404 | 18 | •.974 |
| 1976–Tucson | P. C. | SS | 139 | •570 | 78 | 170 | 19 | 4 | 5 | 54 | .298 | 220 | 429 | 22 | •.967 |

Invited to Oakland A's 1977 spring camp.

## LOUIS VICTOR PINIELLA
Name pronounced Pin-ELLA.
### (Lou)

Born August 28, 1943, at Tampa, Fla.
Height, 6.02. Weight, 190.
Throws and bats righthanded.
Hobbies–Fishing and golf.
Attended University of Tampa, Tampa, Fla.
Named Rookie of the Year in Carolina League, 1963.
Named by Baseball Writers Association as American League Rookie of the Year, 1969.

| Year Club | League | Pos. | G. | AB. | R. | H. | 2B. | 3B. | HR. | RBI. | B.A. | PO. | A. | E. | F.A. |
|---|---|---|---|---|---|---|---|---|---|---|---|---|---|---|---|
| 1962–Selma† | Ala.-Fl. | OF | 70 | 278 | 40 | 75 | 10 | 5 | 8 | 44 | .270 | 94 | 6 | 9 | .917 |
| 1963–Peninsula | Carol. | OF | 143 | 548 | 71 | 170 | 29 | 4 | 16 | 77 | .310 | 271 | •23 | 8 | .974 |
| 1964–Aberdeen‡ | North. | OF | 20 | 74 | 8 | 20 | 8 | 3 | 0 | 12 | .270 | 37 | 1 | 1 | .974 |

| Year | Club | League | Pos. | G. | AB. | R. | H. | 2B. | 3B. | HR. | RBI. | B.A. | PO. | A. | E. | F.A. |
|------|------|--------|------|----|-----|----|----|-----|-----|-----|------|------|-----|----|----|------|
| 1964—Baltimore | | Amer. | PH | 4 | 1 | 0 | 0 | 0 | 0 | 0 | 0 | .000 | 0 | 0 | 0 | .000 |
| 1965—Elmira§ | | East. | OF | 126 | 490 | 64 | 122 | 29 | 6 | 11 | 64 | .249 | 176 | 5 | 7 | .963 |
| 1966—Portland | | P. C. | OF | 133 | 457 | 47 | 132 | 22 | 3 | 7 | 52 | .289 | 177 | 11 | 11 | .945 |
| 1967—Portland | | P. C. | OF | 113 | 396 | 49 | 122 | 20 | 1 | 8 | 56 | .308 | 199 | 7 | 6 | .972 |
| 1968—Portland | | P. C. | OF | 88 | 331 | 49 | 105 | 15 | 3 | 13 | 62 | .317 | 167 | 6 | 7 | .961 |
| 1968—Cleveland xy | | Amer. | OF | 6 | 5 | 1 | 0 | 0 | 0 | 0 | 1 | .000 | 1 | 0 | 0 | 1.000 |
| 1969—Kansas City | | Amer. | OF | 135 | 493 | 43 | 139 | 21 | 6 | 11 | 68 | .282 | 278 | 13 | 7 | .977 |
| 1970—Kansas City | | Amer. | OF-1B | 144 | 542 | 54 | 163 | 24 | 5 | 11 | 88 | .301 | 250 | 6 | 4 | .985 |
| 1971—Kansas City z | | Amer. | OF | 126 | 448 | 43 | 125 | 21 | 5 | 3 | 51 | .279 | 201 | 6 | 3 | .986 |
| 1972—Kansas City | | Amer. | OF | 151 | 574 | 65 | 179 | •33 | 4 | 11 | 72 | .312 | 275 | 8 | 7 | .976 |
| 1973—Kansas City a | | Amer. | OF | 144 | 513 | 53 | 128 | 28 | 1 | 9 | 69 | .250 | 196 | 9 | 3 | .986 |
| 1974—New York | | Amer. | OF-1B | 140 | 518 | 71 | 158 | 26 | 0 | 9 | 70 | .305 | 270 | 16 | 3 | .990 |
| 1975—New York b | | Amer. | OF | 74 | 199 | 7 | 39 | 4 | 1 | 0 | 22 | .196 | 65 | 5 | 1 | .986 |
| 1976—New York | | Amer. | O-DH-PH | 100 | 327 | 36 | 92 | 16 | 6 | 3 | 38 | .281 | 199 | 10 | 4 | .981 |
| Major League Totals | | | | 1024 | 3620 | 373 | 1023 | 173 | 28 | 57 | 479 | .282 | 1735 | 73 | 32 | .983 |

†Drafted by Washington Senators from Jacksonville (Cleveland Indians' organization), November 26, 1962.
‡Reinstated from Military List by Washington Senators, July 20, 1964 and assigned to Baltimore Orioles to complete deal for Pitcher Lester (Buster) Narum, August 4, 1964; Orioles optioned him to Aberdeen.
§Traded by Baltimore Orioles to Cleveland Indians' organization for Catcher Cam Carreon, March 10, 1966.
xSelected by Seattle Pilots from Cleveland Indians in expansion draft, October 15, 1968.
yTraded by Seattle Pilots to Kansas City Royals for Outfielder Steve Whitaker and Pitcher John Gelnar (latter assigned to Vancouver), April 1, 1969.
zOn disabled list May 5 through June 8.
aTraded with Pitcher Ken Wright to New York Yankees for Pitcher Lindy McDaniel, December 7, 1973.
bOn supplemental disabled list, June 17 to July 6, 1975.

### CHAMPIONSHIP SERIES RECORD

| Year | Club | League | Pos. | G. | AB. | R. | H. | 2B. | 3B. | HR. | RBI. | B.A. | PO. | A. | E. | F.A. |
|------|------|--------|------|----|-----|----|----|-----|-----|-----|------|------|-----|----|----|------|
| 1976—New York | | Amer. | DH-PH | 4 | 11 | 1 | 3 | 1 | 0 | 0 | 0 | .273 | 0 | 0 | 0 | .000 |

### WORLD SERIES RECORD

| Year | Club | League | Pos. | G. | AB. | R. | H. | 2B. | 3B. | HR. | RBI. | B.A. | PO. | A. | E. | F.A. |
|------|------|--------|------|----|-----|----|----|-----|-----|-----|------|------|-----|----|----|------|
| 1976—New York | | Amer. | DH-O-PH | 4 | 9 | 1 | 3 | 1 | 0 | 0 | 0 | .333 | 1 | 0 | 0 | 1.000 |

### ALL-STAR GAME RECORD

| Year | League | Pos. | AB. | R. | H. | 2B. | 3B. | HR. | RBI. | B.A. | PO. | A. | E. | F.A. |
|------|--------|------|-----|----|----|-----|-----|-----|------|------|-----|----|----|------|
| 1972—American | | PH | 1 | 0 | 0 | 0 | 0 | 0 | 0 | .000 | 0 | 0 | 0 | .000 |

## LEE PATRICK PITLOCK
### (Skip)

Born November 6, 1947, at Chicago, Ill.
Height, 6.03. Weight, 190.
Throws and bats lefthanded.
Hobbies—Music and golf.
Attended Southern Illinois University, Carbondale, Ill.; received
Bachelor of Science degree in Advertising Journalism.

| Year | Club | League | G. | IP. | W. | L. | Pct. | H. | R. | ER. | SO. | BB. | ERA. |
|------|------|--------|----|-----|----|----|------|----|----|----|----|----|------|
| 1969—Great Falls | | Pioneer | 7 | 41 | 3 | 1 | .750 | 25 | 12 | 9 | 58 | 17 | 1.98 |
| 1969—Fresno | | California | 8 | 57 | 7 | 1 | .875 | 44 | 21 | 15 | 73 | 18 | 2.37 |
| 1970—Phoenix | | P. Coast | 13 | 106 | 10 | 3 | .769 | 78 | 34 | 29 | 92 | 43 | 2.46 |
| 1970—San Francisco | | National | 18 | 87 | 5 | 5 | .500 | 92 | 48 | 45 | 56 | 48 | 4.66 |
| 1971—Phoenix | | P. Coast | 44 | 149 | 7 | 11 | .389 | 193 | 125 | 106 | 103 | 78 | 6.40 |
| 1972—Phoenix† | | P. Coast | 31 | 136 | 8 | 10 | .444 | 131 | 61 | 50 | 106 | 53 | 3.31 |
| 1973—Iowa | | Am. Assoc. | 30 | 131 | 8 | 8 | .500 | 117 | 68 | 59 | 117 | 59 | 4.06 |
| 1974—Chicago | | American | 40 | 106 | 3 | 3 | .500 | 103 | 58 | 52 | 68 | 55 | 4.42 |
| 1975—Denver | | Am. Assoc. | 13 | 46 | 4 | 1 | .800 | 55 | 24 | 20 | 32 | 21 | 3.91 |
| 1975—Chicago‡ | | American | 1 | 0 | 0 | 0 | .000 | 1 | 0 | 0 | 0 | 0 | ...... |
| 1975—Tucson | | P. Coast | 17 | 101 | 4 | 9 | .308 | 102 | 49 | 42 | 56 | 46 | 3.74 |
| 1976—Tuc.§-SLC | | P. Coast | 43 | 76 | 5 | 3 | .625 | 84 | 64 | 57 | 91 | 67 | 6.75 |
| National League Totals | | | 18 | 87 | 5 | 5 | .500 | 92 | 48 | 45 | 56 | 48 | 4.66 |
| American League Totals | | | 41 | 106 | 3 | 3 | .500 | 104 | 58 | 52 | 68 | 55 | 4.42 |
| Major League Totals | | | 59 | 193 | 8 | 8 | .500 | 196 | 106 | 97 | 124 | 103 | 4.52 |

†Traded by San Francisco Giants to Chicago White Sox for Pitcher Chuck Hartenstein and Second Baseman Glenn Redmon, February 7, 1973.
‡Traded with Pitcher Stan Bahnsen to Oakland Athletics for Pitcher Dave Hamilton and Infielder-Outfielder Chet Lemon, June 15, 1975.
§Traded to California Angels' organization for Pitcher Charlie Hudson, May 19, 1976.
Invited to California Angels' 1977 spring camp.

## GAYLEN RICHARD PITTS

Born June 6, 1946, at Wichita, Kan.
Height, 6.01. Weight, 190.
Throws and bats righthanded.
Attended Arkansas State University, Jonesboro, Ark., and
University of Arkansas, Fayetteville, Ark.

| Year Club League | Pos. | G. | AB. | R. | H. | 2B. | 3B. | HR. | RBI. | B.A. | PO. | A. | E. | F.A. |
|---|---|---|---|---|---|---|---|---|---|---|---|---|---|---|
| 1964—Sarasota Cards ..Sar. Rk. | SS | 56 | 176 | 21 | 40 | 2 | 2 | 0 | 8 | .227 | *81 | 92 | 13 | *.930 |
| 1965—Cedar Rapids ....Midw. | SS | 98 | 358 | 44 | 87 | 10 | 3 | 3 | 28 | .243 | 147 | 237 | *49 | .887 |
| 1966—Cedar Rapids† ..Midw. | SS | 15 | 56 | 12 | 13 | 2 | 1 | 1 | 2 | .232 | 20 | 40 | 4 | .938 |
| 1967—Arkansas .........Texas | | | | | (Military Service) | | | | | | | | | |
| 1968—St. Petersburg ..Fla. St. | SS-2B | 17 | 62 | 9 | 14 | 1 | 0 | 0 | 7 | .226 | 35 | 43 | 8 | .907 |
| 1968—Modesto ...........Calif. | ●S-3-2-O | 119 | 398 | 49 | 103 | 18 | 2 | 5 | 43 | .259 | 135 | 269 | ●45 | .900 |
| 1969—Arkansas .........Texas | *3-S-O-2 | 122 | 422 | 56 | 110 | 18 | 3 | 11 | 48 | .261 | 158 | 223 | *28 | .932 |
| 1970—Tulsa‡ .............A.A. | 3-2-S-O | 115 | 364 | 51 | 86 | 14 | 3 | 9 | 39 | .236 | 128 | 236 | 16 | .958 |
| 1971—Tulsa§-Iowa ......A.A. | 3-S-2-O-1 | 83 | 251 | 28 | 58 | 7 | 2 | 5 | 31 | .231 | 88 | 117 | 11 | .949 |
| 1972—Iowa..................A.A. | S-O-3-2 | 114 | 373 | 43 | 82 | 12 | 1 | 10 | 43 | .220 | 131 | 269 | 25 | .941 |
| 1973—Tucson .............P.C. | S-2-3-O-1 | 75 | 202 | 34 | 58 | 8 | 3 | 5 | 22 | .287 | 87 | 174 | 18 | .903 |
| 1974—Tucson .............P.C. | S-3-2 | 67 | 236 | 28 | 58 | 10 | 1 | 4 | 28 | .246 | 117 | 157 | 20 | .932 |
| 1974—Oakland ...........Amer. | 3-2-1 | 18 | 41 | 4 | 10 | 3 | 0 | 0 | 3 | .244 | 22 | 28 | 4 | .926 |
| 1975—Tucson .............P.C. | 3-S-2-1 | 135 | 482 | 74 | 129 | 23 | 2 | 11 | 58 | .268 | 240 | 237 | 20 | .960 |
| 1975—Oakland ...........Amer. | 3-S-2 | 10 | 3 | 1 | 1 | 1 | 0 | 0 | 1 | .333 | 4 | 6 | 1 | .909 |
| 1976—Tucson x .........P.C. | 3-2-S | 106 | 310 | 56 | 81 | 14 | 0 | 12 | 50 | .261 | 125 | 217 | 18 | .950 |
| Major League Totals ...................... | | 28 | 44 | 5 | 11 | 4 | 0 | 0 | 4 | .250 | 26 | 34 | 5 | .923 |

†On temporary inactive list, May 20, 1966. On Military List, June 15, 1966 to March 23, 1968.
‡On disabled list, June 6 to June 19, 1970.
§Traded by St. Louis Cardinals to Oakland Athletics for Pitcher Dennis Higgins, July 21, 1971.
xTraded to Wichita (Chicago Cubs' organization) for Outfielder Jim Tyrone, March 15, 1977.

## WILLIAM FRANCIS PLUMMER
### (Bill)

Born March 21, 1947, at Oakland, Calif.
Height, 6.02. Weight, 200.
Throws and bats righthanded.
Hobby—Hunting.
Attended Shasta College, Redding, Calif., and Sacramento State College,
Sacramento, Calif.
Son of William L. Plummer, minor league pitcher, 1921 through 1927, and
nephew of Earl "Red" Baldwin, minor league catcher, 1915 through 1931.

| Year Club League | Pos. | G. | AB. | R. | H. | 2B. | 3B. | HR. | RBI. | B.A. | PO. | A. | E. | F.A. |
|---|---|---|---|---|---|---|---|---|---|---|---|---|---|---|
| 1965—Cedar Rapids ....Midw. | C | 15 | 2 | 2 | 2 | 1 | 0 | 0 | 0 | .133 | 46 | 3 | 1 | .980 |
| 1965—Sarasota Cards ..Fla. Rk. | C | 42 | 102 | 10 | 27 | 5 | 0 | 0 | 7 | .265 | *189 | 26 | 5 | .977 |
| 1966—Eugene.............Northw. | C | 46 | 125 | 6 | 18 | 3 | 0 | 1 | 11 | .144 | 276 | 29 | 10 | .968 |
| 1967—Modesto† .........Calif. | C-1-3 | 120 | 397 | 48 | 93 | 8 | 6 | 11 | 56 | .234 | 851 | 69 | 18 | .981 |
| 1968—Chicago‡ .........Nat. | C | 2 | 2 | 0 | 0 | 0 | 0 | 0 | 0 | .000 | 2 | 0 | 0 | 1.000 |
| 1969—Indianapolis ......A.A. | *C-O-P | 104 | 355 | 41 | 88 | 8 | 3 | 7 | 41 | .248 | *653 | *64 | 8 | .989 |
| 1970—Indianapolis ......A.A. | *C-O-1 | 115 | 365 | 37 | 95 | 12 | 1 | 7 | 42 | .260 | *653 | 52 | 4 | *.994 |
| 1970—Cincinnati.........Nat. | C | 4 | 8 | 0 | 1 | 0 | 0 | 0 | 0 | .125 | 6 | 0 | 1 | .857 |
| 1971—Indianapolis ......A.A. | *C-3-1 | 104 | 372 | 50 | 99 | 15 | 5 | 17 | 65 | .266 | 569 | *66 | 9 | .986 |
| 1971—Cincinnati.........Nat. | C-3B | 10 | 19 | 0 | 0 | 0 | 0 | 0 | 0 | .000 | 8 | 6 | 0 | 1.000 |
| 1972—Cincinnati§ .......Nat. | C-1-3 | 38 | 102 | 8 | 19 | 4 | 0 | 2 | 9 | .186 | 156 | 9 | 1 | .994 |
| 1973—Cincinnati.........Nat. | C-3B | 50 | 119 | 8 | 18 | 3 | 0 | 2 | 11 | .151 | 172 | 10 | 2 | .989 |
| 1974—Cincinnati.........Nat. | C-3B | 50 | 120 | 7 | 27 | 7 | 0 | 2 | 10 | .225 | 208 | 14 | 6 | .974 |
| 1975—Cincinnati.........Nat. | C | 65 | 159 | 17 | 29 | 7 | 0 | 1 | 19 | .182 | 186 | 14 | 2 | .990 |
| 1976—Cincinnati.........Nat. | C | 56 | 153 | 16 | 38 | 6 | 1 | 4 | 19 | .248 | 235 | 21 | 6 | .977 |
| Major League Totals ..................... | | 275 | 682 | 56 | 132 | 27 | 1 | 11 | 68 | .194 | 973 | 74 | 18 | .983 |

†Drafted by Chicago Cubs from Tulsa (St. Louis Cardinals' organization), November 28, 1967.
‡Released to Indianapolis (with Outfielder Clarence Jones in trade in which Cincinnati also acquired Pitch-
er Ken Myette in exchange for Pitcher Ted Abernathy), January 9, 1969.
§Placed on supplemental disabled list, March 30 through May 5, 1972.

PITCHING RECORD

| Year Club League | | G. | IP. | W. | L. | Pct. | H. | R. | ER. | SO. | BB. | ERA. |
|---|---|---|---|---|---|---|---|---|---|---|---|---|
| 1969—Indianapolis ....................A.A. | | 1 | 2 | 0 | 0 | .000 | 2 | 0 | 0 | 0 | 1 | 0.00 |

## BIFF POCOROBA
Name pronounced poh-koh-ROH-buh.

Born July 25, 1953, at Burbank, Calif.
Height, 5.10. Weight, 175.
Throws right and bats left and righthanded.
Hobbies—Hunting and golf.

| Year Club League | Pos. | G. | AB. | R. | H. | 2B. | 3B. | HR. | RBI. | B.A. | PO. | A. | E. | F.A. |
|---|---|---|---|---|---|---|---|---|---|---|---|---|---|---|
| 1971—Wytheville .......Appal. | C | 42 | 124 | 17 | 37 | 7 | 0 | 3 | 19 | .298 | 262 | 13 | 3 | .989 |
| 1972—Greenwood .......W. Car. | C | 75 | 212 | 25 | 55 | 5 | 0 | 7 | 29 | .259 | 446 | 25 | 10 | *.979 |
| 1972—Richmond..........Int. | PH | 1 | 1 | 0 | 0 | 0 | 0 | 0 | 0 | .000 | 0 | 0 | 0 | .000 |
| 1973—Savannah† ........South. | C | 114 | 368 | 46 | 86 | 13 | 0 | 12 | 46 | .234 | 417 | 38 | 7 | .985 |
| 1974—Savannah‡ ........South. | *C-1B | 79 | 241 | 48 | 75 | 10 | 2 | 9 | 45 | .311 | 435 | 25 | 2 | *.996 |
| 1975—Atlanta.............Nat. | C | 67 | 188 | 15 | 48 | 7 | 1 | 1 | 22 | .255 | 237 | 25 | 8 | .970 |
| 1976—Atlanta§ ...........Nat. | C | 54 | 174 | 16 | 42 | 7 | 0 | 0 | 14 | .241 | 273 | 39 | 7 | .978 |
| Major League Totals ..................... | | 121 | 362 | 31 | 90 | 14 | 1 | 1 | 36 | .249 | 510 | 64 | 15 | .974 |

†On disabled list, July 12 to July 22, 1973.
‡On disabled list, April 26 to June 7, 1974.
§On disabled list, June 2 to July 6 and August 9 to October 4, 1976.

## RICHARD HENRY POLE
### (Dick)

Born October 13, 1950, at Trout Creek, Mich.
Height, 6.02. Weight, 210.
Throws and bats righthanded.
Hobbies—Fishing and hunting.
Attended Northern Michigan University, Marquette, Mich.

Pitched seven-inning, 2-0 no-hit victory against Peninsula, June 23, 1973 (second game).
Tied for International League lead in shutouts with 4 and in complete games with 16 in 1973.
Tied for Western Carolinas League lead in shutouts with 3 and in games started with 25 in 1969.
Named International League Most Valuable Pitcher in 1973.

| Year | Club | League | G. | IP. | W. | L. | Pct. | H. | R. | ER. | SO. | BB. | ERA. |
|---|---|---|---|---|---|---|---|---|---|---|---|---|---|
| 1969—Greenville | | W. Carol. | 25 | 164 | 13 | 10 | .565 | 165 | 83 | 58 | 99 | 45 | 3.18 |
| 1969—Winter Haven | | Florida St. | 2 | 11 | 0 | 2 | .000 | 8 | 3 | 2 | 5 | 4 | 1.64 |
| 1970—Winter Haven† | | Florida St. | 19 | 99 | 6 | 7 | .462 | 72 | 42 | 33 | 79 | 28 | 3.00 |
| 1970—Winston-Salem | | Carolina | 3 | 20 | 1 | 2 | .333 | 1 | 13 | 11 | 18 | 8 | 4.95 |
| 1971—Pawtucket | | Eastern | 21 | 124 | 8 | 7 | .533 | 107 | 44 | 38 | 70 | 36 | 2.76 |
| 1972—Louisville | | Int'national | 27 | 113 | 4 | 5 | .444 | 113 | 59 | 48 | 65 | 49 | 3.82 |
| 1973—Pawtucket | | Int'national | 23 | 182 | 12 | 9 | .571 | 124 | 54 | 41 | *158 | 80 | *2.03 |
| 1973—Boston | | American | 12 | 55 | 3 | 2 | .600 | 70 | 35 | 34 | 24 | 18 | 5.56 |
| 1974—Pawtucket | | Int'national | 16 | 66 | 2 | 8 | .200 | 67 | 36 | 30 | 61 | 36 | 4.09 |
| 1974—Boston | | American | 15 | 45 | 1 | 1 | .500 | 55 | 28 | 21 | 32 | 13 | 4.20 |
| 1975—Boston† | | American | 18 | 90 | 4 | 6 | .400 | 102 | 46 | 44 | 42 | 32 | 4.40 |
| 1976—Boston§ | | American | 31 | 121 | 6 | 5 | .545 | 131 | 62 | 58 | 49 | 48 | 4.31 |
| Major League Totals | | | 76 | 311 | 14 | 14 | .500 | 358 | 171 | 157 | 147 | 111 | 4.54 |

†On temporary inactive list, April 16 to April 30 and July 7 to July 30, 1970.
‡On disabled list, July 1 to September 1, 1975.
§Selected by Seattle Mariners in American League expansion draft, November 5, 1976.

### WORLD SERIES RECORD

| Year | Club | League | G. | IP. | W. | L. | Pct. | H. | R. | ER. | SO. | BB. | ERA. |
|---|---|---|---|---|---|---|---|---|---|---|---|---|---|
| 1975—Boston | | American | 1 | *0 | 0 | 0 | .000 | 0 | 1 | 1 | 0 | 2 | ...... |

*Pitched to two batters in eighth inning of fifth game.

## ROBERT PAUL JOSEPH POLINSKY
### (Bob)

Born June 21, 1951, at Coaldale, Pa.
Height, 6.05. Weight, 200.
Throws and bats righthanded.
Hobby—Audiophile.
Attended Delaware Valley College, Doylestown, Pa.; received Bachelor of
Science degree in Business Administration.

| Year | Club | League | G. | IP. | W. | L. | Pct. | H. | R. | ER. | SO. | BB. | ERA. |
|---|---|---|---|---|---|---|---|---|---|---|---|---|---|
| 1973—Oneonta | | NYP | 13 | 99 | 8 | 3 | .727 | 102 | 40 | 28 | 99 | 34 | 2.55 |
| 1974—West Haven | | Eastern | 25 | 169 | 7 | 11 | .389 | 163 | 87 | 71 | 110 | 73 | 3.78 |
| 1975—West Haven | | Eastern | 24 | 184 | 8 | 13 | .381 | 155 | 84 | 65 | 121 | 60 | 3.18 |
| 1976—Syracuse† | | Int'national | 46 | 93 | 4 | 8 | .333 | 83 | 44 | 34 | 67 | 49 | 3.29 |

†Traded by New York Yankees with Outfielder Oscar Gamble, Pitcher Dewey Hoyt and cash estimated at $250,000 to Chicago White Sox for Shortstop Bucky Dent, April 5, 1977.

## THOMAS ARTHUR POQUETTE
Name pronounced POE-kett.
### (Tom)

Born October 30, 1951, at Eau Claire, Wis.
Height, 5.11. Weight, 175.
Throws right and bats lefthanded.
Hobbies—Fishing, hunting and reading.

Tied for Southern League and in double plays by outfielders with 3 in 1972.

| Year | Club | League | Pos. | G. | AB. | R. | H. | 2B. | 3B. | HR. | RBI. | B.A. | PO. | A. | E. | F.A. |
|---|---|---|---|---|---|---|---|---|---|---|---|---|---|---|---|---|
| 1970—Kingsport | Appal. | | OF | 56 | 209 | 41 | 57 | 7 | 1 | 8 | 18 | .273 | 81 | 5 | 7 | .925 |
| 1971—Waterloo | Midw. | | O-3 | 111 | 381 | 65 | 113 | 21 | 4 | 8 | 60 | .297 | 135 | 41 | 9 | .951 |
| 1972—Jacksonville | South. | | OF | 126 | 451 | 49 | 113 | 25 | 3 | 6 | 51 | .251 | 159 | 13 | 12 | .935 |
| 1973—Omaha | A. A. | | OF | 131 | 478 | 66 | 128 | 22 | 4 | 9 | 50 | .268 | 230 | *17 | *14 | .946 |
| 1973—Kansas City | Amer. | | OF | 21 | 28 | 4 | 6 | 1 | 0 | 0 | 3 | .214 | 19 | 1 | 3 | .870 |
| 1974—Omaha† | A. A. | | OF | 63 | 223 | 42 | 68 | 10 | 3 | 4 | 27 | .305 | 107 | 7 | 7 | .909 |
| 1975—Jacksonville‡ | South. | | OF | 105 | 355 | 50 | 91 | 16 | 0 | 5 | 40 | .256 | 179 | 16 | 3 | .985 |
| 1976—Kansas City§ | Amer. | | OF-DH | 104 | 344 | 43 | 104 | 18 | 10 | 2 | 34 | .302 | 188 | 1 | 4 | .979 |
| Major League Totals | | | | 125 | 372 | 47 | 110 | 19 | 10 | 2 | 37 | .296 | 207 | 2 | 7 | .968 |

†On disabled list, June 22 to September 1, 1974.
‡On disabled list from beginning of season until May 21, 1975.
§On disabled list, June 23 to July 15, 1976.

### CHAMPIONSHIP SERIES RECORD

| Year | Club | League | Pos. | G. | AB. | R. | H. | 2B. | 3B. | HR. | RBI. | B.A. | PO. | A. | E. | F.A. |
|---|---|---|---|---|---|---|---|---|---|---|---|---|---|---|---|---|
| 1976—Kansas City | Amer. | | OF | 5 | 16 | 1 | 3 | 2 | 0 | 0 | 4 | .188 | 13 | 0 | 0 | 1.000 |

# DARRELL RAY PORTER

Born January 17, 1952, at Joplin, Mo.
Height, 6.01. Weight, 195.
Throws right and bats lefthanded.
Hobbies—Hunting, fishing and golf.
Led American League in passed balls with 15 in 1975 and with 12 in 1976.
Led Midwest League in passed balls with 19 in 1971.
Received bonus reported in excess of $70,000 to sign with Milwaukee Brewers in 1970.

| Year | Club | League | Pos. | G. | AB. | R. | H. | 2B. | 3B. | HR. | RBI. | B.A. | PO. | A. | E. | F.A. |
|------|------|--------|------|-----|------|-----|-----|-----|-----|-----|------|------|------|------|-----|------|
| 1970—Clinton | | Midw. | C | 62 | 185 | 24 | 37 | 11 | 0 | 4 | 21 | .200 | 380 | 42 | 10 | .977 |
| 1971—Danville | | Midw. | C | 101 | 332 | 75 | 90 | 9 | 7 | 24 | 70 | .271 | 674 | •69 | •19 | .975 |
| 1971—Milwaukee | | Amer. | C | 22 | 70 | 4 | 15 | 2 | 0 | 2 | 9 | .214 | 108 | 18 | 3 | .977 |
| 1972—Evansville | | A. A. | C | 88 | 255 | 37 | 55 | 7 | 2 | 13 | 45 | .216 | 541 | •56 | 7 | .988 |
| 1972—Milwaukee | | Amer. | C | 18 | 56 | 2 | 7 | 1 | 0 | 1 | 2 | .125 | 113 | 8 | 3 | .976 |
| 1973—Milwaukee | | Amer. | C | 117 | 350 | 50 | 89 | 19 | 2 | 16 | 67 | .254 | 372 | 47 | 10 | .977 |
| 1974—Milwaukee | | Amer. | C | 131 | 432 | 59 | 104 | 15 | 4 | 12 | 56 | .241 | 484 | 60 | 12 | .978 |
| 1975—Milwaukee | | Amer. | C | 130 | 409 | 66 | 95 | 12 | 5 | 18 | 60 | .232 | 532 | 82 | 13 | .979 |
| 1976—Milwaukee† | | Amer. | C-DH | 119 | 389 | 43 | 81 | 14 | 1 | 5 | 32 | .208 | 491 | 52 | 4 | .975 |
| Major League Totals | | | | 537 | 1706 | 224 | 391 | 63 | 12 | 54 | 226 | .229 | 2100 | 267 | 55 | .977 |

†Traded with Jim Colborn to Kansas City Royals for Outfielder Jim Wohlford, Infielder Jamie Quirk and a player to be named later, December 6, 1976; Pitcher Bob McClure was sent to Milwaukee to complete deal, March 15, 1976.

ALL-STAR GAME RECORD

Member of American League All-Star Team in 1974 game; did not play.


# JOHN WESLEY POWELL
## (Boog)

(A "bugger," pronounced "booger," as a toddler—one who gets into mischief. Family shortened nickname to "Boog.")

Born August 17, 1941, at Lakeland, Fla.
Height, 6.04½. Weight, 246.
Throws right and bats lefthanded.
Hobbies—Hunting and fishing.
Stepbrother of Carl Taylor, former catcher-first baseman with Pittsburgh Pirates, St. Louis Cardinals and Kansas City Royals.
Tied major league record for most strikeouts, inning (2), July 19, 1966 (fifth inning).
Tied major league record for fewest 3-base hits, 150 or more games, season (0), 1969 and 1970.
Established American League record for most consecutive seasons, 10 or more intentional bases on balls, 7, 1974.
Tied American League records for most runs batted in, double-header, 11, July 6, 1966 (20 innings); and most seasons, 10 or more intentional bases on balls, 8, 1974.
Hit three home runs in a game on three occasions: August 10, 1963 (consecutive), June 27, 1964 and August 15, 1966.
Led American League in slugging percentage with .606 in 1964.
Led International League in total bases with 288 in 1961.
Named American League Comeback Player of the Year by THE SPORTING NEWS, 1966 and 1975.
Named first baseman on THE SPORTING NEWS American League All-Star Team, 1966-68-69-70.
Named Most Valuable Player in American League, 1970.
Received reported $25,000 bonus to sign with Baltimore Orioles, 1959.

| Year | Club | League | Pos. | G. | AB. | R. | H. | 2B. | 3B. | HR. | RBI. | B.A. | PO. | A. | E. | F.A. |
|------|------|--------|------|-----|------|-----|------|-----|-----|-----|------|------|------|-----|-----|-------|
| 1959—Bluefield | | Appal. | O-1B | 56 | 191 | 39 | 67 | 7 | 0 | 14 | 59 | .351 | 68 | 5 | 7 | .913 |
| 1960—Fox Cities | | I.I.I. | 1B | 136 | 497 | 83 | 155 | 23 | 3 | 13 | 100 | .312 | 1055 | 68 | 19 | •.983 |
| 1961—Rochester | | Int. | 1B-OF | 142 | 486 | 86 | 156 | 26 | 5 | •32 | 92 | .321 | 842 | 43 | 14 | .984 |
| 1961—Baltimore | | Amer. | OF | 4 | 13 | 0 | 1 | 0 | 0 | 0 | 1 | .077 | 3 | 0 | 0 | 1.000 |
| 1962—Baltimore | | Amer. | OF-1B | 124 | 400 | 44 | 97 | 13 | 2 | 15 | 53 | .243 | 194 | 1 | 6 | .970 |
| 1963—Baltimore | | Amer. | OF-1B | 140 | 491 | 67 | 130 | 22 | 2 | 25 | 82 | .265 | 316 | 18 | 9 | .974 |
| 1964—Baltimore | | Amer. | OF-1B | 134 | 424 | 74 | 123 | 17 | 0 | 39 | 99 | .290 | 233 | 19 | 5 | .980 |
| 1965—Baltimore | | Amer. | 1B-OF | 144 | 472 | 54 | 117 | 20 | 2 | 17 | 72 | .248 | 658 | 53 | 5 | .993 |
| 1966—Baltimore | | Amer. | 1B | 140 | 491 | 78 | 141 | 18 | 0 | 34 | 109 | .287 | 1094 | 68 | 13 | .989 |
| 1967—Baltimore | | Amer. | 1B | 125 | 415 | 53 | 97 | 14 | 1 | 13 | 55 | .234 | 903 | 64 | 14 | .986 |
| 1968—Baltimore | | Amer. | 1B | 154 | 550 | 60 | 137 | 21 | 1 | 22 | 85 | .249•1293 | 79 | 14 | .990 | |
| 1969—Baltimore | | Amer. | 1B | 152 | 533 | 83 | 162 | 25 | 0 | 37 | 121 | .304 | 1192 | 84 | 7 | .994 |
| 1970—Baltimore | | Amer. | 1B | 154 | 526 | 82 | 156 | 28 | 0 | 35 | 114 | .297 | 1209 | 89 | 10 | .992 |
| 1971—Baltimore | | Amer. | 1B | 128 | 418 | 59 | 107 | 19 | 0 | 22 | 92 | .256 | 1031 | 67 | 5 | .995 |
| 1972—Baltimore | | Amer. | 1B | 140 | 465 | 53 | 117 | 20 | 1 | 21 | 81 | .252 | 1116 | 70 | •15 | .988 |
| 1973—Baltimore | | Amer. | 1B | 114 | 370 | 52 | 98 | 13 | 1 | 11 | 54 | .265 | 988 | 77 | 12 | .989 |
| 1974—Baltimore† | | Amer. | 1B | 110 | 344 | 37 | 91 | 13 | 1 | 12 | 45 | .265 | 866 | 61 | 4 | .996 |
| 1975—Cleveland | | Amer. | 1B | 134 | 435 | 64 | 129 | 18 | 0 | 27 | 86 | .297 | 997 | 69 | 3 | •.997 |
| 1976—Cleveland‡§ | | Amer. | 1B | 95 | 293 | 29 | 63 | 9 | 0 | 9 | 33 | .215 | 698 | 61 | 10 | .987 |
| Major League Totals | | | | 1992 | 6640 | 889 | 1766 | 270 | 11 | 339 | 1182 | .266 | 12781 | 880 | 132 | .990 |

†Traded with Pitcher Don Hood to Cleveland Indians for Catcher Dave Duncan and Outfielder Alvin McGrew (assigned to Rochester), February 25, 1975.
‡On disabled list, June 7 through June 22, 1976.
§Released, March 30, 1977; signed as free agent with Los Angeles Dodgers, April 5, 1977.

| Year | Club | League | Pos. | G. | AB. | R. | H. | 2B. | 3B. | HR. | RBI. | B.A. | PO. | A. | E. | F.A. |
|------|------|--------|------|-----|-----|-----|-----|-----|-----|-----|------|------|-----|-----|-----|------|
| 1969–Baltimore | | Amer. | 1B | 3 | 13 | 2 | 5 | 0 | 0 | 1 | 1 | .385 | 34 | 0 | 0 | 1.000 |
| 1970–Baltimore | | Amer. | 1B | 3 | 14 | 2 | 6 | 2 | 0 | 1 | 6 | .429 | 24 | 1 | 0 | 1.000 |
| 1971–Baltimore | | Amer. | 1B | 3 | 10 | 4 | 3 | 0 | 0 | 2 | 3 | .300 | 28 | 2 | 0 | 1.000 |
| 1973–Baltimore | | Amer. | 1B | 1 | 4 | 1 | 0 | 0 | 0 | 0 | 0 | .000 | 7 | 0 | 0 | 1.000 |
| 1974–Baltimore | | Amer. | 1B | 2 | 8 | 0 | 1 | 0 | 0 | 0 | 1 | .125 | 22 | 1 | 0 | 1.000 |
| Championship Series Totals | | | 12 | 49 | 9 | 15 | 2 | 0 | 4 | 11 | .306 | 115 | 4 | 0 | 1.000 | |

### WORLD SERIES RECORD

Tied World Series record for most runs scored, 5-game series, 6, in 1970.

| Year | Club | League | Pos. | G. | AB. | R. | H. | 2B. | 3B. | HR. | RBI. | B.A. | PO. | A. | E. | F.A. |
|------|------|--------|------|-----|-----|-----|-----|-----|-----|-----|------|------|-----|-----|-----|------|
| 1966–Baltimore | | Amer. | 1B | 4 | 14 | 1 | 5 | 1 | 0 | 0 | 1 | .357 | 27 | 1 | 0 | 1.000 |
| 1969–Baltimore | | Amer. | 1B | 5 | 19 | 0 | 5 | 0 | 0 | 0 | 0 | .263 | 46 | 2 | 1 | .980 |
| 1970–Baltimore | | Amer. | 1B | 5 | 17 | 6 | 5 | 1 | 0 | 2 | 5 | .294 | 38 | 2 | 0 | 1.000 |
| 1971–Baltimore | | Amer. | 1B | 7 | 27 | 1 | 3 | 0 | 0 | 0 | 1 | .111 | 52 | 4 | 1 | .982 |
| World Series Totals | | | 21 | 77 | 8 | 18 | 2 | 0 | 2 | 7 | .234 | 163 | 9 | 2 | .989 | |

### ALL-STAR GAME RECORD

| Year | League | Pos. | AB. | R. | H. | 2B. | 3B. | HR. | RBI. | B.A. | PO. | A. | E. | F.A. |
|------|--------|------|-----|-----|-----|-----|-----|-----|------|------|-----|-----|-----|------|
| 1968–American | | 1B | 2 | 0 | 0 | 0 | 0 | 0 | 0 | .000 | 2 | 0 | 0 | 1.000 |
| 1969–American | | 1B | 4 | 0 | 1 | 0 | 0 | 0 | 0 | .250 | 9 | 1 | 0 | 1.000 |
| 1970–American | | 1B | 3 | 0 | 0 | 0 | 0 | 0 | 0 | .000 | 5 | 0 | 0 | .000 |
| All-Star Game Totals | | | 9 | 0 | 1 | 0 | 0 | 0 | 0 | .111 | 16 | 1 | 0 | 1.000 |

Named to American League All-Star Team for 1971 game; replaced due to injury.

## MICHAEL JAMES PROLY
### (Mike)

Born December 15, 1950, at Jamaica, N. Y.
Height, 6.00  Weight, 185.
Throws and bats righthanded.
Hobbies–Fishing, swimming and golf.
Attended St. John's University, Jamaica, N. Y.; received Bachelor
of Science degree in Marketing.

| Year | Club | League | G. | IP. | W. | L. | Pct. | H. | R. | ER. | SO. | BB. | ERA. |
|------|------|--------|-----|-----|-----|-----|------|-----|-----|-----|-----|-----|------|
| 1972–St. Petersburg | | Florida St. | 12 | 46 | 3 | 1 | .750 | 28 | 9 | 4 | 41 | 10 | 0.78 |
| 1972–Modesto | | California | 6 | 29 | 1 | 3 | .250 | 41 | 29 | 23 | 16 | 15 | 7.14 |
| 1973–St. Petersburg | | Florida St. | 37 | 164 | 14 | 5 | ∗.737 | 129 | 44 | 32 | 112 | 28 | ∗1.76 |
| 1974–Arkansas | | Texas | 39 | 101 | 8 | 2 | .800 | 101 | 37 | 31 | 51 | 34 | 2.76 |
| 1975–Tulsa | | Am. Assoc. | 55 | 86 | 7 | 10 | .412 | 101 | 42 | 37 | 51 | 43 | 3.87 |
| 1976–St. Louis | | Nat. | 14 | 17 | 1 | 0 | 1.000 | 21 | 9 | 7 | 4 | 6 | 3.71 |
| 1976–Tulsa | | Am. Assoc. | 50 | 67 | 6 | 4 | .600 | 71 | 28 | 20 | 28 | 13 | 2.69 |
| Major League Totals | | | 14 | 17 | 1 | 0 | 1.000 | 21 | 9 | 7 | 4 | 6 | 3.71 |

## RONALD RALPH PRUITT
### (Ron)

Born October 21, 1951, at Flint, Mich.
Height, 6.00. Weight, 185.
Throws and bats righthanded.
Hobbies–Fishing and listening to music.
Attended Michigan State University, East Lansing, Mich.

Led Eastern League catchers in double plays with 13 in 1974.

| Year | Club | League | Pos. | G. | AB. | R. | H. | 2B. | 3B. | HR. | RBI. | B.A. | PO. | A. | E. | F.A. |
|------|------|--------|------|-----|-----|-----|-----|-----|-----|-----|------|------|-----|-----|-----|------|
| 1972–Denver | | A. A. | O-C-2 | 60 | 167 | 22 | 36 | 5 | 0 | 5 | 24 | .216 | 117 | 10 | 4 | .969 |
| 1973–Spokane | | P. C. | O-C-3-1 | 112 | 372 | 68 | 103 | 22 | 7 | 8 | 55 | .277 | 319 | 68 | 11 | .972 |
| 1974–Pittsfield | | East. | ∗C-O-1-3 | 129 | 415 | 74 | 111 | 28 | 2 | 15 | 77 | .267 | ∗693 | ∗91 | ●17 | .979 |
| 1975–Spokane | | P. C. | C-3-O | 77 | 271 | 51 | 75 | 10 | 3 | 9 | 42 | .277 | 183 | 62 | 14 | .946 |
| 1975–Texas† | | Amer. | C-OF | 14 | 17 | 2 | 3 | 0 | 0 | 0 | 0 | .176 | 21 | 5 | 0 | 1.000 |
| 1976–Cleveland | | Amer. | O-C-2-1 | 47 | 86 | 7 | 23 | 1 | 1 | 0 | 5 | .267 | 73 | 16 | 1 | .989 |
| Major League Totals | | | | 61 | 103 | 9 | 26 | 1 | 1 | 0 | 5 | .252 | 94 | 21 | 1 | .991 |

†Traded with Pitcher Stan Thomas to Cleveland Indians for Catcher John Ellis, December 9, 1975.

## GREGORY RUSSELL PRYOR
### (Greg)

Born October 2, 1949, at Marietta, O.
Height, 6.00. Weight, 180.
Throws and bats righthanded.
Hobbies–Music, reading, photography and sailing.
Attended Florida Southern College, Lakeland, Fla.; received Bachelor of
Science Degree in Industrial Management.
Brother of Jeff Pryor, pitcher in California Angels' organization, 1968-72.

Tied for Pacific Coast League lead in double plays by shortstop with 90 in 1976.

| Year Club | League | Pos. | G. | AB. | R. | H. | 2B. | 3B. | HR. | RBI. | B.A. | PO. | A. | E. | F.A. |
|---|---|---|---|---|---|---|---|---|---|---|---|---|---|---|---|
| 1971—Geneva...............NYP | | 3-2-S-O | 60 | 226 | 40 | 64 | 10 | 4 | 4 | 28 | .283 | 76 | 138 | 21 | .911 |
| 1972—Pittsfield .........East. | | SS | 65 | 208 | 23 | 43 | 10 | 2 | 1 | 16 | .207 | 89 | 155 | 29 | .894 |
| 1972—Burlington ........Carol. | | SS-OF | 39 | 119 | 16 | 28 | 2 | 1 | 1 | 15 | .235 | 49 | 110 | 11 | .935 |
| 1973—Rocky Mount ....Carol. | | SS | 126 | 443 | 53 | 130 | 20 | 9 | 2 | 44 | .293 | 183 | 329 | 49 | .913 |
| 1974—Pittsfield .........East. | | 3-S-2 | 122 | 441 | 61 | 104 | 20 | 1 | 5 | 37 | .236 | 113 | 255 | 26 | .934 |
| 1975—Spokane ...........P. C. | | S-3-2 | 135 | 481 | 59 | 117 | 21 | 2 | 5 | 53 | .243 | 184 | 411 | 33 | .947 |
| 1976—Sacramento ......P. C. | | SS | 122 | 495 | 71 | 136 | 21 | 3 | 9 | 51 | .275 | 158 | 409 | 32 | .947 |
| 1976—Texas ...............Amer. | | 2-3-S | 5 | 8 | 2 | 3 | 0 | 0 | 0 | 1 | .375 | 4 | 8 | 0 | 1.000 |
| Major League Totals ..................... | | | 5 | 8 | 2 | 3 | 0 | 0 | 0 | 1 | .375 | 4 | 8 | 0 | 1.000 |

†Traded with Infielder Brian Doyle and cash estimated at $25,000 to New York Yankees for Infielder Sandy Alomar, February 17, 1977.

## TERRY STEPHEN PUHL

Born July 8, 1956, at Melville, Saskatchewan, Canada.
Height, 6.02. Weight, 195.
Throws right and bats lefthanded.
Hobby—Crossword puzzles.

| Year Club | League | Pos. | G. | AB. | R. | H. | 2B. | 3B. | HR. | RBI. | B.A. | PO. | A. | E. | F.A. |
|---|---|---|---|---|---|---|---|---|---|---|---|---|---|---|---|
| 1974—Covington .........Appal. | | OF | 59 | 211 | 42 | 60 | 11 | 0 | 0 | 21 | .284 | 89 | 2 | 2 | .978 |
| 1975—Dubuque...........Midw. | | OF-1B | 104 | 346 | 57 | 115 | 10 | 2 | 0 | 28 | .332 | 230 | 11 | 7 | .971 |
| 1976—Columbus .........South. | | OF | 28 | 98 | 13 | 28 | 5 | 0 | 1 | 14 | .286 | 76 | 1 | 2 | .975 |
| 1976—Memphis ..........Int. | | OF | 105 | 372 | 50 | 99 | 17 | 3 | 1 | 39 | .266 | 191 | 5 | 3 | .985 |

Listed on Houston Astros' 1977 spring roster.

## EDDY WILLIAM PUTMAN
### (Ed)

Born September 25, 1953, at Los Angeles, Calif.
Height, 6.01. Weight, 190.
Throws and bats righthanded.
Hobbies—Fishing, tennis and bicycling.
Attended University of Southern California, Los Angeles, Calif.

Received large bonus to sign with Chicago Cubs, 1975.

| Year Club | League | Pos. | G. | AB. | R. | H. | 2B. | 3B. | HR. | RBI. | B.A. | PO. | A. | E. | F.A. |
|---|---|---|---|---|---|---|---|---|---|---|---|---|---|---|---|
| 1975—Midland ............Tex. | | C | 24 | 68 | 8 | 14 | 1 | 0 | 2 | 6 | .206 | 114 | 23 | 3 | .979 |
| 1975—Key West .........Fla. St. | | C-OF | 92 | 293 | 39 | 65 | 15 | 2 | 2 | 32 | .222 | 284 | 42 | 7 | .979 |
| 1976—Wichita ............A. A. | | C-1B | 12 | 44 | 2 | 12 | 3 | 0 | 1 | 6 | .273 | 79 | 9 | 0 | 1.000 |
| 1976—Midland ...........Texas | | 1-C-O | 97 | 331 | 48 | 97 | 18 | 0 | 7 | 54 | .293 | 379 | 24 | 9 | .978 |
| 1976—Chicago ...........Nat. | | C-1B | 5 | 7 | 0 | 3 | 0 | 0 | 0 | 0 | .429 | 16 | 0 | 0 | 1.000 |
| Major League Totals ..................... | | | 5 | 7 | 0 | 3 | 0 | 0 | 0 | 0 | .429 | 16 | 0 | 0 | 1.000 |

## PATRICK EDWARD PUTNAM
### (Pat)

Born December 3, 1953, at Bethel, Vt.
Height, 6.00. Weight, 205.
Throws right and bats lefthanded.
Attended University of South Alabama, Mobile, Ala.

Led Western Carolina League in total bases with 305, sacrifice flies with 12, and intentional walks with 15 in 1976.
Named Minor League Player of the Year by THE SPORTING NEWS, 1976.

| Year Club | League | Pos. | G. | AB. | R. | H. | 2B. | 3B. | HR. | RBI. | B.A. | PO. | A. | E. | F.A. |
|---|---|---|---|---|---|---|---|---|---|---|---|---|---|---|---|
| 1975—Sara. Ranger ....Gulf C. | | 1B-OF | 18 | 73 | 13 | 21 | 4 | 1 | 2 | 17 | .288 | 144 | 9 | 2 | .981 |
| 1975—Lynchburg ........Carol. | | 1B-OF | 44 | 158 | 15 | 35 | 7 | 0 | 5 | 22 | .222 | 352 | 22 | 3 | .992 |
| 1976—Asheville ..........W. Car. | | •1B-C | 138 | 538 | 100 | •194 | •33 | 3 | •24 | •142 | .361 | 1156 | 97 | 11 | •.991 |

Invited to Texas Rangers' 1977 spring camp.

## JAMES PATRICK QUIRK
### (Jamie)

Born October 22, 1954, at Whittier, Calif.
Height, 6.04. Weight, 190.
Throws right and bats lefthanded.
Hobby—Sports in general.
Attended Whittier College, Whittier, Calif.

Led American Association third basemen in double plays with 31 in 1975.
Led Pioneer League shortstops in double plays with 16 in 1972.

| Year Club | League | Pos. | G. | AB. | R. | H. | 2B. | 3B. | HR. | RBI. | B.A. | PO. | A. | E. | F.A. |
|---|---|---|---|---|---|---|---|---|---|---|---|---|---|---|---|
| 1972—Billings ............Pion. | | SS | 55 | 208 | 29 | 53 | 9 | 4 | 5 | 37 | .255 | •63 | •162 | •28 | •.889 |
| 1973—San Jose...........Calif. | | SS | 132 | 429 | 58 | 99 | 12 | 7 | 8 | 45 | .231 | 160 | 330 | 39 | .926 |
| 1974—Jacksonville ......South. | | SS | 46 | 163 | 16 | 37 | 7 | 2 | 3 | 21 | .227 | 75 | 133 | 20 | .912 |

| Year | Club | League | Pos. | G. | AB. | R. | H. | 2B. | 3B. | HR. | RBI. | B.A. | PO. | A. | E. | F.A. |
|---|---|---|---|---|---|---|---|---|---|---|---|---|---|---|---|---|
| 1974–Omaha ...............A. A. | | | S-3-2 | 53 | 203 | 27 | 57 | 10 | 2 | 10 | 31 | .281 | 64 | 141 | 14 | .936 |
| 1975–Omaha ...............A. A. | | | 3B | 127 | 445 | 62 | 122 | 23 | 4 | 13 | 64 | .274 | 109 | •254 | 16 | •.958 |
| 1975–Kansas City ......Amer. | | | OF-3B | 14 | 39 | 2 | 10 | 0 | 0 | 1 | 5 | .256 | 19 | 3 | 2 | .917 |
| 1976–Kansas City† ....Amer. | | | DH-S-3-1 | 64 | 114 | 11 | 28 | 6 | 0 | 1 | 15 | .246 | 9 | 14 | 2 | .920 |
| Major League Totals ...................... | | | | 78 | 153 | 13 | 38 | 6 | 0 | 2 | 20 | .248 | 28 | 17 | 4 | .918 |

†Traded with Outfielder Jim Wohlford and a player to be named later to Milwaukee Brewers for Pitcher Jim Colborn and Catcher Darrell Porter, December 6, 1976; Pitcher Bob McClure was sent to Milwaukee' to complete deal, March 15, 1977.

CHAMPIONSHIP SERIES RECORD

| Year | Club | League | Pos. | G. | AB. | R. | H. | 2B. | 3B. | HR. | RBI. | B.A. | PO. | A. | E. | F.A. |
|---|---|---|---|---|---|---|---|---|---|---|---|---|---|---|---|---|
| 1976–Kansas City ......Amer. | | | PH-DH | 4 | 7 | 1 | 1 | 0 | 1 | 0 | 2 | .143 | 0 | 0 | 0 | .000 |

## DAVID MARTIN RADER
### (Dave)

Born December 26, 1948, at Claremore, Okla.
Height, 5.11½. Weight, 165.
Throws right and bats lefthanded.
Attended Bakersfield College, Bakersfield, Calif.

Tied for Texas League lead in double plays by catchers with 9 in 1970.
Named THE SPORTING NEWS National League Rookie Player of the Year, 1972.

| Year | Club | League | Pos. | G. | AB. | R. | H. | 2B. | 3B. | HR. | RBI. | B.A. | PO. | A. | E. | F.A. |
|---|---|---|---|---|---|---|---|---|---|---|---|---|---|---|---|---|
| 1967–Salt Lake City ..Pion. | | | •C-3B | 43 | 137 | 23 | 44 | 7 | 3 | 0 | 18 | .321 | 329 | 25 | •13 | .965 |
| 1967–Fresno ..............Calif. | | | C | 15 | 46 | 4 | 11 | 3 | 0 | 0 | 3 | .239 | 112 | 8 | 3 | .976 |
| 1968–Fresno† ............Calif. | | | C | 76 | 269 | 34 | 66 | 9 | 2 | 5 | 19 | .245 | 649 | 29 | 10 | .985 |
| 1969–Amarillo............Texas | | | C-3B | 78 | 236 | 27 | 48 | 13 | 0 | 6 | 31 | .203 | 389 | 50 | 5 | .989 |
| 1970–Amarillo............Texas | | | C | 92 | 282 | 44 | 68 | 9 | 4 | 10 | 41 | .241 | 519 | 63 | •14 | .977 |
| 1971–Phoenix ............P. C. | | | C | 85 | 293 | 41 | 92 | 20 | 5 | 8 | 47 | .314 | 506 | 26 | •14 | .974 |
| 1971–San Francisco ..Nat. | | | C | 3 | 4 | 0 | 0 | 0 | 0 | 0 | 0 | .000 | 1 | 0 | 0 | 1.000 |
| 1972–Phoenix ............P. C. | | | PH | 1 | 1 | 0 | 0 | 0 | 0 | 0 | 0 | .000 | 0 | 0 | 0 | .000 |
| 1972–San Francisco ..Nat. | | | C | 133 | 459 | 44 | 119 | 14 | 1 | 6 | 41 | .259 | 661 | 45 | 11 | .985 |
| 1973–San Francisco ..Nat. | | | C | 148 | 462 | 59 | 106 | 15 | 4 | 9 | 41 | .229 | 701 | 48 | 7 | .991 |
| 1974–San Francisco ..Nat. | | | C | 113 | 323 | 26 | 94 | 16 | 2 | 1 | 26 | .291 | 461 | 38 | 8 | .984 |
| 1975–San Francisco ..Nat. | | | C | 98 | 292 | 39 | 85 | 15 | 0 | 5 | 31 | .291 | 457 | 37 | 8 | .984 |
| 1976–San Francisco‡ ..Nat. | | | C | 88 | 255 | 25 | 67 | 15 | 0 | 1 | 22 | .263 | 349 | 32 | 6 | .984 |
| Major League Totals ...................... | | | | 583 | 1795 | 193 | 471 | 75 | 7 | 22 | 161 | .262 | 2630 | 200 | 40 | .986 |

†On military list from July 25 through end of season.
‡Traded with Pitchers John D'Acquisto and Mike Caldwell to St. Louis Cardinals for Outfielder Willie Crawford, Infielder-Outfielder Vic Harris, and Pitcher John Curtis, October 20, 1976.

## DOUGLAS LEE RADER
### (Doug)

Born July 30, 1944, at Chicago, Ill.
Height, 6.03. Weight, 210.
Throws and bats righthanded.
Hobbies–Fishing, hunting and playing pool.
Attended Illinois Wesleyan University, Bloomington, Ill.

Led National League third basemen in total chances with 479 and tied for lead in double plays with 31 in 1972.
Led National League third basemen in double plays with 39 in 1970.
Named third baseman on THE SPORTING NEWS National League All-Star fielding teams, 1970-71-72-73.
Received reported $25,000 bonus to sign with Houston Astros, 1964.

| Year | Club | League | Pos. | G. | AB. | R. | H. | 2B. | 3B. | HR. | RBI. | B.A. | PO. | A. | E. | F.A. |
|---|---|---|---|---|---|---|---|---|---|---|---|---|---|---|---|---|
| 1965–Durham ............Carol. | | | 3-OF | 112 | 330 | 44 | 69 | 14 | 1 | 14 | 38 | .209 | 111 | 185 | 21 | .934 |
| 1966–Amarillo............Texas | | | 3B | 138 | 527 | 85 | •153 | 21 | 12 | 16 | 74 | .290 | 102 | 240 | 27 | .927 |
| 1967–Oklahoma City ..P. C. | | | 3B | 75 | 273 | 40 | 80 | 23 | 5 | 9 | 44 | .293 | 47 | 110 | 12 | .929 |
| 1967–Houston ............Nat. | | | 1B-3B | 47 | 162 | 24 | 54 | 10 | 4 | 2 | 26 | .333 | 270 | 33 | 8 | .974 |
| 1968–Houston ............Nat. | | | 3B-1B | 98 | 333 | 42 | 89 | 16 | 4 | 6 | 43 | .267 | 130 | 171 | 22 | .932 |
| 1969–Houston ............Nat. | | | OF-3B | 155 | 569 | 62 | 140 | 25 | 3 | 11 | 83 | .246 | 140 | 307 | 26 | .945 |
| 1970–Houston ............Nat. | | | •3B-1B | 156 | 576 | 90 | 145 | 25 | 3 | 25 | 87 | .252 | •149 | •357 | 18 | •.966 |
| 1971–Houston ............Nat. | | | 3B | 135 | 484 | 51 | 118 | 21 | 4 | 12 | 56 | .244 | 93 | 275 | •21 | .946 |
| 1972–Houston ............Nat. | | | 3B | 152 | 533 | 70 | 131 | 24 | 7 | 22 | 90 | .237 | 119 | •340 | 20 | .958 |
| 1973–Houston ............Nat. | | | 3B | 154 | 574 | 79 | 146 | 26 | 0 | 21 | 89 | .254 | •134 | 296 | •25 | .945 |
| 1974–Houston ............Nat. | | | 3B | 152 | 533 | 61 | 137 | 27 | 3 | 17 | 78 | .257 | 128 | 347 | 17 | .965 |
| 1975–Houston† ..........Nat. | | | •3B-SS | 129 | 448 | 41 | 100 | 23 | 2 | 12 | 48 | .223 | 114 | 259 | 11 | •.971 |
| 1976–San Diego ..........Nat. | | | 3B | 139 | 471 | 45 | 121 | 22 | 4 | 9 | 55 | .257 | 109 | 318 | 20 | .955 |
| Major League Totals ...................... | | | | 1317 | 4703 | 565 | 1181 | 219 | 34 | 137 | 655 | .251 | 1386 | 2703 | 188 | .956 |

†Traded to San Diego Padres for Pitchers Joe McIntosh and Larry Hardy, December 11, 1975.

---

### *DID YOU KNOW —*

That Sam Leslie of the New York Giants made 22 hits as a pinch-hitter in 1932? He had 17 singles, four doubles and one home run.

## ERIC JAMES RAICH

Born November 1, 1951, at Detroit, Mich.
Height, 6.04. Weight, 255.
Throws and bats righthanded.
Attended University of Southern California, Los Angeles, Calif.

| Year Club | League | G. | IP. | W. | L. | Pct. | H. | R. | ER. | SO. | BB. | ERA. |
|---|---|---|---|---|---|---|---|---|---|---|---|---|
| 1972—Elmira | Eastern | 22 | 129 | 5 | 12 | .294 | 98 | 55 | 40 | 72 | 56 | 2.79 |
| 1973—San Antonio | Texas | 26 | 178 | 9 | 9 | .500 | 176 | 79 | 71 | 112 | 50 | 3.59 |
| 1974—San Antonio | Texas | 10 | 77 | 5 | 4 | .556 | 69 | 29 | 23 | 47 | 22 | 2.69 |
| 1974—Oklahoma City | Am. Assoc. | 20 | 107 | 5 | 6 | .455 | 159 | 79 | 73 | 70 | 37 | 6.14 |
| 1975—Oklahoma City | Am. Assoc. | 7 | 47 | 1 | 4 | .200 | 53 | 24 | 16 | 23 | 18 | 3.06 |
| 1975—Cleveland | American | 18 | 93 | 7 | 8 | .467 | 118 | 61 | 57 | 34 | 31 | 5.52 |
| 1976—Toledo | Int'national | 29 | 141 | 3 | 9 | .250 | 163 | 87 | 75 | 42 | 46 | 4.79 |
| 1976—Cleveland | American | 1 | 3 | 0 | 0 | .000 | 7 | 5 | 5 | 1 | 0 | 15.00 |
| Major League Totals | | 19 | 96 | 7 | 8 | .467 | 125 | 66 | 62 | 35 | 31 | 5.81 |

## ORLANDO RAMIREZ (LEAL)

Born December 18, 1951, at Cartagena, Colombia.
Height, 5.10. Weight, 175.
Throws and bats righthanded.
Hobby—Swimming.

| Year Club | League | Pos. | G. | AB. | R. | H. | 2B. | 3B. | HR. | RBI. | B.A. | PO. | A. | E. | F.A. |
|---|---|---|---|---|---|---|---|---|---|---|---|---|---|---|---|
| 1972—Shreveport | Texas | SS | 30 | 61 | 4 | 6 | 0 | 0 | 1 | 2 | .098 | 32 | 54 | 9 | .905 |
| 1972—Idaho Falls | Pion. | SS | 35 | 112 | 17 | 14 | 2 | 1 | 0 | 6 | .125 | 55 | 130 | 15 | .925 |
| 1973—Quad Cities | Midw | SS | 106 | 412 | 66 | 107 | 13 | 2 | 3 | 45 | .260 | 144 | 301 | 21 | •.955 |
| 1974—El Paso | Texas | SS | 50 | 196 | 38 | 38 | 9 | 2 | 0 | 20 | .194 | 94 | 163 | 20 | .928 |
| 1974—Salt Lake City | ..P. C. | SS | 55 | 184 | 37 | 62 | 4 | 3 | 0 | 23 | .337 | 86 | 205 | 14 | .954 |
| 1974—California | Amer. | SS | 31 | 86 | 4 | 14 | 0 | 0 | 0 | 7 | .163 | 41 | 90 | 6 | .956 |
| 1975—Salt Lake City† | ..P. C. | SS | 28 | 76 | 9 | 15 | 0 | 1 | 1 | 8 | .197 | 32 | 63 | 4 | .960 |
| 1975—California | Amer. | SS | 44 | 100 | 10 | 24 | 4 | 1 | 0 | 4 | .240 | 62 | 90 | 16 | .905 |
| 1976—Salt Lake City | ..P. C. | SS | 8 | 27 | 4 | 5 | 1 | 0 | 1 | 4 | .185 | 8 | 20 | 4 | .875 |
| 1976—El Paso‡ | Texas | SS-2B | 31 | 133 | 20 | 30 | 4 | 2 | 1 | 14 | .226 | 48 | 82 | 6 | .956 |
| 1976—California | Amer. | SS | 30 | 70 | 3 | 14 | 1 | 0 | 0 | 5 | .200 | 30 | 82 | 4 | .966 |
| Major League Totals | | | 105 | 256 | 17 | 52 | 5 | 1 | 0 | 16 | .203 | 133 | 262 | 26 | .938 |

†On disabled list, August 19 to September 8, 1975.
‡On disabled list, June 7 to August 3, 1976.

## ROBERT LEE RANDALL
### (Bob)

Born June 10, 1949, at Norton, Kan.
Height, 6.02. Weight, 175.
Throws and bats righthanded.
Hobby—Hunting.
Attended Kansas State University, Manhattan, Kan.; received
Bachelor of Science degree in Business Administration.

Led Pioneer League shortstops in double plays with 34 in 1969.
Led Pacific Coast League second basemen in double plays with 115 in 1974.
Led American League second basemen in double plays with 124 in 1976.

| Year Club | League | Pos. | G. | AB. | R. | H. | 2B. | 3B. | HR. | RBI. | B.A. | PO. | A. | E. | F.A. |
|---|---|---|---|---|---|---|---|---|---|---|---|---|---|---|---|
| 1969—Ogden | Pion. | •SS-2B | 71 | 271 | 52 | •90 | 12 | 5 | 1 | 39 | .332 | •123 | •161 | 23 | .925 |
| 1970—Bakersfield† | Calif. | •2B-SS | 98 | 362 | 48 | 97 | 14 | 3 | 3 | 39 | .268 | 176 | 274 | 15 | •.968 |
| 1971—Albuquerque | Tex. | 3-2-S-C | 38 | 94 | 8 | 22 | 3 | 0 | 0 | 7 | .234 | 24 | 40 | 7 | .901 |
| 1971—Bakersfield | Calif. | 2B | 42 | 171 | 26 | 46 | 5 | 1 | 1 | 16 | .269 | 103 | 127 | 13 | .947 |
| 1971—Spokane | P. C. | 2B-SS | 6 | 2 | 0 | 0 | 0 | 0 | 0 | 0 | .000 | 1 | 1 | 1 | .667 |
| 1972—Bakersfield‡ | Calif. | 2B-SS | 135 | •544 | 97 | •184 | 27 | 3 | 5 | 57 | .338 | 258 | 421 | 44 | .939 |
| 1973—Albuquerque | P. C. | 2B | 21 | 47 | 6 | 9 | 3 | 0 | 0 | 3 | .191 | 32 | 36 | 4 | .944 |
| 1973—Waterbury | East. | 2B | 86 | 331 | 60 | 102 | 22 | 1 | 1 | 25 | .308 | 192 | 302 | 13 | .970 |
| 1974—Albuquerque | P. C. | •2B-3B | 140 | 536 | 77 | •181 | 32 | 4 | 3 | 60 | .338 | •278 | •427 | •22 | .970 |
| 1975—Albuquerque§ | ....P. C. | 2B | 107 | 391 | 62 | 114 | 23 | 3 | 2 | 43 | .292 | 253 | 323 | 19 | .968 |
| 1976—Minnesota | Amer. | 2B | 153 | 475 | 55 | 127 | 18 | 4 | 1 | 34 | .267 | 327 | 423 | •24 | .969 |
| Major League Totals | | | 153 | 475 | 55 | 127 | 18 | 4 | 1 | 34 | .267 | 327 | 423 | 24 | .969 |

†On restricted list from beginning of season until May 18, 1970.
‡Player-coach.
§Traded by Los Angeles Dodgers to Minnesota Twins for Outfielder-Catcher Danny Walton, December 23, 1975.

## LEONARD SHENOFF RANDLE
### (Lenny)

Born February 12, 1949, at Long Beach, Calif.
Height, 5.10. Weight, 175.
Throws right and bats left and righthanded.
Hobbies—Photography and collecting wine labels.
Attended Arizona State University, Tempe, Ariz.

| Year Club | League | Pos. | G. | AB. | R. | H. | 2B. | 3B. | HR. | RBI. | B.A. | PO. | A. | E. | F.A. |
|---|---|---|---|---|---|---|---|---|---|---|---|---|---|---|---|
| 1970—Denver | A.A. | 2B-SS | 46 | 101 | 14 | 21 | 3 | 0 | 0 | 5 | .208 | 68 | 92 | 4 | .976 |
| 1971—Denver | A.A. | 2B-OF | 47 | 170 | 32 | 49 | 8 | 2 | 4 | 26 | .288 | 94 | 139 | 4 | .983 |

| Year Club League | Pos. | G. | AB. | R. | H. | 2B. | 3B. | HR. | RBI. | B.A. | PO. | A. | E. | F.A. |
|---|---|---|---|---|---|---|---|---|---|---|---|---|---|---|
| 1971–Washington........Amer. | 2B | 75 | 215 | 27 | 47 | 11 | 0 | 2 | 13 | .219 | 178 | 178 | 12 | .967 |
| 1972–Denver ...............A.A. | 2-S-O | 41 | 161 | 23 | 42 | 3 | 1 | 2 | 10 | .261 | 74 | 149 | 13 | .945 |
| 1972–Texas ................Amer. | 2-S-O | 74 | 249 | 23 | 48 | 13 | 0 | 2 | 21 | .193 | 161 | 177 | 20 | .944 |
| 1973–Spokane ............P.C. | 2-O-3 | 140 | •562 | 118 | 159 | 24 | 7 | 4 | 58 | .283 | 345 | 293 | 17 | .974 |
| 1973–Texas ................Amer. | 2B-OF | 10 | 29 | 3 | 6 | 1 | 1 | 1 | 1 | .207 | 19 | 9 | 2 | .933 |
| 1974–Texas ................Amer. | 3-2-O-S | 151 | 520 | 65 | 157 | 17 | 4 | 1 | 49 | .302 | 218 | 285 | 23 | .956 |
| 1975–Texas ................Amer. | I-C-O | 156 | 601 | 85 | 166 | 24 | 7 | 4 | 57 | .276 | 376 | 270 | 16 | .976 |
| 1976–Texas ................Amer. | I-O-DH | 142 | 539 | 53 | 121 | 11 | 6 | 1 | 51 | .224 | 354 | 324 | 20 | .971 |
| Major League Totals ...... | | 608 | 2153 | 256 | 545 | 77 | 18 | 11 | 192 | .253 | 1306 | 1243 | 93 | .965 |

## WILLIAM LARRY RANDOLPH, JR.
### (Willie)

Born July 6, 1954, at Holly Hill, S. C.
Height, 5.11. Weight, 165.
Throws and bats righthanded.
Hobbies–Bowling, movies and listening to jazz music.

Tied major league record for most assists by second baseman in extra-inning game since 1900 with 13, August 25, 1976 (19 innings).

Established American League record for most chances accepted by second baseman in extra-inning game with 20, August 25, 1976 (19 innings).

Major League stolen bases: 1975 (1), 1976 (37). Total–38.

Led Western Carolinas League batters in walks with 90 and tied for lead in sacrifice flies with 8 in 1973.

Led Eastern League batters in walks with 110 in 1974.

| Year Club League | Pos. | G. | AB. | R. | H. | 2B. | 3B. | HR. | RBI. | B.A. | PO. | A. | E. | F.A. |
|---|---|---|---|---|---|---|---|---|---|---|---|---|---|---|
| 1972–Brad'n Pirates ..Gulf C. | SS-OF | 44 | 167 | 21 | 53 | 6 | 5 | 0 | 10 | .317 | 85 | 116 | 24 | .893 |
| 1973–Charleston ........W. Car. | 2B | 121 | 428 | 93 | 120 | 25 | 6 | 8 | 51 | .280 | •285 | 308 | •24 | .961 |
| 1974–Thetford Mines..East. | 2B | 135 | 461 | •103 | 117 | 28 | 6 | 12 | 53 | .254 | 269 | 319 | 21 | .966 |
| 1975–Charleston ........Int. | 2B | 91 | 313 | 41 | 106 | 13 | 5 | 7 | 42 | .339 | 189 | 250 | 16 | .965 |
| 1975–Pittsburgh† ........Nat. | 2B-3B | 30 | 61 | 9 | 10 | 1 | 0 | 0 | 3 | .164 | 34 | 45 | 6 | .929 |
| 1976–New York..........Amer. | 2B | 125 | 430 | 59 | 115 | 15 | 4 | 1 | 40 | .267 | 307 | 415 | 19 | .974 |
| National League Totals .................. | | 30 | 61 | 9 | 10 | 1 | 0 | 0 | 3 | .164 | 34 | 45 | 6 | .929 |
| American League Totals ............... | | 125 | 430 | 59 | 115 | 15 | 4 | 1 | 40 | .267 | 307 | 415 | 19 | .974 |
| Major League Totals ...... | | 155 | 491 | 68 | 125 | 16 | 4 | 1 | 43 | .254 | 341 | 460 | 25 | .970 |

†Traded with Pitchers Ken Brett and Dock Ellis to New York Yankees for Pitcher Doc Medich, December 11, 1975.

### CHAMPIONSHIP SERIES RECORD

| Year Club League | Pos. | G. | AB. | R. | H. | 2B. | 3B. | HR. | RBI. | B.A. | PO. | A. | E. | F.A. |
|---|---|---|---|---|---|---|---|---|---|---|---|---|---|---|
| 1976–New York..........Amer. | 2B | 5 | 17 | 0 | 2 | 0 | 0 | 0 | 1 | .118 | 8 | 14 | 0 | 1.000 |

### WORLD SERIES RECORD

| Year Club League | Pos. | G. | AB. | R. | H. | 2B. | 3B. | HR. | RBI. | B.A. | PO. | A | E. | F.A. |
|---|---|---|---|---|---|---|---|---|---|---|---|---|---|---|
| 1976–New York..........Amer. | 2B | 4 | 14 | 1 | 1 | 0 | 0 | 0 | 0 | .071 | 13 | 8 | 0 | 1.000 |

## ERIC RALPH RASMUSSEN

Name pronounced ras-MUSS-un.
(Formerly known as Harry)

Born March 22, 1952, at Racine, Wis.
Height, 6.03. Weight, 205.
Throws and bats righthanded.
Hobbies–Music, camping, skeet shooting and movies.
Attended Indian Hills Community College, Centerville, Ia., and
University of New Orleans, New Orleans, La.

Tied for Texas League lead in complete games by pitchers with 13 in 1974.

| Year Club | League | G. | IP. | W. | L. | Pct. | H. | R. | ER. | SO. | BB. | ERA. |
|---|---|---|---|---|---|---|---|---|---|---|---|---|
| 1973–Sarasota Cardinals ............Gulf C. | | 3 | 23 | 2 | 0 | 1.000 | 16 | 4 | 3 | 27 | 4 | 1.17 |
| 1973–St. Petersburg....................Florida St. | | 8 | 52 | 3 | 3 | .500 | 47 | 17 | 13 | 33 | 6 | 2.25 |
| 1974–Arkansas............................Texas | | 22 | 159 | •14 | 5 | .737 | 154 | 65 | 55 | 121 | 32 | 3.11 |
| 1975–Tulsa ................................Am. Assoc. | | 18 | 129 | 10 | 5 | .667 | 133 | 56 | 53 | 89 | 36 | 3.70 |
| 1975–St. Louis ...........................National | | 14 | 81 | 5 | 5 | .500 | 86 | 44 | 34 | 59 | 20 | 3.78 |
| 1976–St. Louis ...........................National | | 43 | 150 | 6 | 12 | .333 | 139 | 67 | 59 | 76 | 54 | 3.54 |
| Major League Totals ........................... | | 57 | 231 | 11 | 17 | .393 | 225 | 111 | 93 | 135 | 74 | 3.62 |

## DOUGLAS JAMES RAU

Last name rhymes with cow.

### (Doug)

Born December 15, 1948, at Columbus, Tex.
Height, 6.02. Weight, 180.
Throws and bats lefthanded.
Hobbies–Fishing, cars, hunting, and golf.
Attended Texas A&M University, College Station, Tex.; received Bachelor of
Science degree in Finance and Economics.

Tied California League record with 21 strikeouts in nine-inning game, July 18, 1970.
Named California League Rookie of the Year in 1970.

| Year Club | League | G. | IP. | W. | L. | Pct. | H. | R. | ER. | SO. | BB. | ERA. |
|---|---|---|---|---|---|---|---|---|---|---|---|---|
| 1970–Bakersfield | California | 15 | 113 | 12 | 2 | .857 | 86 | 34 | 22 | 140 | 18 | 1.75 |
| 1970–Spokane | P. Coast | 1 | 1 | 0 | 0 | .000 | 7 | 6 | 5 | 1 | 0 | 45.00 |
| 1971–Albuquerque | Texas | 15 | 117 | 7 | 5 | .583 | 97 | 34 | 22 | 96 | 29 | 1.69 |
| 1971–Spokane | P. Coast | 13 | 86 | 5 | 5 | .500 | 98 | 48 | 37 | 79 | 30 | 3.87 |
| 1972–Albuquerque | P. Coast | 26 | 172 | 14 | 3 | *.824 | 167 | 80 | 67 | 133 | 70 | 3.51 |
| 1972–Los Angeles | National | 7 | 33 | 2 | 2 | .500 | 18 | 11 | 8 | 19 | 11 | 2.18 |
| 1973–Los Angeles | National | 31 | 64 | 4 | 2 | .667 | 64 | 28 | 28 | 51 | 28 | 3.94 |
| 1974–Los Angeles | National | 36 | 198 | 13 | 11 | .542 | 191 | 90 | 82 | 126 | 70 | 3.73 |
| 1975–Los Angeles | National | 38 | 258 | 15 | 9 | .625 | 227 | 96 | 89 | 151 | 61 | 3.10 |
| 1976–Los Angeles | National | 34 | 231 | 16 | 12 | .571 | 221 | 71 | 66 | 98 | 69 | 2.57 |
| Major League Totals | | 146 | 784 | 50 | 36 | .581 | 721 | 296 | 273 | 445 | 239 | 3.13 |

CHAMPIONSHIP SERIES RECORD

| Year Club | League | G. | IP. | W. | L. | Pct. | H. | R. | ER. | SO. | BB. | ERA. |
|---|---|---|---|---|---|---|---|---|---|---|---|---|
| 1974–Los Angeles | National | 1 | ⅔ | 0 | 1 | .000 | 3 | 5 | 3 | 0 | 1 | 40.50 |

## CLARENCE GEORGE RAUTZHAN

Name pronounced ROTZ-han.

### (Lance)

Born August 20, 1952, at Pottsville, Pa.
Height, 6.01. Weight, 195.
Throws left and bats righthanded.
Hobby–Hunting.
Son of William E. Rautzhan, Sr., first baseman in Chicago White Sox'
organization, 1946 through 1949.

Led Eastern League pitchers in complete games with 21 and tied for lead in games started with 28 in 1975.
Tied for Florida State League lead in complete games by pitchers with 16 in 1971.

| Year Club | League | G. | IP. | W. | L. | Pct. | H. | R. | ER. | SO. | BB. | ERA. |
|---|---|---|---|---|---|---|---|---|---|---|---|---|
| 1970–Ogden | Pioneer | 14 | 85 | 7 | 1 | .875 | 73 | 43 | 25 | 84 | 36 | 2.65 |
| 1971–Daytona Beach | Florida St. | 25 | 173 | 14 | 5 | .737 | 146 | 56 | 40 | 119 | 66 | 2.08 |
| 1972–Bakersfield | California | 24 | 109 | 10 | 9 | .526 | 117 | 68 | 47 | 91 | 56 | 3.88 |
| 1973–Waterbury | Eastern | 26 | 92 | 4 | 7 | .364 | 94 | 54 | 45 | 64 | 50 | 4.40 |
| 1974–Waterbury | Eastern | 25 | 164 | 11 | 11 | .389 | 161 | 78 | 59 | 68 | 57 | 3.24 |
| 1975–Waterbury | Eastern | 28 | *218 | 14 | 10 | .583 | *200 | 73 | 50 | 115 | 62 | 2.06 |
| 1976–Albuquerque | P. Coast | 40 | 81 | 3 | 5 | .375 | 97 | 50 | 38 | 48 | 41 | 4.22 |

Listed on Los Angeles Dodgers' 1977 spring roster.

## SHANE WILLIAM RAWLEY

Born July 27, 1955, at Racine, Wis.
Height, 6.00. Weight, 170.
Throws left and bats righthanded.
Hobby–Airplanes.
Attended Indian Hills Communtiy College, Centerville, Ia.

| Year Club | League | G. | IP. | W. | L. | Pct. | H. | R. | ER. | SO. | BB. | ERA. |
|---|---|---|---|---|---|---|---|---|---|---|---|---|
| 1974–Sarasota Expos | Gulf Coast | 2 | 12 | 0 | 1 | .000 | 12 | 9 | 3 | 16 | 4 | 2.25 |
| 1974–Kinston | Carolina | 5 | 19 | 0 | 2 | .000 | 22 | 15 | 13 | 11 | 12 | 6.16 |
| 1975–West Palm Beach | Florida St. | 24 | 165 | 8 | 12 | .400 | 148 | 80 | 56 | 113 | 73 | 3.05 |
| 1976–Quebec City | Eastern | 25 | 164 | 11 | 7 | .611 | 143 | 55 | 49 | 113 | 79 | 2.69 |

Listed on Montreal Expos' 1977 spring roster.

## PETER IRVING REDFERN

### (Pete)

Born August 25, 1954, at Glendale, Calif.
Height, 6.02. Weight, 195.
Throws and bats righthanded.
Hobbies–Music and water skiing.
Attended University of Southern California, Los Angeles, Calif.

Received reported $40,000 bonus to sign with Minnesota Twins, 1976.

| Year Club | League | G. | IP. | W. | L. | Pct. | H. | R. | ER. | SO. | BB. | ERA. |
|---|---|---|---|---|---|---|---|---|---|---|---|---|
| 1976–Tacoma | P. Coast | 4 | 27 | 2 | 1 | .667 | 23 | 8 | 8 | 18 | 9 | 2.67 |
| 1976–Minnesota | American | 23 | 118 | 8 | 8 | .500 | 105 | 61 | 46 | 74 | 63 | 3.51 |
| Major League Totals | | 23 | 118 | 8 | 8 | .500 | 105 | 61 | 46 | 74 | 63 | 3.51 |

**DID YOU KNOW —**

That Billy Pierce, pitching for the Detroit Tigers, Chicago White Sox and San Francisco Giants, won 211 games during his major league career? He hurled from 1945 to 1964.

## RONALD LEE REED
## (Ron)

Born November 2, 1942, at La Porte, Ind.
Height, 6.06. Weight, 215.
Throws and bats righthanded.
Attended University of Notre Dame, Notre Dame, Ind.
Played professional basketball with Detroit Pistons, 1965-66 and 1966-67.
Led International League in complete games with 17 and tied for lead in shutouts with 5 in 1967.

| Year    Club | League | G. | IP. | W. | L. | Pct. | H. | R. | ER. | SO. | BB. | ERA. |
|---|---|---|---|---|---|---|---|---|---|---|---|---|
| 1965—West Palm Beach | Florida St. | 7 | 43 | 3 | 2 | .600 | 27 | 7 | 7 | 35 | 9 | 1.47 |
| 1966—Kinston | Carolina | 8 | 51 | 5 | 2 | .714 | 43 | 16 | 10 | 39 | 12 | 1.76 |
| 1966—Austin | Texas | 4 | 30 | 3 | 1 | .750 | 19 | 4 | 4 | 22 | 7 | 1.20 |
| 1966—Richmond | Int'national | 14 | 87 | 5 | 2 | .714 | 74 | 36 | 34 | 68 | 26 | 3.52 |
| 1966—Atlanta | National | 2 | 8 | 1 | 1 | .500 | 7 | 2 | 2 | 6 | 4 | 2.25 |
| 1967—Richmond | Int'national | 28 | •222 | 14 | 10 | .583 | 179 | 68 | 62 | 172 | 53 | 2.51 |
| 1967—Atlanta | National | 3 | 21 | 1 | 1 | .500 | 21 | 8 | 7 | 11 | 3 | 3.00 |
| 1968—Atlanta | National | 35 | 202 | 11 | 10 | .524 | 189 | 87 | 75 | 111 | 49 | 3.34 |
| 1969—Atlanta | National | 36 | 241 | 18 | 10 | .643 | 227 | 103 | 93 | 160 | 56 | 3.47 |
| 1970—Shreveport | Texas | 2 | 7 | 0 | 0 | .000 | 5 | 2 | 2 | 6 | 2 | 2.57 |
| 1970—Atlanta† | National | 21 | 135 | 7 | 10 | .412 | 140 | 69 | 66 | 68 | 39 | 4.40 |
| 1971—Atlanta | National | 32 | 222 | 13 | 14 | .481 | 221 | 105 | 92 | 129 | 54 | 3.73 |
| 1972—Atlanta | National | 31 | 213 | 11 | 15 | .423 | 222 | 109 | 93 | 111 | 60 | 3.93 |
| 1973—Atlanta‡ | National | 20 | 116 | 4 | 11 | .267 | 133 | 71 | 57 | 64 | 31 | 4.42 |
| 1974—Atlanta§ | National | 28 | 186 | 10 | 11 | .476 | 171 | 76 | 70 | 78 | 41 | 3.39 |
| 1975—Atlanta x-St. Louis y | National | 34 | 250 | 13 | 13 | .500 | 274 | 118 | 98 | 139 | 53 | 3.53 |
| 1976—Philadelphia | National | 59 | 128 | 8 | 7 | .533 | 88 | 39 | 35 | 96 | 32 | 2.46 |
| Major League Totals | | 301 | 1722 | 97 | 103 | .485 | 1693 | 787 | 688 | 973 | 422 | 3.60 |

†On disabled list, March 24 through June 3, 1970.
‡On disabled list, July 10 to September 11, 1973.
§On disabled list, May 16 to June 25, 1974.
xTraded with a player to be named later to St. Louis Cardinals for Pitchers Elias Sosa and Ray Sadecki, May 28, 1975; Braves sent Outfielder Wayne Nordhagen to Cardinals, June 2, 1975, to complete deal.
yTraded to Philadelphia Phillies for Outfielder Mike Anderson, December 9, 1975.

### CHAMPIONSHIP SERIES RECORD

| Year    Club | League | G. | IP. | W. | L. | Pct. | H. | R. | ER. | SO. | BB. | ERA. |
|---|---|---|---|---|---|---|---|---|---|---|---|---|
| 1969—Atlanta | National | 1 | 1⅔ | 0 | 1 | .000 | 5 | 4 | 4 | 3 | 3 | 21.60 |
| 1976—Philadelphia | National | 2 | 4⅔ | 0 | 0 | .000 | 6 | 4 | 4 | 2 | 2 | 7.20 |
| Championship Series Totals | | 3 | 6⅓ | 0 | 1 | .000 | 11 | 8 | 8 | 5 | 5 | 11.37 |

### ALL-STAR GAME RECORD

| Year    League | IP. | W. | L. | Pct. | H. | R. | ER. | SO. | BB. | ERA. |
|---|---|---|---|---|---|---|---|---|---|---|
| 1968—National | ⅓ | 0 | 0 | .000 | 0 | 0 | 0 | 1 | 0 | 0.00 |

## KENNETH JOHN REITZ
## (Ken)

Born June 24, 1951, at San Francisco, Calif.
Height, 6.00. Weight, 186.
Throws and bats righthanded.
Hobby—Raising horses.
Brother of Roy Reitz, outfielder-first baseman in San Francisco Giants'
organization, 1963 through 1966.
Led American Association third basemen in double plays with 35 in 1972 and led Texas League third basemen with 33 in 1971.
Named third baseman on THE SPORTING NEWS National League All-Star fielding team, 1975.

| Year    Club | League | Pos. | G. | AB. | R. | H. | 2B. | 3B. | HR. | RBI. | B.A. | PO. | A. | E. | F.A. |
|---|---|---|---|---|---|---|---|---|---|---|---|---|---|---|---|
| 1969—Sarasota Cards | Gulf C. | 2B-3 | 11 | 37 | 8 | 12 | 2 | 0 | 0 | 4 | .324 | 17 | 20 | 2 | .949 |
| 1969—Cedar Rapids | Midw. | 1-2-3 | 35 | 136 | 7 | 38 | 8 | 0 | 2 | 15 | .279 | 125 | 33 | 10 | .940 |
| 1970—St. Petersburg | Fla. St. | 3B-1 | 127 | •513 | 51 | 149 | •33 | 1 | 6 | 75 | .290 | 150 | 241 | 27 | .935 |
| 1971—Arkansas | Tex. | 3B | 131 | 505 | 48 | 137 | 29 | 0 | 7 | 53 | .271 | •116 | •316 | 17 | •.962 |
| 1972—Tulsa | A. A. | 3B | 118 | 462 | 52 | 129 | 26 | 1 | 15 | 66 | .279 | •106 | •259 | •25 | .936 |
| 1972—St. Louis | Nat. | 3B | 21 | 78 | 5 | 28 | 4 | 0 | 0 | 10 | .359 | 17 | 26 | 2 | .956 |
| 1973—St. Louis | Nat. | •3B-SS | 147 | 426 | 40 | 100 | 20 | 2 | 6 | 42 | .235 | 88 | 213 | 8 | •.974 |
| 1974—St. Louis | Nat. | •3B-S-2 | 154 | 579 | 48 | 157 | 28 | 2 | 7 | 54 | .271 | 131 | 281 | 12 | •.972 |
| 1975—St. Louis† | Nat. | 3B | 161 | 592 | 43 | 159 | 25 | 1 | 5 | 63 | .269 | 124 | 279 | 23 | .946 |
| 1976—San Francisco‡ | Nat. | 3B-SS | 155 | 577 | 40 | 154 | 21 | 1 | 5 | 66 | .267 | 141 | 304 | 19 | .959 |
| Major League Totals | | | 638 | 2252 | 176 | 598 | 98 | 6 | 23 | 235 | .266 | 501 | 1103 | 64 | .962 |

†Traded to San Francisco Giants for Pitcher Pete Falcone, December 8, 1975.
‡Traded to St. Louis Cardinals for Pitcher Lynn McGlothen, December 10, 1976.

## GERALD PETER REMY
## (Jerry)

Born November 8, 1952, at Fall Rivers, Mass.
Height, 5.09. Weight, 165.
Throws right and bats lefthanded.
Hobby—Reading.
Attended Roger Williams College, Bristol, R. I.

Major League stolen bases: 1975 (4), 1976 (35). Total—69.
Led Midwest League second basemen in double plays with 73 in 1973.
Led California League second basemen in double plays with 86 in 1972.
Named Most Valuable Player in Midwest League, 1973.

| Year | Club | League | Pos. | G. | AB. | R. | H. | 2B. | 3B. | HR. | RBI. | B.A. | PO. | A. | E. | F.A. |
|------|------|--------|------|-----|------|-----|------|-----|-----|-----|------|------|------|------|-----|------|
| 1971—Magic Valley | ....Pion. | | 2B-OF | 32 | 104 | 25 | 32 | 5 | 3 | 0 | 6 | .308 | 61 | 54 | 5 | .958 |
| 1972—Stockton | ...........Calif. | | •2B-SS | 133 | 532 | 59 | 141 | 18 | 3 | 4 | 43 | .265 | 275 | •404 | 28 | .960 |
| 1973—Quad Cities | ......Midw. | | 2B | 117 | 478 | 66 | •160 | 23 | 10 | 4 | 36 | •.335 | •277 | •330 | 24 | .962 |
| 1974—El Paso | ...........Tex. | | 2B | 91 | 394 | 74 | 133 | 34 | 5 | 4 | 46 | .338 | 233 | 267 | 18 | .965 |
| 1974—Salt Lake City | ..P. C. | | 2B | 48 | 195 | 33 | 57 | 6 | 5 | 0 | 21 | .292 | 108 | 135 | 7 | .972 |
| 1975—California | .........Amer. | | 2B | 147 | 569 | 82 | 147 | 17 | 5 | 1 | 46 | .258 | 336 | 427 | 14 | .982 |
| 1976—California | .........Amer. | | 2B-DH | 143 | 502 | 64 | 132 | 14 | 3 | 0 | 28 | .263 | 279 | 406 | 16 | .977 |
| Major League Totals | ..................... | | | 290 | 1071 | 146 | 279 | 31 | 8 | 1 | 74 | .260 | 615 | 833 | 30 | .980 |

†On disabled list, August 12 through remainder of season.


## STEVEN RENKO, JR.
### (Steve)

Born December 10, 1944, at Kansas City, Kan.
Height, 6.05. Weight, 230.
Throws and bats righthanded.
Hobbies—Golf and riding horses.
Attended University of Kansas, Lawrence, Kan.

Led National League in wild pitches with 19 in 1974.
Pitched seven-inning, 1-0 no-hit victory against Albuquerque, July 21, 1968.

| Year | Club | League | G. | IP. | W. | L. | Pct. | H. | R. | ER. | SO. | BB. | ERA. |
|------|------|--------|-----|------|-----|-----|------|------|-----|-----|------|------|------|
| 1966—Williamsport | ......................Eastern | | 1 | 2 | 0 | 0 | .000 | 0 | 0 | 0 | 2 | 1 | 0.00 |
| 1967—Winter Haven† | ....................Florida St. | | 11 | 84 | 8 | 1 | .889 | 44 | 17 | 15 | 109 | 39 | 1.61 |
| 1968—Memphis | ...............................Texas | | 22 | 145 | 7 | 11 | .389 | 116 | 63 | 53 | 106 | 73 | 3.29 |
| 1968—Jacksonville | ......................Int'national | | 7 | 51 | 4 | 1 | .800 | 35 | 20 | 17 | 41 | 17 | 3.00 |
| 1969—Tidewater‡ | .........................Int'national | | 12 | 66 | 3 | 6 | .333 | 56 | 43 | 40 | 57 | 43 | 5.45 |
| 1969—Montreal | ...............................National | | 18 | 103 | 6 | 7 | .462 | 94 | 54 | 46 | 68 | 50 | 4.02 |
| 1970—Montreal | ...............................National | | 41 | 223 | 13 | 11 | .542 | 203 | 121 | 107 | 142 | 104 | 4.32 |
| 1971—Montreal | ...............................National | | 40 | 276 | 15 | 14 | .517 | 256 | 128 | •115 | 129 | 135 | 3.75 |
| 1972—Montreal | ...............................National | | 30 | 97 | 1 | 10 | .091 | 96 | 60 | 56 | 66 | 67 | 5.20 |
| 1973—Montreal | ...............................National | | 36 | 250 | 15 | 11 | .577 | 201 | 94 | 78 | 164 | 108 | 2.81 |
| 1974—Montreal | ...............................National | | 37 | 228 | 12 | 16 | .429 | 222 | 115 | 102 | 138 | 81 | 4.03 |
| 1975—Montreal | ...............................National | | 31 | 170 | 6 | 12 | .333 | 175 | 89 | 77 | 99 | 76 | 4.08 |
| 1976—Mont.§-Chi. | .........................National | | 33 | 176 | 8 | 12 | .400 | 179 | 87 | 78 | 116 | 46 | 3.99 |
| Major League Totals | .............................. | | 266 | 1523 | 76 | 93 | .445 | 1426 | 748 | 659 | 922 | 667 | 3.89 |

†On disabled list from July 30 through end of season with left shoulder separation.

‡Recalled by New York Mets and traded to Montreal Expos with Infielder Kevin Collins (recalled from Tidewater), Pitcher Jay Carden (on Memphis roster) and Pitcher Dave Colon (with Marion) for First Baseman Donn Clendenon, June 15, 1969.

§Traded with Outfielder-First Baseman Larry Biittner to Chicago Cubs for First Baseman Andy Thornton, May 17, 1976.

### RECORD AS FIRST BASEMAN

| Year | Club | League | Pos. | G. | AB. | R. | H. | 2B. | 3B. | HR. | RBI. | B.A. | PO. | A. | E. | F.A. |
|------|------|--------|------|-----|------|-----|------|-----|-----|-----|------|------|------|------|-----|------|
| 1965—Marion | ..............Appal. | | 1-OF | 50 | 169 | 39 | 49 | 3 | 3 | 7 | 32 | .290 | 199 | 11 | 11 | .950 |
| 1966—Auburn | ..............NYP | | 1B | 69 | 246 | 38 | 57 | 10 | 2 | 10 | 42 | .232 | 516 | 33 | 12 | .979 |
| 1966—Williamsport | ......East. | | •1B-P | 59 | 195 | 20 | 33 | 3 | 0 | 7 | 18 | .169 | 450 | 24 | •11 | .977 |
| 1967—Winter Haven | ....Fla. St. | | 1-P-O | 71 | 197 | 27 | 43 | 3 | 1 | 8 | 24 | .218 | 355 | 36 | 8 | .980 |
| 1969—Tidewater | ..........Int. | | P-1B | 18 | 16 | 3 | 5 | 1 | 0 | 1 | 5 | .313 | 15 | 4 | 1 | .950 |
| 1972—Montreal | .........Nat. | | P-1B | 32 | 24 | 0 | 7 | 0 | 0 | 0 | 0 | .292 | 9 | 17 | 1 | .963 |


## MERVIN WELDON RETTENMUND
### (Merv)

Born June 6, 1943, at Flint, Mich.
Height, 5.11. Weight, 195.
Throws and bats righthanded.
Hobbies—Badminton, music and reading.
Attended Ball State University, Muncie, Ind.; received Bachelor of Science degree in Education.

Tied major league record for most bases on balls, inning (2), June 22, 1970, 9th inning.
Tied for American League lead in double plays by outfielders with 4 in 1971.
Led California League outfielders in double plays with 6 in 1965.
Led Eastern League batters in walks with 90 in 1967.
Led International League batters in walks with 85 in 1968.
Named THE SPORTING NEWS Minor League Player of the Year, 1968.
Named as outfielder on THE SPORTING NEWS American League All-Star Team, 1971.

| Year | Club | League | Pos. | G. | AB. | R. | H. | 2B. | 3B. | HR. | RBI. | B.A. | PO. | A. | E. | F.A. |
|------|------|--------|------|-----|------|-----|------|-----|-----|-----|------|------|------|------|-----|------|
| 1965—Stockton | ...........Calif. | | OF | 129 | 361 | 85 | 88 | 13 | 3 | 11 | 38 | .244 | 212 | 16 | 5 | .979 |
| 1966—Stockton | ...........Calif. | | OF | 127 | 440 | 85 | 135 | 16 | 6 | 21 | 69 | .307 | •280 | 6 | 7 | .976 |
| 1967—Elmira | ..............East. | | OF | 131 | 423 | 67 | 121 | 17 | 3 | 4 | 51 | .286 | 246 | 10 | 7 | .973 |
| 1968—Baltimore | .........Amer. | | OF | 31 | 64 | 10 | 19 | 5 | 0 | 2 | 7 | .297 | 29 | 1 | 0 | 1.000 |

| Year Club | League | Pos. | G. | AB. | R. | H. | 2B. | 3B. | HR. | RBI. | B.A. | PO. | A. | E. | F.A. |
|---|---|---|---|---|---|---|---|---|---|---|---|---|---|---|---|
| 1968–Rochester..........Int. | OF | | 114 | 393 | •104 | 130 | 25 | 5 | 22 | 59 | •.331 | 251 | 11 | 4 | .985 |
| 1969–Baltimore..........Amer. | OF | | 95 | 190 | 27 | 47 | 10 | 3 | 4 | 25 | .247 | 107 | 3 | 1 | .991 |
| 1970–Baltimore..........Amer. | OF | | 106 | 338 | 60 | 109 | 17 | 2 | 18 | 58 | .322 | 201 | 6 | 5 | .976 |
| 1971–Baltimore..........Amer. | OF | | 141 | 491 | 81 | 156 | 23 | 4 | 11 | 75 | .318 | 292 | 7 | 7 | .977 |
| 1972–Baltimore†........Amer. | OF | | 102 | 301 | 40 | 70 | 10 | 2 | 6 | 21 | .233 | 174 | 6 | 2 | .989 |
| 1973–Baltimore‡........Amer. | OF | | 95 | 321 | 59 | 84 | 17 | 2 | 9 | 44 | .262 | 196 | 4 | 3 | .985 |
| 1974–Cincinnati..........Nat. | OF | | 80 | 208 | 30 | 45 | 6 | 0 | 6 | 28 | .216 | 103 | 3 | 0 | 1.000 |
| 1975–Cincinnati..........Nat. | OF-3B | | 93 | 188 | 24 | 45 | 6 | 1 | 2 | 19 | .239 | 99 | 2 | 0 | 1.000 |
| 1976–San Diego..........Nat. | OF-PH | | 86 | 140 | 16 | 32 | 7 | 0 | 2 | 11 | .229 | 79 | 6 | 2 | .977 |
| American League Totals | | | 570 | 1705 | 277 | 485 | 82 | 13 | 50 | 230 | .284 | 999 | 27 | 18 | .983 |
| National League Totals | | | 259 | 536 | 70 | 122 | 19 | 1 | 10 | 58 | .228 | 281 | 11 | 2 | .993 |
| Major League Totals | | | 829 | 2241 | 347 | 607 | 101 | 14 | 60 | 288 | .271 | 1280 | 38 | 20 | .985 |

†On supplemental disabled list, August 25 through September 9.

‡Traded with Infielder Junior Kennedy and Catcher Bill Wood to Cincinnati Reds for Pitcher Ross Grimsley and Catcher Wally Williams, December 4, 1973.

§Traded to San Diego Padres for Infielder Rudy Meoli and cash, April 5, 1976.

### CHAMPIONSHIP SERIES RECORD

| Year Club | League | Pos. | G. | AB. | R. | H. | 2B. | 3B. | HR. | RBI. | B.A. | PO. | A. | E. | F.A. |
|---|---|---|---|---|---|---|---|---|---|---|---|---|---|---|---|
| 1969–Baltimore..........Amer. | PH | 1 | 0 | 0 | 0 | 0 | 0 | 0 | 0 | .000 | 0 | 0 | 0 | .000 |
| 1970–Baltimore..........Amer. | OF | 1 | 3 | 1 | 1 | 0 | 0 | 0 | 1 | .333 | 3 | 1 | 0 | 1.000 |
| 1971–Baltimore..........Amer. | PR-OF | 3 | 8 | 0 | 2 | 1 | 0 | 0 | 1 | .250 | 7 | 0 | 0 | 1.000 |
| 1973–Baltimore‡........Amer. | OF | 3 | 11 | 1 | 1 | 0 | 0 | 0 | 0 | .091 | 3 | 0 | 0 | 1.000 |
| 1975–Cincinnati§........Nat. | PH | 2 | 1 | 1 | 0 | 0 | 0 | 0 | 0 | .000 | 0 | 0 | 0 | .000 |
| Championship Series Totals | | 10 | 23 | 3 | 4 | 1 | 0 | 0 | 2 | .174 | 13 | 1 | 0 | 1.000 |

### WORLD SERIES RECORD

Tied World Series record for most hits, inning, 2, October 11, 1971, fifth inning.

| Year Club | League | Pos. | G. | AB. | R. | H. | 2B. | 3B. | HR. | RBI. | B.A. | PO. | A. | E. | F.A. |
|---|---|---|---|---|---|---|---|---|---|---|---|---|---|---|---|
| 1969–Baltimore..........Amer. | PR | 1 | 0 | 0 | 0 | 0 | 0 | 0 | 0 | .000 | 0 | 0 | 0 | .000 |
| 1970–Baltimore..........Amer. | PH-OF | 2 | 5 | 2 | 2 | 0 | 0 | 1 | 2 | .400 | 3 | 0 | 0 | 1.000 |
| 1971–Baltimore..........Amer. | PH-OF | 7 | 27 | 3 | 5 | 0 | 0 | 1 | 4 | .185 | 17 | 0 | 0 | 1.000 |
| 1975–Cincinnati..........Nat. | PH | 3 | 3 | 0 | 0 | 0 | 0 | 0 | 0 | .000 | 0 | 0 | 0 | .000 |
| World Series Totals | | 13 | 35 | 5 | 7 | 0 | 0 | 2 | 6 | .200 | 20 | 0 | 0 | 1.000 |

## PAUL RICHARD REUSCHEL

Name pronounced RUSH-ul.

Born January 12, 1947, at Quincy, Ill.
Height, 6.04. Weight, 225.
Throws and bats righthanded.
Hobby—Reading.
Attended Western Illinois University, Macomb, Ill.; received
Bachelor of Science degree in Physical Education.
Brother of Rick Reuschel, pitcher with Chicago Cubs.

Led American Association in saves with 15 in 1974.

| Year Club | League | G. | IP. | W. | L. | Pct. | H. | R. | ER. | SO. | BB. | ERA. |
|---|---|---|---|---|---|---|---|---|---|---|---|---|
| 1968–Caldwell ..............................Pioneer | 4 | 17 | 0 | 3 | .000 | 19 | 13 | 10 | 15 | 6 | 5.29 |
| 1968–Quincy ..................................Midwest | 11 | 60 | 3 | 5 | .375 | 70 | 39 | 27 | 41 | 10 | 4.05 |
| 1969–Quincy†..................................Midwest | 20 | 127 | 11 | 3 | .786 | 137 | 54 | 40 | 84 | 32 | 2.83 |
| 1970–San Antonio .......................Texas | 32 | 184 | 10 | 10 | .500 | 198 | 80 | 66 | 79 | 59 | 3.23 |
| 1971–Tacoma................................P. Coast | 13 | 38 | 0 | 5 | .000 | 57 | 39 | 35 | 20 | 14 | 8.29 |
| 1971–San Antonio .......................Texas | 17 | 82 | 6 | 8 | .429 | 89 | 44 | 42 | 31 | 20 | 4.61 |
| 1972–Midland................................Texas | 6 | 41 | 2 | 3 | .400 | 56 | 24 | 20 | 16 | 10 | 4.39 |
| 1972–Wichita .............................Am. Assoc. | 22 | 103 | 7 | 4 | .636 | 103 | 38 | 32 | 58 | 28 | 2.80 |
| 1973–Wichita .............................Am. Assoc. | 41 | 89 | 7 | 2 | .778 | 121 | 68 | 53 | 49 | 13 | 5.36 |
| 1974–Wichita .............................Am. Assoc. | •58 | 88 | 5 | 7 | .417 | 109 | 49 | 38 | 67 | 32 | 3.89 |
| 1975–Wichita .............................Am. Assoc. | 35 | 57 | 6 | 4 | .600 | 63 | 35 | 31 | 32 | 28 | 4.89 |
| 1975–Chicago................................National | 28 | 36 | 1 | 3 | .250 | 44 | 15 | 14 | 12 | 13 | 3.50 |
| 1976–Chicago................................National | 50 | 87 | 4 | 2 | .667 | 94 | 46 | 44 | 55 | 33 | 4.55 |
| Major League Totals ............................. | 78 | 123 | 5 | 5 | .500 | 138 | 61 | 58 | 67 | 46 | 4.24 |

†On temporary inactive list, April 27 to May 25, 1969.

## RICKY EUGENE REUSCHEL

Name pronounced RUSH-ul.

### (Rick)

Born May 16, 1949, at Quincy, Ill.
Height, 6.03. Weight, 225.
Throws and bats righthanded.
Attended Western Illinois University, Macomb, Ill.
Brother of Paul Reuschel, pitcher with Chicago Cubs.

Tied major league record for most putouts, pitcher, inning, 3, April 25, 1975, 3rd inning.
Tied National League record for most sacrifice flies allowed in season with 13 in 1976.
Led Northern League pitchers in complete games with 7 and tied for lead in games started with 14 in 1970.

| Year Club | League | G. | IP. | W. | L. | Pct. | H. | R. | ER. | SO. | BB. | ERA. |
|---|---|---|---|---|---|---|---|---|---|---|---|---|
| 1970–Huron .................................Northern | | 14 | 102 | 9 | 2 | .818 | 96 | 52 | 40 | 88 | 22 | 3.52 |
| 1971–San Antonio† ......................Texas | | 16 | 121 | 8 | 4 | .667 | 105 | 40 | 31 | 81 | 15 | 2.31 |
| 1972–Wichita ..............................Am. Assoc. | | 12 | 102 | 9 | 2 | .818 | 78 | 30 | 15 | 72 | 30 | 1.32 |
| 1972–Chicago...............................National | | 21 | 129 | 10 | 8 | .556 | 127 | 46 | 42 | 87 | 29 | 2.93 |
| 1973–Chicago...............................National | | 36 | 237 | 14 | 15 | .483 | 244 | 95 | 79 | 168 | 62 | 3.00 |
| 1974–Chicago...............................National | | 41 | 241 | 13 | 12 | .520 | 262 | 130 | 115 | 160 | 83 | 4.29 |
| 1975–Chicago...............................National | | 38 | 234 | 11 | •17 | .393 | 244 | 116 | 97 | 155 | 67 | 3.73 |
| 1976–Chicago...............................National | | 38 | 260 | 14 | 12 | .538 | 260 | 117 | 100 | 146 | 64 | 3.46 |
| Major League Totals ............................ | | 174 | 1101 | 62 | 64 | .492 | 1137 | 504 | 433 | 716 | 305 | 3.54 |

†On temporary inactive list, July 2, 1971. Transferred to military list, July 8, 1971 through April 10, 1972.

## JERRY REUSS
Name pronounced Royce.

Born June 19, 1949, at St. Louis, Mo.
Height, 6.05. Weight, 200.
Throws and bats lefthanded.
Attended Southern Illinois University, Carbondale, Ill., Central Missouri State College,
Warrensburg, Mo., and University of California at Santa Barbara, Santa Barbara, Calif.
Led National League in hit batsmen with 10 in 1972.
Tied for National League lead in games started by pitchers with 40 in 1973.
Led American Association pitchers in games started with 29 in 1969.
Led Texas League in wild pitches with 16 in 1968.
Received reported $30,000 bonus to sign with St. Louis Cardinals, 1967.

| Year Club | League | G. | IP. | W. | L. | Pct. | H. | R. | ER. | SO. | BB. | ERA. |
|---|---|---|---|---|---|---|---|---|---|---|---|---|
| 1967–Sarasota Cards ...................Gulf Coast | | 2 | 7 | 0 | 0 | .000 | 7 | 6 | 4 | 6 | 3 | 5.14 |
| 1967–Cedar Rapids ......................Midwest | | 9 | 58 | 2 | 5 | .286 | 44 | 20 | 12 | 63 | 19 | 1.86 |
| 1967–Tulsa ..................................P. Coast | | 1 | 1 | 0 | 0 | .000 | 2 | 6 | 6 | 1 | 4 | 54.00 |
| 1968–Arkansas..............................Texas | | 17 | 112 | 7 | 8 | .467 | 75 | 43 | 27 | 86 | 45 | 2.17 |
| 1969–Tulsa ..................................Am. Assoc. | | 30 | •186 | •13 | 11 | .542 | 188 | •112 | 84 | •151 | 116 | 4.06 |
| 1969–St. Louis .............................National | | 1 | 7 | 1 | 0 | 1.000 | 2 | 0 | 0 | 3 | 3 | 0.00 |
| 1970–Tulsa ..................................Am. Assoc. | | 11 | 85 | 7 | 2 | .778 | 69 | 26 | 20 | 69 | 28 | 2.12 |
| 1970–St. Louis .............................National | | 20 | 127 | 7 | 8 | .467 | 132 | 62 | 58 | 74 | 49 | 4.11 |
| 1971–St. Louis† ...........................National | | 36 | 211 | 14 | 14 | .500 | 228 | 125 | 112 | 131 | 109 | 4.78 |
| 1972–Houston ..............................National | | 33 | 192 | 9 | 13 | .409 | 177 | 101 | 89 | 174 | 83 | 4.17 |
| 1973–Houston‡.............................National | | 41 | 279 | 16 | 13 | .552 | 271 | 123 | 116 | 177 | •117 | 3.74 |
| 1974–Pittsburgh............................National | | 35 | 260 | 16 | 11 | .593 | 259 | 115 | 101 | 105 | 101 | 3.50 |
| 1975–Pittsburgh............................National | | 32 | 237 | 18 | 11 | .621 | 224 | 73 | 67 | 131 | 78 | 2.54 |
| 1976–Pittsburgh............................National | | 31 | 209 | 14 | 9 | .609 | 209 | 98 | 82 | 108 | 51 | 3.53 |
| Major League Totals .............................. | | 229 | 1522 | 95 | 79 | .546 | 1502 | 697 | 625 | 903 | 591 | 3.70 |

†Traded to Houston Astros for Pitchers Scipio Spinks and Lance Clemons, April 15, 1972.
‡Traded to Pittsburgh Pirates for Catcher Milt May, October 31, 1972.

### CHAMPIONSHIP SERIES RECORD

| Year Club | League | G. | IP. | W. | L. | Pct. | H. | R. | ER. | SO. | BB. | ERA. |
|---|---|---|---|---|---|---|---|---|---|---|---|---|
| 1974–Pittsburgh............................National | | 2 | 9⅔ | 0 | 2 | .000 | 7 | 4 | 4 | 3 | 8 | 3.72 |
| 1975–Pittsburgh............................National | | 1 | 2⅔ | 0 | 1 | .000 | 4 | 4 | 4 | 1 | 4 | 13.50 |
| Championship Series Totals ..................... | | 3 | 12⅓ | 0 | 3 | .000 | 11 | 8 | 8 | 4 | 12 | 5.84 |

### ALL-STAR GAME RECORD

| Year League | IP. | W. | L. | Pct. | H. | R. | ER. | SO. | BB. | ERA. |
|---|---|---|---|---|---|---|---|---|---|---|
| 1975–National ...................................................... | 3 | 0 | 0 | .000 | 3 | 0 | 0 | 2 | 0 | 0.00 |

## DAVID A. REVERING
### (Dave)

Born February 12, 1953, at Roseville, Calif.
Height, 6.04. Weight, 210.
Throws right and bats lefthanded.
Hobby–Cars.
Led Eastern League batters in walks with 100 and tied for lead in strikeouts with 110 in 1973.
Led Eastern League first basemen in double plays with 105 in 1973.

| Year Club | League | Pos. | G. | AB. | R. | H. | 2B. | 3B. | HR. | RBI. | B.A. | PO. | A. | E. | F.A. |
|---|---|---|---|---|---|---|---|---|---|---|---|---|---|---|---|
| 1971–Brad'ton Reds ..Gulf C | | 1B | 45 | 133 | 24 | 36 | 8 | 3 | •8 | •33 | .271 | •312 | 18 | 2 | •.976 |
| 1972–Tampa ..............Fla. St. | | 1B-O | 126 | 413 | 51 | 112 | •28 | 5 | 8 | 70 | .271 | 1000 | 70 | 24 | .978 |
| 1973–Three Rivers ....East. | | 1B | 117 | 371 | 74 | 97 | 18 | 1 | 16 | 74 | .261 | 958 | 68 | 17 | .984 |
| 1974–Three Rivers ....East. | | 1B | 16 | 47 | 11 | 16 | 3 | 0 | 5 | 12 | .340 | 126 | 10 | 3 | .978 |
| 1974–Indianapolis ......A. A. | | 1B | 94 | 302 | 40 | 80 | 19 | 3 | 15 | 60 | .265 | 707 | 43 | 4 | •.995 |
| 1975–Indianapolis ......A. A. | | 1B | 120 | 382 | 53 | 97 | 15 | 5 | 21 | 71 | .254 | •959 | •91 | 12 | .989 |
| 1976–Indianapolis ......A. A. | | 1B | 123 | 407 | 63 | 118 | 20 | 2 | 27 | 77 | .290 | •1051 | 75 | 7 | .994 |

Listed on Cincinnati Reds' 1977 spring roster.

# GORDON CRAIG REYNOLDS
(Known by middle name.)

Born December 27, 1952, at Houston, Tex.
Height, 6.01. Weight, 175.
Throws right and bats lefthanded.
Hobbies—Golf and bowling.
Attended Houston Baptist College, Houston, Tex.

Led Carolina League shortstops in double plays with 81 in 1973 and tied for International League lead with 64 in 1975.
Tied for Gulf Coast League lead in sacrifice flies with 4 in 1971.

| Year    Club        League | Pos. | G. | AB. | R. | H. | 2B. | 3B. | HR. | RBI. | B.A. | PO. | A. | E. | F.A. |
|---|---|---|---|---|---|---|---|---|---|---|---|---|---|---|
| 1971—Bradenton Pir. ..Gulf C. | SS | 48 | 192 | 26 | 61 | 8 | 0 | 0 | 16 | .318 | •87 | 112 | •25 | .888 |
| 1972—Gastonia† .........W. Car. | SS | 41 | 146 | 18 | 35 | 4 | 1 | 0 | 9 | .240 | 55 | 94 | 12 | .925 |
| 1973—Salem................Carol. | SS-2B | 138 | •558 | 75 | •160 | 18 | 5 | 13 | 86 | .287 | 200 | 395 | 50 | .922 |
| 1973—Charleston ........Int. | SS-3B | 4 | 14 | 2 | 3 | 0 | 0 | 0 | 0 | .214 | 4 | 11 | 1 | .938 |
| 1974—Thetford Mines..East. | SS | 64 | 234 | 31 | 66 | 7 | 0 | 6 | 29 | .282 | 76 | 170 | 13 | .950 |
| 1974—Charleston‡ .....Int. | SS-2B | 36 | 107 | 12 | 36 | 5 | 0 | 0 | 5 | .336 | 40 | 71 | 3 | .974 |
| 1975—Charleston ........Int. | SS | 108 | 425 | 51 | 131 | 22 | 3 | 6 | 42 | .308 | 151 | 287 | 26 | .944 |
| 1975—Pittsburgh ........Nat. | SS | 31 | 76 | 8 | 17 | 3 | 0 | 0 | 4 | .224 | 43 | 82 | 4 | .969 |
| 1976—Charleston .......Int. | SS-2B | 126 | 497 | 57 | 144 | 18 | 1 | 2 | 47 | .290 | 198 | 262 | 31 | .937 |
| 1976—Pittsburgh§........Nat. | SS-2B | 7 | 4 | 1 | 1 | 0 | 0 | 1 | 1 | .250 | 2 | 6 | 1 | .889 |
| Major League Totals ..................... | | 38 | 80 | 9 | 18 | 3 | 0 | 1 | 5 | .225 | 45 | 88 | 5 | .964 |

†On disabled list, June 6 to August 30, 1972.
‡On disabled list, July 31 to August 21, 1974.
§Traded with Infielder Jim Sexton to Seattle Mariners for Pitcher Grant Jackson, December 7, 1976.

# KENNETH LEE REYNOLDS
(Ken)

Born January 4, 1947, at Trevose, Pa.
Height, 5.11. Weight, 180.
Throws and bats lefthanded.
Hobbies—Bowling and golf.
Attended New Mexico Highlands University, Las Vegas, N. M.

Tied National League record for most consecutive games lost at the beginning of season, 12, 1972.
Pitched seven-inning, 3-0 no-hit victory against Sioux Falls, September 2, 1966.
Led Northern League in wild pitches with 18 in 1966.
Led Western Carolinas League in shutouts with 5 and tied for lead in games started with 24 in 1967.
Led American Association pitchers in games started with 32 in 1973.
Tied for Eastern League lead in games started by pitchers with 27 in 1969.

| Year    Club       League | G. | IP. | W. | L. | Pct. | H. | R. | ER. | SO. | BB. | ERA. |
|---|---|---|---|---|---|---|---|---|---|---|---|
| 1966—Huron .....................Northern | 15 | 94 | 9 | 4 | .692 | 72 | 41 | 35 | 124 | •77 | 3.35 |
| 1967—Spartanburg .......................W.Carolinas | 24 | 168 | 13 | 9 | .591 | 123 | 66 | 54 | •215 | •111 | 2.89 |
| 1967—Tidewater ...........................Carolina | 2 | 10 | 0 | 1 | .000 | 10 | 5 | 5 | 10 | 4 | 4.50 |
| 1968—Tidewater ...........................Carolina | 19 | 123 | 10 | 5 | .667 | 97 | 47 | 42 | 132 | 66 | 3.07 |
| 1969—Reading ...........................Eastern | 27 | 192 | •16 | 6 | •.727 | 154 | 91 | 72 | •180 | •110 | 3.38 |
| 1970—Eugene ...........................P. Coast | 29 | 202 | 13 | 10 | .565 | 175 | 95 | 77 | 143 | •106 | 3.43 |
| 1970—Philadelphia .......................National | 4 | 2 | 0 | 0 | .000 | 3 | 0 | 0 | 1 | 4 | 0.00 |
| 1971—Philadelphia .......................National | 35 | 162 | 5 | 9 | .357 | 163 | 89 | 81 | 81 | 82 | 4.50 |
| 1972—Philadelphia† .......................National | 33 | 154 | 2 | 15 | .118 | 149 | 76 | 73 | 87 | 60 | 4.27 |
| 1973—Evansville .......................Am. Assoc. | 33 | •216 | 15 | ●13 | .536 | •209 | 101 | 90 | 135 | 83 | 3.75 |
| 1973—Milwaukee‡ ..........................American | 2 | 7 | 0 | 1 | .000 | 5 | 7 | 6 | 3 | 10 | 7.71 |
| 1974—Tulsa ...............................Am. Assoc. | 24 | 155 | 11 | 9 | .550 | 153 | 71 | 60 | 117 | 74 | 3.48 |
| 1975—Tulsa ...............................Am. Assoc. | 19 | 138 | 10 | 4 | .714 | 106 | 59 | 56 | 103 | 79 | 3.65 |
| 1975—St. Louis§ ...........................National | 10 | 17 | 0 | 1 | .000 | 12 | 4 | 3 | 7 | 11 | 1.59 |
| 1976—San Diego ...........................National | 19 | 32 | 0 | 3 | .000 | 38 | 27 | 23 | 18 | 29 | 6.47 |
| 1976—Syracuse ...........................Int'national | 7 | 11 | 1 | 2 | .333 | 18 | 14 | 12 | 8 | 14 | 9.82 |
| 1976—Hawaii x ...........................P. Coast | 8 | 60 | 5 | 1 | .833 | 58 | 28 | 25 | 44 | 21 | 3.75 |
| National League Totals........................... | 101 | 367 | 7 | 28 | .200 | 365 | 196 | 180 | 194 | 186 | 4.41 |
| American League Totals........................... | 2 | 7 | 0 | 1 | .000 | 5 | 7 | 6 | 3 | 10 | 7.71 |
| Major League Totals ........................... | 103 | 374 | 7 | 29 | .194 | 370 | 203 | 186 | 197 | 196 | 4.48 |

†Traded with Outfielder Joe Lis and Pitcher Ken Sanders to Minnesota Twins for Infielder-Outfielder Cesar Tovar, November 30, 1972; traded by Minnesota Twins to Milwaukee Brewers for Third Baseman Mike Ferraro (assigned to Tacoma), March 27, 1973.
‡Sold to Tulsa (St. Louis Cardinals' organization), October 2, 1973.
§Traded with Pitcher Bob Stewart to San Diego Padres for Pitcher Danny Frisella, April 8, 1976.
xSold to Toronto Blue Jays, March 22, 1977. Released, March 31, 1977.

# RICHARD ALAN RHODEN
(Rick)

Born May 16, 1953, at Boynton Beach, Fla.
Height, 6.04. Weight, 195.
Throws and bats righthanded.
Hobbies—Golf, fishing, hunting and ping pong.

Led Pacific Coast League in hit batsmen with 13 in 1974.

| Year Club | League | G. | IP. | W. | L. | Pct. | H. | R. | ER. | SO. | BB. | ERA. |
|---|---|---|---|---|---|---|---|---|---|---|---|---|
| 1971–Daytona Beach .................Florida St. | | 11 | 61 | 4 | 6 | .400 | 59 | 32 | 27 | 67 | 29 | 3.98 |
| 1972–El Paso...............................Texas | | 13 | 87 | 6 | 4 | .600 | 70 | 36 | 32 | 89 | 30 | 3.31 |
| 1972–Albuquerque ......................P. Coast | | 13 | 80 | 7 | 1 | .875 | 83 | 41 | 34 | 55 | 34 | 3.83 |
| 1973–Albuquerque† .....................P. Coast | | 20 | 116 | 4 | 9 | .308 | 117 | 66 | 58 | 68 | 70 | 4.50 |
| 1974–Albuquerque ......................P. Coast | | 26 | 178 | 9 | 10 | .474 | 197 | 103 | 87 | 106 | 65 | 4.40 |
| 1974–Los Angeles .....................National | | 4 | 9 | 1 | 0 | 1.000 | 5 | 2 | 2 | 7 | 4 | 2.00 |
| 1975–Los Angeles .....................National | | 26 | 99 | 3 | 3 | .500 | 94 | 40 | 34 | 40 | 32 | 3.09 |
| 1976–Los Angeles .....................National | | 27 | 181 | 12 | 3 | .800 | 165 | 66 | 60 | 77 | 53 | 2.98 |
| Major League Totals ............................... | | 57 | 289 | 16 | 6 | .727 | 264 | 108 | 96 | 124 | 89 | 2.99 |

†On disabled list, July 20 to August 15, 1973.

### ALL-STAR RECORD

| Year League | IP. | W. | L. | Pct. | H. | R. | ER. | SO. | BB. | ERA. |
|---|---|---|---|---|---|---|---|---|---|---|
| 1976–National ...................................... | 1 | 0 | 0 | .000 | 1 | 0 | 0 | 0 | 0 | .000 |

## FRANK JOSEPH RICCELLI
Name pronounced ruh-SELL-ee.

Born February 24, 1953, at Syracuse, N. Y.
Height, 6.03. Weight, 205.
Throws and bats lefthanded.
Hobbies–Billiards, hunting and fishing.
Led Pioneer League pitchers in games started with 14 in 1971.
Led Texas League in wild pitches with 13 in 1972.

| Year Club | League | G. | IP. | W. | L. | Pct. | H. | R. | ER. | SO. | BB. | ERA. |
|---|---|---|---|---|---|---|---|---|---|---|---|---|
| 1971–Great Falls† .......................Pioneer | | 14 | 88 | 7 | 3 | .700 | 64 | 39 | 25 | 115 | •61 | 2.56 |
| 1972–Amarillo ...........................Texas | | 25 | 164 | 9 | 9 | .500 | 142 | 74 | 58 | •183 | 76 | 3.18 |
| 1973–Phoenix...............................P. Coast | | 27 | 163 | 10 | 11 | .476 | 171 | 98 | 77 | 124 | 83 | 4.25 |
| 1974–Phoenix‡ ...........................P. Coast | | 19 | 73 | 3 | 7 | .300 | 95 | 65 | 20 | 28 | 49 | 6.16 |
| 1975–Lafayette ...........................Texas | | 26 | •185 | 14 | 6 | .700 | 176 | 87 | 67 | 120 | 87 | 3.26 |
| 1976–Phoenix...............................P. Coast | | 30 | 166 | 9 | 11 | .450 | 181 | 110 | 91 | 95 | 114 | 4.93 |
| 1976–San Francisco ....................National | | 4 | 16 | 1 | 1 | .500 | 16 | 10 | 10 | 11 | 5 | 5.63 |
| Major League Totals ............................... | | 4 | 16 | 1 | 1 | .500 | 16 | 10 | 10 | 11 | 5 | 5.63 |

†Appeared in one game as an outfielder.
‡On disabled list, April 11 to April 21 and June 5 to June 24, 1974.

## JAMES EDWARD RICE
### (Jim)

Born March 8, 1953, at Anderson, S. C.
Height, 6.02. Weight, 200.
Throws and bats righthanded.
Led American League batters in strikeouts with 123 in 1976.
Led Florida State League in total bases with 240 in 1972.
Led International League in total bases with 249 in 1974.
Name leftfielder on THE SPORTING NEWS American League All-Star Team, 1975.
Named Minor League Player of the Year by THE SPORTING NEWS, 1974.
Named International League Most Valuable Player in 1974.

| Year Club League | Pos. | G. | AB. | R. | H. | 2B. | 3B. | HR. | RBI. | B.A. | PO. | A. | E. | F.A. |
|---|---|---|---|---|---|---|---|---|---|---|---|---|---|---|
| 1971–Williamsport......NYP | OF | 60 | 223 | 34 | 57 | 9 | 5 | 5 | 27 | .256 | 86 | 2 | 6 | .936 |
| 1972–Winter Haven ....Fla. St. | OF | 130 | •491 | •80 | •143 | 20 | 13 | 17 | 87 | .291 | 190 | 10 | 9 | .957 |
| 1973–Bristol ............East. | OF | 119 | 423 | 66 | 134 | 25 | 4 | 27 | 93 | •.317 | 169 | 13 | 12 | .938 |
| 1973–Pawtucket ........Int. | OF | 10 | 37 | 7 | 14 | 2 | 0 | 4 | 10 | .378 | 21 | 0 | 0 | 1.000 |
| 1974–Pawtucket ........Int. | OF | 117 | 430 | 69 | 145 | 21 | 4 | •25 | •93 | •.337 | 181 | 10 | 11 | .946 |
| 1974–Boston ............Amer. | OF | 24 | 67 | 6 | 18 | 2 | 1 | 1 | 13 | .269 | 4 | 0 | 1 | .800 |
| 1975–Boston ............Amer. | OF | 144 | 564 | 92 | 174 | 29 | 4 | 22 | 102 | .309 | 162 | 6 | 0 | 1.000 |
| 1976–Boston ............Amer. | OF-DH | 153 | 581 | 75 | 164 | 25 | 8 | 25 | 85 | .282 | 199 | 8 | 7 | .967 |
| Major League Totals ..................... | | 321 | 1212 | 173 | 356 | 56 | 13 | 48 | 200 | .294 | 365 | 14 | 8 | .979 |

## JAMES RODNEY RICHARD
### (J. R.)

Born March 7, 1950, at Vienna, La.
Height, 6.08. Weight, 230.
Throws and bats righthanded.
Hobbies–Pool, dancing, movies, art and outdoor sports.
Attended Arizona State University, Tempe, Ariz.

Tied modern major league record for most strikeouts, first major league game, 15, September 5, 1971 (second game of doubleheader).
Pitched seven-inning, 2-0 no-hit victory against Daytona Beach, August 28, 1970.
Led American Association in wild pitches with 18 and tied for lead in shutouts with 3 in 1971.

| Year Club | League | G. | IP. | W. | L. | Pct. | H. | R. | ER. | SO. | BB. | ERA. |
|---|---|---|---|---|---|---|---|---|---|---|---|---|
| 1969–Covington ...........................Ap'alchian | | 12 | 56 | 5 | 4 | .556 | 51 | 50 | 41 | 71 | •52 | 6.59 |
| 1970–Cocoa ...............................Florida St. | | 19 | 109 | 4 | 11 | .267 | 67 | 53 | 29 | 138 | 68 | 2.39 |

| Year | Club | League | G. | IP. | W. | L. | Pct. | H. | R. | ER. | SO. | BB. | ERA. |
|------|------|--------|----|-----|----|----|------|----|----|-----|-----|-----|------|
| 1971 | Oklahoma City | Am. Assoc. | 24 | 173 | 12 | 7 | .632 | 116 | 55 | 47 | •202 | •105 | •2.45 |
| 1971 | Houston | National | 4 | 21 | 2 | 1 | .667 | 17 | 9 | 8 | 29 | 16 | 3.43 |
| 1972 | Oklahoma City | A.A. | 19 | 128 | 10 | 8 | .556 | 94 | 57 | 43 | 169 | 79 | 3.02 |
| 1972 | Houston | Nat. | 4 | 6 | 1 | 0 | 1.000 | 10 | 9 | 9 | 8 | 8 | 13.50 |
| 1973 | Denver | A.A. | 8 | 52 | 2 | 4 | .333 | 54 | 39 | 33 | 66 | 26 | 5.71 |
| 1973 | Houston | Nat. | 16 | 72 | 6 | 2 | .750 | 54 | 37 | 32 | 75 | 38 | 4.00 |
| 1974 | Columbus | Southern | 13 | 87 | 5 | 8 | .385 | 103 | 65 | 52 | 77 | 61 | 5.38 |
| 1974 | Denver | A.A. | 4 | 33 | 4 | 0 | 1.000 | 15 | 2 | 0 | 26 | 12 | 0.00 |
| 1974 | Houston | Nat. | 15 | 65 | 2 | 3 | .400 | 58 | 31 | 30 | 42 | 36 | 4.15 |
| 1975 | Houston | National | 33 | 203 | 12 | 10 | .545 | 178 | 107 | 99 | 176 | •138 | 4.39 |
| 1976 | Houston | National | 39 | 291 | 20 | 15 | .571 | 221 | 105 | 89 | 214 | 151 | 2.75 |
| | Major League Totals | | 111 | 658 | 43 | 31 | .581 | 538 | 298 | 267 | 544 | 387 | 3.65 |

## EDWARD LOUIS RICKS
### (Ed)

Born January 5, 1951, at Bastrop, La.
Height, 6.04. Weight, 200.
Throws and bats righthanded.
Hobbies—Art and music.
Attended Grambling College, Grambling, La.

Pitched seven-inning, 2-0 no-hit victory against Pompano Beach, June 27, 1973.
Tied for Appalachian League lead in games started by pitchers with 13 in 1972.
Tied for Eastern League lead in shutouts with 5 in 1974.

| Year | Club | League | G. | IP. | W. | L. | Pct. | H. | R. | ER. | SO. | BB. | ERA. |
|------|------|--------|----|-----|----|----|------|----|----|-----|-----|-----|------|
| 1972 | Johnson City | Ap'lachian | 13 | •97 | 6 | 6 | .500 | •100 | •72 | •56 | 94 | 49 | 5.20 |
| 1973 | Ft. Lauderdale | Florida St. | 24 | 142 | 9 | 9 | .500 | 105 | 62 | 45 | 124 | 91 | 2.85 |
| 1974 | West Haven | Eastern | 23 | 159 | 11 | 11 | .500 | 151 | 86 | 77 | 125 | 96 | 4.36 |
| 1974 | Syracuse | Int. | 4 | 27 | 2 | 2 | .500 | 20 | 12 | 12 | 21 | 13 | 4.00 |
| 1975 | Syracuse | Int'national | 26 | 149 | 8 | 7 | .533 | 148 | 82 | 72 | 98 | 83 | 4.35 |
| 1976 | Syracuse† | Int'national | 22 | 123 | 10 | 6 | .625 | 129 | 73 | 58 | 68 | 81 | 4.24 |

†On disabled list, April 17 through April 28, 1976.
Listed on New York Yankees' 1977 spring roster.

## ALLEN STEVENS RIPLEY

Born October 18, 1952, at Norwood, Mass.
Height, 6.03. Weight, 190.
Throws and bats righthanded.
Hobbies—Fishing and golfing.
Son of Walt Ripley, pitcher in Boston Red Sox organization, 1932-1945.

| Year | Club | League | G. | IP. | W. | L. | Pct. | H. | R. | ER. | SO. | BB. | ERA. |
|------|------|--------|----|-----|----|----|------|----|----|-----|-----|-----|------|
| 1973 | Elmira | NYP | 14 | 79 | 5 | 6 | .455 | 74 | 34 | 0 | 64 | 26 | 2.96 |
| 1974 | Winston-Salem | Carolina | 28 | 170 | 10 | 9 | .526 | 166 | 87 | 66 | 114 | 73 | 3.49 |
| 1975 | Winston-Salem | Carolina | 25 | •186 | •14 | 7 | .667 | 150 | 70 | 57 | 120 | 75 | 2.76 |
| 1975 | Bristol | Eastern | 1 | 5 | 1 | 0 | 1.000 | 7 | 2 | 1 | 3 | 1 | 1.80 |
| 1976 | Bristol | Eastern | 21 | 161 | 10 | 10 | .500 | 161 | 67 | 58 | 88 | 39 | 3.22 |
| 1976 | Rhode Island | Int'national | 5 | 39 | 3 | 2 | .600 | 40 | 19 | 17 | 33 | 16 | 3.92 |

Listed on Boston Red Sox' 1977 spring roster.

## JESUS TORRES RIVERA, JR.
### (Bombo)

Born August 2, 1952, at Ponce, Puerto Rico.
Height, 5.10. Weight, 187.
Throws and bats righthanded.
Hobbies—Dancing and fishing.

Led Florida State League outfielders in double plays with 5 in 1972.

| Year | Club | League | Pos. | G. | AB. | R. | H. | 2B. | 3B. | HR. | RBI. | B.A. | PO. | A. | E. | F.A. |
|------|------|--------|------|----|-----|----|----|-----|-----|-----|------|------|-----|----|----|------|
| 1970 | Brad'ton Expos | Gulf C. | OF | 39 | 125 | 25 | 30 | 8 | 1 | 4 | 20 | .240 | 45 | 5 | 7 | .877 |
| 1971 | Quebec City | East. | OF | 37 | 83 | 7 | 15 | 3 | 0 | 1 | 10 | .181 | 35 | 1 | 3 | .923 |
| 1971 | Jamestown | NYP | OF-1B | 55 | 210 | 32 | 52 | 6 | 4 | 3 | 22 | .248 | 102 | 2 | 4 | .963 |
| 1972 | W. Palm Beach | Fla. St. | OF | 125 | 439 | 44 | 114 | 14 | 12 | 3 | 60 | .260 | 186 | 7 | 8 | .960 |
| 1973 | Quebec City | East. | OF-3B | 121 | 408 | 48 | 99 | 14 | 5 | 6 | 45 | .243 | 113 | 84 | 28 | .876 |
| 1974 | Quebec City | East. | O-3-C | 108 | 352 | 47 | 102 | 12 | 1 | 7 | 42 | .290 | 180 | 37 | 11 | .952 |
| 1975 | Memphis† | Int. | OF | 40 | 140 | 22 | 41 | 5 | 1 | 9 | 22 | .293 | 57 | 7 | 4 | .941 |
| 1975 | Montreal | Nat. | OF | 5 | 9 | 1 | 1 | 0 | 0 | 0 | 0 | .111 | 8 | 0 | 1 | .889 |
| 1976 | Montreal | Nat. | OF-PH | 68 | 185 | 22 | 51 | 11 | 4 | 2 | 19 | .276 | 89 | 7 | 5 | .950 |
| | Major League Totals | | | 73 | 194 | 23 | 52 | 11 | 4 | 2 | 19 | .268 | 97 | 7 | 6 | .945 |

†On disabled list, June 10 to August 27, 1975.

## JOHN MILTON RIVERS
### (Mickey)

Born October 31, 1948, at Miami, Fla.
Height, 5.10. Weight, 165.
Throws and bats lefthanded.
Attended Miami-Dade (North) Community College, Miami, Fla.

Major League stolen bases: 1970 (1), 1971 (13), 1972 (4), 1973 (8), 1974 (30), 1975 (70), 1976 (43). Total—169.
Led American League in stolen bases with 70 in 1975.
Led Pacific Coast League in stolen bases with 47 in 1973.
Led Pioneer League batters in bases on balls with 66 in 1969.
Tied for Pacific Coast League lead in double plays by outfielders with 3 in 1971.
Named Most Outstanding Player in Texas League, 1970.
Named as outfielder on THE SPORTING NEWS American League All-Star Team, 1976.

| Year   Club        League | Pos. | G. | AB. | R. | H. | 2B. | 3B. | HR. | RBI. | B.A. | PO. | A. | E. | F.A. |
|---|---|---|---|---|---|---|---|---|---|---|---|---|---|---|
| 1969–Magic Valley†....Pion. | OF | 67 | 225 | 75 | 69 | 13 | 6 | 7 | 41 | .307 | 67 | 8 | •11 | .872 |
| 1970–El Paso ............Texas | OF | 114 | 449 | •99 | •154 | 25 | 10 | 14 | 56 | •.343 | 235 | 13 | 12 | .954 |
| 1970–California.........Amer. | OF | 17 | 25 | 6 | 8 | 2 | 0 | 0 | 3 | .320 | 10 | 0 | 0 | 1.000 |
| 1971–Salt Lake City ..P.C. | OF | 72 | 292 | 54 | 94 | 13 | 11 | 10 | 47 | .322 | 153 | 11 | 8 | .953 |
| 1971–California.........Amer. | OF | 78 | 268 | 31 | 71 | 12 | 2 | 1 | 12 | .265 | 159 | 5 | 4 | .976 |
| 1972–Salt Lake City ..P.C. | OF | 59 | 241 | 50 | 81 | 14 | 3 | 3 | 16 | .336 | 129 | 3 | 5 | .964 |
| 1972–California.........Amer. | OF | 58 | 159 | 18 | 34 | 6 | 2 | 0 | 7 | .214 | 105 | 0 | 2 | .981 |
| 1973–Salt Lake City ..P.C. | OF | 141 | 556 | 113 | •187 | 18 | 14 | 9 | 71 | .336 | •327 | 12 | 7 | .980 |
| 1973–California.........Amer. | OF | 30 | 129 | 26 | 45 | 6 | 4 | 0 | 16 | .349 | 60 | 0 | 6 | .909 |
| 1974–California‡.......Amer. | OF | 118 | 466 | 69 | 133 | 19 | •11 | 3 | 31 | .285 | 309 | 9 | 2 | .994 |
| 1975–California§.......Amer. | OF | 155 | 616 | 70 | 175 | 17 | •13 | 1 | 53 | .284 | 371 | 13 | 9 | .977 |
| 1976–New York.........Amer. | OF | 137 | 590 | 95 | 184 | 31 | 8 | 8 | 67 | .312 | 407 | 6 | 6 | .986 |
| Major League Totals | | 593 | 2253 | 315 | 650 | 93 | 40 | 13 | 189 | .288 | 1421 | 33 | 29 | .980 |

†Traded with Pitcher Clint Compton by Atlanta Braves to California Angels for Pitchers Hoyt Wilhelm and Bob Priddy, September 8, 1969.
‡On disabled list, August 21 through remainder of season.
§Traded with Pitcher Ed Figueroa to New York Yankees for Outfielder Bobby Bonds, December 11, 1975.

### CHAMPIONSHIP SERIES RECORD

| Year   Club        League | Pos. | G. | AB. | R. | H. | 2B. | 3B. | HR. | RBI. | B.A. | PO. | A. | E. | F.A. |
|---|---|---|---|---|---|---|---|---|---|---|---|---|---|---|
| 1976–New York.........Amer. | OF | 5 | 23 | 5 | 8 | 0 | 1 | 0 | 0 | .348 | 11 | 0 | 0 | 1.000 |

### WORLD SERIES RECORD

| Year   Club        League | Pos. | G. | AB. | R. | H. | 2B. | 3B. | HR. | RBI. | B.A. | PO. | A. | E. | F.A. |
|---|---|---|---|---|---|---|---|---|---|---|---|---|---|---|
| 1976–New York.........Amer. | OF | 4 | 18 | 1 | 3 | 0 | 0 | 0 | 0 | .167 | 14 | 0 | 0 | 1.000 |

### ALL-STAR GAME RECORD

| Year   League | Pos. | AB. | R. | H. | 2B. | 3B. | HR. | RBI. | B.A. | PO. | A. | E. | F.A. |
|---|---|---|---|---|---|---|---|---|---|---|---|---|---|
| 1976–American | OF | 2 | 0 | 1 | 0 | 0 | 0 | 0 | .500 | 2 | 0 | 0 | 1.000 |

## DAVID ARTHUR ROBERTS
### (Dave)

Born September 11, 1944, at Gallipolis, O.
Height, 6.03. Weight, 192.
Throws and bats lefthanded.
Hobbies—Golf and fishing.

Led Southern League in complete games with 14 and shutouts with 4 in 1966.

| Year   Club        League | G. | IP. | W. | L. | Pct. | H. | R. | ER. | SO. | BB. | ERA. |
|---|---|---|---|---|---|---|---|---|---|---|---|
| 1963–Spartanburg†...................W. Carolinas | 18 | 126 | 9 | 3 | .750 | 95 | 32 | 25 | 121 | 18 | •1.79 |
| 1964–Asheville...........................Southern | 11 | 59 | 3 | 3 | .500 | 64 | 33 | 30 | 44 | 28 | 4.58 |
| 1964–Kinston .............................Carolina | 16 | 100 | 5 | 7 | .417 | 102 | 47 | 40 | 109 | 34 | 3.60 |
| 1965–Columbus ......................Int'national | 4 | 16 | 0 | 2 | .000 | 20 | 18 | 18 | 12 | 10 | 10.13 |
| 1965–Asheville...........................Southern | 24 | 132 | 9 | 8 | .529 | 108 | 60 | 43 | 114 | 63 | 2.93 |
| 1966–Asheville‡ ........................Southern | 31 | 190 | 14 | 5 | .737 | 153 | 63 | 55 | 157 | 60 | •2.61 |
| 1967–Columbus§ .....................Int'national | 10 | 62 | 5 | 1 | .833 | 55 | 18 | 15 | 37 | 16 | 2.18 |
| 1968–Columbus x.....................Int'national | 27 | 193 | •18 | 5 | •.783 | 189 | 74 | 68 | 133 | 45 | 3.17 |
| 1969–Elmira .............................Eastern | 15 | 121 | 7 | 5 | .583 | 117 | 55 | 47 | 76 | 43 | 3.50 |
| 1969–San Diego ......................National | 22 | 49 | 0 | 3 | .000 | 65 | 30 | 26 | 19 | 19 | 4.78 |
| 1970–San Diego ......................National | 43 | 182 | 8 | 14 | .364 | 182 | 80 | 77 | 102 | 43 | 3.81 |
| 1971–San Diego y....................National | 37 | 270 | 14 | 17 | .452 | 238 | 79 | 63 | 135 | 61 | 2.10 |
| 1972–Houston ........................National | 35 | 192 | 12 | 7 | .632 | 227 | 100 | 96 | 111 | 57 | 4.50 |
| 1973–Houston .........................National | 39 | 249 | 17 | 11 | .607 | 264 | 92 | 79 | 119 | 62 | 2.86 |
| 1974–Houston .........................National | 34 | 204 | 10 | 12 | .455 | 216 | 83 | 77 | 72 | 65 | 3.40 |
| 1975–Houston z .......................National | 32 | 198 | 8 | 14 | .364 | 182 | 98 | 94 | 101 | 73 | 4.27 |
| 1976–Detroit ...........................American | 36 | 252 | 16 | 17 | .485 | 254 | 122 | 112 | 79 | 63 | 4.00 |
| National League Totals............................ | 242 | 1344 | 69 | 78 | .469 | 1374 | 562 | 512 | 659 | 380 | 3.43 |
| American League Totals........................ | 36 | 252 | 16 | 17 | .485 | 254 | 122 | 112 | 79 | 63 | 4.00 |
| Major League Totals ............................ | 278 | 1596 | 85 | 95 | .472 | 1628 | 684 | 624 | 738 | 443 | 3.52 |

†Released on waivers by Philadelphia Phillies to Pittsburgh Pirates, April 6, 1964.
‡Drafted by Kansas City Athletics from Columbus (Pittsburgh Pirates' organization), November 28, 1966; returned to Columbus, April 7, 1967.
§On disabled list for three months of season.

xRecalled by Pittsburgh Pirates; selected by San Diego Padres from Pittsburgh in expansion draft, October 14, 1968.
yTraded to Houston Astros for Infielder Derrel Thomas and Pitchers Bill Greif and Mark Schaeffer, December 3, 1971.
zTraded with Catcher Milt May and Pitcher Jim Crawford to Detroit Tigers for Outfielder Leon Roberts, Catcher Terry Humphrey and Pitchers Gene Pentz and Mark Lemongello, December 6, 1975.

## DAVID WAYNE ROBERTS
### (Dave)
Born February 17, 1951, at Lebanon, Ore.
Height, 6.03. Weight, 205.
Throws and bats righthanded.
Hobbies—Hunting, fishing, scuba diving, water skiing and sandlot football.
Attended University of Oregon, Eugene, Ore., and San Diego State University, San Diego, Calif.

| Year Club | League | Pos. | G. | AB. | R. | H. | 2B. | 3B. | HR. | RBI. | B.A. | PO. | A. | E. | F.A. |
|---|---|---|---|---|---|---|---|---|---|---|---|---|---|---|---|
| 1972—San Diego.........Nat. | | 3-2-S-C | 100 | 418 | 38 | 102 | 17 | 0 | 5 | 33 | .244 | 92 | 198 | 21 | .932 |
| 1973—Hawaii ..............P.C. | | 3B-2B | 22 | 80 | 14 | 30 | 5 | 2 | 1 | 7 | .375 | 13 | 37 | 2 | .962 |
| 1973—San Diego.........Nat. | | 3B-2B | 127 | 479 | 56 | 137 | 20 | 3 | 21 | 64 | .286 | 92 | 276 | 24 | .939 |
| 1974—San Diego.........Nat. | | 3-S-O | 113 | 318 | 26 | 53 | 10 | 1 | 5 | 18 | .167 | 88 | 180 | 13 | .954 |
| 1975—Hawaii ..............P.C. | | 2-3-S | 121 | 442 | 60 | 116 | 31 | 3 | 12 | 71 | .262 | 205 | 314 | 20 | .963 |
| 1975—San Diego.........Nat. | | 3B-2B | 33 | 113 | 7 | 32 | 2 | 0 | 2 | 12 | .283 | 37 | 68 | 8 | .929 |
| 1976—Hawaii† ...........P.C. | | C-1-2 | 106 | 366 | 54 | 91 | 17 | 1 | 10 | 53 | .249 | 579 | 62 | 16 | .976 |
| Major League Totals ...................... | | | 373 | 1328 | 127 | 324 | 49 | 4 | 33 | 127 | .244 | 309 | 722 | 66 | .940 |

†Sold to Toronto Blue Jays, October 22, 1976. Traded to San Diego Padres for Pitcher Jerry Johnson, February 17, 1977.

## LEON KAUFFMAN ROBERTS
Born January 22, 1951, at Vicksburg, Mich.
Height, 6.03. Weight, 200.
Throws and bats righthanded.
Hobbies—Golf and swimming.
Attended University of Michigan, Ann Arbor, Mich.

| Year Club | League | Pos. | G. | AB. | R. | H. | 2B. | 3B. | HR. | RBI. | B.A. | PO. | A. | E. | F.A. |
|---|---|---|---|---|---|---|---|---|---|---|---|---|---|---|---|
| 1972—Lakeland .........Fla. St. | | OF | 74 | 254 | 36 | 78 | 14 | 3 | 5 | 52 | .307 | 162 | 8 | 5 | .971 |
| 1972—Rocky Mount ....Carol. | | OF | 6 | 22 | 4 | 6 | 1 | 0 | 0 | 2 | .273 | 15 | 0 | 0 | 1.000 |
| 1973—Montgomery ......South. | | OF | 133 | 489 | 87 | 144 | •30 | 1 | 14 | 70 | .294 | 276 | 10 | 6 | .979 |
| 1974—Evansville ........A.A. | | OF | 132 | 481 | 74 | 137 | 31 | 4 | 12 | 79 | .285 | 264 | 9 | 9 | .968 |
| 1974—Detroit ..............Amer. | | OF | 17 | 63 | 5 | 17 | 3 | 2 | 0 | 7 | .270 | 25 | 0 | 2 | .926 |
| 1975—Detroit† ...........Amer. | | OF | 129 | 447 | 51 | 115 | 17 | 5 | 10 | 38 | .257 | 268 | 10 | 5 | .982 |
| 1976—Houston ...........Nat. | | OF-PH | 87 | 235 | 31 | 68 | 11 | 2 | 7 | 33 | .289 | 99 | 1 | 2 | .980 |
| American League Totals ................ | | | 146 | 510 | 56 | 132 | 20 | 7 | 10 | 45 | .259 | 293 | 10 | 7 | .977 |
| National League Totals ................ | | | 87 | 235 | 31 | 68 | 11 | 2 | 7 | 33 | .289 | 99 | 1 | 2 | .980 |
| Major League Totals ...................... | | | 233 | 745 | 87 | 200 | 31 | 9 | 17 | 78 | .268 | 392 | 11 | 9 | .978 |

†Traded with Catcher Terry Humphrey and Pitchers Gene Pentz and Mark Lemongello to Houston Astros for Catcher Milt May and Pitchers Jim Crawford and Dave Roberts, December 6, 1975.

## BROOKS CALBERT ROBINSON, JR.
Born May 18, 1937, at Little Rock, Ark.
Height, 6.01. Weight, 190.
Throws and bats righthanded.
Hobbies—Hunting and fishing.
Attended Little Rock Junior College, Little Rock, Ark.

Established following major league records: most years leading league in games, third baseman (8), 1970; most double plays, third baseman, lifetime, 616, 1976; most games, third baseman, lifetime 2,855, 1976; most putouts, third baseman, lifetime, 2,691, 1976; most assists, third baseman, lifetime, 6,177, 1976; most chances accepted, third baseman, lifetime, 8,868, 1976; highest fielding average, third baseman, lifetime, .971, 1976; most seasons leading league, assists, third baseman, 8, 1974; and most seasons, third baseman, 22, 1976.

Tied following major league records: most home runs with bases filled, two consecutive games (2), May 6 and 9, 1962; fewest stolen bases, season, 150 or more games (0), 1971; fewest caught stealing, season, 150 or more games, 0, 1972; most consecutive seasons leading league in games (4), 1961 through 1964; and most consecutive seasons, 150 or more games, 14, 1974; most seasons, one club, 22, 1976; most consecutive seasons, one club, 22, 1976.

Established American League records for most games played, third baseman, 162-game schedule (163), 1961 and 1964; most home runs, third baseman, lifetime, 266, 1976; most years 150 or more games, league, 14, 1974; most times grounding into double play, career, 290, 1975; most seasons leading league, fielding, third baseman, 11, 1975; and most sacrifice flies, lifetime, 113, 1976.

Tied American League record for most seasons leading league, chances accepted, third baseman, 8, 1974.

Led American League third basemen in double plays with 43 in 1963, 40 in 1964 and 44 in 1974.

Tied for American League lead in sacrifice flies with 8 in 1967 and 8 in 1968.

Named third baseman on THE SPORTING NEWS American League All-Star Teams, 1961-62-64-65-66-67-68-71-72.

Named third baseman on THE SPORTING NEWS American League All-Star fielding teams, 1960-61-62-63-64-65-66-67-68-69-70-71-72-73-74-75.

Named Most Valuable Player in American League, 1964.

— 318 —

Named American League Player of the Year by THE SPORTING NEWS, 1964.

| Year | Club | League | Pos. | G. | AB. | R. | H. | 2B. | 3B. | HR. | RBI. | B.A. | PO. | A. | E. | F.A. |
|---|---|---|---|---|---|---|---|---|---|---|---|---|---|---|---|---|
| 1955—York | ...............Pied. | | 2B-3B | 95 | 354 | 72 | 117 | 17 | 3 | 11 | 67 | .331 | 184 | 226 | 14 | .967 |
| 1955—Baltimore | .........Amer. | | 3B | 6 | 22 | 0 | 2 | 0 | 0 | 0 | 1 | .091 | 2 | 8 | 2 | .833 |
| 1956—San Antonio | ......Tex. | | •3B-2B | 154 | 577 | 72 | 157 | 28 | 6 | 9 | 74 | .272 | •213 | 396 | 26 | •.959 |
| 1956—Baltimore | .........Amer. | | 3B-2B | 15 | 44 | 5 | 10 | 4 | 0 | 1 | 1 | .227 | 9 | 25 | 2 | .944 |
| 1957—San Antonio | ......Tex. | | 3B-SS | 33 | 124 | 10 | 33 | 5 | 1 | 1 | 9 | .266 | 34 | 59 | 4 | .959 |
| 1957—Baltimore† | .......Amer. | | 3B | 50 | 117 | 13 | 28 | 6 | 1 | 2 | 14 | .239 | 34 | 66 | 3 | .971 |
| 1958—Baltimore | .........Amer. | | •3B-2B | 145 | 463 | 31 | 110 | 16 | 3 | 3 | 32 | .238 | •157 | 283 | 22 | .952 |
| 1959—Vancouver | ........P. C. | | 3B | 42 | 163 | 20 | 54 | 9 | 2 | 6 | 30 | .331 | 54 | 93 | 8 | .948 |
| 1959—Baltimore | .........Amer. | | 3B-2B | 88 | 313 | 29 | 89 | 15 | 2 | 4 | 24 | .284 | 92 | 187 | 13 | .955 |
| 1960—Baltimore | .........Amer. | | •3B-2B | 152 | 595 | 74 | 175 | 27 | 9 | 14 | 88 | .294 | •174 | •330 | 12 | •.977 |
| 1961—Baltimore | .........Amer. | | •3B-2-S | •163 | •668 | 89 | 192 | 38 | 7 | 7 | 61 | .287 | 155 | 334 | 14 | .972 |
| 1962—Baltimore | .........Amer. | | •3-S-2B | •162 | 634 | 77 | 192 | 29 | 9 | 23 | 86 | .303 | 165 | 340 | 11 | •.979 |
| 1963—Baltimore | .........Amer. | | •3B-SS | •161 | 589 | 67 | 148 | 26 | 4 | 11 | 67 | .251 | 153 | •331 | 12 | •.976 |
| 1964—Baltimore | .........Amer. | | 3B | •163 | 612 | 82 | 194 | 35 | 3 | 28 | •118 | .317 | •153 | •327 | 14 | •.972 |
| 1965—Baltimore | .........Amer. | | 3B | 144 | 559 | 81 | 166 | 25 | 2 | 18 | 80 | .297 | 144 | 296 | 15 | .967 |
| 1966—Baltimore | .........Amer. | | 3B | 157 | 620 | 91 | 167 | 35 | 2 | 23 | 100 | .269 | 174 | •313 | 12 | •.976 |
| 1967—Baltimore | .........Amer. | | 3B | 158 | 610 | 88 | 164 | 25 | 5 | 22 | 77 | .269 | 147 | •405 | 11 | •.980 |
| 1968—Baltimore | .........Amer. | | 3B | •162 | 608 | 65 | 154 | 36 | 6 | 17 | 75 | .253 | 168 | •353 | 16 | •.970 |
| 1969—Baltimore | .........Amer. | | 3B | 156 | 598 | 73 | 140 | 21 | 3 | 23 | 84 | .234 | 163 | •370 | 13 | •.976 |
| 1970—Baltimore | .........Amer. | | 3B | 158 | 608 | 84 | 168 | 31 | 4 | 18 | 94 | .276 | 157 | 321 | 17 | .966 |
| 1971—Baltimore | .........Amer. | | 3B | 156 | 589 | 67 | 160 | 21 | 1 | 20 | 92 | .272 | 131 | 354 | 16 | .968 |
| 1972—Baltimore | .........Amer. | | 3B | 153 | 556 | 48 | 139 | 23 | 2 | 8 | 64 | .250 | 129 | 333 | 11 | •.977 |
| 1973—Baltimore | .........Amer. | | 3B | 155 | 549 | 53 | 141 | 17 | 2 | 9 | 72 | .257 | 129 | 354 | 15 | .970 |
| 1974—Baltimore | .........Amer. | | 3B | 153 | 553 | 46 | 159 | 27 | 0 | 7 | 59 | .288 | 115 | •410 | 18 | .967 |
| 1975—Baltimore | .........Amer. | | 3B | 144 | 482 | 50 | 97 | 15 | 1 | 6 | 53 | .201 | 96 | 326 | 9 | •.979 |
| 1976—Baltimore | .........Amer. | | 3B | 71 | 218 | 16 | 46 | 8 | 2 | 3 | 11 | .211 | 59 | 126 | 6 | .969 |
| Major League Totals | ................... | | | 2872 | 10607 | 1229 | 2841 | 480 | 68 | 267 | 1353 | .269 | 2706 | 6192 | 264 | .971 |

†On disabled list from April 28 through June 24.

## CHAMPIONSHIP SERIES RECORD

| Year | Club | League | Pos. | G. | AB. | R. | H. | 2B. | 3B. | HR. | RBI. | B.A. | PO. | A. | E. | F.A. |
|---|---|---|---|---|---|---|---|---|---|---|---|---|---|---|---|---|
| 1969—Baltimore | .........Amer. | | 3B | 3 | 14 | 1 | 7 | 1 | 0 | 0 | 0 | .500 | 6 | 10 | 0 | 1.000 |
| 1970—Baltimore | .........Amer. | | 3B | 3 | 12 | 3 | 7 | 2 | 0 | 0 | 1 | .583 | 3 | 5 | 0 | 1.000 |
| 1971—Baltimore | .........Amer. | | 3B | 3 | 11 | 2 | 4 | 1 | 0 | 1 | 3 | .364 | 4 | 7 | 0 | 1.000 |
| 1973—Baltimore | .........Amer. | | 3B | 5 | 20 | 1 | 5 | 2 | 0 | 0 | 2 | .250 | 2 | 14 | 1 | .941 |
| 1974—Baltimore | .........Amer. | | 3B | 4 | 12 | 1 | 1 | 0 | 0 | 1 | 1 | .083 | 4 | 13 | 0 | 1.000 |
| Championship Series Totals | ............ | | | 18 | 69 | 8 | 24 | 6 | 0 | 2 | 7 | .348 | 19 | 49 | 1 | .986 |

## WORLD SERIES RECORD

Hit home run in first World Series at-bat, first inning, October 5, 1966.
Tied World Series record for most hits, 5-game series, 9, in 1970.

| Year | Club | League | Pos. | G. | AB. | R. | H. | 2B. | 3B. | HR. | RBI. | B.A. | PO. | A. | E. | F.A. |
|---|---|---|---|---|---|---|---|---|---|---|---|---|---|---|---|---|
| 1966—Baltimore | .........Amer. | | 3B | 4 | 14 | 2 | 3 | 0 | 0 | 1 | 1 | .214 | 4 | 6 | 0 | 1.000 |
| 1969—Baltimore | .........Amer. | | 3B | 5 | 19 | 0 | 1 | 0 | 0 | 2 | 2 | .053 | 1 | 16 | 0 | 1.000 |
| 1970—Baltimore | .........Amer. | | 3B | 5 | 21 | 5 | 9 | 2 | 0 | 2 | 6 | .429 | 9 | 14 | 1 | .958 |
| 1971—Baltimore | .........Amer. | | 3B | 7 | 22 | 2 | 7 | 0 | 0 | 0 | 5 | .318 | 6 | 17 | 2 | .920 |
| World Series Totals | ...................... | | | 21 | 76 | 9 | 20 | 2 | 0 | 3 | 14 | .263 | 35 | 37 | 3 | .960 |

## ALL-STAR GAME RECORD

| Year | League | Pos. | AB. | R. | H. | 2B. | 3B. | HR. | RBI. | B.A. | PO. | A. | E. | F.A. |
|---|---|---|---|---|---|---|---|---|---|---|---|---|---|---|
| 1960—American (both games) | ...... | 3B | 3 | 0 | 0 | 0 | 0 | 0 | 0 | .000 | 0 | 0 | 0 | .000 |
| 1961—American (both games) | ...... | 3B | 5 | 0 | 1 | 0 | 0 | 0 | 0 | .200 | 0 | 5 | 0 | 1.000 |
| 1962—American (both games) | ...... | 3B | 1 | 1 | 0 | 0 | 0 | 0 | 0 | .000 | 0 | 2 | 0 | 1.000 |
| 1963—American | ..................... | 3B | 2 | 0 | 2 | 0 | 0 | 0 | 0 | 1.000 | 1 | 1 | 0 | 1.000 |
| 1964—American | ..................... | 3B | 4 | 0 | 2 | 0 | 1 | 0 | 2 | .500 | 1 | 2 | 0 | 1.000 |
| 1965—American | ..................... | 3B | 4 | 1 | 1 | 0 | 0 | 0 | 0 | .250 | 1 | 2 | 0 | 1.000 |
| 1966—American | ..................... | 3B | 4 | 1 | 3 | 0 | 1 | 0 | 0 | .750 | 4 | 4 | 0 | 1.000 |
| 1967—American | ..................... | 3B | 6 | 1 | 1 | 0 | 0 | 1 | 1 | .167 | 0 | 6 | 0 | 1.000 |
| 1968—American | ..................... | 3B | 2 | 0 | 0 | 0 | 0 | 0 | 0 | .000 | 0 | 1 | 0 | 1.000 |
| 1969—American | ..................... | 3B | 1 | 0 | 0 | 0 | 0 | 0 | 0 | .000 | 1 | 1 | 0 | 1.000 |
| 1970—American | ..................... | 3B | 3 | 1 | 2 | 0 | 1 | 0 | 2 | .667 | 1 | 1 | 0 | 1.000 |
| 1971—American | ..................... | 3B | 3 | 0 | 1 | 0 | 0 | 0 | 0 | .333 | 1 | 3 | 0 | 1.000 |
| 1972—American | ..................... | 3B | 2 | 0 | 0 | 0 | 0 | 0 | 0 | .000 | 0 | 1 | 0 | 1.000 |
| 1973—American | ..................... | 3B | 2 | 0 | 0 | 0 | 0 | 0 | 0 | .000 | 1 | 3 | 0 | 1.000 |
| 1974—American | ..................... | 3B | 3 | 0 | 0 | 0 | 0 | 0 | 0 | .000 | 0 | 0 | 0 | .000 |
| All-Star Game Totals | ..................... | | 45 | 5 | 13 | 0 | 3 | 1 | 5 | .289 | 11 | 32 | 0 | 1.000 |

# CRAIG GEORGE ROBINSON

Born August 21, 1948, at Abington, Pa.
Height, 5.10. Weight, 165.
Throws and bats righthanded.
Hobbies—Reading and all sports.
Attended Wake Forest University, Winston-Salem, N. C.; received Bachelor of
Arts degree in History. Did graduate work at Emory University, Atlanta, Ga.
Led Pacific Coast League shortstops in total chances with 740 and tied for lead in double plays with 89 in 1972.

Led Pacific Coast League shortstops in double plays with 91 and in total chances with 697 in 1971.

| Year | Club | League | Pos. | G. | AB. | R. | H. | 2B. | 3B. | HR. | RBI. | B.A. | PO. | A. | E. | F.A. |
|---|---|---|---|---|---|---|---|---|---|---|---|---|---|---|---|---|
| 1970—Reading | ............ | East. | SS | 89 | 272 | 34 | 57 | 7 | 5 | 1 | 16 | .210 | 142 | 282 | 10 | .977 |
| 1971—Eugene | ............... | P.C. | SS | ●145 | 581 | 70 | 156 | 18 | 8 | 7 | 33 | .269 | •238 | •426 | 33 | •.953 |
| 1972—Eugene | ............... | P.C. | •SS-3B | 146 | 579 | 65 | 131 | 17 | 4 | 7 | 48 | .226 | •232 | •485 | 25 | •.966 |
| 1972—Philadelphia | ...... | Nat. | SS | 5 | 15 | 0 | 3 | 1 | 0 | 0 | 0 | .200 | 4 | 16 | 0 | 1.000 |
| 1973—Eugene | ............... | P.C. | SS | 98 | 398 | 59 | 110 | 16 | 8 | 3 | 37 | .276 | 168 | 303 | 27 | .946 |
| 1973—Philadelphia† | .... | Nat. | SS-2B | 46 | 146 | 11 | 33 | 7 | 0 | 0 | 7 | .226 | 70 | 112 | 10 | .948 |
| 1974—Atlanta | ............. | Nat. | SS | 145 | 452 | 52 | 104 | 4 | 6 | 0 | 29 | .230 | 238 | 395 | 29 | .956 |
| 1975—Atl.‡-S.F. | ......... | Nat. | SS-2B | 39 | 46 | 5 | 3 | 1 | 0 | 0 | 0 | .065 | 34 | 37 | 4 | .947 |
| 1976—S.F.§-Atl. | ......... | Nat. | 2-3-S | 30 | 30 | 8 | 8 | 1 | 0 | 0 | 5 | .267 | 12 | 36 | 5 | .906 |
| 1976—Richmond | ......... | Int. | SS | 26 | 67 | 4 | 11 | 1 | 0 | 0 | 4 | .164 | 40 | 89 | 5 | .963 |
| Major League Totals | ...... | | | 265 | 689 | 76 | 151 | 14 | 6 | 0 | 41 | .219 | 358 | 596 | 48 | .952 |

†Traded with Pitcher Barry Lersch to Atlanta Braves for Pitcher Ron Schueler, December 3, 1973; Braves traded Infielder Gil Garrido to Phillies for First Baseman-Outfielder Bob Beall, December 10, 1973, to complete deal.

‡Traded to San Francisco Giants for First Baseman-Third Baseman Ed Goodson, June 11, 1975.

§Traded with First Baseman Willie Montanez, Outfielder Jake Brown, and Infielder Mike Eden to Atlanta Braves for Third Baseman-First Baseman Darrell Evans and Shortstop Marty Perez, June 13, 1976.

## WILLIAM HENRY ROBINSON, JR.
### (Bill)

Born June 26, 1943, at McKeesport, Pa.
Height, 6.02. Weight, 200.
Throws and bats righthanded.
Hobbies—Fishing, basketball and reading.

| Year | Club | League | Pos. | G. | AB. | R. | H. | 2B. | 3B. | HR. | RBI. | B.A. | PO. | A. | E. | F.A. |
|---|---|---|---|---|---|---|---|---|---|---|---|---|---|---|---|---|
| 1961—Wellsville | ......... | NYP | OF | 67 | 251 | 37 | 60 | 15 | 4 | 2 | 25 | .239 | 107 | 7 | 8 | .934 |
| 1962—Eau Claire | ........ | North. | OF | 23 | 63 | 3 | 9 | 1 | 1 | 0 | 3 | .143 | 27 | 2 | 0 | 1.000 |
| 1962—Dublin | .............. | Ga.-Fla. | OF | 62 | 207 | 46 | 63 | 9 | 4 | 8 | 37 | .304 | 71 | 1 | 5 | .935 |
| 1963—Waycross | ......... | Ga.-Fla. | OF | 113 | 418 | 69 | •132 | 18 | •10 | 10 | 62 | .316 | •225 | 10 | 8 | •.967 |
| 1964—Yakima | ......... | Northw. | OF | 104 | 400 | 81 | 139 | 24 | 5 | 18 | 81 | •.348 | •247 | 21 | 10 | .964 |
| 1965—Atlanta | .............. | Int. | OF | 133 | 407 | 41 | 109 | 17 | 2 | 10 | 37 | .268 | 228 | 8 | 12 | .952 |
| 1966—Richmond | .......... | Int. | OF-2-3 | 139 | 509 | 86 | 159 | 30 | 4 | 20 | 79 | .312 | 283 | 14 | 2 | .993 |
| 1966—Atlanta† | ............ | Nat. | OF | 6 | 11 | 1 | 3 | 0 | 1 | 0 | 3 | .273 | 4 | 0 | 1 | .800 |
| 1967—New York | ......... | Amer. | OF | 116 | 342 | 31 | 67 | 6 | 1 | 7 | 29 | .196 | 169 | 10 | 6 | .968 |
| 1968—New York | ......... | Amer. | OF | 107 | 342 | 34 | 82 | 16 | 7 | 6 | 40 | .240 | 195 | 3 | 3 | .985 |
| 1969—New York | ......... | Amer. | OF-1B | 87 | 222 | 23 | 38 | 11 | 2 | 3 | 21 | .171 | 103 | 5 | 4 | .964 |
| 1970—Syracuse‡ | ......... | Int. | OF-3B | 115 | 372 | 68 | 96 | 20 | 0 | 13 | 43 | .258 | 166 | 6 | 2 | .989 |
| 1971—Tucson§ | ............ | P.C. | OF-3-1 | 133 | 495 | 75 | 136 | 33 | 6 | 14 | 81 | .275 | 328 | 26 | 6 | .983 |
| 1972—Eugene | ............... | P.C. | OF | 65 | 240 | 47 | 73 | 9 | 2 | 20 | 66 | .304 | 140 | 3 | 3 | .979 |
| 1972—Philadelphia | ...... | Nat. | OF | 82 | 188 | 19 | 45 | 9 | 1 | 8 | 21 | .239 | 109 | 2 | 2 | .982 |
| 1973—Philadelphia x | .. | Nat. | OF-3B | 124 | 452 | 62 | 130 | 32 | 1 | 25 | 65 | .288 | 234 | 18 | 8 | .969 |
| 1974—Philadelphia y | .. | Nat. | OF | 100 | 280 | 32 | 66 | 14 | 1 | 5 | 29 | .236 | 162 | 8 | 5 | .971 |
| 1975—Pittsburgh | ....... | Nat. | OF | 92 | 200 | 26 | 56 | 12 | 2 | 6 | 33 | .280 | 107 | 3 | 1 | .991 |
| 1976—Pittsburgh | ....... | Nat. | O-3-1 | 122 | 393 | 55 | 119 | 22 | 3 | 21 | 64 | .303 | 185 | 53 | 8 | .967 |
| American League Totals | ............... | | 310 | 906 | 88 | 187 | 33 | 10 | 16 | 90 | .206 | 467 | 18 | 13 | .974 |
| National League Totals | ................ | | 526 | 1524 | 195 | 419 | 89 | 9 | 65 | 215 | .275 | 801 | 84 | 25 | .972 |
| Major League Totals | ...................... | | 836 | 2430 | 283 | 606 | 122 | 19 | 81 | 305 | .249 | 1268 | 102 | 38 | .973 |

†Traded with Pitcher Chi-Chi Olivo (transferred from Richmond to Syracuse) to New York Yankees for Third Baseman Clete Boyer and player to be named later, November 29, 1966.

‡Traded by New York Yankees to Chicago White Sox for Pitcher Barry Moore, December 3, 1970.

§Traded by Chicago White Sox to Philadelphia Phillies for Catcher Jerry Rodriguez, December 13, 1971.

xOn disabled list, June 2 to June 25, 1973.

yTraded to Pittsburgh Pirates for Pitcher Wayne Simpson, April 5, 1975.

### PITCHING RECORD

| Year | Club | League | G. | IP. | W. | L. | Pct. | H. | R. | ER. | SO. | BB. | ERA. |
|---|---|---|---|---|---|---|---|---|---|---|---|---|---|
| 1962—Dublin | ............................... | Ga.-Fla. | 1 | 3 | 0 | 0 | .000 | 5 | 6 | 5 | 0 | 1 | 15.00 |

### CHAMPIONSHIP SERIES RECORD

| Year | Club | League | Pos. | G. | AB. | R. | H. | 2B. | 3B. | HR. | RBI. | B.A. | PO. | A. | E. | F.A. |
|---|---|---|---|---|---|---|---|---|---|---|---|---|---|---|---|---|
| 1975—Pittsburgh | ........ | Nat. | PH | 2 | 2 | 0 | 0 | 0 | 0 | 0 | 0 | .000 | 0 | 0 | 0 | .000 |

## PATRICK EDWARD ROCKETT
### (Pat)

Born January 9, 1955, at San Antonio, Tex.
Height, 5.11. Weight, 170.
Throws and bats righthanded.
Hobbies—Water skiing and music recording.
Attended San Antonio College, San Antonio, Tex.

| Year | Club | League | Pos. | G. | AB. | R. | H. | 2B. | 3B. | HR. | RBI. | B.A. | PO. | A. | E. | F.A. |
|---|---|---|---|---|---|---|---|---|---|---|---|---|---|---|---|---|
| 1973—Wytheville | ........ | Appal. | SS | 56 | 197 | 34 | 55 | 9 | 0 | 5 | 31 | .279 | 82 | 147 | 29 | .888 |
| 1974—Greenwood | ........ | W. Car. | SS | 119 | 436 | 77 | 133 | 14 | 0 | 7 | 63 | .305 | •204 | 368 | •53 | .915 |
| 1975—Savannah | .......... | South. | SS | 130 | 453 | 50 | 115 | 8 | 1 | 2 | 35 | .254 | 215 | 391 | 36 | .944 |
| 1976—Savannah | .......... | South. | SS | 42 | 144 | 13 | 32 | 1 | 1 | 1 | 13 | .222 | 62 | 119 | 11 | .943 |
| 1976—Richmond | ......... | Int. | SS-PH | 66 | 200 | 34 | 49 | 8 | 0 | 6 | 25 | .245 | 94 | 186 | 21 | .930 |
| 1976—Atlanta | .............. | Nat. | SS-PH | 4 | 5 | 0 | 1 | 0 | 0 | 0 | 0 | .200 | 0 | 1 | 0 | 1.000 |
| Major League Totals | ...................... | | 4 | 5 | 0 | 1 | 0 | 0 | 0 | 0 | .200 | 0 | 1 | 0 | 1.000 |

# AURELIO RODRIGUEZ (ITUARTE)

Born December 28, 1947, at Cananea, Sonora, Mexico.
Height, 5.10. Weight, 180.
Throws and bats righthanded.
Brother of Francisco Rodriguez, former shortstop in St. Louis Cardinals' organization and presently playing in Mexican League with Aquascalientes.
Tied major league record for most games played with two clubs, season (159), California (17)—Washington (142), 1970.
Tied American League record for most long hits, inning, 2, August 20, 1972 (sixth inning).
Led American League third basemen in total chances with 514 in 1972 and with 536 in 1975.
Led American League third basemen in double plays with 41 in 1970 and 42 in 1969.
Led Mexican League third basemen in double plays with 35 in 1966.
Named Mexican League Rookie of the Year, 1966.
Named third baseman on THE SPORTING NEWS American League All-Star fielding team, 1976.

| Year Club | League | Pos. | G. | AB. | R. | H. | 2B. | 3B. | HR. | RBI. | B.A. | PO. | A. | E. | F.A. |
|---|---|---|---|---|---|---|---|---|---|---|---|---|---|---|---|
| 1965—Fresnillo | Mex. C | 3-O-2 | 138 | 552 | 103 | 162 | 26 | 9 | 25 | 104 | .293 | 197 | 263 | 31 | .937 |
| 1965—Jalisco | Mex. | 3B | 15 | 50 | 5 | 13 | 1 | 1 | 0 | 3 | .260 | 7 | 23 | 5 | .857 |
| 1966—Jalisco | Mex. | •3B-SS | 135 | 480 | 64 | 140 | 17 | •16 | 3 | 53 | .292 | •115 | •316 | •30 | .935 |
| 1966—Seattle | P.C. | SS-3B | 17 | 59 | 6 | 15 | 0 | 2 | 0 | 6 | .254 | 23 | 34 | 5 | .919 |
| 1967—El Paso | Texas | 3B | 79 | 309 | 49 | 101 | 20 | 9 | 11 | 47 | .327 | •69 | 148 | 6 | .973 |
| 1967—Seattle | P.C. | 3B | 51 | 185 | 18 | 57 | 12 | 0 | 2 | 17 | .308 | 36 | 79 | 3 | .975 |
| 1967—California | Amer. | 3B | 29 | 130 | 14 | 31 | 3 | 1 | 1 | 8 | .238 | 19 | 75 | 1 | .989 |
| 1968—California | Amer. | 3B-2B | 76 | 223 | 14 | 54 | 10 | 1 | 1 | 16 | .242 | 65 | 116 | 15 | .923 |
| 1968—Seattle | P.C. | S-3B-2B | 46 | 181 | 21 | 45 | 8 | 0 | 3 | 15 | .249 | 65 | 99 | 9 | .948 |
| 1969—California | Amer. | 3B | 159 | 561 | 47 | 130 | 17 | 2 | 7 | 49 | .232 | 145 | 352 | •24 | .954 |
| 1970—Cal.†-Wash.‡ | Amer. | •3B-SS | 159 | 610 | 70 | 152 | 33 | 7 | 19 | 83 | .249 | 127 | •398 | 18 | .967 |
| 1971—Detroit | Amer. | 3B-SS | 154 | 604 | 68 | 153 | 30 | 7 | 15 | 39 | .253 | 128 | 344 | 23 | .954 |
| 1972—Detroit | Amer. | •3B-SS | 153 | 601 | 65 | 142 | 23 | 5 | 13 | 56 | .236 | •150 | 350 | 17 | .967 |
| 1973—Detroit | Amer. | 3B-SS | 160 | 555 | 46 | 123 | 27 | 3 | 9 | 58 | .222 | 137 | 338 | 14 | .971 |
| 1974—Detroit | Amer. | 3B | 159 | 571 | 54 | 127 | 23 | 5 | 5 | 49 | .222 | 132 | 389 | 21 | .961 |
| 1975—Detroit | Amer. | 3B | 151 | 507 | 47 | 124 | 20 | 6 | 13 | 60 | .245 | 136 | 375 | 25 | .953 |
| 1976—Detroit§ | Amer. | 3B | 128 | 480 | 40 | 115 | 13 | 2 | 8 | 50 | .240 | 120 | 280 | 9 | •.978 |
| Major League Totals | | | 1328 | 4842 | 465 | 1151 | 199 | 39 | 91 | 468 | .238 | 1159 | 3017 | 167 | .962 |

†Traded with Outfielder Rick Reichardt to Washington Senators for Third Baseman Ken McMullen, April 26, 1970.

‡Traded with Shortstop Ed Brinkman and Pitchers Joe Coleman and Jim Hannan to Detroit Tigers for Pitcher Denny McLain, Third Baseman Don Wert, Pitcher Norm McRae and Infielder-Outfielder Elliott Maddox, October 9, 1970.

§On disabled list, August 30 through October 4, 1976.

## CHAMPIONSHIP SERIES RECORD

| Year Club | League | Pos. | G. | AB. | R. | H. | 2B. | 3B. | HR. | RBI. | B.A. | PO. | A. | E. | F.A. |
|---|---|---|---|---|---|---|---|---|---|---|---|---|---|---|---|
| 1972—Detroit | Amer. | 3B | 5 | 16 | 0 | 0 | 0 | 0 | 0 | 0 | .000 | 2 | 14 | 1 | .941 |

# EDUARDO RODRIGUEZ (REYES)

Born March 6, 1952, at Barceloneta, Puerto Rico.
Height, 6.00. Weight, 185.
Throws and bats righthanded.
Hobby—Bicycling.

| Year Club | League | G. | IP. | W. | L. | Pct. | H. | R. | ER. | SO. | BB. | ERA. |
|---|---|---|---|---|---|---|---|---|---|---|---|---|
| 1972—Danville | Midwest | 40 | 85 | 9 | 6 | .600 | 61 | 31 | 20 | 98 | 38 | 2.12 |
| 1973—Shreveport | Texas | 10 | 26 | 2 | 1 | .667 | 11 | 3 | 1 | 28 | 16 | 0.35 |
| 1973—Evansville | Am. Assoc. | 5 | 37 | 1 | 1 | .500 | 28 | 16 | 10 | 26 | 14 | 2.43 |
| 1973—Milwaukee | American | 30 | 76 | 9 | 7 | .563 | 71 | 33 | 28 | 49 | 47 | 3.32 |
| 1974—Milwaukee | American | 43 | 112 | 7 | 4 | .636 | 97 | 49 | 45 | 58 | 51 | 3.62 |
| 1975—Milwaukee | American | 43 | 88 | 7 | 0 | 1.000 | 77 | 37 | 34 | 65 | 44 | 3.48 |
| 1976—Milwaukee | American | 45 | 136 | 5 | 13 | .278 | 124 | 68 | 55 | 77 | 65 | 3.64 |
| Major League Totals | | 161 | 412 | 28 | 24 | .538 | 369 | 187 | 162 | 249 | 207 | 3.54 |

# ELISEO C. RODRIGUEZ
## (Ellie)

Born May 24, 1946, at Fajardo, Puerto Rico.
Height, 5.11. Weight, 185.
Throws and bats righthanded.
Hobby—Bowling.

Tied major league record for most chances accepted, catcher, game (since 1900), 20, August 12, 1974.
Established American League record for most putouts, catcher, extra-inning game, 21, June 14, 1974 (15 innings).
Tied American League record for most putouts, catcher, game, 19, August 12, 1974.
Led American League catchers in total chances with 864 in 1974.
Led Appalachian League in passed balls with 20 in 1964.
Led Southern League catchers in double plays with 9 in 1966.

| Year Club | League | Pos. | G. | AB. | R. | H. | 2B. | 3B. | HR. | RBI. | B.A. | PO. | A. | E. | F.A. |
|---|---|---|---|---|---|---|---|---|---|---|---|---|---|---|---|
| 1964—Daytona Beach | Fla. St. | C | 17 | 42 | 6 | 10 | 0 | 0 | 0 | 5 | .238 | 37 | 5 | 1 | .977 |
| 1964—Wytheville† | Appal. | C | 56 | 181 | 54 | 64 | 10 | 6 | 4 | 34 | .354 | •407 | •39 | 9 | •.980 |

| Year Club League | Pos. | G. | AB. | R. | H. | 2B. | 3B. | HR. | RBI. | B.A. | PO. | A. | E. | F.A. |
|---|---|---|---|---|---|---|---|---|---|---|---|---|---|---|
| 1965-Greensboro........Carol. | C | 108 | 342 | 49 | 93 | 14 | 4 | 2 | 45 | .272 | 591 | 57 | 10 | .985 |
| 1966-Columbus .........South. | C | 110 | 335 | 35 | 78 | 14 | 2 | 2 | 37 | .233 | 616 | 78 | 5 | *.993 |
| 1967-Syracuse .........Int. | C | 83 | 266 | 27 | 66 | 4 | 0 | 2 | 26 | .248 | 461 | 46 | 4 | .992 |
| 1967-Binghamton ......East. | C | 14 | 39 | 3 | 9 | 1 | 0 | 0 | 4 | .231 | 76 | 5 | 2 | .976 |
| 1968-Syracuse‡.........Int. | C | 45 | 127 | 18 | 37 | 8 | 1 | 0 | 5 | .291 | 237 | 24 | 0 | 1.000 |
| 1969-New York§ ........Amer. | C | 9 | 24 | 1 | 5 | 0 | 0 | 0 | 1 | .208 | 41 | 3 | 0 | 1.000 |
| 1969-Kansas City ......Amer. | C | 95 | 267 | 27 | 63 | 10 | 0 | 2 | 20 | .236 | 433 | 39 | 5 | .990 |
| 1970-Kansas City x....Amer. | C | 80 | 231 | 25 | 52 | 8 | 2 | 1 | 15 | .225 | 451 | 32 | 6 | .988 |
| 1971-Milwaukee .......Amer. | C | 115 | 319 | 28 | 67 | 10 | 1 | 1 | 30 | .210 | 520 | 67 | 5 | .992 |
| 1972-Milwaukee .......Amer. | C | 116 | 355 | 31 | 101 | 14 | 2 | 2 | 35 | .285 | 542 | 54 | 10 | .983 |
| 1973-Milwaukee y......Amer. | C | 94 | 290 | 30 | 78 | 8 | 1 | 0 | 30 | .269 | 324 | 40 | 5 | .986 |
| 1974-California.........Amer. | C | 140 | 395 | 48 | 100 | 20 | 0 | 7 | 36 | .253 | *782 | •75 | 7 | .992 |
| 1975-California z a....Amer. | C | 90 | 226 | 20 | 53 | 6 | 0 | 3 | 27 | .235 | 492 | 33 | 5 | .991 |
| 1976-Los Angeles b....Nat. | C | 36 | 66 | 10 | 14 | 0 | 0 | 0 | 9 | .212 | 128 | 17 | 2 | .986 |
| Major League Totals ...................... | | 775 | 2173 | 220 | 533 | 76 | 6 | 16 | 203 | .245 | 3713 | 360 | 45 | .989 |

†Drafted by New York Yankees from Dallas (Kansas City Athletics' organization), November 30, 1964.
‡On disabled list, April 10 through May 3, and from June 16 through July 2, 1968.
§Selected by Kansas City Royals from New York Yankees in expansion draft, October 15, 1968.
xTraded to Milwaukee Brewers for First Baseman-Outfielder Carl Taylor, February 2, 1971.
yTraded with Pitchers Skip Lockwood and Gary Ryerson and Outfielders Ollie Brown and Joe Lahoud to California Angels for Pitchers Clyde Wright and Steve Barber, Outfielder Ken Berry, Catcher Art Kusnyer and a player to be named later, October 22, 1973.
zOn supplemental disabled list, May 3 to June 1, 1975.
aTraded to Los Angeles Dodgers for Outfielder Orlando Alvarez and cash, March 21, 1976.
bOn disabled list, August 30 through September 14, 1976.

ALL-STAR GAME RECORD

Member of American League All-Star Team for the 1969 and 1972 games; did not play.

### GARY STEVEN ROENICKE
Name pronounced Reh-NICK-ee.
Born December 5, 1954, at Covina, Calif.
Height, 6.03. Weight, 205.
Throws and bats righthanded.
Hobbies—Water skiing and fishing.
Attended California Poly State University, Pomona, Calif., and
Whittier College, Whittier, Calif.

Tied for Florida State League lead in double plays by third basemen with 32 in 1974.

| Year Club League | Pos. | G. | AB. | R. | H. | 2B. | 3B. | HR. | RBI. | B.A. | PO. | A. | E. | F.A. |
|---|---|---|---|---|---|---|---|---|---|---|---|---|---|---|
| 1973-Jamestown.......NYP | 3B | 68 | 255 | 48 | 76 | 17 | 6 | 3 | 40 | .298 | *71 | 92 | 11 | *.937 |
| 1974-W. Palm Beach Fla. St. | 3-O-1 | 131 | 470 | 68 | 130 | 24 | 0 | 14 | *82 | .277 | 152 | 216 | 31 | .922 |
| 1974-Quebec City ......East. | 3B | 1 | 3 | 0 | 1 | 0 | 0 | 0 | 0 | .333 | 1 | 2 | 0 | 1.000 |
| 1975-Quebec City ......East. | OF | 131 | 466 | 67 | 133 | 23 | 0 | 14 | *74 | .285 | 223 | *22 | 10 | .961 |
| 1976-Denver..............A. A. | OF | 77 | 252 | 56 | 73 | 11 | 5 | 12 | 44 | .290 | 110 | 9 | 5 | .960 |
| 1976-Montreal .........Nat. | OF-PH | 29 | 90 | 9 | 20 | 3 | 1 | 2 | 5 | .222 | 39 | 3 | 2 | .955 |
| Major League Totals ...................... | | 29 | 90 | 9 | 20 | 3 | 1 | 2 | 5 | .222 | 39 | 3 | 2 | .955 |

### RANDELL WYNN ROGERS
(Randy)
Born August 16, 1956, at Texarkana, Ark.
Height, 6.00. Weight, 175.
Throws and bats righthanded.

| Year Club League | Pos. | G. | AB. | R. | H. | 2B. | 3B. | HR. | RBI. | B.A. | PO. | A. | E. | F.A. |
|---|---|---|---|---|---|---|---|---|---|---|---|---|---|---|
| 1974-Bellingham........Midw. | SS | 59 | 175 | 27 | 41 | 4 | 0 | 1 | 16 | .234 | 84 | 144 | 22 | .912 |
| 1975-Danville ...........Midw. | SS | 124 | 443 | 72 | 102 | 19 | 2 | 0 | 27 | .230 | 166 | 356 | 47 | .917 |
| 1976-Waterbury ........East. | SS | 125 | 399 | 36 | 93 | 9 | 2 | 2 | 27 | .233 | 192 | 372 | 41 | .932 |

Listed on Los Angeles Dodgers' 1977 spring roster.

### STEPHEN DOUGLAS ROGERS
(Steve)
Born October 26, 1949, at Jefferson City, Mo.
Height, 6.01. Weight, 177.
Throws and bats righthanded.
Hobbies—Golf and collecting coins, stamps and Indian arrowheads.
Attended Tulsa University, Tulsa, Okla.; received Bachelor of Science
degree in Petroleum Engineering.

Named National League Rookie Pitcher of the Year by THE SPORTING NEWS, 1973.

| Year Club League | G. | IP. | W. | L. | Pct. | H. | R. | ER. | SO. | BB. | ERA. |
|---|---|---|---|---|---|---|---|---|---|---|---|
| 1971-Winnipeg...........................Int'national | 15 | 102 | 3 | 10 | .231 | 109 | 51 | 45 | 67 | 40 | 3.97 |
| 1972-Peninsula† ........................Int'national | 13 | 64 | 2 | 6 | .250 | 75 | 32 | 29 | 39 | 25 | 4.08 |
| 1973-Quebec City ......................Eastern | 11 | 77 | 4 | 5 | .444 | 61 | 29 | 23 | 64 | 33 | 2.69 |
| 1973-Peninsula .........................Int'national | 4 | 29 | 3 | 1 | .750 | 18 | 6 | 6 | 22 | 8 | 1.86 |
| 1973-Montreal ...........................National | 17 | 134 | 10 | 5 | .667 | 93 | 28 | 23 | 64 | 49 | 1.54 |

| Year    Club | League | G. | IP. | W. | L. | Pct. | H. | R. | ER. | SO. | BB. | ERA. |
|---|---|---|---|---|---|---|---|---|---|---|---|---|
| 1974-Montreal | National | 38 | 254 | 15 | •22 | .405 | 255 | •139 | •126 | 154 | 80 | 4.46 |
| 1975-Montreal | National | 35 | 252 | 11 | 12 | .478 | 248 | 104 | 92 | 137 | 88 | 3.29 |
| 1976-Montreal | National | 33 | 230 | 7 | 17 | .292 | 212 | 93 | 82 | 150 | 69 | 3.21 |
| Major League Totals | | 123 | 870 | 43 | 56 | .434 | 808 | 364 | 323 | 505 | 286 | 3.34 |

†On temporary inactive list, April 14 to June 9, 1972.

## ALL-STAR GAME RECORD

Member of National League All-Star Team in 1974 game; did not play.

## OCTAVIO ROJAS (RIVAS)

Name pronounced ROW-hass.

### (Cookie)

Born March 6, 1939, at Havana, Cuba.
Height, 5.10. Weight, 171.
Throws and bats righthanded.
Hobby—Movies

Tied major league record for fewest triples, season, 500 or more at bats, 0, 1968.
Led National League in sacrifice hits with 16 in 1967.
Led National League second basemen in double plays with 110 in 1968.
Led International League second basemen in double plays with 89 in 1961.
Named second baseman on THE SPORTING NEWS American League All-Star Team, 1971.

| Year    Club | League | Pos. | G. | AB. | R. | H. | 2B. | 3B. | HR. | RBI. | B.A. | PO. | A. | E. | F.A. |
|---|---|---|---|---|---|---|---|---|---|---|---|---|---|---|---|
| 1956-W. Palm Beach | Fla. St. | 2B | 129 | 476 | 75 | 131 | 19 | 6 | 1 | 43 | .275 | 297 | 344 | 34 | .950 |
| 1958-Savannah | Sally | INF | 134 | 527 | 74 | 134 | 24 | 2 | 10 | 44 | .254 | 343 | 335 | 26 | .963 |
| 1959-Havana | Int. | 2B | 99 | 318 | 30 | 74 | 12 | 1 | 3 | 13 | .233 | 212 | 176 | 13 | .968 |
| 1960-Hav'a-Jer. City | Int. | 2B | 110 | 276 | 19 | 62 | 8 | 1 | 1 | 24 | .225 | 213 | 211 | •18 | .959 |
| 1961-Jersey City | Int. | 2B | 150 | 567 | 62 | 150 | 25 | 6 | 1 | 44 | .265 | •350 | •382 | •24 | •.968 |
| 1962-Cincinnati | Nat. | 2B-3B | 39 | 86 | 9 | 19 | 2 | 0 | 0 | 6 | .221 | 60 | 52 | 6 | .949 |
| 1963-Philadelphia | Nat. | 2B-OF | 64 | 77 | 18 | 17 | 0 | 1 | 1 | 2 | .221 | 43 | 68 | 1 | .991 |
| 1964-Philadelphia | Nat. | O-S-C | 109 | 340 | 58 | 99 | 19 | 5 | 2 | 31 | .291 | 164 | 76 | 7 | .972 |
| 1964-Philadelphia | Nat. | O-IF-C | 109 | 340 | 58 | 99 | 19 | 5 | 2 | 31 | .291 | 164 | 76 | 7 | .972 |
| 1966-Philadelphia | Nat. | 2-OF-SS | 156 | 626 | 77 | 168 | 18 | 1 | 6 | 55 | .268 | 319 | 295 | 13 | .979 |
| 1967-Philadelphia | Nat. | I-O-C-P | 147 | 528 | 60 | 137 | 21 | 2 | 4 | 45 | .259 | 297 | 360 | 15 | .978 |
| 1968-Philadelphia | Nat. | •2B-C | 152 | 621 | 53 | 144 | 19 | 0 | 9 | 48 | .232 | •365 | 424 | 10 | •.987 |
| 1969-Philadelphia‡ | Nat. | 2B-OF | 110 | 391 | 35 | 89 | 11 | 1 | 4 | 30 | .228 | 260 | 229 | 11 | .978 |
| 1970-St. Louis§ | Nat. | 2-O-S | 23 | 47 | 2 | 5 | 0 | 0 | 0 | 2 | .106 | 24 | 30 | 0 | 1.000 |
| 1970-Kansas City | Amer. | 2B | 98 | 384 | 36 | 100 | 13 | 3 | 2 | 28 | .260 | 217 | 283 | 9 | .982 |
| 1971-Kansas City x | Amer. | •2-S-O | 115 | 414 | 56 | 124 | 22 | 2 | 6 | 59 | .300 | 254 | 293 | 5 | •.991 |
| 1972-Kansas City | Amer. | 2-3-S | 137 | 487 | 49 | 127 | 25 | 0 | 3 | 53 | .261 | 265 | 368 | 9 | .986 |
| 1973-Kansas City | Amer. | 2B | 139 | 551 | 78 | 152 | 29 | 3 | 6 | 69 | .276 | 302 | 424 | 13 | .982 |
| 1974-Kansas City | Amer. | 2B | 144 | 542 | 52 | 147 | 17 | 1 | 6 | 60 | .271 | 292 | 368 | 9 | •.987 |
| 1975-Kansas City | Amer. | 2B | 120 | 406 | 34 | 103 | 18 | 2 | 2 | 37 | .254 | 233 | 303 | 11 | .980 |
| 1976-Kansas City | Amer. | 2-3-1 | 63 | 132 | 11 | 32 | 6 | 0 | 0 | 16 | .242 | 53 | 52 | 1 | .990 |
| American League Totals | | | 816 | 2916 | 316 | 785 | 130 | 11 | 5 | 322 | .269 | 1616 | 2091 | 57 | .985 |
| National League Totals | | | 942 | 3237 | 390 | 836 | 115 | 13 | 29 | 261 | .258 | 1806 | 1789 | 72 | .980 |
| Major League Totals | | | 1758 | 6153 | 706 | 1621 | 245 | 24 | 54 | 583 | .263 | 3422 | 3880 | 129 | .983 |

†Recalled by Cincinnati Reds; traded to Philadelphia Phillies for Pitcher Jim Owens, November 27, 1962.
‡Traded with First Baseman-Outfielder Richie Allen and Pitcher Jerry Johnson to St. Louis Cardinals for Catcher Tim McCarver, Outfielders Curt Flood and Byron Browne and Pitcher Joe Hoerner, October 7, 1969. Flood refused to report and the Cardinals sent First Baseman Guillermo Montanez and a player to be named later to Philadelphia to complete the deal, April 7, 1970. (Pitcher James Robert Browning was sent from St. Louis to Philadelphia as "the player to be named later.")
§Traded to Kansas City Royals for Outfielder Fred Rico (assigned from Omaha to Tusla), June 13, 1970.
xOn disabled list, August 22 to September 13, 1971.

## CHAMPIONSHIP SERIES RECORD

| Year    Club | League | Pos. | G. | AB. | R. | H. | 2B. | 3B. | HR. | RBI. | B.A. | PO. | A. | E. | F.A. |
|---|---|---|---|---|---|---|---|---|---|---|---|---|---|---|---|
| 1976-Kansas City | Amer. | PH-2B | 4 | 9 | 2 | 3 | 0 | 0 | 0 | 1 | .333 | 4 | 6 | 0 | 1.000 |

## ALL-STAR GAME RECORD

| Year    League | Pos. | AB. | R. | H. | 2B. | 3B. | HR. | RBI. | B.A. | PO. | A. | E. | F.A. |
|---|---|---|---|---|---|---|---|---|---|---|---|---|---|
| 1965-National | PH | 1 | 0 | 0 | 0 | 0 | 0 | 0 | .000 | 0 | 0 | 0 | .000 |
| 1971-American | 2B | 1 | 0 | 0 | 0 | 0 | 0 | 0 | .000 | 1 | 1 | 0 | 1.000 |
| 1972-American | PH-2B | 1 | 1 | 1 | 0 | 0 | 1 | 2 | 1.000 | 3 | 1 | 0 | 1.000 |
| 1973-American | 2B | 0 | 0 | 0 | 0 | 0 | 0 | 0 | .000 | 1 | 1 | 0 | 1.000 |
| All-Star Game Totals | | 3 | 1 | 1 | 0 | 0 | 1 | 2 | .333 | 5 | 3 | 0 | 1.000 |

Member of American League All-Star Team in 1974 game; did not play.

## PITCHING RECORD

| Year    Club | League | G. | IP. | W. | L. | Pct. | H. | R. | ER. | SO. | BB. | ERA. |
|---|---|---|---|---|---|---|---|---|---|---|---|---|
| 1967-Philadelphia | Nat. | 1 | 1 | 0 | 0 | .000 | 1 | 0 | 0 | 0 | 0 | 0.00 |

## DID YOU KNOW —

That the Cleveland Indians won the World Series in 1920?

## ENRIQUE ROMO (NAVARRO)

Born July 15, 1947, at Santa Rosalia, Baja Calif., Mexico.
Height, 5.11. Weight, 185.
Throws and bats righthanded.
Brother of Vicente Romo, former pitcher with Cleveland Indians and Boston
Red Sox and now with Cordoba in Mexican League.

| Year    Club | League | G. | IP. | W. | L. | Pct. | H. | R. | ER. | SO. | BB. | ERA. |
|---|---|---|---|---|---|---|---|---|---|---|---|---|
| 1966–Puerto Mexico.................Mex. S.E. | | 22 | 61 | 1 | 2 | .333 | 65 | 28 | 21 | 32 | 15 | 3.10 |
| 1967–Puerto Mexico.................Mex. S.E. | | 18 | 82 | 4 | 5 | .444 | 65 | 42 | 34 | 51 | 35 | 3.74 |
| 1968–Jalisco ............................Mexican | | 23 | 106 | 9 | 9 | .500 | 94 | 44 | 33 | 48 | 25 | 2.80 |
| 1969–Jalisco ............................Mexican | | 33 | 161 | 8 | 9 | .471 | 180 | 73 | 63 | 95 | 47 | 3.52 |
| 1970–Jalisco ............................Mexican | | 36 | 155 | 10 | 9 | .526 | 159 | 67 | 48 | 79 | 50 | 2.79 |
| 1971–Jalisco ............................Mexican | | 35 | 149 | 10 | 9 | .526 | 148 | 54 | 50 | 89 | 48 | 3.02 |
| 1972–Gomez Palacio ...................Mexican | | 38 | 186 | 11 | 8 | .579 | 133 | 65 | 42 | 104 | 52 | 2.03 |
| 1973–Mexico Reds .......................Mexican | | 36 | 163 | 11 | 9 | .550 | 172 | 72 | 57 | 117 | 36 | 3.15 |
| 1974–Mexico Reds .......................Mexican | | 32 | 193 | 17 | 9 | .654 | 197 | 85 | 66 | 130 | 49 | 3.08 |
| 1975–Mexico Reds .......................Mexican | | 30 | 219 | 13 | 8 | .619 | 194 | 71 | 57 | 146 | 52 | 2.34 |
| 1976–Mexico Reds† .....................Mexican | | 29 | 233 | 20 | 4 | •.833 | 169 | 60 | 49 | •239 | 56 | 1.89 |

†Traded to Seattle Mariners for cash estimated at $75,000 and a player to be named later.

## GILBERT RONDON

Born November 18, 1953, at Bronx, N. Y.
Height, 6.02. Weight, 200.
Throws and bats righthanded.

| Year    Club | League | G. | IP. | W. | L. | Pct. | H. | R. | ER. | SO. | BB. | ERA. |
|---|---|---|---|---|---|---|---|---|---|---|---|---|
| 1973–Bluefield ............................Ap'alachian | | 14 | 79 | 4 | 6 | .400 | 66 | 47 | 28 | 76 | 41 | 3.19 |
| 1974–Miami† ...............................Florida St. | | 14 | 35 | 2 | 2 | .500 | 30 | 17 | 15 | 32 | 14 | 3.86 |
| 1975–Salinas ..............................California | | 29 | 82 | 6 | 1 | .857 | 63 | 28 | 24 | 84 | 40 | 2.63 |
| 1975–El Paso‡ ............................Texas | | 9 | 31 | 4 | 1 | .800 | 32 | 20 | 20 | 24 | 25 | 5.81 |
| 1976–Houston§ ............................National | | 19 | 54 | 2 | 2 | .500 | 70 | 37 | 34 | 21 | 39 | 5.67 |
| Major League Totals ............... | | 19 | 54 | 2 | 2 | .500 | 70 | 37 | 34 | 21 | 39 | 5.67 |

†Released by Balitmore Orioles' organization, June 12, 1974; signed as free agent by California Angels' organization, January 3, 1975.
‡Drafted from Salt Lake City (California Angels' organization) by Houston Astros, December 8, 1975.
§On disabled list July 9 through August 5, 1976.

## PHILLIP ANTHONY ROOF
## (Phil)

Born March 5, 1941, at Paducah, Ky.
Height, 6.03. Weight, 205.
Throws and bats righthanded.
Hobbies—Hunting and golf.
Brother of Paul Roof, former pitcher in Milwaukee Braves' organization, Adrian Roof,
former pitcher in St. Louis Cardinals' organization, and David Roof, former pitcher
in Minnesota Twins' organization.

Led Three-I League catchers in double plays with 14 and in passed balls with 27 in 1960.
Tied for American Association lead in double plays by catchers with 10 and in passed balls with 17 in 1962.
Received reported $35,000 bonus to sign with Milwaukee Braves, 1959.

| Year    Club | League | Pos. | G. | AB. | R. | H. | 2B. | 3B. | HR. | RBI. | B.A. | PO. | A. | E. | F.A. |
|---|---|---|---|---|---|---|---|---|---|---|---|---|---|---|---|
| 1959–Midland ...........Soph. | | C-OF | 52 | 140 | 22 | 36 | 6 | 0 | 3 | 18 | .257 | 179 | 7 | 4 | .979 |
| 1960–Cedar Rapids ....I.I.I. | | C | 123 | 429 | 41 | 98 | 13 | 2 | 8 | 42 | .228 | •900 | •98 | 15 | .985 |
| 1961–Milwaukee .......Nat. | | C | 1 | 0 | 0 | 0 | 0 | 0 | 0 | 0 | .000 | 2 | 0 | 0 | 1.000 |
| 1961–Yakima ...........Northw. | | •C-O-3-1 | 114 | 379 | 43 | 99 | 17 | 3 | 6 | 49 | .261 | 593 | 59 | 9 | •.985 |
| 1962–Louisville .........A.A. | | C | 125 | 390 | 45 | 89 | 12 | 2 | 8 | 34 | .228 | •707 | •77 | •15 | .981 |
| 1963–Denver ............P.C. | | C | 107 | 346 | 54 | 77 | 18 | 1 | 11 | 51 | .223 | 705 | •59 | 9 | .988 |
| 1963–Toronto ...........Int. | | C | 23 | 62 | 2 | 8 | 1 | 1 | 0 | 5 | .129 | 105 | 11 | 3 | .975 |
| 1964–Denver ............P. C. | | C-1B | 74 | 218 | 24 | 41 | 8 | 1 | 4 | 28 | .188 | 389 | 39 | 4 | .991 |
| 1964–Milwaukee† .....Nat. | | C | 1 | 2 | 0 | 0 | 0 | 0 | 0 | 0 | .000 | 8 | 0 | 0 | 1.000 |
| 1965–Cal.‡-Clev.§ ......Amer. | | C | 52 | 74 | 4 | 12 | 1 | 0 | 0 | 3 | .162 | 214 | 23 | 2 | .992 |
| 1966–Kansas City ......Amer. | | C-1B | 127 | 369 | 33 | 77 | 14 | 3 | 7 | 44 | .209 | 684 | 52 | 11 | .985 |
| 1967–Kansas City ......Amer. | | C | 114 | 327 | 23 | 67 | 14 | 5 | 6 | 24 | .205 | 677 | 55 | 7 | .991 |
| 1968–Oakland x.........Amer. | | C | 34 | 64 | 5 | 12 | 0 | 0 | 1 | 2 | .188 | 116 | 6 | 4 | .968 |
| 1969–Oakland y.........Amer. | | C | 106 | 247 | 19 | 58 | 6 | 1 | 2 | 19 | .235 | 493 | 40 | 9 | .983 |
| 1970–Milwaukee ........Amer. | | C-1B | 110 | 321 | 39 | 73 | 7 | 1 | 13 | 37 | .227 | 596 | 47 | 8 | .988 |
| 1971–Mil.z-Minn .......Amer. | | C | 72 | 201 | 12 | 43 | 6 | 1 | 1 | 16 | .214 | 359 | 38 | 8 | .980 |
| 1972–Minnesota .......Amer. | | C | 61 | 146 | 16 | 30 | 11 | 1 | 3 | 12 | .205 | 257 | 11 | 6 | .978 |
| 1973–Minnesota .......Amer. | | C | 47 | 117 | 10 | 23 | 4 | 1 | 1 | 15 | .197 | 218 | 17 | 2 | .992 |
| 1974–Minnesota .......Amer. | | C | 44 | 97 | 10 | 19 | 1 | 0 | 2 | 13 | .196 | 200 | 24 | 0 | 1.000 |
| 1975–Minnesota .......Amer. | | C | 63 | 126 | 18 | 38 | 2 | 0 | 7 | 21 | .302 | 245 | 30 | 3 | .989 |
| 1976–Minn. a-Chi. b ..Amer. | | C-PH-DH | 22 | 55 | 1 | 11 | 3 | 0 | 0 | 4 | .200 | 76 | 12 | 3 | .967 |
| 1976–Iowa.................A.A. | | C | 10 | 25 | 2 | 6 | 1 | 0 | 2 | 5 | .240 | 42 | 4 | 0 | 1.000 |
| American League Totals ............... | | | 852 | 2144 | 190 | 463 | 69 | 13 | 43 | 210 | .216 | 4135 | 355 | 63 | .986 |
| National League Totals ............... | | | 2 | 2 | 0 | 0 | 0 | 0 | 0 | 0 | .000 | 10 | 0 | 0 | 1.000 |
| Major League Totals .................... | | | 854 | 2146 | 190 | 463 | 69 | 13 | 43 | 210 | .216 | 4145 | 355 | 63 | .986 |

†Traded to Los Angeles Angels with Pitcher Ron Piche, October 14, 1964, with Angels sending Pitcher Dan Osinski to Milwaukee Braves, November 29, 1964, to complete deal.

‡Traded with Pitcher Jack Spring to Cleveland Indians for a player to be named later, June 15, 1965, to complete deal in which Angels obtained Shortstop Jackie Hernandez, May 15, 1965. Outfielder Bubba Morton was transferred from Portland to Seattle, September 15, 1965.

§Traded to Kansas City Athletics for Outfielder Jim Landis, December 1, 1965. Trade included swap of two minor league players, Pitcher Jim Rittwage going to Indians' organization for Outfielder Joe Rudi.

xOn disabled list with pulled muscle in left arm from April 21 through June 4.

yTraded with Pitcher Lew Krausse, Outfielder Mike Hershberger and Pitcher Ken Sanders (latter transferred from Des Moines to Portland) to Seattle Pilots for First Baseman Don Mincher and Infielder Ron Clark, January 15, 1970.

zTraded to Minnesota Twins for Catcher Paul Ratliff, July 8, 1971.

aUnconditionally released, April 3, 1976; signed as free agent by Chicago White Sox, August 9, 1976.

bTraded to Toronto Blue Jays for Pitcher Larry Anderson, January 5, 1976.

## JAMES PHILLIP ROOKER
### (Jim)

Born September 23, 1942, at Lakeview, Ore.
Height, 6.00. Weight, 195.
Throws left and bats righthanded.
Hobbies—Golf, fishing, hunting and gun collecting.

| Year Club | League | G. | IP. | W. | L. | Pct. | H. | R. | ER. | SO. | BB. | ERA. |
|---|---|---|---|---|---|---|---|---|---|---|---|---|
| 1962—Jamestown | NYP | 3 | 10 | 0 | 0 | .000 | 11 | 10 | 9 | 3 | 8 | 8.10 |
| 1964—Duluth-Superior | Northern | 11 | 63 | 3 | 4 | .429 | 49 | 46 | 37 | 51 | 60 | 5.28 |
| 1965—Montgomery | Southern | 13 | 47 | 1 | 4 | .200 | 34 | 30 | 22 | 45 | 28 | 4.21 |
| 1965—Rocky Mount | Carolina | 15 | 68 | 1 | 7 | .125 | 58 | 39 | 31 | 50 | 42 | 4.10 |
| 1966—Montgomery | Southern | 5 | 7 | 0 | 0 | .000 | 12 | 11 | 8 | 8 | 6 | 10.29 |
| 1966—Rocky Mount | Carolina | 23 | 145 | 12 | 5 | .706 | 98 | 44 | 33 | 99 | 75 | 2.05 |
| 1967—Montgomery | Southern | 8 | 56 | 5 | 2 | .714 | 50 | 22 | 18 | 45 | 22 | 2.89 |
| 1967—Toledo | Int'national | 19 | 100 | 5 | 5 | .500 | 98 | 48 | 42 | 92 | 51 | 3.78 |
| 1968—Toledo | Int'national | 25 | 190 | 14 | 8 | .636 | 144 | 67 | 55 | •206 | 72 | 2.61 |
| 1968—Detroit†‡ | American | 2 | 5 | 0 | 0 | .000 | 4 | 2 | 2 | 4 | 1 | 3.60 |
| 1969—High Point | Carolina | 2 | 18 | 2 | 0 | 1.000 | 11 | 4 | 0 | 27 | 1 | 0.00 |
| 1969—Omaha | Am. Assoc. | 2 | 18 | 2 | 0 | 1.000 | 12 | 3 | 3 | 16 | 3 | 1.50 |
| 1969—Kansas City | American | 28 | 158 | 4 | 16 | .200 | 136 | 80 | 66 | 108 | 73 | 3.76 |
| 1970—Kansas City§ | American | 38 | 204 | 10 | 15 | .400 | 190 | 99 | 80 | 117 | 102 | 3.53 |
| 1971—Omaha | Am. Assoc. | 6 | 46 | 2 | 3 | .400 | 52 | 22 | 14 | 38 | 13 | 2.74 |
| 1971—Kansas City | American | 20 | 54 | 2 | 7 | .222 | 59 | 35 | 32 | 31 | 24 | 5.33 |
| 1972—Omaha | Am. Assoc. | 8 | 62 | 3 | 5 | .375 | 57 | 18 | 12 | 53 | 12 | 1.73 |
| 1972—Kansas City x | American | 18 | 72 | 5 | 6 | .455 | 78 | 37 | 35 | 44 | 24 | 4.38 |
| 1973—Pittsburgh | National | 41 | 170 | 10 | 6 | .625 | 143 | 59 | 54 | 122 | 52 | 2.86 |
| 1974—Pittsburgh | National | 33 | 263 | 15 | 11 | .577 | 228 | 93 | 81 | 139 | 83 | 2.77 |
| 1975—Pittsburgh | National | 28 | 197 | 13 | 11 | .542 | 177 | 80 | 65 | 102 | 76 | 2.97 |
| 1976—Pittsburgh | National | 30 | 199 | 15 | 8 | .652 | 201 | 83 | 74 | 92 | 72 | 3.35 |
| American League Totals | | 106 | 493 | 21 | 44 | .323 | 467 | 253 | 215 | 304 | 224 | 3.92 |
| National League Totals | | 132 | 829 | 53 | 36 | .596 | 749 | 315 | 274 | 455 | 283 | 2.97 |
| Major League Totals | | 238 | 1322 | 74 | 80 | .480 | 1216 | 568 | 489 | 759 | 507 | 3.33 |

†Sold to New York Yankees, September 30, 1968.

‡Selected by Kansas City Royals from New York Yankees in expansion draft, October 15, 1968.

§Played one game in outfield.

xReleased to Pittsburgh Pirates (in trade which sent Pitcher Gene Garber from Charleston to Kansas City), October 25, 1972.

### CHAMPIONSHIP SERIES RECORD

| Year Club | League | G. | IP. | W. | L. | Pct. | H. | R. | ER. | SO. | BB. | ERA. |
|---|---|---|---|---|---|---|---|---|---|---|---|---|
| 1974—Pittsburgh | National | 1 | 7 | 0 | 0 | .000 | 6 | 2 | 2 | 4 | 5 | 2.57 |
| 1975—Pittsburgh | National | 1 | 4 | 0 | 1 | .000 | 7 | 4 | 4 | 5 | 0 | 9.00 |
| Championship Series Record | | 2 | 11 | 0 | 1 | .000 | 13 | 6 | 6 | 9 | 5 | 4.91 |

### RECORD AS OUTFIELDER-FIRST BASEMAN

Led NYP League batters in strikeouts with 164 in 1961 and led Northern League with 127 in 1963.

| Year Club | League | Pos. | G. | AB. | R. | H. | 2B. | 3B. | HR. | RBI. | B.A. | PO. | A. | E. | F.A. |
|---|---|---|---|---|---|---|---|---|---|---|---|---|---|---|---|
| 1960—Decatur | Midw. | OF | 69 | 254 | 33 | 56 | 11 | 3 | 1 | 18 | .220 | 133 | 11 | 7 | .954 |
| 1961—Jamestown | NYP | OF | 125 | 451 | 83 | 121 | 16 | •13 | 10 | 88 | .268 | •283 | •17 | 13 | •.958 |
| 1962—Jamestown | NYP | OF-P | 119 | 455 | 101 | 128 | 15 | 8 | 16 | 80 | .281 | •214 | •23 | 10 | .960 |
| 1963—Dul.-Sup. | North. | OF | 115 | 412 | 82 | 112 | 12 | •11 | 19 | 78 | .272 | 276 | •20 | 11 | .964 |
| 1964—Knoxville | South. | OF | 27 | 79 | 5 | 14 | 3 | 0 | 3 | 11 | .177 | 40 | 4 | 4 | .917 |
| 1964—Dul.-Sup. | North. | O-1-P | 77 | 251 | 35 | 57 | 6 | 1 | 10 | 40 | .227 | 249 | 25 | 8 | .972 |
| 1967—Toledo | Int. | P-O-1B | 31 | 52 | 3 | 9 | 1 | 0 | 1 | 2 | .173 | 6 | 17 | 0 | 1.000 |
| 1968—Toledo | Int. | P-OF | 34 | 77 | 8 | 16 | 1 | 1 | 3 | 11 | .208 | 12 | 29 | 1 | .976 |

```
D I D   Y O U   K N O W —
```
That in 1963 not a single player in the American League played in every one of his club's games?

# PETER EDWARD ROSE
## (Pete)

Born April 14, 1942, at Cincinnati, O.
Height, 5.10½. Weight, 195.
Throws right and bats right and lefthanded.
Hobby—Sports.
Brother of David Rose, minor league pitcher in Cincinnati Reds' organization, 1967–1970.

Established major league records for most hits, switch hitter, season, 230, and most singles, switch hitter, season, 181, in 1973; and most plate appearances, season, 771, in 1974.

Tied major league records for most consecutive seasons leading majors in hits, 2, 1973; most consecutive seasons leading majors in games, 2, 1975; most seasons, 600+ at bats, 12, 1976; and most seasons, consecutive, leading major leagues in runs, 3, 1974-76.

Established National League record for highest fielding percentage, outfielder, career (1,000 or more games), .9919, 1975.

Tied modern National League records for highest batting average, switch hitter, season, 100 or more games, .348, in 1969; most seasons, 600 or more at bats, 11, 1975; most consecutive seasons leading league in runs, 3, 1974-76; most seasons leading league in hits, 6, 1976; most seasons, 200+ hits, 8, 1976.

Led Florida State League in total bases with 246 in 1961.

Named National League Rookie Player of the Year by THE SPORTING NEWS and National League Rookie of the Year by the Baseball Writers' Association, 1963.

Named THE SPORTING NEWS National League Player of the Year, 1968.

Named as second baseman on THE SPORTING NEWS National League All-Star Team, 1965-66.

Named as outfielder on THE SPORTING NEWS National League All-Star Team, 1968 and 1973.

Named outfielder on THE SPORTING NEWS National League All-Star fielding team, 1969 and 1970.

Named National League Most Valuable Player, 1973.

| Year | Club | League | Pos. | G. | AB. | R. | H. | 2B. | 3B. | HR. | RBI. | B.A. | PO. | A. | E. | F.A. |
|---|---|---|---|---|---|---|---|---|---|---|---|---|---|---|---|---|
| 1960–Geneva | | NYP | 2B | 85 | 321 | 60 | 89 | 8 | 5 | 1 | 43 | .277 | 198 | 193 | •36 | .916 |
| 1961–Tampa | | Fla. St. | 2B | 130 | 484 | 105 | •160 | 20 | •30 | 2 | 77 | .331 | 256 | 294 | 21 | .963 |
| 1962–Macon | | Sally | 2B | 139 | 540 | •136 | 178 | 31 | •17 | 9 | 71 | .330 | 317 | 368 | 24 | .966 |
| 1963–Cincinnati† | | Nat. | 2B-OF | 157 | 623 | 101 | 170 | 25 | 9 | 6 | 41 | .273 | 360 | 366 | 22 | .971 |
| 1964–Cincinnati | | Nat. | 2B | 136 | 516 | 64 | 139 | 13 | 2 | 4 | 34 | .269 | 263 | 301 | 12 | .979 |
| 1965–Cincinnati | | Nat. | 2B | 162 | •670 | 117 | •209 | 35 | 11 | 11 | 81 | .312 | •382 | 403 | 20 | .975 |
| 1966–Cincinnati | | Nat. | 2B-3B | 156 | 654 | 97 | 205 | 38 | 5 | 16 | 70 | .313 | 409 | 374 | 18 | .978 |
| 1967–Cincinnati | | Nat. | OF-2B | 148 | 585 | 86 | 176 | 32 | 8 | 12 | 76 | .301 | 287 | 93 | 11 | .972 |
| 1968–Cincinnati‡ | | Nat. | •O-2-1 | 149 | 626 | 94 | •210 | 42 | 6 | 10 | 49 | •.335 | 270 | •20 | 3 | .990 |
| 1969–Cincinnati | | Nat. | OF-2B | 156 | 627 | •120 | 218 | 33 | 11 | 16 | 82 | •.348 | 317 | 10 | 4 | .988 |
| 1970–Cincinnati | | Nat. | OF | 159 | 649 | 120 | •205 | 37 | 9 | 15 | 52 | .316 | 309 | 8 | 1 | •.997 |
| 1971–Cincinnati | | Nat. | OF | 160 | 632 | 86 | 192 | 27 | 4 | 13 | 44 | .304 | 306 | 13 | 2 | .994 |
| 1972–Cincinnati | | Nat. | OF | •154 | •645 | 107 | •198 | 31 | 11 | 6 | 57 | .307 | 330 | •15 | 2 | .994 |
| 1973–Cincinnati | | Nat. | OF | 160 | •680 | 115 | •230 | 36 | 8 | 5 | 64 | •.338 | 343 | 15 | 3 | .992 |
| 1974–Cincinnati | | Nat. | OF | •163 | 652 | •110 | 185 | •45 | 7 | 3 | 51 | .284 | 346 | 11 | 1 | •.997 |
| 1975–Cincinnati | | Nat. | 3B-OF | •162 | 662 | •112 | 210 | •47 | 4 | 7 | 74 | .317 | 161 | 230 | 14 | .965 |
| 1976–Cincinnati | | Nat. | •3B-OF | 162 | 665 | •130 | •215 | •42 | 6 | 10 | 63 | .323 | 115 | 293 | 13 | .969 |
| Major League Totals | | | | 2184 | 8886 | 1459 | 2762 | 483 | 101 | 134 | 838 | .311 | 4198 | 2152 | 126 | .980 |

†On military list, October 1, 1963, through March 14, 1964.
‡On disabled list, July 6 through July 27, 1968.

## CHAMPIONSHIP SERIES RECORD

| Year | Club | League | Pos. | G. | AB. | R. | H. | 2B. | 3B. | HR. | RBI. | B.A. | PO. | A. | E. | F.A. |
|---|---|---|---|---|---|---|---|---|---|---|---|---|---|---|---|---|
| 1970–Cincinnati | | Nat. | OF | 3 | 13 | 1 | 3 | 0 | 0 | 0 | 1 | .231 | 3 | 0 | 0 | 1.000 |
| 1972–Cincinnati | | Nat. | OF | 5 | 20 | 1 | 9 | 4 | 0 | 0 | 2 | .450 | 10 | 0 | 0 | 1.000 |
| 1973–Cincinnati | | Nat. | OF | 5 | 21 | 3 | 8 | 1 | 0 | 2 | 2 | .381 | 10 | 1 | 0 | 1.000 |
| 1975–Cincinnati | | Nat. | 3B | 3 | 14 | 3 | 5 | 0 | 0 | 1 | 2 | .357 | 2 | 1 | 0 | 1.000 |
| 1976–Cincinnati | | Nat. | 3B | 3 | 14 | 3 | 6 | 2 | 1 | 0 | 2 | .429 | 2 | 5 | 1 | .875 |
| Championship Series Totals | | | | 19 | 82 | 11 | 31 | 7 | 1 | 3 | 9 | .378 | 27 | 7 | 1 | .971 |

## WORLD SERIES RECORD

| Year | Club | League | Pos. | G. | AB. | R. | H. | 2B. | 3B. | HR. | RBI. | B.A. | PO. | A. | E. | F.A. |
|---|---|---|---|---|---|---|---|---|---|---|---|---|---|---|---|---|
| 1970–Cincinnati | | Nat. | OF | 5 | 20 | 2 | 5 | 1 | 0 | 1 | 2 | .250 | 14 | 1 | 1 | .938 |
| 1972–Cincinnati | | Nat. | OF | 7 | 28 | 3 | 6 | 0 | 0 | 1 | 2 | .214 | 14 | 1 | 0 | 1.000 |
| 1975–Cincinnati | | Nat. | 3B | 7 | 27 | 3 | 10 | 1 | 1 | 0 | 2 | .370 | 7 | 9 | 0 | 1.000 |
| 1976–Cincinnati | | Nat. | 3B | 4 | 16 | 1 | 3 | 1 | 0 | 0 | 1 | .188 | 6 | 3 | 0 | 1.000 |
| World Series Totals | | | | 23 | 91 | 9 | 24 | 3 | 1 | 2 | 7 | .264 | 41 | 14 | 1 | .982 |

## ALL-STAR GAME RECORD

| Year | League | Pos. | AB. | R. | H. | 2B. | 3B. | HR. | RBI. | B.A. | PO. | A. | E. | F.A. |
|---|---|---|---|---|---|---|---|---|---|---|---|---|---|---|
| 1965–National | | 2B | 2 | 0 | 0 | 0 | 0 | 0 | 0 | .000 | 2 | 4 | 0 | 1.000 |
| 1967–National | | 2B | 1 | 0 | 0 | 0 | 0 | 0 | 0 | .000 | 1 | 0 | 0 | 1.000 |
| 1969–National | | OF | 1 | 0 | 0 | 0 | 0 | 0 | 0 | .000 | 2 | 0 | 0 | 1.000 |
| 1970–National | | OF | 3 | 1 | 1 | 0 | 0 | 0 | 0 | .333 | 3 | 0 | 0 | 1.000 |
| 1971–National | | OF | 0 | 0 | 0 | 0 | 0 | 0 | 0 | .000 | 0 | 0 | 0 | .000 |
| 1973–National | | OF | 3 | 1 | 0 | 0 | 0 | 0 | 0 | .000 | 1 | 0 | 0 | 1.000 |
| 1974–National | | OF | 2 | 0 | 0 | 0 | 0 | 0 | 0 | .000 | 1 | 0 | 0 | 1.000 |
| 1975–National | | OF | 4 | 0 | 2 | 0 | 0 | 0 | 1 | .500 | 4 | 0 | 0 | 1.000 |
| 1976–National | | 3B | 3 | 1 | 2 | 0 | 1 | 0 | 0 | .667 | 0 | 1 | 0 | 1.000 |
| All-Star Game Totals | | | 19 | 3 | 5 | 0 | 1 | 0 | 1 | .263 | 14 | 5 | 0 | 1.000 |

Named to National League All-Star Team for 1968 game; replaced due to injury.

## DAVID ROSELLO (RODRIGUEZ)
### (Dave)

Born June 26, 1950, at Mayaguez, Puerto Rico.
Height, 6.00. Weight, 160.
Throws and bats righthanded.
Led American Association shortstops in total chances with 686 in 1972.
Tied for American Association lead in double plays by shortstops with 88 in 1972.

| Year | Club | League | Pos. | G. | AB. | R. | H. | 2B. | 3B. | HR. | RBI. | B.A. | PO. | A. | E. | F.A. |
|---|---|---|---|---|---|---|---|---|---|---|---|---|---|---|---|---|
| 1969–Quincy | | Midw. | S-O | 99 | 297 | 38 | 56 | 8 | 3 | 1 | 26 | .189 | 151 | 234 | 37 | .912 |
| 1970–Quincy | | Midw. | SS | 51 | 165 | 33 | 42 | 6 | 0 | 4 | 16 | .255 | 78 | 172 | 23 | .916 |
| 1970–San Antonio | | Texas | SS | 64 | 209 | 22 | 49 | 7 | 1 | 3 | 16 | .234 | 101 | 192 | 18 | .942 |
| 1971–San Antonio | | Texas | SS | 125 | 487 | 44 | 111 | 11 | 7 | 2 | 38 | .228 | 187 | 384 | 40 | .935 |
| 1972–Wichita | | A. A. | SS | •137 | 451 | 52 | 122 | 22 | 4 | 2 | 46 | .271 | •215 | •436 | •35 | .945 |
| 1972–Chicago | | Nat. | SS | 5 | 12 | 2 | 3 | 0 | 0 | 1 | 3 | .250 | 11 | 11 | 4 | .846 |
| 1973–Wichita | | A. A. | SS-2B | 99 | 367 | 54 | 115 | 15 | 3 | 8 | 51 | .313 | 157 | 304 | 34 | .931 |
| 1973–Chicago | | Nat. | 2B-SS | 16 | 38 | 4 | 10 | 2 | 0 | 0 | 2 | .263 | 30 | 29 | 3 | .952 |
| 1974–Wichita | | A. A. | SS-2B | 22 | 92 | 18 | 33 | 7 | 1 | 0 | 15 | .359 | 31 | 69 | 6 | .943 |
| 1974–Chicago | | Nat. | 2B-SS | 62 | 148 | 9 | 30 | 7 | 0 | 0 | 10 | .203 | 97 | 114 | 8 | .963 |
| 1975–Wichita | | A. A. | SS | 135 | •522 | 100 | 134 | 29 | 2 | 7 | 46 | .257 | 225 | •435 | 32 | .954 |
| 1975–Chicago | | Nat. | SS | 19 | 58 | 7 | 15 | 2 | 0 | 1 | 8 | .259 | 27 | 53 | 4 | .952 |
| 1976–Chicago | | Nat. | SS-2B | 91 | 227 | 27 | 55 | 5 | 1 | 1 | 11 | .242 | 129 | 217 | 12 | .966 |
| Major League Totals | | | | 193 | 483 | 49 | 113 | 16 | 1 | 3 | 34 | .234 | 294 | 424 | 31 | .959 |

## GARY DOUGLAS ROSS

Born September 16, 1947, at McKeesport, Pa.
Height, 6:01. Weight, 189.
Throws and bats righthanded.
Hobby–Riding horses.
Attended Grand View Junior College, Des Moines, Ia.
Pitched five-inning 19-0 no-hit victory against Salt Lake City, May 19, 1975.
Tied for Pacific Coast League lead in shutouts with 3 in 1975.

| Year | Club | League | G. | IP. | W. | L. | Pct. | H. | R. | ER. | SO. | BB. | ERA. |
|---|---|---|---|---|---|---|---|---|---|---|---|---|---|
| 1967–Quincy | | Midwest | 23 | 146 | 13 | 7 | .650 | 130 | 80 | 52 | 112 | 67 | 3.21 |
| 1967–Tacoma | | P. Coast | 5 | 19 | 0 | 3 | .000 | 25 | 16 | 16 | 7 | 10 | 7.58 |
| 1968–San Antonio | | Texas | 14 | 108 | 6 | 7 | .462 | 92 | 31 | 25 | 90 | 42 | 2.08 |
| 1968–Tacoma | | P. Coast | 5 | 31 | 3 | 1 | .750 | 23 | 7 | 6 | 20 | 18 | 1.74 |
| 1968–Chicago | | National | 13 | 41 | 1 | 1 | .500 | 44 | 22 | 19 | 31 | 25 | 4.17 |
| 1969–Chicago†-San Diego | | National | 48 | 112 | 3 | 12 | .200 | 105 | 61 | 54 | 60 | 58 | 4.34 |
| 1970–Salt Lake City | | P. Coast | 8 | 45 | 1 | 4 | .200 | 63 | 34 | 29 | 24 | 16 | 5.80 |
| 1970–San Diego | | National | 33 | 62 | 2 | 3 | .400 | 72 | 37 | 36 | 39 | 36 | 5.23 |
| 1971–Hawaii | | P. Coast | 20 | 113 | 7 | 11 | .389 | 141 | 72 | 68 | 90 | 39 | 5.42 |
| 1971–San Diego | | National | 13 | 24 | 1 | 3 | .250 | 27 | 10 | 8 | 13 | 11 | 3.00 |
| 1972–San Diego | | National | 60 | 92 | 4 | 3 | .571 | 87 | 35 | 25 | 46 | 49 | 2.45 |
| 1973–San Diego | | National | 58 | 76 | 4 | 4 | .500 | 93 | 51 | 46 | 44 | 33 | 5.45 |
| 1974–Hawaii‡ | | P. Coast | 13 | 66 | 4 | 4 | .500 | 62 | 38 | 33 | 46 | 28 | 4.50 |
| 1974–San Diego | | National | 9 | 18 | 0 | 0 | .000 | 23 | 10 | 9 | 11 | 6 | 4.50 |
| 1975–Hawaii§ | | P. Coast | 27 | 188 | •16 | 8 | .667 | 170 | 70 | 52 | 123 | 44 | 2.49 |
| 1975–California | | American | 1 | 5 | 0 | 1 | .000 | 6 | 3 | 3 | 4 | 1 | 5.40 |
| 1976–California | | American | 34 | 225 | 8 | 16 | .333 | 224 | 89 | 75 | 100 | 58 | 3.00 |
| National League Totals | | | 234 | 425 | 15 | 26 | .366 | 451 | 226 | 197 | 244 | 218 | 4.17 |
| American League Totals | | | 35 | 230 | 8 | 17 | .320 | 230 | 92 | 78 | 104 | 59 | 3.05 |
| Major League Totals | | | 269 | 655 | 23 | 43 | .348 | 681 | 318 | 275 | 348 | 277 | 3.78 |

†Traded with Pitcher Joe Niekro and Infielder Francisco Libran to San Diego Padres for Pitcher Dick Selma, April 24, 1969. Libran remained with Cubs' San Antonio farm team but became San Diego property.
‡On disabled list, June 4 to June 22 and July 11 to July 28, 1974.
§Traded by San Diego Padres to California Angels for Outfielder-Infielder Bobby Valentine and a player to be named later, September 17, 1975; Angels sent Infielder Rudy Meoli to Padres, November 4, 1975, to complete deal.

## JERON KENNIS ROYSTER
### (Jerry)

Born October 18, 1952, at Sacramento, Calif.
Height, 6:00. Weight, 165.
Throws and bats righthanded.
Hobbies–Water skiing and swimming.
Attended Healds Business College, Sacramento, Calif.
Tied for National League lead in double plays by third basemen with 35 in 1976.
Led Texas League third basemen in double plays with 26 in 1972.
Named Pacific Coast League Player of the Year in 1975.

| Year | Club | League | Pos. | G. | AB. | R. | H. | 2B. | 3B. | HR. | RBI. | B.A. | PO. | A. | E. | F.A. |
|---|---|---|---|---|---|---|---|---|---|---|---|---|---|---|---|---|
| 1971–Bakersfield | | Calif. | 3B | 7 | 20 | 2 | 2 | 1 | 0 | 0 | 2 | .100 | 1 | 5 | 1 | .857 |
| 1971–Daytona Beach | | Fla. St. | 3-S-2 | 111 | 371 | 68 | 100 | 13 | 7 | 8 | 42 | .270 | 90 | 265 | 29 | .924 |
| 1972–El Paso | | Texas | •3-S-O | 127 | 479 | •89 | 123 | 28 | 3 | 18 | 59 | .257 | 103 | 209 | •35 | .899 |
| 1973–Albuquerque | | P. C. | 3-S-O | 122 | 463 | 78 | 140 | 24 | 11 | 6 | 68 | .302 | 167 | 222 | 24 | .942 |

| Year | Club | League | Pos. | G. | AB. | R. | H. | 2B. | 3B. | HR. | RBI. | B.A. | PO. | A. | E. | F.A. |
|------|------|--------|------|-----|-----|-----|-----|-----|-----|-----|------|------|-----|-----|-----|------|
| 1973–Los Angeles | | Nat. | 3B-2B | 10 | 19 | 1 | 4 | 0 | 0 | 0 | 2 | .211 | 3 | 14 | 3 | .850 |
| 1974–Albuquerque | | P. C. | •3-2-S | 125 | 458 | 69 | 126 | 19 | 1 | 10 | 65 | .275 | 121 | 257 | 14 | •.964 |
| 1974–Los Angeles | | Nat. | 2-O-3 | 6 | 0 | 2 | 0 | 0 | 0 | 0 | 0 | .000 | 0 | 3 | 0 | 1.000 |
| 1975–Albuquerque | | P. C. | SS-3B | 133 | 487 | •91 | 162 | 31 | 7 | 10 | 65 | •.333 | 183 | 349 | 38 | .933 |
| 1975–Los Angeles† | | Nat. | O-2-3-S | 13 | 36 | 2 | 9 | 2 | 1 | 0 | 1 | .250 | 12 | 15 | 2 | .931 |
| 1976–Atlanta | | Nat. | •3B-SS | 149 | 533 | 65 | 132 | 13 | 1 | 5 | 45 | .248 | •158 | 310 | 19 | .961 |
| Major League Totals | | | | 178 | 588 | 70 | 145 | 15 | 2 | 5 | 48 | .246 | 173 | 342 | 24 | .955 |

†Traded with Outfielder Jimmy Wynn, Second Baseman Lee Lacy and First Baseman-Outfielder Tom Paciorek to Atlanta Braves for Outfielder Dusty Baker and First Baseman-Third Baseman Ed Goodson, November 17, 1975.

## DAVID SCOTT ROZEMA
### (Dave)

Born August 5, 1956, at Grand Rapids, Mich.
Height, 6:04. Weight, 185.
Throws and bats righthanded.

Tied for Midwest League lead in shutouts with 5 in 1975.
Tied for Southern League lead in shutouts with 4 in 1976.

| Year | Club | League | G. | IP. | W. | L. | Pct. | H. | R. | ER. | SO. | BB. | ERA. |
|------|------|--------|-----|-----|-----|-----|------|-----|-----|-----|-----|-----|------|
| 1975–Clinton | | Midwest | 27 | 164 | 14 | 5 | .737 | 128 | 50 | 38 | 123 | 32 | 2.09 |
| 1976–Montgomery† | | Southern | 19 | 126 | 12 | 4 | .750 | 98 | 29 | 22 | 96 | 15 | •1.57 |

†On disabled list May 9 through June 21, 1976.
Invited to Detroit Tigers' 1977 spring camp.

## JOSEPH ODEN RUDI
### (Joe)

Born September 7, 1946, at Modesto, Calif.
Height, 6.02½. Weight, 200.
Throws and bats righthanded.
Hobbies–Hunting and golf.
Attended Modesto Junior College, Modesto, Calif., and Chabot College, Hayward, Calif.

Led American League in total bases with 287 in 1974.
Named outfielder on THE SPORTING NEWS American League All-Star Team, 1972, 1974 and 1976.
Named as outfielder on THE SPORTING NEWS American League All-Star fielding team, 1974, 1975 and 1976.

| Year | Club | League | Pos. | G. | AB. | R. | H. | 2B. | 3B. | HR. | RBI. | B.A. | PO. | A. | E. | F.A. |
|------|------|--------|------|-----|-----|-----|-----|-----|-----|-----|------|------|-----|-----|-----|------|
| 1964–Wytheville | | Appal. | OF | 8 | 28 | 10 | 12 | 3 | 0 | 1 | 15 | .429 | 8 | 13 | 0 | 1.000 |
| 1964–Daytona Beach† | | Fla. St. | 3-O | 48 | 166 | 20 | 37 | 9 | 0 | 5 | 26 | .223 | 49 | 44 | 15 | .861 |
| 1965–Dubuque‡ | | Midw | •3-O | 110 | 374 | 55 | 95 | 21 | 2 | 16 | 58 | .254 | •123 | 145 | •37 | .879 |
| 1966–Modesto | | Calif. | OF-3B | 101 | 381 | 67 | 113 | 19 | 4 | 24 | 85 | .297 | 161 | 18 | 4 | .978 |
| 1967–Kansas City | | Amer. | 1-OF | 19 | 43 | 4 | 8 | 2 | 0 | 0 | 1 | .186 | 69 | 1 | 1 | .986 |
| 1967–Birmingham | | South. | 1-OF | 121 | 437 | 62 | 126 | 26 | 3 | 13 | 70 | .288 | 921 | 60 | 17 | .983 |
| 1968–Vancouver | | P. C. | OF | 16 | 60 | 9 | 19 | 3 | 0 | 3 | 7 | .317 | 23 | 1 | 1 | .960 |
| 1968–Oakland | | Amer. | OF | 68 | 181 | 10 | 32 | 5 | 1 | 1 | 12 | .177 | 77 | 1 | 1 | .987 |
| 1969–Des Moines | | A. A. | OF-1-3B | 57 | 240 | 42 | 85 | 15 | 2 | 11 | 65 | .354 | 436 | 39 | 8 | .983 |
| 1969–Oakland | | Amer. | OF-1B | 35 | 122 | 10 | 23 | 3 | 1 | 2 | 6 | .189 | 134 | 9 | 3 | .979 |
| 1970–Oakland | | Amer. | OF-1B | 106 | 350 | 40 | 108 | 23 | 2 | 11 | 42 | .309 | 302 | 18 | 4 | .988 |
| 1971–Oakland | | Amer. | OF-1B | 127 | 513 | 62 | 137 | 23 | 4 | 10 | 52 | .267 | 280 | 7 | 2 | .993 |
| 1972–Oakland | | Amer. | OF-3B | 147 | 593 | 94 | •181 | 32 | •9 | 19 | 75 | .305 | 247 | 9 | 2 | .992 |
| 1973–Oakland | | Amer. | OF-1B | 120 | 437 | 53 | 118 | 25 | 1 | 12 | 66 | .270 | 231 | 6 | 2 | .992 |
| 1974–Oakland | | Amer. | OF-1B | 158 | 593 | 73 | 174 | •39 | 4 | 22 | 99 | .293 | 416 | 18 | 5 | .989 |
| 1975–Oakland§ | | Amer. | 1B-OF | 126 | 468 | 66 | 130 | 26 | 6 | 21 | 75 | .278 | 804 | 37 | 7 | .992 |
| 1976–Oaklandx | | Amer. | OF-1-DH | 130 | 500 | 54 | 135 | 32 | 3 | 13 | 94 | .270 | 270 | 7 | 3 | .989 |
| Major League Totals | | | | 1036 | 3800 | 466 | 1046 | 210 | 31 | 111 | 522 | .275 | 2830 | 113 | 30 | .990 |

†Sold by Kansas City Athletics to Cleveland Indians, May 3, 1965 (the deal was designed to protect Rudi and Jim Rittwage, an Indian farmhand, from the first-year bonus draft rules then in effect). Transaction included swap of Catcher Phil Roof of Indians to Athletics for Outfielder Jim Landis, December 1, 1965.
‡Returned by Cleveland Indians' organization to Kansas City Athletics' organization, December 2, 1965.
§On disabled list, August 11 to September 11, 1975.
xPlayed out option year and granted free agency, November 1, 1976; signed as free agent by California Angels, November 17, 1976.

### CHAMPIONSHIP SERIES RECORD

| Year | Club | League | Pos. | G. | AB. | R. | H. | 2B. | 3B. | HR. | RBI. | B.A. | PO. | A. | E. | F.A. |
|------|------|--------|------|-----|-----|-----|-----|-----|-----|-----|------|------|-----|-----|-----|------|
| 1971–Oakland | | Amer. | OF | 2 | 7 | 0 | 1 | 1 | 0 | 0 | 0 | .143 | 4 | 0 | 0 | 1.000 |
| 1972–Oakland | | Amer. | OF | 5 | 20 | 1 | 5 | 1 | 0 | 0 | 2 | .250 | 11 | 0 | 0 | 1.000 |
| 1973–Oakland | | Amer. | OF | 5 | 18 | 1 | 4 | 0 | 0 | 1 | 3 | .222 | 11 | 0 | 0 | 1.000 |
| 1974–Oakland | | Amer. | OF | 4 | 13 | 0 | 2 | 0 | 1 | 0 | 1 | .154 | 5 | 0 | 0 | 1.000 |
| 1975–Oakland | | Amer. | 1B-OF | 3 | 12 | 1 | 3 | 2 | 0 | 0 | 0 | .250 | 22 | 2 | 0 | 1.000 |
| Championship Series Totals | | | | 19 | 70 | 3 | 15 | 4 | 1 | 1 | 6 | .214 | 53 | 2 | 0 | 1.000 |

### WORLD SERIES RECORD

Tied World Series records for most putouts, first baseman, inning, 3, October 16, 1974, 6th inning, and most putouts, left fielder, game, 6, October 12, 1974.

| Year Club League | Pos. | G. | AB. | R. | H. | 2B. | 3B. | HR. | RBI. | B.A. | PO. | A. | E. | F.A. |
|---|---|---|---|---|---|---|---|---|---|---|---|---|---|---|
| 1972–Oakland ...........Amer. | OF | 7 | 25 | 1 | 6 | 0 | 0 | 1 | 1 | .240 | 20 | 0 | 0 | 1.000 |
| 1973–Oakland ...........Amer. | OF | 7 | 27 | 3 | 9 | 2 | 0 | 0 | 4 | .333 | 20 | 2 | 0 | 1.000 |
| 1974–Oakland ...........Amer. | OF-1B | 5 | 18 | 1 | 6 | 0 | 0 | 1 | 4 | .333 | 28 | 0 | 0 | 1.000 |
| World Series Totals ....................... | | 19 | 70 | 5 | 21 | 2 | 0 | 2 | 9 | .300 | 68 | 2 | 0 | 1.000 |

### ALL-STAR GAME RECORD

| Year League | Pos. | AB. | R. | H. | 2B. | 3B. | HR. | RBI. | B.A. | PO. | A. | E. | F.A. |
|---|---|---|---|---|---|---|---|---|---|---|---|---|---|
| 1972–American ........................... | OF | 1 | 0 | 1 | 1 | 0 | 0 | 0 | 1.000 | 0 | 0 | 0 | .000 |
| 1974–American ......................... | OF | 2 | 0 | 0 | 0 | 0 | 0 | 0 | .000 | 1 | 0 | 0 | 1.000 |
| 1975–American ........................ | OF | 3 | 0 | 1 | 0 | 0 | 0 | 0 | .333 | 5 | 0 | 0 | 1.000 |
| All-Star Game Totals ...................... | | 6 | 0 | 2 | 1 | 0 | 0 | 0 | .333 | 6 | 0 | 0 | 1.000 |

## KENNETH VICTOR RUDOLPH
### (Ken)

Born December 29, 1946, at Rockford, Ill.
Height, 6.01. Weight, 185.
Throws and bats righthanded.
Hobbies–Golf and sketching.
Attended Los Angeles City College, Los Angeles, Calif., and Florissant Valley
Community College, St. Louis, Mo.

| Year Club League | Pos. | G. | AB. | R. | H. | 2B. | 3B. | HR. | RBI. | B.A. | PO. | A. | E. | F.A. |
|---|---|---|---|---|---|---|---|---|---|---|---|---|---|---|
| 1965–Treas. Valley ....Pion. | C | 19 | 73 | 9 | 15 | 2 | 1 | 3 | 15 | .205 | 85 | 18 | 2 | .981 |
| 1965–Quincy ..............Midw. | C | 34 | 127 | 14 | 35 | 8 | 0 | 3 | 15 | .276 | 252 | 30 | 6 | .979 |
| 1966–Lodi .................Calif. | C | 71 | 243 | 24 | 64 | 13 | 4 | 6 | 35 | .263 | 528 | 37 | ∗17 | .971 |
| 1967–Lodi† ...............Calif. | C | 48 | 115 | 12 | 28 | 5 | 0 | 4 | 14 | .243 | 181 | 22 | 6 | .971 |
| 1968–San Antonio‡ ....Texas | C-1-O | 45 | 138 | 11 | 28 | 0 | 0 | 4 | 17 | .203 | 229 | 38 | 10 | .967 |
| 1968–Tacoma ...........P. C. | C-OF | 13 | 36 | 2 | 5 | 0 | 0 | 0 | 0 | .139 | 35 | 4 | 0 | 1.000 |
| 1969–San Antonio ......Tex. | C | 6 | 23 | 2 | 8 | 1 | 0 | 1 | 4 | .348 | 28 | 3 | 0 | 1.000 |
| 1969–Chicago§ .........Nat. | C-OF | 27 | 34 | 7 | 7 | 1 | 0 | 1 | 6 | .206 | 43 | 3 | 1 | .978 |
| 1970–San Antonio ......Texas | C | 36 | 120 | 11 | 30 | 6 | 1 | 0 | 7 | .250 | 203 | 17 | 5 | .978 |
| 1970–Chicago x .........Nat. | C | 20 | 40 | 1 | 4 | 1 | 0 | 0 | 2 | .100 | 67 | 6 | 0 | 1.000 |
| 1971–Tacoma y .........P. C. | C-OF | 57 | 179 | 19 | 51 | 13 | 0 | 3 | 32 | .285 | 350 | 33 | 2 | .995 |
| 1971–Chicago ...........Nat. | C | 25 | 76 | 5 | 15 | 3 | 0 | 0 | 7 | .197 | 153 | 16 | 0 | 1.000 |
| 1972–Chicago ...........Nat. | C | 42 | 106 | 10 | 25 | 1 | 1 | 2 | 9 | .236 | 178 | 23 | 7 | .966 |
| 1973–Chicago z .........Nat. | C | 64 | 170 | 12 | 35 | 8 | 1 | 2 | 17 | .206 | 259 | 28 | 9 | .970 |
| 1974–San Francisco a Nat. | C | 57 | 158 | 11 | 41 | 3 | 0 | 0 | 10 | .259 | 253 | 25 | 1 | .996 |
| 1975–St. Louis .........Nat. | C | 44 | 80 | 5 | 16 | 2 | 0 | 1 | 6 | .200 | 93 | 11 | 3 | .972 |
| 1976–St. Louis b ........Nat. | C-PH | 27 | 50 | 1 | 8 | 3 | 0 | 0 | 5 | .160 | 61 | 2 | 4 | .940 |
| Major League Totals ..................... | | 306 | 714 | 52 | 151 | 22 | 2 | 6 | 62 | .211 | 1103 | 114 | 25 | .980 |

†On disabled list from June 18 through August 14.
‡On temporary inactive list, May 20 to May 28 and June 6 to June 29, 1968.
§On military list, July 11 to July 29, 1969.
xOn military list, July 10 to July 26, 1970.
yOn temporary inactive list, July 7 to July 26, 1971.
zOn supplemental disabled list, August 22 to September 6, 1973. Traded to San Francisco Giants for Pitcher
Willie Prall, March 19, 1974.
aTraded with Pitcher Elias Sosa to St. Louis Cardinals for Catcher Marc Hill, October 14, 1974.
bSold to San Francisco Giants, March 31, 1977.

## VERNON GERALD RUHLE
### (Vern)

Born January 25, 1951, at Coleman, Mich.
Height, 6.01. Weight, 185.
Throws and bats righthanded.
Attended Olivet College, Olivet, Mich.

| Year Club League | G. | IP. | W. | L. | Pct. | H. | R. | ER. | SO. | BB. | ERA. |
|---|---|---|---|---|---|---|---|---|---|---|---|
| 1972–Bristol ...............................Ap'lachian | 4 | 28 | 0 | 2 | .000 | 24 | 6 | 4 | 30 | 5 | 1.29 |
| 1972–Rocky Mount.....................Carolina | 13 | 72 | 5 | 8 | .385 | 87 | 53 | 38 | 53 | 28 | 4.75 |
| 1973–Lakeland...........................Florida St. | 15 | 96 | 6 | 5 | .545 | 81 | 27 | 22 | 67 | 24 | 2.06 |
| 1973–Montgomery ......................Southern | 10 | 81 | 6 | 2 | .750 | 72 | 33 | 26 | 34 | 17 | 2.89 |
| 1974–Montgomery ......................Southern | 5 | 45 | 5 | 0 | 1.000 | 29 | 6 | 3 | 32 | 12 | 0.60 |
| 1974–Evansville..........................Am. Assoc. | 22 | 156 | 13 | 5 | .722 | 178 | 80 | 70 | 94 | 42 | 4.04 |
| 1974–Detroit ..............................American | 5 | 33 | 2 | 0 | 1.000 | 35 | 13 | 10 | 10 | 6 | 2.73 |
| 1975–Detroit ..............................American | 32 | 190 | 11 | 12 | .478 | 199 | 104 | 85 | 67 | 65 | 4.03 |
| 1976–Detroit ..............................American | 32 | 200 | 9 | 12 | .429 | 227 | 99 | 87 | 88 | 59 | 3.92 |
| Major League Totals ........................... | 69 | 423 | 22 | 24 | .478 | 461 | 216 | 182 | 165 | 130 | 3.87 |

## WILLIAM ELLIS RUSSELL
### (Bill)

Born October 21, 1948, at Pittsburg, Kan.
Height, 6.00. Weight, 180.
Throws and bats righthanded.
Attended Kansas State College, Pittsburg, Kan.

Tied major league record for most strikeouts, game, 5, June 9, 1971.

Led National League shortstops in total chances with 834 in 1973.
Tied for California League lead in double plays by outfielders with 4 in 1968.
Named shortstop on THE SPORTING NEWS National League All-Star Team, 1973.

| Year | Club | League | Pos. | G. | AB. | R. | H. | 2B. | 3B. | HR. | RBI. | B.A. | PO. | A. | E. | F.A. |
|------|------|--------|------|----|-----|----|----|-----|-----|-----|------|------|-----|----|----|------|
| 1966–Ogden | ............... | Pion. | OF | 39 | 87 | 19 | 31 | 5 | 1 | 3 | 21 | .356 | 25 | 3 | 2 | .933 |
| 1967–Dubuque | ........... | Midw. | OF | 67 | 263 | 29 | 58 | 11 | 1 | 5 | 21 | .221 | 98 | 11 | 10 | .916 |
| 1968–Bakersfield | ........ | Calif. | OF | 115 | 439 | 76 | 123 | 16 | 3 | 17 | 55 | .280 | 255 | •22 | 7 | .975 |
| 1969–Los Angeles | ...... | Nat. | OF | 98 | 212 | 35 | 48 | 6 | 2 | 5 | 15 | .226 | 132 | 4 | 3 | .978 |
| 1970–Spokane | ........... | P.C. | O-3-SS | 55 | 237 | 48 | 86 | 13 | 5 | 3 | 30 | .363 | 112 | 39 | 6 | .962 |
| 1970–Los Angeles | ...... | Nat. | OF-SS | 81 | 278 | 30 | 72 | 11 | 9 | 0 | 28 | .259 | 167 | 10 | 3 | .983 |
| 1971–Los Angeles | ...... | Nat. | 2B-O-S | 91 | 211 | 29 | 48 | 7 | 4 | 2 | 15 | .227 | 131 | 124 | 8 | .970 |
| 1972–Los Angeles | ...... | Nat. | •SS-OF | 129 | 434 | 47 | 118 | 19 | 5 | 4 | 34 | .272 | 202 | 439 | •34 | .950 |
| 1973–Los Angeles | ...... | Nat. | SS | •162 | 615 | 55 | 163 | 26 | 3 | 4 | 56 | .265 | 243 | •560 | 31 | .963 |
| 1974–Los Angeles | ...... | Nat. | •SS-OF | 160 | 553 | 61 | 149 | 17 | 6 | 5 | 65 | .269 | 194 | 491 | •39 | .946 |
| 1975–Los Angeles† | | Nat. | SS | 84 | 252 | 24 | 52 | 9 | 2 | 0 | 14 | .206 | 94 | 230 | 11 | .967 |
| 1976–Los Angeles | ...... | Nat. | SS | 149 | 554 | 53 | 152 | 17 | 3 | 5 | 65 | .274 | 251 | 476 | 28 | .963 |
| Major League Totals | ...................... | | | 954 | 3109 | 334 | 802 | 113 | 34 | 25 | 292 | .258 | 1414 | 2334 | 157 | .960 |

†On disabled list, April 13 to May 6 and May 11 to June 30, 1975.

CHAMPIONSHIP SERIES RECORD

| Year | Club | League | Pos. | G. | AB. | R. | H. | 2B. | 3B. | HR. | RBI. | B.A. | PO. | A. | E. | F.A. |
|------|------|--------|------|----|-----|----|----|-----|-----|-----|------|------|-----|----|----|------|
| 1974–Los Angeles | ...... | Nat. | SS | 4 | 18 | 1 | 7 | 0 | 0 | 0 | 3 | .389 | 13 | 16 | 0 | 1.000 |

WORLD SERIES RECORD

| Year | Club | League | Pos. | G. | AB. | R. | H. | 2B. | 3B. | HR. | RBI. | B.A. | PO. | A. | E. | F.A. |
|------|------|--------|------|----|-----|----|----|-----|-----|-----|------|------|-----|----|----|------|
| 1974–Los Angeles | ...... | Nat. | SS | 5 | 18 | 0 | 4 | 0 | 1 | 0 | 2 | .222 | 4 | 11 | 1 | .938 |

ALL-STAR GAME RECORD

| Year | League | Pos. | AB. | R. | H. | 2B. | 3B. | HR. | RBI. | B.A. | PO. | A. | E. | F.A. |
|------|--------|------|-----|----|----|-----|-----|-----|------|------|-----|----|----|------|
| 1973–National | ............................ | SS | 2 | 0 | 0 | 0 | 0 | 0 | 0 | .000 | 0 | 2 | 0 | 1.000 |
| 1976–National | ............................ | SS | 1 | 0 | 0 | 0 | 0 | 0 | 0 | .000 | 1 | 2 | 0 | 1.000 |
| All-Star Game Totals | ...................... | | 3 | 0 | 0 | 0 | 0 | 0 | 0 | .000 | 1 | 4 | 0 | 1.000 |

## RICHARD DAVID RUTHVEN
### (Dick)

Born March 27, 1951, at Sacramento, Calif.
Height, 6.02. Weight, 195.
Hobbies–Reading, electronics, fishing, skiing and music.
Attended Fresno State University, Fresno, Calif.
Brother-in-law of Tommy Hutton, first baseman-outfielder with
Philadelphia Phillies.

| Year | Club | League | G. | IP. | W. | L. | Pct. | H. | R. | ER. | SO. | BB. | ERA. |
|------|------|--------|----|-----|----|----|------|----|----|-----|-----|-----|------|
| 1973–Philadelphia† | ..................... | National | 25 | 128 | 6 | 9 | .400 | 125 | 69 | 60 | 98 | 75 | 4.22 |
| 1974–Philadelphia | ....................... | National | 35 | 213 | 9 | 13 | .409 | 182 | 106 | 95 | 153 | 116 | 4.01 |
| 1975–Toledo | ............................... | Int'national | 23 | 153 | 10 | 12 | .455 | 148 | 72 | 54 | 114 | 69 | 3.18 |
| 1975–Philadelphia‡ | ..................... | National | 11 | 41 | 2 | 2 | .500 | 37 | 22 | 19 | 26 | 22 | 4.17 |
| 1976–Atlanta | ............................... | National | 36 | 240 | 14 | 17 | .452 | 255 | 112 | 112 | 142 | 90 | 4.20 |
| Major League Totals | ............................. | | 107 | 622 | 31 | 41 | .430 | 599 | 309 | 286 | 419 | 313 | 4.14 |

†On disabled list, August 3 to September 1, 1973.
‡Traded with Pitcher Roy Thomas and Infielder-Outfielder Alan Bannister to Chicago White Sox for Pitcher Jim Kaat and Shortstop Mike Buskey, December 10, 1975. Traded with Outfielder Ken Henderson and Pitcher Danny Osborn by Chicago White Sox to Atlanta Braves for Outfielder Ralph Garr and Infielder Larvell
Blanks, December 12, 1975.

## LYNN NOLAN RYAN, JR.
### (Known by middle name.)

Born January 31, 1947, at Refugio, Tex.
Height, 6.02. Weight, 190.
Throws and bats righthanded.
Hobby–Hunting.
Attended Alvin Junior College, Alvin, Tex.

Established major league records for most strikeouts, season (since 1900), 383, 1973; most games, 10 or
more strikeouts, season, 23, 1973; most seasons, 300 or more strikeouts, 4, 1976; most consecutive seasons, 300
or more strikeouts (since 1900), 3, 1974; most strikeouts, two consecutive games, 32, August 7 and 12, 1974;
most strikeouts, three consecutive games, 41, August 7-12-16, 1974; and most strikeouts, three consecutive
games (including extra innings), 47, August 12-16-20, 1974 (27⅓ innings).
Tied following major league records: struck out side on 9 pitches, April 19, 1968 (third inning) and July 9,
1972; most no-hit games, season, 2 1973; most strikeouts, game, 19, August 12, 1974; most no-hit games, life-
time, 4, 1975; and most consecutive seasons leading majors, bases on balls allowed, 3, 1974.
Established American League record for most clubs shut out (won or tied), season, 8, in 1972 (all clubs ex-
cept Kansas City, New York and Oakland).
Tied American League record for most strikeouts, consecutive, game, 8, July 9, 1972 and August 7, 1973.
Pitched 4-0 no-hit victory against Minnesota Twins, September 28, 1974.
Pitched 3-0 no-hit victory against Kansas City Royals, May 15, 1973.
Pitched 6-0 no-hit victory against Detroit Tigers, July 15, 1973.

Pitched 1-0 no-hit victory against Baltimore Orioles, June 1, 1975.
Led American League in shutouts with 9 in 1972 and with 7 in 1976.
Led American League in wild pitches with 18 in 1972.
Led Western Carolinas League pitchers in games started with 28 in 1966.
Tied for Appalachian League lead in hit batsmen with 8 in 1965.
Named Outstanding Pitcher in Western Carolinas League, 1966.

| Year Club | League | G. | IP. | W. | L. | Pct. | H. | R. | ER. | SO. | BB. | ERA. |
|---|---|---|---|---|---|---|---|---|---|---|---|---|
| 1965—Marion | Ap'lachian | 13 | 78 | 3 | 6 | .333 | 61 | 47 | 38 | 115 | 56 | 4.38 |
| 1966—Greenville | W. Carolinas | 29 | 183 | •17 | 2 | .895 | 109 | 59 | 51 | •272 | •127 | 2.51 |
| 1966—Williamsport | Eastern | 3 | 19 | 0 | 2 | .000 | 9 | 6 | 2 | 35 | 12 | 0.95 |
| 1966—New York | National | 2 | 3 | 0 | 1 | .000 | 5 | 5 | 5 | 6 | 3 | 15.00 |
| 1967—Winter Haven† | Florida St. | 1 | 4 | 0 | 0 | .000 | 1 | 1 | 1 | 5 | 2 | 2.25 |
| 1967—Jacksonville‡ | Int'national | 3 | 7 | 1 | 0 | 1.000 | 3 | 1 | 0 | 18 | 3 | 0.00 |
| 1968—New York§ | National | 21 | 134 | 6 | 9 | .400 | 93 | 50 | 46 | 133 | 75 | 3.09 |
| 1969—New York | National | 25 | 89 | 6 | 3 | .667 | 60 | 38 | 35 | 92 | 53 | 3.54 |
| 1970—New York | National | 27 | 132 | 7 | 11 | .389 | 86 | 59 | 50 | 125 | 97 | 3.41 |
| 1971—New York x | National | 30 | 152 | 10 | 14 | .417 | 125 | 78 | 67 | 137 | 116 | 3.97 |
| 1972—California | American | 39 | 284 | 19 | 16 | .543 | 166 | 80 | 72 | •329 | •157 | 2.28 |
| 1973—California | American | 41 | 326 | 21 | 16 | .568 | 238 | 113 | 104 | •383 | •162 | 2.87 |
| 1974—California | American | 42 | •333 | 22 | 16 | .579 | 221 | 127 | 107 | •367 | •202 | 2.89 |
| 1975—California | American | 28 | 198 | 14 | 12 | .538 | 152 | 90 | 76 | 186 | 132 | 3.45 |
| 1976—California | American | 39 | 284 | 17 | 18 | .486 | 193 | 117 | 106 | •327 | 183 | 3.36 |
| National League Totals | | 105 | 510 | 29 | 38 | .433 | 369 | 230 | 203 | 493 | 344 | 3.58 |
| American League Totals | | 189 | 1425 | 93 | 78 | .544 | 970 | 527 | 465 | 1592 | 836 | 2.94 |
| Major League Totals | | 294 | 1935 | 122 | 116 | .513 | 1339 | 757 | 668 | 2085 | 1180 | 3.11 |

†On military list from beginning of season through May 13.
‡Suffered elbow injury; on disabled list July 16 through August 30.
§On disabled list with blisters on pitching hand from July 30 through August 30.
xTraded with Pitcher Don Rose, Outfielder Leroy Stanton and Catcher Francisco Estrada to California Angels for Infielder Jim Fregosi, December 10, 1971.

CHAMPIONSHIP SERIES RECORD

| Year Club | League | G. | IP. | W. | L. | Pct. | H. | R. | ER. | SO. | BB. | ERA. |
|---|---|---|---|---|---|---|---|---|---|---|---|---|
| 1969—New York | National | 1 | 7 | 1 | 0 | 1.000 | 3 | 2 | 2 | 7 | 2 | 2.57 |

WORLD SERIES RECORD

| Year Club | League | G. | IP. | W. | L. | Pct. | H. | R. | ER. | SO. | BB. | ERA. |
|---|---|---|---|---|---|---|---|---|---|---|---|---|
| 1969—New York | National | 1 | 2⅓ | 0 | 0 | .000 | 1 | 0 | 0 | 3 | 2 | 0.00 |

ALL-STAR GAME RECORD

| Year League | IP. | W. | L. | Pct. | H. | R. | ER. | SO. | BB. | ERA. |
|---|---|---|---|---|---|---|---|---|---|---|
| 1973—American | 2 | 0 | 0 | .000 | 2 | 2 | 2 | 2 | 2 | 9.00 |

Member of American League All-Star Team for the 1972 and 1975 games; did not play.

## RAYMOND MICHAEL SADECKI

Name pronounced Suh-DECK-ee.

### (Ray)

Born December 26, 1940, at Kansas City, Kan.
Height, 5.11. Weight, 195.
Throws and bats lefthanded.
Received reported $50,000 bonus to sign with St. Louis Cardinals, 1958.

| Year Club | League | G. | IP. | W. | L. | Pct. | H. | R. | ER. | SO. | BB. | ERA. |
|---|---|---|---|---|---|---|---|---|---|---|---|---|
| 1958—Winnipeg | Northern | 19 | 132 | 9 | 7 | .563 | 72 | 59 | 49 | 174 | 129 | 3.34 |
| 1959—Omaha | Am. Assoc. | 31 | 193 | 13 | 9 | .591 | 164 | 98 | 87 | 175 | •145 | 4.06 |
| 1960—Rochester | Int'national | 6 | 41 | 2 | 1 | .667 | 27 | 14 | 8 | 23 | 27 | 1.76 |
| 1960—St. Louis | National | 26 | 157 | 9 | 9 | .500 | 148 | 76 | 66 | 95 | 86 | 3.78 |
| 1961—St. Louis | National | 31 | 223 | 14 | 10 | .583 | 196 | 100 | 92 | 114 | 102 | 3.71 |
| 1962—St. Louis | National | 22 | 102 | 6 | 8 | .429 | 121 | 74 | 63 | 50 | 43 | 5.56 |
| 1962—Atlanta | Int'national | 9 | 60 | 7 | 1 | .875 | 51 | 18 | 17 | 39 | 34 | 2.55 |
| 1963—St. Louis | National | 36 | 193 | 10 | 10 | .500 | 198 | 100 | 88 | 136 | 78 | 4.10 |
| 1964—St. Louis | National | 37 | 220 | 20 | 11 | .645 | 232 | 104 | 90 | 119 | 60 | 3.68 |
| 1965—St. Louis | National | 36 | 173 | 6 | 15 | .286 | 192 | 107 | 100 | 122 | 64 | 5.20 |
| 1966—St. Louis†-San Francisco | National | 31 | 129 | 5 | 8 | .385 | 141 | 91 | 69 | 83 | 48 | 4.81 |
| 1967—San Francisco | National | 35 | 188 | 12 | 6 | .667 | 165 | 65 | 58 | 145 | 58 | 2.78 |
| 1968—San Francisco | National | 38 | 254 | 12 | •18 | .400 | 225 | 94 | 82 | 206 | 70 | 2.91 |
| 1969—San Francisco‡ | National | 29 | 138 | 5 | 8 | .385 | 137 | 73 | 65 | 104 | 53 | 4.24 |
| 1970—New York | National | 28 | 139 | 8 | 4 | .667 | 134 | 67 | 60 | 89 | 52 | 3.88 |
| 1971—New York | National | 34 | 163 | 7 | 7 | .500 | 139 | 56 | 53 | 120 | 44 | 2.93 |
| 1972—New York | National | 34 | 76 | 2 | 1 | .667 | 73 | 33 | 26 | 38 | 31 | 3.08 |
| 1973—New York‡ | National | 31 | 117 | 5 | 4 | .556 | 109 | 47 | 44 | 87 | 41 | 3.38 |
| 1974—New York§ | National | 34 | 103 | 8 | 8 | .500 | 107 | 49 | 39 | 46 | 35 | 3.41 |
| 1975—St. Louis x-Atlanta y | National | 33 | 77 | 3 | 3 | .500 | 86 | 46 | 35 | 32 | 28 | 4.09 |
| 1975—Kansas City | American | 5 | 3 | 1 | 0 | 1.000 | 5 | 2 | 1 | 0 | 3 | 3.00 |
| 1976—K.C. z-Milw. a | American | 39 | 42 | 2 | 0 | 1.000 | 45 | 20 | 18 | 28 | 23 | 3.86 |
| National League Totals | | 515 | 2452 | 132 | 130 | .504 | 2403 | 1182 | 1030 | 1586 | 893 | 3.78 |
| American League Totals | | 44 | 45 | 3 | 0 | 1.000 | 50 | 22 | 19 | 28 | 26 | 3.80 |
| Major League Totals | | 559 | 2497 | 135 | 130 | .509 | 2453 | 1204 | 1049 | 1614 | 919 | 3.78 |

†Traded to San Francisco Giants for First Baseman Orlando Cepeda, May 8, 1966.
‡Traded with Outfielder Dave Marshall to New York Mets for Infielder Bob Heise and Outfielder Jim Gosger, December 12, 1969.
§Traded with Pitcher Tommy Moore to St. Louis Cardinals for First Baseman-Third Baseman Joe Torre, October 13, 1974.
xTraded with Pitcher Elias Sosa to Atlanta Braves for Pitcher Ron Reed and a player to be named later, May 28, 1975; Braves sent Outfielder Wayne Nordhagen to Cardinals, June 2, 1975, to complete deal.
yTraded to Kansas City Royals for Pitchers Al Autry and Norm Angelini, September 4, 1975, to complete deal in which Braves acquired Pitcher Bruce Dal Canton on waivers from Royals, June 20, 1975.
zReleased, May 5, 1976; signed as free agent with Milwaukee Brewers, May 13, 1976.
aReleased, December 14, 1976; signed as free agent by New York Mets, March 31, 1977.

WORLD SERIES RECORD

| Year Club | League | G. | IP. | W. | L. | Pct. | H. | R. | ER. | SO. | BB. | ERA. |
|---|---|---|---|---|---|---|---|---|---|---|---|---|
| 1964—St. Louis | National | 2 | 6⅓ | 1 | 0 | 1.000 | 12 | 7 | 6 | 2 | 5 | 8.53 |
| 1973—New York | National | 4 | 4⅔ | 0 | 0 | .000 | 5 | 1 | 1 | 6 | 1 | 1.93 |
| World Series Totals | | 6 | 11 | 1 | 0 | 1.000 | 17 | 8 | 7 | 8 | 6 | 5.73 |

## MICHAEL GEORGE SADEK
Name pronounced SAY-deck.
### (Mike)
Born May 30, 1946, at Minneapolis, Minn.
Height, 5.10. Weight, 167.
Throws and bats righthanded.
Hobby—Sports in general.
Attended University of Minnesota, Minneapolis, Minn., and St. Cloud
State College, St. Cloud, Minn.

| Year Club | League | Pos. | G. | AB. | R. | H. | 2B. | 3B. | HR. | RBI. | B.A. | PO. | A. | E. | F.A. |
|---|---|---|---|---|---|---|---|---|---|---|---|---|---|---|---|
| 1967—St. Cloud | North. | C | 53 | 177 | 37 | 41 | 5 | 0 | 0 | 17 | .232 | 401 | 32 | •14 | .969 |
| 1968—Orlando | Fla. St. | O-C-3-2 | 60 | 162 | 29 | 43 | 3 | 0 | 0 | 12 | .265 | 107 | 21 | 5 | .962 |
| 1969—Charlotte† | South. | C-2B | 81 | 224 | 28 | 43 | 9 | 3 | 0 | 25 | .192 | 384 | 41 | 5 | .988 |
| 1970—Amarillo | Texas | C | 17 | 46 | 6 | 9 | 2 | 0 | 0 | 3 | .196 | 116 | 17 | 2 | .985 |
| 1970—Phoenix | P.C. | •C-O-3 | 74 | 197 | 29 | 48 | 5 | 3 | 1 | 25 | .244 | 354 | 37 | •10 | .975 |
| 1971—Phoenix | P.C. | C | 76 | 220 | 30 | 68 | 8 | 4 | 1 | 32 | .309 | 473 | 33 | •14 | .973 |
| 1972—Phoenix | P.C. | C-3-S-O-2 | 78 | 212 | 25 | 52 | 9 | 1 | 1 | 24 | .245 | 409 | 42 | 7 | .985 |
| 1973—San Francisco‡ | Nat. | C | 39 | 66 | 6 | 11 | 1 | 1 | 0 | 4 | .167 | 146 | 7 | 3 | .981 |
| 1974—Phoenix | P.C. | C | 117 | 371 | 50 | 93 | 17 | 5 | 1 | 38 | .251 | 615 | •61 | 14 | .980 |
| 1975—Phoenix | P.C. | C | 50 | 160 | 29 | 43 | 8 | 6 | 2 | 28 | .269 | 293 | 48 | 3 | .991 |
| 1975—San Francisco | Nat. | C | 42 | 106 | 14 | 25 | 5 | 2 | 0 | 9 | .236 | 207 | 10 | 1 | .995 |
| 1976—San Francisco | Nat. | C-PH | 55 | 93 | 8 | 19 | 2 | 0 | 0 | 7 | .204 | 191 | 11 | 3 | .985 |
| Major League Totals | | | 136 | 265 | 28 | 55 | 8 | 3 | 0 | 20 | .208 | 544 | 28 | 7 | .988 |

†Drafted by San Francisco Giants from Denver (Minnesota Twins' organization), December 1, 1969.
‡On supplemental disabled list, June 25 to July 10, 1973.

## JAMES MICHAEL SADOWSKI
### (Jim)
Born August 7, 1951, at Pittsburgh, Pa.
Height, 6.03. Weight, 195.
Throws and bats righthanded.
Hobbies—Bowling, paddle ball and golf.
Attended Manatee Junior College, West Bradenton, Fla.
Nephew of Ted Sadowski, former pitcher and scout with Washington-Minnesota franchise; Ed Sadowski, former catcher with Boston Red Sox and Los Angeles Angels and minor league instructor for Montreal Expos, and Bob Sadowski, former pitcher with Milwaukee-Atlanta franchise.

| Year Club | League | G. | IP. | W. | L. | Pct. | H. | R. | ER. | SO. | BB. | ERA. |
|---|---|---|---|---|---|---|---|---|---|---|---|---|---|
| 1970—Gastonia | W. Carol. | 17 | 104 | 4 | 7 | .364 | 96 | 69 | 49 | 77 | 65 | 4.24 |
| 1970—Bradenton Pirates | Gulf C. | 4 | 33 | 3 | 1 | .750 | 25 | 13 | 10 | 32 | 8 | 2.73 |
| 1971—Salem | Carolina | 19 | 114 | 4 | 7 | .364 | 91 | 65 | 50 | 94 | 72 | 3.95 |
| 1971—Waterbury | Eastern | 2 | 18 | 2 | 0 | 1.000 | 5 | 2 | 2 | 13 | 14 | 1.00 |
| 1972—Salem | Carolina | 30 | 104 | 7 | 8 | .467 | 94 | 55 | 45 | 91 | 68 | 3.89 |
| 1973—Sherbrooke | Eastern | 39 | 124 | 11 | 5 | .688 | 94 | 61 | 46 | 135 | 95 | 3.34 |
| 1974—Charleston | Int'national | 30 | 94 | 4 | 10 | .286 | 72 | 48 | 42 | 87 | 45 | 4.02 |
| 1974—Pittsburgh | National | 4 | 9 | 0 | 1 | .000 | 7 | 6 | 6 | 1 | 9 | 6.00 |
| 1975—Charleston | Int'national | 27 | 126 | 6 | 12 | .333 | 124 | 70 | 58 | 70 | 76 | 4.14 |
| 1976—Charleston† | Int'national | 28 | 163 | 9 | 8 | .529 | 160 | 86 | 75 | 74 | 95 | 4.14 |
| Major League Totals | | 4 | 9 | 0 | 1 | .000 | 7 | 6 | 6 | 1 | 9 | 6.00 |

†Traded to Cincinnati Reds' organization for Pitcher Tom Carroll, November 6, 1976.

## DID YOU KNOW —
That Willie Mays scored 20 runs in All-Star Game competition? It's the all-time All-Star Game record for runs scored.

## JOSEPH CHARLES SAMBITO

Name pronounced sam-BEET-oh.

### (Joe)

Born June 28, 1952, at Brooklyn, N.Y.
Height, 6.01. Weight, 185.
Throws and bats lefthanded.
Hobbies—Fishing and all sports.
Attended Adelphi University, Garden City, N.Y.

Led Southern League in wild pitches with 14 and tied for lead in games started with 28 in 1975.
Tied for Appalachian League lead in shutouts with 2 in 1973.

| Year Club | League | G. | IP. | W. | L. | Pct. | H. | R. | ER. | SO. | BB. | ERA. |
|---|---|---|---|---|---|---|---|---|---|---|---|---|
| 1973–Columbus ............................Southern | | 1 | 2 | 0 | 0 | .000 | 4 | 4 | 4 | 2 | 1 | 18.00 |
| 1973–Covington ............................Ap'lachian | | 11 | 55 | 4 | 2 | .667 | 32 | 18 | 9 | 57 | 13 | 1.47 |
| 1974–Cedar Rapids .....................Midwest | | 23 | 156 | 11 | 8 | .579 | 133 | 59 | 52 | 182 | 49 | 3.00 |
| 1975–Columbus ............................Southern | | 30 | *209 | 12 | 9 | .571 | *200 | 85 | 70 | *140 | 85 | 3.01 |
| 1976–Memphis............................Int'national | | 5 | 27 | 3 | 0 | 1.000 | 37 | 19 | 19 | 17 | 13 | 6.33 |
| 1976–Columbus ............................Southern | | 12 | 100 | 8 | 2 | .800 | 77 | 27 | 20 | 61 | 23 | 1.80 |
| 1976–Houston ............................National | | 20 | 53 | 3 | 2 | .600 | 45 | 21 | 21 | 26 | 14 | 3.57 |
| Major League Totals ............................ | | 20 | 53 | 3 | 2 | .600 | 45 | 21 | 21 | 26 | 14 | 3.57 |

## KENNETH GEORGE SANDERS, JR.

### (Ken)

Born July 8, 1941, at St. Louis, Mo.
Height, 5.11. Weight, 185.
Throws and bats righthanded.
Hobbies—Golf, hunting and fishing.
Attended St. Louis University, St. Louis, Mo.

Established major league record for most games finished, season (77), 1971.
Established American League record for most clubs, pitcher, lifetime, 8, 1976.
Led American League in saves with 31 in 1971.
Led Florida State League pitchers in complete games with 22 in 1960.
Named by THE SPORTING NEWS as American League Fireman of the Year, 1971.

| Year Club | League | G. | IP. | W. | L. | Pct. | H. | R. | ER. | SO. | BB. | ERA. |
|---|---|---|---|---|---|---|---|---|---|---|---|---|
| 1960–Sanford................................Florida St. | | 34 | *241 | *19 | 10 | .655 | *209 | 107 | *86 | 191 | 83 | 3.22 |
| 1961–Portsmouth ..........................Sally | | 32 | 166 | 13 | 8 | .619 | 157 | 90 | 73 | 84 | 66 | 3.96 |
| 1962–Portland ............................P. Coast | | 7 | 24 | 0 | 4 | .000 | 26 | 18 | 16 | 9 | 13 | 6.00 |
| 1962–Albuquerque .....................Texas | | 6 | 14 | 0 | 3 | .000 | 35 | 24 | 23 | 4 | 4 | 14.79 |
| 1962–Binghamton.......................Eastern | | 25 | 121 | 3 | 11 | .214 | 137 | 74 | 54 | 66 | 39 | 4.02 |
| 1963–Nashville...........................Sally | | 7 | 29 | 1 | 1 | .500 | 36 | 15 | 12 | 13 | 9 | 3.72 |
| 1963–Binghamton.......................Eastern | | 28 | 119 | 5 | 6 | .455 | 115 | 61 | 48 | 74 | 46 | 3.63 |
| 1964–Birmingham .....................Southern | | 41 | 75 | 9 | 1 | .900 | 66 | 23 | 19 | 67 | 33 | 2.28 |
| 1964–Kansas City.......................American | | 21 | 27 | 0 | 2 | .000 | 23 | 12 | 11 | 18 | 17 | 3.67 |
| 1965–Vancouver†.........................P. Coast | | •57 | 92 | 8 | 6 | .571 | 75 | 29 | 28 | 63 | 51 | 2.74 |
| 1966–Boston‡-Kansas City ...........American | | 62 | 113 | 6 | 10 | .375 | 95 | 50 | 47 | 74 | 76 | 3.74 |
| 1967–Vancouver..........................P. Coast | | 50 | 84 | 9 | 6 | .600 | 75 | 25 | 19 | 68 | 14 | 2.04 |
| 1968–Vancouver..........................P. Coast | | 35 | 58 | 2 | 4 | .333 | 53 | 24 | 22 | 43 | 16 | 3.41 |
| 1968–Oakland ............................American | | 7 | 11 | 0 | 1 | .000 | 8 | 5 | 4 | 6 | 8 | 3.27 |
| 1969–Iowa§x .............................Am. Assoc. | | 29 | 114 | 6 | 7 | .462 | 117 | 55 | 43 | 49 | 34 | 3.39 |
| 1970–Portland y..........................P. Coast | | 14 | 34 | 4 | 1 | .800 | 21 | 5 | 4 | 21 | 10 | 1.06 |
| 1970–Milwaukee .........................American | | 50 | 92 | 5 | 2 | .714 | 64 | 19 | 18 | 64 | 25 | 1.76 |
| 1971–Milwaukee .........................American | | *83 | 136 | 7 | 12 | .368 | 111 | 35 | 29 | 80 | 34 | 1.92 |
| 1972–Milwaukee za .....................American | | 62 | 92 | 2 | 9 | .182 | 88 | 38 | 32 | 51 | 31 | 3.13 |
| 1973–Minnesota b-Cleveland.........American | | 42 | 72 | 7 | 5 | .583 | 71 | 37 | 35 | 33 | 30 | 4.38 |
| 1974–Cleveland c-California .........American | | 18 | 21 | 0 | 1 | .000 | 31 | 17 | 15 | 8 | 8 | 6.43 |
| 1974–Salt Lake City d .................P. Coast | | 19 | 34 | 3 | 1 | .750 | 37 | 15 | 13 | 22 | 13 | 3.44 |
| 1975–Tidewater ..........................Int'national | | 28 | 52 | 6 | 1 | .857 | 44 | 10 | 8 | 33 | 10 | 1.38 |
| 1975–New York e........................National | | 29 | 43 | 1 | 1 | .500 | 31 | 11 | 11 | 8 | 14 | 2.30 |
| 1976–New York f .........................National | | 31 | 47 | 1 | 2 | .333 | 39 | 16 | 15 | 16 | 12 | 2.87 |
| 1976–Kansas City g......................American | | 3 | 3 | 0 | 0 | .000 | 3 | 0 | 0 | 2 | 0 | .000 |
| American League Totals.......................... | | 348 | 567 | 27 | 42 | .391 | 494 | 213 | 191 | 336 | 229 | 3.03 |
| National League Totals............................ | | 60 | 90 | 2 | 3 | .400 | 70 | 27 | 26 | 24 | 26 | 2.60 |
| Major League Totals ............................ | | 408 | 657 | 29 | 45 | .392 | 564 | 240 | 217 | 360 | 255 | 2.97 |

†Drafted by Boston Red Sox from Vancouver (Kansas City Athletics' organization), November 29, 1965.

‡Traded with Pitcher Guido Grilli and Outfielder Jim Gosger to Kansas City Athletics for Outfielder Jose Tartabull and Pitchers John Wyatt and Roland Sheldon, June 13, 1966.

§Temporary inactive list April 10 through May 22.

xReleased to Portland (part of six-player deal in which Oakland acquired First Baseman Don Mincher from Seattle), January 15, 1970.

yReleased to Milwaukee Brewers, May 30, 1970.

zTraded with Pitchers Jim Lonborg, Ken Brett and Earl Stephenson to Philadelphia Phillies for Infielders Don Money and John Vukovich and Pitcher Billy Champion, October 31, 1972.

aTraded with Pitcher Ken Reynolds and Outfielder Joe Lis by Philadelphia Phillies to Minnesota Twins for Infielder-Outfielder Cesar Tovar, November 30, 1972.

bReleased on waivers to Cleveland Indians, August 3, 1973.

cReleased, June 17, 1974; signed as free agent by California Angels, June 24, 1974.

dTraded by California Angels to New York Mets for Catcher Ike Hampton, March 22, 1975.

eOn disabled list, August 10 to September 1, 1975.
fSold to Kansas City Royals, September 17, 1976.
gUnconditionally released, December 13, 1976; signed as free agent with Milwaukee Brewers, January 4, 1977.

## THOMAS JAMES SANDT
### (Tom)
Born December 22, 1950, at Brooklyn, N. Y.
Height, 5.11. Weight, 180.
Throws and bats righthanded.
Hobby—Golf

Named Northwest League Player of the Year in 1969.

| Year | Club | League | Pos. | G. | AB. | R. | H. | 2B. | 3B. | HR. | RBI. | B.A. | PO. | A. | E. | F.A. |
|------|------|--------|------|----|-----|----|----|----|----|----|------|------|----|----|----|------|
| 1969—Tri-City | | N'west | •SS-2B | 60 | 243 | •63 | 77 | 10 | 1 | 1 | 24 | .317 | 93 | 141 | 19 | •.925 |
| 1970—Burlington† | | Midw. | SS | 29 | 118 | 18 | 34 | 4 | 0 | 0 | 4 | .288 | 50 | 89 | 16 | .897 |
| 1971—Burlington | | Midw. | SS | 70 | 279 | 42 | 73 | 7 | 0 | 0 | 20 | .262 | 93 | 159 | 25 | .910 |
| 1971—Birmingham | | South. | SS | 29 | 84 | 10 | 18 | 2 | 1 | 0 | 2 | .214 | 27 | 62 | 5 | .947 |
| 1972—Birmingham | | South. | SS | 109 | 386 | 40 | 85 | 11 | 2 | 1 | 14 | .220 | 150 | 307 | 17 | •.964 |
| 1973—Birmingham | | South. | SS | 18 | 74 | 11 | 18 | 3 | 0 | 0 | 5 | .243 | 34 | 51 | 7 | .924 |
| 1973—Burlington | | Midw. | S-2-P | 92 | 359 | 77 | 108 | 10 | 6 | 6 | 54 | .301 | 138 | 240 | 22 | .945 |
| 1974—Tucson | | P. C. | S-2-3 | 81 | 206 | 31 | 49 | 8 | 0 | 0 | 14 | .238 | 102 | 164 | 15 | .947 |
| 1975—Tucson | | P. C. | •S-2-O | 116 | 391 | 62 | 121 | 20 | 0 | 2 | 49 | .309 | 193 | 287 | 22 | •.956 |
| 1975—Oakland | | Amer. | 2B | 1 | 0 | 0 | 0 | 0 | 0 | 0 | 0 | .000 | 0 | 0 | 0 | .000 |
| 1976—Oakland‡ | | Amer. | S-2-3 | 41 | 67 | 6 | 14 | 1 | 0 | 0 | 3 | .209 | 44 | 60 | 3 | .972 |
| Major League Totals | | | | 42 | 67 | 6 | 14 | 1 | 0 | 0 | 3 | .209 | 44 | 60 | 3 | .972 |

†On Military list from beginning of season until July 14, 1970.
‡Sold to St. Louis Cardinals, March 26, 1977.

### PITCHING RECORD

| Year | Club | League | G. | IP. | W. | L. | Pct. | H. | R. | ER. | SO. | BB. | ERA. |
|------|------|--------|----|-----|----|----|------|----|----|----|-----|-----|------|
| 1973—Burlington | | Midwest | 1 | 1 | 0 | 0 | .000 | 0 | 0 | 0 | 0 | 1 | 0.00 |

## MANUEL deJESUS SANGUILLEN
Name pronounced San-GHEE-yen.
### (Manny)
Born March 21, 1944, at Colon, Panama.
Height, 6.00. Weight, 193.
Throws and bats righthanded.
Hobbies—Fishing and playing guitar.

Tied major league record for most triples with bases filled, season, 3, 1971.
Tied for National League lead in double plays by catchers with 12 in 1971.
Led NYP League catchers in double plays with 9 in 1965.
Led Carolina League in passed balls with 17 in 1966 and International League with 9 in 1968.
Named catcher on THE SPORTING NEWS National League All-Star Team, 1971.

| Year | Club | League | Pos. | G. | AB. | R. | H. | 2B. | 3B. | HR. | RBI. | B.A. | PO. | A. | E. | F.A. |
|------|------|--------|------|----|-----|----|----|----|----|----|------|------|----|----|----|------|
| 1965—Batavia | | NYP | C | 99 | 340 | 45 | 80 | 8 | 2 | 6 | 36 | .235 | 689 | •69 | 10 | .987 |
| 1966—Raleigh | | Carol. | C | 115 | 400 | 62 | 131 | 19 | 3 | 8 | 49 | .328 | 683 | •87 | 16 | .980 |
| 1966—Columbus | | Int. | C | 9 | 26 | 1 | 6 | 0 | 0 | 0 | 0 | .231 | 37 | 12 | 0 | 1.000 |
| 1967—Columbus | | Int. | C | 71 | 240 | 28 | 62 | 6 | 2 | 9 | 29 | .258 | 409 | 48 | •10 | .979 |
| 1967—Pittsburgh | | Nat. | C | 30 | 96 | 6 | 26 | 4 | 0 | 0 | 8 | .271 | 133 | 11 | 2 | .986 |
| 1968—Columbus | | Int. | C-1B-O | 105 | 377 | 45 | 119 | 16 | 5 | 8 | 60 | .316 | 592 | 60 | 8 | .988 |
| 1969—Pittsburgh | | Nat. | C | 129 | 459 | 62 | 139 | 21 | 6 | 5 | 57 | .303 | 825 | 71 | •17 | .981 |
| 1970—Pittsburgh | | Nat. | C | 128 | 486 | 63 | 158 | 19 | 9 | 7 | 61 | .325 | 775 | 66 | 10 | .988 |
| 1971—Pittsburgh | | Nat. | C | 138 | 533 | 60 | 170 | 26 | 5 | 7 | 81 | .319 | 712 | •72 | 5 | .994 |
| 1972—Pittsburgh | | Nat. | C-OF | 136 | 520 | 55 | 155 | 18 | 8 | 7 | 71 | .298 | 724 | 50 | 9 | .989 |
| 1973—Pittsburgh | | Nat. | C-OF | 149 | 589 | 64 | 166 | 26 | 7 | 12 | 65 | .282 | 632 | 41 | 17 | .975 |
| 1974—Pittsburgh | | Nat. | C | 151 | 596 | 77 | 171 | 21 | 4 | 7 | 68 | .287 | 713 | 76 | 12 | .985 |
| 1975—Pittsburgh | | Nat. | C | 133 | 481 | 60 | 158 | 24 | 4 | 9 | 58 | .328 | 650 | 53 | 9 | .987 |
| 1976—Pittsburgh† | | Nat. | C | 114 | 389 | 52 | 113 | 16 | 6 | 2 | 36 | .290 | 518 | 52 | •13 | .978 |
| Major League Totals | | | | 1108 | 4149 | 499 | 1256 | 175 | 49 | 56 | 505 | .303 | 5682 | 492 | 94 | .985 |

†Traded with cash estimated at $100,000 to Oakland A's for Manager Chuck Tanner, November 5, 1976.

### CHAMPIONSHIP SERIES RECORD

| Year | Club | League | Pos. | G. | AB. | R. | H. | 2B. | 3B. | HR. | RBI. | B.A. | PO. | A. | E. | F.A. |
|------|------|--------|------|----|-----|----|----|----|----|----|------|------|----|----|----|------|
| 1970—Pittsburgh | | Nat. | C | 3 | 12 | 0 | 2 | 0 | 0 | 0 | 0 | .167 | 13 | 1 | 1 | .983 |
| 1971—Pittsburgh | | Nat. | C | 4 | 15 | 1 | 4 | 0 | 0 | 0 | 1 | .267 | 30 | 1 | 0 | 1.000 |
| 1972—Pittsburgh | | Nat. | C-PH | 5 | 16 | 4 | 5 | 1 | 0 | 1 | 2 | .313 | 22 | 0 | 1 | .957 |
| 1974—Pittsburgh | | Nat. | C | 4 | 16 | 0 | 4 | 1 | 0 | 0 | 0 | .250 | 19 | 2 | 2 | .913 |
| 1975—Pittsburgh | | Nat. | C | 3 | 12 | 0 | 2 | 0 | 0 | 0 | 0 | .167 | 29 | 1 | 1 | .968 |
| Championship Series Totals | | | | 19 | 70 | 5 | 17 | 2 | 0 | 1 | 3 | .243 | 113 | 5 | 5 | .959 |

### WORLD SERIES RECORD

| Year | Club | League | Pos. | G. | AB. | R. | H. | 2B. | 3B. | HR. | RBI. | B.A. | PO. | A. | E. | F.A. |
|------|------|--------|------|----|-----|----|----|----|----|----|------|------|----|----|----|------|
| 1971—Pittsburgh | | Nat. | C | 7 | 29 | 3 | 11 | 1 | 0 | 0 | 0 | .379 | 37 | 0 | 0 | 1.000 |

| Year League | Pos. | AB. | R. | H. | 2B. | 3B. | HR. | RBI. | B.A. | PO. | A. | E. | F.A. |
|---|---|---|---|---|---|---|---|---|---|---|---|---|---|
| 1972—National .......................... | C | 2 | 0 | 1 | 0 | 0 | 0 | 0 | .500 | 6 | 0 | 0 | 1.000 |

Member of National League All-Star Team for 1971 and 1975 games; did not play.

## MANUEL EDUARDO SARMIENTO (APONTE)
Name pronounced sar-mee-EN-toh.
### (Manny)
Born February 2, 1956, at Cagua, Aragua, Venezuela.
Height, 6.00. Weight, 170.
Throws and bats righthanded.
Hobbies—Listening to music and playing basketball.
Led Northwest League in saves with 14 in 1973 and Eastern League with 15 in 1975.

| Year Club | League | G. | IP. | W. | L. | Pct. | H. | R. | ER. | SO. | BB. | ERA. |
|---|---|---|---|---|---|---|---|---|---|---|---|---|
| 1972—Bradenton Reds.................. | G. Coast | 18 | 40 | 2 | 6 | .250 | 40 | 22 | 13 | 34 | 15 | 2.93 |
| 1973—Seattle .............................. | Northwest | *36 | 67 | 2 | 6 | .250 | 53 | 22 | 16 | 60 | 24 | 2.15 |
| 1974—Tampa ............................. | Florida St. | 39 | 126 | 10 | 9 | .526 | 112 | 42 | 40 | 80 | 47 | 2.86 |
| 1975—Three Rivers...................... | Eastern | *64 | 129 | 6 | 8 | .429 | 104 | 41 | 37 | 114 | 51 | 2.58 |
| 1976—Indianapolis ..................... | Am. Assoc. | 43 | 65 | 11 | 5 | .688 | 49 | 21 | 20 | 51 | 24 | 2.77 |
| 1976—Cincinnati ........................ | National | 22 | 44 | 5 | 1 | .833 | 36 | 14 | 10 | 20 | 12 | 2.05 |
| Major League Totals ............................ | | 22 | 44 | 5 | 1 | .833 | 36 | 14 | 10 | 20 | 12 | 2.05 |

CHAMPIONSHIP SERIES RECORD

| Year Club | League | G. | IP. | W. | L. | Pct. | H. | R. | ER. | SO. | BB. | ERA. |
|---|---|---|---|---|---|---|---|---|---|---|---|---|
| 1976—Cincinnati .......................... | National | 1 | 1 | 0 | 0 | .000 | 2 | 2 | 2 | 0 | 1 | 18.00 |

## RICHARD CLYDE SAWYER
### (Rick)
Born April 7, 1948, at Bakersfield, Calif.
Height, 6.02. Weight, 205.
Throws and bats righthanded.
Hobby—Sports in general.
Attended Bakersfield Junior College, Bakersfield, Calif., and
California State University, Northridge, Calif.

| Year Club | League | G. | IP. | W. | L. | Pct. | H. | R. | ER. | SO. | BB. | ERA. |
|---|---|---|---|---|---|---|---|---|---|---|---|---|
| 1968—Reno.................................. | California | 4 | 10 | 0 | 1 | .000 | 12 | 10 | 9 | 10 | 6 | 8.10 |
| 1968—Sarasota Indians ................ | Gulf Coast | 7 | 30 | 2 | 3 | .400 | 31 | 12 | 10 | 25 | 11 | 3.00 |
| 1969—Reno.................................. | California | 26 | 100 | 7 | 7 | .500 | 106 | 43 | 35 | 99 | 33 | 3.15 |
| 1970—Reno.................................. | California | 23 | 130 | 10 | 5 | .667 | 125 | 60 | 49 | 122 | 42 | 3.39 |
| 1971—Jacksonville†...................... | Southern | 19 | 138 | 8 | 3 | .727 | 121 | 62 | 49 | 112 | 47 | 3.20 |
| 1972—Portland ............................ | P. Coast | 29 | 130 | 7 | 9 | .438 | 138 | 72 | 66 | 83 | 54 | 4.57 |
| 1972—Reno.................................. | California | 1 | 5 | 0 | 0 | .000 | 10 | 4 | 3 | 4 | 1 | 5.40 |
| 1973—San Antonio‡...................... | Texas | 27 | 179 | *18 | 5 | .783 | 159 | 73 | 56 | 124 | 66 | 2.81 |
| 1974—Syracuse ........................... | Int'national | 24 | 164 | 8 | 7 | .533 | 131 | 65 | 51 | 136 | 59 | 2.80 |
| 1974—New York .......................... | American | 1 | 2 | 0 | 0 | .000 | 2 | 3 | 3 | 1 | 1 | 13.50 |
| 1975—Syracuse ........................... | Int'national | 25 | 175 | 13 | 9 | .591 | 134 | 53 | 48 | 96 | 47 | 2.47 |
| 1975—New York .......................... | American | 4 | 6 | 0 | 0 | .000 | 7 | 4 | 2 | 3 | 2 | 3.00 |
| 1976—Syracuse§ .......................... | Int'national | 19 | 134 | 9 | 4 | .692 | 125 | 55 | 41 | 65 | 38 | 2.75 |
| 1976—San Diego ......................... | National | 13 | 82 | 5 | 3 | .625 | 84 | 24 | 23 | 33 | 38 | 2.52 |
| National League Totals........................ | | 13 | 82 | 5 | 3 | .625 | 84 | 24 | 23 | 33 | 38 | 2.52 |
| American League Totals........................ | | 5 | 8 | 0 | 0 | .000 | 9 | 7 | 5 | 4 | 3 | 5.63 |
| Major League Totals .............................. | | 18 | 90 | 5 | 3 | .625 | 93 | 31 | 28 | 37 | 41 | 2.80 |

†On temporary inactive list, July 8 through July 30, 1971.
‡Traded by Cleveland Indians with Outfielder Walt Williams to New York Yankees as part of deal where Yankees sent Catcher Jerry Moses to Detroit Tigers and Detroit sent Pitcher Jim Perry to Cleveland and Pitcher Ed Farmer to New York, March 19, 1974.
§Assigned to San Diego Padres, July 31, 1976, to complete deal which sent Outfielder Gene Locklear to New York Yankees' organization, July 10, 1976.

## JAMES PATRICK SCANLON
### (Pat)
Born September 23, 1952, at Minneapolis, Minn.
Height, 6.01. Weight, 180.
Throws right and bats lefthanded.
Hobby—Golf.
Attended St. Petersburg Junior College, St. Petersburg, Fla., and
University of Minnesota, Minneapolis, Minn.
Son of Paul F. Scanlon, Jr., former catcher in Chicago Cubs' organization.
Tied for Eastern League lead in strikeouts by batters with 110 in 1973.

| Year Club League | Pos. | G. | AB. | R. | H. | 2B. | 3B. | HR. | RBI. | B.A. | PO. | A. | E. | F.A. |
|---|---|---|---|---|---|---|---|---|---|---|---|---|---|---|
| 1970—Watertown ........North. | 3B | 39 | 131 | 21 | 36 | 6 | 2 | 4 | 26 | .275 | 36 | 69 | 17 | .861 |
| 1970—Brad'ton Expos..Gulf C. | 3B | 12 | 39 | 5 | 7 | 2 | 1 | 1 | 9 | .179 | 12 | 14 | 5 | .839 |

| Year Club | League | Pos. | G. | AB. | R. | H. | 2B. | 3B. | HR. | RBI. | B.A. | PO. | A. | E. | F.A. |
|---|---|---|---|---|---|---|---|---|---|---|---|---|---|---|---|
| 1971—W. Palm Beach | Fla.St. | 3B-2B | 121 | 355 | 38 | 75 | 6 | 5 | 10 | 43 | .211 | 82 | 215 | 24 | .925 |
| 1972—W. Palm Beach | Fla.St. | *3B-1B | 120 | 398 | 45 | 109 | 19 | 6 | 2 | 50 | .274 | 210 | 256 | 18 | *.963 |
| 1972—Quebec City | ......East. | 3B | 8 | 16 | 0 | 2 | 1 | 0 | 0 | 1 | .125 | 6 | 9 | 1 | .938 |
| 1973—Quebec City | ......East. | *1-3-C | 132 | 395 | 57 | 98 | 25 | 5 | 15 | 79 | .248 | 657 | *165 | 22 | .974 |
| 1974—Memphis | ..........Int. | 3B-1B | 112 | 297 | 51 | 84 | 10 | 4 | 18 | 60 | .283 | 156 | 132 | 15 | .950 |
| 1974—Montreal | ..........Nat. | 3B | 2 | 4 | 1 | 1 | 0 | 0 | 0 | 0 | .250 | 0 | 3 | 0 | 1.000 |
| 1975—Memphis | ..........Int. | 3B-1B | 29 | 85 | 14 | 15 | 4 | 1 | 3 | 14 | .176 | 32 | 53 | 8 | .914 |
| 1975—Montreal | ..........Nat. | 3B-1B | 60 | 109 | 5 | 20 | 3 | 1 | 2 | 15 | .183 | 12 | 57 | 3 | .958 |
| 1976—Montreal | ..........Nat. | 3B-1B | 11 | 27 | 2 | 5 | 1 | 0 | 1 | 2 | .185 | 11 | 12 | 3 | .885 |
| 1976—Denver† | ............A.A. | 3B-PH | 103 | 312 | 65 | 96 | 21 | 2 | 18 | 78 | .308 | 59 | 179 | 17 | .933 |
| Major League Totals | ..................... | | 73 | 140 | 8 | 26 | 4 | 1 | 3 | 17 | .186 | 23 | 72 | 6 | .940 |

†Traded with Pitcher Steve Dunning and Outfielder Tony Scott by Montreal Expos to St. Louis Cardinals for Pitchers Bill Greif and Angel Torres, and Outfielder Sam Mejias, November 6, 1976.

## RANDY JAMES SCARBERY

Born June 22, 1952, at Fresno, Calif.
Height, 6.01. Weight, 185.
Throws and bats righthanded.
Hobbies—Golf and painting.
Attended University of Southern California, Los Angeles, Calif.

| Year Club | League | G. | IP. | W. | L. | Pct. | H. | R. | ER. | SO. | BB. | ERA. |
|---|---|---|---|---|---|---|---|---|---|---|---|---|
| 1973—Birmingham | ......................Southern | 7 | 43 | 1 | 6 | .143 | 44 | 28 | 23 | 29 | 25 | 4.81 |
| 1973—Tucson | ...............................P. Coast | 10 | 58 | 3 | 3 | .500 | 74 | 39 | 33 | 39 | 26 | 5.12 |
| 1974—Tucson | ...............................P. Coast | 32 | 189 | 11 | 13 | .458 | *247 | *140 | *122 | 104 | 74 | 5.81 |
| 1975—Tucson† | ...............................P. Coast | 12 | 44 | 1 | 1 | .500 | 56 | 39 | 28 | 18 | 17 | 5.73 |
| 1975—Birmingham | ......................Southern | 17 | 116 | 6 | 10 | .375 | 121 | 66 | 50 | 51 | 42 | 3.88 |
| 1976—Chattanooga | ......................Southern | 9 | 65 | 6 | 2 | .750 | 55 | 18 | 17 | 29 | 12 | 2.35 |
| 1976—Tucson | ...............................P. Coast | 18 | 69 | 4 | 8 | .333 | 97 | 58 | 43 | 48 | 33 | 5.61 |

†On disabled list from beginning of season until April 29, 1975.
Listed on Oakland Athletics' 1977 spring roster.

## MICHAEL JACK SCHMIDT
### (Mike)

Born September 27, 1949, at Dayton, O.
Height, 6.02. Weight, 195.
Throws and bats righthanded.
Hobby—Golf.
Attended Ohio University, Athens, O.; received Bachelor of Arts degree in Business Administration.

Tied following major league records: most home runs extra inning game, 4, April 17, 1976 (10 innings); most consecutive home runs in extra inning game, 4, April 17, 1976 (10 innings); most home runs in consecutive plate appearances, 4, April 17, 1976; most home runs in two consecutive games, 5, April 17-18, 1976; most home runs in three consecutive games, 6, April 17-20, 1976; most home runs in month of April, 11; most consecutive seasons leading major leagues in strikeouts, 3, 1974-1976.
Established National League record for most assists, third baseman, season, 404, in 1974.
Tied National League record for most home runs, bases full, one month, 2, June, 1973.
Major league stolen bases: 1972 (0), 1973 (8), 1974 (23), 1975 (29), 1976 (14). Total—74.
Led National League in total bases with 306 in 1976.
Led National League in slugging percentage with a mark of .546 in 1974.
Led National League batters in strikeouts with 138 in 1974, 180 in 1975 and 149 in 1976.
Led Pacific Coast League batters in strikeouts with 145 in 1972.
Named third baseman on THE SPORTING NEWS National League All-Star Team, 1974 and 1976.
Named third baseman on THE SPORTING NEWS National League All-Star fielding team, 1976.

| Year Club | League | Pos. | G. | AB. | R. | H. | 2B. | 3B. | HR. | RBI. | B.A. | PO. | A. | E. | F.A. |
|---|---|---|---|---|---|---|---|---|---|---|---|---|---|---|---|---|
| 1971—Reading | ............East. | SS-3B | 74 | 237 | 27 | 50 | 7 | 1 | 8 | 31 | .211 | 100 | 224 | 23 | .934 |
| 1972—Eugene | ..............P.C. | 2-3-SS | 131 | 436 | 80 | 127 | 23 | 6 | 26 | 91 | .291 | 271 | 324 | 25 | .960 |
| 1972—Philadelphia† | ....Nat. | 3B-2B | 13 | 34 | 2 | 7 | 0 | 0 | 1 | 3 | .206 | 10 | 25 | 2 | .946 |
| 1973—Philadelphia | ......Nat. | 3-2-1-S | 132 | 367 | 43 | 72 | 11 | 0 | 18 | 52 | .196 | 119 | 256 | 18 | .954 |
| 1974—Philadelphia | ......Nat. | 3B | 162 | 568 | 108 | 160 | 28 | 7 | *36 | 116 | .282 | 134 | *404 | 26 | .954 |
| 1975—Philadelphia | ......Nat. | 3B-SS | 158 | 562 | 93 | 140 | 34 | 3 | *38 | 95 | .249 | 139 | 390 | 26 | .953 |
| 1976—Philadelphia | ......Nat. | 3B | 160 | 584 | 112 | 153 | 31 | 4 | *38 | 107 | .262 | 139 | *377 | 21 | .961 |
| Major League Totals | ..................... | | 625 | 2115 | 358 | 532 | 104 | 14 | 131 | 373 | .252 | 541 | 1452 | 93 | .955 |

†On disabled list, August 21 through September 2, 1972.

### CHAMPIONSHIP SERIES RECORD

| Year Club | League | Pos. | G. | AB. | R. | H. | 2B. | 3B. | HR. | RBI. | B.A. | PO. | A. | E. | F.A. |
|---|---|---|---|---|---|---|---|---|---|---|---|---|---|---|---|---|
| 1976—Philadelphia | ......Nat. | 3B | 3 | 13 | 1 | 4 | 2 | 0 | 0 | 2 | .308 | 4 | 9 | 1 | .929 |

### ALL-STAR GAME RECORD

| Year League | Pos. | AB. | R. | H. | 2B. | 3B. | HR. | RBI. | B.A. | PO. | A. | E. | F.A. |
|---|---|---|---|---|---|---|---|---|---|---|---|---|---|
| 1974—National | ............... PH-3B | 0 | 1 | 0 | 0 | 0 | 0 | 0 | .000 | 0 | 1 | 0 | 1.000 |
| 1976—National | ............... 3B | 1 | 0 | 0 | 0 | 0 | 0 | 0 | .000 | 0 | 0 | 0 | .000 |
| All-Star Game Totals | ....................... | 1 | 1 | 0 | 0 | 0 | 0 | 0 | .000 | 0 | 1 | 0 | 1.000 |

## RONALD RICHARD SCHUELER
Name pronounced SHOO-lur.
### (Ron)

Born April 18, 1948, at Hays, Kan.
Height, 6.04. Weight, 205.
Throws and bats righthanded.
Attended Fort Hays State College, Hays, Kan.
Pitched 2-0 no-hit victory against San Antonio, September 7, 1970.

| Year Club | League | G. | IP. | W. | L. | Pct. | H. | R. | ER. | SO. | BB. | ERA. |
|---|---|---|---|---|---|---|---|---|---|---|---|---|
| 1967–Kinston | Carolina | 23 | 137 | 9 | 9 | .500 | 152 | 90 | 82 | 87 | 63 | 5.39 |
| 1968–Greenwood | W. Carol. | 11 | 31 | 1 | 3 | .250 | 36 | 21 | 17 | 30 | 25 | 4.94 |
| 1968–Richmond | Int'national | 2 | 14 | 1 | 1 | .500 | 13 | 4 | 4 | 3 | 2 | 2.57 |
| 1968–Shreveport | Texas | 18 | 59 | 5 | 3 | .625 | 73 | 47 | 39 | 37 | 21 | 5.95 |
| 1969–Shreveport† | Texas | 134 | 95 | 5 | 7 | .417 | 70 | 35 | 33 | 71 | 57 | 3.13 |
| 1970–Shreveport | Texas | 26 | 115 | 6 | 10 | .375 | 112 | 66 | 57 | 93 | 61 | 4.46 |
| 1971–Savannah | Southern | 13 | 80 | 5 | 6 | .455 | 78 | 32 | 29 | 68 | 17 | 3.26 |
| 1971–Richmond | Int'national | 13 | 74 | 4 | 4 | .500 | 54 | 31 | 23 | 49 | 32 | 2.80 |
| 1972–Atlanta | National | 37 | 145 | 5 | 8 | .385 | 122 | 68 | 59 | 96 | 60 | 3.66 |
| 1973–Atlanta‡ | National | 39 | 186 | 8 | 7 | .533 | 179 | 91 | 80 | 124 | 66 | 3.87 |
| 1974–Philadelphia | National | 44 | 203 | 11 | 16 | .407 | 202 | 91 | 84 | 109 | 98 | 3.72 |
| 1975–Philadelphia | National | 46 | 93 | 4 | 4 | .500 | 88 | 55 | 54 | 69 | 40 | 5.23 |
| 1976–Philadelphia§ | National | 35 | 50 | 1 | 0 | 1.000 | 44 | 18 | 16 | 43 | 16 | 2.88 |
| Major League Totals | | 201 | 677 | 29 | 35 | .453 | 635 | 323 | 293 | 441 | 280 | 3.90 |

†Played one game in outfield.
‡Traded to Philadelphia Phillies for Pitcher Barry Lersch and Shortstop Craig Robinson, December 3, 1973; Phillies traded First Baseman-Outfielder Bob Beall to Braves for Infielder Gil Garrido, December 10, 1973, to complete deal.
§Sold to Minnesota Twins, March 31, 1977.

## CHARLES BUDD SCHULTZ
### (Buddy)

Born September 19, 1950, at Cleveland, O.
Height, 6.00. Weight, 170.
Throws left and bats righthanded.
Hobby–Coin collecting.
Attended Miami University, Oxford, O.; received Bachelor of
Science degree in Education

| Year Club | League | G. | IP. | W. | L. | Pct. | H. | R. | ER. | SO. | BB. | ERA. |
|---|---|---|---|---|---|---|---|---|---|---|---|---|
| 1972–Bradenton Cubs | Gulf Coast | 11 | 52 | 2 | 2 | .500 | 52 | 22 | 19 | 75 | 18 | 3.29 |
| 1973–Quincy | Midwest | 14 | 88 | 7 | 4 | .636 | 82 | 41 | 30 | 104 | 28 | 3.07 |
| 1973–Midland | Texas | 9 | 65 | 3 | 4 | .429 | 67 | 26 | 24 | 39 | 15 | 3.32 |
| 1974–Midland | Texas | 29 | 67 | 9 | 6 | .600 | 71 | 36 | 27 | 58 | 19 | 3.63 |
| 1974–Wichita | Am. Assoc. | 10 | 15 | 3 | 0 | 1.000 | 12 | 3 | 3 | 20 | 3 | 1.80 |
| 1975–Wichita | Am. Assoc. | 47 | 60 | 2 | 8 | .200 | 62 | 38 | 27 | 48 | 21 | 4.05 |
| 1975–Chicago | National | 6 | 6 | 2 | 0 | 1.000 | 11 | 6 | 4 | 4 | 5 | 6.00 |
| 1976–Chicago | National | 29 | 24 | 1 | 1 | .500 | 37 | 19 | 16 | 15 | 9 | 6.00 |
| 1976–Wichita† | Am. Assoc. | 13 | 32 | 1 | 1 | .500 | 28 | 15 | 12 | 22 | 15 | 3.38 |
| Major League Totals | | 35 | 30 | 3 | 1 | .750 | 48 | 25 | 20 | 19 | 14 | 6.00 |

†Traded to New Orleans (St. Louis Cardinals' organization) for Pitcher Mark Covert, February 28, 1977.

## ANTHONY SCOTT
### (Tony)

Born September 18, 1951, at Cincinnati, O.
Height, 6.00. Weight, 175.
Throws right and bats right and lefthanded.
Hobbies–Cards, music and racing cars.

| Year Club | League | Pos. | G. | AB. | R. | H. | 2B. | 3B. | HR. | RBI. | B.A. | PO. | A. | E. | F.A. |
|---|---|---|---|---|---|---|---|---|---|---|---|---|---|---|---|
| 1969–Braden. Expos | Gulf C. | OF | 38 | 95 | 13 | 17 | 1 | 2 | 0 | 7 | .179 | 53 | 6 | 5 | .922 |
| 1970–W. Palm Beach | Fla. St. | OF | 3 | 2 | 0 | 1 | 0 | 0 | 0 | 0 | .500 | 1 | 0 | 0 | 1.000 |
| 1970–Watertown | North. | OF | 63 | 243 | 41 | 61 | 9 | 2 | 10 | 46 | .251 | 108 | •12 | 9 | .930 |
| 1971–W. Palm Beach | Fla. St. | OF | 47 | 84 | 21 | 19 | 3 | 2 | 1 | 9 | .226 | 28 | 2 | 1 | .968 |
| 1971–Jamestown | NYP | OF | 69 | 258 | 41 | 68 | 13 | 3 | 2 | 22 | .264 | •173 | 8 | 6 | .968 |
| 1972–Quebec City | East. | OF | 135 | 412 | 47 | 88 | 9 | 0 | 2 | 39 | .214 | 296 | 15 | 14 | .957 |
| 1973–Quebec City | East. | OF | 128 | 379 | 48 | 97 | 14 | 4 | 5 | 38 | .256 | 231 | 21 | 4 | .984 |
| 1973–Montreal | Nat. | OF | 11 | 1 | 2 | 0 | 0 | 0 | 0 | 0 | .000 | 0 | 0 | 1 | .000 |
| 1974–Quebec City | East. | OF | 109 | 359 | 76 | 102 | 8 | 4 | 10 | 38 | .284 | 193 | 5 | 4 | •.980 |
| 1974–Memphis | Int. | OF | 11 | 6 | 2 | 0 | 0 | 0 | 0 | 0 | .000 | 0 | 0 | 0 | .000 |
| 1974–Montreal | Nat. | OF | 19 | 7 | 2 | 2 | 0 | 0 | 0 | 1 | .286 | 7 | 0 | 0 | 1.000 |
| 1975–Montreal | Nat. | OF | 92 | 143 | 19 | 26 | 4 | 2 | 0 | 11 | .182 | 94 | 6 | 4 | .962 |
| 1976–Denver† | A. A. | OF-PH | 106 | 328 | 63 | 102 | 21 | 9 | 8 | 45 | .311 | 162 | 7 | 0 | 1.000 |
| Major League Totals | | | 122 | 151 | 23 | 28 | 4 | 2 | 0 | 12 | .185 | 101 | 6 | 5 | .955 |

†Traded with Pitcher Steve Dunning and Infielder Pat Scanlon by Montreal Expos to St. Louis Cardinals for Pitchers Bill Greif and Angel Torres, and Outfielder Sam Mejias, November 6, 1976.

# GEORGE C. SCOTT, JR.

Born March 23, 1944, at Greenville, Miss.
Height, 6.02. Weight, 215.
Throws and bats righthanded.

Tied major league records for most games (162), and most strikeouts (152), rookie season, 1966.
Led American League batters in strikeouts with 152 in 1966.
Led American League first basemen in double plays with 130 in 1966, 115 in 1967 and 137 in 1974.
Led American League first basemen in total chances with 1471 in 1974.
Led American League in total bases with 318 in 1975 and tied for lead with 295 in 1973.
Led Eastern League in total bases with 290 and led third basemen in double plays with 25 in 1965.
Named Most Valuable player in Eastern League, 1965.
Named first baseman on THE SPORTING NEWS American League All-Star fielding teams, 1967-68-71-72-73-74-75-76.

| Year | Club | League | Pos. | G. | AB. | R. | H. | 2B. | 3B. | HR. | RBI. | B.A. | PO. | A. | E. | F.A. |
|---|---|---|---|---|---|---|---|---|---|---|---|---|---|---|---|---|
| 1962 | Olean | NYP | 3B-2B | 63 | 223 | 31 | 53 | 8 | 1 | 5 | 28 | .238 | 79 | 116 | 18 | .915 |
| 1963 | Wellsville | NYP | 3B-SS | 106 | 426 | 82 | 125 | 12 | 9 | 15 | 74 | .293 | 94 | 151 | 27 | .901 |
| 1964 | Winston-Salem | Carol. | •3B | 55 | 156 | 24 | 45 | 7 | 2 | 10 | 30 | .288 | 28 | 65 | 6 | .939 |
| 1965 | Pittsfield | East. | •3B-1 | 140 | •523 | 91 | •167 | •30 | •9 | •25 | •94 | .319 | •140 | •283 | •31 | .932 |
| 1966 | Boston | Am. | •1B-3B | 162 | 601 | 73 | 147 | 18 | 7 | 27 | 90 | .245 | •1362 | 121 | 16 | .989 |
| 1967 | Boston | Amer. | •1-3B | 159 | 565 | 74 | 171 | 21 | 7 | 19 | 82 | .303 | •1321 | 94 | •19 | .987 |
| 1968 | Boston | Amer. | 1B-3B | 124 | 350 | 23 | 60 | 14 | 0 | 3 | 25 | .171 | 810 | 65 | 11 | .988 |
| 1969 | Boston | Amer. | 3B-1B | 152 | 549 | 63 | 139 | 14 | 5 | 16 | 52 | .253 | 542 | 226 | 18 | .977 |
| 1970 | Boston† | Amer. | 3B-1B | 127 | 480 | 50 | 142 | 24 | 5 | 16 | 63 | .296 | 551 | 149 | 18 | .975 |
| 1971 | Boston‡ | Amer. | 1B | 146 | 537 | 72 | 141 | 16 | 4 | 24 | 78 | .263 | 1256 | 75 | 11 | .992 |
| 1972 | Milwaukee | Amer. | 1B-3B | 152 | 578 | 71 | 154 | 24 | 4 | 20 | 88 | .266 | 1223 | 119 | 15 | .989 |
| 1973 | Milwaukee | Amer. | 1B | 158 | 604 | 98 | 185 | 30 | 4 | 24 | 107 | .306 | 1388 | •118 | 9 | .994 |
| 1974 | Milwaukee | Amer. | 1B | 158 | 604 | 74 | 170 | 36 | 2 | 17 | 82 | .281 | •1345 | •114 | 12 | •.992 |
| 1975 | Milwaukee | Amer. | •1B-3B | 158 | 617 | 86 | 176 | 26 | 4 | •36 | •109 | .285 | 1205 | •116 | 15 | .989 |
| 1976 | Milwaukee§ | Amer. | 1B | 156 | 606 | 73 | 166 | 21 | 5 | 18 | 77 | .274 | 1393 | 107 | 13 | .991 |
| | Major League Totals | | | 1652 | 6091 | 757 | 1651 | 244 | 47 | 220 | 853 | .271 | 12396 | 1304 | 157 | .989 |

†On disabled list July 18 through August 17.
‡Traded with Catcher Don Pavletich, Pitchers Ken Brett and Jim Lonborg and Outfielders Billy Conigliaro and Joe Lahoud to Milwaukee Brewers for Pitchers Marty Pattin and Lew Krausse and Outfielders Tommy Harper and Pat Skrable, October 11, 1971.
§Traded with Outfielder Bernie Carbo to Boston Red Sox for First Baseman Cecil Cooper, December 6, 1976.

## WORLD SERIES RECORD

| Year | Club | League | Pos. | G. | AB. | R. | H. | 2B. | 3B. | HR. | RBI. | B.A. | PO. | A. | E. | F.A. |
|---|---|---|---|---|---|---|---|---|---|---|---|---|---|---|---|---|
| 1967 | Boston | Amer. | 1B | 7 | 26 | 3 | 6 | 1 | 1 | 0 | 0 | .231 | 70 | 3 | 0 | 1.000 |

## ALL-STAR GAME RECORD

| Year | League | Pos. | AB. | R. | H. | 2B. | 3B. | HR. | RBI. | B.A. | PO. | A. | E. | F.A. |
|---|---|---|---|---|---|---|---|---|---|---|---|---|---|---|
| 1966 | American | 1B | 2 | 0 | 0 | 0 | 0 | 0 | 0 | .000 | 4 | 1 | 0 | 1.000 |
| 1975 | American | 1B | 2 | 0 | 0 | 0 | 0 | 0 | 0 | .000 | 5 | 0 | 0 | 1.000 |
| | All-Star Game Totals | | 4 | 0 | 0 | 0 | 0 | 0 | 0 | .000 | 9 | 1 | 0 | 1.000 |

# JOHN HENRY SCOTT

Born January 24, 1952, at Jackson, Miss.
Height, 6.02. Weight, 175.
Throws and bats righthanded.

Tied for Northwest League lead in total bases with 159 in 1971 and tied for lead in sacrifice flies with 5 in 1970.

| Year | Club | League | Pos. | G. | AB. | R. | H. | 2B. | 3B. | HR. | RBI. | B.A. | PO. | A. | E. | F.A. |
|---|---|---|---|---|---|---|---|---|---|---|---|---|---|---|---|---|
| 1970 | Tri-City | Northw. | O-S-3 | 65 | 215 | 31 | 58 | 12 | 2 | 4 | 31 | .270 | 75 | 34 | 13 | .893 |
| 1971 | Lodi | Calif. | OF | 24 | 68 | 12 | 22 | 1 | 0 | 4 | .324 | 20 | 2 | 2 | .917 |
| 1971 | Tri-City | Northw. | O-SS | 77 | •312 | 65 | •109 | 12 | •7 | 8 | 55 | .349 | 107 | 85 | 22 | .897 |
| 1972 | Alexandria | Texas | O-S-1 | 107 | 347 | 46 | 89 | 10 | 2 | 13 | 46 | .256 | 218 | 6 | 7 | .970 |
| 1973 | Alexandria | Texas | OF | 130 | 461 | 62 | 136 | 19 | 6 | 5 | 45 | .295 | 256 | 15 | 11 | .961 |
| 1974 | Hawaii | P.C. | OF | 141 | •582 | 93 | 159 | 23 | 5 | 12 | 59 | .273 | 296 | 7 | 9 | .971 |
| 1974 | San Diego | Nat. | OF | 14 | 15 | 3 | 1 | 0 | 0 | 0 | 0 | .067 | 8 | 1 | 0 | 1.000 |
| 1975 | Alexandria | Texas | OF | 61 | 239 | 40 | 64 | 11 | 1 | 3 | 37 | .268 | 114 | 9 | 8 | .939 |
| 1975 | San Diego | Nat. | PR-OF | 25 | 9 | 6 | 0 | 0 | 0 | 0 | 0 | .000 | 0 | 0 | 0 | .000 |
| 1976 | Hawaii† | P.C. | OF | 133 | 517 | 83 | 163 | 25 | 4 | 15 | 82 | .315 | 209 | 13 | 14 | .941 |
| | Major League Totals | | | 39 | 24 | 9 | 1 | 0 | 0 | 0 | 0 | .042 | | | | 1.000 |

†Sold to Toronto Blue Jays, October 22, 1976.

# RALPH ROBERT SCOTT
## (Mickey)

Born July 25, 1947, at Weimar, West Germany.
Height, 6.00. Weight, 165.
Throws and bats lefthanded.
Hobbies—Basketball, golf and football.

Led International League in saves with 17 in 1974.
Tied for New York-Pennsylvania League lead in games started by pitchers with 24 in 1966.

| Year Club | League | G. | IP. | W. | L. | Pct. | H. | R. | ER. | SO. | BB. | ERA. |
|---|---|---|---|---|---|---|---|---|---|---|---|---|
| 1965—Sarasota Yankees ............... | Florida Rk. | 9 | 39 | 3 | 2 | .600 | 31 | 14 | 8 | 31 | 9 | 1.85 |
| 1965—Ft. Lauderdale ................... | Florida St. | 4 | 29 | 0 | 1 | .000 | 23 | 8 | 5 | 29 | 15 | 1.55 |
| 1966—Binghamton...................... | NYP | 24 | 170 | •15 | 5 | .750 | 137 | 64 | 52 | •190 | 67 | 2.75 |
| 1967—New York .......................... | American | | | | | (In Military Service) | | | | | | |
| 1968—Binghamton† ...................... | Eastern | 18 | 115 | 8 | 6 | .571 | 83 | 44 | 33 | 74 | 41 | 2.58 |
| 1969—Syracuse‡ ......................... | Int'national | 21 | 119 | 6 | 5 | .545 | 140 | 69 | 63 | 63 | 25 | 4.76 |
| 1970—Rochester§ ......................... | Int'national | 43 | 65 | 6 | 3 | .667 | 73 | 43 | 36 | 43 | 25 | 4.98 |
| 1971—Rochester ........................... | Int'national | 54 | 72 | 9 | 1 | .900 | 64 | 27 | 27 | 54 | 24 | 3.38 |
| 1972—Baltimore ......................... | American | 15 | 23 | 0 | 1 | .000 | 23 | 7 | 7 | 11 | 5 | 2.74 |
| 1973—Baltimore x.......................... | American | 1 | 2 | 0 | 0 | .000 | 2 | 1 | 1 | 2 | 2 | 4.50 |
| 1973—Montreal y ......................... | National | 22 | 24 | 1 | 2 | .333 | 27 | 14 | 14 | 11 | 9 | 5.25 |
| 1974—Rochester z......................... | Int'national | •57 | 91 | 8 | 2 | .800 | 61 | 14 | 10 | 55 | 23 | 0.99 |
| 1975—California ........................ | American | 50 | 68 | 4 | 2 | .667 | 59 | 34 | 25 | 31 | 18 | 3.31 |
| 1976—California a....................... | American | 33 | 39 | 3 | 0 | 1.000 | 47 | 17 | 14 | 10 | 12 | 3.23 |
| American League Totals.......................... | | 99 | 132 | 7 | 3 | .700 | 131 | 59 | 47 | 54 | 37 | 3.20 |
| National League Totals.......................... | | 22 | 24 | 1 | 2 | .333 | 27 | 14 | 14 | 11 | 9 | 5.25 |
| Major League Totals .................... | | 121 | 156 | 8 | 5 | .615 | 158 | 73 | 61 | 65 | 46 | 3.52 |

†On temporary inactive list, July 8 to August 10, 1968.
‡On temporary inactive list, July 26 to August 12, 1969; traded with cash by New York Yankees to Chicago White Sox for Infielder-Outfielder Pete Ward, December 18, 1969; option transferred to Rochester, April 14, 1970.
§Traded by Chicago White Sox to Baltimore Orioles for Infielder Mickey McGuire, September 23, 1970.
xPurchased by Montreal Expos, May 22, 1973.
yReleased to Rochester (Baltimore Orioles' organization), April 5, 1974, to complete deal in which Expos obtained Pitcher John Montague from Orioles, April 13, 1973.
zAssigned by Baltimore Orioles to California Angels, October 3, 1974, to complete deal in which Orioles obtained Infielder-Outfielder Bob Oliver on waivers from Angels, September 11, 1974.
aOn disabled list, April 5 to May 5, 1976.

## RODNEY DARRELL SCOTT

Born October 16, 1953, at Indianapolis, Ind.
Height, 6.00. Weight, 160.
Throws and bats righthanded.

Led Pioneer League in stolen bases with 26 in 1973.

| Year Club | League | Pos. | G. | AB. | R. | H. | 2B. | 3B. | HR. | RBI. | B.A. | PO. | A. | E. | F.A. |
|---|---|---|---|---|---|---|---|---|---|---|---|---|---|---|---|
| 1972—Sarasota Royals | Gulf C. | S-3-O-2 | 35 | 125 | 23 | 47 | 4 | 2 | 1 | 14 | .376 | 51 | 64 | 8 | .935 |
| 1973—San Jose........... | Calif. | 2B | 48 | 159 | 23 | 35 | 3 | 2 | 2 | 15 | .220 | 90 | 102 | 12 | .941 |
| 1973—Billings ............ | Pion. | •SS-2B | 64 | 236 | 51 | 70 | 10 | 2 | 0 | 21 | .297 | 91 | 144 | 26 | •.900 |
| 1974—Waterloo .......... | Midw. | S-2-O | 58 | 221 | 43 | 57 | 6 | 1 | 1 | 16 | .258 | 86 | 169 | 22 | .921 |
| 1974—San Jose........... | Calif. | SS | 63 | 230 | 38 | 69 | 6 | 2 | 1 | 15 | .300 | 108 | 205 | 27 | .921 |
| 1975—Jacksonville ......South. | SS | 20 | 77 | 19 | 26 | 2 | 0 | 0 | 8 | .338 | 34 | 49 | 7 | .922 |
| 1975—Omaha .............. | A.A. | 2B-SS | 12 | 37 | 6 | 10 | 1 | 1 | 0 | 1 | .270 | 13 | 18 | 5 | .861 |
| 1975—Kansas City† | ....Amer. | 2B-SS | 48 | 15 | 13 | 1 | 0 | 0 | 0 | 0 | .067 | 8 | 12 | 2 | .909 |
| 1976—Denver .............. | A.A. | S-2-O | 114 | 375 | 75 | 115 | 20 | 6 | 1 | 26 | .307 | 164 | 285 | 27 | .943 |
| 1976—Montreal ........... | Nat. | 2B-SS | 7 | 10 | 3 | 4 | 0 | 0 | 0 | 0 | .400 | 6 | 8 | 0 | 1.000 |
| American League Totals ...................... | | | 48 | 15 | 13 | 1 | 0 | 0 | 0 | 0 | .067 | 8 | 12 | 2 | .909 |
| National League Totals ................. | | | 7 | 10 | 3 | 4 | 0 | 0 | 0 | 0 | .400 | 6 | 8 | 0 | 1.000 |
| Major League Totals ...................... | | | 55 | 25 | 16 | 5 | 0 | 0 | 0 | 0 | .200 | 14 | 20 | 2 | .944 |

†Sold to Montreal Expos, December 12, 1975, to complete deal in which Royals obtained Catcher Bob Stinson from Expos, March 31, 1975.
‡Traded to Texas Rangers for Pitcher Jeff Terpko, March 15, 1977; traded with Pitcher Jim Umbarger and cash estimated at $100,000 to Oakland A's for Outfielder Claudell Washington, March 26, 1977.

## WAYNE ALLISON SCRIVENER
### (Chuck)
(Nicknamed by father.)

Born October 3, 1947, at Alexandria, Va.
Height, 5.09. Weight, 170.
Throws and bats righthanded.
Hobbies—Music and sports in general.
Attended Community College of Baltimore, Baltimore, Md., and
University of Baltimore, Baltimore, Md.

Son of John Scrivener, Jr., who played in Washington Senators' organization, 1935 and 1936. Nephew of Jack Crouch, Sr., catcher with St. Louis Browns and Cincinnati Reds, 1930-31-33. Cousin of Jack Crouch, Jr., infielder in Detroit Tigers' organization, 1958 and 1959.

Led American Association shortstops in double plays with 98 in 1975.

| Year Club | League | Pos. | G. | AB. | R. | H. | 2B. | 3B. | HR. | RBI. | B.A. | PO. | A. | E. | F.A. |
|---|---|---|---|---|---|---|---|---|---|---|---|---|---|---|---|
| 1968—Lakeland .......... | Fla. St. | SS-3B | 66 | 223 | 22 | 56 | 3 | 2 | 3 | 22 | .251 | 96 | 162 | 24 | .915 |
| 1969—Montgomery† | ....South. | SS | 18 | 62 | 5 | 12 | 4 | 0 | 0 | 5 | .194 | 18 | 61 | 4 | .952 |
| 1969—Rocky Mount | ....Carol. | SS | 63 | 226 | 18 | 48 | 6 | 3 | 0 | 14 | .212 | 95 | 220 | 17 | .949 |
| 1970—Rochy Mount‡ | ..Carol. | SS-2B | 11 | 23 | 2 | 2 | 1 | 0 | 0 | 0 | .087 | 17 | 28 | 3 | .938 |
| 1970—Montgomery ......South. | SS | 82 | 243 | 31 | 57 | 13 | 1 | 5 | 25 | .235 | 102 | 243 | 11 | .969 |
| 1971—Toledo ............. | Int. | SS-2B | 14 | 27 | 5 | 4 | 0 | 1 | 0 | 2 | .148 | 11 | 22 | 5 | .868 |
| 1971—Montgomery§ | ....South. | SS | 51 | 140 | 13 | 33 | 4 | 0 | 0 | 16 | .236 | 68 | 147 | 14 | .939 |

| Year    Club           League | Pos. | G. | AB. | R. | H. | 2B. | 3B. | HR. | RBI. | B.A. | PO. | A. | E. | F.A. |
|---|---|---|---|---|---|---|---|---|---|---|---|---|---|---|
| 1972–Toledo x............Int. | SS-2B | 104 | 253 | 33 | 64 | 8 | 1 | 4 | 27 | .253 | 160 | 237 | 20 | .952 |
| 1973–Toledo y............Int. | 2-S-3 | 66 | 182 | 15 | 39 | 6 | 2 | 1 | 15 | .214 | 90 | 151 | 13 | .949 |
| 1974–Evansville ........A.A. | S-2-3 | 99 | 249 | 44 | 61 | 10 | 5 | 8 | 28 | .245 | 130 | 249 | 8 | .979 |
| 1975–Evansville ........A.A. | SS | 131 | 447 | 65 | 112 | 23 | 6 | 10 | 62 | .251 | 208 | 427 | 17 | .974 |
| 1975–Detroit .............Amer. | 3B-SS | 4 | 16 | 0 | 4 | 1 | 0 | 0 | 0 | .250 | 2 | 8 | 0 | 1.000 |
| 1976–Detroit .............Amer. | 2-S-3 | 80 | 222 | 28 | 49 | 7 | 1 | 2 | 16 | .221 | 137 | 230 | 12 | .968 |
| Major League Totals ..................... | | 84 | 238 | 28 | 53 | 8 | 1 | 2 | 16 | .223 | 139 | 238 | 12 | .969 |

†On restricted list from beginning of season until June 16, 1969.
‡On disabled list, April 21 to May 12, 1970.
§On disabled list, May 27 to July 19, 1971.
xOn disabled list from beginning of season until May 15, 1972.
yOn disabled list, July 7 to August 13, 1973.

## RODNEY GRANT SCURRY
### (Rod)

Born March 17, 1956, at Sacramento, Calif.
Height, 6.02. Weight, 180.
Throws and bats lefthanded.
Hobbies–Golf and basketball.

| Year    Club           League | G. | IP. | W. | L. | Pct. | H. | R. | ER. | SO. | BB. | ERA. |
|---|---|---|---|---|---|---|---|---|---|---|---|
| 1974–Niagara Falls .....................NYP | 14 | 89 | 5 | 6 | .455 | 55 | 36 | 34 | 102 | 74 | 3.44 |
| 1975–Salem ................................Carolina | •26 | 150 | 9 | 12 | .429 | 128 | 79 | 61 | 143 | 118 | 3.66 |
| 1976–Shreveport .........................Texas | 24 | 123 | 8 | 8 | .500 | 120 | 71 | 53 | 83 | 83 | 3.88 |

Listed on Pittsburgh Pirates' 1977 spring roster.

## RANDALL LEE SEALY
### (Randy)

Born September 6, 1954, at Freeport, Tex.
Height, 6.02. Weight, 200.
Throws and bats righthanded.

Named Most Outstanding Pitcher in Western Carolinas League, 1974.

| Year    Club           League | G. | IP. | W. | L. | Pct. | H. | R. | ER. | SO. | BB. | ERA. |
|---|---|---|---|---|---|---|---|---|---|---|---|
| 1973–Bradenton Pirates ................Gulf Coast | 10 | 44 | 1 | 6 | .143 | 42 | 40 | •37 | 46 | 47 | 7.57 |
| 1974–Charleston .........................W. Carol. | 22 | 155 | 12 | 5 | .706 | 99 | 44 | 34 | 132 | 45 | •1.97 |
| 1975–Shreveport .........................Texas | 23 | 139 | 10 | 5 | .667 | 152 | 85 | 67 | 84 | 66 | 4.34 |
| 1976–Shreveport .........................Texas | 15 | 80 | 5 | 5 | .500 | 83 | 35 | 31 | 40 | 28 | 3.49 |
| 1976–Charleston†‡ ......................Int'national | 5 | 25 | 1 | 2 | .333 | 32 | 21 | 15 | 13 | 11 | 5.40 |

†On disabled list, July 25 through August 9, 1976.
‡Sold to California Angels, April 4, 1977.

## GEORGE THOMAS SEAVER
### (Tom)

Born November 17, 1944, at Fresno, Calif.
Height, 6.01. Weight, 195.
Throws and bats righthanded.
Hobbies–Golf, hunting and bridge.
Attended Fresno City College, Fresno, Calif., and University of Southern California,
Los Angeles, Calif.; received Bachelor of Science degree.

Established major league records for lowest earned run average, lifetime (2,000 or more innings), 2.47,
1976; and most consecutive seasons, 200 or more strikeouts, 9, 1968 through 1976.
Tied major league record for most strikeouts, game, 19, April 22, 1970 against San Diego Padres.
Established following National League records: most strikeouts, consecutive, game (10), April 22, 1970;
most strikeouts, righthanded pitcher, season (289), 1971.
Tied for National League lead in complete games by pitchers with 18 in 1973.
Led International League in games started by pitchers with 32 in 1966.
Named National League Rookie of the Year by the Baseball Writers' Association of America, 1967.
Won National League Cy Young Memorial Award, 1969, 1973 and 1975.
Named righthanded pitcher on THE SPORTING NEWS National League All-Star Team, 1969, 1973 and 1975.
Named National League Pitcher of the Year by THE SPORTING NEWS, 1969, 1973 and 1975.
Signed by Atlanta Braves to Richmond contract for reported $40,000 bonus, February, 1966; subsequently,
Commissioner William Eckert nullified the contract because the signing violated the college rule. However,
since the University of Southern California then declared Seaver ineligible, Eckert decreed that any club other
than the Braves which was willing to match terms of his Richmond contract would be eligible to draw for nego-
tiation rights. Cleveland Indians, Philadelphia Phillies and New York Mets expressed that willingness, and
Eckert drew the name of the Mets in a special drawing, April 3, 1966; Mets then signed Seaver to Jacksonville
contract for reported $50,000 bonus.

| Year    Club           League | G. | IP. | W. | L. | Pct. | H. | R. | ER. | SO. | BB. | ERA. |
|---|---|---|---|---|---|---|---|---|---|---|---|
| 1966–Jacksonville .......................Int'national | 34 | 210 | 12 | 12 | .500 | 184 | 87 | 73 | 188 | 66 | 3.13 |
| 1967–New York ..........................National | 35 | 251 | 16 | 13 | .552 | 224 | 85 | 77 | 170 | 78 | 2.76 |
| 1968–New York ..........................National | 36 | 278 | 16 | 12 | .571 | 224 | 73 | 68 | 205 | 48 | 2.20 |
| 1969–New York ..........................National | 36 | 273 | •25 | 7 | .781 | 202 | 75 | 67 | 208 | 82 | 2.21 |
| 1970–New York ..........................National | 37 | 291 | 18 | 12 | .600 | 230 | 103 | 91 | •283 | 83 | •2.81 |

| Year | Club | League | G. | IP. | W. | L. | Pct. | H. | R. | ER. | SO. | BB. | ERA. |
|------|------|--------|----|----|----|----|------|----|----|-----|-----|-----|------|
| 1971–New York | | National | 36 | 286 | 20 | 10 | .667 | 210 | 61 | 56 | •289 | 61 | •1.76 |
| 1972–New York | | National | 35 | 262 | 21 | 12 | .636 | 215 | 92 | 85 | 249 | 77 | 2.92 |
| 1973–New York | | National | 36 | 290 | 19 | 10 | .655 | 219 | 74 | 67 | •251 | 64 | •2.08 |
| 1974–New York | | National | 32 | 236 | 11 | 11 | .500 | 199 | 89 | 84 | 201 | 75 | 3.20 |
| 1975–New York | | National | 36 | 280 | •22 | 9 | .710 | 217 | 81 | 74 | •243 | 88 | 2.38 |
| 1976–New York | | National | 35 | 271 | 14 | 11 | .560 | 211 | 83 | 78 | •235 | 77 | 2.59 |
| Major League Totals | | | 354 | 2718 | 182 | 107 | .630 | 2151 | 816 | 747 | 2334 | 733 | 2.47 |

### CHAMPIONSHIP SERIES RECORD

| Year | Club | League | G. | IP. | W. | L. | Pct. | H. | R. | ER. | SO. | BB. | ERA. |
|------|------|--------|----|----|----|----|------|----|----|-----|-----|-----|------|
| 1969–New York | | National | 1 | 7 | 1 | 0 | 1.000 | 8 | 5 | 5 | 2 | 3 | 6.43 |
| 1973–New York | | National | 2 | 16⅔ | 1 | 1 | .500 | 13 | 4 | 3 | 17 | 5 | 1.62 |
| Championship Series Totals | | | 3 | 23⅔ | 2 | 1 | .667 | 21 | 9 | 8 | 19 | 8 | 3.04 |

### WORLD SERIES RECORD

| Year | Club | League | G. | IP. | W. | L. | Pct. | H. | R. | ER. | SO. | BB. | ERA. |
|------|------|--------|----|----|----|----|------|----|----|-----|-----|-----|------|
| 1969–New York | | National | 2 | 15 | 1 | 1 | .500 | 12 | 5 | 5 | 9 | 3 | 3.00 |
| 1973–New York | | National | 2 | 15 | 0 | 1 | .000 | 13 | 4 | 4 | 18 | 3 | 2.40 |
| World Series Totals | | | 4 | 30 | 1 | 2 | .333 | 25 | 9 | 9 | 27 | 6 | 2.70 |

### ALL-STAR GAME RECORD

| Year | League | IP. | W. | L. | Pct. | H. | R. | ER. | SO. | BB. | ERA. |
|------|--------|-----|----|----|------|----|----|-----|-----|-----|------|
| 1967–National | | 1 | 0 | 0 | .000 | 0 | 0 | 0 | 1 | 1 | 0.00 |
| 1968–National | | 2 | 0 | 0 | .000 | 2 | 0 | 0 | 5 | 0 | 0.00 |
| 1970–National | | 3 | 0 | 0 | .000 | 1 | 0 | 0 | 4 | 0 | 0.00 |
| 1973–National | | 1 | 0 | 0 | .000 | 0 | 0 | 0 | 0 | 1 | 0.00 |
| 1975–National | | 1 | 0 | 0 | .000 | 2 | 3 | 3 | 2 | 1 | 27.00 |
| 1976–National | | 2 | 0 | 0 | .000 | 2 | 1 | 1 | 1 | 1 | 4.50 |
| All-Star Game Totals | | 10 | 0 | 0 | .000 | 7 | 4 | 4 | 13 | 4 | 3.60 |

Member of National League All-Star Team for 1969, 1971 and 1972 games; did not play.

## DIEGO PABLO SEGUI (GONZALEZ)
Name pronounced Suh-GHEE.

Born August 17, 1938, at Holguin, Oriente, Cuba.
Height, 6.00. Weight, 190.
Throws and bats righthanded.
Hobby–Fishing.
Brother of Dario Segui, former pitcher in Kansas City Athletics' organization.

| Year | Club | League | G. | IP. | W. | L. | Pct. | H. | R. | ER. | SO. | BB. | ERA. |
|------|------|--------|----|----|----|----|------|----|----|-----|-----|-----|------|
| 1958–Graceville† | | Ala.-Fla. | 0 | 0 | 0 | 0 | .000 | 0 | 0 | 0 | 0 | 0 | ....... |
| 1958–Tucson‡ | | Ariz.-Mex. | 39 | 106 | 7 | 5 | .583 | 140 | 83 | 68 | 82 | 43 | 5.77 |
| 1959–Pocatello | | Pioneer | 44 | 204 | 12 | 14 | .462 | •231 | 131 | 100 | 156 | 62 | 4.41 |
| 1960–Sioux City | | I.I.I. | 21 | 154 | 12 | 9 | .571 | 153 | 81 | 68 | 108 | 60 | 3.97 |
| 1961–Hawaii | | P. Coast | 40 | 167 | 5 | 10 | .333 | 187 | 96 | 82 | 86 | 65 | 4.42 |
| 1962–Kansas City | | American | 37 | 117 | 8 | 5 | .615 | 89 | 53 | 50 | 71 | 46 | 3.85 |
| 1963–Kansas City | | American | 38 | 167 | 9 | 6 | .600 | 173 | 84 | 70 | 116 | 73 | 3.77 |
| 1964–Kansas City | | American | 40 | 217 | 8 | •17 | .320 | 219 | 118 | 110 | 155 | 94 | 4.56 |
| 1965–Kansas City§ | | American | 40 | 163 | 5 | 15 | .250 | 166 | 102 | 84 | 119 | 67 | 4.64 |
| 1966–Washington | | American | 21 | 72 | 3 | 7 | .300 | 82 | 42 | 40 | 54 | 24 | 5.00 |
| 1966–Hawaii x-Vancouver | | P. Coast | 13 | 47 | 4 | 3 | .571 | 44 | 25 | 21 | 36 | 16 | 4.02 |
| 1967–Vancouver | | P. Coast | 7 | 56 | 4 | 2 | .667 | 38 | 11 | 8 | 35 | 12 | 1.29 |
| 1967–Kansas City | | American | 36 | 70 | 3 | 4 | .429 | 62 | 30 | 24 | 52 | 31 | 3.09 |
| 1968–Oakland y | | American | 52 | 83 | 6 | 5 | .545 | 51 | 25 | 22 | 72 | 32 | 2.39 |
| 1969–Seattle z | | American | 66 | 142 | 12 | 6 | .667 | 127 | 62 | 53 | 113 | 61 | 3.36 |
| 1970–Oakland | | American | 47 | 162 | 10 | 10 | .500 | 130 | 54 | 46 | 95 | 68 | •2.56 |
| 1971–Oakland a | | American | 26 | 146 | 10 | 8 | .556 | 122 | 59 | 51 | 81 | 63 | 3.14 |
| 1972–Oakland a | | American | 7 | 23 | 0 | 1 | .000 | 25 | 10 | 9 | 11 | 7 | 3.52 |
| 1972–St. Louis | | National | 33 | 56 | 3 | 1 | .750 | 47 | 23 | 19 | 54 | 32 | 3.05 |
| 1973–St. Louis b | | National | 65 | 100 | 7 | 6 | .538 | 78 | 35 | 31 | 93 | 53 | 2.79 |
| 1974–Boston | | American | 58 | 108 | 6 | 8 | .429 | 106 | 54 | 48 | 76 | 49 | 4.00 |
| 1975–Boston c | | American | 33 | 71 | 2 | 5 | .286 | 71 | 41 | 38 | 45 | 43 | 4.82 |
| 1976–Hawaii d e | | P. Coast | 21 | 147 | 11 | 5 | .688 | 117 | 64 | 52 | 105 | 51 | •3.18 |
| American League Totals | | | 501 | 1541 | 82 | 97 | .458 | 1423 | 734 | 645 | 1060 | 658 | 3.77 |
| National League Totals | | | 98 | 156 | 10 | 7 | .588 | 125 | 58 | 50 | 147 | 85 | 2.88 |
| Major League Totals | | | 599 | 1697 | 92 | 104 | .469 | 1548 | 792 | 695 | 1207 | 743 | 3.69 |

†Released by Cincinnati Reds' organization, April 21, 1958; signed as free agent by Tucson, April 30, 1958.
‡Sold to Kansas City Athletics for $1,500, September 26, 1958.
§Sold to Washington Senators, April 13, 1966.
xTraded by Washington Senators to Kansas City Athletics (assigned to Vancouver) for Pitcher Jim Duckworth (assigned to Hawaii), July 30, 1966.
ySelected by Seattle Pilots from Oakland Athletics in expansion draft, October 15, 1968.
zTraded with Shortstop Ray Oyler to Oakland A's for Pitcher George Lauzerique and Shortstop Ted Kubiak, December 7, 1969.
aTraded to St. Louis Cardinals for a player to be named later, June 7, 1972; Athletics traded Pitcher Steve Easton to Cardinals for Outfielder Matty Alou, August 27, 1972, to complete deal.
bTraded with Pitcher Reggie Cleveland and Infielder Terry Hughes to Boston Red Sox for Pitchers John Curtis, Mike Garman and Lynn McGlothen, December 7, 1973.

cUnconditionally released, April 7, 1976; signed as free agent with Hawaii (San Diego Padres' organization), May 29, 1976.
dOn suspended list, September 7 through remainder of season.
eSold to Seattle Mariners, October 23, 1976.

## CHAMPIONSHIP SERIES RECORD

| Year | Club | League | ∖G. | IP. | W. | L. | Pct. | H. | R. | ER. | SO. | BB. | ERA. |
|---|---|---|---|---|---|---|---|---|---|---|---|---|---|
| 1971—Oakland | | American | 1 | 4⅔ | 0 | 1 | .000 | 6 | 3 | 3 | 4 | 6 | 5.79 |

## RONALD WILLIAM SELAK
### (Ron)

Born March 25, 1955, at Berkeley, Calif.
Height, 6.02. Weight, 175.
Throws and bats righthanded.
Hobbies—Golf, fishing and softball.

| Year | Club | League | G. | IP. | W. | L. | Pct. | H. | R. | ER. | SO. | BB. | ERA. |
|---|---|---|---|---|---|---|---|---|---|---|---|---|---|
| 1973—Sarasota Cardinals | | Gulf Coast | 8 | 41 | 3 | 1 | .750 | 26 | 11 | 9 | 58 | 11 | 1.98 |
| 1973—Arkansas | | Texas | 5 | 27 | 1 | 2 | .333 | 18 | 6 | 3 | 24 | 3 | 1.00 |
| 1974—Arkansas† | | Texas | 20 | 135 | 9 | 8 | .529 | 124 | 60 | 49 | 86 | 31 | 3.07 |
| 1974—Columbus | | Southern | 2 | 11 | 0 | 1 | .000 | 14 | 9 | 7 | 7 | 3 | 5.73 |
| 1975—Columbus | | Southern | 6 | 49 | 4 | 2 | .667 | 44 | 13 | 12 | 30 | 7 | 2.20 |
| 1975—Iowa | | Am. Assoc. | 16 | 96 | 4 | 8 | .333 | 97 | 43 | 36 | 76 | 45 | 3.38 |
| 1976—Memphis | | Int'national | 31 | 163 | 4 | 12 | .250 | 162 | 100 | 94 | 112 | 105 | 5.19 |

†Traded with a player to be named later by St. Louis Cardinals to Houston Astros for Pitcher Claude Osteen, August 15, 1974; Cardinals assigned Pitcher Dan Larson to Astros, October 4, 1974, to complete deal.
Listed on Houston Astros' 1977 spring roster.

## MICHAEL DAVID SEMBER
### (Mike)

Born February 24, 1953, at Hammond, Ind.
Height, 6.00. Weight, 185.
Throws and bats righthanded.
Hobbies—Tennis and music.
Attended University of Tulsa, Tulsa, Okla., received Bachelor of Science degree in Communications.
Led Texas League shortstops in total chances with 623 in 1975.

| Year | Club | League | Pos. | G. | AB. | R. | H. | 2B. | 3B. | HR. | RBI. | B.A. | PO. | A. | E. | F.A. |
|---|---|---|---|---|---|---|---|---|---|---|---|---|---|---|---|---|
| 1974—Midland† | | Texas | SS | 62 | 183 | 29 | 42 | 4 | 2 | 6 | 17 | .230 | 102 | 190 | 21 | .933 |
| 1975—Midland | | Texas | *SS-3B | 125 | 402 | 64 | 101 | 13 | 5 | 9 | 59 | .251 | *220 | 410 | 42 | *.937 |
| 1976—Wichita | | A. A. | SS-OF | 69 | 216 | 26 | 52 | 5 | 0 | 1 | 16 | .241 | 82 | 143 | 22 | .910 |
| 1976—Midland | | Texas | SS-OF | 54 | 187 | 25 | 47 | 2 | 2 | 3 | 23 | .251 | 71 | 86 | 18 | .897 |

†On disabled list, June 25 through July 5, 1974; released, April 4, 1977.
Listed on Chicago Cubs' 1977 spring roster.

## MANUEL MODESTO SEOANE

Name pronounced Soh-AHN-ay.
### (Manny)

Born June 26, 1955, at Tampa, Fla.
Height, 6.03. Weight, 187.
Throws and bats righthanded.
Attended Hillsborough Community College, Tampa, Fla.

| Year | Club | League | G. | IP. | W. | L. | Pct. | H. | R. | ER. | SO. | BB. | ERA. |
|---|---|---|---|---|---|---|---|---|---|---|---|---|---|
| 1973—Pulaski | | Ap'lachian | 16 | 106 | 8 | 5 | .615 | 89 | 40 | 35 | *101 | 25 | 2.97 |
| 1974—Rocky Mount | | Carolina | 28 | 177 | 8 | 11 | .421 | *200 | 102 | *82 | 128 | 47 | 4.17 |
| 1975—Reading† | | Eastern | 17 | 128 | 6 | 4 | .692 | 120 | 43 | 35 | 64 | 28 | 2.46 |
| 1976—Oklahoma City‡ | | Am. Assoc. | 21 | 117 | 8 | 7 | .533 | 144 | 69 | 62 | 69 | 24 | 4.77 |

†On disabled list, July 31 through September 29, 1975.
‡On disabled list, July 1 through July 30, 1976.
Listed on Philadelphia Phillies' 1977 spring roster.

## JIMMY DALE SEXTON

Born December 15, 1951, at Mobile, Ala.
Height, 5.10. Weight, 175.
Throws and bats righthanded.
Hobbies—Hunting and fishing.
Led Texas League in stolen bases with 48 in 1975.

| Year | Club | League | Pos. | G. | AB. | R. | H. | 2B. | 3B. | HR. | RBI. | B.A. | PO. | A. | E. | F.A. |
|---|---|---|---|---|---|---|---|---|---|---|---|---|---|---|---|---|
| 1970—Braden. Pirates | Gulf C | | S-2-3 | 33 | 113 | 17 | 32 | 2 | 0 | 0 | 7 | .283 | 40 | 68 | 12 | .900 |
| 1971—Braden. Pirates | Gulf C | | 3-2-S | 35 | 119 | 23 | 29 | 2 | 1 | 0 | 11 | .244 | 45 | 54 | 1 | .990 |
| 1972—Niagara Falls | NYP | | SS | 69 | 212 | 41 | 61 | 2 | 3 | 0 | 23 | .288 | 86 | 178 | 13 | *.953 |
| 1973—Salem | Carol. | | *2B-SS | 124 | 446 | 86 | 120 | 17 | 3 | 3 | 39 | .269 | 240 | 323 | *33 | .945 |
| 1974—Thetford Mines | East. | | *3-S-2 | 115 | 350 | 53 | 87 | 14 | 1 | 3 | 32 | .249 | 97 | 197 | 18 | *.942 |

| Year | Club | League | Pos. | G. | AB. | R. | H. | 2B. | 3B. | HR. | RBI. | B.A. | PO. | A. | E. | F.A. |
|---|---|---|---|---|---|---|---|---|---|---|---|---|---|---|---|---|
| 1975–Shreveport | ........Tex. | | SS | 103 | 383 | 82 | 105 | 23 | 5 | 3 | 28 | .274 | 148 | 279 | 34 | .926 |
| 1976–Shreveport | ........Tex. | | SS-PH | 59 | 207 | 43 | 67 | 14 | 2 | 4 | 30 | .324 | 76 | 159 | 21 | .918 |
| 1976–Charleston† | ......Int. | | 2B-SS | 49 | 154 | 21 | 42 | 8 | 1 | 3 | 12 | .273 | 85 | 109 | 6 | .970 |

†Traded with Infielder Craig Reynolds to Seattle Mariners for Pitcher Grant Jackson, December 7, 1976.

## PAUL GREGORY SHANAHAN, JR.
### (Greg)
Born December 11, 1947, at Eureka, Calif.
Height, 6.02. Weight, 190.
Throws and bats righthanded.
Hobby–Outdoor activities.
Attended University of California, Santa Barbara, Calif., and
Humboldt State College, Arcata, Calif.

Tied for Pacific Coast League lead in complete games by pitchers with 14 in 1973.

| Year | Club | League | G. | IP. | W. | L. | Pct. | H. | R. | ER. | SO. | BB. | ERA. |
|---|---|---|---|---|---|---|---|---|---|---|---|---|---|
| 1970–Medford | ............................Northwest | | 14 | 86 | 5 | 5 | .500 | 76 | 46 | 35 | 85 | 25 | 3.66 |
| 1971–Bakersfield | ........................California | | 27 | 164 | 8 | 10 | .444 | 176 | 104 | 73 | 182 | 78 | 4.01 |
| 1972–Bakersfield | ........................California | | 11 | 44 | 3 | 0 | 1.000 | 28 | 13 | 12 | 58 | 17 | 2.45 |
| 1972–El Paso | ...............................Texas | | 21 | 127 | 10 | 8 | .556 | 113 | 54 | 44 | 129 | 32 | 3.11 |
| 1973–Albuquerque | .......................P. Coast | | 29 | 198 | 12 | 12 | .500 | 197 | 97 | 92 | 160 | 90 | 4.18 |
| 1973–Los Angeles | ........................National | | 7 | 16 | 0 | 0 | .000 | 14 | 6 | 6 | 11 | 4 | 3.38 |
| 1974–Albuquerque | .......................P. Coast | | 18 | 117 | 4 | 11 | .267 | 142 | 80 | 70 | 80 | 55 | 5.38 |
| 1974–Los Angeles | ........................National | | 4 | 7 | 0 | 0 | .000 | 7 | 3 | 3 | 2 | 5 | 3.86 |
| 1975–Albuquerque† | .....................P. Coast | | 29 | 203 | 9 | 13 | .409 | 219 | 118 | 95 | •147 | 73 | 4.21 |
| 1976–Mexico Reds‡ | .....................Mexican | | 22 | 173 | 12 | 8 | .600 | 175 | 67 | 45 | 133 | 47 | 2.34 |
| Major League Totals | ............................. | | 11 | 23 | 0 | 0 | .000 | 21 | 9 | 9 | 13 | 9 | 3.52 |

†Released by Los Angeles Dodgers, April 16, 1976; signed as free agent with Mexico City Reds, April 24, 1976.

‡Released, September 21, 1976; signed as free agent by Kansas City Royals' organization, February 2, 1977.

## WILLIAM HOWARD SHARP
### (Bill)
Born January 18, 1950, at Lima, O.
Height, 5.10. Weight, 180.
Throws and bats lefthanded.
Attended Ohio State University, Columbus, O.

| Year | Club | League | Pos. | G. | AB. | R. | H. | 2B. | 3B. | HR. | RBI. | B.A. | PO. | A. | E. | F.A. |
|---|---|---|---|---|---|---|---|---|---|---|---|---|---|---|---|---|
| 1971–Asheville | ..........South. | | OF | 56 | 160 | 20 | 36 | 3 | 2 | 5 | 21 | .255 | 85 | 3 | 1 | .989 |
| 1972–Knoxville† | ........South. | | OF | 44 | 137 | 20 | 39 | 8 | 5 | 2 | 24 | .285 | 77 | 3 | 4 | .952 |
| 1973–Iowa | ..................A. A. | | OF | 39 | 145 | 32 | 40 | 7 | 2 | 3 | 13 | .276 | 61 | 7 | 2 | .971 |
| 1973–Chicago | ............Amer. | | OF | 77 | 196 | 23 | 54 | 8 | 3 | 4 | 22 | .276 | 146 | 10 | 3 | .981 |
| 1974–Iowa | ..................A. A. | | OF | 37 | 150 | 24 | 50 | 6 | 3 | 5 | 26 | .333 | 85 | 3 | 3 | .967 |
| 1974–Chicago | ............Amer. | | OF | 100 | 320 | 45 | 81 | 13 | 2 | 4 | 24 | .253 | 210 | 3 | 3 | .986 |
| 1975–Chi.‡-Milw. | ........Amer. | | OF | 143 | 408 | 38 | 102 | 27 | 3 | 1 | 38 | .250 | 310 | 12 | 3 | .991 |
| 1976–Milwaukee | ........Amer. | | O-DH-PH | 78 | 180 | 16 | 44 | 4 | 0 | 1 | 11 | .244 | 108 | 7 | 3 | .975 |
| Major League Totals | ...................... | | | 398 | 1104 | 122 | 281 | 52 | 8 | 9 | 95 | .254 | 774 | 32 | 12 | .985 |

†On military list, February 18 to June 17, 1972.
‡Traded to Milwaukee Brewers for Outfielder Bob Coluccio, May 8, 1975.

## BOB MITCHELL SHELDON
Born November 27, 1950, at Montebello, Calif.
Height, 6.01. Weight, 170.
Throws right and bats lefthanded.
Hobby–Hunting.
Attended Loyola Marymount University, Los Angeles, Calif.

| Year | Club | League | Pos. | G. | AB. | R. | H. | 2B. | 3B. | HR. | RBI. | B.A. | PO. | A. | E. | F.A. |
|---|---|---|---|---|---|---|---|---|---|---|---|---|---|---|---|---|
| 1972–Newark | ...........NYP | | SS | 68 | 248 | 44 | 69 | 9 | 2 | 1 | 24 | .278 | 94 | 149 | 13 | .949 |
| 1973–Shreveport | ........Texas | | 2-S-3 | 131 | 498 | 55 | 114 | 21 | 2 | 1 | 37 | .229 | 252 | 392 | 21 | .968 |
| 1974–Sacramento† | .....P. C. | | 2B | 75 | 301 | 64 | 100 | 11 | 1 | 11 | 37 | .332 | 161 | 224 | 15 | .963 |
| 1974–Milwaukee | .......Amer. | | 2B | 10 | 17 | 4 | 2 | 1 | 1 | 0 | 0 | .118 | 1 | 4 | 0 | 1.000 |
| 1975–Sacramento | ......P. C. | | 2B | 82 | 327 | 44 | 102 | 10 | 0 | 5 | 23 | .312 | 193 | 245 | 12 | .973 |
| 1975–Milwaukee | ........Amer. | | 2B | 53 | 181 | 17 | 52 | 3 | 3 | 0 | 14 | .287 | 87 | 122 | 5 | .977 |
| 1976–Spokane‡ | .......P. C. | | 1B-2B | 75 | 260 | 56 | 72 | 12 | 1 | 1 | 19 | .277 | 629 | 55 | 5 | .993 |
| Major League Totals | ...................... | | | 63 | 198 | 21 | 54 | 4 | 4 | 0 | 14 | .273 | 88 | 126 | 5 | .977 |

†On disabled list, August 8 to September 3, 1974.
‡On disabled list, May 31 to July 9, 1976.
Listed on Milwaukee Brewers' 1977 spring roster.

# DENNIS LEE SHERRILL

Born March 3, 1956, at Miami, Fla.
Height, 6.00. Weight, 165.
Throws and bats righthanded.
Hobbies—Fishing, golf, basketball and football.

| Year | Club | League | Pos. | G. | AB. | R. | H. | 2B. | 3B. | HR. | RBI. | B.A. | PO. | A. | E. | F.A. |
|------|------|--------|------|----|-----|----|----|-----|-----|-----|------|------|-----|----|----|------|
| 1974—Ft. Lauderdale | ..Fla. St. | | SS | 58 | 183 | 25 | 33 | 7 | 2 | 1 | 18 | .180 | 114 | 155 | 21 | .928 |
| 1975—West Haven | ......East. | | SS | 113 | 335 | 47 | 74 | 10 | 5 | 1 | 34 | .221 | 159 | 332 | 39 | .926 |
| 1976—Syracuse | .........Int. | | SS | 5 | 10 | 0 | 0 | 0 | 0 | 0 | 0 | .000 | 8 | 11 | 0 | 1.000 |
| 1976—West Haven† | ....East. | | SS | 37 | 109 | 12 | 20 | 2 | 0 | 0 | 4 | .183 | 64 | 115 | 13 | .932 |

†On disabled list, July 11 through September 10, 1976.
Listed on New York Yankees' 1977 spring roster.

# ROBERT CHARLES SHIRLEY
## (Bob)

Born June 25, 1954, at Oklahoma City, Okla.
Height, 5.11. Weight, 180.
Throws right and bats lefthanded.
Attended University of Oklahoma, Norman, Okla.

| Year | Club | League | G. | IP. | W. | L. | Pct. | H. | R. | ER. | SO. | BB. | ERA. |
|------|------|--------|----|----|----|----|------|----|----|----|----|----|------|
| 1976—Amarillo | .............................Texas | | 16 | 111 | 9 | 5 | .643 | 113 | 55 | 41 | 90 | 39 | 3.32 |
| 1976—Hawaii | ................................P. Coast | | 13 | 81 | 5 | 5 | .500 | 91 | 62 | 47 | 47 | 24 | 5.22 |

Invited to San Diego Padres' 1977 spring camp.

# THOMAS MICHAEL SHOPAY

Name pronounced Show-PAY.

## (Tom)

Born February 21, 1945, at Bristol, Conn.
Height, 5.09. Weight, 160.
Throws right and bats lefthanded.
Hobbies—Golf, coin collecting and antiques.
Attended Dean Junior College, Franklin, Mass., University of Bridgeport,
Bridgeport, Conn., and Suffolk University, Boston, Mass.

| Year | Club | League | Pos. | G. | AB. | R. | H. | 2B. | 3B. | HR. | RBI. | B.A. | PO. | A. | E. | F.A. |
|------|------|--------|------|----|-----|----|----|-----|-----|-----|------|------|-----|----|----|------|
| 1965—Binghamton | ......NYP | | OF | 67 | 218 | 45 | 70 | 9 | 6 | 5 | 30 | .321 | 91 | 7 | 1 | .990 |
| 1966—Greensboro | ........Carol. | | OF | 71 | 243 | 37 | 65 | 11 | 4 | 1 | 14 | .267 | 95 | 3 | 4 | .961 |
| 1967—Syracuse | .........Int. | | OF | 138 | •542 | 70 | 150 | 18 | •13 | 9 | 45 | .277 | 222 | 10 | 4 | .983 |
| 1967—New York | .........Amer. | | OF | 8 | 27 | 2 | 8 | 1 | 0 | 2 | 6 | .296 | 9 | 2 | 1 | .917 |
| 1968—Syracuse | .........Int. | | OF-3B | 125 | 458 | 40 | 112 | 20 | 8 | 2 | 35 | .245 | 217 | 11 | 3 | .987 |
| 1969—Syracuse | .........Int. | | OF | 65 | 242 | 43 | 62 | 9 | 5 | 7 | 32 | .256 | 108 | 4 | 3 | .974 |
| 1969—New York† | .......Amer. | | OF | 28 | 48 | 2 | 4 | 0 | 1 | 0 | 0 | .083 | 26 | 0 | 0 | 1.000 |
| 1970—Rochester‡ | .......Int. | | OF | 88 | 343 | 76 | 111 | 14 | 6 | 7 | 34 | .324 | 159 | 12 | 3 | .983 |
| 1971—Baltimore§ | .........Amer. | | OF | 47 | 74 | 10 | 19 | 2 | 0 | 0 | 5 | .257 | 18 | 1 | 0 | 1.000 |
| 1972—Baltimore | .........Amer. | | OF | 49 | 40 | 3 | 9 | 0 | 0 | 2 | .225 | 4 | 0 | 0 | 1.000 |
| 1973—Rochester | .........Int. | | •OF-3B | 131 | 478 | 63 | 127 | 23 | 4 | 7 | 33 | .266 | 269 | 12 | 2 | •.993 |
| 1974—Rochester | .........Int. | | OF | 103 | 352 | 62 | 110 | 16 | 0 | 10 | 36 | .313 | 192 | 5 | 3 | .985 |
| 1975—Baltimore | .........Amer. | | OF-C | 40 | 31 | 4 | 5 | 1 | 0 | 0 | 2 | .161 | 17 | 3 | 0 | 1.000 |
| 1976—Rochester | .........Int. | | O-C-3-2 | 55 | 173 | 29 | 60 | 9 | 1 | 4 | 19 | .347 | 85 | 5 | 3 | .968 |
| 1976—Baltimore | .........Amer. | | OF-C | 14 | 20 | 4 | 4 | 0 | 0 | 0 | 1 | .200 | 14 | 1 | 0 | 1.000 |
| Major League Totals | ...................... | | | 186 | 240 | 25 | 49 | 4 | 1 | 2 | 16 | .204 | 88 | 7 | 1 | .990 |

†Drafted by Baltimore Orioles from Syracuse (New York Yankees' organization), December 1, 1969.
‡On disabled list, July 22 through September 4, 1970.
§On disabled list, May 24 through July 6, 1971.

### WORLD SERIES RECORD

| Year | Club | League | Pos. | G. | AB. | R. | H. | 2B. | 3B. | HR. | RBI. | B.A. | PO. | A. | E. | F.A. |
|------|------|--------|------|----|-----|----|----|-----|-----|-----|------|------|-----|----|----|------|
| 1971—Baltimore | .........Amer. | | PH | 5 | 4 | 0 | 0 | 0 | 0 | 0 | 0 | .000 | 0 | 0 | 0 | .000 |

# PAUL EDWARD SIEBERT

Born June 5, 1953, at Minneapolis, Minn.
Height, 6.02. Weight, 205.
Throws and bats lefthanded.
Son of Dick Siebert, former first baseman with Brooklyn Dodgers,
St. Louis Cardinals and Philadelphia Athletics.

Led Appalachian League in shutouts with 3 in 1971.
Led Southern League in complete games with 18 and tied for lead in shutouts with 3 in 1974.
Named Outstanding Pitcher in Southern League, 1974.

| Year | Club | League | G. | IP. | W. | L. | Pct. | H. | R. | ER. | SO. | BB. | ERA. |
|------|------|--------|----|----|----|----|------|----|----|----|----|----|------|
| 1971—Covington | .............................Ap'achian | | 13 | 87 | 5 | 2 | .714 | 74 | 25 | 20 | 96 | 24 | 2.07 |
| 1972—Cocoa | ................................Florida St. | | 24 | 164 | 8 | 9 | .471 | 142 | 67 | 50 | 131 | 70 | 2.74 |
| 1973—Columbus | .............................Southern | | 23 | 140 | 8 | 6 | .571 | 142 | 73 | 61 | 88 | 51 | 3.92 |
| 1974—Columbus | .............................Southern | | 26 | •211 | •15 | 7 | .682 | 188 | 73 | 60 | 120 | 67 | 2.56 |

| Year Club | League | G. | IP. | W. | L. | Pct. | H. | R. | ER. | SO. | BB. | ERA. |
|---|---|---|---|---|---|---|---|---|---|---|---|---|
| 1974—Houston | National | 5 | 25 | 1 | 1 | .500 | 21 | 12 | 10 | 10 | 11 | 3.60 |
| 1975—Iowa | Am. Assoc. | 30 | 194 | 12 | 12 | .500 | 200 | 90 | 84 | 115 | 55 | 3.90 |
| 1975—Houston | National | 7 | 18 | 0 | 2 | .000 | 20 | 7 | 6 | 6 | 6 | 3.00 |
| 1976—Memphis | Int'national | 18 | 94 | 8 | 3 | .727 | 104 | 43 | 39 | 47 | 7 | 3.73 |
| 1976—Houston† | National | 19 | 26 | 0 | 2 | .000 | 29 | 10 | 9 | 10 | 18 | 3.12 |
| Major League Totals | | 31 | 69 | 1 | 5 | .167 | 70 | 29 | 25 | 26 | 35 | 3.26 |

†Traded to San Diego Padres for Pitcher Mike Allen, January 25, 1977.

## LUIS PASCUAL SILVERIO

Name pronounced Sil-VAIR-ee-o.

Born October 23, 1956, at Villas Gonzalez, Santiago, Dominican Republic.
Height, 5.11. Weight, 165.
Throws and bats righthanded.
Hobby—Music.

| Year Club | League | Pos. | G. | AB. | R. | H. | 2B. | 3B. | HR. | RBI. | B.A. | PO. | A. | E. | F.A. |
|---|---|---|---|---|---|---|---|---|---|---|---|---|---|---|---|
| 1974—Sara K. C. | Gulf C. | OF | 48 | 157 | 39 | 47 | 5 | 4 | 3 | 28 | .299 | 76 | 7 | 4 | .954 |
| 1975—Waterloo | Midw. | OF | 12 | 26 | 2 | 3 | 1 | 1 | 0 | 3 | .115 | 15 | 0 | 0 | 1.000 |
| 1975—Sarasota Royals | Gulf C. | OF | 44 | 150 | 20 | 35 | 5 | 3 | ∗5 | 29 | .233 | 61 | 6 | 2 | .971 |
| 1976—Waterloo | Midw. | OF | 122 | 463 | 75 | 126 | 20 | 3 | 14 | 82 | .272 | ∗270 | 9 | 6 | ∗.979 |

Listed on Kansas City Royals' 1977 spring roster.

## TED LYLE SIMMONS

Born August 9, 1949, at Highland Park, Mich.
Height, 5.11. Weight, 195.
Throws right and bats left and righthanded.
Hobby—Riding motorcycles.
Attended University of Michigan, Ann Arbor, Mich.

Led National League catchers in total chances with 928 in 1972, 975 in 1973 and 880 in 1975.
Led National League in passed balls with 25 in 1973 and 28 in 1975.
Named Rookie of the Year and Most Valuable Player in California League, 1968.
Received reported $50,000 bonus to sign with St. Louis Cardinals, 1967.

| Year Club | League | Pos. | G. | AB. | R. | H. | 2B. | 3B. | HR. | RBI. | B.A. | PO. | A. | E. | F.A. |
|---|---|---|---|---|---|---|---|---|---|---|---|---|---|---|---|
| 1967—Sarasota Cards | Gulf C. | C | 6 | 20 | 5 | 7 | 1 | 1 | 2 | 8 | .350 | 33 | 0 | 0 | 1.000 |
| 1967—Cedar Rapids | Midw. | OF-C | 47 | 171 | 15 | 46 | 11 | 2 | 4 | 34 | .269 | 119 | 8 | 3 | .977 |
| 1968—Modesto | Calif. | ∗C-O | 136 | 493 | 86 | 163 | 30 | 2 | 28 | ∗117 | ∗.331 | ∗989 | 79 | ∗16 | .985 |
| 1968—St. Louis | Nat. | C | 2 | 3 | 0 | 1 | 0 | 0 | 0 | 0 | .333 | 3 | 1 | 0 | 1.000 |
| 1969—Tulsa | A. A. | C-3-O-1 | 129 | 499 | 80 | 158 | 33 | 4 | 16 | 88 | .317 | 463 | 92 | 19 | .967 |
| 1969—St. Louis† | Nat. | C | 5 | 14 | 0 | 3 | 0 | 1 | 0 | 3 | .214 | 22 | 0 | 1 | .957 |
| 1970—Tulsa | A. A. | C | 15 | 51 | 10 | 19 | 4 | 1 | 1 | 8 | .373 | 99 | 7 | 0 | 1.000 |
| 1970—St. Louis | Nat. | C | 82 | 284 | 29 | 69 | 8 | 2 | 3 | 24 | .243 | 466 | 37 | 5 | .990 |
| 1971—St. Louis‡ | Nat. | C | 133 | 510 | 64 | 155 | 32 | 4 | 7 | 77 | .304 | 747 | 52 | 9 | .989 |
| 1972—St. Louis | Nat. | ∗C-1B | 152 | 594 | 70 | 180 | 36 | 6 | 16 | 96 | .303 | ∗967 | ∗93 | 13 | .988 |
| 1973—St. Louis | Nat. | ∗C-1-O | 161 | 619 | 62 | 192 | 36 | 2 | 13 | 91 | .310 | ∗932 | 78 | 14 | .986 |
| 1974—St. Louis | Nat. | C-1B | 152 | 599 | 66 | 163 | 33 | 6 | 20 | 103 | .272 | 813 | 87 | 15 | .983 |
| 1975—St. Louis | Nat. | ∗C-1-O | 157 | 581 | 80 | 193 | 32 | 3 | 18 | 100 | .332 | 818 | 64 | ∗15 | .983 |
| 1976—St. Louis | Nat. | C-1-O-3 | 150 | 546 | 60 | 159 | 35 | 3 | 5 | 75 | .291 | 726 | 88 | 10 | .988 |
| Major League Totals | | | 994 | 3750 | 431 | 1115 | 212 | 27 | 82 | 569 | .297 | 5494 | 500 | 82 | .986 |

†On military list, December 12, 1969 through May 9, 1970.
‡On military list, June 19 through July 4, 1971.

### ALL-STAR GAME RECORD

| Year League | Pos. | AB. | R. | H. | 2B. | 3B. | HR. | RBI. | B.A. | PO. | A. | E. | F.A. |
|---|---|---|---|---|---|---|---|---|---|---|---|---|---|
| 1973—National | PH-C | 1 | 0 | 0 | 0 | 0 | 0 | 0 | .000 | 1 | 1 | 0 | 1.000 |

Member of National League All-Star Team in 1972 and 1974 games; did not play.

## JOE ALLEN SIMPSON

Born December 31, 1951, at Purcell, Okla.
Height, 6.03. Weight, 180.
Throws and bats lefthanded.
Hobbies—Photography, listening to music and other sports.
Attended University of Oklahoma, Norman, Okla.

| Year Club | League | Pos. | G. | AB. | R. | H. | 2B. | 3B. | HR. | RBI. | B.A. | PO. | A. | E. | F.A. |
|---|---|---|---|---|---|---|---|---|---|---|---|---|---|---|---|
| 1973—Albuquerque | P. C. | OF | 15 | 54 | 10 | 12 | 0 | 0 | 0 | 6 | .222 | 40 | 1 | 4 | .911 |
| 1973—Bakersfield | Calif. | OF | 61 | 227 | 37 | 69 | 4 | 1 | 1 | 24 | .304 | 127 | 4 | 3 | .978 |
| 1974—Waterbury | East. | OF | 117 | 406 | 59 | 121 | 18 | 6 | 1 | 30 | .298 | 256 | 16 | 14 | .951 |
| 1974—Albuquerque | P. C. | OF | 13 | 43 | 2 | 7 | 1 | 1 | 0 | 0 | .163 | 29 | 2 | 0 | 1.000 |
| 1975—Albuquerque† | P. C. | OF | 133 | 514 | 84 | 142 | 24 | 6 | 2 | 49 | .276 | 289 | 8 | 5 | .983 |
| 1975—Los Angeles | Nat. | OF | 9 | 6 | 3 | 2 | 0 | 0 | 0 | 0 | .333 | 5 | 0 | 0 | 1.000 |
| 1976—Albuquerque | P. C. | OF-1B | 108 | 419 | 77 | 131 | 19 | 7 | 4 | 60 | .313 | 193 | 15 | 8 | .961 |
| 1976—Los Angeles | Nat. | OF | 23 | 30 | 2 | 4 | 1 | 3 | 0 | 0 | .133 | 24 | 0 | 0 | 1.000 |
| Major League Totals | | | 32 | 36 | 5 | 6 | 1 | 3 | 0 | 0 | .167 | 29 | 0 | 0 | 1.000 |

†On disabled list, April 10 to April 20, 1975.

## WAYNE KIRBY SIMPSON

Born December 2, 1948, at Los Angeles, Calif.
Height, 6.04. Weight, 215.
Throws and bats righthanded.
Hobby—Listening to jazz.

Pitched seven-inning, 3-0 no-hit victory against Syracuse, June 20, 1975 (first game of doubleheader).
Led American Association in hit batsmen with 11 and in wild pitches with 22 in 1969.
Tied for Northern League lead in wild pitches with 15 in 1967 and led Southern League with 24 in 1968.

| Year Club | League | G. | IP. | W. | L. | Pct. | H. | R. | ER. | SO. | BB. | ERA. |
|---|---|---|---|---|---|---|---|---|---|---|---|---|
| 1967—Sioux Falls | Northern | 12 | 81 | 4 | 3 | .571 | 59 | 39 | 26 | 68 | *71 | 2.89 |
| 1968—Asheville | Southern | 26 | 131 | 7 | 9 | .438 | 122 | 70 | 57 | 97 | *86 | 3.92 |
| 1969—Indianapolis | Am. Assoc. | 27 | 162 | 7 | *13 | .350 | 145 | 102 | 88 | 120 | 102 | 4.89 |
| 1970—Cincinnati | National | 26 | 176 | 14 | 3 | *.824 | 125 | 73 | 59 | 119 | 81 | 3.02 |
| 1971—Indianapolis | Am. Assoc. | 6 | 34 | 2 | 0 | 1.000 | 34 | 16 | 14 | 24 | 21 | 3.67 |
| 1971—Cincinnati | National | 22 | 117 | 4 | 7 | .364 | 106 | 66 | 62 | 61 | 77 | 4.77 |
| 1972—Indianapolis | Am. Assoc. | 3 | 15 | 0 | 2 | .000 | 15 | 9 | 9 | 11 | 10 | 5.40 |
| 1972—Cincinnati† | National | 24 | 130 | 8 | 5 | .615 | 124 | 63 | 60 | 70 | 49 | 4.15 |
| 1973—Omaha | Am. Assoc. | 9 | 61 | 3 | 5 | .375 | 57 | 29 | 25 | 37 | 27 | 3.69 |
| 1973—Kansas City‡ | American | 16 | 60 | 3 | 4 | .429 | 66 | 39 | 38 | 29 | 35 | 5.70 |
| 1974—Charleston§ | Int'national | 25 | 160 | 9 | 10 | .474 | 139 | 68 | 59 | 109 | 67 | 3.32 |
| 1975—Toledo | Int'national | 26 | 170 | 12 | 7 | .632 | 131 | 58 | 41 | 110 | 56 | 2.17 |
| 1975—Philadelphia x | National | 7 | 31 | 1 | 0 | 1.000 | 31 | 11 | 11 | 19 | 11 | 3.19 |
| 1976—Salt Lake City | P. Coast | 28 | 174 | 13 | 6 | .684 | 189 | 98 | 82 | 131 | 72 | 4.24 |
| National League Totals | | 79 | 454 | 27 | 15 | .643 | 386 | 213 | 192 | 269 | 218 | 3.81 |
| American League Totals | | 16 | 60 | 3 | 4 | .429 | 66 | 39 | 38 | 29 | 35 | 5.70 |
| Major League Totals | | 95 | 514 | 30 | 19 | .612 | 452 | 252 | 230 | 298 | 253 | 4.03 |

†Traded with Outfielder Hal McRae to Kansas City Royals for Pitcher Roger Nelson and Outfielder Richie Scheinblum, November 30, 1972.
‡Traded to Pittsburgh Pirates for Pitcher Jim Foor, March 28, 1974.
§Traded by Pittsburgh Pirates to Philadelphia Phillies for Outfielder Bill Robinson, April 5, 1975.
xSold to California Angels, April 7, 1976.
Listed on California Angels' 1977 spring roster.

ALL-STAR GAME RECORD
Member of National League All-Star Team in 1970 game; did not play.

## WILLIAM ROBERT SINGER
### (Bill)

Born April 24, 1944, at Los Angeles, Calif.
Height, 6.04. Weight, 200.
Throws and bats righthanded.
Hobbies—Swimming, dancing and water skiing.

Pitched 5-0 no-hit victory against Philadelphia Phillies, July 20, 1970.
Pitched seven-inning, 3-0 no-hit victory against Dallas, April 23, 1964.
Led Pacific Coast League pitchers in complete games with 17 in 1965.
Received reported $50,000 bonus to sign with Los Angeles Dodgers, 1961.

| Year Club | League | G. | IP. | W. | L. | Pct. | H. | R. | ER. | SO. | BB. | ERA. |
|---|---|---|---|---|---|---|---|---|---|---|---|---|
| 1962—Reno | California | 19 | 127 | 9 | 3 | .750 | 128 | 80 | 61 | 136 | 82 | 4.32 |
| 1963—Albuquerque | Texas | 24 | 95 | 6 | 7 | .462 | 101 | 65 | 61 | 90 | 54 | 5.78 |
| 1964—Spokane | P. Coast | 32 | 173 | 11 | 10 | .524 | 171 | 94 | 80 | 76 | 81 | 4.16 |
| 1964—Los Angeles | National | 2 | 14 | 0 | 1 | .000 | 11 | 5 | 5 | 3 | 12 | 3.21 |
| 1965—Spokane | P. Coast | 33 | 211 | 14 | 15 | .483 | 213 | 115 | *106 | 127 | 91 | 4.52 |
| 1965—Los Angeles | National | 2 | 1 | 0 | 0 | .000 | 2 | 0 | 0 | 1 | 2 | 0.00 |
| 1966—Spokane | P. Coast | 33 | 233 | 13 | 11 | .542 | 205 | 105 | 90 | *217 | 87 | 3.48 |
| 1966—Los Angeles | National | 3 | 4 | 0 | 0 | .000 | 4 | 0 | 0 | 4 | 2 | 0.00 |
| 1967—Los Angeles | National | 32 | 204 | 12 | 8 | .600 | 185 | 68 | 60 | 169 | 61 | 2.65 |
| 1968—Los Angeles | National | 37 | 256 | 13 | 17 | .433 | 227 | 97 | 82 | 227 | 78 | 2.88 |
| 1969—Los Angeles | National | 41 | 316 | 20 | 12 | .625 | 244 | 96 | 82 | 247 | 74 | 2.34 |
| 1970—Los Angeles† | National | 16 | 106 | 8 | 5 | .615 | 79 | 39 | 37 | 93 | 32 | 3.14 |
| 1971—Los Angeles | National | 31 | 203 | 10 | 17 | .370 | 195 | 103 | 94 | 144 | 71 | 4.17 |
| 1972—Los Angeles‡§ | National | 26 | 169 | 6 | 16 | .273 | 148 | 84 | 69 | 101 | 60 | 3.67 |
| 1973—California | American | 40 | 316 | 20 | 14 | .588 | 280 | 124 | 113 | 241 | 130 | 3.22 |
| 1974—California x | American | 14 | 109 | 7 | 4 | .636 | 102 | 48 | 36 | 77 | 43 | 2.97 |
| 1975—California y | American | 29 | 179 | 7 | 15 | .318 | 171 | 107 | 99 | 78 | 81 | 4.98 |
| 1976—Tex. z-Minn. a | American | 36 | 237 | 13 | 10 | .565 | 233 | 119 | 97 | 97 | 96 | 3.68 |
| National League Totals | | 190 | 1273 | 69 | 76 | .476 | 1095 | 492 | 429 | 989 | 392 | 3.03 |
| American League Totals | | 119 | 841 | 47 | 43 | .522 | 786 | 398 | 345 | 493 | 350 | 3.69 |
| Major League Totals | | 309 | 2114 | 116 | 119 | .494 | 1881 | 890 | 774 | 1482 | 742 | 3.30 |

†On disabled list, April 22 through June 14 and August 12 through September 8.
‡On disabled list, June 24 through July 15, 1972.
§Traded with Outfielder Frank Robinson, Infielders Billy Grabarkewitz and Bob Valentine and Pitcher Mike Strahler to California Angels for Pitcher Andy Messersmith and Third Baseman Ken McMullen, November 28, 1972.
xOn emergency disabled list, June 9 through remainder of season.
yTraded to Texas Rangers for First Baseman Jim Spencer and an estimated $100,000, December 10, 1975.
zTraded with Infielders Roy Smalley and Mike Cubbage, Pitcher Jim Gideon and $250,000 cash to Minnesota Twins for Pitcher Bert Blyleven and Shortstop Danny Thompson, June 1, 1976.
aSelected by Toronto Blue Jays in American League expansion draft, November 5, 1976.

| Year League | IP. | W. | L. | Pct. | H. | R. | ER. | SO. | BB. | ERA. |
|---|---|---|---|---|---|---|---|---|---|---|
| 1969—National | 2 | 0 | 0 | .000 | 0 | 0 | 0 | 0 | 0 | 0.00 |
| 1973—American | 2 | 0 | 0 | .000 | 3 | 3 | 3 | 2 | 1 | 13.50 |
| All-Star Game Totals | 4 | 0 | 0 | .000 | 3 | 3 | 3 | 2 | 1 | 6.75 |

## KENNETH WAYNE SINGLETON
### (Ken)

Born June 10, 1947, at New York, N. Y.
Height, 6.04. Weight, 210.
Throws right and bats left and righthanded.
Attended Hofstra University, Hempstead, N. Y.

Tied National League record for most home runs, switch-hitting, one month, 9, July, 1973.
Led Florida State League batters in walks with 87 in 1967.
Led California League in sacrifice flies with 6 in 1968.

| Year Club League | Pos. | G. | AB. | R. | H. | 2B. | 3B. | HR. | RBI. | B.A. | PO. | A. | E. | F.A. |
|---|---|---|---|---|---|---|---|---|---|---|---|---|---|---|
| 1967—Winter Haven ....Fla. St. | O-1B | 102 | 278 | 49 | 77 | 17 | 1 | 4 | 41 | .277 | 222 | 7 | 5 | .979 |
| 1968—Raleigh-Durham Carol. | 1B-OF | 26 | 74 | 21 | 19 | 3 | 0 | 3 | 12 | .257 | 176 | 8 | 5 | .974 |
| 1968—Visalia .............Calif. | OF-1B | 80 | 263 | 61 | 83 | 5 | 0 | 11 | 35 | .316 | 187 | 12 | 7 | .966 |
| 1968—Jacksonville ......Int. | OF-1B | 29 | 78 | 12 | 16 | 5 | 1 | 2 | 10 | .205 | 34 | 0 | 2 | .944 |
| 1969—Memphis ..........Tex. | OF-1B | 115 | 366 | 65 | 113 | 16 | 6 | 10 | 65 | .309 | 234 | 10 | 3 | .988 |
| 1970—Tidewater..........Int. | OF | 64 | 219 | 48 | 85 | 16 | 1 | 17 | 46 | .388 | 92 | 4 | 2 | .980 |
| 1970—New York.........Nat. | OF | 69 | 198 | 22 | 52 | 8 | 0 | 5 | 26 | .263 | 90 | 1 | 3 | .968 |
| 1971—New York.........Nat. | OF | 115 | 298 | 34 | 73 | 5 | 0 | 13 | 46 | .245 | 143 | 5 | 4 | .974 |
| 1972—Montreal†.........Nat. | OF | 142 | 507 | 77 | 139 | 23 | 2 | 14 | 50 | .274 | 236 | 9 | 7 | .972 |
| 1973—Montreal .........Nat. | OF •162 | 560 | 100 | 169 | 26 | 2 | 23 | 103 | .302 | 278 | •20 | 5 | .983 |
| 1974—Montreal‡.........Nat. | OF | 148 | 511 | 68 | 141 | 20 | 2 | 9 | 74 | .276 | 224 | 7 | 11 | .955 |
| 1975—Baltimore.........Amer. | OF | 155 | 586 | 88 | 176 | 37 | 4 | 15 | 55 | .300 | 283 | 9 | 3 | .990 |
| 1976—Baltimore.........Amer. | OF-DH | 154 | 544 | 62 | 151 | 25 | 2 | 13 | 70 | .278 | 278 | 9 | 5 | .983 |
| National League Totals | | 636 | 2074 | 301 | 574 | 82 | 6 | 64 | 299 | .277 | 971 | 42 | 30 | .971 |
| American League Totals | | 309 | 1130 | 150 | 327 | 62 | 6 | 28 | 125 | .289 | 561 | 18 | 8 | .986 |
| Major League Totals | | 945 | 3204 | 451 | 901 | 144 | 12 | 92 | 424 | .281 | 1532 | 60 | 38 | .977 |

†Traded with First Baseman Mike Jorgensen and Infielder Tim Foli To Montreal Expos for Outfielder Rusty Staub, April 6, 1972.

‡Traded with Pitcher Mike Torrez to Baltimore Orioles for Pitchers Dave McNally and Bill Kirkpatrick and Outfielder Rich Coggins, December 4, 1974.

## TED CRAWFORD SIZEMORE

Born April 15, 1945, at Gadsden, Ala.
Height, 5.10. Weight, 170.
Throws and bats righthanded.
Hobbies—Golf, chess and cards.
Attended University of Michigan, Ann Arbor, Mich.; received Bachelor of Science degrees in Education and Marketing.

Established major league record for longest errorless game by second baseman, 25 innings, September 11, 1974.
Tied major league records for most triples with bases filled, season, 3, 1969; and most errors, second baseman, inning 3, April 17, 1975, 6th inning.
Led National League in sacrifice hits with 25 in 1973.
Led Texas League in sacrifice flies with 9 in 1967.
Selected by Baseball Writers' Association as National League Rookie of the Year, 1969.
Named Player of the Year in Northwest League, 1966.

| Year Club League | Pos. | G. | AB. | R. | H. | 2B. | 3B. | HR. | RBI. | B.A. | PO. | A. | E. | F.A. |
|---|---|---|---|---|---|---|---|---|---|---|---|---|---|---|
| 1966—Tri-City ...........N'west | C | 58 | 191 | 34 | 63 | 8 | 2 | 4 | 37 | .330 | 393 | 38 | 7 | •.984 |
| 1967—Albuquerque ......Texas | C-O-IN | 131 | 440 | 53 | 130 | 21 | 4 | 5 | 61 | .295 | 693 | 58 | 11 | .986 |
| 1968—Spokane ...........P. C. | OF-C | 81 | 258 | 35 | 81 | 11 | 4 | 0 | 34 | .314 | 192 | 13 | 7 | .967 |
| 1969—Los Angeles .....Nat. | 2-S-O | 159 | 590 | 69 | 160 | 20 | 5 | 4 | 46 | .271 | 347 | 469 | 24 | .971 |
| 1970—Los Angeles†‡....Nat. | 2-O-S | 96 | 340 | 40 | 104 | 10 | 1 | 1 | 34 | .306 | 209 | 239 | 9 | .980 |
| 1971—St. Louis .........Nat. | 2-S-O-3 | 135 | 478 | 53 | 126 | 14 | 5 | 3 | 42 | .264 | 277 | 379 | 18 | .973 |
| 1972—St. Louis .........Nat. | 2B | 120 | 439 | 53 | 116 | 17 | 4 | 2 | 38 | .264 | 222 | 342 | 14 | .976 |
| 1973—St. Louis§ .........Nat. | 2B-3B | 142 | 521 | 69 | 147 | 22 | 1 | 1 | 54 | .282 | 313 | 463 | 15 | .981 |
| 1974—St. Louis x .......Nat. | 2-S-O | 129 | 504 | 68 | 126 | 17 | 0 | 2 | 47 | .250 | 336 | 412 | 16 | .979 |
| 1975—St. Louis y .......Nat. | 2B | 153 | 562 | 56 | 135 | 23 | 1 | 3 | 49 | .240 | 329 | 405 | 21 | .972 |
| 1976—Los Angeles z....Nat. | 2-3-C | 84 | 266 | 18 | 64 | 8 | 1 | 0 | 18 | .241 | 178 | 191 | 7 | .981 |
| Major League Totals | | 1018 | 3700 | 426 | 978 | 131 | 18 | 16 | 328 | .264 | 2211 | 2900 | 124 | .976 |

†On disabled list, June 12 through July 11, 1970.

‡Traded with Catcher Bob Stinson to St. Louis Cardinals for First Baseman Dick Allen, October 5, 1970.

§On supplemental disabled list, April 26 to May 15, 1973.

xOn supplemental disabled list, July 4 to July 20, 1974.

yTraded to Los Angeles Dodgers for Outfielder Willie Crawford, March 2, 1976.

zTraded to Philadelphia Phillies for Catcher Johnny Oates and a player to be named later, December 20, 1976; Pitcher Quency Hill was assigned to Albuquerque to complete deal, January 4, 1977.

# DAVID LINDSEY SKAGGS
## (Dave)
Born June 12, 1951, at Santa Monica, Calif.
Height, 6.02. Weight, 200.
Throws and bats righthanded.
Hobbies–Golf, bowling and horse racing.

| Year | Club | League | Pos. | G. | AB. | R. | H. | 2B. | 3B. | HR. | RBI. | B.A. | PO. | A. | E. | F.A. |
|---|---|---|---|---|---|---|---|---|---|---|---|---|---|---|---|---|
| 1969–Aberdeen | | North. | C | 62 | 220 | 21 | 69 | 11 | 1 | 4 | 31 | .314 | •506 | 44 | 11 | .980 |
| 1970–Aberdeen | | North. | | | | | (On Military List) | | | | | | | | | |
| 1971–Stockton | | Calif. | C-OF | 77 | 184 | 23 | 35 | 2 | 0 | 3 | 13 | .190 | 395 | 45 | 12 | .973 |
| 1972–Miami | | Fla. St. | C-O-3 | 72 | 239 | 25 | 50 | 3 | 1 | 3 | 23 | .209 | 433 | 55 | 10 | .980 |
| 1973–Lodi | | Calif. | C-3-1-O | 82 | 260 | 33 | 66 | 9 | 5 | 1 | 37 | .254 | 419 | 48 | 15 | .969 |
| 1974–Asheville | | South. | C | 110 | 363 | 41 | 91 | 16 | 2 | 5 | 38 | .251 | 531 | •66 | 4 | .993 |
| 1975–Asheville | | South. | C-1B | 59 | 199 | 26 | 53 | 8 | 1 | 0 | 24 | .266 | 297 | 40 | 5 | .985 |
| 1975–Rochester | | Int. | C-1B | 41 | 99 | 4 | 22 | 8 | 0 | 0 | 10 | .222 | 177 | 18 | 4 | .980 |
| 1976–Rochester | | Int. | C | 85 | 252 | 40 | 61 | 8 | 2 | 2 | 27 | .242 | 408 | 50 | 5 | .989 |

†On disabled list, May 26 to June 24, 1976.
Listed on Baltimore Orioles' 1977 spring roster.

# JAMES MICHAEL SLATON
## (Jim)
Born June 19, 1950, at Long Beach, Calif.
Height, 6.00. Weight, 185.
Throws and bats righthanded.
Hobby–Water skiing.
Attended Antelope Valley College, Lancaster, Calif.

Pitched 5-0 no-hit victory against Wichita, August 3, 1972.

| Year | Club | League | G. | IP. | W. | L. | Pct. | H. | R. | ER. | SO. | BB. | ERA. |
|---|---|---|---|---|---|---|---|---|---|---|---|---|---|
| 1969–Billings | | Pioneer | 2 | 8 | 1 | 0 | 1.000 | 1 | 0 | 0 | 16 | 0 | 0.00 |
| 1969–Clinton | | Midwest | 13 | 82 | 6 | 3 | .667 | 65 | 27 | 26 | 83 | 34 | 2.85 |
| 1970–Clinton† | | Midwest | 2 | 18 | 1 | 1 | .500 | 9 | 4 | 3 | 15 | 5 | 1.50 |
| 1971–Evansville | | Am. Assoc. | 4 | 32 | 1 | 0 | 1.000 | 22 | 9 | 5 | 26 | 9 | 1.39 |
| 1971–Milwaukee | | American | 26 | 148 | 10 | 8 | .556 | 140 | 67 | 62 | 63 | 71 | 3.77 |
| 1972–Evansville | | Am. Assoc. | 16 | 114 | 11 | 2 | .846 | 97 | 39 | 37 | 68 | 37 | 2.92 |
| 1972–Milwaukee | | American | 9 | 44 | 1 | 6 | .143 | 50 | 31 | 27 | 17 | 21 | 5.52 |
| 1973–Milwaukee | | American | 38 | 276 | 13 | 15 | .464 | 266 | 127 | 114 | 134 | 99 | 3.72 |
| 1974–Milwaukee | | American | 40 | 250 | 13 | 16 | .448 | 255 | 117 | 109 | 126 | 102 | 3.92 |
| 1975–Milwaukee | | American | 37 | 217 | 11 | 18 | .379 | 238 | 129 | 109 | 119 | 90 | 4.52 |
| 1976–Milwaukee | | American | 38 | 293 | 14 | 15 | .483 | 287 | 126 | 112 | 138 | 94 | 3.44 |
| Major League Totals | | | 188 | 1228 | 62 | 78 | .443 | 1236 | 597 | 533 | 597 | 477 | 3.91 |

†On military list, May 8 through remainder of season.

# ROY FREDERICK SMALLEY, III
Born October 25, 1952, at Los Angeles, Calif.
Height, 6.01. Weight, 185.
Throws right and bats left and righthanded.
Attended Los Angeles City Community College, Los Angeles, Calif., and
University of Southern California, Los Angeles, Calif.
Son on Roy Smalley, Jr., former infielder with Chicago Cubs, Milwaukee Braves and
Philadelphia Phillies. Nephew of Gene Mauch, manager of Minnesota Twins.
Tied major league record for most strikeouts in two consecutive games with 8, August 28-29, 1976.
Led American League batters in sacrifice hits with 25 in 1976.
Received reported $100,000 bonus to sign with Texas Rangers, 1974.

| Year | Club | League | Pos. | G. | AB. | R. | H. | 2B. | 3B. | HR. | RBI. | B.A. | PO. | A. | E. | F.A. |
|---|---|---|---|---|---|---|---|---|---|---|---|---|---|---|---|---|
| 1974–Pittsfield | | East. | SS | 125 | 406 | 74 | 102 | 22 | 5 | 14 | 42 | .251 | 146 | 376 | •42 | .926 |
| 1975–Spokane | | P. C. | SS-2B | 43 | 162 | 26 | 55 | 8 | 1 | 2 | 19 | .340 | 88 | 151 | 10 | .960 |
| 1975–Texas | | Amer. | S-2-C | 78 | 250 | 22 | 57 | 8 | 0 | 3 | 33 | .228 | 108 | 232 | 20 | .944 |
| 1976–Tex.†–Minn. | | Amer. | SS-2B | 144 | 513 | 61 | 133 | 18 | 3 | 3 | 44 | .259 | 274 | 447 | 26 | .965 |
| Major League Totals | | | .222 | 763 | 83 | 190 | 26 | 3 | 6 | 77 | .249 | 382 | 679 | 46 | .958 |

†Traded with Pitchers Bill Singer and Jim Gideon, Infielder Mike Cubbage, and $250,000 cash to Minnesota Twins for Pitcher Bert Blyleven and Shortstop Danny Thompson, June 1, 1976.

# BILLY EDWARD SMITH
Born July 14, 1953, at Jonesboro Hodge, La.
Height, 6.02½. Weight, 185.
Throws right and bats left and righthanded.
Hobbies–Music and sports in general.

Tied for Pioneer League lead in stolen bases with 17 in 1971.

| Year | Club | League | Pos. | G. | AB. | R. | H. | 2B. | 3B. | HR. | RBI. | B.A. | PO. | A. | E. | F.A. |
|---|---|---|---|---|---|---|---|---|---|---|---|---|---|---|---|---|
| 1971–Idaho Falls | | Pion. | SS | 59 | 231 | 29 | 53 | 5 | 2 | 0 | 17 | .229 | •87 | •179 | •36 | .881 |
| 1972–Stockton | | Calif. | S-2-3 | 127 | 455 | 58 | 105 | 15 | 10 | 5 | 31 | .231 | 216 | 340 | 53 | .913 |
| 1973–Salinas | | Calif. | SS-2B | 64 | 236 | 44 | 71 | 11 | 5 | 2 | 27 | .301 | 115 | 187 | 27 | .918 |

| Year    Club         League | Pos. | G. | AB. | R. | H. | 2B. | 3B. | HR. | RBI. | B.A. | PO. | A. | E. | F.A. |
|---|---|---|---|---|---|---|---|---|---|---|---|---|---|---|
| 1973—El Paso†............Texas | SS | 46 | 166 | 32 | 55 | 6 | 2 | 4 | 18 | .331 | 69 | 140 | 13 | .941 |
| 1974—Salt Lake City‡..P. C. | SS | 40 | 126 | 15 | 26 | 5 | 0 | 0 | 11 | .206 | 53 | 148 | 18 | .918 |
| 1974—El Paso ...........Tex. | 2B-1B | 62 | 227 | 32 | 76 | 6 | 3 | 1 | 22 | .335 | 292 | 131 | 15 | .966 |
| 1975—Salt Lake City ..P. C. | S-3-1-2 | 64 | 226 | 37 | 67 | 11 | 1 | 3 | 34 | .296 | 103 | 156 | 16 | .942 |
| 1975—California.........Amer. | S-1-3 | 59 | 143 | 10 | 29 | 5 | 1 | 0 | 14 | .203 | 95 | 99 | 14 | .933 |
| 1976—Salt Lake City ..P. C. | 1-3-S-2-O | 115 | 396 | 64 | 114 | 16 | 9 | 3 | 60 | .288 | 416 | 171 | 11 | .982 |
| 1976—California§ ........Amer. | SS-DH | 13 | 8 | 0 | 3 | 0 | 0 | 0 | 0 | .375 | 0 | 5 | 3 | .625 |
| Major League Totals ...................... | | 72 | 151 | 10 | 32 | 5 | 1 | 0 | 14 | .212 | 95 | 104 | 17 | .921 |

†On disabled list, August 17 to October 25, 1973.

‡On disabled list, June 7 to June 28, 1974.

§Played out option year and granted free agency, November 1, 1976; signed as free agent with Baltimore Orioles, February 8, 1977.

## CARL REGINALD SMITH
### (Reggie)

Born April 2, 1945, at Shreveport, La.
Height, 6.00. Weight, 190.
Throws right and bats right and lefthanded.
Hobbies—Working with plastics and all sports.
Attended Compton Community College, Compton, Calif.

Tied National League record for most games, switch-hitting home runs, lifetime, 2, in 1975.
Led American League in total bases with 302 in 1971.
Named outfielder on THE SPORTING NEWS American League All-Star fielding team, 1968.
Named outfielder on THE SPORTING NEWS American League All-Star Team, 1970.

| Year    Club         League | Pos. | G. | AB. | R. | H. | 2B. | 3B. | HR. | RBI. | B.A. | PO. | A. | E. | F.A. |
|---|---|---|---|---|---|---|---|---|---|---|---|---|---|---|
| 1963—Wytheville†........Appal. | SS | 66 | •253 | 59 | 65 | 8 | 3 | 8 | 37 | .257 | 88 | •146 | •41 | .851 |
| 1964—Reading ............East. | 3B | 17 | 47 | 6 | 6 | 1 | 0 | 0 | 4 | .128 | 7 | 20 | 9 | .750 |
| 1964—Waterloo ..........Midw. | 3-OF | 87 | 308 | 63 | 98 | 18 | 5 | 15 | 60 | .318 | 84 | 67 | 19 | .888 |
| 1965—Pittsfield .........East. | OF-2-3 | 130 | 499 | 85 | 129 | 23 | 14 | 8 | 64 | .259 | 263 | 107 | 21 | .946 |
| 1966—Toronto ...........Int. | •OF-S-2 | 143 | 506 | 86 | 162 | 30 | 9 | 18 | 80 | •320 | 303 | 49 | •17 | .954 |
| 1966—Boston ..............Amer. | OF | 6 | 26 | 1 | 4 | 1 | 0 | 0 | 0 | .154 | 17 | 0 | 1 | .944 |
| 1967—Boston ..............Amer. | OF-2B | 158 | 565 | 78 | 139 | 24 | 6 | 15 | 61 | .246 | 353 | 32 | 7 | .982 |
| 1968—Boston ..............Amer. | OF | 155 | 558 | 78 | 148 | •37 | 5 | 15 | 69 | .265 | •390 | 8 | 6 | .985 |
| 1969—Boston ..............Amer. | OF | 143 | 543 | 87 | 168 | 29 | 7 | 25 | 93 | .309 | 321 | 8 | 14 | .959 |
| 1970—Boston ..............Amer. | OF | 147 | 580 | 109 | 176 | 32 | 7 | 22 | 74 | .303 | 361 | •15 | 9 | .977 |
| 1971—Boston ..............Amer. | OF | 159 | 618 | 85 | 175 | •33 | 2 | 30 | 96 | .283 | 386 | 15 | •14 | .966 |
| 1972—Boston ..............Amer. | OF | 131 | 467 | 75 | 126 | 25 | 4 | 21 | 74 | .270 | 247 | 8 | 5 | .981 |
| 1973—Boston‡ ...........Amer. | OF-1B | 115 | 423 | 79 | 128 | 23 | 2 | 21 | 69 | .303 | 282 | 8 | 5 | .983 |
| 1974—St. Louis .........Nat. | OF-1B | 143 | 517 | 79 | 160 | 26 | 9 | 23 | 100 | .309 | 286 | 9 | 7 | .977 |
| 1975—St. Louis .........Nat. | O-1-3 | 135 | 477 | 67 | 144 | 26 | 3 | 19 | 76 | .302 | 650 | 39 | 15 | .979 |
| 1976—St. L.§-L.A. ......Nat. | OF-1-3 | 112 | 395 | 55 | 100 | 15 | 5 | 18 | 49 | .253 | 314 | 48 | 4 | .989 |
| National League Totals ................. | | 390 | 1389 | 201 | 404 | 67 | 17 | 60 | 225 | .291 | 1250 | 96 | 26 | .981 |
| American League Totals ................ | | 1014 | 3780 | 592 | 1064 | 204 | 33 | 149 | 536 | .281 | 2357 | 94 | 61 | .976 |
| Major League Totals ..................... | | 1404 | 5169 | 793 | 1468 | 271 | 50 | 209 | 761 | .284 | 3607 | 190 | 87 | .978 |

†Drafted by Boston Red Sox from Dallas-Fort Worth (Minnesota Twins' organization), December 2, 1963.

‡Traded with Pitcher Ken Tatum to St. Louis Cardinals for Pitcher Rick Wise and Outfielder Bernie Carbo, October 26, 1973.

§Traded to Los Angeles Dodgers for Catcher-Outfielder Joe Ferguson, Outfielder Bob Detherage, and Infielder Freddie Tisdale (latter assigned from Lodi to St. Petersburg), June 15, 1976.

### WORLD SERIES RECORD

Tied World Series record for most putouts, inning, outfielder (3), October 11, 1967, seventh inning.

| Year    Club         League | Pos. | G. | AB. | R. | H. | 2B. | 3B. | HR. | RBI. | B.A. | PO. | A. | E. | F.A. |
|---|---|---|---|---|---|---|---|---|---|---|---|---|---|---|
| 1967—Boston ..............Amer. | OF | 7 | 24 | 3 | 6 | 1 | 0 | 2 | 3 | .250 | 14 | 2 | 2 | 1.000 |

### ALL-STAR GAME RECORD

| Year    League | Pos. | AB. | R. | H. | 2B. | 3B. | HR. | RBI. | B.A. | PO. | A. | E. | F.A. |
|---|---|---|---|---|---|---|---|---|---|---|---|---|---|
| 1969—American ........................... | OF | 2 | 1 | 0 | 0 | 0 | 0 | 0 | .000 | 0 | 0 | 0 | .000 |
| 1972—American ........................... | PH | 1 | 0 | 0 | 0 | 0 | 0 | 0 | .000 | 0 | 0 | 0 | .000 |
| 1974—National ........................... | OF | 2 | 1 | 1 | 0 | 0 | 1 | 1 | .500 | 2 | 0 | 0 | 1.000 |
| 1975—National ........................... | OF | 2 | 1 | 1 | 0 | 0 | 0 | 0 | .500 | 0 | 0 | 0 | .000 |
| All-Star Game Totals ...................... | | 7 | 3 | 2 | 0 | 0 | 1 | 1 | .286 | 2 | 0 | 0 | 1.000 |

## LONNIE SMITH

Born December 22, 1955, at Chicago, Ill.
Height, 5.09. Weight, 170
Throws and bats righthanded.
Hobby—Fishing.

Led Western Carolinas League in stolen bases with 56 in 1975.

| Year    Club         League | Pos. | G. | AB. | R. | H. | 2B. | 3B. | HR. | RBI. | B.A. | PO. | A. | E. | F.A. |
|---|---|---|---|---|---|---|---|---|---|---|---|---|---|---|
| 1974—Auburn.............NYP | OF | 61 | 210 | 48 | 60 | 10 | 4 | 5 | 27 | .286 | 143 | 6 | •9 | .943 |
| 1975—Spartanburg ......W. Car. | OF | 131 | 465 | •114 | •150 | 23 | 4 | 7 | 40 | .323 | •317 | 9 | 11 | .967 |
| 1976—Oklahoma City ..A.A. | OF | 134 | 483 | •93 | 149 | 24 | 9 | 8 | 54 | .308 | 200 | 4 | •14 | .936 |

Listed on Philadelphia Phillies' 1977 spring roster.

## MYRL THOMAS SMITH, JR.

Born March 22, 1952, at Baltimore, Md.
Height, 6.03. Weight, 190.
Throws and bats righthanded.

Led Appalachian League in hit batsmen with 7 and wild pitches with 16 and tied for lead in games started with 13 in 1971.

| Year Club | League | G. | IP. | W. | L. | Pct. | H. | R. | ER. | SO. | BB. | ERA. |
|---|---|---|---|---|---|---|---|---|---|---|---|---|
| 1971—Bluefield | Appal. | 13 | 77 | 5 | 6 | .455 | 58 | 44 | 39 | 72 | *49 | 4.56 |
| 1972—Miami | Florida St. | 23 | 133 | 7 | 7 | .500 | 103 | 58 | 45 | 114 | 65 | 3.05 |
| 1973—Asheville | Southern | 26 | 167 | 9 | 10 | .474 | 154 | 89 | *86 | 99 | 80 | 4.63 |
| 1974—Asheville | Southern | 13 | 81 | 4 | 6 | .400 | 76 | 37 | 29 | 52 | 52 | 3.22 |
| 1974—Miami | Florida St. | 10 | 66 | 4 | 3 | .571 | 60 | 33 | 22 | 59 | 27 | 3.00 |
| 1975—Asheville | Southern | 35 | 74 | 7 | 1 | .875 | 58 | 14 | 12 | 66 | 22 | 1.46 |
| 1975—Rochester | Int'national | 2 | 3 | 0 | 2 | .000 | 6 | 3 | 3 | 2 | 1 | 9.00 |
| 1976—Charlotte† | Southern | 24 | 47 | 5 | 3 | .625 | 38 | 15 | 14 | 34 | 18 | 2.68 |

†On disabled list, June 18 through July 14, 1976.
Listed on Baltimore Orioles' 1977 spring roster.


## TOMMY ALEXANDER SMITH

Born August 1, 1948, at Albermarle, N. C.
Height, 6.03. Weight, 210.
Attended North Carolina State University, Raleigh, N. C.; received Bachelor of Arts degree in History. Did graduate studies at Appalachian State University, Boone, N. C.

| Year Club | League | Pos. | G. | AB. | R. | H. | 2B. | 3B. | HR. | RBI. | B.A. | PO. | A. | E. | F.A. |
|---|---|---|---|---|---|---|---|---|---|---|---|---|---|---|---|
| 1970—Sumter | W. Car. | OF | 53 | 183 | 27 | 67 | 10 | 6 | 3 | 43 | .366 | 37 | 1 | 7 | .844 |
| 1970—Savannah | South. | OF | 4 | 17 | 1 | 5 | 0 | 0 | 1 | 5 | .294 | 3 | 0 | 0 | 1.000 |
| 1971—Jacksonville† | South. | OF-1B | 72 | 251 | 28 | 66 | 11 | 2 | 3 | 19 | .263 | 138 | 5 | 2 | .986 |
| 1972—Elmira | East. | OF | 102 | 346 | 36 | 96 | 13 | 3 | 5 | 35 | .277 | 170 | 6 | 6 | .967 |
| 1973—Oklahoma City | A.A. | OF | 128 | 482 | 82 | 165 | 28 | 7 | 4 | 63 | .342 | 149 | 6 | 10 | .953 |
| 1973—Cleveland | Amer. | OF | 14 | 41 | 6 | 10 | 2 | 0 | 2 | 3 | .244 | 27 | 0 | 0 | 1.000 |
| 1974—Oklahoma City‡ | A.A. | OF | 93 | 381 | 59 | 119 | 23 | ●9 | 10 | 67 | .312 | 176 | 6 | 5 | .973 |
| 1974—Cleveland | Amer. | OF | 23 | 31 | 4 | 3 | 1 | 0 | 0 | 0 | .097 | 29 | 1 | 2 | .938 |
| 1975—Oklahoma City | A.A. | OF | 130 | 497 | 65 | 150 | 23 | 5 | 4 | 63 | .302 | 251 | 15 | 2 | .993 |
| 1975—Cleveland | Amer. | OF | 8 | 8 | 0 | 1 | 0 | 0 | 0 | 2 | .125 | 4 | 0 | 0 | 1.000 |
| 1976—Toledo | Int. | OF | 69 | 284 | 58 | 95 | 18 | 9 | 9 | 54 | .335 | 162 | 4 | 4 | .976 |
| 1976—Cleveland§ | Amer. | OF-DH | 55 | 164 | 17 | 42 | 3 | 1 | 2 | 12 | .256 | 90 | 4 | 2 | .979 |
| Major League Totals | | | 100 | 244 | 27 | 56 | 6 | 1 | 4 | 17 | .230 | 150 | 5 | 4 | .975 |

†On military list from beginning of season to May 19; on temporary inactive list, June 1 to June 28, 1971.
‡On temporary inactive list, April 16 to April 30, 1974.
§Selected by Seattle Mariners in American League expansion draft November 5, 1976.


## ERIC THANE SODERHOLM

Name pronounced Sod-er-holm.

Born September 24, 1948, Cortland, N. Y.
Height, 6.00. Weight, 187.
Hobbies—Bowling, golf and sports in general.
Attended South Georgia Junior College, Douglas, Ga., University of South Florida, Tampa, Fla., and University of Tampa, Tampa, Fla.
Brother of Dale Soderholm, shortstop in Minnesota Twins' organization.

Tied American League record with Jay Johnstone for most home runs, game, both clubs, pinch-hitters, 2, October 4, 1972 (both in sixth inning).
Named Florida State League Player of the Year in 1968.

| Year Club | League | Pos. | G. | AB. | R. | H. | 2B. | 3B. | HR. | RBI. | B.A. | PO. | A. | E. | F.A. |
|---|---|---|---|---|---|---|---|---|---|---|---|---|---|---|---|
| 1968—Orlando | Fla. St. | SS | 84 | 293 | 51 | 80 | 12 | 4 | 12 | 39 | .273 | 115 | 272 | 17 | .958 |
| 1969—Orlando | Fla. St. | SS | 51 | 192 | 39 | 53 | 9 | 2 | 6 | 43 | .276 | 75 | 177 | 13 | .951 |
| 1969—Red Springs | Carol. | SS | 20 | 68 | 8 | 20 | 4 | 1 | 1 | 4 | .294 | 38 | 66 | 7 | .937 |
| 1969—Charlotte | South. | SS-3 | 48 | 145 | 26 | 33 | 10 | 1 | 3 | 23 | .228 | 71 | 131 | 9 | .959 |
| 1970—Orlando | Fla. St. | 3B | 25 | 90 | 17 | 20 | 4 | 1 | 1 | 9 | .222 | 20 | 55 | 4 | .949 |
| 1970—Evansville | A.A. | SS-3B | 98 | 310 | 44 | 77 | 11 | 3 | 15 | 42 | .248 | 168 | 279 | 18 | .961 |
| 1971—Portland | P.C. | 3B-1B | 132 | 454 | 80 | 125 | 28 | 3 | 22 | 83 | .275 | 91 | 286 | 26 | .935 |
| 1971—Minnesota | Amer. | 3B | 21 | 64 | 9 | 10 | 4 | 0 | 1 | 4 | .156 | 17 | 48 | 4 | .942 |
| 1972—Minnesota | Amer. | 3B | 93 | 287 | 28 | 54 | 10 | 0 | 13 | 39 | .188 | 66 | 163 | 14 | .942 |
| 1973—Tacoma | P.C. | 3B-SS | 116 | 390 | 60 | 93 | 27 | 5 | 10 | 55 | .238 | 113 | 252 | 20 | .948 |
| 1973—Minnesota | Amer. | 3B-SS | 35 | 111 | 22 | 33 | 7 | 2 | 1 | 9 | .297 | 26 | 67 | 8 | .921 |
| 1974—Minnesota | Amer. | 3B-SS | 141 | 464 | 63 | 128 | 18 | 3 | 10 | 51 | .276 | 101 | 273 | 17 | .957 |
| 1975—Minnesota† | Amer. | 3B | 117 | 419 | 62 | 120 | 17 | 2 | 11 | 58 | .286 | 94 | 277 | 12 | .969 |
| 1976—Minnesota‡ | Amer. | | | | | (Did Not Play) | | | | | | | | | |
| Major League Totals | | | 407 | 1345 | 184 | 345 | 56 | 7 | 36 | 161 | .257 | 304 | 828 | 55 | .954 |

†On supplemental disabled list, August 21 through November 20, 1976.
‡On disabled list, March 31 through October 4, 1976. Played out option year and granted free agency November 1, 1976; signed as free agent with Chicago White Sox, November 26, 1976.

# TOLIA SOLAITA
Name pronounced So-lee-ta.
## (Tony)
Born January 15, 1947, at Nuuuila, Tutuila, American Samoa.
Height, 6.00. Weight, 210.
Throws and bats lefthanded.
Attended Mira Costa College, Oceanside, Calif.
Led Gulf Coast League first basemen in double plays with 27 in 1966.
Led Carolina League in total bases with 314, in walks with 113 and led first basemen in double plays with 127 in 1968.
Named Player of the Year in Carolina League, 1968.
Named Player of the Year in Gulf Coast League, 1966.

| Year Club | League | Pos. | G. | AB. | R. | H. | 2B. | 3B. | HR. | RBI. | B.A. | PO. | A. | E. | F.A. |
|---|---|---|---|---|---|---|---|---|---|---|---|---|---|---|---|
| 1965—Sarasota Yanks | Fla. Rk. | 1B | 45 | 110 | 12 | 28 | 4 | 0 | 1 | 14 | .255 | 231 | 15 | 2 | .992 |
| 1966—Greensboro | Carol. | 1B | 15 | 36 | 3 | 4 | 0 | 0 | 0 | 3 | .111 | 82 | 6 | 1 | .989 |
| 1966—Binghamton | NYP | 1B | 33 | 96 | 15 | 22 | 4 | 1 | 2 | 17 | .229 | 238 | 26 | 8 | .971 |
| 1966—Sarasota Yanks | Gulf C. | 1B | 45 | 145 | 20 | 47 | •9 | 0 | 2 | •40 | •.324 | 346 | 23 | 3 | •.992 |
| 1967—Ft. Lauderdale | Fla. St. | 1B | 128 | 400 | 53 | 98 | 9 | 4 | 14 | 64 | .243 | 1137 | 62 | 17 | .986 |
| 1968—High Pt.-Thoms | Carol. | •1B-O | 138 | 467 | •106 | 141 | 20 | 3 | •49 | •122 | .302 | 1103 | 95 | •20 | .984 |
| 1968—New York | Amer. | 1B | 1 | 1 | 0 | 0 | 0 | 0 | 0 | 0 | .000 | 5 | 0 | 0 | 1.000 |
| 1969—Syracuse | Int. | 1B | 19 | 58 | 7 | 14 | 3 | 0 | 2 | 5 | .241 | 132 | 6 | 6 | .958 |
| 1969—Tucson | P.C. | 1B | 32 | 72 | 13 | 14 | 0 | 0 | 6 | 19 | .194 | 161 | 13 | 4 | .978 |
| 1969—Columbus | South. | 1B | 59 | 191 | 30 | 50 | 6 | 4 | 15 | 38 | .262 | 523 | 46 | 4 | .993 |
| 1970—Syracuse | Int. | 1B | 130 | 396 | 62 | 122 | 24 | 2 | 19 | 87 | .308 | 1097 | 69 | •16 | .986 |
| 1971—Syracuse | Int. | 1B | 117 | 349 | 72 | 82 | 15 | 2 | 19 | 54 | .235 | 917 | 56 | 10 | .990 |
| 1972—Syracuse | Int. | 1B | 39 | 112 | 11 | 23 | 2 | 0 | 3 | 16 | .205 | 267 | 32 | 6 | .980 |
| 1972—West Haven† | East. | 1B | 86 | 269 | 50 | 65 | 11 | 2 | 12 | 44 | .242 | 777 | 62 | 6 | .993 |
| 1973—Charleston‡ | Int. | 1B | 132 | 438 | 71 | 126 | 18 | 2 | 23 | 74 | .288 | 1021 | •129 | 14 | .988 |
| 1974—Kansas City | Amer. | 1B-OF | 96 | 239 | 31 | 64 | 12 | 0 | 7 | 30 | .268 | 508 | 40 | 5 | .991 |
| 1975—Kansas City | Amer. | 1B | 93 | 231 | 35 | 60 | 11 | 0 | 16 | 44 | .260 | 282 | 28 | 2 | .994 |
| 1976—K.C.§-Calif. | Am. | 1-DH-PH | 94 | 283 | 29 | 74 | 13 | 0 | 9 | 42 | .261 | 485 | 57 | 2 | .996 |
| Major League Totals | | | 284 | 754 | 95 | 198 | 36 | 0 | 32 | 116 | .262 | 1280 | 125 | 9 | .994 |

†Traded by New York Yankees to Pittsburgh Pirates for First Baseman George Kopacz, February 28, 1973.
‡Drafted from Charleston (Pittsburgh Pirates' organization) by Kansas City Royals, December 3, 1973.
§Sold (via waivers) to California Angels, July 14, 1976.


# DENNIS SOLARI
Born November 12, 1954, at Stockton, Calif.
Height, 6.00. Weight, 177.
Throws and bats righthanded.

| Year Club | League | G. | IP. | W. | L. | Pct. | H. | R. | ER. | SO. | BB. | ERA. |
|---|---|---|---|---|---|---|---|---|---|---|---|---|
| 1972—Marion | Ap'lachian | 20 | 54 | 2 | 4 | .333 | 57 | 31 | 19 | 45 | 22 | 3.17 |
| 1973—Pompano Beach | Florida St. | 24 | 169 | 8 | 11 | .421 | 158 | 69 | 49 | 122 | 31 | 2.61 |
| 1973—Visalia | Calif. | 2 | 12 | 2 | 0 | 1.000 | 8 | 2 | 2 | 6 | 2 | 1.50 |
| 1974—Victoria | Texas | 21 | 135 | 7 | 5 | .583 | 150 | 70 | 56 | 50 | 35 | 3.73 |
| 1975—Jackson | Texas | 21 | 115 | 7 | 7 | .500 | 126 | 68 | 52 | 69 | 40 | 4.07 |
| 1976—Tidewater | Int'national | 42 | 86 | 6 | 4 | .600 | 84 | 33 | 26 | 45 | 22 | 2.72 |

Listed on New York Mets' 1977 spring roster.


# ELIAS SOSA (MARTINEZ)
First name pronounced E-lee-us.
Born June 10, 1950, at La Vega, Dominican Republic.
Height, 6.02. Weight, 186.
Throws and bats righthanded.

| Year Club | League | G. | IP. | W. | L. | Pct. | H. | R. | ER. | SO. | BB. | ERA. |
|---|---|---|---|---|---|---|---|---|---|---|---|---|
| 1968—Salt Lake City | Pioneer | 8 | 18 | 0 | 5 | .000 | 33 | 32 | 16 | 15 | 14 | 8.00 |
| 1969—Decatur | Midwest | 9 | 22 | 0 | 1 | .000 | 27 | 13 | 11 | 24 | 17 | 4.50 |
| 1969—Great Falls | Pioneer | 14 | 27 | 0 | 2 | .000 | 22 | 21 | 18 | 38 | 22 | 6.00 |
| 1970—Amarillo | Texas | 3 | 5 | 0 | 0 | .000 | 3 | 2 | 1 | 2 | 4 | 1.80 |
| 1970—Fresno | California | 21 | 102 | 6 | 8 | .429 | 119 | 66 | 58 | 95 | 39 | 5.12 |
| 1971—Fresno | California | 31 | 152 | 12 | 9 | .571 | 140 | 68 | 56 | 124 | 48 | 3.32 |
| 1972—Phoenix | P. Coast | 55 | 120 | 10 | 2 | .833 | 123 | 40 | 39 | 92 | 44 | 2.93 |
| 1972—San Francisco | National | 8 | 16 | 0 | 1 | .000 | 10 | 4 | 4 | 10 | 12 | 2.25 |
| 1973—San Francisco | National | 71 | 107 | 10 | 4 | .714 | 95 | 42 | 39 | 70 | 41 | 3.28 |
| 1974—San Francisco | National | 68 | 101 | 9 | 7 | .563 | 94 | 54 | 39 | 48 | 45 | 3.48 |
| 1975—St. Louis‡-Atlanta | National | 57 | 90 | 2 | 5 | .286 | 92 | 49 | 43 | 46 | 43 | 4.30 |
| 1976—Atl.§-L.A. | National | 45 | 69 | 6 | 8 | .429 | 71 | 42 | 34 | 52 | 25 | 4.43 |
| Major League Totals | | 249 | 383 | 27 | 25 | .519 | 362 | 191 | 159 | 226 | 166 | 3.74 |

†Traded with Catcher Ken Rudolph to St. Louis Cardinals for Catcher Marc Hill, October 14, 1974.
‡Traded with Pitcher Ray Sadecki to Atlanta Braves for Pitcher Ron Reed and a player to be named later, May 28, 1975; Braves sent Outfielder Wayne Nordhagen to Cardinals, June 2, 1975, to complete deal.
§Traded (via waivers) with Infielder Lee Lacy to Los Angeles Dodgers for Pitcher Mike Marshall, June 23, 1976.

## JOSE YNOCENCIO SOSA

Born December 28, 1952, at Santo Domingo, Dominican Republic.
Height, 5.11. Weight, 165.
Throws and bats righthanded.
First cousin of Felipe, Matty and Jesus Alou, former major league outfielders.
Led Midwest League in hit batsmen with 14 in 1974.

| Year Club | League | G. | IP. | W. | L. | Pct. | H. | R. | ER. | SO. | BB. | ERA. |
|---|---|---|---|---|---|---|---|---|---|---|---|---|
| 1970–Covington | Ap'lachian | 10 | 55 | 3 | 5 | .375 | 42 | 31 | 21 | 50 | 40 | 3.44 |
| 1971–Columbus† | Southern | 15 | 82 | 3 | 8 | .273 | 66 | 56 | 44 | 83 | 80 | 4.83 |
| 1972–Columbus | Southern | 9 | 50 | 2 | 7 | .222 | 55 | 46 | 39 | 38 | 51 | 7.02 |
| 1972–Cocoa | Florida St. | 7 | 35 | 1 | 4 | .200 | 33 | 27 | 23 | 34 | 34 | 5.91 |
| 1973–Cedar Rapids‡ | Midwest | 7 | 38 | 4 | 1 | .800 | 33 | 17 | 16 | 37 | 28 | 3.79 |
| 1974–Cedar Rapids | Midwest | 22 | 124 | 6 | 12 | .333 | 121 | 75 | 52 | 88 | 67 | 3.77 |
| 1975–Columbus | Southern | 29 | 49 | 6 | 2 | .750 | 33 | 8 | 6 | 46 | 26 | 1.10 |
| 1975–Houston | National | 25 | 47 | 1 | 3 | .250 | 51 | 21 | 21 | 31 | 23 | 4.02 |
| 1976–Memphis | Int'national | 41 | 80 | 4 | 10 | .286 | 86 | 54 | 50 | 56 | 51 | 5.63 |
| 1976–Houston | National | 9 | 12 | 0 | 0 | .000 | 16 | 9 | 9 | 5 | 6 | 6.75 |
| Major League Totals | | 34 | 59 | 1 | 3 | .250 | 67 | 30 | 30 | 36 | 29 | 4.58 |

†On disabled list, August 2 through remainder of season.
‡On disabled list, July 21 through remainder of season.

## MARIO MELVIN SOTO

Born July 12, 1956, Bani, Dominican Republic.
Height, 6.00. Weight, 174.
Throws and bats righthanded.

| Year Club | League | G. | IP. | W. | L. | Pct. | H. | R. | ER. | SO. | BB. | ERA. |
|---|---|---|---|---|---|---|---|---|---|---|---|---|
| 1974–Billings† | Pioneer | .. | .. | .. | .. | .... | .. | .. | .. | .. | .. | .... |
| 1975–Eugene | Northwest | 5 | 30 | 2 | 3 | .400 | 33 | 21 | 14 | 11 | 18 | 4.20 |
| 1976–Tampa | Florida St. | 26 | 197 | 13 | 7 | .650 | 142 | 54 | 41 | 124 | 80 | 1.87 |

†On disabled list, July 1 through September 17, 1974.
Listed on Cincinnati Reds' 1977 spring roster.

## JEFFREY BLAKE SOVERN
### (Jeff)

Born September 12, 1951, at Battle Creek, Mich.
Height, 6.01. Weight, 190.
Throws and bats righthanded.
Hobbies–Bowling, golf and basketball.
Attended Central Michigan University, Mt. Pleasant, Mich.;
received Bachelor of Science degree in Accounting.

| Year Club | League | Pos. | G. | AB. | R. | H. | 2B. | 3B. | HR. | RBI. | B.A. | PO. | A. | E. | F.A. |
|---|---|---|---|---|---|---|---|---|---|---|---|---|---|---|---|
| 1973–Appleton | Midw. | 3-S-C | 68 | 258 | 36 | 74 | 16 | 4 | 9 | 55 | .287 | 75 | 117 | 12 | .941 |
| 1974–Iowa | A.A. | C | 1 | 4 | 1 | 2 | 0 | 0 | 1 | 1 | .500 | 10 | 1 | 1 | .917 |
| 1974–Knoxville | South. | C-O-1 | 108 | 346 | 46 | 71 | 18 | 0 | 8 | 34 | .205 | 556 | 62 | 15 | .976 |
| 1975–Denver† | A.A. | *C-1-3 | 106 | 334 | 52 | 98 | 13 | 0 | 17 | 65 | .293 | 473 | *72 | 11 | .980 |
| 1976–Indianapolis | A.A. | C-1-O-3 | 103 | 328 | 30 | 68 | 8 | 0 | 6 | 33 | .207 | 524 | 55 | 12 | .980 |

†Traded with Pitcher Rich Hinton by Chicago White Sox to Cincinnati Reds for Pitcher Clay Carroll, December 12, 1975.
Listed on Cincinnati Reds' 1977 spring roster.

## HORACE ARTHUR SPEED, III

Born October 4, 1951, at Los Angeles, Calif.
Height, 6.01. Weight, 180.
Throws and bats righthanded.
Hobbies–Billiards and table tennis.
Led Pioneer League outfielders in double plays with 3 in 1969.

| Year Club | League | Pos. | G. | AB. | R. | H. | 2B. | 3B. | HR. | RBI. | B.A. | PO. | A. | E. | F.A. |
|---|---|---|---|---|---|---|---|---|---|---|---|---|---|---|---|
| 1969–Great Falls | Pion. | OF-1B | 48 | 141 | 28 | 28 | 9 | 0 | 4 | 24 | .199 | 53 | 5 | 5 | .921 |
| 1970–Decatur | Midw. | OF | 109 | 363 | 46 | 96 | 14 | 5 | 11 | 46 | .264 | 233 | 9 | 13 | .949 |
| 1971–Fresno | Calif. | OF | 118 | 385 | 65 | 104 | 20 | 4 | 18 | 74 | .270 | 173 | 7 | 11 | .942 |
| 1972–Amarillo | Tex. | OF | 103 | 341 | 38 | 86 | 10 | 4 | 10 | 36 | .252 | 135 | 9 | 7 | .954 |
| 1973–Amarillo | Tex. | OF | 120 | 406 | 77 | 124 | 20 | 5 | 25 | 88 | .305 | 247 | 13 | 9 | .967 |
| 1974–Phoenix | P.C. | OF | 141 | 505 | 67 | 138 | 28 | 10 | 14 | 83 | .273 | 282 | 12 | 7 | .977 |
| 1975–Phoenix | P.C. | OF | 92 | 305 | 54 | 83 | 16 | 5 | 12 | 38 | .272 | 143 | 10 | 5 | .968 |
| 1975–San Francisco | Nat. | OF | 17 | 15 | 2 | 2 | 1 | 0 | 0 | 1 | .133 | 9 | 0 | 1 | .900 |
| 1976–Phoenix | P.C. | OF | 134 | 448 | 75 | 109 | 19 | 5 | 18 | 73 | .243 | 268 | 12 | 12 | .959 |
| Major League Totals | | | 17 | 15 | 2 | 2 | 1 | 0 | 0 | 1 | .133 | 9 | 0 | 1 | .900 |

## DID YOU KNOW —

That John (Red) Murray of the New York Giants was the home run leader of the National League in 1909? He hit six round-trippers that season.

# CHRIS EDWARD SPEIER
Name pronounced Spire.

Born June 28, 1950, at Alameda, Calif.
Height, 6.01. Weight, 175.
Throws and bats righthanded.
Attended University of Santa Barbara, Santa Barbara, Calif.
Named shortstop on THE SPORTING NEWS National League All-Star Team, 1972.

| Year Club | League | Pos. | G. | AB. | R. | H. | 2B. | 3B. | HR. | RBI. | B.A. | PO. | A. | E. | F.A. |
|---|---|---|---|---|---|---|---|---|---|---|---|---|---|---|---|
| 1970–Amarillo............Tex. | | •SS-3-O | 129 | 460 | 44 | 130 | 20 | 5 | 6 | 66 | .283 | •224 | •327 | 38 | .935 |
| 1971–San Francisco ..Nat. | | SS | 157 | 601 | 74 | 141 | 17 | 6 | 8 | 46 | .235 | 239 | 517 | •33 | .953 |
| 1972–San Francisco ..Nat. | | SS | 150 | 562 | 74 | 151 | 25 | 2 | 15 | 71 | .269 | 243 | •517 | 20 | .974 |
| 1973–San Francisco ..Nat. | | •SS-2B | 153 | 542 | 58 | 135 | 17 | 4 | 11 | 71 | .249 | 255 | 471 | •33 | .957 |
| 1974–San Francisco ..Nat. | | SS-2B | 141 | 501 | 55 | 125 | 19 | 5 | 9 | 53 | .250 | 215 | 453 | 21 | .970 |
| 1975–San Francisco ..Nat. | | SS-3B | 141 | 487 | 60 | 132 | 30 | 5 | 10 | 69 | .271 | 247 | 421 | 12 | •.982 |
| 1976–San Francisco ..Nat. | | S-2-3-1 | 145 | 495 | 51 | 112 | 18 | 4 | 3 | 40 | .226 | 241 | 464 | 19 | .974 |
| Major League Totals ..................... | | | 887 | 3188 | 372 | 796 | 126 | 26 | 56 | 350 | .250 | 1440 | 2843 | 138 | .968 |

CHAMPIONSHIP SERIES RECORD

| Year Club | League | Pos. | G. | AB. | R. | H. | 2B. | 3B. | HR. | RBI. | B.A. | PO. | A. | E. | F.A. |
|---|---|---|---|---|---|---|---|---|---|---|---|---|---|---|---|
| 1971–San Francisco ..Nat. | | SS | 4 | 14 | 4 | 5 | 1 | 0 | 1 | 1 | .357 | 3 | 14 | 1 | .944 |

ALL-STAR GAME RECORD

| Year League | | Pos. | AB. | R. | H. | 2B. | 3B. | HR. | RBI. | B.A. | PO. | A. | E. | F.A. |
|---|---|---|---|---|---|---|---|---|---|---|---|---|---|---|
| 1972–National ............................ | | SS | 2 | 0 | 0 | 0 | 0 | 0 | 0 | .000 | 1 | 5 | 0 | 1.000 |
| 1973–National ............................ | | SS | 2 | 0 | 0 | 0 | 0 | 0 | 0 | .000 | 1 | 1 | 0 | 1.000 |
| All-Star Game Totals ..................... | | | 4 | 0 | 0 | 0 | 0 | 0 | 0 | .000 | 2 | 6 | 0 | 1.000 |

Member of National League All-Star Team in 1974 game; did not play.


# GERALD WAYNE SPENCER
(Jerry)

Born October 30, 1951, at San Antonio, Tex.
Height, 6.02. Weight, 195.
Throws and bats righthanded.
Hobbies–Fishing and hunting.
Attended Southwest Texas State University, San Marcos, Tex.
Led Carolina League in hit batsmen with 12 in 1972.

| Year Club | League | G. | IP. | W. | L. | Pct. | H. | R. | ER. | SO. | BB. | ERA. |
|---|---|---|---|---|---|---|---|---|---|---|---|---|
| 1970–Jamestown ..........................NYP | | 12 | 81 | 5 | 6 | .455 | 66 | 34 | 28 | 78 | 32 | 3.11 |
| 1971–Greenville...........................W. Carol. | | 19 | 48 | 4 | 2 | .667 | 46 | 24 | 19 | 49 | 20 | 3.56 |
| 1972–Winston-Salem ...................Carolina | | 26 | 145 | 6 | 12 | .333 | 157 | 74 | 60 | 107 | 40 | 3.72 |
| 1973–Winston-Salem† ...................Carolina | | 22 | 105 | 6 | 6 | .500 | 107 | 47 | 42 | 61 | 33 | 3.60 |
| 1974–Winston-Salem ...................Carolina | | 29 | 214 | 11 | 7 | .611 | 195 | 90 | 70 | 115 | 70 | 2.94 |
| 1975–Bristol ...............................Eastern | | 14 | 99 | 8 | 6 | .571 | 86 | 33 | 26 | 42 | 28 | 2.36 |
| 1975–Pawtucket...........................Int'national | | 8 | 39 | 1 | 1 | .500 | 39 | 18 | 15 | 19 | 15 | 3.46 |
| 1976–Rhode Island......................Int'national | | 7 | 35 | 1 | 2 | .333 | 34 | 21 | 20 | 17 | 20 | 5.14 |

†On disabled list, June 25 to July 20, 1973.
Listed on Boston Red Sox' 1977 spring roster.


# HUBERT THOMAS SPENCER
(Tommy)

Born February 28, 1951, at Gallipolis, O.
Height, 6.00. Weight, 170.
Throws and bats righthanded.
Hobbies–Hockey, fishing and skiing.
Attended Rio Grande College, Rio Grande, O.
Led American Association batters in sacrifice hits with 10 in 1976.
Tied for Eastern League lead in double plays by outfielders with 6 in 1972.

| Year Club | League | Pos. | G. | AB. | R. | H. | 2B. | 3B. | HR. | RBI. | B.A. | PO. | A. | E. | F.A. |
|---|---|---|---|---|---|---|---|---|---|---|---|---|---|---|---|
| 1970–Tampa ..............Fla. St. | | OF | 130 | 471 | 52 | 134 | 13 | 5 | 3 | 50 | .285 | 294 | 11 | 8 | .974 |
| 1971–Three Rivers† ..East. | | OF | 79 | 289 | 41 | 75 | 13 | 0 | 9 | 26 | .260 | 146 | 6 | 7 | .956 |
| 1972–Indianapolis ......A.A. | | OF | 51 | 158 | 11 | 36 | 6 | 1 | 1 | 12 | .228 | 77 | 6 | 1 | .988 |
| 1972–Three Rivers ....East. | | OF | 83 | 315 | 53 | 88 | 13 | 5 | 5 | 28 | .279 | 185 | 7 | 2 | .990 |
| 1973–Indianapolis ......A.A. | | OF | 7 | 10 | 1 | 2 | 0 | 0 | 0 | 1 | .200 | 4 | 1 | 0 | 1.000 |
| 1973–Three Rivers ....East. | | •OF-2B | 124 | 470 | 69 | 128 | 23 | 3 | 4 | 50 | .272 | •282 | 12 | 9 | .970 |
| 1974–Indianapolis ......A.A. | | OF | 125 | 437 | 66 | 127 | 20 | 8 | 14 | 54 | .291 | •272 | 6 | 5 | •.982 |
| 1975–Indianapolis ......A.A. | | OF | 129 | 434 | 68 | 116 | 19 | 7 | 7 | 41 | .267 | 265 | 16 | 2 | •.993 |
| 1976–Indianapolis‡ ....A.A. | | OF | 126 | 419 | 47 | 100 | 17 | 4 | 7 | 43 | .239 | 268 | 11 | 6 | .979 |

†On disabled list, August 2 through remainder of season.
‡Traded from Cincinnati Reds' organization to Chicago White Sox' organization for Infielder Hugh Young, November 6, 1976.

## JAMES LLOYD SPENCER
### (Jim)

Born July 30, 1947, at Hanover, Pa.
Height, 6.02. Weight, 195.
Throws and bats lefthanded.
Hobbies—Golf and hunting.
Grandson of L. Benjamin Spencer, outfielder in minor leagues
from 1911-29; played with Washington in 1913.

Led American League first basemen in double plays with 131 in 1970.
Led Texas League in total bases with 267, in sacrifice flies with 10 and led first basemen in double plays with 109 in 1968.
Named first baseman on THE SPORTING NEWS American League All-Star fielding team, 1970.
Received reported $20,000 bonus to sign with California Angels, 1965.

| Year | Club | League | Pos. | G. | AB. | R. | H. | 2B. | 3B. | HR. | RBI. | B.A. | PO. | A. | E. | F.A. |
|------|------|--------|------|----|-----|----|----|-----|-----|-----|------|------|-----|----|----|------|
| 1965–Quad Cities | ......Midw. | | 1B | 76 | 269 | 25 | 60 | 10 | 4 | 2 | 25 | .223 | 562 | 16 | 10 | .983 |
| 1966–El Paso | ............Texas | | 1B | 133 | 488 | 72 | 129 | 22 | 7 | 16 | 53 | .264•1174 | | 62 | 12 | .990 |
| 1967–El Paso | ............Texas | | •1-O | 134 | 480 | 75 | 134 | 27 | 5 | 19 | 73 | .279 | 1042 | 81 | 7 | •.994 |
| 1968–El Paso | ............Texas | | •1B-O | 135 | 493 | •85 | 144 | 29 | 5 | •28 | •96 | .292•1170 | | •80 | 11 | •.991 |
| 1968–California | .........Amer. | | 1B | 19 | 68 | 2 | 13 | 1 | 0 | 0 | 5 | .191 | 152 | 18 | 1 | .994 |
| 1969–Hawaii | .............P.C. | | 1B | 47 | 172 | 30 | 45 | 8 | 0 | 6 | 22 | .262 | 433 | 39 | 4 | .992 |
| 1969–California | .........Amer. | | 1B | 113 | 386 | 39 | 98 | 14 | 3 | 10 | 31 | .254 | 926 | 66 | 9 | .991 |
| 1970–California | .........Amer. | | 1B | 146 | 511 | 61 | 140 | 20 | 4 | 12 | 68 | .274•1212 | | 85 | 7 | •.995 |
| 1971–California | .........Amer. | | 1B | 148 | 510 | 50 | 121 | 21 | 2 | 18 | 59 | .237•1296 | | •93 | 5 | •.996 |
| 1972–California | .........Amer. | | 1B-OF | 82 | 212 | 13 | 47 | 5 | 0 | 1 | 14 | .222 | 289 | 23 | 3 | .990 |
| 1973–Calif.†-Texas | ....Amer. | | 1B | 131 | 439 | 45 | 115 | 16 | 5 | 6 | 54 | .262 | 994 | 74 | 1 | •.999 |
| 1974–Texas | ................Amer. | | 1B | 118 | 352 | 36 | 98 | 11 | 4 | 7 | 44 | .278 | 389 | 27 | 1 | .998 |
| 1975–Texas‡ | ............Amer. | | 1B | 132 | 403 | 50 | 107 | 18 | 1 | 11 | 47 | .266 | 844 | 70 | 5 | .995 |
| 1976–Chicago | ............Amer. | | 1B-OF | 150 | 518 | 53 | 131 | 13 | 2 | 14 | 70 | .253 | 1206 | •112 | 2 | •.998 |
| Major League Totals | ..................... | | | 1039 | 3399 | 349 | 870 | 119 | 21 | 79 | 392 | .256 | 7308 | 568 | 34 | .996 |

†Traded with Pitcher Lloyd Allen to Texas Rangers for First Baseman Mike Epstein, Pitcher Rich Hand and Catcher Rick Stelmaszek (latter assigned to Salt Lake City), May 20, 1973.

‡Traded with an estimated $100,000 to California Angels for Pitcher Bill Singer, December 10, 1975. Traded with Outfielder Morris Nettles by California Angels to Chicago White Sox for Third Baseman Bill Melton and Pitcher Steve Dunning, December 11, 1975.

### ALL-STAR GAME RECORD

| Year | League | Pos. | AB. | R. | H. | 2B. | 3B. | HR. | RBI. | B.A. | PO. | A. | E. | F.A. |
|------|--------|------|-----|----|----|-----|-----|-----|------|------|-----|----|----|------|
| 1973–American | ......................... | PH | 1 | 0 | 0 | 0 | 0 | 0 | 0 | .000 | 0 | 0 | 0 | .000 |

## ROBERT WALTER SPERRING
### (Rob)

Born October 10, 1949, at San Francisco, Calif.
Height, 6.01. Weight, 185.
Throws and bats righthanded.
Hobbies—Hunting and fishing.
Attended University of the Pacific, Stockton, Calif.; received Bachelor
of Arts degree in Physical Education.

Led Texas League second basemen in double plays with 78 in 1973.

| Year | Club | League | Pos. | G. | AB. | R. | H. | 2B. | 3B. | HR. | RBI. | B.A. | PO. | A. | E. | F.A. |
|------|------|--------|------|----|-----|----|----|-----|-----|-----|------|------|-----|----|----|------|
| 1971–Caldwell | ............Pion. | | O-S-1 | 31 | 123 | 21 | 31 | 4 | 0 | 5 | 20 | .252 | 43 | 16 | 6 | .908 |
| 1971–Quincy | ..............Midw. | | OF-SS | 35 | 131 | 18 | 33 | 11 | 2 | 1 | 15 | .252 | 48 | 22 | 18 | .795 |
| 1972–Midland | ............Texas | | 3-2-S | 128 | 469 | 56 | 119 | 21 | 3 | 9 | 50 | .254 | 124 | 247 | 24 | .939 |
| 1973–Wichita | ............A. A. | | 2B-3B | 10 | 34 | 7 | 6 | 0 | 0 | 0 | 3 | .176 | 18 | 22 | 3 | .930 |
| 1973–Midland | ............Tex. | | •2B-3B | 116 | 451 | 72 | 133 | 23 | 3 | 14 | 56 | .295 | •309 | •378 | •27 | .962 |
| 1974–Wichita | ............A. A. | | 2-S-3 | 107 | 367 | 56 | 93 | 16 | 4 | 5 | 36 | .253 | 203 | 315 | 15 | .972 |
| 1974–Chicago | ............Nat. | | 2B-SS | 42 | 107 | 9 | 22 | 3 | 0 | 1 | 5 | .206 | 64 | 101 | 10 | .943 |
| 1975–Chicago | ............Nat. | | 3-2-S-O | 65 | 144 | 25 | 30 | 4 | 1 | 1 | 9 | .208 | 70 | 115 | 12 | .939 |
| 1976–Wichita | ............A. A. | | S-2-1-O-3 | 94 | 298 | 34 | 71 | 13 | 3 | 13 | 38 | .238 | 173 | 217 | 17 | .958 |
| 1976–Chicago† | .........Nat. | | 3-S-2-O | 43 | 93 | 8 | 24 | 3 | 0 | 0 | 7 | .258 | 36 | 40 | 1 | .987 |
| Major League Totals | ..................... | | | 150 | 344 | 42 | 76 | 10 | 1 | 2 | 21 | .221 | 170 | 256 | 23 | .949 |

†Traded with Third Baseman Bill Madlock to San Francisco Giants for Outfielder Bobby Murcer, Infielder Steve Ontiveros and Pitcher Andrew Muhlstock, February 11, 1976; traded with Outfielder Willie Crawford to Houston Astros for Second Baseman Rob Andrews and a player to be named later, March 26, 1977.

## LESLIE CHARLES SPIKES
### (Charlie)

Born January 23, 1951, at Bogalusa, La.
Height, 6.03. Weight, 220.
Throws and bats righthanded.
Hobby—Basketball.
Brother of William Spikes, former outfielder in Pittsburgh Pirates' organization.
Led Carolina League hitters in strikeouts with 117 in 1971 and Florida State League with 157 in 1970.

| Year Club League | Pos. | G. | AB. | R. | H. | 2B. | 3B. | HR. | RBI. | B.A. | PO. | A. | E. | F.A. |
|---|---|---|---|---|---|---|---|---|---|---|---|---|---|---|
| 1969–Johnson City ....Appal. | *3-OF | 47 | 163 | 29 | 33 | 2 | 0 | 8 | 21 | .202 | 33 | 65 | *29 | .772 |
| 1970–Ft. Lauderdale ..Fla. St. | 3-O | 127 | 422 | 71 | 100 | 12 | 2 | 19 | 62 | .237 | 132 | 135 | 40 | .870 |
| 1971–Kinston ...........Carol. | OF | 127 | 423 | 77 | 114 | 16 | 1 | *22 | 79 | .270 | 151 | 14 | *15 | .917 |
| 1972–West Haven ......East. | OF | 126 | 427 | 83 | 132 | 27 | 5 | 26 | 83 | .309 | 191 | 12 | 14 | .935 |
| 1972–New York† ........Amer. | OF | 14 | 34 | 2 | 5 | 1 | 0 | 0 | 3 | .147 | 14 | 1 | 0 | 1.000 |
| 1973–Cleveland .........Amer. | OF | 140 | 506 | 68 | 120 | 12 | 3 | 23 | 73 | .237 | 202 | 13 | 8 | .964 |
| 1974–Cleveland .........Amer. | OF | 155 | 568 | 63 | 154 | 23 | 1 | 22 | 80 | .271 | 284 | 16 | 10 | .968 |
| 1975–Cleveland .........Amer. | OF | 111 | 345 | 41 | 79 | 13 | 3 | 11 | 33 | .229 | 176 | 13 | 5 | .974 |
| 1976–Cleveland .........Amer. | OF-DH | 101 | 334 | 34 | 79 | 11 | 5 | 3 | 31 | .237 | 185 | 7 | 3 | .985 |
| Major League Totals ..................... | | 521 | 1787 | 208 | 437 | 60 | 12 | 59 | 220 | .244 | 861 | 50 | 26 | .972 |

†Traded with Outfielder Rosendo Torres, Catcher-First Baseman John Ellis, and Infielder Jerry Kenney to Cleveland Indians for Catcher Jerry Moses and Third Baseman Graig Nettles, November 27, 1972.

## DANIEL RAY SPILLNER
### (Dan)

Born November 27, 1951, at Casper, Wyo.
Height, 6.01. Weight, 195.
Throws and bats righthanded.
Hobby–Hunting.
Attended Green River Community College, Auburn, Wash.

| Year Club League | G. | IP. | W. | L. | Pct. | H. | R. | ER. | SO. | BB. | ERA. |
|---|---|---|---|---|---|---|---|---|---|---|---|
| 1970–Tri-City...............................Northwest | 7 | 29 | 1 | 1 | .500 | 37 | 21 | 18 | 21 | 15 | 5.59 |
| 1971–Lodi ..................................California | 25 | 148 | 10 | 5 | .667 | 177 | 102 | 87 | 96 | 55 | 5.29 |
| 1972–Alexandria .......................Texas | 27 | 180 | 16 | 7 | .696 | 156 | 75 | 68 | 126 | *85 | 3.41 |
| 1973–Hawaii .............................P. Coast | 32 | 188 | 10 | 11 | .476 | 188 | 105 | 86 | 124 | 85 | 4.12 |
| 1974–Hawaii .............................P. Coast | 7 | 54 | 4 | 2 | .667 | 49 | 24 | 22 | 47 | 18 | 3.67 |
| 1974–San Diego .........................National | 30 | 148 | 9 | 11 | .450 | 153 | 78 | 66 | 95 | 70 | 4.01 |
| 1975–San Diego ..........................National | 37 | 167 | 5 | 13 | .278 | 194 | 93 | 79 | 104 | 63 | 4.26 |
| 1976–San Diego ..........................National | 32 | 107 | 2 | 11 | .154 | 120 | 70 | 60 | 57 | 55 | 5.05 |
| Major League Totals ............................... | 99 | 422 | 16 | 35 | .314 | 467 | 241 | 205 | 256 | 188 | 4.37 |

## PAUL WILLIAM SPLITTORFF, JR.

Name pronounced split-orf.

Born October 8, 1946, at Evansville, Ind.
Height, 6.03. Weight, 205.
Throws and bats lefthanded.
Attended Morningside College, Sioux City, Ia.; received Bachelor of
Science degree in Business Administration.

Led New York-Pennsylvania League in wild pitches with 17 and complete games with 11 in 1968.
Tied for American Association lead in complete games by a pitcher with 11 in 1969.

| Year Club League | G. | IP. | W. | L. | Pct. | H. | R. | ER. | SO. | BB. | ERA. |
|---|---|---|---|---|---|---|---|---|---|---|---|
| 1968–Corning.................................NYP | 16 | ●120 | 8 | 5 | .615 | *127 | 56 | 46 | ●136 | 47 | 3.45 |
| 1969–Omaha ................................Am. Assoc. | 28 | 174 | 12 | 10 | .545 | 201 | 101 | 88 | 101 | 63 | 4.55 |
| 1970–Omaha ................................Am. Assoc. | 28 | 162 | 8 | 12 | .400 | 192 | 87 | 69 | 91 | 55 | 3.83 |
| 1970–Kansas City...........................American | 2 | 9 | 0 | 1 | .000 | 16 | 9 | 7 | 10 | 5 | 7.00 |
| 1971–Omaha ................................Am. Assoc. | 8 | 61 | 5 | 2 | .714 | 51 | 16 | 10 | 51 | 10 | 1.48 |
| 1971–Kansas City...........................American | 22 | 144 | 8 | 9 | .471 | 129 | 49 | 43 | 80 | 35 | 2.69 |
| 1972–Kansas City...........................American | 35 | 216 | 12 | 12 | .500 | 189 | 81 | 75 | 140 | 67 | 3.13 |
| 1973–Kansas City...........................American | 38 | 262 | 20 | 11 | .645 | 279 | 135 | 116 | 110 | 78 | 3.98 |
| 1974–Kansas City...........................American | 36 | 226 | 13 | 19 | .406 | 252 | 122 | 103 | 90 | 75 | 4.10 |
| 1975–Kansas City...........................American | 35 | 159 | 9 | 10 | .474 | 156 | 75 | 56 | 76 | 56 | 3.17 |
| 1976–Kansas City†.........................American | 26 | 159 | 11 | 8 | .579 | 169 | 79 | 70 | 59 | 59 | 3.96 |
| Major League Totals ............................... | 194 | 1175 | 73 | 70 | .510 | 1190 | 550 | 470 | 565 | 375 | 3.60 |

†On disabled list, July 28 through September 4, 1976.

### CHAMPIONSHIP SERIES RECORD

| Year Club League | G. | IP. | W. | L. | Pct. | H. | R. | ER. | SO. | BB. | ERA. |
|---|---|---|---|---|---|---|---|---|---|---|---|
| 1976–Kansas City......................American | 2 | 9⅓ | 1 | 0 | 1.000 | 7 | 2 | 2 | 2 | 5 | 1.93 |

## STEPHEN ROBERT STAGGS
### (Steve)

Born May 6, 1951, Anchorage, Alaska.
Height, 5.09. Weight, 150.
Throws and bats righthanded.
Hobbies–Handball and basketball.
Attended Cerritos Junior College, Norwalk, Calif.

Led Pioneer League in bases on balls with 86 in 1971.
Led California League in bases on balls with 92 in 1972.

| Year Club League | Pos. | G. | AB. | R. | H. | 2B. | 3B. | HR. | RBI. | B.A. | PO. | A. | E. | F.A. |
|---|---|---|---|---|---|---|---|---|---|---|---|---|---|---|
| 1971–Billings ............Pion. | 2B-1B | 67 | 198 | *72 | 59 | 10 | 1 | 9 | 46 | .298 | *139 | 160 | *30 | .909 |
| 1972–San Jose...........Calif. | 2B | 121 | 385 | 71 | 100 | 10 | 5 | 10 | 50 | .260 | 234 | 357 | *40 | .937 |
| 1973–Key West .........Fla. St. | 2B | 74 | 248 | 48 | 69 | 16 | 2 | 2 | 15 | .278 | 151 | 187 | 20 | .944 |

| 1973–Waterloo .........Midw. | 3B-2B | 50 | 177 | 39 | 52 | 11 | 4 | 1 | 21 | .294 | 50 | 111 | 22 | .880 |
|---|---|---|---|---|---|---|---|---|---|---|---|---|---|---|
| 1974–Jacksonville ......South. | 2B | 127 | 466 | 70 | 118 | 19 | 4 | 13 | 83 | .253 | 296 | 351 | •31 | .954 |
| 1975–Omaha .............A. A. | 2B | 122 | 428 | 64 | 108 | 17 | 4 | 7 | 39 | .252 | 254 | 348 | 23 | .963 |
| 1976–Omaha† ...........A. A. | 2B | •136 | 492 | 92 | 139 | 20 | 14 | 5 | 50 | .283 | 273 | 389 | •30 | .957 |

†Selected by Toronto Blue Jays in American League expansion draft, November 5, 1976.

## ROY JOSEPH STAIGER, JR.

Name Pronounced STAY-gur.

Born January 6, 1950, at Tulsa, Okla.
Height, 5.11. Weight, 190.
Throws and bats righthanded.
Hobbies–Hunting and fishing.
Attended Bacone Junior College, Bacone, Okla.

Led International League third basemen in double plays with 34 in 1973 and 31 in 1974.
Led California League third basemen in double plays with 24 in 1971.

| Year Club League | Pos. | G. | AB. | R. | H. | 2B. | 3B. | HR. | RBI. | B.A. | PO. | A. | E. | F.A. |
|---|---|---|---|---|---|---|---|---|---|---|---|---|---|---|
| 1970–Visalia .............Calif. | S-2-3 | 76 | 297 | 37 | 71 | 13 | 0 | 7 | 34 | .239 | 120 | 194 | 12 | .963 |
| 1971–Visalia .............Calif. | •3-S-2 | 139 | 524 | 91 | 148 | 18 | 5 | 19 | 83 | .282 | 150 | •307 | 22 | •.954 |
| 1972–Memphis† .........Texas | 3B | 81 | 277 | 24 | 78 | 10 | 4 | 3 | 38 | .282 | 57 | 130 | 12 | .940 |
| 1973–Tidewater .........Int. | 3B | 136 | 434 | 49 | 108 | 13 | 1 | 8 | 55 | .249 | •98 | •252 | •20 | .946 |
| 1974–Tidewater .........Int. | 3B | 136 | 452 | 34 | 123 | 21 | 1 | 3 | 38 | .272 | •120 | •279 | 16 | .961 |
| 1975–Tidewater .........Int. | •3-2-S | 136 | 468 | 51 | 132 | 29 | 4 | 9 | •81 | .282 | •144 | •323 | 6 | •.987 |
| 1975–New York .........Nat. | 3B | 13 | 19 | 2 | 3 | 1 | 0 | 0 | 0 | .158 | 5 | 11 | 0 | 1.000 |
| 1976–New York .........Nat. | 3B-SS | 95 | 304 | 23 | 67 | 8 | 1 | 2 | 26 | .220 | 55 | 209 | 9 | .967 |
| Major League Totals ..................... | | 108 | 323 | 25 | 70 | 9 | 1 | 2 | 26 | .217 | 60 | 220 | 9 | .969 |

†On disabled list, July 25 to August 22, 1972.

## KEVIN BRUCE STANFIELD

Born December 19, 1955, at Huron, S. D.
Height, 6.00. Weight, 190.
Throws and bats lefthanded.
Hobbies–Hunting and fishing.
Attended San Bernardino Valley Junior College, San Bernardino, Calif.

| Year Club League | G. | IP. | W. | L. | Pct. | H. | R. | ER. | SO. | BB. | ERA. |
|---|---|---|---|---|---|---|---|---|---|---|---|
| 1976–Elizabethton .......................Ap'lachian | 9 | 21 | 2 | 3 | .400 | 23 | 7 | 6 | 19 | 8 | 2.57 |
| 1976–Wisconsin Rapids ................Midwest | 17 | 23 | 3 | 1 | .750 | 25 | 13 | 5 | 16 | 11 | 1.96 |

Invited to Minnesota Twins' 1977 spring camp.

## DONALD JOSEPH STANHOUSE
## (Don)

Born February 12, 1951, at Du Quoin, Ill.
Height, 6.03. Weight, 187.
Throws and bats righthanded.
Hobby–Golf.
Attended Mesa Community College, Mesa, Ariz.

Tied for Northwest League lead in shutouts with 2 in 1969.

| Year Club League | G. | IP. | W. | L. | Pct. | H. | R. | ER. | SO. | BB. | ERA. |
|---|---|---|---|---|---|---|---|---|---|---|---|
| 1969–Tri-City ...................Northwest | 12 | 61 | 5 | 1 | .833 | 50 | 25 | 21 | •88 | 31 | 3.10 |
| 1970–Birmingham .......................Southern | 16 | 84 | 7 | 5 | .583 | 57 | 27 | 21 | 80 | 42 | 2.25 |
| 1971–Iowa† ................................Am. Assoc. | 22 | 154 | 7 | 4 | .636 | 143 | 71 | 64 | 104 | 85 | 3.73 |
| 1972–Denver‡ ............................Am. Assoc. | 5 | 35 | 2 | 2 | .500 | 28 | 17 | 15 | 32 | 27 | 3.86 |
| 1972–Texas ...............................American | 24 | 105 | 2 | 9 | .182 | 83 | 48 | 44 | 78 | 73 | 3.77 |
| 1973–Spokane ............................P. Coast | 12 | 66 | 3 | 5 | .375 | 80 | 56 | 54 | 55 | 42 | 7.36 |
| 1973–Texas ...............................American | 21 | 70 | 1 | 7 | .125 | 70 | 41 | 37 | 42 | 44 | 4.76 |
| 1974–Spokane ............................P. Coast | 12 | 48 | 4 | 5 | .444 | 38 | 16 | 13 | 40 | 27 | 2.44 |
| 1974–Texas§ ..............................American | 18 | 31 | 1 | 1 | .500 | 38 | 20 | 17 | 26 | 17 | 4.94 |
| 1975–Memphis x ........................Int'national | 13 | 80 | 6 | 5 | .545 | 67 | 27 | 17 | 47 | 30 | 1.91 |
| 1975–Montreal ...........................National | 4 | 13 | 0 | 0 | .000 | 19 | 12 | 12 | 5 | 11 | 8.31 |
| 1976–Montreal ...........................National | 34 | 184 | 9 | 12 | .429 | 182 | 84 | 77 | 79 | 92 | 3.77 |
| American League Totals.......................... | 63 | 206 | 4 | 17 | .190 | 191 | 109 | 98 | 146 | 134 | 4.28 |
| National League Totals............................. | 38 | 197 | 9 | 12 | .429 | 201 | 96 | 89 | 84 | 103 | 4.07 |
| Major League Totals ............................. | 101 | 403 | 13 | 29 | .310 | 392 | 205 | 187 | 230 | 237 | 4.18 |

†Traded by Oakland A's with Pitcher Jim Panther to Texas Rangers for Pitcher Denny McLain, March 4, 1972.
‡On disabled list, Arpil 30 through May 31, 1972.
§Traded with Infielder Pete Mackanin to Montreal Expos for Outfielder Willie Davis, December 5, 1974.
xOn disabled list, July 24 through August 3, 1975.

### RECORD AS INFIELDER

| Year Club League | Pos. | G. | AB. | R. | H. | 2B. | 3B. | HR. | RBI. | B.A. | PO. | A. | E. | F.A. |
|---|---|---|---|---|---|---|---|---|---|---|---|---|---|---|
| 1969–Tri-City ...........Northw. | 3-P-S | 53 | 165 | 19 | 44 | 10 | 0 | 2 | 36 | .269 | 47 | 70 | 17 | .873 |

## STEPHEN CHARLES STANILAND
Name pronounced STAN-uh-lun.
### (Steve)
Born May 14, 1955, at Peoria, Ill.
Height, 6.05. Weight, 215.
Throws and bats righthanded.
Hobbies—Fishing and basketball.
Attended University of Santa Clara, Santa Clara, Calif.
Son of Charles Staniland, former catcher in St. Louis Cardinals' organization.

| Year    Club | League | G. | IP. | W. | L. | Pct. | H. | R. | ER. | SO. | BB. | ERA. |
|---|---|---|---|---|---|---|---|---|---|---|---|---|
| 1973—Lewiston | Northwest | 16 | 79 | 4 | ●8 | .333 | 85 | 60 | 47 | 67 | 58 | 5.35 |
| 1974—Burlington | Midwest | 19 | 119 | 9 | 4 | .692 | 105 | 50 | 43 | 110 | 55 | 3.25 |
| 1975—Modesto‡ | California | 6 | 41 | 2 | 2 | .500 | 29 | 25 | 15 | 35 | 25 | 3.29 |
| 1975—St. Petersburg | Florida St. | 2 | 15 | 1 | 1 | .500 | 12 | 4 | 2 | 15 | 2 | 1.20 |
| 1975—Arkansas | Texas | 13 | 77 | 6 | 4 | .600 | 68 | 39 | 28 | 60 | 40 | 3.27 |
| 1975—Tulsa | Am. Assoc. | 4 | 19 | 0 | 2 | .000 | 19 | 19 | 18 | 11 | 20 | 8.52 |
| 1976—Arkansas | Texas | 27 | 147 | 6 | 11 | .353 | 151 | 88 | 69 | 121 | 62 | 4.22 |

†On disabled list, May 22 to June 13, 1974.
‡Traded with a player to be named later by Oakland Athletics to St. Louis Cardinals for Infielder Teddy Martinez, May 18, 1975; Athletics assigned Pitcher Mike Barlow to Cardinals, May 23, 1975, to complete deal.
Listed on St. Louis Cardinals' 1977 spring roster.

## FREDERICK BLAIR STANLEY
### (Fred)
Born August 13, 1947, at Farnhamville, Ia.
Height, 5.11. Weight, 170.
Throws and bats righthanded.
Hobbies—Hunting and fishing.
Attended Rio Hondo Junior College, Whittier, Calif.

| Year    Club | League | Pos. | G. | AB. | R. | H. | 2B. | 3B. | HR. | RBI. | B.A. | PO. | A. | E. | F.A. |
|---|---|---|---|---|---|---|---|---|---|---|---|---|---|---|---|
| 1966—Salisbury | W. Car. | SS | 52 | 174 | 24 | 42 | 3 | 1 | 0 | 8 | .241 | 92 | 131 | 24 | .903 |
| 1966—Bism.-Mandan | North | SS | 12 | 46 | 5 | 12 | 0 | 0 | 0 | 0 | .261 | 12 | 28 | 6 | .870 |
| 1967—Covington | Appal. | | | | | (In Military Service) | | | | | | | | | |
| 1968—Dallas-Ft. W. | Tex. | ●SS-2B | 106 | 337 | 26 | 66 | 8 | 4 | 1 | 26 | .196 | 165 | 336 | 27 | ●.949 |
| 1969—Savannah | South. | SS | 80 | 257 | 28 | 70 | 7 | 1 | 1 | 22 | .272 | 129 | 194 | 28 | .920 |
| 1969—Okla. City† | A. A. | 2B-SS | 24 | 81 | 14 | 25 | 2 | 1 | 0 | 8 | .309 | 55 | 71 | 4 | .969 |
| 1969—Seattle | Amer. | SS-2B | 17 | 43 | 2 | 12 | 2 | 1 | 0 | 4 | .279 | 22 | 29 | 2 | .962 |
| 1970—Portland | P. C. | S-2-O | 88 | 291 | 26 | 78 | 8 | 4 | 0 | 33 | .268 | 148 | 223 | 13 | .966 |
| 1970—Milwaukee‡ | Amer. | 2B | 6 | 0 | 1 | 0 | 0 | 0 | 0 | 0 | .000 | 1 | 1 | 0 | 1.000 |
| 1971—Wichita | A. A. | SS-2B | 32 | 114 | 12 | 28 | 8 | 1 | 1 | 8 | .246 | 56 | 101 | 10 | .940 |
| 1971—Cleveland | Amer. | SS-2B | 60 | 129 | 14 | 29 | 4 | 0 | 2 | 12 | .225 | 61 | 145 | 6 | .972 |
| 1972—Cleveland§ | Amer. | SS-2 | 6 | 12 | 1 | 2 | 1 | 0 | 0 | 0 | .167 | 5 | 7 | 1 | .923 |
| 1972—San Diego x | Nat. | 2-S-3 | 39 | 85 | 15 | 17 | 2 | 0 | 0 | 2 | .200 | 63 | 68 | 2 | .985 |
| 1973—Syracuse | Int. | SS-C | 111 | 322 | 57 | 80 | 15 | 1 | 2 | 30 | .248 | 190 | 344 | 23 | .959 |
| 1973—New York | Amer. | SS-2B | 26 | 66 | 6 | 14 | 0 | 1 | 1 | 5 | .212 | 42 | 72 | 2 | .983 |
| 1974—Syracuse y | Int. | SS | 72 | 225 | 21 | 58 | 11 | 0 | 1 | 21 | .258 | 101 | 196 | 9 | .971 |
| 1974—New York | Amer. | SS-2B | 33 | 38 | 2 | 7 | 0 | 0 | 0 | 3 | .184 | 32 | 59 | 1 | .989 |
| 1975—New York | Amer. | S-2-3 | 117 | 252 | 34 | 56 | 5 | 1 | 0 | 15 | .222 | 161 | 249 | 9 | .979 |
| 1976—New York | Amer. | SS-2B | 110 | 260 | 32 | 62 | 2 | 2 | 1 | 20 | .238 | 148 | 251 | 7 | .983 |
| American League Totals | | | 375 | 800 | 92 | 182 | 14 | 5 | 4 | 59 | .228 | 473 | 813 | 28 | .979 |
| National League Totals | | | 39 | 85 | 15 | 17 | 2 | 0 | 0 | 2 | .200 | 63 | 68 | 2 | .985 |
| Major League Totals | | | 414 | 885 | 107 | 199 | 16 | 5 | 4 | 61 | .225 | 536 | 881 | 30 | .979 |

†Recalled by Houston Astros and sold to Seattle Pilots, September 8, 1969.
‡Sold to Cleveland Indians' organization, March 26, 1971.
§Traded to San Diego Padres for Pitcher Mike Kilkenny, June 11, 1972.
xTraded to Syracuse (New York Yankees' organization) for Catcher George Pena, October 24, 1972.
yOn disabled list, April 23 to May 3, 1974.

### CHAMPIONSHIP SERIES RECORD

| Year    Club | League | Pos. | G. | AB. | R. | H. | 2B. | 3B. | HR. | RBI. | B.A. | PO. | A. | E. | F.A. |
|---|---|---|---|---|---|---|---|---|---|---|---|---|---|---|---|
| 1976—New York | Amer. | SS | 5 | 15 | 1 | 5 | 2 | 0 | 0 | 0 | .333 | 7 | 15 | 1 | .957 |

### WORLD SERIES RECORD

| Year    Club | League | Pos. | G. | AB. | R. | H. | 2B. | 3B. | HR. | RBI. | B.A. | PO. | A. | E. | F.A. |
|---|---|---|---|---|---|---|---|---|---|---|---|---|---|---|---|
| 1976—New York | Amer. | SS | 4 | 6 | 1 | 1 | 1 | 0 | 0 | 1 | .167 | 4 | 7 | 1 | .917 |

## MITCHELL JACK STANLEY
### (Mickey)
Born July 20, 1942, at Grand Rapids, Mich.
Height, 6.01  Weight, 195.
Throws and bats righthanded.
Hobby—Hunting.
Attended Grand Rapids Junior College, Grand Rapids, Mich.

Established major league record for highest fielding percentage, outfielder, lifetime, .992, 1976.
Tied major league record for highest fielding average, season, outfielder, 100 or more games (1.000), 1968 and 1970.

Tied American League record for most putouts, game, center fielder, 11, July 13, 1973.
Tied for International League lead in double plays by outfielder with 5 in 1965.
Named outfielder on THE SPORTING NEWS American League All-Star fielding team, 1968-69-70-73.

| Year—Club | League | Pos. | G. | AB. | R. | H. | 2B. | 3B. | HR. | RBI. | B.A. | PO. | A. | E. | F.A. |
|---|---|---|---|---|---|---|---|---|---|---|---|---|---|---|---|
| 1961—Duluth-Superior | North. | OF | 44 | 157 | 29 | 35 | 7 | 2 | 2 | 22 | .223 | 90 | 5 | 3 | .969 |
| 1961—Decatur ............ | Midw. | OF-1B | 76 | 258 | 42 | 72 | 14 | 6 | 7 | 54 | .279 | 286 | 19 | 8 | .974 |
| 1962—Duluth-Superior | North. | OF | 123 | 466 | 72 | 133 | 21 | 7 | 4 | 43 | .285 | •286 | 12 | 7 | .977 |
| 1963—Knoxville .......... | Sally | OF | 112 | 404 | 56 | 102 | 19 | 2 | 5 | 51 | .252 | 259 | 5 | 7 | .974 |
| 1964—Syracuse .......... | Int. | OF | 19 | 50 | 1 | 8 | 1 | 0 | 0 | 5 | .160 | 27 | 0 | 0 | 1.000 |
| 1964—Knoxville .......... | South. | OF | 90 | 345 | 43 | 105 | 20 | 3 | 8 | 51 | .304 | 191 | 9 | 3 | .985 |
| 1964—Detroit ............. | Amer. | OF | 4 | 11 | 3 | 3 | 0 | 0 | 0 | 1 | .273 | 5 | 0 | 0 | 1.000 |
| 1965—Syracuse .......... | Int. | OF | 144 | 541 | 68 | 152 | 26 | 7 | 10 | 73 | .281 | •344 | 8 | 3 | •.992 |
| 1965—Detroit ............. | Amer. | OF | 30 | 117 | 14 | 28 | 6 | 0 | 3 | 13 | .239 | 69 | 1 | 1 | .986 |
| 1966—Detroit† .......... | Amer. | OF | 92 | 235 | 28 | 68 | 15 | 4 | 3 | 19 | .289 | 163 | 6 | 0 | 1.000 |
| 1967—Detroit ............. | Amer. | OF-1B | 145 | 333 | 38 | 70 | 7 | 3 | 7 | 24 | .210 | 264 | 7 | 4 | .985 |
| 1968—Detroit ............. | Amer. | •O-1-S-2 | 153 | 583 | 88 | 151 | 16 | 6 | 11 | 60 | .259 | 405 | 40 | 4 | •.991 |
| 1969—Detroit ............. | Amer. | OF-S-1 | 149 | 592 | 73 | 139 | 28 | 1 | 16 | 70 | .235 | 342 | 138 | 10 | .980 |
| 1970—Detroit ............. | Amer. | •OF-1 | 142 | 568 | 83 | 143 | 21 | 11 | 13 | 47 | .252 | 384 | 9 | 1 | •.997 |
| 1971—Detroit ............. | Amer. | OF | 139 | 401 | 43 | 117 | 14 | 5 | 7 | 41 | .292 | 315 | 10 | 4 | .988 |
| 1972—Detroit ............. | Amer. | OF | 142 | 435 | 45 | 102 | 16 | 6 | 14 | 55 | .234 | 309 | 9 | 2 | .994 |
| 1973—Detroit ............. | Amer. | OF | 157 | 602 | 81 | 147 | 23 | 5 | 17 | 57 | .244 | 420 | 10 | 3 | ·.993 |
| 1974—Detroit‡ ............. | Amer. | O-1-2 | 99 | 394 | 40 | 87 | 13 | 2 | 8 | 34 | .221 | 341 | 14 | 4 | .989 |
| 1975—Detroit§ .......... | Amer. | O-1-3 | 52 | 164 | 26 | 42 | 7 | 3 | 3 | 19 | .256 | 183 | 22 | 2 | .990 |
| 1976—Detroit ............. | Amer. | O-1-3-2 | 84 | 214 | 34 | 55 | 17 | 1 | 4 | 29 | .257 | 187 | 45 | 5 | .979 |
| Major League Totals ..................... | | | 1388 | 4649 | 596 | 1152 | 183 | 47 | 106 | 469 | .248 | 3387 | 311 | 40 | .989 |

†Suffered broken hand, May 13; on disabled list from May 16 through June 17.
‡On disabled list, July 31 to September 13, 1974.
§On emergency disabled list, July 29 to September 26, 1975.

### CHAMPIONSHIP SERIES RECORD

| Year—Club | League | Pos. | G. | AB. | R. | H. | 2B. | 3B. | HR. | RBI. | B.A. | PO. | A. | E. | F.A. |
|---|---|---|---|---|---|---|---|---|---|---|---|---|---|---|---|
| 1972—Detroit ............. | Amer. | O-PH | 4 | 6 | 0 | 2 | 0 | 0 | 0 | 0 | .333 | 7 | 0 | 0 | 1.000 |

### WORLD SERIES RECORD

Tied following World Series records: Most runs, inning (2), and most at-bats, inning (2), third inning, October 9, 1968; most putouts, shortstop, inning (3), sixth inning, October 10, 1968.

| Year—Club | League | Pos. | G. | AB. | R. | H. | 2B. | 3B. | HR. | RBI. | B.A. | PO. | A. | E. | F.A. |
|---|---|---|---|---|---|---|---|---|---|---|---|---|---|---|---|
| 1968—Detroit ............. | Amer. | SS-OF | 7 | 28 | 4 | 6 | 0 | 1 | 0 | 0 | .214 | 15 | 16 | 2 | .939 |

## ROBERT WILLIAM STANLEY
### (Bob)

Born November 10, 1954, at Portland, Me.
Height, 6.04. Weight, 210.
Throws and bats righthanded.

Led New York-Pennsylvania League pitchers in games started with 15 in 1974.
Tied for Florida State and Eastern League lead in games started with 27 in 1975 and 27 in 1976.

| Year—Club | League | G. | IP. | W. | L. | Pct. | H. | R. | ER. | SO. | BB. | ERA. |
|---|---|---|---|---|---|---|---|---|---|---|---|---|
| 1974—Elmira ................................ | NYP | 15 | 86 | 6 | 6 | .500 | 94 | 57 | 44 | 45 | 40 | 4.60 |
| 1975—Winter Haven ..................... | Florida St. | 27 | 169 | 5 | •17 | .227 | 136 | 76 | 55 | 73· | 74 | 2.93 |
| 1976—Bristol† ................................ | Eastern | 27 | 186 | 15 | 9 | .625 | 176 | 76 | 55 | 78 | 83 | 2.66 |

†On disabled list, June 19 through June 24, 1976.
Listed on Boston Red Sox' 1977 spring roster.

## LEROY BOBBY STANTON
### (Lee)

Born April 10, 1946, at Latta, S. C.
Height, 6.01. Weight, 200.
Throws and bats righthanded.
Hobbies—Billiards and music.

Hit three hom runs in a game, July 10, 1973, against Baltimore Orioles.
Led Texas League in sacrifice flies with 8 in 1969 and International League with 8 in 1971.

| Year—Club | League | Pos. | G. | AB. | R. | H. | 2B. | 3B. | HR. | RBI. | B.A. | PO. | A. | E. | F.A. |
|---|---|---|---|---|---|---|---|---|---|---|---|---|---|---|---|
| 1965—Greenville† ........ | W. Car. | OF | 39 | 149 | 18 | 43 | 4 | 7 | 2 | 19 | .289 | 53 | 3 | 5 | .918 |
| 1965—Marion .............. | Appal. | OF | 14 | 48 | 3 | 11 | 2 | 0 | 1 | 3 | .229 | 18 | 0 | 1 | .947 |
| 1966-67—‡ | | | | | (In Military Service) | | | | | | | | | | |
| 1968—Raleigh-Durham | Carol. | OF | 133 | 467 | 73 | 124 | 22 | 10 | 12 | 75 | .266 | 214 | 16 | 6 | .974 |
| 1969—Memphis .......... | Texas | OF | 127 | 459 | 47 | 122 | 15 | •10 | 4 | 52 | .266 | 229 | 15 | 6 | .976 |
| 1970—Tidewater.......... | Int. | OF | 133 | 498 | 66 | 151 | 20 | 5 | 19 | 94 | .303 | 233 | 8 | 6 | .976 |
| 1970—New York.......... | Nat. | OF | 4 | 4 | 0 | 1 | 0 | 1 | 0 | 0 | .250 | 1 | 0 | 0 | 1.000 |
| 1971—Tidewater.......... | Int. | OF | •139 | 500 | 84 | 162 | •31 | 4 | 23 | 101 | .324 | 216 | 16 | 6 | .975 |
| 1971—New York§ ........ | Nat. | OF | 5 | 21 | 2 | 4 | 1 | 0 | 0 | 2 | .190 | 9 | 0 | 0 | 1.000 |
| 1972—California .......... | Amer. | OF | 127 | 402 | 44 | 101 | 15 | 3 | 12 | 39 | .251 | 225 | 6 | 4 | .983 |
| 1973—California .......... | Amer. | OF | 119 | 306 | 41 | 72 | 9 | 2 | 8 | 34 | .235 | 160 | 5 | 6 | .965 |
| 1974—California x ...... | Amer. | OF | 118 | 415 | 48 | 111 | 21 | 2 | 11 | 62 | .267 | 226 | 11 | 6 | .975 |

| Year Club League | Pos. | G. | AB. | R. | H. | 2B. | 3B. | HR. | RBI. | B.A. | PO. | A. | E. | F.A. |
|---|---|---|---|---|---|---|---|---|---|---|---|---|---|---|
| 1975–California.........Amer. | OF | 137 | 440 | 67 | 115 | 20 | 3 | 14 | 82 | .261 | 230 | •16 | 10 | .961 |
| 1976–California y ......Amer. | O-PH-DH | 93 | 231 | 12 | 44 | 13 | 1 | 2 | 25 | .190 | 128 | 1 | 2 | .985 |
| American League Totals ............... | | 594 | 1794 | 212 | 443 | 78 | 11 | 47 | 242 | .247 | 969 | 39 | 28 | .973 |
| National League Totals ................. | | 9 | 25 | 2 | 5 | 1 | 1 | 0 | 2 | .200 | 10 | 0 | 0 | 1.000 |
| Major League Totals ..................... | | 603 | 1819 | 214 | 448 | 79 | 12 | 47 | 244 | .246 | 979 | 39 | 28 | .973 |

†On disabled list from May 13 through June 16 after being hit by pitch.
‡On military list, April 1, 1966 through March 15, 1968.
§Traded with Pitchers Nolan Ryan and Don Rose and Catcher Francisco Estrada to California Angels for Infielder Jim Fregosi, December 10, 1971.
xOn disabled list, April 23 to May 28, 1974.
ySelected by Seattle Mariners in American League expansion draft, November 5, 1976.

## MICHAEL THOMAS STANTON
### (Mike)

Born September 25, 1952, at St. Louis, Mo.
Height, 6.02. Weight, 200.
Throws and bats righthanded.
Hobbies–Canoeing, playing the guitar and making tables.
Attended Miami-Dade (South) Community College, Miami, Fla.

Tied for Southern League lead in games started by pitchers with 27 in 1974.

| Year Club | League | G. | IP. | W. | L. | Pct. | H. | R. | ER. | SO. | BB. | ERA. |
|---|---|---|---|---|---|---|---|---|---|---|---|---|
| 1973–Covington ...........................Ap'lachian | | 7 | 51 | 2 | 3 | .400 | 34 | 26 | 11 | 70 | 21 | 1.94 |
| 1973–Cedar Rapids .....................Midwest | | 7 | 53 | 3 | 2 | .600 | 40 | 16 | 8 | 59 | 18 | 1.36 |
| 1974–Columbus ...........................Southern | | 27 | 179 | 11 | •15 | .423 | 158 | 85 | 61 | •146 | •121 | 3.07 |
| 1975–Iowa ...................................Am. Assoc. | | 18 | 107 | 5 | 11 | .313 | 95 | 56 | 49 | 105 | 66 | 4.12 |
| 1975–Houston .............................National | | 7 | 17 | 0 | 2 | .000 | 20 | 14 | 14 | 16 | 20 | 7.41 |
| 1975–Columbus ...........................Southern | | 10 | 39 | 2 | 3 | .400 | 31 | 13 | 10 | 41 | 19 | 2.31 |
| 1976–Memphis .............................Int'national | | 21 | 128 | 6 | 11 | .353 | 135 | 88 | 69 | 101 | 67 | 4.85 |
| Major League Totals ............................. | | 7 | 17 | 0 | 2 | .000 | 20 | 14 | 14 | 16 | 20 | 7.41 |

Listed on Houston Astros' 1977 spring roster.

## WILVER DORNEL STARGELL
### (Willie)

Born March 6, 1941, at Earlsboro, Okla.
Height, 6.03. Weight, 220.
Throws and bats lefthanded.
Hobbies–Bowling and dancing.
Attended Santa Rosa Junior College, Santa Rosa, Calif.

Established major league records for most consecutive seasons 10 or more intentional bases on balls (10), 1974; most seasons, 100 or more strikeouts (12), 1976; and most consecutive seasons, 100 or more strikeouts (12), 1976.

Tied following major league records: most long hits, game (5), August 1, 1970; most times, three or more home runs in a game, season, 2, April 10 and April 21, 1971; and most home runs month of April 11, in 1971.

Established following National League records: most games, 4 or more long hits, lifetime (4), 1973; most strikeouts, lifetime, 1,598, 1976.

Tied National League record for most strikeouts in two consecutive games (7), September 24-25, 1964.

Hit three home runs in a game, June 24, 1965, May 22, 1968, April 10 and April 21, 1971.

Led National League in slugging percentage with .646 in 1973.

Led National League batters in strikeouts with 154 in 1971.

Named as outfielder on THE SPORTING NEWS National League All-Star Team, 1965, 1966 and 1971.

Named first baseman on THE SPORTING NEWS National League All-Star Team, 1972.

| Year Club League | Pos. | G. | AB. | R. | H. | 2B. | 3B. | HR. | RBI. | B.A. | PO. | A. | E. | F.A. |
|---|---|---|---|---|---|---|---|---|---|---|---|---|---|---|
| 1959–S. A'gelo-R'well Soph. | 1B | 118 | 431 | 66 | 118 | 28 | 6 | 7 | 87 | .274 | 842 | 22 | •37 | .959 |
| 1960–Grand Forks......North. | OF | 107 | 396 | 63 | 103 | 19 | 1 | 11 | 61 | .260 | 224 | 12 | 13 | .948 |
| 1961–Asheville .........Sally | OF | 130 | 453 | 78 | 131 | 21 | 8 | 22 | 89 | .289 | 264 | 14 | •19 | .936 |
| 1962–Columbus ..........Int. | OF-1B | 138 | 497 | 97 | 137 | 21 | 8 | 27 | 82 | .276 | 354 | 18 | 13 | .966 |
| 1962–Pittsburgh .......Nat. | OF | 10 | 31 | 1 | 9 | 3 | 1 | 0 | 4 | .290 | 12 | 1 | 1 | .929 |
| 1963–Pittsburgh .......Nat. | OF-1B | 108 | 304 | 34 | 74 | 11 | 6 | 11 | 47 | .243 | 226 | 12 | 9 | .964 |
| 1964–Pittsburgh .......Nat. | OF-1B | 117 | 421 | 53 | 115 | 19 | 7 | 21 | 78 | .273 | 565 | 24 | 10 | .983 |
| 1965–Pittsburgh .......Nat. | OF-1B | 144 | 533 | 68 | 145 | 25 | 8 | 27 | 107 | .272 | 268 | 14 | 8 | .972 |
| 1966–Pittsburgh .......Nat. | OF-1B | 140 | 485 | 84 | 153 | 30 | 0 | 33 | 102 | .315 | 300 | 13 | 11 | .966 |
| 1967–Pittsburgh .......Nat. | OF-1B | 134 | 462 | 54 | 125 | 18 | 6 | 20 | 73 | .271 | 447 | 27 | 11 | .977 |
| 1968–Pittsburgh .......Nat. | OF-1B | 128 | 435 | 57 | 103 | 15 | 1 | 24 | 67 | .237 | 254 | 19 | 9 | .968 |
| 1969–Pittsburgh .......Nat. | OF-1B | 145 | 522 | 89 | 160 | 31 | 6 | 29 | 92 | .307 | 333 | 14 | 7 | .980 |
| 1970–Pittsburgh .......Nat. | •OF-1B | 136 | 474 | 70 | 125 | 18 | 3 | 31 | 85 | .264 | 184 | •17 | 5 | .976 |
| 1971–Pittsburgh .......Nat. | OF | 141 | 511 | 104 | 151 | 26 | 0 | •48 | 125 | .295 | 237 | 8 | 4 | .984 |
| 1972–Pittsburgh .......Nat. | •1B-OF | 138 | 495 | 75 | 145 | 28 | 2 | 33 | 112 | .293 | 931 | 41 | •17 | .983 |
| 1973–Pittsburgh .......Nat. | OF | 148 | 522 | 106 | 156 | •43 | 3 | •44 | •119 | .299 | 261 | 14 | 7 | .975 |
| 1974–Pittsburgh .......Nat. | OF-1B | 140 | 508 | 90 | 153 | 37 | 4 | 25 | 96 | .301 | 256 | 8 | 9 | .967 |
| 1975–Pittsburgh .......Nat. | 1B | 124 | 461 | 71 | 136 | 32 | 2 | 22 | 90 | .295 | 1121 | 54 | 10 | .992 |
| 1976–Pittsburgh .......Nat. | 1B | 117 | 428 | 54 | 110 | 20 | 3 | 20 | 65 | .257 | 1037 | 53 | 13 | .988 |
| Major League Totals ..................... | | 1870 | 6592 | 1010 | 1860 | 356 | 52 | 388 | 1262 | .282 | 6432 | 319 | 131 | .981 |

| Year Club League | Pos. | G. | AB. | R. | H. | 2B. | 3B. | HR. | RBI. | B.A. | PO. | A. | E. | F.A. |
|---|---|---|---|---|---|---|---|---|---|---|---|---|---|---|
| 1970–Pittsburgh ........Nat. | OF | 3 | 12 | 0 | 6 | 1 | 0 | 0 | 1 | .500 | 4 | 0 | 0 | 1.000 |
| 1971–Pittsburgh ........Nat. | OF | 4 | 14 | 1 | 0 | 0 | 0 | 0 | 0 | .000 | 6 | 0 | 0 | 1.000 |
| 1972–Pittsburgh ........Nat. | 1B-OF | 5 | 16 | 1 | 1 | 1 | 0 | 0 | 1 | .063 | 32 | 3 | 0 | 1.000 |
| 1974–Pittsburgh .......Nat. | OF | 4 | 15 | 3 | 6 | 0 | 0 | 2 | 4 | .400 | 13 | 0 | 0 | 1.000 |
| 1975–Pittsburgh ........Nat. | 1B | 3 | 11 | 1 | 2 | 1 | 0 | 0 | 0 | .182 | 15 | 0 | 0 | 1.000 |
| Championship Series Totals ............ | | 19 | 68 | 6 | 15 | 3 | 0 | 2 | 6 | .221 | 70 | 3 | 0 | 1.000 |

## WORLD SERIES RECORD

| Year Club League | Pos. | G. | AB. | R. | H. | 2B. | 3B. | HR. | RBI. | B.A. | PO. | A. | E. | F.A. |
|---|---|---|---|---|---|---|---|---|---|---|---|---|---|---|
| 1971–Pittsburgh ........Nat. | OF | 7 | 24 | 3 | 5 | 1 | 0 | 0 | 1 | .208 | 11 | 1 | 0 | 1.000 |

## ALL-STAR GAME RECORD

| Year League | Pos. | AB. | R. | H. | 2B. | 3B. | HR. | RBI. | B.A. | PO. | A. | E. | F.A. |
|---|---|---|---|---|---|---|---|---|---|---|---|---|---|
| 1964–National ............................. | PH | 1 | 0 | 0 | 0 | 0 | 0 | 0 | .000 | 0 | 0 | 0 | .000 |
| 1965–National ............................. | OF | 3 | 2 | 2 | 0 | 0 | 1 | 2 | .667 | 1 | 0 | 0 | 1.000 |
| 1966–National ............................. | PH | 1 | 0 | 0 | 0 | 0 | 0 | 0 | .000 | 0 | 0 | 0 | .000 |
| 1971–National ............................. | OF | 2 | 1 | 0 | 0 | 0 | 0 | 0 | .000 | 2 | 0 | 0 | 1.000 |
| 1972–National ............................. | OF | 1 | 0 | 0 | 0 | 0 | 0 | 0 | .000 | 0 | 0 | 0 | .000 |
| 1973–National ............................. | PH-OF | 1 | 0 | 0 | 0 | 0 | 0 | 0 | .000 | 1 | 0 | 0 | 1.000 |
| All-Star Game Totals ...................... | | 9 | 3 | 2 | 0 | 0 | 1 | 2 | .222 | 4 | 0 | 0 | 1.000 |

### DANIEL JOSEPH STAUB
### (Rusty)
(Named by nurses in hospital of birth for his hair.)

Born April 1, 1944, at New Orleans, La.
Height, 6.02. Weight, 205.
Throws right and bats lefthanded.
Hobbies—Golf, coin and stamp collecting.

Tied for National League lead in double plays by outfielders with 5 in 1971, with 5 in 1973 and with 5 in 1974.
Led Carolina League first basemen in double plays with 123 in 1962.
Named Rookie of the Year and Player of the Year in Carolina League, 1962.
Received reported $100,000 bonus to sign with Houston Astros, 1961.

| Year Club League | Pos. | G. | AB. | R. | H. | 2B. | 3B. | HR. | RBI. | B.A. | PO. | A. | E. | F.A. |
|---|---|---|---|---|---|---|---|---|---|---|---|---|---|---|
| 1962–Durham ............Carol. | 1B | ●140 | 509 | 61 | 149 | 20 | 4 | 23 | 93 | .293 | ●1247 | ●76 | ●20 | .985 |
| 1963–Houston ............Nat. | 1B-OF | 150 | 513 | 43 | 115 | 17 | 4 | 6 | 45 | .224 | 963 | 63 | 11 | .989 |
| 1964–Houston ............Nat. | 1B-OF | 89 | 292 | 26 | 63 | 10 | 2 | 8 | 35 | .216 | 512 | 30 | 9 | .984 |
| 1964–Oklahoma City ..P.C. | OF-1B | 71 | 226 | 55 | 71 | 13 | 1 | 20 | 45 | .314 | 306 | 22 | 5 | .985 |
| 1965–Houston ............Nat. | OF-1B | 131 | 410 | 43 | 105 | 20 | 1 | 14 | 63 | .256 | 203 | 12 | 11 | .951 |
| 1966–Houston ............Nat. | OF-1B | 153 | 554 | 60 | 155 | 28 | 3 | 13 | 81 | .280 | 291 | 15 | 12 | .962 |
| 1967–Houston ............Nat. | OF | 149 | 546 | 71 | 182 | ●44 | 1 | 10 | 74 | .333 | 269 | 10 | 11 | .962 |
| 1968–Houston† ............Nat. | 1B-OF | 161 | 591 | 54 | 172 | 37 | 1 | 6 | 72 | .291 | 1336 | 94 | 13 | .991 |
| 1969–Montreal ..........Nat. | OF | 158 | 549 | 89 | 166 | 26 | 5 | 29 | 79 | .302 | 265 | ●16 | 10 | .966 |
| 1970–Montreal ..........Nat. | OF | 160 | 569 | 98 | 156 | 23 | 7 | 30 | 94 | .274 | 308 | 14 | 5 | .985 |
| 1971–Montreal‡ ..........Nat. | OF | ●162 | 599 | 94 | 186 | 34 | 6 | 19 | 97 | .311 | 290 | ●20 | ●18 | .945 |
| 1972–New York§ ........Nat. | OF | 66 | 239 | 32 | 70 | 11 | 0 | 9 | 38 | .293 | 108 | 4 | 2 | .982 |
| 1973–New York..........Nat. | OF | 152 | 585 | 77 | 163 | 36 | 1 | 15 | 76 | .279 | 297 | 17 | 7 | .978 |
| 1974–New York..........Nat. | OF | 151 | 561 | 65 | 145 | 22 | 2 | 19 | 78 | .258 | 262 | ●●19 | 5 | .983 |
| 1975–New York x ...... Nat. | OF | 155 | 574 | 93 | 162 | 30 | 4 | 19 | 105 | .282 | 267 | ●15 | 4 | .986 |
| 1976–Detroit ............Amer. | OF-DH | 161 | 589 | 73 | 176 | 28 | 3 | 15 | 96 | .299 | 218 | 8 | 7 | .970 |
| American League Totals ................. | | 161 | 589 | 73 | 176 | 28 | 3 | 15 | 96 | .299 | 218 | 8 | 7 | .970 |
| National League Totals ........... | | 1873 | 6582 | 845 | 1840 | 338 | 37 | 197 | 937 | .280 | 5371 | 329 | 118 | .980 |
| Major League Totals ...................... | | 1998 | 7171 | 918 | 2016 | 366 | 40 | 212 | 1033 | .281 | 5589 | 337 | 125 | .979 |

†Traded to Montreal Expos for First Baseman Donn Clendenon and Outfielder Jesus Alou, January 22, 1969. Clendenon refused to report to Houston; Pitchers John Billingham and Drannon (Skip) Guinn and cash sent to Houston to complete deal, April 8, 1969.

‡Traded to New York Mets for Outfielder Ken Singleton, First Baseman Mike Jorgensen and Infielder Tim Foli, April 6, 1972.

§On disabled list, July 21 through September 1, 1972.

xTraded with Pitcher Bill Laxton to Detroit Tigers for Pitcher Mickey Lolich and Outfielder Billy Baldwin, December 12, 1975.

## CHAMPIONSHIP SERIES RECORD

| Year Club League | Pos. | G. | AB. | R. | H. | 2B. | 3B. | HR. | RBI. | B.A. | PO. | A. | E. | F.A. |
|---|---|---|---|---|---|---|---|---|---|---|---|---|---|---|
| 1973–New York..........Nat. | OF | 4 | 15 | 4 | 3 | 0 | 0 | 3 | 5 | .200 | 10 | 0 | 0 | 1.000 |

## WORLD SERIES RECORD

| Year Club League | Pos. | G. | AB. | R. | H. | 2B. | 3B. | HR. | RBI. | B.A. | PO. | A. | E. | F.A. |
|---|---|---|---|---|---|---|---|---|---|---|---|---|---|---|
| 1973–New York..........Nat. | OF-PH | 7 | 26 | 1 | 11 | 2 | 0 | 1 | 6 | .423 | 5 | 0 | 0 | 1.000 |

## ALL-STAR GAME RECORD

| Year League | Pos. | AB. | R. | H. | 2B. | 3B. | HR. | RBI. | B.A. | PO. | A. | E. | F.A. |
|---|---|---|---|---|---|---|---|---|---|---|---|---|---|
| 1967–National ............................. | PH | 1 | 0 | 1 | 0 | 0 | 0 | 0 | 1.000 | 0 | 0 | 0 | .000 |
| 1968–National ............................. | PH | 1 | 0 | 0 | 0 | 0 | 0 | 0 | .000 | 0 | 0 | 0 | .000 |
| 1970–National ............................. | PH | 1 | 0 | 0 | 0 | 0 | 0 | 0 | .000 | 0 | 0 | 0 | .000 |
| 1976–American ............................. | OF | 2 | 0 | 2 | 0 | 0 | 0 | 0 | 1.000 | 1 | 0 | 0 | 1.000 |
| All-Star Game Totals ...................... | | 5 | 0 | 3 | 0 | 0 | 0 | 0 | .600 | 1 | 0 | 0 | 1.000 |

Member of National League All-Star Team for 1969 and 1971 games; did not play.

## JOHN HARDIN STEARNS

Born August 21, 1951, at Denver, Colo.
Height, 6.00. Weight, 185.
Throws and bats righthanded.
Hobby—Listening to music.
Attended University of Colorado, Boulder, Colo.
Brother of Bill Stearns, catcher in New York Yankees' organization.
Tied for Carolina League lead in double plays by catchers with 9 in 1974.

| Year Club League | Pos. | G. | AB. | R. | H. | 2B. | 3B. | HR. | RBI. | B.A. | PO. | A. | E. | F.A. |
|---|---|---|---|---|---|---|---|---|---|---|---|---|---|---|
| 1973—Reading ...........East. | C-O-3-1 | 67 | 166 | 28 | 40 | 7 | 4 | 3 | 24 | .241 | 232 | 33 | 4 | .985 |
| 1974—Rocky Mount ....Carol. | C-O-1 | 62 | 230 | 41 | 79 | 16 | 4 | 4 | 38 | .343 | 400 | 62 | 13 | .973 |
| 1974—Toledo ..............Int. | C-3B | 77 | 278 | 34 | 74 | 9 | 2 | 3 | 28 | .266 | 414 | 49 | 5 | .989 |
| 1974—Philadelphia† ....Nat. | C | 1 | 2 | 0 | 1 | 0 | 0 | 0 | 0 | .500 | 1 | 0 | 0 | 1.000 |
| 1975—New York.........Nat. | C | 59 | 169 | 25 | 32 | 5 | 1 | 3 | 10 | .189 | 297 | 40 | 2 | .994 |
| 1976—New York.........Nat. | C-PH | 32 | 103 | 13 | 27 | 6 | 0 | 2 | 10 | .262 | 200 | 20 | 3 | .987 |
| 1976—Tidewater.........Int. | C-3B | 102 | 332 | 64 | 103 | 17 | 2 | 10 | 45 | .310 | 416 | 100 | 14 | .974 |
| Major League Totals ...................... | | 92 | 274 | 38 | 60 | 11 | 1 | 5 | 20 | .219 | 498 | 60 | 5 | .991 |

†Traded with Outfielder Del Unser and Pitcher Mac Scarce to New York Mets for Pitcher Tug McGraw and Outfielders Don Hahn and Dave Schneck, December 3, 1974.

## WILLIAM ALLEN STEIN

Name pronounced stine.

### (Bill)

Born January 21, 1947, at Battle Creek, Mich.
Height, 5.10. Weight, 175.
Throws and bats righthanded.
Hobbies—Bowling, basketball and golf.
Attended Brevard Junior College, Cocoa, Fla., and Southern Illinois
University, Carbondale, Ill.
Led American Association in total bases with 274 in 1974.

| Year Club League | Pos. | G. | AB. | R. | H. | 2B. | 3B. | HR. | RBI. | B.A. | PO. | A. | E. | F.A. |
|---|---|---|---|---|---|---|---|---|---|---|---|---|---|---|
| 1969—Tulsa ................A. A. | 2-3-S | 62 | 183 | 24 | 54 | 11 | 5 | 1 | 20 | .295 | 81 | 97 | 9 | .952 |
| 1970—Arkansas ..........Texas | 2-O-S | 114 | 429 | 56 | 124 | 21 | 2 | 8 | 52 | .289 | 179 | 198 | 17 | .957 |
| 1971—Tulsa† ..............A. A. | O-3-2-P | 103 | 389 | 50 | 106 | 22 | 4 | 8 | 67 | .272 | 154 | 86 | 13 | .949 |
| 1972—Tulsa ...............A. A. | O-2-3-1 | 103 | 360 | 49 | 100 | 26 | 4 | 5 | 36 | .278 | 146 | 52 | 5 | .975 |
| 1972—St. Louis ..........Nat. | 3B-OF | 14 | 35 | 2 | 11 | 0 | 1 | 2 | 3 | .314 | 5 | 4 | 0 | 1.000 |
| 1973—St. Louis ..........Nat. | OF-1-3 | 32 | 55 | 4 | 12 | 2 | 0 | 0 | 2 | .218 | 37 | 1 | 0 | 1.000 |
| 1973—Tulsa‡§..............A. A. | 3B | 21 | 81 | 12 | 23 | 2 | 1 | 0 | 8 | .284 | 8 | 37 | 1 | .978 |
| 1974—Iowa.................A. A. | 3B-OF | •135 | 543 | *107 | *178 | 32 | 8 | 16 | 74 | .328 | 89 | 204 | 13 | .958 |
| 1974—Chicago ...........Amer. | 3B | 13 | 43 | 5 | 12 | 1 | 0 | 0 | 5 | .279 | 7 | 20 | 4 | .871 |
| 1975—Chicago ...........Amer. | 2-3-O | 76 | 226 | 23 | 61 | 7 | 1 | 3 | 21 | .270 | 87 | 118 | 9 | .958 |
| 1976—Chicago x .........Amer. | 2-3-1-S-O | 117 | 392 | 32 | 105 | 15 | 2 | 4 | 36 | .268 | 161 | 243 | 19 | .955 |
| American League Totals ................ | | 206 | 661 | 60 | 178 | 23 | 3 | 7 | 62 | .269 | 255 | 381 | 32 | .952 |
| National League Totals .................. | | 46 | 90 | 6 | 23 | 2 | 1 | 2 | 5 | .256 | 42 | 5 | 0 | 1.000 |
| Major League Totals ...................... | | 252 | 751 | 66 | 201 | 25 | 4 | 9 | 67 | .268 | 297 | 386 | 32 | .955 |

†On temporary inactive list, July 1 through July 12, 1971.
‡Traded by Tulsa (St. Louis Cardinals' organization) to Salt Lake City (California Angels' organization) for Infielder Jerry DaVanon, September 25, 1973.
§Sold by California Angels to Chicago White Sox, April 3, 1974; White Sox sent Pitcher Steve Blateric to Angels, August 1, 1974, to complete deal.
xSelected by Seattle Mariners in American League expansion draft, November 5, 1976.

PITCHING RECORD

| Year Club | League | G. | IP. | W. | L. | Pct. | H. | R. | ER. | SO. | BB. | ERA. |
|---|---|---|---|---|---|---|---|---|---|---|---|---|
| 1971—Tulsa ..................................Am. Assoc. | | 1 | 6 | 0 | 0 | .000 | 8 | 3 | 3 | 6 | 0 | 4.50 |

## WILLIAM RANDOLPH STEIN
### (Randy)

Born March 7, 1953, at Pomona, Calif.
Height, 6.04. Weight, 210.
Throws and bats righthanded.

| Year Club | League | G. | IP. | W. | L. | Pct. | H. | R. | ER. | SO. | BB. | ERA. |
|---|---|---|---|---|---|---|---|---|---|---|---|---|
| 1971—Aberdeen ..........................Northern | | 6 | 40 | 2 | 3 | .400 | 27 | 21 | 17 | 28 | 23 | 3.83 |
| 1972—Miami................................Florida St. | | 20 | 142 | 11 | 5 | .688 | 111 | 43 | 28 | 110 | 60 | 1.77 |
| 1973—Asheville...........................Southern | | 20 | 156 | 14 | 6 | .700 | 133 | 66 | 49 | 73 | 54 | 2.83 |
| 1973—Rochester .........................Int'national | | 6 | 36 | 1 | 2 | .333 | 36 | 19 | 14 | 19 | 15 | 3.50 |
| 1974—Rochester† ........................Int'national | | 6 | 34 | 3 | 1 | .750 | 39 | 19 | 16 | 17 | 12 | 4.24 |
| 1975—Rochester‡ ........................Int'national | | 21 | 110 | 8 | 2 | .800 | 91 | 47 | 38 | 59 | 62 | 3.11 |
| 1976—Rochester§ ........................Int'national | | 24 | 110 | 5 | 6 | .455 | 120 | 71 | 67 | 51 | 58 | 5.48 |

†On disabled list, June 7 to October 25, 1974.
‡On disabled list, May 20 to June 19, 1975.
§On disabled list, May 3 to May 23, 1976.
Listed on Baltimore Orioles' 1977 spring roster.

# RENALDO ANTONIO STENNETT
## (Rennie)

Born April 5, 1951, at Colon, Panama.
Height, 6.00. Weight, 178.
Throws and bats righthanded.
Hobbies—Basketball, dancing, sports and movies.
Brother of Fernando Stennett, infielder in Pittsburgh Pirates' organization, 1973-76.

Established following major league records; most hits, game, since 1900, 7, September 16, 1975; most consecutive hits, game, since 1900, 7, September 16, 1975; and most hits, two consecutive games, since 1900, 10, September 16 and 17, 1975.

Tied following major league records: most times on base, game, since 1900, 7, September 16, 1975; most at bats, game, since 1900, 7, September 16, 1975; and most innings, 2 or more hits, game, 2, September 16, 1975.

Tied National League record for most hits, 3 consecutive games, since 1900, 12, September 16 through September 18, 1975.

Led National League shortstops in total chances with 950 in 1976.

Led Carolina League in total bases with 229 in 1970.

Led Western Carolinas League outfielders in double plays with 5 in 1969.

| Year | Club | League | Pos. | G. | AB. | R. | H. | 2B. | 3B. | HR. | RBI. | B.A. | PO. | A. | E. | F.A. |
|------|------|--------|------|----|-----|----|----|-----|-----|-----|------|------|-----|----|----|------|
| 1969—Gastonia | W. Car. | ★O-3B | 107 | 396 | 51 | 114 | 17 | ●7 | 3 | 49 | .288 | 150 | ★14 | 8 | .953 |
| 1970—Salem | Carol. | OF | 131 | ★540 | 65 | ★176 | 20 | ★9 | 5 | 50 | ★.326 | 201 | 13 | 10 | .955 |
| 1970—Columbus | Int. | 2B | 1 | 4 | 1 | 2 | 1 | 0 | 0 | 0 | .500 | 5 | 1 | 1 | .857 |
| 1971—Charleston | Int. | 2B | 80 | 323 | 61 | 111 | 17 | 10 | 3 | 39 | .344 | 172 | 224 | 17 | .959 |
| 1971—Pittsburgh | Nat. | 2B | 50 | 153 | 24 | 54 | 5 | 4 | 1 | 15 | .353 | 82 | 106 | 9 | .954 |
| 1972—Pittsburgh | Nat. | 2-O-S | 109 | 370 | 43 | 106 | 14 | 5 | 3 | 30 | .286 | 197 | 173 | 10 | .974 |
| 1973—Pittsburgh | Nat. | 2-S-O | 128 | 466 | 45 | 113 | 18 | 3 | 10 | 55 | .242 | 281 | 348 | 14 | .978 |
| 1974—Pittsburgh | Nat. | ★2B-OF | 157 | 673 | 84 | 196 | 29 | 3 | 7 | 56 | .291 | ★444 | 475 | 19 | .980 |
| 1975—Pittsburgh | Nat. | 2B | 148 | 616 | 89 | 176 | 25 | 7 | 7 | 62 | .286 | 379 | 463 | 18 | .979 |
| 1976—Pittsburgh | Nat. | ★2B-SS | 157 | 654 | 59 | 168 | 31 | 9 | 2 | 60 | .257 | ★432 | 506 | 19 | .980 |
| Major League Totals | | | 749 | 2932 | 344 | 813 | 122 | 31 | 30 | 278 | .277 | 1815 | 2071 | 89 | .978 |

### CHAMPIONSHIP SERIES RECORD

| Year | Club | League | Pos. | G. | AB. | R. | H. | 2B. | 3B. | HR. | RBI. | B.A. | PO. | A. | E. | F.A. |
|------|------|--------|------|----|-----|----|----|-----|-----|-----|------|------|-----|----|----|------|
| 1972—Pittsburgh | Nat. | OF-2B | 5 | 21 | 2 | 6 | 0 | 0 | 0 | 1 | .286 | 17 | 1 | 0 | 1.000 |
| 1974—Pittsburgh | Nat. | 2B | 4 | 16 | 1 | 1 | 0 | 0 | 0 | 0 | .063 | 10 | 10 | 1 | .952 |
| 1975—Pittsburgh | Nat. | 2B-SS | 3 | 14 | 0 | 3 | 0 | 0 | 0 | 0 | .214 | 3 | 8 | 0 | 1.000 |
| Championship Series Totals | | | 12 | 51 | 3 | 10 | 0 | 0 | 0 | 1 | .196 | 30 | 19 | 1 | .980 |


# ROYLE ELDON STILLMAN

Born January 2, 1951, at Santa Monica, Calif.
Height, 5.10. Weight, 175.
Throws and bats lefthanded.
Hobbies—Art and surfing.
Attended El Camino College, Torrance, Calif.

Tied for California League lead in sacrifice flies with 8 in 1970.

| Year | Club | League | Pos. | G. | AB. | R. | H. | 2B. | 3B. | HR. | RBI. | B.A. | PO. | A. | E. | F.A. |
|------|------|--------|------|----|-----|----|----|-----|-----|-----|------|------|-----|----|----|------|
| 1969—Ogden | Pion. | OF | 62 | 191 | 39 | 63 | 14 | 3 | 6 | 38 | .330 | 71 | 4 | 6 | .926 |
| 1970—Bakersfield† | Calif. | OF | 103 | 336 | 68 | 115 | 15 | 4 | 9 | 76 | .342 | 139 | 3 | 4 | .973 |
| 1971—Albuquerque‡ | Texas | OF-1B | 133 | 438 | 59 | 117 | 26 | 8 | 8 | 64 | .267 | 602 | 35 | 6 | .991 |
| 1972—Asheville | South. | OF | 137 | 481 | 83 | 143 | 27 | 2 | 23 | 83 | .297 | ★256 | 9 | 9 | .967 |
| 1973—Rochester§ | Int. | OF | 94 | 322 | 35 | 114 | 16 | 4 | 1 | 41 | .354 | 123 | 7 | 5 | .963 |
| 1974—Rochester x | Int. | OF | 111 | 366 | 50 | 107 | 22 | 1 | 7 | 49 | .292 | 140 | 7 | 3 | .980 |
| 1975—Rochester | Int. | 1B-OF | 126 | 444 | 65 | 139 | ●30 | 2 | 14 | 75 | .313 | 598 | 38 | 6 | .991 |
| 1975—Baltimore | Amer. | OF | 13 | 14 | 1 | 6 | 0 | 0 | 0 | 1 | .429 | 3 | 0 | 0 | 1.000 |
| 1976—Baltimore | Amer. | PH-1B | 20 | 22 | 0 | 2 | 0 | 0 | 0 | 1 | .091 | 2 | 0 | 0 | 1.000 |
| 1976—Rochester y | Int. | O-1-PH | 56 | 185 | 26 | 54 | 8 | 1 | 5 | 44 | .292 | 56 | 4 | 1 | .984 |
| Major League Totals | | | 33 | 36 | 1 | 8 | 0 | 0 | 0 | 2 | .222 | 5 | 0 | 0 | 1.000 |

†On disabled list, May 4 through May 26, 1970.

‡Traded by Los Angeles Dodgers with Pitchers Doyle Alexander and Bob O'Brien and Catcher Sergio Robles to Baltimore Orioles for Outfielder Frank Robinson and Pitcher Pete Richert, December 2, 1971.

§On disabled list June 11 to July 5, 1973.

xOn temporary inactive list from beginning of season until April 30, 1974.

yPlayed out option year and granted free agency, November 1, 1976; signed as free agent with Chicago White Sox December 5, 1976.


# GORRELL ROBERT STINSON, III
## (Bob)

Born October 11, 1945, at Elkin, N. C.
Height, 5.11. Weight, 180.
Throws right and bats left and righthanded.
Hobbies—Hunting, fishing and horseback riding.
Attended Miami-Dade (North) Junior College, Miami, Fla.

Led Pioneer League outfielders in double plays with 4 in 1966.

Tied for Pacific Coast League in passed balls with 18 in 1969.

| Year Club League | Pos. | G. | AB. | R. | H. | 2B. | 3B. | HR. | RBI. | B.A. | PO. | A. | E. | F.A. |
|---|---|---|---|---|---|---|---|---|---|---|---|---|---|---|
| 1966—Santa Barbara ..Calif. | OF | 5 | 12 | 0 | 3 | 0 | 0 | 0 | 1 | .250 | 6 | 0 | 0 | 1.000 |
| 1966—Ogden ..............Pion. | OF | 56 | 176 | 34 | 50 | 7 | 2 | 5 | 33 | .284 | 71 | •8 | •11 | .878 |
| 1967—Albuquerque......Tex. | O-C-P | 120 | 387 | 47 | 92 | 15 | 3 | 6 | 42 | .238 | 234 | 6 | 7 | .972 |
| 1968—Albuquerque......Tex. | C-O-3 | 96 | 291 | 37 | 83 | 10 | 0 | 4 | 25 | .285 | 500 | 64 | 9 | .984 |
| 1969—Spokane ...........P. C. | C-OF | 117 | 349 | 47 | 98 | 9 | 5 | 6 | 54 | .281 | 477 | 51 | 8 | .985 |
| 1969—Los Angeles ......Nat. | C | 4 | 8 | 1 | 3 | 0 | 0 | 0 | 2 | .375 | 20 | 0 | 1 | .952 |
| 1970—Spokane ...........P. C. | •C-O-3 | 101 | 315 | 56 | 94 | 19 | 4 | 6 | 53 | .298 | 471 | 47 | 9 | •.983 |
| 1970—Los Angeles† ....Nat. | C | 4 | 3 | 1 | 0 | 0 | 0 | 0 | 0 | .000 | 3 | 0 | 0 | 1.000 |
| 1971—Tulsa ................A. A. | C-O-3-1 | 87 | 299 | 54 | 97 | 21 | 3 | 7 | 46 | .324 | 344 | 42 | 13 | .967 |
| 1971—St. Louis‡ .........Nat. | C-OF | 17 | 19 | 3 | 4 | 1 | 0 | 0 | 1 | .211 | 36 | 0 | 1 | .973 |
| 1972—Houston§ .........Nat. | C-OF | 27 | 35 | 3 | 6 | 1 | 0 | 0 | 2 | .171 | 26 | 2 | 1 | .966 |
| 1973—Montreal .........Nat. | C-3B | 48 | 111 | 12 | 29 | 6 | 1 | 3 | 12 | .261 | 174 | 9 | 4 | .979 |
| 1974—Montreal x y......Nat. | C | 38 | 87 | 4 | 15 | 2 | 0 | 1 | 6 | .172 | 122 | 14 | 0 | 1.000 |
| 1975—Kansas City ......Amer. | C-2-O-1 | 63 | 147 | 18 | 39 | 9 | 1 | 1 | 9 | .265 | 257 | 33 | 2 | .993 |
| 1976—Kansas City z ....Amer. | C | 79 | 209 | 26 | 55 | 7 | 1 | 2 | 25 | .263 | 304 | 30 | 7 | .979 |
| National League Totals ................. | | 138 | 263 | 24 | 57 | 10 | 1 | 4 | 23 | .217 | 381 | 25 | 7 | .983 |
| American League Totals ............... | | 142 | 356 | 44 | 94 | 16 | 2 | 3 | 34 | .264 | 561 | 63 | 9 | .986 |
| Major League Totals ..................... | | 280 | 619 | 68 | 151 | 26 | 3 | 7 | 57 | .244 | 942 | 88 | 16 | .985 |

†Traded with Infielder Ted Sizemore to St. Louis Cardinals for First Baseman Richie Allen, October 5, 1970.

‡Traded to Houston Astros for Infielder Orlando Martinez, November 3, 1971.

§Sold to Montreal Expos, March 27, 1973.

xOn supplemental disabled list from beginning of season until May 13, 1974.

ySold to Kansas City Royals, March 31, 1975; Royals sold Shortstop Rodney Scott to Expos, December 12, 1975, to complete deal.

zSelected by Seattle Mariners in American League expansion draft, November 5, 1976.

### CHAMPIONSHIP SERIES RECORD

| Year Club League | Pos. | G. | AB. | R. | H. | 2B. | 3B. | HR. | RBI. | B.A. | PO. | A. | E. | F.A. |
|---|---|---|---|---|---|---|---|---|---|---|---|---|---|---|
| 1976—Kansas City ......Amer. | PH-C | 2 | 1 | 0 | 0 | 0 | 0 | 0 | 0 | .000 | 0 | 0 | 0 | .000 |

### PITCHING RECORD

| Year Club League | G. | IP. | W. | L. | Pct. | H. | R. | ER. | SO. | BB. | ERA. |
|---|---|---|---|---|---|---|---|---|---|---|---|
| 1967—Albuquerque .....................Texas | 1 | 1 | 0 | 0 | .000 | 3 | 4 | 4 | 0 | 1 | 36.00 |

## TIMOTHY PAUL STODDARD
### (Tim)

Born January 24, 1953, at East Chicago, Ind.
Height, 6.07. Weight, 235.
Throws and bats righthanded.
Hobbies—Basketball and listening to music.
Attended North Carolina State University, Raleigh, N. C.

| Year Club League | G. | IP. | W. | L. | Pct. | H. | R. | ER. | SO. | BB. | ERA. |
|---|---|---|---|---|---|---|---|---|---|---|---|
| 1975—Knoxville ...........................Southern | 31 | 66 | 3 | 4 | .429 | 66 | 40 | 31 | 37 | 43 | 4.23 |
| 1975—Chicago................................American | 1 | 1 | 0 | 0 | .000 | 2 | 1 | 1 | 0 | 0 | 9.00 |
| 1976—Knoxville ...........................Southern | 20 | 140 | 9 | 8 | .529 | 147 | 55 | 45 | 62 | 60 | 2.89 |
| 1976—Iowa ................................Am. Assoc. | 12 | 29 | 0 | 2 | .000 | 37 | 20 | 18 | 20 | 15 | 5.59 |
| Major League Totals ............................ | 1 | 1 | 0 | 0 | .000 | 2 | 1 | 1 | 0 | 0 | 9.00 |

Listed on Chicago White Sox' 1977 spring roster.

## GERARD THOMAS STONE
### (Jerry)

Born May 6, 1952, at Burbank, Calif.
Height, 5.11. Weight, 180.
Throws right and bats left and righthanded.
Hobbies—Tennis and swimming.
Attended Loyola Marymount University, Los Angeles, Calif.

Led Texas League catchers in double plays with 8 in 1975.
Led Texas League catchers in passed balls with 24 and tied for lead in double plays with 9 in 1974.
Led Northwest League batters in walks with 80 in 1973.
Led Northwest League catchers in double plays with 6 in 1973.

| Year Club League | Pos. | G. | AB. | R. | H. | 2B. | 3B. | HR. | RBI. | B.A. | PO. | A. | E. | F.A. |
|---|---|---|---|---|---|---|---|---|---|---|---|---|---|---|
| 1973—Walla Walla ......N'west | C | 77 | 240 | 50 | 65 | 18 | 1 | •10 | 47 | .271 | •444 | •66 | 3 | •.994 |
| 1974—Alexandria ........Tex. | C | 123 | 404 | 47 | 109 | 21 | 1 | 4 | 43 | .270 | 388 | 43 | 8 | .982 |
| 1975—Alexandria ........Tex. | •C-3B | 120 | 389 | 34 | 111 | 21 | 2 | 4 | 58 | .285 | 385 | 37 | 6 | •.986 |
| 1976—Hawaii ..............P. C. | C | 61 | 179 | 27 | 46 | 4 | 2 | 4 | 22 | .257 | 290 | 22 | 5 | .984 |

Listed on San Diego Padres' 1977 spring roster.

---

## *DID YOU KNOW* —

That shortstop Tommy Thevenow of the St. Louis Cardinals had 10 hits in the 1926 World Series? His batting average was .416.

## STEVEN MICHAEL STONE
### (Steve)
Born July 14, 1947, at Cleveland, O.
Height, 5.10. Weight, 175.
Throws and bats righthanded.
Hobbies—Chess, reading, sports cars and golf.
Attended Kent State University, Kent, O.; received Bachelor of Science degree
in Education.

| Year    Club | League | G. | IP. | W. | L. | Pct. | H. | R. | ER. | SO. | BB. | ERA. |
|---|---|---|---|---|---|---|---|---|---|---|---|---|
| 1969–Fresno ..................California | California | 27 | 167 | 12 | ●13 | .480 | 170 | 82 | 67 | 184 | 57 | 3.61 |
| 1970–Amarillo ..............................Texas | Texas | 19 | 114 | 9 | 5 | .643 | 103 | 55 | 50 | 108 | 59 | 3.95 |
| 1970–Phoenix.............................P. Coast | P. Coast | 8 | 58 | 5 | 3 | .625 | 46 | 13 | 11 | 50 | 23 | 1.71 |
| 1971–Phoenix.............................P. Coast | P. Coast | 10 | 61 | 6 | 3 | .667 | 60 | 29 | 27 | 57 | 23 | 3.98 |
| 1971–San Francisco .....................National | National | 24 | 111 | 5 | 9 | .357 | 110 | 56 | 51 | 63 | 55 | 4.14 |
| 1972–San Francisco† ..................National | National | 27 | 124 | 6 | 8 | .429 | 97 | 48 | 41 | 85 | 49 | 2.98 |
| 1973–Chicago‡ ..............................American | American | 36 | 176 | 6 | 11 | .353 | 163 | 87 | 83 | 138 | .82 | 4.24 |
| 1974–Chicago...............................National | National | 38 | 170 | 8 | 6 | .571 | 185 | 92 | 78 | 90 | 64 | 4.13 |
| 1975–Chicago...............................National | National | 33 | 214 | 12 | 8 | .600 | 198 | 103 | 94 | 139 | 80 | 3.95 |
| 1976–Chicago§ ..........................National | National | 17 | 75 | 3 | 6 | .333 | 70 | 36 | 34 | 33 | 21 | 4.08 |
| National League Totals............................ | | 139 | 694 | 34 | 37 | .479 | 660 | 335 | 298 | 410 | 269 | 3.86 |
| American League Totals......................... | | 36 | 176 | 6 | 11 | .353 | 163 | 87 | 83 | 138 | 82 | 4.24 |
| Major League Totals ................................ | | 175 | 870 | 40 | 48 | .454 | 823 | 422 | 381 | 548 | 351 | 3.94 |

†Traded with Outfielder Ken Henderson to Chicago White Sox for Pitcher Tom Bradley, November 29, 1972.
‡Traded with Pitcher Ken Frailing, Catcher Steve Swisher and a player to be named later to Chicago Cubs for Third Baseman Ron Santo, December 11, 1973; White Sox sent Pitcher Jim Kremmel to Cubs, December 18, 1973, to complete deal.
§On disabled list, April 25 through July 2, 1976; played out option year and granted free agency, November 1, 1976; signed as free agent with Chicago White Sox, November 24, 1976.

## BRENT TERRY STROM
Born October 14, 1948, at San Diego, Calif.
Height, 6.03. Weight, 190.
Throws left and bats righthanded.
Attended San Diego City College, San Diego, Calif., and University of Southern California,
Los Angeles, Calif.; received Bachelor of Arts degree in Physical Education.

| Year    Club | League | G. | IP. | W. | L. | Pct. | H. | R. | ER. | SO. | BB. | ERA. |
|---|---|---|---|---|---|---|---|---|---|---|---|---|
| 1970–Visalia ...................California | California | 10 | 72 | 4 | 5 | .444 | 65 | 32 | 30 | 79 | 22 | 3.75 |
| 1971–Tidewater ..........................Int'national | Int'national | 11 | 74 | 6 | 2 | .750 | 65 | 24 | 21 | 60 | 22 | 2.55 |
| 1971–Memphis ...........................Texas | Texas | 15 | 106 | 7 | 3 | .700 | 100 | 43 | 36 | 87 | 35 | 3.06 |
| 1972–Tidewater ..........................Int'national | Int'national | 21 | 142 | 6 | 7 | .462 | 135 | 61 | 52 | 101 | 47 | 3.30 |
| 1972–New York† ..........................National | National | 11 | 30 | 0 | 3 | .000 | 34 | 25 | 23 | 20 | 15 | 6.90 |
| 1973–Cleveland‡ ..........................American | American | 27 | 123 | 2 | 10 | .167 | 134 | 73 | 63 | 91 | 47 | 4.61 |
| 1974–Oklahoma City §x .............Am. Assoc. | Am. Assoc. | 9 | 50 | 3 | 4 | .429 | 48 | 33 | 29 | 39 | 22 | 5.22 |
| 1974–Hawaii ..............................P. Coast | P. Coast | 13 | 68 | 3 | 7 | .300 | 75 | 54 | 52 | 60 | 32 | 6.88 |
| 1975–Hawaii ..............................P. Coast | P. Coast | 12 | 90 | 8 | 3 | .727 | 70 | 22 | 15 | 85 | 22 | 1.50 |
| 1975–San Diego ...........................National | National | 18 | 120 | 8 | 8 | .500 | 103 | 42 | 34 | 56 | 33 | 2.55 |
| 1976–San Diego ..........................National | National | 36 | 211 | 12 | 16 | .429 | 188 | 100 | 77 | 103 | 73 | 3.28 |
| National League Totals............................ | | 65 | 361 | 20 | 27 | .426 | 325 | 167 | 134 | 179 | 121 | 3.34 |
| American League Totals......................... | | 27 | 123 | 2 | 10 | .167 | 134 | 73 | 63 | 91 | 47 | 4.61 |
| Major League Totals ................................ | | 92 | 484 | 22 | 37 | .373 | 459 | 240 | 197 | 270 | 168 | 3.66 |

†Traded with Pitcher Bob Rauch to Cleveland Indians for Pitcher Phil Hennigan, November 27, 1972.
‡On disabled list, August 13 to September 6, 1973.
§On disabled list, April 16 to April 30, 1974.
xTraded with Pitcher Terry Ley by Cleveland Indians to San Diego Padres, June 21, 1974, to complete deal in which Indians obtained Pitcher Steve Arlin from Padres for two players to be named later, June 15, 1974.

## JOHN J. SUMMERS
### (Champ)
(Nicknamed by his father, an ex-boxer in the navy.)
Born June 15, 1948, at Bremerton, Wash.
Height, 6.02. Weight, 205.
Throws right and bats lefthanded.
Hobby—Billiards.
Attended Nicholls State University, Thibodaux, La., and Southern Illinois University at
Edwardsville, Edwardsville, Ill.

| Year    Club    League | Pos. | G. | AB. | R. | H. | 2B. | 3B. | HR. | RBI. | B.A. | PO. | A. | E. | F.A. |
|---|---|---|---|---|---|---|---|---|---|---|---|---|---|---|
| 1971–C. Bay-N. Bend..Northw. | OF | 65 | 222 | 36 | 56 | 8 | 5 | 3 | 34 | .252 | 90 | 6 | 6 | .941 |
| 1972–Burlington ........Midw. | OF-1B | 97 | 273 | 43 | 84 | 20 | 0 | 10 | 54 | .308 | 210 | 13 | 9 | .961 |
| 1973–Tucson .............P.C. | OF-1-3 | 94 | 288 | 49 | 96 | 15 | 5 | 8 | 45 | .333 | 97 | 4 | 3 | .971 |
| 1974–Tucson .............P.C. | OF | 94 | 334 | 49 | 88 | 13 | 6 | 10 | 59 | .263 | 139 | 4 | 3 | .979 |
| 1974–Oakland ...........Amer. | OF | 20 | 24 | 2 | 3 | 1 | 0 | 0 | 3 | .125 | 6 | 0 | 0 | 1.000 |
| 1975–Tucson† ...........P.C. | OF | 17 | 54 | 5 | 17 | 0 | 2 | 0 | 6 | .315 | 21 | 0 | 0 | 1.000 |
| 1975–Chicago ...........Nat. | OF | 76 | 91 | 14 | 21 | 5 | 1 | 1 | 16 | .231 | 16 | 0 | 2 | .889 |
| 1976–Chicago‡ .........Nat. | 1-OF-C | 83 | 126 | 11 | 26 | 2 | 0 | 3 | 13 | .206 | 95 | 5 | 1 | .990 |
| National League Totals ................. | | 159 | 217 | 25 | 47 | 7 | 1 | 4 | 29 | .216 | 111 | 5 | 3 | .975 |
| American League Totals ............... | | 20 | 24 | 2 | 3 | 1 | 0 | 0 | 3 | .125 | 6 | 0 | 0 | 1.000 |
| Major League Totals .................... | | 179 | 241 | 27 | 50 | 8 | 1 | 4 | 32 | .207 | 117 | 5 | 3 | .976 |

## JAMES HOWARD SUNDBERG
### (Jim)

Born May 18, 1951, at Galesburg, Ill.
Height, 6.00. Weight, 190.
Throws and bats righthanded.
Hobby—Hunting.
Attended University of Iowa, Iowa City, Iowa.

Tied American League record for most games, catcher, season, 155, in 1975.
Led American League catchers in double plays with 15 in 1974 and with 11 in 1976.
Led American League catchers in total chances with 909 in 1975 and with 822 in 1976.
Named catcher on THE SPORTING NEWS American League All-Star fielding team, 1976.

| Year Club | League | Pos. | G. | AB. | R. | H. | 2B. | 3B. | HR. | RBI. | B.A. | PO. | A. | E. | F.A. |
|---|---|---|---|---|---|---|---|---|---|---|---|---|---|---|---|
| 1973—Pittsfield | East. | C | 91 | 242 | 39 | 72 | 14 | 0 | 5 | 40 | .298 | 449 | 52 | 3 | •.994 |
| 1974—Texas | Amer. | C | 132 | 368 | 45 | 91 | 13 | 3 | 3 | 36 | .247 | 722 | 69 | 8 | .990 |
| 1975—Texas | Amer. | C | 155 | 472 | 45 | 94 | 9 | 0 | 6 | 36 | .199 | •791 | •101 | 17 | .981 |
| 1976—Texas | Amer. | C | 140 | 448 | 33 | 102 | 24 | 2 | 3 | 34 | .228 | •719 | •96 | 7 | •.991 |
| Major League Totals | | | 427 | 1288 | 123 | 287 | 46 | 5 | 12 | 106 | .223 | 2232 | 266 | 32 | .987 |

### ALL-STAR GAME RECORD
Member of American League All-Star Team in 1974 game; did not play.

## RICHARD LEE SUTCLIFFE
### (Rick)

Born June 21, 1956, at Independence, Mo.
Height, 6.07. Weight, 215.
Throws right and bats lefthanded.
Hobbies—Basketball and football.

Tied for Northwest League lead in shutouts with 2 in 1974.

| Year Club | League | G. | IP. | W. | L. | Pct. | H. | R. | ER. | SO. | BB. | ERA. |
|---|---|---|---|---|---|---|---|---|---|---|---|---|
| 1974—Bellingham | Northwest | 17 | 95 | 10 | 3 | .769 | 79 | 42 | 35 | 69 | 48 | 3.32 |
| 1975—Bakersfield | California | •28 | 193 | 8 | •16 | .333 | •214 | •115 | •89 | 91 | 68 | 4.15 |
| 1976—Waterbury | Eastern | 30 | 187 | 10 | 11 | .476 | •187 | 90 | 66 | 121 | 45 | 3.18 |
| 1976—Los Angeles | National | 1 | 5 | 0 | 0 | .000 | 2 | 0 | 0 | 3 | 1 | .000 |
| Major League Totals | | 1 | 5 | 0 | 0 | .000 | 2 | 0 | 0 | 3 | 1 | .000 |

## GARY LYNN SUTHERLAND

Born September 27, 1944, at Glendale, Calif.
Height, 6.00. Weight, 185.
Throws and bats righthanded.
Hobby—Golf.
Attended University of Southern California, Los Angeles, Calif.
Son of Ralph Sutherland, former pitcher in St. Louis Cardinals' organization, and brother of Darrell Sutherland, former pitcher with New York Mets and Cleveland Indians.

Led National League second basemen in double plays with 110 in 1969.
Led American Association second basemen in double plays with 114 in 1973.

| Year Club | League | Pos. | G. | AB. | R. | H. | 2B. | 3B. | HR. | RBI. | B.A. | PO. | A. | E. | F.A. |
|---|---|---|---|---|---|---|---|---|---|---|---|---|---|---|---|
| 1965—Chattanooga | South. | 2B | •141 | 540 | 59 | 154 | 25 | 5 | 3 | 60 | .285 | 297 | 372 | 20 | .971 |
| 1966—San Diego | P.C. | •SS-2B | 140 | 532 | 57 | 135 | 27 | 1 | 4 | 54 | .254 | 215 | 445 | •38 | .946 |
| 1966—Philadelphia | Nat. | SS | 3 | 3 | 0 | 0 | 0 | 0 | 0 | 0 | .000 | 1 | 2 | 0 | 1.000 |
| 1967—Philadelphia | Nat. | SS-OF | 103 | 231 | 23 | 57 | 12 | 1 | 1 | 19 | .247 | 110 | 115 | 15 | .938 |
| 1968—Philadelphia† | Nat. | 2-3-S-OF | 67 | 138 | 16 | 38 | 7 | 0 | 0 | 15 | .275 | 48 | 73 | 3 | .976 |
| 1969—Montreal | Nat. | 2-SS-OF | 141 | 544 | 63 | 130 | 26 | 1 | 3 | 35 | .239 | 328 | 389 | 21 | .972 |
| 1970—Montreal | Nat. | 2-SS-3 | 116 | 359 | 37 | 74 | 10 | 0 | 3 | 26 | .206 | 182 | 264 | 12 | .974 |
| 1971—Montreal | Nat. | 2-S-O-3 | 111 | 304 | 25 | 78 | 7 | 2 | 4 | 26 | .257 | 157 | 253 | 21 | .951 |
| 1972—Peninsula‡ | Int. | 2-3-1 | 53 | 186 | 29 | 53 | 11 | 1 | 3 | 13 | .285 | 115 | 150 | 12 | .957 |
| 1972—Oklahoma City | A.A. | 2B-3B | 79 | 284 | 39 | 85 | 15 | 3 | 0 | 31 | .299 | 165 | 215 | 12 | .969 |
| 1972—Houston | Nat. | 3B-2B | 5 | 8 | 0 | 1 | 0 | 0 | 0 | 1 | .125 | 1 | 2 | 0 | 1.000 |
| 1973—Denver | A.A. | 2B | 134 | •572 | 85 | 168 | •36 | 4 | 3 | 80 | .294 | 307 | •420 | 15 | •.980 |
| 1973—Houston§ | Nat. | 2B-SS | 16 | 54 | 8 | 14 | 5 | 0 | 0 | 3 | .259 | 37 | 31 | 2 | .971 |
| 1974—Detroit | Amer. | 2-SS-3 | 149 | 619 | 60 | 157 | 20 | 1 | 5 | 49 | .254 | 340 | 380 | 18 | .976 |
| 1975—Detroit | Amer. | 2B | 129 | 503 | 51 | 130 | 12 | 3 | 6 | 39 | .258 | 278 | 365 | 21 | .968 |
| 1976—Det. x-Milw. y | Amer. | 2-1-DH | 101 | 232 | 19 | 49 | 7 | 2 | 1 | 15 | .211 | 161 | 204 | 11 | .971 |
| American League Totals | | | 379 | 1354 | 130 | 336 | 39 | 6 | 12 | 103 | .248 | 779 | 949 | 50 | .972 |
| National League Totals | | | 562 | 1641 | 172 | 392 | 67 | 4 | 11 | 125 | .239 | 864 | 1129 | 74 | .964 |
| Major League Totals | | | 941 | 2995 | 302 | 728 | 106 | 10 | 23 | 228 | .243 | 1643 | 2078 | 124 | .968 |

†Selected by Montreal Expos from Philadelphia Phillies in expansion draft, October 14, 1968.
‡Sold by Montreal Expos to Oklahoma City (Houston Astros' organization), June 13, 1972.
§Traded with Pitcher Jim Ray to Detroit Tigers for Pitcher Fred Scherman and a player to be named later, December 3, 1973.
xTraded to Milwaukee Brewers for Second Baseman Pedro Garcia, June 10, 1976.
yOn disabled list, June 20 through July 7, 1976; released, February 17, 1977; signed as free agent with San Diego Padres, April 1, 1977.

# HOWARD BRUCE SUTTER

Name pronounced Suit-er.
(Known by middle name.)

Born January 8, 1953, at Lancaster, Pa.
Height, 6.02. Weight, 190.
Throws and bats righthanded.
Hobby—Hunting.

Tied for Texas League lead in saves with 13 in 1975.

| Year Club | League | G. | IP. | W. | L. | Pct. | H. | R. | ER. | SO. | BB. | ERA. |
|---|---|---|---|---|---|---|---|---|---|---|---|---|
| 1972—Bradenton Cubs | Gulf Coast | 2 | 5 | 0 | 0 | .000 | 3 | 0 | 0 | 4 | 0 | 0.00 |
| 1973—Quincy | Midwest | 40 | 85 | 3 | 3 | .500 | 94 | 52 | 39 | 76 | 27 | 4.13 |
| 1974—Key West† | Florida St. | 18 | 40 | 1 | 5 | .167 | 26 | 9 | 6 | 50 | 13 | 1.35 |
| 1974—Midland | Texas | 8 | 25 | 1 | 2 | .333 | 22 | 6 | 4 | 14 | 6 | 1.44 |
| 1975—Midland | Texas | 41 | 67 | 5 | 7 | .417 | 64 | 26 | 16 | 50 | 21 | 2.15 |
| 1976—Wichita | Am. Assoc. | 7 | 12 | 2 | 1 | .667 | 9 | 3 | 2 | 16 | 4 | 1.50 |
| 1976—Chicago | National | 52 | 83 | 6 | 3 | .667 | 63 | 27 | 25 | 73 | 26 | 2.71 |
| Major League Totals | | 52 | 83 | 6 | 3 | .667 | 63 | 27 | 25 | 73 | 26 | 2.71 |

†On disabled list, May 22, to July 28, 1974.

# DONALD HOWARD SUTTON
## (Don)

Born April 2, 1945, at Clio, Ala.
Height, 6.01. Weight, 190.
Throws and bats righthanded.
Hobbies—All other sports.
Attended Mississippi College, Clinton, Miss., and Whittier College, Whittier, Calif.

Tied National League record for most wild pitches, inning (3), (4th inn.) September 11, 1970.
Led National League in shutouts with 9 in 1972.
Led National League pitchers in games started with 40 in 1974.
Named National League Rookie Pitcher of the Year by THE SPORTING NEWS, 1966.
Named righthanded pitcher on THE SPORTING NEWS National League All-Star Team, 1976.
Named Player of the Year in Texas League, 1965.

| Year Club | League | G. | IP. | W. | L. | Pct. | H. | R. | ER. | SO. | BB. | ERA. |
|---|---|---|---|---|---|---|---|---|---|---|---|---|
| 1965—Santa Barbara | California | 10 | 84 | 8 | 1 | .889 | 59 | 18 | 14 | 101 | 15 | 1.50 |
| 1965—Albuquerque | Texas | 21 | 165 | 15 | 6 | •.714 | 151 | 60 | 51 | 138 | 30 | 2.78 |
| 1966—Los Angeles | National | 37 | 226 | 12 | 12 | .500 | 192 | 82 | 75 | 209 | 52 | 2.99 |
| 1967—Los Angeles | National | 37 | 233 | 11 | 15 | .423 | 223 | 106 | 102 | 169 | 57 | 3.94 |
| 1968—Spokane | P. Coast | 2 | 16 | 1 | 1 | .500 | 11 | 2 | 2 | 19 | 5 | 1.13 |
| 1968—Los Angeles | National | 35 | 208 | 11 | 15 | .423 | 179 | 64 | 60 | 162 | 59 | 2.60 |
| 1969—Los Angeles | National | 41 | 293 | 17 | 18 | .486 | 269 | 123 | 113 | 217 | 91 | 3.47 |
| 1970—Los Angeles | National | 38 | 260 | 15 | 13 | .536 | 251 | 127 | •118 | 201 | 78 | 4.08 |
| 1971—Los Angeles | National | 38 | 265 | 17 | 12 | .586 | 231 | 85 | 75 | 194 | 55 | 2.55 |
| 1972—Los Angeles | National | 33 | 273 | 19 | 9 | .679 | 186 | 78 | 63 | 207 | 63 | 2.08 |
| 1973—Los Angeles | National | 33 | 256 | 18 | 10 | .643 | 196 | 78 | 69 | 200 | 56 | 2.43 |
| 1974—Los Angeles | National | 40 | 276 | 19 | 9 | .679 | 241 | 111 | 99 | 179 | 80 | 3.23 |
| 1975—Los Angeles | National | 35 | 254 | 16 | 13 | .552 | 202 | 87 | 81 | 175 | 62 | 2.87 |
| 1976—Los Angeles | National | 35 | 268 | 21 | 10 | .677 | 231 | 98 | 91 | 161 | 82 | 3.06 |
| Major League Totals | | 402 | 2812 | 176 | 136 | .564 | 2401 | 1039 | 946 | 2074 | 735 | 3.03 |

### CHAMPIONSHIP SERIES RECORD

| Year Club | League | G. | IP. | W. | L. | Pct. | H. | R. | ER. | SO. | BB. | ERA. |
|---|---|---|---|---|---|---|---|---|---|---|---|---|
| 1974—Los Angeles | National | 2 | 17 | 2 | 0 | 1.000 | 7 | 1 | 1 | 13 | 2 | 0.53 |

### WORLD SERIES RECORD

| Year Club | League | G. | IP. | W. | L. | Pct. | H. | R. | ER. | SO. | BB. | ERA. |
|---|---|---|---|---|---|---|---|---|---|---|---|---|
| 1974—Los Angeles | National | 2 | 13 | 1 | 0 | 1.000 | 9 | 4 | 4 | 12 | 3 | 2.77 |

### ALL-STAR GAME RECORD

| Year League | | IP. | W. | L. | Pct. | H. | R. | ER. | SO. | BB. | ERA. |
|---|---|---|---|---|---|---|---|---|---|---|---|
| 1972—National | | 2 | 0 | 0 | .000 | 1 | 0 | 0 | 2 | 0 | 0.00 |
| 1973—National | | 1 | 0 | 0 | .000 | 0 | 0 | 0 | 0 | 0 | 0.00 |
| 1975—National | | 2 | 0 | 0 | .000 | 3 | 0 | 0 | 1 | 0 | 0.00 |
| All-Star Game Totals | | 5 | 0 | 0 | .000 | 4 | 0 | 0 | 3 | 0 | 0.00 |

# JOHNNY IKE SUTTON
## (John)

Born November 13, 1952, at Dallas, Texas.
Height, 5.11. Weight, 185.
Throws and bats righthanded.
Hobbies—Hunting, fishing and other outdoor activities.
Attended University of Plano, Plano, Tex.

| Year Club | League | G. | IP. | W. | L. | Pct. | H. | R. | ER. | SO. | BB. | ERA. |
|---|---|---|---|---|---|---|---|---|---|---|---|---|
| 1974—Gastonia | W. Carol. | 24 | 169 | 12 | 8 | .600 | 157 | 74 | 50 | 130 | 68 | 2.66 |
| 1975—Pittsfield | Eastern | 49 | 81 | 7 | 4 | .636 | 63 | 26 | 22 | 32 | 44 | 2.44 |
| 1976—Sacramento† | P. Coast | •59 | 99 | 10 | 5 | .667 | 116 | 79 | 59 | 47 | 53 | 5.36 |

†Traded by Texas Rangers' organization to St. Louis Cardinals' organization for Pitcher Mike Wallace, October 22, 1976.
Listed on St. Louis Cardinals' 1977 spring roster.

## CRAIG STEVEN SWAN

Born November 30, 1950, at Van Nuys, Calif.
Height, 6.03. Weight, 220.
Throws and bats righthanded.
Attended Arizona State University, Tempe, Ariz.

Led International League in complete games with 13 in 1975.
Tied for International League lead in shutouts with 4 in 1973.

| Year | Club | League | G. | IP. | W. | L. | Pct. | H. | R. | ER. | SO. | BB. | ERA. |
|------|------|--------|-----|-----|----|----|------|----|----|-----|-----|-----|------|
| 1972—Memphis | | Texas | 14 | 108 | 7 | 3 | .700 | 102 | 28 | 27 | 81 | 26 | 2.25 |
| 1973—Tidewater† | | Int'national | 16 | 100 | 7 | 5 | .583 | 88 | 30 | 26 | 79 | 25 | 2.34 |
| 1973—New York | | National | 3 | 8 | 0 | 1 | .000 | 16 | 9 | 8 | 4 | 2 | 9.00 |
| 1974—Tidewater | | Int'national | 9 | 51 | 2 | 3 | .400 | 53 | 29 | 27 | 31 | 17 | 4.76 |
| 1974—New York‡ | | National | 7 | 30 | 1 | 3 | .250 | 28 | 19 | 15 | 10 | 21 | 4.50 |
| 1975—Tidewater | | Int'national | 26 | 165 | 13 | 7 | .650 | 136 | 48 | 44 | 111 | 38 | 2.40 |
| 1975—New York | | National | 6 | 31 | 1 | 3 | .250 | 38 | 22 | 22 | 19 | 13 | 6.39 |
| 1976—New York | | National | 23 | 132 | 6 | 9 | .400 | 129 | 64 | 52 | 89 | 44 | 3.55 |
| Major League Totals | | | 39 | 201 | 8 | 16 | .333 | 211 | 114 | 97 | 122 | 80 | 4.34 |

†On disabled list, June 5 to June 25, 1973.
‡On disabled list, June 14 to July 22, 1974.

## STEVEN EUGENE SWISHER
### (Steve)

Born August 9, 1951, at Parkersburg, W. Va.
Height, 6.02. Weight, 205.
Throws and bats righthanded.
Attended Ohio University, Athens, O.; received Bachelor of science degree in Education.

| Year | Club | League | Pos. | G. | AB. | R. | H. | 2B. | 3B. | HR. | RBI. | B.A. | PO. | A. | E. | F.A. |
|------|------|--------|------|-----|-----|----|----|-----|-----|-----|------|------|-----|----|----|------|
| 1973—Knoxville | | South. | C | 54 | 161 | 19 | 34 | 5 | 0 | 6 | 18 | .211 | 235 | 25 | 4 | .985 |
| 1973—Iowa† | | A. A. | C | 6 | 21 | 1 | 6 | 0 | 0 | 1 | 1 | .286 | 30 | 4 | 0 | 1.000 |
| 1974—Wichita | | A. A. | C | 52 | 153 | 15 | 30 | 4 | 1 | 3 | 13 | .196 | 284 | 33 | •11 | .966 |
| 1974—Chicago | | Nat. | C | 90 | 280 | 21 | 60 | 5 | 0 | 5 | 27 | .214 | 493 | 50 | 7 | .987 |
| 1975—Wichita | | A. A. | C | 7 | 21 | 8 | 6 | 0 | 0 | 4 | 9 | .286 | 27 | 4 | 1 | .969 |
| 1975—Chicago | | Nat. | C | 93 | 254 | 20 | 54 | 16 | 2 | 1 | 22 | .213 | 426 | 36 | 10 | .979 |
| 1976—Chicago | | Nat. | C | 109 | 377 | 25 | 89 | 13 | 3 | 5 | 42 | .236 | 574 | 49 | 11 | .983 |
| Major League Totals | | | | 292 | 911 | 66 | 203 | 34 | 5 | 11 | 91 | .223 | 1493 | 135 | 28 | .983 |

†Traded with Pitchers Ken Frailing and Steve Stone and a player to be named later by Chicago White Sox to Chicago Cubs for Third Baseman Ron Santo, December 11, 1973; White Sox sent Pitcher Jim Kremmel to Cubs, December 18, 1973, to complete deal.

## ROBERT JOSEPH SYKES
### (Bob)

Born December 11, 1954, at Neptune, N. J.
Height, 6.01. Weight, 195.
Throws and bats lefthanded.
Attended Miami-Dade (North) Community College, Miami, Fla.

Led Appalachian League in shutouts with 6 and complete games with 7 in 1974.
Tied for Appalachian League lead in games started with 13 in 1974.

| Year | Club | League | G. | IP. | W. | L. | Pct. | H. | R. | ER. | SO. | BB. | ERA. |
|------|------|--------|-----|-----|----|----|------|----|----|-----|-----|-----|------|
| 1974—Bristol | | Ap'lachian | 14 | •101 | •11 | 0 | •1.000 | 52 | 18 | 12 | 96 | 31 | •1.07 |
| 1975—Montgomery | | Southern | 27 | 191 | •14 | 10 | .583 | 180 | 63 | 67 | 88 | 87 | 3.16 |
| 1976—Evansville† | | Am. Assoc. | 24 | 118 | 8 | 11 | .421 | 137 | 71 | 56 | 70 | 71 | 4.27 |

†On disabled list, June 10 through June 21, 1976.
Invited to Detroit Tigers' 1977 spring camp.

## JERRY LYNN TABB

Born March 17, 1952, at Altus, Okla.
Height, 6.02. Weight, 195.
Throws right and bats lefthanded.
Hobbies—Rock collecting, golf and hunting.
Attended University of Tulsa, Tulsa, Okla., received Bachelor of Science degree in Petroleum Engineering.

| Year | Club | League | Pos. | G. | AB. | R. | H. | 2B. | 3B. | HR. | RBI. | B.A. | PO. | A. | E. | F.A. |
|------|------|--------|------|-----|-----|----|-----|-----|-----|-----|------|------|------|----|----|------|
| 1973—Midland | | Texas | 1B | 76 | 260 | 56 | 71 | 14 | 2 | 12 | 44 | .273 | 772 | 41 | 7 | .991 |
| 1974—Midland | | Texas | 1B | 123 | 460 | 72 | 121 | 16 | 3 | •29 | 105 | .263 | 1079 | 69 | 12 | •.990 |
| 1974—Wichita | | A. A. | 1B | 11 | 47 | 10 | 21 | 3 | 3 | 2 | 7 | .447 | 93 | 3 | 0 | 1.000 |
| 1975—Wichita† | | A. A. | 1B | 97 | 355 | 57 | 86 | 18 | 1 | 7 | 48 | .242 | 785 | 49 | 10 | .988 |
| 1976—Wichita | | A. A. | 1B | 124 | 395 | 60 | 114 | 21 | 1 | 19 | 67 | .289 | 1016 | 46 | 11 | .990 |
| 1976—Chicago‡ | | Nat. | 1B | 11 | 24 | 2 | 7 | 0 | 0 | 0 | 0 | .292 | 52 | 2 | 0 | 1.000 |
| Major League Totals | | | | 11 | 24 | 2 | 7 | 0 | 0 | 0 | 0 | .292 | 52 | 2 | 0 | 1.000 |

†On disabled list, July 8 through August 9, 1975.
‡Sold to Oakland A's, March 15, 1977.

## JOHN FELIX TAMARGO, SR.

Born November 7, 1951, at Tampa, Fla.
Height, 5.10. Weight, 170.
Throws right and bats left and righthanded.
Hobbies—Golf and tennis.
Attended Miami-Dade (North) Community College, Miami, Fla., and
Georgia Southern College, Statesboro, Ga.; received Bachelor
of Arts degree in Business Administration.

| Year | Club | League | Pos. | G. | AB. | R. | H. | 2B. | 3B. | HR. | RBI. | B.A. | PO. | A. | E. | F.A. |
|------|------|--------|------|-----|-----|-----|-----|-----|-----|-----|------|------|------|-----|-----|------|
| 1973—St. Petersburg | ..Fla. St. | | C | 68 | 220 | 24 | 57 | 3 | 2 | 2 | 32 | .259 | 404 | 32 | 4 | .991 |
| 1974—Modesto† | .........Calif. | | C | 26 | 90 | 16 | 24 | 5 | 0 | 2 | 9 | .267 | 166 | 15 | 5 | .973 |
| 1974—Arkansas‡ | ........Tex. | | C | 1 | 1 | 0 | 0 | 0 | 0 | 0 | 0 | .000 | 4 | 1 | 0 | 1.000 |
| 1974—St. Petersburg§ | ..Fla. St. | | DH | 8 | 25 | 5 | 7 | 1 | 0 | 1 | 5 | .280 | 0 | 0 | 0 | .000 |
| 1975—Arkansas | .........Tex. | | C | 39 | 120 | 20 | 31 | 7 | 1 | 1 | 11 | .258 | 167 | 20 | 4 | .979 |
| 1975—Tulsa | ...............A. A. | | C | 53 | 164 | 27 | 47 | 12 | 0 | 5 | 23 | .287 | 231 | 19 | 2 | .992 |
| 1976—Tulsa | ...............A. A. | | C-1B | 113 | 346 | 44 | 96 | 21 | 3 | 8 | 48 | .277 | 663 | 45 | 19 | .974 |
| 1976—St. Louis | .........Nat. | | C | 10 | 10 | 2 | 3 | 0 | 0 | 0 | 1 | .300 | 4 | 0 | 0 | 1.000 |
| Major League Totals | ...................... | | | 10 | 10 | 2 | 3 | 0 | 0 | 0 | 1 | .300 | 4 | 0 | 0 | 1.000 |

†On disabled list, April 29 to June 4, 1974.
‡On disabled list, June 19 to June 30, 1974.
§On disabled list, July 1 to August 9, 1974.

## FRANK DARYL TANANA

Last name rhymes with banana.

Born July 3, 1953, at Detroit, Mich.
Height, 6.03. Weight, 195.
Throws and bats lefthanded.
Hobbies—Golf and all physical activities.
Attended California State University at Fullerton, Calif.
Son of Frank Richard Tanana, former outfielder in Cleveland Indians' organization.

Tied major league record for most strikeouts, lefthanded pitcher, game, 17, June 21, 1975 (1st game of doubleheader).
Led Texas League pitchers in complete games with 15 in 1973.
Named American League Rookie Pitcher of the Year by THE SPORTING NEWS, 1974.
Named Texas League Pitcher of the Year in 1973.
Named lefthanded pitcher on THE SPORTING NEWS American League All-Star Team, 1976.

| Year | Club | League | G. | IP. | W. | L. | Pct. | H. | R. | ER. | SO. | BB. | ERA. |
|------|------|--------|-----|-----|-----|-----|------|-----|-----|-----|-----|-----|------|
| 1971—Idaho Falls† | ........................ | Pioneer | .... | .... | .... | .... | .... | .... | .... | .... | .... | .... | .... |
| 1972—Quad Cities | ......................... | Midwest | 19 | 129 | 7 | 2 | .778 | 111 | 48 | 40 | 134 | 57 | 2.79 |
| 1973—El Paso | .............................. | Texas | 26 | •206 | 16 | 6 | .727 | 170 | 72 | 62 | •197 | 63 | 2.71 |
| 1973—Salt Lake City | ..................... | P. Coast | 2 | 14 | 1 | 0 | 1.000 | 11 | 5 | 4 | 15 | 2 | 2.57 |
| 1973—California | ........................... | American | 4 | 26 | 2 | 2 | .500 | 20 | 11 | 9 | 22 | 8 | 3.12 |
| 1974—California | ........................... | American | 39 | 269 | 14 | 19 | .424 | 262 | 104 | 93 | 180 | 77 | 3.11 |
| 1975—California | ........................... | American | 34 | 257 | 16 | 9 | .640 | 211 | 80 | 75 | •269 | 73 | 2.63 |
| 1976—California | ........................... | American | 34 | 288 | 19 | 10 | .655 | 212 | 88 | 78 | 261 | 73 | 2.44 |
| Major League Totals | ............................... | | 111 | 840 | 51 | 40 | .560 | 705 | 283 | 255 | 732 | 231 | 2.73 |

†Appeared in one game as pinch runner (did not pitch due to a sore arm).

### ALL-STAR GAME RECORD

| Year | League | IP. | W. | L. | Pct. | H. | R. | ER. | SO. | BB. | ERA. |
|------|--------|-----|-----|-----|------|-----|-----|-----|-----|-----|------|
| 1976—American | ..................................................... | 2 | 0 | 0 | .000 | 3 | 3 | 3 | 0 | 1 | 6.00 |

## RANDALL LEE TATE
### (Randy)

Born October 23, 1952, at Florence, Ala.
Height, 6.03. Weight, 190.
Throws and bats righthanded.
Hobbies—Hunting and fishing.
Attended Calhoun Junior College, Decatur, Ala.

Pitched seven-inning, 2-0 no-hit victory against Ft. Lauderdale, June 8, 1973.
Led Appalachian League in wild pitches with 20 in 1972 and Western Carolinas League with 23 in 1974.

| Year | Club | League | G. | IP. | W. | L. | Pct. | H. | R. | ER. | SO. | BB. | ERA. |
|------|------|--------|-----|-----|-----|-----|------|-----|-----|-----|-----|-----|------|
| 1972—Marion | ..................... | Ap'alachian | 14 | 60 | 0 | •9 | .000 | 65 | 68 | 40 | 56 | 54 | 6.00 |
| 1973—Pompano Beach | .................. | Florida St. | 21 | 117 | 4 | 10 | .286 | 105 | 80 | 57 | 82 | 88 | 4.38 |
| 1974—Anderson | ........................... | W. Carol. | 25 | 159 | 7 | 11 | .389 | 111 | 82 | 65 | 153 | •150 | 3.68 |
| 1974—Tidewater | ........................... | Int'national | 2 | 17 | 2 | 0 | 1.000 | 10 | 2 | 2 | 9 | 8 | 1.06 |
| 1975—New York | ........................... | National | 26 | 138 | 5 | 13 | .278 | 121 | 73 | 68 | 99 | 86 | 4.43 |
| 1976—Tidewater | ........................... | Int'national | 27 | 122 | 7 | 14 | .333 | 136 | 96 | 84 | 58 | 93 | 6.20 |
| Major League Totals | ............................... | | 26 | 138 | 5 | 13 | .278 | 121 | 73 | 68 | 99 | 86 | 4.43 |

---

## DID YOU KNOW —

That Moe Drabowsky, pitching for Baltimore, struck out 11 batters in the last six and two-thirds innings of the World Series game played October 5, 1966?

## ALEJANDRO A. TAVERAS (BETANCES)
### (Alex)

Born October 9, 1955, at Tamboril, Santiago, Dominican Republic.
Height, 5.10. Weight, 155.
Throws and bats righthanded.
Led Midwest League in being caught stealing with 14 in 1974.

| Year Club League | Pos. | G. | AB. | R. | H. | 2B. | 3B. | HR. | RBI. | B.A. | PO. | A. | E. | F.A. |
|---|---|---|---|---|---|---|---|---|---|---|---|---|---|---|
| 1974—Cedar Rapids ....Midw. | SS | 110 | 383 | 64 | 109 | 13 | 3 | 1 | 32 | .285 | 163 | 260 | 33 | .928 |
| 1975—Iowa.................A. A. | SS | 135 | 489 | 58 | 125 | 15 | 4 | 0 | 36 | .256 | 207 | 385 | 33 | .947 |
| 1976—Memphis ..........Int. | SS | 128 | 447 | 70 | 103 | 9 | 6 | 0 | 42 | .230 | 211 | 367 | 30 | .951 |
| 1976—Houston ...........Nat. | SS-2B | 14 | 46 | 3 | 10 | 0 | 0 | 0 | 2 | .217 | 26 | 44 | 3 | .960 |
| Major League Totals ..................... | | 14 | 46 | 3 | 10 | 0 | 0 | 0 | 2 | .217 | 26 | 44 | 3 | .960 |

## FRANKLIN TAVERAS (FABIAN)
### (Frank)

Born December 24, 1950, at Villa Vasquez, Dominican Republic.
Height, 6.00. Weight, 160.
Throws and bats righthanded.
Led Western Carolinas League shortstops in double plays with 56 in 1970 and International League with 96 in 1973.
Major League stolen bases: 1974 (13), 1975 (17), 1976 (58). Total—88.

| Year Club League | Pos. | G. | AB. | R. | H. | 2B. | 3B. | HR. | RBI. | B.A. | PO. | A. | E. | F.A. |
|---|---|---|---|---|---|---|---|---|---|---|---|---|---|---|
| 1968—Clinton ..............Midw. | 2-3-S | 21 | 58 | 7 | 12 | 1 | 0 | 0 | 5 | .207 | 28 | 34 | 12 | .838 |
| 1968—Brad'ton Pir. ....Gulf C. | SS | 14 | 50 | 18 | 17 | 0 | 2 | 0 | 8 | .340 | 21 | 36 | 12 | .826 |
| 1968—Salem...............Carol. | 2B-SS | 14 | 26 | 4 | 5 | 0 | 0 | 0 | 2 | .192 | 10 | 19 | 1 | .967 |
| 1969—Salem...............Carol. | 2B | 20 | 57 | 5 | 11 | 0 | 2 | 0 | 4 | .193 | 29 | 46 | 7 | .915 |
| 1969—Gastonia...........W. Car. | 2-S | 80 | 308 | 40 | 63 | 2 | 3 | 0 | 15 | .205 | 147 | 228 | 26 | .935 |
| 1969—Geneva..............NYP | S-2-3 | 13 | 54 | 9 | 19 | 1 | 1 | 0 | 6 | .352 | 17 | 39 | 9 | .862 |
| 1970—Gastonia ..........W. Car. | SS | •122 | 442 | 67 | 115 | 13 | 2 | 1 | 41 | .260 | •193 | •337 | 37 | •.935 |
| 1971—Waterbury ........East. | SS | 87 | 314 | 52 | 65 | 12 | 2 | 2 | 19 | .207 | 112 | 258 | 25 | .937 |
| 1971—Charleston ........Int. | SS | 48 | 146 | 19 | 39 | 2 | 2 | 0 | 11 | .267 | 65 | 127 | 9 | .955 |
| 1971—Pittsburgh ........Nat. | PR | 1 | 0 | 0 | 0 | 0 | 0 | 0 | 0 | .000 | 0 | 0 | 0 | .000 |
| 1972—Charleston ........Int. | SS | 133 | 455 | 52 | 112 | 14 | 3 | 1 | 46 | .246 | 202 | 411 | 30 | •.953 |
| 1972—Pittsburgh ........Nat. | SS | 4 | 3 | 0 | 0 | 0 | 0 | 0 | 0 | .000 | 2 | 2 | 0 | 1.000 |
| 1973—Charleston ........Int. | •S-3-O | 145 | 462 | 51 | 112 | 7 | 3 | 2 | 44 | .242 | •222 | •429 | •43 | .938 |
| 1974—Pittsburgh ........Nat. | SS | 126 | 333 | 33 | 82 | 4 | 2 | 0 | 26 | .246 | 170 | 321 | 31 | .941 |
| 1975—Pittsburgh ........Nat. | SS | 134 | 378 | 44 | 80 | 9 | 4 | 0 | 23 | .212 | 200 | 369 | 28 | .953 |
| 1976—Pittsburgh ........Nat. | SS | 144 | 519 | 76 | 134 | 8 | 6 | 0 | 24 | .258 | 210 | 481 | 35 | .952 |
| Major League Totals ..................... | | 409 | 1233 | 153 | 296 | 21 | 12 | 0 | 73 | .240 | 582 | 1173 | 94 | .951 |

CHAMPIONSHIP SERIES RECORD

| Year Club League | Pos. | G. | AB. | R. | H. | 2B. | 3B. | HR. | RBI. | B.A. | PO. | A. | E. | F.A. |
|---|---|---|---|---|---|---|---|---|---|---|---|---|---|---|
| 1974—Pittsburgh ........Nat. | SS | 2 | 2 | 0 | 0 | 0 | 0 | 0 | 0 | .000 | 2 | 1 | 0 | 1.000 |
| 1975—Pittsburgh ........Nat. | SS | 3 | 7 | 0 | 1 | 0 | 0 | 0 | 1 | .143 | 4 | 6 | 0 | 1.000 |
| Championship Series Totals ........... | | 5 | 9 | 0 | 1 | 0 | 0 | 0 | 1 | .111 | 6 | 7 | 0 | 1.000 |

## BRUCE BELL TAYLOR

Born April 16, 1953, at Holden, Mass.
Height, 6.00. Weight, 178.
Throws and bats righthanded.
Hobbies—Hunting and hiking.
Led Eastern League in saves with 14 in 1974.

| Year Club League | G. | IP. | W. | L. | Pct. | H. | R. | ER. | SO. | BB. | ERA. |
|---|---|---|---|---|---|---|---|---|---|---|---|
| 1973—Tampa ...............................Florida St. | 17 | 74 | 5 | 6 | .455 | 62 | 16 | 12 | 49 | 25 | 1.46 |
| 1973—Three Rivers.......................Eastern | 18 | 34 | 4 | 3 | .571 | 24 | 14 | 12 | 27 | 16 | 3.18 |
| 1974—Three Rivers.......................Eastern | •59 | 101 | 9 | 4 | .692 | 69 | 32 | 24 | 101 | 74 | 2.14 |
| 1974—Indianapolis .......................Am. Assoc. | 13 | 15 | 0 | 2 | .000 | 10 | 4 | 1 | 11 | 7 | 0.60 |
| 1975—Indianapolis† ......................Am. Assoc. | 51 | 81 | 8 | 1 | .889 | 65 | 22 | 20 | 61 | 61 | 2.22 |
| 1976—Evansville ..........................Am. Assoc. | 47 | 68 | 6 | 7 | .462 | 60 | 35 | 31 | 58 | 52 | 4.10 |

†Drafted from Cincinnati Reds' organization by Detroit Tigers, December 8, 1975.
Listed on Detroit Tigers' 1977 spring roster.

## KENTON CHARLES TEKULVE
### (Kent)

Born March 5, 1947, at Cincinnati, O.
Height, 6.04. Weight, 180.
Throws and bats righthanded.
Hobbies—Golf and bowling.
Attended Marietta College, Marietta, O.; received Bachelor of
Science degree in Physical Education.

| Year Club League | G. | IP. | W. | L. | Pct. | H. | R. | ER. | SO. | BB. | ERA. |
|---|---|---|---|---|---|---|---|---|---|---|---|
| 1969—Geneva ...............................NYP | 9 | 53 | 6 | 2 | .750 | 40 | 15 | 10 | 60 | 22 | 1.70 |
| 1970—Salem .................................Carolina | 41 | 79 | 4 | 6 | .400 | 68 | 29 | 17 | 75 | 51 | 1.94 |

| Year    Club | League | G. | IP. | W. | L. | Pct. | H. | R. | ER. | SO. | BB. | ERA. |
|---|---|---|---|---|---|---|---|---|---|---|---|---|
| 1971—Salem ................................Carolina | | 47 | 75 | 11 | 5 | .688 | 77 | 36 | 29 | 62 | 31 | 3.48 |
| 1971—Waterbury..........................Eastern | | 2 | 3 | 0 | 0 | .000 | 3 | 0 | 0 | 0 | 2 | 0.00 |
| 1972—Sherbrooke .......................Eastern | | 31 | 72 | 7 | 6 | .538 | 61 | 24 | 21 | 54 | 22 | 2.63 |
| 1972—Charleston .......................Int'national | | 9 | 22 | 2 | 1 | .667 | 22 | 10 | 10 | 9 | 10 | 4.09 |
| 1973—Sherbrooke .......................Eastern | | •57 | 94 | •12 | 4 | •.750 | 70 | 24 | 16 | 89 | 35 | 1.53 |
| 1974—Charleston .......................Int'national | | 35 | 60 | 6 | 3 | .667 | 50 | 20 | 15 | 38 | 21 | 2.25 |
| 1974—Pittsburgh .......................National | | 8 | 9 | 1 | 1 | .500 | 12 | 6 | 6 | 6 | 5 | 6.00 |
| 1975—Charleston .......................Int'national | | 24 | 71 | 5 | 4 | .556 | 47 | 23 | 14 | 46 | 19 | 1.77 |
| 1975—Pittsburgh .......................National | | 34 | 56 | 1 | 2 | .333 | 43 | 20 | 14 | 28 | 23 | 2.25 |
| 1976—Pittsburgh .......................National | | 64 | 103 | 5 | 3 | .625 | 91 | 30 | 28 | 68 | 25 | 2.45 |
| Major League Totals ................................ | | 106 | 168 | 7 | 6 | .538 | 146 | 56 | 48 | 102 | 53 | 2.57 |

### CHAMPIONSHIP SERIES RECORD

| Year    Club | League | G. | IP. | W. | L. | Pct. | H. | R. | ER. | SO. | BB. | ERA. |
|---|---|---|---|---|---|---|---|---|---|---|---|---|
| 1975—Pittsburgh..........................National | | 2 | 1⅓ | 0 | 0 | .000 | 3 | 1 | 1 | 2 | 1 | 6.75 |

## GARRY LEWIS TEMPLETON

Born March 24, 1956, at Lockey, Tex.
Height, 5.11. Weight, 175.
Throws right and bats left and righthanded.
Brother of Ken Templeton, former minor league outfielder for Oakland A's, 1972-74.
Received reported $40,000 bonus to sign with St. Louis Cardinals, 1974.

| Year    Club | League | Pos. | G. | AB. | R. | H. | 2B. | 3B. | HR. | RBI. | B.A. | PO. | A. | E. | F.A. |
|---|---|---|---|---|---|---|---|---|---|---|---|---|---|---|---|
| 1974—Sarasota Cards ..Gulf C. | | SS | 18 | 71 | 11 | 19 | 1 | 0 | 3 | 10 | .268 | 15 | 41 | 3 | .949 |
| 1974—St. Petersburg ..Fla. St. | | SS | 23 | 95 | 3 | 20 | 1 | 0 | 0 | 2 | .211 | 42 | 64 | 7 | .938 |
| 1975—St. Petersburg ..Fla. St. | | SS | 82 | 349 | 50 | 92 | 7 | 8 | 1 | 32 | .264 | 130 | 253 | 29 | .930 |
| 1975—Arkansas ..........Tex. | | SS | 42 | 177 | 36 | 71 | 9 | 4 | 2 | 20 | .401 | 60 | 131 | 18 | .914 |
| 1976—Tulsa ................A.A. | | •S-3-O | 106 | 443 | 65 | 142 | 24 | •15 | 6 | 38 | .321 | •178 | 319 | 34 | .936 |
| 1976—St. Louis ..........Nat. | | SS | 53 | 213 | 32 | 62 | 8 | 2 | 1 | 17 | .291 | 111 | 172 | 24 | .922 |
| Major League Totals ...................... | | | 53 | 213 | 32 | 62 | 8 | 2 | 1 | 17 | .291 | 111 | 172 | 24 | .922 |

## FURY GENE TENACE

Name pronounced TEN-nis.

(Known by middle name.)
Born October 10, 1946, at Russelton, Pa.
Height, 6.00. Weight, 195.
Throws and bats righthanded.
Hobby—Hunting.

Established major league record for fewest singles, season (150 or more games), 58, in 1974.
Tied major league records for fewest chances accepted and fewest putouts, first baseman, game, 0, September 1, 1974.
Led American League batters in walks with 110 in 1974.
Led Carolina League catchers in double plays with 13 in 1968 and Southern League catchers with 7 in 1969.

| Year    Club | League | Pos. | G. | AB. | R. | H. | 2B. | 3B. | HR. | RBI. | B.A. | PO. | A. | E. | F.A. |
|---|---|---|---|---|---|---|---|---|---|---|---|---|---|---|---|
| 1965—Shelby ..............W. Car. | | OF | 32 | 93 | 10 | 17 | 2 | 1 | 2 | 6 | .183 | 22 | 2 | 1 | .960 |
| 1966—Leesburg ..........Fla. St. | | 1-O-3-P | 91 | 228 | 28 | 48 | 8 | 2 | 1 | 24 | .211 | 310 | 23 | 12 | .965 |
| 1967—Peninsula ..........Carol. | | OF | 3 | 7 | 0 | 0 | 0 | 0 | 0 | 1 | .000 | 2 | 1 | 0 | 1.000 |
| 1967—Leesburg ..........Fla. St. | | C-I-P | 106 | 354 | 47 | 94 | 12 | 2 | 6 | 44 | .266 | 204 | 14 | 11 | .952 |
| 1968—Peninsula ..........Car. | | C-O-3-1 | 132 | 435 | 78 | 123 | 20 | 3 | 21 | 71 | .283 | 639 | 68 | 17 | .977 |
| 1969—Birmingham ......South. | | C-OF-3 | 89 | 276 | 56 | 88 | 20 | 4 | 20 | 74 | .319 | 442 | 51 | 7 | .986 |
| 1969—Oakland ............Amer. | | C | 16 | 38 | 1 | 6 | 0 | 0 | 1 | 2 | .158 | 61 | 6 | 0 | 1.000 |
| 1970—Iowa..................A.A. | | C-OF | 93 | 319 | 54 | 90 | 24 | 1 | 16 | 63 | .282 | 534 | 57 | 9 | .985 |
| 1970—Oakland ............Amer. | | C | 38 | 105 | 19 | 32 | 6 | 0 | 7 | 20 | .305 | 180 | 18 | 2 | .990 |
| 1971—Oakland ............Amer. | | C-OF | 65 | 179 | 26 | 49 | 7 | 0 | 7 | 25 | .274 | 300 | 20 | 2 | .994 |
| 1972—Oakland ............Amer. | | C-O-INF | 82 | 227 | 22 | 51 | 5 | 3 | 5 | 32 | .225 | 329 | 23 | 7 | .981 |
| 1973—Oakland ............Amer. | | 1-C-2 | 160 | 510 | 83 | 132 | 18 | 2 | 24 | 84 | .259 | 1218 | 71 | 14 | .989 |
| 1974—Oakland ............Amer. | | 1-C-2 | 158 | 484 | 71 | 102 | 17 | 1 | 26 | 73 | .211 | 1110 | 83 | 10 | .992 |
| 1975—Oakland ............Amer. | | C-1B | 158 | 498 | 83 | 127 | 17 | 0 | 29 | 87 | .255 | 942 | 84 | 11 | .989 |
| 1976—Oakland† ..........Amer. | | 1B-C-DH | 128 | 417 | 64 | 104 | 19 | 1 | 22 | 66 | .249 | 840 | 56 | 8 | .991 |
| Major League Totals ...................... | | | 805 | 2458 | 369 | 603 | 89 | 7 | 121 | 389 | .245 | 4980 | 361 | 54 | .990 |

†On disabled list, April 30 through May 27, 1976. Played out option year and granted free agency, November 1, 1976; signed as free agent with San Diego Padres, December 14, 1976.

### PITCHING RECORD

| Year    Club | League | G. | IP. | W. | L. | Pct. | H. | R. | ER. | SO. | BB. | ERA. |
|---|---|---|---|---|---|---|---|---|---|---|---|---|---|
| 1966—Leesburg..........................Florida St. | | 3 | 17 | 0 | 1 | .000 | 24 | 7 | 4 | 8 | 6 | 2.12 |
| 1967—Leesburg..........................Florida St. | | 4 | 8 | 0 | 0 | .000 | 4 | 0 | 0 | 8 | 1 | 0.00 |
| 1968—Peninsula .........................Carolina | | 2 | 3 | 0 | 0 | .000 | 4 | 1 | 1 | 0 | 1 | 3.00 |

### CHAMPIONSHIP SERIES RECORD

| Year    Club | League | Pos. | G. | AB. | R. | H. | 2B. | 3B. | HR. | RBI. | B.A. | PO. | A. | E. | F.A. |
|---|---|---|---|---|---|---|---|---|---|---|---|---|---|---|---|
| 1971—Oakland ..........Amer. | | C | 1 | 3 | 0 | 0 | 0 | 0 | 0 | 0 | .000 | 8 | 0 | 0 | 1.000 |
| 1972—Oakland ..........Amer. | | C-2B | 5 | 17 | 1 | 1 | 0 | 0 | 0 | 1 | .059 | 21 | 5 | 1 | .963 |
| 1973—Oakland ..........Amer. | | 1B-C | 5 | 17 | 3 | 4 | 1 | 0 | 0 | 0 | .235 | 40 | 3 | 0 | 1.000 |

| Year | Club | League | Pos. | G. | AB. | R. | H. | 2B. | 3B. | HR. | RBI. | B.A. | PO. | A. | E. | F.A. |
|------|------|--------|------|----|----|----|----|----|----|----|------|------|-----|----|----|------|
| 1974—Oakland | ...........Amer. | | 1B | 4 | 11 | 1 | 0 | 0 | 0 | 0 | 1 | .000 | 35 | 2 | 0 | 1.000 |
| 1975—Oakland | ...........Amer. | | C-1B | 3 | 9 | 0 | 0 | 0 | 0 | 0 | 0 | .000 | 19 | 1 | 0 | 1.000 |
| Championship Series Totals | ............ | | | 18 | 57 | 5 | 5 | 1 | 0 | 0 | 2 | .088 | 123 | 11 | 1 | .993 |

### WORLD SERIES RECORD

Established World Series record for slugging percentage, 7-game series, .913, 1972.
Tied World Series Record for most bases on balls, 7-game series, 11, 1973.
Tied World Series record for most home runs, 7-game series, 4, 1972.
First player to hit two home runs in first two World Series at bats, October 14, 1972.

| Year | Club | League | Pos. | G. | AB. | R. | H. | 2B. | 3B. | HR. | RBI. | B.A. | PO. | A. | E. | F.A. |
|------|------|--------|------|----|----|----|----|----|----|----|------|------|-----|----|----|------|
| 1972—Oakland | ...........Amer. | | C-1B | 7 | 23 | 5 | 8 | 1 | 0 | 4 | 9 | .348 | 48 | 5 | 1 | .981 |
| 1973—Oakland | ...........Amer. | | 1B-C | 7 | 19 | 0 | 3 | 1 | 0 | 0 | 3 | .158 | 57 | 2 | 2 | .967 |
| 1974—Oakland | ...........Amer. | | 1B | 5 | 9 | 0 | 2 | 0 | 0 | 0 | 0 | .222 | 20 | 1 | 0 | 1.000 |
| World Series Totals | ....................... | | | 19 | 51 | 5 | 13 | 2 | 0 | 4 | 12 | .255 | 125 | 8 | 3 | .978 |

### ALL-STAR GAME RECORD

| Year | League | | Pos. | AB. | R. | H. | 2B. | 3B. | HR. | RBI. | B.A. | PO. | A. | E. | F.A. |
|------|--------|--|------|-----|----|----|----|----|----|------|------|-----|----|----|------|
| 1975—American | .......................... | | 1B-C | 3 | 1 | 0 | 0 | 0 | 0 | 0 | .000 | 4 | 0 | 1 | .800 |

## JEFFREY MICHAEL TERPKO
### (Jeff)

Born October 16, 1950, at Sayre, Pa.
Height, 6.00. Weight, 185.
Throws and bats righthanded.
Hobbies—Hunting and fishing.
Nephew of Johnny Stetz, former minor leaguer.

Tied for Pacific Coast League lead in saves with 13 in 1975.

| Year | Club | League | G. | IP. | W. | L. | Pct. | H. | R. | ER. | SO. | BB. | ERA. |
|------|------|--------|----|----|----|----|------|----|----|----|----|----|------|
| 1968—Geneva | ................................ | NYP | 13 | 78 | 6 | 5 | .545 | 61 | 42 | 33 | 103 | 33 | 3.81 |
| 1969—Buffalo | .............................. | Int'national | 22 | 118 | 7 | 7 | .500 | 132 | 67 | 62 | 49 | 40 | 4.73 |
| 1970—Pittsfield†‡ | ......................... | Eastern | 20 | 97 | 6 | 10 | .375 | 92 | 61 | 48 | 78 | 66 | 4.45 |
| 1971—Pittsfield§ | ........................... | Eastern | 10 | 47 | 4 | 3 | .571 | 50 | 22 | 20 | 30 | 17 | 3.83 |
| 1971—Burlington | ........................... | Carolina | 1 | 2 | 0 | 1 | .000 | 2 | 3 | 0 | 0 | 2 | 0.00 |
| 1972—Greenville | ......................... | W. Carolinas | 1 | 6 | 0 | 1 | .000 | 9 | 4 | 4 | 6 | 3 | 6.00 |
| 1972—Burlington x | ....................... | Carolina | 15 | 69 | 4 | 3 | .571 | 61 | 27 | 23 | 69 | 25 | 3.00 |
| 1973—Spokane y | ........................... | P. Coast | | | | | | (Did not play) | | | | | |
| 1974—Pittsfield | ............................ | Eastern | 20 | 37 | 7 | 2 | .778 | 18 | 7 | 5 | 29 | 18 | 1.22 |
| 1974—Spokane | .............................. | P. Coast | 21 | 32 | 4 | 0 | 1.000 | 18 | 6 | 6 | 30 | 21 | 1.69 |
| 1974—Texas | .................................. | American | 3 | 7 | 0 | 0 | .000 | 6 | 1 | 1 | 3 | 4 | 1.29 |
| 1975—Spokane | .............................. | P. Coast | 43 | 70 | 6 | 4 | .600 | 76 | 33 | 32 | 46 | 33 | 4.11 |
| 1976—Texas z | ................................ | American | 32 | 53 | 3 | 3 | .500 | 42 | 15 | 14 | 24 | 29 | 2.38 |
| Major League Totals | .............................. | | 35 | 60 | 3 | 3 | .500 | 48 | 16 | 15 | 27 | 33 | 2.25 |

†Traded on a conditional basis with First Baseman-Catcher Greg Goossen and First Baseman Gene Martin by Washington Senators to Philadelphia Phillies for Outfielder Curt Flood, November 3, 1970.
‡Returned by Philadelphia Phillies to Washington Senators, April 10, 1971.
§On temporary inactive list, May 12 to June 3, 1971.
xOn temporary inactive list, June 10 to June 22, 1972.
yOn suspended list, April 12, 1973. Transferred to restricted list, September 29, 1973 to February 26, 1974.
zTraded to Montreal Expos for Infielder Rodney Scott, March 15, 1977.

## JERRY WAYNE TERRELL

Born July 13, 1946, at Elysian, Minn.
Height, 6.00. Weight, 170.
Throws right and bats left and righthanded.
Hobbies—Numismatics and music.
Attended Mankato State College, Mankato, Minn.; received Bachelor of Arts degree in Accounting.

Led New York-Pennsylvania League second basemen in chances accepted with 350 and double plays with 48 in 1968.
Led Carolina League second basemen in double plays with 81 in 1972.

| Year | Club | League | Pos. | G. | AB. | R. | H. | 2B. | 3B. | HR. | RBI. | B.A. | PO. | A. | E. | F.A. |
|------|------|--------|------|----|----|----|----|----|----|----|------|------|-----|----|----|------|
| 1968—Auburn | ...............NYP | | 2B | 73 | •304 | 65 | 90 | •17 | 5 | 5 | 36 | .296 | •164 | 186 | 18 | .951 |
| 1969—† | | | | | (In Military Service) | | | | | | | | | | |
| 1970—Lynchburg | ........Carol. | | 2B | 118 | 463 | 60 | 129 | 16 | 5 | 1 | 36 | .279 | •332 | 341 | 20 | •.971 |
| 1971—Charlotte | ..........South. | | 2B | 109 | 424 | 61 | 98 | 8 | 1 | 0 | 32 | .231 | 267 | 271 | 15 | .973 |
| 1972—Tacoma | ............P. C. | | 2B | 119 | 496 | 82 | 144 | 20 | 7 | 2 | 35 | .290 | 272 | 321 | 14 | .977 |
| 1973—Minnesota | .......Am. | | S-3-2-O | 124 | 438 | 43 | 116 | 15 | 2 | 1 | 32 | .265 | 170 | 298 | 18 | .963 |
| 1974—Minnesota | .......Am. | | IF-OF | 116 | 229 | 43 | 56 | 4 | 6 | 0 | 19 | .245 | 114 | 179 | 9 | .970 |
| 1975—Tacoma | ............P. C. | | 2B-3B | 45 | 178 | 35 | 57 | 13 | 1 | 2 | 14 | .320 | 88 | 112 | 9 | .957 |
| 1975—Minnesota | .......Amer. | | IF-OF | 108 | 385 | 48• | 110 | 16 | 2 | 1 | 36 | .286 | 267 | 232 | 14 | .973 |
| 1976—Minnesota | .......Amer. | | 2-3-S-O | 89 | 171 | 29 | 42 | 3 | 1 | 0 | 8 | .246 | 82 | 122 | 8 | .962 |
| Major League Totals | ...................... | | | 437 | 1223 | 163 | 324 | 38 | 11 | 2 | 95 | .265 | 633 | 831 | 49 | .968 |

†On military list, May 20 through September 23, 1969.

# DANNY LEE THOMAS
## (Dan)

Born May 9, 1951, at Birmingham, Ala.
Height, 6.02. Weight, 190.
Throws and bats righthanded.
Attended Southern Illinois University, Carbondale, Ill.

Led Texas League in strikeouts with 126 in 1973.
Named Eastern League Most Valuable Player in 1976.

| Year Club | League | Pos. | G. | AB. | R. | H. | 2B. | 3B. | HR. | RBI. | B.A. | PO. | A. | E. | F.A. |
|---|---|---|---|---|---|---|---|---|---|---|---|---|---|---|---|
| 1972–Newark ...........NYP | | 3B | 12 | 48 | 9 | 13 | 4 | 1 | 0 | 7 | .271 | 18 | 20 | 8 | .826 |
| 1972–Evansville ........A. A. | | 3B | 17 | 54 | 4 | 7 | 2 | 0 | 0 | 1 | .130 | 11 | 18 | 4 | .879 |
| 1972–San Antonio ......Texas | | 2-OF-3 | 39 | 121 | 10 | 25 | 7 | 1 | 1 | 13 | .207 | 66 | 63 | 8 | .942 |
| 1973–Shreveport ........Texas | | OF-3B | 132 | 458 | 75 | 122 | 21 | 1 | 9 | 60 | .266 | 171 | 102 | 29 | .904 |
| 1974–Shreveport† ......Texas | | OF | 59 | 188 | 24 | 48 | 7 | 1 | 2 | 26 | .255 | 65 | 5 | 2 | .972 |
| 1975–Thetford Mines‡ East. | | OF | 53 | 191 | 25 | 48 | 11 | 1 | 8 | 23 | .251 | 55 | 3 | 3 | .951 |
| 1976–Pittsfield§.........East. | | OF-1B | 115 | 381 | 78 | 124 | 17 | 3 | •29 | •83 | •.325 | 192 | 13 | 3 | .986 |
| 1976–Milwaukee ........Amer. | | OF | 32 | 105 | 13 | 29 | 5 | 1 | 4 | 15 | .276 | 60 | 3 | 3 | .955 |
| Major League Totals ..................... | | | 32 | 105 | 13 | 29 | 5 | 1 | 4 | 15 | .276 | 60 | 3 | 3 | .955 |

†On disabled list, June 5 through July 13, 1974.
‡On suspended list, June 27 through September 2, 1975.
§On disabled list, July 19 through July 30, 1976.

# DERREL OSBON THOMAS

Born January 14, 1951, at Los Angeles, Calif.
Height, 6.00. Weight, 160.
Throws right and bats right and lefthanded.
Hobbies—Singing and dancing.

| Year Club | League | Pos. | G. | AB. | R. | H. | 2B. | 3B. | HR. | RBI. | B.A. | PO. | A. | E. | F.A. |
|---|---|---|---|---|---|---|---|---|---|---|---|---|---|---|---|
| 1969–Cocoa ...............Fla. St. | | SS | 33 | 114 | 17 | 33 | 5 | 3 | 0 | 8 | .289 | 57 | 75 | 22 | .857 |
| 1969–Okla. City..........A. A. | | SS-OF | 36 | 154 | 21 | 48 | 4 | 6 | 0 | 17 | .312 | 50 | 64 | 11 | .912 |
| 1970–Columbus ..........South. | | SS-2B | 38 | 156 | 24 | 38 | 5 | 4 | 4 | 12 | .244 | 60 | 95 | 14 | .917 |
| 1970–Okla. City..........A. A. | | S-2-O | 75 | 272 | 39 | 73 | 5 | 6 | 4 | 21 | .268 | 126 | 156 | 20 | .934 |
| 1971–Okla. City..........A. A. | | •2B-SS | 122 | 486 | 74 | 139 | 22 | 8 | 3 | 42 | .286 | •257 | 325 | 15 | •.975 |
| 1971–Houston† ..........Nat. | | 2B | 5 | 5 | 0 | 0 | 0 | 0 | 0 | 0 | .000 | 3 | 2 | 0 | 1.000 |
| 1972–Hawaii ..............P. C. | | OF-2B | 6 | 27 | 2 | 4 | 2 | 0 | 0 | 3 | .148 | 13 | 6 | 2 | .905 |
| 1972–San Diego..........Nat. | | 2-S-O | 130 | 500 | 48 | 115 | 15 | 5 | 5 | 36 | .230 | 290 | 357 | 26 | .961 |
| 1973–San Diego..........Nat. | | SS-2B | 113 | 404 | 41 | 96 | 7 | 1 | 0 | 22 | .238 | 211 | 324 | 37 | .935 |
| 1974–San Diego† ........Nat. | | 2-3-O-S | 141 | 523 | 48 | 129 | 24 | 6 | 3 | 41 | .247 | 310 | 336 | 18 | .973 |
| 1975–San Francisco ..Nat. | | 2B-OF | 144 | 540 | 99 | 149 | 21 | 9 | 6 | 48 | .276 | 349 | 372 | 19 | .974 |
| 1976–San Francisco§..Nat. | | 2-O-3-S | 81 | 272 | 38 | 63 | 5 | 4 | 2 | 19 | .232 | 163 | 215 | 15 | .962 |
| Major League Totals ..................... | | | 614 | 2244 | 274 | 552 | 72 | 25 | 16 | 266 | .246 | 1326 | 1606 | 115 | .962 |

†Traded with Pitchers Bill Greif and Mark Schaeffer to San Diego Padres for Pitcher Dave Roberts, December 3, 1971.
‡Traded to San Francisco Giants for Second Baseman Tito Fuentes and Pitcher Butch Metzger, December 6, 1974.
§On disabled list, July 12 through September 15, 1976.

# JAMES GORMAN THOMAS, III
## (Known by middle name.)

Born December 12, 1950, at Charleston, S. C.
Height, 6.02. Weight, 205.
Throws and bats righthanded.
Hobbies—Drag racing, reading and rock music.
Attended Baptist College, Charleston, S. C.

Tied American League record for most consecutive strikeouts (non-pitcher), 8, July 27-29, 1975.
Led Texas League batters in strikeouts with 171 and tied for lead in double plays by outfielders with 4 in 1972.
Led Midwest League batters in strikeouts with 170 in 1971.
Led Pacific Coast League batters in strikeouts with 175 in 1974.

| Year Club | League | Pos. | G. | AB. | R. | H. | 2B. | 3B. | HR. | RBI. | B.A. | PO. | A. | E. | F.A. |
|---|---|---|---|---|---|---|---|---|---|---|---|---|---|---|---|
| 1969–Billings ............Pion. | | SS-1B | 41 | 142 | 23 | 42 | 10 | 3 | 4 | 28 | .296 | 94 | 82 | 27 | .867 |
| 1970–Clinton† ............Midw. | | S-3-2 | 85 | 297 | 36 | 63 | 5 | 4 | 8 | 39 | .212 | 105 | 186 | 28 | .912 |
| 1971–Danville ...........Midw. | | OF-3 | 121 | 457 | 82 | 112 | 20 | 4 | •31 | 83 | .245 | 195 | 14 | 10 | .954 |
| 1972–San Antonio ......Texas | | •O-1 | 135 | 465 | 70 | 112 | 22 | 2 | •26 | 68 | .214 | •305 | •24 | 6 | •.982 |
| 1973–Evansville ........A. A. | | OF | 46 | 146 | 26 | 31 | 6 | 0 | 8 | 18 | .212 | 66 | 3 | 4 | .945 |
| 1973–Milwaukee .......Amer. | | OF-3B | 59 | 155 | 16 | 29 | 7 | 1 | 2 | 11 | .187 | 87 | 1 | 4 | .957 |
| 1974–Sacramento ......P. C. | | OF | 138 | 474 | 117 | 141 | 15 | 1 | 51 | 122 | .297 | 302 | 16 | 10 | .970 |
| 1974–Milwaukee ........Amer. | | OF | 17 | 46 | 10 | 12 | 4 | 0 | 2 | 11 | .261 | 26 | 0 | 0 | 1.000 |
| 1975–Milwaukee ........Amer. | | OF | 121 | 240 | 34 | 43 | 12 | 2 | 10 | 28 | .179 | 215 | 5 | 9 | .961 |
| 1976–Milwaukee ........Amer. | | O-3-DH | 99 | 227 | 27 | 45 | 9 | 2 | 8 | 36 | .198 | 211 | 4 | 4 | .982 |
| Major League Totals ..................... | | | 296 | 668 | 87 | 129 | 32 | 5 | 22 | 86 | .193 | 539 | 10 | 17 | .968 |

†On restricted list, March 4 through May 30, 1970.

## ROY JUSTIN THOMAS

Born June 22, 1953, at Quantico, Va.
Height, 6.05. Weight, 215.
Throws and bats righthanded.
Hobbies—Billiards, basketball and trap shooting.
Attended University of Tampa, Tampa, Fla., and De Anza College, Cupertino, Calif.

Pitched seven-inning, 2-0 no-hit victory against West Haven, August 20, 1974 (2nd game of doubleheader).
Led Eastern League in games started by pitchers with 27 in 1974.
Led Carolina League in shutouts with 6 in 1973.
Led American Association pitchers in wild pitches with 17 in 1976.

| Year | Club | League | G. | IP. | W. | L. | Pct. | H. | R. | ER. | SO. | BB. | ERA. |
|------|------|--------|----|-----|----|----|------|----|----|-----|-----|-----|------|
| 1971—Walla Wall | ....................... | Northwest | 7 | 12 | 0 | 3 | .000 | 19 | 22 | 14 | 8 | 16 | 10.50 |
| 1972—Spartanburg | .................... | W. Carolinas | 24 | 152 | 11 | 7 | .611 | 128 | 67 | 58 | 128 | 62 | 3.43 |
| 1973—Rocky Mount | .................... | Carolina | 26 | 169 | •15 | 8 | .652 | 119 | 53 | 42 | •193 | 77 | •2.24 |
| 1973—Reading | ..................... | Eastern | 2 | 16 | 2 | 0 | 1.000 | 11 | 2 | 2 | 14 | 7 | 1.13 |
| 1974—Reading | ..................... | Eastern | 27 | •191 | 14 | 11 | .560 | 154 | 77 | 55 | •168 | 89 | 2.59 |
| 1974—Toledo | ................... | Int'national | 2 | 7 | 0 | 0 | .000 | 5 | 3 | 1 | 5 | 2 | 1.29 |
| 1975—Toledo | ................... | Int'national | 19 | 119 | 4 | 9 | .308 | 112 | 63 | 53 | 95 | 49 | 4.01 |
| 1975—Reading† | .................... | Eastern | 10 | 67 | 6 | 3 | .667 | 50 | 22 | 19 | 53 | 29 | 2.55 |
| 1976—Iowa‡ | ...................... | Am. Assoc. | 27 | 168 | 6 | 11 | .353 | 167 | 89 | 70 | 103 | 72 | 3.75 |

†Traded with Pitcher Dick Ruthven and Infielder-Outfielder Alan Bannister by Philadelphia Phillies to Chicago White Sox for Pitcher Jim Kaat and Shortstop Mike Buskey, December 10, 1975.
‡Selected by Seattle Mariners in American League expansion draft, November 5, 1976. Traded to Houston Astros for Infielder Larry Milbourne, March 30, 1977.

## STANLEY BROWN THOMAS
### (Stan)

Born July 11, 1949, at Rumford, Me.
Height, 6.01. Weight, 186.
Throws and bats righthanded.
Attended Florida State University, Tallahassee, Fla., and University of
New Haven, West Haven, Conn.; received Bachelor of Science
degree in Law Enforcement.

| Year | Club | League | G. | IP. | W. | L. | Pct. | H. | R. | ER. | SO. | BB. | ERA. |
|------|------|--------|----|-----|----|----|------|----|----|-----|-----|-----|------|
| 1971—Geneva | ............................. | NYP | 18 | 116 | 8 | 5 | .615 | 94 | 34 | 21 | 89 | 25 | •1.63 |
| 1972—Burlington | .......................... | Carolina | 28 | 148 | 7 | 9 | .438 | 145 | 77 | 67 | 98 | 45 | 4.07 |
| 1973—Pittsfield | ........................ | Eastern | 51 | 85 | 7 | 6 | .538 | 85 | 31 | 26 | 68 | 24 | 2.75 |
| 1974—Spokane | ........................ | P. Coast | 23 | 43 | 1 | 0 | 1.000 | 41 | 20 | 17 | 39 | 16 | 3.56 |
| 1974—Texas | ..................... | American | 12 | 14 | 0 | 0 | .000 | 22 | 10 | 10 | 8 | 6 | 6.43 |
| 1975—Texas† | ..................... | American | 46 | 81 | 4 | 4 | .500 | 72 | 36 | 28 | 46 | 34 | 3.11 |
| 1976—Cleveland‡ | ........................ | American | 37 | 106 | 4 | 4 | .500 | 88 | 33 | 27 | 54 | 41 | 2.29 |
| Major League Totals | ............................. | | 95 | 201 | 8 | 8 | .500 | 182 | 79 | 65 | 108 | 81 | 2.91 |

†Traded with Utilityman Ron Pruitt to Cleveland Indians for Catcher John Ellis, December 9, 1975.
‡Selected by Seattle Mariners in American League expansion draft, November 5, 1976.

## GARY LEAH THOMASSON

Name pronounced Tom-as-son.

Born July 29, 1951, at San Diego, Calif.
Height, 6.02. Weight, 190.
Throws and bats lefthanded.
Hobbies—Hunting, fishing and playing the guitar.

Tied for Midwest League lead in double plays by outfielders with 4 in 1970.

| Year | Club | League | Pos. | G. | AB. | R. | H. | 2B. | 3B. | HR. | RBI. | B.A. | PO. | A. | E. | F.A. |
|------|------|--------|------|----|-----|----|----|-----|-----|-----|------|------|-----|----|----|------|
| 1969—Great Falls | ........ | Pion. | OF-1-P | 49 | 117 | 25 | 42 | 7 | 5 | 0 | 12 | .359 | 101 | 5 | 8 | .980 |
| 1970—Decatur | ............ | Midw. | OF | 115 | 424 | 76 | 115 | 18 | 6 | 8 | 53 | .271 | 179 | 14 | 8 | .960 |
| 1971—Amarillo | ............ | Texas | OF | 126 | 418 | 57 | 114 | 14 | 7 | 6 | 55 | .273 | 287 | 7 | 10 | .967 |
| 1972—Phoenix | ............ | P.C. | •1B-OF | 138 | 482 | 88 | 136 | 32 | 8 | 11 | 76 | .282 | 865 | 34 | •14 | .985 |
| 1972—San Francisco | .. | Nat. | 1B-OF | 10 | 27 | 5 | 9 | 1 | 1 | 0 | 1 | .333 | 60 | 1 | 0 | 1.000 |
| 1973—San Francisco | .. | Nat. | 1B-OF | 112 | 235 | 35 | 67 | 10 | 4 | 4 | 30 | .285 | 312 | 15 | 6 | .982 |
| 1974—San Francisco | .. | Nat. | OF-1B | 120 | 315 | 41 | 77 | 14 | 3 | 2 | 29 | .244 | 235 | 17 | 7 | .973 |
| 1975—San Francisco | .. | Nat. | OF-1B | 114 | 326 | 44 | 74 | 12 | 3 | 7 | 32 | .227 | 293 | 18 | 7 | .978 |
| 1976—San Francisco† | .. | Nat. | OF-1-PH | 103 | 328 | 45 | 85 | 20 | 5 | 8 | 38 | .259 | 376 | 20 | 12 | .970 |
| Major League Totals | ..................... | | | 459 | 1231 | 170 | 312 | 57 | 16 | 21 | 130 | .253 | 1276 | 71 | 32 | .977 |

†On disabled list, April 29 through June 2, 1976.

### PITCHING RECORD

| Year | Club | League | G. | IP. | W. | L. | Pct. | H. | R. | ER. | SO. | BB. | ERA. |
|------|------|--------|----|-----|----|----|------|----|----|-----|-----|-----|------|
| 1969—Great Falls | ....................... | Pioneer | 1 | 1 | 0 | 0 | .000 | 0 | 2 | 2 | 1 | 5 | 18.00 |

---

## DID YOU KNOW—

That outfielder Babe Herman of the Brooklyn Dodgers batted .393 in 1930? It was not good enough to win the league batting championship.

# BOBBY LaRUE THOMPSON

Born November 3, 1953, at Charlotte, N. C.
Height, 5.10. Weight, 175.
Throws right and bats left and righthanded.
Hobbies—Football and basketball.

Led Carolina League outfielders in double plays with 6 in 1975.
Led Carolina League in stolen bases with 65 in 1975.

| Year Club | League | Pos. | G. | AB. | R. | H. | 2B. | 3B. | HR. | RBI. | B.A. | PO. | A. | E. | F.A. |
|---|---|---|---|---|---|---|---|---|---|---|---|---|---|---|---|
| 1972—Geneva.............NYP | | OF-SS-3 | 35 | 91 | 15 | 22 | 4 | 0 | 2 | 14 | .242 | 40 | 12 | 7 | .881 |
| 1973—Gastonia...........W. Car. | | OF | 49 | 153 | 19 | 36 | 3 | 1 | 1 | 15 | .235 | 107 | •19 | 4 | .969 |
| 1974—Gastonia...........W. Car. | | OF | 113 | 362 | 51 | 87 | 11 | 5 | 7 | 52 | .240 | 156 | 14 | 10 | .944 |
| 1975—Lynchburg ........Carol. | | OF | 119 | 429 | 87 | 128 | 19 | •10 | 2 | 43 | .298 | •269 | •26 | •18 | .942 |
| 1976—San Antonio ......Texas | | OF | 87 | 320 | 63 | 91 | 5 | 7 | 5 | 24 | .284 | 172 | 10 | 16 | .919 |
| 1976—Sacramento†......P.C. | | OF | 20 | 66 | 17 | 21 | 3 | 0 | 4 | 11 | .318 | 53 | 4 | 3 | .950 |

†On suspended list, June 8 through June 16, 1976.
Listed on Texas Rangers' 1977 spring roster.

# JASON DOLPH THOMPSON

Born July 6, 1954, at Hollywood, Calif.
Height, 6.04. Weight, 200.
Throws and bats lefthanded.
Attended California State University at Northridge, Northridge, Calif.

| Year Club | League | Pos. | G. | AB. | R. | H. | 2B. | 3B. | HR. | RBI. | B.A. | PO. | A. | E. | F.A. |
|---|---|---|---|---|---|---|---|---|---|---|---|---|---|---|---|
| 1975—Montgomery ......South. | | 1B | 75 | 222 | 42 | 72 | 12 | 1 | 10 | 38 | .324 | 633 | 47 | 10 | .986 |
| 1976—Evansville ........A.A. | | 1B | 4 | 16 | 3 | 5 | 0 | 0 | 3 | 6 | .313 | 29 | 7 | 0 | 1.000 |
| 1976—Detroit .............Amer. | | 1B | 123 | 412 | 45 | 90 | 12 | 1 | 17 | 54 | .218 | 1157 | 88 | 8 | .994 |
| Major League Totals ..................... | | | 123 | 412 | 45 | 90 | 12 | 1 | 17 | 54 | .218 | 1157 | 88 | 8 | .994 |

# MICHAEL WAYNE THOMPSON
## (Mike)

Born September 6, 1949, at Denver, Colo.
Height, 6.03. Weight, 205.
Throws and bats righthanded.
Hobbies—Hunting and fishing.
Attended Oklahoma State University, Stillwater, Okla., and
Nebraska Wesleyan University, Lincoln, Neb.

Tied for Western Carolinas League lead in complete games with 9 and led in wild pitches with 42 in 1968.

| Year Club | League | G. | IP. | W. | L. | Pct. | H. | R. | ER. | SO. | BB. | ERA. |
|---|---|---|---|---|---|---|---|---|---|---|---|---|
| 1967—Geneva .............................NYP | | 10 | 55 | 2 | 5 | .286 | 45 | 32 | 23 | 37 | 45 | 3.76 |
| 1968—Salisbury.......................W. Carol. | | 29 | •156 | 7 | •13 | .350 | •141 | •93 | •74 | •136 | •106 | 4.27 |
| 1969—Burlington..........................Carol. | | 18 | 99 | 9 | 5 | .643 | 62 | 35 | 23 | 84 | 68 | 2.09 |
| 1970—Denver ......................Am. Assoc. | | 5 | 13 | 0 | 2 | .000 | 16 | 17 | 15 | 7 | 14 | 10.38 |
| 1970—Pittsfield .........................Eastern | | 19 | 110 | 5 | 9 | .357 | 101 | 70 | 65 | 102 | 77 | 5.32 |
| 1971—Denver ......................Am. Assoc. | | 11 | 60 | 5 | 3 | .625 | 55 | 35 | 28 | 50 | 29 | 4.18 |
| 1971—Washington† .....................American | | 16 | 67 | 1 | 6 | .143 | 53 | 39 | 36 | 41 | 54 | 4.84 |
| 1972—Denver‡ ....................Am. Assoc. | | 20 | 112 | 6 | 8 | .429 | 96 | 59 | 51 | 88 | 64 | 4.09 |
| 1973—Tulsa§...........................Am. Assoc. | | 20 | 99 | 7 | 7 | .500 | 88 | 44 | 31 | 92 | 67 | 2.83 |
| 1973—St. Louis ............................National | | 2 | 4 | 0 | 0 | .000 | 1 | 0 | 0 | 3 | 5 | 0.00 |
| 1974—Tulsa ...........................Am. Assoc. | | 10 | 71 | 5 | 4 | .556 | 56 | 31 | 28 | 78 | 43 | 3.55 |
| 1974—St. Louis x-Atlanta .............National | | 20 | 42 | 0 | 3 | .000 | 44 | 26 | 26 | 27 | 37 | 5.57 |
| 1975—Atlanta y..........................National | | 16 | 52 | 0 | 6 | .000 | 60 | 32 | 27 | 42 | 32 | 4.67 |
| 1976—Indianapolis z .....................Am. Assoc. | | 21 | 93 | 5 | 7 | .417 | 76 | 46 | 41 | 73 | 68 | 3.97 |
| American League Totals.......................'...... | | 16 | 67 | 1 | 6 | .143 | 53 | 39 | 36 | 41 | 54 | 4.84 |
| National League Totals............................ | | 38 | 98 | 0 | 9 | .000 | 105 | 58 | 53 | 72 | 74 | 4.87 |
| Major League Totals ............................... | | 54 | 165 | 1 | 15 | .063 | 158 | 97 | 89 | 113 | 128 | 4.85 |

†On military list June 11 through June 30.
‡Traded by Texas Rangers to St. Louis Cardinals (assigned to Tulsa) for Pitcher Mike Nagy (assigned to Spokane), March 31, 1973.
§On temporary inactive list, June 1 to June 19, 1973.
xSold to Atlanta Braves, September 10, 1974.
yOn disabled list, April 3 to May 2, 1975. Traded to Cincinnati Reds for Outfielder-First Baseman Terry Crowley, April 6, 1976.
zOn disabled list, July 19 to July 22, 1976; traded by Cincinnati Reds' organization to Texas Rangers' organization for Pitcher Art DeFilippis, November 8, 1976.

# VERNON SCOTT THOMPSON

Born December 7, 1955, at Grove City, Pa.
Height, 6.03. Weight, 195.
Throws and bats lefthanded.
Hobbies—Swimming, basketball, bowling and automobiles.
Son of William K. Thompson, first baseman-outfielder in Cincinnati Reds'
organization and Milwaukee Braves' organization, 1953-1962.

| Year Club | League | Pos. | G. | AB. | R. | H. | 2B. | 3B. | HR. | RBI. | B.A. | PO. | A. | E. | F.A. |
|---|---|---|---|---|---|---|---|---|---|---|---|---|---|---|---|
| 1974—Bradenton Cubs | Gulf C. | OF-1B | 47 | 169 | 22 | 43 | 6 | 3 | 1 | 19 | .254 | 86 | 7 | 5 | .948 |
| 1975—Key West .........Fla.St. | | OF-1B | 123 | 424 | 40 | 95 | 6 | 3 | 3 | 41 | .224 | 186 | 10 | •12 | .942 |
| 1976—Midland ...........Texas | | 1B-OF | 116 | 425 | 47 | 121 | 11 | 2 | 7 | 54 | .285 | 766 | 50 | 12 | .985 |

Listed on Chicago Cubs' 1977 spring roster.

## PAUL GAYTON THORMODSGARD
Name pronounced THER-muds-gard.
### (Thor)
Born November 10, 1953, at San Francisco, Calif.
Height, 6.02. Weight, 190.
Throws and bats righthanded.
Attended Mount San Jacinto Junior College, Gilman Hot Springs, Calif.

| Year Club | League | G. | IP. | W. | L. | Pct. | H. | R. | ER. | SO. | BB. | ERA. |
|---|---|---|---|---|---|---|---|---|---|---|---|---|
| 1972–Bradenton Reds...................Gulf Coast | | 12 | 45 | 2 | 2 | .500 | 47 | 27 | 18 | 33 | 19 | 3.60 |
| 1973–Tampa ..............................Florida St. | | 18 | 107 | 7 | 7 | .500 | 112 | 48 | 28 | 69 | 29 | 2.36 |
| 1974–Tampa†...............................Florida St. | | 26 | 135 | 6 | 15 | .286 | 152 | 80 | 70 | 54 | 45 | 4.67 |
| 1975–.......................................... | | | | | | (Out of Organized Baseball) | | | | | | |
| 1976–Reno‡ .................................California | | 16 | 104 | 6 | ,8 | .429 | 119 | 58 | 49 | 67 | 42 | 4.24 |

†Released, December 9, 1974. Did not play in 1975 because of broken thumb on pitching hand.
‡Signed as free agent, with Reno (Minnesota Twins' organization), December 13, 1975; on disabled list, April 14 to June 11, 1976.
Invited to Minnesota Twins' 1977 spring camp.


## ANDRE THORNTON
### (Andy)
Born August 13, 1949, at Tuskegee, Ala.
Height, 6.02. Weight, 205.
Throws and bats righthanded.
Hobbies–Reading and billiards.
Attended Cheyney State College, Cheyney, Pa.

Tied major league record for most assists, first baseman, inning, 3, August 22, 1975, 5th inning.
Led Northwest League first basemen in double plays with 35 in 1968.

| Year Club | League | Pos. | G. | AB. | R. | H. | 2B. | 3B. | HR. | RBI. | B.A. | PO. | A. | E. | F.A. |
|---|---|---|---|---|---|---|---|---|---|---|---|---|---|---|---|
| 1967–Huron† ..............North. | | 3-OF | 19 | 55 | 3 | 10 | 1 | 2 | 1 | 3 | .182 | 7 | 9 | 10 | .615 |
| 1968–Eugene‡ ...........Northw. | | 1B | 56 | 185 | 27 | 46 | 9 | 2 | 5 | 31 | .249 | •427 | •24 | 10 | •.978 |
| 1969–Spartanburg‡‡ ..W. Car. | | •1-3-O | 90 | 299 | 56 | 75 | 13 | 4 | 13 | 51 | .251 | 701 | 45 | •20 | .974 |
| 1970–Peninsula§ ........Carol. | | 1B | 67 | 193 | 24 | 48 | 7 | 2 | 5 | 23 | .249 | 499 | 30 | 5 | .991 |
| 1971–Reading x.........East. | | 1B | 116 | 367 | 67 | 98 | 18 | 1 | 26 | 76 | .267 | 1006 | 48 | 15 | .986 |
| 1972–Eugene x.........P.C. | | 1B-3B | 46 | 141 | 22 | 45 | 8 | 2 | 6 | 29 | .319 | 224 | 46 | 11 | .961 |
| 1972–Richmond z .....Int. | | 1B-OF | 49 | 159 | 30 | 42 | 5 | 0 | 14 | 36 | .264 | 379 | 33 | 6 | .986 |
| 1973–Richmond a .....Int. | | 3-1-0 | 16 | 49 | 8 | 10 | 2 | 0 | 4 | 8 | .204 | 67 | 17 | 5 | .944 |
| 1973–Wichita ...........A.A. | | 1B | 40 | 135 | 34 | 39 | 2 | 0 | 17 | 45 | .289 | 362 | 23 | 1 | .997 |
| 1973–Chicago ...........Nat. | | 1B | 17 | 35 | 3 | 7 | 3 | 0 | 0 | 2 | .200 | 81 | 10 | 1 | .989 |
| 1974–Chicago ...........Nat. | | 1B-3B | 107 | 303 | 41 | 79 | 16 | 4 | 10 | 46 | .261 | 760 | 70 | 7 | .992 |
| 1975–Chicago b .........Nat. | | 1B-3B | 120 | 372 | 70 | 109 | 21 | 4 | 18 | 60 | .293 | 984 | 77 | 13 | .988 |
| 1976–Chi c-Mont. d ....Nat. | | 1B-OF | 96 | 268 | 28 | 52 | 11 | 2 | 11 | 38 | .194 | 542 | 46 | 6 | .990 |
| Major League Totals ..................... | | | 340 | 978 | 142 | 247 | 51 | 10 | 39 | 146 | .252 | 2367 | 203 | 27 | .990 |

†On military list, December 29, 1967 through May 1, 1968.
‡On temporary inactive list, June 1 through July 2.
‡‡On temporary inactive list, June 4 through June 24.
§On temporary inactive list, June 11 through June 30.
xOn temporary inactive list, June 7 through June 26.
yReleased to Richmond (part of deal in which Philadelphia Phillies sent Pitcher Joe Hoerner to Atlanta Braves in trade for Pitchers Jim Nash and Gary Neibauer), June 15, 1972.
zOn temporary inactive list, June 28 through July 1. On disabled list, July 5 through July 16. On temporary inactive list, August 1 through August 4.
aTraded by Atlanta Braves to Chicago Cubs for First Baseman Joe Pepitone, May 19, 1973.
bOn disabled list, April 1 to May 4, 1975.
cTraded to Montreal Expos for Pitcher Steve Renko and Outfielder-First Baseman Larry Biittner, May 17, 1976.
dOn disabled list, June 10 to July 1, 1976; traded to Cleveland Indians for Pitcher Jackie Brown, December 10, 1976.


## LUIS CLEMENTE TIANT (VEGA)
Name pronounced TEE-aunt.

Born November 23, 1940, at Havana, Cuba.
Height, 5.11. Weight, 187.
Throws and bats righthanded.

Established modern major league record for most strikeouts, two consecutive games, 32, June 29, first game (13) and July 3 (19) 1968, 19 innings.
Established American League record for most strikeouts, ten-inning game (19), July 3, 1968.
Pitched 4-0 no-hit victory against Winston-Salem, May 7, 1963.
Led American League in shutouts with 7 in 1974.
Tied for American League lead in shutouts with 5 in 1966 and led with 9 in 1968.
Led Carolina League in shutouts with 6 and in complete games with 17 in 1963.
Named THE SPORTING NEWS American League Comeback Player of the Year, 1972.
Named Player of the Year in Pacific Coast League, 1964.

| Year Club | League | G. | IP. | W. | L. | Pct. | H. | R. | ER. | SO. | BB. | ERA. |
|---|---|---|---|---|---|---|---|---|---|---|---|---|
| 1959–Mexico City Tigers ............Mexican | | 41 | 184 | 5 | 19 | .208 | 214 | *139 | 121 | 98 | 107 | 5.92 |
| 1960–Mexico City Tigers ............Mexican | | 41 | 180 | ●17 | 7 | *.708 | 194 | 115 | 93 | 107 | *124 | 4.65 |
| 1961–Mexico City Tigers ............Mexican | | 24 | 145 | 12 | 9 | .571 | 138 | 77 | 61 | 141 | 106 | 3.79 |
| 1962–Jacksonville .......................Int'national | | 1 | 1 | 0 | 0 | .000 | 0 | 0 | 0 | 0 | 1 | 0.00 |
| 1962–Charleston ........................Eastern | | 29 | 139 | 7 | 8 | .467 | 141 | 75 | 56 | 99 | 72 | 3.63 |
| 1963–Burlington..........................Carolina | | 31 | 204 | 14 | 9 | .609 | 151 | 68 | 58 | *207 | 81 | 2.56 |
| 1964–Portland ............................P. Coast | | 17 | 137 | 15 | 1 | *.938 | 88 | 37 | 31 | 154 | 40 | 2.04 |
| 1964–Cleveland ...........................American | | 19 | 127 | 10 | 4 | .714 | 94 | 41 | 40 | 105 | 47 | 2.83 |
| 1965–Cleveland ...........................American | | 41 | 196 | 11 | 11 | .500 | 166 | 88 | 77 | 152 | 66 | 3.54 |
| 1966–Cleveland ...........................American | | 46 | 155 | 12 | 11 | .522 | 121 | 50 | 48 | 145 | 50 | 2.79 |
| 1967–Cleveland ...........................American | | 33 | 214 | 12 | 9 | .571 | 177 | 76 | 65 | 219 | 67 | 2.73 |
| 1968–Cleveland ...........................American | | 34 | 258 | 21 | 9 | .700 | 152 | 53 | 46 | 264 | 73 | *1.60 |
| 1969–Cleveland† ........................American | | 38 | 250 | 9 | *20 | .410 | 229 | *123 | 103 | 156 | *129 | 3.71 |
| 1970–Minnesota‡§ .......................American | | 18 | 93 | 7 | 3 | .700 | 84 | 36 | 35 | 50 | 41 | 3.39 |
| 1971–Richmond x-Louisville .........Int'national | | 9 | 54 | 3 | 5 | .375 | 47 | 27 | 25 | 48 | 28 | 4.17 |
| 1971–Boston ...............................American | | 21 | 72 | 1 | 7 | .125 | 73 | 42 | 39 | 59 | 32 | 4.88 |
| 1972–Boston ...............................American | | 43 | 179 | 15 | 6 | .714 | 128 | 45 | 38 | 123 | 65 | *1.91 |
| 1973–Boston ...............................American | | 35 | 272 | 20 | 13 | .606 | 217 | 105 | 101 | 206 | 78 | 3.34 |
| 1974–Boston ...............................American | | 38 | 311 | 22 | 13 | .629 | 281 | 106 | 101 | 176 | 82 | 2.92 |
| 1975–Boston ...............................American | | 35 | 260 | 18 | 14 | .563 | 262 | 126 | 116 | 142 | 72 | 4.02 |
| 1976–Boston ...............................American | | 38 | 279 | 21 | 12 | .636 | 274 | 107 | 95 | 131 | 64 | 3.06 |
| Major League Totals ..............................  | | 439 | 2666 | 179 | 132 | .576 | 2258 | 998 | 904 | 1928 | 866 | 3.05 |

†Traded with Pitcher Stan Williams to Minnesota Twins for Pitchers Dean Chance and Bob Miller, Outfielder Ted Uhlaender and Outfielder-Third Baseman Graig Nettles, December 12, 1969.
‡On disabled list June 1 through August 3.
§Unconditionally released, March 31, 1971; signed as free agent by Atlanta Braves, April 16, 1971.
xReleased by Atlanta Braves, May 15, 1971; signed as free agent by Boston Red Sox, May 17, 1971.

## CHAMPIONSHIP SERIES RECORD

| Year Club | League | G. | IP. | W. | L. | Pct. | H. | R. | ER. | SO. | BB. | ERA. |
|---|---|---|---|---|---|---|---|---|---|---|---|---|
| 1970–Minnesota ..........................American | | 1 | ⅔ | 0 | 0 | .000 | 1 | 2 | 1 | 0 | 0 | 13.50 |
| 1975–Boston ...............................American | | 1 | 9 | 1 | 0 | 1.000 | 3 | 1 | 0 | 8 | 3 | 0.00 |
| Championship Series Totals ...................... | | 2 | 9⅔ | 1 | 0 | 1.000 | 4 | 3 | 1 | 8 | 3 | 0.93 |

## WORLD SERIES RECORD

| Year Club | League | G. | IP. | W. | L. | Pct. | H. | R. | ER. | SO. | BB. | ERA. |
|---|---|---|---|---|---|---|---|---|---|---|---|---|
| 1975–Boston ...............................American | | 3 | 25 | 2 | 0 | 1.000 | 25 | 10 | 10 | 12 | 8 | 3.60 |

## ALL-STAR GAME RECORD

| Year League | IP. | W. | L. | Pct. | H. | R. | ER. | SO. | BB. | ERA. |
|---|---|---|---|---|---|---|---|---|---|---|
| 1968–American ....................................................: | 2 | 0 | 1 | .000 | 2 | 1 | 0 | 2 | 2 | 0.00 |
| 1974–American .................................................... | 2 | 0 | 1 | .000 | 4 | 3 | 2 | 0 | 1 | 9.00 |
| 1976–American .................................................... | 2 | 0 | 0 | .000 | 1 | 0 | 0 | 1 | 0 | .000 |
| All-Star Game Totals.................................... | 6 | 0 | 2 | .000 | 7 | 4 | 2 | 3 | 3 | 3.000 |

## RICHARD WILLIAM TIDROW
### (Dick)

Born May 14, 1947, at San Francisco, Calif.
Height, 6.04. Weight, 215.
Throws and bats' righthanded.
Hobbies—Music and sports in general.
Attended Chabot College, Hayward, Calif.
Named THE SPORTING NEWS American League Rookie Pitcher of the Year, 1972.

| Year Club | League | G. | IP. | W. | L. | Pct. | H. | R. | ER. | SO. | BB. | ERA. |
|---|---|---|---|---|---|---|---|---|---|---|---|---|
| 1967–Reno....................................California | | 7 | 19 | 0 | 1 | .000 | 20 | 16 | 14 | 18 | 10 | 6.63 |
| 1967–Rock Hill ............................W. Carolinas | | 4 | 16 | 0 | 1 | .000 | 15 | 10 | 10 | 9 | 9 | .563 |
| 1968–Reno† ..................................California | | 6 | 8 | 1 | 0 | 1.000 | 3 | 0 | 0 | 11 | 4 | 0.00 |
| 1969–Reno ....................................California | | 25 | 187 | 15 | 6 | .714 | 170 | 71 | 55 | 189 | 48 | 2.65 |
| 1970–Wichita ................................Am. Assoc. | | 18 | 83 | 3 | 4 | .429 | 99 | 49 | 47 | 71 | 29 | 5.10 |
| 1970–Reno ....................................California | | 6 | 35 | 2 | 2 | .500 | 35 | 16 | 10 | 33 | 12 | 2.57 |
| 1971–Wichita ................................Am. Assoc. | | 20 | 124 | 8 | 6 | .571 | 123 | 61 | 57 | 81 | 45 | 4.15 |
| 1971–Reno ....................................California | | 7 | 38 | 4 | 0 | 1.000 | 38 | 16 | 14 | 29 | 11 | 3.32 |
| 1972–Cleveland ...........................American | | 39 | 237 | 14 | 15 | .483 | 200 | 83 | 73 | 123 | 70 | 2.77 |
| 1973–Cleveland ...........................American | | 42 | 275 | 14 | 16 | .467 | 289 | 150 | 135 | 138 | 95 | 4.42 |
| 1974–Cleveland‡-New York .........American | | 37 | 210 | 12 | 12 | .500 | 226 | 116 | 97 | 108 | 66 | 4.16 |
| 1975–New York§ ..........................American | | 37 | 69 | 6 | 3 | .667 | 65 | 27 | 24 | 38 | 31 | 3.13 |
| 1976–New York ...........................American | | 47 | 92 | 4 | 5 | .444 | 80 | 29 | 27 | 65 | 24 | 2.64 |
| Major League Totals ..............................  | | 202 | 883 | 50 | 51 | .495 | 860 | 405 | 356 | 472 | 286 | 3.63 |

†On military list from beginning of season until August 13.
‡Traded with First Baseman Chris Chambliss and Pitcher Cecil Upshaw to New York Yankees for Pitchers Fritz Peterson, Fred Beene, Steve Kline and Tom Buskey, April 26, 1974.
§On disabled list from beginning of season until April 19 and from August 19 through remainder of season.

## CHAMPIONSHIP SERIES RECORD

| Year Club | League | G. | IP. | W. | L. | Pct. | H. | R. | ER. | SO. | BB. | ERA. |
|---|---|---|---|---|---|---|---|---|---|---|---|---|
| 1976–New York ...........................American | | 3 | 7⅓ | 1 | 0 | 1.000 | 6 | 4 | 3 | 0 | 4 | 3.68 |

| Year | Club | League | G. | IP. | W. | L. | Pct. | H. | R. | ER. | SO. | BB. | ERA. |
|------|------|--------|-----|-----|----|----|------|----|----|-----|-----|-----|------|
| 1976—New York ...........................Americal | | American | 2 | 2⅓ | 0 | 0 | .000 | 5 | 2 | 2 | 1 | 1 | 7.71 |

## JACKSON A. TODD

Born November 20, 1951, at Tulsa, Okla.
Height, 6.02. Weight, 180.
Throws and bats righthanded.
Hobbies—Outdoor sports.
Attended University of Oklahoma, Norman, Okla.
Pitched 3-0 no-hit victory against Arkansas, May 14, 1974.

| Year | Club | League | G. | IP. | W. | L. | Pct. | H. | R. | ER. | SO. | BB. | ERA. |
|------|------|--------|-----|-----|----|----|------|----|----|-----|-----|-----|------|
| 1973—Memphis ...........................Texas | | Texas | 14 | 76 | 6 | 5 | .545 | 69 | 29 | 24 | 57 | 20 | 2.84 |
| 1974—Victoria† ...........................Texas | | Texas | 23 | 173 | 11 | 8 | .579 | 165 | 78 | 62 | 115 | 43 | 3.23 |
| 1975—Jackson‡ ...........................Texas | | Texas | 13 | 54 | 3 | 4 | .429 | 52 | 29 | 19 | 31 | 20 | 3.17 |
| 1976—Tidewater ...........................Int'national | | Int'national | 26 | •201 | 13 | 9 | .520 | 204 | 75 | 65 | 125 | 53 | 2.91 |

†Played one game at shortstop.
‡On temporary inactive list, April 10 through June 19, 1975.
Listed on New York Mets' 1977 spring roster.

## JAMES RICHARD TODD, JR.
### (Jim)

Born September 21, 1947, at Lancaster, Pa.
Height, 6.02. Weight, 190.
Throws right and bats lefthanded.
Hobby—Sports in general.
Attended Parsons College, Fairfield, Ia., and Millersville State College, Millersville, Pa.

| Year | Club | League | G. | IP. | W. | L. | Pct. | H. | R. | ER. | SO. | BB. | ERA. |
|------|------|--------|-----|-----|----|----|------|----|----|-----|-----|-----|------|
| 1969—Huron ...............................Northern | | Northern | 17 | 103 | 6 | •8 | .429 | 108 | 54 | 32 | 68 | 43 | 2.80 |
| 1970—Quincy ...............................Northwest | | Northwest | 11 | 82 | 7 | 2 | .778 | 65 | 28 | 17 | 67 | 21 | 1.87 |
| 1970—San Antonio .......................Texas | | Texas | 18 | 106 | 5 | 6 | .455 | 107 | 50 | 34 | 48 | 36 | 2.89 |
| 1971—San Antonio .......................Texas | | Texas | 23 | 168 | 11 | 9 | .550 | 149 | 65 | 47 | 87 | 34 | 2.51 |
| 1971—Tacoma...............................P. Coast | | P. Coast | 8 | 51 | 3 | 3 | .500 | 52 | 24 | 21 | 30 | 18 | 3.71 |
| 1972—Wichita† .............................Am. Assoc. | | Am. Assoc. | 26 | 142 | 9 | 7 | .563 | 157 | 78 | 69 | 81 | 50 | 4.37 |
| 1973—Wichita ............................Am. Assoc. | | Am. Assoc. | 26 | 156 | 12 | 8 | .600 | 169 | 87 | 79 | 79 | 62 | 4.55 |
| 1974—Wichita .............................Am. Assoc. | | Am. Assoc. | 3 | 21 | 1 | 1 | .500 | 16 | 5 | 4 | 7 | 6 | 1.71 |
| 1974—Chicago‡ .............................National | | National | 43 | 88 | 4 | 2 | .667 | 82 | 45 | 38 | 42 | 41 | 3.89 |
| 1975—Tucson ...............................P. Coast | | P. Coast | 2 | 13 | 1 | 0 | 1.000 | 11 | 3 | 3 | 9 | 4 | 2.08 |
| 1975—Oakland .............................American | | American | 58 | 122 | 8 | 3 | .727 | 104 | 40 | 31 | 50 | 33 | 2.29 |
| 1976—Oakland§...............................American | | American | 49 | 83 | 7 | 8 | .467 | 87 | 43 | 35 | 22 | 34 | 3.80 |
| | National League Totals............................ | | 43 | 88 | 4 | 2 | .667 | 82 | 45 | 38 | 42 | 41 | 3.89 |
| | American League Totals.......................... | | 107 | 205 | 15 | 11 | .577 | 191 | 83 | 66 | 72 | 67 | 2.90 |
| | Major League Totals ............................. | | 150 | 293 | 19 | 13 | .594 | 273 | 128 | 104 | 114 | 108 | 3.19 |

†Appeared as an outfielder.
‡Traded to Oakland Athletics for a player to be named later, April 6, 1975; Athletics sent Outfielder John (Champ) Summers to Cubs, April 29, 1975, to complete deal.
§Traded to Chicago Cubs for Pitcher Joe Coleman, March 15, 1977.

| Year | Club | League | G. | IP. | W. | L. | Pct. | H. | R. | ER. | SO. | BB. | ERA. |
|------|------|--------|-----|-----|----|----|------|----|----|-----|-----|-----|------|
| 1975—Oakland ...........................American | | American | 3 | 1 | 0 | 0 | .000 | 3 | 1 | 1 | 0 | 0 | 9.00 |

## ROBERT TOLAN
### (Bobby)

Born November 19, 1945, at Los Angeles, Calif.
Height, 5.11. Weight, 180.
Throws and bats lefthanded.
Hobby—Basketball.

Major League stolen bases: 1965 (2), 1966 (1), 1967 (12), 1968 (9), 1969 (26), 1970 (57), 1972 (42), 1973 (15), 1974 (7), 1975 (11), 1976 (10). Total—192.
Led National League in stolen bases with 57 in 1970.
Led National League outfielders in total chances with 414 in 1972.
Named outfielder on THE SPORTING NEWS National League All-Star team, 1970.
Named THE SPORTING NEWS National League Comeback Player of the Year, 1972.

| Year | Club | League | Pos. | G. | AB. | R. | H. | 2B. | 3B. | HR. | RBI. | B.A. | PO. | A. | E. | F.A. |
|------|------|--------|------|-----|-----|----|-----|-----|-----|-----|------|------|-----|----|----|------|
| 1963—Reno† ...............Calif. | | Calif. | 1B-OF | 75 | 299 | 63 | 81 | 12 | 5 | 8 | 42 | .271 | 564 | 27 | 11 | .982 |
| 1964—Tulsa ................Texas | | Texas | •OF-1B | 130 | 475 | 74 | 141 | 27 | 10 | 9 | 68 | .297 | 241 | 19 | •10 | .963 |
| 1965—Jacksonville ......Int. | | Int. | OF-1B | 145 | •558 | 86 | 162 | 25 | •10 | 8 | 48 | .290 | 320 | 10 | 8 | .976 |
| 1965—St. Louis .........Nat. | | Nat. | OF | 17 | 69 | 8 | 13 | 2 | 0 | 0 | 6 | .188 | 32 | 0 | 1 | .970 |
| 1966—Tulsa ...............P. C. | | P. C. | 1B-OF | 44 | 171 | 28 | 57 | 6 | 3 | 4 | 26 | .333 | 260 | 9 | 7 | .975 |
| 1966—St. Louis‡ ........Nat. | | Nat. | OF-1B | 43 | 93 | 10 | 16 | 5 | 1 | 1 | 6 | .172 | 41 | 1 | 2 | .955 |
| 1967—St. Louis .........Nat. | | Nat. | OF-1B | 110 | 265 | 35 | 67 | 7 | 3 | 6 | 32 | .253 | 225 | 9 | 1 | .996 |
| 1968—St. Louis .........Nat. | | Nat. | OF-1B | 92 | 278 | 28 | 64 | 12 | 1 | 5 | 17 | .230 | 199 | 12 | 4 | .981 |

| Year Club League | Pos. | G. | AB. | R. | H. | 2B. | 3B. | HR. | RBI. | B.A. | PO. | A. | E. | F.A. |
|---|---|---|---|---|---|---|---|---|---|---|---|---|---|---|
| 1969–Cincinnati§ ........Nat. | OF | 152 | 637 | 104 | 194 | 25 | 10 | 21 | 93 | .305 | ●362 | 6 | 10 | .974 |
| 1970–Cincinnati..........Nat. | OF | 152 | 589 | 112 | 186 | 34 | 6 | 16 | 80 | .316 | 349 | 7 | 8 | .978 |
| 1971–Cincinnati x ......Nat. | | | | | (Injured; did not play.) | | | | | | | | | |
| 1972–Cincinnati..........Nat. | OF | 149 | 604 | 88 | 171 | 28 | 5 | 8 | 82 | .283 | •401 | 9 | 4 | .990 |
| 1973–Cincinnati y ......Nat. | OF | 129 | 457 | 42 | 94 | 14 | 2 | 9 | 51 | .206 | 279 | 9 | 10 | .966 |
| 1974–San Diego z ......Nat. | OF | 95 | 357 | 45 | 95 | 16 | 1 | 8 | 40 | .266 | 161 | 5 | 5 | .971 |
| 1975–San Diego a ......Nat. | OF-1B | 147 | 506 | 58 | 129 | 19 | 4 | 5 | 43 | .255 | 336 | 20 | 7 | .981 |
| 1976–Philadelphia ......Nat. | 1B-OF | 110 | 272 | 32 | 71 | 7 | 0 | 5 | 35 | .261 | 395 | 14 | 5 | .988 |
| Major League Totals ...................... | | 1196 | 4127 | 562 | 1100 | 169 | 33 | 84 | 485 | .266 | 2775 | 92 | 57 | .980 |

†Drafted by St. Louis Cardinals from Columbus (Pittsburgh Pirates' organization), December 2, 1963.
‡On military list, August 29 through December 28.
§Traded with Pitcher Wayne Granger to Cincinnati Reds for Outfielder Vada Pinson, October 11, 1968.
xOn disabled list, March 21, 1971 through April 15, 1972.
yTraded with Pitcher Dave Tomlin to San Diego Padres for Pitcher Clay Kirby, November 9, 1973.
zOn disabled list, July 19 to September 15, 1974.
aReleased, February 12, 1976; signed as a free agent by Philadelphia Phillies, March 22, 1976.

### CHAMPIONSHIP SERIES RECORD

| Year Club League | Pos. | G. | AB. | R. | H. | 2B. | 3B. | HR. | RBI. | B.A. | PO. | A. | E. | F.A. |
|---|---|---|---|---|---|---|---|---|---|---|---|---|---|---|
| 1970–Cincinnati..........Nat. | OF | 3 | 12 | 3 | 5 | 0 | 0 | 1 | 2 | .417 | 5 | 0 | 0 | 1.000 |
| 1972–Cincinnati..........Nat. | OF | 5 | 21 | 3 | 5 | 1 | 1 | 0 | 4 | .238 | 13 | 0 | 0 | 1.000 |
| 1976–Philadelphia ......Nat. | PH-OF-1 | 3 | 2 | 0 | 0 | 0 | 0 | 0 | 0 | .000 | 1 | 0 | 0 | 1.000 |
| Championship Series Totals ............ | | 11 | 35 | 6 | 10 | 1 | 1 | 1 | 6 | .286 | 19 | 0 | 0 | 1.000 |

### WORLD SERIES RECORD

| Year Club League | Pos. | G. | AB. | R. | H. | 2B. | 3B. | HR. | RBI. | B.A. | PO. | A. | E. | F.A. |
|---|---|---|---|---|---|---|---|---|---|---|---|---|---|---|
| 1967–St. Louis ..........Nat. | PH | 3 | 2 | 1 | 0 | 0 | 0 | 0 | 0 | .000 | 0 | 0 | 0 | .000 |
| 1968–St. Louis ..........Nat. | PH | 1 | 1 | 0 | 0 | 0 | 0 | 0 | 0 | .000 | 0 | 0 | 0 | .000 |
| 1970–Cincinnati..........Nat. | OF | 5 | 19 | 5 | 4 | 1 | 0 | 1 | 1 | .211 | 4 | 0 | 1 | .800 |
| 1972–Cincinnati..........Nat. | OF | 7 | 26 | 2 | 7 | 1 | 0 | 0 | 6 | .269 | 11 | 0 | 1 | .917 |
| World Series Totals ...................... | | 16 | 48 | 8 | 11 | 2 | 0 | 1 | 7 | .229 | 15 | 0 | 2 | .882 |

## DAVID ALLEN TOMLIN
### (Dave)

Born June 22, 1949, at Maysville, Ky.
Height, 6.02. Weight, 185.
Throws and bats lefthanded.
Hobbies–Hunting and horses.

Led Appalachian League pitchers in games started with 13 and tied for lead in complete games with 6 in 1967.

| Year Club League | G. | IP. | W. | L. | Pct. | H. | R. | ER. | SO. | BB. | ERA. |
|---|---|---|---|---|---|---|---|---|---|---|---|
| 1967–Wytheville.............................Ap'alchian | 14 | 85 | ●7 | 6 | .538 | •93 | 55 | 41 | 47 | 43 | 4.34 |
| 1968–Tampa ...............................Florida St. | 37 | 56 | 6 | 3 | .667 | 47 | 19 | 15 | 38 | 16 | 2.41 |
| 1969–Tampa ...............................Florida St. | 23 | 44 | 5 | 1 | .833 | 34 | 18 | 14 | 25 | 22 | 2.86 |
| 1970–Asheville..............................Southern | 25 | 139 | 6 | 10 | .375 | 135 | 62 | 48 | 73 | 58 | 3.11 |
| 1971–Indianapolis .......................Am. Assoc. | 41 | 61 | 7 | 4 | .636 | 46 | 19 | 15 | 50 | 24 | 2.23 |
| 1972–Indianapolis .......................Am. Assoc. | 36 | 90 | 5 | 6 | .455 | 83 | 30 | 28 | 86 | 36 | 2.79 |
| 1972–Cincinnati ..........................National | 3 | 4 | 0 | 0 | .000 | 7 | 4 | 4 | 2 | 1 | 9.00 |
| 1973–Indianapolis .......................Am. Assoc. | 25 | 31 | 1 | 3 | .250 | 29 | 15 | 12 | 26 | 11 | 3.52 |
| 1973–Cincinnati† .........................National | 16 | 28 | 1 | 2 | .333 | 24 | 15 | 15 | 20 | 15 | 4.82 |
| 1974–Hawaii ..............................P. Coast | 25 | 48 | 5 | 1 | .833 | 33 | 10 | 9 | 48 | 20 | 1.69 |
| 1974–San Diego ..........................National | 47 | 58 | 2 | 0 | 1.000 | 59 | 29 | 28 | 29 | 30 | 4.34 |
| 1975–San Diego ..........................National | 67 | 83 | 4 | 2 | .667 | 87 | 38 | 30 | 48 | 31 | 3.25 |
| 1976–San Diego ..........................National | 49 | 73 | 0 | 1 | .000 | 62 | 24 | 23 | 43 | 20 | 2.84 |
| Major League Totals ............................... | 182 | 246 | 7 | 5 | .583 | 239 | 110 | 100 | 142 | 97 | 3.66 |

†Traded with Outfielder Bobby Tolan to San Diego Padres for Pitcher Clay Kirby, November 9, 1973.

### CHAMPIONSHIP SERIES RECORD

| Year Club League | G. | IP. | W. | L. | Pct. | H. | R. | ER. | SO. | BB. | ERA. |
|---|---|---|---|---|---|---|---|---|---|---|---|
| 1973–Cincinnati ..........................National | 1 | 1⅔ | 0 | 0 | .000 | 5 | 3 | 3 | 1 | 1 | 16.20 |

## THOMAS HOWARD TOMS
### (Tommy)

Born October 15, 1951, at Charlottesville, Va.
Height, 6.04. Weight, 195.
Throws and bats righthanded.
Hobbies–Camping, hiking, backpacking, golf and basketball.
Attended East Carolina University, Greensville, N. C.; received bachelor of
Science degree in Health and Physcial Education.

| Year Club League | G. | IP. | W. | L. | Pct. | H. | R. | ER. | SO. | BB. | ERA. |
|---|---|---|---|---|---|---|---|---|---|---|---|
| 1973–Great Falls .........................Pioneer | 21 | 34 | 3 | 2 | .600 | 27 | 12 | 9 | 41 | 9 | 2.38 |
| 1973–Fresno ...............................California | 4 | 15 | 0 | 1 | .000 | 18 | 10 | 4 | 9 | 3 | 2.40 |
| 1974–Amarillo ..............................Texas | 36 | 85 | 7 | 4 | .636 | 87 | 44 | 26 | 69 | 25 | 2.75 |

| Year Club | League | G. | IP. | W. | L. | Pct. | H. | R. | ER. | SO. | BB. | ERA. |
|---|---|---|---|---|---|---|---|---|---|---|---|---|
| 1974—Phoenix | P. Coast | 10 | 23 | 3 | 1 | .750 | 25 | 11 | 8 | 21 | 6 | 3.13 |
| 1975—Phoenix | P. Coast | 40 | 74 | 1 | 4 | .200 | 63 | 27 | 17 | 45 | 28 | 2.07 |
| 1975—San Francisco | National | 7 | 10 | 0 | 1 | .000 | 13 | 8 | 7 | 6 | 6 | 6.30 |
| 1976—Phoenix | P. Coast | 51 | 72 | 4 | 6 | .400 | 68 | 24 | 17 | 56 | 21 | 2.13 |
| 1976—San Francisco | National | 7 | 9 | 0 | 1 | .000 | 13 | 7 | 6 | 4 | 1 | 6.00 |
| Major League Totals | | 14 | 19 | 0 | 2 | .000 | 26 | 15 | 13 | 10 | 7 | 6.16 |

## JOSEPH PAUL TORRE
### (Joe)

Born July 18, 1940, at Brooklyn, N. Y.
Height, 6.01. Weight, 210.
Throws and bats righthanded.
Hobbies—Popular music and golf.
Brother of Frank Torre, former first baseman with Milwaukee Braves and Philadelphia Phillies.

Tied major league record for most consecutive times grounded into double play, 4, July 21, 1975.
Led National League first basemen in double plays with 144 in 1974.
Led National League catchers in double plays with 12 in 1967.
Led National League in total bases with 352 in 1971.
Hit for cycle, game (single, double, triple, home run), June 27, 1973.
Named catcher on THE SPORTING NEWS National League All-Star Teams, 1964-65-66.
Named catcher on THE SPORTING NEWS National League All-Star fielding team, 1965.
Named third baseman on THE SPORTING NEWS National League All-Star Team, 1971.
Named Major League Player of the Year by THE SPORTING NEWS, 1971.
Most Valuable Player in the National League, 1971.

| Year Club | League | Pos. | G. | AB. | R. | H. | 2B. | 3B. | HR. | RBI. | B.A. | PO. | A. | E. | F.A. |
|---|---|---|---|---|---|---|---|---|---|---|---|---|---|---|---|
| 1960—Eau Claire | North. | C | 117 | 369 | 63 | 127 | 23 | 3 | 16 | 74 | •.344 | 636 | 64 | 9 | .987 |
| 1960—Milwaukee | Nat. | PH | 2 | 2 | 0 | 1 | 0 | 0 | 0 | 0 | .500 | 0 | 0 | 0 | .000 |
| 1961—Louisville | A. A. | C | 27 | 111 | 18 | 38 | 8 | 2 | 3 | 24 | .342 | 185 | 14 | 2 | .990 |
| 1961—Milwaukee | Nat. | C | 113 | 406 | 40 | 113 | 21 | 4 | 10 | 42 | .278 | 494 | 50 | 10 | .982 |
| 1962—Milwaukee | Nat. | C | 80 | 220 | 23 | 62 | 8 | 1 | 5 | 26 | .282 | 325 | 39 | 5 | .986 |
| 1963—Milwaukee | Nat. | C-1-OF | 142 | 501 | 57 | 147 | 19 | 4 | 14 | 71 | .293 | 919 | 76 | 6 | .994 |
| 1964—Milwaukee | Nat. | •C-1B | 154 | 601 | 87 | 193 | 36 | 5 | 20 | 109 | .321 | 1081 | 94 | 7 | •.994 |
| 1965—Milwaukee | Nat. | C-1B | 148 | 523 | 68 | 152 | 21 | 1 | 27 | 80 | .291 | 1022 | 73 | 8 | .993 |
| 1966—Atlanta | Nat. | C-1B | 148 | 546 | 83 | 172 | 20 | 3 | 36 | 101 | .315 | 874 | 87 | 12 | .988 |
| 1967—Atlanta | Nat. | C-1B | 135 | 477 | 67 | 132 | 18 | 1 | 20 | 68 | .277 | 785 | 81 | 8 | .991 |
| 1968—Atlanta† | Nat. | •C-1B | 115 | 424 | 45 | 115 | 11 | 2 | 10 | 55 | .271 | 733 | 48 | 2 | •.997 |
| 1969—St. Louis | Nat. | 1B-C | 159 | 602 | 72 | 174 | 29 | 6 | 18 | 101 | .289 | 1360 | 91 | 7 | .995 |
| 1970—St. Louis | Nat. | C-3-1B | •161 | 624 | 89 | 203 | 27 | 9 | 21 | 100 | .325 | 651 | 162 | 13 | .984 |
| 1971—St. Louis | Nat. | 3B | 161 | 634 | 97 | •230 | 34 | 8 | 24 | •137 | •.363 | •136 | 271 | •21 | .951 |
| 1972—St. Louis | Nat. | 3B-1B | 149 | 544 | 71 | 157 | 26 | 6 | 11 | 81 | .289 | 336 | 198 | 15 | .973 |
| 1973—St. Louis | Nat. | 1B-3B | 141 | 519 | 67 | 149 | 17 | 2 | 13 | 69 | .287 | 881 | 128 | 12 | .988 |
| 1974—St. Louis‡ | Nat. | •1B-3B | 147 | 529 | 59 | 149 | 28 | 1 | 11 | 70 | .282 | 1173 | •121 | 14 | .989 |
| 1975—New York | Nat. | 3B-1B | 114 | 361 | 33 | 89 | 16 | 3 | 6 | 35 | .247 | 172 | 157 | 15 | .956 |
| 1976—New York | Nat. | 1-3B-PH | 114 | 310 | 36 | 95 | 10 | 3 | 5 | 31 | .306 | 593 | 52 | 7 | .989 |
| Major League Totals | | | 2183 | 7823 | 994 | 2333 | 341 | 59 | 251 | 1176 | .298 | 11535 | 1728 | 162 | .988 |

†Traded to St. Louis Cardinals for First Baseman Orlando Cepeda, March 17, 1969.
‡Traded to New York Mets for Pitchers Tommy Moore and Ray Sadecki, October 13, 1974.

### ALL-STAR GAME RECORD

| Year League | Pos. | AB. | R. | H. | 2B. | 3B. | HR. | RBI. | B.A. | PO. | A. | E. | F.A. |
|---|---|---|---|---|---|---|---|---|---|---|---|---|---|
| 1964—National | C | 2 | 0 | 0 | 0 | 0 | 0 | 0 | .000 | 5 | 0 | 0 | 1.000 |
| 1965—National | C | 4 | 1 | 1 | 0 | 0 | 1 | 2 | .250 | 5 | 1 | 0 | 1.000 |
| 1966—National | C | 3 | 0 | 0 | 0 | 0 | 0 | 0 | .000 | 5 | 0 | 0 | 1.000 |
| 1967—National | C | 2 | 0 | 0 | 0 | 0 | 0 | 0 | .000 | 4 | 1 | 0 | 1.000 |
| 1970—National | PH | 1 | 0 | 0 | 0 | 0 | 0 | 0 | .000 | 0 | 0 | 0 | .000 |
| 1971—National | 3B | 3 | 0 | 0 | 0 | 0 | 0 | 0 | .000 | 1 | 0 | 0 | 1.000 |
| 1972—National | 3B | 3 | 0 | 1 | 0 | 0 | 0 | 0 | .333 | 1 | 2 | 0 | 1.000 |
| 1973—National | 1B-3B | 3 | 0 | 0 | 0 | 0 | 0 | 0 | .000 | 5 | 0 | 0 | 1.000 |
| All-Star Game Totals | | 21 | 1 | 2 | 0 | 0 | 1 | 2 | .095 | 26 | 4 | 0 | 1.000 |

Member of National League All-Star Team for the 1963 game; did not play.

## PABLO ARNOLDO TORREALBA
Name pronounced torr-ay-AHL-buh.

Born April 28, 1948, at Barquisimeto, Venezuela.
Height, 5.10. Weight, 173.
Throws and bats righthanded.

Pitched seven-inning, 6-0 no-hit victory against Salisbury, May 25, 1968.
Led International League in saves with 15 in 1975.

| Year Club | League | G. | IP. | W. | L. | Pct. | H. | R. | ER. | SO. | BB. | ERA. |
|---|---|---|---|---|---|---|---|---|---|---|---|---|
| 1967—Sarasota Braves | Gulf Coast | 8 | 29 | 1 | 4 | .200 | 20 | 16 | 14 | 23 | 21 | 4.34 |
| 1967—West Palm Beach | Florida St. | 2 | 10 | 0 | 0 | .000 | 16 | 11 | 9 | 11 | 3 | 8.10 |
| 1968—Greenwood | W. Carolinas | 44 | 103 | 10 | 7 | .588 | 82 | 34 | 30 | 91 | 34 | 2.62 |
| 1968—Richmond | Int'national | 4 | 6 | 0 | 1 | .000 | 11 | 6 | 6 | 4 | 3 | 9.00 |
| 1969—Greenwood | W. Carolinas | 40 | 86 | 8 | 5 | .615 | 74 | 32 | 24 | 81 | 37 | 2.51 |

| Year Club | League | G. | IP. | W. | L. | Pct. | H. | R. | ER. | SO. | BB. | ERA. |
|---|---|---|---|---|---|---|---|---|---|---|---|---|
| 1970–Greenwood | W. Carolinas | 40 | 76 | 7 | 3 | .700 | 65 | 41 | 33 | 78 | 22 | 3.91 |
| 1971–Jalisco | Mexican | 29 | 149 | 13 | 8 | .619 | 145 | 61 | 44 | 94 | 47 | 2.66 |
| 1972–Savannah† | Southern | 20 | 39 | 3 | 3 | .500 | 33 | 13 | 9 | 31 | 15 | 2.08 |
| 1973–Savannah | Souhern | 30 | 103 | 8 | 6 | .571 | 82 | 30 | 16 | 72 | 24 | 1.40 |
| 1973–Richmond | Int'national | 21 | 60 | 0 | 3 | .000 | 62 | 30 | 21 | 44 | 16 | 3.15 |
| 1974–Richmond | Int'national | 53 | 113 | 4 | 8 | .333 | 115 | 53 | 43 | 115 | 35 | 3.42 |
| 1975–Richmond | Int'national | 64 | 137 | 12 | 9 | .571 | 97 | 30 | 22 | 114 | 48 | •1.44 |
| 1975–Atlanta | National | 6 | 7 | 0 | 1 | .000 | 7 | 2 | 1 | 5 | 3 | 1.29 |
| 1976–Atlanta‡§ | National | 36 | 53 | 0 | 2 | .000 | 67 | 25 | 21 | 33 | 22 | 3.57 |
| Major League Totals | | 42 | 60 | 0 | 3 | .000 | 74 | 27 | 22 | 38 | 25 | 3.30 |

†Placed on suspension list by Southern League President, June 16 through October 27, 1972.
‡On disabled list, May 31 through June 20, 1976.
§Sold to Oakland A's, March 30, 1977.

## ANGEL RAFAEL TORRES (RUIZ)

Born October 24, 1952, at Azua, Dominican Republic.
Height, 5.11. Weight, 168.
Throws and bats lefthanded.

| Year Club | League | G. | IP. | W. | L. | Pct. | H. | R. | ER. | SO. | BB. | ERA. |
|---|---|---|---|---|---|---|---|---|---|---|---|---|
| 1971–Sarasota Cardinals | Gulf Coast | 9 | 45 | 1 | 5 | .167 | 43 | 21 | 16 | 41 | 14 | 3.20 |
| 1972–St. Petersburg | Florida St. | 28 | 155 | 10 | 4 | .714 | 136 | 56 | 44 | 104 | 51 | 2.55 |
| 1973–Modesto | California | 33 | 77 | 6 | 6 | .500 | 72 | 42 | 24 | 67 | 32 | 2.81 |
| 1973–Arkansas | Texas | 16 | 44 | 3 | 6 | .333 | 41 | 20 | 13 | 24 | 25 | 2.66 |
| 1974–Arkansas | Texas | 6 | 21 | 0 | 0 | .000 | 20 | 12 | 10 | 19 | 7 | 4.29 |
| 1974–St. Petersburg | Florida St. | 21 | 122 | 8 | 5 | .615 | 108 | 43 | 40 | 75 | 58 | 2.95 |
| 1975–Arkansas† | Texas | 30 | 134 | 5 | 7 | .417 | 126 | 64 | 48 | 62 | 61 | 3.22 |
| 1976–Arkansas‡ | Texas | 48 | 95 | 2 | 5 | .286 | 82 | 50 | 36 | 77 | 60 | 3.41 |

†On disabled list, May 12 to May 21, 1975.
‡Traded by St. Louis Cardinals' organization with Pitcher Bill Greif and Outfielder Sam Mejias to Montreal Expos for Pitcher Steve Dunning, Infielder Pat Scanlon and Outfielder Tony Scott, November 6, 1976. Listed on Montreal Expos' 1977 spring roster.

## HECTOR EPITACIO TORRES (MARROQUIN)

Born September 16, 1945, at Monterrey, Nuevo Leon, Mexico.
Height, 6.00. Weight, 175.
Throws and bats righthanded.
Son of Epitacio (LaMala) Torres, former minor league manager.
Led California League shortstops in double plays with 72 in 1964.

| Year Club | League | Pos. | G. | AB. | R. | H. | 2B. | 3B. | HR. | RBI. | B.A. | PO. | A. | E. | F.A. |
|---|---|---|---|---|---|---|---|---|---|---|---|---|---|---|---|
| 1962–Decatur | Midw. | SS | 96 | 304 | 44 | 58 | 6 | 3 | 3 | 33 | .191 | 122 | 203 | 49 | .869 |
| 1963–Fresno† | Calif. | SS | 104 | 343 | 38 | 62 | 11 | 2 | 4 | 38 | .181 | 142 | 317 | 29 | •.941 |
| 1964–Fresno | Calif. | SS | 139 | 511 | 69 | 114 | 16 | 4 | 18 | 60 | .223 | •228 | •371 | 37 | .942 |
| 1965–Springfield | East. | SS | 44 | 150 | 6 | 28 | 4 | 1 | 2 | 10 | .187 | 65 | 115 | 7 | .963 |
| 1965–Decatur‡ | Midw. | SS | 64 | 241 | 25 | 62 | 6 | 0 | 5 | 35 | .257 | 84 | 178 | 20 | .929 |
| 1966–Seattle | P. C. | SS | 102 | 346 | 34 | 86 | 9 | 3 | 3 | 24 | .249 | 152 | 267 | 22 | .950 |
| 1967–Seattle§ | P. C. | SS | 139 | 472 | 29 | 101 | 14 | 7 | 2 | 39 | .214 | 235 | 431 | 27 | .961 |
| 1968–Houston | Nat. | SS-2B | 128 | 466 | 44 | 104 | 11 | 1 | 1 | 24 | .223 | 159 | 393 | 24 | .958 |
| 1969–Oklahoma City | A. A. | SS | 29 | 105 | 13 | 25 | 3 | 0 | 0 | 5 | .238 | 41 | 78 | 3 | .975 |
| 1969–Houston x | Nat. | SS | 34 | 69 | 5 | 11 | 1 | 0 | 1 | 8 | .159 | 30 | 38 | 4 | .944 |
| 1970–Oklahoma City | A. A. | SS | 38 | 151 | 15 | 46 | 7 | 3 | 2 | 20 | .305 | 65 | 126 | 9 | .955 |
| 1970–Houston y | Nat. | SS-2B | 31 | 65 | 6 | 16 | 1 | 2 | 0 | 5 | .246 | 34 | 51 | 4 | .955 |
| 1971–Chicago z | Nat. | SS-2B | 31 | 58 | 4 | 13 | 3 | 0 | 0 | 2 | .224 | 12 | 45 | 3 | .950 |
| 1972–Montreal a | Nat. | 2-S-O-3-P | 83 | 181 | 14 | 28 | 4 | 1 | 2 | 7 | .155 | 112 | 167 | 9 | .969 |
| 1973–Houston b | Nat. | SS-2B | 38 | 66 | 3 | 6 | 1 | 0 | 0 | 2 | .091 | 32 | 75 | 5 | .955 |
| 1974–Hawaii c | P. C. | SS | 123 | 425 | 41 | 110 | 14 | 1 | 7 | 47 | .259 | 211 | 347 | 23 | •.960 |
| 1975–San Diego | Nat. | S-3-2 | 112 | 352 | 31 | 91 | 12 | 0 | 5 | 26 | .259 | 128 | 338 | 13 | .973 |
| 1976–San Diego d | Nat. | S-3-2 | 74 | 215 | 8 | 42 | 6 | 0 | 4 | 15 | .195 | 72 | 168 | 12 | .952 |
| Major League Totals | | | 531 | 1472 | 115 | 311 | 39 | 4 | 13 | 89 | .211 | 579 | 1275 | 74 | .962 |

†On disabled list from July 11 through August 14.
‡Traded by San Francisco Giants to California Angels for Outfielder Dave Marshall, April 6, 1966.
§Sent to Houston Astros by California Angels, November 21, 1967, to complete deal in which Angels obtained Pitcher Jim Weaver from Oklahoma City, August 7, 1967.
xOn disabled list June 11 through July 2.
yTraded to Chicago Cubs for Shortstop Roger Metzger, October 12, 1970.
zTraded to Montreal Expos for Pitcher Dan McGinn (First Baseman Hal Breeden was optioned to Peninsula by Chicago Cubs as part of the deal), April 7, 1971.
aSold to Houston Astros, April 4, 1973.
bTraded to Chicago White Sox for a player to be named later, October 23, 1973; White Sox sent Pitcher Dan Neumeier to Houston, December 4, 1973, to complete deal.
cSold to San Diego Padres, April 3, 1975.
dTraded with Outfielder Johnny Grubb and Catcher Fred Kendall to Cleveland Indians for Outfielder George Hendrick, December 8, 1976. Traded to Toronto Blue Jays for Outfielder-First Baseman John Lowenstein, March 29, 1977.

## RECORD AS PITCHER

| Year Club | League | G. | IP. | W. | L. | Pct. | H. | R. | ER. | SO. | BB. | ERA. |
|---|---|---|---|---|---|---|---|---|---|---|---|---|
| 1972–Montreal .......................... National | | 1 | 1 | 0 | 0 | .000 | 5 | 2 | 2 | 0 | 0 | 18.00 |

## ROSENDO TORRES, JR.
### (Rusty)

Born September 30, 1948, at Aquadilla, Puerto Rico.
Height, 5.11. Weight, 180.
Throw right and bats right and lefthanded.
Hobby–Repairing racing cars.
Led Carolina League outfielders in double plays with 5 in 1969.

| Year Club | League | Pos. | G. | AB. | R. | H. | 2B. | 3B. | HR. | RBI. | B.A. | PO. | A. | E. | F.A. |
|---|---|---|---|---|---|---|---|---|---|---|---|---|---|---|---|
| 1967–Greensboro........Carol. | | OF | 13 | 15 | 1 | 3 | 1 | 0 | 0 | 0 | .200 | 4 | 0 | 0 | 1.000 |
| 1967–Ft. Lauderdale† Fla. St. | | OF | 6 | 19 | 1 | 2 | 0 | 0 | 0 | 0 | .105 | 10 | 0 | 1 | .909 |
| 1967–Oneonta ............NYP | | OF | 8 | 13 | 5 | 3 | 0 | 0 | 0 | 0 | .231 | 11 | 0 | 0 | 1.000 |
| 1967–Johnson City ....Appal. | | OF | 48 | 127 | 23 | 35 | 8 | 0 | 3 | 22 | .276 | 60 | 1 | 7 | .897 |
| 1968–Ft. Lauderdale ..Fla. St. | | •O-2 | 125 | 340 | 47 | 78 | 6 | •13 | 3 | 26 | .229 | 169 | 29 | •15 | .930 |
| 1969–Kinston ............Carol. | | OF | 139 | 507 | •96 | 137 | 26 | 11 | 13 | 49 | .270 | 319 | •21 | 11 | .969 |
| 1970–Manchester‡......East. | | OF | 41 | 127 | 21 | 31 | 5 | 0 | 3 | 16 | .244 | 86 | 2 | 3 | .967 |
| 1971–Syracuse .........Int. | | OF | 133 | 441 | 91 | 128 | 25 | 7 | 19 | 71 | .290 | 256 | 16 | 5 | •.982 |
| 1971–New York.........Amer. | | OF | 9 | 26 | 5 | 10 | 3 | 0 | 2 | 3 | .385 | 13 | 0 | 0 | 1.000 |
| 1972–Syracuse .........Int. | | OF | 19 | 57 | 6 | 19 | 3 | 1 | 1 | 3 | .333 | 25 | 2 | 0 | 1.000 |
| 1972–New York§ .......Amer. | | OF | 80 | 199 | 15 | 42 | 7 | 0 | 3 | 13 | .211 | 86 | 4 | 2 | .978 |
| 1973–Cleveland .........Amer. | | OF | 122 | 312 | 31 | 64 | 8 | 1 | 7 | 28 | .205 | 191 | 9 | 5 | .976 |
| 1974–Cleveland x .......Amer. | | OF | 108 | 150 | 19 | 28 | 2 | 0 | 3 | 12 | .187 | 110 | 8 | 5 | .959 |
| 1975–Salt Lake C. y ..P. C. | | OF | 107 | 369 | 59 | 113 | 18 | •9 | 8 | 64 | .306 | 290 | 10 | 5 | .984 |
| 1976–California .........Amer. | | OF-3-DH | 120 | 264 | 37 | 54 | 16 | 3 | 6 | 27 | .205 | 195 | 5 | 2 | .990 |
| Major League Totals ..................... | | | 439 | 951 | 107 | 198 | 36 | 4 | 21 | 83 | .208 | 595 | 26 | 14 | .978 |

†On disabled list, May 18 through June 20.
‡On disabled list, April 24 through May 12. On temporary inactive list, May 25 through August 8.
§Traded with Catcher-First Baseman John Ellis, Infielder Jerry Kenney and Outfielder Charlie Spikes to Cleveland Indians for Catcher Jerry Moses and Infielder-Outfielder Graig Nettles, November 27, 1972.
xTraded with Catcher Ken Suarez to California Angels, December 4, 1974, to complete deal in which Indians acquired Outfielder Frank Robinson on waivers from Angels, September 12, 1974.
yOn disabled list, April 10 to May 10, 1975.

## MICHAEL AUGUSTINE TORREZ
### (Mike)

Born August 28, 1946, at Topeka, Kan.
Height, 6:05. Weight, 220.
Throws and bats righthanded.
Hobbies–Hunting, fishing, billiards and entering car shows.
Received reported $20,000 bonus to sign with St. Louis Cardinals, 1965.

| Year Club | League | G. | IP. | W. | L. | Pct. | H. | R. | ER. | SO. | BB. | ERA. |
|---|---|---|---|---|---|---|---|---|---|---|---|---|
| 1965–Raleigh ...............................Carolina | | 20 | 94 | 4 | 8 | .333 | 92 | 66 | 50 | 81 | 75 | 4.79 |
| 1966–Rock Hill ............................W. Carol. | | 15 | 90 | 7 | 4 | .636 | 63 | 35 | 25 | 85 | 37 | 2.50 |
| 1966–Arkansas...........................Texas | | 15 | 79 | 3 | 9 | .250 | 73 | 44 | 23 | 65 | 42 | 2.62 |
| 1967–Tulsa ................................P. Coast | | 29 | 190 | 10 | 10 | .500 | 152 | 82 | 70 | 155 | •108 | 3.32 |
| 1967–St. Louis ...........................National | | 3 | 6 | 0 | 1 | .000 | 5 | 2 | 2 | 5 | 1 | 3.00 |
| 1968–St. Louis ...........................National | | 5 | 19 | 2 | 1 | .667 | 20 | 7 | 6 | 6 | 12 | 2.84 |
| 1968–Tulsa ................................P. Coast | | 16 | 86 | 8 | 2 | .800 | 74 | 33 | 31 | 82 | 36 | 3.24 |
| 1969–St. Louis ...........................National | | 24 | 108 | 10 | 4 | .714 | 96 | 47 | 43 | 61 | 62 | 3.58 |
| 1970–St. Louis ...........................National | | 30 | 179 | 8 | 10 | .444 | 168 | 96 | 84 | 100 | 103 | 4.22 |
| 1971–Winnipeg...........................Int'national | | 18 | 75 | 2 | 4 | .333 | 96 | 72 | 68 | 45 | 52 | 8.16 |
| 1971–St. Louis†-Montreal .............National | | 10 | 39 | 1 | 2 | .333 | 45 | 27 | 24 | 10 | 31 | 5.54 |
| 1972–Montreal ...........................National | | 34 | 243 | 16 | 12 | .571 | 215 | 97 | 90 | 102 | 103 | 3.33 |
| 1973–Montreal ...........................National | | 35 | 208 | 9 | 12 | .429 | 207 | 116 | 103 | 90 | 115 | 4.46 |
| 1974–Montreal‡ ..........................National | | 32 | 186 | 15 | 8 | .652 | 184 | 90 | 74 | 92 | 84 | 3.58 |
| 1975–Baltimore§ .........................American | | 36 | 271 | 20 | 9 | •.690 | 238 | 103 | 92 | 119 | •133 | 3.06 |
| 1976–Oakland ............................American | | 39 | 266 | 16 | 12 | .571 | 231 | 93 | 74 | 115 | 87 | 2.50 |
| American League Totals.......................... | | 75 | 537 | 36 | 21 | .632 | 469 | 196 | 166 | 234 | 220 | 2.78 |
| National League Totals........................... | | 173 | 988 | 61 | 50 | .550 | 940 | 482 | 426 | 476 | 511 | 3.88 |
| Major League Totals ...... | | 248 | 1525 | 97 | 71 | .577 | 1409 | 678 | 592 | 710 | 731 | 3.49 |

†Traded to Montreal Expos' organization for Pitcher Bob Reynolds, June 15, 1971.
‡Traded with Outfielder Ken Singleton to Baltimore Orioles for Outfielder Rich Coggins and Pitchers Dave McNally and Bill Kirkpatrick, December 4, 1974.
§Traded with Outfielder Don Baylor and Pitcher Paul Mitchell to Oakland Athletics for Outfielder Reggie Jackson and Pitchers Ken Holtzman and Bill Van Bommel, April 2, 1976.

---

**DID YOU KNOW —**

That first baseman Bill Terry of the New York Giants won the National League batting championship in 1930 with a mark of .401?

---

## RANDOLPH ALVIN TRAPP
### (Randy)

Born August 6, 1952, at Chicago, Ill.
Height, 6:02. Weight, 190.
Throws and bats righthanded.
Hobbies—Fishing and bowling.
Attended Eastern Illinois University, Charleston, Ill.;
received Bachelor of Business Administration degree.

| Year | Club | League | Pos. | G. | AB. | R. | H. | 2B. | 3B. | HR. | RBI. | B.A. | PO. | A. | E. | F.A. |
|------|------|--------|------|-----|-----|-----|-----|-----|-----|-----|------|------|-----|-----|-----|------|
| 1973—Batavia | | NYP | OF-3B | 63 | 227 | 42 | 70 | 10 | 2 | •12 | 44 | .308 | 61 | 37 | 14 | .875 |
| 1974—Victoria | | Tex. | 3B-P | 135 | 498 | 89 | 132 | 31 | 4 | 18 | 79 | .265 | 97 | 250 | 25 | .933 |
| 1975—Tidewater | | Int. | 3B-2B | 47 | 123 | 11 | 25 | 6 | 1 | 0 | 12 | .203 | 28 | 68 | 9 | .914 |
| 1975—Jackson | | Tex. | 3-2-O | 77 | 261 | 50 | 67 | 16 | 2 | 7 | 38 | .257 | 64 | 154 | 14 | .940 |
| 1976—Tidewater | | Int. | •3-O-2 | 130 | 385 | 64 | 90 | 11 | 2 | 11 | 38 | .234 | 117 | 182 | 16 | •.949 |

Listed on New York Mets' 1977 spring roster.

### PITCHING RECORD

| Year | Club | League | G. | IP. | W. | L. | Pct. | H. | R. | ER. | SO. | BB. | ERA. |
|------|------|--------|-----|-----|-----|-----|------|-----|-----|-----|-----|-----|------|
| 1974—Victoria | | Texas | 1 | 1 | 0 | 0 | .000 | 1 | 1 | 1 | 0 | 1 | 9.00 |

## WILLIAM EDWARD TRAVERS
### (Bill)

Born October 27, 1952, at Norwood, Mass.
Height, 6:04. Weight, 187.
Throws and bats lefthanded.
Hobbies—Bowling, fishing and golf.
Pitched 16-1 no-hit victory against Quad Cities, May 30, 1971.
Tied for Pacific Coast League lead in shutouts with 3 in 1975.

| Year | Club | League | G. | IP. | W. | L. | Pct. | H. | R. | ER. | SO. | BB. | ERA. |
|------|------|--------|-----|-----|-----|-----|------|-----|-----|-----|-----|-----|------|
| 1970—Clinton | | Midwest | 10 | •48 | 1 | 6 | .143 | 53 | 35 | 30 | 38 | 26 | 5.63 |
| 1971—Danville | | Midwest | 21 | 137 | 7 | 8 | .467 | 126 | 63 | 46 | 98 | 33 | 3.02 |
| 1972—San Antonio | | Texas | 17 | 89 | 3 | 7 | .300 | 87 | 37 | 29 | 77 | 26 | 2.93 |
| 1973—Evansville† | | Am. Assoc. | 2 | 3 | 0 | 0 | .000 | 4 | 3 | 3 | 3 | 3 | 9.00 |
| 1974—Sacramento | | P. Coast | 5 | 23 | 2 | 3 | .400 | 19 | 22 | 17 | 16 | 20 | 6.65 |
| 1974—Milwaukee | | American | 23 | 53 | 2 | 3 | .400 | 59 | 29 | 29 | 31 | 30 | 4.92 |
| 1975—Sacramento | | P. Coast | 12 | 61 | 3 | 3 | .500 | 55 | 24 | 20 | 46 | 31 | 2.95 |
| 1975—Milwaukee | | American | 28 | 136 | 6 | 11 | .353 | 130 | 78 | 65 | 57 | 60 | 4.30 |
| 1976—Milwaukee | | American | 34 | 240 | 15 | 16 | .484 | 211 | 92 | 75 | 120 | 95 | 2.81 |
| Major League Totals | | | 85 | 429 | 23 | 30 | .434 | 400 | 199 | 169 | 208 | 185 | 3.55 |

†On disabled list, April 13 to May 16 and June 17 to September 4, 1973.

## STEPHEN ROBERT TRELLA
### (Steve)

Born December 8, 1953, at Brooklyn, N. Y.
Height, 6:05. Weight, 205.
Throws and bats righthanded.
Hobbies—Scuba diving and automotive mechanics.
Attended Fullerton College, Fullerton, Calif.
Pitched seven inning, 1-0 no-hit victory against Jacksonville, April 24, 1976 (first game of doubleheader).
Tied for Midwest League lead in shutouts with 5 in 1975.

| Year | Club | League | G. | IP. | W. | L. | Pct. | H. | R. | ER. | SO. | BB. | ERA. |
|------|------|--------|-----|-----|-----|-----|------|-----|-----|-----|-----|-----|------|
| 1973—Bristol | | Ap'lachian | 6 | 13 | 0 | 2 | .000 | 18 | 14 | 10 | 9 | 13 | 6.92 |
| 1973—Anderson | | W. Carol. | 9 | 22 | 0 | 4 | .000 | 26 | 28 | 22 | 13 | 28 | 9.00 |
| 1974—Lakeland† | | Florida St. | 14 | 63 | 2 | 2 | .500 | 55 | 22 | 19 | 46 | 37 | 2.71 |
| 1975—Clinton | | Midwest | 24 | 164 | 11 | 9 | .550 | 116 | 46 | 32 | 136 | 77 | 1.76 |
| 1975—Montgomery | | Southern | 2 | 10 | 1 | 0 | 1.000 | 10 | 3 | 3 | 4 | 7 | 2.70 |
| 1976—Montgomery‡ | | Southern | 23 | 124 | 9 | 7 | .563 | 101 | 64 | 57 | 94 | 72 | 4.14 |

†On disabled list, April 16 to June 5, 1974.
‡On disabled list, June 23 to July 3, 1976.
Listed on Detroit Tigers' 1977 spring roster.

## JESUS MANUEL TRILLO (MARCANO)
Name pronounced TREE-yo.
### (Manny)

Born December 25, 1950, at Caripito, Managas, Venezuela.
Height, 6:01. Weight, 160.
Throws and bats righthanded.
Hobbies—Movies and all sports.
Led Pacific Coast League second basemen in double plays with 113 in 1973.

| Year Club | League | Pos. | G. | AB. | R. | H. | 2B. | 3B. | HR. | RBI. | B.A. | PO. | A. | E. | F.A. |
|---|---|---|---|---|---|---|---|---|---|---|---|---|---|---|---|
| 1968—Huron† | North. | S-3-C | 35 | 92 | 8 | 24 | 2 | 1 | 0 | 4 | .261 | 35 | 48 | 5 | .943 |
| 1969—Spartanburg‡ | W. Car. | 3-C-S-2 | 83 | 275 | 41 | 77 | 18 | 0 | 1 | 26 | .280 | 188 | 98 | 12 | .960 |
| 1970—Birmingham | South. | 3-2-S | 84 | 241 | 26 | 63 | 10 | 1 | 2 | 19 | .261 | 101 | 130 | 14 | .943 |
| 1971—Birmingham§ | South. | 3B-SS | 107 | 371 | 37 | 104 | 18 | 1 | 5 | 44 | .280 | 110 | 212 | 31 | .912 |
| 1972—Iowa | A. A. | 3-2-S | 133 | 509 | 67 | 153 | 27 | 6 | 9 | 53 | .301 | 176 | 304 | 28 | .945 |
| 1973—Tucson | P. C. | •2B-OF | 135 | 519 | 76 | 162 | 25 | 7 | 8 | 78 | .312 | •304 | •373 | 19 | •.973 |
| 1973—Oakland | Amer. | 2B | 17 | 12 | 0 | 3 | 2 | 0 | 0 | 3 | .250 | 15 | 17 | 2 | .941 |
| 1974—Tucson | P. C. | 2B | 85 | 320 | 31 | 81 | 19 | 1 | 2 | 39 | .253 | 198 | 256 | 12 | .974 |
| 1974—Oakland x | Amer. | 2B | 21 | 33 | 3 | 5 | 0 | 0 | 0 | 2 | .152 | 31 | 43 | 4 | .949 |
| 1975—Chicago | Nat. | •2B-SS | 154 | 545 | 55 | 135 | 12 | 2 | 7 | 70 | .248 | 350 | •509 | •29 | .967 |
| 1976—Chicago | Nat. | •2B-SS | 158 | 582 | 42 | 139 | 24 | 3 | 4 | 59 | .239 | 350 | •527 | 17 | .981 |
| American League Totals | | | 38 | 45 | 3 | 8 | 2 | 0 | 0 | 5 | .178 | 46 | 60 | 6 | .946 |
| National League Totals | | | 312 | 1127 | 97 | 274 | 36 | 5 | 11 | 129 | .243 | 700 | 1036 | 46 | .974 |
| Major League Totals | | | 350 | 1172 | 100 | 282 | 38 | 5 | 11 | 134 | .241 | 746 | 1096 | 52 | .972 |

†On disabled list, August 16 through September 3, 1968.

‡Drafted by Birmingham (Oakland Athletics' organization) from Raleigh-Durham (Philadelphia Phillies' organization), December 1, 1969.

§On disabled list, May 1 through May 20, 1971.

xTraded with Pitchers Darold Knowles and Bob Locker to Chicago Cubs for First Baseman-Outfielder Billy Williams, October 23, 1974.

## CHAMPIONSHIP SERIES RECORD

| Year Club | League | Pos. | G. | AB. | R. | H. | 2B. | 3B. | HR. | RBI. | B.A. | PO. | A. | E. | F.A. |
|---|---|---|---|---|---|---|---|---|---|---|---|---|---|---|---|
| 1974—Oakland | Amer. | PR | 1 | 0 | 1 | 0 | 0 | 0 | 0 | 0 | .000 | 0 | 0 | 0 | .000 |

## RICKY JOHN TRONERUD

Name pronounced TRON-un-rood.

### (Rick)

Born September 18, 1953, at Minneapolis, Minn.
Height, 6.02. Weight, 200.
Throws and bats righthanded.
Hobbies—Fishing and golf.

Tied for Midwest League lead in saves with 10 in 1974.

| Year Club | League | G. | IP. | W. | L. | Pct. | H. | R. | ER. | SO. | BB. | ERA. |
|---|---|---|---|---|---|---|---|---|---|---|---|---|
| 1972—Coos Bay-North Bend | Northwest | 20 | 52 | 1 | 5 | .167 | 70 | 40 | 30 | 41 | 25 | 5.19 |
| 1973—Burlington | Midwest | 29 | 105 | 5 | 9 | .357 | 107 | 62 | 51 | 57 | 44 | 4.37 |
| 1974—Burlington | Midwest | 46 | 76 | 5 | 3 | .625 | 56 | 27 | 25 | 84 | 39 | 2.96 |
| 1975—Birmingham | Southern | 28 | 59 | 3 | 4 | .429 | 55 | 27 | 19 | 29 | 22 | 2.90 |
| 1976—Chattanooga† | Southern | 22 | 46 | 4 | 1 | .800 | 49 | 17 | 17 | 25 | 16 | 3.33 |
| 1976—Tucson‡ | P. Coast | 4 | 6 | 0 | 0 | .000 | 3 | 1 | 1 | 3 | 3 | 1.50 |

†On disabled list, May 5 through May 15, 1976.

‡On disabled list, August 7 through August 17, 1976.

Listed on Oakland A's 1977 spring roster.

## DARRELL WAYNE TURNER

Born March 30, 1955, at Winter Garden, Fla.
Height, 6.03. Weight, 190.
Throws and bats righthanded.
Hobby—Music.

| Year Club | League | G. | IP. | W. | L. | Pct. | H. | R. | ER. | SO. | BB. | ERA. |
|---|---|---|---|---|---|---|---|---|---|---|---|---|
| 1973—Bradenton | Gulf Coast | 9 | 31 | 1 | 2 | .333 | 29 | 16 | 8 | 22 | 18 | 2.32 |
| 1974—Key West | Florida St. | 26 | 135 | 3 | •18 | .143 | 143 | •96 | 56 | 70 | 75 | 3.73 |
| 1975—Key West | Florida St. | 24 | 127 | 8 | 9 | .471 | 123 | 66 | 59 | 47 | 65 | 4.18 |
| 1975—Wichita | Am. Assoc. | 5 | 25 | 1 | 1 | .500 | 39 | 23 | 18 | 8 | 11 | 6.48 |
| 1976—Midland | Texas | 25 | 123 | 4 | 12 | .250 | 144 | 83 | 71 | 57 | 66 | 5.20 |

Listed on Chicago Cubs' 1977 spring roster.

## JOHN WEBBER TURNER

### (Jerry)

Born January 17, 1954, at Texarkana, Ark.
Height, 5.10. Weight, 175.
Throws and bats lefthanded.
Hobbies—Fishing and bowling.

| Year Club | League | Pos. | G. | AB. | R. | H. | 2B. | 3B. | HR. | RBI. | B.A. | PO. | A. | E. | F.A. |
|---|---|---|---|---|---|---|---|---|---|---|---|---|---|---|---|
| 1972—Tri-City | Northw. | OF | 66 | 199 | 44 | 75 | 7 | 3 | 6 | 47 | •.377 | 69 | •10 | 12 | .868 |
| 1973—Alexandria† | Texas | OF | 75 | 269 | 30 | 69 | 15 | 1 | 7 | 28 | .257 | 103 | 6 | 8 | .932 |
| 1974—Alexandria | Texas | OF | 130 | 472 | 77 | 154 | 24 | 5 | 18 | 68 | .326 | 247 | 13 | •21 | .925 |
| 1974—San Diego | Nat. | OF | 17 | 48 | 4 | 14 | 1 | 0 | 0 | 2 | .292 | 14 | 1 | 0 | 1.000 |
| 1975—Hawaii | P.C. | OF | 142 | 535 | 88 | •176 | 27 | 3 | 11 | 91 | .329 | 195 | 9 | •16 | .927 |
| 1975—San Diego | Nat. | OF | 11 | 22 | 1 | 6 | 0 | 0 | 0 | 0 | .273 | 10 | 0 | 1 | .909 |
| 1976—San Diego | Nat. | OF-PH | 105 | 281 | 41 | 75 | 16 | 5 | 5 | 37 | .267 | 115 | 6 | 5 | .960 |
| Major League Totals | | | 133 | 351 | 46 | 95 | 17 | 5 | 5 | 39 | .271 | 139 | 7 | 6 | .960 |

†On disabled list, July 22 through September 7, 1973.

## WAYNE LEE TWITCHELL

Born March 10, 1948, at Portland, Ore.
Height, 6.06. Weight, 220.
Throws and bats righthanded.
Hobbies—Hunting and fishing.
Attended Portland Community College, Portland, Ore.

Tied major league record for most consecutive strikeouts, two consecutive games (18 innings), 8, May 16 (4), May 22 (4), 1973.

| Year | Club | League | G. | IP. | W. | L. | Pct. | H. | R. | ER. | SO. | BB. | ERA. |
|------|------|--------|----|-----|----|----|------|----|----|-----|-----|-----|------|
| 1966—Bismarck-Mandan | | Northern | 13 | 64 | 4 | 1 | .800 | 48 | 18 | 10 | 77 | 21 | 1.41 |
| 1966—Oklahoma City | | P. Coast | 3 | 5 | 0 | 2 | .000 | 10 | 13 | 6 | 5 | 9 | 10.80 |
| 1967—Asheville | | Carolina | 16 | 67 | 2 | 4 | .333 | 60 | 34 | 26 | 65 | 42 | 3.49 |
| 1968—Greensboro | | Carolina | 19 | 102 | 6 | 5 | .545 | 68 | 42 | 31 | 115 | 48 | 2.74 |
| 1968—Dallas-Fort Worth | | Texas | 8 | 54 | 4 | 4 | .500 | 48 | 21 | 15 | 47 | 34 | 2.50 |
| 1969—Oklahoma City†‡ | | Am. Assoc. | 19 | 68 | 2 | 5 | .286 | 65 | 50 | 36 | 54 | 55 | 4.76 |
| 1970—Portland | | P. Coast | 27 | 144 | 9 | 12 | .429 | 163 | 106 | 87 | 103 | 93 | 5.44 |
| 1970—Milwaukee§ | | American | 2 | 2 | 0 | 0 | .000 | 3 | 2 | 2 | 5 | 1 | 9.00 |
| 1971—Eugene | | P. Coast | 37 | 95 | 6 | 9 | .400 | 83 | 58 | 51 | 116 | 56 | 4.83 |
| 1971—Philadelphia | | National | 6 | 16 | 1 | 0 | 1.000 | 8 | 4 | 0 | 15 | 10 | 0.00 |
| 1972—Philadelphia | | National | 49 | 140 | 5 | 9 | .357 | 138 | 72 | 63 | 112 | 56 | 4.05 |
| 1973—Philadelphia | | National | 34 | 223 | 13 | 9 | .591 | 172 | 71 | 62 | 169 | 99 | 2.50 |
| 1974—Philadelphia x | | National | 25 | 112 | 6 | 9 | .400 | 122 | 71 | 65 | 72 | 65 | 5.22 |
| 1975—Philadelphia | | National | 36 | 134 | 5 | 10 | .333 | 132 | 82 | 66 | 101 | 78 | 4.43 |
| 1976—Philadelphia | | National | 26 | 62 | 3 | 1 | .750 | 55 | 18 | 12 | 67 | 18 | 1.74 |
| American League Totals | | | 2 | 2 | 0 | 0 | .000 | 3 | 2 | 2 | 5 | 1 | 9.00 |
| National League Totals | | | 176 | 687 | 33 | 38 | .465 | 627 | 318 | 268 | 536 | 326 | 3.51 |
| Major League Totals | | | 178 | 689 | 33 | 38 | .465 | 630 | 320 | 270 | 541 | 327 | 3.53 |

†On disabled list, June 4 to July 16, 1969.
‡Sold by Houston Astros to Seattle Pilots, November 21, 1969.
§Traded to Philadelphia Phillies for Outfielder Pat Skrable, April 5, 1971.
xOn disabled list from beginning of season until May 23, 1974.

### ALL-STAR GAME RECORD

| Year | League | IP. | W. | L. | Pct. | H. | R. | ER. | SO. | BB. | ERA. |
|------|--------|-----|----|----|------|----|----|-----|-----|-----|------|
| 1973—National | | 1 | 0 | 0 | .000 | 1 | 0 | 0 | 1 | 0 | 0.00 |

## JAMES VERNON TYRONE
### (Jim)

Born January 29, 1949, at Alice, Tex.
Height, 6.01. Weight, 185.
Throws and bats righthanded.
Hobbies—Fishing, hunting and bowling.
Attended Ranger Junior College, Ranger, Tex., and Pan American University, Edinburg, Tex.
Brother of Wayne Tyrone, infielder-outfielder in Chicago Cubs' organization.

| Year | Club | League | Pos. | G. | AB. | R. | H. | 2B. | 3B. | HR. | RBI. | B.A. | PO. | A. | E. | F.A. |
|------|------|--------|------|----|-----|----|----|-----|-----|-----|------|------|-----|----|----|------|
| 1971—Quincy | | Midw. | OF-SS | 61 | 238 | 48 | 72 | 9 | 4 | 14 | 36 | .303 | 127 | 10 | 9 | .938 |
| 1972—Midland | | Texas | OF | 128 | 472 | 63 | 133 | 17 | 5 | 16 | 71 | .282 | 210 | 15 | •16 | .934 |
| 1972—Chicago | | Nat. | OF | 13 | 8 | 1 | 0 | •0 | 0 | 0 | 0 | .000 | 6 | 1 | 0 | 1.000 |
| 1973—Wichita | | A.A. | OF-3B | 20 | 83 | 9 | 16 | 1 | 1 | 1 | 5 | .193 | 24 | 3 | 3 | .900 |
| 1973—Midland | | Texas | OF | 108 | 388 | 73 | 107 | 16 | 5 | 13 | 68 | .276 | 181 | 9 | 10 | .950 |
| 1974—Wichita | | A.A. | OF | 18 | 71 | 10 | 26 | 3 | 2 | 0 | 7 | .366 | 22 | 5 | 1 | .964 |
| 1974—Chicago | | Nat. | OF-3B | 57 | 81 | 19 | 15 | 0 | 1 | 3 | 3 | .185 | 26 | 2 | 1 | .966 |
| 1975—Wichita | | A.A. | OF-3B | 120 | 449 | 71 | 135 | 21 | 2 | 13 | 73 | .301 | 180 | 37 | 13 | .943 |
| 1975—Chicago | | Nat. | OF | 11 | 22 | 0 | 5 | 0 | 1 | 0 | 3 | .227 | 7 | 1 | 0 | 1.000 |
| 1976—Wichita† | | A.A. | OF-3B | 124 | 459 | 72 | 123 | 14 | 1 | 20 | 57 | .268 | 192 | 12 | 6 | .971 |
| Major League Totals | | | | 81 | 111 | 20 | 20 | 0 | 2 | 3 | 6 | .180 | 39 | 4 | 1 | .977 |

†Traded to Tucson (Oakland A's organization) for Infielder Gaylen Pitts, March 15, 1977.

## MICHAEL RAY TYSON
### (Mike)

Born January 13, 1950, at Rocky Mount, N. C.
Height, 5.09. Weight, 175.
Throws and bats righthanded.
Hobby—Golf.
Attended Indian River Community College, Ft. Pierce, Fla.

Led National League shortstops in double plays with 108 in 1974.
Led American Association second basemen in double plays with 97 in 1972.

| Year | Club | League | Pos. | G. | AB. | R. | H. | 2B. | 3B. | HR. | RBI. | B.A. | PO. | A. | E. | F.A. |
|------|------|--------|------|----|-----|----|----|-----|-----|-----|------|------|-----|----|----|------|
| 1970—St. Petersburg | | Fla.St. | SS-2B | 109 | 400 | 47 | 98 | 10 | 3 | 4 | 37 | .245 | 177 | 279 | 35 | .929 |
| 1971—Modesto | | Calif. | 2-S-3-O | 107 | 326 | 46 | 78 | 12 | 1 | 2 | 26 | .239 | 179 | 208 | 19 | .953 |
| 1972—Tulsa | | A.A. | •2B-SS | 132 | 444 | 39 | 103 | 14 | 3 | 3 | 50 | .232 | •319 | 335 | 13 | •.981 |
| 1972—St. Louis | | Nat. | 2B-SS | 13 | 37 | 1 | 7 | 1 | 0 | 0 | 0 | .189 | 26 | 36 | 3 | .954 |
| 1973—St. Louis | | Nat. | •SS-2B | 144 | 469 | 48 | 114 | 15 | 4 | 1 | 33 | .243 | 239 | 401 | •33 | .951 |
| 1974—St. Louis | | Nat. | SS-2B | 151 | 422 | 35 | 94 | 14 | 5 | 1 | 37 | .223 | 247 | 434 | 31 | .956 |

| Year Club League | Pos. | G. | AB. | R. | H. | 2B. | 3B. | HR. | RBI. | B.A. | PO. | A. | E. | F.A. |
|---|---|---|---|---|---|---|---|---|---|---|---|---|---|---|
| 1975–St. Louis ..........Nat. | SS-2-3 | 122 | 368 | 45 | 98 | 16 | 3 | 2 | 37 | .266 | 184 | 308 | 15 | .970 |
| 1976–St. Louis† .........Nat. | 2B | 76 | 245 | 26 | 70 | 12 | 9 | 3 | 28 | .286 | 158 | 237 | 12 | .971 |
| Major League Totals ...................... | | 506 | 1541 | 155 | 383 | 58 | 21 | 7 | 135 | .248 | 854 | 1416 | 94 | .960 |

†On disabled list, April 14 to May 9 and July 18 to September 1, 1976.

## JAMES HAROLD UMBARGER
### (Jim)

Born February 17, 1953, at Burbank, Calif.
Height, 6.06. Weight, 205.
Throws and bats lefthanded.
Hobbies–Music, all sports, reading, driving, people and traveling.
Attended Arizona State University, Tempe, Ariz.

Tied major league record for pitchers by recording an unassisted double play, August 19, 1975.
Tied for Eastern League lead in shutouts with 5 in 1974.

| Year Club League | G. | IP. | W. | L. | Pct. | H. | R. | ER. | SO. | BB. | ERA. |
|---|---|---|---|---|---|---|---|---|---|---|---|
| 1974–Pittsfield............................Eastern | 14 | 97 | 7 | 4 | .636 | 74 | 24 | 18 | 74 | 27 | 1.67 |
| 1975–Texas ................................American | 56 | 131 | 8 | 7 | .533 | 134 | 63 | 60 | 50 | 59 | 4.12 |
| 1976–Texas† ...............................American | 30 | 197 | 10 | 12 | .455 | 208 | 86 | 69 | 105 | 54 | 3.15 |
| Major League Totals ............................... | 86 | 328 | 18 | 19 | .486 | 342 | 149 | 129 | 155 | 113 | 3.54 |

†Traded with Infielder Rodney Scott and cash estimated at $100,000 to Oakland A's for Outfielder Claudell Washington, March 26, 1977.

## THOMAS GERALD UNDERWOOD
### (Tom)

Born December 22, 1953, at Kokomo, Ind.
Height, 5.11. Weight, 170.
Throws left and bats righthanded.
Hobbies–Golf and hunting.
Son of John Underwood, former minor leaguer in Philadelphia Phillies' organization.

Named Most Valuable Pitcher in Western Carolinas League, 1973.

| Year Club League | G. | IP. | W. | L. | Pct. | H. | R. | ER. | SO. | BB. | ERA. |
|---|---|---|---|---|---|---|---|---|---|---|---|
| 1973–Spartanburg ........................W. Carol. | 26 | 193 | 13 | 6 | .684 | 137 | 66 | 45 | •187 | 79 | •2.10 |
| 1974–Reading .............................Eastern | 23 | 165 | 14 | 5 | •.737 | 134 | 65 | 46 | 157 | 69 | 2.51 |
| 1974–Toledo................................Int'national | 3 | 9 | 0 | 1 | .000 | 8 | 4 | 4 | 11 | 4 | 4.00 |
| 1974–Philadelphia ........................National | 7 | 13 | 1 | 0 | 1.000 | 15 | 8 | 7 | 8 | 5 | 4.85 |
| 1975–Philadelphia .......................National | 35 | 219 | 14 | 13 | .519 | 221 | 110 | 101 | 123 | 84 | 4.15 |
| 1976–Philadelphia .......................National | 33 | 156 | 10 | 5 | .667 | 154 | 63 | 61 | 94 | 63 | 3.52 |
| Major League Totals ............................... | 75 | 388 | 25 | 18 | .581 | 390 | 181 | 169 | 225 | 152 | 3.92 |

CHAMPIONSHIP SERIES RECORD

| Year Club League | G. | IP. | W. | L. | Pct. | H. | R. | ER. | SO. | BB. | ERA. |
|---|---|---|---|---|---|---|---|---|---|---|---|
| 1976–Philadelphia ........................National | 1 | ⅓ | 0 | 0 | .000 | 1 | 0 | 0 | 0 | 2 | .000 |

## DELBERT BERNARD UNSER
### (Del)

Born December 9, 1944, at Decatur, Ill.
Height, 6.00. Weight, 180.
Throws and bats lefthanded.
Hobby–Golf.

Attended Mississippi State University, Starkville, Miss., and Eastern Illinois University,
Charleston, Ill.; received Bachelor of Arts degree in Mathematics. Did post-graduate
work in physical education at University of Maryland.
Son of Al Unser, major league catcher with Detroit Tigers and Cincinnati
Reds, 1942 through 1945, and now scout with Cleveland Indians.

Established major league record for fewest triples, season, for league leader in triples, 8, in 1969.
Led American League outfielders in double plays with 10 in 1968.
Tied for lead in double plays by Eastern League outfielders with 10 in 1967.
Named THE SPORTING NEWS American League Rookie Player of the Year, 1968.
Received reported $25,000 bonus to sign with Washington Senators, 1966.

| Year Club League | Pos. | G. | AB. | R. | H. | 2B. | 3B. | HR. | RBI. | B.A. | PO. | A. | E. | F.A. |
|---|---|---|---|---|---|---|---|---|---|---|---|---|---|---|
| 1966–York ................East. | OF | 39 | 123 | 11 | 27 | 4 | 1 | 3 | 11 | .220 | 58 | 3 | 5 | .924 |
| 1967–York ................East. | OF | 138 | 507 | 56 | 117 | 14 | 7 | 6 | 32 | .231 | 269 | •20 | 8 | .973 |
| 1968–Washington........Amer. | •OF-1 | 156 | 635 | 66 | 146 | 13 | 7 | 1 | 30 | .230 | 392 | •22 | 5 | .988 |
| 1969–Washington........Amer. | OF | 153 | 581 | 69 | 166 | 19 | •8 | 7 | 57 | .286 | 339 | 8 | 10 | .972 |
| 1970–Washington........Amer. | OF | 119 | 322 | 37 | 83 | 5 | 1 | 5 | 30 | .258 | 173 | 8 | 3 | .984 |
| 1971–Washington†......Amer. | OF | 153 | 581 | 63 | 148 | 19 | 6 | 9 | 41 | .255 | 394 | 10 | 8 | .981 |
| 1972–Cleveland‡ .......Amer. | OF | 132 | 383 | 29 | 91 | 12 | 0 | 1 | 17 | .238 | 248 | 10 | 3 | .989 |
| 1973–Philadelphia ......Nat. | OF | 136 | 440 | 64 | 127 | 20 | 4 | 11 | 52 | .289 | 329 | 14 | 4 | .988 |
| 1974–Philadelphia§ ....Nat. | OF | 142 | 454 | 72 | 120 | 18 | 5 | 11 | 61 | .264 | 300 | 13 | 6 | .981 |

| Year | Club | League | Pos. | G. | AB. | R. | H. | 2B. | 3B. | HR. | RBI. | B.A. | PO. | A. | E. | F.A. |
|---|---|---|---|---|---|---|---|---|---|---|---|---|---|---|---|---|
| 1975—New York | | Nat. | OF | 147 | 531 | 65 | 156 | 18 | 2 | 10 | 53 | .294 | 362 | 13 | 5 | .987 |
| 1976—N.Y. x-Mont. | | Nat. | OF | 146 | 496 | 57 | 113 | 19 | 4 | 12 | 40 | .228 | 288 | 10 | 3 | .990 |
| American League Totals | | | | 713 | 2502 | 264 | 634 | 68 | 22 | 23 | 175 | .253 | 1546 | 58 | 29 | .982 |
| National League Totals | | | | 571 | 1921 | 258 | 516 | 75 | 15 | 44 | 206 | .269 | 1279 | 50 | 18 | .987 |
| Major League Totals | | | | 1284 | 4423 | 522 | 1150 | 143 | 37 | 67 | 381 | .260 | 2825 | 108 | 47 | .984 |

†Traded with Pitchers Gary Jones, Terry Ley and Dennis Riddleberger to Cleveland Indians for Pitchers Mike Paul and Rich Hand, Catcher Ken Suarez and Outfielder Roy Foster, December 2, 1971.

‡Traded with Infielder Terry Wedgewood to Philadelphia Phillies for Outfielders Oscar Gamble and Roger Freed, November 30, 1972.

§Traded with Pitcher Mac Scarce and Catcher John Stearns to New York Mets for Pitcher Tug McGraw and Outfielders Don Hahn and Dave Schneck, December 3, 1974.

xTraded with Infielder Wayne Garrett to Montreal Expos for Outfielders Jim Dwyer and Jose (Pepe) Mangual, July 21, 1976.

## JOHN GODOY URREA

Name pronounced yur-REE-uh.

Born February 9, 1955, Los Angeles, Calif.
Height, 6.03. Weight, 200.
Throws and bats righthanded.
Attended Rio Hondo Junior College, Whittier, Calif.

| Year | Club | League | G. | IP. | W. | L. | Pct. | H. | R. | ER. | SO. | BB. | ERA. |
|---|---|---|---|---|---|---|---|---|---|---|---|---|---|
| 1974—St. Petersburg | | Florida St. | 1 | 2 | 0 | 0 | .000 | 2 | 0 | 0 | 0 | 2 | 0.00 |
| 1974—Sarasota Cardinals | | Gulf C. | 6 | 26 | 2 | 1 | .667 | 21 | 5 | 4 | 15 | 6 | 1.38 |
| 1975—St. Petersburg | | Florida St. | 23 | 175 | •14 | 8 | .636 | 138 | 61 | 41 | 108 | 60 | 2.11 |
| 1976—Arkansas | | Texas | 24 | 151 | 11 | 8 | .579 | 167 | 71 | 63 | 113 | 45 | 3.75 |

Listed on St. Louis Cardinals' 1977 spring roster.

## MICHAEL LEWIS VAIL
### (Mike)

Born November 10, 1951, at San Francisco, Calif.
Height, 6.00. Weight, 185.
Throws and bats righthanded.
Hobbies—Collecting stamps and coins and breeding Persian cats.
Attended De Anza College, Cupertino, Calif.

Tied National League record for most consecutive games, 1 or more hits, rookie season, since 1900, 23, August 22 through September 15, 1975.
Tied for California League lead in double plays by outfielders with 3 in 1973.
Named Player of the Year in International League, 1975.

| Year | Club | League | Pos. | G. | AB. | R. | H. | 2B. | 3B. | HR. | RBI. | B.A. | PO. | A. | E. | F.A. |
|---|---|---|---|---|---|---|---|---|---|---|---|---|---|---|---|---|
| 1971—Sarasota Cards | | Gulf C. | 3B-2B | 35 | 95 | 6 | 24 | 4 | 1 | 0 | 17 | .253 | 18 | 53 | 5 | .934 |
| 1972—Modesto | | Calif. | 3B | 42 | 136 | 15 | 32 | 5 | 0 | 4 | 17 | .235 | 30 | 57 | 15 | .853 |
| 1972—Cedar Rapids | | Midw. | 3B-OF | 61 | 202 | 19 | 49 | 7 | 1 | 7 | 37 | .243 | 48 | 50 | 14 | .875 |
| 1972—Arkansas | | Texas | 3B-OF | 19 | 65 | 4 | 12 | 6 | 0 | 1 | 7 | .185 | 23 | 14 | 1 | .974 |
| 1973—Modesto | | Calif. | *OF-3B | 134 | 479 | 81 | 133 | •31 | 9 | 15 | 80 | .278 | 150 | *23 | 12 | .935 |
| 1974—Modesto | | Calif. | OF | 62 | 221 | 37 | 79 | 15 | 3 | 7 | 41 | .357 | 113 | 2 | 6 | .950 |
| 1974—Arkansas† | | Texas | OF | 73 | 261 | 31 | 82 | 7 | 4 | 8 | 35 | .314 | 116 | 6 | 4 | .968 |
| 1975—Tidewater | | Int. | OF | 115 | 409 | 53 | 140 | 23 | *9 | 7 | 79 | *.342 | 182 | 9 | 2 | .990 |
| 1975—New York | | Nat. | OF | 38 | 162 | 17 | 49 | 8 | 1 | 3 | 17 | .302 | 92 | 9 | 3 | .971 |
| 1976—New York‡ | | Nat. | OF-PH | 53 | 143 | 8 | 31 | 5 | 1 | 0 | 9 | .217 | 63 | 1 | 4 | .941 |
| Major League Totals | | | | 91 | 305 | 25 | 80 | 13 | 2 | 3 | 26 | .262 | 155 | 10 | 7 | .959 |

†Traded with Infielder Jack Heidemann by St. Louis Cardinals to New York Mets for Infielder Teddy Martinez, December 11, 1974.

‡On disabled list, April 1 to June 15, 1976.

## ELLIS CLARENCE VALENTINE

Born July 30, 1954, at Helena, Ark.
Height, 6.04. Weight, 205.
Throws and bats righthanded.
Hobbies—Music, billiards and chess.

Led International League in total bases with 226 in 1975.
Led Eastern League outfielders in double plays with 5 in 1974.

| Year | Club | League | Pos. | G. | AB. | R. | H. | 2B. | 3B. | HR. | RBI. | B.A. | PO. | A. | E. | F.A. |
|---|---|---|---|---|---|---|---|---|---|---|---|---|---|---|---|---|
| 1972—Cocoa Expos | | Fl. E.C. | OF | 53 | 177 | 24 | 47 | 8 | 0 | 1 | 18 | .266 | 76 | 4 | 1 | .988 |
| 1973—W. Palm Beach | | Fla. St. | OF | 119 | 403 | 59 | 124 | 18 | 4 | 6 | 61 | .308 | 169 | 11 | 5 | .973 |
| 1974—Quebec City | | East. | OF | 130 | 426 | 46 | 112 | 11 | 7 | 5 | 50 | .263 | 204 | *20 | 10 | .957 |
| 1975—Memphis | | Int. | OF-1B | 139 | 494 | *87 | *151 | •30 | 3 | 13 | 66 | .306 | 266 | 12 | 6 | .979 |
| 1975—Montreal | | Nat. | OF | 12 | 33 | 2 | 12 | 4 | 0 | 1 | 3 | .364 | 12 | 1 | 2 | .867 |
| 1976—Denver | | A.A. | OF | 57 | 204 | 31 | 63 | 9 | 1 | 7 | 32 | .309 | 122 | 8 | 2 | .985 |
| 1976—Montreal | | Nat. | OF-PH | 94 | 305 | 36 | 85 | 15 | 2 | 7 | 39 | .279 | 162 | 12 | 5 | .972 |
| Major League Totals | | | | 106 | 338 | 38 | 97 | 19 | 2 | 8 | 42 | .287 | 174 | 13 | 7 | .964 |

## ROBERT JOHN VALENTINE
### (Bobby)

Born May 13, 1950, at Stamford, Conn.
Height, 5.10. Weight, 185.
Throws and bats righthanded.
Attended University of Southern California, Los Angeles, Calif.

Led Pioneer League in stolen bases with 20 in 1968.
Led Pacific Coast League in total bases with 324, sacrifice flies with 10 and double plays by shortstops with 106 in 1970.
Named Pacific Coast League Player of the Year in 1970.

| Year Club | League | Pos. | G. | AB. | R. | H. | 2B. | 3B. | HR. | RBI. | B.A. | PO. | A. | E. | F.A. |
|---|---|---|---|---|---|---|---|---|---|---|---|---|---|---|---|
| 1968—Odgen ............ | Pion. | *O-S | 62 | 224 | *62 | 63 | 14 | 4 | 6 | 26 | .281 | *111 | •10 | 6 | .953 |
| 1969—Spokane ............ | P.C. | *S-O | 111 | 402 | 61 | 104 | 19 | 5 | 3 | 35 | .259 | 166 | 254 | *38 | .917 |
| 1969—Los Angeles ...... | Nat. | PR | 5 | 0 | 3 | 0 | 0 | 0 | 0 | 0 | .000 | 0 | 0 | 0 | .000 |
| 1970—Spokane ............ | P.C. | *SS-2 | •146 | *621 | *122 | *211 | *39 | *16 | 14 | 80 | *.340 | *217 | 474 | *54 | .928 |
| 1971—Spokane ............ | P.C. | SS | 7 | 30 | 7 | 10 | 2 | 0 | 1 | 2 | .333 | 13 | 18 | 3 | .912 |
| 1971—Los Angeles ...... | Nat. | S-3-2-O | 101 | 281 | 32 | 70 | 10 | 2 | 1 | 25 | .249 | 123 | 176 | 16 | .949 |
| 1972—Los Angeles† .... | Nat. | 2-3-O-S | 119 | 391 | 42 | 107 | 11 | 2 | 3 | 32 | .274 | 178 | 245 | 23 | .948 |
| 1973—California‡ ........ | Amer. | SS-OF | 32 | 126 | 12 | 38 | 5 | 2 | 1 | 13 | .302 | 63 | 75 | 6 | .958 |
| 1974—California§x ...... | Amer. | O-S-3 | 117 | 371 | 39 | 97 | 10 | 3 | 3 | 39 | .261 | 160 | 116 | 17 | .942 |
| 1975—Charleston y...... | Int. | 3B | 56 | 175 | 27 | 41 | 4 | 0 | 1 | 17 | .234 | 44 | 74 | 6 | .952 |
| 1975—Salt Lake City ....P.C. | | 1-0-3-2 | 46 | 147 | 29 | 45 | 6 | 1 | 0 | 17 | .306 | 92 | 14 | 3 | .972 |
| 1975—California z ...... | Amer. | 1-3-O | 26 | 57 | 5 | 16 | 2 | 0 | 0 | 5 | .281 | 27 | 1 | 2 | .933 |
| 1975—San Diego......... | Nat. | OF | 7 | 15 | 1 | 2 | 0 | 0 | 1 | 1 | .133 | 4 | 0 | 0 | 1.000 |
| 1976—Hawaii .............. | P.C. | 1-0-3-S | 120 | 395 | 67 | 120 | 23 | 2 | 13 | 89 | .304 | 578 | 47 | 4 | .994 |
| 1976—San Diego......... | Nat. | OF-1B | 15 | 49 | 3 | 18 | 4 | 0 | 0 | 4 | .367 | 55 | 6 | 0 | 1.000 |
| National League Totals .................. | | | 247 | 736 | 81 | 197 | 25 | 4 | 5 | 62 | .268 | 360 | 427 | 39 | .953 |
| American League Totals ............... | | | 175 | 554 | 56 | 151 | 17 | 5 | 4 | 57 | .273 | 250 | 192 | 25 | .946 |
| Major League Totals ...................... | | | 422 | 1290 | 137 | 348 | 42 | 9 | 9 | 119 | .270 | 610 | 619 | 64 | .950 |

†Traded with Infielder Billy Grabarkewitz, Outfielder Frank Robinson and Pitchers Bill Singer and Mike Strahler to California Angels for Pitcher Andy Messersmith and Third Baseman Ken McMullen, November 28, 1972.

‡On emergency disabled list, May 17 through remainder of season.

§On supplementary disabled list, May 29 to June 13, 1974.

xLoaned to Charleston (Pittsburgh Pirates' organization), April 4, 1975.

yReturned to California Angels' organization, June 20, 1975.

zTraded with a player to be named later to San Diego Padres for Pitcher Gary Ross, September 17, 1975; Angels assigned Infielder Rudy Meoli to Padres to complete deal, November 4, 1975.

## JOHN ANDREW VALLE

Born September 8, 1954, at New York, N.Y.
Height, 6.00. Weight, 185.
Throws and bats righthanded.
Hobbies—Tennis and basketball.

Led Southern League in total bases with 218 in 1975.

| Year Club | League | Pos. | G. | AB. | R. | H. | 2B. | 3B. | HR. | RBI. | B.A. | PO. | A. | E. | F.A. |
|---|---|---|---|---|---|---|---|---|---|---|---|---|---|---|---|
| 1972—Clinton ............. | Midw. | 3B | 49 | 179 | 21 | 45 | 2 | 1 | 4 | 16 | .251 | 43 | 127 | 15 | .919 |
| 1973—Lakeland ......... | Fla. St. | OF | 127 | 425 | 59 | 107 | 14 | 5 | 4 | 48 | .252 | 168 | 9 | 6 | .967 |
| 1974—Montgomery......South. | | O-2-3 | 104 | 348 | 47 | 92 | 20 | 2 | 7 | 32 | .264 | 188 | 22 | 6 | .972 |
| 1974—Evansville ........A.A. | | OF | 7 | 19 | 1 | 1 | 1 | 0 | 0 | 1 | .053 | 10 | 0 | 0 | 1.000 |
| 1975—Montgomery......South. | | OF | 134 | 460 | 76 | 130 | 15 | 2 | 23 | 72 | .283 | 208 | 6 | 4 | .982 |
| 1976—Evansville ........A.A. | | OF | 22 | 68 | 4 | 12 | 3 | 0 | 0 | 8 | .176 | 29 | 0 | 1 | .967 |
| 1976—Montgomery† ....South. | | 3-O-PH | 74 | 232 | 45 | 58 | 11 | 1 | 15 | 53 | .250 | 42 | 97 | 12 | .920 |

†On disabled list, June 12 through June 23, 1976.
Listed on Detroit Tigers' 1977 spring roster.

## WILLIAM JOSEPH VAN BOMMEL
### (Bill)

Born February 15, 1952, at Appleton, Wis.
Height, 6.05. Weight, 215.
Throws and bats righthanded.
Hobbies—Basketball, hunting and fishing.
Attended University of Wisconsin at Oshkosh, Oshkosh, Wis.

| Year Club | League | G. | IP. | W. | L. | Pct. | H. | R. | ER. | SO. | BB. | ERA. |
|---|---|---|---|---|---|---|---|---|---|---|---|---|
| 1971—Burlington.......................... | Midwest | 7 | 24 | 1 | 0 | 1.000 | 21 | 11 | 9 | 8 | 16 | 3.38 |
| 1971—Coos Bay-North Bend .......... | Northwest | 1 | 3 | 0 | 0 | .000 | 2 | 1 | 0 | 2 | 3 | 0.00 |
| 1972—Burlington.......................... | Midwest | 24 | 164 | 9 | 9 | .500 | 149 | 86 | 64 | 142 | 72 | 3.51 |
| 1973—Burlington.......................... | Midwest | 9 | 47 | 2 | 2 | .500 | 43 | 29 | 22 | 35 | 43 | 4.21 |
| 1973—Birmingham ...................... | Southern | 11 | 43 | 0 | 7 | .000 | 56 | 51 | 44 | 24 | 37 | 9.21 |
| 1974—Birmingham ...................... | Southern | 7 | 47 | 4 | 2 | .667 | 41 | 26 | 23 | 45 | 21 | 4.40 |
| 1974—Tucson ............................. | P. Coast | 18 | 108 | 6 | 9 | .400 | 120 | 65 | 62 | 75 | 59 | 5.17 |
| 1975—Birmingham ...................... | Southern | 16 | 118 | 7 | 9 | .438 | 103 | 52 | 38 | 74 | 53 | 2.90 |
| 1975—Tucson† ........................... | P. Coast | 13 | 35 | 0 | 4 | .000 | 51 | 39 | 35 | 15 | 33 | 9.00 |
| 1976—Rochester ......................... | Int'national | 9 | 17 | 0 | 2 | .000 | 20 | 12 | 9 | 7 | 12 | 4.76 |
| 1976—Charlotte............................ | Southern | 16 | 65 | 3 | 3 | .500 | 43 | 18 | 13 | 40 | 22 | 1.80 |

†Traded with Outfielder Reggie Jackson and Pitcher Ken Holtzman by Oakland Athletics to Baltimore Orioles for Outfielder Don Baylor and Pitchers Mike Torrez and Paul Mitchell, April 2, 1976.
Listed on Baltimore Orioles' 1977 spring roster.

## OTONIEL VELEZ (FRANCESCHI)
### (Otto)

Born November 29, 1950, at Ponce, Puerto Rico.
Height, 6.00. Weight, 170.
Throws and bats righthanded.

Led International League hitters in bases on balls with 130 in 1973 and with 87 in 1975.
Named Appalachian League Player of the Year in 1970.

| Year Club | League | Pos. | G. | AB. | R. | H. | 2B. | 3B. | HR. | RBI. | B.A. | PO. | A. | E. | F.A. |
|---|---|---|---|---|---|---|---|---|---|---|---|---|---|---|---|
| 1970–Ft. Lauderdale† | Fla.St. | OF | 20 | 54 | 7 | 9 | 0 | 1 | 0 | 4 | .167 | 27 | 2 | 2 | .935 |
| 1970–Johnson City | ....Appal. | 3-2-OF | 53 | 176 | •49 | 65 | 10 | 4 | 7 | •44 | •.369 | 61 | 83 | 15 | .906 |
| 1971–Kinston | ............Carol. | 3B | 113 | 384 | 82 | 119 | 21 | 4 | 16 | 73 | .310 | 68 | 172 | 25 | .906 |
| 1972–West Haven | ......East. | 3-OF-1 | 122 | 409 | 64 | 102 | 17 | 1 | 13 | 68 | .249 | 102 | 211 | 28 | .918 |
| 1973–Syracuse | ..........Int. | OF-3B | 138 | 409 | 92 | 110 | 19 | 7 | 29 | 98 | .269 | 177 | 11 | 10 | .949 |
| 1973–New York | ..........Amer. | OF | 23 | 77 | 9 | 15 | 4 | 0 | 2 | 7 | .195 | 45 | 2 | 2 | .959 |
| 1974–Syracuse | ..........Int. | 1-2-3 | 65 | 200 | 44 | 62 | 13 | 0 | 13 | 35 | .310 | 474 | 39 | 13 | .975 |
| 1974–New York | ..........Amer. | 1-OF-3 | 27 | 67 | 9 | 14 | 1 | 1 | 2 | 10 | .209 | 140 | 8 | 3 | .980 |
| 1975–Syracuse‡ | ......Int. | 3B-1B | 81 | 244 | 56 | 61 | 18 | 2 | 10 | 35 | .250 | 302 | 90 | 19 | .954 |
| 1975–New York | ..........Amer. | 1B | 6 | 8 | 0 | 2 | 0 | 0 | 0 | 1 | .250 | 11 | 0 | 0 | 1.000 |
| 1976–New York§ | ........Amer. | O-1-3-DH | 49 | 94 | 11 | 25 | 6 | 0 | 2 | 10 | .266 | 89 | 2 | 2 | .978 |
| Major League Totals | ...................... | | 105 | 246 | 29 | 56 | 11 | 1 | 6 | 28 | .228 | 285 | 12 | 7 | .966 |

†On disabled list, May 19 to June 6, 1970.
‡On disabled list, June 10 to August 2, 1975.
§Selected by Toronto Blue Jays in American League expansion draft, November 5, 1976.

### CHAMPIONSHIP SERIES RECORD

| Year Club | League | Pos. | G. | AB. | R. | H. | 2B. | 3B. | HR. | RBI. | B.A. | PO. | A. | E. | F.A. |
|---|---|---|---|---|---|---|---|---|---|---|---|---|---|---|---|
| 1976–New York | .........Amer. | PH | 1 | 1 | 0 | 0 | 0 | 0 | 0 | 0 | .000 | 0 | 0 | 0 | .000 |

### WORLD SERIES RECORD

| Year Club | League | Pos. | G. | AB. | R. | H. | 2B. | 3B. | HR. | RBI. | B.A. | PO. | A. | E. | F.A. |
|---|---|---|---|---|---|---|---|---|---|---|---|---|---|---|---|
| 1976–New York | .........Amer. | PH | 3 | 3 | 0 | 0 | 0 | 0 | 0 | 0 | .000 | 0 | 0 | 0 | .000 |


## JOHN C. VERHOEVEN

Name pronounced Vur-WHO-ven.

Born July 3, 1953, at Long Beach, Calif.
Height, 6.05. Weight, 200.
Throws and bats righthanded.
Attended Westmont College, Santa Barbara, Calif., and La Verne College,
La Verne, Calif.; received Bachelor of Arts Degree in Physical Education.

| Year Club | League | G. | IP. | W. | L. | Pct. | H. | R. | ER. | SO. | BB. | ERA. |
|---|---|---|---|---|---|---|---|---|---|---|---|---|
| 1974–Quad Cities | .........................Midwest | 27 | 43 | 1 | 0 | 1.000 | 37 | 19 | 15 | 52 | 17 | 3.14 |
| 1975–El Paso | ...............................Texas | 31 | 56 | 4 | 0 | 1.000 | 45 | 18 | 10 | 46 | 26 | 1.61 |
| 1975–Salt Lake City | .....................P. Coast | 18 | 26 | 3 | 1 | .750 | 24 | 15 | 13 | 9 | 18 | 4.50 |
| 1976–Salt Lake City | .....................P. Coast | 28 | 60 | 7 | 2 | .778 | 53 | 19 | 15 | 56 | 18 | 2.25 |
| 1976–California | ............................Amer. | 21 | 37 | 0 | 2 | .000 | 35 | 15 | 14 | 23 | 14 | 3.41 |
| Major League Totals | ............................... | 21 | 37 | 0 | 2 | .000 | 35 | 15 | 14 | 23 | 14 | 3.41 |


## THOMAS MARTIN VERYZER

Name pronounced Vuh-RISE-er.

### (Tom)

Born February 11, 1953, at Islip, N.Y.
Height, 6.00. Weight, 175.
Throws and bats righthanded.
Hobbies–Music and basketball.

Tied for Southern League lead in sacrifice flies with 7 in 1972.

| Year Club | League | Pos. | G. | AB. | R. | H. | 2B. | 3B. | HR. | RBI. | B.A. | PO. | A. | E. | F.A. |
|---|---|---|---|---|---|---|---|---|---|---|---|---|---|---|---|
| 1971–Bristol | ..............Appal. | SS | 51 | 169 | 27 | 38 | 7 | 4 | 4 | 20 | .225 | 68 | 137 | 19 | •.915 |
| 1972–Montgomery† | ....South. | SS | 111 | 381 | 36 | 84 | 20 | 4 | 8 | 49 | .220 | 166 | 358 | 26 | .953 |
| 1973–Toledo | ..............Int. | SS | 94 | 284 | 32 | 71 | 11 | 5 | 3 | 26 | .250 | 155 | 239 | 28 | .934 |
| 1973–Detroit | ..............Amer. | SS | 18 | 20 | 1 | 6 | 0 | 1 | 0 | 2 | .300 | 6 | 12 | 3 | .857 |
| 1974–Evansville‡ | ........A.A. | SS | 67 | 223 | 36 | 66 | 7 | 1 | 11 | 36 | .296 | 109 | 207 | 15 | .955 |
| 1974–Detroit | ..............Amer. | SS | 22 | 55 | 4 | 13 | 2 | 0 | 2 | 9 | .236 | 18 | 33 | 4 | .927 |
| 1975–Detroit | ..............Amer. | SS | 128 | 404 | 37 | 102 | 13 | 1 | 5 | 48 | .252 | 215 | 358 | 24 | .960 |
| 1976–Detroit§ | ...........Amer. | SS | 97 | 354 | 31 | 83 | 8 | 2 | 1 | 25 | .234 | 164 | 313 | 17 | .966 |
| Major League Totals | ...................... | | 265 | 833 | 73 | 204 | 23 | 4 | 8 | 84 | .245 | 403 | 716 | 48 | .959 |

†On disabled list, April 11 to April 28, 1972.
‡On disabled list, June 5 to July 6, 1974.
§On disabled list, August 19 to October 4, 1976.

## JAMES MICHAEL VOSK
### (Jim)

Born March 17, 1953, at Red Bank, N. J.
Height, 6.03. Weight, 215.
Throws and bats righthanded.
Hobbies—Golf and bartending.
Attended Montclair State College, Upper Montclair, N. J.

Led Eastern League in saves with 16 in 1976.

| Year Club | League | G. | IP. | W. | L. | Pct. | H. | R. | ER. | SO. | BB. | ERA. |
|---|---|---|---|---|---|---|---|---|---|---|---|---|
| 1971—Williamsport | NYP | 13 | 96 | 8 | 3 | .727 | 77 | 35 | 32 | 87 | 48 | 3.00 |
| 1972—Winter Haven | Florida St. | 17 | 167 | 6 | 13 | .316 | 150 | 68 | 47 | 115 | 81 | 2.53 |
| 1973—Winston-Salem | Carolina | 3 | 4 | 0 | 2 | .000 | 11 | 12 | 7 | 2 | 5 | 15.75 |
| 1973—Winter Haven | Florida St. | 11 | 52 | 3 | 4 | .429 | 64 | 31 | 30 | 37 | 26 | 5.19 |
| 1974—Winston-Salem | Carolina | 27 | 58 | 2 | 5 | .286 | 64 | 45 | 38 | 44 | 50 | 5.90 |
| 1975—Winston-Salem | Carolina | 20 | 124 | 5 | 6 | .455 | 116 | 68 | 48 | 69 | 59 | 3.48 |
| 1976—Bristol | Eastern | 40 | 82 | 2 | 5 | .286 | 56 | 22 | 16 | 50 | 35 | 1.76 |

Listed on Boston Red Sox' 1977 spring roster.


## PETER DENNIS VUCKOVICH
Name pronounced VOO-Ko-vitch.
### (Pete)

Born October 27, 1952, at Johnstown, Pa.
Height, 6.04. Weight, 215.
Throws and bats righthanded.
Attended Clarion State College, Clarion, Pa.

| Year Club | League | G. | IP. | W. | L. | Pct. | H. | R. | ER. | SO. | BB. | ERA. |
|---|---|---|---|---|---|---|---|---|---|---|---|---|
| 1974—Appleton | Midwest | 5 | 15 | 1 | 0 | 1.000 | 10 | 2 | 2 | 22 | 3 | 1.20 |
| 1974—Knoxville | Southern | 13 | 47 | 2 | 5 | .286 | 50 | 32 | 22 | 42 | 29 | 4.21 |
| 1975—Denver | Am. Assoc. | 19 | 116 | 11 | 4 | .733 | 103 | 63 | 56 | 86 | 54 | 4.34 |
| 1975—Chicago | Amer. | 4 | 10 | 0 | 1 | .000 | 17 | 15 | 15 | 5 | 7 | 13.50 |
| 1976—Chicago† | Amer. | 33 | 110 | 7 | 4 | .636 | 122 | 59 | 57 | 62 | 60 | 4.66 |
| Major League Totals | | 37 | 120 | 7 | 5 | .583 | 139 | 74 | 72 | 67 | 67 | 5.40 |

†Selected by Toronto Blue Jays in American League expansion draft, November 5, 1976.


## JOHN CHRISTOPHER VUKOVICH
Name pronounced VOO-koe-vich.

Born July 31, 1947, at Sacramento, Calif.
Height, 6.01. Weight, 190.
Throws and bats righthanded.
Hobbies—Hunting and fishing.
Attended American River College, Sacramento, Calif.

Led Pacific Coast League third basemen in double plays with 29 in 1970 and tied for lead with 24 in 1972.

| Year Club | League | Pos. | G. | AB. | R. | H. | 2B. | 3B. | HR. | RBI. | B.A. | PO. | A. | E. | F.A. |
|---|---|---|---|---|---|---|---|---|---|---|---|---|---|---|---|
| 1966—Huron | North. | SS | 67 | 241 | 30 | 62 | 5 | 2 | 2 | 35 | .257 | 56 | 103 | 12 | *.930 |
| 1967—Spartanburg† | W. Car. | 3B | 74 | 261 | 35 | 66 | 12 | 1 | 4 | 40 | .253 | 50 | 120 | 16 | .914 |
| 1968—Spartanburg | W. Car. | 3B | 37 | 134 | 23 | 42 | 11 | 0 | 3 | 20 | .313 | 37 | 78 | 5 | .958 |
| 1968—Tidewater | Carol. | 3B-2B | 66 | 225 | 23 | 65 | 12 | 0 | 4 | 34 | .280 | 69 | 99 | 9 | .949 |
| 1969—Reading | East. | 3B | 110 | 372 | 39 | 94 | 9 | 4 | 6 | 45 | .253 | 114 | 187 | 15 | *.953 |
| 1970—Eugene | P.C. | *3B-1B | 138 | 520 | 58 | 143 | 21 | 3 | 22 | 96 | .275 | *124 | *334 | 22 | *.954 |
| 1970—Philadelphia | Nat. | SS-3B | 3 | 8 | 1 | 1 | 0 | 0 | 0 | 0 | .125 | 4 | 8 | 2 | .857 |
| 1971—Eugene | P.C. | 3B | 58 | 221 | 31 | 68 | 16 | 2 | 5 | 35 | .308 | 55 | 104 | 14 | .919 |
| 1971—Philadelphia | Nat. | 3B | 74 | 217 | 11 | 36 | 5 | 0 | 0 | 14 | .166 | 58 | 137 | 9 | .956 |
| 1972—Eugene‡ | P.C. | 3-2-SS | 139 | 539 | 84 | 141 | 32 | 2 | 13 | 68 | .262 | 194 | 364 | 19 | .967 |
| 1973—Milwaukee | Amer. | 3-1-SS | 55 | 128 | 10 | 16 | 3 | 0 | 2 | 9 | .125 | 86 | 67 | 5 | .968 |
| 1974—Milwaukee§ | Amer. | S-3-2-1 | 38 | 80 | 5 | 15 | 1 | 0 | 3 | 11 | .188 | 46 | 68 | 5 | .958 |
| 1975—Cincinnati | Nat. | 3B | 31 | 38 | 4 | 8 | 3 | 0 | 0 | 2 | .211 | 12 | 37 | 4 | .925 |
| 1975—Indianapolis x | A.A. | INF-OF | 49 | 152 | 6 | 21 | 7 | 0 | 0 | 12 | .138 | 89 | 88 | 6 | .967 |
| 1975—Toledo | Int. | 3B-OF | 26 | 97 | 6 | 22 | 5 | 0 | 0 | 10 | .227 | 26 | 49 | 2 | .974 |
| 1976—Reading y | East. | 2-SS-3 | 47 | 171 | 15 | 41 | 9 | 0 | 5 | 16 | .240 | 68 | 140 | 8 | .963 |
| 1976—Philadelphia | Nat. | 3B-1B | 4 | 8 | 2 | 1 | 0 | 0 | 1 | 2 | .125 | 6 | 2 | 0 | 1.000 |
| National League Totals | | | 112 | 271 | 18 | 46 | 8 | 0 | 1 | 18 | .170 | 80 | 184 | 15 | .946 |
| American League Totals | | | 93 | 208 | 15 | 31 | 4 | 0 | 5 | 20 | .149 | 132 | 135 | 10 | .964 |
| Major League Totals | | | 205 | 479 | 33 | 77 | 12 | 0 | 6 | 38 | .161 | 212 | 319 | 25 | .955 |

†On temporary inactive list, June 17 through June 28. On military list, July 29, 1967 through February 6, 1968.

‡Traded by Philadelphia Phillies with Pitcher Billy Champion and Infielder Don Money to Milwaukee Brewers for Pitchers Jim Lonborg, Ken Brett, Ken Sanders and Earl Stephenson, October 31, 1972.

§Traded to Cincinnati Reds for Pitcher Pat Osburn, October 22, 1974.

xTraded by Cincinnati Reds to Philadelphia Phillies for Outfielder Dave Schneck, August 5, 1975.

yOn suspended list (on Oklahoma City roster), April 16 to June 29, 1976; on disabled list, August 1 to August 12, 1976.

## MARK DUANE WAGNER

Born March 4, 1954, at Conneaut, O.
Height, 6.00. Weight, 165.
Throws and bats righthanded.
Hobbies—Basketball, handball and playing the guitar.

| Year    Club | League | Pos. | G. | AB. | R. | H. | 2B. | 3B. | HR. | RBI. | B.A. | PO. | A. | E. | F.A. |
|---|---|---|---|---|---|---|---|---|---|---|---|---|---|---|---|
| 1972–Bristol ..............Appal. | | 2-S-3 | 56 | 196 | 35 | 40 | 5 | 2 | 2 | 13 | .204 | 106 | 142 | 19 | .929 |
| 1973–Clinton ..............Midw.  • | | SS | 122 | 451 | 51 | 125 | 16 | 1 | 1 | 48 | .277 | 169 | •348 | 34 | .938 |
| 1974–Lakeland†.........Fla. St. | | SS | 23 | 77 | 12 | 21 | 1 | 1 | 0 | 10 | .273 | 27 | 70 | 9 | .915 |
| 1975–Clinton ..............Midw. | | SS | 119 | 436 | 52 | 111 | 11 | 4 | 1 | 50 | .255 | •175 | 339 | 31 | •.943 |
| 1976–Evansville ........A. A. | | SS | 107 | 304 | 32 | 79 | 9 | 5 | 1 | 22 | .260 | 148 | 297 | •36 | .925 |
| 1976–Detroit ..............Amer. | | SS | 39 | 115 | 9 | 30 | 2 | 3 | 0 | 12 | .261 | 60 | 135 | 11 | .947 |
| Major League Totals ..................... | | | 39 | 115 | 9 | 30 | 2 | 3 | 0 | 12 | .261 | 60 | 135 | 11 | .947 |

†On disabled list, May 10 through remainder of season.

## MICHAEL RICHARD WAITS
### (Ricky)

Born May 15, 1952, at Atlanta, Ga.
Height, 6.03. Weight, 195.
Throws left and bats left and righthanded.
Hobbies—Singing, writing, reading and golf.
Attended Clayton Junior College and Atlanta Baptist College, Chamblee, Ga.

| Year    Club | League | G. | IP. | W. | L. | Pct. | H. | R. | ER. | SO. | BB. | ERA. |
|---|---|---|---|---|---|---|---|---|---|---|---|---|
| 1970–Anderson ...........................W. Carolinas | | 9 | 42 | 2 | 3 | .400 | 27 | 25 | 22 | 37 | 33 | 4.71 |
| 1971–Pittsfield...........................Eastern | | 25 | 139 | 5 | 9 | .357 | 123 | 65 | 50 | 98 | 82 | 3.24 |
| 1972–Pittsfield...........................Eastern | | 25 | 116 | 8 | 8 | .500 | 104 | 66 | 40 | 84 | 82 | 3.10 |
| 1973–Spokane ...........................P. Coast | | 28 | 154 | 14 | 7 | .667 | 153 | 96 | 67 | 99 | 103 | 3.92 |
| 1973–Texas ...........................American | | 1 | 1 | 0 | 0 | .000 | 1 | 1 | 1 | 0 | 1 | 9.00 |
| 1974–Spokane ...........................P. Coast | | 26 | 153 | 12 | 6 | .667 | 152 | 98 | 75 | 90 | 95 | 4.41 |
| 1975–Spokane†...........................P. Coast | | 11 | 67 | 5 | 4 | .556 | 76 | 46 | 36 | 38 | 37 | 4.84 |
| 1975–Oklahoma City ...................Am. Assoc. | | 9 | 53 | 1 | 5 | .167 | 55 | 29 | 26 | 31 | 27 | 4.42 |
| 1975–Cleveland ...........................American | | 16 | 70 | 6 | 2 | .750 | 57 | 25 | 23 | 34 | 25 | 2.96 |
| 1976–Cleveland‡ ...........................Amer. | | 26 | 124 | 7 | 9 | .438 | 143 | 60 | 55 | 65 | 54 | 3.99 |
| Major League Totals ............................... | | 43 | 195 | 13 | 11 | .542 | 201 | 86 | 79 | 99 | 80 | 3.65 |

†Traded with Pitchers Jim Bibby and Jackie Brown and an estimated $100,000 by Texas Rangers to Cleveland Indians for Pitcher Gaylord Perry, June 12, 1975.
‡On disabled list, April 30 through May 29, 1976.

## ROBERT THOMAS WALKER
### (Tom)

Born November 7, 1948, at Tampa, Fla.
Height, 6.01. Weight, 190.
Throws and bats righthanded.
Hobbies—Reading and teaching small children.
Attended Brevard Junior College, Cocoa, Fla., and University of Tampa, Tampa, Fla.;
received Bachelor of Science degree in Physical Education.

Pitched fifteen-inning, 1-0 no-hit victory against Albuquerque, August 4, 1971.

| Year    Club | League | G. | IP. | W. | L. | Pct. | H. | R. | ER. | SO. | BB. | ERA. |
|---|---|---|---|---|---|---|---|---|---|---|---|---|
| 1968–Miami...................Fla. St. | | 18 | 103 | 7 | 4 | .636 | 92 | 34 | 30 | 67 | 29 | 2.62 |
| 1969–Miami...................Fla. St. | | 16 | 118 | 9 | 5 | .643 | 93 | 42 | 37 | 83 | 33 | 2.82 |
| 1970–Stockton ...................California | | 21 | 125 | 8 | 8 | .500 | 113 | 53 | 39 | 129 | 39 | 2.81 |
| 1971–Dallas-Ft. Worth† ...............Texas | | 31 | 168 | 13 | 9 | .591 | 130 | 61 | 42 | 123 | 36 | 2.25 |
| 1972–Montreal ...........................National | | 46 | 75 | 2 | 2 | .500 | 71 | 27 | 24 | 42 | 22 | 2.88 |
| 1973–Montreal ...........................National | | 54 | 92 | 7 | 5 | .583 | 95 | 52 | 37 | 68 | 42 | 3.62 |
| 1974–Memphis...........................Int'national | | 5 | 40 | 5 | 0 | 1.000 | 26 | 6 | 6 | 37 | 7 | 1.35 |
| 1974–Montreal‡ ...........................National | | 33 | 92 | 4 | 5 | .444 | 96 | 45 | 39 | 70 | 28 | 3.82 |
| 1975–Detroit§ ...........................American | | 36 | 115 | 3 | 8 | .273 | 116 | 69 | 57 | 60 | 40 | 4.46 |
| 1976–Tulsa x ...........................Am. Assoc. | | 21 | 115 | 9 | 5 | .643 | 132 | 62 | 48 | 80 | 24 | 3.76 |
| 1976–St. Louis ...........................National | | 10 | 20 | 1 | 2 | .333 | 22 | 10 | 9 | 11 | 3 | 4.05 |
| National League Totals............................ | | 143 | 279 | 14 | 14 | .500 | 284 | 134 | 109 | 191 | 95 | 3.52 |
| American League Totals......................... | | 36 | 115 | 3 | 8 | .273 | 116 | 69 | 57 | 60 | 40 | 4.46 |
| Major League Totals ............................... | | 179 | 394 | 17 | 22 | .436 | 400 | 203 | 166 | 251 | 135 | 3.79 |

†Drafted by Montreal Expos from Rochester (Baltimore Orioles' organization), November 29, 1971.
‡Traded with Catcher Terry Humphrey to Detroit Tigers for Pitcher Woodie Fryman, December 4, 1974.
§Sold to St. Louis Cardinals, February 4, 1976.
xOn disabled list, April 16 through May 31, 1976.

## STANLEY ARTHUR WALL
### (Stan)

Born June 16, 1951, at Butler, Mo.
Height, 6.01. Weight, 175.
Throws and bats lefthanded.
Hobbies—Bowling, golf, swimming and hunting.

Led Pioneer League in saves with 7 and in wild pitches with 11 in 1969.

| Year Club | League | G. | IP. | W. | L. | Pct. | H. | R. | ER. | SO. | BB. | ERA. |
|---|---|---|---|---|---|---|---|---|---|---|---|---|
| 1969—Ogden | Pioneer | •36 | 71 | 8 | 4 | .667 | 68 | 38 | 24 | 80 | 36 | 3.04 |
| 1970—Daytona Beach | Florida St. | 23 | 150 | 11 | 6 | .647 | 141 | 62 | 43 | 120 | 64 | 2.58 |
| 1971—Albuquerque | Texas | 35 | 132 | 8 | 6 | .571 | 123 | 67 | 53 | 84 | 40 | 3.61 |
| 1972—Albuquerque | P. Coast | 28 | 125 | 6 | 8 | .429 | 120 | 75 | 64 | 71 | 53 | 4.61 |
| 1973—Albuquerque | P. Coast | 13 | 32 | 1 | 2 | .333 | 47 | 26 | 24 | 21 | 20 | 6.75 |
| 1973—Waterbury | Eastern | 16 | 55 | 2 | 5 | .286 | 70 | 41 | 38 | 40 | 34 | 6.22 |
| 1974—Albuquerque | P. Coast | 36 | 105 | 8 | 10 | .444 | 105 | 57 | 42 | 94 | 59 | 3.60 |
| 1975—Albuquerque | P. Coast | 23 | 106 | 9 | 5 | .643 | 105 | 44 | 28 | 66 | 42 | 2.38 |
| 1975—Los Angeles | National | 10 | 16 | 0 | 1 | .000 | 12 | 6 | 3 | 6 | 7 | 1.69 |
| 1976—Los Angeles | National | 31 | 50 | 2 | 2 | .500 | 50 | 21 | 20 | 27 | 15 | 3.60 |
| Major League Totals | | 41 | 66 | 2 | 3 | .400 | 62 | 27 | 23 | 33 | 22 | 3.14 |

## MICHAEL SHERMAN WALLACE
### (Mike)

Born February 3, 1951, at Gastonia, N. C.
Height, 6.02. Weight, 200.
Throws and bats lefthanded.
Hobby—Reading.
Attended Arizona State University, Tempe, Ariz., and Virginia
Commonwealth University, Richmond, Va.

Pitched seven-inning, 2-0 no-hit victory against Manchester, August 28, 1971.
Led Western Carolinas League pitchers in games started with 25 in 1970.
Led Appalachian League pitchers in games started with 14 and tied for lead in complete games with 7 in 1969.
Tied for Pacific Coast League lead in games started with 31 and wild pitches with 14 in 1972.

| Year Club | League | G. | IP. | W. | L. | Pct. | H. | R. | ER. | SO. | BB. | ERA. |
|---|---|---|---|---|---|---|---|---|---|---|---|---|
| 1969—Pulaski | Ap'achian | 14 | •102 | 6 | 6 | .500 | •102 | 54 | •45 | •123 | 47 | 3.97 |
| 1970—Spartanburg | W. Carolina | 25 | 167 | 8 | 8 | .500 | 150 | 95 | 68 | 157 | 72 | 3.66 |
| 1971—Reading | Eastern | 28 | 184 | 10 | 14 | .417 | 181 | •91 | •72 | 138 | 62 | 3.52 |
| 1972—Eugene | P. Coast | 32 | 203 | •16 | 7 | .696 | •202 | 103 | 78 | 128 | 91 | 3.46 |
| 1973—Eugene | P. Coast | 15 | 106 | 6 | 5 | .545 | 120 | 67 | 55 | 68 | 39 | 4.67 |
| 1973—Reading | Eastern | 3 | 14 | 2 | 0 | 1.000 | 11 | 5 | 4 | 6 | 7 | 2.57 |
| 1973—Philadelphia | National | 20 | 33 | 1 | 1 | .500 | 38 | 16 | 14 | 20 | 15 | 3.82 |
| 1974—Philadelphia† | National | 8 | 8 | 1 | 0 | 1.000 | 12 | 6 | 5 | 1 | 2 | 5.63 |
| 1974—Syracuse | Int'national | 5 | 10 | 1 | 1 | .500 | 8 | 5 | 1 | 11 | 2 | 0.90 |
| 1974—New York | American | 23 | 52 | 6 | 0 | 1.000 | 42 | 18 | 14 | 34 | 35 | 2.42 |
| 1975—New York‡ | American | 3 | 4 | 0 | 0 | .000 | 11 | 7 | 7 | 2 | 1 | 15.75 |
| 1975—Tulsa | Am. Assoc. | 21 | 75 | 5 | 6 | .455 | 80 | 41 | 37 | 62 | 43 | 4.44 |
| 1975—St. Louis | National | 9 | 9 | 0 | 0 | .000 | 9 | 2 | 2 | 6 | 5 | 2.00 |
| 1976—St. Louis§ | National | 49 | 66 | 3 | 2 | .600 | 66 | 34 | 30 | 40 | 39 | 4.09 |
| American League Totals | | 26 | 56 | 6 | 0 | 1.000 | 53 | 25 | 21 | 36 | 36 | 3.38 |
| National League Totals | | 86 | 116 | 5 | 3 | .625 | 125 | 58 | 51 | 67 | 61 | 3.96 |
| Major League Totals | | 112 | 172 | 11 | 3 | .786 | 178 | 83 | 72 | 103 | 97 | 3.77 |

†Traded to New York Yankees for Pitcher Ken Wright, May 3, 1974.
‡Sold to St. Louis Cardinals, June 13, 1975.
§Traded to Texas Rangers for Pitcher Johnny Ike Sutton, October 22, 1976.

## DENNIS MARTIN WALLING
### (Denny)

Born April 17, 1954, at Neptune, N. J.
Height, 6.01. Weight, 185.
Throws right and bats lefthanded.
Hobby—Hunting.
Attended Brookdale Community College, Lincroft, N. J., and
Clemson University, Clemson, S. C.
Brother of Gregory Walling, outfielder-first baseman in Houston
Astros' organization, 1967.

Received large bonus to sign with Oakland Athletics, 1975.

| Year Club | League | Pos. | G. | AB. | R. | H. | 2B. | 3B. | HR. | RBI. | B.A. | PO. | A. | E. | F.A. |
|---|---|---|---|---|---|---|---|---|---|---|---|---|---|---|---|
| 1975—Oakland | Amer. | OF | 6 | 8 | 0 | 1 | 1 | 0 | 0 | 2 | .125 | 3 | 0 | 0 | 1.000 |
| 1976—Chattanooga | South. | OF-PH | 115 | 369 | 48 | 95 | 15 | 5 | 9 | 42 | .257 | 241 | 8 | 2 | •.992 |
| 1976—Oakland | Amer. | OF | 3 | 11 | 1 | 3 | 0 | 0 | 0 | 0 | .273 | 8 | 0 | 1 | .889 |
| Major League Totals | | | 9 | 19 | 1 | 4 | 1 | 0 | 0 | 2 | .210 | 11 | 0 | 1 | .917 |

## HAROLD JOSEPH WALLIS
### (Joe)

Born January 9, 1952, at East St. Louis, Ill.
Height, 5.10. Weight, 190.
Throws right and bats lefthanded.
Attended Southern Illinois University, Carbondale, Ill.

| Year Club | League | Pos. | G. | AB. | R. | H. | 2B. | 3B. | HR. | RBI. | B.A. | PO. | A. | E. | F.A. |
|---|---|---|---|---|---|---|---|---|---|---|---|---|---|---|---|
| 1973—Quincy | Midw. | OF | 12 | 47 | 11 | 20 | 4 | 0 | 6 | 18 | .426 | 18 | 0 | 2 | .900 |
| 1973—Midland | Midw. | OF | 55 | 198 | 23 | 39 | 5 | 0 | 4 | 11 | .197 | 108 | 6 | 5 | .958 |

| Year | Club | League | Pos. | G. | AB. | R. | H. | 2B. | 3B. | HR. | RBI. | B.A. | PO. | A. | E. | F.A. |
|------|------|--------|------|-----|------|-----|------|-----|-----|-----|------|------|------|-----|-----|------|
| 1974—Key West | ........ | Fla.St. | OF-2-P | 82 | 281 | 37 | 62 | 8 | 4 | •16 | 39 | .221 | 155 | 36 | 7 | .965 |
| 1974—Midland | ........... | Texas | OF | 37 | 108 | 11 | 22 | 2 | 0 | 3 | 10 | .204 | 69 | 5 | 1 | .987 |
| 1975—Midland | ........... | Texas | OF | 102 | 348 | 53 | 99 | 23 | 5 | 7 | 59 | .284 | 198 | 14 | 7 | .968 |
| 1975—Wichita | ........... | A.A. | OF | 34 | 120 | 22 | 40 | 15 | 5 | 2 | 24 | .333 | 89 | 6 | 2 | .979 |
| 1975—Chicago | ........... | Nat. | OF | 16 | 56 | 9 | 16 | 2 | 2 | 1 | 4 | .286 | 31 | 1 | 0 | 1.000 |
| 1976—Chicago | ........... | Nat. | OF | 121 | 338 | 51 | 86 | 11 | 5 | 5 | 21 | .254 | 193 | 11 | 5 | .976 |
| Major League Totals | ...................... | | | 137 | 394 | 60 | 102 | 13 | 7 | 6 | 25 | .259 | 224 | 12 | 5 | .979 |

PITCHING RECORD

| Year | Club | League | G. | IP. | W. | L. | Pct. | H. | R. | ER. | SO. | BB. | ERA. |
|------|------|--------|-----|-----|-----|-----|------|-----|-----|-----|-----|-----|------|
| 1974—Key West | ........................... | Florida St. | 1 | 1 | 0 | 0 | .000 | 1 | 1 | 1 | 0 | 3 | 9.00 |

## DANIEL DEAN WARTHEN
### (Dan)

Born December 1, 1952, at Omaha, Neb.
Height, 6.00. Weight, 200.
Throws left and bats righthanded.
Hobbies—Hunting and fishing.
Led Northern League pitchers in complete games with 10 in 1971.

| Year | Club | League | G. | IP. | W. | L. | Pct. | H. | R. | ER. | SO. | BB. | ERA. |
|------|------|--------|-----|-----|-----|-----|------|-----|-----|-----|-----|-----|------|
| 1971—Watertown | ......................... | Northern | 14 | 109 | 9 | 3 | .750 | •109 | 64 | 48 | 101 | 49 | 3.96 |
| 1972—Quebec City† | ....................... | Eastern | 10 | 46 | 3 | 4 | .429 | 40 | 24 | 21 | 38 | 20 | 4.11 |
| 1973—Quebec City | ....................... | Eastern | 36 | 141 | 8 | 6 | .571 | 106 | 71 | 56 | 102 | 107 | 3.57 |
| 1974—Quebec City | ....................... | Eastern | 14 | 91 | 5 | 6 | .455 | 81 | 40 | 31 | 56 | 57 | 3.07 |
| 1974—Memphis | ............................. | Int'national | 14 | 86 | 6 | 2 | .750 | 79 | 39 | 31 | 70 | 41 | 3.24 |
| 1975—Memphis | ............................. | Int'national | 8 | 54 | 2 | 5 | .286 | 32 | 16 | 14 | 48 | 30 | 2.33 |
| 1975—Montreal | ............................. | National | 40 | 168 | 8 | 6 | .571 | 130 | 62 | 58 | 128 | 87 | 3.11 |
| 1976—Denver | .............................. | Am. Assoc. | 8 | 34 | 4 | 0 | 1.000 | 22 | 17 | 12 | 34 | 20 | 3.18 |
| 1976—Montreal | ............................. | National | 23 | 90 | 2 | 10 | .167 | 76 | 59 | 53 | 67 | 66 | 5.30 |
| Major League Totals | ............................. | | 63 | 258 | 10 | 16 | .385 | 206 | 121 | 111 | 195 | 153 | 4.22 |

†On disabled list, June 12 to July 1, 1972. On temporary inactive list, July 1 to September 5, 1972.

## CLAUDELL WASHINGTON

Born August 31, 1954, at Los Angeles, Calif.
Height, 6.00. Weight, 190.
Throws and bats lefthanded.
Brother of Don Washington, outfielder in Los Angeles Dodgers' organization.
Major League stolen bases: 1974 (6), 1975 (40), 1976 (37). Total—83.
Led Midwest League in total bases with 218 in 1973.

| Year | Club | League | Pos. | G. | AB. | R. | H. | 2B. | 3B. | HR. | RBI. | B.A. | PO. | A. | E. | F.A. |
|------|------|--------|------|-----|------|-----|------|-----|-----|-----|------|------|------|-----|-----|------|
| 1972—C's Bay-N. Bend | | Northw. | OF | 33 | 111 | 13 | 31 | 3 | 2 | 2 | 15 | .279 | 37 | 1 | 6 | .864 |
| 1973—Burlington | ........ | Midw. | OF | 108 | 447 | •92 | 144 | 25 | 5 | 13 | 81 | .322 | 149 | 10 | •15 | .914 |
| 1974—Birmingham | ...... | South. | OF | 74 | 294 | 64 | 106 | 23 | 3 | 11 | 55 | .361 | 116 | 5 | 13 | .903 |
| 1974—Oakland | ........... | Amer. | OF | 73 | 221 | 16 | 63 | 10 | 5 | 0 | 19 | .285 | 63 | 2 | 1 | .985 |
| 1975—Oakland | ........... | Amer. | OF | 148 | 590 | 86 | 182 | 24 | 7 | 10 | 77 | .308 | 305 | 8 | 7 | .978 |
| 1976—Oakland† | ......... | Amer. | OF-DH | 134 | 490 | 65 | 126 | 20 | 6 | 5 | 53 | .257 | 276 | 10 | •11 | .963 |
| Major League Totals | ...................... | | | 355 | 1301 | 167 | 371 | 54 | 18 | 15 | 149 | .285 | 644 | 20 | 19 | .972 |

†On disabled list, August 16 through September 1, 1976; traded to Texas Rangers for Pitcher Jim Umbarger, Infielder Rodney Scott and cash estimated at $100,000, March 26, 1977.

CHAMPIONSHIP SERIES RECORD

| Year | Club | League | Pos. | G. | AB. | R. | H. | 2B. | 3B. | HR. | RBI. | B.A. | PO. | A. | E. | F.A. |
|------|------|--------|------|-----|------|-----|------|-----|-----|-----|------|------|------|-----|-----|------|
| 1974—Oakland | ........... | Amer. | OF-PH | 4 | 11 | 1 | 3 | 1 | 0 | 0 | 0 | .273 | 11 | 0 | 0 | 1.000 |
| 1975—Oakland | ........... | Amer. | OF-DH | 3 | 12 | 1 | 3 | 1 | 0 | 0 | 1 | .250 | 1 | 0 | 2 | .333 |
| Championship Series Totals | ........... | | | 7 | 23 | 2 | 6 | 2 | 0 | 0 | 1 | .261 | 12 | 0 | 2 | .857 |

WORLD SERIES RECORD

| Year | Club | League | Pos. | G. | AB. | R. | H. | 2B. | 3B. | HR. | RBI. | B.A. | PO. | A. | E. | F.A. |
|------|------|--------|------|-----|------|-----|------|-----|-----|-----|------|------|------|-----|-----|------|
| 1974—Oakland | ........... | Amer. | OF-PH | 5 | 7 | 1 | 4 | 0 | 0 | 0 | 0 | .571 | 3 | 0 | 0 | 1.000 |

ALL-STAR GAME RECORD

| Year | League | Pos. | AB. | R. | H. | 2B. | 3B. | HR. | RBI. | B.A. | PO. | A. | E. | F.A. |
|------|--------|------|------|-----|-----|-----|-----|-----|------|------|------|-----|-----|------|
| 1975—American | ........................... | PR-OF | 1 | 0 | 1 | 0 | 0 | 0 | 0 | 1.000 | 1 | 0 | 0 | 1.000 |

## U. L. WASHINGTON

Born October 27, 1953, at Atoka, Okla.
Height, 5.11. Weight, 175.
Throws and bats righthanded.
Attended Murray State College, Tishomingo, Okla.
Led American Association batters in strikeouts with 145 in 1975.
Led Appalachian League shortstops in double plays with 29 in 1973.
Led Appalachain League in sacrifice flies with 8 in 1973.

| Year Club | League | Pos. | G. | AB. | R. | H. | 2B. | 3B. | HR. | RBI. | B.A. | PO. | A. | E. | F.A. |
|---|---|---|---|---|---|---|---|---|---|---|---|---|---|---|---|
| 1973—Kingsport ..........Appal. | | SS | 68 | 244 | 47 | 69 | 14 | 4 | 5 | 51 | .283 | 89 | 176 | 36 | .880 |
| 1974—San Jose............Calif. | | SS-2B | 68 | 245 | 38 | 61 | 9 | 2 | 6 | 21 | .249 | 81 | 201 | 34 | .892 |
| 1974—Jacksonville .....South. | | SS | 47 | 167 | 29 | 43 | 11 | 1 | 2 | 20 | .257 | 71 | 172 | 17 | .935 |
| 1975—Omaha .............A.A. | | SS | 128 | 475 | 60 | 113 | 11 | 8 | 5 | 37 | .238 | 195 | 367 | *46 | .924 |
| 1976—Omaha† ..........A.A. | | SS | 30 | 120 | 20 | 30 | 3 | 2 | 4 | 16 | .250 | 48 | 102 | 15 | .909 |

†On disabled list, May 21 through September 6, 1976.
Listed on Kansas City Royals' 1977 spring roster.

## STEVEN CRAIG WATERBURY
### (Steve)

Born April 6, 1952, at Marion, Ill.
Height, 6.05. Weight, 190.
Throws and bats righthanded.
Hobbies—Hunting, fishing, taxidermy and Labrador field trial dogs.

| Year Club | League | G. | IP. | W. | L. | Pct. | H. | R. | ER. | SO. | BB. | ERA. |
|---|---|---|---|---|---|---|---|---|---|---|---|---|
| 1971—Cedar Rapids .....................Midwest | | 21 | 117 | 6 | 10 | .375 | 107 | 56 | 46 | 89 | 72 | 3.54 |
| 1972—St. Petersburg....................Florida St. | | 26 | 155 | 11 | 10 | .524 | 122 | 52 | 42 | 113 | 84 | 2.44 |
| 1973—Modesto .............................California | | 30 | 127 | 4 | 8 | .333 | 136 | 89 | 64 | 121 | 85 | 4.54 |
| 1974—Modesto .............................California | | 21 | 143 | 8 | 9 | .471 | 128 | 70 | 57 | 105 | 74 | 3.59 |
| 1974—Arkansas............................Texas | | 2 | 15 | 0 | 2 | .000 | 15 | 7 | 6 | 6 | 8 | 3.60 |
| 1975—Arkansas............................Texas | | 11 | 69 | 7 | 4 | .636 | 50 | 31 | 29 | 32 | 32 | 3.78 |
| 1975—Tulsa .................................Am. Assoc. | | 11 | 75 | 4 | 2 | .667 | 68 | 36 | 33 | 41 | 45 | 3.96 |
| 1976—Tulsa .................................Am. Assoc. | | 28 | 123 | 6 | 10 | .375 | 162 | 97 | 80 | 91 | 79 | 5.85 |
| 1976—Arkansas............................Texas | | 1 | 3 | 0 | 1 | .000 | 4 | 5 | 5 | 1 | 5 | 15.00 |
| 1976—St. Louis ............................National | | 5 | 6 | 0 | 0 | .000 | 7 | 4 | 4 | 4 | 3 | 6.00 |
| Major League Totals ............................. | | 5 | 6 | 0 | 0 | .000 | 7 | 4 | 4 | 4 | 3 | 6.00 |

Listed on St. Louis Cardinals' 1977 spring roster.

## JOHN DAVID WATHAN

Born October 4, 1949, at Cedar Rapids, Ia.
Height, 6.02. Weight, 205.
Throws and bats righthanded.
Hobbies—Reading, flying and all sports.
Attended University of San Diego, San Diego, Calif., and
Mount Mercy College, Cedar Rapids, Ia.

| Year Club | League | Pos. | G. | AB. | R. | H. | 2B. | 3B. | HR. | RBI. | B.A. | PO. | A. | E. | F.A. |
|---|---|---|---|---|---|---|---|---|---|---|---|---|---|---|---|
| 1971—San Jose............Calif. | | C-OF | 64 | 215 | 37 | 56 | 11 | 2 | 1 | 29 | .260 | 438 | 31 | 14 | .971 |
| 1971—Waterloo ..........Midw. | | C-O-1 | 43 | 147 | 31 | 41 | 4 | 4 | 3 | 21 | .279 | 282 | 18 | 1 | .997 |
| 1972—San Jose† .........Calif. | | C-1-3 | 48 | 148 | 25 | 40 | 8 | 0 | 4 | 15 | .270 | 324 | 31 | 3 | .992 |
| 1972—Omaha .............A. A. | | C | 18 | 51 | 8 | 15 | 1 | 1 | 0 | 2 | .294 | 94 | 5 | 1 | .990 |
| 1972—Jacksonville .....South. | | C | 16 | 54 | 6 | 17 | 3 | 1 | 0 | 3 | .315 | 111 | 7 | 4 | .967 |
| 1973—Jacksonville‡ .....South. | | C-1-3 | 65 | 233 | 20 | 58 | 8 | 3 | 5 | 34 | .249 | 294 | 28 | 4 | .988 |
| 1974—Jacksonville .....South. | | 1-O-C | 120 | 428 | 63 | 105 | 14 | 2 | 7 | 47 | .245 | 760 | 50 | 7 | .991 |
| 1975—Omaha .............A. A. | | C-OF | 104 | 360 | 42 | 109 | 14 | 4 | 8 | 46 | .303 | 532 | 45 | 10 | .983 |
| 1976—Omaha .............A. A. | | C-OF | 24 | 84 | 4 | 13 | 5 | 0 | 0 | 6 | .155 | 128 | 14 | 4 | .973 |
| 1976—Kansas City ......Amer. | | C | 27 | 42 | 5 | 12 | 1 | 0 | 0 | 5 | .286 | 57 | 4 | 1 | .984 |
| Major League Totals ...................... | | 27 | 42 | 5 | 12 | 1 | 0 | 0 | 5 | .286 | 57 | 4 | 1 | .984 |

†On disabled list, May 5 to May 30, 1972.
‡On disabled list, May 25 to June 28, 1973.
§On disabled list, July 29 to September 1, 1976.

CHAMPIONSHIP SERIES RECORD

| Year Club | League | Pos. | G. | AB. | R. | H. | 2B. | 3B. | HR. | RBI. | B.A. | PO. | A. | E. | F.A. |
|---|---|---|---|---|---|---|---|---|---|---|---|---|---|---|---|
| 1976—Kansas City ......Amer. | | C | 1 | 0 | 0 | 0 | 0 | 0 | 0 | 0 | .000 | 0 | 0 | 0 | .000 |

## ROBERT JOSE WATSON
### (Bob)

Born April 10, 1946, at Los Angeles, Calif.
Height, 6.01½. Weight, 201.
Throws and bats righthanded.
Attended Los Angeles Harbor College, Los Angeles, Calif.

Led Florida State League catchers in double plays with 14 in 1966.

| Year Club | League | Pos. | G. | AB. | R. | H. | 2B. | 3B. | HR. | RBI. | B.A. | PO. | A. | E. | F.A. |
|---|---|---|---|---|---|---|---|---|---|---|---|---|---|---|---|
| 1965—Salisbury ..........W. Car. | | C | 80 | 309 | 51 | 88 | 20 | 3 | 12 | 55 | .285 | 476 | 25 | 15 | .971 |
| 1966—Cocoa...............Fla. St. | | C-OF | 105 | 348 | 56 | 105 | 21 | 8 | 10 | 55 | .302 | 529 | 36 | 13 | .978 |
| 1966—Houston ...........Nat. | | PH | 1 | 1 | 0 | 0 | 0 | 0 | 0 | 0 | .000 | 0 | 0 | 0 | .000 |
| 1967—Amarillo...........Texas | | *1B-OF | 96 | 351 | 73 | 98 | 14 | 5 | 14 | 60 | .279 | 778 | 41 | *17 | .980 |
| 1967—Oklahoma City ..P. C. | | OF-1B | 41 | 148 | 18 | 39 | 4 | 2 | 5 | 15 | .264 | 64 | 3 | 3 | .957 |
| 1967—Houston ...........Nat. | | 1B | 6 | 14 | 1 | 3 | 0 | 0 | 1 | 2 | .214 | 21 | 2 | 1 | .958 |
| 1968—Oklahoma City ..P. C. | | OF | 20 | 76 | 14 | 30 | 7 | 2 | 5 | 16 | .395 | 34 | 0 | 2 | .944 |
| 1968—Houston† ..........Nat. | | OF | 45 | 140 | 13 | 32 | 7 | 0 | 2 | 8 | .229 | 46 | 0 | 6 | .885 |

| Year Club | League | Pos. | G. | AB. | R. | H. | 2B. | 3B. | HR. | RBI. | B.A. | PO. | A. | E. | F.A. |
|---|---|---|---|---|---|---|---|---|---|---|---|---|---|---|---|
| 1969–Savannah .........South. | | C-1B | 26 | 96 | 19 | 25 | 4 | 0 | 4 | 10 | .260 | 178 | 12 | 5 | .974 |
| 1969–Oklahoma City ...A. A. | | C-1-O-2 | 61 | 223 | 41 | 91 | 14 | 4 | 7 | 48 | .408 | 369 | 25 | 9 | .978 |
| 1969–Houston ..........Nat. | | O-1-C | 20 | 40 | 3 | 11 | 3 | 0 | 0 | 3 | .275 | 46 | 3 | 0 | 1.000 |
| 1970–Houston‡ .........Nat. | | 1-C-OF | 97 | 327 | 48 | 89 | 19 | 2 | 11 | 61 | .272 | 707 | 40 | 6 | .992 |
| 1971–Houston§ .........Nat. | | OF-1B | 129 | 468 | 49 | 135 | 17 | 3 | 9 | 67 | .288 | 470 | 18 | 7 | .986 |
| 1972–Houston ...........Nat. | | OF-1B | 147 | 548 | 74 | 171 | 27 | 4 | 16 | 86 | .312 | 231 | 7 | 5 | .979 |
| 1973–Houston ...........Nat. | | OF-1-C | 158 | 573 | 97 | 179 | 24 | 3 | 16 | 94 | .312 | 433 | 11 | 12 | .974 |
| 1974–Houston ...........Nat. | | OF-1B | 150 | 524 | 69 | 156 | 19 | 4 | 11 | 67 | .298 | 237 | 12 | 4 | .984 |
| 1975–Houston ...........Nat. | | 1B-OF | 132 | 485 | 67 | 157 | 27 | 1 | 18 | 85 | .324 | 1089 | 70 | 8 | .993 |
| 1976–Houston ...........Nat. | | 1B | 157 | 585 | 76 | 183 | 31 | 3 | 16 | 102 | .313 | 1395 | 96 | 15 | .990 |
| Major League Totals ..................... | | | 1042 | 3705 | 497 | 1116 | 174 | 20 | 100 | 575 | .301 | 4675 | 259 | 64 | .987 |

†Suffered broken ankle July 31; on disabled list from August 3 through end of season.
‡On military list, August 8 through August 24, 1970.
§On military list, July 17 through August 2, 1971.

### ALL-STAR GAME RECORD

| Year League | Pos. | AB. | R. | H. | 2B. | 3B. | HR. | RBI. | B.A. | PO. | A. | E. | F.A. |
|---|---|---|---|---|---|---|---|---|---|---|---|---|---|
| 1973–National ................. | OF | 0 | 0 | 0 | 0 | 0 | 0 | 0 | .000 | 0 | 0 | 0 | .000 |
| 1975–National ................. | PH | 1 | 0 | 0 | 0 | 0 | 0 | 0 | .000 | 0 | 0 | 0 | .000 |
| All-Star Game Totals ...................... | | 1 | 0 | 0 | 0 | 0 | 0 | 0 | .000 | 0 | 0 | 0 | .000 |

## STEPHAN MICHAEL WEATHERS
### (Mike)

Born November 25, 1949, Lynwood, Calif.
Height, 6.02. Weight, 180
Throws and bats righthanded.
Hobby–Golf.
Attended Cerritos Junior College, Norwalk, Calif., and Chapman College, Orange, Calif.,
received Bachelor of Arts degree in History.

| Year Club | League | Pos. | G. | AB. | R. | H. | 2B. | 3B. | HR. | RBI. | B.A. | PO. | A. | E. | F.A. |
|---|---|---|---|---|---|---|---|---|---|---|---|---|---|---|---|
| 1971–C's Bay-N. Bend | Northw. | 2B | 48 | 152 | 33 | 38 | 10 | 0 | 0 | 23 | .250 | 104 | 121 | 15 | .938 |
| 1972–Burlington ........ | Midw. | 2B | 13 | 40 | 9 | 8 | 1 | 0 | 1 | 9 | .200 | 25 | 39 | 2 | .970 |
| 1973–Birmingham ...... | South. | 2B | 81 | 273 | 24 | 68 | 12 | 2 | 2 | 19 | .249 | 181 | 222 | 19 | .955 |
| 1973–Burlington ........ | Midw. | 2B | 16 | 63 | 14 | 18 | 2 | 1 | 1 | 6 | .286 | 30 | 42 | 4 | .947 |
| 1973–Birmingham† .... | South. | 2B | 77 | 239 | 10 | 36 | 4 | 0 | 0 | 15 | .151 | 177 | 201 | 17 | .957 |
| 1974–Tucson‡ .......... | P. C. | SS-2B | 34 | 73 | 10 | 14 | 4 | 0 | 0 | 4 | .192 | 30 | 60 | 13 | .874 |
| 1974–Birmingham ...... | South. | SS | 48 | 160 | 19 | 42 | 10 | 1 | 2 | 18 | .263 | 70 | 136 | 13 | .941 |
| 1975–Tucson .......... | P. C. | 2B-SS-3B | 106 | 297 | 36 | 75 | 17 | 1 | 1 | 35 | .253 | 172 | 233 | 17 | .960 |
| 1976–Tucson§ .......... | P. C. | 2B-3B | 112 | 370 | 38 | 97 | 18 | 2 | 3 | 34 | .262 | 220 | 306 | 18 | .967 |

†On temporary inactive list, July 3 through July 22, 1973.
‡On disabled list, April 12 through May 20, 1974.
§Selected by Toronto Blue Jays from Oakland Athletics in American League expansion draft, November 5, 1976; traded with cash estimated at $30,000 to Oakland A's for First Baseman Ron Fairly, February 24, 1977

## HENRY GAYLON MATTHEW WEBB
### (Hank)

Born May 21, 1950, at Amityville, N. Y.
Height, 6.02. Weight, 175.
Throws and bats righthanded.
Attended Hofstra University, Hempstead, N. Y., and State University of New York at New Paltz.

Pitched seven-inning, 1-0 no-hit victory against Rochester, June 7, 1974 (2nd game of doubleheader).
Tied for Texas League lead in shutouts with 4 in 1972.

| Year Club | League | G. | IP. | W. | L. | Pct. | H. | R. | ER. | SO. | BB. | ERA. |
|---|---|---|---|---|---|---|---|---|---|---|---|---|
| 1969–Marion........................ | Ap'lachian | 12 | 77 | 6 | 2 | .750 | 73 | 30 | 25 | 54 | 16 | *2.92 |
| 1970–Pompano Beach.................. | Florida St. | 11 | 58 | 5 | 2 | .714 | 57 | 26 | 18 | 43 | 27 | 2.79 |
| 1971–Memphis...................... | Texas | 8 | 24 | 0 | 4 | .000 | 29 | 24 | 18 | 20 | 19 | 6.75 |
| 1971–Pompano Beach.................. | Florida St. | 19 | 115 | 9 | 5 | .643 | 90 | 51 | 40 | 85 | 48 | 3.13 |
| 1972–Visalia...................... | California | 12 | 45 | 3 | 3 | .500 | 45 | 30 | 22 | 54 | 28 | 4.40 |
| 1972–Memphis...................... | Texas | 16 | 115 | 9 | 5 | .643 | 94 | 37 | 29 | 97 | 35 | 2.28 |
| 1972–New York..................... | Nat. | 6 | 18 | 0 | 0 | .000 | 18 | 9 | 9 | 15 | 9 | 4.50 |
| 1973–Tidewater..................... | Int'national | 22 | 127 | 8 | 9 | .471 | 110 | 60 | 43 | 101 | 52 | 3.05 |
| 1973–New York..................... | National | 2 | 2 | 0 | 0 | .000 | 2 | 2 | 2 | 1 | 2 | 9.00 |
| 1974–Tidewater..................... | Int'national | 25 | 152 | 10 | 8 | .556 | 123 | 65 | 58 | 130 | 72 | 3.43 |
| 1974–New York..................... | National | 3 | 10 | 0 | 2 | .000 | 15 | 9 | 8 | 8 | 10 | 7.20 |
| 1975–Tidewater..................... | Int'national | 3 | 15 | 1 | 0 | 1.000 | 9 | 1 | 1 | 6 | 6 | 0.60 |
| 1975–New York..................... | National | 29 | 115 | 7 | 6 | .538 | 102 | 58 | 52 | 38 | 62 | 4.07 |
| 1976–New York..................... | National | 8 | 16 | 0 | 1 | .000 | 17 | 9 | 8 | 7 | 7 | 4.50 |
| 1976–Tidewater†..................... | Int'national | 19 | 81 | 2 | 9 | .182 | 104 | 65 | 55 | 50 | 47 | 6.11 |
| Major League Totals...................... | | 48 | 161 | 7 | 9 | .438 | 154 | 87 | 79 | 69 | 90 | 4.42 |

†Traded with Pitcher Rick Sanders to Los Angeles Dodgers for Infielder Rick Auerbach, February 7, 1977.

## DAVID THOMAS WEHRMEISTER
### (Dave)

Born November 9, 1952, at Berwyn, Ill.
Height, 6.04. Weight, 195.
Throws and bats righthanded.
Hobby—Golf.
Attended Northwest Missouri State College, Kirksville, Mo.

| Year Club | League | G. | IP. | W. | L. | Pct. | H. | R. | ER. | SO. | BB. | ERA. |
|---|---|---|---|---|---|---|---|---|---|---|---|---|
| 1973—Alexandria | Texas | 23 | 137 | 8 | 12 | .400 | 110 | 64 | 49 | 84 | 60 | 3.22 |
| 1974—Hawaii | P. Coast | 4 | 12 | 0 | 3 | .000 | 17 | 13 | 12 | 7 | 9 | 9.00 |
| 1974—Alexandria | Texas | 18 | 130 | 5 | 10 | .333 | 119 | 73 | 59 | 90 | 65 | 4.08 |
| 1975—Alexandria† | Texas | 17 | 105 | 5 | 8 | .385 | 103 | 54 | 40 | 58 | 36 | 3.43 |
| 1975—Hawaii | P. Coast | 10 | 52 | 3 | 5 | .375 | 63 | 37 | 37 | 31 | 24 | 6.40 |
| 1976—San Diego | National | 7 | 19 | 0 | 4 | .000 | 27 | 17 | 16 | 10 | 11 | 7.58 |
| 1976—Hawaii | P. Coast | 23 | 112 | 6 | 11 | .353 | 137 | 85 | 72 | 61 | 54 | 5.79 |
| Major League Totals | | 7 | 19 | 0 | 4 | .000 | 27 | 17 | 16 | 10 | 11 | 7.58 |

†On disabled list, May 2 to May 17, 1975.
Listed on San Diego Padres' 1977 spring roster.


## DONALD PAUL WERNER
### (Don)

Born March 8, 1953, at Appleton, Wis.
Height, 6.01. Weight, 180.
Throws and bats righthanded.

| Year Club | League | Pos. | G. | AB. | R. | H. | 2B. | 3B. | HR. | RBI. | B.A. | PO. | A. | E. | F.A. |
|---|---|---|---|---|---|---|---|---|---|---|---|---|---|---|---|
| 1971—Brad'ton Reds | Gulf C. | C-3B | 10 | 21 | 7 | 7 | 1 | 1 | 0 | 5 | .333 | 45 | 2 | 1 | .979 |
| 1971—Tampa | Fla. St. | C | 36 | 122 | 10 | 21 | 3 | 1 | 0 | 16 | .172 | 186 | 22 | 1 | .995 |
| 1972—Tampa | Fla. St. | C | 116 | 377 | 42 | 97 | 8 | 1 | 1 | 31 | .257 | 736 | 75 | 15 | .982 |
| 1973—Three Rivers | East. | C-OF | 110 | 284 | 31 | 57 | 9 | 1 | 5 | 34 | .201 | 452 | 47 | 11 | .978 |
| 1974—Tampa | Fla. St. | C | 120 | 397 | 44 | 92 | 13 | 1 | 2 | 38 | .232 | 580 | 71 | 3 | •.995 |
| 1975—Indianapolis | A. A. | C | 86 | 228 | 39 | 64 | 11 | 5 | 9 | 34 | .281 | 423 | 51 | 7 | •.985 |
| 1975—Cincinnati | Nat. | C | 7 | 8 | 0 | 1 | 0 | 0 | 0 | 0 | .125 | 10 | 2 | 1 | .923 |
| 1976—Indianapolis | A. A. | C | 38 | 112 | 14 | 23 | 4 | 1 | 1 | 12 | .205 | 201 | 28 | 6 | .974 |
| 1976—Richmond | Int. | C-OF | 49 | 151 | 19 | 40 | 1 | 1 | 2 | 21 | .265 | 215 | 22 | 5 | .979 |
| 1976—Cincinnati | Nat. | C | 3 | 4 | 0 | 2 | 1 | 0 | 0 | 1 | .500 | 7 | 2 | 0 | 1.000 |
| Major League Totals | | | 10 | 12 | 0 | 3 | 1 | 0 | 0 | 1 | .250 | 17 | 4 | 1 | .954 |


## CLAUDE WILLIAM WESTMORELAND

Born April 21, 1953, at Aurora, Colo.
Height, 6.03. Weight, 210.
Throws and bats righthanded.
Hobbies—Fishing, hunting, cars and audiophile.
Attended University of California, Berkeley, Calif.

Led Western Carolinas League in total bases with 231 in 1974.

| Year Club | League | Pos. | G. | AB. | R. | H. | 2B. | 3B. | HR. | RBI. | B.A. | PO. | A. | E. | F.A. |
|---|---|---|---|---|---|---|---|---|---|---|---|---|---|---|---|
| 1974—Orangeburg | W. Caf. | 1B-OF | 129 | 442 | 82 | 131 | 25 | 6 | 21 | 74 | .296 | 692 | 49 | 29 | .962 |
| 1974—Bakersfield | Calif. | OF | 11 | 38 | 8 | 12 | 2 | 0 | 2 | 6 | .316 | 7 | 4 | 4 | .733 |
| 1975—Bakersfield | Calif. | OF-1B | 136 | 485 | 90 | 121 | 19 | 7 | •20 | 81 | .249 | 219 | 20 | 18 | .930 |
| 1976—Waterbury | East. | OF | 37 | 128 | 13 | 23 | 3 | 1 | 1 | 6 | .180 | 82 | 6 | 4 | .957 |
| 1976—Lodi | Calif. | 3B-OF | 76 | 288 | 55 | 88 | 12 | 3 | 11 | 58 | .306 | 83 | 71 | 24 | .865 |

Listed on Los Angeles Dodgers' 1977 spring roster.


## GARY RICHARD WHEELOCK

Born November 29, 1951, at Bakersfield, Calif.
Height, 6.03. Weight, 205.
Throws and bats righthanded.
Attended Fullerton College, Fullerton, Calif., and University of California at Irvine,
Irvine, Calif.; Received Bachelor of Arts degree in Social Science.

| Year Club | League | G. | IP. | W. | L. | Pct. | H. | R. | ER. | SO. | BB. | ERA. |
|---|---|---|---|---|---|---|---|---|---|---|---|---|
| 1974—Salinas | California | 2 | 3 | 0 | 0 | .000 | 3 | 0 | 0 | 3 | 1 | 0.00 |
| 1974—Quad Cities | Midwest | 25 | 68 | 3 | 3 | .500 | 57 | 25 | 18 | 79 | 15 | 2.38 |
| 1975—Salt Lake City | P. Coast | 31 | 120 | 7 | 6 | .538 | 113 | 56 | 41 | 68 | 47 | 3.08 |
| 1976—Salt Lake City† | P. Coast | 27 | 201 | •15 | 8 | .652 | 206 | 100 | 85 | •138 | 154 | 3.81 |
| 1976—California‡ | American | 2 | 2 | 0 | 0 | .000 | 6 | 6 | 6 | 2 | 1 | 27.00 |
| Major League Totals | | 2 | 2 | 0 | 0 | .000 | 6 | 6 | 6 | 2 | 1 | 27.00 |

†On disabled list June 15 to June 28, 1976.
‡Selected by Seattle Mariners in American League expansion draft, November 5, 1976.

## FRANK WHITE, JR.

Born September 4, 1950, at Greenville, Miss.
Height, 5.11. Weight, 170.
Throws and bats righthanded.
Hobbies—Hunting and listening to music.

Led Gulf Coast League in stolen bases with 18 and led shortstops in double plays with 27 in 1971.

| Year | Club | League | Pos. | G. | AB. | R. | H. | 2B. | 3B. | HR. | RBI. | B.A. | PO. | A. | E. | F.A. |
|------|------|--------|------|-----|------|-----|-----|-----|-----|-----|------|------|-----|------|-----|-------|
| 1971—Sara. Royals | | Gulf C. | SS | 50 | 158 | 31 | 39 | 6 | 3 | 1 | 21 | .247 | 70 | •149 | 17 | •.928 |
| 1972—San Jose | | Calif. | SS | 49 | 187 | 44 | 55 | 7 | 2 | 10 | 26 | .294 | 77 | 138 | 14 | .939 |
| 1972—Jacksonville | | South. | SS | 91 | 333 | 34 | 84 | 12 | 2 | 2 | 23 | .252 | 124 | 306 | 31 | .933 |
| 1973—Omaha | | A. A. | 2B-SS | 86 | 348 | 49 | 92 | 19 | 2 | 4 | 32 | .264 | 163 | 221 | 21 | .948 |
| 1973—Kansas City | | Amer. | SS-2B | 51 | 139 | 20 | 31 | 6 | 1 | 0 | 5 | .223 | 71 | 121 | 12 | .941 |
| 1974—Kansas City | | Amer. | 2-S-3 | 99 | 204 | 19 | 45 | 6 | 3 | 1 | 18 | .221 | 119 | 189 | 12 | .963 |
| 1975—Kansas City | | Amer. | 2-S-3-C | 111 | 304 | 43 | 76 | 10 | 2 | 7 | 36 | .250 | 182 | 275 | 12 | .974 |
| 1976—Kansas City | | Amer. | 2B-SS | 152 | 446 | 39 | 102 | 17 | 6 | 2 | 46 | .229 | 296 | 479 | 23 | .971 |
| Major League Totals | | | | 413 | 1093 | 121 | 254 | 39 | 12 | 10 | 105 | .232 | 668 | 1064 | 59 | .967 |

### CHAMPIONSHIP SERIES RECORD

| Year | Club | League | Pos. | G. | AB. | R. | H. | 2B. | 3B. | HR. | RBI. | B.A. | PO. | A. | E. | F.A. |
|------|------|--------|------|-----|-----|-----|-----|-----|-----|-----|------|------|-----|-----|-----|-------|
| 1976—Kansas City | | Amer. | 2B-PR | 4 | 8 | 2 | 1 | 0 | 0 | 0 | 0 | .125 | 6 | 11 | 0 | 1.000 |

## JEROME CARDELL WHITE
### (Jerry)

Born August 23, 1952, at Shirley, Mass.
Height, 5.10. Weight, 165.
Throws right and bats left and righthanded.
Hobbies—Football, ping pong and basketball.
Attended City College of San Francisco, San Francisco, Calif.

| Year | Club | League | Pos. | G. | AB. | R. | H. | 2B. | 3B. | HR. | RBI. | B.A. | PO. | A. | E. | F.A. |
|------|------|--------|------|-----|------|-----|-----|-----|-----|-----|------|------|-----|-----|-----|-------|
| 1970—Brad'ton Expos | | Gulf C. | OF | 55 | 201 | 32 | 58 | 10 | 2 | 1 | 16 | .289 | 102 | 5 | 5 | .955 |
| 1971—W. Palm Beach | | Fla. St. | OF | 130 | 505 | 71 | 132 | 17 | 4 | 2 | 32 | .261 | 222 | 4 | •13 | .946 |
| 1972—Quebec City† | | East. | OF | 26 | 56 | 4 | 13 | 1 | 0 | 0 | 2 | .232 | 46 | 1 | 0 | 1.000 |
| 1972—W. Palm Beach | | Fla. St. | OF | 27 | 96 | 13 | 28 | 1 | 1 | 1 | 13 | .292 | 63 | 1 | 2 | .970 |
| 1973—Peninsula‡ | | Int. | OF | 112 | 360 | 50 | 99 | 10 | 6 | 1 | 30 | .275 | 182 | 7 | 5 | .974 |
| 1974—Quebec City | | East. | OF | 21 | 69 | 13 | 17 | 2 | 2 | 0 | 5 | .246 | 35 | 2 | 1 | .974 |
| 1974—Memphis | | Int. | OF | 77 | 175 | 28 | 45 | 6 | 2 | 3 | 17 | .257 | 87 | 5 | 1 | .989 |
| 1974—Montreal | | Nat. | OF | 9 | 10 | 0 | 4 | 1 | 1 | 0 | 2 | .400 | 6 | 0 | 0 | 1.000 |
| 1975—Memphis | | Int. | OF | 98 | 354 | 44 | 105 | 16 | 5 | 10 | 45 | .297 | 223 | 6 | 6 | .974 |
| 1975—Montreal | | Nat. | OF | 39 | 97 | 14 | 29 | 4 | 1 | 2 | 7 | .299 | 81 | 1 | 2 | .976 |
| 1976—Montreal | | Nat. | OF | 114 | 278 | 32 | 68 | 11 | 1 | 2 | 21 | .245 | 157 | 4 | 3 | .982 |
| Major League Totals | | | | 162 | 385 | 46 | 101 | 16 | 3 | 4 | 30 | .262 | 244 | 5 | 5 | .980 |

†On temporary inactive list, April 22 to June 24, 1972.
‡On temporary inactive list, July 28 to August 14, 1973.

## ROY HILTON WHITE

Born December 27, 1943, at Los Angeles, Calif.
Height, 5.11. Weight, 170.
Throws right and bats left and righthanded.
Hobby—Reading.
Attended Compton Junior College, Compton, Calif.

Tied the following major league records: most times switch hitting 2 home runs, game, 1, May 7, 1970; most times switch hitting 2 triples, game, 1, September 8, 1970; fewest three-base hits, season, 150 or more games, 0, 1972.
Established American League record for most sacrifice flies, season, 17, 1971.
Led American League in sacrifice flies with 11 in 1969.
Tied for American League lead in total bases on balls with 99 in 1972.
Led Southern League in total bases with 279 in 1965.
Named Most Valuable Player in Southern League, 1965.

| Year | Club | League | Pos. | G. | AB. | R. | H. | 2B. | 3B. | HR. | RBI. | B.A. | PO. | A. | E. | F.A. |
|------|------|--------|------|-----|------|------|------|-----|-----|-----|------|------|-----|-----|-----|-------|
| 1962—Greensboro | | Carol. | 2B | 25 | 93 | 17 | 19 | 5 | 0 | 1 | 1 | .204 | 73 | 66 | 8 | .946 |
| 1962—Ft. Lauderdale | | Fla.St. | 2B | 98 | 367 | 54 | 105 | 12 | 6 | 3 | 41 | .286 | 200 | 282 | 28 | .945 |
| 1963—Greensboro | | Carol. | 2B | •146 | 554 | •117 | 171 | 25 | 10 | 9 | 66 | .309 | 326 | 350 | •33 | .953 |
| 1964—Columbus† | | South. | 2B | 110 | 376 | 55 | 95 | 13 | 6 | 9 | 41 | .253 | 206 | 275 | 16 | .968 |
| 1965—Columbus | | South. | 2B | 139 | •560 | •103 | •168 | 26 | •14 | 19 | 56 | .300 | 309 | 374 | •27 | .962 |
| 1965—New York | | Amer. | OF-2B | 14 | 42 | 7 | 14 | 2 | 0 | 0 | 3 | .333 | 16 | 4 | 0 | 1.000 |
| 1966—New York‡ | | Amer. | OF-2B | 115 | 316 | 39 | 71 | 13 | 2 | 7 | 20 | .225 | 159 | 6 | 7 | .959 |
| 1967—Spokane | | P.C. | 3B | 84 | 306 | 49 | 105 | 24 | 4 | 6 | 48 | .343 | 64 | 139 | 18 | .919 |
| 1967—New York | | Amer. | OF-3B | 70 | 214 | 22 | 48 | 8 | 0 | 2 | 18 | .224 | 79 | 29 | 10 | .915 |
| 1968—New York | | Amer. | OF | 159 | 577 | 89 | 154 | 20 | 7 | 17 | 62 | .267 | 283 | 14 | 1 | .997 |
| 1969—New York§ | | Amer. | OF | 130 | 448 | 55 | 130 | 30 | 5 | 7 | 74 | .290 | 267 | 9 | 3 | .989 |
| 1970—New York | | Amer. | OF | •162 | 609 | 109 | 180 | 30 | 6 | 22 | 94 | .296 | 315 | 6 | 2 | .994 |
| 1971—New York | | Amer. | OF | 147 | 524 | 86 | 153 | 22 | 7 | 19 | 84 | .292 | 306 | 8 | 0 | •1.000 |
| 1972—New York | | Amer. | OF | 155 | 556 | 76 | 150 | 29 | 0 | 10 | 54 | .270 | 323 | 8 | 2 | .994 |
| 1973—New York | | Amer. | OF | •162 | •639 | 88 | 157 | 22 | 3 | 18 | 60 | .246 | 339 | 4 | 8 | .977 |

| Year Club | League | Pos. | G. | AB. | R. | H. | 2B. | 3B. | HR. | RBI. | B.A. | PO. | A. | E. | F.A. |
|---|---|---|---|---|---|---|---|---|---|---|---|---|---|---|---|
| 1974—New York.........Amer. | | OF | 136 | 473 | 68 | 130 | 19 | 8 | 7 | 43 | .275 | 141 | 2 | 1 | .993 |
| 1975—New York.........Amer. | | OF-1B | 148 | 556 | 81 | 161 | 32 | 5 | 12 | 59 | .290 | 361 | 12 | 6 | .984 |
| 1976—New York.........Amer. | | OF | 156 | 626 | 104 | 179 | 29 | 3 | 14 | 65 | .286 | 380 | 9 | 5 | .987 |
| Major League Totals ...................... | | | 1554 | 5580 | 824 | 1527 | 256 | 46 | 135 | 636 | .273 | 2869 | 111 | 45 | .985 |

†On disabled list, July 7 through July 29, 1964.

‡Optioned to Spokane as part of deal in which New York Yankees traded Pitcher Jack Cullen, Outfielder-Infielder John Miller and $25,000 cash to Los Angeles Dodgers for Infielder John Kennedy, April 3, 1967.

§On military list, June 27 through July 12.

### CHAMPIONSHIP SERIES RECORD

| Year Club | League | Pos. | G. | AB. | R. | H. | 2B. | 3B. | HR. | RBI. | B.A. | PO. | A. | E. | F.A. |
|---|---|---|---|---|---|---|---|---|---|---|---|---|---|---|---|
| 1976—New York.........Amer. | | OF | 5 | 17 | 4 | 5 | 3 | 0 | 0 | 3 | .294 | 17 | 0 | 0 | 1.000 |

### WORLD SERIES RECORD

| Year Club | League | Pos. | G. | AB. | R. | H. | 2B. | 3B. | HR. | RBI. | B.A. | PO. | A. | E. | F.A. |
|---|---|---|---|---|---|---|---|---|---|---|---|---|---|---|---|
| 1976—New York.........Amer. | | OF | 4 | 15 | 0 | 2 | 0 | 0 | 0 | 0 | .133 | 13 | 0 | 0 | 1.000 |

### ALL-STAR GAME RECORD

| Year League | | Pos. | AB. | R. | H. | 2B. | 3B. | HR. | RBI. | B.A. | PO. | A. | E. | F.A. |
|---|---|---|---|---|---|---|---|---|---|---|---|---|---|---|
| 1969—American ........................... | | PH | 1 | 0 | 0 | 0 | 0 | 0 | 0 | .000 | 0 | 0 | 0 | .000 |

Member of the American League All-Star Team in 1970 game; did not play.

## TERRY BERTLAND WHITFIELD

Born January 12, 1953, at Blythe, Calif.
Height, 6.02½. Weight, 195.
Throws right and bats lefthanded.
Hobbies—Assembling toys and working puzzles.

Tied for International League lead in double plays by outfielders with 3 in 1976.
Led International League batters in strikeouts with 129 in 1974.
Led Appalachian League in total bases with 125 in 1971.
Led Carolina League in total bases with 234 in 1973.
Named Carolina League Player of the Year in 1973.
Named Appalachian League Player of the Year in 1971.

| Year Club | League | Pos. | G. | AB. | R. | H. | 2B. | 3B. | HR. | RBI. | B.A. | PO. | A. | E. | F.A. |
|---|---|---|---|---|---|---|---|---|---|---|---|---|---|---|---|
| 1971—Johnson City ....Appal. | | OF | 67 | 252 | 42 | 73 | 14 | 4 | •10 | •43 | .290 | 104 | 6 | •9 | .924 |
| 1972—Ft. Lauderdale ..Fla.St. | | OF | 49 | 153 | 21 | 25 | 3 | 5 | 1 | 15 | .163 | 57 | 4 | 5 | .924 |
| 1972—Oneonta ...........NYP | | OF | •70 | 256 | •65 | 70 | 6 | •11 | 7 | 47 | .273 | 120 | 7 | 3 | .977 |
| 1973—Kinston ............Carol. | | OF | 129 | 451 | 94 | 151 | 25 | 2 | •18 | 81 | •.335 | 197 | 9 | 11 | .949 |
| 1974—Syracuse ..........Int. | | OF | 140 | 499 | 71 | 129 | 25 | 4 | 17 | 71 | .259 | •345 | 12 | 5 | .986 |
| 1974—New York.........Amer. | | OF | 2 | 5 | 0 | 1 | 0 | 0 | 0 | 0 | .200 | 0 | 0 | 0 | .000 |
| 1975—Syracuse ..........Int. | | OF | 111 | 390 | 47 | 106 | 24 | 4 | 11 | 69 | .272 | 208 | 10 | 10 | .956 |
| 1975—New York.........Amer. | | OF | 28 | 81 | 9 | 22 | 1 | 1 | 0 | 7 | .272 | 42 | 3 | 1 | .978 |
| 1976—Syracuse ..........Int. | | OF-DH | 138 | 525 | 81 | 152 | 25 | 6 | 16 | 89 | .290 | 208 | 13 | 15 | .936 |
| 1976—New York† ........Amer. | | OF | 1 | 0 | 0 | 0 | 0 | 0 | 0 | 0 | .000 | 0 | 0 | 0 | .000 |
| Major League Totals ...................... | | | 31 | 86 | 9 | 23 | 1 | 1 | 0 | 7 | .267 | 42 | 3 | 1 | .978 |

†Traded to San Francisco Giants for Second Baseman Marty Perez, March 14, 1977.

## EDWARD JAMES WHITSON
### (Eddie)

Born May 19, 1955, at Johnson City, Tenn.
Height, 6.03. Weight, 195.
Throws and bats righthanded.

| Year Club | League | G. | IP. | W. | L. | Pct. | H. | R. | ER. | SO. | BB. | ERA. |
|---|---|---|---|---|---|---|---|---|---|---|---|---|
| 1974—Bradenton Pirates ................Gulf Coast | | 8 | 44 | 1 | 4 | .200 | 45 | 28 | 21 | 25 | 15 | 4.30 |
| 1975—Charleston ..........................W. Carol. | | 24 | 142 | 8 | •15 | .348 | 140 | •96 | •80 | 120 | 99 | 5.07 |
| 1976—Salem ..................................Carolina | | 26 | •203 | •15 | 9 | .625 | 168 | 75 | 57 | •186 | 65 | 2.53 |

Listed on Pittsburgh Pirates' 1977 spring roster.

## LEO ERNEST WHITT
### (Ernie)

Born June 13, 1952, Detroit, Mich.
Height, 6.02. Weight, 200.
Throws right and bats lefthanded.
Hobbies—Hunting and fishing.
Attended Macomb County Community College, Warren, Mich.

| Year Club | League | Pos. | G. | AB. | R. | H. | 2B. | 3B. | HR. | RBI. | B.A. | PO. | A. | E. | F.A. |
|---|---|---|---|---|---|---|---|---|---|---|---|---|---|---|---|
| 1972—Williamsport......NYP | | 1B | 1 | 4 | 1 | 2 | 1 | 0 | 0 | 0 | .500 | 8 | 1 | 0 | 1.000 |
| 1972—Winter Haven ....Fla.St. | | C-1B-OF | 31 | 82 | 3 | 15 | 1 | 1 | 0 | 7 | .183 | 151 | 14 | 5 | .971 |
| 1973—Winston-Salem ..Carol. | | C-OF-1B | 130 | 424 | 63 | 123 | 23 | 3 | 1 | 50 | .290 | 686 | 70 | 15 | .980 |
| 1974—Bristol .............East. | | C-OF-1B | 111 | 385 | 55 | 96 | 10 | 1 | 9 | 56 | .249 | 557 | 50 | 6 | .990 |
| 1975—Bristol† ...........East. | | C-OF | 82 | 252 | 29 | 64 | 9 | 1 | 2 | 19 | .254 | 357 | 36 | 7 | .982 |
| 1976—Bristol .............East. | | C | 26 | 87 | 12 | 19 | 2 | 3 | 1 | 10 | .218 | 127 | 25 | 1 | .993 |

| Year | Club | League | Pos. | G. | AB. | R. | H. | 2B. | 3B. | HR. | RBI. | B.A. | PO. | A. | E. | F.A. |
|------|------|--------|------|-----|------|-----|-----|-----|-----|-----|------|------|------|-----|-----|-------|
| 1976–Rhode Island | ....Int. | | C-1B | 90 | 304 | 33 | 81 | 16 | 2 | 7 | 42 | .266 | 456 | 58 | 8 | .985 |
| 1976–Boston‡ | ...........Amer. | | C | 8 | 18 | 4 | 4 | 2 | 0 | 1 | 3 | .222 | 24 | 0 | 0 | 1.000 |
| Major League Totals ...................... | | | | 8 | 18 | 4 | 4 | 2 | 0 | 1 | 3 | .222 | 24 | 0 | 0 | 1.000 |

†On disabled list, April 11 through June 13, 1975.
‡Selected by Toronto Blue Jays in American League expansion draft, November 5, 1976.

## MILTON EDWARD WILCOX
### (Milt)

Born April 20, 1950, at Honolulu, Hawaii.
Height, 6.02. Weight, 185.
Throws and bats righthanded.
Hobby–Bowling.

Pitched seven-inning, 2-0 no-hit victory against Evansville, July 4, 1970.
Led American Association in shutouts with 5 in 1970 and tied for lead with 3 in 1971.

| Year | Club | League | G. | IP. | W. | L. | Pct. | H. | R. | ER. | SO. | BB. | ERA. |
|------|------|--------|-----|------|-----|-----|------|------|-----|-----|------|------|------|
| 1968–Tampa | ...................Florida St. | | 8 | 47 | 3 | 3 | .500 | 28 | 11 | 7 | 48 | 18 | 1.34 |
| 1968–Sarasota Reds | .....................Gulf Coast | | 6 | 33 | 3 | 2 | .600 | 24 | 10 | 4 | 33 | 11 | 1.09 |
| 1969–Tampa† | .........................Florida St. | | 15 | 46 | 4 | 1 | .800 | 53 | 30 | 28 | 38 | 29 | 5.48 |
| 1970–Indianapolis | .................Am. Assoc. | | 28 | 168 | 12 | 10 | .545 | 144 | 58 | 53 | 110 | 53 | 2.84 |
| 1970–Cincinnati | ..........................National | | 5 | 22 | 3 | 1 | .750 | 19 | 6 | 6 | 13 | 7 | 2.45 |
| 1971–Indianapolis | .................Am. Assoc. | | 16 | 102 | 8 | 5 | .615 | 84 | 29 | 25 | 62 | 22 | 2.20 |
| 1971–Cincinnati‡ | ..........................National | | 18 | 43 | 2 | 2 | .500 | 43 | 22 | 16 | 21 | 17 | 3.35 |
| 1972–Cleveland | ...........................American | | 32 | 156 | 7 | 14 | .333 | 145 | 67 | 59 | 90 | 72 | 3.40 |
| 1973–Cleveland§ | ..........................American | | 26 | 134 | 8 | 10 | .444 | 143 | 90 | 87 | 82 | 68 | 5.84 |
| 1974–Cleveland x | ..........................American | | 41 | 71 | 2 | 2 | .500 | 74 | 42 | 37 | 33 | 24 | 4.69 |
| 1975–Wichita | ................................Am. Assoc. | | 8 | 48 | 4 | 3 | .571 | 56 | 31 | 23 | 18 | 15 | 4.31 |
| 1975–Chicago | ................................National | | 25 | 38 | 0 | 1 | .000 | 50 | 27 | 24 | 21 | 17 | 5.68 |
| 1976–Wichita y-Evansville | ...........Am. Assoc. | | 27 | 130 | 6 | 7 | .462 | 141 | 72 | 55 | 94 | 63 | 3.81 |
| National League Totals............................ | | | 48 | 103 | 5 | 4 | .556 | 112 | 55 | 46 | 55 | 41 | 4.02 |
| American League Totals............................ | | | 99 | 361 | 17 | 26 | .395 | 362 | 199 | 183 | 205 | 164 | 4.56 |
| Major League Totals ...................... | | | 147 | 464 | 22 | 30 | .423 | 474 | 254 | 229 | 260 | 205 | 4.44 |

†On military list, April 16 to May 9; on temporary inactive list, June 11 to July 1, 1969.
‡Traded to Cleveland Indians for Outfielder Ted Uhlaender, December 6, 1971.
§On military list, June 16 to June 30; on disabled list, July 24 to August 15, 1973.
xOn military list, July 20 to August 4, 1974. Traded to Chicago Cubs for Pitcher Dave LaRoche and Outfielder Brock Davis, February 28, 1975.
ySold to Detroit Tigers, June 10, 1976.

### CHAMPIONSHIP SERIES RECORD

| Year | Club | League | G. | IP. | W. | L. | Pct. | H. | R. | ER. | SO. | BB. | ERA. |
|------|------|--------|-----|------|-----|-----|------|------|-----|-----|------|------|------|
| 1970–Cincinnati | ...........................National | | 1 | 3 | 1 | 0 | 1.000 | 1 | 0 | 0 | 5 | 2 | 0.00 |

### WORLD SERIES RECORD

| Year | Club | League | G. | IP. | W. | L. | Pct. | H. | R. | ER. | SO. | BB. | ERA. |
|------|------|--------|-----|------|-----|-----|------|------|-----|-----|------|------|------|
| 1970–Cincinnati | ...........................National | | 2 | 2 | 0 | 1 | .000 | 3 | 2 | 2 | 2 | 0 | 9.00 |

## MARK EUGENE WILEY

Born February 28, 1949, at San Diego, Calif.
Height, 6.01. Weight, 200.
Throws and bats righthanded.
Hobby–Fishing.
Attended California Poly State University, Pomona, Calif.; received
Bachelor of Science degree in Physical Education.

Led Pacific Coast League in games started with 31 in 1976.
Led Pacific Coast League in saves with 16 in 1974.
Led New York-Pennsylvania League in games started with 15, complete games with 14 and shutouts with 6 in 1970.
Named New York-Pennsylvania League Player of the Year in 1970.

| Year | Club | League | G. | IP. | W. | L. | Pct. | H. | R. | ER. | SO. | BB. | ERA. |
|------|------|--------|-----|------|-----|-----|------|------|-----|-----|------|------|------|
| 1970–Auburn | ................................NYP | | 15 | •127 | •10 | 3 | .769 | 87 | 29 | 21 | •144 | 33 | 1.49 |
| 1971–Portland | ............................P. Coast | | 15 | 73 | 3 | 10 | .231 | 96 | 70 | 63 | 51 | 40 | 7.77 |
| 1971–Charlotte | ............................Southern | | 14 | 86 | 5 | 2 | .714 | 80 | 30 | 26 | 67 | 24 | 2.72 |
| 1972–Charlotte | ............................Southern | | 17 | 85 | 7 | 6 | .538 | 93 | 46 | 43 | 41 | 27 | 4.55 |
| 1972–Tacoma | ...............................P. Coast | | 11 | 62 | 4 | 6 | .400 | 62 | 30 | 25 | 51 | 21 | 3.63 |
| 1973–Orlando | ...............................Southern | | 19 | 103 | 8 | 7 | .533 | 122 | 52 | 48 | 84 | 37 | 4.19 |
| 1973–Tacoma | ...............................P. Coast | | 10 | 54 | 4 | 5 | .444 | 53 | 34 | 24 | 38 | 26 | 4.00 |
| 1974–Tacoma | ...............................P. Coast | | •56 | 77 | 8 | 5 | .615 | 106 | 61 | 45 | 52 | 44 | 5.26 |
| 1975–Tacoma | ...............................P. Coast | | 17 | 92 | 9 | 1 | .900 | 72 | 28 | 22 | 47 | 24 | 2.15 |
| 1975–Minnesota | .............................American | | 15 | 39 | 1 | 3 | .250 | 50 | 30 | 26 | 15 | 13 | 6.00 |
| 1976–Tacoma | ...............................P. Coast | | 34 | •219 | •15 | •15 | .500 | •267 | 116 | 90 | 96 | 39 | 3.70 |
| Major League Totals ............................. | | | 15 | 39 | 1 | 3 | .250 | 50 | 30 | 26 | 15 | 13 | 6.00 |

# ROBERT DONALD WILFONG
## (Rob)

Born September 1, 1953, at Pasadena, Calif.
Height, 6.01. Weight, 180.
Throws right and bats lefthanded.
Hobbies—Hunting, fishing and golf.
Attended Mount San Antonio Junior College, Walnut, Calif.

| Year Club | League | Pos. | G. | AB. | R. | H. | 2B. | 3B. | HR. | RBI. | B.A. | PO. | A. | E. | F.A. |
|---|---|---|---|---|---|---|---|---|---|---|---|---|---|---|---|
| 1972—Charlotte† | ........W. Car. | 2B | 102 | 363 | 64 | 107 | 18 | 2 | 2 | 35 | .295 | 212 | 224 | 16 | .965 |
| 1973—Lynchburg | ........Carol. | 2B | 131 | 520 | 94 | 143 | 13 | 9 | 7 | 37 | .275 | ∗323 | 326 | 18 | .973 |
| 1974—Orlando | ............South. | 2B | 109 | 403 | 58 | 99 | 7 | 4 | 3 | 23 | .246 | 249 | 303 | 8 | ∗.986 |
| 1975—Orlando | ............South. | 2B | 125 | 403 | 54 | 99 | 14 | 1 | 4 | 37 | .246 | 274 | 347 | 16 | .975 |
| 1976—Tacoma | ............P.C. | 2B | 69 | 220 | 41 | 67 | 8 | 3 | 3 | 16 | .305 | 163 | 191 | 6 | .983 |

†On disabled list, May 22 to June 2, 1972.
Listed on Minnesota Twins' 1977 spring roster.

# JAMES WEBSTER WILHELM
## (Jim)

Born September 20, 1952, at Greenbrae, Calif.
Height, 6.03. Weight, 190.
Throws and bats righthanded.
Attended University of Santa Clara, Santa Clara, Calif.; received
Bachelor of Arts degree in Economics.

| Year Club | League | Pos. | G. | AB. | R. | H. | 2B. | 3B. | HR. | RBI. | B.A. | PO. | A. | E. | F.A. |
|---|---|---|---|---|---|---|---|---|---|---|---|---|---|---|---|
| 1974—Walla Walla | ......Northw. | OF-1B | 82 | 295 | 58 | 83 | 7 | 5 | 3 | 32 | .281 | 189 | 12 | 9 | .957 |
| 1975—Alexandria | ........Texas | OF | 119 | 415 | 61 | 108 | 12 | 1 | 3 | 37 | .260 | 289 | 10 | 8 | .974 |
| 1976—Amarillo | ............Texas | OF | 132 | 495 | 92 | 154 | 32 | 7 | 7 | 76 | .311 | ∗317 | 7 | 8 | .976 |

Listed on San Diego Padres' 1977 spring roster.

# CHARLES PROSEK WILLIAMS
## (Charlie)

Born October 11, 1947, at Flushing, N.Y.
Height, 6.03. Weight, 195.
Throws and bats righthanded.
Hobbies—Golf, fishing and hunting.
Attended Parsons College, Fairfield, Ia.

Led Pacific Coast League in sacrifice hits with 12 in 1972.

| Year Club | League | G. | IP. | W. | L. | Pct. | H. | R. | ER. | SO. | BB. | ERA. |
|---|---|---|---|---|---|---|---|---|---|---|---|---|
| 1968—Mankato | ...........Northern | 11 | 67 | 5 | 1 | .833 | 56 | 24 | 18 | 57 | 32 | 2.42 |
| 1969—Memphis | ...........Texas | 10 | 32 | 1 | 3 | .250 | 36 | 16 | 16 | 25 | 15 | 4.50 |
| 1969—Visalia | ...............California | 16 | 91 | 3 | 6 | .333 | 114 | 54 | 48 | 91 | 37 | 4.75 |
| 1970—Memphis | ...........Texas | 26 | 158 | 12 | 5 | .706 | 136 | 67 | 57 | 128 | 61 | 3.25 |
| 1971—New York | ...........National | 31 | 90 | 5 | 6 | .455 | 92 | 53 | 48 | 53 | 41 | 4.80 |
| 1972—Tidewater† | ...........Int'national | 5 | 36 | 3 | 2 | .600 | 36 | 18 | 18 | 33 | 17 | 4.50 |
| 1972—Phoenix‡ | ...........P. Coast | 23 | 139 | 10 | 10 | .500 | 143 | 76 | 71 | 94 | 57 | 4.60 |
| 1972—San Francisco | ...........National | 3 | 9 | 0 | 2 | .000 | 14 | 10 | 9 | 3 | 3 | 9.00 |
| 1973—Phoenix‡ | ...........P. Coast | 15 | 76 | 5 | 5 | .500 | 81 | 40 | 34 | 50 | 24 | 4.03 |
| 1973—San Francisco | ...........National | 12 | 23 | 3 | 0 | 1.000 | 32 | 19 | 17 | 11 | 7 | 6.65 |
| 1974—San Francisco | ...........National | 39 | 100 | 1 | 3 | .250 | 93 | 38 | 31 | 48 | 31 | 2.79 |
| 1975—San Francisco | ...........National | 55 | 98 | 5 | 3 | .625 | 94 | 41 | 38 | 45 | 66 | 3.49 |
| 1976—San Francisco | ...........National | 48 | 85 | 2 | 0 | 1.000 | 80 | 33 | 28 | 34 | 39 | 2.96 |
| Major League Totals | ...........  | 188 | 405 | 16 | 14 | .533 | 405 | 194 | 171 | 194 | 187 | 3.80 |

†Traded by New York Mets with cash to San Francisco Giants for Outfielder Willie Mays, May 11, 1972.
‡Played one game at first base.

# EARL CRAIG WILLIAMS, JR.

Born July 14, 1948, at Newark, N. J.
Height, 6.03. Weight, 225.
Throws and bats righthanded.
Hobbies—Reading and listening to phonograph records.
Attended Ithaca College, Ithaca, N. Y.

Led National League in passed balls with 28 in 1972.
Led Western Carolinas League in total bases with 252 in 1969.
Named by The Sporting News as National League Rookie Player of the Year, 1971.
Named by the Baseball Writers' Association as National League Rookie of the Year, 1971.
Named Western Carolinas League Most Valuable Player in 1969.

| Year Club | League | Pos. | G. | AB. | R. | H. | 2B. | 3B. | HR. | RBI. | B.A. | PO. | A. | E. | F.A. |
|---|---|---|---|---|---|---|---|---|---|---|---|---|---|---|---|
| 1966—Sarasota Braves | Gulf C. | 1B-P | 31 | 90 | 8 | 19 | 4 | 0 | 1 | 10 | .211 | 153 | 19 | 2 | .989 |
| 1967—W. Palm B'ch. | ..Fla. St. | O-1 | 85 | 287 | 33 | 72 | 6 | 3 | 7 | 27 | .251 | 376 | 21 | 4 | .990 |
| 1968—Greenwood† | ......W. Car. | OF | 8 | 29 | 5 | 8 | 0 | 0 | 1 | 3 | .276 | 6 | 2 | 2 | .800 |
| 1968—W. Palm B'ch. | ..Fla. St. | 1-O | 50 | 144 | 14 | 34 | 8 | 0 | 0 | 12 | .236 | 309 | 22 | 6 | .982 |
| 1969—Greenwood | ........W. Car. | 1B | 103 | 382 | 83 | 130 | 19 | 2 | ∗33 | 107 | ∗.340 | ∗1002 | 54 | 15 | .986 |
| 1970—Shreveport | ........Texas | 3-1-S | 89 | 330 | 53 | 105 | 21 | 2 | 19 | 63 | .318 | 151 | 122 | 21 | .929 |
| 1970—Richmond | ..........Int. | OF-3-1 | 22 | 68 | 10 | 18 | 1 | 0 | 5 | 15 | .265 | 27 | 17 | 2 | .957 |

| Year | Club | League | Pos. | G. | AB. | R. | H. | 2B. | 3B. | HR. | RBI. | B.A. | PO. | A. | E. | F.A. |
|------|------|--------|------|-----|------|-----|-----|-----|-----|-----|------|------|------|-----|-----|------|
| 1970–Atlanta..............Nat. | | | 1B-3B | 10 | 19 | 4 | 7 | 4 | 0 | 0 | 5 | .368 | 23 | 8 | 0 | 1.000 |
| 1971–Atlanta..............Nat. | | | C-3-1 | 145 | 497 | 64 | 129 | 14 | 1 | 33 | 87 | .260 | 596 | 117 | 18 | .975 |
| 1972–Atlanta‡ ...........Nat. | | | C-3-1 | 151 | 565 | 82 | 146 | 24 | 2 | 28 | 87 | .258 | 620 | 219 | 31 | .964 |
| 1973–Baltimore..........Amer. | | | C-1B | 132 | 459 | 58 | 109 | 18 | 1 | 22 | 83 | .237 | 733 | 52 | 8 | .990 |
| 1974–Baltimore§ ........Amer. | | | C-1B | 118 | 413 | 47 | 105 | 16 | 0 | 14 | 52 | .254 | 707 | 50 | 8 | .990 |
| 1975–Atlanta..............Nat. | | | 1B-C | 111 | 383 | 42 | 92 | 13 | 0 | 11 | 50 | .240 | 896 | 56 | 12 | .988 |
| 1976–Atl. x-Mont. y ....Nat. | | | 1B-C | 122 | 374 | 35 | 84 | 13 | 2 | 17 | 55 | .225 | 715 | 64 | 9 | .988 |
| National League Totals ................. | | | | 539 | 1838 | 217 | 458 | 68 | 5 | 89 | 284 | .249 | 2850 | 464 | 70 | .979 |
| American League Totals ............... | | | | 250 | 872 | 105 | 214 | 34 | 1 | 36 | 135 | .245 | 1440 | 102 | 16 | .990 |
| Major League Totals ...................... | | | | 789 | 2710 | 322 | 672 | 102 | 6 | 125 | 419 | .248 | 4290 | 566 | 86 | .982 |

†On restricted list April 4 through June 12.
‡Traded with Infielder Taylor Duncan to Baltimore Orioles for Pitchers Pat Dobson and Roric Harrison, Catcher Johnny Oates and Infielder Dave Johnson, November 30, 1972.
§Traded to Atlanta Braves for Pitcher Jimmy Freeman and an estimated $75,000, April 17, 1975.
xSold to Montreal Expos, July 2, 1976.
ySold (via Waivers) to Oakland A's, March 28, 1977.

### CHAMPIONSHIP SERIES RECORD

| Year | Club | League | Pos. | G. | AB. | R. | H. | 2B. | 3B. | HR. | RBI. | B.A. | PO. | A. | E. | F.A. |
|------|------|--------|------|-----|------|-----|-----|-----|-----|-----|------|------|------|-----|-----|------|
| 1973–Baltimore..........Amer. | | | 1B-C | 5 | 18 | 2 | 5 | 2 | 0 | 1 | 4 | .278 | 43 | 2 | 0 | 1.000 |
| 1974–Baltimore..........Amer. | | | 1B | 2 | 6 | 0 | 0 | 0 | 0 | 0 | 0 | .000 | 16 | 1 | 1 | .944 |
| Championship Series Totals ............ | | | | 7 | 24 | 2 | 5 | 2 | 0 | 1 | 4 | .208 | 59 | 3 | 1 | .984 |

### PITCHING RECORD

| Year | Club | League | G. | IP. | W. | L. | Pct. | H. | R. | ER. | SO. | BB. | ERA. |
|------|------|--------|-----|-----|-----|-----|------|-----|-----|-----|-----|-----|------|
| 1966–Sarasota Braves ..................Gulf Coast | | | 11 | 61 | 1 | 0 | 1.000 | 60 | 26 | 21 | 32 | 22 | 3.10 |

## MARK WESTLEY WILLIAMS

Born July 28, 1953, at Elmira, N. Y.
Height, 6.00. Weight, 180.
Throws and bats lefthanded.
Hobbies—Music, fishing, swimming and tennis.
Attended Manatee Junior College, Bradenton, Fla.

| Year | Club | League | Pos. | G. | AB. | R. | H. | 2B. | 3B. | HR. | RBI. | B.A. | PO. | A. | E. | F.A. |
|------|------|--------|------|-----|------|-----|-----|-----|-----|-----|------|------|------|-----|-----|------|
| 1972–Sarasota Royals Gulf C. | | | OF-1B | 48 | 183 | 32 | 55 | 4 | 5 | 0 | 23 | .301 | 113 | 8 | 1 | .991 |
| 1973–Waterloo ..........Midw. | | | OF | 109 | 374 | 56 | 117 | 21 | 3 | 6 | 67 | .313 | 159 | 6 | 8 | .954 |
| 1974–San Jose............Calif. | | | OF-1B | 48 | 153 | 23 | 42 | 4 | 0 | 3 | 30 | .275 | 71 | 2 | 2 | .973 |
| 1974–Jacksonville ......South. | | | OF | 17 | 63 | 9 | 19 | 5 | 0 | 1 | 4 | .302 | 20 | 2 | 2 | .917 |
| 1974–Omaha ..............A. A. | | | OF | 44 | 177 | 19 | 48 | 11 | 0 | 3 | 15 | .271 | 113 | 4 | 2 | .983 |
| 1975–Omaha† ............A. A. | | | OF | 103 | 333 | 35 | 75 | 15 | 1 | 2 | 28 | .225 | 198 | 7 | 6 | .972 |
| 1976–Modesto ...........Calif. | | | OF | 36 | 111 | 15 | 29 | 3 | 0 | 2 | 12 | .261 | 33 | 0 | 1 | .971 |
| 1976–Chattanooga‡ ....South. | | | OF | 46 | 170 | 17 | 60 | 11 | 0 | 1 | 17 | .353 | 101 | 6 | 5 | .955 |

†Traded by Kansas City Royals to Oakland A's for Infielder Rick Ingalls, September 15, 1975.
‡On disabled list, June 7 through July 10, 1976.
Listed on Oakland A's 1977 spring roster.

## MICHAEL HENRY WILLIS
### (Mike)

Born December 26, 1950, at Oklahoma City, Okla.
Height, 6.02. Weight, 205.
Throws and bats lefthanded.
Hobbies—Fishing and golf.
Attended Vanderbilt University, Nashville, Tenn.

Pitched 4-0 no-hit victory against Pulaski, June 28, 1972.
Tied for International League lead in shutouts with 4 in 1974.

| Year | Club | League | G. | IP. | W. | L. | Pct. | H. | R. | ER. | SO. | BB. | ERA. |
|------|------|--------|-----|-----|-----|-----|------|-----|-----|-----|-----|-----|------|
| 1972–Bluefield ............Ap'achian | | | 12 | 86 | 7 | 4 | .636 | 67 | 42 | 29 | 98 | 33 | 3.03 |
| 1973–Miami ................Florida St. | | | 18 | 125 | 9 | 6 | .600 | 88 | 36 | 27 | 87 | 34 | 1.94 |
| 1973–Asheville............Southern | | | 9 | 69 | 5 | 3 | .625 | 68 | 30 | 26 | 30 | 18 | 3.39 |
| 1974–Asheville............Southern | | | 7 | 36 | 3 | 0 | 1.000 | 34 | 16 | 12 | 18 | 11 | 3.00 |
| 1974–Rochester ...........Int'national | | | 21 | 143 | 9 | 4 | .692 | 117 | 49 | 42 | 74 | 42 | 2.64 |
| 1975–Rochester ...........Int'national | | | 32 | 175 | ●14 | 8 | .636 | 151 | 71 | 50 | 84 | 54 | 2.57 |
| 1976–Rochester† ........Int'national | | | 27 | 156 | 12 | 6 | .667 | 161 | 81 | 73 | 80 | 39 | 4.21 |

†Selected by Toronto Blue Jays in American League expansion draft, November 5, 1976.

## JAMES ARTHUR WILLOUGHBY
### (Jim)

Born January 31, 1949, at Salinas, Calif.
Height, 6.02. Weight, 200.
Throws and bats righthanded.
Hobbies—Photography, model rocketry and cars.
Attended Phoenix College, Phoenix, Ariz., Fresno State College, Fresno, Calif., and University of California, Berkeley, Calif.

Led Pacific Coast League pitchers in complete games with 12 and shutouts with 4 in 1971.

| Year Club | League | G. | IP. | W. | L. | Pct. | H. | R. | ER. | SO. | BB. | ERA. |
|---|---|---|---|---|---|---|---|---|---|---|---|---|
| 1967—Salt Lake City | Pioneer | 17 | 70 | 3 | 3 | .500 | 57 | 47 | 31 | 72 | 31 | 3.99 |
| 1968—Fresno | California | 6 | 10 | 1 | 1 | .500 | 10 | 7 | 6 | 11 | 4 | 4.91 |
| 1968—Medford | Northwest | 12 | 56 | 4 | 6 | .400 | 60 | 48 | 33 | 48 | 18 | 5.30 |
| 1969—Fresno | California | 20 | 156 | 12 | 4 | *.750 | 126 | 44 | 35 | 160 | 38 | 2.02 |
| 1970—Phoenix | P. Coast | 29 | 190 | 11 | 9 | .550 | 211 | 84 | 69 | 116 | 39 | 3.27 |
| 1971—Phoenix | P. Coast | 31 | 204 | 14 | 9 | .609 | 189 | 91 | 76 | 140 | 79 | 3.35 |
| 1971—San Francisco | National | 2 | 4 | 0 | 1 | .000 | 8 | 4 | 4 | 3 | 1 | 9.00 |
| 1972—Phoenix | P. Coast | 26 | 164 | 9 | 8 | .529 | 172 | 104 | 85 | 115 | 53 | 4.66 |
| 1972—San Francisco | National | 11 | 88 | 6 | 4 | .600 | 72 | 25 | 23 | 40 | 14 | 2.35 |
| 1973—San Francisco | National | 39 | 123 | 4 | 5 | .444 | 138 | 74 | 64 | 60 | 37 | 4.68 |
| 1974—Phoenix | P. Coast | 15 | 94 | 6 | 6 | .500 | 122 | 66 | 61 | 39 | 24 | 5.84 |
| 1974—San Francisco† | National | 18 | 41 | 1 | 4 | .200 | 51 | 27 | 21 | 12 | 9 | 4.61 |
| 1975—Tulsa‡ | Am. Assoc. | 15 | 114 | 8 | 6 | .571 | 112 | 43 | 41 | 62 | 28 | 3.24 |
| 1975—Boston | American | 24 | 48 | 5 | 2 | .714 | 46 | 25 | 19 | 29 | 16 | 3.56 |
| 1976—Boston | American | 54 | 99 | 3 | 12 | .200 | 94 | 38 | 31 | 37 | 31 | 2.82 |
| American League Totals | | 78 | 147 | 8 | 14 | .364 | 140 | 63 | 50 | 66 | 47 | 3.06 |
| National League Totals | | 70 | 256 | 11 | 15 | .440 | 269 | 130 | 112 | 115 | 61 | 3.94 |
| Major League Totals | | 148 | 403 | 19 | 29 | .396 | 409 | 193 | 162 | 181 | 108 | 3.62 |

†Traded to St. Louis Cardinals for Second Baseman Tom Heintzelman, October 14, 1974.

‡Traded by St. Louis Cardinals to Boston Red Sox, July 4, 1975, to complete deal in which Cardinals obtained Shortstop Mario Guerrero from Red Sox for a player to be named later, April 4, 1975.

WORLD SERIES RECORD

| Year Club | League | G. | IP. | W. | L. | Pct. | H. | R. | ER. | SO. | BB. | ERA. |
|---|---|---|---|---|---|---|---|---|---|---|---|---|
| 1975—Boston | American | 3 | 6⅓ | 0 | 1 | .000 | 3 | 1 | 0 | 2 | 0 | 0.00 |

## ELLIOTT TAYLOR WILLS
### (Bump)

(Nicknamed by father after Bump Elliott.)

Born July 27, 1952, at Washington, D. C.
Height, 5.09 Weight, 172.
Throws right and bats left and righthanded.
Hobby—Playing the guitar.
Attended Arizona State University, Tempe, Ariz.
Son of Maury Wills, infielder with Los Angeles Dodgers, Pittsburgh Pirates and Montreal Expos, 1959 through 1972.

| Year Club | League | Pos. | G. | AB. | R. | H. | 2B. | 3B. | HR. | RBI. | B.A. | PO. | A. | E. | F.A. |
|---|---|---|---|---|---|---|---|---|---|---|---|---|---|---|---|
| 1975—Pittsfield | East. | 2B-SS | 122 | 456 | 72 | *140 | 23 | 2 | 9 | 49 | .307 | 223 | 304 | 26 | .953 |
| 1976—Sacramento | P. C. | 2B | 117 | 432 | 91 | 140 | 20 | 6 | 26 | 95 | .324 | 297 | 350 | 19 | .971 |

Listed on Texas Rangers' 1977 spring roster.

## WILLIE JAMES WILSON

Born July 9, 1955, at Montgomery, Ala.
Height, 6.03. Weight, 190.
Throws right and bats left and righthanded.

Led Gulf Coast League in stolen bases with 24 in 1974.
Led Midwest League in stolen bases with 76 in 1975.
Named Midwest League Most Valuable Player in 1975.

| Year Club | League | Pos. | G. | AB. | R. | H. | 2B. | 3B. | HR. | RBI. | B.A. | PO. | A. | E. | F.A. |
|---|---|---|---|---|---|---|---|---|---|---|---|---|---|---|---|
| 1974—Sarasota Royals | Gulf C. | OF | 47 | 155 | 30 | 39 | 3 | 5 | 1 | 14 | .252 | 92 | 8 | 4 | .962 |
| 1975—Waterloo | Midw. | OF | 127 | 486 | 92 | *132 | 18 | 4 | 8 | 73 | .272 | 249 | *17 | 17 | .940 |
| 1976—Jacksonville | South. | OF | 107 | 388 | 54 | 98 | 13 | 6 | 1 | 35 | .253 | 273 | 5 | 8 | .972 |
| 1976—Kansas City | Amer. | OF-PH | 12 | 6 | 0 | 1 | 0 | 0 | 0 | 0 | .167 | 6 | 1 | 1 | .875 |
| Major League Totals | | | 12 | 6 | 0 | 1 | 0 | 0 | 0 | 0 | .167 | 6 | 1 | 1 | .875 |

## DAVID MARK WINFIELD
### (Dave)

Born October 3, 1951, at St. Paul, Minn.
Height, 6.06. Weight, 220.
Throws and bats righthanded.
Hobbies—Reading, art and fashion.
Attended University of Minnesota, Minneapolis, Minn.

| Year Club | League | Pos. | G. | AB. | R. | H. | 2B. | 3B. | HR. | RBI. | B.A. | PO. | A. | E. | F.A. |
|---|---|---|---|---|---|---|---|---|---|---|---|---|---|---|---|
| 1973—San Diego | Nat. | OF-1B | 56 | 141 | 9 | 39 | 4 | 1 | 3 | 12 | .277 | 65 | 1 | 3 | .957 |
| 1974—San Diego | Nat. | OF | 145 | 498 | 57 | 132 | 18 | 4 | 20 | 75 | .265 | 276 | 4 | *12 | .960 |
| 1975—San Diego | Nat. | OF | 143 | 509 | 74 | 136 | 20 | 2 | 15 | 76 | .267 | 302 | 9 | 9 | .972 |
| 1976—San Diego | Nat. | OF | 137 | 492 | 81 | 139 | 26 | 4 | 13 | 69 | .283 | 304 | *15 | 6 | .982 |
| Major League Totals | | | 481 | 1640 | 221 | 446 | 68 | 11 | 51 | 232 | .272 | 947 | 36 | 30 | .970 |

# RICHARD CHARLES WISE
## (Rick)

Born September 13, 1945, at Jackson, Mich.
Height, 6.02. Weight, 195.
Throws and bats righthanded.
Hobbies—Hunting and fishing.
Brother of Tom Wise, former infielder in Houston Astros' organization, 1970-75.

Tied major league records for most games, two or more home runs by a pitcher in a season (2), 1971; most putouts, game, pitcher, 5, May 15, 1973.
Pitched 4-0 no-hit victory against Cincinnati Reds, June 23, 1971.

| Year | Club | League | G. | IP. | W. | L. | Pct. | H. | R. | ER. | SO. | BB. | ERA. |
|------|------|--------|----|-----|----|----|------|----|----|-----|-----|-----|------|
| 1963—Bakersfield | | California | 12 | 65 | 6 | 3 | .667 | 47 | 26 | 19 | 98 | 23 | 2.63 |
| 1964—Philadelphia | | National | 25 | 69 | 5 | 3 | .625 | 78 | 41 | 31 | 39 | 25 | 4.04 |
| 1965—Arkansas | | P. Coast | 30 | 194 | 8 | •16 | .333 | 195 | 107 | 96 | 148 | 84 | 4.45 |
| 1966—San Diego | | P. Coast | 12 | 55 | 3 | 1 | .750 | 44 | 16 | 14 | 26 | 9 | 2.29 |
| 1966—Philadelphia | | National | 22 | 99 | 5 | 6 | .455 | 100 | 50 | 41 | 58 | 23 | 3.73 |
| 1967—Philadelphia | | National | 36 | 181 | 11 | 11 | .500 | 177 | 69 | 66 | 111 | 45 | 3.28 |
| 1968—Philadelphia | | National | 30 | 182 | 9 | 15 | .375 | 210 | 100 | •92 | 97 | 37 | 4.55 |
| 1969—Philadelphia | | National | 33 | 220 | 15 | 13 | .536 | 215 | 100 | 79 | 144 | 61 | 3.23 |
| 1970—Philadelphia | | National | 35 | 220 | 13 | 14 | .481 | 253 | 115 | 102 | 113 | 65 | 4.17 |
| 1971—Philadelphia† | | National | 38 | 272 | 17 | 14 | .548 | 261 | 110 | 87 | 155 | 70 | 2.88 |
| 1972—St. Louis | | National | 35 | 269 | 16 | 16 | .500 | 250 | 98 | 93 | 142 | 71 | 3.11 |
| 1973—St. Louis‡ | | National | 35 | 259 | 16 | 12 | .571 | 259 | 113 | 97 | 144 | 59 | 3.37 |
| 1974—Boston§ | | American | 9 | 49 | 3 | 4 | .429 | 47 | 23 | 21 | 25 | 16 | 3.86 |
| 1975—Boston | | American | 35 | 255 | 19 | 12 | .613 | 262 | 126 | 112 | 141 | 72 | 3.95 |
| 1976—Boston | | American | 34 | 224 | 14 | 11 | .560 | 218 | 100 | 88 | 93 | 48 | 3.54 |
| American League Totals | | | 78 | 528 | 36 | 27 | .571 | 527 | 249 | 221 | 259 | 136 | 3.77 |
| National League Totals | | | 289 | 1771 | 107 | 104 | .507 | 1803 | 796 | 688 | 1003 | 457 | 3.50 |
| Major League Totals | | | 367 | 2299 | 143 | 131 | .522 | 2330 | 1045 | 909 | 1262 | 593 | 3.56 |

†Traded to St. Louis Cardinals for Pitcher Steve Carlton, February 25, 1972.
‡Traded with Outfielder Bernie Carbo to Boston Red Sox for Outfielder Reggie Smith and Pitcher Ken Tatum, October 26, 1973.
§On disabled list, August 7 to September 1, 1974.

### CHAMPIONSHIP SERIES RECORD

| Year | Club | League | G. | IP. | W. | L. | Pct. | H. | R. | ER. | SO. | BB. | ERA. |
|------|------|--------|----|-----|----|----|------|----|----|-----|-----|-----|------|
| 1975—Boston | | American | 1 | 7⅓ | 1 | 0 | 1.000 | 6 | 3 | 2 | 2 | 3 | 2.45 |

### WORLD SERIES RECORD

| Year | Club | League | G. | IP. | W. | L. | Pct. | H. | R. | ER. | SO. | BB. | ERA. |
|------|------|--------|----|-----|----|----|------|----|----|-----|-----|-----|------|
| 1975—Boston | | American | 2 | 5⅓ | 1 | 0 | 1.000 | 6 | 5 | 5 | 2 | 2 | 8.44 |

### ALL-STAR GAME RECORD

| Year | League | IP. | W. | L. | Pct. | H. | R. | ER. | SO. | BB. | ERA. |
|------|--------|-----|----|----|------|----|----|-----|-----|-----|------|
| 1973—National | | 2 | 1 | 0 | 1.000 | 2 | 1 | 1 | 1 | 0 | 4.50 |

Member of National League All-Star Team in 1971 game; did not play.


# JOHNNY BILTON WOCKENFUSS

Born February 27, 1949, at Welch, W. Va.
Height, 6.00. Weight, 195.
Throws and bats righthanded.
Hobbies—Hunting and fishing.

Led American Association in passed balls with 10 in 1974.
Tied for Eastern League lead in passed balls with 24 in 1972.

| Year | Club | League | Pos. | G. | AB. | R. | H. | 2B. | 3B. | HR. | RBI. | B.A. | PO. | A. | E. | F.A. |
|------|------|--------|------|----|-----|----|----|-----|-----|-----|------|------|-----|----|----|------|
| 1967—Geneva | | NYP | OF | 3 | 7 | 0 | 1 | 0 | 0 | 0 | 1 | .143 | 0 | 0 | 1 | 1.000 |
| 1968—Geneva | | NYP | OF-3B | 39 | 132 | 13 | 26 | 1 | 1 | 4 | 17 | .197 | 50 | 5 | 7 | .887 |
| 1969—Burlington | | Carol. | OF | 62 | 197 | 23 | 33 | 7 | 1 | 4 | 15 | .168 | 110 | 4 | 4 | .966 |
| 1969—Shelby | | W. Car. | OF | 39 | 157 | 26 | 51 | 12 | 0 | 7 | 29 | .325 | 77 | 7 | 4 | .955 |
| 1970—Pittsfield | | East. | •O-3-2 | 123 | 429 | 65 | 106 | 11 | 6 | 15 | 47 | .247 | 219 | 11 | 4 | •.983 |
| 1971—Pittsfield | | East. | OF-C | 103 | 331 | 37 | 77 | 11 | 1 | 9 | 41 | .233 | 182 | 5 | 3 | .984 |
| 1972—Pittsfield | | East. | •C-OF | 125 | 410 | 57 | 118 | 20 | 2 | 9 | 60 | .288 | •772 | •68 | 7 | .992 |
| 1973—Spokane† | | P.C. | C-OF | 20 | 54 | 6 | 11 | 2 | 0 | 1 | 6 | .204 | 64 | 4 | 3 | .953 |
| 1973—Tulsa‡ | | A.A. | C-OF | 60 | 184 | 22 | 49 | 12 | 1 | 2 | 22 | .266 | 298 | 32 | 5 | .985 |
| 1974—Evansville | | A.A. | C | 84 | 233 | 40 | 64 | 11 | 2 | 10 | 43 | .275 | 412 | 41 | 10 | .978 |
| 1974—Detroit | | Amer. | C | 13 | 29 | 1 | 4 | 1 | 0 | 0 | 2 | .138 | 45 | 10 | 4 | .932 |
| 1975—Evansville | | A.A. | C-OF | 43 | 142 | 20 | 41 | 11 | 0 | 6 | 28 | .289 | 174 | 26 | 3 | .985 |
| 1975—Detroit | | Amer. | C | 35 | 118 | 15 | 27 | 6 | 3 | 4 | 13 | .229 | 195 | 23 | 4 | .982 |
| 1976—Detroit | | Amer. | C | 60 | 144 | 18 | 32 | 7 | 2 | 3 | 10 | .222 | 221 | 19 | 15 | .941 |
| Major League Totals | | | | 108 | 291 | 34 | 63 | 14 | 5 | 7 | 25 | .216 | 461 | 52 | 25 | .957 |

†Traded with Pitcher Mike Nagy by Texas Rangers to St. Louis Cardinals for Pitcher Jim Bibby, June 6, 1973.
‡Traded by St. Louis Cardinals to Detroit Tigers for Infielder Larry Elliott, December 3, 1973.

## JAMES EUGENE WOHLFORD
### (Jim)

Born February 28, 1951, at Visalia, Calif.
Height, 5.11. Weight, 1975.
Throws and bats righthanded.
Hobbies—Golf and playing phonograph records.
Attended College of the Sequoias, Visalia, Calif.

Led Pioneer League in stolen bases with 32 in 1970.

| Year | Club | League | Pos. | G. | AB. | R. | H. | 2B. | 3B. | HR. | RBI. | B.A. | PO. | A. | E. | F.A. |
|---|---|---|---|---|---|---|---|---|---|---|---|---|---|---|---|---|
| 1970—Billings | ............ | Pion. | •S-2-3 | 62 | 221 | 42 | 68 | 7 | 2 | 3 | 37 | .308 | 72 | 158 | •36 | .865 |
| 1971—San Jose | ............ | Calif. | 2B-SS | 120 | 491 | 82 | 149 | 27 | 6 | 11 | 41 | .303 | 193 | 327 | 30 | .945 |
| 1972—Omaha | ............. | A.A. | •2-3-O | 132 | 475 | 75 | 138 | 13 | 10 | 7 | 47 | .291 | 247 | 292 | •32 | .944 |
| 1972—Kansas City | ...... | Amer. | 2B | 15 | 25 | 3 | 6 | 1 | 0 | 0 | 0 | .240 | 7 | 12 | 1 | .950 |
| 1973—Omaha | ............. | A.A. | OF | 65 | 246 | 30 | 76 | 9 | 4 | 3 | 30 | .309 | 91 | 5 | 2 | .980 |
| 1973—Kansas City | ...... | Amer. | OF | 45 | 109 | 21 | 29 | 1 | 3 | 2 | 10 | .266 | 31 | 2 | 0 | 1.000 |
| 1974—Kansas City | ...... | Amer. | OF | 143 | 501 | 55 | 136 | 16 | 7 | 2 | 44 | .271 | 273 | 7 | 5 | .982 |
| 1975—Kansas City | ...... | Amer. | OF | 116 | 353 | 45 | 90 | 10 | 5 | 0 | 30 | .255 | 175 | 9 | 9 | .953 |
| 1976—Kansas City† | .... | Amer. | O-2-PH | 107 | 293 | 47 | 73 | 10 | 2 | 1 | 24 | .249 | 190 | 8 | 5 | .975 |
| Major League Totals | ...................... | | | 426 | 1281 | 171 | 334 | 38 | 17 | 5 | 108 | .261 | 676 | 38 | 20 | .973 |

†Traded with Infielder Jamie Quirk and a player to be named later to Milwaukee Brewers for Pitcher Jim Colborn and Catcher Darrell Porter, December 6, 1976; Pitcher Bob McClure was sent to Milwaukee to complete deal, March 15, 1977.

### CHAMPIONSHIP SERIES RECORD

| Year | Club | League | Pos. | G. | AB. | R. | H. | 2B. | 3B. | HR. | RBI. | B.A. | PO. | A. | E. | F.A. |
|---|---|---|---|---|---|---|---|---|---|---|---|---|---|---|---|---|
| 1976—Kansas City | ...... | Amer. | OF-PH | 5 | 11 | 3 | 2 | 0 | 0 | 0 | 0 | .182 | 7 | 0 | 0 | 1.000 |

## WILBUR FORRESTER WOOD, JR.

Born October 22, 1941, at Cambridge, Mass.
Height, 6.00. Weight, 190.
Throws left and bats righthanded.
Hobby—Fishing.

Established major league record for most strikeouts, season, by pitcher as batter, 65, 1972.
Tied major league record for most consecutive seasons leading major leagues in earned runs, 2, 1973.
Established following American League records: Most games pitched, season (88), 1968; most games, season, none complete (88), 1968; most games, season, relief pitcher (88), 1968; most consecutive season leading league, games started, 4, 1975.
Tied following American League records: most seasons leading league, runs allowed, 2, 1973; most consecutive seasons, leading league, runs allowed, 2, 1973; most consecutive seasons, leading league, earned runs, 2, 1973.
Led American League pitchers in games started with 49 in 1972, 48 in 1973, 42 in 1974 and 43 in 1975.
Led Pacific Coast League pitchers in complete games with 19 in 1964.
Led International League in complete games with 15 and shutouts with 8 in 1966.
Tied for Eastern League lead in games started by pitchers with 29 in 1962.
Named THE SPORTING NEWS American League Pitcher of the Year, 1972
Named lefthanded pitcher on THE SPORTING NEWS American League All-Star Team, 1972.
Won THE SPORTING NEWS American League Fireman of the Year Award, 1968.
Received reported $30,000 bonus to sign with Boston Red Sox, 1960.

| Year | Club | League | G. | IP. | W. | L. | Pct. | H. | R. | ER. | SO. | BB. | ERA. |
|---|---|---|---|---|---|---|---|---|---|---|---|---|---|
| 1960—Waterloo | ............................. | Midwest | 4 | 20 | 1 | 0 | 1.000 | 20 | 10 | 6 | 21 | 9 | 2.70 |
| 1960—Raleigh | ............................. | Carolina | 13 | 77 | 3 | 5 | .375 | 85 | 43 | 33 | 59 | 32 | 3.84 |
| 1961—Winston-Salem | ................... | Carolina | 16 | 111 | 8 | 5 | .615 | 99 | 48 | 39 | 103 | 33 | 3.15 |
| 1961—Boston | ............................. | American | 6 | 13 | 0 | 0 | .000 | 14 | 8 | 8 | 7 | 7 | 5.54 |
| 1961—Johnstown | ............................ | Eastern | 10 | 74 | 3 | 7 | .300 | 80 | 40 | 38 | 44 | 15 | 4.62 |
| 1962—York | ............................ | Eastern | 29 | •219 | 15 | 11 | .577 | 198 | 81 | 69 | 178 | 62 | 2.84 |
| 1962—Boston | ............................ | American | 1 | 8 | 0 | 0 | .000 | 6 | 3 | 3 | 3 | 3 | 3.38 |
| 1963—Seattle | ............................. | P. Coast | 8 | 64 | 5 | 2 | .714 | 54 | 15 | 8 | 43 | 10 | 1.13 |
| 1963—Boston | ............................. | American | 25 | 65 | 0 | 5 | .000 | 67 | 35 | 27 | 28 | 13 | 3.74 |
| 1964—Boston | ............................. | American | 4 | 6 | 0 | 0 | .000 | 13 | 11 | 11 | 5 | 3 | 16.50 |
| 1964—Seattle† | ............................ | P. Coast | 28 | 191 | 15 | 8 | .652 | 176 | 61 | 54 | 197 | 49 | 2.30 |
| 1964—Pittsburgh | ............................ | National | 3 | 17 | 0 | 2 | .000 | 16 | 8 | 7 | 7 | 11 | 3.71 |
| 1965—Pittsburgh | ............................ | National | 34 | 51 | 1 | 1 | .500 | 44 | 21 | 18 | 29 | 16 | 3.18 |
| 1966—Columbus‡ | ............................ | Int'national | 31 | •224 | 14 | 8 | .636 | 197 | 69 | 60 | 109 | 38 | •2.41 |
| 1967—Chicago | ............................ | American | 51 | 95 | 4 | 2 | .667 | 95 | 34 | 26 | 47 | 28 | 2.46 |
| 1968—Chicago | ............................ | American | •88 | 159 | 13 | 12 | .520 | 127 | 39 | 33 | 74 | 33 | 1.87 |
| 1969—Chicago | ............................ | American | •76 | 120 | 10 | 11 | .476 | 113 | 48 | 40 | 73 | 40 | 3.00 |
| 1970—Chicago | ............................ | American | •77 | 122 | 9 | 13 | .409 | 118 | 50 | 38 | 85 | 36 | 2.80 |
| 1971—Chicago | ............................ | American | 44 | 334 | 22 | 13 | .629 | 272 | 95 | 71 | 210 | 62 | 1.91 |
| 1972—Chicago | ............................ | American | 49 | •377 | •24 | 17 | .585 | •325 | •119 | •105 | 193 | 74 | 2.51 |
| 1973—Chicago | ............................ | American | 49 | •359 | •24 | 20 | .545 | •381 | •166 | •138 | 199 | 91 | 3.46 |
| 1974—Chicago | ............................ | American | 42 | 320 | 20 | 19 | .513 | 305 | 143 | 128 | 169 | 80 | 3.60 |
| 1975—Chicago | ............................ | American | 43 | 291 | 16 | •20 | .444 | 309 | •148 | •133 | 140 | 92 | 4.11 |
| 1976—Chicago§ | ............................ | American | 7 | 56 | 4 | 3 | .571 | 51 | 24 | 14 | 31 | 11 | 2.25 |
| American League Totals | ......................... | | 562 | 2325 | 146 | 135 | .520 | 2196 | 923 | 775 | 1264 | 573 | 3.00 |
| National League Totals | ......................... | | 37 | 68 | 1 | 3 | .250 | 60 | 29 | 25 | 36 | 27 | 3.31 |
| Major League Totals | ............................. | | 599 | 2393 | 147 | 138 | .516 | 2256 | 952 | 800 | 1300 | 600 | 3.01 |

†Purchased from Boston Red Sox by Pittsburgh Pirates, September 6, 1964.
‡Sold by Pittsburgh Pirates to Chicago White Sox, October 12, 1966; White Sox sold Pitcher Juan Pizarro to Pirates, November 28, 1966, to complete deal.
§On disabled list, May 12 through October 12, 1976.

## ALL-STAR GAME RECORD

| Year League | IP. | W. | L. | Pct. | H. | R. | ER. | SO. | BB. | ERA. |
|---|---|---|---|---|---|---|---|---|---|---|
| 1972—American | 2 | 0 | 0 | .000 | 2 | 1 | 1 | 1 | 1 | 4.50 |

Member of American League All-Star Team in 1971 and 1974 games; did not play.

## ALVIS WOODS
### (Al)

Born August 8, 1953, at Oakland, Calif.
Height, 6.03. Weight, 190.
Throws and bats lefthanded.
Hobbies—Listening to music, the outdoors and crafts.
Attended Laney College, Oakland, Calif.

| Year Club | League | Pos. | G. | AB. | R. | H. | 2B. | 3B. | HR. | RBI. | B.A. | PO. | A. | E. | F.A. |
|---|---|---|---|---|---|---|---|---|---|---|---|---|---|---|---|
| 1973—Geneva | NYP | OF | 35 | 116 | 17 | 35 | 6 | 1 | 2 | 10 | .302 | 47 | 3 | 5 | .909 |
| 1974—Wis. Rapids | Midw. | OF | 111 | 405 | 87 | 126 | 17 | 5 | 18 | 77 | .311 | 207 | 6 | 5 | .977 |
| 1975—Orlando† | South. | OF | 123 | 411 | 55 | 108 | 11 | 4 | 6 | 50 | .263 | 248 | 9 | 4 | .985 |
| 1976—Tacoma‡ | P. C. | OF | 121 | 416 | 60 | 118 | 15 | 4 | 6 | 74 | .284 | 219 | 11 | 9 | .962 |

†On disabled list, May 29 to June 8, 1975.
‡On disabled list, April 17 to April 27, 1976; selected by Toronto Blue Jays in American League expansion draft, November 5, 1976.

## GARY LEE WOODS

Born July 20, 1954, at Santa Barbara, Calif.
Height, 6.02. Weight, 185.
Throws and bats righthanded.
Hobbies—Skiing and volleyball.
Attended Santa Barbara City Junior College, Santa Barbara, Calif.

| Year Club | League | Pos. | G. | AB. | R. | H. | 2B. | 3B. | HR. | RBI. | B.A. | PO. | A. | E. | F.A. |
|---|---|---|---|---|---|---|---|---|---|---|---|---|---|---|---|
| 1973—Lewiston | Northw. | OF | 63 | 220 | 23 | 45 | 7 | 3 | 2 | 15 | .205 | 87 | 2 | 7 | .927 |
| 1974—Burlington | Midw. | OF | 117 | 405 | 68 | 115 | •30 | 3 | 11 | 59 | .284 | 228 | 4 | 8 | .967 |
| 1975—Birmingham | South. | OF | 134 | 484 | 76 | 126 | 15 | 6 | 1 | 43 | .260 | •366 | •20 | 7 | .982 |
| 1976—Tucson | P. C. | •OF-3B | 137 | 526 | 79 | 162 | 22 | 6 | 8 | 67 | .308 | •355 | 14 | 13 | .966 |
| 1976—Oakland† | Amer. | OF-PH | 6 | 8 | 0 | 1 | 0 | 0 | 0 | 0 | .125 | 7 | 0 | 0 | 1.000 |
| Major League Totals | | | 6 | 8 | 0 | 1 | 0 | 0 | 0 | 0 | .125 | 7 | 0 | 0 | 1.000 |

†Selected by Toronto Blue Jays in American League expansion draft, November 5, 1976.

## JAMES CLIFTON WRIGHT
### (Jim)

Born December 21, 1950, at Reed City, Mich.
Height, 6.01. Weight, 170.
Throws and bats righthanded.

| Year Club | League | G. | IP. | W. | L. | Pct. | H. | R. | ER. | SO. | BB. | ERA. |
|---|---|---|---|---|---|---|---|---|---|---|---|---|
| 1969—Jamestown | NYP | 13 | 54 | 2 | 5 | .286 | 66 | 44 | 32 | 37 | 20 | 5.33 |
| 1970—Jamestown† | NYP | 3 | 8 | 0 | 0 | .000 | 3 | 1 | 1 | 8 | 2 | 1.13 |
| 1971—Greenville‡ | W. Carol. | 24 | 83 | 6 | 7 | .462 | 85 | 48 | 39 | 74 | 32 | 4.23 |
| 1971—Winston-Salem | Carolina | 3 | 4 | 0 | 0 | .000 | 2 | 0 | 0 | 0 | 1 | 0.00 |
| 1972—Anderson§ | W. Carol. | 15 | 42 | 0 | 4 | .000 | 59 | 43 | 35 | 35 | 24 | 7.50 |
| 1973—Winston-Salem | Carolina | 35 | 126 | 7 | 4 | .636 | 117 | 64 | 43 | 103 | 50 | 3.07 |
| 1974—Bristol | Eastern | 25 | 164 | 9 | 8 | .529 | 153 | 70 | 50 | 131 | 58 | 2.74 |
| 1975—Bristol | Eastern | 10 | 69 | 7 | 1 | .875 | 61 | 28 | 27 | 66 | 30 | 3.52 |
| 1975—Pawtucket | Int'national | 17 | 102 | 1 | 10 | .091 | 105 | 51 | 40 | 69 | 46 | 3.53 |
| 1976—Rhode Island | Int'national | 37 | 136 | 6 | 12 | .333 | 162 | 90 | 76 | 74 | 44 | 5.03 |

†On Military List from beginning of season until August 24, 1970.
‡On temporary inactive list, July 24 to August 18, 1971.
§On temporary inactive list, July 6 to July 28, 1972.
Listed on Boston Red Sox' 1977 spring roster.

## HAROLD DELANO WYNEGAR, JR.
Name pronounced WY-nuh-ger.
### (Butch)
(Nicknamed by grandmother.)

Born March 14, 1956, at York, Pa.
Height, 6.01. Weight, 190.
Throws right and bats left and righthanded.
Hobbies—Astronomy, music and coins.

Led Appalachian League catchers in double plays with 9 in 1974.
Led California League batters in walks with 142 in 1975.
Named American League Rookie Player of the Year by THE SPORTING NEWS, 1976.

| Year Club | League | Pos. | G. | AB. | R. | H. | 2B. | 3B. | HR. | RBI. | B.A. | PO. | A. | E. | F.A. |
|---|---|---|---|---|---|---|---|---|---|---|---|---|---|---|---|
| 1974—Elizabethton | Appal. | C | 60 | 191 | 32 | 66 | 10 | 0 | 8 | 51 | •.346 | 344 | 39 | 5 | •.987 |
| 1975—Reno | Calif. | C •139 | 468 | 106 | 147 | 18 | 6 | 19 | •112 | .314 | •734 | •99 | 9 | .989 | |
| 1976--Minnesota | Amer. | C-DH | 149 | 534 | 58 | 139 | 21 | 2 | 10 | 69 | .260 | 650 | 78 | •16 | .978 |
| Major League Totals | | | 149 | 534 | 58 | 139 | 21 | 2 | 10 | 69 | .260 | 650 | 78 | 16 | .978 |

### ALL-STAR GAME RECORD

| Year League | Pos. | AB. | R. | H. | 2B. | 3B. | HR. | RBI. | B.A. | PO. | A. | E. | F.A. |
|---|---|---|---|---|---|---|---|---|---|---|---|---|---|
| 1976—American | PH | 0 | 0 | 0 | 0 | 0 | 0 | 0 | .000 | 0 | 0 | 0 | .000 |

## JAMES SHERMAN WYNN
### (Jimmy)

Born March 12, 1942, at Cincinnati, O.
Height, 5.09. Weight, 170.
Throws and bats righthanded.
Hobbies—Jazz music, reading and sports.
Attended Central State College, Wilberforce, O.

Tied the following National League records: most bases on balls in a season, 148 in 1969; most bases on balls, intentional, game (3), July 11, 1970.
Hit three home runs in a game, June 15, 1967, and May 11, 1974.
Major League stolen bases: 1963 (4), 1964 (5), 1965 (43), 1966 (13), 1967 (16), 1968 (11), 1969 (23), 1970 (24), 1971 (10), 1972 (17), 1973 (14), 1974 (18), 1975 (7), 1976 (16). Total—221.
Led National League batters in strikeouts with 137 in 1967.
Led National League outfielders in double plays with 8 in 1968 and tied for lead with 5 in 1971.
Named as outfielder on THE SPORTING NEWS National League All-Star Team, 1967 and 1974.
Named National League Comeback Player of the Year by THE SPORTING NEWS, 1974.

| Year Club | League | Pos. | G. | AB. | R. | H. | 2B. | 3B. | HR. | RBI. | B.A. | PO. | A. | E. | F.A. |
|---|---|---|---|---|---|---|---|---|---|---|---|---|---|---|---|---|
| 1962—Tampa† | Fla. St. | •3-O-2 | 120 | 400 | 93 | 116 | 10 | 5 | •14 | •81 | .290 | •181 | 194 | 29 | •.928 |
| 1963—San Antonio | Texas | SS-3B | 78 | 302 | 57 | 87 | 15 | 11 | 16 | 49 | .288 | 139 | 185 | 28 | .920 |
| 1963—Houston | Nat. | O-S-3B | 70 | 250 | 31 | 61 | 10 | 5 | 4 | 27 | .244 | 124 | 33 | 8 | .952 |
| 1964—Houston | Nat. | OF | 67 | 219 | 19 | 49 | 7 | 0 | 5 | 18 | .224 | 129 | 8 | 6 | .958 |
| 1964—Oklahoma City | P. C. | OF-3B | 82 | 282 | 51 | 77 | 9 | 5 | 10 | 40 | .273 | 160 | 24 | 3 | .984 |
| 1965—Houston | Nat. | OF | 157 | 564 | 90 | 155 | 30 | 7 | 22 | 73 | .275 | •382 | 13 | 9 | .978 |
| 1966—Houston‡ | Nat. | OF | 105 | 418 | 62 | 107 | 21 | 1 | 18 | 62 | .256 | 259 | 6 | 6 | .978 |
| 1967—Houston | Nat. | OF | 158 | 594 | 102 | 148 | 29 | 3 | 37 | 107 | .249 | •364 | 4 | 12 | .968 |
| 1968—Houston | Nat. | OF | 156 | 542 | 85 | 146 | 23 | 5 | 26 | 67 | .269 | 298 | •20 | 4 | .988 |
| 1969—Houston | Nat. | OF | 149 | 495 | 113 | 133 | 17 | 1 | 33 | 87 | .269 | 318 | 9 | 5 | .985 |
| 1970—Houston | Nat. | OF | 157 | 554 | 82 | 156 | 32 | 2 | 27 | 88 | .282 | 293 | 14 | 4 | .987 |
| 1971—Houston | Nat. | OF | 123 | 404 | 38 | 82 | 16 | 0 | 7 | 45 | .203 | 232 | 9 | 3 | .988 |
| 1972—Houston | Nat. | OF | 145 | 542 | 117 | 148 | 29 | 3 | 24 | 90 | .273 | 284 | 8 | 5 | .983 |
| 1973—Houston§ | Nat. | OF | 139 | 481 | 90 | 106 | 14 | 5 | 20 | 55 | .220 | 270 | 9 | 4 | .986 |
| 1974—Los Angeles | Nat. | OF | 150 | 535 | 104 | 145 | 17 | 4 | 32 | 108 | .271 | 365 | 10 | 3 | .992 |
| 1975—Los Angeles x | Nat. | OF | 130 | 412 | 80 | 102 | 16 | 0 | 18 | 58 | .248 | 282 | 6 | 5 | .983 |
| 1976—Atlanta y | Nat. | OF | 148 | 449 | 75 | 93 | 19 | 1 | 17 | 66 | .207 | 287 | 17 | 9 | .971 |
| Major League Totals | | | 1854 | 6459 | 1088 | 1631 | 280 | 37 | 290 | 951 | .252 | 3887 | 166 | 83 | .980 |

†Drafted by Houston Colts from San Diego (Cincinnati Reds' system), November 26, 1962.
‡Crashed into outfield wall August 1; on disabled list from August 5 through end of season.
§Traded to Los Angeles Dodgers for Pitchers Claude Osteen and Dave Culpepper, December 6, 1973.
xTraded with Second Baseman Lee Lacy, First Baseman-Outfielder Tom Paciorek and Infielder Jerry Royster to Atlanta Braves for Outfielder Dusty Baker and First Baseman-Third Baseman Ed Goodson, November 17, 1975.
ySold to New York Yankees, November 29, 1976.

### CHAMPIONSHIP SERIES RECORD

| Year Club | League | Pos. | G. | AB. | R. | H. | 2B. | 3B. | HR. | RBI. | B.A. | PO. | A. | E. | F.A. |
|---|---|---|---|---|---|---|---|---|---|---|---|---|---|---|---|---|
| 1974—Los Angeles | Nat. | OF | 4 | 10 | 4 | 2 | 2 | 0 | 0 | 2 | .200 | 11 | 0 | 0 | 1.000 |

### WORLD SERIES RECORD

| Year Club | League | Pos. | G. | AB. | R. | H. | 2B. | 3B. | HR. | RBI. | B.A. | PO. | A. | E. | F.A. |
|---|---|---|---|---|---|---|---|---|---|---|---|---|---|---|---|---|
| 1974—Los Angeles | Nat. | OF | 5 | 16 | 1 | 3 | 1 | 0 | 1 | 2 | .188 | 5 | 0 | 0 | 1.000 |

### ALL-STAR GAME RECORD

| Year League | Pos. | AB. | R. | H. | 2B. | 3B. | HR. | RBI. | B.A. | PO. | A. | E. | F.A. |
|---|---|---|---|---|---|---|---|---|---|---|---|---|---|
| 1967—National | PH | 1 | 0 | 1 | 0 | 0 | 0 | 0 | 1.000 | 0 | 0 | 0 | .000 |
| 1974—National | OF | 3 | 1 | 1 | 0 | 0 | 0 | 0 | .333 | 0 | 0 | 0 | .000 |
| 1975—National | OF | 2 | 1 | 1 | 0 | 0 | 1 | 1 | .500 | 1 | 0 | 0 | 1.000 |
| All-Star Game Totals | | 6 | 2 | 3 | 0 | 0 | 1 | 1 | .500 | 1 | 0 | 0 | 1.000 |

---

### DID YOU KNOW —
That Lou Boudreau, now a broadcaster for the Chicago Cubs, managed the Cleveland Indians to victory in the World Series in 1948?

## HUGH YANCY, JR.

Born October 16, 1950, at Sarasota, Fla.
Height, 5.11. Weight, 180.
Throws and bats righthanded.
Hobbies—Fishing and basketball.
Attended Manatee Junior College, West Bradenton, Fla.

Led Northern League in stolen bases with 22 in 1970.
Led Southern League third basemen in double plays with 32 in 1971.

| Year Club | League | Pos. | G. | AB. | R. | H. | 2B. | 3B. | HR. | RBI. | B.A. | PO. | A. | E. | F.A. |
|---|---|---|---|---|---|---|---|---|---|---|---|---|---|---|---|
| 1968–Sara. W. Sox | ....Gulf C. | S-O-3-2 | 55 | 182 | 30 | 50 | 5 | 4 | 0 | 19 | .275 | 74 | 108 | 29 | .863 |
| 1969–Appleton | Midw. | 3-SS | 41 | 101 | 8 | 14 | 2 | 1 | 0 | 12 | .139 | 29 | 63 | 11 | .893 |
| 1969–Duluth-Super. | ....North. | SS-2 | 6 | 21 | 5 | 6 | 1 | 1 | 1 | 5 | .286 | 8 | 17 | 1 | .962 |
| 1969–Sara. W. Sox | ....Gulf C. | SS | 18 | 52 | 5 | 21 | 3 | 0 | 0 | 6 | .404 | 20 | 37 | 3 | .950 |
| 1970–Appleton | Midw. | S-2-3 | 28 | 74 | 12 | 21 | 1 | 0 | 0 | 10 | .284 | 33 | 50 | 12 | .874 |
| 1970–Duluth-Super. | ....North. | 3-O-S | 66 | 243 | 56 | 81 | 11 | •6 | 3 | 40 | .333 | 73 | 74 | 25 | .855 |
| 1971–Asheville | ........South. | 3-2-S | 133 | 467 | 71 | 129 | 20 | 2 | 5 | 37 | .276 | •125 | •308 | •37 | .921 |
| 1972–Knoxville | ........South. | •3-2-S | 134 | 500 | 82 | 147 | 16 | 5 | 6 | 60 | .294 | 127 | 295 | •33 | .927 |
| 1972–Chicago | ...........Amer. | 3B | 9 | 0 | 1 | 0 | 0 | 0 | 0 | 0 | .111 | 2 | 6 | 0 | 1.000 |
| 1973–Iowa | ...............A. A. | •2B-SS | 134 | 535 | 92 | 156 | 29 | 1 | 9 | 57 | .292 | •324 | 369 | 22 | .969 |
| 1974–Iowa | ...............A. A. | 2B | 122 | 450 | 75 | 129 | 25 | 1 | 6 | 40 | .287 | 241 | 293 | •26 | .954 |
| 1974–Chicago | ...........Amer. | DH | 1 | 0 | 0 | 0 | 0 | 0 | 0 | 0 | .000 | 0 | 0 | 0 | .000 |
| 1975–Denver† | ...........A. A. | 3B-2B | 56 | 208 | 43 | 58 | 14 | 0 | 9 | 36 | .279 | 36 | 85 | 12 | .910 |
| 1975–Syracuse | .........Int. | 3-2-O | 60 | 198 | 26 | 56 | 11 | 3 | 0 | 16 | .283 | 62 | 112 | 10 | .946 |
| 1976–Toledo | .............Int. | 3B | 34 | 136 | 22 | 40 | 12 | 0 | 2 | 21 | .294 | 30 | 78 | 7 | .939 |
| 1976–Iowa | ...............A. A. | 2-S-3 | 73 | 258 | 31 | 73 | 11 | 2 | 4 | 44 | .283 | 130 | 200 | 12 | .965 |
| 1976–Chicago‡ | .........Amer. | 2B | 3 | 10 | 0 | 1 | 1 | 0 | 0 | 0 | .100 | 8 | 4 | 0 | 1.000 |
| Major League Totals | ...................... | | 7 | 19 | 0 | 2 | 1 | 0 | 0 | 0 | .105 | 10 | 10 | 0 | 1.000 |

†Option transferred by Chicago White Sox' organization to Syracuse, June 20, 1975.
‡Traded to Cincinnati Reds' organziation for Outfielder Tommy Spencer, November 6, 1976.

## CARL MICHAEL YASTRZEMSKI

Name pronounced Yah-STREM-skee.

Born August 22, 1939, at Southampton, N. Y.
Height, 6.00. Weight, 180.
Throws right and bats lefthanded.
Attended Notre Dame University, Notre Dame, Ind., and Merrimack College,
North Andover, Mass.; received Bachelor of Science degree in Business Administration.

Established major league records for lowest batting average, season, leader in batting (.301), 1968, and most years leading league in assists by outfielders, 6, 1971.
Tied following major league records: fewest triples, season (150 or more games), 0, 1970; most home runs, two consecutive games—5, May 19-20, 1976.
Won American League Triple Crown, 1967.
Led American League batters in walks with 95 in 1963 and 119 in 1968; led in slugging percentage with .536 in 1965, .622 in 1967 and .592 in 1970; led in total bases with 360 in 1967 and 335 in 1970; led in sacrifice flies with 9 in 1972.
Tied for American League lead in double plays by outfielders with 4 in 1971.
Named Most Valuable Player in Carolina League, 1959.
Named outfielder on THE SPORTING NEWS American League All-Star Teams, 1963-65-67.
Named as outfielder on THE SPORTING NEWS American League All-Star fielding team 1963-65-67-68-69-71.
Named Most Valuable Player in American League, 1967.
Named American League Player of the Year by THE SPORTING NEWS, 1967.
Named No. 1 Major League Player by THE SPORTING NEWS, 1967.
Received reported $100,000 bonus to sign with Boston Red Sox, 1958.

| Year Club | League | Pos. | G. | AB. | R. | H. | 2B. | 3B. | HR. | RBI. | B.A. | PO. | A. | E. | F.A. |
|---|---|---|---|---|---|---|---|---|---|---|---|---|---|---|---|
| 1959–Raleigh | ............Car. | •2B-SS | 120 | 451 | 87 | •170 | •34 | 6 | 15 | 100 | •.377 | •255 | 284 | •45 | •.923 |
| 1960–Minneapolis | ......A. A. | OF | 148 | 570 | 84 | •193 | 36 | 8 | 7 | 69 | .339 | 243 | 18 | 5 | .981 |
| 1961–Boston | .............Amer. | OF | 148 | 583 | 71 | 155 | 31 | 6 | 11 | 80 | .266 | 248 | 12 | 10 | .963 |
| 1962–Boston | .............Amer. | OF | 160 | 646 | 99 | 191 | 43 | 6 | 19 | 94 | .296 | 329 | •15 | •11 | .969 |
| 1963–Boston | .............Amer. | OF | 151 | 570 | 91 | •183 | •40 | 3 | 14 | 68 | •.321 | 283 | •18 | 6 | .980 |
| 1964–Boston | .............Amer. | •OF-3B | 151 | 567 | 77 | 164 | 29 | 9 | 15 | 67 | .289 | 372 | •24 | 11 | .973 |
| 1965–Boston | .............Amer. | OF | 133 | 494 | 78 | 154 | •45 | 3 | 20 | 72 | .312 | 222 | 11 | 3 | .987 |
| 1966–Boston | .............Amer. | OF | 160 | 594 | 81 | 165 | •39 | 2 | 16 | 80 | .278 | 310 | •15 | 5 | .985 |
| 1967–Boston | .............Amer. | OF | 161 | 579 | •112 | •189 | 31 | 4 | •44 | •121 | •.326 | 297 | 13 | 7 | .978 |
| 1968–Boston | .............Amer. | OF-1B | 157 | 539 | 90 | 162 | 32 | 2 | 23 | 74 | •.301 | 315 | 13 | 3 | .991 |
| 1969–Boston | .............Amer. | OF-1B | •162 | 603 | 96 | 154 | 28 | 2 | 40 | 111 | .255 | 427 | •38 | 6 | .987 |
| 1970–Boston | .............Amer. | 1B-OF | 161 | 566 | •125 | 186 | 29 | 0 | 40 | 102 | .329 | 816 | 64 | 14 | .984 |
| 1971–Boston | .............Amer. | OF | 148 | 508 | 75 | 129 | 21 | 2 | 15 | 70 | .254 | 281 | •16 | 2 | .993 |
| 1972–Boston† | ...........Amer. | OF-1B | 125 | 455 | 70 | 120 | 18 | 2 | 12 | 68 | .264 | 498 | 43 | 8 | .985 |
| 1973–Boston | .............Amer. | 1-3-O | 152 | 540 | 82 | 160 | 25 | 4 | 19 | 95 | .296 | 979 | 119 | 18 | .984 |
| 1974–Boston | .............Amer. | 1B-OF | 148 | 515 | •93 | 155 | 25 | 2 | 15 | 79 | .301 | 806 | 46 | 6 | .993 |
| 1975–Boston | .............Amer. | 1B-OF | 149 | 543 | 91 | 146 | 30 | 1 | 14 | 60 | .269 | 1217 | 88 | 5 | .996 |
| 1976–Boston | .............Amer. | 1B-OF | 155 | 546 | 71 | 146 | 23 | 2 | 21 | 102 | .267 | 922 | 55 | 4 | .996 |
| Major League Totals | ..................... | | 2421 | 8849 | 1402 | 2559 | 489 | 50 | 338 | 1343 | .289 | 8322 | 590 | 119 | .987 |

†Placed on supplemental disabled list, May 10 through June 9, 1972.

### CHAMPIONSHIP SERIES RECORD

| Year Club | League | Pos. | G. | AB. | R. | H. | 2B. | 3B. | HR. | RBI. | B.A. | PO. | A. | E. | F.A. |
|---|---|---|---|---|---|---|---|---|---|---|---|---|---|---|---|
| 1975–Boston | ..............Amer. | OF | 3 | 11 | 4 | 5 | 1 | 0 | 1 | 2 | .455 | 7 | 2 | 0 | 1.000 |

| Year | Club | League | Pos. | G. | AB. | R. | H. | 2B. | 3B. | HR. | RBI. | B.A. | PO. | A. | E. | F.A. |
|------|------|--------|------|----|-----|----|----|-----|-----|-----|------|------|-----|----|----|------|
| 1967—Boston | | Amer. | OF | 7 | 25 | 4 | 10 | 2 | 0 | 3 | 5 | .400 | 16 | 2 | 0 | 1.000 |
| 1975—Boston | | Amer. | OF-1B | 7 | 29 | 7 | 9 | 0 | 0 | 0 | 4 | .310 | 35 | 1 | 0 | 1.000 |
| World Series Totals | | | | 14 | 54 | 11 | 19 | 2 | 0 | 3 | 9 | .352 | 51 | 3 | 0 | 1.000 |

## ALL-STAR GAME RECORD

| Year | League | Pos. | AB. | R. | H. | 2B. | 3B. | HR. | RBI. | B.A. | PO. | A. | E. | F.A. |
|------|--------|------|-----|----|----|-----|-----|-----|------|------|-----|----|----|------|
| 1963—American | | OF | 2 | 0 | 0 | 0 | 0 | 0 | 0 | .000 | 1 | 0 | 0 | 1.000 |
| 1967—American | | OF | 4 | 0 | 3 | 1 | 0 | 0 | 0 | .750 | 2 | 0 | 0 | 1.000 |
| 1968—American | | OF | 4 | 0 | 0 | 0 | 0 | 0 | 0 | .000 | 0 | 0 | 0 | .000 |
| 1969—American | | OF | 1 | 0 | 0 | 0 | 0 | 0 | 0 | .000 | 1 | 0 | 0 | 1.000 |
| 1970—American | | OF-1B | 6 | 1 | 4 | 1 | 0 | 0 | 1 | .667 | 8 | 0 | 0 | 1.000 |
| 1971—American | | OF | 3 | 0 | 0 | 0 | 0 | 0 | 0 | .000 | 0 | 0 | 0 | .000 |
| 1972—American | | OF | 3 | 0 | 0 | 0 | 0 | 0 | 0 | .000 | 3 | 0 | 0 | 1.000 |
| 1974—American | | 1B | 1 | 0 | 0 | 0 | 0 | 0 | 0 | .000 | 5 | 0 | 0 | 1.000 |
| 1975—American | | PH | 1 | 1 | 1 | 0 | 0 | 1 | 3 | 1.000 | 0 | 0 | 0 | .000 |
| 1976—American | | OF | 2 | 0 | 0 | 0 | 0 | 0 | 0 | .000 | 0 | 0 | 0 | .000 |
| All-Star Totals | | | 27 | 2 | 8 | 2 | 0 | 1 | 4 | .296 | 20 | 0 | 0 | 1.000 |

Member of American League All-Star Team in 1966; did not play. Named to American League All-Star Teams for 1965 and 1973 games; replaced due to injury.

## STEPHEN WAYNE YEAGER

Name pronounced YAY-gur.

### (Steve)

Born November 24, 1948, at Huntington, W. Va.
Height, 6.00. Weight, 195.
Throws and bats righthanded.
Hobbies—Arts, hunting, fishing and auto mechanics.

Tied major league record for most putouts, extra-inning game, catcher, 22, August 8, 1972 (19 innings).
Set National League record for most chances accepted, extra-inning game, catcher, 24, August 8, 1972 (19 innings).

| Year | Club | League | Pos. | G. | AB. | R. | H. | 2B. | 3B. | HR. | RBI. | B.A. | PO. | A. | E. | F.A. |
|------|------|--------|------|----|-----|----|----|-----|-----|-----|------|------|-----|----|----|------|
| 1967—Ogden | | Pion. | C | 1 | 0 | 0 | 0 | 0 | 0 | 0 | 0 | .000 | 0 | 0 | 0 | .000 |
| 1967—Dubuque | | Midw. | C-1B | 14 | 35 | 0 | 6 | 0 | 0 | 0 | 2 | .171 | 67 | 3 | 3 | .959 |
| 1968—Daytona Beach | | Fla. St. | C | 59 | 144 | 17 | 22 | 3 | 1 | 1 | 6 | .153 | 314 | 23 | 9 | .974 |
| 1969—Bakersfield | | Calif. | C | 22 | 65 | 8 | 10 | 1 | 0 | 0 | 2 | .154 | 145 | 26 | 4 | .977 |
| 1969—Albuquerque | | Texas | PH | 1 | 1 | 0 | 0 | 0 | 0 | 0 | 0 | .000 | 0 | 0 | 0 | .000 |
| 1970—Albuquerque | | Texas | C-O-3 | 55 | 151 | 23 | 42 | 5 | 1 | 3 | 24 | .278 | 224 | 29 | 5 | .981 |
| 1971—Albuquerque | | Texas | C | 107 | 339 | 49 | 93 | 16 | 5 | 8 | 53 | .274 | 678 | 84 | *14 | .982 |
| 1972—Albuquerque | | P. C. | C | 82 | 257 | 46 | 72 | 6 | 6 | 13 | 45 | .280 | 494 | 26 | 9 | .983 |
| 1972—Los Angeles | | Nat. | C | 35 | 106 | 18 | 29 | 0 | 1 | 4 | 15 | .274 | 220 | 19 | 4 | .984 |
| 1973—Los Angeles | | Nat. | C | 54 | 134 | 18 | 34 | 5 | 0 | 2 | 10 | .254 | 230 | 24 | 5 | .981 |
| 1974—Los Angeles | | Nat. | C | 94 | 316 | 41 | 84 | 16 | 1 | 12 | 41 | .266 | 552 | 58 | 5 | .992 |
| 1975—Los Angeles | | Nat. | C | 135 | 452 | 34 | 103 | 16 | 1 | 12 | 54 | .228 | *806 | 62 | 7 | .992 |
| 1976—Los Angeles | | Nat. | C | 117 | 359 | 42 | 77 | 11 | 3 | 11 | 35 | .214 | 522 | *77 | 9 | .985 |
| Major League Totals | | | | 435 | 1367 | 153 | 322 | 48 | 6 | 41 | 155 | .236 | 2330 | 240 | 30 | .988 |

### CHAMPIONSHIP SERIES RECORD

| Year | Club | League | Pos. | G. | AB. | R. | H. | 2B. | 3B. | HR. | RBI. | B.A. | PO. | A. | E. | F.A. |
|------|------|--------|------|----|-----|----|----|-----|-----|-----|------|------|-----|----|----|------|
| 1974—Los Angeles | | Nat. | C | 3 | 9 | 1 | 0 | 0 | 0 | 0 | 0 | .000 | 14 | 1 | 0 | 1.000 |

### WORLD SERIES RECORD

| Year | Club | League | Pos. | G. | AB. | R. | H. | 2B. | 3B. | HR. | RBI. | B.A. | PO. | A. | E. | F.A. |
|------|------|--------|------|----|-----|----|----|-----|-----|-----|------|------|-----|----|----|------|
| 1974—Los Angeles | | Nat. | C | 4 | 11 | 0 | 4 | 1 | 0 | 0 | 1 | .364 | 32 | 4 | 1 | .973 |

## JOEL RANDOLPH YOUNGBLOOD, III

Born August 28, 1951, at Houston, Tex.
Height, 6.00. Weight, 180.
Throws and bats righthanded.
Hobbies—Hunting and fishing.

| Year | Club | League | Pos. | G. | AB. | R. | H. | 2B. | 3B. | HR. | RBI. | B.A. | PO. | A. | E. | F.A. |
|------|------|--------|------|----|-----|----|----|-----|-----|-----|------|------|-----|----|----|------|
| 1970—Tampa | | Fla. St. | SS | 17 | 54 | 7 | 12 | 0 | 0 | 0 | 3 | .222 | 22 | 40 | 9 | .873 |
| 1970—Sioux Falls | | North. | 2-3-S | 65 | 236 | 27 | 53 | 11 | 1 | 0 | 17 | .225 | 110 | 134 | 26 | .904 |
| 1971—Tampa | | Fla. St. | 3-S-O | 136 | 443 | 75 | 113 | 25 | 4 | 5 | 44 | .255 | 159 | 207 | 26 | .934 |
| 1972—Three Rivers | | East. | OF-3B | 104 | 366 | 57 | 106 | 15 | 5 | 12 | 60 | .290 | 118 | 80 | 30 | .868 |
| 1973—Indianapolis | | A. A. | O-S-3 | 124 | 451 | 88 | 143 | 24 | 9 | 11 | 50 | .317 | 136 | 112 | 28 | .899 |
| 1974—Indianapolis† | | A. A. | OF | 103 | 316 | 55 | 90 | 17 | 4 | 13 | 49 | .285 | 115 | 6 | 4 | .968 |
| 1975—Indianapolis | | A. A. | OF-2B | 123 | 418 | 65 | 110 | 21 | •9 | 6 | 51 | .263 | 201 | 13 | 7 | .968 |
| 1976—Cincinnati‡ | | Nat. | I-O-C-PH | 55 | 57 | 8 | 11 | 1 | 1 | 0 | 1 | .193 | 15 | 3 | 1 | .947 |
| Major League Totals | | | | 55 | 57 | 8 | 11 | 1 | 1 | 0 | 1 | .193 | 15 | 3 | 1 | .947 |

†On disabled list, June 7 to June 19, 1974.
‡Traded to St. Louis Cardianls for Pitcher Bill Caudill, March 28, 1977.

# ROBIN R. YOUNT

Born September 16, 1955, at Danville, Ill.
Height, 6.01. Weight, 170.
Throws and bats righthanded.
Hobbies—Golf, fishing and motorcycles.
Brother of Larry Yount, former minor league pitcher in Houston Astros', Milwaukee Brewers'
and Pittsburgh Pirates' organizations, 1968-1976.
Led American League shortstops in total chances with 831 and double plays with 104 in 1976.

| Year Club | League | Pos. | G. | AB. | R. | H. | 2B. | 3B. | HR. | RBI. | B.A. | PO. | A. | E. | F.A. |
|---|---|---|---|---|---|---|---|---|---|---|---|---|---|---|---|
| 1973–Newark ...........NYP | | SS | 64 | 242 | 29 | 69 | 15 | 3 | 3 | 25 | .285 | 43 | 85 | 18 | .877 |
| 1974–Milwaukee .......Amer. | | SS | 107 | 344 | 48 | 86 | 14 | 5 | 3 | 26 | .250 | 148 | 327 | 19 | .962 |
| 1975–Milwaukee .......Amer. | | SS | 147 | 558 | 67 | 149 | 28 | 2 | 8 | 52 | .267 | 273 | 402 | •44 | .939 |
| 1976–Milwaukee .......Amer. | | SS | 161 | 638 | 59 | 161 | 19 | 3 | 2 | 54 | .252 | •290 | 510 | 31 | .963 |
| Major League Totals ..................... | | | 415 | 1540 | 174 | 396 | 61 | 10 | 13 | 132 | .257 | 711 | 1239 | 94 | .954 |

# PATRICK PAUL ZACHRY
## (Pat)

Born April 24, 1952, at Richmond, Tex.
Height, 6.05. Weight, 180.
Throws and bats righthanded.
Named National League Rookie of the Year by Baseball Writers Association of America, 1976.

| Year Club | League | G. | IP. | W. | L. | Pct. | H. | R. | ER. | SO. | BB. | ERA. |
|---|---|---|---|---|---|---|---|---|---|---|---|---|
| 1970–Bradenton Reds....................Gulf Coast | | 9 | 54 | 1 | 4 | .200 | 53 | 29 | 15 | 55 | 24 | 2.50 |
| 1970–Sioux Falls .....................Northern | | 3 | 21 | 2 | 1 | .677 | 20 | 9 | 8 | 19 | 5 | 3.43 |
| 1971–Tampa† ................................Florida St. | | 22 | 143 | 12 | 4 | .750 | 125 | 58 | 51 | 115 | 72 | 3.21 |
| 1972–Three Rivers......................Eastern | | 25 | 133 | 7 | 7 | .500 | 110 | 55 | 39 | 102 | 79 | 2.64 |
| 1973–Three Rivers......................Eastern | | 42 | 178 | •12 | 12 | .500 | 158 | 81 | 65 | 130 | •127 | 3.29 |
| 1974–Indianapolis .....................Am. Assoc. | | 33 | 151 | 10 | 7 | .588 | 129 | 69 | 59 | 98 | 71 | 3.52 |
| 1975–Indianapolis .....................Am. Assoc. | | 27 | 159 | 10 | 7 | .588 | 120 | 52 | 43 | 100 | 70 | •2.44 |
| 1976–Cincinnati ..........................National | | 38 | 204 | 14 | 7 | .667 | 170 | 70 | 62 | 143 | 83 | 2.74 |
| Major League Totals ............................... | | 38 | 204 | 14 | 7 | .667 | 170 | 70 | 62 | 143 | 83 | 2.74 |

†Appeared in one game as second baseman.

## CHAMPIONSHIP SERIES RECORD

| Year Club | League | G. | IP. | W. | L. | Pct. | H. | R. | ER. | SO. | BB. | ERA. |
|---|---|---|---|---|---|---|---|---|---|---|---|---|
| 1976–Cincinnati ...........................National | | 1 | 5 | 1 | 0 | 1.000 | 6 | 2 | 2 | 3 | 3 | 3.60 |

## WORLD SERIES RECORD

| Year Club | League | G. | IP. | W. | L. | Pct. | H. | R. | ER. | SO. | BB. | ERA. |
|---|---|---|---|---|---|---|---|---|---|---|---|---|
| 1976–Cincinnati ...........................National | | 1 | 6⅔ | 1 | 0 | 1.000 | 6 | 2 | 2 | 6 | 5 | 2.70 |

# GEOFFREY CLAYTON ZAHN
## (Jeff)

Born December 19, 1946, at Baltimore, Md.
Height, 6.01. Weight, 185.
Throws and bats lefthanded.
Attended University of Michigan, Ann Arbor, Mich.; received Bachelor
of Science degree in Education.

Pitched 1-0 no-hit loss against St. Petersburg, June 30, 1968.

| Year Club | League | G. | IP. | W. | L. | Pct. | H. | R. | ER. | SO. | BB. | ERA. |
|---|---|---|---|---|---|---|---|---|---|---|---|---|
| 1968–Daytona Beach† .................Florida St. | | 21 | 138 | 8 | 9 | .471 | 97 | 44 | 32 | 108 | 38 | 2.09 |
| 1969–Albuquerque‡§.....................Texas | | 15 | 98 | 9 | 3 | .750 | 103 | 42 | 38 | 44 | 29 | 3.49 |
| 1970–Spokane x ...........................P. Coast | | 27 | 53 | 1 | 1 | .500 | 67 | 41 | 32 | 22 | 32 | 5.43 |
| 1971–Albuquerque y.....................Texas | | 29 | 164 | 8 | 12 | .400 | 155 | 77 | 39 | 126 | 50 | 2.14 |
| 1972–El Paso...............................Texas | | 9 | 73 | 7 | 2 | .778 | 54 | 21 | 15 | 77 | 17 | 1.85 |
| 1972–Albuquerque ......................P. Coast | | 18 | 109 | 10 | 1 | .909 | 126 | 66 | 57 | 80 | 30 | 4.71 |
| 1973–Albuquerque z.....................P. Coast | | 25 | 177 | 13 | 8 | .619 | 185 | 81 | 60 | 103 | 66 | 3.05 |
| 1973–Los Angeles ......................National | | 6 | 13 | 1 | 0 | 1.000 | 5 | 2 | 2 | 9 | 2 | 1.38 |
| 1974–Los Angeles ......................National | | 21 | 80 | 3 | 5 | .375 | 78 | 28 | 18 | 33 | 16 | 2.03 |
| 1975–Los Angeles a-Chicago b ......National | | 18 | 66 | 2 | 8 | .200 | 69 | 40 | 34 | 22 | 31 | 4.64 |
| 1976–Wichita ...............................Am. Assoc. | | 21 | 137 | 8 | 8 | .500 | 142 | 81 | 65 | 66 | 61 | 4.27 |
| 1976–Chicago c ...........................National | | 3 | 8 | 0 | 1 | .000 | 16 | 10 | 10 | 4 | 2 | 11.25 |
| Major League Totals ............................... | | 48 | 167 | 6 | 14 | .300 | 168 | 80 | 64 | 68 | 51 | 3.45 |

†On restricted list, April 11 to May 2, 1968.
‡On temporary inactive list, April 22 to June 16, 1969.
§On disabled list, June 16 to July 7, 1969.
xAppeared as first baseman.
yAppeared as an outfielder.
zOn disabled list, June 18 to June 30, 1973.
aTraded with Pitcher Eddie Solomon to Chicago Cubs for Pitcher Burt Hooton, May 2, 1975.
bOn disabled list, July 21 to September 2, 1975.
cReleased, January 17, 1977.
Invited to Minnesota Twins' 1977 spring camp.

## JOSEPH EDMUND ZDEB

Name pronounced Zeb.

### (Joe)

Born June 27, 1953, at Mendota, Ill.
Height, 5.11. Weight, 185.
Throws and bats righthanded.
Hobby—Fishing, snowmobiling and skin diving.
Attended University of Illinois, Champaign, Ill.

| Year | Club | League | Pos. | G. | AB. | R. | H. | 2B. | 3B. | HR. | RBI. | B.A. | PO. | A. | E. | F.A. |
|---|---|---|---|---|---|---|---|---|---|---|---|---|---|---|---|---|
| 1971—Billings | ..... | Pion. | OF-3B | 49 | 147 | 13 | 27 | 4 | 3 | 1 | 12 | .184 | 35 | 9 | 6 | .880 |
| 1972—Kingsport | ..... | Appal. | OF | 69 | *263 | *57 | 84 | 17 | 0 | 12 | 55 | .319 | *114 | 3 | 7 | .944 |
| 1973—San Jose | ..... | Calif. | OF | 57 | 169 | 16 | 33 | 6 | 0 | 1 | 13 | .195 | 68 | 3 | 4 | .947 |
| 1973—Waterloo | ..... | Midw. | OF | 71 | 262 | 44 | 93 | 20 | 3 | 8 | 55 | .355 | 114 | 7 | 3 | .976 |
| 1974—San Jose | ..... | Calif. | OF | 128 | 427 | 60 | 126 | 20 | 3 | 5 | 67 | .295 | 168 | 16 | 6 | .968 |
| 1975—Jacksonville | ..... | South. | OF | 129 | 438 | 60 | 116 | 17 | 4 | 5 | 43 | .265 | 246 | 11 | 3 | .988 |
| 1976—Omaha | ..... | A. A. | OF | 117 | 372 | 57 | 111 | 8 | 6 | 5 | 44 | .298 | 209 | 7 | 7 | .969 |

Listed on Kansas City Royals' 1977 spring roster.


## GEORGE WILLIAM ZEBER

Born August 29, 1950, at Ellwood City, Pa.
Height, 5.11. Weight, 170.
Throws right and bats left and righthanded.
Hobbies—Motorcycling and camping.
Attended Cypress Junior College, Cypress, Calif.

| Year | Club | League | Pos. | G. | AB. | R. | H. | 2B. | 3B. | HR. | RBI. | B.A. | PO. | A. | E. | F.A. |
|---|---|---|---|---|---|---|---|---|---|---|---|---|---|---|---|---|
| 1968—Johnson City | .... | Appal. | 2-SS | 50 | 169 | 26 | 43 | 5 | 1 | 0 | 18 | .254 | 73 | 142 | 13 | .943 |
| 1969—Kinston | ..... | Carol. | 2-S-3 | 132 | 459 | 59 | 111 | 14 | 6 | 3 | 39 | .242 | 235 | 291 | 25 | .955 |
| 1970—† | ..... | | | | | | (In military service.) | | | | | | | | | |
| 1972—West Haven | ..... | East. | *2B-3B | 118 | 393 | 75 | 105 | 14 | 1 | 8 | 27 | .267 | 245 | 285 | *29 | .948 |
| 1973—Syracuse‡ | ..... | Int. | 2B | 67 | 211 | 26 | 36 | 8 | 1 | 3 | 23 | .171 | 142 | 190 | 10 | .971 |
| 1974—Syracuse | ..... | Int. | 3B-2B | 40 | 108 | 14 | 17 | 0 | 0 | 2 | 8 | .157 | 23 | 49 | 10 | .878 |
| 1974—West Haven | ..... | East. | 2B-3B | 73 | 247 | 23 | 60 | 7 | 2 | 3 | 30 | .243 | 145 | 167 | 16 | .951 |
| 1975—Syracuse | ..... | Int. | 2B-3B | 110 | 347 | 33 | 87 | 16 | 2 | 3 | 36 | .251 | 198 | 285 | 18 | .964 |
| 1976—Syracuse | ..... | Int. | 2B | 118 | 397 | 59 | 99 | 16 | 2 | 6 | 43 | .249 | 237 | 377 | 19 | .970 |

†On military list, March 24, 1970 through March 29, 1972.
‡On disabled list, July 17 through remainder of season.
Invited to New York Yankees' 1977 spring camp.


## RICHARD WALTER ZISK

### (Richie)

Born February 6, 1949, at Brooklyn, N. Y.
Height, 6.01. Weight, 205.
Throws and bats righthanded.
Hobbies—Golf, bowling and fishing.
Attended Seton Hall University, South Orange, N. J.

Led International League in total bases with 252 in 1972.
Named as outfielder on THE SPORTING NEWS National League All-Star Team, 1974.
Named Player of the Year in Appalachian League, 1967.

| Year | Club | League | Pos. | G. | AB. | R. | H. | 2B. | 3B. | HR. | RBI. | B.A. | PO. | A. | E. | F.A. |
|---|---|---|---|---|---|---|---|---|---|---|---|---|---|---|---|---|
| 1967—Salem | ..... | Appal. | O-1B | 56 | 189 | 41 | 58 | 9 | 2 | *16 | 51 | .307 | 97 | 6 | 9 | .920 |
| 1968—Gastonia | ..... | W. Car. | OF | 53 | 185 | 32 | 52 | 8 | 1 | 13 | 41 | .281 | 78 | 7 | 5 | .944 |
| 1969—Salem† | ..... | Carol. | OF | 78 | 265 | 43 | 84 | 12 | 5 | 11 | 45 | .317 | 157 | 7 | 2 | .988 |
| 1970—Waterbury | ..... | East. | OF | 125 | 450 | 83 | 133 | 17 | 6 | *34 | 88 | .296 | 175 | 10 | 8 | .959 |
| 1971—Charleston | ..... | Int. | OF | 135 | 424 | 90 | 123 | 15 | 1 | 29 | *109 | .290 | 214 | 6 | 8 | .965 |
| 1971—Pittsburgh | ..... | Nat. | OF | 7 | 15 | 2 | 3 | 1 | 0 | 1 | 2 | .200 | 7 | 0 | 0 | 1.000 |
| 1972—Charleston | ..... | Int. | OF | 122 | 441 | 83 | 136 | 30 | 4 | *26 | 86 | .308 | 220 | 16 | 1 | .996 |
| 1972—Pittsburgh | ..... | Nat. | OF | 17 | 37 | 4 | 7 | 3 | 0 | 0 | 4 | .189 | 14 | 1 | 1 | .938 |
| 1973—Pittsburgh | ..... | Nat. | OF | 103 | 333 | 44 | 108 | 23 | 7 | 10 | 54 | .324 | 139 | 12 | 2 | .987 |
| 1974—Pittsburgh | ..... | Nat. | OF | 149 | 536 | 75 | 168 | 30 | 3 | 17 | 100 | .313 | 312 | 9 | 5 | .985 |
| 1975—Pittsburgh | ..... | Nat. | OF | 147 | 504 | 69 | 146 | 27 | 3 | 20 | 75 | .290 | 264 | 7 | 7 | .975 |
| 1976—Pittsburgh‡ | ..... | Nat. | OF | 155 | 581 | 91 | 168 | 35 | 2 | 21 | 89 | .289 | 300 | 11 | 4 | .987 |
| Major League Totals | ..... | | | 578 | 2006 | 285 | 600 | 119 | 15 | 69 | 324 | .299 | 1036 | 40 | 19 | .983 |

†On restricted list, April 2 through June 7, 1969.
‡Traded with Pitcher Silvio Martinez to Chicago White Sox for Pitchers Terry Forster and Rich Gossage, December 10, 1976.


### CHAMPIONSHIP SERIES RECORD

| Year | Club | League | Pos. | G. | AB. | R. | H. | 2B. | 3B. | HR. | RBI. | B.A. | PO. | A. | E. | F.A. |
|---|---|---|---|---|---|---|---|---|---|---|---|---|---|---|---|---|
| 1974—Pittsburgh | ..... | Nat. | OF-PH | 3 | 10 | 1 | 3 | 0 | 0 | 0 | 0 | .300 | 2 | 0 | 0 | 1.000 |
| 1975—Pittsburgh | ..... | Nat. | OF | 3 | 10 | 0 | 5 | 1 | 0 | 0 | 0 | .500 | 8 | 0 | 0 | 1.000 |
| Championship Series Totals | ..... | | | 6 | 20 | 1 | 8 | 1 | 0 | 0 | 0 | .400 | 10 | 0 | 0 | 1.000 |

**HANK AARON**

— 410 —

# Recently Retired Players

## HENRY LOUIS AARON
### (Hank)

Born February 5, 1934, at Mobile, Ala.
Height, 6.00. Weight, 190.
Threw and batted righthanded.
Hobbies—Hunting and music.
Brother of Tommie Aaron, former infielder-outfielder with Milwaukee-Atlanta
Brave franchise and presently a manager in the Braves' organization.

Established following major league records: most games, lifetime (3,298), 1976; most at-bats, lifetime (12,364), 1976; most home runs, lifetime (755), 1976; most plate appearances, lifetime (13,940), 1976; most years, 100 or more runs scored (15), 1970; most years leading league, total bases (8), 1969; most years, 300 or more total bases (15), 1971; most years, 150 or more games (14), 1970; most consecutive years, 20 or more home runs (20), 1974; most consecutive years, 100 or more extra bases on long hits (19), 1973; most years, 30 or more home runs (15), 1973; most years, 20 or more home runs (20), 1974; most total bases, lifetime (6,856), 1976; most sacrifice flies, lifetime (121), 1976; most intentional bases on balls, lifetime (293), 1976; most runs batted in, lifetime (2,297), 1976; most consecutive seasons, 100 or more games (22), 1976; most long hits, lifetime (1,477), 1976; most seasons, 10 or more intentional bases on balls (16), 1973; most seasons, 100 or more games (22), 1975; and most times grounding into double play, lifetime (328), 1976.

Tied major league record for most consecutive years, 100 or more runs scored (13), 1967.

Established following National League records: most seasons hitting home runs in each league park (9), 1966; most seasons, 100 or more runs batted in (11), 1971; most seasons, 40 or more home runs (8), 1973; most runs scored, lifetime (2,107), 1974; most home runs, bases full, lifetime (16), 1974; and fewest doubles, season, for leader in doubles (34), 1956.

Tied following National League records: most years, leading league in runs batted in (4), 1966; most bases on balls, game, since 1900 (5), July 11, 1972 (15 innings); most consecutive batting streaks, 20 or more games, season, league (4), 1956-59-62-71; and most home runs, runs, season, for runnerup in home runs (47), 1971.

One of five players in major league history to hit 30 home runs and steal 30 bases in the same season (44 home runs and 31 stolen bases in 1963).

Hit three home runs in a game, June 21, 1959.

Led National League outfielders in double plays with 6 in 1960, 5 in 1964 and 5 in 1966.

Led National League in slugging percentage with .636 in 1959, .586 in 1963, .573 in 1967 and .669 in 1971; led in total bases with 340 in 1956; 369 in 1957; 400 in 1959; 334 in 1960; 358 in 1961; 370 in 1963; 344 in 1967; 332 in 1969.

Led Sally League in total bases with 338 in 1953.

Named outfielder on THE SPORTING NEWS All-Star Major League Teams, 1956-58-59.

Named outfielder on THE SPORTING NEWS National League All-Star Teams, 1963-65-67-69-70-71.

Most Valuable Player in National League, 1957.

Named National League Player of the Year by THE SPORTING NEWS, 1956 and 1963.

Named outfielder on THE SPORTING NEWS National League All-Star fielding team, 1958-59-60.

| Year Club | League | Pos. | G. | AB. | R. | H. | 2B. | 3B. | HR. | RBI. | B.A. | PO. | A. | E. | F.A. |
|---|---|---|---|---|---|---|---|---|---|---|---|---|---|---|---|
| 1952—Eau Claire ........North. | SS | 87 | 345 | 79 | 116 | 19 | 4 | 9 | 61 | .336 | 137 | 265 | 35 | .920 |
| 1953—Jacksonville ......Sally | 2B | 137 | 574 | •115 | •208 | •36 | 14 | 22 | •125 | •362 | 330 | •310 | •36 | .947 |
| 1954—Milwaukee† .......Nat. | OF | 122 | 468 | 58 | 131 | 27 | 6 | 13 | 69 | .280 | 223 | 5 | 7 | .970 |
| 1955—Milwaukee .......Nat. | OF-2B | 153 | 602 | 105 | 189 | •37 | 9 | 27 | 106 | .314 | 340 | 93 | 15 | .967 |
| 1956—Milwaukee ........Nat. | OF | 153 | 609 | 106 | •200 | •34 | 14 | 26 | 92 | •328 | 316 | 17 | •13 | .962 |
| 1957—Milwaukee .......Nat. | OF | 151 | 615 | •118 | 198 | 27 | 6 | •44 | •132 | .322 | 346 | 9 | 6 | .983 |
| 1958—Milwaukee .......Nat. | OF | 153 | 601 | 109 | 196 | 34 | 4 | 30 | 95 | .326 | 305 | 12 | 5 | .984 |
| 1959—Milwaukee .......Nat. | OF-3B | 154 | 629 | 116 | •223 | 46 | 7 | 39 | 123 | •355 | 263 | 22 | 5 | .983 |
| 1960—Milwaukee .......Nat. | OF-2B | 153 | 590 | 102 | 172 | 20 | 11 | 40 | •126 | .292 | 321 | 13 | 6 | .982 |
| 1961—Milwaukee .......Nat. | OF-3B | •155 | 603 | 115 | 197 | •39 | 10 | 34 | 120 | .327 | 379 | 15 | 7 | .983 |
| 1962—Milwaukee .......Nat. | OF-1B | 156 | 592 | 127 | 191 | 28 | 6 | 45 | 128 | .323 | 341 | 11 | 7 | .981 |
| 1963—Milwaukee .......Nat. | OF | 161 | 631 | •121 | 201 | 29 | 4 | •44 | •130 | .319 | 267 | 10 | 6 | .979 |
| 1964—Milwaukee .......Nat. | OF-2B | 145 | 570 | 103 | 187 | 30 | 2 | 24 | 95 | .328 | 284 | 28 | 6 | .981 |
| 1965—Milwaukee .......Nat. | OF | 150 | 570 | 109 | 181 | •40 | 1 | 32 | 89 | .318 | 298 | 9 | 4 | .987 |
| 1966—Atlanta .......Nat. | OF-2B | 158 | 603 | 117 | 168 | 23 | 1 | •44 | •127 | .279 | 315 | 12 | 4 | .988 |
| 1967—Atlanta .......Nat. | OF-2B | 155 | 600 | •113 | 184 | 37 | 3 | •39 | 109 | .307 | 322 | 12 | 7 | .979 |
| 1968—Atlanta .......Nat. | OF-1B | 160 | 606 | 84 | 174 | 33 | 4 | 29 | 86 | .287 | 418 | 20 | 5 | .989 |
| 1969—Atlanta .......Nat. | OF-1B | 147 | 547 | 100 | 164 | 30 | 3 | 44 | 97 | .300 | 299 | 13 | 5 | .984 |
| 1970—Atlanta .......Nat. | OF-1B | 150 | 516 | 103 | 154 | 26 | 1 | 38 | 118 | .298 | 319 | 10 | 7 | .979 |
| 1971—Atlanta .......Nat. | 1B-OF | 139 | 495 | 95 | 162 | 22 | 3 | 47 | 118 | .327 | 733 | 40 | 5 | .994 |
| 1972—Atlanta .......Nat. | 1B-OF | 129 | 449 | 75 | 119 | 10 | 0 | 34 | 77 | .265 | 996 | 70 | 17 | .984 |
| 1973—Atlanta .......Nat. | OF | 120 | 392 | 84 | 118 | 12 | 1 | 40 | 96 | .301 | 206 | 5 | 5 | .977 |
| 1974—Atlanta‡ ...........Nat. | OF | 112 | 340 | 47 | 91 | 16 | 0 | 20 | 69 | .268 | 142 | 3 | 2 | .986 |
| 1975—Milwaukee .......Amer. | DH-OF | 137 | 465 | 45 | 109 | 16 | 2 | 12 | 60 | .234 | 2 | 0 | 0 | 1.000 |
| 1976—Milwaukee§ ......Amer. | DH-OF | 85 | 271 | 22 | 62 | 8 | 0 | 10 | 35 | .229 | 1 | 0 | 0 | 1.000 |
| American League Totals ................. | | 222 | 736 | 67 | 171 | 24 | 2 | 22 | 95 | .232 | 3 | 0 | 0 | 1.000 |
| National League Totals ..................... | | 3076 | 11628 | 2107 | 3600 | 600 | 96 | 733 | 2202 | .310 | 7433 | 429 | 144 | .982 |
| Major League Totals ..................... | | 3298 | 12364 | 2174 | 3771 | 624 | 98 | 755 | 2297 | .305 | 7436 | 429 | 144 | .982 |

†Fractured right ankle sliding into third base in game against Cincinnati Reds, September 5, 1954—out for rest of season.

‡Traded to Milwaukee Brewers for Outfielder Dave May and a minor league player to be named later, November 2, 1974; Brewers assigned Pitcher Roger Alexander to Braves, December 2, 1974, to complete deal.

§Placed on voluntary retired list, October 28, 1976.

### CHAMPIONSHIP SERIES RECORD

| Year Club | League | Pos. | G. | AB. | R. | H. | 2B. | 3B. | HR. | RBI. | B.A. | PO. | A. | E. | F.A. |
|---|---|---|---|---|---|---|---|---|---|---|---|---|---|---|---|
| 1969—Atlanta..............Nat. | OF | 3 | 14 | 3 | 5 | 2 | 0 | 3 | 7 | .357 | 4 | 1 | 1 | .833 |

Tied World Series record by making one or more hits in each game, 1957.

| Year | Club | League | Pos. | G. | AB. | R. | H. | 2B. | 3B. | HR. | RBI. | B.A. | PO. | A. | E. | F.A. |
|---|---|---|---|---|---|---|---|---|---|---|---|---|---|---|---|---|
| 1957–Milwaukee | | Nat. | OF | 7 | 28 | 5 | 11 | 0 | 1 | 3 | 7 | .393 | 11 | 0 | 0 | 1.000 |
| 1958–Milwaukee | | Nat. | OF | 7 | 27 | 3 | 9 | 2 | 0 | 0 | 2 | .333 | 14 | 0 | 0 | 1.000 |
| World Series Totals | | | | 14 | 55 | 8 | 20 | 2 | 1 | 3 | 9 | .364 | 25 | 0 | 0 | 1.000 |

## ALL-STAR GAME RECORD

| Year League | Pos. | AB. | R. | H. | 2B. | 3B. | HR. | RBI. | B.A. | PO. | A. | E. | F.A. |
|---|---|---|---|---|---|---|---|---|---|---|---|---|---|
| 1955–National | OF | 2 | 1 | 2 | 0 | 0 | 0 | 1 | 1.000 | 0 | 0 | 0 | .000 |
| 1956–National | OF | 1 | 0 | 0 | 0 | 0 | 0 | 0 | .000 | 0 | 0 | 0 | .000 |
| 1957–National | OF | 4 | 0 | 1 | 0 | 0 | 0 | 0 | .250 | 2 | 0 | 0 | 1.000 |
| 1958–National | OF | 2 | 0 | 0 | 0 | 0 | 0 | 1 | .000 | 2 | 0 | 0 | 1.000 |
| 1959–National (both games) | OF | 7 | 1 | 2 | 0 | 0 | 0 | 2 | .286 | 4 | 0 | 0 | 1.000 |
| 1960–National (both games) | OF | 7 | 0 | 0 | 0 | 0 | 0 | 0 | .000 | 1 | 1 | 0 | 1.000 |
| 1961–National (both games) | PH-OF | 3 | 1 | 1 | 0 | 0 | 0 | 0 | .333 | 1 | 0 | 0 | 1.000 |
| 1962–National (second game) | OF | 2 | 0 | 0 | 0 | 0 | 0 | 0 | .000 | 1 | 0 | 0 | 1.000 |
| 1963–National | OF | 4 | 1 | 0 | 0 | 0 | 0 | 0 | .000 | 3 | 0 | 0 | 1.000 |
| 1964–National | PH | 1 | 0 | 0 | 0 | 0 | 0 | 0 | .000 | 0 | 0 | 0 | .000 |
| 1965–National | OF | 5 | 0 | 1 | 0 | 0 | 0 | 0 | .200 | 0 | 0 | 0 | .000 |
| 1966–National | OF | 4 | 0 | 0 | 0 | 0 | 0 | 0 | .000 | 2 | 0 | 0 | 1.000 |
| 1967–National | OF | 6 | 0 | 1 | 0 | 0 | 0 | 0 | .167 | 2 | 0 | 0 | 1.000 |
| 1968–National | OF | 3 | 0 | 1 | 0 | 0 | 0 | 0 | .333 | 1 | 0 | 0 | 1.000 |
| 1969–National | OF | 4 | 1 | 1 | 0 | 0 | 0 | 0 | .250 | 0 | 0 | 0 | .000 |
| 1970–National | OF | 2 | 0 | 0 | 0 | 0 | 0 | 0 | .000 | 1 | 0 | 0 | 1.000 |
| 1971–National | OF | 2 | 1 | 1 | 0 | 0 | 1 | 1 | .500 | 0 | 0 | 0 | .000 |
| 1972–National | OF | 3 | 1 | 1 | 0 | 0 | 1 | 2 | .333 | 0 | 0 | 0 | .000 |
| 1973–National | 1B | 2 | 0 | 1 | 0 | 0 | 0 | 1 | .500 | 3 | 1 | 0 | 1.000 |
| 1974–National | OF | 2 | 0 | 0 | 0 | 0 | 0 | 0 | .000 | 0 | 0 | 0 | .000 |
| 1975–American | PH | 1 | 0 | 0 | 0 | 0 | 0 | 0 | .000 | 0 | 0 | 0 | .000 |
| All-Star Game Totals | | 67 | 7 | 13 | 0 | 0 | 2 | 8 | .194 | 23 | 2 | 0 | 1.000 |

Named to the National League All-Star Team (first game) in 1962; replaced due to injury.

# HERMAN THOMAS DAVIS, JR.
## (Tommy)

Born March 21, 1939, at Brooklyn, N. Y.
Height, 6.02.  Weight, 200.
Threw and batted righthanded.
Hobby—Modern jazz recordings.

Tied major league record for most clubs, lifetime (10), since 1900.
Tied major league record for fewest triples, season (150 or more games), 0, 1967.
Led Midwest League in total bases with 271 and stolen bases with 68 in 1957. Led Pacific Coast League in total bases with 315 in 1959.
Named outfielder on THE SPORTING NEWS National League All-Star Team, 1962-63.
Named designated hitter on THE SPORTING NEWS American League All-Star Team, 1974.

| Year | Club | League | Pos. | G. | AB. | R. | H. | 2B. | 3B. | HR. | RBI. | B.A. | PO. | A. | E. | F.A. |
|---|---|---|---|---|---|---|---|---|---|---|---|---|---|---|---|---|
| 1956–Hornell | | Pony | OF | 43 | 154 | 14 | 50 | 5 | 1 | 0 | 26 | .325 | 49 | 7 | 4 | .933 |
| 1957–Kokomo | | Midw. | OF-3B | 127 | •518 | •115 | •185 | 23 | 6 | 17 | 104 | •.357 | 179 | 32 | 19 | .917 |
| 1958–Victoria | | Tex. | OF-1B | 122 | 461 | 74 | 140 | 21 | 10 | 13 | 66 | .304 | 261 | 17 | 7 | .975 |
| 1958–Montreal | | Int. | OF-2-3B | 14 | 26 | 3 | 8 | 0 | 1 | 1 | 7 | .308 | 6 | 0 | 1 | .857 |
| 1959–Spokane | | P.C. | OF | •153 | •612 | 90 | •211 | 32 | 9 | 18 | 78 | •.345 | •414 | 15 | •10 | .977 |
| 1959–Los Angeles | | Nat. | PH | 1 | 1 | 0 | 0 | 0 | 0 | 0 | 0 | .000 | 0 | 0 | 0 | .000 |
| 1960–Los Angeles | | Nat. | OF-3B | 110 | 352 | 43 | 97 | 18 | 1 | 11 | 44 | .276 | 153 | 17 | 4 | .977 |
| 1961–Los Angeles | | Nat. | OF-3B | 132 | 460 | 60 | 128 | 13 | 2 | 15 | 58 | .278 | 173 | 91 | 17 | .940 |
| 1962–Los Angeles | | Nat. | OF-3B | 163 | 665 | 120 | •230 | 27 | 9 | 27 | •153 | •.346 | 269 | 60 | 20 | .943 |
| 1963–Los Angeles | | Nat. | OF-3B | 146 | 556 | 69 | 181 | 19 | 3 | 16 | 88 | •.326 | 204 | 67 | 15 | .948 |
| 1964–Los Angeles | | Nat. | OF | 152 | 592 | 70 | 163 | 20 | 5 | 14 | 86 | .275 | 264 | 9 | 5 | .982 |
| 1965–Los Angeles† | | Nat. | OF | 17 | 60 | 3 | 15 | 1 | 1 | 0 | 9 | .250 | 21 | 1 | 0 | 1.000 |
| 1966–Los Angeles‡ | | Nat. | OF-3B | 100 | 313 | 27 | 98 | 11 | 1 | 3 | 27 | .313 | 99 | 9 | 3 | .973 |
| 1967–New York§ | | Nat. | OF-1B | 154 | 577 | 72 | 174 | 32 | 0 | 16 | 73 | .302 | 236 | 7 | 7 | .972 |
| 1968–Chicago x | | Amer. | OF-1B | 132 | 456 | 30 | 122 | 5 | 3 | 8 | 50 | .268 | 211 | 9 | 8 | .965 |
| 1969–Seattle y | | Amer. | OF-1B | 123 | 454 | 52 | 123 | 29 | 1 | 6 | 80 | .271 | 183 | 3 | 7 | .964 |
| 1969–Houston | | Nat. | OF | 24 | 79 | 2 | 19 | 3 | 0 | 1 | 9 | .241 | 27 | 1 | 0 | 1.000 |
| 1970–Hou. a-Chi. | | Nat. | OF | 68 | 255 | 28 | 71 | 14 | 2 | 5 | 38 | .278 | 86 | 4 | 5 | .947 |
| 1970–Oakland b | | Am. | OF-1B | 66 | 200 | 17 | 58 | 9 | 1 | 1 | 27 | .290 | 110 | 4 | 4 | .966 |
| 1971–Oakland c | | Am. | 1-O-2-3 | 79 | 219 | 26 | 71 | 8 | 1 | 3 | 42 | .324 | 275 | 37 | 5 | .984 |
| 1972–Chicago d e | | Nat. | 1B-OF | 15 | 26 | 3 | 7 | 1 | 0 | 0 | 6 | .269 | 31 | 1 | 1 | .970 |
| 1972–Baltimore | | Amer. | OF-1B | 26 | 82 | 9 | 21 | 3 | 0 | 0 | 6 | .256 | 51 | 4 | 0 | 1.000 |
| 1973–Baltimore | | Amer. | 1B | 137 | 552 | 53 | 169 | 20 | 3 | 7 | 89 | .306 | 32 | 2 | 1 | .971 |
| 1974–Baltimore | | Amer. | DH | 158 | 626 | 67 | 181 | 20 | 1 | 11 | 84 | .289 | 0 | 0 | 0 | .000 |
| 1975–Baltimore f | | Amer. | DH | 116 | 460 | 43 | 130 | 14 | 1 | 6 | 57 | .283 | 0 | 0 | 0 | .000 |
| 1976–Calif. g-K.C. h | | Amer. | DH-1B | 80 | 238 | 17 | 63 | 5 | 0 | 3 | 26 | .265 | 4 | 0 | 0 | •1.000 |
| American League Totals | | | | 917 | 3287 | 314 | 938 | 111 | 11 | 45 | 461 | .285 | 866 | 59 | 25· | .974 |
| National League Totals | | | | 1082 | 3936 | 497 | 1183 | 159 | 24 | 108 | 591 | .301 | 1563 | 267 | 77 | .960 |
| Major League Totals | | | | 1999 | 7223 | 811 | 2121 | 272 | 35 | 153 | 1052 | .294 | 2429 | 326 | 102 | .964 |

†Suffered broken ankle against San Francisco Giants, May 1; on disabled list from May 3 through September 22.

‡Traded with Outfielder-Infielder Derrell Griffith to New York Mets for Second Baseman Ron Hunt and Outfielder-Infielder Jim Hickman, November 29, 1966.

§Traded with Pitchers Jack Fisher and Billy Wynne to Chicago White Sox for Outfielder Tommie Agee and Infielder Al Weiss, December 15, 1967. White Sox purchased Catcher Dick Booker from Jacksonville as part of deal.

xSelected by Seattle Pilots from Chicago White Sox in expansion draft, October 15, 1968.

yTraded to Houston Astros for Outfielders Hilario Valdespino and Dan Walton, August 31, 1969.

aSold To Oakland Athletics, June 22, 1970.

bSold to Chicago Cubs, September 16, 1970. Released by Chicago Cubs, December 28, 1970, and signed as free agent by Oakland Athletics, March 29, 1971.

cOn disabled list August 31 through September 15.

dReleased by Oakland A's, March 30, 1972, and signed as free agent by Chicago Cubs, July 6, 1972.

eTraded to Baltimore Orioles for Catcher Ellie Hendricks, August 18, 1972.

fReleased, February 12, 1976; signed as free agent by New York Yankees, February 20, 1976. Released by New York Yankees, April 6, 1976.

gSigned as free agent by California Angels, June 2, 1976; sold to Kansas City Royals, September 20, 1976.

hUnconditionally released, February 8, 1977.

## CHAMPIONSHIP SERIES RECORD

| Year | Club | League | Pos. | G. | AB. | R. | H. | 2B. | 3B. | HR. | RBI. | B.A. | PO. | A. | E. | F.A. |
|------|------|--------|------|----|-----|----|----|-----|-----|-----|------|------|-----|----|----|------|
| 1971–Oakland | ............ | Amer. | PH-1B | 3 | 8 | 1 | 3 | 1 | 0 | 0 | 0 | .375 | 8 | 0 | 0 | 1.000 |
| 1973–Baltimore | ......... | Amer. | DH | 5 | 21 | 1 | 6 | 1 | 0 | 0 | 2 | .286 | 0 | 0 | 0 | .000 |
| 1974–Baltimore | ......... | Amer. | DH | 4 | 15 | 0 | 4 | 0 | 0 | 0 | 1 | .267 | 0 | 0 | 0 | .000 |
| Championship Series Totals | ............ | | | 12 | 44 | 2 | 13 | 2 | 0 | 0 | 3 | .295 | 8 | 0 | 0 | 1.000 |

## WORLD SERIES RECORD

Tied World Series records for most three-base hits, game (2), October 3, 1963; most three-base hits, four-game Series (2), 1963; most putouts, game, by left fielder (6), October 3, 1963–and in same game most putouts by outfielder, inning (3), seventh inning.

| Year | Club | League | Pos. | G. | AB. | R. | H. | 2B. | 3B. | HR. | RBI. | B.A. | PO. | A. | E. | F.A. |
|------|------|--------|------|----|-----|----|----|-----|-----|-----|------|------|-----|----|----|------|
| 1963–Los Angeles | ...... | Nat. | OF | 4 | 15 | 0 | 6 | 0 | 2 | 0 | 2 | .400 | 6 | 0 | 0 | 1.000 |
| 1966–Los Angeles | ...... | Nat. | OF | 4 | 8 | 0 | 2 | 0 | 0 | 0 | 0 | .250 | 3 | 0 | 0 | 1.000 |
| World Series Totals | ...................... | | | 8 | 23 | 0 | 8 | 0 | 2 | 0 | 2 | .348 | 9 | 0 | 0 | 1.000 |

## ALL-STAR GAME RECORD

| Year | League | Pos. | AB. | R. | H. | 2B. | 3B. | HR. | RBI. | B.A. | PO. | A. | E. | F.A. |
|------|--------|------|-----|----|----|-----|-----|-----|------|------|-----|----|----|------|
| 1962–National (both games) | ........ | OF | 5 | 0 | 0 | 0 | 0 | 0 | 0 | .000 | 2 | 1 | 1 | .750 |
| 1963–National | ............................. | OF | 3 | 1 | 1 | 0 | 0 | 0 | 0 | .333 | 2 | 1 | 0 | 1.000 |
| All-Star Game Totals | ...................... | | 8 | 1 | 1 | 0 | 0 | 0 | 0 | .125 | 4 | 2 | 1 | .857 |

# WILLIAM ASHLEY FREEHAN
## (Bill)

Born November 29, 1941, at Detroit, Mich.
Height, 6.03. Weight, 208.
Threw and batted righthanded.
Hobbies—Golf, football and hunting.
Attended University of Michigan, Ann Arbor, Mich.; received Bachelor of Science
degree in History.

Established major league records for highest fielding average, catcher, lifetime, .9933, 1976; and putouts, catcher, lifetime (9,941), 1976; and most chances accepted, catcher, lifetime (10,662), 1976.

Tied major league record for most times hit by pitcher, game (3), August 16, 1968.

Established following American League records: most putouts, game, nine innings, catcher (19), June 15, 1965; most putouts, catcher, season (971), 1968; and most chances accepted, catcher, season (1,044), 1968.

Tied American League record for most times hit by pitcher, season (24), 1968.

Hit three home runs in a game, August 9, 1971.

Tied for American League lead in double plays by catchers with 15 in 1968.

Tied for American Association lead in passed balls with 17 in 1962.

Named catcher on THE SPORTING NEWS American League All-Star fielding teams, 1965-66-67-68-69.

Named catcher on THE SPORTING NEWS American League All-Star Teams, 1967-68-69-71.

Received reported $100,000 bonus to sign with Detroit Tigers, 1961.

| Year | Club | League | Pos. | G. | AB. | R. | H. | 2B. | 3B. | HR. | RBI. | B.A. | PO. | A. | E. | F.A. |
|------|------|--------|------|----|-----|----|----|-----|-----|-----|------|------|-----|----|----|------|
| 1961–Duluth-Sup'ior | ..North. | C | 30 | 99 | 22 | 34 | 5 | 1 | 7 | 26 | .343 | 166 | 22 | 6 | .969 |
| 1961–Knoxville | ..........Sally | C | 47 | 159 | 29 | 46 | 6 | 3 | 4 | 29 | .289 | 260 | 18 | 6 | .979 |
| 1961–Detroit | ..............Amer. | C | 4 | 10 | 1 | 4 | 0 | 0 | 0 | 4 | .400 | 14 | 4 | 0 | 1.000 |
| 1962–Denver | ..............A. A. | •C-1B | 113 | 392 | 47 | 111 | 22 | 2 | 9 | 58 | .283 | 684 | 55 | 11 | •.985 |
| 1963–Detroit | ..............Amer. | C-1B | 100 | 300 | 37 | 73 | 12 | 2 | 9 | 36 | .243 | 554 | 38 | 3 | .995 |
| 1964–Detroit | ..............Amer. | C-1B | 144 | 520 | 69 | 156 | 14 | 8 | 18 | 80 | .300 | 930 | 61 | 7 | .993 |
| 1965–Detroit | ..............Amer. | C | 130 | 431 | 45 | 101 | 15 | 0 | 10 | 43 | .234 | •865 | 57 | 4 | .996 |
| 1966–Detroit | ..............Amer. | •C-1B | 136 | 492 | 47 | 115 | 22 | 0 | 12 | 46 | .234 | •942 | 60 | 4 | •.996 |
| 1967–Detroit | ..............Amer. | •C-1B | 155 | 517 | 66 | 146 | 23 | 1 | 20 | 74 | .282• | 1027 | 68 | 8 | .993 |
| 1968–Detroit | ..............Amer. | •C-1-O | 155 | 540 | 73 | 142 | 24 | 2 | 25 | 84 | .263• | 1133 | 83 | 7 | .994 |
| 1969–Detroit | ..............Amer. | •C-1 | 143 | 489 | 61 | 128 | 16 | 3 | 16 | 49 | .262 | •959 | 56 | 10 | .990 |
| 1970–Detroit† | ..........Amer. | C | 117 | 395 | 44 | 95 | 17 | 3 | 16 | 52 | .241 | 742 | 42 | 2 | •.997 |
| 1971–Detroit | ..............Amer. | •C-O | 148 | 516 | 57 | 143 | 26 | 4 | 21 | 71 | .277 | •912 | 50 | 4 | .996 |
| 1972–Detroit | ..............Amer. | C-1 | 111 | 374 | 51 | 98 | 18 | 2 | 10 | 56 | .262 | 654 | 60 | 8 | .989 |
| 1973–Detroit | ..............Amer. | •C-1B | 110 | 380 | 33 | 89 | 10 | 1 | 6 | 29 | .234 | 638 | 53 | 3 | •.996 |
| 1974–Detroit | ..............Amer. | 1B-C | 130 | 445 | 58 | 132 | 17 | 5 | 18 | 60 | .297 | 902 | 81 | 9 | .991 |

| Year Club | League | Pos. | G. | AB. | R. | H. | 2B. | 3B. | HR. | RBI. | B.A. | PO. | A. | E. | F.A. |
|---|---|---|---|---|---|---|---|---|---|---|---|---|---|---|---|
| 1975–Detroit | Amer. | *C-1B | 120 | 427 | 42 | 105 | 17 | 3 | 14 | 47 | .246 | 635 | 66 | 6 | *.992 |
| 1976–Detroit†‡ | Amer. | C-1-DH | 71 | 237 | 22 | 64 | 10 | 1 | 5 | 27 | .270 | 328 | 34 | 6 | .984 |
| Major League Totals | | | 1774 | 6073 | 706 | 1591 | 241 | 35 | 200 | 758 | .262 | 11235 | 813 | 81 | .993 |

†On disabled list August 31 to end of season.
‡Released, December 12, 1976.

## CHAMPIONSHIP SERIES RECORD

| Year Club | League | Pos. | G. | AB. | R. | H. | 2B. | 3B. | HR. | RBI. | B.A. | PO. | A. | E. | F.A. |
|---|---|---|---|---|---|---|---|---|---|---|---|---|---|---|---|
| 1972–Detroit | Amer. | C | 3 | 12 | 2 | 3 | 1 | 0 | 1 | 3 | .250 | 24 | 3 | 0 | 1.000 |

## WORLD SERIES RECORD

| Year Club | League | Pos. | G. | AB. | R. | H. | 2B. | 3B. | HR. | RBI. | B.A. | PO. | A. | E. | F.A. |
|---|---|---|---|---|---|---|---|---|---|---|---|---|---|---|---|
| 1968–Detroit | Amer. | C | 7 | 24 | 0 | 2 | 1 | 0 | 0 | 2 | .083 | 45 | 6 | 2 | .962 |

## ALL-STAR GAME RECORD

| Year League | Pos. | G. | AB. | R. | H. | 2B. | 3B. | HR. | RBI. | B.A. | PO. | A. | E. | F.A. |
|---|---|---|---|---|---|---|---|---|---|---|---|---|---|---|
| 1965–American | C | 1 | 0 | 1 | 0 | 0 | 0 | 0 | 1.000 | 4 | 0 | 0 | 1.000 |
| 1966–American | C | 2 | 0 | 1 | 0 | 0 | 0 | 0 | .500 | 4 | 0 | 0 | 1.000 |
| 1967–American | C | 5 | 0 | 0 | 0 | 0 | 0 | 0 | .000 | 13 | 0 | 0 | 1.000 |
| 1968–American | C | 2 | 0 | 0 | 0 | 0 | 0 | 0 | .000 | 4 | 0 | 0 | 1.000 |
| 1969–American | C | 2 | 1 | 2 | 0 | 0 | 1 | 2 | 1.000 | 4 | 0 | 0 | 1.000 |
| 1970–American | C | 1 | 0 | 0 | 0 | 0 | 0 | 0 | .000 | 4 | 0 | 0 | 1.000 |
| 1971–American | C | 3 | 0 | 0 | 0 | 0 | 0 | 0 | .000 | 6 | 1 | 0 | 1.000 |
| 1972–American | C | 1 | 1 | 0 | 0 | 0 | 0 | 0 | .000 | 3 | 0 | 0 | 1.000 |
| All-Star Game Totals | | 17 | 2 | 4 | 0 | 0 | 1 | 2 | .235 | 42 | 1 | 0 | 1.000 |

Member of American League All-Star Team in 1964, 1973 and 1975 games; did not play.

# TOMMY HARPER

Born October 14, 1940, at Oak Grove, La.
Height, 5.09. Weight, 160.
Threw and batted righthanded.
Attended San Francisco State College, San Francisco, Calif., and
Santa Rosa Junior College, Santa Rosa, Calif.

One of five players in major league history to hit 30 home runs and steal 30 bases in the same season (31 home runs and 38 stolen bases in 1970).
Led American League in stolen bases with 73 in 1969 and 54 in 1973.
Major League stolen bases: 1962 (1), 1963 (12), 1964 (24), 1965 (35), 1966 (29), 1967 (23), 1968 (11), 1969 (73), 1970 (38), 1971 (25), 1972 (25), 1973 (54), 1974 (28), 1975 (26), 1976 (4). Total—408.
Led Three I League in stolen bases with 31 in 1961.
Led Three I League batters in walks with 136 in 1961 and Pacific Coast League batters with 105 in 1962.
Named Most Valuable Player in Three I League, 1961.

| Year Club | League | Pos. | G. | AB. | R. | H. | 2B. | 3B. | HR. | RBI. | B.A. | PO. | A. | E. | F.A. |
|---|---|---|---|---|---|---|---|---|---|---|---|---|---|---|---|
| 1960–Topeka† | I. I. I. | 2B | 79 | 252 | 65 | 64 | 14 | 3 | 5 | 36 | .254 | 162 | 203 | 28 | .929 |
| 1961–Topeka | I. I. I. | 2B | 124 | 426 | *131 | 138 | 27 | *11 | 15 | 65 | .324 | 285 | 315 | 23 | *.963 |
| 1962–Cincinnati | Nat. | 3B | 6 | 23 | 1 | 4 | 0 | 0 | 0 | 1 | .174 | 6 | 7 | 1 | .929 |
| 1962–San Diego | P. C. | 3B-OF | 144 | 499 | *120 | 166 | 24 | 8 | 26 | 84 | .333 | 106 | 233 | 34 | .909 |
| 1963–Cincinnati | Nat. | OF-3B | 129 | 408 | 67 | 106 | 12 | 3 | 10 | 37 | .260 | 224 | 7 | 4 | .983 |
| 1964–Cincinnati | Nat. | OF-3B | 102 | 317 | 42 | 77 | 5 | 2 | 4 | 22 | .243 | 149 | 6 | 1 | .994 |
| 1965–Cincinnati | Nat. | OF-3-2B | 159 | 646 | *126 | 166 | 28 | 3 | 18 | 64 | .257 | 279 | 10 | 5 | .983 |
| 1966–Cincinnati | Nat. | OF | 149 | 553 | 85 | 154 | 22 | 5 | 5 | 31 | .278 | 257 | 5 | 1 | .996 |
| 1967–Cincinnati‡§ | Nat. | OF | 103 | 365 | 55 | 82 | 17 | 3 | 7 | 22 | .225 | 208 | 6 | 1 | .995 |
| 1968–Cleveland x | Am. | OF-2B | 130 | 235 | 26 | 51 | 15 | 2 | 6 | 26 | .217 | 121 | 1 | 2 | .984 |
| 1969–Seattle | Am. | 2-3-OF | 148 | 537 | 78 | 126 | 10 | 2 | 9 | 41 | .235 | 232 | 268 | 22 | .958 |
| 1970–Milwaukee | Am. | *3-2-OF | 154 | 604 | 104 | 179 | 35 | 4 | 31 | 82 | .296 | 192 | 330 | *28 | .949 |
| 1971–Milwaukee y | Am. | O-3-2 | 152 | 585 | 79 | 151 | 26 | 3 | 14 | 52 | .258 | 227 | 118 | 18 | .950 |
| 1972–Boston | Am. | OF | 144 | 556 | 92 | 141 | 29 | 2 | 14 | 49 | .254 | 321 | 4 | 5 | .985 |
| 1973–Boston | Am. | OF | 147 | 566 | 92 | 159 | 23 | 3 | 17 | 71 | .281 | 251 | 13 | 4 | .985 |
| 1974–Boston z | Am. | OF | 118 | 443 | 66 | 105 | 15 | 3 | 5 | 24 | .237 | 105 | 2 | 2 | .982 |
| 1975–Calif. a–Oak. b | Am. | 1-O-3 | 123 | 354 | 51 | 90 | 14 | 1 | 5 | 38 | .254 | 249 | 10 | 6 | .977 |
| 1976–Baltimore c | Amer. | DH-1-OF | 46 | 77 | 8 | 18 | 5 | 0 | 1 | 7 | .234 | 2 | 0 | 0 | 1.000 |
| American League Totals | | | 1162 | 3957 | 596 | 1020 | 172 | 20 | 102 | 390 | .258 | 1700 | 746 | 87 | .966 |
| National League Totals | | | 648 | 2312 | 376 | 589 | 84 | 16 | 44 | 177 | .255 | 1123 | 41 | 13 | .989 |
| Major League Totals | | | 1810 | 6269 | 972 | 1609 | 256 | 36 | 146 | 567 | .257 | 2823 | 787 | 100 | .973 |

†On temporary inactive list, May 28 through June 16.
‡Suffered fractured right wrist May 28 after crashing into wall; on disabled list through July 26.
§Traded to Cleveland Indians for First Baseman Fred Whitfield and Pitcher George Culver, November 21, 1967. Outfielder Bob Raudman was assigned from Chicago Cubs to Reds as part of deal.
xSelected by Seattle Pilots from Cleveland Indians in expansion draft, October 15, 1968.
yTraded with Pitchers Marty Pattin and Lew Krausse and Outfielder Pat Skrable to Boston Red Sox for Catcher Don Pavletich, Pitchers Ken Brett and Jim Lonborg, First Baseman George Scott and Outfielders Billy Conigliaro and Joe Lahoud, October 11, 1971.
zTraded to California Angels for Infielder Bob Heise, December 2, 1974.
aSold to Oakland Athletics, August 13, 1975.
bReleased, November 20, 1975; signed as free agent by Baltimore Orioles, April 9, 1976.
cReleased March 25, 1977.

| Year | Club | League | Pos. | G. | AB. | R. | H. | 2B. | 3B. | HR. | RBI. | B.A. | PO. | A. | E. | F.A. |
|------|------|--------|------|-----|-----|-----|-----|-----|-----|-----|------|------|-----|-----|-----|------|
| 1975–Oakland | | Amer. | PH | 1 | 0 | 0 | 0 | 0 | 0 | 0 | 0 | .000 | 0 | 0 | 0 | .000 |

## ALL-STAR GAME RECORD

| Year | League | Pos. | AB. | R. | H. | 2B. | 3B. | HR. | RBI. | B.A. | PO. | A. | E. | F.A. |
|------|--------|------|-----|-----|-----|-----|-----|-----|------|------|-----|-----|-----|------|
| 1970–American | | PR | 0 | 0 | 0 | 0 | 0 | 0 | 0 | .000 | 0 | 0 | 0 | .000 |

## DERON ROGER JOHNSON

Born July 17, 1938, at San Diego, Calif.
Height, 6.02. Weight, 209.
Threw and batted righthanded.
Hobbies–Golf and bowling.

Established major league record for fewest chances accepted (excludes errors) by first baseman, season, 150 or more games, 1251, in 1970.

Tied major league records for most home runs, consecutive appearances (4), July 10-11, 1971; fewest triples, season (150 or more games), 0, 1971; and most strikeouts, inning, 2, September 23, 1973, fifth inning.

Hit three home runs in a game, July 11, 1971.

Led Nebraska State League in total bases with 167 in 1956 and Eastern League with 279 in 1957.

Tied for Nebraska State League lead in double plays by outfielders with 4 in 1956.

Named as third baseman on THE SPORTING NEWS National League All-Star Team, 1965.

| Year | Club | League | Pos. | G. | AB. | R. | H. | 2B. | 3B. | HR. | RBI. | B.A. | PO. | A. | E. | F.A. |
|------|------|--------|------|-----|-----|-----|-----|-----|-----|-----|------|------|-----|-----|-----|------|
| 1956–Kearney | | Neb. St. | OF | 63 | 243 | *70 | 80 | 9 | 3 | *24 | *78 | .329 | 104 | 9 | 4 | .966 |
| 1957–Binghamton | | East. | OF | 137 | 501 | *103 | 152 | 23 | 13 | *26 | 102 | .303 | 253 | 13 | 6 | .978 |
| 1958–Richmond | | Int. | OF-3B | 154 | 570 | 79 | 148 | 27 | 5 | 27 | 103 | .260 | 248 | 33 | 7 | .976 |
| 1959–Richmond | | Int. | OF-3B | 154 | 556 | 85 | 155 | 23 | 6 | 25 | 90 | .279 | 195 | 153 | 18 | .951 |
| 1960–New York | | Am. | 3B | 6 | 4 | 0 | 2 | 1 | 0 | 0 | 0 | .500 | 0 | 3 | 1 | .750 |
| 1960–Richmond | | Int. | 3B-OF | 151 | 552 | 79 | 135 | 23 | 6 | 27 | 92 | .245 | 172 | 249 | 15 | .966 |
| 1961–N. Y.†–K. C. | | Am. | O-3-1B | 96 | 302 | 32 | 63 | 11 | 3 | 8 | 44 | .209 | 134 | 66 | 9 | .957 |
| 1962–Kansas City‡§ | | Am. | 1-3B-O | 17 | 19 | 1 | 2 | 1 | 0 | 0 | 0 | .105 | 5 | 1 | 1 | .857 |
| 1963–San Diego | | P. C. | OF-IN | 129 | 481 | 85 | 133 | 22 | 3 | *33 | 91 | .277 | 360 | 55 | 14 | .967 |
| 1964–Cincinnati | | Nat. | 1B-O-3B | 140 | 477 | 63 | 130 | 24 | 4 | 21 | 79 | .273 | 952 | 84 | 10 | .990 |
| 1965–Cincinnati | | Nat. | 3B | 159 | 616 | 92 | 177 | 30 | 7 | 32 | 130 | .287 | 132 | 266 | 22 | .948 |
| 1966–Cincinnati | | Nat. | OF-1-3 | 142 | 505 | 75 | 130 | 25 | 3 | 24 | 81 | .257 | 339 | 36 | 5 | .987 |
| 1967–Cincinnati x | | Nat. | 1B-3B | 108 | 361 | 39 | 81 | 18 | 1 | 13 | 53 | .224 | 606 | 73 | 4 | .994 |
| 1968–Atlanta y | | Nat. | 1B-3B | 127 | 342 | 29 | 71 | 11 | 1 | 8 | 33 | .208 | 759 | 78 | 4 | .995 |
| 1969–Philadelphia | | Nat. | OF-3-1B | 138 | 475 | 51 | 121 | 19 | 4 | 17 | 80 | .255 | 250 | 99 | 11 | .969 |
| 1970–Philadelphia | | Nat. | 1B-3B | 159 | 574 | 66 | 147 | 28 | 3 | 27 | 93 | .256 | 1180 | 74 | 6 | .995 |
| 1971–Philadelphia | | Nat. | 1B-3B | 158 | 582 | 74 | 154 | 29 | 0 | 34 | 95 | .265 | 1233 | 123 | 12 | .991 |
| 1972–Philadelphia z | | Nat. | 1B | 96 | 230 | 19 | 49 | 4 | 1 | 9 | 31 | .213 | 479 | 24 | 9 | .982 |
| 1973–Philadelphia a | | Nat. | 1B | 12 | 36 | 3 | 6 | 2 | 0 | 1 | 5 | .167 | 77 | 6 | 2 | .976 |
| 1973–Oakland | | Am. | 1B | 131 | 464 | 61 | 114 | 14 | 2 | 19 | 81 | .246 | 167 | 6 | 1 | .994 |
| 1974–Oa.b–Mil.c–Bo.d | | Am. | 1B | 110 | 351 | 30 | 60 | 4 | 2 | 13 | 43 | .171 | 220 | 10 | 4 | .983 |
| 1975–Chi. e–Boston | | Am. | 1B | 151 | 565 | 68 | 135 | 25 | 1 | 19 | 75 | .239 | 475 | 24 | 3 | .994 |
| 1976–Boston f | | Am. | DH-1B | 15 | 38 | 3 | 5 | 1 | 1 | 0 | 6 | .132 | 30 | 1 | 0 | 1.000 |
| American League Totals | | | | 526 | 1743 | 195 | 381 | 57 | 9 | 59 | 243 | .218 | 1031 | 111 | 19 | .984 |
| National League Totals | | | | 1239 | 4198 | 511 | 1066 | 190 | 24 | 186 | 680 | .254 | 6007 | 863 | 85 | .988 |
| Major League Totals | | | | 1765 | 5941 | 706 | 1447 | 247 | 33 | 245 | 923 | .244 | 7038 | 974 | 104 | .987 |

†Traded to Kansas City Athletics with Pitcher Art Ditmar for Pitcher Bud Daley, June 14, 1961.
‡Sold to Cincinnati Reds' organization, April 5, 1963.
§On military list through July 31.
xTraded to Atlanta Braves for Outfielder Mack Jones, Pitcher Jay Ritchie and First Baseman Jim Beauchamp, October 10, 1067. Ritchie and Beauchamp assigned to Buffalo.
ySold to Philadelphia Phillies, December 3, 1968.
zOn supplemental disabled list, June 15 through July 1.
aTraded to Oakland Athletics for Third Baseman-Outfielder Jack Bastable (assigned from Birmingham to Rocky Mount), May 2, 1973.
bOn supplemental disabled list, April 11 to April 26, 1974. Released on waivers to Milwaukee Brewers, June 24, 1974; Brewers assigned Pitcher Bill Parsons to Athletics, July 1, 1974, to complete deal.
cSold to Boston Red Sox, September 7, 1974.
dReleased, October 25, 1974; signed as free agent by Chicago White Sox, April 5, 1975.
eTraded to Boston Red Sox for cash and a player to be named later, September 21, 1975; Red Sox sent Catcher Chuck Erickson to White Sox, October 21, 1975, to complete deal.
fReleased, June 4, 1976.

## CHAMPIONSHIP SERIES RECORD

| Year | Club | League | Pos. | G. | AB. | R. | H. | 2B. | 3B. | HR. | RBI. | B.A. | PO. | A. | E. | F.A. |
|------|------|--------|------|-----|-----|-----|-----|-----|-----|-----|------|------|-----|-----|-----|------|
| 1973–Oakland | | Am. | DH | 4 | 10 | 0 | 1 | 0 | 0 | 0 | 0 | .100 | 0 | 0 | 0 | .000 |

## WORLD SERIES RECORD

| Year | Club | League | Pos. | G. | AB. | R. | H. | 2B. | 3B. | HR. | RBI. | B.A. | PO. | A. | E. | F.A. |
|------|------|--------|------|-----|-----|-----|-----|-----|-----|-----|------|------|-----|-----|-----|------|
| 1973–Oakland | | Am. | PH-1B | 6 | 10 | 0 | 3 | 1 | 0 | 0 | 0 | .300 | 8 | 1 | 0 | 1.000 |

**BILLY WILLIAMS**

## MICHAEL STEPHEN LOLICH
### (Mickey)

Born September 12, 1940, at Portland, Ore.
Height, 6.01. Weight, 207.
Threw left and batted righthanded.
Hobby—Hunting.
Attended Clark Junior College, Vancouver, Wash.
First cousin of Ron Lolich, former outfielder with Chicago White Sox and Cleveland
Indians, and Frank Lolich, former pitcher in New York Mets' organization.

Established American League record for most strikeouts, lefthanded pitcher, lifetime (2,679), 1975.
Tied American League record for most seasons, 200 or more strikeouts, 7, 1974.
Pitched first five innings of 4-3 no-hit loss against Asheville, June 4, 1961.
Led American League in hit batsmen with 12 in 1965.
Led American League pitchers in games started with 45 and complete games with 29 in 1971.
Tied American League lead in shutouts with 6 in 1967.

| Year | Club | League | G. | IP. | W. | L. | Pct. | H. | R. | ER. | SO. | BB. | ERA. |
|---|---|---|---|---|---|---|---|---|---|---|---|---|---|
| 1959—Knoxville | | Sally | 11 | 67 | 3 | 6 | .333 | 51 | 29 | 19 | 42 | 53 | 2.55 |
| 1959—Durham | | Carolina | 9 | 37 | 1 | 2 | .333 | 27 | 22 | 17 | 24 | 45 | 4.14 |
| 1960—Knoxville | | Sally | 4 | 15 | 0 | 1 | .000 | 17 | 13 | 13 | 14 | 20 | 7.63 |
| 1960—Durham | | Carolina | 25 | 113 | 5 | 10 | .333 | 111 | 71 | 51 | 135 | 87 | 4.06 |
| 1961—Knoxville | | Sally | 15 | 72 | 3 | 5 | .375 | 49 | 50 | 41 | 93 | 76 | 5.10 |
| 1961—Durham | | Carolina | 18 | 102 | 5 | 5 | .500 | 92 | 42 | 34 | 102 | 73 | 2.99 |
| 1962—Denver | | Am. Assoc. | 9 | 12 | 0 | 4 | .000 | 26 | 24 | 22 | 10 | 10 | 16.50 |
| 1962—Portland | | P. Coast | 23 | 130 | 10 | 9 | .526 | 116 | 66 | 57 | 138 | 57 | 3.95 |
| 1963—Detroit | | American | 33 | 144 | 5 | 9 | .357 | 145 | 64 | 57 | 103 | 56 | 3.56 |
| 1963—Syracuse | | Int'national | 6 | 22 | 0 | 2 | .000 | 21 | 11 | 6 | 21 | 10 | 2.45 |
| 1964—Detroit | | American | 44 | 232 | 18 | 9 | .667 | 196 | 88 | 84 | 192 | 64 | 3.26 |
| 1965—Detroit | | American | 43 | 244 | 15 | 9 | .625 | 216 | 103 | 93 | 226 | 72 | 3.43 |
| 1966—Detroit | | American | 40 | 204 | 14 | 14 | .500 | 204 | 119 | 108 | 173 | 83 | 4.76 |
| 1967—Detroit | | American | 31 | 204 | 14 | 13 | .519 | 165 | 71 | 69 | 174 | 56 | 3.04 |
| 1968—Detroit | | American | 39 | 220 | 17 | 9 | .654 | 178 | 84 | 78 | 197 | 65 | 3.19 |
| 1969—Detroit | | American | 37 | 281 | 19 | 11 | .633 | 214 | 111 | 98 | 271 | 122 | 3.14 |
| 1970—Detroit | | American | 40 | 273 | 14 | •19 | .424 | 272 | 125 | •115 | 230 | 109 | 3.79 |
| 1971—Detroit | | American | 45 | •376 | •25 | 14 | .641 | •336 | 133 | 122 | •308 | 92 | 2.92 |
| 1972—Detroit | | American | 41 | 327 | 22 | 14 | .611 | 282 | 100 | 91 | 250 | 74 | 2.50 |
| 1973—Detroit | | American | 42 | 309 | 16 | 15 | .516 | 315 | 143 | 131 | 214 | 79 | 3.82 |
| 1974—Detroit | | American | 41 | 308 | 16 | •21 | .432 | 310 | 155 | 142 | 202 | 78 | 4.15 |
| 1975—Detroit† | | American | 32 | 241 | 12 | 18 | .400 | 260 | 119 | 101 | 139 | 64 | 3.77 |
| 1976—New York‡ | | National | 31 | 193 | 8 | 13 | .381 | 184 | 83 | 69 | 120 | 52 | 3.22 |
| American League Totals | | | 508 | 3363 | 207 | 175 | .542 | 3093 | 1415 | 1289 | 2679 | 1014 | 3.45 |
| National League Totals | | | 31 | 193 | 8 | 13 | .381 | 184 | 83 | 69 | 120 | 52 | 3.22 |
| Major League Totals | | | 539 | 3556 | 215 | 188 | .533 | 3277 | 1498 | 1358 | 2799 | 1066 | 3.44 |

†Traded with Outfielder Billy Baldwin to New York Mets for Outfielder Rusty Staub and Pitcher Bill Laxton, December 12, 1975.
‡Placed on voluntary retired list, February 7, 1977.

### CHAMPIONSHIP SERIES RECORD

| Year | Club | League | G. | IP. | W. | L. | Pct. | H. | R. | ER. | SO. | BB. | ERA. |
|---|---|---|---|---|---|---|---|---|---|---|---|---|---|
| 1972—Detroit | | American | 2 | 19 | 0 | 1 | .000 | 14 | 4 | 3 | 10 | 5 | 1.42 |

### WORLD SERIES RECORD

Tied World Series records for most games won Series (3), and most games won, Series, no losses (3), 1968.
Hit home run first World Series at bat, October 3, 1968, third inning.

| Year | Club | League | G. | IP. | W. | L. | Pct. | H. | R. | ER. | SO. | BB. | ERA. |
|---|---|---|---|---|---|---|---|---|---|---|---|---|---|
| 1968—Detroit | | American | 3 | 27 | 3 | 0 | 1.000 | 20 | 5 | 5 | 21 | 6 | 1.67 |

### ALL-STAR GAME RECORD

| Year | League | IP. | W. | L. | Pct. | H. | R. | ER. | SO. | BB. | ERA. |
|---|---|---|---|---|---|---|---|---|---|---|---|
| 1971—American | | 2 | 0 | 0 | .000 | 1 | 1 | 1 | 1 | 0 | 4.50 |
| 1972—American | | 2 | 0 | 0 | .000 | 1 | 0 | 0 | 1 | 0 | 0.00 |
| All-Star Game Totals | | 4 | 0 | 0 | .000 | 2 | 1 | 1 | 2 | 0 | 2.25 |

Member of American League All-Star Team in 1969 game; did not play.


## BILLY LEO WILLIAMS

Born June 15, 1938, at Whistler, Ala.
Height, 6.01½. Weight, 170.
Threw and batted lefthanded.
Hobbies—Football, fishing, hunting and swimming.

Tied major league records for most home runs two consecutive games (5), September 8 and 10, 1968, most consecutive doubles in one game, 4, April 9, 1969, and most times, four long hits, game, season, 2, April 9 and September 5, 1969.
Established the following National League records: most games played consecutive, league, 1,117, September 22, 1963 through September 2, 1970; most games by outfielder, season (164), 1965.
Tied National League record for most consecutive years, 600-or-more at-bats (9), 1970.
Hit three home runs in game, September 10, 1968.
Led National League in total bases with 321 in 1968, 373 in 1970, and 348 in 1972.

Led National League in slugging percentage with .606 in 1972.
Named National League Rookie Player of the Year by THE SPORTING NEWS and National League Rookie of the Year by the Baseball Writers' Association, 1961.
Named THE SPORTING NEWS Major League Player of the Year, 1972.
Named THE SPORTING NEWS National League Player of the Year, 1972.
Named outfielder on THE SPORTING NEWS National League All-Star Teams, 1964-68-70-72.

| Year Club League | Pos. | G. | AB. | R. | H. | 2B. | 3B. | HR. | RBI. | B.A. | PO. | A. | E. | F.A. |
|---|---|---|---|---|---|---|---|---|---|---|---|---|---|---|
| 1956—Ponca City† ......Soo. St. | OF | 13 | 17 | 4 | 4 | 0 | 0 | 0 | 4 | .235 | 6 | 0 | 1 | .857 |
| 1957—Ponca City ........Soo. St. | OF | ●126 | 451 | 87 | 140 | *40 | 3 | 17 | 95 | .310 | 211 | 21 | *25 | .903 |
| 1958—Pueblo‡ ...........West. | OF | 21 | 80 | 9 | 20 | 2 | 1 | 2 | 11 | .250 | 30 | 1 | 2 | .939 |
| 1958—Burlington ........I.I.I. | OF | 61 | 214 | 38 | 65 | 7 | 0 | 10 | 38 | .304 | 93 | 4 | 4 | .960 |
| 1959—San Antonio ......Tex. | 1B-OF | 94 | 371 | 57 | 118 | 22 | 7 | 10 | 79 | .318 | 578 | 54 | 21 | .968 |
| 1959—Fort Worth ........A.A. | OF | 5 | 21 | 7 | 10 | 4 | 1 | 1 | 5 | .476 | 10 | 2 | 1 | .923 |
| 1959—Chicago ...........Nat. | OF | 18 | 33 | 0 | 5 | 0 | 1 | 0 | 2 | .152 | 18 | 0 | 0 | 1.000 |
| 1960—Houston§ .........A.A. | OF | 126 | 473 | 74 | 153 | 28 | 3 | 26 | 80 | .323 | 207 | 7 | 7 | .968 |
| 1960—Chicago ...........Nat. | OF | 12 | 47 | 4 | 13 | 0 | 2 | 2 | 7 | .277 | 25 | 0 | 1 | .962 |
| 1961—Chicago ...........Nat. | OF | 146 | 529 | 75 | 147 | 20 | 7 | 25 | 86 | .278 | 220 | 9 | *11 | .954 |
| 1962—Chicago ...........Nat. | OF | 159 | 618 | 94 | 184 | 22 | 8 | 22 | 92 | .298 | 273 | 18 | 10 | .967 |
| 1963—Chicago ...........Nat. | OF | 161 | 612 | 87 | 175 | 36 | 9 | 25 | 95 | .286 | 298 | 13 | 4 | .987 |
| 1964—Chicago ...........Nat. | OF | 162 | 645 | 100 | 201 | 39 | 2 | 33 | 98 | .312 | 233 | 14 | 13 | .950 |
| 1965—Chicago ...........Nat. | OF | ●164 | 645 | 115 | 203 | 39 | 6 | 34 | 108 | .315 | 296 | 10 | 10 | .968 |
| 1966—Chicago ...........Nat. | OF | ●162 | 648 | 100 | 179 | 23 | 5 | 29 | 91 | .276 | 319 | 9 | 8 | .976 |
| 1967—Chicago ...........Nat. | OF | 162 | 634 | 92 | 176 | 21 | 12 | 28 | 84 | .278 | 271 | 3 | 3 | .989 |
| 1968—Chicago ...........Nat. | OF | *163 | 642 | 91 | 185 | 30 | 8 | 30 | 98 | .288 | 261 | 4 | 9 | .967 |
| 1969—Chicago ...........Nat. | OF | *163 | 642 | 103 | 188 | 33 | 10 | 21 | 95 | .293 | 250 | 15 | 12 | .957 |
| 1970—Chicago ...........Nat. | OF | ●161 | 636 | *137 | ●205 | 34 | 4 | 42 | 129 | .322 | 259 | 13 | 3 | .989 |
| 1971—Chicago ...........Nat. | OF | 157 | 594 | 86 | 179 | 27 | 5 | 28 | 93 | .301 | 284 | 8 | 7 | .977 |
| 1972—Chicago ...........Nat. | OF-1B | 150 | 574 | 95 | 191 | 34 | 6 | 37 | 122 | *.333 | 275 | 13 | 4 | .986 |
| 1973—Chicago ...........Nat. | OF-1B | 156 | 576 | 72 | 166 | 22 | 2 | 20 | 86 | .288 | 420 | 34 | 6 | .987 |
| 1974—Chicago xy ........Nat. | 1B-OF | 117 | 404 | 55 | 113 | 22 | 0 | 16 | 68 | .280 | 635 | 53 | 11 | .984 |
| 1975—Oakland ...........Amer. | DH-1B | 155 | 520 | 68 | 127 | 20 | 1 | 23 | 81 | .244 | 30 | 3 | 1 | .971 |
| 1976—Oakland z .........Amer. | DH-OF | 120 | 351 | 36 | 74 | 12 | 0 | 11 | 41 | .211 | 0 | 0 | 0 | .000 |
| National League Totals ................. | | 2213 | 8479 | 1306 | 2510 | 402 | 87 | 392 | 1354 | .296 | 4337 | 216 | 112 | .976 |
| American League Totals .............. | | 275 | 871 | 104 | 201 | 32 | 1 | 34 | 122 | .231 | 30 | 3 | 1 | .971 |
| Major League Totals ................. | | 2488 | 9350 | 1410 | 2711 | 434 | 88 | 426 | 1476 | .290 | 4367 | 219 | 113 | .976 |

†On disabled list, July 17 to August 18, 1956.
‡On temporary inactive list, June 7 to July 2, 1958.
§On disabled list, August 8 to September 5, 1960.
xOn supplemental disabled list, August 19 to September 3, 1974.
yTraded to Oakland Athletics for Pitchers Darold Knowles and Bob Locker and Second Baseman Manny Trillo, October 23, 1974.
zReleased, November 9, 1976.

CHAMPIONSHIP SERIES RECORD

| Year Club League | Pos. | G. | AB. | R. | H. | 2B. | 3B. | HR. | RBI. | B.A. | PO. | A. | E. | F.A. |
|---|---|---|---|---|---|---|---|---|---|---|---|---|---|---|
| 1975—Oakland ............Amer. | DH-PH | 3 | 8 | 0 | 0 | 0 | 0 | 0 | 0 | .000 | 0 | 0 | 0 | .000 |

ALL-STAR GAME RECORD

| Year League | Pos. | AB. | R. | H. | 2B. | 3B. | HR. | RBI. | B.A. | PO. | A. | E. | F.A. |
|---|---|---|---|---|---|---|---|---|---|---|---|---|---|
| 1962—National (second game) ...... | OF | 1 | 0 | 0 | 0 | 0 | 0 | 1 | .000 | 2 | 0 | 0 | 1.000 |
| 1964—National ............................. | OF | 4 | 1 | 1 | 0 | 0 | 1 | 1 | .250 | 1 | 0 | 0 | 1.000 |
| 1965—National ............................. | PH | 1 | 0 | 0 | 0 | 0 | 0 | 0 | .000 | 0 | 0 | 0 | .000 |
| 1968—National ............................. | PH | 1 | 0 | 0 | 0 | 0 | 0 | 0 | .000 | 0 | 0 | 0 | .000 |
| 1972—National ............................. | OF | 2 | 1 | 1 | 0 | 0 | 0 | 0 | .500 | 0 | 0 | 0 | .000 |
| 1973—National ............................. | OF | 2 | 0 | 1 | 0 | 0 | 0 | 0 | .500 | 0 | 0 | 0 | .000 |
| All-Star Game Totals ...................... | | 11 | 2 | 3 | 0 | 0 | 1 | 2 | .273 | 3 | 0 | 0 | 1.000 |

# CHAMPIONSHIP . . . WORLD SERIES SCHEDULE

The 1977 Major League baseball season closes on Sunday, October 2, and this year there will not be a long wait for the start of the League Championship Series. The American League Championship Series will commence on Tuesday, October 4 in the home park of the American League East Champions and the National League Series will commence on the same date in the home park of the National League West titlist. The first two games are scheduled for October 4 and 5 with October 6 as a travel date and the remaining games, as necessary, in the A.L. West stadium and the N.L.'s East home park on October 7, 8 and 9.

The 1977 World Series—74th between the two leagues—will open in the American League champion's home park on Tuesday, October 11. Games are scheduled in the A.L. stadium on October 11 and 12 with the travel date on Thursday, October 13. The series will resume in the N.L.'s championship city on Friday, Saturday and Sunday, October 14, 15 and 16. The 17th would be a travel date and the remaining games, as needed, would be in the A.L. city on Tuesday and Wednesday, October 18 and 19.

# Major League Managers

## JOSEPH SALVADOR ALTOBELLI
### (Alto)
### San Francisco Giants

Born May 26, 1932, at Detroit, Mich.
Height, 6.00. Weight, 180.
Threw and batted lefthanded.
Hobby—Hunting.

Led American Association first basemen in double plays with 146 in 1954, with 126 in 1955, and with 160 in 1962.

Named by THE SPORTING NEWS as Minor League Manager of the Year, 1974.

| Year | Club | League | Pos. | G. | AB. | R. | H. | 2B. | 3B. | HR. | RBI. | B.A. | PO. | A. | E. | F.A. |
|------|------|--------|------|-----|------|-----|-----|-----|-----|-----|------|------|------|-----|-----|------|
| 1951 | Daytona Beach | Fla. St. | 1B | •140 | 598 | 118 | 204 | •40 | 19 | 8 | 101 | .341 | •1259 | •90 | •45 | .967 |
| 1952 | Reading | East. | 1B | 128 | 436 | 49 | 118 | 9 | 7 | 2 | 37 | .271 | 1036 | 63 | •20 | .982 |
| 1953 | Reading | East. | 1B | 148 | 528 | 76 | 155 | 28 | 9 | 4 | 65 | .294 | 1092 | •83 | 19 | .984 |
| 1954 | Indianapolis | A.A. | 1B | 149 | 551 | 73 | 158 | 31 | 10 | 6 | 79 | .287 | 1120 | 84 | 12 | .990 |
| 1955 | Indianapolis | A.A. | 1B | 98 | 395 | 58 | 107 | 24 | 1 | 7 | 53 | .271 | 322 | 61 | 14 | .984 |
| 1955 | Cleveland | Amer. | 1B | 42 | 75 | 8 | 15 | 3 | 0 | 2 | 5 | .200 | 224 | 11 | 2 | .992 |
| 1956 | Indianapolis | A.A. | 1B | 145 | 528 | 69 | 134 | 18 | 10 | 19 | 81 | .254 | 1181 | 100 | 15 | .988 |
| 1957 | Cleveland | Amer. | 1B-OF | 83 | 87 | 9 | 18 | 3 | 2 | 0 | 9 | .207 | 158 | 9 | 1 | .994 |
| 1957 | Columbus | Int. | 1B | 22 | 77 | 16 | 18 | 5 | 1 | 2 | 10 | .234 | 176 | 20 | 3 | .985 |
| 1958 | Indianapolis† | A.A. | •1B-OF | 133 | 463 | 60 | 133 | 24 | 4 | 12 | 74 | .287 | 1012 | 83 | 14 | •.987 |
| 1959 | Toronto‡ | Int. | 1B | 148 | 518 | 71 | 131 | 17 | 6 | 17 | 61 | .253 | 1244 | 87 | 13 | .990 |
| 1960 | Montreal | Int. | 1B | 154 | 552 | 79 | 141 | 25 | 5 | •31 | •105 | .255 | •1401 | 101 | 14 | .991 |
| 1961 | Syracuse | Int. | 1B-OF | 96 | 351 | 50 | 90 | 11 | 4 | 10 | 47 | .256 | 396 | 31 | 13 | .968 |
| 1961 | Minnesota§ | Amer. | OF-1B | 41 | 95 | 10 | 21 | 2 | 1 | 3 | 14 | .221 | 54 | 1 | 2 | .965 |
| 1962 | Omaha | A.A. | 1B | 141 | 502 | 81 | 136 | 23 | 7 | 13 | 67 | .271 | •1247 | •89 | 12 | .991 |
| 1963 | Rochester x | Int. | 1B-OF | 97 | 315 | 45 | 77 | 13 | 0 | 15 | 44 | .244 | 361 | 31 | 4 | .990 |
| 1964 | Rochester | Int. | 1B | 122 | 345 | 35 | 86 | 11 | 1 | 11 | 52 | .249 | 680 | 51 | 3 | .996 |
| 1965 | Rochester y | Int. | 1B | 117 | 393 | 51 | 116 | 11 | 3 | 20 | 59 | .295 | 884 | 74 | 15 | .985 |
| 1966 | Rochester y | Int. | OF | 25 | 60 | 5 | 14 | 5 | 0 | 1 | 5 | .233 | 24 | 1 | 0 | 1.000 |
| 1967 | Elmira | East. | 1B | 3 | 7 | 0 | 1 | 0 | 0 | 0 | 2 | .143 | 17 | 2 | 0 | 1.000 |
| 1970 | Dal.-Ft. Worth | Tex. | 1B-P | 11 | 11 | 1 | 4 | 0 | 0 | 0 | 3 | .364 | 17 | 1 | 2 | .917 |
| | Major League Totals | | | 166 | 257 | 27 | 54 | 8 | 3 | 5 | 28 | .210 | 436 | 21 | 5 | .989 |

### RECORD AS PITCHER

| Year | Club | League | G. | IP. | W. | L. | Pct. | H. | R. | ER. | SO. | BB. | ERA. |
|------|------|--------|-----|-----|-----|-----|------|-----|-----|-----|-----|-----|------|
| 1970 | Dallas-Ft. Worth | Texas | 2 | 4 | 0 | 0 | .000 | 5 | 8 | 6 | 1 | 3 | 13.50 |

†Sold by Cleveland Indians' organization to Toronto (International) for a reported $20,000, January 13, 1959.
‡Traded to Los Angeles Dodgers' organization for Third Baseman Clyde Parris, April 1, 1960.
§Released outright by Minnesota Twins' organization to Los Angeles Dodgers' organization, October 12, 1961.
xOn disabled list, May 13 to May 29 and July 19 to August 14, 1963.
yPlayer-coach.

### RECORD AS MANAGER

| Year | Club | League | Position | W. | L. | Year | Club | League | Position | W. | L. |
|------|------|--------|----------|-----|-----|------|------|--------|----------|-----|-----|
| 1966 | Bluefield | Appal. | Third | 38 | 33 | 1971 | Rochester | Int. | †First | 86 | 54 |
| 1967 | Bluefield | Appal. | First | 42 | 25 | 1972 | Rochester | Int. | Fourth | 76 | 68 |
| 1968 | Stockton | Calif. | Seventh | 29 | 41 | 1973 | Rochester | Int. | ‡First (A) | 79 | 67 |
| | (Second Half) | | Second | 38 | 32 | 1974 | Rochester | Int. | §First (N) | 88 | 56 |
| 1969 | Dallas-Ft. Worth | Texas | Second (W) | 75 | 58 | 1975 | Rochester | Int. | Second | 85 | 56 |
| 1970 | Dallas-Ft. Worth | Texas | Third (W) | 63 | 73 | 1976 | Rochester | Int. | xFirst | 88 | 50 |

†Won playoffs by defeating Syracuse, three games to one and Tidewater, three games to two; won Junior World Series against Denver (American Association), four games to three.
‡Lost championship playoff to Charleston, three games to none.
§Won Governor's Cup by defeating Syracuse, four games to three, won League Championship by defeating Memphis, four games to two.
xLost semifinal playoff series to Richmond, three games to one.

## GEORGE LEE ANDERSON
### (Sparky)
### Cincinnati Reds

Born February 22, 1934, at Bridgewater, S. D.
Height, 5:09. Weight, 168.
Threw and batted righthanded.

Led California League shortstops in double plays with 83 in 1953.

Led Texas League second basemen in double plays with 117 in 1955, Pacific Coast League with 135 in 1957 and International League with 104 in 1958 and 89 in 1960.

Led Western League in sacrifice hits with 20 in 1954 and International League with 15 in 1960; tied for Texas League lead with 22 in 1955 and International League lead with 15 in 1960.

| Year Club League | Pos. | G. | AB. | R. | H. | 2B. | 3B. | HR. | RBI. | B.A. | PO. | A. | E. | F.A. |
|---|---|---|---|---|---|---|---|---|---|---|---|---|---|---|
| 1953–Santa Barbara ..Calif. | SS | •141 | •598 | 98 | 157 | 21 | 4 | 5 | 55 | .263 | •277 | 395 | 32 | .955 |
| 1954–Pueblo ..............West. | 2B | 147 | 497 | 72 | 147 | 13 | 5 | 0 | 62 | .296 | •397 | 432 | 20 | •.976 |
| 1955–Fort Worth .......Texas | 2B | 158 | 594 | 86 | 158 | 24 | 1 | 0 | 42 | .266 | •456 | •469 | 18 | •.981 |
| 1956–Montreal ..........Int. | 2B | 140 | 453 | 65 | 135 | 17 | 5 | 0 | 47 | .298 | 372 | 391 | 15 | .981 |
| 1957–Los Angeles ......P.C. | •2B-SS | •168 | 619 | 74 | 161 | 15 | 0 | 2 | 35 | .260 | •524 | •488 | •15 | •.985 |
| 1958–Montreal† .........Int. | 2B | •155 | 580 | 78 | 156 | 35 | 5 | 2 | 56 | .269 | •387 | •464 | 10 | .983 |
| 1959–Philadelphia ......Nat. | 2B | 152 | 477 | 42 | 104 | 9 | 3 | 0 | 34 | .218 | 343 | 403 | 12 | .984 |
| 1960–Toronto ............Int. | 2B | 148 | 543 | 67 | 123 | 11 | 5 | 5 | 21 | .227 | 319 | •416 | 12 | .984 |
| 1961–Toronto ............Int. | 2B | 97 | 275 | 30 | 66 | 17 | 0 | 0 | 22 | .240 | 189 | 203 | 6 | .985 |
| 1962–Toronto ............Int. | 2B | 124 | 432 | 56 | 111 | 18 | 2 | 2 | 38 | .257 | 282 | 327 | 8 | •.987 |
| 1963–Toronto ............Int. | 2B | 116 | 358 | 56 | 89 | 12 | 5 | 3 | 25 | .249 | 226 | 256 | 6 | •.988 |
| Major League Totals ..................... | | 152 | 477 | 42 | 104 | 9 | 3 | 0 | 34 | .218 | 343 | 403 | 12 | .984 |

†Recalled by Los Angeles Dodgers; traded to Philadelphia Phillies for Pitchers Jim Golden and Gene Snyder and Outfielder Eldon (Rip) Repulski, December 23, 1958.

## RECORD AS MANAGER

| Year Club League | Position | W. | L. | Year Club League | Position | W. | L. |
|---|---|---|---|---|---|---|---|
| 1964–Toronto ..............Int. | Fifth | 80 | 72 | 1968–Asheville ............South. | First | 86 | 54 |
| 1965–Rock Hill............W. Carol. | Eighth | 24 | 40 | 1970–Cincinnati .........Nat. | First (W) | 102 | 60 |
| (Second Half) | †First | 35 | 23 | 1971–Cincinnati .........Nat. | yFourth(W) | 79 | 83 |
| 1966–St. Petersburg ....Fla. St. | Second | 42 | 24 | 1972–Cincinnati .........Nat. | First(W) | 95 | 59 |
| (Second Half) | ‡First | 49 | 21 | 1973–Cincinnati .........Nat. | First(W) | 99 | 63 |
| 1967–Modesto ............Calif. | §Second | 38 | 32 | 1974–Cincinnati .........Nat. | Second(W) | 98 | 64 |
| (Second Half) | xFirst | 41 | 29 | 1975–Cincinnati .........Nat. | First(W) | 108 | 54 |
| | | | | 1976–Cincinnati .........Nat. | First(W) | 102 | 60 |

†Won playoff against Salisbury (First Half winner), two games to none.
‡Lost playoff against Leesburg (First Half winner), three games to two.
§Tied for position with Santa Barbara.
xLost playoff against San Jose (First Half winner), two games to none.
yTied for position with Houston Astros.
Coach, San Diego Padres, 1969.

## CHAMPIONSHIP SERIES RECORD

| Year Club League | W. | L. |
|---|---|---|
| 1970–Cincinnati ..........National | 3 | 0 |
| 1972–Cincinnati ..........National | 3 | 2 |
| 1973–Cincinnati ..........National | 2 | 3 |
| 1975–Cincinnati ..........National | 3 | 0 |
| 1976–Cincinnati ..........National | 3 | 0 |

## WORLD SERIES RECORD

| Year Club League | W. | L. |
|---|---|---|
| 1970–Cincinnati ..........National | 1 | 4 |
| 1972–Cincinnati ..........National | 3 | 4 |
| 1975–Cincinnati ..........National | 4 | 3 |
| 1976–Cincinnati ..........National | 4 | 0 |

## JAMES DAVID BRISTOL
### (Dave)
### Atlanta Braves

Born June 23, 1933, at Macon, Ga.
Height, 5.11. Weight, 175.
Threw and batted righthanded.
Hobbies–Bird hunting and golf.
Attended University of North Carolina, Chapel Hill, N. C., and Western Carolina College, Cullowhee, N. C.; received Bachelor of Science degree in Education.

Led New York-Pennsylvania League second basemen in double plays with 86 in 1958 and led Florida State League second basemen with 93 in 1960.

| Year Club League | Pos. | G. | AB. | R. | H. | 2B. | 3B. | HR. | RBI. | B.A. | PO. | A. | E. | F.A. |
|---|---|---|---|---|---|---|---|---|---|---|---|---|---|---|
| 1951–Welch...............Appal. | 2B | 64 | 270 | 55 | 73 | 12 | 3 | 0 | 22 | .270 | 136 | 172 | 22 | .933 |
| 1952–Ogden ..............Pion. | 2B | 73 | 285 | 39 | 67 | 5 | 5 | 1 | 26 | .235 | 182 | 176 | 22 | .942 |
| 1953–Ogden ..............Pion. | 2B | 55 | 220 | 32 | 57 | 10 | 5 | 2 | 37 | .259 | 125 | 145 | 6 | .978 |
| 1954–Columbia ..........Sally | | | | | (In Military Service) | | | | | | | | | |
| 1955–Sunbury ...........Pied. | 2B | 115 | 409 | 58 | 101 | 17 | 3 | 5 | 37 | .247 | 308 | 275 | 16 | .973 |
| 1956–W. Palm Beach Fla. St. | 3B | 117 | 441 | 72 | 121 | 21 | 6 | 4 | 57 | .274 | 127 | 188 | 32 | .908 |
| 1957–Wausau ............North. | 2-S-3 | 21 | 75 | 12 | 25 | 5 | 0 | 2 | 8 | .333 | 46 | 47 | 6 | .939 |
| 1957–Hornell .............NYP | 2B | 85 | 331 | 61 | 110 | 22 | 1 | 5 | 46 | .332 | 243 | 207 | 27 | .943 |
| 1958–Geneva.............NYP | 2B | 120 | 464 | 69 | 145 | 26 | 2 | 10 | 81 | .312 | •312 | 291 | 16 | •.974 |
| 1959–Visalia .............Calif. | 2B | 138 | 543 | 100 | 157 | 33 | 7 | 13 | 97 | .289 | •370 | 382 | •19 | .975 |
| 1960–Palatka ............Fla. St. | •2-1B | 137 | 499 | 97 | 147 | 26 | 2 | •15 | 95 | .295 | •427 | 321 | 15 | •.980 |
| 1961–Topeka ..............I.I.I. | INF-OF | 59 | 146 | 28 | 41 | 8 | 2 | 9 | 32 | .281 | 54 | 52 | 4 | .964 |

## PITCHING RECORD

| Year Club League | G. | IP. | W. | L. | Pct. | H. | R. | ER. | SO. | BB. | ERA. |
|---|---|---|---|---|---|---|---|---|---|---|---|
| 1957–Hornell ...................NYP | 1 | .... | 0 | 0 | .000 | .... | .... | .... | .... | .... | ....... |
| 1958–Geneva ...................NYP | 3 | .... | 0 | 0 | .000 | .... | .... | .... | .... | .... | ....... |
| 1959–Visalia ...................Calif. | 3 | .... | 0 | 0 | .000 | .... | .... | .... | .... | .... | ....... |
| 1960–Palatka .................Fla. St. | 6 | .... | 0 | 0 | .000 | .... | .... | .... | .... | .... | ....... |
| 1961–Topeka .....................I.I.I. | 1 | .... | 0 | 0 | .000 | .... | .... | .... | .... | .... | ....... |

## RECORD AS MANAGER

| Year Club | League | Position | W. | L. | Year Club | League | Position | W. | L. |
|---|---|---|---|---|---|---|---|---|---|
| 1957—Hornell ..............NYP | | Seventh | 38 | 59 | 1964—San Diego ..........P. C. | | §First(W) | 91 | 67 |
| 1958—Geneva ..............NYP | | †Second | 69 | 57 | 1965—San Diego ..........P. C. | | xThird(E) | 70 | 78 |
| 1959—Visalia ..............Calif. | | Fifth | 33 | 37 | 1966—Cincinnati y........Nat. | | Seventh | 39 | 36 |
| (Second Half) | | Fourth | 30 | 40 | 1967—Cincinnati ..........Nat. | | Fourth | 87 | 75 |
| 1960—Palatka ..............Fla. St. | | Second | 38 | 29 | 1968—Cincinnati ..........Nat. | | Fourth | 83 | 79 |
| (Second Half) | | ‡First | 43 | 27 | 1969—Cincinnati ..........Nat. | | Third(W) | 89 | 73 |
| 1961—Topeka ..............I.I.I. | | First | 79 | 50 | 1970—Milwaukee..........Amer. | | Fifth(W) | 65 | 97 |
| 1962—Macon ................Sally | | Third | 80 | 59 | 1971—Milwaukee..........Amer. | | Sixth(W) | 69 | 92 |
| 1963—Macon ................Sally | | Second | 39 | 27 | 1972—Milwaukee z ......Amer. | | Sixth(E) | 10 | 20 |
| (Second Half) | | Third | 42 | 32 | 1976—Atlanta ..............Nat. | | Sixth(W) | 70 | 92 |

†Won playoffs by defeating Olean, two games to none and Wellsville, three games to none.
‡Won playoff by defeating Lakeland (First Half winner), three games to one.
§Defeated Arkansas (Eastern Division champion) in playoffs, four games to three.
xTied for position.
yReplaced Don Heffner, July 13.
zReplaced by Del Crandall, May 27.
Coach, Cincinnati Reds, 1966, until named manager, July 13, 1966; Montreal Expos, 1973 through 1975.

## HERMAN LOUIS FRANKS
### Chicago Cubs

Born January 4, 1914, at Price, Utah.
Height, 5.11. Weight, 200.
Threw right and batted lefthanded.
Attended University of Utah, Salt Lake City, Utah.

| Year Club | League | Pos. | G. | AB. | R. | H. | 2B. | 3B. | HR. | RBI. | B.A. | PO. | A. | E. | F.A. |
|---|---|---|---|---|---|---|---|---|---|---|---|---|---|---|---|
| 1932—Hollywood ........P. C. | | C | 16 | 36 | 3 | 11 | 2 | 0 | 1 | 5 | .306 | 35 | 7 | 1 | .977 |
| 1933—Hollywood ........P. C. | | C | 4 | 8 | 1 | 3 | 0 | 0 | 1 | .... | 375 | 11 | 3 | 1 | .933 |
| 1934—Omaha ..............West. | | C | 2 | 3 | 1 | 1 | 0 | 1 | 0 | 1 | .333 | 4 | 0 | 1 | .833 |
| 1935—Jacksonville ......W. Dixie | | C | 128 | 482 | 55 | 137 | 24 | 1 | 6 | 83 | .284 | ★552 | ★119 | 12 | .982 |
| 1936—Houston ...........Tex. | | C | 97 | 312 | 33 | 81 | 12 | 8 | 5 | 48 | .260 | 436 | 70 | 16 | .969 |
| 1937—Houston ...........Tex. | | C | 10 | 23 | 3 | 3 | 1 | 0 | 0 | 3 | .130 | 34 | 5 | 1 | .975 |
| 1937—Sacramento ......P. C. | | C | 96 | 313 | 41 | 83 | 14 | 5 | 3 | 39 | .265 | 372 | 51 | 11 | .975 |
| 1938—Sacramento ......P. C. | | C | 143 | 470 | 55 | 129 | 29 | 3 | 9 | 67 | .274 | 557 | 82 | 7 | .898 |
| 1939—St. Louis ..........Nat. | | C | 17 | 17 | 1 | 1 | 0 | 0 | 0 | 3 | .059 | 34 | 2 | 1 | .973 |
| 1939—Columbus† ........A. A. | | C | 58 | 175 | 22 | 52 | 5 | 0 | 4 | 18 | .297 | 222 | 36 | 3 | .989 |
| 1940—Brooklyn .........Nat. | | C | 65 | 131 | 11 | 24 | 4 | 0 | 1 | 14 | .183 | 183 | 22 | 2 | .990 |
| 1941—Montreal .........Int. | | C | 46 | 120 | 17 | 35 | 9 | 1 | 4 | 18 | .292 | 216 | 27 | 2 | .992 |
| 1941—Brooklyn .........Nat. | | C | 57 | 139 | 10 | 28 | 7 | 0 | 1 | 11 | .201 | 191 | 21 | 3 | .986 |
| 1942—Montreal .........Int. | | C | 17 | 52 | 2 | 15 | 4 | 0 | 1 | 7 | .288 | 64 | 11 | 4 | .949 |
| 1942-45—Brooklyn ....Nat. | | | | | | (In Military Service) | | | | | | | | | |
| 1946—Montreal .........Int. | | C | 100 | 289 | 52 | 81 | 16 | 2 | 14 | 67 | .280 | 421 | 40 | 4 | .991 |
| 1947—St. Paul ...........A. A. | | C | 49 | 102 | 3 | 21 | 3 | 2 | 2 | 16 | .206 | 125 | 33 | 6 | .963 |
| 1947—Philadelphia ......Amer. | | C | 8 | 15 | 2 | 3 | 0 | 1 | 0 | 1 | .200 | 12 | 1 | 0 | 1.000 |
| 1948—Philadelphia‡ ....Amer. | | C | 40 | 98 | 10 | 22 | 7 | 1 | 1 | 14 | .224 | 113 | 17 | 3 | .977 |
| 1949—New York.........Nat. | | C | 1 | 3 | 1 | 2 | 0 | 0 | 0 | 0 | .667 | 4 | 1 | 0 | 1.000 |
| National League Totals ................. | | | 140 | 290 | 23 | 55 | 11 | 0 | 2 | 28 | .190 | 412 | 46 | 6 | .987 |
| American League Totals .............. | | | 48 | 113 | 12 | 25 | 7 | 2 | 1 | 15 | .221 | 125 | 18 | 3 | .979 |
| Major League Totals ...................... | | | 188 | 403 | 35 | 80 | 18 | 2 | 3 | 43 | .199 | 537 | 64 | 9 | .985 |

†Recalled by St. Louis Cardinals and sold to Brooklyn Dodgers, February 6, 1940.
‡Unconditionally released by Philadelphia Athletics at close of season.

## WORLD SERIES RECORD

| Year Club | League | Pos. | G. | AB. | R. | H. | 2B. | 3B. | HR. | RBI. | B.A. | PO. | A. | E. | F.A. |
|---|---|---|---|---|---|---|---|---|---|---|---|---|---|---|---|
| 1941—Brooklyn ..........Nat. | | C | 1 | 1 | 0 | 0 | 0 | 0 | 0 | 0 | .000 | 0 | 1 | 0 | 1.000 |

## RECORD AS MANAGER

| Year Club | League | Position | W. | L. |
|---|---|---|---|---|
| 1947—St. Paul† ...........A. A. | | Seventh | 52 | 74 |
| 1961—Salt Lake City‡ ..P. C. | | Eighth | 2 | 6 |
| 1965—San Francisco ....Nat. | | Second | 95 | 67 |
| 1966—San Francisco ....Nat. | | Second | 93 | 68 |
| 1967—San Francisco ....Nat. | | Second | 91 | 71 |
| 1968—San Francisco ....Nat. | | Second | 88 | 74 |

†Replaced as manager by Curt Davis when sold to Philadelphia Athletics, August 21, 1947.
‡Resigned as manager to devote full time to general manager's duties; replaced as manager by Freddy Fitzsimmons, April 30, with club in eighth place.
Coach, New York Giants, 1949 through 1955; scout, New York Giants, 1957; coach, San Francisco Giants, 1958; scout, San Francisco Giants, 1959-60; coach, San Francisco Giants, 1964; coach, Chicago Cubs, part of 1970.

---

## *DID YOU KNOW —*

That Frank Frisch, the Fordham Flash, had a lifetime batting average of .316? He played in the National League from 1919 to 1937. He never spent a day in the minors.

# JOSEPH FILMORE FRAZIER
## (Joe)
## New York Mets

Born October 6, 1923, at Liberty, N. C.
Height, 6.00. Weight, 181.
Threw right and batted lefthanded.
Hobbies—Hunting, fishing and golf.

Led Texas League in total bases with 307 in 1953.
Named Texas League Player of the Year in 1953.
Named Minor League Manager of the Year by THE SPORTING NEWS, 1975.

| Year | Club | League | Pos. | G. | AB. | R. | H. | 2B. | 3B. | HR. | RBI. | B.A. | PO. | A. | E. | F.A. |
|---|---|---|---|---|---|---|---|---|---|---|---|---|---|---|---|---|
| 1941—Leaksville | ........Bi.St. | | 3B | 110 | 463 | 96 | 143 | 31 | 11 | 10 | 55 | .309 | 132 | 222 | •40 | .898 |
| 1942—Cedar Rapids | ....III | | O-SS-3 | 116 | 444 | 89 | 140 | •35 | 3 | 8 | 71 | .315 | 182 | 118 | 30 | .909 |
| 1943-44-45—W.-Barre | ..East. | | | | | | (In Military Service) | | | | | | | | | |
| 1946—Wilkes-Barre | ....East. | | OF | 135 | 503 | 82 | 151 | 25 | 8 | 5 | 91 | .300 | 223 | 16 | 7 | .972 |
| 1947—Okla. City | .........Tex. | | OF-2B | 133 | 471 | 69 | 130 | 27 | 5 | 5 | 66 | .276 | 214 | 24 | 7 | .971 |
| 1947—Cleveland† | ........Amer. | | OF | 9 | 14 | 1 | 1 | 1 | 0 | 0 | 0 | .071 | 6 | 0 | 1 | .857 |
| 1948—San Antonio | ......Tex. | | OF | 139 | 472 | 86 | 126 | 24 | 8 | 9 | 57 | .267 | 250 | 11 | 8 | .970 |
| 1949—Baltimore | ..........Int. | | OF | 23 | 80 | 9 | 14 | 1 | 1 | 0 | 5 | .175 | 34 | 1 | 2 | .946 |
| 1949—San Antonio | .....Tex. | | OF | 120 | 405 | 65 | 117 | 26 | 8 | 11 | 64 | .289 | 213 | 15 | 9 | .962 |
| 1950—San Antonio | .....Tex. | | OF | 133 | 487 | 88 | 129 | 27 | 3 | 12 | 67 | .265 | 251 | 13 | 4 | .985 |
| 1951—San Antonio | .....Tex. | | OF-1B | 25 | 73 | 14 | 17 | 3 | 1 | 1 | 12 | .233 | 44 | 0 | 3 | .936 |
| 1951—Memphis | .........South. | | OF | 113 | 394 | 67 | 106 | 26 | 6 | 13 | 86 | .269 | 217 | 9 | 5 | .978 |
| 1952—Okla. City | .........Tex. | | OF | 156 | 574 | 82 | 169 | •48 | 1 | 14 | 93 | .294 | 321 | 15 | 10 | .971 |
| 1953—Okla. City‡ | ........Tex. | | OF | 152 | 548 | •109 | 182 | •55 | 2 | 22 | 113 | •.332 | 290 | 16 | 6 | .981 |
| 1954—St. Louis | .........Nat. | | OF-1B | 81 | 88 | 8 | 26 | 5 | 2 | 3 | 18 | .295 | 16 | 1 | 1 | .944 |
| 1955—St. Louis | .........Nat. · | | OF | 58 | 70 | 12 | 14 | 1 | 0 | 4 | 9 | .200 | 16 | 0 | 0 | 1.000 |
| 1956—St. L.§-Cinn.x | ...Nat. | | OF | 24 | 36 | 3 | 8 | 2 | 0 | 2 | 6 | .222 | 4 | 0 | 1 | .800 |
| 1956—Baltimore | .........Amer. | | OF | 45 | 74 | 7 | 19 | 6 | 0 | 1 | 12 | .257 | 31 | 2 | 0 | 1.000 |
| 1957—Vancouver | ........P.C. | | OF | 147 | 471 | 62 | 121 | 23 | 2 | 15 | 72 | .257 | 248 | 12 | 3 | .989 |
| 1958—Vancouver | ........P.C. | | OF-P | 117 | 357 | 55 | 98 | 13 | 0 | 14 | 70 | .275 | 178 | 4 | 3 | .984 |
| 1959—Vancouver y | ........P.C. | | OF | 101 | 293 | 28 | 64 | 12 | 0 | 4 | 25 | .219 | 117 | 6 | 5 | .961 |
| 1960—Spokane | ............P.C. | | OF-P | 56 | 100 | 6 | 21 | 2 | 0 | 0 | 8 | .210 | 26 | 2 | 2 | .933 |
| American League Totals | ................ | | | 54 | 88 | 8 | 20 | 7 | 0 | 1 | 12 | .227 | 37 | 2 | 1 | .975 |
| National League Totals | ................. | | | 163 | 194 | 23 | 48 | 8 | 2 | 9 | 33 | .247 | 36 | 1 | 2 | .949 |
| Major League Totals | ..................... | | | 217 | 282 | 31 | 68 | 15 | 2 | 10 | 45 | .241 | 73 | 3 | 3 | .962 |

†Traded to St. Louis Browns with Pitcher Bryan Stephens, Outfielder Dick Kokos and reported $25,000 for Pitcher Bob Muncrief and Outfielder Walt Judnich, November 20, 1947.
‡Traded to St. Louis Cardinals for Catcher Les Fusselman and cash, October 12, 1953.
§Traded to Cincinnati Reds with Shortstop Alex Grammas for Infielder Chuck Harmon, May 16, 1956.
xReleased on waivers to Baltimore Orioles, June 26, 1956.
yOn disabled list, June 8 to June 18, 1959.

## PITCHING RECORD

| Year | Club | League | G. | IP. | W. | L. | Pct. | H. | R. | ER. | SO. | BB. | ERA. |
|---|---|---|---|---|---|---|---|---|---|---|---|---|---|
| 1958—Vancouver | ............................P.C. | | 1 | .... | 0 | 0 | .000 | .... | .... | .... | .... | .... | ....... |
| 1960—Spokane | .............................P.C. | | 4 | .... | 0 | 1 | .000 | .... | .... | .... | .... | .... | ....... |

## RECORD AS MANAGER

| Year | Club | League | Position | W. | L. |
|---|---|---|---|---|---|
| 1965—Brad'ton Astros | ..Fla. Rookie | First | 36 | 21 |
| 1966—Cocoa | ...............Fla. St. | Third | 39 | 26 |
| (Second Half) | | Fourth | 42 | 29 |
| 1968—Mankato | ...........Northern | Second | 42 | 27 |
| 1969—Pompano B'ch | ....Fla. St. | †Third(E) | 67 | 63 |
| 1970—Visalia | ...........Calif. | Sixth | 33 | 37 |
| (Second Half) | | Sixth | 33 | 37 |
| 1971—Visalia | ..............Calif. | †Third | 35 | 34 |
| (Second Half) | | ‡First | 46 | 24 |
| 1972—Visalia | ..............Calif. | Fifth | 33 | 37 |
| (Second Half) | | †Second | 40 | 30 |
| 1973—Memphis | ...........Texas | §First(E) | 77 | 61 |
| 1974—Victoria | ..............Texas | xFirst(E) | 79 | 57 |
| 1975—Tidewater | ..........Int. | yFirst | 86 | 55 |
| 1976—New York | ..........Nat. | Third(E) | 86 | 76 |

†Tied for position.
‡Won playoff against Fresno (First Half winner), two games to none.
§Won playoff against San Antonio, three games to two.
xWon playoff against El Paso, three games to none.
yWon league championship by defeating Rochester in one-game playoff, 8-0. Won playoffs by defeating Charleston, three games to none and Syracuse, three games to one. Lost Junior World Series to Evansville (American Association), four games to one.
Scout, Houston Colt .45s, 1961 through 1964; Batting Instructor, Houston Astros, 1967.

# ALEXANDER PETER GRAMMAS
Name pronounced GRAMM-uss.
## (Alex)
## Milwaukee Brewers

Born April 3, 1927, at Birmingham, Ala.
Height, 6.00. Weight, 176.
Threw and batted righthanded.
Hobby—Fishing.
Attended Mississippi State University, State College, Miss.;
received Bachelor of Science degree in Business.

| Year Club League | Pos. | G. | AB. | R. | H. | 2B. | 3B. | HR. | RBI. | B.A. | PO. | A. | E. | F.A. |
|---|---|---|---|---|---|---|---|---|---|---|---|---|---|---|
| 1949—Muskegon ..........Cent. | 3B | 87 | 294 | 42 | 96 | 12 | 3 | 0 | 30 | .327 | 120 | 217 | 24 | .934 |
| 1950—Memphis .........South. | *SS-3B | 135 | 457 | 49 | 102 | 16 | 6 | 1 | 41 | .223 | 247 | 381 | 24 | *.963 |
| 1951—Memphis .........South. | 3B | 52 | 185 | 35 | 47 | 6 | 1 | 2 | 16 | .254 | 54 | 88 | 12 | .922 |
| 1951—Tulsa ................Tex. | SS-3B | 88 | 302 | 29 | 83 | 10 | 3 | 2 | 32 | .275 | 146 | 256 | 27 | .937 |
| 1952—Tulsa ................Tex. | SS-2B | 158 | 602 | 80 | 146 | 28 | 9 | 2 | 51 | .243 | 314 | 536 | 37 | .958 |
| 1953—Kansas City† ....A.A. | SS | 140 | 584 | 93 | 179 | 29 | 3 | 2 | 62 | .307 | *262 | *438 | 24 | .967 |
| 1954—St. Louis .........Nat. | SS-3B | 142 | 401 | 57 | 106 | 17 | 4 | 2 | 29 | .264 | 253 | 432 | 24 | .966 |
| 1955—St. Louis .........Nat. | 3B | 128 | 366 | 32 | 88 | 19 | 2 | 3 | 25 | .240 | 235 | 340 | 19 | .968 |
| 1956—St. L.‡-Cinn. ......Nat. | 3-S-2 | 83 | 152 | 18 | 37 | 11 | 0 | 0 | 17 | .243 | 60 | 105 | 5 | .971 |
| 1957—Cincinnati.........Nat. | S-2-3 | 73 | 99 | 14 | 30 | 4 | 0 | 0 | 8 | .303 | 60 | 75 | 3 | .978 |
| 1958—Cincinnati§.......Nat. | S-3-2 | 105 | 216 | 25 | 47 | 8 | 0 | 0 | 12 | .218 | 125 | 174 | 6 | .980 |
| 1959—St. Louis .........Nat. | SS | 131 | 368 | 43 | 99 | 14 | 2 | 3 | 30 | .269 | 216 | 373 | 22 | .964 |
| 1960—St. Louis .........Nat. | S-2-3 | 102 | 196 | 20 | 48 | 4 | 1 | 4 | 17 | .245 | 102 | 171 | 9 | .968 |
| 1961—St. Louis .........Nat. | S-2-3 | 89 | 170 | 23 | 36 | 10 | 1 | 0 | 21 | .212 | 112 | 182 | 10 | .967 |
| 1962—St. L.x-Chi........Nat. | S-2-3 | 44 | 78 | 3 | 16 | 3 | 0 | 0 | 4 | .205 | 34 | 66 | 2 | .980 |
| 1963—Chicago ............Nat. | SS | 16 | 27 | 1 | 5 | 0 | 0 | 0 | 0 | .185 | 8 | 13 | 1 | .955 |
| Major League Totals .................... | | 913 | 2073 | 236 | 512 | 90 | 10 | 12 | 163 | .247 | 1206 | 1931 | 101 | .969 |

†On option to Kansas City by Cincinnati Reds; Traded to St. Louis Cardinals for Pitcher Jack Crimian and reported $100,000, December 2, 1953.

‡Traded to Cincinnati Redlegs with Outfielder Joe Frazier for Infielder Chuck Harmon, May 16, 1956.

§Traded to St. Louis Cardinals with Pitcher Alex Kellner and First Baseman George Crowe for Pitcher Bobby Mabe, Shortstop Eddie Kasko and Outfielder Del Ennis, October 3, 1958.

xTraded to Chicago Cubs with Outfielder Don Landrum for Infielder Daryl Robertson and Outfielder Bobby Gene Smith, June 5, 1962.

### RECORD AS MANAGER

| Year Club | League | Position | W. | L. |
|---|---|---|---|---|
| 1964—Ft. Worth ..........Texas | | Sixth | 51 | 89 |
| 1969—Pittsburgh† ........Nat. | | Third(E) | 4 | 1 |
| 1976—Milwaukee..........Amer. | | Sixth(E) | 66 | 95 |

†Replaced Larry Shepard, September 26.

Coach, Pittsburgh Pirates, 1965 through 1969; Cincinnati Reds, 1970 through 1975.

## ROY THOMAS HARTSFIELD
### Toronto Blue Jays

Born October 25, 1925, at Chattahoochee, Ga.
Height, 5.09. Weight, 165.
Threw and batted righthanded.
Brother of Robert Hartsfield, former infielder in Atlanta Braves'
system and now manager of Bradenton Cubs of the Gulf Coast League.

Led Texas League batters in strikeouts with 121 in 1948.
Led American Association second basemen in double plays with 125 in 1949 and 113 in 1955.

| Year Club League | Pos. | G. | AB. | R. | H. | 2B. | 3B. | HR. | RBI. | B.A. | PO. | A. | E. | F.A. |
|---|---|---|---|---|---|---|---|---|---|---|---|---|---|---|
| 1954—Fort Worth ........Texas | 2B | 83 | 297 | 38 | 83 | 21 | 3 | 7 | 33 | .280 | 195 | 184 | 11 | .972 |
| 1943—Atlanta..............So. | *SS-3-OF | 136 | 502 | 62 | 133 | 17 | 2 | 1 | 38 | .265 | 227 | 370 | *65 | .902 |
| 1944-45—Atlanta ........South. | | | | | (In Military Service) | | | | | | | | | |
| 1946—Atlanta..............South. | SS | 2 | 6 | 3 | 0 | 0 | 0 | 0 | 1 | .000 | 2 | 3 | 1 | .833 |
| 1946—Charleston ........Sally | 2B | 108 | 414 | 72 | 105 | 14 | 5 | 5 | 39 | .254 | 254 | 272 | 46 | .920 |
| 1947—Atlanta..............South. | 2B | 13 | 40 | 7 | 12 | 2 | 0 | 0 | 2 | .300 | 23 | 31 | 3 | .947 |
| 1947—Charleston ........Sally | 2B | 131 | 551 | 97 | 156 | 36 | 9 | 6 | 59 | .283 | 348 | 436 | *53 | .937 |
| 1948—Dallas ..............Tex. | 2B | 148 | 601 | 97 | 150 | 29 | 3 | 16 | 58 | .250 | 416 | 407 | 40 | .954 |
| 1949—Milwaukee .......A. A. | 2B | •154 | *640 | 120 | *203 | 27 | 8 | 12 | 86 | .317 | *471 | *537 | *37 | .965 |
| 1950—Boston .............Nat. | 2B | 107 | 419 | 62 | 116 | 15 | 2 | 7 | 24 | .277 | 236 | 247 | *26 | .949 |
| 1951—Boston .............Nat. | 2B | 120 | 450 | 63 | 122 | 11 | 2 | 6 | 31 | .271 | 336 | 293 | 20 | .969 |
| 1952—Boston .............Nat. | 2B | 38 | 107 | 13 | 28 | 4 | 3 | 0 | 4 | .262 | 61 | 73 | 7 | .950 |
| 1952—Milwaukee .......A. A. | 2B | 23 | 84 | 15 | 20 | 3 | 1 | 1 | 5 | .238 | 57 | 55 | 5 | .957 |
| 1952—Baltimore .........Int. | 2B | 55 | 219 | 26 | 49 | 5 | 1 | 2 | 17 | .224 | 135 | 144 | 10 | .965 |
| 1953—Montreal ..........Int. | 2B | 135 | 538 | 74 | 125 | 30 | 8 | 3 | 46 | .232 | 276 | 395 | 18 | .974 |
| 1954—Montreal ..........Int. | 2B | 34 | 104 | 15 | 19 | 6 | 0 | 0 | 8 | .183 | 69 | 85 | 10 | .939 |
| 1954—Fort Worth ........Texas | 3B | 83 | 297 | 38 | 83 | 21 | 3 | 7 | 33 | .280 | 71 | 162 | 11 | .962 |
| 1955—St. Paul ..........A. A. | 2B | 145 | 564 | 90 | 146 | 21 | 5 | 26 | 85 | .259 | •347 | *429 | 22 | .972 |
| 1956—St. Paul ..........A. A. | 2B-OF | 140 | 502 | 66 | 144 | 24 | 3 | 19 | 80 | .287 | 250 | 316 | 15 | .974 |
| 1957—Los Angeles ......P. C. | 3B-OF | 149 | 459 | 63 | 129 | 24 | 2 | 7 | 63 | .281 | 113 | 178 | 18 | .942 |
| 1958—Des Moines ......West. | 2B | 102 | 281 | 45 | 78 | 17 | 5 | 3 | 34 | .281 | 141 | 177 | 14 | .958 |
| 1958—Des Moines .....West. | 2B | 102 | 281 | 45 | 79 | 17 | 5 | 3 | 34 | .281 | 141 | 177 | 14 | .958 |
| 1960—Panama City .....Ala.-Fl. | PH | 9 | 9 | 1 | 1 | 0 | 0 | 0 | 0 | .111 | 0 | 0 | 0 | .000 |
| Major League Totals .................... | | 265 | 976 | 138 | 266 | 30 | 7 | 13 | 59 | .273 | 633 | 613 | 53 | .959 |

### RECORD AS MANAGER

| Year Club League | Position | W. | L. | Year Club League | Position | W. | L. |
|---|---|---|---|---|---|---|---|
| 1958—Des Moines ........West. | Eighth | 61 | 83 | 1965—Albuquerque ......Texas | First | 77 | 63 |
| 1959—Odessa ..............Soph. | Third(S) | 54 | 69 | 1966—Spokane ............P. C. | Third(W) | 75 | 73 |
| 1960—Panama City ......Ala.-Fla. | First | 74 | 44 | 1967—Spokane ............P. C. | †First(W) | 80 | 68 |
| 1961—Greenville .........Sally | Third | 72 | 66 | 1968—Spokane ............P. C. | ‡First(W) | 85 | 60 |
| 1962—Greenville .........Sally | Fifth | 65 | 75 | 1973—Hawaii ..............P. C. | §Second(W) | 70 | 74 |
| 1963—St. Petersburg ....Fla. St. | Second | 33 | 27 | 1974—Hawaii ..............P. C. | Third(W) | 67 | 77 |
| (Second Half) | Fifth | 31 | 50 | 1975—Hawaii ..............P. C. | xFirst(W) | 88 | 56 |
| 1964—St. Petersburg ....Fla. St. | Second | 42 | 27 | 1976—Hawaii ..............P. C. | yFirst(W) | 77 | 68 |
| (Second Half) | First | 41 | 28 | | | | |

†Lost Championship playoff to San Diego, four games to two.
‡Lost Championship playoff to Tulsa, four games to one.
§Replaced Rocky Bridges, May 20, with club in fourth place.
xWon Championship playoff by defeating Salt Lake City, four games to two.
yWon Championship playoff by defeating Salt Lake City, three games to two.
Coach, Los Angeles Dodgers, 1969-72; Atlanta Braves, 1973.

## DORREL NORMAN ELVERT HERZOG
### (Relly and Whitey)
(Named "Relly" by mother from his first name; "Whitey" by Bill Speith, McAlester sportscaster, because of light hair.)
### KANSAS CITY ROYALS
Born November 9, 1931, at New Athens, Ill.
Height, 5.11½. Weight, 187
Threw and batted lefthanded.

| Year | Club | League | Pos. | G. | AB. | R. | H. | 2B. | 3B. | HR. | RBI. | B.A. | PO. | A. | E. | F.A. |
|---|---|---|---|---|---|---|---|---|---|---|---|---|---|---|---|---|
| 1949—McAlester | | Soo. St. | OF | 96 | 398 | 53 | 111 | 19 | 7 | 0 | 31 | .279 | 22 | 14 | 0 | •1.000 |
| 1950—McAlester | | Soo. St. | OF | 132 | 467 | 107 | 164 | 36 | 10 | 4 | 85 | .351 | 272 | 15 | 7 | •.976 |
| 1951—Norfolk | | Pied. | OF | 5 | 17 | 5 | 1 | 0 | 0 | 0 | 2 | .059 | 13 | 0 | 1 | .926 |
| 1951—Joplin | | W.A. | OF-1B | 113 | 418 | 99 | 119 | 14 | 8 | 7 | 48 | .285 | 454 | 19 | 9 | .981 |
| 1952—Beaumont | | Texas | OF | 35 | 121 | 11 | 24 | 4 | 1 | 0 | 9 | .198 | 83 | 3 | 5 | .945 |
| 1952—Quincy | | I.I.I. | OF | 68 | 225 | 53 | 65 | 9 | 6 | 7 | 44 | .289 | 131 | 9 | 5 | .966 |
| 1952—Kansas City | | A.A. | OF-1B | 14 | 27 | 5 | 8 | 1 | 0 | 1 | 5 | .296 | 21 | 1 | 1 | .957 |
| 1953-54 | | | | | | | | (In MIlitary Service.) | | | | | | | | |
| 1955—Denver† | | A.A. | OF-1B | 149 | 515 | 101 | 149 | 24 | 7 | 21 | 98 | .289 | 324 | 10 | 4 | .988 |
| 1956—Washington | | Amer. | OF-1B | 117 | 421 | 49 | 103 | 13 | 7 | 4 | 35 | .245 | 274 | 10 | 7 | .976 |
| 1957—Washington | | Amer. | OF | 36 | 78 | 7 | 13 | 3 | 0 | 0 | 4 | .167 | 53 | 0 | 1 | .981 |
| 1957—Miami | | Int. | OF | 77 | 257 | 48 | 70 | 14 | 5 | 2 | 25 | .272 | 114 | 5 | 4 | .967 |
| 1958—Wash.‡-K. C. | | Amer. | OF-1B | 96 | 101 | 11 | 23 | 1 | 2 | 0 | 9 | .228 | 146 | 6 | 3 | .981 |
| 1959—Kansas City | | Amer. | OF-1B | 38 | 123 | 25 | 36 | 7 | 1 | 1 | 9 | .293 | 87 | 2 | 3 | .967 |
| 1960—Kansas City§ | | Amer. | OF-1B | 83 | 252 | 43 | 67 | 10 | 2 | 8 | 38 | .266 | 137 | 6 | 4 | .973 |
| 1961—Baltimore | | Amer. | OF | 113 | 323 | 39 | 94 | 11 | 6 | 5 | 35 | .291 | 143 | 2 | 0 | 1.000 |
| 1962—Baltimore x | | Amer. | OF | 99 | 263 | 34 | 70 | 13 | 1 | 7 | 35 | .266 | 132 | 4 | 3 | .978 |
| 1963—Detroit | | Amer. | 1B-OF | 52 | 53 | 5 | 8 | 2 | 1 | 0 | 7 | .151 | 44 | 1 | 1 | .978 |
| Major League Totals | | | | 634 | 1614 | 213 | 414 | 60 | 20 | 25 | 172 | .257 | 1016 | 31 | 22 | .979 |

†Traded to Washington Senators with Pitcher Bob Wiesler, Catcher Lou Berberet, Second Baseman Herb Plews and Outfielder Dick Tettelbach for pitcher Maury McDermott and Shortstop Bob Kline (assigned to the Yankees' American Association farm club—Denver). Other players in deal assigned February 8, 1956; Herzog, April 2, 1956.
‡Sold to Kansas City Athletics, May 14, 1958.
§Traded to Baltimore Orioles with Outfielder Russ Snyder and a player to be named at later date, for Pitcher Jim Archer, Catcher Clint Courtney, First Baseman Bob Boyd, Infielder Wayne Causey and Outfielder Al Pilarcik, January 24, 1961; Courtney returned to the Orioles, April 15, 1961, to complete deal.
xTraded to Detroit Tigers with Catcher Gus Triandos for Catcher Dick Brown, November 26, 1962.

### RECORD AS MANAGER

| Year | Club | League | Position | W. | L. |
|---|---|---|---|---|---|
| 1973—Texas | | Amer. | †Sixth(W) | 47 | 91 |
| 1974—California‡ | | Amer. | Sixth(W) | 2 | 2 |
| 1975—Kansas City§ | | Amer. | Second(W) | 41 | 25 |
| 1976—Kansas City | | Amer. | First(W) | 90 | 72 |

†Replaced by interim manager Del Wilber, September 7.
‡Served as interim manager, June 27 through June 30 after Dick Williams replaced Bobby Winkles, June 26.
§Replaced Jack McKeon, July 24.
Scout, Kansas City Athletics, 1964.
Coach, Kansas City Athletics, 1965; New York Mets, 1966; California Angels, 1974 and part of 1975.
Director of Player Development, New York Mets, 1967 through 1972.

### CHAMPIONSHIP SERIES RECORD

| Year | Club | League | W. | L. |
|---|---|---|---|---|
| 1976—Kansas City | | Amer. | 2 | 3 |

## RALPH GEORGE HOUK
### Detroit Tigers
Born August 9, 1919, at Lawrence, Kan.
Height, 5.11. Weight, 198.
Threw and batted righthanded.
Hobbies—Hunting and fishing.
Named Major League Manager of the Year by THE SPORTING NEWS, 1961.

| Year | Club | League | Pos. | G. | AB. | R. | H. | 2B. | 3B. | HR. | RBI. | B.A. | PO. | A. | E. | F.A. |
|---|---|---|---|---|---|---|---|---|---|---|---|---|---|---|---|---|
| 1939—Neosho | | Ak.Mo. | C | 119 | 427 | 69 | 122 | 15 | 6 | 1 | 56 | .286 | 634 | •79 | 13 | •.982 |
| 1940—Joplin | | W.A. | C | 110 | 364 | 53 | 114 | 18 | 7 | 0 | 63 | .313 | 517 | 78 | 10 | •.983 |
| 1941—Binghamton | | East. | C | 5 | 9 | 3 | 3 | 0 | 0 | 0 | 0 | .333 | 9 | 1 | 1 | .909 |
| 1941—Augusta | | Sally | C | 97 | 340 | 37 | 92 | 11 | 5 | 1 | 48 | .271 | 542 | 62 | 12 | .981 |
| 1942-45—Bing'ton | | East. | | | | | (In Military Service) | | | | | | | | | |
| 1946—Kansas City | | A.A. | C | 8 | 23 | 5 | 8 | 2 | 0 | 1 | 1 | .348 | 28 | 5 | 0 | 1.000 |

— 424 —

| Year Club | League | Pos. | G. | AB. | R. | H. | 2B. | 3B. | HR. | RBI. | B.A. | PO. | A. | E. | F.A. |
|---|---|---|---|---|---|---|---|---|---|---|---|---|---|---|---|
| 1946–Beaumont..........Tex. | | C-OF | 87 | 279 | 38 | 82 | 20 | 2 | 0 | 40 | .294 | 297 | 45 | 9 | .974 |
| 1947–New York.........Amer. | | C | 41 | 92 | 7 | 25 | 3 | 1 | 0 | 12 | .272 | 138 | 13 | 2 | .987 |
| 1948–Kansas City ......A.A. | | •C-3B | 103 | 364 | 54 | 110 | 24 | 5 | 1 | 49 | .302 | 464 | •72 | 7 | .987 |
| 1948–New York.........Amer. | | C | 14 | 29 | 3 | 8 | 2 | 0 | 0 | 3 | .276 | 41 | 5 | 0 | 1.000 |
| 1949–New York.........Amer. | | C | 5 | 7 | 0 | 4 | 0 | 0 | 0 | 1 | .571 | 8 | 0 | 1 | .889 |
| 1949–Kansas City ......A.A. | | C | 95 | 313 | 47 | 86 | 18 | 1 | 0 | 36 | .275 | 398 | 48 | 7 | .985 |
| 1950–New York.........Amer. | | C | 10 | 9 | 0 | 1 | 1 | 0 | 0 | 1 | .111 | 12 | 1 | 1 | .929 |
| 1951–New York.........Amer. | | C | 3 | 5 | 0 | 1 | 0 | 0 | 0 | 2 | .200 | 2 | 1 | 0 | 1.000 |
| 1952–New York.........Amer. | | C | 9 | 6 | 0 | 2 | 0 | 0 | 0 | 0 | .333 | 10 | 1 | 1 | .917 |
| 1953–New York.........Amer. | | C | 8 | 9 | 2 | 2 | 0 | 0 | 0 | 1 | .222 | 10 | 0 | 0 | 1.000 |
| 1954–New York.........Amer. | | PH | 1 | 1 | 0 | 0 | 0 | 0 | 0 | 0 | .000 | 0 | 0 | 0 | .000 |
| 1955–Denver ...........A.A. | | C | 15 | 26 | 1 | 4 | 3 | 0 | 0 | 4 | .154 | 33 | 1 | 3 | .919 |
| 1956–Denver .............A.A. | | C | 1 | 4 | 0 | 0 | 0 | 0 | 0 | 0 | .000 | 7 | 1 | 0 | 1.000 |
| Major League Totals ..................... | | | 91 | 158 | 12 | 43 | 6 | 1 | 0 | 20 | .272 | 221 | 21 | 5 | .980 |

## WORLD SERIES RECORD

| Year Club | League | Pos. | G. | AB. | R. | H. | 2B. | 3B. | HR. | RBI. | B.A. | PO. | A. | E. | F.A. |
|---|---|---|---|---|---|---|---|---|---|---|---|---|---|---|---|
| 1947–New York.........Amer. | | PH | 1 | 1 | 0 | 1 | 0 | 0 | 0 | 0 | 1.000 | 0 | 0 | 0 | .000 |
| 1952–New York.........Amer. | | PH | 1 | 1 | 0 | 0 | 0 | 0 | 0 | 0 | .000 | 0 | 0 | 0 | .000 |
| World Series Totals ..................... | | | 2 | 2 | 0 | 1 | 0 | 0 | 0 | 0 | .500 | 0 | 0 | 0 | .000 |

## RECORD AS MANAGER

| Year Club | League | Position | W. | L. | Year Club | League | Position | W. | L. |
|---|---|---|---|---|---|---|---|---|---|
| 1955–Denver ..............A.A. | | †Third | 83 | 71 | 1969–New York ..........Amer. | | Fifth(E) | 80 | 81 |
| 1956–Denver ..............A.A. | | Second | 87 | 67 | 1970–New York ..........Amer. | | Second(E) | 93 | 69 |
| 1957–Denver ..............A.A. | | ‡Second | 90 | 64 | 1971–New York ..........Amer. | | Fourth(E) | 82 | 80 |
| 1961–New York .........Amer. | | First | 109 | 53 | 1972–New York ..........Amer. | | Fourth(E) | 79 | 76 |
| 1962–New York .........Amer. | | First | 96 | 66 | 1973–New York ..........Amer. | | Fourth(E) | 80 | 82 |
| 1963–New York .........Amer. | | First | 104 | 57 | 1974–Detroit ..............Amer. | | Sixth(E) | 72 | 90 |
| 1966–New York§ ........Amer. | | Tenth | 66 | 73 | 1975–Detroit ..............Amer. | | Sixth(E) | 57 | 102 |
| 1967–New York .........Amer. | | Ninth | 72 | 90 | 1976–Detroit ..............Amer. | | Fifth(E) | 74 | 87 |
| 1968–New York .........Amer. | | Fifth | 83 | 79 | | | | | |

†Tied for position.

‡Won playoffs by defeating Minneapolis, four games to none and St. Paul, four games to two; won Junior World Series against Buffalo (International League), four games to one.

§Replaced Johnny Keane, May 7.

Coach, New York Yankees, part of 1953 and 1954 seasons and 1958 through 1960; vice-president-general manager, New York Yankees, 1964 through May 6, 1966.

## WORLD SERIES RECORD

| Year Club | League | W. | L. |
|---|---|---|---|
| 1961–New York ..........American | | 4 | 1 |
| 1962–New York ..........American | | 4 | 3 |
| 1963–New York ..........American | | 0 | 4 |

## DARRELL DEAN JOHNSON
### Seattle Mariners

Born August 25, 1927, at Ord, Neb.
Height, 6.01. Weight, 190.
Threw and batted righthanded.
Hobbies–Hunting and golf.

Tied for American Association lead in double plays by catchers with 11 in 1956 and tied for International League lead with 11 in 1959.

Named Major League Manager of the Year by THE SPORTING NEWS, 1975.

| Year Club | League | Pos. | G. | AB. | R. | H. | 2B. | 3B. | HR. | RBI. | B.A. | PO. | A. | E. | F.A. |
|---|---|---|---|---|---|---|---|---|---|---|---|---|---|---|---|
| 1949–Redding ...........F. West | | C-O | 88 | 322 | 60 | 89 | 19 | 1 | 9 | 58 | .276 | 589 | 60 | 17 | .974 |
| 1950–Marshall...........E. Tex. | | •C-O | 131 | 493 | 77 | 162 | •36 | 9 | 13 | 105 | .329 | •608 | 79 | 15 | •.979 |
| 1951–San Antonio ......Tex. | | C-OF | 49 | 169 | 23 | 45 | 8 | 1 | 3 | 24 | .266 | 200 | 32 | 4 | .983 |
| 1951–Wichita Falls ....Big St. | | C-OF | 71 | 288 | 47 | 89 | 11 | 2 | 2 | 38 | .309 | 275 | 62 | 10 | .971 |
| 1952–San Antonio ......Tex. | | C-OF | 24 | 83 | 9 | 27 | 3 | 0 | 3 | 15 | .325 | 106 | 12 | 2 | .983 |
| 1952–St. Louis‡-Chi. ..Amer. | | C | 51 | 115 | 12 | 26 | 2 | 1 | 0 | 10 | .226 | 161 | 23 | 5 | .974 |
| 1953–Memphis‡ ........South. | | C | 113 | 370 | 50 | 92 | 15 | 1 | 4 | 44 | .249 | 506 | 61 | 12 | .979 |
| 1954–Richmond§ ........Int. | | C | 90 | 291 | 32 | 76 | 10 | 0 | 6 | 37 | .261 | 377 | 54 | 6 | .986 |
| 1955–Denver.............A.A. | | C | 152 | 555 | 56 | 170 | 26 | 4 | 4 | 49 | .306 | •822 | •87 | 12 | .987 |
| 1956–Denver .............A.A. | | •C-3-O | 107 | 367 | 61 | 117 | 20 | 3 | 7 | 48 | .319 | 561 | 46 | •14 | .977 |
| 1957–New York.........Amer. | | C | 21 | 46 | 4 | 10 | 1 | 0 | 1 | 8 | .217 | 75 | 8 | 0 | 1.000 |
| 1958–New York.........Amer. | | C | 5 | 16 | 1 | 4 | 0 | 0 | 0 | 0 | .250 | 22 | 3 | 0 | 1.000 |
| 1959–Richmond x ......Int. | | C | 94 | 316 | 22 | 69 | 8 | 0 | 4 | 28 | .218 | 502 | 56 | 11 | .981 |
| 1960–St. Louis .........Nat. | | C | 8 | 2 | 0 | 0 | 0 | 0 | 0 | 0 | .000 | 10 | 1 | 0 | 1.000 |
| 1961–Phila.y-Cinn. ....Nat. | | C | 41 | 115 | 7 | 31 | 3 | 0 | 1 | 9 | .270 | 198 | 23 | 2 | .991 |
| 1962–Cincinnati z ......Nat. | | C | 2 | 4 | 0 | 0 | 0 | 0 | 0 | 0 | .000 | 16 | 2 | 0 | 1.000 |
| 1962–Baltimore.........Amer. | | C | 6 | 22 | 0 | 4 | 0 | 0 | 0 | 1 | .182 | 30 | 2 | 0 | 1.000 |
| American League Totals ................ | | | 83 | 199 | 17 | 44 | 3 | 1 | 1 | 19 | .221 | 288 | 36 | 5 | .985 |
| National League Totals ................ | | | 51 | 121 | 7 | 31 | 3 | 0 | 1 | 9 | .256 | 224 | 26 | 2 | .992 |
| Major League Totals ................ | | | 134 | 320 | 24 | 75 | 6 | 1 | 2 | 28 | .234 | 512 | 62 | 7 | .988 |

†Sold with Outfielder Jim Rivera to Chicago White Sox; St. Louis purchased Outfielder Ray Coleman from Chicago and Outfielder-Catcher J. W. Porter from Colorado Springs in same deal, July 28, 1952.

‡Traded with Pitcher Lou Kretlow and $75,000 to St. Louis Browns for Pitcher Virgil Trucks and Third Baseman Bob Elliott, June 13, 1953. Johnson reported at close of season, others transferred on date of trade.

§Recalled by Baltimore Orioles and traded with Pitchers Mike Blyzka, Don Larsen and Bob Turley, First Baseman Dick Kryhoski, Shortstop Billy Hunter and Outfielders Ted del Guercio and Jim Fridley to New York Yankees for Pitchers Harry Byrd, Jim McDonald and Bill Miller, Catchers Hal Smith and Gus Triandos, Second Baseman Don Leppert, Third Baseman Kal Segrist, Shortstop Willie Miranda and Outfielder Gene Woodling. Yankees assigned Blyzka, del Guercio, Johnson and Fridley to minor league teams. Byrd, McDonald, Smith, Triandos, Miranda, Woodling, Larsen, Turley and Hunter transferred November 18; others on December 3, 1954.

xDrafted by St. Louis Cardinals from Richmond (New York Yankees' organization), November 30, 1959.

yStarted season as St. Louis Cardinals' coach, released July 8, 1961; signed as player by Philadelphia Phillies, July 9, 1961; sold to Cincinnati Reds, August 14, 1961.

zReleased by Cincinnati Reds; signed as player-coach by Baltimore Orioles, April 24, 1962; released as player by Baltimore, June 12, 1962.

## WORLD SERIES RECORD

| Year | Club | League | Pos. | G. | AB. | R. | H. | 2B. | 3B. | HR. | RBI. | B.A. | PO. | A. | E. | F.A. |
|------|------|--------|------|-----|-----|-----|-----|-----|-----|-----|------|------|-----|-----|-----|------|
| 1961–Cincinnati | ........... | Nat. | C | 2 | 4 | 0 | 2 | 0 | 0 | 0 | 0 | .500 | 8 | 1 | 0 | 1.000 |

## RECORD AS MANAGER

| Year | Club | League | Position | W. | L. | Year | Club | League | Position | W. | L. |
|------|------|--------|----------|-----|-----|------|------|--------|----------|-----|-----|
| 1963–Rochester | ..........Int. | | Third(N) | 75 | 76 | 1972–Louisville | ..........Int. | | ‡First | 81 | 63 |
| 1964–Rochester | ..........Int. | | †Fourth | 82 | 72 | 1973–Pawtucket | ..........Int. | | §Second(A) | 78 | 68 |
| 1965–Rochester | ..........Int. | | Fifth | 73 | 74 | 1974–Boston | ................Amer. | | Third(E) | 84 | 78 |
| 1966–Elmira | ..............East. | | First | 88 | 51 | 1975–Boston | ................Amer. | | First(E) | 95 | 65 |
| 1971–Louisville | ..........Int. | | Fifth | 71 | 69 | 1976–Boston x | ...........Amer. | | Third(E) | 41 | 45 |

†Won playoffs by defeating Jacksonville, four games to none and Syracuse, four games to two.

‡Lost playoff final series to Tidewater, three games to two after defeating Rochester in semifinals, two games to one.

§Won playoffs by defeating Tidewater, three games to two and Charleston, three games to two; won Junior World Series against Tulsa (American Association), four games to one.

xReplaced by Don Zimmer, July 19, 1976.

Coach, St. Louis Cardinals, August 5, 1960 through July 8, 1961; coach, Baltimore Orioles, 1962; scout, New York Yankees, 1967; coach, Boston Red Sox, 1968 and 1969; instructor and special assignment scout, Boston Red Sox, 1970.

## CHAMPIONSHIP SERIES RECORD

| Year | Club | League | W. | L. |
|------|------|--------|-----|-----|
| 1975–Boston | ...............American | | 3 | 0 |

## WORLD SERIES RECORD

| Year | Club | League | W. | L. |
|------|------|--------|-----|-----|
| 1975–Boston | ...............American | | 3 | 4 |

## THOMAS CHARLES LASORDA
Name pronounced Luh-SORR-duh.
### (Tom)
### Los Angeles Dodgers

Born September 22, 1927, at Morristown, Pa.
Height, 5.09. Weight, 175.
Threw and batted lefthanded.
Hobby—Making home movies.

Tied National League record by making three wild pitches in an inning, first inning, May 5, 1955.
Struck out 25 batters while pitching a 15-inning, 6-5 victory over Amsterdam, May 31, 1948.
Led International League in complete games with 16 and tied for lead in shutouts with 5 in 1958.
Led Canadian-American League in wild pitches with 20 in 1948 and led International League with 14 in 1953.
Named International League Most Valuable Pitcher in 1958.
Named by THE SPORTING NEWS as Minor League Manager of the Year, 1970.

| Year | Club | League | G. | IP. | W. | L. | Pct. | H. | R. | ER. | SO. | BB. | ERA. |
|------|------|--------|-----|-----|-----|-----|------|-----|-----|-----|-----|-----|------|
| 1945–Concord | ...........................N. C. St. | | 27 | 121 | 3 | 12 | .200 | 115 | 84 | 55 | 91 | 100 | 4.09 |
| 1946-47–† | ..........................................E. Shore | | (In Military Service) | | | | | | | | | | |
| 1948–Schenectady‡§ | .....................Can.-Am. | | 32 | 192 | 9 | 12 | .429 | 180 | 122 | 99 | 195 | 153 | 4.64 |
| 1949–Greenville | ............................Sally | | 45 | 178 | 7 | 7 | .500 | 141 | 81 | 58 | 151 | 138 | 2.93 |
| 1950–Montreal | ............................Int. | | 31 | 146 | 9 | 4 | .692 | 136 | 73 | 60 | 85 | 82 | 3.70 |
| 1951–Montreal | ............................Int. | | 31 | 165 | 12 | 8 | .600 | 145 | 75 | 64 | 80 | 87 | 3.49 |
| 1952–Montreal | ............................Int. | | 33 | 182 | 14 | 5 | .737 | 156 | 90 | 74 | 77 | 93 | 3.66 |
| 1953–Montreal | ............................Int. | | 36 | 208 | 17 | 8 | .680 | 171 | 77 | 65 | 122 | 94 | 2.81 |
| 1954–Montreal | ............................Int. | | 23 | 154 | 14 | 5 | .737 | 142 | 66 | 60 | 75 | 79 | 3.51 |
| 1954–Brooklyn | ............................Nat. | | 4 | 9 | 0 | 0 | .000 | 8 | 5 | 5 | 5 | 5 | 5.00 |
| 1955–Brooklyn | ............................Nat. | | 4 | 4 | 0 | 0 | .000 | 5 | 6 | 6 | 4 | 6 | 13.50 |
| 1955–Montreal x | ............................Int. | | 22 | 143 | 9 | 8 | .529 | 125 | 58 | 52 | 92 | 62 | 3.27 |
| 1956–Kansas City y | ............................Amer. | | 18 | 45 | 0 | 4 | .000 | 40 | 38 | 31 | 28 | 45 | 6.20 |
| 1956–Denver | ............................A.A. | | 16 | 83 | 3 | 4 | .429 | 94 | 54 | 46 | 54 | 34 | 4.99 |
| 1957–Denver z | ............................A.A. | | 6 | .... | 0 | 2 | .000 | | | | | | |
| 1957–Los Angeles | ............................P.C. | | 29 | 132 | 7 | 10 | .412 | 134 | 73 | 57 | 72 | 59 | 3.90 |
| 1958–Montreal | ............................Int. | | 34 | *230 | *18 | 6 | .750 | 191 | 77 | 64 | 126 | 76 | 2.50 |

| Year Club | League | G. | IP. | W. | L. | Pct. | H. | R. | ER. | SO. | BB. | ERA. |
|---|---|---|---|---|---|---|---|---|---|---|---|---|
| 1959—Montreal | Int. | 29 | 188 | 12 | 8 | .600 | 192 | 93 | 80 | 64 | 77 | 3.83 |
| 1960—Montreal a | Int. | 12 | 45 | 2 | 5 | .286 | 79 | 48 | 41 | 17 | 24 | 8.20 |
| American League Totals | | 18 | 45 | 0 | 4 | .000 | 40 | 38 | 31 | 28 | 45 | 6.20 |
| National League Totals | | 8 | 13 | 0 | 0 | .000 | 13 | 11 | 11 | 9 | 11 | 7.62 |
| Major League Totals | | 26 | 58 | 0 | 4 | .000 | 53 | 49 | 42 | 37 | 56 | 6.52 |

†On National Defense list, May 14, 1946 through February 2, 1948.
‡On disabled list, July 9 through July 19.
§Drafted by Nashua (Brooklyn Dodgers' organization) from Philadelphia Phillies' organization, November 24, 1948.
xSold by Brooklyn Dodgers' organization to Kansas City Athletics for an estimated $35,000, March 2, 1956.
yTraded to New York Yankees for Pitcher Wally Burnette and cash, July 11, 1956.
zSold by New York Yankees' organization to Brooklyn Dodgers' organization, May 26, 1957.
aReleased by Montreal, July 9, 1960.

## RECORD AS MANAGER

| Year Club | League | Position | W. | L. | Year Club | League | Position | W. | L. |
|---|---|---|---|---|---|---|---|---|---|
| 1966—Ogden | Pioneer | First | 39 | 27 | 1970—Spokane | P.C. | †First(N) | 94 | 52 |
| 1967—Ogden | Pioneer | First | 41 | 25 | 1971—Spokane | P.C. | Third(N) | 69 | 76 |
| 1968—Ogden | Pioneer | First | 39 | 25 | 1972—Albuquerque | P.C. | ‡First(E) | 92 | 56 |
| 1969—Spokane | P.C. | Second(N) | 71 | 73 | 1976—Los Angeles§ | Nat. | Second(W) | 2 | 2 |

†Won championship playoff against Hawaii, four games to none.
‡Won championship playoff against Eugene, three games to one.
§Replaced retiring Walter Alston, September 30, 1976.
Scout, Los Angeles Dodgers, 1961 through 1965; manager Los Angeles farm team in Arizona Instructional League, 1969; coach, Los Angeles Dodgers, 1973 through 1976.

# ROBERT GRANVILLE LEMON
## (Bob)
## Chicago White Sox

Born September 22, 1920, at San Bernardino, Calif.
Height, 6.00. Weight, 180.
Threw right and batted lefthanded.
Hobby—Golf.

Established major league record for most double plays, season, pitcher, 15, 1953.
Pitched 2-0 no-hit victory against Detroit Tigers, June 30, 1948.
Led American League pitchers in complete games with 20 in 1948 and 28 in 1952.
Led American League in shutouts with 10 in 1948.
Tied for American League lead in complete games with 22 in 1950, 21 in 1954 and 21 in 1956.
Tied for American League lead in games started by pitchers with 36 in 1952.
Named Outstanding American League Pitcher by THE SPORTING NEWS, 1948-50-54.
Named as pitcher on THE SPORTING NEWS All-Star Major League Teams, 1948-50-54.
Named Minor League Manager of the Year by THE SPORTING NEWS, 1966.
Elected to Hall of Fame in 1976.

## PITCHING RECORD

| Year Club | League | G. | IP. | W. | L. | Pct. | H. | R. | ER. | SO. | BB. | ERA. |
|---|---|---|---|---|---|---|---|---|---|---|---|---|
| 1938—Oswego | Can.-Am. | 1 | 1 | 0 | 0 | .000 | 1 | 0 | 0 | 1 | 0 | 0.00 |
| 1941—Wilkes-Barre | Eastern | 1 | 1 | 0 | 1 | .000 | 0 | 1 | 1 | 0 | 3 | 9.00 |
| 1946—Cleveland | Amer. | 32 | 94 | 4 | 5 | .444 | 77 | 40 | 26 | 39 | 68 | 2.49 |
| 1947—Cleveland | Amer. | 37 | 167 | 11 | 5 | .688 | 150 | 68 | 64 | 65 | 97 | 3.45 |
| 1948—Cleveland | Amer. | 43 | •294 | 20 | 14 | .588 | 231 | 104 | 92 | 147 | 129 | 2.82 |
| 1949—Cleveland | Amer. | 37 | 280 | 22 | 10 | .688 | 211 | 101 | 93 | 138 | 137 | 2.99 |
| 1950—Cleveland | Amer. | 44 | •288 | •23 | 11 | .676 | •281 | 144 | 123 | •170 | 146 | 3.84 |
| 1951—Cleveland | Amer. | 42 | 263 | 17 | ●14 | .548 | •244 | •119 | 103 | 132 | 124 | 3.52 |
| 1952—Cleveland | Amer. | 42 | •310 | 22 | 11 | .667 | 236 | 104 | 86 | 131 | 105 | 2.50 |
| 1953—Cleveland | Amer. | 41 | •287 | 21 | 15 | .583 | •283 | 119 | 107 | 98 | 110 | 3.36 |
| 1954—Cleveland | Amer. | 36 | 258 | ●23 | 7 | .767 | 228 | 95 | 78 | 110 | 92 | 2.72 |
| 1955—Cleveland | Amer. | 35 | 211 | ●18 | 10 | .643 | 218 | 103 | 91 | 100 | 74 | 3.88 |
| 1956—Cleveland | Amer. | 39 | 255 | 20 | 14 | .588 | 230 | 103 | 86 | 94 | 89 | 3.04 |
| 1957—Cleveland | Amer. | 21 | 117 | 6 | 11 | .353 | 129 | 70 | 60 | 45 | ˙64 | 4.62 |
| 1958—Cleveland | Amer. | 11 | 25 | 0 | 1 | .000 | 41 | 15 | 15 | 8 | 16 | 5.40 |
| 1958—San Diego | P.C. | 12 | 56 | 2 | 5 | .286 | 67 | 32 | 27 | 19 | 22 | 4.34 |
| Major League Totals | | 460 | 2849 | 207 | 128 | .618 | 2559 | 1185 | 1024 | 1277 | 1251 | 3.23 |

## WORLD SERIES RECORD

Established World Series record for most bases on balls by pitcher, four-game series, 8, in 1954.

| Year Club | League | G. | IP. | W. | L. | Pct. | H. | R. | ER. | SO. | BB. | ERA. |
|---|---|---|---|---|---|---|---|---|---|---|---|---|
| 1948—Cleveland | Amer. | 2 | 16⅓ | 2 | 0 | 1.000 | 16 | 4 | 3 | 6 | 7 | 1.65 |
| 1954—Cleveland | Amer. | 2 | 13⅓ | 0 | 2 | .000 | 16 | 11 | 10 | 11 | 8 | 6.75 |
| World Series Totals | | 4 | 29⅔ | 2 | 2 | .500 | 32 | 15 | 13 | 17 | 15 | 3.94 |

## ALL-STAR GAME RECORD

| Year League | IP. | W. | L. | Pct. | H. | R. | ER. | SO. | BB. | ERA. |
|---|---|---|---|---|---|---|---|---|---|---|
| 1950—American | 3 | 0 | 0 | .000 | 1 | 0 | 0 | 2 | 0 | 0.00 |
| 1951—American | 1 | 0 | 0 | .000 | 2 | 0 | 0 | 1 | 1 | 0.00 |
| 1952—American | 2 | 0 | 1 | .000 | 2 | 2 | 2 | 0 | 2 | 9.00 |
| 1954—American | ⅔ | 0 | 0 | .000 | 1 | 0 | 0 | 0 | 0 | 0.00 |
| All-Star Game Totals | 6⅔ | 0 | 1 | .000 | 6 | 2 | 2 | 3 | 3 | 2.70 |

## BATTING RECORD

| Year Club | League | Pos. | G. | AB. | R. | H. | 2B. | 3B. | HR. | RBI. | B.A. | PO. | A. | E. | F.A. |
|---|---|---|---|---|---|---|---|---|---|---|---|---|---|---|---|
| 1938—Springfield ........M.-Atl. | INF-OF | 7 | 18 | 1 | 4 | 1 | 0 | 0 | 2 | .222 | 4 | 5 | 2 | .818 |
| 1938—Oswego ............C.-A. | O-SS-P | 75 | 282 | 44 | 88 | 6 | 6 | 7 | 34 | .312 | 97 | 52 | 12 | .925 |
| 1939—Springfield ........M.-Atl. | SS-O | 80 | 307 | 44 | 90 | 14 | 3 | 3 | 39 | .293 | 106 | 103 | 25 | .893 |
| 1939—New Orleans ........South. | OF-3B | 52 | 207 | 30 | 64 | 9 | 6 | 0 | 22 | .309 | 65 | 33 | 13 | .883 |
| 1940—Wilkes-Barre ....East. | 3B-OF | 92 | 321 | 37 | 82 | 14 | 3 | 2 | 53 | .255 | 132 | 68 | 16 | .926 |
| 1941—Wilkes-Barre ....East. | •3-SS-P | •141 | •562 | •109 | •169 | 15 | 13 | 4 | 43 | .301 | •179 | 268 | 36 | .925 |
| 1941—Cleveland ........Amer. | 3B | 5 | 4 | 0 | 1 | 0 | 0 | 0 | 0 | .250 | 1 | 1 | 0 | 1.000 |
| 1942—Baltimore ........Int. | •3B-SS | 148 | 596 | 95 | 160 | 23 | 8 | 21 | 80 | .268 | •159 | •349 | •33 | .939 |
| 1942—Cleveland ........Amer. | 3B | 5 | 5 | 0 | 0 | 0 | 0 | 0 | 0 | .000 | 0 | 1 | 1 | .500 |
| 1943-44-45—Cleveland..Amer. | | | | | (In Military Service) | | | | | | | | | |
| 1946—Cleveland ........Amer. | P-OF | 55 | 89 | 9 | 16 | 3 | 0 | 1 | 4 | .180 | 46 | 30 | 2 | .974 |
| 1947—Cleveland ........Amer. | P-OF | 47 | 56 | 11 | 18 | 4 | 3 | 2 | 5 | .321 | 13 | 46 | 1 | .983 |
| 1948—Cleveland ........Amer. | P | 52 | 119 | 20 | 34 | 9 | 0 | 5 | 21 | .286 | •23 | •86 | 4 | .965 |
| 1949—Cleveland ........Amer. | P | 46 | 108 | 17 | 29 | 6 | 2 | 7 | 19 | .269 | •34 | •71 | 4 | .963 |
| 1950—Cleveland ........Amer. | P | 72 | 136 | 21 | 37 | 9 | 1 | 6 | 26 | .272 | 22 | 66 | 4 | .957 |
| 1951—Cleveland ........Amer. | P | 56 | 102 | 11 | 21 | 4 | 1 | 3 | 13 | .206 | 21 | •60 | 2 | .976 |
| 1952—Cleveland ........Amer. | P | 54 | 124 | 14 | 28 | 5 | 0 | 2 | 9 | .226 | •32 | •79 | 2 | .982 |
| 1953—Cleveland ........Amer. | P | 51 | 112 | 12 | 26 | 9 | 1 | 2 | 17 | .232 | •31 | •74 | 3 | .972 |
| 1954—Cleveland ........Amer. | P | 40 | 98 | 11 | 21 | 4 | 1 | 2 | 10 | .214 | •22 | 57 | 3 | .963 |
| 1955—Cleveland ........Amer. | P | 49 | 78 | 11 | 19 | 0 | 0 | 1 | 9 | .244 | 16 | 43 | 1 | .983 |
| 1956—Cleveland ........Amer. | P | 43 | 93 | 8 | 18 | 0 | 0 | 5 | 12 | .194 | 24 | •61 | •6 | .934 |
| 1957—Cleveland ........Amer. | P | 25 | 46 | 2 | 3 | 1 | 0 | 1 | 1 | .065 | 12 | 31 | 0 | 1.000 |
| 1958—Cleveland ........Amer. | P | 15 | 13 | 1 | 3 | 0 | 0 | 0 | 1 | .231 | 1 | 7 | 0 | 1.000 |
| 1958—San Diego..........P.C. | OF-P | 32 | 69 | 2 | 18 | 4 | 0 | 0 | 7 | .261 | 25 | 9 | 0 | 1.000 |
| Major League Totals ..................... | | 615 | 1183 | 148 | 274 | 54 | 9 | 37 | 147 | .232 | 298 | 713 | 33 | .968 |

## RECORD AS MANAGER

| Year Club | League | Position | W. | L. | Year Club | League | Position | W. | L. |
|---|---|---|---|---|---|---|---|---|---|
| 1964—Hawaii ..............P.C. | Sixth(W) | 60 | 98 | | 1971—Kansas City........Amer. | Second(W) | 85 | 76 | |
| 1965—Seattle...............P.C. | Second(W) | 79 | 69 | | 1972—Kansas City........Amer. | Fourth(W) | 76 | 78 | |
| 1966—Seattle...............P.C. | †First(W) | 83 | 65 | | 1974—Sacramento ........P.C. | Fourth(W) | 66 | 78 | |
| 1969—Vancouver .........P.C. | ‡Second(N) | 71 | 73 | | 1975—Richmond x........Int. | Sixth | 33 | 45 | |
| 1970—Kansas City§ ......Amer. | ‡Fourth(W) | 46 | 64 | | | | | | |

†Won playoff by defeating Tulsa, four games to three.
‡Tied for position.
§Replaced Charlie Metro with club in fifth place, June 9.
xReplaced Clint Courtney with club in fifth place, June 16.
 Scout, Cleveland Indians, 1959; coach, Cleveland Indians, start of season through May 7, 1960; coach, Philadelphia Phillies, 1961; coach, California Angels, 1967 and 1968; coach, Kansas City Royals, part of 1970; special assignments scout, Kansas City Royals, 1973; special assignments scout, Atlanta Braves, part of 1975; coach, New York Yankees, 1976.

# FRANK JOSEPH LUCCHESI
Name pronounced Lou-CASEY.
## Texas Rangers
Born April 24, 1926, at San Francisco, Calif.
Height, 5.08. Weight, 175.
Threw and batted righthanded.

| Year Club | League | Pos. | G. | AB. | R. | H. | 2B. | 3B. | HR. | RBI. | B.A. | PO. | A. | E. | F.A. |
|---|---|---|---|---|---|---|---|---|---|---|---|---|---|---|---|
| 1945—Portland...........P. C. | OF | 60 | 118 | 17 | 29 | 5 | 2 | 0 | 16 | .246 | 95 | 4 | 0 | 1.000 |
| 1946—Salem...............W. Int. | OF | 53 | 197 | 38 | 51 | 3 | 2 | 1 | 26 | .259 | 122 | 4 | 4 | .969 |
| 1947—Salem-Victoria ..W. Int. | OF | 59 | 183 | 40 | 45 | 6 | 2 | 1 | 15 | .246 | 99 | 8 | 3 | .973 |
| 1947—Bisbee ..............A.-Tex. | IF-OF | 38 | 137 | 28 | 52 | 4 | 4 | 0 | 14 | .380 | 73 | 63 | 13 | .913 |
| 1948—Ventura ..........Calif. | OF | 133 | 538 | 103 | 142 | 25 | 5 | 3 | 41 | .264 | 308 | •22 | 8 | .976 |
| 1949—Ventura ..........Calif. | OF | 135 | 550 | 115 | 140 | 19 | 5 | 5 | 44 | .255 | •370 | 17 | 4 | •.990 |
| 1950—Twin Falls .......Pion. | OF | 120 | 475 | 105 | 115 | 14 | 0 | 8 | 45 | .242 | 303 | 15 | 4 | •.988 |
| 1951—Medford ..........Far W. | OF | 113 | 440 | 93 | 122 | 24 | 5 | 2 | 68 | .277 | 220 | •20 | 5 | •.980 |
| 1952—Thomasville .....Ga.-Fla. | OF | 138 | 524 | 87 | 161 | 29 | 3 | 1 | 59 | .307 | •339 | 17 | 1 | •.997 |
| 1953—Pine Bluff .......Cot. St. | OF | 123 | 433 | 84 | 144 | 20 | 1 | 15 | 70 | .333 | 283 | 9 | 9 | .970 |
| 1954—Pine Bluff .......Cot. St. | OF-PH | 10 | 24 | 4 | 10 | 2 | 0 | 0 | 4 | .417 | .... | .... | .. | ....... |
| 1955—Pocatello .........Pion. | OF | 118 | 435 | 63 | 120 | 10 | 1 | 0 | 56 | .276 | 250 | 11 | 5 | .981 |
| 1956—Salt Lake City ..Pion. | OF | 48 | 176 | 24 | 36 | 5 | 1 | 0 | 13 | .205 | 105 | 6 | 0 | 1.000 |
| 1957—High Point .......Caro. | PH | 1 | 1 | 0 | 1 | 0 | 0 | 0 | 0 | 1.000 | .... | .... | .. | ....... |

## RECORD AS MANAGER

| Year Club | League | Position | W. | L. | Year Club | League | Position | W. | L. |
|---|---|---|---|---|---|---|---|---|---|
| 1951—Medford ............Far West | Fourth | 25 | 30 | | 1963—Arkansas............Int. | Third(S) | 78 | 73 | |
| (Second Half) | Fifth | 22 | 37 | | 1964—Arkansas............P. C. | yFirst(E) | 95 | 61 | |
| 1952—Thomasville........Geo.-Fla. | Sixth | 66 | 74 | | 1965—Little Rock ........P. C. | Fifth(E) | 67 | 79 | |
| 1953—Pine Bluff .........Cot. St. | Third | 65 | 60 | | 1966—San Diego .........P. C. | Fifth(W) | 72 | 75 | |
| 1954—Pine Bluff .........Cot. St. | Fifth | 47 | 71 | | 1967—Reading..............East. | Third(W) | 70 | 69 | |
| 1955—Pocatello ...........Pion. | Third | 72 | 59 | | 1968—Reading..............East. | zSecond | 81 | 59 | |
| 1956—Salt Lake City ....Pion. | †Second | 70 | 62 | | 1969—Eugene ..............P. C. | aFirst(S) | 88 | 58 | |
| 1957—High Point.........Carol. | Fourth | 33 | 33 | | 1970—Philadelphia .....Nat. | Fifth(E) | 73 | 88 | |
| (Second Half) | ‡First | 46 | 28 | | 1971—Philadelphia ......Nat. | Sixth(E) | 67 | 95 | |
| 1958—High Point.........Carol. | Second | 76 | 63 | | 1972—Philadelphia b ....Nat. | Sixth(E) | 26 | 50 | |
| 1959—Williamsport ......East. | Third | 81 | 60 | | 1973—Oklahoma City ..A. A. | Third(W) | 61 | 74 | |
| 1960—Williamsport ......East. | §Fifth | 76 | 62 | | 1975—Texas c ..............Amer. | Third(W) | 35 | 32 | |
| 1961—Chattanooga ......So. Ass'n | First | 90 | 62 | | 1976—Texas ................Amer. | Fifth(W) | 76 | 86 | |
| 1962—Williamsport ......East. | xFirst | 83 | 57 | | | | | | |

†Tied for position with Billings.

‡Lost championship playoff to Durham (first half winner), four games to three.

§Defeated Reading, two games to none in championship playoff semifinals; led Springfield, one game to none, in best-of-five finals when series was ended because of rain, with both clubs being declared playoff co-champions.

xLost championship playoff finals to Elmira, three games to one after defeating Springfield in semifinals, two games to one.

yLost championship playoff to San Diego (Western Division winner), four games to three.

zWon championship playoff by defeating Binghamton, two games to none and Pittsfield, three games to one.

aLost championship playoff to Tacoma, three games to two.

bReplaced by General Manager Paul Owens, July 10.

cReplaced Billy Martin with club in fourth place, July 21.

Coach, Texas Rangers, 1974 and part of 1975.

# ALFRED MANUEL MARTIN
## (Billy)
### New York Yankees

Born May 16, 1928, at Berkeley, Calif.
Height, 5.11. Weight, 170.
Threw and batted righthanded.
Hobbies—Hunting and golf.

Tied major league record for most clubs, league, season, as manager, 2 (Detroit and Texas), 1973. Led American League second basemen in double plays with 121 in 1953 and led league in sacrifice hits with 13 in 1958.

| Year  Club | League | Pos. | G. | AB. | R. | H. | 2B. | 3B. | HR. | RBI. | B.A. | PO. | A. | E. | F.A. |
|---|---|---|---|---|---|---|---|---|---|---|---|---|---|---|---|
| 1946—Idaho Falls | Pion. | 3B-2B | 32 | 114 | 13 | 29 | 7 | 0 | 0 | 12 | .254 | 33 | 55 | 16 | .846 |
| 1947—Phoenix | Ar.-Tex. | 3B | 130 | •586 | 141 | •230 | •48 | 12 | 9 | •174 | •.392 | •207 | •317 | •55 | .905 |
| 1947—Oakland | P.C. | 3B-2B | 15 | 53 | 3 | 12 | 3 | 0 | 0 | 5 | .226 | 23 | 24 | 5 | .904 |
| 1948—Oakland | P.C. | INF | 132 | 401 | 60 | 111 | 28 | 2 | 3 | 42 | .277 | 301 | 288 | 21 | .966 |
| 1949—Oakland | P.C. | •2B-SS | 172 | 623 | 90 | 178 | 27 | 3 | 12 | 92 | .286 | •454 | 475 | •37 | .962 |
| 1950—Kansas City | A.A. | 2B | 29 | 118 | 15 | 33 | 6 | 2 | 4 | 10 | .280 | 68 | 80 | 8 | .949 |
| 1950—New York | Amer. | 2B-3B | 34 | 36 | 10 | 9 | 1 | 0 | 1 | 8 | .250 | 24 | 16 | 1 | .976 |
| 1951—New York | Amer. | 2-S-3-O | 51 | 58 | 10 | 15 | 1 | 2 | 0 | 2 | .259 | 45 | 62 | 4 | .964 |
| 1952—New York | Amer. | 2B | 109 | 363 | 32 | 97 | 13 | 3 | 3 | 33 | .267 | 244 | 323 | 9 | .984 |
| 1953—New York | Amer. | 2B-SS | 149 | 587 | 72 | 151 | 24 | 6 | 15 | 75 | .257 | 389 | 409 | 14 | .983 |
| 1954—New York | Amer. | (In Military Service) | | | | | | | | | | | | | |
| 1955—New York† | Amer. | 2B-SS | 20 | 70 | 8 | 21 | 2 | 0 | 1 | 9 | .300 | 46 | 50 | 3 | .970 |
| 1956—New York | Amer. | 2B-3B | 121 | 458 | 76 | 121 | 24 | 5 | 9 | 49 | .264 | 253 | 288 | 15 | .973 |
| 1957—N. Y.‡-K. C.§ | Amer. | 2-3-S | 116 | 410 | 45 | 103 | 14 | 5 | 10 | 39 | .251 | 220 | 232 | 13 | .972 |
| 1958—Detroit x | Amer. | SS-3B | 131 | 498 | 56 | 127 | 19 | 1 | 7 | 42 | .255 | 206 | 288 | 20 | .961 |
| 1959—Cleveland y | Amer. | 2B-3B | 73 | 242 | 37 | 63 | 7 | 0 | 9 | 24 | .260 | 150 | 153 | 2 | .993 |
| 1960—Cincinnati z | Nat. | 2B | 103 | 317 | 34 | 78 | 17 | 1 | 3 | 16 | .246 | 228 | 207 | 11 | .975 |
| 1961—Milwaukee a | Nat. | PH | 6 | 6 | 1 | 0 | 0 | 0 | 0 | 0 | .000 | 0 | 0 | 0 | .000 |
| 1961—Minnesota | Amer. | 2B-SS | 108 | 374 | 44 | 92 | 15 | 5 | 6 | 36 | .246 | 217 | 224 | 17 | .963 |
| American League Totals | | | 912 | 3096 | 390 | 799 | 120 | 27 | 61 | 317 | .258 | 1794 | 2028 | 98 | .976 |
| National League Totals | | | 109 | 323 | 35 | 78 | 17 | 1 | 3 | 16 | .241 | 228 | 207 | 11 | .975 |
| Major League Totals | | | 1021 | 3419 | 425 | 877 | 137 | 28 | 64 | 333 | .257 | 2022 | 2235 | 109 | .976 |

†In Military Service most of season.

‡Traded to Kansas City Athletics with Pitcher Ralph Terry and Outfielders Woodie Held and Bob Martyn for Pitcher Ryne Duren and Outfielders Jim Pisoni and Harry Simpson, June 15, 1957. Duren and Pisoni were assigned to their Denver (American Association) farm club.

§Traded to Detroit Tigers with Pitchers Maury McDermott and Tom Morgan, Catcher Tim Thompson and Outfielders Lou Skizas and Gus Zernial for Pitchers Duke Maas and John Tsitouris, Catcher Frank House, First Basemen Kent Hadley and Jim McManus and Outfielders Jim Small and Bill Tuttle. All players but Hadley and McManus transferred November 20, 1957; Hadley added January 8, 1958, and McManus, April 2.

xTraded to Cleveland Indians with Pitcher Al Cicotte for Pitchers Don Mossi and Ray Narleski and Infielder Ossie Alvarez, November 30, 1958.

yTraded to Cincinnati Reds with Pitcher Cal McLish and First Baseman Gordon Coleman for Second Baseman Johnny Temple, December 15, 1959.

zSold to Milwaukee Braves, December 3, 1960.

aTraded to Minnesota Twins for Infielder Billy Consolo (latter assigned to Vancouver) and cash, June 1, 1961.

## WORLD SERIES RECORD

Tied following World Series records: Highest batting average 6-game Series (.500), 1953; one or more hits in each game, 6-game Series, 1953; most three-base hits, 6-game Series (2), 1953; most long hits (5) in 6-game Series, 1953; one or more hits, each game, 7-game Series, 1956; most times caught stealing, game, 2, September 28, 1955.

| Year  Club | League | Pos. | G. | AB. | R. | H. | 2B. | 3B. | HR. | RBI. | B.A. | PO. | A. | E. | F.A. |
|---|---|---|---|---|---|---|---|---|---|---|---|---|---|---|---|
| 1951—New York | Amer. | PR | 1 | 0 | 1 | 0 | 0 | 0 | 0 | 0 | .000 | 0 | 0 | 0 | .000 |
| 1952—New York | Amer. | 2B | 7 | 23 | 2 | 5 | 0 | 0 | 1 | 4 | .217 | 16 | 16 | 1 | .970 |
| 1953—New York | Amer. | 2B | 6 | 24 | 5 | 12 | 1 | 2 | 2 | 8 | .500 | 13 | 14 | 0 | 1.000 |
| 1955—New York | Amer. | 2B | 7 | 25 | 2 | 8 | 1 | 1 | 0 | 4 | .320 | 17 | 20 | 0 | 1.000 |
| 1956—New York | Amer. | 2B-3B | 7 | 27 | 5 | 8 | 0 | 2 | 2 | 3 | .296 | 14 | 20 | 0 | 1.000 |
| World Series Totals | | | 28 | 99 | 15 | 33 | 2 | 5 | 5 | 19 | .333 | 60 | 70 | 1 | .992 |

| Year League | Pos. | AB. | R. | H. | 2B. | 3B. | HR. | RBI. | B.A. | PO. | A. | E. | F.A. |
|---|---|---|---|---|---|---|---|---|---|---|---|---|---|
| 1956—American ........................... | PH | 1 | 0 | 0 | 0 | 0 | 0 | 0 | .000 | 0 | 0 | 0 | .000 |

## RECORD AS MANAGER

| Year Club | League | Position | W. | L. | Year Club | League | Position | W. | L. |
|---|---|---|---|---|---|---|---|---|---|
| 1968—Denver† ............P.C. | Fourth(E) | 65 | 50 | | 1973—Texas§ ...............Amer. | | Sixth(W) | 9 | 14 |
| 1969—Minnesota .........Amer. | First(W) | 97 | 65 | | 1974—Texas ................Amer. | | Second(W) | 84 | 76 |
| 1971—Detroit ..............Amer. | Second(E) | 91 | 71 | | 1975—Texas x ..............Amer. | | Fourth(W) | 44 | 51 |
| 1972—Detroit ..............Amer. | First(E) | 86 | 70 | | 1975—New York y........Amer. | | Third(E) | 30 | 26 |
| 1973—Detriot‡..............Amer. | Third(E) | 71 | 65 | | 1976—New York .........Amer. | | First(E) | 97 | 62 |

†Replaced John Goryl with club in sixth place, May 27.
‡Replaced by interim manager Joe Schultz, September 1.
§Replaced interim manager Del Wilber, September 8.
xReplaced by Frank Lucchesi, July 20.
yReplaced Bill Virdon, August 1.
Scout, Minnesota Twins, 1962 through 1964; coach, Minnesota Twins, 1965 through May 26, 1968.

## CHAMPIONSHIP SERIES RECORD

| Year Club | League | W. | L. |
|---|---|---|---|
| 1969—Minnesota .........Amer. | | 0 | 3 |
| 1972—Detroit ..............Amer. | | 2 | 3 |
| 1976—New York .........Amer. | | 3 | 2 |

## WORLD SERIES RECORD

| Year Club | League | W. | L. |
|---|---|---|---|
| 1976—New York .........Amer. | | 0 | 4 |

## GENE WILLIAM MAUCH
### Minnesota Twins

Born November 18, 1925, at Salina, Kan.
Height, 5.10. Weight, 173.
Threw and batted righthanded.
Hobby—Golf.
Brother-in-law of Roy Smalley, Jr., infielder with Chicago Cubs, Milwaukee Braves and
Philadelphia Phillies, 1948 through 1958. Uncle of Roy Smalley III,
infielder with Minnesota Twins.

Named Major League Manager of the Year by THE SPORTING NEWS, 1973.

| Year Club | League | Pos. | G. | AB. | R. | H. | 2B. | 3B. | HR. | RBI. | B.A. | PO. | A. | E. | F.A. |
|---|---|---|---|---|---|---|---|---|---|---|---|---|---|---|---|
| 1943—Durham ............Pied. | | SS | 32 | 115 | 19 | 37 | 5 | 1 | 0 | 14 | .322 | 77 | 81 | 19 | .893 |
| 1943—Montreal ..........Int. | | 2B-SS | 31 | 77 | 5 | 13 | 1 | 0 | 0 | 4 | .169 | 36 | 41 | 12 | .865 |
| 1944—Brooklyn ..........Nat. | | SS | 5 | 15 | 2 | 2 | 1 | 0 | 0 | 2 | .133 | 7 | 9 | 0 | 1.000 |
| 1944—Montreal†..........Int. | | SS | 14 | 53 | 12 | 15 | 0 | 0 | 0 | 2 | .283 | 25 | 39 | 8 | .889 |
| 1945—Brooklyn ..........Nat. | | | | | | (In Military Service) | | | | | | | | | |
| 1946—St. Paul‡ ..........A.A. | | SS | 149 | 536 | 74 | 133 | 19 | 3 | 6 | 55 | .248 | 296 | *417 | *64 | .918 |
| 1947—Pittsburgh ........Nat. | | 2B-SS | 16 | 30 | 8 | 9 | 0 | 0 | 0 | 1 | .300 | 18 | 20 | 3 | .927 |
| 1947—Indianapolis§ ....A.A. | | 2B | 58 | 217 | 37 | 65 | 13 | 4 | 0 | 16 | .300 | 176 | 174 | 12 | .967 |
| 1948—Brook.x-Chicago Nat. | | 2B-SS | 65 | 151 | 19 | 30 | 3 | 2 | 1 | 7 | .199 | 90 | 105 | 12 | .942 |
| 1949—Chicago y .........Nat. | | 2-S-3 | 72 | 150 | 15 | 37 | 6 | 2 | 1 | 7 | .247 | 98 | 125 | 9 | .961 |
| 1950—Boston ..............Nat. | | 2-3-S | 48 | 121 | 17 | 28 | 5 | 0 | 1 | 15 | .231 | 83 | 85 | 7 | .960 |
| 1951—Boston ..............Nat. | | S-3-2 | 19 | 20 | 5 | 2 | 0 | 0 | 0 | 1 | .100 | 16 | 16 | 1 | .970 |
| 1951—Milwaukee z a ..A.A. | | INF | 37 | 109 | 30 | 33 | 2 | 0 | 1 | 16 | .303 | 76 | 89 | 7 | .959 |
| 1952—St. Louis b .......Nat. | | SS | 7 | 3 | 0 | 0 | 0 | 0 | 0 | 0 | .000 | 1 | 0 | 1 | .500 |
| 1952—Milwaukee ........A.A. | | SS-2B | 102 | 327 | 58 | 106 | 24 | 3 | 4 | 60 | .324 | 202 | 258 | 12 | .975 |
| 1953—Atlanta c .........South. | | 2B | 111 | 340 | 65 | 91 | 23 | 3 | 9 | 51 | .268 | 200 | 239 | 18 | .961 |
| 1954—Los Angeles .....P.C. | | 2B | 153 | 565 | 81 | 162 | 26 | 2 | 11 | 58 | .287 | 354 | 380 | 19 | .975 |
| 1955—Los Angeles .....P.C. | | *2B-3B | 155 | 584 | 93 | 173 | 37 | 4 | 8 | 49 | .296 | *436 | 375 | 18 | .978 |
| 1956—Los Angeles d....P.C. | | 2B-3B | 146 | 566 | 123 | 197 | 29 | 3 | 20 | 84 | .348 | 348 | 403 | 24 | .969 |
| 1956—Boston ..............Amer. | | 2B | 7 | 25 | 4 | 8 | 0 | 0 | 0 | 1 | .320 | 12 | 17 | 2 | .935 |
| 1957—Boston ..............Amer. | | 2B | 65 | 222 | 23 | 60 | 10 | 3 | 2 | 28 | .270 | 127 | 153 | 11 | .962 |
| 1958—Minneapolis .....A.A. | | 2B-3B | 65 | 210 | 25 | 51 | 12 | 2 | 3 | 29 | .243 | 108 | 136 | 16 | .938 |
| 1959—Minneapolis .....A.A. | | PH | 8 | 8 | 1 | 4 | 0 | 0 | 0 | 0 | .500 | 0 | 0 | 0 | .000 |
| American League Totals ................ | | | 72 | 247 | 27 | 68 | 10 | 3 | 2 | 29 | .275 | 139 | 170 | 13 | .960 |
| National League Totals ................. | | | 232 | 490 | 66 | 108 | 15 | 4 | 3 | 33 | .220 | 313 | 360 | 33 | .953 |
| Major League Totals ...................... | | | 304 | 737 | 93 | 176 | 25 | 7 | 5 | 62 | .239 | 452 | 530 | 46 | .955 |

†Entered Military Service in May.
‡Recalled by Brooklyn Dodgers and traded to Pittsburgh Pirates with Pitchers Kirby Higbe and Cal McLish and Catcher Homer (Dixie) Howell for Outfielder Al Gionfriddo and reported $100,000, May 3, 1947.
§Recalled by Pittsburgh Pirates and traded to Brooklyn Dodgers with Pitcher Elwin (Preacher) Roe and Shortstop Billy Cox for Pitchers Hal Gregg and Vic Lombardi and Outfielder Fred (Dixie) Walker, December 7, 1947.
xSold to Chicago Cubs, June 17, 1948.
yTraded to Boston Braves with cash for Pitcher Bill Voiselle, December 14, 1949.
zDrafted by New York Yankees from Milwaukee (Boston Braves' organization), November 19, 1951.
aSold via waivers by New York Yankees to St. Louis Cardinals, March 26, 1952.
bReturned by Cardinals to Milwaukee (Boston Braves' organization), May 21, 1952.
cReleased to Los Angeles (Chicago Cubs' organization), September 28, 1953.
dReleased to Boston Red Sox, September 10, 1956.

| Year | Club | League | Position | W. | L. |
|---|---|---|---|---|---|
| 1953—Atlanta | South. | | Third | 84 | 70 |
| 1958—Minneapolis | A.A. | | †Third | 82 | 71 |
| 1959—Minneapolis | A.A. | | ‡Second(E) | 95 | 67 |
| 1960—Philadelphia§ | Nat. | | Eighth | 58 | 94 |
| 1961—Philadelphia | Nat. | | Eighth | 47 | 107 |
| 1962—Philadelphia | Nat. | | Seventh | 81 | 80 |
| 1963—Philadelphia | Nat. | | Fourth | 87 | 75 |
| 1964—Philadelphia | Nat. | | xSecond | 92 | 70 |
| 1965—Philadelphia | Nat. | | Sixth | 85 | 76 |
| 1966—Philadelphia | Nat. | | Fourth | 87 | 75 |

| Year | Club | League | Position | W. | L. |
|---|---|---|---|---|---|
| 1967—Philadelphia | Nat. | | Fifth | 82 | 80 |
| 1968—Philadelphia y | Nat. | | Fifth | 28 | 27 |
| 1969—Montreal | Nat. | | Sixth(E) | 52 | 110 |
| 1970—Montreal | Nat. | | Sixth(E) | 73 | 89 |
| 1971—Montreal | Nat. | | Fifth(E) | 71 | 90 |
| 1972—Montreal | Nat. | | Fifth(E) | 70 | 86 |
| 1973—Montreal | Nat. | | Fourth(E) | 79 | 83 |
| 1974—Montreal | Nat. | | Fourth(E) | 79 | 82 |
| 1975—Montreal | Nat. | | xFifth(E) | 75 | 87 |
| 1976—Minnesota | Amer. | | Third(W) | 85 | 77 |

†Won playoffs by defeating Wichita, four games to two and Denver, four games to none; won Junior World Series by defeating Montreal (International League), four games to none.

‡Won playoffs by defeating Omaha, four games to two and Fort Worth, four games to three; lost Junior World Series to Havana (International League), four games to three.

§Replaced Eddie Sawyer, who resigned after managing Phils in season opener (Coach Andy Cohen served as acting manager for second game), April 15, 1960.

xTied for position.

yReplaced by Bob Skinner, June 16.

## JOHN ALOYSIUS McKEON
### (Jack)
### Oakland A's

Born November 23, 1930, at South Amboy, N. J.
Height, 5.08. Weight, 205.
Threw and batted righthanded.
Hobbies—Poetry, modern art and music.
Attended Seton Hall University, South Orange, N. J., and Elon College, Elon, N. C.;
received Bachelor of Science degree in Physical Education.
Brother of Bill McKeon, former catcher in Milwaukee Braves' organization.

Led Alabama State League catchers in double plays with 9 in 1949.
Set Carolina League record for double plays by a catcher with 17 in 1953.
Named Carolina League Manager of the Year, 1961.
Named American Association Manager of the Year, 1969.

| Year | Club | League | Pos. | G. | AB. | R. | H. | 2B. | 3B. | HR. | RBI. | B.A. | PO. | A. | E. | F.A. |
|---|---|---|---|---|---|---|---|---|---|---|---|---|---|---|---|---|
| 1949—Greenville | Ala. St. | | C | 116 | 390 | 54 | 98 | 12 | 1 | 1 | 49 | .251 | *806 | 65 | 13 | *.985 |
| 1950—York | Int. | | C | 1 | 3 | .... | 1 | .... | .... | .... | .... | .333 | figures unavailable | | | |
| 1950—Gloversville | C.-Am. | | C | 72 | 209 | 18 | 45 | 5 | 0 | 0 | 14 | .215 | 281 | 30 | 15 | .954 |
| 1951— | | | | | | | (In Military Service.) | | | | | | | | | |
| 1952—Hutchison | W. Assn | | C | 116 | 358 | 42 | 78 | 10 | 1 | 4 | 40 | .218 | 756 | 68 | 11 | .987 |
| 1953—Burlington | Carolina | | C | 140 | 474 | 46 | 86 | 19 | 2 | 6 | 52 | .181 | *836 | *82 | 21 | .978 |
| 1954—Burlington | Carolina | | C | 17 | 30 | 1 | 4 | 0 | 0 | 0 | 2 | .133 | 60 | 9 | 0 | 1.000 |
| 1954—Hutchison† | W. Assn | | C | 46 | 140 | 18 | 29 | 5 | 0 | 1 | 13 | .207 | 273 | 33 | 4 | .987 |
| 1955—Fay.-Greens.-Fayetteville‡ | Carolina | | C | 59 | 172 | 20 | 29 | 3 | 0 | 1 | 17 | .169 | 292 | 20 | 6 | .981 |
| 1956—Missoula§ | Pioneer | | C | 113 | 370 | 44 | 63 | 8 | 0 | 0 | 29 | .170 | 630 | 78 | 9 | .987 |
| 1957—Missoula§ | Pioneer | | C | 102 | 299 | 37 | 65 | 7 | 0 | 4 | 40 | .217 | 645 | 55 | 10 | .986 |
| 1958—Missoula§ | Pioneer | | C | 108 | 354 | 49 | 93 | 16 | 0 | 8 | 51 | .263 | 739 | 64 | 12 | .985 |
| 1959—Fox Cities | Three-I | | C | 11 | 20 | 1 | 2 | 0 | 0 | 0 | 1 | .100 | figures unavailable | | | |

†Released by Pittsburgh Pirates' organization, September 28, 1954.

‡Played 10 games with Fayetteville, 5 games with Greensboro, and was a player-manager with Fayetteville for 44 games.

§Player-manager.

### PITCHING RECORD

| Year | Club | League | G. | IP. | W. | L. | Pct. | H. | R. | ER. | SO. | BB. | ERA. |
|---|---|---|---|---|---|---|---|---|---|---|---|---|---|
| 1956—Missoula | Pioneer | 8 | .... | 0 | 0 | .000 | .... | .... | .... | .... | .... | ....... |
| 1957—Missoula | Pioneer | 6 | .... | 0 | 0 | .000 | .... | .... | .... | .... | .... | ....... |
| 1958—Missoula | Pioneer | 2 | .... | 0 | 0 | .000 | .... | .... | .... | .... | .... | ....... |

### RECORD AS MANAGER

| Year | Club | League | Position | W. | L. |
|---|---|---|---|---|---|
| 1955—Fayetteville† | Carol. | | Third | 70 | 67 |
| 1956—Missoula | Pioneer | | Seventh | 61 | 71 |
| 1957—Missoula | Pioneer | | Sixth | 26 | 35 |
| (Second Half) | | | Third | 36 | 29 |
| 1958—Missoula | Pioneer | | Fourth | 34 | 29 |
| (Second Half) | | | Third | 36 | 30 |
| 1959—Fox Cities | Three-I | | Seventh | 26 | 39 |
| (Second Half) | | | Fourth | 33 | 28 |
| 1960—Wilson | Carolina | | Third | 36 | 34 |
| (Second Half) | | | Second | 37 | 31 |
| 1961—Wilson | Carolina | | First | 41 | 28 |
| (Second Half) | | | First | 42 | 28 |

| Year | Club | League | Position | W. | L. |
|---|---|---|---|---|---|
| 1962—Vancouver | P.C. | | Seventh | 72 | 79 |
| 1963—Dallas-Ft. W. | P.C. | | Third(S) | 79 | 79 |
| 1964—Atlanta‡ | Int. | | Eighth | 19 | 42 |
| 1968—H. Pt.-Thom. | Carol. | §Second(W) | 69 | 71 |
| 1969—Omaha | A.A. | | First | 85 | 55 |
| 1970—Omaha | A.A. | | xFirst(E) | 73 | 65 |
| 1971—Omaha | A.A. | | Third(E) | 69 | 70 |
| 1972—Omaha | A.A. | | Second(E) | 71 | 69 |
| 1973—Kansas City | Amer. | | Second(W) | 88 | 74 |
| 1974—Kansas City | Amer. | | Fifth(W) | 77 | 85 |
| 1975—Kansas City | Amer. | | Second(W) | 50 | 46 |
| 1976—Richmond | Int. | | zFourth | 69 | 71 |

†Replaced Aaron Robinson on June 11. Replaced by John Sanford on August 6 because of hand injury with team tied for first (record is for full season).

‡Replaced by Peter Appleton on June 21.

§Won playoffs by defeating Greensboro, one game to none, Lynchburg, two games to none and Raleigh-Durham, two games to one.

xWon playoff by defeating Denver, four games to one; lost Junior World Series to Syracuse, four games to one.

yReplaced by Whitey Herzog, July 24, 1975.

Managed Sampson Air Force Base team to Air Force Championship, 1951.

Scout, Minnesota Twins, 1965 through 1967.

## JOHN FRANCIS McNAMARA
### San Diego Padres

Born June 4, 1932, at Sacramento, Calif.
Height, 5.10. Weight, 175.
Threw and batted righthanded.
Attended Sacramento State College, Sacramento, Calif.
Led Northwest League catchers in double plays with 15 in 1958, 10 in 1959 and 14 in 1962.
Led Northwest League in sacrifice hits with 18 in 1959.

| Year Club | League | Pos. | G. | AB. | R. | H. | 2B. | 3B. | HR. | RBI. | B.A. | PO. | A. | E. | F.A. |
|---|---|---|---|---|---|---|---|---|---|---|---|---|---|---|---|
| 1951−Fresno | Calif. | C | 60 | 182 | 20 | 38 | 2 | 0 | 0 | 12 | .209 | 284 | 46 | 11 | .968 |
| 1952−Houston | Texas | ... | 6 | 13 | 0 | 1 | 0 | 0 | 0 | 0 | .077 | .... | .... | .... | .... |
| 1952−Lynchburg | Pied. | C | 102 | 303 | 25 | 54 | 8 | 0 | 0 | 19 | .178 | 489 | 57 | 8 | ⋆.986 |
| 1953−Winston-Salem | Carol. | | | | | (In Military Service) | | | | | | | | | |
| 1954−Omaha† | West. | | | | | (In Military Service) | | | | | | | | | |
| 1955−Lewiston | N'west | C | 129 | 427 | 49 | 102 | 24 | 4 | 1 | 54 | .239 | 544 | ⋆93 | ●15 | .977 |
| 1956−Sacramento | P. C. | C | 76 | 181 | 22 | 31 | 5 | 1 | 1 | 18 | .171 | 256 | 25 | 0 | 1.000 |
| 1956−Albuquerque | West. | C | 29 | 83 | 11 | 23 | 2 | 2 | 1 | 9 | .277 | 191 | 23 | 1 | .995 |
| 1957−Tulsa | Texas | C | 19 | 47 | 5 | 7 | 2 | 0 | 0 | 5 | .149 | 92 | 9 | 2 | .981 |
| 1957−Amarillo | West. | C | 43 | 93 | 17 | 26 | 8 | 0 | 0 | 21 | .280 | 177 | 13 | 3 | .984 |
| 1958−Lewiston | N'west | C | 133 | 439 | 62 | 117 | 20 | 2 | 2 | 63 | .276 | ⋆892 | ⋆76 | 9 | ⋆.991 |
| 1959−Lewiston | N'west | C | 141 | 491 | 74 | 122 | 25 | 4 | 1 | 44 | .248 | 714 | ⋆84 | 8 | .990 |
| 1960−Lewiston | N'west | C | 120 | 387 | 62 | 98 | 19 | 2 | 0 | 42 | .253 | ⋆726 | 48 | 7 | ⋆.991 |
| 1961−Lewiston | N'west | C | 77 | 204 | 28 | 54 | 6 | 0 | 0 | 27 | .265 | 368 | 37 | 4 | .990 |
| 1962−Lewiston | N'west | C | 93 | 281 | 41 | 77 | 11 | 2 | 1 | 33 | .274 | 670 | 74 | 8 | ⋆.989 |
| 1963−Binghamton | East. | C | 69 | 199 | 19 | 45 | 10 | 1 | 0 | 24 | .226 | 483 | 34 | 2 | .996 |
| 1964−Dallas | P. C. | C-3B | 13 | 13 | 1 | 6 | 0 | 0 | 0 | 1 | .194 | 58 | 7 | 0 | 1.000 |
| 1965−Birmingham | South. | | | | | (Did Not Play) | | | | | | | | | |
| 1966−Mobile | South. | C | 8 | 17 | 3 | 4 | 0 | 0 | 0 | 0 | .235 | 44 | 1 | 0 | 1.000 |
| 1967−Birmingham | South. | C | 2 | 6 | 1 | 0 | 0 | 0 | 0 | 1 | .000 | 10 | 1 | 0 | 1.000 |

†Released by St. Louis Cardinals' organization, April 16, 1955.

### PITCHING RECORD

| Year Club | League | G. | IP. | W. | L. | Pct. | H. | R. | ER. | SO. | BB. | ERA. |
|---|---|---|---|---|---|---|---|---|---|---|---|---|
| 1960−Lewiston | Northwest | 5 | .... | 0 | 0 | .000 | .... | .... | .... | .... | .... | ....... |
| 1961−Lewiston | Northwest | 4 | .... | 0 | 0 | .000 | .... | .... | .... | .... | .... | ....... |
| 1962−Lewiston | Northwest | 4 | 9 | 0 | 0 | .000 | 13 | 6 | 6 | 3 | 2 | 6.00 |
| 1963−Binghamton | Eastern | 1 | 1 | 0 | 0 | .000 | 0 | 0 | 0 | 0 | 0 | 0.00 |

### RECORD AS MANAGER

| Year Club | League | Position | W. | L. | Year Club | League | Position | W. | L. |
|---|---|---|---|---|---|---|---|---|---|
| 1959−Lewiston | N'west | Second | 36 | 34 | 1965−Birmingham | South. | Eighth | 54 | 85 |
| (Second Half) | | Third | 39 | 32 | 1966−Mobile | South. | First | 88 | 52 |
| 1960−Lewiston | N'west | Third | 38 | 29 | 1967−Birmingham | South. | First | 84 | 55 |
| (Second Half) | | Third | 40 | 34 | 1969−Oakland‡ | Am. | Second(W) | 8 | 5 |
| 1961−Lewiston | N'west | †First | 41 | 25 | 1970−Oaklnd | Am. | Second(W) | 89 | 73 |
| (Second Half) | | Second | 43 | 31 | 1974−San Diego | Nat. | Sixth(W) | 60 | 102 |
| 1962−Lewiston | N'west | Fifth | 31 | 38 | 1975−San Diego | Nat. | Fourth(W) | 71 | 91 |
| (Second Half) | | Fourth | 35 | 37 | 1976−San Diego | Nat. | Fifth(W) | 73 | 89 |
| 1963−Binghamton | East. | Fourth | 65 | 75 | | | | | |
| 1964−Dallas | P. C. | Sixth(E) | 53 | 104 | | | | | |

†Won playoff by defeating Yakima (Second Half winner), four games to one.

‡Replaced Hank Bauer, September 19, 1969.

Coach, Oakland Athletics, 1968 and 1969; San Francisco Giants, 1971 through 1973.

## DANIEL LEONARD OZARK
### (Danny)
### Philadelphia Phillies

Born November 26, 1923, at Buffalo, N.Y.
Height, 6.03. Weight, 210.
Threw and batted righthanded.
Hobbies—Taking movies and carpentry.
Brother of Norm Ozark, former infielder in Brooklyn Dodger and
Milwaukee Brave organizations.
Named Pacific Coast League Manager of the Year in 1963.
Named Major League Manager of the Year by THE SPORTING NEWS, 1976.

| Year Club | League | Pos. | G. | AB. | R. | H. | 2B. | 3B. | HR. | RBI. | B.A. | PO. | A. | E. | F.A. |
|---|---|---|---|---|---|---|---|---|---|---|---|---|---|---|---|
| 1942−Olean | Pony | 2B | 103 | 369 | 72 | 91 | 19 | 6 | 6 | 45 | .247 | 208 | 281 | 31 | .940 |
| 1943-44-45 | | | | | | (In Military Service) | | | | | | | | | |
| 1946−Abilene | WT-NM | 1B | 133 | 526 | 133 | 171 | 34 | 6 | 31 | 142 | .325 | 1193 | ⋆70 | 18 | .986 |

| Year Club League | Pos. | G. | AB. | R. | H. | 2B. | 3B. | HR. | RBI. | B.A. | PO. | A. | E. | F.A. |
|---|---|---|---|---|---|---|---|---|---|---|---|---|---|---|
| 1947—Fort Worth ........Tex. | 1B-3B | 131 | 436 | 58 | 107 | 18 | 0 | 14 | 58 | .245 | 637 | 142 | 40 | .951 |
| 1948—St. Paul ............A.A. | 1B | 23 | 62 | 13 | 14 | 1 | 0 | 5 | 12 | .226 | 106 | 8 | 4 | .966 |
| 1948—Newport News ..Pied. | 1B | 116 | 414 | 64 | 124 | 25 | 2 | 15 | 78 | .300 | 996 | 91 | 21 | .981 |
| 1949—St. Paul ............A.A. | 1B | 92 | 277 | 53 | 85 | 14 | 2 | 13 | 48 | .307 | 559 | 68 | 15 | .977 |
| 1950—St. Paul ............A.A. | 1B | 24 | 54 | 9 | 10 | 0 | 0 | 1 | 6 | .185 | 82 | 8 | 2 | .978 |
| 1950—Elmira ............East. | 1B | 94 | 328 | 67 | 101 | 19 | 4 | 6 | 46 | .308 | 736 | 83 | 21 | .975 |
| 1951—St. Paul ............A.A. | 1B | 125 | 376 | 64 | 98 | 21 | 1 | 15 | 74 | .261 | 867 | 92 | 15 | .985 |
| 1952—St. Paul ............A.A. | 1B | 112 | 334 | 58 | 77 | 18 | 0 | 17 | 62 | .231 | 720 | 76 | 11 | .986 |
| 1953—St. Paul ............A.A. | PH | 2 | 1 | 0 | 1 | 0 | 0 | 0 | 0 | 1.000 | 0 | 0 | 0 | .000 |
| 1953—Fort Worth ........Texas | 1B | 134 | 494 | 90 | 148 | 25 | 2 | 23 | 89 | .300 | 1016 | 85 | 10 | .991 |
| 1954—Fort Worth ........Tex. | 1B-3B | 121 | 428 | 85 | 114 | 22 | 3 | 23 | 73 | .266 | 617 | 123 | 19 | .975 |
| 1955—Fort Worth ........Texas | 1B | 140 | 447 | 69 | 121 | 24 | 2 | 18 | 79 | .271 | 1069 | 85 | 10 | .991 |
| 1956—Wichita Falls ....Big St. | 1B | 113 | 386 | 92 | 135 | 23 | 3 | •32 | 101 | .350 | 761 | 85 | 25 | .971 |
| 1957—Cedar Rapids ....I.I.I. | 1B | 95 | 290 | 49 | 77 | 13 | 1 | 19 | 64 | .266 | 526 | 49 | 12 | .980 |
| 1958—Macon ..............Sally | PH | 17 | 18 | 0 | 2 | 0 | 0 | 0 | 1 | .111 | 0 | 0 | 0 | .000 |
| 1959—Macon ..............Sally | 1B-3B | 8 | 16 | 0 | 5 | 2 | 0 | 0 | 1 | .313 | 5 | 7 | 3 | .800 |
| 1960—St. Paul ............A.A. | PH | 1 | 1 | 0 | 0 | 0 | 0 | 0 | 0 | .000 | 0 | 0 | 0 | .000 |
| 1961—Omaha ..............A.A. | PH | 1 | 0 | 0 | 0 | 0 | 0 | 0 | 0 | .000 | 0 | 0 | 0 | .000 |
| 1963—Spokane ............P.C. | | 3 | 4 | 0 | 1 | 0 | 0 | 0 | 0 | .250 | | | | |

## PITCHING RECORD

| Year Club | League | G. | IP. | W. | L. | Pct. | H. | R. | ER. | SO. | BB. | ERA. |
|---|---|---|---|---|---|---|---|---|---|---|---|---|
| 1957—Cedar Rapids .................I.I.I. | | 3 | .... | 0 | 0 | .000 | ... | ... | ... | ... | ... | ... |
| 1958—Macon................................Sally | | 1 | .... | 0 | 0 | .000 | ... | ... | ... | ... | ... | ... |

## RECORD AS MANAGER

| Year Club League | Position | W. | L. |
|---|---|---|---|
| 1956—Wichita Falls ......Big State | Fourth | 76 | 64 |
| 1957—Cedar Rapids......I.I.I. | Sixth | 49 | 79 |
| 1958—Macon ..............Sally | †Third | 70 | 70 |
| 1959—Macon ..............Sally | Eighth | 63 | 76 |
| 1960—St. Paul..............A.A. | ‡Third | 83 | 71 |
| 1961—Omaha ..............A.A. | Sixth | 62 | 87 |
| 1962—Omaha ..............A.A. | Second | 79 | 68 |
| 1963—Spokane ............P.C. | §First(N) | 98 | 60 |
| 1964—Spokane ............P.C. | Third(W) | 85 | 73 |
| 1973—Philadelphia ......Nat. | Sixth(E) | 71 | 91 |
| 1974—Philadelphia ......Nat. | Third(E) | 80 | 82 |
| 1975—Philadelphia ......Nat. | Second(E) | 86 | 76 |
| 1976—Philadelphia ......Nat. | First(E) | 101 | 61 |

†Won playoffs by defeating Augusta, one game to none and Jacksonville, two games to none.
‡Tied for position.
§Lost playoff to Oklahoma City, four games to three.
Coach, Los Angeles Dodgers, 1965 through 1972.

## CHAMPIONSHIP SERIES RECORD

| Year Club | League | W. | L. |
|---|---|---|---|
| 1976—Philadelphia ......National | | 0 | 3 |

# VERNON FRED RAPP
## (Vern)

Born May 11, 1928, at St. Louis, Mo.
Height, 6.00. Weight, 195.
Threw and batted righthanded.
Hobbies—Hunting and fishing.

Named by THE SPORTING NEWS as Minor League Manager of the Year, 1976.

| Year Club League | Pos. | G. | AB. | R. | H. | 2B. | 3B. | HR. | RBI. | B.A. | PO. | A. | E. | F.A. |
|---|---|---|---|---|---|---|---|---|---|---|---|---|---|---|
| 1946—Marion ..............Ohio St. | C-OF | 115 | 375 | 86 | 118 | 16 | 8 | 14 | 89 | .315 | 452 | 73 | 30 | .946 |
| 1947—St. Joseph ........W.A. | C | 101 | 365 | 59 | 103 | 21 | 9 | 6 | 81 | .282 | 532 | 76 | 15 | .976 |
| 1948—Omaha ..............West. | C | 56 | 186 | 30 | 61 | 12 | 1 | 9 | 31 | .328 | 298 | 40 | 15 | .958 |
| 1948—Columbus ..........A.A. | C | 7 | 19 | 6 | 7 | 0 | 0 | 1 | 3 | .368 | | | | |
| 1949—Columbus ..........A.A. | C | 77 | 249 | 30 | 64 | 14 | 5 | 6 | 29 | .257 | 313 | 40 | 14 | .962 |
| 1950—Houston ............Texas | C | 72 | 186 | 19 | 35 | 5 | 4 | 4 | 21 | .188 | 217 | 25 | 8 | .968 |
| 1951-52—Columbus......A.A. | (In Military Service) | | | | | | | | | | | | | |
| 1953—Rochester† ........Int. | C | 97 | 282 | 35 | 71 | 15 | 9 | 1 | 30 | .252 | 290 | 33 | 6 | .982 |
| 1954—Kansas City‡ ....A.A. | C | 28 | 66 | 9 | 17 | 3 | 0 | 1 | 9 | .258 | 128 | 10 | 0 | 1.000 |
| 1955—Charleston§x ....A.A. | C | 70 | 192 | 17 | 46 | 5 | 1 | 7 | 19 | .240 | 171 | 26 | 6 | .970 |
| 1956—Minneapolis y ....A.A. | C | 85 | 205 | 28 | 62 | 8 | 2 | 11 | 32 | .302 | 263 | 26 | 9 | .970 |
| 1957—Louisville z........A.A. | C | 77 | 246 | 58 | 13 | 1 | 4 | 4 | 31 | .236 | 514 | 42 | 7 | .988 |
| 1958—Denver a ..........A.A. | 1B-C | 93 | 274 | 48 | 78 | 12 | 2 | 14 | 55 | .285 | 436 | 39 | 10 | .979 |
| 1959—Denver a ..........A.A. | C | 89 | 212 | 18 | 53 | 10 | 3 | 4 | 31 | .250 | 194 | 30 | 4 | .982 |
| 1960—Denver ab ..........A.A. | C | 36 | 99 | 9 | 14 | 4 | 0 | 2 | 12 | .141 | 146 | 12 | 2 | .988 |
| 1961—Modesto§ ..........Calif. | PH | 3 | 1 | 0 | 1 | 0 | 0 | 0 | 0 | 1.000 | .... | .... | .... | .... |
| 1966—Little Rock§ ......Tex. | PH | 1 | 1 | 0 | 1 | 0 | 0 | 0 | 0 | 1.000 | .... | .... | .... | .... |
| 1976—Denver§ ............A.A. | C | 1 | 1 | 0 | 0 | 0 | 0 | 0 | 1 | 1.000 | 0 | 0 | 0 | .000 |

†Loaned by St. Louis Cardinals' organization to New York Yankees' organization, May 24, 1954.
‡Returned by Yankees' organization to Cardinals' organization, July 26, 1954. On disabled list, August 12 to September 30, 1954. Released by St. Louis Cardinals' organization, September 30, 1954; signed as free agent by Charleston, December 11, 1954.
§Player-manager.
xReleased, December 14, 1955; signed as free agent by New York Giants' organization, January 10, 1956.
yReleased by New York Giants' organization to Louisville, January 12, 1957.
zReleased to Denver (N.Y. Yankees' organization), April 2, 1958.
aPlayer-coach.
bReleased to Detroit Tigers' organization, October 12, 1960.

## RECORD AS MANAGER

| Year Club | League | Position | W. | L. | Year Club | League | Position | W. | L. |
|---|---|---|---|---|---|---|---|---|---|
| 1955—Charleston† ........A.A. | | Eighth | 19 | 40 | 1969—Indianapolis........A.A. | | Third | 74 | 66 |
| 1961—Modesto ............Calif. | | Fourth | 30 | 39 | 1970—Indianapolis........A.A. | | Third(E) | 71 | 69 |
| (Second Half) | | Sixth | 27 | 43 | 1971—Indianapolis........A.A. | | zFirst(E) | 84 | 55 |
| 1962—Greensboro‡ ......Carol. | | Fifth | 65 | 75 | 1972—Indianapolis........A.A. | | Fourth(E) | 61 | 79 |
| 1965—Tulsa.................Texas | | §First(E) | 81 | 60 | 1973—Indianapolis........A.A. | | Second(E) | 74 | 62 |
| 1966—Arkansas...........Texas | | xFirst | 81 | 59 | 1974—Indianapolis........A.A. | | aFirst(E) | 78 | 57 |
| 1967—Arkansas...........Texas | | Fifth | 63 | 77 | 1975—Indianapolis........A.A. | | Second(E) | 71 | 64 |
| 1968—Arkansas...........Texas | | yFirst(E) | 82 | 58 | 1976—Denver .............A.A. | | bFirst | 86 | 50 |

†Replaced Danny Murtaugh, July 16, 1955.
‡Replaced by Steven Souchock, August 11, 1962.
§Lost playoff to Albuquerque, three games to one.
xLost playoff to Austin, two games to one.
yLost playoff to El Paso, three games to one.
zLost playoff to Denver, four games to three.
aLost playoff to Tulsa, four games to three.
bWon playoff by defeating Omaha, four games to two.

## FRANK ROBINSON
### Cleveland Indians

Born August 31, 1935, at Beaumont, Tex.
Height, 6.01. Weight, 194.
Throws and bats righthanded.
Hobbies—Movies and music.
Attended Xavier University, Cincinnati, O.

Established major league records for most major league parks, one or more home runs, 32, 1956 through 1973, and most times hit by pitch, rookie season, 20, 1956.

Tied the following major league records: Most home runs, bases filled, game (2), June 26, 1970; most home runs, bases filled, two successive at bats (2), June 26, 1970; most runs batted in, two successive innings (8), June 26, 1970, (5th, 6th); fewest putouts, first baseman, 9 innings (0), July 1, 1971; most home runs, rookie season, 38, 1956.

Established National League record, most years leading league, hit by pitcher (6), 1965.

Hit three home runs in a game, August 22, 1959.

Won American League Triple Crown, 1966.

Led National League in slugging percentage with .595 in 1960, .611 in 1961 and .624 in 1962; led league's first basemen in double plays with 111 in 1959.

Led American League in total bases with 367 and in slugging percentage with .637 in 1966.

Named National League Rookie of the Year by the Baseball Writers' Association and THE SPORTING NEWS, 1956.

Named outfielder on THE SPORTING NEWS National League All-Star fielding team, 1958.

Named Most Valuable National League Player, 1961.

Named Outstanding National League Player by THE SPORTING NEWS, 1961.

Named as outfielder on THE SPORTING NEWS National League All-Star Team, 1961-62.

Named as outfielder on THE SPORTING NEWS American League All-Star Team, 1966-67.

Named American League Player of the Year by THE SPORTING NEWS, 1966.

Named Major League Player of the Year by THE SPORTING NEWS, 1966.

Named Most Valuable American League Player, 1966.

| Year Club | League | Pos. | G. | AB. | R. | H. | 2B. | 3B. | HR. | RBI. | B.A. | PO. | A. | E. | F.A. |
|---|---|---|---|---|---|---|---|---|---|---|---|---|---|---|---|
| 1953—Ogden .............Pion. | | O-3B-1B | 72 | 270 | 70 | 94 | 20 | 6 | 17 | 83 | .348 | 105 | 28 | 18 | .881 |
| 1954—Tulsa .................Tex. | | 2B-3B | 8 | 30 | 4 | 8 | 0 | 0 | 0 | 1 | .267 | 17 | 15 | 1 | .970 |
| 1954—Columbia ..........Sally | | OF-3-2B | 132 | 491 | *112 | 165 | 32 | 9 | 25 | 110 | .336 | 258 | 63 | 18 | .947 |
| 1955—Columbia ..........Sally | | OF-1B | 80 | 243 | 50 | 64 | 15 | 7 | 12 | 52 | .263 | 203 | 3 | 4 | .981 |
| 1956—Cincinnati.........Nat. | | OF | 152 | 572 | *122 | 166 | 27 | 6 | 38 | 83 | .290 | 323 | 5 | 8 | .976 |
| 1957—Cincinnati.........Nat. | | OF-1B | 150 | 611 | 97 | 197 | 29 | 5 | 29 | 75 | .322 | 487 | 36 | 6 | .989 |
| 1958—Cincinnati.........Nat. | | OF-3B | 148 | 554 | 90 | 149 | 25 | 6 | 31 | 83 | .269 | 314 | 24 | 6 | .983 |
| 1959—Cincinnati.........Nat. | | 1B-OF | 146 | 540 | 106 | 168 | 31 | 4 | 36 | 125 | .311 | 1049 | 78 | 18 | .984 |
| 1960—Cincinnati.........Nat. | | 1-OF-3 | 139 | 464 | 86 | 138 | 33 | 6 | 31 | 83 | .297 | 775 | 62 | 10 | .988 |
| 1961—Cincinnati.........Nat. | | OF-3B | 153 | 545 | 117 | 176 | 32 | 7 | 37 | 124 | .323 | 284 | 15 | 3 | .990 |
| 1962—Cincinnati.........Nat. | | OF | 162 | 609 | *134 | 208 | *51 | 2 | 39 | 136 | .342 | 315 | 10 | 2 | .994 |
| 1963—Cincinnati.........Nat. | | OF-1B | 140 | 482 | 79 | 125 | 19 | 3 | 21 | 91 | .259 | 238 | 13 | 4 | .984 |
| 1964—Cincinnati.........Nat. | | OF | 156 | 568 | 103 | 174 | 38 | 6 | 29 | 96 | .306 | 279 | 7 | 4 | .986 |
| 1965—Cincinnati.........Nat. | | OF | 156 | 582 | 109 | 172 | 33 | 5 | 33 | 113 | .296 | 282 | 5 | 3 | .990 |
| 1966—Baltimore‡ .........Am. | | OF-1B | 155 | 576 | *122 | 182 | 34 | 2 | *49 | *122 | *.316 | 282 | 6 | 5 | .983 |
| 1967—Baltimore.........Am. | | OF-1B | 129 | 479 | 83 | 149 | 23 | 7 | 30 | 94 | .311 | 207 | 8 | 2 | .991 |
| 1968—Baltimore.........Am. | | OF-1B | 130 | 421 | 69 | 113 | 27 | 1 | 15 | 52 | .268 | 193 | 5 | 7 | .966 |
| 1969—Baltimore.........Am. | | OF-1B | 148 | 539 | 111 | 166 | 19 | 5 | 32 | 100 | .308 | 367 | 19 | 5 | .987 |
| 1970—Baltimore.........Am. | | OF-1B | 132 | 471 | 88 | 144 | 24 | 1 | 25 | 78 | .306 | 262 | 11 | 4 | .986 |
| 1971—Baltimore‡ .......Am. | | OF-1B | 133 | 455 | 82 | 128 | 16 | 2 | 28 | 99 | .281 | 449 | 20 | 11 | .977 |
| 1972—Los Angeles§ ....Nat. | | OF | 103 | 342 | 41 | 86 | 6 | 1 | 19 | 59 | .251 | 168 | 6 | 6 | .967 |
| 1973—California .........Amer. | | OF | 147 | 534 | 85 | 142 | 29 | 0 | 30 | 97 | .266 | 38 | 3 | 1 | .976 |
| 1974—Calif.x-Cleve. ....Amer. | | 1B-OF | 144 | 477 | 81 | 117 | 27 | 3 | 22 | 68 | .245 | 23 | 0 | 1 | .958 |
| 1975—Cleveland y ......Amer. | | DH-PH | 49 | 118 | 19 | 28 | 5 | 0 | 9 | 24 | .237 | 0 | 0 | 0 | .000 |
| 1976—Cleveland y ......Amer. | | 1B-OF | 15 | 67 | 5 | 15 | 0 | 0 | 3 | 10 | .224 | 11 | 0 | 0 | 1.000 |
| National League Totals | | | 1605 | 5869 | 1084 | 1759 | 324 | 51 | 343 | 1068 | .300 | 4514 | 261 | 70 | .986 |
| American League Totals | | | 1182 | 4137 | 745 | 1184 | 204 | 21 | 243 | 744 | .286 | 1832 | 72 | 36 | .981 |
| Major League Totals | | | 2787 | 10006 | 1829 | 2943 | 528 | 72 | 586 | 1812 | .294 | 6346 | 333 | 106 | .984 |

†Traded to Baltimore Orioles for Outfielder Dick Simpson and Pitchers Milt Pappas and Jack Baldschun, December 9, 1965.

‡Traded with Pitcher Pete Richert to Los Angeles Dodgers for Pitchers Doyle Alexander and Bob O'Brien, Catcher Sergio Robles and First Baseman-Outfielder Royle Stillman, December 2, 1971.
§Traded with Infielders Billy Grabarkewitz and Bob Valentine and Pitchers Bill Singer and Mike Strahler to California Angels for Third Baseman Ken McMullen and Pitcher Andy Messersmith, November 28, 1972.
xReleased on waivers to Cleveland Indians, September 12, 1974; Indians assigned Outfielder Rusty Torres and Catcher Ken Suarez to Angels, December 4, 1974, to complete deal.
yPlayer-manager.

## CHAMPIONSHIP SERIES RECORD

| Year Club League | Pos. | G. | AB. | R. | H. | 2B. | 3B. | HR. | RBI. | B.A. | PO. | A. | E. | F.A. |
|---|---|---|---|---|---|---|---|---|---|---|---|---|---|---|
| 1969–Baltimore.........Amer. | OF | 3 | 12 | 1 | 4 | 2 | 0 | 1 | 2 | .333 | 2 | 0 | 1 | .667 |
| 1970–Baltimore.........Amer. | OF | 3 | 10 | 3 | 2 | 0 | 0 | 1 | 2 | .200 | 2 | 0 | 0 | 1.000 |
| 1971–Baltimore.........Amer. | OF | 3 | 12 | 2 | 1 | 1 | 0 | 0 | 1 | .083 | 7 | 0 | 0 | 1.000 |
| Championship Series Totals ............ | | 9 | 34 | 6 | 7 | 3 | 0 | 2 | 5 | .206 | 11 | 0 | 1 | .917 |

## WORLD SERIES RECORD

Tied World Series record for most times hit by pitcher, game (2), October 8, 1961.
Hit home run in first World Series at bat, October 5, 1966.

| Year Club League | Pos. | G. | AB. | R. | H. | 2B. | 3B. | HR. | RBI. | B.A. | PO. | A. | E. | F.A. |
|---|---|---|---|---|---|---|---|---|---|---|---|---|---|---|
| 1961–Cincinnati..........Nat. | OF | 5 | 15 | 3 | 3 | 2 | 0 | 1 | 4 | .200 | 5 | 0 | 0 | 1.000 |
| 1966–Baltimore.........Amer. | OF | 4 | 14 | 4 | 4 | 0 | 1 | 2 | 3 | .286 | 6 | 0 | 0 | 1.000 |
| 1969–Baltimore.........Amer. | OF | 5 | 16 | 2 | 3 | 0 | 0 | 1 | 1 | .188 | 13 | 0 | 0 | 1.000 |
| 1970–Baltimore.........Amer. | OF | 5 | 22 | 5 | 6 | 0 | 0 | 2 | 4 | .273 | 7 | 0 | 0 | 1.000 |
| 1971–Baltimore.........Amer. | OF | 7 | 25 | 5 | 7 | 0 | 0 | 2 | 2 | .280 | 12 | 0 | 0 | 1.000 |
| World Series Totals ........................ | | 26 | 92 | 19 | 23 | 2 | 1 | 8 | 14 | .250 | 43 | 0 | 0 | 1.000 |

## ALL-STAR GAME RECORD

| Year League | Pos. | AB. | R. | H. | 2B. | 3B. | HR. | RBI. | B.A. | PO. | A. | E. | F.A. |
|---|---|---|---|---|---|---|---|---|---|---|---|---|---|
| 1956–National ............................ | OF | 2 | 0 | 0 | 0 | 0 | 0 | 0 | .000 | 1 | 0 | 0 | 1.000 |
| 1957–National ............................ | OF | 2 | 0 | 1 | 0 | 0 | 0 | 0 | .500 | 5 | 0 | 0 | 1.000 |
| 1959–National (second game) ...... | 1B | 3 | 1 | 3 | 0 | 0 | 1 | 1 | 1.000 | 3 | 0 | 1 | .750 |
| 1961–National (first game) ......... | OF | 1 | 0 | 1 | 0 | 0 | 0 | 0 | 1.000 | 2 | 0 | 0 | 1.000 |
| 1962–National (second game) ...... | OF | 3 | 0 | 0 | 0 | 0 | 0 | 0 | .000 | 1 | 0 | 0 | 1.000 |
| 1965–National ............................ | PH | 1 | 0 | 0 | 0 | 0 | 0 | 0 | .000 | 0 | 0 | 0 | .000 |
| 1966–American ........................... | OF | 4 | 0 | 0 | 0 | 0 | 0 | 0 | .000 | 2 | 0 | 0 | 1.000 |
| 1969–American ........................... | OF | 2 | 0 | 0 | 0 | 0 | 0 | 0 | .000 | 0 | 0 | 0 | .000 |
| 1970–American ........................... | OF | 3 | 0 | 0 | 0 | 0 | 0 | 0 | .000 | 1 | 0 | 0 | 1.000 |
| 1971–American ........................... | OF | 2 | 1 | 1 | 0 | 0 | 1 | 2 | .500 | 2 | 0 | 0 | 1.000 |
| 1974–American ........................... | PH | 1 | 0 | 0 | 0 | 0 | 0 | 0 | .000 | 0 | 0 | 0 | .000 |
| All-Star Game Totals ....................... | | 24 | 2 | 6 | 0 | 0 | 2 | 3 | .250 | 17 | 0 | 1 | .944 |

Member of National League All-Star Team in 1959 (first game) and 1961 (second game); did not play. Named to American League Team for 1967 game; replaced due to injury.

## RECORD AS MANAGER

| Year Club | League | Position | W. | L. |
|---|---|---|---|---|
| 1975–Cleveland .........Amer. | | Fourth(E) | 79 | 80 |
| 1976–Cleveland .........Amer. | | Fourth(E) | 81 | 78 |

# NORMAN BURT SHERRY
## (Norm)
### California Angels

Born July 16, 1931, at New York, N.Y.
Height, 5.11. Weight, 180.
Threw and batted righthanded.
Brother of Larry Sherry, pitcher with Los Angeles Dodgers, Detroit Tigers, Houston Astros and California Angels, 1958 through 1968, and now coach with Pittsburgh Pirates.
Brother of George Sherry, pitcher in Pittsburgh Pirates' organization, 1951.

| Year Club League | Pos. | G. | AB. | R. | H. | 2B. | 3B. | HR. | RBI. | B.A. | PO. | A. | E. | F.A. |
|---|---|---|---|---|---|---|---|---|---|---|---|---|---|---|
| 1950–Santa Barbara ..Calif. | C-OF | 96 | 294 | 35 | 71 | 12 | 1 | 4 | 32 | .241 | 394 | 43 | 23 | .950 |
| 1951–Fort Worth.......Tex. | C | 25 | 65 | 1 | 5 | 2 | 0 | 0 | 3 | .077 | 90 | 14 | 12 | .897 |
| 1951–Newport News ..Pied. | C | 72 | 214 | 41 | 50 | 2 | 0 | 2 | 22 | .234 | 292 | 33 | 14 | .959 |
| 1952-53–Fort Worth....Tex. | | | | | (In Military Service) | | | | | | | | | |
| 1954–Fort Worth.......Tex. | C | 5 | 5 | 3 | 2 | 0 | 0 | 0 | 0 | .400 | 14 | 1 | 1 | .938 |
| 1954–Newport News ..Pied. | C-P | 122 | 382 | 56 | 98 | 13 | 3 | 12 | 47 | .257 | •727 | 63 | 21 | •.974 |
| 1955–Fort Worth.......Tex. | C | 67 | 165 | 28 | 43 | 10 | 1 | 4 | 26 | .261 | 221 | 18 | 5 | .980 |
| 1956–Fort Worth† ......Tex. | C | 2 | 4 | 0 | 0 | 0 | 0 | 0 | 0 | .000 | 7 | 0 | 0 | 1.000 |
| 1956–Buffalo ............Int. | C-OF | 64 | 181 | 14 | 39 | 5 | 0 | 2 | 7 | .215 | 244 | 16 | 7 | .974 |
| 1957–St. Paul‡ .........A.A. | C-1-O | 60 | 193 | 18 | 47 | 9 | 3 | 2 | 29 | .244 | 303 | 25 | 4 | .988 |
| 1958–Spokane ...........P.C. | C | 131 | 417 | 34 | 116 | 27 | 2 | 2 | 41 | .278 | 551 | •75 | •10 | .984 |
| 1959–Los Angeles ......Nat. | C | 2 | 3 | 0 | 1 | 0 | 0 | 0 | 2 | .333 | 4 | 0 | 0 | 1.000 |
| 1959–Spokane ...........P.C. | C | 108 | 332 | 35 | 84 | 15 | 1 | 7 | 47 | .253 | 433 | 52 | 9 | .982 |
| 1960–Los Angeles ......Nat. | C | 47 | 138 | 22 | 39 | 4 | 1 | 8 | 19 | .283 | 282 | 15 | 2 | .993 |
| 1961–Los Angeles§ ....Nat. | C | 47 | 121 | 10 | 31 | 2 | 0 | 5 | 21 | .256 | 253 | 16 | 2 | .993 |
| 1962–Los Angeles x....Nat. | C | 35 | 88 | 7 | 16 | 2 | 0 | 3 | 16 | .182 | 221 | 13 | 2 | .992 |
| 1963–New York .........Nat. | C | 63 | 147 | 6 | 20 | 1 | 0 | 2 | 11 | .136 | 265 | 26 | 3 | .981 |
| 1964–Buffalo y .........Int. | C | 100 | 289 | 34 | 67 | 13 | 0 | 4 | 43 | .232 | 447 | 38 | 7 | .986 |
| 1965–Santa Barbara z Calif. | C | 33 | 86 | 7 | 23 | 4 | 0 | 2 | 15 | .267 | 154 | 9 | 4 | .976 |

| Year Club League | Pos. | G. | AB. | R. | H. | 2B. | 3B. | HR. | RBI. | B.A. | PO. | A. | E. | F.A. |
|---|---|---|---|---|---|---|---|---|---|---|---|---|---|---|
| 1966—Santa Barbara z Calif. | PH | 2 | 2 | 0 | 2 | 0 | 0 | 0 | 0 | 1.000 | .... | .... | .... | .... |
| 1967—Santa Barbara z Calif. | C | 15 | 34 | 2 | 5 | 3 | 0 | 0 | 4 | .147 | 53 | 2 | 1 | .982 |
| Major League Totals .................... | | 194 | 497 | 45 | 107 | 9 | 1 | 18 | 69 | .215 | 525 | 70 | 9 | .985 |

†On disabled list, April 13 to May 22 and May 26 to June 13, 1956.
‡On disabled list, May 21 to July 24, 1957.
§On disabled list, July 12 to August 14, 1961.
xSold to New York Mets, October 11, 1962.
yReleased by New York Mets' organization, October 15, 1964.
zPlayer-manager.

## PITCHING RECORD

| Year Club | League | G. | IP. | W. | L. | Pct. | H. | R. | ER. | SO. | BB. | ERA. |
|---|---|---|---|---|---|---|---|---|---|---|---|---|
| 1954—Newport News....................Piedmont | | 1 | ⅓ | 0 | 0 | .000 | 1 | 0 | 0 | 0 | 0 | 0.00 |

## RECORD AS MANAGER

| Year Club League | Position | W. | L. | Year Club League | Position | W. | L. |
|---|---|---|---|---|---|---|---|
| 1965—Santa Barbara ....Calif. | Sixth | 30 | 40 | 1969—Idaho Falls ........Pioneer | Sixth | 30 | 42 |
| (Second Half) | †Fifth | 31 | 39 | 1972—Shreveport ........Tex. | Fourth(E) | 64 | 76 |
| 1966—Santa Barbara ....Calif. | Fifth | 35 | 35 | 1973—El Paso ..............Tex. | Second(W) | 69 | 71 |
| (Second Half) | †Fifth | 34 | 36 | 1974—Salt Lake City ....P.C. | Third(E) | 69 | 73 |
| 1967—Santa Barbara ....Calif. | †Second | 38 | 32 | 1975—Salt Lake City ....P.C. | ‡First(E) | 80 | 64 |
| (Second Half) | Third | 39 | 31 | 1976—California§ ........Amer. | Fourth(W) | 37 | 29 |

†Tied for position.
‡Lost playoff to Hawaii, four games to two.
Scout, New York Yankees, 1968; coach, California Angels, 1970, 1971 and 1976.
§Replaced Dick Williams, July 23, 1976.

## CHARLES WILLIAM TANNER, JR.
### (Chuck)
### Pittsburgh Pirates

Born July 4, 1929, at New Castle, Pa.
Height, 6.00. Weight, 185.
Threw and batted lefthanded.
Father of Mark Tanner, former minor league pitcher in Chicago Cubs' and
Texas Rangers' organizations, 1972-76.

Tied major league record by hitting home run in first time at bat in major leagues, eighth inning, April 12, 1955. Hit ball on first pitch, the second player in major league history to accomplish this feat. He was at bat at the time as a pinch-hitter.
Named THE SPORTING NEWS Major League Manager of the Year, 1972.

| Year Club League | Pos. | G. | AB. | R. | H. | 2B. | 3B. | HR. | RBI. | B.A. | PO. | A. | E. | F.A. |
|---|---|---|---|---|---|---|---|---|---|---|---|---|---|---|
| 1946—Evansville ........I.I.I. | OF | 2 | 1 | 0 | 0 | 0 | 0 | 0 | 0 | .000 | 0 | 0 | 1 | .000 |
| 1946—Owenboro..........Kitty | OF | 23 | 80 | 15 | 20 | 3 | 1 | 0 | 7 | .250 | 50 | 3 | 4 | .930 |
| 1947—Owensboro .......Kitty | OF | 25 | 104 | 32 | 35 | 9 | 3 | 0 | 20 | .337 | 47 | 3 | 2 | .962 |
| 1947—Eau Claire ........North. | OF | 40 | 151 | 29 | 49 | 6 | 3 | 7 | 27 | .325 | 76 | 3 | 9 | .898 |
| 1948—Eau Claire ........North. | OF | 67 | 263 | 60 | 95 | 22 | 5 | 7 | 52 | .361 | 89 | 4 | 9 | .912 |
| 1948—Pawtucket ........N. Eng. | OF | 46 | 171 | 26 | 47 | 1 | 6 | 2 | 20 | .275 | 60 | 6 | 5 | .930 |
| 1949—Denver .............West. | OF | 124 | 467 | 92 | 146 | 32 | 5 | 5 | 53 | .313 | 206 | 13 | 12 | .948 |
| 1950—Denver .............West. | OF | 154 | 619 | 111 | *195 | 34 | 9 | 7 | 86 | .315 | 248 | 16 | 14 | .950 |
| 1951—Atlanta.............South. | OF | 134 | 506 | 84 | 161 | 28 | 6 | 4 | 44 | .318 | 286 | 6 | 4 | .986 |
| 1952—Milwaukee ........A.A. | OF | 11 | 27 | 2 | 4 | 1 | 1 | 0 | 4 | .148 | 11 | 1 | 0 | 1.000 |
| 1952—Atlanta.............South. | OF | 117 | 440 | 64 | 152 | 18 | 11 | 2 | 65 | .345 | 212 | 9 | 6 | .974 |
| 1953—Toledo ..............A.A. | OF | 17 | 52 | 5 | 10 | 3 | 0 | 2 | 5 | .192 | 29 | 2 | 0 | 1.000 |
| 1953—Atlanta.............South. | OF | 126 | 465 | 71 | 148 | 29 | 11 | 6 | 57 | .318 | 220 | 8 | 3 | .987 |
| 1954—Atlanta.............South. | OF ●155 | | 594 | 109 | 192 | 35 | 12 | 20 | 101 | .323 | 290 | 21 | 7 | .978 |
| 1955—Milwaukee ........Nat. | OF | 97 | 243 | 27 | 60 | 9 | 3 | 6 | 27 | .247 | 101 | 4 | 2 | .981 |
| 1956—Milwaukee ........Nat. | OF | 60 | 63 | 6 | 15 | 2 | 0 | 1 | 4 | .238 | 4 | 0 | 1 | .800 |
| 1957—Mil.†-Chi. .........Nat. | OF | 117 | 387 | 47 | 108 | 19 | 2 | 9 | 48 | .279 | 191 | 5 | 2 | .990 |
| 1958—Chicago‡ .........Nat. | OF | 73 | 103 | 10 | 27 | 6 | 0 | 4 | 17 | .262 | 21 | 0 | 1 | .955 |
| 1959—Minneapolis§ ....A.A. | OF | 152 | 549 | 79 | 175 | *41 | 10 | 12 | 78 | .319 | 194 | 5 | 4 | .980 |
| 1959—Cleveland .........Amer. | OF | 14 | 48 | 6 | 12 | 2 | 0 | 1 | 5 | .250 | 18 | 0 | 0 | 1.000 |
| 1960—Cleveland .........Amer. | OF | 21 | 25 | 2 | 7 | 1 | 0 | 0 | 4 | .280 | 5 | 0 | 0 | 1.000 |
| 1960—Toronto ............Int. | OF | 28 | 92 | 13 | 27 | 5 | 2 | 4 | 14 | .293 | 40 | 1 | 0 | 1.000 |
| 1961—Toronto x ..........Int. | OF | 70 | 218 | 19 | 49 | 5 | 3 | 6 | 22 | .225 | 84 | 7 | 3 | .968 |
| 1961—Dallas-Ft.Worth A.A. | OF | 48 | 170 | 28 | 51 | 12 | 5 | 1 | 18 | .300 | 74 | 5 | 5 | .940 |
| 1961—Los Angeles .....Amer. | OF | 7 | 8 | 0 | 1 | 0 | 0 | 0 | 0 | .125 | 0 | 0 | 0 | .000 |
| 1962—Los Angeles .....Amer. | OF | 7 | 8 | 0 | 1 | 0 | 0 | 0 | 0 | .125 | 0 | 0 | 0 | .000 |
| 1962—Dallas-Ft.Worth A.A. | OF | 114 | 359 | 43 | 113 | 28 | 2 | 5 | 41 | .315 | 181 | 16 | 8 | .961 |
| 1968—El Paso ............Texas | PH | 1 | 1 | 0 | 0 | 0 | 0 | 0 | 0 | .000 | 0 | 0 | 0 | .000 |
| American League Totals ................ | | 49 | 89 | 8 | 21 | 3 | 0 | 1 | 9 | .236 | 23 | 0 | 0 | 1.000 |
| National League Totals ................ | | 347 | 796 | 90 | 210 | 36 | 5 | 20 | 96 | .264 | 317 | 9 | 6 | .982 |
| Major League Totals .................... | | 396 | 885 | 98 | 231 | 39 | 5 | 21 | 105 | .261 | 340 | 9 | 6 | .983 |

†Sold on waivers to Chicago Cubs, June 8, 1957.
‡Traded to Boston Red Sox for Pitcher Robert W. Smith, March 9, 1959.
§Purchased from Boston Red Sox by Cleveland Indians, September 9, 1959.
xSold by Cleveland Indians to Los Angeles Angels, September 8, 1961.

| Year | Club | League | Position | W. | L. |
|------|------|--------|----------|----|----|
| 1963–Quad Cities | Midwest | | Fourth | 29 | 32 |
| (Second Half) | | | Second | 37 | 25 |
| 1964–Quad Cities | Midwest | | Eighth | 24 | 31 |
| (Second Half) | | | Second | 38 | 25 |
| 1965–El Paso | Texas | | Third(W) | 53 | 87 |
| 1966–El Paso | Texas | | Fifth | 62 | 78 |
| 1967–Seattle | P.C. | | Fifth(W) | 69 | 79 |
| 1968–El Paso | Texas | | †First(W) | 77 | 60 |
| 1969–Hawaii | P.C. | | Third(S) | 74 | 72 |

| Year | Club | League | Position | W. | L. |
|------|------|--------|----------|----|----|
| 1970–Hawaii | P.C. | | ‡First(S) | 98 | 48 |
| 1970–Chicago§ | Amer. | | Sixth(W) | 3 | 13 |
| 1971–Chicago | Amer. | | Third(W) | 79 | 83 |
| 1972–Chicago | Amer. | | Second(W) | 87 | 67 |
| 1973–Chicago | Amer. | | Fifth(W) | 77 | 85 |
| 1974–Chicago | Amer. | | Fourth(W) | 80 | 80 |
| 1975–Chicago | Amer. | | Fifth(W) | 75 | 86 |
| 1976–Oakland | Amer. | | Second(W) | 87 | 74 |

†Won playoff by defeating Arkansas, three games to one.
‡Lost playoff to Spokane, four games to none.
§Replaced Don Gutteridge, September 14, 1970. (Billy Adair served as interim manager from September 3 until Tanner's arrival.)
Traded to Pittsburgh Pirates for Catcher Manny Sanguillen and $100,000 cash, November 5, 1976.

# WILLIAM CHARLES VIRDON
Name pronounced VER-done.
## (Bill)
### Houston Astros

Born June 9, 1931, at Royal Oak Township, Mich.
Height, 6.00. Weight, 185.
Threw right and batted lefthanded.
Hobbies–Golf and hunting.
Attended Drury College, Springfield, Mo.

Tied major league record for most clubs managed, season, 2, in 1975.
Tied major league record for most assists by an outfielder, inning (2), second inning, second game, August 10, 1958; tied National League record for fewest triples, season, for leader in triples, 10, in 1962; led National League outfielders in double plays (5), 1959.
Named National League Rookie of the Year by THE SPORTING NEWS, 1955.
Named outfielder on THE SPORTING NEWS National League All-Star fielding team, 1962.
Named Major League Manager of the Year by THE SPORTING NEWS, 1974.

| Year | Club | League | Pos. | G. | AB. | R. | H. | 2B. | 3B. | HR. | RBI. | B.A. | PO. | A. | E. | F.A. |
|------|------|--------|------|----|-----|----|----|-----|-----|-----|------|------|-----|----|----|------|
| 1950–Independence | K-O-M | OF | 119 | •501 | 82 | 134 | 29 | 10 | 6 | 76 | .267 | 215 | •20 | 12 | .951 |
| 1950–Kansas City | A.A. | OF | 14 | 41 | 3 | 14 | 3 | 0 | 0 | 3 | .341 | 13 | 1 | 1 | .933 |
| 1951–Norfolk | Pied. | OF | 118 | 486 | 91 | 139 | 20 | 4 | 6 | 48 | .286 | 297 | 19 | 10 | .969 |
| 1952–Binghamton | East. | OF | 122 | 467 | 57 | 122 | 13 | 9 | 2 | 46 | .261 | 300 | •18 | 11 | .967 |
| 1953–Kansas City | A.A. | OF | 95 | 330 | 51 | 77 | 13 | 4 | 6 | 25 | .233 | 174 | 8 | 7 | .963 |
| 1953–Birmingham† | South. | OF | 42 | 164 | 27 | 52 | 7 | 2 | 3 | 14 | .317 | 96 | 7 | 4 | .963 |
| 1954–Rochester | Int. | OF | 139 | 505 | 85 | 168 | 28 | 11 | 22 | 98 | •.333 | 361 | 6 | 14 | .963 |
| 1955–St. Louis‡ | Nat. | OF | 144 | 534 | 58 | 150 | 18 | 6 | 17 | 68 | .281 | 339 | 7 | 12 | .966 |
| 1956–St. L.‡-Pitts. | Nat. | OF | •157 | 580 | 77 | 185 | 23 | 10 | 10 | 46 | .319 | 387 | 12 | 5 | .988 |
| 1957–Pittsburgh | Nat. | OF | 144 | 604 | 75 | 161 | 24 | 11 | 9 | 46 | .267 | 401 | 11 | 3 | .993 |
| 1958–Pittsburgh | Nat. | OF | 144 | 519 | 67 | 132 | 24 | 2 | 8 | 41 | .254 | 404 | 16 | 9 | .979 |
| 1959–Pittsburgh | Nat. | OF | 120 | 409 | 60 | 108 | 16 | 9 | 8 | 40 | .264 | 272 | 10 | 5 | .983 |
| 1960–Pittsburgh | Nat. | OF | 146 | 599 | 81 | 156 | 22 | 8 | 9 | 58 | .260 | 384 | 6 | 6 | .985 |
| 1961–Pittsburgh | Nat. | OF | 156 | 663 | 82 | 164 | 27 | •10 | 6 | 47 | .247 | 360 | 11 | 9 | .976 |
| 1962–Pittsburgh | Nat. | OF | 142 | 554 | 58 | 149 | 22 | 6 | 8 | 53 | .269 | 323 | 6 | 4 | .988 |
| 1963–Pittsburgh | Nat. | OF | 145 | 473 | 59 | 115 | 11 | 3 | 3 | 27 | .243 | 243 | 5 | 6 | .976 |
| 1964–Pittsburgh | Nat. | OF | 135 | 481 | 58 | 134 | 22 | 5 | 4 | 24 | .279 | 260 | 3 | 8 | .970 |
| 1965–Pittsburgh | Nat. | OF | 144 | 561 | 59 | 141 | 28 | 11 | 8 | 50 | .251 | 403 | 13 | 6 | .986 |
| 1966–Williamsport | East. | OF | 5 | 7 | 0 | 0 | 0 | 0 | 0 | 0 | .000 | 1 | 0 | 0 | 1.000 |
| 1967– | | | | | | | (Did Not Play) | | | | | | | | | |
| 1968–Pittsburgh | Nat. | OF | 6 | 3 | 1 | 1 | 0 | 0 | 1 | 2 | .333 | 1 | 0 | 0 | 1.000 |
| Major League Totals | | | | 1583 | 5980 | 735 | 1596 | 237 | 81 | 91 | 502 | .267 | 3777 | 100 | 73 | .981 |

†Traded to St. Louis Cardinals by New York Yankees with Pitcher Mel Wright and Outfielder Emil Tellinger for Outfielder Enos (Country) Slaughter, April 11, 1954.
‡Traded to Pittsburgh Pirates for Pitcher Dick Littlefield and Outfielder Bobby Del Greco, May 17, 1956.

## WORLD SERIES RECORD

| Year | Club | League | Pos. | G. | AB. | R. | H. | 2B. | 3B. | HR. | RBI. | B.A. | PO. | A. | E. | F.A. |
|------|------|--------|------|----|-----|----|----|-----|-----|-----|------|------|-----|----|----|------|
| 1960–Pittsburgh | Nat. | OF | 7 | 29 | 2 | 7 | 3 | 0 | 0 | 5 | .241 | 18 | 0 | 1 | .947 |

## RECORD AS MANAGER

| Year | Club | League | Position | W. | L. |
|------|------|--------|----------|----|----|
| 1966–Williamsport | East | | Fourth | 68 | 72 |
| 1967–Jacksonville | Int. | | Fifth | 66 | 73 |
| 1972–Pittsburgh | Nat. | | First(E) | 96 | 59 |
| 1973–Pittsburgh† | Nat. | | Third(E) | 67 | 69 |

| Year | Club | League | Position | W. | L. |
|------|------|--------|----------|----|----|
| 1974–New York | Amer. | | Second(E) | 89 | 73 |
| 1975–New York‡ | Amer. | | Third(E) | 53 | 51 |
| 1975–Houston§ | Nat. | | Sixth(W) | 17 | 17 |
| 1976–Houston | Nat. | | Third(W) | 80 | 82 |

†Replaced by Danny Murtaugh with club in second place, September 7.
‡Replaced by Billy Martin, August 1.
§Replaced Preston Gomez, August 19.
Coach, Pittsburgh Pirates, 1968 through 1971.

## CHAMPIONSHIP SERIES RECORD

| Year | Club | League | W. | L. |
|------|------|--------|----|----|
| 1972–Pittsburgh | Nat. | | 2 | 3 |

## EARL SIDNEY WEAVER
### Baltimore Orioles

Born August 14, 1930, at St. Louis, Mo.
Height, 5.07. Weight, 180.
Threw and batted righthanded.

Led Western League second basemen in double plays with 112 in 1953 and Southern League with 110 in 1955.
Led Western League batters in hit by pitch with 13 in 1954.
Named Most Valuable Player in Illinois State League, 1948.

| Year Club | League | Pos. | G. | AB. | R. | H. | 2B. | 3B. | HR. | RBI. | B.A. | PO. | A. | E. | F.A. |
|---|---|---|---|---|---|---|---|---|---|---|---|---|---|---|---|
| 1948–West Frankfort..Ill. St. | | 2B | ●120 | 447 | 96 | 120 | 20 | 4 | 2 | 49 | .268 | •302 | 323 | 21 | •.967 |
| 1949–St. Joseph ........W. Assn | | 2B | 138 | 500 | 80 | 141 | 22 | 4 | 2 | 101 | .282 | 307 | 369 | 26 | .963 |
| 1950–Winston-Salem ..Carol. | | 2B | 127 | 439 | 57 | 121 | 20 | 0 | 3 | 60 | .276 | 352 | 345 | 16 | •.978 |
| 1951–Houston ............Texas | | 2B | 13 | 43 | 9 | 10 | 4 | 0 | 0 | 2 | .233 | 43 | 40 | 2 | .976 |
| 1951–Omaha ..............West. | | 2B | 142 | 506 | 81 | 141 | 35 | 2 | 0 | 52 | .279 | 330 | 393 | 25 | .967 |
| 1952–Houston ............Texas | | 2B | 57 | 201 | 24 | 44 | 7 | 1 | 2 | 21 | .219 | 148 | 128 | 11 | .962 |
| 1952–Omaha ..............West. | | 2B | 97 | 353 | 63 | 98 | 15 | 0 | 0 | 34 | .278 | 239 | 267 | 16 | .969 |
| 1953–Omaha† ............West. | | 2B | 141 | 478 | 57 | 116 | 16 | 0 | 3 | 47 | .243 | 344 | 389 | 17 | •.977 |
| 1954–Denver ..............West. | | 2B | 143 | 541 | 124 | 153 | 30 | 2 | 6 | 59 | .283 | 325 | 409 | 18 | .976 |
| 1955–New Orleans ....South. | | 2B | 119 | 392 | 77 | 109 | 19 | 2 | 6 | 69 | .278 | 294 | 342 | 10 | •.985 |
| 1956–New Orleans ....South. | | 2B | 26 | 101 | 11 | 23 | 4 | 0 | 0 | 8 | .228 | 60 | 69 | 5 | .963 |
| 1956–Mont.-Knox. ......Sally | | 2B | 113 | 417 | 47 | 99 | 10 | 3 | 4 | 22 | .237 | 300 | 309 | 11 | •.982 |
| 1957–Fitzgerald ........Ga.-Fla. | | 2B | 112 | 354 | 70 | 102 | 15 | 3 | 6 | 38 | .288 | 321 | 289 | 19 | .970 |
| 1958–Dublin ..............Ga.-Fla. | | 2B | 37 | 85 | 27 | 25 | 6 | 0 | 4 | 21 | .294 | 54 | 41 | 3 | .969 |
| 1959–Aberdeen ..........North. | | 2B | 13 | 35 | 8 | 7 | 2 | 0 | 0 | 3 | .200 | 40 | 25 | 2 | .970 |
| 1960–Fox Cities ........I.I.I. | | 2-OF | 30 | 3 | 7 | 1 | 0 | 0 | 4 | .233 | 10 | 20 | 1 | .968 |
| 1965–Elmira ..............East. | | 2B | 1 | 0 | 0 | 0 | 0 | 0 | 0 | 0 | .000 | 0 | 0 | 0 | .000 |

†Released by St. Louis Cardinals' organization to Pittsburgh Pirates' organization, September 23, 1953.

### PITCHING RECORD

| Year Club | League | G. | IP. | W. | L. | Pct. | H. | R. | ER. | SO. | BB. | ERA. |
|---|---|---|---|---|---|---|---|---|---|---|---|---|
| 1957–Fitzgerald ...........................Ga.-Fla. | | 5 | .... | 1 | 0 | 1.000 | .... | .... | .... | .... | .... | ....... |
| 1958–Dublin...............................Ga.-Fla. | | 2 | .... | 0 | 0 | .000 | .... | .... | .... | .... | .... | ....... |
| 1959–Aberdeen ...........................Northern | | 1 | .... | 0 | 0 | .000 | .... | .... | .... | .... | .... | ....... |

### RECORD AS MANAGER

| Year Club | League | Position | W. | L. | Year Club | League | Position | W. | L. |
|---|---|---|---|---|---|---|---|---|---|
| 1956–Knoxville† .........Sally | | Eighth | 10 | 24 | 1966–Rochester ..........Int. | | §First | 83 | 64 |
| 1957–Fitzgerald .........Ga.-Fla. | | Fourth | 37 | 33 | 1967–Rochester ..........Int. | | Second | 80 | 61 |
| (Second Half) | | Sixth | 28 | 41 | 1968–Baltimore x ........Amer. | | Second | 48 | 34 |
| 1958–Dublin ................Ga.-Fla. | | Third | 37 | 28 | 1969–Baltimore ..........Amer. | | First(E) | 109 | 53 |
| (Second Half) | | Third | 35 | 28 | 1970–Baltimore ..........Amer. | | First(E) | 108 | 54 |
| 1959–Aberdeen............North. | | Second | 69 | 55 | 1971–Baltimore ..........Amer. | | First(E) | 101 | 57 |
| 1960–Fox Cities ..........I.I.I. | | First | 82 | 56 | 1972–Baltimore ..........Amer. | | Third(E) | 80 | 74 |
| 1961–Fox Cities ..........I.I.I. | | Fourth | 67 | 62 | 1973–Baltimore ..........Amer. | | First(E) | 97 | 65 |
| 1962–Elmira ..............East. | | ‡Second | 72 | 68 | 1974–Baltimore ..........Amer. | | First (E) | 91 | 71 |
| 1963–Elmira ..............East. | | Second | 76 | 64 | 1975–Baltimore ..........Amer. | | Second(E) | 90 | 69 |
| 1964–Elmira ..............East. | | First | 82 | 58 | 1976–Baltimore ..........Amer. | | Second(E) | 88 | 74 |
| 1965–Elmira ..............East. | | Second | 83 | 55 | | | | | |

†Replaced Dick Bartell, August 8.
‡Won playoffs by defeating York, two games to one and Williamsport, three games to one.
§Lost in playoffs to Richmond, three games to one.
xReplaced Hank Bauer with club in third place, July 11.
Coach, Baltimore Orioles, 1968 (through July 10).

### CHAMPIONSHIP SERIES RECORD

| Year Club | League | W. | L. |
|---|---|---|---|
| 1969–Baltimore .........Amer. | | 3 | 0 |
| 1970–Baltimore .........Amer. | | 3 | 0 |
| 1971–Baltimore .........Amer. | | 3 | 0 |
| 1973–Baltimore .........Amer. | | 2 | 3 |
| 1974–Baltimore .........Amer. | | 1 | 3 |

### WORLD SERIES RECORD

| Year Club | League | W. | L. |
|---|---|---|---|
| 1969–Baltimore .........Amer. | | 1 | 4 |
| 1970–Baltimore .........Amer. | | 4 | 1 |
| 1971–Baltimore .........Amer. | | 3 | 4 |

## RICHARD HIRSHFELD WILLIAMS
### (Dick)
### Montreal Expos

Born May 7, 1929, at St. Louis, Mo.
Height, 6.00. Weight, 190.
Threw and batted righthanded.
Hobby–Golf.
Attended Pasadena City College, Pasadena, Calif.
Named Major League Manager of the Year by THE SPORTING NEWS, 1967.

| Year Club | League | Pos. | G. | AB. | R. | H. | 2B. | 3B. | HR. | RBI. | B.A. | PO. | A. | E. | F.A. |
|---|---|---|---|---|---|---|---|---|---|---|---|---|---|---|---|
| 1947—Santa Barbara ..Calif. | | OF-3B | 79 | 313 | 47 | 77 | 20 | 2 | 4 | 50 | .246 | 165 | 36 | 5 | .976 |
| 1948—Santa Barbara ..Calif. | | OF | 97 | 385 | 82 | 129 | 29 | 2 | 16 | 90 | .335 | 245 | 19 | 9 | .967 |
| 1948—Fort Worth .......Tex. | | OF-3B | 41 | 140 | 16 | 29 | 1 | 0 | 4 | 16 | .207 | 60 | 2 | 1 | .984 |
| 1949—Fort Worth .......Tex. | | •OF-2-3B | 154 | 562 | 109 | 174 | 30 | 6 | 23 | 114 | .310 | •446 | 18 | 8 | .983 |
| 1950—Fort Worth .......Tex. | | OF | 144 | 510 | 69 | 153 | 30 | 1 | 11 | 72 | .300 | 401 | 20 | 6 | .986 |
| 1951—Brooklyn† .........Nat. | | OF | 23 | 60 | 5 | 12 | 3 | 1 | 1 | 5 | .200 | 21 | 1 | 0 | 1.000 |
| 1952—Brooklyn .........Nat. | | OF-1-3B | 36 | 68 | 13 | 21 | 4 | 1 | 0 | 11 | .309 | 51 | 3 | 0 | 1.000 |
| 1953—Brooklyn .........Nat. | | OF | 30 | 55 | 4 | 12 | 2 | 0 | 2 | 5 | .218 | 24 | 0 | 2 | .923 |
| 1953—Montreal .........Int. | | OF | 66 | 230 | 28 | 64 | 12 | 1 | 2 | 33 | .278 | 111 | 3 | 2 | .983 |
| 1954—Brooklyn .........Nat. | | OF | 16 | 34 | 5 | 5 | 0 | 0 | 1 | 2 | .147 | 12 | 0 | 0 | 1.000 |
| 1954—St. Paul ............A.A. | | OF-1B | 49 | 162 | 23 | 40 | 8 | 0 | 6 | 18 | .247 | 212 | 15 | 3 | .987 |
| 1955—Fort Worth .......Tex. | | OF-1B | 153 | 596 | 82 | 189 | 29 | 4 | 24 | 91 | .317 | 580 | 22 | 7 | .989 |
| 1956—Brooklyn .........Nat. | | PH | 7 | 7 | 0 | 2 | 0 | 0 | 0 | 0 | .286 | 0 | 0 | 0 | .000 |
| 1956—Montreal‡ .........Int. | | 1B | 13 | 50 | 3 | 13 | 3 | 0 | 0 | 6 | .260 | 106 | 17 | 4 | .969 |
| 1956—Baltimore .........Am. | | O-1-2-3 | 87 | 353 | 45 | 101 | 18 | 4 | 11 | 37 | .286 | 249 | 17 | 4 | .985 |
| 1957—Balt.§-Cleve.x ....Am. | | O-3-1B | 114 | 372 | 49 | 97 | 17 | 2 | 7 | 34 | .261 | 244 | 72 | 8 | .975 |
| 1958—Baltimore y ......Am. | | O-3-1-2 | 128 | 409 | 36 | 113 | 17 | 0 | 4 | 32 | .276 | 359 | 61 | 8 | .981 |
| 1959—Kansas City ......Am. | | 3-1-O-2 | 130 | 488 | 72 | 130 | 33 | 1 | 16 | 75 | .266 | 349 | 181 | 13 | .976 |
| 1960—Kansas City z ....Am. | | 3-1B-OF | 127 | 420 | 47 | 121 | 31 | 0 | 12 | 65 | .288 | 376 | 131 | 11 | .979 |
| 1961—Baltimore .........Am. | | O-1-3B | 103 | 310 | 37 | 64 | 15 | 2 | 8 | 24 | .206 | 209 | 16 | 3 | .987 |
| 1962—Baltimore a b ....Am. | | OF-1-3B | 82 | 178 | 20 | 44 | 7 | 1 | 1 | 18 | .247 | 180 | 13 | 0 | 1.000 |
| 1963—Boston .............Am. | | 3-1B-OF | 79 | 136 | 15 | 35 | 8 | 0 | 2 | 12 | .257 | 64 | 28 | 1 | .989 |
| 1964—Boston .............Am. | | 1-3-OF | 61 | 69 | 10 | 11 | 2 | 0 | 5 | 11 | .159 | 50 | 21 | 1 | .986 |
| American League Totals ................. | | | 911 | 2735 | 331 | 716 | 148 | 10 | 66 | 308 | .262 | 2080 | 540 | 49 | .982 |
| National League Totals ................. | | | 112 | 224 | 27 | 52 | 9 | 2 | 4 | 23 | .232 | 108 | 4 | 2 | .982 |
| Major League Totals ...................... | | | 1023 | 2959 | 358 | 768 | 157 | 12 | 70 | 331 | .260 | 2188 | 544 | 51 | .982 |

†On National Defense Service List, February 7 to May 29, 1951.
‡Recalled by Brooklyn Dodgers and sold to Baltimore Orioles, June 25, 1956.
§Traded to Cleveland Indians for Outfielder Jim Busby, June 13, 1957.
xTraded with Pitcher Bud Daley and Outfielder Gene Woodling to Baltimore Orioles for Pitcher Don Ferrarese and Outfielder Larry Doby, April 1, 1958.
yTraded to Kansas City Athletics for Shortstop Chico Carrasquel, October 2, 1958.
zTraded with Pitcher Dick Hall to Baltimore Orioles for Pitcher Jerry Walker and Outfielder Chuck Essegian, April 13, 1961.
aSold to Houston Colts, October 12, 1962.
bTraded by Houston Colts to Boston Red Sox for Outfielder Carroll Hardy, December 10, 1962.

## WORLD SERIES RECORD

| Year Club | League | Pos. | G. | AB. | R. | H. | 2B. | 3B. | HR. | RBI. | B.A. | PO. | A. | E. | F.A. |
|---|---|---|---|---|---|---|---|---|---|---|---|---|---|---|---|
| 1953—Brooklyn ..........Nat. | | PH | 3 | 2 | 0 | 1 | 0 | 0 | 0 | 0 | .500 | 0 | 0 | 0 | .000 |

## RECORD AS MANAGER

| Year Club | League | Position | W. | L. |
|---|---|---|---|---|
| 1965—Toronto .............Int. | | †Third | 81 | 64 |
| 1966—Toronto .............Int. | | ‡Second | 82 | 65 |
| 1967—Boston...............Amer. | | First | 92 | 70 |
| 1968—Boston...............Amer. | | Fourth | 86 | 76 |
| 1969—Boston§ .............Amer. | | Third(E) | 82 | 71 |
| 1971—Oakland.............Amer. | | First(W) | 101 | 60 |
| 1972—Oakland.............Amer. | | First(W) | 93 | 62 |
| 1973—Oakland x.........Amer. | | First(W) | 94 | 68 |
| 1974—California y ........Amer. | | Sixth(W) | 36 | 48 |
| 1975—California z .......Amer. | | Sixth(W) | 72 | 89 |
| 1976—California .........Amer. | | Fourth(W) | 39 | 57 |

†Won playoffs by defeating Atlanta, four games to none and Columbus, four games to one.
‡Tied for position during regular season. Won playoffs by defeating Columbus, three games to two and Richmond, four games to one.
§Replaced by interim manager Eddie Popowski, September 23, 1969.
xQuit as manager of the Oakland Athletics following 1973 World Series. Signed contract to manage New York Yankees but American League President Joe Cronin ruled that Williams must honor the two years remaining on his Oakland contract.
yReplaced Bobby Winkles as manager, June 26, 1974. (Whitey Herzog served as interim manager, June 27 through June 30.)
zReplaced by Norm Sherry, July 23, 1976.
Coach, Montreal Expos, 1970.

## CHAMPIONSHIP SERIES RECORD

| Year Club | League | W. | L. |
|---|---|---|---|
| 1971—Oakland.............Amer. | | 0 | 3 |
| 1972—Oakland.............Amer. | | 3 | 2 |
| 1973—Oakland.............Amer. | | 3 | 2 |

## • WORLD SERIES RECORD

| Year Club | League | W. | L. |
|---|---|---|---|
| 1967—Boston...............Amer. | | 3 | 4 |
| 1972—Oakland.............Amer. | | 4 | 3 |
| 1973—Oakland.............Amer. | | 4 | 3 |

# DONALD WILLIAM ZIMMER
## (Don)
### Boston Red Sox

Born January 17, 1931, at Cincinnati, O.
Height, 5.09½. Weight, 188.
Threw and batted righthanded.
Hobbies—Golf and fishing.
Father of Tom Zimmer, manager of Wisconsin Rapids (Minnesota Twins' organization).

| Year Club | League | Pos. | G. | AB. | R. | H. | 2B. | 3B. | HR. | RBI. | B.A. | PO. | A. | E. | F.A. |
|---|---|---|---|---|---|---|---|---|---|---|---|---|---|---|---|
| 1949—Cambridge | E. Shore | SS | 71 | 304 | 56 | 69 | 14 | 3 | 4 | 30 | .227 | 162 | 171 | 27 | .925 |
| 1950—Hornell | Pony | •SS-3B | 123 | 518 | •146 | 163 | 34 | 5 | •23 | 122 | .315 | •269 | •367 | 45 | •.934 |
| 1951—Elmira | East. | SS | 137 | 546 | 94 | 149 | 28 | 2 | 9 | 70 | .273 | •326 | 414 | 38 | •.951 |
| 1952—Mobile | South. | SS | 153 | 613 | 107 | 190 | 32 | 7 | 17 | 91 | .310 | •355 | •517 | •52 | .944 |
| 1953—St. Paul† | A.A. | SS | 81 | 320 | 57 | 96 | 14 | 4 | 23 | 63 | .300 | 165 | 264 | 21 | .953 |
| 1954—St. Paul | A.A. | SS | 73 | 268 | 54 | 78 | 9 | 6 | 17 | 53 | .291 | 152 | 200 | 16 | .957 |
| 1954—Brooklyn | Nat. | SS | 24 | 33 | 3 | 6 | 0 | 1 | 0 | 0 | .182 | 14 | 32 | 3 | .939 |
| 1955—Brooklyn | Nat. | 2-S-3 | 88 | 280 | 38 | 67 | 10 | 1 | 15 | 50 | .239 | 184 | 207 | 12 | .970 |
| 1956—Brooklyn‡ | Nat. | S-3-2 | 17 | 20 | 4 | 6 | 1 | 0 | 0 | 2 | .300 | 10 | 11 | 1 | .955 |
| 1957—Brooklyn | Nat. | 3-S-2 | 84 | 269 | 23 | 59 | 9 | 1 | 6 | 19 | .219 | 114 | 186 | 15 | .952 |
| 1958—Los Angeles | Nat. | S-3-2-O | 127 | 455 | 52 | 119 | 15 | 2 | 17 | 60 | .262 | 281 | 395 | 26 | .963 |
| 1959—Los Angeles x | Nat. | S-3-2 | 97 | 249 | 21 | 41 | 7 | 1 | 4 | 28 | .165 | 120 | 240 | 10 | .973 |
| 1960—Chicago | Nat. | 2-3-S-O | 132 | 368 | 37 | 95 | 16 | 7 | 6 | 35 | .258 | 211 | 274 | 16 | .968 |
| 1961—Chicago y | Nat. | 2-3-OF | 128 | 477 | 57 | 120 | 25 | 4 | 13 | 40 | .252 | 284 | 332 | 20 | .969 |
| 1962—N.Y. z-Cinn. a | Nat. | 3-2-S | 77 | 244 | 19 | 52 | 12 | 2 | 2 | 17 | .213 | 77 | 129 | 11 | .949 |
| 1963—Los Angeles b | Nat. | 3-2-S | 22 | 23 | 4 | 5 | 1 | 0 | 1 | 2 | .217 | 3 | 14 | 2 | .895 |
| 1963—Washington | Am. | 3B-2B | 83 | 298 | 37 | 74 | 12 | 1 | 13 | 44 | .248 | 90 | 177 | 18 | .937 |
| 1964—Washington | Am. | 3-OF-C-2 | 121 | 341 | 38 | 84 | 16 | 2 | 12 | 38 | .246 | 72 | 144 | 10 | .956 |
| 1965—Washington c | Am. | C-3-2 | 95 | 226 | 20 | 45 | 6 | 0 | 2 | 17 | .199 | 181 | 81 | 12 | .956 |
| 1966—Toei | Pacific | 3B-SS | 87 | 203 | 14 | 37 | 2 | 0 | 9 | 20 | .182 | 101 | 143 | 11 | .957 |
| 1967—Knoxville | So. | P-3-1-C | 25 | 49 | 2 | 10 | 3 | 0 | 0 | 5 | .204 | 21 | 12 | 6 | .846 |
| 1967—Buffalo | Int. | 3B-OF | 16 | 33 | 2 | 6 | 2 | 0 | 1 | 2 | .182 | 4 | 9 | 3 | .813 |
| American League Totals | | | 299 | 865 | 95 | 203 | 34 | 3 | 27 | 99 | .235 | 343 | 402 | 40 | .949 |
| National League Totals | | | 796 | 2418 | 258 | 570 | 96 | 19 | 64 | 253 | .236 | 1298 | 1820 | 116 | .964 |
| Major League Totals | | | 1095 | 3283 | 353 | 773 | 130 | 22 | 91 | 352 | .235 | 1641 | 2222 | 156 | .961 |

†Was leading American Association in home runs and runs batted in July 7, 1953, when he was struck in the head by Pitcher Jim Kirk of Columbus; out of action for rest of season.

‡Suffered cheek bone fracture when he was struck by a pitch from Hal Jeffcoat of Cincinnati Redlegs, June 23, 1956; out of action for rest of season.

xTraded to Chicago Cubs for Pitcher Ron Perranoski, Infielder John Goryl, Outfielder Lee Handley and reported $25,000, April 8, 1960; players acquired by Dodgers were from the Cubs' farm system and assigned by Los Angeles to minor league clubs.

ySelected by New York Mets in Expansion Draft, October 10, 1961.

zTraded to Cincinnati Reds for Pitcher Robert G. Miller and Third Baseman Cliff Cook May 6, 1962.

aTraded to Los Angeles Dodgers for Pitcher Scott Breeden, January 24, 1963.

bSold to Washington Senators, June 24, 1963.

cReleased, November 19, 1965; went on to play one year of professional baseball in Japan with Toei Flyers.

### PITCHING RECORD

| Year Club | League | G. | IP. | W. | L. | Pct. | H. | R. | ER. | SO. | BB. | ERA. |
|---|---|---|---|---|---|---|---|---|---|---|---|---|
| 1967—Knoxville | Southern | 12 | 27 | 0 | 0 | .000 | 33 | 15 | 14 | 8 | 7 | 4.67 |

### WORLD SERIES RECORD

| Year Club | League | Pos. | G. | AB. | R. | H. | 2B. | 3B. | HR. | RBI. | B.A. | PO. | A. | E. | F.A. |
|---|---|---|---|---|---|---|---|---|---|---|---|---|---|---|---|
| 1955—Brooklyn | Nat. | 2B | 4 | 9 | 0 | 2 | 0 | 0 | 0 | 2 | .222 | 4 | 8 | 2 | .857 |
| 1959—Los Angeles | Nat. | SS | 1 | 1 | 0 | 0 | 0 | 0 | 0 | 0 | .000 | 0 | 1 | 0 | 1.000 |
| World Series Totals | | | 5 | 10 | 0 | 2 | 0 | 0 | 0 | 2 | .200 | 4 | 9 | 2 | .867 |

### ALL-STAR GAME RECORD

| Year League | Pos. | AB. | R. | H. | 2B. | 3B. | HR. | RBI. | B.A. | PO. | A. | E. | F.A. |
|---|---|---|---|---|---|---|---|---|---|---|---|---|---|
| 1961—National (first game) | 2B | 1 | 0 | 0 | 0 | 0 | 0 | 0 | .000 | 0 | 0 | 1 | .000 |

### RECORD AS MANAGER

| Year Club | League | Position | W. | L. |
|---|---|---|---|---|
| 1967—Knoxville | South. | †Sixth | 26 | 46 |
| 1967—Buffalo | Int. | †Seventh | 33 | 40 |
| 1968—Indianapolis | P.C. | Fifth(E) | 66 | 78 |
| 1969—Key West | Fla. St. | ‡Th'd(S) | 67 | 63 |
| 1970—Salt Lake City | P.C. | Fourth(S) | 44 | 99 |
| 1972—San Diego§ | Nat. | Sixth(W) | 54 | 88 |
| 1973—San Diego | Nat. | Sixth(W) | 60 | 102 |
| 1976—Boston x | Amer. | Third(E) | 42 | 34 |

†Transferred by Cincinnati Reds' Organization from Knoxville to Buffalo, July 5.
‡Tied for position with Pompano Beach.
§Replaced Preston Gomez, April 27, 1972.
xReplaced Darrell Johnson, July 19, 1976.
Coach, Montreal Expos, 1971; San Diego Padres, 1972; Boston Red Sox, 1974 to July, 1976.

# Major League Coaches

## CHARLES DWIGHT ADAMS
### (Red)
### Los Angeles Dodgers

Born October 7, 1921, at Parlier, Calif.
Height, 6.02. Weight, 200.
Threw and batted righthanded.
Hobbies—Movies and musicals.

| Year   Club | League | G. | IP. | W. | L. | Pct. | H. | R. | ER. | SO. | BB. | ERA. |
|---|---|---|---|---|---|---|---|---|---|---|---|---|
| 1939—Bisbee | Ariz.-Tex. | 27 | 216 | 16 | 8 | .667 | 244 | 148 | 111 | 116 | 62 | 4.63 |
| 1940—Bisbee | Ariz.-Tex. | 31 | •240 | 13 | 12 | .520 | 188 | •176 | •141 | 191 | 68 | 5.29 |
| 1941—Vancouver | W. Int'tional | 32 | 171 | 6 | 15 | .286 | 207 | 115 | 94 | 95 | 67 | 4.95 |
| 1942—Los Angeles | P. Coast | 11 | 67 | 6 | 4 | .600 | 69 | 31 | 31 | 21 | 31 | 4.16 |
| 1942—Tulsa | Texas | 10 | 90 | 4 | 8 | .333 | 93 | 50 | 44 | 44 | 37 | 4.40 |
| 1943— | | | | | (Out of Organized Ball) | | | | | | | |
| 1944—Los Angeles | P. Coast | •44 | 186 | 10 | 7 | .588 | 176 | 88 | 74 | 87 | 56 | 3.58 |
| 1945—Los Angeles | P. Coast | 41 | 298 | 21 | 15 | .583 | 269 | 104 | 90 | 160 | 90 | 2.72 |
| 1946—Los Angeles | P. Coast | 17 | 104 | 9 | 4 | .692 | 96 | 39 | 31 | 61 | 25 | 2.68 |
| 1946—Chicago | National | 8 | 12 | 0 | 1 | .000 | 18 | 12 | 11 | 8 | 7 | 8.25 |
| 1947—Los Angeles | P. Coast | 34 | 236 | 14 | 12 | .538 | 230 | 97 | 92 | 134 | '57 | 3.51 |
| 1948—Los Angeles | P. Coast | 32 | 226 | 14 | 11 | .560 | 234 | 98 | 89 | 102 | 61 | 3.54 |
| 1949—Los Angeles†-San Diego‡ | P. Coast | 24 | 161 | 8 | 7 | .533 | 173 | 74 | 69 | 73 | 58 | 3.86 |
| 1950—Portland | P. Coast | 41 | 181 | 9 | 10 | .474 | 172 | 107 | 93 | 92 | 76 | 4.62 |
| 1951—Portland‡ | P. Coast | 37 | 153 | 11 | 9 | .550 | 149 | 96 | 69 | 80 | 53 | 4.06 |
| 1952—Portland | P. Coast | 37 | 269 | 15 | 16 | .484 | 211 | 74 | 65 | 162 | 67 | •2.17 |
| 1953—Portland | P. Coast | 37 | 177 | 9 | 10 | .474 | 176 | 92 | 86 | 82 | 63 | 4.38 |
| 1954—Portland | P. Coast | 34 | 129 | 7 | 11 | .389 | 152 | 80 | 73 | 62 | 48 | 5.11 |
| 1955—Portland | P. Coast | 28 | 220 | 12 | 12 | .500 | 184 | 61 | 50 | 108 | 33 | 2.05 |
| 1956—Portland§-Los Angeles | P. Coast | 18 | 100 | 6 | 4 | .600 | 125 | 59 | 50 | 36 | 21 | 4.49 |
| 1957—Los Angeles x | P. Coast | 9 | 54 | 2 | 5 | .286 | 55 | 29 | 25 | 15 | 17 | 4.19 |
| 1957—Miami | Int'national | 16 | 43 | 1 | 2 | .333 | 46 | 24 | 18 | 19 | 15 | 3.77 |
| 1958—Sacramento | P. Coast | 4 | 10 | 0 | 1 | .000 | 15 | 8 | 8 | 2 | 4 | 7.20 |
| Major League Totals | | 8 | 12 | 0 | 1 | .000 | 18 | 12 | 11 | 8 | 7 | 8.25 |

†Traded by Chicago Cubs' organization to Cleveland Indians' organization, April 20, 1949.
‡Traded by Cleveland Indians' organization to Brooklyn Dodgers' organization, December 15, 1949.
§Released, June 18, 1956; signed as free agent by Los Angeles (Pacific Coast League), June 19, 1956.
xReleased, July 16, 1957.
Scout, Los Angeles Dodgers, 1959 through 1968; coach, Los Angeles Dodgers, 1969 through 1977.

## JOHN JOSEPH AMALFITANO
Name pronounced UH-mal-fuh-TONN-oh.
### (Joe)
### San Diego Padres

Born January 23, 1934, at San Pedro, Calif.
Height, 5.11. Weight, 179.
Threw and batted righthanded.
Attended Loyola University, Los Angeles, Calif., and University of
Southern California, Los Angeles, Calif.; received Bachelor
of Arts degree in Accounting.

Received reported $35,000 bonus to sign with New York Giants, 1954.

| Year   Club | League | Pos. | G. | AB. | R. | H. | 2B. | 3B. | HR. | RBI. | B.A. | PO. | A. | E. | F.A. |
|---|---|---|---|---|---|---|---|---|---|---|---|---|---|---|---|
| 1954—New York | Nat. | 3B-2B | 9 | 5 | 2 | 0 | 0 | 0 | 0 | 0 | .000 | 2 | 5 | 0 | 1.000 |
| 1955—New York | Nat. | SS-3B | 36 | 22 | 8 | 5 | 1 | 1 | 0 | 1 | .227 | 12 | 19 | 3 | .912 |
| 1956—Minneapolis | A.A. | 2B | 44 | 121 | 23 | 31 | 4 | 1 | 0 | 8 | .256 | 76 | 90 | 6 | .965 |
| 1956—Johnstown | East. | 3B-SS | 64 | 257 | 36 | 75 | 14 | 2 | 4 | 30 | .292 | 81 | 144 | 18 | .926 |
| 1957—Dallas | Texas | INF | 98 | 359 | 40 | 105 | 14 | 6 | 3 | 27 | .292 | 99 | 183 | 20 | .934 |
| 1958—Phoenix† | P.C. | INF-OF | 114 | 372 | 62 | 106 | 28 | 4 | 9 | 51 | .285 | 195 | 207 | 21 | .950 |
| 1959—Toronto‡ | Int. | 2B | 115 | 380 | 62 | 117 | 19 | 6 | 7 | 43 | .308 | 240 | 274 | 9 | .983 |
| 1960—San Francisco | Nat. | 3-2-S-O | 106 | 328 | 47 | 91 | 15 | 3 | 1 | 27 | .277 | 103 | 187 | 14 | .954 |
| 1961—San Francisco§ | Nat. | 2B-3B | 109 | 384 | 64 | 98 | 11 | 4 | 2 | 23 | .255 | 204 | 236 | 13 | .971 |
| 1962—Houston x | Nat. | 2B-3B | 117 | 380 | 44 | 90 | 12 | 5 | 1 | 27 | .237 | 231 | 270 | 18 | .965 |
| 1963—San Francisco | Nat. | 2B-3B | 54 | 137 | 11 | 24 | 3 | 0 | 1 | 7 | .175 | 61 | 92 | 3 | .981 |
| 1963—Tacoma y | P.C. | 2B-SS | 24 | 86 | 8 | 20 | 4 | 0 | 1 | 12 | .233 | 51 | 64 | 5 | .958 |
| 1964—Chicago | Nat. | 2-SS-1 | 100 | 324 | 51 | 78 | 19 | 6 | 4 | 27 | .241 | 201 | 254 | 17 | .964 |
| 1965—Chicago | Nat. | 2B-SS | 67 | 96 | 13 | 26 | 4 | 0 | 0 | 8 | .271 | 31 | 67 | 2 | .980 |
| 1966—Chicago | Nat. | 2-3-SS | 41 | 38 | 8 | 6 | 2 | 0 | 0 | 3 | .158 | 23 | 19 | 1 | .977 |
| 1966—Tacoma | P.C. | SS-3B | 17 | 66 | 9 | 16 | 4 | 0 | 1 | 4 | .242 | 32 | 56 | 4 | .957 |
| 1967—Chicago | Nat. | PH | 4 | 1 | 0 | 0 | 0 | 0 | 0 | 0 | .000 | .... | .... | .. | ...... |
| Major League Totals | | | 643 | 1715 | 248 | 418 | 67 | 19 | 9 | 123 | .244 | 868 | 1149 | 71 | .966 |

†Assigned outright to Toronto by San Francisco Giants, December 5, 1958.
‡Drafted by San Francisco Giants, November 30, 1959.
§Selected by Houston Colts in National League expansion draft, October 10, 1961.
xTraded to San Francisco Giants for Pitcher Dick LeMay and Outfielder Manuel Mota, November 30, 1962.

ySold by San Francisco Giants to Chicago Cubs, March 29, 1964.
Coach, Chicago Cubs, 1967 through 1971; San Francisco Giants, 1972 through 1975; San Diego Padres, 1976 and 1977.

## GEORGE IRVIN BAMBERGER
### Baltimore Orioles

Born August 1, 1925, at Staten Island, N.Y.
Height, 5.11½. Weight, 190.
Threw right and batted left and righthanded.
Hobbies—Golf and oil painting.

Established Pacific Coast League record for most innings pitched without issuing a base on balls, 68⅔, from July 10 to August 14, 1958.
Pitched 1-0 no-hit victory against Toronto, June 17, 1951.
Led International League in wild pitches with 11 in 1949.
Led Pacific Coast League in wild pitches with 13 in 1950.
Tied for International League lead in shutouts with 5 in 1949 and tied for Pacific Coast League lead with 5 in 1958.

| Year | Club | League | G. | IP. | W. | L. | Pct. | H. | R. | ER. | SO. | BB. | ERA. |
|---|---|---|---|---|---|---|---|---|---|---|---|---|---|
| 1946—Erie | ............... | Mid. Atl. | 26 | 160 | 13 | 3 | .813 | 121 | 52 | 24 | 107 | 87 | •1.35 |
| 1947—Manchester | ..................... | N. England | 33 | 165 | 12 | 11 | .522 | 135 | 87 | 64 | 134 | 99 | 3.49 |
| 1948—Jersey City | ................... | Int'national | 25 | 65 | 2 | 2 | .500 | 83 | 52 | 46 | 28 | 4 | 6.37 |
| 1949—Jersey City | ................... | Int'national | 32 | 194 | 14 | 11 | .560 | 193 | 119 | 97 | 98 | 87 | 4.50 |
| 1950—Oakland | ........................... | P. Coast | 39 | 236 | 17 | 13 | .567 | 226 | 120 | 111 | 133 | 112 | 4.23 |
| 1951—New York | ......................... | National | 2 | 2 | 0 | 0 | .000 | 4 | 4 | 4 | 1 | 2 | 18.00 |
| 1951—Ottawa | ............................ | Int'national | 26 | 174 | 11 | 11 | .500 | 158 | 75 | 65 | 68 | 57 | 3.36 |
| 1952—New York | ......................... | National | 5 | 4 | 0 | 0 | .000 | 6 | 4 | 4 | 0 | 6 | 9.00 |
| 1952—Oakland | .......................... | P. Coast | 27 | 150 | 14 | 6 | .700 | 129 | 59 | 48 | 67 | 36 | 2.88 |
| 1953—Oakland | .......................... | P. Coast | 47 | 245 | 15 | 16 | .484 | 289 | •146 | •136 | 111 | 100 | 5.00 |
| 1954—Oakland | .......................... | P. Coast | 40 | 179 | 11 | 8 | .579 | 170 | 75 | 70 | 61 | 81 | 3.53 |
| 1955—Oakland | .......................... | P. Coast | 35 | 180 | 12 | 14 | .462 | 182 | 87 | 83 | 70 | 61 | 4.15 |
| 1956—Vancouver | ........................ | P. Coast | 30 | 186 | 9 | 14 | .391 | 215 | 101 | 84 | 69 | 45 | 4.07 |
| 1957—Vancouver | ........................ | P. Coast | 34 | 200 | 14 | 12 | .538 | •244 | 98 | 89 | 73 | 46 | 4.01 |
| 1958—Vancouver | ........................ | P. Coast | 31 | 184 | 15 | 11 | .577 | 183 | 58 | 50 | 71 | 26 | •2.45 |
| 1959—Baltimore | ........................ | American | 3 | 8 | 0 | 0 | .000 | 15 | 7 | 7 | 2 | 2 | 7.88 |
| 1959—Vancouver | ........................ | P. Coast | 25 | 160 | 11 | 7 | .611 | 167 | 60 | 53 | 75 | 27 | 2.98 |
| 1960—Vancouver | ........................ | P. Coast | 35 | 206 | 12 | 12 | .500 | 238 | 111 | 87 | 89 | 34 | 3.80 |
| 1961—Vancouver | ........................ | P. Coast | 31 | 196 | 12 | 6 | .667 | 195 | 97 | 82 | 105 | 42 | 3.77 |
| 1962—Vancouver | ........................ | P. Coast | 34 | 228 | 12 | 12 | .500 | 227 | 98 | 80 | 135 | 37 | 3.16 |
| 1963—Dallas-Ft. Worth | ................. | P. Coast | 35 | 169 | 7 | 15 | .318 | 205 | 101 | 85 | 86 | 29 | 4.53 |
| National League Totals | ............................ | | 7 | 6 | 0 | 0 | .000 | 10 | 8 | 8 | 1 | 8 | 12.00 |
| American League Totals | ........................... | | 3 | 8 | 0 | 0 | .000 | 15 | 7 | 7 | 2 | 2 | 7.88 |
| Major League Totals | ................................ | | 10 | 14 | 0 | 0 | .000 | 25 | 15 | 15 | 3 | 10 | 9.64 |

Player-Coach, Vancouver, Pacific Coast League, 1960 through 1962; Dallas-Ft. Worth, Pacific Coast League, 1963; Minor League Pitching Instructor, Baltimore Orioles, 1964 through 1967; Coach, Baltimore Orioles, 1968 through 1977.

## ROMANUS BASGALL
### (Monty)
### Los Angeles Dodgers

Born, February 8, 1923, at Pfeifer, Kan.
Height, 5.10½. Weight, 185.
Threw and batted righthanded.
Hobbies—Hunting and fishing.
Attended Sterling College, Sterling, Kan.

Led Pacific Coast League in sacrifice hits with 27 in 1952.

| Year | Club | League | Pos. | G. | AB. | R. | H. | 2B. | 3B. | HR. | RBI. | B.A. | PO. | A. | E. | F.A. |
|---|---|---|---|---|---|---|---|---|---|---|---|---|---|---|---|---|
| 1942—Valdosta | ............ | Ga.-Fla. | 2B | 126 | 502 | 71 | 127 | 14 | 7 | 1 | 65 | .253 | 427 | 502 | 35 | .964 |
| 1943-44-45—Durham | .... | Pied. | | | | | (In Military Service) | | | | | | | | | |
| 1946—Fort Worth | ........ | Texas | 2B-P | 155 | 545 | 60 | 123 | 22 | 2 | 1 | 45 | .226 | 432 | 457 | 41 | .956 |
| 1947—Fort Worth† | ...... | Texas | 2B-SS | 153 | 599 | 75 | 163 | 30 | 5 | 3 | 71 | .272 | 460 | 422 | 30 | .967 |
| 1948—Pittsburgh | ........ | Nat. | 2B | 38 | 51 | 12 | 11 | 1 | 0 | 2 | 6 | .216 | 37 | 35 | 0 | 1.000 |
| 1948—New Orleans | .... | South. | 2B | 23 | 94 | 25 | 34 | 9 | 1 | 1 | 12 | .362 | 51 | 66 | 2 | .983 |
| 1949—Pittsburgh | ........ | Nat. | 2B-3B | 107 | 308 | 25 | 67 | 9 | 1 | 2 | 26 | .218 | 224 | 225 | 13 | .972 |
| 1950—Indianapolis | ...... | A.A. | 2B | 133 | 462 | 63 | 130 | 29 | 4 | 13 | 58 | .281 | 331 | 286 | 25 | .961 |
| 1951—Pittsburgh | ........ | Nat. | 2B | 55 | 153 | 15 | 32 | 5 | 2 | 0 | 9 | .209 | 140 | 144 | 9 | .969 |
| 1951—Indianapolis | ...... | A.A. | SS | 37 | 106 | 15 | 27 | 5 | 1 | 1 | 13 | .255 | 42 | 73 | 11 | .913 |
| 1952—Hollywood | ........ | P.C. | 2B | 149 | 578 | 89 | 161 | 22 | 0 | 8 | 63 | .279 | 379 | 345 | 24 | .968 |
| 1953—Hollywood | ........ | P.C. | 2B | 162 | 578 | 63 | 144 | 28 | 4 | 10 | 77 | .249 | 417 | 429 | •31 | .965 |
| 1954—Hollywood | ........ | P.C. | 2B | 145 | 457 | 57 | 115 | 18 | 1 | 4 | 59 | .252 | 323 | •356 | 16 | .977 |
| 1955—Seattle‡ | .......... | P.C. | 2B-3B | 132 | 420 | 59 | 103 | 25 | 1 | 8 | 42 | .245 | 266 | 297 | 25 | .957 |
| 1956—Waco§ | ............. | Big St. | 2B | 54 | 154 | 20 | 50 | 8 | 0 | 4 | 24 | .325 | 86 | 94 | 12 | .938 |
| 1957—Beaumont§ | ....... | Big St. | 2B | 36 | 80 | 10 | 27 | 4 | 1 | 0 | 17 | .338 | 55 | 52 | 3 | .973 |
| 1958—Lincoln§ | .......... | West. | INF | 6 | 10 | 1 | 2 | 1 | 0 | 0 | 2 | .200 | figures unavailable | | | |
| Major League Totals | ..................... | | | 200 | 512 | 52 | 110 | 15 | 3 | 4 | 41 | .215 | 401 | 404 | 22 | .973 |

†Drafted from Montreal (Brooklyn Dodgers' organization) by Pittsburgh Pirates, December 3, 1947.
‡Released, September 19, 1955.
§Player-manager.

— 442 —

## RECORD AS PITCHER

| Year    Club | League | G. | IP. | W. | L. | Pct. | H. | R. | ER. | SO. | BB. | ERA. |
|---|---|---|---|---|---|---|---|---|---|---|---|---|
| 1946—Fort Worth ........................Texas | | 1 | 1 | 0 | 0 | .000 | 3 | 4 | 2 | 1 | 1 | 18.00 |

## RECORD AS MANAGER

| Year    Club | League | Position | W. | L. | Year    Club | League | Position | W. | L. |
|---|---|---|---|---|---|---|---|---|---|
| 1956—Waco.................Big St. | | †Second | 78 | 62 | 1958—Lincoln .............West. | | Third | 75 | 71 |
| 1957—Beaumont .........Big St. | | Fourth | 31 | 33 | 1971—Albuquerque ......Tex. | | Third(W) | 67 | 75 |
| (Second Half) | | Second | 30 | 30 | 1972—El Paso‡ ............Tex. | | Second(W) | 33 | 31 |

†Tied for position with Port Arthur.
‡Replaced by Stan Wasiak, June 22, 1972.
Scout, Los Angeles Dodgers, 1959 through 1970, and from July 20, 1972 through the end of the season; coach, Los Angeles Dodgers, 1973 through 1977.


# VERNON ADAIR BENSON
## (Vern)
## Atlanta Braves

Born September 19, 1924, at Granite Quarry, N. C.
Height, 5.11.  Weight, 185.
Threw right and batted lefthanded.
Hobbies—Fishing and golf.
Attended Catawba College, Salisbury, N. C.
Father of Randy Benson, former pitcher in St. Louis Cardinals' and Baltimore Orioles' organization.

| Year    Club | League | Pos. | G. | AB. | R. | H. | 2B. | 3B. | HR. | RBI. | B.A. | PO. | A. | E. | F.A. |
|---|---|---|---|---|---|---|---|---|---|---|---|---|---|---|---|
| 1943—Philadelphia ......Amer. | | PH | 2 | 2 | 0 | 0 | 0 | 0 | 0 | 0 | .000 | 0 | 0 | 0 | .000 |
| 1944-45—Philadelphia..Amer. | | | | | (In Military Service) | | | | | | | | | | |
| 1946—Toronto ............Int. | | OF | 26 | 71 | 15 | 11 | 2 | 1 | 3 | 8 | .155 | 42 | 5 | 1 | .979 |
| 1946—Savannah ..........Sally | | OF | 65 | 210 | 19 | 35 | 5 | 5 | 1 | 24 | .167 | 128 | 7 | 6 | .957 |
| 1946—Philadelphia† ....Amer. | | OF | 7 | 5 | 1 | 0 | 0 | 0 | 0 | 0 | .000 | 4 | 0 | 0 | 1.000 |
| 1947—Rochester..........Int. | | OF | 87 | 186 | 35 | 51 | 11 | 1 | 6 | 30 | .274 | 119 | 4 | 3 | .976 |
| 1948—Rochester..........Int. | | INF-OF | 97 | 228 | 39 | 56 | 12 | 2 | 4 | 38 | .246 | 118 | 119 | 14 | .944 |
| 1949—Rochester..........Int. | | INF | 20 | 54 | 7 | 11 | 2 | 0 | 1 | 10 | .204 | 26 | 30 | 9 | .862 |
| 1949—Houston ............Tex. | | O-3B-S | 90 | 290 | 61 | 67 | 14 | 5 | 1 | 25 | .231 | 179 | 10 | 3 | .984 |
| 1950—Columbus ..........A. A. | | OF-2B | 119 | 363 | 75 | 92 | 18 | 7 | 8 | 55 | .253 | 207 | 31 | 6 | .975 |
| 1951—Columbus ..........A. A. | | 3-2-O | 138 | 467 | 95 | 144 | 25 | 6 | 18 | 89 | .308 | 172 | 229 | 24 | .944 |
| 1951—St. Louis ..........Nat. | | 3B-OF | 13 | 46 | 8 | 12 | 3 | 1 | 1 | 7 | .261 | 10 | 19 | 2 | .935 |
| 1952—Columbus ..........A. A. | | 3B-OF | 58 | 213 | 31 | 51 | 11 | 0 | 4 | 30 | .239 | 62 | 52 | 6 | .950 |
| 1952—St. Louis ..........Nat. | | 3B | 20 | 47 | 6 | 9 | 2 | 0 | 2 | 5 | .191 | 5 | 27 | 4 | .889 |
| 1953—St. Louis ..........Nat. | | PH | 13 | 4 | 2 | 0 | 0 | 0 | 0 | 0 | .000 | 0 | 0 | 0 | .000 |
| 1953—Houston ............Tex. | | 3B-O-S | 58 | 194 | 32 | 48 | 7 | 2 | 7 | 22 | .247 | 76 | 83 | 8 | .952 |
| 1953—Rochester..........Int. | | SS | 49 | 175 | 44 | 53 | 12 | 3 | 6 | 34 | .303 | 79 | 150 | 7 | .970 |
| 1954—Rochester..........Int. | | O-3-2B | 93 | 263 | 53 | 63 | 16 | 2 | 6 | 31 | .240 | 132 | 80 | 11 | .951 |
| 1954—Columbus ..........A. A. | | OF-2B | 46 | 154 | 21 | 37 | 5 | 4 | 5 | 14 | .240 | 63 | 35 | 1 | .990 |
| 1955—Rochester..........Int. | | S-O-3B | 125 | 344 | 54 | 78 | 10 | 3 | 14 | 45 | .227 | 139 | 204 | 15 | .958 |
| 1956—Winnipeg‡.........North. | | IN-O | 109 | 329 | 66 | 85 | 14 | 3 | 7 | 46 | .258 | 122 | 231 | 28 | .927 |
| 1956—Omaha ...............A. A. | | 3B | 1 | 4 | 0 | 2 | 0 | 0 | 0 | 0 | .500 | 1 | 3 | 0 | 1.000 |
| 1957—Winnipeg‡.........North. | | 3B-S | 99 | 256 | 59 | 57 | 12 | 1 | 6 | 35 | .223 | 72 | 189 | 23 | .919 |
| 1958—Winston-Salem‡ Carol. | | 2B | 50 | 82 | 16 | 23 | 8 | 0 | 3 | 22 | .280 | 26 | 27 | 4 | .930 |
| 1959—Tulsa‡ .............Tex. | | PH | 2 | 2 | 0 | 0 | 0 | 0 | 0 | 0 | .000 | 0 | 0 | 0 | .000 |
| American League Totals ................ | | | 9 | 7 | 1 | 0 | 0 | 0 | 0 | 0 | .000 | 4 | 0 | 0 | 1.000 |
| National League Totals ................... | | | 46 | 97 | 16 | 21 | 5 | 1 | 3 | 12 | .216 | 15 | 46 | 6 | .910 |
| Major League Totals ..................... | | | 55 | 104 | 17 | 21 | 5 | 1 | 3 | 12 | .202 | 19 | 46 | 6 | .915 |

†Released to Rochester (St. Louis Cardinals' organization), September 30, 1946.
‡Player-manager.

## PITCHING RECORD

| Year    Club | League | G. | IP. | W. | L. | Pct. | H. | R. | ER. | SO. | BB. | ERA. |
|---|---|---|---|---|---|---|---|---|---|---|---|---|
| 1957—Winnipeg............................Northern | | 1 | .... | 0 | 0 | .000 | .... | .... | .... | .... | .... | ....... |
| 1958—Winston-Salem ....................Carolina | | 1 | .... | 0 | 0 | .000 | .... | .... | .... | .... | .... | ....... |

## RECORD AS MANAGER

| Year    Club | League | Position | W. | L. | Year    Club | League | Position | W. | L. |
|---|---|---|---|---|---|---|---|---|---|
| 1956—Winnipeg ............North. | | Second | 63 | 55 | 1959—Tulsa.................Texas | | Third | 77 | 67 |
| 1957—Winnipeg ...........North. | | Fourth | 34 | 29 | 1960—Tulsa.................Texas | | ‡Third | 76 | 68 |
| (Second Half) | | †First | 35 | 24 | 1961—Portland§ ..........P. C. | | Fourth | 42 | 36 |
| 1958—Wins.-Salem ......Carol. | | Fifth | 69 | 68 | | | | | |

†Won playoff against Duluth-Superior (First Half winner), two games to one.
‡Won playoffs by defeating San Antonio, three games to one and Victoria, three games to none.
§Assigned to coaching job with St. Louis Cardinals; replaced by Ray Katt, July 6.
Coach, St. Louis Cardinals, July 6, 1961 through 1964; New York Yankees, 1965 through May 7, 1966; Cincinnati Reds, July 15, 1966, through 1969; St. Louis Cardinals, July 17, 1970, through 1975; Atlanta Braves, 1976 and 1977.

## CARROLL JAMES BERINGER
## (C. B.)
### Philadelphia Phillies

Born August 14, 1928, at Bellwood, Neb.
Height, 6.00. Weight, 195.
Threw and batted righthanded.
Hobby–Photography.

Tied for Texas League lead in complete games by pitchers with 19 in 1959.
Named Pitcher of the Year in Texas League, 1959.

| Year  Club | League | G. | IP. | W. | L. | Pct. | H. | R. | ER. | SO. | BB. | ERA. |
|---|---|---|---|---|---|---|---|---|---|---|---|---|
| 1946–Cambridge | E. Shore | 29 | 192 | 8 | 13 | .381 | 198 | 106 | 66 | 114 | 54 | 3.09 |
| 1947–Cambridge | E. Shore | 31 | 237 | 22 | 6 | .786 | 225 | 85 | 67 | 179 | 65 | 2.55 |
| 1948–Newport News | Piedmont | 22 | 170 | 11 | 9 | .550 | 150 | 67 | 53 | 101 | 57 | 2.81 |
| 1949–Fort Worth | Texas | 48 | 94 | 6 | 4 | .600 | 83 | 35 | 30 | 45 | 45 | 2.87 |
| 1950–Fort Worth | Texas | 45 | 83 | 6 | 2 | .750 | 69 | 22 | 15 | 41 | 27 | 1.63 |
| 1951-52–Montreal | Int'national | | | | | (In Military Service) | | | | | | |
| 1953–Fort Worth | Texas | 26 | 91 | 7 | 2 | .773 | 70 | 21 | 19 | 61 | 36 | 1.88 |
| 1954–Fort Worth | Texas | 34 | 127 | 8 | 8 | .500 | 120 | 56 | 47 | 67 | 35 | 3.33 |
| 1955–Fort Worth | Texas | 42 | 230 | 14 | 9 | .609 | 208 | 81 | 70 | 87 | 49 | 2.74 |
| 1956–Fort Worth | Texas | 44 | 176 | 13 | 10 | .565 | 190 | 89 | 75 | 79 | 47 | 3.83 |
| 1957–Fort Worth | Texas | 36 | 183 | 11 | 9 | .550 | 183 | 65 | 59 | 92 | 36 | 2.90 |
| 1958–Victoria | Texas | 21 | 100 | 10 | 1 | .909 | 98 | 35 | 34 | 59 | 18 | 3.06 |
| 1959–Victoria | Texas | 29 | 196 | •19 | 5 | •.792 | 206 | 83 | 73 | 109 | 22 | 3.34 |
| 1960–St. Paul | Am. Assoc. | 33 | 150 | 10 | 4 | .714 | 162 | 76 | 63 | 86 | 22 | 3.78 |

Batting practice pitcher, Los Angeles Dodgers, 1961 through 1966; coach, Los Angeles Dodgers, 1957 through 1972; coach, Philadelphia Phillies, 1973 through 1977.


## LAWRENCE PETER BERRA, SR.
## (Yogi)

(Named by boyhood pals on The Hill, the heavily-populated Italian
section of St. Louis. A Yogi was considered an odd character–
later in life the term grew to one of affection.)

### New York Yankees

Born May 12, 1925, at St. Louis, Mo.
Height, 5.08. Weight, 191.
Threw right and batted lefthanded.
Hobby–Sports.
Father of Larry Berra, Jr., former catcher in New York Mets' organization, Tim Berra,
former wide receiver with New York Giants and Baltimore Colts, and Dale Berra,
third baseman in Pittsburgh Pirates' organization.

Established following major league records: Most years leading league in games as catcher (8); most put-outs, catcher, career (8711); most chances accepted, catcher, career (9493); most consecutive errorless games, catcher (148) and most consecutive chances accepted, no errors (950), July 28, 1957 (second game), to May 10, 1959 (second game).
Tied major league record for most years leading league in double plays, catcher (6).
Established American League records for most home runs, catcher, season (30), 1952 and 1956, and most putouts, catcher, career (8696).
Led American League catchers in double plays with 18 in 1949, 16 in 1950, 25 in 1951, 10 in 1952, 14 in 1954 and 15 in 1956.
Led American League catchers in passed balls with 7 in 1950.
Named American League Most Valuable Player, 1951-54-55.
Named catcher on THE SPORTING NEWS Major League All-Star Teams, 1950-52-54-56.
Elected to Hall of Fame, 1972.

| Year  Club | League | Pos. | G. | AB. | R. | H. | 2B. | 3B. | HR. | RBI. | B.A. | PO. | A. | E. | F.A. |
|---|---|---|---|---|---|---|---|---|---|---|---|---|---|---|---|
| 1940–Norfolk | Pied. | C | 111 | 376 | 52 | 95 | 17 | 8 | 7 | 56 | .253 | •480 | 75 | •16 | .972 |
| 1944-45–Kansas City | A. A. | | | | | (In Military Service) | | | | | | | | | |
| 1946–Newark | Int. | C-OF | 77 | 277 | 41 | 87 | 14 | 1 | 15 | 59 | .314 | 344 | 45 | 11 | .973 |
| 1946–New York | Amer. | C | 7 | 22 | 3 | 8 | 1 | 0 | 2 | 4 | .364 | 28 | 6 | 0 | 1.000 |
| 1947–New York | Amer. | C-OF | 83 | 293 | 41 | 82 | 15 | 3 | 11 | 54 | .280 | 307 | 18 | 9 | .973 |
| 1948–New York | Amer. | C-OF | 125 | 469 | 70 | 143 | 24 | 10 | 14 | 98 | .305 | 390 | 40 | 9 | .979 |
| 1949–New York | Amer. | C | 116 | 415 | 59 | 115 | 20 | 2 | 20 | 91 | .277 | 544 | 60 | 7 | .989 |
| 1950–New York | Amer. | C | 151 | 597 | 116 | 192 | 30 | 6 | 28 | 124 | .322 | •777 | •64 | 13 | .985 |
| 1951–New York | Amer. | C | 141 | 547 | 92 | 161 | 19 | 4 | 27 | 88 | .294 | •693 | •82 | •13 | .984 |
| 1952–New York | Amer. | C | 142 | 534 | 97 | 146 | 17 | 1 | 30 | 98 | .273 | •700 | •73 | 6 | .992 |
| 1953–New York | Amer. | C | 137 | 503 | 80 | 149 | 23 | 5 | 27 | 108 | .296 | 566 | 64 | 9 | .986 |
| 1954–New York | Amer. | •C-3B | 151 | 584 | 88 | 179 | 28 | 6 | 22 | 125 | .307 | •718 | 64 | 8 | .990 |
| 1955–New York | Amer. | C | 147 | 541 | 84 | 147 | 20 | 3 | 27 | 108 | .272 | •721 | 54 | •13 | .984 |
| 1956–New York | Amer. | •C-OF | 140 | 521 | 93 | 155 | 29 | 2 | 30 | 105 | .298 | •733 | 57 | •11 | .986 |
| 1957–New York | Amer. | •C-OF | 134 | 482 | 74 | 121 | 14 | 2 | 24 | 82 | .251 | •707 | 61 | 4 | •.995 |
| 1958–New York | Amer. | •C-OF-1 | 122 | 433 | 60 | 115 | 17 | 3 | 22 | 90 | .266 | 558 | 44 | 2 | •.997 |
| 1959–New York | Amer. | •C-OF | 131 | 472 | 64 | 134 | 25 | 1 | 19 | 69 | .284 | •706 | 62 | 4 | •.995 |
| 1960–New York | Amer. | C-OF | 120 | 359 | 46 | 99 | 14 | 1 | 15 | 62 | .276 | 312 | 24 | 5 | .985 |
| 1961–New York | Amer. | OF-C | 119 | 395 | 62 | 107 | 11 | 0 | 22 | 61 | .271 | 237 | 15 | 2 | .992 |
| 1962–New York | Amer. | C-OF | 86 | 232 | 25 | 52 | 8 | 0 | 10 | 35 | .224 | 238 | 17 | 6 | .977 |
| 1963–New York† | Amer. | C | 64 | 147 | 20 | 43 | 6 | 0 | 8 | 28 | .293 | 244 | 13 | 3 | .988 |
| 1964–New York‡ | Amer. | | | | | (Did not play–served as manager.) | | | | | | | | | |

– 444 –

| Year | Club | League | Pos. | G. | AB. | R. | H. | 2B. | 3B. | HR. | RBI. | B.A. | PO. | A. | E. | F.A. |
|---|---|---|---|---|---|---|---|---|---|---|---|---|---|---|---|---|
| 1965–New York | | Nat. | C | 4 | 9 | 1 | 2 | 0 | 0 | 0 | 0 | .222 | 15 | 1 | 1 | .941 |
| American League Totals | | | | 2116 | 7546 | 1174 | 2148 | 321 | 49 | 358 | 1430 | .285 | 9179 | 818 | 124 | .988 |
| National League Totals | | | | 4 | 9 | 1 | 2 | 0 | 0 | 0 | 0 | .222 | 15 | 1 | 1 | .941 |
| Major League Totals | | | | 2120 | 7555 | 1175 | 2150 | 321 | 49 | 358 | 1430 | .285 | 9194 | 819 | 125 | .988 |

†Player-coach.

‡Released by New York Yankees, October 16, 1964; signed as coach with New York Mets, November 17, 1964.

### WORLD SERIES RECORD

Established following World Series records: Most Series played (14); most games (75); most times on winning team (10); most at-bats (259); Most hits (71); most one-base hits (49); most Series played by catcher (12); most games caught (63); most putouts by catcher (457); most Series, one or more runs batted in (11).

Tied for the following World Series records: First player to hit pinch home run in World Series, October 2, 1947; hit home run with bases loaded, second inning, October 5, 1956—which also gave him a tie for most runs batted in, inning (4); made one or more hits in a game, seven-game Series, 1955; hit by pitcher twice in a game, October 2, 1953; most two-base hits, total Series (10).

| Year | Club | League | Pos. | G. | AB. | R. | H. | 2B. | 3B. | HR. | RBI. | B.A. | PO. | A. | E. | F.A. |
|---|---|---|---|---|---|---|---|---|---|---|---|---|---|---|---|---|
| 1947–New York | | Amer. | C-OF | 6 | 19 | 2 | 3 | 0 | 0 | 1 | 2 | .158 | 21 | 2 | 2 | .920 |
| 1949–New York | | Amer. | C | 4 | 16 | 2 | 1 | 0 | 0 | 0 | 1 | .063 | 37 | 3 | 0 | 1.000 |
| 1950–New York | | Amer. | C | 4 | 15 | 2 | 3 | 0 | 0 | 1 | 2 | .200 | 30 | 1 | 0 | 1.000 |
| 1951–New York | | Amer. | C | 6 | 23 | 4 | 6 | 1 | 0 | 0 | 0 | .261 | 27 | 3 | 1 | .968 |
| 1952–New York | | Amer. | C | 7 | 28 | 2 | 6 | 1 | 0 | 2 | 3 | .214 | 59 | 7 | 1 | .985 |
| 1953–New York | | Amer. | C | 6 | 21 | 3 | 9 | 1 | 0 | 1 | 4 | .429 | 36 | 3 | 0 | 1.000 |
| 1955–New York | | Amer. | C | 7 | 24 | 5 | 10 | 1 | 0 | 1 | 2 | .417 | 40 | 4 | 0 | 1.000 |
| 1956–New York | | Amer. | C | 7 | 25 | 5 | 9 | 2 | 0 | 3 | 10 | .360 | 50 | 3 | 0 | 1.000 |
| 1957–New York | | Amer. | C | 7 | 25 | 5 | 8 | 1 | 0 | 1 | 2 | .320 | 44 | 2 | 1 | .979 |
| 1958–New York | | Amer. | C | 7 | 27 | 3 | 6 | 3 | 0 | 0 | 2 | .222 | 60 | 6 | 0 | 1.000 |
| 1960–New York | | Amer. | C-OF-PH | 7 | 22 | 6 | 7 | 0 | 0 | 1 | 8 | .318 | 18 | 1 | 0 | 1.000 |
| 1961–New York | | Amer. | OF | 4 | 11 | 2 | 3 | 0 | 0 | 1 | 3 | .273 | 11 | 0 | 1 | .917 |
| 1962–New York | | Amer. | C | 2 | 2 | 0 | 0 | 0 | 0 | 0 | 0 | .000 | 6 | 1 | 0 | 1.000 |
| 1963–New York | | Amer. | PH | 1 | 1 | 0 | 0 | 0 | 0 | 0 | 0 | .000 | 0 | 0 | 0 | .000 |
| World Series Totals | | | | 75 | 259 | 41 | 71 | 10 | 0 | 12 | 39 | .274 | 439 | 36 | 6 | .988 |

### ALL-STAR GAME RECORD

| Year | League | Pos. | AB. | R. | H. | 2B. | 3B. | HR. | RBI. | B.A. | PO. | A. | E. | F.A. |
|---|---|---|---|---|---|---|---|---|---|---|---|---|---|---|
| 1949–American | | C | 3 | 0 | 0 | 0 | 0 | 0 | 0 | .000 | 2 | 1 | 0 | 1.000 |
| 1950–American | | C | 2 | 0 | 0 | 0 | 0 | 0 | 0 | .000 | 2 | 0 | 0 | 1.000 |
| 1951–American | | C | 4 | 1 | 1 | 0 | 0 | 0 | 0 | .250 | 4 | 2 | 1 | .857 |
| 1952–American | | C | 2 | 0 | 0 | 0 | 0 | 0 | 0 | .000 | 6 | 0 | 0 | 1.000 |
| 1953–American | | C | 4 | 0 | 0 | 0 | 0 | 0 | 0 | .000 | 4 | 0 | 0 | 1.000 |
| 1954–American | | C | 4 | 2 | 2 | 0 | 0 | 0 | 0 | .500 | 5 | 0 | 0 | 1.000 |
| 1955–American | | C | 6 | 1 | 1 | 0 | 0 | 0 | 0 | .167 | 8 | 2 | 0 | 1.000 |
| 1956–American | | C | 2 | 0 | 2 | 0 | 0 | 0 | 0 | 1.000 | 10 | 1 | 0 | 1.000 |
| 1957–American | | C | 3 | 0 | 1 | 0 | 0 | 0 | 1 | .333 | 6 | 0 | 0 | 1.000 |
| 1958–American | | C | 2 | 0 | 0 | 0 | 0 | 0 | 0 | .000 | 3 | 0 | 0 | 1.000 |
| 1959–American (second game) | | C | 3 | 1 | 1 | 0 | 0 | 1 | 2 | .333 | 2 | 0 | 0 | 1.000 |
| 1960–American (both games) | | C | 4 | 0 | 0 | 0 | 0 | 0 | 0 | .000 | 9 | 1 | 0 | 1.000 |
| 1961–American (first game) | | C | 1 | 0 | 0 | 0 | 0 | 0 | 0 | .000 | 0 | 0 | 0 | .000 |
| 1962–American (second game) | | PH | 1 | 0 | 0 | 0 | 0 | 0 | 0 | .000 | 0 | 0 | 0 | .000 |
| All-Star Game Totals | | | 41 | 5 | 8 | 0 | 0 | 1 | 3 | .195 | 61 | 7 | 1 | .986 |

Member of American League All-Star Team in 1948, 1959 (first game) and 1961 (second game); did not play.

### RECORD AS MANAGER

| Year | Club | League | Position | W. | L. | Year | Club | League | Position | W. | L. |
|---|---|---|---|---|---|---|---|---|---|---|---|
| 1964–New York | | Amer. | First | 99 | 63 | 1974–New York | | Nat. | Fifth(E) | 71 | 91 |
| 1972–New York | | Nat. | Third(E) | 83 | 73 | 1975–New York† | | Nat. | Third (E) | 56 | 53 |
| 1973–New York | | Nat. | First(E) | 82 | 79 | | | | | | |

†Replaced by Roy McMillan, August 5.
Coach, New York Mets, 1965 through 1971; New York Yankees, 1976 and 1977.

| CHAMPIONSHIP SERIES RECORD | | | | | WORLD SERIES RECORD | | | | |
|---|---|---|---|---|---|---|---|---|---|
| Year | Club | League | W. | L. | Year | Club | League | W. | L. |
| 1973–New York | National | | 3 | 2 | 1964–New York | American | | 3 | 4 |
| | | | | | 1973–New York | National | | 3 | 4 |

## STEPHEN BOROS, JR.
Name pronounced Boris.
### (Steve)
### Kansas City Royals
Born September 3, 1936, at Flint, Mich.
Height, 6.00. Weight, 185.

Threw and batted righthanded.
Hobbies–Reading and going to theatre.
Attended University of Michigan, Ann Arbor, Mich.; received
Bachelor of Arts degree in Literature.

Hit three home runs in one game, August 6, 1962.
Led American Association in total bases with 329 in 1960.
Led Southern Association in stolen bases with 23 in 1959.
Tied American League record for most errors, third baseman, nine-inning game, 4, August 23, 1962.
Named Most Valuable Player in American Association, 1960.
Received reported $25,000 bonus to sign with Detroit Tigers, 1957.

| Year | Club | League | Pos. | G. | AB. | R. | H. | 2B. | 3B. | HR. | RBI. | B.A. | PO. | A. | E. | F.A. |
|---|---|---|---|---|---|---|---|---|---|---|---|---|---|---|---|---|
| 1957–Detroit | ..............Amer. | | 3B-SS | 24 | 41 | 4 | 6 | 1 | 0 | 0 | 2 | .146 | 8 | 27 | 3 | .921 |
| 1958–Birmingham | ......South. | | INF | 44 | 138 | 24 | 36 | 3 | 2 | 6 | 17 | .261 | 81 | 68 | 11 | .931 |
| 1958–Charleston | ........A. A. | | 2B-3B | 6 | 13 | 1 | 1 | 0 | 0 | 0 | 0 | .077 | 7 | 8 | 1 | .938 |
| 1958–Augusta | ...........Sally | | INF | 77 | 269 | 53 | 69 | 7 | 2 | 14 | 36 | .257 | 72 | 157 | 25 | .902 |
| 1958–Detroit | ..............Amer. | | 2B | 6 | 2 | 0 | 0 | 0 | 0 | 0 | 0 | .000 | 2 | 0 | 0 | 1.000 |
| 1959–Birmingham | ......South. | | O-3-2 | 147 | 522 | 89 | 159 | 24 | 7 | 16 | 85 | .305 | 171 | 154 | 15 | .956 |
| 1960–Denver | ..............A. A. | | 3B | 151 | 571 | •128 | 181 | 42 | 8 | 30 | •119 | .317 | 110 | •275 | •31 | .925 |
| 1961–Detroit† | ..........Amer. | | 3B | 116 | 396 | 51 | 107 | 18 | 2 | 5 | 62 | .270 | 115 | 192 | 15 | .953 |
| 1962–Detroit‡ | ..........Amer. | | 3B-2B | 116 | 356 | 46 | 81 | 14 | 1 | 16 | 47 | .228 | 118 | 163 | 21 | .930 |
| 1963–Chicago§ | ..........Nat. | | 1B-OF | 41 | 90 | 9 | 19 | 5 | 1 | 3 | 7 | .211 | 126 | 7 | 4 | .971 |
| 1964–San Diego | ..........P. C. | | 3B | 26 | 100 | 18 | 30 | 8 | 0 | 3 | 15 | .300 | 13 | 39 | 1 | .981 |
| 1964–Cincinnati | ..........Nat. | | 3B | 117 | 370 | 31 | 95 | 12 | 3 | 2 | 31 | .257 | 95 | 204 | 12 | .961 |
| 1965–Cincinnati | ..........Nat. | | 3B | 2 | 0 | 0 | 0 | 0 | 0 | 0 | 0 | .000 | 0 | 1 | 0 | 1.000 |
| 1965–San Diego | ..........P. C. | | 3-S-O | 117 | 420 | 73 | 113 | 28 | 6 | 12 | 30 | .269 | 108 | 217 | 12 | .964 |
| 1966–Buffalo | ..............Int. | | S-3-O | 106 | 330 | 51 | 92 | 16 | 1 | 13 | 40 | .279 | 113 | 113 | 20 | .919 |
| 1967–Buffalo x | ........Int. | | 2-3-O | 107 | 290 | 29 | 55 | 5 | 0 | 10 | 23 | .190 | 155 | 182 | 17 | .952 |
| 1968–Ind.-Van. y | ........P. C. | | 3-2-1 | 100 | 320 | 24 | 85 | 15 | 0 | 1 | 32 | .266 | 78 | 149 | 10 | .958 |
| 1969–Omaha z | ..........A. A. | | INF-O-S | 103 | 309 | 56 | 84 | 13 | 5 | 4 | 53 | .272 | 113 | 110 | 6 | .974 |
| | American League Totals | ................. | | 262 | 795 | 101 | 194 | 33 | 3 | 21 | 111 | .244 | 243 | 382 | 39 | .941 |
| | National League Totals | ................. | | 160 | 460 | 40 | 114 | 17 | 4 | 5 | 38 | .248 | 221 | 212 | 16 | .964 |
| | Major League Totals | ..................... | | 422 | 1255 | 141 | 308 | 50 | 7 | 26 | 149 | .245 | 464 | 594 | 55 | .951 |

†On disabled list with broken collarbone, July 24 to September 1, 1961.
‡Traded to Chicago Cubs for Pitcher Bob Anderson, November 28, 1962.
§Sold to San Diego (Cincinnati Reds' organization), December 13, 1963.
xOn disabled list, July 7 to July 19, 1967.
yReleased by Cincinnati Reds' organization, April 9, 1969; signed as free agent by Omaha (Kansas City Royals' organization), April 16, 1969.
zReleased by Kansas City Royals' organization, October 20, 1969.

RECORD AS MANAGER

| Year | Club | League | Position | W. | L. | Year | Club | League | Position | W. | L. |
|---|---|---|---|---|---|---|---|---|---|---|---|
| 1970–Waterloo | ............Midwest | Tenth | 25 | 37 | | (Second Half) | | | Second(N) | 35 | 27 |
| | (Second Half) | | Tenth | 24 | 36 | 1973–San Jose | ............Calif. | | †Third | 36 | 34 |
| 1971–Waterloo | ............Midwest | Fifth(N) | 20 | 37 | | (Second Half) | | | Second | 39 | 31 |
| | (Second Half) | | †Second(N) | 35 | 27 | 1974–San Jose | ............Calif. | | †Fourth | 36 | 34 |
| 1972–Waterloo | ............M'west | Second(N) | 37 | 26 | | (Second Half) | | | ‡First | 45 | 25 |

†Tied for position.
‡Lost playoff to Fresno (First Half winner), three game to two.
Coach, Kansas City Royals, 1975 through 1977.

## CLOYD VICTOR BOYER
### (Junior)
### New York Yankees

Born September 1, 1927, at Alba, Mo.
Height, 6.01. Weight, 188.
Threw and batted righthanded.
Hobbies–Hunting and fishing.
Brother of Ken Boyer, Baltimore minor league manager (Rochester), and Clete Boyer, former third baseman with Kansas City, New York Yankees, and Atlanta, 1955-71

| Year | Club | League | G. | IP. | W. | L. | Pct. | H. | R. | ER. | SO. | BB. | ERA. |
|---|---|---|---|---|---|---|---|---|---|---|---|---|---|
| 1945–Lynchburg | .........................Piedmont | | 2 | 2 | 0 | 0 | .000 | 6 | 7 | 7 | 2 | 7 | 31.50 |
| 1945–Johnson City | .........................Ap'alachian | | 13 | 72 | 4 | 7 | .364 | 70 | 56 | 40 | 55 | 49 | 5.00 |
| 1945-46–Johnson City | ...................Ap'alachian | | | | | | (In Military Service) | | | | | | |
| 1946–Carthage | .........................K-O-M | | 5 | 26 | 3 | 1 | .750 | 25 | .... | 12 | 35 | 24 | 4.15 |
| 1947–Duluth | .........................Northern | | 32 | •228 | 16 | 9 | .640 | 199 | 89 | 62 | •239 | 106 | 2.45 |
| 1948–Houston | .........................Texas | | 30 | 223 | 16 | 10 | .615 | 191 | 97 | 78 | •188 | 126 | 3.15 |
| 1949–Rochester | .........................Int'national | | 31 | 190 | 15 | 10 | .600 | 147 | 77 | 66 | 143 | 110 | 3.13 |
| 1949–St. Louis | .........................National | | 4 | 3 | 0 | 0 | .000 | 5 | 4 | 4 | 0 | 7 | 12.00 |
| 1950–St. Louis | .........................National | | 36 | 120 | 7 | 7 | .500 | 105 | 52 | 47 | 82 | 49 | 3.53 |
| 1951–Columbus | .........................Am. Assoc. | | 5 | 40 | 2 | 3 | .400 | 29 | 12 | 9 | 44 | 22 | 2.03 |
| 1951–St. Louis | .........................National | | 19 | 63 | 2 | 5 | .286 | 68 | 42 | 37 | 40 | 46 | 5.29 |
| 1952–St. Louis | .........................National | | 23 | 110 | 6 | 6 | .500 | 108 | 56 | 52 | 44 | 47 | 4.25 |
| 1953–Houston | .........................Texas | | 28 | 65 | 4 | 2 | .667 | 64 | 26 | 20 | 31 | 3 | 2.77 |
| 1954–Rochester | .........................Int'national | | 12 | 30 | 0 | 0 | .000 | .... | .... | .... | 21 | 24 | 4.50 |
| 1954–Columbus† | .........................Am. Assoc. | | 10 | 39 | 2 | 3 | .400 | 41 | 18 | 16 | 20 | 20 | 3.69 |
| 1955–Kansas City | .........................American | | 30 | 98 | 5 | 5 | .500 | 107 | 81 | 68 | 32 | 66 | 6.24 |
| 1956–Sacramento | .........................P. Coast | | 26 | 164 | 10 | 9 | .526 | 173 | 91 | 72 | 64 | 77 | 3.95 |

| Year Club | League | G. | IP. | W. | L. | Pct. | H. | R. | ER. | SO. | BB. | ERA. |
|---|---|---|---|---|---|---|---|---|---|---|---|---|
| 1957—Sacramento‡ | P. Coast | 11 | 42 | 1 | 4 | .200 | 53 | 36 | 25 | 18 | 24 | 5.31 |
| 1957—Indianapolis | Am. Assoc. | 26 | 90 | 6 | 4 | .600 | 93 | 42 | 37 | 35 | 41 | 3.70 |
| 1958—Indianapolis | Am. Assoc. | 28 | 182 | 13 | 8 | .619 | 171 | 79 | 60 | 83 | 67 | 2.97 |
| 1959—Indianapolis | Am. Assoc. | 34 | 202 | 10 | 14 | .417 | 186 | 95 | 74 | 85 | 59 | 3.30 |
| 1960—Indianapolis | Am. Assoc. | 32 | 209 | 12 | 8 | .600 | 215 | 100 | 90 | 78 | 65 | 3.88 |
| 1961—Indianapolis | Am. Assoc. | 29 | 61 | 3 | 5 | .375 | 83 | 59 | 46 | 17 | 36 | 6.79 |
| National League Totals | | 82 | 296 | 15 | 18 | .454 | 286 | 154 | 140 | 166 | 149 | 4.26 |
| American League Totals | | 30 | 98 | 5 | 5 | .500 | 107 | 81 | 68 | 32 | 66 | 6.24 |
| Major League Totals | | 112 | 394 | 20 | 23 | .465 | 393 | 235 | 208 | 198 | 215 | 4.75 |

†Drafted by Kansas City A'S, November 22, 1954.
‡Sold to Indianapolis (Chicago White Sox' organization), June 6, 1957.

### RECORD AS MANAGER

| Year Club | League | Position | W. | L. |
|---|---|---|---|---|
| 1962—Shelby† | W. Carol. | Third | 21 | 30 |
| 1963—Ft. Lauderdale‡ | Fla. St. | Third | 31 | 28 |
| 1968—Binghamton§ | East. | Fourth | 67 | 72 |

†Replaced Joe Abernethy for second half of season, June 26, 1962.
‡Replaced Steve Shouchock for second half of season, June 30, 1963.
§Replaced Frank Verdi, June 14, 1968.
Coach, Richmond (New York Yankees' organization), 1962; New York Yankees' minor league pitching coach, 1963-64, 74-76; Scout, New York Yankees 1964-74; Coach, New York Yankees, 1977.

## JAMES ALTON BRAGAN, SR.
### (Jimmy)
### Milwaukee Brewers

Born March 12, 1929, at Birmingham, Ala.
Height, 6.00. Weight, 198.
Threw and batted righthanded.
Hobbies—Hunting, fishing and golf.
Attended Mississippi State University, Starksville, Miss.; received
Bachelor of Science degree in Education.
Brother of Bobby Bragan, former major league infielder-catcher and manager
and presently President of National Association; and Frank Bragan,
former infielder in Chicago White Sox' organization.

| Year Club | League | Pos. | G. | AB. | R. | H. | 2B. | 3B. | HR. | RBI. | B.A. | PO. | A. | E. | F.A. |
|---|---|---|---|---|---|---|---|---|---|---|---|---|---|---|---|
| 1950—Elmira | East. | 2B | 59 | 218 | 28 | 58 | 7 | 1 | 0 | 22 | .266 | 120 | 141 | 19 | .932 |
| 1951—Fort Worth | Texas | 2B | 20 | 62 | 5 | 9 | 1 | 1 | 0 | 3 | .145 | 40 | 44 | 7 | .923 |
| 1951—Newport News | Pied. | 2B | 115 | 432 | 60 | 111 | 12 | 2 | 1 | 34 | .257 | 306 | 338 | 23 | .966 |
| 1952—Miami | Fla.-Int. | 2B | 146 | 563 | 63 | 140 | 11 | 1 | 0 | 44 | .249 | 339 | 410 | 14 | *.982 |
| 1953—Fort Worth | Texas | INF | 36 | 70 | 3 | 20 | 3 | 0 | 0 | 6 | .286 | 53 | 27 | 4 | .952 |
| 1954—Fort Worth | Texas | 2B-3B | 79 | 243 | 28 | 59 | 1 | 0 | 3 | 22 | .243 | 161 | 166 | 9 | .973 |
| 1954—Mobile† | South. | 2B | 37 | 142 | 24 | 44 | 3 | 0 | 1 | 11 | .310 | 67 | 93 | 4 | .976 |
| 1955—Columbia | Sally | 2B | 131 | 533 | 99 | 164 | 25 | 2 | 3 | 51 | .308 | 319 | *332 | 23 | .963 |
| 1956—Nashville | South. | 2B | 15 | 46 | 2 | 10 | 0 | 0 | 0 | 5 | .217 | 21 | 34 | 1 | .982 |
| 1956—Savannah | Sally | 2B | 124 | 486 | 51 | 126 | 18 | 3 | 3 | 37 | .259 | 319 | 330 | 15 | .977 |
| 1957—Monterrey‡ | Mex. | 2B | 2 | 1 | 0 | 0 | 0 | 0 | 0 | 0 | .000 | 0 | 0 | 0 | .000 |
| 1957—Macon§ | Sally | 2B | 13 | 48 | 5 | 11 | 2 | 0 | 0 | 0 | .229 | 40 | 47 | 2 | .978 |

†Released by Brooklyn Dodgers' organization, April 6, 1955; signed as free agent by Cincinnati Reds' organization, April 22, 1955.
‡Released by Cincinnati Reds' organization, April 30, 1957; signed as free agent by Brooklyn Dodgers' organization, May 23, 1957.
§On disabled list, June 3 to June 14, 1957. Released by Brooklyn Dodgers' organization, June 14, 1957.

### RECORD AS MANAGER

| Year Club | League | Position | W. | L. |
|---|---|---|---|---|
| 1957—Bluefield | Appal. | First | 47 | 20 |
| 1971—Winnipeg† | Int. | Eighth | 12 | 38 |

†Replaced Clyde McCullough, July 19.
Scout, Cincinnati Reds, 1958 through 1966; coach, Cincinnati Reds, 1967 through 1969; coach, Montreal Expos, 1970 through 1972; scout, Montreal Expos, 1973; coach, Milwaukee Brewers, 1976 and 1977.
Assistant baseball coach at Mississippi State University, 1974; head coach in 1975 when team compiled record of 16 wins and 24 losses.

## JAMES THOMAS BREWER
### (Jim)
### Montreal Expos

Born November 17, 1937, at Merced, Calif.
Height, 6.02. Weight, 186.
Threw and batted lefthanded.
Hobbies—Hunting and fishing.

Tied National League records for most home runs allowed with bases full, season, 3, in 1970; and most home runs allowed with bases full, lifetime, 8, 1975.

| Year Club | League | G. | IP. | W. | L. | Pct. | H. | R. | ER. | SO. | BB. | ERA. |
|---|---|---|---|---|---|---|---|---|---|---|---|---|
| 1956—Ponca City ..........................Soo. State | | 33 | 91 | 2 | 4 | .333 | 106 | 84 | 63 | 59 | 54 | 6.23 |
| 1957—Ponca City ..........................Soo. State | | 30 | 146 | 11 | 5 | .688 | 137 | 80 | 65 | 126 | 74 | 4.01 |
| 1958—Burlington..............................I.I.I. | | 39 | 191 | 9 | 8 | .529 | 200 | 96 | 79 | 126 | 91 | 3.72 |
| 1959—Burlington..............................I.I.I. | | 21 | 162 | 10 | 10 | .500 | 138 | 74 | 48 | 140 | 60 | *2.67 |
| 1959—San Antonio ......................Texas | | 10 | 47 | 4 | 1 | .800 | 45 | 29 | 25 | 34 | 31 | 4.79 |
| 1960—Houston .........................Am. Assoc. | | 18 | 120 | 8 | 5 | .615 | 119 | 51 | 45 | 75 | 28 | 3.38 |
| 1960—Chicago† ...........................National | | 5 | 22 | 0 | 3 | .000 | 25 | 14 | 14 | 7 | 6 | 5.73 |
| 1961—Chicago..............................National | | 36 | 87 | 1 | 7 | .125 | 116 | 65 | 56 | 57 | 21 | 5.79 |
| 1962—Salt Lake City.....................P. Coast | | 29 | 209 | 10 | 10 | .500 | 231 | 118 | 100 | 156 | 74 | 4.31 |
| 1962—Chicago...............................National | | 6 | 6 | 0 | 1 | .000 | 10 | 6 | 6 | 1 | 3 | 9.00 |
| 1963—Chicago‡ ............................National | | 29 | 50 | 3 | 2 | .600 | 59 | 32 | 27 | 35 | 15 | 4.86 |
| 1964—Los Angeles ......................National | | 34 | 93 | 4 | 3 | .571 | 79 | 33 | 31 | 63 | 25 | 3.00 |
| 1965—Los Angeles§......................National | | 19 | 49 | 3 | 2 | .600 | 33 | 13 | 10 | 31 | 28 | 1.84 |
| 1966—Los Angeles ......................National | | 13 | 22 | 0 | 2 | .000 | 17 | 9 | 9 | 8 | 11 | 3.68 |
| 1967—Los Angeles ......................National | | 30 | 101 | 5 | 4 | .556 | 78 | 32 | 30 | 74 | 31 | 2.67 |
| 1968—Los Angeles ......................National | | 54 | 76 | 8 | 3 | .727 | 59 | 22 | 21 | 75 | 33 | 2.49 |
| 1969—Los Angeles ......................National | | 59 | 88 | 7 | 6 | .538 | 71 | 30 | 25 | 92 | 41 | 2.56 |
| 1970—Los Angeles ......................National | | 58 | 89 | 7 | 6 | .538 | 66 | 36 | 31 | 91 | 33 | 3.13 |
| 1971—Los Angeles ......................National | | 55 | 81 | 6 | 5 | .545 | 55 | 17 | 17 | 66 | 24 | 1.89 |
| 1972—Los Angeles ......................National | | 51 | 78 | 8 | 7 | .533 | 41 | 16 | 11 | 69 | 25 | 1.27 |
| 1973—Los Angeles ......................National | | 56 | 72 | 6 | 8 | .429 | 58 | 26 | 24 | 56 | 25 | 3.00 |
| 1974—Los Angeles x .....................National | | 24 | 39 | 4 | 4 | .500 | 29 | 14 | 11 | 26 | 10 | 2.54 |
| 1975—Los Angeles y .....................National | | 21 | 33 | 3 | 1 | .750 | 44 | 20 | 19 | 21 | 12 | 5.18 |
| 1975—California ............................American | | 21 | 35 | 1 | 0 | 1.000 | 38 | 9 | 7 | 22 | 11 | 1.80 |
| National League Totals............................ | | 550 | 986 | 65 | 64 | .504 | 840 | 385 | 342 | 772 | 343 | 3.12 |
| American League Totals. ......................... | | 21 | 35 | 1 | 0 | 1.000 | 38 | 9 | 7 | 22 | 11 | 1.80 |
| Major League Totals | | 571 | 1021 | 66 | 64 | .508 | 878 | 394 | 349 | 794 | 354 | 3.08 |

†Suffered broken jaw August 4; on disabled list remainder of season.
‡Traded to Los Angeles Dodgers with Catcher Cuno Barragan for Pitcher Dick Scott, December 13, 1963.
§Underwent surgery for bone chips in right elbow; on disabled list from June 6 through July 18.
xOn disabled list, July 4 to August 10 and August 15 to September 6, 1974.
yReleased on waivers to California Angels, July 15, 1975; Angels sent Pitcher Dave Sells to Dodgers, July 22, 1975, at complete deal.

### WORLD SERIES RECORD

| Year Club | League | G. | IP. | W. | L. | Pct. | H. | R. | ER. | SO. | BB. | ERA. |
|---|---|---|---|---|---|---|---|---|---|---|---|---|
| 1965—Los Angeles ......................National | | 1 | 2 | 0 | 0 | .000 | 3 | 1 | 1 | 1 | 0 | 4.50 |
| 1966—Los Angeles ......................National | | 1 | 1 | 0 | 0 | .000 | 0 | 0 | 0 | 1 | 0 | 0.00 |
| 1974—Los Angeles ......................National | | 1 | ⅓ | 0 | 0 | .000 | 0 | 0 | 0 | 1 | 0 | 0.00 |
| World Series Totals ................................. | | 3 | 3⅓ | 0 | 0 | .000 | 3 | 1 | 1 | 3 | 0 | 2.70 |

### ALL-STAR GAME RECORD

| Year League | IP. | W. | L. | Pct. | H. | R. | ER. | SO. | BB. | ERA. |
|---|---|---|---|---|---|---|---|---|---|---|
| 1973—National ...................................................... | 1 | 0 | 0 | .000 | 0 | 0 | 0 | 2 | 1 | 0.00 |

Coach Montreal Expos, 1977.
Voluntary retired, October 5, 1976.

# DONALD RAY BRYANT
## (Don)
### Seattle Mariners

Born July 13, 1941, at Jasper, Fla.
Height, 6.06. Weight, 225.
Threw and batted righthanded.
Hobby—All sports.

Led New York-Pennsylvania League catchers in double plays with 15 in 1962.

| Year Club | League | Pos. | G. | AB. | R. | H. | 2B. | 3B. | HR. | RBI. | B.A. | PO. | A. | E. | F.A. |
|---|---|---|---|---|---|---|---|---|---|---|---|---|---|---|---|
| 1960—Montgomery ......Ala.-Fl. | | C | 43 | 117 | 10 | 22 | 5 | 0 | 1 | 12 | .188 | 213 | 17 | 8 | .966 |
| 1961—Decatur ...........Midw. | | C | 40 | 129 | 19 | 28 | 4 | 0 | 3 | 20 | .217 | 255 | 26 | 9 | .969 |
| 1961—Montgomery ......Ala.-Fl. | | C | 45 | 147 | 18 | 33 | 5 | 0 | 3 | 14 | .224 | 261 | 12 | 6 | .978 |
| 1962—Jamestown ........NYP | | C | 113 | 404 | 57 | 110 | 13 | 7 | 8 | 65 | .272 | 775 | 61 | *22 | .974 |
| 1963—Knoxville .........Sally | | C | 77 | 243 | 20 | 60 | 9 | 1 | 1 | 21 | .247 | 447 | 29 | 11 | .977 |
| 1964—Syracuse ..........Int. | | C | 2 | 7 | 1 | 2 | 0 | 0 | 0 | 2 | .286 | 15 | 3 | 0 | 1.000 |
| 1964—Knoxville ..........South. | | C | 62 | 184 | 19 | 51 | 8 | 3 | 1 | 19 | .277 | 346 | 19 | 4 | .989 |
| 1965—Salt Lake City ..P. C. | | C | 29 | 86 | 7 | 17 | 4 | 1 | 0 | 11 | .198 | 122 | 7 | 0 | 1.000 |
| 1965—Syracuse† ..........Int. | | C | 57 | 176 | 12 | 30 | 3 | 2 | 0 | 11 | .170 | 364 | 16 | 4 | .990 |
| 1966—Tacoma ...........P. C. | | C | 80 | 277 | 34 | 71 | 14 | 4 | 6 | 35 | .256 | 410 | 49 | 14 | .970 |
| 1966—Chicago‡ ..........Nat. | | C | 13 | 26 | 2 | 8 | 2 | 0 | 0 | 4 | .308 | 42 | 3 | 1 | .978 |
| 1967—Phoenix ...........P. C. | | C | 129 | 442 | 42 | 129 | 16 | 7 | 7 | 58 | .292 | 718 | 56 | *19 | .976 |
| 1968—Phoenix§x..........P. C. | | C-1B | 46 | 149 | 13 | 35 | 4 | 2 | 1 | 12 | .235 | 256 | 15 | 0 | 1.000 |
| 1969—Houston yz .......Nat. | | C | 31 | 59 | 2 | 11 | 1 | 0 | 1 | 6 | .186 | 141 | 7 | 1 | .993 |
| 1970—Columbus ..........South. | | C | 17 | 71 | 6 | 16 | 2 | 0 | 2 | 9 | .225 | 135 | 7 | 1 | .993 |
| 1970—Oklahoma City ..A. A. | | C | 20 | 46 | 5 | 9 | 0 | 0 | 0 | 3 | .196 | 107 | 6 | 0 | 1.000 |
| 1970—Houston a..........Nat. | | C | 15 | 24 | 2 | 5 | 0 | 0 | 0 | 3 | .208 | 42 | 2 | 2 | .957 |
| 1971—Louisville ..........Int. | | C | 69 | 204 | 20 | 52 | 8 | 0 | 1 | 26 | .255 | 422 | 25 | 3 | .993 |
| 1972—Louisville ..........Int. | | C | 24 | 40 | 4 | 6 | 0 | 0 | 1 | 7 | .150 | 76 | 9 | 2 | .977 |
| 1973—Pawtucket .........Int. | | C | 18 | 47 | 1 | 8 | 1 | 0 | 0 | 2 | .170 | 74 | 7 | 4 | .953 |
| Major League Totals ..................... | | | 59 | 109 | 6 | 24 | 3 | 0 | 1 | 13 | .220 | 225 | 12 | 4 | .983 |

†Sold by Detroit Tigers' organization to Tacoma (Chicago Cubs' organization), December 6, 1965.
‡Traded to San Francisco Giants for Catcher Dick Bertell, April 3, 1967.
§On disabled list with broken hand from June 24 through September 8.
xDrafted by Houston Astros from Phoenix (San Francisco Giants' organization), December 2, 1968.
yDrafted by Seattle Pilots from Oklahoma City (Houston Astros' organization), December 1, 1969.
zReturned by Milwaukee Brewers to Oklahoma City (Houston Astros' organization), April 3, 1970.
aSold to Louisville (Boston Red Sox' organization), December 3, 1970.
Player-Coach, Pawtucket (Boston Red Sox' organization), 1973; coach, Boston Red Sox, 1974 through 1976; coach, Seattle Mariners, 1977.

## THOMAS ROLAND BURGESS
### (Tom)
### New York Mets

Born September 1, 1927, at London, Ont., Canada.
Height, 6.00. Weight, 180.
Threw and batted lefthanded.
Hobby—Fishing.
Attended University of Western Ontario, Ont., Canada.

| Year Club | League | Pos. | G. | AB. | R. | H. | 2B. | 3B. | HR. | RBI. | B.A. | PO. | A. | E. | F.A. |
|---|---|---|---|---|---|---|---|---|---|---|---|---|---|---|---|
| 1946—Hamilton | Pony | OF-P | 111 | 402 | 71 | 109 | 16 | 8 | 16 | 65 | .271 | 154 | 10 | 7 | .959 |
| 1947—Allentown | Int.-St. | OF | 106 | 360 | 61 | 126 | 25 | 5 | 13 | 79 | .350 | 160 | 13 | 2 | .989 |
| 1948—Omaha | West. | OF | 20 | 51 | 13 | 12 | 1 | 2 | 1 | 5 | .235 | 26 | 2 | 0 | 1.000 |
| 1948—Columbus | Sally | OF | 67 | 237 | 32 | 56 | 9 | 5 | 1 | 26 | .236 | 114 | 9 | 2 | .984 |
| 1949-50-51—Columbus | Sally | | | | | | (Voluntarily retired) | | | | | | | | |
| 1952—Columbus | Sally | OF-P | 149 | 525 | 98 | 172 | ●40 | 8 | 18 | 89 | .328 | 319 | 12 | 6 | .982 |
| 1953—Rochester | Int. | OF | 122 | 407 | 85 | 141 | 18 | 6 | 22 | 93 | .346 | 180 | 13 | 5 | .975 |
| 1954—St. Louis | Nat. | OF | 17 | 21 | 2 | 1 | 1 | 0 | 0 | 1 | .048 | 3 | 0 | 1 | .750 |
| 1954—Rochester | Int. | OF | 76 | 250 | 28 | 59 | 9 | 0 | 10 | 34 | .236 | 146 | 9 | 1 | .994 |
| 1955—Rochester | Int. | OF | 85 | 309 | 52 | 88 | 12 | 3 | 10 | 50 | .285 | 145 | 2 | 1 | .993 |
| 1956—Rochester | Int. | OF | 132 | 423 | 60 | 119 | 20 | 6 | 10 | 71 | .281 | 232 | 8 | 3 | ●.988 |
| 1957—Rochester | Int. | ●OF-1B | 128 | 422 | 72 | 122 | 29 | 2 | 22 | 72 | .289 | 401 | 16 | 4 | ●.990 |
| 1958—Rochester | Int. | OF-1B | 136 | 467 | 73 | 129 | 22 | 3 | 19 | 63 | .276 | 294 | 19 | 4 | .987 |
| 1959—Columbus | Int. | ●OF-1B | 132 | 406 | 71 | 119 | 14 | 2 | 28 | 96 | .293 | 373 | 29 | ●9 | .978 |
| 1960—Columbus† | Int. | OF | 117 | 349 | 56 | 96 | 20 | 1 | 15 | 59 | .275 | 170 | 5 | 0 | ●1.000 |
| 1961—Dallas-Ft. W. | A. A. | ●1B-OF | 136 | 452 | 66 | 130 | 24 | 5 | 14 | 73 | .288 | 883 | 61 | 6 | ●.994 |
| 1962—Los Angeles‡ | A. L. | 1B-OF | 87 | 143 | 17 | 28 | 7 | 1 | 2 | 13 | .196 | 286 | 15 | 1 | .997 |
| 1963—Richmond§ | Int. | PH | 15 | 28 | 2 | 5 | 0 | 0 | 1 | 2 | .179 | .... | .... | .... | .... |
| National League Totals | | | 17 | 21 | 2 | 1 | 1 | 0 | 0 | 1 | .048 | 3 | 0 | 1 | .750 |
| American League Totals | | | 87 | 143 | 17 | 28 | 7 | 1 | 2 | 13 | .196 | 286 | 15 | 1 | .997 |
| Major League Totals | | | 104 | 164 | 19 | 29 | 8 | 1 | 2 | 14 | .177 | 289 | 15 | 2 | .993 |

†Traded by Pittsburgh Pirates' organization to Los Angeles Angels' organization, December 12, 1960.
‡Traded by Los Angeles Angels' organization to New York Yankees' organization, April 8, 1963.
§On temporary inactive list, April 16 to May 3, 1963. On disabled list, June 2 to July 9, 1963. Released, July 9, 1963.

### RECORD AS MANAGER

| Year Club | League | Position | W. | L. | Year Club | League | Position | W. | L. |
|---|---|---|---|---|---|---|---|---|---|
| 1969—Sarasota | Gulf C. | Seventh | 21 | 33 | 1973—Arkansas | Texas | Third | 69 | 71 |
| 1970—Sarasota | Gulf C. | Fifth | 32 | 28 | 1974—Sarasota | Gulf C. | Fifth | 27 | 21 |
| 1971—Sarasota | Gulf C. | Seventh | 20 | 33 | 1975—Johnson City | Appal. | First(S) | 41 | 27 |
| 1972—Modesto | Calif. | Sixth | 31 | 38 | 1976—Tidewater | Int. | Seventh | 60 | 78 |
| (Second Half) | | †First | 45 | 25 | | | | | |

†Won playoff by defeating Bakersfield, two games to none.
Coach, New York Mets, 1977.

## JAMES FRANKLIN BUSBY
### (Jim)
### Seattle Mariners

Born January 8, 1927, at Kenedy, Tex.
Height, 6.01. Weight, 175.
Threw and batted righthanded.
Hobbies—Hunting and fishing.
Attended Texas Christian University, Fort Worth, Tex.; received Bachelor
of Science degree in Physical Education.
Father of Jim C. Busby, outfielder in Pittsburgh Pirates' organization. Fourth-cousin
of Steve Busby, pitcher with Kansas City Royals.

Tied major league record by hitting grand-slam home runs in two consecutive games, July 5-6, 1956.

| Year Club | League | Pos. | G. | AB. | R. | H. | 2B. | 3B. | HR. | RBI. | B.A. | PO. | A. | E. | F.A. |
|---|---|---|---|---|---|---|---|---|---|---|---|---|---|---|---|
| 1948—Muskegon | Cent. | PH | 2 | 2 | 1 | 1 | 0 | 1 | 0 | 0 | .500 | 0 | 0 | 0 | .000 |
| 1948—Waterloo | I.I.I. | OF | 68 | 293 | 65 | 89 | 11 | 3 | 9 | 40 | .304 | 170 | 8 | 12 | .937 |
| 1949—Muskegon | Cent. | OF | 9 | 30 | 2 | 5 | 1 | 0 | 0 | 1 | .167 | 25 | 1 | 1 | .963 |
| 1949—Waterloo | I.I.I. | OF | 78 | 333 | 62 | 106 | 15 | 5 | 4 | 29 | .318 | 174 | 14 | 7 | .964 |
| 1950—Chicago | Amer. | OF | 18 | 48 | 5 | 10 | 0 | 0 | 0 | 4 | .208 | 25 | 2 | 1 | .964 |
| 1950—Sacramento | P.C. | OF-3B | 111 | 416 | 76 | 129 | 23 | 8 | 3 | 31 | .310 | 283 | 15 | 2 | .993 |
| 1951—Chicago | Amer. | OF | 143 | 477 | 59 | 135 | 15 | 2 | 5 | 68 | .283 | 360 | 16 | 7 | .982 |

— 449 —

| Year | Club | League | Pos. | G. | AB. | R. | H. | 2B. | 3B. | HR. | RBI. | B.A. | PO. | A. | E. | F.A. |
|------|------|--------|------|----|-----|----|----|-----|-----|-----|------|------|-----|----|----|------|
| 1952 | Chicago†-Wash. | Amer. | OF | 145 | 551 | 63 | 130 | 24 | 4 | 2 | 47 | .236 | *472 | 4 | 3 | .994 |
| 1953 | Washington....... | Amer. | OF | 150 | 586 | 68 | 183 | 28 | 7 | 6 | 82 | .312 | *482 | 15 | 6 | .988 |
| 1954 | Washington....... | Amer. | OF | *155 | 628 | 83 | 187 | 22 | 7 | 7 | 80 | .298 | *491 | 6 | 6 | .988 |
| 1955 | Wash.‡-Chi.§...... | Amer. | OF | 146 | 528 | 61 | 126 | 19 | 6 | 7 | 41 | .239 | 375 | 7 | 5 | .987 |
| 1956 | Cleveland ......... | Amer. | OF | 135 | 494 | 72 | 116 | 17 | 3 | 12 | 50 | .235 | 344 | 3 | 4 | .989 |
| 1957 | Cleve.x-Balt. | Amer. | OF | 116 | 362 | 40 | 86 | 12 | 2 | 5 | 23 | .238 | 277 | 9 | 5 | .983 |
| 1958 | Baltimore y ...... | Amer. | *OF-3B | 113 | 215 | 32 | 51 | 7 | 2 | 3 | 19 | .237 | 196 | 1 | 1 | *.995 |
| 1959 | Boston ............. | Amer. | OF | 61 | 102 | 16 | 23 | 8 | 0 | 1 | 5 | .225 | 49 | 1 | 1 | .980 |
| 1960 | Bos.z-Baltimore | Amer. | OF | 80 | 159 | 25 | 41 | 7 | 1 | 0 | 12 | .258 | 133 | 2 | 2 | .985 |
| 1960 | Miami .............. | Int. | OF | 27 | 94 | 13 | 26 | 6 | 1 | 1 | 7 | .277 | 66 | 2 | 2 | .971 |
| 1961 | Baltimore a ...... | Amer. | OF | 75 | 89 | 15 | 23 | 3 | 1 | 0 | 6 | .258 | 76 | 2 | 1 | .987 |
| 1962 | Houston ........... | Nat. | OF-C | 15 | 11 | 2 | 2 | 0 | 0 | 0 | 1 | .182 | 4 | 0 | 0 | 1.000 |
| 1962 | Oklahoma City ..A.A. | | OF | 23 | 77 | 6 | 15 | 1 | 0 | 0 | 2 | .195 | 33 | 0 | 0 | 1.000 |
| | American League Totals | ............... | | 1337 | 4239 | 539 | 1111 | 162 | 35 | 48 | 437 | .263 | 3280 | 80 | 42 | .988 |
| | National League Totals | ............... | | 15 | 11 | 2 | 2 | 0 | 0 | 0 | 1 | .182 | 4 | 0 | 0 | 1.000 |
| | Major League Totals | ............... | | 1352 | 4250 | 541 | 1113 | 162 | 35 | 48 | 438 | .262 | 3284 | 68 | 42 | .988 |

†Traded to Washington Senators with Second Baseman Mel Hoderlein for Outfielder Sam Mele, May 3, 1952.

‡Traded to Chicago White Sox for Pitcher Bob Chakales, Catcher Clint Courtney and Outfielder Johnny Groth, June 7, 1955.

§Traded to Cleveland Indians with Shortstop Alfonso (Chico) Carrasquel for Outfielder Larry Doby, October 25, 1955.

xTraded to Baltimore Orioles for Outfielder Dick Williams, June 13, 1957.

yTraded to Boston Red Sox for Infielder Billy Klaus, December 15, 1958.

zUnconditionally released, April 26, 1960; signed with Miami (Baltimore Orioles' organization), May 16, 1960.

aUnconditionally released, October 9, 1961; signed by Houston Astros, October 16, 1961.

### ALL-STAR GAME RECORD

| Year | League | Pos. | AB. | R. | H. | 2B. | 3B. | HR. | RBI. | B.A. | PO. | A. | E. | F.A. |
|------|--------|------|-----|----|----|-----|-----|-----|------|------|-----|----|----|------|
| 1951 | American ........................... | OF | 0 | 0 | 0 | 0 | 0 | 0 | 0 | .000 | 0 | 0 | 0 | .000 |

Coach, Baltimore Orioles, part of 1961; Houston Astros part of 1962 and 1963 through 1967; Atlanta Braves, 1968 through 1975; Chicago White Sox, 1976; Seattle Mariners, 1977.

## CHRISTOPHER JOHN CANNIZZARO

Name pronounced Can-uh-ZARR-oh.

### (Chris)
### Atlanta Braves

Born May 3, 1938, at Oakland, Calif.
Height, 6.00. Weight, 184.
Threw and batted righthanded.
Hobbies—Golf, hunting and fishing.

Tied major league record for most unassisted double plays, catcher, career, 2, 1965.
Led International League catchers in double plays with 15 in 1967.
Tied International League catchers for lead in passed balls with 14 in 1960.

| Year | Club | League | Pos. | G. | AB. | R. | H. | 2B. | 3B. | HR. | RBI. | B.A. | PO. | A. | E. | F.A. |
|------|------|--------|------|----|-----|----|----|-----|-----|-----|------|------|-----|----|----|------|
| 1956 | Decatur ............ | Midw. | C | 40 | 104 | 9 | 22 | 3 | 0 | 0 | 13 | .212 | 234 | 26 | 7 | .974 |
| 1957 | Ardmore ......... | Soo.St. | C | 32 | 96 | 13 | 27 | 6 | 0 | 1 | 14 | .281 | 188 | 15 | 7 | .967 |
| 1957 | Billings ........... | Pion. | C | 46 | 134 | 18 | 32 | 3 | 1 | 3 | 22 | .239 | 248 | 19 | 7 | .974 |
| 1958 | Omaha ............. | A.A. | C | 110 | 334 | 44 | 91 | 14 | 1 | 6 | 41 | .272 | 620 | 56 | 7 | .990 |
| 1959 | Omaha ............. | A.A. | C | 101 | 268 | 23 | 62 | 6 | 4 | 2 | 21 | .231 | 505 | 41 | 6 | .989 |
| 1960 | St. Louis ......... | Nat. | C | 7 | 9 | 0 | 2 | 0 | 0 | 0 | 1 | .222 | 19 | 3 | 0 | 1.000 |
| 1960 | Rochester......... | Int. | C | 122 | 358 | 38 | 90 | 15 | 5 | 5 | 44 | .251 | *631 | 60 | *14 | .980 |
| 1961 | Portland ......... | P.C. | C-3B | 41 | 133 | 12 | 27 | 3 | 1 | 1 | 12 | .203 | 177 | 20 | 6 | .970 |
| 1961 | St. Louis† | Nat. | C | 6 | 2 | 0 | 1 | 0 | 0 | 0 | 0 | .500 | 5 | 0 | 0 | 1.000 |
| 1962 | New York......... | Nat. | C-OF | 59 | 133 | 9 | 32 | 2 | 1 | 0 | 9 | .241 | 219 | 34 | 7 | .973 |
| 1962 | Rochester......... | Int. | C | 27 | 82 | 15 | 20 | 1 | 1 | 1 | 12 | .244 | 157 | 12 | 4 | .977 |
| 1963 | Buffalo ............ | Int. | C | 93 | 308 | 28 | 82 | 14 | 5 | 7 | 39 | .266 | 472 | 27 | 7 | .986 |
| 1963 | New York......... | Nat. | C | 16 | 33 | 4 | 8 | 1 | 0 | 0 | 4 | .242 | 49 | 6 | 0 | 1.000 |
| 1964 | New York......... | Nat. | C | 60 | 164 | 11 | 51 | 10 | 0 | 0 | 10 | .311 | 225 | 28 | 3 | .988 |
| 1965 | New York‡ | Nat. | C | 114 | 251 | 17 | 46 | 8 | 2 | 0 | 7 | .183 | 435 | 69 | *12 | .977 |
| 1966 | Richmond§ | Int. | C | 101 | 322 | 23 | 73 | 13 | 0 | 8 | 41 | .227 | 609 | 48 | 8 | .988 |
| 1967 | Toledo x ............ | Int. | *C-3-1-O | 98 | 322 | 26 | 82 | 10 | 1 | 8 | 36 | .255 | 544 | 72 | *13 | .979 |
| 1968 | Columbus ......... | Int. | C-1B-3B | 88 | 268 | 29 | 65 | 8 | 1 | 4 | 31 | .243 | 460 | 60 | 7 | .987 |
| 1968 | Pittsburgh y ...... | Nat. | C | 25 | 58 | 5 | 14 | 2 | 2 | 1 | 7 | .241 | 111 | 10 | 3 | .976 |
| 1969 | San Diego......... | Nat. | C | 134 | 418 | 23 | 92 | 14 | 3 | 4 | 33 | .220 | 644 | 69 | 9 | .988 |
| 1970 | San Diego......... | Nat. | C | 111 | 341 | 27 | 95 | 13 | 3 | 5 | 42 | .279 | 559 | 44 | 12 | .980 |
| 1971 | S.D.z-Chicago a | Nat. | C | 92 | 260 | 20 | 54 | 9 | 1 | 6 | 31 | .208 | 425 | 32 | 7 | .985 |
| 1972 | Los Angeles ...... | Nat. | C | 73 | 200 | 14 | 48 | 6 | 0 | 2 | 18 | .240 | 312 | 26 | 6 | .983 |
| 1973 | Los Angeles b.... | Nat. | C | 17 | 21 | 0 | 4 | 0 | 0 | 0 | 3 | .190 | 33 | 0 | 0 | 1.000 |
| 1974 | Denver c ......... | A.A. | 1B-C-3B | 40 | 88 | 12 | 19 | 6 | 0 | 1 | 14 | .216 | 91 | 20 | 7 | .941 |
| 1974 | San Diego......... | Nat. | C | 26 | 60 | 2 | 11 | 1 | 0 | 0 | 4 | .183 | 126 | 12 | 3 | .979 |
| 1975 | Hawaii ............. | P.C. | C | 4 | 5 | 0 | 0 | 0 | 0 | 0 | 0 | .000 | 10 | 0 | 0 | 1.000 |
| | Major League Totals | ...................... | | 740 | 1950 | 132 | 458 | 66 | 12 | 18 | 169 | .235 | 3162 | 333 | 62 | .983 |

†Selected by New York Mets in National League expansion draft, October 10, 1961.

‡Released to Atlanta Braves' organization, April 7, 1966.

— 450 —

§Traded with First Baseman-Outfielder John Herrnstein by Atlanta Braves to Detroit Tigers for Pitchers Julio Navarro and Ed Rakow, December 7, 1966.

xSold by Detroit Tigers' organization to Pittsburgh Pirates' organization, November 29, 1967.

yTraded with Pitcher Tommie Sisk to San Diego Padres for Outfielder Ron Davis and Infielder Bobby Klaus (latter sent to Columbus, O.), March 28, 1969.

zTraded to Chicago Cubs for Infielder Garry Jestadt, May 19, 1971.

aReleased on waivers to Los Angeles Dodgers, December 17, 1971.

bUnconditionally released, October 23, 1973; signed as free agent by Houston Astros' organization, January 7, 1974.

cPlayer-coach. Sold by Houston Astros' organization to San Diego Padres, August 1, 1974.

### PITCHING RECORD

| Year | Club | League | G. | IP. | W. | L. | Pct. | H. | R. | ER. | SO. | BB. | ERA. |
|------|------|--------|----|----|----|----|------|----|----|-----|-----|-----|------|
| 1957—Ardmore | | Sooner St. | 2 | .... | 1 | 0 | 1.000 | .... | .... | .... | .... | .... | ....... |
| 1957—Billings | | Pioneer | 2 | .... | 0 | 0 | .000 | .... | .... | .... | .... | .... | ....... |

### ALL-STAR GAME RECORD

Member of National League All-Star Team in 1969; did not play.

Coach, Atlanta Braves, 1976 and 1977.

## GALEN BERNARD CISCO

Name pronounced SIS-coe.

### Kansas City Royals

Born March 7, 1937, at St. Marys, Ohio.
Height, 6.00. Weight, 197.
Threw and batted righthanded.
Hobbies—Hunting and fishing.
Attended Ohio State University, Columbus, O.; received Bachelor
of Science degree in Education.

Led International League in shutouts with 6 in 1968.

| Year | Club | League | G. | IP. | W. | L. | Pct. | H. | R. | ER. | SO. | BB. | ERA. |
|------|------|--------|----|----|----|----|------|----|----|-----|-----|-----|------|
| 1958—Raleigh | | Carolina | 14 | 29 | 2 | 2 | .500 | 23 | 16 | 14 | 27 | 20 | 4.34 |
| 1958—Corning | | NYP | 18 | 122 | 4 | 10 | .286 | 124 | 71 | 53 | 100 | 64 | 3.91 |
| 1959—Allentown | | Eastern | 2 | 1 | 0 | 1 | .000 | 3 | 2 | 2 | 0 | 1 | 18.00 |
| 1959—Raleigh | | Carolina | 5 | 23 | 2 | 2 | .500 | 22 | 17 | 12 | 16 | 18 | 4.70 |
| 1959—Waterloo | | Midwest | 23 | 182 | 15 | 7 | .682 | 142 | 63 | 45 | 165 | 62 | •2.23 |
| 1960—Minneapolis | | Am. Assoc. | 33 | 138 | 3 | 7 | .300 | 122 | 54 | 45 | 70 | 45 | 2.93 |
| 1961—Seattle | | P. Coast | 9 | 70 | 6 | 1 | .857 | 55 | 20 | 12 | 37 | 20 | 1.54 |
| 1961—Boston | | American | 17 | 52 | 2 | 4 | .333 | 67 | 40 | 39 | 26 | 28 | 6.75 |
| 1962—Boston† | | American | 23 | 83 | 4 | 7 | .364 | 95 | 66 | 62 | 43 | 50 | 6.72 |
| 1962—New York | | National | 4 | 19 | 1 | 1 | .500 | 15 | 7 | 7 | 13 | 11 | 3.32 |
| 1963—New York | | National | 51 | 156 | 7 | 15 | .318 | 165 | 88 | 75 | 81 | 64 | 4.33 |
| 1964—New York | | National | 36 | 192 | 6 | 19 | .240 | 182 | 85 | 77 | 78 | 54 | 3.61 |
| 1965—New York | | National | 35 | 112 | 4 | 8 | .333 | 119 | 63 | 56 | 58 | 51 | 4.50 |
| 1966—Jacksonville‡-Toronto | | Int'national | 30 | 140 | 11 | 6 | .647 | 157 | 71 | 64 | 98 | 40 | 4.11 |
| 1967—Boston | | American | 11 | 22 | 0 | 1 | .000 | 21 | 10 | 9 | 8 | 8 | 3.68 |
| 1967—Pittsfield | | Eastern | 4 | 11 | 0 | 0 | .000 | 5 | 3 | 1 | 7 | 1 | 0.82 |
| 1967—Toronto | | Int'national | 10 | 65 | 3 | 5 | .375 | 63 | 20 | 15 | 46 | 13 | 2.08 |
| 1968—Louisville§ | | Int'national | 29 | 204 | 11 | 12 | .478 | 157 | 58 | 50 | 157 | 60 | •2.21 |
| 1969—Omaha | | Am. Assoc. | 10 | 63 | 3 | 4 | .429 | 77 | 40 | 35 | 42 | 15 | 5.00 |
| 1969—Kansas City | | American | 15 | 22 | 1 | 1 | .500 | 17 | 11 | 9 | 18 | 15 | 3.68 |
| 1970—Omaha | | Am. Assoc. | 24 | 76 | 6 | 3 | .667 | 63 | 25 | 21 | 49 | 17 | 2.49 |
| American League Totals | | | 66 | 179 | 7 | 13 | .350 | 200 | 127 | 119 | 95 | 101 | 5.98 |
| National League Totals | | | 126 | 479 | 18 | 43 | .295 | 481 | 243 | 215 | 230 | 180 | 4.04 |
| Major League Totals | | | 192 | 658 | 25 | 56 | .309 | 681 | 370 | 334 | 325 | 281 | 4.57 |

†Sold to New York Mets, September 7, 1962.

‡Sold by New York Mets' organization to Boston Red Sox' organization, June 6, 1966.

§Sold by Boston Red Sox' organization to Kansas City Royals' organization, August 14, 1968.

Coach, Kansas City Royals, 1971 through 1977.

## ELWOOD ROBERT CLEAR

### (Bob)

### California Angels

Born December 14, 1927, Denver, Colo.

Height, 5.10. Weight, 170.
Threw and batted righthanded.
Hobbies—Fishing and hunting.

Led Far West League Pitchers in complete games with 23 in 1948.
Led Western League in shutouts with 4 in 1950.
Tied for Arizona-Mexico League lead in games started with 31 in 1957.
Led Arizona-Mexico League in complete games with 28 in 1957 and with 22 in 1958.
Tied for Northern League in games started with 27 and shutouts with 3 in 1960.
Lead Northern League in complete games with 23 in 1960.

| Year | Club | League | G. | IP. | W. | L. | Pct. | H. | R. | ER. | SO. | BB. | ERA. |
|------|------|--------|----|----|----|----|------|----|----|-----|-----|-----|------|
| 1946—Bakersfield | | California | 2 | 11 | 1 | 0 | 1.000 | 5 | 3 | .... | 7 | 9 | ...... |
| 1948—Fresno | | California | 3 | 11 | 0 | 1 | .000 | .... | .... | .... | 7 | 6 | ...... |

| Year Club | League | G. | IP. | W. | L. | Pct. | H. | R. | ER. | SO. | BB. | ERA. |
|---|---|---|---|---|---|---|---|---|---|---|---|---|
| 1948—Willows | Far West | 36 | •219 | 17 | 12 | .586 | 190 | 125 | 84 | 143 | 102 | 3.45 |
| 1949—Lynchburg | Piedmont | 5 | 12 | 0 | 1 | .000 | .... | .... | .... | 4 | 10 | .... |
| 1949—Pocatello | Pioneer | 24 | 151 | 11 | 6 | .647 | 183 | 116 | 98 | 108 | 103 | 5.84 |
| 1950—Omaha | Western | 31 | 224 | 16 | 7 | .696 | 182 | 102 | 84 | 129 | 119 | 3.38 |
| 1951—Rochester | Int'national | 4 | 5 | 0 | 1 | .000 | .... | .... | .... | 2 | 4 | 0.00 |
| 1951—Columbus | Am. Assoc. | 11 | 22 | 0 | 4 | .000 | .... | .... | 24 | 15 | 23 | 9.82 |
| 1951—Houston | Texas | 9 | 31 | 1 | 2 | .333 | .... | .... | 28 | 11 | 18 | 8.13 |
| 1952—Houston | Texas | 35 | 193 | 9 | 12 | .429 | 177 | 86 | 74‡ | 84 | 102 | 3.44 |
| 1953—Houston | Texas | 40 | 113 | 4 | 6 | .400 | 100 | 53 | 42 | 79 | 69 | 3.35 |
| 1954—Omaha | Western | 39 | 267 | •20 | 11 | .645 | 236 | 107 | 87 | 145 | 114 | 2.93 |
| 1955—Omaha | Am. Assoc. | 27 | 57 | 1 | 10 | .091 | 51 | 34 | 28 | 39 | 33 | 4.42 |
| 1956—Omaha | Am. Assoc. | 3 | 7 | 0 | 0 | .000 | .... | .... | .... | .... | .... | .... |
| 1956—Sioux City§ | Western | 22 | 78 | 5 | 4 | .556 | 95 | 56 | 52 | 60 | 44 | 6.00 |
| 1957—Douglas§ | Ariz.-Mex. | 37 | 268 | •20 | 11 | .645 | 133 | 108 | 228 | 83 | 3.63 |
| 1958—Douglas§ | Ariz.-Mex. | 30 | 216 | 18 | 8 | •.692 | 227 | 132 | 106 | 193 | 84 | 4.42 |
| 1959—Idaho Falls§ | Pioneer | 26 | 176 | 13 | 8 | .619 | 156 | 82 | 55 | 189 | 45 | 2.81 |
| 1960—Grand Forks§x | Northern | 27 | •216 | •21 | 6 | .778 | •193 | 83 | 60 | •183 | 64 | 2.50 |
| 1961—Grand Forks§ | Northern | 12 | 66 | 4 | 5 | .444 | 81 | 60 | 37 | 50 | 35 | 5.05 |
| 1967—Clinton§ | Midwest | 2 | 11 | 1 | 0 | 1.000 | 6 | 2 | 2 | 12 | 2 | 1.64 |

### RECORD AS INFIELDER

| Year Club | League | Pos. | G. | AB. | R. | H. | 2B. | 3B. | HR. | RBI. | B.A. | PO. | A. | E. | F.A. |
|---|---|---|---|---|---|---|---|---|---|---|---|---|---|---|---|
| 1945—Batavia | Pony | SS-3B | 119 | 472 | 80 | 105 | 27 | 2 | 0 | 46 | .222 | 184 | 367 | 70 | .887 |
| 1946—Bakersfield† | Calif. | 3B | 66 | 218 | 31 | 58 | 13 | 0 | 0 | 20 | .266 | 58 | 118 | 34 | .838 |
| 1947—Decatur‡ | I.I.I. | 3B-2B | 64 | 231 | 24 | 48 | 7 | 1 | 5 | 30 | .208 | 47 | 108 | 16 | .906 |
| 1947—Lynchburg | Pied. | | 16 | 45 | 3 | 9 | 1 | 1 | 0 | 8 | .200 | .... | .... | .... | ...... |

†On temporary inactive list, June through September, 1946.
‡On disabled list, July 22 through July 31, 1947.
§Player-manager.
xOn disabled list, July 2 through July 12, 1960.

### RECORD AS MANAGER

| Year Club | League | Position | W. | L. | Year Club | League | Position | W. | L. |
|---|---|---|---|---|---|---|---|---|---|
| 1956—Sioux City† | Western | Eighth | 18 | 36 | 1965—Kinston | Carolina | Third(E) | 72 | 71 |
| (Second Half) | | Eighth | 27 | 43 | 1966—Gastonia | W. Carol. | Fifth | 34 | 31 |
| 1957—Douglas | Ariz.-Mex. | Fourth | 32 | 36 | (Second Half) | | Third | 33 | 26 |
| (Second Half) | | Third | 36 | 33 | 1967—Clinton | Midwest | Seventh | 27 | 31 |
| 1958—Douglas | Ariz.-Mex. | First | 68 | 52 | (Second Half) | | Tenth | 24 | 38 |
| 1959—Idaho Falls | Pioneer | Third | 64 | 65 | 1968—Clinton | Midwest | Sixth | 28 | 32 |
| 1960—Grand Forks | Northern | Fifth | 61 | 62 | (Second Half) | | Ninth | 26 | 35 |
| 1961—Grand Forks | Northern | Fourth | 60 | 66 | 1969—Geneva | N.Y.P. | Eighth | 27 | 46 |
| 1962—Batavia | N.Y.P. | Fifth | 51 | 67 | 1970—Idaho Falls | Pioneer | First | 44 | 26 |
| 1963—Gastonia | ‡W. Carol. | Second | 31 | 26 | 1971—Idaho Falls | Pioneer | Third | 36 | 34 |
| (Second Half) | | Second | 42 | 26 | 1972—Idaho Falls | Pioneer | Fourth | 27 | 45 |
| 1964—Gastonia§ | W. Carol. | Eighth | 24 | 39 | 1973—Idaho Falls | Pioneer | Fourth | 23 | 48 |
| 1964—Asheville x | Southern | Eighth | 52 | 86 | | | | | |

†Replaced Harold Olt, May 16, 1956.
‡Lost playoff to Greenville, two games to none.
§Replaced June 11, 1964.
xReplaced July 10, 1964.
Scout, California Angels, 1969-1975; Coach, California Angels, July 23, 1976, to date.


## ROCCO DOMENICO COLAVITO

Name pronounced Coll-A-VEE-toe.

### (Rocky)
### Cleveland Indians

Born August 10, 1933, at New York, N. Y.
Height, 6.03. Weight, 198.
Threw and batted righthanded.
Hobbies—Billiards and hunting.

Tied following major league records: Fewest errors, season, 150 or more games, outfielder (0), 1965, and highest fielding percentage by outfielder, season, 150 or more games (1.000), 1965.
Tied major league record for most consecutive home runs in a game (4), June 10, 1959; also tied major league mark for most home runs in a game (4), June 10, 1959; tied American League standard for most total bases in a game (16), June 10, 1959; tied A. L. mark for most home runs in a doubleheader (4), hitting one in first game and three in the nightcap, August 27, 1961.
Established American League record for most consecutive errorless games (234), September 6, 1964, through June 15, 1966; most years leading outfielders in games played (5), 1965.
Led American League in slugging percentage with .620 in 1958; led league in total bases with 301 in 1959 and 309 in 1962; led league's outfielders in double plays with 6 in 1958 and 5 in 1960; led league in walks with 93 in 1965; tied for league lead in grounding into double plays with 25 in 1966.
Hit three home runs in game, August 27, 1961 (second game) and July 5, 1962.
Named as outfielder on THE SPORTING NEWS American League All-Star Team, 1961.

| Year Club | League | Pos. | G. | AB. | R. | H. | 2B. | 3B. | HR. | RBI. | B.A. | PO. | A. | E. | F.A. |
|---|---|---|---|---|---|---|---|---|---|---|---|---|---|---|---|
| 1951—Daytona Beach | Fla. St. | OF-P | •140 | 506 | 98 | 139 | 35 | 3 | •23 | 111 | .275 | •303 | 19 | •20 | .942 |
| 1952—Cedar Rapids | I.I.I. | OF | 32 | 94 | 14 | 16 | 1 | 1 | 8 | 21 | .170 | 49 | 4 | 1 | .981 |

| Year Club League | Pos. | G. | AB. | R. | H. | 2B. | 3B. | HR. | RBI. | B.A. | PO. | A. | E. | F.A. |
|---|---|---|---|---|---|---|---|---|---|---|---|---|---|---|
| 1952–Spartanburg ......Tri.-St. | OF | 66 | 226 | 42 | 57 | 14 | 1 | 11 | 55 | .252 | 100 | 4 | 1 | .990 |
| 1953–Reading ............East. | OF | 146 | 528 | 89 | 143 | 21 | 6 | •28 | •121 | .271 | 263 | 12 | 5 | .982 |
| 1954–Indianapolis ......A. A. | OF | 149 | 528 | 94 | 143 | 30 | 3 | •38 | 116 | .271 | 271 | 16 | 7 | .976 |
| 1955–Indianapolis ......A. A. | OF | 150 | 555 | 92 | 149 | 30 | 3 | 30 | 104 | .268 | 314 | •23 | 10 | .971 |
| 1955–Cleveland ........Amer. | OF | 5 | 9 | 3 | 4 | 2 | 0 | 0 | 0 | .444 | 7 | 1 | 0 | 1.000 |
| 1956–San Diego.........P. C. | OF | 35 | 133 | 31 | 49 | 10 | 1 | 12 | 32 | .368 | 50 | 3 | 3 | .946 |
| 1956–Cleveland .........Amer. | OF | 101 | 322 | 55 | 89 | 11 | 4 | 21 | 65 | .276 | 177 | 6 | 6 | .968 |
| 1957–Cleveland .........Amer. | OF | 134 | 461 | 66 | 116 | 26 | 0 | 25 | 84 | .252 | 268 | 12 | •11 | .962 |
| 1958–Cleveland .........Amer. | O-1B-P | 143 | 489 | 80 | 148 | 26 | 3 | 41 | 113 | .330 | 327 | 15 | 9 | .974 |
| 1959–Cleveland† ........Amer. | OF | 154 | 588 | 90 | 151 | 24 | 0 | •42 | 111 | .257 | 319 | 7 | 5 | .985 |
| 1960–Detroit .............Amer. | OF | 145 | 555 | 67 | 138 | 18 | 1 | 35 | 87 | .249 | 271 | 11 | 7 | .976 |
| 1961–Detroit .............Amer. | OF | •163 | 583 | 129 | 169 | 30 | 2 | 45 | 140 | .290 | 329 | •16 | 9 | .975 |
| 1962–Detroit .............Amer. | OF | 161 | 601 | 90 | 164 | 30 | 2 | 37 | 112 | .273 | 359 | 10 | 3 | .992 |
| 1963–Detroit‡ ...........Amer. | OF | 160 | 597 | 91 | 162 | 29 | 2 | 22 | 91 | .271 | 319 | 10 | 4 | .988 |
| 1964–Kansas City§ ....Amer. | OF | 160 | 588 | 89 | 161 | 31 | 2 | 34 | 102 | .274 | 275 | 10 | 8 | .973 |
| 1965–Cleveland .........Amer. | OF | •162 | 592 | 92 | 170 | 25 | 2 | 26 | •108 | .287 | 265 | 9 | 0 | •1.000 |
| 1966–Cleveland .........Amer. | OF | 151 | 533 | 68 | 127 | 13 | 0 | 30 | 72 | .238 | 261 | 10 | 5 | .982 |
| 1967–Cleve. x-Chi. y ..Amer. | OF | 123 | 381 | 30 | 88 | 13 | 1 | 8 | 50 | .231 | 158 | 4 | 5 | .970 |
| 1968–Los Angeles z ....Nat. | OF | 40 | 113 | 8 | 23 | 3 | 0 | 3 | 11 | .204 | 45 | 2 | 0 | 1.000 |
| 1968–New York.........Amer. | OF-P | 39 | 91 | 13 | 20 | 2 | 2 | 5 | 13 | .220 | 27 | 1 | 2 | .933 |
| American League Totals ................ | | 1801 | 6390 | 963 | 1707 | 280 | 21 | 371 | 1148 | .267 | 3362 | 122 | 74 | .979 |
| National League Totals .................. | | 40 | 113 | 8 | 23 | 3 | 0 | 3 | 11 | .204 | 45 | 2 | 0 | 1.000 |
| Major League Totals ...................... | | 1841 | 6503 | 971 | 1730 | 283 | 21 | 374 | 1159 | .266 | 3407 | 124 | 74 | .979 |

†Traded to Detroit Tigers for Outfielder Harvey Kuenn, April 17, 1960.

‡Traded to Kansas City Athletics with Pitcher Bob Anderson and reported $50,000 for Pitchers Ed Rakow and Dave Wickersham and Second Baseman Jerry Lumpe, November 18, 1963.

§Traded to Chicago White Sox for Outfielders Jim Landis and Mike Hershberger and a pitcher to be named later, January 20, 1965, as part of three-way deal which saw White Sox immediately send Colavito and Catcher Camilo Carreon to Cleveland Indians for Pitcher Tommy John, Catcher John Romano and Outfielder Tommie Agee; White Sox assigned Pitcher Fred Talbot to Athletics, February 10, 1965, to complete deal.

xTraded to Chicago White Sox for Outfielder Jim King and player to be named later, July 29, 1967; Infielder Marv Staehle assigned to Portland to complete deal, July 29, 1967.

ySold to Los Angeles Dodgers March 26, 1968.

zReleased by Los Angeles Dodgers, July 11, 1968; signed as free agent by New York Yankees, July 15, 1968.

### ALL-STAR GAME RECORD

| Year League | Pos. | AB. | R. | H. | 2B. | 3B. | HR. | RBI. | B.A. | PO. | A. | E. | F.A. |
|---|---|---|---|---|---|---|---|---|---|---|---|---|---|
| 1959–American (both games) ...... | OF | 5 | 1 | 2 | 0 | 0 | 1 | 1 | .400 | 1 | 0 | 0 | 1.000 |
| 1961–American (both games) ...... | OF | 8 | 1 | 1 | 0 | 0 | 1 | 2 | .125 | 4 | 0 | 0 | 1.000 |
| 1962–American (both games) ...... | OF | 5 | 1 | 1 | 0 | 0 | 1 | 4 | .200 | 3 | 0 | 0 | 1.000 |
| 1964–American ............................ | PH-OF | 2 | 0 | 1 | 1 | 0 | 0 | 0 | .500 | 0 | 0 | 0 | .000 |
| 1965–American ............................ | OF | 4 | 0 | 1 | 0 | 0 | 0 | 1 | .250 | 1 | 0 | 0 | 1.000 |
| 1966–American ............................ | PH | 1 | 0 | 0 | 0 | 0 | 0 | 0 | .000 | 0 | 0 | 0 | .000 |
| All-Star Game Totals ...................... | | 25 | 3 | 6 | 1 | 0 | 3 | 8 | .240 | 9 | 0 | 0 | 1.000 |

### PITCHING RECORD

| Year Club League | G. | IP. | W. | L. | Pct. | H. | R. | ER. | SO. | BB. | ERA. |
|---|---|---|---|---|---|---|---|---|---|---|---|
| 1951–Daytona Beach ....................Florida St. | 1 | 4 | 0 | 0 | .000 | 1 | 1 | 1 | 3 | 3 | 2.52 |
| 1958–Cleveland ............................American | 1 | 3 | 0 | 0 | .000 | 0 | 0 | 0 | 3 | 0 | 0.00 |
| 1968–New York ............................American | 1 | 3 | 1 | 0 | 1.000 | 1 | 0 | 0 | 1 | 2 | 0.00 |
| Major League Totals ............................. | 2 | 6 | 1 | 0 | 1.000 | 1 | 0 | 0 | 2 | 5 | 0.00 |

Scout, New York Yankees, 1969; coach, Cleveland Indians, 1973, 1976 and 1977.

## PATRICK CORRALES

Name pronounced Corr-AL-ees.

### (Pat)

### Texas Rangers

Born March 20, 1941, at Los Angeles, Calif.
Height, 6.00½. Weight, 195.
Threw and batted righthanded.
Hobby–Hunting.

Established major league record for most times awarded first base, season, on catcher's interference, 6, in 1965.

Tied major league record for most times awarded first base, game, on catcher's interference, 2, September 29, 1965.

Led Florida State League catchers in double plays with 18 in 1960 and tied for Sally League lead with 10 in 1963.

| Year Club League | Pos. | G. | AB. | R. | H. | 2B. | 3B. | HR. | RBI. | B.A. | PO. | A. | E. | F.A. |
|---|---|---|---|---|---|---|---|---|---|---|---|---|---|---|
| 1959–Bakersfield........Calif. | C | 5 | 5 | 0 | 0 | 0 | 0 | 0 | 0 | .000 | 4 | 2 | 1 | .857 |
| 1959–Johnson City ....Appal. | C | 23 | 74 | 10 | 18 | 4 | 0 | 2 | 13 | .243 | 124 | 5 | 3 | .977 |
| 1960–Tampa ..............Fla. St. | C | 128 | 386 | 73 | 95 | 18 | 5 | 1 | 60 | .246 | •1011 | 83 | 23 | .979 |
| 1961–Des Moines ........I.I.I. | C | 104 | 333 | 33 | 103 | 18 | 0 | 3 | 36 | .309 | 707 | 42 | •19 | .975 |
| 1962–Dallas-Ft. W. ....A. A. | C | 42 | 121 | 10 | 27 | 6 | 1 | 2 | 14 | .223 | 180 | 16 | 3 | .985 |
| 1962–Williamsport......East. | C-OF | 42 | 136 | 9 | 26 | 1 | 0 | 1 | 10 | .191 | 237 | 24 | 7 | .974 |
| 1963–Chattanooga ......Sally | C | 127 | 415 | 42 | 108 | 15 | 1 | 3 | 51 | .260 | 715 | 59 | 17 | .979 |

| Year | Club | League | Pos. | G. | AB. | R. | H. | 2B. | 3B. | HR. | RBI. | B.A. | PO. | A. | E. | F.A. |
|------|------|--------|------|-----|------|-----|------|-----|-----|-----|------|------|------|-----|-----|------|
| 1964–Arkansas | .........P. C. | C | 101 | 335 | 36 | 102 | 19 | 1 | 9 | 48 | .304 | 682 | 51 | 7 | .991 |
| 1964–Philadelphia | ......Nat. | PH | 2 | 1 | 1 | 0 | 0 | 0 | 0 | 0 | .000 | 0 | 0 | 0 | .000 |
| 1965–Philadelphia | ......Nat. | C | 63 | 174 | 16 | 39 | 8 | 1 | 2 | 15 | .224 | 358 | 24 | 7 | .982 |
| 1965–Arkansas | .........P. C. | C | 28 | 85 | 6 | 16 | 4 | 0 | 0 | 4 | .188 | 181 | 14 | 2 | .990 |
| 1966–St. Louis | .........Nat. | C | 28 | 72 | 5 | 13 | 2 | 0 | 0 | 3 | .181 | 133 | 23 | 4 | .975 |
| 1967–Tulsa‡ | ..............P. C. | C-1B | 130 | 435 | 55 | 119 | 18 | 1 | 10 | 54 | .274 | 714 | 69 | 8 | .990 |
| 1968–Indianapolis | ......P. C. | C-1B | 77 | 242 | 26 | 66 | 11 | 3 | 6 | 34 | .273 | 461 | 42 | 5 | .990 |
| 1968–Cincinnati | .........Nat. | C | 20 | 56 | 3 | 15 | 4 | 0 | 6 | 6 | .268 | 101 | 8 | 1 | .991 |
| 1969–Cincinnati | .........Nat. | C | 29 | 72 | 10 | 19 | 5 | 0 | 1 | 5 | .264 | 133 | 7 | 2 | .986 |
| 1970–Cincinnati | .........Nat. | C | 43 | 106 | 9 | 25 | 5 | 1 | 1 | 10 | .236 | 167 | 11 | 3 | .983 |
| 1971–Cincinnati | .........Nat. | C | 40 | 94 | 6 | 17 | 2 | 0 | 0 | 6 | .181 | 145 | 4 | 3 | .980 |
| 1972–Indianapolis | ......A. A. | C | 30 | 98 | 9 | 31 | 4 | 0 | 1 | 12 | .316 | 193 | 10 | 0 | 1.000 |
| 1972–Cinn.§-S. Diego | ..Nat. | C | 46 | 120 | 6 | 23 | 0 | 0 | 0 | 6 | .192 | 251 | 23 | 2 | .993 |
| 1973–San Diego | .........Nat. | C | 29 | 72 | 7 | 15 | 2 | 1 | 0 | 3 | .208 | 130 | 6 | 2 | .986 |
| 1974–Hawaii x | ...........P. C. | C | 53 | 169 | 21 | 42 | 6 | 0 | 5 | 24 | .249 | 324 | 17 | 3 | .991 |
| 1975–Alexandria | ........Tex. | C-1B | 1 | 0 | 0 | 0 | 0 | 0 | 0 | 0 | .000 | 4 | 0 | 0 | 1.000 |
| Major League Totals | ..................... | | 300 | 767 | 63 | 166 | 28 | 3 | 4 | 54 | .216 | 1418 | 106 | 24 | .984 |

†Traded with Pitcher Art Mahaffey and Outfielder Alex Johnson to St. Louis Cardinals for First Baseman Bill White, Shortstop Dick Groat and Catcher Bob Uecker, October 27, 1965.

‡Recalled by St. Louis Cardinals; traded to Cincinnati Reds' organization with Infielder Jim Williams for Catcher John Edwards, February 8, 1968.

§Traded to San Diego Padres for Catcher Bob Barton, June 11, 1972.

xReleased by San Diego Padres' organization, September 27, 1974.

### WORLD SERIES RECORD

| Year | Club | League | Pos. | G. | AB. | R. | H. | 2B. | 3B. | HR. | RBI. | B.A. | PO. | A. | E. | F.A. |
|------|------|--------|------|-----|------|-----|------|-----|-----|-----|------|------|------|-----|-----|------|
| 1970–Cincinnati | .........Nat. | PH | 1 | 1 | 0 | 0 | 0 | 0 | 0 | 0 | .000 | 0 | 0 | 0 | .000 |

### RECORD AS MANAGER

| Year | Club | League | Position | W. | L. |
|------|------|--------|----------|-----|-----|
| 1975–Alexandria | ........Texas | Fourth(E) | 58 | 72 |

Coach, Texas Rangers, part of 1975 through 1977.

## ROBERT JOE COX
### (Bobby)
### New York Yankees

Born May 21, 1941, at Tulsa, Okla.

Height, 6.00. Weight, 185.
Threw and batted righthanded.
Hobby–Golf.
Attended Reedley Junior College, Reedley, Calif.

Led Alabama-Florida League shortstops in double plays with 71 in 1961.
Received reported $40,000 bonus to sign with Los Angeles Dodgers, 1959.

| Year | Club | League | Pos. | G. | AB. | R. | H. | 2B. | 3B. | HR. | RBI. | B.A. | PO. | A. | E. | F.A. |
|------|------|--------|------|-----|------|-----|------|-----|-----|-----|------|------|------|------|-----|------|
| 1960–Reno | ...............Calif. | 2B | 125 | 440 | 99 | 112 | 20 | 5 | 13 | 75 | .255 | 282 | •385 | •39 | .945 |
| 1961–Salem | ...............Northw. | 2B | 14 | 44 | 3 | 9 | 2 | 0 | 0 | 2 | .205 | 25 | 25 | 2 | .962 |
| 1961–Panama City | ....Ala.-Fl. | 2B | 92 | 335 | 66 | 102 | 27 | 4 | 17 | 73 | .304 | 220 | 247 | 8 | •.983 |
| 1962–Salem | ...............Northw. | 3-2B | •141 | 514 | 83 | 143 | 26 | 7 | 16 | 82 | .278 | 174 | 296 | 28 | .944 |
| 1963–Albuquerque | ......Texas | 3B | 17 | 53 | 5 | 15 | 2 | 0 | 2 | 5 | .283 | 8 | 27 | 1 | .972 |
| 1963–Great Falls | ........Pion. | 3B | 109 | 407 | 103 | 137 | •31 | 4 | 19 | 85 | .337 | 82 | 211 | 21 | •.933 |
| 1964–Albuquerque | ......Texas | 2B | 138 | 523 | 98 | 152 | 29 | 13 | 16 | 91 | .291 | •322 | •415 | •28 | .963 |
| 1965–Salt Lake City | ..P. C. | •3B-2B | 136 | 473 | 58 | 125 | 32 | 1 | 12 | 55 | .264 | 133 | 337 | 22 | •.955 |
| 1966–Tacoma | ............P. C. | 3B-2B | 10 | 34 | 2 | 4 | 1 | 0 | 0 | 4 | .118 | 23 | 15 | 0 | 1.000 |
| 1966–Austin | .............Texas | 2-3B | 92 | 339 | 35 | 77 | 11 | 1 | 7 | 30 | .227 | 140 | 216 | 12 | .967 |
| 1967–Richmond† | ...........Int. | 3B-1B | 99 | 350 | 52 | 104 | 17 | 4 | 14 | 51 | .297 | 84 | 136 | 8 | .965 |
| 1968–New York | .........Amer. | 3B | 135 | 437 | 33 | 100 | 15 | 1 | 7 | 41 | .229 | 98 | 279 | 17 | .957 |
| 1969–New York | .........Amer. | 3B-2B | 85 | 191 | 17 | 41 | 7 | 1 | 2 | 17 | .215 | 50 | 147 | 11 | .947 |
| 1970–Syracuse‡ | .........Int. | 3B-SS | 90 | 251 | 34 | 55 | 15 | 0 | 9 | 30 | .219 | 86 | 163 | 13 | .950 |
| 1971–Ft. Lauderdale§ | Fla. St. | 2B | 4 | 9 | 1 | 1 | 0 | 0 | 0 | 0 | .111 | 3 | 3 | 0 | 1.000 |
| Major League Totals | ..................... | | 220 | 628 | 50 | 141 | 22 | 2 | 9 | 58 | .224 | 148 | 426 | 28 | .953 |

†Recalled by Atlanta Braves; traded to New York Yankees for Catcher Bob Tillman and Pitcher Dale Roberts (latter transferred to Richmond), December 7, 1967.

‡On disabled list, May 28 through June 18, 1970.

§Player-manager.

### RECORD AS MANAGER

| Year | Club | League | Position | W. | L. | Year | Club | League | Position | W. | L. |
|------|------|--------|----------|-----|-----|------|------|--------|----------|-----|-----|
| 1971–Ft. Lauderdale | ..Fla. St. | Fourth(E) | 71 | 70 | 1974–Syracuse | ............Int. | Second(N) | 74 | 70 |
| 1972–West Haven | ........†East. | First (A.) | 84 | 56 | 1975–Syracuse | ............Int. | Third | 72 | 64 |
| 1973–Syracuse | ............Int. | Third(Am.) | 76 | 70 | 1976–Syracuse | ............‡Int. | Second | 82 | 57 |

†Defeated Three Rivers in playoff, three games to none.

‡Won playoffs by defeating Memphis, three games to none; and Richmond (finals), three games to one.
New York Yankees' minor league instructor 1972-76; coach, New York Yankees, 1977.

## ROGER LEE CRAIG
### San Diego Padres

Born February 17, 1931, at Durham, N. C.
Height, 6.04. Weight, 196.
Threw and batted righthanded.
Hobby—Sports.
Attended North Carolina State College, Raleigh, N. C.

Tied major league record for most 1-0 games lost, season (5), 1963; tied National League mark for most consecutive losses, season (18), May 4 through August 4, 1963, inclusive.
Tied for National League lead in shutouts with 4 in 1959.

| Year | Club | League | G. | IP. | W. | L. | Pct. | H. | R. | ER. | SO. | BB. | ERA. |
|---|---|---|---|---|---|---|---|---|---|---|---|---|---|
| 1950—Newport News | | Piedmont | 6 | 19 | 0 | 1 | .000 | 22 | 17 | 15 | 7 | 23 | 7.11 |
| 1950—Valdosta | | Ga.-Fla. | 23 | 167 | 14 | 7 | .667 | 136 | 86 | 58 | 152 | 150 | 3.13 |
| 1951—Newport News | | Piedmont | 38 | 21 | 14 | 11 | .560 | 175 | 109 | 90 | 119 | ∗175 | 3.67 |
| 1952-53—Elmira | | Eastern | | | | | (In Military Service) | | | | | | |
| 1954—Elmira | | Eastern | 3 | 2 | 0 | 0 | .000 | 4 | 6 | 2 | 1 | 2 | 9.00 |
| 1954—Pueblo | | Western | 6 | 14 | 1 | 1 | .500 | 14 | 17 | 15 | 8 | 19 | 9.64 |
| 1954—Newport News | | Piedmont | 20 | 125 | 8 | 3 | .727 | 107 | 44 | 35 | 108 | 56 | 2.50 |
| 1955—Montreal | | Int'national | 22 | 117 | 10 | 2 | .833 | 105 | 48 | 46 | 68 | 64 | 3.54 |
| 1955—Brooklyn | | National | 21 | 91 | 5 | 3 | .625 | 81 | 37 | 28 | 48 | 43 | 2.77 |
| 1956—Brooklyn | | National | 35 | 199 | 12 | 11 | .522 | 169 | 90 | 82 | 109 | 87 | 3.71 |
| 1957—Brooklyn | | National | 32 | 111 | 6 | 9 | .400 | 102 | 58 | 57 | 69 | 47 | 4.62 |
| 1958—Los Angeles | | National | 9 | 32 | 2 | 1 | .667 | 30 | 20 | 16 | 16 | 12 | 4.50 |
| 1958—St. Paul | | Am. Assoc. | 28 | 182 | 5 | ∗17 | .227 | 180 | 100 | 79 | 119 | 77 | 3.91 |
| 1959—Spokane | | P. Coast | 14 | 96 | 6 | 7 | .462 | 86 | 39 | 34 | 46 | 26 | 3.19 |
| 1959—Los Angeles | | National | 29 | 153 | 11 | 5 | .688 | 122 | 49 | 35 | 76 | 45 | 2.06 |
| 1960—Los Angeles | | National | 21 | 116 | 8 | 3 | .727 | 99 | 48 | 42 | 69 | 43 | 3.26 |
| 1961—Los Angeles† | | National | 40 | 113 | 5 | 6 | .455 | 130 | 87 | 77 | 63 | 52 | 6.13 |
| 1962—New York | | National | 42 | 233 | 10 | ∗24 | .294 | 261 | 133 | 117 | 118 | 70 | 4.52 |
| 1963—New York‡ | | National | 46 | 236 | 5 | ∗22 | .185 | 249 | 117 | 99 | 108 | 58 | 3.78 |
| 1964—St. Louis§ | | National | 39 | 166 | 7 | 9 | .438 | 180 | 76 | 60 | 84 | 35 | 3.25 |
| 1965—Cincinnati x | | National | 40 | 64 | 1 | 4 | .200 | 74 | 33 | 26 | 30 | 25 | 3.66 |
| 1966—Philadelphia | | National | 14 | 23 | 2 | 1 | .667 | 31 | 15 | 14 | 13 | 5 | 5.48 |
| 1966—Seattle | | P. Coast | 6 | 22 | 0 | 1 | .000 | 15 | 11 | 6 | 11 | 9 | 2.45 |
| 1968—Albuquerque | | Texas | 1 | 4 | 0 | 0 | .000 | 3 | 0 | 0 | 2 | 2 | 0.00 |
| Major League Totals | | | 368 | 1537 | 74 | 98 | .430 | 1528 | 763 | 653 | 803 | 522 | 3.82 |

†Selected by New York Mets in National League expansion draft, October 10, 1961.
‡Traded to St. Louis Cardinals for Pitcher Bill Wakefield and Outfielder George Altman, November 4, 1963.
§Traded to Cincinnati Reds with Outfielder Charlie James for Pitcher Bob Purkey and a player to be named later, December 14, 1964.
xReleased by Cincinnati Reds and signed by Philadelphia Phillies, April 11, 1966.

### WORLD SERIES RECORD

| Year | Club | League | G. | IP. | W. | L. | Pct. | H. | R. | ER. | SO. | BB. | ERA. |
|---|---|---|---|---|---|---|---|---|---|---|---|---|---|
| 1955—Brooklyn | | National | 1 | 6 | 1 | 0 | 1.000 | 4 | 2 | 2 | 4 | 5 | 3.00 |
| 1956—Brooklyn | | National | 2 | 6 | 0 | 1 | .000 | 10 | 8 | 8 | 4 | 3 | 12.00 |
| 1959—Los Angeles | | National | 2 | 9⅓ | 1 | 1 | .000 | 15 | 9 | 9 | 8 | 5 | 8.68 |
| 1964—St. Louis | | National | 2 | 5 | 1 | 0 | 1.000 | 2 | 0 | 0 | 9 | 3 | 0.00 |
| World Series Totals | | | 7 | 26⅓ | 2 | 2 | .500 | 31 | 19 | 19 | 25 | 16 | 6.49 |

### RECORD AS MANAGER

| Year | Club | League | Position | W. | L. |
|---|---|---|---|---|---|
| 1968—Albuquerque | | Texas | Second(W) | 70 | 69 |

Scout, Los Angeles Dodgers, 1967; coach, San Diego Padres, 1969 through 1972; minor league pitching instructor, Los Angeles Dodgers, 1973; coach, Houston Astros, 1974 and 1975; coach, San Diego Padres, 1976 and 1977.

## DELMAR WESLEY CRANDALL
### (Del)
### California Angels

Born March 5, 1930, at Ontario, Calif.
Height, 6.01½. Weight, 202.
Threw and batted righthanded.
Hobby—Photography.

Tied major league record for most years leading league, catchers in assists (6), 1960.
Led National League catchers in double plays, 1953-59; led in passed balls, 1960.
Received Gold Glove award as outstanding National League fielding catcher, 1958-59-60-62.
Named as catcher on THE SPORTING NEWS All-Star Major League Team, 1958-60.
Named as catcher on THE SPORTING NEWS All-Star National League Team, 1962.

| Year | Club | League | Pos. | G. | AB. | R. | H. | 2B. | 3B. | HR. | RBI. | B.A. | PO. | A. | E. | F.A. |
|---|---|---|---|---|---|---|---|---|---|---|---|---|---|---|---|---|
| 1948—Leavenworth | | W. A. | C | 123 | 425 | 81 | 129 | 27 | 4 | 15 | 84 | .304 | 575 | 71 | 16 | .976 |
| 1948—Milwaukee | | A. A. | C | 5 | 12 | 1 | 1 | 0 | 0 | 0 | 0 | .083 | 17 | 1 | 0 | 1.000 |
| 1949—Evansville | | I.I.I. | C | 38 | 154 | 28 | 54 | 13 | 3 | 8 | 36 | .351 | 250 | 29 | 3 | .989 |
| 1949—Boston | | Nat. | C | 67 | 228 | 21 | 60 | 10 | 1 | 4 | 34 | .263 | 287 | 39 | 6 | .982 |
| 1950—Boston | | Nat. | C-1B | 79 | 255 | 21 | 56 | 11 | 0 | 4 | 37 | .220 | 319 | 41 | 12 | .968 |
| 1951-52—Boston | | Nat. | | | | | (In Military Service) | | | | | | | | | |

| Year Club League | Pos. | G. | AB. | R. | H. | 2B. | 3B. | HR. | RBI. | B.A. | PO. | A. | E. | F.A. |
|---|---|---|---|---|---|---|---|---|---|---|---|---|---|---|
| 1953–Milwaukee .......Nat. | C | 116 | 382 | 55 | 104 | 13 | 1 | 15 | 51 | .272 | 556 | •62 | 9 | .986 |
| 1954–Milwaukee .......Nat. | C | 138 | 463 | 60 | 112 | 18 | 2 | 21 | 64 | .242 | •665 | •79 | 8 | .989 |
| 1955–Milwaukee .......Nat. | C | 133 | 440 | 61 | 104 | 15 | 2 | 26 | 62 | .236 | 611 | 67 | •10 | .985 |
| 1956–Milwaukee .......Nat. | C | 112 | 311 | 37 | 74 | 14 | 2 | 16 | 48 | .238 | 448 | 44 | 2 | •.996 |
| 1957–Milwaukee .......Nat. | •C-O-1B | 118 | 383 | 45 | 97 | 11 | 2 | 15 | 46 | .253 | 429 | •60 | 7 | .986 |
| 1958–Milwaukee .......Nat. | C | 131 | 427 | 50 | 116 | 23 | 1 | 18 | 63 | .272 | •659 | •64 | 7 | •.990 |
| 1959–Milwaukee .......Nat. | C | 150 | 518 | 62 | 133 | 19 | 2 | 21 | 72 | .257 | 783 | •71 | 5 | •.994 |
| 1960–Milwaukee .......Nat. | C | 142 | 537 | 81 | 158 | 14 | 1 | 19 | 77 | .294 | •764 | •70 | 10 | .988 |
| 1961–Milwaukee† .....Nat. | C | 15 | 30 | 3 | 6 | 3 | 0 | 0 | 1 | .200 | 17 | 3 | 0 | 1.000 |
| 1962–Milwaukee .......Nat. | •C-1B | 107 | 350 | 35 | 104 | 12 | 3 | 8 | 45 | .297 | 488 | 55 | 3 | •.995 |
| 1963–Milwaukee‡ ......Nat. | C-1B | 86 | 259 | 18 | 52 | 4 | 0 | 3 | 28 | .201 | 459 | 43 | 4 | .992 |
| 1964–San Francisco ..Nat. | C | 69 | 195 | 12 | 45 | 8 | 1 | 3 | 11 | .231 | 402 | 30 | 3 | .993 |
| 1965–Pittsburgh x .....Nat. | C | 60 | 140 | 11 | 30 | 2 | 0 | 2 | 10 | .214 | 248 | 23 | 1 | .996 |
| 1966–Cleveland y ......Amer. | C | 50 | 108 | 10 | 25 | 2 | 0 | 4 | 8 | .231 | 304 | 15 | 3 | .991 |
| 1969–Albuquerque z ..Tex. | .... | 1 | 2 | 0 | 1 | 0 | 0 | 0 | 0 | .500 | .... | .... | .... | ...... |
| 1970–Albuquerque z ..Tex. | P-3B | 2 | 4 | 0 | 0 | 0 | 0 | 0 | 0 | .000 | 0 | 0 | 0 | .000 |
| National League Totals ................. | | 1523 | 4918 | 575 | 1251 | 177 | 18 | 175 | 649 | .254 | 7145 | 751 | 87 | .989 |
| American League Totals ............... | | 50 | 108 | 10 | 25 | 2 | 0 | 4 | 8 | .231 | 304 | 15 | 3 | .991 |
| Major League Totals ...................... | | 1573 | 5026 | 585 | 1276 | 179 | 18 | 179 | 657 | .254 | 7449 | 766 | 90 | .989 |

†On disabled list most of season due to arm trouble.

‡Traded to San Francisco Giants with Pitchers Bob Hendley and Bob Shaw for Pitcher Billy Hoeft, Catcher Ed Bailey, Infielder Ernie Bowman and Outfielder Felipe Alou. All players but Bowman changed clubs December 3, 1963—he being promised added player in deal and transferred January 8, 1964.

§Traded to Pittsburgh Pirates for Pitchers Bob Priddy and Oufielder-First Baseman Bob Burda, February 11, 1965; Burda was transferred from Columbus roster to Giants' Tacoma farm club.

xReleased by Pittsburgh Pirates and signed by Cleveland Indians, November 30, 1965.

yOn disabled list, June 4 through June 24, Released, October 14, 1966.

zPlayer-manager.

## PITCHING RECORD

| Year Club League | G. | IP. | W. | L. | Pct. | H. | R. | ER. | SO. | BB. | ERA. |
|---|---|---|---|---|---|---|---|---|---|---|---|
| 1970–Albuquerque ........................Texas | 2 | 3 | 1 | 0 | 1.000 | 2 | 0 | 0 | 2 | 2 | 0.00 |

## WORLD SERIES RECORD

Tied World Series record for most double plays started by catcher in seven-game series (2), 1957.

| Year Club League | Pos. | G. | AB. | R. | H. | 2B. | 3B. | HR. | RBI. | B.A. | PO. | A. | E. | F.A. |
|---|---|---|---|---|---|---|---|---|---|---|---|---|---|---|
| 1957–Milwaukee .......Nat. | C | 6 | 19 | 1 | 4 | 0 | 0 | 1 | 1 | .211 | 21 | 4 | 0 | 1.000 |
| 1958–Milwaukee .......Nat. | C | 7 | 25 | 4 | 6 | 0 | 0 | 1 | 3 | .240 | 43 | 5 | 0 | 1.000 |
| World Series Totals ...................... | | 13 | 44 | 5 | 10 | 0 | 0 | 2 | 4 | .227 | 64 | 9 | 0 | 1.000 |

## ALL-STAR GAME RECORD

| Year League | Pos. | AB. | R. | H. | 2B. | 3B. | HR. | RBI. | B.A. | PO. | A. | E. | F.A. |
|---|---|---|---|---|---|---|---|---|---|---|---|---|---|
| 1955–National ............................. | C | 1 | 0 | 0 | 0 | 0 | 0 | 0 | .000 | 1 | 0 | 0 | 1.000 |
| 1958–National ............................. | C | 4 | 0 | 0 | 0 | 0 | 0 | 0 | .000 | 5 | 0 | 0 | 1.000 |
| 1959–National (both games) ........ | C | 5 | 1 | 2 | 0 | 0 | 0 | 1 | .400 | 17 | 1 | 0 | 1.000 |
| 1960–National (both games) ........ | C | 5 | 1 | 2 | 0 | 0 | 1 | 1 | .400 | 7 | 0 | 0 | 1.000 |
| 1962–National (both games) ........ | C | 5 | 0 | 0 | 0 | 0 | 0 | 0 | .000 | 8 | 0 | 0 | 1.000 |
| All-Star Game Totals ...................... | | 20 | 2 | 4 | 0 | 0 | 1 | 2 | .200 | 38 | 1 | 0 | 1.000 |

## RECORD AS MANAGER

| Year Club League | Position | W. | L. | Year Club League | Position | W. | L. |
|---|---|---|---|---|---|---|---|
| 1969–Albuquerque ......Tex. | Fourth(W) | 67 | 69 | 1972–Milwaukee‡ ........Amer. | Sixth(E) | 54 | 70 |
| 1970–Albuquerque ......Tex. | †First(W) | 83 | 52 | 1973–Milwaukee..........Amer. | Fifth(E) | 74 | 88 |
| 1971–Evansville ..........A. A. | Fourth(E) | 60 | 78 | 1974–Milwaukee..........Amer. | Fifth(E) | 76 | 86 |
| 1972–Evansville ..........A. A. | Second(E) | 21 | 17 | 1975–Milwaukee§ ........Amer. | Fifth(E) | 67 | 94 |

†Won playoff against Memphis, three games to one.

‡Replaced Dave Bristol, May 30, 1972.

§Replaced by Harvey Kuenn, September 28, 1975.

Minor League Instructor, California Angels, 1976; coach, California Angels, 1977.


## ALVIN RALPH DARK
### Chicago Cubs

Born January 7, 1922, at Comanche, Okla.
Height, 5.11. Weight, 185.
Threw and batted righthanded.
Hobby—Golf.
Attended Louisiana State University, Baton Rouge, La., and
Southwestern Louisiana Institute, Lafayette, La.

Led National League shortstops in double plays with 114 in 1951, 116 in 1952 and 105 in 1957.
Named Major League Rookie of the Year by the Baseball Writers Association, 1948.
Named as shortstop on THE SPORTING NEWS Major League All-Star Team, 1954.

| Year Club League | Pos. | G. | AB. | R. | H. | 2B. | 3B. | HR. | RBI. | B.A. | PO. | A. | E. | F.A. |
|---|---|---|---|---|---|---|---|---|---|---|---|---|---|---|
| 1946–Boston ..............Nat. | SS-OF | 15 | 13 | 0 | 3 | 3 | 0 | 1 | .231 | 6 | 14 | 2 | .900 |
| 1947–Milwaukee ........A. A. | SS | 149 | •614 | •121 | 186 | •49 | 7 | 10 | 66 | .303 | •290 | •454 | •46 | .942 |
| 1948–Boston ..............Nat. | SS | 137 | 543 | 85 | 175 | 39 | 6 | 3 | 48 | .322 | 253 | 393 | 25 | .983 |

| Year Club League | Pos. | G. | AB. | R. | H. | 2B. | 3B. | HR. | RBI. | B.A. | PO. | A. | E. | F.A. |
|---|---|---|---|---|---|---|---|---|---|---|---|---|---|---|
| 1949—Boston† ............Nat. | SS-3B | 130 | 529 | 74 | 146 | 23 | 5 | 3 | 53 | .276 | 233 | 395 | 26 | .960 |
| 1950—New York.........Nat. | SS | 154 | 587 | 79 | 164 | 36 | 5 | 16 | 67 | .279 | 288 | 465 | 30 | .962 |
| 1951—New York.........Nat. | SS | 156 | 646 | 114 | 196 | •41 | 7 | 14 | 69 | .303 | •295 | •465 | •45 | .944 |
| 1952—New York.........Nat. | SS | 151 | 589 | 92 | 177 | 29 | 3 | 14 | 73 | .301 | •324 | 423 | 27 | .965 |
| 1953—New York.........Nat. | IF-O-P | 155 | •647 | 126 | 194 | 41 | 6 | 23 | 88 | .300 | 325 | 433 | 24 | .969 |
| 1954—New York.........Nat. | SS | •154 | •644 | 98 | 189 | 26 | 6 | 20 | 70 | .293 | 289 | 487 | •36 | .956 |
| 1955—New York.........Nat. | SS | 115 | 475 | 77 | 134 | 20 | 3 | 9 | 45 | .282 | 213 | 324 | 21 | .962 |
| 1956—N. Y.‡-St. Louis Nat. | SS | 148 | 619 | 73 | 170 | 26 | 7 | 6 | 54 | .275 | 267 | 424 | 29 | .960 |
| 1957—St. Louis .........Nat. | •SS-3B | 140 | 583 | 80 | 169 | 25 | 8 | 4 | 64 | .290 | •276 | 421 | 25 | .965 |
| 1958—St. L.§-Chicago..Nat. | 3B-SS | 132 | 528 | 61 | 156 | 16 | 4 | 4 | 48 | .295 | 121 | 260 | 21 | .948 |
| 1959—Chicago x .........Nat. | 3-1-SS | 136 | 477 | 60 | 126 | 22 | 9 | 6 | 45 | .264 | 138 | 260 | 21 | .950 |
| 1960—Phila. y-Mil. z....Nat. | 3-O-1-2 | 105 | 339 | 45 | 90 | 11 | 3 | 4 | 32 | .265 | 146 | 90 | 10 | .959 |
| Major League Totals ...................... | | 1828 | 7219 | 1064 | 2089 | 358 | 72 | 126 | 757 | .289 | 3174 | 4854 | 342 | .959 |

†Traded to New York Giants with Second Baseman Eddie Stanky for Pitcher Sam Webb, Third Baseman Sid Gordon, Shortstop John (Buddy) Kerr and Outfielder Willard Marshall, December 14, 1949.

‡Traded to St. Louis Cardinals with Pitcher Don Liddle, Catcher Ray Katt and Outfielder-First Baseman Whitey Lockman for Pitchers Gordon Jones and Dick Littlefield, Catcher Bill Sarni, Second Baseman Al Schoendienst and Outfielder Jack Brandt. All players but Jones exchanged clubs June 14, 1956—Jones being assigned to Giants October 1, 1956.

§Traded to Chicago Cubs for Pitcher Jim Brosnan, May 20, 1958.

xTraded to Philadelphia Phillies with Pitcher John Buzhardt and Third Baseman Jim Woods for Outfielder Richie Ashburn, January 11, 1960.

yTraded to Milwaukee Braves for Third Baseman Joe Morgan and cash, June 23, 1960.

zTraded to San Francisco Giants for Infielder Andre Rodgers, October 31, 1960.

## WORLD SERIES RECORD

Tied World Series record for most one-base hits in a 4-game series (7), and tied mark by making one or more hits in each series game, 1954.

| Year Club League | Pos. | G. | AB. | R. | H. | 2B. | 3B. | HR. | RBI. | B.A. | PO. | A. | E. | F.A. |
|---|---|---|---|---|---|---|---|---|---|---|---|---|---|---|
| 1948—Boston ..............Nat. | SS | 6 | 24 | 2 | 4 | 1 | 0 | 0 | 0 | .167 | 7 | 12 | 3 | .064 |
| 1951—New York.........Nat. | SS | 6 | 24 | 5 | 10 | 3 | 0 | 1 | 4 | .417 | 10 | 16 | 0 | 1.000 |
| 1954—New York.........Nat. | SS | 4 | 17 | 2 | 7 | 0 | 0 | 0 | 0 | .412 | 7 | 12 | 1 | .950 |
| World Series Totals ....................... | | 16 | 65 | 9 | 21 | 4 | 0 | 1 | 4 | .323 | 24 | 40 | 4 | .941 |

## ALL-STAR GAME RECORD

| Year League | Pos. | AB. | R. | H. | 2B. | 3B. | HR. | RBI. | B.A. | PO. | A. | E. | F.A. |
|---|---|---|---|---|---|---|---|---|---|---|---|---|---|
| 1951—National ............................. | SS | 5 | 0 | 1 | 0 | 0 | 0 | 0 | .200 | 0 | 3 | 0 | 1.000 |
| 1954—National ............................. | SS | 5 | 0 | 1 | 0 | 0 | 0 | 0 | .200 | 1 | 2 | 0 | 1.000 |
| All-Star Game Totals ....................... | | 10 | 0 | 2 | 0 | 0 | 0 | 0 | .200 | 1 | 5 | 0 | 1.000 |

Member of National League All-Star Team for 1952 game; did not play.

## PITCHING RECORD

| Year Club | League | G. | IP. | W. | L. | Pct. | H. | R. | ER. | SO. | BB. | ERA. |
|---|---|---|---|---|---|---|---|---|---|---|---|---|
| 1953—New York ...........................National | | 1 | 1 | 0 | 0 | .000 | 1 | 2 | 2 | 0 | 1 | 18.00 |

## RECORD AS MANAGER

| Year Club League | Position | W. | L. | Year Club League | Position | W. | L. |
|---|---|---|---|---|---|---|---|
| 1961—San Francisco ....Nat. | Third | 85 | 69 | 1968—Cleveland ..........Amer. | Third | 86 | 75 |
| 1962—San Francisco ....Nat. | †First | 103 | 62 | 1969—Cleveland ..........Amer. | Sixth(E) | 62 | 99 |
| 1963—San Francisco ....Nat. | Third | 88 | 74 | 1970—Cleveland ..........Amer. | Fifth(E) | 76 | 86 |
| 1964—San Francisco ....Nat. | Fourth | 90 | 72 | 1971—Cleveland§.........Amer. | Sixth(E) | 42 | 61 |
| 1966—Kansas City........Amer. | Seventh | 74 | 86 | 1974—Oakland.............Amer. | First(W) | 90 | 72 |
| 1967—Kansas City‡ ......Amer. | Tenth | 52 | 69 | 1975—Oakland.............Amer. | First(W) | 98 | 64 |

†Defeated Los Angeles two games to one in playoff for championship.

‡Replaced by Luke Appling, August 20.

§Replaced by Johnny Lipon, July 30.

Coach, Chicago Cubs, 1965 and 1977.

## CHAMPIONSHIP SERIES RECORD

| Year Club | League | W. | L. |
|---|---|---|---|
| 1974—Oakland..............American | | 3 | 1 |
| 1975—Oakland..............American | | 0 | 3 |

## WORLD SERIES RECORD

| Year Club | League | W. | L. |
|---|---|---|---|
| 1962—San Francisco ....National | | 3 | 4 |
| 1974—Oakland..............American | | 4 | 1 |

# JAMES HOUSTON DAVENPORT
## (Jim)
### San Francisco Giants

Born August 17, 1933, at Siluria, Ala.
Height, 5.11. Weight, 183.
Threw and batted righthanded.
Hobbies—Hunting, fishing and golf.
Attended Mississippi Southern College, Hattiesburg, Mass.

Established major league record for most consecutive errorless games by third baseman, league, 97, July 29, 1966 through April 28, 1968 (209 chances accepted–played other positions during streak).

Established National League record for most consecutive errorless games by third baseman, season, 64, May 22 through September 30, 1967, first game (137 chances accepted–played other positions during streak).

Tied for National League lead in sacrifice hits with 17 in 1958.

Led Cotton States League in total bases with 239 in 1955.

Received Gold Glove award as outstanding fielding third baseman in National League, 1962.

| Year Club | League | Pos. | G. | AB. | R. | H. | 2B. | 3B. | HR. | RBI. | B.A. | PO. | A. | E. | F.A. |
|---|---|---|---|---|---|---|---|---|---|---|---|---|---|---|---|
| 1955–El Dorado ........ | Cot. St. | 3B | 105 | 405 | 102 | •147 | 29 | 6 | 17 | 76 | •.363 | •113 | •190 | 23 | .929 |
| 1956–Dallas .............. | Tex. | 3B-SS | 154 | 577 | 97 | 154 | 28 | 6 | 14 | 74 | .267 | 125 | 349 | 24 | .952 |
| 1957–Minneapolis ...... | A. A. | 3B-SS | 148 | 529 | 68 | 154 | 28 | 3 | 10 | 53 | .291 | 123 | 252 | 15 | .962 |
| 1958–San Francisco .. | Nat. | 3B-SS | 134 | 434 | 70 | 111 | 22 | 3 | 12 | 41 | .256 | 96 | 232 | 14 | .959 |
| 1959–San Francisco .. | Nat. | •3B-SS | 123 | 469 | 65 | 121 | 16 | 3 | 6 | 38 | .258 | 91 | 222 | 7 | •.978 |
| 1960–San Francisco .. | Nat. | •3B-SS | 112 | 363 | 43 | 91 | 15 | 3 | 6 | 38 | .251 | 83 | 178 | 10 | •.963 |
| 1961–San Francisco .. | Nat. | 3B | 137 | 436 | 64 | 121 | 28 | 4 | 12 | 65 | .278 | 119 | 235 | 13 | •.965 |
| 1962–San Francisco .. | Nat. | 3B | 144 | 485 | 83 | 144 | 25 | 5 | 14 | 58 | .297 | 125 | 256 | 19 | .953 |
| 1963–San Francisco .. | Nat. | 3-2-S | 147 | 460 | 40 | 116 | 19 | 3 | 4 | 36 | .252 | 152 | 230 | 13 | .967 |
| 1964–San Francisco .. | Nat. | S-3-2 | 116 | 297 | 24 | 70 | 10 | 6 | 2 | 26 | .236 | 138 | 237 | 11 | .972 |
| 1965–San Francisco .. | Nat. | 3-SS-2 | 106 | 271 | 29 | 68 | 14 | 3 | 4 | 31 | .251 | 97 | 147 | 14 | .950 |
| 1966–San Francisco .. | Nat. | S-3-2-1 | 111 | 305 | 42 | 76 | 6 | 2 | 9 | 30 | .249 | 107 | 201 | 14 | .957 |
| 1967–San Francisco .. | Nat. | 3-S-2B | 124 | 295 | 42 | 81 | 10 | 3 | 5 | 30 | .275 | 83 | 192 | 4 | .986 |
| 1968–San Francisco .. | Nat. | 3-SS-2 | 113 | 272 | 27 | 61 | 1 | 1 | 1 | 17 | .224 | 57 | 137 | 8 | .961 |
| 1969–San Francisco .. | Nat. | 3-1-O-S | 112 | 303 | 20 | 73 | 10 | 1 | 2 | 42 | .241 | 84 | 158 | 8 | .968 |
| 1970–San Francisco .. | Nat. | 3B | 22 | 37 | 3 | 9 | 1 | 0 | 0 | 4 | .243 | 7 | 7 | 0 | 1.000 |
| Major League Totals ..................... | | | 1501 | 4427 | 552 | 1142 | 177 | 37 | 77 | 456 | .258 | 1314 | 2432 | 135 | .965 |

## WORLD SERIES RECORD

Established World Series records for most double plays, third baseman, 7-game Series (4), 1962, and most double plays started, third baseman, 7-game Series (4), 1962.

| Year Club | League | Pos. | G. | AB. | R. | H. | 2B. | 3B. | HR. | RBI. | B.A. | PO. | A. | E. | F.A. |
|---|---|---|---|---|---|---|---|---|---|---|---|---|---|---|---|
| 1962–San Francisco .. | Nat. | 3B | 7 | 22 | 1 | 3 | 1 | 0 | 0 | 1 | .136 | 6 | 12 | 3 | .857 |

## ALL-STAR GAME RECORD

| Year League | Pos. | AB. | R. | H. | 2B. | 3B. | HR. | RBI. | B.A. | PO. | A. | E. | F.A. |
|---|---|---|---|---|---|---|---|---|---|---|---|---|---|
| 1962–National (first game) .......... | 3B | 1 | 0 | 1 | 0 | 0 | 0 | 0 | 1.000 | 0 | 1 | 0 | 1.000 |

Member of National League All-Star Team in 1962 (second game); did not play.

## RECORD AS MANAGER

| Year Club | League | Position | W. | L. |
|---|---|---|---|---|
| 1971–Phoenix.............. | P. C. | Second(S) | 74 | 70 |
| 1972–Phoenix.............. | P. C. | Second(E) | 81 | 67 |
| 1973–Phoenix.............. | P. C. | Third(E) | 70 | 73 |

Coach, San Francisco Giants, July 13, 1970 to close of season; coach, San Diego Padres, 1974 and 1975; coach, San Francisco Giants, 1976 and 1977.

# WILLIAM LESTER DeMARS
## (Billy)
### Philadelphia Phillies

Born August 26, 1925, at Brooklyn, N. Y.
Height, 5.10. Weight, 170.
Threw and batted righthanded.

| Year Club | League | Pos. | G. | AB. | R. | H. | 2B. | 3B. | HR. | RBI. | B.A. | PO. | A. | E. | F.A. |
|---|---|---|---|---|---|---|---|---|---|---|---|---|---|---|---|
| 1943–Olean ................ | Pony | SS | 50 | 189 | 27 | 51 | 12 | 1 | 0 | 29 | .270 | 88 | 131 | 16 | .932 |
| 1943–Lancaster.......... | Int.-St. | SS | 21 | 82 | 13 | 19 | 2 | 1 | 0 | 6 | .232 | 42 | 73 | 7 | .943 |
| 1944-45–Durham ........ | Pied. | | (In Military Service) | | | | | | | | | | | | |
| 1946–Nashua.............. | N. Eng. | SS | 98 | 321 | 43 | 76 | 9 | 8 | 1 | 42 | .237 | 170 | 275 | 38 | .921 |
| 1947–Asheville† ......... | Tri-St. | SS | 112 | 427 | 85 | 140 | 21 | 4 | 5 | 88 | .328 | 203 | 321 | 33 | .941 |
| 1948–Philadelphia ...... | Amer. | S-3-2B | 18 | 29 | 3 | 5 | 0 | 0 | 0 | 1 | .172 | 18 | 25 | 3 | .935 |
| 1949–Buffalo‡ ............ | Int. | SS | 109 | 378 | 49 | 105 | 18 | 1 | 6 | 56 | .278 | 228 | 329 | 28 | .952 |
| 1950–St. Louis .......... | Amer. | SS-3B | 61 | 178 | 25 | 44 | 5 | 1 | 0 | 13 | .247 | 118 | 129 | 19 | .929 |
| 1951–San Antonio ...... | Texas | SS | 129 | 408 | 46 | 100 | 14 | 2 | 3 | 30 | .245 | 251 | 254 | 30 | .944 |
| 1951–St. Louis .......... | Amer. | SS | 1 | 4 | 1 | 1 | 0 | 0 | 0 | 0 | .250 | 1 | 4 | 0 | 1.000 |
| 1952–Toronto ............ | Int. | 3B-SS | 141 | 524 | 70 | 148 | 23 | 6 | 4 | 45 | .282 | 174 | 283 | 21 | .956 |
| 1953–Toronto ............ | Int. | •SS-3B | 148 | 545 | 69 | 142 | 23 | 3 | 3 | 52 | .261 | 272 | 400 | 24 | •.966 |
| 1954–Toronto ............ | Int. | SS | 40 | 134 | 17 | 40 | 9 | 2 | 0 | 9 | .299 | 62 | 84 | 7 | .954 |
| 1955–Toronto ............ | Int. | 2B-SS | 67 | 184 | 24 | 52 | 10 | 0 | 3 | 17 | .283 | 115 | 123 | 7 | .971 |
| 1956–Buffalo ............. | Int. | SS | 104 | 320 | 26 | 78 | 9 | 0 | 1 | 22 | .244 | 153 | 244 | 12 | .971 |
| 1957–Portland .......... | P. C. | 3-S-2B | 137 | 356 | 35 | 86 | 16 | 1 | 3 | 34 | .242 | 136 | 281 | 10 | .977 |
| 1958–Port.-Vancouver | P. C. | PH | 2 | 1 | 0 | 0 | 0 | 0 | 0 | 0 | .000 | 0 | 0 | 0 | .000 |
| 1958–Aberdeen .......... | No. | S-3-OF | 81 | 240 | 28 | 62 | 5 | 0 | 4 | 30 | .258 | 78 | 158 | 13 | .948 |
| 1959–Stockton .......... | Calif. | 3B-P | 2 | 5 | 0 | 1 | 0 | 0 | 0 | 1 | .200 | 0 | 1 | 0 | 1.000 |
| 1960–Stockton .......... | Calif. | 3B-P | 7 | 14 | 3 | 3 | 0 | 0 | 0 | 1 | .214 | 1 | 3 | 0 | 1.000 |
| Major League Totals ..................... | | | 80 | 211 | 29 | 50 | 5 | 1 | 0 | 14 | .237 | 137 | 158 | 22 | .931 |

†Drafted by Philadelphia Athletics from Mobile (Brooklyn Dodgers' organization), November 10, 1947.

‡Recalled by Philadelphia Athletics; traded with Third Baseman Frank Gustine, Outfielders Ray Coleman and Rocky Ippolito and $100,000 to St. Louis Browns for Third Baseman Bob Dillinger and Outfielder Paul Lehner, December 13, 1949.

| Year Club | League | G. | IP. | W. | L. | Pct. | H. | R. | ER. | SO. | BB. | ERA. |
|---|---|---|---|---|---|---|---|---|---|---|---|---|
| 1959–Stockton ...........................California | | 1 | .... | 1 | 0 | 1.000 | .... | .... | .... | .... | .... | .... |
| 1960–Stockton ...........................California | | 3 | .... | 0 | 0 | .000 | .... | .... | .... | .... | .... | .... |

## RECORD AS MANAGER

| Year Club | League | Position | W. | L. | Year Club | League | Position | W. | L. |
|---|---|---|---|---|---|---|---|---|---|
| 1958–Aberdeen† .........North | | Eighth | 37 | 63 | (Second Half) | | Eighth | 27 | 33 |
| 1959–Stockton ............Calif. | | Fourth | 35 | 34 | 1964–Fox Cities .........Midwest | | Second | 39 | 22 |
| (Second Half) | | Third | 41 | 29 | (Second Half) | | First | 42 | 21 |
| 1960–Stockton ............Calif. | | Sixth | 27 | 43 | 1965–Fox Cities .........Midwest | | Eighth | 25 | 35 |
| (Second Half) | | Second | 39 | 31 | (Second Half) | | Fifth | 30 | 28 |
| 1961–Leesburg‡ .........Fla. St. | | Seventh | 15 | 41 | 1966–Miami ...............Fla. St. | | Seventh | 31 | 36 |
| 1961–Tri-Cities§ ..........Northw. | | Sixth | 9 | 18 | (Second Half) | | Third | 44 | 27 |
| (Second Half) | | Sixth | 27 | 42 | 1967–Elmira ..............East. | | xFirst(W) | 74 | 65 |
| 1962–Aberdeen............North. | | Fourth | 64 | 60 | 1968–Rochester ..........Int. | | Third | 77 | 69 |
| 1963–Fox Cities .........Midwest | | Fifth | 28 | 32 | | | | | |

†Replaced Bernie Lutz with club in eighth place, May 25.
‡Replaced by Cal Ripken, June 7.
§Replaced Whitey McDowell with club in sixth place, June 10.
xLost playoff to Binghamton (Eastern Division winner), three games to one.
Coach, Philadelphia Phillies, 1969 through 1977.


# LAWRENCE EUGENE DOBY
## (Larry)
### Chicago White Sox

Born December 13, 1924, at Camden, S. C.
Height, 6.01, Weight, 200.
Threw right and batted lefthanded.
Attended Long Island University, Brooklyn, N.Y., New York University,
New York, N.Y., and Virginia Union University, Richmond, Va.

Hit three home runs in a game, August 2, 1950; hit for cycle, June 4, 1952.
Led American League in slugging percentage with .541 in 1952.
Tied for American League lead in double plays by outfielders with 6 in 1954.
Named by Baseball Writers' Association of America as center fielder on THE SPORTING NEWS All-Star Major League Team, 1950.

| Year Club | League | Pos. | G. | AB. | R. | H. | 2B. | 3B. | HR. | RBI. | B.A. | PO. | A. | E. | F.A. |
|---|---|---|---|---|---|---|---|---|---|---|---|---|---|---|---|
| 1947–Cleveland .........Amer. | | 2-1-SS | 29 | 32 | 3 | 5 | 1 | 0 | 0 | 2 | .156 | 11 | 4 | 0 | 1.000 |
| 1948–Cleveland .........Amer. | | OF | 121 | 439 | 83 | 132 | 23 | 9 | 14 | 66 | .301 | 287 | 12 | •14 | .955 |
| 1949–Cleveland .........Amer. | | OF | 147 | 547 | 106 | 153 | 25 | 3 | 24 | 85 | .280 | 355 | 7 | 9 | .976 |
| 1950–Cleveland .........Amer. | | OF | 142 | 503 | 110 | 164 | 25 | 5 | 25 | 102 | .326 | 367 | 2 | 5 | .987 |
| 1951–Cleveland .........Amer. | | OF | 134 | 447 | 84 | 132 | 27 | 5 | 20 | 69 | .295 | 321 | 12 | 8 | .977 |
| 1952–Cleveland .........Amer. | | OF | 140 | 519 | •104 | 143 | 26 | 8 | •32 | 104 | .276 | 398 | 11 | 6 | .986 |
| 1953–Cleveland .........Amer. | | OF | 149 | 513 | 92 | 135 | 18 | 5 | 29 | 102 | .263 | 354 | 10 | 6 | .984 |
| 1954–Cleveland .........Amer. | | OF | 153 | 577 | 94 | 157 | 18 | 4 | •32 | •126 | .272 | 411 | 14 | 2 | .995 |
| 1955–Cleveland† ........Amer. | | OF | 131 | 491 | 91 | 143 | 17 | 5 | 26 | 75 | .291 | 313 | 6 | 2 | .994 |
| 1956–Chicago .........Amer. | | OF | 140 | 504 | 89 | 135 | 22 | 3 | 24 | 102 | .268 | 371 | 4 | 5 | .987 |
| 1957–Chicago‡§ .........Amer. | | OF | 119 | 416 | 57 | 120 | 27 | 2 | 14 | 79 | .288 | 255 | 3 | 4 | .985 |
| 1958–Cleveland x ......Amer. | | OF | 89 | 247 | 41 | 70 | 10 | 1 | 13 | 45 | .283 | 141 | 5 | 0 | 1.000 |
| 1959–Det.y-Chicagoz ..Amer. | | OF-1B | 39 | 113 | 6 | 26 | 4 | 2 | 0 | 13 | .230 | 56 | 3 | 3 | .952 |
| 1960–San Diego..........P.C. | | OF | 9 | 27 | 2 | 6 | 0 | 1 | 0 | 3 | .222 | 7 | 0 | 0 | 1.000 |
| 1962–Chunichi............Cent. | | 1B-OF | 72 | 240 | 27 | 54 | 9 | 1 | 10 | 35 | .225 | 326 | 11 | 3 | .991 |
| Major League Totals ......................... | | | 1533 | 5348 | 960 | 1515 | 243 | 52 | 253 | 970 | .283 | 3640 | 93 | 64 | .983 |

†Traded to Chicago White Sox for Shortstop Alfonso (Chico) Carrasquel and Outfielder Jim Busby, October 25, 1955.

‡Traded to Baltimore Orioles with Pitcher Jack Harshman and First Baseman Jim Marshall for Pitcher Ray Moore, First Baseman-Outfielder Tito Francona and Infielder-Outfielder Billy Goodman, December 3, 1957; White Sox sent Pitcher Russ Heman to Orioles, January 31, 1958, to complete deal.

§Traded by Baltimore Orioles to Cleveland Indians with Pitcher Don Ferrarese for Pitcher Bud Daley and Outfielders Dick Williams and Gene Woodling, April 1, 1958.

xTraded to Detroit Tigers for Outfielder Tito Francona, March 3, 1959.

ySold to Chicago White Sox for an estimated $30,000, May 13, 1959.

zReleased by Chicago White Sox' organization, April 15, 1960; went on to play one year of professional baseball in Japan with Chunichi Dragons.

## WORLD SERIES RECORD

| Year Club | League | Pos. | G. | AB. | R. | H. | 2B. | 3B. | HR. | RBI. | B.A. | PO. | A. | E. | F.A. |
|---|---|---|---|---|---|---|---|---|---|---|---|---|---|---|---|
| 1948–Cleveland .........Amer. | | OF | 6 | 22 | 1 | 7 | 1 | 0 | 1 | 2 | .318 | 11 | 0 | 1 | .917 |
| 1954–Cleveland .........Amer. | | OF | 4 | 16 | 0 | 2 | 0 | 0 | 0 | 0 | .125 | 7 | 0 | 0 | 1.000 |
| World Series Totals ....................... | | | 10 | 38 | 1 | 9 | 1 | 0 | 1 | 2 | .237 | 18 | 0 | 1 | .947 |

## ALL-STAR GAME RECORD

| Year League | Pos. | AB. | R. | H. | 2B. | 3B. | HR. | RBI. | B.A. | PO. | A. | E. | F.A. |
|---|---|---|---|---|---|---|---|---|---|---|---|---|---|
| 1949–American .......................... | OF | 1 | 0 | 0 | 0 | 0 | 0 | 0 | .000 | 2 | 0 | 0 | 1.000 |
| 1950–American .......................... | OF | 6 | 1 | 2 | 1 | 0 | 0 | 0 | .333 | 9 | 0 | 0 | 1.000 |
| 1951–American .......................... | PH | 1 | 0 | 0 | 0 | 0 | 0 | 0 | .000 | 0 | 0 | 0 | .000 |

| Year League | Pos. | AB. | R. | H. | 2B. | 3B. | HR. | RBI. | B.A. | PO. | A. | E. | F.A. |
|---|---|---|---|---|---|---|---|---|---|---|---|---|---|
| 1952—American ........................... | OF | 0 | 0 | 0 | 0 | 0 | 0 | 0 | .000 | 0 | 0 | 0 | .000 |
| 1953—American ........................... | OF | 1 | 0 | 0 | 0 | 0 | 0 | 0 | .000 | 1 | 1 | 0 | 1.000 |
| 1954—American ........................... | OF | 1 | 1 | 1 | 0 | 0 | 1 | 1 | 1.000 | 0 | 0 | 0 | .000 |
| All-Star Game Totals ................. | | 10 | 2 | 3 | 1 | 0 | 1 | 1 | .300 | 12 | 1 | 0 | 1.000 |

Member of American League All-Star team in 1955 game; did not play.

Scout, Montreal Expos, 1969; minor league instructor, Montreal Expos, 1970; coach, Montreal Expos, 1971 through 1973; coach, Cleveland Indians, 1974; coach, Montreal Expos, 1976; coach, Chicago White Sox, 1977.

## ROBERT PERSHING DOERR
### (Bobby)
### Toronto Blue Jays

Born April 7, 1918, at Los Angeles, Calif.
Height, 5.11. Weight, 185.
Threw and batted righthanded.
Hobbies—Hunting and fishing.

Established following American League records: most consecutive errorless games, season, second baseman (73) and most consecutive chances accepted, season, no errors, second baseman (414), June 24, 1948, first game, to September 19, 1948, first game; most years leading second basemen in double plays (5), 1947.

Led American League second basemen in double plays with 118 in 1938, 118 in 1940, 132 in 1943, 129 in 1946 and 118 in 1947.

Established World Series record for most assists, second baseman, 7-game Series (31), 1946.

Named Most Valuable Player in the American League by THE SPORTING NEWS, 1944.

Named as second baseman on the major league All-Star Team by THE SPORTING NEWS, 1944.

| Year Club League | Pos. | G. | AB. | R. | H. | 2B. | 3B. | HR. | RBI. | B.A. | PO. | A. | E. | F.A. |
|---|---|---|---|---|---|---|---|---|---|---|---|---|---|---|
| 1934—Hollywood ........P.C. | 2B | 67 | 210 | 12 | 52 | 6 | 0 | 0 | 11 | .259 | 135 | 164 | 14 | .955 |
| 1935—Hollywood ........P.C. | 2B | 172 | 647 | 87 | 205 | 22 | 8 | 4 | 74 | .317 | 444 | 466 | 38 | .960 |
| 1936—San Diego .........P.C. | 2B | 175 | 695 | 100 | •238 | 37 | 12 | 2 | 77 | .342 | 399 | •504 | 33 | .965 |
| 1937—Boston ..............Amer. | 2B | 55 | 147 | 22 | 33 | 5 | 1 | 2 | 14 | .224 | 94 | 124 | 6 | .973 |
| 1938—Boston ..............Amer. | 2B | 145 | 509 | 70 | 147 | 26 | 7 | 5 | 80 | .289 | 372 | 420 | 26 | .968 |
| 1939—Boston ..............Amer. | 2B | 127 | 525 | 75 | 167 | 28 | 2 | 12 | 73 | .318 | 336 | 431 | 19 | .976 |
| 1940—Boston ..............Amer. | 2B | 151 | 595 | 87 | 173 | 37 | 10 | 22 | 105 | .291 | •401 | 480 | 21 | •.975 |
| 1941—Boston ..............Amer. | 2B | 132 | 500 | 74 | 141 | 28 | 4 | 16 | 93 | .282 | 290 | 389 | 20 | .971 |
| 1942—Boston ..............Amer. | 2B | 144 | 545 | 71 | 158 | 35 | 5 | 15 | 102 | .290 | 376 | 453 | 21 | •.975 |
| 1943—Boston ..............Amer. | 2B •155 | 604 | 78 | 163 | 32 | 3 | 16 | 75 | .270 | •415 | •490 | 9 | •.990 |
| 1944—Boston ..............Amer. | 2B | 125 | 468 | 95 | 152 | 30 | 10 | 15 | 81 | .325 | 341 | 363 | 17 | .976 |
| 1945—Boston .............. | | | | | | (In Military Service) | | | | | | | | |
| 1946—Boston ..............Amer. | 2B | 151 | 583 | 95 | 158 | 34 | 9 | 18 | 116 | .271 | •420 | •483 | 13 | •.986 |
| 1947—Boston ..............Amer. | 2B | 146 | 561 | 79 | 145 | 23 | 10 | 17 | 95 | .258 | 376 | •466 | 16 | .981 |
| 1948—Boston ..............Amer. | 2B | 140 | 527 | 94 | 150 | 23 | 6 | 27 | 111 | .285 | 366 | 430 | 6 | •.993 |
| 1949—Boston ..............Amer. | 2B | 139 | 541 | 91 | 167 | 30 | 9 | 18 | 109 | .309 | 395 | 439 | 17 | .980 |
| 1950—Boston ..............Amer. | 2B | 149 | 586 | 103 | 172 | 29 | •11 | 27 | 120 | .294 | •443 | 431 | 11 | •.988 |
| 1951—Boston ..............Amer. | 2B | 106 | 402 | 60 | 116 | 21 | 2 | 13 | 73 | .289 | 303 | 311 | 12 | .981 |
| Major League Totals ..................... | | 1865 | 7093 | 1094 | 2042 | 381 | 89 | 223 | 1247 | .288 | 4928 | 5710 | 214 | .980 |

### WORLD SERIES RECORD

| Year Club League | Pos. | G. | AB. | R. | H. | 2B. | 3B. | HR. | RBI. | B.A. | PO. | A. | E. | F.A. |
|---|---|---|---|---|---|---|---|---|---|---|---|---|---|---|
| 1946—Boston ..............Amer. | 2B | 6 | 22 | 1 | 9 | 1 | 0 | 1 | 3 | .409 | 18 | 31 | 0 | 1.000 |

### ALL-STAR GAME RECORD

| Year League | Pos. | AB. | R. | H. | 2B. | 3B. | HR. | RBI. | B.A. | PO. | A. | E. | F.A. |
|---|---|---|---|---|---|---|---|---|---|---|---|---|---|
| 1941—American ........................... | 2B | 3 | 0 | 0 | 0 | 0 | 0 | 0 | .000 | 0 | 0 | 0 | .000 |
| 1943—American ........................... | 2B | 4 | 1 | 2 | 0 | 0 | 1 | 3 | .500 | 3 | 3 | 0 | 1.000 |
| 1944—American ........................... | 2B | 3 | 0 | 0 | 0 | 0 | 0 | 0 | .000 | 4 | 1 | 1 | .833 |
| 1946—American ........................... | 2B | 2 | 0 | 0 | 0 | 0 | 0 | 0 | .000 | 1 | 1 | 0 | 1.000 |
| 1947—American ........................... | 2B | 2 | 1 | 1 | 0 | 0 | 0 | 0 | .500 | 0 | 2 | 0 | 1.000 |
| 1948—American ........................... | 2B | 2 | 0 | 0 | 0 | 0 | 0 | 0 | .000 | 0 | 3 | 0 | 1.000 |
| 1950—American ........................... | 2B | 3 | 0 | 0 | 0 | 0 | 0 | 0 | .000 | 1 | 4 | 0 | 1.000 |
| 1951—American ........................... | 2B | 1 | 0 | 1 | 0 | 0 | 0 | 0 | 1.000 | 1 | 0 | 0 | 1.000 |
| All-Star Game Totals ....................... | | 20 | 2 | 4 | 0 | 0 | 1 | 3 | .200 | 10 | 14 | 1 | .960 |

Member of American League All-Star team in 1942; did not play.

Scout, Boston Red Sox, 1957 through 1966; coach, Boston Red Sox, 1967 through 1969; coach, Toronto Blue Jays, 1977.

## CALVIN COOLIDGE ERMER
### Oakland A's

Born November 10, 1923, at Baltimore, Md.
Height, 6.02. Weight, 190.
Threw and batted righthanded.
Hobbies—Golf and fishing.

Named Minor League Manager of the Year by THE SPORTING NEWS in 1958.

| Year Club League | Pos. | G. | AB. | R. | H. | 2B. | 3B. | HR. | RBI. | B.A. | PO. | A. | E. | F.A. |
|---|---|---|---|---|---|---|---|---|---|---|---|---|---|---|
| 1942—Orlando ............F.E.C. | 2B | 19 | 69 | 12 | 20 | 2 | 1 | 0 | 12 | .290 | .... | .... | .... | ....... |
| 1942—Jacksonville ......Sally | | | | | (No Record Available) | | | | | | | | | |
| 1942—Burlington ........BI-St. | 2B | 95 | 368 | 46 | 76 | 17 | 1 | 6 | 30 | .207 | •233 | 240 | 17 | •.965 |

| Year Club League | Pos. | G. | AB. | R. | H. | 2B. | 3B. | HR. | RBI. | B.A. | PO. | A. | E. | F.A. |
|---|---|---|---|---|---|---|---|---|---|---|---|---|---|---|
| 1943-44-45—Chatt'ooga South. | | | | | | (In Military Service) | | | | | | | | |
| 1946—Orlando ............Fla.St. | 2B | 93 | 352 | 73 | 92 | 17 | 5 | 4 | 47 | .261 | 276 | 274 | 18 | .968 |
| 1947—Charlotte ..........Tri-St. | 2B | 136 | 488 | 72 | 136 | 27 | 8 | 7 | 82 | .279 | 336 | •417 | 29 | •.963 |
| 1947—Washington........Amer. | 2B | 1 | 3 | 0 | 0 | 0 | 0 | 0 | 0 | .000 | 4 | 3 | 0 | 1.000 |
| 1948—Charlotte ..........Tri-St. | 2B | 44 | 158 | 25 | 30 | 3 | 0 | 0 | 27 | .191 | 124 | 141 | 18 | .936 |
| 1948—Hagerstown ......Int.-St. | 3B | 83 | 334 | 68 | 95 | 18 | 4 | 3 | 38 | .284 | 84 | 172 | 19 | .931 |
| 1949—Savannah .........Sally | 2B | 153 | •612 | 84 | 141 | 28 | 6 | 0 | 60 | .230 | •414 | •420 | 24 | .961 |
| 1950—Orlando ............Fla.St. | 3B | •140 | 474 | 84 | 115 | 30 | 5 | 8 | 86 | .243 | •227 | •298 | 29 | •.948 |
| 1951—Charlotte ..........Tri-St. | 2B | 128 | 418 | 80 | 124 | 23 | 4 | 6 | 77 | .297 | 284 | 416 | 21 | •.971 |
| Major League Totals ..................... | | 1 | 3 | 0 | 0 | 0 | 0 | 0 | 0 | .000 | 4 | 3 | 0 | 1.000 |

### RECORD AS MANAGER

| Year Club League | Position | W. | L. | Year Club League | Position | W. | L. |
|---|---|---|---|---|---|---|---|
| 1950—Orlando..............Fla.St. | First | 88 | 52 | 1960—Columbus ..........Int. | Sixth | 69 | 84 |
| 1951—Charlotte............Tri-State | First | 100 | 40 | 1961—Richmond ..........Int. | Sixth | 71 | 83 |
| 1952—Chattanooga ......South. | First | 86 | 66 | 1965—Denver ..............P.C. | †Second | 83 | 62 |
| 1953—Chattanooga ......South. | Sixth | 73 | 81 | 1966—Denver ..............P.C. | †Fourth | 79 | 68 |
| 1954—Chattanooga ......South. | First | 75 | 76 | 1967—Denver‡ ............P.C. | †Sixth | 21 | 25 |
| 1955—Chattanooga ......South. | Third | 80 | 74 | 1967—Minnesota§ ........Amer. | xSecond | 66 | 46 |
| 1956—Chattanooga ......South. | Sixth | 76 | 78 | 1968—Minnesota ..........Amer. | Seventh | 79 | 83 |
| 1957—Chattanooga ......South. | Fourth | 83 | 70 | 1974—Tacoma..............P.C. | Second(W) | 75 | 66 |
| 1958—Birmingham ......South. | First | 91 | 62 | 1975—Tacoma§..............P.C. | Second(W) | 73 | 69 |
| 1959—Columbus ..........Int. | Second | 84 | 70 | 1976—Tacoma..............P.C. | Second(W) | 76 | 69 |

†Eastern Division.
‡Replaced by John Goryl, June 9.
§Replaced Sam Mele, June 9, with team in sixth place.
xTied for position.

Coach, Baltimore Orioles, 1962; scout, Baltimore Orioles, 1963-64; Minnesota Twins, 1969; coach, Milwaukee Brewers, 1970-71; scout, Milwaukee Brewers, 1972-73; scout, Minnesota Twins, 1973; coach, Oakland A's, 1977.

## JAMES GOTTFRIED FREY
### (Jim)
### Baltimore Orioles

Born May 26, 1931, at Cleveland, O.
Height, 5.09. Weight, 170.
Threw and batted lefthanded.
Hobbies—Golf and bowling.
Attended Ohio State University, Columbus, O.

Led Texas League in total bases with 294 and tied for lead in stolen bases with 21 in 1957.
Named Most Valuable Player in Texas League, 1957.

| Year Club League | Pos. | G. | AB. | R. | H. | 2B. | 3B. | HR. | RBI. | B.A. | PO. | A. | E. | F.A. |
|---|---|---|---|---|---|---|---|---|---|---|---|---|---|---|
| 1950—Evansville ........I.I.I. | | | | (appeared in less than 10 games; no record available) | | | | | | | | | | |
| 1950—Paducah............M.O.V. | OF | 106 | 412 | 73 | 134 | 21 | 11 | 1 | 58 | .325 | 180 | 17 | 6 | .970 |
| 1951—Evansville ........I.I.I. | OF | 119 | 447 | 69 | 145 | 24 | 9 | 1 | 58 | .324 | 197 | 18 | 10 | .956 |
| 1952—Hartford...........East. | OF | 20 | 80 | 12 | 21 | 8 | 0 | 0 | 7 | .263 | 23 | 2 | 0 | 1.000 |
| 1952—Evansville ........I.I.I. | OF | 90 | 307 | 66 | 103 | 25 | 3 | 2 | 54 | .336 | 145 | 15 | 6 | .964 |
| 1953—Jacksonville ......So. Atl. | OF | 117 | 429 | 64 | 136 | 25 | 4 | 2 | 37 | .317 | 241 | 18 | 2 | •.992 |
| 1954—Jacksonville ......So. Atl. | OF | 139 | 529 | 89 | 167 | •40 | 4 | 11 | 65 | .316 | 314 | 18 | 5 | .985 |
| 1955—Toledo ............A. A. | OF | 142 | 486 | 88 | 137 | 36 | 0 | 4 | 54 | .282 | 209 | 17 | 11 | .954 |
| 1956—Atlanta.............S. A. | OF | 25 | 87 | 14 | 22 | 4 | 0 | 1 | 11 | .253 | 39 | 5 | 2 | .957 |
| 1956—Austin†-Ft. W.‡..Texas | OF | 126 | 447 | 63 | 125 | 20 | 2 | 6 | 39 | .280 | 224 | 7 | 10 | .959 |
| 1957—Tulsa§ ..............Texas | OF | •155 | 589 | •102 | •198 | •50 | •11 | 8 | 74 | •.336 | 310 | 16 | 12 | .964 |
| 1958—Omaha ..............A. A. | OF | 117 | 420 | 63 | 119 | 19 | 7 | 4 | 45 | .283 | 211 | 8 | 6 | .973 |
| 1959—Rochester..........Int. | OF | 114 | 338 | 56 | 100 | 17 | 2 | 11 | 42 | .296 | 157 | 7 | 4 | .976 |
| 1960—Rochester x ......Int. | OF | 125 | 441 | 78 | 140 | 21 | 4 | 16 | 66 | •.317 | 199 | 12 | 8 | .963 |
| 1961—Buffalo ............Int. | OF | 115 | 354 | 49 | 93 | 17 | 1 | 10 | 47 | .263 | 180 | 8 | 4 | .979 |
| 1962—Buffalo y .........Int. | OF | 134 | 448 | 67 | 121 | 18 | 1 | 16 | 59 | .270 | 196 | 17 | 5 | .977 |
| 1963—Col.z-Atl.a ........Int. | OF | 62 | 108 | 11 | 28 | 3 | 0 | 2 | 12 | .259 | 29 | 2 | 3 | .912 |

†Traded by Milwaukee Braves' organization to Brooklyn Dodgers' organization for Outfielder Ray Shearer, July 4, 1956.
‡Sold by Brooklyn Dodgers' organization to Tulsa, April 12, 1957.
§Sold to St. Louis Cardinals' organization, July 31, 1957, to be announced after the season was over.
xReleased by St. Louis Cardinals' organization to Buffalo, October 5, 1960.
yReleased to Pittsburgh Pirates' organization, December 3, 1962.
zReleased by Pittsburgh Pirates' organization, May 7, 1963; signed as free agent by St. Louis Cardinals' organization, May 18, 1963.
aOn disabled list, July 8 to July 29, 1963. Released, October 15, 1963.

### PITCHING RECORD

| Year Club | League | G. | IP. | W. | L. | Pct. | H. | R. | ER. | SO. | BB. | ERA. |
|---|---|---|---|---|---|---|---|---|---|---|---|---|
| 1956—Austin ...............................Texas | | 1 | .... | 0 | 0 | .000 | .... | .... | .... | .... | .... | ...... |
| 1957—Tulsa ..................................Texas | | 4 | .... | 0 | 0 | .000 | .... | .... | .... | .... | .... | ...... |
| 1960—Rochester ..........................Int'national | | 1 | .... | 0 | 0 | .000 | .... | .... | .... | .... | .... | ...... |
| 1961—Buffalo ...............................Int'national | | 2 | .... | 0 | 0 | .000 | .... | .... | .... | .... | .... | ...... |

| Year | Club | League | Position | W. | L. |
|------|------|--------|----------|----|----|
| 1964—Bluefield | ...........Appal. | | Fourth | 27 | 44 |
| 1965—Bluefield | ...........Appal. | | Fifth | 31 | 38 |

Scout, Baltimore Orioles, 1966 through 1969; coach, Baltimore Orioles, 1970 through 1977.

## DAVID GARCIA
### (Dave)
### California Angels

Born September 15, 1920, at East St. Louis, Ill.
Height, 6.00. Weight, 180.
Threw and batted righthanded.
Led Wisconsin State League in total bases with 259 in 1951.

| Year | Club | League | Pos. | G. | AB. | R. | H. | 2B. | 3B. | HR. | RBI. | B.A. | PO. | A. | E. | F.A. |
|------|------|--------|------|----|-----|----|----|-----|-----|-----|------|------|-----|-----|----|------|
| 1939—Lake Charles† | ..Evan. | | 2B-OF | 4 | 8 | 0 | 1 | 0 | 0 | 0 | 0 | .125 | 2 | 0 | 0 | 1.000 |
| 1940— | ...................... | | | | | | | (Out of Organized Baseball) | | | | | | | | |
| 1941—G.F.-E.C. | ............North. | | 2B | 43 | 143 | 16 | 32 | 7 | 0 | 3 | 25 | .224 | 78 | 78 | 8 | .951 |
| 1942—Eau Claire | ........North. | | 3B-2B | 123 | 487 | 83 | 156 | 25 | 9 | 18 | 107 | .320 | 89 | 183 | 33 | .892 |
| 1943-44-45— | ................. | | | | | | | (In U. S. Army Air Corps) | | | | | | | | |
| 1946—Minneapolis | ......A. A. | | 3B | 20 | 65 | 8 | 17 | 6 | 0 | 1 | 9 | .262 | 14 | 37 | 7 | .879 |
| 1946—Little Rock | ........S. A. | | 3B | 20 | 42 | 5 | 5 | 0 | 0 | 0 | 2 | .119 | 21 | 32 | 5 | .914 |
| 1946—Wilkes-Barre | ....East. | | 3B-2B | 68 | 216 | 24 | 46 | 9 | 1 | 1 | 20 | .213 | 35 | 51 | 8 | .915 |
| 1947—Sioux City | ......West. | | •2B-3B | 130 | 533 | 85 | 157 | 19 | 10 | 13 | 71 | .295 | 325 | •343 | 45 | .937 |
| 1948—Jersey City | ........Int. | | 2B-3B | 7 | 14 | 1 | 3 | 2 | 0 | 0 | 1 | .214 | 2 | 8 | 2 | .833 |
| 1948—Knoxville | ..........T.-S. | | 3-2B-P | 95 | 347 | 54 | 98 | 16 | 3 | 16 | 59 | .282 | 111 | 178 | 25 | .920 |
| 1949—Oshkosh | ...........W.S. | | 2-3B-SS | 116 | 391 | 75 | 128 | 34 | 2 | 10 | 82 | .327 | 310 | 281 | 32 | .949 |
| 1950—Oshkosh | ...........W.S. | | 2B-SS-P | 119 | 421 | 89 | 139 | 20 | 5 | 22 | 130 | .330 | 262 | 256 | 27 | .950 |
| 1951—Oshkosh | ...........W.S. | | 2B-3B | 118 | 426 | 97 | •157 | 27 | 3 | •23 | •127 | •.369 | 226 | 286 | 28 | .948 |
| 1952—Oshkosh | ...........W.S. | | 2-3B-SS | 117 | 404 | 82 | 132 | 30 | 2 | 15 | 82 | .327 | 192 | 255 | 26 | .945 |
| 1953—Oshkosh | ...........W.S. | | 2B-P-OF | 119 | 436 | 79 | 138 | 27 | 3 | 15 | 90 | .317 | 295 | 277 | 27 | .955 |
| 1954—Sioux City | ........West. | | 2B-3B | 126 | 421 | 47 | 112 | 20 | 3 | 10 | 52 | .266 | 322 | 315 | 24 | .964 |
| 1955—Mayfield | ...........Kitty | | 2B | 91 | 237 | 64 | 112 | 19 | 2 | 19 | 81 | .332 | 176 | 199 | 11 | .972 |
| 1955—Minneapolis | ......A. A. | | 2B | 5 | 12 | 2 | 3 | 1 | 0 | 0 | 0 | .250 | 1 | 1 | 0 | 1.000 |
| 1956—Minneapolis | ......A. A. | | 2B-3B | 5 | 3 | 0 | 1 | 0 | 0 | 0 | 0 | .333 | 2 | 5 | 1 | .875 |
| 1957—Danville | ...........Carol. | | 2B | 27 | 76 | 8 | 20 | 3 | 0 | 1 | 8 | .263 | 22 | 55 | 3 | .975 |

†Released by St. Louis Browns' organization, September 1939.

### RECORD AS PITCHER

| Year | Club | League | G. | IP. | W. | L. | Pct. | H. | R. | ER. | SO. | BB. | ERA. |
|------|------|--------|----|-----|----|----|------|----|----|-----|-----|-----|------|
| 1948—Knoxville | ..........................Tri-State | | 1 | 5 | 0 | 0 | .000 | 3 | 1 | 1 | 2 | 2 | 1.80 |
| 1950—Oshkosh | ..........................Wis. State | | 4 | 13 | 0 | 1 | .000 | 15 | 21 | 19 | 6 | 17 | 9.69 |
| 1953—Oshkosh | ..........................Wis. State | | 4 | 5 | 0 | 0 | .000 | 3 | 2 | 1 | 2 | 5 | 1.80 |

### RECORD AS MANAGER

| Year | Club | League | Position | W. | L. | Year | Club | League | Position | W. | L. |
|------|------|--------|----------|----|----|------|------|--------|----------|----|----|
| 1948—Knoxville† | ..........Tri-St. | | Sixth | 51 | 44 | 1957—Danville | ...........Carol. | | Fifth | 28 | 39 |
| 1949—Oshkosh | ...........Wis. St. | | First | 72 | 49 | (Second Half)§ | | | Fifth | 10 | 18 |
| 1950—Oshkosh | ...........Wis. St. | | ‡First | 74 | 49 | 1964—El Paso | ..............Texas | | Fourth | 67 | 73 |
| 1951—Oshkosh | ...........Wis. St. | | Second | 65 | 55 | 1967—Fresno | ..............Calif. | | Fifth | 35 | 35 |
| 1952—Oshkosh | ...........Wis. St. | | Third | 63 | 58 | (Second Half) | | | Sixth | 32 | 37 |
| 1953—Oshkosh | ...........Wis. St. | | Eighth | 17 | 38 | 1968—Fresno | ..............Calif. | | Fourth | 36 | 34 |
| (Second Half) | | | Third | 40 | 28 | (Second Half) | | | xFirst | 43 | 26 |
| 1954—Sioux City | .........West. | | Fifth | 78 | 75 | 1969—Salt Lake City | ....Pion. | | Fourth | 37 | 34 |
| 1955—Mayfield | ...........Kitty | | Second | 65 | 43 | 1974—El Paso | ..............Texas | | yFirst(W) | 76 | 61 |

†Replaced Dale Alexander, June 8, with club in eighth place.
‡Won playoffs by defeating Fond du Lac, three games to one and Janesville, four games to two.
§Replaced by Jack Pollitt, July 22.
xWon playoff by defeating San Jose (First Half winner), two games to one.
yLost playoff to Victoria (Eastern Division winner), three games to none.
Coach, Minneapolis (American Association), 1956; scout, San Francisco Giants, 1957 through 1963 and 1965 and 1966; coach, San Diego Padres, 1970 through 1973; coach, Cleveland Indians, 1975 and 1976; coach, California Angels, 1977.

## WILLIAM FREDERICK GARDNER
### (Billy)
### Montreal Expos

Born July 19, 1927, at New London, Conn.
Height, 6.00. Weight, 180.
Threw and batted righthanded.
Hobbies—Fishing, hunting and basketball.

Established major league record for most putouts by second baseman in extra-inning game (12), 16-inning game, May 21, 1957; holds major league record for fewest assists by second baseman season playing 150 or more games (350), 1959.
Led American League second basemen in double plays, 1959.

| Year Club League | Pos. | G. | AB. | R. | H. | 2B. | 3B. | HR. | RBI. | B.A. | PO. | A. | E. | F.A. |
|---|---|---|---|---|---|---|---|---|---|---|---|---|---|---|
| 1945–Bristol .............Appal. | 3B | 74 | 304 | 67 | 100 | 16 | 6 | 5 | 56 | .329 | *107 | *132 | 11 | *.956 |
| 1945–Jersey City........Int. | 3B-OF | 49 | 172 | 16 | 47 | 4 | 2 | 1 | 20 | .273 | 55 | 75 | 8 | .942 |
| 1946–Jersey City ......Int. | | | | | (In Military Service) | | | | | | | | | |
| 1947–Jacksonville ......Sally | 3B-SS | 110 | 423 | 55 | 111 | 18 | 5 | 1 | 41 | .262 | 129 | 191 | 32 | .909 |
| 1948–Jacksonville ......Sally | 3B | •154 | 548 | 66 | 140 | 26 | 4 | 3 | 66 | .255 | *150 | 262 | *36 | .920 |
| 1949–Minneapolis ....A. A. | 3B | 17 | 28 | 7 | 5 | 0 | 0 | 2 | 6 | .179 | 5 | 16 | 4 | .840 |
| 1949–Jersey City...........Int. | 3B | 17 | 45 | 6 | 11 | 1 | 0 | 0 | 1 | .244 | 18 | 25 | 4 | .915 |
| 1950–Sioux City ........West. | 3B | 154 | 581 | 96 | 176 | 32 | 7 | 22 | 118 | .303 | *159 | *335 | *48 | .911 |
| 1951–Ottawa .............Int. | 3B | 150 | 555 | 56 | 128 | 19 | 6 | 3 | 37 | .231 | •182 | 279 | *36 | .928 |
| 1952–Minneapolis ......A. A. | INF-OF | 93 | 224 | 29 | 58 | 15 | 1 | 1 | 15 | .259 | 109 | 165 | 23 | .923 |
| 1953–Nashville ..........Sou. | *SS-3B | 153 | 591 | 88 | 182 | •42 | 5 | 10 | 71 | .308 | 255 | 444 | *42 | .943 |
| 1954–New York..........Nat. | INF | 62 | 108 | 10 | 23 | 5 | 0 | 1 | 7 | .213 | 42 | 82 | 2 | .984 |
| 1955–New York..........Nat. | INF | 59 | 187 | 26 | 38 | 10 | 1 | 3 | 17 | .203 | 76 | 139 | 13 | .943 |
| 1955–Minneapolis† ....A. A. | INF | 73 | 290 | 55 | 90 | 15 | 1 | 17 | 48 | .310 | 161 | 210 | 17 | .956 |
| 1956–Baltimore..........Amer. | INF | 144 | 515 | 53 | 119 | 16 | 2 | 11 | 50 | .231 | 301 | 386 | 18 | .974 |
| 1957–Baltimore..........Amer. | *2B-SS | 154 | *644 | 79 | 169 | *36 | 3 | 6 | 55 | .262 | 406 | 450 | 12 | *.986 |
| 1958–Baltimore..........Amer. | 2B-SS | 151 | 560 | 32 | 126 | 28 | 2 | 3 | 33 | .225 | 354 | 356 | 11 | .985 |
| 1959–Baltimore†........Amer. | *2-SS-3 | 140 | 401 | 34 | 87 | 13 | 2 | 6 | 27 | .217 | 334 | 393 | *18 | .976 |
| 1960–Washington...........Amer. | *2B-SS | 145 | 592 | 71 | 152 | 26 | 5 | 9 | 56 | .257 | 360 | 418 | *21 | .974 |
| 1961–Minn.§-N. Y........Amer. | 2B-3B | 86 | 253 | 24 | 57 | 14 | 0 | 2 | 13 | .225 | 121 | 160 | 11 | .962 |
| 1962–N. Y.x-Boston ....Amer. | INF | 57 | 200 | 23 | 54 | 9 | 2 | 0 | 12 | .270 | 80 | 125 | 10 | .953 |
| 1963–Boston y...........Amer. | 2B-3B | 36 | 84 | 4 | 16 | 2 | 1 | 0 | 1 | .190 | 37 | 59 | 1 | .990 |
| 1964–Seattle z............P. C. | 2B | 101 | 308 | 23 | 69 | 8 | 4 | 1 | 28 | .224 | 173 | 226 | 11 | .973 |
| American League Totals ................ | | 913 | 3249 | 320 | 780 | 144 | 17 | 37 | 247 | .240 | 1993 | 2347 | 102 | .997 |
| National League Totals ................. | | 121 | 295 | 36 | 61 | 15 | 1 | 4 | 24 | .207 | 118 | 221 | 15 | .958 |
| Major League Totals ..................... | | 1034 | 3544 | 356 | 841 | 159 | 18 | 41 | 271 | .237 | 2111 | 2568 | 117 | .976 |

†Started 1956 season with New York Giants; sold to Baltimore Orioles for reported $20,000, April 21, 1956.
‡Traded to Washington Senators for Catcher Clint Courtney and Infielder Ron Samford, April, 1960.
§Traded to New York Yankees for Pitcher Danny McDevitt, June 14, 1961.
xTraded to Boston Red Sox for cash and transfer of Outfielder Tom Umphlett from Seattle, Pacific Coast League, to Richmond, International League, June 21, 1962.
yReleased by Boston Red Sox, October 2, 1963.
zPlayer-coach.

## WORLD SERIES RECORD

| Year Club League | Pos. | G. | AB. | R. | H. | 2B. | 3B. | HR. | RBI. | B.A. | PO. | A. | E. | F.A. |
|---|---|---|---|---|---|---|---|---|---|---|---|---|---|---|
| 1961–New York..........Amer. | PH | 1 | 1 | 0 | 0 | 0 | 0 | 0 | 0 | .000 | 0 | 0 | 0 | .000 |

## RECORD AS MANAGER

| Year Club | League | Position | W. | L. | Year Club | League | Position | W. | L. |
|---|---|---|---|---|---|---|---|---|---|
| 1967–Pittsfield ............East. | | Second(E) | 75 | 62 | 1972–Jacksonville ......South. | | Fourth(E) | 64 | 75 |
| 1968–Pittsfield ............East. | | †First | 84 | 55 | 1973–Jacksonville ......South. | | ‡First(E) | 76 | 60 |
| 1969–Pittsfield ............East. | | Fourth | 68 | 72 | 1974–Jacksonville ......South. | | §First(E) | 78 | 60 |
| 1970–Louisville ..........Int. | | Sixth | 69 | 71 | 1975–Omaha ..............A. A. | | Third(E) | 67 | 69 |
| 1971–Pawtucket..........East. | | Third(Am.) | 63 | 76 | 1976–Omaha ..............A. A. | | xFirst(E) | 78 | 58 |

†Lost playoff to Reading, three games to one.
‡Lost playoff to Montgomery, three games to one.
§Lost playoff to Knoxville, three games to two.
xLost playoff to Denver, four games to one.
Coach, Boston Red Sox' organization, October 1964 though 1966; coach, Montreal Expos, 1977.

# JAMES GILLIAM
## (Junior)

(Named by members of the Baltimore Elite Giants since he was the youngest player on the club.)

### Los Angeles Dodgers

Born October 17, 1928, at Nashville, Tenn.
Height, 5.11½. Weight, 180.
Threw right and batted right and lefthanded.
Hobby–Billiards.

Established modern major league record for most assists by second baseman, game (12), July 21, 1956.
Established National League record for most bases on balls, season, by a rookie (100), 1953; led league in bases on balls (96), 1959.
Named as second baseman on The Sporting News National League All-Star Team, 1963.
Named as National League Rookie of the Year by the Baseball Writers' Association and The Sporting News, 1953.

| Year Club League | Pos. | G. | AB. | R. | H. | 2B. | 3B. | HR. | RBI. | B.A. | PO. | A. | E. | F.A. |
|---|---|---|---|---|---|---|---|---|---|---|---|---|---|---|
| 1951–Montreal ..........Int. | 2-OF-3 | 152 | 565 | *117 | 162 | 22 | 9 | 7 | 73 | .287 | 386 | 247 | 17 | .974 |
| 1952–Montreal ..........Int. | *2-O-3B | 151 | 561 | *111 | 169 | 39 | 9 | 9 | 112 | .301 | 343 | 362 | 9 | *.987 |
| 1953–Brooklyn ..........Nat. | 2B | 151 | 605 | 125 | 168 | 31 | *17 | 6 | 63 | .278 | 332 | 426 | 19 | .976 |
| 1954–Brooklyn ..........Nat. | 2B-OF | 146 | 607 | 107 | 171 | 28 | 8 | 13 | 52 | .282 | 349 | 388 | 17 | .977 |
| 1955–Brooklyn ..........Nat. | 2B-OF | 147 | 538 | 110 | 134 | 20 | 8 | 7 | 40 | .249 | 309 | 271 | 19 | .968 |
| 1956–Brooklyn ..........Nat. | 2B-OF | 153 | 594 | 102 | 178 | 23 | 8 | 6 | 43 | .300 | 340 | 332 | 12 | .982 |
| 1957–Brooklyn ..........Nat. | *2B-OF | 149 | 617 | 89 | 154 | 26 | 4 | 2 | 37 | .250 | *416 | 390 | 11 | •.987 |
| 1958–Los Angeles ......Nat. | OF-3-2 | 147 | 555 | 81 | 145 | 25 | 5 | 2 | 43 | .261 | 245 | 176 | 12 | .972 |

| Year Club League | Pos. | G. | AB. | R. | H. | 2B. | 3B. | HR. | RBI. | B.A. | PO. | A. | E. | F.A. |
|---|---|---|---|---|---|---|---|---|---|---|---|---|---|---|
| 1959–Los Angeles ......Nat. | OF-3-2 | 145 | 553 | 91 | 156 | 18 | 4 | 3 | 34 | .282 | 143 | 258 | 17 | .959 |
| 1960–Los Angeles ......Nat. | 3B-2B | 151 | 557 | 96 | 138 | 20 | 2 | 5 | 40 | .248 | 152 | 331 | 16 | .968 |
| 1961–Los Angels .......Nat. | 2B-3B-O | 144 | 439 | 74 | 107 | 26 | 3 | 4 | 32 | .244 | 195 | 283 | 13 | .974 |
| 1962–Los Angeles .....Nat. | 2B-3B-O | 160 | 588 | 83 | 159 | 24 | 1 | 4 | 43 | .270 | 243 | 388 | 20 | .969 |
| 1963–Los Angeles ......Nat. | 2B-3B | 148 | 525 | 77 | 148 | 27 | 4 | 6 | 49 | .282 | 267 | 243 | 13 | .975 |
| 1964–Los Angeles ......Nat. | 3B-2B-O | 116 | 334 | 44 | 76 | 8 | 3 | 2 | 27 | .228 | 101 | 171 | 18 | .938 |
| 1965–Los Angeles ......Nat. | 3B-O-2B | 111 | 372 | 54 | 104 | 19 | 4 | 4 | 39 | .280 | 85 | 142 | 10 | .958 |
| 1966–Los Angeles ......Nat. | 3-2-1B | 88 | 235 | 30 | 51 | 9 | 0 | 1 | 16 | .217 | 43 | 103 | 7 | .954 |
| Major League Totals .................... | | 1956 | 7119 | 1163 | 1889 | 304 | 71 | 65 | 558 | .265 | 3220 | 3902 | 204 | .972 |

## WORLD SERIES RECORD

Tied World Series record for making most long hits (5) in six-game Series, 1953; tied Series mark for most hits, game (4), October 6, 1959.

| Year Club League | Pos. | G. | AB. | R. | H. | 2B. | 3B. | HR. | RBI. | B.A. | PO. | A. | E. | F.A. |
|---|---|---|---|---|---|---|---|---|---|---|---|---|---|---|
| 1953–Brooklyn ..........Nat. | 2B | 6 | 27 | 4 | 8 | 3 | 0 | 2 | 4 | .296 | 15 | 16 | 1 | .969 |
| 1956–Brooklyn ..........Nat. | 2B | 7 | 24 | 2 | 2 | 0 | 0 | 0 | 2 | .083 | 19 | 17 | 0 | 1.000 |
| 1959–Los Angeles .....Nat. | 3B | 6 | 25 | 2 | 6 | 0 | 0 | 0 | 0 | .240 | 4 | 10 | 0 | 1.000 |
| 1963–Los Angeles .....Nat. | 3B | 4 | 13 | 3 | 2 | 0 | 0 | 0 | 0 | .154 | 2 | 2 | 0 | 1.000 |
| 1965–Los Angeles .....Nat. | 3B | 7 | 28 | 2 | 6 | 1 | 0 | 0 | 2 | .214 | 4 | 7 | 2 | .846 |
| 1966–Los Angeles .....Nat. | 3B | 2 | 6 | 0 | 0 | 0 | 0 | 0 | 1 | .000 | 3 | 4 | 1 | .875 |
| World Series Totals ....................... | | 39 | 147 | 15 | 31 | 5 | 0 | 2 | 12 | .211 | 55 | 69 | 4 | .969 |

## ALL-STAR GAME RECORD

| Year League | Pos. | AB. | R. | H. | 2B. | 3B. | HR. | RBI. | B.A. | PO. | A. | E. | F.A. |
|---|---|---|---|---|---|---|---|---|---|---|---|---|---|
| 1959–National (second game) ...... | 3B | 2 | 1 | 1 | 0 | 0 | 1 | 1 | .500 | 0 | 0 | 0 | .000 |

Member of National League All-Star Team in 1956; did not play.
Coach, Los Angeles Dodgers, 1965 through 1977.


# FRED EARL GLADDING
## Detroit Tigers

Born June 28, 1936, at Flat Rock, Mich.
Height, 6.01. Weight, 225.
Threw right and batted lefthanded.
Hobbies—Fishing and hunting.

Led National League in saves with 29 in 1969.
Pitched seven-inning, 7-0 no-hit victory against Macon, May 28, 1958.
Tied for Georgia-Florida League lead in complete games with 16 and in shutouts with 5 in 1957.

| Year Club | League | G. | IP. | W. | L. | Pct. | H. | R. | ER. | SO. | BB. | ERA. |
|---|---|---|---|---|---|---|---|---|---|---|---|---|
| 1956–Valdosta ............................Ga.-Fla. | | 35 | 199 | 11 | 9 | .550 | 166 | 83 | 61 | 167 | 86 | 2.76 |
| 1957–Valdosta ............................Ga.-Fla. | | 37 | 217 | 16 | 8 | .667 | 185 | 73 | 51 | 185 | 93 | •.2.12 |
| 1958–Birmingham ......................Southern | | 3 | 7 | 0 | 1 | .000 | 8 | 7 | 6 | 6 | 6 | 7.71 |
| 1958–Augusta ............................Sally | | 30 | 163 | 12 | 7 | .632 | 136 | 67 | 55 | 101 | 68 | 3.08 |
| 1959–Birmingham ......................Southern | | 7 | 39 | 2 | 3 | .400 | 39 | 26 | 24 | 22 | 30 | 5.54 |
| 1959–Knoxville ............................Sally | | 20 | 81 | 6 | 2 | .750 | 92 | 42 | 32 | 52 | 42 | 3.56 |
| 1960–Birmingham ......................Southern | | 1 | 1 | 0 | 0 | .000 | 5 | 5 | 5 | 0 | 2 | 45.00 |
| 1960–Knoxville ............................Sally | | 23 | 122 | 9 | 5 | .643 | 102 | 43 | 33 | 100 | 45 | 2.43 |
| 1960–Denver ...............................Am. Assoc. | | 14 | 65 | 3 | 2 | .600 | 57 | 18 | 17 | 44 | 14 | 2.35 |
| 1961–Denver ...............................Am. Assoc. | | 17 | 86 | 7 | 3 | .700 | 80 | 25 | 21 | 73 | 26 | 2.20 |
| 1961–Detroit ...............................American | | 8 | 16 | 1 | 0 | 1.000 | 18 | 7 | 6 | 11 | 11 | 3.38 |
| 1962–Denver ...............................Am. Assoc. | | 46 | 113 | 6 | 12 | .333 | 121 | 68 | 48 | 78 | 50 | 3.82 |
| 1962–Detroit ...............................American | | 6 | 5 | 0 | 0 | .000 | 3 | 0 | 0 | 4 | 2 | 0.00 |
| 1963–Syracuse ...........................Int'national | | 37 | 71 | 4 | 2 | .667 | 74 | 32 | 31 | 72 | 20 | 3.39 |
| 1963–Detroit ...............................American | | 22 | 27 | 1 | 1 | .500 | 19 | 6 | 6 | 24 | 14 | 2.00 |
| 1964–Syracuse ...........................Int'national | | 7 | 17 | 2 | 1 | .667 | 9 | 4 | 3 | 18 | 6 | 1.59 |
| 1964–Detroit ...............................American | | 42 | 67 | 7 | 4 | .636 | 57 | 23 | 23 | 59 | 27 | 3.09 |
| 1965–Detroit ...............................American | | 46 | 70 | 6 | 2 | .750 | 63 | 22 | 22 | 43 | 29 | 2.83 |
| 1966–Detroit ...............................American | | 51 | 74 | 5 | 0 | 1.000 | 62 | 33 | 27 | 57 | 29 | 3.28 |
| 1967–Detroit† ...............................American | | 42 | 77 | 6 | 4 | .600 | 62 | 20 | 17 | 64 | 19 | 1.99 |
| 1968–Houston‡ ...........................National | | 7 | 4 | 0 | 0 | .000 | 8 | 7 | 7 | 2 | 3 | 15.75 |
| 1969–Houston ...........................National | | 57 | 73 | 4 | 8 | .333 | 83 | 39 | 34 | 40 | 27 | 4.19 |
| 1970–Houston ...........................National | | 63 | 71 | 7 | 4 | .636 | 84 | 39 | 32 | 46 | 24 | 4.06 |
| 1971–Houston ...........................National | | 48 | 51 | 4 | 5 | .444 | 51 | 17 | 12 | 17 | 22 | 2.12 |
| 1972–Houston ...........................National | | 42 | 49 | 5 | 6 | .455 | 38 | 16 | 15 | 18 | 12 | 2.76 |
| 1973–Denver ...............................Am. Assoc. | | 20 | 19 | 0 | 2 | .000 | 28 | 12 | 10 | 9 | 5 | 4.74 |
| 1973–Houston§ ...........................National | | 16 | 16 | 1 | 0 | 1.000 | 18 | 8 | 8 | 9 | 4 | 4.50 |
| American League Totals.......................... | | 217 | 336 | 26 | 11 | .703 | 284 | 111 | 101 | 262 | 131 | 2.71 |
| National League Totals.......................... | | 233 | 264 | 22 | 23 | .489 | 282 | 126 | 108 | 132 | 92 | 3.68 |
| Major League Totals .............................. | | 450 | 600 | 48 | 34 | .585 | 566 | 237 | 209 | 394 | 223 | 3.13 |

†Traded with cash to Houston Astros for Third Baseman Eddie Mathews. Mathews went to Tigers, August 17, 1967, and Gladding to Astros on November 22, 1967.
‡On disabled list from May 3 through June 6 and July 2 through end of season with elbow trouble.
§Released, October 9, 1973.
Minor league instructor, Detroit Tigers, 1974 and 1975; coach, Detroit Tigers, 1976 and 1977.

## PEDRO W. GOMEZ (MARTINEZ)
### (Preston)
### Los Angeles Dodgers

Born April 20, 1923, at Central Preston, Oriente, Cuba.
Height, 5.11. Weight, 185.
Threw and batted righthanded.
Hobbies—Fishing and golf.
Attended Mexico City College, Mexico City, Mexico, and Florida Southern, Lakeland, Fla.

| Year | Club | League | Pos. | G. | AB. | R. | H. | 2B. | 3B. | HR. | RBI. | B.A. | PO. | A. | E. | F.A. |
|------|------|--------|------|-----|-----|-----|-----|-----|-----|-----|------|------|-----|-----|-----|------|
| 1944—Washington† | ......Amer. | | 2B-SS | 8 | 7 | 2 | 2 | 1 | 0 | 0 | 2 | .286 | 4 | 1 | 1 | .833 |
| 1945—Buffalo | ..............Int. | | SS | 108 | 375 | 52 | 101 | 19 | 2 | 3 | 23 | .269 | 202 | 288 | 43 | .919 |
| 1946—Vicksburg | ..........So'east | | SS | 22 | 76 | 3 | 8 | 1 | 0 | 0 | 3 | .105 | 26 | 69 | 8 | .922 |
| 1947—Vicksburg | ..........So'east | | SS | 14 | 48 | 5 | 14 | 1 | 1 | 1 | 11 | .292 | 17 | 37 | 5 | .915 |
| 1947—New London | ......Col. | | SS | 90 | 332 | 53 | 95 | 8 | 3 | 9 | 55 | .286 | 133 | 246 | 56 | .871 |
| 1948—Florence | ............Tri-St. | | SS | 51 | 187 | 21 | 34 | 9 | 0 | 1 | 15 | .182 | 68 | 147 | 24 | .900 |
| 1949—Saginaw | ............Cent. | | SS | 105 | 358 | 42 | 76 | 17 | 3 | 3 | 42 | .212 | 174 | 258 | 35 | .925 |
| 1950—Saginaw | ............Cent. | | | (On voluntary retired list) | | | | | | | | | | | | |
| 1951—Three Rivers | ....Prov. | | SS | 125 | 448 | 58 | 120 | 21 | 1 | 9 | 58 | .268 | 175 | 348 | 41 | .927 |
| 1952—Tol.-Charleston | ..A.A. | | SS | 18 | 52 | 4 | 10 | 1 | 0 | 0 | 5 | .192 | 20 | 37 | 5 | .919 |
| 1952—Havana | ..............Fla. Int. | | SS | 9 | 33 | 3 | 6 | 1 | 0 | 0 | 4 | .182 | 11 | 18 | 3 | .906 |
| 1953— | | | | (Out of Organized Baseball) | | | | | | | | | | | | |
| 1954—Yakima | ............W. Int. | | | 12 | 27 | 3 | 5 | 0 | 0 | 1 | 2 | .185 | 6 | 28 | 3 | .906 |
| Major League Totals | ..................... | | | 8 | 7 | 2 | 2 | 1 | 0 | 0 | 2 | .286 | 4 | 1 | 1 | .833 |

†Released, March 1945.

### RECORD AS MANAGER

| Year | Club | League | Position | W. | L. | Year | Club | League | Position | W. | L. |
|------|------|--------|----------|-----|-----|------|------|--------|----------|-----|-----|
| 1957—Fresnillo | ............Cen. Mex. | Second | 6 | 4 | 1964—Richmond | ..........Int. | Seventh | 65 | 88 |
| 1957—Mex. C. Reds† | ....Mexican | Second | 59 | 50 | 1969—San Diego | ..........Nat. | Sixth (W) | 52 | 110 |
| 1958—Mex. C. Reds‡ | ....Mexican | Second | 48 | 43 | 1970—San Diego | ..........Nat. | Sixth (W) | 63 | 99 |
| 1959—Havana | ..............Int. | §Third | 80 | 73 | 1971—San Diego | ..........Nat. | Sixth (W) | 61 | 100 |
| 1960—Spokane | ............P.C. | First | 92 | 61 | 1972—San Diego y | .......Nat. | Fourth (W) | 4 | 7 |
| 1961—Spokane | ............P.C. | xSixth | 68 | 86 | 1974—Houston | ..............Nat. | Fourth(W) | 81 | 81 |
| 1962—Spokane | ............P.C. | Eighth | 58 | 96 | 1975—Houston z | ..........Nat. | Sixth(W) | 47 | 80 |
| 1963—Richmond | ..........Int. | Fifth | 66 | 81 | | | | | | |

†Replaced Lazaro Salazar following latter's death with Reds in first place, May 1, 1957. Won playoffs by defeating Monterrey, four games to none and Mexico City Tigers, four games to three.
‡Replaced by Molinero Montes de Oca, August 1, 1958.
§Won playoffs by defeating Columbus in semifinals, four games to none and defeating Richmond in finals, four games to two. Won Junior World Series by defeating Minneapolis of American Association, four games to three.
xTied for position with Hawaii.
yReplaced by Don Zimmer, April 27.
zReplaced by Bill Virdon, August 18.
Coach, Los Angeles Dodgers, 1965 through 1968, 1977; coach, Houston Astros, 1973; coach, St. Louis Cardinals, 1976.

## GEORGE EDWIN HAAS
### (Eddie)
### Atlanta Braves

Born May 26, 1935, at Paducah, Ky.
Height, 5.11. Weight, 178.
Threw right and batted lefthanded.
Hobbies—Hunting and fishing.
Brother of Lou Haas, former infielder in Milwaukee Braves' organization.
Cousin of Phil Roof, catcher with Minnesota Twins, and Paul Roof,
former pitcher in Milwaukee Braves' organization.

| Year | Club | League | Pos. | G. | AB. | R. | H. | 2B. | 3B. | HR. | RBI. | B.A. | PO. | A. | E. | F.A. |
|------|------|--------|------|-----|-----|-----|-----|-----|-----|-----|------|------|-----|-----|-----|------|
| 1953—Hickory | ............T. Heel | | OF | 7 | 12 | 4 | 0 | 0 | 0 | 0 | 1 | .000 | 5 | 0 | 0 | 1.000 |
| 1953—Gainesville† | ......Soo. St. | | OF | 24 | 75 | 15 | 22 | 1 | 2 | 0 | 10 | .293 | 30 | 2 | 3 | .914 |
| 1954—Gainesville‡ | ......Soo. St. | | OF | 122 | 455 | 102 | 152 | 29 | 11 | 16 | 92 | .334 | 200 | 15 | 16 | .931 |
| 1955—Des Moines§ | ......West. | | OF | 75 | 260 | 50 | 84 | 16 | 1 | 12 | 50 | .323 | 136 | 11 | 5 | .967 |
| 1956—Los Angeles | ......P. C. | | OF | 41 | 149 | 34 | 41 | 5 | 1 | 4 | 19 | .275 | 72 | 8 | 6 | .930 |
| 1956—Des Moines | ......West. | | OF | 98 | 359 | 82 | 115 | 25 | 3 | 11 | 54 | .320 | 233 | 9 | 11 | .957 |
| 1957—Fort Worth | ........Tex. | | OF | 130 | 459 | 72 | 128 | 26 | 8 | 9 | 53 | .279 | 307 | 11 | 12 | .964 |
| 1957—Chicago x | .........Nat. | | OF | 14 | 24 | 1 | 5 | 1 | 0 | 0 | 4 | .208 | 4 | 0 | 0 | 1.000 |
| 1958—Milwaukee | .......Nat. | | OF | 9 | 14 | 2 | 5 | 0 | 0 | 0 | 1 | .357 | 5 | 0 | 0 | 1.000 |
| 1958—Wichita | ..........A. A. | | OF | 89 | 313 | 55 | 102 | 26 | 6 | 10 | 46 | .326 | 120 | 9 | 6 | .956 |
| 1959—Milwaukee y | Nat. | | | (Did not play) | | | | | | | | | | | | |
| 1960—Louisville z | ......A. A. | | OF | 21 | 68 | 9 | 18 | 8 | 0 | 0 | 10 | .265 | 29 | 0 | 1 | .967 |
| 1960—Milwaukee | ........Nat. | | OF | 32 | 32 | 4 | 7 | 2 | 0 | 1 | 5 | .219 | 2 | 0 | 0 | 1.000 |
| 1961—Vancouver | ..........P. C. | | OF | 124 | 357 | 58 | 86 | 16 | 6 | 9 | 62 | .241 | 145 | 4 | 8 | .949 |
| 1962—Louisville | ..........A. A. | | OF | 16 | 29 | 1 | 8 | 0 | 0 | 0 | 5 | .276 | figures unavailable | | | |
| 1962—Hawaii | ..........P. C. | | OF | 86 | 218 | 37 | 52 | 4 | 2 | 12 | 32 | .239 | 102 | 6 | 6 | .947 |
| 1963—Denver | ..............P. C. | | OF-P | 78 | 118 | 21 | 44 | 7 | 2 | 3 | 13 | .373 | 37 | 1 | 2 | .950 |
| 1964—Denver a | ..........P. C. | | OF | 79 | 113 | 7 | 24 | 4 | 0 | 3 | 20 | .212 | 34 | 1 | 1 | .972 |
| Major League Totals | ..................... | | | 55 | 70 | 7 | 17 | 3 | 0 | 1 | 10 | .243 | 11 | 0 | 0 | 1.000 |

†On disabled list, July 3 to August 11, 1953.
‡On disabled list, July 19 to August 4, 1954.
§On disabled list, May 21 to June 3 and August 8 to September 18, 1955.
xTraded to Milwaukee Braves with Pitchers Don Kaiser and Bob Rush for Pitcher Taylor Phillips and Catcher Sam Taylor, December 5, 1957.
yMissed entire season because of a broken ankle.
zOn disabled list, May 16 to June 3, 1960.
aReleased, September 30, 1964.

## PITCHING RECORD

| Year   Club              | League  | G. | IP. | W. | L. | Pct. | H. | R. | ER. | SO. | BB. | ERA. |
|--------------------------|---------|----|-----|----|----|------|----|----|-----|-----|-----|------|
| 1963—Denver              | P. Coast | 2 | 4 | 0 | 0 | .000 | 3 | 0 | 0 | 1 | 0 | 0.00 |

## RECORD AS MANAGER

| Year   Club | League | Position | W. | L. | Year   Club | League | Position | W. | L. |
|-------------|--------|----------|----|----|-------------|--------|----------|----|----|
| 1966—Yakima | N'west | Third | 39 | 44 | (Second Half) | | Third | 32 | 29 |
| 1967—W. Palm Beach | Fla. St. | Fourth(E) | 28 | 40 | 1970—Greenwood | W. Car. | ‡Second | 37 | 29 |
| (Second Half) | | Fifth(E) | 23 | 41 | (Second Half) | | Third | 33 | 31 |
| 1968—Richmond | Int. | Eighth | 59 | 87 | 1971—Savannah | South. | Fifth | 57 | 84 |
| 1969—Greenwood | W. Car. | †First | 37 | 26 | 1972—Wythesville | Appal. | Second(N) | 35 | 30 |

†Won playoff by defeating Shelby (Second Half winner), two games to one.
‡Lost 1-0 to Greenville on June 27 in playoff for first half championship.
Minor League Instructor, Atlanta Braves, 1973 and part of 1974; coach, Atlanta Braves, August 27, 1974 through 1977.

# HARVEY HADDIX, JR.
## Cleveland Indians

Born September 18, 1925, at Medway, O.
Height, 5.09. Weight, 161.
Threw and batted lefthanded.
Hobbies—Hunting and fishing.
Brother of Ben Haddix, former catcher in New York Giants' organization and
Fred Haddix, former pitcher in Boston Red Sox' organization.

Established major league record for most consecutive batters retired, game (36), May 26, 1959, against Milwaukee Braves. Lost, 1-0, in thirteenth inning.
Tied National League record for most wild pitches, inning (3), sixth inning, August 21, 1963.
Led National League in shutouts with 6 in 1953.
Led American Association pitchers in complete games with 17 in 1950.
Named pitcher on THE SPORTING NEWS National League All-Star fielding team, 1958-59-60.

| Year   Club | League | G. | IP. | W. | L. | Pct. | H. | R. | ER. | SO. | BB. | ERA. |
|-------------|--------|----|-----|----|----|------|----|----|-----|-----|-----|------|
| 1947—Winston-Salem | Carolina | 27 | 204 | 19 | 5 | •.792 | 144 | 62 | 43 | 268 | 70 | •1.90 |
| 1948—Columbus | Am. Assoc. | 32 | 186 | 11 | 9 | .550 | 199 | 109 | 99 | 144 | 67 | 4.79 |
| 1949—Columbus | Am. Assoc. | 35 | 219 | 13 | 13 | .500 | 206 | 98 | 85 | 177 | 94 | 3.49 |
| 1950—Columbus | Am. Assoc. | 30 | 217 | •18 | 6 | .750 | 192 | 76 | 65 | •160 | 59 | •2.70 |
| 1951—St. Louis | National | | | | | (In Military Service) | | | | | | |
| 1952—St. Louis | National | 7 | 42 | 2 | 2 | .500 | 31 | 18 | 13 | 31 | 10 | 2.79 |
| 1953—St. Louis | National | 36 | 253 | 20 | 9 | .690 | 220 | 97 | 86 | 163 | 69 | 3.06 |
| 1954—St. Louis | National | 43 | 260 | 18 | 13 | .581 | 247 | 114 | 103 | 184 | 77 | 3.57 |
| 1955—St. Louis | National | 37 | 208 | 12 | 16 | .429 | 216 | 111 | 103 | 150 | 62 | 4.46 |
| 1956—St. Louis†-Philadelphia | National | 35 | 230 | 13 | 8 | .619 | 224 | 113 | 94 | 170 | 65 | 3.68 |
| 1957—Philadelphia | National | 27 | 171 | 10 | 13 | .435 | 176 | 84 | 77 | 136 | 39 | 4.05 |
| 1958—Cincinnati§ | National | 29 | 184 | 8 | 7 | .533 | 191 | 79 | 72 | 110 | 43 | 3.52 |
| 1959—Pittsburgh | National | 31 | 224 | 12 | 12 | .500 | 189 | 88 | 78 | 149 | 49 | 3.13 |
| 1960—Pittsburgh | National | 29 | 172 | 11 | 10 | .524 | 189 | 87 | 76 | 101 | 38 | 3.98 |
| 1961—Pittsburgh | National | 29 | 156 | 10 | 6 | .625 | 159 | 72 | 71 | 99 | 41 | 4.10 |
| 1962—Pittsburgh | National | 28 | 141 | 9 | 6 | .600 | 146 | 74 | 66 | 101 | 42 | 4.21 |
| 1963—Pittsburgh x | National | 49 | 70 | 3 | 4 | .429 | 67 | 27 | 26 | 70 | 20 | 3.34 |
| 1964—Baltimore | American | 49 | 90 | 5 | 5 | .500 | 68 | 26 | 23 | 90 | 23 | 2.30 |
| 1965—Baltimore | American | 24 | 34 | 3 | 2 | .600 | 31 | 22 | 13 | 21 | 23 | 3.44 |
| American League Totals | | 73 | 124 | 8 | 7 | .533 | 99 | 48 | 36 | 111 | 46 | 2.61 |
| National League Totals | | 380 | 2111 | 128 | 106 | .547 | 2055 | 964 | 865 | 1464 | 555 | 3.69 |
| Major League Totals | | 453 | 2235 | 136 | 113 | .546 | 2154 | 1012 | 901 | 1575 | 601 | 3.63 |

†Traded to Philadelphia Phillies with Pitchers Ben Flowers and Stu Miller for Pitchers Murry Dickson and Herman Wehmeier, May 11, 1956.
‡Traded to Cincinnati Redlegs for Outfielder Wally Post, December 6, 1957.
§Traded to Pittsburgh Pirates with Catcher Forrest (Smoky) Burgess and Third Baseman Don Hoak for Pitcher Charles (Whammy) Douglas, Infielders-Outfielders Jim Pendleton and Frank Thomas and Outfielder Johnny Powers, January 31, 1959.
xTraded to Baltimore Orioles for Shortstop Dick Yencha and cash, December 14, 1963.

## WORLD SERIES RECORD

| Year   Club | League | G. | IP. | W. | L. | Pct. | H. | R. | ER. | SO. | BB. | ERA. |
|-------------|--------|----|-----|----|----|------|----|----|-----|-----|-----|------|
| 1960—Pittsburgh | National | 2 | 7⅓ | 2 | 0 | 1.000 | 6 | 2 | 2 | 6 | 2 | 2.45 |

## ALL-STAR GAME RECORD

| Year   League | IP. | W. | L. | Pct. | H. | R. | ER. | SO. | BB. | ERA. |
|---------------|-----|----|----|------|----|----|-----|-----|-----|------|
| 1955—National | 3 | 0 | 0 | .000 | 3 | 1 | 1 | 2 | 0 | 3.00 |

Member of National League All-Star Team in 1953 and 1954; did not play in 1953 and replaced due to injury in 1954.

Coach, New York Mets, 1966 and 1967; coach, Cincinnati Reds, 1969; minor league pitching coach, Pittsburgh Pirates, 1968 and 1970; coach, Boston Red Sox, 1971; coach, Cleveland Indians, 1975 through 1977.

## THOMAS FRANK HALLER
### San Francisco Giants

Born June 23, 1937, at Lockport, Ill.
Height, 6.04. Weight, 205.
Threw righthanded and batted lefthanded.
Attended University of Illinois, Champaign, Ill, bachelor of
science degree in physical education.
Brother of Bill Haller, American League umpire.

Established National League record for most double plays, season, catcher (23), 1968.
Led Pacific Coast League catchers in passed balls with 19 in 1958.
Led Eastern League catchers in double plays with 23 in 1968.
Received reported $54,000 bonus to sign with San Francisco Giants, 1958.

| Year Club | League | Pos. | G. | AB. | R. | H. | 2B. | 3B. | HR. | RBI. | B.A. | PO. | A. | E. | F.A. |
|---|---|---|---|---|---|---|---|---|---|---|---|---|---|---|---|
| 1958—Phoenix ...........| P. C. | C | 105 | 298 | 42 | 68 | 14 | 1 | 16 | 54 | .228 | 447 | 39 | 7 | .986 |
| 1959—Springfield ........| East. | •C-O-1 | 110 | 348 | 45 | 96 | 19 | 2 | 5 | 50 | .276 | 661 | 47 | 7 | .990 |
| 1960—Tacoma ...........| P. C. | C | 127 | 342 | 39 | 86 | 15 | 5 | 13 | 42 | .251 | •637 | •62 | 8 | .989 |
| 1961—San Francisco ..| Nat. | C | 30 | 62 | 5 | 9 | 1 | 0 | 2 | 8 | .145 | 117 | 7 | 0 | 1.000 |
| 1961—Tacoma ...........| P. C. | C-OF | 56 | 161 | 21 | 33 | 5 | 4 | 4 | 20 | .205 | 282 | 27 | 2 | .994 |
| 1962—San Francisco ..| Nat. | C | 99 | 272 | 53 | 71 | 13 | 1 | 18 | 55 | .261 | 472 | 38 | 4 | .992 |
| 1963—San Francisco ..| Nat. | C-OF | 98 | 298 | 32 | 76 | 8 | 1 | 14 | 44 | .255 | 506 | 39 | 4 | .993 |
| 1964—San Francisco ..| Nat. | C-OF | 117 | 388 | 43 | 98 | 14 | 3 | 16 | 48 | .253 | 739 | 50 | 9 | .989 |
| 1965—San Francisco ..| Nat. | C | 134 | 422 | 40 | 106 | 4 | 3 | 16 | 49 | .251 | •864 | 50 | •12 | .987 |
| 1966—San Francisco ..| Nat. | C-1B | 142 | 471 | 74 | 113 | 19 | 2 | 27 | 67 | .240 | 830 | 59 | 8 | .991 |
| 1967—San Francisco† ..| Nat. | C-OF | 141 | 455 | 54 | 114 | 23 | 5 | 14 | 49 | .251 | 797 | 64 | 3 | .997 |
| 1968—Los Angeles ......| Nat. | C | 144 | 474 | 37 | 135 | 27 | 5 | 4 | 53 | .285 | 863 | 81 | 6 | .994 |
| 1969—Los Angeles ......| Nat. | C | 134 | 445 | 46 | 117 | 18 | 3 | 6 | 39 | .263 | 800 | 48 | 7 | .992 |
| 1970—Los Angeles ......| Nat. | C | 112 | 325 | 47 | 93 | 16 | 6 | 10 | 47 | .286 | 524 | 26 | 4 | .993 |
| 1971—Los Angeles‡ ....| Nat. | C | 84 | 202 | 23 | 54 | 5 | 0 | 5 | 32 | .267 | 320 | 34 | 8 | .978 |
| 1972—Detroit§ ...........| Amer. | C | 59 | 121 | 7 | 25 | 5 | 2 | 2 | 13 | .207 | 220 | 15 | 0 | 1.000 |
| National League Totals ................ | | | 1235 | 3814 | 454 | 986 | 148 | 29 | 132 | 491 | .259 | 6832 | 496 | 65 | .991 |
| American League Totals ................ | | | 59 | 121 | 7 | 25 | 5 | 2 | 2 | 13 | .207 | 220 | 15 | 0 | 1.000 |
| Major League Totals ..................... | | | 1294 | 3935 | 461 | 1011 | 153 | 31 | 134 | 504 | .257 | 7052 | 511 | 65 | .991 |

†Traded with Pitcher Frank Kasheta (assigned from Phoenix to Spokane) to Los Angeles Dodgers for Second Baseman Ron Hunt and Infielder Nate Oliver, February 13, 1968.

‡Traded to Detroit Tigers for cash and a player to be named later, December 2, 1971. Detroit assigned Pitcher Bernie Beckman to El Paso to complete the deal, March 31, 1972.

§Released to Philadelphia Phillies, October 25, 1972.

### CHAMPIONSHIP SERIES RECORD

| Year Club | League | Pos. | G. | AB. | R. | H. | 2B. | 3B. | HR. | RBI. | B.A. | PO. | A. | E. | F.A. |
|---|---|---|---|---|---|---|---|---|---|---|---|---|---|---|---|
| 1972—Detroit ..............| Amer. | PH | 1 | 1 | 0 | 0 | 0 | 0 | 0 | 0 | .000 | 0 | 0 | 0 | .000 |

### WORLD SERIES RECORD

| Year Club | League | Pos. | G. | AB. | R. | H. | 2B. | 3B. | HR. | RBI. | B.A. | PO. | A. | E. | F.A. |
|---|---|---|---|---|---|---|---|---|---|---|---|---|---|---|---|
| 1962—San Francisco ..| Nat. | C | 4 | 14 | 1 | 4 | 1 | 0 | 1 | 3 | .286 | 29 | 2 | 0 | 1.000 |

### ALL-STAR GAME RECORD

| Year League | Pos. | AB. | R. | H. | 2B. | 3B. | HR. | RBI. | B.A. | PO. | A. | E. | F.A. |
|---|---|---|---|---|---|---|---|---|---|---|---|---|---|
| 1967—National ............................. | C | 1 | 0 | 0 | 0 | 0 | 0 | 0 | .000 | 7 | 0 | 0 | 1.000 |
| 1968—National ............................. | C | 2 | 0 | 0 | 0 | 0 | 0 | 0 | .000 | 6 | 0 | 0 | 1.000 |
| All-Star Game Totals ....................... | | 3 | 0 | 0 | 0 | 0 | 0 | 0 | .000 | 13 | 0 | 0 | 1.000 |

Member of National League All-Star team in 1966 game; did not play.
Coach, San Francisco Giants, 1977.

## FRED JAMES HATFIELD
### Detroit Tigers

Born March 18, 1925, at Lanett, Ala.
Height, 6.00. Weight, 200.
Threw righthanded and batted lefthanded.
Hobbies—Fishing and hunting.
Attended Troy (Ala.) State Teachers College; received Bachelor of
Science degree in Physical Education.

| Year Club | League | Pos. | G. | AB. | R. | H. | 2B. | 3B. | HR. | RBI. | B.A. | PO. | A. | E. | F.A. |
|---|---|---|---|---|---|---|---|---|---|---|---|---|---|---|---|
| 1942—Canton ..............| Mid.Atl. | 3B | 12 | 36 | 3 | 6 | 0 | 0 | 0 | 1 | .167 | 3 | 24 | 5 | .844 |
| 1942—D'ville-Sch'field | Bi-St. | 3B | 81 | 335 | 31 | 87 | 13 | 3 | 1 | 37 | .260 | 119 | 192 | 28 | .917 |
| 1943-44-45—Louisville ..| A.A. | | | | | (In Military Service) | | | | | | | | | |
| 1946—Roanoke ...........| Pied. | 3B-P | 114 | 440 | 66 | 118 | 7 | 9 | 3 | 42 | .268 | 124 | 203 | 25 | .929 |
| 1947—Scranton...........| East. | 3B-SS | 137 | 525 | 72 | 143 | 22 | 8 | 7 | 74 | .272 | 198 | 303 | 44 | .919 |
| 1948—Louisville ..........| A.A. | 3B | 39 | 155 | 12 | 39 | 8 | 2 | 0 | 12 | .252 | 35 | 75 | 10 | .917 |

| Year | Club | League | Pos. | G. | AB. | R. | H. | 2B. | 3B. | HR. | RBI. | B.A. | PO. | A. | E. | F.A. |
|------|------|--------|------|-----|-----|-----|-----|-----|-----|-----|------|------|-----|------|-----|------|
| 1948—Lynn | ................ | N.Eng. | 3B | 108 | 402 | 104 | 114 | 20 | 6 | 14 | 74 | .284 | 116 | 230 | 18 | •.951 |
| 1949—Birmingham | ..... | South. | 3B | 154 | 597 | 98 | 156 | 21 | 13 | 25 | 101 | .261 | 155 | •344 | 20 | •.961 |
| 1950—Birmingham | ..... | South. | 3B | 141 | 544 | 113 | 163 | 22 | 9 | 27 | 101 | .300 | •170 | •286 | 15 | •.968 |
| 1950—Boston | ............. | Amer. | 3B | 10 | 12 | 3 | 3 | 0 | 0 | 0 | 2 | .250 | 4 | 9 | 0 | 1.000 |
| 1951—Boston | ............. | Amer. | 3B | 80 | 163 | 23 | 28 | 4 | 2 | 2 | 14 | .172 | 40 | 124 | 7 | .959 |
| 1952—Bos.†-Detroit | .... | Amer. | •3B-SS | 131 | 466 | 48 | 112 | 13 | 3 | 3 | 28 | .240 | 132 | •289 | 14 | •.968 |
| 1953—Detroit | ............. | Amer. | INF | 109 | 311 | 41 | 79 | 11 | 1 | 3 | 19 | .254 | 120 | 208 | 9 | .973 |
| 1954—Detroit | ............. | Amer. | 2B-3B | 81 | 218 | 31 | 64 | 12 | 0 | 2 | 25 | .294 | 129 | 152 | 11 | .962 |
| 1955—Detroit | ............. | Amer. | INF | 122 | 413 | 51 | 96 | 15 | 3 | 8 | 33 | .232 | 252 | 324 | 21 | .965 |
| 1956—Det.‡-Chicago | .... | Amer. | INF | 114 | 333 | 48 | 87 | 9 | 1 | 7 | 35 | .261 | 91 | 197 | 11 | .963 |
| 1957—Chicago§ | ......... | Amer. | 3B | 69 | 114 | 14 | 23 | 3 | 0 | 0 | 8 | .202 | 23 | 74 | 5 | .951 |
| 1958—Cleveland x | ...... | Amer. | 3B | 3 | 8 | 0 | 1 | 0 | 0 | 1 | 1 | .125 | 1 | 6 | 0 | 1.000 |
| 1958—Cincinnati | .......... | Nat. | 2B-3B | 3 | 1 | 0 | 0 | 0 | 0 | 0 | 0 | .000 | 0 | 0 | 0 | .000 |
| 1958—San Diego | ......... | P.C. | 3B-2B | 106 | 374 | 55 | 101 | 17 | 5 | 10 | 37 | .270 | 153 | 215 | 21 | .946 |
| 1959—S.D.-Spokane | ..... | P.C. | 3B | 130 | 421 | 58 | 95 | 16 | 2 | 8 | 49 | .226 | 105 | 202 | 14 | .956 |
| 1960—Little Rock y | ..... | So.Assn. | 3B-2B | 114 | 336 | 73 | 93 | 12 | 3 | 14 | 52 | .277 | 128 | 228 | 12 | .967 |
| 1961—Little Rock y | ..... | So.Assn. | 3B-SS | 115 | 292 | 43 | 92 | 19 | 2 | 6 | 56 | .315 | 67 | 146 | 18 | .922 |
| 1962—Modesto y | ......... | Calif. | 3B-1B | 93 | 250 | 44 | 83 | 11 | 0 | 8 | 51 | .332 | 88 | 79 | 14 | .923 |
| 1963—Denver z | .......... | P.C. | ......... | 9 | 16 | 1 | 3 | 0 | 0 | 0 | 0 | .188 | 0 | 0 | 0 | .000 |
| 1963—Jamestown y | .... | NYP | ......... | 3 | 11 | 2 | 4 | 0 | 0 | 0 | 4 | .364 | 0 | 0 | 0 | .000 |
| American League Totals | ................ | | | 719 | 2038 | 259 | 493 | 67 | 10 | 25 | 165 | .242 | 792 | 1383 | 78 | .965 |
| National League Totals | ................... | | | 3 | 1 | 0 | 0 | 0 | 0 | 0 | 0 | .000 | 0 | 0 | 0 | .000 |
| Major League Totals | ...................... | | | 722 | 2039 | 259 | 493 | 67 | 10 | 25 | 165 | .242 | 792 | 1383 | 78 | .965 |

†Traded to Detroit Tigers with Pitcher Bill Wight, First Baseman Walter Dropo, Shortstop Johnny Pesky and Outfielder Don Lenhardt for Pitcher Paul (Dizzy) Trout, Third Baseman George Kell, Shortstop Johnny Lipon and Outfielder Walter (Hoot) Evers, June 3, 1952.

‡Traded with Outfielder Jim Delsing to Chicago White Sox for Pitcher Harry Byrd and Infielders Jim Brideweser and Bob Kennedy, May 15, 1956.

§Traded to Cleveland Indians with Outfielder Minnie Minoso for Pitcher Early Wynn and Infielder-Outfielder Al Smith, December 4, 1957.

xTraded to Cincinnati Redlegs for Pitcher Bob Kelly, April 23, 1958.

yPlayer-manager.

zPlayer-coach.

### RECORD AS MANAGER

| Year | Club | League | Position | W. | L. | Year | Club | League | Position | W. | L. |
|------|------|--------|----------|----|----|------|------|--------|----------|----|----|
| 1960—Little Rock | ........ | So.Assn. | Third | 82 | 69 | 1972—Montgomery | ......South. | §First(W) | 78 | 61 |
| 1961—Little Rock | ..... | So.Assn. | Third | 80 | 73 | 1973—Montgomery | ......South. | xFirst(W) | 80 | 58 |
| 1962—Modesto | ............ | Calif. | †Second | 37 | 36 | 1974—Evansville | ..........A.A. | Fourth(E) | 68 | 67 |
| (Second Half) | | | Second | 38 | 29 | 1975—Evansville | ..........A.A. | yFirst(E) | 77 | 59 |
| 1963—Jamestown‡ | ........ | NYP | Fourth | 62 | 68 | 1976—Evansville | ..........A.A. | Fourth(E) | 55 | 81 |
| 1970—Lewiston | ............ | N'west | First(N) | 43 | 37 | | | | | | |

†Tied for second with Visalia.

‡Replaced Max Macon, June 26, 1963.

§Won playoff by defeating Asheville, three games to none.

xWon playoff by defeating Jacksonville, three games to one.

yWon playoff by defeating Denver, four games to two.

St. Louis minor league instructor, 1968-71; coach, Detroit Tigers, 1977.

## JAMES EDWARD HEGAN
### (Jim)
### Detroit Tigers

Born August 3, 1920, at Lynn, Mass.
Height, 6.02. Weight, 195.
Threw and batted righthanded.
Father of Mike Hegan, Milwaukee Brewers' first baseman-outfielder.

Tied major league record for catchers by making unassisted double play in game, June 21, 1949; caught three no-hit games; Don Black's win over the Philadelphia Athletics, July 10, 1947, Bob Lemon's effort over Detroit Tigers, June 30, 1948, and Bob Feller's third no-hitter of his career, July 1, 1951, when he beat the Detroit Tigers.

Established American League records for highest fielding average, catcher, season (150 or more games), .990, in 1949, and fewest errors by catcher, season (150 or more games), 7, in 1949.

Led American League catchers in double plays with 17 in 1948.

Tied for American League lead in double plays by catchers with 14 in 1947 and 12 in 1955.

| Year | Club | League | Pos. | G. | AB. | R. | H. | 2B. | 3B. | HR. | RBI. | B.A. | PO. | A. | E. | F.A. |
|------|------|--------|------|-----|-----|-----|-----|-----|-----|-----|------|------|-----|------|-----|------|
| 1938—Springfield | ........ | Mid Atl. | C-OF | 62 | 185 | 33 | 54 | 10 | 3 | 5 | 19 | .292 | 256 | 33 | 6 | .980 |
| 1939—Springfield | ........ | Mid Atl. | C-OF | 103 | 342 | 46 | 83 | 13 | 1 | 13 | 53 | .243 | 616 | 57 | 15 | .978 |
| 1940—Wilkes-Barre | .... | East. | C | 32 | 78 | 7 | 19 | 3 | 3 | 0 | 7 | .244 | 108 | 13 | 4 | .968 |
| 1940—Oklahoma City | .. | Texas | C | 44 | 138 | 16 | 39 | 7 | 3 | 2 | 18 | .283 | 161 | 15 | 3 | .983 |
| 1941—Oklahoma City | .. | Texas | C | 77 | 256 | 30 | 62 | 9 | 7 | 1 | 26 | .242 | 322 | 62 | 9 | .977 |
| 1941—Wilkes-Barre | .... | East. | C | 34 | 98 | 9 | 23 | 2 | 4 | 2 | 12 | .235 | 116 | 22 | 4 | .972 |
| 1941—Cleveland | ......... | Amer. | C | 16 | 47 | 4 | 15 | 2 | 0 | 1 | 5 | .319 | 63 | 10 | 2 | .973 |
| 1942—Baltimore | ......... | Int. | C | 4 | 8 | 1 | 2 | 1 | 0 | 0 | 0 | .250 | 10 | 0 | 0 | 1.000 |
| 1942—Cleveland | ......... | Amer. | C | 68 | 170 | 10 | 33 | 5 | 0 | 0 | 11 | .194 | 227 | 32 | 6 | .977 |
| 1943-44-45—Cleveland | .. | Amer. | | | | | | | (In Military Service) | | | | | | | | |
| 1946—Cleveland | ......... | Amer. | C | 88 | 271 | 29 | 64 | 11 | 5 | 0 | 17 | .236 | 386 | 47 | 5 | .989 |
| 1947—Cleveland | ......... | Amer. | C | 135 | 378 | 38 | 94 | 14 | 5 | 4 | 42 | .249 | •566 | 54 | 7 | .989 |
| 1948—Cleveland | ......... | Amer. | C | 144 | 472 | 60 | 117 | 21 | 6 | 14 | 61 | .248 | •637 | •76 | 7 | .990 |

| Year | Club | League | Pos. | G. | AB. | R. | H. | 2B. | 3B. | HR. | RBI. | B.A. | PO. | A. | E. | F.A. |
|---|---|---|---|---|---|---|---|---|---|---|---|---|---|---|---|---|
| 1949–Cleveland | Amer. | | C | 152 | 468 | 54 | 105 | 19 | 5 | 8 | 55 | .224 | *651 | *73 | 7 | .990 |
| 1950–Cleveland | Amer. | | C | 131 | 415 | 53 | 91 | 16 | 5 | 14 | 58 | .219 | 656 | ●64 | 5 | .993 |
| 1951–Cleveland | Amer. | | C | 133 | 416 | 60 | 99 | 17 | 5 | 6 | 43 | .238 | 597 | 66 | 6 | *.991 |
| 1952–Cleveland | Amer. | | C | 112 | 333 | 39 | 75 | 17 | 2 | 4 | 41 | .225 | 498 | 53 | 7 | .987 |
| 1953–Cleveland | Amer. | | C | 112 | 299 | 37 | 65 | 10 | 1 | 9 | 37 | .217 | 399 | 42 | *11 | .976 |
| 1954–Cleveland | Amer. | | C | 139 | 423 | 56 | 99 | 12 | 7 | 11 | 40 | .234 | 661 | 49 | 4 | *.994 |
| 1955–Cleveland | Amer. | | C | 116 | 304 | 30 | 67 | 5 | 2 | 9 | 40 | .220 | 583 | 34 | 2 | *.997 |
| 1956–Cleveland | Amer. | | C | 122 | 315 | 42 | 70 | 15 | 2 | 6 | 34 | .222 | 648 | 28 | 10 | .985 |
| 1957–Cleveland† | Amer. | | C | 58 | 148 | 14 | 32 | 7 | 0 | 4 | 15 | .216 | 287 | 14 | 0 | 1.000 |
| 1958–Detroit‡ | Amer. | | C | 45 | 130 | 14 | 25 | 6 | 0 | 1 | 7 | .192 | 211 | 19 | 1 | .996 |
| 1958–Philadelphia | Nat. | | C | 25 | 59 | 5 | 13 | 6 | 0 | 0 | 6 | .220 | 104 | 8 | 1 | .991 |
| 1959–Phila.§-San F.x | Nat. | | C | 46 | 81 | 1 | 14 | 2 | 0 | 0 | 8 | .173 | 156 | 17 | 3 | .983 |
| 1960–Chicago y | Nat. | | C | 24 | 43 | 4 | 9 | 2 | 1 | 1 | 5 | .209 | 76 | 9 | 2 | .977 |
| American League Totals | | | | 1571 | 4589 | 540 | 1051 | 177 | 45 | 91 | 506 | .229 | 7070 | 661 | 80 | .990 |
| National League Totals | | | | 95 | 183 | 10 | 36 | 10 | 1 | 1 | 19 | .197 | 336 | 34 | 6 | .984 |
| Major League Totals | | | | 1666 | 4772 | 550 | 1087 | 187 | 46 | 92 | 525 | .228 | 7406 | 695 | 86 | .989 |

†Traded to Detroit Tigers with Pitcher Hank Aguirre for Pitcher Hal Woodeshick and Catcher-Outfielder J. W. Porter, February 18, 1958.

‡Traded to Philadelphia Phillies for cash and Catcher John Turk (assigned from Tulsa to Lancaster), July 27, 1958.

§Sold to San Francisco Giants, June 14, 1959.

xUnconditionally released by San Francisco Giants, January 21, 1960; signed with Chicago Cubs, May 28, 1960.

yUnconditionally released by Chicago Cubs, July 30, 1960; signed with New York Yankees as coach, July 31, 1960.

### WORLD SERIES RECORD

| Year | Club | League | Pos. | G. | AB. | R. | H. | 2B. | 3B. | HR. | RBI. | B.A. | PO. | A. | E. | F.A. |
|---|---|---|---|---|---|---|---|---|---|---|---|---|---|---|---|---|
| 1948–Cleveland | Amer. | | C | 6 | 19 | 2 | 4 | 0 | 0 | 1 | 5 | .211 | 25 | 5 | 0 | 1.000 |
| 1954–Cleveland | Amer. | | C | 4 | 13 | 1 | 2 | 1 | 0 | 0 | 0 | .154 | 27 | 3 | 0 | 1.000 |
| World Series Totals | | | | 10 | 32 | 3 | 6 | 1 | 0 | 1 | 5 | .188 | 52 | 8 | 0 | 1.000 |

### ALL-STAR GAME RECORD

| Year | League | Pos. | AB. | R. | H. | 2B. | 3B. | HR. | RBI. | B.A. | PO. | A. | E. | F.A. |
|---|---|---|---|---|---|---|---|---|---|---|---|---|---|---|
| 1950–American | | C | 3 | 0 | 0 | 0 | 0 | 0 | 0 | .000 | 7 | 1 | 0 | 1.000 |
| 1951–American | | PH | 1 | 0 | 1 | 1 | 0 | 0 | 0 | 1.000 | 0 | 0 | 0 | .000 |
| All-Star Game Totals | | | 4 | 0 | 1 | 1 | 0 | 0 | 0 | .250 | 7 | 1 | 0 | 1.000 |

Member of American League All-Star Team in 1947, 1949 and 1952; did not play.

Coach, New York Yankees, July 31, 1960, through 1973; coach, Detroit Tigers, 1974 through 1977.

## CHARLES JOSEPH HILLER
### (Chuck)
### Kansas City Royals

Born October 1, 1935, at Johnsburg, Ill.
Height, 5.11. Weight, 172.
Threw right and batted lefthanded.
Hobbies—Bowling and all other sports.
Attended St. Thomas College, St. Paul, Minn.; received Bachelor of Arts degree in Business Administration.

| Year | Club | League | Pos. | G. | AB. | R. | H. | 2B. | 3B. | HR. | RBI. | B.A. | PO. | A. | E. | F.A. |
|---|---|---|---|---|---|---|---|---|---|---|---|---|---|---|---|---|
| 1957–Cocoa | Fla.St. | | 2B-SS | 133 | 505 | 99 | 148 | 21 | 9 | 11 | 51 | .293 | 252 | 370 | 46 | .931 |
| 1958–Minot† | North. | | 2B | 120 | 455 | 89 | 128 | 23 | 12 | 8 | 58 | .281 | *339 | 308 | 26 | .961 |
| 1959–Eugene | Northw. | | 2B | 139 | 487 | 92 | *166 | 24 | ●9 | 13 | 99 | .341 | *309 | *395 | 22 | *.970 |
| 1960–Rio Grande Val. | Texas | | 2B | 144 | 560 | 89 | *187 | *47 | 4 | 3 | 74 | *.334 | *365 | *438 | 16 | *.980 |
| 1961–San Francisco | Nat. | | 2B | 70 | 240 | 38 | 57 | 12 | 1 | 2 | 12 | .238 | 133 | 158 | 8 | .973 |
| 1961–Tacoma | P.C. | | 2B | 73 | 281 | 54 | 91 | 15 | 3 | 5 | 32 | .324 | 163 | 188 | 14 | .962 |
| 1962–San Francisco | Nat. | | 2B | 161 | 602 | 94 | 166 | 22 | 2 | 3 | 48 | .276 | 367 | 417 | *29 | .964 |
| 1963–San Francisco | Nat. | | 2B | 111 | 417 | 44 | 93 | 10 | 2 | 6 | 33 | .223 | 224 | 277 | 19 | .963 |
| 1964–San Francisco | Nat. | | 2B-3B | 80 | 208 | 21 | 37 | 8 | 1 | 1 | 17 | .180 | 113 | 145 | 7 | .974 |
| 1965–S.F.‡-New York | Nat. | | 2-OF-3 | 107 | 293 | 25 | 69 | 11 | 1 | 6 | 22 | .235 | 151 | 183 | 14 | .960 |
| 1966–New York | Nat. | | 2-3-OF | 108 | 254 | 25 | 71 | 8 | 2 | 2 | 14 | .280 | 110 | 153 | 5 | .981 |
| 1967–N.Y.§x-Phila.y | Nat. | | 2B | 56 | 97 | 4 | 18 | 4 | 0 | 0 | 5 | .186 | 33 | 46 | 3 | .963 |
| 1968–Pittsburgh | Nat. | | 2B | 11 | 13 | 2 | 5 | 1 | 0 | 0 | 1 | .385 | 4 | 2 | 1 | .857 |
| 1968–Columbus z | Int. | | 3-2-1-OF | 84 | 273 | 33 | 75 | 10 | 2 | 3 | 36 | .275 | 208 | 142 | 10 | .972 |
| Major League Totals | | | | 704 | 2121 | 253 | 516 | 76 | 9 | 20 | 152 | .243 | 1135 | 1381 | 86 | .967 |

†Drafted from Cleveland Indians' organization by Eugene (San Francisco Giants' organization), December 2, 1958.

‡Sold to New York Mets, May 12, 1965.

§Suffered fractured finger when hit by a line drive, May 3; on disabled list through June 11.

xTraded to Philadelphia Phillies for Infielder Phil Linz, May 11, 1967.

yDrafted by Pittsburgh Pirates from San Diego (Philadelphia Phillies' organization), November 28, 1967.

zReleased by Pittsburgh Pirates' organization, December 20, 1968.

### WORLD SERIES RECORD

Tied World Series record by hitting a home run with the bases full, seventh inning, October 8, 1962—giving him a tie for most runs batted in, inning (4). Hiller was the first National League player to achieve this distinction.

| Year Club | League | Pos. | G. | AB. | R. | H. | 2B. | 3B. | HR. | RBI. | B.A. | PO. | A. | E. | F.A. |
|---|---|---|---|---|---|---|---|---|---|---|---|---|---|---|---|
| 1962—San Francisco ..Nat. | | 2B | 7 | 26 | 4 | 7 | 3 | 0 | 1 | 5 | .269 | 16 | 22 | 1 | .974 |

## RECORD AS MANAGER

| Year Club | League | Position | W. | L. | Year Club | League | Position | W. | L. |
|---|---|---|---|---|---|---|---|---|---|
| 1969—Salem ...............Carol. | | †First(W) | 78 | 66 | 1972—Marion .............Appal. | | Fourth(S) | 22 | 45 |
| 1970—Tidewater .........Int. | | Fourth | 74 | 66 | 1974—Marion .............Appal. | | Second(N) | 33 | 35 |
| 1971—Marion .............Appal. | | Second(S) | 33 | 35 | 1975—Marion .............Appal. | | First(N) | 35 | 33 |

†Lost playoff semifinals to Burlington, two games to none after defeating High Point-Thomasville in quarterfinals, two games to none.

Coach, Texas Rangers, 1973; coach, Kansas City Royals, 1976 and 1977.

# ELSTON GENE HOWARD
## New York Yankees

Born February 23, 1929, at St. Louis, Mo.
Height, 6.02. Weight, 210.
Threw and batted righthanded.
Hobbies—Hunting and modern jazz.

Tied major league record for most bases on balls, inning (2), September 26, 1964, second inning.
Named Most Valuable Player in International League, 1954.
Named Most Valuable Player in American League, 1963.
Named as catcher on THE SPORTING NEWS American League All-Star Teams, 1961-63-64.
Named at catcher on THE SPORTING NEWS American League All-Star fielding team, 1963-64.

| Year Club | League | Pos. | G. | AB. | R. | H. | 2B. | 3B. | HR. | RBI. | B.A. | PO. | A. | E. | F.A. |
|---|---|---|---|---|---|---|---|---|---|---|---|---|---|---|---|
| 1950—Muskegon..........Cent. | | OF | 54 | 184 | 22 | 52 | 6 | 2 | 9 | 42 | .283 | 61 | 8 | 3 | .958 |
| 1951-52—Binghamton ..East. | | (In Military Service) | | | | | | | | | | | | | |
| 1953—Kansas City ......A.A. | | OF-C | 139 | 497 | 58 | 142 | 22 | 9 | 10 | 70 | .286 | 228 | 20 | 10 | .961 |
| 1954—Toronto ............Int. | | *C-OF | 138 | 497 | 78 | 164 | 21 | *16 | 22 | 109 | .330 | *588 | 42 | 8 | .987 |
| 1955—New York..........Amer. | | OF-C | 97 | 279 | 33 | 81 | 8 | 7 | 10 | 43 | .290 | 147 | 13 | 3 | .982 |
| 1956—New York..........Amer. | | OF-C | 98 | 290 | 35 | 76 | 8 | 3 | 5 | 34 | .262 | 205 | 16 | 1 | .995 |
| 1957—New York..........Amer. | | O-C-1B | 110 | 356 | 33 | 90 | 13 | 4 | 8 | 44 | .253 | 266 | 19 | 6 | .979 |
| 1958—New York..........Amer. | | C-O-1B | 103 | 376 | 45 | 118 | 19 | 5 | 11 | 66 | .314 | 447 | 29 | 2 | .996 |
| 1959—New York..........Amer. | | 1B-C-O | 125 | 443 | 59 | 121 | 24 | 6 | 18 | 73 | .273 | 712 | 49 | 10 | .987 |
| 1960—New York..........Amer. | | C-OF | 107 | 323 | 29 | 79 | 11 | 3 | 6 | 39 | .245 | 410 | 40 | 6 | .987 |
| 1961—New York..........Amer. | | C-1B | 129 | 446 | 64 | 155 | 17 | 5 | 21 | 77 | .34b | 725 | 47 | 6 | .992 |
| 1962—New York..........Amer. | | C | 136 | 494 | 63 | 138 | 23 | 5 | 21 | 91 | .279 | 713 | 44 | 4 | *.995 |
| 1963—New York..........Amer. | | C | 135 | 487 | 75 | 140 | 21 | 6 | 28 | 85 | .287 | 786 | 51 | 5 | *994 |
| 1964—New York..........Amer. | | C | 150 | 550 | 63 | 172 | 27 | 3 | 15 | 84 | .313 | *939 | 67 | 2 | *998 |
| 1965—New York..........Amer. | | C-1-O | 110 | 391 | 38 | 91 | 15 | 1 | 9 | 45 | .233 | 644 | 44 | 6 | .991 |
| 1966—New York..........Amer. | | C-1B | 126 | 410 | 38 | 105 | 19 | 2 | 6 | 35 | .256 | 665 | 52 | 9 | .988 |
| 1967—N.Y.†-Boston ....Amer. | | C-1B | 108 | 315 | 22 | 56 | 9 | 0 | 4 | 28 | .178 | 536 | 40 | 6 | .990 |
| 1968—Boston‡ ...........Amer. | | C | 71 | 203 | 22 | 49 | 4 | 0 | 5 | 18 | .241 | 377 | 30 | 2 | .995 |
| Major League Totals ...................... | | | 1605 | 5363 | 619 | 1471 | 218 | 50 | 167 | 762 | .274 | 7572 | 541 | 68 | .992 |

†Traded to Boston Red Sox for cash and players to be named later, August 3, 1967. Pitcher Ron Klimkowski assigned from Toronto to Syracuse as part payment August 8, 1967, and Pitcher Pete Magrini assigned to Syracuse, October 14, 1967 to complete deal.

‡Released, October 29, 1968.

## WORLD SERIES RECORD

Hit homer in first World Series at-bat, September 28, 1955.
Tied following World Series records: Most hits, inning (2), October 6, 1960, sixth inning; most long hits, five-game Series (4), 1961; most passed balls, game, nine innings (2), October 7, 1964.

| Year Club | League | Pos. | G. | AB. | R. | H. | 2B. | 3B. | HR. | RBI. | B.A. | PO. | A. | E. | F.A. |
|---|---|---|---|---|---|---|---|---|---|---|---|---|---|---|---|
| 1955—New York..........Amer. | | OF | 7 | 26 | 3 | 5 | 0 | 0 | 1 | 3 | .192 | 11 | 1 | 0 | 1.000 |
| 1956—New York..........Amer. | | OF | 1 | 5 | 1 | 2 | 1 | 0 | 1 | 1 | .400 | 2 | 0 | 0 | 1.000 |
| 1957—New York..........Amer. | | 1B-PH | 6 | 11 | 2 | 3 | 0 | 0 | 1 | 3 | .273 | 22 | 1 | 1 | .958 |
| 1958—New York..........Amer. | | OF-PH | 6 | 18 | 4 | 4 | 0 | 0 | 0 | 2 | .222 | 14 | 2 | 0 | 1.000 |
| 1960—New York..........Amer. | | C-PH | 5 | 13 | 4 | 6 | 1 | 1 | 1 | 4 | .462 | 11 | 6 | 0 | 1.000 |
| 1961—New York..........Amer. | | C | 5 | 20 | 5 | 5 | 3 | 0 | 1 | 1 | .250 | 31 | 0 | 0 | 1.000 |
| 1962—New York..........Amer. | | C | 6 | 21 | 1 | 3 | 1 | 0 | 0 | 1 | .143 | 37 | 1 | 0 | 1.000 |
| 1963—New York..........Amer. | | C | 4 | 15 | 0 | 5 | 0 | 0 | 0 | 1 | .333 | 30 | 2 | 0 | 1.000 |
| 1964—New York..........Amer. | | C | 7 | 24 | 5 | 7 | 1 | 0 | 0 | 2 | .292 | 40 | 2 | 1 | .997 |
| 1967—Boston .............Amer. | | C | 7 | 18 | 0 | 2 | 0 | 0 | 0 | 1 | .111 | 23 | 1 | 0 | 1.000 |
| World Series Totals ....................... | | | 54 | 171 | 25 | 42 | 7 | 1 | 5 | 19 | .246 | 221 | 10 | 2 | .991 |

## ALL-STAR GAME RECORD

| Year League | Pos. | AB. | R. | H. | 2B. | 3B. | HR. | RBI. | B.A. | PO. | A. | E. | F.A. |
|---|---|---|---|---|---|---|---|---|---|---|---|---|---|
| 1960—American (first game) ........ | C | 1 | 0 | 0 | 0 | 0 | 0 | 0 | .000 | 4 | 0 | 0 | 1.000 |
| 1961—American (both games) ...... | C | 2 | 0 | 0 | 0 | 0 | 0 | 0 | .000 | 6 | 0 | 0 | 1.000 |
| 1962—American (second game) .... | C | 2 | 0 | 0 | 0 | 0 | 0 | 0 | .000 | 2 | 0 | 0 | 1.000 |
| 1963—American ........................... | C | 1 | 0 | 0 | 0 | 0 | 0 | 0 | .000 | 5 | 0 | 0 | 1.000 |
| 1964—American ........................... | C | 3 | 1 | 0 | 0 | 0 | 0 | 0 | .000 | 9 | 0 | 0 | 1.000 |
| All-Star Game Totals ...................... | | 9 | 1 | 0 | 0 | 0 | 0 | 0 | .000 | 26 | 0 | 0 | 1.000 |

Member of American League All-Star Team in 1957, 1958, 1959 (second game), 1960 (second game), 1962 (first game) and 1965; did not play.

Coach New York Yankees, 1969 through 1977.

## FRANK OLIVER HOWARD
### (The Horse)

(Tagged by Bobby Lillis when he was with the Dodgers, for his size, in exchange of nicknames, dubbing Lillis "The Flea."

### Milwaukee Brewers
Born August 8, 1936, at Columbus, O.

Height, 6.07. Weight, 250.
Threw and batted righthanded.
Attended Ohio State University, Columbus, O.

Established following major league records: Most home runs, one week (10), May 12 through May 18, 1968; most home runs, five consecutive games, (8), May 12 through May 17, 1968; most home runs, six consecutive games (10), May 12 through May 18, 1968; most years, 100 or more strikeouts, lifetime, 10, 1971.

Tied the following major league records: most consecutive strikeouts, 9 inning game (5), September 19, 1970, first game; most strikeouts, two consecutive games (7), July 9, 1965 (doubleheader); most unassisted putouts, first baseman, inning, 3, September 9, 1972 (first inning).

Tied American League record for most home runs, four consecutive games (7), May 12 through May 16, 1968.

Led Three-I League in total bases with 311 and strikeouts with 129 in 1958.

Tied American League record for most consecutive games, hitting homer each game (6), 1968.

Led American League batters in strikeouts with 155 in 1967.

Led American League in total bases with 330 and slugging percentage with .552 in 1968; and led in total bases with 340 in 1969.

Led the American League in grounding into double plays, 29, in 1969.

Led American League batters in walks with 132 in 1970.

Named Minor League Player of the Year by THE SPORTING NEWS, 1959.

Named National League Rookie of the Year by the Baseball Writers' Association and THE SPORTING NEWS, 1960.

Named an outfielder on THE SPORTING NEWS American League All-Star Team, 1968-69-70.

Received reported $108,000 bonus to sign with Los Angeles Dodgers, 1958.

| Year | Club | League | Pos. | G. | AB. | R. | H. | 2B. | 3B. | HR. | RBI. | B.A. | PO. | A. | E. | F.A. |
|---|---|---|---|---|---|---|---|---|---|---|---|---|---|---|---|---|
| 1958–Green Bay | | I.I.I. | OF-P | •129 | 487 | 104 | 162 | 34 | 2 | •37 | •119 | .333 | 186 | 6 | 8 | .960 |
| 1958–Los Angeles | | Nat. | OF | 8 | 29 | 3 | 7 | 1 | 0 | 1 | 2 | .241 | 12 | 1 | 0 | 1.000 |
| 1959–Victoria | | Tex. | OF-3B | 63 | 261 | 59 | 93 | 13 | 0 | 27 | 79 | .356 | 99 | 16 | 5 | .958 |
| 1959–Spokane | | P.C. | OF-1B | 76 | 295 | 43 | 94 | 19 | 2 | 16 | 47 | .319 | 243 | 16 | 6 | .977 |
| 1959–Los Angeles | | Nat. | OF | 9 | 21 | 2 | 3 | 0 | 1 | 1 | 6 | .143 | 10 | 0 | 0 | 1.000 |
| 1960–Spokane | | P.C. | 1B | 26 | 97 | 17 | 36 | 11 | 0 | 4 | 24 | .371 | 233 | 19 | 8 | .969 |
| 1960–Los Angeles | | Nat. | OF-1B | 117 | 448 | 54 | 120 | 15 | 2 | 23 | 77 | .268 | 196 | 11 | 4 | .981 |
| 1961–Los Angeles | | Nat. | OF-1B | 92 | 267 | 36 | 79 | 10 | 2 | 15 | 45 | .296 | 122 | 10 | 8 | .943 |
| 1962–Los Angeles | | Nat. | OF | 141 | 493 | 80 | 146 | 25 | 6 | 31 | 119 | .296 | 187 | 19 | 6 | .972 |
| 1963–Los Angeles | | Nat. | OF | 123 | 417 | 58 | 114 | 16 | 1 | 28 | 64 | .273 | 190 | 4 | 8 | .960 |
| 1964–Los Angeles† | | Nat. | OF | 134 | 433 | 60 | 98 | 13 | 2 | 24 | 69 | .226 | 183 | 2 | 4 | .979 |
| 1965–Washington | | Amer. | OF | 149 | 516 | 53 | 149 | 22 | 6 | 21 | 84 | .289 | 204 | 5 | 4 | .981 |
| 1966–Washington | | Amer. | OF | 146 | 493 | 52 | 137 | 19 | 4 | 18 | 71 | .278 | 216 | 5 | 4 | .982 |
| 1967–Washington | | Amer. | OF-1B | 149 | 519 | 71 | 133 | 20 | 2 | 36 | 89 | .256 | 225 | 6 | 3 | .987 |
| 1968–Washington | | Amer. | OF-1B | 158 | 598 | 79 | 164 | 28 | 3 | *44 | 106 | .274 | 576 | 52 | 19 | .971 |
| 1969–Washington | | Amer. | OF-1B | 161 | 592 | 111 | 175 | 17 | 2 | 48 | 111 | .296 | 602 | 34 | 14 | .978 |
| 1970–Washington | | Amer. | OF-1B | 161 | 566 | 90 | 160 | 15 | 1 | *44 | *126 | .283 | 601 | 31 | 11 | .983 |
| 1971–Washington | | Amer. | OF-1B | 153 | 549 | 60 | 153 | 25 | 2 | 26 | 83 | .279 | .555 | 65 | 5 | .992 |
| 1972–Tex.‡-Det. | | Amer. | 1B-OF | 109 | 320 | 29 | 78 | 10 | 0 | 10 | 38 | .244 | 521 | 32 | 13 | .977 |
| 1973–Detroit§ | | Amer. | 1B | 85 | 227 | 26 | 58 | 9 | 1 | 12 | 29 | .256 | 12 | 0 | 1 | .923 |
| American League Totals | | | | 1271 | 4380 | 571 | 1207 | 165 | 21 | 259 | 737 | .276 | 3512 | 230 | 74 | .981 |
| National League Totals | | | | 624 | 2108 | 293 | 567 | 80 | 14 | 123 | 382 | .269 | 900 | 47 | 30 | .969 |
| Major League Totals | | | | 1895 | 6488 | 864 | 1774 | 245 | 35 | 382 | 1119 | .273 | 4412 | 277 | 104 | .978 |

†Traded to Washington Senators with Pitchers Phil Ortega and Pete Richert and Infielder Ken McMullen for Pitcher Claude Osteen, Infielder John Kennedy and cash estimated at $100,000, December 4, 1964; deal was completed with transfer of First Baseman Dick Nen to Senators, December 15, 1964.

‡Sold to Detroit Tigers, August 31, 1972.

§Unconditionally released, October 25, 1973.

### WORLD SERIES RECORD

| Year | Club | League | Pos. | G. | AB. | R. | H. | 2B. | 3B. | HR. | RBI. | B.A. | PO. | A. | E. | F.A. |
|---|---|---|---|---|---|---|---|---|---|---|---|---|---|---|---|---|
| 1963–Los Angeles | | Nat. | OF | 3 | 10 | 2 | 3 | 1 | 0 | 1 | 1 | .300 | 4 | 0 | 0 | 1.000 |

### ALL-STAR GAME RECORD

| Year | League | Pos. | AB. | R. | H. | 2B. | 3B. | HR. | RBI. | B.A. | PO. | A. | E. | F.A. |
|---|---|---|---|---|---|---|---|---|---|---|---|---|---|---|
| 1968–American | | OF | 2 | 0 | 0 | 0 | 0 | 0 | 0 | .000 | 0 | 0 | 0 | .000 |
| 1969–American | | OF | 1 | 1 | 1 | 0 | 0 | 1 | 1 | 1.000 | 0 | 0 | 1 | .000 |
| 1970–American | | OF | 2 | 0 | 0 | 0 | 0 | 0 | 0 | .000 | 0 | 0 | 0 | .000 |
| 1971–American | | PH | 1 | 0 | 0 | 0 | 0 | 0 | 0 | .000 | 0 | 0 | 0 | .000 |
| All-Star Game Totals | | | 6 | 1 | 1 | 0 | 0 | 1 | 1 | .167 | 0 | 0 | 1 | .000 |

### PITCHING RECORD

| Year | Club | League | G. | IP. | W. | L. | Pct. | H. | R. | ER. | SO. | BB. | ERA. |
|---|---|---|---|---|---|---|---|---|---|---|---|---|---|
| 1958–Green Bay | | I.I.I. | 1 | 1 | 0 | 0 | .000 | 0 | 0 | 0 | 1 | 0 | 0.00 |

### RECORD AS MANAGER

| Year | Club | League | Position | W. | L. |
|---|---|---|---|---|---|
| 1976–Spokane | | P.C. | Fourth (W) | 65 | 78 |

Minor League Instructor, Milwaukee Brewers, 1975; coach, Milwaukee Brewers, 1977.

# RICHARD DALTON HOWSER
## (Dick)
## New York Yankees

Born May 14, 1937, at Miami, Fla.
Height, 5.09. Weight, 155.
Threw and batted righthanded.
Hobby—Sports
Attended Florida State University, Tallahassee, Fla.; received Bachelor
of Science degree in Education.

Tied American League record for most games played by shortstop, season (162), 1964.
Tied for American League lead in sacrifice hits with 6 in 1964.
Led Three-I League in stolen bases with 31 in 1959.
Named American League Rookie of the Year by THE SPORTING NEWS, 1961.
Received reported $21,000 bonus to sign with Kansas City Athletics, 1958.

| Year | Club | League | Pos. | G. | AB. | R. | H. | 2B. | 3B. | HR. | RBI. | B.A. | PO. | A. | E. | F.A. |
|---|---|---|---|---|---|---|---|---|---|---|---|---|---|---|---|---|
| 1958 | Winona | I.I.I. | SS | 83 | 333 | 80 | 96 | 16 | 1 | 6 | 30 | .288 | 152 | 233 | 28 | .932 |
| 1959 | Sioux City | I.I.I. | 2B-SS | 111 | 392 | •107 | 109 | 17 | 5 | 4 | 39 | .278 | 240 | 289 | 33 | .941 |
| 1960 | Sioux City | I.I.I. | SS | 44 | 149 | 59 | 52 | 15 | 1 | 5 | 21 | .349 | 63 | 130 | 20 | .906 |
| 1960 | Shreveport | South. | SS | 88 | 331 | 78 | 112 | 20 | 6 | 4 | 38 | .338 | 189 | 270 | 31 | .937 |
| 1961 | Kansas City | Amer. | SS | 158 | 611 | 108 | 171 | 29 | 6 | 3 | 45 | .280 | *299 | 427 | *38 | .950 |
| 1962 | Kansas City† | Amer. | SS | 83 | 286 | 53 | 68 | 8 | 3 | 6 | 34 | .238 | 138 | 191 | 13 | .962 |
| 1963 | K.C.‡-Cleve. | Amer. | SS | 64 | 203 | 29 | 48 | 5 | 0 | 1 | 11 | .236 | 101 | 113 | 11 | .951 |
| 1964 | Cleveland | Amer. | SS | 162 | 637 | 101 | 163 | 23 | 4 | 3 | 52 | .256 | 291 | 463 | 20 | .974 |
| 1965 | Cleveland | Amer. | SS-2B | 107 | 307 | 47 | 72 | 8 | 2 | 1 | 6 | .235 | 144 | 211 | 7 | .981 |
| 1966 | Cleveland§ | Amer. | SS-2B | 67 | 140 | 18 | 32 | 9 | 1 | 2 | 4 | .229 | 53 | 95 | 5 | .967 |
| 1967 | New York x | Amer. | 2-3-SS | 63 | 149 | 18 | 40 | 6 | 0 | 0 | 10 | .268 | 64 | 76 | 3 | .979 |
| 1968 | New York | Amer. | 2-3-SS | 85 | 150 | 24 | 23 | 2 | 1 | 0 | 3 | .153 | 61 | 106 | 3 | .982 |
| | Major League Totals | | | 789 | 2483 | 398 | 617 | 90 | 17 | 16 | 165 | .248 | 1151 | 1682 | 100 | .966 |

†Suffered broken bone in left hand on tag of Luis Aparicio of White Sox, June 24, 1962; returned to lineup, September 15.

‡Traded to Cleveland Indians with Catcher Jose Azcue for Catcher Howard Edwards and reported $100,000, May 25, 1963.

§Traded to New York Yankees for Pitcher Gil Downs (transferred from Syracuse to Portland) and cash, December 20, 1966.

xFractured bone in wrist July 16; on disabled list through August 31.

### ALL-STAR GAME RECORD

| Year | League | Pos. | AB. | R. | H. | 2B. | 3B. | HR. | RBI. | B.A. | PO. | A. | E. | F.A. |
|---|---|---|---|---|---|---|---|---|---|---|---|---|---|---|
| 1961 | American (first game) | 3B | 1 | 0 | 0 | 0 | 0 | 0 | 0 | .000 | 0 | 1 | 0 | 1.000 |

Member of American League All-Star Team in 1961 (second game); did not play.

Coach, New York Yankees, 1969 through 1977.


# WALTER JOHN HRINIAK
Name pronounced RIN-ee-ack.
## (Walt)
## Boston Red Sox

Born May 2, 1943, at Natick, Mass.
Height, 5.11. Weight, 180.
Threw right and batted lefthanded.
Hobbies—Hunting, fishing and golf.

Led Texas League catchers in passed balls with 16 in 1968.
Led Texas League shortstops in double plays with 67 in 1966.
Received reported $50,000 bonus to sign with Milwaukee Braves, 1961.

| Year | Club | League | Pos. | G. | AB. | R. | H. | 2B. | 3B. | HR. | RBI. | B.A. | PO. | A. | E. | F.A. |
|---|---|---|---|---|---|---|---|---|---|---|---|---|---|---|---|---|
| 1961 | Eau Claire | North. | SS | 76 | 267 | 35 | 83 | 14 | 1 | 2 | 50 | .311 | 120 | 216 | 22 | .939 |
| 1962 | Yakima | Northw. | SS | 139 | 444 | 64 | 133 | 21 | 7 | 2 | 54 | .300 | *204 | *352 | 30 | .949 |
| 1963 | Austin | Tex. | 2B | 117 | 370 | 47 | 98 | 11 | 4 | 3 | 45 | .265 | 233 | 295 | 17 | .969 |
| 1964 | Austin† | Tex. | 3B-2B | 52 | 175 | 19 | 41 | 5 | 1 | 0 | 11 | .234 | 63 | 95 | 10 | .940 |
| 1965 | Austin | Tex. | 2B-3B | 10 | 28 | 5 | 3 | 1 | 0 | 0 | 0 | .107 | 18 | 18 | 2 | .947 |
| 1965 | Yakima | Northw. | S-2B | 116 | 390 | 60 | 100 | 17 | 4 | 10 | 57 | .256 | 190 | 303 | 26 | .950 |
| 1966 | Austin | Tex. | SS | 134 | 455 | 48 | 107 | 16 | 3 | 0 | 38 | .235 | 230 | *388 | 20 | *.969 |
| 1967 | Austin | Tex. | 2-3-S-C | 83 | 282 | 50 | 76 | 11 | 3 | 8 | 40 | .270 | 140 | 172 | 12 | .963 |
| 1967 | Richmond | Int. | 2B-C | 24 | 40 | 4 | 11 | 1 | 1 | 0 | 7 | .275 | 34 | 14 | 2 | .960 |
| 1968 | Shreveport | Tex. | C-3-O-2 | 107 | 345 | 40 | 108 | 11 | 1 | 6 | 47 | .313 | 453 | 100 | 8 | .986 |
| 1968 | Atlanta | Nat. | C | 9 | 26 | 0 | 9 | 0 | 0 | 0 | 3 | .346 | 57 | 1 | 2 | .967 |
| 1969 | Atl.‡-San Diego | Nat. | C | 38 | 73 | 4 | 16 | 0 | 0 | 0 | 1 | .219 | 105 | 7 | 2 | .982 |
| 1970 | Salt Lake City§ | P. C. | 2B-C | 121 | 410 | 49 | 101 | 21 | 4 | 2 | 35 | .246 | 285 | 330 | 19 | .970 |
| 1971 | Savannah xy | So. | 3-C-2-P | 48 | 114 | 8 | 16 | 0 | 0 | 0 | 5 | .140 | 93 | 38 | 6 | .956 |
| 1971 | Winnipeg | Int. | C-2-3-O | 9 | 23 | 3 | 7 | 3 | 0 | 1 | 5 | .304 | 25 | 6 | 3 | .912 |
| 1972 | Quebec City z | East. | 1-3-C-2 | 36 | 88 | 10 | 29 | 5 | 2 | 0 | 15 | .330 | 183 | 14 | 4 | .980 |
| 1973 | Peninsula z | Int. | 3B | 17 | 50 | 2 | 7 | 0 | 0 | 0 | 2 | .140 | 4 | 10 | 1 | .933 |
| | Major League Totals | | | 47 | 99 | 4 | 25 | 0 | 0 | 0 | 4 | .253 | 162 | 8 | 4 | .977 |

†On disabled list from May 22 through August 3 after suffering injuries in auto accident which killed teammate Jerry Hummitzsch.

‡On disabled list, April 7 to April 28, 1969. Traded with Outfielder Andy Finlay and Infielder Van Kelly to San Diego Padres for Outfielder Tony Gonzalez, June 13, 1969.

§Traded by San Diego Padres to Atlanta Braves for Pitcher Rick Wilson, April 3, 1971.

xOn disabled list, June 7 to June 30, 1971.

yUnconditionally released by Atlanta Braves' organization, July 23, 1971; signed as free agent by Montreal Expos' organization, August 24, 1971.

zSelected by Montreal Expos' organization to manage Jamestown (New York-Pennsylvania League).

### PITCHING RECORD

| Year   Club | League | G. | IP. | W. | L. | Pct. | H. | R. | ER. | SO. | BB. | ERA. |
|---|---|---|---|---|---|---|---|---|---|---|---|---|
| 1971—Savannah ..........................Southern | | 1 | 1 | 0 | 0 | .000 | 2 | 1 | 1 | 0 | 0 | 9.00 |

### RECORD AS MANAGER

| Year   Club | League | Position | W. | L. |
|---|---|---|---|---|
| 1972—Jamestown ........NYP | | Third | 42 | 28 |
| 1973—Jamestown ........NYP | | Third | 41 | 28 |

Player-coach, Quebec City (Montreal Expos' organization), part of 1972; coach, Montreal Expos, 1974 and 1975; minor league coach and instructor, Montreal Expos, 1976; coach, Boston Red Sox, 1977.

## SIDNEY CHARLES HUDSON
### (Sid)
### Texas Rangers

Born January 3, 1915, at Coalfield, Tenn.
Height, 6.04. Weight, 192.
Threw and batted righthanded.
Hobbies—Golf and woodworking.

| Year   Club | League | G. | IP. | W. | L. | Pct. | H. | R. | ER. | SO. | BB. | ERA. |
|---|---|---|---|---|---|---|---|---|---|---|---|---|
| 1938—Sanford .............................Florida St. | | 27 | 174 | 11 | 7 | .611 | 135 | 64 | 39 | 136 | 68 | 2.02 |
| 1939—Sanford .............................Florida St. | | 29 | 250 | •24 | 4 | •.857 | 207 | 64 | 50 | •192 | 63 | 1.80 |
| 1940—Washington .........................American | | 38 | 252 | 17 | 16 | .515 | 272 | 149 | 128 | 96 | 81 | 4.57 |
| 1941—Washington .........................American | | 33 | 250 | 13 | 14 | .481 | 242 | 124 | 96 | 108 | 97 | 3.46 |
| 1942—Washington .........................American | | 35 | 239 | 10 | 17 | .370 | 266 | •140 | 116 | 72 | 70 | 4.37 |
| 1943-44-45—Washington .................American | | | | | | (In Military Service) | | | | | | |
| 1946—Washington .........................American | | 31 | 142 | 8 | 11 | .421 | 160 | 75 | 57 | 35 | 37 | 3.61 |
| 1947—Washington .........................American | | 20 | 106 | 6 | 9 | .400 | 113 | 66 | 66 | 37 | 58 | 5.60 |
| 1948—Washington .........................American | | 39 | 182 | 4 | 16 | .200 | 217 | 128 | 119 | 53 | 107 | 5.88 |
| 1949—Washington .........................American | | 40 | 209 | 8 | •17 | .320 | 234 | 117 | 98 | 54 | 91 | 4.22 |
| 1950—Washington .........................American | | 30 | 238 | 14 | 14 | .500 | 261 | 129 | 108 | 75 | 98 | 4.08 |
| 1951—Washington .........................American | | 23 | 139 | 5 | 12 | .294 | 168 | 90 | 79 | 43 | 52 | 5.12 |
| 1952—Washington†-Boston.............American | | 28 | 197 | 10 | 13 | .435 | 204 | 86 | 73 | 74 | 65 | 3.34 |
| 1953—Boston ....................,.......American | | 30 | 156 | 6 | 9 | .400 | 164 | 65 | 61 | 60 | 49 | 3.52 |
| 1954—Boston .............................American | | 33 | 71 | 3 | 4 | .429 | 83 | 43 | 35 | 27 | 30 | 4.44 |
| Major League Totals ............................ | | 380 | 2181 | 104 | 152 | .406 | 2384 | 1212 | 1036 | 734 | 835 | 4.28 |

†Traded to Boston Red Sox for Pitchers Randy Gumpert and Walt Masterson, June 10, 1952.

### ALL-STAR GAME RECORD

| Year   League | IP. | W. | L. | Pct. | H. | R. | ER. | SO. | BB. | ERA. |
|---|---|---|---|---|---|---|---|---|---|---|
| 1941—American ...................................................... | 1 | 0 | 0 | .000 | 3 | 2 | 2 | 1 | 1 | 18.00 |

Member of American League All-Star Team in 1942; did not play.

Scout, Boston Red Sox, 1955 through 1960; coach, Washington Senators, 1961 through April 29, 1965; minor league pitching coach, Washington Senators, 1966 and 1967; coach, Washington Senators, 1968 through 1971; minor league pitching coach, Texas Rangers, 1973 through 1975; coach, Texas Rangers, 1972 and 1977.

## CECIL RANDOLPH HUNDLEY, JR.
### (Randy)
### Chicago Cubs

Born June 1, 1942, at Martinsville, Va.
Height, 6.00. Weight, 165.
Threw and batted righthanded.
Hobby—golf

Established following major league records: Most home runs, catcher, rookie season (19), 1966; most games, catcher, season (160), 1968; highest fielding average, catcher, season (150 or more games), .996, in 1967; fewest errors by catcher, season (150 or more games), 4, in 1967.

Led National League catchers in double plays with 17 in 1969.

Tied for Appalachian League lead in double plays by catcher with 4 in 1960.

Named as catcher on THE SPORTING NEWS National League All-Star fielding team, 1967.

Received reported $110,000 bonus to sign with San Francisco Giants, 1960.

| Year   Club | League | Pos. | G. | AB. | R. | H. | 2B. | 3B. | HR. | RBI. | B.A. | PO. | A. | E. | F.A. |
|---|---|---|---|---|---|---|---|---|---|---|---|---|---|---|---|
| 1960—Salem.................Appal. | | C | 44 | 153 | 32 | 41 | 10 | 3 | 3 | 15 | .268 | 324 | 28 | 10 | .972 |
| 1961—Fresno .............Calif. | | C-OF | 88 | 273 | 36 | 68 | 12 | 1 | 6 | 45 | .249 | 658 | 56 | 10 | .986 |
| 1962—Fresno .............Calif. | | C-3-O | 105 | 331 | 42 | 79 | 12 | 3 | 8 | 39 | .239 | 624 | 74 | 14 | .980 |
| 1963—El Paso .............Tex. | | •C-3B | 115 | 379 | 66 | 123 | 30 | 3 | 23 | 81 | .325 | 703 | 58 | 11 | •.986 |
| 1964—Tacoma ...........P. C. | | C | 21 | 62 | 6 | 16 | 4 | 0 | 2 | 8 | .258 | 103 | 13 | 3 | .975 |
| 1964—Atlanta.............Int. | | •C-OF | 113 | 374 | 40 | 81 | 10 | 1 | 13 | 40 | .217 | 621 | 50 | •14 | .980 |

— 473 —

| Year   Club          League | Pos. | G. | AB. | R. | H. | 2B. | 3B. | HR. | RBI. | B.A. | PO. | A. | E. | F.A. |
|---|---|---|---|---|---|---|---|---|---|---|---|---|---|---|
| 1964—San Francisco ..Nat. | C | 2 | 1 | 1 | 0 | 0 | 0 | 0 | 0 | .000 | 0 | 0 | 0 | .000 |
| 1965—Tacoma ...........P. C. | C | 90 | 279 | 20 | 67 | 19 | 2 | 3 | 29 | .240 | 491 | 45 | 9 | .983 |
| 1965—San Francisco†..Nat. | C | 6 | 15 | 0 | 1 | 0 | 0 | 0 | 0 | .067 | 34 | 9 | 0 | 1.000 |
| 1966—Chicago ............Nat. | C | 149 | 526 | 50 | 124 | 22 | 3 | 19 | 63 | .236 | 871 | •85 | 14 | .986 |
| 1967—Chicago ............Nat. | C | 152 | 539 | 68 | 144 | 25 | 3 | 14 | 60 | .267 | •865 | 59 | 4 | .996 |
| 1968—Chicago ............Nat. | C | 160 | 553 | 41 | 125 | 18 | 4 | 7 | 65 | .226 | 885 | 81 | 5 | .995 |
| 1969—Chicago ............Nat. | C | 151 | 522 | 67 | 133 | 15 | 1 | 18 | 64 | .255 | 978 | •79 | 8 | .992 |
| 1970—Chicago‡ .........Nat. | C | 73 | 250 | 13 | 61 | 5 | 0 | 7 | 36 | .244 | 455 | 26 | 5 | .990 |
| 1971—Chicago§ .........Nat. | C | 9 | 21 | 1 | 7 | 1 | 0 | 0 | 2 | .333 | 43 | 3 | 1 | .979 |
| 1972—Chicago ............Nat. | C | 114 | 357 | 23 | 78 | 12 | 0 | 5 | 30 | .218 | 569 | 53 | 3 | •.995 |
| 1973—Chicago x .........Nat. | C | 124 | 368 | 35 | 83 | 11 | 1 | 10 | 43 | .226 | 648 | 59 | 5 | .993 |
| 1974—Minnesota y .....Amer. | C | 32 | 88 | 2 | 17 | 2 | 0 | 0 | 3 | .193 | 148 | 17 | 6 | .965 |
| 1975—San Diego ......National | C | 74 | 180 | 7 | 37 | 5 | 1 | 2 | 14 | .206 | 237 | 20 | 8 | .970 |
| 1976—Chicago ............Nat. | C | 13 | 18 | 3 | 3 | 2 | 0 | 0 | 1 | .167 | 22 | 2 | 2 | .923 |
| National League Totals ................. | | 1027 | 3350 | 309 | 796 | 116 | 13 | 82 | 378 | .237 | 5607 | 476 | 55 | .991 |
| American League Totals ................ | | 32 | 88 | 2 | 17 | 2 | 0 | 0 | 3 | .193 | 148 | 17 | 6 | .965 |
| Major League Totals ...................... | | 1059 | 3438 | 311 | 813 | 118 | 13 | 82 | 381 | .236 | 5755 | 493 | 61 | .990 |

†Traded with Pitcher Bill Hands to Chicago Cubs for Pitcher Lindy McDaniel and Outfielder Don Landrum, December 2, 1965.
‡On disabled list April 22 through July 10.
§On disabled list April 15 through May 11 and May 31 through September 15.
xTraded to Minnesota Twins for Catcher George Mitterwald, December 6, 1973.
yReleased, October 25, 1974; signed as free agent by San Diego Padres, April 3, 1975.
zReleased, April 4, 1976; signed as a free agent by Chicago Cubs, April 13, 1976.

### ALL-STAR GAME RECORD

| Year   League | Pos. | AB. | R. | H. | 2B. | 3B. | HR. | RBI. | B.A. | PO. | A. | E. | F.A. |
|---|---|---|---|---|---|---|---|---|---|---|---|---|---|
| 1969—National .............................. | C | 1 | 1 | 0 | 0 | 0 | 0 | 0 | .000 | 3 | 0 | 0 | 1.000 |

Coach, Chicago Cubs, 1977.


## GORDON WILLIAM HUNTER
### (Billy)
### Baltimore Orioles

Born June 4, 1928, at Punxsutawney, Pa.
Height, 5.11. Weight, 190.
Threw and batted righthanded.
Hobby—Sports.
Attended Indiana State Teachers College, Indiana, Pa.

Led Canadian-American League shortstops in double plays with 83 in 1948.
Led Texas League shortstops in double plays with 135 in 1952.
Named Texas League Player of the Year in 1952.

| Year   Club          League | Pos. | G. | AB. | R. | H. | 2B. | 3B. | HR. | RBI. | B.A. | PO. | A. | E. | F.A. |
|---|---|---|---|---|---|---|---|---|---|---|---|---|---|---|
| 1948—Three Rivers ....Ca.-Am. | •S-3 | 138 | 541 | 71 | 132 | 17 | 3 | 4 | 64 | .244 | •264 | 355 | 44 | •.934 |
| 1949—Nashua..............N. Eng. | SS | 95 | 362 | 39 | 85 | 15 | 3 | 1 | 44 | .235 | 146 | 260 | 27 | .938 |
| 1949—Newport News ..Pied. | SS | 12 | 51 | 3 | 11 | 1 | 0 | 0 | 1 | .216 | 28 | 31 | 2 | .967 |
| 1950—Pueblo ..............West. | SS-2B | 137 | 497 | 80 | 125 | 23 | 5 | 5 | 50 | .252 | 282 | 361 | 36 | .947 |
| 1951—Fort Worth ........Tex. | •SS-2B | 141 | 480 | 43 | 121 | 17 | 6 | 1 | 49 | .252 | 245 | 425 | 31 | •.956 |
| 1952—Fort Worth†.......Tex. | •SS-P | 161 | 610 | 81 | 174 | 25 | 5 | 3 | 75 | .285 | •339 | •577 | 32 | .966 |
| 1952—Fort Worth† ......Tex. | •SS-P | 161 | 610 | 81 | 174 | 25 | 5 | 3 | 75 | .285 | •339 | •577 | 32 | .966 |
| 1953—St. Louis ...........Amer. | SS | 154 | 567 | 50 | 124 | 18 | 1 | 1 | 37 | .219 | 284 | •512 | •25 | .970 |
| 1954—Baltimore‡ ........Amer. | SS | 125 | 411 | 28 | 100 | 9 | 5 | 2 | 27 | .243 | 249 | 333 | •32 | .948 |
| 1955—New York..........Amer. | SS | 98 | 255 | 14 | 58 | 7 | 1 | 3 | 20 | .227 | 115 | 249 | 16 | .958 |
| 1955—Denver§ ............A.A. | SS | 13 | 48 | 7 | 16 | 3 | 1 | 0 | 1 | .333 | 20 | 37 | 1 | .983 |
| 1956—New York x .......Amer. | SS-3B | 39 | 75 | 8 | 21 | 3 | 4 | 0 | 11 | .280 | 51 | 64 | 0 | 1.000 |
| 1957—Kansas City .......Amer. | 2-S-3 | 116 | 319 | 39 | 61 | 10 | 4 | 8 | 29 | .191 | 175 | 263 | 18 | .961 |
| 1958—K.C.y-Cleve. ......Amer. | S-2-3 | 98 | 248 | 27 | 46 | 11 | 3 | 2 | 20 | .185 | 148 | 216 | 19 | .950 |
| 1959—San Diego..........P.C. | 2B | 136 | 465 | 51 | 116 | 23 | 3 | 8 | 47 | .249 | 322 | 313 | 11 | •.983 |
| Major League Totals ...................... | | 630 | 1875 | 166 | 410 | 58 | 18 | 16 | 144 | .219 | 1022 | 1637 | 110 | .960 |

†Sold to St. Louis Browns by Brooklyn Dodgers for reported $90,000 and Pitcher Bob Mahoney, Shortstop Stan Rojek and Outfielder Ray Coleman, October 14, 1952.
‡Traded to New York Yankees with Pitchers Mike Blyzka, Don Larsen and Bob Turley, Catcher Darrell Johnson, First Baseman Dick Kryhoski and Outfielders Ted del Guercio and Jim Fridley for Pitchers Harry Byrd, Jim McDonald and Bill Miller, Catchers Hal Smith and Gus Triandos, Second Baseman Don Leppert, Third Baseman Kal Segrist, Shortstop Willie Miranda and Outfielder Gene Woodling. Yankees assigned Blyzka, Johnson, del Guercio and Fridley to their minor league organization. Trade started November 18 with transfer of Byrd, McDonald, Smith, Triandos, Woodling, Larsen, Turley and Hunter—completed December 3, 1954 with assignment of other players.
§Fractured left leg near ankle sliding into second base in game against Omaha, August 19, 1955; out for rest of season.
xTraded to Kansas City Athletics with Pitchers Walter (Rip) Coleman, Tom Morgan and Maury McDermott, Second Baseman Milt Graff and Outfielder Irv Noren for Pitchers Art Ditmar, Bobby Shantz and Jack McMahan, First Baseman Wayne Belardi and Second Baseman Cletis Boyer, February 19, 1957. Commissioner Ford Frick voided Boyer being included in trade, ruling he must complete his bonus term with Athletics. Cletis transferred to Yanks June 4, 1957, and assigned to Binghamton (Western) farm club.
yTraded to Cleveland Indians for Infielder Alfonso Carrasquel, June 12, 1958.

| Year League | Pos. | AB. | R. | H. | 2B. | 3B. | HR. | RBI. | B.A. | PO. | A. | E. | F.A. |
|---|---|---|---|---|---|---|---|---|---|---|---|---|---|
| 1953-American | PR | 0 | 0 | 0 | 0 | 0 | 0 | 0 | .000 | 0 | 0 | 0 | .000 |

### RECORD AS MANAGER

| Year Club | League | Position | W. | L. |
|---|---|---|---|---|
| 1962-Bluefield | Appal. | First | 47 | 23 |
| 1963-Bluefield | Appal. | First | 45 | 24 |

Scout, Cleveland Indians, 1961; coach, Baltimore Orioles, 1964 through 1977.

## ALVIN NEIL JACKSON
### (Jack)
(Named by friends after last name.)
### Boston Red Sox
Born December 25, 1935, at Waco, Tex.
Height, 5.09½. Weight, 163.
Threw and batted lefthanded.
Attended Wiley College, Marshall, Tex., and Paul Quinn College, Waco, Tex.

| Year Club | League | G. | IP. | W. | L. | Pct. | H. | R. | ER. | SO. | BB. | ERA. |
|---|---|---|---|---|---|---|---|---|---|---|---|---|
| 1955-Waco | Big State | 15 | 116 | 8 | 5 | .615 | 102 | 42 | 36 | 88 | 65 | 2.79 |
| 1956-Mexico City Tigers | Mexican | 37 | 207 | 14 | 10 | .583 | 179 | 78 | 66 | 114 | 95 | 2.87 |
| 1957-Columbus | Int'national | 5 | 13 | 0 | 2 | .000 | 14 | 11 | 9 | 10 | 7 | 6.23 |
| 1957-Mexico City Tigers | Mexican | 24 | 84 | 7 | 6 | .538 | 82 | 47 | 36 | 38 | 35 | 3.86 |
| 1957-Lincoln | Western | 3 | 11 | 0 | 1 | .000 | 14 | 9 | 8 | 6 | 14 | 6.55 |
| 1958-Lincoln | Western | 31 | 230 | 18 | 9 | .667 | 189 | 99 | 53 | 162 | 101 | *2.07 |
| 1959-Pittsburgh | National | 8 | 18 | 0 | 0 | .000 | 30 | 14 | 13 | 13 | 8 | 6.50 |
| 1959-Columbus | Int'national | 26 | 162 | 15 | 4 | .789 | 130 | 47 | 42 | 111 | 51 | 2.33 |
| 1960-Columbus | Int'national | 35 | 197 | 10 | 14 | .417 | 159 | 81 | 67 | 122 | 58 | 3.06 |
| 1961-Columbus | Int'national | 31 | 196 | 12 | 7 | .632 | 187 | 80 | 63 | 166 | 44 | 2.89 |
| 1961-Pittsburgh† | National | 3 | 24 | 1 | 0 | 1.000 | 20 | 10 | 9 | 15 | 4 | 3.38 |
| 1962-New York | National | 36 | 231 | 8 | 20 | .286 | 244 | 132 | 113 | 118 | 78 | 4.40 |
| 1963-New York | National | 37 | 227 | 13 | 17 | .433 | 237 | *128 | 100 | 142 | 84 | 3.96 |
| 1964-New York | National | 40 | 213 | 11 | 16 | .407 | 229 | 115 | 101 | 112 | 60 | 4.27 |
| 1965-New York‡ | National | 37 | 205 | 8 | 20 | .286 | 217 | 111 | 99 | 120 | 61 | 4.35 |
| 1966-St. Louis | National | 36 | 233 | 13 | 15 | .464 | 222 | 82 | 65 | 90 | 45 | 2.51 |
| 1967-St. Louis§ | National | 38 | 107 | 9 | 4 | .692 | 117 | 61 | 47 | 43 | 29 | 3.95 |
| 1968-New York | National | 25 | 93 | 3 | 7 | .300 | 88 | 42 | 38 | 59 | 17 | 3.68 |
| 1969-New York x-Cincinnati | National | 42 | 38 | 1 | 0 | 1.000 | 45 | 30 | 29 | 26 | 21 | 6.87 |
| Major League Totals | | 302 | 1386 | 67 | 99 | .404 | 1449 | 725 | 614 | 738 | 407 | 3.99 |

†Selected by New York Mets in National League expansion draft, October 10, 1961.

‡Traded with Third Baseman Charlie Smith to St. Louis Cardinals for Third Baseman Ken Boyer, October 20, 1965.

§Sent to New York Mets, October 13, 1967, to complete deal in which St. Louis Cardinals obtained Pitcher Jack Lamabe, July 16, 1967.

xSold to Cincinnati Reds, June 13, 1969.

yReleased by Cincinnati Reds' organization, April 13, 1970.

### RECORD AS MANAGER

| Year Club | League | Position | W. | L. |
|---|---|---|---|---|
| 1976-Marion | Appal. | Fourth(N) | 28 | 42 |

Minor league pitching instructor, New York Mets, 1976; coach, Boston Red Sox, 1977.

## GROVER WILLIAM JONES, JR.
### (Deacon)
(Father was Deacon in Union Baptist Church-named for this association.)
### Houston Astros
Born April 18, 1934, at White Plains, N. Y.
Height, 5.10. Weight, 190.
Threw right and batted lefthanded.
Hobby-Singing.
Attended Ithaca College, Ithaca, N. Y.; received Bachelor of Science degree in Physiotherapy.

Led Sally League in sacrifice flies with 13 in 1962.
Led Sally League first basemen in double plays with 103 in 1962.

| Year Club | League | Pos. | G. | AB. | R. | H. | 2B. | 3B. | HR. | RBI. | B.A. | PO. | A. | E. | F.A. |
|---|---|---|---|---|---|---|---|---|---|---|---|---|---|---|---|
| 1955-Waterloo | I.I.I. | 2B | 78 | 267 | 64 | 85 | 11 | 7 | 9 | 58 | .318 | 194 | 219 | 18 | .958 |
| 1956-Dubuque | Midw. | *2-1B | 100 | 330 | 105 | 135 | 25 | 6 | 26 | *120 | *.409 | 308 | 209 | 16 | *.970 |
| 1956-Waterloo | I.I.I. | 3B-2B | 18 | 50 | 12 | 12 | 1 | 2 | 0 | 6 | .240 | 28 | 30 | 7 | .982 |
| 1957-58-Colo. Springs | West. | | | | | | (In Military Service) | | | | | | | | |
| 1959-Lincoln | I.I.I. | 1B-2B | 122 | 428 | 92 | 128 | 31 | 2 | 11 | 76 | .299 | 802 | 91 | 18 | .980 |
| 1960-San Diego† | P.C. | IF-OF | 80 | 144 | 25 | 43 | 2 | 4 | 5 | 27 | .299 | 127 | 53 | 7 | .963 |
| 1961-Charleston | Sally | 1B | 132 | 427 | 81 | 121 | 19 | 5 | 13 | 78 | .283 | 1106 | 48 | 16 | .986 |

| Year | Club | League | Pos. | G. | AB. | R. | H. | 2B. | 3B. | HR. | RBI. | B.A. | PO. | A. | E. | F.A. |
|---|---|---|---|---|---|---|---|---|---|---|---|---|---|---|---|---|
| 1962—Savannah | Sally | | 1B | 136 | 499 | 119 | 159 | 30 | 5 | 26 | ★101 | .319 | ★1145 | ★73 | 10 | ★.992 |
| 1962—Chicago | Amer. | | 1B | 18 | 28 | 3 | 9 | 2 | 0 | 0 | 8 | .321 | 46 | 4 | 2 | .962 |
| 1963—Chicago | Amer. | | 1B | 17 | 16 | 4 | 3 | 0 | 1 | 1 | 2 | .183 | 6 | 1 | 0 | 1.000 |
| 1963—Indianapolis | Int. | | 1B | 97 | 338 | 64 | 116 | 17 | 3 | 19 | 73 | .343 | 766 | 44 | 7 | .991 |
| 1964—Indianapolis | Int. | | 1B | 49 | 163 | 26 | 31 | 7 | 2 | 3 | 17 | .190 | 387 | 33 | 2 | .995 |
| 1964—Lynchburg | South. | | 1B | 86 | 311 | 53 | 93 | 20 | 2 | 11 | 62 | .299 | 768 | 52 | 8 | .990 |
| 1965—Sarasota‡ | Fla. St. | | 1B-2B | 100 | 320 | 48 | 104 | 15 | 8 | 8 | 59 | .325 | 527 | 128 | 12 | .981 |
| 1966—Fox Cities§ | Midw. | | 1B-OF | 114 | 368 | 77 | 130 | ★36 | 4 | 18 | ★80 | ★.353 | 554 | 53 | 12 | .981 |
| 1966—Chicago | Amer. | | PH | 5 | 5 | 0 | 2 | 0 | 0 | 0 | 0 | .400 | .... | .... | .... | .... |
| 1967—Appleton§x | Midw. | | OF-1B | 45 | 122 | 31 | 43 | 13 | 0 | 5 | 20 | .352 | 89 | 9 | 0 | 1.000 |
| Major League Totals | | | | 40 | 49 | 7 | 14 | 2 | 1 | 1 | 10 | .286 | 52 | 5 | 2 | .966 |

†On disabled list, July 4 to July 16, 1960.
‡On disabled list, July 6 to July 27, 1965.
§Player-coach.
xOn disabled list, June 20 to July 14, 1967. Released by Chicago White Sox' organization, September 30, 1967.

### RECORD AS MANAGER

| Year | Club | League | Position | W. | L. |
|---|---|---|---|---|---|
| 1973—Appleton | | Midwest | Fifth(N) | 17 | 41 |
| (Second Half) | | | Fifth(N) | 27 | 35 |

Scout and minor league instructor, Chicago White Sox, 1968 through 1972 and 1974 and 1975; coach, Houston Astros, 1976 and 1977.

## THEODORE BERNARD KLUSZEWSKI
Name pronounced Kluh-ZOO-skee.
### (Ted)
### Cincinnati Reds

Born, September 10, 1924, at Argo, Ill.
Height, 6.02. Weight, 240.
Threw and batted lefthanded.
Hobbies—Golf and fishing.
Attended University of Indiana, Bloomington, Ind.

Established major league record for first basemen by leading in fielding five consctive seasons, 1955; tied major league records for fewest triples, season (150 or more games), 0, 1955; set National League records for most consecutive games scoring runs (17), August 27-September 13, 1954, inclusive, and most home runs, season, at home grounds, 34, in 1954; tied National League records for most home runs, season, for runner-up in home runs, 47, 1955, and most home runs, one week (Sunday through Saturday), 8, July 1, first game, through July 7, 1956, 7 games; led N. L. first basemen in double plays, 1953-54-55-56, tying Frank McCormick's (Cincinnati Reds, 1939-40-41-42) major league mark.

Hit three home runs in a game, first game, July 1, 1956.

Named as first baseman on THE SPORTING NEWS All-Star Major League Teams, 1954-55-56.

| Year | Club | League | Pos. | G. | AB. | R. | H. | 2B. | 3B. | HR. | RBI. | B.A. | PO. | A. | E. | F.A. |
|---|---|---|---|---|---|---|---|---|---|---|---|---|---|---|---|---|
| 1946—Columbia | Sally | | 1B-OF | 90 | 335 | 59 | 118 | 24 | 5 | 11 | 87 | ★.352 | 525 | 20 | 15 | .973 |
| 1947—Cincinnati | Nat. | | 1B | 9 | 10 | 1 | 1 | 0 | 0 | 0 | 2 | .100 | 10 | 0 | 0 | 1.000 |
| 1947—Memphis | South. | | 1B | 115 | 427 | 80 | 161 | 32 | 9 | 7 | 68 | ★.377 | 931 | 60 | 19 | .981 |
| 1948—Cincinnati | Nat. | | 1B | 113 | 379 | 49 | 104 | 23 | 4 | 12 | 57 | .274 | 833 | 65 | 9 | .990 |
| 1949—Cincinnati | Nat. | | 1B | 136 | 531 | 63 | 164 | 26 | 2 | 8 | 68 | .309 | 1140 | 65 | 14 | .989 |
| 1950—Cincinnati | Nat. | | 1B | 134 | 538 | 76 | 165 | 37 | 0 | 25 | 111 | .307 | 1123 | 61 | 15 | .987 |
| 1951—Cincinnati | Nat. | | 1B | 154 | 607 | 74 | 157 | 35 | 2 | 13 | 77 | .259 | ★1381 | 88 | 5 | ★.997 |
| 1952—Cincinnati | Nat. | | 1B | 135 | 497 | 62 | 159 | 24 | 11 | 16 | 86 | .320 | 1121 | 66 | 8 | ★.993 |
| 1953—Cincinnati | Nat. | | 1B | 149 | 570 | 97 | 180 | 25 | 0 | 40 | 108 | .316 | 1285 | 58 | 7 | ★.995 |
| 1954—Cincinnati | Nat. | | 1B | 149 | 573 | 104 | 187 | 28 | 3 | ★49 | ★141 | .326 | 1237 | 101 | 5 | ★.996 |
| 1955—Cincinnati | Nat. | | 1B | 153 | 612 | 116 | ★192 | 25 | 0 | 47 | 113 | .314 | ★1388 | 86 | 8 | ★.995 |
| 1956—Cincinnati | Nat. | | 1B | 138 | 517 | 91 | 156 | 14 | 1 | 35 | 102 | .302 | 1166 | 89 | 13 | .990 |
| 1957—Cincinnati† | Nat. | | 1B | 69 | 127 | 12 | 34 | 7 | 0 | 6 | 21 | .268 | 161 | 15 | 2 | .989 |
| 1958—Pittsburgh | Nat. | | 1B | 100 | 301 | 29 | 88 | 13 | 4 | 4 | 37 | .292 | 591 | 36 | 4 | .994 |
| 1959—Pittsburgh‡ | Nat. | | 1B | 60 | 122 | 11 | 32 | 10 | 1 | 2 | 17 | .262 | 151 | 12 | 0 | 1.000 |
| 1959—Chicago | Amer. | | 1B | 31 | 101 | 11 | 30 | 2 | 1 | 2 | 10 | .297 | 220 | 10 | 0 | 1.000 |
| 1960—Chicago§ | Amer. | | 1B | 81 | 181 | 20 | 53 | 9 | 0 | 5 | 39 | .293 | 325 | 19 | 1 | .997 |
| 1961—Los Angeles | Amer. | | 1B | 107 | 263 | 32 | 64 | 12 | 0 | 15 | 39 | .243 | 520 | 28 | 6 | .989 |
| American League Totals | | | | 219 | 545 | 63 | 147 | 23 | 1 | 22 | 88 | .270 | 1065 | 57 | 7 | .994 |
| National League Totals | | | | 1499 | 5384 | 785 | 1619 | 267 | 28 | 257 | 940 | .301 | 11587 | 742 | 90 | .993 |
| Major League Totals | | | | 1718 | 5929 | 848 | 1766 | 290 | 29 | 279 | 1028 | .298 | 12652 | 799 | 97 | .993 |

†Traded to Pittsburgh Pirates for First Baseman Dee Fondy, December 28, 1957.
‡Released to Chicago White Sox in waiver deal for Infielder Bob Sagers and Outfielder-First Baseman Harry Simpson, August 25, 1959. Sagers, playing for Indianapolis, American Association, transferred to Columbus, International League, at close of season.
§Selected in expansion draft by Los Angeles Angels, December 14, 1960.

### WORLD SERIES RECORD

Established World's Series record for most runs batted in six-game Series (10), 1959; this ten RBIs ties mark for Series of any length; tied Series standard for most runs batted in, game (5), October 1, 1959.

| Year | Club | League | Pos. | G. | AB. | R. | H. | 2B. | 3B. | HR. | RBI. | B.A. | PO. | A. | E. | F.A. |
|---|---|---|---|---|---|---|---|---|---|---|---|---|---|---|---|---|
| 1959—Chicago | Amer. | | 1B | 6 | 23 | 5 | 9 | 1 | 0 | 3 | 10 | .391 | 59 | 3 | 0 | 1.000 |

| Year League | Pos. | AB. | R. | H. | 2B. | 3B. | HR. | RBI. | B.A. | PO. | A. | E. | F.A. |
|---|---|---|---|---|---|---|---|---|---|---|---|---|---|
| 1953—National ............................ | 1B | 3 | 0 | 1 | 0 | 0 | 0 | 0 | .333 | 5 | 0 | 0 | 1.000 |
| 1954—National ............................ | 1B | 4 | 2 | 2 | 0 | 0 | 1 | 3 | .500 | 5 | 0 | 0 | 1.000 |
| 1955—National ............................ | 1B | 5 | 1 | 2 | 1 | 0 | 0 | 0 | .400 | 9 | 2 | 0 | 1.000 |
| 1956—National ............................ | 1B | 2 | 1 | 2 | 2 | 0 | 0 | 1 | 1.000 | 2 | 0 | 0 | 1.000 |
| All-Star Game Totals ........................ | | 14 | 4 | 7 | 3 | 0 | 1 | 4 | .500 | 21 | 2 | 0 | 1.000 |

Coach, Cincinnati Reds, 1970 through 1977.

# ROBERT FRANK KNOOP

Name pronounced "K-NOP."

## (Bobby)

## Chicago White Sox

Born October 18, 1938, at Sioux City, Ia.
Height, 6.01. Weight, 183.
Threw and batted righthanded.
Hobby—Golf.

Established major league records for most double plays, game, 9 innings, second baseman (6), May 1, 1966, and most putouts, 9 innings, second baseman (12), August 30, 1966.

Tied major league record for most double plays, second baseman, double-header (8), May 1, 1966, (first game).

Tied major league record for most games, rookie season (162), 1964.

Led Texas League second basemen in double plays with 128 in 1959 and Pacific Coast League second basemen with 97 in 1963.

Led American League second basemen in double plays with 123 in 1964, 135 in 1966, 91 in 1967 and 94 in 1968.

Named second baseman on THE SPORTING NEWS American League All-Star fielding teams, 1966-67-68.

| Year Club League | Pos. | G. | AB. | R. | H. | 2B. | 3B. | HR. | RBI. | B.A. | PO. | A. | E. | F.A. |
|---|---|---|---|---|---|---|---|---|---|---|---|---|---|---|
| 1956—Leesburg ..........Fla. St. | 2B | 42 | 137 | 12 | 26 | 6 | 1 | 1 | 9 | .190 | 78 | 83 | 10 | .942 |
| 1957—Lawton..............Soo. St. | 2B | 125 | 471 | 61 | 123 | 22 | 4 | 11 | 67 | .261 | •321 | •324 | 26 | •.961 |
| 1958—Cedar Rapids ....I.I.I. | 2B | 121 | 417 | 63 | 114 | 22 | 1 | 7 | 61 | .273 | 265 | 269 | 24 | •.957 |
| 1959—Austin ..............Tex. | 2B •146 | 549 | 44 | 145 | 23 | 7 | 3 | 72 | .264 | •395 | •390 | •30 | .963 | | |
| 1960—Louisville ..........A. A. | 2B | 19 | 72 | 5 | 17 | 2 | 1 | 0 | 2 | .236 | 33 | 50 | 1 | .988 |
| 1960—Austin ..............Tex. | 2B | 88 | 332 | 47 | 93 | 17 | 2 | 5 | 35 | .280 | 209 | 243 | 14 | .970 |
| 1961—San Diego-Van ..P. C. | IN-OF | 114 | 290 | 27 | 58 | 14 | 2 | 4 | 23 | .200 | 211 | 205 | 13 | .970 |
| 1962—Toronto ...........Int. | PH | 7 | 7 | 0 | 0 | 0 | 0 | 0 | 0 | .000 | 0 | 0 | 0 | .000 |
| 1962—Hawaii ..............P. C. | 2B | 95 | 320 | 41 | 84 | 12 | 1 | 11 | 43 | .263 | 212 | 238 | 12 | .974 |
| 1963—Hawaii† ...........P. C. | •2B-SS | 146 | 555 | 72 | 157 | 19 | 1 | 20 | 67 | .283 | 331 | •449 | •29 | .952 |
| 1964—Los Angeles ......Amer. | 2B | 162 | 486 | 42 | 105 | 8 | 1 | 7 | 38 | .216 | 357 | •522 | •20 | .978 |
| 1965—California .........Amer. | 2B | 142 | 465 | 47 | 125 | 24 | 4 | 7 | 43 | .269 | 331 | 402 | •22 | .971 |
| 1966—California .........Amer. | 2B | 161 | 590 | 54 | 137 | 18 | •11 | 17 | 72 | .232 | •381 | •488 | 17 | •.981 |
| 1967—California .........Amer. | 2B | 159 | 511 | 51 | 125 | 18 | 5 | 9 | 38 | .245 | •376 | 392 | 11 | .986 |
| 1968—California .........Amer. | 2B | 152 | 494 | 48 | 123 | 20 | 4 | 3 | 39 | .249 | 350 | 425 | 15 | .981 |
| 1969—Calif.‡-Chi. .......P. C. | •2B-SS | 146 | 555 | 72 | 157 | 19 | 1 | 20 | 67 | .283 | 331 | •449 | •29 | .964 |
| 1970—Chicago§ ..........Amer. | 2B | 130 | 402 | 34 | 92 | 13 | 2 | 5 | 36 | .229 | 276 | 403 | 11 | .984 |
| 1971—Kansas City x......Amer. | 2B | 72 | 161 | 14 | 33 | 8 | 1 | 1 | 11 | .205 | 89 | 120 | 7 | .968 |
| 1972—Kansas City ......Amer. | 2B | 44 | 97 | 8 | 23 | 5 | 0 | 0 | 7 | .237 | 61 | 80 | 4 | .972 |
| Major League Totals ...................... | | 1153 | 3622 | 337 | 856 | 129 | 29 | 56 | 331 | .236 | 2556 | 3218 | 119 | .980 |

†Drafted by Los Angeles Angels from Denver (Milwaukee Braves' organization), December 2, 1963.
‡Traded to Chicago White Sox for Infielder Sandy Alomar and Pitcher Bob Priddy, May 14, 1969.
§Sold to Kansas City Royals, March 24, 1971.
xReleased by Kansas City Royals' organization, October 5, 1972.

| Year League | Pos. | AB. | R. | H. | 2B. | 3B. | HR. | RBI. | B.A. | PO. | A. | E. | F.A. |
|---|---|---|---|---|---|---|---|---|---|---|---|---|---|---|
| 1966—American ............................ | 2B | 2 | 0 | 0 | 0 | 0 | 0 | 0 | .000 | 3 | 1 | 0 | 1.000 |

### RECORD AS MANAGER

| Year Club | League | Position | W. | L. |
|---|---|---|---|---|
| 1975—Quad Cities ........Midwest | | First(S) | 35 | 25 |
| (Second Half) | | †First(S) | 43 | 22 |
| 1976—El Paso.............Texas | | Second(W) | 77 | 56 |

†Lost playoff for League Championship to Waterloo, two games to none.

Minor League Instructor, Calfiornia Angels, part of 1975; coach, Chicago White Sox, 1977.

# FRED CARL KOENIG

Name pronounced CAIN-eg.

## Texas Rangers

Born April 27, 1931, at St. Louis, Mo.
Height, 6.03. Weight, 200.
Threw and batted righthanded.
Attended University of Illinois, Champaign, Ill.

Led Eastern League first basemen in double plays with 124 in 1954.

| Year Club | League | Pos. | G. | AB. | R. | H. | 2B. | 3B. | HR. | RBI. | B.A. | PO. | A. | E. | F.A. |
|---|---|---|---|---|---|---|---|---|---|---|---|---|---|---|---|
| 1951—Hamilton ..........Pony | 1B | 67 | 235 | 31 | 60 | 14 | 2 | 5 | 39 | .255 | 365 | 19 | 12 | .967 |
| 1951—Paducah ...........Kitty | 1B | 29 | 111 | 14 | 29 | 8 | 2 | 2 | 14 | .261 | 199 | 6 | 6 | .972 |
| 1952—Allentown ......Inter. St. | 1B | 15 | 50 | 8 | 12 | 2 | 0 | 0 | 11 | .240 | 126 | 2 | 1 | .992 |
| 1952—Paducah ...........Kitty | 1B | 92 | 358 | 81 | 103 | 24 | 7 | 15 | 90 | .288 | 695 | 41 | 11 | .985 |
| 1953—St. Joseph ........W. A. | 1B | 136 | 486 | 81 | 134 | 32 | 11 | 5 | 81 | .276 | 1102 | 69 | 19 | .984 |
| 1954—Allentown ........East. | 1B | 136 | 484 | 68 | 139 | 28 | 4 | 11 | 83 | .287*1193 | | 78 | 20 | .985 |
| 1955—Omaha ..............A. A. | 1B-OF | 32 | 89 | 14 | 22 | 5 | 0 | 3 | 21 | .247 | 107 | 2 | 2 | .982 |
| 1955—Columbus .........Sally | 1B | 80 | 295 | 38 | 85 | 11 | 1 | 11 | 36 | .288 | 630 | 50 | 13 | .981 |
| 1956—Allentown ........East. | 3B-OF | 112 | 389 | 47 | 93 | 14 | 5 | 11 | 62 | .239 | 99 | 103 | 25 | .900 |
| 1957—Winston-Salem ..Carol. | O-3-1 | 78 | 266 | 49 | 66 | 20 | 4 | 5 | 42 | .248 | 234 | 52 | 9 | .969 |
| 1957—Columbus .........Sally | 3B | 62 | 221 | 41 | 58 | 12 | 2 | 6 | 44 | .262 | 55 | 101 | 16 | .907 |
| 1958—York ...............East. | 3-O-1 | 102 | 334 | 42 | 100 | 14 | 5 | 9 | 58 | .299 | 199 | 75 | 11 | .961 |
| 1959—Omaha ..............A. A. | 3B | 16 | 49 | 4 | 10 | 2 | 0 | 1 | 10 | .204 | 9 | 20 | 3 | .906 |
| 1959—Tulsa ...............Texas | IF-OF | 19 | 66 | 5 | 16 | 1 | 0 | 1 | 5 | .242 | .... | .... | .... | .... |
| 1959—York ...............East. | 1-O-3 | 72 | 264 | 42 | 71 | 14 | 4 | 8 | 26 | .269 | 305 | 55 | 18 | .952 |
| 1960—Tulsa ...............Tex. | O-1-3 | 101 | 271 | 53 | 80 | 18 | 0 | 10 | 31 | .295 | 181 | 33 | 8 | .964 |
| 1961—Tulsa† .............Texas | IF-OF | 90 | 275 | 41 | 74 | 18 | 5 | 12 | 45 | .260 | 212 | 99 | 15 | .954 |
| 1962—Winnipeg†.........North. | 1B | 44 | 98 | 25 | 36 | 10 | 3 | 4 | 23 | .367 | 78 | 6 | 1 | .988 |
| 1963—Winnipeg‡.........North. | .... | 10 | 14 | 3 | 4 | 0 | 0 | 0 | 2 | .286 | .... | .... | .... | .... |

†Released by St. Louis Cardinals' organization, December 9, 1961.
‡Player-manager.

## RECORD AS MANAGER

| Year Club | League | Position | W. | L. | Year Club | League | Position | W. | L. |
|---|---|---|---|---|---|---|---|---|---|
| 1962—Winnipeg ...........Northern | Seventh | 59 | 63 | | 1968—Quad Cities ........Midwest | †First | 35 | 19 |
| 1963—Winnipeg ...........Northern | Fourth | 55 | 64 | | (Second Half) | ‡Sixth | 30 | 31 |
| 1964—Sarasota Cards ..Rookie | Second | 30 | 30 | | 1969—Quad Cities ........Midwest | ‡§First | 35 | 19 |
| 1965—Idaho Falls ........Pioneer | Fourth | 31 | 35 | | (Second Half) | Seventh | 29 | 38 |
| 1967—Quad Cities ........Midwest | Third | 35 | 23 | | 1972—Arkansas ...........Texas | Third(E) | 65 | 74 |
| (Second Half) | Third | 34 | 28 | | 1975—Sarasota Cards ..G. C. | Seventh | 17 | 35 |

†Won playoff against Decatur (Second Half winner), two games to one.
‡Tied for position.
§Appleton defeated Quad Cities in regularly-scheduled game of July 16 and was declared First Half champion by league president.

Coach, California Angels, 1970 and 1971; Director of Player Development, St. Louis Cardinals, 1973 and 1974; coach, St. Louis Cardinals, 1976; Texas Rangers, 1977.

## JOHN THOMAS KROL
### (Jack)
### St. Louis Cardinals
Born July 5, 1936, at Chicago, Ill.
Height, 5.11. Weight, 175.
Threw and batted righthanded.

| Year Club | League | Pos. | G. | AB. | R. | H. | 2B. | 3B. | HR. | RBI. | B.A. | PO. | A. | E. | F.A. |
|---|---|---|---|---|---|---|---|---|---|---|---|---|---|---|---|
| 1954—Ardmore ..........Soo. St. | 3B | 139 | 578 | 131 | 162 | 22 | 5 | 16 | 92 | .280 | 141 | 292 | *56 | .886 |
| 1955—Ardmore ..........Soo. St. | SS-3B | 140 | 534 | 104 | 147 | 31 | 5 | 19 | 77 | .275 | 218 | 305 | 56 | .903 |
| 1956—Fresno .............Calif. | SS | 131 | 503 | 97 | 144 | 24 | 7 | 8 | 79 | .286 | 191 | 368 | *72 | .886 |
| 1957—Winston-Salem ..Carol. | SS | 133 | 503 | 64 | 139 | 28 | 1 | 15 | 72 | .276 | *249 | 345 | *59 | .910 |
| 1958—York ...............East. | 2B-SS | 127 | 458 | 65 | 111 | 17 | 9 | 12 | 62 | .242 | 279 | 314 | 30 | .952 |
| 1959—York ...............East. | 2-3-S | 119 | 453 | 65 | 121 | 18 | 5 | 11 | 49 | .267 | 235 | 278 | 28 | .948 |
| 1960—Memphis .........S. A. | 3-2-S | 122 | 362 | 51 | 103 | 25 | 2 | 3 | 43 | .285 | 148 | 174 | 33 | .910 |
| 1961—Lancaster.........East. | 2B | 109 | 369 | 55 | 92 | 23 | 4 | 12 | 50 | .249 | 216 | 213 | ●23 | .949 |
| 1962—Portsmouth†......S. Atl. | 2B-3B | 120 | 401 | 54 | 99 | 20 | 0 | 13 | 55 | .247 | 218 | 247 | *27 | .945 |
| 1963—Charlotte‡ ........S. Atl. | 2B-1B | 101 | 342 | 45 | 84 | 13 | 1 | 11 | 55 | .246 | 220 | 172 | 15 | .963 |
| 1964—York§ ..............East. | 2B | 99 | 320 | 49 | 79 | 12 | 1 | 13 | 45 | .247 | 270 | 235 | 19 | .964 |
| 1965—Burlington x .....Carol. | 2B | 133 | 446 | 70 | 123 | 22 | 0 | 12 | 54 | .276 | *332 | 332 | 22 | .968 |
| 1966—Rock Hill y .......W. Car. | PH | 1 | 2 | 2 | 2 | 1 | 0 | 0 | 1 | 1.000 | .... | .... | .... | .... |

†Released, December 4, 1962; signed as free agent by Minnesota Twins' organization, April 17, 1963.
‡Released, April 13, 1964; signed as free agent by Washington Senators' organization, April 22, 1964.
§On disabled list, August 17 through September 28, 1964.
xUnconditionally released, January 24, 1976.
yPlayer-manager.

## RECORD AS MANAGER

| Year Club | League | Position | W. | L. | Year Club | League | Position | W. | L. |
|---|---|---|---|---|---|---|---|---|---|
| 1966—Rock Hill...........W. Carol. | Third | 42 | 24 | | 1971—Arkansas...........Texas | ‡First(C) | 75 | 64 |
| (Second Half) | Eighth | 16 | 44 | | 1972—Tulsa.................A. A. | Second(W) | 78 | 62 |
| 1967—Cedar Rapids......Midwest | †Sixth | 27 | 31 | | 1973—Tulsa.................A. A. | §First(W) | 68 | 67 |
| (Second Half) | Ninth | 26 | 36 | | 1974—Little Rock ........Texas | Second(E) | 75 | 59 |
| 1968—Cedar Rapids......Midwest | Second | 32 | 22 | | 1975—St. Petersburg ....Fla. St. | xFirst(N) | 88 | 47 |
| (Second Half) | Fifth | 31 | 31 | | 1976—Little Rock ........Texas | Fourth(E) | 59 | 76 |
| 1969—St. Petersburg ....Fla. St. | Sixth(C) | 54 | 76 | | | | | |
| 1970—Modesto ...........Calif. | †Third | 38 | 32 | | | | | |
| (Second Half) | Fourth | 38 | 32 | | | | | |

†Tied for position.
‡Lost Dixie Series to Charlotte, 3 games to none.
§Won playoff by defeating Iowa, four games to three.
xWon semi-final playoff by defeating Key West, two games to one; won playoff by defeating Tampa, three games to two.

Minor league instructor, St. Louis Cardinals, 1966 through 1976; coach, St. Louis Cardinals, 1977.

# KARL OTTO KUEHL
Name pronounced KEEL.
## Minnesota Twins

Born September 5, 1937, at Monterey Park, Calif.
Height, 5.11. Weight, 175.
Threw and batted lefthanded.

Led Northwest League first basemen in double plays with 102 in 1957.
Led New York-Pennsylvania League first basemen in double plays with 84 in 1961.

| Year | Club | League | Pos. | G. | AB. | R. | H. | 2B. | 3B. | HR. | RBI. | B.A. | PO. | A. | E. | F.A. |
|---|---|---|---|---|---|---|---|---|---|---|---|---|---|---|---|---|
| 1955—Ogden† | | Pion. | 1B | 76 | 310 | 67 | 106 | 16 | 2 | 4 | 37 | .342 | 679 | 31 | 12 | .983 |
| 1956—H.P.-Tho'ville | ....Carol. | | OF-1B | •154 | •613 | 103 | 178 | 27 | 2 | 10 | 45 | .290 | 736 | 42 | 27 | .966 |
| 1957—Salem | | Northw. | 1B | 129 | 435 | 93 | 151 | •31 | 6 | 3 | 86 | •.347 | 1024 | 48 | 14 | .987 |
| 1957—Seattle | | P. C. | .... | 10 | 19 | 2 | 5 | 1 | 0 | 0 | 2 | .263 | figures unavailable | | | |
| 1958—Savannah | | Sally | .... | 18 | 29 | 6 | 7 | 1 | 0 | 1 | 9 | .241 | figures unavailable | | | |
| 1958—Albuquerque | | West. | 1B | 113 | 390 | 76 | 106 | 6 | 10 | 1 | 25 | .272 | 945 | 65 | 19 | .982 |
| 1959—Salem§ | | Northw. | •1-O-P | 128 | 411 | 77 | 110 | 18 | •9 | 3 | 34 | .268 | 883 | 38 | 12 | •.987 |
| 1960—Salme§x | | Northw. | 1-O-P | 113 | 332 | 65 | 114 | 14 | 4 | 6 | 56 | .343 | 589 | 35 | 7 | .989 |
| 1961—Geneva§y | | NYP | •1B-P | 97 | 270 | 80 | 85 | 12 | 4 | 19 | 83 | .315 | 687 | 40 | 7 | •.990 |
| 1962—Geneva§z | | NYP | 1B | 22 | 67 | 18 | 18 | 3 | 2 | 2 | 10 | .269 | 88 | 5 | 2 | .979 |

†On disabled list, August 1 through remainder of season.
‡Released by Cincinnati Reds' organization, March 6, 1959.
§Player-manager.
xOn temporary inactive list, April 30 to May 10, 1960. On disabled list, May 20 to May 30, 1960.
yOn disabled list, May 28 to June 23, 1961.
zOn disabled list, May 27 to August 31, 1962.

### PITCHING RECORD

| Year | Club | League | G. | IP. | W. | L. | Pct. | H. | R. | ER. | SO. | BB. | ERA. |
|---|---|---|---|---|---|---|---|---|---|---|---|---|---|
| 1959—Salem§ | | Northwest | 2 | .... | 0 | 0 | .000 | .... | .... | .... | .... | .... | ...... |
| 1960—Salem§x | | Northwest | 6 | .... | 0 | 0 | .000 | .... | .... | .... | .... | .... | ...... |
| 1961—Geneva§y | | NYP | 4 | .... | 0 | 0 | .000 | .... | .... | .... | .... | .... | ...... |

### RECORD AS MANAGER

| Year | Club | League | Position | W. | L. | Year | Club | League | Position | W. | L. |
|---|---|---|---|---|---|---|---|---|---|---|---|
| 1959—Salem | | Northwest | †First | 43 | 26 | 1970—Clinton | | Midwest | xNinth | 26 | 37 |
| (Second Half) | | | Sixth | 30 | 41 | 1972—Quebec City | | Eastern | Third(N) | 75 | 64 |
| 1960—Salem | | Northwest | Fifth | 22 | 44 | 1973—Quebec City | | Eastern | Fourth(N) | 65 | 72 |
| (Second Half) | | | Fifth | 34 | 42 | 1974—Memphis | | Int. | yFirst(S) | 87 | 55 |
| 1961—Geneva | | NYP | ‡First | 77 | 48 | 1975—Memphis | | Int. | Fifth | 65 | 75 |
| 1962—Geneva | | NYP | Sixth | 44 | 74 | 1976—Montreal z | | National | Sixth(E) | 43 | 85 |
| 1969—Clinton | | Midwest | §Second | 42 | 28 | | | | | | |

†Lost playoff to Yakima (Second Half Winner), four games to one.
‡Lost playoff semifinal series to Olean, two games to one.
§Replaced Sibby Sisti, August 2. Replaced by Tom Giordano, August 25. Record is for complete Second Half of season.
xReplaced Earl Torgeson at close of First Half of season.
yLost league championship playoff to Rochester, four games to two.
zReplaced by Charlie Fox, September 4, 1976.

Scout, Houston Colt .45s and Houston Astros, 1963 through part of 1968; scout, Seattle-Milwaukee franchise, part of 1968 through part of 1971; scout, Montreal Expos, part of 1971; coach, Minnesota Twins, 1977.

# HARVEY EDWARD KUENN
Name pronounced Keen.
## Milwaukee Brewers

Born December 4, 1930, at West Allis, Wis.
Height, 6.02. Weight, 200.
Threw and batted righthanded.
Hobby—Bowling.
Attended University of Wisconsin, Madison, Wis.

Tied major league record by making 200 or more hits in his first full season in the major leagues; broke Johnny Tobin's (St. Louis Browns, 1921) mark of most times at-bat, season (679), 1953; tied A. L. record by making two long hits in an inning, first inning, July 20, 1954, first game; tied major league record for most two-base hits, inning (2), July 24, 1964.

Named American League Rookie of the Year by the Baseball Writers' Association and THE SPORTING NEWS, 1953.

Named as shortstop on THE SPORTING NEWS All-Star Major League Team, 1956.

Received reported $55,000 bonus to sign with Detroit Tigers, 1952.

| Year | Club | League | Pos. | G. | AB. | R. | H. | 2B. | 3B. | HR. | RBI. | B.A. | PO. | A. | E. | F.A. |
|---|---|---|---|---|---|---|---|---|---|---|---|---|---|---|---|---|
| 1952—Davenport | | I.I.I. | SS | 63 | 256 | 46 | 87 | 17 | 3 | 1 | 40 | .340 | 114 | 194 | 26 | .922 |
| 1952—Detroit | | Amer. | SS | 19 | 80 | 2 | 26 | 2 | 2 | 0 | 8 | .325 | 44 | 57 | 4 | .962 |
| 1953—Detroit | | Amer. | SS | 155 | •679 | 94 | •209 | 33 | 7 | 2 | 48 | .308 | •308 | 441 | 21 | .973 |
| 1954—Detroit | | Amer. | SS | •155 | •656 | 81 | •201 | 28 | 6 | 5 | 48 | .306 | •294 | •496 | 28 | .966 |
| 1955—Detroit | | Amer. | SS | 145 | 620 | 101 | 190 | •38 | 5 | 8 | 62 | .306 | 253 | 378 | 29 | .956 |
| 1956—Detroit | | Amer. | •SS-O | 146 | 591 | 96 | •196 | 32 | 7 | 12 | 88 | .332 | 219 | 388 | 20 | •.968 |
| 1957—Detroit | | Amer. | •S-3-1B | 151 | 624 | 74 | 173 | 30 | 6 | 9 | 44 | .277 | 251 | 387 | •30 | .955 |
| 1958—Detroit | | Amer. | OF | 139 | 561 | 73 | 179 | •39 | 3 | 8 | 54 | .319 | •358 | 9 | 6 | .984 |

| Year Club League | Pos. | G. | AB. | R. | H. | 2B. | 3B. | HR. | RBI. | B.A. | PO. | A. | E. | F.A. |
|---|---|---|---|---|---|---|---|---|---|---|---|---|---|---|
| 1959–Detroit† ...........Amer. | OF | 139 | 561 | 99 | •198 | •42 | 7 | 9 | 71 | •.353 | 247 | 6 | 3 | .988 |
| 1960–Cleveland‡ ........Amer. | OF-3B | 126 | 474 | 65 | 146 | 24 | 0 | 9 | 54 | .308 | 222 | 13 | 9 | .963 |
| 1961–San Francisco ..Nat. | O-3-S | 131 | 471 | 60 | 125 | 22 | 4 | 5 | 46 | .265 | 190 | 43 | 10 | .959 |
| 1962–San Francisco ..Nat. | OF-3B | 130 | 487 | 73 | 148 | 23 | 5 | 10 | 68 | .304 | 180 | 47 | 8 | .966 |
| 1963–San Francisco ..Nat. | OF-3B | 120 | 417 | 61 | 121 | 13 | 2 | 6 | 31 | .290 | 115 | 60 | 13 | .931 |
| 1964–San Francisco ..Nat. | OF-1-3 | 111 | 351 | 42 | 92 | 16 | 2 | 4 | 22 | .262 | 136 | 9 | 6 | .960 |
| 1965–S.F.§-Chicago ....Nat. | OF-1B | 77 | 179 | 15 | 40 | 5 | 0 | 0 | 12 | .223 | 81 | 8 | 3 | .967 |
| 1966–Chi. x-Phila. y ..Nat. | OF-1-3 | 89 | 162 | 15 | 48 | 9 | 0 | 0 | 15 | .296 | 130 | 3 | 1 | .993 |
| American League Totals ................ | | 1175 | 4846 | 685 | 1518 | 268 | 43 | 62 | 477 | .313 | 2196 | 2175 | 150 | .967 |
| National League Totals ................. | | 658 | 2067 | 266 | 574 | 88 | 13 | 25 | 184 | .278 | 832 | 170 | 41 | .961 |
| Major League Totals ..................... | | 1833 | 6913 | 951 | 2092 | 356 | 56 | 87 | 671 | .303 | 3028 | 2345 | 191 | .966 |

†Traded to Cleveland Indians for Outfielder Rocky Colavito, April 17, 1960.

‡Traded to San Francisco Giants for Pitcher Johnny Antonelli and Outfielder Willie Kirkland, December 3, 1960.

§Traded with Catcher Ed Bailey and Pitcher Bob Hendley to Chicago Cubs for Catcher Dick Bertell and First Baseman-Outfielder Len Gabrielson, May 29, 1965.

xSold to Philadelphia Phillies, April 23, 1966.

yReleased by Philadelphia Phillies, October 7, 1966.

## WORLD SERIES RECORD

Tied World Series mark for most putouts, game, by left fielder (6), October 4, 1962.

| Year Club League | Pos. | G. | AB. | R. | H. | 2B. | 3B. | HR. | RBI. | B.A. | PO. | A. | E. | F.A. |
|---|---|---|---|---|---|---|---|---|---|---|---|---|---|---|
| 1962–San Francisco ..Nat. | OF | 4 | 12 | 1 | 1 | 0 | 0 | 0 | 0 | .083 | 11 | 0 | 0 | 1.000 |

## ALL-STAR GAME RECORD

| Year League | Pos. | AB. | R. | H. | 2B. | 3B. | HR. | RBI. | B.A. | PO. | A. | E. | F.A. |
|---|---|---|---|---|---|---|---|---|---|---|---|---|---|
| 1953–American ........................... | PH | 1 | 0 | 0 | 0 | 0 | 0 | 0 | .000 | 0 | 0 | 0 | .000 |
| 1955–American ........................... | SS | 3 | 1 | 1 | 0 | 0 | 0 | 0 | .333 | 1 | 0 | 0 | 1.000 |
| 1956–American ........................... | SS | 5 | 0 | 1 | 0 | 0 | 0 | 0 | .200 | 2 | 3 | 0 | 1.000 |
| 1957–American ........................... | SS | 2 | 0 | 0 | 0 | 0 | 0 | 1 | .000 | 0 | 1 | 0 | 1.000 |
| 1959–American (first game) ........ | OF | 1 | 1 | 0 | 0 | 0 | 0 | 0 | .000 | 0 | 0 | 0 | .000 |
| 1960–American (both games) ...... | OF-PH | 4 | 1 | 1 | 0 | 0 | 0 | 0 | .250 | 1 | 0 | 0 | 1.000 |
| All-Star Game Totals ....................... | | 16 | 3 | 3 | 0 | 0 | 0 | 1 | .188 | 4 | 4 | 0 | 1.000 |

## RECORD AS MANAGER

| Year Club | League | Position | W. | L. |
|---|---|---|---|---|
| 1975–Milwaukee† ........Amer. | | Fifth(E) | 1 | 0 |

†Served as interim manager the final game of season after Del Crandall was fired.

Coach, Milwaukee Brewers, 1971 through 1977.

# CHARLES RICHARD LAU

Last name rhymes with "how."

## (Charley)
## Kansas City Royals

Born April 12, 1933, at Romulus, Mich.
Height, 6.00. Weight, 193.
Threw right and batted lefthanded.
Hobbies–Hunting and spear-fishing.

Tied major league record for most doubles, game (4), July 13, 1962.
Tied American League record for most passed balls, inning (3), June 14, 1962, eighth inning.
Led Carolina League catchers in double plays with 15 in 1955.
Led American Association in passed balls with 18 in 1959.

| Year Club League | Pos. | G. | AB. | R. | H. | 2B. | 3B. | HR. | RBI. | B.A. | PO. | A. | E. | F.A. |
|---|---|---|---|---|---|---|---|---|---|---|---|---|---|---|
| 1952–Jamestown ........Pony | C-OF | 92 | 295 | 53 | 98 | 27 | 5 | 7 | 58 | .332 | 406 | 58 | 10 | .979 |
| 1953-54–Buffalo..........Int. | | | | | (In Military Service) | | | | | | | | | |
| 1955–Durham ............Carol. | C | 127 | 396 | 69 | 116 | 18 | 5 | 18 | 75 | .293 | 732 | 77 | 21 | .975 |
| 1956–Charleston ........A. A. | C-3B | 110 | 322 | 32 | 83 | 11 | 4 | 12 | 53 | .258 | 475 | 57 | 10 | .982 |
| 1956–Detroit ..............Amer. | C | 3 | 9 | 1 | 2 | 0 | 0 | 0 | 0 | .222 | 17 | 0 | 0 | 1.000 |
| 1957–Charleston ........A. A. | C | 70 | 202 | 23 | 49 | 14 | 1 | 8 | 25 | .243 | 310 | 36 | 6 | .983 |
| 1958–Charleston ........A. A. | C | 39 | 115 | 10 | 33 | 5 | 0 | 3 | 14 | .287 | 156 | 23 | 3 | .984 |
| 1958–Detroit ..............Amer. | C | 30 | 68 | 8 | 10 | 1 | 2 | 0 | 6 | .147 | 120 | 10 | 2 | .985 |
| 1959–Detroit ..............Amer. | C | 2 | 6 | 0 | 1 | 0 | 0 | 0 | 0 | .167 | 11 | 1 | 0 | 1.000 |
| 1959–Charles.-Louis.† A. A. | C | 121 | 390 | 55 | 114 | 29 | 2 | 20 | 79 | .292 | 609 | 46 | 5 | .992 |
| 1960–Milwaukee ........Nat. | C | 21 | 53 | 4 | 10 | 2 | 0 | 2 | 2 | .189 | 94 | 11 | 0 | 1.000 |
| 1961–Milwaukee ........Nat. | C | 28 | 82 | 3 | 17 | 5 | 0 | 0 | 5 | .207 | 114 | 7 | 4 | .968 |
| 1961–Vancouver‡ ......P. C. | C-O-1 | 45 | 143 | 22 | 42 | 7 | 1 | 6 | 22 | .294 | 227 | 14 | 4 | .984 |
| 1961–Baltimore..........Amer. | C | 17 | 47 | 3 | 8 | 0 | 0 | 1 | 4 | .170 | 90 | 6 | 1 | .990 |
| 1962–Baltimore..........Amer. | C | 81 | 197 | 21 | 58 | 11 | 2 | 6 | 37 | .294 | 269 | 15 | 1 | .996 |
| 1963–Balt.§-Kan. C ....Amer. | C | 91 | 235 | 19 | 64 | 13 | 0 | 3 | 32 | .272 | 306 | 20 | 7 | .979 |
| 1964–K. C.x-Balt. ......Amer. | C | 105 | 276 | 27 | 73 | 22 | 2 | 3 | 23 | .264 | 422 | 25 | 4 | .991 |
| 1965–Baltimore..........Amer. | C | 68 | 132 | 15 | 39 | 5 | 2 | 2 | 18 | .295 | 165 | 9 | 2 | .989 |
| 1966–Baltimore y ......Amer. | PH | 18 | 12 | 1 | 6 | 2 | 1 | 0 | 5 | .500 | 0 | 0 | 0 | .000 |

| Year Club League | Pos. | G. | AB. | R. | H. | 2B. | 3B. | HR. | RBI. | B.A. | PO. | A. | E. | F.A. |
|---|---|---|---|---|---|---|---|---|---|---|---|---|---|---|
| 1967—Baltimore z ......Amer. | PH | 11 | 8 | 0 | 1 | 1 | 0 | 0 | 3 | .125 | 0 | 0 | 0 | .000 |
| 1967—Atlanta.............Nat. | PH | 52 | 45 | 3 | 9 | 1 | 0 | 1 | 5 | .200 | 0 | 0 | 0 | .000 |
| American League Totals ............... | | 426 | 990 | 95 | 262 | 55 | 9 | 15 | 128 | .265 | 1400 | 86 | 17 | .989 |
| National League Totals ................. | | 101 | 180 | 10 | 36 | 8 | 0 | 1 | 12 | .200 | 208 | 18 | 4 | .983 |
| Major League Totals ...................... | | 527 | 1170 | 105 | 298 | 63 | 9 | 16 | 140 | .255 | 1608 | 104 | 21 | .988 |

†Traded to Milwaukee Braves by Detroit Tigers with Pitcher Don Lee for Pitcher Don Kaiser, Catcher Mike Roarke and Infielder Casey Wise, October 15, 1959. Kaiser and Roarke were transferred from Louisville to Charleston, American Association, and Lee from Charleston to Louisville. Wise was assigned to Detroit and Lau to Milwaukee.

‡Sold by Milwaukee Braves to Baltimore Orioles, August 21, 1961.

§Sold to Kansas City Athletics for a reported $20,000, July 1, 1963.

xTraded to Baltimore Orioles for Pitcher Wes Stock, June 15, 1964.

yOn disabled list from May 11 through September 1; underwent surgery for removal of scar tissue on right elbow.

zSold to Atlanta Braves, May 31, 1967.

### RECORD AS MANAGER

| Year Club | League | Position | W. | L. |
|---|---|---|---|---|
| 1968—Shreveport ........Texas | Second(E) | | 78 | 62 |

Coach, Baltimore Orioles, 1969; coach, Oakland Athletics, 1970; coach, Kansas City Royals, 1971 through 1974; minor league instructor, Kansas City Royals, part of 1975; coach, Kansas City Royals, part of 1975 through 1977.

## DONALD GEORGE LEPPERT
### (Don)
### Toronto Blue Jays

Born October 19, 1932, at Indianapolis, Ind.
Height, 6.02. Weight, 215.
Threw and batted righthanded.
Hobbies—Hunting and fishing.
Attended Wabash College, Crawfordsville, Ind.

Hit home run in first time at bat in major leagues, June 18, 1961.
Hit three home runs in a game, April 11, 1963.

| Year Club League | Pos. | G. | AB. | R. | H. | 2B. | 3B. | HR. | RBI. | B.A. | PO. | A. | E. | F.A. |
|---|---|---|---|---|---|---|---|---|---|---|---|---|---|---|
| 1955—Evansville ........I.I.I. | C | 19 | 43 | 11 | 15 | 4 | 0 | 3 | 10 | .349 | 53 | 6 | 2 | .967 |
| 1955—Corpus Christi ..Big St. | C | 58 | 184 | 29 | 44 | 9 | 2 | 10 | 32 | .239 | 250 | 20 | 6 | .978 |
| 1956—Wichita ............A. A. | C | 70 | 165 | 19 | 38 | 8 | 0 | 8 | 21 | .230 | 268 | 20 | 6 | .980 |
| 1957—Austin .............Tex. | C | 119 | 403 | 45 | 94 | 16 | 1 | 20 | 59 | .233 | 521 | 45 | •17 | .971 |
| 1958—Austin .............Tex. | C-OF | 85 | 240 | 25 | 55 | 4 | 0 | 11 | 28 | .229 | 331 | 25 | 9 | .975 |
| 1959—Austin .............Tex. | C | 5 | 13 | 2 | 4 | 0 | 0 | 0 | 1 | .308 | 28 | 2 | 0 | 1.000 |
| 1959—Dallas .............A. A. | C | 132 | 404 | 45 | 109 | 17 | 1 | 13 | 66 | .270 | 479 | 45 | 9 | .983 |
| 1960—Dal.-Ft. Worth ..A. A. | C | 118 | 363 | 41 | 93 | 18 | 0 | 17 | 63 | .256 | 506 | 51 | 19 | .967 |
| 1961—Columbus ..........Int. | C | 39 | 114 | 18 | 44 | 4 | 1 | 6 | 30 | .386 | 217 | 14 | 3 | .987 |
| 1961—Pittsburgh ........Nat. | C | 22 | 60 | 6 | 16 | 2 | 1 | 3 | 5 | .267 | 80 | 11 | 3 | .968 |
| 1962—Pittsburgh†........Nat. | C | 45 | 139 | 14 | 37 | 6 | 1 | 3 | 18 | .266 | 243 | 23 | 3 | .989 |
| 1963—Washington........Amer. | C | 73 | 211 | 20 | 50 | 11 | 0 | 6 | 24 | .237 | 281 | 20 | 5 | .984 |
| 1964—Washington........Amer. | C | 50 | 122 | 6 | 19 | 3 | 0 | 3 | 12 | .156 | 191 | 14 | 2 | .990 |
| 1965—Hawaii .............P. C. | C | 61 | 148 | 13 | 50 | 5 | 0 | 5 | 19 | .338 | 195 | 22 | 3 | .986 |
| 1966—Columbus ..........Int. | C | 66 | 140 | 9 | 32 | 0 | 0 | 3 | 13 | .229 | 206 | 18 | 4 | .982 |
| American League Totals ............... | | 123 | 333 | 26 | 69 | 14 | 0 | 9 | 36 | .207 | 472 | 34 | 7 | .986 |
| National League Totals ................. | | 67 | 199 | 20 | 53 | 8 | 2 | 6 | 23 | .266 | 323 | 34 | 6 | .983 |
| Major League Totals ...................... | | 190 | 532 | 46 | 122 | 22 | 2 | 15 | 59 | .229 | 795 | 68 | 13 | .985 |

†Traded to Washington Senators for Pitcher Ron Honeycutt and cash, December 15, 1962.

### ALL-STAR GAME RECORD

Member of American League All-Star team in 1963; did not play.

### RECORD AS MANAGER

| Year Club | League | Position | W. | L. |
|---|---|---|---|---|
| 1967—Gastonia ...........W. Carol. | Second | | 61 | 59 |

Coach, Pittsburgh Pirates, 1968-76; coach, Toronto Blue Jays, 1977.

## ROBERT PERRY LILLIS
### (Bob)
### Houstoη Astros

Born June 2, 1930, at Altadena, Calif.
Height, 5.11. Weight, 168.
Threw and batted righthanded.
Hobbies—Hunting and fishing.
Attended University of Southern California, Los Angeles, Calif.

| Year Club League | Pos. | G. | AB. | R. | H. | 2B. | 3B. | HR. | RBI. | B.A. | PO. | A. | E. | F.A. |
|---|---|---|---|---|---|---|---|---|---|---|---|---|---|---|
| 1951—Pueblo .............West. | SS | 37 | 141 | 17 | 34 | 6 | 3 | 0 | 13 | .241 | 80 | 104 | 12 | .939 |
| 1951—Newport News ..Pied. | SS | 39 | 136 | 16 | 28 | 1 | 3 | 0 | 12 | .206 | 59 | 110 | 10 | .944 |

| Year Club | League | Pos. | G. | AB. | R. | H. | 2B. | 3B. | HR. | RBI. | B.A. | PO. | A. | E. | F.A. |
|---|---|---|---|---|---|---|---|---|---|---|---|---|---|---|---|
| 1952—Elmira ..............East. | SS | 76 | 310 | 35 | 63 | 15 | 1 | 0 | 18 | .203 | 147 | 221 | 18 | .953 |
| 1953—Newport News ..Pied. | SS | 129 | 523 | •102 | 152 | 25 | 6 | 3 | 60 | .291 | •311 | •443 | •40 | .950 |
| 1954-55—Mobile .........South. | | | | (In Military Service) | | | | | | | | | | |
| 1956—St. Paul ............A. A. | SS | 144 | •590 | 96 | 157 | 33 | 2 | 18 | 65 | .266 | •304 | 395 | 27 | •.963 |
| 1957—St. Paul ............A. A. | SS | •154 | •598 | 72 | 155 | 26 | 5 | 2 | 49 | .259 | •323 | 477 | 30 | •.964 |
| 1958—St. Paul ............A. A. | SS | 67 | 272 | 42 | 74 | 10 | 6 | 3 | 17 | .272 | 136 | 193 | 17 | .951 |
| 1958—Los Angeles ......Nat. | SS | 20 | 69 | 10 | 27 | 3 | 1 | 1 | 5 | .391 | 29 | 52 | 3 | .964 |
| 1959—Los Angeles ......Nat. | SS | 30 | 48 | 7 | 11 | 2 | 0 | 0 | 2 | .229 | 27 | 52 | 7 | .919 |
| 1959—Spokane ............P. C. | SS | 103 | 406 | 50 | 116 | 17 | 6 | 3 | 27 | .286 | 206 | 352 | 17 | •.970 |
| 1960—Los Angeles ......Nat. | SS-3-2 | 48 | 60 | 6 | 16 | 4 | 0 | 0 | 6 | .267 | 40 | 52 | 1 | .989 |
| 1961—L. A.†-St. L.‡ ....Nat. | SS-2-3 | 105 | 239 | 24 | 51 | 4 | 0 | 0 | 22 | .213 | 123 | 201 | 19 | .945 |
| 1962—Houston ............Nat. | SS-2-3 | 129 | 457 | 38 | 114 | 12 | 4 | 1 | 30 | .249 | 223 | 378 | 15 | .976 |
| 1963—Houston ............Nat. | SS-2-3 | 147 | 469 | 31 | 93 | 13 | 1 | 1 | 19 | .198 | 249 | 375 | 26 | .960 |
| 1964—Houston ............Nat. | 2-SS-3 | 109 | 332 | 31 | 89 | 11 | 2 | 0 | 17 | .268 | 169 | 236 | 10 | .976 |
| 1965—Houston ............Nat. | SS-3-2 | 124 | 408 | 34 | 90 | 12 | 1 | 0 | 20 | .221 | 206 | 304 | 16 | .970 |
| 1966—Houston ............Nat. | 2-SS-3 | 68 | 164 | 14 | 38 | 6 | 0 | 0 | 11 | .232 | 99 | 109 | 10 | .954 |
| 1967—Houston ............Nat. | SS-2-3 | 37 | 82 | 3 | 20 | 1 | 0 | 0 | 5 | .244 | 27 | 66 | 7 | .930 |
| Major League Totals ..................... | | 817 | 2328 | 198 | 549 | 68 | 9 | 3 | 137 | .236 | 1192 | 1825 | 114 | .964 |

†Traded to St. Louis Cardinals with Outfielder Carl Warwick for Infielder Daryl Spencer, May 30, 1961.
‡Selected by Houston Colts in National League expansion draft, October 10, 1961.

Scout, Houston Astros, 1968 through 1970; Director of Minor League Instruction, Houston Astros, 1972; coach, Houston Astros, part of 1967 and 1973 through 1977.

## JOSEPH PAUL LONNETT

Name pronounced Lon-NETT.

### (Joe)

### Pittsburgh Pirates

Born February 7, 1927, at Beaver Falls, Pa.
Height, 5.10½. Weight, 185.
Threw and batted righthanded.
Hobby—Photography.

| Year Club | League | Pos. | G. | AB. | R. | H. | 2B. | 3B. | HR. | RBI. | B.A. | PO. | A. | E. | F.A. |
|---|---|---|---|---|---|---|---|---|---|---|---|---|---|---|---|
| 1947—Lockport ..........Pony | OF | 78 | 253 | 45 | 56 | 11 | 4 | 5 | 43 | .221 | 164 | 10 | 7 | .961 |
| 1948—Bradford ..........Pony | C | 124 | 445 | 102 | 138 | 22 | 9 | 11 | 82 | .310 | 579 | •79 | •14 | .979 |
| 1949—Vandergrift ......Mid. Atl. | C | 104 | 398 | 105 | 122 | 33 | 8 | 20 | 93 | .307 | 498 | 59 | 11 | .981 |
| 1949—Utica ................East. | C | 36 | 120 | 14 | 25 | 6 | 1 | 3 | 15 | .208 | 134 | 19 | 9 | .944 |
| 1950—Terre Haute ......I.I.I. | C | 109 | 343 | 62 | 102 | 21 | 7 | 11 | 61 | .297 | •779 | 55 | •13 | •.985 |
| 1951-52—Philadelphia Nat. | | | | (In Military Service) | | | | | | | | | | |
| 1953—Batimore .........Int. | C-O-1-2 | 77 | 162 | 27 | 25 | 3 | 0 | 11 | 25 | .154 | 277 | 27 | 2 | .993 |
| 1954—Syracuse .........Int. | C | 98 | 295 | 63 | 79 | 16 | 1 | 21 | 63 | .268 | 476 | 45 | 9 | .983 |
| 1955—Syracuse .........Int. | C | 26 | 60 | 8 | 17 | 1 | 1 | 2 | 8 | .283 | 94 | 4 | 0 | 1.000 |
| 1956—Philadelphia .....Nat. | C | 16 | 22 | 2 | 4 | 0 | 0 | 0 | 0 | .182 | 24 | 2 | 0 | 1.000 |
| 1957—Philadelphia .....Nat. | C | 67 | 160 | 12 | 27 | 5 | 0 | 5 | 15 | .169 | 305 | 16 | 1 | .997 |
| 1958—Philadelphia .....Nat. | C | 17 | 50 | 0 | 7 | 2 | 0 | 0 | 2 | .140 | 78 | 7 | 1 | .988 |
| 1958—Wichita ............A.A. | C | 52 | 140 | 20 | 28 | 5 | 0 | 2 | 18 | .200 | 261 | 21 | 2 | .993 |
| 1959—Louisville ..........A.A. | C | 32 | 86 | 12 | 25 | 4 | 1 | 4 | 14 | .291 | 135 | 10 | 0 | 1.000 |
| 1959—Buffalo .............Int. | C | 16 | 50 | 8 | 15 | 5 | 0 | 3 | 8 | .300 | 96 | 7 | 2 | .981 |
| 1959—Philadelphia ......Nat. | C | 43 | 93 | 8 | 16 | 1 | 0 | 1 | 10 | .172 | 171 | 4 | 3 | .983 |
| 1960—Buffalo .............Int. | C | 82 | 257 | 38 | 63 | 4 | 0 | 10 | 34 | .245 | 423 | 37 | 9 | .981 |
| 1961—Buffalo† ...........Int. | C | 3 | 5 | 0 | 2 | 1 | 0 | 0 | 0 | .400 | figures unavailable | | | |
| 1962—Buff.-Rochester Int. | C | 69 | 176 | 18 | 32 | 5 | 1 | 6 | 24 | .182 | 317 | 15 | 5 | .985 |
| 1963—Little Rock........Int. | C | 5 | 17 | 2 | 4 | 1 | 0 | 1 | 5 | .235 | figures unavailable | | | |
| Major League Totals ..................... | | 143 | 325 | 22 | 54 | 8 | 0 | 6 | 27 | .166 | 578 | 29 | 5 | .992 |

†On disabled list, May 1 to September 28.

### RECORD AS MANAGER

| Year | Club | League | Position | W. | L. |
|---|---|---|---|---|---|
| 1966—Huron | | ................North. | Third | 32 | 35 |
| 1967—Huron | | ................North. | Sixth | 27 | 40 |

Scout, Philadelphia Phillies, 1963 through 1965 and 1968 through 1970; coach, Chicago White Sox, 1971 through 1975; coach, Oakland Athletics, 1976; coach, Pittsburgh Pirates, 1977.

## HARRY LEE LOWREY

### (Peanuts)

### Chicago Cubs

Born August 27, 1918, at Los Angeles, Calif.
Height, 5.08½. Weight, 170.
Threw and batted righthanded.
Hobbies—Golf, movies, hunting and fishing.

| Year Club | League | Pos. | G. | AB. | R. | H. | 2B. | 3B. | HR. | RBI. | B.A. | PO. | A. | E. | F.A. |
|---|---|---|---|---|---|---|---|---|---|---|---|---|---|---|---|
| 1937—Moline ..............I.I.I. | SS-2B | 45 | 181 | 34 | 55 | 6 | 2 | 3 | | .304 | 73 | 108 | 21 | .896 |
| 1938—Ponca City ........W.A. | SS | 123 | 479 | 105 | 128 | 35 | 5 | 5 | 63 | .267 | 204 | 358 | 63 | .899 |

| Year Club | League | Pos. | G. | AB. | R. | H. | 2B. | 3B. | HR. | RBI. | B.A. | PO. | A. | E. | F.A. |
|---|---|---|---|---|---|---|---|---|---|---|---|---|---|---|---|
| 1939–St. Joseph ........W.A. | | SS | 137 | 517 | 122 | 178 | 39 | 7 | 15 | 108 | .344 | •244 | 367 | •72 | .895 |
| 1940–Tulsa ................Texas | | 3B | 32 | 110 | 24 | 33 | 10 | 0 | 2 | 14 | .300 | 26 | 53 | 7 | .919 |
| 1940–Los Angeles ......P.C. | | SS-3B | 70 | 216 | 36 | 54 | 7 | 1 | 1 | 12 | .250 | 84 | 142 | 16 | .934 |
| 1941–Los Angeles ......P.C. | | OF-3B | 164 | 653 | 110 | 203 | 39 | 4 | 6 | 69 | .311 | 354 | 103 | 27 | .944 |
| 1942–Chicago ..........Nat. | | OF | 27 | 58 | 4 | 11 | 0 | 0 | 1 | 4 | .190 | 43 | 2 | 1 | .978 |
| 1942–Milwaukee .........A.A. | | OF | 9 | 32 | 5 | 9 | 0 | 0 | 0 | 0 | .281 | 17 | 1 | 0 | 1.000 |
| 1942–Los Angeles ......P.C. | | OF | 96 | 393 | 64 | 101 | 17 | 0 | 5 | 39 | .257 | 211 | 13 | 6 | .974 |
| 1943–Chicago ............Nat. | | OF-INF | 130 | 480 | 59 | 140 | 25 | 12 | 1 | 63 | .292 | 341 | 62 | 10 | .976 |
| 1944–Chicago ............Nat. | | | | | (In Military Service) | | | | | | | | | | |
| 1945–Chicago ............Nat. | | OF-SS | 143 | 523 | 72 | 148 | 22 | 7 | 7 | 89 | .283 | 281 | 19 | 5 | .984 |
| 1946–Chicago ............Nat. | | OF-3B | 144 | 540 | 75 | 139 | 24 | 5 | 4 | 54 | .257 | 330 | 49 | 12 | .969 |
| 1947–Chicago ............Nat. | | 3-2-OF | 115 | 448 | 56 | 126 | 17 | 5 | 5 | 37 | .281 | 138 | 200 | 17 | .952 |
| 1948–Chicago ............Nat. | | OF-INF | 129 | 435 | 47 | 128 | 12 | 3 | 2 | 54 | .294 | 238 | 29 | 5 | .982 |
| 1949–Chi.†-Cincinnati Nat. | | OF-3B | 127 | 420 | 66 | 115 | 21 | 2 | 4 | 35 | .274 | 259 | 9 | 4 | .985 |
| 1950–Cin.‡-St. Louis ..Nat. | | OF-2-3 | 108 | 320 | 44 | 75 | 14 | 0 | 2 | 15 | .234 | 184 | 36 | 4 | .982 |
| 1951–St. Louis ..........Nat. | | OF-3-2 | 114 | 370 | 52 | 112 | 19 | 5 | 5 | 40 | .303 | 230 | 25 | 9 | .966 |
| 1952–St. Louis ..........Nat. | | OF-3B | 132 | 374 | 48 | 107 | 18 | 2 | 1 | 48 | .286 | 176 | 20 | 7 | .966 |
| 1953–St. Louis ..........Nat. | | OF-2-3 | 104 | 182 | 26 | 49 | 9 | 2 | 5 | 27 | .269 | 64 | 20 | 3 | .966 |
| 1954–St. Louis§..........Nat. | | OF | 74 | 61 | 6 | 7 | 1 | 2 | 0 | 5 | .115 | 5 | 0 | 0 | 1.000 |
| 1955–Philadelphia x ..Nat. | | O-PH-1 | 54 | 106 | 9 | 20 | 4 | 0 | 0 | 8 | .189 | 42 | 2 | 1 | .978 |
| 1956–Buffalo..............Int. | | OF | 117 | 352 | 41 | 97 | 12 | 1 | 4 | 33 | .276 | 146 | 10 | 1 | .994 |
| 1957–New Orleans ....South. | | OF | 73 | 169 | 38 | 61 | 7 | 1 | 0 | 12 | .361 | 97 | 2 | 1 | .990 |
| 1958–Austin ..............Tex. | | OF | 46 | 103 | 13 | 31 | 3 | 2 | 2 | 13 | .301 | 24 | 1 | 0 | 1.000 |
| 1959–Seattle ............P.C. | | OF-INF | 36 | 79 | 10 | 14 | 4 | 0 | 0 | 6 | .177 | 35 | 30 | 7 | .903 |
| Major League Totals ..................... | | | 1401 | 4317 | 564 | 1177 | 186 | 45 | 37 | 479 | .273 | 2331 | 473 | 78 | .973 |

†Traded to Cincinnati Reds with Outfielder Harry Walker for Outfielders Henry Sauer and Frank Baumholtz, June 15, 1949.

‡Released to St. Louis Cardinals on waivers, September 7, 1950.

§Unconditionally released by St. Louis Cardinals, October 12, 1954; signed by Philadelphia Phillies, February 10, 1955.

xReleased by Philadelphia Phillies, October 3, 1955.

WORLD SERIES RECORD

| Year Club | League | Pos. | G. | AB. | R. | H. | 2B. | 3B. | HR. | RBI. | B.A. | PO. | A. | E. | F.A. |
|---|---|---|---|---|---|---|---|---|---|---|---|---|---|---|---|
| 1945–Chicago ............Nat. | | OF | 7 | 29 | 4 | 9 | 1 | 0 | 0 | 0 | .310 | 21 | 1 | 0 | 1.000 |

ALL-STAR GAME RECORD

| Year League | Pos. | AB. | R. | H. | 2B. | 3B. | HR. | RBI. | B.A. | PO. | A. | E. | F.A. |
|---|---|---|---|---|---|---|---|---|---|---|---|---|---|
| 1946–National ............................ | OF | 2 | 0 | 1 | 0 | 0 | 0 | 0 | .500 | 3 | 0 | 0 | 1.000 |

RECORD AS MANAGER

| Year Club | League | Position | W. | L. |
|---|---|---|---|---|
| 1957–New Orleans ......South. | | Eighth | 60 | 94 |
| 1958–Austin ...:..........Texas | | Fourth | 77 | 76 |
| 1960–Idaho Falls† ......Pion. | | Second | 24 | 15 |

†Succeeded by George Noga, June 1.

Coach, Philadelphia Phillies, June 1, 1960 through 1966; San Francisco Giants, 1967-68; Montreal Expos 1969; Chicago Cubs, 1970-71; California Angels, 1972; Chicago Cubs, 1977.

## CALVIN COOLIDGE JULIUS CEASAR TUSKAHOMA McLISH
### (Cal)
### (Milwaukee Brewers

Born December 1, 1925, at Anadarko, Okla.
Height, 6.01. Weight, 204.
Threw right and batted left and righthanded.
Hobby–Golf.

Tied major league record for most home runs allowed, inning (4), May 22, 1957; led American League in wild pitches (8), 1957.

| Year Club | League | G. | IP. | W. | L. | Pct. | H. | R. | ER. | SO. | BB. | ERA. |
|---|---|---|---|---|---|---|---|---|---|---|---|---|
| 1944–Brooklyn..............National | | 23 | 84 | 3 | 10 | .231 | 110 | 81 | 73 | 24 | 48 | 7.82 |
| 1945–Brooklyn..............National | | | | | (In Military Service) | | | | | | | |
| 1946–Brooklyn†‡ .........National | | 1 | ⅓ | 0 | 0 | .000 | 1 | 2 | 2 | 0 | 0 | 54.00 |
| 1947–Pittsburgh...........National | | 1 | 1 | 0 | 0 | .000 | 2 | 2 | 2 | 0 | 0 | 18.00 |
| 1947–Kansas City.........Am. Assoc. | | 16 | 92 | 6 | 7 | .462 | 104 | 55 | 45 | 40 | 42 | 4.40 |
| 1948–Pittsburgh...........National | | 2 | 5 | 0 | 0 | .000 | 8 | 5 | 5 | 1 | 2 | 9.00 |
| 1948–Indianapolis§.......Am. Assoc. | | 29 | 172 | 12 | 9 | .571 | 199 | 100 | 79 | 71 | 57 | 4.13 |
| 1949–Chicago..............National | | 8 | 23 | 1 | 1 | .500 | 31 | 21 | 15 | 6 | 12 | 5.87 |
| 1949–Los Angeles ......P. Coast | | 29 | 150 | 8 | 11 | .421 | 164 | 95 | 96 | 68 | 107 | 5.76 |
| 1950–Los Angeles ......P. Coast | | 42 | 260 | 20 | 11 | .645 | 243 | 119 | 104 | 129 | 104 | 3.60 |
| 1951–Chicago..............National | | 30 | 146 | 4 | 10 | .286 | 159 | 76 | 72 | 46 | 52 | 4.44 |
| 1952–Los Angeles ......P. Coast | | 34 | 212 | 10 | 15 | .400 | 215 | 106 | 89 | 84 | 60 | 3.78 |
| 1953–Los Angeles ......P. Coast | | 35 | 235 | 16 | 11 | .593 | 239 | 108 | 97 | 114 | 60 | 3.71 |
| 1954–Los Angeles ......P. Coast | | 37 | 245 | 13 | 15 | .464 | 261 | 102 | 96 | 120 | 74 | 3.53 |
| 1955–Los Angeles x-San Diego y ..P. Coast | | 35 | 233 | 17 | 12 | .586 | 230 | 88 | 80 | 116 | 69 | 3.09 |
| 1956–Cleveland §.........American | | 37 | 62 | 2 | 4 | .333 | 67 | 36 | 34 | 27 | 32 | 4.94 |
| 1957–Cleveland ..........American | | 42 | 144 | 9 | 7 | .563 | 118 | 55 | 44 | 88 | 67 | 2.75 |

| Year Club | League | G. | IP. | W. | L. | Pct. | H. | R. | ER. | SO. | BB. | ERA. |
|---|---|---|---|---|---|---|---|---|---|---|---|---|
| 1958—Cleveland | American | 39 | 226 | 16 | 8 | .667 | 214 | 92 | 75 | 97 | 70 | 2.99 |
| 1959—Cleveland z | American | 35 | 235 | 19 | 8 | .704 | •253 | 110 | 95 | 113 | 72 | 3.64 |
| 1960—Cincinnati a | National | 37 | 151 | 4 | 14 | .222 | 170 | 85 | 70 | 56 | 48 | 4.17 |
| 1961—Chicago b | American | 31 | 162 | 10 | 13 | .435 | 178 | 87 | 79 | 80 | 47 | 4.39 |
| 1962—Philadelphia | National | 32 | 155 | 11 | 5 | .688 | 184 | 84 | 73 | 71 | 45 | 4.24 |
| 1963—Philadelphia | National | 32 | 210 | 13 | 11 | .542 | 184 | 85 | 76 | 98 | 56 | 3.26 |
| 1964—Philadelphia c | National | 2 | 5 | 0 | 1 | .000 | 6 | 3 | 2 | 6 | 1 | 3.60 |
| American League Totals | | 184 | 829 | 56 | 40 | .583 | 830 | 380 | 327 | 405 | 288 | 3.55 |
| National League Totals | | 168 | 780 | 36 | 52 | .409 | 855 | 444 | 390 | 308 | 264 | 4.50 |
| Major League Totals | | 352 | 1609 | 92 | 92 | .500 | 1685 | 824 | 717 | 713 | 552 | 4.01 |

†In military service most of season.

‡Traded to Pittsburgh Pirates with Pitcher Kirby Higbe, Catcher Homer Howell and Shortstop Gene Mauch for Outfielder Al Gionfriddo and reported $100,000, May 3, 1947.

§Traded to Chicago Cubs by Pittsburgh Pirates with Third Baseman Frank Gustine for Pitcher Cliff Chambers and Catcher Clyde McCullough, December 8, 1948.

xSold by Chicago Cubs' organization to San Diego, April 27, 1955.

yConditionally released to Cleveland Indians, October 15, 1955.

zTraded to Cincinnati Reds with First Baseman Gordon Coleman and Second Baseman Billy Martin for Second Baseman Johnny Temple, December 15, 1959.

aTraded to Chicago White Sox with Pitcher Juan Pizarro for Third Baseman Gene Freese, December 15, 1960.

bSent to Philadelphia Phillies as replacement for Third Baseman Andy Carey who refused to report to Phils in trade made December 15, 1961; Sox traded Pitcher Frank Barnes and Carey for Pitcher Taylor Phillips and Infielder Bob Sadowski. McLish assigned to Phillies, March 24, 1962.

cPlaced on disabled list with sore arm, April 13; returned to active list, June 29, 1964, and released, July 31, 1964.

### ALL-STAR GAME RECORD

| Year League | IP. | W. | L. | Pct. | H. | R. | ER. | SO. | BB. | ERA. |
|---|---|---|---|---|---|---|---|---|---|---|
| 1959—American (second game) | 2 | 0 | 0 | .000 | 1 | 0 | 0 | 2 | 1 | 0.00 |

Coach, Philadelphia Phillies, 1965 and 1966; scout, Philadelphia Phillies, 1967 and 1968; coach, Montreal Expos, 1969 through 1975; coach, Milwaukee Brewers, 1976 and 1977.

## DONALD JOHN McMAHON
### (Don)
### Minnesota Twins

Born January 4, 1930, at Brooklyn, N. Y.
Height, 6.02. Weight, 210.
Threw and batted righthanded.
Hobby—Photography.

| Year Club | League | G. | IP. | W. | L. | Pct. | H. | R. | ER. | SO. | BB. | ERA. |
|---|---|---|---|---|---|---|---|---|---|---|---|---|
| 1950—Owensboro | Kitty | 33 | 218 | •20 | 9 | .690 | •211 | 104 | 66 | •143 | 119 | •2.72 |
| 1951—Denver† | Western | 4 | 16 | 1 | 0 | 1.000 | 10 | 5 | 4 | 15 | 8 | 2.25 |
| 1952—Milwaukee | Am. Assoc. | | | | | (In Military Service) | | | | | | |
| 1953—Evansville† | I.I.I. | 26 | 114 | 6 | 5 | .545 | 113 | 69 | 57 | 91 | 77 | 4.50 |
| 1954—Atlanta | Southern | 46 | 91 | 8 | 5 | .615 | 87 | 39 | 36 | 90 | 64 | 3.56 |
| 1955—Toledo | Am. Assoc. | 42 | 142 | 2 | 13 | .133 | 149 | 88 | 79 | 93 | 95 | 5.01 |
| 1956—Atlanta | Southern | 14 | 36 | 4 | 2 | .667 | 23 | 9 | 8 | 34 | 17 | 2.00 |
| 1956—Wichita | Am. Assoc. | 40 | 89 | 4 | 4 | .500 | 86 | 48 | 43 | 78 | 40 | 4.35 |
| 1957—Wichita | Am. Assoc. | 21 | 71 | 6 | 2 | .750 | 59 | 25 | 23 | 65 | 38 | 2.92 |
| 1957—Milwaukee | National | 32 | 47 | 2 | 3 | .400 | 33 | 13 | 8 | 46 | 29 | 1.53 |
| 1958—Milwaukee | National | 38 | 59 | 7 | 2 | .778 | 50 | 25 | 24 | 37 | 29 | 3.66 |
| 1959—Milwaukee | National | 60 | 81 | 5 | 3 | .625 | 81 | 26 | 23 | 55 | 37 | 2.56 |
| 1960—Milwaukee | National | 48 | 64 | 3 | 6 | .333 | 66 | 48 | 42 | 50 | 32 | 5.91 |
| 1961—Milwaukee | National | 53 | 92 | 6 | 4 | .600 | 84 | 35 | 29 | 55 | 51 | 2.84 |
| 1962—Milwaukee‡-Houston | National | 53 | 80 | 5 | 6 | .455 | 56 | 16 | 15 | 72 | 33 | 1.69 |
| 1963—Houston§ | National | 49 | 80 | 1 | 5 | .167 | 83 | 38 | 36 | 51 | 26 | 4.05 |
| 1964—Cleveland | American | 70 | 101 | 6 | 4 | .600 | 67 | 31 | 27 | 92 | 52 | 2.41 |
| 1965—Cleveland | American | 58 | 85 | 3 | 3 | .500 | 79 | 36 | 31 | 60 | 37 | 3.28 |
| 1966—Cleveland x-Boston | American | 61 | 90 | 9 | 8 | .529 | 73 | 33 | 27 | 62 | 44 | 2.70 |
| 1967—Boston y-Chicago | American | 63 | 109 | 6 | 2 | .750 | 68 | 29 | 24 | 84 | 40 | 1.98 |
| 1968—Chicago z-Detroit | American | 45 | 82 | 5 | 2 | .714 | 53 | 18 | 18 | 65 | 30 | 1.98 |
| 1969—Detroit a | American | 34 | 37 | 3 | 5 | .375 | 25 | 17 | 16 | 38 | 18 | 3.89 |
| 1969—San Francisco | National | 13 | 24 | 3 | 1 | .750 | 13 | 9 | 8 | 21 | 9 | 3.00 |
| 1970—San Francisco | National | 61 | 94 | 9 | 5 | .643 | 70 | 32 | 31 | 74 | 45 | 2.97 |
| 1971—San Francisco | National | 61 | 82 | 10 | 6 | .625 | 73 | 40 | 37 | 71 | 37 | 4.06 |
| 1972—San Francisco b | National | 44 | 63 | 3 | 3 | .500 | 46 | 26 | 26 | 45 | 21 | 3.71 |
| 1973—San Francisco c | National | 22 | 30 | 4 | 0 | 1.000 | 21 | 5 | 5 | 20 | 7 | 1.50 |
| 1974—San Francisco d | National | 9 | 12 | 0 | 0 | .000 | 13 | 5 | 4 | 5 | 2 | 3.00 |
| National League Totals | | 543 | 808 | 58 | 44 | .569 | 689 | 318 | 288 | 602 | 358 | 3.21 |
| American League Totals | | 331 | 504 | 32 | 24 | .571 | 365 | 164 | 143 | 401 | 221 | 2.55 |
| Major League Totals | | 874 | 1312 | 90 | 68 | .570 | 1054 | 482 | 431 | 1003 | 579 | 2.96 |

†On military list from May 30, 1951, through May 17, 1953.

‡Sold to Houston Colt .45s, May 9, 1962.

§Sold to Cleveland Indians, September 30, 1963.

xTraded with Pitcher Lee Stange to Boston Red Sox for Pitcher Dick Radatz, June 2, 1966.
yTraded with Pitcher Bob Snow (transferred from Pittsfield to Evansville) to Chicago White Sox for Infielder Jerry Adair, June 2, 1967.
zTraded to Detroit Tigers for Pitcher Dennis Ribant, July 26, 1968.
aSold to San Francisco Giants, August 9, 1969.
bReleased, October 10, 1972.
cPlaced on active roster, June 25, 1973; released, October 9, 1973.
dPlaced on active roster, May 21, 1974; released, July 3, 1974.

## CHAMPIONSHIP SERIES RECORD

| Year   Club | League | G. | IP. | W. | L. | Pct. | H. | R. | ER. | SO. | BB. | ERA. |
|---|---|---|---|---|---|---|---|---|---|---|---|---|
| 1971—San Francisco | National | 2 | 3 | 0 | 0 | .000 | 0 | 0 | 0 | 3 | 0 | 0.00 |

## WORLD SERIES RECORD

| Year   Club | League | G. | IP. | W. | L. | Pct. | H. | R. | ER. | SO. | BB. | ERA. |
|---|---|---|---|---|---|---|---|---|---|---|---|---|
| 1957—Milwaukee | National | 3 | 5 | 0 | 0 | .000 | 3 | 0 | 0 | 5 | 3 | 0.00 |
| 1958—Milwaukee | National | 3 | 3⅓ | 0 | 0 | .000 | 3 | 2 | 2 | 5 | 3 | 5.40 |
| 1968—Detroit | American | 2 | 2 | 0 | 0 | .000 | 4 | 3 | 3 | 1 | 0 | 13.50 |
| World Series Totals | | 8 | 10⅓ | 0 | 0 | .000 | 10 | 5 | 5 | 11 | 6 | 4.35 |

## ALL-STAR GAME RECORD

Member of National League All-Star Team in 1958 game; did not play.

Coach, San Francisco Giants, 1973 through 1975; coach, Minnesota Twins, 1976 and 1977.


# ROBERT LANE MILLER
## (Bob)
## Toronto Blue Jays

Born February 18, 1939, at St. Louis, Mo.
Height, 6.01. Weight, 195.
Threw and batted righthanded.
Hobbies—Golf and boating.
Attended St. Louis Univeristy, St. Louis, Mo.
Tied major league record for most clubs played on, lifetime, 10, 1973.
Received reported $20,000 bonus to sign with St. Louis Cardinals, 1957.

| Year   Club | League | G. | IP. | W. | L. | Pct. | H. | R. | ER. | SO. | BB. | ERA. |
|---|---|---|---|---|---|---|---|---|---|---|---|---|
| 1957—St. Louis | National | 5 | 9 | 0 | 0 | .000 | 13 | 9 | 7 | 5 | 7 | 7.00 |
| 1958—Rochester | Int'national | 5 | 15 | 1 | 1 | .500 | 15 | 12 | 11 | 15 | 12 | 6.60 |
| 1958—Houston† | Texas | 27 | 160 | 8 | 11 | .421 | 157 | 79 | 63 | 115 | 64 | 3.54 |
| 1959—Rochester | Int'national | 25 | 139 | 8 | 12 | .400 | 144 | 60 | 54 | 76 | 43 | 3.50 |
| 1959—St. Louis | National | 11 | 71 | 4 | 3 | .571 | 66 | 31 | 26 | 43 | 21 | 3.30 |
| 1960—St. Louis | National | 15 | 53 | 4 | 3 | .571 | 53 | 21 | 20 | 33 | 17 | 3.40 |
| 1960—Memphis‡ | Southern | 3 | 11 | 1 | 0 | 1.000 | 10 | 3 | 3 | 8 | 5 | 2.45 |
| 1961—St. Louis‡‡ | National | 34 | 74 | 1 | 3 | .250 | 82 | 41 | 35 | 39 | 46 | 4.26 |
| 1962—New York§ | National | 33 | 144 | 1 | 12 | .077 | 146 | 98 | 78 | 91 | 62 | 4.88 |
| 1963—Los Angeles | National | 42 | 187 | 10 | 8 | .556 | 171 | 71 | 60 | 125 | 65 | 2.89 |
| 1964—Los Angeles | National | •74 | 138 | 7 | 7 | .500 | 115 | 49 | 40 | 94 | 63 | 2.61 |
| 1966—Los Angeles | National | 46 | 84 | 4 | 2 | .667 | 70 | 31 | 26 | 58 | 29 | 2.79 |
| 1967—Los Angeles x | National | 52 | 86 | 2 | 9 | .182 | 88 | 46 | 41 | 32 | 27 | 4.29 |
| 1968—Minnesota | American | 45 | 72 | 0 | 3 | .000 | 65 | 26 | 22 | 41 | 24 | 2.75 |
| 1969—Minnesota yz | American | 48 | 119 | 5 | 5 | .500 | 118 | 42 | 40 | 57 | 32 | 3.03 |
| 1970—Cleve.a-Chicago b | American | 30 | 98 | 6 | 8 | .429 | 123 | 56 | 52 | 51 | 48 | 4.78 |
| 1970—Chicago | National | 7 | 9 | 0 | 0 | .000 | 6 | 5 | 5 | 4 | 6 | 5.00 |
| 1971—Chi. c-S.D. d-Pitt | National | 56 | 99 | 8 | 5 | .615 | 83 | 24 | 18 | 51 | 40 | 1.64 |
| 1972—Pittsburgh e | National | 36 | 54 | 5 | 2 | .714 | 54 | 19 | 16 | 18 | 24 | 2.67 |
| 1973—Detroit g | American | 22 | 42 | 4 | 2 | .667 | 34 | 16 | 16 | 23 | 22 | 3.43 |
| 1973—San Diego f-New York | National | 19 | 32 | 0 | 0 | .000 | 29 | 18 | 14 | 16 | 12 | 3.94 |
| 1974—New York h | National | 58 | 78 | 2 | 2 | .500 | 89 | 39 | 31 | 35 | 39 | 3.58 |
| 1975—Hawaii | P. Coast | 15 | 25 | 0 | 1 | .000 | 32 | 17 | 16 | 9 | 8 | 5.76 |
| National League Totals | | 549 | 1221 | 54 | 63 | .462 | 1147 | 539 | 451 | 723 | 482 | 3.32 |
| American League Totals | | 145 | 331 | 15 | 18 | .455 | 340 | 140 | 130 | 172 | 126 | 3.53 |
| Major League Totals | | 694 | 1552 | 69 | 81 | .460 | 1487 | 679 | 581 | 895 | 608 | 3.37 |

†On military list, October 5, 1958 through March 9, 1959.
‡On disabled list, July 15 through September 2.
‡‡Selected by New York Mets in National League expansion draft, October 10, 1961.
§Traded to Los Angeles Dodgers for First Baseman Tim Harkness and Second Baseman Larry Burright,
December 1, 1962.
xTraded with Pitcher Ron Perranoski and Catcher John Roseboro to Minnesota Twins for Pitcher Jim
Grant and Shortstop Zoilo Versalles, November 28, 1967.
yTraded with Pitcher Dean Chance, Outfielder Ted Uhlaender and Third Baseman-Outfielder Graig Nettles to the Cleveland Indians for Pitchers Luis Tiant and Stan Williams, December 11, 1969.
zOn disabled list, August 9, through September 1.
aTraded with Pitcher R. Barry Moore to Chicago White Sox for Outfielder Charles Bradford and Pitcher
Tommie Sisk, latter assigned to Wichita, June 15, 1970.
bSold to Chicago Cubs, September 1, 1970.
cReleased May 10, 1971; signed as free agent by San Diego Padres, May 11, 1971.
dTraded to Pittsburgh Pirates for Pitcher Ed Acosta and Outfielder John Jeter, August 10, 1971.
eUnconditionally released, March 27, 1973; signed as free agent by San Diego Padres, April 2, 1973.

fPurchased via waivers by Detroit Tigers, June 22, 1973.
gSold to New York Mets, September 23, 1973.
hReleased, October 1, 1974; signed as free agent by Hawaii (San Diego Padres' organization) March 31, 1975.

## CHAMPIONSHIP SERIES RECORD

| Year Club | League | G. | IP. | W. | L. | Pct. | H. | R. | ER. | SO. | BB. | ERA. |
|---|---|---|---|---|---|---|---|---|---|---|---|---|
| 1969—Minnesota | American | 1 | 1⅔ | 0 | 1 | .000 | 5 | 3 | 1 | 0 | 0 | 5.40 |
| 1971—Pittsburgh | National | 1 | 3 | 0 | 0 | .000 | 3 | 2 | 2 | 3 | 3 | 6.00 |
| 1972—Pittsburgh | National | 1 | 1 | 0 | 0 | .000 | 0 | 0 | 0 | 1 | 0 | 0.00 |
| Championship Series Totals | | 3 | 5⅔ | 0 | 1 | .000 | 8 | 5 | 3 | 4 | 3 | 4.76 |

## WORLD SERIES RECORD

| Year Club | League | G. | IP. | W. | L. | Pct. | H. | R. | ER. | SO. | BB. | ERA. |
|---|---|---|---|---|---|---|---|---|---|---|---|---|
| 1965—Los Angeles | National | 2 | 1⅓ | 0 | 0 | .000 | 0 | 0 | 0 | 0 | 0 | 0.00 |
| 1966—Los Angeles | National | 1 | 3 | 0 | 0 | .000 | 2 | 0 | 0 | 1 | 2 | 0.00 |
| 1971—Pittsburgh | National | 3 | 4⅔ | 0 | 1 | .000 | 7 | 2 | 2 | 2 | 1 | 3.86 |
| World Series Totals | | 6 | 9 | 0 | 1 | .000 | 9 | 2 | 2 | 3 | 3 | 2.00 |

## RECORD AS MANAGER

| Year Club | League | Position | W. | L. |
|---|---|---|---|---|
| 1976—Amarillo | Texas | †First | 81 | 54 |

†Won playoff by defeating Shreveport, three games to two.

Coach, Toronto Blue Jays, 1977.

# SATURNINO ORESTES ARRIETA MINOSO (ARMAS)
## (Minnie)
## Chicago White Sox

Born November 29, 1922, at Pefico, Matanzas, Cuba.
Height, 5.11. Weight, 175.
Threw and batted righthanded.
Hobbies—Movies and horseback riding.
Father of Orestes Minoso, Jr., outfielder in Kansas City Royals' organization,
1971 through 1974, now playing in Mexican League.

Led American League in stolen bases (31) 1951, (22) 1952 and (25) 1953.
Established major league records for most consecutive years, leading league, hit by pitcher (6), 1956 through 1961; and most years leading league in hit by pitcher (10), 1961.
Established American League record for most times hit by pitch, career, 189, 1949 through 1964 (except 1950 and 1962).
Led American League in total bases with 304 in 1954.
Named by THE SPORTING NEWS as American League Rookie of the Year, 1951.
Named as outfielder on THE SPORTING NEWS All-Star Major League Teams 1959-60.
Received Gold Glove award as outstanding major league fielder in left field, 1957; received award as outstanding American League fielder in left field, 1959-60.

| Year Club | League | Pos. | G. | AB. | R. | H. | 2B. | 3B. | HR. | RBI. | B.A. | PO. | A. | E. | F.A. |
|---|---|---|---|---|---|---|---|---|---|---|---|---|---|---|---|
| 1948—Dayton | Cent. | 3B-2B | 11 | 40 | 14 | 21 | 7 | 1 | 1 | 8 | .525 | 6 | 26 | 0 | 1.000 |
| 1949—Cleveland | Amer. | OF | 9 | 16 | 2 | 3 | 0 | 0 | 1 | 1 | .188 | 11 | 0 | 0 | 1.000 |
| 1949—San Diego | P.C. | OF | 137 | 532 | 99 | 158 | 19 | 7 | 22 | 75 | .297 | 309 | 10 | 12 | .964 |
| 1950—San Diego | P.C. | *3-OF-SS | 169 | 599 | 130 | 203 | 40 | 10 | 20 | 115 | .339 | 209 | 290 | *33 | .938 |
| 1951—Cleve.†-Chicago | Amer. | O-3-1-S | 146 | 530 | 112 | 173 | 34 | *14 | 10 | 76 | .326 | 264 | 130 | 22 | .947 |
| 1952—Chicago | Amer. | OF-3-SS | 147 | 569 | 96 | 160 | 24 | 9 | 13 | 61 | .281 | 323 | 22 | 7 | .980 |
| 1953—Chicago | Amer. | ●OF-3B | 151 | 556 | 104 | 174 | 24 | 8 | 15 | 104 | .313 | 282 | 29 | ●12 | .963 |
| 1954—Chicago | Amer. | OF-3B | 153 | 568 | 119 | 182 | 29 | *18 | 19 | 116 | .320 | 347 | 25 | 9 | .976 |
| 1955—Chicago | Amer. | OF-3B | 139 | 517 | 79 | 149 | 26 | 7 | 10 | 70 | .288 | 289 | 21 | 9 | .972 |
| 1956—Chicago | Amer. | OF-3-1 | 151 | 545 | 106 | 172 | 29 | ●11 | 21 | 88 | .316 | 287 | 16 | 10 | .968 |
| 1957—Chicago‡ | Amer. | OF-3B | 153 | 568 | 96 | 176 | ●36 | 5 | 12 | 103 | .310 | 293 | 9 | 5 | .984 |
| 1958—Cleveland | Amer. | OF-3B | 149 | 556 | 94 | 168 | 25 | 2 | 24 | 80 | .302 | 301 | 13 | 8 | .975 |
| 1959—Cleveland§ | Amer. | OF | 148 | 570 | 92 | 172 | 32 | 0 | 21 | 92 | .302 | 314 | 14 | 5 | .985 |
| 1960—Chicago | Amer. | OF | *154 | 591 | 89 | *184 | 32 | 4 | 20 | 105 | .311 | 282 | 14 | 6 | .980 |
| 1961—Chicago x | Amer. | OF | 152 | 540 | 91 | 151 | 28 | 3 | 14 | 82 | .280 | 273 | 10 | 13 | .956 |
| 1962—St. Louis yz | Nat. | OF | 39 | 97 | 14 | 19 | 5 | 0 | 1 | 10 | .196 | 33 | 2 | 1 | .972 |
| 1963—Washington a | Amer. | OF-3B | 109 | 315 | 38 | 72 | 12 | 2 | 4 | 30 | .229 | 108 | 26 | 5 | .964 |
| 1964—Chicago b | Amer. | OF | 30 | 31 | 4 | 7 | 0 | 0 | 1 | 5 | .226 | 9 | 0 | 0 | 1.000 |
| 1964—Indianapolis | P.C. | OF-3B | 52 | 178 | 22 | 47 | 11 | 0 | 4 | 26 | .264 | 50 | 36 | 9 | .905 |
| 1965—Jalisco | Mex. | OF-3B | 134 | 469 | *106 | 169 | *35 | 10 | 14 | 82 | .360 | 478 | 19 | 11 | .978 |
| 1966—Jalisco c | Mex. | 1B | 107 | 376 | 70 | 131 | 18 | 1 | 6 | 45 | .348 | 922 | 48 | *19 | .981 |
| 1967—Orizaba d | Mex.SE. | OF-3-1 | 36 | 100 | 20 | 35 | 7 | 3 | 5 | 19 | .350 | 76 | 13 | 7 | .927 |
| 1967—Jalisco | Mex. | 1B-OF | 13 | 37 | 5 | 9 | 1 | 2 | 0 | 3 | .243 | 78 | 2 | 0 | 1.000 |
| 1968—Puerto Mex.d | Mex.SE. | 1-OF-3 | 56 | 145 | 30 | 53 | 17 | 2 | 4 | 23 | .366 | 181 | 9 | 8 | .960 |
| 1968—Jalisco | Mex. | OF-1B | 22 | 54 | 9 | 15 | 5 | 1 | 2 | 13 | .296 | 24 | 2 | 0 | 1.000 |
| 1969—Puerto Mex.d | Mex.SE. | 1B-OF | 74 | 193 | 33 | 58 | 10 | 2 | 2 | 32 | .301 | 448 | 10 | 9 | .981 |
| 1969—Jalisco | Mex. | 1-OF-3 | 36 | 103 | 18 | 33 | 3 | 1 | 2 | 14 | .320 | 214 | 11 | 2 | .991 |
| 1970—Gomez Palacio | Mex. | 1B | 40 | 47 | 6 | 22 | 6 | 0 | 2 | 17 | .468 | 25 | 1 | 1 | .963 |
| 1971—Gomez Palacio | Mex. | 1B-2B | 112 | 336 | 37 | 106 | 15 | 2 | 6 | 57 | .315 | 807 | 29 | 11 | .987 |
| 1972—Gomez Palacio | Mex. | 1B | 121 | 425 | 48 | 121 | 24 | 1 | 12 | 63 | .285 | 1015 | 36 | 10 | .991 |
| 1973—Gomez Palacio | Mex. | 1B-OF | 120 | 407 | 50 | 108 | 15 | 1 | 12 | 83 | .265 | 852 | 29 | 10 | .989 |
| 1976—Chicago | Amer. | PH-DH | 3 | 8 | 0 | 1 | 0 | 0 | 0 | 0 | .125 | 0 | 0 | 0 | .000 |
| American League Totals | | 1794 | 6480 | 1122 | 1944 | 331 | 83 | 185 | 1013 | .300 | 3383 | 329 | 111 | .971 |
| National League Totals | | 39 | 97 | 14 | 19 | 5 | 0 | 1 | 10 | .196 | 33 | 2 | 1 | .972 |
| Major League Totals | | 1833 | 6577 | 1136 | 1963 | 336 | 83 | 186 | 1023 | .299 | 3416 | 331 | 112 | .971 |

†Traded to Chicago White Sox as part of three-club deal in which Indians also shipped Pitcher Sam Zoldak and Catcher Ray Murray to Philadelphia Athletics; Cleveland received Pitcher Lou Brissie from Athletics for their share of the players. Athletics also sent Outfielder Paul Lehner to the White Sox and added Outfielder Dave Philley and Gus Zernial from White Sox, April 30, 1951.

‡Traded to Cleveland Indians with Infielder Fred Hatfield for Pitcher Early Wynn and Outfielder Al Smith, December 4, 1957.

§Traded to Chicago White Sox with Pitchers Don Ferrarese and Jake Striker and Catcher Dick Brown for Catcher John Romano, First Baseman Norm Cash and Third Baseman-Outfielder Bubba Phillips, December 6, 1959.

xTraded to St. Louis Cardinals for First Baseman-Outfielder Joe Cunningham, November 27, 1961.

ySuffered skull fracture and broken right wrist chasing line drive, May 11, 1962; returned to active list, July 19—used sparingly for remainder of season.

zTraded to Washington Senators for an estimated $30,000 and minor league player to be named later, April 2, 1963.

aReleased, October 14, 1963; signed as free agent by Chicago White Sox, April 8, 1964.

bReleased, July 17, 1964.

cOn disabled list, May 21 to June 20, 1966.

dPlayer-manager.

### ALL-STAR GAME RECORD

| Year League | Pos. | AB. | R. | H. | 2B. | 3B. | HR. | RBI. | B.A. | PO. | A. | E. | F.A. |
|---|---|---|---|---|---|---|---|---|---|---|---|---|---|
| 1951—American | OF | 2 | 0 | 0 | 0 | 0 | 0 | 0 | .000 | 2 | 0 | 0 | 1.000 |
| 1952—American | OF | 1 | 1 | 1 | 1 | 0 | 0 | 0 | 1.000 | 0 | 0 | 0 | .000 |
| 1953—American | OF | 2 | 0 | 2 | 0 | 0 | 0 | 1 | 1.000 | 0 | 0 | 0 | .000 |
| 1954—American | OF | 4 | 1 | 2 | 0 | 0 | 0 | 0 | .500 | 1 | 0 | 1 | .500 |
| 1957—American | OF | 1 | 0 | 1 | 1 | 0 | 0 | 1 | 1.000 | 1 | 1 | 0 | 1.000 |
| 1959—American (first game) | OF | 5 | 0 | 0 | 0 | 0 | 0 | 0 | .000 | 0 | 1 | 0 | 1.000 |
| 1960—American (both games) | OF | 5 | 0 | 0 | 0 | 0 | 0 | 0 | .000 | 1 | 0 | 0 | 1.000 |
| All-Star Game Totals | | 20 | 2 | 6 | 2 | 0 | 0 | 2 | .300 | 5 | 2 | 1 | .875 |

### RECORD AS MANAGER

| Year Club | League | Position | W. | L. | Year Club | League | Position | W. | L. |
|---|---|---|---|---|---|---|---|---|---|
| 1967—Orizaba | Mex.SE | Seventh | 40 | 66 | 1970—Gomez Palacio | Mexican | Third(N) | 68 | 82 |
| 1968—Puerto Mexico | Mex.SE | Third | 57 | 36 | 1971—Gomez Palacio | Mex. | Fourth(N) | 72 | 76 |
| 1969—Puerto Mexico | Mex.SE | Fourth | 56 | 59 | 1975—Leon | Mex.C. | Sixth | 28 | 39 |

Coach, Chicago White Sox, 1976 and 1977.

## ALEX MONCHAK
### (Al)
### Pittsburgh Pirates

Born December 22, 1919, at Bayonne, N. J.
Height, 6.00. Weight, 180.
Threw right and batted right and lefthanded.

Led Longhorn League in stolen bases with 36 in 1949 and 48 in 1950.
Led Longhorn League second basemen in double plays with 109 in 1949, 140 in 1950 and 128 in 1951.

| Year Club | League | Pos. | G. | AB. | R. | H. | 2B. | 3B. | HR. | RBI. | B.A. | PO. | A. | E. | F.A. |
|---|---|---|---|---|---|---|---|---|---|---|---|---|---|---|---|
| 1937—Knoxville | South. | ...... | 1 | 3 | 0 | 1 | 0 | 0 | 0 | 0 | .000 | .... | .... | ...... | |
| 1937—Albany | NYP | INF | (Appeared in less than 10 games; no figures available.) | | | | | | | | | | | | |
| 1937—Clarksdale | Cot.St. | SS | 45 | 167 | 25 | 41 | 6 | 1 | 2 | 16 | .246 | 91 | 111 | 19 | .914 |
| 1937—Baltimore | Int. | INF | 14 | 34 | 4 | 6 | 1 | 0 | 0 | 0 | .176 | .... | .... | .... | ...... |
| 1938—Dover | E.Shore | SS | 95 | 390 | 86 | 118 | 21 | 7 | 10 | 46 | .303 | 204 | 314 | 31 | .944 |
| 1939—Dover | E.Shore | SS-3B | 104 | 389 | 88 | 131 | 22 | 6 | 15 | 73 | .337 | 229 | 291 | 32 | .977 |
| 1939—Baltimore | Int. | INF | 3 | 6 | .... | 1 | .... | .... | .... | .... | .167 | .... | .... | .... | ...... |
| 1940—Philadelphia | Nat. | INF | 19 | 14 | 1 | 2 | 0 | 0 | 0 | 0 | .143 | .... | .... | .... | ...... |
| 1940—Portsmouth | Pied. | SS | 43 | 142 | 26 | 38 | 11 | 2 | 4 | 18 | .268 | 80 | 137 | 11 | .952 |
| 1941—Elmira | East. | SS | 92 | 287 | 40 | 61 | 9 | 0 | 3 | 17 | .212 | 154 | 222 | 22 | .945 |
| 1942—Elmira | East. | 2B-SS | 50 | 176 | 21 | 43 | 4 | 2 | 0 | 10 | .244 | 139 | 144 | 16 | .947 |
| 1943-44-45— | | | (In Military Service) | | | | | | | | | | | | |
| 1946—Hartford | East. | 2B | 63 | 215 | 37 | 38 | 5 | 0 | 2 | 15 | .177 | 144 | 185 | 10 | .971 |
| 1947— | | | (Out of Organized Baseball) | | | | | | | | | | | | |
| 1948—Austin | Big St. | 2B | 120 | 446 | 84 | 129 | 20 | 9 | 1 | 64 | .289 | 361 | 364 | 22 | *.971 |
| 1949—Odessa | Long. | 2B | 137 | 522 | *147 | 175 | 37 | 6 | *35 | 125 | .335 | *402 | *455 | 23 | .974 |
| 1950—Odessa | Long. | 2B | 134 | 488 | 126 | 147 | 37 | 5 | 19 | 108 | .301 | *450 | *388 | 27 | *.969 |
| 1951—Roswell | Long. | 2B | 140 | 565 | 113 | 176 | 41 | 5 | 22 | 123 | .311 | *409 | *394 | 25 | *.970 |
| 1952—Roswell | Long. | 2B | 113 | 417 | 80 | 110 | 23 | 3 | 10 | 62 | .264 | 326 | *335 | 21 | *.970 |
| 1953—Lexington | Tar Heel | 2B | 112 | 388 | 61 | 90 | 18 | 5 | 7 | 43 | .232 | *313 | *327 | 20 | *.970 |
| 1954—Portsmouth | Pied. | 2B | 79 | 274 | 23 | 72 | 8 | 5 | 3 | 41 | .265 | 197 | 178 | 11 | .972 |
| 1954—Keokuk | I.I.I. | 2B | 34 | 123 | 17 | 27 | 3 | 1 | 2 | 17 | .220 | 84 | 95 | 7 | .962 |
| 1955—Wellsville | PONY | 2B | 100 | 319 | 50 | 76 | 20 | 1 | 7 | 64 | .238 | 248 | 212 | 11 | *.977 |
| 1956—Wellsville | PONY | 2B | 35 | 99 | 9 | 21 | 3 | 0 | 2 | 12 | .212 | 18 | 25 | 0 | 1.000 |
| 1957—Wellsville | NYP | INF | 4 | 13 | 0 | 0 | 0 | 0 | 0 | 0 | .000 | .... | .... | .... | ...... |
| Major League Totals | | | 19 | 14 | 1 | 2 | 0 | 0 | 0 | | .143 | .... | .... | .... | ...... |

### PITCHING RECORD

| Year Club | League | G. | IP. | W. | L. | Pct. | H. | R. | ER. | SO. | BB. | ERA. |
|---|---|---|---|---|---|---|---|---|---|---|---|---|
| 1954—Portsmouth | Piedmont | 1 | .... | 0 | 0 | .000 | .... | .... | .... | .... | .... | .... |
| 1956—Wellsville | PONY | 1 | .... | 0 | 1 | .000 | .... | .... | .... | .... | .... | .... |

## RECORD AS MANAGER

| Year Club | League | Position | W. | L. | Year Club | League | Position | W. | L. |
|---|---|---|---|---|---|---|---|---|---|
| 1949–Odessa | Long. | Fifth | 66 | 74 | 1957–Wellsville | NYP | zFirst | 74 | 43 |
| 1950–Odessa | Long. | †First | 97 | 55 | 1958–Cedar Rapids | I.I.I. | Fourth | 28 | 40 |
| 1951–Roswell | Long. | Third | 79 | 61 | (Second Half) | | aFirst | 49 | 23 |
| 1952–Roswell | Long. | ‡Fifth | 65 | 75 | 1959–Cedar Rapids | I.I.I. | Fifth | 30 | 30 |
| 1953–Lexington | Tar Heel | §Fourth | 59 | 54 | (Second Half) | | Eighth | 23 | 43 |
| 1954–Portsmouth x | Pied. | Third | 50 | 47 | 1960–Austin | Texas | Fifth | 73 | 71 |
| 1955–Wellsville | PONY | Fourth | 68 | 58 | 1961–Davenport | Midw. | Fourth | 32 | 30 |
| 1956–Wellsville | PONY | yFirst | 74 | 46 | (Second Half) | | Second | 36 | 26 |

†Won playoffs by defeating Vernon, four games to one and Big Spring, four games to three.
‡Tied for position with San Angelo.
§Won playoffs by defeating Rutherford County, four games to two and Marion, four games to two.
xReplaced August 1 by Pepper Martin.
yWon playoffs by defeating Hornell, two games to one and Olean, three games to two.
zLost playoff semifinal series to Batavia, two games to one.
aWon playoff by defeating Davenport (First Half winner), three games to two.

Scout and farm system instructor, California Angels, 1962 through 1970; coach, Chicago White Sox, 1971 through 1975; coach, Oakland Athletics, 1976; coach, Pittsburgh Pirates, 1977.

## JACKIE SPENCER MOORE
### Toronto Blue Jays

Born February 19, 1939, at Jay, Fla.
Height, 6.00, Weight, 181.
Threw and batted righthanded.
Hobbies—Hunting, fishing and golf.

| Year Club | League | Pos. | G. | AB. | R. | H. | 2B. | 3B. | HR. | RBI. | B.A. | PO. | A. | E. | F.A. |
|---|---|---|---|---|---|---|---|---|---|---|---|---|---|---|---|
| 1957–Montgomery | Al.-Fla. | O-C | 71 | 263 | 36 | 62 | 6 | 1 | 7 | 35 | .236 | 237 | 18 | 10 | .962 |
| 1958–Valdosta | Ga.-Fla. | C-3 | 87 | 333 | 61 | 100 | 20 | 3 | 9 | 78 | .300 | 445 | 75 | 11 | .979 |
| 1958–Augusta | Sally | C-OF | 13 | 35 | 4 | 8 | 1 | 1 | 1 | 12 | .229 | 31 | 3 | 0 | 1.000 |
| 1959–Durham | Carol. | C-OF | 94 | 305 | 43 | 79 | 18 | 2 | 8 | 55 | .259 | 407 | 33 | 8 | .982 |
| 1960–Knoxville | Sally | C | 97 | 314 | 40 | 85 | 15 | 3 | 10 | 40 | .271 | 541 | 46 | 10 | .983 |
| 1961–Knoxville | Sally | C-2-3B | 43 | 151 | 14 | 45 | 6 | 3 | 0 | 30 | .298 | 248 | 22 | 2 | .993 |
| 1961–Denver | A. A. | C | 43 | 134 | 8 | 32 | 3 | 0 | 0 | 8 | .239 | 218 | 26 | 3 | .988 |
| 1962–Denver† | A. A. | C-OF | 32 | 98 | 10 | 25 | 3 | 0 | 0 | 14 | .255 | 164 | 10 | 3 | .983 |
| 1962–Toronto | Int. | C | 12 | 29 | 3 | 4 | 0 | 0 | 0 | 2 | .138 | 56 | 6 | 1 | .984 |
| 1963–Syracuse‡ | Int. | C | 73 | 213 | 23 | 63 | 5 | 1 | 7 | 37 | .296 | 371 | 30 | 4 | .990 |
| 1964–Syracuse | Int. | C | 99 | 286 | 34 | 68 | 8 | 1 | 1 | 31 | .238 | 449 | 35 | 6 | .988 |
| 1965–Detroit | Amer. | C | 21 | 53 | 2 | 5 | 0 | 0 | 0 | 2 | .094 | 128 | 6 | 2 | .985 |
| 1965–Syracuse§ | Int. | C | 17 | 50 | 3 | 9 | 2 | 0 | 0 | 4 | .100 | 80 | 4 | 1 | .988 |
| 1966–Syracuse x | Int. | C | 89 | 290 | 24 | 60 | 11 | 2 | 2 | 17 | .207 | 429 | 37 | 4 | •.991 |
| 1967–Toronto y | Int. | C | 100 | 307 | 21 | 61 | 4 | 0 | 3 | 30 | .199 | •643 | 40 | 4 | •.994 |
| Major League Totals | | | 21 | 53 | 2 | 5 | 0 | 0 | 0 | 2 | .094 | 128 | 6 | 2 | .985 |

†On disabled list, June 19 to August 2, 1962.
‡Conditionally released by Detroit Tigers' organization to Los Angeles Angels, October 11, 1963; returned by Angels to Tigers, March 27, 1964.
§On disabled list, July 31 through August 14, 1965.
xAssigned by Detroit Tigers to Boston Red Sox, October 13, 1966, to complete deal in which Tigers obtained Pitcher Bill Monbouquette from Red Sox for Outfielder George Thomas and Infielder George Smith, October 4, 1965.
yReleased by Boston Red Sox' organization, February 21, 1968.

### RECORD AS MANAGER

| Year Club | League | Position | W. | L. |
|---|---|---|---|---|
| 1968–Jamestown | NYP | Seventh | 31 | 44 |
| 1969–Jamestown | NYP | Sixth | 33 | 41 |
| 1975–Pittsfield | Eastern | Fourth | 27 | 32 |
| (Second Half)† | | | 13 | 8 |

†Replaced by Orlando Martinez, July 24.

Coach, Milwaukee Brewers, 1970 through 1972; Texas Rangers, 1973 and 1974, part of 1975 and 1976; Toronto Blue Jays, 1977.

## MAURICE JOSEPH MOZZALI
### (Mo)
### St. Louis Cardinals

Born December 12, 1922, at Louisville, Ky.
Height, 5.10. Weight, 160.
Threw and batted lefthanded.
Hobby—Golf.

| Year Club | League | Pos. | G. | AB. | R. | H. | 2B. | 3B. | HR. | RBI. | B.A. | PO. | A. | E. | F.A. |
|---|---|---|---|---|---|---|---|---|---|---|---|---|---|---|---|
| 1946–Jacksonville | S.A.L. | OF | 18 | 54 | 12 | 10 | 3 | 1 | 0 | 3 | .185 | 11 | 0 | 2 | .846 |
| 1946–Manchester | N.E.L. | OF-1B | 113 | 419 | 104 | 149 | 21 | 10 | 19 | •118 | •.356 | 216 | 15 | 10 | .958 |
| 1947–Minn.†-Colum. | A.A. | OF | 114 | 340 | 71 | 102 | 15 | 3 | 6 | 35 | .300 | 179 | 11 | 3 | .984 |
| 1948–Columbus | A.A. | OF-1B | 98 | 274 | 63 | 80 | 18 | 1 | 2 | 27 | .292 | 220 | 8 | 4 | .974 |
| 1949–Columbus‡ | A.A. | | | | | | (Inactive) | | | | | | | | |

| Year | Club | League | Pos. | G. | AB. | R. | H. | 2B. | 3B. | HR. | RBI. | B.A. | PO. | A. | E. | F.A. |
|------|------|--------|------|-----|-----|-----|-----|-----|-----|-----|------|------|------|-----|-----|------|
| 1950—Columbus | ..........A.A. | | 1B-OF | 115 | 375 | 74 | 115 | 20 | 4 | 4 | 47 | .307 | 597 | 42 | 10 | .985 |
| 1951—Columbus | ..........A.A. | | 1B-OF | 123 | 426 | 81 | 124 | 32 | 3 | 8 | 49 | .291 | 629 | 50 | 7 | .990 |
| 1952—Columbus | ..........A.A. | | OF-1B | 81 | 225 | 41 | 71 | 13 | 5 | 2 | 27 | .278 | 228 | 10 | 2 | .992 |
| 1953—Columbus | ..........A.A. | | 1B | 154 | 534 | 91 | 157 | 27 | 12 | 5 | 72 | .294•1360 | | 116 | 10 | .993 |
| 1954—Columbus | ..........A.A. | | 1B | 152 | 543 | 88 | 157 | 29 | 4 | 11 | 79 | .289 | 1337 | 94 | 15 | .990 |
| 1955—Omaha | ..............A.A. | | 1B-OF | 117 | 319 | 49 | 86 | 15 | 0 | 10 | 53 | .270 | 390 | 40 | 3 | .991 |
| 1956—Omaha | ..............A.A. | | 1B-OF | 132 | 434 | 63 | 131 | 17 | 3 | 5 | 58 | .302 | 567 | 40 | 3 | .995 |
| 1957—Rochester§ | .......Int. | | 1B-OF | 133 | 430 | 52 | 116 | 26 | 2 | 5 | 40 | .270 | 700 | 91 | 6 | .992 |
| 1958—Albany x | ..........Ga.-Fla. | | 1B | 113 | 328 | 100 | 110 | 29 | 1 | 3 | 63 | .335 | 742 | 58 | 9 | .989 |

†Traded to St. Louis Cardinals' organization, July 2, 1947.
‡On suspended list, April 19, 1949. Transferred to restricted list, May 7, 1949 to March 28, 1950.
§Player—coach.
xPlayer—manager. Released by St. Louis Cardinals' organization, January 23, 1959.

## RECORD AS MANAGER

| Year | Club | League | Position | W. | L. |
|------|------|--------|----------|----|----|
| 1958—Albany | ..............Ga.-Fla. | | †First | 42 | 21 |
| (Second Half) | | | ‡First | 44 | 20 |
| 1961—Johnson City | ......Appal. | | Eighth | 26 | 38 |

†Lost to Valdosta, July 9, in playoff to decide first-half title.
‡Lost to Valdosta, three games to one.

Scout, St. Louis Cardinals, 1959 through 1976; coach, St. Louis Cardinals, 1977.

# BILLY ARNOLD MUFFETT
## California Angels

Born September 21, 1930, at Hammond, Ind.
Height, 6.01. Weight, 208.
Threw and batted righthanded.
Hobbies—Hunting, fishing and golf.

Pitched 10-0 no-hit victory against San Antonio in Texas League playoffs, September 12, 1955.
Tied for Cotton States League lead in shutouts with 6 in 1951.
Named Most Valuable Player in Cotton States League, 1951.

| Year | Club | League | G. | IP. | W. | L. | Pct. | H. | R. | ER. | SO. | BB. | ERA. |
|------|------|--------|-----|-----|-----|-----|------|-----|-----|-----|-----|-----|------|
| 1949—Helena | ................................Cotton St. | | 35 | 164 | 10 | 10 | .500 | 187 | 142 | •109 | 71 | 154 | 5.98 |
| 1950—Monroe | ................................Cotton St. | | 27 | 205 | 11 | 13 | .458 | 166 | 95 | 68 | 105 | 139 | 2.98 |
| 1951—Shreveport | ..........................Texas | | 4 | 8 | 0 | 1 | .000 | 7 | 8 | 2 | 7 | 12 | 2.25 |
| 1951—Monroe | ................................Cotton St. | | 35 | 244 | •22 | 9 | •.710 | 173 | 75 | 61 | 159 | 129 | •2.25 |
| 1952-53—Shreveport | ......................Texas | | | | | | | (In Military Service) | | | | | |
| 1954—Shreveport | ..........................Texas | | 34 | 149 | 5 | 11 | .313 | 145 | 90 | 80 | 82 | 92 | 4.83 |
| 1955—Macon | ...................................Sally | | 16 | 59 | 3 | 4 | .429 | 69 | 36 | 32 | 27 | 40 | 4.91 |
| 1955—Shreveport† | ..........................Texas | | 26 | 127 | 10 | 4 | .714 | 111 | 52 | 43 | 57 | 64 | 3.05 |
| 1956—Omaha | ...............................Am. Assoc. | | 5 | 11 | 0 | 0 | .000 | 12 | 11 | 8 | 7 | 8 | 6.55 |
| 1956—Houston | ..............................Texas | | 28 | 171 | 14 | 10 | .583 | 127 | 58 | 51 | 98 | 54 | 2.68 |
| 1957—Houston | ..............................Texas | | 25 | 188 | 14 | 6 | .700 | 142 | 49 | 46 | 139 | 64 | 2.20 |
| 1957—St. Louis | ............................National | | 23 | 44 | 3 | 2 | .600 | 35 | 11 | 11 | 21 | 13 | 2.25 |
| 1958—Omaha | ...............................Am. Assoc. | | 3 | 28 | 2 | 1 | .667 | 19 | 9 | 0 | 16 | 9 | 2.89 |
| 1958—St. Louis‡ | ..........................National | | 35 | 84 | 4 | 6 | .400 | 107 | 52 | 46 | 41 | 42 | 4.93 |
| 1959—Phoenix | ...............................P. Coast | | 12 | 54 | 3 | 2 | .600 | 79 | 45 | 33 | 21 | 17 | 5.50 |
| 1959—San Francisco§ | ...................National | | 5 | 7 | 0 | 0 | .000 | 11 | 6 | 4 | 3 | 3 | 5.14 |
| 1959—Minneapolis | ...........................Am. Assoc. | | 20 | 55 | 4 | 4 | .500 | 55 | 27 | 21 | 35 | 29 | 3.44 |
| 1960—Minneapolis | ...........................Am. Assoc. | | 17 | 96 | 5 | 5 | .500 | 99 | 40 | 28 | 60 | 22 | 2.63 |
| 1960—Boston | ...............................American | | 23 | 125 | 6 | 4 | .600 | 116 | 53 | 45 | 75 | 36 | 3.24 |
| 1961—Boston | ...............................American | | 38 | 113 | 3 | 11 | .214 | 130 | 87 | 71 | 47 | 36 | 5.65 |
| 1962—Boston | ...............................American | | 1 | 4 | 0 | 0 | .000 | 8 | 4 | 4 | 1 | 2 | 9.00 |
| 1962—Seattle x | .............................P. Coast | | 8 | 37 | 1 | 2 | .333 | 33 | 18 | 13 | 19 | 13 | 3.16 |
| 1962—Atlanta y | ............................Int'national | | 17 | 61 | 4 | 6 | .400 | 74 | 28 | 23 | 30 | 21 | 3.39 |
| 1963—Richmond | ..........................Int'national | | 28 | 145 | 10 | 6 | .625 | 129 | 45 | 39 | 79 | 25 | 2.42 |
| 1964—Richmond | ..........................Int'national | | 31 | 136 | 9 | 9 | .500 | 148 | 72 | 64 | 64 | 34 | 4.24 |
| 1965—Tulsa | ..................................Texas | | 8 | 15 | 0 | 1 | .000 | 25 | 11 | 9 | 5 | 2 | 5.40 |
| American League Totals | | | 62 | 242 | 9 | 15 | .375 | 254 | 140 | 120 | 123 | 74 | 4.46 |
| National League Totals | | | 63 | 135 | 7 | 8 | .467 | 153 | 69 | 61 | 65 | 58 | 4.07 |
| Major League Totals | | | 125 | 377 | 16 | 23 | .410 | 407 | 209 | 181 | 188 | 132 | 4.32 |

†Drafted from Los Angeles by St. Louis Cardinals, November 28, 1955.
‡Traded with Catcher Hobie Landrith and Third Baseman Benny Valenzuela to San Francisco Giants for Pitchers Ernie Broglio and Marv Grisson, October 8, 1958.
§Traded to Boston Red Sox for Pitcher Bud Byerly, July 26, 1959.
xReleased by Boston Red Sox' organization to Atlanta (St. Louis Cardinals' organization), June 27, 1962.
yDrafted from Tulsa (St. Louis Cardinals' organization) by Richmond (New York Yankees' organization), November 26, 1962.
zReleased by New York Yankees' organization, September 22, 1964; signed as free agent by Tulsa (St. Louis Cardinals' organization), January 23, 1965.

Coach, Tulsa (Texas League), 1965; minor league pitching coach, St. Louis Cardinals, 1966; coach, St. Louis Cardinals, 1967 through 1970; minor league pitching instructor, California Angeles, 1971 through August 22, 1974; coach, California Angeles, part of 1974; 1975 through 1977.

## RUSSELL EUGENE NIXON
### (Russ)
### Cincinnati Reds

Born February 19, 1935, at Cleves, O.
Height, 6.01. Weight, 190.
Threw right and batted lefthanded.
Hobby—Hunting.
Attended Univeristy of Cincinnati, Cincinnati, O.
Twin brother of Roy Nixon, former first baseman in Cleveland Indians' organization.

Led Florida State League catchers in double plays with 14 and passed balls with 23 in 1954.

| Year Club | League | Pos. | G. | AB. | R. | H. | 2B. | 3B. | HR. | RBI. | B.A. | PO. | A. | E. | F.A. |
|---|---|---|---|---|---|---|---|---|---|---|---|---|---|---|---|
| 1953—Green Bay | Wis. St. | C-OF | 43 | 137 | 17 | 46 | 6 | 5 | 0 | 30 | .336 | 213 | 22 | 6 | .975 |
| 1954—Jack'ville Beach | Fla. St. | C | 125 | 465 | 114 | 180 | •36 | 12 | 6 | 96 | •.387 | •821 | •95 | 22 | .977 |
| 1955—Keokuk | I.I.I. | C | 94 | 358 | 66 | 138 | 29 | 2 | 5 | 77 | •.385 | •718 | 47 | 10 | •.987 |
| 1956—Indianapolis | A. A. | C | 105 | 320 | 38 | 102 | 19 | 5 | 4 | 44 | .319 | 402 | 37 | 9 | .980 |
| 1957—Cleveland | Amer. | C | 62 | 185 | 15 | 52 | 7 | 1 | 2 | 18 | .281 | 268 | 31 | 5 | .984 |
| 1958—Cleveland | Amer. | C | 113 | 376 | 42 | 113 | 17 | 4 | 9 | 46 | .301 | 499 | 31 | 5 | .991 |
| 1959—Cleveland | Amer. | C | 82 | 258 | 23 | 62 | 10 | 3 | 1 | 29 | .240 | 374 | 31 | 6 | .985 |
| 1960—Clev.†-Boston | Amer. | C | 105 | 354 | 30 | 101 | 22 | 3 | 6 | 39 | .285 | 488 | 34 | 6 | .989 |
| 1961—Boston | Amer. | C | 87 | 242 | 24 | 70 | 12 | 2 | 1 | 19 | .289 | 330 | 21 | 9 | .975 |
| 1962—Boston | Amer. | C | 65 | 151 | 11 | 42 | 7 | 2 | 1 | 19 | .278 | 201 | 7 | 0 | 1.000 |
| 1963—Boston | Amer. | C | 98 | 287 | 27 | 77 | 18 | 1 | 5 | 30 | .268 | 483 | 22 | 4 | .992 |
| 1964—Boston | Amer. | C | 81 | 163 | 10 | 38 | 7 | 0 | 1 | 20 | .233 | 273 | 11 | 3 | .990 |
| 1965—Boston | Amer. | C | 59 | 137 | 11 | 37 | 5 | 1 | 0 | 11 | .270 | 200 | 10 | 4 | .981 |
| 1965—Toronto‡ | Int. | C | 31 | 93 | 10 | 30 | 3 | 2 | 0 | 14 | .323 | 195 | 11 | 3 | .986 |
| 1966—Minnesota | Amer. | C | 51 | 90 | 5 | 25 | 2 | 1 | 0 | 7 | .260 | 137 | 5 | 2 | .986 |
| 1967—Minnesota§ | Amer. | C | 74 | 170 | 16 | 40 | 6 | 1 | 1 | 22 | .235 | 306 | 26 | 2 | .994 |
| 1968—Pittsfield | East. | C-OF | 41 | 137 | 15 | 29 | 3 | 2 | 0 | 13 | .212 | 214 | 23 | 3 | .988 |
| 1968—Boston x | Amer. | C | 29 | 85 | 1 | 13 | 2 | 0 | 0 | 6 | .153 | 147 | 6 | 1 | .994 |
| Major League Totals | | | 906 | 2504 | 215 | 670 | 115 | 19 | 27 | 266 | .268 | 3708 | 238 | 47 | .988 |

†Traded with Outfielder Carroll Hardy to Boston Red Sox for Pitcher Ted Bowsfield and Outfielder Marty Keough, June 13, 1960. (Indians had traded Nixon to Red Sox for First Baseman Jim Marshall and Catcher Stan White, March 16, 1960, but deal was cancelled by Commissioner Ford Frick on March 25 because of White's request for voluntary retirement.)

‡Recalled by Boston Red Sox and traded with Infielder Chuck Schilling to Minnesota Twins for Pitcher Dick Stigman and a player to be named later, April 6, 1966; First Baseman Jose Calero assigned to Winston-Salem to complete deal, April 17, 1966.

§Released April 8, 1968, and signed as free agent by Boston Red Sox.

xDrafted from Louisville (Boston Red Sox' organization) by Chicago White Sox, December 2, 1968. Released by Chicago White Sox, April 5, 1969.

### RECORD AS MANAGER

| Year Club | League | Position | W. | L. |
|---|---|---|---|---|
| 1970—Sioux Falls | Northern | Sixth | 24 | 46 |
| 1971—Tampa | Fla. St. | Second(W) | 79 | 61 |
| 1972—Tampa | Fla. St. | Second(W) | 66 | 64 |
| 1973—Tampa | Fla. St. | Fourth(N) | 73 | 71 |
| 1974—Tampa | Fla. St. | †First(N) | 68 | 64 |
| 1975—Tampa | Fla. St. | Second(N) | 72 | 59 |

†Lost semifinal playoff series to West Palm Beach, two games to none.

Coach, Cincinnati Reds, 1976 and 1977.


## JOSEPH RUDOLPH NOSSEK

Name pronounced NAH-sek.

### (Joe)
### Cleveland Indians

Born November 8, 1940, at Cleveland, O.
Height, 6.00. Weight, 175.
Threw and batted righthanded.
Hobbies—Bowling, archery and collecting recordings.
Attended Ohio University, Athens, O.

Led Pacific Coast League outfielders in double plays with 7 in 1968.

| Year Club | League | Pos. | G. | AB. | R. | H. | 2B. | 3B. | HR. | RBI. | B.A. | PO. | A. | E. | F.A. |
|---|---|---|---|---|---|---|---|---|---|---|---|---|---|---|---|
| 1961—Charlotte | Sally | OF-3B | 80 | 303 | 24 | 83 | 9 | 3 | 0 | 27 | .274 | 162 | 33 | 10 | .951 |
| 1962—Charlotte | Sally | O-3-2B | 134 | 521 | 58 | 144 | 17 | 4 | 3 | 56 | .276 | 297 | 25 | 14 | .958 |
| 1963—Dal.-Ft. Worth | .P. C. | OF-3B | 128 | 447 | 38 | 131 | 22 | 2 | 4 | 52 | .293 | 276 | 15 | 9 | .970 |
| 1964—Atlanta | Int. | O-3-2B | 113 | 424 | 47 | 101 | 11 | 2 | 8 | 29 | .238 | 303 | 29 | 12 | .965 |
| 1964—Minnesota | Amer. | OF | 7 | 1 | 1 | 0 | 0 | 0 | 0 | 0 | .000 | 0 | 0 | 0 | .000 |
| 1965—Minnesota | Amer. | OF-3B | 87 | 170 | 19 | 37 | 9 | 0 | 2 | 16 | .218 | 72 | 26 | 4 | .961 |
| 1966—Minn.†-K. C. | Amer. | OF-3B | 91 | 230 | 13 | 60 | 10 | 3 | 1 | 27 | .261 | 161 | 8 | 3 | .983 |
| 1967—Kansas City | Amer. | OF | 87 | 166 | 12 | 34 | 6 | 1 | 0 | 10 | .205 | 105 | 2 | 2 | .982 |
| 1968—Vancouver | .P. C. | •O-3-P | 146 | 539 | 53 | 133 | 15 | 3 | 3 | 36 | .247 | •374 | •39 | 11 | .974 |
| 1969—Oakland | Amer. | OF | 13 | 6 | 0 | 0 | 0 | 0 | 0 | 0 | .000 | 7 | 0 | 0 | 1.000 |
| 1969—Iowa‡-Tulsa | A. A. | OF-3B | 50 | 195 | 26 | 66 | 8 | 0 | 3 | 27 | .338 | 99 | 6 | 5 | .955 |
| 1969—St. Louis | Nat. | OF | 9 | 5 | 2 | 1 | 0 | 0 | 0 | 0 | .200 | 2 | 0 | 0 | 1.000 |

| Year | Club | League | Pos. | G. | AB. | R. | H. | 2B. | 3B. | HR. | RBI. | B.A. | PO. | A. | E. | F.A. |
|---|---|---|---|---|---|---|---|---|---|---|---|---|---|---|---|---|
| 1970—Tulsa ...............A. A. | | | O-3-2-1 | 116 | 356 | 35 | 81 | 11 | 1 | 2 | 30 | .228 | 165 | 40 | 6 | .972 |
| 1970—St. Louis§.........Nat. | | | PH | 1 | 1 | 0 | 0 | 0 | 0 | 0 | 0 | .000 | 0 | 0 | 0 | .000 |
| 1971—Evansville x ......A. A. | | | O-S-3-P-2 | 67 | 157 | 17 | 35 | 4 | 0 | 1 | 17 | .223 | 79 | 16 | 6 | .941 |
| American League Totals ................ | | | | 285 | 573 | 45 | 131 | 25 | 4 | 3 | 53 | .229 | 345 | 36 | 9 | .977 |
| National League Totals ................. | | | | 10 | 6 | 2 | 1 | 0 | 0 | 0 | 0 | .167 | 2 | 0 | 0 | 1.000 |
| Major League Totals ...................... | | | | 295 | 579 | 47 | 132 | 25 | 4 | 3 | 53 | .228 | 347 | 36 | 9 | .977 |

†Sold to Kansas City Athletics, May 11, 1966.
‡Released to Tulsa (St. Louis Cardinals' organization), July 12, 1969, in trade which sent Infielder Robert W. Johnson from St. Louis Cardinals to Oakland A's.
§Sold to Milwaukee Brewers, February 4, 1971.
xPlayer-coach.

### WORLD SERIES RECORD

| Year | Club | League | Pos. | G. | AB. | R. | H. | 2B. | 3B. | HR. | RBI. | B.A. | PO. | A. | E. | F.A. |
|---|---|---|---|---|---|---|---|---|---|---|---|---|---|---|---|---|
| 1965—Minnesota ........Amer. | | | OF-PH | 6 | 20 | 0 | 4 | 0 | 0 | 0 | 0 | .200 | 13 | 0 | 0 | 1.000 |

### PITCHING RECORD

| Year | Club | League | G. | IP. | W. | L. | Pct. | H. | R. | ER. | SO. | BB. | ERA. |
|---|---|---|---|---|---|---|---|---|---|---|---|---|---|
| 1968—Vancouver...........................P. Coast | | | 7 | 7 | 1 | 0 | 1.000 | 6 | 1 | 1 | 2 | 0 | 1.29 |
| 1971—Evansville ...........................Am. Assoc. | | | 1 | 2 | 0 | 0 | .000 | 1 | 1 | 1 | 0 | 3 | 4.50 |

### RECORD AS MANAGER

| | Year | Club | League | Position | W. | L. |
|---|---|---|---|---|---|---|
| | 1972—Danville ............Midwest | | | †First(S) | 73 | 52 |

†Won championship playoff against Appleton, two games to none.
Coach, Milwaukee Brewers, 1973 through 1975; coach, Minnesota Twins, 1976; coach, Cleveland Indians, 1977.

## ANTONIO OLIVA (LOPEZ)
Name pronounced Aw-LEE-vah.
### (Tony)
(Used brother Tony's passport to enter country.)
### Minnesota Twins
Born July 20, 1940, at Pinar del Rio, Cuba.
Height, 6.02. Weight, 192.
Threw right and batted lefthanded.
Hobbies—Swimming and golf.

Tied major league records for most total bases, rookie season (374), 1964, and most consecutive years leading league in hits, 3, 1966.

Established American League records for most hits, rookie season (217), 1964; and most seasons, 10 or more intentional bases on balls, 9, 1975.

Hit three home runs in a game, July 3, 1973 against Kansas City Royals.
Led American League in slugging percentage, .546, in 1971.
Led Appalachian League in total bases with 159 and tied for lead in double plays by outfielders with 3 in 1961.
Named Rookie of the Year in Appalachian League, 1961.
Named American League Rookie of the Year by the Baseball Writers' Association and Rookie Player of the Year by THE SPORTING NEWS, 1964.
Named as outfielder on THE SPORTING NEWS American League All-Star Team, 1964-65-66-70-71.
Named American League Player of the Year by THE SPORTING NEWS, 1965.
Named as outfielder on THE SPORTING NEWS American League All-Star Fielding team, 1966.
Named American League Player of the Year by THE SPORTING NEWS, 1971.

| Year | Club | League | Pos. | G. | AB. | R. | H. | 2B. | 3B. | HR. | RBI. | B.A. | PO. | A. | E. | F.A. |
|---|---|---|---|---|---|---|---|---|---|---|---|---|---|---|---|---|
| 1961—Wytheville ........Appal. | | | OF | 64 | 249 | 55 | •102 | 15 | 6 | 10 | •81 | •.410 | 70 | •12 | 14 | .854 |
| 1962—Charlotte† ........Sally | | | OF | 127 | 469 | 71 | 164 | 35 | 6 | 17 | 93 | .350 | 231 | 13 | •19 | .928 |
| 1962—Minnesota ........Amer. | | | OF | 9 | 9 | 3 | 4 | 1 | 0 | 0 | 3 | .444 | 3 | 0 | 0 | 1.000 |
| 1963—Dal.-Ft. Worth ..P.C. | | | OF | 146 | 536 | 79 | 163 | 30 | 8 | 23 | 74 | .304 | 301 | 14 | 11 | .966 |
| 1963—Minnesota ........Amer. | | | PH | 7 | 7 | 0 | 3 | 0 | 0 | 0 | 1 | .429 | 0 | 0 | 0 | .000 |
| 1964—Minnesota ........Amer. | | | OF | 161 | 672 | •109 | •217 | •43 | 9 | 32 | 94 | •.323 | 313 | 5 | 6 | .981 |
| 1965—Minnesota ........Amer. | | | OF | 149 | 576 | 107 | •185 | 40 | 5 | 16 | 98 | •.321 | 284 | 10 | •11 | .964 |
| 1966—Minnesota ........Amer. | | | OF | 159 | 622 | 99 | •191 | 32 | 7 | 25 | 87 | .307 | 335 | 9 | •10 | .972 |
| 1967—Minnesota ........Amer. | | | OF | 146 | 557 | 76 | 161 | •34 | 6 | 17 | 83 | .289 | 286 | 8 | 4 | .987 |
| 1968—Minnesota ........Amer. | | | OF | 128 | 470 | 54 | 136 | 24 | 5 | 18 | 68 | .289 | 227 | 7 | 4 | .983 |
| 1969—Minnesota ........Amer. | | | OF | 153 | 637 | 97 | •197 | •39 | 4 | 24 | 101 | .309 | 311 | 14 | 6 | .982 |
| 1970—Minnesota ........Amer. | | | OF | 157 | 628 | 96 | •204 | •36 | 7 | 23 | 107 | .325 | 351 | 12 | •12 | .968 |
| 1971—Minnesota ........Amer. | | | OF | 126 | 487 | 73 | 164 | 30 | 3 | 22 | 81 | •.337 | 216 | 6 | 7 | .969 |
| 1972—Minnesota‡ ........Amer. | | | OF | 10 | 28 | 1 | 9 | 1 | 0 | 1 | 1 | .321 | 6 | 0 | 1 | .857 |
| 1973—Minnesota ........Amer. | | | DH | 146 | 571 | 63 | 166 | 20 | 0 | 16 | 92 | .291 | 0 | 0 | 0 | .000 |
| 1974—Minnesota ........Amer. | | | DH | 127 | 459 | 43 | 131 | 16 | 2 | 13 | 57 | .285 | 0 | 0 | 0 | .000 |
| 1975—Minnesota ........Amer. | | | DH | 131 | 455 | 46 | 123 | 10 | 0 | 13 | 58 | .270 | 0 | 0 | 0 | .000 |
| Major League Totals ...................... | | | | 1609 | 6178 | 867 | 1891 | 326 | 48 | 219 | 931 | .306 | 2332 | 71 | 61 | .975 |

†On disabled list, April 13 through April 23, 1962.
‡On disabled list, June 9, 1972. Transferred to emergency disabled list, June 27 through September 27, 1972.

| Year Club League | Pos. | G. | AB. | R. | H. | 2B. | 3B. | HR. | RBI. | B.A. | PO. | A. | E. | F.A. |
|---|---|---|---|---|---|---|---|---|---|---|---|---|---|---|
| 1969—Minnesota ........Amer. | OF | 3 | 13 | 3 | 5 | 2 | 0 | 1 | 2 | .385 | 6 | 1 | 2 | .778 |
| 1970—Minnesota ........Amer. | OF | 3 | 12 | 2 | 6 | 2 | 0 | 1 | 1 | .500 | 10 | 2 | 0 | 1.000 |
| Championship Series Totals ............ | | 6 | 25 | 5 | 11 | 4 | 0 | 2 | 3 | .440 | 16 | 3 | 2 | .905 |

## WORLD SERIES RECORD

Tied World Series records for most putouts, game, nine innings, right fielder (7), October 6, 1965, and most chances accepted, game, nine innings, right fielder (7), October 6, 1965.

| Year Club League | Pos. | G. | AB. | R. | H. | 2B. | 3B. | HR. | RBI. | B.A. | PO. | A. | E. | F.A. |
|---|---|---|---|---|---|---|---|---|---|---|---|---|---|---|
| 1965—Minnesota ........Amer. | OF | 7 | 26 | 2 | 5 | 1 | 0 | 1 | 2 | .192 | 20 | | 1 | .952 |

## ALL-STAR GAME RECORD

| Year League | Pos. | AB. | R. | H. | 2B. | 3B. | HR. | RBI. | B.A. | PO. | A. | E. | F.A. |
|---|---|---|---|---|---|---|---|---|---|---|---|---|---|
| 1964—American ........................... | OF | 4 | 0 | 0 | 0 | 0 | 0 | 0 | .000 | 0 | 0 | 0 | .000 |
| 1965—American ........................... | OF | 2 | 0 | 1 | 1 | 0 | 0 | 0 | .500 | 0 | 0 | 0 | .000 |
| 1966—American ........................... | OF | 4 | 0 | 0 | 0 | 0 | 0 | 0 | .000 | 0 | 0 | 0 | .000 |
| 1967—American ........................... | OF | 6 | 0 | 2 | 0 | 0 | 0 | 0 | .333 | 4 | 0 | 0 | 1.000 |
| 1968—American ........................... | OF | 1 | 0 | 1 | 1 | 0 | 0 | 0 | 1.000 | 2 | 0 | 0 | 1.000 |
| 1970—American ........................... | OF | 2 | 0 | 1 | 1 | 0 | 0 | 0 | .500 | 0 | 0 | 0 | .000 |
| All-Star Game Totals ....................... | | 19 | 0 | 5 | 3 | 0 | 0 | 0 | .263 | 6 | 0 | 0 | 1.000 |

Member of American League All-Star Team for 1969 game; did not play.
Named to American League All-Star Team for 1971 game; replaced due to injury.

Coach, Minnesota Twins, 1977.

## CLAUDE WILSON OSTEEN

Name pronounced OH-steen.

### St. Louis Cardinals

Born August 9, 1939, at Caney Springs, Tenn.
Height, 5.11¾. Weight, 175.
Threw and batted lefthanded.
Hobbies—Golf, hunting and fishing.

| Year Club League | G. | IP. | W. | L. | Pct. | H. | R. | ER. | SO. | BB. | ERA. |
|---|---|---|---|---|---|---|---|---|---|---|---|
| 1957—Nashville....................Southern | 7 | 13 | 1 | 1 | .500 | 7 | 8 | 8 | 13 | 20 | 5.54 |
| 1957—Cincinnati ...........................National | 3 | 4 | 0 | 0 | .000 | 4 | 1 | 1 | 3 | 3 | 2.25 |
| 1958—Wenatchee .......................Northwest | 22 | 151 | 14 | 4 | •.778 | 145 | 61 | 51 | 174 | 67 | 3.04 |
| 1958—Seattle ...........................P. Coast | 12 | 79 | 5 | 4 | .556 | 69 | 38 | 27 | 40 | 42 | 3.08 |
| 1959—Seattle ...........................P. Coast | 28 | 193 | 8 | 12 | .400 | 167 | 82 | 64 | 155 | 78 | 2.98 |
| 1959—Cincinnati ...........................National | 2 | 8 | 0 | 0 | .000 | 11 | 10 | 6 | 3 | 9 | 6.75 |
| 1960—Cincinnati ...........................National | 20 | 48 | 0 | 1 | .000 | 53 | 29 | 27 | 15 | 30 | 5.06 |
| 1961—Cincinnati ...........................National | 1 | ⅓ | 0 | 0 | .000 | 0 | 0 | 0 | 0 | 0 | 0.00 |
| 1961—Indianapolis† ......................Am. Assoc. | 28 | 191 | 15 | 11 | .577 | 184 | 92 | 75 | 132 | 77 | 3.53 |
| 1961—Washington ...........................American | 3 | 18 | 1 | 1 | .500 | 14 | 11 | 10 | 14 | 9 | 5.00 |
| 1962—Washington ...........................American | 28 | 150 | 8 | 13 | .381 | 140 | 62 | 61 | 59 | 47 | 3.66 |
| 1963—Washington ...........................American | 40 | 212 | 9 | 14 | .391 | 222 | 101 | 79 | 109 | 60 | 3.35 |
| 1964—Washington‡ ......................American | 37 | 257 | 15 | 13 | .536 | 256 | 107 | 95 | 133 | 64 | 3.33 |
| 1965—Los Angeles ......................National | 40 | 287 | 15 | 15 | .500 | 253 | 95 | 89 | 162 | 78 | 2.79 |
| 1966—Los Angeles ......................National | 39 | 240 | 17 | 14 | .548 | 238 | 92 | 76 | 137 | 65 | 2.85 |
| 1967—Los Angeles ......................National | 39 | 288 | 17 | 17 | .500 | •298 | 116 | 103 | 152 | 52 | 3.22 |
| 1968—Los Angeles ......................National | 39 | 254 | 12 | •18 | .400 | 267 | •109 | 87 | 119 | 54 | 3.08 |
| 1969—Los Angeles ......................National | 41 | 321 | 20 | 15 | .571 | •293 | 103 | 95 | 183 | 74 | 2.66 |
| 1970—Los Angeles ......................National | 37 | 259 | 16 | 14 | .533 | 280 | 121 | 110 | 114 | 52 | 3.82 |
| 1971—Los Angeles ......................National | 38 | 259 | 14 | 11 | .560 | 262 | 108 | 101 | 109 | 63 | 3.51 |
| 1972—Los Angeles ......................National | 33 | 252 | 20 | 11 | .645 | 232 | 82 | 74 | 100 | 69 | 2.64 |
| 1973—Los Angeles§ ......................National | 33 | 237 | 16 | 11 | .593 | 227 | 97 | 87 | 86 | 61 | 3.30 |
| 1974—Houston x-St. Louis y .........National | 31 | 161 | 9 | 11 | .450 | 184 | 81 | 68 | 51 | 58 | 3.80 |
| 1975—Chicago z ...........................American | 37 | 204 | 7 | 16 | .304 | 237 | 110 | 99 | 63 | 92 | 4.37 |
| American League Totals.......................... | 145 | 841 | 40 | 57 | .412 | 869 | 391 | 344 | 378 | 272 | 3.68 |
| National League Totals ....................... | 396 | 2618 | 156 | 138 | .531 | 2602 | 1044 | 924 | 1234 | 668 | 3.18 |
| Major League Totals ................................ | 541 | 3459 | 196 | 195 | .501 | 3471 | 1435 | 1268 | 1612 | 940 | 3.30 |

†Traded to Washington Senators by Cincinnati Reds in deal first reported as for cash and player to be named later, September 16, 1961; Senators released Pitcher Dave Sisler to Reds. November 28, 1961, to complete deal.

‡Traded to Los Angeles Dodgers with Infielder John Kennedy and cash estimated at $100,000 for Outfielder Frank Howard, Infielder Ken McMullen and Pitchers Phil Ortega and Pete Richert, December 4, 1964; First Baseman Dick Nen was transferred to Senators, December 15, to complete deal.

§Traded with Pitcher Dave Culpepper to Houston Astros for Outfielder Jim Wynn, December 6, 1973.

xTraded to St. Louis Cardinals for Pitcher Ron Selak and a player to be named later, August 15, 1974; Cardinals assigned Pitcher Dan Larson to Astros, October 4, 1974, to complete deal.

yReleased, April 5, 1975; signed as free agent by Chicago White Sox, April 11, 1975.

zReleased, April 5, 1976.

## WORLD SERIES RECORD

| Year Club League | G. | IP. | W. | L. | Pct. | H. | R. | ER. | SO. | BB. | ERA. |
|---|---|---|---|---|---|---|---|---|---|---|---|
| 1965—Los Angeles .......................National | 2 | 14 | 1 | 1 | .500 | 9 | 2 | 1 | 4 | 5 | 0.64 |
| 1966—Los Angeles .......................National | 1 | 7 | 0 | 1 | .000 | 3 | 1 | 1 | 3 | 1 | 1.29 |
| World Series Totals ................................. | 3 | 21 | 1 | 2 | .333 | 12 | 3 | 2 | 7 | 6 | 0.86 |

| Year | League | IP. | W. | L. | Pct. | H. | R. | ER. | SO. | BB. | ERA. |
|------|--------|-----|----|----|------|----|----|-----|-----|-----|------|
| 1970 | National | 3 | 1 | 0 | 1.000 | 3 | 0 | 0 | 0 | 1 | 0.00 |
| 1973 | National | 2 | 0 | 0 | .000 | 2 | 0 | 0 | 1 | 1 | 0.00 |
| All-Star Game Totals | | 5 | 1 | 0 | 1.000 | 5 | 0 | 0 | 1 | 2 | 0.00 |

Member of National League All-Star Team in 1967 game; did not play.

Coach, Reading (Eastern League), 1976; coach, St. Louis Cardinals, 1977.

## ANTONIO ARISTIDES PACHECO

Name pronounced PA-checko.

### (Tony)
### Houston Astros

Born August 9, 1927, at Havana, Cuba.
Height, 6.00. Weight, 190.
Threw and batted righthanded.
Hobby—Music.

| Year | Club | League | Pos. | G. | AB. | R. | H. | 2B. | 3B. | HR. | RBI. | B.A. | PO. | A. | E. | F.A. |
|------|------|--------|------|----|-----|----|----|-----|-----|-----|------|------|-----|----|----|------|
| 1949 | Newport | Mt. St. | SS | 96 | 374 | 67 | 92 | 11 | 2 | 1 | 41 | .246 | 200 | 306 | 43 | .921 |
| 1950 | Newport | Mt. St. | SS | 115 | 450 | 91 | 132 | 26 | 5 | 3 | 51 | .293 | 242 | 336 | 51 | .919 |
| 1951 | Havana | Fla. Int. | 2B | 121 | 373 | 33 | 80 | 14 | 1 | 3 | 34 | .214 | 291 | 303 | 14 | •.977 |
| 1952 | Havana | Fla. Int. | SS-2B | 153 | 527 | 58 | 121 | 19 | 3 | 1 | 31 | .230 | 348 | 419 | 38 | .953 |
| 1953 | Charleston | A.A. | .... | 7 | 18 | 2 | 4 | 1 | 0 | 0 | 3 | .222 | figures unavailable | | | |
| 1953 | Havana | Fla. Int. | 2B-SS | 87 | 262 | 39 | 61 | 11 | 1 | 1 | 39 | .233 | 213 | 224 | 7 | .984 |
| 1954 | Havana†‡ | Int. | 2B | 10 | 28 | 1 | 7 | 1 | 0 | 0 | 3 | .250 | 20 | 28 | 1 | .980 |
| 1954 | W. Palm Beach | Fla. Int. | 2B | 55 | 194 | 35 | 49 | 7 | 3 | 1 | 17 | .253 | 148 | 107 | 3 | .988 |
| 1954 | Cocoa | Fla. St. | 2B | 33 | 121 | 22 | 28 | 2 | 1 | 0 | 12 | .231 | 110 | 109 | 4 | .982 |
| 1955 | Columbia | S. Atl. | 2B | 12 | 36 | 2 | 4 | 0 | 0 | 0 | 3 | .111 | 21 | 25 | 2 | .958 |
| 1955 | HP-Thomas.§ | Carol. | 2B | 53 | 164 | 47 | 33 | 6 | 1 | 0 | 6 | .201 | 121 | 109 | 10 | .958 |
| 1956 | Savannah x | S. Atl. | SS-3B | 53 | 130 | 15 | 22 | 3 | 0 | 3 | 9 | .169 | 45 | 80 | 11 | .919 |
| 1956 | Monterrey | Mex. | 3B-SS | 45 | 148 | 13 | 33 | 9 | 0 | 1 | 17 | .223 | 58 | 109 | 9 | .949 |

†On disabled list, April 20 to April 27 and May 14 to May 24, 1954.

‡Released by Washington Senators' organization, November 22, 1954; signed as free agent by Cincinnati Reds' organization, April 7, 1955.

§On disabled list, June 9 to September 22, 1955.

xReleased by Cincinnati Reds' organization, July 10, 1956.

### RECORD AS MANAGER

| Year | Club | League | Position | W. | L. | Year | Club | League | Position | W. | L. |
|------|------|--------|----------|----|----|------|------|--------|----------|----|----|
| 1958 | Havana† | Int. | Eighth | 65 | 88 | 1968 | Covington | Appal. | xSecond | 39 | 32 |
| 1959 | Palatka‡ | Fla. St. | Fourth | 36 | 33 | 1969 | Peninsula | Carol. | Fourth(E) | 67 | 76 |
| | (Second Half) | | Third | 38 | 29 | 1970 | Cocoa | Fla. St. | Sixth(E) | 43 | 84 |
| 1966 | Bis.-Mandan | North. | Sixth | 16 | 47 | 1971 | Cocoa | Fla. St. | Second(E) | 80 | 59 |
| 1967 | Covington | Appal. | Fourth | 29 | 35 | 1972 | Okla. City y | A.A. | Fourth(W) | 57 | 83 |
| 1968 | Cocoa§ | Fla. St. | Second(E) | 74 | 65 | 1973 | San Antonio | Texas | zFirst(W) | 82 | 57 |
| | | | | | | 1975 | Sarasota Ind. | G.C. | Sixth | 19 | 33 |

†Replaced Napoleon Reyes, July 23.

‡Replaced Clement Koshorek, June 17.

§Replaced by Leo Posada.

xTied for position with Johnson City.

yAlso managed Latin All-Star Team that won World Baseball Classic in Hawaii.

zLost championship playoff to Memphis three games to two.

Scout, Cincinnati Reds, 1957 and 1960; scout, Houston Astros, 1961 through 1965; coach, Cleveland Indians, 1974; coach, Houston Astros, 1976 and 1977.

## JOSE ANTONIO PAGAN

Name pronounced Puh-GAHN.

### Pittsburgh Pirates

Born May 5, 1935, at Barceloneta, Puerto Rico.
Height, 5.09. Weight, 165.
Threw and batted righthanded.
Hobby—Fishing.

Tied major league record for most home runs as pinch-hitter, two consecutive appearances, August 6 and August 12, 1969.

Tied National League record for most errors, third baseman, inning (3), fourth inning, August 18, 1966.

| Year | Club | League | Pos. | G. | AB. | R. | H. | 2B. | 3B. | HR. | RBI. | B.A. | PO. | A. | E. | F.A. |
|------|------|--------|------|----|-----|----|----|-----|-----|-----|------|------|-----|----|----|------|
| 1955 | El Dorado | C. St. | S-O-1 | 97 | 322 | 60 | 88 | 12 | 1 | 3 | 40 | .273 | 121 | 114 | 11 | .955 |
| 1956 | Danville | Carol. | SS | 147 | 566 | 92 | 160 | 30 | 4 | 10 | 67 | .283 | 261 | 274 | 40 | .930 |
| 1957 | Springfield | East. | •2-3-S | 133 | •542 | 67 | 143 | 24 | 7 | 4 | 48 | .264 | •334 | •307 | •28 | .958 |
| 1958 | Springfield | East. | •3-2-S | 126 | 513 | 68 | 153 | 27 | 7 | 5 | 77 | .298 | •151 | •258 | 14 | •.967 |
| 1959 | Phoenix | P. C. | SS | 105 | 445 | 79 | 139 | 29 | 3 | 19 | 55 | .312 | 191 | 334 | •40 | .929 |
| 1959 | San Francisco | Nat. | 3-S-2 | 31 | 46 | 7 | 8 | 1 | 0 | 0 | 1 | .174 | 17 | 26 | 4 | .915 |
| 1960 | Tacoma | P. C. | •S-3-2B | 128 | 519 | 69 | 153 | 22 | 6 | 8 | 51 | .295 | •252 | 329 | 28 | .954 |
| 1960 | San Francisco | Nat. | SS-3B | 18 | 49 | 8 | 14 | 2 | 2 | 0 | 2 | .286 | 16 | 17 | 3 | .917 |
| 1961 | San Francisco | Nat. | SS-OF | 134 | 434 | 38 | 110 | 15 | 2 | 5 | 46 | .253 | 230 | 334 | 21 | .964 |

| Year—Club | League | Pos. | G. | AB. | R. | H. | 2B. | 3B. | HR. | RBI. | B.A. | PO. | A. | E. | F.A. |
|---|---|---|---|---|---|---|---|---|---|---|---|---|---|---|---|
| 1962—San Francisco | ..Nat. | SS | 164 | 580 | 73 | 150 | 25 | 6 | 7 | 57 | .259 | 286 | 461 | 21 | •.973 |
| 1963—San Francisco | ..Nat. | S-2-O | 148 | 483 | 46 | 113 | 12 | 1 | 6 | 39 | .234 | 262 | 375 | 20 | .970 |
| 1964—San Francisco | ..Nat. | SS-OF | 134 | 367 | 33 | 82 | 10 | 1 | 1 | 28 | .223 | 210 | 303 | 22 | .959 |
| 1965—S.F.†-Pitts. | ........Nat. | SS-3B | 68 | 121 | 16 | 26 | 5 | 0 | 0 | 6 | .215 | 47 | 97 | 12 | .923 |
| 1965—Columbus | ..........Int. | 3B | 8 | 34 | 2 | 7 | 1 | 1 | 0 | 3 | .206 | 3 | 14 | 0 | 1.000 |
| 1966—Pittsburgh | ....x..Nat. | 3-S-2-O | 109 | 368 | 44 | 97 | 15 | 6 | 4 | 54 | .264 | 86 | 219 | 18 | .944 |
| 1967—Pittsburgh | ...Nat. | 3-O-S-2-C | 81 | 211 | 17 | 61 | 6 | 2 | 1 | 19 | .289 | 73 | 109 | 7 | .963 |
| 1968—Pittsburgh | ........N. | 3-O-S-2-1 | 80 | 163 | 24 | 36 | 7 | 1 | 4 | 21 | .221 | 40 | 65 | 7 | .938 |
| 1969—Pittsburgh | ........Nat. | 3-O-2 | 108 | 274 | 29 | 78 | 11 | 4 | 9 | 42 | .285 | 56 | 78 | 5 | .964 |
| 1970—Pittsburgh | ........Nat. | 3-O-2-1 | 95 | 230 | 21 | 61 | 14 | 1 | 7 | 29 | .265 | 46 | 91 | 6 | .958 |
| 1971—Pittsburgh‡ | .......Nat. | 3-O-1 | 57 | 158 | 16 | 38 | 1 | 0 | 5 | 15 | .241 | 53 | 62 | 2 | .983 |
| 1972—Pittsburgh§ | ......Nat. | 3B-OF | 53 | 127 | 11 | 32 | 9 | 0 | 3 | 8 | .252 | 27 | 37 | 7 | .901 |
| 1973—Philadelphia x | ..Nat. | 3-1-O-2 | 46 | 78 | 4 | 16 | 5 | 0 | 0 | 5 | .205 | 21 | 18 | 1 | .975 |
| Major League Totals | ...................... | | 1326 | 3689 | 387 | 922 | 138 | 26 | 52 | 372 | .250 | 1470 | 2292 | 156 | .960 |

†Traded to Pittsburgh Pirates for Shortstop Dick Schofield, May 22, 1965.

‡On disabled list August 8 through September 14.

§Released by Pittsburgh Pirates, October 24, 1972. Signed as free agent by Philadelphia Phillies, November 13, 1972.

xUnconditionally released, August 16, 1973.

### CHAMPIONSHIP SERIES RECORD

| Year—Club | League | Pos. | G. | AB. | R. | H. | 2B. | 3B. | HR. | RBI. | B.A. | PO. | A. | E. | F.A. |
|---|---|---|---|---|---|---|---|---|---|---|---|---|---|---|---|
| 1970—Pittsburgh | ........Nat. | 3B | 1 | 3 | 0 | 1 | 0 | 0 | 0 | 0 | .333 | 0 | 4 | 0 | 1.000 |
| 1971—Pittsburgh | ........Nat. | 3B | 1 | 1 | 0 | 0 | 0 | 0 | 0 | 0 | .000 | 1 | 2 | 0 | 1.000 |
| Championship Series Totals | ............ | | 2 | 4 | 0 | 1 | 0 | 0 | 0 | 0 | .250 | 1 | 6 | 0 | 1.000 |

### WORLD SERIES RECORD

| Year—Club | League | Pos. | G. | AB. | R. | H. | 2B. | 3B. | HR. | RBI. | B.A. | PO. | A. | E. | F.A. |
|---|---|---|---|---|---|---|---|---|---|---|---|---|---|---|---|
| 1962—San Francisco | ..Nat. | SS | 7 | 19 | 2 | 7 | 0 | 0 | 1 | 2 | .368 | 8 | 14 | 1 | .957 |
| 1971—Pittsburgh | ........Nat. | 3B | 4 | 15 | 0 | 4 | 2 | 0 | 0 | 2 | .267 | 2 | 8 | 0 | 1.000 |
| World Series Totals | ....................... | | 11 | 34 | 2 | 11 | 2 | 0 | 1 | 4 | .324 | 10 | 22 | 1 | .970 |

Coach, Pittsburgh Pirates, 1974 through 1977.

# JOHN MICHAEL PESKY

(Christened John Paveskovich; legalized to Pesky.)

## (Johnny)

## Boston Red Sox

Born September 27, 1919, at Portland, Ore.
Height, 5.09. Weight, 175.
Threw right and batted lefthanded.

The following major league records: made 200 or more hits in first full season in majors, 205 in 1942; most runs scored, game (6), May 8, 1946; and most at bats, nine-inning game (7), June 8, 1950.

Led American League third basemen in double plays with 35 in 1948 and 48 in 1949.

Led Piedmont League shortstops in double plays with 95 in 1940.

Named as shortstop on THE SPORTING NEWS All-Star Major League Teams, 1942 and 1946.

Named American Association Most Valuable Player in 1941.

| Year—Club | League | Pos. | G. | AB. | R. | H. | 2B. | 3B. | HR. | RBI. | B.A. | PO. | A. | E. | F.A. |
|---|---|---|---|---|---|---|---|---|---|---|---|---|---|---|---|
| 1940—Rocky Mount | ....Pied. | SS | 136 | •576 | 114 | •187 | 28 | •16 | 4 | 55 | .325 | 257 | 435 | 44 | .940 |
| 1941—Louisville | ..........A. A. | SS | 146 | 600 | 93 | •195 | 25 | 5 | 1 | 48 | .325 | •308 | 411 | 32 | .957 |
| 1942—Boston | ...........Amer. | SS | 147 | 620 | 105 | •205 | 29 | 9 | 2 | 51 | .331 | 320 | •465 | 37 | .955 |
| 1943-44-45—Boston | ......Amer. | | | | | (In Military Service) | | | | | | | | | |
| 1946—Boston | ..............Amer. | SS | 153 | •621 | 115 | •208 | 43 | 4 | 2 | 55 | .335 | 296 | 479 | 25 | .969 |
| 1947—Boston | ..............Amer. | SS-3B | 155 | •638 | 106 | •207 | 27 | 8 | 0 | 39 | .324 | 276 | 429 | 17 | .976 |
| 1948—Boston | ..............Amer. | 3B | 143 | 565 | 124 | 159 | 26 | 6 | 3 | 55 | .281 | 121 | 303 | 22 | .951 |
| 1949—Boston | ..............Amer. | 3B | 148 | 604 | 111 | 185 | 27 | 7 | 2 | 69 | .306 | •184 | •333 | 16 | .970 |
| 1950—Boston | ..............Amer. | 3B-SS | 127 | 490 | 112 | 153 | 22 | 6 | 1 | 49 | .312 | 183 | 289 | 13 | .973 |
| 1951—Boston | ..............Amer. | S-3-2 | 131 | 480 | 93 | 150 | 20 | 6 | 3 | 41 | .313 | 223 | 370 | 26 | .958 |
| 1952—Bostont-Detroit.Amer. | | S-2-3 | 94 | 244 | 36 | 55 | 6 | 0 | 1 | 11 | .225 | 126 | 172 | 15 | .952 |
| 1953—Detroit† | ...........Amer. | 2B | 103 | 308 | 43 | 90 | 22 | 1 | 2 | 24 | .292 | 166 | 224 | 3 | .992 |
| 1954—Det.‡-Wash.§ | .....Amer. | 2B-SS | 69 | 175 | 22 | 43 | 4 | 3 | 1 | 10 | .246 | 92 | 91 | 4 | .979 |
| 1955—Denver | ..............A. A. | 3B | 66 | 137 | 32 | 47 | 7 | 2 | 1 | 18 | .343 | 22 | 45 | 7 | .905 |
| 1956—Durham x | .........Carol. | 2B | 17 | 35 | 2 | 6 | 2 | 0 | 1 | 1 | .171 | 26 | 31 | 2 | .966 |
| Major League Totals | ...................... | | 1270 | 4745 | 867 | 1455 | 226 | 50 | 17 | 404 | .307 | 1987 | 3155 | 178 | .967 |

†Traded to Detroit Tigers with Pitcher Bill Wight, First Baseman Walt Dropo, Third Baseman Fred Hatfield and Outfielder Don Lenhardt for Pitcher Paul (Dizzy) Trout, Third Baseman George Kell, Shortstop Johnny Lipon and Outfielder Walter (Hoot) Evers, June 3, 1952.

‡Traded to Washington Senators for Infielder Mel Hoderlein, June 14, 1954.

§Unconditionally released by Washington Senators, November 10, 1954; signed with Baltimore Orioles, December 21, 1954 and released, April 14, 1955.

xPlayer-manager.

### WORLD SERIES RECORD

| Year—Club | League | Pos. | G. | AB. | R. | H. | 2B. | 3B. | HR. | RBI. | B.A. | PO. | A. | E. | F.A. |
|---|---|---|---|---|---|---|---|---|---|---|---|---|---|---|---|
| 1946—Boston | ..............Amer. | SS | 7 | 30 | 2 | 7 | 0 | 0 | 0 | 0 | .233 | 13 | 16 | 4 | .879 |

| Year | League | | Pos. | AB. | R. | H. | 2B. | 3B. | HR. | RBI. | B.A. | PO. | A. | E. | F.A. |
|---|---|---|---|---|---|---|---|---|---|---|---|---|---|---|---|
| 1946—American | ..................... | | SS | 2 | 0 | 0 | 0 | 0 | 0 | 0 | .000 | 1 | 0 | 1 | .500 |

### RECORD AS MANAGER

| Year | Club | League | Position | W. | L. | Year | Club | League | Position | W. | L. |
|---|---|---|---|---|---|---|---|---|---|---|---|
| 1956—Durham | .............. | Carol. | Second | 84 | 69 | 1961—Seattle | ................ | P. C. | Third | 86 | 68 |
| 1957—Birmingham | ...... | South. | Sixth | 74 | 79 | 1962—Seattle | ................ | P. C. | Fourth | 76 | 74 |
| 1958—Lancaster | ......... | East. | Third(S) | 37 | 33 | 1963—Boston | ................ | Amer. | Seventh | 76 | 85 |
| | (Second Half) | | †First(S) | 38 | 24 | 1964—Boston§ | .............. | Amer. | Eighth | 71 | 89 |
| 1959—Knoxville | ........... | Sally | ‡First | 78 | 62 | 1968—Columbus | .......... | Int. | Second | 82 | 64 |
| 1960—Victoria | ............. | Texas | Fourth | 77 | 69 | | | | | | |

†Lost playoff finals to Binghamton, three games to two.
‡Lost playoff semifinal series to Charleston, three games to two.
§Replaced by Billy Herman, October 3, 1964.
Coach, Pittsburgh Pirates, 1965 through 1967; Boston Red Sox, 1975 through 1977.

## JOSEPH BENJAMIN PIGNATANO
Named pronounced Pig-na-TAWN-o.

### (Joe)
### New York Mets

Born August 4, 1929, at Brooklyn, N. Y.
Height, 5.10.   Weight, 180.
Threw and batted righthanded.
Second cousin of Pete Falcone, pitcher with St. Louis Cardinals.

| Year | Club | League | Pos. | G. | AB. | R. | H. | 2B. | 3B. | HR. | RBI. | B.A. | PO. | A. | E. | F.A. |
|---|---|---|---|---|---|---|---|---|---|---|---|---|---|---|---|---|
| 1948—Cairo | ................ | Kitty | C | 3 | 8 | 2 | 3 | 1 | 0 | 0 | 2 | .375 | 14 | 2 | 4 | .800 |
| 1949—Cambridge | ........ | E. Shore | C | 87 | 268 | 51 | 62 | 7 | 4 | 0 | 24 | .231 | 491 | 66 | 23 | .960 |
| 1950—Valdosta | ............ | Ga.-Fla. | C-O | 127 | 424 | 102 | 121 | 17 | 17 | 4 | 77 | .285 | 732 | 80 | 18 | .978 |
| 1951-52—N'port News | ..Pied. | | | | | | (In Military Service) | | | | | | | | | |
| 1953—Asheville | .......... | Tri St. | •C-OF | 121 | 433 | 92 | 137 | 24 | •13 | 6 | 82 | .316 | •580 | 63 | •26 | .961 |
| 1954—Elmira | .............. | East. | C | 118 | 335 | 47 | 83 | 10 | 9 | 2 | 51 | .248 | 485 | •78 | 10 | .983 |
| 1955—Fort Worth | ........ | Tex. | C-OF | 125 | 381 | 49 | 76 | 11 | 5 | 5 | 41 | .199 | 548 | 53 | 10 | .984 |
| 1956—St. Paul | .......... | A. A. | C | 81 | 224 | 37 | 66 | 11 | 1 | 5 | 29 | .295 | 380 | 35 | 3 | .993 |
| 1957—Brooklyn | .......... | Nat. | C | 8 | 14 | 0 | 3 | 1 | 0 | 0 | 1 | .214 | 36 | 1 | 0 | 1.000 |
| 1957—Montreal | .......... | Int. | C | 70 | 211 | 32 | 63 | 7 | 2 | 1 | 17 | .299 | 287 | 32 | 1 | .997 |
| 1958—Los Angeles | ..... | Nat. | C | 63 | 142 | 18 | 31 | 4 | 0 | 9 | 17 | .218 | 286 | 18 | 0 | 1.000 |
| 1959—Los Angeles | ..... | Nat. | C | 52 | 139 | 17 | 33 | 4 | 1 | 1 | 11 | .237 | 322 | 17 | 1 | .997 |
| 1960—Los Angeles† | ....Nat. | | C | 58 | 90 | 11 | 21 | 4 | 0 | 2 | 9 | .233 | 131 | 21 | 4 | .984 |
| 1961—Kansas City‡ | ....Amer. | | C-3B | 92 | 243 | 31 | 59 | 10 | 3 | 4 | 22 | .243 | 380 | 35 | 9 | .979 |
| 1962—S.F.§-N. York | ....Nat. | | C | 34 | 61 | 4 | 14 | 2 | 0 | 0 | 2 | .230 | 107 | 13 | 1 | .992 |
| 1963—Buff.-Rochester | Int. | | C | 86 | 236 | 37 | 56 | 13 | 2 | 3 | 27 | .237 | 454 | 37 | 5 | .990 |
| 1964—Rochester | .......... | Int. | C | 88 | 237 | 19 | 48 | 7 | 1 | 4 | 19 | .203 | 508 | 23 | 3 | •.994 |
| | American League Totals | ................ | | 92 | 243 | 31 | 59 | 10 | 3 | 4 | 22 | .243 | 380 | 35 | 9 | .979 |
| | National League Totals | .................. | | 215 | 446 | 50 | 102 | 15 | 1 | 12 | 40 | .229 | 982 | 92 | 6 | .994 |
| | Major League Totals | ...................... | | 307 | 689 | 81 | 161 | 25 | 4 | 16 | 62 | .234 | 1362 | 127 | 15 | .990 |

†Sold to Kansas City Athletics, January 31, 1961.
‡Traded to San Francisco Giants for Outfielder Jose Tartabull, December 15, 1961.
§Sold to New York Mets, July 13, 1962.

### WORLD SERIES RECORD

| Year | Club | League | Pos. | G. | AB. | R. | H. | 2B. | 3B. | HR. | RBI. | B.A. | PO. | A. | E. | F.A. |
|---|---|---|---|---|---|---|---|---|---|---|---|---|---|---|---|---|
| 1959—Los Angeles | ......Nat. | | C | 1 | 0 | 0 | 0 | 0 | 0 | 0 | 0 | .000 | 1 | 0 | 0 | 1.000 |

Coach, Washington Senators, 1965 through 1967; New York Mets, 1968 through 1977.

## VADA EDWARD PINSON, JR.
### Seattle Mariners

Born August 11, 1938, at Memphis, Tenn.
Height, 5.11. Weight, 187.
Threw and batted lefthanded.

Tied major league record by making 200 or more hits in first full season in majors (205), 1959.
Major League stolen bases: 1958 (2), 1959 (21), 1960 (32), 1961 (23), 1962 (26), 1963 (27), 1964 (8), 1965 (21), 1966 (18), 1967 (26), 1968 (17), 1969 (4), 1970 (7), 1971 (25), 1972 (17), 1973 (5), 1974 (21), 1975 (5). Total—305.
Led California League in total bases with 349 in 1957.
Led Pacific Coast League in stolen bases with 37 in 1958.
Named outfielder on THE SPORTING NEWS National League All-Star fielding team, 1961.

| Year | Club | League | Pos. | G. | AB. | R. | H. | 2B. | 3B. | HR. | RBI. | B.A. | PO. | A. | E. | F.A. |
|---|---|---|---|---|---|---|---|---|---|---|---|---|---|---|---|---|
| 1956—Wausau | ............ | North. | 1B | 75 | 277 | 35 | 77 | 11 | 5 | 2 | 23 | .278 | 626 | 28 | 12 | .982 |
| 1957—Visalia | .............. | Cal. | •OF-1B | 135 | 569 | •165 | •209 | •40 | •20 | 20 | 97 | .367 | 260 | •30 | 16 | .948 |
| 1958—Cincinnati | ......... | Nat. | OF | 27 | 96 | 20 | 26 | 7 | 0 | 1 | 8 | .271 | 50 | 4 | 0 | 1.000 |
| 1958—Seattle | .............. | P.C. | •OF-1 | 124 | 475 | 92 | 163 | 28 | 8 | 11 | 77 | .343 | 385 | 13 | •15 | .964 |
| 1959—Cincinnati | ......... | Nat. | OF | 154 | •648 | •131 | 205 | •47 | 9 | 20 | 84 | .316 | •423 | 11 | 7 | .984 |

| Year Club League | Pos. | G. | AB. | R. | H. | 2B. | 3B. | HR. | RBI. | B.A. | PO. | A. | E. | F.A. |
|---|---|---|---|---|---|---|---|---|---|---|---|---|---|---|
| 1960—Cincinnati.........Nat. | OF | 154 | •652 | 107 | 187 | •37 | 12 | 20 | 61 | .287 | •401 | 11 | 8 | .981 |
| 1961—Cincinnati.........Nat. | OF | 154 | 607 | 101 | •208 | 34 | 8 | 16 | 87 | .343 | •391 | 19 | 10 | .976 |
| 1962—Cincinnati.........Nat. | OF | 155 | 619 | 107 | 181 | 31 | 7 | 23 | 100 | .292 | 344 | 13 | 4 | .989 |
| 1963—Cincinnati.........Nat. | OF | •162 | 652 | 96 | •204 | 37 | •14 | 22 | 106 | .313 | 357 | 9 | 8 | .979 |
| 1964—Cincinnati.........Nat. | OF | 156 | 625 | 99 | 166 | 23 | 11 | 23 | 84 | .266 | 299 | 14 | 9 | .972 |
| 1965—Cincinnati.........Nat. | OF | 159 | 669 | 97 | 204 | 34 | 10 | 22 | 94 | .305 | 354 | 9 | 3 | •.992 |
| 1966—Cincinnati.........Nat. | OF | 156 | 618 | 70 | 178 | 35 | 6 | 16 | 76 | .288 | 344 | 9 | 13 | .964 |
| 1967—Cincinnati.........Nat. | OF | 158 | 650 | 90 | 187 | 28 | •13 | 18 | 66 | .288 | 341 | 4 | 5 | .986 |
| 1968—Cincinnati† | Nat. | OF | 130 | 499 | 60 | 135 | 29 | 6 | 5 | 48 | .271 | 258 | 7 | 6 | .978 |
| 1969—St. Louis‡ | Nat. | OF | 132 | 495 | 58 | 126 | 22 | 6 | 10 | 70 | .255 | 218 | 6 | 1 | •.996 |
| 1970—Cleveland | Amer. | OF-1B | 148 | 574 | 74 | 164 | 28 | 6 | 24 | 82 | .286 | 284 | 9 | 5 | .983 |
| 1971—Cleveland§ | Amer. | OF-1B | 146 | 566 | 60 | 149 | 23 | 4 | 11 | 35 | .263 | 315 | 11 | 7 | .979 |
| 1972—California | Amer. | OF-1B | 136 | 484 | 56 | 133 | 24 | 2 | 7 | 49 | .275 | 207 | 11 | 2 | .991 |
| 1973—California x | Amer. | OF | 124 | 466 | 56 | 121 | 14 | 6 | 8 | 57 | .260 | 210 | 11 | 8 | .965 |
| 1974—Kansas City | Amer. | OF-1B | 115 | 406 | 46 | 112 | 18 | 2 | 6 | 41 | .276 | 198 | 9 | 4 | .981 |
| 1975—Kansas City y | Amer. | OF-1B | 103 | 319 | 38 | 71 | 14 | 5 | 4 | 22 | .223 | 151 | 6 | 1 | .994 |
| American League Totals | | 772 | 2815 | 330 | 750 | 121 | 25 | 60 | 286 | .266 | 1365 | 57 | 27 | .981 |
| National League Totals | | 1697 | 6830 | 1036 | 2007 | 364 | 102 | 196 | 884 | .294 | 3780 | 116 | 74 | .981 |
| Major League Totals | | 2469 | 9645 | 1366 | 2757 | 485 | 127 | 256 | 1170 | .286 | 5145 | 173 | 101 | .981 |

†Traded to St. Louis Cardinals for Outfielder Bob Tolan and Pitcher Wayne Granger, October 11, 1968.

‡Traded to Cleveland Indians for Outfielder Jose Cardenal, November 20, 1969.

§Traded with Outfielder Frank Baker and Pitcher Alan Foster to California Angels for Catcher Jerry Moses and Outfielder Alex Johnson, October 5, 1971.

xTraded to Kansas City Royals for Pitcher Barry Raziano and cash, February 23, 1974.

yReleased, December 17, 1975; signed as free agent by Milwaukee Brewers, January 14, 1976. Released by Milwaukee Brewers, April 4, 1976.

Coach, Seattle Mariners, 1977.

### WORLD SERIES RECORD

| Year Club League | Pos. | G. | AB. | R. | H. | 2B. | 3B. | HR. | RBI. | B.A. | PO. | A. | E. | F.A. |
|---|---|---|---|---|---|---|---|---|---|---|---|---|---|---|
| 1961—Cincinnati..........Nat. | OF | 5 | 22 | 0 | 2 | 1 | 0 | 0 | 0 | .091 | 18 | 1 | 1 | .950 |

### ALL-STAR GAME RECORD

| Year League | Pos. | AB. | R. | H. | 2B. | 3B. | HR. | RBI. | B.A. | PO. | A. | E. | F.A. |
|---|---|---|---|---|---|---|---|---|---|---|---|---|---|
| 1959—National (second game) | PR | 0 | 0 | 0 | 0 | 0 | 0 | 0 | .000 | 0 | 0 | 0 | .000 |
| 1960—National (both games) | OF | 1 | 0 | 0 | 0 | 0 | 0 | 0 | .000 | 1 | 0 | 0 | 1.000 |
| All-Star Game Totals | | 1 | 0 | 0 | 0 | 0 | 0 | 0 | .000 | 1 | 0 | 0 | 1.000 |

Member of National League All-Star Team in 1959 (first game); did not play

### PITCHING RECORD

| Year Club | League | G. | IP. | W. | L. | Pct. | H. | R. | ER. | SO. | BB. | ERA. |
|---|---|---|---|---|---|---|---|---|---|---|---|---|
| 1956—Wausau...............Northern | | 2 | .... | 0 | 0 | .000 | .... | .... | .... | .... | .... | .... |
| 1957—Visalia ...............California | | 1 | .... | 0 | 0 | .000 | .... | .... | .... | .... | .... | .... |

## JAMES HARRISON REESE
### (Jimmie)
#### California Angels

Born October 1, 1905, at New York, N. Y.
Height, 6.00. Weight, 170.
Threw right and batted lefthanded.
Hobby—Woodworking.

Set following Pacific Coast League career records for second baseman: most putouts (4771), most assists (5119), most chances accepted (9890).

Led Pacific Coast League second basemen in total chances accepted with 1273 in 1927, 1189 in 1929, and 1125 in 1934.

| Year Club League | Pos. | G. | AB. | R. | H. | 2B. | 3B. | HR. | RBI. | B.A. | PO. | A. | E. | F.A. |
|---|---|---|---|---|---|---|---|---|---|---|---|---|---|---|
| 1924—Oakland ............P.C. | INF | 8 | 32 | 8 | 6 | 2 | 0 | 0 | .... | .188 | figures unavailable | | | |
| 1925—Oakland ............P.C. | 2B-SS | 136 | 463 | 63 | 115 | 24 | 2 | 0 | 37 | .248 | 342 | 367 | 26 | .965 |
| 1926—Oakland ............P.C. | 2B | 183 | 709 | 113 | 189 | 32 | 11 | 4 | 48 | .267 | •563 | 586 | 36 | .970 |
| 1927—Oakland† ...........P.C. | 2B | 191 | 722 | 113 | 213 | 34 | 17 | 2 | 83 | .295 | •621 | 652 | 21 | •.984 |
| 1928—Oakland ............P.C. | 2B | 132 | 478 | 60 | 118 | 10 | 5 | 1 | 35 | .247 | 406 | 459 | 21 | .976 |
| 1929—Oakland ............P.C. | 2B | 190 | 766 | 142 | 258 | 33 | 9 | 1 | 56 | .337 | •622 | 567 | 25 | •.979 |
| 1930—New York.........Amer. | 2B | 77 | 188 | 44 | 65 | 14 | 2 | 3 | 18 | .346 | 86 | 99 | 5 | .974 |
| 1931—New York.........Amer. | 2B | 65 | 245 | 41 | 59 | 10 | 2 | 3 | 26 | .241 | 173 | 168 | 10 | .972 |
| 1932—St. Paul‡ .........A.A. | 2B | 25 | 61 | 10 | 12 | 2 | 2 | 1 | 5 | .197 | 39 | 61 | 2 | .980 |
| 1932—St. Louis§ .........Nat. | 2B | 90 | 309 | 38 | 82 | 15 | 0 | 2 | 26 | .265 | 209 | 220 | 9 | .979 |
| 1933—Los Angeles ......P.C. | 2B | 104 | 393 | 85 | 130 | 23 | 6 | 5 | 38 | .330 | 258 | 298 | 18 | .969 |
| 1934—Los Angeles ......P.C. | 2B | 180 | 733 | 123 | 228 | 31 | 12 | 3 | 85 | .311 | •541 | 584 | 32 | •.972 |
| 1935—Los Angeles ......P.C. | 2B | 155 | 576 | 79 | 171 | 28 | 8 | 1 | 66 | .297 | 448 | 489 | 36 | .963 |
| 1936—Los Angeles ......P.C. | 2B | 146 | 515 | 57 | 139 | 21 | 3 | 0 | 54 | .270 | 385 | 422 | 26 | .969 |
| 1937—San Diego.........P.C. | 2B | 138 | 506 | 59 | 159 | 23 | 7 | 2 | 78 | .314 | 333 | 442 | 27 | .966 |
| 1938—San Diego.........P.C. | 2B | 146 | 349 | 41 | 81 | 11 | 1 | 0 | 28 | .233 | 284 | 286 | 15 | .974 |
| 1939—Bellingham-Spo. W. Int. | INF | 22 | 39 | 3 | 7 | 1 | 0 | 0 | 4 | .179 | figures unavailable | | | |
| American League Totals | | 142 | 433 | 85 | 124 | 24 | 4 | 6 | 44 | .286 | 259 | 267 | 15 | .972 |
| National League Totals | | 90 | 309 | 38 | 82 | 15 | 0 | 2 | 26 | .265 | 209 | 220 | 9 | .979 |
| Major League Totals | | 232 | 742 | 123 | 206 | 39 | 4 | 8 | 70 | .278 | 468 | 487 | 24 | .975 |

†Sold with Shortstop Lyn Lary to New York Yankees for an estimated $100,000, January, 1928. Reese wasn't to be delivered until 1930.
‡Sold to St. Louis Cardinals, May, 1932.
§Sold to Los Angeles, February, 1933.

### RECORD AS MANAGER

| Year | Club | League | Position | W. | L. |
|------|------|--------|----------|----|----|
| 1939—Bellingham | ........West. Int. | †Sixth | 24 | 44 |
| 1960—San Diego | .........P.C. | ‡Fourth | 34 | 18 |
| 1961—San Diego | .........P.C. | §Fifth | 39 | 44 |

†Replaced Ken Penner, June 8, team in sixth place; released August 17.
‡Replaced George Metkovich, July 23, with team in seventh place. Tied for position.
§Resigned July 6.

Batboy, Los Angeles Angels, 1917 through 1923; coach, Los Angeles Angels, 1940 through 1942; manager, Army service team at Camp Campbell, Kentucky, 1942; scout, Boston Braves, 1945 through 1946; coach, San Diego, 1948 through 1960; coach, Hawaii, 1963 through 1964 and 1969; coach, Seattle, 1965 through 1968; coach, Portland, 1970; scout, Montreal Expos, 1971 through 1972; coach, California Angels, 1973 through 1977.

## CALVIN EDWIN RIPKEN, SR.
### (Cal)
### Baltimore Orioles

Born December 17, 1935, at Aberdeen, Md.
Height, 6.00. Weight, 175.
Threw and batted righthanded.
Hobby—Golf.
Brother of Bill Ripken, former outfielder in Brooklyn Dodgers' organization.

| Year | Club | League | Pos. | G. | AB. | R. | H. | 2B. | 3B. | HR. | RBI. | B.A. | PO. | A. | E. | F.A. |
|------|------|--------|------|----|-----|----|----|-----|-----|-----|------|------|-----|----|----|------|
| 1957—Phoenix | .............Ar.-Mx. | O-C-3 | 112 | 398 | 68 | 109 | 15 | 6 | 7 | 60 | .274 | 220 | 54 | 17 | .942 |
| 1958—Wilson† | .............Carol. | •C-O-3 | 118 | 393 | 40 | 85 | 20 | 2 | 4 | 38 | .216 | 655 | •72 | 5 | •.993 |
| 1959—Pensacola | .........Al.-Fla. | C-P | 61 | 219 | 36 | 64 | 14 | 3 | 2 | 35 | .292 | 378 | 31 | 6 | .986 |
| 1959—Amarillo | ............Tex. | C | 30 | 69 | 6 | 14 | 2 | 0 | 0 | 3 | .203 | 111 | 10 | 0 | 1.000 |
| 1960—Fox Cities | .........I.I.I. | •C-OF | 107 | 356 | 59 | 100 | 20 | 4 | 9 | 74 | .281 | 619 | 34 | 7 | •.989 |
| 1961—Little Rock | ........South. | C | 32 | 81 | 6 | 15 | 2 | 1 | 1 | 8 | .185 | 120 | 12 | 0 | 1.000 |
| 1961—Leesburg‡ | .........Fla. St. | C-P | 52 | 127 | 20 | 30 | 3 | 0 | 1 | 13 | .236 | 286 | 32 | 1 | .997 |
| 1961—Rochester | ..........Int. | C | 11 | 24 | 2 | 2 | 0 | 0 | 1 | 2 | .083 | figures unavailable | | | |
| 1962—Fox Cities‡ | ........Midw. | C-P | 58 | 143 | 25 | 39 | 9 | 0 | 4 | 36 | .273 | 311 | 20 | 4 | .988 |
| 1963—Aberdeen§ | ........North. | | | | | | | (Did not play) | | | | | | | | |
| 1964—Aberdeen‡ | ........North. | | 2 | 1 | 0 | 0 | 0 | 0 | 0 | 0 | .000 | .... | .... | .... | .... |

†Released by Baltimore Orioles' organization, April 20, 1959; re-signed by Baltimore Orioles' organization, April 25, 1959.
‡Player-manager.
§On disabled list, April 27 to September 17, 1963.

### PITCHING RECORD

| Year | Club | League | G. | IP. | W. | L. | Pct. | H. | R. | ER. | SO. | BB. | ERA. |
|------|------|--------|----|-----|----|----|------|----|----|-----|-----|-----|------|
| 1959—Pensacola | ...........................Ala.-Fla. | 1 | .... | 0 | 0 | .000 | .... | .... | .... | .... | .... | .... |
| 1961—Leesburg‡ | ...........................Florida St. | 2 | .... | 0 | 0 | .000 | .... | .... | .... | .... | .... | .... |
| 1962—Fox Cities‡ | .........................Midwest | 3 | 15 | 0 | 0 | .000 | 22 | 15 | 11 | 3 | 7 | 6.60 |

### RECORD AS MANAGER

| Year | Club | League | Position | W. | L. |
|------|------|--------|----------|----|----|
| 1961—Leesburg† | .........Fla. St. | Seventh | 8 | 5 |
| (Second Half)‡ | | Third | 30 | 31 |
| 1962—Fox Cities | ....Midwest | Ninth | 25 | 36 |
| (Second Half) | | Third | 36 | 27 |
| 1963—Aberdeen | ..........Northern | Second | 65 | 55 |
| 1964—Aberdeen | ..........Northern | §First | 80 | 37 |
| 1965—Tri-City | ............Northwest | Fourth | 34 | 36 |
| (Second Half) | | xFirst | 47 | 22 |
| 1966—Aberdeen | ..........Northern | Second | 47 | 22 |

| Year | Club | League | Position | W. | L. |
|------|------|--------|----------|----|----|
| 1967—Miami | ...............Fla. St. | Third(E) | 31 | 39 |
| (Second Half) | | Second(E) | 34 | 37 |
| 1968—Elmira | .............Eastern | Third | 77 | 63 |
| 1969—Rochester | .........Int. | Fifth | 71 | 69 |
| 1970—Rochester | .........Int. | Third | 76 | 64 |
| 1971—Dallas-Ft.W. | ......Texas | Second(W) | 82 | 59 |
| 1972—Asheville | ...........South. | yFirst(E) | 81 | 58 |
| 1973—Asheville | ...........South. | Second(W) | 71 | 69 |
| 1974—Asheville | ...........South. | Second(W) | 70 | 67 |

†Replaced Billy DeMars, June 7.
‡Assigned to Rochester as a player, August 17.
§Won Baukol Playoff (based on last 30 days of regular season) with record of 19 wins, 10 losses, 1 tie.
xWon playoff against Lewiston (First Half winner), three games to none.
yLost playoff to Montgomery, three games to none.

Scout, Baltimore Orioles, 1975; coach, Baltimore Orioles, 1976 and 1977.

## RAYMOND ROY RIPPELMEYER
### (Ray)
### Philadelphia Phillies

Born July 9, 1933, at Valmeyer, Ill.
Height, 6.03. Weight, 200.
Threw and batted righthanded.
Hobbies—Basketball, golf, swimming and photography.

Attended Southeast Missouri State, Cape Girardeau, Mo., and Southern Illinois University, Carbondale, Ill.; received Bachelor of Science degree in Agriculture.

Led Southern Association in complete games by pitchers with 19 in 1959.
Led Pacific Coast League in complete games by pitchers with 17 in 1960.
Tied for American Association lead in shutouts with 3 in 1961.
Tied for Three-I League lead in shutouts with 3 in 1954.

| Year    Club | League | G. | IP. | W. | L. | Pct. | H. | R. | ER. | SO. | BB. | ERA. |
|---|---|---|---|---|---|---|---|---|---|---|---|---|
| 1954—Toledo................ | Am. Assoc. | 1 | 4 | 0 | 0 | .000 | 2 | 2 | 2 | 1 | 7 | 4.50 |
| 1955—Evansville ................ | I.I.I. | 30 | 204 | 16 | 5 | .762 | 190 | 90 | 66 | 104 | 94 | *2.91 |
| 1955—Toledo................ | Am. Assoc. | 1 | 3 | 0 | 1 | .000 | 5 | 2 | 2 | 1 | 3 | 6.00 |
| 1955—Atlanta ................ | So. Assoc. | 39 | 180 | 9 | 11 | .450 | 186 | 110 | 87 | 71 | 77 | 4.35 |
| 1956— | | | | | (In Military Service) | | | | | | |
| 1957—Wichita ................ | Am. Assoc. | 25 | 73 | 2 | 3 | .400 | 80 | 33 | 28 | 41 | 21 | 3.45 |
| 1958—Atlanta ................ | So. Assoc. | 21 | 152 | 11 | 8 | .579 | 128 | 55 | 43 | 71 | 55 | 2.93 |
| 1958—Wichita ................ | Am. Assoc. | 14 | 69 | 4 | 3 | .571 | 70 | 45 | 32 | 30 | 23 | 4.17 |
| 1959—Louisville ................ | Am. Assoc. | 11 | 46 | 3 | 2 | .600 | 61 | 29 | 26 | 18 | 15 | 5.09 |
| 1959—Atlanta† ................ | So. Assoc. | 23 | 188 | 11 | 12 | .478 | 191 | 87 | 67 | 91 | 54 | 3.21 |
| 1960—Seattle ................ | P. Coast | 33 | 229 | 16 | 13 | .552 | 227 | 94 | 69 | 98 | 57 | 2.71 |
| 1961—Indianapolis‡ ................ | Am. Assoc. | 35 | 218 | 13 | 8 | .619 | 227 | 102 | 88 | 97 | 50 | 3.65 |
| 1962—Washington§ ................ | American | 18 | 39 | 1 | 2 | .333 | 47 | 24 | 24 | 17 | 17 | 5.54 |
| 1962—San Diego ................ | P. Coast | 12 | 75 | 3 | 5 | .375 | 79 | 38 | 31 | 30 | 10 | 3.72 |
| 1963—San Diego ................ | P. Coast | 36 | 145 | 11 | 2 | .846 | 133 | 66 | 42 | 62 | 29 | 2.61 |
| 1964—San Diego ................ | P. Coast | 36 | 169 | 14 | 7 | .667 | 178 | 74 | 64 | 72 | 31 | 3.41 |
| 1965—San Diego ................ | P. Coast | 13 | 26 | 1 | 3 | .250 | 44 | 25 | 23 | 18 | 8 | 7.96 |
| Major League Totals ................ | | 18 | 39 | 1 | 2 | .333 | 47 | 24 | 24 | 17 | 17 | 5.54 |

†Drafted from Milwaukee Braves' organization by Seattle (Cincinnati Reds' organization), November 20, 1959.

‡Drafted from Cincinnati Reds' organization by Washington Senators, November 27, 1961.

§Returned to Cicninnati Reds' organization, July 11, 1962.

### RECORD AS MANAGER

| Year    Club | League | Position | W. | L. |
|---|---|---|---|---|
| 1965—Aberdeen............ | Northern | Fourth | 27 | 39 |

Coach, San Diego (Pacific Coast League), 1966 and 1967; minor league pitching instructor, Philadelphia Phillies, 1968 and 1969; coach, Philadelphia Phillies, 1970 through 1977.

# JOHN EDWARD RUBERTO
## (Sonny)
## St. Louis Cardinals

Born January 2, 1946, at Staten Island, N. Y.
Height, 5.11. Weight, 175.
Threw and batted righthanded.
Hobby—Hockey.

| Year    Club | League | Pos. | G. | AB. | R. | H. | 2B. | 3B. | HR. | RBI. | B.A. | PO. | A. | E. | F.A. |
|---|---|---|---|---|---|---|---|---|---|---|---|---|---|---|---|
| 1964—Rock Hill .......... | W. Car. | C | 27 | 70 | 14 | 17 | 2 | 1 | 0 | 4 | .243 | 199 | 21 | 5 | .978 |
| 1964—Sarasota ............ | Sar. Rk. | C | 14 | 24 | 5 | 6 | 1 | 1 | 0 | 6 | .250 | 42 | 16 | 1 | .983 |
| 1964—Winnipeg .......... | North. | C | 17 | 48 | 8 | 14 | 0 | 0 | 3 | 11 | .292 | 88 | 6 | 3 | .969 |
| 1965—Raleigh ............ | Carol. | C-3B | 77 | 183 | 23 | 37 | 8 | 1 | 1 | 14 | .202 | 192 | 58 | 5 | .980 |
| 1966—St. Petersburg†..Fla. St. | | C-2B | 88 | 279 | 40 | 79 | 10 | 1 | 2 | 22 | .283 | 220 | 69 | 2 | .993 |
| 1967—Tulsa ................ | P. C. | C | 1 | 1 | 0 | 0 | 0 | 0 | 0 | 0 | .000 | 0 | 0 | 0 | .000 |
| 1967—Little Rock........ | Texas | C | 1 | 3 | 0 | 1 | 1 | 0 | 0 | 0 | .333 | 4 | 0 | 1 | .800 |
| 1967—Modesto‡ ........ | Calif. | Inf. | 85 | 282 | 32 | 56 | 8 | 3 | 7 | 31 | .199 | 251 | 130 | 19 | .952 |
| 1968—Little Rock........ | Texas | C-3B | 98 | 306 | 30 | 71 | 14 | 4 | 0 | 28 | .232 | 573 | 79 | 16 | .976 |
| 1969—Tulsa§ ............ | A. A. | C-1B | 14 | 49 | 6 | 16 | 2 | 0 | 0 | 7 | .327 | 62 | 11 | 2 | .973 |
| 1969—San Diego.......... | Nat. | C | 19 | 21 | 3 | 3 | 0 | 0 | 0 | 0 | .143 | 38 | 6 | 0 | 1.000 |
| 1970—Lodi x ............. | Calif. | 2B | 1 | 3 | 0 | 0 | 0 | 0 | 0 | 0 | .000 | 5 | 3 | 1 | .889 |
| 1970—Asheville y ....... | South. | 3B-C | 37 | 102 | 4 | 28 | 5 | 0 | 0 | 7 | .275 | 55 | 47 | 5 | .953 |
| 1971—Indianapolis ..... | A. A. | C-Inf | 105 | 322 | 23 | 94 | 11 | 1 | 5 | 37 | .292 | 265 | 153 | 15 | .965 |
| 1972—Indianapolis ..... | A. A. | C-SS-2B | 117 | 367 | 34 | 90 | 11 | 3 | 7 | 43 | .245 | 377 | 130 | 13 | .975 |
| 1972—Cincinnati.......... | Nat. | C | 2 | 3 | 0 | 0 | 0 | 0 | 0 | 0 | .000 | 5 | 0 | 0 | 1.000 |
| 1973—Indianapolis ..... | A. A. | C-Inf | 93 | 287 | 37 | 67 | 9 | 1 | 3 | 25 | .233 | 424 | 60 | 8 | .984 |
| 1974—Indianapolis ..... | A. A. | C | 99 | 280 | 35 | 73 | 10 | 0 | 8 | 37 | .261 | 495 | 58 | 11 | .980 |
| 1975—Indianapolis ..... | A. A. | C-3B | 90 | 260 | 27 | 68 | 12 | 1 | 6 | 25 | .262 | 434 | 62 | 15 | .971 |
| 1976—Indianapolis ..... | A. A. | C-PH | 40 | 83 | 3 | 21 | 2 | 0 | 0 | 6 | .253 | 139 | 17 | 5 | .969 |
| Major League Totals ...................... | | | 21 | 24 | 3 | 3 | 0 | 0 | 0 | 0 | .125 | 43 | 6 | 0 | 1.000 |

†On disabled list, July 19 through July 31, 1966.

‡On disabled list, May 20 through June 3, 1967.

§Traded by St. Louis Cardinals' organization to San Diego Padres' organization, May 23, 1969.

xPlayer-manager.

yTraded by San Diego Padres' organization to Indianapolis (Cincinnati Reds' organization), October 20, 1970.

zPlayer-coach.

### RECORD AS MANAGER

| Year    Club | League | Position | W. | L. |
|---|---|---|---|---|
| 1970—Lodi .................. | Calif. | Eighth | 20 | 50 |
| (Second Half) | | Eighth | 23 | 47 |

Coach, St. Louis Cardinals, 1977.

# CORNELIUS JOSEPH RYAN
## (Connie)
### Texas Rangers

Born February 27, 1920, at New Orleans, La.
Height, 5.11. Weight, 175.
Threw and batted righthanded.
Hobbies—Golf and fishing.
Attended Louisiana State University, Baton Rouge, La.
Made six hits in six times at bat, April 16, 1953.

| Year Club | League | Pos. | G. | AB. | R. | H. | 2B. | 3B. | HR. | RBI. | B.A. | PO. | A. | E. | F.A. |
|---|---|---|---|---|---|---|---|---|---|---|---|---|---|---|---|
| 1940–Atlanta | South. | 2B | 14 | 42 | 1 | 7 | 1 | 0 | 0 | 2 | .167 | 17 | 28 | 4 | .918 |
| 1940–Savannah | Sally | 2B | 113 | 421 | 83 | 133 | 22 | 4 | 13 | 73 | .316 | 261 | 325 | 16 | *.973 |
| 1941–Atlanta | South. | 2B | 151 | 600 | 106 | 180 | 33 | 4 | 5 | 83 | .300 | 323 | 447 | 32 | .960 |
| 1942–New York | Nat. | 2B | 11 | 27 | 4 | 5 | 0 | 0 | 0 | 2 | .185 | 31 | 36 | 4 | .944 |
| 1942–Jersey City† | Int. | 2B | 112 | 374 | 40 | 91 | 11 | 5 | 1 | 51 | .243 | 280 | 321 | 18 | .971 |
| 1943–Boston | Nat. | 2B-3B | 132 | 457 | 52 | 97 | 10 | 2 | 1 | 24 | .212 | 257 | 374 | 24 | .963 |
| 1944–Boston | Nat. | 2B-3B | 80 | 332 | 56 | 98 | 18 | 5 | 4 | 25 | .295 | 233 | 296 | 14 | .974 |
| 1945–Boston | Nat. | | | | | (In Military Service) | | | | | | | | | |
| 1946–Boston | Nat. | 2B-3B | 143 | 502 | 55 | 121 | 28 | 8 | 1 | 48 | .241 | 400 | 367 | 22 | .968 |
| 1947–Boston | Nat. | *2B-SS | 150 | 544 | 60 | 144 | 33 | 5 | 5 | 69 | .265 | 394 | 433 | *23 | .973 |
| 1948–Boston | Nat. | 2B-3B | 51 | 122 | 14 | 26 | 3 | 0 | 0 | 10 | .213 | 91 | 114 | 7 | .967 |
| 1949–Boston | Nat. | INF | 85 | 208 | 28 | 52 | 13 | 1 | 6 | 20 | .250 | 118 | 131 | 8 | .969 |
| 1950–Bos.‡-Cincinnati | Nat. | 2B | 126 | 439 | 57 | 109 | 20 | 5 | 6 | 49 | .248 | 361 | 342 | 16 | .978 |
| 1951–Cincinnati | Nat. | *2-3-1-O | 136 | 473 | 75 | 112 | 17 | 4 | 16 | 53 | .237 | 348 | 353 | *22 | .970 |
| 1952–Philadelphia | Nat. | 2B | ●154 | 577 | 81 | 139 | 24 | 6 | 12 | 49 | .241 | 348 | *462 | *23 | .972 |
| 1953–Philadelphia x | Nat. | 2B-1B | 90 | 247 | 47 | 73 | 14 | 6 | 5 | 26 | .296 | 138 | 168 | 13 | .959 |
| 1953–Chicago y | Amer. | 3B | 17 | 54 | 6 | 12 | 1 | 0 | 0 | 6 | .222 | 20 | 31 | 4 | .927 |
| 1954–Cincinnati | Nat. | PH | 1 | 0 | 0 | 0 | 0 | 0 | 0 | 0 | .000 | 0 | 0 | 0 | .000 |
| 1954–Louisville | A. A. | 2B | 66 | 204 | 27 | 43 | 6 | 2 | 2 | 22 | .211 | 131 | 148 | 4 | .986 |
| 1955–Corpus Christi | Big St. | 3-2B-P | 122 | 403 | 90 | 101 | 15 | 2 | 10 | 56 | .251 | 103 | 227 | 10 | .946 |
| 1956–Austin | Tex. | IN-0-P | 45 | 82 | 10 | 24 | 7 | 0 | 0 | 13 | .293 | 85 | 29 | 2 | .983 |
| American League Totals | | | 17 | 54 | 6 | 12 | 1 | 0 | 0 | 6 | .222 | 20 | 31 | 4 | .927 |
| National League Totals | | | 1167 | 3928 | 529 | 976 | 180 | 42 | 56 | 375 | .248 | 2619 | 3076 | 176 | .970 |
| Major League Totals | | | 1184 | 3982 | 535 | 988 | 181 | 42 | 56 | 381 | .248 | 2639 | 3107 | 180 | .970 |

†Traded by New York Giants to Boston Braves with Catcher Hugh Poland for Catcher Ernie Lombardi, April 27, 1943.

‡Traded to Cincinnati Reds for Catcher Walker Cooper, May 10, 1950.

§Traded to Philadelphia Phillies with Pitcher Howard Fox and Catcher Forrest (Smoky) Burgess for Pitcher Niles Jordan, Catcher Andy Seminick, Infielder Eddie Pellagrini and Outfielder Dick Sisler, December 10, 1951.

xReleased to Chicago White Sox on waivers, August 25, 1953.

yTraded to Cincinnati Reds with Pitcher Saul Rogovin and Third Baseman Rocky Krsnich for Outfielder Willard Marshall, December 10, 1953.

### WORLD SERIES RECORD

| Year Club | League | Pos. | G. | AB. | R. | H. | 2B. | 3B. | HR. | RBI. | B.A. | PO. | A. | E. | F.A. |
|---|---|---|---|---|---|---|---|---|---|---|---|---|---|---|---|
| 1948–Boston | Nat. | PH | 2 | 1 | 0 | 0 | 0 | 0 | 0 | 0 | .000 | 0 | 0 | 0 | .000 |

### ALL-STAR GAME RECORD

| Year League | Pos. | AB. | R. | H. | 2B. | 3B. | HR. | RBI. | B.A. | PO. | A. | E. | F.A. |
|---|---|---|---|---|---|---|---|---|---|---|---|---|---|
| 1944–National | 2B | 4 | 1 | 2 | 0 | 0 | 0 | 0 | .500 | 4 | 4 | 1 | .889 |

### RECORD AS MANAGER

| Year Club | League | Position | W. | L. |
|---|---|---|---|---|
| 1955–Corpus Christi | Big State | First | 45 | 17 |
| (Second Half) | | †First | 48 | 31 |
| 1956–Austin | Texas | Sixth | 72 | 82 |
| 1958–Seattle | P. Coast | Sixth | 72 | 82 |
| 1962–Oklahoma City | Am. Assoc. | Fifth | 66 | 81 |
| 1968–Twin Falls | Pioneer | Fourth | 30 | 31 |
| 1975–Atlanta‡ | National | Fifth | 9 | 18 |

†Won playoffs by defeating Harlingen, four games to one and Waco, four games to none.

‡Replaced Clyde King, August 31, 1975.

Coach, Milwaukee Braves, 1957; Coach, Dallas-Ft. Worth, Texas League, 1960; Scout, Houston Astros, 1961, 63-66; Scout, Kansas City Athletics, 1967; Scout, Atlanta Braves, 1969-70; Coach, Atlanta Braves, 1971; Scout, Atlanta Braves, 1972; Coach, Atlanta Braves, 1973-74; Coach, Texas Rangers, 1977.

# JOHN FRANKLIN SAIN
## (Johnny)
### Atlanta Braves

Born September 25, 1918, at Havana, Ark.
Height, 6.02. Weight, 194.
Threw and batted righthanded.
Hobbies—Hunting and auto and airplane mechanics.

Led National League in sacrifice hits with 16 in 1948.
Led National League pitchers in complete games with 24 in 1946 and 28 in 1948.
Named by Baseball Writers' Association of America as pitcher on THE SPORTING NEWS All-Star Major League Team, 1948.
Named Top Pitcher in National League by THE SPORTING NEWS, 1948.

| Year Club | League | G. | IP. | W. | L. | Pct. | H. | R. | ER. | SO. | BB. | ERA. |
|---|---|---|---|---|---|---|---|---|---|---|---|---|
| 1936—Osceola | No'east Ark. | 11 | 76 | 5 | 3 | .625 | 71 | 34 | 23 | 44 | 32 | 2.72 |
| 1937—Osceola | No'east Ark. | 24 | 135 | 5 | 8 | .385 | 128 | 86 | 62 | 72 | 64 | 4.13 |
| 1938—Newport | No'east Ark. | 21 | 172 | 14 | 4 | .800 | 162 | 74 | 52 | 111 | 48 | 2.72 |
| 1939—Newport | No'east Ark. | 29 | 220 | 18 | 10 | .643 | 214 | 103 | 80 | 175 | 76 | 3.27 |
| 1940—Nashville | Southern | 30 | 97 | 8 | 4 | .667 | 98 | 56 | 48 | 49 | 52 | 4.45 |
| 1941—Nashville | Southern | 41 | 139 | 6 | 12 | .333 | 160 | 84 | 71 | 93 | 71 | 4.60 |
| 1942—Boston | National | 40 | 97 | 4 | 7 | .364 | 79 | 54 | 42 | 68 | 63 | 3.90 |
| 1943-44-45—Boston | National | | | | | (In Military Service) | | | | | | |
| 1946—Boston | National | 37 | 265 | 20 | 14 | .588 | 225 | 80 | 65 | 129 | 87 | 2.21 |
| 1947—Boston | National | 38 | 266 | 21 | 12 | .636 | •265 | 117 | 104 | 132 | 79 | 3.52 |
| 1948—Boston | National | 42 | •315 | •24 | 15 | .615 | •297 | 105 | 91 | 137 | 83 | 2.60 |
| 1949—Boston | National | 37 | 243 | 10 | 17 | .370 | 285 | •150 | •130 | 73 | 75 | 4.81 |
| 1950—Boston | National | 37 | 278 | 20 | 13 | .606 | •294 | 139 | 122 | 96 | 70 | 3.95 |
| 1951—Boston† | National | 26 | 160 | 5 | 13 | .278 | 195 | 88 | 75 | 63 | 45 | 4.22 |
| 1951—New York | American | 7 | 37 | 2 | 1 | .667 | 41 | 17 | 17 | 21 | 8 | 4.14 |
| 1952—New York | American | 35 | 148 | 11 | 6 | .647 | 149 | 70 | 57 | 57 | 38 | 3.47 |
| 1953—New York | American | 40 | 189 | 14 | 7 | .667 | 189 | 68 | 63 | 84 | 45 | 3.00 |
| 1954—New York | American | 45 | 77 | 6 | 6 | .500 | 66 | 27 | 27 | 33 | 15 | 3.16 |
| 1955—New York‡-Kansas City | American | 28 | 50 | 2 | 5 | .286 | 60 | 32 | 31 | 17 | 11 | 5.58 |
| American League Totals | | 155 | 501 | 35 | 25 | .583 | 505 | 214 | 195 | 212 | 117 | 3.50 |
| National League Totals | | 257 | 1624 | 104 | 91 | .533 | 1640 | 733 | 629 | 698 | 502 | 3.49 |
| Major League Totals | | 412 | 2125 | 139 | 116 | .545 | 2145 | 947 | 824 | 910 | 619 | 3.49 |

†Sold to New York Yankees for $50,000 and Pitcher Selva (Lou) Burdette, August 29, 1951.
‡Traded to Kansas City Athletics with Outfielder Enos Slaughter for Pitcher John (Sonny) Dixon and cash, May 11, 1955.

## WORLD SERIES RECORD

| Year Club | League | G. | IP. | W. | L. | Pct. | H. | R. | ER. | SO. | BB. | ERA. |
|---|---|---|---|---|---|---|---|---|---|---|---|---|
| 1948—Boston | National | 2 | 17 | 1 | 1 | .500 | 9 | 2 | 2 | 9 | 0 | 1.06 |
| 1951—New York | American | 1 | 2 | 0 | 0 | .000 | 4 | 2 | 2 | 2 | 2 | 9.00 |
| 1952—New York | American | 1 | 6 | 0 | 1 | .000 | 6 | 2 | 2 | 3 | 3 | 3.00 |
| 1953—New York | American | 2 | 5⅔ | 1 | 0 | 1.000 | 8 | 3 | 3 | 1 | 1 | 4.76 |
| World Series Totals | | 6 | 30⅔ | 2 | 2 | .500 | 27 | 9 | 9 | 15 | 6 | 2.64 |

## ALL-STAR GAME RECORD

| Year League | IP. | W. | L. | Pct. | H. | R. | ER. | SO. | BB. | ERA. |
|---|---|---|---|---|---|---|---|---|---|---|
| 1947—National | 1 | 0 | 1 | .000 | 2 | 1 | 1 | 1 | 0 | 9.00 |
| 1948—National | 1⅔ | 0 | 0 | .000 | 0 | 0 | 0 | 3 | 0 | 0.00 |
| All-Star Game Totals | 2⅔ | 0 | 1 | .000 | 2 | 1 | 1 | 4 | 0 | 3.38 |

Member of American League All-Star Team in 1953; did not play.

Coach, Kansas City Athletics, 1959 (up to August 28); New York Yankees, 1961 through 1963; out of Organized Baseball, 1964; coach, Minnesota Twins, 1965 and 1966; Detroit Tigers, 1967 through 1969; pitching instructor, California Angels, 1970; coach, Chicago White Sox, 1971 through 1975; pitching instructor, Atlanta Braves, 1976; coach, Richmond, 1976; coach, Atlanta Braves, 1977.

# GEORGE RICHARD SCHERGER
## Cincinnati Reds

Born November 10, 1920, at Dickinson, N. D.
Height, 5.08. Weight, 183.
Threw and batted righthanded.
Attended Seton Hall College, South Orange, N. J.

| Year Club | League | Pos. | G. | AB. | R. | H. | 2B. | 3B. | HR. | RBI. | B.A. | PO. | A. | E. | F.A. |
|---|---|---|---|---|---|---|---|---|---|---|---|---|---|---|---|
| 1940—Superior | North. | 2B | 20 | 69 | 16 | 22 | 5 | 1 | 1 | 8 | .319 | 37 | 47 | 2 | .977 |
| 1940—Newport | NE-Ark. | 2B | 29 | 109 | 24 | 26 | 3 | 2 | 0 | 9 | .239 | 88 | 75 | 2 | .988 |
| 1941—Olean | Pony | 2B | 62 | 241 | 45 | 65 | 12 | 1 | 1 | 29 | .270 | 144 | 175 | 15 | .955 |
| 1942—Kingsport | Appal. | 2B | 57 | 209 | 43 | 56 | 9 | 5 | 1 | 19 | .268 | .... | .... | .... | .... |
| 1943-44-45— | | | | | | (In Military Service) | | | | | | | | | |
| 1946—Danville | I.I.I. | 2B | 123 | 478 | 96 | 116 | 13 | 7 | 2 | 44 | .243 | 310 | 353 | 29 | .958 |
| 1947—Kingston | No. Atl. | 2B | 52 | 193 | 39 | 60 | 14 | 5 | 2 | 32 | .311 | 126 | 142 | 2 | .993 |
| 1947—Thomasville | N.C. St. | 2B | 38 | 139 | 20 | 38 | 4 | 5 | 1 | 26 | .273 | 107 | 102 | 12 | .946 |
| 1948—Olean | Pony | 2B | 127 | 497 | 95 | 161 | 49 | 6 | 3 | 60 | .324 | 369 | 353 | 26 | .965 |
| 1949—Three Rivers | Ca.-Am. | 2B | 139 | 478 | 91 | 122 | 23 | 8 | 0 | 53 | .255 | 363 | 306 | 22 | •.968 |
| 1950—Three Rivers | C-A | 2-3-SS | 123 | 370 | 64 | 95 | 13 | 2 | 0 | 39 | .257 | 250 | 310 | 24 | .959 |
| 1951—Ponca City | K-O-M | 2B | 121 | 419 | 103 | 113 | 24 | 13 | 1 | 74 | .270 | 299 | 326 | 13 | •.980 |
| 1952—Santa Barbara | Calif. | 2B | 69 | 238 | 34 | 58 | 12 | 3 | 0 | 30 | .244 | 203 | 175 | 10 | .974 |
| 1953—Santa Barbara | Calif. | 2B | 31 | 79 | 9 | 15 | 1 | 1 | 0 | 8 | .190 | 72 | 55 | 2 | .984 |
| 1954—Newport News | Pied. | 2B | 59 | 141 | 15 | 40 | 3 | 1 | 0 | 19 | .284 | 104 | 106 | 8 | .963 |
| 1955—Newport News | Pied. | IF | 21 | 22 | 1 | 6 | 0 | 0 | 1 | 6 | .273 | figures unavailable | | | |
| 1956—Cedar Rapids | I.I.I. | PH | 3 | 2 | 0 | 0 | 0 | 0 | 0 | 0 | .000 | .... | .... | .... | .... |

| Year Club | League | Position | W. | L. | Year Club | League | Position | W. | L. |
|---|---|---|---|---|---|---|---|---|---|
| 1947—Kingston* | No. Atl. | First | 81 | 48 | 1961—Panama City | Ala.-Fla. | Fifth | 23 | 37 |
| 1947—Thomasville** | N.C. St. | Fifth | 54 | 56 | (Second Half) | | Third | 32 | 27 |
| 1948—Olean | Pony | Seventh | 60 | 66 | 1962—Ozark-And. | Ala.-Fla. | Fifth | 54 | 66 |
| 1949—Three Rivers | Can.-Am. | Third | 75 | 64 | 1963—Salisbury | W.C. | Fourth | 32 | 29 |
| 1950—Three Rivers | Can.-Am. | Eighth | 46 | 90 | (Second Half) | | xFirst | 41 | 24 |
| 1951—Ponca City | K-O-M | †First | 85 | 39 | 1964—Salisbury | W.C. | Second | 36 | 28 |
| 1952—Santa Barbara | Calif. | Second | 74 | 66 | (Second Half) | | yFirst | 41 | 23 |
| 1953—Santa Barbara | Calif. | Third | 74 | 66 | 1965—St. Petersburg | Fla. St. | Third | 38 | 27 |
| 1954—Newport News | Pied. | ‡Second | 76 | 63 | (Second Half) | | Ninth | 30 | 42 |
| 1955—Newport News | Pied. | §First | 77 | 52 | 1967—Tampa | Fla. St. | Third | 29 | 37 |
| 1956—Cedar Rapids | I.I.I. | Seventh | 24 | 22 | (Second Half) | | Fourth | 26 | 34 |
| (Second Half) | | Seventh | 20 | 34 | 1968—Tampa | Fla. St. | Third | 74 | 62 |
| | | | | | 1969—Sarasota Reds | Gulf Coast | Third | 30 | 24 |

*Resigned July 22.
**Became manager July 22.
†Lost playoff semifinal series to Carthage, three games to two.
‡Won playoffs by defeating York, four games to none and Portsmouth, four games to three.
§Lost playoff semifinal series to Portsmouth, three games to one.
xLost playoff against Greenville (First Half winner), two games to none.
yWon playoff against Rock Hill (First Half winner), two games to one.

Coach, Cincinnati Reds, 1970 through 1977.

## ALBERT FRED SCHOENDIENST
Named pronounced SCHAIN-deenst.

### (Red)
(Nicknamed because of color of hair.)

### Oakland A's
Born February 2, 1923, at Germantown, Ill.
Height, 6.01. Weight, 192.
Threw right and batted right and lefthanded.
Hobbies—Hunting, fishing and bowling.

Established major league records for most two-base hits, three consecutive games (8), June 5, 6, 6, 1948, and most long hits, three consecutive games (9), June 5, 6, 6, 1948, 8 doubles, 1 home run.

Tied major league records for most two-base hits, two consecutive games (6), June 5, 6 (first game), 1948, most long hits, doubleheader (6), June 6, 1948, 5 doubles, 1 home run, and most at-bats, doubleheader (more than 18 innings), no hits, 12, June 9, 1947, 24 innings.

Established National League records: Highest fielding average, season, 100 or more games, second baseman (.9934), 1956; most years leading league in fielding average, 100 or more games, second baseman (7); most games, season, pinch-hitter (80), 1962.

Tied following National League records: Most two-base hits, doubleheader (5), June 6, 1948; most double plays started, game, second baseman (4), August 20, 1954; most hits, season, pinch-hitter (22), 1962.

Led National League in stolen bases with 26 in 1945.

Led National League second basemen in double plays with 109 in 1953 and 137 in 1954.

Named second baseman on The Sporting News Major League All-Star teams, 1953 and 1957.

| Year Club | League | Pos. | G. | AB. | R. | H. | 2B. | 3B. | HR. | RBI. | B.A. | PO. | A. | E. | F.A. |
|---|---|---|---|---|---|---|---|---|---|---|---|---|---|---|---|
| 1942—Union City | Kitty | 2B | 6 | 27 | 4 | 11 | 3 | 0 | 0 | 4 | .407 | 16 | 20 | 2 | .947 |
| 1942—Albany | Ga.-Fla. | S-2B | 68 | 264 | 41 | 71 | 7 | 5 | 1 | 28 | .269 | 155 | 209 | 27 | .931 |
| 1943—Lynchburg | Pied. | SS | 9 | 36 | 8 | 17 | 2 | 0 | 0 | 5 | .472 | 18 | 36 | 3 | .947 |
| 1943—Rochester | Int. | SS | 136 | 555 | 81 | •187 | 21 | 5 | 6 | 37 | •.337 | •339 | •438 | 48 | .942 |
| 1944—Rochester† | Int. | SS | 25 | 102 | 26 | 38 | 3 | 2 | 2 | 14 | .373 | 50 | 84 | 17 | .887 |
| 1945—St. Louis | Nat. | OF-S-2 | 137 | 565 | 89 | 157 | 22 | 6 | 1 | 47 | .278 | 302 | 30 | 10 | .971 |
| 1946—St. Louis | Nat. | •2-3-SS | 142 | 606 | 94 | 170 | 28 | 5 | 0 | 34 | .281 | 363 | 379 | 13 | •.983 |
| 1947—St. Louis | Nat. | 2-3-OF | 151 | •659 | 91 | 167 | 25 | 9 | 3 | 48 | .253 | 364 | 417 | 19 | .976 |
| 1948—St. Louis | Nat. | 2B | 119 | 408 | 64 | 111 | 21 | 4 | 4 | 36 | .272 | 230 | 269 | 10 | .980 |
| 1949—St. Louis | Nat. | •2-S3-O | 151 | 640 | 102 | 190 | 25 | 2 | 3 | 54 | .297 | •428 | •471 | 15 | •.984 |
| 1950—St. Louis | Nat. | 2-O-3 | 153 | •642 | 81 | 177 | •43 | 9 | 7 | 63 | .276 | 425 | 437 | 14 | .984 |
| 1951—St. Louis | Nat. | 2B-SS | 135 | 553 | 88 | 160 | 32 | 7 | 6 | 54 | .289 | 354 | 419 | 10 | .987 |
| 1952—St. Louis | Nat. | •2-3-SS | 152 | 620 | 91 | 188 | 40 | 7 | 7 | 67 | .303 | •417 | 460 | 20 | .978 |
| 1953—St. Louis | Nat. | 2B | 146 | 564 | 107 | 193 | 35 | 5 | 15 | 79 | .342 | •365 | •430 | 14 | •.983 |
| 1954—St. Louis | Nat. | 2B | 148 | 610 | 98 | 192 | 38 | 8 | 5 | 79 | .315 | 394 | •477 | 18 | .980 |
| 1955—St. Louis | Nat. | 2B | 145 | 553 | 68 | 148 | 21 | 3 | 11 | 51 | .268 | 296 | 381 | 10 | •.985 |
| 1956—St. L.‡-N. Y. | Nat. | 2B | 132 | 487 | 61 | 147 | 21 | 3 | 2 | 29 | .302 | 298 | 308 | 4 | .993 |
| 1957—N. Y.§-Milw. | Nat. | •2B-OF | 150 | 648 | 91 | •200 | 31 | 8 | 15 | 65 | .309 | 379 | 448 | 12 | •.986 |
| 1958—Milwaukee | Nat. | 2B | 106 | 427 | 47 | 112 | 23 | 1 | 1 | 24 | .262 | 233 | 301 | 7 | •.987 |
| 1959—Milwaukee x | Nat. | 2B | 5 | 3 | 0 | 0 | 0 | 0 | 0 | 0 | .000 | 1 | 1 | 1 | .667 |
| 1960—Milwaukee y | Nat. | 2B | 68 | 226 | 21 | 58 | 9 | 1 | 1 | 19 | .257 | 120 | 148 | 10 | .964 |
| 1961—St. Louis | Nat. | 2B | 72 | 120 | 9 | 36 | 9 | 0 | 1 | 12 | .300 | 43 | 42 | 4 | .955 |
| 1962—St. Louis | Nat. | 2B-3B | 98 | 143 | 21 | 43 | 4 | 0 | 2 | 12 | .301 | 33 | 48 | 1 | .988 |
| 1963—St. Louis | Nat. | PH | 6 | 5 | 0 | 0 | 0 | 0 | 0 | 0 | .000 | 0 | 0 | 0 | .000 |
| Major League Totals | | | 2216 | 8479 | 1223 | 2449 | 427 | 78 | 84 | 773 | .289 | 5045 | 5466 | 192 | .982 |

†Entered Military Service in May.
‡Traded to New York Giants with Pitchers Gordon Jones and Dick Littlefield, Catcher Bill Sarni and Outfielder Jack Brandt for Pitcher Don Liddle, Catcher Ray Katt, Shortstop Al Dark and Outfielder-First Baseman Whitey Lockman. All players but Jones exchanged clubs June 14, 1956—Jones being assigned to Giants, October 1, 1956.

§Traded to Milwaukee Braves for Pitcher Ray Crone, Second Baseman Danny O'Connell and Outfielder Bobby Thomson, June 15, 1957.

xOn disabled list with tuberculosis most of season.

yReleased by Milwaukee Braves, October 14, 1960; signed by St. Louis Cardinals, March 15, 1961.

## WORLD SERIES RECORD

Tied World Series record for most at-bats in nine-inning game, 6, October 10, 1946.

| Year | League | Pos. | G. | AB. | R. | H. | 2B. | 3B. | HR. | RBI. | B.A. | PO. | A. | E. | F.A. |
|------|--------|------|----|-----|----|----|-----|-----|-----|------|------|-----|----|----|------|
| 1946—St. Louis | Nat. | 2B | 7 | 30 | 3 | 7 | 1 | 0 | 0 | 1 | .233 | 17 | 21 | 1 | .974 |
| 1957—Milwaukee | Nat. | 2B | 5 | 18 | 0 | 5 | 1 | 0 | 0 | 2 | .278 | 5 | 10 | 0 | 1.000 |
| 1958—Milwaukee | Nat. | 2B | 7 | 30 | 5 | 9 | 3 | 1 | 0 | 0 | .300 | 18 | 19 | 1 | .974 |
| World Series Totals | | | 19 | 78 | 8 | 21 | 5 | 1 | 0 | 3 | .269 | 40 | 50 | 2 | .978 |

## ALL-STAR GAME RECORD

| Year | League | Pos. | AB. | R. | H. | 2B. | 3B. | HR. | RBI. | B.A. | PO. | A. | E. | F.A. |
|------|--------|------|-----|----|----|-----|-----|-----|------|------|-----|----|----|------|
| 1946—National | | 2B | 2 | 0 | 0 | 0 | 0 | 0 | 0 | .000 | 0 | 2 | 0 | 1.000 |
| 1948—National | | 2B | 4 | 0 | 0 | 0 | 0 | 0 | 0 | .000 | 0 | 1 | 0 | 1.000 |
| 1949—National | | PH | 1 | 0 | 1 | 0 | 0 | 0 | 0 | 1.000 | 0 | 0 | 0 | .000 |
| 1950—National | | 2B | 1 | 1 | 1 | 0 | 0 | 1 | 1 | 1.000 | 1 | 1 | 0 | 1.000 |
| 1951—National | | 2B | 0 | 0 | 0 | 0 | 0 | 0 | 0 | .000 | 0 | 0 | 0 | .000 |
| 1953—National | | 2B | 3 | 0 | 0 | 0 | 0 | 0 | 0 | .000 | 0 | 3 | 0 | 1.000 |
| 1954—National | | 2B | 2 | 0 | 0 | 0 | 0 | 0 | 0 | .000 | 1 | 0 | 0 | 1.000 |
| 1955—National | | 2B | 6 | 0 | 2 | 0 | 0 | 0 | 0 | .333 | 3 | 2 | 0 | 1.000 |
| 1957—National | | 2B | 2 | 0 | 0 | 0 | 0 | 0 | 0 | .000 | 0 | 0 | 1 | .000 |
| All-Star Game Totals | | | 21 | 1 | 4 | 0 | 0 | 1 | 1 | .190 | 5 | 9 | 1 | .933 |

Member of National League All-Star Team in 1952; did not play.

## RECORD AS MANAGER

| Year | Club | League | Position | W. | L. | Year | Club | League | Position | W. | L. |
|------|------|--------|----------|----|----|------|------|--------|----------|----|----|
| 1965—St. Louis | National | Seventh | 80 | 81 | | 1971—St. Louis | Nat. | Second(E) | 90 | 72 |
| 1966—St. Louis | National | Sixth | 83 | 79 | | 1972—St. Louis | Nat. | Fourth(E) | 75 | 81 |
| 1967—St. Louis | National | First | 101 | 60 | | 1973—St. Louis | Nat. | Second(E) | 81 | 81 |
| 1968—St. Louis | National | First | 97 | 65 | | 1974—St. Louis | Nat. | Second(E) | 86 | 75 |
| 1969—St. Louis | Nat. | Fourth(E) | 87 | 75 | | 1975—St. Louis | Nat. | †Third(E) | 82 | 80 |
| 1970—St. Louis | Nat. | Fourth(E) | 76 | 86 | | 1976—St. Louis | Nat. | Fifth(E) | 72 | 90 |

†Tied for position.

Coach, St. Louis Cardinals, 1963 and 1964; coach, Oakland A's, 1977.

## WORLD SERIES RECORD

| Year | Club | League | W. | L. |
|------|------|--------|----|----|
| 1967—St. Louis | National | 4 | 3 |
| 1968—St. Louis | National | 3 | 4 |

# GEORGE WARREN SCHULTZ
## (Barney)
## Chicago Cubs

Born August 15, 1926, at Beverly, N. J.
Height, 6.02. Weight, 200.
Threw and batted righthanded.
Hobby—Following all sports.
Attended University of New Hampshire, Durham, N. H.

| Year | Club | League | G. | IP. | W. | L. | Pct. | H. | R. | ER. | SO. | BB. | ERA. |
|------|------|--------|----|-----|----|----|------|----|----|-----|-----|-----|------|
| 1944—Wilmington | Inter-State | 10 | 28 | 0 | 2 | .000 | 39 | 24 | 16 | 12 | 15 | 5.14 |
| 1944—Bradford | Pony | 6 | 44 | 3 | 3 | .500 | 45 | 23 | 21 | 21 | 18 | 4.30 |
| 1945—Wilmington | Inter-State | 33 | 198 | 11 | 14 | .440 | 215 | 120 | 99 | 121 | 101 | 4.50 |
| 1946—Terre Haute | I.I.I. | 9 | 18 | 0 | 4 | .000 | 19 | 14 | 10 | 12 | 14 | 5.00 |
| 1946—Schenectady† | Can.-Am. | 8 | 27 | 1 | 1 | .500 | 33 | 23 | 17 | 13 | 14 | 5.67 |
| 1947—Hagerstown | Inter-State | 30 | 124 | 5 | 9 | .357 | 152 | 88 | 74 | 59 | 89 | 5.37 |
| 1948—Hagerstown | Inter-State | 40 | •219 | 6 | •19 | .240 | 220 | •144 | 117 | 123 | 114 | 4.81 |
| 1949—Rock Hill | Tri-State | 27 | 180 | 10 | 12 | .455 | 179 | 95 | 75 | 139 | 90 | 3.75 |
| 1950—Macon | Sally | 36 | 237 | 13 | 14 | .481 | 189 | 104 | 94 | 168 | 123 | 3.57 |
| 1951—Des Moines-Denver | Western | 29 | 198 | 11 | 14 | .440 | 193 | 90 | 71 | 122 | 95 | 3.23 |
| 1952—Denver | Western | 34 | 238 | 17 | 9 | .654 | 209 | 97 | 84 | 148 | 96 | 3.18 |
| 1953—Hollywood | P. Coast | 5 | 9 | 0 | 0 | .000 | 11 | 1 | 2 | 9 | 5 | 1.93 |
| 1953—Denver‡ | Western | 31 | 173 | 13 | 7 | .650 | 147 | 99 | 80 | 102 | 84 | 4.16 |
| 1954—Columbus | Am. Assoc. | 41 | 119 | 8 | 8 | .500 | 99 | 59 | 51 | 70 | 49 | 3.86 |
| 1955—St. Louis | National | 19 | 30 | 1 | 2 | .333 | 28 | 27 | 26 | 19 | 15 | 7.80 |
| 1955—Houston | Texas | 19 | 125 | 5 | 7 | .417 | 106 | 52 | 48 | 111 | 42 | 3.46 |
| 1956—Omaha | Am. Assoc. | 45 | 118 | 9 | 12 | .429 | 110 | 67 | 55 | 95 | 41 | 4.19 |
| 1957—Omaha | Am. Assoc. | 44 | 121 | 8 | 7 | .533 | 101 | 43 | 38 | 86 | 39 | 2.83 |
| 1958—Omaha§-Charleston | Am. Assoc. | 39 | 97 | 8 | 5 | .615 | 87 | 44 | 39 | 72 | 26 | 3.62 |
| 1959—Charleston | Am. Assoc. | 36 | 81 | 3 | 5 | .375 | 77 | 40 | 36 | 55 | 24 | 4.00 |
| 1959—Detroit x | American | 13 | 18 | 1 | 2 | .333 | 17 | 12 | 9 | 17 | 14 | 4.50 |
| 1960—Houston | Am. Assoc. | 53 | 146 | 8 | 9 | .471 | 130 | 56 | 49 | 103 | 41 | 3.02 |
| 1961—Houston | Am. Assoc. | 24 | 49 | 6 | 1 | .857 | 37 | 16 | 15 | 40 | 17 | 2.76 |
| 1961—Chicago | National | 41 | 67 | 7 | 6 | .538 | 57 | 32 | 20 | 59 | 25 | 2.69 |

| Year Club | League | G. | IP. | W. | L. | Pct. | H. | R. | ER. | SO. | BB. | ERA. |
|---|---|---|---|---|---|---|---|---|---|---|---|---|
| 1962–Chicago | National | 51 | 78 | 5 | 5 | .500 | 66 | 36 | 33 | 58 | 23 | 3.81 |
| 1963–Chicago y-St. Louis | National | 39 | 63 | 3 | 0 | 1.000 | 61 | 26 | 25 | 44 | 17 | 3.57 |
| 1964–Jacksonville | Int'national | 42 | 86 | 8 | 5 | .615 | 61 | 13 | 10 | 70 | 22 | 1.05 |
| 1964–St. Louis | National | 30 | 49 | 1 | 3 | .250 | 35 | 14 | 9 | 29 | 11 | 1.65 |
| 1965–St. Louis | National | 34 | 42 | 2 | 2 | .500 | 39 | 22 | 18 | 38 | 11 | 3.86 |
| 1965–Jacksonville | Int'national | 10 | 15 | 0 | 1 | .000 | 25 | 10 | 7 | 13 | 5 | 4.20 |
| 1966–Tulsa | P. Coast | 25 | 25 | 2 | 0 | 1.000 | 20 | 9 | 9 | 20 | 12 | 3.24 |
| American League Totals | | 13 | 18 | 1 | 2 | .333 | 17 | 12 | 9 | 17 | 14 | 4.50 |
| National League Totals | | 214 | 329 | 19 | 18 | .514 | 286 | 157 | 131 | 247 | 102 | 3.58 |
| Major League Totals | | 227 | 347 | 20 | 20 | .500 | 303 | 169 | 140 | 264 | 116 | 3.63 |

†Originally signed by Philadelphia Phillies; released, July 1946.
‡Released to Columbus (St. Louis Cardinals' organization), September 23, 1953.
§Released by St. Louis Cardinals' organization to Detroit Tigers' organization, May 26, 1958.
xTraded to Chicago Cubs for Infielders Wayne Connally and J. C. Hartman, April 13, 1960.
yTraded to St. Louis Cardinals for Infielder-Outfielder Leo Burke, June 24, 1963.

### WORLD SERIES RECORD

| Year Club | League | G. | IP. | W. | L. | Pct. | H. | R. | ER. | SO. | BB. | ERA. |
|---|---|---|---|---|---|---|---|---|---|---|---|---|
| 1964–St. Louis | National | 4 | 4 | 0 | 1 | .000 | 9 | 8 | 8 | 1 | 2 | 18.00 |

Minor League Pitching Instructor, St. Louis Cardinals, 1967 through 1970; coach, St. Louis Cardinals, 1971 through 1975; coach, Wichita (Chicago Cubs' organization), 1976; coach, Chicago Cubs, 1977.

## LAWRENCE WILLIAM SHEPARD
### (Larry)
### Cincinnati Reds

Born April 3, 1919, at Lakewood, O.
Height, 5.11. Weight, 180.
Threw and batted righthanded.
Hobbies—Golf, chess, bowling and bridge.
Attended McGill University, Montreal, Quebec, Canada.

| Year Club | League | G. | IP. | W. | L. | Pct. | H. | R. | ER. | SO. | BB. | ERA. |
|---|---|---|---|---|---|---|---|---|---|---|---|---|
| 1941–Three Rivers† | Can.-Am. | 33 | 218 | 15 | 11 | .577 | 210 | 120 | 90 | 110 | 124 | 3.72 |
| 1942-45– | | | | | | (In military service) | | | | | | |
| 1946–Nashua‡ | New Eng. | 28 | 156 | 12 | 5 | .706 | 137 | 68 | 60 | 89 | 74 | 3.46 |
| 1947–Pueblo | Western | 33 | 194 | 15 | 10 | .600 | 193 | 108 | 85 | 105 | 95 | 3.94 |
| 1948–Medford | Far West | 36 | 215 | •22 | 3 | •.880 | 171 | 102 | 69 | 217 | 105 | 2.89 |
| 1949–Billings | Pioneer | 34 | 209 | •21 | 6 | •.778 | 195 | 103 | 84 | 138 | 97 | 3.62 |
| 1950–Billings | Pioneer | 33 | 223 | •22 | 6 | •.786 | 151 | 78 | 63 | 172 | 87 | •2.54 |
| 1951–Billings§ | Pioneer | 40 | 250 | 24 | 11 | .686 | 237 | 110 | 83 | 177 | 112 | 2.99 |
| 1952–Hollywood | P. Coast | 35 | 107 | 6 | 4 | .600 | 96 | 42 | 37 | 32 | 56 | 3.11 |
| 1953–Hollywood | P. Coast | 20 | 35 | 4 | 2 | .667 | 34 | 20 | 20 | 15 | 26 | 5.14 |
| 1953–Charleston | Sally | 30 | 141 | 10 | 8 | .556 | 130 | 56 | 39 | 73 | 39 | 2.49 |
| 1954–Williamsport | Eastern | 34 | 167 | 9 | 10 | .474 | 146 | 73 | 55 | 68 | 64 | 2.96 |
| 1955–Williamsport | Eastern | 37 | 169 | 16 | 7 | .696 | 139 | 70 | 59 | 72 | 72 | 3.14 |
| 1956–Lincoln | Western | 18 | 62 | 3 | 0 | 1.000 | 76 | 53 | 45 | 34 | 23 | 6.53 |
| 1957– | | | | | | (Did Not Play) | | | | | | |
| 1958–Salt Lake CIty | P. Coast | 7 | 16 | 0 | 1 | .000 | 21 | 11 | 9 | 5 | 11 | 5.06 |

†Sold to New York Giants but deal was cancelled since Shepard was inducted in the armed services.
‡Signed as free agent by Brooklyn Dodgers' organization, March 1946.
§Drafted from Brooklyn Dodgers' organization by Hollywood (Pittsburgh Pirates' organization), December 3, 1951.

### RECORD AS MANAGER

| Year Club | League | Position | W. | L. | Year Club | League | Position | W. | L. |
|---|---|---|---|---|---|---|---|---|---|
| 1948–Medford | Far West | Second | 66 | 56 | 1959–Salt Lake C. | P. Coast | First | 85 | 69 |
| 1949–Billings | Pioneer | Second | 77 | 48 | 1960–Salt Lake C. | P. Coast | Third | 80 | 73 |
| 1950–Billings | Pioneer | †Third | 72 | 54 | 1961–Columbus | Int'tional | xFirst | 92 | 62 |
| 1951–Billings | Pioneer | Sixth | 65 | 70 | 1962–Columbus | Int'tional | Fifth | 82 | 72 |
| 1953–Charleston‡ | Sally | Seventh | 43 | 49 | 1963–Columbus | Int'tional | Fourth(S) | 75 | 73 |
| 1954–Williamsport | Eastern | Seventh | 63 | 77 | 1964–Columbus | Int'tional | Sixth | 68 | 85 |
| 1955–Williamsport | Eastern | Fifth | 71 | 66 | 1965–Columbus | Int'tional | yFirst | 85 | 61 |
| 1956–Lincoln | Western | §First | 45 | 27 | 1966–Columbus | Int'tional | Second | 82 | 65 |
| (Second Half) | | Second | 39 | 27 | 1968–Pittsburgh | National | Sixth | 80 | 82 |
| 1957–Lincoln | Western | First | 98 | 56 | 1969–Pittsburgh z | National | Third(E) | 84 | 73 |
| 1958–Salt Lake C. | P. Coast | Fifth | 77 | 77 | | | | | |

†Won playoffs by defeating Pocatello, two games to none and Twin Falls, three games to none.
‡Replaced Norman Shope, June 1.
§Won playoff against Amarillo (Second Half winner), four games to one.
xLost playoff semifinal series against Rochester, four games to one.
yLost playoff finals against Toronto, four games to one after defeating Syracuse in semifinals, four games to two.
zReplaced by Alex Grammas, September 26.
Coach, Philadelphia Phillies, 1967; Cincinnati Reds, 1970 through 1977.

# LAWRENCE SHERRY
## (Larry)
## Pittsburgh Pirates

Born July 25, 1935, at Los Angeles, Calif.
Height, 6.02. Weight, 204.
Threw and batted righthanded.
Hobbies—Bowling and fishing.
Brother Norman, manager of California Angels.

Made unassisted double play as pitcher, tying a major league record, September 4, 1961.
Tied record for most games won by relief pitcher in a World Series (2), 1959.

| Year Club | League | G. | IP. | W. | L. | Pct. | H. | R. | ER. | SO. | BB. | ERA. |
|---|---|---|---|---|---|---|---|---|---|---|---|---|
| 1953—Santa Barbara .....................California | 9 | 42 | 1 | 2 | .333 | 48 | 27 | 21 | 23 | 33 | 4.54 |
| 1954—Great Falls .........................Pioneer | 4 | 13 | 0 | 3 | .000 | 11 | 13 | 11 | 12 | 10 | 7.82 |
| 1954—Bakersfield .....................California | 21 | 110 | 6 | 5 | .545 | 95 | 71 | 63 | 87 | 115 | 5.15 |
| 1955—Newport News...................Piedmont | 32 | 101 | 5 | 10 | .333 | 94 | 78 | 55 | 91 | 71 | 4.90 |
| 1956—Pueblo ............................Western | 33 | 209 | 13 | 13 | .500 | 194 | 117 | 102 | 184 | 132 | 4.39 |
| 1957—Los Angeles .......................P. Coast | 5 | 21 | 0 | 1 | .000 | 22 | 12 | 12 | 17 | 10 | 5.23 |
| 1957—Fort Worth ........................Texas | 27 | 170 | 10 | 10 | .500 | 131 | 65 | 58 | •146 | 89 | 3.07 |
| 1958—Spokane ..........................P. Coast | 29 | 154 | 6 | 14 | .300 | 160 | 97 | 84 | 84 | 88 | 4.91 |
| 1958—Los Angeles .....................National | 5 | 4 | 0 | 0 | .000 | 10 | 7 | 6 | 2 | 7 | 13.50 |
| 1959—St. Paul.......................Am. Assoc. | 15 | 115 | 6 | 7 | .462 | 103 | 49 | 46 | 109 | 53 | 3.60 |
| 1959—Los Angeles .....................National | 23 | 94 | 7 | 2 | .778 | 75 | 27 | 23 | 72 | 43 | 2.20 |
| 1960—Los Angeles .....................National | 57 | 142 | 14 | 10 | .583 | 125 | 65 | 60 | 114 | 82 | 3.80 |
| 1961—Los Angeles .....................National | 53 | 95 | 4 | 4 | .500 | 90 | 48 | 41 | 79 | 39 | 3.88 |
| 1962—Los Angeles .....................National | 58 | 90 | 7 | 3 | .700 | 81 | 40 | 32 | 71 | 44 | 3.20 |
| 1963—Los Angeles†.....................National | 36 | 80 | 2 | 6 | .250 | 82 | 43 | 33 | 47 | 24 | 3.71 |
| 1964—Detroit ............................American | 38 | 66 | 7 | 5 | .583 | 52 | 29 | 27 | 58 | 37 | 3.68 |
| 1965—Detroit ............................American | 39 | 78 | 3 | 6 | .333 | 71 | 30 | 27 | 46 | 40 | 3.12 |
| 1966—Detroit ............................American | 55 | 78 | 8 | 5 | .615 | 66 | 38 | 33 | 63 | 36 | 3.81 |
| 1967—Detroit‡ ...........................American | 20 | 28 | 0 | 1 | .000 | 35 | 22 | 20 | 20 | 7 | 6.43 |
| 1967—Houston ...........................National | 29 | 41 | 1 | 2 | .333 | 53 | 26 | 22 | 32 | 13 | 4.83 |
| 1968—California .........................American | 3 | 3 | 0 | 0 | .000 | 7 | 2 | 2 | 2 | 2 | 6.00 |
| 1968—Hawaii .............................P. Coast | 34 | 88 | 6 | 6 | .500 | 77 | 30 | 28 | 62 | 25 | 2.86 |
| 1969—Tucson .............................P. Coast | 25 | 61 | 6 | 5 | .545 | 83 | 37 | 34 | 45 | 16 | 5.02 |
| 1970—Mobile§xz .........................Southern | 26 | 33 | 4 | 6 | .429 | 36 | 14 | 9 | 24 | 13 | 2.45 |
| National League Totals...................... | 231 | 546 | 35 | 27 | .564 | 516 | 256 | 217 | 417 | 252 | 3.58 |
| American League Texas ..................... | 152 | 250 | 18 | 17 | .514 | 224 | 119 | 107 | 187 | 120 | 3.85 |
| Major League Totals ......................... | 383 | 796 | 53 | 44 | .546 | 740 | 375 | 324 | 604 | 372 | 3.66 |

†Sold to Detroit Tigers, April 9, 1964; Outfielder Lou Johnson was transferred from Syracuse to Spokane, a Dodger farm team, as part of the deal.
‡Traded to Houston Astros' organization for Outfielder Jim Landis, June 30, 1967.
§Player-coach.
xPlayer-manager.
zOn disabled list, July 14 through September 5, 1970.

### WORLD SERIES RECORD

| Year Club | League | G. | IP. | W. | L. | Pct. | H. | R. | ER. | SO. | BB. | ERA. |
|---|---|---|---|---|---|---|---|---|---|---|---|---|
| 1959—Los Angeles .......................National | 4 | 12⅔ | 2 | 0 | 1.000 | 8 | 1 | 1 | 5 | 2 | 0.71 |

### RECORD AS MANAGER

| Year Club | League | Position | W. | L. |
|---|---|---|---|---|
| 1970—Mobile† ..............South. | Seventh | 59 | 78 |
| 1971—Asheville ............South. | Second(E) | 90 | 51 |
| 1972—Tucson ..............P. C. | Fourth(E) | 60 | 88 |
| 1974—Charleston..........W. Carol. | Second | 41 | 30 |
| (Second Half) | | Third | 30 | 30 |

†Replaced Tom Saffell, July 2, 1970.
Minor League Pitching Instructor, Pittsburgh Pirates, 1974 through 1976; coach, Pittsburgh Pirates, 1977.

# ROBERT RALPH SKINNER
## (Bob)
## San Diego Padres

Born October 3, 1931, at LaJolla, Calif.
Height, 6.04½. Weight, 205.
Threw and batted lefthanded.
Hobby—Automobiles.

Named THE SPORTING NEWS Minor League Manager of the Year, 1967.

| Year Club | League | Pos. | G. | AB. | R. | H. | 2B. | 3B. | HR. | RBI. | B.A. | PO. | A. | E. | F.A. |
|---|---|---|---|---|---|---|---|---|---|---|---|---|---|---|---|
| 1951—Waco ...............Big St. | 1B | 98 | 367 | 67 | 104 | 22 | 3 | 9 | 58 | .283 | 679 | 52 | •35 | .954 |
| 1951—Mayfield...........Kitty | 1B | 29 | 106 | 40 | 50 | 9 | 4 | 6 | 29 | .472 | 164 | 10 | 8 | .956 |
| 1952-53—Burlington ...Carol. | | | | (In Military Service) | | | | | | | | | |
| 1954—Pittsburgh ........Nat. | 1B-OF | 132 | 470 | 67 | 117 | 15 | 9 | 8 | 46 | .249 | 1026 | 84 | 16 | .986 |
| 1955—New Orleans ....South. | 1B | 86 | 321 | 62 | 111 | 24 | 6 | 8 | 62 | .346 | 724 | 52 | 16 | .980 |

| Year Club League | Pos. | G. | AB. | R. | H. | 2B. | 3B. | HR. | RBI. | B.A. | PO. | A. | E. | F.A. |
|---|---|---|---|---|---|---|---|---|---|---|---|---|---|---|
| 1956–Pittsburgh ........Nat. | O-1-3 | 113 | 233 | 29 | 47 | 8 | 3 | 5 | 29 | .202 | 217 | 8 | 2 | .991 |
| 1957–Pittsburgh ........Nat. | O-1-3 | 126 | 387 | 58 | 118 | 12 | 6 | 13 | 45 | .305 | 232 | 17 | 8 | .969 |
| 1958–Pittsburgh ........Nat. | OF | 144 | 529 | 93 | 170 | 33 | 9 | 13 | 70 | .321 | 232 | 19 | 6 | .977 |
| 1959–Pittsburgh ........Nat. | OF-1B | 143 | 547 | 78 | 153 | 18 | 4 | 13 | 61 | .280 | 285 | 9 | 11 | .964 |
| 1960–Pittsburgh ........Nat. | OF | 145 | 571 | 83 | 156 | 33 | 6 | 15 | 86 | .273 | 250 | 13 | 5 | .981 |
| 1961–Pittsburgh ........Nat. | OF | 119 | 381 | 61 | 102 | 20 | 3 | 3 | 42 | .268 | 175 | 5 | 5 | .973 |
| 1962–Pittsburgh ........Nat. | OF | 144 | 510 | 87 | 154 | 29 | 7 | 20 | 75 | .302 | 210 | 6 | 9 | .960 |
| 1963–Pitt.†-Cin..........Nat. | OF | 106 | 316 | 43 | 82 | 15 | 7 | 3 | 25 | .259 | 131 | 4 | 1 | .993 |
| 1964–Cin.‡-St. Louis ..Nat. | OF | 80 | 177 | 16 | 45 | 8 | 0 | 4 | 21 | .254 | 62 | 4 | 5 | .930 |
| 1965–St. Louis ..........Nat. | OF | 80 | 152 | 25 | 47 | 5 | 4 | 5 | 26 | .309 | 43 | 0 | 3 | .935 |
| 1966–St. Louis ..........Nat. | PH | 49 | 45 | 2 | 7 | 1 | 0 | 1 | 5 | .156 | 0 | 0 | 0 | .000 |
| Major League Totals ..................... | | 1381 | 4318 | 642 | 1198 | 197 | 58 | 103 | 531 | .277 | 2863 | 169 | 71 | .977 |

†Traded to Cincinnati Reds for Outfielder Jerry Lynch, May 23, 1963.

‡Traded to St. Louis Cardinals for cash and Catcher Jim Saul, June 13, 1964; Saul was transferred from Jacksonville to San Diego.

### WORLD SERIES RECORD

| Year Club League | Pos. | G. | AB. | R. | H. | 2B. | 3B. | HR. | RBI. | B.A. | PO. | A. | E. | F.A. |
|---|---|---|---|---|---|---|---|---|---|---|---|---|---|---|
| 1960–Pittsburgh ........Nat. | OF | 2 | 5 | 2 | 1 | 0 | 0 | 0 | 1 | .200 | 4 | 1 | 0 | 1.000 |
| 1964–St. Louis ..........Nat. | PH | 4 | 3 | 0 | 2 | 1 | 0 | 0 | 1 | .667 | 0 | 0 | 0 | .000 |
| World Series Totals ..................... | | 6 | 8 | 2 | 3 | 1 | 0 | 0 | 2 | .375 | 4 | 1 | 0 | 1.000 |

### ALL-STAR GAME RECORD

| Year League | Pos. | AB. | R. | H. | 2B. | 3B. | HR. | RBI. | B.A. | PO. | A. | E. | F.A. |
|---|---|---|---|---|---|---|---|---|---|---|---|---|---|
| 1958–National ............................. | OF | 3 | 0 | 1 | 0 | 0 | 0 | 1 | .333 | 2 | 0 | 0 | 1.000 |
| 1960–National (both games) ........ | OF | 7 | 1 | 2 | 0 | 0 | 0 | 1 | .286 | 3 | 0 | 0 | 1.000 |
| All-Star Game Totals ....................... | | 10 | 1 | 3 | 0 | 0 | 0 | 2 | .300 | 5 | 0 | 0 | 1.000 |

### RECORD AS MANAGER

| Year Club | League | Position | W. | L. |
|---|---|---|---|---|
| 1967–San Diego ..........P. C. | | †First(E) | 85 | 63 |
| 1968–San Diego‡ ........P. C. | | Fourth(E) | 31 | 28 |
| 1968–Philadelphia§......National | | xSeventh | 48 | 59 |
| 1969–Philadelphia y ....National | | Fifth(E) | 44 | 64 |

†Defeated Spokane in championship playoff, four games to two.

‡Promoted to Philadelphia Phillies, June 15.

§Replaced Gene Mauch with club in fifth place, June 16.

xTied for position with Los Angeles Dodgers.

yReplaced by George Myatt, August 7.

Coach, San Diego Padres, 1970 through 1973; Pittsburgh Pirates, 1974 through 1976; coach, San Diego Padres, 1977.


## HAROLD RAYMOND SMITH
### (Hal)
### Milwaukee Brewers

Born June 1, 1931, at Barling, Ark.
Height, 5.10½. Weight, 198.
Threw and batted righthanded.
Hobbies—Home movies and music.
Attended Fort Smith Junior College, Fort Smith, Ark.
Brother of Tommy Smith, former catcher in St. Louis Cardinal, Houston Astro and Kansas City Royal organizations; and Ron Smith, Jr., former infielder in New York Yankees' organization.

Led National League in passed balls with 17 in 1957.

| Year Club League | Pos. | G. | AB. | R. | H. | 2B. | 3B. | HR. | RBI. | B.A. | PO. | A. | E. | F.A. |
|---|---|---|---|---|---|---|---|---|---|---|---|---|---|---|
| 1949–Albany ..............Ga.-Fla. | C | 99 | 321 | 50 | 72 | 12 | 2 | 1 | 31 | .224 | 542 | 57 | 19 | .969 |
| 1950–Lynchburg ........Pied. | C | 2 | 3 | 0 | 0 | 0 | 0 | 0 | 0 | .000 | 10 | 0 | 0 | 1.000 |
| 1950–Hamilton ..........Pony | C-3B | 79 | 281 | 33 | 63 | 13 | 0 | 0 | 21 | .224 | 281 | 72 | 25 | .934 |
| 1951–Columbus..........Sally | | | | | (In Military Service) | | | | | | | | | |
| 1952–Allentown† ........Int.-St. | C | 11 | 33 | 7 | 7 | 1 | 0 | 0 | 3 | .212 | 62 | 7 | 5 | .933 |
| 1952–Omaha ..............West. | C | 20 | 47 | 2 | 12 | 0 | 0 | 1 | 4 | .255 | 59 | 9 | 1 | .986 |
| 1953–Omaha ..............West. | C-OF | 107 | 339 | 33 | 73 | 10 | 1 | 1 | 21 | .215 | 462 | 50 | 18 | .966 |
| 1954–Houston ............Texas | C | 79 | 270 | 27 | 70 | 9 | 1 | 5 | 39 | .259 | 451 | 43 | 12 | .976 |
| 1955–Houston ............Texas | •C-OF | 139 | 512 | 58 | 153 | 22 | 7 | 8 | 67 | .299 | •761 | •78 | 7 | •.992 |
| 1956–St. Louis ..........Nat. | C | 75 | 227 | 27 | 64 | 12 | 0 | 5 | 23 | .282 | 300 | 34 | 6 | .982 |
| 1957–St. Louis ..........Nat. | C | 100 | 333 | 25 | 93 | 12 | 3 | 2 | 37 | .279 | 168 | 42 | 5 | .990 |
| 1958–St. Louis ..........Nat. | C | 77 | 220 | 13 | 50 | 4 | 1 | 1 | 24 | .227 | 346 | 22 | 4 | .989 |
| 1959–St. Louis ..........Nat. | C | 142 | 452 | 35 | 122 | 15 | 3 | 13 | 50 | .270 | 758 | 60 | 9 | .989 |
| 1960–St. Louis ..........Nat. | C | 127 | 337 | 20 | 77 | 16 | 0 | 2 | 28 | .228 | 664 | 61 | 7 | .990 |
| 1961–St. Louis‡ ..........Nat. | C | 45 | 125 | 6 | 31 | 4 | 1 | 0 | 10 | .248 | 261 | 28 | 2 | .993 |
| 1965–Pittsburgh ........Nat. | C | 4 | 3 | 0 | 0 | 0 | 0 | 0 | 0 | .000 | 13 | 0 | 0 | 1.000 |
| Major League Totals | | 570 | 1697 | 126 | 437 | 63 | 8 | 23 | 172 | .258 | 2810 | 247 | 27 | .989 |

†On voluntary retired list, May 5 to July 4, 1952.

‡Placed on disabled list, June 20, 1961, after suffering from a heart condition; transferred to voluntary retired list, October 2; reinstated May 3, 1962 and named coach of St. Louis Cardinals five days later; released October 1, 1962.

## ALL-STAR GAME RECORD

| Year League | Pos. | AB. | R. | H. | 2B. | 3B. | HR. | RBI. | B.A. | PO. | A. | E. | F.A. |
|---|---|---|---|---|---|---|---|---|---|---|---|---|---|
| 1959—National (second game) ...... | C | 2 | 0 | 0 | 0 | 0 | 0 | 0 | .000 | 5 | 0 | 0 | 1.000 |

Member of National League All-Star team in 1957 and 1959 (first game); did not play.

## RECORD AS MANAGER

| Year Club | League | Position | W. | L. |
|---|---|---|---|---|
| 1964—Rock Hill............ | W. Carol. | †First | 43 | 21 |
| (Second Half) | | Fifth | 33 | 30 |

†Lost playoff to Salisbury (Second Half winner), two games to one.

Coach, St. Louis Cardinals, May 8, 1962, through end of season; minor league instructor, St. Louis Cardinals, 1963; coach, Pittsburgh Pirates, 1965 through 1967; coach, Cincinnati Reds, 1968 and 1969; scout, St. Louis Cardinals, 1970 through 1975; coach, Milwaukee Brewers, 1976 and 1977.

## DENNIS JAMES SOMMERS
### (Denny)
### New York Mets

Born July 12, 1940, at Hortonville, Wis.
Height, 6.02. Weight, 197.
Threw right and batted lefthanded.
Hobbies—Basketball and movies.
Attended Wisconsin State University, Oshkosh, Wis.

| Year Club | League | Pos. | G. | AB. | R. | H. | 2B. | 3B. | HR. | RBI. | B.A. | PO. | A. | E. | F.A. |
|---|---|---|---|---|---|---|---|---|---|---|---|---|---|---|---|
| 1958—Michigan City | Midw. | OF | 37 | 102 | 11 | 17 | 1 | 0 | 1 | 14 | .167 | 44 | 1 | 3 | .938 |
| 1959—Michigan City | Midw. | C-OF | 122 | 406 | 54 | 87 | 14 | 2 | 7 | 47 | .214 | 604 | 51 | 12 | .982 |
| 1960—Eugene | Northw. | C | 108 | 306 | 27 | 75 | 11 | 3 | 3 | 37 | .245 | 515 | 32 | 12 | .979 |
| 1961—Vic.-R.G.V. | Texas | C | 67 | 198 | 18 | 47 | 3 | 1 | 1 | 19 | .237 | 370 | 33 | 1 | .998 |
| 1962—Springfield | East. | C | 78 | 218 | 17 | 52 | 6 | 1 | 0 | 21 | .239 | 392 | 15 | 8 | .981 |
| 1963—Springfield | East. | C | 140 | 464 | 33 | 93 | 12 | 0 | 3 | 47 | .200 | •934 | •93 | •20 | .981 |
| 1964—Springfield | East. | C | 123 | 401 | 27 | 86 | 15 | 0 | 1 | 35 | .214 | •795 | •55 | 10 | .988 |
| 1965—Springfield | East. | C | 88 | 281 | 28 | 68 | 9 | 0 | 1 | 21 | .242 | 616 | 36 | 7 | .989 |
| 1965—Tacoma | P. C. | C | 24 | 79 | 8 | 16 | 2 | 0 | 0 | 7 | .203 | 137 | 11 | 4 | .974 |
| 1966—Phoenix | P. C. | C | 52 | 101 | 8 | 23 | 7 | 0 | 0 | 12 | .228 | 117 | 7 | 0 | 1.000 |
| 1966—Lexington† | W. Car. | PH | 8 | 7 | 0 | 1 | 1 | 0 | 0 | 2 | .143 | .... | .... | .... | ...... |
| 1967—Decatur† | Midw. | PH | 9 | 7 | 0 | 1 | 1 | 0 | 0 | 1 | .143 | .... | .... | .... | ...... |

†Player-manager.

## RECORD AS MANAGER

| Year Club | League | Position | W. | L. | Year Club | League | Position | W. | L. |
|---|---|---|---|---|---|---|---|---|---|
| 1966—Lexington | W. Carol.† | Seventh | 15 | 28 | (Second Half) | | Fifth | 35 | 35 |
| 1967—Decatur | Midwest | Fifth | 27 | 30 | 1971—Fresno | Calif. | §First | 42 | 28 |
| (Second Half) | | Second | 35 | 28 | (Second Half) | | Seventh | 28 | 42 |
| 1968—Decatur | Midwest | Fifth | 29 | 27 | 1972—Amarillo | Texas | Second(W) | 71 | 68 |
| (Second Half) | | ‡First | 40 | 21 | 1973—Amarillo | Texas | Fourth(W) | 64 | 75 |
| 1969—Fresno | California | Second | 38 | 32 | 1974—Amarillo | Texas | Second(W) | 69 | 62 |
| (Second Half) | | Fifth | 34 | 36 | 1975—Lafayette | Texas | xFirst(E) | 72 | 57 |
| 1970—Fresno | California | Fifth | 36 | 33 | 1976—Midland | Texas | Fourth(W) | 62 | 74 |

†Replaced Alex Cosmidis, July 8, 1966.
‡Lost playoff to Quad Cities, two games to one.
§Lost playoff to Visalia, two games to one.
xMidland and Lafayette each won two games in playoff; rain prevented completion of series, and Midland and Lafayette were declared co-champions by league president.

Coach, New York Mets, 1977.

## ALBERT LEE STANGE

Name pronounced STANG.

(Known by middle name.)

### Oakland A's

Born October 27, 1936, at Chicago, Ill.
Height, 5.10. Weight, 170.
Threw and batted righthanded.
Hobbies—Bowling and golf.
Attended Drake University, Des Moines, Ia.

Tied major league record for most strikeouts in one inning by a pitcher (4), seventh inning. September 2, 1964.
Led Carolina League in games started with 35 and complete games with 20 and tied for lead in shutouts with 3 in 1960.

| Year Club | League | G. | IP. | W. | L. | Pct. | H. | R. | ER. | SO. | BB. | ERA. |
|---|---|---|---|---|---|---|---|---|---|---|---|---|
| 1957—Fort Walton Beach | Ala.-Fla. | 22 | 95 | 5 | 6 | .455 | 89 | 64 | 57 | 62 | 74 | 5.40 |
| 1958—Fort Walton Beach | Ala.-Fla. | 32 | 217 | 13 | 12 | .520 | 192 | 100 | 81 | 171 | 120 | 3.36 |
| 1959—Fox Cities | I.I.I. | 34 | 79 | 4 | 6 | .400 | 96 | 62 | 52 | 72 | 53 | 5.92 |
| 1960—Wilson | Carolina | 39 | •251 | •20 | •13 | 606 | •235 | •125 | •100 | 196 | 92 | 3.59 |
| 1961—Minnesota | American | 7 | 12 | 1 | 0 | 1.000 | 15 | 6 | 4 | 10 | 10 | 3.00 |

| Year Club | League | Pos. | G. | AB. | R. | H. | 2B. | 3B. | HR. | RBI. | B.A. | PO. | A. | E. | F.A. |
|---|---|---|---|---|---|---|---|---|---|---|---|---|---|---|---|
| 1961–Syracuse | Int'national | | 56 | 112 | 7 | 12 | .368 | 102 | 56 | 47 | 90 | 47 | 3.78 | | |
| 1962–Minnesota | American | | 44 | 95 | 4 | 3 | .571 | 98 | 57 | 47 | 70 | 39 | 4.45 | | |
| 1963–Dallas-Fort Worth | P. Coast | | 9 | 66 | 7 | 1 | .875 | 53 | 15 | 15 | 74 | 8 | 2.05 | | |
| 1963–Minnesota | American | | 32 | 165 | 12 | 5 | .706 | 145 | 53 | 48 | 100 | 43 | 2.62 | | |
| 1964–Minnesota†-Cleveland | American | | 37 | 171 | 7 | 14 | .333 | 176 | 92 | 84 | 132 | 50 | 4.42 | | |
| 1965–Cleveland | American | | 41 | 132 | 8 | 4 | .667 | 122 | 50 | 49 | 80 | 26 | 3.34 | | |
| 1966–Cleveland‡-Boston | American | | 36 | 169 | 8 | 9 | .471 | 157 | 70 | 62 | 85 | 46 | 3.30 | | |
| 1967–Boston | American | | 35 | 182 | 8 | 10 | .444 | 171 | 64 | 56 | 101 | 32 | 2.77 | | |
| 1968–Boston | American | | 50 | 103 | 5 | 5 | .500 | 89 | 54 | 45 | 53 | 25 | 3.93 | | |
| 1969–Boston | American | | 41 | 137 | 6 | 9 | .400 | 137 | 70 | 56 | 59 | 56 | 3.68 | | |
| 1970–Boston§-Chicago x | American | | 36 | 50 | 3 | 2 | .600 | 62 | 37 | 30 | 28 | 17 | 5.40 | | |
| Major League Totals | | | 359 | 1216 | 62 | 61 | .504 | 1172 | 553 | 481 | 718 | 344 | 3.56 | | |

†Traded to Cleveland Indians with Outfielder George Banks for Pitcher Jim Grant, June 15, 1964.
‡Traded with Pitcher Don McMahon to Boston Red Sox for Pitcher Dick Radatz, June 2, 1966.
§Sold to Chicago White Sox, June 29, 1970.
xUnconditionally released by Chicago White Sox, December 12, 1970.

### WORLD SERIES RECORD

| Year Club | League | G. | IP. | W. | L. | Pct. | H. | R. | ER. | SO. | BB. | ERA. |
|---|---|---|---|---|---|---|---|---|---|---|---|---|
| 1967–Boston | American | 1 | 2 | 0 | 0 | .000 | 3 | 1 | 0 | 0 | 0 | 0.00 |

Coach, Boston Red Sox, 1972 through 1974; coach, Minnesota Twins, 1975; minor league instructor, Oakland A's, 1976; coach, Oakland A's, 1977.

## HERMAN PAUL STARRETTE
Name pronounced Stah-RET.
### (Herm)
### San Francisco Giants
Born November 20, 1938, at Statesville, N. C.
Height, 6.01. Weight, 185.
Threw and batted righthanded.
Hobbies–Hunting and fishing.
Attended Lenoir Rhyne College, Hickory, N. C.

| Year Club | League | G. | IP. | W. | L. | Pct. | H. | R. | ER. | SO. | BB. | ERA. |
|---|---|---|---|---|---|---|---|---|---|---|---|---|
| 1958–Aberdeen | Northern | 21 | 144 | 7 | 9 | .438 | 136 | 70 | 56 | 103 | 58 | 3.50 |
| 1959–Aberdeen | Northern | 32 | 196 | 17 | 7 | .708 | 208 | 94 | 76 | 154 | 54 | 3.49 |
| 1960–Vancouver | P. Coast | 11 | 27 | 0 | 2 | .000 | 35 | 21 | 20 | 10 | 13 | 6.67 |
| 1960–Stockton | California | 24 | 142 | 9 | 7 | .563 | 159 | 66 | 54 | 91 | 31 | 3.42 |
| 1961–Fox Cities | I.I.I. | 35 | 146 | 11 | 7 | .611 | 153 | 64 | 59 | 128 | 54 | 3.64 |
| 1962–Elmira | Eastern | *61 | 163 | 14 | 10 | .583 | 155 | 61 | 48 | 133 | 29 | 2.65 |
| 1963–Rochester | Int'national | 24 | 48 | 6 | 2 | .750 | 40 | 11 | 6 | 28 | 14 | 1.13 |
| 1963–Baltimore | American | 18 | 26 | 0 | 1 | .000 | 26 | 10 | 10 | 13 | 7 | 3.46 |
| 1964–Rochester | Int'national | 30 | 55 | 5 | 2 | .714 | 46 | 14 | 12 | 46 | 11 | 1.96 |
| 1964–Baltimore | American | 5 | 11 | 1 | 0 | 1.000 | 9 | 3 | 2 | 5 | 6 | 1.64 |
| 1965–Rochester | Int'national | 44 | 78 | 3 | 3 | .500 | 79 | 29 | 25 | 43 | 14 | 2.88 |
| 1965–Baltimore | American | 4 | 9 | 0 | 0 | .000 | 8 | 3 | 1 | 3 | 3 | 1.00 |
| 1966–Rochester | Int'national | 14 | 21 | 0 | 1 | .000 | 36 | 23 | 20 | 8 | 5 | 8.57 |
| Major League Totals | | 27 | 46 | 1 | 1 | .500 | 43 | 16 | 13 | 21 | 16 | 2.54 |

Coach, Rochester (International League), 1967; Minor League Pitching Instructor, Baltimore Orioles, 1968 through 1973; coach, Atlanta Braves, 1974 through 1976; San Francisco Giants, 1977.

## WESLEY GAY STOCK
### (Wes)
### Seattle Mariners
Born April 10, 1934, at Longview, Wash.
Height, 6.01½. Weight, 182.
Threw and batted righthanded.
Hobbies–Hunting and golf.
Attended Washington State College, Pullman, Wash.

| Year Club | League | G. | IP. | W. | L. | Pct. | H. | R. | ER. | SO. | BB. | ERA. |
|---|---|---|---|---|---|---|---|---|---|---|---|---|
| 1956–Aberdeen | Northern | 30 | 181 | 14 | 6 | •.700 | 169 | 90 | 67 | •182 | 109 | 3.33 |
| 1957-58–Knoxville | Sally | | | | | (In Military Service) | | | | | | |
| 1959–Baltimore | American | 7 | 13 | 0 | 0 | .000 | 16 | 6 | 5 | 8 | 2 | 3.46 |
| 1959–Miami | Int'national | 6 | 15 | 0 | 1 | .000 | 21 | 19 | 15 | 9 | 13 | 9.00 |
| 1959–Vancouver | P. Coast | 22 | 98 | 6 | 6 | .500 | 87 | 41 | 37 | 59 | 40 | 3.40 |
| 1960–Miami | Int'national | 21 | 128 | 8 | 6 | .571 | 102 | 41 | 32 | 102 | 34 | 2.25 |
| 1960–Baltimore | American | 17 | 34 | 2 | 2 | .500 | 26 | 11 | 11 | 23 | 14 | 2.91 |
| 1961–Baltimore | American | 35 | 72 | 5 | 0 | 1.000 | 58 | 24 | 24 | 47 | 27 | 3.00 |
| 1962–Baltimore | American | 53 | 65 | 3 | 2 | .600 | 50 | 33 | 32 | 34 | 36 | 4.43 |
| 1963–Baltimore | American | 47 | 75 | 7 | 0 | 1.000 | 69 | 41 | 33 | 55 | 31 | 3.96 |
| 1964–Baltimore†-K.C. | American | 64 | 114 | 8 | 3 | .727 | 86 | 30 | 29 | 115 | 42 | 2.29 |
| 1965–Kansas City | American | 62 | 100 | 0 | 4 | .000 | 96 | 62 | 58 | 52 | 40 | 5.22 |
| 1966–Vancouver | P. Coast | 1 | 1 | 0 | 0 | .000 | 0 | 0 | 0 | 1 | 0 | 0.00 |

| Year Club | League | G. | IP. | W. | L. | Pct. | H. | R. | ER. | SO. | BB. | ERA. |
|---|---|---|---|---|---|---|---|---|---|---|---|---|
| 1966—Kansas City.........................American | | 35 | 44 | 2 | 2 | .500 | 30 | 15 | 13 | 31 | 21 | 2.66 |
| 1967—Kansas City.........................American | | 1 | 1 | 0 | 0 | .000 | 3 | 2 | 2 | 0 | 2 | 18.00 |
| Major League Totals .............................. | | 321 | 518 | 27 | 13 | .675 | 434 | 224 | 207 | 365 | 215 | 3.60 |

†Traded to Kansas City Athletics for Catcher Charlie Lau, June 15, 1964.

Coach, Kansas City Athletics, 1967; Minor League Pitching Instructor, New York Mets, 1968 and 1969; coach, Milwaukee Brewers, 1970 through 1972; Oakland Athletics, 1973 through 1976; Seattle Mariners, 1977.

## ANTONIO TAYLOR (SANCHEZ)
### (Tony)
### Philadelphia Phillies

Born December 19, 1935, at Central Alava, Matanzas, Cuba.
Height, 5:09½. Weight, 179.
Threw and batted righthanded.
Hobby—Movies.

Established National League record for fewest assists by second baseman, season, 150 or more games, 358, in 1964.

Led Northern League in stolen bases with 38 in 1955.

| Year Club | League | Pos. | G. | AB. | R. | H. | 2B. | 3B. | HR. | RBI. | B.A. | PO. | A. | E. | F.A. |
|---|---|---|---|---|---|---|---|---|---|---|---|---|---|---|---|
| 1954—Tx.C.-Th'b'd'x ..Evng. | | 3B-SS | 131 | 516 | 104 | 162 | 25 | •12 | 5 | 49 | .314 | 170 | 337 | 60 | .894 |
| 1955—St. Cloud ...........North. | | 3B | 125 | 510 | 103 | 136 | 19 | •10 | 5 | 46 | .267 | 129 | •276 | •37 | .916 |
| 1956—Danville ...........Carol. | | 3B | 150 | 544 | 95 | 145 | 28 | 7 | 13 | 60 | .267 | 153 | 272 | 30 | .934 |
| 1957—Dallas† ..............Tex. | | 3-SS-O | 105 | 368 | 61 | 80 | 11 | 5 | 3 | 31 | .217 | 104 | 190 | 17 | .945 |
| 1958—Chicago ............Nat. | | 2B-3B | 140 | 497 | 63 | 117 | 15 | 3 | 6 | 27 | .235 | 311 | 374 | 23 | .968 |
| 1959—Chicago ............Nat. | | •2B-SS | 150 | 624 | 96 | 175 | 30 | 8 | 8 | 38 | .280 | 355 | •456 | •25 | .970 |
| 1960—Chi.‡-Phila. ......Nat. | | 2B-3B | 146 | 581 | 80 | 165 | 25 | 7 | 5 | 44 | .284 | 321 | 411 | 23 | .970 |
| 1961—Philadelphia .....Nat. | | 2B-3B | 106 | 400 | 47 | 100 | 17 | 3 | 2 | 26 | .250 | 233 | 279 | 10 | .981 |
| 1962—Philadelphia .....Nat. | | 2B-SS | 152 | 625 | 87 | 162 | 21 | 5 | 7 | 43 | .259 | 372 | 385 | 22 | .972 |
| 1963—Philadelphia .....Nat. | | •2B-3B | 157 | 640 | 102 | 180 | 20 | 10 | 5 | 49 | .281 | 325 | 412 | 10 | •.987 |
| 1964—Philadelphia .....Nat. | | 2B | 154 | 570 | 62 | 143 | 13 | 6 | 4 | 46 | .251 | 325 | 358 | 16 | .977 |
| 1965—Philadelphia .....Nat. | | 2B-3B | 106 | 323 | 41 | 74 | 14 | 3 | 3 | 27 | .229 | 169 | 222 | 17 | .958 |
| 1966—Philadelphia .....Nat. | | 2B-3B | 125 | 434 | 47 | 105 | 14 | 8 | 5 | 40 | .242 | 187 | 281 | 9 | .981 |
| 1967—Philadelphia .....Nat. | | 1-3-2-S | 132 | 462 | 55 | 110 | 16 | 6 | 2 | 34 | .238 | 524 | 182 | 9 | 987 |
| 1968—Philadelphia .....Nat. | | 3-2-1B | 145 | 547 | 59 | 137 | 20 | 2 | 3 | 38 | .250 | 115 | 324 | 16 | .965 |
| 1969—Philadelphia .....Nat. | | 3-2-1B | 138 | 557 | 68 | 146 | 24 | 5 | 3 | 30 | .262 | 262 | 294 | 15 | .974 |
| 1970—Philadelphia .....Nat. | | 2-3-O-S | 124 | 439 | 74 | 132 | 26 | 9 | 9 | 55 | .301 | 220 | 215 | 5 | .989 |
| 1971—Philadelphia§ ....Nat. | | 2-3-1 | 36 | 107 | 9 | 25 | 2 | 1 | 1 | 5 | .234 | 58 | 64 | 1 | .992 |
| 1971—Detroit ..............Amer. | | 2B-3B | 55 | 181 | 27 | 52 | 10 | 2 | 3 | 19 | .287 | 115 | 109 | 1 | .996 |
| 1972—Detroit ..............Amer. | | 2-3-1 | 78 | 228 | 33 | 69 | 12 | 4 | 1 | 20 | .303 | 130 | 122 | 8 | .969 |
| 1973—Detroit x .........Am. | | 2-1-3-O | 84 | 275 | 35 | 63 | 9 | 3 | 5 | 24 | .229 | 151 | 168 | 4 | .988 |
| 1974—Philadelphia .....Nat. | | 1-3-2 | 62 | 64 | 5 | 21 | 4 | 0 | 2 | 13 | .328 | 34 | 4 | 0 | 1.000 |
| 1975—Philadelphia .....Nat. | | 3-1-2 | 79 | 103 | 13 | 25 | 5 | 1 | 1 | 17 | .243 | 34 | 35 | 5 | .932 |
| 1976—Philadelphia y ..Nat. | | 3B-2B | 26 | 23 | 2 | 6 | 1 | 0 | 0 | 3 | .261 | 0 | 1 | 0 | 1.000 |
| American League Totals ................ | | 217 | 684 | 95 | 184 | 31 | 9 | 9 | 63 | .269 | 396 | 399 | 13 | .984 | |
| National League Totals ................... | | 1978 | 6996 | 910 | 1823 | 267 | 77 | 66 | 535 | .260 | 3845 | 4297 | 206 | .975 | |
| Major League Totals ...................... | | 2195 | 7680 | 1005 | 2007 | 298 | 86 | 75 | 598 | .261 | 4241 | 4696 | 219 | .976 | |

†Drafted by Chicago Cubs from Dallas (New York Giants' organization), December 2, 1957.

‡Traded to Philadelphia with Catcher Cal Neeman for Pitcher Don Cardwell and First Baseman Ed Bouchee, May 13, 1960.

§Traded to Detroit Tigers for Pitchers Mike Fremuth (assigned from Montgomery to Reading) and Carl Cavanaugh (assigned from Rocky Mount to Peninsula), June 12, 1971.

xUnconditionally released, December 3, 1973; signed as free agent by Philadelphia Phillies, December 19, 1973.

yOn disabled list, April 8 to April 30 and May 15 to July 30, 1976.

### CHAMPIONSHIP SERIES RECORD

| Year Club | League | Pos. | G. | AB. | R. | H. | 2B. | 3B. | HR. | RBI. | B.A. | PO. | A. | E. | F.A. |
|---|---|---|---|---|---|---|---|---|---|---|---|---|---|---|---|
| 1972—Detroit ..............Amer. | | 2B | 4 | 15 | 0 | 2 | 2 | 0 | 0 | 0 | .133 | 5 | 9 | 0 | 1.000 |

### ALL-STAR GAME RECORD

| Year League | Pos. | AB. | R. | H. | 2B. | 3B. | HR. | RBI. | B.A. | PO. | A. | E. | F.A. |
|---|---|---|---|---|---|---|---|---|---|---|---|---|---|
| 1960—National (both games) ........ | PR-2B | 1 | 0 | 1 | 0 | 0 | 0 | 0 | 1.000 | 2 | 1 | 0 | 1.000 |

Coach, Philadelphia Phillies, 1977.

## JEFFREY ALLEN TORBORG
### (Jeff)
### Cleveland Indians

Born November 26, 1941, at Westfield, N. J.
Height, 6.00½. Weight, 195.
Threw and batted righthanded.
Hobby—Sports.

Attended Rutgers University, New Brunswick, N. J.; received Bachelor of Science degree in Education. Did graduate studies at Montclair State College, Montclair, N. J.; earned Masters degree in Athletic Administration.

Received reported $100,000 bonus to sign with Los Angeles Dodgers, 1963.

| Year | Club | League | Pos. | G. | AB. | R. | H. | 2B. | 3B. | HR. | RBI. | B.A. | PO. | A. | E. | F.A. |
|------|------|--------|------|----|----|----|----|-----|-----|-----|------|------|-----|----|----|------|
| 1963–Albuquerque | ...Texas | | C | 64 | 184 | 19 | 41 | 10 | 3 | 1 | 18 | .223 | 349 | 27 | 6 | .984 |
| 1964–Los Angeles | ...Nat. | | C | 28 | 43 | 4 | 10 | 1 | 1 | 0 | 4 | .233 | 80 | 4 | 2 | .977 |
| 1965–Los Angeles | ...Nat. | | C | 56 | 150 | 8 | 36 | 5 | 1 | 3 | 13 | .240 | 300 | 19 | 3 | .991 |
| 1966–Los Angeles | ...Nat. | | C | 46 | 120 | 4 | 27 | 3 | 0 | 1 | 13 | .225 | 269 | 17 | 4 | .986 |
| 1967–Los Angeles | ...Nat. | | C | 76 | 196 | 11 | 42 | 4 | 1 | 2 | 12 | .214 | 413 | 30 | 5 | .989 |
| 1968–Los Angeles | ...Nat. | | C | 37 | 93 | 2 | 15 | 2 | 0 | 0 | 4 | .161 | 206 | 20 | 2 | .991 |
| 1969–Los Angeles | ...Nat. | | C | 51 | 124 | 7 | 23 | 4 | 0 | 0 | 7 | .185 | 251 | 26 | 1 | .996 |
| 1970–Los Angeles† | ...Nat. | | C | 64 | 134 | 11 | 31 | 8 | 0 | 1 | 17 | .231 | 275 | 16 | 5 | .983 |
| 1971–California‡ | ...Amer. | | C | 55 | 123 | 6 | 25 | 5 | 0 | 0 | 5 | .203 | 208 | 17 | 3 | .987 |
| 1972–California‡‡ | ...Amer. | | C | 59 | 153 | 5 | 32 | 3 | 0 | 0 | 8 | .209 | 383 | 28 | 1 | .998 |
| 1973–California§ x | ...Amer. | | C | 102 | 255 | 20 | 56 | 7 | 0 | 1 | 18 | .220 | 611 | 37 | 6 | .991 |
| National League Totals | .................. | | | 358 | 860 | 47 | 184 | 27 | 3 | 7 | 70 | .214 | 1794 | 132 | 22 | .989 |
| American League Totals | ............... | | | 216 | 531 | 31 | 113 | 15 | 0 | 1 | 31 | .213 | 1202 | 82 | 10 | .990 |
| Major League Totals | ...................... | | | 574 | 1391 | 78 | 297 | 42 | 3 | 8 | 101 | .214 | 2996 | 214 | 32 | .990 |

†Sold to California Angels, March 13, 1971.
‡On disabled list, June 25 through July 27.
‡‡On disabled list, May 21 through June 13.
§On disabled list, July 13 to August 10, 1973.
xTraded to St. Louis Cardinals for Pitcher John Andrews, December 6, 1973. Unconditionally released by St. Louis, March 25, 1974.

Coach, Cleveland Indians, 1975 through 1977.

## RICHARD JOSEPH TRACEWSKI

Name pronounced Truh-ZOO-skee.

### (Dick)
### Detroit Tigers

Born February 3, 1935, at Eynon, Pa.
Height, 5.11. Weight, 170.
Threw and batted righthanded.
Hobbies–Bowling, golf and hunting.

Led Tri-State League shortstops in double plays with 83 in 1955.

| Year | Club | League | Pos. | G. | AB. | R. | H. | 2B. | 3B. | HR. | RBI. | B.A. | PO. | A. | E. | F.A. |
|------|------|--------|------|----|----|----|----|-----|-----|-----|------|------|-----|----|----|------|
| 1953–Sheboygan | ........Wis. St. | | SS | 50 | 193 | 57 | 46 | 3 | 3 | 0 | 34 | .238 | 72 | 157 | 36 | .864 |
| 1954–Bakersfield | ........Calif. | | SS | 25 | 87 | 10 | 19 | 1 | 2 | 0 | 8 | .218 | 41 | 67 | 18 | .857 |
| 1954–Hornell | ..............Pony | | SS | 18 | 65 | 16 | 18 | 1 | 1 | 0 | 7 | .277 | 29 | 34 | 10 | .863 |
| 1954–Thomasville | ......Ga.-Fla. | | SS | 72 | 274 | 36 | 76 | 7 | 4 | 3 | 32 | .277 | 138 | 191 | 28 | .922 |
| 1955–Asheville | ..........Tri-St. | | SS | 117 | 443 | 78 | 111 | 15 | 7 | 0 | 45 | .251 | ★240 | ★356 | ★47 | .927 |
| 1956–Fort Worth | ..........Texas | | SS | 66 | 194 | 30 | 46 | 5 | 2 | 0 | 20 | .237 | 115 | 184 | 27 | .917 |
| 1956–Cedar Rapids | ....I.I.I. | | SS | 55 | 212 | 32 | 55 | 9 | 3 | 2 | 15 | .259 | 109 | 174 | 27 | .913 |
| 1957–Pueblo | ..............West. | | SS | 151 | 570 | 93 | 170 | 26 | ●14 | 4 | 69 | .298 | 285 | ★446 | 47 | .940 |
| 1958-59–Montreal | ......Int. | | | | | | | (In Military Service) | | | | | | | | |
| 1960–Atlanta | ..............A. A. | | SS | 149 | 582 | 91 | 152 | 13 | 7 | 1 | 42 | .261 | ★269 | 436 | 43 | .943 |
| 1961–Omaha | ..............South. | | SS | 150 | 532 | 107 | 153 | 22 | 8 | 2 | 58 | .288 | 300 | 389 | 40 | .945 |
| 1962–Los Angeles | ......Nat. | | SS | 15 | 2 | 3 | 0 | 0 | 0 | 0 | 0 | .000 | 1 | 4 | 0 | 1.000 |
| 1962–Spokane | ...........P. C. | | SS-2B | 121 | 467 | 62 | 114 | 25 | 2 | 3 | 28 | .244 | 213 | 346 | 35 | .941 |
| 1963–Los Angeles | ......Nat. | | SS-2B | 104 | 217 | 23 | 49 | 2 | 1 | 1 | 10 | .226 | 105 | 216 | 4 | .958 |
| 1964–Los Angeles | ......Nat. | | 2-3B-SS | 106 | 304 | 31 | 75 | 13 | 4 | 1 | 26 | .247 | 152 | 218 | 15 | .961 |
| 1965–Los Angeles† | ....Nat. | | 3-2B-SS | 78 | 186 | 17 | 40 | 6 | 0 | 1 | 20 | .215 | 51 | 132 | 12 | .938 |
| 1966–Detroit | ..............Amer. | | 2B-SS | 81 | 124 | 15 | 24 | 1 | 1 | 0 | 7 | .194 | 71 | 100 | 10 | .945 |
| 1967–Detroit | ..............Amer. | | SS-2-3B | 74 | 107 | 19 | 30 | 4 | 2 | 1 | 9 | .280 | 54 | 90 | 3 | .980 |
| 1968–Detroit | ..............Amer. | | S-3-2 | 90 | 212 | 30 | 33 | 3 | 1 | 4 | 15 | .156 | 82 | 157 | 5 | .980 |
| 1969–Detroit | ..............Amer. | | SS-2-3 | 66 | 79 | 10 | 11 | 2 | 0 | 0 | 4 | .139 | 59 | 87 | 5 | .967 |
| National League Totals | .................. | | | 303 | 709 | 74 | 164 | 21 | 5 | 3 | 56 | .231 | 309 | 570 | 41 | .955 |
| American League Totals | ............... | | | 311 | 522 | 74 | 98 | 10 | 4 | 5 | 35 | .188 | 266 | 434 | 23 | .968 |
| Major League Totals | ...................... | | | 614 | 1231 | 148 | 262 | 31 | 9 | 8 | 91 | .213 | 575 | 1004 | 64 | .961 |

†Traded to Detroit Tigers for Pitcher Phil Regan, December 15, 1965.

### WORLD SERIES RECORD

| Year | Club | League | Pos. | G. | AB. | R. | H. | 2B. | 3B. | HR. | RBI. | B.A. | PO. | A. | E. | F.A. |
|------|------|--------|------|----|----|----|----|-----|-----|-----|------|------|-----|----|----|------|
| 1963–Los Angeles | ...Nat. | | 2B | 4 | 13 | 1 | 2 | 0 | 0 | 0 | 0 | .154 | 7 | 7 | 1 | .933 |
| 1965–Los Angels | .......Nat. | | PH-2B | 6 | 17 | 0 | 2 | 0 | 0 | 0 | 0 | .118 | 11 | 11 | 1 | .957 |
| 1968–Detroit | ..............Am. | | 3B-PR | 2 | 0 | 1 | 0 | 0 | 0 | 0 | 0 | .000 | 0 | 0 | 0 | .000 |
| World Series Totals | ...................... | | | 12 | 30 | 2 | 4 | 0 | 0 | 0 | 0 | .133 | 18 | 18 | 2 | .947 |

### RECORD AS MANAGER

| Year | Club | League | Position | W. | L. |
|------|------|--------|----------|----|----|
| 1970–Lakeland | ...........Fla. St. | Sec'd(W) | 69 | 64 | |
| 1971–Montgomery | ......South. | Third(E) | 73 | 69 | |

Coach, Detroit Tigers, 1972 through 1977.

---

### *DID YOU KNOW* —

That Hoyt Wilhelm of the Baltimore Orioles pitched a no-hit no-run game against the New York Yankees on September 20, 1958?

# JAMES BARTON VERNON
## (Mickey)
## Montreal Expos

Born April 22, 1918, at Marcus Hook, Pa.
Height, 6.02. Weight, 192.
Threw and batted lefthanded.
Hobbies—Home movies and attending sports events.
Attended Villanova College, Villanova, Pa.

Established major league records for most assists by a first baseman, season (155), 1949; most double plays by first baseman, lifetime (2044), 1959; and most double plays, first baseman, doubleheader (10), August 18, 1943, 23 innings.

Tied major league record for most unassisted double plays, first baseman, game, 2, May 29, 1946.

Established American League records for most games played at first base, lifetime (2,227), 1958; most assist by first baseman, lifetime (1,444), 1958; most putouts by first baseman, lifetime (19,754), 1958.

Named as first baseman on THE SPORTING NEWS All-Star Major League Team, 1953.

| Year | Club | League | Pos. | G. | AB. | R. | H. | 2B. | 3B. | HR. | RBI. | B.A. | PO. | A. | E. | F.A. |
|------|------|--------|------|----|-----|----|----|----|----|----|----|----|----|----|----|----|
| 1937—Easton | | E. Shore | 1B | 83 | 300 | 51 | 86 | 24 | 6 | 10 | 64 | .287 | 814 | 54 | •16 | .982 |
| 1938—Greenville† | | Sally | 1B | 132 | 524 | 84 | 172 | 31 | 12 | 1 | 72 | .328 | 1159 | 74 | •24 | .981 |
| 1939—Springfield | | East. | 1B | 69 | 268 | 52 | 92 | 13 | 7 | 3 | 41 | .343 | 601 | 31 | 6 | .991 |
| 1939—Washington | | Amer. | 1B | 76 | 276 | 23 | 71 | 15 | 4 | 1 | 30 | .257 | 690 | 40 | 11 | .985 |
| 1940—Jersey City | | Int. | 1B | 154 | 569 | 76 | 161 | 2 | 9 | 9 | 65 | .283 | 1305 | 75 | 16 | .989 |
| 1940—Washington | | Amer. | 1B | 5 | 19 | 0 | 3 | 0 | 0 | 0 | 0 | .158 | 41 | 2 | 0 | 1.000 |
| 1941—Washington | | Amer. | 1B | 138 | 531 | 73 | 159 | 27 | 11 | 9 | 93 | .299 | 1186 | 80 | 10 | .992 |
| 1942—Washington | | Amer. | 1B | 151 | 621 | 76 | 168 | 34 | 6 | 9 | 86 | .271 | 1360 | 95 | •26 | .982 |
| 1943—Washington | | Amer. | 1B | 145 | 553 | 89 | 148 | 29 | 8 | 7 | 70 | .268 | 1351 | 75 | 14 | .990 |
| 1944-45—Washington | | Amer. | | | | | (In Military Service) | | | | | | | | | |
| 1946—Washington | | Amer. | 1B | 148 | 587 | 88 | 207 | •51 | 8 | 8 | 85 | •.353 | 1320 | 101 | •15 | .990 |
| 1947—Washington | | Amer. | 1B | 154 | 600 | 77 | 159 | 29 | 12 | 7 | 85 | .265 | 1299 | 105 | •19 | .987 |
| 1948—Washington‡ | | Amer. | 1B | 150 | 558 | 78 | 135 | 27 | 7 | 3 | 48 | .242 | 1297 | 113 | 15 | .989 |
| 1949—Cleveland | | Amer. | 1B | 153 | 584 | 72 | 170 | 27 | 4 | 18 | 83 | .291 | •1438 | •155 | 14 | .991 |
| 1950—Cleve.§-Wash. | | Amer. | 1B | 118 | 417 | 55 | 117 | 17 | 3 | 9 | 75 | .281 | 959 | 78 | 9 | •.991 |
| 1951—Washington | | Amer. | 1B | 141 | 546 | 69 | 160 | 30 | 7 | 9 | 87 | .293 | 1157 | 87 | 8 | •.994 |
| 1952—Washington | | Amer. | 1B | 154 | 569 | 71 | 143 | 33 | 9 | 10 | 80 | .251 | 1291 | 115 | 10 | •.993 |
| 1953—Washington | | Amer. | 1B | 152 | 608 | 101 | 205 | •43 | 11 | 15 | 115 | •.337 | •1376 | 94 | 12 | .992 |
| 1954—Washington | | Amer. | 1B | 151 | 597 | 90 | 173 | •33 | 14 | 20 | 97 | .290 | •1365 | 76 | 11 | •.992 |
| 1955—Washington x | | Amer. | 1B | 150 | 538 | 74 | 162 | 23 | 8 | 14 | 85 | .301 | 1258 | 69 | 8 | .994 |
| 1956—Boston | | Amer. | 1B | 119 | 403 | 67 | 125 | 28 | 4 | 15 | 84 | .310 | 930 | 58 | 11 | .989 |
| 1957—Boston y | | Amer. | 1B | 102 | 270 | 36 | 65 | 18 | 1 | 7 | 38 | .241 | 662 | 51 | 6 | .992 |
| 1958—Cleveland z | | Amer. | 1B | 119 | 355 | 49 | 104 | 22 | 3 | 8 | 55 | .293 | 774 | 50 | 11 | .987 |
| 1959—Milwaukee a | | Nat. | 1B-OF | 74 | 91 | 8 | 20 | 4 | 0 | 3 | 14 | .220 | 65 | 4 | 2 | .972 |
| 1960—Pittsburgh b | | Nat. | PH | 9 | 8 | 0 | 1 | 0 | 0 | 0 | 1 | .125 | 0 | 0 | 0 | .000 |
| American League Totals | | | | 2326 | 8632 | 1188 | 2474 | 486 | 120 | 169 | 1296 | .287 | 19754 | 1444 | 210 | .990 |
| National League Totals | | | | 83 | 99 | 8 | 21 | 4 | 0 | 3 | 15 | .212 | 65 | 4 | 2 | .972 |
| Major League Totals | | | | 2409 | 8731 | 1196 | 2495 | 490 | 120 | 172 | 1311 | .286 | 19819 | 1448 | 212 | .990 |

†Released by St. Louis Browns' organziation and signed as free agent by Washington Senators, September 1938.

‡Traded to Cleveland Indians with Pitcher Early Wynn for Pitchers Joe Haynes and Ed Klieman and First Baseman Eddie Robinson, December 14, 1948.

§Traded to Washington Senators for Pitcher Dick Weik, June 14, 1950.

xTraded to Boston Red Sox with Pitchers Bob Porterfield and Johnny Schmitz and Outfielder Tom Umphlett for Pitchers Dick Brodowski, Truman Clevenger and Al Curtis, Outfielders Neil Christley and Karl Olson, November 8, 1955.

yReleased to Cleveland Indians on waivers, January 29, 1958.

zTraded to Milwaukee Braves for Pitcher Humberto Robinson, April 11, 1959.

aUnconditionally released by Milwaukee Braves, October 13, 1959.

bPlayer-coach.

## ALL-STAR GAME RECORD

| Year | League | Pos. | AB. | R. | H. | 2B. | 3B. | HR. | RBI. | B.A. | PO. | A. | E. | F.A. |
|------|--------|------|-----|----|----|----|----|----|----|----|----|----|----|----|
| 1946—American | | 1B | 2 | 0 | 0 | 0 | 0 | 0 | 0 | .000 | 2 | 1 | 0 | 1.000 |
| 1948—American | | PH | 0 | 1 | 0 | 0 | 0 | 0 | 0 | .000 | 0 | 0 | 0 | .000 |
| 1953—American | | 1B | 3 | 0 | 0 | 0 | 0 | 0 | 0 | .000 | 6 | 0 | 0 | 1.000 |
| 1954—American | | 1B | 1 | 0 | 0 | 0 | 0 | 0 | 0 | .000 | 1 | 0 | 0 | 1.000 |
| 1955—American | | 1B | 5 | 0 | 1 | 0 | 0 | 0 | 1 | .200 | 8 | 0 | 0 | 1.000 |
| 1956—American | | 1B | 2 | 0 | 0 | 0 | 0 | 0 | 0 | .000 | 4 | 0 | 0 | .000 |
| 1958—American | | PH | 1 | 1 | 1 | 0 | 0 | 0 | 0 | 1.000 | 0 | 0 | 0 | .000 |
| All-Star Game Totals | | | 14 | 2 | 2 | 0 | 0 | 0 | 1 | .143 | 21 | 1 | 0 | 1.000 |

## RECORD AS MANAGER

| Year | Club | League | Position | W. | L. | Year | Club | League | Position | W. | L. |
|------|------|--------|----------|----|----|------|------|--------|----------|----|----|
| 1961—Washington | | American | †Ninth | 61 | 100 | 1968—Vancouver | | P. C. | Sixth(W) | 58 | 88 |
| 1962—Washington | | American | Tenth | 60 | 101 | 1969—Richmond | | Int. | Eight | 56 | 83 |
| 1963—Washington | | American‡ | Tenth | 14 | 26 | 1970—Richmond | | Int. | Fifth | 73 | 67 |
| 1966—Vancouver | | P. C. | Second(W) | 77 | 71 | 1971—Manchester | | East. | Fourth(A) | 61 | 75 |
| 1967—Vancouver | | P. C. | Third(W) | 77 | 69 | | | | | | |

†Tied for position.

‡Replaced by Gil Hodges, May 22.

Coach, Pittsburgh Pirates, 1960 and 1964; Coach, St. Louis Cardinals, 1965; minor league batting instructor, Kansas City Royals, 1973 and 1974; minor league batting instructor, Los Angeles Dodgers, 1975 and 1976; Coach, Montreal Expos, 1977.

## OSVALDO JOSEPH VIRGIL
### (Ozzie)
### Montreal Expos

Born May 7, 1933, at Monte Christi, Dominican Republic.
Height, 6.00. Weight, 185.
Threw and batted righthanded.
Hobbies—Hunting, fishing and golf.

Led American Association third basemen in double plays with 39 in 1956 and International League third basemen with 28 in 1963.

| Year | Club | League | Pos. | G. | AB. | R. | H. | 2B. | 3B. | HR. | RBI. | B.A. | PO. | A. | E. | F.A. |
|------|------|--------|------|----|-----|----|----|-----|-----|-----|------|------|-----|----|----|------|
| 1953–St. Cloud | | North. | 3B | 118 | 433 | 63 | 112 | 13 | 4 | 7 | 60 | .259 | 117 | •258 | •41 | .901 |
| 1954–Danville | | Car. | •3B-SS | 137 | 530 | 78 | 154 | 34 | 7 | 9 | 68 | .291 | •201 | 287 | 23 | .955 |
| 1955–Dallas | | Tex. | •3-2-SS | 159 | 614 | 86 | 181 | 31 | 5 | 17 | 79 | .295 | 178 | 368 | 16 | •.972 |
| 1956–Minneapolis | | A. A. | •3B-OF | 152 | 525 | 66 | 139 | 28 | 4 | 10 | 67 | .265 | •180 | •334 | ●23 | .957 |
| 1956–New York | | Nat. | 3B | 3 | 12 | 2 | 5 | 1 | 1 | 0 | 2 | .417 | 3 | 1 | 1 | .800 |
| 1957–New York† | | Nat. | 3-O-S | 96 | 226 | 26 | 53 | 0 | 2 | 4 | 24 | .235 | 63 | 111 | 12 | .936 |
| 1958–Charleston | | A. A. | 3B | 47 | 184 | 23 | 54 | 9 | 5 | 4 | 34 | .293 | 54 | 102 | 7 | .957 |
| 1958–Detroit | | Amer. | 3B | 49 | 193 | 19 | 47 | 10 | 2 | 3 | 19 | .244 | 55 | 101 | 3 | .981 |
| 1959–Charleston | | A. A. | IN-O-C | 154 | 554 | 57 | 149 | 19 | 2 | 8 | 49 | .269 | 341 | 252 | 25 | .960 |
| 1960–Denver | | A. A. | OF-IF | 59 | 202 | 37 | 77 | 11 | 3 | 9 | 55 | .381 | 75 | 53 | 4 | .970 |
| 1960–Detroit | | Amer. | 3-2-S-C | 62 | 132 | 16 | 30 | 4 | 2 | 3 | 13 | .227 | 52 | 85 | 4 | .972 |
| 1961–Detroit‡-K. C.§ | | | 3-C-S-2 | 31 | 51 | 2 | 7 | 0 | 0 | 1 | 1 | .137 | 23 | 17 | 3 | .930 |
| 1962–Baltimore | | Amer. | PH | 1 | 0 | 0 | 0 | 0 | 0 | 0 | 0 | .000 | 0 | 0 | 0 | .000 |
| 1962–Rochester | | Int. | 3B-SS-C | 104 | 365 | 60 | 98 | 14 | 3 | 2 | 58 | .268 | 86 | 172 | 9 | .966 |
| 1963–Rochester x | | Int. | 3B | 149 | 584 | 71 | 179 | 23 | 7 | 11 | 75 | .307 | •140 | 290 | 19 | .958 |
| 1964–Toronto y z | | Int. | 3B | 150 | •608 | 80 | 164 | 29 | 5 | 11 | 48 | .270 | •137 | •311 | 23 | .951 |
| 1965–Pittsburgh a | | Nat. | C-3-2 | 39 | 49 | 3 | 13 | 2 | 0 | 1 | 5 | .265 | 36 | 17 | 1 | .981 |
| 1966–Phoenix | | P. C. | 3B-1B-C | 39 | 153 | 20 | 44 | 10 | 0 | 4 | 26 | .288 | 54 | 61 | 5 | .958 |
| 1966–San Francisco | | Nat. | C-3-1-2-O | 42 | 89 | 7 | 19 | 2 | 0 | 2 | 9 | .213 | 120 | 28 | 3 | .980 |
| 1967–Phoenix | | P. C. | 2-C-3-1B | 117 | 392 | 58 | 125 | 19 | 3 | 4 | 61 | .319 | 400 | 157 | 17 | .970 |
| 1968–Phoenix | | P. C. | C-1-3-2B | 106 | 326 | 26 | 84 | 10 | 2 | 0 | 30 | .258 | 407 | 60 | 5 | .989 |
| 1969–San Francisco | | Nat. | PH | 1 | 1 | 0 | 0 | 0 | 0 | 0 | 0 | .000 | 0 | 0 | 0 | .000 |
| American League Totals | | | | 143 | 376 | 38 | 84 | 14 | 4 | 7 | 33 | .221 | 130 | 203 | 10 | .971 |
| National League Totals | | | | 181 | 377 | 38 | 90 | 5 | 3 | 7 | 40 | .239 | 222 | 157 | 17 | .957 |
| Major League Totals | | | | 324 | 753 | 75 | 174 | 19 | 7 | 14 | 73 | .231 | 352 | 360 | 27 | .963 |

†Traded to Detroit Tigers with First Baseman Gail Harris for Third Baseman Jim Finigan and estimated $25,000, January 28, 1958.

‡Traded to Kansas City Athletics with Pitcher Bill Fischer for Pitcher Gerry Staley and Infielder Reno Bertoia, August 2, 1961.

§Assigned to Portland, October 11, 1961, and drafted by Baltimore Orioles, November 27, 1961.

xTraded by Baltimore Orioles' organization to Milwaukee Braves' organization for Infielder Ted Kazanski, December 13, 1963.

yReleased by Milwaukee Braves' organization to York (Washington Senators' organization), October 13, 1964.

zDrafted from Washington Senators' organization by Columbus (Pittsburgh Pirates' organization), November 30, 1964.

aTraded with Pitcher Joe Gibbon to San Francisco Giants for Outfielder Matty Alou and player to be named later, December 1, 1965.

Coach, San Francisco Giants, 1969 through 1972; scout, 1973; coach, 1974 and 1975; coach, Montreal Expos, 1976 and 1977.

## ALBERT BLUFORD WALKER, JR.
### (Rube)

(Named by old-time player in home town whose nickname also was
"Rube"—passed name along because he was proud of Walker.)

### New York Mets

Born May 16, at Lenior, N. C.
Height, 6.01. Weight, 200.
Threw right and batted lefthanded.
Hobbies—Hunting and fishing.
Brother of Verlon Walker, late Chicago Cubs' coach.

| Year | Club | League | Pos. | G. | AB. | R. | H. | 2B. | 3B. | HR. | RBI. | B.A. | PO. | A. | E. | F.A. |
|------|------|--------|------|----|-----|----|----|-----|-----|-----|------|------|-----|----|----|------|
| 1944–Erwin | | Appal. | C | 55 | 182 | 26 | 48 | 4 | 4 | 1 | 28 | .264 | 304 | 18 | 13 | .961 |
| 1945–Nashville | | South. | C | 20 | 51 | 3 | 11 | 1 | 2 | 0 | 6 | .216 | 46 | 9 | 4 | .932 |
| 1945–Portsmouth | | Pied. | C | 71 | 225 | 31 | 58 | 14 | 1 | 7 | 27 | .258 | 332 | 27 | 15 | .960 |
| 1946–Davenport | | I.I.I. | C | 96 | 356 | 53 | 126 | 18 | 6 | 13 | 85 | •354 | 468 | 55 | 11 | •.979 |
| 1947–Nashville | | South. | C | 128 | 435 | 67 | 144 | 20 | 1 | 22 | 105 | .331 | 435 | 36 | •17 | .965 |
| 1948–Chicago | | Nat. | C | 79 | 171 | 17 | 47 | 8 | 0 | 5 | 26 | .275 | 178 | 22 | 4 | .980 |
| 1949–Chicago | | Nat. | C | 56 | 172 | 11 | 42 | 4 | 1 | 3 | 22 | .244 | 166 | 23 | 7 | .964 |
| 1950–Chicago | | Nat. | C | 74 | 213 | 19 | 49 | 7 | 1 | 6 | 16 | .230 | 240 | •34 | 7 | .975 |
| 1951–Chi.†-Brooklyn | | Nat. | C | 73 | 181 | 15 | 43 | 8 | 0 | 4 | 14 | .238 | 173 | 23 | 6 | .970 |
| 1952–Brooklyn | | Nat. | C | 46 | 139 | 9 | 36 | 8 | 0 | 1 | 19 | .259 | 217 | 16 | 3 | .987 |
| 1953–Brooklyn | | Nat. | C | 43 | 95 | 5 | 23 | 6 | 0 | 3 | 9 | .242 | 120 | 12 | 3 | .978 |
| 1954–Brooklyn | | Nat. | C | 50 | 155 | 12 | 28 | 7 | 0 | 5 | 23 | .181 | 259 | 19 | 1 | .996 |
| 1955–Brooklyn | | Nat. | C | 48 | 103 | 6 | 26 | 5 | 0 | 2 | 13 | .252 | 147 | 10 | 2 | .987 |
| 1956–Brooklyn | | Nat. | C | 54 | 146 | 5 | 31 | 6 | 1 | 3 | 20 | .212 | 184 | 20 | 3 | .986 |

| Year | Club | League | Pos. | G. | AB. | R. | H. | 2B. | 3B. | HR. | RBI. | B.A. | PO. | A. | E. | F.A. |
|---|---|---|---|---|---|---|---|---|---|---|---|---|---|---|---|---|
| 1957—Brooklyn | ..........Nat. | | C | 60 | 166 | 12 | 30 | 8 | 0 | 2 | 23 | .181 | 230 | 20 | 2 | .992 |
| 1958—Los Angeles | ......Nat. | | C | 25 | 44 | 3 | 5 | 2 | 0 | 1 | 7 | .114 | 62 | 5 | 1 | .985 |
| 1959—Hous.-St. Paul | ..A. A. | | C | 103 | 280 | 26 | 75 | 10 | 0 | 5 | 36 | .268 | 338 | 41 | 3 | .992 |
| 1960—Atlanta | ..............South. | | C | 62 | 147 | 22 | 37 | 3 | 0 | 5 | 29 | .252 | 221 | 11 | 4 | .983 |
| Major League Totals | ...................... | | | 608 | 1585 | 114 | 360 | 69 | 3 | 35 | 192 | .227 | 1976 | 204 | 39 | .982 |

†Traded to Brooklyn Dodgers with Pitcher Johnny Schmitz, Second Baseman Wayne Terwilliger and Outfielder Andy Pafko for Pitcher Joe Hatten, Catcher Bruce Edwards, Second Baseman Eddie Miksis and Outfielder Gene Hermanski, June 15, 1951.

## WORLD SERIES RECORD

| Year | Club | League | Pos. | G. | AB. | R. | H. | 2B. | 3B. | HR. | RBI. | B.A. | PO. | A. | E. | F.A. |
|---|---|---|---|---|---|---|---|---|---|---|---|---|---|---|---|---|
| 1956—Brooklyn | ..........Nat. | | PH | 2 | 2 | 0 | 0 | 0 | 0 | 0 | 0 | .000 | 0 | 0 | 0 | .000 |

## RECORD AS MANAGER

| Year | Club | League | Position | W. | L. | Year | Club | League | Position | W. | L. |
|---|---|---|---|---|---|---|---|---|---|---|---|
| 1959—Houston† | ............A.A. | | Fifth | 29 | 41 | 1963—Augusta | ..............Sally | | §First | 41 | 21 |
| 1960—Atlanta | .............Southern | | ‡First | 87 | 67 | (Second Half) | | | Fifth | 34 | 42 |
| 1961—Atlanta | .............Southern | | Fourth | 77 | 74 | 1964—Columbus | .........Southern | . | Seventh | 65 | 74 |
| 1962—Amarillo | ...........Texas | | Sixth | 56 | 84 | | | | | | |

†Replaced by Del Wilber, June 21.
‡Lost playoff semifinal series to Birmingham, three games to two.
§Won playoff against Lynchburg (Second Half winner), three games to two.

Coach, Los Angeles Dodgers, June 24, 1958, to end of season; coach, Washington Senators, 1965 through 1967; New York Mets, 1968 through 1977.

## HARRY CLINTON WARNER
### Toronto Blue Jays

Born December 11, 1928, at Reeders, Pa.
Height, 6.02. Weight, 215.
Threw right and batted lefthanded.
Hobbies—Hunting and fishing.
Attended Muhlenberg College, Allentown, Pa.

Tied for South Atlantic League lead in double plays with 114 in 1957.
Lead South Atlantic League in bases on balls with 96 in 1958, and 106 in 1959.

| Year | Club | League | Pos. | G. | AB. | R. | H. | 2B. | 3B. | HR. | RBI. | B.A. | PO. | A. | E. | F.A. |
|---|---|---|---|---|---|---|---|---|---|---|---|---|---|---|---|---|
| 1946—Stroudsburg | ......N. Atl. | | 2B | 24 | 55 | 7 | 14 | 2 | 1 | 2 | 14 | .255 | 30 | 15 | 2 | .956 |
| 1947—Stroudsburg | ......N. Atl. | | OF | 60 | 244 | 40 | 71 | 8 | 3 | 2 | 36 | .291 | 90 | 2 | 1 | .989 |
| 1948—Stroudsburg | ......N. Atl. | | 1B | 104 | 392 | 71 | 117 | 22 | 8 | 10 | 94 | .298 | 899 | 41 | 13 | .986 |
| 1949—Stroudsburg | ......N. Atl. | | 1B | 127 | 495 | 122 | 172 | 28 | 13 | 17 | 125 | .347 | 1160 | 69 | 15 | .988 |
| 1950—Eau Claire† | ......North. | | 1B | 112 | 424 | 97 | 121 | 20 | 7 | 12 | 90 | .285 | 1026 | 73 | 20 | .982 |
| 1951—Evansville | ........I.I.I. | | 1B | 110 | 392 | 66 | 93 | 14 | 9 | 5 | 54 | .237 | 982 | 65 | 7 | .993 |
| 1952—Evansville | ........I.I.I. | | 1B | 117 | 418 | 87 | 111 | 25 | 11 | 11 | 69 | .266•1126 | •75 | 8 | •.993 |
| 1953—Jacksonville | ......S. Atl. | | 3B-1B | 92 | 263 | 35 | 68 | 16 | 4 | 4 | 48 | .259 | 202 | 89 | 13 | .957 |
| 1954—Salem | ...............West. I. | | 1B | 126 | 432 | 88 | 136 | 32 | 6 | 17 | 87 | .315 | 957 | •92 | 8 | •.992 |
| 1955—Jacksonville | ......S. Atl. | | 1B | 126 | 427 | 58 | 117 | 21 | 6 | 8 | 61 | .274 | 948 | •88 | 14 | .987 |
| 1956—Austin | ...............Texas | | 1B | 29 | 97 | 24 | 26 | 8 | 1 | 4 | 14 | .268 | 239 | 22 | 2 | .992 |
| 1956—Charlotte | .........S. Atl. | | 1B | 99 | 330 | 67 | 89 | 12 | 8 | 8 | 50 | .270 | 931 | 67 | 13 | .987 |
| 1957—Charlotte | .........S. Atl. | | 1B | 145 | 520 | 65 | 124 | 20 | 6 | 6 | 70 | .238 | 1229 | 101 | 11 | •.992 |
| 1958—Charlotte | .........S. Atl. | | 1B | 140 | 506 | 81 | 145 | 22 | 10 | 13 | •88 | .287 | 1170 | 81 | 12 | .990 |
| 1959—Charlotte | .........S. Atl. | | 1B | 138 | 463 | •94 | 121 | 6 | 14 | 14 | 64 | .261•1214 | 76 | 11 | .991 |
| 1960—Erie‡ | ................N.Y.-Pa. | | 1B | 98 | 323 | 79 | 85 | 16 | 4 | 14 | 64 | .263 | 812 | •87 | 6 | •.993 |
| 1961—Erie‡ | ................N.Y.-Pa. | | PH | 11 | 9 | 1 | 1 | 0 | 0 | 0 | 2 | .111 | .... | .... | .... | .... |
| 1962—Wilson‡ | ...........Carol. | | PH | 10 | 12 | 1 | 5 | 0 | 0 | 0 | 3 | .417 | .... | .... | .... | .... |

†On Inactive list, July 13 to July 24, 1950.
‡Player—Manager.

## RECORD AS MANAGER

| Year | Club | League | Position | W. | L. | Year | Club | League | Position | W. | L. |
|---|---|---|---|---|---|---|---|---|---|---|---|
| 1960—Erie | .................N.Y.-Pa. | | †First | 83 | 46 | 1968—Charlotte | ...........Southern | | Third | 72 | 68 |
| 1961—Erie | .................N.Y.-Pa. | | Second | 68 | 57 | 1969—Orlando | ..............Fla. St. | | ‡First(C) | 80 | 52 |
| 1962—Wilson | ..............Carol. | | Fifth(tie) | 65 | 75 | 1970—Charlotte | ...........Southern | | Sixth | 66 | 73 |
| 1963—Orlando | ..............Fla. St. | | Fourth | 31 | 31 | 1971—Charlotte | ...........Southern | | §First(E) | 92 | 50 |
| (Second Half) | | | Second | 33 | 28 | 1972—Tacoma | ..............P. C. | | Third(W) | 65 | 83 |
| 1964—Orlando | ..............Fla. St. | | Eighth | 22 | 47 | 1973—Orlando | ..............Fla. St. | | Fourth(E) | 65 | 70 |
| (Second Half) | | | Second | 38 | 31 | 1974—Lynchburg | ..........Carol. | | Second | 40 | 30 |
| 1965—Orlando | ..............Fla. St. | | Fourth | 34 | 31 | (Second Half) | | | Third | 38 | 32 |
| (Second Half) | | | Second | 43 | 26 | 1975—Reno | .................Calif. | | First | 43 | 27 |
| 1966—Charlotte | ...........Southern | | Sixth | 64 | 74 | (Second Half) | | | | 43 | 27 |
| 1967—Charlotte | ...........Southern | | Fourth | 75 | 65 | 1976—Tacoma | ..............P. C. | | Second(W) | 76 | 69 |

†Won playoff by defeating Corning, two games to none, lost championship series to Wellsville, two games to one in best-of-five finals when series was ended because of rain, with Wellsville declared champion.
‡Lost playoff to Miami, four games to one.
§Won playoff by defeating Asheville, two games to one; won Dixie Association Championship by defeating Arkansas, three games to none.

Coach, Toronto Blue Jays, 1977.

# WILLIAM FREDERICK WIETELMANN

Name pronounced Wee-tel-man.

## (Whitey)

(Named by Casey Stengel because of Wietelmann's white hair.)

### San Diego Padres

Born March 15, 1919, at Zanesville, O.
Height, 5.11½. Weight, 219.
Threw righthanded and batted left and righthanded.
Hobby—Cooking.

| Year Club | League | Pos. | G. | AB. | R. | H. | 2B. | 3B. | HR. | RBI. | B.A. | PO. | A. | E. | F.A. |
|---|---|---|---|---|---|---|---|---|---|---|---|---|---|---|---|
| 1937—Beaver Falls...... | P. St. A. | SS | 88 | 292 | 47 | 68 | 11 | 4 | 5 | 38 | .233 | •144 | 229 | 38 | •.908 |
| 1938—Evansville ........ | I.I.I. | SS | 117 | 389 | 61 | 94 | 14 | 3 | 6 | 59 | .242 | 237 | 318 | 49 | .919 |
| 1939—Hartford........... | East. | SS | 141 | 498 | 51 | 117 | 13 | 6 | 3 | 55 | .235 | •286 | •461 | •63 | .922 |
| 1939—Boston ............. | Nat. | SS | 23 | 69 | 2 | 14 | 1 | 0 | 0 | 5 | .203 | 36 | 66 | 5 | .925 |
| 1940—Boston ............. | Nat. | 2B | 35 | 41 | 3 | 8 | 1 | 0 | 0 | 1 | .195 | 14 | 11 | 1 | .962 |
| 1941—Boston ............. | Nat. | 2-SS-3 | 16 | 33 | 1 | 3 | 0 | 0 | 0 | 0 | .091 | 26 | 29 | 0 | 1.000 |
| 1941—Hartford........... | East. | SS-P | 65 | 211 | 25 | 45 | 7 | 4 | 0 | 22 | .213 | 122 | 156 | 13 | .955 |
| 1942—Boston ............. | Nat. | SS-2B | 13 | 34 | 4 | 7 | 2 | 0 | 0 | 0 | .206 | 19 | 29 | 3 | .941 |
| 1942—Louisville ......... | A. A. | SS | 133 | 527 | 69 | 137 | 21 | 3 | 0 | 35 | .260 | 297 | 388 | 48 | .935 |
| 1943—Boston ............. | Nat. | SS | 153 | 534 | 33 | 115 | 14 | 1 | 0 | 39 | .215 | 307 | •581 | •40 | .957 |
| 1944—Boston ............. | Nat. | SS-2-3 | 125 | 417 | 46 | 100 | 18 | 1 | 2 | 32 | .240 | 269 | 351 | 30 | .954 |
| 1945—Boston ............. | Nat. | 2-S-3-P | 123 | 428 | 53 | 116 | 15 | 3 | 4 | 33 | .271 | 303 | 338 | 21 | .968 |
| 1946—Boston† ........... | Nat. | S-3-2-P | 44 | 78 | 7 | 16 | 0 | 0 | 0 | 5 | .205 | 40 | 39 | 7 | .919 |
| 1947—Pittsburgh ........ | Nat. | S-2-3-1 | 48 | 128 | 21 | 30 | 4 | 1 | 1 | 7 | .234 | 69 | 68 | 13 | .913 |
| 1948—Sacramento ...... | P. C. | 2-SS-1 | 143 | 481 | 64 | 112 | 22 | 1 | 8 | 43 | .233 | 366 | 387 | 31 | .961 |
| 1949—Sac.-San Diego .. | P. C. | SS-2B | 149 | 496 | 67 | 119 | 24 | 2 | 4 | 37 | .240 | 260 | 391 | 36 | .948 |
| 1950—San Diego.......... | P. C. | SS-2B | 138 | 418 | 65 | 109 | 18 | 0 | 2 | 35 | .261 | 205 | 349 | 23 | .960 |
| 1951—San Diego.......... | P. C. | SS-O-3 | 125 | 390 | 53 | 102 | 12 | 5 | 8 | 44 | .262 | 203 | 273 | 25 | .950 |
| 1952—San Diego.......... | P. C. | PH | 23 | 24 | 3 | 5 | 0 | 0 | 0 | 0 | .208 | .... | .... | .... | .... |
| 1953—Wichita Falls .... | Big St. | S-1-P-2 | 98 | 323 | 60 | 90 | 24 | 0 | 8 | 46 | .279 | 321 | 169 | 20 | .961 |
| 1954—Lincoln............. | West. | 2-3-P | 65 | 147 | 14 | 30 | 5 | 0 | 2 | 12 | .204 | 75 | 90 | 6 | .965 |
| 1955—Yuma............... | A.-Mex. | P-2 | 94 | 243 | 47 | 64 | 9 | 2 | 7 | 50 | .263 | 85 | 104 | 12 | .943 |
| 1956—Yuma............... | A.-Mex. | P | 31 | 57 | 6 | 15 | 4 | 0 | 1 | 13 | .263 | 10 | 24 | 0 | 1.000 |
| Major League Totals ..................... | | | 580 | 1762 | 170 | 409 | 55 | 6 | 7 | 122 | .232 | 1083 | 1512 | 120 | .958 |

†Traded with Infielder Billy Herman, Pitcher Elmer Singleton and Outfielder Stan Wentzel to Pittsburgh Pirates for Outfielder Bob Elliott and Catcher Hank Camelli, September 30, 1946.

### PITCHING RECORD

| Year Club | League | G. | IP. | W. | L. | Pct. | H. | R. | ER. | SO. | BB. | ERA. |
|---|---|---|---|---|---|---|---|---|---|---|---|---|
| 1941—Hartford ............................ | Eastern | 3 | 16 | 1 | 1 | .500 | 18 | 0 | 0 | 3 | 11 | 0.00 |
| 1945—Boston ............................... | National | 1 | 1 | 0 | 0 | .000 | 6 | 6 | 6 | 0 | 2 | 54.00 |
| 1946—Boston ............................... | National | 3 | 7 | 0 | 0 | .000 | 9 | 8 | 6 | 2 | 4 | 7.71 |
| 1951—San Diego ........................... | P. Coast | 2 | 9 | 0 | 1 | .000 | 9 | 5 | 4 | 4 | 2 | 4.50 |
| 1952—San Diego ........................... | P. Coast | 4 | 7 | 0 | 0 | .000 | 14 | 15 | 14 | 1 | 5 | 18.00 |
| 1953—Wichita Falls...................... | Big State | 20 | 114 | 8 | 3 | .727 | 115 | 52 | 44 | 57 | 47 | 3.47 |
| 1954—Lincoln ............................... | Western | 14 | 37 | 0 | 2 | .000 | 47 | 37 | 37 | 20 | 24 | 9.00 |
| 1955—Yuma ................................. | Ariz.-Mex. | •50 | 258 | 21 | 13 | .618 | •294 | 158 | 139 | 195 | 97 | 4.86 |
| 1956—Yuma ................................. | Ariz.-Mex. | 25 | 138 | 9 | 7 | .563 | 165 | 116 | 88 | 82 | 57 | 5.74 |
| Major League Totals .............................. | | 4 | 8 | 0 | 0 | .000 | 15 | 14 | 12 | 2 | 6 | 13.50 |

### RECORD AS MANAGER

| Year Club | League | Position | W. | L. | Year Club | League | Position | W. | L. |
|---|---|---|---|---|---|---|---|---|---|
| 1953—Wichita Falls...... | Big State | †First | 85 | 58 | 1956—Yuma§ .............. | Ariz.-Mex. | Eighth | 8 | 18 |
| 1954—Lincoln‡ ............ | Western | Sixth | 50 | 61 | (Second Half) | | xFirst | 37 | 18 |
| 1955—Yuma ................ | Ariz.-Mex. | Second | 83 | 57 | | | | | |

†Won playoffs by defeating Longview, four games to none and Tyler, four games to three.
‡Replaced by Red McQuillen, August 6.
§Replaced by William Harris, May 15; re-signed at start of second half, July 5.
xLost playoff to Cananea (First Half winner), three games to none.

Coach, Sacramento (Pacific Coast League), 1959; San Diego (Pacific Coast League), 1959 through 1965 and 1968; Cincinnati Reds, 1966 and 1967; coach, San Diego Padres, 1969 through 1977.

# DONALD ELLIS WILLIAMS

## (Don)

### San Diego Padres

Born December 24, 1937, at Paragould, Ark.
Height, 5.10. Weight, 185.
Threw and batted righthanded.
Hobby—Hunting.
Attended Arkansas State College, Conway, Ark.

Named the California League's Most Valuable Player, 1961.
Led Midwest League shortstops in double plays with 56 in 1958.
Led Three-I League shortstops in double plays with 68 in 1960.
Led California League shortstops in double plays with 79 in 1961.
Led Texas League shortstops in double plays with 57 in 1967.

| Year Club League | Pos. | G. | AB. | R. | H. | 2B. | 3B. | HR. | RBI. | B.A. | PO. | A. | E. | F.A. |
|---|---|---|---|---|---|---|---|---|---|---|---|---|---|---|
| 1956–Shawnee............Soo. St. | SS | 21 | 76 | 11 | 18 | 2 | 0 | 1 | 3 | .237 | 40 | 45 | 13 | .867 |
| 1957–Shawnee............Soo. St. | SS | 121 | 434 | 74 | 100 | 14 | 5 | 1 | 39 | .230 | 179 | 240 | 42 | .909 |
| 1958–Kokomo ...........Midw. | SS | 118 | 427 | 71 | 121 | 14 | 4 | 9 | 55 | .283 | 159 | •348 | 37 | •.932 |
| 1959–Green Bay ........I.I.I. | SS | 122 | 424 | 53 | 110 | 15 | 5 | 1 | 55 | .259 | 176 | 294 | •42 | .918 |
| 1960–Green Bay ........I.I.I. | SS | 134 | 495 | 68 | 122 | 15 | 6 | 0 | 39 | .246 | 200 | •339 | 30 | •.947 |
| 1961–Reno ...............Calif. | SS | 136 | 542 | •132 | •197 | 32 | 4 | 18 | 97 | •.363 | 222 | •362 | 35 | •.943 |
| 1962–Spokane† .........P. C. | SS | 26 | 60 | 9 | 10 | 1 | 0 | 0 | 5 | .167 | 18 | 23 | 1 | .976 |
| 1963–Spokane ...........P. C. | SS | 72 | 181 | 25 | 44 | 9 | 1 | 2 | 16 | .243 | 31 | 69 | 9 | .917 |
| 1964–Albuquerque.....Texas | SS | 135 | 468 | 62 | 129 | 30 | 7 | 8 | 74 | .276 | •236 | •402 | 34 | •.949 |
| 1965–Albuquerque.....Texas | 2B | 139 | 537 | 73 | 154 | 26 | 8 | 2 | 62 | .287 | •355 | •415 | 15 | .981 |
| 1966–Spokane ...........P. C. | 2B | 108 | 349 | 22 | 72 | 6 | 2 | 0 | 30 | .206 | 237 | 252 | 15 | .970 |
| 1967–Albuquerque.....Texas | S-2-3 | 113 | 390 | 57 | 116 | 18 | 2 | 5 | 38 | .297 | 160 | 283 | 14 | .969 |
| 1968–Bakersfield‡ ......Calif. | PH | 2 | 2 | 0 | 1 | 0 | 0 | 0 | 0 | .500 | .... | .... | .... | ...... |

†On military list October 28, 1961, August 1, 1962.
‡Player–manager.

RECORD AS MANAGER

| Year Club | League | Position | W. | L. |
|---|---|---|---|---|
| 1968–Bakersfield ........California | Sixth | 31 | 39 |
| (Second Half) | | Eighth | 30 | 40 |

Scout, San Diego Padres, 1968 through 1974; minor league instructor, San Diego Padres, 1974 through 1976, coach, San Diego Padres, 1977.

## STANLEY WILSON WILLIAMS
### (Stan)
### Chicago White Sox

Born September 14, 1936, at Enfield, N. J.
Height, 6.04. Weight, 225.
Threw and batted righthanded.

Pitched seven-inning, 9-0 no-hit victory against Quebec City, June 29, 1974 (2nd game of doubleheader).
Led Piedmont League pitchers in games started with 30, complete games with 18 and hit batsmen with 16 in 1955.
Led American Association pitchers in games started with 34 and hit batsmen with 14 and tied for lead in wild pitches with 11 in 1957.

| Year Club | League | G. | IP. | W. | L. | Pct. | H. | R. | ER. | SO. | BB. | ERA. |
|---|---|---|---|---|---|---|---|---|---|---|---|---|
| 1954–Shawnee ...........................Soo. St. | 15 | 61 | 3 | 5 | .375 | 56 | 47 | 31 | 77 | 50 | 4.57 |
| 1955–Newport News.....................Piedmont | 31 | •242 | 18 | 7 | .720 | 160 | 77 | 65 | •301 | •158 | •2.42 |
| 1956–Fort Worth ........................Texas | 9 | 45 | 2 | 2 | .500 | 40 | 33 | 26 | 46 | 32 | 5.20 |
| 1956–St. Paul..............................Am. Assoc. | 24 | 127 | 9 | 7 | .563 | 124 | 76 | 64 | 95 | 70 | 4.54 |
| 1957–St. Paul...............................Am. Assoc. | 35 | 246 | 19 | 7 | .731 | 188 | 92 | 83 | •223 | •148 | 3.04 |
| 1958–St. Paul...............................Am. Assoc. | 8 | 64 | 2 | 3 | .400 | 43 | 22 | 20 | 44 | 28 | 2.81 |
| 1958–Los Angeles ........................National | 27 | 119 | 9 | 7 | .563 | 99 | 58 | 53 | 80 | 65 | 4.01 |
| 1959–Los Angeles ........................National | 35 | 125 | 5 | 5 | .500 | 102 | 64 | 55 | 89 | 86 | 3.96 |
| 1960–Los Angeles ........................National | 38 | 207 | 14 | 10 | .583 | 162 | 84 | 69 | 175 | 72 | 3.00 |
| 1961–Los Angeles ........................National | 41 | 235 | 15 | 12 | .556 | 213 | 114 | 102 | 205 | 108 | 3.91 |
| 1962–Los Angeles† .......................National | 40 | 186 | 14 | 12 | .538 | 184 | 104 | 92 | 108 | 98 | 4.45 |
| 1963–New York ............................American | 29 | 146 | 9 | 8 | .529 | 137 | 59 | 52 | 98 | 57 | 3.21 |
| 1964–New York‡ ..........................American | 21 | 82 | 1 | 5 | .167 | 76 | 39 | 35 | 54 | 38 | 3.84 |
| 1965–Cleveland ............................American | 3 | 4 | 0 | 0 | .000 | 6 | 4 | 3 | 1 | 3 | 6.75 |
| 1965–Seattle ................................P. Coast | 34 | 134 | 6 | 6 | .500 | 115 | 53 | 49 | 106 | 49 | 3.29 |
| 1966–Spokane§..............................P. Coast | 31 | 60 | 4 | 2 | .667 | 52 | 13 | 11 | 39 | 30 | 1.65 |
| 1967–Portland ..............................P. Coast | 31 | 98 | 7 | 6 | .538 | 105 | 53 | 43 | 70 | 30 | 3.95 |
| 1967–Cleveland ............................American | 16 | 79 | 6 | 4 | .600 | 64 | 26 | 23 | 75 | 24 | 2.62 |
| 1968–Cleveland ............................American | 44 | 194 | 13 | 11 | .542 | 163 | 64 | 54 | 147 | 51 | 2.51 |
| 1969–Cleveland x .........................American | 61 | 178 | 6 | 14 | .300 | 155 | 86 | 78 | 139 | 67 | 3.94 |
| 1970–Minnesota ...........................American | 68 | 113 | 10 | 1 | .909 | 85 | 34 | 25 | 76 | 32 | 1.99 |
| 1971–Minnesota y .........................American | 46 | 78 | 4 | 5 | .444 | 63 | 44 | 36 | 47 | 44 | 4.15 |
| 1971–St. Louis z............................National | 10 | 13 | 3 | 0 | 1.000 | 13 | 2 | 2 | 8 | 2 | 1.38 |
| 1972–Salt Lake City a ..................P. Coast | 12 | 29 | 2 | 2 | .500 | 33 | 20 | 15 | 13 | 14 | 4.66 |
| 1972–Louisville ............................Int'national | 26 | 56 | 2 | 3 | .400 | 39 | 18 | 17 | 43 | 19 | 2.73 |
| 1972–Boston b .............................American | 3 | 4 | 0 | 0 | .000 | 5 | 3 | 3 | 3 | 1 | 6.75 |
| 1974–Bristol c .............................Eastern | 5 | 19 | 2 | 0 | 1.000 | 9 | 1 | 1 | 14 | 4 | 0.47 |
| American League Totals........................... | 291 | 878 | 49 | 48 | .505 | 754 | 359 | 309 | 640 | 317 | 3.17 |
| National League Totals............................ | 191 | 885 | 60 | 46 | .566 | 773 | 426 | 373 | 665 | 431 | 3.79 |
| Major League Totals ............................... | 482 | 1763 | 109 | 94 | .537 | 1527 | 785 | 682 | 1305 | 748 | 3.48 |

†Traded to New York Yankees for First Baseman Bill Skowron, November 26, 1962.
‡Sold to Cleveland Indians, March 30, 1965.
§On temporary inactive list, April 21 to June 6, 1966.
xTraded to Minnesota Twins with Pitcher Luis Tiant for Pitchers Dean Chance and Robert L. Miller, Outfielder Ted Uhlaender and Outfielder-Third Baseman Graig Nettles, December 11, 1969.
yTraded to St. Louis Cardinals for two players to be named later, September 1, 1971; Cardinals assigned Outfielder Fred Rico and Pitcher Dan Ford to Twins, September 14, 1971, to complete deal.
zReleased by St. Louis Cardinals, April 9, 1972. Signed as free agent by Salt Lake City (California Angels' organization), April 24, 1972.
aReleased by California Angels' organization, June 1, 1972. Signed as free agent by Louisville (Boston Red Sox' organization), June 13, 1972.
bReleased by Boston Red Sox, September 23, 1972.
cPlayer-manager.

## CHAMPIONSHIP SERIES RECORD

| Year Club | League | G. | IP. | W. | L. | Pct. | H. | R. | ER. | SO. | BB. | ERA. |
|---|---|---|---|---|---|---|---|---|---|---|---|---|
| 1970—Minnesota ...........................American | American | 2 | 6 | 0 | 0 | .000 | 2 | 0 | 0 | 2 | 1 | 0.00 |

## WORLD SERIES RECORD

| Year Club | League | G. | IP. | W. | L. | Pct. | H. | R. | ER. | SO. | BB. | ERA. |
|---|---|---|---|---|---|---|---|---|---|---|---|---|
| 1959—Los Angeles ......................National | National | 1 | 2 | 0 | 0 | .000 | 0 | 0 | 0 | 1 | 2 | 0.00 |
| 1963—New York ...........................American | American | 1 | 3 | 0 | 0 | .000 | 1 | 0 | 0 | 5 | 0 | 0.00 |
| World Series Totals ................................. | | 2 | 5 | 0 | 0 | .000 | 1 | 0 | 0 | 6 | 2 | 0.00 |

## ALL-STAR GAME RECORD

| Year League | IP. | W. | L. | Pct. | H. | R. | ER. | SO. | BB. | ERA. |
|---|---|---|---|---|---|---|---|---|---|---|
| 1960—National (second game) ............................... | 2 | 0 | 0 | .000 | 2 | 0 | 0 | 2 | 1 | 0.00 |

## RECORD AS MANAGER

| Year Club | League | Position | W. | L. |
|---|---|---|---|---|
| 1974—Bristol................Eastern | Eastern | †First(A) | 74 | 61 |

†Lost playoff semifinal series to Thetford Mines, two games to none.

Coach, Boston Red Sox, 1975 and 1976; Chicago White Sox, 1977.

## ROBERT PAUL WINE
### (Bobby)
### Philadelphia Phillies

Born September 17, 1938, at Bronx, N. Y.
Height, 6.01. Weight, 190.
Threw and batted righthanded.
Hobbies—Basketball and model building.

Established major league record for most double plays, shortstop, season (137), 1970.
Named as shortstop on THE SPORTING NEWS National League All-Star fielding team, 1963.

| Year Club | League | Pos. | G. | AB. | R. | H. | 2B. | 3B. | HR. | RBI. | B.A. | PO. | A. | E. | F.A. |
|---|---|---|---|---|---|---|---|---|---|---|---|---|---|---|---|
| 1957—Johnson City ....Appal. | Appal. | SS | 54 | 202 | 53 | 68 | 11 | 6 | 6 | 42 | .337 | 63 | 131 | 24 | .890 |
| 1958—Bakersfield........Calif. | Calif. | SS | 112 | 440 | 78 | 137 | 13 | 11 | 11 | 75 | .311 | 207 | 304 | 26 | •.952 |
| 1959—Williamsport......East. | East. | SS | 120 | 426 | 40 | 89 | 12 | 3 | 5 | 33 | .209 | 216 | •333 | •42 | .929 |
| 1960—Buffalo..............Int. | Int. | SS | 154 | 569 | 61 | 153 | 28 | 5 | 8 | 53 | .269 | •246 | •500 | •33 | .958 |
| 1960→Philadelphia ......Nat. | Nat. | SS | 4 | 14 | 1 | 2 | 0 | 0 | 0 | 0 | .143 | 9 | 10 | 0 | 1.000 |
| 1961—Buffalo..............Int. | Int. | SS | 152 | 534 | 46 | 130 | 18 | 6 | 6 | 48 | .243 | •301 | 430 | 30 | .961 |
| 1962—Buffalo..............Int. | Int. | SS | 24 | 95 | 12 | 23 | 4 | 0 | 3 | 12 | .242 | 38 | 88 | 3 | .977 |
| 1962—Philadelphia ......Nat. | Nat. | SS-3B | 112 | 311 | 30 | 76 | 15 | 0 | 4 | 25 | .244 | 149 | 263 | 8 | .981 |
| 1963—Philadelphia .....Nat. | Nat. | SS-3B | 142 | 418 | 29 | 90 | 14 | 3 | 6 | 44 | .215 | 224 | 369 | 17 | .972 |
| 1964—Philadelphia .....Nat. | Nat. | SS-3B | 126 | 283 | 28 | 60 | 8 | 3 | 4 | 34 | .212 | 159 | 266 | 15 | .966 |
| 1965—Philadelphia .....Nat. | Nat. | SS-1B | 139 | 394 | 31 | 90 | 8 | 1 | 5 | 33 | .228 | 223 | 387 | 21 | .967 |
| 1966—Philadelphia .....Nat. | Nat. | SS-OF | 46 | 89 | 8 | 21 | 5 | 0 | 0 | 5 | .236 | 57 | 91 | 4 | .974 |
| 1967—Philadelphia .....Nat. | Nat. | •SS-1B | 135 | 363 | 27 | 69 | 12 | 5 | 2 | 28 | .190 | 206 | 392 | 12 | •.980 |
| 1968—Philadelphia‡§ ..Nat. | Nat. | SS-3B | 27 | 71 | 5 | 12 | 3 | 0 | 2 | 7 | .169 | 37 | 68 | 3 | .972 |
| 1969—Montreal ..........Nat. | Nat. | SS-1B-3 | 121 | 370 | 23 | 74 | 8 | 1 | 3 | 25 | .200 | 214 | 367 | 31 | .949 |
| 1970—Montreal ..........Nat. | Nat. | SS | 159 | 501 | 40 | 116 | 21 | 3 | 3 | 51 | .232 | 284 | 481 | 19 | .976 |
| 1971—Montreal ..........Nat. | Nat. | SS | 119 | 340 | 25 | 68 | 9 | 0 | 1 | 16 | .200 | 221 | 321 | 10 | .982 |
| 1972—Montreal ..........Nat. | Nat. | 3-SS-2 | 34 | 18 | 2 | 4 | 1 | 0 | 0 | 0 | .222 | 12 | 15 | 1 | .964 |
| Major League Totals ..................... | | | 1164 | 3172 | 249 | 682 | 104 | 16 | 30 | 268 | .215 | 1795 | 3030 | 141 | .972 |

†Suffered wrenched back June 24; on disabled list from July 19 through August 31.
‡Underwent operation for ruptured spinal disc; on disabled list from May 29 through end of season.
§Sent by Philadelphia Phillies to Montreal Expos to replace Larry Ja kson, April 7, 1969. Jackson announced retirement after being taken by Montreal in expansion draft.
xReleased, July 10, 1972.

Coach, Philadelphia Phillies, July 26, 1972 through 1977.

## BOBBY BROOKS WINKLES
### San Francisco Giants

Born March 11, 1932, at Swifton, Ark.
Height, 5.09. Weight, 170.
Threw and batted righthanded.
Hobbies—Golf and fishing.
Attended Illinois Wesleyan University, Bloomington, Ill., and University of Colorado,
Boulder, Colo.; received Bachelor of Arts degree in Philosophy and
Master of Science degree in Physical Education.

Named by THE SPORTING NEWS as College Baseball Coach of the Year, 1965, 1967 and 1969.

| Year Club | League | Pos. | G. | AB. | R. | H. | 2B. | 3B. | HR. | RBI. | B.A. | PO. | A. | E. | F.A. |
|---|---|---|---|---|---|---|---|---|---|---|---|---|---|---|---|
| 1951—Col. Springs ......West. | West. | SS | 104 | 405 | 53 | 118 | 17 | 4 | 3 | 44 | .291 | 196 | 339 | 39 | .932 |
| 1952—Waterloo ..........Ill. | Ill. | SS | 30 | 129 | 17 | 37 | 9 | 1 | 0 | 22 | .287 | 60 | 113 | 7 | .961 |
| 1953— ....................... | | | | | (In U. S. Army) | | | | | | | | | | |
| 1954—Memphis ..........S. A. | S. A. | SS | 52 | 182 | 18 | 41 | 2 | 1 | 0 | 20 | .222 | 92 | 157 | 13 | .950 |
| 1954—Col. Springs ......West. | West. | SS | 81 | 314 | 42 | 92 | 16 | 1 | 1 | 38 | .293 | 153 | 277 | 26 | .943 |
| 1955—Charleston ........A. A. | A. A. | SS | 44 | 142 | 14 | 35 | 3 | 2 | 0 | 10 | .246 | 57 | 116 | 8 | .956 |
| 1955—Col. Springs ......West | West | SS | 108 | 409 | 45 | 117 | 15 | 1 | 0 | 33 | .286 | 176 | 382 | 30 | .949 |

| Year Club League | Pos. | G. | AB. | R. | H. | 2B. | 3B. | HR. | RBI. | B.A. | PO. | A. | E. | F.A. |
|---|---|---|---|---|---|---|---|---|---|---|---|---|---|---|
| 1956—Col. Springs ......West. | 2-S-3 | 131 | 510 | 77 | 152 | 31 | 4 | 5 | 60 | .298 | 248 | 351 | 33 | .948 |
| 1956—Tulsa ...............Texas | SS | 6 | 24 | 0 | 5 | 0 | 0 | 0 | 0 | .208 | figures unavailable |  |  |  |
| 1957—Tulsa ...............Texas | SS | 154 | 639 | 89 | 178 | 18 | 4 | 2 | 48 | .279 | •303 | •513 | 42 | .951 |
| 1958—Indianapolis ......A. A. | SS | 84 | 281 | 30 | 64 | 11 | 2 | 1 | 17 | .228 | 125 | 223 | 17 | .953 |
| 1958—Tulsa ...............Texas | SS | 64 | 255 | 30 | 51 | 8 | 4 | 0 | 5 | .200 | 113 | 227 | 13 | .963 |

RECORD AS MANAGER

| Year Club | League | Position | W. | L. |
|---|---|---|---|---|
| 1973—California ..........Amer. | | Fourth(W) | 79 | 83 |
| 1974—California ..........Amer. | | Sixth(W) | 30 | 44 |

Baseball coach at Arizona State University, 1959 through 1971. Record: 524 wins, 173 losses; won NCAA championship in 1965, 1967 and 1969.

†Replaced by Dick Williams, June 26 (Whitey Herzog served as interim manager, June 27 through June 30).

Coach, California Angels, 1972; coach, Oakland Athletics, part of 1974 and 1975; coach, San Francisco Giants, 1976 and 1977.

## MELVIN JAMES WRIGHT, JR.
### (Mel)
### Houston Astros

Born May 11, 1928, at Manila, Ark.
Height, 6.03. Weight, 205.
Threw and batted righthanded.
Hobbies—Hunting and fishing.
Attended Ouachita Baptist College, Arkadephia, Ark.

| Year Club League | G. | IP. | W. | L. | Pct. | H. | R. | ER. | SO. | BB. | ERA. |
|---|---|---|---|---|---|---|---|---|---|---|---|
| 1950—McAlester ..........................Soo. St. | 32 | 215 | 15 | 7 | .682 | 180 | 87 | 72 | 130 | 59 | 3.01 |
| 1951—Joplin ..............................W. A. | 28 | 206 | 15 | 9 | .625 | 199 | 97 | 84 | 123 | 77 | 3.67 |
| 1952—Binghamton.........................Eastern | •57 | 121 | 7 | 8 | .467 | 95 | 39 | 26 | 45 | 56 | 1.93 |
| 1953—Kansas City† ........................Am. Assoc. | 47 | 111 | 13 | 2 | •.867 | 112 | 47 | 40 | 73 | 35 | 3.24 |
| 1954—St. Louis ...............................National | 9 | 10 | 0 | 0 | .000 | 16 | 15 | 12 | 4 | 11 | 10.80 |
| 1954—Columbus ...........................Am. Assoc. | 28 | 117 | 8 | 8 | .500 | 138 | 55 | 49 | 45 | 21 | 3.77 |
| 1955—Rochester ...........................Int'national | 20 | 49 | 1 | 1 | .500 | 47 | 24 | 15 | 15 | 19 | 2.76 |
| 1955—St. Louis ...............................National | 29 | 36 | 2 | 2 | .500 | 44 | 26 | 25 | 18 | • 9 | 6.25 |
| 1956—Omaha ...............................Am. Assoc. | 15 | 24 | 0 | 0 | .000 | 28 | 9 | 9 | 10 | 7 | 3.38 |
| 1956—Rochester ...........................Int'national | 27 | 56 | 5 | 6 | .455 | 53 | 26 | 19 | 33 | 16 | 3.05 |
| 1957—Rochester ...........................Int'national | 46 | 62 | 5 | 5 | .500 | 58 | 23 | 20 | 27 | 22 | 2.90 |
| 1958—Rochester ...........................Int'national | 41 | 47 | 1 | 2 | .333 | 49 | 21 | 15 | 31 | 12 | 2.87 |
| 1959—Houston‡-Dallas....................Am. Assoc. | 71 | 117 | 10 | 8 | .556 | 113 | 42 | 32 | 74 | 35 | 2.46 |
| 1960—Dallas-Fort Worth ...............Am. Assoc. | 54 | 70 | 5 | 4 | .556 | 61 | 31 | 18 | 60 | 6 | 2.31 |
| 1960—Chicago...............................National | 9 | 16 | 0 | 1 | .000 | 17 | 9 | 9 | 8 | 3 | 5.06 |
| 1961—Chicago...............................National | 11 | 21 | 0 | 1 | .000 | 42 | 26 | 25 | 6 | 4 | 10.71 |
| 1961—Houston ........................Am. Assoc. | 6 | 12 | 0 | 1 | .000 | 11 | 6 | 5 | 8 | 1 | 3.75 |
| Major League Totals ................................. | 58 | 83 | 2 | 4 | .333 | 119 | 76 | 71 | 36 | 27 | 7.70 |

†Assigned to New York Yankees and traded to St. Louis Cardianls with Outfielders Emil Tellinger and Bill Virdon for Outfielder Enos Slaughter, April 11, 1954.

‡Released by St. Louis Cardinals' organization to Dallas (Chicago Cubs' organization), June 24, 1959.

RECORD AS MANAGER

| Year Club | League | Position | W. | L. |
|---|---|---|---|---|
| 1969—Huron ...............Northern | | Fourth | 31 | 39 |

Coach, Salt Lake City (Pacific Coast League), 1962; Chicago Cubs, 1963 and 1964; scout, Chicago Cubs, 1965 through 1967; coach, Tacoma (Pacific Coast League), 1968; scout, Chicago Cubs, 1970 through 1972; coach, Pittsburgh Pirates, 1973; coach, New York Yankees, 1974 and 1975; coach, Houston Astros, 1976 and 1977.

## EDWARD FRED JOSEPH YOST
### (Eddie)
### New York Mets

Born October 13, 1926, at Brooklyn, N. Y.
Height, 5.10. Weight, 182.
Threw and batted righthanded.
Hobbies—Golf and fishing.
Attended New York University, New York City, N. Y.; received Master's degree
in Physical Education.

Tied A. L. mark by playing 157 games at third base, 1952—154-game season; tied A. L. standard for third sackers by starting three double plays in a game, June 5, 1949; holds major league record for most years leading third basemen putouts (8), 1959.

Led American League batters in walks with 141 in 1950, 129 in 1952, 123 in 1953, 151 in 1956, 135 in 1959 and 125 in 1960.

Led American League third basemen in double plays with 45 in 1950 and 31 in 1956.

| Year Club League | Pos. | G. | AB. | R. | H. | 2B. | 3B. | HR. | RBI. | B.A. | PO. | A. | E. | F.A. |
|---|---|---|---|---|---|---|---|---|---|---|---|---|---|---|
| 1944—Washington........Amer. | 3B-SS | 7 | 14 | 3 | 2 | 0 | 0 | 0 | 0 | .143 | 9 | 6 | 2 | .882 |
| 1945-46—Washington ..Amer. | | | | | (In Military Service) | | | | | | | | | |
| 1946—Washington........Amer. | 3B | 8 | 25 | 2 | 2 | 1 | 0 | 0 | 1 | .080 | 7 | 17 | 0 | 1.000 |
| 1947—Washington........Amer. | 3B | 115 | 428 | 52 | 102 | 17 | 3 | 0 | 14 | .238 | 125 | 198 | 14 | .958 |

| Year Club | League | Pos. | G. | AB. | R. | H. | 2B. | 3B. | HR. | RBI. | B.A. | PO. | A. | E. | F.A. |
|---|---|---|---|---|---|---|---|---|---|---|---|---|---|---|---|
| 1948—Washington.......Amer. | | 3B | 145 | 555 | 74 | 138 | 32 | 11 | 2 | 50 | .249 | •189 | 240 | 15 | .966 |
| 1949—Washington.......Amer. | | 3B | 124 | 435 | 57 | 110 | 19 | 7 | 9 | 45 | .253 | 158 | 232 | 19 | .954 |
| 1950—Washington.......Amer. | | 3B | 155 | 573 | 114 | 169 | 26 | 2 | 11 | 58 | .295 | •205 | 307 | •30 | .945 |
| 1951—Washington.......Amer. | | •3B-OF | •154 | 568 | 109 | 161 | •36 | 4 | 12 | 65 | .283 | •209 | 234 | 21 | .955 |
| 1952—Washington.......Amer. | | 3B | •157 | 587 | 92 | 137 | 32 | 3 | 12 | 49 | .233 | •212 | 249 | 18 | .962 |
| 1953—Washington.......Amer. | | 3B | 152 | 577 | 107 | 157 | 30 | 7 | 9 | 45 | .272 | •190 | 300 | 18 | .965 |
| 1954—Washington.......Amer. | | 3B | •155 | 539 | 101 | 138 | 26 | 4 | 11 | 47 | .256 | •170 | •347 | 17 | .968 |
| 1955—Washington.......Amer. | | 3B | 122 | 375 | 64 | 91 | 17 | 5 | 7 | 48 | .243 | 100 | 217 | 19 | .943 |
| 1956—Washington.......Amer. | | •3B-OF | 152 | 515 | 94 | 119 | 17 | 2 | 11 | 53 | .231 | •182 | •303 | 18 | .964 |
| 1957—Washington.......Amer. | | 3B | 110 | 414 | 47 | 104 | 13 | 5 | 9 | 38 | .251 | 109 | 207 | 16 | .952 |
| 1958—Washington† .....Amer. | | •3-O-1 | 134 | 406 | 55 | 91 | 16 | 0 | 8 | 37 | .224 | 122 | 187 | 11 | •.966 |
| 1959—Detroit .............Amer. | | 3B-2B | 148 | 521 | •115 | 145 | 19 | 0 | 21 | 61 | .278 | •168 | 260 | 17 | •.962 |
| 1960—Detroit‡ ...........Amer. | | 3B | 143 | 497 | 78 | 129 | 23 | 2 | 14 | 47 | .260 | 155 | 208 | •26 | .933 |
| 1961—Los Angeles .....Amer. | | 3B | 76 | 213 | 29 | 43 | 4 | 0 | 3 | 15 | .202 | 57 | 103 | 6 | .964 |
| 1962—Los Angeles .....Amer. | | 3B-1B | 52 | 104 | 22 | 25 | 9 | 1 | 0 | 10 | .240 | 69 | 48 | 4 | .967 |
| Major League Totals ..................... | | | 2109 | 7346 | 1215 | 1863 | 337 | 56 | 139 | 683 | .254 | 2436 | 3663 | 271 | .957 |

†Traded to Detroit Tigers with Shortstop Rocky Bridges and Outfielder Neil Chrisley for Third Baseman Reno Bertoia, Shortstop Ron Samford and Outfielder Jim Delsing, December 6, 1958.

‡Selected by Los Angeles Angels in American League expansion draft, December 14, 1960.

## ALL-STAR GAME RECORD

Member of American League All-Star Team in 1952; did not play.

Coach, Los Angeles Dodgers, part of 1962; Washington Senators, 1963 through 1967; coach, New York Mets, 1968 through 1977.

### GERALD ROBERT ZIMMERMAN
(Jerry)
**Minnesota Twins**

Born September 21, 1934, at Omaha, Neb.
Height, 6.02. Weight, 185.
Threw and batted righthanded.
Hobby—Bowling.

Led California League catchers in double plays with 11 in 1953.
Led Eastern League catchers in double plays with 15 in 1956.
Received reported $77,000 bonus to sign with Boston Red Sox, 1952.

| Year Club | League | Pos. | G. | AB. | R. | H. | 2B. | 3B. | HR. | RBI. | B.A. | PO. | A. | E. | F.A. |
|---|---|---|---|---|---|---|---|---|---|---|---|---|---|---|---|
| 1952—San Jose...........Calif. | | C | 72 | 261 | 21 | 60 | 11 | 1 | 0 | 22 | .230 | 513 | 41 | 11 | .981 |
| 1953—San Jose...........Calif. | | C | 101 | 328 | 31 | 87 | 15 | 2 | 2 | 58 | .265 | •699 | 63 | 13 | •.983 |
| 1954—Corning ...........Pony | | C | 113 | 374 | 62 | 113 | 22 | 4 | 7 | 69 | .302 | •779 | 44 | 9 | •.989 |
| 1955—Greensboro........Carol. | | C | 100 | 305 | 38 | 84 | 13 | 1 | 6 | 49 | .275 | 619 | 50 | 11 | .984 |
| 1956—Albany .............East. | | C | 111 | 350 | 30 | 81 | 20 | 0 | 3 | 36 | .231 | 698 | •80 | 6 | •.992 |
| 1957—Oklahoma City ..Tex. | | C | 119 | 357 | 32 | 95 | 15 | 1 | 4 | 28 | .266 | 604 | 54 | 13 | .981 |
| 1958—Minneapolis .......A. A. | | C | 57 | 168 | 18 | 42 | 6 | 0 | 2 | 16 | .250 | 276 | 27 | 0 | 1.000 |
| 1959—Minneapolis† ....A. A. | | C | 20 | 59 | 6 | 11 | 3 | 0 | 1 | 6 | .186 | 101 | 15 | 1 | .991 |
| 1959—Vancouver‡ ......P. C. | | C | 44 | 125 | 11 | 22 | 5 | 0 | 0 | 9 | .176 | 215 | 19 | 1 | .996 |
| 1960—Seattle .............P. C. | | C | 82 | 222 | 22 | 62 | 9 | 0 | 6 | 26 | .279 | 370 | 37 | 2 | .995 |
| 1961—Cincinnati§ ........Nat. | | C | 76 | 204 | 8 | 42 | 5 | 0 | 0 | 10 | .206 | 374 | 22 | 10 | .975 |
| 1962—Minnesota .......Amer. | | C | 34 | 62 | 8 | 17 | 4 | 0 | 0 | 7 | .274 | 111 | 9 | 1 | .992 |
| 1963—Minnesota .......Amer. | | C | 39 | 56 | 3 | 13 | 1 | 0 | 0 | 3 | .232 | 116 | 8 | 0 | 1.000 |
| 1964—Minnesota .......Amer. | | C | 63 | 120 | 6 | 24 | 3 | 0 | 0 | 12 | .200 | 264 | 22 | 2 | .993 |
| 1965—Minnesota .......Amer. | | C | 83 | 154 | 8 | 33 | 1 | 1 | 1 | 11 | .214 | 321 | 22 | 1 | •.997 |
| 1966—Minnesota .......Amer. | | C | 60 | 119 | 11 | 30 | 4 | 1 | 1 | 15 | .252 | 264 | 16 | 1 | .996 |
| 1967—Minnesota .......Amer. | | C | 104 | 234 | 13 | 39 | 3 | 0 | 1 | 12 | .167 | 572 | 44 | 5 | .992 |
| 1968—Minnesota x .......Amer. | | C | 24 | 45 | 3 | 5 | 1 | 0 | 0 | 2 | .111 | 109 | 7 | 1 | .991 |
| American League Totals ............... | | | 407 | 790 | 52 | 161 | 17 | 2 | 3 | 62 | .204 | 1757 | 128 | 11 | .994 |
| National League Totals ................. | | | 76 | 204 | 8 | 42 | 5 | 0 | 0 | 10 | .206 | 374 | 22 | 10 | .975 |
| Major League Totals ..................... | | | 483 | 994 | 60 | 203 | 22 | 2 | 3 | 72 | .204 | 2131 | 150 | 21 | .991 |

†Released by Boston Red Sox' organization to Baltimore Orioles' organization, July 16, 1959.

‡Released by Baltimore Orioles' organization to Cincinnati Reds' organization, September 25, 1959.

§Traded to Minnesota Twins for Outfielder Dan Dobbek, January 30, 1962.

xReleased, March 18, 1969.

## WORLD SERIES RECORD

| Year Club | League | Pos. | G. | AB. | R. | H. | 2B. | 3B. | HR. | RBI. | B.A. | PO. | A. | E. | F.A. |
|---|---|---|---|---|---|---|---|---|---|---|---|---|---|---|---|
| 1961—Cincinnati..........Nat. | | C | 2 | 0 | 0 | 0 | 0 | 0 | 0 | 0 | .000 | 4 | 0 | 0 | 1.000 |
| 1965—Minnesota .......Amer. | | C | 2 | 1 | 0 | 0 | 0 | 0 | 0 | 0 | .000 | 2 | 1 | 0 | 1.000 |
| World Series Totals ..................... | | | 4 | 1 | 0 | 0 | 0 | 0 | 0 | 0 | .000 | 6 | 1 | 0 | 1.000 |

Scout, Montreal Expos, 1969; coach, Montreal Expos, 1970 through 1975; coach, Minnesota Twins, 1976 and 1977.

---

### DID YOU KNOW —

That Hank Aaron hit the last home run of his major league career (No. 755) on July 20, 1976, off of pitcher Dick Drago of the California Angels? It was the 10th round-tripper of the season for Hammerin' Henry.

# Major League Umpires

## LAWRENCE ROBERT BARNETT
### (Larry)

Born January 3, 1943, at Nitro, W. Va.
Height, 6.03. Weight, 190.
Hobbies—Golf and swimming.

Umpire, Midwest League, 1964 and 1965; Texas League, 1966 through 1968; American League, 1969 through 1977.
Championship Series umpire, 1972 and 1976.
World Series umpire, 1975.

## NICHOLAS GREGORY BREMIGAN
### (Nick)

Born April 4, 1945, at Philadelphia, Pa.
Height, 6.01. Weight, 195.
Hobby—Chess.
Attended State University of New York at Buffalo, Buffalo, N. Y.; received
Bachelor of Science degree in History and Education.

Umpire, Florida State League, 1969 and 1970; Eastern League, 1971; International League, 1972 and 1973; American League, 1974 through 1977.

## JOSEPH NORBERT BRINKMAN
### (Joe)

Born April 9, 1944, at Little Falls, Minn.
Height, 6.02. Weight, 200.
Attended St. Cloud State College, St. Cloud, Minn.

Umpire, Midwest League, 1968; Southern League, 1969 and 1970; American Association, 1971 and 1972; American League, 1973 through 1977.
Championship Series umpire, 1976.

## NESTOR CHYLAK, JR.

Name pronounced SHY-lack.

Born May 11, 1922, at Olyphant, Pa.
Height, 6.00. Weight, 190.
Hobby—Photography.
Attended Scranton University, Scranton, Pa., and Rutgers University,
New Brunswick, N. J.

Umpire, Pony League, 1947 and 1948; Canadian-American League, 1949; Eastern League, 1950 and 1951; International League, 1952 and 1953; American League, 1954 through 1977.
All-Star Game umpire, 1957, 1960 (both games), 1964 and 1973.
World Series umpire, 1957, 1960, 1966 and 1971.
Championship Series umpire, 1969, 1972 and 1973.

## ALAN MARSHALL CLARK
### (Al)

Born January 9, 1948, at Trenton, N. J.
Height, 6.01. Weight, 235.
Attended Eastern University, Richmond, Ky., and
Mercer County Community College, Trenton, N. J.

Umpire, Midwest League, 1972; Texas League, 1973; American Association, 1974 and 1975; American League, 1976 and 1977.

## NICHOLAS COLOSI
### (Nick)

Born November 22, 1927, at Sicily, Italy.
Height, 6.00. Weight, 175.
Hobby—Photography.

Umpire, Florida State League, 1962; South Atlantic League, 1963; Southern League, 1964 and 1965; International League, 1966 through 1968; National League, September 15, 1968, through 1977.
All-Star Game umpire, 1971.
Championship Series umpire, 1974.
World Series umpire, 1975.

## TERRANCE JOSEPH COONEY
### (Terry)

Born April 12, 1933, at Condon, Ore.
Height, 6.00. Weight, 205.
Hobbies—Golfing, hunting and fishing.
Attended Oregon College of Education, Monmouth, Ore., and
Modesto Junior College, Modesto, Calif.

Umpire, California League, 1969 and part of 1970; Texas League, May 4, 1970, through remainder of season; Pacific Coast League, 1971 through 1974; American League, 1975 through 1977.

## GERALD JOSEPH CRAWFORD
### (Gerry)

Born August 13, 1947, at Philadelphia, Pa.
Height, 5.11. Weight, 185.
Son of Shag Crawford, former National League umpire, 1956 through 1975.

Umpire, Florida State League, 1970; Carolina League, 1971; Eastern League, 1972; International League, 1973 through 1975; National League, May 15, 1976, through 1977.

## JERRY PARKER DALE

Born April 3, 1933, at Evansville, Ind.
Height, 6.00. Weight, 200.
Threw and batted righthanded.
Hobby—Basketball.
Attended California State Poly College, Pomona, Calif.; received
Master of Science degree in Physical Education.

Umpire, Pioneer League, 1963; Pacific Coast League, 1964 through 1970; National League, 1971 through 1977.

All-Star Game umpire, 1972. Championship Series umpire, 1973 and 1976.

| Year | Club | League | G. | IP. | W. | L. | Pct. | H. | R. | ER. | SO. | BB. | ERA. |
|------|------|--------|----|-----|----|----|------|----|----|-----|-----|-----|------|
| 1951—Fulton | | Kitty | 29 | 153 | 10 | 9 | .526 | 167 | 107 | 86 | 61 | 119 | 5.06 |
| 1952—Fulton† | | Kitty | 29 | 114 | 9 | 14 | .391 | 137 | 111 | 70 | 57 | 63 | 5.51 |
| 1953-54 | | | | | | | (National Defense List) | | | | | | |
| 1955—Clovis | | W. T.-N. M. | 41 | 196 | 13 | 10 | .565 | 299 | ●188 | •155 | 85 | 75 | 7.11 |
| 1956—El Paso | | S'western | 10 | 43 | 2 | 2 | .500 | 69 | 48 | 43 | 21 | 19 | 9.00 |

†Released by Washington Senators' organization, September 13, 1952.

## DAVID LEROY DAVIDSON
### (Satch)
(Named by classmates in school because he was a fan of Satch in the
Bowery Boys movies.)

Born January 18, 1936, at London, O.
Height, 6.02. Weight, 215.
Threw right and batted lefthanded.
Attended Wilmington College, Wilmington, O.

Umpire, New York-Pennsylvania League, 1966; Eastern League, 1967 and 1968; National League, 1969 through 1977.
All-Star Game umpire, 1976. Championship Series umpire, 1971 and 1974. World Series umpire, 1975.

| Year | Club | League | Pos. | G. | AB. | R. | H. | 2B. | 3B. | HR. | RBI. | B.A. | PO. | A. | E. | F.A. |
|------|------|--------|------|----|-----|----|----|-----|-----|-----|------|------|-----|----|----|------|
| 1961—Columbus† | | Int. | C | 2 | 3 | 0 | 0 | 0 | 0 | 0 | 0 | .000 | 4 | 0 | 0 | 1.000 |

## WILLIAM EDWARD JOHN DEEGAN
### (Bill)

Born April 13, 1935, at Camden, N. J.
Height, 6.02. Weight, 225.
Attended LaSalle College, Philadelphia, Pa.

Umpire, Midwest League, 1967 and part of 1968; Carolina League, June 17, 1968, through remainder of season; Southern League, 1969 and 1970; American League, 1971 through 1977.
Championship Series umpire, 1974.
World Series umpire, 1976.

## DONALD ANTON DENKINGER
Name pronounced Den-KING-er.
### (Don)

Born August 28, 1936, at Cedar Falls, Ia.
Height, 6.01. Weight, 185.
Hobby—Golf.
Attended Wartburg College, Waverly, Ia.

Umpire, Alabama-Florida League, 1960; Northwest League, 1961 and 1962; Texas League, 1963 through 1965; International League, 1966 through 1968; American League, 1969 through 1977.
World Series umpire, 1974.
Championship Series umpire, 1972 and 1975.
All-Star Game umpire, 1971 and 1976.

## LOUIS JOHN DiMURO
Name pronounced De-MEW-row.
### (Lou)

Born April 24, 1932, at Brooklyn, N. Y.
Height, 6.01. Weight, 180.
Hobbies—Bowling and fishing.
Attended Jersey City Junior College, Jersey City, N. J.

Umpire, Kitty League, 1955; Northern League, 1956; Eastern League, 1957; International League, 1958 through 1962; American League, 1963 through 1977.
World Series umpire, 1969 and 1976.
All-Star Game umpire, 1965, 1967 and 1972.
Championship Series umpire, 1971 and 1975.

# ROBERT ALLEN ENGEL
## (Bob)

Born October 11, 1933, at Atascadero, Calif.
Height, 5.10. Weight, 200.
Attended Bakersfield College, Bakersfield, Calif.

Umpire, Sooner State League, 1956; California League, 1957 through 1961; Pacific Coast League, 1962 through August 20, 1965; National League, August 21, 1965, through 1977.
World Series umpire, 1972.
All-Star Game umpire, 1966 and 1973.
Championship Series umpire, 1970 and 1973.

# JAMES BREMOND EVANS
## (Jim)

Born November 5, 1946, at Longview, Tex.
Height, 6.00. Weight, 185.
Attended Kilgore College, Kilgore, Tex., and University of Texas, Austin, Tex.;
received Bachelor of Science degree in Political Science.

Umpire, Florida State League, 1968; Texas League, 1969 and 1970; American Association, 1971; American League, 1972 through 1977.
Championship Series umpire, 1975.
All-Star Game umpire, 1976.

# ROBERT DALE FORD
## (Known by middle name.)

Born July 6, 1942, at Jonesboro, Tenn.
Height, 6.00. Weight, 190.
Hobbies—Writing poetry, raising cattle and officiating basketball.
Attended East Tennessee State University, Johnson City, Tenn.

Umpire, Florida State League, 1970; Carolina League, 1971; Southern League, 1972; American Association, 1973 through part of 1975; American League, part of 1975 through 1977.

# ARTHUR FRANK FRANTZ
## (Art)

Born March 1, 1921, at Chicago, Ill.
Height, 6.00. Weight, 205.
Threw and batted righthanded.
Hobbies—Bowling, skating, table tennis and billiards.

Umpire, New York-Pennsylvania League, 1958 through 1962; Pacific Coast League, 1963 through 1968; American League, 1969 through 1977.
All-Star Game umpire, 1974.
World Series umpire, 1975.

| Year Club League | Pos. | G. | AB. | R. | H. | 2B. | 3B. | HR. | RBI. | B.A. | PO. | A. | E. | F.A. |
|---|---|---|---|---|---|---|---|---|---|---|---|---|---|---|
| 1940—Caruth.-Batesv ..NE Ark. | P-SS | 57 | 157 | 14 | 24 | 4 | 0 | 0 | 0 | .153 | 44 | 39 | 8 | .912 |
| 1941—Asheville .........Pied. | P | 30 | 39 | 6 | 7 | 0 | 1 | 0 | 5 | .179 | 6 | 31 | 6 | .860 |
| 1942—Decatur ...........I.I.I. | P | 11 | 10 | 2 | 1 | 0 | 0 | 0 | 0 | .000 | 2 | 8 | 2 | .833 |
| 1942—Decatur ...........I.I.I. | P | 11 | 10 | 2 | 1 | 0 | 0 | 0 | 0 | .100 | 2 | 8 | 2 | .833 |
| 1942—Allentown ..........Int.-St. | 3-P | 58 | 255 | 23 | 65 | 10 | 2 | 3 | 35 | .255 | 40 | 91 | 15 | .897 |
| 1943—Hamilton............Pony | | | | | | (In Military Service) | | | | | | | | |
| 1944—Columbus .........A.A. | P | 12 | 11 | 2 | 4 | 0 | 0 | 0 | 0 | .364 | .... | .... | .... | ...... |
| 1944—Mobile .............South. | SS | 40 | 140 | 17 | 42 | 11 | 1 | 1 | 16 | .300 | 82 | 89 | 24 | .877 |
| 1945—Allentown..........Int.-St. | S-P | 65 | 257 | 47 | 76 | 13 | 5 | 7 | 47 | .296 | 123 | 187 | 28 | .917 |
| 1945—Rochester† ........Int. | SS-P | 58 | 190 | 18 | 40 | 4 | 2 | 0 | 17 | .211 | 102 | 162 | 31 | .895 |
| 1946—Niagara Falls ....Mid-A. | O-S-P-3 | 106 | 368 | 52 | 108 | 16 | 11 | 1 | 60 | .293 | 110 | 28 | 11 | .926 |
| 1947— ...................... | | | | | | (Out of Organized Ball) | | | | | | | | |
| 1948—Watertown ........Bor. | ∗SS-OF | 122 | 455 | 77 | 140 | 22 | 9 | 5 | 90 | .308 | ∗270 | 304 | 49 | .921 |
| 1949—Watertown ........Bor. | OF | 102 | 347 | 65 | 95 | 19 | 2 | 6 | 53 | .274 | 68 | 4 | 4 | .947 |
| 1950—St. Jean............Prov. | OF | 19 | 36 | 5 | 7 | 1 | 1 | 0 | 6 | .194 | 12 | 0 | 1 | .923 |
| 1951-52 ...................... | | | | | | (Out of Organized Ball) | | | | | | | | |
| 1953—Batavia ...........Pony | P | 1 | .... | .... | .... | .... | .... | .... | .... | .000 | .... | .... | .... | ....... |

## RECORD AS PITCHER

| Year Club League | G. | IP. | W. | L. | Pct. | H. | R. | ER. | SO. | BB. | ERA. |
|---|---|---|---|---|---|---|---|---|---|---|---|
| 1940—Caruthersville-Batesville ......NE Ark. | 23 | 152 | 10 | 9 | .526 | 161 | 87 | 59 | 129 | 55 | 3.49 |
| 1941—Decatur.................I.I.I. | 4 | 16 | 0 | 3 | .000 | 21 | 16 | .... | 9 | 16 | ....... |
| 1941—Asheville.................Piedmont | 30 | 141 | 8 | 7 | .533 | 138 | 64 | 46 | 66 | 76 | 2.94 |
| 1942—Decatur.................I.I.I. | 10 | 25 | 1 | 4 | .200 | 34 | 25 | .... | 13 | 16 | ....... |
| 1942—Asheville.................Piedmont | 4 | 29 | 1 | 2 | .333 | 35 | 29 | .... | 11 | 13 | ....... |
| 1942—Allentown .............Inter-St. | 13 | 88 | 3 | 7 | .300 | 85 | 41 | 28 | 46 | 60 | 2.86 |
| 1943—Hamilton.................Pony | | | | | (In Military Service) | | | | | | |
| 1944—Columbus .............Am. Assoc. | 8 | 28 | 1 | 2 | .333 | 38 | 15 | 12 | 14 | 11 | 3.86 |
| 1945—Allentown .............Inter-St. | 2 | 5 | 0 | 0 | .000 | .... | .... | .... | .... | .... | ....... |
| 1945—Rochester† .................Int'national | 1 | .... | 0 | 1 | .000 | .... | .... | .... | .... | .... | ....... |
| 1946—Niagara Falls .................Mid-Atl. | 10 | 69 | 6 | 2 | .750 | 61 | 33 | 20 | 54 | 35 | 2.61 |
| 1953—Batavia .................Pony | 1 | .... | 0 | 0 | .000 | .... | .... | .... | .... | .... | ....... |

†Released by St. Louis Cardinals' organization, March 1946.

## BRUCE NEAL FROEMMING

Born September 28, 1939, at Milwaukee, Wis.
Height, 5.08. Weight, 185.

Umpire, Nebraska State League, 1958; Northern League, 1959 and 1960; Northwest League, 1963; Texas League, 1965 and part of 1966; Pacific Coast League, June 15, 1966, through 1970; National League, 1971 through 1977.
Championship Series umpire, 1973.
All-Star Game umpire, 1975.
World Series umpire, 1976.

## RICHARD RAUL GARCIA
### (Rich)

Born May 22, 1942, at Key West, Fla.
Height, 5.09. Weight, 175.
Hobbies—Swimming and fishing.

Umpire, Florida State League, 1970 and 1971; Southern League, 1972; International League, 1973 and 1974; American League, 1975 through 1977.

## RUSSELL LOUIS GOETZ
### (Russ)

Born May 31, 1930, at McKeesport, Pa.
Height, 6.02. Weight, 205.

Umpire, Georgia State League, 1955 and 1956; Carolina League, 1957 and 1958; South Atlantic League, 1959 through 1961; Pacific Coast League, 1962 through 1967; American League, 1968 through 1977.
World Series umpire, 1973.
All-Star Game umpire, 1970 and 1975.
Championship Series umpire, 1970 and 1974.

## WILLIAM EDWARD HALLER
### (Bill)

Born February 28, 1935, at Joliet, Ill.
Height, 6.04. Weight, 205.
Hobby—Hunting.
Attended Joliet Junior College, Joliet, Ill.
Brother of Tom Haller, coach with San Francisco Giants.

Pacific Coast League, August 5, 1960 through September 10, 1961; American League, September 11, 1961 Pacific Coast League, August 5, 1960, through September 10, 1961; American League, September 11, 1961.
World Series umpire, 1968 and 1972.
All-Star Game umpire, 1963, 1970 and 1975.
Championship Series umpire, 1970, 1973 and 1976.

## HAROLD DOUGLAS HARVEY
### (Doug)

Born March, 13, 1930, at South Gate, Calif.
Height, 6.02. Weight, 195.
Hobby—Golf.
Attended San Diego State College, San Diego, Calif.

Umpire, California League, 1958 through 1960; Pacific Coast League, 1961; National League, 1962 through 1977.
World Series umpire, 1968 and 1974.
All-Star Game umpire, 1963, 1964 and 1971.
Championship Series umpire, 1970, 1972 and 1976.

## KENNETH JOHN KAISER
### (Ken)

Born July 26, 1945.
Height, 6.01. Weight, 220.
Attended Al Somers Umpire School.

Umpire, Florida Rookie League, 1965; Western Carolinas League, 1966; New York-Pennsylvania League, 1966 and 1967; Northern League, 1967; Carolina League, 1969 and 1970; Eastern League, 1970 and 1971; International League, 1972 through 1976; American League, 1977.

## JOHN WILLIAM KIBLER

Born January 9, 1929, at Piseco, N. Y.
Height, 6.00. Weight, 200.

Umpire, Georgia-Florida League, 1958; Pioneer League, 1959; Sally League, 1960 and 1961; American Association, 1962; International League, 1963; National League, September, 1963, through 1977.
All-Star Game umpire, 1965 and 1974.
Championship Series umpire, 1972 and 1975.
World Series umpire, 1971.

## GREGORY JOHN KOSC

Name pronounced KOSK.

### (Greg)

Born April 27, 1949, at Bridgeport, Conn.
Height, 6.01. Weight, 240.
Hobby—Weight lifting.
Attended University of Texas at El Paso, El Paso, Tex.; received
Bachelor of Business Administration degree.

Umpire, Western Carolinas League, 1972; Carolina League, 1973; Southern League, 1974; Pacific Coast League, 1975; American League, 1976 and 1977.

## WILLIAM GUSTAVE KUNKEL

### (Bill)

Born July 7, 1936, at Hoboken, N. J.
Height, 6.01. Weight, 190.
Threw and batted righthanded.
Hobbies—Fishing and bowling.

Umpire, Florida State League, 1966; Southern League, 1967 and 1968; American League, September 16, 1968, through 1977.
World Series umpire, 1974.
All-Star Game umpire, 1972.
Championship Series umpire, 1971 and 1975.

| Year | Club | League | G. | IP. | W. | L. | Pct. | H. | R. | ER. | SO. | BB. | ERA. |
|------|------|--------|----|-----|----|----|------|----|----|-----|-----|-----|------|
| 1955—Bluefield† | | Ap'lachian | 2 | 10 | 0 | 2 | .000 | 13 | 13 | 11 | 9 | 10 | 9.90 |
| 1956—Shawnee | | Soo. St. | 40 | 166 | 9 | 13 | .409 | 181 | 122 | 83 | 150 | 87 | 4.50 |
| 1957-58—Thomasville | | Ga.-Fla. | | | | | (In Military Service) | | | | | | |
| 1959—Great Falls | | Pioneer | 43 | 189 | 14∗ | 12 | .538 | 199 | 114 | 88 | 160 | 92 | 4.19 |
| 1960—Montreal‡ | | Int'national | 51 | ∗210 | 8 | ∗19 | .296 | ∗212 | 107 | 90 | 98 | 79 | 3.86 |
| 1961—Kansas City | | American | 58 | 89 | 3 | 4 | .429 | 103 | 58 | 51 | 46 | 32 | 5.16 |
| 1962—Kansas City | | American | 9 | 8 | 0 | 0 | .000 | 8 | 7 | 3 | 6 | 4 | 3.38 |
| 1962—Portland§ | | P. Coast | 10 | 51 | 3 | 2 | .600 | 62 | 29 | 29 | 32 | 7 | 5.12 |
| 1962—Toronto x | | Int'national | 15 | 46 | 6 | 1 | .867 | 38 | 13 | 12 | 22 | 9 | 2.35 |
| 1963—New York | | American | 22 | 46 | 3 | 2 | .600 | 42 | 15 | 14 | 31 | 13 | 2.74 |
| 1964—Toronto | | Int'national | 27 | 55 | 0 | 4 | .000 | 55 | 21 | 19 | 30 | 20 | 3.11 |
| 1964—Denver | | P. Coast | 29 | 66 | 3 | 5 | .375 | 55 | 30 | 27 | 49 | 24 | 3.68 |
| 1965—Rochester-Syracuse | | Int'national | 42 | 80 | 3 | 4 | .429 | 88 | 40 | 33 | 50 | 30 | 3.71 |
| Major League Totals | | | 89 | 143 | 6 | 6 | .500 | 153 | 80 | 68 | 83 | 49 | 4.28 |

†Released by Boston Red Sox' organization, May 19, 1955; signed as free agent by Hornell (Brooklyn Dodgers' organization), October 24, 1955.
‡Drafted by Kansas City Athletics from Montreal (Los Angeles Dodgers' organization), November 28, 1960.
§Released by Kansas City Athletics' organization to Milwaukee Braves' organization, August 4, 1962.
xDrafted by New York Yankees from Toronto (Milwaukee Braves' organization), November 28, 1962.

## RONALD MICHAEL LUCIANO

### (Ron)

Born June 28, 1937, at Endicott, N. Y.
Height, 6.04. Weight, 240.
Attended Syracuse University, Syracuse, N. Y.; received Bachelor of
Science degree in Mathematics.
Selected in 3rd round of 1959 NFL draft by Detroit Lions as a tackle.

Umpire, Florida State League, 1964; Eastern League, 1965; International League, 1966 through 1968; American League, 1969 through 1977.
World Series umpire, 1974.
All-Star Game umpire, 1973.
Championship Series umpire, 1971 and 1975.

## GEORGE PATRICK MALONEY

Born February 28, 1928, at New York, N. Y.
Height, 6.02. Weight, 205.

Umpire, Florida State League, 1952 through 1954; Carolina League, 1955; Sophomore League, 1960 and 1961; Eastern League, 1962 and 1963; Pacific Coast League, 1964 through 1969; American League, 1970 through 1977.
All-Star Game umpire, 1974.
Championship Series, umpire, 1973 and 1976.
World Series umpire, 1975.

## LARRY SANDERS McCOY

Born May 19, 1941, at Essex, Mo.
Height, 5.11. Weight, 188.

Umpire, Midwest League, 1966; Carolina League, 1967; Texas League, 1968 through 1970; American League, 1971 through 1977.
Championship Series umpire, 1973 and 1976.

## JAMES GILBERT McKEAN
### (Jim)

Born May 26, 1945, at Montreal, Quebec, Canada.
Height, 6.02. Weight, 225.
Attended Sir George Williams University, Montreal, Quebec, Canada;
received degree in Physical Education.
Played professional football in Canadian Football League with Montreal Alouettes and
Saskatchewan Roughriders, 1964 through 1966.

Umpire, Florida State League, 1970 and part of 1971 season; Eastern League, June 25, 1971, to May 15, 1972;
International League, 1972 and 1973; American League, 1974 through 1977.

## JOHN PATRICK McSHERRY

Born September 11, 1944, at New York, N. Y.
Height, 6.03. Weight, 235.

Umpire, Carolina League, 1967 and 1968; International League, 1969 through part of 1971; National League,
June 1, 1971, through 1977.
All-Star Game umpire, 1975.
Championship Series umpire, 1974.

## EDWIN DURWOOD MERRILL
(Known by middle name.)

Born March 12, 1938.
Height, 5.10. Weight, 215.

Umpire, California League, 1972; Texas League, 1973 and 1974; American Association, 1974 through 1976;
American League, 1977.

## EDWARD MICHAEL MONTAGUE
### (Eddie)

Born November 3, 1948, at San Francisco, Calif.
Height, 5.11. Weight, 170.
Hobbies—Guitar, racquet ball and banjo.
Attended City College of San Francisco, San Francisco, Calif.
Son of Edward Francis Montague, former infielder with Cleveland Indians
and presently a scout for San Francisco Giants.

Umpire, California League, 1972; Pacific Coast League, 1973 through 1975; National League, 1976 and 1977.

## JEROME A. NEUDECKER
Name pronounced NEW-deck-er.
### (Jerry)

Born August 13, 1930, at Marine, Ill.
Height, 6.00. Weight, 185.
Hobby—Bowling.

Umpire, Georgia-Alabama League, 1950; Evangeline League, 1951; South Atlantic League, 1956; Georgia-
Florida League, 1957; South Atlantic League, 1960 through 1962; Southern League, 1963 through 1965; Ameri-
can League, 1966 through 1977.
Military Service, 1952 through 1955.
World Series umpire, 1973.
All-Star Game umpire, 1966, 1972 and 1976.
Championship Series umpire, 1970 and 1974.

## ANDREW HOLGER OLSEN
### (Andy)

Born November 30, 1931, at Brooklyn, N. Y.
Height, 6.01. Weight, 195.
Threw and batted lefthanded.
Hobbies—Boating and fishing.

Umpire, Sophomore League, 1959; Northern League, 1960 through 1962; Eastern League, 1963 through part
of 1965; Pacific Coast League, June 7, 1965, through 1968; National League, September 13, 1968, through 1977.
World Series umpire, 1974.
All-Star Game umpire, 1976.
Championship Series umpire, 1971 and 1975.

| Year    Club | League | G. | IP. | W. | L. | Pct. | H. | R. | ER. | SO. | BB. | ERA. |
|---|---|---|---|---|---|---|---|---|---|---|---|---|
| 1949—Andalusia | Ala. St. | 29 | 155 | 11 | 7 | .611 | 138 | 86 | 72 | 106 | 98 | 4.18 |
| 1950—Andalusia† | Ala. St. | 38 | 260 | 18 | 12 | .600 | 235 | 141 | 107 | 184 | 160 | 3.70 |
| 1951—Burlington | Carolina | 3 | 15 | 0 | 2 | .000 | .... | .... | 14 | .... | .... | 8.40 |
| 1951—Salisbury | N. Car. St. | 9 | 63 | 3 | 5 | .375 | 71 | 52 | 35 | 47 | 36 | 5.00 |
| 1951—Hutchinson | W. Assoc. | 13 | 50 | 3 | 2 | .600 | 63 | 44 | 33 | 26 | 48 | 5.94 |
| 1952-53—Brunswick | Ga.-Fla. | | | | | (In Military Service) | | | | | | |
| 1954—Burlington-Graham | Carolina | 37 | 146 | 11 | 4 | .733 | 123 | 80 | 72 | 140 | 84 | 4.44 |

| | | | | | | | | | | |
|---|---|---|---|---|---|---|---|---|---|---|
| 1955–Hollywood ...........................P. Coast | 4 | 2 | 0 | 0 | .000 | 2 | 2 | 0 | 0 | 1 | 0.00 |
| 1955–Burlington-Graham .............Carolina | 34 | 145 | 6 | 10 | .375 | 161 | 93 | 68 | 104 | 70 | 4.22 |
| 1956–Lincoln ...............................Western | 15 | 46 | 2 | 1 | .667 | 40 | 24 | 19 | 40 | 26 | 3.72 |
| 1956–Waco‡ ................................Big State | 22 | 119 | 10 | 6 | .625 | 116 | 69 | 64 | 124 | 57 | 4.84 |

†Drafted by Burlington (Pittsburgh Pirates' organization), November 1950.

‡Released by Pittsburgh Pirates' organization to Mexico City Blues, September 28, 1956. Released by Mexico City Blues, April 16, 1957.

## STEPHEN MICHAEL PALERMO
### (Steve)

Born October 9, 1949, at Worcester, Mass.
Height, 6.02. Weight, 175.
Hobbies–Golf and basketball.
Attended Worcester State College, Worcester, Mass.

Umpire, New York-Pennsylvania League, 1972; Carolina League, 1973; Eastern League, 1973 and 1974; American Association, 1975 and 1976; American League, 1977.

## DAVID ROBERT PHILLIPS
### (Dave)

Born October 8, 1943, at St. Louis, Mo.
Height, 5.11. Weight, 180.
Attended Southeast Missouri State University, Cape Girardeau, Mo.
Son of Robert E. Phillips, minor league umpire, 1946 through 1956.

Umpire, Midwest League, 1964 and 1965; Texas League, 1966; International League, 1967 through 1970; American League, 1971 through 1977.
Championship Series umpire, 1974.
World Series umpire, 1976.

## JOHN PAUL PRYOR
### (Known by middle name.)

Born July 10, 1927, at Woonsocket, R. I.
Height, 6.02. Weight, 220.
Threw and batted lefthanded.
Hobby–Coaching high school athletic teams.
Attended High Point College, High Point, N. C., and University of South Dakota, Vermillion, S. D.; received Bachelor of Arts degree in Education.

Umpire, Tri-State League, 1953; Carolina League, 1954 through part of 1959; Sally League, June 19, 1959, through 1960; American Association, 1961; National League, September 20, 1961, through 1977.
World Series umpire, 1967 and 1973.
All-Star Game umpire, 1963 and 1971.
Championship Series umpire, 1970 and 1974.

| Year Club | League | G. | IP. | W. | L. | Pct. | H. | R. | ER. | SO. | BB. | ERA. |
|---|---|---|---|---|---|---|---|---|---|---|---|---|
| 1945–Johnson City ........................Ap'lachian | 10 | 56 | 3 | 3 | .500 | 48 | 30 | 27 | 38 | 50 | 4.34 |
| 1945–Allentown ...........................Inter-State | 1 | 4 | 0 | 0 | .000 | .... | .... | .... | .... | .... | ...... |
| 1946–Portland .............................N. England | 14 | 68 | 0 | 7 | .000 | 116 | 81 | 62 | 12 | 54 | 8.21 |
| 1946–Galax ................................Blue Ridge | 5 | 15 | 0 | 1 | .000 | 36 | 41 | .... | 6 | 25 | ...... |
| 1946–Bloomingdale .....................N. Atlantic | 1 | .... | 1 | 0 | 1.000 | .... | .... | .... | .... | .... | ...... |
| 1946–Sanford...............................Tobacco St. | 5 | 17 | 1 | 0 | 1.000 | 18 | 13 | .... | 5 | 10 | ...... |
| 1947–Waterbury...........................Colonial | .... | .... | 0 | 0 | .000 | .... | .... | .... | .... | .... | ...... |
| 1947–Leaksville-Greensboro .........Carolina | .... | .... | .... | .... | ..... | .... | .... | .... | .... | .... | ...... |
| 1948–North Wilkesboro ...............Blue Ridge | 17 | 85 | 4 | 6 | .400 | 94 | 63 | 42 | 19 | 38 | 4.45 |
| 1953–Fayetteville.........................Carolina | .... | .... | 0 | 0 | .000 | .... | .... | .... | .... | .... | ...... |
| 1953–Asheville.............................Tri-State | .... | .... | 0 | 0 | .000 | .... | .... | .... | .... | .... | ...... |

## FRANK VICTOR PULLI

Born March 22, 1935 at Easton, Pa.
Height, 5.11. Weight, 185.

Umpire, Midwest League, 1968; Eastern League, 1969; International League, 1970 and 1971; National League, 1972 through 1977.
Championship Series umpire, 1975.

## JAMES EDWARD QUICK
### (Jim)

Born September 6, 1943, at Sacramento, Calif.
Height, 6.00. Weight, 218.
Hobbies–Duck and pheasant hunting.
Attended Yuba Community College, Marysville, Calif.

Umpire, Northwest League, 1968; California League, 1969; Texas League, 1970; Pacific Coast League, 1971 through 1975; National League, 1976 and 1977.

## LAURENCE HENRY RENNERT, JR.
### (Dutch)
(Named after Emil "Dutch" Leonard, former major league pitcher.)

Born June 12, 1930, at Oshkosh, Wis.
Height, 5.09. Weight, 175.

Umpire, Alabama-Florida League, 1957; Pioneer League, 1958; Three-I League, 1959 and 1960; Southern Association, 1961; Texas League, 1962 through 1964; Pacific Coast League, 1965 through 1973; National League, 1974 through 1977.


## PAUL EDWARD RUNGE

Born October 20, 1940, at St. Catharines, Ontario, Canada.
Height, 6.01. Weight, 190.
Threw right and batted lefthanded.
Attended Arizona State University, Tempe, Ariz.; received
Bachelor of Arts degree in Education.
Son of Edward Paul Runge, former American League umpire.

Umpire, California League, 1965 and 1966; Eastern League, 1967; Pacific Coast League, 1968 through 1972; National League, August 24, 1972 through 1977.

| Year | Club | League | Pos. | G. | AB. | R. | H. | 2B. | 3B. | HR. | RBI. | B.A. | PO. | A. | E. | F.A. |
|------|------|--------|------|-----|-----|-----|-----|-----|-----|-----|------|------|-----|-----|-----|------|
| 1962—Modesto† | | Calif. | OF-C | 55 | 143 | 23 | 39 | 7 | 1 | 1 | 1 | .273 | 163 | 10 | 8 | .956 |
| 1963—Durham | | Carol. | OF-1 | 50 | 149 | 14 | 33 | 5 | 0 | 0 | 15 | .221 | 110 | 5 | 1 | .991 |
| 1963—Modesto‡ | | Calif. | OF | 55 | 190 | 13 | 48 | 9 | 1 | 0 | 23 | .253 | 52 | 6 | 3 | .951 |
| 1964—Tri-City§ | | Northw. | C | 18 | 46 | 4 | 8 | 0 | 0 | 0 | 2 | .174 | 117 | 8 | 1 | .992 |

†On disabled list, July 16 through July 27, 1962.
‡Released by Houston Colts' organization, April 5, 1964; signed as free agent by Los Angeles Angels' organization, April 15, 1964.
§Released by Los Angeles Angels' organization, June 2, 1964.


## MARTIN JOHN SPRINGSTEAD
### (Marty)

Born July 9, 1937, at Nyack, N. Y.
Height, 6.00. Weight, 180.
Hobby—Golf.
Attended Fairleigh Dickinson University, Teaneck, N. J.

Umpire, Northern League, 1960; Southern League, 1963 through 1965; American League, 1966 through 1977.
Military Service, 1961 and 1962.
World Series umpire, 1973.
All-Star Game umpire, 1969 and 1975.
Championship Series umpire, 1970 and 1974.


## RICHARD JACK STELLO
### (Dick)

Born July 20, 1934, at Boston, Mass.
Height, 5.11. Weight, 195.
Hobbies—Golf and fishing.
Attended Merrimack College, Andover, Mass.

Umpire, Georgia-Florida League, 1963; Texas League, 1964 and 1965; International League, 1966 through 1968; National League, September 20, 1968 through 1977.
Championship Series umpire, 1971 and 1976.
World Series umpire, 1975.


## EDWARD LAWRENCE SUDOL
Name pronounced Soo-doll.
### (Ed)

Born September 13, 1920, at Passaic, N. J.
Height, 6.02. Weight, 210.
Threw and batted righthanded.
Hobbies—Swimming and dancing.
Attended Fairleigh-Dickinson University, Rutherford, N. J.

Umpire, Tri-State League, part of 1953 and all of 1954  International League, 1955 through part of 1957; National League, June 27, 1957, through 1977.
World Series umpire, 1965 and 1971.
All-Star Game umpire, 1961 (second game), 1964 and 1974.
Championship Series umpire, 1969, 1973 and 1976.

| Year | Club | League | Pos. | G. | AB. | R. | H. | 2B. | 3B. | HR. | RBI. | B.A. | PO. | A. | E. | F.A. |
|------|------|--------|------|-----|-----|-----|-----|-----|-----|-----|------|------|-----|-----|-----|------|
| 1940—Po'ke C.-Cam. | | E. Shore | 1B | 44 | 164 | 20 | 33 | 8 | 0 | 4 | 20 | .201 | 236 | 24 | 12 | .956 |
| 1941—Tarboro | | C. Plan | 1B | 107 | 421 | 61 | 131 | 19 | 9 | 2 | 63 | .311 | 919 | 49 | 22 | .978 |
| 1942—Wilmington | | Int.-St. | 1B | 23 | 75 | 5 | 17 | 1 | 0 | 0 | 4 | .227 | 156 | 5 | 0 | 1.000 |

| Year | Club | League | Pos. | G. | AB. | R. | H. | 2B. | 3B. | HR. | RBI. | B.A. | PO. | A. | E. | F.A. |
|---|---|---|---|---|---|---|---|---|---|---|---|---|---|---|---|---|
| 1942–Jacksonville | ......Sally | | 2B | 26 | 94 | 18 | 33 | 3 | 1 | 1 | 11 | .351 | 36 | 25 | 4 | .938 |
| 1943–Baltimore | ..........Int. | | PH | 8 | 8 | 1 | 1 | 0 | 0 | 0 | 1 | .125 | 0 | 0 | 0 | .000 |
| 1943–Wilkes-Barre† | ....East. | | OF | 42 | 154 | 26 | 52 | 9 | 4 | 0 | 20 | .338 | 55 | 2 | 1 | .983 |
| 1944–Baltimore | ..........Int. | | | | | | (In Military Service) | | | | | | | | | |
| 1945–Wi'es†-Hart. | ......East. | | O-1B | 98 | 363 | 44 | 93 | 17 | 10 | 2 | 53 | .256 | 290 | 23 | 10 | .969 |
| 1946–Allentown | ..........Int.-St. | | 1B | 139 | 519 | 98 | 178 | 30 | 13 | 28 | 132 | .343 | 1103 | 63 | •28 | .977 |
| 1947–Stam.-Pough. | ....Col. | | OF-1B | 121 | 479 | 88 | 142 | 19 | 10 | 12 | 87 | .296 | 515 | 31 | 16 | .972 |
| 1948–Savannah | ..........Sally | | 1B | 35 | 119 | 17 | 29 | 5 | 1 | 1 | 19 | .244 | 232 | 15 | 9 | .965 |
| 1948–El Dorado | ........Cot. St. | | 1B | 91 | 352 | 61 | 108 | 14 | 9 | 7 | 41 | .307 | 758 | 54 | 14 | .983 |
| 1949–El Dorado | ........Cot. St. | | 1B | 134 | 512 | 106 | 154 | 30 | 7 | 9 | 79 | .301 | •1171 | 67 | 23 | •.982 |
| 1950–Greenville | ........Cot. St. | | 1B | 127 | 512 | 71 | 136 | 29 | 5 | 6 | 89 | .266 | 1158 | 53 | 15 | •.988 |
| 1951–Greenville | ........Cot. St. | | 1B | 31 | 108 | 9 | 30 | 5 | 0 | 0 | 14 | .278 | 229 | 15 | 2 | .992 |
| 1952–Pampa | ..............WT-NM | | 1B | 113 | 417 | 67 | 122 | 29 | 1 | 21 | 85 | .293 | 688 | 32 | 10 | .986 |
| 1953–Charleston | ........Sally | | ... | 9 | .... | .... | .... | .... | .... | .... | .... | .107 | .... | .... | .... | ........ |
| 1953–Rock Hill | ..........Tri-St. | | 1B | 62 | 236 | 42 | 62 | 10 | 0 | 11 | 46 | .263 | 498 | 30 | 6 | .989 |

†In Military Service most of season.

## TERRY ANTHONY TATA

Born April 24, 1940, at Waterbury, Conn.
Height, 5.10. Weight, 180.
Hobbies–Photography, reading, and all sports.

Umpire, Midwest League, 1960; Northern League, 1961 through 1964; Texas League, 1965 and 1966; International League, 1967 through 1972; National League, 1973 through 1976.
Championship Series umpire, 1976.

## EDWARD PAUL VARGO
## (Ed)

Born April 30, 1930, at Butler, Pa.
Height, 5.10. Weight, 180.

Umpire, Georgia-Florida League, 1953 and 1954; Piedmont League, 1955; Georgia-Florida League, 1956; Eastern League, part of 1957; International League, July 22, 1957, through 1959; National League, 1960 through 1977.
World Series umpire, 1965 and 1971.
All-Star Game umpire, 1961 (first game), 1966 and 1974.
Championship Series umpire, 1969, 1973 and 1976.

## VITO HENRY VOLTAGGIO
## (Vic)

Born March 17, 1941, at Vineland, N. J.
Height, 6.04. Weight, 210.
Hobbies–Fishing and cabinet making.
Attended East Carolina College, Greenville, N. C.; and
Cumberland Community College, Vineland, N. J.

Umpire, Midwest League, 1973; Carolina League, 1974; Southern League, 1975; Pacific Coast League, 1976; American League, 1977.

## HARRY HUNTER WENDELSTEDT, JR.

Born July 27, 1938, at Baltimore, Md.
Height, 6.02. Weight, 240.
Hobby–Fishing.
Attended Essex Community College, Essex, Md., and University of Maryland,
College Park, Md.; received Bachelor of Science degree in education.

Umpire, Georgia-Florida League, 1962; Northwest League, 1963; Texas League, 1964; International League, 1965; National League, 1966 through 1977.
World Series umpire, 1973.
All-Star Game umpire, 1968 and 1976.
Championship Series umpire, 1972.

## LEE HOWARD WEYER
Name pronounced Wire.

Born September 3, 1936, at Imlay City, Mich.
Height, 6.06. Weight, 250.
Hobbies–Bowling, golf and billiards.

Umpire, Midwest League, 1956 and 1957; Southern Association, 1958 and 1959; International League, 1960 and part of 1961 (out of service for almost entire year because of auto accident); National League, September, 1961; entered Service in 1962 and was re-instated in July–divided balance of season between International League and National League; National League, 1963 through 1977.
World Series umpire, 1969 and 1976.
All-Star Game umpire, 1965 and 1972.
Championship Series umpire, 1971 and 1974.

## ARTHUR WILLIAMS
## (Art)

Born February 24, 1934, at Camden, Ark.
Height, 6.02. Weight, 218.
Threw and batted righthanded.
Hobbies—All sports, fishing, listening to music and watching "cowboy" movies.
Attended Bakersfield College, Bakersfield, Calif.

Umpire, Pioneer League, 1969; Midwest League, 1970; Texas League, part of 1971 and 1972 seasons; International League, June 1, 1971, through remainder of season; National League, June 6, 1972, through 1977.
Championship Series umpire, 1975.

| Year Club | League | G. | IP. | W. | L. | Pct. | H. | R. | ER. | SO. | BB. | ERA. |
|---|---|---|---|---|---|---|---|---|---|---|---|---|
| 1953—Bakersfield ..........................California | | 20 | 163 | 11 | 6 | .647 | 150 | 74 | 59 | 99 | 66 | 3.25 |
| 1954—Idaho Falls ..........................Pioneer | | 25 | 118 | 9 | 3 | .750 | 116 | 75 | 63 | 86 | 77 | 4.81 |
| 1955—Visalia† ...............................California | | 33 | 186 | 7 | 16 | .304 | 201 | 124 | 117 | 127 | 98 | 5.65 |
| 1956—Bakersfield‡-Stockton ..........California | | 55 | 242 | 9 | 16 | .360 | 277 | 189 | 142 | 135 | 125 | 5.28 |
| 1957—Stockton§ ............................California | | 6 | 37 | 3 | 0 | 1.000 | 41 | 19 | 17 | 24 | 24 | 4.14 |

†On suspended list, April 20 through May 15, 1955.
‡Released by Detroit Tigers' organization to Stockton, August 20, 1956.
§Released, May 2, 1957.

## WILLIAM GEORGE WILLIAMS, SR.
## (Billy)

Born September 19, 1930, at Brooklyn, N. Y.
Height, 5.11½. Weight, 185.
Hobbies—Woodworking and hunting.
Father of Billy Williams, Jr., general manager of Spartanburg
(Philadelphia Phillies' organization).

Umpire, Evangeline League, 1956, Southwestern League, 1957; Sally League, 1958 through part of 1959; International League, July 31, 1959, through July, 1963; National League, August, 1963, through 1977.
World Series umpire, 1970 and 1976.
Championship Series umpire, 1972 and 1975.
All-Star Game umpire, 1965 and 1973.

# UNASSISTED TRIPLE PLAYS

Neal Ball, shortstop, Cleveland A.L., vs. Boston at Cleveland, July 19, 1909, first game, second inning. Ball caught McConnell's liner, touched second, retiring Wagner, who was on his way to third base, and then tagged Stahl as he came up to second.

William A. Wambsganss, second baseman, Cleveland A.L., vs. Brooklyn N.L., in World Series game at Cleveland, October 10, 1920, fifth inning. Wambsganss caught Mitchell's line drive, stepped on second to retire Kilduff, then tagged Miller coming from first.

George H. Burns, first baseman, Boston A.L., vs. Cleveland at Boston, September 14, 1923, second inning. Burns caught Brower's liner, tagged Lutzke off first and then ran to second and reached that bag before Stephenson could return from third base.

Ernest K. Padgett, shortstop, Boston N.L., vs. Philadelphia at Boston, October 6, 1923, second game, fourth inning. Padgett caught Holke's liner, ran to second to retire Tierney, then tagged Lee before he could return to first.

F. Glenn Wright, shortstop, Pittsburgh N.L., vs. St. Louis at Pittsburgh, May 7, 1925, ninth inning. Wright caught Bottomley's liner, ran to second to retire Cooney and then tagged Hornsby, who was en route to second.

James E. Cooney, shortstop, Chicago N.L., vs. Pittsburgh at Pittsburgh, May 30, 1927, morning game, fourth inning. Cooney caught Paul Waner's liner, stepped on second to retire Lloyd Waner, then tagged Barnhart off first.

John H. Neun, first baseman, Detroit A.L., vs. Cleveland at Detroit, May 31, 1927, ninth inning. Neun caught Summa's liner, ran over and tagged Jamieson between first and second and then touched second base before Myatt could return.

Ronald L. Hansen, shortstop, Washington A.L., vs. Cleveland at Cleveland, July 30, 1968, night game, first inning. With the count 3 and 2 on Azcue, Nelson broke for third base. Hansen caught Azcue's liner, stepped on second to double Nelson and then tagged Snyder going into second base.

(All above unassisted triple plays made with runners on first and second bases only.)

# ACTIVE PLAYERS

## A

| | |
|---|---|
| Aase, Don | 3 |
| Abbott, Glenn | 3 |
| Adams, Glenn | 3 |
| Adams, Bob | 4 |
| Aikens, Willie | 4 |
| Albert, Jeff | 4 |
| Albury, Vic | 4 |
| Alcala, Santo | 5 |
| Alexander, Doyle | 5 |
| Alexander, Gary | 5 |
| Alexander, Matt | 6 |
| Alfano, Don | 6 |
| Allen, Mike | 6 |
| Allen, Dick | 6 |
| Almon, Bill | 8 |
| Alomar, Sandy | 8 |
| Alston, Wendell | 9 |
| Alvarado, Luis | 9 |
| Andersen, Larry | 9 |
| Anderson, Larry | 9 |
| Anderson, Mike | 10 |
| Andrews, Fred | 10 |
| Andrews, Rob | 10 |
| Andujar, Jack | 11 |
| Angelini, Norm | 11 |
| Apodaca, Bob | 11 |
| Armas, Tony | 12 |
| Armbrister, Ed | 12 |
| Arnold, John | 13 |
| Arroyo, Fred | 13 |
| Ashby, Alan | 13 |
| Ashford, Tom | 13 |
| Asselstine, Brian | 14 |
| Atkinson, Bill | 14 |
| Auerbach, Rick | 14 |
| Augustine, Jerry | 15 |
| Ault, Doug | 15 |
| Ausman, Paul | 15 |
| Autry, Al | 15 |
| Aviles, Ramon | 16 |
| Ayala, Benny | 16 |

## B

| | |
|---|---|
| Bacsik, Mike | 16 |
| Baez, Jose | 17 |
| Bahnsen, Stan | 17 |
| Bailey, Bob | 17 |
| Bailor, Bob | 18 |
| Bair, Doug | 18 |
| Baker, Jack | 18 |
| Baker, Dusty | 19 |
| Baldwin, Rick | 19 |
| Baldwin, Billy | 19 |
| Bando, Sal | 20 |
| Bane, Eddie | 20 |
| Bannister, Alan | 21 |
| Bannister, Floyd | 21 |
| Bare, Ray | 21 |
| Barker, Jeff | 22 |
| Barker, Len | 22 |
| Barr, Jim | 22 |
| Barr, Steve | 22 |
| Barrios, Francisco | 23 |

| | |
|---|---|
| Bass, Randy | 23 |
| Batton, Chris | 23 |
| Baylor, Don | 24 |
| Beamon, Charlie | 24 |
| Beard, Mike | 24 |
| Beare, Gary | 25 |
| Belanger, Mark | 25 |
| Bell, Buddy | 26 |
| Bell, Kevin | 26 |
| Belloir, Rob | 26 |
| Bench, Johnny | 27 |
| Beniquez, Juan | 28 |
| Bergman, Dave | 28 |
| Bernal, Vic | 28 |
| Bernard, Dwight | 28 |
| Bernhardt, Juan | 29 |
| Berra, Dale | 29 |
| Bevacqua, Kurt | 29 |
| Bibby, Jim | 30 |
| Biittner, Larry | 30 |
| Billingham, Jack | 30 |
| Bird, Doug | 31 |
| Blackwell, Tim | 32 |
| Blair, Dennis | 32 |
| Blair, Paul | 32 |
| Blanks, Larvell | 33 |
| Blomberg, Ron | 33 |
| Blue, Vida | 34 |
| Blyleven, Bert | 34 |
| Bochte, Bruce | 35 |
| Boggs, Tom | 35 |
| Boisclair, Bruce | 35 |
| Boitano, Danny | 36 |
| Bonds, Bobby | 36 |
| Bonham, Bill | 37 |
| Bonnell, Barry | 37 |
| Boone, Bob | 37 |
| Borbon, Pedro | 38 |
| Borgmann, Glenn | 38 |
| Bosetti, Rick | 38 |
| Bosley, Thaddis | 39 |
| Bosman, Dick | 39 |
| Bostock, Lyman | 39 |
| Boswell, Ken | 40 |
| Bowa, Larry | 40 |
| Bowling, Steve | 41 |
| Braun, Steve | 41 |
| Brett, George | 42 |
| Brett, Ken | 42 |
| Briggs, Dan | 43 |
| Briles, Nelson | 43 |
| Broberg, Pete | 44 |
| Brock, Lou | 44 |
| Brohamer, Jack | 45 |
| Brown, Jackie | 45 |
| Brown, Ollie | 46 |
| Bruno, Tom | 47 |
| Brusstar, Warren | 47 |
| Bryant, Derek | 47 |
| Brye, Steve | 47 |
| Buckner, Bill | 48 |
| Bulling, Terry | 48 |
| Bumbry, Al | 48 |
| Burgmeier, Tom | 49 |
| Burke, Glenn | 49 |

| | |
|---|---|
| Burleson, Rick | 50 |
| Burris, Ray | 50 |
| Burroughs, Jeff | 50 |
| Burton, Jim | 51 |
| Busby, Steve | 51 |
| Buskey, Mike | 51 |
| Buskey, Tom | 52 |
| Byrd, Jeff | 52 |

## C

| | |
|---|---|
| Cabell, Enos | 52 |
| Cacek, Craig | 53 |
| Caldwell, Mike | 53 |
| Camp, Rick | 53 |
| Campaneris, Bert | 54 |
| Campbell, Bill | 55 |
| Camper, Cardell | 55 |
| Candelaria, John | 55 |
| Cannon, Joe | 56 |
| Capilla, Doug | 56 |
| Cappuzzello, George | 56 |
| Capra, Buzz | 56 |
| Carbo, Bernie | 57 |
| Cardenal, Jose | 57 |
| Carew, Rod | 58 |
| Carlton, Steve | 59 |
| Carrithers, Don | 59 |
| Carroll, Clay | 60 |
| Carroll, Tom | 61 |
| Carter, Gary | 61 |
| Carty, Rico | 61 |
| Cash, Dave | 62 |
| Castillo, Esteban | 63 |
| Castro, Bill | 63 |
| Caudill, Bill | 63 |
| Caughey, Wayne | 63 |
| Cedeno, Cesar | 64 |
| Cerone, Rick | 64 |
| Cey, Ron | 64 |
| Chalk, Dave | 65 |
| Chambliss, Chris | 65 |
| Champion, Mike | 66 |
| Chaney, Darrell | 66 |
| Chant, Charlie | 67 |
| Chevez, Tony | 67 |
| Chiles, Rich | 67 |
| Christenson, Larry | 67 |
| Clancy, Jim | 68 |
| Clarey, Doug | 68 |
| Clark, Jack | 68 |
| Clay, Kenny | 68 |
| Cleveland, Reggie | 69 |
| Clines, Gene | 69 |
| Clyde, David | 70 |
| Coe, Roger | 70 |
| Colbert, Nate | 70 |
| Colborn, Jim | 71 |
| Coleman, Dave | 72 |
| Coleman, Joe | 72 |
| Collins, Dave | 72 |
| Collins, Don | 73 |
| Coluccio, Bob | 73 |
| Concepcion, Dave | 73 |
| Cooper, Cecil | 74 |
| Corcoran, Tim | 74 |

# RECENTLY RETIRED PLAYERS

# MAJOR LEAGUE MANAGERS

# MAJOR LEAGUE COACHES

# MAJOR LEAGUE UMPIRES

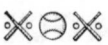

## SCOREBOARD Of MAJORS' ALL-STAR GAMES

1933—At Comiskey Park, Chicago, July 6. Americans 4, Nationals 2.
1934—At Polo Grounds,. New York, July 10. Americans 9, Nationals 7.
1935—At Municipal Stadium, Cleveland, July 8. Americans 4, Nationals 1.
1936—At Braves Field, Boston, July 7. Nationals 4, Americans 3.
1937—At Griffith Stadium, Washington, July 7. Americans 8, Nationals 3.
1938—At Crosley Field, Cincinnati, July 6. Nationals 4, Americans 1.
1939—At Yankee Stadium, New York, July 11. Americans 3, Nationals 1.
1940—At Sportsman's Park, St. Louis, July 9. Nationals 4, Americans 0.
1941—At Briggs Stadium, Detroit, July 8. Americans 7, Nationals 5.
1942—At Polo Grounds, New York, July 6. Americans 3, Nationals 1.
1943—At Shibe Park, Philadelphia, July 13 (night game). Americans 5, Nationals 3.
1944—At Forbes Field, Pittsburgh, July 11 (night game). Nationals 7, Americans 1.
1945—No game played.
1946—At Fenway Park, Boston, July 9, Americans 12, Nationals 0.
1947—At Wrigley Field, Chicago, July 8. Americans 2, Nationals 1.
1948—At Sportsman's Park, St. Louis, July 13. Americans 5, Nationals 2.
1949—At Ebbets Field, Brooklyn, July 12. Americans 11, Nationals 7.
1950—At Comiskey Park, Chicago, July 11. Nationals 4, Americans 3 (14 innings).
1951—At Briggs Stadium, Detroit, July 10. Nationals 8, Americans 3.
1952—At Shibe Park, Philadelphia, July 18. Nationals 3, Americans 2 (five innings, rain).
1953—At Crosley Field, Cincinnati, July 14. Nationals 5, Americans 1.
1954—At Municipal Stadium, Cleveland, July 13. Americans 11, Nationals 9.
1955—At County Stadium, Milwaukee, July 12. Nationals 6, Americans 5 (12 innings).
1956—At Griffith Stadium, Washington, D. C., July 10. Nationals 7, Americans 3.
1957—At Busch Stadium, St. Louis, July 9. Americans 6, Nationals 5.
1958—At Memorial Stadium, Baltimore, July 8. Americans 4, Nationals 3.
1959—At Forbes Field, Pittsburgh, July 7. Nationals 5, Americans 4.
　　　At Memorial Coliseum, Los Angeles, August 3. Americans 5, Nationals 3.
1960—At Municipal Stadium, Kansas City, July 11. Nationals 5, Americans 3.
　　　At Yankee Stadium, New York, July 13. Nationals 6, Americans 0.
1961—At Candlestick Park, San Francisco, July 11. Nationals 5, Americans 4 (10 inn.).
　　　At Fenway Park, Boston, July 31. Americans 1, Nationals 1 (nine innings, rain).
1962—At District of Columbia Stadium, Washington, July 10. Nationals 3, Americans 1.
　　　At Wrigley Field, Chicago, July 30. Americans 9, Nationals 4.
1963—At Municipal Stadium, Cleveland, July 9. Nationals 5, Americans 3.
1964—At Shea Stadium, New York, July 7. Nationals 7, Americans 4.
1965—At Metropolitan Stadium, Bloomington, Minn., July 13. Nationals 6, Americans 5.
1966—At Busch Memorial Stadium, St. Louis, Mo., July 12. Nationals 2, Americans 1.
1967—At Anaheim Stadium, Anaheim, Calif., July 11. Nationals 2, Americans 1 (15 inn.).
1968—At Astrodome, Houston, Texas, July 9. Nationals 1, Americans 0.
1969—At Kennedy Memorial Stadium, Washington, July 23. Nationals 9, Americans 3.
1970—At Riverfront Stadium, Cincinnati, July 14. Nationals 5, Americans 4 (12 innings).
1971—At Tiger Stadium, Detroit, July 13. Americans 6, Nationals 4.
1972—At Atlanta Stadium, Atlanta, July 25. Nationals 4, Americans 3 (10 innings).
1973—At Royals Stadium, Kansas City, July 24. Nationals 7, Americans 1.
1974—At Three Rivers Stadium, Pittsburgh, July 23. Nationals 7, Americans 2.
1975—At County Stadium, Milwaukee, July 15. Nationals 6, Americans 3
1976—At Veterans Stadium, Philadelphia, July 13. Nationals 7, Americans 1.

# NOTES